ARS COLOR CLASSIFICATIONS

w	White, Near White and White Blend
ly	Light Yellow
my	Medium Yellow
dy	Deep Yellow
yb	Yellow Blend
ab	Apricot and Apricot Blend
ob	Orange and Orange Blend
op	Orange Pink
or	Orange Red
lp	Light Pink
mp	Medium Pink
dp	Deep Pink
pb	Pink Blend
mr	Medium Red
dr	Dark Red
rb	Red Blend
m	Mauve and Mauve Blend
r	Russet

AWARDS

Generally only Gold Medals (GM) or their equivalent are listed for the various awarding agencies throughout the world.

All-American Rose Selection (AARS)
American Rose Society Awards:
    James Alexander Gamble Rose Fragrance Award
    John Cook Medal
    Gertrude M. Hubbard GM
    Dr. W. Van Fleet Medal
    David Fuerstenberg Prize
    National GM Certificate
    Award of Excellence (AOE) for Miniature Roses
    American Rose Center Trial Ground Gold, Silver and Bronze Certificates
ADR Anerkannte Deutsche Rose (Germany)
Baden-Baden GM
Bagatelle (Paris) GM
Belfast GM
Copenhagen GM
Dublin GM
Geneva GM
Genova (Genoa, Italy) GM
Glasgow (Tollcross, Scotland) GM
The Hague GM and the Golden Rose
Le Roeuix (Belgium) GM
Lyon GM
Madrid GM
Monza GM
PIT President's International Trophy (England)
Royal National Rose Society of Great Britain (RNRS) GM
RNRS James Mason Medal
New Zealand GM
Orleans GM
Portland (Oregon, USA) GM
Rome GM
ROTY—Rose of The Year, Great Britain
Toyko GM
World Federation of Rose Societies (WFRS) Rose of the Year

MODERN ROSES
10

MODERN ROSES 10

The Comprehensive List of Roses
of
Historical and Botanical Importance
including
All Modern International Rose Registrations

EDITOR
Thomas Cairns, Ph.D., D.Sc.
Studio City
California, USA

The American Rose Society
Shreveport, Louisiana
1993

Front Cover:
Gourmet Popcorn
A floriferous white miniature, semi-double, twice voted top of the list in garden display in Roses in Review — in 1991 a score of 8.2 and in 1992, 8.4. A sport of **Popcorn** discovered by Luis Desamero in 1986, this miniature rose boasts of pure white flowers in massive clusters, with a slight fragrance, on an upright and bushy plant. The growth habit of this variety is also admired for its dark green disease resistant foliage. The variety is universally accepted because of its ease of adaptation to various planting styles — looks great in containers, hanging baskets and as trees. Distributed by Weeks Roses, Upland, California.

Library of Congress Cataloging-in-Publication Data

Modern Roses 10/editor, Thomas Cairns

   p. cm.—(Modern Roses 10)
Includes references and index.
ISBN 0-9636340-0-3
1. Roses—Registration. I. Cairns, Thomas

This book represents information obtained from authentic registration files and from past issues of **Modern Roses**, updated as required by changes approved by the appropriate ARS Committees. Every effort has been made to give reliable data and information, but the publisher cannot assume responsibility for the validity of all materials or for the consequences of their use.

Direct all inquires to the American Rose Society, P.O. 30,000, Shreveport, Louisiana 71130-0030.

©1993 by American Rose Society
International Standard Book Number 0-9636340-0-3
Printed in the United States
Printed on acid-free paper

PREFACE

In 1955, the American Rose Society (ARS) was formally designated as the International Registration Authority for Roses (IRAR) by the International Society for Horticulture Science. Then in 1981 ARS was designated to serve as The Registrar for Communauté Internationale des Obtenteurs de Plantes Ornementales et Fruitières de Reproduction Asexuée (CIOPORA). Rose registrations of all approved new registrations and/or change, corrections, deletions are first published in abbreviated form in *The American Rose* magazine, followed by more detailed listings with narrative descriptions in *The American Rose Annual*. From time to time, however, complete lists of comprehensive descriptions of such registrations are published as part of editions of *'Modern Roses.'*

The last such cumulative listing, *Modern Roses 9*, listed only those cultivars still in cultivation or of botanical importance. Therefore, consultation with *Modern Roses 8* was necessary to have a complete and comprehensive listing of all cultivars. Because of an overwhelming need, expressed by rosarians everywhere, to have one definitive volume containing comprehensive information, this current edition of *Modern Roses 10* was undertaken.

As with any publication of this size and importance, particular care has been taken to avoid mistakes. However, infallibility is a goal rarely reached. It should be stressed that this edition reflects only authorized ARS registration data and subsequent changes that have already appeared in *The American Rose* magazine or *The American Rose Annual* up to December 1992. However, during the preparation of this edition many color classes were assigned to cultivars, particularly with Old Garden Roses, where no color class was previously indicated or a change in color class was in order based on new color classes recently approved by the ARS Board of Directors. This phase of assigning color classes, outside of the normal practice of pre-publication, was approved by the ARS Classification Committee and Registration Committee working with the hybridizer/introducer where possible.

Lastly, I am honored to have been given this challenge to design the computer software to convert the rose registration system to a data base format as well as serve as Editor with a team of distinguished rosarians in bringing you, the reader, this comprehensive compilation of roses of historical or botanical importance including all modern rose registrations to date.

Studio City, California   Tommy Cairns
January 1993

ACKNOWLEDGMENTS

Financial Support by All-America Rose Selections (AARS) Members
Since the inception of this project, various individuals representing the All-America Rose Selections (AARS) organization have contributed financially to assist ARS in buying the appropriate computer equipment and funding a staff person for data entry. The contributions of the following AARS members are gratefully acknowledged: Conklin Brothers, Weeks Wholesale Roses Inc., Devor Nurseries, Bear Creek Gardens, Montebello Rose Co. Inc., Paramount Nursery Packing Co., Joseph H. Hill Co., Co-Operative Rose Growers, H.C. Downham Nursery, Nor'East Miniature Roses, Moorestown Gardens, Springhill Nursery and Conard-Pyle.

International Editorial Advisory Board
The art of managing and editing such a herculean task as *Modern Roses 10* could not have been accomplished without a great deal of initial planning assistance and guidance from the members of the Editorial Advisory Board:

Dr. Ray C. Allen, *Tucson, Arizona, USA*
David Austin, *Wolverhampton, England, UK*
John Baxter, *Northampton, England, UK*
Leonie Bell, *Conshohocken, Pennsylvania, USA*
Claudia Bonnett, *Albuquerque, New Mexico, USA*
Larry Burks, *Tyler, Texas, USA*
Tom Carruth, *Altadena, California, USA*
Jack Harkness, OBE, *Suffolk, England, UK*
Malcolm Lowe, *Nashua, New Hampshire, USA*
Sam McGredy, *Auckland, New Zealand*
Grace E. Seward, *Altadena, California, USA*
Jan Shivers, *Indianapolis, Indiana, USA*

ARS Members
Without my friend and, in many instances, my mentor, Dr. Ray C. Allen, Chairman of the Registration Committee, I would have found the task insurmountable. His constant advice and counsel must be considered a necessary ingredient to the success of this publication.

In the final stages of preparing for publication, the Chairman of the Old Garden Rose Committee, H. Scott Hansen, Immediate Past ARS President, Dr. Charles Jeremias, and ARS Vice President, Pete Haring, were invaluable in processing the establishment of color classes for many OGRs, as well as color class changes for more modern cultivars and in proof reading the final copy before publication.

The Combined Rose List 1992, compiled and edited by Beverly R. Dobson and Peter Schneider, was relied upon for verification of valid dates of registration and most recently published official changes, as well as for other essential information about roses.

ARS Staff in Shreveport
I would also like to express my gratitude to the following ARS staff, Kris McKnight, Susan Moreland and Carol Spiers for their constant help and assistance in quickly solving problems as they arose. In particular, the diligence of Carol Spiers, who assumed the data entry responsibility in the final stages, deserves special recognition.

ARS Judges and Exhibitors
Lastly, I would like to thank all my friends and colleagues in the rose world, at home and abroad, who have given me such strong support and help over the past two years to get the job done. Having finished the task, I can only hope that I have served you all faithfully in the shared pride of accomplishment.

T.C.

ABOUT THIS EDITION

Modern Roses 10 can be considered a technical advance. In previous editions of *Modern Roses*, the records on all cultivars have been maintained and sorted manually on a card index. This process of hand sorting over thousands of records to prepare a new edition was therefore slow, cumbersome, time consuming and subject to transcription errors.

Database
With the advent of low cost computers, all rose registration records are now entered into a permanent data base system. Development of this data base system will faciltate the preparation of future editions of *Modern Roses* as well as provide a valuable data base for participating hybridizers, introducers and scholars. The system could be set up as a bulletin board to be interrogated by off site modem-computer hook up to ask many different specific questions. Apart from the obvious question *"Has the name already been assigned?"*, other questions such as *"List all hybrid teas with Pristine as pollen parent,"* can be posed since the structure of the data base has been designed to ask such questions dealing with all definitions included in the registration package.

This phase of the project represents a giant step forward in managing the commitment of ARS to its trusted function as The Registrar for the world of roses. The dictionary format for the entries was chosen to highlight the fundamental information most frequently used by rose growers, judges and exhibitors.

System of Measurements
In the descriptive entries for the cultivars, petal dimensions and growth height are often listed in inches or centimeters. Rather than attempt to bring absolute consistency and convert all dimensions into the metric system, it was decided to leave the original dimensions as indicated in the registration documents.

Code Names
Within the main list there are a number of registered cultivars beginning with a set of capital letters, usually three, followed by lower case letters. This coined word was intended to be, but is not always pronounceable. The capital letters indicate the hybridizer or introducer, and the lower case letters indicate the specific cultivar, which in most cases has been assigned one or more trade names.

Both IRAR and CIOPORA require that this code name be part of the registration file. Many countries require that a different trade name be assigned to a cultivar in order to accord it plant protection rights, hence the proliferation of alternate names. Infrequently the capital letters appear elsewhere than at the beginning of the code name as for example, Lolita, LitaKOR.

Parentage
In the case of the parentage of cultivars, it was decided to print this part of the entry in italics to allow the reader to easily spot this information. This choice of italics for parents does not infer botanical significance, merely a typographical style for ease of identification within the narrative.

Extinct Cultivars
Another innovation within this edition is the inclusion of those older cultivars declared extinct, thereby allowing re-use of the name for a more modern cultivar. To perserve the historical importance of such information as well as the parentage information, many of the cultivars declared extinct have been included and appear, when appropriate, just before the entry of the modern cultivar bearing the same name. In this manner, the serious rose scholar now has access to information previously not appearing in editions of *Modern Roses.*

Appendices
At the end of the main registered rose list, there are three Appendices to help the reader with additional information. The first Appendix is a list of synonyms to permit location of the main descriptive record via its correct registered name, i.e. its official ARS rose show name. The second Appendix is a list of unregistered cultivars to assist ARS judges and exhibitors in confirming that a cultivar cannot be shown. The third Appendix is a list of hybridizers and introducers with addresses.

MODERN ROSES 10

Aafje Heynis HT, *mr*, 1964, *Prima Ballerina* × *Salvo*; Buisman. Flowers bright red, well-shaped, large; foliage glossy, light green; vigorous, upright.

Aalsmeer Gold® HT, *dy*, 1978, (Bekola); *Berolina* × *Seedling*; Kordes. Bud long, pointed; flowers deep yellow, dbl. (23 petals), high centered, borne singly; slight fragrance; foliage glossy; vigorous, upright, bushy growth.

Abaillard G (OGR), *pb*, 1845, (Abalard); Raised at Angers; Flowers rose marbled, full.

Abasanta HT, *dp*, 1956, *Red Columbia* × *(Red Columbia* × *Tausendschön sport)*; Motose. Bud pointed, cerise; flowers carmine, occasionally streaked white, semi-dbl. (15-25 petals), fragrant, medium (3½ in.); foliage dark; compact growth.

Abba Dabba Min, *mr*, 1979, *Red Can Can* × *Seedling*; Lyon. Bud long, pointed; flowers medium red, dbl. (38 petals), borne 1-5 per cluster; slight fragrance; foliage small, medium green; tiny, curved prickles; compact, bushy growth.

Abbé Girardin B (OGR), *mp*, 1881, *Louise Odier* × *Hermosa*; Bernaix, A. Flowers carmine-pink, center darker, full, large; fragrant.

Abbeyfield Rose HT, *dp*, 1983, (COCbrose); *National Trust* × *Silver Jubilee*; Cocker, A.; Cocker, 1985. Flowers rose red, dbl. (35 petals), large; slight fragrance; foliage medium, medium green, semi-glossy; bushy growth. Glasgow Golden Prize, 1990.

Abbotswood HCan (OGR), *mp*, 1954, *Chance hybrid of R. canina* × *Unknown garden variety*; Hilling. Flowers pink, dbl.; habit similar to R. canina.

Abel Carrière HP (OGR), *dr*, 1875, *Baron de Bonstetten* × *Seedling*; Verdier, E. Flowers velvety crimson, brighter center, dbl. (45 petals), large.

Abendröte HP (OGR), *op*, 1919, *Frau Karl Druschki* × *Juliet*; Ebeling; Teschendorff. Flowers light coral-red; compact.

Aberdonian F, *rb*, 1974, (*Evelyn Fison* × *Manx Queen)* × *(Sabine* × *Circus)*; Cocker. Flowers golden bronze and scarlet, dbl. (20 petals), large; slightly fragrant; foliage glossy.

Abhisarika HT, *rb*, 1977, *Induced mutant* × *Kiss of Fire*; Indian Agric. Research Inst. Bud long, pointed; flowers red blend, striped, dbl. (48 petals), high-centered, small (2½-3 in.); slightly fragrant; foliage glossy, yellowish; vigorous growth.

Abiding Faith HT, *dp*, 1954, *La France sport* × *(Senator* × *Florex)*; Motose. Bud semi-ovoid; flowers deep rose-pink, dbl. (20-35 petals), large (4-5 in.); very fragrant; vigorous, upright growth. A forcing variety.

Abiding Faith, Climbing Cl HT, *dp*, 1957, Motose.

Abol HT, *w*, 1927, Evans; Beckwith. Flowers ivory-white tinted blush, full, large; very fragrant.

Abracadabra HT, *pb*, 1991, (JACbute); *White Masterpiece* × *Tribute*; Warriner, William; Bear Creek Gardens, 1993. Flowers purple pink, tan and yellow, full (26-40 petals), large blooms borne mostly singly; very fragrant; foliage large, dark green, semi-glossy; some prickles; medium (90-120 cms), upright, bushy growth.

Abricot HT, *ab*, 1929, *Mrs. Aaron Ward* × *Jean C.N. Forestier*; Barbier. Flowers apricot and coral-salmon, reverse coral-red.

Abricoté T (OGR), *ab*, Prior to 1848. Flowers apricot, margins flesh, dbl., cupped.

Abundance F, *mp*, 1974, *Seedling* × *Firecracker*; Gandy. Flowers medium pink, dbl. (30 petals), large (4½ in.); slightly fragrant; foliage dark; low, bushy growth.

Academy® Min, *pb*, 1983, (MACgutsy); *Anytime* × *Matangi*; McGredy, 1982. Flowers pink blend, dbl. (20 petals), patio, small; slight fragrance; foliage small, medium green, semi-glossy; bushy growth.

Acadian Ch (OGR), *dp*, 1986, *R. nitida* × *R. chinensis semperflorens*; James, John. Flowers deep, bright pink, single (5 petals), medium; very fragrant; foliage small, medium green, matt; fine prickles; upright, bushy, hardy growth.

A Capella HT, *mr*, 1984, *Command Performance* × *Tiffany*; Stoddard, Louis. Flowers medium red, dbl. (35 petals), large blooms borne singly; slight fragrance; foliage large, medium green, matt; upright growth. ARC TG (B), 1984.

Acapulco F, *yb*, 1962, *Seedling* × *Masquerade*; Abrams, Von; Peterson & Dering. Bud pointed; flowers yellow and light orange, often flushed pink, dbl. (30-40 petals), cupped, medium, cluster; slightly fragrant; foliage dark, glossy; bushy, compact growth.

Accent F, *mr*, 1977, *Marlena* × *Seedling*; Warriner; J&P. Bud ovoid; flowers cardinal-red, dbl. (25 petals), flat, medium (2-2½ in.); slightly fragrant; foliage small, dark, leathery; bushy, compact growth.

Acclaim HT, *ob*, 1982, (JACaim); *Sunfire* × *Spellbinder*; Warriner; J&P, 1986. Flowers orange, dbl. (34 petals), large; slight fragrance; foliage medium green, semi-glossy; upright, bushy.

Accolade HT, *rb*, 1979, *(Daily Sketch × Charles Mallerin) × Peter Frankenfeld*; Dawson, G.; Rainbow Roses. Bud ovoid; flowers bright red, shaded darker, dbl. (48 petals), exhibition form, borne mostly singly; slight fragrance; foliage dark, matt; hooked, brown prickles; vigorous growth.

Accord F, *ab*, 1965, *Circus × Seedling*; Mason, P.G. Flowers apricot-peach, reverse carmine, well formed, high-centered, cluster; fragrant; foliage dark; bushy growth.

Acey Deucy™ Min, *mr*, 1982, (SAVathree); *(Yellow Jewel × Tamango) × Sheri Anne*; Saville; Nor'East Min. Roses. Flowers medium red, dbl. (20 petals), high-centered, HT form, small; fragrant; foliage small, medium green, semi-glossy; bushy growth.

Achievement R, *dp*, 1925, *Dorcas sport*; English. Foliage variegated.

Acidalie B (OGR), *w*, 1838, Rousseau. Flowers white with blush center, full, globular, large; vigorous; recurrent.

Acqua Cheta HT, *rb*, 1962, *Crimson Glory × Peace*; Giacomasso. Flowers magenta-red, reverse silvery, dbl. (50 petals); foliage dark; compact growth.

Actrice HT, *rb*, 1966, *Tzigane × Kordes' Perfecta*; Verschuren, A.; A.J. van Engelan. Bud ovoid; flowers red and light pink, dbl., large; foliage dark.

Ada Perry Min, *op*, 1978, *Little Darling × Coral Treasure seedling*; Bennett, Dee; Tiny Petals Nursery. Bud ovoid; flowers soft coral-orange, dbl. (40 petals), exhibition form, medium; slightly fragrant; foliage dark; vigorous, upright growth.

Adagio HT, *dr*, 1971, *Seedling × Uncle Walter*; Lens. Bud very long, pointed; flowers blood-red, dbl. (28-35 petals), globular, large (3½-4 in.); foliage dark; vigorous, bushy growth.

Adair Roche HT, *pb*, 1968, *Paddy McGredy × Femina seedling*; McGredy, S., IV; McGredy. Flowers deep pink, reverse silver, dbl. (30 petals), well-formed, large; slightly fragrant; foliage glossy. GM, Belfast, 1971.

Adam T (OGR), *mp*, 1838, (President); Adam. Flowers rich rosy-salmon, full, globular, very large.

Adam Messerich B (OGR), *mr*, 1920, *Frau Oberhofgärtner Singer × (Louise Odier seedling × Louis Phillippe)*; Lambert, P. Flowers rose-red, semi-dbl., cupped; foliage glossy, light; vigorous, bushy growth; recurrent bloom.

Adam's Smile™ Min, *dp*, 1987, (SAVArend; SAVasmile); *(Rise 'n' Shine × Sheri Anne) × Rainbow's End*; Saville, F. Harmon; Nor'East Miniature Roses, 1991. Flowers deep pink, dbl. (23-27 petals), high-centered, exhibition, medium, borne usually singly and in sprays of 3-5; no fragrance; foliage medium, medium green, semi-glossy; prickles long, thin, pointed slightly downward, gray-red; fruit none; upright, bushy, medium growth.

Added Touch Min, *or*, 1984, (LYOad); *Dandy Lyon × Seedling*; Lyon. Bud small; flowers orange-red, touch of yellow in the center and back of petals, dbl. (20 petals), small; fragrant; foliage small, medium green, semi-glossy; upright, bushy growth.

Adélaide d'Orléans HSem (OGR), *w*, 1826, Jacques. Bud very small, well-formed; flowers pale rose, yellow stamens, semi-dbl., borne in clusters; vigorous (15 ft.) growth.

Adelaide Hoodless S, *dp*, 1975, *Fire King × (J.W. Fargo × Assiniboine)*; Marshall, H.H.; Canadian Ornamental Plant Foundation, 1972. Bud ovoid; flowers light red, semi-dbl., medium; slightly fragrant; foliage glossy; vigorous, bushy growth; repeat bloom.

Adelaide Lee Min, *pb*, 1986, *Gene Boerner × Magic Carrousel*; Stoddard, L. Flowers white with red petal edges, dbl. (25 petals), urn-shaped, 1 in. blooms borne singly; slight fragrance; foliage medium green, matt; few, green, straight prickles; upright growth.

Adélaïde Moullé R, *pb*, 1902, *R. wichuraiana × Souv. de Catherine Guillot*; Barbier. Flowers lilac-pink, center carmine, cluster; midseason bloom.

Adèle HT, *dy*, 1935, *Roselandia × Clarice Goodacre*; Lens. Flowers clear gold, base deeper.

Adèle Courtoise G (OGR), *dp*. Flowers rosy red, very dbl., small.

Adèle Crofton HT, *yb*, 1928, Dickson, A. Flowers yellow overlaid scarlet-orange, dbl.; fragrant.

Adèle Descemet G (OGR), Descemet, prior to 1814.

Adèle Prévost G (OGR), *lp*, Prior to 1848. Flowers blush, center pink, dbl., large; vigorous, upright growth.

Adeline C (OGR), *pb*, 1830, Vibert. Flowers vivid rose, paler toward edge, full; foliage dark; compact, branching growth.

Adeline M (OGR), *dp*, Bud well mossed; flowers lilac-rose, dbl., medium (2 in.); foliage light green; compact, well-branched growth.

Adeline Genée F, *my*, 1967, *Paddy McGredy × Seedling*; Harkness. Bud plump; flowers medium yellow, dbl. (50 petals), large (4 in.) blooms in clusters; slightly fragrant; foliage glossy; low, bushy growth.

A. Denis HT, *my*, 1935, *Gorgeous × Marion Cran*; Böhm. Flowers lemon-yellow, streaked carmine, full, large; very fragrant.

Adieu de Bordier G (OGR), *mr.* Flowers vivid red, very dbl.

Admirable Min, *w*, 1991, (SEArodney); *Seedling × Admiral Rodney*; McCann, Sean; Justice Miniature Roses, 1992. Bud ovoid, sharply pointed sepals; fl. soft pink with darker accent, rev. ivory with pink accent, fades to creamy white with pink at hinge, dbl. (38 self cleaning, rounded petals), no quilling, high-centered, exh., large (6 cms), borne usually singly; long, straight stems; heavy, fruity fragrance; fol. lg., med. green, semi-glossy; upright, tall.

Admiral Rodney HT, *pb*, 1973, Trew, C.; Warley Rose Gardens. Flowers pale rose-pink, reverse deeper, dbl. (45 petals), large (4-4½ in.); very fragrant; foliage large, glossy, dark; vigorous growth.

Admiral Schley HT, *r*, 1901, *Col. Joffé × Général Jacqueminot*; Cook, J. Flowers red.

Admiral Ward HT, *rb*, 1915, *Seedling × Château de Clos Vougeot*; Pernet-Ducher. Flowers crimson-red, shaded fiery red and velvetypurple, dbl., globular, large; fragrant.

Admiration HT, *rb*, 1922, McGredy. Flowers cream, shaded vermilion, dbl., pointed, large; very fragrant; foliage light green; moderately bushy growth.

Admired Miranda® S, *lp*, 1983, (AUSmira); *The Friar × The Friar*; Austin, D., 1982. Flowers light pink, dbl. (40+ petals), opening flat, then reflexing, large; very fragrant; foliage medium, medium green, semi-glossy; upright growth.

Adolf Deegen HT, *pb*, 1935, *Ophelia × Wilhelm Kordes*; Böhm. Flowers rosy pink with fiery streaks, large; fragrant.

Adolf Grille F, *dp*, 1940, *Dance of Joy × (Cathrine Kordes × E.G. Hill)*; Kordes; J&P. Bud pointed, ovoid; flowers scarlet-carmine, dbl. (25 petals), cupped, large (4-5 in.), in clusters; slightly fragrant; foliage leathery, dark, wrinkled; vigorous, bushy, compact growth.

Adolf Horstmann® HT, *yb*, 1971, (Adolph Horstmann); *Colour Wonder × Dr. A.J. Verhage*; Kordes, R.; Kordes. Flowers yellow-orange, dbl., classic HT form, large (5 in.); slightly fragrant; foliage glossy; vigorous, upright growth.

Adolf Kärger HT, *my*, 1918, *Cissie Easlea × Sunburst*; Kordes, H. Flowers golden yellow, fading; slightly fragrant.

Adolf Koschel HT, *ab*, 1918, *Harry Kirk × Louise Catherine Breslau*; Kordes, H. Flowers orange-yellow; fragrant.

Adolph Gude HT, *pb*, 1941, *Red Radiance sport*; Gude. Flowers rose-pink, reverse

darker, dbl. (30 petals), high-centered, large (5½-6 in.); fragrant; very vigorous growth.

Adonis HT, *ly*, 1921, *Sunburst × American Beauty*; Bees. Flowers ivory-yellow, shaded lemon, dbl.; fragrant. NRS Gold Medal, 1920.

Adora Pol, *mp*, 1936, Beckwith. Bud deep flame-pink; Flowers rose-pink, dbl.; very fragrant; vigorous, dwarf growth.

Adorable HT, *lp*, 1930, *Columbia sport*; Eichholz. Flowers flesh-pink.

Adoration HT, *op*, 1940, (Île de France); *(Mme. Joseph Perraud × Seedling) × Seedling*; Gaujard; J&P. Bud long, pointed; flowers bright salmon, dbl. (22 petals), large (5 in.); fragrant; foliage leathery; vigorous, bushy growth.

Adorn Min, *pb*, 1986, *Seedling × Seedling*; McDaniel, E.; McDaniel's Min. Roses. Flowers medium pink blending lighter, reverse medium pink, dbl. (30 petals), urn-shaped, exhibition, medium blooms borne singly; no fragrance; foliage medium, dark, semi-glossy; slender, light prickles; medium, upright, bushy growth.

Adrian Bailey F, *op*, 1972, *Fragrant Cloud × Evelyn Fison*; Bailey. Bud globular; flowers orange-scarlet, dbl. (28 petals), large (3½ in.); foliage glossy; bushy, upright growth.

Adrie Stokman HT, *mp*, 1948, *Raised from Parel van Aalsmeer*; Stokman. Flowers darker pink than Briarcliff.

Adrienne Leal F, *dp*, 1965, *Roundelay sport*; Leal. Bud ovoid; flowers deep pink to soft mauve, full, medium; slightly fragrant; foliage dark, leathery; vigorous, upright.

Adrienne Martin HT, *dp*, 1930, *Recuerdo de Angel Peluffo × The Queen Alexandra Rose*; Buatois. Flowers carmine, base yellow, very dbl., cupped; fragrant; foliage glossy, dark; vigorous, bushy, low growth.

Advance HT, *rb*, 1940, *Comtesse Vandal × Mrs. Sam McGredy*; LeGrice; C-P. Flowers orange-flame, shaded cerise, reverse cerise, dbl., large; long, strong stem; slightly fragrant; foliage leathery, dark; vigorous, bushy growth.

Advocate HT, *mr*, 1928, Dickson, A. Flowers crimson-scarlet, dbl.; fragrant.

A. Dvorak HT, *op*, 1933, *Mme. Butterfly × Gorgeous*; Böhm. Flowers light pinkish orange, open, large; foliage glossy, dark; bushy growth.

Aëlita S, *w*, 1952, *New Dawn seedling*; Shtanko, E.E. Flowers white tinted green, dbl. (50 petals), large; very fragrant; foliage glossy; vigorous growth.

Aenne Burda HT, *mr*, 1973, Kordes. Flowers blood-red, dbl., high-centered, large; slightly fragrant; foliage large, glossy; vigorous, upright, bushy growth.

Aenne Kreis HT, *ab*, 1930, *Wilhelm Kordes sport*.; Kreis. Flowers orange-yellow, reverse lighter, dbl., well formed; vigorous, branching growth.

Aflame F, *op*, 1954, *(Poulsen's Pink × Ellinor LeGrice) × Mrs. Pierre S. duPont*; LeGrice. Flowers orange-strawberry, semi-dbl., large (4 in.) blooms in clusters; very fragrant; foliage dark, glossy; vigorous, low, spreading growth.

A Fleurs Gigantesques G (OGR), *mp*, 1813, Raised at Sèvres. Flowers rich deep pink, very dbl., large; very fragrant; bushy. The rose imported by Bobbink & Atkins and distributed as 'Marie Louise' appears to be this variety.

Africa Star HT, *m*, 1965, West; Harkness. Flowers mauve, dbl. (65 petals), large (3½-4 in.); foliage coppery; bushy growth.

Africa Star HT, *m*, 1965, West; Harkness. Flowers mauve, dbl. (65 petals), large (3½-4 in.); foliage coppery; bushy growth.

African Sunset HT, *ab*, 1966, *Sutter's Gold × Chantré*; Herholdt, J.A. Flowers apricot-orange, dbl., pointed, large (4½ in.); fragrant; free growth.

After Midnight™ Min, *dr*, 1990, (KINnight); *(B.C. × Scamp) × Black Jade*; King, Gene, 1986; AGM Miniature Roses, 1991. Bud ovoid; flowers dark red, tips show darker edge, outer petals darker, dbl. (28 petals), high-centered, exhibition, medium, borne singly; no fragrance; foliage medium, medium green, semi-glossy; medium, upright growth.

Afterglow HT, *ab*, 1930, *Seedling × Souv. de Claudius Pernet*; Hill, J.H., Co. Flowers apricot-yellow, dbl.; very fragrant. A florists' variety, not distributed for outdoor use.

Afterglow HT, *ob*, 1938, (Sam Buff); *Mrs. Sam McGredy sport*; LeGrice. Bud long, pointed, orange; flowers golden yellow, reverse golden orange, dbl., large, long stem; slightly fragrant; foliage bluish green, glossy; vigorous, bushy growth.

Afternoon Delight Min, *mp*, 1991, (JOLaft); *Party Girl × Fashion Flame*, Jolly, Marie; Rosehill Farm, 1992-93. Flowers medium pink, moderately full (21 petals), medium (4-7 cms) blooms borne mostly singly and in small clusters; slight fragrance; foliage medium, medium green, matt; few prickles; tall (45 cms), upright, spreading, vigorous growth.

Agar G (OGR), *pb*, 1843, Raised at Angers. Flowers dark rose, spotted, dbl., medium.

A. G. A. Rappard HT, *op*, 1934, (A.G.A. Ridder van Rappard); Buisman. Flowers salmon, verging on neyron pink, dbl., well

shaped; slightly fragrant; foliage glossy, bright green; vigorous, bushy growth.

Agate Pourpre HT, *mr*, 1965, *Impeccable × Rome Glory*; Delbard-Chabert; Cuthbert. Flowers currant-red, dbl., cupped, large (5-6 in.); foliage dark, serrated; intermittent bloom.

Agatha G (OGR), *lp*, 1818, (R. gallica agatha (Thory) Loiseleur). Flowers light pink, dbl., inner petals concaved.

Agatha Christie F, *dp*, 1966, Buisman. Bud ovoid; flowers pink-red, dbl., medium blooms in clusters; foliage dark; compact growth.

Agathe Incarnata G (OGR), *mp*, Cultivated before 1815. Flowers pink, quartered; habit intermediate between the Gallicas and the Damasks.

Agathe Roses G (OGR), *lp*, (R. gallica agatha); Origin unknown. Flowers pale colors, very full, compact, outer petals spreading, inner ones concaved; foliage curled.

Age Tendre HT, *dp*, 1966, *Queen Elizabeth × Spartan*; Croix, P. Bud long, pointed; flowers rose, dbl., high-centered, large; strong stem; vigorous growth.

Agénay® HT, *op*, 1966, (DELcus); *Chic Parisien × (Michèle Meilland × Mme. Joseph Perraud)*; Delbard-Chabert. Bud long, pointed; flowers salmon-pink, dbl., large; fragrant; foliage glossy, leathery; vigorous, bushy growth.

Agénor G (OGR), *m*, 1832, Vibert or Robert. Flowers reddish purple, full, medium.

A. G. Furness HT, *mr*, 1941, *Sensation seedling*; Clark, A. Flowers rich red; semi-climber growth.

Aglaia HMult (OGR), *ly*, 1896, (Yellow Rambler); *R. multiflora × Rêve d'Or*; Schmitt; Lambert, P. Flowers straw-yellow to white, dbl., in clusters; fragrant; foliage glossy; vigorous.

Agnes HRg (S), *ly*, 1900, *R. rugosa × R. foetida persiana*; Saunder, 1900; Central Exp. Farm, 1922. Flowers pale amber, center deeper, dbl.; fragrant; foliage light green, glossy, rugose; vigorous (6ft.), bushy growth; non-recurrent bloom; (21).

Agnes HRg (S), *my*, 1900, *R. rugosa × R. foetida persiana*; Saunders; Central Exp. Farm, 1922. Flowers pale amber, center deeper, dbl., open, short stem; fragrant; foliage light, glossy, wrinkled; vigorous (6 ft.), bushy; profuse, non-recurrent bloom; very hardy; (21).

Agnès Ageron HT, *mr*, 1958, *Mme. Méha Sabatier × Léonce Colombier*; Arles; Roses-France. Flowers cerise-red, reverse tinted currant-red, well formed; very vigorous.

Agnes Barclay HT, *yb*, 1927, Clark, A.; NRS Victoria. Flowers yellow and reddish salmon; fragrant.

Agnes De Puy HT, *dp*, 1930, *Lady Battersea × (Honeymoon × Mme. Butterfly)*; De Puy. Flowers geranium-red veined gold, dbl. (22 petals), high-centered, large blooms on long stem; fragrant; very vigorous; hardy.

Agnes Emily Carman HRg (S), *mr*, 1898, *R. rugosa × R. × harisonii*; Carman. Flowers bright crimson, dbl., large; foliage large, rugose; vigorous (5 ft.) growth; some repeat bloom.

Agnes Glover HT, *dr*, 1924, *Admiral Ward × George Dickson*; Chaplin Bros. Flowers deep velvety crimson; fragrant.

Agnes Kruse F, 1936, *Mme. Edouard Herriot × Eblouissant*; Tantau. Flowers velvety red, fiery, large; vigorous.

Agnes Laura Blackburn F, *yb*, 1989, *City of Portsmouth × Seedling*; Cants of Colchester, Ltd. Bud pointed; flowers bicolor yellow, single (5 petals), medium, borne in sprays.

Agnes Lucké HT, *pb*, 1959, *Happiness × Peace, Climbing*; Armbrust; Langbecker. Bud long, pointed; flowers cerise-pink, reverse whitish pink, dbl. (50 petals), high-centered, large to medium size; fragrant; foliage leathery; vigorous, upright growth.

Agnes Marguerite HT, *or*, 1953, Bide. Flowers reddish orange, shaded apricot; foliage glossy.

Agnes Roggen HT, *pb*, 1926, Leenders, M. Flowers pale pink, reverse carmine, dbl.; fragrant.

Agnes Winchel HT, *pb*, 1989, *Dorothy Anne × Seedling*; Winchel, Joseph F.; Coiner Nursery, 1990. Bud pointed; flowers light pink with deep pink border, dbl. (28 petals), high-centered, exhibition, medium, borne singly; slight, fruity fragrance; foliage medium, dark green, semi-glossy; prickles slightly hooked, medium, green; fruit globular, medium, orange; upright, medium growth.

Agreement F, *pb*, 1971, *Unknown*; LeGrice. Flowers deep glowing pink, base golden, dbl. (30 petals), HT form, large (3 in.); foliage glossy, bright green; tall, very free growth.

Ahlin F, *ob*, 1979, *Seedling × Little Darling*; Fong. Bud ovoid; flowers orange, 15 petals, high-centered, borne 4-6 per cluster; slight fragrance; foliage large, leathery; hooked prickles; upright growth.

Ahoi F, *or*, 1964, Tantau, Math. Bud urn shaped; flowers bright orange-red, dbl., blooms in clusters; low, bushy growth.

Aïcha HSpn (OGR), *dy*, 1966, *Souv. de Jacques Verschuren × Guldtop*; Petersen. Bud long, pointed; flowers deep yellow, semi-dbl., large; very fragrant; foliage light green; vigorous, bushy growth.

Aïda HT, *mr*, 1956, *Crimson Glory × Signora*; Mansuino, A.; J&P. Bud urn shaped; flowers clear rose-red, dbl. (25 petals), cupped, large (5 in.); very fragrant; foliage leathery; vigorous, upright, symmetrical growth.

Aiglon HT, *rb*, 1961, *Viola × Opera seedling*; Gaujard. Bud long, pointed; flowers coppery red, reverse yellow, dbl, (38 petals), large; fragrant; foliage glossy, light green; vigorous, upright growth.

Aileen F, *ab*, 1975, *Elizabeth of Glamis sport*; Wood. Flowers light apricot, peach blended, full, large (3½ in.); fragrant; upright, free growth.

Aimable Amie G (OGR), *dp*, Flowers dark pink, dbl., medium.

Aimée Vibert N (OGR), *w*, 1828, (Bouquet de la Mariée; Nivea); *Champneys' Pink Cluster × R. sempervirens hybrid*; Vibert. Flowers pure white, dbl., medium blooms in small clusters; vigorous growth; recurrent bloom.

Ain't Misbehavin' Min, *dr*, 1990, (SEAbla); *Oonagh × (Pot Black × Black Jade)*; McCann, Sean, 1991. Flowers dark red, single (5 petals); slight fragrance; foliage small, green, semi-glossy; bushy growth.

Air France HT, *dr*, 1958, *Seedling × Poinsettia*; Asseretto, A.; Pin-Blanchon. Flowers red to cherry-red, dbl., cupped, medium; fragrant; Vigorous bushy. RULED EXTINCT 9/82 ARM.

Air France Min, *yb*, 1982, (MEIfinaro; Rosy Meillandina; American Independence; Air France Meillandina); *Minijet × (Darling Flame × Perle de Montserrat)*; Meilland, M.L., 1983. Flowers yellow, pink petal edges, dbl. (40+ petals), small; no fragrance; foliage small, dark, matt; bushy.

Airborne F, *dp*, 1949, *Donald Prior × Rosamunde*; Leenders, M. Flowers deep pink, dbl., large; fragrant; vigorous growth.

Aisling F, *w*, 1966, *Queen Elizabeth × Allgold*; Slattery. Flowers ivory-cream, dbl., large (4 in.); slightly fragrant; foliage small, glossy; very vigorous growth.

Ajanta HT, *m*, 1978, *Lady X seedling × Memoriam*; Thakur; Doon Valley Roses. Bud tapered; flowers mauve, dbl. (35-40 petals), high-centered, very large (5-5½ in.); fragrant (spicy); foliage large, glossy; bushy growth.

Akebono HT, *yb*, 1964, *Ethel Sanday × Narzisse*; Kawai. Flowers light yellow flushed carmine, dbl. (56 petals), high pointed, large; foliage dark, glossy; vigorous, upright.

Akemi F, *or*, 1977, *(Sarabande × Hawaii) × (Sarabande × Ruby Lips)*; Keisei Rose Nursery. Bud ovoid; flowers orange-red, dbl. (33 petals), cupped, medium (2-2½ in.); slightly fragrant; foliage dark; vigorous, upright growth.

Akito F, *w*, 1974, (TANito); *Zorina × Nordia*; Tantau. Bud ovoid; flowers white, dbl., medium blooms in clusters; slightly fragrant; foliage medium, medium green; upright, bushy.

Alabama HT, *pb*, 1976, *Mexicana × Tiffany*; Weeks, 1977. Bud long, pointed; flowers deep pink, reverse near white, dbl. (25 petals), high-centered to cupped, large (3½-4 in.); fragrant (tea); foliage dark, leathery; upright growth.

Alabaster HT, *w*, 1961, *Blanche Mallerin × McGredy's Ivory*; Wyant. Flowers white, dbl. (70-80 petals), high-centered, large (5 in.); fragrant; moderate, upright growth.

Aladdin F, *mr*, 1965, *Miracle × Edith Piaf*; Verbeek. Bud ovoid; flowers red, very dbl., medium blooms in clusters; foliage dark; many prickles.

Alain F, *mr*, 1948, *(Guineé × Skyrocket) × Orange Triumph*; Meilland, F.; C-P. Bud ovoid; flowers bright carmine-red, semi-dbl., medium blooms in clusters; slightly fragrant; foliage glossy, dark; upright, bushy growth; (28). GM, Geneva, 1948.

Alain Blanchard G (OGR), *m*, 1839, *Probably R. centifolia × R. gallica*; Vibert. Flowers purplish-crimson, color becoming mottled giving a spotted look, golden stamens, semi-dbl., cupped, large; fragrant; foliage medium green; vigorous, medium growth.

Alain, Climbing Cl F, *mr*, 1957, (Grimpant Alain); Delforge.

Alain, Climbing Cl F, *mr*, 1957, Roth.

Alamein F, *mr*, 1963, *Spartan × Queen Elizabeth*; McGredy, S. IV; McGredy. Flowers scarlet, semi-dbl. (10 petals), flat, large (3 in.) blooms in clusters; slightly fragrant; foliage dark; vigorous, bushy growth.

Alanna Holloway HT, *dr*, 1974, *Uncle Walter* sport; Holloway. Flowers dark red, ovoid; slightly fragrant; foliage glossy, leathery; very vigorous.

Alaska HT, *w*, 1949, *Peace × Blanche Mallerin*; Meilland, F. Flowers ivory-white, dbl. (50 petals), well-formed, large; fragrant; vigorous, upright growth.

Alaska Centennial Gr, *dr*, 1967, *Siren × Avon*; Morey; Country Garden Nursery. Bud long, pointed; flowers dark blood-red-scarlet, dbl., high-centered, large (3½-5 in.); fragrant; foliage dark, leathery, glossy; vigorous, upright growth.

Alba Maxima A (OGR), *w*, (R. alba maxima; Maxima; Great Double White; The Jacobite Rose); Prior to 1867. Flowers similar to Maiden's Blush, but center creamy; height 6-8 ft. This has sported to Alba Semi-plena.

Alba Meidiland™ S, *w*, 1987, (MEIflopan; Alba Meillandécor; Meidiland Alba); *R. sempervirens × Marthe Carron*; Meilland, Mrs. Marie-Louise, 1985. Flowers white, dbl. (over 40 petals), medium; no fragrance; foliage medium, medium green, glossy; spreading growth; can be propagated on own roots.

Alba Meillandina® Min, *w*, 1988, (MEInabron); *MEIdonq × (Darling × Jack Frost)*; Meilland, M.L.; SNC Meilland & Cie, 1987. Flowers white, very dbl. (over 40 petals), medium; no fragrance; foliage small, medium green, semi-glossy; bushy growth.

Alba Odorata HBc (OGR), *w*, 1834, (R. bracteata alba odorata, R. microphylla alba odorata); *Probably a hybrid of R. bracteata and a Tea rose*; Mariani. Flowers white, anthers yellow, large; fragrant; foliage 5-7 oval leaflets; wood greenish-purple; straight prickles.

Alba Semi-plena A (OGR), *w*, (R. alba semi-plena); Prior to 1867; A very old form that has been observed as a sport from Alba Maxima. Flowers white, golden stamens, semi-dbl. (8-12 petals); large crop of red hips in fall.

Alba Suaveolens A (OGR), *w*, (R. alba suaveolens Dieck); Cultivated prior to 1750. Flowers white, semi-dbl., 2 in. diam.; source of attar of roses.

Albast HT, *op*, 1928, *Morgenglans × Mrs. Wemyss Quin*; Van Rossem. Bud ovoid; flowers salmon-pink, dbl., open, large; slightly fragrant; foliage bronze, glossy; vigorous growth.

Albéric Barbier R, *ly*, 1900, *R. wichuraiana × Shirley Hibberd*; Barbier. Bud small, yellow; flowers creamy white, center yellow, dbl., borne in clusters; fragrant; foliage glossy, dark; vigorous growth; non-recurrent bloom. Do not confuse with Mme. Albert Barbier. (14).

Albert F, *op*, 1962, Jones; Hennessey. Flowers orange salmon, dbl. (50 petals), high-centered, medium blooms in clusters; foliage glossy, bronze; vigorous, bushy, compact growth.

Albert Edwards S, *ly*, 1961, *R. spinosissima altaica × R. hugonis*; Hillier. Flowers creamy yellow, single (5 petals), medium (1½-2 in.); fragrant; vigorous growth.

Albert Gilles HT, *op*, 1943, *Julien Potin × Mme. Joseph Perraud*; Mallerin; A. Meilland. Flowers pink tinted coral.

Albert Maumené HHug (S), *or*, 1934, *Mme. Edouard Herriot × R. hugonis*; Sauvageot. Bud large, pointed, ovoid, copper-red; flowers carroty red shaded copper, semi-dbl., cupped, globular; foliage glossy, dark; very vigorous, bushy, open habit; profuse, recurrent bloom.

Albert Payé HP (OGR), *lp*, 1873, Touvais. Flowers flesh-pink, large; vigorous.

Albert Pike HT, *dp*, 1926, *Columbia sport*; Vestal. Flowers glowing cerise, flushed peach at times.

Alberta Hunter F, *ly*, 1985, *Eleanor Perenyi × Lillian Gish*; French, R. Flowers light yellow, red stamens, dbl. (25 petals), cupped, large blooms borne singly; fragrant; foliage medium, dark, semi-glossy; small, straight, red prickles; fruit small, dull orange, globular; medium, upright, bushy growth.

Albertan S, *mp*, 1962, *Athabasca seedling*; Erskine. Flowers bright pink, semi-dbl. (15-18 petals); (14).

Albertine LCl, *op*, 1921, *R. wichuraiana × Mrs. Arthur Robert Waddell*; Barbier. Bud ovoid; flowers light salmon pink, dbl., cupped, large blooms in clusters; fragrant; vigorous growth; non-recurrent bloom.

Albion HT, *mp*, 1969, *Frileuse × Seedling*; Poulsen, N.D.; Vilmorin-Andrieux. Flowers medium pink, dbl., urn-shaped, large, borne singly; slight fragrance; foliage semi-glossy; bushy.

Albion S, *w*, *R. laxa hybrid*; Skinner. Bud cream; flowers white, dbl.; foliage firm, dark; leaflets small; height 4 ft.; recurrent bloom; hardy.

Alcazar F, *or*, 1961, *Jolie Princesse × (Opera × Miss France)*; Gaujard. Bud pointed; flowers coppery red, semi-dbl. (18 petals), large (3 in.); slightly fragrant; foliage glossy, bronze; bushy growth.

Alchymist S, *ab*, 1956, (Alchemist; Alchymiste); *Golden Glow × R. eglanteria hybrid*; Kordes. Bud ovoid; flowers yellow shaded orange, pink and red, very dbl., large; fragrant; foliage glossy, bronze; vigorous, upright (6 ft.) growth; heavy, non-recurrent bloom.

Alcine G (OGR), *dp*, Flowers deep rosy pink, spotted white, edged lilac-blush, dbl., cupped, large; vigorous, upright growth.

Alec Rose F, *or*, 1969, *Hassan × John Church*; McGredy, S., IV; McGredy. Flowers scarlet, well-formed, blooms in trusses; free growth.

Alec's Red® HT, *mr*, 1973, (COred); *Fragrant Cloud × Dame de Coeur*; Cocker, 1970. Flowers medium red, dbl. (45 petals), large (6 in.); fragrant; foliage matt, green; vigorous, upright growth. Edland Fragrance Medal, 1969; GM, RNRS, 1970; RNRS PIT, 1970; ADR, 1973

Alec's Red, Climbing® Cl HT, *mr*, 1975, *Alec's Red sport*; Harkness.

Alegrias F, *rb*, 1978, *Seedling × Unnamed Charleston seedling*; Barni-Pistoia, Rose. Bud globular; flowers medium yellow, reverse orange-red, 23 petals, shallow-cupped blooms borne 3-6 per cluster; no fragrance; foliage medium, glossy; straight, reddish-green prickles; upright, bushy growth.

Alena Gr, *ob*, 1970, *Seedling × Tropicana*; Raffel; Port Stockton Nursery. Flowers orange, dbl., cupped, large; fragrant; foliage large, glossy, dark; vigorous, upright, bushy growth.

Alexander® HT, *or*, 1972, (HARlex); (Alexandra); *Tropicana × (Ann Elizabeth × Allgold)*; Harkness. Bud pointed; flowers bright vermilion-red, dbl. (25 petals), high-centered, large (5 in.); slightly fragrant; foliage glossy; tall, vigorous growth. GM, Hambourg, 1973, Belfast, 1974; ADR, 1974; RNRS, James Mason Medal, 1987.

Alexander Emslie HT, *dr*, 1918, Dickson, A. Flowers deep crimson, base slightly white; fragrant.

Alexander Hill Gray T (OGR), *dy*, 1911, (Yellow Maman Cochet; Yellow Cochet); Dickson, A. Flowers deep lemon-yellow, aging deeper, large; very fragrant; vigorous growth.

Alexander Marghiloman HT, *w*, 1928, *Harry Kirk seedling*; Mühle. Flowers cream-white, center salmon.

Alexander Milne Min, *lp*, 1987, (LAVmilne); *Corn Silk × Ice Princess*; Laver, Keith G.; Springwood Roses. Flowers light pink, reverse cream, dbl. (35 petals), high-centered, small, borne singly; no fragrance; foliage small, medium green, semi-glossy; straight, light brown prickles; fruit rounded, orange; bushy, low growth.

Alexander von Humboldt K (S), *mr*, 1960, *R. kordesii × Cleopatra*; Kordes, R.; Kordes. Flowers scarlet, borne in large clusters; foliage glossy; vigorous (9-12 ft.) growth.

Alexandra® T (OGR), *yb*, 1900, Paul, W. Flowers buff and yellow.

Alexandre Dumas D (OGR), *lp*, 1969, *Ma Perkins × R. damascena versicolor*; Fankhauser. Flowers light pink, very dbl., cupped, medium blooms in clusters; very fragrant (damask); foliage small, light green, glossy, leathery; vigorous, upright (6-8 ft.) growth; abundant, non-recurrent bloom.

Alexandre Girault LCl, *pb*, 1909, *R. wichuraiana × Papa Gontier*; Barbier. Flowers carmine-red, base salmon, dbl., large; fragrant; vigorous growth; non-recurrent bloom.

Alexandre Laquement G (OGR), *m*, (Alexander Laquemont); Prior to 1906. Flowers violet spotted with red.

Alexandria Rose S, *rb*, 1988, (WILalex; City of Alexandria; The Alexandria Rose) *(Queen Elizabeth × Kordes' Perfecta) × Mount Shasta*; Williams, J. Benjamin. Flowers ivory to white with light red washing on petal edge, deeper yellow at base and heart, dbl. (26-40 petals), large; foliage large, dark green, glossy, disease resistant; upright, bushy, vigorous, strong, hardy growth.

Alexandrine Chapuis HT, *my*, 1935, *Feu Joseph Looymans × Seedling*; Vially. Bud long, pointed, yellow, shaded carmine; flowers yellow, full, well formed, large; foliage bright green.

Alexia F, *pb*, 1984, (CANlot); *Jubilant × Seedling*; Cants of Colchester. Flowers cream blended pink, dbl. (20 petals), medium; fragrant; foliage medium, medium green, semi-glossy; upright growth.

Alexia Wilson F, *ob*, 1972, *Elizabeth of Glamis sport*; Horner. Flowers cream veined orange.

Alezane HT, *ab*, 1935, *Angèle Pernet × Comtesse de Castilleja*; Pahissa; J&P. Bud urn shaped, reddish brown; flowers deep apricot, dbl., cupped, large; fragrant (fruity); foliage glossy, bronze, dark; very vigorous growth.

Alfi™ Min, *dp*, 1985, (POUlfi; Elfin; Alfie); *Mini-Poul × Harriet Poulsen*; Olesen, M.&P.; Poulsen's, 1981. Flowers deep pink, semi-dbl. (10-15 petals), small blooms in large trusses; no fragrance; foliage small, light green, glossy; compact growth.

Alfie Luv Min, *op*, 1991, (TALalf); *Azure Sea × Seedling*; Taylor, Pete & Kay; Taylor's Roses, 1992. Flowers orange-pink with lavender hue, reverse same, yellow base, full (15-25 petals), medium (4-7 cms), blooms borne mostly singly; slight fragrance; foliage medium, medium green, semi-glossy; some prickles; upright, medium (60 cms) growth.

Alfred A. Buckwell HT, *mr*, 1952, *Hector Deane × Betty Uprichard*; Buckwell. Flowers red, dbl. (30 petals), high-centered, medium (3 in.); very fragrant; foliage dark, leathery; vigorous growth.

Alfred Colomb HP (OGR), *dp*, 1865, *Général Jacqueminot × Seedling*; Lacharme. Flowers strawberry-red, reflexes crimson-carmine, full (45 petals), globular, high-centered, large; very fragrant; growth dense; recurrent bloom.

Alfred de Dalmas M (OGR), *lp*, 1855, (Mousseline); Laffay. Buds rose-colored; flowers light pink with blush edges, of poor quality, dbl., small, in corymbs; fragrant; very prickly; vigorous, straggling growth; some

recurrent bloom. Name used erroneously as a synonym for 'Mousseline', which see.

Alfred de Rougemont HP (OGR), *dr*, 1863, *Général Jacqueminot seedling*; Lacharme. Flowers crimson-magenta, full, well formed, very large; vigorous, upright growth.

Alfred K. Williams HP (OGR), *mr*, 1877, *Général Jacqueminot sport*; Schwartz, J. Flowers carmine-red, changing to magenta.

Alfred Newton HT, *yb*, 1959, *Moonbeam × Karl Herbst*; Kemp, M.L. Flowers pale yellow edged crimson, dbl. (35-40 petals), high-centered, large (5 in.); very fragrant; foliage dark; vigorous growth.

Alfred Pétot HT, *dr*, 1935, *Jeanne Excoffier × Yves Druhen*; Buatois. Bud elongated; flowers crimson, full, well formed, large blooms on strong stems; very fragrant; foliage dark; very vigorous.

Alfred W. Mellersh HT, *op*, 1918, Paul, W. Flowers salmon-yellow, shaded rose, center amber.

Alfredo Moreira da Silva HT, *yb*, 1946, *Dr. Kirk × Peace*; Mallerin; A. Meilland. Bud long, pointed; flowers golden yellow tinted coral, semi-dbl., large; foliage dark; very vigorous, upright growth.

Alger HT, *op*, 1943, Gaujard. Bud pointed; flowers clear pink, reverse salmon-pink, dbl., very large; foliage leathery; vigorous growth.

Algonquin S, *pb*, 1928, *R. rubrifolia × R. rugosa hybrid seedling*; Central Exp. Farm. Flowers purplish rose, center white, single, flat, large; foliage dull, yellow-green; fruit large, red, bottle shaped; very vigorous (10 ft.) growth; non-recurrent bloom; hardy.

Ali-Baba F, *or*, 1963, *(Corail × Baccará) × Seedling*; Croix, P. Flowers orange-red, semi-dbl. (15-20 petals), large blooms in clusters.

Alibi F, *w*, 1960, *Kaiserin Auguste Viktoria × Pink Fragrance*; deRuiter. Flowers white, dbl. (30 petals), well formed, large (3-4 in.); vigorous growth.

Alice Pol, 1925, *Echo × Orléans Rose*; Spek. Flowers pink, fringed, borne in large clusters. RULED EXTINCT 11/80 ARM.

Alice 1935, *R. macounii hybrid*; Wright, P. H. Similar to Mary L. Evans but more nearly dbl. and softer pink. RULED EXTINCT 11/80 ARM.

Alice HT, *lp*, 1978, *Royal Highness × Christian Dior*; Allender, R.W. Bud long; flowers light pink, darker center, dbl. (45 petals), high-centered, borne singly; no fragrance; foliage large; long, red prickles; spreading (to about 4 ft.) growth; shy bloomer.

Alice Aldrich HRg (S), *lp*, 1901, *R. rugosa × Caroline de Sansal*; Lovett, J.T. Conard &

Jones. Flowers clear, bright pink, dbl., large; repeat bloom.

Alice Amos F, *pb*, 1922, *Tip-Top × Seedling*; Spek; Prior. Bud long, pointed; flowers cerise, white eye, single, blooms in clusters on strong stem; very vigorous growth.

Alice Faye Min, *rb*, 1992, (SEAodd); *Seedling × Seedling*; McCann, Sean; Justice Miniature Roses, 1992. Flowers a full circle of red with distinct yelloweye from the bottom view, yellow reverse ages to creamy yellow, dbl. (22-24 petals), urn-shaped, loose, large (6 cms) blooms borne singly; no fragrance; foliage large, medium green, semi-glossy; upright, tall growth.

Alice Gray Ayr (OGR), *w*, *R. arvensis hybrid*; Origin unknown; P.T., 1848. Flowers creamy white, semi-dbl; moderately vigorous growth.

Alice Harding HT, *my*, 1937, *Souv. de Claudius Pernet × Mrs. Pierre S. duPont*; Mallerin; J&P. Bud ovoid; flowers golden yellow, dbl., large; fragrant; foliage glossy, dark; vigorous growth.

Alice Kaempff HT, *pb*, 1921, *Gen. MacArthur × Radiance*; Felberg-Leclerc. Flowers silvery rose-pink, center coppery yellow, dbl.; fragrant.

Alice King Cl F, *mr*, 1988, *Dublin Bay × Seedling*; Harrison, G. Flowers medium, luminous red, aging lighter, verydbl. (40-50 petals), small, borne in sprays of 1-3; no fragrance; foliage light green, glossy; prickles small, medium red; vigorous, slight perpetual growth.

Alice Lee Min, *pb*, 1991, (TALali); *Azure Sea × Seedling*; Taylor, Pete & Kay, 1986; Taylor's Roses, 1990. Bud pointed; flowers pink with color getting lighter towards edge of petals giving a lavender cast, whitish-pink reverse, aging darker, dbl. (15-18 petals), high-centered, exhibition, medium, borne singly; slight fragrance; foliage medium, medium green, semi-glossy; upright, bushy, medium growth.

Alice Leroi M (OGR), *pb*, 1842, Vibert. Flowers lilac-blush shaded rose, center deep rose, well-mossed, dbl., very large; vigorous growth.

Alice Manley HT, *my*, 1958, *Seedling × Golden Rapture*; Hill, J.H., Co. Bud long, pointed; flowers mimosa-yellow, dbl. (45-50 petals), high-centered, large (3½-4 in.); slightly fragrant; foliage leathery; vigorous, upright, bushy growth. A florists' variety, not distributed for outdoor use.

Alice Marion Whyte HT, *lp*, 1932, Evans. Flowers soft pink, fading pure white; fragrant.

Alice Pat F, *rb*, 1981, *Seedling × Seedling*; Jerabek. Bud ovoid; flowers red shading to white, reverse white shaded pink, dbl. (38 petals), opening flat, borne 1-6 per cluster; light fragrance; foliage dark, glossy; slightly hooked, reddish-tan prickles; upright, short growth. ARC TG (B), 1983.

Alice Stern HT, *w*, 1926, *Grange Colombe × Sunburst*; Gillot, F. Bud long, pointed; flowers white, center cream, sometimes salmon, dbl. (30-40 petals), large; fragrant; foliage dark, bronze; vigorous, bushy growth.

Alice Vena G (OGR), *m*, *Thought to have some R. gallica and R. centifolia in its parentage*; Original name and date unknown. Flowers plum-purple, large blooms in clusters.

Alice Wieman Pol, *dp*, 1965, *Seedling × Rita Sammons*; Bodley. Flowers pink, dbl., open, small; fragrant; growth moderate, bushy; continuous bloom.

Alicia HT, *pb*, 1972, *Golden Scepter × Ena Harkness*; Lees. Flowers rose-pink, edged cream, dbl. (36 petals), full, large (3½ in.); fragrant; foliage dark; vigorous growth.

Alida HT, *mr*, 1938, *Charles P. Kilham × E.G. Hill*; Lens. Bud long, pointed; flowers medium red, very full, well formed; foliage bright; vigorous, bushy growth.

Alida Lovett LCl, *lp*, 1905, *Souv. du Prés. Carnot × R. wichuraiana*; Van Fleet, 1905; J.T. Lovett. Bud long, pointed; flowers shell-pink, base shaded sulphur, dbl., large blooms in clusters; slightly fragrant; foliage glossy; vigorous, climbing growth; seasonal bloom.

Aliette HT, 1958, *Pres. Herbert Hoover × Signora*; Arles; Roses-France. Flowers salmon-pink tinted orange, well formed; slightly fragrant; vigorous, bushy growth.

Alika G (OGR), *mr*, 1906, (Gallica Grandiflora; *R. gallica grandiflora*); Hansen, N.E. Brought from Russia in 1906; In commerce, 1930. Flowers brilliant red with no purple, many stamens, petalage variable — single to dbl., large; fragrant; vigorous growth.

Aline HT, *or*, 1950, *Picture sport*; Astolat Nursery. Flowers peach, dbl. (22 petals), compact, large (4 in.); fragrant; foliage dark; vigorous growth.

Alison Wheatcroft F, *ab*, 1959, *Circus sport*; Wheatcroft Bros. Flowers apricot flushed crimson.

Alistair Sheridan HT, *ob*, 1992, (PEArich); *F seedling (HO79) × HT seedling (315)*; Pearce, C., 1986; The Limes New Roses, 1991. Flowers orange, reverse orange, aging pinky orange, urn-shaped, dbl., medium (12 cms) blooms borne usually singly; slight fragrance; foliage large, medium green, glossy; upright growth.

Alister Stella Gray N (OGR), *ly*, 1894, (Golden Rambler); Gray, A.H. Bud long, pointed; flowers pale yellow, center orange, fading to white, full blooms in clusters; fragrant; vigorous climbing growth; recurrent bloom; (14).

All That Jazz™ S, *op*, 1991, (TWOadvance); *Gitte × Seedling*; Twomey, Jerry, 1983; DeVor Nurseries, 1991. Bud pointed; flowers coral salmon blend, semi-dbl. (12-13 petals), cupped, loose, large, borne in sprays of 3-5; moderate, damask fragrance; foliage medium, dark green, glossy; upright, bushy, medium growth. AARS, 1992.

Allamand-Ho S, *pb*, 1984, *(Hawkeye Belle × Prairie Star) × Iobelle*; Buck; Iowa State University. Bud ovoid; flowers pink and yellow blend, petals edged ruby red, color intensifying and spreading with age, dbl. (38 petals), shallow-cupped, large blooms in clusters of 1-6; sweet fragrance; foliage dark, leathery, semi-glossy; awl-like, red-brown prickles; erect, bushy growth; repeat bloom; hardy.

Allard Sp (OGR), *dy*, (R. xanthina Allard); *R. xanthina form or hybrid*; Prior to 1936. Flowers chrome-yellow, dbl.

Allégresse HT, *mr*, 1952, *Fantaisie × Sensation*; Robichon; Vilmorin-Andrieux. Flowers red, becoming lighter, very dbl., well formed on strong stem; vigorous, upright growth.

Allegretto HT, *or*, 1975, *Fragrant Cloud × Sutter's Gold*; Huber. Bud long, pointed; flowers orange-red, semi-dbl. (14-17 petals), shallow, large (4 in.); slightly fragrant; foliage leathery; upright growth.

Allegro® HT, *or*, 1962, (MEIarlo); *(Happiness × Independence) × Soraya*; Meilland, A.; URS, 1962 & C-P, 1964. Flowers orange-red, dbl. (30 petals), high-centered to cupped, large (3½-4½ in.); slightly fragrant; foliage leathery, glossy; vigorous, bushy growth. GM, Rome & The Hague, 1962.

Allelulia® HT, *rb*, 1982, (DELatur; Hallelujah); *((Impeccable × Papa Meilland) × (Gloire de Rome × Impeccable)) × Corrida*; Delbard, G., 1980. Flowers velvety deep red, silver reverse, dbl. (30 petals), large blooms of heavy substance; foliage deep green, glossy.

Allen Chandler Cl HT, mr, 1923, *Hugh Dickson × Seedling*; Chandler; Prince. Bud long, pointed; flowers brilliant crimson, single to semi-dbl., large blooms borne 3-4 per cluster; slightly fragrant; foliage dark, leathery, glossy; vigorous, pillar growth; recurrent bloom; (28). GM, NRS, 1923.

Allen's Fragrant Pillar Cl HT, rb, 1931, *Paul's Lemon Pillar × Souv. de Claudius Denoyel*; Allen. Bud long, pointed; flowers cerise, base flushed yellow, dbl., open, large blooms on long, strong stem; foliage glossy, bronze; moderate climbing growth; recurrent bloom.

Allen's Golden Climber LCl, *ob*, 1933, Allen; Flowers orange, dbl., large; foliage glossy; non-recurrent bloom.

Allgold® F, *my*, 1958, (All Gold®); *Goldilocks × Ellinor LeGrice*; LeGrice, 1956. Flowers bright buttercup-yellow, 15-22 petals, large (3 in.) blooms borne singly and in large trusses; slightly fragrant; foliage small, glossy, dark; vigorous growth. GM, NRS, 1956.

Allgold, Climbing Cl F, *my*, 1961, (Grimpant All Gold; Grimpant Allgold;) *Allgold sport*; Gandy.

Alliance F, *dp*, 1966, *Rosita × Queen Elizabeth*; Delforge. Bud ovoid; flowers light red and deep pink, dbl., large blooms on strong stems; fragrant; foliage soft; very vigorous, bushy growth.

Allison Sweetie Gr, *mr*, 1975, *Tropicana × Mister Lincoln*; Miller, F. Bud long, pointed, oval; flowers medium red, dbl. (21-25 petals), exhibition form, large (3-3½ in.); fragrant; foliage large, glossy, dark; tall, vigorous growth.

Alliswell HT, *w*, 1956, *Neige Parfum × (Charlotte Armstrong × Blanche Mallerin)*; Motose. Bud ovoid; flowers white overcast pink, center cameo-pink, dbl. (50-60 petals), peony shaped, large (5-6 in.); fragrant; vigorous, bushy growth.

Allotria® F, *or*, 1958, (TANal); *Fanal × Cinnabar seedling*; Tantau, Math. Flowers orange-scarlet, dbl., flat, large (3 in.) blooms in large clusters; foliage dark, glossy; vigorous.

Allspice HT, *my*, 1977, (AROall); *Buccaneer × Peace*; Armstrong, D.L.; Armstrong Nursery. Bud ovoid, pointed, deep yellow; flowers medium yellow, dbl. (35 petals), large (4½ in.); fragrant (honey and tea rose); foliage large, olive-green; vigorous, upright, bushy growth.

Allure HT, *pb*, 1950, *Mrs. Pierre S. duPont × Charlotte Armstrong*; Swim; Inter-State Nursery. Bud long, pointed, carmine-rose; flowers neyron rose, base yellow, dbl. (28-30 petals), high-centered, large (5-6 in.); slightly fragrant; foliage leathery, glossy, light green; very vigorous, upright growth.

Alma F, *dr*, *Orange Triumph × Eutin*; Riethmuller. Flowers dark crimson, dbl., medium blooms in large clusters; dwarf growth.

Alma Mater HT, *lp*, 1929, *Columbia sport*; Good & Reese. Flowers lighter in color.

Almirante Américo Tomás HT, *rb*, 1955, (Miramar); *Sultane × Peace*; Moreira da Silva. Flowers geranium-red, reverse old-gold, dbl., large; very vigorous growth.

Almond Glory Min, *ab*, 1991, (ZIPalm); *Rise 'n' Shine × High Spirits*; Zipper, Herbert; Magic Moment Miniatures, 1992. Flowers deep apricot, full (26-40 petals), exhibition form, small (0-4 cms) blooms borne in small clusters; fragrant; foliage small, dark green, glossy; some prickles; medium (30 cms), compact growth.

Almondeen HT, *pb*, 1982, (AROfrap); *Angel Face × First Prize*, Christensen; Armstrong Nursery, 1984. Flowers almond and pink blend, dbl. (40+ petals), good form, large; slight fragrance; foliage large, medium green, semi-glossy; upright, bushy growth.

Aloha Cl HT, *mp*, 1949, *Mercedes Gallart × New Dawn*; Boerner; J&P. Bud ovoid; flowers rose-pink, reverse deeper, dbl. (58 petals), cupped, large (3½ in.); fragrant; foliage leathery, dark; vigorous, pillar (8-10 ft.) growth; recurrent bloom.

Alois Jirásek HT, *ob*, 1931, *Mme. Butterfly × Mrs. George Shawyer*; Böhm. Bud long, pointed; flowers dark orange, tinted brownish yellow, dbl., large; fragrant; foliage glossy; vigorous.

A Longs Pédoncules M (OGR), *lp*, 1854, Robert. Bud pale green, mossy; flowers pink, flushed lilac, many petalled, long peduncles, small blooms nodding in clusters; foliage small, round, soft green; vigorous growth.

Alouette Pol, *op*, 1971, *Ambassadeur Baert × Seedling*; Delforge. Bud long, pointed; flowers salmon-orange, semi-dbl., cupped, medium; slightly fragrant; foliage leathery; vigorous, bushy growth; profuse, continuous bloom.

Aloysia Kaiser S, *my*, 1937, *Miss G. Mesman × Belle Doria*; Lambert, P. Bud ochre-yellow; flowers reddish bright yellow, round, full, large blooms in clusters; vigorous growth; seasonal bloom.

Alpha HT, *or*, 1975, (MEInastur); *((Show Girl × Baccará) × Romantica) × (Romantica × Tropicana)*; Paolino; URS. Flowers bright vermilion, dbl. (20 petals), large (4 in.); foliage leathery; vigorous; greenhouse variety.

Alphonse de Lamartine HP (OGR), *lp*, 1853, Ducher. Flowers rosy blush, full, medium; moderate growth.

Alphonse Karr T (OGR), *m*, 1878, *Duchess of Edinburgh seedling*; Nabonnand, G. Flowers crimson-purple, center lighter, full, large.

Alpin LCl, *or*, 1960, *Spectacular × Seedling*; Combe; Minier. Flowers bright orange-red,

dbl., large; slightly fragrant; foliage dark, glossy; vigorous growth; recurrent bloom.

Alpine HT, *my*, 1954, *Sunnymount sport*; Grillo. Bud long, pointed; flowers clear yellow, dbl. (30 petals), open, large (5½ in.); fragrant; foliage leathery; vigorous, upright growth.

Alpine Glow F, *or*, 1954, (Alpenglühen); *Cinnabar × (Cinnabar × Käthe Duvigneau)*; Tantau, Math.; J&P. Bud deep orange-red; flowers vermilion-red, dbl. (28 petals), cupped, large (3-4 in.) blooms in clusters of 4-10; fragrant; foliage glossy; vigorous, bushy.

Alpine Sunset® HT, *ab*, 1973, *Dr. A.J. Verhage × Irish Gold*; Cants of Colchester, 1974. Flowers peach-pink, apricot reverse, dbl. (30 petals), large (7-8 in.); fragrant; foliage glossy, medium green; vigorous, upright.

Alsace HT, *op*, 1946, *Peace × Mme. Joseph Perraud*; Meilland, F. Flowers salmon-pink, base gold, dbl., large (6 in.); fragrant; foliage dark; free growth.

Alsace-Lorraine HP (OGR), *dr*, 1879, Duval. Flowers dark velvety red, large.

Alt Wien HT, *pb*, 1965, *Queen of Bermuda sport*; Prinz; Wohlt. Flowers carmine-rose, dbl., large (4 in.); foliage dark, glossy; compact growth.

Altalaris S, *w*, 1941, *R. spinosissima altaica × R. acicularis*; Skinner. Bud large, pointed; flowers white, sometimes flushed pink, single, open; foliage leathery; fruit bright red, apple shaped; vigorous, bushy, prickly growth; abundant, non-recurrent bloom.

Altesse HT, *dp*, 1950, *Vercors × Léonce Colombier*; Meilland, F.; URS. Bud ovoid; flowers strawberry-red, dbl. (35-40 petals), globular, large; vigorous, upright growth.

Althea HT, *mr*, 1930, Pemberton; Bentall. Flowers glowing crimson; fragrant (damask).

Altissimo® LCl, *mr*, 1966, (DELmur; Altus); *Ténor × Seedling*; Delbard-Chabert; Cuthbert. Flowers blood-red, single (7 petals), cupped to flat, large (4-5 in.); slightly fragrant; foliage dark, serrated; tall growth; repeat bloom.

Altmärker HT, *yb*, 1908, *Kaiserin Auguste Viktoria × Luciole*; Türke. Flowers ochre-yellow tinted garnet, full, large; fragrant; vigorous growth.

Altonia Sp (OGR), *mp*, 1835, *R. setigera natural variation*; Found in Illinois, 1835. Flowers brilliant pink, single or semi-dbl. (over 5 petals).

Alvares Cabral F, *mr*, *Pinocchio × Alain*; Moreira da Silva. Flowers bright red.

Always HT, *dr*, 1959, (*Charlotte Armstrong × Applause*) *× Ena Harkness*; Leon. Bud long, pointed; flowers dark cardinal-red, dbl. (28 petals), large (6 in.); fragrant; foliage leathery; vigorous growth.

Always A Lady Min, *m*, 1988, (TINlady); *Deep Purple* × *Dilly Dilly*; Bennett, Dee. Tiny Petals Nursery, 1987. Flowers pale mauve to lavender, dbl. (25-30 petals), high-centered, exhibition, medium, borne usually singly or in sprays of 3-5; moderate, damask fragrance; foliage medium, medium green, semi-glossy; prickles hooked slightly downward, pale yellow; fruit globular, green to brown; bushy, medium growth.

Always Mine™ HT, *dr*, 1989, (DEVsiem); *Visa* × *Sassy*; Marciel, Stanley G.; DeVor Nursery. Bud pointed, tapering; flowers deep red, dbl. (39 petals), cupped, large, borne singly; heavy, spicy fragrance; foliage large, dark green, glossy; prickles declining, pea green with cinnamon tinges; upright, tall growth.

Ama F, *or*, 1955, *Obergärtner Wiebicke* × *Independence*; Kordes. Bud ovoid; flowers deep orange-scarlet, dbl., high-centered, large blooms in clusters (up to 20); foliage dark, glossy, leathery; vigorous, bushy growth.

A. MacKenzie S, *rb*, 1985, (Alexander MacKenzie); *Queen Elizabeth* × *(Red Dawn* × *Suzanne)*; Svejda, F.; Agriculture Canada, 1984. Bud ovoid; flowers medium red, reverse lighter, dbl. (45 petals), cupped, 3 inch blooms in clusters of 6-12; fragrant; foliage yellow-green, glossy, leathery; purple prickles; upright growth; repeat bloom.

Amadis Bslt (OGR), *dr*, 1829, (Crimson Boursault); *R. chinensis* × *R. pendulina*; Laffay. Flowers deep crimson-purple, semi-dbl., cupped, large; young wood whitish green, old wood red-brown; no prickles; vigorous, upright growth; excellent pillar; once popular as an understock.

Amalfi Pol, *dy*, 1971, Delforge. Bud long, pointed; flowers deep yellow to salmon-pink, dbl., cupped, small; slightly fragrant; foliage small, dark; moderate, bushy growth; abundant, continuous bloom.

Amalia Jung HT, *mr*, 1934, *Mrs. Henry Winnett* × *Lady Helen Maglona*; Leenders, M. Flowers crimson-red, dbl., large; fragrant; foliage glossy, cedar-green; vigorous growth.

Amalie de Greiff HT, *pb*, 1912, *Herrin von Lieser* × *Mme. Mélanie Soupert*; Lambert, P. Flowers brick-rose, center salmon and orange-yellow, dbl.

Amami HT, *op*, 1927, Easlea. Flowers peachpink, semi-dbl. (12-15 petals), very large; foliage light; very vigorous.

Amanda F, *my*, 1979, (BEEsian); *Arthur Bell* × *Zambra*; Bees Ltd. Bud globular; flowers medium yellow, dbl. (25 petals), high-cen-

tered, large (3½ in.); slightly fragrant; foliage small, light green; upright growth.

Amanda Kay Min, *w*, 1991, (JUSamanda); *Seedling* × *Seedling*; Justice, Jerry, 1990; Justice Miniature Roses. Bud ovoid; flowers white to near white, some pinkshading, dbl., high-centered, exhibition, small blooms borne singly; heavy, spicy fragrance; foliage small, medium green, glossy; bushy, low growth.

Amanda Marciel™ HT, *lp*, 1989, (DEVnina; AmandaTM); *Seedling* × *Pink Puff*; Marciel, Stanley G.; DeVor Nursery. Bud slender and tapering; flowers very delicate pink, dbl. (26 petals), cupped, large, borne singly; slight, spicy fragrance; foliage medium, dark green, glossy; prickles none; upright, tall growth.

Amarante Pol, *mr*, 1916, Barbier. Flowers dark crimson, sometimes striped white, blooms in clusters of 25-70.

Amarillo HT, *dy*, 1961, *Buccaneer* × *Lowell Thomas*; Abrams, Von; Peterson & Dering. Bud pointed; flowers deep yellow, dbl. (30 petals), large (5 in.); fragrant; foliage leathery, light green; vigorous, upright growth.

Amateur E. Biron HT, *op*, 1928, Biron. Flowers shrimp-pink, center tinted copper, reverse old-rose, camellia shaped.

Amatsu-Otome HT, *yb*, 1960, *Chrysler Imperial* × *Doreen*; Teranishi; Itami Rose Nursery. Flowers golden yellow edged deep orange, dbl. (48 petals), high-centered to cupped, large (4½-5 in.); slightly fragrant; foliage semi-glossy; vigorous, compact growth.

Amaury Fonseca Pol, *w*, 1914, Soupert & Notting. Flowers white, suffused light pink in fall, well formed.

Amazing Grace HT, *mp*, 1973, *Carina* × *Mischief*; Anderson's Rose Nursery. Flowers rich pink, dbl. (43 petals), high pointed, large (5 in.); slightly fragrant.

Amazone LCl, *mr*, 1961, *Spectacular sport*; Delforge. Flowers bright red.

Amazone T (OGR), *my*, 1872, *Safrano* × *Seedling*; Ducher. Flowers yellow, reverse veined rose, well formed.

Ambassadeur Baert F, *op*, 1964, *Sumatra* × *Seedling*; Delforge. Flowers salmon; foliage bronze; low, compact growth.

Ambassadeur Nemry F, *dp*, 1949, Leenders, M. Flowers deep rose-pink, reverse salmon-carmine, dbl., large; fragrant; vigorous growth.

Ambassador HT, *ob*, 1930, *Mme. Butterfly* × *Souv. de Claudius Pernet*; Premier Rose Gardens. Bud long, pointed; flowers bronze-salmon, dbl., large; fragrant; foliage leathery, dark; vigorous, bushy growth.

Ambassador® HT, *ob*, 1979, (MEInuzeten); *Seedling* × *Whisky Mac*; Meilland; C-P. Bud conical; flowers orange-red, reverse blended with golden yellow (orange-apricot), dbl. (33 petals), cupped, large (4 in.); foliage dark, glossy.

Amber R, 1908, *Jersey Beauty seedling*; Paul, W. Flowers pale amber, single; low growth; early bloom. RULED EXTINCT.

Amber HT, 1930, *Ophelia sport*; Jordan, B.L.; Beckwith. Flowers amber. RULED EXTINCT.

Amber Beauty F, *pb*, 1962, *Goldilocks × Lavender Pinocchio*; Leenders, J. Flowers pink tinted brown, dbl.; very fragrant.

Amber Flash™ Min, *ob*, 1982, (WILdak); *Zorina × Starina*; Williams, J.B.; C-P. Flowers orange blend, 15-25 petals, medium; fragrant; foliage medium, dark, semi-glossy.

Amber Gold HT, *dy*, 1962, *Golden Rapture × Golden Scepter*; Moro; J&P. Bud ovoid; flowers deep golden yellow, dbl. (40-45 petals), cupped, large (5 5½ in.); fragrant; foliage leathery; vigorous, upright growth. A greenhouse variety for cut-flower purposes.

Amber Queen® F, *ab*, 1983, (HARroony); *Southampton × Typhoon*; Harkness, 1984. Bud plump; flowers amber yellow, dbl. (40 petals), cupped, large blooms in clusters of 3-7; fragrant; foliage large, copper red to medium green, semi-glossy; reddish prickles; low, bushy growth. ROTY, 1984; GM, Genoa, 1986 & Orléans, 1987; AARS, 1988.

Amber Ribbon Min, *ab*, 1991, (ZIPamb); *Rise 'n' Shine × Pot 'o Gold*; Zipper, Herbert; Magic Moment Miniatures, 1992. Bud pointed; flowers deep apricot to deep yellow at base, reverse deep apricot to deep yellow, aging to deep yellow on edge, light yellow at base (butterscotch), dbl. (22 petals), high-centered, exhibition, medium (4-4.5 cms), borne usually singly or in sprays of 2-5; slight fragrance; foliage medium, dark green, semi-glossy; upright, tall growth.

Amber Sands Min, *ab*, 1984, *Fragrant Cloud × Poker Chip*; Hardgrove, Donald & Mary; Rose World Originals. Flowers apricot, dbl. (35 petals), high-centered, exhibition form, large; slight fragrance; foliage medium, medium green, semi-glossy; upright, bushy.

Amberglo™ Min, *r*, 1988, (MINapco); *Tom Brown × Twilight Trail*; Williams, Ernest. Flowers russet, dbl. (34 petals), small; very fragrant; foliage small, dark green, semi-glossy; bushy, sturdy growth.

Amberlight F, *yb*, 1961, (Amber Light); *(Seedling × Lavender Pinocchio) × Marcel Bourgouin*; LeGrice, 1962. Flowers clear amber, dbl. (26 ruffled petals), large (3½-4 in.) blooms in open clusters; very fragrant (fruity); vigorous, upright, bushy growth.

Ambiance HT, *lp*, 1955, *Comtesse Vandal × Pres. Macia*; Delforge. Bud long, pink, passing to cream.

Ambossfunken HT, *rb*, 1961, (Anvil Sparks); Meyer; Kordes. Flowers coral-red streaked golden yellow, dbl. (33 petals), well-formed, large; fragrant; bushy growth.

Ambra® F, *ob*, 1982, *Seedling × Seedling*; Barni-Pistoia, Rose. Flowers orange blend, dbl. (20 petals), deep cupped, large blooms in clusters of 3-5; light fragrance; foliage medium, brownish-green, glossy; reddish prickles; upright, bushy.

Ambre HT, *ob*, 1950, *Peace × Seedling*; Gaujard. Bud ovoid; flowers brilliant orange and yellow, dbl., very large; fragrant; foliage glossy, dark; very vigorous, bushy growth.

Ambre Solaire Pol, *pb*, 1966, *Masquerade × Seedling*; Ebben. Bud ovoid; flowers red, pink and yellow, dbl., medium blooms in clusters; slightly fragrant; foliage dark.

Ambrosia F, *ob*, 1962, *Seedling × Shepherd's Delight*; Dickson, P.; A. Dickson. Flowers amber, single (7-10 petals), flat, large (2½-3 in.) blooms in large clusters; foliage dark; vigorous, bushy growth.

Amdo HRg (S), *mp*, 1927, *Tetonkaha × La Mélusine*; Hansen, N.E. Flowers pink, semi-dbl. (16 petals), in clusters of 7-10; non-recurrent bloom.

Amélia A (OGR), *mp*, Prior to 1823; Flowers bright pink, anthers deep yellow, dbl., large; fragrant; non-recurrent bloom.

Amelia Barter HT, *mr*, 1963, *Queen Elizabeth × Claude*; Barter. Flowers bright scarlet tinted silvery, dbl. (34 reflexed petals), large (5½ in.); foliage dark, glossy.

Amelia Earhart HT, *yb*, 1932, (Président Charles Hain); *Souv. de Claudius Pernet × (Louise Catherine Breslau × Paul Neyron)*; Reymond; J&P. Flowers golden yellow, center flushed pink, dbl., large; very fragrant; vigorous growth.

Amélie de Bethune HT, *rb*, 1923, Pernet-Ducher; Flowers coral-red shaded carmine, dbl.

Amélie de Mansfield G (OGR), *mp*, Flowers vivid pink, dbl., medium.

Amélie Gravereaux HRg (OGR), *mr*, 1903, *(Général Jacqueminot × Maréchal Niel) × Conrad Ferdinand Meyer*; Gravereaux. Bud ovoid; flowers medium red, fading, dbl.; foliage dark, rugose; vigorous, spiny growth; recurrent bloom.

America R, *mp*, 1915, (Walsh's Rambler); *R. wichuraiana × R. multiflora*; Walsh. Flowers pink, center white, single blooms in large clusters (often to 75).

America LCl, *op*, 1976, (JACclam); *Fragrant Cloud × Tradition*; Warriner; J&P. Bud ovoid, pointed; flowers salmon, reverse lighter, dbl. (43 petals), imbricated, medium (3½-4½ in.); very fragrant. AARS, 1976.

American Banner T (OGR), *pb*, 1879, *Bon Silène sport*; Cartwright; P. Henderson. Flowers carmine striped white, semi-dbl., small.

American Beauty HP (OGR), *dp*, 1875, (Mme. Ferdinand Jamin); *Parentage unknown*; Lédéchaux, 1875; Bancroft and Field Bros., 1886. Bud globular; flowers deep pink, full (50 petals), cupped, large; very fragrant; vigorous growth; sometimes recurrent; a famous greenhouse variety.

American Beauty, Climbing LCl, *dp*, 1909, *(R. wichuraiana × Marion Dingee) × American Beauty*; Hoopes, Bro. & Thomas; Not a sport of American Beauty. Flowers deep rose-pink, cupped, large; fragrant; height 12-15 ft.; non-recurrent bloom.

American Dawn HT, *rb*, 1976, *Personality × Seedling*; Warriner; J&P. Bud ovoid; flowers rose-red, base white, dbl. (30 petals), high-centered, large (4-5 in.); slightly fragrant; foliage glossy, dark; upright growth.

American Dream™ HT, *dr*, 1987, (WINbur); *(My Dream × Charles Mallerin) × Seedling*; Winchel, Joe; Co-Operative Rose Growers, 1990. Flowers deep red, dbl. (25 petals), high-centered, exhibition, large, borne singly; slight, damask fragrance; foliage medium, medium green, semi-glossy; average, dark brown, slightly recurred prickles; fruit round, average, medium orange; upright, tall growth. ARC TG (G), 1986.

American Fantasy™ HT, *op*, 1989, (TWOfan); *Sonia × Seedling*; Twomey, Jerry; DeVor Nursery, 1991. Bud ovoid; flowers salmon pink, reverse lighter, dbl. (32 petals), cupped, large, borne singly; moderate, fruity fragrance; foliage medium, dark green, glossy; prickles declining, yellow with red tinge; upright, medium growth.

American Flagship HT, *mr*, 1946, *Crimson Glory × Self*; Lammerts; C.R. Burr. Bud urn-shaped; flowers bright scarlet, semi-dbl. (15 petals), large (3½-4½ in.); slightly fragrant (spicy); foliage leathery; vigorous, upright, bushy growth.

American Girl HT, *mr*, 1929, *Hollywood sport*; Maton. Flowers red, dbl., high-centered, large blooms on long stem; fragrant; foliage leathery, dark; vigorous growth.

American Glory HT, *dr*, 1991, (TWOadmire); *Portland Trailblazer × Seedling*; Twomey, Jerry, 1983; DeVor Nurseries, 1991. Bud ovoid, pointed; flowers cardinal red, dbl. (28 petals), cupped, large, borne usually singly; very slight, damask fragrance; foliage medium, dark green, semi-glossy; upright, bushy, medium growth.

American Heritage® HT, *yb*, 1965, (LAMlam); *Queen Elizabeth × Yellow Perfection*; Lammerts, W.E.; Germain's. Bud long, pointed; flowers ivory and salmon blend, becoming salmon, dbl., high-centered, large; foliage dark, leathery; tall growth. AARS, 1966.

American Heritage, Climbing Cl HT, *yb*, 1971, Arora, Bal Raj; The Rosery, India.

American Home HT, *dr*, 1960, *Chrysler Imperial × New Yorker*; Morey; J&P. Flowers dark red, dbl. (30 petals), cupped, large (4½ in.); very fragrant; foliage leathery; vigorous, upright growth.

American Pillar R, *pb*, 1902, *(R. wichuraiana × R. setigera) × Red Hybrid Perpetual*; Van Fleet, 1902; Conard & Jones, 1908. Flowers carmine-pink, white eye, golden stamens, single blooms in large clusters; foliage leathery, glossy; fruit red; vigorous (15-20 ft.) growth; non-recurrent bloom; (21).

American Pride HT, 1928, *Grillodale sport*; Grillo. Bud long, pointed; Flowers pure white, outside petals occasionally tinted pink, dbl. (35 petals), large (4½ in) blooms; fragrant; Foliage leathery; Very vigorous growth. RULED EXTINCT 2/79 ARM.

American Pride HT, *dr*, 1978, (JACared); Warriner; J&P, 1974. Bud pointed, ovoid; flowers dark red, dbl. (33 petals), high-centered, large (4-5 in.); slightly fragrant; foliage large, dark; tall, upright growth.

American Rose Centennial™ Min, *pb*, 1991, (SAVars; A.R.S. Centennial); *High Spirits × Rainbow's End*; Saville, F. Harmon; Nor'East Miniature Roses, 1992. Bud ovoid; flowers pink blend, very dbl. (50-55 petals), excellent hybrid tea form, exhibition, high-centered, medium (3½ cms) blooms borne singly or in sprays of 3-5; slight fragrance; foliage medium, dark green, semi-glossy; bushy, medium growth. Named in honor of the American Rose Society Centennial.

American Roseate E (OGR), *dp*, Prince Nursery, prior to 1846. Flowers bright rose, semi-dbl.; vigorous growth.

American Spirit HT, *mr*, 1988, (JACtred; Medal of Honor); *Seedling × American Pride*; Warriner; J&P. Flowers medium red, dbl. (35 petals), high-centered, large blooms borne usually singly; no fragrance; foliage medium, medium green, semi-glossy; upright, tall growth.

American White E (OGR), *w*, Prince Nursery, about 1840. Flowers creamy white, semi-dbl.; vigorous growth.

Americana HT, *mr*, 1961, *Poinsettia seedling* × *New Yorker*; Boerner; J&P. Bud ovoid; flowers bright red, dbl. (28 petals), high-centered, large (5½ in.); fragrant; foliage leathery; vigorous, upright growth.

America's Junior Miss F, *lp*, 1964, (Junior Miss); *Seventeen* × *Demure seedling*; Boerner; J&P. Bud ovoid; flowers soft coral-pink, dbl., medium; fragrant; foliage glossy; vigorous, bushy growth; sometimes improperly abbreviated to Junior Miss.

Ames 5 HBlanda (S), *mp*, 1932, (Ames Climber); *R. multiflora* × *R. blanda*; Maney; Iowa State College. Flowers pink, good size, in clusters; thornless stems, red in winter; very vigorous; non-recurrent bloom; very hardy, much hardier than *R. multiflora*. Introduced as a rose inderstock.

Ames 6 HBlanda (S), *mp*, Very similar to Ames 5, but more fertile; (14).

Améthyste R, *m*, 1911, *Non Plus Ultra sport*; Nonin. Flowers violet-crimson.

Ami Desvignes HT, *mr*, 1954, Privat. Flowers red, base of petals veined coral, semi-dbl., petals waved, large; foliage glossy; vigorous growth.

Ami F. Mayery HT, *mr*, 1938, *Huguette Vincent* × *Seedling*; Denoyel, Mme.; C. Chambard. Bud long, pointed, vermilion-red; flowers poppy-red, dbl., cupped, very large blooms on stiff stems; foliage dark; vigorous growth.

Ami Léon Chenault F, *mr*, 1929, *Lafayette sport*; Nonin. Flowers dark garnet, slightly striated white, blooms in clusters.

Ami Léon Pin HT, *ly*, 1947, Gaujard. Bud long, pointed; flowers pale yellow, reverse pink, dbl., very large; fragrant; Foliage dark; very vigorous growth.

Ami L. Cretté HT, *rb*, 1931, Chambard, C.; C-P. Bud long, pointed, coppery oriental red; flowers crimson-red, reverse light coral-rose and yellow, semi-dbl., cupped, medium to large; fragrant; foliage dark; very vigorous, bushy growth.

Ami Quinard HT, *dr*, 1927, *Mme. Méha Sabatier* × *(Mrs. Edward Powell* × *R. foetida bicolor*; Gaujard, 1927; C-P, 1930. Bud long, pointed; flowers blackish garnet and coppery scarlet, semi-dbl. (17 petals), cupped, medium; fragrant; foliage leathery; vigorous growth.

Ami René Badel F, *mr*, 1961, *Belle Créole* × *(Gloire du Midi* × *Paul Crampel)*; Arles; Roses-France. Bud pointed; flowers carthamus-red, dbl. (36 petals), high-centered; very fragrant; foliage bronze.

Amiable Rouge G (OGR), Godefroy, prior to 1845.

Amica HT, 1966, *Coup de Foudre* × *Lampo*; Cazzaniga; F. Giuseppe. Flowers cinnabar-red, large; fragrant; foliage light green.

Amiga Mia S, *mp*, 1978, *Queen Elizabeth* × *Prairie Princess*; Buck; Iowa State University. Bud ovoid, pointed; flowers empire-rose, dbl. (30 petals), high-centered, large (4-5 in.); fragrant; foliage large, dark, leathery; vigorous, upright, bushy growth.

Amigo F, *mr*, 1951, *World's Fair* × *Adolf Grille*; Whisler; Germain's. Bud short, pointed; flowers currant-red, semi-dbl. (17-20 petals), cupped, large (3-3½ in.); fragrant (spicy); foliage leathery; upright, bushy growth.

Amiral Gravina HP (OGR), *m*, 1860, Moreau-Robert. Flowers blackish purple, shaded with scarlet.

Amistad Sincera HT, *w*, 1963, (Sincera); *Alaska* × *Virgo*; Camprubi; C-P. Bud ovoid; flowers pure white, dbl. (55 petals), high-centered to cupped, large (4-4½ in.); foliage leathery; vigorous, well-branched growth.

Amitié HT, *ob*, 1951, *Mandalay* × *Schéhérazade*; Mallerin; EFR. Flowers coppery orange-yellow, dbl., well shaped, large; vigorous, branching growth.

Amleger HT, *mr*, 1972, *Baccará sport*; Molina; URS. Flowers blood-red to cardinal-red, dbl. (40 petals), cupped, imbricated, large (4½ in.); slightly fragrant (tea); foliage dark, leathery; vigorous growth.

Amor F, *mp*, 1957, *(Golden Rapture* × *Floribunda seedling)* × *Self*; deRuiter; Blaby Rose Gardens. Bud pointed; flowers clear pink, dbl. (22 petals), medium; vigorous, bushy growth.

Amore F, *mp*, 1957, *Orange Triumph* × *Spring Song (F)*; Riethmuller. Flowers rosy pink, reverse lighter, dbl., medium; fragrant; foliage semi-glossy; moderate growth.

Amorette Min, *w*, 1980, (AmoRU; Amoretta®; Snowdrop); *Rosy Jewel* × *Zorina*; deRuiter; Fryer's Nursery, 1979. Bud pointed; flowers white, ivory center, dbl. (33 reflexed petals), patio, borne 10-15 per cluster; slight fragrance; foliage light, mid-green; long, narrow, red prickles; short, dense, bushy growth.

Amorous HT, *lp*, 1986, (JACarina); *White Masterpiece* × *Marina*; Warriner; J&P. Flowers shell pink, dbl. (30 petals), high-centered, medium blooms borne singly; slight, fruity fragrance; foliage large, medium green, glossy; upright, tall; greenhouse variety.

Amourette Ch (OGR), *mp,* Flowers rose-pink, edged lighter, large, pointed, petals recurving; foliage dark; stems red.

Amoureuse HT, *ab,* 1966, *Peace × Unnamed Rose Gaujard seedling;* Gaujard. Flowers coppery yellow, dbl. (34 petals), large, borne singly; foliage large, medium green.

Ampère HT, *or,* 1937, *Charles P. Kilham × Condesa de Sástago;* Meilland, F. Flowers nasturtium-red, edges lighter, reverse orange-yellow, dbl., very large; very fragrant; foliage bright green.

Amruda Min, *dr,* 1979, (Amanda; Red Ace); *Scarletta × Seedling;* deRuiter, 1977; Fryer's Nursery, 1982. Flowers dark red, dbl. (20 petals), medium; slight fragrance; foliage small, medium green, semi-glossy; bushy growth.

Amsterdam® F, *or,* 1972, (HAVam); *Europeana × Parkdirektor Riggers;* Verschuren, T.; Verschuren. Bud ovoid; flowers clear orange-red, semi-dbl. (12-15 petals), large (2½ in.); foliage glossy, brown-red; vigorous growth. GM, The Hague, 1972.

Amulett HT, *mr,* 1932, *Mrs. Henry Winnett × Johanniszauber;* Tantau; C-P. Bud ovoid; flowers fiery red, very dbl., high-centered; fragrant; foliage dark, glossy; vigorous, bushy growth.

Amurensis Sp (OGR), *mp,* A semi-dbl. fld. triploid form of *R. blanda carpohispida.* Flowers medium pink, large; wood red; tall, sparsely armed growth.

Amurensis Sp (OGR), *mp,* Seems to be a dbl.-fld. form of *R. blanda carpohispida.* Flowers pink, semi-dbl., large; wood red; tall, sparsely armed.

Amy F, *mp,* 1954, *Show Girl × Fashion;* Abrams, Von; Peterson & Dering. Bud ovoid; flowers carmine-rose, dbl. (38 petals), high-centered, large (2½-3 in.) blooms in loose clusters; fragrant; foliage leathery; compact, dwarf growth.

Amy Brown® F, *ob,* 1979, (HARkushi); *Orange Sensation × ((Highlight × Colour Wonder) × (Parkdirektor Riggers × Piccadilly));* Harkness. Bud ovoid; flowers burnt-orange to fire-red, dbl. (28 petals), rounded, large (2½-3 in.); fragrant (fruity); foliage large, dark; low, bushy growth.

Amy Johnson LCl, *mp,* 1931, *Souv. de Gustave Prat × Seedling;* Clark, A.; NRS Victoria. Bud ovoid; flowers pink, dbl., cupped, large; fragrant; foliage wrinkled; vigorous (12-15 ft.).

Amy Rebecca Min, *dy,* 1986, *Rise 'n' Shine × Summer Butter;* Jolly, M.; Rosehill Farm, 1987. Flowers deep yellow, dbl. (38 petals), high-centered, small blooms borne usually singly; slightly fragrant; foliage small, me-

dium green, semi-glossy; small, brown prickles; medium, upright growth.

Amy Robsart E (OGR), *dp,* 1894, *R. eglanteria × HP or B;* Penzance; Keynes, Williams & Co. Flowers deep rose, semi-dbl., large; fragrant; foliage fragrant; vigorous; summer bloom.

Amy Vanderbilt F, *m,* 1956, *Lavender Pinocchio seedling × Lavender Pinocchio;* Boerner; J&P. Bud globular; flowers lavender-lilac, dbl. (70 petals), cupped, large (3 in.) blooms in pyramidal clusters; fragrant; foliage dark, glossy; upright, bushy.

Amy's Delight Min, *mp,* 1980, *Little Darling × Little Chief;* Williams, E.D. Bud ovoid; flowers clear medium pink, dbl. (60 petals), opening imbricated, borne usually singly; no fragrance; foliage small, medium green, very glossy; straight, tan prickles; compact, bushy growth.

Anabell® F, *ob,* 1972, (KORbell; Annabelle; Kordes' Rose Anabel); *Zorina × Colour Wonder;* Kordes; Dicksons of Hawlmark. Flowers orange and silvery blend, dbl. (30 petals), well-formed, large (4 in.); fragrant; foliage small.

Anaïs B (OGR), *mp,* Flowers pink.

Anaïs Ségalas G (OGR), *pb,* 1837, Vibert. Flowers rosy crimson, edged rosy lilac, full, expanded, large; branching growth.

Anastasia HT, *w,* 1980, *John F. Kennedy × Pascali;* Greff, N.P. Bud ovoid, pointed; flowers white, dbl. (30 petals), exhibition form, borne usually singly; no fragrance; foliage large, dark; bronze prickles, turning brown with age; vigorous, dense growth.

Anatole de Montesquieu HSem (OGR), *w,* 1860, Van Houtte. Flowers white.

Anci Böhmova R, *mp,* 1929, (Anci Böhm); *Marietta Silva Tarouca sport;* Böhm. Like parent in form, fullness and color but brighter.

Ancient Art Min, *op,* 1985, *Rise 'n' Shine × Picnic;* Hardgrove, Donald L.; Rose World Originals. Flowers orange-pink blend, yellow reverse, dbl. (60+ petals), medium; slight fragrance; foliage medium, medium green, matt; upright, bushy growth.

Anda Pol, *rb,* 1980, (LENda); *(Britannia × R. moschata) × (Little Angel × Europeana);* Lens. Flowers dark red, white eye, single (5 petals), 2in. blooms in clusters of 18-24; fruity fragrance; purple prickles; bushy growth.

Andalusien® F, *mr,* 1976, (KORdalu); *Seedling × Zorina;* Kordes, 1977. Bud long, pointed; flowers red, dbl. (34 petals), cupped, large (3 in.); vigorous, bushy growth. ADR, 1976.

Andante S, *op,* 1962, *Sea of Fire × (Josef Rothmund × R. laxa);* Buck; Iowa State University. Bud ovoid, pointed; flowers light salmon-pink, dbl., cupped, medium; slightly fragrant; foliage dark, bronze, leathery; vigorous (5-6 ft.), upright, arching growth; repeat bloom.

Andante HT, *mr*, 1962, Laperrière; EFR. Flowers red, dbl. (40 petals), large; foliage bronze; vigorous, bushy growth.

Andenken an Franz Heinsohn F, *dr*, 1938, *D.T. Poulsen × Seedling*; Poulsen, S. Flowers dark red, dbl., urn-shaped, medium, in clusters; slight fragrance; upright, bushy.

Andenken an Gartendirektor Siebert R, *pb*, 1923, *Eisenach × Polyantha seedling*; Kiese. Flowers carmine-rose, with yellow, blooms in clusters.

Andersen's Yellow HT, *my*, 1984, *Queen Elizabeth × Seedling*; Walter, J.C.; Kimbrew-Walter Roses. Flowers medium yellow, dbl. (40+ petals), large; slight fragrance; foliage medium, dark, semi-glossy.

Andersonii HCan (OGR), *mp*, 1935, *Chance hybrid of R. canina × possibly R. arvensis*. Flowers pink, single, medium (2-2½ in.); spreading habit.

Andorra HT, *ab*, 1973, *Dr. A.J. Verhage × Seedling*; Kordes; Fey. Bud long, pointed; flowers apricot blend, dbl. (24 petals), high-centered, large; very fragrant; foliage glossy, dark; vigorous, upright, bushy growth.

André Gamon HT, *mp*, 1908, Pernet-Ducher. Flowers carmine.

André le Troquer HT, *ob*, 1946, Mallerin; A. Meilland. Flowers orange shading to apricot, dbl. (30 petals), cupped, large (5 in.); very fragrant; foliage very dark; very vigorous, upright growth.   GM, Bagatelle, 1946 & NRS, 1951.

André Leroy d'Angers HP (OGR), *mr*, 1862, Trouillard; Standish. Flowers crimson, shaded with violet, full, often ill-formed, large; vigorous.

André Louis R, *w*, 1920, Tanne; Turbat. Flowers white, center flesh-pink.

André Pernet HT, *mr*, 1956, *Peace × Mme. Elie Dupraz seedling*; Gaujard. Bud long; flowers red, becoming lighter at center and purplish on outer petals, full, well formed, large; foliage dark; very vigorous growth.

André Schwartz T (OGR), *mr*, 1883, Schwartz, J. Flowers crimson, sometimes striped white.

Andrea Min, *pb*, 1971, *Little Darling × Seedling*; Moore, R.S.; Sequoia Nursery, 1978. Bud pointed; flowers deep pink, silver reverse, dbl. (20 petals), high-centered, small (1½ in.); foliage dark; vigorous, bushy, spreading growth.

Andrée Joubert HT, *op*, 1952, *Soeur Thérèse × Duquesa de Peñaranda*; Mallerin; EFR. Bud

very long, dark orange-coral; flowers pastel salmon, large.

Andrée Lenoble Pol, *dp*, 1915, Turbat; Flowers unfading rose or red.

Andrée Palthey HT, *mr*, 1946, *Mme. Joseph Perraud × Seedling*; Gaujard. Bud long, pointed; flowers bright red, very full, large; fragrant; foliage bronze; vigorous growth.

Andrée Perrier HT, *ob*, 1932, *Souv. de F. Bohé × Seedling*; Chambard, C. Bud long; flowers orange-yellow, shaded carmine, dbl., cupped, very large.

Andrée Roux HT, *rb*, 1927, Pernet-Ducher; Gaujard. Flowers coral-red, tipped carmine, reverse yellow.

Andrée Vanderschrick R, *w*, 1935, Buatois. Bud greenish; flowers white, very dbl., opening well, small blooms in clusters; fragrant; foliage dark; very vigorous, climbing growth; profuse seasonal bloom.

Andrée-Sophie Girard F, *mr*, 1958, *Alain × Independence*; Arles; Roses-France. Flowers currant-red, edged silvery, dbl.

Andres Batlle HT, *dr*, 1951, *Comtesse Vandal × Sensation*; Camprubi. Bud long, pointed; flowers crimson, dbl., high-centered, large blooms on strong stems; slightly fragrant; vigorous growth.

Andulka HT, *op*, 1935, Brada; Böhm. Bud long, pointed; flowers pink to salmon-pink, full, large; vigorous, bushy growth.

Anemone HLaev (OGR), *lp*, 1896, (*R. × anemonoides* Rehder; Anemone Rose; Pink Cherokee); *Possibly R. laevigata × Tea*; J.C. Schmidt. Flowers silver pink, single (5 petals), large (4 in.); fragrant; foliage glossy; vigorous, bushy growth; spring bloom, then scattered bloom; (14).

Angara HT, *rb*, 1983, *Montezuma sport*; Gupta, Dr. M.N. & Shukla, R.; National Botanical Research Institute. Flowers dark red with hues of orange.

Angel™ S, *w*, 1982, (DEVite); *(Queen Elizabeth × Seedling) × Jack Frost*; DeVor, P. Flowers white, dbl. (35 petals), flora-tea, small; slight fragrance; foliage medium, light green, semi-glossy; upright growth; greenhouse variety.

Angel Bells® HT, *rb*, 1964, (HERmela); *Peace × Rina Herholdt*; Herholdt, J.A.; Herholdt's Nursery. Flowers ivory, flushed orange and red, dbl. (30+ petals), well-formed, large blooms borne singly; slight fragrance; foliage dark, glossy; bushy growth.

Angel Cream F, *w*, 1989, *Angel Face sport*; Ravi, Professor N., 1988. Bud broadly ovate; flowers creamy white, turning pure white.

Angel Darling Min, *m*, 1976, *Little Chief* × *Angel Face*; Moore, R.S.; Sequoia Nursery. Flowers lavender, 10 petals, small (1½ in.); slightly fragrant; foliage leathery; vigorous.

Angel Delight HT, *ab*, 1976, *Femina sport*; Fryer's Nursery. Flowers peach shaded salmon.

Angel Dust Min, *w*, 1978, *Magic Carrousel* × *Magic Carrousel*; Bennett, Dee; Tiny Petals Nursery. Bud ovoid; flowers white, 18-20 petals, exhibition, small; foliage dark; vigorous, upright, spreading growth.

Angel Eyes Min, *dp*, 1978, Lyon. Bud ovoid; flowers spinel-red, semi-dbl. (10 petals), small (1 in.); slightly fragrant; foliage small; very compact, bushy growth.

Angel Face F, *m*, 1968, *(Circus* × *Lavender Pinocchio)* × *Sterling Silver*; Swim & Weeks; C-P. Bud pointed; flowers deep mauve-lavender, petal edges darker, dbl. (30 wavy petals), high-centered, large (3½-4 in.); very fragrant; foliage dark, leathery, glossy; vigorous, upright, bushy growth. AARS, 1969; ARS John Cook Medal, 1971.

Angel Girl HT, *pb*, 1973, (WElan); *Bel Ange sport*; Wyant. Flowers peach-pink.

Angel Guimera HT, *my*, 1926, *Frau Karl Druschki* × *Souv. de Claudius Pernet*; Dot, P.; S. Dot. Flowers amber-yellow, dbl.

Angel Pink Cl Min, *op*, 1987, (MORgel; Pink Angel); *Little Darling* × *Eleanor*; Moore, Ralph S. Flowers pink to soft coral pink, holds color, dbl., high-centered, exhibition, borne in sprays of 3-7; slight fragrance; foliage medium, light green, semi-glossy; medium, brown prickles, slightly hooked downwards; fruit none; upright, tall, climbing (5-7 ft.) growth.

Angel Wings HT, *yb*, 1958, *Golden Rapture* × *Girona*; Lindquist; Howard Rose Co. Bud ovoid; flowers yellow, shading to white, edged pink, (23 petals), cupped to flat, large (3½-4 in.); fragrant; foliage leathery; upright. GM, Portland, 1959.

Angela F, *yb*, 1957, *Masquerade* × *Golden Scepter*; Kordes; Morse. Flowers golden yellow shaded crimson, dbl. (28 petals), medium (2½ in.), slightly fragrant; truss of 15-20; foliage glossy, dark; vigorous, upright; very free bloom.

Angela Rippon® Min, *mp*, 1978, (OcaRU; Ocarina); *Rosy Jewel* × *Zorina*; deRuiter; Fryer's Nursery. Flowers salmon-pink, patio, small; fragrant; dwarf, compact growth.

Angela's Choice F, *pb*, 1973, *Dainty Maid* × *Anna Wheatcroft*; Gobbee. Flowers light pink, reverse deep pink, semi-dbl. (15 petals), large (3 in.); foliage matt; vigorous, upright.

Angèle HT, *w*, 1933, *Seedling* × *Kaiserin Auguste Viktoria*; Vestal. Bud ovoid; flowers creamy white, dbl., large blooms in clusters on long stems; fragrant; foliage leathery; vigorous, bushy growth.

Angèle Pernet HT, *ob*, 1924, *Bénédicte Seguin* × *HT*; Pernet-Ducher. Bud ovoid; flowers reddish-orange shaded yellow, dbl., globular, large; fragrant (fruity); foliage dark, bronze, leathery; vigorous, bushy. GM, Bagatelle, 1924 & NRS, 1925.

Angelglo™ Min, *m*, 1982, (MINaco); *Angel Face* × *(Angel Face* × *Over the Rainbow)*; Williams, E.D.; Mini-Roses. Flowers lavender, dbl. (35 ruffled petals), micro-mini, small; slight fragrance; foliage small, dark, semi-glossy; bushy growth.

Angelica F, *dp*, 1984, (KORday; Angela®); *Yesterday* × *Peter Frankenfeld*; Kordes. Flowers deep pink, dbl. (35 petals), cupped, medium blooms borne singly and in clusters; no fragrance; foliage medium, medium green, glossy; bushy growth. ADR, 1982.

Angelina S, *pb*, 1976, *(Tropicana* × *Carine)* × *(Cläre Grammerstorf* × *Frühlingsmorgen)*; Cocker, 1975. Flowers rose-pink, white eye and reverse, 11 petals, large (3 in.) blooms in clusters; fragrant; foliage matt, light green; bushy, spreading growth.

Angeline Lauro HT, *or*, 1967, (Angelina Lauro); Lens, 1968; Spek. Flowers orange-red, dbl., medium; foliage dark.

Angelique F, *op*, 1961, *World's Fair* × *Pinocchio*; Swim; C.R. Burr. Bud ovoid; flowers coral-pink to salmon-pink, dbl. (20-25 petals), open, large (2½-3 in.), in clusters; slightly fragrant; vigorous, spreading growth.

Angelis HT, *w*, 1960, *Virgo* × *Ibiza*; Dot, P. Bud long; flowers white, single (8-10 petals); very fragrant; upright, bushy growth.

Angelita® Min, *w*, 1981, (MACangel; MACangeli; Snowball); *Moana* × *Snow Carpet*; McGredy, S., 1982. Flowers white, very dbl., small; slight fragrance; foliage small, dark, glossy; spreading.

Angelita Ruaix HT, *ob*, 1940, *Duquesa de Peñaranda* × *Pres. Herbert Hoover*; Dot, P. Flowers orange-yellow, dbl., high-centered, large; foliage glossy, dark; very vigorous growth.

Angels Mateu HT, *ab*, 1934, *Magdalena de Nubiola* × *Duquesa de Peñaranda*; Dot, P.; C-P. Bud ovoid; flowers salmon, overlaid gold, dbl. (40 petals), globular, large; fragrant (blackberry); foliage dark; vigorous, bushy growth. GM, Bagatelle & Rome, 1934.

Angelus HT, *w*, 1921, *Columbia* × *Ophelia seedling*; Lemon. Flowers white, center cream, dbl. (40-45 petals), large; fragrant; foliage leathery, dark; vigorous growth.

Angelus, Climbing Cl HT, *w*, 1933, Dixie Rose Nursery;

Angkor® HT, *mr*, 1967, (DELtrac); *Belle Rouge × (Rome Glory × Gratitude)*; Delbard-Chabert. Flowers carmine-red, dbl., globular, large; slightly fragrant; foliage bronze, glossy, leathery; vigorous, bushy growth.

Angle Ayr (OGR), *lp*, (Jessica; Rose Angle); Prior to 1848. Flowers flesh tinged with rose, semi-dbl., large.Not to be confused with Rose Angle (E).

Anglica Minor A (OGR), *w*, (Maxima version). Flowers white, center muddled, dbl.; foliage dark gray-green; dwarf.

Angola F, *dr*, *Seedling × Alain*; Moreira da Silva. Flowers dark red.

Angus MacNeil F, *op*, 1967, *The Optimist × Ma Perkins*; Vincent. Flowers salmon-pink and cream, well formed, in clusters; foliage dark; free growth.

Anibal David HT, *my*, 1961, Moreira da Silva. Flowers yellow.

A Night in June HT, *or*, 1935, *Evening Star* sport; Elmer's Nursery. Flowers coral-red, dbl., very large; slightly fragrant; foliage leathery; vigorous, bushy growth.

Animo F, *yb*, 1962, *Masquerade × Beauté*; deRuiter. Flowers yellow, becoming copperred, semi-dbl. (12-16 petals), open, medium (2½ in.) blooms in clusters; bushy growth.

Anita F, *pb*, 1982, *Rumba × Marmalade*; Swim, H.C. & Christensen, J.E.; Armstrong Nursery. Bud ovoid, pointed; flowers pink blend, dbl. (43 petals), large blooms in cluster of 3-7; light teafragrance; foliage large, glossy; large prickles; medium growth.

Anita Charles™ Min., *op*, 1981, (MORnita); *Golden Glow (Brownell) × Over the Rainbow*; Moore, R.S. Bud pointed; flowers bright pink, reverse lighter pink-yellow blend, dbl. (43 petals), high-centered, borne singly, sometimes 2-3 per cluster; tea fragrance; foliage small, leathery, matt; straight prickles; vigorous, upright, spreading growth.

Anita Stahmer F, *dp*, 1973, *Zorina* sport; Kordes. Bud long, pointed; flowers deep pink, dbl. (27 petals), high-centered, large (2½ in.); slightly fragrant; foliage soft; vigorous, upright, bushy growth.

Ankara HT, *op*, 1940, *Joanna Hill × Mme. Joseph Perraud*; Meilland, F.; A. Meilland. Flowers salmon-orange, center coppery, dbl., cupped, very large; slightly fragrant; foliage leathery; vigorous, upright growth.

Ankori HT, *ob*, 1985, (KORangeli; Angelique®; Kordes' Rose Angelique); *Mercedes × Seedling*; Kordes, 1980. Flowers orange, dbl. (40 petals), well-formed, large; slight fragrance; foliage medium, medium green, matt; bushy growth.

Ann Aberconway F, *ab*, 1976, *Arthur Bell × Seedling*; Mattock. Flowers apricot-orange, dbl. (20 petals), large (3 in.); fragrant; foliage dark, leathery.

Ann Barter HT, *mr*, 1962, *Peace × Ena Harkness*; Barter. Flowers cerise, semi-dbl. (18 petals), large (5 in.); fragrant; foliage dark; vigorous growth.

Ann Elizabeth F, *mp*, 1962, Norman; Harkness. Flowers clear rose-pink, semi-dbl. (15 petals), large, open cluster; slightly fragrant; foliage glossy; vigorous, quite tall.

Ann Endt HRg (S), *dr*, 1978, *R. rugosa × R. foliolosa*; Nobbs. Bud long-sepaled; flowers dark red, single (5 petals), medium; fragrant (cinnamon); foliage small, soft.

Ann Factor HT, *ab*, 1975, *Duet × Jack O'Lantern*; Ellis & Swim; Armstrong Nursery. Bud ovoid; flowers pastel apricot, very dbl., high-centered to cupped, large; very fragrant; foliage large, glossy, bronze, leathery; vigorous, bushy growth.

Ann Holbrook Min., *yb*, 1981, *Patricia Scranton × Little Darling*; Dobbs, Annette. Bud globular; flowers yellow-pink blend, 15-25 petals, small; slight fragrance; foliage small, medium green, glossy; spreading growth.

Ann Moore Min., *or*, 1981, (MORberg); *Little Darling × Fire Princess*; Moore, R.S. Bud long, pointed; flowers orange-red, dbl. (30 petals), high-centered, borne usually singly; fragrant; foliage leathery, semi-glossy; long prickles; vigorous, bushy, upright growth.

Anna Chartron T (OGR), *w*, 1896, *Kaiserin Auguste Viktoria × Luciole*; Vve. Schwartz Flowers white tinted pink.

Anna de Diesbach HP (OGR), *dp*, 1858, (Anna Von Diesbach; Gloire de Paris; Glory of Paris); *La Reine × Seedling*; Lacharme. Bud long, pointed; flowers deep pink, center darker, dbl. (40 petals), cupped, large (5-6 in.); very fragrant; vigorous, tall.

Anna de Noailles HT, *dr*, 1941, *Étoile de Hollande × Seedling*; Gaujard. Flowers crimson-red, semi-dbl., high-centered, medium; very fragrant; very vigorous, bushy growth.

Anna Ford® Min., *ob*, 1980, (HARpiccolo); *Southampton × Darling Flame*; Harkness. Flowers deep orange, yellow eye, semi-dbl. (18 petals), patio, small blooms in large clusters; slight fragrance; foliage small, glossy;

small prickles; low, bushy. GM, RNRS, 1981 & Genoa, 1987; RNRS PIT, 1981.

Anna Hartmannová HT, *w*, 1933, *Frau Luise Kiese sport*; Brada; Böhm. Flowers cream-white, very full; fragrant.

Anna Louisa F, *lp*, 1967, *Highlight × Valeta*; deRuiter. Flowers soft pink, dbl., medium (2½ in.) blooms in large clusters; vigorous, low, bushy growth.

Anna Marie S, *dp*, 1843, Feast. Flowers pale rose, dbl., large blooms in clusters.

Anna Marie HT, *dp*, 1948, *Soeur Thérèse × (Duquesa de Peñaranda × Mrs. Pierre S. duPont)*; Ohlhus; C-P. Bud ovoid; flowers rosy pink, dbl. (40-70 petals), high-centered, large (5 in.); very fragrant; foliage leathery, dark; vigorous, upright growth.

Anna Müller-Idserda F, *mp*, 1966, *Duet × Juliette E. van Beuningen*; Buisman. Bud ovoid; flowers pink, dbl., medium; very fragrant; foliage dark.

Anna Neagle HT, *rb*, 1937, McGredy. Flowers bright currant-red, base sunflower-yellow, dbl.; foliage dark; free, branching growth.

Anna Olivier T (OGR), *pb*, 1872, Ducher. Flowers yellowish flesh, shaded salmon, reverse rose, full, well-formed, large; vigorous growth; (14).

Anna Rübsamen R, *mp*, 1904, Weigand, C. Flowers clear pink, dbl., large blooms in compact clusters; vigorous growth.

Anna Soupert HT, *yb*, 1934, *Sunburst × Prince de Bulgarie*; Soupert, G.; C. Soupert. Flowers yellow, center orange, dbl., very large, cactus-dahlia form; slightly fragrant; foliage bronze, dark; dwarf growth.

Anna Stave HT, *w*, 1973, *Pink Parfait × Kordes' Perfecta*; Curtis, E.C.; Kimbrew. Bud ovoid; flowers white, tipped pink, dbl., high-centered, medium; very fragrant; foliage dark, soft; moderate, upright growth.

Anna Wheatcroft F, *or*, 1958, *Cinnabar seedling × Seedling*; Tantau; Wheatcroft Bros. Flowers light vermilion, gold stamens, single, large (4 in.) blooms in clusters; slightly fragrant; foliage dark, glossy; vigorous growth.

Anna Zinkeisen S, *ly*, 1982, (HARquhling); *Seedling × Frank Naylor*; Harkness, 1983. Bud plump; flowers light yellow, dbl. (30 petals), medium blooms in clusters of 3-7; musky fragrance; foliage small, light green, semi-glossy; small prickles; medium, spreading, dense growth.

Annabella HT, 1940, *Joanna Hill sport*; Grillo. Flowers light buff-gold, dbl. (55 petals), large (5 in.); fragrant. RULED EXTINCT 5/83 ARM.

Annabella® HT, *my*, 1981, *Ambassador × Seedling*; Barni-Pistoia, Rose. Bud ovoid; flowers medium yellow, dbl. (35 petals), deeply cupped, medium, borne singly; no fragrance; foliage medium, dark, matt; straight, light yellow prickles; upright.

Annaroy HT, *pb*, 1951, *Pink Princess × Los Angeles*; Shepherd; Bosley Nursery. Bud ovoid; flowers pink with slight salmon undertone, very dbl. (110 petals), imbricated; foliage glossy.

Annchen Müller Pol, *dp*, 1907, (AEnnchen Müller; Annie Mueller); *Crimson Rambler × Georges Pernet*; Schmidt, J.C. Flowers warm rose, fading, dbl., cupped, large blooms in clusters; slightly fragrant; foliage glossy; vigorous, bushy growth.

Anne HT, *mr*, 1925, Pemberton. Flowers cherry-red, full, globular, large; fragrant (damask); foliage leathery; vigorous, bushy, compact growth.

Anne Cocker® F, *op*, 1970, *Highlight × Colour Wonder*; Cocker, A.; Cocker, 1971. Flowers vermilion, dbl. (36 petals), medium (2½ in.); foliage glossy, light to medium green; vigorous, upright.

Anne de Bretagne® S, *dp*, 1979, (MEI-turaphar; Meilland Decor Rose; Decor Rose); *(Malcair × Danse des Sylphes) × ((Zambra × Zambra) × Centenaire de Lourdes)*; Meilland, M.L., 1976. Bud conical; flowers deep pink, dbl. (20 petals), shallow-cupped; foliage semi-glossy; vigorous, upright growth.

Anne d'Ornano HT, *m*, 1967, *John S. Armstrong × Rose Gaujard*; Gaujard. Bud long, pointed; flowers bright purple-crimson, dbl., very large; fragrant; foliage dark, leathery; vigorous, bushy growth.

Anne Farnworth HT, *rb*, 1964, *Tzigane sport*; Court. Flowers like parent, in sunset shades.

Anne Harkness® F, *ab*, 1979, (HARkaramel); *Bobby Dazzler × ((Manx Queen × Prima Ballerina) × (Chanelle 128Mö Piccadilly))*; Harkness, 1980. Bud globular; flowers deep apricot, dbl. (28 ruffled petals), cupped, medium blooms in trusses; slightly fragrant; foliage medium green, semi-glossy; vigorous, upright, tall growth.

Anne Jackson LCl, *dp*, 1973, *Spectacular × LCl*; Jackson, J.R. Flowers cerise, dbl. (30-35 petals), cupped to flat, medium; fragrant; foliage glossy, bronze; vigorous growth.

Anne Kercher HT, *dp*, 1980, (SIMjezbel); *First Prize × Seedling*; Simpson, J.W. Bud long, pointed; flowers deep pink, dbl. (30 petals), classic HT form, borne singly or 3 per cluster; foliage large, dense, medium green; straight prickles; vigorous, very bushy, compact growth.

Anne Laferrère HP (OGR), *dr*, 1916, Nabonnand, C. Flowers deep velvety blood-red; vigorous growth.

Anne Letts HT, *pb*, 1954, *Peace × Charles Gregory*; Letts; Flowers rose-pink, reverse silvery, dbl. (28 petals), pointed, large (4½ in.); fragrant; foliage glossy; bushy growth.

Anne Leygues T (OGR), *lp*, 1905, *Gén. Schablikine × Comtesse Bardi*; Nabonnand, P.&C. Flowers flesh-pink.

Anne Marie Trechslin® HT, *dp*, 1968, (MEIfour; Anne Marie); *Sutter's Gold × (Demain × Peace)*; Meilland; URS. Bud long, pointed; flowers deep pink, dbl., high-centered, large; very fragrant; foliage dark, leathery; vigorous, branching growth.

Anne McDonald F, *pb*, 1992, *Granada × Kordes Perfecta*; Spriggs, Ian Raymond, 1984; Treloar Roses, 1991. Flowers rose pink and creamy yellow, hybrid tea type, classical (30 petals), large (8 cm) blooms borne in clusters of 10-30; slightly fragrant; foliage medium green, glossy; medium to tall (1-3 m), upright growth.

Anne of Geierstein E (OGR), *dr*, 1894, *R. eglanteria × HP or B*; Penzance; Keynes, Williams & Co. Flowers deep crimson, single; fragrant; foliage fragrant; fruit bright scarlet; vigorous growth; summer bloom.

Anne Poulsen F, *mr*, 1935, (Anne-Mette Poulsen); *Ingar Olsson × Seedling*; Poulsen, S.; McGredy & J&P, 1935. Bud long, pointed; flowers bright crimson-red, darkening, dbl., large blooms in clusters; fragrant; vigorous growth.

Anne Scranton F, *lp*, 1971, *Queen Elizabeth × Katherine T. Marshall*; Dobbs, Annette. Bud ovoid; flowers light pink, center flesh-white, dbl., medium; foliage leathery; vigorous, upright growth.

Anne Vanderbilt HT, *or*, 1941, *Seedling × Stargold*; Brownell. Bud pointed; flowers reddish orange, dbl. (28 petals), open, large (4-5 in.); very fragrant; foliage leathery, glossy; very vigorous, bushy growth.

Anne Watkins HT, *ab*, 1962, *Ena Harkness × Grand'mère Jenny*; Watkins Roses. Flowers deep cream shaded yellow, reverse apricot, dbl. (30 petals), well-shaped, large (5 in.); foliage dark, glossy; vigorous, upright growth.

Anneka HT, *yb*, 1990, (HARronver); *Goldbonnet × Silver Jubilee*; Harkness, R.; R. Harkness & Co., Ltd. Bud ovoid; flowers yellow blend, very dbl. (45 petals), high-centered to cupped to reflexed, medium, borne usually singly or

in sprays of 3-5; fruity fragrance; foliage medium, medium green, glossy; prickles slightly curved, medium, dark reddish; fruit ovoid, medium to large, green; upright, medium growth.

Anneke Doorenbos F, *pb*, 1956, *Buisman's Triumph sport*; Doorenbos; Boerma. Flowers silver-pink, reverse darker.

Anneke Koster Pol, *dr*, 1927, *Greta Kluis sport*; Koster, D.A.; Flowers deep red.

Anne-Marie de Montravel Pol, *w*, 1879, (Anna-Maria de Montravel); *Dbl. flowered Multiflora × Mme. de Tartas*; Rambaux. Flowers pure white, dbl., of irregular form when fully open, sometimes showing a few stamens, small(1½ in.) blooms in clusters of up to 60; fragrant (lily-of-the-valley); foliage dark green above, grayish beneath, glossy, 3-5 leaflets; very few prickles; dwarf, compact growth.

Anne-Marie Milliat HT, *w*, 1939, Gaujard. Bud very long; flowers white, very full, large; very vigorous growth.

Annemarie van Onsem F, *mr*, 1971, *Circus × Korona*; Inst. of Orn. Plant Growing. Bud ovoid; flowers vivid red, semi-dbl., open, medium; foliage large, glossy, dark; very vigorous, upright, bushy.

Anne's Delight Min, *dp*, 1981, *Little Darling × Over the Rainbow*; Williams, E.D.; MiniRoses. Bud pointed; flowers dark pink, dbl. (40 petals), high-centered, borne usually singly; slight fragrance; foliage small, dark, glossy; long, thin prickles; upright, bushy growth.

Annette HT, *op*, 1952, *Charlotte Armstrong × Contrast*; Swim; Earl May Seed Co. Bud long, pointed; flowers salmon-pink, dbl. (20-25 petals), high-centered, large (4-4½ in.); fragrant; foliage glossy, leathery, dark; vigorous, compact growth.

Annette Dobbs Min, *op*, 1991, (MORnet); *Anytime × Playgirl*; Moore, Ralph S., 1986; Sequoia Nursery, 1990. Bud pointed; flowers coral red, lighter reverse, ages slightly lighter, semi-dbl. (15 petals), flat with petal edges turning up, medium blooms borne in sprays of 3-5; no fragrance; foliage medium, medium green, semi-glossy; bushy, medium growth.

Annette Gatward HT, *ab*, 1954, *Mrs. Charles Lamplough × Barbara Richards*; Gatward. Flowers peach, full, large; fragrant; foliage light green; upright growth.

Annette Gravereaux HT, *my*, 1929, *Mev. C. van Marwijk Kooy × Golden Emblem*; Leenders, M. Flowers lemon-yellow, shaded orange, dbl.

Anni Jebens HT, *dy*, 1932, *Charles P. Kilham* × *Mev. G.A. van Rossem*; Kordes. Bud large, long, pointed, golden yellow; flowers blood-red, reverse golden yellow, dbl., high-centered; fragrant; foliage leathery, glossy, bronze; bushy, dwarf growth.

Anni Welter M (OGR), *mp*, 1906, *Crested Moss* × *La France*; Welter. Flowers medium pink, large; fragrant; resembles seed parent slightly.

Annie Brandt HT, *op*, 1932, *Mrs. Pierre S. du-Pont* × *Colette Clément*; Mallerin; C-P. Bud long, pointed; flowers pink tinted coral, semi-dbl., open, large; fragrant; foliage leathery, glossy; very vigorous, bushy growth.

Annie Burgess HP (OGR), *lp*, 1926, *Lyon Rose* × *Frau Karl Druschki*; Burgess, S.W. Flowers pale pink, in clusters; early bloom.

Annie Cook T (OGR), *rb*, 1888, *Bon Silène sport*; Cook, J. Flowers blush-tinted.

Annie Crawford HP (OGR), *mp*, 1915, (Miss Annie Crawford); Hall. Flowers bright pink, dbl. (30-35 petals), high-centered, very large; vigorous growth; recurrent bloom. GM, NRS, 1914.

Annie de Metz HT, *or*, 1932, *Golden Emblem* × *R. foetida bicolor seedling*; Mallerin; C-P. Bud large; flowers orange-red, full, high-centered.

Annie Drevet HT, *rb*, 1939, *Charles P. Kilham* × *(K. of K.* × *Mari Dot)*; Caron, B.; A. Meilland, 1939 & Port Stockton Nursery, 1941. Bud long, yellow; flowers fiery red, reverse yellow, semi-dbl., cupped, large; slightly fragrant; foliage leathery, glossy, dark; vigorous growth.

Annie Dupeyrat HT, *op*, 1935, *Mrs. T. Hillas* × *Elvira Aramayo*; Mallerin; C-P. Bud ovoid; flowers orange-pink, dbl., very large; fragrant; foliage leathery; bushy growth.

Annie Laurie HT, *pb*, 1918, (Double Mme. Butterfly); *Ophelia sport*; Stuppy Floral Co. Bud long, pointed; flowers flesh-pink, base yellow, dbl., cupped, large; fragrant; foliage glossy; very vigorous.

Anniversary HT, 1961, *Mary Jo* × *Lamplighter*; Hill, J. H. Co. Bud ovoid; Flowers yellow, dbl. (55-60 petals), high centered to open, strong stem, large (4-5 in.); fragrant; Foliage leathery, dark; Vigorous, upright growth. A greenhouse variety. RULED EXTINCT 5/81 ARM.

Anniversary HT, *dr*, 1981, *Love Affair* × *Seedling*; Hoy, Lowel L.; Joseph H. Hill Co. Bud long, pointed; flowers dark red, dbl. (23 petals), high-centered, borne 1-3 per cluster; fragrant; foliage medium to large; prickles hooked down; upright.

Ann's Wedding HT, *my*, 1975, *Whisky Mac sport*; Rosemount Nursery. Flowers yellow,

dbl. (40 petals), very full, large (4 in.); fragrant; foliage glossy, dark; free growth.

Anny Min, *w*, 1949, *Rouletii* × *Perla de Montserrat*; Dot, P. Flowers pale pink fading white, dbl. (30 petals), micro-mini, very small (½ in.); long, leafy sepals; height 6 in.

Anny Brandt HT, *yb*, 1951, Mallerin; EFR. Bud pointed; flowers creamy yellow, edge and reverse tinted lilac, full, petals waved, large; vigorous growth.

Anthea HT, *yb*, 1949, *McGredy's Yellow* × *Phyllis Gold*; Bees. Flowers pale yellow flushed rose, dbl. (20-25 petals), compact, large (4-5 in.); slightly fragrant; foliage dark; vigorous growth.

Anthea Fortescue F, *pb*, 1992, (PEAshine); F seedling (P135) × F seedling (N147); Pearce, C.A., 1987; The Limes New Roses, 1991. Flowers pink, yellow center, buff reverse, dbl., urn-shaped, medium (6 cms) blooms borne in sprays of 3-9; slight fragrance; foliage small, medium green, glossy, immune to powdery mildew; low, spreading growth.

Anthéor HT, *ab*, 1948, *(Joanna Hill* × *Duquesa de Peñaranda)* × *(Charles P. Kilham* × *Mme. Joseph Perraud)*; Meilland, F. Bud long, furled; flowers reddish apricot, dbl.; very fragrant.

Anticipation HT, *rb*, 1990, (MEIdinro; Rodin; Altesse); *Seedling* × *Seedling*; Meilland, 1980; Co-Operative Rose Growers, 1991. Flowers red with silver/white reverse, semi-dbl. (35 petals), exhibition, high-centered, medium, borne singly; slight fragrance; foliage medium, medium green, semi-glossy; bushy growth.

Antigone® HT, *yb*, 1969, (GAUti); *Rose Gaujard* × *Guitare*; Gaujard. Bud pointed; flowers yellow shaded red, dbl., large; fragrant; foliage light green, soft; vigorous, upright growth. GM, Bagatelle, 1967.

Antigua HT, *ab*, 1974, (JACtig); *South Seas* × *Golden Masterpiece*; Warriner; J&P. Bud ovoid; flowers apricot blend, dbl., high-centered, large; slightly fragrant; foliage leathery; vigorous, upright, bushy growth. GM, Geneva, 1972.

Antinea HT, *op*, 1934, *Julien Potin* × *Seedling*; Gaujard; H&S & Dreer. Flowers salmon-orange, base yellow, dbl., very large; fragrant; foliage glossy; very vigorous, bushy growth.

Antique F, *rb*, 1967, *Honeymoon* × *Circus*; Kordes; A. Dickson. Flowers crimson and gold, blooms in clusters; bushy growth.

Antique Lace F, *mp*, 1991, *Seedling* × *Little Cameo*; Strahle, Glenn, 1985; Coyier's Roses, 1990. Bud ovoid; flowers medium pink, light pink center, semi-dbl. (25-35 petals), urn-shaped, medium; foliage medium, dark green, semi-glossy; bushy, medium growth.

Antique Rose™ Min, *mp*, 1980, (MORcara; MORcana); *Baccará × Little Chief*; Moore, R.S. Bud pointed; flowers rose pink, dbl. (38 petals), high-centered, mini-flora, medium, borne usually singly; slight fragrance; foliage dark, semi-glossy; straight, brown prickles; vigorous, upright.

Antique Silk F, *w*, 1985, (KORampa; Champagner®; Kordes' Rose Champagner); *Anabell seedling × Seedling*; Kordes, 1982. Flowers near white, dbl. (20 petals), flora-tea, large; slight fragrance; foliage medium, medium green, semi-glossy; upright, bushy growth.

Antique Tapestry Min, *rb*, 1991, (CLEtape); *Redgold × Seedling*; Clements, John; Heirloom Old Garden Roses, 1990. Flowers burgandy and gold, moderately full (15-25 petals), exhibition, medium (4-7 cms) blooms borne mostly singly; slight fragrance; foliage medium, dark green, semi-glossy; few prickles; medium (40 cms), upright growth.

Antoine Ducher HP (OGR) *rb*, 1866, Ducher. Flowers violet-red, large. When crossed with *R. foetida persiana* this rose yielded Soliel d'Or, from which the Pernetiana class originated (now incorporated with the Hybrid Teas). (28)

Antoine Noailly HT, *mr*, 1958, *Seedling × Mme. G. Forest-Colcombet*; Croix, P. Bud long; flowers clear red, scalloped petals.

Antoine Rivoire HT, *lp*, 1895, *Dr. Grill × Lady Mary Fitzwilliam*; Pernet-Ducher. Bud ovoid; flowers light pink shaded darker, dbl., imbricated; fragrant; foliage dark; vigorous.

Antoine Verdier HP (OGR), *pb*, 1871, Jamain. Flowers pink, shaded muddy lilac, dbl.

Antoinette HT, *ab*, 1968, *Queen Elizabeth × Peace*; Patterson; Patterson Roses. Bud long, pointed; flowers apricot blend, dbl., open, medium size; fragrant; foliage large, glossy, leathery; vigorous, upright growth.

Antonella HT, *mp*, 1964, Mondial Roses. Bud globular; flowers camellia-pink, dbl., high-centered, large (5 in.) on strong stems; fragrant; vigorous growth.

Antonelliana HT, *ob*, 1952, *Gaiezza × Margaret McGredy*; Giacomasso. Flowers orange and deep yellow tipped, dbl., well formed; foliage glossy; vigorous growth.

Antonia F, *w*, 1979, *Tantau's Tip Top sport*; Bazeley, B.L.; Highfield Nursery. Bud long, pointed; flowers blushed white, palest pink flush, dbl., well-formed blooms in large clusters; slight fragrance; vigorous, bushy, low growth.

Antonia d'Ormois G (OGR), *lp*, Prior to 1848. Flowers blush, fading at edge, full, cupped, medium.

Antonia Pahissa HT, *ob*, 1935, Pahissa. Bud long, pointed; flowers rich orange, dbl., cupped, large blooms on long stems; fragrant; foliage glossy, dark; very vigorous, bushy growth.

Antonia Ridge® HT, *mr*, 1976, (MEIparadon); *(Chrysler Imperial × Karl Herbst) × Seedling*; Paolino; URS. Flowers cardinal-red, dbl. (30 petals), high-centered, large (4-4½ in.); slightly fragrant; vigorous growth.

Antonia Rolleri de Peluffo HT, *dr*, 1926, *Gen. MacArthur × Mme. Edouard Herriot*; Soupert & Notting. Flowers brilliant red, center darker, dbl.; fragrant.

Antonietta Ingegnoli Pol, *pb*, 1923, *R. wichuraiana × R. chinensis*; Ingegnoli. Flowers golden pink, opening in two distinct tones on same plant, dbl.; fragrant.

Anurag HT, *pb*, 1980, *Sweet Afton × Gulzar*; Div. of Veg. Crops & Floriculture. Bud long, pointed; flowers tyrian rose, dbl. (54 petals), high-centered, borne singly; strong fragrance; foliage large, smooth, light green; hooked, brown prickles; upright, bushy.

Anuschka® F, *or*, 1978, (TANkanusch); Tantau, 1977. Bud ovoid; flowers orange-red, dbl. (23 petals), large; slightly fragrant; foliage large; bushy, upright growth.

Anusheh F, *rb*, 1992, (PAYable); *Len Turner × Seedling*; Payne, A.J. Flowers red with yellow reverse, full (26-40 petals), medium (4-7 cms) blooms borne in large clusters; slight fragrance; foliage medium, dark green, glossy; many prickles; medium, upright growth.

A. N. W. B. Rose HT, *w*, 1933, *Frau Karl Druschki × Souv. de Claudius Pernet*; Buisman. Flowers white, tinted yellow, dbl., open, large; slightly fragrant; very vigorous growth.

Anytime Min, *op*, 1973, *New Penny × Elizabeth of Glamis*; McGredy, S., IV; McGredy. Flowers salmon-orange, purplish eye, semi-dbl. (12 petals), small (½-1 in.); fragrant; foliage dark.

Anzac HT, *op*, 1943, *Miss Rowena Thom × Seedling*; Howard, F.H.; H&S. Flowers azalea-pink with coppery scarlet sheen, dbl. (42-50 petals), camellia form; large (5 in.) on long stems; fragrant (fruity); foliage leathery; very vigorous, upright, compact growth.

Aorangi F, *w*, 1979, *Arthur Bell × Red Devil*; Murray, N. Bud pointed; flowers cream, dbl. (41 petals), high-centered, large (3 in.); slightly fragrant; foliage large; upright growth.

Aotearoa-New Zealand HT, *lp*, 1989, (MACgenev; New Zealand); *Harmonie × Auckland Metro*; McGredy, Sam, 1991. Flowers light pink, dbl. (34 petals), large; very fragrant; foliage large, medium green, semi-glossy.

Aozora HT, *m*, 1973, (Blue Sky); *Sterling Silver seedling × Seedling*; Suzuki; Keisei Rose Nursery, 1972. Flowers deep lilac-blue, dbl., high-centered, large; fragrant; foliage large, leathery; vigorous, upright growth.

Apache S, *yb*, 1961, *Fred Howard × Buccaneer*; Abrams, Von; Peterson & Dering. Bud ovoid, flushed red; flowers medium to buff-yellow, dbl. (60 petals), large (5-6 in.); very fragrant; foliage leathery; vigorous (5-6 ft.), spreading, open growth.

Apache Belle HT, *rb*, 1969, *The Alamo sport*; Sitton; Co-Operative Rose Growers. Bud ovoid; flowers orange-red, very dbl., large (5 in.); slightly fragrant; foliage glossy; vigorous, upright, compact growth.

Apache Princess Min, *or*, 1989, (TWOmin); *(Cricket × Christ 78) × Seedling*; Twomey, Jerry; DeVor Nursery, 1990. Bud ovoid; flowers bright orange-red, dbl. (38 petals), cupped, medium, borne singly; slight, fruity fragrance; foliage medium, medium green, semi-glossy; prickles declining, purple; upright, medium growth.

Apache Tears F, *rb*, 1971, *Karl Herbst × China Doll*; Pikiewicz; Edmunds. Flowers cream to creamy pink, petals edged red, dbl., high-centered, medium; slightly fragrant; foliage large, light; vigorous, bushy growth.

Apache Wells F, *yb*, 1971, *Circus × The Optimist*; Williams, J.B. Bud ovoid; flowers canary-yellow, washed pink, dbl., high-centered to cupped, medium-small; slightly fragrant; foliage leathery; vigorous, bushy growth.

Apeles Mestres LCl, *dy*, 1931, *Frau Karl Druschki × Souv. de Claudius Pernet*; Dot, P.; C-P. Flowers sunflower-yellow, dbl., globular, large; fragrant; foliage dark, glossy; vigorous, climbing-growth.

Apéritif F, *pb*, 1972, *Seedling × Starbright*; Boerner; J&P. Bud ovoid; flowers ivory, petals edged rose-pink, dbl., high-centered, medium; slightly fragrant; foliage leathery; vigorous, upright, bushy growth.

Aphrodite HT, *or*, 1928, *Hortulanus Budde × Toison d'Or*; Easlea. Bud long, pointed; flowers coral-red, shaded gold, semi-dbl., large; very fragrant; foliage dark, glossy; vigorous, bushy growth.

Aphrodite, Climbing Cl HT, *or*, 1933, Hillock.

Apogée® HT, *ob*, 1966, (DELbaf; DELbal; DELbat); *(Queen Elizabeth × Provence) × (Sultane seedling × Mme. Joseph Perraud)*; Delbard-Chabert. Bud ovoid; flowers coppery, dbl., cupped, large; slightly fragrant; foliage bronze, glossy; vigorous, upright growth.

Apolline B (OGR), *mp*, 1848, *Pierre de St. Cyr seedling*; Verdier, V. Flowers bright rose-pink, cupped.

Apollo® HT, *my*, 1971, (ARMolo); *High Time × Imperial Gold*; Armstrong, D.L.; Armstrong Nursery. Bud long, pointed; flowers medium yellow, dbl., large; fragrant; foliage large, glossy, dark, leathery; vigorous, upright, bushy growth. AARS, 1972.

Apollo HT, *dy*, 1941, *Mme. Joseph Perraud sport*; Armstrong, J.A.; Armstrong Nursery. Flowers golden yellow.

Apothecary's Rose G (OGR), *dp*, (*R. gallica officinalis* Thory; *R. provincialis* Miller; *R. gallica plena* Regel; *R. gallica maxima* hort.; *R. officinalis* (Thory) Kirschleger; *R. centifolia provincialis*; (The) Apothecary's Rose of Provins; Double French Rose; Red Rose of Lancaster; Officinalis). Probably cultivated before 1600. Flowers deep pink, yellow stamens, semi-dbl.; foliage dark; few prickles; branching growth.

Apotheker Franz Hahne S, *op*, 1919, Müller, F. Flowers salmon-rose on orange-yellow ground.

Apotheose F, *yb*, 1963, *Arc-en-Ciel × Seedling*; Delforge. Flowers indian yellow edged red, becoming garnet-red; vigorous growth.

Appeal HT, *mp*, 1957, *Ena Harkness × Treasure*; Fletcher; Tucker. Flowers clean pink, dbl., blooms on long stem; very fragrant; vigorous, bushy growth.

Applause HT, *dp*, 1949, *Contrast × Charlotte Armstrong*; Swim; Armstrong Nursery. Bud long, pointed; flowers light red, dbl. (50 petals) high-centered, large (4-4½ in.), slightly fragrant; foliage leathery, dark; vigorous, upright, bushy growth. GM, Bagatelle, 1947.

Apple Blossom HMult (OGR), *lp*, 1932, *Dawson × R. multiflora*; Burbank; Stark Bros. Flowers light pink, center lighter, full, petals crinkled, borne in huge clusters; vigorous.

Appleblossom S, *lp*, 1963, Skinner. Flowers appleblossom-pink, loosely dbl., cupped; bushy (2 ft.) growth; recurrent bloom.

Appledore F, *lp*, 1962, *Karl Herbst × Pink Charming*; Allen, E.M. Flowers light pink, dbl. (24 petals), medium; fragrant; foliage glossy; vigorous growth.

Applejack S, *pb*, 1973, *Goldbusch × (Josef Rothmund × R. laxa* Retzius)*; Buck; Iowa State University. Bud small, long, pointed, ovoid;

flowers neyron rose, stippled crimson, semi-dbl., large; very fragrant; foliage leathery; vigorous, upright, bushy growth; repeat bloom.

Appleton's Limelight HT, *dy*, 1934, *Lady Forteviot sport*; Appleton. Bud long, pointed; flowers deep golden yellow, semi-dbl., open, large; foliage leathery, glossy; vigorous, bushy.

Appreciation HT, *mr*, 1971, *Queen Elizabeth × Seedling*; Gregory. Flowers light red shading crimson, dbl. (27 petals), pointed, large (4 in.); slightly fragrant; foliage glossy; vigorous growth.

Apricot Brandy F, *ab*, 1972, Fryer's Nursery. Flowers apricot, base yellow, dbl. (22 petals), large (4 in.); slightly fragrant; foliage bronze-green.

Apricot Charm™ Min, *ab*, 1986, (MINaeco); *Gingersnap × Anita Charles*; Williams, E.; Mini-Roses. Flowers apricot, reverse slightly deeper, blending to yellow at base, dbl. (42 petals), high-centered, exhibition, small, borne usually singly; slight fragrance; foliage small, dark green, glossy; few, long, thin, short, light tan prickles; no fruit; bushy, spreading, medium growth.

Apricot Crème Min, *ab*, 1988, *Yellow Doll, Climbing sport*; Bell, Douglas & Judy; Michigan Miniature Roses, 1989. Bud pointed; flowers light apricot, edges cream, reverse apricot to cream.

Apricot Dawn HT, *ab*, 1938, *Golden Dawn sport*; Wyant. Flowers apricot, base yellow; fragrant.

Apricot Doll Min, *ab*, 1990, (LAVdoll); *Painted Doll × Painted Doll*; Laver, Keith, 1986; Springwood Roses, 1991. Bud ovoid; flowers apricot, yellow center, reverse lighter, aging light apricot, dbl. (30-35 petals), urn-shaped, medium, borne usually singly and in sprays of 1-4; moderate fragrance; foliage small, medium green, matt; spreading, low growth.

Apricot Glow LCl, *ab*, 1936, *(Emily Gray × Dr. W. Van Fleet) × Jacotte*; Brownell; B&A, 1936, C-P, 1937 & Dreer. Flowers apricot, turning apricot-pink, dbl., large truss on long stems; very fragrant; foliage very glossy; very vigorous (20 ft.) growth.

Apricot Medinette Min, *ab*, 1985, (POUlcot; Apricot Midinette; Patio Flame); *Mini-Poul × Mary Sumner*; Olesen, M.&P.; Ludwig Roses, 1983. Flowers apricot-orange, dbl. (20 petals), well-formed, small blooms in clusters; slight fragrance; foliage leathery, glossy; brown prickles; spreading growth.

Apricot Mist™ Min, *ab*, 1987, (SAVamist); *Fantasia × Baby Katie*; Saville, F. Harmon;

Nor'East Miniature Roses. Flowers apricot with tones of pink and yellow, very dbl. (40-45 petals), high-centered, exhibition, medium, borne singly and in sprays of 3-20; slight fragrance; foliage small, dark green, glossy; long, thin, straight, brown prickles; no fruit; bushy, low, profuse, compact, symmetrical growth.

Apricot Nectar F, *ab*, 1965, *Seedling × Spartan*; Boerner; J&P. Bud ovoid; flowers pink-apricot, base golden, dbl.; cupped, large (4-4½ in.); very fragrant (fruity); foliage glossy, dark; vigorous, bushy growth. AARS, 1966.

Apricot Parfait HT, *ab*, 1978, *Seedling × South Seas*; Warriner; J&P. Bud ovoid; flowers apricot-pink blend, dbl. (53 petals), high-centered, large (4 in.); slightly fragrant; foliage large, dark; upright growth.

Apricot Perfection Min, *ab*, 1992, (CLEperf); *My Louisa × Seedling*; Clements, John K.; Heirloom Old Garden Roses, 1990. Flowers soft apricot, moderately full (15-25 petals), high centered, exhibition, small (0-4 cms.) blooms borne mostly singly; slight fragrance; foliage, small, medium green, matt; some prickles; tall(50 cms.), upright, bushy growth.

Apricot Queen HT, *ab*, 1940, *Mrs. J.D. Eisele × Glowing Sunset*; Howard, F.H.; H&S. Bud pointed; flowers salmon-pink, base apricot-orange, dbl. (45 petals), large; foliage leathery; very vigorous, bushy growth. AARS, 1941.

Apricot Queen, Climbing Cl HT, *ab*, 1950, Maranda; Introduced in Australia.

Apricot Silk HT, *ab*, 1965, *Souv. de Jacques Verschuren × Seedling*; Gregory. Flowers apricot, dbl., high-centered, large; fragrant; foliage dark, glossy; vigorous, upright growth.

Apricot Spice HT, *ab*, 1985, (SANspic); *City of Gloucester × Seedling*; Sanday, John. Flowers apricot, dbl. (35 petals), medium; slight fragrance; foliage medium, medium green, matt; bushy growth.

Apricot Wine F, *ab*, 1978, *Allgold × Seedling*; Slack. Flowers burnt apricot, semi-dbl. (12 petals); foliage dark, glossy; low, compact growth.

Apriheart Min, *ab*, 1983, *Picnic × Rise 'n' Shine*; Hardgrove, Donald L. Bud small; flowers light apricot, center deeper, dbl. (40+ petals), small blooms borne singly; very fragrant; foliage small, medium green, semi-glossy; very few prickles; bushy growth.

April Hamer HT, *pb*, 1983, *Mount Shasta × Prima Ballerina*; Bell, R.J.; Treloars Roses. Flowers shell pink with bright pink edges, dbl. (40 petals), exhibition, large; fragrant; foliage dark; vigorous, upright growth.

April Moon S, *my*, 1984, *Serendipity* × *(Tickled Pink* × *Maytime)*; Buck, Dr. G.J.; Iowa State University. Bud small; flowers lemon yellow, dbl. (28 petals), shallow-cupped, medium blooms, borne 5-10 per cluster; sweet fragrance; foliage dark, leathery; awl-like, tan prickles; erect, short, bushy growth; repeat bloom; hardy.

Aprilia HT, *dp*, 1937, Cazzaniga. Bud ovoid; flowers old-rose, full, open, very large; slightly fragrant; foliage leathery; vigorous, upright growth. GM, Rome, 1937.

Apsara F, 1966, Pal; Indian Agric. Research Institute. Bud ovoid; Flowers salmon-pink, semi-dbl., open, medium; Foliage glossy; Vigorous, upright, open growth. RULED EXTINCT 3/84 ARM.

Apsara HT, *op*, 1983, *Sonia* × *Sabine*; Pal; K.S.G. Sons, 1982. Flowers light pink shaded salmon, dbl. (75 petals), flat, medium; strong fragrance; foliage medium, roundish, leathery; hooked, brown prickles; upright growth.

Aquarelle F, *dy*, 1969, *Gold Strike* × *Golden Garnette*; Lens. Bud ovoid; flowers deep yellow, dbl. (18-25 petals), flat, open, medium (2 in.); fragrant (fruity); foliage dark; very vigorous growth.

Aquarius Gr, *pb*, 1971, (ARMaq); *(Charlotte Armstrong* × *Contrast)* × *(Fandango* × *(World's Fair* × *Floradora))*; Armstrong, D.L.; Armstrong Nursery. Bud ovoid; flowers medium pink blend, dbl., high-centered, medium; slightly fragrant; foliage large, leathery; vigorous, upright, bushy growth. GM, Geneva, 1970; AARS, 1971.

Aquilla Bright HT, *ob*, 1988, *Sunblest* × *Matador*; Lea, R.F.G. Flowers orange blend, dbl. (26-40 petals), medium, slight fragrance; foliage medium, medium green, semi-glossy; upright growth.

Ara Pacis HT, *w*, 1955, *Peace* × *Marguerite Chambard*; Giacomasso. Bud tubular, well formed; flowers ivory-white edged reddish purple, dbl. (50 petals), very large on long stems; foliage glossy, bright green; vigorous growth; best in hot climates.

Arabella HT, *dp*, 1918, *Mme. Caroline Testout* sport; Tantau. Flowers crimson-pink, pointed, large; fragrant; vigorous growth.

Arabesque F, *lp*, 1978, *(Gavotte* × *Tropicana)* × *Tropicana*; Sanday. Bud pointed; flowers soft pink, 10 petals, large (3 in.); slightly fragrant; vigorous growth.

Arabian Nights F, *op*, 1963, *Spartan* × *Beauté*; McGredy, S. IV; McGredy. Flowers light salmon-orange, dbl. (25 petals), well-formed, large (4½ in.); fragrant; vigorous.

Araby Gr, *lp*, 1973, *Honey Chile* × *Rose Merk*; Thomson. Bud long, pointed; flowers light orchid-pink, center white, dbl., open, large; very fragrant; foliage large, glossy, dark, leathery; vigorous, upright growth.

Araceli Leyva HT, *op*, 1940, *Mme. Butterfly* × *Comtesse Vandal*; Dot, P. Bud long, pointed; flowers rose-salmon, dbl., cupped, large blooms on strong stems; fragrant; foliage leathery; vigorous, upright growth.

Arakan F, *lp*, 1968, *Pink Parfait* × *Ivory Fashion*; Harkness. Flowers light pink, dbl., blooms in trusses; slightly fragrant.

Aramis F, *dr*, 1964, *Bel Ami* × *(Java* × *Alain)*; Laperrière; EFR. Flowers bright scarlet, semi-dbl., large (3 in.) blooms in clusters of 7-8; foliage dark; very bushy, compact growth.

Aratama HT, *yb*, 1976, *Kordes' Perfecta* × *(Garden Party* × *Christian Dior)*; Takahashi. Bud pointed; flowers yellow and red, dbl. (25 petals), high-centered, very large (6 in.); slightly fragrant; foliage glossy, light green; vigorous growth.

Arc de Triomphe HT, *yb*, 1955, Buyl Frères. Bud globular; flowers yellow-copper, dbl., large; fragrant; foliage glossy, olive-green; upright growth. RULED EXTINCT 1/86.

Arcadia R, *dr*, 1913, Walsh. Flowers crimson-scarlet, dbl., rosette form, blooms in clusters; very vigorous growth.

Arcadia HT, *rb*, 1938, Gaujard. Bud ovoid; flowers reddish copper, dbl., very large on long stems; foliage glossy; vigorous growth.

Arc-en-Ciel F, *pb*, 1961, *Masquerade* × *Maria Delforge*; Delforge. Flowers rich yellow to salmon-pink, carmine and crimson, dbl. (65-70 petals), tight cluster; foliage dark; growth moderate.

Archangel S, *lp*, 1979, *Little Darling* × *Gypsy Moth*; Hawker, U. Flowers delicate pink, single (9-10 petals), frilled, large (3½ in.); slightly fragrant; foliage light green; tall growth.

Archduchess Charlotte Ch (OGR), *dp*, 1975, *Archduke Charles* sport; Earing, F.E.; Kern Rose Nursery. Bud pointed; flowers intense deep solid pink, very dbl. (76 petals), cupped, large (2½-3 in.); fragrant; foliage glossy, smooth; climbing growth; profuse bloom early summer.

Archduke Charles Ch (OGR), *rb*, Laffay, prior to 1837. Flowers rose with paler edges, aging to rich crimson; moderate growth.

Archiduc Joseph T (OGR), *pb*, 1892, *Mme. Lombard* seedling; Nabonnand, G. Flowers purplish pink, center flesh-pink; vigorous growth; (14).

Archiduchesse Elisabeth d'Autriche H P (OGR), *mp*, 1881, Moreau-Robert. Flowers rose-pink, fully dbl.

Archiduchesse Elisabeth-Marie Pol,   *ly*, 1898, *Mignonette × Luciole*; Soupert & Notting. Flowers canary-yellow fading white, full, imbricated, medium; very fragrant; vigorous growth.

Archie Gray HT, *dr*, 1920, Dickson, H. Flowers deep crimson, shaded scarlet, dbl.

Arch. Reventós HT, *ab*, 1935, Leenders, M. Bud ovoid, apricot; flowers cream-yellow, dbl., large; foliage glossy, dark; vigorous, bushy.

Arctic Emerald S, *w*, 1982, *Thérèse Bugnet × Europeana*; James, John. Bud globular, pointed; flowers white, with yellow-green center, semi-dbl. (12 petals), small to medium blooms borne 1-5 per cluster; slight fragrance; foliage small, light green; low, compact growth; repeat bloom.

Arctic Flame HT, *mr*, 1955, *(Queen o' the Lakes × Pink Princess) × Mirandy*; Brownell; Stern's Nursery. Bud pointed; flowers bright red, dbl. (55 petals), large (5 in.); fragrant; vigorous, bushy growth.

Arctic Glow S, *rb*, 1982, *Pike's Peak × Show Girl*; James, John. Bud globular, pointed; flowers scarlet shading towhite center, dbl. (28 petals), large blooms borne singly; slight fragrance; foliage dark, rough; compact growth; repeat bloom.

Arctic Pink F, *lp*, 1966, *Dearest sport*; Smith, E. Flowers pink fading lighter, cupped, large (3 in.) blooms in trusses; very fragrant; vigorous growth.

Arctic Snow™ Min, *w*, 1983, (MINlco); *Seedling × Over the Rainbow*; Williams, E.D.; Mini-Roses. Flowers white, dbl. (40+ petals), exhibition, small; slight fragrance; foliage small, dark, glossy; upright, bushy growth.

Arctic Sunrise Min, *w*, 1989, (BARarcsun); *Snow Carpet × Tranquillity*; Barrett, F.H., 1991. Bud pointed; flowers white, dbl. (30 petals), flat, small, borne in sprays of 40-60; no fragrance; foliage small, medium green, glossy; prickles long thin, small, pale tan; fruit none; spreading, low growth.

Ardelle HT, *w*, 1957, *Mrs. Charles Lamplough × Peace*; Eddie; Harkness; Wyant. Bud long, pointed; flowers creamy white, dbl. (72 petals), high-centered, large (5 in.); fragrant; foliage glossy; very vigorous, compact growth.

Ardente Cl F, *op*, *Seedling × Alain*; Moreira da Silva. Flowers salmon and orange.

Ardoisée de Lyon HP (OGR), *m*, 1858, Damaizin. Flowers violet-rose; vigorous.

Ardon R, *mp*, 1925, Turbat. Flowers bright neyron rose, stained white, borne in pyramidal clusters of 30-40.

Ardore HT, *mr*, 1973, *Seedling × Ninfa*; Calvino. Bud ovoid, globular; flowers orient red, dbl., cupped, large; fragrant; foliage large, dark, leathery; very vigorous, upright, bushy growth.

Ards Beauty F, *my*, 1984, (DICjoy); *(Eurorose × Whisky Mac) × Bright Smile*; Dickson, P., 1986. Bud large; flowers medium yellow, dbl. (20 petals), HT type, large; fragrant; foliage medium, medium green, glossy; bushy growth. GM, RNRS, 1983.

Ards Rover Cl HP (OGR), *dr*, 1898, Dickson, A. Flowers crimson, shaded maroon, dbl. (25 stiff petals), large; fragrant; pillar growth; sometimes recurrent bloom.

Arend Herwig F, *ob*, 1966, *Korona × Heureux Anniversaire*; Buisman. Bud ovoid; flowers orange-red, dbl., medium; foliage dark.

Arethusa Ch (OGR), *yb*, 1903, Paul, W. Flowers yellow, tinted apricot; vigorous growth.

Argentina F, *ab*, 1941, *Mev. Nathalie Nypels × Orange Glory*; Leenders, M. Flowers reddish apricot, semi-dbl.; fragrant.

Argentine Cramon HT, *w*, 1915, Chambard, C. Flowers white, center tinted salmon-rose.

Argosy HT, *op*, 1938, *Souv. de Gustave Prat × Seedling*; Clark, A.; NRS New South Wales. Flowers salmon, flushed pink, dbl., long stem.

Argyle HT, *w*, 1921, *Mme. Caroline Testout × Marquise de Sinéty*; Dobbie. Flowers pure white; vigorous growth.

Aria F, *op*, 1957, *Duchess of Rutland × Fashion*; deRuiter. Flowers salmon shaded pink, dbl., large; bushy growth.

Ariadne Ch (OGR), *rb*, 1918, Paul, W. Flowers bright crimson, center shaded yellow.

Ariake HT, *w*, 1976, *(Lady X × Garden Party) × Seedling*; Teranishi, K.; Itami Rose Nursery. Bud globular; flowers ivory, dbl. (47-50 petals), cupped, very large (5 in.); fragrant; foliage light green; vigorous, upright growth.

Arianna® HT, *pb*, 1968, (MEIdali); *Charlotte Armstrong × (Peace × Michèle Meilland)*; Meilland, M.L.; URS. Flowers carmine-rose suffused coral, dbl. (35 petals), high-centered, large; slightly fragrant; foliage dark, leathery; vigorous, upright, open growth. GM, Bagatelle, Rome & The Hague, 1965.

Aribau HT, *mr*, 1936, *K. of K. × Director Rubió*; Dot, P.; H. Guillot. Bud long, pointed; flowers brilliant red, dbl., large blooms on long stems; foliage glossy; very vigorous growth.

Ariel HT, *my*, 1921, *Mme. Edouard Herriot* × *Natalie Boettner*; Bees. Flowers golden yellow, streaked crimson, dbl., globular, large blooms on long stems; fragrant; foliage dark; vigorous, bushy growth. GM, NRS, 1920.

Arioso HT, *or*, 1970, (MEIhud); *(Paris-Match* × *Baccará)* × *Marella*; Paolino; URS. Flowers light vermilion, dbl. (25 petals), full, very large (5 in.); slightly fragrant (fruity); foliage glossy, dark; very vigorous, upright.

Ariste HT, *my*, 1960, *Joanna Hill* × *Souv. de Mme. Boullet*; Jones; Hennessey. Bud very pointed, deep yellow; flowers light yellow, single (5 petals), medium; fragrant; foliage dark, leathery; vigorous, bushy growth.

Aristide Briand R, *m*, 1928, *Yseult Guillot* × *Seedling*; Penny. Flowers mauve-pink, borne in clusters of 10-29; fragrant.

Aristobule M (OGR), *dp*, 1849, Flowers dark rose with touches of clear rose, full; growth good.

Aristocrat HT, *pb*, 1949, *Pink Delight sport*; Holmes, M.A.; Avansino; Mortensen. Bud long, pointed; flowers clear light pink, reverse darker, dbl. (28-35 petals), high-centered, large (4½-5 in.); fragrant; foliage leathery, dark; very vigorous, upright growth.

Arizona Gr, *ob*, 1975, (WErina; Tocade); *((Fred Howard* × *Golden Scepter)* × *Golden Rapture)* × *((Fred Howard* × *Golden Scepter)* × *Golden Rapture)*; Weeks; C-P. Bud ovoid; flowers golden bronze, dbl., high-centered, medium; very fragrant; foliage glossy, dark, leathery; vigorous, upright, bushy growth. AARS, 1975.

Arizona Sunset Min, *yb*, 1985, *(Orange Sweetheart* × *Zinger)* × *Party Girl*; Jolly, Nelson F.; Rosehill Farm. Flowers light yellow, flushed orange-red, dbl. (20 petals), cupped, medium; slight fragrance; foliage small, medium green, semi-glossy; prickles slanted downward; bushy, spreading growth.

Arjun HT, *or*, 1980, *Blithe Spirit* × *Montezuma*; Div. of Veg. Crops & Floriculture. Bud long, pointed; flowers orange-red, dbl. (35 petals), cupped blooms borne singly or 8 per cluster; slight fragrance; foliage large, smooth; hooked prickles; tall, upright.

Arkansas HT, *or*, 1980, *Seedling* × *Seedling*; Weeks. Bud ovoid, pointed; flowers orange-red, dbl. (48 petals), urn-shaped blooms borne singly or 2-4 per cluster; slight, spicy fragrance; foliage leathery; long, oval-based prickles, hooked downward; upright, vigorous growth.

Arkansas Sunshine F, *my*, 1962, *Goldilocks* × *Seedling*; Jones; Hennessey. Flowers golden yellow, dbl. (30 petals), cupped, medium blooms in clusters; foliage dark, leathery; vigorous, bushy growth.

Arkle HT, *or*, 1977, *Whisky Mac sport*; Hughes Roses. Bud cupped; flowers dark tangerine, dbl. (45-50 petals), cupped, large (4 in.); very fragrant; foliage glossy; vigorous growth.

Arlene Francis HT, *my*, 1957, *Eclipse seedling* × *Golden Scepter*; Boerner; J&P. Bud long, pointed; flowers golden yellow, dbl. (30 petals), high-centered, large (5 in.); very fragrant; foliage dark, glossy; vigorous growth.

Arlequin HT, *ob*, 1945, Gaujard. Flowers orange-yellow and coppery red, dbl., globular, very large; fragrant; foliage dark, glossy; bushy growth.

Armada® S, *mp*, 1988, (HARuseful); *New Dawn* × *Silver Jubilee*; Harkness, R.; R. Harkness & Co. Flowers medium pink, aging slightly paler, dbl. (17 petals), cupped, medium, borne in sprays of up to 12; moderate fragrance; foliage medium, medium green, glossy; prickles slightly recurred, medium green; fruit rounded, medium green; spreading, allgrowth; repeats.

Armagh HT, *ab*, 1950, *Sam McGredy* × *Admiration*; McGredy. Flowers creamy pink, apricot and buff, dbl. (49 petals), pointed; large; slightly fragrant; foliage dark; free growth.

Arménie HT, *ab*, 1936, *Rhea Reid* × *Yves Druhen*; Buatois. Bud purple-garnet; flowers blood-red, shaded, very dbl., large; fragrant; very vigorous, bushy growth.

Arminda HT, *op*, 1956, *Peace* × *Symphonie*; Camprubi. Bud ovoid; flowers bright pink tinted coral, very dbl., globular, large blooms on strong stems; fragrant; foliage glossy; vigorous growth.

Armonia HT, *mr*, 1951, Cazzaniga. Bud long, pointed; flowers bright red, dbl., high-centered, medium blooms on long stems; fragrant; foliage dark, leathery; very vigorous, upright growth.

Arm-Roy Beauty HT, *mr*, 1945, *Better Times sport*; Armacost & Royston; Very vigorous, tall growth.

Arndt LCl, *lp*, 1913, *Hélène* × *Gustav Grünerwald*; Lambert, P. Bud yellowish red; flowers pale pink, dbl., in large clusters; foliage dark; half climbing growth; recurrent.

Arnelda Mae Min, *lp*, 1983, *Sheri Anne* × *Seedling*; Pencil, Paul S. Bud small; flowers light pink, dbl. (30 petals), high-centered, small blooms borne singly and in clusters up to 7; slight fragrance; foliage small, light green, matt; bushy growth.

Arnhem Glory HT, *dr*, 1959, Verschuren. Flowers deep velvety red, large; very fragrant; vigorous growth.

Arnold HRg (S), *mr*, 1893, (Arnoldiana); *R. rugosa* × *Général Jacqueminot*; Dawson; Eastern Nursery. Flowers scarlet, single; vigorous growth; some recurrent bloom.

Arnold Greensitt HT, *yb*, 1986, (NOStarn); *E.H. Morse* × *Summer Sunshine*; Greensitt, J.A.; Nostell Priory Rose Gardens. Flowers yellow blend, full (26-40 petals), medium, very fragrant; foliage large, light green, matt; bushy growth.

Aroha HT, *mp*, 1986, (MURha); *Rifleman* × *Pascali*; Murray, N. Flowers medium, soft pink, dbl. (43 petals), elongated blooms, borne in sprays of 3-5; slight fragrance; foliage medium, light green; pointed, brown prickles; tall growth.

Aroma HT, *mr*, 1931, Cant, B.R.; J&P. Bud ovoid; flowers crimson, dbl., large; vigorous, bushy growth.

AROwago HT, *rb*, 1986, (Showoff; Show Off); *Typhoo Tea* × *Snowfire*; Christensen; Armstrong Nursery. Flowers velvety brilliant red, reverse silvery blend, dbl. (35 petals), large; slightly fragrant; foliage large, dark, semi-glossy; upright, bushy growth.

Arpeggio F, *dp*, 1961, Abrams, Von; Peterson & Dering. Bud pointed; flowers light red, semi-dbl. (12-18 petals), large (3 in.) blooms in clusters; slightly fragrant; foliage dark, glossy; vigorous, compact growth.

Arras Pol, *mr*, 1924, *Triomphe Orléanais sport*; Turbat. Flowers crimson-red.

Arrillaga HP (OGR), *lp*, 1929, (*R. centifolia* × *Mrs. John Laing*) × *Frau Karl Druschki*; Schoener; B&A. Flowers light pink, base golden, dbl. (50 petals), large; fragrant; vigorous growth.

Arrogance HT, *pb*, 1970, *Mischief* × *John S. Armstrong*; Poulsen, N.D.; Poulsen. Flowers coral-pink, dbl. (25 petals), large (4 in.), slightly fragrant; foliage dark, leathery; compact growth.

Artama HT, *yb*, 1978, *Kordes' Perfecta* × *(Garden Party* × *Christian Dior)*; Takahashi, Takeshi. Bud pointed; flowers yellow blend, 25 petals, high-centered; light fragrance; foliage light green, pointed, glossy; few prickles; sturdy growth.

Arthur Bell F, *my*, 1965, *Cläre Grammerstorf* × *Piccadilly*; McGredy, S. IV; McGredy. Flowers yellow to creamy yellow, semi-dbl. (15 petals), large; very fragrant; foliage heavily veined; vigorous growth.

Arthur Bell, Climbing Cl F, *my*, 1979, Pearce, C.; Limes Rose Nursery.

Arthur Cook HT, *dr*, 1924, McGredy. Bud long, pointed; flowers deep crimson, dbl., large blooms on long, strong stems; fragrant;

foliage light, glossy; vigorous, bushy, compact growth. GM, NRS, 1925.

Arthur de Sansal P (OGR), *m*, 1855, Cochet, Sc. Flowers rich crimson-purple, fully dbl., damask-like.

Arthur Hillier HMoy (S), *dp*, 1961, *R. macrophylla* × *R. moyesii*; Hillier. Flowers rose-crimson, single (5 petals), large (2¹/₂-3 in.); slightly fragrant; vigorous growth; repeat bloom.

Arthur R. Goodwin HT, *or*, 1909, *Seedling* × *Soleil d'Or*; Pernet-Ducher. Flowers coppery orange-red, passing to salmon-pink.

Arthur R. Goodwin, Climbing Cl HT, *or*,

Arthur Scargill Min, *mr*, 1985, *Amruda sport*; Thompson, M. Flowers medium red.

Arthur Schulte HT, *rb*, 1986, *Unnamed Colorama seedling* × *Chrysler Imperial*; Williams, J. Benjamin; Krider Nursery, 1989. Flowers cherry to blood red with ivory white at base of petals, dbl. (43 petals), high-centered, exhibition, large, borne singly and in sprays of 1-3; moderate, damask fragrance; foliage large, dark green, semi-glossy, disease resistant; medium-large, light green-bronze prickles; fruit rounded, medium, pumpkin-orange; upright, bushy, medium, very vigorous, some interbranching growth.

Arthur Young M (OGR), *m*, 1863, Portemer. Flowers dark purple, cupped, large; vigorous growth; recurrent.

Artistic F, *ob*, 1971, LeGrice. Flowers orange, fading red, semi-dbl. (10-15 petals), pointed, medium (2 in.); fragrant; foliage small.

Aruba-Caribe HT, *pb*, 1967, *Diamond Jubilee seedling* × *Fashion seedling*; Boerner; J&P. Bud ovoid; flowers rose-pink and ivory, dbl. (38 petals), high-centered, large (5 in.); very fragrant (fruity); foliage leathery; vigorous, upright growth.

Aruna HT, *or*, 1968, *Independence* × *Seedling*; Pal; Indian Agricultural Research Institute. Flowers bright orange-scarlet, dbl., cupped, medium; foliage glossy; bushy, compact.

Arunima F, *dp*, 1975, *Frolic* × *Seedling*; Indian Agricultual Research Institute. Bud ovoid; flowers deep pink, dbl. (50 petals), medium (2 in.); foliage glossy; vigorous, bushy, compact.

Asaborake HT, *dy*, 1979, *(Golden Scepter* × *Narzisse)* × *Kordes' Perfecta*; Ota, Kaichiro. Flowers deep yellow, sometimes tipped pink, dbl. (30 petals), high-centered, large; slight fragrance; foliage medium green, semi-glossy; bushy, upright growth.

Asagumo HT, *yb*, 1973, (Oriental Dawn); *Peace seedling* × *Charleston seedling*; Suzuki; Keisei Rose Nursery. Bud ovoid; flowers yellow blend, dbl., cupped, globular, large; fragrant;

foliage glossy, dark; vigorous, upright growth.

Asbach F, *or*, 1960, *Ambassadeur Nemry × Cinnabar*; Leenders, M. Flowers orange-red.

Aschenbrödel Pol, 1903, *Petite Léonie × R. foetida bicolor*; Lambert, P. Flowers rose with salmon, full, small; fragrant; bushy, dwarf growth.

Aschermittwoch LCl, *w*, 1955, (Ash Wednesday); *R. rubiginosa hybrid*; Kordes. Bud silvery gray; flowers snow-white, dbl., large blooms in large trusses; vigorous growth.

Aschersoniana S, *m*, 1880, (R. × *aschersoniana* *Graebner*); *R. blanda × R. chinensis*; Orig. ca. 1880. Flowers bright, light purple, very numerous, small; growth 6 ft.; (14).

Ascot F, *ab*, 1962, Brownie × *Seedling*; Dickson, P.; Dickson, A. Flowers salmon-coral, semi-dbl. (18 petals), large (4 in.) blooms in clusters; low growth.

Asepala M (OGR), *w*, Prior to 1846. Flowers white, shaded flesh, sometimes edged rose, full, petal edges curled, small; compact, erect growth.

Ashgrove Jubilee HT, *pb*, 1990, (WELco); *Mascot × ((Seedling × Red Lion) × Silver Lining)*; Welsh, Eric, 1985; Rose Hill Roses, 1990. Flowers cream, shading to deep rose at edges, 30 petals, classic HT form, borne singly; slight fragrance; foliage thick, shiny, dark green, obtuse at base; tall, upright growth.

Asmodée G (OGR), *mr*, 1849, Vibert. Flowers rosy crimson, full, large.

Aspirant Marcel Rouyer HT, *ab*, 1919, *Sunburst × Seedling*; Pernet-Ducher. Bud long, pointed; flowers apricot, tinted salmon-flesh, veined yellow, dbl., large blooms on long, strong stems; fragrant; foliage glossy, bronze; very vigorous growth.

Aspirant Marcel Rouyer, Climbing Cl HT, *ab*, 1934, Brenier, E.C.

Assemblage des Beautes G (OGR), *dr*, 1823, Flowers brilliant crimson, dbl., medium; erect growth.

Assiniboine HSuf (S), *dp*, 1962, *Donald Prior × R. arkansana*; Marshall, H.H.; Canada Dept. of Agric. Flowers purplish red, semi-dbl., large to medium blooms with weak stems; slightly fragrant; foliage glossy; vigorous growth; intermittent bloom.

Asso di Cuori® HT, *dr*, 1983, (KORred; Ace of Hearts; Toque Rouge); *Parentage unknown*; Kordes, W.; John Mattock, 1981. Bud large, ovoid; flowers dark red, dbl. (30 petals), cupped; fragrant; foliage large, dark; dark green prickles; bushy growth.

Asso Francesco Baracca HT, *pb*, 1936, *Julien Potin × Seedling*; Giacomasso. Bud long; flowers golden salmon, center deeper, dbl., well formed, long stems; very fragrant; vigorous growth.

Asterix® Min, *or*, 1980, (LENpon); *(Little Red × (Little Angel × Robin Hood)) × Idée Fixe*; Lens. Flowers orange-red, dbl. (65 petals), flat, small blooms in clusters of 12-22; no fragrance; hooked, brown prickles; bushy growth.

Astolat Charm HT, *pb*, 1951, *McGredy's Salmon sport*; Astolat Nursery. Flowers flesh-pink, base apricot, dbl. (30 petals), large (4 in.); very fragrant; foliage dark; vigorous growth.

Astoria HT, *ob*, 1963, *Opera × Demoiselle*; Delforge. Bud pointed; flowers bright orange shaded coral; fragrant; foliage bronze, glossy.

Astra™ Min, *mp*, 1982, (WILsma); *Pinafore × (Lilibet × Fairy Queen)*; Williams, J.B.; C-P. Flowers pink, bright yellow stamens, single (5 petals), small; slight fragrance; foliage small, medium green, semi-glossy; upright growth.

Astral HT, *dp*, 1976, *Tropicana × Pink Favorite*; Bees. Flowers deep rose-pink, dbl. (24 petals), low-centered, large (4 in.); very fragrant; foliage glossy, dark; vigorous.

Astrée HT, *pb*, 1956, *Peace × Blanche Mallerin*; Croix, P. Flowers medium pink, reverse shaded orange, dbl., large; very fragrant.

Astrorose HT, *mr*, 1971, *Helene Schoen × Chrysler Imperial*; Porter; General Bionomics. Bud long, pointed; flowers cardinal-red to crimson, dbl., medium; fragrant; foliage large, dark, bronze, leathery; vigorous growth.

Asturias F, *rb*, 1956, *Méphisto × Coralín*; Dot, M. Flowers red, reverse carmine, dbl. (40 petals), large blooms borne in corymbs on strong stems; foliage glossy; very vigorous.

Asun Galindez de Chapa HT, *pb*, 1923, *Mons. Paul Lédé × Jacques Vincent*; Ketten Bros. Flowers salmon-pink, reverse darker, base yellow.

Atalanta LCl, 1927, *Paul Ploton × William Allen Richardson*; Williams, A.H. Bud coppery pink; flowers flesh-pink, dbl.; fragrant.

Atalante F, *mr*, 1958, Buyl Frères. Flowers geranium-red, large; very vigorous growth.

Atara HT, *rb*, 1975, *Suspense sport*; Nevo, Motke; Maoz Haim Nursery, 1974. Flowers medium red, flecked and striped near white, reverse near white with red veins.

Athabasca Sp (OGR), *dp*, 1930, *R. macounii variant*; Found in Alberta, Canada. Flowers deep pink, semi-dbl.; very vigorous; non-recurrent; hardy.

Athalin B (OGR), *mr*, 1830, Jacques. Flowers cherry-red. Important progenitor of the early Hybrid Perpetuals. (28).

Athene HT, *lp*, 1975, *Peace* × *Diamond Jubilee*; Murray & Hawken; Rasmussen's. Bud green; flowers porcelain-pink, base yolk-yellow, dbl. (37 petals), large (5½ in.); very fragrant (apple); foliage large; moderate, bushy growth.

Atherton HT, *my*, 1981, *Seedling* × *Sunblest*; Perry, Astor. Bud long, pointed; flowers medium yellow, 35 petals, urn-shaped, blooms borne 1-3 per cluster; fruity fragrance; foliage medium, matt; small, recurred prickles; medium growth.

Athlete HT, *rb*, 1964, *Tzigane* × *Claude*; Barter. Flowers nasturtium-red shaded gold, semi-dbl. (16 petals), medium; slightly fragrant; foliage light green; bushy growth.

Athlone F, *yb*, 1965, *Circus* × *Cinnabar*; McGredy, S., IV. Flowers cream edged orange-scarlet, open, blooms in clusters; slightly fragrant; foliage small, dark; free growth.

Athos® F, *ob*, 1965, (LAPwon); *Coup de Foudre* × *Soleil*; Laperrière; EFR. Flowers bright orange, dbl. (28 petals), large; foliage dark; bushy growth.

Atida HT, *dr*, 1941, *Mme. Van de Voorde* × *Dance of Joy*; Sauvageot, H.; Sauvageot. Flowers velvety dark scarlet, semi-dbl., well formed, quite large; fragrant; very vigorous growth.

Atlanta HT, *dy*, 1992, (WEKdoclem); *Honor* × *Gingersnap*; Lemrow, Maynard; Weeks Roses, 1996. Flowers deep clear yellow, long-lasting color, moderately full (15-25 petals), large (7+ cms) blooms borne mostly singly, abundant blooms; slight fragrance; foliage medium, medium green, matt; some prickles; medium (90-120 cms), upright, bushy, full growth.

Atlantic® F, *or*, 1959, (GAval); *Peace* × *Seedling*; Gaujard. Flowers orange-red, semi-dbl., medium; slightly fragrant; foliage glossy, dark.

Atlantida HT, *op*, 1939, Pahissa. Flowers coppery salmon, shaded peach; vigorous growth.

Atlantis F, *m*, 1970, *Orangeade* × *Lilac Charm*; Harkness. Flowers deep mauve, single (5 petals), large (3 in.); fragrant; foliage glossy, purple tinted. GM, Rome, 1969.

Atlas® HT, *dr*, 1966, (DELkort); *Chic Parisien* × *Provence*; Delbard-Chabert. Bud long, pointed; flowers magenta-red edged darker, dbl., cupped, large; foliage dark, glossy; vigorous, upright, bushy growth.

Atombombe F, *mr*, 1953, (Atom Bomb; Atomflash; Velvet Robe); *Obergärtner Wiebicke* × *Independence*; Kordes. Bud pointed; flowers deep scarlet-orange, dbl. (28 petals), medium (2½ in.), cluster; very vigorous.

Atomic White HT, *ly*, 1948, *Pink Princess* × *Shades of Autumn*; Brownell. Bud long, pointed; flowers white, center tinted yellow, dbl., high-centered, large; fragrant; vigorous, bushy growth.

Atropurpurea HRg (S), *mr*, 1899, *R. rugosa* × *R. damascena*; Paul. Flowers carmine-crimson, single, blooms in clusters; vigorous (3-5 ft.) growth.

Atropurpurea Pol, *m*, 1910, *Mme. Norbert Levavasseur* × *Perle des Rouges*; Levavasseur. Flowers purple-red.

Attar of Roses HT, *w*, 1936, Cant, B.R. Bud globular; flowers creamy white, edged pink, dbl., cupped, borne on long, strong stems; fragrant; foliage glossy, bronze; vigorous, bushy, compact growth.

Attila A (OGR), *dp*, Flowers deep pink, semi-dbl., cupped, large.

Attraction HT, *yb*, 1931, Dickson, A. Flowers yellow and orange, dbl., globular; slightly fragrant; foliage glossy, bronze; dwarf, bushy growth.

Attraktion® F, *op*, 1963, Tantau, M. Bud long, pointed; flowers salmon-copper, reverse golden yellow, dbl., blooms in large clusters; very fragrant; foliage glossy, dark; vigorous, bushy growth.

Aubade HT, *ob*, 1963, *Docteur Valois* × *Seedling*; Verbeek. Flowers yellow-orange, dbl., medium; foliage dark.

Aubrey Cobden HT, *my*, 1948, *Oswald Sieper* × *Seedling*; Mee; Fryer's Nursery. Flowers clear yellow, dbl. (30 petals), medium; very fragrant; foliage glossy, stems red; free growth.

Auckland Metro HT, *w*, 1987, (MACbucpal; Métro); *Sexy Rexy* × *(Seedling* × *Ferry Porsche)*; McGredy, Sam; Sam McGredy Roses International, 1988. Flowers white, dbl. (26-40 petals), large; very fragrant; foliage large, dark green, semi-glossy; bushy growth.

Audie Murphy HT, *mr*, 1957, *Charlotte Armstrong* × *Grande Duchesse Charlotte*; Lammerts; Roseway Nursery. Bud long, pointed, crimson; flowers medium red, dbl. (20 petals), high-centered, flat, large (4½-5½ in.); fragrant (spicy); foliage semi-glossy, dark, bronze; vigorous, upright, bushy growth. GM, Portland, 1957.

Audine HT, *lp*, 1950, *Percy Izzard* × *William Moore*; Gatward. Flowers shell-pink, dbl. (22 petals), reflexed, high-centered; fragrant; foliage dark; vigorous, upright growth.

Audrey HT, *dr*, 1922, Paul, W. Flowers deep crimson, high-centered, well formed; fragrant.

Audrey Harrison Cl HT, *ab*, 1969, *Shot Silk sport*; Harrison; Harkness. Flowers pale apricot, semi-dbl., large (4 in.); very fragrant; foliage glossy, dark; free bloom, early.

Audrey Hepburn HT, *lp*, 1991, (TWOadore); *Evening Star* × *Seedling*; Twomey, Jerry, 1983; DeVor Nursery, 1992. Bud pointed; flowers blush pink, fading to lighter pink, dbl. (30-32 petals), large; moderate, fruity fragrance; foliage medium, dark green, glossy; upright, bushy, medium growth.

Audrey Stell HT, *pb*, 1937, *Soeur Thérèse sport*; Stell; Stell Rose Nursery. Flowers soft strawberry-pink, reverse sulphur-yellow, semi-dbl., long, strong stems; foliage light; vigorous, bushy growth.

August Noack HT, *dr*, 1928, *Columbia sport*; Kordes. Bud long, pointed; flowers deep scarlet, dbl., open, high-centered, large; fragrant; foliage bronze, dark; vigorous, bushy growth.

August Noack, Climbing Cl HT, *dr*, 1935, Lens;

August Seebauer F, *dp*, 1944, (The Queen Mother); *Break o' Day (HT)* × *Else Poulsen*; Kordes. Bud long, pointed; flowers deep rose-pink, dbl., high-centered, large blooms in clusters; foliage glossy; vigorous growth; (28).

Auguste Delobel R, *mr*, 1924, Turbat. Flowers carmine, large white eye, yellow stamens, borne in clusters of 25-50.

Auguste Finon R, *yb*, 1923, *Goldfinch* × *Seedling*; Turbat. Flowers golden yellow passing to coppery and salmon, borne in clusters; fragrant.

Auguste Gervais LCl, *ab*, 1918, *R. wichuraiana* × *Le Progrès*; Barbier. Flowers coppery yellow and salmon, fading white, semi-dbl., large (4-5 in.) blooms in clusters of 10-20; fragrant; very vigorous, climbing growth; seasonal bloom.

Auguste Kordes Cl F, *mr*, 1928, (Lafayette, Climbing); *Lafayette sport*; Kordes. Flowers light scarlet, borne in clusters; vigorous, climbing growth; fine seasonal bloom, later intermittent.

Auguste Roussel LCl, *pb*, 1913, *R. macrophylla* × *Papa Gontier*; Barbier. Flowers salmon-pink to flesh-pink, semi-dbl., well-formed, petals undulated, large blooms in clusters of 5-12; very vigorous, climbing growth; seasonal bloom.

Auguste Vermare HT, *or*, 1958, *Comtesse Vandal* × *Seedling*; Arles; Roses-France. Bud pointed; flowers coral-red; vigorous, upright growth.

Augustine Guinoiseau HT, *w*, 1889, (White La France); *La France sport*; Guinoiseau. Flowers white, tinted light flesh.

Augustus Hartmann HT, *dp*, 1914, Cant, B.R. Flowers tyrian rose, dbl., large; slightly fragrant; foliage rich green, leathery; vigorous growth. GM, NRS, 1914.

Auld Lang Syne HT, *ob*, 1956, *Tawny Gold* × *(Talisman* × *Tawny Gold)*; Motose. Bud ovoid; flowers orange edged pale orange-yellow, dbl. (35-45 petals), large (4 in.); fragrant (fruity); bushy growth.

Aunt Gerry HT, *ly*, 1992, *Lanvin sport*; Sheldon, John & Jennifer; Trophy Roses, 1992. Flowers golden yellow, more golden yellow than Lanvin, full (35 petals), slight petal quill, high spiraled center, large (7+ cms) blooms borne mostly singly; mild, spicy fragrance; foliage medium, medium green, semi-glossy; prickly peduncle; medium (90-120 cms), upright, very vigorous growth.

Aunt Harriet R, *rb*, 1918, *Apolline* × *R. wichuraiana*; Van Fleet; Phila. Farm Journal. Flowers scarlet-crimson, white eye, yellow stamens; vigorous growth.

Aunt Honey S, *mp*, 1984, *Music Maker* × *Habanera*; Buck, Dr. G.J.; Iowa State University. Bud large, ovoid; flowers medium pink, dbl. (38 petals), high-centered blooms borne 5-10 per cluster; damask-like fragrance; foliage medium, dark olive-green; awl-like, tan prickles; erect, short, bushy growth; repeat bloom; hardy.

Aunty Dora F, *m*, 1970, *Dearest* × *Lilac Charm*; Deamer; Warley Rose Gardens. Flowers magenta, semi-dbl., medium blooms in trusses; slightly fragrant; low growth.

Aurea HT, *yb*, 1948, Dot. Flowers yellow, reverse red, well formed; fragrant (fruity); foliage glossy; vigorous growth.

Aureate HT, *ob*, 1932, Dickson, A. Flowers orange and scarlet to yellow, dbl., large; fragrant; foliage bronze; vigorous, bushy growth. GM, NRS, 1929.

Aurelia Capdevila HT, *pb*, 1933, Dot, P. Flowers pink, base salmon; fragrant; foliage dark; vigorous growth.

Aurélien Igoult R, *m*, 1924, *Veilchenblau* × *Seedling*; Igoult; Bruant. Flowers purple; vigorous, climbing growth.

Aureola HT, *my*, 1934, *Mev. G.A. van Rossem sport*; Böhm. Flowers golden yellow.

Auréole HT, *ob*, 1951, Gaujard. Bud large; flowers orange-yellow, semi-dbl.; fragrant; foliage glossy, dark; very vigorous growth.

Aurora LCl, *ob*, 1956, *R. kordesii hybrid*; Kordes. Flowers orange-yellow, dbl., large; vigorous growth.

Aurora HMsk (S), *ly*, 1928, *Danaë × Miriam*; Pemberton. Flowers yellow, passing to creamy white, semi-single; fragrant.

Aurora F, *op*, 1941, *Mev. Nathalie Nypels × Seedling*; Leenders, M. Flowers salmon-pink tinted golden yellow and orange, dbl.; fragrant. GM, Bagatelle, 1940.

Aurora Sp (OGR), *dp*, *R. acicularis variety*; Found by Erskine in Alberta, Canada, about 1950. Flowers red, single (5 wide, thick petals); foliage red and purple in fall. An attractive shrub.

Aurora Boreal HT, *rb*, 1935, *Étoile de Hollande × (Ville de Paris × Sensation)*; Munné, B. Flowers geranium, shaded fiery red, semi-dbl.; foliage dark; very vigorous growth.

Aurore Ch (OGR), *yb*, Flowers yellow passing to salmon-pink, loose form; recurrent bloom; (14).

Aurore HT, *pb*, 1936, Capiago. Flowers pink, base yellow, dbl.; fragrant; vigorous growth.

Aurore d'Espagne HT, *pb*, 1966, *Zambra × Queen Elizabeth*; Dot; Minier. Bud long, pointed; flowers salmon-pink to nankeen yellow, semi-dbl., cupped, medium; slightly fragrant; vigorous growth.

Aurore Sand LCl, *pb*, 1964, *Mme. Moisans × Odette Joyeux*; Robichon. Flowers two-tone soft pink and copper, well formed; fragrant; vigorous growth; recurrent bloom. GM, Bagatelle, 1963.

AUSbuff S, *ab*, 1990, (English Garden); *Lilian Austin × (Seedling × Iceberg)*; Austin, David; Delbard, 1988. Flowers soft apricot yellow, cup form, very large; strong fragrance; foliage clear green; bushy, vigorous growth.

AUSburn S, *lp*, 1986, (Robbie Burns); *Wife of Bath × R. pimpinellifolia*; Austin, David, 1985. Flowers light pink, white center, single (5 petals), small; fragrant; foliage small, medium green, matt; bushy, strong growth.

AUScot S, *op*, 1990, (Abraham Darby); *Yellow Cushion × Aloha*; Austin, David; Delbard, 1985. Flowers pink peach-apricot, cup form, very large; strong fragrance; foliage dark green; vigorous, bushy growth.

AUSlight S, *mp*, 1990, (Claire Rose); *Charles Austin × (Seedling × Iceberg)*; Austin, David; Delbard, 1988. Flowers medium pink, cup form, very large; strong fragrance; foliage clear green; bushy, vigorous growth.

AUSlo S, *mr*, 1990, (Othello); *Lilian Austin × The Squire*; Austin, David; Delbard, 1989.

Flowers clear red, cup form, very large; very fragrant; foliage dark green; vigorous, bushy growth.

Ausonius HMsk (S), *pb*, 1932, *(Chamisso × Léonie Lamesch) × (Geheimrat Dr. Mittweg × Tip-Top)*; Lambert, P. Bud oval, yellow-red; flowers yellowish pink, center white, semi-dbl., borne in pyramidal truss of 20-50; fragrant; foliage leathery; semi-climbing, bushy growth; free, recurrent bloom.

Australia Felix HT, *pb*, 1919, *Jersey Beauty × La France*; Clark, A. Bud small, globular; flowers pink and silver shaded lavender, semi-dbl., cupped; very fragrant; foliage dark, glossy; vigorous, bushy growth.

Australian Gold® F, *ab*, 1980, (KORmat; Mona Lisa); Kordes; John Mattock, 1985. Bud ovoid; flowers apricot-peach, dbl. (20 petals), blooms borne 5 per cluster; moderate fragrance; foliage dark, leathery; red prickles; bushy growth.

AUSwhite S, *w*, 1987, (Swan); *Charles Austin × (Seedling × Iceberg)*; Austin, David. Flowers white, tinged buff, reverse white, very dbl. (40 petals), rosette, large, borne usually singly; moderate, fruity fragrance; foliage large, light green, semi-glossy; hooked, medium, red prickles; no fruit; upright, tall growth; repeat bloom.

Autocrat HT, *pb*, 1925, Beckwith. Flowers ochre to flesh-pink, reverse prawn-red, large.

Autumn HT, *ob*, 1928, *Sensation × Souv. de Claudius Pernet*; Coddington. Flowers burnt-orange, streaked red, dbl. (70 petals), cupped; fragrant; foliage dark, glossy.

Autumn Bouquet S, *mp*, 1948, *New Dawn × Crimson Glory*; Jacobus; B&A. Bud long, pointed; flowers carmine-rose-pink, dbl., large; very fragrant; foliage leathery; vigorous, upright, compact growth; recurrent bloom.

Autumn, Climbing Cl HT, *ob*, 1951, DeVor, W.L.; Amling-DeVor Nursery.

Autumn Damask D (OGR), *mp*, *(R. damascena semperflorens* (Duhamel de Courset) Rowley; *R. bifera* Persoon; *R. damascena bifera* hort., not Regel; *R. bifera semperflorens* Duhamel de Courset; *R.semperflorens* Duhamel de Courset in part; Rose des Quatre Saisons; Four Seasons, Quatre Saisons, Rose of Castille; Castilian; Old Castilian); Prior to 1819; Like Summer Damask, but tending to bloom in autumn as well as early summer. One parent of the Hybrid Perpetual roses. Probably the Four-Seasons Rose of Paestum mentioned by classical writers. Perpetual White Moss is a sport of this. (28).

Autumn Delight HMsk (S), *w*, 1933, Bentall. Flowers white, stamens red, almost single, borne in large clusters.

Autumn Dusk Gr, *pb*, 1976, *Music Maker × (Dornröschen × Peace)*; Buck; Iowa State University. Bud ovoid, pointed; flowers pale Tyrian rose and white, dbl. (33 petals), high-centered, large (3½-4½ in.); fragrant; foliage leathery; upright, bushy growth.

Autumn Fire Min, *or*, 1983, (MORanium); *Little Chief × Anytime*; Moore, R.S., 1982. Flowers orange-red, semi-dbl., small; no fragrance; foliage small, medium green, semi-glossy; bushy, very spreading growth.

Autumn Flame HT, *ob*, 1953, *Ednah Thomas × Autumn*; Thomson. Bud long, pointed; flowers orange-yellow tinted red, dbl. (35-40 petals), cupped, large (4 in.); foliage dark, leathery; upright, bushy, compact growth.

Autumn Frost Min, *w*, 1983, (LITlin); *Seedling × Seedling*; Rose, Euie; Little Gems Mini Rose Nursery. Flowers white, dbl. (35 petals), exhibition form, medium; slight fragrance; foliage medium, medium green, semi-glossy; bushy growth.

Autumn Glow HT, *ob*, 1978, *Pascali × Bayadère*; Anderson's Rose Nursery. Bud pear shaped; flowers yellow-orange, dbl. (55 petals), exhibition form, large (5 in.); slightly fragrant; foliage small; bushy growth.

Autumn Gold HT, *yb*, 1969, *Seedling × Seedling*; Weeks. Bud pointed; flowers brown-butterscotch-yellow, dbl. (42 petals), globular, large (3½-4 in.); fragrant; foliage glossy, dark, leathery; tall, upright growth.

Autumn Hues F, *ob*, 1962, *Pinocchio × Fred Edmunds*; Abrams, Von; Peterson & Dering. Bud pointed; flowers orange, yellow and scarlet, dbl. (35 petals), high-centered, large (3-3½ in.) blooms in clusters; slightly fragrant; foliage glossy; upright growth.

Autumn Leaves S, *ob*, 1985, (AUSleaf); Austin, David. Flowers orange blend, dbl. (40+ long, twisted petals), large; fragrant; foliage medium, medium green, semi-glossy; upright growth.

Autumn Magic Min, *ob*, 1987, (FOUtum); *Confetti × Anita Charles*; Jacobs, Betty; Four Seasons Rose Nursery. Flowers bright golden-orange, with red at petal tips, reverse yellow, fading orange-red to red, dbl. (35 petals), high-centered, exhibition, medium, borne usually singly; very long feathery sepals; no fragrance; foliage medium, dark green, semi-glossy; very few prickles; no fruit; bushy, medium growth.

Autumn Queen HT, *ob*, 1933, (Vice-President Curtis); Vestal. Bud long, pointed; flowers burnt-orange, pink, gold, semi-dbl., open; slightly fragrant; foliage leathery, bronze; vigorous, bushy growth.

Autumn Spray F, *yb*, 1964, *Masquerade × Isobel Harkness*; Norman; Harkness. Flowers gold edged red, dbl. (40 petals), flat, large (3 in.); foliage glossy.

Autumn Sunlight LCl, *or*, 1965, *Spectacular × Goldilocks, Climbing*; Gregory. Flowers orange-vermilion, dbl. (30 petals), semi-globular, medium blooms in clusters; fragrant; foliage glossy, bright green.

Autumn Sunset S, *ab*, 1986, *Westerland sport*; Lowe, Malcolm; Lowe's Own Root Roses, 1988. Flowers medium apricot, with touches of orange and golden yellow, fading lighter, dbl. (20 petals), cupped, loose, large, borne in sprays of 5-15; heavy, fruity fragrance; foliage medium, medium green, glossy, disease resistant; curved, medium, red prickles; fruit round, medium, orange; bushy, tall growth; repeat bloom.

Avalanche HT, *w*, 1922, Lippiatt. Flowers creamy white, center deeper, dbl.

Avalanche HT, *w*, 1936, Chambard, C. Bud long; flowers white, large; foliage slightly bronze; vigorous, bushy, compact growth.

Avalanche Rose® F, *mr*, 1986, (DELaval); *(François et Joseph Guy × Sultane seedling) × (Alain × Étoilede Hollande)*; Delbard, 1977. Flowers medium red, dbl. (25 wavy petals), large; no fragrance; vigorous, bushy growth.

Avalon HT, *ab*, 1935, *Duchess of Atholl sport*; Western Rose Co.; Germain's. Bud ovoid; flowers apricot-yellow, center deeper, dbl., globular, very large; slightly fragrant; foliage glossy, bronze; vigorous, bushy growth.

Avandel Min, *yb*, 1977, (MORvandel); *Little Darling × New Penny*; Moore, R.S.; Sequoia Nursery. Bud long, pointed; flowers pink-yellow blend, dbl. (23 petals), cupped to flat, small (1-1½ in.); fragrant (fruity); foliage medium to dark green, leathery; upright, bushy growth. AOE, 1978.

Avanti HT, *dr*, 1990, (JACsay); *Royalty × Samantha*; Warriner, William A. & Zary, Keith W., 1986; Bear Creek Gardens, Inc., 1992. Bud ovoid, pointed; flowers dark red, hint of blue reverse, aging dark, dark red, very dbl. (25-30 petals), urn-shaped, high-centered, exhibition, large blooms borne singly; slight, fruity fragrance; foliage medium to large, dark green, matt to semi-glossy; upright, bushy, tall growth.

Ave Maria HT, *w*, 1957, *Seedling × Break o' Day, Climbing*; Brownell; Stern's Nursery. Flowers pure white, dbl., well-formed, large (4-6 in.); vigorous, bushy growth.   RULED EXTINCT 12/85.

Ave Maria® HT, *op*, 1985, (KORav; Sunburnt Country); *Uwe Seeler × Sonia*; Kordes, W., 1981. Flowers orange-salmon, dbl. (35 petals), high-centered, large blooms borne singly; fragrant; foliage large, medium green, semi-glossy; small prickles; upright growth.

Avenant G (OGR), *lp*, Prior to 1848. Flowers deep flesh-pink, fading, very dbl., large; erect growth.

Aventure HT, *or*, 1964, (Adventure); *(Corail × Baccará) × Seedling*; Croix, P., 1964; C-P, 1965. Flowers orange-red, dbl. (55 petals), high-centered, large; slightly fragrant; foliage leathery, glossy; vigorous, upright, bushy growth.

Aviateur Blériot R, *yb*, 1910, *R. wichuraiana × William Allen Richardson*; Fauque. Flowers pale orange-yellow, fading white, dbl. (34 petals), borne in clusters; fragrant (magnolia); foliage glossy, dark; vigorous, climbing growth; non-recurrent bloom.

Aviator Parmentier HT, *op*, 1941, *Seedling × Briarcliff*; Verschuren-Pechtold; J. Parmentier. Bud long, pointed; flowers peach-pink to orange, dbl. (30-35 petals), high-centered, large (4-4½in.); foliage glossy; very vigorous growth.

Avignon F, *my*, 1974, *Zambra × Allgold*; Cants of Colchester. Flowers medium yellow, dbl. (23 petals), medium (2 in.); slightly fragrant; foliage light, glossy; vigorous growth.

Aviora HT, *mr*, 1960, *Happiness × Seedling*; Verbeek. Flowers clear red, dbl. (40 petals); very large; foliage glossy, dark.

Avô Albina HT, *rb*, 1956, *Peace × Crimson Glory*; Moreira da Silva. Flowers crimson, reverse silvery, high-centered, large; very vigorous.

Avô Alfredo HT, *rb*, 1956, *Seedling × Independence*; Moreira da Silva. Flowers spectrum-red, reverse carmine.

Avoca HT, *mr*, 1907, Dickson, A. Flowers crimson-scarlet, dbl., high-centered, large; fragrant; very vigorous growth.

Avocet F, *ob*, 1983, (HARpluto); *Dame of Sark × Seedling*; Harkness, R., 1984. Bud pointed; flowers orange edged vermilion, semi-dbl. (13 wavy petals), large blooms in large clusters; fragrant; foliage dark, glossy; many, dark prickles; medium, bushy growth.

Avon® HT, *dr*, 1961, *Nocturne × Chrysler Imperial*; Morey; J&P. Bud ovoid; flowers dark red, dbl. (23 petals), high-centered, large (4½-5½ in.); very fragrant; foliage leathery; vigorous, upright growth.

Avon, Climbing Cl HT, *dr*, 1975, Kumar.

Avril Sherwood F, *my*, 1975, *Pink Parfait × Allgold*; Sherwood; F. Mason. Bud ovoid; flowers golden yellow fading to buttercup-yellow, semi-dbl. (18 petals), large (3-3½ in.); slightly fragrant; foliage glossy, dark, leathery; upright growth.

Awakening LCl, *lp*, 1992, *New Dawn sport*; Peter Beales Roses; Hortico, Inc., 1992. Flowers light pink, fully dbl. (26-40 petals), quartered, medium to large (4-7 cms.) blooms; fragrant; foliage light green, glossy; 10' × 8' growth; brought from Czechoslovakia by Mr. D. Balfour to England, where it was introduced by Peter Beales Roses.

Award HT, *mr*, 1953, *Will Rogers × Mme. Henri Guillot*; Taylor, C.A. Flowers velvety red, borne on short stems; very fragrant; foliage very glossy, dark; vigorous growth.

A. W. Jessep HT, *dp*, 1952, Clark, A. Flowers rich cerise-pink, dbl. (38 petals), large; fragrant; vigorous growth.

Ayako™ Gr, *ly*, 1991, (MALmiya); *Sonia sport*; Maltagliati, Mark G.; Nino-miya Nursery Co., 1990. Flowers pale yellow cream, full (26-40 petals), large; flora-tea; slight fragrance; foliage medium, medium green, semi-glossy; medium, upright growth.

Aylsham HNit (S), *dp*, 1948, *Hansa × R. nitida*; Wright, P.H. Bud ovoid; flowers deep pink, dbl., large; slightly fragrant; foliage light green, glossy; sets fruit; vigorous (to 5 ft.); non-recurrent bloom.

Ayrshire Queen Ayr (OGR), *dr*, 1835, *Blush Ayrshire × Tuscany*; Rivers. Flowers purplish crimson, semi-dbl.

Ayrshire Rose (*R. arvensis ayreshirea* Seringe; *R. capreolata* Neill; *R. arvensis capreolata* (Neill) Bean); A group composed of hybrids of *R. arvensis*.

Azalea Rose Pol, *mp*, 1940, *Ellen Poulsen sport*; Griffing Nursery. Flowers bright rose-pink, resemble azaleas.

Azeez F, *op*, 1965, Pal; Indian Agric. Research Inst. Bud pointed; flowers coral-pink, reverse lighter, dbl., high-centered, medium; foliage leathery; upright, compact growth.

Azelda HT, *op*, 1963, *Queen Elizabeth × Rosenelfe*; Matthews. Bud long, pointed; flowers coral-rose, dbl., cupped, borne on long stems; very fragrant; foliage glossy, light green; vigorous, upright growth.

Aztec HT, *or*, 1957, *Charlotte Armstrong × Seedling*; Swim; Armstrong Nursery. Bud long, pointed; flowers scarlet-orange, dbl. (25 petals), high-centered, large (4-5 in.); fragrant; foliage glossy, leathery; vigorous, spreading growth.

Azur F, *m*, 1967, *Sterling Silver × (Gold Strike × Golden Garnette)*; Lens. Bud ovoid; flowers deep lavender-mauve, semi-dbl. (15 petals), pointed, large (2½-3 in.); very fragrant; foliage dark reddish-green; vigorous, compact, bushy growth.

Azure Sea HT, *m*, 1983, (AROlala); *(Angel Face × First Prize) × Lady X*; Christensen; Armstrong Nursery. Flowers silvery lavender, petals edged ruby, deeper reverse, dbl. (30 petals), well-formed, large; slight fragrance; foliage large, dark, matt; upright, bushy growth.

Babe Ruth HT, *op*, 1950, *Los Angeles × Seedling*; Howard, F.H.; H&S. Bud ovoid; flowers coral, reverse rose-coral, dbl. (35-40 petals), cupped, large (4-4½ in.); fragrant; foliage leathery, glossy, bronze; vigorous, upright growth.

Babette F, *m*, 1969, *Seedling × Eminence*; Gaujard. Flowers lavender-pink, single, cupped, small; slightly fragrant; foliage leathery, small; vigorous, bushy growth.

Babt Deitz Pol, *or*, 1924, Opdebeeck. Flowers oriental red, edged salmon, full.

Baby Alan Pol, *mp*, 1930, Kessler; J.T. Lovett. Flowers shining pink, very dbl., resembling English daisy in form, borne in clusters.

Baby Alberic Pol, *ly*, 1932, Chaplin Bros. Bud yellow; flowers creamy white, dbl., small; vigorous; recurrent bloom.

Baby Ashley™ Min, *yb*, 1985, (KINash); King, Gene; AGM Min. Roses. Flowers light yellow, petals edged light pink, dbl. (24 petals), medium blooms borne singly and in clusters of 3-5; no fragrance; foliage small, dark, matt; straight, small, light brown prickles; bushy growth.

Baby Baccará® Min, *or*, 1965, (MEIbyba); *Callisto × Perla de Alcañada*; Meilland, Alain; URS; Wheatcroft Bros. Flowers orange-scarlet, dbl., small (1½ in.); slightly fragrant; foliage dark.

Baby Betsy McCall Min, *lp*, 1960, *Cécile Brünner × Rosy Jewel*; Morey, Dennison; J&P. Flowers light pink, dbl. (20 petals), cupped, micro-mini, small (1 in.); fragrant; foliage leathery, light green; vigorous, dwarf, compact (8 in.) growth.

Baby Bettina Min, *or*, 1977, (MEIdacinu); *(Callisto × Perla de Alcañada) × Starina*; Meilland, M.L.; Meilland Et Cie. Bud ovoid; flowers vermilion, reverse carmine, 15-20 petals, deep cupped, mini-flora, borne 3-11 per cluster; slight fragrance; foliage matt, dense; vigorous.

Baby Betty Pol, *mp*, 1929, *Eblouissant × Comtesse du Cayla*; Burbage Nursery. Bud ovoid, yellow, tinged red; flowers pink, baselighter, full, cupped, small; fragrant; foliage leathery, dark, bronze; vigorous, compact, bushy growth; abundant, recurrent bloom.

Baby Bio F, *dy*, 1977, *Golden Treasure × Seedling*; Smith, E.; Rosemont Nursery. Flowers deep golden yellow, dbl. (28 petals), patio, large (3 in.); slightly fragrant; foliage glossy. GM, Rome, 1976.

Baby Blaze F, *mr*, 1954, (Lund's Jubiläum); *World's Fair × Hamburg*; Kordes, W.; J&P. Bud ovoid; flowers cherry-red, white eye, dbl. (33 petals), semi-cupped, large (3 in.) blooms in clusters of 10-25; fragrant; foliage light, glossy; vigorous, bushy, compact.

Baby Bunting Min, *dp*, 1953, *Ellen Poulsen × Tom Thumb*; deVink, J.; T. Robinson, Porchester Nursery. Flowers deep pink, dbl. (20 petals), small (1¼in.); fragrant.

Baby Cécile Brunner Min, *lp*, 1981, (MORcebru); *Cécile Brünner, Climbing × Fairy Princess*; Moore, Ralph S.; Moore Min. Roses. Flowers soft pink, small; slight fragrance; foliage small, medium green, matt; flowers and plant similar to Cécile Brunner, only in miniature; upright, bushy growth.

Baby Château F, *mr*, 1936, (Château; Baby Vougeot); *Aroma × (Eva × Ami Quinard)*; Kordes. Bud ovoid, crimson; flowers red shaded garnet, dbl., large; fragrant; foliage glossy, bronze; very vigorous, bushy growth; (28).

Baby Cheryl Min, *lp*, 1965, *Spring Song (Min) × Seedling*; Williams, E.D.; Mini-Roses. Bud pointed; flowers light pink, reverse lighter, dbl., micro-mini, small; fragrant (spicy); foliage leathery; vigorous, dwarf growth.

Baby Darling Min, *ab*, 1964, *Little Darling × Magic Wand*; Moore, R.S.; Sequoia Nursery. Bud pointed; flowers apricot-orange, dbl. (20 petals), small; dwarf, bushy (12 in.).

Baby Darling, Climbing Cl Min, *ab*, 1972, Trauger, F.; Sequoia Nursery.

Baby Diana™ Min, *or*, 1986, (SAVadi); *Zorina × (Sheri Anne × Glenfiddich)*; Saville, F. Harmon; Nor'East Min. Roses. Flowers orange-red, yellow reverse, dbl. (20 petals), high-centered, exhibition, small blooms borneusually singly; moderate fragrance; foliage small, medium green, semi-glossy; long, thin, hooked, brown prickles; bushy growth.

Baby Dominic Min, *op*, 1992, (JUDnic); *Centergold × Cuddles*; Bell, Judy; Michigan Mini Roses. Flowers light orange-coral pink, moderately full (15-25 petals), fringed sepals, exhibition, micro-mini, dime-sized blooms borne in small clusters; slight fragrance; foliage small, light green, matt; few prickles; low, compact, bushy growth.

Baby Eclipse™ Min, *ly*, 1984, (MORecli); *(R. wichuraiana × Floradora) × Yellow Jewel*; Moore, Ralph S.; Moore Min. Roses. Bud small; flowers light yellow, semi-dbl., mini-flora, small; slight fragrance; foliage small, medium green, matt; bushy, spreading growth. AOE, 1984.

Baby Elegance Pol, *ab*, 1912, Hobbies. Flowers pale yellow-orange, single.

Baby Face™ Min, *lp*, 1982, (LAVaby); *Popcorn* × *Popcorn*; Laver, Keith. Bud tapered; flowers light pink, dbl. (35 petals), very small blooms in sprays of many; slight fragrance; foliage small, light green, matt; compact growth.

Baby Faurax Pol, *m*, 1924, Lille, L. Flowers violet, dbl., small blooms in large clusters; fragrant; dwarf growth.

Baby Garnette Min, *mr*, 1962, *Red Imp* × *Sparkler*; Morey, Dennison; J&P. Flowers blood-red, dbl., small; foliage dark; vigorous (10-12 in.), compact growth.

Baby Gloria Pol, *or*, 1936, *Gloria Mundi sport*; Böhm. Flowers salmon-red, larger than parent; very dwarf (6-8 in.) growth.

Baby Gold Star Min, *dy*, 1940, (Estrellita de Oro); *Eduardo Toda* × *Rouletii*; Dot, Pedro; C-P. Bud pointed; flowers golden yellow, semi-dbl. (14 petals); slightly fragrant; foliage small, soft.

Baby Gold Star, Climbing Cl Min, *dy*, 1964, Williams, E.D.; Mini-Roses.

Baby Jayne Cl Min, *mp*, 1957, (Fairy Hedge; Pixie Hedge); *Violette* × *Zee*; Moore, R.S.; Germain's. Flowers soft pink, dbl. (45 petals), very small blooms in clusters; foliage small, glossy; height 3-4 ft.

Baby Katie™ Min, *pb*, 1978, *Sheri Anne* × *Watercolor*; Saville, F.H.; Nor'East Min. Roses. Bud ovoid, pointed; flowers cream and pink blend, dbl. (28 petals), high-centered, small; slightly fragrant; foliage matt, green; vigorous, compact, bushy growth.

Baby Lilian Min, Flowers begonia-rose, base tinted orange-yellow, dbl., rather large for the class; slightly fragrant; foliage small, light, glossy; vigorous (12-15 in.) growth; good for indoor potting.

Baby Love Min, *dy*, 1992, *Sweet Magic* × *Miniature Seedling*; Scrivens, Len. Flowers buttercup yellow, single (5 petals), small (0-4 cms) blooms borne mostly singly; slight fragrance; foliage small, medium green, semi-glossy; some prickles; low (400 cms), compact growth.

Baby Lyon Rose Pol, *rb*, 1916, Turbat. Flowers coral-rose, shaded chrome-yellow or shrimp-red, dbl.

Baby Masquerade® Min, *rb*, 1956, (TANba; TANbakede; Baby Carnaval; Baby Carnival; Baby Maskarade; Baby Mascarade®; Baby Maskerade®); *Tom Thumb* × *Masquerade*; Tan-

tau, M.; J&P, 1955. Bud ovoid; flowers yellow aging red, dbl. (23 petals), small (1 in.); slightly fragrant (fruity); foliage leathery; vigorous, compact (8 in. tall).

Baby Masquerade, Climbing Cl Min, *rb*, 1974, Sykes, R.O.; Mini-Roses.

Baby Michael Min, *dp*, 1991, (JUSmichael); *Seedling* × *Seedling*; Justice, Jerry, 1990; Justice Miniature Roses. Bud pointed; flowers deep rose pink, reverse medium pink with a touch of silver at base, very dbl. (38-40 petals), high-centered, medium blooms borne singly; slight, spicy fragrance; foliage medium, dark green, semi-glossy; upright, medium growth.

Baby Mine Pol, *my*, 1929, *Cécile Brunner, Climbing seedling*; Moore, R.S. Flowers sulphur to butter-yellow.

Baby Ophelia Min, *lp*, 1961, *(R. wichuraiana* × *Floradora)* × *Little Buckaroo*; Moore, R.S.; Sequoia Nursery. Bud pointed; flowers soft pink, dbl. (33 petals), small (1 in.); fragrant; foliage glossy; vigorous, bushy (8-12 in.) growth.

Baby Peace Min, *yb*, 1962, *Peace sport*; De Mott & Johnson, G.E. Bud urn shaped; flowers ivory-yellow tipped pink, dbl. (50-55 petals), small (½-1 in.); slightly fragrant; very vigorous growth.

Baby Pinocchio Min, *pb*, 1967, *Golden Glow* × *Little Buckaroo*; Moore, R.S.; Sequoia Nursery; Mini-Roses. Bud ovoid; flowers salmon-pink blend, dbl., small; fragrant; foliage glossy, leathery; vigorous, bushy growth.

Baby Rosamunde Pol, *mp*, 1930, Kessler; J.T. Lovett. Flowers rose-pink, semi-dbl.

Baby Sunbeam LCl, *ab*, 1934, Burbank; Stark Bros. Flowers light apricot, passing to cream-yellow, large yellow center, borne in large cluster; foliage bronze; very vigorous growth.

Baby Sunrise Min, *ab*, 1984, (MACparlez; Gold Fever); *Dorola* × *Moana*; McGredy, Sam; John Mattock Roses. Bud small; flowers copper apricot, semi-dbl., small; slight fragrance; foliage small, medium green, semi-glossy; bushy growth.

Baby Sylvia F, *op*, 1959, *Lady Sylvia* × *Seedling*; Fryer's Nursery. Flowers flesh-salmon-pink, dbl. (25-30 petals), large (3 in.); very vigorous growth.

Baby Talk F, *m*, 1980, *Plain Talk* × *Angel Face*; Weeks. Bud small, ovoid, pointed; flowers dusty mauve-pink, dbl. (26 petals), patio, blooms borne mostly singly; tea fragrance; foliage small to medium, moderately thin; low to medium, compact, dense growth.

Baby Typhoon Min, *ab*, 1988, *Gold Coin sport*; Halevi, A.M., 1987. Flowers bright, clear apricot, center golden-yellow, dbl. (35-40 petals), cupped, exhibition, medium, borne singly or in sprays of 3-5; moderate, damask fragrance; foliage medium, dark green, semiglossy; prickles pointed, large, straw; bushy, spreading, tall growth.

Babylon HT, *op*, 1976, *Tropicana × Pink Favorite*; Bees Ltd.; Sealand Nursery. Flowers deep coral-pink, dbl. (36 petals), low-centered, large (5 in.); very fragrant; foliage glossy, dark; moderately vigorous growth.

Bacardi HT, *ob*, 1987, *Seedling self pollination*; Weeks, O.L.; Weeks Roses, 1988. Flowers uniform iridescent coral-orange, fading lighter, dbl. (30 petals), high-centered, exhibition, small, borne singly; slight, fruity fragrance; foliage medium, medium green, semi-glossy; straight, small, reddish prickles; upright, medium growth.

Baccará® HT, *or*, 1954, (MEger; Jacqueline); *Happiness × Independence*; Meilland, F.; URS, 1954; C-P, 1957. Flowers bright orange-red, dbl. (75 petals), cupped to flat, medium (3 in.); foliage dark, leathery; bushy, upright growth.

Baccará, Climbing® Cl HT, *or*, 1965, (MEgersar); URS.

Bacchus HT, *dp*, 1951, Dickson, A. Flowers cherry-pink, dbl. (25 petals), medium; fragrant; vigorous growth. GM, NRS, 1952.

Bad Füssing® F, *mr*, 1980, (KORbad); *Gruss an Bayern × Seedling*; Kordes, W. Bud large; flowers medium red, dbl. (23 petals), cupped, blooms in clusters; fragrant; foliage glossy, dark; few prickles; vigorous, upright, bushy growth.

Bad Neuenahr K (S), *mr*, 1958, Kordes, W. Bud ovoid; flowers scarlet, dbl. (50 petals), cupped, large (4 in.) blooms in clusters (to 15); fragrant; foliage dark, leathery; vigorous (6 ft.) growth.

Bad Pyrmont F, *or*, 1976, *Duftwolke × Seedling*; Kordes; Horstmann. Bud pointed; flowers orange-red; dbl. (40 petals), large (4 in.), high centered; slightly fragrant; foliage dark, soft; vigorous, upright, bushy; abundant bloom.

Bad Wörishofen® F, *mr*, 1972, (Gruss an Worishofen); *Sarabande × Marlena*; Kordes, W. Bud ovoid; flowers medium red, semi-dbl. (18 petals), cupped, medium (2½ in.); slightly fragrant; foliage dark, soft; vigorous, bushy growth.

Baden-Baden HT, *dr*, 1952, *Poinsettia × Crimson Glory*; Kordes. Flowers deep crimson, dbl., large; very fragrant; foliage dark, leathery; vigorous, upright growth.

Badinage HT, *op*, 1951, *Peace × Seedling*; Gaujard, J. Flowers salmon-pink flushed cop-

pery, dbl. (30 petals), large (4-4½ in.); fragrant; foliage leathery, dark; vigorous.

Bagatelle HT, *mr*, 1943, Gaujard. Bud large, oval; flowers bright red, very dbl.; fragrant; foliage leathery; very vigorous, bushy growth.

Bagdad HT, *or*, 1953, *Charlotte Armstrong × Signora*; Swim. Bud ovoid to urn shape; flowers nasturtium-red toorange, dbl. (48-55 petals), high-centered, becoming cupped, large (4½ in.); very fragrant; foliage glossy; very vigorous, bushy growth.

Bagheera F, *or*, 1976, (KORgera); *Nordia × Seedling*; Kordes, W. Bud ovoid; flowers orange-red, dbl. (35 petals), high-centered, large (4 in.); slightly fragrant; foliage glossy, dark; vigorous, upright growth.

Bagliore HT, *mr*, 1955, Aicardi, D. Flowers crimson-red; very fragrant; stiff stem; very vigorous growth.

Bahama F, *dr*, 1968, *Fidélio × Hanne*; Soenderhousen. Flowers dark red, semi-dbl.; very fragrant; vigorous, low growth.

Bahia F, *ob*, 1974, *Rumba × Tropicana*; Lammerts, Dr. W.E.; Armstrong Nursery. Bud ovoid; flowers orange, dbl., cupped, medium; fragrant (spicy); foliage glossy, dark, leathery; vigorous, upright, bushy growth. AARS, 1974.

Bahrs Lieveling F, *mr*, 1950, *Donald Prior × Orange Triumph*; Leenders, M. Flowers velvety crimson-red.

Baiser HT, *w*, 1953, *Mme. Joseph Perraud × Independence*; Mallerin; EFR. Flowers pearly white, edges tinted pink, dbl. (40 petals), high-centered, medium (3 in.); fragrant; vigorous growth.

Bajazzo HT, *rb*, 1961, Kordes, R.; Kordes. Flowers velvety blood-red, reverse white, well-formed, large; very fragrant; vigorous, upright growth.

Balalaika F, *dr*, 1978, Hubner; O. Baum. Bud ovoid; flowers blood-red, dbl.; fragrant; foliage glossy; low, bushy growth.

Balcon LCl, *or*, 1960, *Spectacular × Seedling*; Combe; Minier. Bud ovoid; flowers geranium-red, dbl., open, medium; slightly fragrant; foliage dark, glossy; very vigorous growth.

Balduin HT, *pb*, 1896, (Crimson Maman Cochet; Red Maman Cochet;); Helen Gould *Charles Darwin × Marie van Houtte*; Lambert, P., 1896; Dingee & Conard, 1901. Flowers pink, edged darker, dbl., large; fragrant; vigorous growth.

Baléares HT, *w*, 1957, *Peace × Flambee*; Dot, S. Bud pointed; flower base and reverse of petals white suffused carmine, deeper at edges, dbl. (35 petals); stiff stem; very fragrant; foliage dark, glossy; upright growth.

Bali Pol, 1960, *Masquerade × Golden Rain*; Leenders, J. Flowers orange-yellow, single (6 petals), open, large; foliage glossy, light green; bushy growth.

Bali-Hi HT, *mp*, 1959, Lowe. Flowers peach-pink to shell-pink, high-centered, medium; fragrant; foliage glossy; vigorous, upright growth.

Balinese HT, *m*, 1963, *Grey Pearl × Brownie*; Boerner; J&P. Bud ovoid; flowers brown and lavender tones, dbl. (35-40 petals), cupped, large (4½-5 in.); very fragrant (fruity); foliage glossy; vigorous, upright growth.

Baljit HT, *dp*, 1979, *Velsheda sport*; Lucknow. Bud pointed; flowers spirea-red, dbl. (30-40 petals), open but full, large (5 in.); foliage dark, leathery; free growth; long-lasting, profuse bloom.

Ballade F, *op*, 1960, *Signal Red × Polyantha seedling*; deRuiter. Flowers deep orange-salmon, dbl. (25 petals), well formed blooms borne in clusters; bushy growth.

Ballerina HMsk (S), *mp*, 1937, Bentall. Flowers bright soft pink, white eye, single, small blooms in very large clusters; vigorous (3 ft.) growth.

Ballerina F, *my*, 1941, Leenders, M. Flowers naples yellow, dbl., large; fragrant.

Ballerine HT, *w*, 1955, Buyl Frères; Delforge. Bud long; flowers satiny snow-white, dbl., open, medium; very fragrant; foliage glossy; vigorous, bushy growth.

Ballet® HT, *dp*, 1958, (KORflot); *Florex × Karl Herbst*; Kordes, R.; A. Dickson; McGredy. Flowers deep pink, dbl. (52 petals), large (5 in.); slightly fragrant; foliage gray-green; vigorous, bushy growth.

Ballet, Climbing Cl HT, *w*, 1962, Kordes.

Baltimore HT, *lp*, 1898, *Mme. Antoine Rivoire × Lady Mary Fitzwilliam*; Cook, J.; Blush tinted.

Baltimore Beauty LCl, *ly*, 1927, Schluter. Flowers buff-yellow, fading white, single and semi-dbl., borne in clusters on long, strong stems; fragrant.

Baltimore Belle HSet (OGR), *lp*, 1843, (Belle de Baltimore); *Probably R. setigera × Noisette*; Feast. Flowers pale blush to rose-white, very dbl., borne in clusters; fragrant; vigorous growth; non-recurrent bloom.

Bambey HT, *mr*, 1979, (*Fragrant Cloud × Peace*) *× Alec's Red*; Perry, Astor, 1981. Bud long, pointed; flowers medium red, dbl. (60 petals), classic HT form; intense, fruity fragrance; foliage matt; small, recurred prickles; medium growth.

Bambi F, *mp*, 1962, *The Optimist × Korona*; Watkins Roses. Flowers bright pink, dbl. (24 petals), medium (2 in.) blooms in clusters; slightly fragrant; foliage dark; vigorous, bushy, low growth.

Bambi F, *mp*, 1962, Abrams, Von; Peterson & Dering. Bud pointed; flowers light apricot-pink, semi-dbl. (20 petals), cupped, large (3 in.) blooms in clusters; slightly fragrant; foliage glossy; vigorous, bushy, compact.

Bambina F, *w*, 1962, *Seedling × Virgo*; Moreira da Silva. Bud yellow; flowers white, semi-dbl., large, borne in clusters.

Bambino Min, *mp*, 1953, *Perla de Alcañada pink sport*; Dot, P.

Bambula® F, *op*, 1970, Tantau; Wheatcroft & Sons, 1969. Flowers orange-pink, dbl. (28 petals), large (5 in.); slightly fragrant; foliage glossy, dark.

Banana Split Min, *yb*, 1987, (ZIPban); *Little Darling × Poker Chip*; Zipper, Herbert; Magic Moment Miniatures. Flowers creamy yellow blushed with pink, moderately full (15-25 petals), medium; no fragrance; foliage medium, medium green, semi-glossy; upright, bushy growth.

Banaras Dawn HT, *ab*, 1977, Saxena; Doon Valley Roses. Bud tapered; flowers apricot-buff, dbl. (30 petals), high-centered, large (4½ in.); very fragrant (fruity); foliage glossy, light green; vigorous growth.

Banater Rose HT, *w*, 1927, *Harry Kirk seedling*; Mühle. Flowers cream-white, center orange-yellow, dbl.; slightly fragrant.

Banbridge F, *pb*, 1967, *Mme. Léon Cuny × Cläre Grammerstorf*; McGredy, S. IV. Flowers rose-red and yellow, well shaped, large (3 in.) blooms in clusters; slightly fragrant.

Banco HT, *op*, 1956, *Peace × Seedling*; Laperrière; EFR. Flowers salmon-pink becoming gold tinted, dbl. (50 petals), well-formed, large; foliage bright green; vigorous, upright growth.

Bangor F, *or*, 1972, *Jubilant × Marlena*; Dickson, A. Flowers geranium-lake, dbl. (24 petals), ovate, large (3½ in.); slightly fragrant; foliage leathery; free growth.

Banjaran F, *yb*, 1969, Pal; KSG Son. Flowers gold and orange-red, dbl., cupped, small blooms in clusters; slightly fragrant; foliage leathery; vigorous, upright, compact growth.

Banksiaeflora R, *w*, *Possibly R. arvensis × Noisette hybrid*. Flowers white, center cream, very dbl., small.

Banner HT, *pb*, 1951, *Charlotte Armstrong sport*; Raffel; Port Stockton Nursery. Flowers deep pink, striped white.

Banshee S, *mp*, Origin unknown, 1928. Flowers pink, troubled by balling, very dbl., of poor texture; fragrant; non-recurrent.

Bantry Bay® LCl, *mp*, 1967, *New Dawn × Korona*; McGredy, S. IV; McGredy. Flowers soft pink, reverse bright pink, large (4 in.) blooms in clusters; slightly fragrant.

Banzai HT, *rb*, 1961, (MEIlimona); *Radar × Caprice (Meilland)*; Meilland, M.L.; C-P. Bud ovoid; flowers red, pink and cream blend, dbl. (30 petals), high-centered to cupped, medium (3½ in.); slightly fragrant; foliage leathery, dark; vigorous, bushy growth.

Banzai HT, *my*, 1976, (MEIlimona; Banzai '76); *Coed × ((Seedling × Seedling) × Verla)*; Paolino; Meilland. Flowers canary-yellow, dbl. (35 petals), full, deeply cupped, large (4 in.); slightly fragrant; vigorous growth.

Barbara HT, *rb*, 1923, Paul, W. Flowers bright red, base yellow, reverse pale yellow.

Barbara HT, *yb*, 1962, Gaujard; Gandy. Flowers amber-yellow lightly flushed pink, semi-dbl. (20 petals), high-centered, large (5 in.); foliage dark; very vigorous growth.

Barbara Bush™ HT, *pb*, 1990, (JACbush); *Pristine × Antigua*; Warriner, William; Bear Creek Gardens, 1991. Flowers salmon pink where exposed to sun, lighter pink to ivory white where unexposed, reverse pink near margin, near white at base, dbl. (25-30 petals), high-centered, large, borne singly; heavy, damask fragrance; foliage medium, medium green, glossy; tall, upright, spreading growth.

Barbara Frietchie HT, *dp*, 1959, *Heart's Desire × The Chief*; Silva; Plant Hybridizers of Calif. Bud long, pointed; flowers rose-red, dbl., open, large; vigorous, upright growth.

Barbara Mandrell™ Min, *ab*, 1990, (KINbarb); *(Seedling × Party Girl) × Party Girl*; King, Gene, 1980; AGM Miniature Roses, 1991. Bud pointed; flowers dark apricot changing to apricot-pink at ¼ open, yellow base, aging to white, dbl. (28 petals), high-centered, exhibition, medium, borne singly or in sprays of 3-10; slight fragrance; foliage medium, medium green, matt; upright, medium growth.

Barbara Mason HT, *my*, 1947, *Eclipse × Luis Brinas*; Moss; F. Mason. Bud long, pointed; flowers yellow, semi-dbl., high-centered, medium; fragrant; foliage glossy; vigorous, upright growth. A florists' variety.

Barbara Meyer Gr, *or*, 1971, *Queen Elizabeth × Tropicana*; Meyer, H.M.; Aloe Vera Nursery. Bud ovoid; flowers orange-red, very dbl., high-centered, medium; slightly fragrant; foliage glossy, dark; vigorous, upright growth.

Barbara Richards HT, *yb*, 1930, Dickson, A. Flowers yellow, reverse flushed pink, dbl., very large; weak neck; fragrant; vigorous, bushy growth.

Barbara Robinson HT, *w*, 1925, Dickson, A. Bud long, pointed; flowers creamy white, dbl., high-centered, large; slightly fragrant.

Barbara Straus HT, *dr*, 1978, *Mister Lincoln × Seedling*; Schwartz, E.; Flora World, Inc. Bud long, pointed; flowers dark red, dbl. (22 petals), blooms borne singly; slight fragrance; foliage glossy; spreading, upright growth.

Barbara Ward HT, *mr*, 1931, *Royal Red × Columbia*; Ward, F.B. Flowers crimson-scarlet, dbl. (42 petals), large; fragrant; vigorous growth.

Barbarella Min, *pb*, 1981, *Seedling × Seedling*; Barni-Pistoia, Rose. Flowers deep pink, reverse creamy yellow, dbl. (20 petals), small; light fragrance; foliage small, dark, matt; bushy growth.

Barbarossa HP (OGR), *m*, 1906, *(Frau Karl Druschki × Captain Hayward) × Princesse de Béarn*; Welter. Flowers carmine-purple, full (55 petals), large; fragrant; vigorous.

Barbecue F, *mr*, 1961, *Seedling × Lilli Marleen*; Dickson, P.; A. Dickson. Flowers rich red, dbl. (30 petals), flat, large (4 in.) blooms in large clusters; fragrant; foliage dark; vigorous, upright, bushy growth.

Barbie F, *mp*, 1977, *Escort × Jazz Fest*; Swim & Ellis; Armstrong Nursery. Bud pointed, ovoid; flowers medium pink, dbl. (35-40 petals), sweetheart, medium (2½ in.); slightly fragrant; foliage small, glossy; upright growth.

Barcarolle HT, *mr*, 1959, *Paulette × Tonnerre*; Laperrière; EFR. Flowers crimson tinted geranium-red, dbl. (50 petals), large; vigorous, bushy growth.

Barcelona HT, *dr*, 1932, *(Sensation × Templar) × Lord Charlemont*; Kordes. Bud long, pointed; flowers crimson, dbl. (75 petals), large; fragrant (spicy); foliage dark; vigorous growth.

Bardou Job B (OGR), *dr*, 1887, *Gloire des Rosomanes × Général Jacqueminot*; Nabonnand, G. Flowers crimson, shaded blackish, semi-dbl.; vigorous, semi-climbing growth.

Barillet M (OGR), *mr*, 1850, Verdier, V. Flowers dark carmine, dbl., cupped, large.

Barkhatnaia Krasavitsa HT, *dr*, 1938, (Velvet Beauty); Gubonen. Flowers velvety red, semi-dbl., cupped, medium; fragrant; foliage dark; low growth.

Barn Dance S, *op*, 1975, *Tickled Pink × Prairie Princess*; Buck; Iowa State University. Bud ovoid, long, pointed; flowers light salmon-pink, dbl. (23 petals), shallowly cupped, large (2½-3½ in.); slightly fragrant; foliage light to dark, leathery.

Baron de Bonstetten HP (OGR), *dr*, 1871, *Général Jacqueminot × Géant des Batailles*; Liabaud. Flowers dark velvety crimson, dbl. (80 petals), large; fragrant; vigorous, compact growth; sometimes recurrent bloom.

Baron de Wassenaer M (OGR), *dp*, 1854, Verdier, V. Flowers light crimson, cupped blooms in clusters; vigorous growth.

Baron Girod de l'Ain HP (OGR), *rb*, 1897, *Eugène Furst sport*; Reverchon. Flowers bright red, petals edged white.

Baron Jacques Riston HT, *op*, 1936, *Mme. Butterfly × (Rev. David R. Williamson × Gorgeous)*; Ketten Bros. Bud long, pointed; flowers salmon-pink, dbl. (45-50 petals), well shaped, large; fragrant; very vigorous growth.

Baron Meillandina® Min, *rb*, 1987, (MEItifran; Baron Sunblaze); *Magic Carrousel × ((Alain × R. mutabilis) × (Medar × Caprice))*; Meilland, M.L.; Meilland Et Cie, 1989. Flowers white with red edges, dbl. (40+ petals), umbrella-shaped, medium; no fragrance; foliage small, medium green, glossy; bushy growth.

Baron T'Kind de Roodenbecke HP (OGR), *m*, 1897, Lévêque. Flowers shaded purple.

Baronesa de Ovilar HT, 1935, *Sensation × Souv. de Claudius Pernet*; Munné, B. Flowers carmine tinted yellow, dbl., very large on strong stems; very fragrant; foliage dark; very vigorous growth.

Baroness Krayenhoff HT, *pb*, 1931, *Mrs. Henry Bowles × Lady Roundway*; Buisman. Flowers peach-pink, center orange, dbl., very large on long stems; fragrant; foliage light green; vigorous, compact growth.

Baroness Rothschild HP (OGR), *lp*, 1868, (Baronne Adolphe de Rothschild); *Souv. de la Reine d'Angleterre sport*; Pernet Père. Flowers very soft rose, tinted white, dbl. (40 petals), cupped, large; vigorous, erect growth; some recurrent bloom.

Baronesse A. van Hövell tôt Westerflier HT, *m*, 1933, Leenders, M. Flowers carmine-purple, base yellow, dbl., large; fragrant; foliage bronze; very vigorous, bushy growth.

Baronesse H. von Geyr HT, *pb*, 1928, *(Farbenkonigin × Juliet) × Sunburst*; Leenders, M. Flowers pale flesh and vermilion-red, dbl.; fragrant.

Baronesse Manon F, *mp*, 1938, *Else Poulsen × Dame Edith Helen*; Poulsen, S.; C-P, 1952. Flowers clear pink, firm petals, large (3 in.); fragrant; foliage glossy, holly-like; vigorous, bushy growth.

Baronesse M. van Tuyll van Serooskerken HT, *pb*, 1922, *Jonkheer J.L. Mock × Mme. Mélanie Soupert*; Leenders, M. Flowers rose and lilac-white, base apricot, semi-dbl.

Baronesse S.H.W. van Dedem HT, yb, 1923, Leenders, M. Flowers yellow and coppery, semi-dbl., open, large; fragrant; foliage dark, glossy; vigorous, bushy growth.

Baronesse van Ittersum R, rb, 1910, Crimson Rambler × *Mme. Laurette Messimy*; Leenders, M. Flowers light crimson, shaded deeper, semi-dbl., open, borne in clusters; slightly fragrant; foliage dark, glossy; vigorous climbing (15 ft.); free, non-recurrent bloom.

Baronne Charles d'Huart HT, *pb*, 1910, *Pharisaer × Seedling*; Ketten Bros. Flowers lilac-rose suffused white, dbl., reflexed.

Baronne de Maynard N (OGR), *w*, 1865, *Blanche Lafitte × Sappho (an unrecorded variety)*; Lacharme. Flowers white, edges tinged pink, cupped; moderately vigorous.

Baronne de Stael G (OGR), *ob*, 1820, Vibert. Flowers salmon-pink, full, open, large; vigorous, branching growth.

Baronne de Vivario Pol, *w*, 1925, *Orléans Rose × Jeanny Soupert*; Soupert & Notting. Flowers white, dbl., in clusters.

Baronne Edmond de Rothschild® HT, *rb*, 1968, (MEIgriso; Baronne de Rothschild); *(Baccará × Crimson King) × Peace*; Meilland; URS, 1969. Flowers ruby-red, whitish reverse, dbl. (40 petals), high-centered, large; very fragrant; foliage glossy, leathery; vigorous growth. GM, Rome & Lyon, 1968.

Baronne Edmond de Rothschild, Climbing® Cl HT, *rb*, 1974, (MEIgrisosar; Baronne de Rothschild, Climbing; Grimpant Baronne de Rothschild); Meilland, M.L.

Baronne Finaz HT, *mp*, 1961, *Peace seedling × Opera*; Gaujard. Flowers bright pink, dbl. (35 petals), large blooms on long stems; fragrant; foliage glossy, dark; very vigorous, upright growth.

Baronne Henriette de Loew T (OGR), *w*, 1888, Nabonnand, G. Flowers pinkish white, center yellow, full; fragrant.

Baronne Henriette de Snoy T (OGR), *pb*, 1897, (Baroness Henrietta Snoy; Baroness Henriette Snoy); *Gloire de Dijon × Mme. Lombard*; Bernaix, A. Flowers flesh, reverse carmine-pink, dbl., well-formed, large; vigorous growth.

Baronne Prévost HP (OGR), *mp*, 1842, Desprez. Flowers rose-pink, shading lighter, full, flat, large; fragrant; vigorous, erect growth; recurrent bloom.

Barrie F, *pb*, 1973, *Sumatra* × *Fashion*; Schloen, J. Bud ovoid; flowers salmon-pink, dbl., cupped, medium, slightly fragrant; foliage flossy, light; free bloom.

Barter's Pink HT, *ob*, 1963, *Queen Elizabeth* × *Claude*; Barter. Flowers bright coral-pink, deeply veined, dbl. (48 reflexed petals), large (4 in.); slightly fragrant; foliage light green; vigorous, bushy growth.

Bashful Pol, *pb*, 1955, (Giesebrecht); deRuiter; Gregory & Willicher Baumschulen. Flowers reddish pink, white eye, single, small blooms in trusses; bushy, compact growth.

Basildon Belle F, *or*, 1964, *Anna Wheatcroft sport*; Maarse, G.; Basildon Rose Garden. Flowers vermilion.

Basildon Bond HT, *ab*, 1980, (HARjosine); *(Sabine* × *Circus)* × *(Yellow Cushion* × *Glory of Ceylon)*; Harkness, R. Flowers apricot, dbl. (27 petals), loose form, borne 1-3 per cluster; fragrant; foliage large, medium green, very glossy; large, straight prickles; medium, upright growth. GM, Belfast, 1982.

Bastogne HT, *or*, Grandes Roseraies. Flowers vermilion, shaded darker, well formed; fragrant; foliage dark; very vigorous.

Battle of Britain HT, *yb*, 1970, *Miss Ireland* × *Summer Sunshine*; Gandy; Wheatcroft & Sons. Flowers yellow-orange, dbl. (30 petals), medium; fragrant.

Bayadère HT, *ab*, 1954, *R.M.S. Queen Mary* × *Seedling*; Mallerin; EFR. Flowers salmon-pink to canary yellow, tinted pink, dbl. (52 petals), high-centered, large; slight fragrance; foliage dark, bronze; vigorous, bushy growth. GM, NRS, 1954.

B.C.™ Min, *dr*, 1986, (KINbee); *Evelyn Fison* × *Magic Mist*; King, Gene; AGM Min. Roses. Flowers dark red, reverse darker, dbl. (24 petals), high-centered, exhibition blooms borne singly; slight fragrance; foliage small, medium green, matt; long, hooked, brown prickles; fruit globular; medium, upright, bushy growth.

Be Glad HT, *rb*, 1988, *Paradise* × *Color Magic*; McMillan, Tom. Flowers white changing to red, reverse white, aging deep pink, dbl. (25-30 petals), high-centered, exhibition, medium, borne singly; moderate, fruity fragrance; foliage medium, dark green, glossy; prickles normal; fruit none; upright, medium growth. 1988 ARC TG (S).

Beach Boy Min, *my*, 1981, *Tom Brown* × *Seedling*; Williams, Ernest; Mini-Roses. Bud pointed; flowers golden buff, dbl. (48 petals), high-centered blooms borne usually singly; slight fragrance; foliage small, dark, slightly glossy; short, tan prickles; upright, bushy growth.

Beachcomber F, *r*, 1986, (MAClapaz); *Seedling* × *Colorbreak*; McGredy, S. Flowers russet, semi-dbl. (6-14 petals), medium; slight fragrance; foliage medium, medium green, semi-glossy; bushy growth.

Beacon Belle R, *lp*, 1919, *Orléans Rose* × *(Katharina Zeimet* × *R. arvensis hybrid)*; Farquhar. Flowers flesh passing to white, dbl., borne in clusters; fragrant.

Beacon Lodge HT, *dr*, 1976, *Chopin* × *Ena Harkness*; Ellick. Flowers deep red, dbl. (40-45 petals), full, large (4-5 in.); fragrant; foliage glossy, dark; very vigorous growth.

Beatrice F, *dp*, 1968, *Paddy McGredy* × *(Kordes' Perfecta* × *Montezuma)*; McGredy, S., IV. Flowers deep rose pink, dbl., in large sprays; slightly fragrant.

Beatrice Boeke HT, *dp*, 1966, *Montezuma* × *Detroiter*; Buisman. Bud ovoid; flowers pink-red, dbl., large.

Beatrice McGregor HT, *dr*, 1938, *Sensation* × *Seedling*; Clark, A.; NRS Victoria. Flowers dark red, dbl., large; very fragrant.

Beau Narcisse G (OGR), *m*, 1850, Miellez. Flowers purple, striped.

Beaucaire Pol, *rb*, 1937, Grandes Roseraies. Flowers edges chamois-pink, center coppery yellow, reverse coppery-red, dbl., large; vigorous, dwarf growth.

Beaujolais HT, *mr*, 1932, *Hadley* × *Laurent Carle*; Croibier. Flowers crimson-carmine, dbl., globular, very large; very fragrant; very vigorous.

Beaulieu Abbey F, *ab*, 1964, *Masquerade* × *Docteur Valois*; Cobley; Blaby Rose Gardens. Flowers creamy yellow suffused pink, dbl., well formed, large (4 in.); fragrant; foliage dark, glossy, leathery; vigorous growth.

Beauté HT, *ab*, 1953, *Mme. Joseph Perraud* × *Seedling*; Mallerin; EFR. Bud long; flowers light apricot, dbl., well-formed, large; fragrant; vigorous growth.

Beauté d'Automne Pol, *dp*, 1918, *Phyllis* × *Seedling*; Turbat. Flowers bright rose-pink, dbl., borne in clusters of 50-70.

Beauté de France HT, *w*, 1920, *Mme. Mélanie Soupert* × *Kaiserin Auguste Viktoria*; Toussaint Mille Fils. Flowers creamy white to pure white, inside yellow, dbl.; fragrant.

Beauté de France HT, 1952, *(Comtesse Vandal* × *Seedling)* × *Seedling*; Gaujard. Bud long, pointed; flowers brick flushed coppery, dbl.; medium; fragrant; foliage leathery, dark; upright growth.

Beauté de Lyon HP (OGR), *or*, 1910, *Seedling* × *Soliel d'Or*; Pernet-Ducher. Flowers coral-red, tinted yellow, dbl.; fragrant. GM, Bagatelle, 1911.

Beauté Inconstante T (OGR), *ob*, 1892, Pernet-Ducher. Flowers orange to coppery red, shaded carmine and yellow; fragrant; vigorous growth.

Beauté Lyonnaise HT, *w*, 1895, Pernet-Ducher. Flowers white tinted pale yellow, large.

Beaute Orléanaise R, *w*, 1919, Turbat. Flowers white to flesh-pink, dbl., borne in clusters of 20-25; slightly fragrant.

Beauté Spatiale® HT, *mr*, 1966, (DELdrop); *Walko × Impeccable*; Delbard-Chabert. Flowers velvety red, semi-dbl., high-centered, medium; slightly fragrant; foliage bronze, soft; moderate, bushy growth.

Beautiful Britain F, *or*, 1983, (DICfire); *Red Planet × Eurorose*; Dickson, P.; Dickson Nurseries, Ltd. Flowers orange-red, reverse deeper, dbl. (20 petals), medium, in clusters; slight fragrance; foliage medium, medium green, semi-glossy; upright, bushy. ROTY, 1983.

Beautiful Doll Min, *mp*, 1982, *Seedling × Zinger*; Jolly, Betty; Rosehill Farm. Flowers medium pink, dbl. (25 petals), exhibition form, borne singly and in small clusters; fragrant; foliage small, dark, semi-glossy; bushy, spreading growth.

Beautiful Dreamer F, *ob*, 1977, *Seedling × Seedling*; Herholdt, J.A. Flowers orange to sunset-gold, dbl. (35 petals), full, pointed, medium (2-2½ in.); slightly fragrant; foliage glossy.

Beautiful Sunday Min, *mr*, 1977, *Camelot × Unnamed Camelot seedling*; Takatori; Japan Rose Nursery. Bud ovoid; flowers bright geranium-red, very dbl. (60 petals), cupped, small; fragrant; foliage glossy, dark, leathery; compact, bushy growth.

Beauty HT, *mr*, 1931, *(Crusader × Premier) × American Beauty*; Ward, F.B. Flowers American Beauty red, but darker, dbl., very large on long stems; fragrant; vigorous.

Beauty Cream F, *w*, 1956, Verschuren; Gandy. Flowers cream, large; fragrant; foliage dark; vigorous, upright growth.

Beauty of Dropmore S, *w*, 1956, *R. spinosissima altaica × R. spinosissima cultivar*; Skinner. Flowers white, dbl.; bushy, erect growth; non-recurrent bloom.

Beauty of Hurst R, *w*, 1926, Hicks. Flowers creamy buff; fragrant; foliage full, dark; very vigorous.

Beauty of New South Wales Pol, *rb*, 1931, *Orléans Rose × Alice Amos*; Knight, G. Flowers bright crimson, center white, single, small blooms in clusters of 20-60; fragrant; bushy, dwarf growth.

Beauty of Rosemawr T (OGR), *pb*, 1903, Conard & Jones. Flowers carmine rose veined vermilion and white, full, medium.

Beauty of Stapleford HT, *rb*, 1879, *Mme. Bravy × Comtesse d'Oxford*; Bennett. Flowers red and violet, well formed, large; moderate growth.

Beauty of Waltham HP (OGR), *mr*, 1862, Paul, W. Flowers rosy crimson, full, large; fragrant; vigorous growth; recurrent bloom.

Beauty Queen F, *mp*, 1984, (CANmiss); *English Miss × Seedling*; Cants of Colchester. Flowers medium pink, dbl. (40+ petals), medium; very fragrant; foliage large, dark, glossy.

Beauty Secret Min, *mr*, 1965, *Little Darling × Magic Wand*; Moore, R.S.; Sequoia Nursery. Bud pointed; flowers cardinal-red, dbl., high-centered, small (1½ in.); very fragrant; foliage small, glossy, leathery; vigorous, bushy growth. AOE, 1975.

Beautyglo™ Min, *lp*, 1985, (MINwco); *Tom Brown × Black Jack*; Williams, Ernest; Mini-Roses. Flowers light pink, dbl. (35 petals), high-centered, exhibition form, small; slight fragrance; foliage small, dark, semi-glossy; bushy growth.

Beauty's Blush HRg (S), *dp*, 1955, *Tetonkaha × Pink Pearl*; Univ. of Saskatchewan. Flowers deep pink, becoming lighter, dbl.; fragrant; vigorous (6 ft.); non-recurrent bloom; hardy on the Canadian prairies.

Bébé Blanc Pol, *w*, 1922, Turbat. Flowers white, dbl., borne in large clusters; dwarf growth.

Bébé Leroux Pol, *w*, 1901, *Mignonette × Archiduchesse Elisabeth-Marie*; Soupert. Flowers white, medium, in trusses of 20-40; fragrant; compact growth.

Becky HT, *dp*, 1925, Beckwith. Flowers glowing rose-pink, single; vigorous.

Bedford Crimson HT, *dr*, 1926, *Richmond × Château de Clos Vougeot*; Laxton Bros. Flowers velvety crimson, dbl. (40 petals), well formed; fragrant.

Bedfordia HT, *pb*, 1931, Laxton Bros. Flowers pink, outer petals lighter, center salmon, dbl. (52 petals); fragrant; vigorous growth.

Bedrich Smetana HT, *w*, 1933, *Modesty × Ophelia*; Böhm. Flowers pearly white, semi-dbl., open, very large; vigorous, bushy growth.

Bee's Frolic S, *lp*, 1976, *Schneezwerg × Clair Matin*; Dawnay, Mrs. E. Bud small, pointed; flowers light pink, semi-dbl. (14 petals), borne 2-3 per cluster; very fragrant; foliage medium, matt; small prickles; upright, strong growth; repeat bloom.

Bel Ami® F, *mr*, 1958, (LAPci); *Michèle Meilland* × *Tonnerre*; Laperrière; EFR. Flowers red, dbl., large blooms in clusters of 7-8; bushy growth.

Bel Ami F, *mr*, 1958, *Michele Meilland* × *Tonnerre*; Laperrière; EFR. Flowers red, dbl., large, borne in clusters of 7-8; bushy growth.

Bel Ange HT, *mp*, 1962, (Bella Epoca; Belle Epoque; Belle Ange); *(Independence* × *Papillon Rose)* × *(Charlotte Armstrong* × *Floradora)*; Lens; J&P, 1965. Flowers soft pink, reverse darker, dbl. (35 petals), large (4¹/₂ in.); fragrant; foliage dark; vigorous growth. GM, Kortrijk, 1965.

Bel Canto HT, *or*, 1964, Mondial Roses. Flowers bright geranium-red, well formed; foliage coppery; upright growth.

Belfast Belle HT, *dy*, 1990, (DICrobot); *Seedling* × *Pot o'Gold*; Dickson, Patrick; Dickson Nurseries, Ltd., 1991. Flowers dark yellow, full (26-40 petals), large; slight fragrance; foliage medium, medium green, semi-glossy; upright, bushy growth.

Belgica HT, *dr*, 1929, Buyl Frères. Flowers crimson-red, shaded garnet, very dbl., large; vigorous growth.

Belinda HMsk (S), *mp*, 1936, Bentall. Flowers medium pink, semi-dbl., borne in very large, erect trusses; fragrant; vigorous (4-6 ft.) growth; good hedge or pillar rose.

Belinda's Dream S, *mp*, 1992, (Belinda's Rose); *Jersey Beauty* × *Tiffany*; Basye, Robert, 1988. Flowers medium pink, very full (41+ petals), large (8-11 cms) blooms borne in small clusters; fruity, raspberry fragrance; foliage medium, medium green, matt; medium (5x4'), bushy growth; repeats.

Bell Charmer Min, *ob*, 1992, (BELcharm); *(Cherish* × *Avandel)* × *Seedling*; Bell, Charles E., Jr.; Kimbrew-Walter Roses, 1993. Flowers distinctive soft orange with light yellow petal base and reverse, full (26-40 petals), well-formed, medium (4-7 cms) blooms borne singly and in clusters of 3-7; slight fragrance; foliage medium, medium green, semi-glossy; some prickles; medium (45-55 cms), upright, bushy growth.

Bell Ringer Min, *dp*, 1989, (Bellringer); *(Fragrant Cloud* × *Avandel)* × *Bonny*; Bell, Charles E., Jr.; Kimbrew-Walter Roses, 1989. Flowers deep pink, silver at base, dbl. (34 petals), small; slight, fruity fragrance; foliage medium, medium green, semi-glossy; upright, bushy growth.

Bella Donna D (OGR), *lp*, Prior to 1848. Flowers soft lilac-pink, dbl., large.

Bella Donna F, *mr*, 1964, *Baccará seedling* × *Miracle*; Verbeek. Bud ovoid; flowers bright red; dbl., medium, in clusters; foliage dark.

Bella Doria G (OGR), *pb*, Flowers pink with red flecks and stripes, cupped.

Bella Rosa® F, *mp*, 1981, (KORwonder; KORwondis; Kordes' Rose Bella Rosa; Toynbee Hall); *Seedling* × *Traümerei*; Kordes, W., 1982. Flowers medium pink, dbl. (34 petals), miniflora, large; slight fragrance; foliage small, medium green, glossy; bushy growth. GM, Copenhagen, 1981 & Baden-Baden, 1983.

Bella Via Min, *w*, 1991, (ZIPvia); *Rise 'n' Shine* × *Olympic Gold*; Zipper, Herbert; Magic Moment Miniatures, 1992. Flowers white, full (26-40 petals), exhibition form, medium (4-7 cms) blooms borne mostly singly; fragrant; foliage medium, dark green, matt; few prickles; medium (40 cms), upright growth.

Bellard A (OGR), Prior to 1857.

Belle Adélaide G (OGR), *dp*, Miellez. Flowers cerise-red, very dbl., flat.

Belle Amour A (OGR), *lp*, Original name and date unknown; Found at a convent at Elboeuf in the 1940's. May have some relationship to 'Splendens' (Ayr); Flowers soft pink with salmon tones, prominent yellow stamens, semi-dbl.; fragrant (myrrh); height 5-6 ft.

Belle Aurore HAlba (OGR), *lp*, *R. alba hybrid*; Descemet, about 1815. Flowers flesh shaded purple, very dbl., large.

Belle Blanca LCl, *w*, Probably a Belle Portugaise white sport; After 1903.

Belle Blonde HT, *my*, 1955, (MEnap); *Peace* × *Lorraine*; Meilland, F.; URS. Flowers yellow, center darker, well-formed; fragrant; foliage glossy; bushy growth.

Belle Clementine HAlba (OGR), *lp*, *R. alba hybrid*; Prior to 1845. Flowers mottled flesh-color.

Belle Créole F, *rb*, 1958, *(Gruss an Teplitz* × *Independence)* × *(Floradora* × *Independence)*; Arles; Roses-France. Flowers variegated red and brick-red, borne in clusters; foliage dark; vigorous, upright growth.

Belle Cuivrée HT, *or*, 1924, Pernet-Ducher. Flowers coral-red, shaded coppery yellow, semi-dbl.

Belle de Bordeaux T (OGR), *pb*, 1861, (Gloire de Bordeaux; Gloire de Bordeau); Lartay. Flowers pink with crimson center, full, large; vigorous.

Belle de Crécy G (OGR), *m*, Roeser, prior to 1829. Flowers cerise and purple, becoming lavender-gray, center green, full, flat, center petals incurved, large; fragrant; lax growth.

Belle de Marly G (OGR), *dp*, Flowers bright rose, shaded violet, full, large.

Belle de Parme F, *mp*, 1962, *(Lafayette × (Gruss an Teplitz × Independence))* × *R. rugosa rubra*; Arles; Roses-France. Flowers lilac-mauve; low, spreading growth.

Belle de Provins HT, *dr*, 1954, *Crimson Glory × E.G. Hill*; Robichon. Flowers velvety dark red, dbl., well formed, large; very fragrant; vigorous growth.

Belle de Ségur A (OGR), *lp*, (Joséphine Beauharnais); Vibert, prior to 1848. Flowers soft rosy flesh, edges blush, dbl., cupped; foliage dark; vigorous, upright growth.

Belle de Yèbles G (OGR), *mr*, Desprez. Flowers bright red.

Belle des Jardins G (OGR), *m*, 1872, *Village Maid × Seedling*; Guillot Fils. Flowers purplish violet-red, variegated carmine, striped white, dbl.; vigorous growth.

Belle Doria G (OGR), *m*, Flowers dull lilac spotted white, center carmine, dbl., medium.

Belle d'Orléans LCl, *or*, 1958, *Seedling × Independence*; Robichon. Flowers orange-red, dbl., large blooms in clusters; foliage glossy; vigorous growth; recurrent bloom.

Belle Époque HT, *pb*, 1962, (Royale); *Peace × Independence*; Kriloff; Cramphorn's Nursery. Flowers fuchsia-pink, reverse creamy, dbl. (40 petals), large (6 in.); fragrant; foliage glossy; vigorous, upright growth.

Belle Étoile Gr, *my*, 1961, *Joanna Hill × Tawny Gold*; Lens. Bud long, pointed; flowers golden yellow, dbl. (25 petals), well formed, medium blooms in clusters of 5-7 on long stems; vigorous, upright growth.

Belle Isis G (OGR), *lp*, 1845, Parmentier. Flowers pale flesh-pink, dbl.

Belle Lyonnaise Cl T (OGR), *ly*, 1870, *Gloire de Dijon seedling*; Levet, F. Flowers canary yellow, fading white, full, large; fragrant; vigorous, climbing growth.

Belle Meillandina® Min, *dr*, 1984, (MEIdanego; Belle Sunblaze); *Meillandina sport*; Meilland, M.L.; Meilland Et Cie, 1980. Flowers dark red.

Belle Normande HP (OGR), *w*, 1865, *La Reine sport*; Oger. Flowers white.

Belle of Punjab F, *mp*, 1965, *Montezuma × Flamenco*; Pal; Indian Agricultural Research Institute. Bud ovoid; flowers pink, dbl., high-centered; slightly fragrant; foliage dark, glossy; very vigorous, compact growth.

Belle of Tasmania F, *or*, 1968, *Korona × Étoile de Hollande*; Holloway. Bud pointed; flowers velvety scarlet, center darker, dbl., high-centered, medium; foliage glossy; vigorous, tall, compact growth.

Belle Poitevine HRg (S), *mp*, 1894, Bruant. Bud long, pointed; flowers rose-pink to magenta-pink, semi-dbl., large; foliage dark, rugose; vigorous (3½-4 ft.), bushy growth; recurrent bloom; (14).

Belle Portugaise LCl, *lp*, 1903, (Belle of Portugal); *R. gigantea × Reine Marie Henriette*; Cayeux. Bud very long, pointed (to 4 in.); flowers light flesh-pink, semi-dbl., large (4-6 in.); foliage glossy; very vigorous (20 ft.) growth; long spring bloom; not hardy north; common in Calif.; (21).

Belle Rosine G (OGR), *dp*, Flowers deep pink, edged lighter, full, open, large; erect growth.

Belle Rouge HT, *dr*, 1956, *Happiness seedling × Impeccable*; Delbard-Chabert. Flowers dark velvety red becoming carmine-purple, large.

Belle Story® S, *lp*, 1985, (AUSelle; AUSspry; Bienenweide); *(Chaucer × Parade)* × *(The Prioress × Iceberg)*; Austin, David; David Austin Roses, 1984. Flowers light pink, yellow stamens, dbl. (35 petals), cupped, large; very fragrant; foliage medium, medium green, semi-glossy; bushy growth.

Belle Vichysoise N (OGR), *lp*, 1897, Found at Vichy; Lévêque. Flowers pink or pinkish white, small blooms in clusters of 20-50; very vigorous growth.

Belles and Beaus S, *rb*, 1987, (ADAbel); *Little Darling × Seedling*; Adams, Neil D. Flowers red-white bicolor, dbl. (15-25 petals), HT-formed, floribunda type, medium; no fragrance; foliage medium, dark green, glossy; disease resistant; upright, moderately hardy growth.

Bellevue® HT, *yb*, 1976, (POUlena; Jarlina); *(Tropicana × Piccadilly)* × *Fru Jarl*; Poulsen, N.D.; Poulsen. Flowers dark yellow and apricot, edged red, dbl. (23 petals), large (6 in.); foliage glossy, leathery; vigorous, upright growth.

Bellina F, *op*, 1959, *Pinocchio × (Fashion × Orange Triumph)*; Abrams, Von; Peterson & Dering. Flowers shrimp-pink, dbl. (40 petals), high-centered, medium (2-2½ in.) blooms in large clusters; fragrant; foliage glossy; low, compact growth.

Bellissima Min, *or*, 1988, (ZIPbell); *Pink Petticoat × Lady Rose*; Zipper, Herbert; Magic Moment Miniatures, 1989. Flowers orange-red, darker along edges, dbl. (over 40 petals), exhibition, medium, borne singly; no fragrance; foliage medium, medium green, semi-glossy; upright growth.

Bellona F, *my*, 1976, (KORilona); *New Day × Minigold*; Kordes, R.; J&P. Bud ovoid; flowers golden yellow, dbl. (27 petals), pointed, large (3 in.); slightly fragrant; foliage light; very vigorous, upright growth.

Beloved HT, *w*, 1978, *Memoriam* sport; Hill, E.H.; Shropshire Roses. Bud tinted pink; flowers white, dbl. (33-35 petals), reflexing, very large (6-7 in.); fragrant; foliage glossy.

Belvédère F, *dr*, 1928, *Eblouissant × Château de Clos Vougeot*; Kiese. Flowers velvety dark red, dbl., large; vigorous, dwarf growth.

Belvédère HT, *dr*, 1955, *Reine Elisabeth × Christopher Stone*; Delforge. Flowers dark red.

Ben Arthur Davis HT, *yb*, 1935, *Edith Nellie Perkins* sport; Bostick. Flowers yellow, reverse pinkish gold, dbl, cupped; foliage leathery, glossy, dark; bushy growth.

Ben Cant HP (OGR), *dr*, 1902, *Suzanne-Marie Rodocanachi × Victor Hugo*; Cant, B.R. Flowers crimson, center darker, dbl. (25 petals), high-centered, very large; very fragrant; vigorous growth.

Ben Stad LCl, *pb*, 1925, (Rev. Floris Ferwerda); *Silver Moon × Mme. Jules Grolez*; Undritz; B&A. Flowers pink, center yellow, edged white, reverse flesh-pink.

Bendigold F, *or*, 1979, *Rumba × Redgold*; Murley; Brundrett. Bud globular; flowers orange-red, dbl., large (3 in.); fragrant; foliage glossy, bronze; vigorous, upright growth.

Bénédicte Seguin HT, *ob*, 1918, Pernet-Ducher. Flowers ochre, shaded coppery orange, dbl.

Benedictus XV HT, *w*, 1917, *Jonkheer J.L. Mock × Marquise de Sinéty*; Leenders, M. Flowers rosy white, dbl.; fragrant.

Benedikt Roezl HRg (S), *lp*, 1925, *R. rugosa seedling × La France*; Berger, V.; Faist. Flowers light carmine-rose, very dbl., large; fragrant; foliage rugosa-like; vigorous, very bushy growth.

Benelux F, *dr*, 1949, *Donald Prior × Rosamunde*; Leenders, M. Flowers crimson-red, semi-dbl.; fragrant.

Benevolence HT, *or*, 1985, (SANolence); *Vera Dalton × Seedling*; Sanday, John, 1986. Flowers orange-red, dbl. (35 petals), large; fragrant; foliage large, dark, semi-glossy; long, narrow prickles; bushy growth.

Bengale Rouge Ch (OGR), *mr*, 1955, *Gruss an Teplitz × Seedling*; Gaujard. Bud ovoid; flowers bright carmine-red, open, very large; foliage abundant; very vigorous growth; recurrent bloom.

Bengali® F, *or*, 1969, (KORal); *Dacapo × Seedling*; Kordes; Buisman, 1969. Bud ovoid; flowers red-orange, dbl., medium; foliage dark.

Bengt M. Schalin S, *dp*, 1956, *R. kordesii × Eos*; Kordes. Flowers rose-red, semi-dbl., me-

dium blooms in clusters (up to 10); slightly fragrant; foliage lightgreen, leathery, glossy; very vigorous growth; non-recurrent bloom.

Ben-Hur Gr, *mr*, 1960, *Charlotte Armstrong × (Charlotte Armstrong × Floradora)*; Lammerts; Germain's. Bud long, pointed; flowers crimson, dbl. (23 petals), high-centered, large (4-5 in.); fragrant; foliage leathery, glossy; vigorous.

Benjamin Franklin HT, *lp*, 1969, Abrams, Von. Bud ovoid; flowers dawn-pink, dbl. (55 petals), high-centered, large; slightly fragrant; foliage dark, leathery; upright.

Bennett's Seedling Ayr (OGR), *w*, 1840, (Thoresbyana); Raised by Bennett, gardener for Lord Manners; Lord Manners at Thoresby, England. A dbl. form or hybrid of *R. arvensis*; Flowers pure white, expanded form, medium; fragrant.

Benoit Friart HT, *m*, 1978, *Fragrant Cloud × Astée*; Rijksstation Voor Sierplantenteelt. Flowers rosy lilac, dbl. (47 petals), flat, medium blooms borne 1-7 per cluster; very fragrant; foliage matt; upright growth.

Benson & Hedges Gold® HT, *yb*, 1979, (MACgem); *Yellow Pages × (Arthur Bell × Cynthia Brooke)*; McGredy, S. IV; Mattock. Bud ovoid; flowers deep golden yellow flushed coppery red, dbl. (33 petals), medium; fragrant; bushy growth.

Bentall's Scarlet HT, *or*, 1935, Bentall. Flowers bright scarlet; slightly fragrant; very vigorous growth.

Bentveld HT, *op*, 1932, *Charles P. Kilham* sport; Posthuma; Low. Flowers carmine-orange, edges lighter than parent; vigorous growth.

Benvenuto® LCl, *mr*, 1967, (MEIelpa); *(Alain × Guinée) × Cocktail*; Meilland; URS. Flowers rose-red, semi-dbl., medium; slightly fragrant; vigorous, climbing growth; recurrent bloom.

Bérangère M (OGR), *lp*, 1849, Vibert. Flowers delicate pink, full, large.

Berceuse HT, *my*, 1950, *Signora × Mrs. Pierre S. duPont*; Robichon. Bud globular, yellow; flowers chamois, very dbl., very large; very fragrant; foliage leathery; very vigorous, upright growth.

Bérénice G (OGR), *rb*, 1818, Vibert. Flowers rose and crimson, shaded with slate, full, globular, large; pendulous habit.

Bergers Erfolg HRg (S), *mr*, 1925, *R. rugosa seedling × Richmond*; Berger, V.; Pfitzer. Flowers fire-red, stamens yellow, single, large (3-4 in.) blooms in clusters; foliage dark; very vigorous, bushy growth; occasionally recurrent bloom.

Bergrat Otto Berger HT, *w*, 1924, *Pharisaer* × *Prince de Bulgarie*; Berger, V.; Faist. Flowers creamy white to sulphur, center deeper, dbl.; fragrant.

Berkeley Beauty™ Min, *m*, 1988, (MORberk); *Pink Petticoat* × *Make Believe*; Moore, Ralph S.; Sequoia Nursery, 1987. Flowers picotee white, edged lavender to pink (striped), dbl., high centered, exhibition, small, medium, borne usually singly; moderate fragrance; foliage medium, medium green, semi-glossy, abundant; prickles varying green to brown; bushy, medium, neat growth.

Berlin S, *ob*, 1949, *Eva* × *Peace*; Kordes. Bud long, pointed; flowers orange-scarlet, center golden, single, large blooms in large clusters; fragrant; foliage leathery, dark; prickles large; very vigorous, upright growth; repeat bloom; (28).

Bermuda Pink HT, *lp*, 1974, *Queen of Bermuda* × *Montezuma*; Golik; Dynarose. Bud ovoid; flowers flesh-pink, dbl. (35-40 petals), globular, large (4-5 in.); slightly fragrant (rose); foliage glossy, light; compact, moderate growth.

Bermudiana HT, *mp*, 1966, *Golden Masterpiece seedling* × *Golden Masterpiece seedling*; Boerner; J&P. Bud ovoid; flowers pink, dbl. (35-60 petals), high-centered, large (5-6 in.); fragrant; foliage leathery; vigorous, upright growth.

Bern® HT, *dp*, 1975, *Crimson Glory* × *Lilac Charm*; Huber. Bud long, pointed; flowers deep pink, dbl. (24 petals), shallow, large (4 in.); very fragrant (spicy); foliage dark, leathery; spreading growth.

Bernadette HT, *lp*, 1964, *Peace sport*; Kelly. Flowers light pink, dbl., high-centered, large; slightly fragrant; foliage dark, leathery; vigorous, bushy.

Bernadette Chirac® HRg (S), *ab*, 1979, (DELbéchir); *R. rugosa* × (*First Edition* × *Floradora*); Delbard-Chabert. Flowers apricot, yellow and orange blend, dbl. (23 petals), cupped, 3½ in.; slightly fragrant; foliage rugose; vigorous, bushy growth.

Bernaix, Climbing Cl HT, *dr*, 1935, *Souv. d'Alexandre Bernaix sport*; Shamburger, C.S.

Bernalia S, *mp*, 1961, *Mosqueta* × *Cecilia*; Bernal. Flowers pink, center white, semi-dbl. (about 10 petals), small blooms in clusters; fragrant; foliage bright green; vigorous growth; recurrent bloom.

Bernard P (OGR), *op*, 1846, (Pompon Perpetual); *Rose du Roi sport*. Flowers salmon-pink.

Bernard Verlot HP (OGR), *rb*, 1868, Baron-Veillard. Flowers red-scarlet, center violet.

Bernd Clüver F, *mp*, 1974, *Nordia* × *Sans Souci*; Reinold. Bud pointed; flowers medium pink, large (2½-3 in.); fragrant (fruity); moderate, upright growth.

Bernice HT, *mp*, 1927, Pemberton. Flowers carmine-pink on yellow base, semi-dbl.; fragrant.

Bernice Pol, *mp*, 1937, *Baby Tausendschon (probably Echo)* × *Gloria Mundi*; Nicolas; J&P. Bud ovoid; flowers brilliant cerise-pink, dbl., globular, small blooms in clusters; very fragrant; foliage glossy, light; dwarf growth; recurrent bloom.

Berolina F, *my*, 1977, *Mabella* × *Seedling*; Kordes. Bud long, pointed; flowers medium yellow, dbl. (24 petals), high-centered, large (3½ in.); slightly fragrant; foliage dark, soft; vigorous, upright growth.

Bersagliera HT, *dp*, 1960, Luigi. Bud globular; flowers crimson, phlox-pink and fuchsia-pink, dbl., medium to large blooms on strong stems; vigorous growth.

Bertha S, *lp*, 1946, (*R. rugosa* × *Hybrid Perpetual*) × (*R. multiflora* × *R. blanda*); Wright, P.H. Flowers delicate pink, single, very large, borne like hollyhock flowers on erect stems; height 8 ft.; non-recurrent bloom.

Bertha Aikman HT, *op*, 1977, *Gypsy Moth* × *Percy Thrower*; Simpson, J.W.; Manawatu Rose Soc. Bud high pointed; flowers two-toned salmon-pink, dbl. (45 petals), large (4 in.); fragrant; foliage matt; moderate, slightly spreading growth.

Bertha Gorst HT, *mr*, 1933, *Autumn sport*; Beckwith. Flowers crimson-cerise, base gold, veined bronze, dbl., very large; very fragrant; foliage bronze.

Bertha Turner HT, *op*, 1925, Pemberton. Flowers salmon-peach; fragrant.

Berthe Baron HP (OGR), *lp*, 1869, *Jules Margottin* × *Seedling*; Baron-Veillard. Flowers delicate rose shaded with white, full, large.

Berthe Mallerin HT, *or*, 1960, Mallerin. Flowers red tinted orange, dbl., on strong stems; vigorous growth.

Bertram Park HT, *mr*, 1929, (Coquette); *Eblouissant* × *Mme. Edouard Herriot*; Burbage Nursery. Flowers rosy crimson, base yellow, single; slightly fragrant.

Berwick HSpn (OGR), *pb*, *R. spinosissima hybrid*. Flowers rose shading to white at edges, semi-dbl., large; dwarf growth.

Beryl Ainger HT, *w*, 1955, *The Doctor sport*; F. Cant. Flowers cream, base golden yellow; fragrant.

Beryl Bach HT, *yb*, 1985, (HARtesia); *Sunsprite* × *Silver Jubilee*; Harkness, R.; R. Harkness & Co. Flowers yellow, blended pink, dbl. (40 petals), large; fragrant; foliage large, light green, matt; tall, upright growth.

Beryl Formby HT, *yb*, 1948, *McGredy's Sunset sport*; Fryer's Nursery. Flowers golden yellow shaded crimson, dbl. (36-40 petals); very fragrant; foliage glossy; bushy growth.

Beryl Formby, Climbing Cl HT, *yb*, 1956, Letts.

Beryl Wearmouth F, *mp*, 1973, *(Ann Elizabeth × Orange Sensation) × Sea Pearl*; Harkness. Flowers medium pink, semi-dbl. (19 petals), large (4½ in.); foliage light green, matt.

Bess Lovett LCl, *dp*, 1915, Van Fleet; J.T. Lovett. Flowers light red, dbl., cupped, well-formed blooms in clusters; fragrant; foliage glossy, dark; vigorous, climbing growth.

Bessie Brown HT, *ly*, 1899, Dickson, A. Flowers yellowish white, very dbl., large; fragrant; foliage light, leathery, glossy.

Bessie Chaplin HT, *mp*, 1921, *Lady Pirrie × Gorgeous*; Chaplin Bros. Flowers bright pink, center deeper, very dbl; slightly fragrant. GM, NRS, 1923.

Best Regards HT, *pb*, 1944, *Soeur Thérèse × Signora*; Morris; Germain's. Flowers pink bicolor, dbl. (50-60 petals), dahlia form, very large (6-7 in.); fragrant; foliage leathery, dark; very vigorous, compact growth.

Best Regards, Climbing Cl HT, *pb*, 1940, Elmer, C.A.; Germain's.

Best Wishes HT, *dp*, 1959, Fisher, G.; Arnold-Fisher Co. Bud long, pointed; flowers currant-red, dbl. (25-35 petals), high-centered, large (5½-6 in.) on strong stems; fragrant; foliage leathery; very vigorous growth; a greenhouse variety.

Betano Beach F, *rb*, 1966, *Ma Perkins × Detroiter*; Fankhauser; A. Ross & Son. Bud long, pointed; flowers light salmon-pink, reverse scarlet and burnt crimson, dbl., high-centered, medium; foliage glossy, dark, leathery; vigorous, upright growth.

Beth F, *ly*, 1966, *Elizabeth of Glamis sport*; O'Connell; Rumsey. Flowers buff-yellow.

Betinho HT, *rb*, 1958, *Charles Mallerin × Monte Carlo*; Moreira da Silva. Flowers velvety red and brown.

Betsie Jane HT, *ab*, 1976, *Bewitched sport*; Tresise. Bud long, pointed; flowers soft apricot-pink, dbl., full, large; fragrant; foliage light green; tall, vigorous growth.

BETsue F, *or*, 1987, (Sue Betts); *Europeana sport*; Betts, John; Wisbech Plant Co., 1987. Flowers orange-red, long lasting color, dbl. (30+petals), cupped, large blooms borne in sprays of 65-12; moderate fragrance; foliage medium, medium green, semi-glossy; prick-

les sharp, thin, brown; fruit round, red; bushy, low growth.

Betsy McCall F, *op*, 1956, *Seedling × Fashion*; Boerner; J&P. Bud ovoid; flowers shrimp-pink, dbl. (25-30 petals), open, large (3-3½ in.) in large clusters; fragrant; foliage glossy; vigorous, bushy growth.

Betsy Ross HT, *dr*, 1969, (DELup; La Passionata); *(Gloire de Rome × La Vaudoise) × Divine*; Delbard; Trioreau & Stark Bros. Flowers deep red, dbl., high-centered, large; slightly fragrant; foliage light green, upright growth.

Betsy Ross HT, *ob*, 1931, *Talisman sport*.; Samtmann Bros. Flowers like parent but marked russet-orange.

Bette Irene S, *ab*, 1986, *Dairy Maid × Seedling*; Schneider, Peter. Flowers apricot, reverse deeper, fading light pink, semi-dbl (9 petals), imbricated, medium, borne in sprays of 3-24; moderate fragrance; foliage medium, dark green, matt; awl-like, medium, brown prickles; fruit rounded, medium, bright red, ornamental hips; upright, medium-tall growth; repeat bloom.

Better Homes & Gardens HT, *pb*, 1976, *Tropicana × Peace*; Warriner; J&P. Bud ovoid; flowers rose, ivory reverse, dbl. (38 petals), high-centered, medium (3-3½ in.); slightly fragrant; foliage glossy, dark; medium-tall, upright.

Better Times HT, *mr*, 1934, *Briarcliff sport*; Hill, J.H. Co. Flowers cerise, dbl., high-centered, large; slightly fragrant; foliage dark, leathery; very vigorous, compact growth.

Better Times, Climbing Cl HT, *mr*, 1937, Parmentier, J.

Bettie Herholdt HT, *w*, 1976, (HERtie; Betty Herholdt; Messagere); *(White Swan × Seedling) × Pascali*; Herholdt, J.A. Bud pointed; flowers ivory-white, dbl. (50 petals), large (5½ in.); fragrant; vigorous growth.

Bettina® HT, *op*, 1953, (MEpal; MEIpal); *Peace × (Mme. Joseph Perraud × Demain)*; Meilland, F.; URS. Flowers salmon-orange, veined, dbl. (37 petals), well-formed, large (4 in.); fragrant; foliage dark, glossy, bronze; vigorous growth.

Bettina, Climbing® Cl HT, *op*, 1958, (MEpalsar; Grimpant Bettina); Meilland, F.; URS. GM, Geneva, 1959.

Bett's White Delight Min, *w*, 1992, *Pink Petticoat × Seedling*; Walters, Betty & Richard, 1987. Flowers creamy white opening to pure white, very full (58-86 petals), rosette, 65 mm blooms borne in clusters of 5; slight fragrance; foliage medium to dark green, matt; tall, compact growth.

Betty HT, *pb*, 1905, Dickson, A. Flowers coppery rose, shaded yellow, dbl., large; fragrant; very vigorous.

Betty Alden R, *lp*, 1919, *Orléans Rose × (Katharina Zeimet × R. arvensis hybrid)*; Farquhar. Flowers appleblossom-pink passing to white, single.

Betty Baum HT, *lp*, 1927, *Premier sport*; Baum. Flowers delicate pink, base yellow, dbl.; fragrant.

Betty Bee™ Min, *pb*, 1983, (BLAbee); *Little Darling × Toy Clown*; Blazey, Daniel; Nor'East Min. Roses. Flowers pink, white reverse, dbl. (35 ruffled petals), HT form, small; no fragrance; foliage small, medium green, semi-glossy; compact, bushy growth.

Betty Berkeley T (OGR), *mr*, 1904, Bernaix, A. Flowers bright red.

Betty Bland HBlanda (S), *dp*, 1925, *R. blanda × HP*; Skinner. Flowers deep rose, fading pink, center deeper, dbl.; fragrant; foliage rich green, soft; twigs ruby-red; vigorous (6 ft.), bushy growth; non-recurrent bloom; very hardy; (14).

Betty Blossom R, *mp*, 1923, *R. wichuraiana × Mrs. W.J. Grant*; Dawson; Eastern Nursery. Flowers clear rose-pink, semi-dbl., loose cluster; vigorous pillar or bush.

Betty, Climbing Cl HT, *pb*, 1926, Hohman.

Betty Cuthbert HT, *or*, 1964, *Roundelay sport*; Palmer; Palmer & Engall. Bud long, pointed; flowers orange-red, very dbl., medium; very fragrant; foliage soft, glossy; very vigorous, upright growth.

Betty Driver F, *pb*, 1982, (GANdri); *Seedling × Topsi*; Gandy, Douglas; Gandy Roses. Flowers pale peach and gold blend, yellow stamens, semi-dbl., patio, large blooms in clusters; slight fragrance; foliage medium, light green, semi-glossy; low, bushy growth.

Betty Free F, *mp*, 1950, *Fortschritt sport*; LeGrice. Bud pointed; flowers neyron rose, dbl. (25 petals), borne in clusters; slightly fragrant; vigorous growth.

Betty Grace Clark HT, *ob*, 1933, *Marie Adélaide sport*; Clarks' Rose Nursery. Flowers orange-yellow, reverse streaked red, high-centered; fragrant; vigorous, bushy growth.

Betty Hulton HT, *dy*, 1923, Dickson, A. Flowers deep saffron-yellow, dbl.; fragrant. GM, NRS, 1923.

Betty May Wood HT, *ab*, 1968, *Mischief sport*; Wood. Flowers apricot to buff, reverse coral-salmon, dbl. (30 petals), well formed; foliage light green; free growth.

Betty Morse HT, *mr*, 1950, *Crimson Glory × (Crimson Glory × Cathrine Kordes)*; Kordes; Morse. Bud long, pointed; flowers red, dbl. (25 petals), large (4 in.); slightly fragrant; foliage olive-green; vigorous growth.

Betty Neuss HT, *mp*, 1973, *Tropicana*; Dawson, G.; C. Brundrett. Bud small, long, pointed; flowers pure pink, dbl., medium; slightly fragrant; foliage small; very vigorous, upright growth.

Betty Paul HT, *mp*, 1988, *Queen Elizabeth × (Tiffany × Tropicana)*; Warner, A.J. Flowers medium pink blend, dbl. (20-25 petals), high-centered, exhibition, medium, borne usually singly or in sprays of 1-3; slight fragrance; foliage medium, medium green, semi-glossy; disease resistant; prickles straight, medium, light brown; fruit ovoid, small, yellow-orange; upright, medium, tall growth. 1987 ARC TG (B).

Betty Pearson HT, *w*, 1929, Burbage Nursery. Flowers cream, center apricot, petals shell shaped, large.

Betty Prior F, *mp*, 1935, *Kirsten Poulsen × Seedling*; Prior; J&P, 1938. Bud ovoid, dark carmine; flowers carmine-pink, single (5 petals), cupped, borne in clusters; fragrant; vigorous, bushy growth. GM, NRS, 1933.

Betty Stielow HT, *dp*, 1928, *Premier sport*; Stielow Bros. Flowers dark pink, almost red at times, dbl., fragrant.

Betty Sutor HT, *pb*, 1929, McGredy. Flowers pale pink, veined rose, reverse rosy, dbl., large; fragrant; foliage light, glossy; vigorous, bushy growth.

Betty Uprichard HT, *ab*, 1922, Dickson, A. Flowers delicate salmon-pink, reverse carmine with coppery sheen, dbl. (20 petals), large; very fragrant; foliage light, leathery, glossy; very vigorous, tall growth. GM, NRS, 1921.

Betty Uprichard, Climbing Cl HT, *ab*, 1936, Krause.

Betty Will S, *pb*, 1963, *George Will × Betty Bland*; Erskine. Flowers bright pink, lighter reverse, dbl. (35 petals); foliage dark, leathery; some large prickles; tall red canes.

Betty Wright™ Gr, *m*, 1988, (BURbet); *Angel Face × Seedling*; Burks, Larry; Co-Operative Rose Growers. Flowers lilac-mauve, darker at tips, aging lighter lilac, semi-dbl., cupped, urn-shaped, medium, borne usually singly or in sprays of 3-5; slight, fruity fragrance; foliage medium, medium green, matt; prickles slight recurve, average, brown; fruit globular, average, orange-yellow; bushy, medium growth.

Betzel's Pink HT, *op*, 1955, *Pres. Herbert Hoover sport*; Betzel; Edmunds. Bud long; flowers coral-pink, dbl. (55-60 petals), high-centered, large (5 in.) blooms on strong stems; fragrant; foliage leathery, glossy; vigorous, bushy growth.

Beverley Anne Ch (OGR), *mr*, 1987, *Seedling × Seedling*; Nobbs, Kenneth J., 1986. Flowers red-purple, dbl. (21 petals), open, flat, borne in sprays of 3-7; slight fragrance; foliage pivoted, serrated; no prickles; semi-dwarf growth.

Beverly Hills HT, *ob*, 1986, (DELmator; Malicorne); *(Zambra × Orange Sensation) × (Zambra × (Orange Triumph × Floradora))*; Delbard, G., 1982. Flowers dark orange, blooms in clusters, greenhouse variety.

Beverly Nicols HT, *op*, 1939, Burbage Nursery. Flowers cream, reverse salmon, well formed, high-centered, large; fragrant; vigorous growth.

Bewitched HT, *mp*, 1967, *Queen Elizabeth × Tawny Gold*; Lammerts; Germain's. Flowers rose bengal, dbl. (27 petals), high-centered, large (5 in.); fragrant (damask); foliage glossy; vigorous growth.   GM, Portland, 1967; AARS, 1967.

Bhagmati F, *mr*, 1977, *Charleston × ((Roman Holiday × Flamenco) × Goldgleam)*; Viraraghaven; Gopalsinamiengar. Bud ovoid; flowers medium red, 15-20 petals, cupped, large (2½-3 in.); slightly fragrant; foliage glossy, light green; dwarf, vigorous, bushy growth.

Bharani Min, *m*, 1979, (Bharami); *Seedling × Seedling*; Goralaswamiengar, K.S.; Gandy Roses Ltd., 1973. Flowers mauve, semi-dbl., small; slight fragrance; foliage small, light green, matt; upright growth.

Bhim HT, *dr*, 1970, *Charles Mallerin × Delhi Princess*; Indian Agric. Research Inst.; Div. of Vegetable Crops & Flori. Bud long, pointed; flowers scarlet-red, very dbl., open, large; fragrant; vigorous, upright growth; abundant, intermittent bloom.

Bianca HT, 1913, *None listed*; Paul, W. Bud long, pointed; Flowers pale peach tinted pink and violet, center shaded rose, dbl. RULED EXTINCT 3/83 ARM.

Bianca HT, 1927, *None listed*; Pemberton. Flowers white, sometimes lightly flushed cream or pink, dbl., well-formed; fragrant. RULED EXTINCT 3/83 ARM.

Bianca Camelia HT, *w*, 1933, *Nuntius Pacelli × Sachsengruss*; San Remo Exp. Sta. Bud ovoid, pointed; flowers snow-white, center light blush-yellow, dbl. (23-25 petals), very large; very fragrant; foliage light green; very vigorous, upright growth.

Bianco Min, *w*, 1983, (COCblanco); *Darling Flame × Jack Frost*; Cocker, James; Cocker & Sons. Flowers white, dbl. (35 petals), patio,

small; no fragrance; foliage medium, medium green, semi-glossy; bushy growth.

Bicentennial F, *rb*, 1975, Meyer, C.; C-P. Flowers deep pink and red blend, dbl., high-centered, medium; slightly fragrant; foliage leathery; vigorous, upright, bushy growth.

Bichette HT, *mp*, 1968, *Diamond Jubilee × Seedling*; Verschuren, A.; Stassen. Flowers persian rose, full (20-25 petals), large; foliage dark, leathery; vigorous, upright growth.

Bienvenu Gr, *ob*, 1969, *Camelot × (Montezuma × War Dance)*; Swim & Weeks; Weeks Wholesale Rose Grower. Bud long, pointed; flowers reddish orange, dbl. (70 petals), high-centered, large; very fragrant; foliage leathery, matt; vigorous, upright growth.

Big Apple HT, *mr*, 1983, *Mister Lincoln × (Suspense × King's Ransom)*; Weeks, O.L.; Weeks Roses, 1984. Flowers medium red, dbl. (40+ petals), large; fragrant; foliage large, medium green, matt to semi-glossy; upright, spreading growth.

Big Bang® F, *or*, 1980, *Sarabande × Sarabande seedling*; Barni-Pistoia, Rose. Bud pointed; flowers deep orange-red, semi-dbl. (13 petals), shallow-cupped blooms borne 5-10 per cluster; no fragrance; foliage matt, light green; reddish-green prickles; bushy.

Big Ben HT, *dr*, 1964, *Ena Harkness × Charles Mallerin*; Gandy. Flowers dark red, well-formed, large (5-6 in.); very fragrant; foliage dark; tall growth.

Big Duke HT, *dp*, 1991, (Duke Wayne); *The Duke × Seedling*; Weddle, Von C., 1984. Bud pointed; flowers deep pink, silvery pink reverse, dbl, high-centered, exhibition, large blooms borne usually singly; moderate, fruity fragrance; foliage large, medium green, semi-glossy; upright, tall growth.

Big John Min, *mr*, 1979, *Starburst × Over the Rainbow*; Williams, E.D.; Mini-Roses. Bud pointed; flowers deep medium red, base yellow, dbl. (42 petals), high-centered, 1-1½ in.; foliage small, glossy, bronze; upright, bushy growth.

Big Red HT, *dr*, 1967, *Chrysler Imperial × Seedling*; Meilland, M.L.; C-P. Bud pointed; flowers dark red, dbl. (52 petals), high-centered, large (4½-6 in.); slightly fragrant; foliage leathery; vigorous, upright, bushy growth.

Big Splash Cl HT, *rb*, 1969, *Buccaneer × Bravo*; Armstrong, D.L.; Armstrong Nursery. Bud pointed; flowers flame-red, reverse lighter, base yellow, dbl., high-centered, large; fragrant; foliage glossy, leathery; vigorous, climbing (8-10 ft.) growth.

Biggi HT, *yb*, 1975, *Dr. A.J. Verhage × Seedling*; Kordes; Fey. Bud ovoid; flowers yellow blend, dbl. (27 petals), high-centered, large (4½ in.); fragrant; foliage glossy, dark; vigorous, upright growth; intermittent bloom.

Bijou Pol, *lp*, 1932, deRuiter; Sliedrecht & Co. Flowers old rose.

Bijou Superior Pol, *lp*, *Bijou sport*; deRuiter. Flowers have more lasting color.

Bikini Red HT, *mr*, 1974, *Queen of Bermuda* × *Peace*; Golik; Dynarose. Bud ovoid; flowers rose-red, tinged white, dbl. (40 petals), ruffled, large (5 in.); fragrant (fruity); foliage glossy, dark.

Bilitis F, *or*, 1969, *Tabarin* × *Golden Slippers*; Gaujard. Flowers vermilion-red, center yellow.

Bill Beaumont F, *mr*, 1982, *Evelyn Fison* × *Redgold*; Fryer, G.R.; Fryer's Nurseries. Flowers crimson, dbl. (20 petals), slight fragrance; foliage medium, medium green, matt; bushy growth.

Bill Cone Min, *mr*, 1989, (MICone); *Heartland* × *Anita Charles*; Williams, Michael C.; The Rose Garden. Bud ovoid; flowers medium red, dbl. (35 petals), cupped, medium, borne usually singly; no fragrance; foliage medium, medium green, semi-glossy; prickles light green, globular; fruit round, green to orange-yellow; upright, tall growth.

Bill Hunt HT, *op*, 1976, *Mischief* × *Serenade*; Blakemore. Flowers deep coral, dbl. (30 petals), full, medium; fragrant; foliage glossy; fairly vigorous growth.

Bill Slim F, *op*, 1987, (HARquito); *Seedling* × *Silver Jubilee*; Harkness, 1989. Bud globular; flowers salmon, deep pink reverse, dbl. (30 petals), large blooms borne singly or in clusters; slightly fragrant; foliage glossy; bushy, spreading growth.

Bill Temple HT, *w*, 1975, *Crimson Halo* × *Piccadilly*; Harkness. Flowers cream, dbl. (30 petals), large (5-6 in.); slightly fragrant; foliage glossy, dark.

Billard et Barré Cl T (OGR), *my*, 1898, *Mlle. Alice Furon* × *Duchesse d'Auerstadt*; Pernet-Ducher. Flowers golden yellow, dbl.; very fragrant.

Billie Teas Min, *dr*, 1992, (HOOtea); *Seedling* × *Merrimac*; Hooper, John C.; Kimbrew-Walter Roses, 1992. Flowers dark red, full (26-40 petals), small (0-4 cms.) blooms borne mostly singly; no fragrance; foliage medium, medium green, matt; some prickles; medium (38-45 cms.), upright growth. AOE, 1993.

Billionaire HT, *mr*, 1972, *Fragrant Cloud* × *Proud Land*; Warriner; J&P. Bud ovoid, long, pointed; flowers medium red, dbl., high-centered, large; slightly fragrant; foliage leathery; vigorous, upright growth.

Billy Boiler Cl HT, *mr*, 1927, Clark, A.; NRS Victoria. Flowers medium red; vigorous, tall.

Billy Boy HT, *my*, 1926, *Golden Emblem* × *Christine*; McGredy; Beckwith. Flowers sunflower-yellow, semi-dbl.

Billy Boy Min, *mr*, 1990, (MORboy); *Anytime* × *Happy Hour*; Moore, Ralph S.; Sequoia Nursery. Bud pointed, short; flowers medium red, full (15-18 petals), cupped, small blooms borne usually singly; slight fragrance; foliage small, medium green, matt, dense; prickles slender, straight, small, brownish; bushy, low to medium, compact growth.

Bimboro® HT, *dr*, 1978, *Seedling* × *Kardinal*; Kordes, W., Sons; Willemse. Bud globular; flowers dark red, dbl. (46 petals), high-centered, medium (3-3½ in.); fragrant; foliage glossy; vigorous, bushy, upright growth.

Bing Crosby HT, *ob*, 1980, *Seedling* × *First Prize*; Weeks. Bud ovoid; flowers strong orange, dbl. (45 petals), cupped blooms borne mostly singly; slight fragrance; foliage medium, heavy, leathery, wrinkled, dark; long prickles hooked downward; vigorous, upright, bushy growth. AARS, 1981.

Bingo HT, *dr*, 1955, (Dyna); *(Hadley seedling* × *Ami Quinard)* × *Crimson Glory*; Robichon; Ilgenfritz Nursery. Bud pointed; flowers cardinal-red, dbl. (55 petals), high-centered, large (4-5 in.); very fragrant; foliage glossy; upright growth.

Bird of Fire F, *yb*, 1992, (TAYbird); *Fragrant Delight* × *Sunsilk*; Taylor, Thomas E., 1993; National Kirtland's Warbler Recovery Team. Flowers yellow blending to reddish edges, reverse yellow, aging light yellow to reddish pink, dbl. (25-30 petals), high centered, exhibition, medium (10-12 cms) blooms borne usually singly and in sprays of 3-5; moderate fragrance; foliage medium, dark green, semi-glossy, leathery, reddish when young, disease resistant; upright, bushy, medium growth

Birdie Blye S, *mp*, 1904, *Helene* × *Bon Silene*; Van Fleet; Conard & Jones. Bud long, pointed, carmine; flowers rose-pink, dbl., cupped, large blooms in clusters; slightly fragrant; foliage light; vigorous (4-5 ft.) growth; recurrent bloom.

Birdsong LCl, *mp*, 1991, Seward, Grace. Flowers medium pink, semi-dbl. (6-14 petals), small (0-4 cms) blooms borne in very large clusters; fragrant; foliage small to medium, medium green, semi-glossy; few prickles; tall (300+ cms), spreading, large, rambling growth.

Birgitta HT, *dr*, 1961, de Boer. Bud ovoid; flowers dark red, dbl., large.

Bir-Hackeim HT, *mr*, 1946, Mallerin; A. Meilland. Bud long, pointed; flowers fiery red, semi-dbl., open, cupped; very vigorous, upright, bushy growth.

Birmingham Boerner F, *w*, 1975, *Gene Boerner sport*; Schoepfle. Flowers light flesh-pink turning white.

Birmingham Post F, *dp*, 1968, *Queen Elizabeth × Wendy Cussons*; Watkins Roses. Flowers deep pink, full, large; very fragrant; foliage leathery; vigorous growth.

Birthday Party Min, *mp*, 1979, *Attraktion × Sheri Anne*; Strawn; Pixie Treasures. Bud ovoid; flowers pink, dbl. (28 petals), exhibition form, medium (1½-2 in.); fragrant; foliage dark; upright, spreading growth.

Birthday Present Cl HT, *dr*, 1950, *Guinee × Rouge Mallerin*; Toogood. Bud ovoid; flowers dark red, dbl. (20 petals), high-centered; very fragrant; foliage dark, leathery; vigorous, climbing; non-recurrent bloom.

Biscay Min, *mp*, 1988, *Summer Spice × Seedling*; Bridges, Dennis; Bridges Roses, 1989. Bud ovoid; flowers medium pink, reverse slightly darker, dbl. (26 petals), high-centered, medium, borne usually singly; slight fragrance; foliage medium, medium green, semi-glossy; prickles slightly downward pointed, medium, deep pink; upright, medium growth.

Bischof Dr. Korum HP (OGR), *pb*, 1921, *Frau Karl Druschki × Laurent Carle*; Lambert, P. Flowers yellowish rose, dbl.; fragrant.

Bischofsstadt Paderborn® S, *or*, 1964, (Fire Pillar); Kordes, R. Flowers cinnabar-scarlet, single to semi-dbl., saucer shaped; vigorous (3-4 ft.), bushy growth. ADR, 1968.

Bishop Darlington HMsk (S), *ab*, 1926, *Aviateur Bleriot × Moonlight*; Thomas; Dreer; H&S, 1928. Bud ovoid; flowers cream to flesh-pink, with yellow glow, semi-dbl. (17 petals), cupped, large; fragrant (fruity); foliage bronze, soft; semi-climbing growth; recurrent bloom.

Bishop of Sherwood HT, *op*, 1976, *Mischief × (Wendy Cussons × Peace)*; Bracegirdle. Flowers pale salmon flushed pink, dbl. (34 petals), full, large (5 in.); very fragrant; vigorous, upright growth.

Bishop's Rose C (OGR), *pb*, *Apparently R. gallica × R. centifolia*; Originator and date unknown; Form like *R. centifolia*, pink to rich deep carmine; vigorous (to 5 ft.) growth.

Bit o' Gold Min, *dy*, 1981, *Seedling × Golden Angel*; Williams, Ernest D.; Mini-Roses. Bud ovoid; flowers deep yellow, dbl. (40 petals), imbricated form, micro-mini; fragrant; foliage small, dark, semi-glossy; compact, bushy growth.

Bit o' Magic Min, *pb*, 1979, *Over the Rainbow × Over the Rainbow*; Williams, E.D.; Mini-

Roses. Bud pointed; flowers deep pink, reverse nearly white, dbl. (50 petals), high-centered, micro-mini, small (1 in.); foliage small, dark, glossy; compact, spreading growth.

Bit o' Spring Min, *pb*, 1980, *Tom Brown × Golden Angel*; Williams, E.D. Bud long, pointed; flowers medium buffy pink, reverse lighter yellow-pink, dbl. (45 petals), high-centered, borne usually singly; fragrant; foliage deep green, matt; thin, tan prickles curved down; upright, bushy growth.

Bit o' Sunshine Min, *dy*, 1956, (Little Bit o' Sunshine); *Copper Glow × Zee*; Moore, R.S.; Sequoia Nursery. Flowers bright buttercup-yellow, 18-20 petals, small (1½ in.); fragrant; bushy (12-14 in.), compact growth.

Bit of Honey Min, *dy*, 1980, *Sunnydew sport*; Vastine, Gilbert; Gulf Stream Nursery. Same as parent except increased petalage, dbl. (48 petals).

Blaby Courier HT, *mr*, 1956, Verschuren; Blaby Rose Gardens. Bud deep crimson; flowers vivid scarlet on strong stems; fragrant.

Blaby Monarch HT, *lp*, 1960, *Briarcliff × Seedling*; Verschuren; Blaby Rose Gardens. Flowers rose-pink, dbl. (40 petals), high-centered, large (5-6 in.); very fragrant; foliage light green; vigorous growth.

Black Beauty HT, *dr*, 1973, *(Gloire de Rome × Impeccable) × Papa Meilland*; Delbard; Bees. Flowers garnet-red, dbl., large; slightly fragrant; bushy growth.

Black Bess F, *dr*, 1939, *Dance of Joy × Crimson Glory*; Kordes; Morse. Bud long, pointed; flowers blackish crimson, semi-dbl, high-centered, borne in clusters; slightly fragrant; foliage dark, bronze; vigorous, bushy growth.

Black Boy LCl, *dr*, 1919, (Blackboy); *Étoile de France × Bardou Job*; Clark, A.; NRS South Australia. Flowers very dark red, semi-dbl., large; fragrant; foliage sparse, wrinkled, light; vigorous growth.

Black Boy M (OGR), *dr*, 1958, *World's Fair × Nuits de Young*; Kordes. Bud ovoid, lightly mossed; flowers deep crimson, very dbl., large; very fragrant; foliage light green, leathery; vigorous, upright, bushy growth; non-recurrent bloom.

Black Fire Pol, *dr*, 1969, *Red Favorite × Seedling*; Delforge. Bud ovoid; flowers dark red, dbl., open, medium; slightly fragrant; foliage dark, soft; vigorous, bushy growth.

Black Garnet HT, *dr*, 1980, *Mister Lincoln × Mexicana*; Weeks. Bud ovoid, pointed; flowers dark black-red, dbl. (50 petals), high-centered, borne singly or 2-3 per cluster; foliage medium to large, moderately leathery, dark grayish-green; short to medium prickles, hooked downward; bushy, upright, branching growth.

Black Ice F, *dr*, 1971, *(Iceberg × Europeana) × Megiddo*; Gandy. Flowers dark red, dbl. (24 petals), large (4 in.); slightly fragrant; foliage glossy, dark.

Black Jack™ Min, *dr*, 1983, (MINkco); *Tom Brown × Over the Rainbow*; Williams, E.D.; Mini-Roses. Flowers deep red, golden stamens, dbl. (40 petals), high-centered, exhibition, small; slight fragrance; foliage small, dark, semi-glossy; bushy growth.

Black Jade™ Min, *dr*, 1985, (BENblack); *Sheri Anne × Laguna*; Benardella, Frank; Nor'East Min. Roses. Bud near black; flowers deep red, dbl. (35 petals), high-centered, medium; no fragrance; foliage medium, dark, semi-glossy; upright growth. AOE, 1985.

Black Knight HT, *dr*, 1934, *Ami Quinard × Château de Clos Vougeot*; Hillock. Flowers crimson shaded blackish, dbl. (30-35 petals); fragrant; foliage glossy, dark; vigorous growth.

Black Lady® HT, *dr*, 1976, (TANblady); Tantau. Bud globose; flowers blackish-red, dbl., medium; very fragrant; foliage matt; bushy growth.

Black Magic LCl, *dr*, 1953, *Guinee seedling*; Hamilton. Flowers blackish crimson, medium; very fragrant; occasional repeat bloom.

Black Night® HT, *dr*, 1975, (HUBar); *Fragrant Cloud × Pharaoh*; Huber. Bud long; flowers dark red, dbl. (26 petals), shallow, large (4 in.); foliage dark, leathery; vigorous, upright growth.

Black Opal HT, *dr*, 1957, *Mirandy × Tassin*; Ulrick. Flowers dark velvety red.

Black Prince HP (OGR), *dr*, 1866, Paul, W. Flowers dark crimson shaded black, full, cupped, large; very fragrant; vigorous growth; recurrent bloom.

Black Ruby HT, *dr*, 1965, *Rome Glory × Impeccable*; Delbard-Chabert; Cuthbert. Flowers dark red, center crimson, dbl. (40 petals), cupped, large; tall growth.

Black Satin HT, *dr*, 1987, (BETsat); *Folklore × Loving Memory*; Betts, John; Wisbech Plant Co., 1987. Flowers dark red, dbl. (30 petals), exhibition, medium blooms borne singly; slight fragrance; foliage medium, dark green, semi-glossy; prickles few, pointed slightly down, small, light brown; fruit rounded, medium, red; upright, medium growth.

Black Taquin LCl, *dr*, 1955, *Honour Bright × Guinee*; Eacott. Flowers dark crimson-maroon; vigorous growth.

Black Tea HT, *r*, 1973, *Hawaii × (Aztec × (Goldilocks × Fashion))*; Okamoto, K.; K. Hirakata Nursery. Flowers brown, dbl. (32 petals), urn-shaped, medium blooms borne usually singly; slight fragrance; foliage medium, dark, semi-glossy; deep brown, hooked prickles; medium, bushy growth.

Black Velvet HT, *dr*, 1960, *New Yorker × Happiness*; Morey; J&P. Bud ovoid; flowers dark red, dbl. (28 petals), high-centered, large (5-5½ in.); very fragrant; foliage leathery, dark; vigorous, upright growth.

Blairii No. 1 HCh (OGR), *mp*, *Parks' Yellow Tea-scented China × Hardy rose*; Blair, prior to 1844. Flowers bright rose, sometimes tinged red, semi-dbl., cupped, large; very fragrant; branching growth; liable to injury from severe cold (less hardy than Blairii No. 2).

Blairii No. 2 HCh (OGR), *lp*, 1845, *Parks' Yellow Tea-scented China × Hardy rose*; Blair. Flowers rosy blush, dbl., large; fragrant; vigorous (up to 15 ft.) growth; hardy.

Blakeney's Red HT, *mr*, 1962, *Karl Herbst × Peace*; Blakeney; Eddie. Bud long, pointed; flowers currant-red, base yellow, dbl. (45 petals), high-centered, large (5 in.); fragrant; foliage leathery; moderate, bushy growth.

Blanc de Vibert P (OGR), *w*, 1847, Vibert. Flowers white, dbl.; foliage light green; sometimes recurrent.

Blanc Double de Coubert HRg (S), *w*, 1892, *R. rugosa × Sombreuil*; Cochet-Cochet; Half-open bud pleasing; flowers white, fairly dbl., large; very fragrant (even at night); foliage very rugose; vigorous (5-7 ft.) growth; repeat bloom.

Blanc Parfait A (OGR), *w*, *R. alba miniature form*. Flowers white, small, pompon form; height 12-18 in.

Blanca F, *w*, 1965, *Purpurine × (Papillon Rose × Sterling Silver)*; Lens. Flowers pure white, dbl., large blooms in clusters; slightly fragrant; vigorous growth.

Blanche Amiet HT, *op*, 1921, Turbat. Flowers coppery salmon, passing to clear rose.

Blanche Comète HT, *w*, 1980, (DELoblan; White Comet); *(Virgo × Peace) × (Goldilocks × Virgo)*; Delbard, Georges; Delbard Roses. Flowers white, dbl., blooms in clusters.

Blanche de Belgique HAlba (OGR), *w*, (Blanche Superbe); *R. alba hybrid*; Prior to 1848. Flowers pure white, dbl., very large.

Blanche Dot HT, *w*, 1962, (Blanc Dot); *White Knight × Virgo*; Dot, P. Flowers snow-white, dbl. (33 petals), well-formed, large; slightly fragrant.

Blanche Frowein R, *yb*, 1916, Leenders, M. Flowers coppery yellow; fragrant.

Blanche Lafitte B (OGR), *w*, 1851, Pradel. Flowers rosy white, full, medium blooms in clusters; vigorous; repeats in autumn.

Blanche Mallerin HT, *w*, 1941, *Edith Krause × White Briarcliff*; Mallerin; A. Meilland & C-P. Bud long, pointed; flowers pure white, full (33 petals), high-centered, large (4 in.); foliage leathery, glossy; vigorous growth.

Blanche Messigny HT, *ly*, 1923, Gillot, F. Flowers creamy yellow, dbl. (45 petals), large; fragrant; vigorous, bushy growth.

Blanche Moreau M (OGR), *w*, 1880, *Comtesse de Murinais × Perpetual White Moss*; Moreau-Robert. Bud well mossed; flowers pure white, dbl., large blooms in clusters; fragrant; lax growth; repeat bloom.

Blanche Nabonnand T (OGR), *w*, 1883, Nabonnand, G. Flowers creamy white tinged lemon or flesh, dbl., globular; fragrant.

Blanche Odorante HT, *w*, 1952, *Pole Nord × Neige Parfum*; Caron, B.; EFR. Bud very long, pointed; flowers purest white, quite dbl., large; very fragrant; vigorous growth.

Blanche Rebatel Pol, *pb*, 1889, Bernaix, A. Flowers carmine and white.

Blanche Wimer Min, *pb*, 1986, *Pink Petticoat × Seedling*; Shaw, Dr. John, 1985. Flowers light yellow and pink blend, dbl. (66 petals), cupped, medium blooms borne usually singly; slight, fruity fragrance; foliage medium, medium green, semi-glossy; slightly hooked, reddish-green prickles; fruit none; tall, upright growth.

Blanchefleur C (OGR), *w*, 1835, Vibert. Flowers white tinted blush, dbl.; vigorous.

Blarney Cl HT, *mp*, 1934, *Irish Charm sport*; Howard Rose Co. Flowers pink, base apricot, dbl.; fragrant; foliage leathery, dark; vigorous, climbing growth; recurrent bloom.

Blatná HT, *dr*, 1927, *Lieut. Chaure × Oskar Cordel*; Böhm. Flowers velvety dark red, dbl.; slightly fragrant; dwarf growth.

Blauwe Donau F, *m*, 1971, (Blue Danube); *Orangeade × Sterling Silver*; Verschuren, T.; Verschuren. Bud ovoid; flowers mauve, semi-dbl. (10-12 petals), full, open, large (3 in.); very fragrant; foliage glossy; bushy growth; abundant bloom lasting well.

Blaydon Races F, *yb*, 1976, *Bobby Shafto × (Arthur Bell × Piccadilly)*; Wood. Flowers scarlet shading to yellow, medium (2½ in.); slightly fragrant; foliage glossy, dark, leathery; vigorous, tall, upright growth.

Blaze LCl, *mr*, 1932, *Paul's Scarlet Climber × Gruss an Teplitz*; Kallay; J&P. Flowers bright scarlet, semi-dbl., cupped, medium (2-3 in.) blooms in large clusters; slightly fragrant;

foliage leathery, dark; very vigorous, climbing growth; recurrent bloom.

Blaze Away F, *or*, 1979, *(Karl Herbst × Crimson Glory) × Sarabande*; Sanday. Bud pointed; flowers scarlet-vermilion, single (7 petals), large (3½ in.); slightly fragrant; vigorous, bushy growth.

Blesma Soul HT, *lp*, 1982, *Pascali × Fragrant Cloud*; Anderson Rose Nursery. Bud long, pointed; flowers light pink, dbl. (36 petals), borne singly or in small clusters; very fragrant; foliage light green; large based, reddish-brown prickles; upright growth.

Bless My Time Gr, *lp*, 1983, *Queen Elizabeth sport*; Orr, Rudolph F. Flowers clear light pink, veins sometimes darker.

Blessings® HT, *op*, 1967, *Queen Elizabeth × Seedling*; Gregory, 1968. Flowers medium coral-salmon, dbl. (30 petals), high-centered, large; fragrant.

Bleu Magenta R, *m*, Originator and date unknown. Flowers dark crimson-purple, dbl., borne in clusters; slightly fragrant; foliage dark.

Blithe Spirit HT, *lp*, 1964, *Fandango × Seedling*; Armstrong, D.L. & Swim; Armstrong Nursery. Flowers light pink, dbl., medium; slightly fragrant; foliage leathery; vigorous, spreading, upright growth.

Blizzard Min, *w*, 1991, (JACdrift); *Petticoat × Orange Honey*; Warriner, William A.; Bear Creek Gardens. Bud pointed; flowers white, full (26-40 petals), medium; no fragrance; foliage small, dark green, glossy; low, spreading, compact growth.

Blöhm & Voss F, *or*, *An improved Independence*. Flowers bright orange-scarlet; good truss.

Blondie F, *my*, 1987, (JACliy; JACliv); *(Bridal Pink × Golden Wave) × Gold Rush*; Warriner, William; J&P. Flowers medium yellow, fading slightly, dbl. (25 petals), high-centered, medium, borne usually singly or in sprays of 3-5; slight, fruity fragrance; foliage medium, light green, semi-glossy; straight, medium prickles; no fruit; upright, bushy, medium growth.

Blondine HT, *lp*, 1954, *Catalina sport*; Grillo. Bud pointed, globular; flowers blush-pink, dbl. (60 petals), large (4 in.); fragrant; foliage leathery; upright growth.

Blondine Cl HT, *w*, *Comtesse Vandal, Climbing × Michèle Meilland, Climbing*; Arles; Roses-France. Flowers pearl-white, well formed, large; very fragrant; foliage clear green; vigorous.

Bloodstone HT, *or*, 1951, *The Queen Alexandra Rose × Lord Charlemont*; McGredy. Flowers orange-red, dbl. (24 petals), high-centered, large; slightly fragrant; foliage dark, coppery green; vigorous growth.

Bloomer Girl Min, *op*, 1983, (TINgirl); *Futura × Pink Petticoat*; Bennett, Dee; Tiny Petals Nursery. Flowers soft vermilion to medium pink, dbl. (35 petals), small; slight fragrance; foliage medium, medium green, semi-glossy; upright, bushy growth.

Bloomfield Abundance F, *lp*, 1920, *Sylvia (probably R.) × Dorothy Page-Roberts*; Thomas; B&A. Flowers light salmon-pink, dbl.; foliage glossy, dark; bushy growth; similar to Cecile Brunner, but hardier and flowers larger. Note: This rose is apparently lost. The rose distributed under this name is a sport of 'Cecile Brunner', probably 'Spray Cécile Brunner'. GM, Portland, 1919.

Bloomfield Beverly HT, *or*, 1924, *Mary, Countess of Ilchester × Mme. Edouard Herriot*; Thomas. Flowers orange-crimson, dbl.; fragrant; vigorous growth.

Bloomfield Brilliant LCl, *op*, 1931, *Mme. Abel Chatenay × Kitty Kininmonth*; Thomas; H&S. Flowers light salmon with orange glow, semi-dbl. (18 petals), large; fragrant; vigorous growth.

Bloomfield Comet HMsk (S), *op*, 1924, *Duchess of Wellington × Danaë*; Thomas; B&A. Bud long, pointed, reddish orange; flowers orange, base yellow, single (5 petals), large (3½ in.); fragrant; foliage sparse, light bronze, soft.

Bloomfield Completeness HMsk (S), *ab*, 1931, *Bloomfield Perfection × Mme. Butterfly*; Thomas. Flowers deep orange-yellow, dbl.; fragrant.

Bloomfield Courage R, *rb*, 1925, Thomas; B&A; H&S. Flowers dark velvety red, center white, prominent yellow stamens, single, small blooms in good-sized clusters; foliage dark; vigorous, climbing or pillar (20 ft.) growth; non-recurrent bloom.

Bloomfield Culmination HMsk (S), *pb*, 1924, *Sheila Wilson × Danaë*; Thomas; B&A. Bud long, pointed; flowers rose-pink, center white, single, large (3 in.); slightly fragrant; foliage leathery; moderately vigorous growth; recurrent bloom.

Bloomfield Dainty HMsk (S), *my*, 1924, *Danaë × Mme. Edouard Herriot*; Thomas; B&A. Bud long, pointed, deep orange; flowers clear canary-yellow, single, medium (2 in.); fragrant; foliage glossy; moderately vigorous growth.

Bloomfield Dawn HMsk (S), *pb*, 1931, *Seedling, Climbing × Bloomfield Progress*; Thomas; Armstrong Nursery. Bud long, slender, rose-pink; flowers light pink, base yellow, reverse

deep pink, semi-dbl., large blooms on long, strong stems; fragrant.

Bloomfield Decoration HMsk (S), *pb*, 1925, *Sylvia × Arndt*; Thomas; B&A & H&S, 1927. Flowers cerise-pink, center white, prominent golden stamens, single, open, small; fragrant; foliage glossy.

Bloomfield Discovery HMsk (S), *pb*, 1925, *Danaë × (Frau Karl Druschki × Mme. Caroline Testout)*; Thomas; B&A. Flowers pink, reverse darker, single; foliage dark; moderately vigorous growth.

Bloomfield Exquisite Cl HT, *mp*, 1924, *Gloire de Dijon × Gruss an Teplitz*; Thomas; H&S. Flowers clear pink, dbl.; fragrant; vigorous growth; recurrent bloom.

Bloomfield Fascination HMsk (S), *ly*, 1924, *Danaë × Mme. Lautette Messimy*; Thomas; B&A. Flowers light canary yellow, dbl., small; slightly fragrant; foliage rich bronze green, soft.

Bloomfield Favorite HMsk (S), *w*, 1924, *Debutante × Moonlight*; Thomas. Flowers pinkish cream, dbl.; slightly fragrant.

Bloomfield Flame HT, *rb*, 1930, *Louise Crette × Mme. Charles Lutaud*; Thomas; H&S. Bud long, pointed, flame-red; flowers crimson-flame, center orange-yellow, dbl. (22 petals), large; fragrant (spicy); foliage leathery, glossy, dark bronze; vigorous, bushy growth.

Bloomfield Lustre LCl, *op*, 1931, *Hortulanus Budde × Souv. de Mme. Léonie Viennot*; Thomas; H&S. Flowers salmon-pink, base yellow, dbl.; fragrant.

Bloomfield Magic LCl, *op*, 1924, *Gloire de Dijon × Frau Berta Gurtler*; Thomas. Flowers light salmon to cream, flat; fragrant; moderately vigorous growth.

Bloomfield Mystery LCl, *lp*, 1924, *Blanche Frowein × Bloomfield Abundance*; Thomas; B&A. Flowers silver-pink, tinged yellow, flat, medium (2 in.); fragrant; moderately vigorous growth.

Bloomfield Perfection HMsk (S), *w*, 1925, *Danaë × Bloomfield Abundance*; Thomas; B&A, 1927. Flowers cream-yellow suffused lilac, dbl.; slightly fragrant; recurrent bloom.

Bloomfield Perpetual HP (OGR), *w*, 1920, *Iceberg × Frau Karl Druschki*; Thomas; B&A. Flowers white, single, resembling the Cherokee Rose.

Bloomfield Progress HT, *mr*, 1920, *Mary, Countess of Ilchester × Gen. MacArthur*; Thomas; B&A. Flowers glowing red, dbl.; very fragrant; vigorous growth.

Bloomfield Quakeress Cl T (OGR), *ly*, 1931, *Chance Safrano seedling*; Thomas; Armstrong Nursery. Flowers light yellow, semi-dbl., small blooms on long stems; foliage glossy, light; vigorous growth; free recurrent bloom.

Bloomfield Rocket LCl, *dp*, 1925, *Mme. Caroline Testout × Ulrich Brunner Fils*; Thomas; B&A. Flowers dark pink, center lighter, single, very large; slightly fragrant; very vigorous (6-8 ft.) growth.

Bloomin' Easy™ S, *mr*, 1988, (AROtrusim; Blooming Easy); *Trumpeter × Simplicity*; Christensen, Jack; Armstrong Roses, 1987. Flowers clear, bright red, semi-dbl. (22-25 petals), urn-shaped, medium, borne singly; moderate, tea fragrance; foliage large, medium green, glossy; prickles hooked slightly downward, medium, red; fruit round, medium, bright red-orange; upright, bushy, medium growth; repeats.

Bloomsday F, *ob*, 1981, *Belinda × (Maxi × Joyfullness)*; McCann, Sean; Hughes Roses. Flowers orange, marked brown, reverse deep gold, dbl. (28 petals), loose, 4-5 per cluster; fragrant; foliage matt, green; straight, red-brown prickles; vigorous, upright growth.

Blossom HT, *pb*, 1925, Beckwith. Flowers red over peach-pink, reverse pinkish yellow.

Blossom Hill F, *ob*, 1957, Kordes; Morse. Flowers orange; single (10 petals), cupped, medium (2½ in.) in clusters; slightly fragrant; foliage dark, glossy; vigorous, upright, bushy growth.

Blossomtime LCl, *mp*, 1951, *New Dawn × Seedling*; O'Neal; Bosley Nursery. Bud pointed; flowers pink, reverse deeper, dbl. (38 petals), high-centered, large (4 in.) blooms in clusters of 3-8; very fragrant; tall shrub or moderate climbing (6-7 ft.) growth; repeat bloom.

Blue Angel F, *m*, 1992, (RENangel); *Lavonde × Shocking Blue*; Rennie, Bruce; Rennie Roses. Flowers mauve, moderately full (15-25 petals), medium (4-7 cms) blooms borne mostly singly; fragrant; foliage medium, dark green, semi-glossy; few prickles; medium, bushy growth.

Blue Boy S, *m*, 1958, *Louis Grimmard × Independence*; Kordes. Bud ovoid; flowers deep reddish violet, dbl., high-centered, large; very fragrant; foliage light green, glossy; vigorous (3 ft.), upright, bushy growth; non-recurrent bloom.

Blue Chip F, *m*, 1983, (JACave); *Heirloom × Angel Face*; Warriner, W.; J&P. Flowers mauve, dbl. (20 petals), medium; very fragrant; foliage medium, medium green, semi-glossy; bushy, upright growth; cut flower.

Blue Diamond HT, *m*, 1963, *Purpurine × (Purpurine × Royal Tan)*; Lens. Flowers lavender,

dbl. (35 petals), large (4 in.); fragrant; foliage dark, coppery; vigorous, compact, bushy.

Blue Glow HT, *m*, 1982, *Silent Night × Blue Moon*; Cattermole, R.F. Bud pointed; flowers pinkish-mauve, dbl. (45 petals), exhibition form, large blooms borne singly and 3-5 per cluster; very strong fragrance; foliage light green; light brown, triangular prickles; upright, branching growth.

Blue Heaven HT, *m*, 1971, *(Sterling Silver × Simone) × Song of Paris*; Whisler, D.; Gro-Plant Industries. Bud ovoid; flowers mauve, dbl., high-centered, large; very fragrant; foliage large, glossy; vigorous, upright growth.

Blue Mist Min, *m*, 1970, *Seedling × Seedling*; Moore, R.S.; Sequoia Nursery. Bud short, rounded; flowers soft pink to lavender, dbl. (23 petals), micro-mini, small; very fragrant; foliage soft; vigorous, bushy, rounded growth.

Blue Moon® HT, *m*, 1965, (TANnacht; TANsi; Blue Monday; Mainzer Fastnacht; Sissi); *Sterling Silver seedling × Seedling*; Tantau, Math., 1964. Bud long, pointed; flowers lilac, dbl. (40 petals), large (4 in.); very fragrant; vigorous growth. GM, Rome, 1964; ADR, 1964.

Blue Moon, Climbing Cl HT, *m*, 1981, (Blue Monday, Climbing; Mainzer Fastnacht, Climbing; Sissi, Climbing); *Blue Moon sport*; Mungia, Fred A., Sr.; Montebello Rose Co., Inc.

Blue Nile® HT, *m*, 1981, (DELnible; Nil Bleu®); *(Holstein × Bayadere) × (Prelude × Saint-Exupery)*; Delbard, G.; Armstrong Nursery, 1976. Bud ovoid, pointed; flowers lavender, dbl. (28 petals), borne singly or 2-3 per cluster; strong fragrance; foliage large, olive green; short prickles, hooked downward; tall, upright, spreading growth. GM, Bagatelle.

Blue Parfum® HT, *m*, 1978, (TANfifum; TANifume; TANtifum; Blue Perfume; Tantau. Bud ovoid; flowers mauve-blush, dbl., large; very fragrant; foliage glossy; bushy, upright growth.

Blue Peter Min, *m*, 1983, (RUIblun; Azulabria; Bluenette); *Little Flirt × Seedling*; deRuiter, G.; Fryer's Nursery. Flowers lilac-purple, semi-dbl., patio, small; slight fragrance; foliage small, light green, semi-glossy; bushy growth.

Blue Ribbon HT, *m*, 1984, (AROlical); *(Angel Face × First Prize) × Blue Nile*; Christensen, Jack E.; Armstrong Nursery, 1986. Flowers lavender, dbl. (35 petals), well-formed, large (5-6 in.); very fragrant; foliage very large, dark, semi-glossy; upright growth.

Blue River HT, *m*, 1973, *Mainzer Fastnacht* × *Silver Star*; Kordes; Horstmann. Bud long, pointed; Flowers mauve-magenta, dbl., cupped, large; very fragrant; Foliage glossy; Vigorous, upright growth. RULED EXTINCT 6/84 ARM.

Blue River® HT, *m*, 1984, (KORsicht); *Blue Moon* × *Zorina*; Kordes, W. Bud large; flowers lilac, shaded deeper at petal edges, dbl. (35 petals), high-centered, exhibition, large; very fragrant; foliage medium, medium green, semi-glossy; upright growth. Baden-Baden GM.

Blue Skies HT, *m*, 1983, (BUCblu); *((Sterling Silver* × *Intermezzo)* × *(Sterling Silver* × *Simone))x (Music Maker* × *(Blue Moon* × *Tom Brown))*; Buck, Griffith J.; J.B. Roses, 1988. Flowers mauve, dbl. (35 petals), large; fragrant; foliage large, semi-glossy; upright, bushy growth.

Blue Star, Climbing Cl HT, *m*, 1963, *Parentage unknown, presumably a chance seedling*; Thompson, M.L. Flowers lavender-blue, dbl., flat, small blooms in cluster; slightly fragrant; foliage glossy; vigorous (8 ft.) growth; profuse, non-recurrent bloom.

Blueblood™ Min, *mr*, 1982, (LAVblu); *Dwarfking '78* × *Hokey Pokey*; Laver, Keith. Flowers medium red, dbl. (55 petals), velvety texture, small; foliage small, deep green, semi-glossy; spreading growth.

Bluesette® F, *m*, 1984, (LENmau); *Little Angel* × *(Westmauve* × *Blue Diamond)*; Lens, Louis. Flowers lilac, dbl. (50 petals), flat, 2 in. blooms in clusters of 3-18; lightly fragrant; dark green prickles; bushy growth.

Blumenschmidt T (OGR), *yb*, 1906, *Mlle. Franziska Kruger sport*; Schmidt, J.C. Flowers primrose-yellow, outer petals rose-pink.

Blumenschmidt's Elfenkönigin HT, *w*, 1939, *Ophelia* × *Julien Potin*; Weigand, C.; Schmidt, J.C. Flowers ivory-white, center orange, dbl., high-centered, very large on long, strong, stems; fragrant (lily-of-the-valley); bushy, dwarf growth.

Blush Belgique A (OGR), *lp*, *R. alba* × *R. canina*. Flowers blush, semi-dbl., large.

Blush Boursault Bslt (OGR), *pb*, (Calypso); Prior to 1848. Flowers blush, center deep flesh, very dbl., globular, very large blooms, tending to ball; foliage remains longer than other Boursaults; pendulous habit.

Blush Damask D (OGR), *lp*, 1759, Flowers center rose, shading to pale blush on outside petals, full, small.

Blush Hip HAlba (OGR), *lp*, Prior to 1846. Flowers soft pink, green eye, dbl.; vigorous.

Blush Moss M (OGR), *lp*, Prior to 1844. Flowers blush, center pinkish when first open, well-mossed, full, cupped, large; moderate branching growth.

Blush Noisette N (OGR), *w*, 1817, *Champneys' Pink Cluster seedling*; Noisette. Flowers pinkish white. (14).

Blush Queen HT, *lp*, 1924, Cant, F. Flowers blush-pink, dbl.; fragrant.

Blush Rambler R, *lp*, 1903, *Crimson Rambler* × *The Garland*; Cant, B.R. Flowers blush-pink, semi-dbl., cupped blooms in clusters; vigorous, climbing (10-12 ft.) growth; non-recurrent bloom.

Blushing Beauty LCl, *lp*, 1934, Burbank; Stark Bros. Flowers three-toned shell-pink, very large; very vigorous growth.

Blushing Blue Min, *m*, 1988, (RENblue); *Shocking Blue* × *Twilight Trail*; Rennie, Bruce F.; Rennie Roses, 1989. Flowers lavender with magenta edge, yellow-tan atbase, dbl. (30-35 petals), high-centered, exhibition, medium, borne usually singly; no fragrance; foliage medium, medium green, semi-glossy; prickles straight, medium, transparent yellow-green; fruit rounded, medium, orange; upright, bushy growth; repeats.

Blushing Bride HT, *w*, 1918, Dickson, H. Flowers white, center blush, dbl. RULED EXTINCT 5/90.

Blushing Bride HT, *W*, 1930, *Mme. Butterfly* × *Premier*; Hill, J.H., Co. Flowers white tinged pink, dbl., large; very fragrant; vigorous growth; a greenhouse variety for forcing purposes. RULED EXTINCT 5/90.

Blushing Bride HT, *w*, 1990, (GREblub); *Silverado sport*; Greenwood, Chris, 1991. Flowers white, moderately full (15-25 petals), large blooms; very fragrant; foliage large, dark green, semi-glossy; upright, bushy growth.

Blushing Dawn Min, *pb*, 1983, (WEEblush); *Jeanne Lajoie* × *Eyepaint*; Weeks, Michael W.J. Flowers creamy white, peach pink eye, yellow stamens, petals painted peach pink, edged white, reverse white, single (7-8 petals), medium blooms borne singly or in small clusters; fragrant; foliage medium, dark, matt; low, bushy growth.

Blushing Groom Min, *w*, 1983, (SEAgru); *Rise 'n' Shine* × *Karl Herbst*; McCann, Sean. Flowers near white, dbl. (35 petals), small; slight fragrance; foliage small, dark, semi-glossy; upright growth.

Blushing Jewel Min, *lp*, 1958, *Dick Koster sport* × *Tom Thumb*; Morey; J&P. Bud ovoid; flowers blush-pink, overcast rose-pink, dbl. (45-50 petals), open, small (½ - ¾ in.); fragrant; low, compact growth.

Blushing Lucy LCl, *lp*, 1938, Williams, A.H. Flowers pale pink, white eye, semi-dbl., large cluster; very fragrant; foliage glossy; vigorous growth; profuse, late bloom.

Blushing Queen Gr, *w*, 1976, *Queen Elizabeth sport*; Baker, L. Bud pointed; flowers near white, center blush-pink, dbl. (38-40 petals), high-centered; fragrant; vigorous, upright growth.

Bob Collard F, *mr*, 1986, *Happiness × Copenhagen*; Turley, V.G., 1987. Flowers very luminous, brilliant red, reverse deeper red, single (11 petals), cupped, medium, borne singly and in sprays of 5-10; slight, fruity fragrance; foliage medium, medium green, glossy; fruit round, cupped, average, red; upright, bushy, medium growth.

Bob Hope HT, *mr*, 1966, *Friedrich Schwartz × Kordes' Perfecta*; Kordes, R.; J&P. Bud urn-shaped; flowers scarlet, dbl. (38 petals), high-centered, large (6 in.); very fragrant; foliage dark, leathery; vigorous, tall growth.

Bob Woolley HT, *ab*, 1970, *Gavotte × Golden Scepter*; Sanday. Flowers peach-pink, reverse lemon, dbl. (60 petals), large (5 in.); slightly fragrant; foliage matt, green.

Bobbie James R, *w*, 1961, Sunningdale Nursery. Flowers creamy white, single (7-9 petals), cupped, small (2 in.) blooms in trusses; very fragrant; foliage glossy; vigorous.

Bobbie Lucas F, *op*, 1967, *Margot Fonteyn × Elizabeth of Glamis*; McGredy, S., IV. Flowers deep salmon-orange, well-formed, large (3½ in.) blooms in clusters; slightly fragrant; foliage dark.

Bobbink White Climber LCl, *w*, 1951, *Dream Girl × Seedling*; Jacobus; B&A. Flowers creamy yellow to pure white, dbl. (45-50 petals), large (3 in.); fragrant; foliage dark, glossy; vigorous climbing growth; recurrent bloom when established.

Bobby Charlton HT, *pb*, 1974, *Royal Highness × Prima Ballerina*; Fryer, G.; Fryer's Nursery. Flowers deep pink, reverse silver, dbl. (38 petals), well-formed, large (6 in.); fragrant (spicy); foliage dark, leathery. GM, Baden-Baden, 1976 & Portland, 1980.

Bobby Dazzler F, *ab*, 1972, (Rosella); *(Vera Dalton × Highlight) × (Ann Elizabeth × Circus)*; Harkness, 1973. Flowers blush, shaded rich apricot, dbl. (50 petals), large (3 in.); slightly fragrant; foliage small, matt.

Bobby Shafto HT, *my*, 1967, *Piccadilly sport*; Wood. Flowers yellow.

Bobo HT, *mr*, 1979, Perry, Astor, 1981. Bud long; flowers medium red, dbl. (30 petals), urn-shaped blooms borne singly; intense, fruity fragrance.

Bobolink Min, *dp*, 1959, *(R. wichuraiana × Floradora) × (Oakington Ruby × Floradora)*; Moore, R.S.; Sequoia Nursery. Flowers rose-pink, base near white, dbl. (50 petals), small (1-1½ in.); slightly fragrant (fruity); foliage leathery, glossy; vigorous, bushy (18 in.) growth.

Bocca Negra R, *dr*, 1910, Dubreuil. Flowers purple-crimson, center white, cupped, borne in clusters of 15-20; vigorous growth.

Boccaccio F, *or*, 1963, *Atombombe × Seedling*; Verschuren, A.; Stassen. Flowers bright scarlet-red, dbl. (30-40 petals), large blooms in clusters; foliage glossy; vigorous, upright growth.

Bochre HT, *pb*, 1990, *Prima Ballerina × Alec's Red*; Rodgers, Shafner. Flowers pink blend, very full (over 40 petals with over 100 small petals), medium blooms; slight fragrance; foliage medium, medium green, matt; upright growth.

Bohemia HT, *mp*, 1928, *Mrs. Franklin Dennison × Mrs. Henry Morse seedling*; Böhm. Flowers pure rose-pink, semi-dbl.; fragrant.

Bohémienne HT, *or*, 1954, Mallerin; EFR. Flowers orange-red, dbl. (45 petals); bushy growth.

Böhm Junior HT, *dp*, 1935, *Laurent Carle × (Paul's Scarlet Climber × Ethel Somerset)*; Böhm. Flowers carmine-red, full; very fragrant; foliage glossy; bushy growth.

Böhmorose HT, *mp*, 1935, *Gen. MacArthur × Laurent Carle*; Böhm. Flowers rosy carmine to light rose-pink, full, very large; foliage glossy, dark; very vigorous growth.

Böhmova Popelka Pol, *dr*, 1934, Böhm. Flowers dark blood-red; foliage curiously variegated.

Böhm's Triumph HT, *dr*, 1934, *Vaterland × Lord Charlemont*; Böhm. Flowers dark red, semi-dbl., high-centered, very large; foliage dark; vigorous, bushy growth.

Bojangles Min, *dy*, 1981, (JACsun); *Spanish Sun × Calgold*; Warriner, W.; J&P, 1983. Flowers deep yellow, dbl. (20 petals), small; no fragrance; foliage small, light green, semi-glossy; upright, bushy growth.

Boksburg Fantasia HT, *mr*, 1987, (KORnitzel); *Seedling × Seedling*; Kordes, W., Sohne; Ludwigs Roses, 1988. Flowers medium red, dbl. (23 petals), large, borne in sprays of 1-3; moderate fragrance; foliage medium green; prickles needle point, brown; tall, well branched growth.

Boléro HT, *rb*, 1937, Gaujard. Flowers nasturtium-red and gold, dbl., long stems; foliage leathery; very vigorous, bushy growth.

Boléro F, *ob*, 1958, Buyl Frères. Bud pointed; flowers orange, dbl., large; very vigorous growth.

Bon Accord HT, *pb*, 1967, *Prima Ballerina × Percy Thrower*; Anderson's Rose Nursery. Flowers pink shaded silver, high-pointed, large (4½ in.); fragrant; foliage glossy.

Bon Silène T (OGR), *dp*, Hardy, before 1837. Bud well-formed; flowers deep rose, dbl., large; fragrant; vigorous growth; recurrent bloom.

Bon Silène Blanc T (OGR), *ly*, 1885, (White Bon Silène); Morat. Flowers pale yellow to creamy white, large.

Bon Voyage HT, 1960, (Voeux de Bonheur); Delbard-Chabert; Stark Bros., 1969. Common syn. for Voeux de Bonheur.

Bonanza HT, 1957, Verbeek. Flowers yellow shaded red; slightly fragrant; Foliage dark; Vigorous growth. RULED EXTINCT 5/82 ARM.

Bonanza® S, *yb*, 1982, (KORmarie; Miss Pam Ayres); *Seedling × Arthur Bell*; Kordes, W., 1983. Flowers yellow tipped red, dbl. (20 petals), large; slight fragrance; foliage medium, dark, glossy; upright. ADR, 1984.

Bonavista HRg (S), *lp*, 1977, *Schneezwerg × Nemesis*; Svejda; Canada Dept. of Agric. Bud ovoid; flowers light pink, dbl. (20 petals), open, medium (2 in.); very fragrant; foliage yellow-green; upright, bushy growth; abundant, repeat bloom.

Bon-Bon F, *pb*, 1974, *Bridal Pink × Seedling*; Warriner; J&P. Bud ovoid; flowers deep rose-pink, reverse white, semi-dbl., large; slightly fragrant; foliage dark; vigorous, bushy growth. AARS, 1974.

Bond Street HT, *op*, 1965, *Radar × Queen Elizabeth*; McGredy, S., IV; McGredy. Flowers deep salmon-pink, dbl. (75 petals), large (4½ in.); very fragrant.

Bonfire R, *mr*, 1928, *Crimson Rambler × R. wichuraiana*; Turbat. Flowers scarlet, dbl., in clusters of 20-25; foliage light; very vigorous.

Bonfire Night® F, *rb*, 1971, *Tiki × Variety Club*; McGredy, S., IV; McGredy. Flowers red, shaded yellow-orange, 19 petals, globular, large (3½ in.); slightly fragrant; foliage matt.

Bonhomme Min, *w*, 1986, (LAVhomme); *Blueblood sport*; Laver, Keith. Flowers white.

Bonica® F, *or*, 1958, *(Alain × Independence) × Moulin Rouge*; Meilland, F.; URS & C-P. Flowers scarlet, dbl. (70 petals), high-centered to cupped, medium blooms in clusters; slightly fragrant; foliage dark, leathery; vigorous, bushy growth.

Bonita LCl, *dr*, 1958, Knight, A.T. Flowers crimson, semi-dbl. (15 petals), medium, in clusters of 3-8; fragrant; foliage dark, glossy; vigorous (10-15 ft.) growth.

Bonjour Gr, *mr*, 1965, *Mignonne × Miss Universe*; Gaujard. Flowers bright red, dbl., medium; slightly fragrant; foliage leathery; very vigorous, bushy growth.

Bonn HMsk (S), *or*, 1950, *Hamburg × Independence*; Kordes. Flowers orange-scarlet, dbl. (25 petals), large (4 in.) blooms in trusses of 10; fragrant (musk); foliage glossy; upright, bushy (4-5 ft.) growth; (29).

Bonne Chere S, *rb*, 1985, (*R. nutkana × Baronne Prevost) × Alika*; James, John. Flowers bright velvet red, creamy eye, single (5 petals), large (3½ in.) blooms in large clusters; slight fragrance; foliage medium, dark, leathery; vigorous, arching (to 4 ft.) growth; repeats.

Bonne Fête HT, *or*, 1960, *Independence × Barcelona*; Delbard-Chabert. Bud long, pointed; flowers orange-coral, dbl. (25-30 petals), large blooms on strong stems; slightly fragrant; foliage leathery, glossy; vigorous, bushy growth.

Bonne Nuit HT, *dr*, 1966, Combe; Wyant, 1956. Bud pointed; flowers blackish red, dbl., high-centered, medium; fragrant; foliage sparse, glossy; bushy growth.

Bonne Nuit, Climbing Cl HT, *dr*, 1964, Kashimoto; Itami Rose Nursery.

Bonnie HNit (S), *dp*, 1956, *Hansa × R. nitida*; Wright, P.H. Similar to Aylsham but taller and more rapid and vigorous in growth.

Bonnie Anne HT, *pb*, 1975, *Prima Ballerina × Wendy Cussons*; MacLeod. Flowers pink, reverse yellow and pink, dbl. (30 petals), medium (3-3½ in.); fragrant; foliage large, dark, glossy.

Bonnie Belle R, *mp*, 1911, Walsh. Flowers rose, single, large; slightly fragrant; height 8-10 ft.

Bonnie Bess HT, *op*, 1929, *Wilhelm Kordes × (Crusader × Sunburst)*; Dale. Flowers deep coral-pink, suffused copper, dbl.; slightly fragrant.

Bonnie Hamilton F, *or*, 1976, *Anne Cocker × Allgold*; Cocker. Flowers vermilion-red, dbl. (26 petals), well-formed, medium (2½ in.); slightly fragrant; foliage dark.

Bonnie Jean HT, *rb*, 1933, Archer. Flowers carmine-cerise, base white, single, large; vigorous growth.

Bonnie Maid F, *pb*, 1951, LeGrice. Flowers silvery pink reverse deep pink, semi-dbl (17 petals), large (3 in.) blooms in clusters of 5-8;

foliage leathery, dark; vigorous, bushy growth. GM, NRS, 1955.

Bonnie Pink F, *lp*, 1964, *White Garnette seedling × Hawaii*; Boerner; J&P. Bud ovoid; flowers geranium-pink overcast begonia-rose, dbl. (35-40 petals), high-centered to flat with upright center petals, large (4½ in.); fragrant; foliage glossy; vigorous, upright growth.

Bonnie Prince R, *w*, 1916, *Tausendschön × Seedling*; Cook, T.N.; Portland Rose Soc., 1924. Flowers white, center tinged yellow, dbl.; fragrant; excellent pillar.

Bonnie Prince Charlie HT, *mr*, 1960, Cuthbert. Bud pointed; flowers bright red, dbl., well formed; fragrant.

Bonnie Scotland HT, *dp*, 1976, *Wendy Cussons × Percy Thrower*; Anderson's Rose Nursery. Flowers light red, dbl. (43 petals), high-centered, large (5 in.); very fragrant (damask); foliage glossy.

Bonny Min, *mp*, 1974, *Zorina × Seedling*; Kordes. Flowers deep pink, lighter reverse, dbl., globular; slightly fragrant; foliage small, light, wrinkled; dwarf growth.

Bonsoir HT, *mp*, 1968, (DICbo); Dickson, A. Bud ovoid; flowers peach-pink, full, large (6 in.); very fragrant; foliage glossy.

Booker T. Washington R, *dr*, 1930, Turbat; C-P. Flowers deep maroon, borne in clusters.

Boomerang Min, *rb*, 1992, (SPOboom); *Seedling × Seedling*; Spooner, Ray; Oregon Miniature Roses, Inc., 1993. Flowers red and white, full (26-40 petals), medium (4-7 cms.) blooms borne in small clusters; no fragrance; foliage medium, medium green, semi-glossy; some prickles; medium, bushy growth. AOE, 1993.

Bo-Peep Min, *mp*, 1950, *Cécile Brunner × Tom Thumb*; deVink; C-P. Bud ovoid, pointed; flowers rose-pink, dbl. (28 petals), cupped, micro-mini, very small; slightly fragrant; foliage small, glossy; bushy, dwarf (5-8 in.) growth.

Bordeaux R, *mr*, 1908, *Crimson Rambler × Blanche Rebatel*; Soupert & Notting. Flowers wine-red, dbl., small blooms in large cluster; very vigorous growth.

Border Beauty F, *mr*, 1957, *Floribunda seedling × Signal Red*; deRuiter; Gregory. Flowers bright scarlet, semi-dbl., medium (2-2½ in.) in very large truss (10-12 in.); foliage dark, glossy; vigorous, upright growth.

Border Coral F, *op*, 1957, *Signal Red × Fashion*; deRuiter; Gregory. Flowers coral-salmon, semi-dbl., medium (2-2½ in.) blooms in trusses; foliage dark, glossy; vigorous, spreading growth.

Border Coral, Climbing Cl F, *op*, 1966, Sanday; Gregory.

Border Gem F, *pb*, 1961, *(Navajo × Golden Dawn) × Pinocchio*; Morey; J&P. Bud ovoid; flowers geranium-pink, center light salmon-orange, dbl. (20 petals), large (2½-3 in.) blooms in clusters; fragrant; foliage leathery; compact, low growth.

Border Gold F, *dy*, 1966, *Allgold × Pigmy Gold*; Morey; Country Garden Nursery. Bud ovoid; flowers medium to deep yellow, very dbl.; slightly fragrant; foliage dark, leathery; vigorous, low, bushy growth.

Border King Pol, *mr*, 1952, (Roi des Bordures); deRuiter; Gregory. Flowers bright strawberry-red, semi-dbl. (16 petals), small; large truss; foliage dark, glossy; very vigorous growth.

Border King, Climbing Cl Pol, *mr*, 1960, Gregory.

Border Princess F, *op*, 1951, Verschuren-Pechtold; Bentley. Flowers coral-pink shaded orange, dbl. (22 petals), high-centered, reflexed, large (3 in.); foliage light, glossy; vigorous growth.

Border Queen F, *op*, 1951, (Reine des Bordures); deRuiter; Harkness; Gregory. Flowers salmon-pink, center paler, reverse darker, single (9 petals), medium (2½ in.), large truss; foliage leathery, olive-green; vigorous, compact growth; (28). GM, NRS, 1950.

Borderer Pol, *pb*, 1918, *Jersey Beauty seedling*; Clark, A.; NRS Victoria. Flowers salmon, fawn and pink, semi-dbl. to dbl.; slightly fragrant; dwarf, spreading growth.

Bordure Nacrée® Min, *ly*, 1973, (DELcrouf; Bordure de Nacrée); *(Orléans Rose × Francois et Joseph Guy) × (Goldilocks × DELtorche)*; Delbard. Flowers creamy light yellow, dbl. (38 petals), small; no fragrance; low, bushy growth. GM, Baden-Baden, 1972.

Bordure Rose® F, *pb*, 1986, (DELbara; Roslyne; Strawberry Ice); *((Goldilocks × Virgo) × (Orange Triumph × Yvonne Rabier)) × Fashion*; Delbard, 1975. Flowers medium pink blending to white at base, dbl. (25 petals), cupped, 3-4 in.; no fragrance; foliage thick and bright; low, compact growth. GM, Baden-Baden, 1973.

Borealis K (S), *w*, 1980, *Blanche Mallerin × Leverkusen*; James, John. Bud globular, pointed; flowers white, dbl. (27 petals), high-centered blooms borne singly; sweet fragrance; foliage shiny; gray prickles; bushy growth; repeat blooming.

Born Free Min, *or*, 1978, *Red Pinocchio × Little Chief*; Moore, R.S.; Sequoia Nursery. Bud long, pointed; flowers brilliant orange-red, dbl. (20 petals), small (1½ in.); foliage dark; bushy, upright growth.

Boryana HT, *dr*, 1977, *Tallyho × Spartan*; Staikov, Prof. Dr. V.; Kalaydjiev and Chorbadjiiski. Flowers dark red, dbl. (55 petals), large; foliage dark, glossy; vigorous, upright.

Boscobel™ Min, *ob*, 1990, (KINbosco); *(Cheers × Rainbow's End) × Breezy*; King, Gene; AGM Miniature Roses. Flowers orange to burnt orange, moderately full (15-25 petals), small, borne mostly singly; no fragrance; foliage medium, light green, matt; upright, medium growth.

Bossa Nova HT, *dy*, 1964, *Leverkusen × Buccaneer*; McGredy, S., IV; McGredy. Flowers deep golden yellow, dbl. (28 petals), high-centered, large (4 in.); foliage dark.

Bossuet G (OGR), *mr*, 1857, Flowers scarlet, edges darker.

Boston HT, *kp*, 1917, *Mrs. George Shawyer × Seedling*; Montgomery Co. Flowers medium pink, dbl.; very fragrant.

Boston Beauty R, *mp*, 1919, *Orléans Rose × (Katharina Zeimet × Old Ayrshire rose)*; Farquhar. Flowers clear pink, dbl.; fragrant.

Botaniste Henri Grimm F, *my*, 1958, *Goldilocks × Fashion*; Gaujard, R.; G. Truffaut. Flowers golden to straw-yellow, becoming pink tinted, large blooms in cluster; vigorous growth.

Botzaris D (OGR), *w*, 1856, Flowers creamy white, dbl., flat; foliage light green.

Boudoir HT, *pb*, 1942, (Paul Fromont); *Ampere × (Charles P. Kilham × Margaret McGredy)*; Meilland, F.; C-P. Flowers tyrian rose, reverse white, dbl. (50 petals), high-centered, large; foliage leathery; vigorous, upright, bushy growth.

Bougainville N (OGR), *pb*, 1822, Cochet, P. Bud red; flowers pink in center, becoming paler and tinged with lilac at the circumference, very dbl., cupped, medium; calyx smooth, obconical; foliage narrow, glossy; branches very prickly.

Boule de Neige B (OGR), *w*, 1867, *Blanche Lafitte × Sappho (Vibert's)*; Lacharme. Flowers pure white, full, compact; fragrant; foliage dark; occasional recurrent bloom.

Bountiful F, *pb*, 1972, *Vesper × Seedling*; LeGrice. Flowers strawberry-salmon, reverse deeper, dbl. (33 petals), HT type, large (3 in.); fragrant; foliage small; tall, erect.

Bouquet F, *dp*, 1940, (Lied; Siegeslied); *Ingar Olsson × Heidekind*; Tantau; C-P. Flowers deep pink, dbl. (33 petals), cupped; slightly fragrant; foliage dark, leathery; vigorous, bushy, compact.

Bouquet Charmant G (OGR), *mp*, Flowers rosy purple, full, large.

Bouquet d'Or N (OGR), *yb*, 1872, *Gloire de Dijon × Seedling*; Ducher. Flowers yellow, center coppery salmon, full, large.

Bouquet d'Or HT, *ly*, 1922, Lippiatt. Flowers light golden yellow, well formed; vigorous growth.

Bouquet Fait S, *pb*, 1985, (Len 1); *R. mollis × Complicata*; Lens, Louis. Flowers medium pink, white eye, semi-dbl., 2 in. blooms in clusters of 1-5; very fragrant; foliage grayish green, hairy; bushy (to 5 ft.) growth; non-recurrent bloom.

Bouquet Rose Pol, *lp*, 1928, Granger-Gaucher; Turbat. Flowers flesh-pink and peach-blossom, clusters of 30-40.

Bouquet Rouge F, *mr*, 1963, *(Gruss an Teplitz × Independence) × (Independence × Floradora)*; Arles; Roses-France. Flowers red, dbl. (45 petals), large blooms in clusters of 14-16; vigorous growth.

Bourbon Rose 1817, (*R. × borboniana* Desportes; *R. borboniana* Chaix; *R. canina borboniana* Thory); A group of hybrids derived from the cross of *R. chinensis × R. damascena semperflorens*. Flowers pink, red or purple, dbl. or semi-dbl., 3 in. diam., solitary or in few-fld. corymbs; some are recurrent.

Boursault Rose (*R. l'heritierana* Thory; *R. reclinata* Thory; *R. boursaultii* hort.); A group of hybrids supposedly derived from the cross of *R. chinensis × R. pendulina*.; Originated prior to 1820. Flowers pink, to purple, nodding, semi-dbl. or dbl., in corymbs; fruit subglobose, smooth climbing to 12 ft.; non-recurrent.

Boutonniere HT, *op*, 1940, *Lulu × Mrs. Sam McGredy*; Lammerts; Armstrong Nursery. Flowers salmon-pink, dbl. (40-50 petals), medium (3 in.); foliage dark, glossy, bronze; vigorous, bushy, compact growth.

Bouzloudja HT, *mr*, 1974, *Sarah Arnot × Rina Herholdt*; Staikov, Prof. Dr. V.; Kalaydjiev and Chorbadjiiski. Flowers medium red, dbl. (40 petals), large; slightly fragrant; foliage dark, glossy; vigorous, bushy growth.

Boy Crazy S, *dp*, 1992, (DICrevival); *Sweet Magic × DICmerlin*; Dickson, Patrick; Bear Creek Gardens, 1992. Flowers deep pink, petal base has cream colored "half moon", moderately full (15-25 petals), heavy petal substance, medium (4-7 cms) blooms borne in small clusters; patio; foliage medium, dark green, glossy; some prickles; medium (90 cms), upright, bushy growth.

Boy Scout HT, *or*, 1946, (Scout); *Joanna Hill × Olympiad*; Duehrsen; California Roses. Bud long, pointed; flowers flame, dbl., high-centered, large; fragrant; foliage dark, glossy; very vigorous, upright, bushy growth.

Boys' Brigade® Min, *mr*, 1983, (COCdinkum); *(Darling Flame × Saint Alban) × (Little Flirt × Marlena)*; Cocker, Ann G.; Cocker & Sons, 1984. Flowers medium red, single (5 petals), medium, patio, blooms in clusters; no fragrance; foliage small, medium green, semi-glossy; bushy.

Bozena Nemcová HT, *dp*, 1931, *Sylvia × Priscilla*; Böhm. Flowers pure dark pink, dbl., cupped, very large on strong stems; very fragrant; foliage bronze, thick; vigorous growth.

Bradgate HT, *yb*, 1970, *Piccadilly sport*; Worth; Lowe. Flowers yellow and deep red bicolor, dbl. (27 petals), pointed, large (4-5 in.); slightly fragrant; foliage dark; free growth.

Bradley Craig® F, *or*, 1986, (MACstewar; Bradley Graig); *Tojo × Montana*; McGredy, S. Flowers scarlet, dbl. (15-25 petals), medium; slight fragrance; foliage medium, medium green, glossy; bushy growth.

Braiswick Charm R, *ob*, 1914, Cant, F. Flowers orange-yellow, edges almost white, cluster on long, strong stems; fragrant; foliage dark, glossy, leathery; very vigorous growth.

Brandenburg HT, *or*, 1965, *(Spartan × Prima Ballerina) × Karl Herbst*; Kordes, R.; McGredy. Flowers deep salmon, reverse darker, dbl. (40 petals), high-centered, large (5 in.); vigorous, upright growth.

Brandenburg Gate HT, *mr*, 1991, (JACgate); *Seedling × Madras*; Warriner, William A.; Bear Creek Gardens, 1990. Flowers red with light reverse, full (26-40 petals), large; fragrant; foliage large, medium green, matt; tall, upright growth.

Brandon LCl, *mr*, 1964, Combe. Bud long, pointed; flowers dark carmine-red, dbl., large; vigorous growth; very free, recurrent bloom.

Brandy™ HT, *ab*, 1981, (AROcad); *First Prize × Dr. A.J. Verhage*; Swim, H.C. & Christensen, J.E.; Armstrong Nursery. Bud long, pointed; flowers deep apricot, dbl. (28 petals), blooms borne mostly singly; mild tea fragrance; foliage large; straight prickles; vigorous, medium growth. AARS, 1982.

Brandy Butter HT, *ob*, 1982, *Fred Gibson × Royal Gold*; Northfield, G. Bud long, pointed; flowers pale gold, dbl. (28 petals), high-centered blooms borne 4-5 per cluster; fragrant; foliage mid-green; thick, triangular-shaped prickles; tall, upright growth.

Brandywine HT, *ly*, 1941, *Seedling × Souvenir*; Thompson's, J.H., Sons; C-P; J&P. Bud long, pointed; flowers buff-yellow, dbl. (25-30 pet-

als), large (4-5 in.); slightly fragrant; foliage olive-green, leathery; very vigorous, upright. ARS John Cook Medal, 1945.

Brasilia HT, *rb*, 1968, *Kordes' Perfecta × Piccadilly*; McGredy, S., IV; McGredy. Flowers scarlet, reverse gold, dbl., large (4 in.); slightly fragrant.

Brass Ring Min, *ob*, 1981, (DICgrow; Peek a Boo); *Memento × Nozomi*; Dickson, P.; J&P. Bud pointed; flowers coppery orange, fading to rose pink, dbl. (21 small petals), flat, patio, blooms in large clusters; foliage small, pointed, glossy; upright, arching growth.

Bravado F, *dr*, 1987, (JACro); *Seedling × Gabriella*; Warriner; J&P. Flowers dark red, dbl. (26 petals), cupped to high-centered, medium blooms are borne usually singly; slight fragrance; foliage medium, dark, semi-glossy; medium, red to brown prickles, hooked downward; medium, upright growth; greenhouse variety.

Bravo HT, *mr*, 1951, *World's Fair × Mirandy*; Swim; Armstrong Nursery. Bud ovoid; flowers cardinal-red, dbl. (35 petals), high-centered, large (4-5 in.), borne in clusters; slightly fragrant; foliage leathery; vigorous, upright, moderately bushy growth.

Brazier HT, *mr*, 1937, (Brasier); *Charles P. Kilham × Seedling*; Mallerin; A. Meilland & C-P. Flowers flame-scarlet, dbl., large; slightly fragrant; foliage glossy; very vigorous, bushy growth.

Brazil HT, *rb*, 1947, Caron, B.; URS. Bud long, pointed; flowers saturn-red, reverse saffron-yellow, dbl., well shaped; foliage light green.

Bread 'n' Butter Min, *ob*, 1985, (TINbutt); *Arizona × Orange Honey*; Bennett, Dee; Tiny Petals Nursery. Flowers golden orange blended yellow, dbl. (28 petals), HT form, medium; fragrant; foliage medium, medium green, semi-glossy; upright, bushy growth.

Break o' Dawn Cl Min, *pb*, 1982, (MINfco); *Little Darling × Over the Rainbow*; Williams, E.D.; Mini-Roses. Flowers white with deep pink edges, white reverse, dbl. (35 petals), small; slight fragrance; foliage small, dark, glossy; upright, bushy, climbing growth.

Break o' Day Pol, *pb*, 1937, Archer. Flowers copper-pink, center yellow, fading to shell-pink, semi-dbl., cupped blooms in clusters; vigorous growth; recurrent bloom.

Break o' Day HT, *ob*, 1939, (Delta); *Seedling × Glenn Dale*; Brownell. Flowers orange shades, dbl. (50 petals), large; very fragrant; vigorous growth.

Break o'Day, Climbing Cl HT, *ob*, 1944, Brownell.

Breakaway Min, *mr*, 1980, *Dandy Lyon* × *Seedling*; Lyon, Lyndon. Bud ovoid, pointed; flowers medium red, dbl. (23 petals), borne singly; slight fragrance; foliage small, medium green; straight, tiny, brownish-green prickles; compact, upright, bushy.

Breath of Life LCl, *ab*, 1980, (HARquanne); *Red Dandy* × *Alexander*; Harkness, R., 1982. Bud plump; flowers apricot to apricot-pink, dbl. (33 petals), borne 1-3 per cluster; fragrant; foliage semi-glossy; large, straight, reddish prickles; upright (to 8 ft.) growth.

Breathtaking HT, *dp*, 1982, (LEObretak); *Pink Silk seedling* × *(Pink Parfait* × *Wendy Cussons)*; Leon, Charles F., Sr. Bud ovoid, long, pointed; flowers deep pink, dbl. (40 petals), exhibition form; very fragrant (damask); foliage medium to large, medium green, semiglossy; upright, bushy growth.

Bredon® S, *ab*, 1985, (AUSbred); *Wife of Bath* × *Lilian Austin*; Austin, David; David Austin Roses, 1984. Flowers apricot, dbl. (40+ petals), medium; fragrant; foliage small, light green, matt; upright growth; repeat bloom.

Breeze Hill LCl, *ab*, 1926, *R. wichuraiana* × *Beauté de Lyon*; Van Fleet; ARS. Flowers flesh tinted apricot, center rose, paling, dbl. (55 petals), cupped, large (3 in.) blooms in clusters; fragrant; bushy growth, heavy canes; non-recurrent bloom.

Breezy™ Min, *ob*, 1984, (SAVabrez); *Sheri Anne* × *Seedling*; Saville, F.H.; Nor'East Min. Roses. Bud small; flowers bright orange-red, yellow reverse, dbl. (20 petals), HT form, small blooms in sprays; fragrant; foliage small, medium green, semi-glossy; upright growth.

Bregina F, *or*, 1965, *Mandrina sport*; deRuiter. Flowers vermilion-red.

Brenda E (OGR), *lp*, 1894, Penzance; Keynes, Williams & Co. Flowers peach-blossom-pink; foliage fragrant; very vigorous growth.

Brenda Ann HT, *dy*, 1974, *Piccadilly sport*; Watts. Flowers amber-yellow, dbl. (37 petals), full, large (5 in.); slightly fragrant; foliage glossy, tinted bronze; vigorous, tall, upright growth.

Brenda Colvin R, *lp*, 1970, (*R. filipes* 'Brenda Colvin'); Colvin; Sunningdale Nursery. Flowers light pink, single (5 petals), small (1 in.) blooms in trusses; very fragrant; foliage dark, glossy; very vigorous growth.

Brenda Lee Min, *yb*, 1991, (MIClee); *Rise 'n' Shine* × *Rainbow's End*; Williams, Michael C., 1988; The Rose Garden. Bud pointed; flowers red edge to yellow base, dbl. (20 petals), urn-shaped, exhibition, small; foliage small, medium green, semi-glossy; bushy, low, compact growth.

Brenda of Tasmania F, *w*, 1971, *Queen Elizabeth sport*; Holloway. Bud ovoid; flowers white, center pink, dbl., cupped, large; fragrant; foliage large, glossy; upright, bushy growth.

Brenda's Fragrance HT, *pb*, 1967, *Lieut. Chaure* × *Hector Deane*; Smith, W.H. Flowers cerise edged white, high-centered; very fragrant; foliage leathery; vigorous growth.

Brennus HCh (OGR), *dr*, 1830, Laffay. Flowers deep red, shaded with violet.

Bresilienne Pol, *dr*, 1971, *Red Favorite* × *Ena Harkness*; Delforge. Bud long, pointed; flowers deep red, dbl., cupped, medium; slightly fragrant; foliage bronze, leathery; vigorous, dwarf, bushy growth.

Brian Donn Min, *dr*, 1991, (TINdonn); *Intrique* × *Big John*; Bennett, Dee, 1985; Tiny Petals Nursery, 1990. Bud ovoid; flowers darkest ruby red to maroon, dark ruby red reverse, ages only slightly lighter at base of petals, very dbl. (35-45 petals), high-centered, exhibition, medium; moderate, damask fragrance; foliage medium, medium green, semi-glossy; bushy, medium growth.

Brian Lee Min, *m*, 1986, (TINlee); *Carrousel* × *Plum Duffy*; Bennett, Dee; Tiny Petals Nursery. Flowers dark red, aging mauve, dbl. (28 petals), urn-shaped, exhibition, mini-flora, medium blooms borne singly and in sprays of 3-4; fragrant; foliage medium, dark, semi-glossy; small reddish prickles; fruit 5/8 in., globular, brown-green; medium, upright, bushy growth.

Briand-Paneuropa HT, *mp*, 1931, *Franklin* × *Willowmere*; Böhm. Flowers carmine-rose, base yellow, dbl., very large; slightly fragrant; vigorous growth.

Brianna HT, *ly*, 1992, (DEVcarlos); *Seedling 82249-1 (75062-1* × *Excitement)* × *Seedling (75062-1* × *Cocktail)*; Marciel, Stanley; DeVor Nurseries. Flowers canary yellow, full (26-40 petals), large (7+ cms) blooms borne mostly singly; fragrant; foliage large, medium green, semi-glossy; few prickles; upright (152 cms) growth.

Brian's Song S, *op*, 1977, *Independence* × *Pike's Peak*; Smith, R.L.; Smith's Greenhouse & Nursery. Flowers orange-pink, dbl. (35 petals), high-centered to cupped, large (4 in.); fragrant; foliage large, glossy, dark; intermittent bloom.

Briarcliff HT, *pb*, 1926, *Columbia sport*; Pierson, P.M. Flowers center deep rose-pink, outer petals lighter; a popular greenhouse variety.

Briarcliff Brilliance HT, *dp*, 1932, *Briarcliff sport*; Pierson, P.M. Flowers rose to rose-red, dbl., large; vigorous growth.

Briarcliff, Climbing Cl HT, *pb*, 1929, Parmentier, J.

Briarcliff Supreme HT, *pb*, 1947, *Briarcliff sport*; Hinner, P.; Bauské Bros. & Hinner. Bud long, pointed; flowers Briarcliff pink, dbl., very large; very fragrant; foliage dark; very vigorous, upright growth.

Bridal Bouquet HT, *w*, 1976, *Lady Sylvia sport*; Ormerod. Flowers white, dbl. (23 petals), medium (3-4 in.); slightly fragrant; foliage matt, green; vigorous, compact growth.

Bridal Pink™ F, *mp*, 1967, (JACbri); *Summertime seedling × Spartan seedling*; Boerner; J&P. Bud ovoid, pointed; flowers pink, dbl., high-centered, large; fragrant; foliage leathery; vigorous, upright, bushy growth; a cut flower variety.

Bridal Robe HT, *w*, 1955, *McGredy's Pink × Mrs. Charles Lamplough*; McGredy. Flowers ivory-white, dbl. (54 petals), high-pointed, large (4 in.); fragrant; foliage glossy, olive-green; vigorous growth. GM, NRS, 1953.

Bridal Veil F, *ly*, 1954, *Pinocchio seedling × Pigmy Gold*; Boerner; Stark Bros. Bud ovoid, cream; flowers white overcast seafoam-yellow, dbl. (75-80 petals), open, medium (2½ in.) in clusters; very fragrant; vigorous, bushy growth.

Bridal White™ F, *w*, 1970, (JACwhy); *Bridal Pink sport*; Warriner; J&P. Flowers ivory-white.

Bride's Blush HT, *w*, 1923, *Columbia sport*; Amling Co. Flowers creamy white, at times blush-pink, single (6 petals); fragrant.

Bride's Dream HT, *lp*, 1985, (KORoyness; Fairy Tale Queen; Marchenkonigin); *Royal Highness × Seedling*; Kordes, R., 1984; Ludwig Roses, 1986. Flowers very pale pink, dbl. (32 petals), high-centered, large; slight fragrance; foliage deep green; dark brown prickles; tall, upright growth.

Bride's White F, *w*, 1968, Mansuino, Q.; Carlton Rose Nursery. Flowers pure white, dbl., cupped, small; vigorous, upright, bushy growth.

Bridesmaid T (OGR), *lp*, 1893, *Catherine Mermet sport*; Moore. Flowers light pink.

Bridesmaid, Climbing Cl T (OGR), *p*, 1893, Moore.

Bridget HT, *op*, 1947, *Mrs. Henry Bowles × Phyllis Gold*; Fletcher; Tucker. Bud long, pointed; flowers brilliant orange-scarlet, base bright golden yellow, dbl. (35-40 petals), flattish, large (4-5 in.); foliage glossy, bright green.

Bridgwater Pride F, *op*, 1982, *Vera Dalton × Allgold*; Sanday, John; Sanday Roses, Ltd. Flowers rich salmon, dbl. (20 petals), medium; fragrant; foliage medium, dark, semi-glossy; bushy, compact growth.

Brigadeiro França Borges F, *or*, 1960, *Independence × Seedling*; Moreira da Silva. Flowers bright orange-red.

Brigadoon™ HT, *pb*, 1991, (JACpal); *Seedling × Pristine*; Warriner, William A., 1983; Bear Creek Gardens, 1992. Bud ovoid, pointed; flowers pink near center, coral pink at petal margin, rose pink and cream blendreverse, ages to coral pink, very dbl. (35-40 petals), urn-shaped, high centered, exhibition, medium; moderate, spicy fragrance; foliage medium, dark green, semi-glossy; upright, spreading, tall growth. AARS, 1992.

Bright Angel S, *yb*, 1977, *Dornroschen × Golden Wings*; Smith, R.L.; Smith's Greenhouse & Nursery. Bud ovoid; flowers light yellow, edged pink, dbl. (48 petals), high-centered, large (4 in.); very fragrant; foliage large, glossy, dark; vigorous, bushy growth; intermittent bloom.

Bright Beam Gr, *pb*, 1972, *Peace × Little Darling*; Fuller; Wyant. Bud ovoid; flowers cream, edged pink, dbl., cupped, large; fragrant; voliage glossy, dark; very vigorous, upright growth; profuse, intermittent bloom.

Bright Eyes F, 1948, *Joanna Hill × (Heidekind × Betty Uprichard)*; Duehrsen; H & S. Bud ovoid; Flowers light yellow to primrose, dbl. (25 petals), medium, large truss; slightly fragrant; Foliage leathery, glossy, dark; Dwarf growth RULED EXTINCT 6/83 ARM.

Bright Eyes F, *or*, 1983, (SANmar); *Seedling × Circus*; Sanday, John; John Sanday Roses. Flowers orange-red, yellow stamens, dbl., medium; slight fragrance; foliage medium, dark, matt; bushy growth.

Bright Fire Cl HT, *dr*, 1977, *Parkdirektor Riggers × Guinee*; Pearce. Flowers crimson, shaded darker, semi-dbl. (15 petals), large (4½ in.); slightly fragrant; foliage glossy, dark; free growth.

Bright Garbs F, *or*, 1977, *Orangeade × Seedling*; Hardikar. Bud pointed; flowers orange-red, semi-dbl. (12 petals), large (2½ in.); fragrant; foliage large; dwarf growth.

Bright Jewel Min, *pb*, Bud pointed; flowers rose-pink, white center, semi-dbl., very small blooms in clusters; low, compact growth.

Bright Melody S, *mr*, 1984, *Carefree Beauty × (HerzAs × Cuthbert Grant)*; Buck, Dr. Griffith; Iowa State University. Bud ovoid, pointed; flowers medium red, dbl. (30 petals), shallow-cupped, large blooms borne 1-10 per cluster; light fragrance; foliage medium-large, dark olive green, leathery; awl-like, tan prickles; erect, bushy growth; repeat bloom.

Bright Morning HT, *my*, 1958, Ratcliffe. Flowers golden yellow; fragrant.

Bright Red Pol, *dr*, 1938, deRuiter. Flowers velvety dark red, dbl., large cluster; bushy growth.

Bright Smile® F, *my*, 1980, (DICdance); *Eurorose × Seedling*; Dickson, P., 1981. Bud pointed; flowers empire yellow, semi-dbl. (15 petals), flat, patio, convex blooms borne 15 per cluster; slight fragrance; foliage dense, mid-green; concave, purple prickles; bushy, medium growth. GM, Belfast, 1982.

Bright Wings HT, *op*, 1942, (Gitane); *Mme. Arthaud × Annie Drevet*; Mallerin; A. Meilland; C-P. Bud long, pointed, rosy orange; flower centers orange shading to pink, dbl. (22 petals), cupped, large strong stems; fragrant (fruity); foliage bronze; vigorous, bushy growth.

Brightness HT, *rb*, 1958, *Doreen sport*; Fryer's Nursery. Bud long, pointed; flowers scarlet, reverse golden yellow, merging to orange, dbl. (28-35 petals), high-centered to open, large (4½-5½ in.); very fragrant; foliage leathery, glossy; bushy, moderately vigorous growth.

Brightside Min, *or*, 1974, *Persian Princess × Persian Princess*; Moore, R.S.; Park Seed Co. Flowers orange-red, dbl. (25 petals), high-centered, small (1 in.); fragrant; foliage small, matt; upright, bushy growth.

Brightside Cream N (OGR), *w*, Flowers creamy white, yellow stamens, semi-dbl. (18 petals), 3 in. blooms in clusters on short stems; foliage dark; vigorous growth, long canes. Well established in Bermuda.

Brigitte Jourdan F, *or*, 1960, *Belle Créole × Independence*; Arles; Roses-France. Bud ovoid; flowers pomegranate-red, dbl., globular, large; slightly fragrant; foliage dark, glossy; vigorous, bushy growth.

Brilliance F, *or*, 1958, *Seedling × Independence*; Boerner; J&P. Bud ovoid; flowers coral, dbl. (50 petals), cupped, medium (2 in.); fragrant; foliage glossy; compact growth; for pot forcing.

Brilliancy HT, *or*, 1936, *Étoile de Hollande × Daily Mail Scented Rose*; LeGrice. Flowers brilliant scarlet, dbl., short stems; very fragrant; foliage leathery; bushy growth.

Brilliant Echo Pol, *mp*, 1927, *Echo sport*; Western Rose Co. Flowers rosy pink.

Brilliant King F, *mr*, 1961, *Cocorico × Orange Delight*; Leenders, J. Flowers bright red, dbl. (32 petals), shallow cupped, large (4 in.); slightly fragrant.

Brilliant Red HT, *mr*, 1938, *Charles P. Kilham × Étoile de Hollande*; Lens. Bud very long, pointed; flowers brilliant red, full, well formed, very large; foliage bright green; vigorous, bushy growth.

Brilliant Star F, *mr*, 1965, *Masquerade × Dicksons Flame*; Watkins Roses. Flowers bright red, center shaded yellow, semi-dbl. (12-20 petals), large (2½-3 in.) blooms in clusters; foliage glossy; vigorous growth.

Brindis LCl, *rb*, 1962, *Orange Triumph, Climbing × (Phyllis Bide × Baccará)*; Dot, S. Flowers geranium-red, center yellow, single; foliage dark; vigorous growth.

Brise Parfumée F, *mr*, 1950, *Böhm's Triumph × Baby Chateau*; Truffaut, G. Bud pointed; flowers red, dbl., borne in clusters; very fragrant; foliage glossy, bronze; bark and twigs reddish brown; many spines; very vigorous growth.

Bristol HT, *rb*, 1968, *Gavotte × Tropicana*; Sanday. Flowers bright crimson, reverse lighter, dbl., large; fragrant; foliage dark; compact growth.

Bristol Post HT, *op*, 1972, *Vera Dalton × Parasol*; Sanday. Flowers pale salmon-pink, base orange, dbl. (29 petals), pointed, large (4½ in.); slightly fragrant; foliage slightly glossy, dark; upright growth.

Britannia Pol, *rb*, 1929, *Coral Cluster × Eblouissant*; Burbage Nursery. Flowers crimson, center white, single, small, borne in clusters of 30-40; foliage small, leathery, light; compact, bushy growth; recurrent bloom.

Britestripe Min, *rb*, 1991, (CLEbrite; Britestripes); *Pinstripe × Seedling*; Clements, John; Heirloom Old Garden Roses, 1990. Flowers soft pink, striped bright red, full (26-40 petals), small (0-4 cms), blooms borne in small clusters; no fragrance; foliage small, medium green, semi-glossy; some prickles; medium (30 cms), bushy, compact growth.

British Columbia Centennial HT, *pb*, 1971, *Pink Masterpiece × Seedling*; Boerner; Pan American Bulb Co. Bud ovoid; flowers light rose-pink, reverse white, dbl., high-centered, large; slightly fragrant; foliage leathery; vigorous growth.

British Queen HT, *w*, 1912, McGredy. Flowers creamy white, center flushed, dbl., open, long, weak stems; slightly fragrant; foliage light green, soft; bushy growth. GM, NRS, 1912.

Brno HT, *ob*, 1933, *Souv. de George Beckwith × Rosemary*; Böhm. Flowers maroon, orange, gold, semi-dbl., open, large; foliage glossy; vigorous, bushy growth.

Broadcaster Gr, *or*, 1969, *Queen Elizabeth* × *Circus*; Perry; Conklin. Bud ovoid; flowers orange-red, dbl., medium; slightly fragrant; foliage dark; vigorous growth.

Broadway™ HT, *yb*, 1985, (BURway); *(First Prize × Gold Glow) × Sutter's Gold*; Perry, Anthony; Cooperative Rose Growers, 1986. Flowers golden yellow, blended pink, dbl. (35 petals), well-formed, medium; fragrant; foliage medium to large, dark, semi-glossy; upright growth. AARS, 1986.

Brocade HT, *pb*, 1960, (Jeune Fille); *Charlotte Armstrong × Baiser*; Combe; Hémeray-Aubert. Bud ovoid; flowers soft rose, base cream-white, dbl. (54 petals), cupped, large (4-5 in.); fragrant; foliage leathery; vigorous, upright growth.

Brög's Canina Sp (OGR), *lp*, Brög. Vigorous, almost thornless strain of *R. canina*; in use as an under stock. Comes fairly true from seed.

Bronze Beauty F, *ob*, 1974, *Electra × Woburn Abbey*; Warriner; J&P. Bud ovoid-pointed; flowers golden yellow to orange-yellow, dbl. (27 petals), open, large (4 in.); slightly fragrant; foliage large, leathery; vigorous growth.

Bronze Bedder HT, *yb*, 1920, Paul, W. Flowers bronzy yellow, single, large.

Bronze Masterpiece HT, *ab*, 1960, (Bronce Masterpiece); *Golden Masterpiece × Kate Smith*; Boerner; J&P. Bud long; flowers bronze-apricot, becoming orange-yellow, dbl. (48 petals), high-centered, large (5½-6 in.); fragrant; foliage leathery, glossy; vigorous, upright growth. GM, Geneva, 1958.

Brook Song S, *my*, 1985, *Prairie Star × Tom Brown*; Buck, Dr. Griffith; Iowa State University, 1984. Flowers medium yellow, dbl. (40 petals), imbricated form, large blooms borne 1-8 per cluster; fragrant; foliage leathery, dark; awl-like, tan prickles; erect; repeat bloom; hardy.

Brookville HT, *ly*, 1942, *Leonard Barron sport*; Brookville Nursery. Flowers cream-yellow.

Brother Wilfrid HT, *mp*, 1976, *Alec's Red sport*; Wood. Flowers medium pink.

Brown County Splendor™ S, *yb*, 1985, (WILkbsp); *Paul's Lemon Pillar × (Garden Party × Command Performance)*; Williams, J.B.; Krider Nursery. Flowers ivory to yellow blended with peach to orange-red, dbl. (35 petals), large; very fragrant; foliage large, dark, semi-glossy; upright, spreading growth.

Brown Velvet F, *r*, 1983, (MACultra; Colorbreak); *Mary Sumner × Kapai*; McGredy, S., 1982. Flowers orange, tinged brownish, dbl. (35 petals), medium; slight fragrance; foliage medium, dark, glossy; upright growth. GM, NZ, 1979.

Brownell Yellow Rambler R, *my*, 1942, (Yellow Rambler); *(Emily Gray × Ghislaine de Feligonde) × Golden Glow*; Brownell. Flowers yellow, dbl., petals recurred, borne in more open cluster than Dorothy Perkins; slightly fragrant.

Brownie F, *r*, 1959, *Lavender Pinocchio seedling × Grey Pearl*; Boerner; J&P. Bud ovoid, tan shades, edged pinkish; flowers brownish tan, reverse yellow, dbl. (38 petals), cupped to flat, large (3½-4 in.) blooms in small clusters; fragrant; foliage leathery; vigorous, upright, bushy growth.

Brunette F, *yb*, 1970, *(Purpurine × Lavender Pinocchio × Fillette) × (Gold Strike × Golden Garnette)*; Lens; Spek. Bud ovoid; flowers amber-yellow to orange, dbl. (25 petals), cupped, medium (1½-2½ in.); foliage glossy; for greenhouse use.

Bruocsella® HT, *dy*, 1980, (LENbru); *Peace × Golden Garnette*; Lens, Louis. Flowers golden yellow, dbl. (35 petals), urn-shaped, exhibition, large blooms borne singly or in small clusters; very fragrant; dark green prickles; upright, bushy growth.

B.S. Bhatcharji HT, *my*, 1933, Dickson, A. Flowers buttercup-yellow, well formed, large; foliage glossy, dark; vigorous growth.

Bubbles Min, *yb*, 1986, (ZIPbub); *(Little Darling × (Roundabout × Redgold)) × (Maytime × Poker Chip)*; Zipper, H.; Magic Moment Min. Flowers medium yellow, shaded pink and coral, dbl. (35 petals), medium blooms borne singly and in small clusters; fragrant; foliage medium, medium green, semi-glossy; upright, spreading growth.

Buccaneer Gr, *my*, 1952, *Golden Rapture × (Max Krause × Capt. Thomas)*; Swim; Armstrong Nursery. Bud urn-shaped; flowers buttercup-yellow, dbl. (30 petals), cupped, medium (3-3½ in.); fragrant; foliage dark, leathery; vigorous, upright, tall growth. GM, Geneva, 1952.

Buckeye Belle HHug (S), *pb*, 1956, *R. hugonis × Seedling*; Garwood. Bud globular; flowers pale to deep pink, semi-dbl. (15 petals), open, small (1½ in.), borne in compact clusters; fragrant; foliage dark; vigorous, upright, bushy; abundant, recurrent bloom.

Buenos Aires F, *r*, 1957, *Mme. Henri Guillot × Pinocchio*; Silva. Flowers burnt brick to dark red-ochre, dbl.; low growth.

Buff Beauty HMsk (S), *ab*, 1939, *William Allen Richardson × Seedling*; Bentall, Ann. Flowers apricot-yellow, dbl. (50 petals), 4 in. blooms in clusters of 12; fragrant; foliage large, medium green, semi-glossy; vigorous (to 6 ft.) growth; (21).

Buff King LCl, *ab*, 1939, Horvath; Wayside Gardens Co. Bud ovoid, deep amber; flowers amber and buff, cupped, large, long, strong stems; foliage glaucous green; very vigorous (10-12 ft.) growth.

Buffy™ Min, *ab*, 1986, (KINbuff); *Vera Dalton × Party Girl*; King, Gene; AGM Miniature Roses, 1987. Flowers light apricot, reverse deeper, darker towards center, dbl. (20 petals), high-centered, exhibition, medium, borne usually singly and in sprays of 5-7; mini-flora; slight fragrance; foliage medium green, matt; slightly hooked, light brown prickles; fruit oval, green; bushy spreading growth.

Bugle Boy™ F, *dy*, 1988, (AROglofy); *Sunsprite × (Unnamed Katherine Loker seedling × Gingersnap)*; Christensen, Jack; Bear Creek Gardens, 1988. Bud ovoid, pointed; flowers deep yellow, dbl. (35 petals), good substance, cupped, medium, borne insprays of 5-6; slight tea fragrance; foliage medium, medium green, very glossy; prickles hooked slightly downward, medium, red to tan; fruit unknown; bushy, medium growth.

Buisman's Glory F, *mr*, 1952, *Karen Poulsen × Sangerhausen*; Buisman. Flowers currant-red, single, open, medium; foliage light green.

Buisman's Triumph F, *mp*, 1952, *Käthe Duvigneau × Cinnabar*; Buisman. Flowers bright pink, becoming lighter, semi-dbl. (13 petals), large; foliage dark; vigorous growth.

Buisson Ardent Gr, *mr*, 1956, *Peace × Seedling*; Gaujard. Flowers bright red, medium; fragrant; foliage dark.

Buisson d'Or HFt (OGR), *my*, 1928, *Mme. Edouard Herriot × R. × harisonii*; Barbier. Flowers canary-yellow, dbl.; fragrant; height 3-5 ft.; good seasonal bloom.

Bullata C (OGR), *mp*, (*R. centifolia bullata*; Rose à Feuilles de Laitue); Orig. before 1815. Flowers medium pink, very dbl., with overlapping petals, globular, 3 in. blooms, solitary or in clusters on long, slender pediculus; very fragrant; foliage very large and crinkled like lettuce; summer bloom; (28).

Bulls Red HT, *mr*, 1977, (MACrero); *Sympathie × Irish Rover*; McGredy, S., IV; McGredy Roses International. Bud ovoid; flowers medium red, dbl. (28 petals), large (4 in.); foliage dark; tall, upright growth.

Bunker Hill HT, *dp*, 1949, *Rome Glory × Better Times*; Fisher, G.; Arnold-Fisher Co. Bud pointed; flowers rose-red, dbl. (25-40 petals), high-centered becoming cupped, large; very fragrant; foliage leathery, dark; very vigorous, bushy growth.

Burbank T (OGR), *mp*, 1900, *Hermosa × Bon Silene*; Burbank; Burpee. Flowers bright rose-pink shading lighter, dbl.; fragrant.

Burgemeester Berger HT, *lp*, 1934, *Dame Edith Helen sport*; Leenders Bros. Flowers soft pink, marked white; vigorous growth.

Burgemeester Sandberg HT, *op*, 1920, *Pharisaer × Lady Alice Stanley*; Van Rossem. Flowers silvery pink, shaded coral-rose-pink, dbl.; fragrant.

Burgemeester van Oppen HT, *my*, 1939, *Golden Ophelia × Pardinas Bonet*; Leenders, M. Flowers golden yellow; fragrant.

Burgund® HT, *dr*, 1977, (KORgund); *Henkell Royal × Seedling*; Kordes, W. Bud long, pointed; flowers dark red, dbl. (30 petals), high-centered, large (4 in.); very fragrant; vigorous, bushy growth.

Burgundian Rose C (OGR), *pb*, 1664, (Burgundy Rose; Parvifolia; Pompon de Bourgogne; *R. centifolia parvifolia* (Ehrhart) Rehder; *R. parvifolia* Ehrhart, not Pallas; *R. burgundensis* Weston; *R. burgundica* Ehrhart; *R. remensis* De Candolle; *R. ehrrhartiana* Trattinnick; *R. pomponia* Thory ex Redouté, not Roessig; *R. gallica remensis* Wallroth; Pompon de Burgogne). Flowers deep pink suffused purple, center paler, dbl., rosette form, 1 in. diam.; foliage dark gray-green; few prickles; 3-5 ft. growth.

Burgundy HT, *mr*, 1939, *Vaterland × Seedling*; H&S. Flowers wine-red, fully dbl., broad, evenly arranged petals; very vigorous growth.

Burma Star F, *ab*, 1974, *Arthur Bell × Manx Queen*; Cocker. Flowers light apricot yellow, dbl. (22 petals), large (3½ in.); fragrant; foliage large, glossy.

Burnaby HT, *w*, 1954, (Golden Heart; Gold Heart); *Phyllis Gold × Pres. Herbert Hoover*; Eddie; Peterson & Dering. Flowers creamy white, dbl. (56 petals), high-centered, large (4-6 in.); slightly fragrant; foliage dark, glossy; vigorous, bushy growth. GM, NRS, 1954 & Portland, 1957.

Burning Love Gr, *mr*, 1956, (Amour Ardent; Brennende Liebe); *Fanal × Crimson Glory*; Tantau, Math. Flowers scarlet, dbl. (22 petals), large (4 in.) blooms in trusses of 3-5; fragrant; foliage dark, glossy; vigorous, bushy growth. GM, Baden-Baden, 1954.

Burnt Orange F, *ob*, 1973, *Woburn Abbey sport*; Hamilton. Flowers deep orange.

Burr's Multiflora Sp (OGR), *Clone of R. multiflora*. For use as an understock.

Burwah Cl HT, *dp*, 1953, *Editor McFarland × Black Boy (Cl HT)*; Ulrick. Flowers deep rose-pink, dbl., cupped, large; very vigorous climbing growth.

Bush Baby Min, *pb*, 1983, (PEAnob); Pearce, C.A.; Limes Rose Nursery. Flowers pink blend, dbl. (35 petals), small; slight fragrance; foliage small, medium green, matt; bushy growth.

Bushfire R, *mr*, 1917, Clark, A. Flowers bright crimson, yellow zone around center, dbl., small, very large truss.

Bushu HT, *ob*, 1984, *Dolce Vita × Roklea*; Yasuda, Yuji. Bud ovoid; flowers orange-red, reverse lighter, dbl. (35 petals), high-centered, large; no fragrance; foliage medium, dark, semi-glossy; prickles slanted downward; tall, vigorous, upright growth.

Busy Lizzie F, *mp*, 1971, (HARbusy); *(Pink Parfait × Masquerade) × Dearest*; Harkness. Flowers pink, semi-dbl. (12 petals), medium (2 in.); slightly fragrant; foliage glossy, dark.

Busy Lizzie F, *mp*, 1970, (HARbusy); *(Pink Parfait × Masquerade) × Dearest*; Harkness. Flowers pink, semi-dbl. (12 petals), medium (2 in.); slightly fragrant; foliage glossy, dark; free growth.

Busybody HT, *dy*, 1929, *Georges Schwartz × Lena*; Clark, A.; Hazlewood Bros. Flowers rich chrome-yellow, small.

Buta HT, *w*, Cant, B.R. Flowers pure white, well formed; very fragrant.

Butterball S, *ly*, 1950, *R. spinosissima altaica hybrid*; Skinner. Flowers creamy yellow, single; foliage small, *R. spinosissima* type; fruit large, round, reddish; prickly, arching branches; height 6 ft.; non-recurrent bloom.

Buttercup HT, *my*, 1930, Dobbie. Flowers buttercup-yellow, semi-dbl., well-formed; fragrant; vigorous growth.

Buttercup HT, *ab*, 1929, Towill. Flowers apricot-yellow, dbl., cupped.

Butterflies of Gold HT, *my*, 1939, *Mrs. Arthur Curtis James seedling*; Brownell. Flowers yellow. Discontinued.

Butterfly Glow HT, *or*, 1969, *Centre Court × Carla*; Barter. Flowers vermilion, dbl. (20 petals), full, large (3½ in.); slightly fragrant; foliage dark; free growth.

Butterfly Wings F, *pb*, 1976, *Dainty Maid × Peace*; Gobbee; Harkness. Flowers ivory, petals edged pink, semi-dbl. (12 petals), flat, large (4-4½ in.) blooms in clusters; fragrant; foliage large.

Buttermere R, *yb*, 1932, Chaplin Bros. Flowers creamy yellow flushed pink, large truss; foliage glossy; vigorous, erect growth.

Butterscotch HT, *yb*, 1942, *Souv. de Claudius Pernet × R.M.S. Queen Mary*; Hill, J.H., Co.; Wayside Gardens Co.; H&S, 1946. Bud long, pointed; flowers lemon-chrome, reverse pale orange-yellow, dbl. (28 petals), large (4½

-5½ in.); slightly fragrant; foliage leathery, glossy, dark; upright, compact growth.

Buttons Min, *w*, 1980, (LEMbut); *Seedling × Seedling*; Lemrow, Dr. Maynard. Bud globular; flowers white, dbl. (35 petals), borne singly; no fragrance; foliage very tiny, smooth; no prickles; compact growth.

Buttons 'n' Bows Min, *dp*, 1981, (Felicity II; Teeny-Weeny); *Mini-Poul × Harriet Poulsen*; Poulsen, D.T.; Windy Hill Nursery, 1982. Bud small; flowers deep pink, dbl. (28 petals), high-centered and cupped, reflexing at maturity, borne singly or in sprays; fruity fragrance; straight prickles; compact, upright growth.

Buzby F, *or*, 1976, *Irish Mist × Topsi*; Plumpton. Flowers light vermilion, semi-dbl. (11 petals), conical, small (1½ in.); slightly fragrant; dwarf, compact, upright growth.

B. W. Price HT, *mp*, 1943, *Night × Mme. Butterfly*; McGredy; J&P. Bud long, pointed; flowers cerise-pink, single (6-8 petals), open, large; foliage soft; vigorous, upright, bushy growth.

Byala Valentina Gr, *w*, 1974, *Queen Elizabeth × Seedling*; Staikov, Prof. Dr. V.; Kalaydjiev and Chorbadjiiski. Flowers creamy white, dbl. (25 petals), large; delicate tea fragrance; foliage dark, glossy; vigorous, upright growth.

By Appointment F, *ab*, 1989, (HARvolute); *Anne Harkness × Letchworth Garden City*; Harkness, R., 1990. Bud ovoid; flowers pale buff apricot, aging paler, dbl. (22 petals), urn-shaped becoming cupped, medium, borne in sprays of 3-15; slight fragrance; foliage medium, dark green, semi-glossy; prickles rather narrow, medium, dark reddish-green; upright, medium growth.

By Design Min, *ob*, 1992, (LAVsign; LAVrange); *(Breezy × Julie Ann) × (June Laver × Painted Doll)*; Laver, Keith G.; Springwood Roses. Flowers orange, full (26-40 petals), exhibition, medium (4-7 cms) blooms borne in small clusters; slight fragrance; foliage medium, medium green, semi-glossy; some prickles; medium (40-50 cms), bushy growth.

By Joe Min, *w*, 1990, *Pink Petticoat × Pink Petticoat*; Gatty, Joe, 1990; Keith Keppel, 1990. Bud pointed; flowers ivory white, dbl. (25 petals), high-centered, medium blooms borne singly; no fragrance; foliage medium, dark green, matt; upright, bushy, tall growth.

Cabaret F, *or*, 1963, *Dacapo × Floribunda seedling*; de Ruiter; Blaby Rose Gardens. Flowers vermilion-salmon, dbl. (35-40 petals), camellia shaped, medium (2½ in.), borne in clusters; Vigorous, upright growth. RULED EXTINCT 6/83 ARM.

Cabaret Min, *dr*, 1983, (JACaret); *(Fire Princess × Mary DeVor) × (Seedling × Caliente)*; Warriner, W.; J&P. Bud small; flowers dark red, dbl. (35 petals), small; fragrant; foliage small, medium green, semi-glossy; upright, bushy growth; cut flower.

Cabbage Rose C (OGR), *mp*, (*R. centifolia* Linnaeus; *R. gallica centifolia* Regel; Provence Rose) Cult. 1596. Flowers medium pink, very dbl. with overlapping petals, 3 in. blooms borne singly or in clusters, nodding on long, slender pediculus; fragrant; summer blooming. This entry refers to more than one clone.

Cacaphony HT, *op*, 1974, *Baccará × Golden Showers*; Golik; Dynarose. Flowers pink tinged orange, dbl. (28 petals), large (4 in.); fragrant (fruity); foliage glossy, dark.

Cactus Blanc® Pol, *w*, 1967, (DELtrob); *(Orléans Rose × Orléans Rose) × ((Francais × Lafayette) × (Orleans Rose × Goldilocks))*; Delbard-Chabert. Bud globular; flowers creamy white, dbl., cupped, small, borne in clusters; foliage light green, glossy; moderate, bushy growth.

Caddy HT, *my*, 1943, *Soeur Thérèse × Prof. Deaux*; Meilland, F. Bud large, well formed, yellow; vigorous growth.

Cadenza LCl, *dr*, 1967, *New Dawn × Embers, Climbing*; Armstrong, D.L.; Armstrong Nursery. Bud ovoid; flowers dark red, dbl., medium (2½-3 in.) blooms in clusters; slightly fragrant; foliage glossy, dark, leathery; compact, moderate growth; recurrent bloom.

Cadette F, *ab*, 1971, *Poupee × Fillette*; Lens. Bud pointed; flowers pastel pink-apricot, dbl. (35 petals), cupped, medium (2 in.); fragrant (fruity); foliage glossy, dark; vigorous, upright growth; for greenhouse use.

Caesar HT, *mr*, 1981, (VARbole, Carambole); *Ilona × Seedling*; van Veen, Jan; Carlton Rose Nursery. Bud ovoid; flowers cardinal red, dbl. (33 petals), high-centered, globular blooms borne 2-3 per cluster; slight tea fragrance; foliage leathery, medium green, semi-glossy; red prickles; upright, branched growth.

Café F, *r*, 1956, *(Golden Glow × R. kordesii) × Lavender Pinocchio*; Kordes; McGredy. Flowers coffee-with-cream color, very dbl., flat blooms in clusters; fragrant; foliage olive-green; vigorous growth.

Café Olé Min, *r*, 1990, (MORolé); *Winter Magic sport*; Moore, Ralph S.; Sequoia Nursery. Bud pointed; flowers russet, very dbl. (40-50+ petals), cupped, medium to large blooms, borne singly or in sprays of 3-5; moderate, spicy fragrance; foliage medium to large, medium green, dull to semi-glossy;

prickles slender, hooked downward, brown; fruit round, orangish; upright, bushy, tall, vigorous growth.

C. A. Fletcher HT, *dp*, 1947, *May Wettern × Mrs. Henry Bowles*; Fletcher; Tucker. Flowers clear rose-crimson, dbl. (35-40 petals), well formed, large (5-6 in.); slightly fragrant; vigorous growth.

Cafougnette HT, *op*, 1956, *Happiness × Peace*; Dorieux; Pin. Flowers soft orange-salmon, reverse carmine-red, open, well shaped, large, strong stems; foliage dark.

Caid Pol, *ob*, 1971, (DELsirp); *Orangeade × Seedling*; Delforge. Bud ovoid; flowers orange, dbl., medium; slightly fragrant; foliage leathery; vigorous, bushy; repeat bloom.

Cairngorm F, *ob*, 1973, *Anne Cocker × Arthur Bell*; Cocker. Flowers tangerine and gold, dbl. (25 petals), medium (2½ in.); slightly fragrant; foliage glossy, dark; upright.

Caitlin Min, *w*, 1986, (TRAcait); *Fairy Moss × Fairy Moss*; Travis, Louis, 1987. Flowers flesh pink fading white, dbl. (12-15 petals), urn-shaped, small, borne in sprays of 4-5; slight, spicy fragrance; foliage small, medium green, semi-glossy; straight, tan-brown prickles; no fruit; bushy, low growth.

Cal Poly Min, *my*, 1991, (MORpoly); *(Little Darling × Yellow Magic) × Gold Badge*; Moore, Ralph S.; Sequoia Nursery, 1992. Flowers medium yellow, long lasting color, non-fading, moderately full (15-25 petals), medium (4-7 cms), blooms borne in small clusters; slight fragrance; foliage medium, medium green, semi-glossy; few prickles; medium (24 cms), upright, bushy growth. AOE, 1992.

Calay Min, *my*, 1982, (TRObelle); *Rumba × New Penny*; Robinson, Thomas; T. Robinson, Ltd. Flowers lemon yellow, semi-dbl., small; fragrant; foliage small, dark, glossy; upright, bushy growth.

Caledonia HT, *w*, 1928, *None listed*; Dobbie. Bud long, pointed; Flowers white, dbl. (25 petals), high centered, large; slightly fragrant; Foliage leathery, dark; Vigorous growth. RULED EXTINCT 7/83 ARM.

Caledonia, Climbing Cl HT, *w*, 1936, Bel.

Caledonian HT, *ly*, 1983, *Kordes' Perfecta × Irish Gold*; Mayle, W.J. Flowers creamy yellow, dbl. (40+ petals), large; slight fragrance; foliage medium, medium green, semi-glossy; bushy growth.

Calgold Min, *dy*, 1977, *Golden Glow (Brownell) × Peachy White*; Moore, R.S.; Sequoia Nursery. Bud pointed; flowers deep clear yellow, dbl. (23 petals), small (1½ in.); slightly fragrant; foliage small to medium, glossy; bushy growth.

Calico HT, *pb*, 1976, *Seedling × Granada*; Weeks; Weeks Roses. Flowers pink, yellow reverse, dbl. (38 ruffled petals), globular, large (3½-4 in.); slightly fragrant (tea); foliage dark; vigorous, upright to spreading growth.

Calico Doll Min, *ob*, 1979, (SAVadoll); *Rise 'n' Shine × Glenfiddich*; Saville; Nor'East Min. Roses. Bud ovoid, pointed; flowers orange, striped yellow, semi-dbl. (18 petals), cupped to flat, small (1-1½ in.); foliage dark; compact growth.

Calico Star F, *yb*, 1977, *Circus × Lavender Girl*; Fong; United Rose Growers. Bud ovoid; flowers golden yellow, edged red, dbl. (25-30 petals), high-centered, large (4 in.); slightly fragrant; upright growth.

Caliente F, *dr*, 1974, *Seedling × Seedling*; Warriner; J&P. Bud ovoid-pointed; flowers deep pure red, dbl., high-centered, medium; slightly fragrant; foliage large, leathery; very vigorous, bushy growth.

California HT, *ob*, 1940, *Miss Rowena Thom × Lady Forteviot*; Howard, F.H.; H&S. Bud long, pointed; flowers ruddy orange, reverse overlaid pink, dbl. (30 petals), large (5-6 in.); fragrant (fruity); foliage leathery, glossy; vigorous, bushy, spreading growth. AARS, 1941.

California HT, *ob*, 1916, H&S. Flowers deep orange, base golden yellow.

California Beauty HT, *my*, 1926, Pacific Rose Co. Flowers yellow.

California Beauty HT, *dp*, 1935, *Dame Edith Helen × Hollywood*; Proietti. Bud long, pointed to ovoid; flowers deep bright pink, dbl., very large; foliage leathery, dark; vigorous growth.

California Centennial HT, *dr*, 1949, *Tango × Mauna Loa*; Howard, F.H.; H&S. Bud long, pointed; flowers dark red, dbl. (28 petals), high-centered, large (3½-4 in.); very fragrant; foliage leathery, bronze; vigorous, upright growth.

California, Climbing Cl HT, *ob*, 1953, Howard, A.P.; H&S.

California Dreaming Min, *mr*, 1987, (RENove); *Julie Ann × Black Jack*; Rennie, Bruce; Rennie Roses. Flowers medium red, reverse lighter, dbl. (28 petals), exhibition, medium blooms borne usually singly; fruity fragrance; foliage medium, dark, semi-glossy; tiny, maroon prickles; fruit globular, yellow-orange; medium, bushy growth.

California Girl Min, *ab*, 1986, (RENirl); *Julie Ann × Red Love*; Rennie, Bruce; Rennie Roses, 1987. Flowers apricot, reverse yellow blend, dbl. (28 petals), high-centered, exhibition, medium blooms borne singly; fruity

fragrance; foliage medium to large, medium green, semi-glossy; small prickles; fruit orange-red; bushy, spreading growth.

California Gold Pol, *ab*, 1934, *Gloria Mundi sport*; Smith, J. Flowers orange-yellow, full, globular, clusters on long stems; slightly fragrant; foliage leathery, light; very vigorous, bushy growth.

California Sun Min, *ab*, 1988, (RENsun); *Shocking Blue × Rise 'n' Shine*; Rennie, Bruce F.; Rennie Roses, 1989. Flowers golden apricot, opening to golden center, reverse lighter, aging purplish-pink edging, dbl. (30-35 petals), high-centered, large, borne singly; patio; no fragrance; foliage large, medium green, matt; prickles straight, medium, pinking; fruit rounded, medium, yellow-orange; upright, tall growth.

California Surf Min, *w*, 1987, (RENurf); *Seedling × Seedling*; Rennie, Bruce F.; Rennie Roses, 1988. Flowers creamy white with peachy-pink edging, dbl. (20 petals), urn-shaped, small, borne usually singly; slight fragrance; foliage small, medium green, semi-glossy; prickles straight, small, reddish-brown; fruit round, small, yellow-orange; upright growth.

California's Favorite HT, *op*, 1949, *Stockton Beauty sport*; Raffel; Port Stockton Nursery. Bud long, pointed; flowers light salmon-pink, base yellow, large; fragrant; foliage soft; vigorous, bushy growth.

Caline HT, *op*, 1958, Ducher, Ch.; EFR. Flowers soft geranium-red, dbl. (33 petals), medium; foliage clear green; vigorous, upright growth.

Callisto HMsk (S), *my*, 1920, *William Allen Richardson × Self*; Pemberton. Flowers golden yellow, rosette form, borne in clusters; height 3-4 ft.; recurrent bloom.

Calocarpa HRg (S), *mp*, (*R. × calocarpa* (André) Willmott; *R. rugosa calocarpa* André); *R. rugosa × Form of R. chinensis*; Orig. prior to 1891. Flowers rose-colored, single; fruit handsome, in abundance.

Calumet Min, *yb*, 1985, (SOCapan); *Golden Angel × Golden Angel*; Eagle, Barry & Dawn; Southern Cross Nursery. Flowers creamy yellow, petals edged with pink, dbl. (30 petals), HT form, medium blooms borne 1-3 per cluster; fragrant; foliage medium green, semi-glossy; very few, small, red prickles; upright, bushy growth.

Calypso D (OGR), *lp*, Vibert, prior to 1848. Flowers rosy blush with paler edges, full, cupped, large.

Calypso F, *or*, 1957, *Geranium Red × Fashion*; Boerner; Stuart. Bud globular; flowers orange-red, reverse red, semi-dbl. (18 petals), loosely cupped, large (3-3½ in.) blooms in large pyramidal trusses; very fragrant (damask); foliage dark, leathery; vigorous, bushy growth.

Camaieux G (OGR), *m*, 1830. Flowers white and pale rosy purple, striped, dbl., well-shaped; very fragrant; vigorous, rather dwarf growth.

Camara® HT, *or*, 1978, (DELcama); *((Chic Parisien × Tropicana) × (Gloire de Rome × Impeccable)) × (Tropicana × Samourai)*; Delbard. Flowers orange-vermilion, dbl. (33 petals), recurred, large (4-5 in.): slightly fragrant.

Camay HT, *dp*, 1959, *Ena Harkness × C.A. Fletcher*; Fletcher; Tucker. Flowers deep rose-pink to carmine, dbl. (40 petals), large (5 in.); fragrant; foliage light green; vigorous growth.

Cameleon F, *yb*, 1961, *Masquerade × Seedling*; Verschuren, A.; van Engelen. Flowers yellow, pink and orange, dbl. (22-27 petals), large clusters; very fragrant; foliage dark, glossy; upright, compact, bushy, symmetrical growth.

Camélia HT, *or*, 1948, *Vainqueur × (Charles P. Kilham × Katharine Pechtold)*; Heizmann & Co. Bud pointed; flowers fiery vermilion-red, semi-dbl., cupped, medium; fragrant; foliage glossy, dark; vigorous, bushy growth. GM Geneva, 1948.

Camelia F, *dp*, 1953, *Pinocchio × Seedling*; Klyn. Flowers cerise-pink, medium, clusters on strong stems; moderate growth.

Cameliarose F, *lp*, 1960, *Mme. Joseph Perraud × Incendie*; Croix, P.; Minier. Flowers soft pink, camellia form; upright growth; very free bloom, especially in autumn.

Camellia Rose Bslt (OGR), Prevost, prior to 1830.

Camelot Gr, *op*, 1964, *Circus × Queen Elizabeth*; Swim & Weeks; C-P. Bud ovoid; flowers shrimp-pink, dbl. (48 petals), cupped, large (3½-4 in.) blooms in clusters; fragrant (spicy); foliage leathery, glossy, dark; vigorous, tall growth. AARS, 1965.

Cameo Pol, *op*, 1932, *Orléans Rose sport*; deRuiter; J&P. Flowers salmon-pink, turning soft orange-pink.

Cameo Queen Min, *pb*, 1986, *Heartland × Seedling*; Bridges, Dennis A. Flowers light pink, reverse blends of pink, dbl. (34 petals), high-centered, mini-flora, medium blooms are borne usually singly; slight fragrance; foliage large, medium green, semi-glossy; medium, long, light prickles; medium, bushy growth.

Cameo Superior Pol, *mp*, *Cameo sport*; deRuiter. Flowers have more lasting color.

Camilla HT, *dp*, 1954, *Fiamma × Talisman*; Aicardi, D.; Olivieri. Bud ovoid; flowers strawberry-red, dbl. (30-36 petals), loosely formed, large; fragrant; very vigorous growth.

Camillo Schneider HT, *mr*, 1922, *Lieut Chaure × Comte G. de Rochemur*; Kordes. Flowers clear blood-red, dbl.; slightly fragrant.

Camoëns HT, *mp*, 1881, *Antoine Verdier × Seedling*; Schwartz, J. Flowers bright rose, center shaded yellow; fragrant; moderately vigorous growth.

Campanile® LCl, *dp*, 1967, (DELtrut; Campanela); *(Queen Elizabeth × Provence) × (Sultane seedling × Mme. Joseph Perraud)*; Delbard-Chabert. Bud globular; flowers deep magenta-pink, dbl., large; fragrant; foliage glossy, leathery, bronze; vigorous, climbing growth; repeats.

Campfire Cl Pol, *or*, 1956, *Cameo sport*; Fryer's Nursery. Flowers orange-scarlet, rosette shape, small, borne in clusters; vigorous (6-8 ft.)

Campfire Min, *or*, 1990, (WILcamp); *Marina × Starina*; Williams, J. Benjamin; White Rose Nurseries, Ltd., 1990. Bud pointed; flowers fiery orange neon red, reverse same, ages deeper, dbl. (26 petals), high-centered, exhibition, medium, borne singly; moderate, damask fragrance; foliage medium, dark green, semi-glossy; upright, bushy growth.

Campfire Girl HT, *op*, 1946, *Joanna Hill × Gruss an Aachen*; Duehrsen; California Roses. Bud long, pointed; flowers deep salmon, dbl., high-centered, large; fragrant; foliage dark, leathery; vigorous, upright, bushy growth.

Camphill Glory HT, *pb*, 1980, (HARkreme); *Elizabeth Harkness × Kordes' Perfecta*; Harkness, R., 1982. Flowers creamy pink, dbl. (54 petals), high-centered, exhibition, large blooms borne singly; slightly fragrant; foliage medium green, matt; many prickles; vigorous, branching growth.

Campina HT, *lp*, 1937, *Comtesse Vandal × White Briarcliff*; Lens. Bud long; flowers flesh-pink; very vigorous.

Camping Pol, *pb*, 1967, *Paul Crampel sport*; Grabezewski. Flowers deep lavender-pink with white eye, single, globular, small, borne in large clusters; foliage small, olive-green; low, bushy growth.

Canadian Centennial F, *or*, 1965, *Pinocchio seedling × Spartan*; Boerner; J&P. Bud ovoid; flowers coral-red, dbl., cupped, medium; fragrant; foliage glossy; vigorous, upright, compact.

Canadian Jubilee HT, *op*, 1927, *Priscilla × Commonwealth*; Dunlop. Flowers indian red to pink, base orange, dbl.; slightly fragrant.

Canadian Northlight HT, *dp*, 1984, *(Fragrant Cloud × Diamond Jubilee) × Super Sun*; Mander, George. Flowers deep pink, dbl. (28 petals), high-centered, HT form, large blooms in clusters of 6-9; light fragrance; foliage medium green, leathery; dark red prickles; spreading growth.

Canadian White Star® HT, *w*, 1980, (C.W.S.®; Dr. Wolfgang Pöschl); *Blanche Mallerin × Pascali*; Mander, George, 1980; Hortico, 1985. Flowers white, dbl. (43 petals), high-centered, opening to multi-pointed star, borne singly; slight fragrance; foliage dark, leathery, glossy; slightly hooked prickles; vigorous, upright growth.

Canarias HT, *mr*, 1964, Dot, P.; Minier. Flowers bright red, large.

Canarienvogel Pol, 1903, (Sunset Glow); *Étoile de Mai × Souv. de Catherine Guillot*; Welter. Flowers saffron-yellow and amber-yellow stained pink and purple, semi-dbl., strong stems; vigorous growth.

Canary T (OGR), *my*, 1852, Guillot Père. Bud small, well formed; flowers canary-yellow; growth rather weak.

Canary HT, *ly*, 1929, Dickson, A. Bud golden yellow, edges flushed; flowers light yellow, deepening, spiral, high-centered; fragrant; branching growth.

Canary Min, *my*, Flowers primuline-yellow, semi-dbl., star shaped.

Canary Bird S, *dy*, 1907, (*R. xanthina* 'Canary Bird'); *Probably R. hugonis × R. xanthina*. Flowers yellow, yellow stamens, paler than *R. xanthina spontanea*, with which it is often confused, single (5 petals); fruit blackish purple.

Canary Charm HT, *my*, 1969, *Wiener Charme* sport; Knight, G. Flowers yellow, dbl., high-centered, very large; foliage dark, leathery; free growth.

Canasta HT, *mr*, 1966, *Karl Herbst × Miss Universe*; Gaujard. Bud long, pointed; flowers bright red, dbl., high-centered, large; fragrant; very vigorous, upright growth.

Canberra Pol, *op*, 1935, *Gloria Mundi* sport; Knight, G. Flowers salmon-coral-pink.

Canberra HT, *op*, 1927, *Donald MacDonald × The Queen Alexandra Rose*; Burbage Nursery. Flowers carmine, reverse buff at base, shading to salmon-pink.

Canberra HT, *mp*, 1928, Harrison. Flowers pink, very full.

Cancan F, *ob*, 1969, (Diorette); Jelly; E.G. Hill Co. Bud short, pointed; flowers mandarin-red, dbl., small; fragrant (spicy); foliage leathery; greenhouse variety.

Candella® HT, *rb*, 1990, (MACspeego); *Howard Morrison × Esmeralda*; McGredy, Sam; Sam McGredy Roses International. Flowers red blend, moderately full (15-25 petals), large blooms; slight fragrance; foliage large, dark green, glossy; bushy growth.

Candeur® F, *w*, 1978, (DELcande); *((Robin Hood × Virgo) × (Frau Karl Druschki × (Queen Elizabeth × Provence)) × (Virgo × Peace)*; Delbard. Flowers white, dbl. (30 petals), high-centered, 3¹/₂ in.; no fragrance; low, upright. GM, Baden-Baden, 1978.

Candeur Lyonnaise HP (OGR), *w*, 1914, *Frau Karl Druschki seedling*; Croibier. Bud long, pointed; flowers white, sometimes tinted pale yellow, dbl., large; vigorous.

Candeur Lyonnaise HP (OGR), *ly*, 1914, *Frau Karl Druschki seedling*; Croibier. Bud long, pointed; flowers white, sometimes tinged pale yellow, dbl., very large; very vigorous growth.

Candice Min, *pb*, 1987, (ZIPcan); *Libby × Queen Elizabeth*; Zipper, Herbert; Magic Moment Miniatures. Flowers pink blend, dbl. (over 40 petals), medium; slight fragrance; foliage medium, medium green, semi-glossy; upright growth.

Candida HT, *yb*, 1964, *Tawny Gold × Golden Scepter*; Leenders, J. Flowers creamy yellow, center salmon, well formed.

Candleflame Min, *yb*, 1956, *(Soeur Thérèse × Julien Potin) × (Eblouissant × Zee)*; Moore, R.S.; Sequoia Nursery. Bud slender; flowers red, yellow and orange, single (5 petals); foliage leathery; vigorous (10 in.), bushy growth.

Candleglow HT, *yb*, 1951, *Golden Rapture × (Seedling × Joanna Hill)*; Whisler; Germain's. Bud long, pointed; flowers yellow washed shrimp-pink, dbl. (38 petals), cupped, large (5-6 in.); slightly fragrant; foliage glossy, dark; vigorous, upright growth.

Candlelight HT, 1932, *Souv. de Claudius Pernet × Mme. Butterfly*; Horvath; Bosley Nursery. Flowers yellow, deeper in hot weather, dbl., high centered, large; fragrant; Foliage glossy; Bushy growth. RULED EXTINCT 9/81 ARM.

Candlelight™ HT, *dy*, 1982, (AROwedye); *Shirley Laugharn × (Bewitched × King's Ransom)*; Christensen, J.E. & Swim, H.C.; Armstrong Nursery. Bud ovoid, pointed; flowers deep yellow, dbl. (30 petals), spiraled, borne mostly singly; mild fragrance; foliage large, semi-glossy; large-based prickles; medium-tall, upright, branching growth.

Candy HT, *ob*, 1950, *Pink Princess* × *Shades of Autumn*; Brownell. Bud long, pointed; flowers apricot-orange, dbl., high-centered, medium; fragrant; vigorous, upright, compact, bushy growth.

Candy Apple Gr, *mr*, 1966, *Jack O'Lantern* × *(Seedling* × *El Capitan)*; Weeks, O.L.; Weeks Roses. Bud ovoid; flowers bright cherry, dbl. (45 petals), semi-cupped, large (5 in.); slightly fragrant (tea); foliage matt, olive-green; upright.

Candy Cane Cl Min, *pb*, 1958, *Seedling* × *Zee*; Moore, R.S.; Sequoia Nursery. Flowers deep pink, striped white, semi-dbl. (13 petals), medium (1½ in.) blooms in loose clusters; vigorous, upright (to 4 ft.) growth.

Candy Favorite HT, *pb*, 1971, *Pink Favorite sport*; Heath, W.L. Flowers carmine, striped pale rose, dbl. (25 petals), full, large (4½-5 in.); slightly fragrant; foliage very glossy; vigorous growth.

Candy Floss F, *lp*, 1959, *Lilibet* × *Seedling*; Fryer's Nursery. Flowers bright pink, dbl. (40 petals), rosette shape, large (3 in.) borne in large clusters; slightly fragrant; very vigorous growth.

Candy Pink Min, *lp*, 1969, *(R. wichuraiana* × *Floradora)* × *(Oakington Ruby* × *Floradora)*; Moore, R.S.; Sequoia Nursery. Bud ovoid; flowers light pink, dbl., small; foliage small, leathery; vigorous, dwarf, bushy growth.

Candy Rose® S, *rb*, 1982, (MEIranovi); *(R. sempervirens* × *Mlle. Marthe Carron)* × *((Lilli Marleen* × *Evelyn Fison)* × *(Orange Sweetheart* × *Fruhlingsmorgen))*; Meilland, M.L., 1980; Meilland Et Cie, 1983. Flowers deep pink, reverse medium red, dbl. (20 petals), medium; no fragrance; foliage small, medium green, semi-glossy; spreading growth.

Candy Stripe HT, *pb*, 1963, *Pink Peace sport*; McCummings; C-P. Flowers dusty pink streaked (striped) lighter.

Candy Sunblaze™ Min, *dp*, 1991, (MEIdanclar; Romantique Meillandina); *Lady Sunblaze sport*; Selection Meilland, 1988; C-P, 1992. Flowers deep pink, very full, medium blooms; slight fragrance; foliage medium, dark green, glossy; tall, upright growth.

Candystick HT, *pb*, 1978, (Candy Stick; Red 'n' White Glory); *Better Times sport*; Williams, J.B.; Lakeland Nursery Sales. Flowers deep pink striped white.

Canigó w, 1927, *Antoine Rivoire* × *Mme. Ravary*; Dot, P. Flowers white, dbl.; slightly fragrant.

Cannes Festival HT, *yb*, 1951, *Peace* × *Prinses Beatrix*; Meilland, F.; URS. Flowers indian yellow veined amber, dbl. (35 petals),

pointed, large (4 in.); fragrant; foliage dark; vigorous, upright, branching growth.

Cantab HNut (S), *dp*, 1927, *R. nutkana* × *Red-Letter Day*; Hurst. Bud long, pointed; flowers deep pink, base white, stamens yellow, single, saucer-shaped, large (3½ in.); foliage dark, 7-9 leaflets; height 6-8 ft.; non-recurrent bloom.

Cantabile S, *lp*, 1962, *Harmonie* × *(Josef Rothmund* × *R. laxa)*; Buck; Iowa State University. Bud ovoid; flowers light camellia-rose shaded darker, dbl. (25 petals), medium; fragrant; foliage leathery, bronze; vigorous, upright (5 ft.) growth; repeat bloom.

Cantabrigiensis S, *ly*, (R. × *pteragonis cantabrigiensis* (Weaver) Rowley; *R.* × *cantabrigiensis* Weaver; The Cambridge Rose); *R. hugonis* × *R. sericea hookeri*; Cult. before 1945. Flowers pale yellow, single, 2¼ in. diam.

Cantate F, *ob*, 1959, *Red Favorite sport*; van de Water; Spek. Flowers orange.

Canterbury S, *mp*, 1969, *(Monique* × *Constance Spry)* × *Seedling*; Austin, D. Flowers rose-pink, semi-dbl. (12 petals), medium; very fragrant; repeat bloom.

Canterbury Pride Min, *r*, 1992, (REYcantpri); *Hot Chocolate* × *Miniature seedling*; Reynolds, Ted; Reynolds Roses. Flowers russet, very full (41+ petals), small (0-4 cms) blooms; slight fragrance; foliage small, medium green, semi-glossy; low (28 cms), upright growth.

Canzonetta F, *or*, 1953, *Lawrence Johnston* × *Fashion*; San Remo Exp. Sta; Sgaravatti. Bud ovoid, cardinal-red; flowers orange-red, reverse yellow suffused red, semi-dbl. (10-12 petals), open, large, borne in clusters of 25-40; fragrant; foliage dark, glossy, leathery; vigorous, bushy growth.

Cape Coral HT, *ab*, 1964, *Spartan* × *Golden Masterpiece*; Boerner; J&P. Bud ovoid; flowers orange-coral, dbl. (50-55 wavy petals), cupped, large (5 in.), long, strong stems; fragrant; foliage leathery, glossy, veined red; vigorous, bushy growth.

Cape Hatteras Min, *w*, 1988, *Rise 'n' Shine* × *Seedling*; Bridges, Dennis; Bridges Roses. Flowers white, dbl. (40 petals), high-centered, exhibition, medium, borne singly; slight, spicy fragrance; foliage medium, dark green, glossy; prickles long, pointed, medium pink-tan; upright, medium, vigorous growth.

Capeline LCl, *mp*, 1965, *Etendard* × *Diane d'Urfe*; Hémeray-Aubert. Flowers tyrian rose, semi-dbl., high-centered; foliage leathery; vigorous growth; recurrent bloom.

Caper F, *dr*, 1976, *Seedling* × *Mary DeVor*; Warriner; J&P. Bud long, pointed; flowers dark red, dbl. (25 petals), open, medium (2-2½ in.);

slightly fragrant; foliage dark; upright growth.

Capistrano HT, *mp*, 1949, Morris; Germain's. Bud ovoid; flowers bright pink, dbl. (36 petals), globular, large (6 in.); fragrant; foliage leathery; vigorous, upright.   AARS, 1950.

Capistrano, Climbing Cl HT, *mp*, 1952, Germain's.

Capitaine Basroger M (OGR), *rb*, 1890, Moreau-Robert. Flowers bright carmine-red, shaded purple, full, large; very vigorous, almost climbing growth.

Capitaine Georges Dessirier HT, *dr*, 1919, *Seedling × Château de Clos Vougeot*; Pernet-Ducher. Flowers dark velvety red, shaded crimson, dbl.; fragrant.

Capitaine John Ingram M (OGR), *m*, 1854, Laffay. Bud well mossed; flowers variously described as dark purple, velvety crimson and reddish purple, full; vigorous growth.

Capitaine Millet T (OGR), *mr*, 1901, *Gén. Schablikine × Mme. Etienne*; Ketten Bros. Flowers bright red, reverse purplish, base golden, full, large; fragrant.

Capitaine Sisolet HP (OGR), *mp*, Prior to 1848. Flowers rose, very dbl., cupped, large; good seedbearer; vigorous, branching growth.

Cappa Magna® F, *mr*, 1965, (DELsap); *Tenor seedling*; Delbard-Chabert; Cuthbert, 1967. Flowers medium red, yellow stamens, 8-10 wavy petals, cupped, large (4 in.) blooms in clusters of 20-30; foliage dark, glossy, large; upright growth.

Capri F, *op*, 1956, *Fashion × Floradora*; Fisher, G.; Arnold-Fisher Co. Bud conical; flowers bright coral, reverse lighter, dbl. (38 petals), high-centered to cupped, large (3-3½ in.) blooms in small clusters; slightly fragrant; foliage bright green, glossy, leathery; vigorous growth.

Caprice HT, *pb*, 1948, (Lady Eve Price); *Peace × Fantastique*; Meilland, F.; C-P. Bud ovoid; flowers deep pink, reverse cream, dbl. (24 petals), large; slightly fragrant; foliage dark, leathery; vigorous, upright, bushy growth.

Caprice HT, *or*, 1934, *Seedling × Gwyneth Jones*; Leenders, M. Bud long, pointed; flowers orient red and peach-red, dbl., large; slightly fragrant; foliage glossy, light; vigorous growth.

Caprice, Climbing Cl HT, 1951, Lens.

Capricorn F, *rb*, 1961, Verschuren; Blaby Rose Gardens. Flowers scarlet, reverse silver, semi-dbl. (16 petals), medium (2 in.), borne in large clusters; slightly fragrant; foliage dark, dull, leathery; very vigorous growth.

Capriole F, *mp*, 1956, *Red Favorite × Fanal*; Tantau, Math. Bud cherry-red; flowers vivid pink, stamens prominent, semi-dbl., medium, in large clusters (up to 40); foliage dark, semi-glossy; vigorous, dwarf, bushy growth.

Captain Bligh HT, *mp*, 1939, *Gustav Grünerwald × Betty Uprichard*; Fitzhardinge; Hazlewood Bros. Bud long, pointed; flowers silvery rose, very dbl., large; foliage leathery, dark; very vigorous growth.

Captain Blood HT, *dr*, 1938, *Gen. MacArthur × E.G. Hill*; Melville Bros.; R. Murrell. Bud ovoid; flowers scarlet and crimson, dbl., cupped; very fragrant; foliage leathery; vigorous, bushy growth.

Captain Christy HT, *lp*, 1873, *Victor Verdier × Safrano*; Lacharme. Flowers soft flesh-pink, center darker, full (40 petals), globular, large; slightly fragrant; wide, compact growth.

Captain Christy, Climbing Cl HT, *lp*, 1881, Ducher.

Captain Cook F, *op*, 1977, (MACal); *Irish Mist × Seedling*; McGredy; Mattock. Flowers orange-salmon, 10 petals, large (4 in.); fragrant; foliage glossy.

Captain F. Bald HT, *dr*, 1919, Dickson, A. Flowers scarlet-crimson, velvety black sheen, dbl.; slightly fragrant.

Capt. F. S. Harvey-Cant HT, *pb*, 1923, Cant, F. Bud long, pointed; flowers peach-pink, reverse deep pink, dbl., very large; fragrant; foliage dark, leathery; vigorous, bushy growth.   GM, NRS, 1922.

Captain Glisson HT, *dy*, 1935, *Joanna Hill × Sweet Adeline*; Hill, J.H., Co. Bud long, pointed; flowers dark yellow, edged lighter, dbl. (28-30 petals), large; very vigorous, compact growth; a florists' variety, not distributed for outdoor use.

Captain Harry Stebbings HT, *dp*, 1980, *Seedling sport*; Stebbings; Country Garden Nursery. Bud long, pointed; flowers deep pink, dbl. (43 petals), high-centered, large (5-6½ in.); very fragrant (fruity); foliage large, leathery; upright, bushy.

Captain Hayward HP (OGR), *dp*, 1893, *Triomphe de l'Exposition seedling*; Bennett. Flowers light crimson, edged lighter, dbl. (25 petals), high-centered, large; fragrant; fruit large, orange; vigorous growth; sparsely recurrent; (28).

Captain Hayward, Climbing Cl HP (OGR), *dp*, 1906, Paul.

Captain Kidd HSet (OGR), *mr*, 1934, *R. setigera seedling × Hoosier Beauty*; Horvath. Flowers blood-red, dbl., open, cupped, large, borne on long, strong stems; fragrant; foliage leathery, dark; very vigorous, climbing or tall pillar growth.

Captain Kilbee Stuart HT, *dr*, 1922, Dickson, A. Bud long, pointed; flowers scarlet-crimson, dbl., very large; very fragrant; moderate growth. GM, NRS, 1922.

Captain Kilby F, *mr*, 1955, deRuiter; Gandy. Flowers blood-red, semi-dbl., medium, large truss; fragrant; foliage glossy, parsley-green; very vigorous.

Capt. Robinson Sp (OGR), *dp*, (Wild rose discovered in the sand dunes of Porter County, Ind., in June, 1924 by C.H. Robinson). Flowers dark pink, semi-dbl. (13 petals); fragrant; foliage small, dark; few prickles; height 1 ft.; non-recurrent bloom.

Capt. Ronald Clerk HT, *or*, 1923, McGredy. Flowers vermilion-scarlet, semi-dbl.; slightly fragrant.

Capt. Ronald Clerk, Climbing Cl HT, *or*, 1935, Austin & McAslan.

Captain Samuel Holland S, *mr*, 1991, *(R. kordesii × (Red Dawn × Suzanne)) × (R. kordesii × (Red Dawn × Suzanne) × (Red Dawn × Suzanne))*; Ogilvie, Ian S.; Agriculture Canada, 1992. Flowers medium red, moderately full (15-25 petals), medium; slight fragrance; foliage medium, medium green, glossy; spreading, medium growth.

Captain Sassoon HT, *dr*, 1938, Gaujard. Flowers dark crimson; fragrant; vigorous growth.

Captain Thomas Cl HT, *w*, 1935, *Bloomfield Completeness × Attraction*; Thomas; Armstrong Nursery, 1938. Bud long, pointed; flowers lemon to cream, single blooms in clusters; fragrant; foliage glossy, light; climbing or pillar (10 ft.) growth; recurrent bloom.

Captain Williams G (OGR), *dr*, Flowers dark red, very dbl., medium.

Captain Woodward HP (OGR), *dp*, Flowers light red.

Captivation™ Min, *or*, 1991, (KINcap); *(Arthur Bell × Little Jackie) × Little Jackie*; King, Gene; AGM Miniature Roses, 1992. Flowers orange-red, full, medium blooms borne mostly singly; slight fragrance; foliage medium, light green, matt; some prickles; upright (60-70 cms), bushy growth.

Captivator HT, *mp*, 1942, *Better Times sport*; Hill, J.H., Co. Flowers pink; a florists' variety, not distributed for outdoor use.

Capucine Chambard HFt (OGR), Unissued seedling of R. foetida bicolor, used in hybridizing.

Cara Mia HT, *mr*, 1969, (Dearest One; Maja Mauser; Natacha; Danina); McDaniel, G.K.; Carlton Rose Nursery. Bud ovoid; flowers red, dbl., large; fragrant; foliage dark; vigorous, upright growth.

Carabella F, *yb*, 1960, *Gartendirektor Otto Linne × Seedling*; Riethmuller. Bud pointed, apricot; flowers cream edged pink, single, open, borne in clusters; fragrant; foliage glossy, light green; moderate, bushy growth.

Caramba® HT, *rb*, 1966, (TANca); Tantau, Math. Bud pointed; flowers bright red, reverse white, dbl. (45 petals), well-formed, large; foliage glossy; upright growth.

Caramel Creme HT, *my*, 1980, *(Sunbonnet × Mister Lincoln) × Oldtimer*; Weeks, O.L. Bud ovoid; flowers caramel yellow, dbl. (30 petals), cupped blooms borne singly; slight, spicy fragrance; foliage finely serrated; long prickles, hooked downward; bushy, moderate growth.

Caravelle HT, *mr*, 1964, *Better Times × Seedling*; Mondial Roses. Flowers bright cherry-red, dbl., high-centered, large, strong stems; vigorous, upright growth.

Cardeal de Rohan F, *dr*, 1957, Moreira da Silva. Flowers deep red, semi-dbl.

Cardinal HT, 1904, *Liberty × Red seedling*; Cook, J. Flowers red; One of the parents of Radiance. RULED EXTINCT 12/85 ARM.

Cardinal de Richelieu G (OGR), *m*, 1840, (Cardinal Richelieu); Laffay. Flowers dark purple, dbl., large; bushy growth. Usually credited to Laffay but may have been originated in Holland by Van Sian and originally named Rose Van Sian.

Cardinal Hume® S, *m*, 1984, (HARregale); *((Seedling × (Orange Sensation × Allgold) × R. californica)) × Frank Naylor*; Harkness, R. Bud pointed; flowers violet-purple, dbl. (31 petals), cupped, medium blooms in clusters of 3 to many; musky scent; foliage variable shades of green, matt; small prickles; medium, spreading growth; repeat bloom.

Cardinal Mercier HT, *op*, 1930, Lens. Flowers salmon-pink tinted orange, globular, very large; foliage bronze; vigorous growth.

Cardinale de la Puma HT, *dp*, 1938, *Mgr. Lemmens × Lord Charlemont*; Leenders, M. Flowers carmine-red, semi-dbl., large; slightly fragrant; foliage glossy; vigorous, bushy growth. GM, Rome, 1937.

Cardinals Hat HT, *mr*, 1960, *Souv. de Jacques Verschuren × Charles Mallerin*; Leenders, J. Flowers red.

Care Deeply Min, *ab*, 1982, (LYOca); *Honey Hill × Seedling*; Lyon, Lyndon; Lyon Greenhouse. Flowers apricot, dbl. (35 petals), medium; fragrant; foliage medium, medium green, semi-glossy; upright, bushy growth.

Carefree F, *dp*, 1959, *Alain* × *Pinocchio*; Fletcher. Flowers rose bengal, dbl. (75 petals), camellia form, medium, clusters; foliage dark; free growth.

Carefree Beauty™ S, *mp*, 1977, (BUCbi; Audace®); *Seedling* × *Prairie Princess*; Buck; C-P. Bud ovoid, long, pointed; flowers light rose, 15-20 petals, large (4½ in.); fragrant; foliage olive-green, smooth; vigorous, upright, spreading growth; repeat bloom.

Carefree Wonder™ S, *pb*, 1990, (MEIpitac); *(Prairie Princess* × *Nirvana)* × *(Eyepaint* × *Rustica)*; Selection Meilland, 1978; The Conard-Pyle Company, 1991. Bud pointed; flowers medium pink with light pink reverse, aging to medium pink, dbl. (26 petals), cupped, large blooms borne in sprays of 1-4; slight fragrance; foliage medium, medium green, semi-glossy; very good disease resistance and hardiness; prickles narrow, reddish; fruit oval, reddish-brown; bushy, medium growth, suitable for hedges. AARS, 1991.

Careless Love HT, *pb*, 1955, *Red Radiance* sport; Conklin; Golden State Nursery. Flowers deep pink, streaked (striped) and splashed white.

Careless Moment Min, *pb*, 1977, *Little Darling* × *Over the Rainbow*; Williams, E.D.; Mini-Roses. Bud long, pointed; flowers white, lightly edged pink, dbl. (45 petals), high-centered, small (1-1½ in.); fragrant; foliage small; bushy, spreading growth.

Caress HT, *yb*, 1935, Dickson, A. Flowers pale buttercup yellow, tinted rose, edged salmon-carmine, rather full; fragrant; foliage bright green, leathery; vigorous growth.

Caribbean Gr, *ab*, 1992, (KORbirac); *Mercedes* × *(New Day* × *Seedling)*; Kordes, W.; Bear Creek Gardens, Inc., 1994. Flowers apricot orange/yellow blend, full (26-40 petals), large (7+ cms) blooms borne in small clusters; fragrant; foliage large, dark green, semi-glossy, has pronounced red mid-vein and leaf margin on new foliage; many prickles; medium (110-125 cms), upright, bushy growth. AARS, 1994.

Caribbean Queen Min, *r*, 1987, (RENeen); *Sunday Brunch* × *Gold Mine*; Rennie, Bruce; Rennie Roses. Flowers apricot-copper, reverse yellow, dbl. (33 petals), exhibition, medium blooms borne singly; slightly fragrant; foliage small to medium, medium green, semi-glossy; medium, orange-red prickles; fruit ovoid yellow; vigorous, bushy growth.

Caribe Min, *ab*, 1982, (JACibe); *Bridal Pink* × *Fire Princess*; Warriner, W.; J&P, 1983. Flowers apricot, semi-dbl.; slight fragrance; foliage

small, light green, semi-glossy; upright, bushy.

Caribou HRg (S), *w*, 1946, *Ross Rambler* × *(R. rugosa* × *R. eglanteria)* × *Seedling)*; Preston; Central Exp. Farm. Bud pointed; flowers white, single (5 petals), flat, large; slightly fragrant; fruit ornamental; foliage glossy, leathery, dark, rugose, scented like sweetbrier; bushy, vigorous growth; non-recurrent bloom; very hardy.

Carillon HT, *or*, 1935, *Charles P. Kilham* × *Mrs. Pierre S. duPont*; Nicolas; J&P. Bud long, pointed, scarlet-orange; flowers brilliant flame, paling, semi-dbl., large; foliage glossy, light; bushy growth.

Carillon HT, *dy*, 1953, (*Soeur Thérèse* × *Orange Nassau)* × *Orange Nassau*; Moulin-Epinay; Vilmorin-Andrieux. Bud long, pointed, deep yellow spotted carmine; flowers deep yellow, dbl. (30-35 petals), medium; vigorous growth.

Carina® HT, *mp*, 1963, (MEIchim); *White Knight* × *(Happiness* × *Independence)*; Meilland, Alain; URS, 1963; C-P; J.H. Hill Co., 1964. Flowers medium pink, dbl. (40 petals), high-centered, large (5 in.); fragrant; foliage leathery; upright, bushy growth. ADR, 1966.

Carina, Climbing® Cl HT, *mp*, 1968, (MEIchimsar; Grimpant Carina); Meilland; URS.

Carina Superior HT, *w*, 1978, *Carina* sport; Takatori; Japan Rose Nursery. Bud pointed; flowers white, reverse light pink, dbl. (35-40 petals), high-centered, large (5 in.); fragrant; foliage leathery; upright, bushy growth.

Carine HT, *op*, 1911, Dickson, A. Bud long, pointed; flowers orange-carmine tinted bff, well formed, strong stems; very fragrant; vigorous growth.

Carioca HT, *ab*, 1942, *Talisman* sport; Chase; J&P. Bud long; flowers apricot, dbl. (25-38 petals), high-centered, large (4½ in.); slightly fragrant; foliage dark, glossy, leathery; vigorous, upright growth; a greenhouse cut flower.

Carioca HT, *ob*, 1951, *Rubin* × *Mme. Henri Guillot*; Lens. Bud semi-ovoid; flowers tangerine-orange, dbl., globular, large, long-strong stems; fragrant; foliage bright bronze green; very vigorous growth.

Carissima R, *lp*, 1905, Walsh. Flowers delicate flesh, dbl., carnation-like; fragrant.

Carito MacMahon HT, *my*, 1934, *Mrs. Pierre S. duPont* × *Cayetana Stuart*; Dot, P. Bud large, ovoid; flowers yellow, dbl., cupped, strong stems; fragrant; foliage glossy, dark; vigorous growth.

Carl Kempkes F, *dr*, 1937, *Dance of Joy* × *Mary Hart*; Kordes; Späth. Bud long, pointed; flowers crimson, semi-dbl., open, large, borne in clusters on strong stems; slightly fragrant; foliage glossy, dark; vigorous, bushy growth.

Carla HT, *op*, 1963, *Queen Elizabeth* × *The Optimist*; deRuiter; Ball, 1968. Flowers soft salmon-pink, dbl. (26 petals), large (3½-5 in.); fragrant; foliage dark; vigorous.

Carla S, *mr*, 1963, *Will Alderman* × *Hansa*; Erskine; Much like Hansa but brighter color; (14).

Carla, Climbing Cl HT, *mr*, 1969, Ross, A., & Son.

Carlea S, *mp*, 1965, *Betty Bland seedling*; Wright, P.H. Flowers medium pink, similar to Victory Year but darker and more free blooming; non-recurrent bloom.

Carlos Beauty Sp (OGR), *mp*, *R. acicularis variety*; Found by Erskine in Alberta, Canada, about 1960. Flowers bright pink, semi-dbl. (12-15 petals); very fragrant.

Carlos Reis Cl HT, *mr*, *Étoile de Hollande, Climbing* × *Pres. Herbert Hoover*; Moreira da Silva. Flowers purplish red.

Carl's Rose Min, *m*, 1985, (LEMcar); *Parentage unknown*; Lemrow, Dr. Maynard. Flowers mauve, dbl. (35 petals), exhibition, small blooms in sprays; no fragrance; foliage small, medium green, semi-glossy; low, upright growth.

Carlsham S, *mp*, 1964, *Hansa* × *R. nitida*; Erskine. Flowers rose-pink, dbl. (25 petals), large; foliage glossy; recurrent bloom; (14).

Carmagnole® F, *w*, 1991, (DELrobla); *(Milrose* × *Legion d'Honneur)* × *(Zambra* × *Orange Sensation)*; Delbard & Chabert, 1990. Flowers white cream with soft pink, moderately full (20-25 petals), cup shaped, medium blooms; light fragrance; foliage dark green; bushy (80-100 cms) growth.

Carmel Bice F, *pb*, 1959, *Gartendirektor Otto Linne* × *Seedling*; Riethmuller. Bud ovoid; flowers pink, reverse lighter, semi-dbl. to dbl., medium blooms in clusters; very fragrant; foliage leathery, glossy; vigorous, upright growth.

Carmela Min, *ob*, 1980, *Fairy Moss* × *Yellow Jewel*; Moore, R.S.; Moore Min. Roses. Buds lightly mossed; flowers orange, yellow center, semi-dbl. (15 petals), small blooms in sprays of 3-5; slight fragrance; foliage small, light green, matt; small, brownish prickles; fruit small, ovoid to globular, orange; medium, bushy, spreading growth.

Carmelita HT, *mr*, 1933, *Matchless* × *Milady*; Spanbauer. Bud ovoid; flowers vivid red, dbl., high-centered, large; foliage dark; very vigorous, bushy.

Carmen HRg (S), *mr*, 1907, *R. rugosa rosea* × *Princesse de Bearn*; Lambert, P. Flowers crimson, stamens yellow, single, large blooms in clusters; foliage dark; vigorous growth.

Carmen HT, *dr*, 1956, *Crimson Glory* × *Seedling*; Delforge. Flowers deep red, dbl., well-formed, large; very fragrant; foliage dark; moderate growth.

Carmen Papandrea Min, *dp*, 1989, *Magic Carrousel sport*; Papandrea, John T. Flowers deep pink.

Carmen Sistachs Pol, 1936, Dot, P. Flowers rose-pink, base old-gold, dbl., cluster; small; foliage sparse, small, soft, light; vigorous, bushy growth.

Carmen Talón HT, *dr*, 1953, *Charles Mallerin* × *Satan*; Dot, P. Bud oval; flowers velvety dark red, dbl. (35 petals), large, strong stems; fragrant; vigorous growth.

Carmen Tessier HT, *dr*, 1964, *Seedling* × *Independence*; Mondial Roses. Bud long, pointed; flowers crimson-red, dbl., open; slightly fragrant; foliage leathery; vigorous, bushy growth.

Carmencita Min, *w*, 1954, *Lady Sylvia* × *Perla de Alcanada*; Camprubi. Bud ovoid; flowers pure white, dbl. (55 petals); foliage clear green; vigorous growth.

Carmenetta S, *lp*, 1923, *R. rubrifolia* × *R. rugosa*; Central Exp. Farm. Flowers pale pink, single, borne in clusters; slightly fragrant; foliage leathery, reddish; vigorous (7 ft.), spreading (11 ft.) growth; very hardy; (28).

Carnaval® F, *rb*, 1987, (KORfrilla; Carnival); *Seedling* × *(Die Krone* × *Simona)*; Kordes, W., 1986. Flowers white with red edges, dbl. (26-40 petals), large; no fragrance; foliage medium, dark green, matt; bushy growth.

Carnaval de Rio® F, *ob*, 1982, (DELorfeu); *(Zambra* × *Orange Sensation)* × *(Zambra* × *(Seedling of Orange Triumph* × *Floradora))*; Delbard, G.; Delbard Roses. Flowers orange, dbl., blooms in clusters.

Carne M (OGR), *lp*, Robert. Flowers flesh-pink, full, large.

Carnival HT, *op*, 1939, Archer. Flowers glowing orange to soft cerise, dbl.; foliage glossy, light; vigorous growth. RULED EXTINCT, 1/88.

Carnival Glass Min, *ob*, 1979, *Seedling* × *Over the Rainbow*; Williams, E.D.; Mini-Roses. Bud pointed; flowers yellow-orange blend, dbl. (38 petals), small (1-1½ in.); slightly fragrant; foliage small, glossy, bronze; bushy, spreading growth.

Carnival Parade Min, *yb*, 1978, *Starburst* × *Over the Rainbow*; Williams, E.D.; Mini-Roses. Bud long, pointed; flowers golden yellow, edged red, dbl. (45 petals), high-centered, small (1 in.); slightly fragrant; foliage small, dark, glossy; upright, bushy growth.

Carnival Queen HT, *mr*, 1965, *(Tassin × Priscilla) × Charlotte Armstrong*; Armbrust; Langbecker. Bud long, pointed; flowers luminous red, semi-dbl., large; fragrant; vigorous.

Carol HT, *pb*, 1964, *Queen Elizabeth × Confidence*; Herholdt, J.A.; Herholdt's Nursery. Flowers cyclamen-rose, becoming orchid at edge, center apricot, dbl. (45 petals), well-formed, medium; slightly fragrant; no prickles on stem; moderate growth.

Carol Amling F, *mp*, 1953, (Carol; Garnette Carol; Garnette Pink); *Garnette sport*; Amling, C.M. & Beltran; Amling Roses. Flowers deep rose-pink, edged lighter.

Carol Ann Pol, *op*, 1940, *Marianne Kluis Superior sport*; Kluis; Klyn. Flowers orange-salmon, dbl. (35-45 petals), cupped, small (1-1½ in.), tight clusters; dwarf (12 in. or less) growth; recurrent bloom.

Carol Howard HT, *mp*, 1935, Pfitzer; P.J. Howard. Bud long, pointed; flowers rose-pink, peony shape, very large; fragrant; foliage dark; vigorous growth.

Carolina Classic HT, *pb*, 1992, (BRIclass); *Just Lucky × Flaming Beauty*; Bridges, Dennis A.; Bridges Roses. Flowers medium pink edged deeper pink, very full (41+ petals), large (7+ cms) blooms borne mostly single; slight fragrance; foliage medium, medium green, matt; few prickles; medium (90-100 cms), upright growth.

Carolina Moon HT, *my*, 1989, *Just Lucky × Thriller*; Bridges, Dennis A.; Bridges Roses, 1990. Bud pointed; flowers medium yellow, fading slightly, dbl. (28 petals), high-centered, exhibition, borne singly; heavy, fruity fragrance; foliage medium, medium green, semi-glossy; prickles pointed slightly downward, medium, deep pink; upright, tall, vigorous growth.

Carolina Morning Min, *rb*, 1989, (MICam; MICar); *Rise 'n' Shine × Rainbow's End*; Williams, Michael C.; The Rose Garden, 1990. Bud pointed; flowers red with yellow center, aging red, dbl. (20 petals), high-centered, small, borne singly and in sprays of 4-7; no fragrance; foliage small, medium green, semi-glossy; prickles straight, small, red; fruit round, orange; bushy, medium growth.

Carolina Sunset LCl, *rb*, 1990, *Seedling × Seedling*; Jeremias, Lephon L. Bud ovoid; flowers crimson, gold reverse, dbl. (35+ petals), cupped blooms borne in sprays of 3-7; slight fragrance; foliage average, dark green, matt; upright, tall growth with 10-12 ft. canes; variety has to be arched and tied down for more blooms.

Caroline HT, *op*, 1955, *Peace × Seedling*; Gaujard. Flowers cinnabar-salmon, dbl. (70 petals), very large; fragrant; foliage dark, glossy, leathery; very vigorous, bushy growth.

Caroline Budde R, *dr*, 1913, (Lien Budde); *Crimson Rambler × Léonie Lamesch*; Leenders, M. Flowers crimson-red, full, large; foliage dark; vigorous growth.

Caroline Davison F, *op*, 1980, (HARhester); *Tip Top × Kim*; Harkness, R. Flowers medium salmon-pink, semi-dbl. (16 petals), mini-flora, small blooms in clusters of 3-7; slight fragrance; foliage small, dark reddish-green; straight, dark green prickles; low, bushy growth.

Caroline de Sansal HP (OGR), *mp*, 1849, Desprez. Flowers pink, center darker, full, flat, large; vigorous growth; recurrent bloom.

Caroline Emmons F, *rb*, 1962, *(Geranium Red × Fashion) × (Diamond Jubilee × Fashion)*; Boerner; Home Nursery Products Corp. Bud ovoid; flowers scarlet-red, dbl. (55-60 petals), cupped, large (3½ in.); very fragrant (geranium); foliage leathery; vigorous, upright, bushy growth.

Caroline Esberg LCl, *mp*, 1926, Diener. Flowers dull rose, dbl., cluster.

Caroline Kaart HT, *op*, 1964, *Bayaderè × Ballet*; Buisman. Flowers salmon-pink veined dark red, large; foliage glossy; upright growth.

Caroline Marniesse N (OGR), *w*, 1848, Roeser. Flowers creamy white, dbl.

Caroline Plumpton F, *dp*, 1975, *Red Lion × Seedling*; Plumpton. Flowers deep neyron rose, edged lighter, dbl. (20-25 petals), moderately full, medium (2½ in.); slightly fragrant; foliage matt, green; very free growth.

Carol-Jean Min, *dp*, 1977, (Indian Meillandina; Indian Sunblaze); *Pinocchio × Little Chief*; Moore, R.S.; Sequoia Nursery. Bud pointed; flowers deep pink, dbl. (22 petals), small (1 in.); slightly fragrant; foliage small to medium, dark; upright, very bushy growth.

Carolyn Ann Min, *mp*, 1985, *Gene Boerner × Baby Katie*; Hooper, Clint; Kimbrew Walter Roses. Flowers medium pink, dbl. (20 petals), small; fragrant; foliage medium, medium green, semi-glossy; bushy growth.

Carolyn Dean R, *mp*, 1941, *Étoile Luisante × Sierra Snowstorm*; Moore, R.S.; Sequoia Nursery. Bud long, pointed; flowers bright pink, single (5 crinkled petals), small (1¼ in.), borne in clusters; foliage glossy; height 5 ft.; recurrent bloom.

Carolyn Dianne F, *lp*, 1964, *Ma Perkins × Pinocchio*; Patterson; Patterson Roses. Flowers light pink, dbl., medium; fragrant; foliage glossy; vigorous, compact growth.

Caron F, *pb*, 1972, *Kordes' Perfecta* × *Saratoga*; Langdale, G.W.T. Flowers white and pink, dbl. (38 petals), large (3 in.); slightly fragrant; foliage semi-glossy; upright growth.

Caroubier R, *mr*, 1912, Nonin. Flowers very bright light crimson-scarlet, single; early bloom.

Carouge HT, *dr*, 1976, *Marylene* × *Credo*; Gaujard. Flowers crimson-red, full; fall growth.

Carpet of Gold LCl, *my*, 1939, *(Emily Gray* × *Yellow Rambler)* × *Golden Glow*; Brownell. Flowers yellow, dbl., medium (2-3 in.); trailing growth.

Carrie Corl Gr, *mr*, 1969, *Queen Elizabeth* × *(Queen Elizabeth seedling* × *Happiness)*; Germain's; Flower of the Month. Bud ovoid; flowers medium red, dbl., large; fragrant; foliage dark, leathery; vigorous growth.

Carrie Jacobs Bond HT, *mp*, 1935, *Premier Supreme* × *Lady Leslie*; Howard, F.H.; Dreer. Bud ovoid; flowers rose-pink, center flushed crimson, very dbl., large, long stems; very fragrant; foliage leathery, dark; vigorous growth.

Carrie Jacobs Bond, Climbing Cl HT, *mp*, 1940, H&S.

Carrot Top Min, *ob*, 1991, (POUltop); *Floribunda seedling* × *Miniature seedling*; Olesen, M.&P.; Weeks Roses, 1994. Flowers orange, clear lasting color, moderately full (15-25 petals), well-formed, small (0-4 cms) blooms borne mostly singly; prolific bloom; slight fragrance; foliage medium, medium green, matt; few prickles; low (40-50 cms), bushy, compact growth.

Carrousel Gr, *mr*, 1950, *Seedling* × *Margy*; Duehrsen; Elmer Roses Co. Flowers medium red, dbl. (20 petals), medium; fragrant; foliage leathery, dark, glossy; vigorous, upright, bushy growth. GM, Portland, 1955 & ARS, 1956.

Carrousel, Climbing Cl Gr, *mr*, 1958, Weeks; Elmer Roses Co.

Carry Nation F, *w*, 1959, *Pinocchio* × *Katharina Zeimet*; Silva; Plant Hybridizers of Calif. Bud ovoid; flowers white, center cream, semi-dbl., globular, small, borne in clusters; slightly fragrant; foliage soft, glossy; vigorous, low growth.

Carte Blanche™ HT, *w*, 1975, (MEIringa); *(Carina* × *White Knight)* × *Jack Frost*; Paolino; URS. Flowers white, dbl. (38 petals), floratea, large (4 in.); foliage matt; vigorous growth.

Cartwheel Min, *rb*, 1989, (JACcart); *Libby* × *Seedling*; Warriner, William A.; Bear Creek

Gardens (J&P), 1990. Bud ovoid; flowers red and white picotee, dbl. (20 petals), cupped, small, borne singly; slight fragrance; foliage small, medium green, matt; prickles hooked, small, tan; low, bushy growth.

Cary Grant™ HT, *ob*, 1987, (MEImainger; Bushveld Dawn); *(Pharaoh* × *Königin der Rosen)* × *((Zambra* × *Suspense)* × *King's Ransom)*; Meilland, Mrs. Marie-Louise; Wayside Gardens, 1987; Conard-Pyle, 1989. Flowers vivid orange blend, luminous yellow-orange at petal base, scarlet-orange at petal margin, very dbl. (35-40 petals), high-centered, exhibition, large, borne usually singly; heavy, spicy fragrance; foliage medium, dark green, glossy; slightly recurred, light green-straw prickles; fruit ovoid, green, red-orange; upright, medium growth.

Caryatide HT, *dr*, 1955, *Hens Verschuren* × *Poinsettia*; Buyl Frères. Bud long, pointed; flowers dark red, semi-dbl., strong stems; upright growth.

Casa Blanca LCl, *w*, 1968, *New Dawn* × *Fashion*; Sima. Bud tinged carmine-pink; flowers white, semi-dbl., medium blooms in clusters; slightly fragrant; foliage dark, glossy; vigorous, climbing growth; intermittent bloom.

Casanova HT, *ly*, 1964, *Queen Elizabeth* × *Kordes' Perfecta*; McGredy, S., IV; Fisons Horticulture. Flowers straw-yellow, dbl. (38 petals), high-centered, large (6 in.); fragrant.

Cascabel F, *rb*, 1957, *Méphisto* × *Perla de Alcañada*; Dot, P. Flowers red, reverse pearly, passing to carmine, dbl. (45-50 petals), globular, opening flat, borne in clusters of 4; foliage glossy; very vigorous, upright, compact growth.

Cascade LCl, *mr*, 1951, *Holstein* × *American Pillar*; Mallerin; EFR. Flowers bright crimson, almost single, large, in very full clusters; very vigorous growth.

Cascadia HMsk (S), *lp*, 1927, *Mme. d'Arblay* × *Bloomfield Abundance*; Thomas; B&A. Flowers blush-pink paling to white, semi-dbl. (15 petals), small (1 in.), borne in clusters; slightly fragrant; foliage glossy, dark; tall growth; recurrent bloom. GM, Portland, 1922.

Cashmere HT, *ab*, 1980, *Tanya* × *Jack O'Lantern*; Weeks, O.L. Bud pointed; flowers soft apricot, dbl. (30 petals), globular, borne singly and 3-5 per cluster; slight, spicy fragrance; foliage leathery, dark; long, hooked prickles; vigorous, bushy growth.

Casimir Moullé R, *pb*, 1910, *R. wichuraiana* × *Mme. Norbert Levavasseur*; Barbier. Flowers purplish pink, reverse silvery pink.

Casino® LCl, *ly*, 1963, (MACca; Gerbe d'Or); *Coral Dawn × Buccaneer*, McGredy, S., IV; McGredy. Flowers soft yellow, dbl., well-formed, large; fragrant; foliage dark, glossy; vigorous (10 ft.) growth; recurrent bloom. GM, NRS, 1963.

Casque d'Or® HT, *my*, 1979, (DELcascor); *(Zambra × Jean de la Lune) × (Michèle Meilland × Tahiti)*; Delbard. Flowers medium yellow, dbl. (30 petals), well-shaped, 4 in.; no fragrance; vigorous, upright, bushy growth.

Cassandra HT, *mr*, 1966, *(Karl Herbst × Ena Harkness) × (Christian Dior × Peace)*; Dorieux; Bees. Flowers cherry, high-centered, large (4½ in.); slightly fragrant; foliage dull, serrated; free growth.

Casta Diva® HT, *w*, 1982, *Pascali × Seedling*; Barni-Pistoia, Rose. Flowers white, dbl. (35 petals), cupped, large; no fragrance; foliage large, dark, glossy; flat, yellow prickles; upright growth.

Castanet F, *op*, 1960, *Chic × Garnette seedling*; Boerner; J&P. Bud ovoid; flowers orange-pink, reverse lighter, dbl. (45 petals), large (3½ in.); fragrant; upright, bushy.

Castella® S, *mr*, 1985, (TANallet); Tantau, M., 1984. Flowers medium red, semi-dbl., medium; no fragrance; foliage large, dark, semi-glossy; upright growth.

Castle Hill Min, *dp*, 1989, (ZIPhill); *Sheri Anne × Red Devil*; Zipper, Herbert; Magic Moment Miniatures, 1990. Bud pointed; flowers deep pink with mauve undertones, shading lighter towards base, dbl. (25 quilled petals), high-centered, exhibition, medium, borne usually singly and in sprays of 2-3; no fragrance; foliage medium, medium green, semi-glossy, highly mildew resistant; prickles curved, small, tan; fruit round, small, light orange; bushy, low growth .

Castle of Mey F, *ob*, 1992, (COClucid); *Anne Cocker × (Yellow Pages × Silver Jubilee)*; Cocker, James; James Cocker & Sons. Flowers orange gold, moderately full (15-25 petals), medium (4-7 cms) blooms borne in small clusters; fragrant; foliage medium, dark green, semi-glossy; some prickles; medium (76.20 cms), bushy growth.

Catalina HT, *pb*, 1939, *Pres. Herbert Hoover × Katharine Pechtold*; San Remo Exp. Sta. Bud long, pointed, carmine, reverse salmon; flowers carmine suffused yellow and rose, dbl. (23 petals), very large; very fragrant; foliage dark, glossy; very vigorous.

Catalina HT, *op*, 1940, *Joanna Hill sport*; Grillo. Bud very long, coral-pink edged old-rose; flowers salmon to shrimp-pink, dbl. (25-30 petals), high-centered, large (4½ in.); fragrant; very vigorous, upright growth.

Catalonia HT, *or*, 1933, *(Shot Silk × Mari Dot) × Jean C.N. Forestier*; Dot, P.; C-P. Flowers bright orange-crimson, shaded gold, very dbl., globular, large; foliage dark; bushy growth.

Catalunya Cl HT, *mr*, 1918, *Gruss an Teplitz sport*; Nonin; Similar to parent but more vigorous.

Caterpillar® Min, *lp*, 1985, (POULcat; Kiki Rose®; Pink Drift); *Temple Bells × Seedling*; Olesen, M.&P.; D.T. Poulsen, 1984. Flowers light pink, semi-dbl., small blooms in large trusses; no fragrance; foliage small, dark, glossy; low, spreading growth; ground cover.

Catharina Klein HT, *pb*, 1930, *Mrs. Franklin Dennison × Hadley*; Berger, V.; Münch & Haufe. Bud ovoid; flowers bright pink, yellow background, very dbl., large; fragrant; foliage rich green; very vigorous growth.

Cathay F, *ly*, 1957, *Fandango × Pinocchio*; Swim. Flowers light yellow, dbl. (35-40 petals), high-centered to cupped, large (3½-4½ in.); very fragrant; foliage glossy, leathery; vigorous, compact growth.

Cathcart Bedder HT, *op*, 1939, Austin & McAslan. Flowers salmon-shrimp-pink; foliage bronze; vigorous, bushy growth.

Cathedral F, *ab*, 1975, (Coventry Cathedral; Houston); *Little Darling × (Goldilocks × Irish Mist)*; McGredy. Flowers apricot shading salmon, dbl. (22 petals), large (4-5 in.); slightly fragrant; foliage glossy, olive-green; bushy growth. GM, NZ & Portland, 1974; AARS, 1976.

Catherine Cookson HT, *lp*, 1986, (NOScook); *Gavotte × King's Ransom*; Greensitt, J.A.; Nostell Priory Rose Gardens. Flowers light pink, dbl. (26-40 petals), large; fragrant; foliage large, dark green, glossy; bushy growth.

Catherine de Würtemberg M (OGR), *lp*, 1843, Robert. Bud well mossed; flowers soft pink, very full, globular, large; vigorous growth.

Catherine Guillot B (OGR), *dp*, 1860, *Louise Odier seedling*; Guillot. Flowers carmine-rose, full, large; vigorous.

Catherine Langeais HT, *mr*, 1965, *Michele Meilland × Berthe Mallerin*; Hémeray-Aubert. Flowers carmine-red, dbl. (46 petals), high-centered, well formed; vigorous, upright growth.

Catherine Marie HT, *mp*, 1991, *Pristine × Captain Harry Stebbings*; Wambach, Alex A., 1990. Bud pointed; flowers medium to shell pink, dbl. (26 petals), exhibition; heavy fragrance; foliage medium, medium green, semi-glossy.

Catherine Mermet T (OGR), *lp*, 1869, Guillot Fils. Bud well-shaped; flowers flesh-pink, edges tinted lilac-pink, dbl., large; fragrant; vigorous; was long grown under glass.

Catherine Seyton E (OGR), *lp*, 1894, Penzance; Keynes, Williams & Co. Flowers soft pink, yellow stamens, single; fragrant; foliage fragrant (apple); vigorous; non-recurrent; (35).

Cathrine Kordes HT, *dr*, 1930, *(Mme Caroline Testout × Willowmere) × Sensation*; Kordes; Dreer; H&S. Bud long, pointed, blood-red, shaded black; flowers dark scarlet, dbl., large; fragrant; foliage dark (blood-red when young), leathery; very vigorous growth.

Cathrine Kordes, Climbing Cl HT, *dr*, 1938, Krohn; Kordes.

Cathy Anne HT, *r*, 1990, *Judith Morton × Sylvia*; Wilson, George D., 1986. Bud pointed; flowers russet, semi-dbl. (25 petals), high-centered, blooms borne singly; no fragrance; foliage small, dark green; long, straight stems; prickles long, slender, red; medium growth.

Catinat G (OGR), *m*, Robert, ca. 1850. Flowers violet, spotted.

Catorce de Abril HT, *yb*, 1932, Padrosa. Flowers yellow streaked red.

Cauldron HT, *pb*, 1971, Waterhouse Nursery. Flowers rose-pink to yellow, dbl. (23 petals), large (4½ in.); fragrant; Foliage glossy, dark. RULED EXTINCT 6/83 ARM.

Cauldron S, *mp*, 1984, *R. rubrifolia × R. nutkana*; Holliger, Franc. Flowers medium pink, single (5 petals), small; slight fragrance; foliage medium, mid-green, matt; upright growth.

Cavalcade F, *rb*, 1950, Verschuren-Pechtold; Stuart. Bud ovoid; flowers oxblood-red and yellow, changing daily to crimson, carmine and silvery pink, dbl. (32 petals), medium; very fragrant (fruity); foliage glossy, dark; vigorous, bushy growth.

Cavalcade, Climbing Cl F, *rb*, 1957, Gandy.

Cavalier HT, *ob*, 1939, *Mrs. Franklin D. Roosevelt sport*; Samtmann Bros. Flowers burnt-orange to cream-buff, dbl.; fragrant.

Cayenne HT, *ob*, 1966, *South Seas × Seedling*; Warriner; J&P. Bud short, pointed; flowers deep orange, dbl. (38 petals), medium (3-4 in.); slightly fragrant; upright growth.

Cayetana Stuart HT, *my*, 1931, *Isabel Llorach × (Constance × Sunburst)*; Dot, P.; C-P. Bud long, pointed; flowers yellow, dbl., cupped, very large; fragrant; foliage dark, glossy; very vigorous, bushy. GM, Bagatelle, 1930.

C. Chambard HT, 1934, Bel. Flowers deep yellow, reverse tinted red, dbl., cupped; foliage dark; vigorous growth.

Cechoslavia HT, *w*, 1921, *Pharisaer × Mme. Antoine Mari*; Berger, V.; A. Berger. Flowers milky white suffused salmon-carmine, center golden yellow, dbl.; fragrant.

Cecil HT, *my*, 1926, Cant, B.R. Flowers golden yellow, single (5 petals), large (4 in.) blooms in large clusters; bushy growth.

Cecil, Climbing Cl HT, *my*, 1940, Chaffin; Armstrong Nursery.

Cécile Brunner Pol, *lp*, 1881, (Mme. Cécile Brunner; Mlle. Cécile Brunner; Mignon; Sweetheart Rose) Ducher, Vve.; Pernet-Ducher. Bud long, pointed; flowers bright pink on yellow ground, dbl., small blooms in clusters; fragrance like Souv. d'un Ami; foliage sparse, soft, dark, 3-5 leaflets; very few prickles; growth like a Tea, dwarf; intermediate between Paquerette and Anne-Marie de Montravel; Said to be Dbl. fld. Multiflora × Souv. d'un Ami; (14).

Cécile Brunner, Climbing Cl Pol, *lp*, 1894, (Mme. Cécile Brunner, Climbing; Mlle. Cécile Brunner, Climbing; Mignon, Climbing; Sweetheart Rose, Climbing). Hosp.

Cécile Brunner, Climbing Cl Pol, *lp*, 1904, Ardagh.

Cecile Custers HT, *pb*, 1914, *Mme. Abel Chatenay × Violet Liddell*; Leenders, M. Flowers lilac-rose, reverse deep rose-pink, dbl.

Cécile Mann HT, *mr*, 1939, *Mrs. Albert Nash × Seedling*; Clark, A.; Brundrett. Flowers red; vigorous growth.

Cécile Ratinckx HT, *my*, 1924, *Louise Catherine Breslau × Mme. Edouard Herriot*; Vandevelde. Flowers coppery yellow.

Cécile Verlet HT, *yb*, 1926, *Marianna Rolfs × Nordlicht (HT)*; Walter, L. Flowers yellow, passing to rose-pink.

Cécile Walter HT, *op*, 1926, *(Mme. Mélanie Soupert × Mme. Edouard Herriot) × Seedling*; Mallerin; C-P. Bud long, pointed; flowers coral-pink to coppery pink, base gold, dbl. (28 petals), cupped, very large; slightly fragrant; foliage rich green, leathery; vigorous growth.

Cecilia S, *pb*, 1980, *(R. wichuraiana × Baronne Prevost) × (R. × odorata)*; James, John. Bud globular, pointed; flowers light pink blended darker pink, dbl. (25 petals), carnation-like form, borne singly or 3-5 per cluster; spicy fragrance; foliage small, pointed, glossy; hooked prickles; vigorous, compact, bushy growth.

Cecilio Rodriguez HT, *dr*, 1950, *Tassin × Eugenio d'Ors*; Camprubi. Bud long, pointed;

flowers dark velvety red, dbl., high-centered, large, strong stems; very fragrant; foliage dark; very vigorous growth.

Cecily Gibson F, *rb*, 1991, (EVEbright; EVErbright); *Southampton × ((Arthur Bell × Maigold) × Glenfiddich)*; Everitt, Derrick, 1990. Bud ovoid; flowers current red, yellow base, dbl. (35 petals), cupped, medium blooms borne in sprays of 3-6; slight to moderate fragrance; foliage medium to large, dark green, glossy; bushy, medium to tall growth.

Cedar Crest College F, *dy*, 1992, (WILcrest); *Ivory Fashion × Sunsprite*; Williams, J. Benjamin, 1993. Flowers deep golden yellow, semi-dbl. (6-14 petals), medium (4-7 cms) blooms borne in small clusters; slight fragrance; foliage medium, dark green, glossy; few prickles; medium (3-4 ft.), upright, bushy growth.

Cedric Adams HT, *dr*, 1949, *Pink Princess × Crimson Glory*; Brownell. Bud ovoid; flowers scarlet to carmine, dbl., high-centered, large; fragrant; foliage dark, bronze; vigorous.

Cee Dee Moss S, *pb*, 1990, (MORceedee); *Carolyn Dean × Seedling*; Moore, Ralph S., 1981; Sequoia Nursery. Bud pointed; flowers pink with occasional white striped, lighter reverse, ages lighter, semi-dbl. (15-25 petals), cupped, loose, medium (6-8 cms), borne in sprays of 3-5; slight fragrance; foliage medium, light green, glossy; bushy, spreading, medium growth.

Celebrate America™ HT, *mr*, 1991, (TANcressor); *Seedling × Seedling*; Rosen Tantau; Bear Creek Gardens, 1990. Flowers medium red, dbl. (45-55 petals), high-centered, large (10-12 cms) blooms borne usually singly; slight fragrance; foliage large, medium green, semi-glossy; upright, spreading, medium growth.

Celebration F, *op*, 1961, *Dickson's Flame × Circus*; Dickson, P.; A. Dickson. Flowers salmon-pink, reverse lighter, dbl. (30 petals), cupped, large (3 in.) blooms in clusters; slightly fragrant; foliage light green; vigorous, bushy growth.

Celebrity HT, *pb*, 1945, (Lustrous); *Golden Rapture × Carmelita*; Hill, E.G., Co. Bud pointed; flowers pink, base shaded yellow, dbl. (30-35 petals), high-centered, very large (6-7 in.); fragrant (spicy); foliage leathery, dark; vigorous, bushy growth.   RULED EXTINCT 1/88.

Celebrity HT, *dy*, 1988, *(Sunbonnet × Mister Lincoln) × Yello Yo Yo*; Weeks, O. L.; Weeks Roses, 1989. Flowers deep yellow, aging clear yellow, dbl. (30-35 petals), high-centered, exhibition, large, borne usually singly, abun-

dant; moderate, fruity fragrance; foliage large, dark green, glossy; prickles pointed slightly downward, small, yellow-brown; upright, bushy, medium height.

Celeste Mahley F, *pb*, 1972, *Seventeen × Gemini*; Byrum; J.H. Hill Co. Bud long, pointed; flowers pink blend, dbl., medium; slightly fragrant; foliage leathery; vigorous, upright, bushy.

Celestial A (OGR), *lp*, (Céleste); *R. alba hybrid*; Prior to 1848. Flowers light blush, golden stamens, dbl.; fragrant; foliage bluish; vigorous (to 6 ft.) growth; non-recurrent bloom.

Celestial HSpn (OGR), *lp*, *R. eglanteria × R. spinosissima*. Flowers pale flesh, dbl., small; very fragrant; low growth.

Celestial HT, *lp*, 1924, *Premier sport*; Myers & Samtmann. Flowers light pink, edged paler, dbl.; fragrant.

Celestial Star F, *or*, 1965, Pal; Indian Agric. Research Institute. Bud ovoid; flowers orange-red, dbl., borne in clusters; foliage glossy; vigorous, compact growth.

Celia Walker F, *rb*, 1962, *Alain × Golden Scepter*; Fletcher; Tucker. Flowers cherry-red, reverse silver, semi-dbl. (15-20 petals), large (3 in.), clusters; slightly fragrant; foliage dark, glossy; vigorous, upright growth.

Célina M (OGR), *m*, 1855, Hardy. Bud heavily mossed; flowers reddish-purple, center occasionally streaked white, dbl., large.

Céline HBour (OGR), *mp*, Laffay, about 1825. Flowers pale rose, dbl., cupped, large; large cluster; very vigorous; does not repeat. First used as understock by Henry Curtis about 1840.

Céline Delbard® F, *ob*, 1986, (DELcélit; DELceli; DELcet); *Seedling × (Milrose × Legion d'Honneur)*; Delbard-Chabert, 1983. Flowers salmon, silver reverse, dbl. (23 petals), cupped, large; no fragrance; bushy growth. GM, Monza.

Céline Forestier N (OGR), *ly*, 1858, Leroy, A. Flowers pale yellow, dbl., large blooms in clusters of 3-4; fragrant; foliage dark, glossy; vigorous (to 6 ft.) growth. repeats; (14).

Celsiana D (OGR), *lp*, Prior to 1750. Flowers pale pink, semi-dbl., petals crinkled, large (4 in.) blooms in cluster of 3-4; fragrant; foliage smooth, grayish, fragrant; vigorous, upright(4-5 ft.) growth.

Cendrillon HT, *mp*, 1951, Gaujard. Bud very large; flowers salmon, dbl.; very fragrant; foliage leathery; very vigorous, upright growth.

Centenaire de Lourdes® F, *mp*, 1958, (DELge; Centennaire de Lourdes; Mrs. Jones); *(Frau Karl Druschki × Seedling) × Seedling*; Delbard-

Chabert. Flowers soft rose, semi-dbl. (15 wavy petals), large (3½-4 in.) blooms in clusters of 5-10; vigorous, bushy growth.

Centenaire du Vesinet Gr, *op*, 1977, (PIronia); *Sonia × Prominent*; Pineau; Searn. Bud pointed; flowers salmon-orange, dbl. (32 petals), large (3 in.); slightly fragrant; vigorous, upright.

Centenary College HT, *dr*, 1982, (AROblaveet); *Angel Face × Typhoo Tea*; Christensen, J.E.; Armstrong Nursery. Flowers deep red, dbl. (35 petals), large; very fragrant; foliage large, medium green, matt; vigorous, upright, tall growth.

Centennial HT, *ob*, 1953, *Seedling × Orange Nassau*; Mallerin; J&P. Bud ovoid; flowers peach-red, reverse orange-buff, dbl. (40-45 petals), high-centered, large (4-4½ in.); fragrant; foliage rich green; vigorous, bushy growth.

Centennial Miss Min, *dr*, 1952, *Oakington Ruby × Self*; Moore, R.S.; Sequoia Nursery. Flowers deep wine-red, base tinged white, dbl. (60 petals), small (1 in.); fragrant; foliage small, dark, leathery, glossy; no prickles; dwarf (10-12 in.), bushy growth.

Centennial Sweetheart Cl F, *mr*, 1959, *Alain sport*; Greene. Bud globular; flowers bright red, dbl. (25 petals), large (3½ in.), borne in large clusters; very fragrant; foliage glossy, light green; very vigorous growth.

Center Gold™ Min, *dy*, 1981, (SAVacent; Atkins Beauty); *Rise 'n' Shine × Kiskadee*; Saville, F. Harmon; American Rose Foundation. Bud pointed; flowers deep yellow, sometimes near white, dbl. (60 petals), high-centered, borne singly or up to 12 per cluster; spicy fragrance; foliage glossy, textured; long, thin prickles, slanted downward; upright, compact growth. AOE, 1982.

Centerpiece™ Min, *mr*, 1984, (SAVapiece; Centre Piece); *(Sheri Anne × Tamango) × (Sheri Anne × (Yellow Jewel × Tamango))*; Saville, F. Harmon; Nor'East Min. Roses, 1985. Flowers deep medium red, dbl. (35 petals), high-centered, small; slight fragrance; foliage small, dark, semi-glossy; bushy growth. AOE, 1985.

Centifolia Minima C (OGR), *mp*, (*R. centifolia minima*); Origin and date unknown. Flowers pink with darker center, dbl.,½ in. diameter

Centifolia Minima C (OGR), *lp*. Flowers soft pink, very dbl. (80-100 petals); fragrant; height 8-15 in., branching; non-recurrent bloom; possibly identical with Gracilis (C); A form or hybrid of Pompon de Bourgogne.

Centifolia Muscosa M (OGR), *mp*, (*R. centifolia muscosa* (Aiton) Seringe; *R. muscosa* Aiton; Moss Rose); Cultivated prior to 1750. Flowers pink, dbl., large, peduncles and calyx glandular, mossy; (See endpapers; 28).

Centifolia Rosea HP (OGR), *mp*, 1863, Touvais. Flowers bright rose, cupped, large; foliage crinkled, light green wood with many red prickles; vigorous.

Centifolia Variegata C (OGR), *pb*, (*R. centifolia variegata*; Belle Villageois; Cottage Maid); Original name and date unknown. Flowers creamy white, striped with pale lilac pink, globular; fragrant.

Centre Court HT, *w*, 1964, *Eden Rose × Ena Harkness*; Barter. Flowers white, center tan, dbl. (38 petals), well shaped, large (4 in.); fragrant; foliage dark; vigorous growth.

Centrex Gold F, *my*, 1975, *Alison Wheatcroft × Chinatown*; Smith, E.; Wheatcroft. Flowers medium yellow, dbl. (25 petals), large (3in.); slightly fragrant; foliage matt, green.

Centro de Lectura HT, *mr*, 1959, *Texas Centennial × Peace*; Dot, M. Flowers crimson, dbl. (40 petals), long, strong stems; fragrant; foliage glossy, bright green; vigorous growth.

Centurio® HT, *dr*, 1974, (HAVop); *Orangeade × Baccará*; Verschuren, T.; Verschuren. Flowers dark red, lasting well; moderate, bushy growth.

Centurion F, *dr*, 1975, *Evelyn Fison × Seedling*; Mattock. Flowers blood-red, shaded crimson, dbl. (30 petals), large (3 in.); slightly fragrant; foliage glossy, dark.

Century Two HT, *mp*, 1971, *Charlotte Armstrong × Duet*; Armstrong, D.L.; Armstrong Nursery. Bud long, pointed; flowers medium pink, dbl., cupped, large; fragrant; foliage leathery; vigorous, upright, bushy growth.

Century 21 HT, *lp*, 1962, *Condessa de Sástago × Soeur Therese*; Morey; J&P. Bud ovoid; flowers shell-pink, reverse slightly darker, dbl., high-centered, large; fragrant; foliage glossy; vigorous growth. Registration refused by ARS because the name was in violation of its rules of nomenclature. Name considered inadmissable under the 1961 International Code (Art. 21).

Ceremony F, *w*, 1970, *Tiara × Pascali*; Lens. Bud cupped; flowers pure white, dbl. (40-45 petals), medium (2½ in.); foliage leathery; very bushy growth; for greenhouse use.

Ceres HMsk (S), *lp*, 1914, Pemberton. Flowers pale blush, tinted light yellow, stamens bright yellow, semi-dbl.; shrub; profuse seasonal bloom.

Ceres HT, *ob*, 1922, *Sunburst × Mme. Edmond Rostand*; Spek. Flowers deep orange, center salmon.

Cerise HT, *dp*, 1945, *Crimson Glory* × *Sterling*;
Tantau. Flowers deep pink, dbl. (25 petals),
large; very fragrant; foliage dark, leathery;
vigorous, upright.

Cerise Bouquet S, *dp*, 1958, *R. multibracteata*
× *Crimson Glory*; Kordes. Flowers cerise-crimson, semi-dbl., flat; fragrant; foliage small,
grayish; open, arching growth.

Cerise Dawn™ HT, *dr*, 1989, (DEVrise);
Carina × *Angel Face*; Marciel, Stanley G.;
DeVor Nursery. Bud urn-shaped; flowers
magenta, reverse tyrian purple, aging no discoloration, dbl. (30 petals), globular, large,
borne singly; slight, damask fragrance; foliage large, dark green, semi-glossy; prickles
declining and well spaced apart, pea green;
upright, tall growth.

Cerise d'Orlin G (OGR), *dp*, Flowers deep
pink, reverse silver, semi-dbl., loose.

Cerise Talisman HT, *dp*, 1933, *Talisman sport*;
Clarks' Rose Nursery. Flowers cerise.

Ceská Pohadka Pol, *rb*, 1933, *Golden Salmon
sport*; Böhm. Flowers red, salmon, rose and
white, borne in clusters; very vigorous, dwarf
growth.

Césonie D (OGR), *dp*, Prior to 1848. Flowers
deep rose, full, large; compact growth.

Cestiflora HSpn (OGR), *ly*, *R. spinosissima hybrid or form*. Flowers sulphur-yellow; fruit
glossy, black; foliage finely divided; height
3-4 ft.; early bloom.

Cha Cha® Min, *ob*, 1982, (COCarum); *(Wee
Man* × *Manx Queen)* × *Darling Flame*; Cocker,
James; Cocker & Sons, 1983. Flowers orange-
red with yellow eye, dbl. (20 small, patio
petals); slight fragrance; foliage small, medium green, semi-glossy; bushy growth.

Chablis HT, *w*, 1983, *Seedling* × *Louisiana*;
Weeks, O.L.; Weeks Roses, 1984. Flowers
creamy white, dbl. (40+ petals), exhibition,
medium-large; slight fragrance; foliage large,
medium green, matt; upright growth.

Chacita F, *dr*, 1947, *Pinocchio* × *Crimson Glory*;
Boerner. Bud ovoid, globular; flowers deep
red, dbl., cupped, medium, borne in clusters;
fragrant; foliage dark, leathery; vigorous,
bushy growth.

Chalice HT, *ab*, 1959, *Orange Delight* × *Golden
Rapture*; Verschuren-Pechtold; J&P. Bud
ovoid, pointed; flowers apricot-yellow, dbl.
(55-60 petals), high-centered, large (5½-6 in.);
very fragrant; foliage leathery, glossy; vigorous, upright growth; a greenhouse variety for
cut-flower purposes.

Challenge F, *dr*, 1962, *Alain* × *Pinocchio*;
Fletcher; Tucker. Flowers deep blood-red,
semi-dbl. (20 petals), camellia shape, medium

(2 in.), borne in clusters; foliage dark; bushy,
low growth.

Challenger HT, *dr*, 1938, Cant, B.R. Flowers
dark crimson, dbl., high-centered, very large,
long stems; very fragrant; foliage leathery,
dark; vigorous, bushy growth. RULED EX-
TINCT, 6/89.

Challenger™ HT, *dr*, 1989, (HILred); *Jacqueline* × *Seedling*; Tracy, Daniel; DeVor Nursery, 1987. Bud ovoid; flowers dark red,
reverse medium red, dbl. (25 petals), urn-
shaped, high-centered, medium, borne in
sprays of 2-3; moderate fragrance; foliage
medium, semi-glossy; prickles angle downward, small, orange blend; fruit pear-shaped,
small, orange blend; upright, medium
growth.

Challis Gold HT, *dy*, 1986, (NOSchal); *Gold
Dot sport*; Greensitt, J.A.; Nostell Priory Rose
Gardens. Flowers deep yellow, dbl. (15-20
petals), medium; slight fragrance; foliage medium, medium green, glossy; spreading
growth.

Chamba Princess F, *op*, 1969, Indian Council
of Agric. Flowers salmon-pink, semi-dbl.,
open, medium; slightly fragrant; foliage
leathery; moderate, bushy growth; intermittent bloom.

Chambe di Kali HT, *mp*, 1983, *Bewitched* ×
Seedling; Pal, Dr. B.P.; K.S.G. Sons. Flowers
medium pink, dbl. (22 petals), high-centered,
large blooms borne singly; slight fragrance;
foliage large, dark, glossy; green to brown
prickles; medium, compact growth.

Chambord F, *mp*, 1960, *Roquebrune* × *Queen
Elizabeth*; Delforge. Bud pointed; flowers
pink, becoming darker, dbl., open, large,
borne in clusters; slightly fragrant; foliage
bronze; bushy growth.

Chameleon HT, *or*, 1918, *Lyon Rose seedling*;
Dickson, A. Flowers flame, edged cerise.

Chami HMsk (S), *mp*, 1929, Pemberton. Flowers bright rose-pink, stamens yellow, semi-
single; very fragrant; bushy growth; recurrent
bloom.

Chamisso R, *pb*, 1922, *Geheimrat Dr. Mittweg* ×
Tip-Top; Lambert, P. Flowers flesh-pink, center yellowish white, semi-dbl., borne in clusters on long stems; fragrant; foliage bronze;
vigorous, trailing growth; profuse, recurrent
bloom.

Champ Weiland HT, *mp*, 1915, *Killarney
sport*; Weiland & Risch. Flowers clear pink;
foliage glowing, reddish.

Champagne HT, *yb*, 1961, *Charlotte Armstrong*
× *Duquesa de Peñaranda*; Lindquist; Howard
Rose Co. Bud pointed, ovoid; flowers buff
shaded apricot, dbl. (28 petals), high-cen-

tered, large (4-5 in.); fragrant; foliage leathery, dark; vigorous, upright, bushy.

Champagne Cocktail F, *yb*, 1983, (HOR-flash); *Old Master × Southampton*; Horner, Colin P., 1985. Flowers pale yellow, flecked and splashed pink, yellow reverse, dbl. (20 petals), medium; fragrant; foliage medium, medium green, glossy; bushy growth. GM, Glasgow, 1990.

Champion HT, *yb*, 1976, *Irish Gold × Whisky Mac*; Fryer, G.; Fryer's Nursery. Flowers yellow-cream, flushed red and pink, dbl. (50-55 petals), very large (7-8 in.); fragrant; foliage large, light.

Champion of the World HP (OGR), *mp*, 1894, (Mrs. DeGraw; Mrs. de Graw); *Hermosa × Magna Charta*; Woodhouse. Flowers rose-pink, dbl., large; fragrant; vigorous growth; seasonal bloom.

Champlain K (S), *dr*, 1982, *(R. kordesii × Seedling) × (Red Dawn × Suzanne)*; Svejda, Felicitas; Agriculture Canada. Flowers dark red, dbl. (30 petals), large; slight fragrance; foliage small, dark yellow-green; straight, yellow-green prickles; bushy growth; repeat bloom; hardy.

Champneys' Pink Cluster N (OGR), *lp*, (Champneys' Rose); *R. chinensis × R. moschata*; Champneys, ca. 1811. Flowers pink, dbl., borne in large clusters; moderately vigorous growth; moderately hardy; recurrent. The first Noisette; also see *R. × noisettiana; (14)*.

Champs-Elysées® HT, *dr*, 1957, (MEIcarl; MEIcari); *Monique × Happiness*; Meilland, F.; URS. Flowers rich crimson-red, dbl. (35 petals), cupped, large; slightly fragrant; vigorous, bushy growth. GM, Madrid, 1957.

Champs-Elysées, Climbing® Cl HT, *dr*, 1969, (MEIcarlsar); Meilland; URS.

Chandelle F, *lp*, 1958, *Gretel Greul × (Lady Sylvia × Fashion)*; Lens. Flowers light pink, reverse darker, dbl., well formed, medium, borne in clusters; very fragrant; foliage bronze; vigorous, compact growth.

Chanderi HT, *lp*, 1968, *Peace × Seedling*; Singh. Bud long, pointed; flowers light pink, edged deeper, dbl., high-centered; medium; slightly fragrant; foliage soft; moderate, upright, compact growth.

Chandrama F, *w*, 1980, *White Bouquet × Virgo*; Division of Veg. Crops & Floriculture. Bud pointed; flowers white, dbl. (25 petals), borne in clusters of 3-6; mild fragrance; foliage dark; straight, brown prickles; spreading growth.

Chanelle F, *op*, 1959, *Ma Perkins × (Fashion × Mrs. William Sprott)*; McGredy, S., IV; McGredy. Flowers peach-pink shaded rose-pink, dbl. (20 petals), well-formed, large (3 in.) blooms in clusters; fragrant; foliage dark, glossy, pointed; vigorous, bushy growth. GM, Madrid, 1959.

Chanoine Tuaillon HT, *dp*, 1931, *Betty Uprichard × Lucie Nicolas Meyer*; Gillot, F. Bud persian red; flowers carmine, dbl., globular, very large; fragrant; very vigorous growth.

Chantal HT, *w*, 1958, *Mme. Charles Sauvage × Carillon*; Moulin-Epinay. Bud long, ovoid; flowers ivory, center yellow, edged carmine, dbl. (60 petals), very large; fragrant; vigorous, bushy, upright growth.

Chanteclerc F, *mr*, 1956, *Peace × Seedling*; Gaujard. Flowers bright red, large; foliage bright green; bushy growth.

Chantilly HT, *or*, 1964, *Baccará × Seedling*; Verschuren, A.; van Engelen. Flowers orange to red-lead, dbl. (40 petals), strong stems; foliage glossy, dark; vigorous growth.

Chantilly Lace HT, *m*, 1978, *Blue Moon × Angel Face*; DeVor, P.; DeVor Nursery. Bud long; flowers red-purple, dbl. (35 petals), high-centered, large (4-5 in.); very fragrant; foliage glossy; vigorous; greenhouse variety.

Chantré HT, *ob*, 1958, *Fred Streeter × Antheor*; Kordes, R. Bud long, pointed; flowers orange and golden yellow, dbl. (20-25 petals), high-centered, large (5 in.); fragrant; foliage dark, leathery; very vigorous, upright, bushy growth.

Chapelain d'Arenberg G (OGR), *mp*, Flowers bright pink.

Chaperon Rouge F, *mr*, 1951, *Crimson Glory × (Baby Chateau × Seedling)*; Vilmorin-Andrieux. Bud globular; flowers velvety crimson, center darker, very dbl., open, medium; fragrant; foliage glossy, bronze, dark; vigorous, upright growth.

Chaplin's Crimson Glow LCl, *rb*, 1930, Chaplin Bros.; Like Paul's Scarlet Climber except color. Flowers deep crimson, base white, full, large.

Chaplin's Pink Climber LCl, *mp*, 1928, *Paul's Scarlet Climber × American Pillar*; Chaplin Bros. Flowers bright pink, stamens golden yellow, semi-dbl., flat, large blooms in large clusters; very vigorous growth; non-recurrent bloom; (28). GM, NRS, 1928.

Chaplin's Pink Companion LCl, *lp*, 1961, *Chaplin's Pink Climber × Opera*; Chaplin, H.J.; Chaplin & Sons. Flowers silvery pink, dbl. (22 petals), medium (2in.) blooms in clusters of up to 30; fragrant; foliage glossy; vigorous growth.

Chaplin's Triumph HT, *dr*, 1936, Chaplin Bros. Bud long, pointed; flowers deep velvety crimson; very fragrant; foliage dark; vigorous growth.

Charade F, *op*, 1965, *Queen Elizabeth × Seedling*; Herholdt, J.A. Flowers coral-cerise tinted salmon, dbl., pointed, large (3 in.), borne in clusters; foliage glossy; free growth.

Charade™ F, *dr*, 1988, *Cindy × Sassy*; Hill, Joseph H., Co.; DeVor Nursery, 1988. Flowers cardinal-red, dbl. (20-25 petals), high-centered, small, borne in sprays of 2-5; mini flora; slight fragrance; foliage medium, dark green, semi-glossy; prickles straight, medium, lilac; bushy, profuse growth

Chariot of Roses Min, *dr*, 1986, *Seedling × Fairy Moss*; Fischer, C.&H.; Alpenflora Gardens. Flowers dark red, dbl. (25 petals), medium blooms borne singly; no fragrance; foliage small, dark, matt; small, nearly straight, reddish prickles; fruit small, globular; long, pendulous growth.

Charisma HT, *or*, 1973, Meilland. Flowers orange-red. RULED EXTINCT 3/77 ARM.

Charisma F, *rb*, 1977, (JELroganor; Surprise Party); *Gemini × Zorina*; Hill, E.G., Co.; C-P. Bud ovoid; flowers scarlet and yellow, dbl. (40 petals), high-centered, medium (2-2½ in.); slightly fragrant; foliage glossy, leathery; vigorous, bushy, upright growth. GM, Portland, 1976; AARS, 1978.

Charity HT, *mr*, 1953, *Will Rogers × Mme. Henri Guillot*; Taylor, C.A. Flowers bright velvety red, dbl. (40-50 petals), high-centered, large (5 in.); fragrant; foliage glossy; vigorous, upright, bushy growth.

Charivari S, *yb*, 1971, (KORub); *Königin der Rosen × Goldrausch*; Kordes, R. Bud ovoid; flowers golden yellow to salmon, dbl., cupped, large; fragrant; foliage glossy; vigorous, upright, bushy growth.

Charles Albanel HRg (S), *mr*, 1982, *Souv. de Philemon Cochet × Seedling*; Svejda, Felicitas; Agriculture Canada. Flowers medium red, dbl. (20 petals), medium; fragrant; foliage yellow-green, rugose; straight, gray-green prickles; low, spreading growth; repeat bloom; ground cover.

Charles Austin® S, *ab*, 1981, *Chaucer × Aloha*; Austin, David; David Austin Roses, 1973. Bud globular; flowers apricot tinged pink, fadingto light pink, dbl. (70 petals), rosette, borne 1-7 per cluster; fragrant; foliage medium green, dense; hooked, red prickles; vigorous, upright, bushy growth.

Charles Bonnet HP (OGR), *dp*, 1884, Bonnet. Flowers dark rose, dbl., medium; repeats.

Charles Cretté HT, *mp*, 1917, Chambard, C. Flowers velvety rose, large.

Charles Darwin HP (OGR), *mp*, 1879, *Mme. Julian Daran seedling*; Laxton Bros.; W. Paul. Flowers brownish crimson, large.

Charles de Gaulle® HT, *m*, 1974, (MEIlanein; Katherine Mansfield); *(Sissi × Prelude) × (Kordes' Sondermeldung × Caprice)*; Meilland, M.L.; URS. Flowers lilac, dbl. (38 petals), globular, then cupped, large (3½-4 in.); very fragrant; vigorous.

Charles de Lapisse HT, *lp*, 1910, *Mme. Caroline Testout sport*; Laroulandie. Flowers pale blush-pink.

Charles de Mills G (OGR), *m*, (Bizarre Triomphante); Original name and date unknown. Flowers dark crimson and purple, many petaled, quartered, large (4½ in.); very few prickles; height to 5 ft.

Charles Dickens F, *op*, 1970, *Paddy McGredy × Elizabeth of Glamis*; McGredy, S., IV; McGredy. Flowers rosy salmon, semi-dbl. (16 petals), large (3 in.); slightly fragrant.

Charles Dillon F, *mp*, 1970, *Orangeade × Piccadilly*; Wood; Homedale Nursery. Flowers soft pink, dbl. (24 petals), large; slightly fragrant; foliage dark; low, bushy growth.

Charles Duval HP (OGR), *mr*, 1847, Laffay. Flowers scarlet, full, cupped; vigorous growth.

Charles E. Shea HT, *mp*, 1917, *Mrs. George Shawyer sport*; Hicks. Flowers rich pink.

Charles F. Warren HT, *mr*, 1957, *Wilfred Pickles × Karl Herbst*; Mee. Flowers rose-pink, dbl. (40 petals), well-formed, large; fragrant; vigorous growth.

Charles Gater HP (OGR), *mr*, 1893, Paul. Flowers red, dbl. (40 petals), globular; fragrant; vigorous.

Charles Gregory HT, *ob*, 1947, Verschuren; Gregory. Flowers vermilion, shaded gold, dbl. (22 petals), well-formed; fragrant; foliage dark, glossy; vigorous.

Charles Gregory, Climbing Cl HT, *ob*, 1960, Gregory.

Charles Henry HT, *mr*, 1967, *Ena Harkness × Lady Sylvia*; Hooney. Flowers crimson; fragrant; foliage dark; vigorous, upright growth.

Charles H. Rigg HT, *mr*, 1931, Chaplin Bros. Flowers bright red fading to pink; full, large; stout, erect stems; fragrant; vigorous growth.

Charles J. Grahame HT, *mr*, 1905, Dickson, A. Flowers dazzling scarlet, well formed, large; very fragrant; vigorous growth.

Charles K. Douglas HT, *mr*, 1919, Dickson, H. Bud long, pointed; flowers medium red, dbl. (28 petals), large; fragrant; foliage dark; vigorous growth.

Charles K. Douglas, Climbing Cl HT, *mr*, 1934, Leenders Bros.

Charles Lawson B (OGR), *dp*, 1853, Lawson. Flowers vivid rose; vigorous, compact growth.

Charles Lefèbvre HP (OGR), *dr*, 1861, *Général Jacqueminot* × *Victor Verdier*; Lacharme. Flowers reddish crimson shaded purple, full (70 petals), cupped, large; fragrant; vigorous, tall growth; bloom often recurrent.

Charles Mallerin HT, *dr*, 1951, *(Rome Glory* × *Congo)* × *Tassin*; Meilland, F.; C-P. Flowers blackish crimson, dbl. (38 petals), flat, large (6 in.); very fragrant; foliage leathery, dark; vigorous, irregular growth.

Charles Mallerin, Climbing Cl HT, *dr*, 1960, Balducci & Figli.

Charles P. Kilham HT, *or*, 1926, McGredy; Beckwith. Flowers red-orange, fading to lincoln red, dbl. (32 petals), well formed, large; slightly fragrant; vigorous, bushy growth. GM, NRS, 1927.

Charles P. Kilham, Climbing Cl HT, *or*, 1931, Howard Rose Co.

Charles P. Kilham, Climbing Cl HT, *or*, 1934, Morse.

Charles Quint G (OGR), *m*, 1880, Moreau-Robert. Flowers lilac-rose and white.

Charles Rovalli T (OGR), *dp*, 1876, Pernet Père. Flowers carmine-rose; moderate growth.

Charles William HT, *pb*, 1989, *Bradenburg* × *Command Performance*; Cattermole, R.F. Bud urn-shaped; flowers carmine rose, reverse lighter, yellow at base of petals, very dbl. (56 petals), pointed, reflexing bloom, large, borne usually singly; very little fragrance; foliage matt, medium green, large; prickles light brown; upright, tall growth.

Charleston F, *yb*, 1963, (MEIridge); *Masquerade* × *(Radar* × *Caprice)*; Meilland, Alain; URS, Wheatcroft Bros.; Wheatcroft & Sons. Bud pointed; flowers yellow flushed crimson, becoming crimson, dbl. (20 petals), large (3 in.) blooms in clusters; slightly fragrant; foliage dark, leathery, glossy; upright, compact growth.

Charleston, Climbing Cl F, *yb*, 1966, Rumsey.

Charlie™ Min, *mr*, 1984, (KINcha); *Seedling* × *Big John*; King, Gene. Flowers medium red, dbl. (35 petals), exhibition, small; no fragrance; foliage small, dark, matt; upright, bushy.

Charlie McCarthy F, *w*, 1955, *Mrs. Dudley Fulton* × *Mermaid*; Wiseman; H&S. Bud creamy white; flowers pure white, dbl. (28 petals), medium (1½-2 in.) blooms in clus-

ters; fragrant; foliage glossy, leathery, dark; dwarf, compact growth.

Charlie Perkins HT, *dr*, 1970, *Carrousel* × *Circus*; Zombory; General Bionomics. Bud long, pointed; flowers dark red, overlaid black, semi-dbl., full, large; fragrant; foliage large, glossy, dark, bronze, leathery; very vigorous, upright, bushy growth.

Charlie's Aunt HT, *pb*, 1965, *Golden Masterpiece* × *Karl Herbst*; McGredy. S., IV; Geest Industries. Flowers cream, heavily suffused rose, dbl. (65 petals), high-pointed, large (5 in.); fragrant; foliage dark.

Charlie's Uncle HT, *rb*, 1975, *Charlie's Aunt* sport; Haynes. Flowers cream, suffused carmine, dbl. (40 petals), full, high-centered, very large (5-6 in.); slightly fragrant; foliage large, leathery.

Charlotte HT, *op*, 1941, *Joanna Hill* × *Golden Dawn*; Duehrsen; California Roses. Bud long, pointed; flowers salmon-pink and coral, base gold, dbl., high-centered; very fragrant; foliage glossy; vigorous, bushy growth.

Charlotte Armstrong HT, *dp*, 1940, *Soeur Thérèse* × *Crimson Glory*; Lammerts; Armstrong Nursery. Bud long, pointed, blood-red; flowers deep pink, dbl. (35 petals), large (3-4 in.); fragrant; foliage dark, leathery; vigorous, compact growth.AARS, 1941; ARS John Cook Medal, 1941; ARS David Fuerstenberg Prize, 1941; GM, Portland, 1941; ARS Gertrude M. Hubbard, 1945; & NRS, 1950

Charlotte Armstrong, Climbing Cl HT, *dp*, 1942, Morris; Armstrong Nursery, 1942; Mon Reve Nursery, 1950.

Charlotte Chevalier HT, *dy*, 1916, *Arthur R. Goodwin* sport; Chambard, C. Flowers dark canary-yellow.

Charlotte Elizabeth Gr, *dp*, 1965, Norman; Harkness. Flowers deep rose-pink, dbl. (26 petals), high-centered, large (3-4 in.) blooms in clusters; foliage glossy.

Charlotte E. van Dedem HT, *my*, 1937, *Roselandia* × *Ville de Paris*; Buisman. Bud long, pointed; flowers yellow, semi-dbl., large; foliage glossy; vigorous. GM, Portland, 1938.

Charlotte Ives F, *pb*, 1965, *Ma Perkins* × *Rose Gaujard*; Warren. Bud globular; flowers rose-pink, center light yellow, single, open, medium, borne in clusters; slightly fragrant; compact, upright, bushy growth.

Charlotte Klemm Ch (OGR), *or*, 1905, Türke. Flowers red shaded orange, semi-dbl., medium.

Charlotte Pate HT, *yb*, 1971, *Wendy Cussons* × *Golden Sun*; MacLeod. Bud globular; flowers pink, yellow reverse, dbl. (25 petals), medium (3½ in.); very fragrant; foliage medium, medium green, glossy.

Charlotte von Rathlef R, *lp*, 1936, *Frageze-ichen* × *American Pillar*; Vogel, M.; Heinemann. Flowers light pink, very dbl.; foliage leathery, dark; vigorous climbing growth; abundant seasonal bloom.

Charlotte Wheatcroft F, *mr*, 1957, Wheatcroft Bros. Flowers bright scarlet, single, large, large truss; foliage dark, glossy; vigorous, tall growth.

Charlotte Wierel Pol, *w*, 1926, *Bebe Leroux* × *Helene Videnz*; Walter, L. Flowers cream-white, center bright rose-pink; vigorous growth.

Charm HT, *op*, 1920, Paul, W. Bud reddish orange, shaded pink and copper; flowers coppery yellow.

Charm Bracelet Min, *dy*, 1992, (JACfog); *Fool's Gold* × *Seedling*; Christensen, Jack; Bear Creek Gardens, 1992. Flowers dark yellow, aging to pink, red blush on petal tips of outer guard petals, very full (41+ petals), good bud and flower form, small (0-4 cms) blooms borne mostly singly; slight fragrance; foliage small, dark green, semi-glossy; some prickles; low (45 cms), bushy, compact growth.

Charm of Paris HT, *mp*, 1965, *Prima Ballerina* × *Montezuma*; Tantau, Math. Flowers pink, dbl. (48 petals), medium (3½ in.); fragrant; vigorous growth. Edland Fragrance Medal, 1966.

Charmaine Pol, *mp*, 1929, *Evelyn Thornton seedling*; Burbage Nursery. Flowers pink tinged salmon, dbl., open, sprays on long stems; fragrant; foliage bright, glossy; very vigorous, bushy growth; recurrent bloom.

Charmant® Min, *mr*, 1987, (KORzimko); *((Seedling* × *Tornado)* × *KORkonig)* × *Trumpeter*; Kordes, W. Flowers medium red, dbl. (40 petals), small; no fragrance; foliage small, medium green, semi-glossy; bushy growth.

Charme HT, *dp*, 1930, (Charm; Germania); Rice Bros. Co. Bud long, pointed; flowers cherry-red, dbl., large; fragrant; foliage glossy; vigorous growth.

Charmente HT, *lp*, 1975, *Fragrant Cloud* × *Ena Harkness*; Huber. Bud globular; flowers light pink, dbl. (42 petals), shallow, large (4 in.); foliage bright green, leathery; upright, spreading growth.

Charmer HT, *lp*, 1923, *Pharisaer seedling* × *Joseph Hill*; Schoener; Doyle. Flowers silvery pink.

Charmer HT, *lp*, 1934, Dickson, A. Flowers light pink, center shaded salmon, full, high-

centered, large; fragrant; foliage leathery; vigorous, free branching growth. GM, NRS, 1932.

Charmglo Min, *pb*, 1980, *Seedling* × *Over the Rainbow*; Williams, Ernest D.; Mini-Roses. Bud long, pointed; flowers creamy white painted deep pink, reverse lighter, dbl. (35 petals), high-centered, borne usually singly; some fragrance; foliage small, medium to dark green, slightly matt; long, thin, brown prickles, curved down; bushy, compact growth.

Charmian® S, *mp*, 1983, (AUSmian); *Seedling* × *Lilian Austin*; Austin, David; David Austin Roses, 1982. Flowers medium pink, dbl. (40+ petals), large; very fragrant; foliage medium, medium green, semi-glossy; spreading growth.

Charming HT, *mp*, 1922, *Alexander Hill Gray* × *Mme. Edouard Herriot*; Van Rossem. Flowers salmon-pink, reverse coral-pink, semi-dbl.; slightly fragrant.

Charming Maid F, *ob*, 1953, *Dainty Maid* × *Mrs. Sam McGredy*; LeGrice. Bud orange-salmon; flowers salmon, base golden, single (5-6 petals), large (4-4½ in.) blooms in trusses; fragrant; foliage dark, glossy. GM, NRS, 1953.

Charming Princess HT, *yb*, 1926, *The Queen Alexandra Rose sport*; Hancock. Flowers deep yellow, edged vermilion; full, large; foliage dark; vigorous growth.

Chartreuse HT, *my*, 1940, *Soeur Thérèse* × *Angels Mateu*; Mallerin; A. Meilland. Bud long; flowers canary-yellow, dbl.; fragrant; foliage glossy; bushy growth.

Chase Beauty HT, *dr*, 1947, *Better Times sport*; Chase; Chase Gardens. Bud long; flowers rich dark red, dbl. (35-45 petals), high-centered, large (5½ in.), slightly fragrant; foliage dark; very vigorous, tall growth.

Chasin' Rainbows™ Min, *rb*, 1988, (SAVachase; Chasing Rainbows); *Zorina* × *Rainbow's End*; Saville, F. Harmon; Nor'East Miniature Roses, 1990. Bud ovoid; flowers very brilliant yellow, edged red with scarlet becoming more prominent when bloom opens, dbl. (21 petals), high-centered, exhibition, small, borne singly and in sprays of 3-24 or more; micro-mini; slight, spicy fragrance; foliage small, dark green, semi-glossy; prickles long, thin, angle, light brown; fruit none; bushy, low growth.

Chastity Cl HT, *w*, 1924, Cant, F. Flowers pure white, base lemon, dbl., high-centered; foliage light, glossy; vigorous; non-recurrent bloom.

Château d'Amboise® HT, *rb*, 1988, (DELrouvel); *Tropicana seedling* × *(Rome Glory* ×

Impeccable) × *(Rouge Meilland × Soraya)*; Delbard & Chabert. Flowers dark red, opening bright, dbl. (23-30 petals), long; slight fragrance; foliage bright; vigorous, semi-raised growth.

Château de Chenonceaux HT, *mp*, 1973, *Americana × Queen Elizabeth*; Gaujard. Flowers brilliant pink, dbl. (45 petals), large; tall growth.

Château de Clos Vougeot HT, *dr*, 1908, Pernet-Ducher. Flowers deep velvety red, dbl. (75 petals); very fragrant (damask); foliage dark, leathery; sprawling growth.

Château de Clos Vougeot, Climbing Cl HT, *dr*, 1920, Morse.

Château de Vaire S, *dr*, 1934, (Vaire); *Charles K. Douglas × R. macrophylla*; Sauvageot. Flowers deep red, dbl., cupped; foliage bronze, dark; height 3½-6½ ft., bushy; non-recurrent bloom.

Château La Salle HT, *yb*, 1966, *Joanna Hill × Ellinor LeGrice*; Morey; Country Garden Nursery. Bud long, pointed; flowers buff-yellow, dbl., high-centered, large; very fragrant; foliage dark, leathery; vigorous, bushy, compact growth.

Château Pelles HT, *lp*, 1927, *Harry Kirk seedling*; Mühle. Bud cream-white; flowers soft pink, shaded salmon, dbl; slightly fragrant.

Châtelaine F, *op*, 1957, *(Peace × Seedling) × Fashion*; Lens. Bud pointed; flowers coral overcast salmon, dbl. (32 petals), well formed, large (3 in.), borne in small clusters; fragrant; foliage glossy, coppery; vigorous growth.

Châtelet HT, *mp*, 1952, (Airain); *Yvonne Plassat × Seedling*; Moulin-Epinay; Vilmorin-Andrieux. Bud globular, coral; flowers pink heavily tinted simon, very dbl., medium.

Chatillon Rambler R, *mp*, 1913, *Dorothy Perkins × Crimson Rambler*; Nonin. Flowers salmon-pink, semi-dbl., small; slightly fragrant; height 15-20 ft.

Chatillon Rose Pol, *mp*, 1923, *Orléans Rose × Seedling*; Nonin. Flowers bright pink, semi-dbl., cupped blooms in large clusters; fragrant; foliage glossy; bushy (1-2 ft.).

Chattem Centennial™ Min, *or*, 1979, *Orange Sensation × Zinger*; Jolly, B.; Rosehill Farm. Bud ovoid; flowers orange-red, dbl. (38 petals), cupped, medium; slightly fragrant (fruity); upright, bushy growth.

Chattem Centennial, Climbing Cl Min, *or*, 1990, *Chattem Centennial sport*; Jolly, Marie; Rosehill Farm, 1991. Bud ovoid; flowers orange-red, orange-red reverse, aging light orange, dbl. (38 petals), cupped, loose, medium, borne usually singly or in sprays of

3-5; slight, fruity fragrance; foliage medium, light green, matt; tall (4-6 ft.) growth.

Chatter F, *mr*, 1947, *World's Fair × Betty Prior*; Boerner; J&P. Flowers velvety bright crimson, semi-dbl. (14 petals), cupped, medium blooms in large clusters; fragrant; bushy, compact growth; (28).

Chatter, Climbing Cl F, *mr*, 1960, Schmidt, K.

Chatterbox F, *ob*, 1973, *Sarabande × Circus*; Sanday. Flowers bright orange-vermilion, semi-dbl. (16 petals), rosette, medium (2 in.); foliage glossy; dwarf.

Chaucer® S, *mp*, 1981, *Seedling × Constance Spry*; Austin, David; David Austin Roses, 1970. Bud globular; flowers medium pink, cupped, quartered, blooms borne 1-5 per cluster; very fragrant; foliage medium green; slightly hooked, red prickles; vigorous, upright, bushy growth.

Checkers Min, *mr*, 1990, (PIXchek); *Deep Purple × Happy Hour*; Chaffin, Lauren M.; Pixie Treasures Miniature Roses. Bud pointed; flowers medium red, aging darker, semi-dbl. (20 petals), high-centered, medium blooms borne singly; slight, spicy fragrance; foliage small, medium green, semi-glossy; prickles needle-shaped, tan; fruit rarely forms; bushy, low growth.

Cheer F, *mp*, 1941, *Dance of Joy × Golden Rapture*; Kordes; J&P. Flowers deep rose-pink, semi-dbl., open, large (4 in.), cluster; fragrant; foliage leathery; vigorous, upright growth. RULED EXTINCT 1/84 ARM.

Cheer Up Min, *ob*, 1986, (TINcheer); *Futura × Bread 'n' Butter*; Bennett, Dee; Tiny Petals Nursery. Flowers deep orange, dbl. (28 petals), urn-shaped to high-centered, exhibition, medium blooms borne usually singly and in sprays of 3-4; slight fragrance; foliage medium, dark, semi-glossy; small, red prickles; fruit globular,½ in., green and brown; medium, upright, bushy growth.

Cheerful HT, *ob*, 1915, McGredy. Flowers orange-flame, base yellow, dbl., very large; fragrant; foliage rich green, glossy.

Cheerfulness F, *op*, 1981, *Seedling × Seedling*; Everett, D.; Gandy Roses, Ltd. Flowers orange, pink and yellow blend, 8 petals, borne 10 per cluster; slight fragrance; foliage small; small, brown prickles; compact growth.

Cheerleader™ Min, *dr*, 1986, (MORcheer); *Fairy Moss × Orange Honey*; Moore, R.S.; Moore Min. Roses, 1985. Flowers dark red, very dbl., small blooms in sprays of 5-10; no fragrance; foliage small, medium green, semi-glossy; fruit none; bushy, spreading growth.

Cheers™ Min, *ob*, 1984, (SAValot); *Poker Chip × Zinger*; Saville, F. Harmon; Nor'East Min. Roses. Flowers orange-red, cream reverse, dbl. (20 petals); slight fragrance; foliage small, medium green, semi-glossy; compact, bushy growth.

Cheery Chatter Min, *mr*, 1984, (LYOter); *Dandy Lyon × Seedling*; Lyon, Lyndon; Lyon Greenhouse. Flowers medium red, dbl. (20 petals), medium; fragrant; foliage small, medium green, semi-glossy; upright, bushy growth.

Chelsea HT, *mr*, 1950, LeGrice. Flowers carmine shaded orient red, dbl., large (4 in.); fragrant; vigorous, compact growth. RULED EXTINCT 6/86.

Chelsea Min, *mp*, 1986, (MORsea); *(Little Darling × Yellow Magic) × Crested Jewel*; Moore, R.S.; Sequoia Nursery. Flowers medium pink, dbl. (25 petals), cupped, small blooms with lacy sepals, borne in clusters of 5 or more; slightly fragrant; foliage small to medium, medium green, semi-glossy; fruit few, globular, medium, orange; upright, bushy growth. First Miniature with sepals like Crested Moss.

Chelsea Belle Min, *mr*, 1991, (TALchelsea); *Azure Sea × Party Girl*; Taylor, Pete & Kay, 1987; Taylor's Roses, 1990. Bud ovoid; glowers medium red with white base, whitish reverse, ages lighter, dbl. (28-30 petals), high-centered, exhibition, medium, borne singly; moderate fragrance; foliage medium, medium green, semi-glossy; upright, bushy, medium growth.

Chelsea Gold F, *ab*, 1985, (LANwool); *Arthur Bell × Elizabeth of Glamis*; Sealand Nurseries, Ltd. Flowers apricot, dbl. (20 petals), medium; slight fragrance; foliage medium, medium green, semi-glossy; many prickles; bushy growth.

Chelsea Pensioner Min, *mr*, 1982, (MATtche); *Gold Pin seedling × Seedling*; Mattock, John; John Mattock, Ltd. Flowers scarlet, dbl. (20 petals), patio, small; slight fragrance; foliage small, dark, semi-glossy; bushy growth.

Chénédolé HCh (OGR), *or*, Thierry, prior to 1848. Flowers light vermilion, dbl., cupped, very large; fragrant; good seed bearer; shoots very prickly; vigorous, upright growth.

Cheré Michelle Min, *op*, 1986, (Cherie Michelle); *Sheri Anne × Anita Charles*; Jolly, Marie; Rosehill Farm, 1987. Flowers white with coral pink petal edges, reverse same, dbl. (30 petals), high-centered, exhibition, small blooms borne singly and in sprays of 2-3; slightly fragrant; foliage medium, medium green, semi-glossy; small, cream to light brown prickles, slightly hooked downward; fruit medium, globular, orange-green; medium, upright growth.

Chérie F, *mp*, 1931, (Cheerio; Cheerie); *Else Poulsen sport*; Morse. Flowers bright rose-pink, dbl., cupped, small, borne in clusters; fragrant; foliage leathery; vigorous, bushy growth.

Chérie F, *ob*, 1964, Gaujard. Bud long; flowers bright orange, reverse coppery, dbl., well formed.

Cherish F, *op*, 1980, (JACsal); *Bridal Pink × Matador*; Warriner; J&P. Bud short, flat; flowers coral-pink, dbl. (28 petals), high-centered, large (3 in.); slightly fragrant; foliage large, dark; compact, spreading growth. AARS, 1980.

Cherokee Fire Min, *dr*, 1982, (LYOch); *Merry Christmas × Seedling*; Lyon, Lyndon; Lyndon Lyon Greenhouse. Flowers deep red, semi-dbl., medium; no fragrance; foliage medium green, semi-glossy; upright, bushy growth.

Cherrio F, *dp*, 1937, Archer. Flowers carmine-cerise, semi-dbl., cupped, large, borne in clusters; slightly fragrant; vigorous, compact growth.

Cherrio F, *mp*, 1948, (Planten un Blomen); *Holstein × Sapho*; Kordes. Flowers light pink, reverse darker, semi-dbl.; vigorous, bushy growth.

Cherry HT, *pb*, 1928, McGredy. Flowers brilliant carmine-pink flushed yellow, lower half yellow, dbl., high-centered, large; fragrant; vigorous, bushy growth.

Cherry Blossom F, *mp*, 1964, *Fashion × Seedling*; Verschuren, A.; van Engelen. Bud orient red; flowers rose-pink to camellia-pink, dbl. (26 petals), borne in clusters; foliage glossy, dark; compact growth.

Cherry Bomb Min, *ob*, 1991, (JOLcher); *Fashion Flame × Sheri Anne*; Jolly, Marie; Rosehill Farm, 1991-92. Flowers orange, very full (41+ petals), small (0-4 cms), blooms borne mostly singly; no fragrance; foliage small, medium green, semi-glossy; few prickles; medium, upright growth.

Cherry Brandy® HT, *ob*, 1965, Tantau, Math. Flowers orange, dbl. (30 petals), large (5 in.); fragrant; foliage dark, glossy, leathery; very vigorous, upright growth.

Cherry Charm LCl, *pb*, 1976, *Norwich Salmon × (Yellow sport × Peeping Tom)*; MacLeod. Flowers deep pink, reverse silver pink, dbl. (25 petals), large (5 in.); slightly fragrant; foliage dark; non-recurrent.

Cherry, Climbing Cl HT, *pb*, 1934, Savage Nursery.

Cherry Glow Gr, *mr*, 1959, *Floradora × First Love*; Swim; C.R. Burr. Flowers cherry-red, dbl. (23 petals), cupped, large (3-4 in.); fragrant (spicy); foliage leathery, glossy; vigorous, upright growth.

Cherry Jubilee S, *mr*, 1991, (JACsos); *Seedling × Simplicity*; Warriner, William A.; Bear Creek Gardens, Inc. Flowers light to medium red, moderately full (15-25 petals), medium; no fragrance; foliage medium, medium green, semi-glossy; upright, bushy growth.

Cherry Magic™ Min, *dr*, 1988, (MORchermag); *Anytime × Lavender Jewel*; Moore, Ralph S.; Sequoia Nursery. Flowers deep red, reverse lighter red with silver sheen, aging lighter, dbl. (25 petals), high-centered, small, borne singly or in sprays of 3-7 or more, abundant; no fragrance; foliage small, medium green, matt; prickles short, small, brown; Fruit round, small, orange to red; bushy, spreading, low growth.

Cherry Page HT, *pb*, 1914, *Duchess of Bedford × Le Progres*; Easlea. Flowers carmine-pink, base yellow.

Cherry Pie HT, *dp*, 1965, Gaujard; Gandy. Flowers deep rose-pink, dbl., high-centered, large (4½ in.); slightly fragrant.

Cherry Ripe F, *mr*, 1949, *Orange Triumph sport*; Heers; Pacific Nursery. Flowers scarlet, dbl. (70 petals), small; vigorous growth; intermittent bloom.

Cherry Velvet® HT, *dp*, 1988, (POUltress); *Vision × Seedling*; Olesen, Mogens & Pernille; Poulsen Roser ApS, 1986. Flowers deep pink, dbl. (20 petals), large; fragrant; foliage large, medium green, glossy; upright, vigorous growth.

Cherryade S, *dp*, 1961, *New Dawn × Red Wonder*; deRuiter. Flowers deep pink, dbl. (40 petals), well-formed, large (4 in.); fragrant; foliage dark; vigorous, tall growth.

Cherry-Rose HT, *mp*, 1946, *Pink Princess × Crimson Glory*; Brownell. Bud long, pointed; flowers cherry-rose, dbl., high-centered, very large; fragrant; foliage glossy; very vigorous, upright, compact growth.

Cherry-Vanilla Gr, *pb*, 1973, (ARMilla); *Buccaneer × El Capitan*; Armstrong, D.L.; Armstrong Nursery. Bud pointed; flowers pink, center creamy yellow, dbl., cupped, medium; fragrant; foliage dark, leathery; vigorous, upright, bushy growth.

Cherub R, *pb*, 1923, *Claire Jacquier seedling*; Clark, A.; Brundrett. Flowers pink and salmon, semi-dbl., cupped, small; foliage rich green, glossy, wrinkled; very vigorous, climbing growth; profuse, non-recurrent bloom.

Chervena Ghita HT, *mr*, 1974, *General Stefanik × Peace*; Staikov, Prof. Dr. V.; Kalaydjiev and Chorbadjiiski. Flowers bright cerise, dbl. (75 petals), large blooms in clusters; foliage dark, glossy; vigorous, upright growth.

Cheryl's Delight™ Min, *pb*, 1984, (MINrco); *Little Darling × Over the Rainbow*; Williams, Ernest D.; Mini-Roses. Flowers medium pink, reverse white, dbl. (35 petals), small; slight fragrance; foliage small, dark, semi-glossy; bushy growth.

Chesapeake Min, *lp*, 1984, *Rise 'n' Shine × (Helen Traubel × First Prize)*; Jolly, Nelson F.; Rosehill Farm. Flowers light pink, dbl. (50 petals), small; slight fragrance; foliage medium, medium green, semi-glossy; bushy growth.

Cheshire Cream F, *w*, 1975, *(Anna Wheatcroft × Ivory Fashion) × (Buff Beauty × Masquerade)*; Holmes, R.; Fryer's Nursery. Flowers soft buff, becoming cream, dbl. (50 petals), medium (2½ in.); fragrant (spicy); foliage small, glossy; low growth.

Cheshire Lady HT, *pb*, 1968, *Fragrant Cloud × Gavotte*; Dale, F. Flowers bright pink to scarlet, dbl. (30-40 petals), large; free growth.

Cheshire Life HT, *or*, 1972, *Prima Ballerina × Princess Michiko*; Fryer, G.; Fryer's Nursery. Flowers vermilion, dbl. (36 petals), spiral, large (5 in.); slightly fragrant; foliage dark, leathery.

Cheshunt Hybrid HT, *mr*, 1872, *Believed to be Mme. de Tartas × Prince Camille de Rohan*; Paul. Flowers red shaded violet, full, large; vigorous growth. Possibly the first English Hybrid Tea.

Chessum's Choice Sp (OGR), *w*, 1988, (CHEstock); *Pfander's Canina sport*; Chessum, Paul; Alan Thompson. For use as a stem of (standard) tree roses.

Chester F, *my*, 1976, *Arthur Bell × Zambra*; Bees. Flowers golden yellow, semi-dbl. (15 petals), large (3 in.); slightly fragrant; foliage glossy, dark; vigorous growth.

Chester Cathedral HT, *ab*, 1990, (FRAnshine); *Honey Favorite × Piccadilly*; Cowlishaw, Frank R., 1989. Bud pointed; flowers light apricot with cream/very light gold reverse, dbl., high-centered, medium, borne usually singly; slight fragrance; foliage medium, dark green, glossy; low, bushy growth.

Chevreul M (OGR), *mp*, 1887, Moreau-Robert. Flowers salmon-pink, well mossed; fruit large, colorful in fall.

Chevy Chase R, *dr*, 1939, *R. soulieana × Eblouissant*; Hansen, N.J.; B&A. Flowers dark crimson, dbl. (65 petals), small blooms in clusters of 10-20; fragrant; foliage soft, light green, wrinkled; vigorous, climbing (to 15 ft.); non-recurrent bloom. ARS Dr. W. Van Fleet Medal, 1941.

Cheyenne Cl HT, *lp*, 1962, *Queen Elizabeth* × *Seedling*; Abrams, Von; Peterson & Dering. Bud long, pointed; Flowers light pink, base coral pink, dbl. (30-40 petals), high centered, large (4-5 in.); slightly fragrant; Foliage leathery; Vigorous (6-7 ft.). RULED EXTINCT 1/85 ARM.

Cheyenne Min, *ab*, 1985, (SPOchey); *Rise 'n' Shine* × *Center Gold*; Spooner, Raymond A.; Oregon Min. Roses, Inc. Flowers golden apricot, dbl. (20 petals), medium blooms borne singly; very fragrant; foliage medium, medium green, semi-glossy; upright growth.

Cheyenne Frontier HT, *w*, 1971, *(Charlotte Armstrong* × *Vogue)* × *Peace*; Adams, M.R. Bud large; flowers white, slowly changing to red, dbl., high-centered, medium; slightly fragrant; foliage large, glossy, dark; moderate, upright growth.

Chez Vito HT, *mr*, 1972, *Paris-Match* × *(Baccará* × *Happiness)*; Meilland. Bud ovoid; flowers medium red, reverse lighter, dbl., high-centered, medium; fragrant; foliage large, leathery; vigorous, upright, bushy growth.

Chi lo Sà? HT, *yb*, 1965, *(Peace* × *Fiaba)* × *Seedling*; Giacomasso; Fratelli. Flowers yellow suffused red.

Chianti S, *m*, 1967, *Dusky Maiden* × *Tuscany*; Austin, D.; Sunningdale Nursery, 1965. Flowers purplish maroon, semi-dbl., borne in small clusters; slightly fragrant; foliage dark, glossy; vigorous growth; repeat bloom.

Chiarastella HT, *rb*, 1948, *Julien Potin* × *Mme. G. Forest-Colcombet*; Giacomasso; Fratelli. Flowers rose-red and yellow bicolor, dbl., well formed, large, strong stems; foliage glossy; vigorous growth.

Chic F, *pb*, 1953, *Pinocchio seedling* × *Fashion*; Boerner; J&P. Bud ovoid; flowers geranium-pink, dbl. (68 petals), cupped, medium (2½ in.) blooms in clusters; fragrant; vigorous, branching growth.

Chic Parisien F, *op*, 1956, Delbard-Chabert. Flowers coral-pink, center darker, dbl., well-formed blooms in clusters of 4-8; slightly fragrant; foliage dark; vigorous growth.

Chicago HT, *m*, 1928, *Premier sport*; Aldous. Flowers soft mauve-pink, dbl.; very fragrant.

Chicago Peace® HT, *pb*, 1962, (JOHnago); *Peace sport*; Johnston; C-P; URS. Flowers phlox-pink, base canary-yellow. GM, Portland, 1961.

Chick-a-dee Min, *mp*, 1990, (MORchick); *Cécile Brunner* × *(Dortmund* × *(Fairy Moss* × *(Little Darling* × *Ferdinand Pichard)))*; Moore, Ralph S.; Sequoia Nursery. Bud pointed; flowers medium pink with occasional white stripes, reverse similar, fading to slightly lighter, dbl. (40-50 petals), high-centered, exhibition blooms borne usually singly or in sprays of 3-9; slight fragrance; foliage small, medium green, matt to semi-glossy; prickles small, hooked downward, brownish; bushy, low, compact, rounded growth.

Chief Justice Holmes Cl HT, *dr*, 1935, *Jules Margottin* × *Château de Clos Vougeot*; Schoener. Flowers very dark red. GM, Portland, 1936.

Chief Seattle HT, *yb*, 1951, *Charlotte Armstrong* × *Signora*; Swim; Armstrong Nursery. Bud conical; flowers buff and old-gold, center shrimp-red, dbl. (55 petals), high-centered, large (4-5 in.); fragrant; foliage glossy; tall growth.

Chieftain HT, *rb*, 1936, *Hadley* × *Talisman*; Montgomery Co. Bud ovoid; flowers brilliant red, base yellow, dbl., high-centered, large; foliage leathery, dark; vigorous growth; a greenhouse variety.

Chiffon HT, *lp*, 1940, *Regina Elena sport*; Grillo. Flowers blush-pink, tinted light lavender, dbl. (30 petals), large (5½ in.); fragrant.

Child's Play Min, *w*, 1991, (SAVachild); *(Yellow Jewel* × *Tamango)* × *Party Girl*; Saville, F. Harmon; Nor'East Miniature Roses. Flowers pink/white bicolor, semi-dbl. (20+ petals), high-centered, medium (4 cms) blooms borne singly or in sprays of 3+; moderate, sweet fragrance; foliage medium, dark green, matt; upright, medium growth. AOE, 1993; AARS, 1993.

Chimo® S, *mr*, 1992, (INTercher); *Seedling* × *Immensee*; Ilsink, Peter; Interplant B.V. & W. Kordes, 1989. Flowers red aging dark red, single (5 petals), cupped, small (3 cms) blooms borne singly; slight fragrance; foliage medium, medium green, glossy; low(90 cms); spreading growth; repeats.

China Belle HCh (OGR), *pb*, 1980, *(Doubloons* × *Holiday)* × *Slater's Crimson China*; James, John. Bud ovoid; flowers light and medium pink blend with yellow, dbl. (26 frilled petals), cupped blooms borne 5-7 per cluster on short stems; mild fruity fragrance; foliage glossy; curved, red prickles; compact, bushy, upright growth.

China Doll Pol, *mp*, 1946, *Mrs. Dudley Fulton* × *Tom Thumb*; Lammerts; Armstrong Nursery. Bud pointed; flowers china-rose, base mimosa-yellow, dbl. (24 petals), cupped, small (1-2 in.) blooms in large trusses; slightly fragrant; foliage leathery, with mostly 5 leaflets (similar to Pinkie, which see); dwarf (18 in.), bushy growth.

China Doll, Climbing Cl Pol, *mp*, 1977, (Weeping China Doll); Weeks; Weeks Roses.

Chinatown® F, *dy*, 1963, (Ville de Chine); *Columbine* × *Clare Grammerstorf*; Poulsen, N.D.; A. Dickson & McGredy. Flowers yellow, sometimes edged pink, dbl., large (4 in.) blooms in clusters; very fragrant; foliage dark; vigorous, tall, bushy. GM, NRS, 1962.

Chinese Lantern Min, *rb*, 1986, (FOUchin); *Avandel* × *Old Master*; Jacobs, B.A.; Four Seasons Rose Nursery. Fl. red, yellow and white hand painting, reverse light pink, fading red and white, more solid color in summer, semi-dbl. (15 petals), large, borne usually singly and in sprays of up to 3; slight, spicy fragrance; foliage medium, medium green, red when young, glossy; fruit round, medium, red-orange; bushy, spreading, medium growth.

Chingari F, *yb*, 1976, *Charleston* × *Seedling*; Pal; Laveena Roses. Bud pointed; flowers aural in to currant-red, semi-dbl. (17 petals), open, large (3 in.); slightly fragrant; foliage glossy; vigorous, bushy, compact growth.

Chipie F, *ab*, 1974, (POUbicarbe); *((Elizabeth of Glamis* × *(Heidelberg* × *8366-2))* × *((Pernille Poulswn* × *(Danish Gold* × *Mischief))*; Poulsen, N.D.; Vilmorin-Andrieux. Flowers rose-begonia to apricot, dbl. (24 petals), open, large (4 in.); foliage light green; bushy growth.

Chipmunk Min, *r*, 1991, (PIXichip; Chipmonk; Peanut Butter & Jelly); *Deep Purple* × *Rainbow's End*; Chaffin, Lauren M.; Pixie Treasures Miniature Roses, 1992. Flowers tannish brown blending with mauve when full blown, full (26-40 petals), medium (4-7 cms) blooms borne mostly singly; fragrant; foliage medium, medium green, semi-glossy; few prickles; medium (30 cms), bushy, neat, compact growth.

Chipper Min, *ab*, 1966, (*Dany Robin seedling* × *Fire King*) × *Perla de Montserrat*; Meilland, Alain; C-P. Bud ovoid; flowers salmon-pink, dbl., small; slightly fragrant; foliage glossy, leathery; vigorous, dwarf growth.

Chippewa S, *mp*, Central Exp. Farm. Flowers rose-pink, semi-dbl. borne in clusters; foliage leathery, bronze.

Chiquita R, *op*, 1938, *Sierra Snowstorm* × *Étoile Luisante*; Moore, R.S.; Brooks & Son. Flowers orange-yellow to coppery orange and salmon-pink, base yellow, well formed, small; very fragrant. RULED EXTINCT 1/88.

Chiquita™ Min, *dr*, 1988, (MORkita); *Anytime* × *Happy Hour*; Moore, Ralph S.; Sequoia Nursery. Flowers rich, dark red with fluores-

cent glow, semi-dbl. (20 petals), flat, borne singly; slight fragrance; foliage small, medium green, matt; prickles hooked, short, brown; fruit few to none; upright, bushy, medium growth.

Chiraz® HT, *pb*, 1986, *Kordes' Perfecta* × *Peace*; Kriloff, M. Flowers creamy white, flushed pink, petals edged carmine red, large; foliage dark; dense growth.

Chiripa F, *mr*, 1957, *Radar* × *(Rosalia Riviera* × *Independence)*; de Dot, G.F. Bud pointed; flowers red, reverse carmine, dbl. (26 petals), borne in clusters of 3-5; foliage bright green; upright, compact growth.

Chivalry® HT, *rb*, 1977, (MACpow); *Peer Gynt* × *Brasilia*; McGredy, S., IV; Mattock. Flowers red, yellowish reverse, dbl. (35 petals), large; foliage glossy, dark.

Chiyo HT, *dp*, 1975, *Karl Herbst* × *Chrysler Imperial*; Ota; Eastern Roses, 1970. Bud long, pointed; flowers deep pink, dbl. (25 petals), high-centered, large (4-4½ in.); slightly fragrant (fruity); foliage glossy, medium to dark green; vigorous, upright growth.

Chloris A (OGR), *lp*, (Rosée du Matin); Prior to 1848. Flowers soft pink, many petaled, reflexing with a button eye; foliage dark, leathery; few prickles; vigorous (to 4-5 ft.) growth.

C.H. Middleton HT, *dr*, 1939, Cant, B.R. Flowers dark crimson, very dbl., high centered, large, long stems; very fragrant; foliage glossy; vigorous, bushy.

Choo-Choo Centennial Min, *lp*, 1980, *Rise 'n' Shine* × *Grand Opera*; Jolly, Betty J.; Rosehill Farm. Bud ovoid; flowers light pink, edged darker, reverse white, dbl. (68 petals), high-centered to flat, small blooms borne 1-5 per cluster; slight fragrance; foliage matt, light green; straight prickles; compact, bushy growth.

Choo-Choo's Baby Min, *rb*, 1980, *Watercolor* × *Watercolor seedling*; Jolly, Betty J.; Rosehill Farm. Bud urn-shaped; flowers red, shaded to yellow at base, dbl. (26 petals), flat, borne usually 1-2 per cluster; little fragrance; foliage tiny, light green; no prickles; low, branching, dense growth.

Chopin HT, *mr*, 1968, *Montezuma* × *Christian Dior*; Ellick. Flowers medium red, dbl. (38 petals), large (4-6 in.); fragrant; foliage medium to light green; vigorous growth.

Chorale S, *lp*, 1978, (*Ruth Hewitt* × *Queen Elizabeth*) × (*Morning Stars* × *Suzanne*); Buck; Iowa State University. Bud ovoid, pointed; flowers pale pink, dbl. (48 petals), high-centered, large (3½ in.); fragrant; foliage dark, leathery; vigorous, upright, bushy growth.

Chorus® F, *or*, 1977, (MEIjulito; MEIjalita; MEImore); *Tamango × (Sarabande × Zambra)*; Paolino; URS, 1975. Flowers vermilion-red, dbl. (35 petals), large (4 in.); slightly fragrant (fruity); foliage glossy; vigorous. ADR, 1977.

Chorus Girl F, *or*, 1970, *Highlight × Seedling*; Robinson, H.; Victoria Nursery. Flowers vermilion, semi-dbl. (16 petals), HT shape, large (3 in.); fragrant; foliage dark, coppery.

Chorus Line S, *dr*, 1992, (JACdaz); *Razzle Dazzle × Seedling*; Zary, Keith & Warriner, William; Bear Creek Gardens. Flowers red, cream base, moderately full (16-20 petals), large (7+ cms) blooms borne in small clusters; fragrant; foliage large, dark green, semiglossy; some prickles; medium (120-135 cms), upright, bushy, very vigorous growth.

Chot Pestitele HP (OGR), *mp*, 1932, *Frau Karl Druschki sport*; Böhm. Bud oblong; flowers rose-pink, dbl. (22 petals), flat, large (6 in.); fragrant; foliage glossy.

Chota F, *or*, 1975, *Violet Carson × Korona*; Sheen. Flowers light vermilion, dbl. (50 petals), very full, large (3½ in.); slightly fragrant; foliage small, semi-glossy; moderately low growth.

Chouette Pol, *dr*, 1969, *Atlantic × Seedling*; Delforge. Bud ovoid; flowers dark fire-red, dbl., full, large; foliage dark, soft; vigorous, bushy growth.

Chris Jolly Min, *or*, 1985, *(Orange Sweetheart × Zinger) × Rise 'n' Shine*; Jolly, Nelson F.; Rosehill Farm. Flowers orange-red, dbl. (40 petals), high-centered, medium; slight fragrance; foliage medium, medium green, semi-glossy; upright, bushy g

Chriss and Dianni Sp (OGR), *w*, *R. multiflora clone*; Widely used as an understock.

Chrissie MacKellar HT, *op*, 1913, Dickson, A. Bud crimson-carmine on deep madder; flowers orange-pink, reverse deeply zoned orange, semi-dbl.; fragrant.

Christian Curle R, *lp*, 1910, *Dorothy Perkins sport*; Cocker. Flowers flesh-pink.

Christian Dior HT, *mr*, 1958, (MEIlie); *(Independence × Happiness) × (Peace × Happiness)*; Meilland, F.; URS, 1958 & C-P, 1961. Bud ovoid, pointed; flowers medium red, dbl. (55 petals), high-centered to cupped, large (4-4½ in.); slightly fragrant; foliage leathery, glossy; vigorous, upright, bushy growth. GM, Geneva, 1958; AARS, 1962.

Christian Dior, Climbing Cl HT, *mr*, 1966, Chang, Chi-Siang.

Christiana Wood HT, *mr*, 1975, *Tropicana Sport*; Wood, J. Bud ovoid; flowers red, dbl.

(31 petals), large (3½ in.); fragrant; upright, bushy growth.

Christina HT, *pb*, 1959, *Granat × Radiance*; Crouch; Roseglen Nursery. Flowers pink, reverse currant red, dbl.; Very vigorous. RULED EXTINCT 12/85 ARM.

Christina HT, *pb*, 1977, *Rina Herboldt × Seedling*; Staikov, Prof. Dr. V.; Kalaydjiev and Chorbadjiiski. Flowers deep pink, reverse light pink, dbl. (45 petals), large; foliage leathery, glossy; vigorous, upright growth.

Christina Atherton HT, *op*, 1978, (MACsev); *Tiki × Seedling*; McGredy, S., IV. Flowers salmon-pink, dbl. (33 petals), classic form, large (4 in.); slightly fragrant; free growth.

Christine HT, *dy*, 1918, McGredy. Flowers deep golden yellow, well-shaped, small; fragrant; foliage dark, glossy. GM, NRS, 1916.

Christine, Climbing Cl HT, *dy*, 1936, Willink.

Christine Gandy F, *dp*, 1958, *Polyantha seedling × Fashion*; deRuiter; Gandy. Flowers deep pink, semi-dbl., large (3 in.) blooms in small clusters; fragrant; foliage dark; vigorous.

Christine Prior HT, *rb*, 1924, McGredy. Flowers deep rosy red, flushed yellow and peach, base yellow, semi-dbl. to dbl.; fragrant.

Christine Weinert Min, *or*, 1976, *(Little Darling × Eleanor) × (Little Darling × Eleanor)*; Moore, R.S.; Sequoia Nursery. Flowers brilliant scarlet, shaded deeper, dbl. (25 petals), flat to rounded, small (1 in.); fragrant; foliage small, leathery; upright, bushy growth.

Christine Wright LCl, *mp*, 1909, *Seedling × Mme. Caroline Testout*; Hoopes, Bro. & Thomas. Flowers wild-rose-pink, semi-dbl., cupped, very large, long stems; fragrant; foliage glossy; height 12-15 ft.

Christine Wunderlich HT, *op*, 1934, *Golden Ophelia sport*; Wunderlich. Flowers yellowish orange-pink, large; fragrant; very vigorous growth.

Christingle F, *or*, 1985, (HARvalex); *Bobby Dazzler × Alexander*; Harkness, R., 1987. Flowers orange-red, dbl. (35 petals), large; slight fragrance; foliage medium, dark, semiglossy; bushy.

Christmas Beauty HT, *dr*, 1942, *Better Times sport*; Krowka. Flowers darker red than parent, dbl. (25-30 petals), large (4½-5 in.); fragrant; foliage blue-green, leathery; vigorous growth.

Christmas Cheer HT, *mr*, 1957, *Sister Kenny × Happiness*; Hill, J.H., Co. Bud long, pointed; flowers cherry-red, dbl. (45-50 petals), high-centered, large (4½-5½ in.); slightly fragrant; foliage dark, leathery; vigorous, upright growth; a florists' variety, not distributed for outdoor use.

Christmas Red HT, *mr*, 1948, *Pink Princess × Crimson Glory*; Brownell. Bud large, long, pointed; flowers spectrum-red, dbl., open; fragrant; foliage glossy; bushy, dwarf growth.

Christobel HT, *ab*, 1937, *Frau Karl Druschki × Mme. Butterfly*; Croibier. Flowers apricot-yellow shaded salmon, dbl., very large; foliage glossy; very vigorous, bushy growth.

Christoph Weigand HT, *lp*, 1928, *Frau Karl Druschki × Souv. de Claudius Pernet*; Weigand, C. Flowers light pink, dbl., high-centered, very large; slightly fragrant; foliage rich green, wrinkled; vigorous growth.

Christopher Min, *mr*, 1988, (TINchris); *Futura × Big John*; Bennett, Dee; Tiny Petals Nursery. Flowers medium red, dbl. (30-35 petals), cupped, exhibition, medium, borne usually singly or in sprays of 3-5; foliage medium, medium green, semi-glossy; prickles hooked slightly downward, yellow-red; fruit globular, green to brown; upright, medium growth.

Christopher Columbus HT, *ob*, 1992, (MEInronsse; MEIronsse; Christoph Columbus; Christoph Colomb; Cristobal Colon; Cristoforo Colombo); *MEIgurani × (Ambassador × MEInaregi)*; Selection Meilland; France, 1990; Italy & Spain 1991; Germany; C-P. Flowers orange blend/copper, full (26-40 petals), large (7+ cms) blooms borne mostly singly; slight fragrance; foliage large, dark green, semi-glossy; many prickles; medium (120-140 cms), upright growth.

Christopher Milton HT, *dp*, 1965, *Christian Dior sport*; Martin, W.A. Bud long, pointed, light red; flowers medium pink, edged lighter, dbl., high-centered, large; foliage dark, glossy; very vigorous, upright growth.

Christopher Stone HT, *mr*, 1935, *Reported to be Étoile de Hollande × Hortulanus Budde*; Robinson, H.; Wheatcroft Bros., 1935 & C-P, 1936. Bud long, pointed; flowers medium red, dbl. (30 petals), large; fragrant (damask); foliage bright green; vigorous. GM, NRS, 1934 & Portland, 1937.

Christopher Stone, Climbing Cl HT, *mr*, 1942, Marsh's Nursery.

Chromatella N (OGR), *ly*, 1843, (Cloth of Gold); *Lamarque seedling*; Coquereau. Flowers creamy white, center yellow, very dbl., globular, large; fragrant; vigorous, climbing; shy bloom until well established.

Chrysler Imperial HT, *dr*, 1952, *Charlotte Armstrong × Mirandy*; Lammerts; Germain's. Bud long, pointed; flowers deep red, dbl. (45 petals), high-centered, large (4½-5 in.); very fragrant; foliage dark, semi-glossy; vigorous, compact growth. GM, Portland, 1951; AARS, 1953; ARS National GM Cert., 1956; ARS John Cook Medal, 1964; James Alexander Gamble Rose Fragrance Medal, 1965.

Chrysler Imperial, Climbing Cl HT, *dr*, 1957, (Grimpant Chrysler Imperial); Begonia, P.B.; Germain's.

Chrystelle HT, *or*, 1975, (GODialing); *(Lady Zia × Wizo) × Silver Lining*; Godin. Bud oval; flowers orange-red, dbl. (30-35 petals), deep cupped, medium (3½ in.); foliage dark.

Chryzia HT, *dp*, 1970, *Chrysler Imperial × Lady Zia*; Wyant. Bud long, pointed; flowers light red, dbl., large; fragrant; vigorous, upright, bushy growth.

Chuckles F, *dp*, 1958, *(Jean Lafitte × New Dawn) × Orange Triumph*; Shepherd; Bosley Nursery. Bud long, pointed; flowers deep pink, white eye, semi-dbl. (11 petals), large (3½ in.) blooms in large clusters; fragrant; foliage dark, leathery; vigorous, bushy.

Chula Vista Min, *dr*, 1992, (TINchula); *Christian Dior × Brian Lee*; Bennett, Dee; Tiny Petals Nursery, 1993. Flowers dark red, full (26-40 petals), HT form, small (0-4 cms) blooms borne mostly single; long stems; slight fragrance; foliage small, medium green semi-glossy, disease resistant; some prickles; medium (60-80 cms), bushy growth.

Church Mouse Min, *r*, 1989, (FOUmouse); *Angel Face × Plum Duffy*; Jacobs, Betty A.; Sequoia Nursery, 1989. Bud pointed; flowers tan-brown, with yellow at base, aging light lavender-brown, dbl. (20 petals), urn-shaped, loose, large, borne usually singly and in sprays of up to 3; moderate, sweet fragrance; foliage large, medium green, matt; prickles slightly declining, small, red to tan; fruit none; low, bushy, compact growth.

Cibles HRg (S), *mr*, 1893, *R. rugosa rubra × Perle de Lyon*; Kaufmann. Flowers bright red, base yellow; vigorous, upright growth.

Cicely O'Rorke Cl HT, *mp*, 1937, *Souv. de Gustave Prat × Seedling*; Clark, A.; NRS Victoria. Flowers pink, shaded salmon, semi-dbl., cupped, large, borne on long stems; very vigorous, climbing or pillar growth; recurrent bloom.

Cidade de Lisboa LCl, *pb*, 1939, *Belle Portugaise × Mme. Edouard Herriot*; Moreira da Silva. Bud long, pointed; flowers salmon-pink, edged yellow, semi-dbl., high-centered, large, borne on long stems; slightly fragrant; vigorous growth.

Cider Cup Min, *ob*, 1987, (DICladida); *Memento × (Liverpool Echo × Woman's Own)*; Dickson, Patrick, 1988. Flowers orange blend, dbl. (15-25 petals), medium; patio; slight fragrance; foliage medium, medium green, glossy.

Cilly Michel HT, *or*, 1928, *Mme. Mélanie Soupert × Felbergs Rosa Druschki*; Felberg-Leclerc. Flowers nasturtium-red, full, large; fragrant.

Cimarron HT, *pb*, 1938, *Nellie E. Hillock × Golden Dawn*; Hillock. Bud spiraled, almost red; flowers ruffled, salmon, reverse deep pink; vigorous, compact growth.

Cina HT, *ob*, 1973, *Premiere Ballerine × Femina*; Gaujard. Bud full; flowers brilliant coral, flushed salmon; foliage large.

Cinderella Min, *w*, 1953, *Cécile Brunner × Tom Thumb*; deVink; C-P. Flowers satiny white tinged pale flesh, dbl. (55 petals), micro-mini, small (1 in.); fragrant (spicy); no prickles; upright growth.

Cinderella R, *dp*, 1909, Walsh. Flowers deep pink, dbl., petal tips quilled, small, borne in large clusters; vigorous growth; free, non-recurrent bloom.

Cinderella, Climbing Cl Min, *w*, 1975, Sequoia Nursery.

Cinderella's Midnight Rose HT, *mp*, 1976, England. Flowers rich pink, large (4-5 in.); slightly fragrant; foliage glossy; vigorous growth.

Cindy™ Min, *dp*, 1985, (MINaaco); *Tom Brown × Over the Rainbow*; Williams, Ernest D.; Mini-Roses. Flowers deep pink, dbl. (40+ petals), well-formed, small; slight fragrance; foliage small, dark, glossy.

Cineraire Ch (OGR), *rb*, E. Murrell, prior to 1964. Flowers rich red, center white, single (5 petals), cupped, very small blooms in trusses.

Cinerama HT, *pb*, 1966, *Seedling × Tzigane*; Herholdt, J.A. Flowers salmon, reverse buffyellow, pointed, large (4½-5 in.); slightly fragrant; vigorous growth.

Cineraria Pol, *m*, 1934, *Miss Edith Cavell × Tip-Top*; Leenders; M. Flowers carmine-purple, center white, semi-dbl., open, large; slightly fragrant; foliage soft; vigorous, bushy growth.

Cingallegra HT, *yb*, 1958, *Golden Scepter × Crimson Glory*; Cazzaniga. Bud well shaped; flowers lemon-yellow, edged pinkish, dbl., long, strong stems.

Cinnabar F, *or*, 1945, (Tantau's Triumph); *Baby Chateau × R. roxburghii*; Tantau. Bud small, globular; flowers scarlet, semi-dbl., cupped blooms in clusters; slightly fragrant; foliage leathery; bushy, upright growth.

Cinnabar Improved F, *or*, 1951, (Verbesserte Tantau's Triumph); *(Cinnabar × Kathe Duvigneau) × Cinnabar*; Tantau. Flowers orange-scarlet, semi-dbl., borne in trusses; bushier and freer bloom than Cinnabar; (28).

Cinnamon Toast™ Min, *r*, 1986, (SAVacin); *Zorina × (Sheri Anne × Glenfiddich)*; Saville, F.H.; Nor'East Min. Roses. Flowers russet brown, dbl. (28 petals), high-centered, exhibition, small; slightly fragrant; foliage small, medium green, semi-glossy; small, red prickles; low, upright, bushy growth.

Circé F, *or*, 1978, (GAUmova); *Guitare × Prominent*; Gaujard. Bud long; flowers brilliant orange-red, semi-dbl. (16 petals), small (1½-2 in.); foliage large, dark; vigorous, compact.

Circus F, *yb*, 1956, *Fandango × Pinocchio*; Swim; Armstrong Nursery. Bud urn-shaped; flowers yellow marked pink, salmon and scarlet, dbl. (45-58 petals), high-centered, large (2½-3 in.) blooms in large clusters; fragrant (tea to spicy); foliage semi-glossy, leathery; bushy growth. GM, Geneva & NRS, 1955; AARS, 1956.

Circus, Climbing Cl F, *yb*, 1961, House; Armstrong Nursery.

Circus Clown Min, *rb*, 1991, (MORpico); *Pink Petticoat × Make Believe*; Moore, Ralph S.; Sequoia Nursery, 1992. Flowers red blend, semi-dbl. (6-14 petals), small (0-4 cms) blooms borne mostly singly or in small clusters; slight fragrance; foliage small, medium green, semi-glossy; few prickles; low (18-22 cms), bushy, compact growth.

Circus Knie® HT, *yb*, 1975, *Moulin Rouge × Peace*; Huber. Bud long, pointed; flowers yellow blend, dbl. (32-38 petals), cupped, large (3½-4 in.); slightly fragrant; foliage dark, leathery.

Circus Parade F, *yb*, 1963, *Circus sport*; Begonia, F.B. & DeVor, P.; Armstong Nursery. Flowers multicolor, redder than Circus.

Cissie Min, *mp*, 1979, *Gene Boerner × Elfinesque*; Bennett, Dee; Tiny Petals Nursery. Bud long, pointed; flowers medium pink, 18-20 petals, exhibition, small (1 in.) blooms borne singly; slightly fragrant; foliage deep green with touches of red and bronze on edges; small, thin prickles; bushy, upright growth.

Cissie Easlea HT, *my*, 1913, *Melanie Soupert × Rayon d'Or*; Pernet-Ducher. Flowers yellow.

Citation Gr, *dr*, 1982, *Seedling × Seedling*; Hoy, Lowel L.; Joseph H. Hill, Co. Flowers dark red, reverse lighter, dbl. (35 petals), high-centered, medium blooms in sprays of 2-3; foliage large, dark, semi-glossy; short, lilac prickles, hooked downward; fruit globular, light orange; medium, bushy growth; greenhouse variety.

Citron HT, *ly*, 1942, *Julien Potin × Seedling*; Gaujard; J&P. Flowers buff, shaded copper, dbl. (28 petals), cupped; fragrant; foliage reddish; vigorous growth.

City of Auckland HT, *ob*, 1981, (MACtane); *Benson & Hedges Gold × Whisky Mac*; McGredy, Sam; McGredy International, 1982. Flowers orange blend, dbl., large; very fragrant; foliage medium green, semi-glossy; bushy growth.

Citronella F, *ly*, 1946, *Mev. Nathalie Nypels × Donald Prior*; Leenders, M.; Longley. Flowers lemon-yellow, semi-dbl. (15 petals), globular, borne in clusters; fragrant; foliage glossy; branching growth.

City of Bath HT, *pb*, 1969, *Gavotte × Buccaneer*; Sanday. Flowers deep candy-pink, reverse lighter, dbl. (55 petals), large (4 in.); fragrant; foliage matt, green.

City of Belfast® F, *or*, 1968, (MACci); *Evelyn Fison × (Circus × Korona)*; McGredy, S., IV; McGredy. Flowers bright red, dbl., cupped, medium blooms in trusses; foliage glossy. GM, RNRS & NZ, 1967, Belfast, 1970 & The Hague, 1976; RNRS PIT, 1.967

City of Benalla HT, *op*, 1983, *My Choice × Extravaganza*; Dawson, George; Rainbow Roses. Bud globular, pointed; flowers carmine, opening with outer petals paling, inner petals coral, dbl. (45 petals), high-centered, large blooms borne singly; light fragrance; foliage dark, dense, glossy; brown prickles, hooked down; vigorous, tall growth.

City of Bradford F, *or*, 1986, (HARrotang); *(Manx Queen × Whisky Mac) × ((Highlight × Colour Wonder) 128Mö (Parkdirektor Riggers × Piccadilly))*; Harkness. Flowers orange-red, semi-dbl. (15 wavy petals), cupped, small to medium blooms in large clusters; slightly fragrant; foliage dark, semi-glossy; medium, upright.

City of Cardiff HT, *rb*, 1992, *Lady Sylvia × Chicago Peace*; Poole, Lionel, 1993. Flowers red blend, very full (41+ petals), large (7+ cms) blooms borne mostly singly; fragrant; foliage medium, medium green, matt; some prickles; medium, upright growth.

City of Gisborne HT, *op*, 1968, *Prima Ballerina × Prima Ballerina*; Appleyard. Bud long, pointed; flowers pink shaded orange-yellow, semi-dbl., high-centered, large; very fragrant; foliage glossy; vigorous, upright growth.

City of Glasgow HT, *ab*, 1970, *Femina sport*; Haynes. Flowers apricot, suffused pink.

City of Gloucester HT, *dy*, 1969, *Gavotte × Buccaneer*; Sanday, 1970. Flowers saffron-yellow shaded gold, dbl., high-centered, large; vigorous growth.

City of Hamilton F, *ob*, 1972, *Innisfree × Elizabeth of Glamis*; Dickson, A. Flowers or-

ange and gold, dbl. (26 ovate petals), large (3½ in.); slightly fragrant; foliage dull; free growth.

City of Harvey R, *op*, 1944, *R. wichuraiana × Orléans Rose*; Wiseman. Flowers pink tinted orange, semi-dbl., cupped, small, borne in clusters; slightly fragrant; foliage dark, glossy; height 12 ft.; profuse bloom, not repeated.

City of Hereford HT, *mp*, 1967, *Wellworth × Spartan*; LeGrice. Flowers carmine-pink, pointed, large (6 in.); very fragrant; foliage dark.

City of Kingston F, *or*, 1973, *Malibu × Independence*; Schloen, J. Bud ovoid; flowers orange-red, very dbl., globular, medium; slightly fragrant; foliage dark, leathery; moderate, bushy growth.

City of Leeds F, *op*, 1966, *Evelyn Fison × (Spartan × Red Favorite)*; McGredy, S., IV; McGredy. Flowers salmon, semi-dbl. (19 petals), large (4½ in.) blooms in clusters; slightly fragrant; foliage dark. GM, RNRS, 1965.

City of Little Rock HT, *mp*, 1924, Hill, E.G., Co.; Vestal. Flowers hydrangea-pink, semi-dbl., open; fragrant; vigorous growth.

City of London® F, *lp*, 1986, (HARukfore); *Radox Bouquet × Margaret Merril*; Harkness, R.; The Rose Gardens, 1988. Flowers light pink, fading to blush, dbl. (15-25 petals), large; very fragrant; foliage medium, medium green, glossy, ovate to pointed; small, reddish, sparse prickles; bushy growth. GM, LeRoeulx, 1985.

City of Manchester HT, *pb*, 1986, (NOSman); *Gavotte × Red Lion*; Greensitt, J.A.; Nostell Priory Rose Gardens. Flowers pink blend, dbl. (over 40 petals), large; fragrant; foliage large, dark green, semi-glossy; bushy growth.

City of Newcastle HT, *yb*, 1976, *Arthur Bell × Mischief*; Wood. Flowers yellow, tinged salmon-orange, dbl. (35 petals), large (5 in.); very fragrant; foliage semi-glossy, vigorous, tall, upright growth.

City of Norwich HT, *mr*, 1949, *Crimson Glory × (Crimson Glory × Cathrine Kordes)*; Kordes; Morse. Bud ovoid; flowers scarlet-crimson, dbl. (35 petals), well formed, large (6 in.); fragrant; foliage leathery.

City of Nottingham F, *or*, 1962, *Seedling × Moulin Rouge*; deRuiter. Flowers orange-scarlet, dbl. (30-40 petals), rosette shape, medium (2½ in.), borne in clusters; slightly fragrant; foliage dark; vigorous, bushy, compact growth.

City of Portland F, *mr*, 1977, *Seedling × Cocktail seedling*; Takatori; Japan Rose Nursery. Bud pointed; flowers geranium-red, base primrose-yellow, single (5 petals), large (2½ -3½ in.); slightly fragrant; foliage glossy; very free growth.

City of Portsmouth F, *ob*, 1975, Cants of Colchester. Flowers copper, dbl. (25 petals), large (3-4 in.); fragrant; foliage bronze; tall growth.

City of Sheffield HT, *yb*, 1986, (NOSshef); *Diorama sport*; Greensitt, J.A.; Nostell Priory Rose Gardens. Flowers yellow blend, dbl. (15-25 petals), medium; very fragrant; foliage medium, medium green, matt; spreading growth.

City of Springfield F, *rb*, 1988, *Pink Parfait × Roman Holiday*; Pencil, Paul, 1989. Flowers red blend, non-fading, dbl. (34 petals), medium, borne in sprays of 6-10; bushy, hardy growth.

City of Worcester HT, *mr*, 1983, *Red Planet × (Ena Harkness × Fragrant Cloud)*; Crivens, L. Flowers medium red, dbl. (35 petals), high-centered, large; fragrant; foliage medium, medium green, matt.

City of York LCl, *w*, 1945, (Direktör Benschop); *Prof. Gnau × Dorothy Perkins*; Tantau; C-P. Flowers creamy white, semi-dbl. (15 petals), cupped, large, in clusters of 7-15; fragrant; foliage glossy, leathery; vigorous, climbing. ARS National GM Certificate, 1950.

Ciudad de Oviedo C (OGR), *mp*, (*R. centifolia simplex* Thory); Prior to 1824. Flowers medium pink, single; (28).

Clair de Lune HT, *m*, 1967, *Eminence × Viola*; Gaujard. Bud pointed; flowers mauve, dbl., large; fragrant; foliage leathery; vigorous, upright growth.

Clair Matin® LCl, *mp*, 1960, (MEImont; Grimpant Clair Matin®); *Fashion × ((Independence × Orange Triumph) × Phyllis Bide)*; Meilland, M.L.; URS, 1960 & C-P, 1963. Bud pointed; flowers pink, semi-dbl. (15 petals), cupped to flat, medium (2-3 in.) blooms in rounded clusters; fragrant (sweetbrier); foliage dark, leathery; vigorous (10-12 ft.), well-branched growth. GM, Bagatelle, 1960.

Claire Desmet HT, *my*, 1932, *Margaret Dickson Hamill × Souv. de Claudius Pernet*; Buatois. Flowers golden yellow, very dbl., cupped, long, strong stems; fragrant; foliage leathery, bronze; vigorous, bushy growth.

Claire Jacquier N (OGR), *ly*, 1888, *Possibly R. multiflora × Tea rose*; Bernaix, A. Flowers yellow, fading to creamy yellow; very vigorous growth.

Claire Scotland Min, *ab*, 1992, (COCdimity); *(National Trust × Wee Man) × Darling Flame*; Cocker, James; James Cocker & Sons, 1990.

Flowers light apricot pink, moderately full (15-25 petals), medium (4-7 cms) blooms borne in small clusters; patio; slight fragrance; foliage medium, medium green, semi-glossy; some prickles; low (50.80 cms), bushy growth.

Claire-France HT, *mp*, 1964, Mondial Roses. Bud pointed; flowers clear pink, dbl. (40 petals), high-centered, large; slightly fragrant; foliage glossy; vigorous, upright growth.

Clara Bow Cl HT, *yb*, 1927, (Clara Bow, Climbing); *Golden Emblem sport*; Padella Rose Co.; Germain's. Flowers yellow stained crimson, dbl.; slightly fragrant; height 12-15 ft.

Clara Curtis HT, *my*, 1922, Dickson, A. Flowers rich golden yellow, very dbl.; very fragrant. GM, NRS, 1919.

Clara Munger R, *m*, Munger. Flowers lavender, similar in size, shape and cluster to *R. multiflora*.

Clara Watson HT, *w*, 1894, Prince. Flowers mother-of-pearl white, center peach, dbl.; fragrant.

Clare HT, *pb*, 1972, *Ethel Sanday × Rose Gaujard*; MacLeod. Flowers cream, edged rose-pink, dbl. (35 petals), exhibition, large (5½ in.); slightly fragrant; foliage large, medium green, semi-glossy; vigorous, tall.

Clare de Escofet HT, *w*, 1920, Easlea. Flowers delicate flesh-white, dbl.

Cläre Grammserstorf F, *dy*, 1957, *Harmonie × R. eglanteria seedling*; Kordes. Bud ovoid; flowers yellow, dbl., high-centered, large; foliage leathery, glossy; vigorous, bushy.

Clare Helen HT, *lp*, 1985, *Gail Borden sport*; Owen, Fred. Flowers light pink.

Claret Min, *m*, 1977, *Little Chief × Little Chief*; Saville; Nor'East Min. Roses. Bud short, pointed; flowers mauve, dbl. (48 petals), cupped, small (1 in.); very compact, spreading.

Claret Cup Min, *rb*, 1962, *Spring Song (Min) × Eutin*; Riethmuller; Hazlewood Bros. Bud globular; flowers dark red, white eye, dbl., small blooms in clusters; fragrant; foliage leathery, dark; vigorous, bushy, compact growth.

Clarice Goodacre HT, *w*, 1916, Dickson, A. Bud pointed; flowers ivory-white, shaded chrome, dbl., high-centered; fragrant; foliage dark, soft; vigorous, bushy growth.

Clarissa® Min, *ab*, 1982, (HARprocrustes); *Southampton × Darling Flame*; Harkness, R.; Harkness & Co., 1983. Flowers apricot, dbl. (43 petals), high-centered, HT form, small blooms in large clusters; slightly fragrant; foliage small, dark, glossy; small prickles; tall, upright growth. NZ Gold Star.

Clarissa Dana HT, *pb*, 1933, *(HT× La France)* × *Marechal Niel*; Nicolas; J&P. Flowers brilliant pink with amber glow, dbl., high-centered, large; fragrant; vigorous.

Clarita HT, *or*, 1971, (MEIbyster; Atoll); *Tropicana* × *(Zambra* × *Romantica)*; Meilland. Flowers vermilion, dbl. (30-35 petals), high-centered, large (5 in.); slightly fragrant; foliage matt, dark; very vigorous, upright growth. GM, Lyon & Geneva, 1971.

Clarke's Multiflora Sp (OGR), *w, R. multiflora clone*; Thornless; used as an understock.

Class Act F, *w*, 1988, (JACare; First Class; White Magic). *Sun Flare* × *Seedling*; Warriner, William; J & P Co. Flowers white, semi-dbl., loose, flat, borne in sprays of 3-6; slight, fruity fragrance; foliage medium, dark green, semi-glossy; prickles long, narrow; upright, bushy, medium growth. GM, Portland, 1989; AARS, 1989.

Classic Chick Min, *ob*, 1986, *Seedling* × *Seedling*; McDaniel, Earl; McDaniel's Min. Roses. Flowers orange, dbl. (35 petals), high-centered, exhibition, medium blooms borne usually singly; no fragrance; foliage medium, dark, semi-glossy; few, slender prickles; medium, upright growth.

Classic Love Min, *mp*, 1983, (LYOcl); *Baby Betsy McCall* × *Seedling*; Lyon, Lyndon; Lyon Greenhouse. Flowers medium pink, dbl. (20 petals), small blooms in clusters; no fragrance; foliage small, medium green, semi-glossy; upright, bushy growth.

Classic Touch HT, *lp*, 1991, *Touch of Class* sport; Hefner, John; Co-Operative Rose Growers, 1993. Flowers light pink, full (26-40 petals), large blooms borne mostly singly; slight fragrance; foliage large, medium green, semi-glossy; tall, upright growth.

Classical Velvet HT, *mr*, 1992, (JOHillstar); *Anniversary* × *Seedling*; Hoy, Lowell (Joseph H. Hill Co.); DeVor Nurseries. Flowers medium red, semi-dbl. (25 petals), large (13 cms) blooms borne in sprays of 4-5; no fragrance; foliage medium, dark green, semi-glossy; upright, bushy, tall growth.

Classie Lassie™ Gr, *pb*, 1990, *Touch of Class* × *Seedling*; Winchel, Joseph; Co-Operative Rose Growers, Specialty Roses, 1991. Bud pointed; flowers ivory pink, with salmon pink edges, aging to salmon, semi-dbl. (25-30 petals), high-centered, exhibition, oval-shaped, medium blooms borne usually singly or in sprays of up to 3; moderate, fruity fragrance; foliage medium, medium green, glossy, disease resistant; prickles average, brown green, slight recurve; bushy, medium growth.

Classy Min, *yb*, 1987, (TRAcla); *Yellow Jewel* × *Yellow Jewel*; Travis, Louis. Flowers yellow with pink overlay, dbl. (13-18 petals), exhibition, small, borne singly; heavy, spicy fragrance; foliage small, medium green, semi-glossy; straight, very few, tan-brown prickles; fruit round, green-orange; bushy, low growth.

Claude HT, *mr*, 1950, *(Comtesse Vandal* × *Brazier)* × *Seedling*; Mallerin; EFR & Wheatcroft Bros. Flowers bright orient red, dbl. (35 petals), very large (6-7 in.); fragrant; foliage glossy, dark; vigorous, upright growth.

Claude Petit HT, *mp*, 1936, *Mlle. Marie Mascuraud* × *Beauté de Lyon*; Buatois. Flowers soft salmon-pink, stamens yellow, very dbl., high-centered; very fragrant; vigorous growth.

Claude Rabbe LCl, *dp*, 1941, Buatois. Flowers carmine-pink, medium, borne in clusters of 6-10.

Claudia F, *pb*, 1959, *Ma Perkins* × *Geranium Red*; Broadley; Roseglen Nursery. Flowers deep cherry-coral, dbl.; vigorous growth.

Claudy Chapel HT, *yb*, 1930, Beaumez; Delhaye. Flowers deep yellow and coppery, to salmon-pink, dbl., large; fragrant; vigorous growth.

Claus Groth HSpn (OGR), *ob*, 1951, (Klaus Groth); *R.M.S. Queen Mary* × *R. spinosissima*; Tantau. Flowers salmon-orange shaded apricot-yellow, full, large; very fragrant (spinosissima); fruit large; foliage dark; vigorous, bushy (5 ft.) growth.

Clematis R, *rb*, 1924, Turbat. Flowers dark red, prominent white eye, single, small, borne in clusters; vigorous, climbing growth.

Clemence Robert M (OGR), *mp*, 1863, Robert et Moreau. Flowers pink, heavily mossed; sometimes recurrent bloom.

Clément Pacaud HT, *dp*, 1916, Chambard, C. Flowers brilliant carmine.

Clementina HT, *pb*, 1961, *Grand Gala* × *Vicky Marfá*; Dot, P.; Flower carmine and rosy white bicolor.

Clementine E (OGR), Prior to 1838. Flowers rosy blush. This rose is apparently not in cultivation. Its name has been used erroneously as a synonym of Janet's Pride.

Clementine Duval B (OGR), *mp*, 1847, Laffay. Flowers bright rose, cupped.

Clémentine Séringe HP (OGR), *mp*, 1840, Wood. Flowers rose-pink, dbl.

Cleo HT, *lp*, 1981, (BEEbop); *Kordes' Perfecta* × *Prima Ballerina*; Bees Ltd. Flowers soft light pink, dbl. (37 petals), high-centered blooms borne 1-2 per cluster; slight fragrance; foliage light green, semi-matt; red prickles; strong, bushy growth.

Cleopatra HT, *rb*, 1955, (Kleopatra); *(Walter Bentley × Condesa de Sástago) × Golden Scepter*; Kordes. Flowers scarlet, reverse old-gold, dbl. (45 petals), well-formed, medium; fragrant; foliage dark, glossy; vigorous growth. GM, NRS, 1955.

Cleora Min, *mp*, 1977, *Fairy Moss × Fairy Moss*; Dobbs; Port Stockton Nursery. Bud globular; flowers medium pink, reverse darker, dbl. (50 petals), flat, small (1½ in.); foliage small, light, leathery; vigorous growth.

Cleveland HT, *pb*, 1916, (H.P. Pinkerton); Dickson, H. Flowers reddish copper on old-rose, base coppery yellow., dbl.; fragrant.

Cleveland Bouquet HT, *op*, 1940, Horvath. Flowers shrimp-pink with salmon-pink undertone, semi-dbl., open.

Climbing Roses. All varieties having the word Climbing as part of their name are listed under their basic name rather than under Climbing. Climbing sports that are not described have flowers like their parent. Climbing sports of the Polyanthas are rarely recurrent, but most Climbing Hybrid Teas, Climbing Grandifloras and Climbing Floribundas do repeat.

Climentina HT, *mp*, 1955, *Independence × Peace*; Klimenko. Flowers rosy pink, large; slightly fragrant.

Clinora Cl HT, *dy*, 1978, *Sunblest sport*; Orard; Pekmez. Bud pointed; flowers deep yellow, well shaped, large (3½ in.); very fragrant.

Clio HP (OGR), *lp*, 1894, Paul, W. Flowers flesh, very dbl., globular, large blooms in clusters; fragrant; foliage rich green; vigorous growth; seasonal bloom.

Clivia® HT, *ob*, 1985, (KORtag); *Mercedes × (Sonia × Uwe Seeler)*; Kordes, W., 1979. Bud ovoid; flowers salmon orange-red blend, dbl. (30 petals), high-centered, exhibition, medium blooms borne singly; fragrant; foliage medium, medium green, matt; brown prickles; upright, bushy.

Clochermerle® HT, *mr*, 1988, (DELpétri); *Seedling × (Michele Meilland × Karla) × Seedling*; Delbard & Chabert. Flowers medium red, dbl. (38 petals), cupped, large; slight fragrance; foliage matt; vigorous, bushy growth.

Clos de la Pellerie HT, *or*, 1987, (DELclopel); *(Spartan × Baccará) × Seedling*; Delbard-Chabert, 1988. Flowers medium vermilion red, dbl. (25-35 petals), long, large; light fragrance; foliage large; good, vigorous, bushy growth.

Clos Fleuri Blanc® F, *w*, 1988, (DELblan); *(Milrose × Legion d'Honneur) × Candeur*; Delbard & Chabert, 1990. Flowers white, dbl.

(40 petals), large; slight fragrance; foliage bright; semi-climbing, vigorous growth.

Clos Fleuri Jaune® F, *my*, 1988, (DELjaune); *(Orléans Rose × Goldilocks) × Parure d'Or*; Delbard & Chabert, 1990. Flowers yellow, shaded ochre, opening to yellow-amber, dbl. (18 petals), large; slight fragrance; foliage bright; raised, semi-climbing, vigorous growth.

Clos Fleuri Rose® F, *mp*, 1988, (DELpomp); *(Zambra × Orange Sensation) × (Robin Hood × Virgo)*; Delbard & Chabert, 1990. Flowers medium pink, dbl. (30 petals), medium; slight fragrance; foliage bright; bushy, vigorous growth.

Clos Fleuri Rouge® F, *mr*, 1988, (DELecla); *Orléans Rose × Queen Elizabeth*; Delbard & Chabert, 1990. Flowers medium red, dbl. (20 petals), medium, flat; slight fragrance; foliage bright; bushy, vigorous growth.

Clos Vougeot® F, *mr*, 1983, (DELific; Red Prolific; Rouge Prolific); *(Alain × Charles Mallerin) × (Lafayette × Walko)*; Delbard-Chabert. Flowers medium red, dbl. (28 petals), medium; no fragrance; bushy growth.

Clotaria HT, *mr*, 1936, (Red Gruss an Coburg); *Gruss an Coburg × J.C. Thornton*; San Remo Exp. Sta. Flowers bright fuchsia-red, dbl. (26-28 petals), well formed, medium; very fragrant; foliage dark, glossy; vigorous, upright, bushy growth.

Clotilde Soupert Pol, *w*, 1890, *Said to be Mignonette × Mme. Damaizin*; Soupert & Notting. Flowers pearly white, center soft rose-pink, verydbl., large blooms in clusters; fragrant; foliage rich green, soft; bushy (10-20 in.) growth.

Clotilde Soupert, Climbing Cl Pol, *w*, 1902, Dingee & Conard.

Clotilde Soupert, Climbing Cl Pol, *w*, 1896, Berckmans, P.J., Co.

Cloud Nine Min, *w*, 1982, (JAClite); *Bon Bon × Calgold*; Warriner, W.A.; J&P. Flowers white, semi-dbl., medium; foliage light green, matt; spreading growth.

Clovelly HT, *dp*, 1924, Hicks. Flowers carmine-pink, well formed; fragrant; vigorous growth. GM, NRS, 1924.

Club F, *mr*, 1957, *Peace × Opera seedling*; Gaujard. Flowers bright red, single, open, medium; slightly fragrant; foliage glossy, bronze; very vigorous, bushy growth.

Clubrose Scala F, *rb*, 1973, (Scala); *Marlena × Seedling*; Kordes. Flowers blood-red and orange, dbl., globular, medium; slightly fragrant; foliage glossy, dark, leathery, bronze; vigorous, upright, bushy growth.

Clydebank Centenary F, *or*, 1988, (COC-dazzle); *((Highlight × Colour Wonder) × (Parkdirector Riggers × Piccadilly)) × Darling Flame*; Cocker, J. & Sons, 1987. Flowers orange-vermilion red, dbl. (15-25 fimbriated petals), medium; slight fragrance; foliage medium, medium green, matt; upright growth.

Clytemnestra HMsk (S), *op*, 1915, *Trier × Liberty*; Pemberton. Bud copper; flowers salmon-chamois, ruffled, small blooms in clusters; fragrant; foliage leathery, dark; bushy (3-4 ft.), spreading growth; recurrent bloom. GM, NRS, 1914.

Cnos X HT, *my*, 1957, *Bettina seedling*; Bronisze (Poland) State Nursery. Flowers golden yellow tinged copper; fragrant; vigorous growth.

Coalite Flame HT, *or*, 1974, *Fragrant Cloud × Red Planet*; Dickson, A. Flowers orange-red, dbl. (60 petals), large (5 in.); fragrant; foliage large, matt.

Coby Fankhauser HT, *my*, 1971, *John S. Bloomfield × Elizabeth Fankhauser*; Fankhauser. Flowers buttercup-yellow, dbl., high-centered, large; fragrant; foliage leathery; vigorous, upright, bushy growth.

COCagold HT, *my*, 1981, (Golden Jubilee); *Peer Gynt × Gay Gordons*; Cocker, James. Flowers medium yellow, dbl. (29 petals), exhibition blooms borne 1-3 per cluster; tea fragrance; foliage large, matt green, glossy; narrow, red-brown prickles.

Cocarde Jaune HT, *pb*, 1933, *Diana × Marie Adélaide*; Ketten Bros. Bud large, long, pointed, reddish salmon; flowers yellowish salmon, base yellow, reverse coral-red, dbl., cupped; fragrant; foliage dark; vigorous, bushy growth.

COCbonne HT, *or*, 1989, (Ena Baxter); *HARkrispin × Silver Jubilee*; Cocker, James & Sons. Bud pointed; flowers salmon pink, reverse salmon red, dbl. (26 petals), high-centered, medium, borne in sprays of 5-9; slight fragrance; foliage large, medium green, glossy; prickles triangular, average, green; fruit urn-shaped, large, brown; bushy, medium growth.

COCceleste F, *mp*, 1988, (Rosabell); *(National Trust × Wee Man) × Darling Flame*; Cocker, J., & Sons, 1986. Flowers medium pink, dbl., medium; patio; slight fragrance; foliage medium, medium green, semi-glossy; bushy growth.

Coccinelle LCl, *or*, 1956, Buyl Frères. Flowers bright geranium-red.

COCdana HT, *yb*, 1988, (Fulton MacKay; Maribel); *Silver Jubilee × Jana*; Cocker, J., 1989. Flowers yellow blend, dbl. (20 petals), large; fragrant; foliage large, medium green, glossy; bushy growth.

Cochineal Glory HT, *mr*, 1937, Leenders, M. Bud pointed; flowers red, semi-dbl., open, large; vigorous, bushy growth.

Cockle Shells Min, *pb*, 1985, (LEOcok); *(Kathy Robinson × Seedling) × (Janna × Seedling)*; Leon, Charles F., Sr. Flowers pale yellow tinged deep pink, dbl. (35 petals), medium; slight fragrance; foliage medium; bushy, spreading growth.

Cocktail S, *rb*, 1961, *(Independence × Orange Triumph) × Phyllis Bide*; Meilland, F.; URS, 1957; C-P, 1961. Bud pointed; Flowers geranium red, base primrose yellow, single (5 petals), medium (2½ in.) borne in clusters; slightly fragrant (spicy); Foliage leathery, glossy; Vigorous, semi-cl., shrub or hedge growth. RULED EXTINCT 10/78 ARM.

Cocktail® S, *rb*, 1957, (MEImick); *(Independence × Orange Triumph) × Phyllis Bide*; Meilland, F.; URS, 1957; C-P, 1961. Bud pointed; flowers geranium-red, base primrose-yellow, single (5 petals), medium (2½ in.) blooms in clusters; slightly fragrant (spicy); foliage leathery, glossy; vigorous, semi-climbing growth.

Coco F, *yb*, 1975, *Pernille Poulsen × Redgold*; Fryer, G.; Fryer's Nursery. Flowers deep golden yellow to orange-pink, dbl. (20-25 petals), large (3 in.); fragrant; foliage glossy, bright; vigorous, free growth.

Coconut Ice HT, *pb*, 1991, *Alexander × Vol de Nuit*; Walker, D.R., 1981. Bud large, pointed; flowers pink blend with mauve headings, full, high-centered, medium blooms borne 1-3 per stem; light fragrance; foliage medium green, semi-glossy; tall, vigorous growth.

Cocorico F, *or*, 1951, *Alain × Orange Triumph*; Meilland, F.; URS, 1951; C-P, 1953. Bud pointed; flowers geranium red, single (8 petals), large (3 in.) blooms in clusters; fragrant (spicy); foliage glossy, bright; vigorous, upright, bushy; (28). GM, Geneva & NRS, 1951.

Cocorico, Climbing Cl F, *or*, 1964, Ruston.

Cocotte HT, *mp*, 1958, *Peace × (Fashion × Vogue)*; Gaujard. Flowers bright salmon, dbl., large; fragrant; foliage bronze; upright growth.

Coed™ F, *my*, 1969, (JELlo); *Golden Garnette × Seedling*; Jelly; E.G. Hill Co. Bud short, pointed; flowers yellow, dbl., high-centered, mini-flora, medium; slightly fragrant; foliage dark, leathery; vigorous, upright growth.

Coelina Dubos D (OGR), *lp*, 1849, Dubos. Flowers pale pink; sometimes recurrent bloom.

Cognac F, *ab*, 1956, *Alpine Glow × Mrs. Pierre S. duPont*; Tantau, Math. Flowers apricot, reverse darker, stamens dark amber, dbl., large, borne in small clusters; foliage glossy, dark olive-green; moderate growth.

Cognac, Climbing Cl F, *ab*, 1962, Kordes.

Coimbra HT, *dp*, 1953, *Heinrich Wendland × Crimson Glory*; Moreira da Silva. Flowers cerise-pink, dbl., high-centered, large; very fragrant.

Colbert® HT, *pb*, 1991, (DELcolb); *((Peace × Bettina) × (President Herbert Hoover × Tropicana)) × Chateau de Versailles*; Delbard & Chabert, 1990. Flowers white cream, delicately shaded porcelain pink, full (27-35 petals), cup shaped, large blooms; light fragrance; foliage dark green, flat; bushy (80-100 cms) growth.

Colcestria Cl HT, *pb*, 1916, Cant, B.R. Flowers rose to silver-pink, full, petals reflexed, large; very fragrant; foliage light.

Colchester Beauty F, *dp*, 1992, (CANsend); *English Miss × Seedling*; Pawsey, P.R.; Cants of Colchester Ltd., 1989. Flowers candy pink, semi-dbl. (6-14 petals), medium (4-7 cms) blooms borne mostly singly; very fragrant; foliage medium, dark green, semi-glossy; some prickles; medium (60-80 cms), bushy growth.

Colchester Gazette F, *mr*, 1972, *Evelyn Fison × Etendard*; Cants of Colchester. Flowers bright red, dbl. (40-50 petals), rosette form, medium (2 in.); slightly fragrant; foliage light; very free growth.

Coleraine HT, *lp*, 1970, *Paddy McGredy × (Mme. Léon Cuny × Columbine)*; McGredy, S., IV; McGredy. Flowers pale pink, dbl. (49 petals), classic form, large (3½ in.); slightly fragrant; foliage light; free growth.

Cole's Pink Lafayette F, *mp*, 1930, *Lafayette sport*; Cole Nursery Co. Flowers rose-pink, semi-dbl.

Coletta Montanelli HT, *dy*, 1975, *Seedling × Peer Gynt*; Kordes; Barni. Bud globular; flowers deep yellow, dbl. (32 petals), high-centered, large (4 in.); slightly fragrant; foliage dark, soft; vigorous, upright, bushy growth.

Colette N (OGR), *pb*, 1932, *William Allen Richardson × Mme. Laurette Messimy*; Schwartz, A. Flowers center nankeen yellow, shaded salmon-pink, large; foliage glossy, light; very vigorous growth. RULED EXTINCT 7/90.

Colette HT, *mp*, 1990, (JACcol); *Lorena × Seedling*; Warriner, William & Zary, Keith, 1986; Bear Creek Gardens, Inc., 1990. Bud ovoid, pointed; flowers medium soft pink, same reverse, aging slightly paler, dbl. (25-30 petals), urn-shaped, high-centered, exhibition, large, borne usually singly; slight, damask fragrance; foliage large, dark green, semi-glossy; upright, bushy, tall growth.

Colette Berges HT, *mr*, 1940, *Red Columbia × Ami Quinard*; Dot, P. Flowers crimson, dbl. (45 petals), high-centered, medium; fragrant (damask); vigorous growth.

Colette Clémente HT, *ob*, 1932, *(Mme. Mélanie Soupert × Mme. Edouard Herriot) × (Mrs. Edward Powell × R. foetida bicolor)*; Mallerin; C-P. Flowers reddish orange, single to semi-dbl., medium; slightly fragrant; foliage glossy, dark; vigorous.

Colette Jelot F, *yb*, 1942, Ampere × *((Charles P. Kilham) × (Charles P. Kilham × Capucine Chambard))*; Meilland, F.; A. Meilland. Flowers amber-yellow shaded currant-red, semi-dbl., open, medium, borne in clusters; slightly fragrant; foliage soft; dwarf growth.

Colibri Min, *ob*, 1958, (MEImal; Colibre); *Goldilocks × Perla de Montserrat*; Meilland, F.; URS. Bud ovoid; flowers bright orange-yellow, dbl., small blooms in clusters; slightly fragrant; foliage glossy; bushy growth. Golden Rose of The Hague, 1962.

Colibri Pol, *ly*, 1898, Lille. Flowers soft yellow, fading.

Colin Kelly HT, *dp*, 1945, *E.G. Hill × The Queen Alexandra Rose*; Krebs; Marsh's Nursery. Bud pointed; flowers cerise-red, dbl., very large; very fragrant; foliage leathery; upright, bushy growth.

Colin Kelly, Climbing Cl HT, *dp*, Marsh's Nursery.

Colisée F, *mr*, 1965, (Colysée); *Atlantic × Circus*; Gaujard; Ilgenfritz Nursery. Bud pointed; flowers coppery pink, semi-dbl., open, medium; foliage dark, glossy; very vigorous, bushy growth.

Colleen HT, *mp*, 1914, McGredy. Bud high pointed; flowers bright rose shaded rose-pink, dbl., large; fragrant; vigorous growth. GM, NRS, 1913.

Colleen Little Min, *my*, 1992, (LEEcal); *Luis Desamero × Cheyenne*; Little, Lee W.; Oregon Miniature Roses, 1992. Flowers medium yellow, full (26-40 petals), high centered, small (0-4 cms) blooms borne usually singly or in sprays of 5-7; slight fragrance; foliage small, dark green, semi-glossy, disease resistant; some prickles; medium (26-30 cms), upright, bushy growth.

Colleen Moore HT, *dr*, 1944, *((De Luxe × Senior) × Premier)) × Chieftain*; Hill, J.H., Co.; Bosley Nursery. Flowers velvety carmine, semi-dbl. (15-25 petals), open, large (4-4½ in.), strong stems; very fragrant; foliage leathery, dark; vigorous, upright growth.

Colonel Campbell Watson HT, *mp*, 1936, *Joan Howarth × Portadown*; Bees. Bud pointed; flowers salmon-pink, dbl., high-centered, long stems; foliage soft; vigorous growth. GM NRS, 1935.

Colonel Dazier HT, *w*, 1927, *Le Progrès × Jonkheer J.L. Mock*; Ketten Bros. Flowers rosy white, reverse bright rose, base golden yellow, dbl.; very fragrant.

Colonel Gravereaux HT, *op*, 1940, Mallerin; A. Meilland. Flowers salmon-coral, reverse yellow, strong stems; vigorous, upright growth.

Colonel Joffé T (OGR), *mr*, 1893, Liabaud. Flowers purplish red, flat, petals wrinkled.

Colonel Leclerc HT, *mp*, 1909, *Mme. Caroline Testout × Horace Vernet*; Pernet-Ducher. Flowers tyrian pink, dbl.; fragrant.

Colonel Lindbergh Pol, *op*, 1928, *Juliana Rose sport*; Ouden, Den. Flowers salmon-orange.

Colonel Nicolas Meyer HT, *mr*, 1934, *La Maréchale Petain × Edouard Mignot*; Sauvageot. Bud pointed; flowers brilliant velvety red, dbl., open, strong stems; fragrant; foliage leathery; vigorous, bushy growth.

Colonel Oswald Fitzgerald HT, *dr*, 1917, Dickson, A. Flowers dark velvety crimson, dbl., well formed; vigorous, branching growth.

Colonel Robert Lefort M (OGR), *mr*, 1864, Verdier, E. Flowers purple-red.

Colonel R.S. Williamson HT, *lp*, 1907, Dickson, A. Flowers white, center deep blush, dbl., high-centered, large; fragrant; foliage glossy, dark; vigorous, open growth.

Colonel Sharman-Crawford HT, *mr*, 1933, Dickson, A. Flowers rich velvety crimson, dbl., high-centered, large, long, strong stems; very fragrant; foliage leathery; vigorous, bushy growth. GM, NRS, 1931.

Colonial White LCl, *w*, 1959, *New Dawn × Mme. Hardy*; Wyant. Bud ovoid; flowers white, dbl., flat, medium (3 in.); fragrant; foliage light green; vigorous, recurrent.

Color Girl F, *pb*, 1966, *Little Darling × Cocorico*; Fuller; Wyant. Bud ovoid; flowers whitish, edged deep pink, dbl., high-centered, medium; very fragrant; foliage dark, leathery; bushy, low growth.

Color Guard Min, *mp*, 1991, (JOLcol); *Anita Charles × Poker Chip*; Jolly, Marie; Rosehill Farm, 1993. Flowers medium pink, moderately full (25 self cleaning petals), medium (5 cms) blooms borne mostly singly; no fragrance; foliage medium, medium green, matt; few prickles; upright (20 cms), bushy, very hardy growth.

Color Magic HT, *pb*, 1978, (JACmag); *Seedling × Spellbinder*; Warriner; J&P. Bud long; flowers ivory to deep rose, dbl. (25 petals), semi-flat, large (5 in.); slightly fragrant; foliage large, dark; upright growth. AARS, 1978.

Color Purple Min, *m*, 1991, (CLEpurp); *Angel Face × Seedling*; Clements, John; Heirloom Old Garden Roses, 1990. Flowers rich deep purple, very full (41+ petals), small (0-4 cms), blooms borne mostly singly; fragrant; foliage medium, dark green, holly-like, glossy; few prickles; low (25 cms), spreading, compact growth.

Colorama HT, *rb*, 1968, (MEIrigalu; Colourama; Dr. R. Maag); *Suspense × Confidence*; Meilland, M.L.; C-P. Bud ovoid; flowers red and yellow, dbl., cupped, large; fragrant; foliage very glossy; vigorous, upright, bushy growth.

Coloranja HT, *or*, 1963, (Mustang); *Fandango × (Independence × Papillon Rose)*; Lens. Bud ovoid; flowers orange-red, dbl., high-centered, large to medium; foliage dark, leathery; vigorous, bushy growth.

Coloso HT, *mp*, 1962, *Chrysler Imperial × (Peace × Queen Elizabeth)*; Dot, S. Flowers pink, dbl. (50 petals); fragrant; very vigorous growth.

Colour Carnival F, *yb*, 1962, LeGrice; Wayside Gardens Co. Flowers primrose-yellow edged pink, dbl. (50 petals), well formed, large (3 in.), borne in clusters; slightly fragrant; vigorous, low, bushy growth.

Colour Glow F, *ob*, 1969, *Tropicana × Masquerade*; Butter; Wood End Gardens. Flowers orange, reddening to flame, dbl. (36 petals), globular, large (3½ in.); slightly fragrant; vigorous growth.

Colour Parade F, *yb*, 1991, (LAVcoat); *Breezy × Julie Ann*; Laver, Keith G.; Springwood Roses, 1992. Flowers yellow turning to red, full (26-40 petals), small (0-4 cms), blooms borne in small clusters; slight fragrance; foliage medium, medium green, glossy; few prickles; low (45 cms), bushy growth.

Colour Sergeant F, *or*, 1972, *Queen Elizabeth × (Ann Elizabeth × Circus)*; Harkness. Flowers orange-red, dbl. (20 petals), large (4 in.); slightly fragrant; foliage glossy.

Colour Wonder HT, *ob*, 1964, (KORbico; Königin der Rosen; Queen of Roses; Reine des Roses); *Kordes' Perfecta × Tropicana*; Kordes, R.; A. Dickson; McGredy, 1964; Wyant, 1966. Bud ovoid; flowers orange-coral, reverse cream, dbl. (50 petals), large; slightly fragrant; foliage glossy, bronze; many, large prickles; vigorous, bushy. ADR, 1964; GM, Belfast, 1966.

Columbia HT, *mp*, 1916, *Ophelia* × *Mrs. George Shawyer*; Hill, E.G., Co. Bud long, pointed; flowers glistening rose-pink, dbl. (65 petals), large; very fragrant; foliage dark; vigorous. A famous parent.   GM, ARS Gertrude M. Hubbard & Portland, 1919.

Columbia R, *mp*, 1903, *Seedling* × *Mme. Caroline Testout*; Hooper, Bro. & Thomas. Flowers pink; moderately vigorous growth; non-recurrent bloom.

Columbia, Climbing Cl HT, *mp*, 1923, Vestal, 1923 & Lens, 1929.

Columbine F, *yb*, 1956, (Colombine); *Danish Gold* × *Frensham*; Poulsen, S.; McGredy. Flowers creamy yellow tinged pink, well-formed blooms in open clusters; very fragrant; foliage glossy; vigorous growth.

Columbus™ F, *dp*, 1990, (WEKuz); *Seedling* × *Bridal Pink*; Carruth, Tom; Weeks Roses, 1991. Bud ovoid, pointed; flowers deep rose pink, very little fading, dbl. (28 petals), high-centered, exhibition, large blooms borne usually singly or in sprays of 3-5; foliage large, medium green, dull; prickles almost straight, slightly hooked, medium, pinkish-brown; bushy, medium growth.

Columbus Queen HT, *pb*, 1962, *La Jolla* × *Seedling*; Armstrong, D.L.; Armstrong Nursery. Bud ovoid, pointed; flowers light pink, reverse darker, dbl. (24-30 petals), high-centered to cupped, large (4 in.); slightly fragrant; foliage leathery, dark; vigorous, upright growth.   GM, Geneva, 1961.

Comanche Gr, *or*, 1968, *Spartan* × *(Carrousel* × *Happiness)*; Swim & Weeks; C-P. Bud pointed; flowers orange-red, dbl., high-centered, medium; slightly fragrant; foliage leathery; vigorous, upright, bushy growth. AARS, 1969.

Comendador Nogueira da Silva HT, *rb*, 1961, *Confidence* × *Independence*; Moreira da Silva. Flowers dark red, reverse silvery.

Comet Cl F, *pb*, 1934, *Gruss an Aachen sport*; Mesman; Bosley Nursery. Flowers flesh pink, shades salmon-yellow, very dbl., large, short, strong stems; slightly fragrant; foliage leathery.

Command Performance HT, *or*, 1970, *Tropicana* × *Hawaii*; Lindquist; Howard Rose Co. Bud ovoid; flowers orange-red, dbl., high-centered, medium; very fragrant; foliage leathery; vigorous, tall, bushy growth.   AARS, 1971.

Commandant Beaurepaire B (OGR), *pb*, 1874, Moreau-Robert. Flowers bright rose-pink streaked (striped) purple-violet and marbled white, dbl., large; fragrant; foliage light green; vigorous growth; occasional repeats.

Commandant Félix Faure HP (OGR), *mr*, 1901, Boutigny. Flowers light crimson-red, tinted vermilion, dbl. (25 petals), cupped; fragrant; vigorous, upright growth.

Commandant L. Bartre HT, *rb*, 1920, *Lady Ashtown* × *Louis van Houtte*; Schwartz, A. Flowers dark carmine-red, tinted brilliant pink, dbl.; vigorous growth.

Commandatore Francesco Ingegnoli Cl HT, *or*, 1923, Ingegnoli. Flowers geranium-red.

Commandeur Jules Gravereaux HP (OGR), *mr*, 1908, *Frau Karl Druschki* × *Liberty*; Croibier. Bud pointed; flowers dazzling red, center shaded maroon, dbl., large, peony-like; very fragrant; vigorous growth.

Commandeur Jules Gravereaux, Climbing Cl HP (OGR), *mr*, 1925, Belouet; Grandes Roseraies.

Commando HT, *op*, 1945, *Mrs. J.D. Eisele* × *Glowing Sunset*; Howard, F.H.; H&S. Bud long, pointed; flowers orange-buff, suffused pink, dbl. (30-35 petals), camellia form, large (5 in.); fragrant; foliage leathery, glossy; upright, bushy growth.

Commonwealth HT, *dp*, 1923, *Ophelia* × *Seedling*; Montgomery Co.; A.N. Pierson. Bud pointed; flowers deep pink, dbl., large; fragrant; foliage leathery, rich green.

Commonwealth F, *pb*, 1948, (Herzblut); *Col. Nicolas Meyer* × *Holstein*; Kordes; Morse. Flowers crimson with white eye, semi-dbl. (10 petals), borne in clusters; slightly fragrant; foliage leathery.

Communis M (OGR), *mp*, (Centifolia Muscosa; Common Moss; Mousseau Ancien; Old Pink Moss; Pink Moss; *R. centifolia muscosa*); Appeared in southern France about 1696. Bud mossed; flowers pale rose, very dbl., globular; vigorous growth. One of the best Moss roses.

Compassion® LCl, *op*, 1972, (Belle de Londres); *White Cockade* × *Prima Ballerina*; Harkness, 1973. Flowers salmon pink shaded apricot, dbl. (36 petals), large blooms borne singly or in 3's; sweet fragrance; foliage large, dark; large, reddish prickles; medium, bushy growth.   GM, Baden-Baden, 1973; Orleans & Geneva, 1979; Edland Fragrance Medal., 1973; ADR, 1976

Complicata G (OGR), *pb*, *Possibly a hybrid of R. macrantha hort.*; Origin and date unknown. Flowers deep pink, white eye, yellow stamens, single, large; rampant (to 6 ft.).

Comrade HT, *mr*, 1948, Dickson, A. Flowers scarlet-crimson, well formed, medium; fragrant.

Comte Boula de Nanteuil G (OGR), *m*, (Boule de Nanteuil; Comte de Nanteuil);

Roeser, ca. 1834. Flowers crimson purple, center sometimes fiery crimson, full, compact, large; branching growth.

Comte de Chambord P (OGR), *pb*, 1860, Robert & Moreau. Flowers pink tinted lilac, very full, flat; very fragrant; vigorous, erect growth.

Comte de Mortemart HP (OGR), *mp*, 1880, (Comtesse de Mortemart); Margottin. Flowers clear pink; very fragrant.

Comte de Nanteuil HP (OGR), *pb*, 1852, Quietier. Flowers light rose with darker edges, sometimes with a green center, full, cupped, large; vigorous.

Comte F. de Chavanac HT, *mp*, *Antoine Rivoire × Zephirine Drouhin*. Flowers peach-blossom-pink, center rosy carmine.

Comte F. de Chavanac, Climbing Cl HT, *mp*, 1929, Siret-Pernet.

Comte Foy de Rouen G (OGR), *lp*, Savoureux. Flowers pale rose, dbl., cupped, very large.

Comte G. de Rochemur HT, 1911, *Xavier Olibo × Gruss an Teplitz*; Schwartz, A. Flowers bright scarlet, dbl., large; fragrant.

Comte Raimbaud HP (OGR), *mr*, 1867, Rolland. Flowers crimson, large.

Comtesse Anne de Bruce HT, *pb*, 1937, *Charles P. Kilham × (Mrs. Pierre S. duPont × R. foetida bicolor seedling)*; Mallerin; H. Guillot. Bud pointed; flowers coppery pink to nasturtium-red, semi-dbl., cupped, very large; fragrant; foliage glossy; very vigorous growth.

Comtesse Bardi T (OGR), *pb*, 1896, Soupert & Notting. Flowers reddish fawn.

Comtesse Cécile de Chabrilliant HP (OGR), *pb*, 1858, Marest. Flowers satiny pink, silvery reverse, full, globular, medium; fragrant; foliage dark, leathery; numerous small, dark prickles.

Comtesse Cécile de Forton Cl T (OGR), *pb*, 1916, Nabonnand, G. Flowers rose-peach, dbl., very large; fragrant.

Comtesse d'Ansembourg HT, *ly*, 1918, *Étoile de France × Marquise de Sinéty*; Leenders, M. Flowers yellowish white, dbl.; very fragrant.

Comtesse de Bouchaud N (OGR), *my*, 1890, Guillot Fils. Flowers yellow, very large.

Comtesse de Caserta T (OGR), *mr*, 1877, Nabonnand, G. Flowers coppery-red, large.

Comtesse de Cassagne HT, *mp*, 1919, Guillot, M. Flowers coppery rose, shaded bright rose, sometimes entirely yellow, dbl.; fragrant.

Comtesse de Castilleja HT, *op*, 1926, *(Mme. Edouard Herriot × Juliet) × Seedling*; Chambard, M. Bud orange; flowers coral, cupped,

strong stems; very fragrant; foliage dark; very vigorous growth.

Comtesse de Chaponay LCl, *lp*, 1924, *R. gigantea × Mme. Hoste*; Nabonnand, G. Flowers cream-rose to salmon, dbl.; very fragrant; very vigorous.

Comtesse de Frigneuse T (OGR), *my*, 1885, *Mme. Damaizin × Seedling*; Guillot Fils. Flowers yellow, large, full; fragrant.

Comtesse de la Morandière HT, *op*, 1929, Chambard, C. Flowers shrimp-pink, reverse coral-red, dbl.; fragrant.

Comtesse de Lacépède G (OGR), *lp*, 1840, Flowers silvery blush, center sometimes rosy, dbl., large; moderate growth.

Comtesse de Martel HT, *mp*, 1939, *Charles P. Kilham × Margaret McGredy*; Meilland, F. Flowers carnation-pink, center coppery, very large; fragrant; very vigorous growth.

Comtesse de Murinais M (OGR), *w*, 1843, (White Moss); Vibert. Flowers flesh, opening white, dbl., large; fragrant; height 4-5 ft.; non-recurrent bloom.

Comtesse de Murinais C (OGR), *mp*, 1843, Robert. Flowers pink.

Comtesse de Serenye HP (OGR), *lp*, 1874, *Said to be La Reine seedling*; Lacharme. Flowers soft pink.

Comtesse Doria M (OGR), *m*, 1854, Portemer. Flowers purple-pink, shaded salmon, heavily mossed.

Comtesse d'Oxford HP (OGR), *dp*, 1869, (Countess of Oxford); Guillot Père. Flowers deep pink, dbl., globular; fragrant; recurrent bloom.

Comtesse du Cayla Ch (OGR), *ob*, 1902, Guillot, P. Flowers nasturtium-red, tinted orange, semi-dbl., flat; fragrant; foliage dark, glossy; vigorous growth; recurrent bloom.

Comtesse Fressinet de Belanger HP (OGR), *mp*, 1886, Lévêque. Flowers rose.

Comtesse Icy Hardegg HT, *dp*, 1911, *Mrs. W.J. Grant × Liberty*; Soupert & Notting. Flowers carmine, full, large.

Comtesse Mélanie de Pourtales HT, *w*, 1914, *Frau Karl Druschki × Mme. Ravary*; Walter. Flowers creamy white, outer petals shaded red.

Comtesse Moens de Fernig HT, *dr*, 1961, *Poinsettia × Seedling*; Verbeek. Flowers wine-red, dbl. (25 petals); fragrant; vigorous growth.

Comtesse O'Gorman HP (OGR), *rb*, 1888, Lévêque. Flowers red and violet.

Comtesse Prozor LCl, *pb*, 1922, *R. gigantea × Comtesse de Bouchaud*; Nabonnand, P. Flowers salmon-rose, reverse coral red.

Comtesse Riza du Parc T (OGR), *mp*, 1876, (Comtesse Risa du Parc); *Duchesse de Brabant seedling*; Schwartz, J. Flowers rose to carmine, full, globular, large; fragrant.

Comtesse Vandal HT, *pb*, 1932, (Comtesse Vandale; Countess Vandal); *(Ophelia × Mrs. Aaron Ward) × Souv. de Claudius Pernet*; Leenders, M.; J&P. Flowers salmon-pink, reverse coppery pink, dbl. (30 petals), high-centered, large; fragrant; foliage leathery; bushy growth; . GM, Bagatelle, 1931.

Comtesse Vandal, Climbing Cl HT, *op*, 1936, (Comtesse Vandale, Climbing; Countess Vandal, Climbing; Grimpant Comtesse Vandal) J&P.

Concertino® F, *or*, 1976, (MEIbinosor); *((Fidélio × Fidélio) × (Zambra × Zambra)) × Marlena*; Meilland, M.L.; Meilland. Flowers cherry-red, dbl. (20 petals), flat-cupped, medium; slightly fragrant; foliage matt, dark; vigorous, bushy growth.

Concerto F, *mr*, 1953, *Alain × Floradora*; Meilland, F.; URS. Bud ovoid, pointed; flowers medium red, semi-dbl. (12-15 petals), loosely cupped, medium (2-2½ in.); slightly fragrant; foliage dark; upright, bushy growth. GM, NRS, 1953; RNRS PIT, 1953.

Concerto, Climbing Cl F, *mr*, 1968, Truffant, G.; URS.

Conchita Pol, *mp*, 1935, Jordan, H.; Low. Flowers clear salmon, dbl., cupped, borne in clusters; slightly fragrant; foliage glossy; vigorous growth.

Concordia HT, *mp*, 1924, Brix; Teschendorff. Flowers glowing pink, edged silver-pink, semi-dbl.; fragrant.

Concordia HT, *rb*, 1946, *Charles P. Kilham × Crimson Glory*; Giacomasso. Flowers red, reverse deep yellow, dbl., well formed; fragrant; vigorous growth.

Condesa de Benahavis HT, *mp*, 1949, *Étoile de Hollande × Sensation*; La Florida. Flowers salmon-pink, well formed; very fragrant.

Condesa de Glimes F, *pb*, Bofill; Torre Blanca. Flowers begonia-pink, center ochre-yellow, single.

Condesa de Mayalde HT, *rb*, 1956, *Peace × Flambee*; Dot, P. Bud pointed; flowers white edged carmine, dbl. (30 petals), high-centered; foliage glossy; compact, upright growth.

Condesa de Mayalde, Climbing Cl HT, *w*, 1964, Samuels.

Condesa de Munter HT, *or*, 1932, *Souv. de Josefina Plà × Souv. de Claudius Pernet*; Munné, B. Flowers geranium-red, tinted orange-yellow, semi-dbl., cupped, large, long, strong stems; vigorous growth.

Condesa de Saldanha HT, *ob*, 1961, Munné, M. Flowers reddish orange, mottled yellow, dbl. (45 petals), large; fragrant; vigorous growth.

Condesa de Sástago HT, *pb*, 1932, *(Souv. de Claudius Pernet × Maréchal Foch) × Margaret McGredy*; Dot, P.; C-P. Bud ovoid; flowers deep pink, reverse yellow, dbl. (55 petals), cupped, large; fragrant; foliage glossy, dark; vigorous, tall growth; (28). GM, Rome, 1933.

Condesa de Sástago, Climbing Cl HT, *pb*, 1936, Vestal.

Condesa de Villarrea HT, *mr*, 1960, *Chrysler Imperial × Texas Centennial*; Dot, M. Flowers crimson, reverse cardinal-red, dbl. (35 petals), large, long, stiff stems; vigorous growth.

Conditorum G (OGR), *dr*, (*R gallica conditorum* Dieck; Tidbit Rose; Hungarian Rose); Flowers dark red-purple, paler reverse, semi-dbl. Perhaps identical with Parkinson's Hungarian Rose, 1629; (28).

Conestoga S, *w*, 1946, *Betty Bland × Seedling*; Preston; Central Exp. Farm. Bud ovoid; flowers white, full (30 petals), open, medium (2 in.), borne in clusters; slightly fragrant; foliage soft, sparse, small; upright, vigorous growth; non-recurrent bloom; hardy.

Confection Min, *mp*, 1988, (JACute); *Seedling × Seedling*; Warriner, William; Bear Creek Gardens. Bud ovoid, pointed; flowers pink with yellow to cream base, very dbl. (100+ petals), high-centered to flat, medium, borne usually singly and in sprays of 2-3; micromini; slight fragrance; foliage medium, dark green, matt; prickles straight to slightly hooked, light green aging to tan or light brown; low, bushy growth.

Confederation HT, *mp*, 1964, *Queen o' the Lakes × Serenade*; Golik; Ellesmere Nursery. Flowers medium pink, dbl. (70 petals), compact, large; very fragrant; foliage dark, glossy; moderate, vigorous growth.

Conference 63 HT, *dr*, 1965, Quentin. Flowers deep crimson, dbl., large (4½ in.); slightly fragrant; foliage light green; tall growth; free bloom under glass.

Confetti F, *rb*, 1980, (AROjechs); *Jack O'Lantern × Zorina*; Swim, H.C. & Christensen, J.E.; Armstrong Nursery, 1983. Bud ovoid; flowers deep yellow, aging orange-red, 18-25 petals, HT form, borne 3-7 per cluster; slight, tea fragrance; foliage medium green; prickles hooked downward; upright growth.

Confidence HT, *pb*, 1951, *Peace × Michèle Meilland*; Meilland, F.; URS, 1951 & C-P, 1953. Bud ovoid; flowers pearly light pink to yellow blend, dbl. (28-38 petals), high-centered, large; fragrant; foliage dark, leathery; vigorous, upright, bushy growth. GM, Bagatelle, 1951.

Confidence, Climbing Cl HT, *pb*, 1961, Hendrickx; URS.

Congo HT, *dr*, 1943, *Admiral Ward × Lemania*; Meilland, F.; A. Meilland. Bud long, pointed; flowers velvety maroon, dbl., open, medium; very fragrant; foliage leathery, bronze; bushy, dwarf growth.

Congolaise HT, *dr*, Tantau. Flowers velvety dark red, dbl., well formed, large; fragrant; vigorous growth.

Congratulations HT, *op*, 1979, (KORlift; Sylvia; Kordes' Rose Sylvia); *Carina × Seedling*; Kordes, W., Sons. Bud long, pointed; flowers medium pink, dbl. (42 petals), high-centered, large (4½ in.); fragrant; vigorous, upright, bushy growth. ADR, 1977.

Connie Min, *dy*, 1991, Jerabek, Paul. Bud pointed; flowers dark yellow fading to light yellow, semi-dbl. (11 petals), flat blooms borne singly or in sprays of 2-7; slight fragrance; foliage medium, dark green, glossy; bushy, medium (36 cms), very dense growth.

Connie Mack F, *dr*, 1952, *Seedling × Margy*; Duehrsen; H&S. Flowers dark velvety crimson, dbl. (25 petals), medium, borne in clusters; slightly fragrant; foliage glossy, dark; vigorous growth.

Conqueror HT, *ly*, 1929, Chaplin Bros. Flowers saffron-yellow, fading pale yellow, semi-dbl. (15 petals); fragrant; vigorous, bushy growth.

Conqueror's Gold F, *yb*, 1986, (HARtwiz); *Amy Brown × Judy Garland*; Harkness, R. Flowers yellow, petals edged orange-red, 18 petals, cupped, medium blooms in clusters of up to 7; slightly fragrant; foliage medium, dark semi-glossy; medium, bushy.

Conrad Ferdinand Meyer HRg (S), *lp*, 1899, *R. rugosa hybrid × Gloire de Dijon*; Müller, F. Flowers silver pink, dbl., cupped, large blooms in clusters; very fragrant; foliage leathery; vigorous (8-10 ft.), good pillar rose, bushy growth; repeat bloom.

Conrad Hilton F, *my*, 1962, (*R. × dupontii × Pinocchio) × (Goldilocks × Feu Pernet-Ducher)*; Shepherd; Bosley Nursery. Bud ovoid; flowers golden yellow, outer petals sometimes white, dbl. (30-45 petals), flat, medium (2½ in.); fragrant; foliage leathery, dark, glossy, crinkled; very vigorous, upright, bushy growth.

Conrad O'Neal S, *dp*, 1966, *Blossomtime seedling × Don Juan*; O'Neal; Wyant. Bud ovoid; flowers deep pink, very dbl., medium; very fragrant; foliage dark, glossy; vigorous, upright.

Conrad's Crimson S, *rb*, 1972, *Sweet Sultan × Conrad F. Meyer*; Eacott. Flowers crimson, shaded purple, dbl. (30 petals), flat, large (3 in.); fragrant; foliage light green to bronze; early bloom.

Conservation Min, *pb*, 1986, (COCdimple); *((Sabine × Circus) × Maxi) × Darling Flame*; Cocker, James & Sons, 1988. Flowers pink blend, semi-dbl., patio, medium; slight fragrance; foliage small, light green, semi-glossy; bushy growth. GM, Dublin Gold, 1986.

Consolata HT, *yb*, 1936, Capiago. Bud pointed; flowers yellow and coppery nasturtium-red, long, strong stems; foliage bronze.

Conspicuous HT, *mr*, 1930, Dickson, A.; B&A, 1932. Flowers glowing scarlet, dbl., very large; vigorous growth.

Constance HT, *my*, 1915, *Rayon d'Or × Seedling*; Pernet-Ducher. Flowers yellow to golden yellow, dbl., high-centered; slightly fragrant; foliage rich green, glossy; bushy growth. GM, Bagatelle, 1916.

Constance Casson HT, *pb*, 1920, *Queen Mary × Gorgeous*; Cant, B.R. Flowers carmine, flushed apricot, dbl.; fragrant.

Constance, Climbing Cl HT, *my*, 1927, Pacific Rose Co.

Constance Morley HT, *ob*, 1981, *Piccadilly × Seedling*; Gregory, C. & Sons, Ltd. Flowers orange-gold tinged red, dbl. (39 petals), diffused center, borne singly; some fragrance; foliage dark, glossy; elongated, orange prickles; spreading, bushy.

Constance Spry® S, *lp*, 1961, (Constanze Spry); *Belle Isis × Dainty Maid*; Austin, D.; Sunningdale Nursery. Flowers pink, dbl., cupped, large (5 in.) blooms in clusters; fragrant (myrrh); foliage dark; vigorous (5-6 ft.) growth.

Constantia HT, *mp*, 1960, *Baccará × Grace de Monaco*; Herholdt, J.A.; Herholdt's Nursery. Bud pointed; flowers neyron rose, dbl. (40 petals), well formed; large (4-4½ in.); fragrant; moderate growth.

Constanze HT, *ob*, 1966, Tantau, Math. Bud pointed; flowers orange, dbl. (25-30 petals), well-formed, large; foliage dark, glossy; upright, bushy growth.

Constellation HT, *ob*, 1949, *Peace × Seedling*; Gaujard. Bud long, pointed; flowers coppery orange, well formed, very large; very vigorous, erect growth.

Contempo F, *ob*, 1971, *Spartan × (Goldilocks × (Fandango × Pinocchio))*; Armstrong, D.L.; Armstrong Nursery. Bud ovoid; flowers orange blending to gold, dbl., high-centered, medium; fragrant; foliage light, leathery; vigorous, bushy growth.

Contentment HT, *pb*, 1956, *(Red seedling × Lilette Mallerin) × Orange Delight*; Boerner; J&P. Bud globular; flowers soft pink suffused yellow, dbl. (65-70 petals), high-centered, large (5½ in.); very fragrant; foliage glossy, leathery; vigorous, upright growth.

Contessa S, *dp*, 1987, (JACris); *Sunsprite × Seedling*; Warriner, William; J&P. Flowers deep pink with yellow center, reverse deep pink, fading slightly, semi-dbl. (6-10 petals), loose, flat, medium, borne usually singly or in sprays of 3-5; slight, spicy fragrance; foliage medium, medium green, semi-glossy; straight, long, green-brown prickles; upright, tall growth; fast cycle.

Continental HT, *mr*, 1966, *Baccará × Yuletide*; Lammerts; Amling-DeVor Nursery. Bud ovoid; flowers cardinal-red, dbl., large; fragrant (fruity); foliage leathery; vigorous, upright growth; a greenhouse variety.

Contrast HT, *pb*, 1937, *Seedling × Talisman*; H&S. Flowers china-pink and bronze, reverse white and bronze, dbl., high-centered; fragrant; foliage leathery, glossy; very vigorous, bushy, compact growth.

Cool Wave Min, *w*, 1987, (ZIPcool); *Poker Chip × Pink Parfait*; Zipper, Herbert; Magic Moment Miniatures. Flowers white with hints of yellow at petal base, dbl. (15-25 petals), high-centered, exhibition, medium; no fragrance; foliage medium, medium green, matt.

Coolness F, *w*, 1958, *Glacier seedling × Starlite seedling*; Boerner; J&P. Bud ovoid, cream; flowers white, dbl. (55-60 petals), large (2½-3 in.); fragrant; foliage leathery, glossy; vigorous, bushy, compact growth; for pot forcing.

Coon Carnival® F, *yb*, 1981, (KORcoon); *Seedling × Seedling*; Kordes, R.; Ludwigs Roses Pty. Ltd. Bud ovoid; flowers yellow, changing to pink and red, dbl. (56 petals), large blooms borne 1-7 per cluster; slight fragrance; foliage matt, green; straight, brown prickles; medium high, bushy growth.

Cooper's Burmese HLaev (S), *w*, 1927, (*R. × cooperi; Gigantea Cooperi*); *Possibly a natural hybrid of R. gigantea × R. laevigata*. Flowers near white, single, large; foliage glossy; vigorous (to 20 ft.) growth.

Cooran F, *dp*, 1953, *Mrs. Tom Henderson × Ming Toy*; Ulrick. Bud long, pointed; flowers deep rose-pink, very large, borne in clusters; very fragrant; very vigorous growth.

Cooroy F, *mp*, 1953, *Mrs. Tom Henderson × Self*; Ulrick. Flowers rose-pink, very dbl., high-centered, borne in clusters.

Copacabana LCl, *or*, 1966, *Coup de Foudre × Seedling*; Dorieux; Bees. Flowers orange-red, dbl. (40 petals), globular, large (3½ in.); slightly fragrant; foliage dark.

Copenhagen Cl HT, *mr*, 1964, *Seedling × Ena Harkness*; Poulsen, N.D.; McGredy. Flowers scarlet, dbl., large (5 in.); fragrant; foliage coppery; vigorous.

Copia F, *mr*, 1964, *(Independence × Seedling) × Tour de France*; Mondial Roses. Flowers bright cardinal-red, semi-dbl., large; vigorous, bushy growth.

Coppélia HT, *ob*, 1952, *Peace × Europa*; Meilland, F. Flowers rosy shades, deepening to orange, dbl. (28 petals), cupped, medium; slightly fragrant; foliage leathery; vigorous, upright growth.

Copper Climber LCl, *op*, 1938, Burbank; Stark Bros. Bud pointed, coppery; flowers glowing coppery salmon, edged pink, large.

Copper Coronet HT, *ab*, 1986, *Ginger Rogers × Royal Highness*; Strange, J.F. Flowers coppery amber, reverse blush pink, fading amber and cream, very dbl. (60 petals), high centered, exhibition, large, borne usually singly; slight fragrance; foliage medium green, semiglossy; upright, medium growth.

Copper Crown S, *op*, 1992, (WILcrown); *Westerland × Orange Velvet*; Williams, J. Benjamin; Hortico, Inc., 1992-93. Flowers orange pink, single (5 petals), large (7+cms.) blooms; slight fragrance; foliage medium, dark green, semi-glossy; upright (4x4'), bushy growth.

Copper Delight F, *ob*, 1956, *Goldilocks × Ellinor LeGrice*; LeGrice. Flowers clear orange, semi-dbl. (14 petals), large blooms in large clusters; fragrant; foliage olive-green; vigorous, upright, bushy growth.

Copper Glow LCl, *ob*, 1940, *Golden Glow × Break o' Day*; Brownell. Flowers copper, dbl. (27 petals), large (4 in.); very fragrant; foliage glossy; vigorous, climbing (20 ft.), open habit; seasonal bloom.

Copper Kettle F, *ob*, 1978, *Queen Elizabeth × Golden Slippers*; Williams, J.B.; J.B. Williams & Associates. Bud elongated; flowers brilliant copper-orange and yellow, dbl. (28 petals), high-centered, large (2½-3½ in.); fragrant; foliage glossy, bronze, dark; upright growth.

Copper King HT, *dy*, 1982, (HERcop); *Vienna Charm × Seedling*; Herholdt, J.A. Flowers copper-gold, dbl. (35 petals), large; no fragrance; foliage dark, glossy; upright.

Copper Luster HT, *op*, 1945, *Better Times × Orange Nassau*; Roberts; Totty. Flowers coppery pink, dbl. (23 petals), loosely cupped, large; slightly fragrant; foliage glossy, bronze; vigorous, upright growth.

Copper Nugget HT, *op*, 1942, *Charles P. Kilham* × *Capt. Thomas*; Lammerts; Armstrong Nursery. Bud ovoid to urn shaped; flowers orange-salmon, dbl. (50-60 petals), high-centered, small, strong stems; slightly fragrant; foliage leathery, glossy, dark; dwarf, bushy growth.

Copper Pot F, *ob*, 1968, (DICpe); *Seedling* × *Golden Scepter*; Dickson, A. Flowers orange-yellow, deeper reverse, semi-dbl. (15 petals), large blooms in trusses; fragrant; foliage glossy, bronze; tall.

Copper Ruffles Min, *or*, 1982, *Anytime* × *Sheri Anne*; Dobbs, Annette. Flowers orange-red, dbl. (35 ruffled petals), HT-form, small; slight fragrance; foliage small, medium-green, semi-glossy; upright growth.

Copper Sunset Min, *ob*, 1988, (SAVacop); *Acey Deucy* × *Rainbow's End*; Saville, F. Harmon. Bud pointed; Flowers coppery-orange, flushed orange-red, reverse medium red, dbl. (21 petals), high-centered, exhibition, long, pointed, medium, borne in sprays of 3-15; slight fragrance; foliage medium, dark green, semi-glossy; prickles long, thin, slanted, gray-red; fruit ovoid, orange; upright, medium, angular growth.

Copperkins HT, *ob*, 1957, *Mme. Henri Guillot* × *Golden Scepter*; Ratcliffe. Bud long, pointed, dark orange-flame; flowers orange, dbl. (25 petals), well formed; very fragrant (fruity); foliage glossy; vigorous growth.

Coppery Heart S, *yb*, 1958, *Peace* × *Conrad Ferdinand Meyer*; Gaujard. Flowers coppery yellow shaded red, dbl., large, long stems; fragrant; foliage dark, glossy; very vigorous growth; repeat bloom.

Copy Cat Min, *mp*, 1986, (MORcat); *Beauty Secret sport*; Moore, R.S.; Moore Min. Roses, 1985. Flowers medium pink.

Coq de Roche HT, *dr*, 1945, *Duquesa de Peñaranda* × *J. B. Meilland*; Meilland, F. Flowers blood-red, very dbl., large; very vigorous growth.

Coquette HT, *w*, 1976, (JACco); *Seedling* × *Seedling*; Warriner; J&P. Bud long; flowers white, dbl. (30-35 petals), high-centered, large (4 in.); slightly fragrant; foliage light green, reddish underneath; upright growth.

Coquette HT, *lp*, 1929, Dobbie. Flowers pale flesh-pink, well formed; slightly fragrant; vigorous growth.

Coquette de Lyon HP (OGR), *lp*, 1859, Lacharme. Flowers flesh-pink.

Coquette de Lyon T (OGR), *ly*, 1872, (La Coquette de Lyon); Ducher. Flowers canary-yellow, medium size.

Coquette des Alpes B (OGR), *w*, 1867, *Blanche Lafitte* × *Sappho (Vibert's)*; Lacharme. Flowers white tinged blush, semi-cupped, medium to large; vigorous growth.

Coquette des Blanches B (OGR), *w*, 1871, *Blanche Lafitte* × *Sappho (Vibert's)*; Lacharme. Flowers white, lightly washed pink, dbl., somewhat flat, cupped; fragrant; vigorous growth.

Coquina R, *pb*, 1909, Walsh. Flowers rose-pink fading lighter, base creamy white, single, cupped, borne in large clusters on long strong stems; fragrant; foliage dark, almost evergreen; very vigorous (20-24 ft.) growth.

Cora Marie HT, *mr*, 1987, (KORlimit; Dallas); *Ankori* × *Seedling*; Kordes, W., 1986. Flowers medium red, dbl. (15-25 petals), large; no fragrance; foliage large, dark green, semi-glossy; upright growth.

Corail LCl, *pb*, 1931, *William Allen Richardson* × *Orléans Rose*; Schwartz, A. Flowers light peach-blossom-pink, reverse coral-pink and carmine, dbl., opening well; foliage bright, glossy; very vigorous growth; recurrent bloom.

Coral R, *mp*, *R. sinowilsonii* × *Seedling*; F.C. Stern. Flowers pink; foliage massive; vigorous climbing like *R. sinowilsonii*; half-hardy.

Coral HT, *pb*, 1931, Dickson, A. Flowers bright coral, base buttercup-yellow, dbl., globular, large, wiry, erect stems; fragrant; vigorous growth.

Coral Anne Griffiths HT, *mp*, 1978, *Red Devil sport*; Henson. Bud very tight; flowers medium pink, very dbl. (72 petals); very large (6 in.); fragrant; foliage glossy, dark; very vigorous growth.

Coral Bay HT, *op*, 1971, *Seedling* × *Seedling*; Swim & Weeks; Weeks Roses. Bud ovoid; flowers silvery coral-orange, dbl., cupped, medium; fragrant; foliage glossy, leathery; vigorous.

Coral Beauty Pol, *mp*, 1941, *Sport of Orléans Rose sport*; deRuiter; J&P. Flowers spinel-pink, dbl., flat, small (1½ in.) borne in clusters; vigorous, branching growth; a florists' pot plant.

Coral Belle F, *ob*, 1962, *Stoplite* × *Orange Sweetheart*; Jelly; E.G. Hill Co. Bud pointed, ovoid; flowers vermilion, dbl. (45 petals), high-centered, medium (1½-2½ in.), strong stems; fragrant; foliage leathery; vigorous, upright growth; a greenhouse variety.

Coral Cameo Min, *dp*, 1986, (MORcalyn); *Little Darling* × *Anytime*; Moore, R.S.; Moore Min. Roses, 1982. Flowers deep pink, dbl., high-centered, exhibition, borne singly and in small sprays; slight fragrance; foliage small, medium green, semi-glossy; very few prickles; fruit small, orange, globular; medium, upright, bushy growth.

Coral Cascade F, *or*, 1980, *Van Bergen × Pink Hot Spot*; James, John. Flowers coral-red, dbl. (50-75 petals), globular blooms borne singly or 3-5 per cluster; light carnation fragrance; foliage opens russet, turning dark green, glossy; reddish-gray prickles; vigorous, compact, bushy growth.

Coral Cluster Pol, *op*, 1920, *Orléans Rose sport*; Murrell, R. Flowers coral-pink. GM, NRS, 1921.

Coral Creeper LCl, *dp*, 1938, *(Dr. W. Van Fleet × Emily Gray) × Jacotte*; Brownell. Bud deep red; flowers coral to light pink, semi-dbl., large (4 in.), 1-15 on upright stems; very fragrant; foliage leathery; very vigorous growth.

Coral Crown F, *or*, 1960, *Else Poulsen × (Fashion × Orange Triumph)*; Abrams, Von; Peterson & Dering. Flowers coral-red, dbl. (35 petals), high-centered to almost flat, large (3 in.) blooms in clusters; fragrant; foliage glossy; low, compact growth.

Coral Cup Pol, *op*, 1936, *Gloria Mundi sport*; B&A. Flowers soft coral, very dbl., cupped, borne in clusters; slightly fragrant; very vigorous, bushy growth; profuse, recurrent bloom.

Coral Dawn® LCl, *mp*, 1952, *(New Dawn seedling × Yellow Hybrid Tea) × Orange-red Polyantha*; Boerner; J&P. Bud ovoid; flowers rose-pink, dbl. (30-35 petals), cupped, large (5 in.) blooms in clusters; fragrant; foliage leathery; vigorous (8-12 ft.).

Coral Destiny HT, *op*, 1984, *Joanna Hill × Queen Elizabeth*; Perry, Anthony; Ball Seed Co. Flowers medium coral pink, dbl. (35 petals), large; slight fragrance; foliage medium green, semi-glossy; upright growth.

Coral Drops HMoy (S), *op*, *R. moyesii hybrid*. Flowers pale coral-pink, single; non-recurrent bloom.

Coral Fantasy Min, *ab*, 1982, (LYOco); *Dandy Lyon × Seedling*; Lyon, Lyndon; Lyon Greenhouse. Flowers apricot, dbl. (34 petals), medium; fragrant; foliage medium green, semi-glossy; vigorous, upright, bushy growth.

Coral Fiesta® HT, *or*, 1983, (DOTrames; Maria Teresa de Esteban; Mme. Teresa Estaban); *Seedling × Seedling*; Dot, Simon; Barni-Pistoia, Rose. Flowers orange-red, dbl. (45 petals), cupped, large; no fragrance; foliage large, dark, matt; light yellow prickles; bushy growth.

Coral Gem F, *pb*, 1958, *((Pinocchio × Mrs. Sam McGredy, Climbing) × (Pinocchio × Mrs. Sam McGredy, Climbing)) × Fashion*; Boerner; J&P. Bud ovoid; flowers light coral-pink, dbl. (40-45 petals), open to cupped, medium (2½ in.), borne in clusters; fragrant (fruity); foliage leathery, dark; vigorous, bushy growth.

Coral Glow LCl, *op*, 1964, *Spectacular × Seedling*; Croix, P.; Minier. Flowers salmon-pink blooms in clusters.

Coral Mist HT, *op*, 1966, *Spartan × Good News*; Patterson; Patterson Roses. Bud ovoid; flowers coral-pink, dbl., high-centered; fragrant; foliage glossy, light green; vigorous, bushy, open growth.

Coral Pillar Cl HT, *mr*, 1945, *Crimson Glory × Capt. Thomas*; Lammerts; Univ. of Calif. Flowers geranium-pink, dbl., high-centered, large; very fragrant; foliage glossy, dark; very vigorous, upright growth.

Coral Princess F, *ob*, 1966, *(Fashion seedling × Garnette seedling) × Spartan*; Boerner; J&P. Bud ovoid; flowers coral-orange, dbl. (25 petals), cupped, large; fragrant; foliage leathery; vigorous, bushy growth.

Coral Queen HT, *or*, 1928, *The Queen Alexandra Rose sport*; Reeves. Flowers coral-red, dbl., cupped, globular, large, long, strong stems; slightly fragrant; foliage dark, glossy; vigorous, bushy growth.

Coral Queen Elizabeth F, *op*, 1966, *Queen Elizabeth × Seedling*; Gregory. Flowers coral-salmon, dbl., large (3 in.), borne in clusters; fragrant; foliage glossy; very vigorous growth.

Coral Reef HT, *mp*, 1948, *Joanna Hill × R.M.S. Queen Mary*; Hill, J.H., Co. Bud long, pointed; flowers pink, dbl. (25-30 petals), medium; fragrant; foliage leathery, wrinkled, dark; vigorous, upright, bushy growth; for both forcing under glass and outdoor use. RULED EXTINCT 4/86.

Coral Reef Min, *op*, 1986, (COCdarlee); *(Darling Flame × St. Albans) × Silver Jubilee*; Cocker, Ann G.; Cocker & Sons. Flowers orange, semi-dbl., patio, medium; slight fragrance; foliage small, medium green, glossy; bushy growth.

Coral Sand HT, *op*, 1990, (RENsand); *Paul Shirville × Shocking Blue*; Rennie, Bruce; Rennie Roses, 1991-92. Flowers coral, full (26-40 petals), large, borne singly; very fragrant; foliage medium, medium green, semi-glossy; bushy growth.

Coral Satin LCl, *op*, 1960, *New Dawn × Fashion*; Zombory; J&P. Bud ovoid; flowers coral, dbl. (25 petals), high-centered, large (3½-4 in.); fragrant; foliage leathery, glossy; vigorous (6-8 ft.) growth.

Coral Sea HT, *dp*, 1942, *Katharine Pechtold × R.M.S. Queen Mary*; Hill, J.H., Co. Bud globular, old-rose; flowers light red, dbl. (40-45 petals), high-centered, large, long, strong stems; slightly fragrant; foliage leathery, dark; vigorous, upright, much branched growth; a florists' variety, not distributed for outdoor use.

Coral Silk F, *op*, 1972, Gregory. Flowers coral and peach, semi-dbl. (18 petals), flat, large (3 in.); fragrant; foliage glossy, dark; very free growth.

Coral Sprite™ Min, *mp*, 1988, (JACoral); *Merci × Party Girl*; Warriner, William; Bear Creek Gardens, 1989. Bud ovoid, pointed; flowers medium pink, very dbl., urn-shaped, medium, borne in sprays of 3-18; no fragrance; foliage medium, dark green, matt; prickles straight to slightly angled downward, yellow-green; bushy, spreading, low growth.

Coral Star HT, *op*, 1967, *Tropicana × Stella*; Robinson, H. Flowers coral-pink, well-formed, medium; very fragrant; vigorous, upright growth.

Coral Sunset HT, *or*, 1966, (Coucher de Soleil); *Garnette seedling × Hawaii*; Boerner; J&P. Bud ovoid; flowers coral-red, dbl., large; fragrant; foliage dark, leathery; vigorous growth.

Coral Treasure Min, *ob*, 1971, *Seedling × Little Buckaroo*; Moore, R.S.; Sequoia Nursery. Bud ovoid; flowers coral-orange, dbl., medium; foliage glossy, leathery; dwarf, bushy.

CoralGlo F, *op*, 1960, *Independence × Fashion*; Boerner; Stark Bros. Bud ovoid; flowers orange-rose, dbl. (42 petals), cupped, large; slightly fragrant; foliage bronze; bushy.

Corali LCl, *rb*, 1931, Dot, P. Flowers coral-red to rosy salmon; foliage bright green; vigorous growth; profuse seasonal bloom.

Coralie M (OGR), *lp*, Miellez, prior to 1848. Flowers flesh, dbl., well-formed, medium.

Coralie D (OGR), *lp*, Prior to 1848. Flowers soft pink, cupped; foliage grayish; vigorous.

Coralie LCl, *pb*, 1919, *Hiawatha × Lyon Rose*; Paul, W. Flowers coral-red to deep pink, dbl.; foliage glossy; vigorous; non-recurrent bloom.

Coralin Min, *or*, 1955, (Carolin; Carolyn; Karolyn); *Méphisto × Perla de Alcañada*; Dot, M. Flowers coral-red, dbl. (40 petals); low, compact.

Coralín Superb Min, *dr*, 1958, *Coralín sport*; Will; Kordes. Flowers dark red.

Coralita LCl, *or*, 1964, *(New Dawn × Geranium Red) × Fashion*; Zombory; J&P. Bud ovoid, deep red; flowers orange-coral, dbl. (40-45 petals), large (4 in.); fragrant; foliage dark,

leathery; vigorous (6-8 ft.). ARS David Fuerstenberg Prize, 1968.

Corallina T (OGR), *rb*, 1900, Paul, W. Flowers coppery red, full, large.

Coralline Pol, *or*, 1938, *Gloria Mundi × Golden Salmon Superieur*; Smith, J.; Eddie. Flowers orange-red, very large clusters; very rampant; profuse, recurrent bloom.

Corbeille Royale HT, *mp*, 1956, Buyl Frères. Bud globular; flowers salmon-pink, dbl.; fragrant; vigorous, upright growth.

Cordelia HT, *ab*, 1975, LeGrice. Flowers peach shaded deeper, dbl. (20 petals), pointed, large (4-4½ in.); fragrant; foliage dark; tall growth.

Cordial HT, *mp*, 1965, *Satisfaction × Seedling*; Verbeek. Bud ovoid; flowers pink, dbl., medium, in clusters; foliage dark.

Cordon Bleu HT, *ab*, 1990, (HARubasil); *Basildon Bond × Silver Jubilee*; Harkness, R.; R. Harkness & Co., Ltd., 1992. Bud pointed; flowers apricot with begonia pink reverse, deepening of apricot with aging, dbl. (20 petals), cupped, medium blooms borne usually single in sprays of 3; moderate, fruity fragrance; foliage medium to large, dark green, glossy; prickles decurving, average, reddish; upright, medium growth.

Cordula® F, *or*, 1972, (KORtri); *Europeana × Marlena*; Kordes, R.; Kordes. Bud globular; flowers red-orange, dbl., medium; slightly fragrant; foliage dark, bronze, leathery; vigorous, dwarf, bushy growth.

Corehead HT, *mr*, 1960, *Ena Harkness × Hazel Alexander*; Dicksons & Co. Flowers bright crimson; very fragrant.

Corina HT, *pb*, 1992, (JACvep); *Bridal Pink × Kardinal*; Warriner, William A. & Zary, Keith W.; Bear Creek Gardens, Inc., 1993. Flowers salmon pink with lighter almost cream reverse, yellow crescent at petal base, full (26-40 petals), very high-centered, large (7+ cms) blooms borne mostly singly; fragrant; foliage large, dark green, matt; few prickles; medium (150 cms), upright growth.

Corinium F, *m*, 1970, *Alamein sport*; Cooper. Flowers mauvish pink, dbl. (48-50 petals), full rosette form, large (3 in.); very fragrant; foliage semi-glossy.

Corky F, *rb*, 1991, (ZIPcork); *Tamango × Seedling*; Zipper, Herbert; Magic Moment Miniatures, 1992. Flowers white with red edges, white reverse, full(26-40 petals), large (7+ cms), blooms borne in small clusters; slight fragrance; foliage large, dark green, semi-glossy; few prickles; medium (100 cms), bushy growth.

Corlia HT, *or*, 1921, Bees. Flowers terra-cotta; fragrant; moderate growth.

Cornelia HMsk (S), *pb*, 1925, Pemberton. Flowers strawberry flushed yellow, dbl., rosette form, small blooms in flattish sprays; fragrant; foliage dark bronze, leathery, glossy; very vigorous growth; recurrent bloom; (14).

Cornelia HT, *pb*, 1919, *Ophelia* × *Mrs. Aaron Ward*; Scott, R. Flowers light pink, base orange, dbl.; fragrant.

Cornélie Koch T (OGR), *w*, 1855, (Cornelia Cook); *Devoniensis seedling*; Koch. Flowers creamy white, tinged lemon-yellow and flesh, dbl., well formed, very large; fragrant; vigorous growth.

Cornelis Timmermans HT, *pb*, 1919, *Pharisaer* × *Le Progres*; Timmermans. Flowers clear pink, edged deep yellow, dbl.; fragrant.

Corner HT, *pb*, 1945, *Soeur Thérèse* × *Seedling*; Wyant. Bud pointed; flowers cerise, base yellow, reverse yellow washed pink, semi-dbl. (20 petals), large (4½ in.); fragrant; foliage leathery, glossy, dark; vigorous, bushy growth.

Cornet HP (OGR), *m*, 1845, Lacharme. Flowers rose tinted with purple, very dbl., cupped, very large; centifolia fragrance; vigorous, branching growth.

Cornsilk™ Min, *ly*, 1982, (SAVasilk); *Rise 'n' Shine* × *Sheri Anne*; Saville, F. Harmon; Nor'East Min. Roses. Flowers pastel yellow, dbl. (40 petals), HT form, small; fragrant; foliage medium, medium green, semi-glossy; vigorous, bushy growth. AOE, 1983.

Corolle LCl, *mr*, 1962, *Spectacular* × *Cocktail*; Dot, S. Flowers red, semi-dbl. (12 petals), medium; vigorous growth.

Coronado HT, *rb*, 1961, *(Multnomah* × *Peace)* × *(Multnomah* × *Peace)*; Abrams, Von; Peterson & Dering. Bud long, pointed; flowers red, reverse yellow, dbl. (40 petals), high-centered, large (5-6 in.); fragrant; foliage glossy, dark; vigorous, upright growth.

Coronation R, *rb*, 1911, Turner. Flowers red, lightly striped white, small, large clusters.

Coronation HP (OGR), *mp*, 1913, Dickson, H. Flowers flesh, shaded bright shrimp-pink, dbl. (50 petals), well formed, large; fragrant; smooth wood; vigorous growth; recurrent bloom. GM, NRS, 1912.

Coronation Gold HT, *yb*, 1954, *Signora* × *Peace*; Cox. Flowers golden yellow flushed crimson, large; very fragrant (damask); foliage glossy; vigorous growth. RULED EXTINCT 1980.

Coronation Gold F, *ab*, 1978, (Maja Oetker); *(Sabine* × *Circus)* × *(Anne Cocker* × *Arthur Bell)*; Cocker, A.; Cocker. Bud globular; flowers golden yellow to apricot, dbl. (27 petals), large (4 in.); slightly fragrant; foliage glossy; vigorous, upright growth.

Coronet F, *dr*, 1957, *Independence* × *Red Wonder*; deRuiter; Blaby Rose Gardens. Flowers deep crimson, semi-dbl. (17 petals), large (3 in.) blooms in clusters; foliage dark, glossy; vigorous, upright growth.

Coronet Supreme HT, *mp*, 1955, *Seedling* × *Golden Rapture*; Jelly; E.G. Hill Co. Bud short, pointed; flowers rose-pink, dbl. (45-65 petals), large (4-5 in.); fragrant; foliage dark, glossy; very vigorous, upright growth; a greenhouse variety.

Corpus Christi HT, *dr*, 1985, *Seedling* × *Night Time*; Weeks, O.L.; Weeks Roses. Flowers dark red, dbl. (35 petals), large; fragrant; foliage large, medium green, semi-glossy; upright, bushy, spreading growth.

Corrie Koster Pol, *dp*, 1923, *Juliana Rose sport*; Koster, M.; Royer. Flowers light coral-red, opening to deep pink, semi-dbl., borne in clusters; slightly fragrant.

Corroboree HT, *m*, 1962, *Baccará* × *My Choice*; Fankhauser. Bud long, pointed; flowers lilac-mauve, dbl. (45 fimbriated petals), open, very large; very fragrant (damask); foliage glossy; vigorous, upright growth.

Corsage F, *w*, 1965, *Blanche Mallerin* × *White Swan*; Belden; Wyant. Flowers white, semi-dbl., globular, small blooms in clusters; slightly fragrant; foliage soft; vigorous, bushy.

Corsair F, *or*, 1985, (SANroc); *(Vera Dalton* × *Stephen Langdon)* × *Fiesta Flame*; Sanday, John; Sanday Roses Ltd. Flowers orange-red, dbl. (20 petals), medium; slight fragrance; foliage medium, dark, glossy; bushy growth.

Corsica F, *pb*, 1964, Verschuren, A.; van Engelen. Flowers salmon-pink edged dark pink to red, semi-dbl. (20 petals); very fragrant; foliage dark, glossy; vigorous, bushy growth.

Corso® HT, *ob*, 1976, *Anne Cocker* × *Dr. A.J. Verhage*; Cocker. Flowers coppery orange, dbl. (33 petals), large (4½ in.); slightly fragrant; foliage glossy, dark.

Corso Fleuri F, *dr*, 1956, *Red Favorite sport*; Mondial Roses. Flowers scarlet-red, semi-dbl., petals waved; dwarf, compact growth.

Coryana S, *mp*, (R. × *coryana* Hurst); *R. roxburghii* × *R. macrophylla*; Hurst, C.C., ca. 1926. Flowers rich pink, single, 2½ in. diam.; tall, sparingly prickly shrub.

Corylus HNit (S), *mp*, 1988, *R. nitida* × *R. rugosa rubra*; LeRougetel, Hazel; Peter Beales, 1988. Flowers medium pink, single, open, medium, borne usually singly or in sprays of 1-4; slight fragrance; foliage medium, dark green, deep veined; prickles small, light brown; fruit round, medium, scarlet; bushy growth.

Cosetta® F, *ob*, 1984, *Zorina* × *Sole di San Remo*; Bartolomeo, E. Flowers light orange, reverse deeper with reddish shadings, dbl. (30 petals), medium; no fragrance; foliage medium, dark, matt.

Cosette F, *mp*, 1986, (HARquillypond; Blue Carpet); *Seedling* × *Esther's Baby*; Harkness, R., 1983. Flowers pink, dbl. (58 flat, quilled petals); patio; slight fragrance; foliage, small, medium green, matt; small, dark prickles; low, spreading growth.

Cosima® F, *or*, 1982, (TANcofeuma); *Parentage not listed*; Tantau, M., 1981. Flowers orange-red, dbl. (20 petals), medium; no fragrance; foliage large, dark, glossy.

Cosimo Ridolfi G (OGR), *m*, 1842, Vibert. Flowers old-rose to lilac, spotted crimson, cupped, medium; foliage soft green; compact growth.

Cosmopolitan F, *mp*, 1955, (Cosmopoliet; Cosmopolit); *Silberlachs* × *Seedling*; Buisman. Flowers pink, large clusters; bushy growth.

Cotillion F, *yb*, 1967, *Rumba* × *Golden Garnette*; Hill, J.H., Co. Bud ovoid; flowers yellow, edged pink, high-centered, medium; slightly fragrant; foliage leathery; vigorous, upright growth; greenhouse variety.

Coton Gold HT, *dy*, 1984, (BABs); *Whisky Mac sport*; Babb, J.T. Flowers glowing yellow.

Cotorrita Real Pol, *pb*, 1931, Padrosa. Flowers white, rose and yellow, very dbl., globular, small, borne in clusters; slightly fragrant; vigorous growth; profuse, recurrent bloom.

Cotswold Charm HT, *dp*, 1967, *Ophelia seedling* × *William Moore*; Bennett, V.G.T. Flowers magenta, high-centered; foliage dark, leathery; moderate growth.

Cotswold Gold Min, *ob*, 1992, (JAYcot); *Tony Jacklin* × *Judy Fischer*; Jellyman, J.S., 1993. Flowers orange, semi-dbl. (6-14 petals), small (0-4 cms) blooms borne in small clusters; slight fragrance; foliage small, medium green, semi-glossy; few prickles; low (20 cms), bushy growth.

Cotswold Sunset F, *pb*, 1992, (JAYsun); *Cairngorm* × *Seedling (Alexander* × *Wembley)*; Jellyman, J.S., 1993. Flowers gold, pink edge, pale pink, moderately full (15-25 petals), HT type, large (7+ cms) blooms borne in small clusters; slight fragrance; foliage medium, dark green, glossy; some prickles; medium (80-90 cms), upright, compact growth.

Cottage Garden Min, *ob*, 1992, (HARyamber); *Clarissa* × *Amber Queen*; Harkness, R.; Harkness New Roses Ltd. Flowers deep rich orange, full (26-40 petals), medium (4-7 cms)

blooms borne in large clusters; foliage small, dark green, glossy; some prickles; low (60 cms), upright growth.

Cotton Candy R, *mp*, 1952, *R. wichuraiana* × *Floribunda Seedling with R. multibracteata-ancestry*; Moore, R.S.; Sequoia Nursery. Bud well-formed; flowers pink, very dbl., medium (2½ in.) blooms in clusters; foliage very glossy, turning to autumn colors; vigorous (10-15 ft.) growth, profuse bloom.

Cotton Top F, *w*, 1962, *Seedling* × *White Butterfly*; Hill, J.H., Co. Bud short, pointed; flowers white, dbl. (45-50 petals), flat, medium (2-3 in.); slightly fragrant; foliage leathery; vigorous, upright, well-branched growth; a greenhouse variety.

Cottontail Min, *w*, 1983, (TINtail); *Pink Petticoat* × *Pink Petticoat*; Strawn, Leslie; Pixie Treasures Nursery. Flowers white, dbl. (33 petals), small blooms in large clusters; slight fragrance; foliage medium, medium green, semi-glossy; upright, bushy growth.

Couleur de Brennus G (OGR), *mr*, Flowers red, full, medium; slender shrub.

Countess Cadogan HT, *lp*, 1978, *Carlita sport*; Buss; H. Buss Nursery. Bud long, pointed; flowers light pink, dbl. (40-45 petals), high-centered, large (4½ in.); slightly fragrant; foliage light green, leathery; very vigorous, upright growth.

Countess Clanwilliam HT, *mr*, 1915, Dickson, H. Flowers pinkish cherry-red, dbl., high-centered; fragrant; foliage rich green; bushy growth. GM, NRS, 1913.

Countess Mary Cl HT, *mp*, 1933, *Mary, Countess of Ilchester Climbing sport*; Dixie Rose Nursery.

Countess of Dalkeith F, *rb*, 1957, *Fashion sport*; Dobbie. Flowers vermilion flushed orange, very dbl.; very fragrant; vigorous growth.

Countess of Elgin HT, *op*, 1925, *Mme. Edouard Herriot sport*; Ferguson. Flowers salmon-pink, reverse deep rose-pink; vigorous growth.

Countess of Gosford HT, *op*, 1906, McGredy. Flowers salmon-pink, full, long pointed, large. GM, NRS, 1905.

Countess of Lieven Ayr (OGR), *w*, *R. arvensis hybrid*. Flowers creamy white, semi-dbl., cupped, medium.

Countess of Lonsdale HT, *dy*, 1919, Dickson, H. Flowers deep yellow, dbl.; fragrant.

Countess of Pembroke HT, *pb*, Flowers pink shaded darker, very full, large; vigorous growth.

Countess of Stradbroke Cl HT, *dr*, 1928, *Walter C. Clark* × *Seedling*; Clark, A.; Hazlewood Bros. Bud ovoid; flowers dark glowing crimson, dbl., well shaped, globular, very large; very fragrant; foliage rich green, wrinkled; vigorous growth; free, recurrent bloom.

Countess of Warwick HT, *my*, 1919, Easlea. Flowers lemon-yellow, edged pink, large.

Country Dancer S, *dp*, 1973, *Prairie Princess × Johannes Boettner*, Buck; Iowa State University. Bud ovoid; flowers rose-red, dbl., large; fragrant; foliage large, glossy, dark, leathery; vigorous, dwarf, upright, bushy growth; repeat bloom.

Country Doctor HT, *lp*, 1952, *Pink Princess × Crimson Glory*, Brownell. Bud long, pointed to ovoid; flowers silvery pink, dbl., high-centered, large; fragrant; foliage glossy; vigorous, bushy growth.

Country Girl F, *mr*, 1958, *Independence × Salmon Perfection*; Temmerman; Schraven. Bud ovoid; flowers geranium-red, dbl., medium; vigorous growth.

Country Girl, Climbing Cl F, *mr*, 1962, Buyl Frères.

Country Joy Min, *pb*, 1984, (MORcojo); *Pinocchio × Yellow Jewel*; Moore, R.S.; Moore Min. Roses. Flowers light pink, yellow reverse, dbl. (40+ petals), small; slight fragrance; foliage small, medium green, matt; compact growth.

Country Lady HT, *ob*, 1987, (HARtsam); *Alexander × Bright Smile*; Harkness, R. Flowers burnt range, reverse suffused pale scarlet, fading orange-salmon, paling pinker, dbl. (25 petals), urn-shaped, loose, medium, borne usually singly; slight, spicy fragrance; foliage medium, medium green, semi-glossy; decurved, medium, reddish prickles; fruit ovoid, medium, green; bushy, medium, high-shouldered growth.

Country Maid F, *lp*, 1971, *Tip Top sport*; Whartons Roses; Deamer. Flowers light pink; slightly fragrant; low, compact growth.

Country Morning Min, *yb*, 1986, (FLOmor); *Avandel × Young Love*; Florac, M.; MB Farm. Flowers light yellow, blended pink, dbl., exhibition, medium blooms borne singly; spicy fragrance; foliage medium, medium green, semi-glossy; small, reddish prickles; medium, upright growth.

Country Music S, *dp*, 1973, *Paddy McGredy × ((World's Fair × Floradora) × Applejack))*; Buck; Iowa State University. Bud ovoid; flowers neyron rose, dbl., large; fragrant; foliage large, leathery; vigorous, dwarf, upright, bushy growth; intermittent bloom.

Country Song S, *lp*, 1984, *Carefree Beauty × The Yeoman*; Buck; Iowa State University. Bud ovoid; flowers light pink, dbl. (28 petals), shallow-cupped, large blooms borne 1-5 per cluster; myrrh fragrance; foliage leathery, dark; awl-like, brown prickles; erect, bushy growth; repeat flowering; hardy.

Countryman S, *pb*, 1978, (Improved Lafayette × Independence) × *Maytime*; Buck; Iowa State University. Bud ovoid, pointed; flowers light rose-bengal, dbl. (25-30 petals), cupped, large (4-5 in.); fragrant; foliage large, dark, leathery; vigorous, upright, spreading, bushy.

Countrywoman HT, *my*, 1978, *Seedling × Peace*; Dawson, G.; Australian Roses. Bud globular; flowers lemon-yellow, dbl., medium; fragrant; foliage leathery; bushy growth.

County Fair F, *mp*, 1960, *Frolic × Pink Bountiful*; Swim; Armstrong Nursery. Bud ovoid, pointed; flowers medium to dark pink, fading much lighter, 8-10 petals, flat, large (2½-3 in.) blooms in clusters; slightly fragrant; foliage leathery, dark, semi-glossy; vigorous, bushy.

Coup de Foudre F, *or*, 1956, (Peace × Independence) × *Oiseau de Feu*; Hémeray-Aubert. Bud well-formed; flowers fiery red, cupped; foliage glossy, bronze; vigorous growth.

Coupe d'Hébé HBour (OGR), *dp*, 1840, *Bourbon × R. chinensis hybrid*; Laffay. Flowers deep pink, very dbl., waxy texture, cupped, large; very fragrant; foliage glossy; vigorous, erect growth.

Coupe d'Or LCl, *my*, 1930, *Jacotte seedling*; Barbier. Flowers canary-yellow, dbl., open, cupped; fragrant; foliage rich green, leathery, glossy; vigorous, climbing or trailing growth.

Courage HT, *dr*, 1923, McGredy. Flowers deep brilliant maroon-crimson, dbl., high-centered, very large; very fragrant; foliage rich green, leathery; bushy, dwarf growth.

Courage HT, *rb*, 1941, *Seedling × Brazier*; Mallerin; A. Meilland. Flowers red tinted yellow, dbl., open, very large; slightly fragrant; vigorous, bushy growth.

Courier LCl, *pb*, 1930, Clark, A.; Brundrett. Flowers pink on white ground, borne in clusters; vigorous, climbing growth; blooms on old wood.

Court Jester F, *ob*, 1980, Cants of Colchester. Flowers orange, reverse yellow, HT-shaped blooms borne 5-7 per cluster; slight fragrance; foliage mid-green, glossy; large hooked, red-brown prickles; tall, upright growth.

Courtney Page HT, *dr*, 1922, McGredy. Flowers velvety dark scarlet-crimson, dbl.; very fragrant. GM, NRS, 1920.

Courtoisie® F, *ob*, 1984, (DELcourt); *Avalanche Rose × Fashion seedling*; Delbard-

Chabert, G. Flowers orange, reverse orange blended with yellow, dbl. (20 petals), large; fragrant; foliage medium, medium green; bushy growth.

Courtship HT, *mp*, 1955, *Mme. Henri Guillot* × *Peace*; Shepherd; Bosley Nursery. Bud conical; flowers cerise-pink, reverse lighter, dbl. (28 petals), high-centered to cupped, large (4-5 in.); foliage dark; vigorous, bushy growth.

Courvoisier® F, *dy*, 1970, (MACsee); *Elizabeth of Glamis* × *Casanova*; McGredy, S., IV; McGredy. Flowers deep yellow, dbl. (49 petals), HT-type, large (3½ in.); very fragrant; foliage glossy, dark.

Cova da Iria HT, *rb*, 1963, *Seedling* × *Crimson Glory*; Moreira da Silva. Flowers light red, reverse gold.

Covent Garden HT, *rb*, 1919, Cant, B.R. Flowers rich deep crimson flushed plumblack on reverse; very fragrant; foliage leathery, glossy; vigorous growth.   GM, NRS, 1918.

Coventrian F, *dp*, 1962, *Highlight* × *Seedling*; Robinson, H. Flowers ruby-cerise, dbl. (30 petals), well formed, large (3-3½ in.), borne in large clusters; foliage dark, glossy; vigorous, bushy growth.

Cover Girl HT, *ob*, 1960, *Sutter's Gold* × *(Mme. Henri Guillot* × *Seedling)*; Abrams, Von; Peterson & Dering. Bud long, pointed; flowers orange, copper and gold, dbl. (28-35 petals), high-centered, large (5 in.); slightly fragrant; foliage glossy, dark; upright, bushy growth.

Cowichan Super Cl HT, *op*, 1975, Tamarack Roses. Flowers orange-salmon, dbl. (30-35 petals), large (5 in.); very fragrant; foliage glossy; tall, very vigorous growth; bloom repeats.

Coy Colleen HT, *w*, 1953, (Blushing Rose); *(Modesty* × *Portadown Glory)* × *Phyllis Gold*; McGredy. Bud pointed, rosy white; flowers milky white, well formed, borne in clusters; slightly fragrant; foliage glossy; vigorous growth.

Crackerjack F, *rb*, 1959, *Fashion* × *Masquerade*; Fryer's Nursery. Flowers scarlet flushed yellow, semi-dbl. (20 petals), borne in clusters; fragrant; free growth.

Craigweil HT, *pb*, 1929, *Mme. Abel Chatenay seedling*; Hicks. Flowers silvery cerise-pink, reverse deeper, dbl., strong stems; fragrant; vigorous growth.

Cramoisi des Alpes G (OGR), *mr*, Flowers bright purplish red, full; heavy, non-recurrent bloom.

Cramoisi Foncé Velouté M (OGR), *dr*, Flowers deep velvety crimson.

Cramoisi Picoté G (OGR), *rb*, 1834, Vibert. Flowers crimson, streaked and mottled (striped & spotted) darker, very full, medium (2 in.).

Cramoisi Supérieur Ch (OGR), *mr*, 1832, (Agrippina; Lady Brisbane); Coquereau. Flowers crimson-red, dbl., cupped, small blooms in large clusters; vigorous growth; recurrent bloom; (21).

Cramoisi Supérieur, Climbing Cl Ch (OGR), *mr*, 1885, (Agrippina, Climbing; Lady Brisbane, Climbing); Couturier.

Crarae HT, *yb*, 1981, *Piccadilly* × *Fred Gibson*; McKirdy, J.M.; John Sanday Roses. Flowers deep yellow marked with scarlet, dbl. (35 petals), large; slight fragrance; foliage medium, dark, glossy; bushy growth.

Crathes Castle F, *mp*, 1980, (COCathes); *Dreamland* × *Topsi*; Cocker, James. Flowers medium pink, 18 petals, borne 12-15 per cluster; fragrant; foliage large, dark, glossy; triangular prickles; rounded, bushy growth.

Crazy Dottie Min, *ob*, 1988, (SEAdot); *Rise 'n' Shine* × *(Sheri Anne* × *Picasso)*; McCann, Sean. Flowers orange-red with star shaped copper center, single (5 petals), small; slight fragrance; foliage small, medium green, semi-glossy; bushy growth.

Crazy Quilt Min, *rb*, 1980, (MORtrip); *Little Darling* × *Miniature seedling*; Moore, R.S.; Sequoia Nursery. Bud pointed; flowers red and white striped, dbl. (25+ petals), flat, borne 1-3 or more per cluster; foliage medium green; small, straight prickles; compact, bushy growth.

Cream Cracker HT, *lp*, 1933, Dickson, A. Flowers creamy buff, reverse shaded salmon, full, large; vigorous growth.   RULED EXTINCT 10/78 ARM.

Cream Cracker HT, *w*, 1979, *Columbine* × *Iceberg*; Murray, N.; Rasmussen's. Bud pointed; flowers cream, dbl. (38 petals), classical pointed form, large (4½ in.) blooms borne singly; very fragrant (apple); foliage large, matt; often without prickles; bushy growth.

Cream Delight Gr, *lp*, 1983, (SUNcredel; Darling); *Sonia sport*; Schuurman, Frank B.; Flower light pink.

Cream Gold Min, *my*, 1978, *Golden Glow (LCl)* × *Seedling*; Moore, R.S.; Sequoia Nursery. Bud long, pointed; flowers medium yellow, dbl. (38 petals), high-centered, small (1½ in.); fragrant; compact, spreading growth.

Cream Peach F, *w*, 1975, *Paddy McGredy* × *Seedling*; Sheridan. Flowers cream, edged pink, semi-dbl. (15-20 petals), full, large (3-4 in.); slightly fragrant; foliage large, glossy; very free growth.

Cream Puff Min, *pb*, 1981, *Little Darling × Elfinesque*; Bennett, Dee; Tiny Petals Nursery. Bud ovoid; flowers cream blushed pink, semi-dbl. (18 petals), borne singly or in clusters of 3; fragrant; foliage dark, semi-glossy; long prickles; spreading, bushy.

Credo HT, *mr*, 1965, *Eminence × John S. Armstrong*; Gaujard. Flowers purplish red, dbl., high-centered, medium; fragrant; foliage leathery; vigorous, upright growth.

Cree S, *lp*, *R. rugosa albo-plena × R. spinosissima hispida*; Central Exp. Farm. Flowers pale pink fading to white, single, large; foliage glossy, bright green; vigorous growth; early bloom, non-recurrent.

Creeping Everbloom LCl, *mr*, 1939, *Frederick S. Peck × (Général Jacqueminot × Dr. W. Van Fleet)*; Brownell. Flowers red, dbl. (30 petals), large (4 in.), borne in clusters; fragrant; canes 3 ft. long; recurrent bloom.

Creina Murland HT, *dy*, 1934, Dickson, A. Flowers sunflower-yellow, deepening, full; slightly fragrant; foliage glossy; very vigorous growth.

Crème Glacée Min, *ly*, 1988, (LAVcreme); *June Laver × Summer Butter*; Laver, Keith; Springwood Roses, 1990. Bud pointed; flowers light yellow, dbl. (23 petals), urn-shaped, small, borne singly; slight fragrance; foliage small, medium green, matt; prickles pointed and straight out, white-beige; fruit globular, orange; bushy growth.

Créole HT, *dr*, 1962, *Peace × Josephine Bruce*; Gaujard. Bud long, pointed; flowers purplish, red base coppery, dbl., large; slightly fragrant; foliage dark, glossy; very vigorous, bushy growth.

Crêpe de Chine® HT, *mr*, 1983, (DELtop); *Joyeux Noel × (Gloire de Rome × Impeccable)*; Delbard-Chabert, 1970. Flowers medium red, dbl. (20 petals), large; light fragrance; foliage glossy, clear green, dense; bronze-red prickles; vigorous, upright, bushy growth. GM, Madrid, 1970.

Crepe Myrtle F, *mr*, 1937, (Harold Ickes); *Permanent Wave sport*; Dixie Rose Nursery. Flowers identical; height 5 ft.

Crepe Suzette Min, *ob*, 1986, (TRAsuz); *Orange Honey × Orange Honey*; Travis, Louis, 1987. Flowers deep yellow with orange overlay, fading white with orange-red overlay, dbl. (25-30 petals), centered, exhibition, small, borne usually singly or in sprays of 3-4; moderate, fruity fragrance; foliage small, medium green, semi-glossy; bowed, tan-brown prickles; no fruit; bushy, low growth.

Crépuscolo HT, *ob*, 1955, *Julien Potin × Sensation*; Aicardi, D.; Giacomasso. Flowers copper, dbl., pointed, strong stems; upright growth.

Crépuscule N (OGR), *ab*, 1904, Dubreuil. Flowers orange, fading to apricot-yellow; makes a tall hedge.

Crescendo HT, *rb*, Flowers bright red, base touched with white, dbl., well formed, large; fragrant; tall growth.

Cresset Gr, *mr*, 1961, *Queen Elizabeth × Cocorico*; Francis; F. Mason. Bud long, pointed; flowers scarlet, semi-dbl., high-centered, medium blooms in clusters; fragrant; foliage leathery, glossy, dark; vigorous, bushy growth.

Cressida S, *ab*, 1992, (AUScress); Austin, David; David Austin Roses, 1983. Flowers apricot peach, very full (41+ petals), large (7+ cms) blooms borne in small clusters; very fragrant; foliage small, light green, semi-glossy; some prickles; tall (180 cms), upright growth.

Crested Jewel M (OGR), *mp*, 1971, *Little Darling × Crested Moss*; Moore, R.S.; Sequoia Nursery. Bud long, pointed, "mossed" similar to Crested Moss, but shorter; flowers bright rose-pink, semi-dbl., high-centered, medium; foliage leathery; vigorous.

Crested Moss M (OGR), *mp*, 1827, (Chapeau de Napoléon; Cristata; *R. centifolia cristata*; *R. centifolia muscosa cristata* (Prevost) Hooker; Crested Provence Rose); Discovered on the wall of a convent near Fribourg; Vibert. Flowers similar to *Centifolia Muscosa*, but the mossy excrescences confined to the edges of the sepals.

Crested Sweetheart LCl, *mp*, 1988, (MORsweet); *Little Darling × Crested Moss*; Moore, Ralph S.; Wayside Gardens, 1988. Flowers medium rose pink, very dbl. (80+ petals), cupped, large, borne in sprays of 3-5; heavy, damask fragrance; foliage large, medium green, matt, rugose; prickles small, gray to brown; upright, tall growth.

Cricket™ Min, *ob*, 1978, (AROket); *Anytime × Katherine Loker*; Christensen; Armstrong Nursery. Bud ovoid; flowers light orange to yellow, dbl. (25 petals), globular, small (1-1½ in.); slightly fragrant; foliage dark; upright, bushy growth.

Cricri® Min, *ob*, 1958, (MEIcri; Gavolda; Cri-Cri); *(Alain × Independence) × Perla de Alcañada*; Meilland, F.; URS. Flowers salmon shaded coral, dbl., small; foliage leathery; dwarf, very bushy growth.

Crimson Beauty HT, *dr*, 1930, *Hoosier Beauty × Crimson Champion*; Dingee & Conard. Flowers crimson, dbl.; very vigorous growth.

Crimson Beauty HT, *dr*, 1935, *Daily Mail Scented Rose* × *Étoile de Hollande*; LeGrice. Flowers red, shaded scarlet and maroon, dbl., large; very fragrant; foliage leathery; vigorous growth.

Crimson Brocade HT, *dr*, 1962, Robinson, H. Flowers bright scarlet-crimson, high-centered, large, strong stems; fragrant; vigorous growth.

Crimson Champion HT, *dr*, 1916, *Étoile de France* × *Crimson seedling*; Cook, J. Flowers velvety crimson-red, dbl.; fragrant; dwarf growth.

Crimson Chatenay HT, *dr*, 1915, *Mme. Abel Chatenay* × *Leuchtfeuer (HCh)*; Merryweather; Like Mme. Abel Chatenay, but bright crimson; fragrant.

Crimson Conquest Cl HT, *dr*, 1931, *Red-Letter Day sport*; Chaplin Bros. Flowers velvety scarlet crimson, semi-dbl., small (2½ in.); foliage light green; vigorous growth.

Crimson Dawn F, *rb*, 1970, *(Anne Poulsen × Dainty Maid)* × *(Bonn × Opera)*; Ellick. Flowers crimson to carmine, dbl. (20 petals), full, large (3½-4½ in.); fragrant; foliage dark; vigorous growth.

Crimson Delight S, *mr*, 1992, (JOHillgolf); *Volare* × *Seedling*; Hoy, Lowell (Joseph H. Hill Co.); DeVor Nurseries. Flowers medium red, dbl., small (6 cms) blooms borne in sprays of 3-4; no fragrance; foliage medium, medium green, semi-glossy; upright, bushy, low growth.

Crimson Descant LCl, *mr*, 1972, *Dortmund* × *Etendard*; Cants of Colchester. Flowers crimson, dbl. (30 petals), large (5 in.); slightly fragrant.

Crimson Diamond HT, *dr*, 1947, *Crimson Glory* × *Charlotte Armstrong*; Lammerts; L.C. Lovett. Bud long, pointed; flowers crimson-red, dbl. (35-40 petals), open, large; fragrant; bushy growth.

Crimson Duke HT, *mr*, 1963, *(Happiness × Independence)* × *Peace*; Meilland, Alain; C-P. Bud ovoid; flowers crimson, dbl. (45-50 petals), high-centered to cupped, large (4-5 in.); fragrant; foliage leathery, dark; vigorous, upright, bushy growth.

Crimson Elegance HT, *dr*, 1990, (LEOcrel); *Big Red* × *Swarthmore*; Leon, Charles F.; Oregon Grown Roses, 1990-91. Bud rounded; flowers crimson/scarlet, crimson reverse, aging darker red, dbl. (40 petals), high-centered, exhibition, medium blooms borne usually singly; moderate fragrance; foliage medium, medium green, semi-glossy; upright, bushy, tall growth.

Crimson Emblem HT, *dr*, 1916, McGredy. Flowers brilliant crimson-scarlet, dbl., cupped, large; vigorous growth.

Crimson Fragrance HT, *dr*, 1979, *Fragrant Cloud* × *Seedling*; Wright, R. & Sons. Bud long, slender; flowers dark red, dbl. (38 petals), borne singly; very fragrant; foliage slender, mid-green; reddish-bronze prickles; branching, upright growth.

Crimson Gem Min, *dr*, 1974, (Flammette); *Lillan* × *Polyantha seedling*; deRuiter; C-P. Bud ovoid; flowers deep red, very dbl., cupped, medium; slightly fragrant; foliage bronze, soft; vigorous, bushy growth.

Crimson Globe M (OGR), *dr*, 1890, Paul, W. Flowers deep crimson, full, globular, large; vigorous growth.

Crimson Glory HT, *dr*, 1935, *Cathrine Kordes seedling* × *W.E. Chaplin*; Kordes; Dreer; J&P. Bud long, pointed; flowers deep velvety crimson, dbl. (30 petals), cupped, large; very fragrant (damask); foliage leathery; vigorous, bushy, spreading growth. GM, NRS, 1936; James Alexander Gamble Rose Fragrance Medal, 1961.

Crimson Glory, Climbing Cl HT, *dr*, 1946, (Grimpant Crimson Glory); J&P.

Crimson Glow Pol, *dr*, 1945, *Night* × *Mrs. Dudley Fulton*; Lammetts; Univ. of Calif. Flowers oxblood-red, semi-dbl., cupped; very fragrant; foliage glossy, dark; vigorous, upright growth.

Crimson Halo HT, *dr*, 1964, *Karl Herbst* × *Crimson Glory*; Park; Harkness. Flowers deep rose-red, dbl. (30 petals), globular, large (5 in.); very fragrant; vigorous growth.

Crimson King HT, *dr*, 1943, (Liebesglut); *Crimson Glory* × *Kardinal*; Kordes; C-P. Bud ovoid, long, pointed; flowers deep velvety crimson, dbl., high-centered, large; very fragrant (damask); foliage leathery; vigorous, bushy growth.

Crimson Medinette Min, *dr*, 1984, (POUlcrim; Crimson Midinette; Patio Prince); *Seedling* × *Pygmae*; Olesen, M.&P.; Ludwigs Roses. Flowers dark red, dbl. (33 petals), small blooms in clusters of 3-5; no fragrance; foliage small, leathery; straight brown prickles; dense growth.

Crimson Mme. Desprez B (OGR), *dr*, Flowers crimson, cupped, large.

Crimson Moss M (OGR), *dr*, A clergyman of Tinwell, Rutlandshire, England; Lee, prior to 1846. Flowers crimson, dbl.; vigorous growth.

Crimson Orléans Pol, *dr*, 1922, *Orléans Rose sport*; Koster, M. Flowers dark red.

Crimson Queen HT, *dr*, 1912, *(Liberty × Richmond)* × *Gen. MacArthur*; Montgomery, A. Flowers rich crimson, turning blue with age, dbl., globular, very large; very fragrant; vigorous growth.

Crimson Rambler HMult (OGR), *mr*, 1893, (The Engineers Rose; Turner's Crimson Rambler; Shi Tz-mei; Ten Sisters; Soukara-Ibara); Turner, 1893; Ellwanger & Barry, 1895. Flowers bright crimson, fading toward blue, dbl., irregular blooms in large, pyramidal clusters; foliage light, leathery, disposed to mildew; very vigorous, climbing (15-24 ft.) growth; heavy, non-recurrent bloom.

Crimson Rosette F, *dr*, 1948, Krebs; H&S. Bud small, ovoid; flowers dark crimson, dbl. (30 petals), rosette, medium (1-1½ in.) blooms in clusters; slightly fragrant; foliage leathery, dark; vigorous, bushy, dwarf growth.

Crimson Shower R, *mr*, 1951, *Excelsa seedling*; Norman; Harkness. Flowers clear crimson, dbl. (20 petals), pompon, small (1¼ in.); slightly fragrant; foliage glossy, light; vigorous (10 ft.) growth.

Crimson Tide HT, *mr*, 1983, (MACmota); *Seedling × Seedling*; McGredy, Sam; Roses by Fred Edmunds. Flowers crimson, dbl. (35 petals), exhibition, large blooms borne singly; slight fragrance; foliage large, dark, leathery; upright growth.

Crimson Wave F, *mr*, 1971, (MEIperator; Imperator); *Zambra × (Sarabande × (Goldilocks × Fashion))*; Meilland. Flowers cardinal-red, shaded cherry, dbl. (25-30 petals), large (4-5 in.); slightly fragrant; foliage large, semi-matt, dark; vigorous, upright growth.

Crinkles Min, *w*, 1989, (FROcrin); *Rise 'n' Shine × Seedling*; Frock, Marshall J., 1990. Bud ovoid; flowers white, aging with flecks of red, slow to fade, very dbl. (60 petals), exhibition, crinkled center, large, borne usually singly; slight fragrance; foliage medium, dark green, semi-glossy; prickles straight, short, red; fruit none observed; upright, bushy, medium growth.

Crinoline LCl, *or*, 1964, *Diane d'Urfe × Étendard*; Hémeray-Aubert. Flowers orange-red, semi-dbl., cupped; foliage bronze; vigorous, climbing growth; recurrent bloom.

Crispin-Morwenna Min, *or*, 1980, (HARkitten); *(Vera Dalton × (Chanelle × Piccadilly)) × Little Buckaroo*; Harkness, R. Flowers salmon-red, dbl. (25 petals), cupped, small blooms borne 3-7 per cluster; slight, spicy fragrance; foliage small, dark, glossy; reddish prickles; low, spreading growth.

Crissy Min, *ob*, 1979, *Liverpool Echo × Sheri Anne*; Strawn; Pixie Treasures. Bud pointed; flowers deep bright coral, dbl. (20-25 petals), medium (1½-2 in.); slightly fragrant; foliage dark.

Cristal HT, *ob*, 1937, *Julien Potin × Seedling*; Gaujard. Bud long, pointed; flowers orange-yellow, dbl., large; foliage leathery, light; vigorous, bushy growth.

Cristoforo Colombo HT, *yb*, 1953, (Christophe Colomb); *Julien Potin × Frau Karl Druschki*; Aicardi, D.; V. Asseretto. Bud long; flowers reddish yellow, reverse tinged pink, dbl. (25-35 petals), large, long stems; slightly fragrant; foliage glossy; very vigorous growth. RULED EXTINCT 4/92.

Criterion HT, *dp*, 1966, *(Independence × Signal Red) × Peace*; deRuiter. Flowers rose-red, dbl., large (5 in.); fragrant; foliage dark; vigorous, tall growth.

Crock O' Gold HT, *my*, 1970, *Beauté sport*; Anderson's Rose Nurs. Flowers clear golden yellow, dbl. (30-35 petals), large (4½ in), classic form.

Croft Original HT, *RB*, 1971, Cocker; Wheatcroft Bros. Flowers old-gold and red, dbl. (30 petals), full, large (5 in.); fragrant; foliage light.

Crown Jewel F, *or*, 1964, *Pink Bountiful × Spartan*; Boerner; J&P. Flowers bright orange-red, dbl., medium, in clusters; fragrant; foliage dark, leathery; moderate growth.

Crown of Gold HT, *yb*, 1937, *Seedling × Joanna Hill*; Duehrsen; H&S. Bud, pointed; Flowers deep gold, edged lemon-yellow, dbl. high-centered, large; foliage light green, leathery; vigorous growth.

Crown Prince HP (OGR), *rb*, 1880, Paul, W., & Son. Flowers reddish crimson tinged with purple.

Crusader HT, *dr*, 1920, Montgomery Co.; A.N. Pierson. Flowers crimson-red, center brighter, dbl. (65 petals), large; slightly fragrant; foliage leathery, rich green; vigorous growth.

Crystal Min, *pb*, 1985, *Zinger × Seedling*; Bridges, Dennis A.; Bridges Roses. Flowers light pink, deep pink reverse, dbl. (35 petals), exhibition, small; fragrant; foliage large, dark, glossy; bushy growth.

Crystal White HT, *w*, 1965, *Princess White × White Queen*; Boerner; J&P. Flowers clear white, dbl., high-centered, large; fragrant; foliage leathery; moderate, bushy growth; greenhouse variety.

Crystalline™ HT, *w*, 1987, (ARObipy; Valerie Swane); *Bridal Pink × (Blue Nile × (Ivory Tower × Angel Face))*; Christensen, Jack & Carruth, Tom; Armstrong Roses, 1986. Flowers white, dbl. (30-35 petals), high-centered, exhibition, large, borne usually singly; moderate, spicy fragrance; foliage medium, medium green, semi-glossy; normal, light green-tan prickles; fruit globose, large, orange; upright, bushy, tall growth.

Cuba HT, *rb*, 1926, Pernet-Ducher. Flowers cardinal-red, tinted yellow, fading quickly, semi-dbl., globular, large; very fragrant; foliage dark, bronze; very vigorous growth.

Cuddle Up Min, *yb*, 1991, (TINcuddle); *Lagerfeld* × *My Delight*; Bennett, Dee, 1987; Tiny Petals Nursery, 1990. Bud ovoid; flowers creamy yellow with coral pink blush, dbl. (25-30 petals), high-centered, exhibition, medium; moderate, fruity fragrance; foliage medium, medium green, semi-glossy; bushy, medium growth.

Cuddles Min, *op*, 1978, *Zorina* × *Seedling*; Schwartz, E.W.; Nor'East Min. Roses. Bud ovoid; flowers deep coral-pink, dbl. (55-60 petals), high-centered, small (1-1½ in.); slightly fragrant; compact growth. AOE, 1979.

Culverbrae S, *dr*, 1973, *Scabrosa* × *Francine*; Gobbee. Flowers crimson-purple, dbl. (58 petals), large (3½-4 in.); very fragrant; foliage light; vigorous; some repeat bloom.

Cumberland Belle Cl M (OGR), *lp*, 1900, (Le Poilu); *Princesse Adélaide sport*; Dreer. Flowers silvery pink, very dbl., well mossed, small; very fragrant.

Cup Final HT, *or*, 1987, (MACsingap); *Benson & Hedges Gold* × *(Kalahari* × *Papa Meilland)*; McGredy, Sam; McGredy Roses International, 1988. Flowers orange-red, dbl. (15-25 petals), large; slight fragrance; foliage medium, medium green, semi-glossy; upright growth.

Cupcake™ Min, *mp*, 1981, (SPIcup); *Gene Boerner* × *(Gay Princess* × *Yellow Jewel)*; Spies, Mark C.; Nor'East Min. Roses. Bud ovoid; flowers clear medium pink, dbl. (60 petals), high-centered blooms borne 1-5 per cluster; no fragrance; foliage glossy; no prickles; compact, bushy growth. AOE, 1983.

Cupid Cl HT, *lp*, 1915, Cant, B.R. Flowers glowing flesh tinted peach, single, large; fruit large, orange; vigorous, pillar growth.

Cupido Min, *lp*, Maarse, G. Flowers shell-pink; height 6 in.

Cupidon F, *dr*, 1966, *Chanteclerc* × *Red Favorite*; Gaujard. Flowers brilliant crimson, semi-dbl., cupped, small; slightly fragrant; foliage leathery; vigorous, bushy growth.

Cupid's Beauty Min, *ob*, 1978, *Seedling* × *Over the Rainbow*; Williams, E.D.; Mini-Roses. Bud long, pointed; flowers light orange and cream, dbl. (40-45 petals), high-centered,

small (1½ in.); fragrant; foliage small, dark; compact, spreading growth.

Cupid's Charm F, *pb*, 1964, *Little Darling* × *First Love*.; Fuller; Wyant. Bud pointed; flowers salmon-pink, dbl. (22 petals), medium; fragrant; vigorous, bushy growth.

Cupie Doll Min, *lp*, 1983, (TINcupie); *Seedling* × *Coral Treasure*; Bennett, Dee; Tiny Petals Nursery. Flowers light pink with fine coral edging of petals, dbl. (25 petals), heavy substance, exhibition, small; slight fragrance; foliage small, medium green, semi-glossy; upright, bushy growth.

Curiosity HT, *rb*, 1971, (COCty); *Cleopatra sport*; Cocker. Flowers scarlet, reverse gold, dbl. (35 petals), cupped, large (4 in.); slightly fragrant; variegated foliage (only rose to date with this property).

Curly Locks Min, *lp*, 1954, Robinson, T. Flowers soft pink; dwarf, compact growth.

Curly Pink HT, *mp*, 1948, *Pink Princess* × *Crimson Glory*; Brownell. Bud long, pointed, rose-red; flowers medium pink, dbl. (50 petals, curled outward), large (3½-5 in.); fragrant; foliage glossy, dark; vigorous, compact growth.

Current Affair Min, *dr*, 1991, *Red Ace* × *Seedling*; Gruenbauer, Richard, 1984; Flowers 'n' Friends Miniature Roses, 1993. Flowers red, reverse red with yellow, ages dark pink, very dbl. (80 petals), cupped, medium; no fragrance; foliage medium, dark green, semi-glossy; upright, medium growth.

Curtain Call HT, *dp*, 1977, *First Prize* × *Seedling*; Weeks; Weeks Roses. Bud pointed; flowers cherry-red, dbl. (32-35 petals), high-centered, globular, large (4-5 in.); slightly fragrant; foliage dark, leathery; vigorous, upright growth.

Curtis Yellow HT, *my*, 1973, *Golden Scepter* × *Miss Hillcrest*; Curtis, E.C.; Kimbrew. Flowers clear yellow, dbl., high-centered, large; fragrant; foliage light, leathery; vigorous, upright growth.

Cuthbert Grant HSuf (S), *dr*, 1967, (Crimson Glory × Assiniboine) × Assiniboine; Marshall, H.H.; Canada Dept. of Agriculture. Bud ovoid; flowers deep purplish red, semi-dbl., cupped, large; slightly fragrant; foliage glossy; vigorous, bushy growth; intermittent bloom.

Cutie Min, *mp*, 1952, *Dancing Doll* × *Oakington Ruby*; Moore, R.S.; Sequoia Nursery. Bud pointed; flowers clear pink, base white, semi-dbl. (16 petals), flat, small (1 in.); slightly fragrant; foliage small, glossy, bright green; very few prickles; dwarf (10 in.), bushy.

Cutie Pie Min, *ly*, 1988, (RENpie); *Tangerine Mist × California Girl*; Rennie, Bruce F.; Rennie Roses, 1989. Bud ovoid; flowers light to medium yellow, dbl. (23 petals), high-centered, small, borne usually singly and in sprays of 2-3; moderate, fruity fragrance; foliage small, dark green, glossy; prickles straight, small, yellow-red; fruit globular, very small, yellow to orange; bushy, low growth.

C. V. Haworth HT, *dr*, 1917, Dickson, A. Flowers intense black-scarlet with rich crimson bloom, massive shell-shaped petals, large; fragrant; vigorous growth. GM, NRS, 1919.

C. V. Haworth, Climbing Cl HT, *dr*, 1932, Cant, F.

C. W. Cowan HT, *mr*, 1912, Dickson, A. Flowers warm carmine-cerise, dbl.; fragrant.

Cyclamen F, *mp*, 1959, (DELbre); *(Frau Karl Druschki seedling × Orange Triumph seedling) × (Orange Triumph seedling × Tonnerre)*; Delbard-Chabert. Bud long; flowers medium pink, semi-dbl. (12 wavypetals), large (3 in.) blooms in sprays of 4-6; vigorous, bushy growth.

Cymbaline S, *lp*, 1983, (AUSlean; Cymbelene; Cymbeline); *Seedling × Lilian Austin*; Austin, David; David Austin Roses, 1982. Flowers light pink, dbl. (35 petals), medium; very fragrant; foliage medium, medium green, semi-glossy; spreading growth.

Cynosure HT, *rb*, 1973, *Scarlet Knight × Festival Beauty*; Hardikar. Bud ovoid; flowers red, striped pink, dbl. (50 petals), large (4½ in.); very fragrant; foliage glossy, soft; vigorous, upright growth.

Cynthia HT, *mr*, 1934, Verschuren-Pechtold; Dreer & H&S. Flowers rich oriental red, full.

Cynthia HT, *dp*, 1975, (WARdrosa; Chanterelle); *Seedling × Bob Hope*; Warriner; J&P. Bud long; flowers deep pink, dbl. (35 petals), high-centered, large (5 in.); fragrant; foliage large, matt, light; tall, upright growth.

Cynthia Ann Parker HT, *w*, 1929, Vestal. Flowers white tinged yellow or cream, dbl. fragrant.

Cynthia Brooke HT, *yb*, 1943, *Le Progres × (Mme. Mélanie Soupert × Le Progres)*; McGredy; J&P. Flowers empire yellow, reverse light salmon, dbl (45 petals), globular, large (4 in.); fragrant (fruity); foliage leathery, dark; moderate, compact, bushy growth.

Cynthia E. Hollis R, *lp*, Dawson; Eastern Nursery. Flowers pale pink, dbl.; foliage small, glossy.

Cynthie G (MRG), *lp*, Descemet, prior to 1848. Flowers pale rose, circumference almost blush, full, cupped, large; erect, moderate growth.

Cyprienne Pol, *mr*, 1969, *Sumatra × Fashion*; Delforge. Bud ovoid; flowers light brilliant red, dbl., full, large; slightly fragrant; foliage glossy, light; moderate, bushy growth; abundant, continuous bloom.

Cyrano HT, *rb*, 1954, *(Opera × Seedling) × Seedling*; Gaujard. Flowers bright red shaded purple, dbl., large, long stems; fragrant; very vigorous, upright growth.

Cyril Fletcher HT, *w*, 1983, (BEEril); *Fragrant Cloud × Whisky Mac*; Bees Ltd. Flowers creamy white, dbl. (35 petals), cabbage rose form, large; very fragrant; foliage medium, dark, semi-glossy; upright, bushy growth.

Czardas HT, *rb*, 1956, *Tango × Seedling*; Delforge. Flowers red, becoming pink; vigorous growth.

Dab HT, *ab*, 1984, *Lady X × Flaming Beauty*; Bridges, Dennis A.; Bridges Roses, 1985. Flowers apricot center, pink reverse, petals tipped deep pink, dbl. (35 petals), exhibition, large; no fragrance; foliage large, dark, glossy; bushy growth.

Dacapo F, *op*, 1960, *Fashion × Floribunda seedling*; deRuiter; Horstmann. Flowers deep salmon-pink, dbl. (28 petals), large (3-4 in.) blooms in clusters; slightly fragrant; vigorous, compact, bushy growth.

Daddies Girl HT, *yb*, 1963, *McGredy's Ivory × Peace*; McTeer, G. Flowers milky white flushed pink, base golden, dbl. (40 petals), large (5-6 in.); fragrant; foliage dark; vigorous, spreading growth.

Dady® F, *mp*, 1975, (GAUzine); *Mignonne × Seedling*; Gaujard. Flowers pink; very fragrant.

Dagenham Show F, *ob*, 1976, *Elizabeth of Glamis × Seedling*; Warley Rose Gardens. Flowers salmon-orange, dbl. (25 petals), large (3½ in.); very fragrant; foliage matt; bushy growth.

Dagmar Späth F, *w*, 1936, (White Lafayette; Blanc Lafayette); *Lafayette sport*; Wirtz & Eicke; Spath. Flowers white, edge flushed pink, fading pure white.

Dagmar Späth, Climbing Cl F, *w*, 1940, Buisman.

Dagmar Späth, Climbing Cl F, *w*, 1943, Howard Rose Co.

Dagmar Späth, Climbing Cl F, *w*, 1961, Huber.

D'Aguesseau G (OGR), *mr*, 1837, Vibert. Flowers fiery crimson, occasionally shaded dark purple, full, large; compact, erect growth.

Dahlila F, *yb*, 1962, *Golden Perfume × Peace*; Leenders, J. Flowers yellow, becoming red.

Daidala® F, *m*, 1975, *Seedling × Silver Star*; Kordes; Willemse. Bud ovoid; flowers mauve, dbl. (35 petals), high-centered, large (4 in.); slightly fragrant; foliage dark, soft; vigorous, upright, bushy growth.

Daily Herald HT, *yb*, 1942, Robinson, T.; J&P. Bud pointed; flowers yellowish orange, dbl., cupped, large (4-5 in.); foliage glossy, dark; vigorous, upright growth.

Daily Mail Scented Rose HT, *rb*, 1927, *Château de Clos Vougeot × K. of K.*; Archer. Flowers crimson, shaded maroon and vermilion, reverse dark crimson, petals imbricated; very fragrant (damask). Daily Mail Cup for Best New Scented Seedling, 1927.

Daily Mail Scented Rose, Climbing Cl HT, 1930, Archer.

Daily Sketch F, *pb*, 1961, (MACai); *Ma Perkins × Grand Gala*; McGredy, S., IV; McGredy. Flower petals silver, edged deep pink, dbl. (46 petals), well-formed, large (3½ in.) blooms in clusters; fragrant; foliage dark; vigorous, bushy growth. GM, NRS, 1960.

Daimonji HT, *or*, 1981, *Seedling × (Miss Ireland × Polynesian Sunset)*; Shibata, T.; K. Hirakata Nursery. Flowers orange-red, dbl. (48 petals), high-centered, large blooms borne usually singly; slight fragrance; foliage medium, dark; medium, bushy growth.

Dainty HT, *pb*, 1921, Dickson, H. Flowers rosy apricot, tinted cherry-pink, edges and reverse deeper pink, dbl., large; fragrant.

Dainty Pol, *op*, 1931, deRuiter. Flowers salmon-pink, cupped.

Dainty Bess HT, *lp*, 1925, *Ophelia × K. of K.*; Archer. Flowers soft rose-pink, very distinct maroon stamens, single (5 broad, fimbriated petals), medium; fragrant; foliage leathery; vigorous growth. GM, NRS, 1925.

Dainty Bess, Climbing Cl HT, *lp*, 1935, van Barneveld; California Roses.

Dainty Dawn Pol, *mp*, 1931, *Amaury Fonseca × Annchen Müller*; Knight, G. Flowers cerise-pink to mauve, semi-dbl., cupped blooms in clusters; fragrant; foliage bronze.

Dainty Delight Cl HT, *mp*, 1949, *Ednah Thomas × Dainty Bess*; Duehrsen; California Roses. Bud ovoid; flowers darker pink than Dainty Bess, semi-dbl., globular, medium, borne in clusters; slightly fragrant; foliage glossy; vigorous (6-8 ft.) growth.

Dainty Dinah Min, *op*, 1981, (COCamond); *Anne Cocker × Wee Man*; Cocker, James; Cocker & Sons. Flowers medium salmon-pink, semi-dbl., patio, small; slight fragrance; foliage small, medium green, semi-glossy; bushy growth.

Dainty Lady HT, *mp*, 1959, *(Girona × Pres. Herbert Hoover) × Michèle Meilland*; Peden. Bud long, pointed; flowers pink, dbl., high-centered, medium; fragrant; foliage leathery; vigorous, upright, compact growth.

Dainty Lady F, *op*, 1963, *Baby Sylvia × Seedling*; Fryer's Nursery. Flowers coppery salmon-pink, well formed, borne in clusters; moderate growth.

Dainty Maid F, *pb*, 1940, *D.T. Poulsen × Seedling*; LeGrice; C-P. Bud pointed, cerise; flowers silvery pink, reverse carmine, single, blooms in clusters; foliage leathery, dark; vigorous, compact, bushy growth; (28). GM, Portland, 1941.

Dainty Superior Pol, *op*, *Dainty (Pol) sport*; deRuiter. Flowers have more lasting color.

Dairy Maid F, *ly*, 1957, *(Poulsen's Pink × Ellinor LeGrice) × Mrs. Pierre S. duPont*; LeGrice. Bud yellow, splashed carmine; flowers cream, fading white, single (5 petals), large (3½ in.) blooms in large clusters; foliage glossy; vigorous growth.

Daisy HT, *ob*, 1923, *Mme. Edouard Herriot sport*; Hicks. Flowers orange-flamed.

Daisy Brasileir R, *rb*, 1918, Turbat. Flowers bright red and purple-red, anthers yellow, single, borne in clusters; slightly fragrant.

Daisy Bud HT, *pb*, 1933, Dickson, A. Bud well shaped; flowers rosy pink, shaded carmine and silver, large; fragrant.

Daisy Doll Min, *pb*, 1977, *Little Amy × Seedling*; Lyon; L. Lyon Greenhouses. Bud long, pointed; flowers rose-pink, dbl. (20-25 petals), open, small (1½ in.); slightly fragrant; foliage tiny; compact, upright growth.

Daisy Dumas HT, *rb*, 1962, *Seedling × (Tzigane × Seedling)*; White; A. Ross & Son. Flowers bright red, reverse gold edged red, dbl., medium; slightly fragrant; foliage dark; bushy growth.

Daisy Hill HMacrantha (S), *mp*, 1906, *R. × waitziana macrantha hybrid*; Kordes. Flowers pink, single, large; fragrant; fruit abundant; height 8 ft. An important parent rose.

Daisy Hillary F, *op*, 1963, *Spartan sport*; Mell. Bud pointed; flowers salmon-pink, dbl., high-centered, large, borne in clusters; foliage leathery; vigorous, bushy growth.

Daisy Mae HT, *dy*, 1987, *Golden Showers × Golden Sun*; Stoddard, Louis. Flowers deep yellow, reverse medium yellow, single (6 petals), flat, large, borne singly; foliage large, dark green, semi-glossy; large, red down-curved prickles, fading gray-tan; fruit round, ovoid, russet-yellow; upright, tall growth.

Daisy Rose F, *pb*, 1982, (KORdaisy); *Robin Hood × Topsi*; Kordes, W. Flowers pink with white eye, single (5 petals), small blooms in large clusters; foliage medium, medium green, semi-glossy; bushy growth.

Dakar HT, *pb*, 1932, *Julien Potin* × *Seedling*; Gaujard. Flowers silvery pink, striped rose-pink, large, long, strong stems; very fragrant.

Dakota Min, *mr*, 1991, (MACsalem); *Volare* × *Eyeopener*; McGredy, Sam; Oregon Miniature Roses, 1992. Flowers bright clear red, showing golden stamens, semi-dbl. (6-14 petals), small (0-4 cms) blooms borne singly or with two side buds; slight fragrance; foliage small, medium green, semi-glossy; bushy(32 cms) growth.

Dale Farm F, *or*, 1973, Smith, E.; Wheatcroft & Sons. Flowers vermilion, dbl. (25 petals), large (3 in.); fragrant; foliage dark; vigorous growth.

Dale's Sunrise® Min, *yb*, 1990, (KINsun); *(B.C. × Scamp)* × *Rainbow's End* × *Tobo*; King, Gene; AGM Miniature Roses, 1991. Flowers yellow tipped medium pink, fading pink, full (15-25 petals), small, borne mostly singly; slight fragrance; foliage small, medium green, semi-glossy; upright, bushy, medium growth.

Dalila HT, *rb*, 1943, *Souv. de Claudius Pernet* × *Seedling*; Gaujard. Bud long; pointed; flowers brilliant coppery red, semi-dbl., large; fragrant; foliage leathery; vigorous, erect growth.

Dalila F, *ob*, 1958, Buyl Frères. Flowers orange, dbl.

Dallas HT, *rb*, 1963, *Peace sport*; Hunter; Waterhouse Nursery, 1963. Flowers crimson-carmine, base primrose-yellow, dbl. (40 petals), very large; foliage dark, glossy; vigorous growth.

Dallas Gold HT, *yb*, 1987, *Seedling* × *Flaming Beauty*; Winchel, Joseph; Kimbrew-Walter Roses, 1987. Flowers yellow blend, dbl. (25 petals), large, heavy blooms; slight fragrance; foliage medium, darkgreen, glossy; bushy growth. ARC TG (S), 1984.

Dalli Dalli® F, *dr*, 1977, (TANlilida); Tantau. Bud ovoid; flowers dark red, dbl., cupped, medium; slightly fragrant; foliage very glossy; upright, bushy growth. ADR, 1975.

Dalvey HT, *dp*, 1971, *Peeping Tom* × *Seedling*; MacLeod. Flowers deep pink, exhibition form, large (5½ in.); very fragrant; foliage medium, light green, matt; vigorous.

Damas Franklin D (OGR), *pb*, 1853, Robert, 1853 or 1856. Flowers flesh-pink, shading to silver.

Dame Blanche R, *w*, 1923, Turbat. Flowers greenish white, stamens yellow, single, borne in clusters; vigorous growth, non-recurrent bloom.

Dame Blanche HT, *w*, 1927, (White Lady); *Stadtrat Glaser seedling*; Mühle. Flowers white tinged green, dbl.; fragrant.

Dame Catherine HT, *dy*, 1937, Cant, B.R. Bud ovoid; flowers golden yellow, dbl., high-centered, large, long stems; foliage glossy; vigorous, bushy growth.

Dame de Coeur HT, *mr*, 1958, (Herz-Dame; Queen of Hearts; Dama di Cuori); *Peace* × *Independence*; Lens. Flowers cherry-red, dbl., large; fragrant; foliage dark, glossy; vigorous growth.

Dame de Coeur, Climbing Cl HT, *mr*, 1984, *Dame de Coeur sport*; Mungia, Fred A.

Dame Edith Helen HT, *mp*, 1926, Dickson, A. Flowers glowing pink, dbl., cupped, very large; long, strong stems; fragrant; foliage leathery; vigorous, bushy growth; not very free bloom. GM, NRS, 1926.

Dame Edith Helen, Climbing Cl HT, *mp*, 1930, H&S.

Dame Joyce Frankland HT, *my*, 1988, (HORnewgram); *(Honey Favorite × Dr. A.J. Verhage)* × *Pot O'Gold*; Horner, Colin P. Bud globular, greenish-yellow; flowers medium yellow, dbl. (32 petals), urn-shaped, borne singly; slight fragrance; foliage large, medium green, glossy; prickles straight, medium, light brown; fruit ovoid, large, yellow; bushy growth.

Dame of Sark F, *ob*, 1976, *(Pink Parfait × Masquerade)* × *Tablers' Choice*; Harkness. Flowers orange flushed red, reverse yellow, dbl. (33 petals), large (4½ in.); slightly fragrant; foliage large, dark.

Dame Prudence S, *lp*, 1969, *Ivory Fashion* × *(Constance Spry × Ma Perkins)*; Austin, D. Flowers soft pink, reverse lighter, dbl. (65 petals), flat, medium; very fragrant.

Dame Vera Lynn F, *or*, 1986, (PEAmax; Dame Vera); *Seedling* × *Seedling*; Pearce, C.A.; Limes Rose Nursery. Flowers brick red, dbl. (20 petals), large; slightly fragrant; foliage medium, dark, semi-glossy; upright growth.

Damon Runyon HT, *mr*, 1955, *Major Shelley* × *Heart's Desire*; Duehrsen; H&S. Bud ovoid; flowers crimson, dbl. (50 petals), high-centered, large (4-5½ in.); fragrant; foliage glossy, coppery green; vigorous, upright, bushy growth.

Dana HT, *mp*, 1982, *White Satin* × *Bewitched*; Swim, H.C. & Ellis, A.E.; Armstrong Nursery. Bud long, pointed; flowers medium pink, dbl. (38 petals), spiraled, formal blooms borne singly, sometimes 3 per cluster; mild carnation fragrance; foliage large, semi-glossy; long, straight prickles; tall, upright, bushy growth.

Danaë HMsk (S), *ly*, 1913, *Reputedly Trier × Gloire de Chedane-Guinoiseau*; Pemberton. Flowers pale buff-yellow, fading white, in clusters; height 6 ft.; recurrent bloom; (14).

D. Ana Guedes HT, *ob*, 1938, *Angèle Pernet × Mme. Méha Sabatier*; Moreira da Silva. Bud ovoid; flowers orange and salmon-pink, veined yellow, dbl., cupped, large; slightly fragrant; foliage soft; vigorous, bushy growth.

Dance of Joy F, *mr*, 1931, *Paul's Scarlet Climber × Seedling*; Sauvageot. Flowers vivid scarlet-crimson, dbl., large; fragrant; foliage dark; vigorous growth; (28). GM, Bagatelle, 1931.

Dancing Doll Cl F, *dp*, 1952, *Étoile Luisante × Seedling*; Moore, R.S.; Marsh's Nursery. Bud small, pointed; flowers deep rose-pink, semi-dbl. (10-14 petals), cupped, borne in clusters; very fragrant; foliage leathery, glossy; vigorous climbing or spreading (10 ft.) growth; profuse, recurrent bloom.

Dancing Silk HT, *op*, 1966, *Ena Harkness × McGredy's Yellow*; Barter. Flowers coral-pink, reflexed, large (5 in.); slightly fragrant; foliage light green; vigorous growth.

Dandee Min, *dr*, 1983, *Seedling × Libby*; Meredith, E.A. & Rovinski, M.E.; Casa de Rosa Domingo. Bud globular; flowers dark red, dbl. (35 petals), flat, medium blooms borne singly; fragrant; foliage medium, dark, semi-glossy; upright growth.

Dandy Pol, *op*, 1945, *Gloria Mundi × Unidentified Species rose*; Wiseman. Flowers light orange-pink, semi-dbl., cupped, small; slightly fragrant; foliage wrinkled, glossy, dark; very vigorous growth; profuse, non-recurrent bloom.

Dandy Dick F, *mp*, 1967, *Pink Parfait × Red Dandy*; Harkness. Flowers medium pink, dbl. (25 petals), well-formed, large blooms in clusters; spicy fragrance; foliage light.

Dandy Lyon Min, *dy*, 1978, *Seedling × Sunspot*; Lyon. Bud long, pointed; flowers buttercup-yellow, dbl. (30 petals), medium (2 in.); fragrant; foliage small, dark, glossy; compact, bushy growth.

D. Angelica Pereira da Rosa HT, *pb*, 1936, *Angèle Pernet × Edith Nellie Perkins*; Moreira da Silva. Flowers pink, shaded golden orange, reverse red, dbl., open, very large; foliage light.

Daniel HT, *rb*, 1943, Mallerin; A. Meilland. Bud long, pointed; flowers capucine-red on golden yellow base, dbl., cupped; foliage dark, glossy; vigorous, bushy growth.

Daniel Lacombe R, *yb*, 1885, *R. multiflora × Général Jacqueminot*; Allard. Flowers yellow washed pink, full, flat, medium; vigorous growth.

Danielle Darrieux HT, *pb*, 1948, Gaujard. Bud long, pointed; flowers salmon suffused yellow, reverse salmon-orange-pink, dbl., very large; fragrant; very vigorous, bushy growth.

Danielle Robyn HT, *rb*, 1971, *Grand Gala × Western Sun*; Hastie. Bud globular; flowers pinky red and creamy white bicolor, dbl., high-centered, large; slightly fragrant; foliage glossy, dark; bushy growth; intermittent bloom.

Daniphyl HT, *mr*, 1978, *Puccini × Chopin*; Ellick; Excelsior Roses. Flowers mandarin-red, dbl. (45-50 petals), full, large (4-5 in.); fragrant; foliage semi-glossy, light; vigorous, upright growth.

Danish Gold F, *yb*, 1949, *(Golden Salmon × Souv. de Claudius Pernet) × Julien Potin*; Poulsen, S.; McGredy. Flowers yellow fading to creamy white, single (5-9 petals), large (2½-3 in.); fragrant (spicy); foliage glossy; vigorous, compact growth. GM, NRS, 1949.

Danish Pink F, *dp*, 1965, Soenderhousen; Hoersholm Nursery. Flowers deep pink, almost single, medium (2-2½in.), borne in large clusters; fragrant (fruity); vigorous, tall growth.

Danny Boy LCl, *or*, 1969, *Uncle Walter × Milord (HT)*; McGredy, S., IV; McGredy. Flowers orange-red, well-formed; very fragrant; foliage dark; recurrent bloom.

Danny Thomas Min, *mr*, 1980, *Rose Hills Red × Self*; Wells, V.W.; Lou McGuire. Flowers medium red, yellow stamens, dbl. (35 petals), borne usually singly; fragrant; foliage dark; straight prickles; compact growth.

Danse Azteque Min, *yb*, 1985, (Rigobec 3); *Baby Masquerade × Seedling*; Gailloux, Gilles. Flowers yellow-pink blend, semi-dbl., flat, medium; slight fragrance; foliage medium, medium green, semi-glossy; vigorous, upright growth.

Danse des Étoiles F, *or*, 1973, (GODsensor); *Orangeade × Orange Sensation*; Godin. Bud ovoid; flowers red-orange, semi-dbl. (15-18 petals), deep cupped, large (2½ in.); foliage light green.

Danse des Sylphes® LCl, *or*, 1959, (MALcair; Grimpant Danse des Sylphes®); *Spectacular × (Peace × Independence)*; Mallerin; URS. Flowers rich red suffused geranium-red, globular, medium blooms in large clusters; foliage glossy; very vigorous growth.

Danubio Azul HT, *m*, 1957, *Tristesse × Independence*; Camprubi. Flowers lilac, dbl., cupped, medium; slightly fragrant; upright growth.

Dany Robin F, *op*, 1958, *Goldilocks × Fashion*; Meilland, F.; URS. Bud pointed; flowers salmon-pink, dbl. (25 wavy petals), open, medium, borne in clusters; slightly fragrant; foliage leathery; vigorous, compact growth.

Danzig HT, *dr*, 1940, *Hadley × Kardinal*; Tantau. Flowers shining dark red, dbl., medium, borne in clusters; upright growth.

Daphne HMsk (S), *lp*, 1912, Pemberton. Flowers blush-pink, semi-dbl., blooms in clusters; fragrant; vigorous growth.

Daphne HT, *lp*, 1925, Dobbie. Flowers soft pink, flushed rose, dbl., well-formed; fragrant.

Daphne B (OGR), *mr*, Flowers bright red, cupped.

Daphne Gandy F, *mr*, 1952, *Farida × Crimson Glory*; Leenders, M.; Gandy. Flowers bloodred, large (3 in.) blooms in large trusses; slightly fragrant; foliage dark; vigorous.

Daphnis HT, *mp*, 1974, *Marylène × Mignonne*; Gaujard. Flowers brilliant pink, very large; upright growth.

Dara HT, *ob*, 1991, *Olympiad × Just Joey*; Wambach, Alex A. Flowers orange blend, dbl. (30 petals), exhibition, medium blooms borne usually singly; heavy fragrance; foliage medium, medium green, semi-glossy; upright growth.

Darcelle Min, *w*, 1991, (SPOdarc); *(Whistle Stop × Popcorn) × Nozomi*; Spooner, Ray; Oregon Miniature Roses. Flowers white, single (5 petals), small (0-4 cms), blooms borne in sprays of 3-5; slight fragrance; foliage small, medium green, semi-glossy; bushy, low (13 cms), very compact growth.

Dardanelle HT, *mr*, 1926, *Premier × Ophelia*; Vestal. Flowers cherry-rose, dbl.; fragrant; foliage wrinkled, dark; bushy growth.

Darius G (OGR), *mr*. Flowers vivid red, full, large.

Dark Boy HT, *dr*, 1965, *Nigrette × Seedling*; Pal; Indian Agric. Research Inst. Bud ovoid; flowers velvety dark maroon-red, dbl., medium; slightly fragrant; foliage soft; moderate, upright, open growth.

Dark Secret HT, *dr*, 1937, *Radiance × Hollywood*; Amling Co. Flowers dark red, dbl., globular, large, short stems; very fragrant; foliage leathery; dwarf growth.

Darling HT, *lp*, 1958, *Pink Princess × Charlotte Armstrong*; Taylor, C.A.; California Nursery Co. Bud ovoid; flowers light pink, dbl., large; fruity fragrance; foliage dark, glossy; vigorous, bushy growth.

Darling Annabelle HT, *w*, 1992, *South Seas × Peace*; Perry, Astor; Hortico, Inc., 1993. Flowers white with faint pink center, full (26-40 petals), excellent exhibition potential, large (over 7 cms) blooms; fragrant; foliage large, medium green, matt; upright (170 cms) growth.

Darling Flame Min, *or*, 1971, (MEIlucca; Minuetto; Minuette); *(Rimosa × Josephine Wheatcroft) × Zambra*; Meilland. Flowers mandarin-red to vermillion red, yellow anthers, dbl. (25 petals), globular, small (1½ in.); slightly fragrant (fruity); foliage glossy, dark; vigorous.

D'Artagnan D (OGR), *dr*, 1969, *Ma Perkins × York and Lancaster*; Fankhauser. Flowers wine-red, dbl., cupped, medium blooms in clusters; very fragrant (damask); foliage dark, leathery, wrinkled; vigorous, upright (6 ft.) growth; non-recurrent bloom.

D'Assas HP (OGR), *pb*, 1850, Vibert. Flowers dark pink, tinged crimson, dbl., petals somewhat fringed, medium or small; vigorous, straggling growth.

Daughter Margaret S, *w*, 1985, (NOBam); *Mutabilis × Cornelia*; Nobbs, K.J. Flowers peach, fading to white, dbl. (48 petals), borne in clusters of 2-6; slight fragrance; foliage typical China; broad, pink prickles; compact growth; repeat bloom.

Dauntless HT, *pb*, 1949, *Crimson Glory × Feu Pernet-Ducher*; Davis. Bud long, pointed; flowers pink, reverse yellow, dbl. (60 petals), high-centered, large; fragrant; foliage leathery, dark; upright growth.

Dauphine F, *op*, 1955, *Seedling × Opera seedling*; Gaujard. Bud ovoid; flowers pink shaded salmon, dbl., open, large, borne in clusters; fragrant; very vigorous growth.

Dauphine, Climbing Cl F, *op*, 1959, Gaujard.

Dave Davis HT, *dr*, 1964, *Seedling × Charles Mallerin*; Davis; Wyant. Bud long, pointed; flowers dark velvety red, dbl. (60 petals), high-centered, large; very fragrant; foliage leathery; moderate growth.

Dave Hessayon HT, *mp*, 1990, (DRIscobruce); *Silver Jubilee × Pink Favorite*; Driscoll, Bill; Rosemary Roses, 1989. Flowers medium pink, full (26-40 petals), medium blooms; fragrant; foliage medium, medium green, glossy; bushy growth.

David Arnot HT, *rb*, Flowers bright scarlet, reverse old-gold; vigorous growth. An improvement on The Queen Alexandra Rose.

David Charles Armstrong HT, *mr*, 1992, (DRIscogeorge); *Silver Jubilee × Fragrant Cloud*; Driscoll, W.E., 1993. Flowers coral red, full (26-40 petals), large (7+cms) blooms borne mostly singly; slight fragrance; foliage medium, medium green, semi-glossy; some prickles; tall (106 cms), upright growth.

David Gilmore HT, *mr*, 1923, Dickson, H. Flowers brilliant scarlet.

David Gold HT, *rb*, 1957, *Shot Silk* × *Peace*; Robinson, H. Flowers cherry-cerise tinted golden yellow, high-centered, very large (6 in.); very fragrant; foliage dark, glossy; very vigorous growth.

David McKee HT, *mr*, 1933, Dickson, A. Flowers carmine-red, dbl., high-centered, large; very fragrant; foliage leathery; vigorous, bushy growth.

David O. Dodd HT, *mr*, 1926, Vestal. Flowers rich crimson flushed scarlet, dbl., large; very fragrant; foliage glossy; bushy growth.

David O. Dodd, Climbing Cl HT, *mr*, 1937, Howard Rose Co.

David Thompson HRg (S), *mr*, 1979, *(Schneezwerg* × *Frau Dagmar Hartopp)* × *Seedling*; Svejda; Canada Dept. of Agric. Bud ovoid; flowers medium red, yellow stamens, dbl. (25 petals), large (2½ in.); very fragrant; upright growth.

Davy Crockett F, *dr*, 1956, *Étoile de Hollande* × *Floribunda seedling*; deRuiter; Gandy. Flowers dark red, dbl., large; vigorous growth.

Dawn HT, *op*, 1953, Jelly; E.G. Hill Co. Bud long, pointed; flowers salmon-pink, base yellow, dbl. (28-36 petals), high-centered, large (5-6 in.); fragrant (spicy); vigorous, upright growth.

Dawn Fragrance LCl, *op*, 1969, *Blossomtime* × *Blossomtime seedling*; Mason, P.G. Flowers salmon-flesh, flushed rose-pink, well formed, cupped; very fragrant; foliage dark, leathery; vigorous growth; intermittent bloom.

Dawn Mist F, *pb*, 1962, *(Goldilocks* × *Pinocchio)* × *Vogue*; Boerner; Home Nursery Products Corp. Bud ovoid; flowers reddish pink, base yellow, dbl. (30-35 petals), cupped, large (3 in.); very fragrant (spicy); foliage leathery, glossy; vigorous, bushy, compact.

Dawn Pink F, *mp*, 1962, *Magenta* × *Ma Perkins*; Anderson's Rose Nursery. Bud apricot; flowers pink, dbl. (45-50 petals), rosette form, large (3½ in.), borne in clusters; fragrant; foliage light green; vigorous, upright growth.

Dawnglow HT, *pb*, 1937, Burbank. Flowers flesh-pink, dbl., high-centered, medium (3½ in.); fragrant.

Dawning, Climbing LCl, *op*, 1956, *New Dawn* × *Margaret McGredy*; Bennett, H.; Pedigree Nursery. Flowers salmon-pink; fragrant; foliage glossy; vigorous growth.

Dawnlight F, *pb*, 1958, *Summer Snow, Climbing* × *Summer Snow*; Motose; G.B. Hart, Inc. Bud ovoid; flowers soft pink, dbl. (30-35 petals), flat, medium (2-2½ in.); slightly fragrant; foliage leathery, light green; thornless; vigorous, bushy growth.

Dawns Early Light HT, *w*, 1972, *Vesuvius* × *Vesuvius*; Linscott. Bud long, palest pink; flowers white, faintly edged pale pink, single (6 petals), pointed, large (3½-4 in.); very fragrant; foliage light; tall growth; bloom lasts well.

Dawson HMult (OGR), *mp*, 1888, *R. multiflora* × *Général Jacqueminot*; Dawson; Strong. Flowers bright rose-pink, dbl., small blooms in clusters of 10-20; vigorous (10-25 ft.) growth.

Day Dream HT, *dp*, 1969, *Helen Traubel* × *Tiffany*; Armstrong, D.L.; Armstrong Nursery. Bud long, pointed; flowers deep pink, dbl., large; foliage glossy, leathery; vigorous, upright, bushy growth.

Day Glow Min, *dp*, 1988, (JACrink); *Petticoat* × *Red Jewel*; Warriner, William; Bear Creek Gardens, 1989. Bud ovoid, pointed; flowers deep pink, fading lighter, very dbl. (60 petals), high-centered to flat, medium, borne usually singly; slight fragrance; foliage medium, dark green, matt; prickles straight, short; low growth.

Day Is Done HT, *or*, 1985, *Die Welt* × *Rosalynn Carter*; Schneider, Peter. Flowers orange-red, dbl. (35 petals), exhibition, large; slight fragrance; foliage large, dark, semi-glossy.

Day Light® F, *ab*, 1992, (INTerlight; Daylight); *Seedling* × *New Year*; Ilsink, G.P., 1985; Interplant B.V., 1991. Flowers apricot-yellow, apricot and light pink reverse, aging to champagne color, urn-shaped, dbl. (15-25 petals), medium (8 cms) blooms borne in sprays of 5-8; no fragrance; foliage medium, dark green, matt; upright, medium (+/- 48 cms) growth.

Day of Triumph HT, *mp*, 1953, (Rendezvous); *Peace* × *Europa*; Meilland, F.; URS, 1953 & Breedlove Nursery, 1955. Bud ovoid; flowers pink edged lighter, dbl. (50-65 petals), cupped, large (5½ in.); fragrant; foliage leathery; vigorous, upright, bushy growth.

Daybreak R, *op*, 1909, *R. wichuraiana* × *R. chinensis*; Dawson; Eastern Nursery. Flowers deep salmon-pink, borne in clusters; late bloom.

Daybreak HMsk (S), *my*, 1918, (Day Break); *Trier* × *Liberty*; Pemberton. Flowers golden yellow, near single; foliage dark; vigorous, bushy growth; recurrent bloom.

Daybreak HT, *pb*, 1935, *Violet Simpson × Ivy May*; Laxton Bros. Bud large, long, pointed; flowers salmon-pink and yellow, very dbl., high-centered; slightly fragrant; foliage leathery; long stems; very vigorous growth.

Daybreak S, *dp*, 1960, *Hansa × R. macounii*; Erskine. Flowers deep pink, dbl. (25-30 petals).

Daylight HT, *pb*, 1939, *Grange Colombe × Los Angeles*; Hansen, N. J.; B & A. Flowers creamy blush-pink, base yellow, very dbl., cupped, high centered, large (4 in.); fragrant; Foliage soft; Vigorous growth. RULED EXTINCT 4/92 ARM.

Daylight Katy F, *my*, 1987, *Bright Smile × (Princess Michael of Kent × Party Girl)*; Schneider, Peter. Flowers bright yellow, fading slightly paler, dbl. (22 petals), urn-shaped, medium, borne in sprays of 3-15; slight fragrance; foliage medium, bronze-green, semiglossy; pointed, medium, reddish prickles; fruit round, small, red; bushy, low growth.

Dazla HT, *rb*, 1930, Cant, B.R. Bud long, pointed; flowers orange-scarlet, base and reverse golden yellow, semi-dbl., wavy petals, large (nearly 6 in.); foliage dark; vigorous.

Dazla, Climbing Cl HT, *rb*, 1950, Cant, B.R.

Dean Collins Gr, *dp*, 1953, *Charlotte Armstrong × Floradora*; Lammerts; Roseway Nursery. Bud ovoid, red; flowers deep pink, dbl. (53 petals), large (4½-5 in.); slightly fragrant; foliage dark, glossy, leathery; vigorous growth.

Dean Hole HT, *pb*, 1904, Dickson, A. Flowers silvery carmine, shaded salmon, dbl.; fragrant.

Dearest F, *pb*, 1960, *Seedling × Spartan*; Dickson, A. Flowers rosy salmon-pink, gold stamens, dbl. (30 petals), well-formed, large (3½ in.) blooms in clusters; fragrant; foliage dark, glossy; vigorous, bushy growth. GM, NRS, 1961.

Debbie Min, *yb*, 1966, *Little Darling × Zee*; Moore, R.S.; Sequoia Nursery. Flowers yellow, edges becoming pink, dbl., small; fragrant; foliage small, leathery; bushy, low, sometimes semi-climbing growth.

Debbie Lynn HT, *dr*, 1992, Jerabek, Paul, 1986. Flowers dark red, dbl. (36 petals), urn-shaped, high-centered, medium (12 cms) blooms borne usually singly; moderate fragrance; foliage medium, dark green, semiglossy; upright, bushy, medium growth.

Debbie-Karen HT, *mp*, 1983, *Seedling × Seedling*; Burdett, H.J., 1984. Flowers medium pink, dbl. (50+ petals), exhibition, large (4½-5½ in.) blooms borne singly; slight fragrance; foliage large, light green, semi-glossy; vigorous, upright growth.

Debidue™ Min, *dp*, 1991, (MICdeb); *Jazz Fest × Party Girl*; Williams, Michael C.; The Rose Garden; Mini Rose Nursery, 1992. Flowers magenta, full (26-40 petals), small (0-4 cms) blooms borne mostly singly; slight fragrance; foliage medium, dark green, semi-glossy; some prickles; medium (12 cms), upright growth. AOE, 1992.

Debonair HT, *my*, 1946, *Golden Rapture × Seedling*; Lammerts; Armstrong Nursery. Bud ovoid; flowers primrose-yellow, dbl. (28-35 petals), high-centered, large (3-4½ in.); fragrant; foliage leathery, glossy, dark; very vigorous, upright, bushy growth.

Deborah Moncrief™ HT, *pb*, 1991, (WILdeb); *Carla × Sonia*; Williams, J. Benjamin, 1988. Flowers pink with ivory blend, full (26-40 petals), large blooms borne mostly singly; very fragrant; few prickles; foliage large, dark green, matt; medium (12-18 in.), bushy, spreading growth.

Debra Gaye Min, *op*, 1985, (TINdeb); *Futura × Fairest of Fair*; Bennett, Dee; Tiny Petals Nursery. Flowers orange-pink, soft yellow reverse, dbl. (38 petals), HT form, medium; slight fragrance; foliage medium, medium green, semi-glossy; bushy, upright growth.

Deb's Delight F, *pb*, 1983, (LEGsweet); *Tip Top × Seedling*; LeGrice, E.B., 1982. Flowers silvery salmon-pink blend, dbl. (35 petals), patio, medium; fragrant; foliage medium, medium green, semi-glossy; low, bushy growth.

Debut™ Min, *rb*, 1988, (MEIbarke; Douce Symphonie; Sweet Symphony); *Coppelia × Magic Carrousel*; Selection Meilland; C-P Co., 1989. Flowers luminous scarlet blending to cream to yellow at base, aging fades to cherry-red, white at base, dbl. (15-18 petals), exhibition, medium, borne usually singly; no fragrance; foliage medium, dark green, semiglossy; prickles slender, few, straw; fruit ovoid, few, dull orange-red; bushy growth. 1989 AARS.

Debutante R, *lp*, 1902, *R. wichuraiana × Baroness Rothschild*; Walsh. Flowers rose-pink, fading to cameo-pink, dbl., borne in clusters of 4-6 on short stems; fragrant (sweetbrier); foliage dark, glossy; height 6-8 ft.; non-recurrent bloom.

De Candolle M (OGR), *lp*, 1857, Portemer. Flowers soft pink or rose-tinted, full, large.

Decea Ann F, *ab*, 1975, *Queen Elizabeth × Elizabeth of Glamis*; Horsfield. Flowers flushed peach-pink, dbl. (26 petals), full, large (3½-4 in.); very fragrant; foliage dark, leathery; upright growth.

Deception HT, *dp*, 1923, Beckwith. Flowers deep rose, large; fragrant. GM, NRS, 1923.

Décor LCl, *or*, 1951, (Record); *(Love × Paul's Scarlet Climber) × Demain*; Mallerin; URS. Flowers bright scarlet, semi-dbl., medium blooms in clusters; foliage leathery; vigorous growth.

Decorator HT, *rb*, 1936, Dickson, A. Flowers brilliant carmine, base orange-yellow; foliage glossy; very vigorous growth.

Dedication F, *ly*, 1968, *Pink Parfait × Circus*; Harkness. Flowers creamy ivory, dbl., borne in trusses; slightly fragrant; foliage glossy.

Dee Bennett™ Min, *ob*, 1988, (SAVadee); *Zorina × (Sheri Anne × (Yellow Jewel × Tamango))*; Saville, F. Harmon; Nor'East Miniature Roses, 1989. Flowers yellow and orange becoming orange-yellow, dbl. (25 petals), high-centered, medium, borne usually singly and in sprays of 3-8; slight, fruity fragrance; foliage medium, dark green, semi-glossy; prickles long, thin, curved, gray-orange; fruit none; bushy, medium growth. 1989 AOE.

Deep Purple F, *m*, 1980, *Zorina × Silver Star*; Kordes, R.; Armstrong Nursery. Bud ovoid, pointed; flowers mauve-pink, dbl. (30-45 petals), imbricated, large (3-4 in.); fragrant; foliage glossy, dark; vigorous, upright, bushy growth.

Deep Secret HT, 1946, *Matchless × seedling*; Hildebrandt. Flowers rich red becoming darker, compact; very fragrant; Not introduced. RULED EXTINCT 4/77 ARM.

Deep Secret HT, *dr*, 1977, (Mildred Scheel); Tantau; Wheatcroft, 1979. Flowers deep crimson, dbl. (40 petals), large (4 in.); very fragrant; foliage glossy, dark; vigorous, upright growth. ADR, 1978.

Deep Velvet™ Min, *dr*, 1981, *(Grand Opera × Jimmy Greaves) × Baby Katie*; Jolly, Betty; Rosehill Farm. Flowers dark red, dbl. (33 petals), high-centered, urn-shaped blooms borne singly and 2-3 per cluster; slight fragrance; foliage tiny, medium green; straight prickles; bushy, compact growth.

Deepika F, *rb*, 1975, *Shepherd's Delight × Seedling*; Indian Agric. Research Inst. Bud pointed; flowers red blend, semi-dbl. (15 petals), medium (2 in.); foliage glossy, dark; vigorous, upright, open growth; free bloom, fairly lasting.

Deepshikha F, *mr*, 1975, *Sea Pearl × Shola*; Indian Agric. Research Inst. Bud pointed; flowers red, dbl. (35 petals), open, large (2½ in.); slightly fragrant (tea); foliage glossy, light; vigorous, compact, bushy growth; very lasting.

Déesse HT, *rb*, 1957, (Goddess); *Peace × Seedling*; Gaujard. Bud long, pointed, white; flowers red spreading from outside to center petals, ending crimson, dbl., medium; vigorous, upright growth.

Defiance HT, *dr*, 1914, *Gruss an Teplitz × Étoile de France*; Kress. Flowers dark velvety red, dbl., large (5-6 in.); very fragrant; foliage dark; vigorous growth.

DeGrazia's Pink Min, *mp*, 1983, (MINhco); *(Seedling × Over the Rainbow) × (Seedling × Over the Rainbow*; Williams, E.D.; Mini-Roses. Flowers medium pink, dbl. (40+ petals), heavy substance, small; slight fragrance; foliage small, dark, glossy; bushy growth.

De Greeff's Jubilee F, *dr*, 1980, (Fellowship); *Diablotin × Gisselfeld*; Verschuren, Ted; Verschuren & Sons. Flowers dark red, semi-dbl., large; slight fragrance; foliage medium, dark, semi-glossy; bushy growth.

Déjà Vous Min, *ab*, 1987, *Anita Charles × Sheri Anne*; Jolly, Nelson & Marie; Rosehill Farm. Bud pointed; flowers light apricot, aging lighter, dbl. (50 petals), high-centered, exhibition, large blooms borne usually singly; slight fragrance; foliage medium, medium green, semi-glossy; no prickles; fruit none; medium, upright, spreading growth.

De la Grifferaie HMult (OGR), *dp*, 1845, *Parentage uncertain, possibly a hybrid between R. multiflora and a Gallica or Damascena*; Vibert. Flowers carmine to pink, fully dbl., medium; robust growth. Once popular as an understock.

Delambre P (OGR), *dp*, 1863, Moreau & Robert. Flowers carmine.

Delbard's Orange Climber LCl, *or*, 1966, (DELpar; Grimpamt Delbard); *Spectacular × (Rome Glory × La Vaudoise)*; Delbard-Chabert, 1963; Armstrong Nursery, 1963. Bud ovoid; flowers orange-red, dbl., high-centered, medium; slightly fragrant; foliage dark, glossy, leathery; vigorous, climbing, well branched growth, repeat bloom.

Delhi Apricot HT, *ab*, 1964, Pal; Indian Agric. Research Inst. Bud pointed; flowers apricot-yellow, dbl., medium; slightly fragrant; foliage light green, soft; moderate, bushy growth.

Delhi Brightness F, *op*, 1963, Pal; Indian Agric. Research Inst. Flowers orange-pink, semi-dbl., open, medium; foliage glossy; vigorous, upright growth.

Delhi Daintiness F, *lp*, 1963, Pal; Indian Agric. Research Inst. Bud pointed; flowers light pink, reverse darker, semi-dbl., medium; foliage glossy; vigorous, upright, compact growth.

Delhi Maid F, *ob*, 1963, Pal; Indian Agric. Research Inst. Bud pointed; flowers flame-orange, base gold, single, open, medium; foliage dark, glossy; vigorous, upright, compact growth.

Delhi Pink Pearl R, *lp*, 1962, *Echo sport*; Pal; Indian Agric. Research Inst. Bud ovoid; flowers pearly pink, semi-dbl., open, medium; foliage glossy, light green; very vigorous, climbing growth.

Delhi Prince F, *dp*, 1963, Pal; Indian Agric. Research Inst. Bud pointed; flowers glowing deep pink, semi-dbl., open, medium; slightly fragrant; foliage glossy; vigorous, bushy growth.

Delhi Princess F, *mp*, 1963, Pal; Indian Agric. Research Inst. Bud ovoid, cerise-red; flowers deep pink, semi-dbl., open, large, borne in clusters; slightly fragrant; foliage glossy, bronze; very vigorous, compact growth.

Delhi Rosette F, *ob*, 1965, Pal; Indian Agric. Research Inst. Bud ovoid; flowers bright orange-scarlet, dbl. (28 petals), open, medium; foliage dark, glossy; vigorous, compact growth.

Delhi Sherbet F, *mp*, 1963, *Gruss an Teplitz* × *Seedling*; Pal; Indian Agric. Research Inst. Bud ovoid; flowers deep rose-pink, dbl., medium; very fragrant; foliage glossy; vigorous, bushy, compact growth.

Delhi Starlet Min, *ly*, 1963, *Goudvlinder* × *Seedling*; Pal; Indian Agric. Research Inst. Bud pointed; flowers light yellow, semi-dbl. open, small; slightly fragrant (musk); foliage small, glossy; dwarf, compact growth.

Delhi Sunshine HT, *yb*, 1963, *Mme. Charles Sauvage* × *Seedling*; Pal; Indian Agric. Research Inst. Bud pointed; flowers deep cream, reverse flushed pink, dbl., medium; foliage light green; bushy, open growth.

Delhi White Pearl LCl, *w*, 1963, *Prosperity* × *Seedling*; Pal; Indian Agric. Research Institute. Bud ovoid; flowers pearly white, dbl., medium blooms in clusters; slightly fragrant; foliage glossy; vigorous; repeat bloom.

Delicado HT, *op*, 1954, Lowe. Flowers shell-pink shaded peach, well shaped, very large (6 in.); moderate growth.

Delicata HRg (S), *lp*, 1898, Cooling. Flowers soft lilac-pink, semi-dbl., large; vigorous growth; recurrent bloom.

Délie Communaudat HT, *yb*, 1933, *Mme. Charles Detreaux* × *Mme. Edouard Herriot*; Buatois. Flowers naples yellow, shaded and edged carmine, dbl., cupped; fragrant; foliage leathery; very vigorous, bushy growth.

Delight R, *rb*, 1904, Walsh. Flowers bright carmine, base white, stamens yellow, single to semi-dbl., cupped, medium to large, large clusters on long stems; foliage glossy; very vigorous, climbing (15-20 ft.) growth.

Delightful HT, *pb*, 1931, *George Dickson seedling*; McGredy. Flowers rose, base yellow, reverse amber-yellow, dbl., high-centered, large; fragrant; foliage glossy; vigorous growth.

Delightful HT, *yb*, 1956, *Curly Pink* × *Shades of Autumn*; Brownell. Bud pointed; flowers straw-yellow, base shaded red, dbl. (35-50 petals), high-centered, large (4-5 in.); fragrant; upright, compact growth.

Delightful Kiwi HT, *lp*, 1989, *Silent Night* × *(Prima Ballerina* × *Irish Mist)*; Cattermole, R.F.; South Pacific Rose Nursery, 1988. Bud tapering; flowers blush pink aging to creamy pink, dbl. (45 petals), urn-shaped, medium, borne singly and in sprays of up to 5; slight fragrance; foliage light green, large, shiny; prickles light brown, very few; upright, branching growth.

Delightful Lady HT, *lp*, 1982, *Pascali* × *Merry Widow*; Attfield, B.B. Flowers light pink, dbl. (30-35 petals), high-centered, exhibition, large, borne singly in spring, 3-5 per cluster in autumn; slight fragrance; foliage semi-glossy; brown prickles; medium-tall.

Delightful Pink F, *mp*, 1958, *Chic* × *Demure*; Boerner; J&P. Bud ovoid; flowers pink, dbl. (40-45 petals), cupped, medium, borne in clusters; fragrant; vigorous, upright growth; for pot forcing.

Delille M (OGR), *w*, 1852, Robert. Flowers blush-white, semi-dbl., nicely mossed; may repeat.

DELjofem HT, *pb*, 1982, (Tendresse); *(Michèle Meilland* × *Bayadère)* × *(Grace de Monaco* × *Present Filial)*; Delbard, G.; Delbard Roses, 1980. Flowers light pink, reverse apricot-pink, dbl., exhibition, large; fragrant; foliage dense.

DELsamo HT, *dp*, 1974, (Paris 2000); *((Deltorche* × *(Sultane* × *Mme. Joseph Perraud))* × *(Queen Elizabebeth* × *Provence)*; Delbard. Flowers deep pink, dbl. (28 petals), cupped, large; no fragrance; vigorous, upright, bushy growth.

DELsatel HT, *or*, 1982, (Satellite®); *((Tropicana* × *Samourai)* × *(Tropicana* × *(Rome Glory* × *Impeccable)))* × *Granada*; Delbard, G. Flowers orange-red, dbl. (28 petals), medium; fragrant; foliage medium, medium green, semi-glossy.

DELsulan HT, *mp*, 1988, (Europe 92R); *Seedling* × *(Michele Meilland* × *Karla)*; Delbard & Chabert. Flowers pink magenta, dbl. (11 petals), long, large; slight fragrance; foliage bright; vigorous, bushy growth.

Delta Gamma HT, *ly*, 1977, *Queen Elizabeth* × *Mount Shasta*; Kimbrew-Walter Roses. Bud pointed; flowers creamy white, base pale yellow, dbl. (38 petals), high-centered, large (4-4½ in.); fragrant (spicy); foliage dark; vigorous, upright, bushy growth.

Delta Gold™ HT, *yb*, 1988, (BURdel); *Arizona* × *World Peace*; Perry, Anthony; Co-Operative Rose Growers, 1989. Flowers red and yellow blend, reverse red-yellow, semi-dbl. (35 petals), urn-shaped, medium, borne singly; strong stems; slight fragrance; foliage medium, dark green, glossy; prickles slight recurve, average, dark; fruit round, average, orange; bushy, medium growth.

De Luxe HT, *rb*, 1931, *Premier sport*; White Bros.; Liggit. Flowers bright velvety scarlet, reverse red, semi-dbl.; slightly fragrant.

DELzen LCl, *or*, 1982, (Zenith®); *(Spectacular* × *Tenor seedling)* × *(Floradora* × *Incendie)*; Delbard, G.; Delbard Roses. Flowers orange-red, semi-dbl., medium blooms in clusters; climbing (to 8 ft.) growth.

Demain HT, *mr*, 1945, *Mrs. Pierre S. duPont* × *Dr. Kirk*; Mallerin; A. Meilland. Bud pointed; flowers brilliant cardinal-red, reverse saffron-yellow, semi-dbl., cupped; very vigorous, upright growth.

Dembrosky HP (OGR), *dr*, 1849, (Dembrowski); Vibert. Flowers deep crimson-violet.

Demoiselle HT, *pb*, 1960, *Peace* × *Opera*; Delforge. Flowers soft pink becoming darker, dbl. (25-30 petals), open, medium; slightly fragrant; foliage bronze; vigorous, bushy growth.

Demokracie LCl, *dr*, 1935, (Blaze Superier); Böhm; Like Blaze but more intense red and of better form; said to be recurrent.

Démone HT, *dr*, 1965, Tantau, Math. Bud ovoid; flowers dark red, dbl., medium; very fragrant; foliage dark.

Demure F, *dp*, 1952, *Garnette* × *Yellow seedling*; Boerner; J&P. Bud ovoid; flowers rose-pink, dbl. (52 petals), flat, medium (2 in.), borne in clusters; fragrant; foliage leathery; vigorous, compact growth; a greenhouse cut flower.

Denis Hélie HP (OGR), *mr*, 1864, Gautreau. Flowers rosy crimson; vigorous growth.

Denise HT, *my*, 1955, *Peace* × *Brandywine*; Buyl Frères; Delforge. Bud oval; flowers citron-yellow, dbl., open, large; slightly fragrant; foliage glossy, clear green; vigorous, bushy growth.

Denise Cassegrain Pol, *w*, 1922, Grandes Roseraies. Flowers snow-white, very dbl., clusters of 30-40; very fragrant.

Denise Chambard HT, *yb*, 1940, Chambard, C.; Orard. Bud long, carmine-yellow; flowers sulphur-yellow, shaded carmine, cupped, large, strong stems; foliage bright green; vigorous, upright growth.

Denise Dewar HT, *dr*, 1968, *Isabelle de France* × *Karl Herbst*; Trew. Flowers crimson, pointed; foliage bronze-green; free growth.

Denise Lefeuvre HT, *rb*, 1930, Chambard, C. Flowers nasturtium-red, center yellow, reverse bright red, dbl., cupped, large, strong stems; very vigorous growth.

Denise McClelland HT, *dr*, 1964, *Amy Johnson* × *New Yorker*; Riethmuller; Akhurst. Flowers claret-red, dbl. (30 petals), large; fragrant; foliage dark, leathery, glossy; vigorous, upright, bushy growth.

Denise-Anne F, *op*, 1973, *(Memoriam* × *Orange Sensation)* × *(Peace* × *Memoriam)*; Ellick; Radway Roses. Flowers blush-pink to orange-apricot, dbl. (30-35 petals), full, large (4 in.); very fragrant; foliage small, glossy, dark; vigorous growth.

Denman HT, *ly*, 1988, (LANden); *Mildred Reynolds* × *Arthur Bell*; Sealand Nurseries, Ltd. Flowers creamy yellow, dbl. (35 petals), urn-shaped, large, borne in sprays of 2-3; heavy fragrance; foliage large, dark green, glossy; prickles medium, red; upright growth.

Denny Boy F, *yb*, 1949, *Pinocchio* × *Mrs. Erskine Pembroke Thom*; Marsh; Marsh's Nursery. Bud small, ovoid; flowers orange-yellow, becoming redder, reverse sulphur-yellow, very dbl., cupped; slightly fragrant; very vigorous, bushy, dwarf growth.

Der Krad HT, *dr*, 1962, *Ami Quinard* × *Crimson Glory*; Wyant. Bud long, pointed; flowers maroon-red, striped darker, dbl., high-centered, large (3½ in.); very fragrant; foliage glossy; vigorous, bushy growth.

Derby F, *or*, 1963, *Miss France* × *Seedling*; Gaujard. Bud ovoid; flowers orange-red, semi-dbl., medium; fragrant; foliage light green, soft; very vigorous, bushy growth.

Dereham Pride Pol, *dr*, 1932, *Éblouissant* × *Orange King*; Norfolk Nursery. Flowers darkest crimson; vigorous, dwarf growth.

Derek Nimmo HT, *ob*, 1981, (MACwhenu); *Seedling* × *Seedling*; McGredy, Sam; John Mattock, Ltd. Bud ovoid; flowers orange-red, silvery reverse, dbl. (30 petals), borne 1-3 per cluster; fragrant; foliage medium green; red prickles; vigorous.

Dernburg HT, *pb*, 1916, Krüger. Flowers bright rose, shaded coral-red and yellow, dbl., large.

DeRuiter's Herald Pol, *dr*, 1949, (Herald); *Orange Triumph* × *Seedling*; deRuiter; Gregory.

Flowers blood-red, prominent yellow stamens, single (6 petals), small, borne in large trusses; foliage glossy, dark; vigorous, bushy growth. GM, NRS, 1948.

Descanso Pillar LCl, *pb*, 1952, *Crimson Glory* × *Capt. Thomas*; Lammerts; Germain's. Bud urn-shaped, carmine to scarlet-red; flowers begonia-rose to deep rose-pink, inside varying to scarlet, dbl. (33 petals), high-centered, large (4½-5 in.); fragrant; foliage dark, glossy; height 6-7 ft.; recurrent bloom.

Deschamps N (OGR), *mr*, 1877, Deschamps. Flowers cherry-red, cupped, large; vigorous.

Desdechardo HT, *dp*, 1980, *Red Lion sport*; Taylor, W.J. Flowers deep pink.

Desert Charm Min, *dr*, 1973, *Baccará* × *Magic Wand*; Moore, R.S.; Sequoia Nursery. Flowers deep red, dbl., high-centered, medium; slightly fragrant; foliage dark, leathery; vigorous, dwarf, bushy.

Desert Dance F, *ob*, 1975, *Impala* × *Seedling*; Herholdt, J.A. Bud pointed; flowers orange, reverse gold, semi-dbl. (15-18 petals), cupped, large (3 in.); slightly fragrant; foliage glossy; moderately tall growth.

Desert Dream HT, *lp*, 1955, *R.M.S. Queen Mary* × *Mrs. Sam McGredy*; McGredy; Kordes. Flowers buff-pink, high pointed, large (5 in.); slightly fragrant; foliage light green; very vigorous growth.

Desert Peace HT, *yb*, 1992, (MEInomad); *(Sonia × Rumba)* × *(Piccadilly × Chicago Peace)*; Selection Meilland; C-P. Flowers yellow tinged with red, moderately full (15-25 petals), medium (4-7 cms) blooms borne mostly singly; slight fragrance; foliage large, dark green, glossy; tall (120-130 cms), upright growth.

Desert Sands F, *ab*, 1976, *Arthur Bell* × *Elizabeth of Glamis*; Bees. Flowers deep apricot, dbl. (30 petals), full, large (4½ in.); very fragrant; vigorous growth.

Desert Song HT, *rb*, 1948, *Mrs. Sam McGredy* × *Golden Dawn*; Fletcher; Tucker. Flowers glowing reddish copper, dbl. (40-45 petals), peony form, large (4-5 in.); very fragrant; foliage glossy, bronze.

Desert Storm Min, *op*, 1991, *Libby* × *Rise 'n' Shine*; Gruenbauer, Richard, 1984; Flowers 'n' Friends Miniature Roses, 1991. Bud ovoid; flowers orange in summer, pink in coldweather, dbl., urn-shaped, medium blooms borne singly; foliage medium, dark green, semi-glossy; upright, medium growth.

Desert Sunset Gr, *or*, 1962, *Floradora* × *Chrysler Imperial*; Booy, H.; Booy Rose Nursery. Bud ovoid; flowers orange-red, single (10 petals), cupped, large (3-4 in.); foliage glossy; upright growth.

Designer's Choice™ Gr, *yb*, 1989, (Hi Teen); *Prominent* × *Bengali*; DeVor Nursery; Co-Operative Rose Growers, 1989. Bud pointed; flowers yellow marked orange, dbl. (30 petals), high-centered, exhibition, medium, borne usually singly and in sprays of 1-3; slight fragrance; foliage medium, dark green, glossy; prickles slight recurve, small, brown; fruit ovoid, small, orange; upright, medium growth.

Désir HT, *rb*, 1945, Gaujard. Flowers purplish red, dbl., large; very fragrant; foliage glossy; very vigorous, bushy growth.

Desire HT, *mr*, 1953, *Pink Delight (HT) sport*; Obertello; Amling-DeVor Nursery. Bud ovoid; flowers cardinal-red, dbl. (35-45 petals), high-centered to open, large (5 in.); fragrant; foliage dark; upright, compact growth.

Désiré Bergera R, *pb*, 1910, *R. wichuraiana* × *Aurore*; Barbier. Flowers coppery rose, center brighter, dbl.; vigorous growth; seasonal bloom.

Désirée® HT, *lp*, 1985, (TANerised); Tantau, M., 1986. Flowers light pink, dbl. (35 petals), large; slight fragrance; foliage large, dark, semi-glossy; upright growth.

Désirée Parmentier G (OGR), *lp*, Prior to 1848. Flowers vivid pink, full, flat, large; bushy.

Desmond Gatward HT, *mr*, 1966, *Karl Herbst* × *Dicksons Red*; Kemp, M.L. Flowers cerise-crimson, well formed, large (4½ in.); slightly fragrant; foliage red-bronze; free-growth.

Desmond Johnston HT, *mr*, 1927, McGredy. Flowers brilliant scarlet, base orange, reverse veined orange, dbl., high-centered, large, short stems; fragrant; foliage rich green, leathery, glossy bushy growth. GM, NRS, 1927.

Desperado F, *yb*, 1968, *Pink Parfait* × *Masquerade*; Harkness. Flowers yellow shaded pink, semi-dbl., borne in trusses; slightly fragrant.

Destino HT, *pb*, Camprubi. Flowers salmon-pink, becoming lilac-pink, dbl. (45 petals), well formed; foliage dark; upright growth.

Destiny HT, *dr*, 1935, Beckwith. Bud long, pointed, well shaped; flowers rich crimson-scarlet shaded blackish, full; foliage dark, leathery; vigorous, bushy growth.

Detroiter HT, *dr*, 1952, (Brilliant; Schlosser's Brilliant); *Poinsettia* × *Crimson Glory*; Kordes; J&P. Bud long, pointed; flowers dark red, dbl. (23 petals), high-centered, large (5½ in.);

fragrant; vigorous, upright, bushy growth. GM, NRS, 1952.

Detroiter, Climbing Cl HT, *dr*, 1960, J&P.

Deuil de Paul Fontaine M (OGR), *m*, 1873, (Paul de Fontainne); Fontaine. Bud somewhat mossy; flowers purple-red, reverse mahogany, cupped; very prickly; vigorous growth; repeat bloom.

Deutsche Hoffnung HT, *yb*, 1920, *Mme. Caroline Testout × Grossherzogin Feodora von Sachsen*; Kiese. Flowers salmon-yellow to apricot-yellow.

Devil Dancer HT, *mr*, 1979, *Sonora × Matangi*; Hawken, U. Bud ovoid; flowers brilliant brick-red, single (5 petals), large (4 in.); slightly fragrant; foliage dark; bushy growth.

Devon Maid LCl, *pb*, 1982, *Casino × Elizabeth of Glamis*; Warner, C.H.; Warner's Roses. Flowers light pink, reverse medium pink, dbl. (22 petals), large blooms in clusters of 3-4; fruity fragrance; foliage large, medium green, glossy; large, curved, orange prickles; fruit orange, ovoid; vigorous, spreading, tall growth; needs support.

Devoniensis T (OGR), *w*, 1838, (Magnolia Rose); *Parentage uncertain, perhaps Elinthii × Yellow China*; Foster; Lucombe, Prince & Co., 1841. Flowers creamy white, center sometimes tinged blush, dbl., very large; fragrant; very vigorous growth; recurrent bloom.

Devoniensis, Climbing Cl T (OGR), *w*, 1858, *Devoniensis sport*; Pavitt; Curtis.

Devotion F, *pb*, 1971, *Orange Sensation × Peace*; Harkness. Flowers light pink, flushed deeper, dbl. (32 petals), large (4½ in.); fragrant; foliage light.

Dewdrop HT, *lp*, 1921, *None listed*; McGredy. Flowers pale pink to pale rose; fragrant. RULED EXTINCT 11/91 ARM.

Dew Drop Min, *rb*, 1991, (ZIPdew); *Sheri Anne × Priscilla Burton*; Zipper, Herbert; Magic Moment Miniatures, 1992. Flowers red with white eye, single (5 petals), small (0-4 cms) blooms borne mostly singly; slight fragrance; foliage small, dark green, semi-glossy, very disease-resistant; few prickles; low (30 cms), compact growth.

D.H. Lawrence HT, *yb*, 1985, (ROSlaw); *Gay Gordons sport*; McCarthy, Mrs. Rosemary; Rosemary Roses. Flowers yellow blend.

Diablotin® F, *mr*, 1961, (DELpo; Little Devil); *Orléans Rose × Fashion*; Delbard-Chabert. Flowers medium red, semi-dbl. (17 petals), 2-3 in. blooms in small clusters; no fragrance; bushy, compact growth.

Diablotin, Climbing® Cl F, *mr*, 1970, (DELposar; Little Devil, Climbing; Grimpant Diablotin; *Diablotin sport*; Delbard; GM, Rome, Paris & Geneva, 1970.

Diabolo F, *op*, 1958, *Jolie Princess × (Alain × Miss France)*; Gaujard. Flowers bright salmon, semi-dbl., cupped, medium, short stems; slightly fragrant; foliage bronze; very vigorous, bushy growth.

Diadem HT, *ob*, 1922, McGredy. Flowers orange-crimson suffused salmon and yellow, dbl., high-centered, very large; fragrant; foliage rich green, leathery, glossy; vigorous, bushy growth.

Diamant® F, *or*, 1962, (KOReb); Kordes, R.; A. Dickson & McGredy. Bud ovoid; flowers bright orange-scarlet, dbl. (40 petals), well-formed, large blooms in clusters of 3-7; slightly fragrant; foliage dark, glossy; vigorous, upright growth.

Diamantina HT, *op*, 1949, *Julien Potin × Ophelia*; Giacomasso. Flowers salmon and rose, large, strong stems.

Diamond Jewel Min, *w*, 1958, *Dick Koster sport × Tom Thumb*; Morey; J&P. Bud globular; flowers white, overcast blush-pink, dbl. (45-50 petals), cupped, small (½-¾ in.); compact, low, open growth.

Diamond Jubilee HT, *ly*, 1947, *Maréchal Niel × Feu Pernet-Ducher*; Boerner; J&P. Bud ovoid; flowers buff-yellow, dbl. (28 petals), cupped, large (5-6 in.); fragrant; foliage leathery; upright, compact growth. AARS, 1948.

Dian Min, *dp*, 1957, *(R. wichuraiana × Floradora) × (Oakington Ruby × Floradora)*; Moore, R.S.; Sequoia Nursery. Flowers soft red, dbl. (45 petals), small (1 in.); fragrant (apple); foliage small, dark, glossy; vigorous (15 in.), bushy growth.

Diana® F, *my*, 1977, (TANdinadi); Tantau. Bud globular; flowers medium yellow, dbl., medium; slightly fragrant; foliage medium, glossy; vigorous, upright.

Diana HT, *mp*, 1921, *Mrs. Frank Workman × Sunburst*; Bees. Flowers malmaison pink, dbl., globular, very large; fragrant; vigorous growth.

Diana Pol, *op*, 1922, Spek. Flowers bright orange shaded pink, semi-dbl., large.

Diana Allen HT, *op*, 1939, *Mrs. Aaron Ward × Seedling*; Clark, A.; NRS New South Wales. Flowers salmon-pink, dbl., small, short stems; bushy, compact.

Diana Armstrong HT, *dy*, 1992, *Seedling × Prima Ballerina*; Thompson, R.; Battersby Roses, 1993. Flowers deep yellow, full (26-40 petals), medium (4-7 cms) blooms borne mostly singly; very fragrant; foliage medium, medium green, semi-glossy; some prickles; upright (80 cms) growth.

Diana Cant HT, *rb*, 1928, *Isobel × Seedling*; Cant, B.R. Flowers carmine-red, base flushed orange, dbl.; fragrant.

Diana Maxwell HT, *ob*, 1957, *Ena Harkness × Sam McGredy*; Kemp, M.L. Flowers orange-cerise, dbl. (45 petals), high pointed, large (5 in.); very fragrant; foliage bronze; vigorous growth.

Diana Menuhin HT, *dy*, 1963, *(Golden Masterpiece × Ellinor LeGrice) × Forward*; LeGrice. Flowers deep buttercup-yellow, dbl. (30 petals), globular, large (5½ in.); foliage dark, glossy; vigorous, upright growth.

Diana Rowden LCl, *op*, 1976, *Mrs. Sam McGredy, Climbing × Red Dandy*; Hawker; Harkness. Flowers deep copper-salmon to rose-pink, dbl. (30 petals), large (5-6 in.); very fragrant; foliage large, copper to green; profuse, continuous bloom.

Diane HT, *yb*, 1958, *Peace × (Seedling × Opera)*; Gaujard. Flowers clear yellow, center orange-yellow, well formed, large; vigorous growth.

Diane de Broglie HT, *ob*, 1929, Chambard, C. Flowers coral-orange, dbl., cupped, very large, strong stems; fragrant; foliage dark; very vigorous growth.

Diane d'Urfé HT, *w*, 1958, *Peace × Incendie*; Croix, A.; Minier. Flowers white, becoming red-edged; vigorous growth.

Dianna Kay Min, *or*, 1981, *Anytime × Sheri Anne*; Dobbs, Annette. Flowers orange-red, dbl. (20 petals), small; no fragrance; foliage small, medium green, semi-glossy; upright.

Dianne Feinstein HT, *yb*, 1979, *McGredy's Yellow × Sutter's Gold*; Fong, William P. Bud ovoid; flowers yellow blend, dbl. (23 petals), high-centered, cupped blooms borne singly; fragrant; foliage dark; triangular prickles; vigorous, spreading growth.

Diany Binny LCl, *w*, 1976, *Kiftsgate × R. rubrifolia (?)*; Binny. Flowers white, single (5 petals), small (2 in.); very fragrant; foliage purplish.

Diapason® HT, *mp*, 1966, (DELpoc); *Chic Parisien × (Sultane seedling × Mme. Joseph Perraud)*; Delbard-Chabert. Flowers porcelain pink, dbl. (40 petals), globular, medium; fragrant; foliage bronze, glossy; very vigorous, bushy growth.

DICdip HT, *pb*, 1974, *Eurorose × Typhoon*; Dickson, P. Flowers pink blend, dbl. (32 petals), large; fragrant; foliage medium, purple when young; upright, bushy growth.

DICfate F, *mp*, 1975, *Futura × (Pye Colour × Prominent)*; Dickson, P. Flowers medium pink, 18 petals, medium; slight fragrance; foliage medium, medium green; upright, bushy.

DICjoon HT, *rb*, 1984, *Bonfire × Typhoon*; Dickson, P. Flowers medium red, yellow reverse, dbl. (20 petals), large, borne singly and in trusses of 5; no fragrance; foliage medium, dark, glossy; bushy growth.

Dick Koster Pol, *dp*, 1929, *Anneke Koster sport*; Koster, D.A. Flowers deep pink.

Dick Koster Fulgens Pol, *dp*, 1940, Koster, M. Flowers light red, semi-dbl., borne in clusters; low, compact growth.

Dick Koster Superior Pol, *mr*, 1955, *Dick Koster sport*; Koster, D.A. Flowers rosy red.

Dick Wilcox HT, *dr*, 1949, *Pink Princess × Crimson Glory*; Brownell. Bud long, pointed to ovoid; flowers rose-red, dbl. (50-60 petals), high-centered, large (4-5½ in.); fragrant; foliage dark; vigorous growth.

Dickson's Bouquet HT, *ab*, 1938, Dickson, A. Flowers salmon, carmine and apricot, blended saffron, full, long, wiry stems; fragrant; vigorous growth.

Dickson's Centennial HT, *mr*, 1936, Dickson, A.; Dreer; J&P, 1937. Bud pointed; flowers crimson to scarlet, loosely formed, very large; long, strong stems; fragrant; foliage bronze; vigorous, bushy growth.

Dickson's Delight HT, *ob*, 1938, Dickson, A. Flowers vivid orange, heavily shaded scarlet-orange; fragrant; foliage bronze-green; vigorous growth.

Dickson's Flame F, *or*, 1958, *Independence seedling × Nymph*; Dickson, A. Flowers scarlet-flame, dbl., large (3½ in.) blooms in trusses; slightly fragrant; vigorous growth. GM, NRS, 1958; NRS PIT, 1958.

Dickson's Perfection HT, *pb*, 1937, Dickson, A.; Port Stockton Nursery. Flowers shrimp-pink, base orange-yellow, full, large; very fragrant; very vigorous growth.

Dickson's Red HT, *dr*, 1938, (Dr. F.G. Chandler); Dickson, A. Flowers velvety crimson-scarlet, semi-dbl. (18 petals), cupped, large; very fragrant (spicy); foliage leathery, dark; vigorous, bushy. GM, NRS, 1939 & Portland, 1941; AARS, 1940.

Dicky® F, *op*, 1984, (DICkimono; Anisley Dickson; München Kindl); *Cathedral × Memento*; Dickson, P., 1983. Flowers reddish salmon-pink, reverse lighter, dbl. (35 petals), large; slight fragrance; foliage medium, medium green, glossy; bushy growth. GM, RNRS, 1984; RNRS PIT, 1984.

DICmickey Min, *or*, 1986, (Buttons); *(Liverpool Echo × Woman's Own) × Memento*; Dickson, P., 1987. Flowers orange-red, dbl. (15-25 petals), medium; patio; slight fragrance; foliage small, medium green, glossy; bushy growth.

Die Präsidentin HT, *w*, 1928, *Harry Kirk seedling*; Mühle. Flowers marble white, center soft yellow, semi-dbl. to dbl.; slightly fragrant.

Die Welt® HT, *ob*, 1976, (DieKOR; The World); *Seedling × Peer Gynt*; Kordes. Bud long, pointed; flowers orange, red and yellowblend, dbl. (25 petals), high-centered, large (4½ in.); slightly fragrant; foliage glossy; vigorous, upright, very tall, bushy growth.

Diener's Blue R, *m*, 1926, Diener. Flowers violet, dbl., medium (2 in.), large, heavy clusters; almost thornless; vigorous growth.

Diener's Rose Understock R, *rb*, 1932, *Veilchenblau × Veilchenblau sport*; Diener. Bud long; flowers rose-red shaded purple, stamens yellowish, single (10 petals), medium (2 in.), borne in clusters; foliage small, notched; climbing or trailing, producing much new wood in a season; suitable for use as an understock.

Dieter Wolf Pol, *or*, 1969, *Tropicana × Jiminy Cricket*; Buisman. Flowers salmon-orange, semi-dbl.; foliage glossy, dark; vigorous, compact growth.

Dignity HT, *w*, 1940, LeGrice. Bud long, pointed; flowers creamy white, dbl.; very fragrant; foliage leathery; vigorous, bushy, compact growth.

Dilly Dilly Min, *m*, 1985, (TINdilly); *Chrysler Imperial × Plum Duffy*; Bennett, Dee; Tiny Petals Nursery. Flowers lavender, dbl. (35 petals), HT form, medium; fragrant; foliage medium, medium green, semi-glossy; upright growth.

Dilys Allen HT, *ob*, 1952, *Mrs. Sam McGredy × Seedling*; Norman; Harkness. Bud long, pointed, ovoid; flowers orange-red, base saffron, large (4 in.); slightly fragrant; foliage glossy, dark bluish green; vigorous, bushy growth.

Dimity HT, *pb*, 1956, *Peace × Seedling*; Taylor, C.A. Bud ovoid, pointed; flowers ivory to pure white, edged pink, dbl., cupped, large; fragrant; foliage dark, leathery; upright, bushy growth.

Dimples F, *ly*, 1968, LeGrice. Flowers canary-yellow to ivory, semi-dbl., borne in trusses; slightly fragrant; foliage glossy.

Dinah HT, *dr*, 1920, Paul, W. Flowers deep crimson, shaded darker.

Dinah Shore HT, *dp*, 1942, *Jewel sport*; Grillo. Flowers cerise-pink, dbl. (65 petals), globular, large (5 in.); very fragrant; foliage glossy, dark; vigorous, upright growth.

Dinky Min, *or*, 1986, *Sheri Anne × Seedling*; Bridges, Dennis A. Flowers orange-red, reverse orange, dbl. (20 petals), urn-shaped, medium blooms borne usually singly; slight fragrance; foliage medium, medium green, semi-glossy; long, light red prickles; upright.

Diny Hage HT, *dr*, 1956, *Ambassadeur Nemry × Crimson Glory*; Leenders, M. Flowers crimson-red, dbl., large; very fragrant; vigorous growth.

Diorama HT, *yb*, 1965, *Peace × Beauté*; deRuiter. Flowers apricot-yellow, dbl., high-centered, large (4½ in.); fragrant; vigorous, upright growth.

Dioressence® Gr, *m*, 1984, (DELdiore); *((Holstein × Bayadère) × Prelude) × Seedling*; Delbard-Chabert. Flowers lavender, dbl. (35 petals), well-formed, large; very fragrant; foliage large, medium green, semi-glossy; bushy growth.

Diplomat HT, *dr*, 1962, *(Poinsettia × Tawny Gold) × Detroiter*; Boerner; Home Nursery Products Corp. Bud ovoid; flowers current red edged blood-red, dbl. (50-55 petals), cupped, large (3½-4 in.); fragrant; foliage leathery, dark; vigorous, upright.

Diputacion de Tarragona HT, *ob*, 1967, (Tarragona); *Baccará × (Chrysler Imperial × Soraya)*; Dot, P.; Rosas Dot. Bud pointed; flowers orange-coral, dbl. (35 petals), high-centered, large; fragrant; foliage glossy, bronze; upright, compact growth.

Directeur Alphand HP (OGR), *m*, 1883, Lévêque. Flowers blackish purple, full, large.

Directeur Donatien Lelievre F, *ob*, 1959, Privat. Flowers coppery orange, dbl., medium.

Directeur Guérin HT, *ob*, 1935, Gaujard. Flowers orange-yellow, center coppery, dbl., very large, long stems; foliage light; very vigorous growth.

Director Rubió HT, *rb*, 1929, *O. Junyent × Jean C.N. Forestier*; Dot, P.; C-P. Flowers magenta-red, semi-dbl., very large, stiff stems; fragrant; dwarf, bushy growth.

Direktor Hjelm Pol, *rb*, 1927, *Prasident Hindenburg sport*; Koster, D.A. Flowers red.

Direktor Rebhuhn HT, *ob*, 1929, *Mme. Butterfly × Angèle Pernet*; Kordes. Flowers orange, center reddish, dbl.; very fragrant.

Direktor Rikala F, *mp*, 1934, *Lafayette sport*; Koster, D.A. Flowers pink.

Direktor Struve Pol, *w*, 1924, *Echo sport*; van Nes. Flowers white.

Dirigent® S, *mr*, 1956, (The Conductor); *Fanal × Karl Weinhausen*; Tantau, Math. Bud pointed; flowers blood-red, semi-dbl., medium blooms in clusters of up to 28; slightly fragrant; foliage leathery; vigorous (4 ft.) growth; recurrent bloom. ADR, 1958.

Disco HT, *rb*, 1980, *Sunrise-Sunset × Seedling*; Weeks, O.L. Bud medium to long, pointed; flowers medium red, reverse cream, dbl. (30 petals), high-centered, globular blooms borne singly and 2-4 per cluster; some spicy fragrance; foliage leathery, dark; prickles hooked downward; tall, upright growth. GM, Baden-Baden.

Disco Dancer® F, *or*, 1984, (DICinfra); *Cathedral × Memento*; Dickson, P., 1983. Flowers orange scarlet, semi-dbl., medium; slight fragrance; foliage medium, medium green, glossy; bushy growth. GM, The Hague, 1982.

Discovery Gr, *pb*, 1958, *(Peace × Christopher Stone) × Floribunda seedling*; deRuiter; Blaby Rose Gardens. Flowers soft pink shaded apricot, dbl., large (5-6 in.); very fragrant; vigorous growth.

Discretion HT, *pb*, 1952, *Peace × Seedling*; Gaujard. Flowers salmon-pink shaded copper, dbl. (28 petals), large; fragrant; foliage glossy.

Display F, *pb*, 1956, *Orange Triumph × Golden Scepter*; Arnot; Croll. Flowers salmon-pink, becoming cherry-pink, semi-dbl. (13 petals), well formed, medium (2½ in.), borne in large clusters; slightly fragrant; foliage glossy, bronze-green; very vigorous growth.

Disraeli S, *mr*, 1987, (ADAdisres); *Hamburger Phoenix × Seedling*; Adams, Neil D. Flowers medium red, dbl. (26-40 petals), medium; no fragrance; foliage large, dark green, glossy, upright, bushy, tall, broad, growth.

Distant Drums S, *m*, 1985, *September Song × The Yeoman*; Buck; Iowa State University. Bud ovoid, pointed; flowers rose-purple, dbl. (40 petals), imbricated, large blooms borne 1-10 per cluster; intense myrrh fragrance; foliage medium-large, dark, leathery; awl-like, brown prickles; vigorous, erect, bushy growth; repeat bloom.

Distinct F, *rb*, 1953, *Triomphe Orléanais × Mrs. Pierre S. duPont*; Boerner; J&P. Flowers spectrum-red with white eye, dbl. (25-30 petals), imbricated, cupped, small, rounded clusters; fragrant; foliage glossy; vigorous, compact growth; good pot plant.

Distinction F, *dp*, 1927, *Lafayette sport*; Turbat. Flowers deep rose-pink, center brighter.

Distinction, Climbing Cl F, *dp*, 1935, Lens.

Ditto Min, *dr*, 1986, (LYOdit); *Baby Betsy McCall × Seedling*; Lyon, L.; MB Farm Min. Roses. Flowers dark red, semi-dbl. (14 petals), very small blooms borne usually singly; no fragrance; foliage small, medium green, matt; no prickles; low, bushy.

Diva HT, *dr*, 1976, *Sonia × Gisselfeld*; Poulsen. Flowers dark velvety red, dbl. (30 petals), very large (6 in.); slightly fragrant; foliage dark; spreading growth; for greenhouse use.

Dividend HT, *dy*, 1931, *Franz Deegen × Seedling*; Clark, A.; NRS Victoria. Flowers rich yellow, dbl., globular; slightly fragrant; foliage dark; dwarf growth.

Divine HT, *mr*, 1964, Delbard-Chabert. Bud dark purplish; flowers cardinal-red, dbl. (45 petals), well formed, large, strong stems; foliage bright green; vigorous, upright growth. GM, Geneva, 1964.

Divine Lady F, *op*, 1965, *Circus × Queen Elizabeth*; Lens. Flowers salmon-pink suffused brownish, dbl.; very vigorous, dense growth.

Dixie HT, *op*, 1925, *Radiance sport*; Gray, W.R. Flowers salmon-pink, cupped, more dbl., large; very fragrant.

Dixie Belle HT, *lp*, 1963, *Golden Masterpiece × Seedling*; Boerner; J&P. Bud ovoid, rose-pink; flowers light pink, dbl. (38 petals), cupped, large (5-5½ in.); fragrant; foliage leathery; vigorous, upright growth.

Dixie Climber Cl HT, *ob*, 1935, *Gov. Alfred E. Smith sport*; Watkins, A.F.; Dixie Rose Nursery; J&P. Flowers salmon and gold.

Dixie Dazzle™ Min, *ob*, 1991, (KINdixie); *(Rainbow's End × Miss Dovey) × Jennie Anne*; King, Gene, 1986; AGM Miniature Roses, 1990. Bud ovoid; flowers orange-red to yellow, dbl. (16 petals), high-centered, exhibition, small; no fragrance; foliage small, medium green, semi-glossy; upright, low growth.

Dixie Holiday HT, *mr*, 1968, *Étoile de Hollande sport*; Garrison; Kimbrew. Bud long, pointed; flowers red, dbl., high-centered to cupped, medium; slightly fragrant; foliage bronze, leathery; very vigorous growth.

Dixieland Min, *rb*, 1992, (BRIdixie); *Fancy Pants × Seedling*; Bridges, Dennis A.; Bridges Roses. Flowers in shades of vibrant pink, red and white intensifying with sun, moderately full (15-25 petals), high centered, medium (4-7 cms) blooms borne mostly single; slight fragrance; foliage medium, medium green, semi-glossy; no prickles; tall (50-60 cms), upright growth.

D. Laura Pinto d'Azevedo HT, *pb*, 1936, *Pink Pearl × Constance*; Moreira da Silva. Flowers shrimp-pink, center coral-red, base orange-yellow, dbl., high-centered, very large; foliage light, soft.

D. Maria Antonia Pacheco HT, *mp*, 1935, *Mme. Butterfly × Johanniszauber*; Moreira da Silva. Flowers deep carmine-pink, well formed, full, large; foliage rich green, glossy; vigorous growth.

D. Maria do Carmo de Fragoso Carmona HT, *pb*, 1939, *Charles P. Kilham × Souv. de Claudius Pernet*; Moreira da Silva. Bud long, pointed; flowers flesh-pink, edged yellow, dbl., high-centered, large, long stems; foliage glossy; vigorous growth.

D. Maria José de Melo HT, *op*, Moreira da Silva. Flowers salmon-pink.

D. Maria Navarro HT, *rb*, 1962, *First Love × Paramount*; Moreira da Silva. Flowers carmine.

Doc Pol, *mp*, 1954, (Degenhard); *Robin Hood × Polyantha seedling*; deRuiter; Gregory, & Willicher Baumschulen, 1954. Flowers phlox-pink, semi-dbl. (15 petals), small blooms in large trusses; compact growth.

Docteur Louis Escarras HT, *rb*, 1922, *Constance × Seedling*; Nabonnand, C. Flowers dark salmon-red shaded carmine-pink, very dbl. (120 petals).

Docteur Marjolin M (OGR), *mp*, 1860, Robert et Moreau. Flowers shell-pink.

Docteur Morel HT, *m*, 1946, *Edith Nellie Perkins × Pres. Herbert Hoover*; Laperrière. Flowers carmine with chrome-yellow reflections, dbl. (40-45 petals), large; foliage dark; vigorous, upright growth.

Docteur Reymond R, *w*, 1907, Mermet. Flowers pure white on pale green base, dbl., pyramidal cluster.

Docteur Robert Salmont HT, *yb*, 1946, Gaujard. Bud pointed; flowers capucine and yellow, reverse tinted chrome, base coppery; foliage dark; vigorous growth.

Docteur Valois HT, *rb*, 1950, *(Annie Drevet × Condesa de Sástago) × Vive la France*; Mallerin; URS. Flowers geranium shaded vermilion, reverse yellow, semi-dbl., large (4 in.); fragrant; foliage dark, glossy; vigorous, bushy growth.

Dr. Adam Christman™ Gr, *dr*, 1986, (WILdac); *Queen Elizabeth × Chrysler Imperial*; Williams, J.B. Flowers dark crimson red to scarlet, full (26-40 petals), large, borne in large sprays and on individual cutting canes; slight fragrance; foliage large, dark green, semi-glossy.

Dr. A. Hermans HT, *ly*, 1906, Verschuren. Flowers yellowish white.

Dr. A. I. Petyt HT, *rb*, 1924, *George Dickson seedling × Edward Mawley*; Burrell. Flowers maroon-crimson shaded scarlet, dbl., high-centered, large; vigorous, bushy growth.

Dr. A. J. Verhage HT, *dy*, 1963, (Golden Wave); *Tawny Gold × (Baccará × Seedling)*; Verbeek; Carlton Rose Nursery. Flowers deep yellow, dbl. (22-30 wavy petals), large; very fragrant; foliage dark, glossy; vigorous, bushy growth.

Dr. A. J. Verhage, Climbing Cl HT, *dy*, 1968, Blaby Rose Gardens.

Dr. Albert Schweitzer HT, *pb*, 1961, *Chic Parisien × Michele Meilland*; Delbard-Chabert. Flowers opal-pink, reverse rose-red, dbl. (30-35 petals), well-formed, large (5-6 in.); fragrant; foliage leathery, glossy; vigorous, upright; bushy growth.

Dr. Andrew Carnegie HT, *pb*, 1927, *Mrs. Henry Morse sport*; Ferguson, R.C.; Dreer, 1930. Flowers light silvery pink, base yellowish.

Dr. Andry HP (OGR), *mr*, 1864, Verdier, E. Flowers rosy crimson, dbl. (45 petals), semi-cupped, medium; foliage glossy; vigorous, upright growth.

Dr. A. S. Thomas HT, *rb*, 1951, Clark, A.; NRS Victoria. Bud long, pointed; flowers dark crimson shaded darker, dbl. (60 petals), high-centered, large; very fragrant; foliage leathery, dark; vigorous, fairly compact growth.

Dr. A. Svehla HT, *rb*, 1935, *Col. Leclerc × Gen. MacArthur*; Böhm. Flowers dark carmine, dbl., very large; bushy growth.

Dr. Augustin Wibbelt HT, *yb*, 1928, *Los Angeles sport*; Leenders, M. Flowers golden yellow, shaded orange, semi-dbl.; fragrant.

Dr. Augusto de Castro HT, *rb*, 1954, *Sultane × Peace*; Moreira da Silva. Flowers bright red, reverse yellow.

Dr. A. von Erlach HT, *pb*, 1932, *Prince de Bulgarie × Mrs. S.K. Rindge*; Soupert & Notting. Bud nankeen yellow and salmon; flowers pink and straw-yellow, stamens yellow, semi-dbl., cupped, stiff stems; very fragrant; vigorous growth.

Dr. Barnardo F, *dr*, 1968, *Vera Dalton × Red Dandy*; Harkness. Flowers crimson, dbl. (30 petals), large blooms in trusses; slightly fragrant; upright, bushy growth.

Dr. B. Benacerraf Min, *pb*, 1988, (MILben); *(Double Delight × Simplex) × Magic Carrousel*; Miller, F. Flowers white to light pink, dark pink borders, opening to light pink, aging darker, dbl. (15-20 petals), informal, borne usually singly or in sprays of 1-5; slight fragrance; foliage ovoid, medium green, matt, disease resistant; vigorous, compact growth.

Doctor Behring HT, *m*, 1978, (DOTemibe); *Amanecer × Tanya*; Dot, S. Bud pointed; flowers red-purple, dbl. (35 petals), deeply cupped, large (4 in.); fragrant; foliage dark; tall, upright growth.

Dr. Belville Cl HT, *ob*, 1931, *Barbara × Sunstar*; Thomas; H&S. Flowers orange-crimson, base yellow, semi-dbl., open, large; fragrant; very vigorous (12 ft.) growth; profuse spring bloom, then scattering.

Dr. B. P. Pal HT, *m*, 1980, *Seedling × Seedling*; Division of Veg. Crops & Floriculture. Bud long, pointed; flowers solferino purple, dbl. (70 petals), high-centered blooms borne singly; light fragrance; foliage dark, leathery; straight, brown prickles; upright growth.

Dr. Branscom HT, *ab*, 1947, *Pink Dawn sport*; Danegger; J.T. Lovett. Bud pointed; flowers peach-blossom flushed apricot-pink, dbl., large; fragrant (spicy); upright growth.

Dr. Brownell HT, *yb*, 1964, *Helen Hayes × Peace*; Brownell, H.C.; Brownell. Bud long, pointed; flowers buff, center chrome-yellow, dbl. (34 petals), high-centered, large (5½ in.); very fragrant; foliage glossy, dark; vigorous, upright growth.

Dr. Burt LCl, *rb*, 1942, *Coral Creeper × Seedling*; Brownell. Bud long, pointed; flowers deep red to pink flushed orange, dbl. (45 petals), large; foliage glossy, light; very vigorous, climbing (to 20 ft.), branching growth; nonrecurrent bloom.

Dr. Carbonaro HT, *pb*, 1958, *Happiness × Grand'mere Jenny*; Moreira da Silva. Flowers rose, reverse silver.

Dr. Carneiro Pacheco HT, *rb*, 1938, *Mev. G.A. van Rossem × Sir David Davis*; Moreira da Silva. Flowers carmine, dbl., open, large; foliage glossy, light; vigorous, bushy growth.

Dr. Cathrall HT, *pb*, 1966, *Hector Deane sport*; Hills. Flowers deep pink, reverse lighter, large (4½-5 in.); very fragrant; foliage dark, leathery; vigorous growth.

Dr. Darley HT, *mp*, 1980, (HARposter); *Red Planet × (Carina × Pascali)*; Harkness, R., 1982. Flowers rose bengal, dbl. (45 petals), globular blooms borne usually singly; slight fragrance; foliage mid-green, semi-glossy; narrow, reddish prickles; upright, bushy growth. GM, Munich, 1983.

Dr. Debat HT, *pb*, 1952, (Dr. F. Debat; La Rosée; Docteur F. Debat); *Peace × Mrs. John Laing*; Meilland, F.; C-P. Bud ovoid, pointed; flowers bright pink tinted coral, dbl. (25-30 petals), high-centered, large (5-6 in.); fragrant; foliage leathery, dark; vigorous, upright. GM, NRS, 1950.

Dr. Debat, Climbing Cl HT, *pb*, 1955, Barni; URS.

Dr. D. F. Malan HT, *dr*, 1960, *Happiness × Mirandy*; Herholdt, J.A.; Herholdt's Nursery. Bud pointed; flowers very dark maroon, dbl. (45-50 petals), large; fragrant; upright growth.

Doctor Dick HT, *op*, 1985, (COCbaden; Dr. Dick); *Fragrant Cloud × Corso*; Cocker, James, & Sons, 1986. Flowers orange-coral, dbl. (40+ petals), exhibition, large; slight fragrance; foliage large, medium green, matt; upright growth.

Dr. Domingos Pereira Cl T (OGR), *pb*, 1925, de Magalhaes. Flowers lilac-rose, center yellow, dbl.; fragrant.

Dr. Eckener HRg (S), *pb*, 1930, *Golden Emblem × Hybrid Rugosa*; Berger, V.; Teschendorff, 1930; C-P, 1931. Flowers coppery rose on yellow ground, aging soft pink, semi-dbl., cupped, large; fragrant; vigorous (5-6 ft.) growth; repeat bloom.

Dr. Edvard Benes HT, *rb*, 1935, *Étoile de France sport*; Böhm. Flowers red with many white streaks, dbl., very large; fragrant; bushy growth.

Dr. Edward Deacon HT, *ob*, 1926, *Mme. Edouard Herriot × Gladys Holland*; Morse. Flowers deep salmon-orange to shrimp-pink, dbl., globular, large; fragrant; vigorous, bushy.

Doctor Eldon Lyle Gr, *dr*, 1968, *Pres. Eisenhower × Suspense*; Mackay; Texas Rose Research Foundation. Bud pointed; flowers dark red, dbl., high-centered, medium; fragrant; foliage soft, bronze; vigorous, compact growth.

Dr. E. M. Mills HHug (S), *yb*, 1926, *R. hugonis × Radiance*; Van Fleet; ARS. Flowers primrose suffused pink, becoming darker, semi-dbl., globular, medium (2-2½ in.); foliage small, dark; vigorous growth; early bloom.

Dr. Ernst Mühle HT, *pb*, 1928, *Mme. Edmée Metz seedling*; Mühle. Flowers rose-pink, with salmon-white reflex, very dbl., very large.

Dr. Felix Guyou T (OGR), *dy*, 1901, Mari. Flowers deep yellow.

Dr. Fleming HT, *pb*, 1960, *Queen Elizabeth × Baleares*; Dot, M. Flowers soft pink, flushed crimson, dbl. (40 petals), well-formed; vigorous.

Dr. Ferrandiz HT, *ob*, Camprubi. Flowers deep orange-red; vigorous growth.

Dr. F. Weigand HT, *mr*, 1930, *Mme. Caroline Testout × Hadley*; Weigand, C. Flowers cherry-red, dbl.; slightly fragrant.

Dr. Gallwey LCl, *w*, 1937, Reiter. Flowers snow-white, single, medium (2 in.), borne in large clusters; very vigorous growth; profuse bloom.

Dr. G. Krüger HT, *dr*, 1913, *Mme. Victor Verdier × Seedling*; Ulbrich; Kiese. Flowers crimson.

Doctor Goldberg HT, *my*, 1989, (GANgo; GANdol); *Royal Dane × Dutch Gold*; Gandy,

Douglas L.; Gandy's Roses, 1988. Flowers medium yellow, dbl. (26-40 petals), large; very fragrant; foliage large, dark green, matt; upright growth.

Dr. Grill T (OGR), *op*, 1886, *Ophirie × Souv. de Victor Hugo*; Bonnaire. Flowers rose shaded coppery; fragrant.

Dr. Guarnero HT, *dp*, 1958, *Happiness × Grand'mere Jenny*; Moreira da Silva. Flowers deep rose, dbl., well formed, large; very fragrant; vigorous, bushy growth.

Dr. Guilherme Pereira da Rosa HT, *mr*, 1955, *Charles Mallerin × Lisboa*; Moreira da Silva. Flowers cherry-red, well formed; moderate growth.

Dr. Heinrich Lumpe HT, *pb*, 1928, *Constance × Admiral Ward*; Berger, V.; A. Berger. Flowers light rose-pink, base yellow, dbl., high-centered, large, strong stems; fragrant; very vigorous, bushy growth.

Dr. Helfferich HT, *pb*, 1919, *Gustav Grunerwald × Mrs. Aaron Ward*; Lambert, P. Flowers rose, center yellowish orange, edged silvery, dbl.; fragrant.

Dr. Henri Neuprez R, *ly*, 1913, *R. wichuraiana × Mme. Barthélemy Levet*; Tanne. Flowers canary-yellow to sulphur-white.

Dr. Herbert Hawkesworth HT, *dr*, 1927, Bees. Flowers deep crimson, center almost black; fragrant.

Dr. H. E. Rumble Min, *mr*, 1981, *Born Free × Westmont*; Hooper, J.C. Flowers scarlet red, dbl. (30 petals), cupped to flat, small; no fragrance; foliage large, light green; small, brown prickles; vigorous, upright growth.

Dr. Hess von Wichdorf HT, *rb*, 1936, *Frank W. Dunlop sport*; Vogel, M.; Heinemann. Flowers red, shaded rose-lilac, dbl., high-centered, large; very fragrant; vigorous, bushy growth.

Dr. H. I. Gallagher HT, *yb*, 1989, *Spellbinder × Irish Gold*; Anderson, Mrs. Etta S. Bud ovoid; flower yellow with bright pink on petal tips, reverse same, aging very slight, dbl. (35-50 petals), high-centered, exhibition, medium, borne singly on long straight canes; heavy, spicy fragrance; foliage medium, bronze-medium green, semi-glossy; heavy, disease/pest resistant; prickles medium, bronze-green; bushy, medium to tall growth. ARC TG (B), 1989.

Dr. Homi Bhabha HT, *w*, 1968, *Virgo × Seedling*; Pal; Indian Agricultural Research Institute. Bud long, pointed; flowers white, center sometimes tinted cream, very dbl., high-centered, large; slightly fragrant; foliage leathery; vigorous, upright growth.

Dr. Homi Bhabha, Climbing Cl HT, *w*, 1976, IARI.

Dr. Huey LCl, *dr*, 1914, (Shafter); *Ethel × Gruss an Teplitz*; Thomas; B&A, 1920; A.N. Pierson, 1920. Flowers crimson-maroon, anthers light yellow, semi-dbl. (15 petals), small (2 in.) blooms in clusters of 3 or 4; slightly fragrant; foliage rich green. Used as understock under the name Shafter. GM, ARS Gertrude M. Hubbard GM, 1924.

Doctor Jackson S, *mr*, 1992, (AUSdoctor); Austin, David; David Austin Roses, 1987. Flowers scarlet, golden stamens, single (5 petals), medium (4-7 cms) blooms borne mostly singly; no fragrance; foliage medium, medium green, semi-glossy; few prickles; medium (120 cms), spreading growth.

Dr. Jaime Lopes Dias HT, *mp*, 1961, *Confidence × Juno*; Moreira da Silva. Flowers pink, large.

Dr. J. G. Fraser HT, *ab*, 1926, *St. Helena × Muriel Dickson*; Easlea. Flowers salmon-apricot, suffused vermilion-pink; vigorous growth.

Dr. J. H. Nicolas LCl, *mp*, 1940, *Charles P. Kilham × Georg Arends*; Nicolas; J&P. Flowers rose-pink, dbl. (50 petals), globular, large (5 in.) blooms in clusters of 3 or 4; fragrant; foliage dark, leathery; vigorous, pillar (8 ft.) growth; recurrent bloom.

Dr. John Snow HT, *w*, 1979, *Helen Traubel × Seedling*; Gandy. Flowers creamy white, dbl. (35 petals), exhibition, large (5 in.); fragrant; foliage light green; tall growth.

Dr. Joseph Drew HT, *yb*, 1918, *Mme. Mélanie Soupert seedling × Comtesse Icy Hardegg*; Page; Easlea. Flowers salmon-yellow, suffused pink, dbl.; fragrant.

Dr. Kater Pol, *dr*. Flowers dark red.

Dr. K. C. Chan Min, *my*, 1987, (TINchan); *Irish Gold × Rise 'n' Shine*; Bennett, Dee; Tiny Petals Nursery, 1986. Flowers medium yellow, fading pale yellow, dbl. (25-30 petals), urn-shaped, medium, borne usually singly; mini-flora; slight fragrance; foliage medium, medium green, semi-glossy; slender, straight, reddish prickles; fruit globular, medium, brown; upright, bushy, medium growth.

Dr. Kirk HT, *op*, 1940, *Charles P. Kilham × Unnamed R. foetida bicolor hybrid*; Mallerin; A. Meilland; C-P. Bud long, pointed; flowers coral, shaded nasturtium-yellow, dbl. (35 petals), high-centered, very large; slightly fragrant; vigorous growth.

Dr. Manuel Alves de Castro HT, *rb*, Moreira da Silva. Flowers red, reverse golden yellow.

Dr. Margaretha F, *dr*, 1960, *Red Pinocchio seedling × Alain*; Maarse, G. Flowers velvety dark red, dbl., medium, in large clusters; vigorous, bushy growth.

Dr. Maximo de Carvalho HT, *dr*, 1960, *Crimson Glory* × *Charles Mallerin*; Moreira da Silva. Flowers crimson-red.

Dr. McAlpine F, *dp*, 1981, (PEAfirst; Seafirst); Pearce, C.A.; Limes Rose Nursery, 1983. Flowers deep rose-pink, dbl. (30 petals), HT form, patio, large blooms borne 1-10 per cluster; very strong fragrance; foliage dark; straight, red prickles; low, bushy growth.

Dr. Mendes Correia HT, *mr*, 1938, *Frau Margarete Oppenheim* × *Hortulanus Budde*; Moreira da Silva. Bud pointed; flowers bright red, dbl., very large; very fragrant; foliage soft; vigorous, bushy growth.

Dr. Mengelberg F, *dr*, 1952, Leenders, M. Flowers deep blood-red, semi-dbl., large; very vigorous growth.

Dr. Merkeley Sp (OGR), *dp*, 1924, *Similar to R. spinosissima*; Discovered in eastern Siberia and named in compliment to Dr. Merkeley, Winnipeg, Man., Canada, who first grew it in North America and encouraged Skinner to introduce it in 1924. Flowers deep pink, dbl.; fragrant; low to medium growth; nonrecurrent bloom.

Dr. M. Euwe HT, *pb*, 1936, Buisman. Bud pointed; flowers salmon tinted yellow and pink, dbl.; very fragrant; foliage leathery, bronze; bushy growth.

Dr. Miroslav Tyrs HP (OGR), *rb*, 1932, *Anna de Diesbach sport*; Böhm. Flowers crimson, shaded darker, very large; fragrant.

Dr. O'Donel Browne HT, *pb*, 1908, Dickson, A. Flowers carmine-rose, full, large, well formed; very fragrant; vigorous growth.

Dr. Oliveira Salazar HT, *ob*, 1955, *Mme. Marie Curie* × *Peace*; Moreira da Silva. Flowers salmon and yellow shaded carmine, very dbl., large; very fragrant.

Dr. Rafael Duque HT, *rb*, 1938, *Frau Margarete Oppenheim* × *Hortulanus Budde*; Moreira da Silva. Flowers velvety purplish red, large; fragrant.

Dr. Richard Legler HT, *pb*, Flowers shrimppink changing to old-rose and orange; fragrant (fruity); moderate growth.

Dr. Scott Sp (OGR), *w*, *R. multiflora strain*; Mildew-resistant strain selected as an under stock.

Dr. Trigo de Negreiros HT, *dr*, 1954, *Charles Mallerin* × *Lisboa*; Moreira da Silva. Bud long, pointed; flowers deep red, large; very vigorous growth.

Dr. van de Plassche Pol, *mp*, 1968, *Heureux Anniversaire* × *Allotria*; Buisman. Bud ovoid;

flowers pink, semi-dbl., medium; foliage dark.

Dr. van Rijn HT, *my*, 1952, Leenders, M. Bud ovoid; flowers lemon-yellow, dbl., high-centered, large; fragrant; foliage light green, glossy; vigorous, bushy growth.

Dr. Vazquez HT, *op*, 1935, *Duchess of Atholl* × *Margaret McGredy*; Camprubi. Flowers salmon, semi-dbl., open, medium; foliage glossy; upright growth.

Dr. W. E. Hadden HT, *rb*, 1934, McGredy. Flowers raspberry-red, flushed yellow, deepening at base, well formed, borne on long, strong stems; foliage dark; vigorous growth.

Dr. W. Van Fleet LCl, *lp*, 1910, *(R. wichuraiana* × *Safrano)* × *Souv. du Prés. Carnot*; Van Fleet; P. Henderson. Bud pointed; flowers cameo-pink fading flesh-white, dbl., large; fragrant; foliage dark, glossy; vigorous, climbing (15-20 ft.) growth; non-recurrent bloom; blooms mostly on old wood.

Dr. Zamenhof R, *rb*, 1935, *R. wichuraiana* × *Seedling*; Brada; Böhm. Flowers crimson-red, base yellow, very large, borne in clusters; very fragrant; very vigorous growth.

Doctor's Wife HT, *op*, 1967, Abrams, Von; Edmunds. Bud long, pointed; flowers salmon-pink, dbl., high-centered, large; slightly fragrant; foliage dark, glossy, leathery; vigorous, upright growth.

Dolce Vita® HT, *op*, 1986, (DELdal; Niagara Pride); *Voeux de Bonheur* × *(Chic Parisien* × *(Michele Meilland* × *Mme. Joseph Perraud))*; Delbard, 1971. Flowers rosy salmon, dbl. (37 petals), high-centered, exhibition, large; slightly fragrant; vigorous, upright, bushy growth.

Dollie B Min, *rb*, 1982, (TRObee); *Park direktor Riggers* × *Darling Flame*; Robinson, Thomas, 1983. Flowers medium red, silver reverse, dbl. (35 petals), small; no fragrance; foliage small, dark green, red edges, glossy; bushy growth.

Dolly® F, *dp*, 1975, (Springs 75); *(Nordia* × *Queen Elizabeth)* × *(Seedling* × *Mischief)*; Poulsen, N.D.; Poulsen. Flowers dark pink, dbl. (20 petals), large (2½-3 in.); foliage glossy, dark; bushy growth.   GM, Baden-Baden, 1973; ADR, 1987.

Dolly Brownell F, *lp*, 1926, *Dr. W. Van Fleet seedling*; Brownell; Flower color same as Dr. W.V.F.

Dolly Darling HT, *mp*, 1949, *Pink Princess* × *Crimson Glory*; Brownell. Bud long, pointed, red; flowers lustrous pink, semi-dbl. (20 petals), open, large (4-5 in.); fragrant; foliage glossy; vigorous, compact growth.

Dolly Madison HT, *dy*, 1935, (Super-Dupont); *Mrs. Pierre S. duPont climbing sport seedling*; Hillock. Flowers golden yellow; vigorous growth.

Dolly Parton HT, *or*, 1984, *Fragrant Cloud × Oklahoma*; Winchel, Joseph; C-P, 1983. Flowers luminous orange-red, dbl. (35 petals), large; very fragrant; foliage medium, medium green, semi-glossy; upright growth.   ARC TG (B), 1982.

Dolly Varden HRg (S), *ab*, 1914, Paul. Flowers light apricot-pink, base yellow, large; vigorous growth; recurrent bloom.

Dolly Varden Pol, *mp*, 1930, deRuiter. Flowers clear pink, dbl.

Dolly's Sister HT, *op*, 1989, *Dolly Parton sport*; Taylor, Thomas E.; Michigan Miniature Roses, 1989. Flowers medium coral-pink.

Dolomiti HT, *ab*, 1933, Ingegnoli.   Bud pointed; flowers flesh, with yellow reflex, dbl., very large, strong stems; fragrant; foliage dark; vigorous growth.

Dominant HT, *op*, 1964, *Golden Masterpiece × Spartan*; Boerner; Spek. Bud ovoid; flowers salmon-pink, dbl., medium, borne in clusters; slightly fragrant; foliage dark.

Dominator F, *mp*, 1961, *New Yorker × The Optimist*; deRuiter. Flowers pink, semi-dbl., large (3 in.) blooms in clusters; fragrant; vigorous, upright growth.

Dominie Sampson HSpn (OGR), *lp*, *R. spinosissima hybrid*; Prior to 1848. Flowers soft pink, semi-dbl.; foliage finely divided; fruit glossy, black; dense, shrubby (3-4 ft.) growth; non-recurrent bloom.

Dominique Min, *lp*, 1981, *Electron × Little Chief*; Bennett, Dee; Tiny Petals Nursery. Bud ovoid; flowers light peachy pink, dbl. (30 petals), exhibition blooms borne singly and in clusters of 5-7; strong apple fragrance; foliage medium green, arrow-shaped; curved prickles; upright growth.

Domino HT, *dr*, 1956, *Peace × Seedling*; Gaujard. Bud long, pointed; flowers dark crimson, medium; slightly fragrant; foliage dark.

Domkapitular Dr. Lager HT, *pb*, 1903, *Mme. Caroline Testout × Princesse de Bassaraba de Brancovan*; Lambert, P. Flowers rose and carmine; fragrant.

Domus Aurea HT, *my*, 1940, *Julien Potin × Yellow seedling*; Aicardi, D.; Giacomasso. Flowers pure yellow, strong stems; foliage dark, glossy; very vigorous growth.

Don Bradman HT, *rb*, 1938, Wheatcroft Bros. Bud long, shapely; flowers coppery claret, fading to silvery pink, dbl. (40-50 petals).

Don Charlton HT, *pb*, 1991, *Silver Jubilee × (Chicago Peace × Doris Tysterman Seedling)*;

Thompson, R.; Battersby Roses, 1992. Flowers deep rose pink with silver reverse, very full, large blooms; fragrant; foliage large, dark green, glossy; upright growth.

Don Don Min, *dr*, 1976, *Seedling × Over the Rainbow*; Williams, E.D.; Mini-Roses. Flowers red, reverse blending near white at base, dbl. (60 petals), small (1-1½ in.); fragrant; foliage small, glossy, bronze; upright, bushy growth.

Don José HT, *op*, 1922, *Archiduc Joseph × Seedling*; Clark, A.; NRS Victoria.   Flowers salmon-pink, semi-dbl.; slightly fragrant.

Don Juan LCl, *dr*, 1958, *New Dawn seedling × New Yorker*; Malandrone; J&P. Bud ovoid; flowers velvety dark red, dbl. (35 petals), cupped, large (5 in.); very fragrant; foliage dark, glossy, leathery; height 8-10 ft.; recurrent bloom.

Don Marshall Min, *dr*, 1982, (MORblack); *Baccará × Little Chief*; Moore, R.S.; Moore Min. Roses. Flowers medium red, reverse blackish-red, dbl. (35 petals), HT form, small; slight fragrance; foliage small, dark, matt; bushy, spreading growth.

Don Quichotte F, *rb*, 1964, *Charles Gregory × Marcelle Auclair*; Robichon; Ilgenfritz Nursery.   Flowers cherry-red, base yellow, dbl., well formed, large, borne in clusters of 6-12; slightly fragrant; foliage glossy, leathery; vigorous, upright growth.

Don Rose HT, *pb*, 1943, *Souer Thérèse × Seedling*; Mallerin; C-P. Bud long, pointed, carmine-red; flowers coppery pink, dbl. (40 petals), open, cupped, large; slightly fragrant; foliage leathery, bluish green; vigorous, upright, bushy, rather compact growth.

Doña Clara HT, *m*, 1965, Camprubi. Bud ovoid; flowers purplish pink, dbl. (50 petals), high-centered, large; vigorous growth.

Donald Davis F, *or*, 1992, (CHEWbeaut); *Anne Harkness × Beautiful Britain*; Warner, C.H. Flowers vermilion, moderately full (15-25 petals), medium (4-7 cms) blooms borne in small clusters; slight fragrance; foliage medium, medium green, semi-glossy; few prickles; medium (90 cms), upright growth.

Donald Macdonald HT, *ob*, 1916, Dickson, A. Flowers orange-carmine, semi-dbl., borne in clusters; fragrant; dwarf growth.   GM, NRS, 1916.

Donald Prior F, *mr*, 1938, *Seedling × D.T. Poulsen*; Prior; J&P. Bud ovoid; flowers bright scarlet flushed crimson, semi-dbl. (11 petals), cupped, large (3 in.) blooms in large clusters; fragrant; foliage leathery, dark; vigorous, bushy growth; (28).

Donald Prior, Climbing Cl F, *mr*, Farr.

Donaldo HT, *rb*, 1979, *Honey Favorite* × *Rose Gaujard*; Murray, N. Bud ovoid; flowers red to pink, dbl. (35 petals), shapely, large (4 in.); foliage large, glossy, dark; tall growth.

Donna Clara HT, *pb*, Leenders, M. Flowers buff, reverse strawberry-pink.

Donna Faye Min, *lp*, 1976, *Ma Perkins* × *Baby Betsy McCall*; Schwartz, E.W.; Nor'East Min. Roses. Bud pointed; flowers light pink, dbl. (27 petals), high-centered, small (1 in.); fragrant; upright growth.

Donna Jean F, *m*, 1991, (TALdon); *Azure Sea* × *Party Girl*; Taylor, Pete & Kay; Taylor's Roses. Flowers mauve with white eye, semi-dbl. (6-14 petals), medium blooms borne singly and in small clusters; no fragrance; foliage medium, dark green, semi-glossy; medium, upright, bushy growth.

Donna Marie HSem (OGR), *w*, 1830, (Donna Maria); *R. sempervirens hybrid*; Vibert. Flowers pure white, very dbl., small.

Dooryard Delight HT, *pb*, 1940, *R. setigera* × *Lady Alice Stanley*; Horvath; Wyant. Bud short, pointed, spiraled; flowers light pink, reverse rose-pink, dbl., petals sharply pointed, medium (2½ in.), large truss; slightly fragrant; foliage leathery; vigorous, bushy growth; recurrent bloom.

Dopey Pol, *mr*, 1954, (Eberwein); *Robin Hood* × *Polyantha seedling*; deRuiter; Gregory; Willicher Baumschulen, 1954. Flowers crimson-red, semi-dbl., small blooms in trusses; compact growth.

Dora HT, *or*, 1975, *Tanagra* × *Rubens*; Gaujard. Bud long; flowers brilliant orange-red, dbl.; foliage bronze.

Dora Delle Min, *pb*, 1991, (TALdor); *Azure Sea* × *Jean Kenneally*; Taylor, Pete & Kay; Taylor's Roses, 1991. Flowers light pink with lavender hue, lighter in center, reverse creamy white, full, high-centered, exhibition, medium blooms borne usually singly; fragrant; foliage medium, medium green, semi-glossy; medium, upright growth.

Dora Hansen HT, *mp*, 1908, Jacobs. Bud long, pointed; flowers thulite-pink, dbl., open, large; slightly fragrant.

Dora Stober HT, *w*, 1925, Leenders, M. Flowers white shaded yellow, dbl.; fragrant.

Dorcas R, *pb*, 1922, English. Flowers deep rose-pink to coral-pink, base yellow, full, borne in large clusters; vigorous growth.   RULED EXTINCT 1/85.

Dorcas S, *pb*, 1984, *Minigold* × *Freckle Face*; Buck; Iowa State University. Bud ovoid, pointed; flowers light pink, pale yellow blend, flecked deeper pink, dbl. (40 petals), shallow-cupped, large blooms borne 8-10 per cluster; light fragrance; foliage dark, leathery; awl-like, tan prickles; erect, bushy growth; repeat bloom; hardy.

Doreen HT, *ob*, 1951, *Lydia* × *McGredy's Sunset*; Robinson, H.; Baker's Nursery. Flowers deep golden orange flushed scarlet, well-formed; fragrant; foliage dark; vigorous.

Doreen Johnson HT, *lp*, 1977, (*Great Venture* × *Fort Vancouver*) × *Memoriam*; Dawson, G.; Australian Roses. Bud long, pointed; flowers pale pink, dbl.; slightly fragrant; foliage large, light; vigorous, bushy growth.

Doreen Thorn HT, *pb*, 1934, Cant, F. Flowers deep pink, base yellow, full, well shaped, large; fragrant; vigorous.

Doreen Wells F, *or*, 1970, *Soraya* × *Circus*; Watkins Roses. Flowers orange-scarlet, dbl. (25 petals), flat, large (3 in.); fragrant; foliage glossy, dark; low, bushy growth.

Doric F, *yb*, 1963, *Masquerade* × *Korona*; Le-Grice. Flowers golden salmon, dbl. (40 petals), large, borne in well-spaced clusters; foliage glossy; vigorous, compact growth.

Dorienne HT, *mr*, 1958, *Mrs. Nieminen* × *Seedling*; Buyl Frères. Bud short; flowers red, dbl. (34 petals), cupped, large; bushy, spreading growth.

Dorina Neave HT, *pb*, 1926, Pemberton. Flowers silvery pink, full, globular, large, stiff stems; very fragrant; compact growth.

Doris HT, *rb*, 1939, *Briarcliff sport*; Spand-ikow. Flowers cerise striped white; not in commerce.

Doris Ann Min, *dr*, 1986, *Black Jade* × *Tiki*; Wambach, Alex A. Flowers dark red, dbl. (26-40 petals), small; foliage small, medium green, matt.

Doris Archer F, *rb*, 1962, *Circus* × *Seedling*; Fryer's Nursery. Flowers yellow, bronze and red, dbl. (30-35 petals), well formed, large (4 in.), borne in clusters; fragrant; foliage glossy; vigorous, compact growth.

Doris Dickson HT, *ob*, 1924, Dickson, S. Flowers orange-cream, veined cherry-red, stiff, wiry stems; fragrant; foliage very dark; vigorous growth.

Doris Downes LCl, *pb*, 1932, Clark, A.; NRS Victoria. Flowers pink, shaded red, semi-dbl., cupped, very large; very fragrant; climbing growth; early bloom.

Doris Findlater HT, *ab*, 1936, Dickson, A. Flowers light apricot, reverse flushed reddish salmon and carmine, full, well formed; vigorous growth.

Doris Grace Robinson HT, *w*, 1943, Bees. Bud pointed; flowers creamy white, well shaped, large; foliage olive-green; vigorous, upright growth.

Doris Howard F, *mr*, 1957, Wheatcroft Bros. Flowers blood-red, borne in large clusters; vigorous, bushy growth.

Doris Norman F, *or*, 1958, *Paul's Scarlet Climber* × *Mary*; Norman; Harkness. Flowers bright orange, dbl. (30 petals), high-centered to open, medium (2 in.), borne in small clusters; foliage purplish to dull green; vigorous, bushy growth.

Doris Osborne HT, *mr*, 1937, *Mme. Abel Chatenay* × *Seedling*; Clark, A.; NRS Victoria. Bud pointed; flowers ruby-cerise, semi-dbl.; bushy growth.

Doris Pleasance HT, *w*, 1978, *Queen Elizabeth sport*; Brewer. Flowers blush-pink to white.

Doris Ryker Pol, *ob*, 1942, (Dorus Rijkers); Leenders, M.; Klyn. Flowers salmon-pink, dbl., medium blooms in clusters; fragrant; foliage light green; vigorous, upright; recurrent.

Doris Trayler HT, *yb*, 1924, McGredy. Bud pointed, orange; flowers yellow, reverse flushed crimson and orange, dbl., high-centered, large; fragrant; foliage light green, leathery, glossy; bushy, dwarf, compact growth.

Doris Tysterman® HT, *ob*, 1975, *Peer Gynt* × *Seedling*; Wisbech Plant Co. Flowers tangerine and gold, dbl. (28 petals), large (4-5 in.); slightly fragrant; foliage glossy; upright.

Dornröschen S, *pb*, 1960, *Pike's Peak* × *Ballet*; Kordes, R. Bud well-shaped; flowers salmon to deep pink, reverse yellow, dbl., large blooms in clusters (up to 10); fragrant; upright, well-branched growth; recurrent bloom.

Dorola® Min, *dy*, 1982, (MACshana; Benson & Hedges Special; Parkay); *Darling Flame* × *New Day*; McGredy, Sam; McGredy International, 1983. Flowers deep yellow, dbl. (26 petals), medium; fragrant; foliage small, medium green, semi-glossy; bushy growth.

Dorothe® HT, *my*, 1979, (LEGga; Midas); *Irish Gold* × *Dr. A.J. Verhage*; LeGrice, E.B., 1980. Bud pointed; flowers medium yellow, dbl. (48 petals), borne singly; slight fragrance; foliage glossy, medium green; large, curved, light brown prickles; vigorous, upright growth.

Dorothea Howard HT, *pb*, 1978, *First Prize* × *Roundelay*; Barclay, Hilary M. Flowers light pink, deeper pink reverse, dbl. (30 petals), well-formed, large blooms borne singly; tea fragrance; foliage medium green, glossy; many hooked, brown prickles.

Dorothy Anderson HT, *lp*, 1949, *Sam McGredy* × *George Dickson*; McGredy. Flowers light pink, dbl. (33 petals), high-centered, large; slightly fragrant; free growth.

Dorothy Anne HT, *pb*, 1985, *First Prize* × *Lady X*; Winchel, Joseph; Kimbrew-Walter Roses. Flowers white blending to deep pink at edges, dbl. (35 petals), large; no fragrance; foliage medium, dark, semi-glossy; upright growth.

Dorothy A. Golik HT, *ob*, 1973, *Tropicana* × *Peace*; Golik; Dynarose. Bud ovoid; flowers orange to flaming red, dbl. (35 petals), high pointed, large (4 in.); fragrant (spicy); foliage glossy; moderate growth.

Dorothy Broster HT, *mp*, 1978, *Blue Moon* × *Karl Herbst*; Ellick; Excelsior Roses. Flowers azalea-pink, dbl. (45 petals), full, large (5 in.); fragrant; foliage dark; very vigorous growth.

Dorothy, Climbing Cl HT, *pb*, 1935, *Dorothy Page-Roberts sport*; Bostick.

Dorothy Dennison R, *lp*, 1909, *Dorothy Perkins sport*; Dennison. Flowers pale pink.

Dorothy Dix Pol, *mp*, 1923, Hicks. Flowers rose-pink, borne in clusters.

Dorothy Douglas HT, *rb*, 1924, Dobbie. Flowers vivid cerise-pink.

Dorothy Drowne R, *pb*, 1924, *Sodenia seedling*; Brownell. Flowers white to pink, center crimson and scarlet.

Dorothy Fowler HRg (S), *mp*, 1938, *R. rugosa* × *(R. acicularis* × *R. spinosissima)*; Skinner. Flowers clear pink, semi-dbl., well formed, medium (3-3½ in.); very fragrant; height 3 ft.; non-recurrent bloom.

Dorothy Goodwin HT, *yb*, 1954, (Perfect Peace); *Peace sport*; Goodwin; Gregory. Flowers yellow tipped cerise-pink, dbl. (32 petals), well formed; large (4 in.); fragrant; foliage dark holly-green; vigorous growth.

Dorothy Grace Cl Min, *yb*, 1986, *Sport of Little Darling* × *Rise 'n' Shine*; Dobbs, Annette; Port Stockton Nursery. Flowers yellow with pink petal edges, dbl. (25 petals), exhibition, small blooms in sprays of 3-5; no fragrance; foliage small, medium green, semi-glossy; very few, brown prickles, hooked downward; upright, climbing (to 6 ft.).

Dorothy Hodgson HT, *ob*, 1930, Cant, F. Flowers orange-cerise, veined darker, well formed, large; slightly fragrant; vigorous growth.

Dorothy Howarth Pol, *op*, 1921, *Léonie Lamesch* × *Annchen Müller*; Bees. Flowers coral-pink, tinted salmon, full, open, borne in clusters; fragrant; foliage dark; bushy growth.

Dorothy James HT, *pb*, 1939, *Golden Dawn sport*; C-P. Flowers peach-pink reverse deep rose; good habit.

Dorothy King HT, *rb*, 1924, King. Flowers scarlet-crimson and maroon, semi-dbl.

Dorothy Lee HT, *pb*, 1929, Morse. Flowers silvery shell-pink, base golden yellow, dbl.

Dorothy Marie HT, *dp*, 1935, *Talisman sport*; Scittine; Lainson. Flowers dark pink.

Dorothy May Cooper Min, *w*, 1975, *R. roulettii* × *Memoriam*; Ellick. Flowers pure white, dbl. (25-30 petals), full, small (1-2 in.); foliage dark; very vigorous growth.

Dorothy McGredy HT, *rb*, 1936, McGredy. Flowers deep vermilion, base and reverse yellow, well shaped, strong stems; fragrant; foliage cedar-green; vigorous growth.

Dorothy Mollison HT, *dr*, 1930, *Mrs. R.C. Bell × Seedling*; Clark, A.; NRS Victoria. Flowers dark crimson.

Dorothy Page-Roberts HT, *pb*, 1907, Dickson, A. Flowers coppery pink, suffused yellow, dbl., open, very large; slightly fragrant; vigorous growth.

Dorothy Peach HT, *yb*, 1957, *Lydia* × *Peace*; Robinson, H. Flowers deep yellow flushed pink, dbl. (37 petals), high-centered, large (5 in.); fragrant; foliage dark, glossy; vigorous. GM, NRS, 1959.

Dorothy Peach, Climbing Cl HT, *yb*, 1963, Watkins Roses.

Dorothy Perkins R, *lp*, 1901, *R. wichuraiana* × *Mme. Gabriel Luizet*; J&P. Flowers rose-pink, full; fragrant; foliage dark, glossy; very vigorous (10-20 ft.) growth.

Dorothy Ratcliffe HT, *rb*, 1910, McGredy. Flowers coral-red shaded fawn-yellow; vigorous growth.

Dorothy Wheatcroft F, *mr*, 1960, Tantau; Wheatcroft Bros. Flowers oriental red shaded darker, semi-dbl. (18 petals), large (3½ in.) blooms in clusters of 13; slightly fragrant; foliage bright green; vigorous, bushy growth. GM, NRS, 1961.

Dorothy's Regal Red HT, *mr*, 1984, Jerabek, Paul. Flowers medium red, dbl. (58 petals), large blooms in small clusters; very fragrant; foliage medium. dark, glossy; bushy growth.

Dorotka Darling Min, *pb*, 1991, *Orange Darling* × *Seedling*; Sudol, Julia, 1992. Flowers pink & cream blend, full (26-40 petals), well-formed, small (0-4 cms) blooms borne mostly singly, sometimes in small clusters; slight fragrance; foliage medium, dark green, semi-glossy, clean and abundant; few prickles; tall (60-80 cms), upright growth.

Dorrit F, *ob*, 1968, *Seedling* × *Folie d'Espagne*; Soenderhousen. Flowers orange-yellow, dbl. (30-40 petals), flat, large blooms in trusses.

D'Orsay Rose Misc OGR (OGR), *dp*, *Thought to be R. carolina hybrid*; Prior to 1850. Buds deep pink, with long sepals; flowers deep pink, outer petals fading to pale pink, dbl.; fragrant; receptacle wide, glandular; leaflets 5-7, leaden green; prickles paired below each leaf; stipules and leaflets narrower than those of 'Rose d'Amour' with which this is confused; erect growth to 5 ft.; summer bloom.

Dortmund® K (S), *mr*, 1955, *Seedling* × *R. kordesii*; Kordes. Bud long, pointed; flowers red, white eye, single, large blooms in large clusters; fragrant; foliage dark, very glossy; vigorous, climbing growth; recurrent bloom. ADR, 1954; GM, Portland, 1971.

Do-Si-Do S, *mp*, 1984, *(Autumn Dusk × Solitude)* × *Wanderin' Wind*; Buck; Iowa State University. Flowers medium lavender-pink, cupped, large blooms borne 3-10 per cluster; fragrant; foliage dark olive green, leathery, glossy; awl-like, tan prickles; vigorous, erect, bushy growth; repeat bloom; hardy.

Dothan HT, *mp*, 1983, *Koppies* × *King of Hearts*; Perry, Astor; Perry Roses, 1984. Flowers medium pink, dbl. (35 petals), exhibition, large; slight fragrance; foliage large, medium green, matt; upright growth.

Dotty HT, *dy*, 1931, *Souv. de Claudius Pernet* × *R. foetida bicolor seedling*; Towill. Flowers bronze-yellow, semi-dbl., globular, large, long stems; fragrant; foliage glossy; very vigorous growth.

Dotty Bass HT, *dr*, 1968, Bass; DeVor Nursery. Bud long, pointed; flowers dark red, dbl., medium; foliage dark, leathery; vigorous, upright growth; a greenhouse variety.

Double Blush Burnet HSpn (OGR), *pb*. Prior to 1846. Flowers center blush, fading at edges, reverse white.

Double Brique G (OGR), *pb*, Flowers rosy pink, shading silver toward outside, dbl.

Double Dark Marbled HSpn (OGR), *rb*, (Petite Red Scotch); *R. spinosissima hybrid*; Prior to 1822. Flowers red mottled purple, semi-dbl., small; early bloom.

Double Delight™ HT, *rb*, 1977, (ANdeli); *Granada* × *Garden Party*; Swim & Ellis; Armstrong Nursery. Bud long, pointed to urn-shaped; flowers creamy white becoming strawberry-red, dbl. (30-45 petals), high-centered, large (5½ in.); fragrant (spicy); upright, spreading, bushy growth. GM, Baden-Baden & Rome, 1976; AARS, 1977; James Alexander Gamble.Rose Fragrance Medal, 1986

Double Delight, Climbing Cl HT, *rb*, 1982, (AROclidd; Grimpant Double Delight); *Double Delight sport*; Christensen, Jack; Armstrong Nursery 1985.

Double Feature Gr, *m*, 1976, (Lakeland's Pride); *Angel Face × Granada*; Williams, J.B.; Lakeland Nursery Sales. Bud pointed; flowers reddish purple, reverse yellow, dbl. (28 petals), high-centered, large (4 in.); slightly fragrant (damask); foliage large, dark; vigorous, upright growth.

Double Joy Min, *op*, 1979, *Little Darling × New Penny*; Moore, R.S.; Sequoia Nursery. Bud long, pointed; flowers pink, dbl. (35 petals), medium (1½ in.); fragrant; foliage small, matt, green; bushy growth.

Double Ophelia HT, *lp*, 1916, *Ophelia × Seedling*; Hill, E.G., Co.; Similar to Ophelia but twice as many petals.

Double Orléans Pol, *mr*, 1924, *Orléans Rose* sport; Hicks. Flowers rosy crimson, center white.

Double Perfection™ HT, *rb*, 1988, (BURwin); *(My Dream × First Prize) × Seedling*; Winchel, Joseph; Co-Operative Rose Growers, 1987. Flowers red, reverse white, aging darker red, reverse cream, semi-dbl., high-centered, exhibition, medium, borne usually singly or in sprays of 1-3; slight fragrance; foliage medium, dark green, semiglossy; prickles slight recurve, average, brown; fruit round, average, orange; bushy, medium growth.

Double Scarlet E (OGR), *mr*, Flowers bright rosy red, dbl.; very fragrant; weak growth.

Double Star Min, *w*, 1978, *Fairy Moss × Fairy Moss*; Dobbs, Annette; Small World Min. Roses. Bud ovoid; flowers white, 10 petals, borne 2-5 per cluster; slight fragrance; foliage small, firm, disease-resistant; no prickles; vigorous growth.

Double Talk F, *rb*, 1980, *Plain Talk × Suspense*; Weeks, O.L. Bud ovoid, pointed; flowers medium red, creamy white reverse, dbl. (48 petals), flat, cupped petals, rolled loosely outward, borne mostly singly; slight, spicy fragrance; foliage glossy, slightly wrinkled, dark; long prickles, hooked downward; compact growth.

Double Treat Min, *yb*, 1986, (MORtreat); *Arizona × ((Fairy Moss × Fairy Moss) × (Little Darling × Ferdinand Pichard))*; Moore, R.S.; Sequoia Nursery, 1985. Bud mossy; flowers bright red and orange-yellow, striped, dbl., cupped, medium blooms borne usually singly and in sprays of 3-5; slight fragrance; foliage small to medium, medium green, semi-glossy; slender, brown prickles; fruit small, orange, globular with numerous spines; medium, upright, bushy growth.

Double White E (OGR), *w*, Flowers flesh-white, dbl.; vigorous growth.

Double White Burnet HSpn (OGR), *w*, Flowers white; very fragrant; vigorous growth.

Doubloons LCl, *my*, 1934, *R. setigera hybrid × R. foetida bicolor hybrid*; Horvath; J&P. Bud ovoid, deep saffron-yellow; flowers rich gold, dbl., cupped, large blooms in clusters; fragrant; foliage glossy; vigorous; intermittent. ARS David Fuerstenberg Prize, 1936.

Doué Rambler R, *mp*, 1921, Begault-Pigné. Flowers bright pink, borne in well-filled clusters.

Douglas MacArthur HT, *pb*, 1943, *Mrs. J.D. Eisele × Glowing Sunset*; Howard, F.H.; H&S. Bud long, pointed; flowers delft rose, base slightly bronze, dbl. (24-30 petals), high-centered, large (4-4½ in.), long stems; foliage leathery; vigorous, upright, bushy, compact growth.

Douglas MacArthur, Climbing Cl HT, *pb*, 1949, Howard, F.H.; H&S.

Douglass Ch (OGR), *dr*, 1848, Verdier, V. Flowers crimson, medium; vigorous growth.

Doulce France F, *pb*, 1964, *(Peace × Seedling) × Lady Sylvia*; Mondial Roses. Bud round; flowers clear pink flushed apricot, dbl., large; vigorous, upright growth.

Dourada HT, *dy*, 1957, *Mme. Marie Curie × Julien Potin*; Moreira da Silva. Flowers deep yellow, dbl., well formed; very vigorous growth.

Dove S, *lp*, 1986, (AUSdove; Dovedale); *Wife of Bath × Iceberg seedling*; Austin, David, 1984. Flowers light pink, dbl. (40+ petals), medium; slightly fragrant; foliage medium, dark, semi-glossy; spreading growth.

Dovedale HT, *rb*, 1975, *Fragrant Cloud × Stella*; Moorhouse & Thornley. Flowers cream, petals edged carmine, dbl. (42 petals), large (5 in.); foliage dark; low, bushy.

Downland Cherry HT, *mr*, 1954, *Vanessa × Shot Silk*; Ratcliffe. Flowers light cerise shaded scarlet; very fragrant (spicy); foliage dark, leathery, dull green; vigorous growth.

Downland Lustre HT, *yb*, 1955, *Vanessa × Shot Silk*; Ratcliffe. Bud bronzy gold; flowers maize-yellow, reverse orange, dbl. (25 short petals), medium; very fragrant (spicy); compact, bushy growth.

Dragon's Eye HCh (OGR), *dr*, 1992, (CLEdrag; Eye of the Dragon; The Dragon's Eye); *Seedling × Seedling*; Clements, John K.; Heirloom Old Garden Roses, 1991. Flowers dark red, very full (41+ petals), exhibition, medium (4-7 cms.) blooms borne mostly singly; fragrant; foliage small, dark green, semi-glossy; some prickles; medium (70 cms.), bushy, compact growth.

Drambuie HT, *rb*, 1973, *Whisky Mac sport*; Anderson's Rose Nursery. Flowers orange-red, reverse red, dbl. (28-30 petals), full, high pointed, large (5 in.); very fragrant; foliage glossy; vigorous, bushy growth.

Dream HT, *op*, 1938, *Better Times sport*; Dramm; Flower geranium-pink, dbl. (50-60 petals), large (4½ in.), strong stems; fragrant.

Dream Cloud S, *pb*, 1984, (AROpiclu); *Zorina* × *Gartendirektor Otto Linne*; Christensen, Jack; Armstrong Nursery, 1985. Flowers light to dark salmon-pink, dbl. (20 petals), medium blooms in large pyramidal clusters; slight fragrance; foliage medium, long, narrow, medium green, matt; spreading, bushy growth; semi-pendulous habit.

Dream Dust F, *mp*, 1969, *Lavender Girl seedling* × *Little Darling seedling*; Gardner, B.C. Bud pointed; flowers medium pink, dbl., small, borne in clusters; slightly fragrant; foliage leathery; very vigorous, spreading growth.

Dream Girl LCl, *pb*, 1944, (Dreamgirl); *Dr. W. Van Fleet* × *Senora Gari*; Jacobus; B&A. Flowers salmon-pink overlaid apricot, dbl. (55-65 petals), large (3½ in.); very fragrant; foliage glossy; recurrent bloom; good pillar rose; (28).

Dream Parade HT, *op*, 1938, *Condesa de Sástago sport*; Hillock. Flowers amber in spring, seashell-pink in hot weather, burnt-orange in fall, dbl., large; fragrant; vigorous growth.

Dream Time HT, *mp*, 1977, (Dreamtime); *Kordes' Perfecta* × *Prima Ballerina*; Bees. Flowers medium pink, dbl. (38 petals), high-centered, large (5 in.); very fragrant; foliage light green; moderately vigorous growth.

Dream Waltz F, *dr*, 1969, Tantau, Math. Flowers dark red, dbl., large blooms in trusses; foliage glossy.

Dreamboat Min, *my*, 1981, (Dream Boat); *Rise 'n' Shine* × *Grand Opera*; Jolly, Betty; Rosehill Farm, 1982. Flowers medium yellow, dbl. (60-70 petals), high-centered, medium; slight fragrance; bushy, spreading growth.

Dreamer™ Min, *mp*, 1990, (SAVadream); *Baby Katie* × *Shocking Blue*; Saville, F. Harmon; Nor'East Miniature Roses, 1991. Bud ovoid, pointed; flowers dusty pink, dbl. (20 petals), cupped, medium, borne singly or in sprays of 3-5; no fragrance; foliage medium, dark green, semi-glossy; upright, bushy, medium growth.

Dreamglo Min, *rb*, 1978, *Little Darling* × *Little Chief*; Williams, E.D.; Mini-Roses. Bud long, pointed; flowers white, tipped and blended red, dbl. (50 petals), high-centered, small (1 in.); slightly fragrant; foliage small, dark; upright growth.

Dreaming Spires LCl, *dy*, 1973, *Buccaneer* × *Arthur Bell*; Mattock. Flowers bright golden yellow, dbl. (25 petals), HT form, medium (3 in.); very fragrant; foliage dark; repeat bloom. GM, Belfast, 1977.

Dreamsicle Min, *ob*, 1992, (TALdre); *Poker Chip* × *Party Girl*; Taylor, Pete & Kay; Taylor's Roses, 1993. Flowers creamy white edged with orangish pink edges, reverse same, moderately full (15-25 petals), when fully open has star shape, medium (4-7 cms) blooms borne mostly singly and in small clusters; slight fragrance; foliage small, medium green, semi-glossy; some prickles; medium (36 cms), compact growth.

Dreamy Min, *yb*, 1987, (TINdream); *Irish Gold* × *Party Girl*; Bennett, Dee; Tiny Petals Nursery. Flowers cream, edges blushed pink, reverse cream with more intense blushing, aging blush invades all petals, dbl. (20-25 petals), urn-shaped, medium, borne usually singly; slight fragrance; foliage medium, medium green, semi-glossy; slender, small, reddish prickles, slanted downward; fruit globular, medium, brown; upright, medium growth.

Dresden HT, *w*, 1961, (Mathé Altéry); *Ophelia* × *Cathrine Kordes*; Robichon; Ilgenfritz Nursery. Bud ovoid; flowers white lightly suffused pink, dbl. (60 petals), high-centered, large (4-5 in.); very fragrant; foliage leathery, dark; very vigorous, upright growth.

Dresden Doll Min, *lp*, 1975, *Fairy Moss* × *Moss seedling*; Moore, R.S.; Sequoia Nursery. Bud mossy; flowers soft pink, semi-dbl. (18 petals), cupped, mini-moss, small (1½ in.); fragrant; foliage glossy, leathery; low, bushy, compact growth.

Dries Verschuren HT, *my*, 1961, (Blaby Jubilee); *Golden Rapture* × *Seedling*; Verschuren, A.; Blaby Rose Gardens. Bud pointed; flowers buttercup-yellow, dbl. (25 petals), well formed, large; fragrant; foliage glossy, bronze; vigorous, upright, bushy growth.

Drifter's Escape F, *or*, 1971, *Orangeade* × *Orange Sensation*; Greenway. Flowers vermilion, semi-dbl. (10 petals), large (3-3½ in.); foliage glossy, reddish when young; free growth.

Dronning Alexandrine HT, *dp*, 1926, Poulsen, S.; Poulsen. Flowers deep pink, dbl., urn-shaped, medium; no fragrance; foliage medium green, semi-glossy; medium, bushy growth.

Dropmore Yellow HFt (OGR), *my*, *R. foetida* × *R. spinosissima altaiaca*; Skinner. Flowers yellow; not introduced.

Droujba F, *yb*, 1975, *Masquerade* × *Rumba*; Staikov, Prof. Dr. V.; Kalaydjiev and Chorbadjiiski. Flowers yellow, shaded red, dbl.

(42 petals), cupped, small blooms in clusters of 5-30 per stem; tea fragrance; foliage dark, glossy; bushy growth.

Dru Min, *dy*, 1985, Hunt, W. Henry, 1986. Flowers deep yellow, dbl. (35 petals), HT form, small; slight fragrance; foliage medium, medium green, semi-glossy; upright, bushy growth.

Drummer Boy F, *mp*, 1965, *Pinocchio × Queen Elizabeth*; Lammerts; Germain's. Bud ovoid; flowers soft carmine-rose, dbl., small, borne in large clusters; slightly fragrant; foliage leathery; vigorous, tall growth.

Drummer Boy F, *dr*, 1987, (HARvacity); *(Wee Man × (Southampton × Darling Flame)) × Red Sprite*; Harkness, R., 1987-88. Flowers deep, vivid, bright scarlet, fading slightly paler, semi-dbl. (15 petals), cupped, loose, small, borne in sprays of 3+; patio; slight, spicy fragrance; foliage small, medium green, semi-glossy, oval-pointed; fairly straight, small, purplish-red prickles; fruit ovoid, small, greenish; spreading, low growth.

D. Silvia Ferreira HT, *ob*, Moreira da Silva. Flowers salmon and red, reverse old-gold.

D.T. Poulsen F, *mr*, 1930, *Orléans Rose × Vesuvius*; Poulsen, S. Flowers bright blood-red, semi-dbl., open; slightly fragrant; foliage dark, leathery; bushy growth; (21).

D.T. Poulsen Improved F, *mr*, 1940, Van der Vis; C-P. Bud small, globular, blood-red; flowers solid cherry-red, dbl. (30-35 petals), open, short, strong stems; foliage leathery, wrinkled, dark; vigorous, compact, bushy growth.

Dublin HT, *mr*, 1982, *(Seedling × Mister Lincoln) × Ann Letts*; Perry, Astor; Perry Roses, 1983. Flowers medium red, dbl. (35 petals), exhibition, large; strong raspberry fragrance; foliage large, medium green, matt, fragrant; upright growth.

Dublin Bay® LCl, *mr*, 1975, (MACdub); *Bantry Bay × Altissimo*; McGredy, S., IV; McGredy Roses International, 1974. Bud ovoid; flowers red, dbl. (25 petals), large (4½ in.); fragrant; climbing growth.

Dubonnet Pol, *dr*, 1958, *Stoplite sport*; Jelly; E.G. Hill Co. Bud small; flowers cardinal-red, dbl.; slightly fragrant; foliage leathery; vigorous growth; a greenhouse variety.

Duc d'Anjou HP (OGR), *dr*, 1862, Boyau. Flowers deep red.

Duc de Bordeaux G (OGR), *pb*, 1820, Vibert. Flowers rosy lilac, full, large.

Duc de Cambridge D (OGR), *m*, 1800, Flowers deep purplish rose, dbl., large; foliage dark, edged reddish brown when young.

Duc de Cazes HP (OGR), *m*, 1861, *Général Jacqueminot × Seedling*; Touvais. Flowers velvety purple, full, cupped; fragrant.

Duc de Fitzjames G (OGR), *dr*, Origin and date unknown. Flowers very dark crimson, shaded purple.

Duc de Guiche G (OGR), *m*, Prior to 1838. Flowers light reddish-violet, dbl., large.

Duc de Magenta T (OGR), *ab*, 1860, Margottin. Flowers flesh shaded fawn, full, large.

Duc de Valmy G (OGR), *m*, Flowers light purplish rose, marbled purple, full, cupped, large.

Ducher Ch (OGR), *w*, 1869, Ducher. Flowers pure white, dbl., flat, small to medium; vigorous.

Duchess HT, *mp*, 1976, *White Satin × Seedling*; Van Veen; Carlton Rose Nursery. Bud ovoid; flowers cameo-pink shaded deeper, full, high-centered, large (4-4½ in.); fragrant; foliage glossy, leathery; bushy, upright growth.

Duchess of Abercorn HT, *pb*, 1919, Dickson, H. Flowers creamy white edged bright rose, dbl.

Duchess of Albany HT, *dp*, 1888, (Red La France); *La France sport*; Paul, W. Flowers deep pink.

Duchess of Atholl HT, *ob*, 1928, Dobbie. Flowers vivid orange, flushed old-rose, dbl., cupped, large; very fragrant; foliage bronze, leathery; vigorous growth.

Duchess of Atholl, Climbing Cl HT, *ob*, 1933, Howard Rose Co.

Duchess of Bedford HP (OGR), *mr*, 1879, Postans, R.B.; W. Paul & Sons. Flowers bright medium red, full, globular, large.

Duchess of Connaught HT, *pb*, 1879, *Adam × Duchesse de Vallombrosa*; Bennett. Flowers deep silvery pink, globular, large; very fragrant; dwarf growth.

Duchess of Edinburgh T (OGR), *dr*, 1874, (Prince Wasiltchikoff); *Souv. de David d'Angers seedling*; Nabonnand, G.; Veitch. Flowers crimson, becoming lighter, full, large; moderate growth.

Duchess of Kent T (OGR), *ly*, Origin and date unknown. Flowers yellowish white.

Duchess of Kent F, *dp*, 1968, *Katharine Worsley sport*; Waterhouse, W.P.; Waterhouse Nursery. Flowers rose-neyron-red, cupped blooms in trusses; low, bushy growth.

Duchess of Marlborough HT, *pb*, 1922, *Jonkheer J.L. Mock seedling × Beauté de Lyon*; Nabonnand, P. Flowers brilliant lilac-rose, reverse carmine-crimson, dbl.

Duchess of Montrose HT, *rb*, 1929, Dobbie. Flowers vermilion-crimson, large.

Duchess of Normandy HT, *pb*, 1912, *Dean Hole sport*; Le Cornu. Flowers soft salmon-flesh, overlaid yellow, dbl., high-centered, large; vigorous, branching growth.

Duchess of Paducah HT, *w*, 1971, *Kordes' Perfecta × Peace*; Williams, J.B. Bud ovoid; flowers white, edge flushed red, dbl., high-centered, large; very fragrant; foliage large, glossy, dark, leathery; vigorous, upright growth.

Duchess of Portland P   (OGR),   *mr*, (Duchesse de Portland; Portland Rose); About 1800. Flowers bright scarlet. The first of the Portland class (Damask hybrids with some recurrence).

Duchess of Rutland F, *dp*, 1956, deRuiter; Gandy. Flowers rich carmine-pink, semi-dbl., small, borne on large truss; vigorous growth.

Duchess of Sutherland HP (OGR), *lp*, 1839, Laffay. Flowers rosy pink, full, large; fragrant; vigorous growth.

Duchess of Sutherland HT, *pb*, 1912, Dickson, A. Flowers rose-pink shaded lemon on white base, dbl., high-centered, large; fragrant (sweetbriar); foliage glossy, olive-green; vigorous.

Duchess of Wellington HT, *ly*, 1909, Dickson, A. Bud pointed; flowers buff-yellow, deeper toward center, semi-dbl. (17 petals), open, large; long, strong stems; fragrant; foliage leathery; bushy growth.

Duchess of Wellington, Climbing Cl HT, *ly*, 1924, Howard Rose Co.

Duchess of Westminster HT, *pb*, 1879, *Adam × Marquise de Castellane*; Bennett. Flowers pink shaded carmine, dbl., large; slightly fragrant; moderate growth.

Duchess of Westminster HT, *mp*, 1911, Dickson, A. Flowers clear rose-pink, dbl.; fragrant.

Duchess of York HT, *yb*, 1925, Dickson, S. Flowers deep golden yellow, center tangerine, very full, well formed, large; vigorous growth.

Duchesse d'Albe T (OGR), *yb*, 1903, Lévêque. Flowers yellowish salmon, shaded coppery purple rose, base golden yellow, full, globular, large.

Duchesse d'Angoulême G (OGR), *lp*, (Duc de Angoulême; Wax Rose); *Probably Gallica × Centifolia hybrid*; Prior to 1846. Flowers blush, center pink, full, cupped, medium; moderate, upright.

Duchesse d'Anjou HT, *mr*, 1976, (GOD-zoty); *Wizo × Soraya*; Godin. Bud pointed; flowers crimson-red, deeply cupped, medium (3-3½ in.); slightly fragrant; foliage dark; Vigorous growth.

Duchesse d'Auerstädt N (OGR), *my*, 1888, *Reve d'Or sport*; Bernaix, A. Flowers golden yellow.

Duchesse de Brabant T (OGR), *lp*, 1857, (Comtesse de Labarathe; Comtesse Ouwaroff); Bernède. Flowers soft rosy pink, dbl. (45 petals), cupped, large; very fragrant; vigorous, spreading growth.

Duchesse de Buccleugh G (OGR), *rb*, 1846, Robert. Flowers lively crimson, edges tinged lavender, full, cupped, large; vigorous growth.

Duchesse de Cambacérès HP (OGR), *m*, 1854, Fontaine. Flowers lilac-rose, dbl.; vigorous.

Duchesse de Caylus HP (OGR), *dp*, 1864, *Alfred Colomb seedling*; Verdier, C. Flowers brilliant carmine-pink, well formed, globular, large; fragrant; moderate growth.

Duchesse de Galliera HP (OGR), *pb*, 1847. Flowers bright rose shaded flesh, full, cupped, large.

Duchesse de Grammont N (OGR), *w*, Prior to 1906. Flowers flesh.

Duchesse de Montebello G (OGR), *lp*, Laffay, prior to 1838. Flowers rosy pink, changing to flesh-pink, full, medium; fragrant; erect, compact; originally classed as HChina.

Duchesse de Rohan HP (OGR), *pb*, (Duc de Rohan); Prior to 1848. Flowers rosy crimson, margined with lilac, full, compact, large.

Duchesse de Talleyrand HT, *yb*, 1944, *Mme. Joseph Perraud × Fred Edmunds*; Meilland, F. Bud pointed; flowers egg-yolk-yellow to chrome-yellow, full; fragrant; well branched growth.

Duchesse de Thuringe B (OGR), *w*, 1847, Père Guillot. Flowers white tinted lilac.

Duchesse de Vallombrosa HP (OGR), *ab*, 1876, *Jules Margottin seedling*; Schwartz, J. Flowers flesh shaded rose, full, large.

Duchesse de Vendome HT, *rb*, 1924, *Souv. de Gilbert Nabonnand × Juliet*; Nabonnand, P. Flowers crimson, coppery reflexes, reverse yellow, dbl.; fragrant.

Duchesse de Verneuil M (OGR), *pb*, 1856, Portemer. Bud heavily mossed; flowers flesh-pink deepening to salmon-pink, camellia form.

Duchesse Marie Salviati T (OGR), *ob*, 1890, *Mme. Lombard × Mme. Maurice Kuppenheim*; Soupert & Notting. Flowers orange-yellow tinted pink.

Duet HT, *mp*, 1960, *Fandango × Roundelay*; Swim; Armstrong. Bud ovoid; flowers light pink, reverse dark pink, dbl. (25-30 petals), high-centered, large (4 in.); slightly fragrant;

foliage leathery; vigorous, upright growth. GM, Baden-Baden, 1959; AARS, 1961.

Duet Supreme HT, *pb*, 1990, *Duet sport*; Patterson, William, 1988; Roses Unlimited, 1990. Bud rounded; flowers light to medium pink blend, medium pink reverse, dbl. (35 petals), urn-shaped, loose, medium blooms borne singly; slight fragrance; foliage medium, dark green, semi-glossy.

Duffey's Delight HT, *dr*, 1976, *Norman Hartnell sport*; Duffey. Bud long, pointed; flowers velvety dark red, very dbl. (60 petals), high-centered, very large (5-6 in.); slightly fragrant; foliage dark; very vigorous, upright growth.

Duftbella® F, *dr*, 1973, *Fragrant Cloud × (Monique × Mardi Gras)*; Hetzel; GAWA. Bud ovoid; flowers dark velvet red, center lighter, dbl., large; very fragrant; vigorous, bushy growth.

Duftrausch F, *mp*, 1972, (TANrausch); Tantau; Horstmann. Bud globular; Flowers pink, semi-dbl; very fragrant; Foliage soft; Upright growth. RULED EXTINCT 4/85 ARM.

Duftrausch® HT, *mp*, 1985, (TANschaubud; Senteur Royale®; Olde Fragrance); *Parentage not listed*; Tantau, M., 1986. Flowers medium pink, dbl. (40+ petals), large; very fragrant; foliage medium, medium green, semi-glossy; upright growth.

Duftstar HT, *dr*, 1974, *Seedling × Papa Meilland*; Kordes; Dehner & Co. Bud long, pointed; flowers dark red, dbl. (24 petals), high-centered, large (4 in.); very fragrant; foliage dark, soft; vigorous, upright growth.

Duftwunder F, *ob*, 1972, *Fragrant Cloud × Goldmarie*; Hetzel. Flowers yellowish orange, very dbl., large; very fragrant; moderate, upright growth.

Duftzauber HT, *mr*, 1969, (KORdu; Fragrant Charm); *Prima Ballerina × Kaiserin Farah*; Kordes, R.; Kordes. Bud ovoid; flowers rose-red, dbl., high-centered, large; very fragrant; foliage light, soft; moderate, upright growth.

Dukat LCl, *my*, 1955, *Mrs. Pierre S. duPont × Golden Glow*; Tantau, Math. Flowers golden yellow, dbl., large; fragrant; foliage glossy, leathery; vigorous (10-16 ft.), upright growth.

Duke of Connaught HP (OGR), *rb*, 1875, Paul. Flowers dark velvety crimson flushed brighter, dbl., large; very fragrant; vigorous growth.

Duke of Connaught HT, *mr*, 1879, *Adam × Louis van Houtte*; Bennett. Flowers rose-crimson, dbl., very large; moderate growth.

Duke of Edinburgh HP (OGR), *dr*, 1868, *Général Jacqueminot × Seedling*; Paul. Flowers deep red, full, large; fragrant; vigorous, erect growth.

Duke of Normandy HT, *lp*, 1921, *St. Helena × George Dickson*; Jersey Nursery. Flowers silvery pink.

Duke of Paducah HT, *rb*, 1970, *Grand Gala × Josephine Bruce*; Williams, J.B. Bud ovoid; flowers dark velvety crimson, dbl., full, large; slightly fragrant; foliage large, glossy, dark, leathery; vigorous, bushy growth.

Duke of Teck HP (OGR), *dp*, 1880, *Duke of Edinburgh × Seedling*; Paul. Flowers deep pink, dbl. (40 petals), globular; fragrant; vigorous growth.

Duke of Wellington HP (OGR), *dr*, 1864, (Duc de Wellington); Granger. Flowers velvety crimson-red; full, cupped, large; very fragrant; vigorous growth.

Duke of Windsor HT, *ob*, 1969, (Herzog von Windsor); Tantau, Math. Bud pointed; flowers orange, dbl. (27 petals), well-formed, large; very fragrant; foliage dark, glossy; very vigorous, upright growth.   Edland Fragrance Medal, 1968; ADR, 1970.

Duke of York C (OGR), *pb*, 1894, Paul, W. Flowers rosy-pink and white to crimson, variable.

Dulcinea HT, *mr*, 1963, *Condesa de Sástago × Seedling*; Verschuren, A.; Stassen. Flowers oriental red, edged darker, reverse yellow, dbl. (50-55 petals), large; foliage dark, glossy; upright, bushy growth.

Dumbo F, *mr*, 1956, *Mme. G. Forest-Colcombet × Independence*; Combe. Flowers bright cherry-red, semi-dbl., very large; foliage dark; very vigorous growth.

Dumortier G (OGR), *pb*, Flowers light red with silvery reflex, very dbl., flat, medium.

Dundee HSpn (OGR), *w*, *R. spinosissima hybrid*; Austin, R., prior to 1832. Flowers white blotched pink, reverse pure white, dbl., cupped; moderate growth.

Dundee Rambler Ayr (OGR), *w*, *Thought to be R. arvensis × Noisette*; Martin, prior to 1837. Flowers white, compact, medium blooms in large clusters.

Dunkerque HT, *op*, 1940, *Charles P. Kilham × Seedling*; Laperrière. Bud pointed, ovoid; flowers bright pink, slightly coppery, dbl. (30 petals), very large; long, strong stems; fragrant; foliage clear olive-green; vigorous, upright, branching growth.   GM, Bagatelle, 1940.

Dunkirk HT, *mr*, 1947, Dickson, A. Flowers rose-red, dbl. (36 petals), large (4-5 in.); fragrant; foliage glossy.

Dunton Gold HT, *ob*, 1966, *Tzigane sport*; Dunton Nursery. Flowers deep golden yellow-orange and pink tipped, high-centered, large (6 in.); fragrant; foliage glossy; vigorous growth.

Duo F, *or*, 1955, *Peace × Seedling*; Gaujard. Flowers coppery orange, single, open, petals fringed, medium; fragrant; foliage dark; very vigorous growth.

Duplex Misc. OGR (OGR), *mp*, (*R. pomifera* duplex; Wolley-Dod's Rose); *Chance garden hybrid of R. pomifera × Unidentified garden rose*; Vibert, prior to 1838. Flowers clear pink, semi-dbl.; foliage downy, gray-green; heavy prickles.

Dupontii Misc. OGR (OGR), *w*, 1817, (*R. × dupontii* Déséglise, *R. moschata nivea* Lindley; *R. freudiana* (Graebner). Perhaps descended from *R. gallica × R. moschata* hybrid. Flowers white, larger than *R. moschata*. Perhaps identical with the Spanish Musk Rose of 1629.

Dupuy Jamain HP (OGR), *mr*, 1868, Jamain. Flowers cerise-red, dbl. (30 petals), well-formed; fragrant; vigorous growth.

Duquesa de Peñaranda HT, *ob*, 1931, *(Morning Blush)*; *Souv. de Claudius Pernet × Rosella (Dot, P.)*; Dot, P.; C-P. Bud pointed; flowers shades of orange, dbl. (35 petals), cupped, large; fragrant; foliage rich green, glossy; vigorous growth. GM, Portland, 1933.

Duquesa de Peñaranda, Climbing Cl HT, *ob*, 1940, Germain's.

Durban July F, *rb*, 1982, (KORdurban; Durbankor); Kordes, W. Flowers yellow, orange to red, semi-dbl., medium; foliage medium, medium green, semi-glossy.

Durham Pillar R, *mr*, 1958, *Chevy Chase × Seedling*; Risley. Bud globular; flowers rose-red, single, cupped, small, borne in clusters; slightly fragrant; foliage dark, leathery, glossy; moderate climbing or trailing growth; free, recurrent bloom.

Durham Prince Bishops HT, *op*, 1990, *Silver Jubilee × Doris Tysterman*; Thompson, R.; Battersby Roses, 1989. Flowers orange, flushed pink, full (26-40 petals), medium; fragrant; foliage large, dark green, glossy; bushy growth.

Dusky Maiden F, *dr*, 1947, *(Daily Mail Scented Rose × Étoile de Hollande) × Else Poulsen*; Le-Grice. Flowers deep crimson scarlet, single, large (3 in.) blooms in trusses; fragrant; foliage dark; vigorous growth. GM, NRS, 1948.

Dusky Red HT, *dr*, 1972, *Karl Herbst × Big Red*; Wyant. Flowers medium red, veined, dbl., high-centered, globular, large; very fragrant; foliage dark, leathery; vigorous, upright, bushy growth; intermittent bloom.

Düsterlohe R, *dp*, 1931, *Venusta Pendula × Miss C.E. van Rossem*; Kordes. Flowers rose-red,

single, large (3 in.); slightly fragrant; vigorous, climbing growth; non-recurrent bloom.

Dusty Pink F, *lp*, 1961, *Garnette × Garnette seedling*; Jelly; E.G. Hill Co. Bud ovoid, long, pointed; flowers light pink, dbl. (50-60 petals), high-centered, large (3-3½ in.); fragrant; vigorous, upright; greenhouse variety.

Dusty Rose Min, *m*, 1974, *Amy Vanderbilt × Cécile Brunner*; Morey; Pixie Treasures. Flowers reddish purple, dbl. (40-50 petals), high-centered, small (1½ in.); fragrant (spicy); foliage dark; upright growth.

Dutch Gold® HT, *my*, 1978, *Peer Gynt × Whisky Mac*; Wisbech Plant Co. Flowers golden yellow, dbl. (32-34 petals), large (6 in.); fragrant; foliage glossy, dark; vigorous.

Dutch Hedge HRg (S), *lp*, 1958, (*R. rugosa rubra × R. cinnamomea) × R. nitida*; Nyveldt. Flowers light pink, single, small; fruit orange-red; compact, upright growth.

Dutch Miss Min, *pb*, 1986, *Summer Spice × Seedling*; Bridges, Dennis, 1987. Flowers light pink veining to white base, fading slightly, dbl. (22 petals), high-centered, medium, borne singly; slight fragrance; foliage medium, dark green, glossy; straight, pointed, medium, tan prickles; upright, medium growth.

Dutch Provence C (OGR), *mp*, Prior to 1848. Flowers rose, globular, large, resembling 'Cabbage Rose', but blooms are larger.

Dwarfking Min, *mr*, 1957, (Dwarf King; Zwergkönig); *World's Fair × Tom Thumb*; Kordes; J&P. Flowers carmine, dbl. (25 petals), cupped, then flat, small blooms borne singly and in clusters; slightly fragrant; foliage glossy; compact (8-10 in.) growth.

Dynamite LCl, *dr*, 1992, (JACsat); *Seedling × Simpathie*; Warriner, William; Bear Creek Gardens. Flowers dark red, full (40 petals), large (10+ cms) blooms borne in small clusters; slight fragrance; foliage large, dark green, glossy, resistant to powdery mildew; some prickles; tall (150-185 cms), upright, spreading, arching growth.

Dynasty™ HT, *ob*, 1989, (JACyo); *Seedling × Seedling*; Warriner, William A.; Bear Creek Gardens, 1991. Bud pointed; flowers bright orange with yellow blending at petal base, aging to coral-pink, dbl. (30 petals), cupped, medium, borne in sprays of 1-5; no fragrance; foliage medium, medium green, semi-glossy; prickles hooked down slightly, red to yellow-green; upright, spreading, tall growth.

Eads F, *pb*, 1991, *(Seedling × Pinocchio) × Seedling*; Burks, Larry; Specialty Roses, 1991. Flowers pink and yellow, semi-dbl., medium blooms borne in small clusters; slight fragrance; foliage medium, medium green, semi-glossy; low, compact growth.

Eagle® HT, *dr*, 1984, (HAVeal); *Centurio* × *Red Planet*; Verschuren, Ted; H.A. Verschuren. Flowers dark red, dbl. (28 petals), cupped, large blooms in sprays of 3-5; moderate fragrance; foliage large, dark, semi-glossy; bushy, tall growth.

Eagle Wings® F, *m*, 1982, (LENsim); *Seedling* × *Picasso*; Lens, Louis. Flowers white, shaded lilac, single (5 petals), 2 in. blooms in clusters of 3-24; spicy fragrance; foliage very dark; hooked, brown prickles; bushy growth.

Earl Beatty HT, *dr*, 1923, *Hoosier Beauty* × *George Dickson*; Chaplin Bros. Flowers deep crimson, full, cupped, large; bushy growth.

Earl Godard Bentinck HT, *mr*, 1931, *Pharisaer* × *Covent Garden*; Buisman. Flowers red, base orange, dbl., large; slightly fragrant; very vigorous growth.

Earl Haig HT, *mr*, 1921, Dickson, A. Flowers brick-red, full, large; fragrant; few thorns; vigorous, bushy growth. GM, NRS, 1920.

Earl of Dufferin HP (OGR), *dr*, 1887, Dickson, A. Flowers velvety crimson, shaded chestnut-red, full (53 petals), globular, very large; fragrant; vigorous growth.

Earl of Eldon N (OGR), *ob*, 1872, Eldon-Coppin. Flowers coppery orange.

Earl of Warwick HT, *lp*, 1904, *Souv. de S.A. Prince* × *Mrs. W.J. Grant*; Paul, W. Flowers pale pinkish buff, reverse livid pink, dbl., large; fragrant.

Earldomensis S, *my*, 1934, *R. hugonis* × *R. sericea pteracantha*; Page. Flowers bright yellow; height 6 ft.

Early Bird F, *mp*, 1965, *Circus* × *Fritz Thiedemann*; Dickson, P.; A. Dickson. Flowers rose-opal, dbl., well formed, large (4 in.); fragrant; free growth.

Early Mist Min, *w*, 1971, de Yssel, Van; Warmerdam. Flowers cream, dbl. (25 petals), globular, medium (2 in.); slightly fragrant; foliage dull, light; vigorous growth.

Early Morn HT, *lp*, 1944, *(Dr. W. Van Fleet* × *Général Jacqueminot)* × *Break O'Day*; Brownell. Flowers shell-pink, dbl. (over 50 petals), high-centered, large; long stems; fragrant; foliage glossy; vigorous growth.

Earth Song Gr, *dp*, 1975, *Music Maker* × *Prairie Star*; Buck; Iowa State University. Bud long, pointed to urn-shaped; flowers Tyrian red to tyrian rose, dbl. (25-30 petals), cupped, large (4-4¹/₂ in.); fragrant; foliage glossy, dark, leathery; upright, bushy growth.

Earthquake™ Min, *rb*, 1983, (MORquake); *Golden Angel* × *Seedling*; Moore, R.S.; Moore Min. Roses, 1984. Flowers striped red and

yellow, reverse yellow, dbl. (40+ petals), small; no fragrance; foliage small, medium green, semi-glossy; upright, bushy.

Earthquake, Climbing Cl Min, *rb*, 1990, (MORshook); *Earthquake sport*; Moore, Ralph S.; Sequoia Nursery, 1991. Bud rounded; flowers red/yellow stripes, yellow reverse, aging similar, dbl. (40+ petals), urn-shaped, medium, borne usually singly or in sprays of 3-5; no fragrance; foliage small, medium green, semi-glossy; upright, tall growth.

Easlea's Golden Rambler LCl, *yb*, 1932, (Golden Rambler); Easlea; Totty. Flowers rich buff-yellow marked crimson, dbl. (35 petals), large (4 in.) blooms in clusters; fragrant; foliage leathery, rich olive-green; vigorous, climbing growth; non-recurrent bloom. GM, NRS, 1932.

East Anglia HT, *mp*, 1939, *Golden Dawn sport*; Morse. Flowers aurora-pink.

Easter Bonnet HT, *op*, 1982, (BURstein; Super Derby); *Queen Elizabeth sport*; Burks, Joe; Co-Operative Rose Growers, Inc. Same as parent except for medium salmon-pink color and shorter growth.

Easter Morning Min, *w*, 1960, (Easter Morn); *Golden Glow (Brownell)* × *Zee*; Moore, R.S.; Sequoia Nursery. Bud pointed; flowers ivory-white, dbl. (60-70 petals), small (1¹/₂ in.); foliage leathery, glossy; vigorous, dwarf (12-16 in.) growth.

Easter Parade F, *yb*, 1951, *Sunshine* × *Herrenhausen*; Whisler; Germain's. Bud ovoid, golden yellow; flowers salmon-pink and cerise, reverse yellow, becoming light carmine, dbl. (50-55 petals), large (2¹/₂-3¹/₂ in.); slightly fragrant; foliage dark, glossy, bronze; vigorous, bushy growth.

Easter Rose (Rubus coronarius, Rubus rosaefolius coronarius); Having rose-like foliage and very double white blooms, this plant is often mistaken for a rose. However, it is a blackberry relative and can be distinguished from a rose by its grooved or fluted stems.

Easy Min, *rb*, 1992, (ZIPeasy); *Pink Petticoat* × *Banana Split*; Zipper, Herbert; Magic Moment Miniatures. Flowers red and white, very full (41+ petals), small (0-4 cms) blooms borne in small clusters; no fragrance; foliage small, dark green, glossy; few prickles; medium (35 cms), bushy growth.

Ebb Tide HT, *ab*, 1961, *(Sutter's Gold* × *Seedling)* × *Peace*; Abrams, Von; Peterson & Dering. Bud long, pointed; flowers light yellowish pink, dbl. (28 petals), high-centered, large (5 in.); slightly fragrant; foliage glossy; vigorous, upright, compact growth.

Éblouissant Pol, *dr*, 1918, *Seedling* × *Cramoisi Superieur*; Turbat. Flowers dazzling deep red, very dbl., globular blooms in clusters; slightly fragrant; foliage bronze, glossy; bushy growth.

Ebony Gr, *dr*, 1960, *Carrousel* × *Charles Mallerin*; Abrams, Von; Peterson & Dering. Bud ovoid; flowers velvety dark red, dbl. (20-30 petals), high-centered to flat, large (3-4 in.); slightly fragrant; foliage glossy; vigorous, upright growth.

Éboracum LCl, *w*, 1977, *Casino* × *Ice White*; Powell. Flowers creamy white, base yellow, dbl. (30-35 petals), full, small (2½-3 in.); fragrant; foliage glossy; strong growth; repeated bloom.

Écarlate HT, *mr*, 1907, *Camoens* × *Seedling*; Boytard. Flowers brilliant scarlet, somewhat like Gruss anTeplitz, semi-dbl., open, small; scentless; foliage rich green, glossy; vigorous, bushy growth.

Echo HMult (OGR), *pb*, 1914, (Baby Tausendschön); *Tausendschön sport*; Lambert, P. Flowers varying (like Tausendschon) from dark pink to almost white, semi-dbl., cupped, large blooms in clusters; bushy growth.

Éclair HP (OGR), *dr*, 1883, *Général Jacqueminot* × *Seedling*; Lacharme. Flowers very dark red shaded blackish, dbl., well-shaped, small; fragrant; tall growth.

Eclipse HT, *ly*, 1935, *Joanna Hill* × *Federico Casas*; Nicolas; J&P. Bud remarkably long, pointed, deep gold, with long, narrow, branching sepals; flowers golden yellow, dbl. (28 petals), loose blooms; fragrant; foliage leathery, dark; vigorous, bushy growth. GM, Portland & Rome, 1935, Bagatelle, 1936; ARS David Fuerstenberg Prize, 1938.

Ecstasy HT, *yb*, 1935, Dickson, A. Flowers pale yellow shaded bronze and cerise, full; very fragrant; erect, branching growth.

Edda S, *mr*, 1969, *Lichterloh* × *Scharlachglut*; Lundstad. Flowers clear rose-red, semi-dbl. (16 petals), open, medium, borne in clusters; foliage dark, glossy, leathery; vigorous growth; profuse, recurrent bloom.

Eddie's Advent HT, *lp*, 1938, *Mrs. Sam McGredy* × *Edith Krause*; Eddie. Flowers pale buff, tipped pink, fading almost white, dbl., high-centered, large; slightly fragrant; foliage leathery; vigorous growth.

Eddie's Cream F, *w*, 1956, *Golden Rapture* × *Lavender Pinocchio*; Eddie; Harkness. Flowers cream, dbl., large, borne in clusters; fragrant (apricot); vigorous growth.

Eddie's Crimson HMoy (S), *mr*, 1956, *Donald Prior* × *R. moyesii hybrid*; Eddie. Flowers blood-red, semi-dbl., large (4-5 in.); fruit large, globular; vigorous (9-10 ft.) growth; non-recurrent bloom.

Eddie's Jewel HMoy (S), *mr*, 1962, *Donald Prior* × *R. moyesii hybrid*; Eddie. Flowers fiery red; bark red; few prickles; vigorous (8-9 ft.) growth; recurrent bloom.

Edel HT, *w*, 1919, *Frau Karl Druschki* × *Niphetos*; McGredy. Flowers ivory-white, passing to pure white, dbl., well formed, very large; fragrant; vigorous growth.

Eden Ellen F, *ab*, 1984, *Seedling* × *Seedling*; Schneider, Peter. Flowers apricot, dbl. (35 petals), medium; slight fragrance; foliage medium, medium green, matt; bushy growth.

Eden Rose® HT, *dp*, 1950, *Peace* × *Signora*; Meilland, F.; URS, 1950 & C-P, 1953. Bud ovoid; flowers tyrian rose, dbl. (50-60 petals), cupped, large (4½ in.); very fragrant; foliage glossy, bright dark green; vigorous, upright growth. GM, NRS, 1950.

Eden Rose, Climbing® Cl HT, *dp*, 1962, Meilland, Alain; URS.

Eden Sungold F, *my*, 1976, *Seedling* × *Seedling*; Herholdt, J.A. Flowers pure yellow, dbl. (30-35 petals), large (3 in.); slightly fragrant; semi-dwarf growth.

Edgar Andreu LCl, *mr*, 1912, *R. wichuraiana* × *Cramoisi Supérieur*; Barbier. Flowers bright blood-red, dbl., large, borne in clusters of 7-15; foliage dark, glossy.

Edgar M. Burnett HT, *pb*, 1914, McGredy. Flowers flesh-pink, center dark pink, dbl.; fragrant. GM, NRS, 1913.

Edina HT, *w*, 1934, Dobbie. Flowers white, occasionally flushed pink, well formed; very fragrant; foliage bronze red passing to green; vigorous growth.

Edith Bellenden E (OGR), *mp*, 1895, Penzance. Flowers pale rose, single; foliage fragrant; vigorous growth; very hardy.

Edith Cavell HT, *ly*, 1918, Chaplin Bros. Flowers pale lemon-white, dbl.

Edith Clark HT, *mr*, 1928, *Mme. Abel Chatenay* × *Seedling*; Clark, A.; Hackett. Flowers fiery red, dbl., globular; slightly fragrant; foliage rich green; dwarf growth.

Edith de Martinelli® F, *op*, 1958, *(Gruss an Teplitz* × *Independence)* × *Floradora*; Arles; Roses-France. Flowers salmon-pink, well-formed; vigorous. GM, Geneva, 1958.

Edith de Martinelli, Climbing® Cl F, *op*, 1983, (ORAdit); Orard, Joseph; Pekmez.

Edith Dennett F, *op*, 1973, Holmes, R.; Fryer's Nursery. Flowers salmon-pink, dbl. (24-30 petals), rosette form, large (2-3 in.); slightly fragrant; foliage glossy; free growth.

Edith Felberg HT, *w*, 1931, *Seedling* × *Souv. de H.A. Verschuren*; Felberg-Leclerc. Flowers cream, center slightly darker, rather dbl., cupped; foliage leathery.

Edith Hayward Cl HT, *lp*, 1967, *Fontanelle ×Gen. MacArthur*; Hayward. Flowers pastel pink, dbl., high-centered, large; fragrant; foliage glossy, dark; vigorous growth; recurrent bloom.

Edith Hazelrigg HT, *ob*, 1953, Cant, F. Flowers orange-cerise, dbl. (25 petals), pointed; fragrant; foliage dark; vigorous growth.

Edith Holden F, *r*, 1988, (CHEWlegacy; Edwardian Lady; The Edwardian Lady); *Belinda × ((Elizabeth of Glamis × (Galway Bay × Sutters Gold))*; Warner, C.H.; E.B. LeGrice Roses, Ltd., 1988. Flowers russet-brown with yellow center, reverse slightly paler, aging slate gray, semi-dbl. (15 petals), urn-shaped, medium, borne in sprays of 10-20; slight fragrance; foliage medium, medium green, glossy; prickles very few; fruit rounded, small, orange; upright, tall, robust growth.

Edith Krause HT, *w*, 1930, *Mrs. Charles Lamplough × Souv. de H.A. Verschuren*; Krause; J&P. Flowers greenish white, dbl. (30 petals), high-centered, large; fragrant; very vigorous growth.

Edith Mary Mee HT, *or*, 1936, Mee; Beckwith. Flowers vivid orient red, flushed orange, base yellow, full; fragrant; foliage dark, leathery; vigorous, bushy, compact growth.

Edith Nellie Perkins HT, *op*, 1928, Dickson, A. Flowers salmon-pink, flushed orange, reverse orange-red, shaded orange, dbl. (35-40 petals); fragrant; few prickles; vigorous, bushy growth.

Edith Nellie Perkins, Climbing Cl HT, *op*, 1936, H&S; Howard Rose Co.

Edith Oliver HT, *lp*, 1980, *Pink Parfait × Seedling*; Singleton, C.H. Flowers soft light pink, dbl. (35 petals), large blooms in clusters of 4; fragrant; foliage medium, medium green, semi-glossy; brownish-red prickles; bushy growth.

Edith Part HT, *pb*, 1913, McGredy. Flowers rich red, suffused deep salmon and coppery yellow; fragrant.

Edith Piaf HT, *m*, 1964, *Poinsettia × (Baccará × Seedling)*; Verbeek. Bud ovoid; flowers purple-red, dbl., large; slightly fragrant; foliage dark; a greenhouse variety.

Edith Roberts HT, *ab*, 1969, *Dorothy Peach* sport; Roberts, P.D. Flowers apricot, high-centered, large (5 in.); fragrant; foliage glossy, dark.

Edith Schurr S, *yb*, 1976, (*Wendy Cussons × Gavotte) × Leverkusen*; Stanard; Edmunds. Bud globular, sulfur-yellow; flowers light yellow, center pink, dbl. (60 petals), large (5 in.);

very fragrant (damask); foliage glossy; spreading growth; recurrent bloom.

Edith Willkie HT, *pb*, 1943, *Joanna Hill × R.M.S. Queen Mary*; Hill, J.H., Co., 1943; Wayside Gardens; H&S, 1946. Bud long, pointed; flowers livid pink, base lemon-chrome, dbl. (25-30 petals), large (4½-5 in.); slightly fragrant; foliage leathery, dark; vigorous, upright, compact growth.

Edith Yorke R, *lp*, 1953, *Havering Rambler × Seedling*; Miller, A.I.; Jackman. Flowers light almond-pink, semi-dbl., rosette form, borne in trusses; very fragrant; foliage light green; very vigorous growth.

Editor McFarland HT, *mp*, 1931, *Pharisaer × Lallita*; Mallerin; C-P. Flowers glowing pink, slightly suffused yellow, dbl. (30 petals), large; very fragrant; vigorous, bushy.

Editor McFarland, Climbing Cl HT, *mp*, 1948, Roseglen Nursery.

Editor Stewart HT, *mr*, 1939, Clark, A.; NRS Victoria. Flowers deep cherry-red, semi-dbl., open, large; long stem; foliage bronze; vigorous pillar or large bush.

Editor Tommy Cairns HT, *pb*, 1991, *Seedling × Seedling*; Winchel, Joseph F., 1992. Flowers bright pink, light pink reverse, full (26-40 petals), medium blooms borne mostly singly; slight fragrance; foliage medium, medium green, semi-glossy; upright, medium growth.

Edmond Proust LCl, *mr*, 1903, *R. wichuraiana × Souv. de Catherine Guillot*; Barbier. Flowers pale rose and carmine, very dbl., large, borne in clusters of 3-6 on short stems; fragrant; foliage glossy; height 5-8 ft.; sparse seasonal bloom.

Edmund M. Mills HT, *ob*, 1927, *Red Radiance × Padre*; Hieatt. Flowers rosy flame, base deep gold, semi-dbl., open, large; very fragrant; foliage dark, leathery; very vigorous, upright growth.

Edmund Rice HT, *dp*, 1992, (WELpin); *Red Lion × Pink Silk*; Welsh, Eric, 1989; Christian Bros. College, 1992. Bud classic HT form; flowers light red, non-fading, full (45-50 pointed, reflexed petals), exhibition, 5" blooms borne 5-7 per cluster and singly; good fragrance; foliage very red when young, dark green, shiny, leathery; bushy, upright (4') growth; repeats quickly.

Edna Kaye HT, *lp*, 1959, *Directeur Guerin × Mirandy*; Kemp, M.L. Flowers light pink tinted buff, dbl. (56 petals), large (5 in.); foliage bronze; free growth.

Edna Marie Min, *lp*, 1988, (MORed); *Pinocchio × Peachy White*; Moore, Ralph S.; Sequoia Nursery. Flowers very soft pink, soft yellow base, aging becomes near white, dbl. (20 petals), high-centered, exhibition, small, borne singly or in sprays of 3-5, abundant; slight, fruity fragrance; foliage small, light green, semi-glossy; prickles small, brown; upright, bushy, medium growth.

Edna Wilson HT, *my*, 1973, (GRIfed); *Beauté sport*; Griffiths, Trevor; T. Griffiths, Ltd. Flowers medium yellow, full, large; medium to strong fragrance; foliage glossy; upright, vigorous growth.

Edna-Chris F, *w*, 1977, *Gene Boerner sport*; Ogden. Bud pointed; flowers off-white, dbl. (30 petals), large (3½ in.); slightly fragrant; foliage matt, green; tall, upright growth.

Ednah Thomas Cl HT, *op*, 1931, (Bloomfield Improvement); *Seedling climber × Bloomfield Progress*; Thomas; H&S. Flowers salmon-rose, dbl., large, strong stems; fragrant; vigorous, climbing growth; recurrent bloom.

Edo Bergsma HT, *ly*, 1932, *Capt. F.S. Harvey-Cant × Étoile de Hollande*; Buisman. Bud pointed; flowers bright flesh and peach, large; very fragrant.

Edouard Mignot HT, *m*, 1927, Sauvageot; F. Gillot. Flowers purplish garnet-red, reverse amaranth, full; fragrant; bushy growth.

Edouard Renard HT, *mr*, 1933, Dot, P. Flowers carmine, base yellow; long, stiff stems.

Eduard Schill HT, *or*, 1931, *Charles P. Kilham × Mev. G.A. van Rossem*; Kordes. Flowers brick-red shaded nasturtium-yellow, semi-dbl., cupped, very large; slightly fragrant; foliage glossy; vigorous growth.

Eduardo Toda HT, *my*, 1947, *Ophelia × Julien Potin*; Dot, P. Bud pointed; flowers sunflower-yellow; slightly fragrant.

Edward Behrens HT, *dr*, 1921, *Richmond × Admiral Ward*; Kordes. Flowers very dark velvety crimson, full, very large; fragrant.

Edward Colston F, *dr*, 1990, (SANcol); *Vera Dalton × Stephen Langdon*; Sanday, John, 1982; John Sanday Roses, Ltd. Bud rounded; flowers dark red with medium red reverse, aging dark red, very dbl. (40-45 petals), cupped, medium blooms borne in sprays of 3-5; slight, fruity fragrance; foliage medium, medium green, matt; prickles barbed, red; no fruit; upright, medium growth.

Edward Mawley HT, *dr*, 1911, McGredy. Bud almost black; flowers dark crimson, semi-dbl. (18 petals), high-centered, large; fragrant; bushy growth. GM, NRS, 1910.

Edward Morren HP (OGR), *mr*, 1868, *Jules Margottin seedling*; Granger. Flowers deep cherry-rose, full, flat, large; vigorous growth.

Edward VII Pol, *mp*, 1911, *Mme. Norbert Levavasseur sport*; Low. Flowers clear pink, small.

Edwin Markham HT, *mp*, 1923, *Ophelia × Hoosier Beauty*; Clarke Bros. Flowers bright rose-pink suffused silvery; dbl.

Edwin T. Meredith HT, *ob*, 1979, *Futura × First Prize*; Warriner; J&P. Bud ovoid, pointed; flowers coral-pink, dbl. (30 petals), flat, large (5 in.); slightly fragrant; bushy, upright growth.

Effective LCl, *mr*, 1913, *Gen. MacArthur seedling × Paul's Carmine Pillar*; Hobbies. Bud long; flowers crimson, cupped; fragrant; very vigorous growth.

Effekt HT, *rb*, 1935, *I Zingari × Seedling*; Krause. Flowers scarlet-red, reverse flushed golden yellow, dbl., cupped, large; slightly fragrant; vigorous, bushy growth.

Egalité F, *m*, 1946, *Irene × Seedling*; Leenders, M.; Longley. Bud pointed; flowers pale lilac-rose, dbl. (25 petals), large (4 in.), borne in trusses; fragrant; foliage bronze; vigorous, branching growth.

Egeskov® F, *mp*, 1982, *Tornado × Matangi*; Olesen, M.&P.; D.T. Poulsen. Flowers bright medium pink, dbl. (20 petals), cupped, medium blooms in large clusters; slight fragrance; foliage medium, light green, glossy; bushy growth.

E. Godfrey Brown HT, *dr*, 1919, Dickson, H. Flowers deep reddish crimson, full; fragrant.

E. G. Hill HT, *mr*, 1929, *Parentage unknown*; Hill, E.G., Co. Bud ovoid; flowers dazzling scarlet, dbl., well formed, very large; very fragrant (damask); vigorous growth.

E. G. Hill, Climbing Cl HT, *mr*, 1942, Marlin.

Eglantine Pol, *dp*, 1930, *Amaury Fonseca × Rodhatte*; Soupert & Notting. Flowers carmine, center white, many yellow stamens; single, small; fragrant; vigorous, dwarf, bushy growth.

Egyptian Treasure S, *ob*, 1973, (*Coup de Foudre × S'Agaro*) × *Vagabonde*; Gandy. Flowers orange, semi-dbl. (16 petals), large (4 in.); slightly fragrant; foliage dark, glossy.

E. I. Farrington F, *mr*, 1953, *Queen o' the Lakes × Seedling*; Brownell. Flowers cardinal-red to blood-red, turning almost crimson, dbl. (50-60 petals), high-centered, large (3½ in.); fragrant; vigorous, spreading growth.

Eiffel Tower HT, *mp*, 1963, (Eiffelturm; Tour Eiffel); *First Love × Seedling*; Armstrong, D.L., & Swim; Armstrong Nursery. Bud long, urn-shaped; flowers medium pink, dbl. (35 petals), high-centered, large (3½-5 in.); very fragrant; foliage leathery, semi-glossy; vigorous, upright growth. GM, Geneva & Rome, 1963.

Eiffel Tower, Climbing Cl HT, *mp*, 1967, Laveena Roses.

Eiko HT, *yb*, 1978, *(Peace × Charleston) × Kagayaki*; Suzuki; Keisei Rose Nursery. Bud pointed; flowers yellow and scarlet, dbl. (30-35 petals), pointed, large (5-6 in.); slightly fragrant; foliage large, glossy, light green; vigorous growth.

Eileen Boxall HT, *dr*, 1948, *Betty Uprichard sport*; Boxall. Flowers cerise, semi-dbl. (18 petals), large (5 in.); fragrant; foliage dark; vigorous growth.

Eileen Dorothea HT, *mr*, 1931, Dickson, A. Bud pointed; flowers crimson-scarlet, edged darker, base yellow, dbl., high-centered; very fragrant; foliage deeply serrated; vigorous growth.

Eileen Louise HT, *mp*, 1985, *Admiral Rodney sport*; Brown, Harry G.L.S. Flowers medium pink.

Eisenach R, *mr*, 1910, Kiese. Flowers bright red, single, borne in clusters; very vigorous growth.

E. J. Baldwin HT, *my*, 1952, *Phyllis Gold × Seedling*; Robinson, H.; Baker's Nursery. Flowers rich golden yellow, dbl. (30-40 petals), high pointed; well formed, large; foliage dark; vigorous, upright, branching growth.

E. J. Ludding HT, *pb*, 1931, *Ophelia × Hill's America*; Van Rossem; Prior & C-P. Flowers carmine-pink shaded coral-red and salmon, dbl., open, large; slightly fragrant; bushy growth.

E. J. Moller HT, *dr*, 1924, *George Dickson seedling*; Moller. Flowers intense red, deepening toward black, full.

Ekta G (OGR), *mp*, 1927, *Alika × American Beauty*; Hansen, N.E. Flowers pink, single; non-recurrent bloom.

El Capitan Gr, *mr*, 1959, *Charlotte Armstrong × Floradora*; Swim; Armstrong Nursery. Flowers cherry to rose-red, dbl. (30 petals), high-centered, large (3½-4½ in.) blooms in small clusters; slightly fragrant; foliage dark, glossy; vigorous, upright, bushy growth. GM, Portland, 1959.

El Capitan, Climbing Cl Gr, *mr*, 1963, Armstrong, D.L.

El Catalá Gr, *rb*, 1981, *Wanderin' Wind × ((Dornroschen × Peace) × Brasilia)*; Buck; Iowa State University. Bud ovoid, pointed; flowers medium red, reverse light pink, dbl. (35 petals), slightly cupped blooms borne 1-8 per cluster; light fragrance; foliage large, glossy; awl-like prickles; erect, slightly bushy growth.

El Cid HT, *or*, 1969, *Fandango × Roundelay*; Armstrong, D.L.; Armstrong Nursery. Bud ovoid; flowers orange-red, dbl., high-centered to cupped, large; foliage soft; vigorous, upright, bushy growth. GM, Rome, 1969.

El Dorado HT, *yb*, 1972, *Manitou × Summer Sunshine*; Armstrong, D.L.; Armstrong Nursery. Flowers golden yellow, edged reddish, dbl., open, high-centered, large; very fragrant; foliage large, glossy, leathery; vigorous, upright growth.

El Paso HT, *yb*, 1988, *First Prize × Arlene Francis*; Ohlson, John. Flowers light yellow on outer petals, deep yellow on inner petals, reverse light yellow, dbl. (30 petals), high-centered, exhibition, medium, borne usually singly; slight, spicy fragrance; foliage medium, medium green, semi-glossy; prickles straight, medium, greenish-brown; bushy, medium, floriferous growth. 1988 ARC TG (B).

Elaina Min, *m*, 1991, (ZIPela); *Blue Nile × Big John*; Zipper, Herbert; Magic Moment Miniatures, 1992. Flowers mauve, full (26-40 petals), exhibition form, small (0-4 cms) blooms borne in small clusters; fragrant; foliage small, dark green, semi-glossy; few prickles; medium (35 cms), bushy growth.

Elaine HT, *mp*, 1950, *Mrs. A.R. Barraclough × Lady Sylvia*; Robinson, H.; Baker's Nursery. Flowers rose-pink, very dbl., high-centered, large; fragrant.

Elaine HT, *ab*, 1951, *Eclipse × R.M.S. Queen Mary*; Boerner; J&P. Bud pointed; flowers apricot, dbl. (35-45 petals), high-centered, large (4½ in.); slightly fragrant; foliage leathery; very vigorous, upright growth; a greenhouse cut flower.

Elaine Holman HT, *pb*, 1975, *Red Devil × Avon*; Watson. Bud long, pointed; flowers pink blend, dbl. (50 petals), high-centered, large (3½-4 in.); fragrant; foliage soft; vigorous growth.

Elaine Stuart HT, *w*, 1932, *Antoine Rivoire × Lillian Moore*; Edwards. Flowers cream, center yellow, long stems.

Elaine White F, *w*, 1959, *Gartendirektor Otto Linne × Seedling*; Riethmuller. Bud pointed; flowers cream, white and pink, semi-dbl., open, small, borne in clusters; fragrant; foliage leathery; very vigorous, upright growth.

Elaine's Choice F, *pb*, 1972, *Orange Sensation × Peace*; Ellick. Flowers pale pink-apricot, yellow blend, dbl. (40 petals), full, large (5 in.); very fragrant; foliage semi-glossy; vigorous growth.

Elation HT, *dy*, 1974, *Buccaneer × Seedling*; Warriner; Spek. Bud long, pointed; flowers deep yellow, dbl., large; slightly fragrant; foliage large, glossy, dark, leathery; vigorous, upright.

Elba HT, *dr*, 1963, *Confidence × Crimson Glory*; Moreira da Silva. Flowers deep red, reverse gold.

Eldora Harvey HT, *pb*, 1930, *Red Radiance × Maman Cochet*; Harvey. Flowers pink, center tinted lavender, reverse dark pink, dbl.; fragrant.

Eldorado HT, *ob*, 1923, *Seedling × Mme. Edouard Herriot*; H&S. Flowers copper, suffused orange and salmon, dbl., very large; fragrant; bushy growth.

Eleanor Min, *op*, 1960, *(R. wichuraiana × Floradora) × (Seedling × Zee)*; Moore, R.S.; Sequoia Nursery. Bud long, pointed; flowers coral-pink, aging darker, dbl. (20-30 petals), small (1 in.); foliage leathery, glossy; upright, bushy, 12 in. growth.

Eleanor Frances HT, *dy*, 1971, *Vienna Charm × Seedling*; Green Acres Rose Nursery. Flowers deep aureolin-yellow, dbl. (28 petals), full, large (5 in.); fragrant; foliage glossy, leathery; vigorous, tall, upright growth.

Eleanor Henning HT, *op*, 1920, Easlea. Bud pointed; flowers salmon-pink.

Eleanor Perenyi Gr, *yb*, 1985, *America × Sunsong*; French, Richard. Flowers yellow flushed apricot, reverse yellow flushed salmon, dbl. (25 petals), loose, wavy form, medium blooms borne singly and in sprays of 3-9; fruity fragrance; foliage medium, dark, semi-glossy; very few, hooked, small, red prickles; fruit small, globular, orange-red; medium, upright growth.

Electra HT, *my*, 1970, *Eclipse × Seedling*; Boerner; J&P. Flowers medium yellow, dbl., open, large; slightly fragrant; foliage large, glossy, leathery; vigorous, upright growth.

Electra R, *ly*, 1900, *R. multiflora × William Allen Richardson*; Veitch. Flowers yellow, fading white, dbl., globular; slightly fragrant; foliage rich green, glossy; very vigorous, climbing growth.

Electron® HT, *dp*, 1970, (Mullard Jubilee); *Paddy McGredy × Prima Ballerina*; McGredy, S., IV; McGredy. Flowers rose-pink, dbl. (32 petals), classic form, large (5 in.); very fragrant. GM, RNRS, 1969, The Hague, 1970, Belfast, 1972 & Portland, 1973; AARS, 1973

Elegance LCl, *my*, 1937, *Glenn Dale × (Mary Wallace × Miss Lolita Armour)*; Brownell. Flowers yellow, fading white at edges, dbl. (48 petals), large (6 in.); fragrant; foliage dark, glossy; vigorous growth.

Elégance HT, *pb*, 1955, Buyl Frères. Bud globular; flowers rose-copper, dbl., large; fra-

grant; foliage dark, leathery; moderate growth.

Elegans R, *w*, (Double White); *R. arvensis hybrid*. Flowers white, semi-dbl, borne in large clusters; very vigorous.

Elegant Beauty HT, *ly*, 1982, (KORgatum; Delicia®; Kordes' Rose Delicia); *New Day × Seedling*; Kordes, W. Flowers light yellow flushed pink, dbl. (20 petals), large; foliage large, dark, matt; upright bushy growth.

Elegant Pearl® Min, *w*, 1983, (INTergant); *Seedling × Nozomi*; Interplant. Flowers creamy white, dbl. (40+ petals), patio, medium blooms in large clusters; slight fragrance; foliage small, medium green, glossy; few, medium prickles; bushy growth.

Elégante HT, *ly*, 1918, Pernet-Ducher. Bud pointed; flowers creamy yellow, full, globular, large; branching growth.

Elégante, Climbing LCl, *w*, LeGrice. Bud long, slender; flowers white, center creamy yellow; foliage dull.

Eleghya Gr, *dr*, 1975, *Spectacular × Seedling*; Staikov, Prof. Dr. V.; Kalaydjiev and Chorbadjiiski. Flowers deep blackish-red, very dbl. (80 petals), cupped, medium blooms in clusters of 2-5; foliage dark; bushy growth.

Elegy HT, *or*, 1971, (MEIlucre; Arturo Toscanini); *((Happiness × Independence) × Sutter's Gold) × ((Happiness × Independence) × Suspense))*; Meilland. Flowers vermilion, dbl. (30 petals), globular, large (5½ in.); slightly fragrant; foliage semi-matt, dark; vigorous.

Elena Castello HT, *pb*, 1932, *Mme. Butterfly × Angèle Pernet*; Munné, B. Flowers apricot-yellow to rose, semi-dbl.; vigorous growth.

Eleta HT, *mp*, 1934, *Sensation × Seedling*; Dahlgren; Kemble-Smith Co. Bud pointed; flowers clear rose-pink, dbl. (65 petals), high-centered, large; vigorous growth.

Elettra HT, *op*, 1940, *Julien Potin × Sensation*; Aicardi, D.; Giacomasso. Flowers copper-pink suffused reddish yellow, dbl., high-centered, large; fragrant; foliage leathery; very vigorous growth.

Elfe F, *w*, 1951, *Swantje × Hamburg*; Tantau. Bud pointed; flowers white tinted rose, shell shaped (5 large and 5 small petals), large, borne in clusters to 25; very fragrant; foliage glossy, dark; vigorous, upright, bushy growth. RULED EXTINCT 4/85.

Elfe® HT, *lp*, 1985, (TANelfe); Tantau, M., 1972. Flowers light pink, dbl. (20 petals), medium; slight fragrance; foliage medium, medium green, matt; upright growth.

Elfe Supreme F, *mp*, *Rosenelfe sport*. Flowers rose-pink.

Elfenreigen HMacrantha (S), *dp*, 1939, *Daisy Hill* × *Seedling*; Krause. Flowers deep rose-pink, center brighter, single, petals shell shaped; large umbel; foliage reddish orange, later gray-green; very vigorous (5 ft.); profuse, non-recurrent bloom.

Elfin F, *or*, 1939, Archer. Flowers cherry-rose shaded orange-salmon, dbl., large (4½ in.), borne in clusters; low growing.   RULED EXTINCT 12/85.

Elfin Charm Min, *pb*, 1974, *(R. wichuraiana* × *Floradora)* × *Fiesta Gold*; Moore, R.S.; Sequoia Nursery. Bud short, pointed; flowers phlox-pink, dbl. (65 petals), small (1 in.); fragrant; foliage small, glossy, leathery; bushy, compact growth.

Elfinesque Min, *op*, 1974, *Little Darling seedling* × *Yellow Bantam*; Morey; Pixie Treasures, 1973. Bud pointed; flowers coral-orange to bright pink, semi-dbl., small; slightly fragrant; foliage small, glossy, leathery; vigorous, dwarf, upright, bushy growth.

Elfinglo Min, *m*, 1977, *Little Chief* × *Little Chief*; Williams, E.D.; Mini-Roses. Bud ovoid; flowers red-purple, dbl. (25-40 petals), cupped to flat, small (½ in.); fragrant; foliage small, glossy; compact.

Eliane HT, *ab*, 1954, *Mme. Joseph Perraud* × *R. foetida bicolor hybrid*; Gaujard; Gandy, 1959. Flowers bright salmon, well formed, large; fragrant; foliage dark; vigorous growth.

Elida HT, *or*, 1966, Tantau, Math. Flowers vermilion, dbl. (30 petals), high-centered, large; fragrant; foliage dark, glossy; vigorous, branching growth.

Elie Beauvillain Cl T (OGR), *mp*, 1887, *Gloire de Dijon* × *Ophirie*; Beauvillain. Flowers coppery pink, full, large; vigorous growth.

Elina® HT, *ly*, 1984, (DICjana; Peaudouce); *Nana Mouskouri* × *Lolita*; Dickson, P., 1983. Flowers pale yellow to ivory, dbl. (35 petals), large; slight fragrance; foliage large, dark, glossy; vigorous, tall growth.   ADR, 1987; GM, NZ (Gold Star), 1987.

Elisa® HT, *mp*, 1981, *Seedling* × *Blessings*; Barni-Pistoia, Rose. Flowers medium pink, dbl. (40 petals), cupped, large; no fragrance; foliage large, light green, matt; upright growth.

Elisa Boëlle HP (OGR), *w*, 1869, (Elise Boelle); Guillot Père. Flowers white, tinted with rose; vigorous.

Elisa Robichon R, *mp*, 1901, *R. wichuraiana* × *L'Ideal*; Barbier. Flowers salmon-pink, fading pinkish buff, semi-dbl., open, large, borne in clusters on short, strong stems; slightly fragrant; vigorous, climbing (10 ft.), or trailing growth.

Elisa Rovella G (OGR), *mp*, Flowers rosy pink, dbl., medium; tall growth.

Elisa Sauvage T (OGR), *yb*, Miellez. Flowers orange to yellow, sometimes yellow to white.

Elisabeth Didden HT, *mr*, 1918, *Mme. Caroline Testout* × *Gen. MacArthur*; Leenders, M. Flowers glowing carmine-red and scarlet, semi-dbl.; fragrant.

Elisabeth Faurax HT, *w*, 1937, *Caledonia* × *Mme. Jules Bouche*; Meilland, F. Bud pointed; flowers white, lightly shaded ivory, very dbl., large, long stems; upright growth.

Elise HT, *w*, 1969, *Prima Ballerina sport*; Edmunds. Bud long, pointed; flowers white, dbl., high centered, large; fragrant; foliage dark, leathery; vigorous, tall growth.

Elise Noelle LCl, *mr*, 1991, *Dublin Bay* × *Burgund*; Alde, Robert O. Flowers medium red, moderately full (15-25 petals), medium (4-7 cms) blooms borne in small clusters; slight fragrance; foliage medium, medium green, semi-glossy; climbing (300 cms) growth.

Eliska Krásnohorská HP (OGR), *mp*, 1932, *Capt. Hayward* × *Una Wallace*; Böhm. Flowers brilliant pink, semi-dbl., high-centered, large; fragrant; foliage soft, bronze; bushy growth.

Elite HT, *yb*, 1936, *Charles P. Kilham* × *Pres. Herbert Hoover*; Tantau; J&P, 1941. Bud pointed, red; flowers salmon-pink and yellow blend, dbl., high-centered, very large; foliage leathery, light; upright growth.

Eliza S, *mp*, 1961, *R. laxa hybrid*; Skinner. Flowers clear pale rose, borne in clusters; foliage dark, glossy; bushy, erect (3 ft.) growth; non-recurrent bloom.

Eliza Balcombe HP (OGR), *pb*, 1842, Laffay. Flowers pale flesh; foliage gray-green.

Elizabeth Pol, *mp*, 1937, Letts. Flowers rich salmon, semi-dbl., borne in large clusters.

Elizabeth Abler Min, *mr*, 1991, (TINabler); *(Christian Dior* × *Brian Lee)* × *Seedling*; Bennett, Dee; Tiny Petals Nursery, 1992. Flowers medium red, opening to paler red at center, semi-dbl. (6-14 petals), HT form, micro-mini, small (0-4 cms) blooms borne mostly singly; fragrant; foliage small, medium green, semi-glossy; no prickles; low (20-30 cms), bushy, compact growth.

Elizabeth Arden HT, *w*, 1929, *Edith Part* × *Mrs. Herbert Stevens*; Prince. Flowers pure white, full; very fragrant.   GM, NRS, 1929.

Elizabeth Cone HT, *lp*, 1954, *Picture sport*; Cone; Roger. Flowers flesh-pink, well shaped; vigorous, low growth.

Elizabeth Cullen HT, *mr*, 1921, Dickson, A. Flowers rich scarlet-crimson, semi-dbl.; very fragrant.   GM, NRS, 1917.

Elizabeth Hamlin R, *pb*, 1987, *Seedling × Seedling*; Nobbs, Kenneth J., 1986. Flowers blush pink, fading to white, single (5 petals), cupped, small, borne in mass clusters of up to 62; very slight fragrance; foliage pennate, 5-7 leaflets, medium; few prickles; rampant growth.

Elizabeth Harbour HT, *pb*, 1985, (HABone); *Elizabeth of Glamis × Unnamed dark red HT seedling*; Harbour, E.R. Bud pointed; flowers light pink, dark pink reverse, dbl. (30 petals), well-formed, large (3 in.) blooms borne singly; slightly fragrant; foliage medium, medium green, semi-glossy; upright (3 ft.), bushy growth.

Elizabeth Harkness® HT, *ly*, 1969, *Red Dandy × Piccadilly*; Harkness. Flowers off-white to creamy buff, often with pastel yellow and pink tones, dbl. (28 petals), large; fragrant; foliage dark; upright, bushy growth.

Elizabeth Harkness, Climbing® Cl HT, *w*, 1975, Harkness.

Elizabeth Hassefras Pol, *mp*, 1951, B&A. Flowers buttercup form, glistening rose-pink with many stamens.

Elizabeth Lee HT, *dr*, 1935, Chaplin Bros. Flowers dark velvety red, well shaped; fragrant.

Elizabeth of Glamis® F, *op*, 1964, (MACel; Irish Beauty); *Spartan × Highlight*; McGredy, S., IV; McGredy, 1964; Edmunds, 1965. Flowers light orange-salmon, dbl. (35 petals), flat, large (4 in.) blooms in clusters; very fragrant; vigorous, compact bushy growth. GM, NRS, 1963; NRS PIT, 1963.

Elizabeth of York HT, *dp*, 1928, Dobbie. Bud large, pointed, cerise; flowers cerise-pink, dbl. (27 petals), high-centered; very fragrant; foliage dark, glossy; few thorns.

Elizabeth Philp F, *ab*, 1976, *Liverpool Echo sport*; Philp, J.B. & Son. Flowers creamy peach.

Elizabeth Rowe M (OGR), *dp*, Bud large, well mossed, deep pink.

Elizabeth Scholtz™ Gr, *yb*, 1988, (WILscso); *(Granada × Oregold) × (Arizona × Sunblest)*; Williams, J. Benjamin. Flowers deep yellow with orange washing, reverse yellow with orange streaking, aging yellow-orange blend, dbl. (26-40 petals), exhibition, medium; damask fragrance; foliage large, plum-red to dark green, glossy; upright, bushy growth.

Elizabeth Taylor HT, *dp*, 1985, *First Prize × Swarthmore*; Weddle, Von C. Flowers deep pink, dbl. (35 petals), high-centered, exhibition, medium blooms borne usually singly; fragrant; foliage large, dark, semi-glossy; upright growth.

Elizabeth W. Adam HT, *dp*, 1926, Adam & Craigmile. Flowers pink veined crimson, base yellow, dbl. (50 petals).

Elizabeth Zeigler R, *dp*, 1917, *Dorothy Perkins sport*; Pierson, A.N. Flowers deep rose-pink.

Elka Gaarlandt Pol, *dp*, 1966, *Hobby × Kathleen Ferrier*; Buisman. Bud ovoid; flowers dark pink, dbl., medium, borne in large clusters; foliage dark.

Ella Guthrie HT, *mp*, 1937, *Premier × Seedling*; Clark, A.; NRS Victoria. Flowers pink, full, large; very fragrant; vigorous growth.

Ella McClatchy R, *mp*, 1926, Diener. Flowers rose, single, borne in clusters; thornless; sometimes recurrent bloom.

Ella Scott R, *dp*, 1925, *Orléans Rose × Chance seedling*; Scott, G.J.; Brundrett; NRS Victoria. Flowers deep rose-pink, approaching red, dbl., borne in clusters of 15-20; few thorns; vigorous, climbing growth.

Ellamae™ Min, *ab*, 1986, (SAVamae); *Zorina × (Sheri Anne × Glenfiddich)*; Saville, F. Harmon; Nor'East Min. Roses. Flowers apricot, dbl. (35 petals), high-centered, exhibition, medium blooms borne singly and in sprays of 3-5; fragrant; foliage medium, dark, glossy; long, thin prickles; medium, upright, bushy growth.

Elle S, *dp*, 1980, *Schneezwerg × Splendens*; Lundstad, Arne; Agricultural University of Norway. Bud pointed; flowers deep pink, semi-dbl. (16 petals), borne 3-5 per cluster; very fragrant; foliage light green, 5-7 leaflets; curved gray prickles; vigorous, upright dense growth; non-recurrent.

Ellen HT, *dp*, 1929, *Premier sport*; Hinner, P.; Gould. Bud pointed; flowers unvarying dark pink, very dbl., large; very fragrant; bushy growth. RULED EXTINCT 12/85.

Ellen® S, *ab*, 1985, (AUScup); Austin, David, 1984. Flowers apricot, dbl. (40+ petals), old rose form, large; very fragrant; foliage large, medium green, semi-glossy; bushy growth.

Ellen Griffin Min, *lp*, 1988, *Uwe Seeler × Party Girl*; Hefner, John; Kimbrew-Walter Roses, 1988. Flowers light pink, dbl. (15-25 petals), medium; slight fragrance; foliage medium, medium green, semi-glossy; upright, bushy growth.

Ellen Mary HT, *dr*, 1963, *Wellworth × Independence*; LeGrice. Flowers dark red, dbl. (34 petals), well-formed, large (5 in.); fragrant; vigorous, upright growth.

Ellen Poulsen Pol, *mp*, 1911, *Mme. Norbert Levavasseur × Dorothy Perkins*; Poulsen, D.; Teschendorff. Flowers bright cherry-pink, dbl., large blooms in clusters; fragrant; foliage glossy, dark; bushy growth; recurrent bloom; (14).

Ellen Poulsen Mork Pol, *dr*, 1928, *Ellen Poulsen sport*; Poulsen, S. Flowers dark red.

Ellen Terry HT, *ly*, 1925, Chaplin Bros. Flowers soft sulphurry cream, outer petals soft peach, well shaped, high pointed; fragrant; upright, vigorous growth.

Ellen Willmott HT, *yb*, 1936, *Dainty Bess × Lady Hillingdon*; Archer. Flowers creamy lemon, flushed rosy pink, single, large; foliage leathery, dark; vigorous, upright growth.

Ellen Willmott HT, *lp*, 1898, Bernaix, A. Flowers silvery flesh to shell-pink, dbl., cupped; very vigorous growth.

Ellen Zinnow HT, *my*, 1930, *Souv. de H.A. Verschuren × Sunstar*; Krause. Flowers yellow, shaded coppery orange and pink, dbl.; fragrant.

Ellen's Joy S, *lp*, 1989, *Vera Dalton × (Dornroschen × (Tickled Pink × Applejack))*; Buck, Dr. Griffith J.; Kimbrew-Walter Roses & Historical Roses, 1991. Bud ovoid; flowers light shell pink, aging lighter, dbl. (23 petals), cupped, medium, borne singly and in sprays of 5-8; fruity fragrance; foliage medium, medium green, semi-glossy; prickles awl-like, rusty-green; fruit globular, orange-red; upright, bushy, spreading, medium, winter hardy growth; repeats.

Ellesmere HT, *w*, 1927, *Ophelia seedling*; Allen. Flowers ivory-white to pure white; fragrant; few thorns.

Elli Hartmann HT, *my*, 1913, *(Souv. du Prés. Carnot × Mme. Mélanie Soupert) × Maréchal Niel*; Welter. Flowers yellowish old-gold, dbl.; fragrant.

Elli Knab HT, *pb*, 1934, *Cathrine Kordes × W.E. Chaplin*; Kordes. Flowers flesh-cream flushed bright rose, veined vermilion, dbl., high-centered, very large; slightly fragrant; foliage leathery; upright, very vigorous growth.

Elli Knab, Climbing Cl HT, *pb*, 1953, Tantau.

Ellinor LeGrice HT, *my*, 1949, *Mrs. Beatty × Yellowcrest*; LeGrice. Bud ovoid; flowers yellow, dbl. (50 petals), cupped, large (5-5½ in.); fragrant (fruity); foliage leathery, glossy, dark; vigorous, upright growth.

Ellinor LeGrice, Climbing Cl HT, *my*, 1959, LeGrice.

Ellis Wood F, *yb*, 1983, *Arthur Bell sport*; Gateshead Metro. Borough Council. Flowers yellow blend, moderately full, medium; foliage medium, medium green, semi-glossy; growth to 75 cms.

Elmhurst HT, *pb*, 1985, *Granada × Helmut Schmidt*; Perry, Astor; Perry Roses. Flowers pink blend, dbl. (35 petals), exhibition, large; fragrant; foliage medium, medium green, matt; upright growth.

Elmira HRg (S), *mr*, 1977, *Schneezwerg × Old Blush*; Svejda; Canada Dept. of Agric. Bud ovoid; flowers bright red, dbl. (25 petals), open, medium (1½-2 in.); very fragrant; foliage yellow-green; upright, bushy growth.

Elmshorn S, *dp*, 1951, *Hamburg × Verdun*; Kordes; Morse. Flowers deep pink, dbl. (20 petals), cupped, pompom type, small (1 in.) blooms in large trusses (to 40); slightly fragrant; foliage glossy, wrinkled, light green; recurrent bloom; (21). ADR, 1950.

Elnar Tonning HT, *dp*, 1926, *Ophelia sport*; Gyllin. Flowers fuller and darker.

Eloira HT, *my*, 1981, (VARiora); *Elvira × Seedling*; van Veen, Jan; G. Verbeek. Flowers medium yellow, dbl. (35 petals), large; no fragrance; foliage medium, medium green, semi-glossy; upright growth.

Eloquence F, *m*, 1986, (JACsil; Little Silver); *(Merci × Fabergé) × Angel Face*; Warriner; J&P. Flowers lavender, dbl. (20 petals), flat, miniflora, small blooms borne singly and in clusters of 3-5; slight, spicy fragrance; foliage medium, medium green, matt; upright, bushy growth; greenhouse variety.

Elsa Arnot HT, *pb*, 1960, *Ena Harkness × Peace*; Arnot; Croll. Flower golden yellow shaded pink and cerise, dbl. (32 petals), large (4 in.); very fragrant; foliage glossy; vigorous, upright growth. GM, NRS, 1959.

Elsa Knoll HT, *op*, 1966, *First Love × Castanet*; Morey; Country Gardens Nursery. Flowers shrimp-pink, dbl. (30 petals), high-centered, large; very fragrant; foliage dark, glossy, leathery; vigorous, upright growth.

Elsbeth F, *lp*, 1962, *Valeta sport*; deRuiter. Flowers soft pink, dbl., borne in clusters; foliage dark; a forcing variety.

Else Chaplin Pol, *dp*, 1937, Chaplin Bros. Flowers deep rich pink, semi-dbl., borne in large trusses; vigorous growth.

Else Kreis Pol, *dp*, 1913, Kreis. Flowers shining deep pink.

Else Poulsen F, *mp*, 1924, (Joan Anderson); *Orléans Rose × Red Star*; Poulsen, S. Flowers bright rose-pink, 10 petals, medium (2 in.) blooms in clusters; slightly fragrant; foliage dark, bronze, glossy; vigorous, bushy growth; (21).

Else Poulsen, Climbing Cl F, *mp*, 1932, Ley.

Else Poulsen Meldugsfri F, *mp*, 1937, *Else Poulsen sport*; Poulsen, S.; Poulsen's Roses. Same as parent except disease (mildew) free.

Else Poulsen Morkrod F, *dr*, 1934, *Else Poulsen sport*; Poulsen, S. Flowers dark red.

Else's Rival F, *mr*, 1938, (Double Else Poulsen); *Else Poulsen sport*; Boer Bros. Flowers carmine red, more dbl.; healthier growth; (21)

Elsie LCl, *lp*, 1934, Chaplin Bros. Flowers soft pink, single; foliage dark, glossy; very vigorous growth.

Elsie Allen HT, *lp*, 1971, *Montezuma sport*; Allen, L.C.; E.T. Welsh. Flowers pale pink, dbl., high-centered, medium; slightly fragrant; vigorous, bushy growth.

Elsie Beckwith HT, *mp*, 1922, *Ophelia seedling × Mev. Dora van Tets*; Beckwith. Flowers rich rosy pink, center deeper, full, high-centered, large; very fragrant; foliage dark, shaded red, leathery; upright growth.

Elsie Boldick Min, *mr*, 1978, *Fairy Moss × Fairy Moss*; Dobbs, A.; Small World Min. Roses. Bud ovoid, mossy; flowers medium red, single, borne 1-5 per cluster; no fragrance; foliage small, soft; height 15 in.

Elsie Devy F, *m*, 1967, *Ma Perkins × Detroiter*; Fankhauser. Bud ovoid; flowers soft lavender-pink, reverse mauve-pink, dbl., high-centered; slightly fragrant; foliage light green, leathery; very vigorous, upright, bushy growth.

Elsie Melton HT, *pb*, 1991, *Pristine × King of Hearts*; Wambach, Alex A.; Alex A. Wambach, 1990. Bud pointed; flowers pink blend, dbl., high-centered, large blooms borne usually singly; fruity fragrance; foliage large, dark green, semi-glossy; upright, tall growth.

Elsie Warren F, *ab*, 1989, (MILsweet); *Arthur Bell × Arthur Bell*; Milner, William; Battersby Roses, 1990. Flowers apricot with lemon yellow eye, dbl. (15-25 petals), medium; fragrant; foliage large, medium green, semi-glossy; upright growth.

Elsie Wright F, *dr*, 1982, *Crimson Glory × Crimson Glory*; Cattermole, R.F. Bud long, pointed; flowers dark red, 15 petals, large blooms borne usually singly, sometimes 3 per cluster; strong damask fragrance; foliage medium, medium green, glossy; light brown prickles; upright growth.

Elsiemae Min, *op*, 1986, *Anne Scranton × Patricia Scranton*; Dobbs, Annette; Port Stockton Nursery. Flowers light coral pink, dbl. (25 petals), exhibition, medium blooms in sprays of 2-4; slight fragrance; foliage medium, medium green, semi-glossy; very few straight, light brown prickles; tall, bushy growth.

Elsinore F, *mr*, 1957, (Helsingör); *Floradora × Pinocchio*; Lindquist; Poulsen. Flowers bright scarlet, semi-dbl., borne in large, open clusters. Similar to Moulin Rouge. GM, NRS, 1957.

Elveshörn® S, *mp*, 1985, (KORbotaf); *The Fairy × Seedling*; Kordes, W. Flowers medium pink, dbl. (35 petals), medium; slight fragrance; foliage medium, dark, semi-glossy; bushy, spreading growth.

Elvira HT, *ab*, 1978, (VARelvi); *Zorina × Dr. A. J. Verhage*; van Veen, Jan; G. Verbeek. Flowers apricot, dbl. (35 petals), large; no fragrance; foliage medium, medium green, semi-glossy; upright growth.

Elvira E (OGR), *lp*, Flowers flesh, semi-dbl., medium; vigorous growth.

Elvira Aramayo HT, *mr*, 1922, *Feu Joseph Looymans × (Leslie Holland × Rayon d'Or)*; Looymans. Flowers indian red, dbl.; bushy growth. GM, Bagatelle, 1922.

Elvira Aramayo, Climbing Cl HT, *mr*, 1933, Ingegnoli.

Elvire Popesco HT, *my*, 1949, *Comtesse Vandal × Seedling*; Gaujard. Bud long, pointed; flowers golden yellow, dbl. (25 petals), large; fragrant; foliage bronze; very vigorous, upright growth.

Elvis Min, *mr*, 1978, *Judy Fischer × Seedling*; Wells, V.W., Jr. Bud pointed; flowers medium red, base white, dbl. (65 petals), high-centered, small (1 in.); slightly fragrant; foliage dark; vigorous growth.

Elysium® F, *mp*, 1961, (KORumelst); Kordes, R. Bud pointed; flowers salmon-pink, dbl. (35 petals), well-formed, cupped, large; fragrant; foliage glossy; vigorous, tall, growth.

Emaline Rouge HT, *dr*, 1938, *Better Times sport*; Hofmann. Flowers deep red.

Emanuel® S, *ab*, 1992, (AUSuel; Emmanuelle); *(Chaucer × Parade) × (Seedling × Iceberg)*; Austin, David; David Austin Roses, 1985. Flowers apricot pink, flat, opening rosette, very full (100+ petals), large (7+ cms) blooms borne in small clusters; very fragrant; foliage small, medium green, semi-glossy; some prickles; medium (110 cms), bushy growth.

Embajador Lequerica HT, *pb*, 1962, La Florida. Bud pointed; flowers strawberry-pink, reverse indian yellow at base passing to brick-red at edge, dbl. (30 petals); vigorous growth.

Embassy HT, *yb*, 1967, *Gavotte × (Magenta × Golden Scepter)*; Sanday. Flowers light gold veined and edged carmine, dbl., pointed, large; fragrant; foliage glossy.

Embassy Regal HT, *pb*, 1976, *(Gavotte × Ethel Sanday) × (Crimson Glory × Seedling)*; Sanday. Flowers cream overlaid peach-pink, dbl. (30 petals), large (5 in.); fragrant.

Emberglow HT, *mp*, 1935, *Souvenir sport*; Grillo. Flowers rich salmon-pink, dbl. (50 petals), large (5 in.), long stems; foliage leathery; vigorous growth.

Embers F, *mr*, 1953, *World's Fair* × *Floradora*; Swim; Armstrong Nursery. Bud ovoid; flowers scarlet, dbl. (19-25 petals), high-centered to cupped, large (2½-3 in.) blooms in clusters; fragrant (spicy); foliage dark, semiglossy; vigorous, bushy, compact growth.

Emblem™ HT, *my*, 1981, (JACblem); *Seedling* × *Sunshine*; Warriner; J&P. Flowers medium yellow, dbl. (25 petals), high-centered blooms borne singly; very little fragrance; foliage glossy, dark; straight, long, light green prickles; upright growth.

Embrace Pol, *lp*, 1972, *Seventeen* × *Jack Frost*; Byrum; J.H. Hill Co. Flowers light pink, very dbl., high-centered, medium; slightly fragrant; foliage leathery; vigorous, upright, bushy growth.

Embrasement F, *mr*, 1956, (CHAgip); Delbard-Chabert. Flowers fiery red, dbl., in clusters of 8-12; foliage bronze; vigorous.

Emerald Dream F, *w*, 1976, *Pinafore* × *Ivory Fashion*; Williams, J.B.; Lakeland Nursery Sales. Bud pointed, light to apple green; flowers white, center green, to ivory, semidbl. (12 petals), flat to loose cup, small (1½-2 in.); slightly fragrant (fruity); foliage dull, very dark, leathery; low, compact growth.

Emeraude d'Or HT, *yb*, 1965, *Sultane* × *Queen Elizabeth*; Delbard-Chabert; Cuthbert. Flowers yellow suffused carmine-pink, petals serrated, large (5 in.); vigorous growth.

Emil Kruisius F, *my*, 1943, *Golden Rapture* × *(Johanna Tantau* × *Eugenie Lamesch)*; Tantau. Bud long, pointed; flowers yellow, dbl. (25-30 petals), large, borne in clusters; slightly fragrant; foliage glossy, light green; vigorous, bushy growth.

Emile Charles HT, *or*, 1922, *Mme. Edouard Herriot sport*; Bernaix, P. Flowers coral-red.

Emile Cramon HT, *or*, 1937, Chambard, C. Bud pointed; flowers coppery carmine, stamens chrome-yellow, very large; foliage dull green; very vigorous growth.

Emile Fortépaule R, *w*, 1902, *R. wichuraiana* × *Souv. de Catherine Guillot*; Barbier. Flowers white, flushed salmon, dbl., borne in large clusters; foliage dark; vigorous growth.

Emile Hausburg HP (OGR), *m*, 1868, Lévêque. Flowers lilac-rose, full, large.

Emile J. Le Duc HT, *mr*, 1931, *Scott's Columbia sport*; Le Duc. Flowers scarlet-crimson, larger and stronger than the parent.

Emilie M (OGR), *w*, Prior to 1906. Flowers white.

Emily HT, *lp*, 1949, *Mme. Butterfly* × *Mrs. Henry Bowles*; Baines; F. Cant. Flowers soft rose pink, dbl. (40 petals), large (5-6 in.); fragrant; foliage dark; vigorous, upright.

Emily Dodd HT, *w*, 1927, Dickson, A. Flowers milk-white, center cream, full, large; slightly fragrant.

Emily Gray LCl, *dy*, 1918, *Jersey Beauty* × *Comtesse du Cayla*; Williams, A.H.; B.R. Cant. Flowers deep golden buff, stamens yellow, dbl. (25 petals), blooms in clusters; fragrant; foliage very glossy, dark, bronze; vigorous, climbing growth; not very free bloom. GM, NRS, 1916.

Emily Hough HT, *lp*, 1991, (HOUemily); *Touch of Class sport*; Hough, Robin, 1993. Flowers white, blushing pink toward center, more pink in cooler weather, moderately full (15-25 petals), form similar to Touch of Class but not as consistent in exhibition quality, large (7+ cms) blooms borne mostly singly; slight fragrance; foliage large, medium green, semi-glossy; some prickles; medium, upright growth.

Emily Post HT, *mp*, 1974, (Omega); *Eternal Sun* × *Carina*; Byrum; J.H. Hill Co. Flowers medium pink, dbl. (48 petals), high-centered, large (3½-4 in.); fragrant; upright, bushy growth.

Emily Rhodes LCl, *mp*, 1937, *Golden Ophelia* × *Zephirine Drouhin*; Clark, A.; NRS Victoria. Flowers pink, dbl., cupped, large; fragrant; vigorous, climbing or pillar growth.

Éminence® HT, *m*, 1962, (GAxence); *Peace* × *(Viola* × *Seedling)*; Gaujard; Ilgenfritz Nursery, 1965. Flowers lavender, dbl. (40 petals), large; very fragrant; foliage leathery, light green; vigorous, upright growth.

Emir HT, *rb*, 1960, *Seedling* × *Peace*; Verbeek. Flowers yellow with orange-red, dbl. (45 petals), very large (6 in.); foliage glossy; free growth.

Emjay Skiba Min, *mp*, 1989, *Sonia* × *Pink Petticoat*; Skiba, Norman A., 1990. Bud pointed; flowers medium pink, outer petals lighter, dbl. (45 petals), high-centered, exhibition, large, borne usually singly; moderate, fruity fragrance; foliage large, dark green, edged red, semi-glossy; prickles sharp, pointed slightly downward, light green; fruit round, dark green to orange; bushy, tall growth.

Emma F, *dp*, 1980, *Chanelle* × *Prima Ballerina*; Pearce, C.A.; Limes Rose Nursery. Flowers deep pink, dbl. (70 petals), medium blooms borne 6-10 per cluster; very fragrant; foliage dark, glossy; large prickles; upright, branching growth.

Emma Jane F, *op*, 1970, *Vera Dalton × (Masquerade × Independence seedling)*; Sanday. Flowers salmon-pink, base orange, semi-dbl. (16 petals), large (3 in.).

Emma Kate F, *mr*, 1992, (JAYemm); *Tony Jacklin × Cairngorm*; Jellyman, J.S., 1992-93. Flowers light red with lighter reverse, dbl. (35 petals), full, medium blooms borne 4-10+ per cluster; moderate, fruity fragrance; foliage medium, dark green, glossy; upright, bushy, medium growth.

Emma Mitchell Min, *ob*, 1992, (HORharpdos); *HARpippin × (Southampton × ((New Penny × White Pet) × Stars 'n Stripes)*; Horner, Colin P.; Battersby Roses, 1993. Flowers orange/vermillion striped white, light orange reverse, aging light orange, semi-dbl. (12 petals), small (2.5 cms) blooms borne in sprays of 5-9; slight, fruity fragrance; foliage small, medium green, semi-glossy; bushy, low growth.

Emma Wright HT, *op*, 1918, McGredy. Flowers orange shaded salmon, semi-dbl.; fragrant; foliage rich green, glossy; dwarf growth.

Emma Wright, Climbing Cl HT, *op*, 1932, Cant, F.

Emmanuella de Mouchy LCl, *mp*, 1922, *R. gigantea × Lady Waterlow*; Nabonnand, P. Flowers delicate transparent rose-pink, semi-dbl.; very fragrant.

Emmeline HT, *my*, 1921, Paul, W. Bud pure deep yellow; flowers lemon-yellow.

Emmeloord Pol, *or*, 1973, *Olala × Finale*; Buisman. Bud cupped; flowers orange-red, semi-dbl., round; foliage glossy, dark.

Emmerdale F, *mp*, 1983, *Seedling × Pink Parfait*; Greensitt, J.A.; Nostell Priory Rose Gardens. Flowers medium pink, dbl. (35 petals), medium; fragrant; foliage medium, medium green, semi-glossy; bushy growth.

Emmie Koster Pol, *dr*, 1956, *Dick Koster sport*; Koster, D.A. Flowers deep red.

Empereur du Maroc HP (OGR), *dr*, 1858, *Geant des Batailles seedling*; Guinoisseau; E. Verdier. Flowers crimson, tinged purple, very distinct, dbl. (40 petals), small; fragrant; low, compact growth.

Emperor HT, *dr*, 1958, *Pink Delight (HT) sport*; Kuramoto. Bud urn shaped; flowers rose-red becoming darker, dbl. (35-45 petals), high-centered, medium (3-3½ in.); very fragrant; foliage glossy; vigorous, compact growth.

Empire Granger HT, *mr*, 1970, *Rose Bowl × Hallmark*; Morey. Bud long, pointed; flowers velvety blood-red, dbl., full, very large; fragrant; foliage large, glossy, dark, bronze, leathery; very vigorous, upright, bushy growth.

Empire Queen HT, *mr*, 1925, *Cherry Page × Vanessa*; Easlea. Flowers brilliant cerise, dbl., large; slightly fragrant; upright growth.

Empire State HT, *mr*, 1934, Nicolas; J&P. Bud pointed; flowers velvety scarlet, base golden yellow; dbl., high-centered, large; very fragrant; foliage leathery; vigorous growth.

Empress HT, *dr*, 1933, *Ophelia seedling × Seedling*; Chaplin Bros. Flowers dark cerise and red, well formed; fragrant; vigorous, upright growth.

Empress Josephine Misc. OGR (OGR), *mp*, (Francofurtana; *R. francofurtana* Thory (not Muenchhausen); Imperatrice Josephine; Souv. de l'Imperatrice Josephine); Form of *R. × francofurtana (R. cinnamomea × R. gallica)*; Prior to 1824. Flowers rich pink veined deeper, semi-dbl., loosely shaped, large, wavy petals; height 4 ft., well-branched growth.

Empress Marie of Russia T (OGR), *my*, Flowers canary-yellow, fading, large; fragrant.

Empress of China Cl Ch (OGR), *mp*, 1896, Jackson; Apparently a climbing sport of Old Blush, which it resembles in all but growth habit.

Ena Gladstone HT, *dp*, 1936, Chaplin Bros. Flowers carmine-pink, base yellow, well shaped, large; fragrant.

Ena Harkness HT, *mr*, 1946, *Crimson Glory × Southport*; Norman; Harkness, 1946 & C-P, 1949. Flowers medium red, dbl., high-centered, large; very fragrant; foliage leathery; vigorous, upright growth. GM, NRS, 1945 & Portland, 1955.

Ena Harkness, Climbing Cl HT, *mr*, 1954, (Grimpant Ena Harkness); Gurteen & Ritson; Murrell.

Enchanted Autumn Gr, *ob*, 1976, *(Queen Elizabeth × Ruth Hewitt) × Whisky*; Buck; Iowa State University. Bud ovoid, pointed; flowers orange, dbl. (30-35 petals), shallow-cupped, large (4-4½ in.); very fragrant; foliage glossy, dark, coppery; upright, bushy growth.

Enchanter HT, *dp*, 1903, *Mme. Caroline Testout × Mlle. Alice Furon*; Cook, J. Flowers deep pink.

Enchantment HT, *pb*, 1946, *R.M.S. Queen Mary × Eternal Youth*; Hill, E.G., Co.; J&P. Bud long, pointed; flowers shell-pink, base yellow, dbl. (35 petals), very large (6 in.); slightly fragrant; foliage leathery; vigorous, upright growth.

Enchantress HRg (S), *dr*, Flowers velvety blood-red, very full; extra strong and hardy.

Enchantress T (OGR), *mp*, 1904, Cook, J. Flowers rose-pink.

Encore F, *mp*, 1958, *Else Poulsen × Capt. Thomas*; Abrams, Von; Peterson & Dering. Bud pointed; Flowers creamy pink, reverse rose-pink, semi-dbl. (10-14 petals), cupped, large (3 in.), large cluster; slightly fragrant (spicy); Foliage glossy; Vigorous, upright, bushy growth. RULED EXTINCT 2/84 ARM.

Encore HT, *dr*, 1984, (JACore); *Seedling × Samantha*; Warriner; J&P. Flowers dark red, dbl. (20 petals), large; no fragrance; foliage medium, dark, semi-glossy; upright growth; greenhouse variety.

Endearment HT, *op*, 1988, *Gladiator × First Prize*; Taylor, Thomas; Michigan Miniature Roses, 1989. Bud pointed; flowers creamy pink, reverse coral pink, semi-dbl. (10 petals), large, borne usually singly and in sprays of 1-3; light, sweet fragrance; foliage large, medium green, matt; prickles straight, medium, light brown; fruit none; upright, tall growth.

Endless Dream™ HT, *mp*, 1989, (TWOdream); *Emily Post × Seedling*; Twomey, Jerry; DeVor Nursery, 1990. Bud pointed; flowers medium, soft pink, dbl. (32 petals), cupped, large, borne singly; moderate, musk fragrance; foliage large, dark green, semi-glossy; prickles declining, grayish-white with black spots; upright, medium growth.

Endless Love Min, *mr*, 1982, (LYOss); *Red Can Can × Seedling*; Lyon, Lyndon. Flowers medium red, dbl. (35 petals), medium; no fragrance; foliage medium, dark, semi-glossy; upright, bushy growth.

Endless Summer Min, *op*, 1988, (RENmer); *Paul Shirville × California Dreaming*; Rennie, Bruce F.; Rennie Roses, 1990. Bud pointed; flowers shrimp-pink, reverse light pink, dbl. (33 petals), high-centered, small, borne singly; slight, spicy fragrance; foliage small, dark green, semi-glossy; prickles straight, small, transparent to brown; fruit none; low, bushy growth.

Endless Tale Cl HT, *my*, 1956, *Lestra Hibberd, Climbing × Lestra Hibbard sport*; Motose. Bud ovoid, deep yellow; flowers amber-yellow, outer petals creamy, dbl. (30-35 petals); very large (6-7 in.); fragrant; foliage leathery; vigorous (20 ft. or more) growth; intermittent bloom.

Endora Min, *pb*, 1991, (ZIPend); *Pristine × High Spirits*; Zipper, Herbert; Magic Moment Miniatures, 1992. Flowers cream, edged deep pink, full (26-40 petals), exhibition, medium (4-7 cms) blooms borne mostly singly; slight fragrance; foliage small, medium green, semi-glossy; few prickles; medium (35 cms), upright growth.

Enemy of War HT, *pb*, 1986, *Festival Beauty × Gynosure*; Hardikar, Dr. M.N. Flowers pink blend, dbl. (50-60 petals), open, slight fragrance; foliage large, dark green, glossy, leathery; beak-shaped, light green to deep brown prickles; very vigorous, profuse growth.

Enfant de France HP (OGR), *lp*, 1860, Lartay. Flowers silvery pink, very dbl.

Enfant d'Orléans Pol, *m*, 1929, Turbat. Flowers neyron rose, tinted purple, fading lighter, borne in clusters of 20-25.

Engagement Gr, *op*, 1969, *Ma Perkins × Montezuma*; Patterson; Patterson Roses. Bud globular; flowers coral-pink, dbl., high-centered, large; slightly fragrant; foliage dark, leathery; vigorous, bushy growth.

English Estates HT, *yb*, 1992, *Whisky Mac × Catherine Cookson*; Thompson, Robert; Battersby Roses, 1991. Flowers deep yellow edged red, full (26-40 petals), medium (4-7 cms) blooms borne mostly singly; very fragrant; foliage medium, dark green, glossy; some prickles; upright (80 cms) growth.

English Hedge HRg (S), *mp*, 1959, (*R. rugosa rubra × R. cinnamomea) × R. nitida*; Nyveldt. Flowers pink, single, small; fruit red; compact, upright growth.

English Holiday F, *yb*, 1977, *Bobby Dazzler × Goldbonnet*; Harkness. Flowers yellow, blended with salmon, dbl. (33 petals), large (4 in.); fragrant; foliage large, glossy.

English Miss F, *lp*, 1977, *Dearest × The Optimist*; Cants of Colchester, 1978. Flowers pale pink, dbl. (60 petals), medium (2½ in.) blooms in clusters; very fragrant; foliage dark purple to dark green.

Eng. Duarte Pacheco HT, *dr*, 1938, *Hadley × Presidente Carmona*; Moreira da Silva. Flowers blackish crimson, very dbl., cupped, large; very fragrant; dwarf growth.

Eng. D. José de Mendia HT, *mp*, Moreira da Silva. Flowers rosy salmon.

Eng. Pereira Caldas HT, *mp*, 1954, Moreira da Silva. Flowers salmon-pink, base yellow.

Eng. Pulido Garcia HT, *yb*, 1961, *Grand'mere Jenny × Michèle Meilland*; Moreira da Silva. Flowers yellow stained pink.

Eng. Vitória Pires HT, *dr*, 1954, Moreira da Silva. Flowers velvety dark red; fragrant.

Enhance S, *ly*, 1992, (SANdaya); *Malmesbury × The Fairy*; Sanday, John; John Sanday Roses Ltd. Flowers soft apricot yellow, moderately full (15-25 petals), small (0-4 cms) blooms borne in large clusters; fragrant; foliage medium, medium green, glossy; some prickles; low (25 cms), spreading growth.

Enid Pol, *lp*, 1936, Prior. Flowers pale pink, borne in clusters; foliage light; upright growth.

Ennio Morlotti F, *mp*, 1973, *Fashion × Queen Elizabeth*; Cazzaniga. Bud globular; flowers clear pink, dbl. (35 petals), high-centered; large (2½-3 in.); very fragrant; foliage glossy; vigorous, upright growth.

Entente Cordiale HT, *w*, 1908, *Mme. Caroline Testout × Soleil d'Or*; Guillot, P. Flowers nasturtium-red, base yellow.

Entente Cordiale HT, *mr*, 1909, *Mme. Abel Chatenay × Kaiserin Auguste Viktoria*; Pernet-Ducher. Flowers creamy white, tinged carmine at edges.

Enterprise F, *pb*, 1957, *Masquerade × Seedling*; Kordes; Morse. Flowers deep pink edged peach, semi-dbl. (20 petals), medium (2 in.) borne in large clusters; fragrant; foliage dark, glossy, vigorous, upright, bushy growth.

Enzo Fumagalli F, *mp*, 1966, *Mount Shasta × Papillon Rose*; Cazzaniga. Bud globular; flowers salmon-pink, very dbl., full, medium; foliage glossy; vigorous, bushy growth; intermittent bloom.

Eos S, *rb*, 1950, *R. moyesii × Magnifica*; Ruys. Bud ovoid; flowers sunset-red becoming brighter, center white, semi-dbl., cupped, medium blooms borne several together; slightly fragrant; foliage leathery, glossy; shrub or pillar (to 6 ft.) growth; non-recurrent bloom.

E. Pemberton Barnes HT, *pb*, 1928, Pemberton. Flowers light pink, shaded cerise.

E. P. H. Kingma HT, *ab*, 1919, *Mme. Edouard Herriot × Duchess of Wellington*; Verschuren. Flowers apricot and orange-yellow, dbl.

Epic F, *mp*, 1989, *Silent Night × Irish Mist*; Cattermole, R.F.; South Pacific Rose Nursery. Bud tapering; flowers medium pink, dbl. (30 wavy petals), flat, medium, borne in sprays of 3-6; spicy fragrance; foliage bronze to dark green, glossy; prickles brown; upright, bushy growth.

Epidor® HT, *dy*, 1981, (DELépi); *(Peace × Marcelle Gret) × (Velizy × Jean de la Lune)*; Delbard-Chabert, G. Flowers deep yellow, dbl. (35 petals), large; slight fragrance; foliage large, medium green, matt; bushy growth. GM, Rome.

Epoca Gr, *dr*, 1966, (LEN 2); *Seedling × Seedling*; Lens, Louis. Flowers very dark red, dbl. (45 petals), exhibition, large blooms in sprays of 3-18; no fragrance; foliage very dark; brown-green prickles; upright, bushy growth.

Eponine HMsk (S), *w*, Flowers white, dbl., cupped; fragrant.

Epos Pol, *mr*, 1971, *Tommy Bright × Seedling*; Delforge. Bud ovoid; flowers red, semi-dbl., cupped, medium; slightly fragrant; foliage bronze, leathery; vigorous, upright growth.

Erato LCl, *w*, 1937, *(Ophelia × R. multiflora) × Florex*; Tantau. Bud pointed; flowers white, semi-dbl., open, borne in clusters on long stems; slightly fragrant; foliage glossy; very vigorous climbing growth.

Erfurt HMsk (S), *pb*, 1939, *Eva × Reveil Dijonnais*; Kordes, 1931. Bud long, pointed; flowers medium pink, yellow toward base, semi-dbl., large blooms in clusters; very fragrant (musk); foliage leathery, wrinkled, bronze; vigorous (5-6 ft.), trailing, bushy growth; recurrent bloom.

Eric F, *mr*, 1965, *Alain × Coup de Foudre*; Hémeray-Aubert. Bud ovoid; flowers red, semi-dbl., cupped, medium; foliage dark, glossy, leathery; vigorous growth.

Eric B. Mee HT, *mr*, 1937, Mee; Beckwith. Flowers vivid cerise, well shaped, small.

Eric Hobbis HT, *pb*, 1966, *Gavotte × Peace*; Sanday. Flowers pink, reverse peach, high-centered, large (4½ in.); low growth.

Eric Holroyd HT, *mr*, 1925, Chaplin Bros. Flowers bright scarlet, base shaded gold; fragrant.

Eric Louw HT, *mr*, 1964, *Queen Elizabeth × Confidence*; Herholdt, J.A.; Herholdt's Nursery. Bud pointed; flowers cyclamen-red, dbl. (35-40 petals), well formed, strong stems; foliage leathery, glossy; vigorous, bushy growth.

Erica F, *or*, 1964, *Seedling × Montezuma*; Herholdt, J.A.; Herholdt's Nursery. Flowers orange-scarlet, semi-dbl., frilled, borne in large clusters.

Erich Frahm F, *mr*, 1939, *Dance of Joy × Mary Hart*; Kordes; Timm. Bud long, pointed, yellowish red; flowers carmine-scarlet, center yellow, shell shaped, open; umbel up to 20; foliage dark, glossy, leathery; vigorous growth, very branching.

Erie S, *lp*, 1946, Preston; Central Exp. Farm. Flowers pale pink, single (5 petals), borne in clusters; fruit bright red, bottle shaped; foliage dark, fragrant (sweetbriar); vigorous, spreading growth; very free, non-recurrent bloom.

Erie Treasure HRg (S), *w*, Souv. de Pierre Leperdrieux × Nova Zembla; Wedrick. Flowers blush to white, dbl.; very fragrant; foliage wrinkled; vigorous (6 ft.), bushy growth; recurrent bloom.

Erik Hjelm HT, *op*, 1929, *Lieut. Chaure × Sachsengruss*; Kordes. Flowers pure salmon-pink, very dbl.; fragrant.

Erika Teschendorff HT, *mr*, 1949, Berger, V.; Teschendorff. Bud long, pointed; flowers fiery scarlet, dbl., open, globular, very large;

slightly fragrant; foliage glossy, dark; very vigorous, upright growth.

Erna Baltzer HT, *my*, 1954, *Tawny Gold × Gaudia*; Leenders, M. Flowers golden yellow, medium; fragrant; vigorous growth.

Erna Doris F, *op*, 1985, (LENdori); *Little Angel × Elizabeth of Glamis*; Lens, Louis. Flowers medium salmon pink, dbl. (24 petals), HT form, medium blooms in clusters of 3-12; slight fragrance; foliage small, medium green; small, hooked, brown-green prickles; upright, bushy growth.

Erna Grootendorst F, *dr*, 1938, *Bergers Erfolg × Gloria Mundi*; Grootendorst, R. Flowers deep velvety crimson, semi-dbl., large; foliage glossy, dark; bushy growth.

Erna Teschendorff Pol, *mr*, 1911, *Mme. Norbert Levavasseur sport*; Teschendorff. Flowers strawberry-red, semi-dbl., open, small; slightly fragrant; foliage rich green, soft; bushy growth.

Ernest H. Morse HT, mr, 1964, Kordes; Morse. Flowers turkey-red, dbl. (30 petals), large (4 in.); very fragrant; foliage leathery; vigorous. GM, RNRS, 1965.

Ernest Metz T (OGR), *mp*, 1888, Guillot Fils. Flowers rose-pink, center darker, full, large.

Ernest Morel HP (OGR), *dr*, 1898, Cochet, P. Flowers bright garnet-red.

Ernestine Cosme R, *rb*, 1926, Turbat. Flowers brilliant red, with large white eye, single, borne in clusters of 75-100; many thorns; very vigorous, climbing growth.

Ernie Min, *m*, 1989, (TINernie); *Blue Nile × Blue Mist*; Bennett, Dee; Tiny Petals Nursery. Bud ovoid; flowers light mauve, dbl. (48 petals), urn-shaped, medium, borne occasionally singly and in sprays of 6-12; moderate, fruity fragrance; foliage medium, medium green, semi-glossy; prickles hooked slightly downward, pale yellow-brown, few; fruit globular, yellow-brown; upright, bushy, tall growth.

Ernie Pyle HT, *mp*, 1946, ((*Royal Red × Talisman*) × *Unnamed red seedling*) × (*Talisman × Nutneyron*); Boerner; J&P. Bud long, pointed; flowers deep rose-pink, reverse deeper, dbl. (35-40 petals), cupped, large (4½-5 in.); very fragrant; foliage leathery; vigorous, upright, bushy growth.

Ernst Grandpierre R, *w*, 1902, *R. wichuraiana × Perle des Jardins*; Weigand, C. Flowers pale cream, base yellow, dbl., open, borne in clusters; slightly fragrant; foliage light, glossy; height 8-10 ft.; sparse bloom.

Eros F, *dp*, 1955, *Pinocchio seedling*; Maarse, G. Flowers deep rosy pink shaded brick-red, base yellow; dwarf, compact growth.

Erotika® HT, *dr*, 1968, (Eroica; Erotica; Eroika); Tantau, Math. Bud ovoid; flowers velvety dark red, dbl. (30-35 petals), well-formed, large; very fragrant; foliage dark, glossy; vigorous, upright growth. ADR, 1969.

Erskine Sp (OGR), *mp*, Hansen, N.E.; Name applied to wild roses dug near Erskine, MN, which apparently represented natural seedlings of R. blanda.

Eruption HT, *mr*, 1934, *Red-Letter Day × Columbia*; Van Rossem. Flowers fiery scarlet-red, semi-dbl., large; foliage sea-green; bushy growth.

Escalade Cl HT, *mr*, 1962, *Spectacular × Charlotte Armstrong*; Combe; Vilmorin-Andrieux. Bud pointed; flowers carmine, high-centered, large; vigorous growth.

Escapade® F, *m*, 1967, (HARpade); *Pink Parfait × Baby Faurax*; Harkness. Flowers magenta-rose, center white, semi-dbl. (12 petals), large (3 in.) blooms in clusters; slightly fragrant; foliage glossy, light green. GM, Belfast & Baden-Baden, 1969; ADR, 1973.

Escort F, *dr*, 1963, *Spartan × Garnette*; Swim & Weeks. Bud pointed to urn-shaped; flowers dark red, dbl. (255-35 petals), high-centered, small to medium; foliage dark, leathery; vigorous, bushy growth; greenhouse variety.

Escultor Clará HT, *m*, 1956, *Lilette Mallerin × Floradora*; Dot, S. Bud pointed; flowers purple-garnet, reverse magenta, dbl. (30 petals), high-centered, large; fragrant; foliage dark, glossy; very vigorous, upright, compact growth.

Escurial® HT, *mr*, 1967, (DELflip); *Gay Paris × Impeccable*; Delbard-Chabert. Flowers velvety cardinal-red, semi-dbl., high-centered to cupped, medium; slightly fragrant; foliage dark, glossy; vigorous, bushy growth.

Eskil HT, *yb*, 1939, *Mrs. Franklin D. Roosevelt sport*; Ringdahl. Flowers light yellow overlaid red and orange.

Esmé HT, *w*, 1920, *Mme. Edouard Herriot × Seedling*; Cant, B.R. Flowers cream-white, edged rosy carmine, dbl.

Esmeralda F, *dp*, 1957, *Gartendirector Otto Linne × Seedling*; Riethmuller. Flowers deep rose-pink, reverse lighter, dbl., small, borne in very large clusters; fragrant; vigorous growth.

Esperanto HT, *my*, 1932, *Miss Lolita Armour sport*; Böhm. Flowers pure yellow, dbl. (60 petals), globular, very large; very fragrant.

Esperanto Jubileo HT, *pb*, 1986, (SANrozo); *Gavotte × Piccadilly*; Sanday, John, 1987. Flowers cream, edged deep rose pink, yellow suffused at base, dbl. (over 40 petals), large;

slight fragrance; foliage medium, medium green, matt; bushy growth.

Espéranza F, *mr*, 1966, *Donald Prior × Reverence*; Delforge. Bud ovoid; flowers bright red, dbl., large blooms in clusters; foliage dark, bronze, leathery, glossy; upright growth. GM, Baden-Baden & The Hague, 1968.

Esplanade HT, *dr*, 1961, *Soraya × Seedling*; Verbeek. Flowers dark red, dbl. (40 petals); fragrant; foliage glossy; vigorous growth.

Espoir F, 1958, *(Oiseau de Feu × Fashion) × (Independence × Seedling)*; Combe; Japan Rose Society. Flowers rich salmon, dbl. (50 petals), rosette shape, large (4½ in.); fragrant; Vigorous, low, bushy growth. RULED EXTINCT 6/83 ARM.

Espoir HT, 1947, *Charles P. Kilham × Neville Chamberlain*; Lens. Bud long, pointed; flowers pink, center light salmon-pink, dbl. (35 petals), large; slightly fragrant; foliage soft; bushy, abundant bloom. RULED EXTINCT 6/83.

Espoir HCh (OGR), *w*, 1984, (Interbec); *HCh seedling × HCh seedling*; Gailloux, Gilles. Flowers white, single (5 petals), small; slight fragrance; foliage very small, medium green, semi-glossy; upright, spreading growth.

Esprit® S, *dr*, 1987, (KORholst; City of Birmingham; Holstein 87; Kordes' Rose Holstein; Petit Marquis); *Seedling × Chorus*; Kordes, W.; J&P, 1989. Flowers deep red, aging darker, semi-dbl. (12 petals), flat, medium, borne in sprays of 5-7; no fragrance; foliage small, medium green, semi-glossy; medium, tan prickles, slightly down pointed; no fruit; upright, bushy, tall growth; repeats.

Essence HT, *dr*, 1930, Cant, B.R. Bud pointed; flowers rich scarlet-crimson, becoming bluish, cupped, outer petals slightly fimbriated; fragrant (damask).

Essence, Climbing Cl HT, *dr*, 1938, Western Rose Co.

Essie Lee Min, *ob*, 1992, (JUDlee); *Tennessee × Tennessee*; Bell, Judy, 1991; Michigan Mini Roses. Flowers white with orange picotee down½ of petals, white to light orange reverse, globular, spiral center, full (26-40 petals), small (0-4 cms) blooms borne mostly singly; no fragrance; foliage small to medium, dark green, semi-glossy; few prickles; upright (46 cms), bushy growth.

Estafette F, *dr*, 1962, *Alain × Elmshorn*; Delforge. Flowers dark red, semi-dbl., open, large (2½-3 in.), borne in clusters; foliage dark, glossy; vigorous growth.

Esther F, *ob*, 1954, *Cocorico × Canzonetta*; San Remo Exp. Sta. Bud pointed, turkey-red; flowers golden orange, reverse lighter, single

(7-8 petals), open, large, borne in clusters of 30-40 on long stems; foliage glossy, bright green; very vigorous, bushy growth.

Esther Geldenhuys HT, *op*, 1987, (KORskipei); *Seedling × Seedling*; Kordes, W., Sohne; Ludwigs Roses, 1988. Flowers light coral pink, dbl. (32 petals), clam-shaped, large, borne singly; moderate fragrance; foliage glossy, purple to medium green; prickles concave, yellow-brown; vigorous, very tall, well-branched growth.

Esther Jerabek F, *mp*, 1978, *The Fairy seedling*; Jerabek. Flowers medium pink, semi-dbl. (18 petals); spreading growth.

Esther Rantzen F, *ob*, 1982, *Spartan × Orangeade*; Dwight, Robert & Son. Flowers orange blend, semi-dbl., medium; fruity fragrance; foliage medium, medium green, semi-glossy; upright, bushy growth.

Esther's Baby® Min, *mp*, 1979, (HARkinder); *(Vera Dalton × (Chanelle × Piccadilly)) × Little Buckaroo*; Harkness. Bud pointed; flowers persian rose, flat, patio, medium; foliage small, glossy; low, spreading growth.

Estrellita Min, *w*, (Pixie Pearl; Estralia); Origin uncertain; Said to have been grown in US since about 1910 or earlier. Flowers white, dbl., large blooms in clusters.

Estru F, *lp*, 1975, *Rosy Jewel × Floribunda seedling*; deRuiter. Flowers light pink, dbl. (50 petals), patio, small (1½ in.); foliage small, glossy, dark; low, compact growth.

Etain R, *op*, 1953, Cant, F. Flowers salmon-pink, borne in trusses; slightly fragrant; foliage glossy, dark, almost evergreen; very vigorous growth.

Étendard LCl, *mr*, 1956, (New Dawn Rouge; Red New Dawn); *New Dawn × Seedling*; Robichon. Flowers bright red, dbl., medium blooms in large clusters; fragrant; foliage very glossy, leathery; vigorous growth; recurrent bloom.

Éterna® HT, *lp*, 1978, (DELic); *((Michèle Meilland × Carla) × (Dr. Schweitzer × Tropicana)) × (Queen Elizabeth × Provence)*; Delbard-Chabert, 1979. Bud long; flowers light carmine pink, dbl. (28-32 petals), large (4-5 in.); slightly fragrant; vigorous, upright growth.

Eternal Flame LCl, *ob*, 1955; *Seedling × Queen o' the Lakes*; Brownell. Flowers light orange, semi-dbl. (12-19 petals), large (3-4 in.); fragrant; upright, climbing growth.

Eternal Sun HT, *or*, 1966, *Seedling × Jacqueline*; Hill, J.H., Co. Bud ovoid; flowers vermilion, dbl., high-centered, large; slightly fragrant; foliage dark, leathery; vigorous, upright, bushy growth; a greenhouse variety.

Eternal Youth HT, *lp*, 1937, (Eterna Giovanezza; Jeunesse Éternelle); *Dame Edith Helen × Julien Potin*; Aicardi, D.; J&P. Bud long, pointed; flowers light pink, suffused orange-salmon, dbl. (50 petals), cupped, large (4-5 in.); very fragrant; foliage leathery; vigorous, upright, bushy growth.

Eternité F, *mr*, 1947, *Mme. Joseph Perraud × Holstein*; Gaujard. Flowers scarlet, dbl. (25 petals), large (4-5 in.); fragrant; foliage dark; very free growth.

Eternity Gr, *rb*, 1991, (TWOetern); *Gitte × Seedling*; Twomey, Jerry; DeVor Nurseries, 1991. Flowers red/cream bicolor, full, medium blooms borne in large clusters; moderately fragrant; foliage medium, dark green; some prickles; tall (183 cms), upright growth.

Ethel R, *lp*, 1912, *Dorothy Perkins seedling*; Turner. Flowers flesh-pink, semi-dbl., borne in clusters; vigorous growth.

Ethel Austin F, *dp*, 1984, (FRYmestin); *Pink Parfait × Redgold*; Fryer's Nursery. Flowers deep pink, dbl. (20 petals); fragrant; foliage large, medium green, semi-glossy; upright.

Ethel Chaplin HT, *my*, 1926, Chaplin Bros. Flowers soft lemon-yellow, dbl.; fragrant.

Ethel Dickson HT, *dp*, 1917, Dickson, H. Flowers deep salmon-rose with silvery flesh reflexes.

Ethel James HT, *dp*, 1921, McGredy. Flowers softer carmine-red than Isobel, flushed orange-scarlet, center yellow, single (5 petals), large; bushy growth. GM, NRS, 1920.

Ethel Malcolm HT, *w*, 1909, McGredy. Flowers ivory-white, very large; vigorous growth. Possibly same as Jackman's White. GM, NRS, 1909.

Ethel Orr™ Min, *mr*, 1987, (MINamco); *Miniature seedling × Big John*; Williams, Ernest; Mini-Roses. Flowers medium red, dbl. (35 petals), high-centered, small, borne usually singly or in sprays of 3-5; slight fragrance; foliage small, medium green, glossy; few, small, tan prickles; no fruit; upright, bushy, medium, profuse growth.

Ethel Sanday HT, *yb*, 1954, *Rex Anderson × Audrey Cobden*; Mee; Sanday. Flowers yellow flushed apricot, dbl. (34 petals), well-formed, large (4-5 in.); slightly fragrant; foliage dark; vigorous, upright growth. GM, NRS, 1953.

Ethel Sloman HT, *mr*, 1966, *Baccará × My Choice*; Fankhauser. Bud ovoid; flowers crimson, very dbl.; slightly fragrant; foliage leathery; compact, bushy growth.

Ethel Somerset HT, *mp*, 1921, Dickson, A. Bud pointed; flowers shrimp-pink, dbl., high-centered; large; very fragrant; vigorous, branching growth.

Ethel Utter LCl, *my*, Wilber. Bud cherry-red; flowers yellow, dbl.

Étienne Levet HP (OGR), *mr*, 1871, *Victor Verdier seedling*; Levet, F. Flowers carmine-red, dbl. (70 petals), large; vigorous, erect growth; sometimes recurrent bloom.

Étienne Rebeillard HT, *pb*, 1924, Pernet-Ducher. Flowers flesh-pink, suffused golden, semi-dbl.; slightly fragrant.

Étincelante HT, *dr*, 1941, *Gruss an Teplitz × Étoile de France*; Chambard, C. Flowers brilliant red, tinted purple, dbl.; fragrant.

Étincelle HT, *or*, 1958, *Crimson Glory × Seedling*; Moulin; Vilmorin-Andrieux. Flowers bright red tinted orange, dbl. (40-45 petals), medium; very fragrant; low, bushy growth.

Etna M (OGR), *dr*, 1845, Laffay. Flowers crimson shaded purple, large, very mossy; fragrant.

Etna HT, *dr*, 1924, *Red-Letter Day × H.V. Machin*; Looymans; Prior. Flowers deep crimson-maroon, semi-dbl.

Étoile d'Alaï HMsk (S), *mr*, 1946, *Skyrocket seedling*; Meilland, F. Flowers brilliant red, prominent golden stamens, quite dbl., medium; bushy growth; repeat bloom.

Étoile de Belgique HT, *mr*, 1946, *Charles P. Kilham × Étoile de Hollande*; Lens. Flowers brilliant red, dbl., very large; slightly fragrant; foliage bronze; vigorous, bushy growth.

Étoile de Belgique HT, *mr*, 1956, *Independence × Happiness*; Buyl Frères. Bud ovoid; flowers geranium-red, dbl., large; bushy, spreading growth.

Étoile de Feu HT, *op*, 1921, Pernet-Ducher. Flowers salmon-pink and coral-red, dbl., globular, large; foliage bronze; vigorous, bushy, branching growth.

Étoile de Feu, Climbing Cl HT, *ob*, 1930, H&S.

Étoile de France HT, *dr*, 1904, *Mme. Abel Chatenay × Fisher Holmes*; Pernet-Ducher. Bud pointed; flowers dark rose-red, center cerise, full, cupped, medium to small; very fragrant; bushy growth.

Étoile de France, Climbing Cl HT, *dr*, 1915, Howard Rose Co.

Étoile de Hollande HT, *mr*, 1919, *Gen. MacArthur × Hadley*; Verschuren. Flowers bright red, dbl. (35-40 petals), cupped, large; very fragrant (damask); foliage soft; moderate, open growth.

Étoile de Hollande, Climbing Cl HT, *mr*, 1931, (Grimpant Étoile de Hollande); Leenders, M.

Étoile de Lyon T (OGR), *my*, 1881, Guillot, P. Flowers golden yellow, dbl., blooms with short, weak stems; fragrant; foliage soft; bushy growth; sparse intermittent bloom.

Étoile de Mai Pol, *ly*, 1893, Gamon. Flowers sulphur-white, dbl., small; very fragrant; vigorous growth.

Étoile de Portugal LCl, *dp*, 1898, *R. gigantea hybrid*; Cayeux. Flowers rose-red, dbl.

Étoile d'Or HT, *yb*, 1931, Pernet-Ducher; Gaujard. Flowers golden yellow, reverse shaded orange, semi-dbl., large; very fragrant; upright, bushy growth.

Étoile Luisante Pol, *mr*, 1918, (Baby Herriot); Turbat; Michell. Bud pointed; flowers cerise-red, shaded coppery, semi-dbl., high-centered, borne in clusters on long stems; slightly fragrant; foliage bronze, glossy; few thorns; bushy growth.

Etty van Best HT, *ly*, 1934, *Pharisaer* × *Souv. de H.A. Verschuren*; Buisman. Flowers white, shaded yellow, full; foliage leathery; vigorous growth.

Étude LCl, *dp*, 1965, *Spectacular* × *New Dawn*; Gregory. Flowers deep rose-pink, semi-dbl., medium blooms in clusters; fragrant; foliage glossy, light green; recurrent bloom.

Eucharis G (OGR), *dp*, Descemet. Flowers bright rose, edged lighter, full, large.

Eugène Barbier HP (OGR), *dy*, 1920, *Frau Karl Druschcki* × *Rayon d'Or*; Barbier. Flowers brilliant canary-yellow, shaded coppery golden yellow, full, globular; fragrant; few thorns; upright growth.

Eugène Boullet HT, *dr*, 1909, Pernet-Ducher. Flowers crimson-red, dbl.; vigorous growth.

Eugène de Beauharnais Ch (OGR), *m*, 1838, (Prince Eugène); Hardy. Flowers purple, full, large; fragrant.

Eugène de Savoie M (OGR), *mr*, 1860, Moreau-Robert. Flowers bright red, shaded, full.

Eugène E. Marlitt B (OGR), *mr*, 1900, (Mme. Eugène Marlitt); Geschwind. Flowers bright carmine shaded scarlet, dbl., large; few prickles; vigorous growth.

Eugène Fürst HP (OGR), *dr*, 1875, *Baron de Bonstetten* × *Seedling*; Soupert & Notting. Flowers crimson-red, shaded purple, full, globular, large; fragrant; recurrent bloom.

Eugène Jacquet R, *mr*, 1916, *Wichuraiana hybrid (red)* × *Multiflora hybrid (pink)*; Turbat. Flowers cherry-red, dbl., borne in clusters of 25-30; fragrant; foliage bright green; vigorous, symmetrical growth; very early bloom.

Eugène Janvier G (OGR), *dp*, Flowers dark pink, paling to lilac, dbl., medium.

Eugène Transon LCl, *or*, 1926, *Mme. Berard* × *Constance*; Barbier. Flowers orange and

copper, reverse orange-red, shaded, borne in clusters of 4-6; vigorous, climbing growth.

Eugène Verdier M (OGR), *dp*, 1872, Verdier, E. Flowers crimson or light red, center deeper, very dbl., well-formed; fragrant.

Eugenia HT, *rb*, 1920, *Mme. Edouard Herriot sport*; Collier. Flowers coral-red to prawn-red, flecked or striped yellow, dbl.; fragrant.

Eugénie Guinoiseau M (OGR), *mr*, 1864, (Eugénie de Guinoiseau); Guinoiseau, B. Flowers reddish cerise, changing to reddish violet, full, large; vigorous growth.

Eugénie Lamesch Pol, *yb*, 1899, *Aglaia* × *William Allen Richardson*; Lambert, P. Flowers ochre-yellow and bright yellow, shaded pink, dbl., blooms in clusters of 5-10; fragrant; foliage glossy; dwarf, compact growth.

Eugenio d'Ors HT, *dr*, 1946, *Sensation* × *Margaret McGredy*; Camprubi. Flowers oxblood-red, dbl., large; very fragrant.

Eugenio Fojo HT, *mr*, 1953, *Texas Centennial* × *Carlos Fargas*; Dot, P. Bud pointed; flowers vermilion-red, dbl. (35 petals), well formed, large; fragrant; vigorous, bushy growth.

Eulalia HT, *mp*, 1934, Verschuren-Pechtold; Dreer & H&S. Flowers pink, lighter toward base, dbl., large; very fragrant; vigorous growth.

Eumundi F, *w*, 1953, *Yvonne Rabier* × *Baby Alberic*; Ulrick. Flowers pure white, very dbl., cupped; foliage light green; vigorous, bushy growth.

Euphrates S, *pb*, 1986, (HARunique); *Hulthemia persica* × *Seedling*; Harkness. Flowers pale salmon red, deep pink eye, single (5 petals), small blooms in clusters of 3-9; slight fragrance; foliage small, variable form (usually long and narrow), light green; prickly stems; low, spreading growth. See Hulthemia.

Euphrosyne R, *mp*, 1895, *R. multiflora* × *Mignonette*; Schmitt. Flowers pure pink, full, small; fragrant; very vigorous growth.

Eureka HT, *mp*, 1914, Hobbies. Flowers bright rose.

Eureka S, *w*, 1956, *Probably Betty Bland* × *Ames 5*; Wright, P.H. Flowers pure white, semi-dbl., small, borne in clusters; less vigorous than Ames 5; intended for trial as a hardy understock.

Europa HT, *mp*, 1928, *Columbia sport*; Keessen; Nieuwesteeg. Flowers bright pink, better.

Europeana® F, *dr*, 1963, *Ruth Leuwerik* × *Rosemary Rose*; deRuiter; C-P, 1968. Flowers dark crimson, dbl., rosette shape, large (3 in.) blooms in large, heavy clusters; slightly fragrant; foliage bronze-green; vigorous growth.

GM, The Hague, 1962 & Portland, 1970; AARS, 1968.

Europeana, Climbing Cl F, *dr*, 1987, (BUReuro); *Europeana sport*; Burks, Joe; Cooperative Rose Growers.

Eurorose F, *yb*, 1973, *Zorina* × *Redgold*; Dickson, A. Flowers yellow-ochre, flushed firered, dbl. (25 petals), globular, large (3½ in.).

Eurosong® HT, *lp*, 1984, (LENoran); *(Queen Elizabeth* × *Seedling)* × *Queen Elizabeth*; Lens, Louis. Flowers light pink, dbl. (38 petals), exhibition, medium blooms borne singly or in three's; slight fragrance; foliage dark reddish-green; large, brownish-red prickles; upright.

Eurovision HT, *dr*, 1961, *Miss France* × *Rosita*; Delforge. Flowers dark red, dbl. (30 petals), large (4 in.); fragrant; foliage dark; vigorous, bushy growth.

Euterpe LCl, *ly*, 1937, *(Ophelia* × *R. multiflora)* × *Florex*; Tantau. Bud pointed; flowers light yellow, semi-dbl., open, borne in clusters on long stems; slightly fragrant; foliage glossy; very vigorous, climbing growth.

Eutin F, *dr*, 1940, (Hoosier Glory); *Eva* × *Solarium*; Kordes. Bud globular, pointed; flowers glowing carmine-red, dbl., cupped blooms in clusters; slightly fragrant; foliage leathery, glossy, dark; vigorous.

Eutin, Climbing Cl F, *dr*, 1957, Lindquist; Howard Rose Co.

Eva HMsk (S), *rb*, 1933, *Robin Hood (Pemberton)* × *J.C. Thornton*; Kordes. Bud pointed; flowers carmine-red, center white, semi-dbl., large blooms in clusters to 75; fragrant; very vigorous growth; intermittent bloom.

Eva Eakins HT, *or*, 1926, McGredy. Flowers scarlet-carmine, flushed orange, base bright yellow, dbl., high-centered, small; slightly fragrant; foliage leathery; bushy growth.

Eva Gabor HT, *dp*, 1983, (POUltal; Sentimental); *Seedling* × *Seedling*; Olesen, M.&P.; Roses by Fred Edmunds. Flowers deep pink, dbl. (40 petals), large; fragrant; foliage large, medium green, glossy; vigorous, upright, bushy growth.

Eva Knott HT, *ob*, 1957, *Ethel Sanday* × *Mrs. Sam McGredy*; Mee. Flowers coppery orange, dbl. (35 petals), well formed; vigorous growth.

Eva Teschendorff HMult (OGR), *w*, 1923, *Echo sport*; Grunewald; Teschendorff. Flowers greenish-white.

Eva Teschendorff, Climbing Cl Pol, *w*, 1926, Opdebeeck.

Evaline Pol, *lp*, 1920, *Orléans Rose* × *Rayon d'Or*; Prosser. Flowers light pink, edged brighter, full, petals quilled, small, borne in clusters; fragrant; bushy growth.

Evangeline R, *pb*, 1906, *R. wichuraiana* × *Crimson Rambler*; Walsh. Flowers rosy white, veined cameo-pink, single, large (2 in.) blooms in clusters on long stems; fragrant; foliage dark, leathery; very vigorous, climbing (12-15 ft.) growth; late seasonal bloom.

Evangeline T (OGR), *w*, 1951, *Mrs. Dudley Cross sport*; Krider Nursery. Bud deep pink; flowers creamy white, edged blush-pink, dbl., medium; fragrant; almost thornless; vigorous, spreading growth.

Evangeline Bruce F, *yb*, 1971, *Colour Wonder* × *Sea Pearl*; Dickson, A. Flowers yellow, flushed pink, dbl. (24 petals), well-formed, large (4½ in.); fragrant; foliage light.

Eve HT, *ob*, 1954, Gaujard. Bud long, pointed; flowers coral-red shaded yellow, dbl., very large; fragrant; foliage glossy; vigorous growth.

Eve Allen HT, *rb*, 1964, *Karl Herbst* × *Gay Crusader*; Allen, E.M.; Sanday. Flowers crimson, reverse and base saffron-yellow, dbl. (26 petals), large (5 in.); fragrant; foliage dark, glossy; vigorous.

Evelien F, *lp*, 1985, (INTerlien); *Seedling* × *Fresh Pink*; Interplant. Flowers light pink, dbl. (35 petals), medium blooms in clusters; slight fragrance; foliage medium, medium green, semi-glossy; greenhouse variety.

Evelina Min, *lp*, 1992, (AMAevelina); *Rosa Maria* × *Seedling (Pink 078)*; Mansuino, Dr. Andrea, 1990. Flowers light pink, full (26-40 petals), medium (4-7 cms) blooms borne mostly singly; no fragrance; foliage medium, medium green, semi-glossy; medium (100-150 cms), bushy growth.

Evelyn HT, *lp*, 1918, *Ophelia sport*; Pierson, A.N. Flowers soft pink, base yellow, dbl. (45-50 petals); fragrant. RULED EXTINCT 1/92.

Evelyn HT, *mp*, 1918, Paul, W. Flowers salmon, shaded and edged rose, base yellow, full, imbricated, large. RULED EXTINCT 1/92.

Evelyn S, *ab*, 1992, (AUSsaucer); *Graham Thomas* × *AUStamora*; Austin, David; David Austin Roses, 1991. Flowers apricot, very full (41+ petals), old fashioned rosette form, large (7+ cms) blooms borne in small clusters; very fragrant; foliage medium, medium green, semi-glossy; some prickles; medium (110 cms), upright, bushy growth.

Evelyn Buchan HT, *pb*, 1959, *Luis Brinas* × *Crimson Glory*; Riethmuller. Flowers pink tinted yellow, dbl. (20-25 petals), high-centered, large (3-4 in.); fragrant; foliage leathery, dark; vigorous, upright growth.

Evelyn Dauntessey HT, *pb*, 1909, McGredy. Flowers salmon stained carmine-rose; moderately vigorous growth.

Evelyn Ellice F, *lp*, 1966, *Queen Elizabeth sport*; Ellice. Flowers light pink, becoming white, pointed, large (3 in.), borne in clusters; foliage light green; vigorous growth.

Evelyn Fison F, *mr*, 1962, (MACev; Irish Wonder); *Moulin Rouge × Korona*; McGredy, S., IV; McGredy, 1962; J&P, 1964. Flowers scarlet, dbl., large (3 in.) blooms in broad clusters; slightly fragrant; foliage dark, glossy; compact, bushy growth. GM, NRS, 1963.

Evelyn May HT, *dp*, 1932, *Lady Alice Stanley × Edith Part*; Edward. Flowers vermilion-pink, full, (65 petals); fragrant; free growth.

Evelyn Murland HT, *pb*, 1923, Dickson, A. Flowers salmon-pink and carmine, veined yellow, reverse veined pink and coral, dbl.; fragrant.

Evelyn Rogers™ Min, *mp*, 1988, (MINarco); *Tom Brown × Over the Rainbow*; Williams, Ernest. Flowers medium pink, dbl. (34 petals), small; slight fragrance; foliage small, medium green, glossy; upright, bushy growth.

Evelyn Thornton Pol, *mp*, 1919, *Léonie Lamesch × Mrs. W.H. Cutbush*; Bees. Flowers shell-pink deepening to salmon and lemon shaded orange, dbl., open, borne in clusters; fragrant; foliage leathery, glossy, dark bronze; bushy growth.

Evening Glow HT, *r*, 1959, *Charlotte Armstrong × Narzisse*; Armbrust; Langbecker. Bud long, pointed; flowers buff, dbl. (35 petals), large; fragrant; foliage leathery; moderate growth.

Evening News HT, *my*, 1927, *Mme. Edouard Herriot sport*; Letts. Flowers apricot-yellow veined rose, base deep buttercup-yellow, dbl., open, borne in clusters; fragrant; foliage glossy, rich green; vigorous, bushy growth.

Evening Shadows Min, *pb*, 1989, (MICeven); *Tiki × Party Girl*; Williams, Michael C.; The Rose Garden, 1990. Bud pointed; flowers pink blend, dbl. (20 petals), high-centered, exhibition, medium, borne usually singly; slight, fruity fragrance; foliage large, medium green, semi-glossy; prickles slight downward curve, small, red; fruit globular, light orange; bushy, medium growth.

Evening Sky HT, *ob*, 1939, *Talisman × Seedling*; Moore, R.S. Flowers orange, tipped scarlet, base yellow, single (6-8 ruffled petals), medium (2½-3 in.); fragrant; foliage bluish green; vigorous growth.

Evening Star® F, *w*, 1974, (JACven); *White Masterpiece × Saratoga*; Warriner; J&P. Flowers white, base shading pale yellow, dbl., high-centered, large; slightly fragrant; foliage large, dark, leathery; vigorous, upright, bushy growth. GM, Belfast & Portland, 1977.

Evening Star HT, *my*, 1919, *Mme. Edouard Herriot sport*; Morse. Flowers golden yellow, shaded apricot, full, large; slightly fragrant; bushy growth.

Evening Telegraph HT, *dy*, 1976, *Whisky Mac sport*; Haynes. Flowers deep yellow.

Evensong HT, *op*, 1963, *Ena Harkness × Sutter's Gold*; Arnot; Croll. Flowers rosy salmon, dbl. (25 petals), well-formed, large (5 in.); foliage dark; vigorous.

Eventail HT, *yb*, 1989, *Sonia × Miyabi*; Kono, Yoshito. Bud ovoid; flowers light yellow to pink, dbl. (50 petals), medium, borne singly; slight fragrance; foliage medium, semi-glossy, slightly denticulated; prickles downward-pointed, reddish-purple; upright, tall growth.

Eventide HT, *dr*, 1948, *Crimson Glory seedling × Rouge Mallerin*; Toogood. Bud ovoid; flowers dark velvety red, dbl., open, medium; fragrant; foliage wrinkled, soft; moderate growth.

Ever Ready LCl, *mr*, 1976, *Aloha × Étoile de Hollande*; MacLeod; Christies Nursery. Flowers bright crimson, dbl. (32 petals), medium (3 in.); fragrant; foliage large, medium green, matt; recurrent bloom.

Everbloom Cl Pol, *dp*, 1939, *Phyllis Bide seedling*; Archer. Flowers deep pink, single, borne in clusters; foliage glossy; height 3-6 ft. first year, 8-10 ft. in about 3 years; recurrent bloom.

Everblooming Pillar No. 122 LCl, *yb*, 1954, *Seedling × Break o' Day*, *Climbing*; Brownell. Flowers light yellow and orange, dbl. (90 petals), large (3½-4½ in.); fragrant; growth like a Hybrid Tea, followed by 4-5 ft. canes that bloom the first season.

Everblooming Pillar No. 126 LCl, *mp*, 1955, *Seedling × Queen o' the Lakes*; Brownell. Flowers pink, base yellow, dbl. (35-50 petals), large (3½-4½ in.), fragrant; bushy, upright growth.

Everblooming Pillar No. 214 LCl, *my*, 1954, *Seedling × Break o' Day*, *Climbing*; Brownell. Flowers amber-yellow, dbl. (75 petals), large (3½ in.); growth like a Hybrid Tea, followed by 4-5 ft. canes that bloom the first season.

Everblooming Pillar No. 340 LCl, *pb*, 1957, *Queen o' the Lakes × Scarlet Sensation*; Brownell. Flowers pink and yellow, dbl. (35-40 petals), high-centered, large (4½-5 in.); fragrant; growth like a Hybrid Tea, followed by longer canes.

Everdream HT, *my*, 1956, *Souv. de Claudius Pernet* × *Kaiserin Auguste Viktoria*; Motose. Bud ovoid; flowers canary-yellow, dbl. (35-40 petals), large (4-5 in.); fragrant; bushy growth.

Everest HP (OGR), *w*, 1927, *Candeur Lyonnaise* × *Mme. Caristie Martel*; Easlea. Flowers cream-white, center tinted green-lemon, dbl. (38 petals), high-centered, very large; fragrant; foliage light; low, spreading growth. GM, NRS, 1927.

Everest Double Fragrance F, *lp*, 1980, *Dearest* × *Elizabeth of Glamis*; Beales, Peter, 1979. Bud pointed; flowers light pink, dbl. (25 petals), borne 3-7 per cluster; very fragrant; foliage dark, heavily veined; large prickles; tall, upright growth.

Evergreen Gem R, *w*, 1899, *R. wichuraiana* × *Maréchal Niel*; Horvath; W.A. Manda. Bud buff; flowers white, dbl., medium (2-3 in.), borne in clusters; fragrant (sweetbriar); foliage almost evergreen; vigorous, climbing or trailing growth.

Evert Regterschot F, *mr*, 1965, *Korona* × *Seedling*; Buisman. Bud ovoid; flowers bright red, semi-dbl., medium; foliage dark.

Evert van Dyk HT, *mp*, 1931, *Ophelia* × *Hill's America*; Van Rossem; H&S. Flowers rose-pink tinted salmon, dbl., high-centered, large; long stems; slightly fragrant; foliage dark; bushy growth.

E. Veyrat Hermanos Cl T (OGR), *pb*, 1895, (E. Veyrath Hermanos; Pillar of Gold); Bernaix, A. Flowers apricot and carmine-pink, reflexes violet-rose, dbl.; very fragrant; vigorous growth.

Evghenya F, *op*, 1975, *Highlight* × *Masquerade*; Staikov, Prof. Dr. V.; Kalaydjiev and Chorbadjiiski. Flowers coral-orange, darker petal edges, base cream, very dbl. (75 petals), large blooms in clusters of 3-12; foliage dark, glossy; vigorous.

Evian Cachat HT, *mp*, 1939, Chambard, C. Flowers bright pink, center copper salmon, dbl., cupped, very large; vigorous growth.

Evita Min, *w*, 1984, (POUlvita); *Mini-Poul* × *Seedling*; Oleson, M.&P.; Poulsen. Flowers white with touch of pale pink, dbl. (20 petals), small blooms in clusters; slight fragrance; foliage small, dark, glossy; bushy growth.

E. V. Lucas HT, *dr*, 1934, McGredy. Flowers dark velvety crimson, semi-dbl., large, borne in sprays; slightly fragrant; foliage dark; vigorous, upright, branching growth.

Evrard Ketten HT, *m*, 1920, *Farbenkönigin* × *Ruhm de Gartenwelt*; Ketten Bros. Flowers bright unshaded carmine-purple, dbl.; very fragrant.

Excalibur F, *mr*, 1967, *Vera Dalton* × *Woburn Abbey*; Harkness. Flowers scarlet, semi-dbl. (14 petals), medium (2½ in.) blooms in clusters; slightly fragrant; foliage dark, glossy; bushy growth.

Excellenz Kuntze S, *ly*, 1909, *Aglaia* × *Souv. de Catherine Guillot*; Lambert, P. Flowers creamy yellow, dbl., small, borne in large clusters; fragrant; foliage dark, glossy; vigorous, upright growth.

Excellenz von Schubert Pol, *dp*, 1909, *Mme. Norbert Levavasseur* × *Frau Karl Druschki*; Lambert, P. Flowers dark carmine-rose, dbl., small blooms in clusters; foliage dark; vigorous growth; late bloom.

Excelsa R, *mr*, 1909, (Red Dorothy Perkins); Walsh. Flowers tyrian rose to bright light crimson, dbl., cupped, irregular blooms in large clusters; foliage rich green, glossy; vigorous, climbing (12-18 ft.) growth; non-recurrent bloom; (14). GM, ARS Gertrude M. Hubbard, 1914.

Excelsior F, *mp*, 1959, *Pinocchio* × *Mrs. Henri Daendels*; Buisman. Flowers salmon, borne in clusters; foliage dark; vigorous, upright growth.

Excitement™ Gr, *dy*, 1985, (HILco); *Golden Fantasie* × *Coed*; Jelly, Robert; E.G. Hill Co. Flowers deep yellow, dbl. (20 petals), high-centered, medium blooms borne usually singly; fragrant; foliage medium, dark, semi-glossy; no prickles; fruit medium, slightly pear-shaped, orange; medium, upright, bushy growth; greenhouse variety.

Exodus Gr, *mp*, 1974, (GODusex); *Kordes' Perfecta* × *Kalinka*; Godin. Bud ovoid; flowers pink, very dbl. (50-52 petals), cupped, large (3 in.); foliage glossy, dark.

Exotic Beauty HT, *op*, 1990, (LEOexbeau); *Silver Jubilee (surmised)* × *Seedling*; Leon, Charles F.; Oregon Grown Roses, 1990-91. Bud rounded; flowers orange blend, reverse pink blend, dbl., high-centered, exhibition, large blooms borne usually singly; slight, fruity fragrance; foliage large, dark green, glossy; upright, bushy, medium growth.

Exploit® LCl, *dp*, 1985, (MEIlider; All In One; Grimpant Exploit); *Fugue* × *Sparkling Scarlet*; Meilland, 1983. Flowers deep pink, dbl. (20 petals), medium; no fragrance; foliage small, medium green, matt; very vigorous, spreading, climbing growth.

Explorer's Dream Min, *op*, 1992, (MICexplore); *Unnamed Miniature seedling* × *Homecoming*; Williams, Michael C.; The Rose Garden; Mini Rose Nursery. Flowers deep orange pink, just a touch of yellow at base of each petal, moderately full (15-25 petals), small (0-4 cms) blooms borne in small clusters; no fragrance; foliage medium, dark green, semi-glossy; some prickles; medium (50 cms), upright growth.

Exquisite HT, *lp*, 1979, *Memoriam* × *((Blanche Mallerin* × *Peace)* × *(Peace* × *Virgo))*; Leon. Bud long, pointed; flowers light pink, dbl. (30 petals), high-centered, large (5½-6 in.); fragrant; vigorous, upright growth.

Exquisite HT, *ly*, 1918, Therkildsen. Flowers creamy yellow, dbl.; slightly fragrant.

Extase HT, *dr*, 1956, *E.G. Hill* × *Seedling*; Delforge. Bud long, dark red; vigorous growth.

Extasis LCl, *dr*, 1963, *Spectacular* × *Cocktail*; Dot, S. Flowers red, shaded darker, single (5 petals), blooms in clusters; vigorous.

Extravaganza F, *pb*, 1974, *Stella* × *(Sabrina* × *Golden Giant)*; Dawson, G.; Neil. Bud ovoid; flowers pink, base cream, dbl., medium; foliage leathery; vigorous, bushy growth.

Eydie Min, *w*, 1981, *Janna* × *Seedling*; Hooper, John; E.M. Brown. Flowers white with pink blush, fading to white, dbl. (50 petals), small blooms in clusters of 5-7; moderate tea fragrance; foliage medium green, purple, when young; beige prickles; vigorous, bushy growth.

Eye Appeal® S, *dr*, 1992, (INTerpeel; Ardennes); *Eyeopener* × *Seedling*; Ilsink, Peter; Interplant B.V., 1991. Flowers dark red, semi-dbl. (8 petals), cupped, medium (5 cms) blooms borne singly; no fragrance; foliage medium, medium green, glossy; spreading, medium (40-60 cms) growth; repeats.

Eye Liner HT, *dr*, 1966, *Queen Elizabeth* × *Montezuma*; Armbrust; Langbecker. Bud long, pointed; flowers blood red, semi-dbl., high-centered, medium; slightly fragrant; foliage dark, leathery; vigorous, upright growth.

Eyecatcher F, *pb*, 1976, *Arthur Bell* × *Pernille Poulsen*; Cants of Colchester, 1977. Flowers pink flushed apricot, reverse silvery cream, dbl. (22 petals), medium (2½ in.); fragrant; foliage glossy, light.

Eyeopener S, *mr*, 1987, (INTerop; Erica; Eye Opener; Tapis Rouge); *(Seedling* × *Eyepaint)* × *(Seedling* × *Dortmund)*; Interplant. Flowers medium red, semi-dbl., small; no fragrance; foliage medium, medium green, glossy; spreading growth.

Eyepaint® F, *rb*, 1975, (MACeye; Eye Paint; Tapis Persan); *Seedling* × *Picasso*; McGredy. Bud ovoid; flowers bright red, whitish eye, gold stamens, single (5-6 petals), medium (2½ in.); slightly fragrant; foliage small, dark; tall, bushy growth. GM, Baden-Baden, 1974 & Belfast, 1978.

E. Y. Teas HP (OGR), *mp*, 1874, (Mons. E.Y. Teas); *Alfred Colomb seedling*; Verdier, E.

Flowers bright red, globular, large; very fragrant.

Fabergé F, *pb*, 1969, *Seedling* × *Zorina*; Boerner; J&P. Bud ovoid; flowers light peach-pink, reverse tinted yellow, dbl., high-centered, large; slightly fragrant; foliage dark, leathery; vigorous, dense, bushy growth.

Fabienne F, *mp*, 1958, *Orange Triumph* × *(Independence* × *Floradora)*; Arles; Roses-France. Flowers reddish salmon, dbl. (35 petals), small; foliage clear green; bushy, low growth.

Fabvier Ch (OGR), *mr*, 1832, Laffay. Flowers crimson-scarlet, semi-dbl., very showy, medium; recurrent.

Facade HT, *mp*, 1970, *Elizabeth Fankhauser* × *Royal Highness*; Fankhauser. Flowers apricot-pink, very dbl. (60 petals), high-centered, very large; very fragrant; foliage glossy, dark, leathery; vigorous, upright growth.

Fackel HT, *dr*, 1937, *Vaterland* × *Barcelona*; Krause. Flowers crimson-red, shaded blackish, very dbl., cupped; slightly fragrant; compact growth.

Faïence HT, *op*, 1935, *Charles P. Kilham* × *Julien Potin*; Van Rossem; C-P, 1937. Flowers peach and apricot, reverse pure yellow, dbl. (45 petals), cupped, large; slightly fragrant; foliage leathery; vigorous, bushy growth.

Faint Heart HT, *w*, 1980, *Hawaii* × *Seedling*; Pavlick, Mike. Flowers cream edged light pink, dbl. (25 petals), exhibition, blooms 1-3 per cluster; slight fragrance; foliage mid to dark, leathery, semi-glossy; straight prickles; medium, branching growth.

Fair Bianca® S, *w*, 1983, (AUSca); Austin, David; David Austin Roses, 1982. Flowers light yellow to white, very dbl., flat, quartered form like Mme. Hardy, medium; fragrant; foliage medium, light green, semi-glossy; upright growth.

Fair Dinkum F, 1966, *Queen Elizabeth* × *Circus*; Small. Flowers peach-salmon, large (3-4 in.), cluster; fragrant; foliage glossy. RULED EXTINCT 6/83 ARM.

Fair Dinkum Min, *pb*, 1983, (TINdink); *Seedling* × *Coral Treasure*; Bennett, Dee; Tiny Petals Nursery. Flowers soft pink, petal margins darker, dbl. (25 petals), HT form, small; slight fragrance; foliage small, medium green, semi-glossy; upright, bushy growth.

Fair Lady HT, *ab*, 1959, *Golden Masterpiece* × *Tawny Gold*; Boerner; J&P. Bud ovoid to pointed; flowers buff overcast pink, dbl. (50 petals), high-centered, large (4½ in.); very fragrant; foliage glossy; vigorous, upright growth; a greenhouse variety.

Fair Maid HT, *mp*, 1940, *Talisman sport*; Peirce. Flowers bright rose to strawberry-pink, changing to deep pink, dbl. (60-75 petals), large (4-5 in.); very fragrant; foliage light green; vigorous, upright growth.

Fair Marjorie Pol, *lp*, 1952, *Katharina Zeimet seedling*; Armstrong, P.M. Bud ovoid, bright pink; flowers blush-pink, lighter in sun, semi-dbl., cupped, medium; very fragrant; vigorous, bushy growth.

Fair Play® S, *m*, 1982, (INTerfair); *Yesterday × Seedling*; Interplant, 1977. Flowers light violet, semi-dbl. (18 petals), medium blooms in large clusters; slight fragrance; foliage medium, dark, matt; dark green prickles; vigorous growth; repeat bloom; ground cover.

Fairest of Fair Min, *ly*, 1982, *Sunbonnet × Rise 'n' Shine*; Bennett, Dee; Tiny Petals Nursery. Flowers medium yellow, 15-18 petals, HT form, borne singly or 3-5 per cluster; slight tea fragrance; foliage small, medium green; very compact, low growth.

Fairhope Min, *ly*, 1989, (TALfairhope); *Azure Sea × Seedling*; Taylor, Franklin T. (Pete) & Kay; Taylor's Roses. Bud pointed; flowers soft, light pastel yellow, reverse same, aging same, color holds well, dbl. (16-28 petals), high-centered, exhibition, medium, borne singly, good substance; slight fragrance; foliage medium, medium green, semi-glossy; prickles straight, medium, red; fruit round, small, green; upright, bushy, medium growth.

Fairlane Min, *ly*, 1980, *Charlie McCarthy × Seedling*; Schwartz, Ernest; Nor'East Min. Roses. Flowers near white flushed pink and yellow, dbl. (20 petals), urn-shaped to high-centered blooms borne 1-5 per cluster; slight fragrance; foliage glossy, medium green, deeply serrated; prickles slanted downward; compact, bushy growth.

Fairlie Rede HT, *op*, 1937, *Mrs. E. Willis × Seedling*; Clark, A.; NRS Victoria. Flowers salmon, flushed fawn, full, large; fragrant; vigorous.

Fairlight F, *op*, 1964, *Joybells × Seedling*; Robinson, H. Flowers coppery salmon to flame, dbl., well-formed, large (3½ in.), in clusters; fragrant; foliage coppery bronze.

Fairy Changeling Pol, *mp*, 1979, (HARnumerous); *The Fairy × Yesterday*; Harkness, 1981. Bud short, plump; flowers pink, dbl. (22 petals), cupped, pompon, medium; slightly fragrant; foliage small, dark; recumbent, spreading growth.

Fairy Cluster F, *mp*, 1935, *Dainty Bess × Ideal*; Archer. Flowers rose-pink, single, borne in clusters on long stems; slightly fragrant; foliage glossy; very vigorous growth.

Fairy Crystal® Pol, *w*, 1980, (HARlittle); *The Fairy × Yesterday*; Harkness, R. Bud squat; flowers white, dbl. (20-25 petals), flat to cupped blooms borne several per cluster; slight fragrance; foliage small, dark, glossy; slender, dark prickles; short, bushy growth.

Fairy Damsel® Pol, *dr*, 1982, (HARneatly; Fairy Red); *The Fairy × Yesterday*; Harkness, R., 1981. Flowers dark red, dbl. (24 petals), cupped to flat, medium; foliage glossy; low, spreading growth.

Fairy Dancers HT, *ab*, 1969, *Wendy Cussons × Diamond Jubilee*; Cocker. Flowers buff-pink, dbl., small; fragrant; low, spreading growth.

Fairy Like Pol, *lp*, 1979, (HARnimble); *The Fairy × Yesterday*; Harkness. Bud short, plump; flowers light rose-pink, dbl. (20 petals), cupped to flat, small; foliage small, glossy; low, spreading growth.

Fairy Magic Min, *mp*, 1979, *Fairy Moss × Miniature Moss seedling*; Moore, R.S.; Sequoia Nursery. Bud mossy, long, pointed; flowers medium pink, semi-dbl. (10-15 petals), medium (1½ in.); fragrant; foliage small, glossy; bushy, upright growth.

Fairy Maid Pol, *lp*, 1981, (HARlassie); *The Fairy × Yesterday*; Harkness. Bud short, plump; flowers light rose-pink, dbl. (20 petals), cupped to flat, medium; foliage glossy; low, bushy growth.

Fairy Moss Min, *mp*, 1969, (Pinocchio × William Lobb) × New Penny; Moore, R.S.; Sequoia Nursery. Bud mossy; flowers medium pink, semi-dbl.; foliage small, light green, leathery; vigorous, bushy, dwarf growth.

Fairy Pompons Min, *w*, 1986, (TRApom); *Fairy Moss × Fairy Moss*; Travis, Louis. Flowers flesh pink fading white, very dbl. (45-60 petals), high-centered, small, borne usually singly; slight spicy fragrance; foliage small, medium green, matt; straight, tan-brown prickles; fruit none; bushy, low growth.

Fairy Prince® Pol, *mr*, 1981, (HARnougette); *The Fairy × Yesterday*; Harkness. Bud short; flowers geranium-lake red, dbl. (25 petals), cupped, medium; foliage glossy; spreading growth. First Prize, Copenhagen.

Fairy Princess Cl Min, *lp*, 1955, *Éblouissant × Zee*; Moore, R.S.; Sequoia Nursery. Bud pointed, salmon-apricot; flowers light pink, very dbl., small (1 in.) blooms in clusters; foliage small, fern-like; height to 2½ ft.

Fairy Queen F, *lp*, 1971, *The Fairy × Queen Elizabeth*; Williams, J.B. Bud ovoid; flowers bluish pink, center coral-pink, dbl., high-centered, small; fragrant; foliage small, glossy, bronze; very vigorous, bushy growth.

Fairy Red Pol, *dr*, 1979, (HARneatly); *The Fairy × Yesterday*; Harkness. Bud short, plump; flowers oxblood-red, dbl. (24 petals), cupped to flat, medium; foliage glossy; low, spreading growth.

Fairy Ring Pol, *mp*, 1979, (HARnicely); Harkness. Bud short, plump; flowers rose-pink, dbl. (20 petals), cupped to flat, medium (2 in.); foliage glossy; low, bushy growth.

Fairy Rose This name has been applied to 'The Fairy,' *R. multiflora nana* and various Miniatures and dwarf China roses.

Fairy Snow Pol, *w*, 1979, (HARlittle); *The Fairy × Yesterday*; Harkness. Bud squat; flowers white, dbl. (20-25 petals), cupped to flattish, medium; low, bushy growth.

Fairy Tale S, *lp*, 1960, *The Fairy × Goldilocks*; Thomson. Bud ovoid; flowers light pink, dbl., open, small; slightly fragrant; foliage dark, glossy; very vigorous, upright (6 ft.) growth.

Fairyland® Pol, *lp*, 1980, (HARlayalong); *The Fairy × Yesterday*; Harkness. Bud short, fat; flowers light pink, dbl. (24 petals), cupped, medium; fragrant; foliage glossy; spreading.

Faithful F, *rb*, 1964, *Dusky Maiden × Tabarin*; Latham. Flowers crimson edged white, becoming velvety crimson, semi-dbl., well shaped, medium, borne in clusters; foliage small, light green; vigorous growth.

Faja Lobbi HT, *mr*, 1963, *Queen Elizabeth × Florence Mary Morse*; Leenders, J. Flowers bright red; vigorous growth.

Falbala HT, *mp*, 1948, Gaujard. Bud long; flowers brilliant salmon; fragrant; foliage glossy, dark; erect growth.

Falkland HSpn (OGR), *w*, *R. spinosissima hybrid*. Flowers pale pink to nearly white, dbl.; low, bushy growth.

Fama HT, *rb*, 1942, Dot, P.; C-P. Flowers amber and red, dbl. (25-30 petals), cupped, large; short stems; foliage soft, light green; vigorous, upright, bushy growth.

Famosa HT, *mp*, 1964, *Tallyho × Flamingo*; Leenders, J. Flowers pink, well formed.

Fan Fare 81 HT, *ob*, 1981, *Cotillion × Hoosier Gold*; Byrum, Roy L.; Joseph H. Hill Co. Bud short, pointed; flowers orange blend, dbl. (23 petals), high-centered blooms borne singly; faint rose fragrance; foliage medium to large; straight, short, broad-based prickles; vigorous growth.

Fan Mail F, *dy*, 1973, *Spanish Sun × Seedling*; Boerner; Spek. Bud long, pointed; flowers deep yellow, dbl., open, medium; fragrant; foliage large, leathery; very vigorous, bushy growth.

Fanal F, *mr*, 1946, *(Johanna Tantau × Heidekind) × Hamburg*; Tantau. Flowers medium red, dbl. (20 petals), large, borne in clusters of 10-15; fragrant; foliage dark, glossy; upright.

Fancy HT, *mr*, 1928, *Souv. de Claudius Pernet × Gen. Smuts*; Van Rossem. Flowers peach shaded cherry-red, base yellow, semi-dbl., open; fragrant.

Fancy Free HT, *pb*, 1922, *Gustav Grünerwald × Seedling*; Clark, A.; NRS New South Wales. Flowers pink, center white, semi-dbl.; fragrant; dwarf growth.

Fancy Lace HT, *mp*, 1967, *Seedling × Queen Elizabeth*; Patterson; Patterson Roses. Bud ovoid; flowers pink tipped silver, dbl., high-centered, large; fragrant; foliage glossy; very vigorous, upright growth.

Fancy Lady Min, *pb*, 1991, (CLElady); *Seedling × Seedling*; Clements, John; Heirloom Old Garden Roses, 1990. Flowers medium pink, white reverse, very full (41+ petals), high pointed, exhibition, small (0-4 cms) blooms borne mostly singly; no fragrance; foliage small, dark green, glossy; few prickles; tall (50 cms), upright growth.

Fancy Pants™ Min, *rb*, 1986, (KINfancy); *Baby Katie × Rose Window*; King, Gene; AGM Miniature Roses, 1987. Flowers deep pink to golden yellow base, edged red, fading deeper pink to slight yellow base, dbl. (40 petals), high-centered, exhibition, medium, borne usually singly or in sprays of 3-5; slight, spicy fragrance; foliage medium, medium green, matt; medium, light red prickles, slightly crooked on end; fr. none observed; upright, bushy, medium growth.

Fancy Talk F, *pb*, 1965, *Spartan × Garnette*; Swim & Weeks; Weeks Wholesale Rose Grower. Bud urn-shaped; flowers pink tinted orange, dbl., high-centered, small blooms in clusters; slightly fragrant; foliage leathery; vigorous, bushy, low growth.

Fancy That Min, *pb*, 1989, *Rise 'n' Shine × Rainbow's End*; Jolly, Marie; Rosehill Farm. Bud pointed; flowers different shades of pink, reverse pink-yellow blend, dbl. (68 petals), high-centered, exhibition, medium, borne usually singly and in sprays of 3-5; slight, spicy fragrance; foliage medium, medium green, semi-glossy; prickles none; fruit globular, green-brown; upright, spreading, medium, vigorous growth.

Fandango HT, *mr*, 1950, *Charlotte Armstrong × Seedling*; Swim; Armstrong Nursery. Bud ovoid, turkey-red, base yellow; flowers orange-red, semi-dbl. (16-25 petals), open, large (3½-4½ in.); fragrant; foliage leathery, glossy, dark; vigorous, upright, bushy growth.

Fanely Revoil HT, *or*, 1962, *Michèle Meilland* × *Seedling*; Orard. Flowers cerise-red, reverse tinted orange, well formed, long stems.

Fanette® HT, *rb*, 1966, (LAPcal); *Jeunesse* × *Souv. du Président Plumecocq*; Laperrière; EFR. Flowers red, reverse white, dbl. (36 petals), high-centered, medium; slightly fragrant; foliage dark, glossy; vigorous, bushy growth.

Fanfare F, *pb*, 1956, *Fandango* × *Pinocchio*; Swim; Armstrong Nursery. Bud urn shaped; flowers orange and salmon to pink, dbl. (20-30 petals), flat cupped to open, large (3-4 in.), borne in large clusters; fragrant (spicy); foliage glossy, leathery; very vigorous, spreading growth. GM, Rome, 1955.

Fanion HT, *dy*, 1961, (Puregold); *Helen Fox* × *(Mrs. Pierre S. duPont* × *Joanna Hill)*; Robichon; Ilgenfritz Nursery. Bud long, pointed; flowers rich yellow, dbl. (30 petals), high-centered, medium (3-3½ in.); very fragrant; foliage leathery, dark, glossy; vigorous, upright growth.

Fanny HT, *mr*, 1935, *Hadley* × *Mrs. Henry Winnett*; Lens. Flowers bright red; vigorous growth.

Fanny Bias G (OGR), *mp*, 1819, Vibert. Flowers blush, center rosy, full, large (3 in.); fragrant; erect, bushy growth.

Fanny Blankers-Koen HT, *ob*, 1949, (Luxembourg); *Talisman* × *Seedling*; Verschuren-Pechtold. Bud long, pointed; flowers orange-yellow, flushed and veined red, semi-dbl. (16 petals), large; very fragrant; foliage glossy; very vigorous, upright, bushy growth.

Fanny Oppenheimer HT, *mr*, 1923, McGredy. Flowers brilliant cardinal, shaded gold; fragrant.

Fantaisie HT, *r*, 1948, Gaujard. Flowers coppery-salmon, base yellow; slightly fragrant; foliage dark; vigorous growth.

Fantan HT, *r*, 1959, (MEImex); *(Pigalle* × *Prélude)* × *Self*; Meilland, F.; URS & C-P. Bud urn-shaped; flowers burnt-orange to yellow-ochre, dbl. (40-55 petals), cupped, large (3½ in.); slightly fragrant; foliage leathery; moderate growth.

Fantan F, *or*, 1956, *Eternité* × *Seedling*; Gaujard. Flowers coppery orange, small; foliage small.

Fantasi™ Min, *w*, 1985, (KINfanta); King, Gene; AGM Min. Roses, 1986. Flowers cream, reverse cream shaded deep pink, dbl. (50 petals), high-centered, exhibition, miniflora, large blooms borne singly; slight fragrance; foliage medium, dark, matt; medium, hooked, brown prickles; fruit none; tall, upright growth.

Fantasia HT, *my*, 1943, *Seedling* × *Lord Lonsdale*; Dickson, A.; J&P. Bud long, pointed; flowers golden to lighter yellow, dbl. (30-35 petals), open, medium, on strong stems; very fragrant; foliage glossy; vigorous, bushy, compact growth; a greenhouse cut flower. RULED EXTINCT.

Fantasia HT, *pb*, 1974, (KORfan); *Silver Star* × *Tradition*; Kordes; Horstmann. Bud ovoid; flowers lilac-red, globular, flora-tea; fragrant; foliage leathery; vigorous growth.

Fantasia, Climbing Cl HT, *my*, 1956, Mell.

Fantastique HT, *yb*, 1943, (Fantasque); *Ampère* × *(Charles P. Kilham* × *(Charles P. Kilham* × *Capucine Chambard))*; Meilland, F.; C-P. Flowers yellow, heavily edged carmine, dbl. (38 petals), cupped, medium (2½-3 in.); fragrant (spicy); foliage dark, leathery, glossy; vigorous, compact growth.

Fantasy HT, *rb*, 1945, *Soeur Thérèse* × *Seedling*; Wyant. Bud long, pointed; flowers cerise, reverse yellow washed pink, semi-dbl. (9-11 petals), open, large (4½ in.) blooms; slender stems; slightly fragrant; foliage leathery, glossy; very vigorous, upright growth. RULED EXTINCT 1/86 ARM.

Fantin-Latour C (OGR), *lp*, Original name, class and date unknown. Flowers blush, full, flat; fragrant; foliage dark, broad; vigorous, bushy growth.

Far Side F, *ob*, 1988, *((Sunsprite* × *(Many Moons* × *Maigold))* × *Eyepaint*; Stoddard, Louis, 1990. Bud ovoid, pointed; flowers orange-vermillion, yellow center, single (5 petals), small, borne in sprays of up to 20; moderate, spicy fragrance; foliage large, medium green, glossy, smooth; prickles straight, medium, stout, pink to brown; fruit globular, medium, vermillion; upright, spreading, tall growth.

Farah HT, *yb*, 1961, *Peace* × *Georges Chesnel*; Gaujard. Flowers coppery yellow, dbl., large, long stems; fragrant; foliage glossy; very vigorous, bushy growth.

Farandole F, *mr*, 1959, *(Goldilocks* × *Moulin Rouge)* × *(Goldilocks* × *Fashion)*; Meilland, M.L.; URS. Bud oval; flowers vermilion, dbl. (25 petals), open, medium, borne in large clusters; foliage leathery; vigorous, well branched growth. GM, Rome, 1959.

Farbenkönigen HT, *mr*, 1902, (Queen of Colors; Reine des Couleurs); *Grand-Duc Adolphe de Luxembourg* × *La France*; Hinner, W. Flowers rosy carmine, dbl.; fragrant.

Farbenspiel F, *rb*, 1960, *Pinocchio* × *Masquerade*; Verschuren, A.; van Engelen. Flowers pink edged red, dbl.; very fragrant; foliage dark; bushy, compact growth.

Farfadet F, *or*, 1955, *Méphisto × Incendie*, Combe. Flowers orange-red, semi-dbl.; very upright growth.

Farida F, *dp*, 1941, *Seedling × Permanent Wave*, Leenders, M. Flowers deep rose-pink, semi-dbl.; fragrant.

Farny Wurlitzer HT, *mr*, 1968, *Poinsettia × Charlotte Armstrong*; Cadey; Ty-Tex Rose Nursery. Bud long, pointed; flowers rich rose red, dbl., large; very fragrant; foliage dark, glossy; vigorous, upright growth.

Farquhar R, *mp*, 1903, (The Farquhar Rose); *R. wichuraiana × Crimson Rambler*, Dawson; Farquhar. Flowers bright clear pink, carnation-like, resembling Lady Gay, dbl., borne in clusters; vigorous, climbing growth; late bloom.

Fascinating HT, *yb*, 1961, *Peace × Orange Nassau*; Fisher, G.; C-P. Bud long, pointed; flowers rose-opal suffused yellow, dbl. (25 petals), high-centered to cupped, large (4½ in.); fragrant; foliage leathery, glossy, dark; upright, bushy growth.

Fascination HT, *pb*, 1927, Chaplin Bros. Flowers rosy cerise, shaded yellow; fragrant; foliage dark, glossy; vigorous growth. RULED EXTINCT 2/81.

Fascination HT, *op*, 1982, (JACoyel); *Seedling × Spellbinder*, Warriner, W.; J&P. Bud nearly globular; flowers orange and rose blend, dbl. (50-60 petals), high-centered blooms borne usually singly; very little fragrance; foliage very large, semi-glossy; long-based prickles, hooked down; upright, heavy branching growth. GM, NZ, 1976.

Fashion F, *pb*, 1949, *Pinocchio × Crimson Glory*; Boerner; J&P. Bud ovoid, deep peach; flowers lively coral-peach, dbl. (23 petals), large (3-3½ in.) blooms in clusters; fragrant; vigorous, bushy growth; (28). GM, NRS, 1948, Bagatelle & Portland, 1949, ARS, 1954; AARS, 1950; ARS David Fuerstenberg Prize, 1950.

Fashion, Climbing Cl F, *pb*, 1951, Boerner.

Fashion, Climbing Cl F, *op*, 1955, Mattock.

Fashion Flame Min, *op*, 1977, *Little Darling × Fire Princess*; Moore, R.S.; Sequoia Nursery. Bud ovoid, pointed; flowers coral-orange, dbl. (35 petals), high-centered, small (1-1½ in.); slightly fragrant; foliage large, leathery; bushy growth.

Fashionette F, *pb*, 1958, *Goldilocks × Fashion*; Boerner; J&P. Bud pointed to ovoid, coral; flowers pinkish coral, dbl. (35-40 petals), cupped, large (3 in.), borne in irregular clusters; fragrant; foliage glossy; vigorous, upright growth.

Fashionette, Climbing Cl F, *pb*, 1962, Noack.

Fat 'n' Sassy Min, *rb*, 1986, (TINsassy); *Carrousel × Sheri Anne*; Bennett, Dee; Tiny Petals Nursery. Flowers white with a reddish border, reverse white, aging reddish blush, dbl. (28 petals), cupped, mini-flora, medium blooms borne singly; slight fragrance; foliage medium, medium green, semi-glossy; small, reddish prickles; fruit globular, 5/8 in. diameter, green-brown; medium, upright, bushy growth.

Fat Tuesday Min, *m*, 1991, (TALfat); *Azure Sea × Lavender Jewel*; Taylor, Pete & Kay; Taylor's Roses, 1992. Flowers lavender with darker edges, blending to lighter center, reverse lighter, full (26-40 petals), medium (4-7 cms) blooms borne mostly singly; no fragrance; foliage medium, medium green, semi-glossy; some prickles; tall (76 cms), upright growth.

Fata Morgana F, *ob*, 1957, *Masquerade × Seedling*; Kordes, R. Flowers orange-yellow, dbl. (28 petals), open, medium (2½ in.), borne in large trusses; slightly fragrant; foliage leathery, glossy; vigorous, upright growth.

Fatima HT, *ob*, 1955, *Opera seedling × Seedling*; Gaujard. Bud long, pointed; flowers orange, reverse bright golden yellow, very large; fragrant; vigorous growth.

Fatime G (OGR), *mp*, 1820, Descemet. Flowers pink, dotted and spotted both lighter and darker, medium, borne in clusters.

Faust F, *yb*, 1957, (Dr. Faust); *Masquerade × Golden Scepter*; Kordes, R.; McGredy & A. Dickson. Flowers golden yellow shaded orange-pink, dbl. (25 petals), medium (2 in.) blooms in large clusters; fragrant; foliage dark, glossy; vigorous, bushy growth. GM, NRS, 1956.

Faust, Climbing Cl F, *yb*, 1963, deRuiter.

Favori F, *op*, 1980, (LEN 3); (Favorite); *Seedling × Seedling*; Lens, Louis. Flowers light salmon-pink, dbl. (23 petals), urn-shaped, 3 in. blooms in clusters of 8-24; very fragrant; foliage dark; hooked, brownish-green prickles; large, bushy growth.

Favorita™ HT, *op*, 1954, *Unnamed HT seedling × Serenade*; Boerner; Stark Bros. Bud ovoid, burnt-orange; flowers salmon overcast orange, dbl. (48 petals), large (5½-6 in.); fragrant; foliage dark; vigorous growth. GM, Rome, 1952.

Fayanne F, *pb*, 1953, *Garnette sport*; Pinchbeck. Flowers deep rose-pink, reverse lighter, dbl. (55 petals), globular to flat, small (2 in.); slightly fragrant; foliage leathery; dwarf, bushy growth.

Faye Reynolds Cl F, *dp*, 1992, (REYfaye); *Westerland* × *Gingersnap*; Reynolds, Ted; Reynolds Roses. Flowers deep pink, full (26-40 petals), large (7+cms.) blooms borne in small clusters; fragrant; foliage sage green, semi-glossy; some prickles; medium (6'6"), upright growth.

F. Cambó HT, *mr*, 1933, *Li Burés* × *Florence L. Izzard*; Dot, P. Flowers carmine, dbl., cupped, large; fragrant; foliage glossy; dwarf growth.

Fear Naught F, *dp*, 1968, *Queen Elizabeth* × *Ena Harkness*; Harkness. Flowers deep pink, dbl.; slightly fragrant.

Federation LCl, *op*, 1938, *(R. setigera* × *Mrs. F.F. Prentiss)* × *Director Rubió*; Horvath; Wayside Gardens Co. Bud pointed; flowers rosy pink, orange undertone, dbl. (24-36 wavy petals), cupped, large (3½ in.); long, strong stems; very fragrant; foliage leathery, glossy, dark; very vigorous climbing (12-14 ft.) growth.

Federico Casas HT, *op*, 1931, *Seedling* × *Eugene Barbier*; Dot, P.; C-P. Flowers coppery pink and orange, semi-dbl., open, very large; very fragrant; foliage dark; vigorous, bushy growth.

Federico Casas, Climbing Cl HT, *op*, 1937, Stell; Stell Rose Nursery.

Fedra F, *mr*, 1959, *(Fiamma* × *Independence)* × *Seedling*; Giacomasso. Flowers brick-red, dbl.; vigorous growth.

Fee F, *or*, 1963, Kordes, R. Flowers orange, dbl., large; strong, wiry stems; moderate growth.

Fée des Champs Pol, *op*, 1965, *Queen Elizabeth* × *Zambra*; Dot; Minier. Flowers salmon-orange, dbl. (20-25 petals); foliage bronze; low growth. GM, Bagatelle, 1965.

Féerie HT, *ob*, 1938, Gaujard. Flowers coppery red, reverse orange-yellow, semi-dbl., open, long stems; fragrant; vigorous, erect growth.

Felberg's Rosa Druschki HP (OGR), *mp*, 1929, *Frau Karl Druschki* × *Farbenkönigin*; Felberg-Leclerc. Flowers bright rose-pink, dbl. (25 petals), large.

Felicia HMsk (S), *pb*, 1928, *Trier* × *Ophelia*; Pemberton. Flowers pink fading to blush and partly white, semi-dbl., large, branching panicles; fragrant (musk); pillar or shrub growth; (21).

Félicité A (OGR), *lp*, Flowers flesh, dbl., medium.

Félicité Bohain M (OGR), *dp*, (Félicité Bohan); 1866. Flowers vivid pink or bright rose, full, large.

Félicité et Perpétue HSem (OGR), *w*, 1828, *Thought to be R. sempervirens* × *Noisette*; Jacques. Flowers pale flesh changing to white, very dbl., flat, fairly large blooms in clusters; foliage almost evergreen; very vigorous growth.

Félicité Parmentier A (OGR), *lp*, 1834. Flowers soft flesh-pink, very dbl., opening flat and then reflexing; very fragrant; foliage gray-green; vigorous, compact growth.

Felicity HT, *mp*, 1919, *Ophelia* × *Hoosier Beauty*; Clarke Bros. Flowers rose-pink suffused silvery, dbl. (50-60 petals), large; fragrant; foliage dark; vigorous, branching growth.

Felicity Kendal HT, *op*, 1985, (LANken); *Fragrant Cloud* × *Mildred Reynolds*; Sealand Nursery. Flowers salmon-orange, dbl. (35 petals), large; foliage large; bushy growth.

Felix Brix HT, *pb*, 1921, *Natalie Boettner* × *Old Gold*; Brix; Teschendorff. Flowers soft rose, suffused yellow, passing to salmon-rose, semi-dbl.

Felix Laporte HT, *m*, 1928, *Yves Druhen* × *Mme. Edouard Herriot*; Buatois. Flowers blackish velvety purple tinged garnet, full, cupped; very fragrant; foliage dark, leathery, glossy; vigorous, bushy growth.

Fellenberg N (OGR), *mr*, (Fellenberg); 1835. Flowers bright crimson, dbl. (36 petals), cupped; foliage dark; vigorous, spreading growth.

Femina HT, *op*, 1963, *Fernand Arles* × *Mignonne*; Gaujard; Ilgenfritz Nursery, 1966. Bud long, pointed; flowers salmon-pink, dbl., large; fragrant; foliage leathery; vigorous, upright.

Femina HT, *lp*, 1957, Poulsen, S. Flowers soft pink, dbl., large; vigorous growth.

Femme HT, *yb*, 1970, (DELvor); *(Gloire de Rome* × *Bayadere)* × *(Queen Elizabeth* × *Provence)*; Delbard-Chabert, G.; Delbard Roses. Flowers ivory yellow, tinted pink, dbl. (28 petals), large; light fragrance; foliage medium, dark, glossy; bronze-red prickles; upright growth.

Fen Queen F, *lp*, 1963, *Queen Elizabeth* × HT *Seedling*; Sharman. Flowers pale flesh, dbl. (25 petals), large; slightly fragrant; foliage light green; vigorous, upright growth.

Ferdinand de Buck G (OGR), *mp*, (Feu de Buck). Flowers brilliant pink, dbl., medium.

Ferdinand Jamin HP (OGR), *mr*, 1888, Lévêque. Flowers vermilion-red.

Ferdinand Pichard HP (OGR), *rb*, 1921, Tanne. Flowers streaked (striped) pink and scarlet, dbl. (25 petals); vigorous, tall growth; recurrent bloom.

Ferdy™ S, *dp*, 1984, (KEItoli; Ferdi); *Climbing seedling* × *Petite Folie seedling*; Suzuki, S.; Keisei Rose Nursery. Flowers deep pink, dbl. (20 petals), small; no fragrance; foliage medium, medium green, matt; spreading (to 5 ft.) growth; ground cover.

Fergie F, *ob*, 1987, (GANfer); *Seedling × Copper Pot*; Gandy, F. Douglas, 1988. Flowers orange blend, dbl. (over 40 petals), large; patio; slight fragrance; foliage medium, medium green, semi-glossy, disease resistant; frostproof; bushy growth.

Feria HT, *op*, 1968, (MEIfrison); *(Grand Gala × Premier Bal) × Love Song*; Meilland; URS. Flowers coral suffused pink, dbl., globular, large; fragrant; foliage leathery; upright.

Fern Kemp HRg (S), *lp*, 1918, *Conrad Ferdinand Meyer × Frau Karl Druschki*; Kemp, J.A. Flowers delicate pink, semi-dbl., large (4 in.); very fragrant; vigorous growth; hardy.

Fern Roehrs LCl, *mp*, 1943, *Paul's Scarlet Climber sport*; Graf; Roehrs. Flowers same as parent but much more dbl.

Fernand Arles HT, *op*, 1949, (Arles); *Mme. Joseph Perraud × Seedling*; Gaujard. Bud long, pointed; flowers orange-salmon shaded red, dbl., very large; fragrant; foliage bronze; very vigorous, bushy growth.

Fernand Point HT, *rb*, 1964, *Peace × Seedling*; Orard. Flowers crimson-red, reverse flesh-pink, base yellow; foliage glossy.

Fernand Rabier R, *dr*, 1918, *Delight × Seedling*; Turbat. Flowers pure deep scarlet, dbl., borne in clusters of 40-50; slightly fragrant; vigorous, climbing or trailer.

Fernand Tanne LCl, *dy*, 1920, Tanne; Turbat. Flowers deep yellow to cream-yellow, dbl., large; very fragrant; vigorous growth.

Fernande Krier R, *pb*, 1925, *Excelsa sport*; Walter, L. Flowers peach-pink, occasionally margined red or sometimes entirely red.

Fernande Lumay HT, *ab*, 1922, *Mrs. Aaron Ward × Seedling*; Buatois. Flowers apricot-nankeen-yellow, edged milk-white, dbl; fragrant.

Fernielea HT, *ab*, 1926, Adam & Craigmile. Flowers apricot, center deeper; fragrant.

Ferris Wheel Min, *yb*, 1984, (AROyumi); *Golden Angel × Cricket*; Christensen, J.; Armstrong Nursery. Flowers yellow, turning pink, orange and red (striped), dbl. (20 petals), medium; slight fragrance; foliage small, dark, semi-glossy; bushy growth.

Ferry Porsche HT, *mr*, 1971, *Tropicana × Americana*; Kordes, W., Sohne. Bud long, pointed; flowers medium red, dbl. (34 petals), high-centered, blooms borne singly and in small clusters; slight fragrance; foliage large, dark, soft; vigorous, upright growth.

Fervid F, *or*, 1960, *Pimpernell × Korona*; LeGrice. Flowers scarlet-orange, single (7 ruffled petals), large (3 in.), in clusters; slightly fragrant; foliage glossy, dark; vigorous, upright.

Festival HT, *mr*, 1943, (Dixie Dream); *E.G. Hill seedling*; Dixie Rose Nursery; Krider Nursery. 1945. Flowers rich red, very dbl.; fragrant; entirely prickle free.

Festival, Climbing Cl HT, *mr*, 1945, *E.G. Hill sport*; Watkins, A.F.; Dixie Rose Nursery. Flowers same red as E.G. Hill, globular, large; very fragrant; foliage glossy; thornless; very vigorous, climbing growth; free, intermittent bloom; hardy in South.

Festival Fanfare F, *pb*, 1982, (BLEstogil); *Fred Loads sport*; Ogilvie, W.D. Flowers dark pink with paler pink stripes, which become nearly white.

Festival Pink™ S, *mp*, 1991, (RUPfespin); *Festival Fanfare sport*; Rupert, Kim L., 1992. Bud pointed; flowers clear medium pink, white petal base, golden stamen, single (5-7 petals), medium (4-7 cms) blooms borne in small and large clusters; slight fragrance; foliage medium, bright green, glossy; many prickles; tall (120-150 cms), bushy, spreading growth.

Festival Queen HT, *lp*, 1968, Lindquist; Edmunds. Bud long, pointed; flowers light pink, edged deeper, well-formed, high-centered; slightly fragrant; foliage dark, leathery; upright, compact growth.

Festival Rouge® F, *dr*, 1980, (DELfesrou; Red Festival); *Walko × (Happiness × Sonia)*; Delbard-Chabert; Delbard Roses. Flowers dark red, semi-dbl., well-formed, blooms in clusters; foliage dark.

Festive Pol, *dr*, 1975, *Bacarrá × Seedling*; Jelly; E.G. Hill Co. Bud short, pointed; flowers dark red, dbl. (27-32 petals), high-centered, large (3-3½ in.); slightly fragrant (sweetbriar); foliage parsley-green; vigorous, upright growth; repeat bloom.

Festivity F, *ob*, 1980, (LENor); *Seedling × Seedling*; Lens, Louis. Flowers orange, dbl. (24 petals), 3 in. blooms in clusters of 3-24; light fragrance; foliage dark; hooked, green prickles; bushy growth.

Fétiche F, *mr*, 1962, *Philippe × Tabarin*; Delforge. Flowers coral-red, center white, semi-dbl. (12 petals), open, medium (2 in.), borne in clusters; foliage dark; moderate, bushy growth.

Feu d'Artifice® LCl, *yb*, 1935, (Fireworks, Climbing); *R. foetida hybrid × Colette Clément*; Mallerin; B&A, 1939. Bud long, pointed, nasturtium-red; flowers yellow, tinted nasturtium-red, semi-dbl., open, borne in clusters on long stems; vigorous, climbing (over 8 ft.) growth.

Feu de Bengale F, *lp*, 1951, *Orange Triumph × Seedling*; Gaujard, R.; G. Truffaut. Flowers pearl-pink, dbl., cupped, large; fragrant; foliage glossy; vigorous growth.

Feu de Joie F, *mr*, 1951, *Orange Triumph × Seedling*; Gaujard, R.; G. Truffaut. Flowers carmine-red, dbl., large, borne in clusters; foliage dark, glossy; vigorous growth.

Feu de Saint-Jean Pol, *dr*, 1951, *Orange Triumph × Seedling*; Gaujard, R.; G. Truffaut. Flowers blackish red, semi-dbl., small, borne in clusters; foliage dark, glossy; vigorous, bushy growth.

Feu d'Enfer F, *or*, 1958, *Orange Triumph × Seedling*; Gaujard, R.; G. Truffaut. Flowers orange-red, dbl., large; upright, well branched growth.

Feu du Ciel Pol, *ob*, 1951, *Orange Triumph × Seedling*; Gaujard, R.; G. Truffaut. Flowers clear orange, semi-dbl., small, borne in clusters; foliage glossy; vigorous, bushy growth.

Feu Follet F, *mp*, 1953, Gaujard, R. Flowers salmon, cupped, fragrant; vigorous growth.

Feu Joseph Looymans HT, *ob*, 1921, *Sunburst × Rayon d'Or*; Looymans. Flowers Indian yellow, dbl., cupped, large blooms with weak stems; foliage leathery; vigorous.

Feu Joseph Looymans, Climbing Cl HT, *ob*, 1935, Western Rose Co.

Feu Magique F, *mr*, 1956, *Independence × Signal Red*; Buyl Frères. Flowers cherry-red, semi-dbl. (18 petals); vigorous growth.

Feu Pernet-Ducher HT, *my*, 1935, *Julien Potin × Margaret McGredy*; Mallerin; A. Meilland; C-P. Flowers bright yellow, center apricot, dbl., large; fragrant (fruity); foliage leathery, dark; vigorous, branching growth. GM, Portland, 1936.

Feu Rouge F, *mr*, 1956, *Red Favorite × Fanal*; Tantau. Bud ovoid; flowers red, semi-dbl., open, large; slightly fragrant; foliage glossy; vigorous growth.

Feudor HT, *yb*, 1963, *Peace × Baccará*; Croix, P.; Minier. Flowers golden yellow shaded vermilion; foliage bright green; vigorous growth.

Feuerball HT, *mr*, 1965, Tantau, Math. Bud globular; flowers red lead color, dbl. (25-30 petals), well formed, large; foliage glossy; very vigorous, bushy.

Feuerland F, *or*, 1977, *Kathe Duvigneau × Topsi*; Kordes, W., Sons. Bud ovoid; flowers orange-red, dbl. (25 petals), cupped, large (2½ in.); slightly fragrant; very vigorous, upright growth.

Feuerreiter F, *mr*, 1968, (Fire-Rider); *Alain × Oskar Scheerer*; Haenchen; Teschendorff. Bud long, pointed; flowers red, semi-dbl., open, large, borne in clusters; slightly fragrant; foliage dark, leathery; very vigorous, upright growth.

Feuerschein F, *mr*, 1930, (Krause's Rote Joseph Guy); *Lafayette sport*; Krause. Flowers brilliant red, not turning blue, full; foliage dark; bushy growth.

Feuerschein, Climbing Cl F, *mr*, 1936, Krause.

Feuerwerk® S, *ob*, 1962, (Feu d'Artifice; Magneet; Fireworks); Tantau, Math. Flowers bright orange, semi-dbl., medium blooms in clusters; foliage glossy; upright, bushy (to 5 ft.) growth. RULED EXTINCT 11/91 ARM.

Feuerzauber® HT, *or*, 1973, (KORfeu; Fire Magic; Magic de Feu); *Fragrant Cloud × Seedling*; Kordes, R., 1974. Flowers orange-red, reverse lighter, dbl., high-centered, medium to large; foliage dark, glossy; vigorous, upright growth.

Feurio F, *or*, 1956, *Rudolph Timm × Independence*; Kordes, R.; J&P, 1957. Bud ovoid; flowers scarlet-red, dbl. (30 petals), cupped, medium (2½ in.), borne in clusters; fragrant; foliage glossy, light green; vigorous, low, bushy growth; a florists' variety.

Feurio, Climbing Cl F, *or*, 1963, Kordes.

Fever F, *dp*, 1982, (PEAfever); Pearce, C.A.; Limes Rose Nursery. Flowers deep pink, very full (40+ petals), large; very fragrant; foliage large, dark; upright.

F. Ferrer LCl, *dr*, 1940, Pahissa; J&P. Bud long, pointed; flowers dark velvety red, open, large; slightly fragrant; foliage leathery; vigorous, climbing growth; somewhat recurrent bloom.

Fiaba HT, *rb*, 1963, (Fiamma × Sovrana) × Seedling; Giacomasso. Flowers bright red tipped yellow; foliage dark, glossy; very vigorous growth.

Fiametta F, *dr*, 1962, *Karl Weinhausen × Goldilocks*; Leenders, J. Flowers velvety red, center yellow; moderate growth.

Fiamma F, *or*, 1948, *Paul's Scarlet Climber × Talisman seedling*; Aicardi, D.; Giacomasso. Flowers vermilion, borne in clusters; vigorous growth. GM, Rome, 1951.

Fiammetta LCl, *ab*, 1922, *R. gigantea × Margaret Molyneux*; Nabonnand, P. Flowers warm amber-yellow, streaked yellow, single; very fragrant; vigorous, climbing growth.

Fiddler's Gold™ Min, *dy*, 1985, (MINzco); *Tom Brown × Golden Angel*; Williams, Ernest D.; Mini-Roses. Flowers deep yellow, dbl. (40+ petals), small; fragrant; foliage small, dark, glossy; bushy growth.

Fidélio® F, *or*, 1964, (MEIchest); *(Radar × Caprice) × Fire King*; Meilland, Alain; URS. Bud long, pointed; flowers turkey-red, reverse crimson red, dbl. (35 petals), high-centered, medium; slightly fragrant; foliage leathery; vigorous, upright growth.

Fidélio F, *ab*, 1961, Horstmann. Bud long, pointed, rosy red; flowers apricot, dbl., borne in large clusters; vigorous growth.

Fidelity HT, *mr*, 1962, *Crimson Glory × Peace*; Abrams, Von. Bud long, pointed; flowers red, dbl., high centered, large; fragrant; foliage glossy; tall. RULED EXTINCT 7/80 ARM.

Fiesta HT, *rb*, 1940, *The Queen Alexandra Rose* sport; Hansen, C.B.; Armstrong Nursery. Bud ovoid; flowers vermilion, splashed bright yellow, dbl., large; fragrant; foliage glossy, dark; vigorous, bushy, compact growth.

Fiesta Brava Min, *or*, 1959, *Méphisto × Perla de Alcañada*; Dot, M.; Combe. Flowers geranium-red, semi-dbl. (14 petals), medium blooms in clusters; foliage glossy; vigorous, upright, bushy growth.

Fiesta Flame F, *mr*, 1978, *Sarabande × Ena Harkness*; Sanday. Bud pointed; flowers intense scarlet, semi-dbl. (15 petals), large (3 in.); slightly fragrant; low, bushy growth.

Fiesta Gold Min, *yb*, 1970, *Golden Glow × Magic Wand*; Moore, R.S.; Mini-Roses. Bud long, pointed; flowers yellow orange, dbl., cupped, small; slightly fragrant; foliage small, glossy, light, leathery; vigorous, dwarf, upright, bushy growth.

Fiesta Ruby Min, *mr*, 1977, *Red Pinocchio × Little Chief*; Moore, R.S.; Sequoia Nursery. Bud ovoid, pointed; flowers medium red, dbl. (35-45 petals), high-centered, small (1 in.); slightly fragrant; foliage dark; bushy, compact growth.

Fiesta Time™ Min, *rb*, 1983, (MINgco); *Starburst × Over the Rainbow*; Williams, Ernest D.; Mini-Roses. Flowers yellow to orange to red, reverse yellow, dbl. (40+ petals), small; slight fragrance; foliage small, dark, glossy; bushy growth.

Fifth Avenue HT, *dp*, 1948, *Orange Nassau* sport; Johnson, W.E. Bud large, ovoid; flowers grenadine-pink, dbl., high-centered; fragrant; vigorous growth.

Figaro HT, *dr*, 1954, *(Crimson Glory × Grande Duchesse Charlotte) × New Yorker*; Lens. Flowers velvety scarlet, dbl. (26 petals), large (4½ in.); very fragrant; vigorous growth.

Figurine HT, *pb*, 1952, *Soeur Thérèse × Seedling*; Lens. Flowers china pink, dbl. (25 petals); fragrant; foliage bluish green; vigorous growth. RULED EXTINCT 11/91 ARM.

Figurine™ Min, *w*, 1991, (BENfig); *Rise 'n' Shine × Laguna*; Benardella, Frank; Weeks Roses, 1992. Flowers ivory white tinged pink, very long buds, delicate coloration,

well-formed, moderately full (15-25 petals), small (0-4 cms) blooms borne mostly singly, some in small clusters; stems suitable for cutting; slight fragrance; foliage medium, dark green, matt; few prickles; medium (40-50 cms), upright, bushy growth. AOE, 1992.

Fiji Gr, *or*, 1965, *Queen Elizabeth × Seedling*; Schwartz, E.W.; Wyant. Bud ovoid; flowers bright orange-red, dbl., cupped, medium; fragrant; vigorous, upright growth.

Filagree Pillar LCl, *dp*, 1962, *Titian × Sterling*; Riethmuller; Hazelwood Bros. Bud ovoid; flowers tyrian rose, heavily veined, reverse lighter, dbl. (50 petals), blooms on strong stems; fragrant; foliage glossy, bronze; vigorous, upright (to 5 ft.) growth.

Fillette F, *mp*, 1965, *Circus × Papillon Rose*; Lens; Spek. Bud ovoid; flowers pink, dbl., medium blooms in clusters; very fragrant; foliage dark.

Fimbriata HRg (S), *lp*, 1891, (Diantheflora; Dianthiflora; Phoebe's Frilled Pink); *R. rugosa × Mme. Alfred Carrière*; Morlet. Flowers light pink, petals carnation-like; very fragrant.

Finale F, *op*, 1964, (Ami des Jardins); *Nordlicht × Meteor (F)*; Kordes, R.; A. Dickson & McGredy. Flowers salmon-rose, dbl. (21 petals), well formed, large (3½ in.), borne in clusters; foliage light green; low, compact growth.

Fine Flare HT, *or*, 1978, *Fragrant Cloud × Mildred Reynolds*; Bees. Bud pointed; flowers vermilion, dbl. (40 petals), rounded, large (4 in.); fragrant; foliage dark; moderately vigorous, upright growth.

Fine Gold HT, *dy*, 1981, (WEEgold); *Seedling × (Hawaii × Seedling)*; Weeks, Michael W.J. Flowers deep golden yellow, dbl. (26 petals), high-centered, medium blooms borne 1-3 per stem; fragrant; foliage medium, dark, glossy; branching, upright growth.

Fine Touch Min, *ab*, 1986, (LYOfin); *Honey Hill × Seedling*; Lyon; MB Farm Min. Roses. Flowers pale apricot, deeper in center, dbl. (37 petals), high-centered, exhibition, large blooms borne singly; slightly fragrant; foliage medium, medium green, matt; few, reddish prickles; fruit globular, medium, orange; medium, upright growth.

Finesse Min, *my*, 1983, *Picnic × Rise 'n' Shine*; Hardgrove, Donald. Flowers medium yellow, dbl. (40+ petals), high-centered, exhibition, small blooms borne 1-3 per stem; no fragrance; foliage small, medium green, semi-glossy; bushy, spreading growth.

Fingerpaint Min, *ob*, 1990, (MORfing); *Orangeade × Little Artist*; Moore, Ralph S.; Sequoia Nursery. Bud short, pointed; flowers orange blend, yellow base, with light yellow reverse, aging orange changing to pink, yellow to white, semi-dbl. (12-14 petals), flat, small blooms borne usually singly and in sprays of 3-5; no fragrance; foliage medium, medium green, semi-glossy; prickles small, brownish, straight; bushy, spreading, low-medium growth.

Finlandia Pol, *op*, 1969, *Greta Kluis sport*; Kraats; Longley. Flowers orange-salmon.

Finstar Min, *op*, 1982, (RUfin; Mini Metro; Finnstar); *Minuette* × *Seedling*; deRuiter, G.; Fryer's Nursery, 1980. Flowers orange-salmon, dbl. (20 petals), small; slight fragrance; foliage small, medium green, semi-glossy; bushy growth.

Fiona F, *mr*, 1976, (KORfi); *Seedling* × *Prominent*; Kordes. Bud long, pointed; flowers medium red, dbl. (24 petals), high centered, large (3 in.); slightly fragrant; foliage wrinkled; vigorous, upright growth. RULED EXTINCT 9/82 ARM.

Fiona® S, *dr*, 1979, (MEIbeluxen); *Sea Foam* × *Picasso*; Meilland, Marie; Meilland Et Cie, 1982. Flowers dark red, dbl. (20 petals), small; slight fragrance; foliage small, dark, semi-glossy; spreading growth.

Fionia R, *lp*, 1914, *Mme. Norbert Levavasseur* × *Dorothy Perkins*; Poulsen, D.; Poulsen. Flowers light pink to rose, small blooms borne in clusters; foliage dark, glossy; vigorous.

Fire Bird F, *rb*, 1992, *Avocet* × *Evelyn Fison*; Strange, J.F. Flowers vermillion, pale yellow center, semi-dbl. (6-14 petals), medium (4-7 cms) blooms borne in large clusters; no fragrance; foliage medium, dark green, leathery; some prickles; medium (70 cms), upright growth.

Fire Chief HT, *mr*, 1942, *Crimson Glory* × *Ami Quinard*; Jacobus; B&A. Bud long, pointed; flowers flame-red, dbl. (24-28 petals), high-centered, large; fragrant; foliage glossy; very vigorous, bushy growth.

Fire Dance HT, *mr*, 1951, *(Ulrich Brunner Fils* × *Westfield Star)* × *(Chieftain* × *Better Times)*; Verschuren; Totty. Bud very long, ovoid; flowers brilliant velvety scarlet, dbl. (25-35 petals), globular, large (4-6 in.); slightly fragrant; foliage glossy, light green; upright, moderately vigorous growth.

Fire Flame F, *or*, 1958, Morse. Flowers scarlet, center orange, single, large (4 in.); moderate growth.

Fire King F, *or*, 1959, (MEIkans); *Moulin Rouge* × *Fashion*; Meilland; URS, 1958 & C-P, 1959. Bud ovoid; flowers fiery scarlet, dbl. (48 petals), high-centered to flat, medium (2½ in.) blooms in clusters; fragrant (musk); foli-

age dark, leathery; vigorous, upright, bushy growth. AARS, 1960.

Fire 'n' Ice™ F, *rb*, 1987, (AROfiric); *Bluhwunder* × *Love*; Christensen, Jack & Carruth, Tom, 1981; Armstrong Roses, 1985. Flowers red, reverse white, fading purplish-red, dbl. (40 petals), high centered, medium, borne usually singly; flora-tea; slight, moderate fragrance; foliage medium, dark green, glossy, very attractive, pointed, few, medium, reddish prickles; fruit none; upright, bushy, tall growth; a greenhouse variety.

Fire Opal F, *or*, 1955, (Fair opal); *Goldilocks* × *Orange Polyantha Seedling*; Boerner; McGredy. Bud ovoid; flowers reddish orange-scarlet, reverse lighter, dbl. (20-25 petals), cupped, medium, borne in clusters; fragrant; foliage glossy; vigorous, open habit; a florists' variety.

Fire Princess Min, *or*, 1969, *Baccará* × *Eleanor*; Moore, R.S.; Sequoia Nursery. Flowers orange-red, dbl., small; foliage small, glossy, leathery; vigorous, bushy growth.

Fire Queen F, *dr*, 1963, *Fusilier* × *(Carrousel* × *Queen o' the Lakes)*; Abrams, Von; Peterson & Dering. Bud ovoid; flowers bright red, dbl., medium, borne in clusters; foliage dark, glossy; vigorous, bushy growth.

Fire Sky HT, *mr*, 1952, *Gen. MacArthur* × *Étoile de Hollande*; Silva. Bud long, pointed; flowers red, cupped, large; foliage dark, glossy; vigorous growth.

Fireball Pol, *or*, 1931, deRuiter. Flowers glowing reddish orange; foliage dark, glossy.

Firebeam F, *rb*, 1960, *Masquerade* × *Seedling*; Fryer's Nursery. Flowers yellow, flame, orange and crimson, semi-dbl. (14 petals), medium (2½ in.), borne in clusters; very fragrant; foliage glossy; vigorous growth.

Firebird F, *ob*, 1960, *Masquerade* × *Mme. Henri Guillot*; Watkins Roses. Flowers bright orange, base golden yellow, semi-dbl. (12-18 petals), large (2½-3 in.), borne in clusters; foliage glossy, light green; vigorous, upright growth. RULED EXTINCT 4/92.

Firebrand HT, *or*, 1938, *Flamingo sport*; Cant, B.R. Flowers bright scarlet.

Firebrand, Climbing Cl HT, *or*, 1953, Raffel; Port Stockton Nursery.

Firecracker F, *mr*, 1956, *Pinocchio seedling* × *Numa Fay seedling*; Boerner; McGredy; A. Dickson, 1956; J&P, 1959. Flowers scarlet, base yellow, semi-dbl. (14 petals), large (4½ in.) blooms in clusters; fragrant; foliage leathery, light green; dwarf, bushy growth.

Firecrest F, *mr*, 1964, *(Cinnabar* × *Marjorie LeGrice)* × *Pimpernell*; LeGrice. Flowers vermillion reverse scarlet, dbl. (35 petals), large (3 in.), in clusters; vigorous, low growth.

Firecrest, Climbing Cl F, *mr*, 1969, LeGrice.

Firedragon HT, *mr*, 1923, Clark, A. Flowers fiery red, full; fragrant.

Firefall Cl Min, *dr*, 1980, (Roy Rumsey); *Dortmund × Little Chief*; Moore, R.S.; Sequoia Nursery. Bud short; flowers dark red, dbl. (35-50 petals), flat, medium (1½ in.) blooms in clusters; foliage small, glossy; trailing, arching growth.

Fireflame F, *mr*, 1954, *Chatter × Red Pinocchio*; Boerner; Stark Bros. Bud ovoid; flowers carmine, dbl. (65-70 petals), large (2½-3 in.), borne in pyramidal clusters; fragrant; vigorous growth.

Fireflash HT, *yb*, 1960, *Marjorie LeGrice × Seedling*; LeGrice; Wayside Gardens Co. Flowers golden yellow splashed scarlet, dbl. (25-30 petals), well formed, large (4½ in.); fragrant; foliage glossy; upright growth.

Firefly F, *yb*, 1975, *Contempo sport*; Joliffe. Bud slightly pointed; flowers medium yellow, dbl. (22 petals), cupped, large (3½ in.); slightly fragrant; foliage dark; upright growth. RULED EXTINCT 4/78 ARM.

Fireglow Pol, *or*, 1929, *Orange King sport*; Wezelenburg. Flowers brilliant vermilion-red, shaded orange, single, blooms in clusters; slightly fragrant; dwarf, compact growth.

Fireglow, Climbing Cl Pol, *or*, 1950, Guillot, M.

Firelight HT, *or*, 1971, *Detroiter × Orange Delbard*; Kordes, R.; J&P. Flowers orange-red, dbl., high-centered, large; fragrant; foliage large, light, leathery; vigorous, upright.

Fireside HT, *yb*, 1977, *Kordes' Perfecta × Belle Blonde*; Lindquist. Bud ovoid; flowers yellow, white, red, dbl. (32-37 petals), imbricated, large (5½-6 in.); slightly fragrant; foliage large, glossy, dark; vigorous, bushy growth.

Firestorm Min, *or*, 1991, (CLEfire); *Seedling × Seedling*; Clements, John; Heirloom Old Garden Roses. Flowers fiery oriental lacquer orange-red, very full (41+ petals), exhibition, small (0-4 cms) blooms borne mostly singly; no fragrance; foliage small, medium green, semi-glossy; few prickles; medium (35 cms), bushy, spreading growth.

Fireworks™ Min, *rb*, 1991, (SAVafire); *(Rise 'n' Shine × Sheri Anne) × Rainbow's End*; Saville, F. Harmon; Nor'East Miniature Roses, 1992. Flowers brilliant orange-yellow bicolor, dbl. (35 petals), high-centered, exhibition, small (3½ cms) blooms borne singly and in sprays of 3-20; slight fragrance; foliage medium, dark green, semi-glossy; bushy, medium growth.

Firmament HT, *dr*, 1971, *Chrysler Imperial × Credo*; Gaujard. Flowers vermilion-crimson, full, large; foliage bronze.

First Blush Pol, *mp*, 1965, *Francais × Orléans Rose*; Delbard-Chabert; Cuthbert. Flowers phlox-pink, cupped, large (3 in.), borne in clusters; foliage dull, light green; moderate growth; intermittent bloom.

First Choice F, *or*, 1958, *Masquerade × Sultane*; Morse. Flowers fiery orange-scarlet, center yellow, single (7 petals), large (5 in.), in trusses; fragrant; tall, spreading.

First Edition F, *op*, 1976, (DELtep; Arnaud Delbard®); *(Zambra × (Orléans Rose × Goldilocks)) × (Orange Triumph seedling × Floradora)*; Delbard-Chabert; C-P. Bud ovoid, pointed; flowers luminous coral, shaded orange, dbl. (28 petals), medium (2-2½ in.); slightly fragrant (tea); foliage glossy, light; upright growth. AARS, 1977.

First Federal HT, *pb*, 1965, *(Radiance × Pageant) × Diamond Jubilee seedling*; Boerner; J&P. Bud ovoid; flowers geranium-pink tinted scarlet, dbl. (35-40 petals), high-centered, large (5-5½ in.), strong stems; very fragrant (rose geranium); vigorous, upright growth.

First Federal Gold HT, *dy*, 1967, *Golden Masterpiece seedling × Golden Masterpiece seedling*; Boerner; J&P. Bud ovoid; flowers gold and yellow, dbl., high-centered, large; fragrant; foliage glossy, leathery; vigorous, upright growth.

First Federal's Renaissance HT, *mp*, 1980, *Seedling × First Prize*; Warriner; J&P. Bud long, pointed; flowers medium pink, tinted lighter, dbl. (20-25 petals), large (5-7 in.); slightly fragrant; foliage large; compact growth; very early bloom.

First Kiss F, *pb*, 1991, (JACling); *Sun Flare × Simplicity*; Warriner, William A.; Bear Creek Gardens, Inc. Flowers light pink, light yellow blend at base, moderately full (15-25 petals), large; slight fragrance; foliage medium, medium green, matt; bushy, compact growth.

First Lady HT, *dp*, 1961, *First Love × Roundelay*; Swim; C.R. Burr. Bud ovoid; flowers rose madder to phlox-pink, semi-dbl. (18-22 petals), cupped, large (3½-4½ in.); slightly fragrant; foliage leathery, dark, semi-glossy; very vigorous, upright growth.

First Lady, Climbing Cl HT, *dp*, 1964, Burr, C.R.

First Lady Nancy HT, *yb*, 1981, *American Heritage × First Prize*; Swim, H.C. & Christensen, J.E.; Armstrong Nursery. Bud ovoid, long, pointed; flowers light yellow tinged light pink, dbl. (32-40 petals), formal, spiraled blooms borne singly; light tea fragrance; foliage semi-glossy, medium; medium prickles; medium, upright, bushy.

First Love HT, *lp*, 1951, (Premier Amour); *Charlotte Armstrong* × *Show Girl*; Swim; Armstrong Nursery. Bud long, pointed; flowers light pink, dbl. (20-30 petals), medium (2½ -3½ in.); slightly fragrant; foliage leathery, light green; moderately bushy growth.

First National Gold Min, *dy*, 1976, *Rise 'n' Shine* × *Yellow Jewel*; Saville; Flora World. Bud pointed; flowers deep yellow, dbl. (38-42 petals), high-centered to flat, small (1-1½ in.); slightly fragrant; foliage small; compact, upright growth.

First National Silver Min, *w*, 1976, *Charlie McCarthy* × *Little Chief*; Schwartz, E.W.; Flora World. Bud ovate; flowers white, very dbl. (50-55 petals), flat, small (1½ in.); slightly fragrant; foliage small, very glossy; compact, spreading growth.

First Offering F, *dr*, 1975, *(Seedling* × *Seedling)* × *Samba*; Viraraghaven. Bud ovoid; flowers dark red, semi-dbl. (15 petals), open, globular, medium (2½ in.); fragrant; foliage large, glossy, bronze, reddish brown when young; vigorous, dwarf, bushy growth; profuse, very lasting bloom.

First Prize HT, *pb*, 1970, *Enchantment seedling* × *Golden Masterpiece seedling*; Boerner; J&P. Bud long, pointed; flowers rose-pink, center blended with old ivory, dbl., high-centered, very large; fragrant; foliage dark, leathery; vigorous, upright growth. AARS, 1970; GM, ARS Gertrude M. Hubbard, 1971.

First Prize, Climbing Cl HT, *pb*, 1976, (JAClist); Reasoner; J&P. Very vigorous, climbing.

First Rose Convention HT, *dr*, 1971, *Flaming Peace* × *Helen Traubel*; Hardikar, Dr. M.N.; The Bombay Rose Society. Bud globular; flowers dark crimson, dbl. (48 petals), flat to cupped, borne singly; no fragrance; foliage red when young, turning dark green; hooked, pale cream prickles; vigorous, upright growth.

Firstar HT, *dy*, 1983, (JACary; Golden Anniversary; Home's Pride; Olympic Spirit); *New Day* × *Oregold*; Warriner, W.; J&P. Flowers deep yellow, dbl. (35 petals), large; fragrant; foliage medium, medium green, glossy; bushy, spreading growth.

Fisher Holmes HP (OGR), *dr*, 1865, (Fisher & Holmes); *Probably Maurice Bernardin self-seedling*; Verdier, E. Bud long, pointed; flowers reddish scarlet, shaded deep velvety crimson, dbl. (30 petals), well-formed, large; upright growth; recurrent bloom; (28).

Fisherman's Friend® S, *dr*, 1987, (AUSchild); *Lilian Austin* × *The Squire*; Austin, David. Flowers deep crimson, reverse lighter, fading crimson-purple, very dbl., cupped, large, borne usually singly and in sprays of 1-3; heavy, damask fragrance; foliage medium, dark green, semi-glossy; broad, straight, large, red-brown prickles; no fruit; bushy growth; repeat bloom.

Five-Colored Rose T (OGR), *w*, 1844, (Fortune's Five-colored Rose; Smith's Parish Fortune). Buds red-tinged; flowers creamy white tinged with pale blush, fading to white, sometimes with a crimson-striped petal, rarely entirely crimson, dbl., medium; foliage light green; vigorous.

F. J. Grootendorst HRg (S), *mr*, 1918, (Grootendorst; Grootendorst Red; Nelkenrose); *R. rugosa rubra* × *Polyantha Seedling*; de Goey; F.J. Grootendorst. Flowers bright red, edges serrated like a carnation, dbl., small blooms in clusters (up to 20); slightly fragrant; foliage small, leathery, wrinkled, dark; vigorous, bushy growth; recurrent bloom.

Flair HT, *op*, 1951, *Lady Sylvia* × *Seedling*; Verschuren-Pechtold; J&P. Bud ovoid; flowers coral-blush, dbl. (30-35 petals), high-centered, large (3½-4½ in.); vigorous growth; a greenhouse cut flower.

Flair HT, *rb*, 1989, *Pristine* × *Ink Spots*; Cummings, Peter E., 1991. Bud pointed; flowers medium red to dark red, reverse lighter, dbl. (38 velvety petals), high-centered, exhibition, medium, borne singly; slight fragrance; foliage medium, dark green, semi-glossy; prickles curved, hooked, reddish-brown, sparse; fruit obovate, one inch, green with red splotch; upright, medium growth.

Flambeau HT, *mr*, 1940, *Royal Red* × *Johannizauber*; Nicolas; J&P. Bud pointed; flowers crimson shaded scarlet, dbl., open, large; strong stems; foliage glossy; vigorous, bushy, open growth.

Flambée F, *or*, 1954, Mallerin; EFR. Flowers orange-red, dbl. (25-30 petals), medium, borne in clusters of 5-6; foliage reddish to bronze; upright, bushy growth. GM, Bagatelle, 1952.

Flamboyant Pol, *mr*, 1931, Turbat. Flowers bright scarlet, aging to crimson-carmine, dbl., large blooms in clusters of 10-20; foliage glossy; dwarf growth.

Flamboyant F, *mr*, *Holstein* × *Incendie*; Croix, P. Flowers bright red; vigorous growth.

Flame R, *op*, 1912, *Crimson Rambler* × *Seedling*; Turner. Flowers bright salmon-pink, semi-dbl., borne in large clusters; foliage dark, glossy; very vigorous, climbing growth.

Flame of Fire HT, *ob*, 1917, McGredy. Flowers orange-flame, full, open, large; fragrant; bushy growth. GM, NRS, 1916.

Flameburst F, *dr*, 1961, *Nearly Wild × Hybrid Tea seedling*; Brownell, H.C. Bud pointed; flowers crimson, center yellow, single (4-5 petals), medium (2 in.), borne in clusters; slightly fragrant; foliage dark, glossy; very vigorous growth.

Flameglo Min, *yb*, 1981, *Starburst × Over the Rainbow*; Williams, E.D.; Mini-Roses. Flowers deep yellow to orange-red, reverse deep yellow, dbl. (40+ petals), small; slight fragrant; foliage small, dark, glossy; upright, bushy growth.

Flamenco F, *lp*, 1960, *Cinnabar × Spartan*; McGredy, S., IV; McGredy. Flowers light salmon-pink, dbl. (21 petals), large (3½ in.) blooms in clusters; slightly fragrant; foliage dark.

Flamina F, *my*, 1964, *(Faust × Peace) × Seedling*; Mondial Roses. Bud pointed, flushed red; flowers golden yellow, dbl., large; foliage clear green; very vigorous, upright, bushy growth.

Flaminaire HT, *ob*, 1960, (Montagny); *Eclipse × Independence*; Dorieux; Pin. Bud globular; flowers orange-flame, semi-dbl., medium; slightly fragrant; foliage dark, glossy; vigorous, bushy growth.

Flaming Arrow F, *or*, 1965, *Montezuma × Nadine*; Schwartz, E.W.; Wyant. Bud long, pointed; flowers bright orange-red, dbl., medium; fragrant; foliage glossy; vigorous, upright growth.

Flaming Beauty HT, *rb*, 1978, *First Prize × Piccadilly*; Winchel; Kimbrew-Walter Roses. Flowers yellow and red-orange, dbl. (35 petals), exhibition, large (4 in.); slightly fragrant; foliage matt, green; bushy growth. ARC TG (S), 1979.

Flaming June Pol, *or*, 1931, (Mrs. A. Hudig); Cutbush. Flowers bright orange-scarlet; vigorous growth.

Flaming Peace HT, *rb*, 1966, (MACbo; Kronenbourg); *Peace sport*; McGredy; Country Garden Nursery, 1966. Flowers bright medium red, reverse straw-yellow veined red.

Flaming Ruby F, *dr*, 1963, *(Eva self × Guinée) × Guinée*; Hennessey. Flowers deep ruby-red, dbl. (60 petals), large (3 in.), borne in clusters; foliage dark, reddish green, small; vigorous growth.

Flaming Sunset HT, *ob*, 1948, *McGredy's Sunset sport*; Eddie. Flowers deep orange, reverse lighter; foliage light bronze.

Flaming Sunset, Climbing Cl HT, *ob*, 1954, Mattock.

Flamingo HT, *dp*, 1929, Dickson, A. Flowers bright geranium-red to rosy cerise, dbl., spiral shape, high-centered; very fragrant; vigorous growth. GM, NRS, 1927.

Flamingo HRg (S), *mp*, 1956, *R. rugosa × White Wings*; Howard, F.H.; Wayside Gardens Co. Bud pointed; flowers rich pink, single (5 petals), cupped, large blooms in clusters; foliage glossy, gray-green; vigorous (3 ft.) growth; recurrent bloom.

Flamingo F, *mp*, 1958, Buyl Frères. Flowers rose; long, strong stems; very vigorous growth.

Flamingo F, *op*, 1961, Horstmann. Bud long, pointed; flowers deep scarlet-pink, dbl. (30 petals), open, borne in clusters; vigorous, upright growth.

Flamingo® HT, *lp*, 1979, (KORflüg; Margaret Thatcher; Porcelain; Veronica; Veronika); *Seedling × Lady Like*; Kordes, W.; Kordes, 1978; Ludwigs Roses, 1983. Bud large, long, pointed; flowers light pink, dbl. (24 petals), high-centered, large blooms borne singly; moderate fragrance; foliage matt, green; many prickles; vigorous, upright, bushy growth.

Flamingo Queen Gr, *dp*, 1972, *Queen Elizabeth sport*; Chan; Canadian Orn. Plant Foundation. Flowers deep pink.

Flammèche F, *ob*, 1959, Combe. Flowers orange, large; vigorous growth.

Flammenrose HT, *ob*, 1921, *Mrs. Joseph Hill × Mme. Edouard Herriot*; Türke; Kiese. Flowers brighter orange-yellow than Mme. Edouard Herriot, semi-dbl. (16 petals).

Flammenspiel S, *mp*, 1974, *Peer Gynt × Seedling*; Kordes; Horstmann. Bud ovoid; flowers salmon-pink, dbl.; foliage large, leathery, dark; vigorous, upright growth.

Flammentanz® LCl, *mr*, 1955, (KORflata; Flame Dance); *R. eglanteria hybrid × R. kordesii*; Kordes. Flowers crimson, dbl., high-centered, very large blooms in clusters; fragrant; foliage dark, leathery; very vigorous (10 ft.) growth; non-recurrent bloom. ADR, 1952.

Flanders Field F, *dp*, 1990, (HORflan); *Prominent × Southampton*; Horner, Heather M., 1992. Bud ovoid; flowers light red aging slightly lighter, semi-dbl., urn-shaped, loose, medium, borne usually singly or in sprays of 5-9; slight fragrance; foliage medium, medium green, semi-glossy; medium to tall, upright growth.

Flandria Pol, *mr*, 1966, Delforge. Bud ovoid; flowers red, semi-dbl., open; fragrant; foliage dark, glossy; bushy growth.

Flash LCl, *rb*, 1938, *Rosella (P. Dot)* × *Margaret McGredy*; Hatton; C-P. Bud ovoid, yellow suffused scarlet; flowers orange-scarlet, reverse and center yellow, dbl., cupped; slightly fragrant; foliage leathery, glossy, bronze; pillar (6-8 ft.), compact growth; long blooming season. GM, Rome, 1939; AARS, 1940.

Flashdance HT, *my*, 1984, (POUlflash); *Berolina* × *Seedling*; Oleson M.&P.; Poulsen Roses. Flowers medium yellow, dbl., urnshaped, large blooms borne singly; slight fragrance; foliage large, medium green, semiglossy; upright growth.

Flashfire LCl, *rb*, 1992, (LEEfir); *Altissimo* × *Playboy*; Little, Lee W.; Heirloom Old Garden Roses, 1992. Flowers brilliant coppery redorange with yellow eye, single (5 petals), large (7+ cms) blooms borne in large clusters of 5-9; slight fragrance; foliage large, dark green, glossy, disease resistant; some prickles; tall (210 cms), upright, spreading growth.

Flashlight F, *or*, 1974, *Vesper* × *Seedling*; LeGrice. Flowers orange-scarlet, dbl. (28 petals), large (3-3½ in.); fragrant; foliage large, bronze; tall growth.

Flavescens HSpn (OGR), *ly*, *R. spinosissima hybrid*; Prior to 1824. Flowers pale lemon, rounded; very hardy.

Flavien Budillon T (OGR), *lp*, Flowers pale flesh, globular, large; very fragrant.

F. L. de Voogd HT, *yb*, 1920, *Mme. Mélanie Soupert* × *Mme. Jenny Gillemot*; Timmermans. Flowers clear reddish yellow, semi-dbl.

Fleet Street HT, *dp*, 1972, *Flaming Peace* × *Prima Ballerina*; McGredy, S., IV; McGredy. Flowers deep rose pink, dbl. (40 petals), wellformed, large (6 in.); very fragrant; foliage large, dark, leathery.

Fleetwood F, *ob*, 1989, *Little Darling* × *Orangeade*; Bridges, Dennis A.; Bridges Roses, 1990. Bud pointed; flowers bright orange, reverse lighter, aging darker on outer petals, dbl. (32 petals), high-centered, exhibition, medium, borne in sprays of 5-10; slight, fruity fragrance; foliage medium, dark green, glossy; prickles straight, medium pink; bushy, medium, vigorous growth.

Flesh Taito F, *ob*, 1988, *Masquerade* × *Matador*; Kikuchi, R., 1989. Flowers yellow at base to vermilion, reverse orange flushed with pink, dbl. (25-30 petals), cupped, large, borne in sprays; moderate fragrance; foliage medium, dark green, undulated; prickles ordinary, green; bushy, medium growth.

Fleur Cowles F, *ly*, 1972, *Pink Parfait* × *Seedling*; Gregory. Flowers cream, center buff, dbl. (35 petals), large (3 in.); fragrant (spicy); foliage glossy, dark.

Fleur de France HT, *my*, 1944, Gaujard. Flowers capucine and yellow, semi-dbl., globular, medium; slightly fragrant; foliage glossy, vigorous, dwarf growth.

Fleurette® S, *lp*, 1977, (INTerette; Flavia); *Yesterday* × *Seedling*; Interplant. Flowers light pink, single (5 petals), 2 in. blooms in clusters; foliage medium green, glossy; few, medium prickles; vigorous (to 4 ft.) growth; ground cover; repeat bloom.

Fliegerheld Boelcke HT, *my*, 1920, *Mme. Caroline Testout* × *Sunburst*; Schmidt, J.C. Flowers nankeen yellow, shaded reddish yellow.

Flighty F, *m*, 1969, *Orangeade* × *Sterling Silver*; Trew; Basildon Rose Gardens. Bud cherryred; flowers light mauve, semi-dbl., medium, borne in trusses; foliage dark; free growth.

Flipper HT, *or*, 1973, *Tanagra* × *John S. Armstrong*; Gaujard. Bud long, pointed; flowers orange-red, large; foliage large.

Flirt F, *mr*, 1952, *Pink Princess* × *Shades of Autumn*; Brownell. Bud pointed; flowers bright cherry-red, reverse yellow, dbl. (35-40 petals), medium, borne in clusters of 25 or more; fragrant; foliage glossy, dark; vigorous, upright growth.

Flirtation HT, *pb*, 1953, *Fiesta* × *Peace*; Shepherd; Bosley Nursery. Bud pointed; flowers begonia-rose, reverse lemon to deep yellow, dbl. (30 petals), high-centered, large (5-6 in.), strong stems; fragrant; foliage dark, leathery; vigorous, bushy, compact growth.

Flon D (OGR), *mr*, 1845, (Gloire des Perpetuelles; La Mienne); Vibert. Flowers bright red; very free bloom, occasionally repeated.

Flor de Torino 61 HT, *w*, 1961, *Monte Carlo* × *Michèle Meilland*; Moreira da Silva. Flowers white edged violet-pink.

Flora HSem (OGR), *m*, (Flore); *R. sempervirens hybrid*; Jacques, ca. 1830. Flowers lilac-pink, center deeper, dbl.; fragrant; seasonal bloom.

Flora HT, *op*, 1957, *Independence* × *Charlotte Armstrong*; Maarse, G. Flowers pink tinted salmon, dbl., large; very fragrant; vigorous, upright growth.

Flora MacLeod LCl, *lp*, 1971, *New Dawn* × *Shot Silk, Climbing*; MacLeod. Flowers pale rose-pink, dbl. (50 petals), large (4½ in.); very fragrant; foliage large, medium green, matt; vigorous; some repeat.

Flora McIvor E (OGR), *pb*, 1894, *R. eglanteria* × *HP or B*; Penzance; Keynes, Williams & Co. Flowers rosy pink, white center, yellow stamens, nearly single, small; very fragrant (foliage and flowers); vigorous growth; summer bloom.

Florabelle F, *op*, 1964, *Ma Perkins × Seedling*; Schwartz, E.W.; Wyant. Flowers soft salmon-pink, dbl. (33 petals), globular, large; fragrant; foliage soft; vigorous, bushy growth.

Floradora F, *or*, 1944, *Baby Château × R. roxburghii*; Tantau; C-P. Bud globular; flowers cinnabar-red, dbl. (25 petals), cupped, medium (2 in.) blooms in sprays of 6-12; slightly fragrant; foliage leathery, glossy; upright, bushy growth. AARS, 1945.

Floradora, Climbing Cl F, *or*, 1951, Shamburger, P.; Shamburger Rose Nursery.

Floral Dance Cl HT, *or*, 1955, *Souv de Mme. Boullet, Climbing × Crimson Glory*; Homan; Roseglen Nursery. Flowers orange-cerise; very vigorous, climbing growth.

Floralies Valenciennoises LCl, *mr*, 1955, *Matador × Soliel d'Orient*; Dorieux; Pin. Bud long, pointed; flowers currant-red, semi-dbl., large; very fragrant; vigorous growth.

Flore Berthelot Pol, *my*, 1921, Turbat. Flowers clear lemon-yellow, passing to white, borne in clusters.

Floréal Pol, *pb*, 1923, *Orléans Rose × Yvonne Rabier*; Turbat. Flowers flesh and rose-pink, dbl.; slightly fragrant.

Floréal HT, *op*, 1944, Gaujard. Bud pointed; flowers coral-pink tinted yellow, dbl., cupped, medium; fragrant; foliage dark, glossy; vigorous growth.

Florence HT, *lp*, 1921, Paul, W. Flowers silvery pink.

Florence HT, *w*, 1961, Dorieux; Pin. Bud long; flowers pure white, large.

Florence Chenoweth HT, *yb*, 1918, (Yellow Herriot); *Mme. Edouard Herriot sport*; Chenoweth. Flowers yellow, shaded coral-red.

Florence Edna HT, *lp*, 1985, *Princesse sport*; Owen, F. Flowers light pink.

Florence Forrester HT, *w*, 1914, McGredy. Flowers white tinged lemon, dbl., large. GM, NRS, 1913.

Florence Haswell Veitch Cl HT, *dr*, 1911, *Mme. Edmée Metz × Victor Hugo*; Paul, W. Flowers bright scarlet, shaded black, full, large; very fragrant; vigorous growth.

Florence Lorraine F, *ab*, 1973, *Royal Highness × (Hawaii × Helen Traubel)*; Middlebrooks; Ellesmere Nursery. Bud ovoid; flowers dark apricot, very dbl., high-centered to cupped, large; fragrant; foliage glossy, dark, leathery, wrinkled; very vigorous, upright, bushy growth.

Florence L. Izzard HT, *dy*, 1923, McGredy. Bud pointed; flowers bright deep golden yellow, dbl., high-centered, large; very fragrant; foliage dark, bronze, leathery, glossy; very vigorous, bushy growth.

Florence Mary HT, *dy*, 1964, *Doreen sport*; Morse. Flowers deep yellow-ochre, well formed, large; fragrant; bushy growth.

Florence Mary Morse S, *mr*, 1951, *Baby Château × Magnifica*; Kordes. Flowers copper-scarlet, semi-dbl. (15 petals), large (3 in.) blooms in trusses to 30; foliage dark, glossy; (28).

Florence Nightingale S, *w*, 1989, (GANflo); *Morgengruss × Seedling*; Gandy, Douglas L.; Gandy's Roses. Bud pointed; flowers glowing white, flushed buff, reverse tinged pink, aging to white, dbl. (32 petals), urn-shaped, medium, borne in sprays; spicy fragrance; foliage medium, medium green, semi-glossy; prickles very pointed, fawn; fruit rounded, green; spreading, medium growth.

Florence Pemberton HT, *w*, 1903, Dickson, A. Flowers creamy white, suffused pink, dbl., high-centered; foliage rich green, leathery; vigorous growth.

Florentia HT, *ob*, 1941, *Julien Potin × Seedling*; Giacomasso. Flowers deep orange, well shaped, large; vigorous, bushy, compact growth. GM, Rome, 1940.

Florentina HT, *dr*, 1973, (Kordes' Rose Florentine); *Liebeszauber × Brandenberg*; Kordes; Horstmann, 1974. Bud large, long, pointed; flowers dark red, high-centered; fragrant; foliage leathery; vigorous. ADR, 1974.

Florentina F, *pb*, 1938, *Seedling × Permanent Wave*; Leenders, M. Flowers hydrangea-pink, reverse rose-red, single, large; long stems; foliage leathery, dark; very vigorous growth.

Florex HT, *op*, 1927, *Mme. Butterfly × Premier*; Geiger; Florex Gardens & A.N. Pierson. Bud pointed; flowers deep coral-salmon, suffused orange-carmine, dbl., high-centered, large; long stems; very fragrant; foliage leathery, glossy, dark; very vigorous growth.

Floriade Gr, *ob*, 1963, *Montezuma sport*; van der Schilden; Armstrong Nursery. Bud urn shaped; flowers bright orange-scarlet, dbl. high-centered to open, large (4 in.); long, strong stems; vigorous growth.

Floricel HT, *or*, 1957, *Carito MacMahon × Luis Brinas*; Dot, P. Bud pointed; flowers red and salmon, dbl. (25 petals), high-centered, large, strong stems; foliage dark, glossy, upright, compact growth.

Florida Red HT, *mr*, 1964, Hennessey. Flowers rich red, dbl. (60 petals), large (5 in.); vigorous growth.

Florida von Scharbeutz F, *ob*, 1957, *Golden Scepter × (München × Peace)*; Kordes, R. Flowers orange-yellow shaded coppery, dbl., high-centered, very large blooms in large clusters;

fragrant; foliage dark, glossy; vigorous, bushy growth.

Florimel F, *mp*, 1958, *Pinocchio × Seedling*; Fryer's Nursery. Flowers silvery pink to deep rose-pink, well formed, borne in clusters; foliage glossy; vigorous growth.

Florinda Norman Thompson HT, *pb*, 1920, Dickson, A. Flowers delicate rose on lemon, base deeper, full; fragrant.

Floron HT, *ab*, 1948, *Comtesse Vandal × Pilar Landecho*; Camprubi. Flowers Indian yellow-orange, inside lighter, dbl., high-centered, very large; slightly fragrant; upright growth.

Florrie Joyce F, *dp*, *Gartendirektor Otto Linne × Borderer*; Riethmuller. Flowers cherry-pink, dbl. (40-45 petals), medium blooms in large clusters; bushy growth.

Flower Carpet™ S, *dp*, 1989, (NOAtraum; Heidetraum); *Immensee × Amanda*; Noack, Werner; Pan-Am Northwest, Inc., 1991. Bud globular; flowers deep pink, reverse lighter, semi-dbl. (15 petals), cupped, small, profuse, borne in sprays of 15-25; slight fragrance; foliage small, dark green, glossy, disease resistant; prickles crooked, dark; fruit globular, small, light red; vigorous, hardy, low, spreading growth. GM, The Hague, 1990.

Flower of Fairfield R, *mr*, 1909, *Crimson Rambler sport*; Ludorf; H. Schultheis. Like Crimson Rambler except that bloom is sometimes recurrent.

Flower Show HT, *rb*, 1980, *Fragrant Cloud × Tropicana*; Bees, Ltd. Bud ovoid, pointed; flowers scarlet, yellow reverse, dbl. (25 petals), borne 3-4 per cluster; fragrant; foliage mid-green, semi-matt; dark red prickles; vigorous, upright growth.

Flower World HT, *or*, 1980, *Baccará × South Seas*; Warriner; Flower World of America. Bud pointed, oval; flowers orange-red, dbl. (20-30 petals), high-centered, large (4 in.); foliage dark, leathery; tall growth.

Fluffy Ruffles F, *pb*, 1935, *Miss Rowena Thom × Seedling*; H&S; Dreer. Flowers silver-pink, reverse deeper rose, semi-dbl., cupped, borne in clusters; slightly fragrant; foliage leathery; vigorous growth.

Fluffy Min, *w*, 1984, (INTerflu; Patio Cloud); *Seedling × Nozomi*; Interplant. Flowers white, shaded creamy pink, semi-dbl. (15 petals), small blooms in clusters; slightly fragrant; foliage dark, glossy; few, medium prickles; spreading growth; ground cover.

Fluorescent® F, *mr*, 1977, (DELflori); *Zambra × ((DELtorche × Tropicana) × (Alain × Souv. de J. Chabert))*; Delbard-Chabert. Flowers medium red, dbl. (33 petals), cupped, medium;

no fragrance; vigorous, bushy, branching growth.

Fluorette F, *or*, 1971, *(Panache × Soprano) × Coloranja*; Lens. Bud pointed; flowers salmon-orange, dbl. (22 petals), cupped, large (3-3½ in.); slightly fragrant; vigorous, upright, bushy growth.

Flush o' Dawn HT, *lp*, 1900, *Margaret Dickson × Sombreuil*; Walsh. Flowers light pink changing to white, full, large; fragrant; vigorous, upright growth.

Flying Colours LCl, *dp*, 1922, *R. gigantea hybrid*; Clark, A.; Hazlewood Bros. Flowers light red, single, large; slightly fragrant; foliage light, leathery, glossy; very vigorous, climbing growth. RULED EXTINCT 8/82 ARM.

Flying Colors™ Min, *rb*, 1982, (SAVapaint); *(Yellow Jewel × Tamango) × Sheri Anne*; Saville, F. Harmon; Nor'East Min. Roses, 1983. Flowers red and yellow blend, aging to pink and white, semi-dbl., micro-mini, small; slight fragrance; foliage medium green, semi-glossy; upright, bushy growth

Flying Tata HT, *dr*, 1983, *Scarlet Knight × Cynosure*; Hardikar, Dr. M.N. Bud ovoid; flowers dark red, dbl. (45 petals), high-centered, medium blooms borne singly; moderate fragrance; foliage medium, dark, glossy; vigorous, upright growth.

F. M. Vokes HT, *my*, 1927, *Ophelia seedling*; Hicks. Flowers yellow, passing to cream; semi-dbl.; fragrant.

Focus HMsk (S), *lp*, 1984, (LENpac); *Marie Pavié × Seedling*; Lens, Louis. Flowers light pink, dbl. (20 petals), small blooms in clusters of 3-50; very fragrant; foliage small, dark; hooked, brownish-green prickles; spreading growth; recurrent bloom.

Foliacée C (OGR), *mp*, 1810, (Caroline de Berry); Descemet. Flowers light rose, full, globular, very large.

Folie d'Espagne F, *yb*, 1965, Soenderhousen. Flowers yellow, orange and scarlet, dbl. (20 petals), flat, medium (2 in.) blooms in cluster; slightly fragrant; foliage dark, glossy.

Folies-Bergère HT, *yb*, 1948, *Souv. de Claudius Pernet × Seedling*; Gaujard. Flowers yellow shaded coppery, dbl., large; fragrant; foliage leathery, light green; very vigorous, erect growth.

Folk Song S, *pb*, 1964, Abrams, Von; Edmunds. Flowers light pink, reverse darker, dbl., medium; foliage glossy; vigorous (3-4 ft.), compact growth; recurrent bloom.

Folkestone F, *dr*, 1936, Archer. Flowers crimson scarlet, semi-dbl., blooms in clusters;

slightly fragrant; foliage dark; bushy, spreading growth; (28).

Folklore® HT, *ob*, 1977, (KORlore); *Fragrant Cloud × Seedling*; Kordes; Barni; Kordes. Bud long, pointed; flowers orange, reverse lighter, dbl. (44 petals), high-centered, large (4½ in.); very fragrant; foliage glossy; very tall and vigorous, upright, bushy growth.

Folksinger S, *yb*, 1985, *Carefree Beauty × Sunsprite*; Buck, Dr. Griffith J.; Iowa State University, 1984. Flowers yellow flushed with dark peach, dbl. (28 petals), slightly cupped, large blooms borne 1-15 per cluster; fragrant; foliage leathery, glossy, coppery mid-green; awl-like, tan prickles; upright, bushy growth; hardy; repeat bloom.

Fondly™ F, *lp*, 1985, (HILset); *Seedling × Seedling*; Jelly, Robert; E.G. Hill Co. Flowers light pink, dbl. (20 petals), high-centered, sweetheart, medium, borne singly and in clusters of 2-4; spicy fragrance; foliage medium, dark, matt; few prickles on peduncles; fruit medium, ovoid, orange-red; medium, upright growth; greenhouse variety.

Fontainebleau® HT, *dp*, 1967, (DELpous; Fontaine Blue); *Dr. Albert Schweitzer × (Bayadère × Rome Glory)*; Delbard-Chabert. Bud long, pointed; flowers magenta-pink, dbl., globular, large; slightly fragrant; foliage dark, glossy, leathery; vigorous, bushy growth.

Fontanelle HT, *my*, 1927, *Souv. de Claudius Pernet × Columbia*; Hill, E.G., Co. Flowers lemon-yellow, center gold, dbl., very large; fragrant; foliage leathery; vigorous growth.

Fontanelle, Climbing Cl HT, *my*, 1935, Johns.

Fontenelle HP (OGR), *mr*, 1877, Moreau-Robert. Flowers bright red, full, very large; very fragrant; vigorous, growth.

Fool's Gold Min, *ob*, 1984, (AROgobi); *Cricket × Dr. A.J. Verhage*; Christensen, Jack; Armstrong Nursery. Flowers gold, reverse bronze, dbl. (20 petals), well-formed, small; slight fragrance; foliage medium, dark, semi-glossy; upright growth.

Fordham Rose™ HT, *dr*, 1989, (WILford); *Chrysler Imperial × Josephine Bruce*; Williams, J. Benjamin; Fordham University, 1990. Bud pointed; flowers deep maroon-red with deep, black, velvety tones, dbl. (32 ruffled petals), urn-shaped, medium, borne singly; moderate fragrance; foliage large, dark green, semiglossy, thick, disease resistant; prickles few, ovoid, curved down, medium, tan; fruit none observed; upright, medium growth.

Forest Fire Min, *or*, 1985, (LEOfire); *((Sheri Anne × Starina) × (Persian Princess × Starina))*

× *((Sheri Anne × Persian Princess) × Starina)*; Leon, Charles F., Sr. Flowers orange-red, dbl. (40+ petals), medium; slight fragrance; foliage medium, medium to dark, semi-glossy; bushy growth.

Forever Amber F, *ob*, 1975, *Arthur Bell × Elizabeth of Glamis*; Bees. Flowers golden amber, suffused fiery orange, semi-dbl. (15 petals), flat, large (4 in.); very fragrant; foliage dark, leathery; vigorous growth.

Forever Scarlet HT, *pb*, 1976, *Wini Edmunds × Mister Lincoln*; Epperson, Richard. Flowers deep pink, reverse lighter, very dbl. (80 petals), exhibition, large blooms borne singly; spicy fragrance; bright red prickles; fruit globular; tall, upright growth.

Forever Yours HT, *dr*, 1964, (Concorde); *Yuletide × Seedling*; Jelly; E.G. Hill Co., 1964; URS, 1967. Bud long, pointed; flowers cardinal-red, dbl. (38 petals), high-centered to flat, large (4-5 in.); fragrant (spicy); vigorous, upright growth; greenhouse variety. ARS John Cook Medal, 1969.

Forevermore Min, *mr*, 1986, (LYOfor); *Seedling × Seedling*; Lyon; M.B. Farm Min. Roses. Flowers medium red, dbl. (38 petals), high-centered, exhibition, large blooms borne singly; very fragrant (spicy); foliage medium, medium green, semi-glossy; few, reddish, small prickles; fruit globular, medium, orange-red; medium, upright growth.

Forez Rose F, *mr*, 1964, *Sumatra × Antoine Noailly*; Croix, P. Flowers geranium-red, becoming old-rose, semi-dbl., borne in clusters; vigorous growth.

Forgotten Dreams HT, *mr*, 1981, *Fragrant Cloud × Teneriffe*; Bracegirdle, D.T.; Arthur Higgs Roses. Bud pointed; flowers cardinal red, dbl. (24 petals), borne singly and in trusses of 3-5; very fragrant; foliage medium green, semi-glossy; straight, red-brown prickles; vigorous, bushy growth.

Formby Favourite HT, *or*, *McGredy's Sunset sport*; Wright, R. Flowers orange-scarlet on golden yellow; said to be identical with Flaming Sunset.

Formby Show HT, *mr*, 1986, *Fragrant Cloud × Elida*; Dwight, Robert & Sons. Flowers medium red, full (26-40 petals), medium; slight fragrance; foliage medium, dark green, semi-glossy; upright growth.

Fornarina G (OGR), *pb*, 1826, Vétillard. Flowers deep rose, marbled white.

Fornarina M (OGR), *mp*, 1862, Moreau-Robert. Flowers deep rose, small; dwarf growth.

Forst HT, *or*, 1937, *Essence × Fritz Schrödter*; Krause. Flowers fiery scarlet red, well formed, very large; vigorous growth.

Forsythe HT, *dp*, 1970, (VERjo); *Miracle × Dr. A. J. Verhage*; Verbeek. Flowers venetian pink, carmine-rose, dbl. (45-50 petals), high-centered, large (4½-5 in.); very fragrant; foliage glossy, dark, leathery; upright growth.

Fort Knox HT, *dy*, 1956, *Seedling × Ville de Paris*; Howard, A.P.; H&S. Bud ovoid; flowers clear yellow, dbl. (20 petals), large (3½-4½ in.); very fragrant; foliage dark, leathery; vigorous, upright, open growth.

Fort Vancouver HT, *mp*, 1956, *Charlotte Armstrong × Times Square*; Swim; Peterson & Dering. Bud long, pointed; flowers medium pink, dbl. (35-50 petals), well-formed, large (5-6 in.); very fragrant (damask); foliage leathery; vigorous growth.

Fortschritt F, *yb*, 1933, (Progress); *Mrs. Pierre S. duPont × Gloria Mundi*; Kordes. Flowers yellow-pink, semi-dbl., open, large borne in clusters; slightly fragrant; foliage glossy, light; vigorous, bushy growth.

Fortuna HT, *mp*, 1927, *Lady Pirrie × Nur Mahal*; Pemberton. Flowers rose-pink becoming lighter, many golden anthers, semi-dbl. (25 petals); fragrant (fruity); dwarf, bushy growth. GM, NRS, 1927; RULED EXTINCT 12/85.

Fortuna® HT, *op*, 1985, (KORtuna); *Sonia × Seedling*; Kordes, W., 1977. Flowers medium salmon-pink, dbl. (30 petals), well-formed, exhibition, large blooms borne singly; fragrant; foliage medium, medium green, semiglossy; medium, upright growth.

Fortune HT, *yb*, 1951, *Phyllis Gold sport*; Watkins Roses. Flowers gold shaded peach, dbl. (60 petals), large (4 in.); fragrant; foliage glossy; vigorous growth. RULED EXTINCT 12/85.

Fortune's Double Yellow Misc OGR (OGR), *yb*, (Beauty of Glazenwood; Gold of Ophir; *R. × odorata pseudindica* Rehder; *R. pseudindica*; *R. chinensis pseudindica*; *R. fortuniana* hort.; San Rafael Rose); 1845. Flowers salmon-yellow, outside tinged red, dbl., blooms in clusters of 3-4; sweet-scented.

Fortuniana Misc OGR (OGR), *w*, (Double Cherokee; Fortuneana; *R. × fortuniana*; *R. fortuneana*); *Supposedly R. banksiae × R. laevigata*; 1850. Flowers white, dbl., large; climbing growth.

Forty-niner HT, *rb*, 1949, *Contrast × Charlotte Armstrong*; Swim; Armstrong Nursery. Bud long, pointed; flowers medium red, reverse yellow, dbl. (25-40 petals), large (3½-4 in.); slightly fragrant; foliage leathery, glossy,

dark; vigorous, upright, compact growth. GM, Portland, 1947; AARS, 1949.

Forty-niner, Climbing Cl HT, *rb*, 1952, Moffet; Armstrong Nursery.

Forum Pol, *mr*, 1969, *Veronique × Independence seedling*; Delforge. Flowers bright red, dbl., open, large; foliage light green, glossy; vigorous, upright growth.

Forward HT, *my*, 1962, *Ethel Sanday × Peace*; LeGrice. Flowers clear primrose-yellow, moderately dbl., large; upright growth.

Forward March HT, *mp*, 1934, *Better Times sport*; Wolfe. Bud pointed, bright old-rose; flowers bright rose-pink, becoming lighter, dbl., large; long stems; foliage dark, bronze, leathery, glossy; very vigorous, bushy growth.

Fosse Way HT, *mp*, 1980, *Colour Wonder × Prima Ballerina*; Langdale, G.W.T. Bud long; flowers rose pink, paler reverse, dbl. (35-40 petals), high-centered blooms borne singly and several together; slight fragrance; foliage matt, light green; hooked prickles; vigorous, tall, upright growth.

Foster's Wellington Cup HT, *w*, 1988, (MACmouhoo; Foster's Melbourne Cup); *Sexy Rexy × Pot O'Gold*; McGredy, Sam; McGredy Roses International, 1991. Flowers white, dbl. (20 petals), medium; fragrant; foliage large, medium green, semi-glossy; bushy growth. GM, NZ, 1991.

Founder's Pride Min, *pb*, 1991, (MICpride); *Seedling × Party Girl*; Williams, Michael C., 1987; The Rose Garden. Bud pointed; flowers deep pink, white center, mostly white reverse, aging deep pink to strawberry red, dbl. (24 petals), high-centered, exhibition, large, borne usually singly; slight, spicy fragrance; foliage large, dark green, semi-glossy; upright growth.

Fountain HT, *mr*, 1970, (Fontaine; Red Prince®); Tantau; Wheatcroft Bros. Flowers crimson, dbl. (35 petals), cupped, large (5 in.); very fragrant; foliage dark, glossy. GM, RNRS, 1971; ADR, 1971; RNRS PIT, 1971.

Fountain of Beauty HT, *ab*, 1974, *Seedling × Colour Wonder*; Golik; Dynarose. Bud ovoid; flowers creamy to salmon, very dbl. (100 petals), medium (3-4 in.); foliage leathery; moderate growth.

Fountain Square™ HT, *w*, 1984, (JACmur); *Pristine sport*; Humenick, Muriel F.; Fountain Square, Inc., 1986. Flowers clear white.

Four Cheers HT, *ob*, 1988, *Daisy Mae × First Prize*; Stoddard, Louis. Bud ovoid; flowers soft orange with yellow center, dbl. (30 petals), urn-shaped, high-centered, medium, borne usually singly and in sprays of 1-3, continuous bloom; slight fragrance; foliage medium, medium green, glossy, smooth, leathery; prickles falcate, moderate, stout, maroon to ivory; fruit globular, medium, orange; spreading, medium growth.

Foxfire HT, *mr*, 1990, *Seedling × First Prize*; Stoddard, Louis, 1991. Bud pointed; flowers medium red, dbl. (30 petals), high-centered, exhibition, medium blooms borne singly; no fragrance; foliage medium, medium green, glossy; prickles straight, green; upright, tall growth.

Foxy Lady™ Min, *op*, 1980, (AROshrim); *Gingersnap × Magic Carrousel*; Christensen; Armstrong Nursery. Bud ovoid, pointed; flowers coral pink and white, dbl. (25 petals), imbricated, medium (1½ in.); foliage small; tall, vigorous, bushy growth.

F. P. Merritt Cl HT, *dr*, 1951, *Hoosier Beauty sport*; Merritt. Flowers bright fiery crimson, dbl. (50-60 petals), high-centered, large (5 in.), very long stems; very fragrant; foliage glossy; very vigorous, climbing (12 ft.) growth.

Fragezeichen R, *mp*, 1910, *Dorothy Perkins × Marie Baumann*; Boettner. Flowers shining pink, dbl. (25 petals), globular, large, in few-flowered trusses; foliage glossy; vigorous; very hardy.

Fragrance HT, *dp*, 1965, *Charlotte Armstrong × Merry Widow*; Lammerts; Germain's. Bud long, pointed; flowers carmine to rose-madder, dbl., high-centered, large; very fragrant; foliage bronze, leathery; vigorous, tall, compact growth.

Fragrance HT, *dr*, 1924, *Hoosier Beauty × George Dickson*; Chaplin Bros. Flowers deep crimson, full, high pointed, large; fragrant; vigorous growth.

Fragrant Air F, *rb*, 1977, Pearce, C.; Limes Rose Nursery. Flowers red changing to magenta-pink, dbl. (20 petals), medium (2½ in.); very fragrant; foliage dark.

Fragrant Beauty S, *dp*, 1950, *(Pharisaer × Conrad Ferdinand Meyer) × Crimson Glory*; Jacobus; B&A. Bud ovoid; flowers carmine, dbl. (22 petals), cupped, large; very fragrant (spicy); foliage glossy; very vigorous (4-5 ft.), upright, compact growth; profuse, recurrent bloom.

Fragrant Bouquet HT, *lp*, 1922, H&S. Flowers shell-pink, base yellow, dbl. (30-35 petals); very fragrant.

Fragrant Cloud HT, *or*, 1967, (TANellis; Duftwolke; Nuage Parfumé); *Seedling × Prima Ballerina*; Tantau, Math., 1963; J&P, 1968. Bud ovoid; flowers coral-red becoming geranium-red, dbl. (25-30 petals), well-formed, large (5 in.); very fragrant; foliage dark, glossy; vigorous, upright growth.   GM, NRS, 1963, Portland, 1967; NRS PIT, 1964;

James Alexander Gamble Rose Fragrance Medal, 1969

Fragrant Cloud, Climbing Cl HT, *or*, 1973, (COLfragrasar; Nuage Parfumé, Climbing); Collin, W.C.; W.H. Collin & Sons.

Fragrant Delight® F, *op*, 1978, (Wisbech Rose Fragrant Delight); *Chanelle × Whisky Mac*; Wisbech Plant Co. Flowers light orange-salmon, reverse deeper, dbl. (22 petals), large (3 in.); very fragrant; foliage glossy, reddish.   Edland Fragrance Medal, 1976; GM, James Mason, 1988.

Fragrant Dream HT, *ab*, 1988, (DICodour); *(Eurorose × Typhoon) × Bonfire*; Dickson, Patrick; Dickson Nursery, 1989. Flowers apricot blended orange, dbl. (20 petals), large; very fragrant; foliage large, medium green, glossy; upright growth.

Fragrant Fantasy™ HT, *ab*, 1992, (DEVfrago); *Seedling 80227-20 × Seedling 82249-1*; Marciel, Stanley & Jeanne; DeVor Nursery. Flowers apricot, moderately full (15-25 petals), large (7+ cms) blooms borne mostly singly; very fragrant; foliage medium, dark green, matt; few prickles; medium (202 cms), upright growth.

Fragrant Glory HT, *dp*, 1950, *Phyllis Gold × Crimson Glory*; Cobley. Bud dark red; flowers deep cyclamen-pink, dbl. (36 petals), high-centered, very large (6 in.), strong stems; very fragrant; vigorous growth.

Fragrant Gold HT, *dy*, 1981, (TANduft; Duftgold); Tantau, M., 1982. Flowers deep yellow, semi-dbl., large; fragrant; foliage medium, dark, glossy; upright growth.

Fragrant Hour HT, *op*, 1973, *Arthur Bell × (Spartan × Grand Gala)*; McGredy. Flowers bronze-pink, dbl. (35 petals), high-pointed, large (4½ in.); very fragrant; foliage light. GM, Belfast, 1975.

Fragrant Lady HT, *mp*, 1991, *Queen Elizabeth × Broadway*; Perry, Anthony; Co-Operative Rose Growers, 1991. Bud ovoid; flowers medium pink, semi-dbl., cupped, urn-shaped, medium blooms borne usually singly; heavy, fruity fragrance; foliage medium, dark green, semi-glossy; upright, medium growth.

Fragrant Love® HT, *mr*, 1979, *Chrysler Imperial × Seedling*; Barni-Pistoia Rose. Bud globular, pointed; flowers medium purplish red, dbl. (45 petals), cupped blooms borne 1-3 per cluster; very fragrant; foliage large, deep green, matt; curved reddish prickles; upright growth.

Fragrant Mist F, *w*, 1984, (SMItsblanc); *Elizabeth of Glamis × Jubilee Celebration*; Smith, Edward. Flowers white, dbl. (35 petals), well-formed, medium; very fragrant; foliage medium, medium green, matt; upright growth.

Fragrant Morning Min, *my*, 1990, (RENmorning); *Sunsprite × Miniature seedling*; Rennie, Bruce; Rennie Roses, International, 1991. Flowers medium yellow, full (26-40 petals), small, borne mostly singly; very fragrant; foliage small, light green, semi-glossy; upright (18 in.) growth.

Fragrant Pink Talisman HT, *pb*, 1938, *Talisman seedling*; Moore, R.S. Flowers pink shades, semi-dbl. (18 petals), slightly larger than Talisman; very fragrant.

Fragrant Surprise HT, *ab*, 1988, (HARverag; Samaritan); *Silver Jubilee × Dr. A.J. Verbage*; Harkness, R.; R. Harkness & Co., 1990. Bud ovoid, reddish-apricot; flowers apricot with pink tints, dbl. (46 quartered petals), cupped, large, borne singly or in sprays of up to 5; fruity fragrance; foliage medium, medium green, semi-glossy; prickles broad, medium, green; bushy, medium growth. Orleans Rose d'Or, 1990.

Fraîcheur R, *lp*, 1921, Turbat. Flowers soft pink, borne in pyramidal clusters; foliage glossy, dark; very vigorous growth.

Fraîcheur HT, *lp*, 1942, *Joanna Hill × Seedling*; Meilland, F.; A. Meilland. Bud long, pointed; flowers soft pink tinted pearl-white, semi-dbl., cupped, medium; slightly fragrant; foliage leathery, light green; vigorous, bushy growth.

Franca F, *pb*, 1961, *Confidence × Seedling*; Moreira; da Silva. Flowers pink and yellow.

Français F, *op*, 1951, *Holstein × Orange Triumph*; Mallerin; EFR. Flowers bright pink tinted orange, semi-dbl., borne in clusters; vigorous growth.

France Inter HT, *mr*, 1969, (DELkri); *(Rome Glory × La Vaudoise) × Divine*; Delbard; Trioreau. Flowers magenta-red, dbl. (35-45 petals), ovoid, large (4-5 in.); slightly fragrant.

France Libre® HT, *ob*, 1990, (DELjaunor); *(Zambra × Orange Sensation) × (Seedling × Seedling)*; Delbard-Chabert, 1981. Flowers nasturtium orange and coppery, yellow and gold reverse, full (25-30 petals), cupped, large; light fragrance; foliage dark green, glossy; upright growth.

Frances Ashton HT, *mp*, 1937, *Lady Battersea × Hawlmark Crimson*; DePuy; Stocking. Bud pointed; flowers carmine, stamens wine-colored, single (5 petals), large; slightly fragrant; foliage leathery; vigorous.

Frances Gaunt HT, *ab*, 1918, Dickson, A. Flowers apricot to salmon-yellow, semi-dbl., cupped, globular, large; very fragrant; foliage

glossy; vigorous, branching growth. GM, Bagatelle, 1920.

Frances Gaunt, Climbing Cl HT, *ab*, 1934, Cazzaniga.

Francesca HMsk (S), *ab*, 1922, *Danaë × Sunburst*; Pemberton. Flowers apricot, single, blooms in large sprays on long stems; slightly fragrant; foliage leathery; vigorous (5-6 ft.) growth; recurrent bloom; (21)

Francesca de Cuixart HT, *rb*, 1960, (F. Cuixart); *Baccará × Golden Masterpiece*; Dot, S.; P. Dot. Bud ovoid; flowers lincoln red, reverse fuchsine-red, dbl. (40 petals), open, large; long stems; very fragrant; foliage glossy, bronze; vigorous, compact growth.

Francesch Matheu HT, *ob*, 1940, *Luis Brinas × Catalonia*; Dot, P. Bud long, pointed; flowers rich golden orange, dbl., cupped, large; strong stems; foliage glossy, dark; very vigorous, upright growth.

Francesco La Scola HT, *or*, 1934, *Hortulanus Budde × Cuba*; Ketten Bros. Flowers bright orange-red, edged Nilsson pink, semi-dbl., large; slightly fragrant; foliage holly-green; vigorous growth; early bloom.

Francette Giraud F, *op*, 1961, *Aloha × (Gloire du Midi × Edith de Martinelli)*; Arles. Flowers bright salmon-pink, dbl., borne in clusters; foliage dark; vigorous growth.

Francie Simms HT, *mp*, 1926, Dickson, A. Flowers rose-pink, marked carmine, base buttercup yellow, dbl.; fragrant.

Francine HT, *rb*, 1961, Kriloff; Cramphorn's Nursery. Bud pointed; flowers crimson, reverse silvery, dbl. (30-35 petals), very large (6 in.); fragrant; foliage glossy; vigorous, bushy growth.

Francine Contier® HT, *my*, 1977, *Peer Gynt × Thalia*; Lens. Bud long, pointed; flowers canary-yellow, dbl. (40-45 petals), high-centered, large (3½-4½ in.); slightly fragrant; foliage glossy, dark; very vigorous growth.

Francis R, *mp*, 1933, *R. wichuraiana hybrid × Crimson Rambler*; Hauser. Flowers rose-pink, dbl.; vigorous growth.

Francis Dubreuil T (OGR), *dr*, 1894, Dubreuil. Bud long; flowers velvety crimson, medium.

Francis E. Lester HMsk (S), *w*, 1946, *Kathleen × Seedling*; Lester Rose Gardens. Flowers white edged pink, single, medium (2 in.) blooms in clusters of 25-30; very vigorous (8-10 ft. in a season) growth; recurrent bloom; very hardy.

Francis Scott Key HT, *pb*, 1913, *Radiance × Seedling*; Cook, J. Flowers deep pink, reverse lighter, dbl., high-centered, very large; long, strong stems; slightly fragrant; foliage dark, leathery, glossy; very vigorous growth.

Francis Scott Key, Climbing Cl HT, *pb*, Discovered by several growers in Tyler, Texas.

Francisco Curbera HT, *pb*, 1923, Dot, P. Flowers salmon-pink and yellow, very dbl., well formed; vigorous growth.

Francita HT, *dp*, 1965, *((Dame Edith Helen × Baccará) × Baccará) × Comtesse Vandal*; Mondial Roses. Flowers light red, very dbl., medium; slightly fragrant; foliage dark.

François Allard HT, *yb*, 1927, *Mme. Mélanie Soupert × Mme. Segond Weber*; Felberg-Leclerc. Flowers creamy yellow, reverse salmon-pink, dbl.

François Bollez HT, *op*, 1935, Gillot, F. Bud shrimp-pink; flowers salmon, base orange, dbl., large.

François Coppée HP (OGR), *dr*, 1895, Lédéchaux. Flowers dark crimson, dbl., large; fragrant.

François Foucard R, *my*, 1900, *R. wichuraiana × L'Ideal*; Barbier. Flowers lemon-yellow, semi-dbl., borne in clusters; very vigorous growth.

François Guillot R, *w*, 1907, *R. wichuraiana × Mme. Laurette Messimy*; Barbier. Flowers milk-white, dbl.; slightly fragrant; foliage light green, glossy; vigorous (15-18 ft.).

François Juranville R, *op*, 1906, *R. wichuraiana × Mme. Laurette Messimy*; Barbier. Flowers bright salmon-pink, base yellow, quite distinct, large; very vigorous growth.

François Laplanche HT, *w*, 1934, *Mme. Charles Détreaux × Mme. Edouard Herriot*; Buatois. Flowers flesh-white on yellow ground, veined and edged carmine, dbl., cupped, large; very fragrant; foliage leathery; bushy growth.

François Levet HP (OGR), *dp*, 1880, Levet, A. Flowers cherry-rose, well formed.

François Michelon HP (OGR), *m*, 1871, *La Reine seedling*; Levet, A. Flowers deep rose tinged lilac, full, globular, large; fragrant; foliage somewhat wrinkled; upright.

François Poisson LCl, *ly*, 1902, *R. wichuraiana × William Allen Richardson*; Barbier. Flowers pale sulphur-yellow, center shaded orange, passing to white, dbl., large; very vigorous growth.

Françoise Blondeau HT, *op*, 1938, *Charles P. Kilham × Colette Clément*; Mallerin; H. Guillot. Flowers coral, full, large; foliage dark; very vigorous growth.

Françoise Crousse Cl T (OGR), *mr*, 1900, Guillot, P. Flowers cerise-crimson shaded darker, full, globular; vigorous growth.

Françoise de Salignac M (OGR), *mp*, 1854, Robert. Flowers rose-pink; vigorous growth.

Frank Macmillan HT, *dr*, 1978, *Uncle Walter × (Ena Harkness × Fragrant Cloud)*; Scrivens. Flowers crimson-red, dbl. (26 petals), full, large (4 in.); very fragrant; foliage semi-glossy; moderately vigorous, spreading growth.

Frank Naylor S, *rb*, 1978, *(((Orange Sensation × Allgold) × ((Little Lady × Lilac Charm) × (Blue Moon × Magenta))) × ((((Cläre Grammerstorf × Frühlingsmorgen) × (Little Lady × Lilac Charm)) × ((Blue Moon × Magenta) × (Cläre Grammerstorf × Frühlingsmorgen)))*; Harkness, 1977. Flowers dark red, yellowish eye, single (5 petals), small (1½ in.); fragrant (musky); foliage small, plum shaded.

Frank Neave HT, *ly*, 1928, Morse. Flowers pale mustard-yellow, dbl.; fragrant.

Frank Penn HT, *pb*, 1970, *Wendy Cussons × Lys Assia*; Clayworth; F. Mason. Bud long, pointed; flowers cerise, reverse pink, dbl., full, large; foliage dark, leathery; very vigorous, upright growth.

Frank Reader HT, *my*, 1927, *Golden Ophelia × Souv. de H.A. Verschuren*; Verschuren; H&S; Dreer. Flowers lemon-yellow, center apricot, fairly full, high-centered, large; strong stems; fragrant; vigorous growth.

Frank Serpa Gr, *op*, 1960, *Pres. Macia × Seedling*; Serpa. Bud pointed; flowers pink tinted salmon, dbl., cupped, large; fragrant; foliage leathery, glossy, dark; very vigorous growth.

Frank W. Dunlop HT, *dp*, 1920, *Mrs. Charles E. Russell × Mrs. George Shawyer*; Dunlop; Totty. Flowers deep bright rose-pink, full (45 petals), high-centered, large; very fragrant.

Frank W. Dunlop, Climbing Cl HT, *dp*, 1933, Dixie Rose Nursery.

Frankenland® F, *or*, 1982, (TANkenfram); Tantau, M.; Tantau Roses. 1978. Bud medium, pointed; flowers brilliant scarlet, dbl. (23 petals), HT form, patio, borne in clusters of many; no fragrance; foliage large, dark, semi-glossy; straight, brown-red prickles; bushy, low growth.

Frankfort Agathé G (OGR), *dp*, Prior to 1906. Flowers cerise.

Frankfurt am Main F, *mr*, 1960, Boerner; Kordes & Tantau. Flowers blood-red shaded scarlet, dbl. (25 petals), well formed, large (2½-3 in.), borne in clusters; slightly fragrant; foliage dark; bushy, upright growth.

Franklin HT, *op*, 1918, Pernet-Ducher. Flowers salmon, shaded yellowish salmon, full.

Franklin D. Roosevelt HT, *mr*, 1939, *Betty Uprichard sport*; McClung. Flowers bright red fading to rose-purple, dbl. (26 petals), cupped, medium; very fragrant; foliage glossy, dark; bush and semi-climbing growth.

Franklin Engelmann F, *dr*, 1970, *Heidelberg × (Detroiter × Seedling)*; Dickson, A. Flowers bright scarlet, dbl. (36 petals), pointed, very large blooms in trusses; vigorous.

Frans Leddy Pol, *op*, 1927, (Frank Leddy); *Kersbergen sport*; Kersbergen; Van Nes. Flowers light orange-red, turning pink, dbl., small.

Franz Deegen HT, *my*, 1901, (Yellow Kaiserin Auguste Viktoria); *Kaiserin Auguste Viktoria × Seedling*; Hinner, W. Flowers soft yellow to golden yellow, full.

Franz Grümmer HT, *or*, 1927, *Mme. Abel Chatenay × Château de Clos Vougeot*; Maass. Flowers coral-red, dbl.

Fraser McLay HT, *mr*, 1974, *Grand Gala × Suspense*; Dawson, G.; Neil. Bud ovoid; flowers glossy medium red, dbl., medium; foliage glossy, leathery; bushy growth.

Fraser's Pink Musk N (OGR), *lp*, 1818, (Blush Musk); Fraser. Flowers blush, semi-dbl., medium, borne in large clusters; very fragrant.

Fraternité F, *pb*, 1946, *Florentina × World's Fair*; Leenders, M.; Longley. Flowers Neyron rose, reverse pale lilac-rose, dbl. (25 petals), globular, large (3 in.), borne in clusters; slightly fragrant; foliage bronze; vigorous growth.

Frau Anny Beaufays F, *mr*, 1962, (Mrs. Annie Beaufays); deRuiter; Beaufays. Bud ovoid; flowers salmon-red, semi-dbl., borne in clusters; slightly fragrant; low growth.

Frau Astrid Späth F, *dp*, 1930, (Astrid Späth; Direktör Rikala); *Lafayette sport*; Spath. Flowers clear carmine-rose; foliage dark glossy; bushy, dwarf, abundant bloom.

Frau Astrid Späth, Climbing Cl F, *dp*, 1935, Lens.

Frau Berta Gürtler R, *lp*, 1913, Gürtler; P. Lambert. Flowers light silky pink, full.

Frau Bertha Kiese HT, *my*, 1914, *Kaiserin Auguste Viktoria × Undine*; Kiese. Flowers pure golden yellow, dbl.

Frau Dagmar Hartopp HRg (S), *mp*, (Frau Dagmar Hastrup; Fru Dagmar Hastrup); ca. 1914. Flowers silvery pink, single (5 petals); foliage crinkled, rich green; low growing; (14).

Frau Dr. Erreth F, *dy*, 1915, *Gruss an Aachen × Mrs. Aaron Ward*; Geduldig. Flowers deep golden yellow, passing to white, dbl., well shaped, borne in sparse clusters; branching growth.

Frau Dr. Krüger HT, *op*, 1919, *Baronne Henriette de Loew × Mme. Caroline Testout*; Kiese. Flowers cream-salmon on golden ground.

Frau Dr. Schricker HCh (OGR), *rb*, 1927, *Gruss an Teplitz × Souv. de Mme. Eugene Verdier*; Felberg-Leclerc. Flowers fiery carmine and coppery-red, dbl., large; very fragrant; dwarf growth.

Frau Eduard Bethge HT, *dr*, 1930, *Hadley × Admiral Ward*; Felberg-Leclerc. Flowers dark crimson and velvety blood-red, dbl., large; very fragrant; foliage light.

Frau Elisabeth Balzer HT, *w*, 1933, *Mrs. Henry Morse sport*; Balzer. Flowers white, base orange-yellow, reverse bright flesh-pink, pointed; vigorous growth.

Frau Elisabeth Münch Pol, *mr*, 1921, *Orléans Rose sport*; Münch & Haufe. Flowers scarlet-cherry-red, with deeper reflexes.

Frau Emmy Hammann HT, *yb*, 1923, *Mme. Caroline Testout × Mme. Hoste*; Weigand, C.; Hammann. Flowers reddish lemon-yellow shaded sunflower-yellow, dbl.

Frau E. Weigand HT, *yb*, 1928, *Mme. Caroline Testout × Souv. de Claudius Pernet*; Weigand, C.; Weigand & H. Schultheis. Flowers canary-yellow, dbl. (70 petals), globular, high-centered, large; strong stems; very fragrant; foliage dark, leathery.

Frau Felberg-Leclerc HT, *my*, 1921, *Louise Catherine Breslau sport*; Felberg-Leclerc. Flowers pure golden yellow, dbl.; slightly fragrant.

Frau Felix Tonnar HT, *mp*, 1924, *Mme. Mélanie Soupert × Mme. Annette Aynard*; Leenders, M. Flowers bright rose, base coppery orange, semi-dbl.

Frau Fritz Pelzer HT, *or*, 1927, *Mme. Edouard Herriot × Edward Mawley*; Leenders, M. Flowers reddish crimson-orange, dbl.

Frau Georg von Simson R, *mp*, 1909, *Helene × Rosel Dach*; Walter. Flowers rose; vigorous growth.

Frau Hedwig Koschel Pol, *w*, 1921, *Ellen Poulsen sport*; Münch & Haufe. Flowers white, slightly shaded yellow, edges tinted rose-pink, full; fragrant.

Frau Hedwig Wagner HT, *mp*, 1919, *Enchantress × Mrs. W.J. Grant*; Krüger; Kiese. Flowers pink, dbl.; fragrant.

Frau Hugo Lauster HT, *dy*, 1932, Lauster; Pfitzer; Dreer. Flowers deep canary-yellow, edged lighter, dbl., well formed; fragrant; vigorous growth.

Frau Ida Münch HT, *ly*, 1919, *Frau Karl Druschki × Billard et Barre*; Beschnidt. Flowers light golden yellow, center deeper, dbl.

Frau Karl Druschki HP (OGR), *w*, 1901, (F.K. Druschkii; Reine des Neiges; Snow Queen; White American Beauty); *Merveille de Lyon × Mme. Caroline Testout*; Lambert, P. Bud pointed, tinged carmine-pink; flowers snow-white, center sometimes blush-pink, dbl. (35 petals), large; scentless; foliage dark; vigorous growth.

Frau Karl Druschki, Climbing Cl HP (OGR), *w*, 1906, (Grimpant Reine des Neiges); Lawrenson.

Frau Lina Strassheim R, *op*, 1907, *Crimson Rambler sport*; Strassheim. Flowers reddish salmon-pink.

Frau Luise Kiese HT, *ly*, 1921, (Luise Kiese); Kiese. Flowers ivory-yellow, sometimes clear yellow, very full.

Frau Luise Lindecke HT, *dr*, 1928, *Columbia sport*; Lindecke; Lindecke; Kordes. Flowers deep claret-red, sometimes crimson, dbl.; very fragrant.

Frau Margarete Oppenheim HT, *rb*, 1928, *Hortulanus Budde × Souv. de Claudius Pernet*; Felberg-Leclerc. Flowers intense carmine-red shaded brick-red and yellow, semi-dbl.

Frau Marie Bromme Pol, *dr*, 1928, *Dr. Kater sport*; Wirtz & Eicke. Flowers bright dark red.

Frau Martha Schmidt HT, *mr*, 1923, *Paula Clegg × Edward Mawley*; Kiese. Flowers carmine-red, dbl.; very fragrant.

Frau Mathilde Bätz HT, *w*, 1929, *Seedling × Ophelia*; Felberg-Leclerc. Flowers pure white, stamens yellow, dbl.; very fragrant.

Frau Math. Noehl HT, *my*, 1913, *Kaiserin Auguste Viktoria × Mme. Ravary*; Welter. Flowers lemon-yellow, dbl.; fragrant.

Frau Mélanie Niedieck HT, *dy*, 1916, *Mme. Jenny Gillemot × Prince de Bulgarie*; Leenders, M. Flowers vivid lemon-yellow, dbl.

Frau Oberhofgärtner Singer HT, *pb*, 1908, *Jules Margottin × Mme. Eugénie Boullet*; Lambert, P. Flowers soft pink edged white; fragrant.

Frau Oberpräsident von Grothe HT, *op*, 1920, *Richmond × Farbenkönigin*; Löbner; P. Lambert. Flowers rose-orange streaked carmine.

Frau Peter Lambert HT, *op*, 1902, *(Kaiserin Auguste Viktoria × Mme. Caroline Testout) × Mme. Abel Chatenay*; Welter. Flowers pink shading to salmon.

Frau Robert Türke HT, *dr*, 1928, *Hadley × Hugh Dickson*; Türke; Teschendorff. Flowers dark crimson, very dbl., long stems; fragrant; foliage dark, glossy; vigorous growth.

Frau Rudolf Schmidt Pol, *dr*, 1919, *Jessie sport*; Schmidt, R. Flowers dark ruby-red without objectionable blue shades; very dwarf growth.

Fräulein Octavia Hesse R, *ly*, 1910, *R. wichuraiana × Kaiserin Auguste Viktoria*; Hesse. Flowers yellowish white, center deeper, dbl., small; fragrant; vigorous, climbing growth; recurrent bloom.

Frazier Annesley HT, *dp*, 1935, McGredy. Bud pointed; flowers carmine, base golden yellow, dbl., high-centered; slightly fragrant; foliage glossy, bronze; very vigorous growth.

Freckle Face S, *pb*, 1976, *(Vera Dalton × Dornroschen) × ((World's Fair × Floradora) × Applejack)*; Buck; Iowa State University. Bud ovoid; flowers light spirea-red, striped dark spirea, dbl. (23 petals), large (3½-4 in.); fragrant (clove); foliage coppery, leathery; bushy, spreading growth.

Freckles S, *pb*, 1976, *Tickled Pink × Country Music*; Buck; Iowa State University. Bud ovoid, pointed to urn-shaped; flowers light scarlet, flushed yellow, dbl. (28 petals), shallowly-cupped, large (4-4½ in.); slightly fragrant; foliage dark, coppery, leathery; upright, bushy growth.

Fred Cramphorn HT, *or*, 1961, (Manola; Samoa); *Peace × Baccará*; Kriloff; Cramphorn's Nursery, 1961; Ilgenfritz Nursery, 1964. Flowers geranium-red, dbl. (40 rounded petals), cupped, large (5-6 in.); foliage dark, glossy; vigorous, upright, bushy growth.

Fred Edmunds HT, *ob*, 1943, (L'Arlésienne); *Duquesa de Peñaranda × Marie-Claire*; Meilland, F.; C-P. Bud long, pointed; flowers coppery orange, dbl. (25 petals), cupped, large (5-5½ in.); very fragrant (spicy); foliage leathery, glossy; bushy, open habit. GM, Portland, 1942; AARS, 1944.

Fred Edmunds, Climbing Cl HT, *ob*, 1989, *Fred Edmunds sport*; Weeks, O.L.; Weeks Roses, 1977.

Fred Fairbrother HT, *dp*, 1974, *(Gavotte × Tropicana) × Fragrant Cloud*; Sanday. Flowers bright cerise, dbl. (40 petals), large (4-5 in.); fragrant; foliage semi-glossy.

Fred Gibson HT, *ab*, 1966, *Gavotte × Buccaneer*; Sanday, 1968. Flowers apricot suffused gold, dbl. (30 petals), large (5 in.); slightly fragrant; foliage dark; tall, vigorous growth.

Fred Howard HT, *yb*, 1952, *Pearl Harbor × Seedling*; Howard, F.H.; H&S. Bud long; flowers golden orange shaded pink, dbl. (55 petals), high-centered, large (4 in.); slightly fragrant; vigorous, upright growth. AARS, 1952.

Fred Howard, Climbing Cl HT, *yb*, 1954, Howard, A.P.; H&S.

Fred J. Harrison HT, *mr*, 1924, Dickson, A. Flowers cardinal-red shaded crimson, dbl.; fragrant. GM, NRS, 1923.

Fred Loads Cl F, *or*, 1968, *Dorothy Wheatcroft × Orange Sensation*; Holmes, R.A.; Fryers Nursery, 1967. Flowers vermilion-orange, single, large (3 in.) blooms in clusters; fragrant; foliage glossy; vigorous, tall growth. GM, RNRS, 1967.

Fred Owen HT, *dy*, 1985, *Jan Guest sport*; Owen, Fred. Flowers deep yellow.

Fred Streeter HT, *my*, 1955, *Luis Brinas × Golden Scepter*; Kordes; Wheatcroft Bros. Bud pointed; flowers clear yellow, dbl. (48 petals), well-formed, large (4 in.); fragrant; foliage dark; vigorous.

Fred Streeter HMoy (S), *dp*, 1951, Jackman. Flowers deep cerise-pink, single, medium, borne in clusters (up to 3); upright, branching growth.

Fred Walker HT, *mp*, 1935, McGredy. Flowers glowing pink, base coppery orange, dbl., high-centered, large; slightly fragrant; foliage soft, light; vigorous growth.

Fred W. Mee HT, *mr*, 1957, (F.W. Mee); *Karl Herbst × The Doctor*; Mee. Flowers scarlet-cerise, dbl. (30 petals), high-centered; very fragrant; vigorous, upright growth.

Freddy F, *op*, 1989, (PEAproof); *Seedling × Seedling*; Pearce, C.A.; Rearsby Roses, 1989. Bud ovoid; flowers deep coral pink, aging pales slightly, dbl. (25 petals), urn-shaped, medium, borne in sprays of 3-21; slight fragrance; foliage medium, medium green, matt; prickles hooked, medium, red; fruit rare; bushy, even growth.

Frédéric Lerr HT, *pb*, 1950, *Crimson Glory × (Mrs. Pierre S. duPont × Signora)*; Sauvageot, H.; Sauvageot. Flowers carmine-red, reverse lighter, dbl., high-centered, large; foliage bronze; very vigorous growth.

Frederica HT, *mr*, Origin unknown; About 1953 in England. Flowers deep crimson, dbl. (30 petals), large (5 in.); fragrant; foliage dark, glossy; vigorous growth.

Frederick S. Peck LCl, *dp*, 1938, *Hybrid creeper × Mrs. Arthur Curtiss James*; Brownell. Flowers deep grenadine-pink, center more yellow, semi-dbl., large (4 in.), slightly arched stems.

Frederick the Second HCh (OGR), *m*, 1847. Flowers rich crimson-purple, dbl., large; vigorous.

Fredericksbergrosen F, *dp*, 1942, *Orléans Rose × Seedling*; Poulsen, S.; Poulsen's Roses. Flowers deep pink, single (5 petals), cupped, medium; no fragrance; foliage medium, medium green, semi-glossy; vigorous, bushy growth.

Fredica S, *w*, 1974, *Indica Major × Multiflora Inermis*; INRA. Bud oval; flowers white, single (5 petals), cupped, medium; thornless; very vigorous, bushy, upright growth; for understock only.

Free Gold HT, 1948, *Pink Princess × Shades of Autumn*; Brownell. Bud long, pointed; flowers yellow, dbl., high centered, open, large; fragrant; foliage glossy; bushy, dwarf growth. RULED EXTINCT 5/83 ARM.

Free Spirit Min, *ab*, 1985, (PIXiree); *Prominent × Gold Pin*; Strawn, Leslie E.; Pixie Treasures Mini Roses, 1984. Flowers apricot, dbl. (20 petals), small; slight fragrance; foliage small, medium green, semi-glossy; upright growth.

Freedom LCl, *w*, 1918, (White American Beauty, Climbing); *Silver Moon × Kaiserin Auguste Viktoria*; Undritz. Flowers white, center yellow, dbl. (75 petals), open, high centered, large (4 in.); long, strong stems; slightly fragrant; foliage dark, bronze, glossy; very vigorous, climbing growth. RULED EXTINCT 3/84 ARM.

Freedom® HT, *dy*, 1984, (DICjem); *(Eurorose × Typhoon) × Bright Smile*; Dickson, Patrick; Dickson Nursery. Flowers chrome yellow, dbl. (35 petals), exhibition, large; fragrant; foliage medium, medium green, glossy; bushy growth. GM, RNRS, 1983.

Freegold® Min, *dy*, 1983, (MACfreego; Free Gold; Penelope Keith); *Seaspray × Dorola*; McGredy, Sam. Flowers deep yellow, gold reverse, dbl. (20 petals), exhibition, small; fragrant; foliage small, light green, semi-glossy; upright growth.

Freeleigh HT, *my*, 1956, *Kingcup × Golden Scepter*; LeGrice. Flowers buttercup-yellow, dbl., well shaped, small; slightly fragrant; foliage glossy, light green; vigorous growth.

Freia HT, *ab*, 1936, *Ville de Paris × Rev. F. Page-Roberts*; Tantau. Flowers sun-yellow tinted orange, base orange, dbl., open, large; foliage leathery, glossy; vigorous, bushy growth.

Freiburg II HT, *pb*, 1917, *Dr. G. Krüger × Frau Karl Druschki*; Krüger. Flowers silver-rose, reverse bright apricot-pink, dbl.

Freiburg II, Climbing Cl HT, *pb*, 1953, Lindecke.

Freifrau Ida von Schubert HT, *dr*, 1912, *Oskar Cordel × Frau Peter Lambert*; Lambert, P. Flowers dark crimson-red, dbl.; fragrant.

Freifrau von Marschall R, *mp*, 1913, *Farquhar × Schneewittchen*; Lambert, P. Flowers fresh pink, dbl., small, borne in immense, loose clusters; vigorous (8-12 ft.) growth; midseason bloom.

Freiheitsglocke HT, *rb*, 1963, (Damas de Yuste; Liberty Bell); *Detroiter × Kordes' Perfecta*; Kordes, R.; A. Dickson; McGredy, 1963; Wyant, 1966. Flowers claret-rose, reverse light cream, dbl. (50 petals), globular, large

(5 in.); fragrant; foliage leathery; vigorous growth.

Freiherr von Marschall T (OGR), *mr*, 1903, *Princesse Alice de Monaco* × *Rose d'Evian*; Lambert, P. Bud pointed; flowers medium red, dbl., large; foliage blood-red when young; vigorous growth.

French Can Can HT, *pb*, 1956, Buyl Frères. Bud well formed; flowers pink, reverse yellow, dbl., large; vigorous, bushy growth.

French Lace F, *w*, 1980, (JAClace); *Dr. A.J. Verhage* × *Bridal Pink*; Warriner, W.A.; J&P. Bud pointed; flowers ivory, pastel apricot to white, dbl. (30 petals, exhibition blooms borne 1-12 per cluster; very little fragrance; foliage small, dark; small prickles; bushy growth. AARS, 1982; GM, Portland, 1984.

French Vanilla Gr, *w*, 1986, *Araby* × *Royal Highness*; Thomson, R. Flowers white and faint pink, reverse same, fading white, dbl., high-centered, medium, borne usually singly; moderate fragrance; foliage medium, dark green, matt; few, moderate, brown prickles; fruit none; spreading growth.

Frensham F, *dr*, 1946, *Floribunda seedling* × *Crimson Glory*; Norman; Harkness, 1946; C-P, 1949. Flowers deep scarlet, semi-dbl. (15 petals), medium blooms in large trusses; slightly fragrant; vigorous growth; (21). GM, NRS, 1943 & ARS, 1955.

Frensham, Climbing Cl F, *dr*, 1958, Bennett, J.A.; Pedigree Nursery.

Frensham's Companion F, *dp*, 1952, *Frensham sport*; Morse. Flowers cerise, semi-dbl. (18 petals), loosely formed, medium, borne in trusses; slightly fragrant; very free growth.

Frenzy F, *rb*, 1970, (MEIhigor; Prince Igor); *(Sarabande* × *Dany Robin)* × *Zambra*; Meilland. Flowers nasturtium-red, reverse yellow, dbl. (25 petals), rounded, medium (2 in.); fragrant (fruity); foliage matt; vigorous, bushy growth.

Fresco® F, *ob*, 1968, (RUIco); *Metropole* × *Orange Sensation*; deRuiter. Flowers orange, reverse golden yellow, well-formed, large (3 in.); slightly fragrant; foliage dark, glossy; vigorous, bushy growth.

Fresh Pink Min, *lp*, 1964, *(R. wichuraiana* × *Floradora)* × *Little Buckaroo*; Moore, R.S.; Sequoia Nursery. Bud ovoid; flowers light pink tipped salmon, dbl. (25 petals), cupped, medium blooms in clusters; slightly fragrant; foliage leathery, glossy; vigorous, bushy.

Fresh Start Min, *mp*, 1986, (FLOsar); *Avandel* × *Little Chief*; Florac, M.; M.B. Farm Min. Roses. Flowers bright medium pink, dbl. (42 pointed petals), globular, medium blooms borne usually singly; no fragrance; foliage

small, medium green, semi-glossy; small, red prickles; low, bushy growth.

Freude® HT, *or*, 1977, (DeKORat; Decorat); *Fragrant Cloud* × *Peer Gynt*; Kordes, W. Sons; Mattock, 1975. Flowers vermilion and gold blend; fragrant; foliage dark; vigorous, bushy growth. ADR, 1975.

Freudenfeuer Pol, *mr*, 1918, Kiese. Flowers bright red; moderate growth.

Freudentanz F, *mr*, 1973, *Fragrant Cloud* × *Goldmarie*; Hetzel; GAWA. Bud pointed; flowers bright red, reverse flamed red, medium; very fragrant; foliage glossy; vigorous, upright, bushy growth.

Freya HT, *dp*, 1956, *Seedling* × *Étoile de Hollande*; Leenders, M. Flowers carmine-red, dbl., large; vigorous growth.

Friction Lights F, *yb*, 1987, (HORlights); *Alexander* × *Champagne Cocktail*; Horner, Colin P.; Battersby Roses, 1987. Flowers canary-yellow edged cherry-red, dbl. (15-25 petals), large; slight fragrance; foliage medium, medium green, semi-glossy; upright growth.

Frieda Krause HT, *or*, 1935, *I Zingari* × *Seedling*; Krause. Flowers orange-scarlet-red, dbl., high-centered, large; foliage leathery, dark; very vigorous, bushy growth.

Friedlanderiana G (OGR), *mp*, *R. gallica hybrid* × *R. canina*. Flowers bright rose-pink, single; non-recurrent bloom.

Friedrich Heyer S, *ob*, 1956, Tantau, Math. Flowers bright orange, 10 petals, large (3½ in.), in large clusters; fragrant; foliage dark, glossy, leathery; vigorous, upright.

Friedrich Schwarz HT, *dr*, 1952, *Poinsettia* × *(Crimson Glory* × *Lord Charlemont)*; Kordes. Flowers crimson, dbl. (30 petals), cupped, large; very fragrant; foliage dark; very tall, branching growth.

Friedrich Wörlein F, *dy*, 1963, *Cläre Grammerstorf* × *Golden Masterpiece*; Kordes; Wörlein. Bud globular; flowers golden yellow, dbl., large; fragrant; foliage dark; vigorous, upright, bushy growth.

Friedrichsruh HT, *dr*, 1908, *Princesse de Bearn* × *Francis Dubreuil*; Türke. Flowers dark crimson, shaded black, turning blue, dbl., open, large; very fragrant; foliage dark, glossy; bushy, open growth.

Friend of Heart HT, *pb*, 1985, *(Festival Beauty* × *Scarlet Knight)* × *Self*; Hardikar, Dr. M.N. Flowers pink blend, dbl. (30 petals), high-centered, large blooms borne singly; slightly fragrant; foliage medium, dark, glossy; deep brown prickles; upright growth.

Friend of Peace HT, *yb*, 1986, *(Scarlet Knight* × *Festival Beauty)* × *Festival Beauty*; Hardikar, Dr. M.N. Flowers yellow blend, dbl. (20-22 petals), globular; very fragrant; foliage large, dark green, glossy, leathery; crescent, light brown prickles; upright, open growth.

Friendship HT, *dp*, 1937, *Templar × Talisman*; Amling Co. Bud pointed; flowers dark red, semi-dbl., high-centered; very fragrant; foliage glossy; vigorous growth. RULED EXTINCT 9/77.

Friendship HT, *dr*, 1938, Dickson, A. Flowers bright strawberry-red, with bright scarlet undertone, full, very large; very vigorous growth. GM, NRS, 1938; RULED EXTINCT 9/77.

Friendship™ HT, *dp*, 1978, (LINrick); *Fragrant Cloud × Miss All-American Beauty*; Lindquist; C-P. Bud ovoid; flowers deep pink, dbl. (28 petals), cupped to flat, large (5½-6 in.); very fragrant; foliage large, dark; vigorous, upright. AARS, 1979.

Friesensöhne® S, *dy*, 1982, (TANsenfrie); Tantau, M.; Tantau Roses, 1981. Flowers deep yellow, semi-dbl., medium; no fragrance; foliage medium, light, glossy.

Frigg S, *m*, 1969, *Schneezwerg × R. nitida*; Lundstad. Flowers mauve, semi-dbl. (15 petals), flat, small, borne in clusters; foliage small, rich green; low growth; free, recurrent bloom.

Frileuse Gr, *mp*, 1966, *Queen Elizabeth × Baronesse Manon*; Poulsen, N.D.; Vilmorin-Andrieux. Flowers medium pink, dbl., urn-shaped, large; slight fragrance; foliage large, light green, glossy; tall, upright, bushy growth.

Frills HT, *op*, 1950, Moss. Flowers deep salmon-pink becoming lighter, petals scalloped, large; compact, bushy growth.

Frilly Dilly F, *dp*, 1986, (MURfri); *Red Lion × Magenta*; Murray, Nola. Flowers light magenta red, full (25 petals), pointed, small, borne in sprays of 5-7; slight fragrance; foliage large, medium green, flat; pointed, brown prickles; upright growth.

Frimousse F, *op*, 1959, *Masquerade × Seedling*; Vilmorin-Andrieux. Flowers orange-pink, base yellow, single, medium, borne in clusters; slightly fragrant; vigorous, very bushy growth.

Friné HT, *dr*, 1961, *Lila Vidri × (Soraya × Vigoro)*; Dot, S. Flowers crimson suffused strawberry-red, dbl. (35 petals), well formed; fragrant; vigorous growth.

Fringette Min, *dp*, 1964, *Seedling × Magic Wand*; Moore, R.S.; Sequoia Nursery. Flowers deep pink, white center, dbl. (25 petals), small; low (8 in.), compact growth.

Frisco® F, *my*, 1987, (KORflapei; Pamela); *((New Day × Minigold) × Banzai) × Antique*

Silk; Kordes, W., 1986. Flowers medium yellow, dbl. (26-40 petals), medium; miniflora; slight fragrance; foliage medium, dark green, semi-glossy; bushy growth.

Frisette F, *or*, 1964, *Seedling × Concerto*; Mondial Roses. Flowers bright scarlet, semi-dbl., open, borne in clusters; vigorous, low to medium height.

Frisky HT, *mr*, 1959, *Charlotte Armstrong × Chrysler Imperial*; Wyant. Flowers velvety red, dbl. (50 petals), open, large; fragrant; foliage dark, glossy; vigorous, bushy growth.

Fritz Höger HT, *dr*, 1934, *(Hadley × Comte G. de Rochemur) × Cathrine Kordes*; Kordes. Bud pointed; flowers pure crimson, dbl., high-centered, large; foliage leathery, dark; very vigorous growth.

Fritz Maydt HT, *w*, 1925, *Mev. C. van Marwijk Kooy × Marquise de Sinéty*; Leenders, M. Flowers coppery flesh-white; fragrant.

Fritz Nobis S, *pb*, 1940, *Joanna Hill × Magnifica*; Kordes. Bud long, pointed, light red; flowers white, reverse reddish salmon-pink, dbl., high-centered, large blooms in clusters; very fragrant; foliage glossy, leathery; vigorous growth; non-recurrent bloom.

Fritz Schrödter HT, *dr*, 1928, *Hortulanus Budde seedling*; Mühle. Flowers brilliant dark scarlet, dbl., large, ; foliage bronze, soft; vigorous, bushy growth.

Fritz Thiedemann HT, *or*, 1959, *Horstmann's Jubiläumsrose seedling × Alpine Glow seedling*; Tantau, Math. Bud pointed; flowers brick-red, dbl. (36 petals), well-shaped, large (4 in.); fragrant; foliage dark; bushy growth.

Fritz Thiedemann, Climbing Cl HT, *or*, 1961, Kordes.

Friuli HT, *ab*, 1933, Ingegnoli. Flowers amber-yellow, cupped, large; vigorous growth.

Frivole F, *mr*, 1958, *Independence × Country Girl*; Buyl Frères. Flowers geranium-red, very dbl.; vigorous, low growth.

Frivolité HT, *or*, 1956, *Peace × Catalonia*; Dot, P. Flowers scarlet shaded orange and salmon, dbl. (50 petals), large; very fragrant; vigorous, compact growth.

Frohsinn® F, *ab*, 1961, (Joyfulness); *Horstmann's Jubiläumsrose × Circus*; Tantau, Math. Bud pointed; flowers apricot, cream and pink blend, dbl. (20 petals), cupped, large blooms in large clusters; slightly fragrant; foliage glossy; vigorous, bushy growth.

Frolic F, *mp*, 1953, *World's Fair × Pinocchio*; Swim; Armstrong Nursery. Flowers bright pink, dbl. (21 petals), medium (2½ in.), in large sprays; slightly fragrant; vigorous, bushy.

Frontenac S, *dp*, 1992, *((Queen Elizabeth × Arthur Bell) × (Simonet Red × von Scharnhorst)) × (R. kordesii × ((Red Dawn × Suzanne) × (Red Dawn × Suzanne)))*; Ogilvie, Ian; Agriculture Canada, 1992. Flowers deep pink, moderately full (15-25 petals), large (7+ cms) blooms borne in small clusters; slight fragrance; foliage medium, dark green, glossy; some prickles; medium (100 cms), upright growth; very winter hardy; grown on own roots.

Frontier Twirl S, *pb*, 1984, *Sevilliana × Just Joey*; Buck, Dr. Griffith J.; Iowa State University. Flowers pink-yellow blend, dbl. (25 petals), shallow-cupped, large blooms borne 1-8 per cluster; fragrant; foliage leathery, medium, bronze green; awl-like, tan prickles; erect, bushy growth; hardy; repeat bloom.

Frostfire Min, *mr*, 1963, *((R. wichuraiana × Floradora) × Seedling) × Little Buckaroo*; Moore, R.S.; Sequoia Nursery. Flowers red, sometimes flecked white, dbl. (30 petals), small (1 in.); foliage dark, glossy; bushy, compact (12-14 in.) growth.

Frosty Min, *w*, 1953, *(R. wichuraiana × Seedling) × Self*; Moore, R.S.; Sequoia Nursery. Bud ovoid, pale pink; flowers clear white, dbl. (45 petals), very small blooms in clusters of 3-10 or more; fragrant (honeysuckle); foliage glossy; vigorous (12-14 in.), compact, spreading growth.

Froufrou HT, *yb*, 1955, *Mme. Joseph Perraud × Yvonne Plassat*; Moulin-Epinay. Flowers chamois-yellow, center carmine, very dbl., large; vigorous, bushy growth.

Frou-Frou HT, *rb*, 1957, *Comtesse Vandal × Seedling*; Laperrière; EFR. Flowers crimson, reverse carmine-pink, dbl. (25 petals), large; moderate growth.

Froy F, *or*, 1972, *Traumland × Poulsen's Pink*; Lundstad; Norges Landbruks-hogskole. Bud ovoid; flowers orange-red, semi-dbl., open, medium; slightly fragrant; foliage glossy, dark; bushy growth.

F. R. Patzer HT, *pb*, 1909, Dickson, A. Flowers creamy buff, reverse warm pink, full, large; branching growth.

Fru Johanne Poulsen HT, *mp*, 1924, *Margrethe Möller seedling*; Poulsen, S. Flowers bright pink, well formed; vigorous growth.

Fru Xenia Jacobsen HT, *dr*, 1925, *Étoile de France × Richmond*; Poulsen, S. Flowers deep red, well shaped, dbl.; fragrant; vigorous growth.

Frühlingsanfang HSpn (OGR), *w*, 1950, *Joanna Hill × R. spinosissima altaica*; Kordes. Bud long, pointed; flowers ivory-white, single, very large (4 in.); fragrant; foliage leath-

ery; very vigorous, bushy (9 ft. in 6 years) growth; intermittent bloom.

Frühlingsduft HSpn (OGR), *pb*, 1949, *Joanna Hill × R. spinosissima altaica*; Kordes. Bud ovoid, golden yellow; flowers lemon-yellow with light pink, dbl., high-centered, very large; very fragrant; foliage large, leathery; very vigorous, upright, bushy growth; non-recurrent bloom.

Frühlingsgold® HSpn (OGR), *my*, 1937, (Spring Gold); *Joanna Hill × R. spinosissima hispida*; Kordes; B&A, 1951. Bud pointed, nasturtium-red; flowers creamy yellow, single (5 petals, sometimes up to 10), large (3 in.); very fragrant; foliage large, light, soft, wrinkled; very vigorous, bushy growth; non-recurrent bloom; (28).

Frühlingsmorgen HSpn (OGR), *pb*, 1942, (Spring Morning); *(E.G. Hill × Catrine Kordes) × R. spinosissima altaica*; Kordes. Flowers cherry-pink, center soft yellow, stamens maroon, single, medium; foliage dark; fruit large, red; free growth (6 ft.); occasionally slightly recurrent bloom; (28).

Frühlingsschnee HSpn (OGR), *w*, 1954, *Golden Glow × R. spinosissima altaica*; Kordes. Bud ovoid; flowers snow-white, single, very large; slightly fragrant; foliage leathery, wrinkled, light green; very vigorous, upright growth.

Fruhlingstag HSpn (OGR), *my*, 1949, *McGredy's Wonder × Frühlingsgold*; Kordes. Bud ovoid; flowers golden yellow, semi-dbl., large, borne in small clusters; fragrant; foliage leathery; many thorns; profuse non-recurrent bloom.

Frühlingszauber HSpn (OGR), *mp*, 1942, *(E.G. Hill × Catrine Kordes) × R. spinosissima altaica*; Kordes. Flowers pink, semi-dbl., medium; foliage dark; fruit large, dark red; vigorous (7 ft.) growth; non-recurrent bloom.

Fryer's Orange HT, *ab*, 1934, *Mrs. Sam McGredy sport*; Fryer's Nursery. Flowers orange-yellow.

FRYjingo HT, *yb*, 1985, (The Lady); *Pink Parfait × Redgold*; Fryer, G.R.; Fryers Nursery. Flowers honey yellow, petals edged salmon, dbl. (35 petals), well-formed, exhibition, large blooms borne singly and in clusters; slight fragrance; foliage medium, medium green, semi-glossy; upright growth. GM, Baden-Baden, 1987.

FRYminicot F, *ab*, 1988, (Sweet Dream); *Seedling × Seedling*; Fryers Nurs., Ltd. Flowers peach-apricot, dbl., medium; mini-flora; fragrant; foliage medium, medium green, semi-glossy; bushy growth. ROTY, 1988.

FRYwilrey HT, *rb*, 1987, (Audrey Wilcox®; *Alpine Sunset* × *Whisky Mac*; Fryers Nursery Ltd., 1985; Flowers cerise red and silver cream, full (26-40 petals), large blooms; very fragrant; foliage large, dark green, glossy.

Fuchsine Guy F, *m*, 1930, *Lafayette sport*; Leenders, M. Flowers lilac-purple, semi-dbl., open, large, borne in clusters; foliage rich green; bushy growth.

Fuëgo F, *or*, 1964, *Aloha* × *Gabychette*; Arles; Roses-France. Bud pointed; flowers Chinese vermilion, dbl. (30 petals), open, medium, borne in clusters; slightly fragrant.

Fuggerstadt Augsburg® F, *or*, 1985, (KORtreu); *Cordula* × *Topsi*; Kordes, W.; Kordes Sons. Flowers orange-red, semi-dbl., medium; slight fragrance; foliage medium, dark, glossy; upright, bushy growth.

Fugitive F, *yb*, 1965, *Mrs. Oakley Fisher* × *Seedling*; Pal; Indian Agric. Research Inst. Bud pointed; flowers apricot-yellow, becoming lighter, semi-dbl., open, borne in clusters; foliage glossy, bronze; vigorous, bushy growth.

Fugue® LCl, *dr*, 1958, (MEItam); *Alain* × *Guinée*; Meilland, M.L.; URS. Bud globular; flowers dark red, dbl. (30 petals), medium blooms in clusters; slightly fragrant; foliage leathery, glossy; vigorous growth. GM, Madrid, 1958.

Fukuyama HT, *op*, 1988, *Pristine* × *Takao*; Tagashira, Kazuso; Hiroshima Rose Nursery, 1988. Bud pointed; flowers salmon-pink, aging dark, dbl. (35 petals), high-centered, large; slight fragrance; foliage red aging dark green, matt, ovoid; prickles red to dark green; fruit round, yellow blend; upright, tall growth.

Fulgens HSpn (OGR), *m*, *R. spinosissima hybrid*. Flowers lilac-pink, semi-dbl.; fruit glossy, black; height 3-4 ft.; early bloom.

Fullcream HT, *ly*, 1959, *Wellworth* × *Diamond Jubilee*; LeGrice. Flowers creamy white, dbl. (28 petals), well formed, large (5-7 in.); very fragrant (honey); foliage glossy; vigorous, low growth.

Fullerton Centennial Min, *or*, 1986, (PIXifull); *Orange Honey* × *Rise 'n' Shine*; Chaffin, L., 1983; Friends of the Fullerton Arboretum, 1987. Flowers orange-red with white base, bright, fading darker, semi-dbl. (20-25 petals), cupped, high-centered, medium, borne singly or in sprays of 2-5; slight fragrance; foliage small, medium green, semi-glossy, disease resistant; needle declining, sparse, light tan prickles; fruit globular, medium green occasionally forms hips; upright, bushy, medium, neat, symmetrical growth.

Fulvia HT, *dp*, 1950, *Mme. Joseph Perraud* × *Mme. Elie Dupraz*; Gaujard. Flowers pink tinted carmine, dbl., medium; slightly fragrant; foliage leathery, light green; vigorous, bushy growth.

Fun Jwan Lo S, *w*, (Odorata 22449; Indica Major); *A Chinese garden variety of R.* × *odorata*; ca. 1924. Flowers white, center pale pink, dbl., small; very vigorous growth; not hardy. Imported by U.S. Dept. of Agriculture for use as an understock.

Funkenmariechen F, *yb*, 1973, *Seedling* × *Samba*; Kordes; Horstmann. Flowers yellow, red, dbl., globular; slightly fragrant; foliage glossy; upright, bushy growth.

Funkuhr® HT, *yb*, 1984, (KORport; Golden Summers; Laser Beam); *Seedling* × *Seedling*; Kordes, W.; Kordes Sons. Flowers yellow, petals edged medium red, aging red, dbl. (35 petals), large; no fragrance; foliage medium, medium green, glossy; upright.

Funny Face Min, *rb*, 1981, *Avandel* × *Zinger*; Jolly, Betty; Rosehill Farm. Flowers white, petals edged red, aging red, dbl. (35 petals), medium; slight fragrance; foliage small, medium green, semi-glossy; upright, bushy growth.

Funny Girl Min, *lp*, 1982, (JACfun); *Bridal Pink* × *Fire Princess*; Warriner, W.A.; J&P, 1983. Flowers light pink, dbl. (20 petals), small; slight fragrance; foliage small, medium green, matt; upright, bushy growth.

Fure-Daiko Cl F, *op*, 1974, (Furedaiko); *(Goldilocks seedling* × *Sarabande)* × *Golden Giant seedling*; Suzuki; Keisei Rose Nursery. Bud ovoid; flowers yellow to light orange-red, dbl., cupped, medium; fragrant; foliage large, glossy, dark; vigorous, climbing growth.

Furore HT, *or*, 1965, *(Baccará* × *Seedling)* × *Miracle*; Verbeek. Flowers scarlet, very dbl., medium; slightly fragrant; foliage dark.

Fürstin Maria Hatzfeldt HT, *dr*, 1927, *Gen. MacArthur* × *Seedling*; Boden. Flowers bright dark red, full; fragrant.

Fürstin von Hohenzollern Infantin T (OGR), *m*, 1898, Brauer, P. Flowers purple rose, center yellowish salmon, full, medium.

Fushino HT, *lp*, 1980, *Utage* × *Ann Letts*; Ota, Kaichiro. Flowers light pink, dbl. (45 petals), high-centered, large; no fragrance; foliage medium green; vigorous, spreading growth.

Fusilier F, *or*, 1957, (Grenadier; Red Soldier); *Red Pinocchio* × *Floradora*; Morey; J&P. Bud globular; flowers orange-scarlet, dbl. (40 petals), large (3-3½ in.) blooms in heavy clusters; slightly fragrant; foliage dark, glossy, leathery; vigorous growth. AARS, 1958.

Futura HT, *or*, 1975, *Seedling × Seedling*; Warriner; J&P. Bud long, pointed; flowers vermilion, dbl., cupped, large; slightly fragrant; foliage glossy, light; vigorous, upright, bushy growth.

F. W. Alesworth HT, *dr*, 1954, (Fred W. Alesworth); *Poinsettia × Crimson Glory*; Robinson, H. Flowers deep crimson, well shaped, large; very fragrant; foliage dark; vigorous growth.

F. W. Lowe HT, *ab*, 1936, Lowe. Flowers rich orange-yellow, well shaped; foliage glossy; vigorous growth.

Fyvie Castle HT, *pb*, 1985, (COCbamber; Amberlight); *(Sunblest × (Sabine × Dr. A.J. Verhage)) × Silver Jubilee*; Cocker, Alexander; Cocker & Sons. Flowers light apricot, amber and pink blend, dbl. (35 petals), well-formed, large; fragrant; foliage large, medium green, semi-glossy; upright growth. GM, NZ (Gold Star), 1985.

Gabi Gr, *or*, 1987, (Gabrielle); *Pink Favorite × Red Dandy*; Poole, Lionel, 1988. Flowers very bright orange-red, fading to lighter orange, dbl. (24 petals), high-centered, classic, medium, borne in sprays of 4-10; moderate fragrance; foliage medium, dark green, glossy; prickles fairly flat, small, dark brown; fruit rounded, small, light brown-green; bushy, medium growth.

Gabriel Lombart HT, *w*, 1932, *Dr. A. Hermans × Rayon d'Or*; Buatois. Flowers flesh-white to cream-white, dbl., cupped, very large; fragrant; vigorous, bushy growth.

Gabriel Noyelle M (OGR), *ab*, 1933, (Gabrielle Noyelle); *Salet × Souv de Mme. Kreuger*; Buatois. Bud ovoid; flowers apricot, dbl., cupped; fragrant; foliage leathery; very vigorous growth; recurrent bloom.

Gabriela Sabatini Min, *or*, 1992, (WILsab); *Marina × Pink Sweetheart*; Williams, J. Benjamin. Flowers bright fire orange-red, moderately full (15-25 petals), small (0-4 cms) blooms borne mostly singly; sweetheart; slight fragrance; foliage small, dark green, semi-glossy; few prickles; low (14-20"), upright, compact, dwarf HT type growth.

Gabriella® F, *mr*, 1977, (BERgme; Gabrielle); *Mercedes sport*; Berggren; W. Kordes Sons. Bud ovoid; flowers medium red, dbl. (33 petals), cupped, large (3 in.); slightly fragrant; foliage glossy; vigorous, bushy.

Gabrielle Privat Pol, *mp*, 1931, Barthelemy-Privat; Turbat. Flowers brilliant carmine-pink, semi-dbl. blooms in pyramidal corymbs of 30-50; bushy growth.

Gabriel's Fire Min, *rb*, 1991, (BRIfire); *Sachet × Seedling*; Bridges, Dennis; Bridges Roses, 1992. Bud pointed; flowers creamy light yellow turning red, semi-dbl. (20-22 petals), urn-shaped, high-centered, exhibition, medium (5 cms) blooms borne usually singly; heavy fragrance; foliage medium, medium green, semi-glossy; bushy, spreading, medium growth.

Gabychette F, *rb*, 1960, *Floradora × Pioupiou*; Arles; Roses-France. Bud ovoid; flowers reddish salmon, base sulphur-yellow, reverse white to rosy white suffused salmon, dbl., high-centered, medium, borne in clusters; slightly fragrant; foliage glossy, light green; low growth.

Gaiata HT, *yb*, 1956, *Boudoir × Peace*; Moreira, da Silva. Flowers indian yellow shaded pink.

Gaiety HT, *ob*, 1926, *Mme. Butterfly × Souv. de Claudius Pernet*; Hill, E.G., Co.; Hill Floral Products Co. Bud pointed; flowers orange, indian red and silver, dbl., cupped, large; foliage light, glossy; vigorous, branching growth.

Gaiety HT, *op*, Archer. Flowers salmon-pink flushed yellow; fragrant; vigorous growth.

Gaiezza HT, *ob*, 1940, *Julien Potin × Mme. G. Forest-Colcombet*; Giacomasso. Flowers orange touched red, center yellow; very fragrant.

Gail Min, *yb*, 1986, (TINgail); *Arizona × Orange Honey*; Bennett, Dee; Tiny Petals Nursery. Flowers golden yellow with orange blush on petal tips, orange spreading with age, dbl. (38 petals), high-centered, exhibition, mini-flora, large blooms borne singly; fragrant; foliage large, medium green, semi-glossy; small reddish prickles; fruit globular, 5/8 in. diameter, light green; medium, bushy, spreading growth.

Gail Borden HT, *pb*, 1957, *R.M.S. Queen Mary × Viktoria Adelheid*; Kordes; J&P. Bud ovoid; flowers deep rose-pink, reverse overcast cream, dbl. (53 petals), high-centered, large (5½ in.); fragrant; foliage dark, glossy, leathery; vigorous, upright growth. GM, NRS, 1957.

Gail Borden, Climbing Cl HT, *pb*, 1960, J&P, 1960.

Gainsborough Cl HT, *lp*, 1903, *Viscountess Folkestone sport*; Good & Reese. Flowers flesh-pink, almost white, dbl., large; long stems; vigorous growth.

Gala F, *pb*, 1973, *Seedling No. 19-64 ps × Seventeen*; Jelly; E.G. Hill Co. Bud short, pointed; flowers light pink, dbl. (28-34 petals), high-centered, large (3-3½ in.); slightly fragrant (spicy); vigorous, upright, free growth.

Gala Day F, *or*, 1966, *Queen Elizabeth × Dicksons Flame*; Watkins Roses. Flowers vermilion-scarlet, pointed, large (4 in.); slightly fragrant; foliage light green; free, upright growth.

Galah HT, *mp*, 1956, Riethmuller. Flowers carmine-pink, base lighter, semi-dbl., large, borne in clusters; fragrant.

Galahad HT, *w*, 1986, *Micaela* × *Lara*; Kriloff, M. Flowers white, dbl., very large; anise fragrance; foliage medium green, semi-glossy.

Galatea HMsk (S), *yb*, 1914, Pemberton. Flowers stone-color, edged pink, small rosette, borne in clusters; recurrent bloom.

Galaty HT, *or*, 1978, (DOTsubebe); *Tropicana* × *Lola Montes*; Dot, S. Flowers orange-red, dbl. (32 petals), deeply cupped, large (4 in.); very fragrant; foliage dark.

Galaxy™ Min, *dr*, 1980, (MORgal); *Fairy Moss* × *Fairy Princess*; Moore, R.S.; Sequoia Nursery. Bud long, pointed; flowers deep velvety red, dbl. (23 petals), high-centered, borne 3, sometimes 5-10 per cluster; little or no fragrance; foliage small to medium; prickles slightly curved; vigorous, bushy, upright growth.

Galaxy R, *dp*, 1906, Walsh. Flowers bright carmine; vigorous growth.

Galia HT, *lp*, 1966, Betzel. Flowers light pink, center darker, very dbl., large; slightly fragrant; foliage dark, leathery; very vigorous, upright growth. RULED EXTINCT 4/81 ARM.

Galia® HT, *or*, 1977, (MEItinirol); *MEIretni* × *Elegy*; Meilland, M.L.; Meilland Et Cie. Flowers orange-red, dbl. (38 petals), cupped blooms borne singly; no fragrance; foliage matt, dense; vigorous growth.

Galileo HT, *mr*, 1971, (MEIgalil); *Ma Fille* × *Love Song*; Meilland. Flowers currant-red to cherry-red, dbl. (30 petals), globular, large (5 in.); foliage large, glossy; vigorous, upright growth.

Gallagher F, *rb*, 1979, *Tropicana*; Murray, N. Bud pointed; flowers cream, edged crimson, dbl. (41 petals), shapely, medium (2½ in.); fragrant (fruity); foliage leathery; bushy growth.

Gallant F, *mr*, 1968, *Tropicana* × *Barbecue*; Dickson, A. Flowers scarlet, dbl. large (3-3½ in.) blooms in clusters; fragrant; foliage glossy.

Galleria HRg (S), *mr*, 1990, (Big John); *The Duke* × *Hansa*; Weddle, V. C.; Hortico, 1990; Bud ovoid; flowers medium watermelon pink, reverse silvery pink, semi-dbl. (13 petals), high centered, large, borne in sprays of 3-5; moderate, spicy, fruity fragrance; foliage large, dark green, glossy; prickles straight, medium, light green to pink; fruit round, small, green to yellow; bushy, tall (8 ft.) growth.

Galleria Borghese HT, *w*, 1954, *Peace* × *Crimson Glory*; Giacomasso. Flowers flesh streaked coral, very large; strong stems; foliage glossy.

Gallica Macrantha Misc. OGR (OGR), *w*, (*R.* × *waitziana macrantha*; *R. macrantha*; *R. gallica macrantha* hort.); *Thought to be a hybrid of R. canina and R. gallica*; Cultivated early in 18th century. Flowers flushed rose at first, changing to nearly white.

Galli-Curci HT, *my*, 1924, *Columbia sport*; Kinsman. Flowers golden yellow.

Gallivarda HT, *rb*, 1977, (Galsar); *Colour Wonder* × *Wiener Charme*; Kordes, W., Sons; Willemse. Bud long, pointed; flowers red, yellow reverse, dbl. (34 petals), high-centered, large (4½ in.); slightly fragrant; foliage glossy; vigorous, upright growth.

Galway Bay® LCl, *op*, 1966, (MACba); *Heidelberg* × *Queen Elizabeth*; McGredy, S., IV. Flowers salmon-pink, well-formed, large (3½ in.) blooms in clusters; slightly fragrant.

G. Amédée Hammond HT, *ab*, 1915, Dickson, A. Flowers apricot-yellow on ivory yellow, dbl.; very fragrant. GM, NRS, 1913.

Gamin de Paris F, *dr*, 1964, *(Orange Triumph* × *Paprika)* × *Seedling*; Mondial Roses. Flowers dark blood-red, dbl., large, borne in large clusters; vigorous, upright growth.

Gamine F, *op*, 1961, *Eclipse* × *Baccará*; Kriloff; Verbeek. Flowers salmon-pink, dbl., medium; fragrant; vigorous growth; a greenhouse variety.

Gamma HT, *pb*, 1972, *Jouvencelle* × *American Heritage*; Gaujard. Bud pointed; flowers pink, suffused vermilion; very fragrant; foliage large.

Gamusin HT, *r*, 1960, *Grey Pearl* × *(Lila Vidri* × *Prelude)*; Dot, P. Flowers cinnamon to pale pink, dbl. (25 petals); very fragrant; vigorous, spreading growth.

Ganga HT, *dy*, 1970, *Sabina* × *Seedling*; Div. of Vegetable Crops & Flori; Indian Agric. Research Inst. Flowers deep golden yellow, , dbl., high-centered, medium; fragrant (tea); vigorous, upright growth; profuse, intermittent bloom.

Ganymed F, *dr*, 1975, *Europeana* × *Seedling*; Kordes. Bud pointed; flowers dark red, dbl. (32 petals), cupped, large (2½ in.); slightly fragrant; foliage glossy; vigorous, upright, bushy growth.

Gardejäger Gratzfeld R, *dp*, 1940, *Rodhatte sport*; Gratzfeld. Flowers carmine-red; vigorous growth.

Garden Delight F, *dp*, 1956, Norman; Harkness. Flowers deep rose-pink, dbl. (34 petals), rosette form, large (3½-4 in.), borne in clusters; fragrant; vigorous, branching growth.

Garden Gem HT, *lp*, 1930, *Mrs. E.T. Stotesbury × Hill's America*; Dingee & Conard. Flowers satiny pink, dbl.; very vigorous growth.

Garden Glow HT, *op*, 1937, Cant, B.R. Flowers scarlet, base copper, dbl.; foliage glossy, bronze; very vigorous, bushy growth.

Garden News HT, *dr*, 1962, *New Yorker × Étoile de Hollande*; Verschuren; Blaby Rose Gardens. Bud pointed; flowers dark crimson-scarlet, dbl. (32 petals), large; strong stems; very fragrant; foliage dull, dark, leathery; moderate growth.

Garden Party® HT, *w*, 1959, *Charlotte Armstrong × Peace*; Swim; Armstrong Nursery. Bud urn-shaped; flowers pale yellow to white, often tinged light pink, dbl. (28 petals), high-centered to cupped, large (4-5 in.); slightly fragrant; foliage semi-glossy; vigorous, bushy, well-branched growth. GM, Bagatelle, 1959; AARS, 1960.

Garden Party, Climbing Cl HT, *w*, 1964, Itami Rose Nursery.

Garden Princess F, *my*, 1961, *Goldilocks × Lavender Pinocchio*; Leenders, J. Flowers yellow, becoming lighter, semi-dbl.; growth moderate.

Garden Queen HT, *op*, 1960, *Ambassadeur Nemry × Tawny Gold*; Leenders, J. Flowers pink to salmon, dbl., large (4 in.); very fragrant; vigorous growth.

Garden State Gr, *mp*, 1964, (MEIgene); *(Happiness × Independence) × White Knight*; Meilland, Alain; C-P. Bud ovoid, pointed; flowers rose-pink, dbl. (42 petals), large (3½-4 in.); fragrant; foliage leathery; vigorous, tall, bushy growth.

Garden Supreme F, *ob*, 1959, Jones; Hennessey. Flowers orange blend shaded reddish, dbl. (32 petals), medium, borne in clusters; foliage leathery, bronze; low, vigorous growth.

Gardener's Sunday F, *my*, 1975, *(Pink Parfait × Masquerade) × Arthur Bell*; Harkness. Flowers yellow, dbl. (20 petals), large (3 in.); fragrant; foliage bright green.

Gardenia R, *w*, 1899, *R. wichuraiana × Perle des Jardins*; Manda, W.A. Bud pointed, yellow; flowers creamy white, center yellow, well-formed blooms in small sprays on short, strong stems; foliage small, dark, glossy; very vigorous growth.

Gardeniaeflora R, *w*, 1901, Benary. Flowers pure white, semi-dbl.; slightly fragrant; early bloom.

Garisenda R, *pb*, 1911, *R. wichuraiana × Souv. de la Malmaison*; Bonfiglioli. Flowers clear rose-pink, tinted silvery, dbl., blooms in clusters.

Garnette F, *dr*, 1951, (Garnette Red; Red Garnette); *(Rosenelfe × Eva) × Heros*; Tantau; J&P. Flowers garnet-red, base light lemon-yellow, dbl. (50 petals), small; slightly fragrant; foliage leathery, dark; bushy growth; greenhouse variety.

Garnette, Climbing Cl F, *dr*, 1954, Soria; Amling-DeVor Nursery.

Garnette Supreme F, *dp*, 1954, *Yellow Pinocchio seedling × Garnette*; Boerner; J&P. Bud ovoid; flowers carmine, dbl. (35-40 petals), cupped, large (2½-3 in.); fragrant; foliage glossy, bronze; vigorous, upright, compact growth; a greenhouse cut flower.

Garnia F, *dp*, 1970, *Lady Sylvia × Garnette*; Butter; Wood End Gardens. Flowers deep pink, dbl. (48 petals), full, large (4½ in.); very fragrant; foliage matt, green; moderately vigorous growth.

Garo LCl, *dr*, 1986, *Uncle Walter × Seedling*; Garelja, Anita, 1978. Flowers blackish-red, very full (48 petals), HT-type, large, borne 1-5 per cluster; very slight fragrance; foliage red turning dark green, semi-glossy; large, brown prickles; upright growth.

Gartendirektor Glocker F, *or*, 1957, *Obergärtner Wiebicke × Independence*; Kordes. Bud ovoid; flowers cinnabar-red, very dbl., large, borne in clusters; fragrant; foliage glossy, leathery; vigorous, bushy growth.

Gartendirektor Julius Schutze HT, *pb*, 1920, *Mme. Jules Gravereaux × Pharisaer*; Kiese. Flowers pale rosy pink and peach-blossom-pink.

Gartendirektor Nose HT, *dr*, 1930, *Royal Red × Templar*; Kordes; Dreer; H&S. Bud pointed; flowers dark crimson, dbl., high-centered, large; fragrant; foliage dark, glossy; vigorous, bushy growth.

Gartendirektor Otto Linne S, *dp*, 1934, *Robin Hood × Rudolph Kluis*; Lambert, P. Flowers dark carmine-pink, edged darker, base yellowish-white, dbl., borne in clusters of 30 on long, strong stems; foliage leathery, light green; vigorous, bushy growth.

Gartenstolz F, *op*, 1945, *Swantje × Hamburg*; Tantau. Flowers rose tinted salmon, single (8-10 petals), large, borne in clusters of 12-15; fragrant; foliage leathery, light green; vigorous, upright, bushy growth.

Gartenzauber F, 1961, (Garden Magic; Magie des Jardins); Kordes, R. Flowers blood-red, tinted cinnabar-red, well formed, large; low growth. RULED EXTINCT 6/81 ARM.

Gartenzauber® F, *mr*, 1984, (KORnacho; Gartenzauber '84); *(Seedling × Tornado) ×*

Chorus; Kordes, W.; Kordes Sons. Flowers medium red, dbl. (35 petals), high-centered, large; slight fragrance; foliage medium, dark, semi-glossy; upright growth.

Garvey HT, *pb*, 1961, *McGredy's Yellow* × *Karl Herbst*; McGredy, S., IV; McGredy. Flowers light geranium, reverse pale red, dbl. (30 petals), globular, large (6 in.); strong stems; fragrant; foliage dark, leathery; vigorous, upright growth.

Gary Lineker F, *ob*, 1991, (PEArobin); *Seedling* × *Seedling*; Pearce, C.; Rearsby Roses, Ltd., 1991. Flowers luminous orange, yellow reverse, single to semi-dbl., medium (4-7 cms) blooms borne in small clusters; slight fragrance; foliage medium, medium green, glossy; many prickles; medium (50-90 cms), upright growth.

Gary Player HT, *ob*, 1968, (Goliath); *Jolie Madame* × *Seedling*; Herholdt, J.A. Flowers orange-vermilion, dbl. (35 petals), high-centered, large (4-4½ in.); foliage glossy, dark; vigorous growth.

Gary Wernett HT, *op*, 1985, *Helen Traubel* × *Helen Traubel*; French, Richard. Flowers medium coral pink, dbl. (28 wavy petals), high-centered to cupped, large blooms borne usually singly; fragrant; foliage medium, medium green, matt; medium, triangular, light red prickles; fruit rare to full term; bushy growth.

Gateshead Festival HT, *op*, 1989, *Doris Tysterman* × *Silver Jubilee*; Thompson, R.; Battersby Roses, 1989. Flowers glowing orange flushed salmon with gold at base of petals, dbl. (26-40 petals), medium; very fragrant; foliage large, dark green, glossy; bushy growth.

GAUbiroc HT, *op*, 1986, (Pénélope®); *(Americana* × *Seedling)* × *Chenonceaux*; Gaujard, J.; Roseraies Gaujard, 1980. Flowers medium salmon pink, dbl. (35 petals), well-formed, large; fragrant; foliage large, medium green, semi-glossy; upright growth.

Gaudia F, *mp*, 1946, *Florentina* × *Talisman*; Leenders, M.; Longley. Flowers rose-pink, base gold and salmon, semi-dbl. (15 petals), large (4 in.), borne in clusters; fragrant; foliage bright green edged red; vigorous, tall growth.

Gauntlet Min, *dr*, 1991, (BRIgaunt); *Kitty Hawk* × *Seedling*; Bridges, Dennis A.; Bridges Roses. Bud ovoid; flowers dark red, lighter reverse, lightens slightly with age, semi-dbl. (20-22 petals), exhibition, medium; slight fragrance; foliage large, medium green, semi-glossy; spreading, medium growth.

Gavá Cl HT, *or*, 1934, *Souv. de Claudius Denoyel* × *Souv. de Claudius Pernet*; Munné, B.; Camprubi. Flowers oriental red shaded rose-pink,

base yellow, dbl., cupped, very large; very fragrant; foliage leathery; very vigorous, climbing growth.

Gavno F, *ob*, 1988, (POUlgav; Bucks Fizz); *Seedling* × *Mary Sumner*; Olesen, Mogens & Pernille; Poulsen Roser ApS. Flowers orange, dbl. (20 petals), medium; no fragrance; foliage medium, dark green, glossy; bushy growth.

Gavotte HT, *pb*, 1963, *Ethel Sanday* × *Lady Sylvia*; Sanday. Flowers pink, reverse light yellow, dbl. (45 petals), large (5 in.); fragrant; foliage dark; vigorous, upright growth.

Gavroche F, *ob*, 1963, Robichon. Flowers orange, center yellow, large; vigorous, bushy growth.

Gay Crusader HT, *rb*, 1948, *Phyllis Gold* × *Catalonia*; Robinson, H.; Baker's Nursery. Flowers red fading to pink, reverse deep yellow, high-centered, large; fragrant; foliage dark.

Gay Dawn HT, *op*, 1958, *Eclipse* × *Mme. Henri Guillot*; Taylor, C.A.; California Nursery Co. Bud pointed; flowers orange-pink, dbl., cupped, large; fragrant (spicy); foliage dark, semi-glossy; very vigorous, upright growth.

Gay Debutante HT, *pb*, 1960, *Peace* sport; Curtis, R.F.; C.R. Burr. Flowers light pink, base yellow, dbl. (40-45 petals), cupped, very large; slightly fragrant; foliage leathery, glossy; vigorous, upright growth.

Gay Dicky F, *ob*, 1956, Verschuren-Pechtold; Gandy. Flowers tangerine-orange; moderate growth.

Gay Gold HT, *my*, 1973, *King's Ransom* × *Piccadilly*; Lowe. Flowers yellow, dbl. (30 petals), large (5½ in.); very fragrant; foliage glossy.

Gay Gordons® HT, *yb*, 1969, *Belle Blonde* × *Karl Herbst*; Cocker. Flowers orange-yellow and red, dbl.; slightly fragrant; foliage dark, glossy; bushy, rather low growth.

Gay Gypsy HT, *dr*, 1949, *Charles K. Douglas* sport; Crane; Bosley Nursery. Bud long, pointed; flowers oxblood-red shaded maroon, semi-dbl. (15-20 petals), open, cupped, large (4½-5 in.); slightly fragrant; foliage leathery; vigorous, upright, bushy growth.

Gay Heart F, *mp*, 1951, *Joanna Hill* × *World's Fair*; Boerner; J&P. Bud ovoid; flowers bright pink, dbl. (25 petals), high-centered, large, borne in large clusters; fragrant; foliage leathery; vigorous, upright growth.

Gay Jewel Min, *lp*, 1958, *Dick Koster* sport × *Tom Thumb*; Morey; J&P. Bud globular; flowers light rose-pink, dbl. (35-40 petals), cupped, small (½ in.); fragrant; foliage glossy; compact (6-8 in.) growth.

Gay Lady HT, *mr*, 1953, *Charlotte Armstrong ×
Piccadilly*; Swim; Breedlove Nursery. Bud
ovoid; flowers currant-red, dbl. (20-28 petals),
open, large (3½-4½ in.); fragrant (spicy); foliage dark, leathery, glossy; very vigorous,
upright growth.

Gay Lyric HT, *mp*, 1971, *Royal Highness × Elizabeth Fankhauser*; Fankhauser. Flowers rose-
pink, very dbl., high-centered, large; fragrant;
foliage glossy, dark, leathery; vigorous, upright growth.

Gay Maid F, *or*, 1969, *Masquerade × Seedling*;
Gregory. Flowers red suffused orange-pink,
dbl. (26 petals), globular, borne in trusses;
foliage light green; very vigorous growth.

Gay Mood LCl, *dp*, 1940, *Joanna Hill × Sanguinaire*; Lammerts; Armstrong Nursery. Bud
large, ovoid to urn shaped, rose-red; flowers
deep rose-pink, semi-dbl. (15-25 petals), open;
foliage glossy, dark; very vigorous, climbing
growth; profuse, recurrent bloom.

Gay Nineties Cl F, *mr*, 1955, *(New Dawn ×
Red Ripples) × Red Ripples*; Sima. Bud ovoid;
flowers rose-red, dbl. (65 petals), medium
(2-2½ in.) blooms in clusters of 5-8; very
fragrant; foliage leathery, glossy; vigorous,
pillar (8 ft.) growth.

Gay Paris HT, *mr*, 1960, *(Floradora × Barcelona) × (Charles Mallerin × Tonnerre)*; Delbard-Chabert. Bud long; flowers bright
crimson, dbl., well-formed, large; fragrant;
foliage bright green; vigorous growth.

Gay Princess F, *lp*, 1967, *Spartan × The
Farmer's Wife*; Boerner; J&P. Bud ovoid;
flowers blush-pink, dbl., cupped, large
blooms in clusters; fragrant; foliage leathery;
vigorous, upright, bushy growth.   AARS.
1967.

Gay Vista S, *lp*, 1957, Riethmuller. Flowers
light pink, single, very large blooms in very
large clusters; height 3½ ft.; repeat bloom.

Gaytime F, *rb*, 1966, *Seedling × Circus*; Armstrong, D.L.; Armstrong Nursery. Bud
ovoid, pointed; flowers red and yellow, dbl.,
cupped, large; slightly fragrant; foliage dark,
glossy, leathery; vigorous, bushy, compact
growth.

Gazelle G (OGR), *lp*, Flowers delicate rose,
large.

Géant des Batailles HP (OGR), *mr*, 1846,
(Giant of Battles); Nérard; Guillot Père.
Flowers deep fiery crimson, full (85 petals);
very fragrant; moderately vigorous growth.

Gee Gee™ Min, *ly*, 1987, (BENgee); *Rise 'n'
Shine × Patricia*; Benardella, Frank, 1981;
Kimbrew-Walter Roses, 1987. Flowers medium yellow, fading lighter, dbl. (20-25 petals), cupped, loose, small, borne usually

singly or in sprays of 3-5; slight, fruity fragrance; foliage medium, light green, matt,
edges toothed; pointed, beige prickles; fruit
none; upright, bushy, medium growth.

Gee Whiz S, *yb*, 1984, *Gingersnap × Sevilliana*;
Buck, Dr. Griffith J.; Iowa State University.
Flowers yellow tinted orange-red, dbl. (23
petals), shallow-cupped, medium blooms
borne 1-10 per cluster; sweet fragrance; foliage medium, leathery, dark olive green; needle-like, brown prickles; low, bushy,
free-branching growth; hardy; repeat bloom.

Geheimrat Dr. Mittweg S, *pb*, 1909, *(Mme.
Norbert Levavasseur × Trier) × R. foetida bicolor*;
Lambert, P. Flowers rose-red, center yellowish white, large, borne in large clusters;
foliage dark; vigorous, bushy growth; recurrent bloom.

Geheimrat Richard Willstätter HT, *ab*, 1931,
Constance × Admiral Ward; Felberg-Leclerc.
Flowers apricot-yellow, veined carmine-red,
stamens yellow, semi-dbl., large; slightly fragrant; foliage bright, thick; vigorous growth.

Geisha® F, *mp*, 1964, (Pink Elizabeth Arden);
Tantau, Math. Bud long; flowers pink, semi-
dbl., large (2½-3in.) blooms in clusters of 20;
foliage dark; bushy, medium height.

Geisha HT, *ob*, 1920, *Mme. Edouard Herriot
sport*; Van Rossem. Bud orange, marked
coral-red; flowers golden yellow.

Geisha Girl F, *my*, 1964, *Gold Cup × McGredy's
Yellow*; McGredy, S., IV; McGredy. Flowers
medium yellow, dbl. (25 petals), large (3½
in.) blooms in clusters; foliage long, pointed;
tall growth.

Gela Gnau HT, *ab*, 1926, Leenders, M. Flowers amber-yellow, reverse apricot, dbl.; fragrant.

Gelbe Holstein F, *ly*, 1951, (Yellow Holstein);
(Eva × Viscountess Charlemont) × Sunmist; Kordes; Wheatcroft Bros. Bud long, pointed;
flowers yellow paling to lemon, dbl. (20
petals), large (3 in.) blooms in large clusters;
slightly fragrant; foliage glossy, light green;
vigorous, upright, bushy growth.

Gelbe Pharisäer HT, *my*, 1927, *Pharisaer ×
Mrs. Aaron Ward*; Hinner, W. Flowers clear
yellow, center deeper; fragrant.

Gem HT, *mp*, 1960, *Ena Harkness × Mme. Butterfly*; Walker. Bud long, pointed; flowers
deep soft pink, semi-dbl., high-centered, medium; fragrant; foliage soft; vigorous, upright growth.

Gem of the Prairies HSet (OGR), *dp*, 1865,
(Bijou des Prairies); *Believed to be Queen of the
Prairies × Mme. Laffay*; Burgess, A. Flowers
rosy red, occasionally blotched white, flat,

large blooms in large clusters; slightly fragrant; vigorous; non-recurrent.

Gemini Pol, *ob*, 1967, *Seedling × Rumba*; Hill, J.H., Co. Bud pointed; flowers orange, dbl., high-centered, small; slightly fragrant; foliage dark, glossy; vigorous, upright, bushy growth; for greenhouse use.

Gemstone HT, *mp*, 1978, *Helen Traubel × Swarthmore*; J&B Roses; Eastern Roses. Bud high-centered; flowers medium pink, dbl. (28 petals), exhibition, large (4 1-2-5 in.); slightly fragrant; foliage matt; vigorous, upright growth.

Gene Boerner F, *mp*, 1968, *Ginger × (Ma Perkins × Garnette Supreme)*; Boerner; J&P. Bud ovoid; flowers deep pink, dbl. (35 petals), high-centered, medium; foliage glossy; vigorous, upright growth. AARS, 1969.

Generaal Smuts HT, *mr*, 1922, *Gen. MacArthur × Mme. Edouard Herriot*; Van Ros-sem. Flowers cherry-red, shaded deep coral-red, dbl.; fragrant.

Generaal Snijders HT, *dp*, 1917, *Mme. Mélanie Soupert × George C. Waud*; Leenders, M. Flowers deep carmine shaded coral-red, dbl.; very fragrant.

Général Baron Berge HP (OGR), *mr*, 1892, Pernet Père. Flowers red, center occasionally striped white, dbl. (50 petals), large; erect, vigorous growth.

Général Berthelot HT, *dp*, 1926, *J.B. Clark × Farbenkönigin*; Walter, L. Flowers dark pink, slightly streaked white, dbl.

General Browne HSpn (OGR), *w*, Flowers blush-white, fading pure white, dbl., quilled; fragrant; foliage dark; twiggy, prickly growth.

Général de Vaulgrenant HT, *dp*, 1926, *Mme. Henriette Schissele × Mme. Adele Gance*; Walter, L. Flowers rose-pink, very full.

General Domingos de Oliveira HT, *ab*, 1939, *Frank Reader × Golden Gleam*; Moreira da Silva. Flowers yellow-apricot tinted flesh-pink, dbl., cupped, large; slightly fragrant; foliage glossy; dwarf growth.

General Don HT, *pb*, 1919, *Mme. Mélanie Soupert × Louise Catherine Breslau*; Le Cornu. Flowers strawberry tinted coppery, base golden yellow, dbl.; fragrant.

Général Donnadieu G (OGR), *mr*, Flowers purplish red, very dbl., compact.

Général Droust M (OGR), *m*, 1847, Vibert. Flowers purplish crimson, not very dbl., medium; vigorous; recurrent.

Général Fetter HT, *m*, 1922, *Jonkheer J.L. Mock × Luise Lilia*; Walter, L. Flowers carmine-purple, very full, glossy.

Général Galliéni T (OGR), *rb*, 1899, *Souv. de Thérèse Levet × Reine Emma des Pays-Bas*;

Nabonnand, G. Flowers coppery red, cupped; vigorous growth.

Général Jacqueminot HP (OGR), *rb*, 1853, (Gén. Jacqueminot; General Jack; Jack Rose); *Probable seedling of Gloire des Rosomanes*; Roussel. Bud scarlet-crimson; flowers dark red, whitish reverse, dbl. (27 petals), blooms with long, strong stems; very fragrant; foliage rich green; vigorous, bushy growth; recurrent bloom. Prototype for HP class.

Gen. John Pershing LCl, *dp*, 1917, (F.R.M. Undritz); *Dr. W. Van Fleet × Mrs. W.J. Grant*; Undritz. Flowers dark pink, dbl. (53 petals), large; fragrant; vigorous, climbing growth.

Général Kléber M (OGR), *mp*, 1856, Robert. Bud well mossed; flowers pink tinted lilac.

General MacArthur HT, *dp*, 1905, E.G. Hill Co. Flowers rose-red, dbl. (20 petals); very fragrant(damask); foliage leathery.

General MacArthur, Climbing Cl HT, *dp*, 1923, Dickson, H.

General Robert E. Lee T (OGR), *my*, 1896, Good & Reese. Bud deep orange-yellow; flowers canary-yellow.

Général Schablikine T (OGR), *op*, 1878, Nabonnand, G. Flowers coppery; vigorous.

Generál Stefánik HP (OGR), *m*, 1933, (Krásná Azurea); *La Brillante × Seedling*; Böhm; J&P. Similar to Reine des Violettes.

Général Tartas T (OGR), *dp*, Bernède. Flowers deep rose, full, large.

General Testard R, *rb*, 1918, Pajotin-Chédane. Flowers red, center white, semi-dbl., small, borne in large clusters.

General Washington HP (OGR), *dr*, 1861, *Triomphe de l'Exposition sport*; Granger. Flowers deep crimson, reflexes maroon, very full (about 150 petals), flat, large; fragrant; moderate growth; occasional recurrent bloom.

General-Superior Arnold Janssen HT, *dp*, 1912, *Farbenkönigin × Gen. MacArthur*; Leenders, M. Bud pointed; flowers deep rose-pink, veined darker, reverse much darker, dbl., large; fragrant.

General-Superior Arnold Janssen, Climbing Cl HT, *dp*, 1931, Böhm.

Generosity HT, *ob*, 1982, *Fred Gibson × Lady Elgin*; Northfield, G. Flowers cream with orange center, dbl. (35 petals), large; fragrant; foliage large, dark, matt; bushy growth.

Genesis Min, *m*, 1991, *Lavender Jade × Angel Face*; Jolly, Marie, 1986; Rosehill Farm, 1992. Bud ovoid; flowers lavender, reverse white, dbl. (45 petals), medium (5 cms) blooms borne singly; moderate fragrance; foliage medium, medium green, semi-glossy; upright growth.

Genève HT, *or*, 1944, *Charles P. Kilham* × *Mme. Joseph Perraud*; Meilland, F. Bud long; flowers salmon-carmine and capucine-red, dbl., high pointed; fragrant; vigorous growth.

Genevieve Min, *yb*, 1982, (SAVagen); *Unnamed Miniature Cl.* × *Miniature seedling*; Saville, F. Harmon; Nor'East Min. Roses, 1983. Flowers yellow, streaked scarlet, scarlet increasing with age, dbl. (35 petals), small; spicy fragrance; foliage medium, medium green, semi-glossy; upright, bushy growth.

Geneviève le Goaster HT, *w*, 1923, Carrette; Richardier. Flowers white, center pale rose, base salmon-rose.

Genius Mendel HT, *mr*, 1935, *Mrs. Henry Winnett* × *Sir David Davis*; Böhm. Bud pointed; flowers light fiery red to pure red, full, high-centered, large; foliage glossy; bushy growth.

Gentle F, *op*, 1960, *Independence* × *(Lady Sylvia* × *Fashion)*; Lens. Flowers salmon-pink, dbl. (26 petals), well formed, large (2½-3 in.), borne in clusters; vigorous, compact, bushy growth.

Gentle Lady HT, *lp*, 1971, *Tiffany* × *Michèle Meilland*; Fuller; Wyant. Bud slender, long, pointed; flowers light pink, dbl. (35 petals), cupped, large (3½ in.); very fragrant; foliage matt, dark, leathery; upright, bushy growth.

Gentle Persuasion S, *yb*, 1984, *Carefree Beauty* × *Oregold*; Buck, Dr. Griffith J.; Iowa State University. Flowers yellow tinted orange, dbl. (28 petals), cupped, medium-large blooms borne 1-5 per cluster; light fragrance; foliage large, leathery, semi-glossy, dark olive green; awl-like, tan prickles; vigorous, bushy, erect growth; repeat bloom; hardy.

Gentle Touch Min, *lp*, 1986, (DIClulu); *(Liverpool Echo* × *Woman's Own)* × *Memento*; Dickson, P. Flowers light pink, moderately full (15-25 petals), small; patio; slight fragrance; foliage small, medium green, semi-glossy; bushy growth. ROTY, 1986.

Genval HT, *mp*, 1963, *Rosita* × *Margaret*; Delforge. Flowers cyclamen-pink; fragrant; foliage bronze, dull; vigorous growth.

Geoff Boycott F, *w*, 1974, *Ice White* × *Tip-Top*; McGredy. Flowers white, dbl. (35 petals), large (3½ in.); slightly fragrant; foliage dark.

Georgie Lad HT, *r*, 1988, (HORkorblush); *Prominent* × *(Champagne Cocktail* × *Alpine Sunset)*; Horner, Colin P.; Battersby Roses, 1990. Bud ovoid, red; flowers mahogany-red, yellow at base, reverse lighter red, dbl., cupped, medium, borne singly and in sprays of 4-6; moderate, fruity fragrance; foliage medium, medium green, matt; prickles

small, light brown; fruit ovoid, medium; upright, medium growth.

Georg Arends HP (OGR), *mp*, 1910, (Fortuné Besson); *Frau Karl Druschki* × *La France*; Hinner, W. Flowers soft pink, full (25 petals), large; very fragrant; vigorous.

George Baker HP (OGR), *dp*, 1881, Paul. Flowers cerise, very full.

George C. Waud HT, *mp*, 1908, Dickson, A. Flowers rose, veined darker, dbl., large (4½ in.); very fragrant; bushy growth.

George Dakin HT, *pb*, 1927, *Ophelia* × *Mrs. Henry Morse*; Burbage Nursery. Flowers silvery pink, flushed apricot, reverse orange to apricot, dbl., high-centered; fragrant; foliage glossy, bronze; vigorous, bushy growth.

George Dickson HT, *mr*, 1912, Dickson, A. Flowers medium red, dbl. (36 petals), large blooms with weak stems; fragrant. GM, NRS, 1911.

George Dickson, Climbing Cl HT, *mr*, 1949, Woodward.

George Elger Pol, *my*, 1912, (Yellow Baby Rambler); Turbat. Bud small, golden yellow; flowers coppery yellow to clear yellow, very dbl., borne in large clusters; slightly fragrant; foliage small, dark, soft; bushy, dwarf growth.

George Elliot HT, *op*, 1970, *Highlight* × *Dorothy Peach*; Wills. Flowers shrimp-pink, dbl. (35 petals), large (4-5 in.); very fragrant; foliage bronze.

George Fox HT, *or*, 1939, *Charles P. Kilham* × *Lady Forteviot*; Savage Nursery. Flowers orange-vermilion, globular, medium; foliage glossy; compact growth.

George Geary HT, *yb*, 1953, *Gwyneth Jones* × *Seedling*; Geary; Burbage Nursery. Flowers golden yellow flushed vermilion, high pointed, large (4 in.); fragrant; foliage dark, bronze; vigorous growth.

George Geuder HT, *yb*, 1931, Schmidt, J.C. Flowers salmon-pink and bright carmine on yellow ground; fragrant; vigorous growth.

George Heers HT, *pb*, 1961, Langbecker. Flowers rich pink, touched apricot and yellow.

George Howarth HT, *dp*, 1928, *Gorgeous* × *The Queen Alexandra Rose*; Bees. Flowers bright carmine, dbl.; fragrant.

George H. Mackereth HT, *dr*, 1924, Dickson, A. Flowers crimson shaded velvety maroon, dbl.; very fragrant.

George R. Hill HT, *w*, 1990, *Admiral Rodney* sport; Varney, Eric; Battersby Roses, Int. 1991. Flowers white, dbl. (45 petals); foliage large, dark green; vigorous growth.

George Thomas HT, *w*, 1975, *Ena Harkness* × *Memoriam*; Ellick. Flowers pure white, tinged pink, dbl. (40 petals), full, very large (6-8 in.); fragrant; foliage dark; vigorous growth.

George Will HRg (S), *dp*, 1939, *(R. rugosa × R. acicularis) × Seedling*; Skinner. Flowers deep pink, dbl., flat, medium (3 in.) blooms in clusters; fragrant (clove); foliage rugose; slender branches; height 3-4 ft.; all-summer bloom.

Georges Cain HRg (S), *dr*, 1909, *Souv. de Pierre Notting × R. rugosa*; Müller, F. Flowers crimson with purple, full, large; very vigorous growth.

Georges Chesnel HT, *dy*, 1935, *Julien Potin seedling × Étoile d'Or*; Pernet-Ducher; Gaujard. Bud pointed; flowers deep golden yellow, veined copper, dbl; foliage glossy.

George's Choice F, *mr*, 1979, *Evelyn Fison × Tabarin*; Ellick; Excelsior Roses. Bud small, ovoid; flowers currant-red, dbl. (35-40 petals), moderately full; fragrant; compact, bushy growth.

Georges Clemenceau HT, *ob*, 1919, *Mme. Edouard Herriot sport*; Lévêque. Flowers bright orange, shaded umber and carmine.

Georges Paquel HT, *my*, 1934, *Seedling × Souv. de Claudius Pernet*; Leenders, M. Flowers saffron-yellow, full, large; slightly fragrant; vigorous, bushy growth.

Georges Perdoux HT, *pb*, 1927, Barbier. Flowers reddish pink tinted coppery red. dbl.; fragrant.

Georges Pernet Pol, *mp*, 1887, *Mignonette × Seedling*; Pernet-Ducher. Flowers bright peach-pink.

Georges Schwartz HT, *my*, 1899, *Kaiserin Auguste Viktoria × Souv. de Mme. Levet*; Vve. Schwartz. Flowers canary-yellow.

Georges Schwartz, Climbing Cl HT, *my*, 1917, Knight, G.

Georges Vibert G (OGR), *rb*, 1853, Robert. Flowers purplish red, streaked (striped) white, dbl., flat, large; fragrant.

Georgette® Min, *mp*, 1981, *Electron × Little Chief*; Bennett, Dee; Tiny Petals Nursery. Bud ovoid; flowers medium pink, veined darker, dbl. (30 petals), exhibition blooms borne singly; very faint fragrance; foliage medium green, dense; straight prickles; upright, compact, bushy growth.

Georgia HT, *ab*, 1980, *Arizona × Seedling*; Weeks, O.L. Bud short, pointed; flowers peach-apricot blend, dbl. (53 petals), borne singly; moderate tea fragrance; foliage large, glossy, leathery; long prickles, hooked downward; tall, upright growth.

Georgianna Doan HT, *pb*, 1942, *Ophelia × Seedling*; Hill, J.H., Co. Bud long, pointed;

flowers two-tone pink, dbl. (25-30 petals), high-centered, medium; very fragrant; foliage leathery, wrinkled, dark; vigorous, upright, much branched growth; a florists' variety, not distributed for outdoor use.

Georgie Anderson F, *ob*, 1982, (ANDgeo); *Elizabeth of Glamis × Seedling*; Andersons' Rose Nursery. Flowers shades of orange, dbl., medium; slight fragrance; foliage medium, dark, semi-glossy; upright growth.

Gerald Hardy HT, *mr*, 1936, Dickson, A. Bud pointed; flowers bright scarlet-red, dbl., spiral, large; strong, erect stems; very fragrant; bushy growth.

Geraldine HT, 1924, *Antoine Rivoire × Marie Adélaide*; Chaplin Bros. Flowers buff, shaded pink, dbl.; fragrant.   RULED EXTINCT 11/82 ARM.

Geraldine F, *ob*, 1982, (PEAhaze); *Seedling × Seedling*; Pearce, C.A.; Limes Rose Nursery, 1984. Flowers orange, dbl. (20 petals), medium; slight fragrance; foliage medium, light green, semi-glossy; upright growth.

Geraldine Hicks HT, *ab*, 1950, *William Moore sport*; Hicks. Flowers bronze-yellow.

Geranium HMoy (S), *mr*, 1938, *R. moyesii variety*; Royal Hort. Soc. Flowers almost scarlet, single, small (2 in.) blooms in clusters (up to 5); fruit crimson; upright (8-10 ft.), compact growth.

Geranium Red F, *or*, 1947, *Crimson Glory × Seedling*; Boerner; J&P. Flowers bright geranium-red, dbl. (50 petals), globular, large (4 in.) blooms in clusters; very fragrant (geranium); foliage dark, glossy; bushy growth.

Gerbe Rose LCl, *lp*, 1904, *R. wichuraiana × Baroness Rothschild*; Fauque; Langue. Flowers delicate pink, dbl., large; slightly fragrant; foliage glossy; vigorous growth.

Gerda Henkel HT, *dr*, 1964, *New Yorker × Prima Ballerina*; Tantau, Math. Flowers deep blood-red, dbl., large; strong stems; foliage dark, leathery; vigorous, upright growth.

Germaine HT, *w*, 1926, *Seedling × Sunburst*; Chambard, C. Flowers creamy white, center salmon.

Germanea HT, *dp*, 1929, *Columbia sport*; Ravenberg. Flowers deep shining rose-pink, dbl., well formed, very large.

Germiston Gold HT, *dy*, 1987, (KORtake); *Seedling × Seedling*; Kordes, W., Sohne; Ludwigs Roses, 1988. Flowers deep golden-yellow, dbl. (36 petals), large, borne in sprays of 1-3; strong fragrance; foliage medium green; prickles concave, brown; medium, well branched, free-flowering growth.

Gert Potgieter HT, 1968, Gowie; Color not reported; foliage light green; vigorous growth.

Gertrud Huck HT, *dp*, 1932, *Wilhelm Kordes sport*; Huck; C-P. Bud pointed; flowers flamingo-red, dbl., cupped, large; fragrant; foliage leathery, bronze; vigorous growth.

Gertrud Schweitzer HT, *ob*, 1973, *Colour Wonder* × *Seedling*; Kordes; Horstmann. Bud long, pointed; flowers apricot-orange, dbl., cupped, large; fragrant; foliage glossy, dark.

Gertrud Westphal F, *or*, 1951, *Baby Château* × *Obergärtner Wiebicke*; Kordes. Flowers orange-scarlet, single (5-7 petals), medium (3 in.); slightly fragrant; foliage glossy, dark reddish green; dwarf, bushy, much branched growth.

Gertrud Westphal, Climbing Cl F, *or*, 1961, Buisman.

Gertrude Gregory HT, *my*, 1957, *Lady Belper sport*; Gregory. Flowers bright golden yellow.

Gertrude Raffel F, *dp*, 1956, Raffel; Port Stockton Nursery. Flowers pink, center rosy, semi-dbl. (15-20 petals), well formed, medium (2-3 in.), borne in large clusters; slightly fragrant; foliage dark; vigorous, bushy growth.

Gertrude Reutener F, *dp*, 1954, Leenders, M. Flowers crimson-pink; vigorous growth.

Gertrude Shilling HT, *dy*, 1988, *Golden Splendour* × *Peer Gynt*; Poole, Lionel; Rearsby Roses, 1989. Flowers bright, deep yellow, aging paler, very dbl. (52 petals), urn-shaped, decorative, large, borne usually singly; moderate, fruity fragrance; foliage large, medium green, matt; prickles broad, fairly flat, large, dark brown; upright, tall, vigorous, good basal growth.

Ghergana Gr, *dr*, 1974, *Spectacular* × *Seedling*; Staikov, Prof. Dr. V.; Kalaydjiev and Chorbadjiiski. Flowers deep blackish-red, dbl. (55 petals), cupped, large blooms in clusters of 2-5; tea fragrance; foliage dark; vigorous, upright growth.

G. H. Davison HT, *mr*, 1988, *Seedling* × *Seedling*; Davison, G.H.; The Central Nursery, 1990. Flowers medium, well-defined red, dbl. (45 petals), high-centered, exhibition, large, borne in sprays of 1-3; slight fragrance; foliage large, dark green, semi-glossy; prickles normal, large, red; fruit oval, large, green; upright growth.

Ghislaine de Féligonde R, *ly*, 1916, *Goldfinch* × *Seedling*; Turbat. Bud bright yellow; flowers yellowish white tinted flesh, borne in clusters of 10-20; vigorous, climbing (8-10 ft.) growth; sometimes flowers are produced on new shoots of the season.

Gibby HT, *dp*, 1977, *Christian Dior sport*; Prof. F. Roses; Ludwig Roses. Bud ovoid, pointed; flowers carmine-pink, dbl. (50 petals), high-centered to cupped, large (4½ in.); foliage dull, dark, leathery; vigorous, upright, bushy growth.

Gidget Min, *op*, 1975, (*R. wichuraiana* × *Floradora*) × *Fire Princess*; Moore, R.S.; Sequoia Nursery. Bud pointed; flowers coral-pink to coral-red, informal shape, small (1 in.); slightly fragrant; foliage small, glossy; vigorous, bushy growth.

Gigantesque HP (OGR), *dp*, 1845, Odier. Flowers deep pink.

Giggles Min, *pb*, 1982, (LYOgi); *Seedling* × *Seedling*; Lyon, L.; Lyon Greenhouse. Bud pointed; flowers medium pink, white center, semi-dbl., small; slight fragrance; foliage small, medium green, semi-glossy; very small, upright, bushy.

Gigi HT, *mp*, 1959, *The Doctor* × *Seedling*; Verschuren; Blaby Rose Gardens. Flowers rose-pink, reverse brighter, dbl., large; long, strong stems; fragrant; foliage light green; vigorous growth.

Gigolette F, *rb*, 1953, Gaujard. Bud ovoid; flowers yellow and red bicolor, semi-dbl., medium, borne in clusters; fragrant; foliage leathery, light green; vigorous growth.

G. I. Joe HT, *dp*, 1943, *Red Better Times sport*; Parmentier, J. Bud long, pointed; flowers rose-red to deep rose-pink, very dbl., large; fragrant; foliage leathery, dark; vigorous growth.

Gilbert F. Levy F, *mr*, 1958, *Moulin Rouge* × *Oiseau de Feu*; Combe. Flowers currant-red, dbl.; very vigorous growth.

Gilda HT, *ab*, 1936, *Souv. de Claudius Pernet* × (*Lady Hillingdon* × *Harry Kirk*); Towill. Bud long, pointed; flowers pure orange-yellow, dbl., large; foliage leathery, dark; vigorous growth. RULED EXTINCT 3/87.

Gilda F, *lp*, 1987, (PEAhigh); *Seedling* × *Seedling*; Pearce, C.A.; The Limes New Roses. Flowers pale shell pink, moderately full (15-25 petals), medium; very fragrant; foliage medium, medium green, matt; upright, spreading growth.

Gillian HT, *op*, 1958, *Michèle Meilland* × *Mme. Butterfly*; Verschuren; Gandy. Bud long, pointed; flowers soft coral-pink; foliage bronze.

Gina F, *dr*, 1960, *Alain* × *Independence*; Kriloff; Cramphorn's Nursery. Flowers velvety dark crimson, single (6 petals), borne in large clusters; slightly fragrant; foliage glossy; vigorous, upright growth.

Gina Louise Min, *op*, 1986, (TRObgina); *Orange Sensation* × *Seedling*; Robinson, T. Flowers bright orange-pink, opening to bright yellow, gold anthers, dbl. (35 petals), cupped, high-centered, large, borne occasionally singly or in sprays of 3-5; heavy, damask, fruity fragrance; foliage small, dark green, semi-glossy; thin, red prickles pointed down; fruit globular, large, orange; bushy, low growth.

Ginette HT, *op*, 1924, *Paul Monnier* × *Souv. de Claudius Pernet*; Buatois. Flowers salmony maize-yellow, dbl.; fragrant.

Ginger F, *or*, 1962, *Garnette seedling* × *Spartan*; Boerner; J&P. Bud ovoid; flowers orange-vermilion, dbl. (28 petals), cupped, large (4 in.) blooms in irregular clusters; fragrant; foliage leathery; vigorous, compact, bushy growth.

Ginger Rogers HT, *op*, 1969, (Salmon Charm); *Tropicana* × *Miss Ireland*; McGredy, S., IV; McGredy. Flowers salmon, dbl. (30 petals), loosely formed, large; fragrant; foliage light green; very tall.

Gingernut F, *r*, 1988, (COCcrazy); *(Sabine* × *Circus)* × *Darling Flame*; Cocker, J. & Sons, 1989. Flowers russet, dbl. (43 petals), medium; patio; fragrant; foliage small, medium green, semi-glossy; bushy growth.

Gingersnap F, *ob*, 1978, (AROsnap; Apricot Prince; Prince Abricot); *(Zambra* × *(Orange Triumph* × *Floradora))* × *(Jean de la Lune* × *(Spartan* × *Mandrina))*; Delbard-Chabert; Armstrong Nursery. Bud long, pointed; flowers pure orange, dbl. (35 petals), imbricated to ruffled, large (4 in.); slightly fragrant; foliage dark; vigorous, upright, bushy growth

Gingia HT, *w*, 1983, *Seedling* × *Seedling*; Fumagalli, Niso. Flowers white, dbl. (35 petals), large; very fragrant; foliage large, light green, glossy; bushy.

Ginny Min, *rb*, 1981, (BISjen); *Little Darling* × *Toy Clown*; Bischoff, Francis J.; Kimbrew-Walter Roses. Bud ovoid; flowers white edged medium red, yellow at hinge, yellow stamens, dbl. (45 petals), high-centered, HT form, opening flat, small blooms borne singly; no fragrance; foliage dark, leathery, reddish tinge on new growth; straight red prickles; upright, compact growth.

Ginny-Lou Min, *mr*, 1983, (TRObinka); *Dollie B.* × *Seedling*; Robinson, Thomas; Thomas Robinson, Ltd., 1984. Flowers bright medium red, dbl. (40+ petals), medium blooms in clusters; no fragrance; foliage small, dark, semi-glossy; bushy growth.

Ginsky F, *pb*, 1983, *Liverpool Echo sport*; Barker; L.E.J. Wood. Flowers light salmon pink opening to pale pink to cream.

Ginza Komachi Cl Min, *pb*, 1980, *Nozomi* × *Seedling*; Kono, Yoshito. Bud globular; flowers deep pink, white eye, yellow stamens,

single (5 petals), small blooms in clusters of 1-10; slight fragrance; foliage medium green, glossy; many, hooked prickles; vigorous growth.

Gioiello Min, *my*, 1984, *Zorina* × *Sole Di San Remo*; Bartolomeo, E. Flowers medium yellow, dbl. (20 petals), small; no fragrance; foliage small, dark, matt.

Gion Cl Min, *pb*, 1979, *Nozomi* × *Seedling*; Onodera, T.; S. Onodera. Bud rounded; flowers pink, single (5 petals), flat, small (1 in.); fragrant; foliage tiny, leathery; bushy, climbing growth; non-recurrent bloom.

Giovane HT, *op*, 1965, *Queen Elizabeth* × *Orient*; Dot, S.; Rosas Dot. Bud pointed; flowers salmon-orange, dbl. (28 petals), high-centered, large; fragrant; foliage glossy, bronze; dense growth.

Giovanezza HT, *rb*, 1933, Ingegnoli. Flowers geranium-red, reverse cream-white, edged lighter; vigorous growth.

Gipsy Boy B (OGR), *dr*, 1909, (Zigeunerknabe); Lambert, P. Flowers dark crimson-red, medium; vigorous (3-5 ft.) growth.

Gipsy Lass HT, *mr*, 1932, (Gypsy Lass); Dickson, A. Flowers scarlet-crimson shaded blackish, dbl., globular; long, willowy stems; very fragrant; bushy growth.

Gipsy Love HT, *or*, 1964, *Chic Parisien* × *Fashion*; Delbard-Chabert; Cuthbert. Flowers orange-vermilion, dbl. (25 petals), large (4 in.); fragrant; vigorous growth.

Gipsy Maid F, *dp*, 1955, LeGrice. Flowers carmine-scarlet, base golden, single, borne in small clusters of 3 or 4; fragrant (sweetbriar); foliage olive-green.

Girasol HT, *my*, 1945, *Joanna Hill* × *Carito MacMahon*; Dot, P. Bud oval; flowers sunflower-yellow, full (25-30 petals); slightly fragrant; foliage dark, glossy; upright, compact growth.

Girl Scout F, *my*, 1961, *Gold Cup* × *Pigmy Gold*; Boerner; J&P. Bud ovoid; flowers golden yellow, dbl. (50 petals), cupped, large (3½-4 in.); fragrant; foliage leathery, glossy; vigorous, medium tall growth.

Girlie Pol, *dr*, 1923, *Orléans Rose sport*; Wezelenburg. Flowers bright scarlet-crimson; bushy growth.

Girona HT, *pb*, 1936, *Li Bures* × *Talisman*; Dot, P.; H. Guillot; C-P, 1939. Flowers soft red and yellow, dbl. (30 petals), high-centered, well-formed, large; very fragrant (damask); foliage bright green; vigorous, spreading growth.

Gisela F, *op*, 1961, *Masquerade* × *Pinocchio*; Verschuren, A.; van Engelen. Flowers salmon-pink, base straw-yellow, dbl. (56 petals), borne in clusters; foliage dark, glossy, bronze; upright, bushy, compact growth.

Gisèle Alday HT, *mp*, 1933, *Mrs. Pierre S. duPont* × *Lallita*; Mallerin; H. Guillot. Bud pointed; flowers bright rose-pink tinted flesh, semi-dbl., cupped, large; slightly fragrant; foliage glossy, dark; vigorous growth.

Giselle Min, *dp*, 1991, (JUSelle); *Crazy Dottie* × *Seedling*; Justice, Jerry; Justice Miniature Roses, 1992. Bud small, pointed with medium green sepals; flowers pink outer edges with very light pink (almost white) at midline of petal, ages to stripe, semi-dbl. (18 self-cleaning petals), urn-shaped, loose, small (3 cms) blooms borne usually singly; no fragrance; foliage small, dark green, glossy, disease resistant; bushy, low growth.

Gisselfeld® HT, *dr*, 1972, *(Tropicana* × *Champs-Elysees)* × *Furore*; Poulsen, N.D.; Poulsen. Flowers dark red, 17-20 petals, large (4-4½ in.); fragrant; foliage dark, leathery; upright.

Gitte HT, *ab*, 1978, (KORita; Peach Melba); *(Fragrant Cloud* × *Peer Gynt)* × *((Dr. A.J. Verhage* × *Colour Wonder)* × *Zorina)*; Kordes, W., Sons; Horstmann. Bud long, pointed; flowers apricot-pink blend, dbl. (33 petals), high-centered, large (4 in.); very fragrant; foliage dark; vigorous, upright, bushy growth.

Giuletta B (OGR), *lp*, 1859, Laurentius.

Giuliana Borgatti HT, *w*, 1936, *Ophelia* × *Ville de Paris*; Borgatti. Flowers white, center shaded rose and salmon, very full, well formed, large; foliage dark ivy-green; vigorous growth.

Giuseppina Papandrea Min, *pb*, 1989, *Petite Folie sport*; Papandrea, John T. Flowers cerise, reverse lighter.

Givenchy™ HT, *rb*, 1986, (AROdousna; Paris Pink); *Gingersnap* × *Double Delight*; Christensen; Armstrong Nursery, 1985. Flowers pink, blushed red, reverse pink, yellow base, dbl. (30 petals), high-centered, exhibition, medium blooms in sprays of 2-5; heavy, spicy fragrance; foliage medium, dark; medium, brown, hooked prickles; fruit none; medium, upright, bushy.

Glacier F, *w*, 1952, *HT Seedling* × *Summer Snow*; Boerner; J&P. Bud ovoid; flowers white, slightly overcast yellow, dbl. (28 petals), cupped, large (4½ in.); fragrant; foliage glossy, dark; vigorous, upright growth.

Glad Tidings F, *dr*, 1988, (TANtide; Lübecker Rotspon; Peter Wessel); *Seedling* × *Seedling*; Tantau, R.; Wheatcroft Ltd., 1989. Bud ovoid; flowers bright crimson, dbl. (20 petals), cupped, medium, borne in sprays; no fragrance; foliage medium, medium green, semi-glossy; upright, medium growth. ROTY, 1989.

Gladiador Cl HT, *dp*, 1954, *Texas Centennial* × *Guinée*; Dot, P. Bud pointed; flowers carmine, dbl., very large; very fragrant; vigorous growth.

Gladiator LCl, *mr*, 1955, *Charlotte Armstrong* × *(Pink Delight* × *New Dawn seedling)*; Malandrone; J&P. Bud ovoid; flowers rose-red, dbl. (35 petals), high-centered, large (4½-5 in.); fragrant; foliage dark, leathery; vigorous (10-12 ft.) growth.

Gladness F, *pb*, 1959, *Sunny Maid* × *Cinnabar*; Fletcher. Bud pointed; flowers light pink edged darker, dbl. (25 petals), large, borne in clusters; foliage dark, glossy; upright growth.

Gladys Benskin HT, *op*, 1929, Dickson, A.; Dreer. Flowers rose-cerise, shaded orange, base deeper orange, full, high-centered, large; fragrant; vigorous growth. GM, NRS, 1929.

Gladys Holland HT, *lp*, 1917, McGredy. Flowers light pink, shaded buff, dbl.; fragrant. GM, NRS, 1916.

Gladys Moncrief HT, *yb*, 1981, *Granada sport*; Jack, J.; Girraween Nursery. Flowers golden yellow to apricot, flushed rose red at petal tips.

Gladys Saavedra HT, *mp*, 1922, *Mme. Abel Chatenay* × *Jonkheer J.L. Mock*; Nabonnand, P. Flowers rosy peach-blossom-pink, full.

Gladys Tweedie HT, *dr*, 1950, *Crimson Glory* × *William Orr*; Toogood. Bud long, pointed; flowers crimson, dbl. (30-35 petals), high-centered, large (5 in.); fragrant; foliage wrinkled; very vigorous, bushy growth.

Glaive HT, *pb*, 1951, Clark, A.; NRS Victoria. Bud long, pointed; flowers cream, center tipped pink, dbl. (25 petals), high-centered, small; slightly fragrant; foliage glossy; vigorous, bushy, compact growth; greenhouse variety.

Glamorous Min, *or*, 1979, *Starburst* × *Over the Rainbow*; Williams, E.D.; Mini-Roses. Bud pointed; flowers orange-red, base yellow, dbl. (35 petals), high-centered, small (1-1½ in.); slightly fragrant; foliage small, glossy, bronze-green; bushy, spreading.

Glamour HT, *op*, 1939, *Comtesse Vandal* × *Pres. Macia*; Leenders, M.; T. Robinson. Bud long, ovoid; flowers salmon-pink, dbl., large; very fragrant; vigorous growth.

Glamour Girl HT, *op*, 1942, *Captain Glisson* × *Justine*; Hill, J.H., Co. Bud pointed, light jasper-red; flowers light salmon, dbl. (45-50 petals), open, large (4-5 in.); strong stems; foliage dark, leathery; very vigorous, upright, much branched growth; a florists' variety, not distributed for outdoor use.

Glarona HT, *w*, 1922, Krüger; Kiese. Flowers creamy flesh, center rose.

Glastonbury S, *rb*, 1981, *The Knight* × *Seedling*; Austin, David; David Austin Roses. Bud globular; flowers dark crimson to deep purple, dbl. (55 petals), borne 1-5 per cluster; very fragrant; foliage medium green, sparse; hooked, red prickles; sparse, spreading growth; repeats.

Gleaming F, *dy*, 1958, *Goldilocks* × *Golden Scepter*; LeGrice. Flowers deep lemon-yellow, single (6-8 petals), large (4 in.), borne in trusses; very fragrant; foliage dark; very free growth.

Glen Almond HT, *pb*, 1973, *Pascali* × *Happy Event*; Wallace. Flowers pale orient pink, dbl. (30 petals), large (3½-4 in.); foliage glossy, leathery; free growth.

Glen Artney HT, *dr*, 1973, *Baccará* × *Sterling Silver*; Wallace. Flowers beetroot-purple, dbl. (40 petals), large (3½-4 in.); slightly fragrant; vigorous growth.

Glenara HT, *dp*, 1951, Clark, A.; NRS Victoria. Bud long, pointed; flowers deep rosy pink, semi-dbl. (18 petals), very large; slightly fragrant; foliage leathery; vigorous, upright bush or pillar growth.

Glenfiddich F, *dy*, 1976, *Arthur Bell* × *(Sabine* × *Circus)*; Cocker. Flowers amber-gold, dbl. (25 petals), large (4 in.); fragrant; foliage glossy, dark.

Glengarry F, *or*, 1969, *Evelyn Fison* × *Wendy Cussons*; Cocker. Flowers vermilion, dbl. (32 petals), large; slightly fragrant; foliage semi-glossy; compact, bushy.

Gleniti Gold HT, *dy*, 1973, *Lady Mandeville* sport; Bone, John, & Son; Trevor Griffiths Ltd. Flowers very deep yellow.

Glenn Dale LCl, *ly*, 1927, *Believed to be R. wichuraiana* × *Isabella Sprunt*; Van Fleet; ARS. Flowers lemon, fading to white, dbl. (40 petals), large blooms in clusters (to 20); slightly fragrant; foliage dark, leathery; vigorous (10 ft.) growth. GM, Portland, 1920.

Glenys Stewart HT, *dp*, 1968, *Montezuma* × *Pink Favorite*; Kemp, M.L.; G. Stewart. Flowers deep rose-pink, full; slightly fragrant; moderate growth; moderate bloom.

Gletscher F, *m*, 1955, *Seedling* × *Lavender Pinocchio*; Kordes. Bud ovoid; flowers pale lilac, dbl., high-centered, large blooms in large trusses; very fragrant; foliage glossy; vigorous, upright, bushy growth.

Glimmer Min, *rb*, 1988, *Party Girl* × *Seedling*; Bridges, Dennis; Bridges Roses, 1989. Bud pointed; flowers bright, medium red, yellow at base, reverse slightly darker, aging darkens edges and dulls color, dbl. (24 petals), high-centered, exhibition, medium, borne usually singly; slight fragrance; foliage medium, medium green, semi-glossy; prickles slightly downward pointed, medium, red; upright, medium growth.

Glitters Cl HT, *mp*, 1934, *Mrs. W.J. Grant* × *Mrs. Sam McGredy*; Smith, J. Bud pointed; flowers brilliant pink, base orange, full, open, globular, very large; long stems; fragrant; foliage leathery; very vigorous growth; recurrent bloom.

Gloaming HT, *pb*, 1935, *Charles P. Kilham* × *Mrs. Pierre S. duPont*; Nicolas; J&P. Bud pointed; flowers luminous pink suffused salmon, reverse lighter, dbl. (36 petals), open, very large; very fragrant; foliage leathery, dark; vigorous, bushy growth.

Globe F, *mr*, 1956, *Fanal* × *Red Favorite*; Tantau. Flowers blood-red, semi-dbl. (20 petals), cupped, medium (2 in.), borne in clusters; fragrant; foliage dark; vigorous, bushy, compact growth.

Globe Hip C (OGR), *w*, Flowers white; much used as a parent.

Gloire de Bruxelles HP (OGR), *m*, 1889, (Gloire de l'Exposition de Bruxelles); *Souv. de William Wood* × *Lord Macaulay*; Soupert & Notting. Flowers very dark, velvety crimson-purple, dbl. (60 petals), large; fragrant; vigorous, upright growth.

Gloire de Chédane-Guinoisseau HP (OGR), *mr*, 1907, *Gloire de Ducher* × *Seedling*; Chédane-Pajotin. Flowers bright crimson-red, dbl. (40 petals), well-formed, cupped, large; fragrant; foliage dark, soft; vigorous growth; occasional recurrent bloom.

Gloire de Cibeins HT, *or*, 1958, *Mme. Méha Sabatier* × *Léonce Colombier*; Arles; Roses-France. Flowers deep vermilion-red, dbl. (30 petals), well formed; long stems; vigorous growth.

Gloire de Dijon Cl T (OGR), *op*, 1853, *Thought to be an unknown Tea* × *Souv. de la Malmaison*; Jacotot. Flowers rich buff-pink shaded orange toward center, full, very large; fragrant; very vigorous, climbing growth; (28).

Gloire de Ducher HP (OGR), *dr*, 1865, Ducher. Flowers dark red, full, very large; fragrant; occasional recurrent bloom.

Gloire de France G (OGR), *lp*, (Fanny Bias); Cultivated 1819. Flowers pale pink, fully dbl.; low.

Gloire de France HT, *or*, 1946, Gaujard. Flowers orange-red variegated copper, full, well formed, large; vigorous growth. GM, Bagatelle, 1945.

Gloire de Guilan D (OGR), *lp*, 1949, *Collected by Miss Nancy Lindsay in Caspian provinces of*

Persia; Original name and date unknown; Hilling, 1949. Flowers clear pink, fully dbl., quartered, center incurved; very fragrant; foliage light green; sprawling shrub (4-5 ft.) growth; spring bloom. Used for making attar of roses.

Gloire de Hollande HT, *dr*, 1918, Verschuren. Flowers dark red.

Gloire de la Brie HT, *mr*, Grandes Roseraies. Bud long; flowers bright red, large.

Gloire de Margottin HP (OGR), *dr*, 1887, Margottin. Flowers dark red, dbl. (60 petals), globular, large; very fragrant; occasional recurrent bloom.

Gloire de Mezel M (OGR), *mp*, Flowers pale rose, very large.

Gloire de Vitry HP (OGR), *mp*, 1854, *La Reine seedling*; Masson. Flowers bright pink, globular, large.

Gloire des Belges HT, *dp*, 1916, Chambard, C. Flowers vivid carmine.

Gloire des Lawranceanas Min, *dr*, 1837, Flowers dark crimson; dwarf growth.

Gloire des Mousseuses M (OGR), *mp*, 1852, (Gloire des Mousseux); Laffay. Bud heavily mossed; flowers clear bright pink, center deeper, full, petals imbricated, large blooms in clusters; foliage light green; vigorous growth.

Gloire des Polyantha Pol, *mp*, 1887, *Mignonette seedling*; Guillot Fils. Flowers bright pink, dbl., well-shaped, small blooms in large clusters; dwarf growth.

Gloire des Rosomanes Ch (OGR), *mr*, 1825, (Ragged Robin; Red Robin); Vibert. Flowers glowing crimson, semi-dbl., very large blooms in large clusters; fragrant; vigorous growth; repeat bloom. Used under the name Ragged Robin as an understock on which to bud roses.

Gloire d'Orient M (OGR), *dr*, 1856, Béluze. Flowers deep red.

Gloire du Bourbonnais® Pol, *rb*, 1987, (DELbourdo; DELbourbo); *(Milrose × Legion d'Honneur) × (Zambra × Sensation)*; Delbard-Chabert, 1988. Flowers center cream, margin carmine, opening turns purple, dbl. (35-40 petals), large; no fragrance; foliage bright; good, dwarf growth.

Gloire du Midi Pol, *or*, 1932, *Gloria Mundi sport*; deRuiter; Sliedrecht & Co.; J&P. Flowers brilliant orange-scarlet.

Gloire du Midi Superior Pol, *or*, *Gloire du Midi sport*; deRuiter. Flowers like parent with more lasting color.

Gloire d'Un Enfant d'Hiram HP (OGR), *mr*, 1899, Vilin. Flowers bright red.

Gloire Lyonnaise HP (OGR), *w*, 1885, *Baroness Rothschild × Mme. Falcot*; Guillot Fils. Flowers white with trace of yellow at center, very dbl. (84 petals), cupped, very large; fragrant; foliage leathery; very vigorous, bushy growth; not very hardy.

Gloria HT, *dr*, 1922, Paul, W. Flowers brilliant scarlet-crimson, full.

Gloria de Grado HT, *mp*, 1950, *Mari Dot × Comtesse Vandal*; La Florida. Flowers pink, tinted carmine, globular; foliage bright green.

Gloria del Llobregat HT, *or*, 1940, *Sensation × Margaret McGredy*; Camprubi. Flowers strawberry-red to vermilion, dbl., cupped, large; fragrant; foliage glossy; very vigorous growth.

Gloria Mundi Pol, *or*, 1929, *Superb (Pol) sport*; deRuiter; Sliedrecht & Co. & Teschendorff. Flowers striking orange-scarlet, dbl., borne in clusters; foliage light, glossy; vigorous, bushy growth.

Gloria Mundi, Climbing Cl Pol, *or*, 1934, Lens.

Gloria Mundi, Climbing Cl Pol, *or*, 1943, Howard Rose Co.

Gloria Mundi Superior Pol, *or*, *Gloria Mundi sport*; deRuiter. Flowers like parent with more lasting color.

Gloria Solis HT, *my*, 1949, *Ville de Paris × Max Krause*; Giacomasso. Flowers yellow, well shaped, large (4-5 in.); foliage dark, glossy; vigorous growth.

Gloriana HT, *my*, 1936, *Condesa de Sástago (probably self seed)*; Hillock. Flowers intense lemon-yellow in heat, deep gold with cerise markings when nights are cool, dbl. (35 petals), cupped; foliage leathery, glossy, dark; vigorous, compact growth.

Glorified La France HT, *lp*, 1916, *Frau Karl Druschki × Mrs. Charles E. Russell*; Cook, J. Flowers silvery pink, deeper than La France, very dbl. (92 petals); slightly fragrant.

Gloriglo Min, *ob*, 1976, *Seedling × Over the Rainbow*; Williams, E.D.; Mini-Roses. Bud pointed; flowers orange, yellow reverse, dbl. (45 petals), high-centered, small (1 in.); slightly fragrant; foliage small, glossy, bronze; upright, bushy growth. AOE, 1978.

Glorio HT, *mr*, 1923, *Premier × Primrose*; Hill, E.G., Co.; Vestal. Flowers scarlet-cerise, dbl.; fragrant.

Gloriosa HT, *w*, 1920, *Kaiserin Auguste Viktoria × Pharisäer*; Kiese. Flowers ivory-white, base yellow; very fragrant.

Glorious F, *dp*, 1947, *(Betty Uprichard × Heidekind) × Heidekind*; Duehrsen; H&S. Bud pointed; flowers salmon scarlet, shaded orange, semi-dbl. (15-17 petals), open, medium, large trusses; slightly fragrant; foliage leathery, dark; vigorous, upright growth. RULED EXTINCT 7/84 ARM.

Glorious HT, *ab*, 1985, (LEOglo); *Seedling × Mirato*; Leon, Charles F., Sr. Flowers medium pink tinted apricot, dbl. (37 petals), well-formed, large; slight fragrance; foliage medium to large, medium green, semi-glossy; upright, bushy growth.

Glorious Easter HT, *op*, 1965, *Seedling × Penelope*; Howard, P.J. Bud ovoid; flowers salmon, dbl., high-centered, medium; foliage leathery; moderate, bushy growth.

Glorious Pernet HT, *r*, 1928, *Souv. de Claudius Pernet sport*; Myers & Samtmann. Flowers copper, center orange.

Glorious Sunset Pol, *rb*, 1931, *Mariposa sport*; Allen. Flowers bronze, suffused red, semi-dbl., small, borne in clusters; slightly fragrant; foliage small, thick; vigorous growth.

Glory Days HT, *mp*, 1991, (JACcor); *Seedling × Showstopper*; Warriner, William A.; Bear Creek Gardens, Inc. Flowers coral pink, full (26-40 petals), large; fragrant; foliage medium, medium green, semi-glossy; tall, upright, bushy growth.

Glory of Ceylon F, *op*, 1967, *Vera Dalton × Masquerade*; Harkness. Flowers orange-yellow blended pink, semi-dbl. (14 petals), medium blooms in clusters; fragrant; foliage dark, glossy.

Glory of Cheshunt HP (OGR), *dr*, 1880, *Charles Lefèvre seedling*; Paul. Flowers rich crimson, cupped; vigorous growth.

Glory of Hurst Pol, *mr*, 1921, *Orléans Rose × Jessie*; Hicks. Flowers cherry-red, semi-dbl., borne in clusters; foliage small, leathery, glossy, rich green; dwarf growth.

Glory of Surrey HT, *my*, 1935, Ley. Flowers golden yellow, semi-dbl.; fragrant; fairly vigorous growth.

Glory of Waltham HP (OGR), *dr*, 1865, Vigneron; W. Paul. Flowers crimson, very dbl., very large; fragrant; vigorous, climbing or pillar.

Glow Worm HT, *or*, 1919, Easlea. Flowers scarlet, suffused coppery orange, semi-dbl.; fragrant.

Glowing Carmine HT, *dp*, 1936, *Miss Rowena Thom × Seedling*; H&S; Dreer. Flowers carmine, dbl., globular, large; slightly fragrant; foliage leathery; vigorous, open habit.

Glowing Embers F, *yb*, 1985, (ANDglo); *Manx Queen × Daily Sketch*; Anderson's Rose Nursery, 1982. Flowers yellow, red reverse, dbl. (35 petals), medium; slight fragrance; foliage medium, medium green, glossy; bushy growth.

Glowing Sunset HT, *ob*, 1933, (Wilhelm Breder); *Fontanelle × Julien Potin*; Kordes; Dreer. Bud long, pointed; flowers orange shaded yellow and pink, dbl., high-centered, very large; very fragrant; foliage leathery, glossy, dark; vigorous growth.

Glowing Velvet HT, *dr*, 1975, Pasley. Flowers deep crimson to scarlet, dbl. (25 petals), large (4 in.); very fragrant; foliage dark; bloom repeats quickly.

Glowry™ Min, *ob*, 1989, (KINglow); *(Arthur Bell × Orange Honey) × Baby Diana*; King, Gene; AGM Miniature Roses. Bud pointed; flowers bright orange-yellow bicolor, dbl. (24 petals), high-centered, exhibition, medium, borne singly; no fragrance; foliage small, medium green, matt; prickles straight, red; fruit none; bushy, low growth.

Glückskind HT, *dp*, 1935, Berger. Flowers deep pink, well formed, large; fragrant.

Glückskind F, *dr*, 1952, Leenders, M. Flowers dark crimson, semi-dbl., medium; very vigorous growth.

Glyndyfrdwy HT, *mp*, 1978, *Gavotte × George Thomas*; Ellick; Excelsior Roses. Flowers neyron rose, dbl. (35 petals), full, large (4-5 in.); fragrant; foliage large, light; very vigorous growth.

Gneisenau S, *w*, 1924, *(Schneelicht × Killarney) × Crimson Rambler*; Lambert, P. Flowers snow-white, stamens yellow, dbl., borne in clusters; height 5-6 ft.; non-recurrent bloom.

Gnome Pol, *ly*, 1936, *Seedling × Mev. Nathalie Nypels*; Leenders, M. Flowers cream-yellow, dbl., large, borne on short stems; very fragrant; foliage leathery, light; bushy, dwarf growth.

Godfrey Winn HT, *m*, 1968, Dot; Wheatcroft & Sons. Flowers purplish, dbl., globular; very fragrant.

Godfrey's Red Petite HT, *dr*, 1966, *Baccará × Audie Murphy*; Godfrey. Flowers deep red, semi-dbl. (15 petals), medium; slightly fragrant; foliage dark; free growth.

Goethe M (OGR), *m*, 1911, Lambert, P. Flowers magenta, single, small; foliage blue-green, rough; new wood bright red; very vigorous growth.

Golconda HT, *ly*, 1968, *Mme. Charles Sauvage × Seedling*; Pal; Indian Agric. Research Inst. Bud ovoid; flowers pale yellow, center deep apricot, dbl., cupped, large; very fragrant; foliage leathery; moderate, bushy, compact growth.

Gold Badge™ F, *my*, 1978, (MEIgronuri; Gold Bunny; Rimosa 79); *Poppy Flash × (Charleston*

× *Allgold*); Paolino; Meilland. Bud conical; flowers lemon-yellow, dbl. (38 petals), cupped, large (3 in.); vigorous growth.

Gold Blaze Min, *yb*, 1980, *Seedling × Seedling*; Lyon. Bud ovoid, pointed; flowers yellow, dipped red, dbl. (23 petals), blooms borne singly or several together; very fragrant; foliage small, glossy, deep green; tiny, straight prickles; compact, upright growth.

Gold Coast Gr, *my*, 1958, (Golden Pride); *Pinocchio × Peace*; Robinson, H.; J&P. Bud ovoid; flowers clear yellow, overcast buff-yellow, dbl. (25-30 petals), cupped, large (4 in.); foliage leathery, glossy; vigorous, upright growth.

Gold Coin Min, *dy*, 1967, *Golden Glow (Brownell) × Magic Wand*; Moore, R.S.; Sequoia Nursery. Flowers buttercup-yellow, dbl., small; fragrant; vigorous, bushy growth.

Gold Country Min, *my*, 1987, (SEAgold); *Rise 'n' Shine × (Rise 'n' Shine × Casino)*; McCann, S. Flowers medium yellow, dbl. (20 petals), exhibition, small blooms borne singly; very fragrant; foliage small, light green, semi-glossy; bushy growth.

Gold Crown HT, *dy*, 1960, (Gold Krone; Goldkrone; Corona de Oro; Couronne d'Or); *Peace × Golden Scepter*; Kordes, R.; McGredy. Flowers golden yellow, dbl. (35 petals), well-formed, large (5 in.); fragrant; foliage leathery, dark; vigorous, upright growth.

Gold Cup F, *dy*, 1957, (Coupe d'Or); *Goldilocks seedling × King Midas seedling*; Boerner; J&P. Bud pointed; flowers golden yellow, dbl. (28 petals), large (4 in.) blooms in clusters; fragrant; foliage dark, glossy; bushy growth. AARS, 1958.

Gold Dame HT, *dy*, 1929, Dobbie. Flowers deep golden yellow, semi-dbl., fragrant; foliage dark, glossy; vigorous, bushy growth.

Gold Dollar HT, *dy*, 1971, (HERdio); *Seedling × Weiner Charme*; Herholdt, J.A.; Herholdt's Nursery. Flowers deep yellow, dbl. (35 petals), large; slightly fragrant; foliage glossy; vigorous.

Gold Dot HT, *my*, 1963, *Queen Elizabeth × Peace*; Dot, S. Flowers medium yellow, dbl. (25 petals), large; vigorous, upright.

Gold Fever Min, *my*, 1990, (MORfever); *Sheri Anne × Gold Badge*; Moore, Ralph S.; Sequoia Nursery. Bud pointed; flowers medium yellow, aging lighter, dbl. (40-50 petals), cupped, exhibition, medium blooms borne usually singly or in sprays of 3-5; spicy fragrance; foliage medium, medium green, semi-glossy; prickles slender, straight, medium to long,

brownish; fruit round, small, orange; upright, bushy, medium growth.

Gold Glow HT, *dy*, 1959, *Fred Howard × Sutter's Gold*; Perry, Anthony; C.R. Burr. Flowers bright yellow, very dbl. (100 petals), large (3½-4 in.); fragrant; foliage leathery, dark, glossy; vigorous, upright growth.

Gold Glow, Climbing Cl HT, *dy*, 1964, Burr, C.R.

Gold Magic F, *dy*, 1990, *Gold Badge × Friessensohne*; Christensen, Jack; Vaughan's Seed Co., 1991. Flowers golden yellow, moderately full (15-25 petals), medium, borne in large clusters; slight fragrance; foliage medium, dark green, glossy; bushy, medium growth.

Gold Medal® Gr, *my*, 1982, (AROyqueli); *Yellow Pages × Shirley Langhorn*; Christensen, J.E.; Armstrong Nursery. Bud ovoid, long, pointed; flowers deep golden yellow sometimes flushed orange, dbl. (38 petals), classic shape, opening formal, spiraled; light tea fragrance; foliage large, dark; tall, upright, bushy growth. GM, NZ (Gold Star), 1983.

Gold Mine HT, *my*, 1925, *Golden Rule × Mrs. Aaron Ward*; Hill, J.H., Co.; J.H. Hill Co.; A.N. Pierson. Flowers indian yellow paling toward edges, base deep orange, dbl.; very fragrant. RULED EXTINCT 9/84.

Gold Mine™ Min, *dy*, 1984, (LAVoro); *Rise 'n' Shine × Yellow seedling*; Laver, Keith. Flowers deep yellow, dbl. (20 petals), small; no fragrance; foliage medium, medium green, semi-glossy; bushy growth.

Gold Moon® Min, *dy*, 1984, (HAVoon); *(Aalsmeer Gold × Seedling) × (Motrea × Golden Times)*; Verschuren, Ted; H.A. Verschuren. Bud ovoid; flowers deep yellow, semi-dbl. (15 petals), small blooms borne singly; slight fragrance; foliage medium, medium green, glossy; no prickles; spreading, low growth; (28).

Gold 'n' Flame Min, *rb*, 1980, *Seedling × Over the Rainbow*; Williams, E.D.; Mini-Roses. Bud long, pointed; flowers medium red, deep golden yellow reverse, dbl. (33 petals), cupped, borne singly; slight fragrance; foliage dark, glossy; very thin, long, tan prickles, curved down; upright, bushy growth.

Gold 'n' Honey HT, *yb*, 1976, *Helen Traubel × (Seedling × Ulster Monarch)*; Leon; Edmunds. Bud long, pointed; flowers yellow and peach, edged rose, dbl. (28 petals), high-centered, large (5-6 in.); very fragrant; vigorous, upright, bushy.

Gold Nugget F, *dy*, 1972, Patterson; Patterson Roses. Flowers bright yellow, dbl., high-centered, medium; fragrant; foliage glossy, abundant; vigorous, upright growth.

Gold Pin Min, *dy*, 1974, Mattock. Flowers bright golden yellow, semi-dbl. (18 petals), small (1 in.); slightly fragrant; foliage bronze.

Gold Pique Min, *my*, 1977, *Seedling × Yellow Jewel*; Lyon. Bud pointed; flowers medium yellow, dbl. (36 petals), small (1½ in.); fragrant; foliage small, dark; compact, bushy growth.

Gold Rush LCl, *yb*, 1941, Duehrsen; H&S. Flowers gold, dbl. (24 petals), high-centered; fragrant; foliage glossy, ivy-green; vigorous, climbing growth; not dependably recurrent.

Gold Spray F, *my*, 1971, *Philippe × Spek's Yellow*; Delforge. Flowers yellow, dbl., full, medium; foliage soft; moderate, bushy growth.

Gold Star HT, *yb*, 1933, *Souv. de Claudius Pernet × Talisman*; Vestal. Bud pointed, orange; flowers golden yellow shaded orange, dbl., large; foliage glossy, bronze, leathery; very vigorous growth. RULED EXTINCT 6/83 ARM.

Gold Strike F, *my*, 1955, *Goldilocks × Pinocchio*; Swim; Armstrong Nursery. Bud urn shaped; flowers lemon-yellow, dbl. (30-35 petals), high-centered, medium (2-2½ in.), borne in rounded clusters; fragrant; foliage leathery; vigorous, bushy, compact growth; a forcing variety for greenhouse use.

Gold Sweetheart Min, *my*, 1984, (WILgosh); *Sunsprite × Rise 'n' Shine*; Williams, J.B.; J.B. Williams & Asso. Flowers deep yellow, dbl. (35 petals), small; slight fragrance; foliage small, medium green, semi-glossy; upright, bushy growth.

Gold Top LCl, *dy*, 1978, Pearce; Limes Rose Nursery. Flowers golden yellow, dbl. (25 petals), full, large (5½ in.); fragrant; foliage large, light matt green; free growth.

Goldbonnet S, *my*, 1973, *(Ann Elizabeth × Allgold) × Golden Showers*; Harkness. Flowers yellow, semi-dbl. (13 petals), large (4 in.); slightly fragrant; foliage large, glossy.

Goldbusch S, *my*, 1954, Kordes. Bud long, pointed; flowers yellow, becoming lighter, semi-dbl., large blooms in clusters (up to 20); foliage leathery, glossy, light green; very vigorous, upright, bushy growth.

Golddigger HT, *dy*, 1963, *Marcelle Gret × Dries Verschuren*; Verschuren, A.; Stassen. Flowers dark saffron-yellow, dbl. (50-55 petals), large; slightly fragrant (spicy); foliage glossy, bronze; upright growth.

Golddust HT, *my*, 1963, *Brandywine × Seedling*; Delforge. Flowers golden yellow; foliage clear green; vigorous growth.

Goldelse HT, *ob*, 1900, *Kaiserin Auguste Viktoria seedling*; Hinner, W. Flowers golden orange.

Golden Altai HSpn (OGR), *ly*, 1943, *R. spinosissima altaica × Harison's Yellow*; Wright, P.H. Flowers cream to pale yellow, single; non-recurrent bloom; very hardy.

Golden Angel Min, *dy*, 1975, *Golden Glow (Brownell) × (Little Darling × Seedling)*; Moore, R.S.; Sequoia Nursery. Bud short, pointed; flowers deep yellow, dbl. (65 petals), small (1 in.); fragrant; foliage matt; bushy, compact growth.

Golden Anniversary HT, *dy*, 1948, *Good News sport*; Mordigan Evergreen Nurs.; C-P. Bud ovoid; flowers yellow, dbl. (50-60 petals), high centered, large (4½-5 in.); very fragrant; foliage leathery; vigorous, upright, bushy growth. RULED EXTINCT 9/82 ARM.

Golden Arctic LCl, *yb*, 1954, *Seedling × Free Gold*; Brownell. Flowers yellow to orange, dbl. (38 petals), large (3½-4 in.); fragrant; growth like a Hybrid Tea, followed by 4-5 ft. canes that bloom the first season.

Golden Bay S, *yb*, 1979, *(Tropicana × Sabine) × Zitronenfalter*; Murray, N. Bud ovoid; flowers deep buff-yellow, dbl. (40 petals), shapely, large (3½ in.); slightly fragrant; foliage large; spreading, bushy growth.

Golden Beauty HT, *ab*, 1937, Van Rossem. Bud very long; flowers orange buff-yellow, stamens golden, semi-dbl., large; foliage clear green, glossy; vigorous, bushy growth.

Golden Beauty Min, *yb*, 1992, (CLEbeau; Golden Girls); *Seedling × Seedling*; Clements, John K.; Heirloom Old Garden Roses, 1990. Flowers gold, edged copper, full (26-40 petals), exhibition, small (0-4 cms.) blooms borne mostly singly; slight fragrance; foliage small, dark green, glossy; few prickles; medium (30 cms.), bushy, spreading growth.

Golden Boy HT, *dy*, 1964, *Golden Masterpiece × Belle Blonde*; McGredy, S., IV; Spek. Flowers deep yellow, dbl. (35 petals), very high-centered, large (5½ in.); foliage long, pointed; moderate growth; a greenhouse variety.

Golden Butterfly HT, *ab*, 1920, *Old Gold seedling*; Therkildsen. Flowers apricot-yellow, shaded carmine, dbl.; fragrant.

Golden California HT, *dy*, 1966, *California sport*; Howard, P.J. Flowers golden, dbl., cupped, large; fragrant; foliage bronze, leathery, glossy; tall, bushy growth.

Golden Cascade LCl, *my*, 1962, *(Capt. Thomas × Joanna Hill) × Lydia*; Morey; J&P. Bud ovoid; flowers chrome-yellow, dbl. (25-30 petals), cupped, large (4½-5 in.); fragrant (fruity); foliage leathery; vigorous (10-12 ft.) growth.

Golden Century Cl Min, *ob*, 1978, *(R. wichuraiana × Floradora) × (Sister Thérèse × Mini-*

ature Seedling); Moore, R.S.; Sequoia Nursery. Bud pointed; flowers cadmium-orange to nasturtium-red, dbl. (35 petals), medium (1½ -2 in.); very fragrant; foliage glossy, leathery; moderate climber.

Golden Chalice HT, *dy*, 1960, *(Starlite × Snow White) × Golden Masterpiece*; Boerner; J&P. Bud ovoid; flowers clear yellow, dbl. (40-45 petals), open, large (4 in.); fragrant; foliage glossy; vigorous, upright growth; a greenhouse variety for cut-flower purposes.

Golden Charm HT, *dy*, 1933, *Talisman sport*; Groshens & Morrison. Flowers deep yellow.

Golden Charm, Climbing Cl HT, *dy*, 1948, Krider Nursery.

Golden Chersonese S, *my*, 1967, (HILgold); *R. ecae × Canary Bird*; Allen, E.F. Flowers yellow, single, small (1½-2 in.) blooms borne singly at each node; fragrant; foliage leaflets 7-9; vigorous growth; early bloom.

Golden Choice HT, *my*, 1967, *My Choice sport*; Bardill Nursery; LeGrice. Flowers lemon-yellow.

Golden City HT, *my*, 1922, *Rayon d'Or × Frau Karl Druschki*; Lippiatt. Bud golden yellow; flowers light buff.

Golden Coach Min, *dy*, 1991, (ZIPgold); *Rise 'n' Shine × Pot O'Gold*; Zipper, Herbert; Magic Moment Miniatures, 1992. Flowers deep yellow, very full (41+ self cleaning petals), small (0-4 cms), blooms borne mostly singly; no fragrance; foliage small, dark green, semi-glossy; few prickles; medium (40 cms), upright, compact growth.

Golden Comet HT, *yb*, 1937, Burbank; Stark Bros. Bud long, pointed; flowers yellow and pink, semi-dbl., open, large; very fragrant; foliage dark, leathery; vigorous growth.

Golden Coronet F, *my*, 1967, *(Lydia × Golden Scepter) × Isobel Harkness*; Morey; Country Garden Nursery. Flowers medium yellow, dbl., high-centered, medium; slightly fragrant; foliage glossy, leathery; vigorous, compact growth.

Golden Crest Cl HT, *my*, 1948, (Gold Crest); Archer. Flowers pure yellow, dbl. large (3-4 in.); fragrant; foliage glossy, dark; good pillar (6 ft.).

Golden Dawn HT, *my*, 1929, *Elegante × Ethel Somerset*; Grant; Hazelwood Bros.; Prior. Bud yellow, flushed pink; flowers medium yellow, dbl. (45 petals), well-formed; very fragrant; low, spreading growth.

Golden Dawn, Climbing Cl HT, *my*, 1937, Knight, G.

Golden Dawn, Climbing Cl HT, *my*, 1935, Armstrong, J.A.

Golden Dawn, Climbing Cl HT, *my*, 1947, LeGrice.

Golden Day HT, *my*, 1931, *Independence Day sport*; Bentley; Harkness. Flowers bright golden yellow, center deeper, larger and fuller; very fragrant; vigorous growth.

Golden Days HT, *dy*, 1982, (RUgolda); *Peer Gynt × Seedling*; deRuiter, G.; Fryer's Nursery, 1980. Flowers deep yellow, dbl. (35 petals), large; slight fragrance; foliage large, medium green, semi-glossy; bushy growth.

Golden Delight F, *my*, 1956, *Goldilocks × Ellinor LeGrice*; LeGrice. Flowers canary-yellow, dbl. (58 petals), large (3in.); fragrant; foliage dark, glossy; dwarf growth.

Golden Diamond HT, *dy*, 1943, Verschuren; L.C. Lovett. Flowers deep yellow, dbl. (30 petals), large; strong stems; foliage leathery, dark; vigorous, upright, compact growth.

Golden Dream HRg (S), *my*, 1932, (Goldener Traum); *Türkes Rugosa Samling × Constance*; Türke; J.C. Schmidt. Bud pointed, streaked red; flowers pure yellow, full, large; very fragrant; very vigorous (6½ ft.) growth; recurrent bloom.

Golden Drop HT, *dy*, 1939, *Mme. Mascuraud × Seedling*; Clark, A. Flowers rich yellow, semi-dbl., small blooms in clusters; tall growth.

Golden Emblem HT, *my*, 1917, *Mme. Mélanie Soupert × Constance*; McGredy. Bud yellow, splashed and shaded red; flowers canary-yellow, dbl., well formed, large; fragrant; foliage dark, glossy, leathery; vigorous growth. GM, NRS, 1915.

Golden Emblem HT, *dy*, 1982, (JACgold); *(Bridal Pink × Dr. A.J. Verhage) × (Golden Sun × South Seas)*; Warriner W.; J&P. Flowers deep yellow, dbl. (20 petals), large; slight fragrance; foliage large, medium green, glossy; upright growth.

Golden Emblem, Climbing Cl HT, *my*, 1927, Armstrong Nursery.

Golden Empire HT, *ob*, 1957, *Orange Everglow × Golden Emblem*; Silva. Flowers orange, dbl.; foliage leathery, glossy.

Golden Fairy Pol, *ly*, 1889, Bennett. Flowers clear buff, yellow and white; dwarf growth.

Golden Fantasie HT, *my*, 1971, (HILgofan; Joan Brickhill®); *Dr. A.J. Verhage × Anniversary*; Byrum; J.H. Hill Co. Flowers yellow, semi-dbl., high-centered, large; very fragrant; foliage large, dark, leathery; vigorous, upright, bushy growth.

Golden Fiction F, *my*, 1958, *Yellow Pinocchio × Moonbeam*; Spek. Flowers yellow; free growth.

Golden Fleece F, *my*, 1955, (Toison d'Or); *Diamond Jubilee* × *Yellow Sweetheart*; Boerner; J&P. Bud ovoid; flowers buff-yellow, dbl. (38 petals), cupped, large (4½ in.), in clusters (to 20); very fragrant; foliage leathery; vigorous, bushy. GM, Bagatelle, 1955.

Golden Frills HT, *my*, 1936, *Feu Joseph Looymans sport*; B&A. Flowers rich golden yellow, dbl., cupped; foliage glossy, wrinkled.

Golden Gardens Min, *my*, 1988, (MORgogard); *(Little Darling* × *Yellow Magic)* × *Gold Badge*; Moore, Ralph S.; Sequoia Nursery, 1989. Bud ovoid; flowers bright, clear medium yellow, reverse slightly lighter, dbl. (28 petals), cupped, informal, medium, borne in sprays of 3-5; no fragrance; foliage medium, medium green, semi-glossy; prickles slender, inclined downward, small, brownish; fruit none; upright, medium growth.

Golden Garnette F, *dy*, 1960, *(Goldilocks seedling* × *Seedling)* × *Tawny Gold*; Boerner; J&P. Bud ovoid; flowers golden yellow, edged lighter, dbl. (33 petals), cupped, large (3-4 in.) blooms in clusters; very fragrant (fruity); foliage leathery, dark, glossy; vigorous, upright, bushy growth.

Golden Gate T (OGR), *w*, 1891, *Safrano* × *Cornelie Koch*; Dingee & Conard. Bud pointed; flowers cream-white, anthers golden yellow, dbl., cupped, globular, very large; fragrant; foliage bright green; vigorous growth.

Golden Gate HT, *my*, 1972, *South Seas* × *King's Ransom*; Warriner; J&P. Bud ovoid; flowers medium yellow, dbl., high-centered, large; slightly fragrant; foliage large, glossy; vigorous, upright, bushy growth.

Golden Gem HT, *my*, 1916, *Lady Hillingdon* × *Harry Kirk*; Towill. Flowers golden yellow.

Golden Giant HT, *dy*, 1961, (KORbi; Fièvre d'Or; Goldrausch); Kordes, R.; A. Dickson; McGredy. Flowers rich golden yellow, dbl. (45 petals), well-formed, large (5 in.); fragrant; foliage dark; vigorous, tall growth. GM, NRS, 1960.

Golden Giant, Climbing Cl HT, *dy*, 1967, Laveena Roses.

Golden Girl Gr, *my*, 1959, (MEIvirgi); *(Joanna Hill* × *Eclipse)* × *Michèle Meilland*; Meilland; C-P. Bud pointed; flowers golden yellow, dbl. (45 petals), high-centered, large (4-4½ in.); fragrant; foliage leathery, light green; upright, vigorous, bushy growth.

Golden Glamour F, *my*, 1951, *Joanna Hill* × *(Mrs. Pierre S. duPont* × *Amelia Earhart)*; Boerner; J&P. Bud pointed; flowers yellow, dbl. (25 petals), high-centered, large; fragrant; foliage glossy; vigorous, upright, bushy growth; a florists' pot plant.

Golden Gleam HT, *my*, 1926, McGredy; Beckwith. Flowers buttercup-yellow, outer petals streaked, dbl. (25 petals); slightly fragrant (fruity); foliage dark.

Golden Glory HT, *dy*, 1931, Dobbie. Flowers deep golden yellow; dbl., large; very fragrant.

Golden Glow HT, *ab*, 1918, *Mme. Edouard Herriot sport*; Chaplin Bros. Flowers apricot, shaded bronzy orange.

Golden Glow LCl, *my*, 1937, *Glenn Dale* × *(Mary Wallace* × *HT)*; Brownell. Flowers yellow, dbl., high-centered, large (3½-5 in.) blooms in clusters; fragrant; foliage leathery, glossy, dark; very vigorous, climbing (20 ft.) growth; non-recurrent bloom.

Golden Halo™ Min, *my*, 1991, (SAVahalo); *Arthur Bell* × *Rainbow's End*; Saville, F. Harmon, 1985; Nor'East Miniature Roses. Bud ovoid, pointed; flowers bright yellow, dbl. (24-26 petals), cupped, medium; slight fragrance; foliage medium, medium green, semi-glossy; upright, bushy growth. AOE, 1991.

Golden Harvest HT, *dy*, 1943, *McGredy's Ivory* × *Seedling*; Mallerin; C-P. Flowers clear yellow, dbl. (35 petals), high-centered, large (4½ in.); fragrant; foliage leathery, glossy, bronze; vigorous growth.

Golden Haze HT, *yb*, 1965, *Peace* × *Golden Rapture*; Verschuren, H.A.M.; J&P. Bud ovoid; flowers light golden yellow, dbl., large; fragrant; foliage glossy; vigorous growth.

Golden Heritage HT, *my*, 1974, *Golden Masterpiece* × *Seedling*; Herholdt, J.A. Flowers canary-yellow, dbl. (25 petals), pointed, large (3½ in.), fragrant (tea); bushy growth.

Golden Hour HT, *ob*, 1952, *Los Angeles* × *California*; Howard, P.J. Bud ovoid; flowers golden yellow, reverse orange, dbl. (45-55 petals), high-centered, large (4-5 in.); very fragrant; foliage leathery, glossy; very vigorous, upright growth.

Golden Ideal HT, *dy*, 1939, *Roselandia* × *Joanna Hill*; Lens. Bud long, pointed; flowers brilliant chrome-yellow, dbl., large; vigorous growth.

Golden Jewel F, *dy*, 1959, (Bijou d'Or; Goldjuwel); *Goldilocks* × *Masquerade seedling*; Tantau, Math. Flowers golden yellow, dbl., large (3 in.) blooms in clusters; fragrant; foliage dark, glossy; vigorous, bushy growth.

Golden Jubilee F, *my*, 1948, *(Mary Wallace* × *Talisman)* × *Mrs. Pierre S. duPont*; Jacobus; B&A. Bud ovoid; flowers golden yellow, becoming buff and chrome, dbl., large (3 in.), in clusters; slightly fragrant; foliage glossy, dark; vigorous, bushy, compact.

Golden Julia HT, *my*, 1992, (RUPgoljul); *Julia's Rose sport*; Rupert, Kim L. Bud long, pointed; flowers medium golden mustard, opening medium golden yellow, fading light yellow with no pink shadings, golden stamen, red stigma, mod. full (18-22 petals), flat, large (7.5-8.75 cms) blooms borne mostly singly, green wood; slight fragrance; foliage medium, medium green, matt; few, yellow prickles; medium (75-90 cms), upright, bushy growth.

Golden King HRg (S), *ly*, 1935, *Dr. Eckener sport*; Beckwith. Flowers pale yellow, semi-dbl., large; very fragrant; slender growth (6-8 ft), not dependably hardy; recurrent.

Golden Lace F, *dy*, 1962, *Goldilocks × (Golden Scepter × Encore)*; Abrams, Von; Peterson & Dering. Bud pointed; flowers deep yellow, dbl. (28 petals), high-centered, large (3 in.) blooms in clusters; fragrant; foliage glossy; vigorous, upright growth.

Golden Leader HT, *ab*, 1961, *Tawny Gold × Seedling*; Leenders, J. Flowers apricot; fragrant.

Golden Leopard F, *my*, 1976, *Golden Slippers seedling × Golden Slippers seedling*; Takatori; Japan Rose Nursery. Bud pointed; flowers daffodil-yellow, dbl. (18-25 petals), high-centered, small (2 in.); fragrant; foliage glossy, leathery; low, compact growth.

Golden Light LCl, *ob*, 1939, Nicolas. Bud pointed; flowers orange-apricot to buff, edged pink, dbl., open, large; strong stems; slightly fragrant; foliage glossy, dark; vigorous, climbing growth.

Golden Lion HSet (OGR), *my*, 1944, *R. setigera hybrid*; Horvath. Flowers clear golden yellow, open, cupped, borne in clusters; foliage light, glossy; height 8-10 ft.; non-recurrent bloom.

Golden Lustre HT, *ab*, 1964, *Kate Smith × Tanya*; Boerner; J&P. Bud ovoid; flowers bronze-apricot overcast yellow, dbl. (60-65 petals), cupped, large (5 in.); fragrant; foliage leathery; moderate growth.

Golden Main HT, *dy*, 1933, (Golden Romance; Golmain; Goldenes Mainz); *Fontanelle × Julien Potin*; Kordes; J&P. Bud golden yellow striped red; flowers golden yellow, dbl., cupped, large; very fragrant; foliage glossy; very vigorous, bushy growth.

Golden Masterpiece HT, *my*, 1954, *Mandalay × Golden Scepter*; Boerner; J&P. Bud long, pointed; flowers golden yellow, dbl. (35 petals), high-centered, very large; fragrant; foliage very glossy; vigorous, upright growth.

Golden Masterpiece, Climbing Cl HT, *my*, 1957, Valdrez.

Golden Medallion HT, *my*, 1981, *Medallion sport*; Permenter; J&P. Bud long, pointed; flowers medium golden yellow, dbl. (40-50 petals), loosely imbricated, very large (7-8 in.); slightly fragrant; foliage large, light; upright growth.

Golden Memories HT, *dy*, 1965, *Golden Rapture sport*; Ravine; Endres Floral Co. Bud long, pointed, canary-yellow tinted coppery; flowers deep canary-yellow, dbl. (28-32 petals), high-centered to open, large (5-6 in.); fragrant (spicy); foliage glossy; vigorous, upright growth.

Golden Mme. Segond Weber HT, *op*, 1923, *Mme. Segond Weber × Primerose*; Soupert & Notting. Flowers salmon, center yellow, full.

Golden Moss M (OGR), *my*, 1932, *Frau Karl Druschki × (Souv. de Claudius Pernet × Blanche Moreau)*; Dot, P.; C-P. Bud globular, peach-yellow, sepals well mossed; flowers tawny yellow, dbl. (37 petals), large blooms in clusters of 3-5; fragrant; foliage almost rugose; vigorous growth; scanty bloom; no repeat.

Golden Ophelia HT, *my*, 1918, *Ophelia seedling*; Cant, B.R. Flowers golden yellow in center, paling slightly on outer petals; foliage glossy; vigorous. GM, NRS, 1918.

Golden Ophelia, Climbing Cl HT, *my*, 1924, Hage; Prior.

Golden Orange Climber LCl, *ob*, 1937, *Mrs. Arthur Curtis James sport*; Brownell. Flowers orange to orange-scarlet, often overlaid golden yellow, semi-dbl. (15 thin, crinkled petals), large (5 in.); vigorous, climbing growth.

Golden Pamela HT, *yb*, 1969, *Wellworth sport*; Wheatley. Bud ovoid; flowers yellow-apricot and pink, dbl., cupped, large; slightly fragrant; foliage large, glossy; vigorous, upright growth.

Golden Peace HT, *my*, 1961, LeGrice. Flowers canary-yellow, dbl. (45 petals), exhibition type, large; fragrant; foliage dark, dull; very vigorous, tall growth.

Golden Pearl HT, *my*, 1967, Warmerdam. Flowers yellow, single, large; slightly fragrant; foliage dark; free growth.

Golden Penny LCl, *yb*, 1981, (COOsyn); *Queen Elizabeth × Scarlet Knight*; Cook, Sylven S. Flowers gold, reverse creamy, dbl. (40+ petals); strong lemon fragrance; foliage medium, medium green, semi-glossy; upright growth (7-8 ft.).

Golden Perfection Pol, *my*, 1937, Leenders, M. Flowers golden yellow, dbl., small; very fragrant; bushy, dwarf growth.

Golden Perfume F, *my*, 1959, *Goldilocks ×
Fashion*; Leenders, J. Flowers orange-yellow
becoming golden yellow, dbl. (50 petals),
large, borne in clusters; fragrant; foliage dark,
glossy, leathery; vigorous, bushy growth.

Golden Perraud HT, *my*, 1946, *Mme. Joseph
Perraud sport*; Lens. Bud long, pointed, well
formed; flowers brilliant golden yellow, dbl.,
large; slightly fragrant; foliage glossy; vigorous growth.

Golden Pheasant F, *ob*, 1951, (Goldfasan);
Prés. Feriér × Dr. Debat; Kordes; Wheatcroft
Bros. Flowers orange and gold, dbl. (40
petals), imbricated, large (4 in.); fragrant;
foliage glossy; low, compact growth.

Golden Phoenix HT, *my*, 1985, (NAKbet);
Bettina sport; Nakashima, T. Flowers yellow.

Golden Picture HT, *yb*, 1967, *Picture seedling
× Marcelle Gret*; Handover, P.&R. Flowers
light yellow tinged pink, medium; slightly
fragrant; foliage leathery; upright growth.

Golden Pirrie HT, *ly*, 1921, *Lady Pirrie sport*;
Dobbie. Flowers yellowish white.

Golden Pixie Min, *my*, 1985, *Yellow Pages ×
Rise 'n' Shine*; Hardgrove, Donald L.; Rose
World Originals. Flowers medium golden
yellow, dbl. (60 petals), medium; slight fragrance; foliage small, medium green, semi-
glossy; vigorous, upright, bushy growth.

Golden Poly Pol, *yb*, 1931, *Angèle Pernet × Orange King*; Pahissa. Flowers pure yellow,
edged carmine, dbl., globular; dwarf growth.

Golden Poly Pol, *my*, 1935, Leenders, M. Bud
yellow with red lines; flowers golden yellow
to yellowish white, semi-dbl., open, large;
slightly fragrant; foliage light, glossy; bushy,
dwarf growth.

Golden Princess S, *yb*, 1984, *Hawkeye Belle ×
(Roundelay × Country Music)*; Buck, Dr. Griffith J.; Iowa State University. Bud ovoid,
pointed; flowers yellow, petals edged deep
pink, dbl. (33 petals), cupped, large blooms
borne 1-5 per cluster; fragrant; foliage medium, olive green, semi-glossy; large, hooked,
tan prickles; upright, bushy growth; hardy;
repeat bloom.

Golden Promise Min, *dy*, 1992, (LAVluv);
June Laver × Potluck Gold; Laver, Keith G.;
Springwood Roses, 1993 Canada. Flowers
deep yellow, full (26-40 petals), small (0-4
cms) blooms borne mostly single; no fragrance; foliage small, dark green, glossy; few
prickles; low (30 cms), bushy growth.

Golden Pyramid LCl, *my*, 1939, Brownell.
Flowers yellow, semi-dbl., large; vigorous
pyramid to 5-6 ft.; free seasonal bloom.

Golden Queen HT, *my*, 1937, *Cross of two
seedlings of Frau Karl Druschki parentage*;

Chambard, C. Bud gold, slightly marked
carmine; flowers golden yellow, dbl., large;
foliage glossy; very vigorous, bushy growth.

Golden Rain F, *my*, 1951, (Goldregen); *Swantje × G. Bentheim*; Tantau. Flowers golden
yellow, semi-dbl. (20 petals), well formed,
large, borne in clusters of 10-15; foliage
glossy; upright, bushy growth.

Golden Rapture HT, *dy*, 1933, (Geheimrat
Duisberg); *Rapture × Julien Potin*; Kordes;
H&S; Dreer, 1934. Bud pointed; flowers
golden yellow, dbl. (40 petals), very large;
fragrant; foliage glossy; vigorous growth.

Golden Rapture, Climbing Cl HT, *dy*, 1941,
Swim; Armstrong Nursery.

Golden Rapture, Climbing Cl HT, *dy*, 1954,
(Climbing Geheimrat Duisberg); Knackfuss.

Golden Rapture No. 5 HT, *my*, *Golden Rapture sport*; Krieter; A.N. Pierson. Bud ovoid;
flowers clear yellow, dbl. (25 petals), high-
centered, large (5 in.); very fragrant; foliage
dark, leathery; vigorous growth; a greenhouse
variety.

Golden Revelry HT, *my*, 1952, *Phyllis Gold ×
Blossom*; McGredy. Flowers golden yellow,
dbl. (21 petals), high pointed; slightly fragrant; foliage glossy, bright green.

Golden Ruffels HT, *my*, 1954, *Orange Ruffels
sport*; Brownell. Bud long, pointed; flowers
golden yellow, dbl., medium; fragrant; upright growth.

Golden Rule HT, *my*, 1918, *Ophelia seedling ×
Sunburst*; Hill, E.G., Co. Flowers clear yellow, dbl.

Golden Salmon Pol, *ob*, 1926, (Goldlachs);
Superb (Pol) sport; deRuiter. Flowers pure
orange, large blooms in huge trusses; vigorous, bushy growth.

Golden Salmon Supérieur Pol, *ob*, 1929,
(Golden Salmon Improved); *Golden Salmon
sport*; deRuiter; Sliedrecht & Co. Flowers
different shades of orange.

Golden Salute HT, *dy*, 1963, *Diamond Jubilee
seedling × Golden Masterpiece*; Boerner; J&P.
Bud ovoid; flowers golden yellow, dbl. (33
petals), cupped, large (5-5½ in.); fragrant;
foliage leathery, glossy; vigorous, moderately
tall growth.

Golden Sam McGredy HT, *yb*, 1935, *Mrs.
Sam McGredy sport*; Lens. Flowers chrome-
yellow, reverse salmon with chrome.

Golden Sástago HT, *dy*, 1938, *Condesa de
Sástago sport*; Dot, P.; C-P. Flowers clear
yellow, dbl., globular, large; fragrant; foliage
soft; vigorous growth.

Golden Scepter HT, *dy*, 1950, (Spek's Yellow);
Golden Rapture × Seedling; Verschuren-
Pechtold; Spek; J&P. Bud pointed; flowers

deep yellow, dbl. (35 petals), high-centered, large (4½ in.); fragrant; foliage leathery, glossy; vigorous, upright.

Golden Scepter, Climbing Cl HT, *dy*, 1956, (Climbing Spek's Yellow); Walters.

Golden Séverine HT, *dy*, 1929, Morse. Flowers deep golden yellow.

Golden Sheen F, *my*, 1966, *Ophelia × Circus*; Swim & Weeks; Carlton Rose Nursery. Bud urn shaped; flowers yellow, edged lighter, dbl., high-centered, borne in clusters; foliage leathery; moderate, upright, bushy growth; for greenhouse use.

Golden Shot F, *dy*, 1973, *Seedling × Allgold*; Martin, J.; Gandy, 1976. Flowers golden yellow, dbl. (24 petals), large (4 in.); slightly fragrant; foliage dark.

Golden Showers® LCl, *my*, 1956, *Charlotte Armstrong × Capt. Thomas*; Lammerts; Germain's. Bud long, pointed; flowers daffodil-yellow, dbl. (27 petals), high-centered to flat, large (4 in.) blooms borne singly and in clusters; fragrant; foliage dark, glossy; vigorous, pillar or climbing (6-10 ft.) growth; recurrent bloom. GM, Portland, 1957; AARS, 1957.

Golden Signora HT, *my*, 1954, *Signora sport*; Lowe. Flowers golden veined orange, dbl. (30 petals), large; fragrant; foliage glossy; vigorous growth.

Golden Slippers F, *yb*, 1961, *Goldilocks × Seedling*; Abrams, Von; Peterson & Dering. Bud pointed; flowers yellow flushed vermilion, center golden yellow, dbl. (23 petals), high-centered, large (3 in.) blooms in clusters; fragrant; foliage leathery, glossy; vigorous, compact, low growth. GM, Portland, 1960; AARS, 1962.

Golden Song Cl Min, *yb*, 1980, *Little Darling × Golden Angel*; Williams, E.D.; Mini-Roses. Bud long, pointed; flowers golden yellow, petals edged pink, dbl. (35 petals), high-centered, flat, blooms borne usually singly; fragrant; foliage small, medium to dark, glossy; long, thin, tan prickles; upright (to about 5 ft.) growth.

Golden Splendor HT, *dy*, 1960, Jones; Hennessey. Bud long, pointed; flowers golden yellow, dbl. (30 petals), high-centered, large (5 in.); foliage glossy; vigorous, tall growth.

Golden Splendour HT, *my*, 1962, *Buccaneer × Golden Sun*; Kordes; Wheatcroft Bros. Flowers clear light yellow, dbl. (40 petals), large; fragrant.

Golden Spray HT, *my*, 1917, Dickson, H. Flowers clear lemon-yellow, huge mass of prominent anthers, semi-dbl., long arching spray. GM, NRS, 1915.

Golden Sprite™ F, *dy*, 1992, (DEVunican); *Golden Fantasie × Excitement*; Marciel, Stanley & Jeanne; DeVor Nursery. Flowers deep yellow, moderately full (15-25 petals), large (7+ cms) blooms borne mostly singly; slight fragrance; foliage medium, dark green, matt; some prickles; medium (197 cms), upright growth.

Golden Star HT, *dy*, 1974, *Whisky Mac sport*; Lowe. Flowers deep yellow, dbl. (32 petals), full, large (4-4½ in.); slightly fragrant; foliage dark; free growth.

Golden State HT, *dy*, 1937, *Souv. de Claudius Pernet × (Charles P. Kilham × Seedling)*; Meilland, F.; C-P, 1938. Flowers golden yellow, dbl., cupped, large; foliage leathery, glossy; vigorous. GM, Bagatelle & Portland, 1937.

Golden Sun HT, *my*, 1957, (Goldene Sonne); *(Walter Bentley × Condesa de Sástago) × Golden Scepter*; Kordes, R. Bud long, pointed; flowers golden yellow, dbl., high-centered, large (5 in.); fragrant; foliage glossy; upright, bushy growth.

Golden Sunburst HT, *yb*, 1967, *Golden Wave sport*; Schneeberg; Carlton Rose Nursery. Bud ovoid; flowers cadmium-orange and saffron-yellow, dbl., large; very fragrant; foliage dark, glossy; vigorous, bushy growth.

Golden Sunset LCl, *my*, 1934, Burbank; Stark Bros. Flowers golden yellow, often tipped orange-red, dbl., cupped, large; long stems; foliage glossy; vigorous growth.

Golden Sunshine HT, *my*, 1964, *Helen Hayes × Golden Masterpiece*; Brownell, H.C.; Brownell. Bud pointed, ovoid, chrome-yellow splashed red; flowers canary-yellow, dbl. (50 petals), high-centered, large (5 in.); very fragrant; vigorous, upright growth.

Golden Surprise F, *my*, 1978, *Woburn Abbey sport*; Hamilton. Flowers medium yellow.

Golden Talisman HT, *my*, 1931, *Talisman sport*; Hill, E.G., Co.; Withdrawn because Mrs. Franklin D. Roosevelt was found to be superior.

Golden Talisman, Climbing Cl HT, *my*, 1935, *Talisman sport*; Elmer's Nursery.

Golden Times HT, *my*, 1970, *Fragrant Cloud × Golden Splendour*; Cocker; Wheatcroft & Sons. Flowers lemon-yellow, dbl. (40 petals), large (4-5 in.); slightly fragrant; foliage glossy.

Golden Treasure, Climbing Cl F, *my*, 1976, Pearson; Burston Nursery.

Golden Tzigane HT, *ob*, 1961, *Tzigane sport*; Gregory. Flowers orange.

Golden Unicorn S, *yb*, 1985, *Paloma Blanca × (Carefree Beauty × Antike)*; Buck, Dr. Griffith J.; Iowa State University, 1984. Flowers yellow, petals edged orange-red, dbl. (28 petals), shallow-cupped, large blooms borne 1-8 per cluster; fragrant; foliage dark olive green, leathery; awl-like, tan prickles; vigorous, upright, bushy, spreading growth; hardy; repeat bloom.

Golden Van Rossem HT, *dy*, 1937, *Mev. G.A. van Rossem sport*; Lens. Flowers chrome yellow.

Golden Vandal HT, *dy*, 1935, *Comtesse Vandal sport*; Lens. Flowers chrome yellow.

Golden Vision LCl, *my*, 1922, *Maréchal Niel × R. gigantea*; Clark, A.; NRS, Victoria. Flowers Marechal Niel yellow, fading nearly white, semi-dbl.; fragrant.

Golden Wedding HT, *my*, 1938, *Souv. de H.A. Verschuren × yellow seedling*; Krebs. Bud pointed, yellow tinted crimson; flowers clear yellow, dbl., large (5 in.); foliage leathery, dark; vigorous growth.

Golden West HT, *my*, 1936, *Duchess of York sport*; Stocking. Bud pointed; flowers golden yellow, semi-dbl., open, large; fragrant; foliage dark, leathery, glossy; vigorous, bushy, spreading growth.

Golden Wings S, *ly*, 1956, *Soeur Thérèse × (R. spinosissima altaica × Ormiston Roy)*; Shepherd; Bosley Nursery. Bud long, pointed; flowers sulphur-yellow, stamens prominent, single (usually 5 petals), large (4-5 in.); slightly fragrant; vigorous, bushy growth; recurrent bloom; very hardy.   GM, ARS (National Gold Medal Certificate), 1958.

Golden Wonder HT, *ab*, 1936, Gunn. Flowers golden apricot suffused pink, globular; fragrant; foliage olive-green; vigorous growth.

Golden Wonder HT, *yb*, 1973, *Miss Ireland × Princess*; Gandy; Morse Roses. Flowers lemon-yellow, edged red, dbl. (36-40 petals), high-centered to cupped, large (4-5 in.); fragrant; foliage dark.

Golden Years® F, *my*, 1988, (HARween); *Sunblest × Amber Queen*; Harkness, R.; R. Harkness & Co., 1990. Bud ovoid; flowers golden yellow, reverse some bronze tint, dbl. (46 petals), cupped, large, borne in sprays of 3-7; slight, fruity fragrance; foliage medium, dark green, semi-glossy; prickles slightly curved, long, thin, greenish-red; fruit none observed; bushy, medium growth.   Hradec Golden Rose, 1989; GM, Orléans, 1990.

Goldendale HT, *my*, 1956, *Annabella sport*; Grillo. Bud long, pointed; flowers golden yellow, dbl. (50 petals), large (5 in.); fragrant.

Goldene Druschki HP (OGR), *my*, 1936, *Frau Karl Druschki × Friedrich Harms*; Lambert, P. Bud pointed; flowers golden yellow, edged lighter turning creamy yellow in hot

weather and full sun, cupped, very large; slightly fragrant; foliage leathery, dark; very vigorous growth.

Goldene Gruss an Aachen F, *ob*, 1935, *Mme. Butterfly × Gloria Mundi*; Kordes.   Bud pointed, red; flowers golden orange, sometimes shaded reddish, dbl., high-centered, very large; fragrant; foliage glossy; bushy growth.

Goldene Johanna Tantau F, *my*, 1945, (Wheatcroft's Golden Polyantha); *Golden Rapture × (Johanna Tantau × Eugénie Lamesch)*; Tantau.   Bud ovoid; flowers clear golden yellow, single, cupped, large (3½ in.), borne in clusters; fragrant; foliage glossy, dark; compact, bushy growth; (28).

Goldener Adler F, *my*, 1965, *Allgold × Seedling*; Verschuren, A.; van Engelen. Bud ovoid; flowers golden yellow, semi-dbl., medium, borne in clusters; foliage light green.

Goldener Olymp® LCl, *dy*, 1984, (KORschnuppe; Olympic Gold); *Seedling × Goldstern*; Kordes, W.; Kordes Sons. Flowers deep yellow, dbl. (20 petals), large; fragrant; foliage large, medium green, matt; upright, bushy (to 7 ft.) growth.

Goldener Reiter F, *my*, 1969, (Golden Rider); *Circus × Golden Giant*; Haenchen; Teschendorff. Flowers golden yellow, dbl. (25 petals), cupped, large; very fragrant; foliage dark; vigorous, upright growth.

Goldenes Herz HT, *dy*, 1975, *Dr. A.J. Verhage × Seedling*; Kordes. Bud ovoid; flowers deep yellow, dbl., cupped, medium; fragrant; foliage glossy, dark, leathery; vigorous, upright, bushy growth.

Goldfinch R, *ly*, 1907, *Helene × Seedling*; Paul. Flowers yellow, aging white, semi-dbl., small blooms in clusters; slightly fragrant; foliage small, wrinkled; vigorous, climbing growth; non-recurrent.

Goldfinger F, *dy*, 1992, (PEAroyal; William David); *(Floribunda seedling × Floribunda Seedling) × (Hybrid Tea Seedling × Climber Seedling)*; Pearce, C.A.; Hewlett-Packard, 1992. Flowers deep yellow, moderately full (15-25 petals), medium (4-7 cms) blooms borne in small clusters; slight fragrance; foliage medium, dark green, glossy; some prickles; low (40 cms), compact growth.

Goldgleam F, *my*, 1966, *Gleaming × Allgold*; LeGrice. Flowers medium yellow, semi-dbl. (18 petals), large (3½-4 in.) blooms in small clusters; very fragrant; foliage dark, glossy; growth moderate.

Goldie F, *my*, 1958, *Goldilocks × Pigmy Gold*; Boerner; J&P. Bud ovoid; flowers golden yellow, edged lighter, dbl. (25-30 petals), large

(4 in.); fragrant; foliage leathery; vigorous, upright, bushy growth; for pot forcing.

Goldilocks F, *my*, 1945, *Seedling × Doubloons*; Boerner; J&P. Flowers deep yellow, fading to cream, dbl. (45 petals), globular, large (3½ in.) blooms in clusters; fragrant; foliage leathery, glossy; vigorous, bushy growth; (28). ARS John Cook Medal, 1947.

Goldilocks, Climbing Cl F, *my*, 1951, Caluya; J&P.

Goldlite™ Gr, *dy*, 1989, (DEVsolear); *Seedling × Excitement*; Marciel, Stanley G.; DeVor Nursery, 1987. Bud urn-shaped; flowers canary yellow, reverse buttercup yellow, aging no discoloration, dbl. (29 imbricated petals), medium, borne usually singly; slight, musk fragrance; foliage medium, dark green, semiglossy; prickles declining, red; fruit round, average, tangerine orange; upright, tall growth.

Goldmarie F, *dy*, 1958, *Masquerade × Golden Main*; Kordes, R. Flowers orange-gold, semidbl., very large, cluster; very fragrant; foliage glossy; very vigorous, upright, bushy growth. RULED EXTINCT 6/84 ARM.

Goldmarie F, *dy*, 1984, (KORfalt; Goldmarie 82); *((Arthur Bell × Zorina) × (Honeymoon × Dr. A.J. Verhage)) × (Seedling × Sunsprite)*; Kordes, W.; Kordes Sons. Flowers deep yellow, red on reverse of outer petal, dbl. (35 petals), large; slight fragrance; foliage medium, medium green, glossy; bushy growth.

Goldmoss F, *my*, 1972, *Rumba × Moss hybrid*; Moore, R.S.; Sequoia Nursery. Bud long, pointed; flowers clear yellow, dbl., medium; very fragrant; foliage light, leathery; vigorous, dwarf, bushy growth.

Goldpoint Min, *my*, 1984, (JACpo); *Rise 'n' Shine × (Fabergé × Precilla)*; Warriner, W.; J&P. Flowers medium yellow, dbl. (20 petals), small; slight fragrance; foliage small, light green, matt; upright, bushy growth.

Goldquelle S, *my*, 1965, Tantau, Math. Bud ovoid; flowers pure golden yellow, dbl., large, borne in clusters on strong stems; slightly fragrant; foliage leathery; upright (4 ft.) growth; recurrent bloom.

Goldschatz F, *my*, 1964, (Golden Treasure); Tantau, Math. Bud pointed; flowers golden yellow, dbl., large blooms in clusters (up to 30); foliage dark, glossy; bushy, upright growth.

Goldstar HT, *dy*, 1983, (CANdide; Gold Star; Goldina; Point du Jour®); *Yellow Pages × Dr. A.J. Verhage*; Cants of Colchester, 1984. Flowers deep yellow, dbl. (35 petals), medium; light fragrance; foliage small, light green, matt; upright growth.   GM, The Hague, 1984.

Goldstern® K (S), *my*, 1966, (TANtern; Gold Star); Tantau, Math. Bud long, pointed; flowers golden yellow, large blooms in clusters; foliage glossy; vigorous, bushy (7-8 ft.) growth; recurrent bloom.

Goldstück F, *my*, 1961, *Goldilocks × Seedling*; Verschuren, A.; van Engelen. Flowers lemon-yellow, dbl. (40-55 petals), borne in clusters; foliage glossy, dark; vigorous, upright growth.

Goldstück S, *my*, 1963, Tantau, Math. Bud long, pointed; flowers golden yellow, large, borne in clusters; very fragrant; vigorous, upright, bushy growth; abundant, non-recurrent bloom.

Goldtopas® F, *my*, 1963, (KORgo; KORtossgo; Gold Topaz; Goldtopaz); Kordes, R. Bud ovoid; flowers amber-yellow, dbl., cupped, large (3½ in.) blooms in clusters (up to 10); foliage glossy; vigorous, bushy. ADR, 1963.

Goldy HT, *dy*, 1981, (KORbeen); *Berolina × Seedling*; Kordes, W.; Kordes Sons. Flowers deep yellow, dbl. (35 petals), large; fragrant; foliage medium, medium green, semi-glossy; upright, bushy growth.

Golestan HT, *or*, 1975, (MEIsadina); *(Tropicana × Tropicana) × ((Seedling × Rouge Meilland) × Independence)*; Meilland, M.L.; Meilland. Bud tapering; flowers vermilion, dbl. (25 petals), high-centered, small; foliage glossy, dark; vigorous, upright growth.

Gondul F, *mr*, 1969, *Lichterloh × Lumina*; Lundstad. Flowers cardinal-red, semi-dbl. (18 petals), open, medium, borne in clusters; foliage dark, glossy; vigorous growth.

Gone Fishin' Min, *ob*, 1992, (SAVafish); *Fairlane × Zorina*; Saville, F. Harmon; Nor'East Miniature Roses, 1993. Flowers bright orange, dbl. (28-35 petals), cupped, medium (3 cms) blooms borne singly and in sprays of 4-10; slight fragrance; foliage medium, dark green, glossy, very disease resistant; bushy, medium growth.

Gonsoli Gaelano HP (OGR), *mp*, 1874, Pernet. Flowers satiny rose.

Good Cheer HT, *dp*, 1937, *Talisman × Templar*; Amling Co. Bud pointed; flowers cerise, dbl., open; long, strong stems; very vigorous growth.

Good Companion F, *mr*, 1961, Dickson, A. Flowers rich red, dbl. (30 petals), flat, large, borne in trusses; fragrant; foliage dark; vigorous growth.

Good Day Sunshine Min, *dy*, 1992, (TALgoo); *Party Girl × Elina*; Taylor, Pete & Kay; Taylor's Roses, 1993. Flowers bright yellow, reverse same, very full (41+ petals), HT form, medium (4-7 cms) blooms borne mostly singly; slight fragrance; foliage medium, medium green, semi-glossy; few prickles; medium (60 cms), upright, bushy, spreading growth.

Good Life F, *or*, 1970, *Elizabeth of Glamis × John Church*; McGredy, S., IV; McGredy. Flowers orange-red, dbl. (30 petals), HT form, medium (2 in.); slightly fragrant; free growth.

Good Morning HT, *w*, 1935, *Premier Supreme sport*; Kaucher; Hill Crest Greenhouses. Flowers white, reverse faintly tinged pink, dbl., very large, borne on long, strong stems; foliage leathery; very vigorous, bushy growth.

Good Morning America™ Min, *my*, 1991, (SAVagood); *Fantasia × Rainbow's End*; Saville, F. Harmon, 1984; Nor'East Miniature Roses. Bud ovoid, urn-shaped; flowers medium yellow, very dbl. (55-60 petals), urn-shaped, exhibition, large blooms; fruity fragrance; foliage medium, dark green, semi-glossy; upright, bushy, tall growth. AOE, 1991.

Good Neighbor HT, *ob*, 1958, *Fred Howard × Seedling*; Warriner; H&S. Flowers burnt-orange, reverse golden, dbl., large; very fragrant; foliage dark; vigorous, upright growth.

Good News HT, *pb*, 1940, (Bonne Nouvelle); *(Radiance × Souv. de Claudius Pernet) × (Joanna Hill × Comtesse Vandal)*; Meilland, F.; C-P. Flowers silvery pink, center tinged apricot, dbl. (50 petals), globular, large (5-6 in.); fragrant; vigorous, bushy growth.

Good Times HT, *pb*, 1977, *Pink Peace × Peace*; Williams, J.B.; Hershey Nursery. Bud ovoid, pointed; flowers ivory to light pink with deep pink edging, dbl. (56 petals), cupped, large (5-5½ in.); slightly fragrant; foliage large, glossy; compact, upright growth.

Gooiland HT, *mp*, 1922, *Sunburst seedling × Red-Letter Day*; Van Rossem. Flowers clear rose-pink, reverse dark coral-rose, dbl.; slightly fragrant.

Gooiland Beauty HT, *ab*, 1924, *Sunburst × Golden Emblem*; Van Rossem; Van Rossem; Prior. Flowers clear golden orange, semi-dbl., open, very large; slightly fragrant; foliage dark, leathery; vigorous, bushy growth. GM, Bagatelle, 1925.

Gooiland Glory HT, *or*, 1925, *Mme. Edouard Herriot × Gen. MacArthur*; Van Rossem; Van Rossem; Prior. Flowers cherry-red shaded coral-red, semi-dbl.; slightly fragrant.

Gopika F, *op*, 1969, *Marlena × Open pollination*; Singh; Gopalaswamiengar. Flowers light salmon-pink, dbl., globular, medium; slightly fragrant; foliage glossy; vigorous, bushy growth.

Gordon Drake F, *dp*, 1956, *Eutin sport*; Williams, G.A. Flowers cerise-pink, dbl., borne in large clusters; very vigorous growth.

Gordon Eddie HT, *ab*, 1949, *Royal Visit × Cynthia Brooke*; Eddie. Flowers deep apricot, edged lighter, dbl. (40 petals), high-centered, very large; fragrant; foliage leathery, glossy; very vigorous, bushy growth. GM, NRS, 1950.

Gordon's College F, *op*, 1992, (COCjabby); *Abbeyfield Rose × Roddy McMillan*; James Cocker & Sons, Ltd. Flowers coral salmon, full (26-40 petals), large (7+ cms.) blooms borne in large clusters; fragrant; foliage large, dark green, glossy, purplish when young; some prickles; medium, upright growth.

Gorgeous HT, *dy*, 1915, Dickson, H. Flowers deep orange-yellow, veined copper, dbl., well-formed, large; fragrant; foliage rich, green, soft; bushy, open growth. GM, NRS, 1913.

Gorgeous HT, *mp*, 1956, *Pink Delight sport*; Franc; Carlton Rose Nursery. Flowers rose-pink, semi-dbl. (18-20 petals), high-centered, large (5 in.); fragrant; foliage leathery; vigorous growth.

Gotenhafen F, *mp*, 1940, *Mev. Nathalie Nypels × Kardinal*; Tantau. Flowers pure bright rose, semi-dbl. (12-15 petals), medium; vigorous, well branched growth.

Gotha HT, *ab*, 1932, (Souv. de H.A. Verschuren × Sunset) × Mev. G.A. van Rossem; Krause. Flowers brownish yellow passing to apricot; fragrant.

Gottfried Keller HFt (OGR), *ab*, 1894, ((Mme. Bérard × R. foetida persiana) × (Pierre Notting × Mme. Bérard)) × R. foetida persiana; Müller, F. Flowers apricot-yellow.

Goudvlinder HT, *ab*, 1926, (Golden Butterfly); *Lady Hillingdon × Souv. de Claudius Pernet*; Van Rossem. Flowers orange-yellow, semi-dbl. (12 petals), small; foliage glossy, brownish red; vigorous, bushy growth.

Gourmet Popcorn Min, *w*, 1986, (WEOpop); *Popcorn sport*; Desamero, Luis; Wee Ones Miniature Roses, 1986; Weeks Roses, 1987. Flowers pure white, semi-dbl. (12-20 petals), medium in large sprays; slight fragrance; foliage large, dark green, glossy; upright, bushy growth, abundant bloom.

Governador Braga da Cruz HT, *ly*, 1954, *Peace × Seedling*; Moreira; da Silva. Flowers light yellow; very vigorous.

Governor Alfred E. Smith HT, *yb*, 1933, *Souv. de F. Bohé seedling × Seedling*; Vve. Denoyel; J&P. Flowers blend of buff, terracotta, gold and salmon, dbl., high-centered, large; foliage glossy; vigorous growth.

Governor Mark Hatfield Gr, *dr*, 1962, *Carrousel × Charles Mallerin*; Abrams, Von; Peterson & Dering. Bud pointed; flowers rich red, dbl. (40 petals), high-centered, large; slightly fragrant; foliage leathery; vigorous, upright growth.

Governor Phillip Cl HT, *mr*, 1939, *Ophelia seedling × Black Boy*; Fitzhardinge; Hazlewood Bros. Flowers ruby-red, flushed darker, very dbl., open, large; long stems; fragrant; foliage leathery, glossy, dark, bronze; vigorous, climbing growth.

Governor Rosellini Gr, *mr*, 1958, *Baby Château × Tiffany*; Lindquist; Howard Rose Co. Flowers rose-red, dbl. (30 petals), high-centered, large (3-4 in.); fragrant (raspberry); foliage dark, leathery; vigorous, upright growth.

Governor's Lady Gloria HT, *m*, 1983, (AROglor); *Sweet Afton × Blue Nile*; Christensen, J.E.; Armstrong Nursery. Flowers pastel mauve, dbl. (35 petals), well-formed, large; very fragrant; foliage large, medium green, matt; upright, bushy growth.

Goya F, *w*, 1976, *Mildred Reynolds × Arthur Bell*; Bees. Flowers cream, dbl. (30 petals), high-centered, large (5 in.); slightly fragrant; foliage dark; vigorous

G. P. & J. Baker F, *op*, 1984, (HARrango); *(Bobby Dazzler × Seedling) × Marion Harkness*; Harkness, R. Flowers salmon orange, reverse lighter, dbl. (36 petals), flat, medium blooms in clusters of 3-11; slight fragrance; foliage dark, glossy; many prickles; medium, bushy growth.

Graaff-Reinet HT, *ab*, 1987, (KORmate); *Seedling × Seedling*; Kordes, W., Sohne; Ludwigs Roses, 1988. Flowers apricot with orange on petal margin, dbl. (36 petals), large, borne in sprays of 1-3; moderate fragrance; foliage dull, medium green; prickles concave, reddish-brown; compact, medium, well branched, free flowering growth.

Grace HRg (S), 1923, *R. rugosa × R. Xharisonii*; Saunders; Central Exp. Farm. Flowers amber, center apricot, very dbl., open; fragrant; foliage wrinkled; bushy (5-6 ft.) growth. RULED EXTINCT ?.

Grace Abounding F, *w*, 1968, *Pink Parfait × Penelope*; Harkness. Flowers ivory, semi-dbl., blooms in trusses; fragrant (musky); foliage glossy.

Grace Darling T (OGR), *w*, 1884, Bennett. Flowers cream-white shaded pink, dbl., globular, large; vigorous.

Grace de Monaco® HT, *lp*, 1956, (MEImit); *Peace × Michèle Meilland*; Meilland, F.; URS. Flowers light rose-pink, dbl., well-formed, large; very fragrant; foliage leathery; vigorous, bushy growth.

Grace Donnelly HT, *op*, 1991, (HORlexstrip); *Alexander × (Southampton × ((New Penny × Little White Pet) × Stars 'n' Stripes))*; Horner, Colin P., 1984; Battersby Roses, 1992. Bud ovoid; flowers pink, orange, yellow striped, dbl., urn-shaped, loose, medium blooms borne singly or in sprays of 5-9; slight, fruity fragrance; foliage medium, medium green, semi-glossy; bushy, tall growth.

Grace Haslam HT, *ob*, *Scarlet Glory × Mrs. Sam McGredy*; Fryer's Nursery. Flowers orange to carmine.

Grace Kimmins F, *mr*, 1973, *Dainty Maid × Red Dandy*; Gobbee. Flowers crimson, dbl. (28 petals), large (3 in.); foliage glossy; vigorous, bushy growth.

Grace Molyneux HT, *ab*, 1909, Dickson, A. Flowers creamy apricot, center flesh, dbl.; slightly fragrant.

Grace Moore HT, *mr*, 1948, (Paul Höltge); *Kardinal × Crimson Glory*; Kordes; C-P. Bud ovoid; flowers crimson-red, dbl., cupped, large; foliage leathery, dark olive-green; vigorous, bushy growth.

Grace Noll Crowell HT, *pb*, 1929, Vestal. Flowers rose-pink, base slightly shaded cream, dbl., high-centered, large; fragrant; foliage soft, light; vigorous, bushy growth.

Grace Note S, *pb*, 1984, *(Tiki × Marigold) × Freckle Face*; Buck, Dr. Griffith J.; Iowa State University. Bud ovoid, pointed; flowers medium pink, freckled red, dbl. (38 petals), imbricated, large blooms borne 3-8 per cluster; moderate fragrance; foliage large, leathery, dark; awl-like, tan prickles; vigorous, erect, bushy growth; hardy; repeat bloom.

Grace Seward Min, *w*, 1991, (TINgrace); *Watercolor × Seedling*; Bennett, Dee; Tiny Petals Nursery. Bud ovoid; flowers white, single (5 petals), medium; moderate, damask fragrance; foliage medium, medium green, semi-glossy; bushy, tall growth.

Grace Wayman Cl HT, *mp*, 1936, Wayman. Flowers pink, dbl., very large; very fragrant; foliage leathery; vigorous, climbing (10 ft.) growth.

Graceful S, *ly*, 1966, *Paul's Lemon Pillar × Marcelle Gret*; Smith, W.H. Flowers yellow fading to cream, full, well formed, large (4 in.); slightly fragrant; foliage glossy; vigorous, bushy growth.

Graceland HT, *my*, 1988, (JACel); *New Day × Seedling*; Warriner, William; Bear Creek Gardens, 1989. Flowers medium yellow, aging lighter at margins, dbl. (30-35 petals), cupped, loose, medium, borne usually singly;

no fragrance; foliage medium, dark green, matt, smooth; prickles medium, reddish-green; upright growth. GM, The Hague, 1988.

Gracie Fields HT, *dy*, 1937, Letts. Flowers vivid buttercup-yellow; fragrant (sweetbriar); foliage glossy; vigorous growth.

Gracilis M (OGR), *dp*, Prévost, prior to 1846. Flowers deep pink, full, globular, well mossed, large; foliage large; vigorous growth; seasonal bloom; good as a standard.

Gracilis Bslt (OGR), *mr*, 1830, Wood. Flowers cherry shaded lilac-blush, semi-dbl., cupped; foliage dark; large, long prickles; vigorous, branching growth.

Gracilis C (OGR), Flowers pale rosy pink, edged lilac-blush, full, compact; branching, low growing. Possibly the same as Centifolia Minima, or at least similar to it.

Gracilis HSet (OGR), *mp*, 1841, *R. setigera hybrid*; Prince Nursery. Flowers pink to rose, very dbl., borne in clusters.

Graciosa HT, *w*, 1957, *Branca × Peace*; Moreira; da Silva. Flowers white edged rose, well formed; very vigorous growth.

Gracious Lady HT, *pb*, 1965, *(Peace seedling × Gail Borden) × Dorothy Peach seedling*; Robinson, H.; J&P. Bud ovoid; flowers peach-pink, base apricot, dbl., high-centered, large; fragrant; foliage glossy, dark; vigorous, bushy growth.

Graf Silva Tarouca HT, *dp*, 1916, *Étoile de France × Lady Mary Fitzwilliam*; Lambert, P. Flowers carmine-red, full, very large; very fragrant; very vigorous growth.

Graf Zeppelin R, *dp*, 1909, *Non Plus Ultra sport*; Boehm. Flowers light red to bright pink, semi-dbl., medium, borne in large clusters; vigorous (6-8 ft.) growth; very free bloom.

Gräfin Minnie Schaffgotsch HT, *w*, 1928, *Clio × Hybrid Tea Seedling*; Mühle. Flowers cream-white, center pink, very dbl.; slightly fragrant.

Grafton Pillar R, *mr*, 1958, *Second generation Skinner's Rambler × Gruss an Aachen*; Risley. Bud globular; flowers bright red, dbl., small, borne in clusters; slightly fragrant; foliage wrinkled; moderate growth; free, recurrent bloom.

Graham HT, *dr*, 1961, *Eclipse × Seedling*; Kriloff; Cramphorn's Nursery. Flowers deep crimson-scarlet, dbl. (35-40 petals), high-centered, large; long stems; fragrant; foliage glossy; vigorous, upright growth.

Graham Thomas™ S, *dy*, 1983, (AUSmas); *Seedling × (Charles Austin × Iceberg seedling)*; Austin, David; David Austin Roses. Flowers

rich deep yellow, dbl. (35 petals), cupped, medium; very fragrant; foliage small, dark, glossy; bushy; recurrent.

Gran Parada F, *my*, 1967, (Grande Parade); *Gold Dot × (Queen Elizabeth × Zambra)*; Dot, S.; Rosas Dot. Flowers yellow, becoming reddish, dbl. (25 petals), open, medium; foliage glossy; vigorous, upright, compact growth.

Granada HT, 1955, *Opera × The Doctor*; Delforge. Flowers deep red, borne in clusters.

Granada HT, *rb*, 1963, (Donatella); *Tiffany × Cavalcade*; Lindquist; Howard Rose Co. Bud urn shaped; flowers blend of rose, nasturtium-red and lemon-yellow, dbl. (18-25 petals), high-centered, large (4-5 in.); fragrant; foliage leathery, crinkled; vigorous, upright growth. AARS, 1964; James Alexander Gamble Rose Fragrance Medal, 1968.

Granada, Climbing Cl HT, *rb*, 1964, Swim & Weeks; Comley.

Granadina Min, *mr*, 1956, (Grenadine); *Granate × Coralín*; Dot, P.; Kordes. Flowers oxblood-red, dbl. (30 petals), globular, small; foliage dark; low, upright growth.

Granat HT, *dr*, 1937, *Barcelona × Château de Clos Vougeot*; Krause. Flowers blackish red, well formed; very vigorous growth.

Granate Min, *dr*, 1947, *Merveille des Rouges × Pompon de Paris*; Dot, P. Flowers velvety oxblood-red, often streaked white, small; almost no prickles; height 6-8 in.

Grand Amour HT, *mr*, 1956, (Côte Rôtie); Delbard-Chabert. Flowers bright red, large; fragrant.

Grand Canary HT, *my*, 1934, *Token sport*; Lowman; U.S. Cut Flower Co. Flowers yellow, dbl., high-centered; foliage glossy; vigorous, compact growth.

Grand Canyon S, *dy*, 1951, *Herrenhausen × Golden Rapture*; Whisler; Germain's. Bud long, pointed, chrome-yellow; flowers yellow, salmon and copper, turning to crimson, open, medium; slightly fragrant; foliage glossy, bronze; very vigorous (6 ft.), arching growth; recurrent bloom.

Grandchild Min, *mp*, 1986, *Unnamed Cécile Brunner seedling × Self*; Garelja, Anita, 1987. Flowers clear, medium pink, dbl. (40 petals), HT-type, small, borne 3-15 per cluster; moderate, sweet fragrance; foliage long, narrow, dense, reddish to medium green; hooked, gray-brown prickles; bushy, shrub-like, tall growth.

Grand Cramoisi G (OGR), *dr*, 1818, Vibert. Flowers crimson; profuse bloom.

Grand-Duc Adolphe de Luxembourg HT, *rb*, 1892, *Triomphe de la Terre des Roses* × *Mme. Loeben Sels*; Soupert & Notting. Flowers brick-red, reverse carmine, dbl., large; weak stems; fragrant; moderate growth.

Grand Duche HT, *m*, 1973, (GODrache); *American Heritage* × *(Seedling* × *Kölner Karneval)*; Godin. Bud ovoid; flowers mauve, dbl. (25 petals), cupped, medium (3-3½ in.); slightly fragrant; foliage dark; vigorous growth.

Grande Duchesse Charlotte HT, *mr*, 1942, Ketten Bros.; C-P. Bud long, pointed; flowers tomato-red, shaded geranium-red, dbl. (25 petals), cactus form, large (5-5½ in.); slightly fragrant; foliage glossy, dark; vigorous, bushy growth. GM, Rome, 1938 & Portland, 1941; AARS, 1943.

Grandee Min, *dr*, 1984, (MAChomai); *Regensberg* × *Ko's Yellow*; McGredy, Sam; Oregon Min. Roses. Flowers dark red, gold stamens, semi-dbl., medium; fragrant; foliage medium, medium green, semi-glossy; upright growth.

Grande Première HT, *yb*, 1959, *Comtesse Vandal* × *Mme. Henri Guillot*; Delbard-Chabert. Bud long, pointed; flowers yellow edged pink, dbl. (38 petals), large; fragrant; foliage bright green, glossy; upright, bushy growth.

Grande Renoncule C (OGR), *mp*, Flowers dull pink, shading to violet, full, medium.

Grande Rouge F, *dr*, 1973, *Seedling* × *Seedling*; Tantau; Ahrens & Sieberz. Bud ovoid; flowers dark red, dbl., medium; slightly fragrant; foliage soft; upright, bushy growth.

Grandeur HT, *dp*, 1954, *Joyance sport*; Grillo. Bud long, pointed; flowers cerise-red, dbl. (70 petals), high-centered, large (4 in.); fragrant; foliage leathery; very vigorous, upright growth.

Grande Walzer® HT, *rb*, 1980, Kordes, W.; Barni-Pistoia, Rose. Bud ovoid; flowers deep orange-red, reverse deep yellow, dbl. (35 petals), cupped blooms borne singly; little fragrance; foliage rather small, light green, glossy; curved, light yellow prickles; upright growth.

Grandezza HT, *mp*, 1962, *Monique* × *Radar*; Herholdt, J.A.; Herholdt's Nursery. Bud spiral, pointed; flowers peach-blossom-pink, dbl., well formed, large; moderate, bushy growth.

Grand Gala HT, *rb*, 1954, *Peace* × *Independence*; Meilland, F.; URS, 1954 & C-P, 1956. Bud globular; flowers rose-red, reverse white suffused pink, dbl. (45-60 petals), high-centered, large (4½-5 in.); slightly fragrant; foliage leathery; vigorous, bushy growth.

Grand Gala, Climbing Cl HT, *rb*, 1961, Yamate; Kakujitsuen.

Grand Hotel® LCl, *mr*, 1972, (MACtel; Grandhotel); McGredy. Flowers scarlet, HT form, large (4 in.); foliage dark; repeat bloom. ADR, 1977.

Grandioso HT, *mr*, 1961, *(Happiness* × *Satisfaction)* × *(Poinsettia* × *Happiness)*; Verbeek. Flowers cherry-red, dbl. (30-40 petals), large (5 in.); fragrant; foliage dark.

Grandissima G (OGR), *m*, (Louis Philippe); Prior to 1848. Flowers rosy crimson, sometimes purplish, very large and full, compact; moderate, branching growth.

Grand Lady HT, *mp*, 1968, *Ma Perkins* × *Peace*; Patterson; Patterson Roses. Bud ovoid; flowers pink, center lighter, dbl., high-centered, large; fragrant; foliage leathery; vigorous, upright, bushy growth.

Grand Marshall™ HT, *mr*, 1989, (AROfuto; City of Warwick); *Futura* × *Olympiad*; Christensen, Jack; Michigan Bulb Co., 1989. Bud ovoid, pointed; flowers medium red, dbl. (35 petals), high-centered, large, borne usually singly; slight fragrance; foliage medium, medium green, semi-glossy; prickles hooked, medium, red to brown; upright, bushy, medium growth.

Grandma's Pink S, *mp*, 1991, (MORbouquet); *Shakespeare Festival* × *Marchioness of Londonderry*; Moore, Ralph S.; Sequoia Nursery. Flowers medium pink, very full, medium blooms borne in small clusters; no fragrance; foliage medium, medium green, matt; medium, upright, bushy growth.

Grandmaster HMsk (S), *ab*, 1954, *Sangerhausen* × *Sunmist*; Kordes; Morse. Bud long, pointed; flowers apricot shaded lemon and pink, semi-dbl. (10 petals), large blooms in clusters; fragrant; foliage light green; bushy growth; recurrent bloom; (28). GM, NRS, 1951.

Grand Masterpiece HT, *mr*, 1978, (JACpie); *Seedling* × *Tonight*; Warriner, W.; J&P. Bud ovoid, pointed; flowers medium red, high-centered, large (5 in.); slightly fragrant; tall, upright.

Grand'mère Jenny HT, *yb*, 1950, (Grem); *Peace* × *(Julien Potin* × *Sensation)*; Meilland, F.; URS, 1950; C-P, 1955. Flowers apricot-yellow, edged and suffused pink, dbl. (30 petals), high-centered, large (4-4½ in.); fragrant; foliage dark, glossy; vigorous growth. GM, NRS, 1950 & Rome, 1955.

Grand'mère Jenny, Climbing Cl HT, *yb*, 1958, (Gremsar; Grimpant Grand'mère Jenny); Meilland, F.; URS.

Grand Mogul HT, *w*, 1965, *Sultane* × *Chic Parisien*; Delbard-Chabert; Cuthbert. Flowers creamy white, dbl. (33 petals), high-centered, large; fragrant; growth moderate.

Grand Nord® HT, *w*, 1986, (DELgrord; Great Nord; Great North); *((Queen Elizabeth* × *Provence)* × *(Virgo* × *Carina))* × *((Voeux de Bonheur* × *Virgo)* × *(Virgo* × *Peace))*; Delbard, 1975. Flowers white, dbl. (28 petals), high-centered, large; slightly fragrant; vigorous, bushy growth. GM, Paris, 1970 & Rome, 1973.

Grand Occasion HT, *pb*, 1970, *Comtesse Vandal* × *Mme. Henri Guillot*; Delbard; Laxton & Bunyard Nursery. Flowers rosy coral shaded yellow, edged carmine, dbl. (30 petals), full, medium (3 in.); very fragrant; foliage glossy, light; vigorous growth.

Grand Opening Min, *rb*, 1991, *Poker Chip* × *Zinger*; Gruenbauer, Richard, 1984; Flowers 'n' Friends Miniature Roses. Bud ovoid; flowers orange-red showing yellow eye, red reverse, ages pale red, eye turns white, dbl. (35 petals), high-centered, medium; moderate, fruity fragrance; foliage medium, dark green, semi-glossy; upright, medium growth.

Grand Opera HT, *pb*, 1964, *Masquerade* × *Peace*; Schwartz, E.W.; Wyant. Bud long, pointed; flowers cream edged pink, becoming pink, dbl. (40 petals), high-centered, large (4-5 in.); fragrant; foliage leathery; vigorous, bushy growth.

Grandpa's Delight F, *ob*, 1984, *Living Fire* × *Seedling*; Pawsey, Roger; Rearsby Roses. Flowers orange-red, yellow center and stamens, semi-dbl., medium; slight fragrance; foliage medium, medium green, glossy; bushy growth.

Grand-Père Lottin R, *op*, 1918, *Lady Godiva* × *Mrs. W.H. Cutbush*; Lottin. Flowers salmony flesh-pink, center brighter, very dbl., borne in clusters.

Grand Prix® HT, *op*, 1968, (DELtuf; DELprima®); *(Chic Parisien* × *(Grande Premiere* × *(Sultane* × *Mme. Joseph Perraud))*; Delbard-Chabert. Flowers coral-pink shaded ochre, semi-dbl., large; slightly fragrant; foliage glossy, leathery; vigorous, upright, bushy growth. GM, Belgium, 1968.

Grand Prize HT, *rb*, 1935, *Red Radiance sport*; Kistler. Flower petals red, white and spotted, dbl., cupped, very large; very fragrant; foliage leathery; very vigorous growth.

Grand Romance HT, *mp*, 1990, (BRIgran); *Lady* × *x Wini Edmunds*; Bridges, Dennis A., 1991; Bridges Roses. Bud ovoid; flowers medium pink, reverse slightly lighter, aging slightly lighter, very dbl. (50 petals), urn-shaped, medium, borne singly; moderate fragrance; foliage medium, dark green, semi-glossy; upright, medium growth.

Grand Siècle® HT, *pb*, 1986, (DELegran; Great Century); *((Queen Elizabeth* × *Provence)* × *(Michèle Meilland* × *Bayadère))* × *((Voeux de Bonheur* × *MEImet)* × *(Peace* × *Dr. Debat))*; Delbard, 1987. Flowers creamy pink blend, dbl. (33 petals), cupped, well-formed, large; light fragrance; foliage large; vigorous, bushy, branching growth.

Grand Slam HT, *mr*, 1963, *Charlotte Armstrong* × *Montezuma*; Armstrong, D.L. & Swim; Armstrong Nursery. Bud urn-shaped; flowers cherry to rose-red, dbl. (28 petals), high-centered to cupped, large (4 in.); slightly fragrant; foliage leathery, dark, semi-glossy; vigorous, upright, spreading growth.

Grange Briar Sp (OGR), *lp*, Selected strain of *R. canina* once used as an understock.

Grange Colombe HT, *w*, 1912, *Mme. Caroline Testout* × *Lady Ashtown*; Guillot, P. Bud pointed; flowers cream-white, center yellow, dbl., cupped, large; fragrant; vigorous growth.

Grannie's Rose S, *my*, Flowers clear pink, semi-dbl., borne in clusters of 5-7; very fragrant; free, non-recurrent bloom. An old variety taken to eastern Canada by early settlers; real name lost. Kills back somewhat but survives Manitoba winters without protection.

Gratia HT, *w*, 1934, *Seedling* × *Pius XI*; Leenders, M. Bud pointed; flowers creamy white, semi-dbl., high-centered, large; fragrant; foliage leathery, dark; vigorous growth.

Gratitude HT, *rb*, 1960, *Impeccable* × *Incendie*; Delbard-Chabert. Bud ovoid; flowers reddish orange, dbl. (25-35 petals), medium (3-3½ in.); slightly fragrant; foliage leathery, dark, glossy; vigorous, upright, bushy growth.

Gravin D'Alcantara HT, *dr*, 1985, *Montezuma* × *Forever Yours*; Rijksstation Voor Sierplantenteelt, 1982. Flowers dark red, dbl. (28 petals), well-formed, cupped, large blooms borne 1-7 per cluster; slight fragrance; foliage matt, dark; red prickles; upright growth.

Grazia HT, *op*, 1941, *Julien Potin* × *Mme. G. Forest-Colcombet*; Giacomasso. Flowers salmon-pink, center darker, very large; long stems; foliage bright green.

Graziella F, *ob*, 1960, *Feu Follet* × *Seedling*; Gaujard, R.; G. Truffaut. Bud globular; flowers orange, dbl., open, medium, borne in clusters; slightly fragrant; foliage glossy, light green; vigorous, bushy growth.

Great Day Min, *dy*, 1982, (MINbco); *(Little Darling × Gold Coin) × (Little Darling × Gold Coin)*; Williams, E.D.; Mini-Roses. Bud long, pointed; flowers deep yellow, dbl. (35 petals), well-formed, small; fragrant; foliage small, light green, glossy; bushy.

Greater Hastings HT, *mp*, 1957, Francis. Flowers pink.

Great Expectations HT, *yb*, 1988, (LANican); *Rosenella × Cassandra*; Sealand Nursery. Flowers light pink, reverse light yellow, aging fading slightly, dbl. (55 petals), high-centered, well shaped, large, borne usually singly; moderate fragrance; foliage medium, medium green, semi-glossy, clean; prickles long, pointed, medium, red; upright growth.

Greatheart HT, *op*, 1921, *Mrs. Walter Easlea sport*; Rosenbluth. Flowers pale flesh, shaded salmon, center deeper, dbl.; fragrant.

Great Maiden's Blush A (OGR), *w*, *(R. alba incarnata; R. incarnata; R. carnea; R. rubicans; R. alba rubicunda; R. alba rubicanda plena*; Cuisse de Nymphe; Cuisse de Nymphe Emue; La Royale; La Seduisante; La Virginale; Maiden's Blush); Cultivated prior to 1738). Flowers white, tinged pink, dbl.

Great News F, *m*, 1973, *Rose Gaujard × City of Hereford*; LeGrice. Flowers plum-purple, reverse silver, dbl. (33 petals), large (4 in.); very fragrant; foliage large, olive-green; moderate growth.

Great News F, *m*, 1973, *Rose Gaujard × City of Hereford*; LeGrice. Flowers plum-purple, reverse silver, dbl. (33 petals), full, large (4 in.); very fragrant; foliage large, olive-green; moderate growth.

Great Scott HT, *mp*, 1991, *Cleo sport*; Ballin, Don & Paula; Edmunds' Roses, 1992. Flowers medium pink, very full (over 40 petals), large blooms; foliage large, medium green, matt; slightly pubescent peduncles, light green with some red coloration on thorns, large thorns, hooked slightly and angled down; upright (120 cms), bushy growth.

Great Venture HT, *yb*, 1970, *Daily Sketch × Suspense*; Dawson, G.; Brundrett. Bud long, pointed; flowers orange-yellow, flushed pink, dbl., medium; very fragrant; foliage large, leathery; vigorous, upright growth.

Great Western HBour (OGR), *m*, 1840, Laffay. Flowers purplish maroon, dbl., large; vigorous growth; blooms mostly in early summer.

Green Bubbles Min, *w*, 1978, Lyon. Bud ovoid; flowers light green, semi-dbl. (12 petals), small (1 in.); slightly fragrant; foliage tiny; very compact, bushy growth.

Green Diamond Min, 1975, *Polyantha Seedling × Sheri Anne*; Moore, R.S.; Sequoia Nursery. Bud pointed, dusty pink; flowers soft green, dbl. (25 petals), cupped, very small ($\frac{1}{2}$ in.); foliage small, leathery; upright, bushy growth.

Green Fire F, *dy*, 1958, *Goldilocks × Seedling*; Swim; Armstrong Nursery. Bud ovoid, pointed; flowers yellow, semi-dbl. (13 petals), flat, large (3 in.) blooms in clusters; slightly fragrant; foliage semi-glossy; vigorous, bushy growth.

Green Ice Min, *w*, 1971, *(R. wichuraiana × Floradora) × Jet Trail*; Moore, R.S.; Sequoia Nursery. Bud pointed; flowers white to soft green, dbl., small; foliage small, glossy, leathery; vigorous, dwarf, bushy growth.

Greenmantle E (OGR), *rb*, 1895, Penzance. Flowers bright rosy red, white eye, golden stamens, single; foliage richly fragrant; very vigorous, tall growth.

Green Rose Ch (OGR), *(R. chinensis viridiflora; R. viridiflora)*; Cultivated prior to 1845. Flowers green, often touched with bronze, dbl., with narrow leaf-like petals, $1\frac{1}{2}$-2 in. blooms borne singly and in clusters; medium, upright growth; recurrent; (14).

Greensleeves F, 1980, (HARlenten); *(Rudolph Timm × Arthur Bell) × ((Pascali × Elizabeth of Glamis) × (Sabine × Violette Dot))*; Harkness. Bud pointed; flowers chartreuse-green, semi-dbl. (15 petals), flat, large; foliage dark; vigorous, upright growth.

Green Snake® S, *w*, 1985, (LENwich; Serpent Vert); *R. arvensis × R. wichuraiana*; Lens, Louis, 1987. Flowers pure white, single (5 petals), small blooms in clusters of 3-24; foliage small, spoon-shaped; hooked, light brownish-green prickles; non-recurrent bloom; groundcover.

Greer Garson HT, *pb*, 1943, Vve. Denoyel; J&P. Bud pointed; flowers begonia-rose, dbl. (35 petals), high-centered, large (5 in.); slightly fragrant; foliage leathery, dark; vigorous, tall, bushy growth.

Greet Koster Pol, *op*, 1933, *Margo Koster sport*; Koster, D.A. Flowers deep pink, shaded salmon.

Grégor Mendel F, *op*, 1955, *Pinocchio seedling*; Maarse, G. Flowers coral-pink shaded yellow and carmine, dbl., well shaped, borne in large clusters; vigorous growth.

Grenadier HT, *mr*, 1930, Dickson, A. Flowers brilliant currant-red shaded scarlet, dbl., cupped; slightly fragrant; foliage rich green, leathery, glossy; vigorous, bushy growth.

Grenoble HT, *mr*, 1927, (Ville de Grenoble); *Capt. F. Bald × Mme. Van de Voorde*; Mallerin;

C-P, 1931. Flowers clear scarlet, dbl. (30-40 petals), high-centered, large (3½ in.); slightly fragrant (spicy); foliage thick; very vigorous growth.

Grenoble, Climbing Cl HT, *mr*, 1939, Western Rose Co.

Greta Kluis Pol, *mr*, 1916, *Echo sport*; Kluis & Koning. Flowers carmine-red.

Greta Kluis Superior Pol, *mr*, 1928, *Tausendschön sport*; Kluis. Flowers deep carmine-red.

Grete Bermbach HT, *pb*, 1925, *Mrs. Aaron Ward* × *Pharisäer*; Leenders Bros. Flowers silvery flesh, center rose, sometimes shaded yellow orange to white, dbl.; fragrant.

Gretel Greul HT, *mr*, 1939, *Rote Rapture sport*; Greul. Similar color but more profuse bloom.

Grethe Poulsen Pol, *dp*, 1928, *Ellen Poulsen* × *Mme. Laurette Messimy*; Poulsen, S. Flowers light cherry-red, base yellow, semi-dbl.; dwarf, well branched growth; early bloom.

Grevinde Rose Danneskjold Samsöe HT, *dr*, 1914, Poulsen, D. Bud dark velvety red; flowers scarlet.

Grevinde Sylvia Knuth R, *w*, 1913, Poulsen, D. Bud yellow; flowers white, center yellow, small, borne in large clusters.

Grey Dawn F, *m*, 1975, *Brownie* × *News*; LeGrice. Flowers gray, reverse flushed pink and gold, dbl. (45 petals), large (3-4 in.); fragrant; foliage glossy; bushy growth.

Grey Pearl HT, *m*, 1945, (The Mouse); *(Mrs. Charles Lamplough* × *Seedling)* × *(Sir David Davis* × *Southport)*; McGredy; J&P. Bud ovoid; flowers lavender-gray, shaded olive and tan, dbl. (43 petals), high-centered, large (4-4½ in.); fragrant; foliage glossy; vigorous growth.

Grey Pearl, Climbing Cl HT, *m*, 1951, Caluya.

Grillodale HT, *lp*, 1926, *Mme. Butterfly sport*; Grillo. Flowers light pink, center deeper, full (50 petals), large (4½ in.); fragrant; foliage dark.

Grimm LCl, *pb*, 1932, (Hiawatha × Altmarker) × (Mme. Leon Pain × Marquise de Sinéty); Lambert, P. Flowers apple-blossom-pink, center white, stamens golden, single, edges fluted, large blooms in clusters of 9-30; vigorous growth; non-recurrent bloom.

Grootendorst Supreme HRg (S), *dr*, 1936, *F.J. Grootendorst sport*; Grootendorst, F.J. Flowers deeper crimson-red.

Gros Choux d'Hollande C (OGR), *lp*, (Great Cabbage of Holland). Flowers soft rose-pink, dbl.; very fragrant; vigorous.

Gros Provins Panaché G (OGR), *m*, Flowers violet-purple streaked white, full.

Grossherzog Ernst Ludwig Cl HT, *mp*, 1888, (Red Marechal Niel); Müller, F. Flowers silvery carmine, very dbl.; very fragrant.

Grossherzogin Feodora von Sachsen HT, *w*, 1914, *Frau Karl Druschki* × *Kaiserin Auguste Viktoria*; Kiese. Flowers creamy white, base deep yellow.

Grumpy Pol, *mp*, 1956, (Burkhardt); *Parentage unknown*; deRuiter; Gregory & Willicher Baumschulen. Flowers pink, dbl., small blooms in long trusses.

Gruppenkönigin F, *pb*, 1935, *Grüss an Aachen* × *Mme. Edouard Herriot*; Kordes, H. Flowers deep bicolor pink, dbl., very large; foliage light, leathery; vigorous, bushy growth.

Gruss an Aachen F, *lp*, 1909, *Frau Karl Druschki* × *Franz Deegen*; Geduldig. Bud orange-red and yellow; flowers flesh-pink fading to creamy white, dbl., large (3 in.); slightly fragrant; foliage rich green, leathery; dwarf growth; (21).

Gruss an Aachen, Climbing Cl F, *lp*, 1937, Kordes.

Gruss an Bayern® F, *mr*, 1971, (KORmun; Baveria); *Messestadt Hannover* × *Hamburg*; Kordes, R.; Kordes. Flowers blood-red, semi-dbl., globular, medium; slightly fragrant; foliage dark, leathery; vigorous, upright growth. ADR, 1973.

Gruss an Berlin HT, *mr*, 1963, (Greetings); Kordes, R. Bud ovoid; flowers pure red, dbl. (40 petals), high-centered, large (5½ in.); slightly fragrant; foliage dark, glossy; vigorous, upright, bushy growth.

Gruss an Coburg HT, *ab*, 1927, *Alice Kaempff* × *Souv. de Claudius Pernet*; Felberg-Leclerc. Flowers apricot-yellow, reverse coppery pink, globular; very fragrant; foliage bronze; vigorous growth.

Gruss an Dresden HT, *mr*, 1913, *Princesse de Bearn seedling*; Türke; Hoyer & Klemm. Flowers fiery red.

Gruss an Freundorf R, *dr*, 1913, *R. wichuraiana hybrid* × *Crimson Rambler*; Praskac; Teschendorff. Flowers dark velvety crimson, center whitish, semi-dbl., stamens bright yellow, large clusters, vigorous, climbing.

Gruss an Hannover LCl, *op*, 1938, Lahmann. Flowers orange-pink, dbl., large; vigorous, upright (10-13 ft.) growth.

Gruss an Koblenz LCl, *mr*, 1963, Kordes, R. Flowers bright scarlet, 20 petals, large (3 in.) blooms in clusters (up to 10); slightly fragrant; vigorous; recurrent bloom.

Gruss an Stuttgart F, *mr*, 1976, (Carina × Seedling) × Sans Souci; Hetzel. Bud ovoid; flowers velvety red, dbl., medium; slightly fragrant; vigorous, bushy growth.

Gruss an Teplitz B (OGR), *mr*, 1897, (Virginia R. Coxe); *((Sir Joseph Paxton × Fellenberg) × Papa Gontier) × Gloire des Rosomanes*; Geschwind; P. Lambert. Bud small, ovoid; flowers light crimson, edges sometimes marked dark garnet, dbl. (33 petals), short, weak stems; very fragrant (spicy); foliage dark(young growth bronze-red); vigorous (6 ft.), bushy growth; recurrent bloom; good for hedges; (28).

Gruss an Teplitz, Climbing Cl HT, *mr*, 1911, (Virginia R. Coxe, Climbing); Storrs & Harrison Co.

Gruss an Weimar HP (OGR), *pb*, 1919, *Frau Karl Druschki × Lyon Rose*; Kiese. Flowers pink on yellowish ground.

Gruss an Zabern R, *w*, 1904, *Euphrosine × Mme. Ocker Ferencz*; Lambert, P. Flowers white.

Grusz an Steinfurth F, *my*, 1961, *Goldilocks × Masquerade*; Leenders, J. Flowers yellow, dbl. (21 petals), open, cupped, borne in large clusters (to 15); moderate growth.

Guadalajara HT, *my*, 1985, (MACdeepo); *New Day × Yellow Bird*; McGredy, Sam; Roses by Fred Edmunds, 1984. Flowers medium yellow, dbl. (24 petals), high-centered, exhibition, large blooms borne singly; fragrant; foliage large, medium green, semi-glossy; large, deltoid, red to brown prickles; fruit never observed; medium, upright growth.

Guardsman HT, *or*, 1937, *Seedling × Shot Silk*; Archer. Flowers bright scarlet, base yellow, dbl., large; slightly fragrant; foliage glossy; vigorous, compact growth.

Guernsey Gold Min, *dy*, 1992, (TRObguern); *Rise 'n' Shine × Seedling*; Robinson, Thomas; Thomas Robinson Ltd., 1990. Flowers golden yellow, full (26-40 petals), urn-shaped, medium (4-7 cms) blooms borne in small clusters; slight fragrance; foliage small, medium green, semi-glossy; some prickles; low (30 cms), upright, bushy growth.

Guernsey Love Min, *dr*, 1986, (TROBlove); *Dollie B. × Seedling*; Robinson, Thomas, 1990. Flowers dark red, dbl. (35 petals), cupped, small blooms in sprays of 4-5; fruity fragrance; foliage small, dark, glossy; thin, red prickles, curving downward; fruit orange-red, globular, medium; upright, bushy growth.

Guerreiro Cl F, *dr*, *Seedling × Alain*; Moreira; da Silva. Flowers dark red.

Guglielmo Marconi HT, *w*, 1934, *Ophelia × Elisabeth Faurax*; Giacomasso. Flowers almost white, tinted flesh.

Guiding Spirit Min, *dp*, 1988, (HARwolave); *(Blue Moon × Seedling) × Little Prince*; Harkness, Jack; R. Harkness & Co., 1989. Bud ovoid; flowers deep pink, reverse lighter, dbl. (22 fluted petals), flat, medium, borne in sprays of 3-9; slight fragrance; foliage small, dark green, semi-glossy; prickles needle-like, very small; low, bushy growth.

Guillaume Kaempff HT, *dr*, 1931, *Hadley × Admiral Ward*; Felberg-Leclerc. Flowers dark crimson-red, edged blackish, dbl., large; very fragrant; foliage thick; vigorous growth.

Guinea Gold HT, *ab*, 1945, *Joanna Hill × Golden Rapture*; Hill, J.H., Co. Bud long, pointed, buff-yellow; flowers apricot-yellow, dbl., open; strong stems; foliage dark, leathery; vigorous, upright, much branched growth; a florists' variety, not distributed for outdoor use.

Guinée Cl HT, *dr*, 1938, *Souv. de Claudius Denoyel × Ami Quinard*; Mallerin; A. Meilland & C-P. Bud pointed; flowers blackish garnet, sometimes mottled scarlet, dbl., large; very fragrant; foliage leathery; height 6½-9 ft.

Guinevere HT, *mp*, 1967, *Red Dandy × Peace*; Harkness. Flowers pink, dbl. (40 petals), large (4½ in.); slightly fragrant; foliage glossy. GM, Baden-Baden.

Guinguette F, *pb*, 1958, *Alain × Feu de Joie*; Gaujard, R.; Hémeray-Aubert. Flowers pink edged darker, well formed, cupped; vigorous growth.

Guirlande Fleurie LCl, *mr*, 1968, *Valenciennes × Paul's Scarlet Climber*; Robichon; Ilgenfritz Nursery. Bud ovoid; flowers bright red, semi-dbl., cupped, large, borne in clusters; slightly fragrant; foliage leathery; very vigorous, climbing growth.

Guiseppe Motta HT, 1936, Heizmann, E. Flowers flesh-pink, reverse red and yellow, semi-dbl., large; very fragrant; vigorous growth.

Guitare® F, *ob*, 1963, (GAegul; GAegui); *Vendome × Golden Slippers*; Gaujard. Bud ovoid; flowers gold and orange-red blend, dbl., medium; very fragrant; foliage light green, leathery; vigorous, bushy growth. GM, Bagatelle, 1966.

Gulab-E-Pal HT, *m*, 1985, *Festival Beauty × (Scarlet Knight × Festival Beauty)*; Hardikar, Dr. M.N. Flowers mauve, blended with yellow, dbl. (70 petals), high-centered, blooms borne singly; fragrant; foliage medium, light green; brown prickles; upright growth.

Guldtop HSpn (OGR), *dy*, *R. Spinosissima seedling*; An unregistered deep golden yellow seedling of *R.spinosissima*, used as a parent of Aicha.

Gulf Breeze Min, *pb*, 1991, (TALgul); *Baby Katie × Poker Chip*; Taylor, Pete & Kay; Taylor's Roses, 1992. Flowers creamy getting darker pink toward edges, reverse same, yellow base, very full (41+ petals), medium (4-7 cms) blooms borne mostly singly; slight fragrance; foliage medium, medium green, semi-glossy; some prickles; upright, medium (35 cms), bushy growth.

Gulliver's Glow S, *mr*, 1954, *Hiawatha × (R. maximowicziana pilosa × Tausendschön)*; Gulliver; Shenandoah Nursery. Flowers bright red, dbl., small, borne in very large clusters; thornless; bushy growth; very hardy.

Gulnare HT, *my*, 1918, Poulsen, D. Flowers golden yellow.

Gumdrop Min, *dr*, 1981, (JACgum); *(San Fernando × Bridal Pink) × (Fire Princess × Mary DeVor)*; Warriner, W.A.; J&P. Bud fat, pointed; flowers dark red, (25 petals), borne 3-12 per cluster; foliage small, semi-glossy; spreading growth.

Gundy F, *dp*, 1966, *Korona mutation*; Schloen, P.; Ellesmere Nursery. Bud ovoid; flowers deep rose-pink, semi-dbl., cupped, borne in clusters; slightly fragrant; foliage dark; vigorous, upright growth.

Gunsei Cl F, *pb*, 1986, *Seedling × Summer Snow*; Kikuchi, R. Flowers white flushed pink on fringe, dbl. (13-15 petals), cupped, borne large number in clusters; slight fragrance; foliage 7 leaflet, green; no prickles; vigorous, upright growth.

Gunston Hall HT, *mr*, 1929, *Seedling × Hoosier Beauty*; U.S. Dept. of Agric.; C-P. Flowers scarlet-crimson.

Gurney Benham HT, *my*, 1935, *Lady Forteviot sport*; Cant, B.R. Flowers buttercup-yellow, dbl., cupped, large; foliage glossy, bronze; vigorous, bushy growth.

Gurney Hill HT, *mr*, 1924, Hill, E.G., Co. Flowers pure red, full; fragrant.

Gussie Min, *pb*, 1979, *Seedling × Seedling*; Lorenzen, Frederick. Bud ovoid; flowers medium red, reverse pale pink and silver, very dbl. (90 petals), high-centered blooms borne singly; slight fragrance; foliage green, leathery; few prickles; bushy, dwarf growth.

Gustav Frahm F, *mr*, 1959, *Fanal × Ama*; Kordes; Timm. Flowers crimson-scarlet, dbl. (25 petals), flat, large (3 in.) blooms in large clusters; slightly fragrant; foliage light, glossy; vigorous, upright growth.

Gustav Grünerwald HT, *pb*, 1903, *Safrano × Mme. Caroline Testout*; Lambert, P. Flowers carmine-pink, center yellow; (28).

Gustave Piganeau HP (OGR), *mr*, 1889, Pernet-Ducher. Flowers bright carmine, full, cupped, very large; growth moderate.

Guy Fawkes F, *yb*, 1975, *My Choice × Masquerade*; Cadle's Roses. Flowers yellow center, reverse shading scarlet, semi-dbl. (15 petals), full, large (3½ in.); very fragrant; foliage glossy.

Guy Laroche HT, *rb*, 1986, (DELricos; Château de Versailles; Gorgeous George; La Tour d'Argent); *Seedling × (Michèle Meilland × Carla)*; Delbard, G.; Armstrong Roses, 1985. Flowers brilliant red, silver reverse, dbl. (30 petals), high-centered, exhibition, large blooms borne usually singly; slight fragrance; foliage medium, medium green, matt; upright, bushy growth.

Guy-Guy F, *ab*, 1966, *(Circus × Circus) × (Circus × Circus)*; Fankhauser. Flowers apricot and pink, edged crimson, dbl., small; fragrant; foliage dark, glossy, leathery; low, compact growth.

Guyscliffe F, *op*, 1984, (LINdliffe); Lindner, Richard; Ludwigs Roses Ltd. Flowers orange-salmon, semi-dbl. (12 petals), cupped, medium blooms borne 3-5 per cluster; strong fragrance; foliage light green; light brown prickles; tall, densely branched growth.

Gwen Marie F, *rb*, 1964, *Dainty Bess seedling*; Robins. Flowers dark red, center light cream, semi-dbl., open, large; very fragrant; foliage soft; tall growth.

Gwen Nash Cl HT, *pb*, 1920, *Rosy Morn × Seedling*; Clark, A.; NRS, New South Wales. Flowers rich pink, center white, semi-dbl., cupped, large; slightly fragrant; foliage glaucous, wrinkled; vigorous, climbing growth.

Gwendoline Collins HT, *mr*, 1937, Clark, A.; NRS Victoria. Flowers cerise shaded cherry, dbl., globular, large; vigorous, bushy growth.

G. W. Peart HT, *mr*, 1948, *Guinée seedling × Rouge Mallerin*; Toogood. Bud ovoid; flowers red, very dbl., medium; foliage leathery, dark; moderate, bushy growth.

Gwyneth Pol, *ly*, 1923, *(Trier × Rayon d'Or) sport × (Gottfried Keller × Entente Cordiale) sport*; Woosman; Easlea. Flowers pale yellow, tinted lemon, changing to nearly white, semi-dbl., open, borne in clusters; fragrant (musk); foliage light, leathery; bushy growth; (21).

Gwyneth HT, *ly*, 1928, *Willowmere × Mrs. Wemyss Quin*; Chaplin Bros. Flowers canary-yellow, without shading.

Gwyneth Jones HT, *op*, 1925, McGredy. Bud pointed; flowers brilliant carmine-orange, semi-dbl., open; slightly fragrant; foliage light, leathery; vigorous, bushy growth. GM, NRS, 1925.

Gwynne Carr HT, *lp*, 1924, Dickson, A. Flowers silvery pink shaded lilac-rose, dbl.

Gwynne Carr, Climbing Cl HT, *lp*, 1934, Easlea.

Gyldenorange F, *ob*, 1952, *Poulsen's Yellow ×
Seedling*; Poulsen, S.; Poulsen. Flowers gold-
en orange, fades to light yellow, dbl., large;
no fragrance; foliage medium, medium
green, semi-glossy; medium growth.

Gympie F, *pb*, 1953, *Yvonne Rabier × Tip-Top*;
Ulrick. Flowers white and pink, very dbl.,
borne in clusters; fragrant; foliage light
green; vigorous, bushy growth.

Gympie Beauty F, *dr*, 1962, Dunstan; Langbecker. Flowers deep red, borne in clusters;
good growth.

Gypsy HT, *or*, 1972, *((Happiness × Chrysler Imperial) × (El Capitan) × Comanche*; Swim &
Weeks; C-P. Bud ovoid; flowers fiery orange-
red, dbl., large; slightly fragrant; foliage large,
glossy, leathery; vigorous, upright, bushy
growth. AARS, 1973.

Gypsy The name appears to have been used for
several roses: HP, (Laxton, 1885); Pol, (Lille,
1898); HT, (Beckwith, 1930); HT, (Van
Rossem, 1931).

Gypsy Fire Min, *or*, 1981, (MORglo); *(R.
wichuraiana × Carolyn Dean) × Fire Princess*;
Moore, R.S.; Moore Min. Roses. Flowers
orange-red, semi-dbl., small blooms in clusters; no fragrance; foliage small, medium
green, semi-glossy to glossy; upright, bushy.

Gypsy Jewel Min, *dp*, 1975, *Little Darling ×
Little Buckaroo*; Moore, R.S.; Park Seed Co.
Flowers deep rose-pink, dbl. (50 petals), high-
centered, small (1½ in.); foliage dark, leathery; vigorous growth.

Gypsy Moth F, *op*, 1968, Tantau, Math. Flowers salmon, dbl. (35 petals), high-centered,
medium blooms in clusters; foliage glossy.

Gypsy Queen R, *mr*, 1929, *Crimson Rambler ×
Seedling*; Moore, R.S. Flowers crimson, dbl.,
small, borne in clusters; vigorous, climbing
growth; resembles Crimson Rambler.

Gypsy's Wine Cup F, *mr*, 1968, *Highlight ×
Seedling*; Austin, D. Flowers deep crimson,
borne in trusses; slightly fragrant; foliage
dark; low, bushy growth.

Gyrene S, *mr*, 1987, *Arctic Glow × ((Pink Hat ×
R. arkansana) × R. arkansana)*; James, John;
Historical Roses, 1987. Flowers bright, medium red, dbl. (15-25 petals), large; moderate
fragrance; foliage medium, medium green,
matt, disease resistant; upright, bushy,
branching, vigorous, hardy growth; repeat
bloom.

Haaksbergen F, *my*, 1961, *Mrs. Pierre S. duPont
× King Boreas*; Buisman. Flowers bright yellow, semi-dbl., medium, borne in clusters;
foliage dark; moderate growth.

Habanera S, *dr*, 1976, *(Vera Dalton × Dornröschen) × ((World's Fair × Floradora) × Apple-

jack)*; Buck; Iowa State University. Bud
ovoid, pointed; flowers dark cardinal-red
edged lighter, dbl. (33 petals), shallow-
cupped, large (4-4½ in.); slightly fragrant;
foliage leathery; upright, bushy growth; repeat bloom.

Hackeburg R, *pb*, 1912, Kiese. Flowers soft
lilac-pink, center white, borne in clusters;
vigorous, climbing growth.

Hadden's Variety S, *m*, 1948, *A chance seedling
similar to R. willmottiae*; Hilling. Flowers rosy
purple, single, borne several together; foliage
small, gray-green; non-recurrent bloom.

Hadley HT, *mr*, 1914, *(Liberty × Richmond) ×
Gen. MacArthur*; Montgomery Co.; A.N. Pierson. Flowers rich crimson, dbl., well-formed,
very large; very fragrant; foliage rich green;
vigorous growth.

Hadley, Climbing Cl HT, *mr*, 1927, Teschendorff.

Hadley Elatior HT, *mr*, 1927, *Hadley sport*;
Teschendorff; More vigor.

Hagoromo LCl, *op*, 1970, *Aztec seedling × New
Dawn seedling*; Suzuki; Keisie Rose Nursery.
Bud ovoid; flowers silvery coral-pink, dbl.,
high-centered, large; fragrant; foliage dark,
leathery; vigorous, climbing growth; free, intermittent bloom.

Haidee S, *pb*, 1953, *R. laxa × R. spinosissima
seedling*; Skinner. Flowers clear pink, center
cream, dbl., cupped, large; foliage small,
dark; wood red, sometimes very prickly; fruit
large, dark red; height 6 ft.; non-recurrent
bloom.

Haiku™ F, *my*, 1987, (AROyefel); *Bridal Pink
× Sunspray*; Christensen, Jack & Carruth,
Tom; Armstrong Roses, 1986. Flowers medium yellow, dbl. (38 petals), high-centered,
medium, borne usually singly or in sprays of
2-3; slight fragrance; foliage medium, dark
green, glossy; normal, light green to tan
prickles; no fruit; upright, bushy, medium
growth.

Haïsha HT, *yb*, 1947, *Peace × Fantastique*; Meilland, F. Flowers gold, edges suffused carmine, dbl. (60 petals), large (6 in.); very
fragrant; foliage leathery, glossy, dark; upright growth.

Hakkoda HT, *pb*, 1983, *Lady × x Izayoi*; Kodoya, Y.; Kogura Rose Nursery, 1986. Flowers white, pink petal edges, dbl. (40 petals),
high-centered, large; very fragrant; foliage
medium green, semi-glossy; broad prickles,
curved downward; bushy growth.

Hakuun F, *w*, 1962, (White Cloud); *Seedling ×
(Pinocchio × Pinocchio)*; Poulsen, N.D.; Poulsen. Bud small; flowers creamy white, semi-
dbl. (15 petals), patio, medium (2 in.); slightly

fragrant; foliage light green; low, compact, bushy growth.

Halali F, *dp*, 1956, *Marchenland* × *Peace*; Tantau, M. Flowers deep pink, semi-dbl., large blooms in clusters; foliage leathery, dense; vigorous (5-6 ft.), spreading growth.

Half Time HT, *rb*, 1976, *((Fandango* × *Roundelay)* × *(Happiness* × *Tiffany))* × *Peace*; Weeks; Weeks Roses. Bud pointed; flowers cherry-red, reverse yellow, dbl. (40 petals), large (3½ -4 in.); fragrant (tea); foliage dark; upright.

Halka HT, *lp*, 1987, Red Queen × *Peace*; Bracegirdle, D.T., 1988. Flowers white blush pink, reverse white-silver, dbl. (30 petals), high-centered, exhibition, large, borne in sprays of 1-5; moderate, damask fragrance; foliage medium, medium green, glossy; straight, medium, red prickles; upright, medium growth.

Hall of Flowers Min, *my*, 1991, (MORmint); *Avandel* × *Gold Badge*; Moore, Ralph S., 1983; Sequoia Nursery. Bud pointed; flowers lemon yellow, similar reverse, aging slightly lighter, dbl., high-centered, medium blooms borne singly; slight fragrance; foliage medium, medium green, semi-glossy; upright, bushy, medium growth.

Halley's Comet F, *mr*, 1986, *Tip Top sport*; Rearsby Roses. Flowers medium red, dbl. (20 petals), medium; slight fragrance; foliage medium, medium green, semi-glossy.

Hallmark HT, *mr*, 1966, *Independence* × *Chrysler Imperial*; Morey; J&P. Bud ovoid; flowers medium red, dbl. (28 petals), cupped, large; fragrant; foliage glossy.

Halloween HT, *yb*, 1962, *(Peace* × *Fred Howard)* × *Seedling*; Howard, A.P.; Great Western Rose Co. Flowers deep yellow, tipped scarlet, dbl. (65 petals), large; very fragrant; foliage glossy, dark, leathery; vigorous, upright growth.

Halo HT, *w*, 1956, *Lady Sylvia* × *(Virgo* × *White Briarcliff)*; Lens; J&P. Bud ovoid; seafoam-green; flowers white, dbl. (25 petals), high-centered, large (4½-5 in.); fragrant; foliage leathery; vigorous, upright growth; a florists' variety, not distributed for outdoor use.

Halo Dolly Min, *pb*, 1992, (MORwateye); *Anytime* × *Seedling (Anytime* × *Angel Face)*; Moore, Ralph S.; Sequoia Nursery, 1993. Flowers bicolor, reddish outside, pink inside with reddish lavender at base of each petal, similar to Harkness Hulthemia hybrids, semi-dbl. (6-14 petals), small (0-4 cms) blooms borne in small clusters; no fragrance; foliage medium, medium green, semi-glossy; few prickles; medium (30-45 cms), upright, bushy, rounded growth.

Halo Star Min, *ob*, 1992, (MORanyface); *Seedling (Anytime* × *Angel Face)* × *Seedling (Anytime* × *Angel Face)*; Moore, Ralph S.; Sequoia Nursery, 1993. Flowers reddish on outside, orange to pink on inside, reddish lavender at base, single (5 petals), small (0-4 cms) blooms; no fragrance; foliage small, medium green, matt; medium (35-40 cms), upright, bushy growth.

Hamburg S, *dr*, 1935, *Eva* × *Daily Mail Scented Rose*; Kordes. Bud pointed; flowers glowing crimson, semi-dbl., very large blooms in clusters; slightly fragrant; foliage large, leathery, glossy; vigorous growth; recurrent bloom; (28).

Hamburger Phoenix K (S), *mr*, 1954, (Hamburger Phonix); *R. kordesii* × *Seedling*; Kordes, 1957. Bud long, pointed; flowers rich red, large blooms in clusters; slightly fragrant; foliage dark, glossy; fruit large, orange-red; vigorous, climbing or trailer growth; repeat bloom.

Hamburg's Love F, *dy*, 1974, *Fragrant Cloud* × *Manx Queen*; Timmerman's Roses. Flowers deep yellow, dbl. (28 petals), large (3 in.); very fragrant; foliage glossy; compact.

Hamish HT, *yb*, 1979, (SIMhaha); *Fairy Dancers* × *Diamond Jubilee*; Simpson, J.W. Bud ovoid; flowers yellow blend, dbl. (50 petals), exhibition blooms borne singly; foliage medium green; dark brown prickles; vigorous, medium, upright to bushy growth.

Hana-Busa F, *or*, 1981, (Hanabusa); *Sarabande* × *(Rumba* × *Olympic Torch)*; Suzuki, S.; Keisei Rose Nursery. Bud ovoid; flowers orange-red, semi-dbl. (18 petals), flat, medium blooms borne 6-10 per cluster; straight prickles; bushy growth.

Hanagasa F, *or*, 1978, *(Hawaii* × *Seedling)* × *Miss Ireland*; Suzuki; Keisei Rose Nursery, 1979. Bud globular; flowers vermilion, dbl. (23 petals), cupped, large (4-4½ in.); fragrant; foliage large, light green; vigorous growth.

Hana-Gasumi F, *w*, 1985, (Hanagasumi); *Europeana* × *(Myo-joh* × *Fidelio)*; Suzuki, S.; Keisei Rose Nursery, 1984. Flowers soft white, aging pink, semi-dbl. (13 petals), flat, medium blooms borne 6-12 per cluster; fragrant; foliage dark, semi-glossy; small, hooked prickles, slanted downward; bushy growth.

Hanaguruma HT, *yb*, 1977, *Kordes' Perfecta* × *(Kordes' Perfecta* × *American Heritage)*; Teranishi, K.; Itami Bara-en. Bud globular; flowers yellow blend, dbl. (58 petals), high-centered, very large (6½-7 in.); slightly fragrant; foliage light green; upright.

Hanakago F, *or*, 1972, *Sarabande seedling* × *Rondo seedling*; Suzuki; Keisei Rose Nursery.

Bud ovoid; flowers deep salmon-vermilion, dbl., cupped, medium; fragrant; foliage glossy, dark; vigorous, bushy growth.

Hana-Kurenai HT, *pb*, 1980, *Big Red × Star Queen*; Ohata, Hatsuo. Bud ovoid; flowers light pink, flushed yellow, reverse deeper, dbl. (33 petals), high-centered blooms borne 1-3 per stem; slightly fragrant; foliage medium, medium green, glossy; few, sickle-shaped prickles; vigorous, upright growth.

Hanami-Gawa Cl Min, *op*, 1986, (Hanamigawa); *Seedling × Petite Folie*; Suzuki, S.; Keisei Rose Nursery, 1985. Flowers soft salmon-pink, shaded orange, dbl. (23 petals), small blooms borne 6-10 per cluster; fragrant; foliage dark, semi-glossy; small, curved prickles, slanted downward; vigorous, very bushy growth.

Hanamori F, *rb*, 1977, *(Tropicana × Karl Herbst) × Lydia*; Teranishi, K; Itami Bara-en. Bud circular; flowers red blend, dbl. (20-25 petals), high-centered, medium (2½ in.); slightly fragrant; foliage glossy, dark; bushy growth.

Handel® LCl, *rb*, 1965, (MACha; Handel; Haendel); *Columbine × Heidelberg*; McGredy, S., IV; McGredy. Flowers cream edged red, dbl. (22 petals), large (3½ in.); foliage glossy, olive-green; recurrent bloom. GM, Portland, 1975.

Handsom Red HT, *mr*, 1954, *(Pink Princess × Mirandy) × Queen o' the Lakes*; Brownell. Flowers spectrum-red, dbl. (45 petals), high-centered, large (4-5 in.); fragrant; upright, bushy growth.

Handy Andy HT, *ab*, 1965, *Kordes' Perfecta × Piccadilly*; McGredy, S., IV; Geest Industries. Flowers apricot edged pink, large (4 in.); slightly fragrant; free growth.

Hanky Panky Min, *ob*, 1991, (TINpanky); *Deep Purple × Party Girl*; Bennett, Dee; Tiny Petals Nursery, 1992. Flowers range from orange to golden peach as they open, full (26-40 petals), medium (4-7 cms), blooms borne mostly singly; fruity fragrance; foliage small, medium green, semi-glossy, disease resistant; some prickles; medium (40-60 cms), bushy, spreading growth.

Hannah Gordon F, *pb*, 1983, (KORweiso; Raspberry Ice); *Seedling × Bordure*; Kordes, W.; John Mattock, Ltd. Flowers white with deep pink petal edges, dbl. (35 petals), large; slight fragrance; foliage large, medium green, semi-glossy; upright, bushy growth.

Hannah Hauxwell F, *op*, 1991, *Seedling × Seedling*; Battersby Roses, 1990. Flowers deep salmon, full (26-40 petals), small; patio; slight fragrance; foliage small, medium green matt; bushy growth.

Hanne HT, *mr*, 1959, *Ena Harkness × Peace*; Soendenhousen; Hoersholm Nursery. Flowers scarlet-crimson, dbl., high-centered, medium to large; very fragrant; foliage leathery; upright growth.

Hans HT, *w*, 1970, *Message × Virgo*; Indian Agric. Research Inst.; Div. of Vegetable Crops & Flori. Flowers white, semi-dbl., open, large; foliage glossy, light; vigorous, upright growth.

Hans Billert HT, *mr*, 1928, *Laurent Carle × Richmond*; Billert; Teschendorff. Flowers brilliant red, very dbl.; fragrant.

Hans Mackart HP (OGR), *rb*, 1884, Verdier, E. Flowers bright deep geranium red, outer petals tinted carmine purple, full, medium; fragrant.

Hans Schmid R, *dp*, 1934, *Fragezeichen × American Pillar*; Vogel, M.; P. Lambert; Heinemann. Flowers deep pink, rather full, well formed, globular, small to medium, borne in clusters of 12-30; foliage large; vigorous, climbing growth.

Hansa HRg (S), *mr*, 1905, Schaum & Van Tol. Flowers mauvy-red, dbl., large blooms with short, weak stems; very fragrant (clove-rose); fruit large, red; vigorous growth; recurrent bloom; hardy.

Hanseat® S, *mp*, 1961, Tantau, Math. Flowers rose-pink, center lighter, single (5 petals), cupped, medium; slightly fragrant; vigorous (6 ft.) growth.

Hansestadt Bremen F, *op*, 1958, *Ama × Fanal*; Kordes, R. Bud ovoid, crimson; flowers deep salmon and reddish pink, dbl. (47 petals), large, borne in clusters (up to 10); fragrant; foliage leathery; very vigorous, bushy growth.

Hansestadt Lübeck F, *mr*, 1962, (Lübeck); Kordes, R.; McGredy. Flowers medium red, dbl., large (3½ in.); slightly fragrant; foliage dark; vigorous, tall growth.

Hansette S, *mr*, 1938, *Hansa × R. rubrifolia*; Wright, P.H. Flowers red, semi-dbl.; non-recurrent bloom.

Hap Renshaw Min, *ab*, 1991, (RENhap); *Party Girl × Lavonde*; Rennie, Bruce; Rennie Roses, International. Flowers apricot, moderately full, small blooms borne mostly singly; slight fragrance; foliage small, dark green, semi-glossy; upright growth.

Happiness HT, *mr*, 1954, (Rim; Rouge Meilland); *(Rome Glory × Tassin) × (Charles P. Kilham × (Charles P. Kilham × Capucine Chambard))*; Meilland, F.; URS, 1949 & C-P, 1951. Bud long, pointed; flowers medium red, dbl. (38 petals), high-centered, large (5-6 in.); slightly fragrant; upright, vigorous growth.

Happiness, Climbing Cl HT, *mr*, 1954, (Rouge Meilland, Climbing); Meilland, F.; URS.

Happy Pol, *mr*, 1954, (Alberich); *Robin Hood × Katharina Zeimet seedling*; deRuiter; Gregory & Willicher Baumschulen. Flowers currant-red, semi-dbl., very small blooms in large trusses; foliage dark, glossy; vigorous, compact (12-15 in.) growth.

Happy Birthday HT, *dp*, 1964, *Peace × The Doctor*; Howard, P.J. Bud ovoid; flowers deep rose, dbl. (25 petals), high-centered, large; very fragrant; foliage leathery; vigorous, upright growth.

Happy Days HT, *or*, 1932, *Briarcliff sport*; Amling, M.C.; Amling Co. Bud pointed; flowers geranium-red, dbl., open, large; long stems; foliage dark; very vigorous growth. RULED EXTINCT 4/87.

Happy Days HT, *dr*, 1962, *Exciting × Grand Gala*; Herholdt, J.A.; Herholdt's Nursery. Bud pointed; flowers oxblood-red, dbl., high-centered, medium (3-3½ in.); long stems; vigorous growth. RULED EXTINCT 4/87.

Happy Day HT, *rb*, 1979, (SIMpalno; Velvet Lustre); *First Prize × Gypsy Moth*; Simpson, J.W. Bud pointed; flowers red blend, dbl. (30 petals), classic HT form blooms borne singly; fragrant; foliage large, dark, semi-glossy; brown prickles; strong, upright, medium growth.

Happy Event F, *pb*, 1964, *(Karl Herbst × Masquerade) × Rose Gaujard*; Dickson, P.; A. Dickson. Flowers light chrome-yellow, flushed rose-opal, semi-dbl. (12 petals), large (3 in.) blooms in clusters; foliage glossy; growth moderate.

Happy Face™ Min, *dp*, 1991, (SAVaface); *(Sheri Anne × Rise 'n' Shine) × Mountie*; Saville, F. Harmon, 1986; Nor'East Miniatures Roses. Bud ovoid; flowers clear rosy pink, very dbl. (35-40 petals), cupped, medium blooms borne usually singly or in sprays of 3-5; no fragrance; foliage medium, dark green, glossy; bushy, medium, compact growth.

Happy Go Lucky™ Min, *ob*, 1987, (SAValuck); *Cheers × (Sheri Ann × (Yellow Jewel × Tamango))*; Saville, F. Harmon; Nor'East Miniature Roses. Flowers brilliant orange-yellow blend, dbl. (17-24 petals), high-centered, exhibition, small, borne usually singly; slight, sweet fragrance; foliage small, dark green, semi-glossy; long, thin pointed prickles; no fruit; bushy, medium growth.

Happy Hour™ Min, *mr*, 1983, (SAVanhour); *(Tamango × Yellow Jewel) × Zinger*; Saville, F. Harmon; Nor'East Min. Roses. Flowers bright medium red, yellow eye, dbl. (20 pet-

als), small; fragrant; foliage small, dark, glossy; bushy, spreading growth.

Happy Red F, *or*, 1960, *Red Favorite × Cocorico*; Leenders, J. Flower bright brick-red, single, borne in clusters; foliage glossy; moderate growth.

Happy Talk F, *mr*, 1973, *Escort × Orange Garnet*; Weeks. Flowers cherry-red, dbl., small; slightly fragrant; foliage glossy, dark; vigorous, upright, bushy growth.

Happy Thought Min, *op*, 1978, *(R. wichuraiana × Floradora) × Sheri Anne*; Moore, R.S.; Sequoia Nursery. Bud pointed; flowers pink blended with coral and yellow, dbl. (40 petals); foliage small, glossy; vigorous, bushy growth.

Happy Time Cl Min, *rb*, 1974, *(R. wichuraiana × Floradora) × (Golden Glow × Zee)*; Moore, R.S.; Sequoia Nursery. Bud short, pointed; flowers yellow overlaid red, dbl. (35 petals), small (1 in.); slightly fragrant; foliage small, glossy, leathery; climbing growth.

Happy Trails Min, *pb*, 1992, (JACcasp); *Immensee × Roller Coaster*; Warriner, William & Zary, Keith; Bear Creek Gardens, 1993. Flowers pink with cream center, very full (41+ petals), small (0-4 cms) blooms borne in small clusters; no fragrance; foliage small, medium to dark green, glossy; some prickles; low (20-30 cms), groundcover, spreading 60-90 cms across.

Happy Wanderer® F, *mr*, 1972, *Seedling × Marlene*; McGredy, S., IV; McGredy, 1974. Flowers scarlet; slightly fragrant.

Happy Wedding Bells HT, *w*, 1966, *White Swan × Virgo*; Morey; Country Garden Nursery. Bud long, pointed; flowers white, dbl. (52 petals), high-centered, large; spicy fragrance; foliage leathery; vigorous, upright growth.

Harbinger LCl, *lp*, 1923, *R. gigantea hybrid*; Clark, A.; Hackett. Bud pointed; flowers soft pink, single, large; slightly fragrant; foliage light; vigorous, climbing growth.

HARdancer F, *ob*, 1976, (Flame Dancer); *Orange Sensation × Alison Wheatcroft*; Harkness; Mason. Flowers orange, red reverse, dbl., cupped, medium; fragrant; foliage dense; large prickles; medium, bushy growth.

Harison Lemon HSpn (OGR), *ly*, 1929, *Harison's Yellow seedling*; Hamblin. Flowers clear lemon-yellow, semi-dbl.; fragrant; bushy (5 ft.) growth; non-recurrent bloom.

Harison Salmon HSpn (OGR), *op*, 1929, (Harison's Salmon); *Harison's Yellow seedling*; Hamblin. Flowers salmon, semi-dbl.; fragrant; non-recurrent bloom.

Harison's Hardy HSpn (OGR), *ly*, 1943, *R. spinosissima altaica* × *Harison's Yellow*; Wright, P.H. Flowers cream, center tinted yellow, semi-dbl.; non-recurrent bloom; very hardy.

Harison's Yellow HFt (OGR), *dy*, (Harisonii; *R* × *harisonii; R. lutea hoggii; R. foetida harisonii*); Probably *Persian Yellow* × *R. spinosissima*; ca. 1830. Flowers bright yellow, yellow stamens, semi-dbl.

Harlequin R, *pb*, 1935, *Excelsa* sport; Cant, F. Flowers half pale pink and half dark red, borne in clusters; very vigorous, climbing growth. RULED EXTINCT 12/83.

Harlow HT, *op*, 1968, *Fragrant Cloud* × *Melrose*; Cocker. Flowers salmon, dbl. (29 petals), large; foliage glossy.

Harmonie S, *pb*, 1954, (Kordes' Harmonie); *R. eglanteria hybrid* × *Peace*; Kordes. Bud ovoid, light red; flowers pink bicolor, large, borne in clusters; fragrant; foliage leathery; very vigorous, upright growth.   RULED EXTINCT 5/80.

Harmonie® HT, *op*, 1981, (KORtember); *Fragrant Cloud* × *Uwe Seeler*; Kordes, W. Bud long, pointed; flowers deep salmon, dbl. (20 petals), high-centered; strong fragrance; foliage slightly glossy; vigorous, upright, bushy. GM, Baden-Baden, 1981.

Harmony Cl HP (OGR), *ab*, 1933, *Rosella (self)*; Nicolas; C-P. Flowers apricot-pink, semi-dbl., high-centered, very large; strong stems; very fragrant; foliage leathery, dark; very vigorous, climbing growth.

Harold Macmillan F, *or*, 1988, (HARwestsun); *Avocet* × *Remember Me*; Harkness, R.; R. Harkness & Co., Ltd., 1989. Flowers orange-red, dbl. (18 petals), cupped, medium, borne in sprays of 3-7; slight fragrance; foliage medium, medium green, glossy, abundant; prickles broad, medium, green; fruit rounded, medium, green; bushy, medium growth.

HARpippin LCl, *ob*, 1984, *Royal Dane* × *((Mischief* × *(Red Dandy* × *Buccaneer))* × *(Sabine* × *Circus))*; Harkness. Flowers pale salmon-red, yellow reverse, dbl. (22 petals), blooms borne singly; slight fragrance; foliage medium, semi-glossy; upright (to 7 ft.).

Harriet Cl HT, *my*, 1931, *Golden Ophelia* sport; Moore, R.S. Flowers golden yellow, edged paler, dbl.; foliage bronze; vigorous, climbing (12-15 ft.) growth; recurrent bloom.

Harriet A. Easlea HT, *rb*, 1922, McGredy. Flowers bright carmine, reverse golden yellow, dbl.; fragrant.

Harriet Elizabeth S, *mp*, 1987, *Paula* × *(Micki* × *Northlander)*; James, John; Historical Roses, 1987. Flowers pure medium pink, dbl. (26-

40 petals), large, borne singly and in clusters; heavy fragrance; foliage medium, red aging dark green, leathery, disease resistant; upright, bushy, vigorous, full; hardy growth; repeat bloom.

Harriet Miller HT, *pb*, 1972, *Helen Hayes* × *Traviata*; Brownell, H.C.; Stern's Nursery. Bud long, pointed; flowers pink, very dbl., globular, large; fragrant; foliage large, glossy; very vigorous, bushy growth.

Harriet Neese S, *op*, 1928, *Ophelia* × *R.* × *harisonii*; Conyers. Flowers coral blended with yellow, base golden yellow, semi-dbl.; slightly fragrant; bushy growth; abundant non-recurrent bloom.

Harriet Poulsen F, *mp*, 1912, *Mme. Norbert Levavasseur* × *Dorothy Perkins*; Poulsen, D. Flowers apple-blossom-pink, single; vigorous growth.

Harriet Shepherd Gr, *mp*, 1982, *Queen Elizabeth* × *Queen Elizabeth*; Shepherd, David. Flowers medium pink, dbl. (35 petals), medium; no fragrance; foliage medium, medium green, holly-like; upright growth.

Harriny HT, *mp*, 1967, *Pink Favorite* × *Lively*; LeGrice. Flowers clear pink, dbl. (40 petals), pointed, large; very fragrant; foliage dark.

Harry Campbell F, *dp*, 1977, Burnet; Benefield's Nursery. Bud small, pointed; flowers cerise-pink shading to white, dbl. (45 petals), large (2½ in.); very fragrant (wild apple); foliage dark, leathery; vigorous, bushy growth.

Harry Edland F, *m*, 1975, *(Lilac Charm* × *Sterling Silver)* × *(Blue Moon* × *(Sterling Silver* × *Africa Star))*; Harkness, 1978. Flowers lilac-pink, dbl. (26 petals), large (4 in.); very fragrant; foliage dark, glossy.   Edland Fragrance Medal, 1975.

Harry G. Hastings HT, *dr*, 1965, (H.G. Hastings); *Gov. Mark Hatfield* × *Helene Schoen*; Abrams, Von. Flowers dark red, dbl., large; slightly fragrant; foliage leathery; vigorous.

Harry Kirk T (OGR), *ly*, 1907, Dickson, A. Bud pointed; flowers light sulphur-yellow, dbl., open; strong stems; fragrant; foliage leathery; vigorous, bushy growth.

Harry Maasz LCl, *rb*, 1939, *Barcelona* × *Daisy Hill*; Kordes. Bud long, pointed; flowers crimson, center white, single, cupped, very large; slightly fragrant; foliage large, leathery, wrinkled, dark; very vigorous, climbing growth.

Harry Wheatcroft HT, *yb*, 1972, (Caribia; Harry®); *Piccadilly* sport; Wheatcroft & Sons, 1973. Flowers yellow striped red, reverse yellow.

Harry Wheatcroft, Climbing Cl HT, *yb*, 1980, (AROmontelib; Caribia, Climbing); Mungia, Fred, Sr.; Montebello Rose Co., Inc.

HARtoflax F, *ob*, 1986, (Harkness Marigold); *Judy Garland* × *Anne Harkness*; Harkness, R. Flowers orange blend, dbl. (35 petals), well-formed, medium blooms in clusters; slight fragrance; foliage medium, medium green, semi-glossy; upright growth.

Haru-Kaze LCl, *op*, 1986, (Harukaze); *Charleston* × *Dorothy Perkins*; Suzuki, S.; Keisei Rose Nursery, 1985. Bud ovoid; flowers salmon yellow to orange-red, dbl. (33 petals), medium blooms borne 6-8 per cluster; foliage dark, glossy, small, curved prickles, slanted downward; bushy, creeping growth.

HARvander Min, *lp*, 1989, (Phoebe); *Clarissa* × *(Seedling* × *Mozart)*; Harkness, R. Bud pointed; flowers pale rose pink, reverse same, aging very little, very dbl. (85 narrow petals), rosette, medium, borne in sprays of 3-15; slight fragrance; foliage small, medium green, semi-glossy; prickles needle-like, long, decurved, small, dark green; fruit not a noticeable feature; bushy, low growth.

Harvard HT, *dr*, 1926, *Hoosier Beauty* × *Seedling*; Vestal. Bud pointed; flowers deep crimson, dbl., open, very large; long stems; very fragrant; foliage soft, bronze.

HARvee Min, *rb*, 1989, (Phoenix); *Clarissa* × *(Wee Man* × *(Southampton* × *Darling Flame)*; Harkness, R. Bud urn-shaped; flowers blood red, with yellow base, reverse same, aging orange-carmine, dbl. (25 long petals), rosette, medium, borne in sprays of 3-9; slight fragrance; foliage small, medium green, semi-glossy, pointed; prickles narrow, recurved, small, green; fruit not a noticeable feature; bushy, low growth.

Harvest Fayre F, *ob*, 1989, (DICnorth); *Seedling* × *Bright Smile*; Dickson, Patrick; Dickson Nursery, 1990. Flowers orange blend, dbl. (15-24 petals), medium; slight fragrance; foliage medium, medium green, glossy; bushy growth. ROTY, 1990.

Harvest Festival HT, *ab*, 1980, *Blessings* × *Sunblest*; Law, M.J. Flowers light apricot-orange, reverse apricot flushed pink, dbl. (28 petals), urn-shaped, medium blooms in sprays of 3-7; slightly fragrant; foliage medium, medium green, semi-glossy; medium, reddish-brown prickles; fruit orange-yellow, globular, large; tall, bushy growth.

Harvest Glow LCl, *rb*, 1941, *Golden Glow* × *Mercedes Gallart*; Brownell. Bud long, pointed, ovoid; flowers red to pink, reverse yellow, dbl. (60 petals), high-centered, large; long stems; foliage light green; vigorous, climbing growth.

Harvest Home® HRg (S), *mp*, 1979, (HARwesi; Harwest Home); *R. rugosa scabrosa* × *Seedling*; Spicer, Mrs. W.E.; Harkness. Bud pointed; flowers mauve-pink, semi-dbl. (14 petals), shallow-cupped, large (4½ in.); slightly fragrant; foliage light green, wrinkled; bushy growth; abundant early bloom, then sporadic.

Harvest Moon HT, *my*, 1976, *Whisky sport*; Mason, A.L.; F. Mason. Bud long, pointed; flowers medium yellow, dbl. (35 petals), large (4-5 in.); slightly fragrant; vigorous.

Harvest Moon HT, *ly*, 1938, Cant, B.R. Flowers cream, single, open, large, borne in clusters on long stems; foliage leathery, dark; vigorous, bushy, compact growth.

Harvest Time Cl HT, *ab*, 1939, *Sophie Thomas* × *Souv. de Claudius Pernet*; Thomas; Armstrong Nursery. Flowers apricot, reverse sometimes pinkish, semi-dbl., open, very large; long stems; fragrant; foliage leathery, dark; very vigorous, climbing (15-20 ft.) growth; free, recurrent bloom.

HARvestal Min, *lp*, 1989, (Pallos); *Clarissa* × *New Penny*; Harkness, R. Bud ovoid; flowers light buff pink, paling to buff white, very dbl. (60 narrow petals), rosette, medium, borne in sprays of 5-17; no fragrance; foliage small, medium green, semi-glossy, pointed, plentiful; prickles narrow, small, dark green; fruit not a noticeable feature; bushy, spreading, low growth.

Harvester HT, *pb*, 1975, *Wendy Cussons* × *Kordes' Perfecta*; Mayhew. Flowers carmine, reverse silver, center lilac, dbl. (35 petals), large (5 in.); very fragrant; foliage large, matt.

HARvool F, *mp*, 1992, (Muriel); *Liverpool Echo* × *Seedling*; Harkness, R.; Harkness New Roses, Ltd. 1991. Flowers medium pink, moderately full (15-25 petals), small (0-4 cms) blooms borne in large clusters; patio; slight fragrance; foliage small, medium green, semi-glossy; few prickles; low (30 cms), bushy growth.

HARwelcome F, *ob*, 1992, (Fellowship); *Southampton* × *Remember Me*; Harkness, R.; Harkness New Roses, Ltd. Flowers orange, moderately full (15-25 petals), medium (4-7 cms) blooms borne in large clusters; slight fragrance; foliage large, dark green, glossy; some prickles; medium (90 cms), bushy growth. GM, RNRS, 1990.

HARwinner Min, *w*, 1989, (Pandora); *Clarissa* × *Darling Flame*; Harkness, R. Bud ovoid; flowers ivory, reverse same, very dbl. (100 petals), rosette, medium, borne in sprays of 3-15; slight fragrance; foliage small, medium green, semi-glossy; prickles thin, small, reddish; fruit not a noticeable feature; bushy, spreading, low, compact growth.

Hassan F, *mr*, 1963, *Tivoli × Independence*; McGredy, S., IV; Fisons Horticulture. Flowers scarlet, dbl. (28 petals), large (4 in.); fragrant; foliage glossy, light green; vigorous, upright growth.

Hassi-Messaoud LCl, *or*, 1961, Hémeray-Aubert. Flowers garnet-red shaded orange, borne in clusters of 12-15; abundant, recurrent bloom.

Hat Pin Min, *m*, 1987, (TINpin); *Angel Face × Angelglo*; Bennett, Dee; Tiny Petals Nursery, 1986. Flowers pale lavender, semi-dbl. (12-15 petals), urn-shaped, small, borne usually singly; micro-mini; fruity fragrance; foliage small, medium green, semi-glossy; straight, extremely small, pale yellow prickles; fruit globular, small, brown; upright, bushy, low growth.

Hat Trick HT, *pb*, 1992, *First Prize × Seedling*; Lienau, David W.; Trophy Roses Ltd., 1993. Flowers pink, darker pink petal edges and reverse, very full (41+ petals), natural recurve, large (7+ cms.) blooms borne mostly singly; slight fragrance; foliage medium, dark green, semi-glossy; few prickles on upper half of stems; medium (90-120 cms.), upright growth.

Hauff R, *m*, 1911, *Aimee Vibert × Crimson Rambler*; Lambert, P. Flowers reddish violet, dbl., borne in clusters; foliage dark, broad; vigorous, climbing growth; recurrent when established.

Hauser HT, *my*, 1975, *Barbara × Guitare*; Gaujard. Flowers yellow-cream, full; vigorous.

Hauser HT, *ly*, 1975, *Barbara × Guitare*; Gaujard. Flowers yellow-cream, full; vigorous growth.

Haute Pink HT, *dp*, 1987, (JAChop); *Bridal Pink × Grand Masterpiece*; Warriner, William; J&P. Flowers rose pink fading little, dbl. (25-30 petals), cupped, loose, medium, borne singly; slight fragrance; foliage medium, medium green, matt; long, narrow, red prickles; no fruit; upright, tall growth.

Havana HT, *pb*, 1950, *Peace × Orange Nassau*; Fisher, G.; Arnold-Fisher Co. Flowers salmon-rose, reverse orange-yellow, dbl. (40 petals), large (5-5½ in.); slightly fragrant; foliage soft; vigorous, compact growth; a greenhouse rose.

Havering HMsk (S), *mp*, 1937, Bentall. Flowers china-pink, large, borne in clusters of 4 or 5; fragrant; vigorous growth.

Havering Rambler R, *mp*, 1920, Pemberton. Flowers almond-blossom-pink, dbl., rosette form, small, borne in large clusters on long stems; very vigorous growth.

HAVipip Min, *pb*, 1981, (Friendship); *(Swany × Mozart) × Mozart*; Verschuren, Ted; H.A. Verschuren. Bud ovoid; flowers pink and white blend, single (5-6 petals), small blooms in sprays of 30-50; no fragrance; foliage medium, light green, semi-glossy; fruit very small; spreading, medium growth; groundcover.

Hawa Mahal HT, *op*, 1976, *Fragrant Cloud × Kordes' Perfecta*; Harkness; Anand Nursery. Flowers salmon-pink, dbl. (25 petals), large (5-6 in.); fragrant; foliage dark.

Hawaii HT, *or*, 1960, *Golden Masterpiece × Seedling*; Boerner; J&P. Bud long, pointed; flowers orange-coral, dbl. (33 petals), high-centered, large (6 in.); very fragrant; foliage leathery; vigorous, upright growth.

Hawaiian Belle Min, *mp*, 1982, *Pink Ribbon × Pink Ribbon*; Dobbs, Annette. Flowers medium pink, aging to pink blend, dbl. (35 petals), small; slight fragrance; foliage small, medium green, matt; bushy growth.

Hawaiian Delight F, *op*, 1968, *Orange Sensation × Circus*; deRuiter; Carlton Rose Nursery. Flowers burnt-orange to pink, dbl., cupped, small; foliage dark, leathery; vigorous, bushy growth.

Hawaiian Sunrise Min, *rb*, 1981, *Seedling × Over the Rainbow*; Williams, E.D.; Mini-Roses. Bud pointed; flowers red and yellow blend, dbl. (40 petals), high-centered blooms borne usually singly; slight fragrance; foliage small, dense, glossy, bronze; thin, reddish prickles; upright growth.

Hawaiian Sunset HT, *ob*, 1962, *Charlotte Armstrong × Signora*; Swim & Weeks; C.R. Burr. Bud ovoid; flowers orange edged yellow, dbl. (45-50 petals), open, large (4-5½ in.); fragrant; foliage leathery, glossy; vigorous, upright, well branched growth.

Hawkeye Belle S, *w*, 1975, (Queen Elizabeth × Pizzicato) × Prairie Princess; Buck; Iowa State University. Bud ovoid; flowers white, tinted azalea-pink, dbl. (38 petals), high-centered, large (4-4½ in.); very fragrant; foliage large, dark, leathery; vigorous, erect, bushy growth.

Hawlmark Crimson HT, *mr*, 1920, Dickson, A. Bud pointed; flowers crimson-scarlet, semi-dbl., fragrant; bushy growth.

Hawlmark Scarlet HT, *mr*, 1923, Dickson, A. Flowers brilliant velvety scarlet-crimson; fragrant. GM, NRS, 1920.

Hazel Alexander HT, *dr*, 1933, *Ophelia seedling*; Dicksons & Co. Flowers deep red; very fragrant.

Hazel Rose HT, *lp*, 1992, *Queen Esther* × *Selfridges*; Poole, Lionel, 1993. Flowers light pink, full (26-40 petals), large (7+ cms) blooms borne singly; slight fragrance; foliage medium, dark green, semi-glossy; few prickles; medium (120 cms), upright growth.

Hazeldean HSpn (OGR), *my*, 1948, *R. spinosissima altaica* × *Persian Yellow*; Wright, P.H. Flowers yellow, more open, of better form than Persian Yellow, with earlier bloom; fragrant; very hardy (to -60); very fertile.

H. C. Andersen® F, *dr*, 1986, (POUlander; America's Choice; Hans Christian Andersen Touraine); *Royal Occasion* × *Seedling*; Olesen, M.&P., 1979; Poulsen Roses, 1986. Flowers dark red, semi-dbl., cupped, large, borne in sprays of 1-25; slight fragrance; foliage medium, dark green, glossy; bushy, tall growth.

H. Chaubert HT, *op*, 1928, *Mrs. Aaron Ward* × *Seedling*; Barbier. Flowers coppery salmon, semi-dbl., open, borne in clusters; slightly fragrant; foliage rich green, glossy; bushy growth.

H. C. Valeton HT, *yb*, 1926, *Golden Ophelia* × *Aspirant Marcel Rouyer*; Verschuren. Flowers golden yellow overspread with rose, large; strong stems; fragrant; vigorous growth.

H. C. Young HT, *op*, 1934, Austin & McAslan. Bud pointed; flowers shrimp-pink, deepening to salmon, base yellow, strong stems; vigorous growth.

H. D. M. Barton HT, *dr*, 1917, Dickson, A. Flowers deep velvety crimson, dbl., large; fragrant; bushy growth.

Headleyensis HHug (S), *ly*, (R. headleyensis); *R. hugonis* × *R. spinosissima altaica*. Flowers creamy yellow, single; vigorous growth.

Headliner HT, *pb*, 1985, (JACtu); *Love* × *Color Magic*; Warriner, W.; J&P. Flower petals white, blending to deep pink at edges, dbl. (40 petals), exhibition, large; slight fragrance; foliage large, medium green, glossy; upright growth.

Heart of England Gr, *dp*, 1978, *Pink Parfait* × *Seedling*; Gregory. Flowers carmine-rose, dbl. (42 petals), high-centered, large (4 in.); fragrant; moderately vigorous growth.

Heart of Gold R, *rb*, 1926, *R. wichuraiana* × *R. moyesii*; Van Fleet; ARS. Flowers crimson, center white, stamens yellow, single, open, borne in clusters; foliage rich green; vigorous (10 ft.) growth.

Heart of T.D.K. HT, *op*, 1983, *Sunblest* × *Red Devil*; Ogawa, Isamu. Bud ovoid; flowers salmon-pink, dbl. (50 petals), large blooms borne singly; slight fragrance; foliage small, light green; heavy hooked prickles; vigorous, upright, tall growth.

Heart Throb F, 1966, *(Circus* × *Circus)* × *(Circus* × *Circus)*; Fankhauser. Bud urn shaped; flowers deep yellow, edges flushed pink, very dbl., medium, cluster; very fragrant; foliage dark, glossy; vigorous, bushy growth. RULED EXTINCT 4/82 ARM.

Heart Throb HT, *mr*, 1982, (LEOnhart); *Norita* × *((Norita* × *Seedling)* × *Papa Meilland)*; Leon, Charles F., Sr. Flowers medium red, dbl. (37 petals), high-centered, medium blooms borne singly and several together; damask fragrance; foliage medium to large, medium green, leathery; vigorous, bushy, tall growth.

Heartbeat F, *op*, 1970, *(Castanet* × *Castanet)* × *(Cornelia* × *Seedling)*; Dickson, P.; A. Dickson. Flowers deep salmon-orange, dbl. (26 petals), globular, large (4½ in.); slightly fragrant; foliage small, dull; very free growth.

Heartbeat HT, *mr*, 1989, *Thriller* × *Wild Cherry*; Bridges, Dennis A.; Bridges Roses, 1990. Bud pointed; flowers medium red, darker outer petals, reverse lighter, dbl. (45 petals), high-centered, medium, borne usually singly; slight, fruity fragrance; foliage medium, medium green, semi-glossy; prickles straight, large, pink to yellow; upright growth.

Heartbreaker Min, *pb*, 1989, (WEKsybil); *Crystalline* × *Magic Carrousel*; Carruth, Tom; Weeks Roses, 1990. Bud pointed; flowers deep pink with white base, dbl., high-centered, exhibition, small, borne in sprays of 3-5; slight fragrance; foliage small, dark green, glossy; prickles nearly straight, small, dark red-brown; fruit globular, small, dark orange; upright, bushy, medium, vigorous growth.

Hearth Glow F, *or*, 1963, *Red Pinocchio* × *(Carrousel* × *Queen o' the Lakes)*; Abrams, Von; Peterson & Dering. Bud ovoid; flowers brick-red, dbl., medium, borne in clusters; foliage soft, light green; vigorous, upright growth.

Heartland™ Min, *op*, 1982, (SAVsay); *Sheri Anne* × *Watercolor*; Saville, F. Harmon; Nor'East Min. Roses. Bud short, pointed; flowers orange-red, dbl. (38 petals), HT form, blooms in clusters; slight fragrance; long, thin prickles; vigorous, upright growth.

Heartlight™ Min, *ob*, 1985, (KINheart); *Golden Slippers* × *Rise 'n' Shine*; King, Gene; AGM Min. Roses, Inc. Flowers orange-yellow, reverse yellow, 16 petals, high-centered, miniflora, large; slight fragrance; foliage medium, medium green, matt; straight, light brown prickles; upright, bushy, medium growth.

Heart's Delight HT, *op*, 1933, *Mrs. Beckwith* sport; Hart, L.P. Flowers apricot-coral-orange, veined red, very dbl., high-centered, large; very fragrant; foliage soft; vigorous, open habit.

Heart's Desire HT, *dr*, 1942, *Seedling × Crimson Glory*; Howard, F.H.; H&S. Bud long, pointed; flowers crimson, dbl. (30 petals), high-centered, large (4½ in.); very fragrant (damask); foliage leathery, dark; vigorous, upright growth.   GM, Portland, 1941; AARS, 1942.

Heart's Desire, Climbing Cl HT, *dr*, 1945, Howard, F.H.; H&S.

Heat Wave F, *or*, 1958, (Mme. Paula Guisez); *Seedling × Roundelay*; Swim; Armstrong Nursery. Bud urn-shaped; flowers orange-scarlet, dbl. (30 petals), cupped, large (3½-4½ in.) blooms in clusters; slightly fragrant; foliage dark, semi-glossy, rounded; vigorous, upright, bushy growth.

Heather Claire HT, *ab*, 1982, *Diamond Jubilee × Bonsoir*; Allender, Robert. Bud long; flowers apricot pink, dbl. (30 petals), blooms borne singly; no fragrance; foliage dark, red reverse; slightly hooked prickles; medium growth.

Heather Honey HT, *ab*, 1988, (HORsilbee); *Silver Jubilee × (Honey Favorite × Southampton)*; Horner, Colin P.; LeGrice Roses, 1991. Bud ovoid, bronze; flowers apricot yellow, reverse apricot; dbl. (25 petals), urn-shaped, medium, borne usually singly and in sprays of 5-7; moderate, fruity fragrance; foliage medium, medium green, glossy; prickles small, greenish-brown; fruit globular, medium, yellow; bushy, medium growth.

Heather Jenkins HT, *mp*, 1968, *Charlotte Armstrong × Ballet*; Watson. Bud globular; flowers pink, reverse darker, dbl., high-centered, medium; slightly fragrant; foliage light green, wrinkled; moderate, upright, open growth.

Heather Leigh Min, *mp*, 1989, (TALheather); *Azure Sea × Miniature seedling*; Taylor, Pete & Kay; Taylor's Roses. Bud pointed; flowers medium pink, reverse slightly darker, aging lighter, holds color well, dbl. (35-40 petals), high-centered, exhibition, medium, borne singly, good substance; no fragrance; foliage medium, medium green, semi-glossy; prickles straight, small, reddish-brown; fruit none; upright, bushy, medium growth.

Heather Muir Sp (OGR), *w*, 1957, *R. sericea* variety; Sunningdale Nursery. Flowers pure white, single, large (3 in.); fragrant; foliage ferny; fruit orange; blooms over a long period.

Heather Paton HT, *mr*, 1934, Austin & McAslan. Flowers carmine, center darker; vigorous growth.

Heaven Scent F, *op*, 1968, *Pernille Poulsen × Isabel de Ortiz*; Poulsen; McGredy. Flowers salmon, dbl. (30 petals), large blooms in trusses; very fragrant.

Heavenly Days™ Min, *op*, 1988, (SAVaday; SAVahe); *Climbing Yellow Miniature seedling × (Sheri Anne × Glenfiddich)*; Saville, F. Harmon; Nor'East Miniature Roses. Flowers glowing indian-orange, reverse lemon yellow, flushed fire-red, aging orange to orange-yellow to pink, dbl. (28-32 petals), cupped, decorative, medium, borne singly or in sprays of 3-7; no fragrance; foliage medium, medium green, glossy, underside matt; bushy, medium, compact growth. AOE, 1988.

Heavenly Fragrance HT, *lp*, 1963, *Tiffany × Mme. Gregoire Staechelin*; Hennessey. Flowers light pink, reverse darker, well formed, large (5 in.); very fragrant; moderate growth.

Hebe F, *dp*, 1941, Leenders, M. Flowers deep pink, reverse lighter.

Hebe HT, *op*, 1949, Dickson, A. Flowers rosy salmon toned orange and apricot-yellow, dbl. (27 petals), high pointed, large (6 in); fragrant; foliage glossy, bronze green; vigorous growth. GM, NRS, 1949.

Hebe's Lip E (OGR), *w*, (Reine Blanche; Rubrotincta; *R. damascena rubrotincta*); Probably *R. damascena × R. eglanteria* hybrid.; Lee, prior to 1846; Re-int. W. Paul, 1912. Flowers creamy white, petals edged pink, semi-dbl., cupped, vigorous growth; non-recurrent bloom.

Hector G (OGR), *m*, Parmentier. Flowers purple, faintly striped with white, dbl., pompon, small.

Hector Deane HT, *rb*, 1938, *McGredy's Scarlet × Lesley Dudley*; McGredy; J&P. Bud pointed; flowers orange, carmine and salmon-pink, dbl., high-centered; very fragrant (fruity); foliage glossy, dark; vigorous, compact growth.

Hedda Hopper HT, *mp*, 1952, *Radiance × Seedling*; Howard, A.P.; H&S. Bud ovoid; flowers light peach passing to pearly pink, dbl. (40 petals), globular, large (3½-4 in.); fragrant; foliage coppery; very vigorous growth.

Hede HT, *my*, 1934, *Prof. Gnau × Mev. G.A. van Rossem*; Tantau. Flowers pure sunflower-yellow, dbl., large; strong stems; slightly fragrant; foliage dark, leathery; vigorous growth.

Hedwig Fulda R, *mr*, 1934, *Orléans Rose × Farbenkönigin*; Leenders Bros. Flowers clear vermilion-red, full, well formed, large, borne in large clusters on long, strong stems; foliage bright, dark; vigorous growth.

Heer HT, *lp*, 1969, *Picture × Open pollination*; Singh; Gopalsinamiengar.   Flowers rose-pink, dbl., high-centered, medium; slightly fragrant; vigorous, upright growth.

Heidegruss F, *pb*, 1937, *Heidekind × Ophelia*; Tantau; Münch & Haufe. Flowers salmon-flesh, base light yellow, very dbl., large, borne in clusters; foliage leathery; vigorous, bushy growth.

Heidekind HRg (S), *dp*, 1931, *Mev. Nathalie Nypels × R. rugosa hybrid*; Berger, V.; Münch & Haufe. Flowers brilliant pink shaded copper-red, dbl., large blooms in clusters; slightly fragrant; foliage thick, rugose.

Heidekönigin® Min, *lp*, 1985, (KORdapt; Palissade Rose; Pheasant); *Zwerkonig '78 × R. wichuraiana seedling*; Kordes, W. Flowers light pink, dbl. (35 petals), large; slight fragrance; foliage small, medium green, glossy; spreading growth; groundcover.

Heidelberg K (S), *mr*, 1959, (KORbe; Grüss an Heidelberg); Kordes, R.; McGredy. Flowers bright crimson, reverse lighter, dbl. (32 petals), high-centered, large (4 in.) blooms in clusters; foliage glossy, leathery; very vigorous, bushy growth.

Heidemarie F, *mr*, 1945, *Hamburg × (Heros × Heidekind)*; Tantau. Flowers carmine-red, single (5-7 petals), large, borne in clusters of 4-6; slightly fragrant; foliage dark, leathery; vigorous, upright, bushy growth.

Heideröslein LCl, *yb*, 1932, *Chamisso × Amalie de Greiff*; Lambert, P. Bud pointed, orange-red; flowers bright yellowish salmon-pink, base sulphur-yellow, single, flat, large blooms in clusters of 29-60; fragrant; broad, bushy growth; recurrent bloom.

Heidesommer® F, *w*, 1985, (KORlirus; Cevennes); *The Fairy × Seedling*; Kordes, W. Flowers white, dbl. (20 petals), medium; very fragrant; foliage small, dark, glossy; upright, bushy growth.

Heidezauber F, *dr*, 1936, *Heidekind × Johanniszauber*; Tantau; Münch & Haufe. Flowers dark red, very dbl., large, borne in clusters; slightly fragrant; foliage dark, leathery; bushy growth.

Heidi™ Min, *mp*, 1978, (ARODi); *Fairy Moss × Iceberg*; Christensen; Armstrong Nursery. Bud mossy; flowers clear medium pink, dbl. (35 petals), mini-moss, small (1½ in.); very fragrant; foliage glossy; very vigorous, bushy growth.

Heidi Jayne HT, *dp*, 1986, *(Piccadilly × Queen Elizabeth) × (Fragrant Cloud × Seedling)*; Esser; Harkness. Flowers bright deep pink, dbl. (32 petals), large; fragrant; foliage large, light green, glossy; numerous prickles; medium, upright growth.

Heimatlos HCan (OGR), *mp*, 1931, *(R. canina × R. roxburghii) × R. canina*; Lohrberg. Bud pointed; flowers rose-pink, single, borne in clusters on short stems; very fragrant; vigorous (5-7 ft.), open habit; non-recurrent bloom; has endured -27.

Hein Evers F, *mr*, 1957, *Red Favorite × Fanal*; Tantau, Math. Bud pointed; flowers bright blood-red, semi-dbl, open, borne in clusters; slightly fragrant; foliage leathery; vigorous, upright growth.

Hein Evers, Climbing Cl F, *mr*, 1963, Kordes.

Hein Mück® S, *dr*, 1961, Tantau, Math. Flowers velvety blood-red, single, cupped, medium blooms in clusters; vigorous (6 ft.) growth.

Heinrich Conrad Soth S, *pb*, 1919, *Geheimrat Dr. Mittweg × R. foetida bicolor*; Lambert, P. Flowers light rosy red, with white eye, single, small, borne in pyramidal clusters on long, strong stems; fragrant; foliage large, glossy, dark; very vigorous, bushy growth; recurrent bloom.

Heinrich Eggers HT, *op*, 1928, *Mrs. Charles E. Russell × Mrs. Wemyss Quin*; Kordes. Flowers orange-copper, often with lighter outer petals, dbl.; fragrant; upright growth.

Heinrich Karsch Pol, *m*, 1927, *Orléans Rose × Joan*; Leenders, M. Flowers violet-rose, semi-dbl.

Heinrich Münch HP (OGR), *mp*, 1911, *Frau Karl Druschki × (Mme. Caroline Testout × Mrs. W.J. Grant)*; Hinner, W.; Münch & Haufe. Flowers soft pink, dbl. (50 petals), very large; fragrant; very vigorous growth; occasional recurrent bloom.

Heinrich Schultheis HP (OGR), *lp*, 1882, *Mabel Morrison × E.Y. Teas*; Bennett. Flowers soft pink, full, well-formed, very large; very fragrant; vigorous growth; occasional recurrent bloom.

Heinrich Wendland HT, *mr*, 1930, *Charles P. Kilham × Mev. G.A. van Rossem*; Kordes; Dreer & H&S. Flowers nasturtium-red, reverse deep golden yellow, dbl., high-centered, very large; very fragrant (fruity); foliage bronze, leathery, glossy; vigorous growth.

Heinrich Wendland, Climbing Cl HT, *mr*, 1937, Stell; Stell Rose Nursery.

Heinsohn's Record HCan (OGR), *lp*, *Derived from R. canina*; Heinsohn-Wedel; Popular understock much used in Germany.

Heinz Erhardt® F, *mr*, 1962, Kordes, R. Flowers medium red, dbl. (25 petals), large (3 in.) blooms in clusters (up to 8); slightly fragrant; foliage coppery; vigorous, bushy growth. GM, Baden-Baden, 1961.

Heinzelmännchen® F, *mr*, 1983, (KORnuma; Red Pixie); *(Satchmo × Seedling) × (Messestadt Hannover × Hamburg)*; Kordes, W., 1984. Flowers medium red, dbl. (35 petals), large; slight fragrance; foliage medium, medium green, glossy; bushy growth.

Heiress HT, *mp*, 1959, Longsdon. Bud pointed; flowers clear rose-pink, well shaped, medium; very fragrant.

Heirloom HT, *m*, 1972, (JACloom); *Seedling × Seedling*; Warriner; J&P. Bud long, pointed; flowers deep lilac, semi-dbl., medium; very fragrant; foliage leathery; vigorous, upright growth.

Heldengruss HT, *dr*, 1920, *Étoile de France × Baron Girod de l'Ain*; Kiese. Flowers pure deep blood-red, dbl.; fragrant.

Helen HT, *pb*, 1930, Ferguson, W. Flowers salmon-pink, base shaded yellow, semi-dbl.; fragrant; vigorous growth.   RULED EXTINCT 11/91.

Helen Min, *mr*, 1991, (TINhelen); *Carrousel × Starina*; Bennett, Dee; Tiny Petals Nursery, 1992. Flowers medium red, full (26-40 petals), HT form, small (0-4 cms) blooms borne mostly singly; long cutting stems; fruity fragrance; foliage small, medium green, semiglossy, disease resistant; few prickles; tall (60-80 cms), upright, bushy growth.

Helen Allen HT, *dr*, 1975, *Evelyn Fison × Vagabonde*; Clayworth. Flowers velvety red, dbl. (20 petals), large (3½-4 in.); fragrant; upright growth.

Helen Bland HBlanda (S), *mp*, 1950, *Betty Bland × R. blanda (St. Hilaire clone)*; Wright, P.H. Flowers rose-pink, center deeper, semidbl., open, medium, borne several together; slightly fragrant; foliage soft; stems redbrown, thornless; vigorous (7-8 ft.), upright growth; profuse non-recurrent bloom.

Helen Boehm Min, *lp*, 1982, (AROprawn); *Foxy Lady × Deep Purple*; Christensen, J.E.; Armstrong Nursery, 1983. Flowers soft pink, dbl. (20 petals), high-centered, small; slight fragrance; foliage small, medium green, semiglossy; upright, bushy growth.

Helen Chamberlain HT, *yb*, 1918, Easlea. Flowers creamy yellow to orange-gold, paling on outer petals.

Helen Fox HT, *my*, 1928, *Mme. Mélanie Soupert × Souv. de Claudius Pernet*; Buatois. Bud pointed, indian yellow; flowers golden yellow, dbl., cupped; slightly fragrant; foliage bronze; vigorous, bushy growth. GM, Bagatelle, 1926.

Helen Good T (OGR), *yb*, 1907, *Maman Cochet sport*; Good & Reese. Bud pointed; flow-

ers delicate yellow suffused pink, edged deeper, dbl.; vigorous growth.

Helen Gould, Climbing Cl HT, *pb*, 1912, *Balduin sport*; Good & Reese.

Helen Hayes HT, *yb*, 1956, *R. wichuraiana hybrid × Sutter's Gold*; Brownell. Bud long, pointed; flowers yellow splashed orange and pink, dbl. (43 petals), high-centered, large (4-5 in.); fragrant; foliage glossy; very vigorous growth.

Helen Keller HP (OGR), *dp*, 1895, Dickson, A. Flowers rosy cerise, petals large, shell shaped; very free bloom. GM, NRS.

Helen Leenders S, *mp*, 1924, *Orléans Rose × R. foetida bicolor*; Leenders, M. Flowers hydrangea-pink, semi-dbl., open, large, borne in clusters; fragrant; foliage large, rich green; very vigorous, (5 ft.), bushy growth; sometimes recurrent bloom.

Helen M. Greig HT, *lp*, *Mrs. A.R. Barraclough × Marmion*; Dobbie. Flowers pastel pink. Was not introduced.

Helen of Troy HT, *mp*, 1956, *Dame Edith Helen × Mrs. Henry Morse*; Stevenson; Waterer. Flowers rose-pink, very dbl.; slightly fragrant (spicy); vigorous, bushy growth.

Helen Taylor HT, *pb*, 1924, Pemberton. Flowers rosy salmon, dbl.; fragrant.

Helen Traubel HT, *pb*, 1951, *Charlotte Armstrong × Glowing Sunset*; Swim; Armstrong Nursery. Bud long, pointed; flowers pink to apricot, dbl. (23 petals), high-centered, flat, large (5-6 in.) blooms with weak necks; fragrant; foliage leathery, matt, green; tall, vigorous growth.   GM, Rome, 1951; AARS, 1952.

Helen Wild HT, *op*, 1959, *Show Girl × Charlotte Armstrong*; Kemp, M.L. Flowers orange-pink veined rose-red, dbl. (35 petals), high-centered, large (5-6 in.); fragrant; foliage light green; free growth.

Helena Van Vliet Pol, *lp*, 1931, *Salmonea sport*; Kersbergen. Flowers soft pink tinted salmon, borne in large trusses; vigorous growth.

Hélène R, *pb*, 1897, *Hybrid Tea seedling × (Aglaia × Crimson Rambler)*; Lambert, P. Flowers soft violet-rose, base yellowish white, single to semi-dbl., borne in clusters of 30-40; slightly fragrant; vigorous, climbing (12-15 ft.) growth.

Hélène Dapples HT, *mr*, 1932, *Mrs. Henry Winnett × Lady Maureen Stewart*; Heizmann, E. Bud pointed, dark; flowers glowing crimson-red; very fragrant; vigorous growth.

Hélène de Montbriand HT, *mr*, 1933, *Reine Marie Henriette × Laurent Carle*; Schwartz, A. Flowers deep carmine-red, shaded vermilion, globular, well formed, large; foliage glossy, dark; vigorous growth.

Hélène de Roumanie HT, *rb*, 1949, *(Mme. Joseph Perraud × Seedling) × (Seedling × Pres. Herbert Hoover)*; Meilland, F. Flowers red to pink, dbl. (35 petals), urn shaped, large (5 in.); slightly fragrant; upright growth. GM, NRS, 1950.

Hélène François HT, *pb*, 1923, *Mme. Edouard Herriot × Viscountess Enfield*; Schwartz, A. Flowers salmon-pink shaded coppery red, center salmon-orange tinted gold, full.

Hélène Granger R, *pb*, 1910, *Tea Rambler × Aglaia*; Granger. Flowers pink, center copper-yellow, borne in clusters of 15-20.

Hélène Robinet HT, *lp*, 1928, *Seedling × Prés. Parmentier*; Sauvageot; F. Gillot. Flowers salmon-white, shaded rose, base yellow, dbl.; slightly fragrant.

Helene Schoen HT, *mr*, 1963, *Multnomah × Charles Mallerin*; Abrams, Von; Peterson & Dering. Bud long, pointed; flowers medium red, dbl. (60 petals), high-centered, large (6 in.); slightly fragrant; foliage leathery, glossy; vigorous, upright growth.

Hélène Vacaresco HT, *pb*, 1939, Chambard, C. Flowers salmon, shaded copper-carmine, cupped, large; foliage dark.

Hélène Valabrègue HT, *lp*, 1953, *Lorraine × Michèle Meilland*; Meilland, F.; URS. Bud pointed; flowers pale rose, dbl., cupped, very large; strong stems; slightly fragrant; foliage leathery; vigorous, bushy growth.

Hélène Videnz Pol, *pb*, 1905, *Euphrosyne × Louis Philippe*; Lambert, P. Flowers salmon-pink, dbl., borne in clusters to 75; vigorous growth.

Helgoland F, *mr*, 1936, *Else Poulsen × Hybrid Tea seedling (dark crimson)*; Kordes. Bud pointed, dark; flowers crimson to carmine, semi-dbl., open, very large, borne in clusters; slightly fragrant; foliage leathery, wrinkled, dark; vigorous, bushy growth.

Helgoland F, *mr*, 1973, Tantau; Horstmann. Bud pointed; flowers copper-red, semi-dbl., medium; slightly fragrant; foliage glossy, light; moderate, upright, bushy growth.

Héliodore Dober G (OGR), *mr*, Flowers deep red edged crimson, ball shaped, quite large.

Helios HT, *dy*, 1935, Leenders, M. Flowers deep sunflower-yellow, semi-dbl., open; foliage leathery, light; vigorous, bushy growth.

Hello Min, *mr*, 1992, (COChello); *Darling Flame × Seedling*; Cocker, James; James Cocker & Sons, 1991. Flowers crimson with white eye, semi-dbl. (6-14 petals), medium (4-7 cms) blooms borne in large clusters;

patio; slight fragrance; foliage medium, medium green, semi-glossy; some prickles; medium (50-80 cms), bushy growth.

Hello There Min, *w*, 1986, (FLOello); *Care Deeply × Red Can Can*; Florac, Marilyn, 1987. Flowers white, light yellow tints in center, very dbl. (108 petals), cupped, good petal retention, small, borne usually singly or in sprays of 3-4; no fragrance; foliage small, medium green, matt; tan, very few prickles; bushy, low growth.

Helmut Schmidt® HT, *my*, 1979, (KORbelma; Goldsmith; Simba); *New Day × Seedling*; Kordes, W. Bud large, long, pointed; flowers medium yellow, dbl. (35 petals), high-centered blooms borne 1-3 per cluster; fragrant; foliage matt; vigorous, upright, bushy growth. GM, Belgium & Geneva, 1979.

Help the Aged HT, *mp*, 1986, *Mischief × Fragrant Cloud*; Bracegirdle, A.J.; Rosemary Roses, 1987. Flowers clear pink, reverse slightly darker, satin two-tone effect, dbl. (23 petals), high-centered, medium, borne in sprays of 6-8; heavy, damask fragrance; foliage medium, light green, semi-glossy; straight, brown, very few prickles; no fruit; bushy, medium growth.

Hen Kauffmann F, *mp*, 1954, Leenders, M. Flowers rosy pink, dbl.; fragrant; vigorous growth.

Henkell Royal® HT, *mr*, 1964, Kordes, R. Bud long; flowers blood-red, well-formed, large; very fragrant; vigorous, bushy growth. GM, Baden-Baden, 1964.

Henri Barruet LCl, *pb*, 1918, Barbier. Flowers coppery yellow, opening to pink and tinted white, borne in clusters of 8-15; vigorous, climbing (8 ft.) growth.

Henri Coupé HP (OGR), *mp*, 1916, *Frau Karl Druschki × Gruss an Teplitz*; Barbier. Flowers pink, dbl.; fragrant.

Henri Declinand LCl, *mr*, 1934, Mermet. Flowers bright magenta-red, quite full, large; foliage dark.

Henri Fouquier G (OGR), *mp*, (Henri Fouquier). Flowers pure rose-pink, dbl., large; fragrant.

Henri Linger LCl, *yb*, 1928, *R. wichuraiana × Benedicte Seguin*; Barbier. Flowers clear yellow-orange, semi-dbl., open; slightly fragrant; foliage light, glossy; very vigorous, climbing growth.

Henri Mallerin HT, *yb*, 1953, *Soeur Thérèse × Duquesa de Peñaranda*; Mallerin; EFR. Bud ovoid; flowers empire-yellow suffused pink, dbl. (55-70 petals), large; slightly fragrant; foliage leathery, glossy; bushy growth.

Henri Martin M (OGR), *mr*, 1863, (Red Moss); Laffay. Bud sparsely mossed; flowers shining crimson, semi-dbl., medium blooms in clusters of 3-8.

Henri Pauthier HT, *mr*, 1933, *Seedling × Edouard Mignot*; Sauvageot; C-P. Flowers bright red, semi-dbl., open, large; fragrant; foliage glossy; bushy growth.

Henrietta HT, *op*, 1917, *Alister Stella Gray × Andre Gamon*; Merryweather. Bud pointed, orange-crimson; flowers soft coral-salmon, semi-dbl., open; fragrant; foliage dark; vigorous growth. RULED EXTINCT 12/85.

Henrietta HT, *ab*, 1984, (POUletta); *Seedling × (Pink Nordia × Sonny Boy)*; Oleson, M.&P.; Poulsen's. Flowers apricot, dbl. (25 petals), urn-shaped, large, borne singly; slight fruity fragrance; foliage large, dark, glossy; vigorous, upright, bushy growth.

Henriette Chandet HT, *op*, 1942, *Rochefort × La Parisienne*; Mallerin; A. Meilland. Bud oval; flowers orange-coral, dbl., large; slightly fragrant; foliage glossy; vigorous, bushy growth.

Henriette Koster Pol, *mr*, 1939, *Dick Koster sport*; Koster, D.A. Flowers red.

Henriette Pechtold HT, *mr*, 1946, *Briarcliff × Katharine Pechtold*; Verschuren-Pechtold. Bud long, pointed; flowers red, reverse salmon-red, dbl., large; fragrant; foliage soft; vigorous, bushy growth.

Henry Field HT, *mr*, 1948, *Pink Princess × Crimson Glory*; Brownell; H. Field. Bud ovoid, long, pointed; flowers crimson-red, dbl. (60 petals), high-centered, large (5 in.); fragrant; foliage glossy; vigorous, bushy growth.

Henry Ford HT, *mp*, 1954, *Pink Dawn, Climbing × The Doctor*; Howard, A.P.; H&S. Bud long; flowers silvery pink, dbl. (30 petals), high-centered, large (4-5 in.); fragrant; vigorous, upright growth.

Henry Ford HT, *my*, 1927, *Mme. Edouard Herriot × Golden Emblem*; Deverman; B&A. Flowers yellow edged salmon-orange, opening to lemon-yellow, semi-dbl.; slightly fragrant.

Henry Hudson HRg (S), *w*, 1976, Svejda; Canada Dept. of Agric. Bud ovoid; flowers white, yellow stamens; dbl. (25 petals), large (2½-3 in.); very fragrant; low, bushy growth; recurrent bloom.

Henry Kelsey K (S), *mr*, 1984, *R. kordesii hybrid × Seedling*; Svejda, F. Flowers medium red, dbl. (28 petals), medium blooms in clusters of 9-18; spicy fragrance; foliage glossy; trailing growth; remontant, very winter hardy.

Henry King Stanford F, *mr*, 1973, *Red Pinocchio × Open pollination*; Sheridan, V.V. Flowers medium red, semi-dbl. (15 petals), small (1½ in.); spreading growth.

Henry Morse F, *dr*, 1958, Kordes; Morse. Flowers deep blood-red shaded scarlet, semi-dbl., large (3 in.), borne in large trusses; free growth.

Henry Nevard HP (OGR), *dr*, 1924, Cant, F. Flowers crimson-scarlet, dbl. (30 petals), cupped, very large; very fragrant; foliage dark, leathery; vigorous, bushy growth; recurrent bloom.

Henry V Ch (OGR), *rb*, Flowers crimson, center white, cupped.

Hens Verschuren HT, *mr*, 1948, *Mary Hart × Seedling*; Verschuren. Bud long; flowers bright red, very large.

Her Majesty HP (OGR), *mp*, 1885, *Mabel Morrison × Canary (T)*; Bennett. Flowers clear rose, with carmine reflexes toward center, dbl., very large; fragrant; very vigorous growth; occasional recurrent bloom.

Hera HT, *mr*, 1924, *Gen. MacArthur × Luise Lilia*; Van Rossem. Flowers brilliant carmine shaded blood-red, dbl. (40 petals); very fragrant.

Heraldo Cl HT, *m*, 1949, *Guinée × Texas Centennial*; Dot, M.; P. Dot. Bud long, pointed; flowers purple-pink, very dbl., large; very fragrant; foliage leathery, dark.

Herbemont's Musk Cluster N (OGR), *w*, Herbemont; prior to 1836. Flowers pure white, dbl., very large blooms in large clusters; recurrent bloom.

Herbert Brunning HT, *mr*, 1940, Clark, A. Flowers brilliant red.

Herbert Wilson F, *w*, 1967, *White Knight × The Optimist*; Latham. Flowers white, well-formed; slightly fragrant; foliage light green.

Herbie Min, *m*, 1987, (TINherb); *Deep Purple × Dilly Dilly*; Bennett, Dee; Tiny Petals Nursery. Flowers rich mauve, outer petals deep mauve at margins, dbl. (25-30 petals), urn-shaped, medium, borne usually singly; slight fragrance; foliage medium, medium green, semi-glossy; slender, straight, average, reddish prickles; fruit globular, medium, brown; upright, bushy, medium growth.

Herbstfeuer E (OGR), *dr*, 1961, (Autumn Fire); Kordes; Kern Rose Nursery. Flowers dark red, semi-dbl., large blooms in clusters (up to 5); fragrant; fruit large, pear-shaped, reddish yellow; vigorous (6 ft.) growth; repeat bloom.

Hercules LCl, *mp*, 1938, *Doubloons × Charles P. Kilham*; Horvath; Wayside Gardens Co. Flowers Dame Edith Helen pink, dbl., cupped, very large; long stems; slightly fragrant; foliage large, glossy, dark; very vigorous, climbing growth.

Herero Gr, *rb*, 1981, (HERbic); *Angel Bells × Southern Sun*; Herholdt, J.A. Flowers yellow, reverse yellow with red overlay, spreading with age, semi-dbl., medium; no fragrance; foliage large, dark, glossy; upright growth.

HERfla HT, *pb*, 1981, (Flamingo); *Seedling × Seedling*; Herholdt, J.A. Flowers light pink, silvery reverse, dbl. (35 petals), cupped, large; fragrant; foliage medium green, semi-glossy; upright growth.

Herfsttooi HT, *dr*, 1919, *Gen. MacArthur seedling × Leuchtfeuer (HCh)*; Van Rossem. Flowers dark crimson, dbl.; fragrant.

H. E. Richardson HT, *mr*, 1913, Dickson, A. Flowers dazzling crimson, full, high-centered; vigorous growth. GM, NRS, 1912.

Heritage® S, *lp*, 1985, (AUSblush); *Seedling × Iceberg seedling*; Austin, David; David Austin Roses, 1984. Flowers light pink, dbl. (40+ petals), cupped, medium; very fragrant; foliage small, dark, semi-glossy; upright, bushy growth; recurrent.

Herman Kegel M (OGR), *m*, 1848, Portemer. Flowers reddish violet, sometimes streaked crimson, full, medium; vigorous growth.

Hermann Eggers HT, *or*, 1930, *(Pink Pearl × Templar) × Florex*; Kordes; Dreer; H&S. Flowers deep orange-scarlet, dbl., high-centered, very large; very fragrant; foliage dark, leathery; very vigorous growth.

Hermann Lindecke HT, *lp*, 1929, *General-Superior Arnold Janssen sport*; Lindecke. Flowers whitish pink, reverse salmon-pink, full, high-centered; large.

Hermann Löns HT, *dp*, 1931, *Ulrich Brunner Fils × Red-Letter Day*; Tantau. Flowers shining light red, single, cupped, large blooms in clusters; fragrant; foliage glossy; vigorous.

Hermann Neuhoff HT, *mr*, 1923, *General-Superior Arnold Janssen sport*; Neuhoff; Kordes. Flower uniform blood-red, dbl.; fragrant.

Hermann Robinow HT, *op*, 1918, *Frau Karl Druschki × Lyon Rose*; Lambert, P. Flowers salmon-orange shaded salmon-rose and dark yellow, full, large; vigorous growth.

Hermann Teschendorff HT, *rb*, 1949, Berger, V.; Teschendorff. Bud ovoid; flowers copper-red, reverse old-gold, dbl., open, cupped, very large; fragrant; foliage glossy, dark, bronze; very vigorous, upright growth.

Hermelia Casas F, *mp*, 1956, *Méphisto × Perla de Alcañada*; Dot, P. Flowers pearly, reverse carmine, dbl. (30 petals), medium, borne in clusters of 3-6; moderate growth.

Hermen Anglada HT, *w*, 1933, Dot, P. Bud very large; flowers white tinted pink, single; very fragrant; very vigorous growth.

Hermione HT, *op*, 1981, (GAUlimor); *Rose Gaujard × Colour Wonder*; Gaujard, J.; Roseraies Gaujard. Flowers deep salmon, dbl. (35 petals), large; fragrant; foliage large, dark, glossy; upright, bushy growth.

Hermosa Ch (OGR), *lp*, (Armosa; Mélanie Lemaire; Mme. Neumann); Marcheseau; Prior to 1837. Bud pointed; flowers light blush-pink, dbl. (35 petals), high-centered; small; fragrant; foliage bluish green; vigorous growth; recurrent bloom; (21).

Hero® S, *mp*, 1983, (AUShero); *The Prioress × Seedling*; Austin, David; David Austin Roses, 1982. Flowers glistening medium pink, dbl. (20 petals), deeply cupped, large; very fragrant; foliage medium, medium green, semi-glossy; spreading growth.

Heroïca HT, *dr*, 1960, *Rome Glory × Independence*; Lens. Flowers deep velvety red, becoming lighter; vigorous growth.

Heroine HT, *op*, 1935, *Wilhelm Kordes × Mrs. Atlee*; Krause. Bud pointed; flowers salmon-shrimp-pink, dbl., high-centered, large; foliage leathery, dark; very vigorous, bushy growth.

Heros HT, *mr*, 1933, *Johanniszauber × Étoile de Hollande*; Tantau. Flowers red, dbl., cupped, very large; very fragrant; foliage leathery, dark; bushy growth.

Herrenhausen HMsk (S), *ly*, 1938, *Eva × Golden Rapture*; Kordes. Bud ovoid, greenish yellow; flowers light yellow, fading white, red tints in sun, dbl., cupped, large, borne in clusters on long stems; fragrant (pansy); foliage leathery, glossy, light; vigorous, bushy growth; profuse, intermittent bloom.

Herrin von Lieser HT, *ly*, 1907, *Frau Karl Druschki × G. Schwartz*; Lambert, P. Flowers cream-yellow, center reddish yellow; very fragrant.

Herself F, *lp*, 1966, *The Optimist × Moulin Rouge*; Vincent; Harkness. Flowers light pink, semi-dbl. (18 petals), large (4 in.), borne in clusters; free growth.

Hertfordshire Glory F, *yb*, 1970, *Isobel Harkness × Circus*; Harkness. Flowers yellow, tinted red, dbl. (20 petals), large; slightly fragrant; foliage glossy.

Herz As® HT, *mr*, 1963, (As de Coeur); Tantau, Math. Bud long, pointed; flowers pure blood-red, dbl., well-formed, large; slightly fragrant; vigorous, upright growth.

Herzensgruss HT, *dr*, 1973, *(Fragrant Cloud × Goldmarie) × Red American Beauty*; Hetzel; GAWA. Bud pointed; flowers dark velvety red, dbl., medium; very fragrant; foliage glossy; vigorous, upright, bushy growth.

Herzog Friedrich II von Anhalt HT, *lp*, 1906, *Souv. du President Carnot* × *Mme. Jules Grolez*; Welter. Flowers soft pink; fragrant.

Hessengruss HT, *dp*, 1928, *Laurent Carle sport*; Thonges. Flowers deep pink, reverse carmine-rose, dbl.; fragrant.

Hessenstar HT, *or*, 1973, *Baccará* × *Prima Ballerina*; Hetzel; GAWA. Bud ovoid; flowers orange-red to geranium-red, dbl. (30-40 petals), medium; fragrant; moderate growth.

Hessie Lowe HT, *op*, 1956, Lowe. Flowers peach-pink, dbl., high-centered; very fragrant; foliage glossy; very vigorous growth.

Hessoise E (OGR), *mp*, Flowers bright rose, semi-dbl.

Heure Mauve HT, *m*, 1962, *Simone* × *Prélude*; Laperrière; EFR. Flowers lilac-mauve tinted blush, dbl. (35 petals), well-formed, large (5 in.); foliage glossy, bright green; vigorous.

Heureux Anniversaire® Gr, *op*, 1960, (DELpre; Happy Anniversary); *(Incendie* × *Chic Parisien)* × *(Floradora* × *Independence)*; Delbard-Chabert; Stark Bros., 1963. Bud urn-shaped; flowers salmon-orange, dbl. (28 petals), large (3 in.); slightly fragrant (spicy); foliage glossy; very vigorous, bushy growth.

Hexham Abbey F, *op*, 1975, *Fairlight* × *Arthur Bell*; Wood. Flowers salmon-pink, base yellow turning copper, large (3½ in.); very fragrant; foliage leathery; vigorous, low to medium height, upright growth.

H. F. Alexander LCl, *ab*, 1952, *Duquesa de Peñaranda* × *Ruth Alexander*; Wilber; Buckley Nursery Co. Flowers apricot, dbl. (30-40 petals), very large; very long stems; foliage glossy; tall, climbing growth.

Hi Ho Cl Min, *op*, 1964, *Little Darling* × *Magic Wand*; Moore, R.S.; Sequoia Nursery. Flowers deep pink, dbl., small, in clusters; foliage glossy; vigorous, climbing.

Hi, Neighbor Gr, *mr*, 1981, *(Queen Elizabeth* × *Prairie Princess)* × *Portrait*; Buck; Iowa State University. Bud ovoid, pointed; flowers medium red, dbl. (43 petals), slightly cupped blooms borne 1-6 per cluster; moderate fragrance; foliage leathery, dark, matt; awl-like prickles; bushy, erect growth.

Hiawatha R, *rb*, 1904, *Crimson Rambler* × *Paul's Carmine Pillar*; Walsh. Flowers deep crimson, center white, anthers golden, single, cupped blooms in large clusters; foliage rich green, leathery, glossy; very vigorous, climbing (15-20 ft.) growth; late bloom.

Hiawatha Recurrent R, *op*, 1931, *Hiawatha* × *Maman Levavasseur*; Sauvageot; C-P. Flowers carmine suffused orange, white eye, small,

borne in clusters on long stems; foliage small, glossy; very vigorous, climbing growth; intermittent bloom.

Hibernica Misc OGR (OGR), *lp*, (R. × *hibernica* Templeton); *R. canina* × *R. spinosissima*; Before 1800 in Great Britain. Flowers pale pink, single, 1 in. diam.; foliage glaucous green; low growth.

Hidalgo® HT, *mr*, 1979, (MEItulandi; Michel Hidalgo); *((Queen Elizabeth* × *Karl Herbst)* × *(Lady* × *x Pharaon))* × *(MEIcesar* × *Papa Meilland)*; Meilland, M.L.; Meilland. Bud conical; flowers currant-red, dbl. (30 petals), cupped, very large; very fragrant; foliage matt, bronze; vigorous, upright growth.

Hidcote Gold Sp (OGR), *my*, 1948, *R. sericea omeiensis variety*; Hilling. Flowers canary-yellow, single blooms borne several together; foliage ferny; non-recurrent bloom.

Hi-de-hi Min, *mp*, 1981, (MACanat); *Anytime* × *Gartendirektor Otto Linne*; McGredy, S. Flowers medium pink, dbl. (20 petals), small; fragrant; foliage small, dark, glossy; bushy growth.

Hi-Fi F, *or*, 1958, *Independence* × *Seedling*; Gregory. Flowers bright orange-scarlet, semi-dbl., borne in clusters; foliage glossy.

High Esteem HT, *pb*, 1961, *(Charlotte Armstrong* × *Mme. Henri Guillot)* × *(Multnomah* × *Charles Mallerin)*; Abrams, Von; Peterson & Dering. Bud pointed; flowers phlox-pink, reverse silvery, dbl. (43 petals), high-centered, large (6 in.); very fragrant (fruity); foliage leathery, light green; vigorous, upright, compact growth.

High Fashion HT, *dp*, 1972, *Queen Elizabeth* × *Peace*; Patterson; Patterson Roses. Bud ovoid; flowers deep pink, dbl., high-centered, medium; very fragrant; foliage glossy, soft; vigorous, upright growth.

High Hope Min, *or*, 1985, (FLOhih); *Young Love* × *Little Chief*; Florac, Marilyn; M.B. Farm Min. Roses, Inc. Flowers bright orange-red, dbl. (45 petals), cupped, small, borne singly and in clusters; no fragrance; foliage medium, light, glossy; vigorous, upright.

High Jinks™ Min, *pb*, 1992, (SAVajinks); *Rise 'n' Shine* × *Sheri Anne*; Saville, F. Harmon; Nor'East Miniature Roses, 1993. Flowers pink blend, dbl. (25-32 petals), high-centered, exhibition, medium (4 cms) blooms borne singly and in sprays of 4-30; slight fragrance; foliage medium, dark green, semi-glossy; upright, bushy, medium to tall growth.

High Noon Cl HT, *my*, 1946, *Soeur Thérèse* × *Capt. Thomas*; Lammerts; Armstrong Nursery. Flowers lemon-yellow, dbl. (28 petals), loosely cupped, medium (3-4 in.); fragrant (spicy); foliage leathery, glossy; upright, vigorous, climbing (8 ft.) growth. AARS, 1948.

High Point Min, *w*, 1986, (MOLhip); *Helen Boehm sport*; Molder, W.A.; Rose Acres. Flowers white.

High Sheriff HT, *or*, 1992, (HARwellington); *Seedling × Silver Jubilee*; Harkness, R.; Harkness New Roses, Ltd. Flowers orange-red, moderately full (15-25 petals), medium (4-7 cms) blooms borne in small clusters; slight fragrance; foliage large, dark green, glossy; few prickles; tall (95 cms), upright growth.

High Society HT, *mr*, 1961, Kordes, R.; A. Dickson. Flowers bright red, dbl. (30 petals), high centered, large (4 in.); slightly fragrant; bushy growth.

High Spirits™ Min, *mr*, 1983, (SAVaspir); *Sheri Anne × Tamango*; Saville, F. Harmon; Nor'East Min. Roses. Flowers medium red, dbl. (35 petals), HT form, small blooms in sprays; slight fragrance; foliage small, dark, semi-glossy; upright growth.

High Stepper Cl Min, *yb*, 1983, (MORclim); *(Little Darling × Yellow Magic) × Magic Wand*; Moore, R.S.; Moore Min. Roses. Flowers yellow overlaid pink, reverse yellow, dbl. (40+ petals), small; slight fragrance; foliage medium, dark, semi-glossy; bushy, spreading (to 5 ft.) growth; needs support.

High Style Min, *mr*, 1983, (LYOhi); *Seedling × Seedling*; Lyon. Flowers cardinal red, dbl. (35 petals), medium blooms in clusters; slight fragrance; foliage medium, medium green, semi-glossy; upright, bushy growth.

High Summer F, *or*, 1978, (DICbee); *Zorina × Ernest H. Morse*; Dickson, P.; Dickson Nursery. Bud ovoid; flowers vermilion, dbl. (26 petals), cupped, large (3 in.); foliage large; bushy growth.

High Tide Min, *ob*, 1986, *Seedling × Seedling*; McDaniel, Earl; McDaniel's Min. Roses. Flowers orange, yellow reverse, dbl. (25 petals), cupped, medium, borne usually singly; slight fragrance; foliage small, dark, semi-glossy; few prickles; upright, bushy.

High Time HT, *pb*, 1959, *Charlotte Armstrong × Signora*; Swim; Roseway Nursery. Bud urn-shaped; flowers claret-rose, reverse gold and pink, dbl. (24 petals), high-centered, cupped, large (4-5 in.); very fragrant (spicy); foliage dark, glossy; vigorous, upright.

Highdownensis S, *mr*, 1928, (R. × *highdownensis* Hillier); *R. moyesii seedling*; Stern, Sir Frederich. Flowers bright medium red, single blooms in clusters; little fragrance; foliage dark, coppery; fruit orange-scarlet; colorful prickles; vigorous, bushy (10x10 ft.) growth.

Highfield® LCl, *ly*, 1980, (HARcomp); *Compassion sport*; Harkness, 1981. Flowers light yellow.

Highland Beauty F, *mr*, 1956, *Signal Red × Red Wonder*; deRuiter; Anderson. Flowers rich red, semi-dbl., large (3 in.), borne in clusters; slightly fragrant; foliage dark, glossy; vigorous growth.

Highland Charm F, *op*, 1956, *Duchess of Rutland × Fashion*; deRuiter; Anderson. Flowers coral-salmon, semi-dbl., large (3½ in.), borne in large clusters; slightly fragrant; foliage leathery; vigorous, bushy growth.

Highland Fling F, *or*, 1971, *Dearest × Elizabeth of Glamis*; Anderson's Rose Nursery. Flowers orange-scarlet, veined black, dbl. (22 petals), large (4-4½ in.); fragrant; foliage glossy.

Highland Glory F, *mr*, 1956, *Sidney Peabody × Floribunda seedling*; deRuiter; Anderson. Flowers crimson-red, semi-dbl., large (3 in.), borne in large clusters; slightly fragrant; foliage coppery; vigorous growth.

Highland Laddie Min, *mr*, 1989, (COCflag); *National Trust × Dainty Dinah*; Cocker, James & Sons. Bud pointed; flowers scarlet red, dbl. (19 petals), cupped, medium, borne in sprays of 5-11; slight fragrance; foliage medium, medium green, glossy; prickles medium, green; fruit urn-shaped, medium, brown; upright growth.

Highland Lass Min, *yb*, 1991, (ZIPhigh); *Rise 'n' Shine × High Spirits*; Zipper, Herbert; Magic Moment Miniatures, 1992. Flowers red and yellow with yellow reverse, semi-dbl. (6-14 petals), small (0-4 cms) blooms borne in small clusters; no fragrance; foliage small, dark green, semi-glossy; few prickles; low (20 cms), compact growth.

Highland Park HT, *op*, 1942, *E.G. Hill × Mme. Henri Guillot*; Mallerin; C-P. Bud tawny salmon; flowers salmon-pink, dbl. (35 petals), open, large; slightly fragrant; foliage leathery; vigorous, upright, bushy growth.

Highland Wedding HT, *w*, 1971, *Virgo × Rose Gaujard*; MacLeod. Flowers white, suffused blush, center light gold, dbl. (30 petals), large (4½ in.); slightly fragrant; foliage large, dark, semi-glossy; vigorous.

Highlight F, *ob*, 1957, *Seedling × Independence*; Robinson, H. Flowers orange-scarlet, dbl. (24 petals), medium (2½ in.) blooms in large clusters; fragrant; vigorous growth. GM, NRS, 1957.

Hightae F, *pb*, 1987, (GREentae); *Duet × Regensberg*; Greenfield, Mrs. P.L.; Hightae Plant Nurs., 1988. Flowers clear, medium pink outer petals, deeper in color at the heart, dbl. (45-50 petals), high-centered, medium, borne usually singly and in sprays of up to 5; strong fragrance; foliage small, bronze aging to medium green, glossy; prickles long, curved slightly downward, red; low, bushy, free-flowering growth.

Hilda HT, *pb*, 1928, Cant, B.R. Flowers salmon-pink, reverse orange-carmine, dbl., globular, very large; long stems; slightly fragrant; foliage leathery; vigorous growth.

Hilda Murrell® S, *mp*, 1985, (AUSmurr); *Seedling × (Parade × Chaucer)*; Austin, David, 1984. Flowers medium pink, dbl. (40+ petals), old rose form, large; very fragrant; foliage large, medium green, matt; bushy growth.

Hilda Phillips HT, *dy*, 1948, *Aureate seedling × Mrs. Sam McGredy*; Bees. Flowers deep golden yellow, well-shaped, medium; fragrant; foliage glossy, bronze.

Hilda Scott HT, *my*, 1955, *Lady Hillingdon seedling*; Glassford; Morse. Flowers butter-yellow, small.

Hilde Apelt HT, *ob*, 1927, *Seedling × Souv. de Claudius Pernet*; Leenders, M. Flowers saffron-yellow, dbl.; fragrant.

Hilde Steinert HT, *rb*, 1926, Leenders, M. Flowers coral-red, reverse reddish salmon and old-gold, semi-dbl.; fragrant.

Hildegarde HT, *ob*, 1946, *Briarcliff sport*; Boerner; J&P. Bud long, pointed; flowers saffron-rose-pink, dbl. (30-35 petals), high-centered, large (5 in.); very fragrant; foliage leathery; very vigorous, upright growth; a greenhouse variety.

Hildenbrandseck HRg (S), *mp*, 1909, *Atropurpurea (HRg) × Frau Karl Druschki*; Lambert, P. Flowers shining clear pink, single, in clusters; vigorous growth; recurrent bloom.

Hill Crest HT, *rb*, 1948, Hill, J.H., Co. Bud short, pointed, oxblood-red; flowers carmine, dbl. (50-55 petals), high-centered, large (3½-4 in.); fragrant; foliage leathery; very vigorous, upright, compact, tall growth; a florists' variety, not distributed for outdoor use.

Hill Top HT, *ab*, 1942, *Joanna Hill × R.M.S. Queen Mary*; Hill, J.H., Co.; Wayside Gardens Co.; H&S, 1946. Bud long, pointed, light coral-red; flowers buff, dbl. (28 petals), globular, large (4-5 in.); fragrant; foliage leathery, dark, wrinkled; vigorous, upright growth.

Hillcrest Pillar S, *my*, 1930, *R. × harisonii seedling*; Hillcrest Gardens. Flowers bright yellow, semi-dbl., medium; pillar (6 ft.) growth.

Hillier Rose S, *dr*, (*R. × pruhoniciana* Schneider; *R. hillieri* Hillier) R. moyesii × R. multibracteata(?); Orig. ca. 1920. Flowers deep red, about 2 in. diam.

Hill's America HT, *mp*, 1921, *Premier × Hoosier Beauty*; Hill, E.G., Co. Flowers rose-pink, dbl. (44 petals); fragrant. GM, NRS, 1924.

Hill's Hillbilly F, *mp*, 1947, *Juanita × Mrs. R.M. Finch*; Wayside Gardens Co.; H&S. Bud ovoid, red; flowers pink, single (5-6 petals), open, small (1-2 in.), borne in clusters; slightly fragrant; foliage leathery, dark; vigorous, upright, bushy growth.

Hill's Victory HT, *rb*, 1942, *Chieftain × Sweet Adeline*; Hill, J.H., Co. Bud red; flowers rose-red to rose-pink, dbl. (50-55 petals), large (5-6 in.); long, strong stems; slightly fragrant; foliage leathery, dark, wrinkled; vigorous, upright, much branched growth.

Himangini F, *w*, 1968, *Saratoga × Seedling*; Indian Agric. Research Inst. Bud ovoid; flowers ivory-white, center light buff, dbl., open, medium; vigorous, bushy, compact growth.

Himatsuri HT, *dr*, 1977, (*Tropicana × Karl Herbst*) × *Mainauperle*; Teranishi, K. Bud circular; flowers dark red, high-centered, large (3½-4 in.); slightly fragrant; foliage small; upright growth.

Hinemoa F, *rb*, 1963, *Circus × Seedling*; Mason, P.G. Flowers buttercup-yellow shading to vermilion, semi-dbl. (17-20 petals), cupped, large (3-3½ in.), borne in clusters; fragrant; foliage bronze, leathery; upright, bushy growth.

Hinrich Gaede HT, *ob*, 1931, *Lady Margaret Stewart × Charles P. Kilham*; Kordes. Bud pointed, nasturtium-red; flowers orange-yellow tinted nasturtium-yellow, dbl., high-centered, very large; fragrant (fruity); foliage glossy, bronze; vigorous growth.

Hinrich Gaede, Climbing Cl HT, *ob*, 1935, Armstrong, J.A.

Hi-Ohgi HT, *or*, 1981, *San Francisco × (Montezuma × Peace)*; Suzuki, S.; Keisei Rose Nursery. Flowers deep orange-red, dbl. (28 petals), large; fragrant; foliage dark, semi-glossy; prickles slanted downward; tall, upright growth.

Hipango F, *yb*, 1983, (MURgo); *Smiley × Una Hawken*; Murray, N. Flowers deep yellow, petals edged orange, reverse yellow, dbl. (21 petals), shapely, large; slight fragrance; foliage medium, medium to light green; vigorous growth.

Hipólito Lázaro LCl, *dr*, Pahissa. Flowers carmine, large; very fragrant.

Hippolyte G (OGR), *m*, Flowers vivid carmine shaded violet, small.

Hippolyte Jamain HP (OGR), *dp*, 1874, Lacharme. Flowers carmine-red, dbl. (38 petals), well-formed, semi-globular; fragrant; foliage red, when young; vigorous, erect growth.

Hiroshima's Children F, *yb*, 1985, (HARmark); Harkness, R. Flowers light yellow, petals edged pink, dbl. (35 petals), HT form, large; slight fragrance; foliage medium, medium green, matt; bushy growth.

His Majesty HT, *dr*, 1909, McGredy. Flowers dark crimson shaded deeper, full, high-centered, very large; long, strong stems; very fragrant; very vigorous growth.

Hisami HT, *lp*, 1988, *Kordes' Perfecta × Christian Dior*; Harada, T. Flowers light cream, flushed crimson at tip, very dbl. (50 petals), high-centered, exhibition, large, borne usually singly; moderate fragrance; foliage medium, dark green, matt; prickles downward curved, red to light green; upright, medium growth.

Hispania HT, *dr*, 1938, Pahissa. Bud pointed; flowers velvety red, dbl., open, very large; long, strong stems; very fragrant; foliage leathery; very vigorous growth.

Hit Parade F, *ob*, 1962, *(Independence × Seedling) × Brownie*; Dickson, P.; A. Dickson. Flowers red, orange and gold, semi-dbl. (16 petals), large (4 in.), borne in large clusters; foliage dark; low growth.

Ho No-o-no-nami LCl, *or*, 1968, (Wave of Flame; Waves of Flame); *Spectacular × Aztec*; Suzuki; Country Garden Nursery, 1967. Bud pointed; flowers orange-red, reverse lighter, dbl., high-centered to open, medium; slightly fragrant; foliage glossy, leathery; vigorous, climbing growth.

Hoagy Carmichael HT, *mr*, 1990, (MACtitir); *(Sir Harry Pilkington × Elegy) × Pounder Star*; McGredy, Sam; McGredy Roses International; Roses by Fred Edmunds, 1990. Flowers medium red, full (26-40 petals), large blooms; fragrant; foliage medium, dark green, matt; upright, bushy growth.

Hobby F, *op*, 1955, (TANob); *Red Favorite × Kathe Duvigneau*; Tantau, Math. Flowers coral-pink, dbl., large blooms in open clusters; slightly fragrant; foliage dark; upright, bushy growth.

Hochsommer F, *dp*, 1960, *Queen Elizabeth × Seedling*; Verschuren, A.; van Engelen. Flowers dark pink, dbl., borne in clusters; foliage dark; low growth.

Hocus-Pocus Gr, *or*, 1975, *Fandango × Simon Bolivar*; Armstrong, D.L.; Armstrong Nursery. Flowers orange-red, dbl. (30 petals), cupped, large (4-4½ in.); slightly fragrant; foliage large, dark; vigorous, upright growth.

Hoddy Toddy™ Min, *dr*, 1989, (KINtoddy); *(Alain × Scamp) × Scamp*; King, Gene; AGM

Miniature Roses. Bud pointed; flowers dark red, petals tipped darker, dbl. (28 petals), cupped, small, borne usually singly and in sprays of 2-3; no fragrance; foliage small, medium green, matt; prickles straight, very small, red; fruit none; bushy, low growth.

Hoffmann von Fallersleben LCl, *rb*, 1917, *Geheimrat Dr. Mittweg × Tip-Top*; Lambert, P. Flowers salmon-red, shaded yellow and ochre, borne in clusters of 5-20; vigorous, climbing growth; sometimes repeats.

Hofgärtner Kalb HCh (OGR), *pb*, 1914, *Souv. de Mme. Eugène Verdier × Gruss an Teplitz*; Felberg-Leclerc. Flowers bright carmine-rose, center yellow, outer petals shaded red, dbl. (35 petals), well-formed, large; fragrant; vigorous, bushy growth.

Hoh-Jun HT, *pb*, 1981, *Granada × Flaming Peace*; Suzuki, S.; Keisei Rose Nursery. Flowers pink flushed rose-red, dbl. (28 petals), cupped blooms in clusters of 2-5; very fragrant; foliage dark, semi-glossy; large prickles; compact growth.

Hokey Pokey Min, *ab*, 1980, *Rise 'n' Shine × Sheri Anne*; Saville, F. Harmon; Nor'East Min. Roses. Bud long, pointed; flowers deep apricot, dbl. (28 petals), high-centered, flat, borne singly; slight spicy fragrance; foliage finely serrated; straight prickles; compact, bushy growth.

Hoku-To HT, *ly*, 1979, (Myoo-Jo × Chicago Peace) × King's Ransom; Suzuki, S.; Keisei Rose Nursery. Flowers soft buff yellow, dbl. (42 petals), high-centered; fragrant; foliage large, light green; vigorous, upright, spreading growth.

Holiday F, 1948, *McGredy's Pillar × Pinocchio*; Boerner; J&P. Bud ovoid, orange-yellow flushed pink; flowers flame-pink, reverse clear yellow, semi-dbl., cupped, large (3-3½ in.), clusters of 3-10; fragrant (clove); foliage glossy; vigorous, bushy, compact growth. RULED EXTINCT 4/83 ARM.

Holiday HT, *mr*, 1981, *Cara Mia × Volare*; Strahle, B. Glen; Carlton Rose Nursery. Flowers medium red, dbl. (35 petals), small; slight fragrance; foliage medium green; upright.

Holiday Cheer Min, *dr*, 1982, (MORliday); *Red Pinocchio × Little Chief*; Moore, R.S.; Moore Min. Roses. Flowers dark red, dbl. (35 petals), small blooms in clusters; no fragrance; foliage small, dark, matt; upright, bushy growth.

Holland Double White Altai Sp (OGR), *w*, *R. spinosissima altaica* form; From Holland; P.H. Wright. Flowers white, dbl.; non-recurrent bloom.

Hollandia Pol, *dr, Believed to be Orléans Rose sport.* Flowers deep red, dbl., rosette form, small.

Hollandia HT, *mr,* 1930, *Aspirant Marcel Rouyer sport;* Zijverden. Flowers brick-red, shaded copper.

Hollandica HRg (S), Thought to have been raised by J. Spek, ca. 1888; Selected Dutch clone of R. rugosa, or perhaps a hybrid with Manettii, widely used as an understock, especially for tree roses.

Hollie Roffey Min, *mp,* 1985, (HARramin); *(Tip Top × (Manx Queen × Golden Masterpiece)) × Darling Flame;* Harkness, R., 1986. Flowers medium pink, dbl. (35 petals), rosette form, small blooms in clusters; slight fragrance; foliage small, pointed, medium green, semi-glossy; spreading growth.

Holly Rochelle HT, *dr,* 1974, *Charlotte Armstrong × Scarlet Knight;* Graham; South Forrest Rose Nursery. Bud pointed; flowers velvety red, very dbl. (60-70 petals), high-centered, large (4 in.); fragrant; very vigorous, upright growth.

Hollybank F, *mr,* 1966, *Independence × United Nations;* Hooney. Flowers vermilion, globular, large (3-3½ in.); slightly fragrant; foliage coppery; upright growth.

Hollywood HT, *rb,* 1930, *Premier sport;* Scittine. Bud pointed; flowers dark rose-red, veined darker, dbl., high-centered; long, strong stems; very fragrant; foliage dark; bushy growth.

Hollywood Beauty HT, *dp,* 1929, *Rose Marie sport;* Pacific Rose Co. Flowers camellia-red, dbl.; fragrant.

Holstein F, *mr,* 1939, (Firefly); *Else Poulsen × Dance of Joy seedling;* Kordes; J&P. Bud pointed, dark crimson; flowers clear crimson, single (6 petals), cupped, large (4 in.) blooms in immense clusters; slightly fragrant; foliage leathery, dark, bronze; very vigorous, bushy growth.   GM, Portland, 1939.

Holstein, Climbing Cl F, *mr,* 1947, Kordes, P.

Holsteinperle® HT, *op,* 1987, (KORdiam; Heidi Kabel; Testa Rossa); *Seedling × Flamingo;* Kordes, W., 1985. Flowers orange pink, dbl. (40+ petals), large; nofragrance; Foliage medium, medium green, semi-glossy; bushy growth.

Holstenrose HT, *mr,* 1937, *Gen. MacArthur × Amulett;* Tantau. Flowers scarlet-red, dbl., cupped, large; fragrant; foliage glossy; vigorous, bushy growth.

Holt Hewitt HT, *rb,* 1925, Beckwith. Flowers rich velvety crimson, flushed and edged scarlet, well shaped, large; very fragrant; vigorous, bushy growth.

Holy Toledo™ Min, *ab,* 1978, (ARObri); *Gingersnap × Magic Carrousel;* Christensen; Armstrong Nursery. Bud ovoid, pointed; flowers brilliant apricot-orange, reverse yellow-orange, dbl. (28 petals), imbricated, medium (1½-2 in.); foliage small, glossy, dark; vigorous, bushy growth. AOE, 1980.

Hombre Min, *pb,* 1983, *Humdinger × Rise 'n' Shine;* Jolly, Nelson F.; Rosehill Farm, 1982. Flowers light apricot pink, reverse light pink, dbl. (40+ petals), high-centered, flat, exhibition, small; slight fragrance; foliage small, medium green, semi-glossy; bushy growth. AOE, 1983.

Home & Country HT, *yb,* 1980, (KRIbatis; Comtesse d'Alcantara); *Seedling × Peace;* Kriloff, Michel; Primavera. Flowers yellow blend, large; fragrant; foliage medium green; glossy; upright growth.

Home Run HT, *pb,* 1956, *Pink Delight sport;* Motose. Bud ovoid; flowers rose-bengal, dbl. (40 petals), high-centered, large (5 in.); fragrant; foliage leathery; vigorous growth.

Home Sweet Home HT, *mp,* 1941, Wood & Ingram; C-P. Flowers rich velvety pink, full; fragrant (damask); foliage glossy, dark; vigorous growth.

Home-Coming Min, *mp,* 1989, (MIChome; Homecoming); *Tiki × Party Girl;* Williams, Michael C.; The Rose Garden. Bud pointed; flowers medium pink with slightly darker petal edges, dbl. (35 petals), high-centered, medium, borne usually singly; no fragrance; foliage medium, medium green, semi-glossy; prickles straight, green; Fruit none; upright, tall growth.

Homeland HT, *pb,* 1951, *Hybrid Tea (red) × Guinée;* LeGrice. Flowers neyron rose, base tinted orange, dbl. (50-60 petals), well formed, large (5½-6 in.); very fragrant; foliage leathery, dark; very free growth.

Homenagem Egas Moniz HT, *mp,* 1959, *Walter × Juno;* Moreira; da Silva. Flowers pink.

Homenagem Gago Coutinho HT, *rb,* 1959, *Confidence × Seedling;* Moreira; da Silva. Flowers crimson-red, reverse yellow.

Homenagem Pinto d'Azevedo HT, *op,* 1959, *Super-Congo × Independence;* Moreira; da Silva. Flowers bright salmon-pink, dbl.

Homère T (OGR), *pb,* 1858, Robert et Moreau. Flowers pink, center flesh-white, full, cupped; fragrant; vigorous, bushy growth.

Hondo HT, *yb,* 1989, *Irish Gold × Las Vegas;* Perry, Astor, 1990. Flowers medium yellow with red-purple on tips, aging red-purple, dbl. (33 petals), large; fragrant; foliage large, dark green, matt; upright growth.

Honest Abe™ Min, *dr*, 1978, (AROn); *Fairy Moss × Rubinette*; Christensen; Armstrong Nursery. Bud mossy; flowers deep velvety crimson-red, dbl. (33 petals), mini-moss, small (1½ in.); slightly fragrant (tea); foliage glossy; vigorous, bushy growth.

Honest Red HT, *mr*, 1991, *Seedling × Sea Pearl*; Wambach, Alex A. Flowers medium red, full (26-40 petals), large blooms borne mostly singly; very fragrant; foliage medium, dark green, semi-glossy; tall, bushy growth.

Honey F, *my*, 1955, *Smiles sport*; Marsh; Marsh's Nursery. Flowers coppery yellow, becoming lemon-yellow, semi-dbl., small.

Honey Bear Min, *ab*, 1987, (PIXihon); *Rise 'n' Shine × Holy Toledo*; Chaffin, Laurie; Pixie Treasures Miniature Roses. Flowers deep apricot, yellow base, reverse light apricot, aging creamy apricot, very dbl. (50-55 petals), cupped, loose, small, borne singly; foliage small, medium green, semi-glossy, disease resistant; needle-like, straight, light tan prickles; bushy, low compact growth.

Honey Bun F, *my*, 1973, *Gold Strike × Golden Garnette*; Ellis; Armstrong Nursery. Bud ovoid; flowers medium yellow, dbl., cupped, medium; very fragrant; foliage dark, leathery; very vigorous, upright, bushy growth.

Honey Bunch F, *dy*, 1971, *Circus × Soraya*; Watkins Roses. Flowers deep gold, shaded peach, dbl. (20 petals), long, pointed, large (3 in.); slightly fragrant; foliage light; moderate, upright growth.

Honey Bunch® F, *yb*, 1989, (COCglen; Honeybunch); *((Sabine × Circus) × Maxi) × Bright Smile*; Cocker, James & Sons. Bud ovoid; flowers yellow with salmon-red, reverse yellow, aging honey-yellow, dbl. (45 petals), cupped, small, borne in sprays of 7-13; patio; moderate fragrance; foliage small, dark green, glossy; prickles small, green; fruit round, small, green; bushy, low growth.

Honey Chile F, *lp*, 1964, *Fashion × Queen Elizabeth*; Thomson; Tillotson. Bud pointed; flowers light pink, dbl., cupped, medium blooms in clusters; slightly fragrant; foliage leathery; vigorous, upright, bushy growth.

Honey Favorite HT, *lp*, 1962, (Honey Favourite); *Pink Favorite sport*; Abrams, Von; Peterson & Dering. Flowers light yellowish pink, base yellow.

Honey Gold F, *my*, 1956, *Yellow Pinocchio × Fashion*; Boerner; J&P. Bud ovoid; flowers maize-yellow overcast buff-yellow, dbl. (43 petals), large (3-3½ in.); fragrant; foliage dark, glossy; vigorous, bushy growth; greenhouse variety.

Honey Hill Min, *ob*, 1981, *Seedling × Seedling*; Lyon. Bud ovoid, pointed; flowers orange, dbl. (48 petals), high-centered, HT form, borne singly or several together; fragrant; foliage medium green, semi-glossy; curved, light brown prickles; vigorous, bushy, upright growth.

Honey Mini-Delite Min, *w*, 1991, (CLEhon); *Seedling × Seedling*; Clements, John; Heirloom Old Garden Roses. Flowers honey cream, full (26-40 petals), small (0-4 cms) blooms borne in small clusters; no fragrance; foliage small, medium green, matt; few prickles; low (25 cms), bushy, compact growth.

Honey Moss Min, *ly*, 1977, (AROnemo); *Fairy Moss × Self*; Sudol. Bud mossy; flowers near white, toward honey, dbl. (52 petals), flat, mini-moss, small (1 in.); fragrant; foliage dark, leathery; spreading growth.

Honey 'n' Spice™ Min, *r*, 1986, (MINagco); *Tom Brown × Over the Rainbow*; Williams, Ernest; Mini-Roses. Flowers tan with red highlights, reverse deeper tan with more red, dbl. (45-49 petals), full, small, borne usually singly; moderate, fresh honey fragrance; foliage small, medium green, semi-glossy; few, short, thin, light tan prickles; no fruit; bushy, medium growth.

Honey Rea HT, *pb*, 1973, Concord Floral Co. Bud ovoid; flowers pink, semi-dbl., high-centered, very large; slightly fragrant; foliage large, dark, leathery; very vigorous, bushy growth.

Honeycomb Min, *ly*, 1974, (*R. wichuraiana × Floradora*) × *Debbie*; Moore, R.S.; Sequoia Nursery. Flowers soft yellow to near white, dbl. (30 petals), high-centered, small (1½ in.); fragrant; foliage small, glossy, light, leathery; dwarf, bushy growth.

Honeyflow F, *pb*, 1957, *Spring Song × Gartendirektor Otto Linne*; Riethmuller. Flowers white edged pink, single, borne in very large clusters; fragrant; foliage glossy; vigorous growth.

Honeyglow F, *yb*, 1956, *Goldilocks × Ellinor LeGrice*; LeGrice. Flowers lemon-yellow, reverse shaded orange, semi-dbl., pointed, medium (2 in.), borne in clusters; foliage glossy; vigorous growth.

Honeypot S, *my*, 1969, *Honigmond × Constance Spry*; Austin, D. Flowers sulphur-yellow, dbl. (40-50 petals), cupped, large (4 in.); very fragrant; foliage dark, semi-glossy; vigorous growth.

Honeysweet S, *op*, 1984, (Honey Sweet); *Serendipity × Wiener Charme*; Buck; Iowa State University. Bud medium-large, ovoid, pointed; flowers yellow-red-orange blend, dbl. (28 petals), cupped, large blooms borne 1-8 per cluster; foliage leathery, dark with copper tints; awl-like, brown-tan prickles; bushy, erect growth; hardy; repeat bloom.

Hong-Kong HT, *rb*, 1962, *Soraya × (Henri Mallerin × Peace)*; Dot, P. Flowers citron-yellow edged currant-red, becoming red, dbl., strong stems; bushy growth.

Honigmond F, *my*, 1960, (Honeymoon); *Cläre Grammerstorf × Golden Scepter*; Kordes, R.; A. Dickson & McGredy. Flowers canary-yellow, dbl. (40 petals), rosette shape, medium blooms in clusters (up to 5); slightly fragrant; foliage dark, veined; vigorous, upright, bushy growth.

Honor™ HT, *w*, 1980, (JAColite; Honour; Michèle Torr); Warriner; J&P. Bud ovoid, pointed; flowers white, dbl. (23 petals), loose, large (5 in.); slightly fragrant; foliage large, dark; upright growth. GM, Portland, 1978; AARS, 1980.

Honorine de Brabant B (OGR), *pb*, Flowers pale lilac-pink, spotted and striped mauve and crimson, dbl., loosely cupped, large; foliage light green; vigorous (to 6 ft.); recurrent bloom.

Honour Bright LCl, *dr*, 1950, *(New Dawn × Allen Chandler) × (Mrs. W.J. Grant, Climbing × Richmond, Climbing)*; Eacott. Flowers brilliant crimson, semi-dbl., medium; fragrant; foliage bright green; very vigorous (4-6 ft.); recurrent bloom.

Hon. Charlotte Knollys HT, *pb*, 1926, *Antoine Rivoire × Willowmere*; Bees. Flowers rose, edged lighter, center creamy yellow, dbl.; slightly fragrant. GM, NRS, 1926.

Hon. Charlotte Knollys HT, *pb*, 1926, *Antoine Rivoire × Willowmere*; Bees. Flowers clear rose, edged lighter, center creamy yellow, dbl.; slightly fragrant. GM, NRS, 1926.

Hon. Edith Gifford T (OGR), *w*, 1882, *Mme. Falcot × Perle des Jardins*; Guillot Fils. Flowers flesh-white tinted rose, full, large.

Hon. George Bancroft HT, *rb*, 1879, *Mme. de St. Joseph × Lord Macaulay*; Bennett. Flowers red shaded violet-crimson; very fragrant; moderate growth.

Hon. Ina Bingham HP (OGR), *mp*, 1905, Dickson, A. Flowers pink, stamens golden yellow, dbl. (23 petals), cupped, large; very fragrant; upright growth.

Hon. Joan Acton HT, *pb*, 1950, *Mrs. Sam McGredy × Golden Dawn*; Marshall, J. Flowers cream edged pink, very dbl. (90 petals), pointed, very large; fragrant; foliage bronze-green; hardy.

Hon. Lady Lindsay S, *pb*, 1939, (Honorine Lady Lindsay); *New Dawn × Rev. F. Page-Roberts*; Hansen, N.J.; B&A, 1938. Flowers pink, reverse darker, dbl. (35 petals); foliage

dark; bushy (3x3 ft.) growth; recurrent bloom; not dependably hardy.

Hon. Violet Douglas Pennant HT, *pb*, 1927, Bees. Flowers blend of cream and rose, dbl.; fragrant.

Hoosier Beauty HT, *rb*, 1915, *Richmond × Château de Clos Vougeot*; Dorner. Bud pointed; flowers glowing crimson shaded darker, dbl., large; very fragrant; foliage sparse, rich green, glossy; bushy growth. GM, NRS, 1915.

Hoosier Beauty, Climbing Cl HT, *rb*, 1925, Gray, W.R.

Hoosier Gold F, *dy*, 1974, *Lydia × Golden Wave*; Byrum; J.H. Hill Co. Bud ovoid; flowers deep yellow, dbl. (30-35 petals), large (2½-3½ in.); slightly fragrant; vigorous growth.

Hoosier Honey HT, *dy*, 1973, *Seedling No. 63-704 × Golden Fantasie*; Byrum; J.H. Hill Co. Bud long, pointed; flowers mimosa-yellow, dbl. (25-30 petals), full, high-centered, large (4-5 in.); very fragrant; foliage dark, leathery; vigorous growth.

Hoosier Honey HT, *my*, 1955, *Anzac × Golden Rapture*; Hill, J.H., Co. Bud ovoid; flowers amber-yellow, dbl. (45-50 petals), open, large (4½-5 in.); fragrant; vigorous, upright, bushy growth.

Hoosier Hysteria S, *dr*, 1981, *Karl Herbst × Simone*; Schwartz, Ernest; Krider Nursery. Bud ovoid; flowers dark red, dbl. (45 petals), high-centered, borne singly or in sprays of 5-7; slight fragrance; foliage dark, leathery; very few, curved, dark green prickles; vigorous, tall, upright growth.

Hoot Owl Min, *rb*, 1990, (MORhoot); *Orangeade × Little Artist*; Moore, Ralph S., 1987; Sequoia Nursery, 1991. Bud pointed; flowers red with white eye, single (5 petals), small, borne usually singly or in sprays of 3-5; no fragrance; foliage small, medium green, semi-glossy; bushy, low growth.

Hope Min, *w*, 1985, *Rise 'n' Shine × Party Girl*; Bridges, Dennis A.; Bridges Roses. Flowers white, dbl. (35 petals), well-formed, small; slight fragrance; foliage large, dark, glossy; bushy growth.

Hopscotch Min, *my*, 1979, (AROyol); *Gingersnap × Magic Carrousel*; Christensen; Armstrong Nursery. Bud ovoid, pointed; flowers golden yellow, dbl. (28 petals), imbricated, small (1½ in.); foliage small; vigorous, bushy growth.

Horace McFarland HT, *op*, 1944, (Président Nomblot); *Mme. Arthaud × Seedling*; Mallerin; A. Meilland & C-P, 1944. Bud mahogany-red; flowers coppery pink, dbl. (43 petals), high-centered, large (4½-5½ in.); fragrant (fruity); foliage leathery, dark; vigorous, bushy growth. AARS, 1945.

Horace Vernet HP (OGR), *dr*, 1866, *Général Jacqueminot* × *Seedling*; Guillot Fils. Flowers deep red, dbl. (40 petals), high-centered, large; very fragrant; moderate, erect growth; repeat bloom.

Horden Hall LCl, *w*, 1928, *R. wichuraiana* × *Frau Karl Druschki*; Conyers. Flowers pure white, with long yellow stamens, single, large; slightly fragrant.

Horizon F, *or*, 1956, *Crimson Glory* × *Cinnabar*; Tantau. Bud pointed; flowers geranium-red, dbl., open, large, borne in large clusters; fragrant; foliage leathery; vigorous, upright, bushy growth.

Horndon Pink HT, *dp*, 1963, *Lady Elgin* × *Independence*; Barter. Flowers old-rose-pink, dbl. (60 petals), large (4½ in.); fragrant; foliage dark.

Horrido® F, *mr*, 1963, (Jockey); Tantau, Math. Bud ovoid; flowers pure blood-red, dbl., cupped blooms in large clusters; foliage dark, glossy; bushy, low growth.

Horstmann's Bergfeuer F, *dr*, 1954, *World's Fair* × *Independence*; Horstmann. Flowers dark blood-red, dbl., well formed, very large, borne in large clusters; moderate growth.

Horstmann's Jubiläumsrose F, *op*, 1954, *Golden Rain* × *Alpine Glow*; Tantau; Horstmann. Flowers pink tinted peach, dbl., well formed, large, borne in clusters of 10-12; foliage glossy, leathery; dwarf growth.

Horstmann's Leuchtfeuer F, *dr*, 1954, *Red Favorite* × *Karl Weinhausen*; Tantau; Horstmann. Flowers blood-red, dbl., large, borne in large clusters; moderate growth.

Horstmann's Rosenresli F, *w*, 1955, *Rudolph Timm* × *Lavender Pinocchio*; Kordes; Horstmann. Flowers pure white, dbl., large blooms in clusters; fragrant; bushy.

Horstmann's Schöne Brünette HT, *or*, 1955, *Independence* × *Hens Verschuren*; Horst-mann. Flowers coppery brick-red, dbl., large; strong stems.

Hortense de Beauharnais G (OGR), *pb*, Flowers rose edged rosy lilac, full.

Hortense Vernet M (OGR), *w*, 1861, Moreau-Robert. Flowers white shaded rose, very dbl.; moderate growth.

Horticultor Vidal HT, *op*, 1952, *Mme. Butterfly* × *Federico Casas*; Dot, P. Bud pointed; flowers salmon-pink, dbl. (35 petals), large; very fragrant; bushy growth.

Hortiflora Pol, *mp*, 1974, Delforge, S. Bud oval; flowers pink, dbl. (45 petals), full, medium (2 in.); slightly fragrant.

Hortulanus Albert Fiet HT, *ab*, 1919, *Mme. Mélanie Soupert* × *Mons. Paul Lédé*; Leenders, M. Flowers apricot and lilac-rose, center coppery orange, dbl.; fragrant.

Hortulanus Budde HT, *mr*, 1919, *Gen. MacArthur* × *Mme. Edouard Herriot*; Verschuren. Bud pointed; flowers medium red, dbl., large; fragrant; foliage dark; vigorous.

Hortulanus Fiet HT, *w*, 1919, *Cissie Easlea* × *Golden Star*; Verschuren. Bud pointed; flowers deep and light cream, dbl., open, very large; slightly fragrant; foliage sparse, glossy, dark; vigorous growth.

Hoshizukuyo HT, *w*, 1990, (*Izayoi* × *Sodōri-Himé*) × *White Success*; Ohtsuki, Hironaka. Bud pointed; flowers ivory, full (35-40 petals), high-centered, large, borne usually singly; heavy, fruity fragrance; foliage medium, light green, semi-glossy; medium, upright growth.

Hostess F, *op*, 1960, *Papillon Rose* × (*Cinnabar* × *Alain*); Lens. Flowers pink tinted salmon, semi-dbl., open, large, borne in clusters of 5-7; vigorous, upright growth.

Hostess Gisela F, *dp*, 1973, *Sympathie* × *Dr. A.J. Verhage*; Hetzel; GAWA. Bud ovoid; flowers dark pink, dbl., medium; very fragrant; foliage very glossy; vigorous, upright, bushy growth.

Hot Lips Min, *op*, 1988, (TINlips); *Futura* × *Why Not*; Bennett, Dee; Tiny Petals Nursery. Flowers deep coral to orange, aging paler, dbl. (25-30 petals), high-centered, exhibition, medium, borne usually singly or in sprays of 3-5; slight, fruity fragrance; foliage medium, medium green, semi-glossy; prickles hooked slightly downward, reddish; fruit globular, green to yellow-brown; upright, bushy, tall growth.

Hot 'n' Spicy F, *or*, 1991, (MACsoda); *Mary Sumner* × *Precious Platinum*; McGredy, Sam; Co-Operative Rose Growers, 1990. Flowers orange-red, semi-dbl. (6-14 petals), medium blooms borne in small clusters; slight fragrance; foliage medium, dark green, glossy; bushy growth.

Hot Pants HT, *or*, 1979, (SIMhopan); *Gypsy Moth* × *Princesse*; Simpson, J.W. Bud high-pointed; flowers orange-red, dbl. (48 petals), exhibition, borne usually 3 per cluster; no fragrance; foliage medium green; few prickles; spreading growth.

Hot Pewter HT, *or*, 1978, (Crucenia; Crucencia); *Alec's Red* × *Red Dandy*; Harkness, R. Flowers brilliant orange-red, dbl. (41 petals), high-centered, borne usually singly; slight fragrance; foliage large, mid-green, semi-glossy; broad, dark prickles; bushy growth.

Hot Shot Min, *or*, 1982, (Hotshot); *Futura ×
Orange Honey*; Bennett, Dee; Tiny Petals
Nursery. Flowers vibrant vermilion, dbl. (28
petals), HT-form, medium; very slight fragrance; foliage small, medium green; upright,
bushy growth. AOE, 1984.

Hot Stuff Min, *mr*, 1978, Lyon. Bud pointed;
flowers turkey-red, semi-dbl. (10 petals),
small (1 in.); slightly fragrant; foliage tiny;
very compact, bushy growth.

Hotel Hershey Gr, *or*, 1977, *Queen Elizabeth ×
Comanche*; Williams, J.B.; Hershey Estates.
Bud long, pointed to urn-shaped; flowers
salmon orange-red, dbl. (34 ruffled petals),
high-centered, large (4-4½ in.); slightly fragrant; foliage dark, leathery; upright growth.

Hôtesse de France HT, *dr*, 1962, *Soraya ×
Seedling*; Hémeray-Aubert. Flowers velvety
deep red, cupped, medium; foliage bronze.

Hotline™ Min, *mr*, 1981, (AROmikeh); *Honest
Abe × Trumpeter*; Christensen; Armstrong
Nursery.   Bud ovoid, pointed, lightly
mossed; flowers bright medium red, dbl. (22
petals), classical HT-form, mini-moss, borne
usually singly; moss fragrance; foliage medium green; straight, thin prickles; compact
(near 12 in.) growth.

Houston HT, *dy*, 1980, *Summer Sunshine × Seedling*; Weeks, O.L. Bud ovoid; flowers deep
bright yellow, dbl. (38 petals), high-centered,
borne singly or 3-4 per cluster; tea fragrance;
foliage leathery, wrinkled, dark; long prickles, hooked downward; vigorous, upright
growth.

Houstonian Gr, *dr*, 1962, *Carrousel × Seedling*;
Patterson; Patterson Roses. Bud ovoid; flowers dark red, dbl. (35 petals), large (4 in.);
fragrant; foliage leathery, glossy, bronze; vigorous, upright, tall growth.

Hovyn de Tronchère T (OGR), *rb*, 1897,
Puyravared. Flowers red with orange depths,
bordered silver.

Howard Jerabek S, *mp*, 1978, Jerabek. Flowers pearl-pink, very dbl. (100 petals); fragrant
(apple-blossom); foliage large, glossy; vigorous growth.

Howard Morrison HT, *dr*, 1983, (MAC-
crackle); *Seedling × Seedling*; McGredy, S.,
1982. Flowers dark red, dbl. (35 petals), large;
slight fragrance; foliage medium, medium
green, semi-glossy; upright, bushy growth.

Hubicka HT, *pb*, 1935, *Grete Bermbach sport*;
Böhm. Flowers alabaster-white, sometimes
rosy, base yellow, dbl., very large; fragrant;
foliage dark; bushy growth.

Hudson HT, *mp*, Mallerin. Flowers pale rose,
well shaped; foliage glossy.

Huette's Dainty Florrie Min, *lp*, 1979, *Sweet
and Low × Mary Marshall*; Schwartz, Ernest;
Men's Garden Club of Virginia. Flowers
light pink, dbl. (24 petals); fragrant; foliage
dark green edged dark red; dark red prickles;
upright, bushy growth.

Hugh Dickson HP (OGR), *mr*, 1905, *Lord
Bacon × Gruss an Teplitz*; Dickson, H. Flowers
medium red, dbl. (38 petals), high-centered,
very large; very fragrant; vigorous growth;
recurrent bloom.

Hugh Watson HP (OGR), *op*, 1905, Dickson,
A. Flowers deep pink tinged salmon and
silver-pink, dbl. (24 petals), flat, very large;
vigorous growth.

Hugo Piller HT, *ab*, 1927, *Ophelia sport*; Leenders, M. Flowers flesh-white, center pale ecru.

Hugo Roller T (OGR), *yb*, 1907, Paul, W.
Flowers lemon-yellow, edged and suffused
crimson, dbl., well-formed blooms with weak
stems; fragrant; foliage small, rich green;
compact, bushy growth.

Hugo Schlösser HT, *op*, 1955, *World's Fair ×
Peace*; Kordes. Bud long, pointed; flowers
salmon-pink, dbl., high-centered, very large;
strong stems; fragrant; foliage leathery; very
vigorous, upright, bushy growth.

Huguette Min, *op*, Flowers shrimp-pink shaded
salmon.

Huguette Despiney R, *yb*, 1911, *Marco sport*;
Girin. Flowers light buff-yellow, edged red,
very dbl., small, borne in large clusters; vigorous growth.

Huguette Duflos HT, *op*, 1937, *Betty Uprichard × Seedling*; Lille. Bud pointed, dark
pink; flowers satiny pink, touched salmon,
dbl. (30-40 petals), large; very fragrant; foliage
dark; vigorous, bushy growth.

Huguette Vincent HT, *op*, 1921, *Mrs. Edward
Powell seedling × Willowmere*; Chambard, C.
Flowers brilliant velvety geranium-red, semi-
dbl.

Hula Girl Min, *ob*, 1975, *Miss Hillcrest × Mabel
Dot*; Williams, E.D.; Mini-Roses & Sequoia
Nursery. Bud long, pointed; flowers bright
orange, dbl. (45 petals), small (1 in.); fragrant
(fruity); foliage small, glossy, embossed;
bushy growth. AOE, 1976.

Hula Hoop HT, *pb*, 1960, Freud; Horstmann.
Flowers striped bright pink and red; very
fragrant. RULED EXTINCT 11/90.

Hula Hoop F, *pb*, 1990, (MORhoop); *(Dortmund × Seedling) × Self*; Moore, Ralph S.;
Sequoia Nursery, 1991. Bud pointed; flowers
white with pink to red edge, similar reverse,
aging less intense, similar color, semi-dbl. (15
petals), opening flat, medium (7-8 cms.),
borne in sprays of 5-15; no fragrance; foliage

medium, medium green, matt; upright, medium growth.

Hullabalou Min, *yb*, 1990, *Rise 'n' Shine* × *Seedling*; Stoddard, Louis. Bud pointed; flowers light orange on yellow with yellow reverse, aging to dull yellow blend, dbl. (20 petals), urn-shaped, small blooms borne in sprays of 2-3; moderate fragrance; foliage small, medium green when new, aging to maroon, semi-glossy; prickles straight, sparse, small, red; bushy, low growth.

HULTHEMIA A monotypic genus closely allied to *Rosa*, and originally included in it by many writers. The one species is distinguished from *Rosa* by the simple leaves without stipules and small, solitary flowers with a dark eye. Iran to Afghanistan.

H. persica (Michaux) Bornmueller *yb*, *(Rosa persica* Michaux; *Rosa berberifolia* Pallas; *Rosa simplicifolia* Salisbury; *Hulthemia berberifolia* (Pallas) Dumortier; *Lowea berberifolia* (Pallas) Lindley). (Int. 1790). Dwarf shrublet with long underground rhizomes. Flowers buttercup-yellow with a scarlet eye like a Cistus, 1 in. diameter blooms; simple, bluish green leaves; Fruit prickly; Curious xerophyte of great botanic interest, exceedingly rare and difficult to cultivate; Propagation by seed only; (14).

× **H. hardii** (Cels) Rowley (*Rosa* × *hardii* Cels); *Hulthemia persica* × *Rosa clinophylla*; Hardy before 1836. Diffuse shrublet with 1-7 narrow leaflets and striking 2 in. yellow flowers with the crimson eye of *Hulthemia*. Unique beauty, hard to maintain in cultivation. Best grown in an airy cold house and sprayed regularly against mildew, to which it is a martyr.

× **Hulthemosa** *Intergeneric hybrids between Hulthemia and Rosa*; Characters intermediate between the two genera. At least two spontaneous crosses (× *H. guzarica Juz.* and × *H. kopetdaghensis (Meff) Juz.) have been reported from the USSR. See also* × *H. hardii, Tigris and Euphrates.*

Humboldt HT, mp, 1922, *Ophelia* × *Seedling*; Hill, E.G., Co.; Cottage Gardens Co. Flowers bright rose-pink, dbl., high-centered; fragrant; foliage glossy, bronze; vigorous growth.

Humdinger Min, *op*, 1976, *Gold Coin seedling* × *Miniature seedling*; Schwartz, E.W.; Nor'East Min. Roses. Bud pointed; flowers orange-red, dbl. (53 petals), high-centered, small (1 in.); slightly fragrant; foliage glossy, dark; upright, bushy. AOE, 1978.

Hume's Blush Tea-scented China T (OGR), *lp*, 1809, *R.* × *odorata variety*; A. Hume. Flowers light pink, dbl.; very fragrant. A famous ancestral rose.

Hummingbird HT, *ob*, 1934, *Talisman sport*; Scittine; Lainson. Bud pointed; flowers bronze-orange, very dbl., medium (3 in.); vigorous growth.

Humoreske Min, *lp*, 1957, *Midget* × *Pixie*; Spek; McGredy. Flowers white, tinged pink, dbl., small, bushy, compact growth.

Humpty-Dumpty Min, *lp*, 1952, *(R. multiflora nana* × *Mrs. Pierre S. duPont F²)* × *Tom Thumb*; deVink; T. Robinson. Flowers soft carmine-pink, center deeper, very dbl. (about 100 petals), blooms in clusters; height 6-8 in.

Hunter HRg (S), *mr*, 1961, (The Hunter); *R. rugosa rubra* × *Independence*; Mattock, R.H.; Mattock. Flowers bright crimson, dbl. (43 petals), medium; foliage rugose; vigorous (4-5 ft.) growth; recurrent bloom.

Hunter's Moon HT, *my*, 1951, *Condesa de Sástago* × *Gorgeous*; McGredy. Flowers yellow, dbl. (30 petals); slightly fragrant; foliage glossy, dark; very vigorous growth.

Huntsman HT, *rb*, 1951, *The Queen Alexandra Rose seedling* × *Crimson Glory*; Robinson, H.; J&P. Flowers spectrum-red, reverse yellow, dbl. (35-40 petals), large (5½ in.); fragrant; foliage dark.

Hurdy Gurdy Min, *rb*, 1986, (MACpluto); *Matangi* × *Stars 'n' Stripes*; McGredy, S. Flowers dark red with white stripes, dbl. (26-40 petals), small; mini-flora; slight fragrance; foliage small, medium green, semi-glossy; upright growth.

Huron S, *lp*, 1932, *Pythagoras* × *R. cinnamomea*; Central Exp. Farm. Flowers white flushed pink, semi-dbl.; fragrant; foliage leathery; vigorous (2½ ft.), compact, bushy growth; nonrecurrent bloom; good hedge rose.

Huron Sunset Min, *my*, 1990, (RENhuron); *Party Girl* × *Golden Rule*; Rennie, Bruce; Rennie Roses, International, 1991. Flowers medium yellow, full (26-40 petals), small, borne in small clusters; no fragrance; foliage small, medium green, semi-glossy; bushy growth.

Hurra® F, *or*, 1962, Tantau, Math. Bud pointed; flowers orange-red, dbl., medium blooms in clusters; foliage glossy; vigorous, bushy growth.

Hurst Charm LCl, *pb*, 1936, Hicks. Flowers pink, slightly tinted mauve, large.

Hurst Crimson Pol, *dr*, 1933, *Ideal sport*; Hicks. Flowers deep crimson, borne in large trusses.

Hurst Delight LCl, *w*, 1936, Hicks. Flowers clear pale cream; fragrant; vigorous growth.

Hurst Favourite LCl, *w*, 1936, Hicks. Flowers pure ivory-white, semi-dbl., very large, borne in clusters; fragrant; very vigorous, climbing growth.

Hurst Gem Pol, *ob*, 1931, *Orléans Rose sport*; Hicks. Flowers brilliant orange-scarlet, semi-dbl., small.

Hurst Glory HT, *ob*, 1936, Hicks. Flowers pale salmon-cerise, flushed yellow, dbl., well shaped, large; fragrant; vigorous growth.

Hurst Scarlet HT, *dr*, 1933, Hicks. Flowers deep scarlet, full, large; fragrant.

Hutton Village HT, *my*, 1973, *Whisky Mac sport*; Deamer; Warley Rose Gardens. Flowers bright yellow.

Hvissinge-Rose F, *pb*, 1943, *Orléans Rose × Seedling*; Poulsen, S. Flowers pinkish with yellow, single, borne in clusters; vigorous growth.

H. V. Machin HT, *dr*, 1914, Dickson, A. Flowers very dark scarlet-crimson, dbl., globular, very large; slightly fragrant; foliage glaucous beech-green. GM, NRS, 1912.

H. V. Machin, Climbing Cl HT, *dr*, 1919, Dickson, H.

H. V. Machin, Climbing Cl HT, *dr*, 1922, H&S.

Hwiezdoslav HT, *rb*, 1936, Böhm. Flowers copper-red to orange-copper-red, dbl., cupped, large; very fragrant; foliage glossy; vigorous, bushy growth.

Hylo F, *mp*, 1961, *Highlight sport*; Cant, B.R. Flowers salmon-pink, dbl. (28 petals), medium (2-2½ in.) borne in clusters; slightly fragrant; bushy growth.

Hymne F, *mp*, 1964, *Miracle × Seedling*; Verbeek. Bud short, pointed; flowers neyron rose, dbl. (38-52 petals), large, borne in large clusters; foliage dark, glossy; vigorous growth.

Hypacia C (OGR), *pb*, (Hypathia); Prior to 1846. Flowers bright rose-pink spotted white, center whitish, dbl., cupped, large; fragrant (damask).

Hythe Cluster Pol, *dp*, 1935, Archer. Flowers glowing deep pink, semi-dbl., cupped, borne in large clusters; foliage small, glossy, light; vigorous growth.

Ian Brinson HT, *dr*, 1945, *Mrs. J.J. Hedley-Willis × J.C. Thornton*; Bees. Flowers crimson, dbl. (30 petals), compact, large (4-5 in.); very fragrant; foliage dark.

Ibis F, *ob*, 1973, (GODeurpan); *Europeana × Orangeade*; Godin. Bud ovoid; flowers orange, semi-dbl. (14-16 petals); foliage dark.

Ibiza HT, *w*, 1938, *Mme. Butterfly × Frau Karl Druschki*; Dot, P. Flowers white, well formed; fragrant; erect growth.

Ice Crystal Min, *w*, 1991, (CLEice); *Seedling × Baby Betsy McCall*; Clements, John; Heirloom Old Garden Roses, 1989. Flowers crystal white, very full (41+ petals), exhibition, small (0-4 cms) blooms borne in small clusters; micro-mini; no fragrance; foliage small, medium green, semi-glossy; some prickles; low (20 cms), bushy, compact growth.

Ice Fairy S, *w*, 1984, (SANmed); *The Fairy sport*; Sanday, John; Sanday Roses Ltd. Flowers white.

Ice Maiden F, *w*, 1977, *Iceberg × Iceberg*; Garelya. Bud pointed; flowers pure white, semi-dbl (15 petals), semi-formal, large (3½ in.); fragrant; foliage narrow, glossy, light green; vigorous, upright growth.

Ice Princess Min, *lp*, 1983, (LAVice); *Pink seedling × Lemon Delight*; Laver, Keith. Flowers light pink, light yellow stamens, finishing white, dbl. (40+ petals), medium; no fragrance; foliage small, medium green, matt.

Ice Queen™ Min, *w*, 1991, (SAVanice); *Cupcake sport*; Saville, F. Harmon, 1983; Nor'East Miniature Roses. Bud ovoid; flowers white, very dbl. (60 petals), high-centered, exhibition, medium; no fragrance; foliage medium, dark green, semi-glossy; bushy, medium growth.

Ice White F, *w*, 1966, (Vision Blanc®); *Mme. Léon Cuny × (Orange Sweetheart × Cinnabar)*; McGredy, S., IV; McGredy. Flowers white, dbl. (25 petals), large (3 in.) blooms in clusters; foliage glossy. GM, Portland, 1970.

Iceberg F, *w*, 1958, (KORbin; Fée des Neiges; Schneewittchen); *Robin Hood × Virgo*; Kordes, R. Bud long, pointed; flowers pure white, dbl., large blooms in clusters; very fragrant; foliage light green, glossy; vigorous, upright, bushy growth. GM, NRS & Baden-Baden, 1958.

Iceberg, Climbing Cl F, *w*, 1968, Cant, B.R.

Iced Ginger F, *ob*, 1971, *Anne Watkins × Seedling*; Dickson, A. Flower petals palest pink, reverse coppery, dbl. (45 petals), large (4½ in.); fragrant; foliage red, veined.

Iced Parfait F, *lp*, 1972, *Pink Parfait × Iceberg*; Xavier, Sister M. Flowers pale pink, dbl. (40 petals), urn-shaped, medium, borne 6 per cluster; fragrant; foliage light green; straight, red prickles; bushy, compact growth.

Iceland Queen LCl, *w*, 1935, Horvath; Wyant. Flowers creamy white, dbl., large; vigorous growth.

ICI Golden Celebration Gr, *dy*, 1988, (PEAquant); *Seedling × Seedling*; Pearce, C.A.; The Limes New Roses. Flowers golden yellow, dbl. (26-40 petals), large; fragrant; foliage medium, medium green, glossy, mildew resistant; bushy, healthy growth.

Ico F, *m*, 1986, *Deep Purple sport*; Patil, B.K.; KSG Sons. Flowers light purple, very dbl. (60-70 petals), globular; slight fragrance; foliage dark green, glossy; brownish-green prickles curving downward; vigorous, upright, bushy growth.

Ico Beauty HT, *pb*, 1986, *Red Planet sport*; Patil, B.K.; KSG Sons. Flowers rose pink, reverse flushed white, dbl. (25-30 petals), high-centered, medium; slight fragrance; foliage glossy; pale green prickles curving downward; upright, bushy growth.

Ida Belle™ Min, *m*, 1989, (MINayco); *(Tom Brown × (Rise 'n' Shine × Watercolor)) × Twilight Trail*; Williams, Ernest D. Flowers lavender with blends of amber, dbl. (33 petals), exhibition, very long-lasting, small; very fragrant; foliage small, medium green, glossy; bushy growth.

Ida Elizabeth HT, *mr*, 1987, (WELiz); *Red Lion × Mainauperle*; Welsh, Eric; Treloar Roses Pty. Ltd., 1990. Flowers medium red, dbl. (30 petals), exhibition, large, borne singly; fragrant; foliage matt; medium, bushy growth.

Ida Klemm R, *w*, 1907, *Crimson Rambler sport*; Walter, L. Flowers snow-white, immense clusters on long, strong stems; vigorous growth.

Ida McCracken HT, *op*, 1952, *Ethel Somerset × Mrs. Sam McGredy*; Norman; Harkness. Flowers salmon and coral, dbl. (25-30 petals), well formed, large (4 in.); fragrant; foliage leathery, dark; free growth.

Ida Scholten HT, *pb*, 1933, *Capt. F.S. Harvey-Cant × Gen. MacArthur*; Buisman. Flowers pink shaded carmine-red, dbl., very large; foliage dark, leathery, glossy; bushy, dwarf, compact growth.

Ideal Pol, *mr*, 1921, *Miss Edith Cavell sport*; Spek. Flowers medium red.

Idée Fixe® F, *or*, 1980, (LENdec); *Seedling × (Seedling × Floradora)*; Lens, Louis. Flowers light orange-red, 15 petals, 2 in. blooms in clusters of 3-18; slight fragrance; foliage small, dark; hooked, light red prickles; low, bushy growth.

Idun F, *mp*, 1969, *Schneewittchen × Fanal*; Lundstad. Flowers neyron rose, dbl. (41 petals), cupped, large, borne in clusters; foliage dark, glossy; bushy growth.

Idylle HT, *pb*, 1959, (Ideal Home); *Monte Carlo × Tonnerre*; Laperrière; EFR. Flowers carmine-pink, base white, dbl. (25-30 petals), well formed, large (5 in.); fragrant; vigorous, upright growth.

Iga 63 HT, *pb*, 1963, *Confidence × Seedling*; Moreira; da Silva. Flowers pink and red.

Igloo HT, *w*, 1969, *Seedling × White Knight*; Verbeek. Bud ovoid; flowers white, dbl., medium; foliage dark.

Ignasi Iglesias HT, *mr*, 1934, *Angel Guimera × (Souv. de Claudius Pernet × Mme. Butterfly)*;

Dot, P. Flowers rose in early season, oriental red in summer, dbl., high-centered; very fragrant; foliage wrinkled; vigorous, bushy growth.

Ignis S, *mr*, 1934, Chotkové Rosarium; Böhm. Flowers fiery red, very large; foliage leathery, dark; vigorous (3¼-6½ ft.) growth; non-recurrent bloom.

Igor *pb*, 1913, Geltsendeger. Flowers carmine-white, dbl. (36 petals), medium; very fragrant; foliage dark; spreading growth.

Ikaruga HT, *yb*, 1975, *McGredy's Ivory × Garden Party*; Ito. Bud ovoid; flowers yellow blend, dbl. (35 petals), high-centered, very large (6 in.); slightly fragrant; vigorous, upright growth.

Ilaria F, *dp*, 1962, *Cinnabar × Fashion*; Borgatti; Sgaravatti. Flowers coral-red, semi-dbl., well formed; foliage dark.

Ildiko F, *mr*, 1971, *Mardi Gras × Paprika*; Inst. of Orn. Plant Growing. Bud ovoid; flowers cherry-red, semi-dbl., cupped, medium; moderate, upright growth; profuse, intermittent bloom.

Île de France R, *rb*, 1922, *American Pillar Seedling*; Nonin. Flowers bright scarlet, center white, semi-dbl., open, borne in clusters on short, strong stems; slightly fragrant; foliage large, leathery, dark; very vigorous (15-20 ft.) growth.

Illinois Gr, *or*, 1969, *Soprano × Tropicana*; Morey; Country Garden Nursery. Bud long, pointed; flowers orange-red, dbl. (25 petals), large; fragrant; foliage leathery; vigorous, bushy growth.

Illumination F, *dy*, 1970, *Cläre Grammerstorf × Happy Event*; Dickson, P.; A. Dickson. Flowers deep sulphur-yellow, semi-dbl. (12 petals), large (3 in.); fragrant; foliage glossy, light; free growth.

Illusion K (S), *mr*, 1961, Kordes, R. Flowers blood-red to cinnabar, dbl., large blooms in large clusters; fragrant; foliage leathery, glossy, light green; vigorous growth.

Illusion HT, *my*, 1961, *Peace × Seedling*; Verbeek. Flowers yellow, dbl. (50 petals); fragrant; foliage glossy; vigorous growth

Ilse Haberland® S, *mp*, 1956, Kordes. Flowers crimson-pink, dbl., high-centered, very large; fragrant; foliage glossy; vigorous, upright, bushy growth.

Ilse Krohn LCl, *w*, 1957, *Golden Glow × R. kordesii*; Kordes. Flowers pure white, very dbl., high-centered, very large; slightly fragrant; foliage glossy, leathery; very vigorous growth; non-recurrent bloom.

Ilse Krohn Superior® K (S), *w*, 1964, Kordes. Flowers pure white, dbl., very fragrant; foliage dark; vigorous (9 ft.) growth.

Ilseta® F, *mp*, 1985, (TANatesil; Ilsetta); *Parentage not given*; Tantau, M., 1983. Flowers medium pink, dbl. (35 petals), medium; no fragrance; foliage medium, medium green, matt; upright growth; greenhouse variety.

I Love You F, *dp*, 1981, *Margaret Thatcher sport*; Takatori, Yoshiho; Japan Rose Nursery. Flowers deep pink.

Imagination HT, *ab*, 1992, (WEKmar); *Marmalade × Seedling*; Winchel, Joe; Weeks Roses, 1993. Buds large, shapely; flowers apricot orange, yellow reverse, good distinct bicoloration, full (26-40 petals), large (7+ cms), shapely blooms borne mostly singly; slight fragrance; foliage large, clean, medium green, semi-glossy; some prickles; medium (100-130 cms), attractive, compact, upright, bushy growth.

Imatra F, *pb*, 1930, *Orléans Rose seedling*; Poulsen, S.; Olsson. Flowers pink to white.

Immaculada Galan F, *w*, 1968, LeGrice. Flowers white, dbl. (60-70 petals), globular, large, borne in trusses; foliage small, bluegray; very free growth.

Immensee® S, *lp*, 1983, (KORimro; Grouse; Lac Rose; Kordes' Rose Immensee); *The Fairy × R. wichuraiana seedling*; Kordes, W., 1982. Flowers light pink to near white, single, small; fragrant; foliage small, dark, glossy; spreading (to 13 ft.) growth; groundcover. GM, RNRS, 1984.

Immortal Juno S, *dp*, 1992, (AUSjuno); Austin, David; David Austin Roses, 1983. Flowers deep pink, very full (41+ petals), large (7+ cms) blooms borne in small clusters; very fragrant; foliage medium, medium green, semi-glossy; some prickles; tall (150 cms), upright growth.

Imogene™ Min, *yb*, 1985, (MINyco); *Little Darling × Over the Rainbow*; Williams, E.D.; MiniRoses. Flowers yellow, marked red, dbl. (45 petals), well-formed, small; slight fragrance; foliage small, dark, glossy; upright, bushy growth.

Imp F, *rb*, 1971, *Daily Sketch × Impeccable*; Dawson, George; Brundrett. Bud globular; flowers red, reverse silver-pink, dbl., small; slightly fragrant; foliage large, dark, leathery; bushy growth.

Impala F, *op*, 1972, (HERpim); *Zambra × Seedling*; Herholdt, J.A. Bud ovoid, pointed; flowers coppery, reverse orange, dbl. (30 petals), cupped, large (2½-3 in.); foliage bright green; bushy growth.

Impatient F, *or*, 1982, (JACdew); *America × Seedling*; Warriner, W.A.; J&P, 1984. Flowers orange-red, semi-dbl., medium; slight fragrance; foliage medium, light green, glossy; upright, bushy growth. AARS, 1984.

Impeccable HT, *dr*, 1955, Delbard-Chabert. Flowers deep velvety red, dbl., well-shaped; very fragrant; foliage dark.

Impératrice Eugénie M (OGR), *m*, 1856, Pere Guillot. Flowers lilac-pink, dbl., medium; fragrant; vigorous growth.

Imperial HT, *rb*, 1957, *Geranium × Opera*; Moreira; da Silva. Flowers cardinal-red, reverse golden yellow, well formed.

Imperial Gold HT, *my*, 1962, (Canadiana); *Charlotte Armstrong × Girona*; Swim; C.R. Burr. Bud ovoid; flowers lemon-yellow to indian yellow, dbl. (30-35 petals), large (3½ -4½ in.); fragrant; foliage leathery, dark, glossy; vigorous, upright growth.

Imperial Pink HT, *mp*, 1942, *Royal Beauty sport*; Coddington. Flowers pink.

Imperial Potentate HT, *mp*, 1921, *Ophelia × Hoosier Beauty*; Clarke Bros. Flowers medium pink, dbl. (45 petals), high-centered, large; foliage dark, leathery; vigorous. GM, Portland, 1921.

Imperial Queen HT, *mr*, 1962, *Queen Elizabeth × Chrysler Imperial*; Lammerts; C.R. Burr. Bud long, pointed; flowers cherry-red, dbl. (21 petals), cupped, large (4½-5 in.); fragrant; foliage leathery, glossy; vigorous, compact growth.

Impress HT, *rb*, 1929, Dickson, A.; Liggit; Dreer. Bud ovoid, cardinal-red, shaded orange; flowers salmon-cerise, tinted golden, dbl. (40-45 petals), very large; foliage dark, glossy; vigorous growth.

Improved Cécile Brünner F, *op*, 1948, (Rosy Morn); *Dainty Bess × R. gigantea*; Duehrsen; H&S. Bud long, pointed; flowers salmon-pink, dbl. (30 petals), high-centered, medium, borne in clusters; slightly fragrant; foliage leathery, dull green; very vigorous, upright growth.

Improved Lafayette F, *mr*, 1935, *E.G. Hill × Seedling*; H&S; Dreer. Flowers medium red, semi-dbl.; slightly fragrant; foliage soft; vigorous, bushy growth.

Improved Peace HT, *yb*, 1959, *Peace sport*; Dean. Bud ovoid; flowers yellow edged and flushed pink, dbl., high-centered, large; slightly fragrant; foliage leathery, wrinkled; very vigorous, bushy growth.

Improved Premier Bal HT, *pb*, Wheatcroft Bros. Flowers pale cream edged deep pink, large; fragrant; foliage leathery; vigorous growth.

Improved Prince Philip Gr, *or*, 1964, *Queen Elizabeth × Prince Philip*; Leenders, J. Flowers orange-red, well formed.

Improved Universal Favorite R, *mp*, 1901, Manda, W.A. Flowers brilliant pink.

Improved Verdun Pol, *dp*, 1946, Kluis; Klyn. Flowers vivid carmine-red, dbl., borne in clusters; foliage leathery; bushy growth.

Impulse Min, *op*, 1986, *Red Ace × Chris Jolly*; Jolly, Marie; Rosehill Farm. Flowers salmon-pink, light yellow reverse, dbl. (38 petals), cupped, small; no fragrance; foliage small, medium green, semi-glossy; long, brownish prickles; fruit not observed; medium, upright growth.

In the Mood Min, *yb*, 1988, (SEAmood); *Rise 'n' Shine × Seedling*; McCann, Sean. Flowers yellow streaked pink, dbl. (20 petals), small; slight fragrance; foliage small, medium green, semi-glossy; bushy growth.

In the Pink F, *mp*, 1988, *Baby Faurax × Seedling*; Ryan, C.; Melville Nursery, 1988. Flowers medium pink, dbl. (60 petals), medium, borne in sprays of 4-5; musk fragrance; foliage greenish-red, glossy; prickles hooked, red; medium, bushy growth.

Inano HT, *dy*, 1978, *Doreen × Goldilocks*; Teranishi, K.; Itami Rose Nursery. Flowers deep yellow, dbl. (40 petals), urn-shaped, medium, borne singly; fruity fragrance; foliage medium, light green; small, brown prickles; medium, bushy growth.

Inata F, *op*, 1967, *Valeta sport*; deRuiter. Flowers pink shaded salmon, semi-dbl., open, borne in trusses; vigorous growth.

Inca de Mallorca F, *mr*, 1958, *Soller × Floradora*; Dot, P. Flowers strawberry-red, dbl. (20 petals), strong stems; compact growth.

Incense HT, *dr*, 1968, *(Karl Herbst × New Yorker) × Konrad Adenauer*; LeGrice. Flowers deep red, full, pointed; very fragrant; vigorous growth.

Inch'Allah HT, *pb*, 1944, *Pres. Macia × Editor McFarland*; Meilland, F. Bud long; flowers bright pink, reverse flesh, stamens yellow, semi-dbl., very large; vigorous growth.

Incomparable HP (OGR), *w*, 1923, Giraud, A. Flowers rosy white, large.

Incredible S, *yb*, 1984, *Gingersnap × Sevilliana*; Buck; Iowa State University. Bud ovoid, pointed; flowers yellow freckled and streaked with orange-red, dbl. (28 petals), urn-shaped, large, borne 1-10 per cluster; fragrant; foliage medium large, leathery, dark olive green, copper tinted when young; awl-like, brown prickles; vigorous, erect growth; hardy; repeat bloom.

Indéfectible Pol, *mr*, 1919, *Annchen Muüler seedling*; Turbat. Flower bright clear red, semi-dbl., fragrant.

Independence F, *or*, 1951, (Geranium; Kordes' Sondermeldung; Reina Elisenda; Sondermeldung); *F2 seedling (Baby Château × Crimson Glory)*; Kordes; J&P. Bud urn-shaped; flowers pure scarlet, dbl. (35 petals), cupped, large (4½ in.) blooms in clusters (up to 10); fragrant; foliage glossy, dark; growth moderate; (28). GM, Bagatelle, 1943, NRS, 1950, Portland, 1953.

Independence, Climbing Cl F, *or*, 1960, Baldacci & Figli.

Independence Day HT, *ab*, 1919, *Mme. Edouard Herriot × Souv. de Gustave Prat*; Bees. Bud pointed; flowers sunflower-gold, stained flame-color and orange-apricot, dbl., globular, high-centered; very fragrant; foliage leathery, glossy, dark; vigorous growth. GM, NRS, 1919.

Independence Day, Climbing Cl HT, *ab*, 1930, Brown, W.&J.; E. Murrell.

Independence '76 F, *mr*, 1974, *Cotillion × Suspense*; Byrum; J.H. Hill Co. Bud short, pointed; flowers medium red, dbl. (22 petals), high-pointed, large (3-4 in.); fragrant (tea); vigorous, upright growth.

Indian Chief HT, *rb*, 1967, *Tropicana × Seedling*; Gregory. Flowers currant-red shaded orange, dbl., pointed; slightly fragrant; foliage dark; very free growth.

Indian Gold F, *yb*, 1961, *Goldilocks × Seedling*; Abrams, Von; Peterson & Dering. Bud ovoid, flushed red; flowers yellow flushed soft pink, dbl. (30-45 petals), high-centered, large (3½ in.) borne in clusters on short stems; fragrant; foliage glossy, light green; upright, compact growth.

Indian Maid HT, *ob*, *Talisman seedling × Souv. de Claudius Pernet*; Padilla. Bud long, pointed; flowers salmon, reverse bronze-yellow, dbl., high-centered; very fragrant; foliage glossy; vigorous growth.

Indian Pink HT, *pb*, 1975, *Seedling × Orange Tango*; McDaniel; Carlton Rose Nursery. Flowers pink blend, dbl. (30-36 petals), globular, large (5 in.); foliage leathery; very vigorous, upright, bushy growth.

Indian Princess Min, *r*, 1982, (PIXiprin); *Yellow Jewel × Golden Cougar*; Strawn, Leslie E.; Pixie Treasures. Flowers tan flushed orange, reverse burnt umber, shaded garnet-brown, dbl. (20 petals), medium; very fragrant; foliage small, dark, semi-glossy; upright.

Indian Red HT, *rb*, 1948, *Pink Princess × Crimson Glory*; Brownell. Bud long, pointed; flowers red shaded deeper, dbl., high-centered, large; fragrant; foliage small, glossy; vigorous, bushy, upright growth; hardy.

Indian Song HT, *pb*, 1971, (MEIhimper; Preziosa); *(Radar × Karl Herbst) × Sabrina*; Meilland. Flowers rose, reverse gold, dbl. (40 petals), high-centered, large (5 in.); slightly fragrant; foliage glossy, dark; vigorous, upright growth.

Indian Summer Cl HT, *ob*, 1938, *Ednah Thomas × Autumn*; Duehrsen; H&S. Bud pointed; flowers orange, streaked red, dbl. (25 petals), large; very fragrant; foliage dark bronze, leathery, glossy; very vigorous (to 12-18 ft.) growth.

Indiana HT, *pb*, 1907, *Rosalind × Frau Karl Druschki*; Hill, E.G., Co. Flowers bright pink, faintly suffused orange, dbl.; bushy growth.

Indianapolis HT, *mp*, 1971, *Coloranja × Seedling*; Schloen, J.; Ellesmere Nursery. Flowers deep yellow-pink, very dbl., cupped, medium; slightly fragrant; foliage glossy, leathery; moderate, upright growth.

Indica Alba Ch (OGR), *lp*, 1802, (White Daily Rose); *Old Blush sport*. Flowers very light blush.

Indira HT, *pb*, 1973, *Baccará × Prima Ballerina*; Hetzel; GAWA. Bud ovoid; flowers pink, reverse lighter, medium; slightly fragrant; foliage soft; vigorous, upright, bushy growth.

Indispensable LCl, *mp*, 1947, *Roserie sport*; Klyn. Bud globular; flowers pink, dbl., high-centered, medium, borne in clusters; slightly fragrant; foliage glossy; moderate, upright, pillar growth.

Indra LCl, *dp*, 1937, *(Ophelia × R. multiflora) × Florex*; Tantau. Bud pointed; flowers rose-pink, semi-dbl., open, borne in clusters on long stems; slightly fragrant; foliage glossy; very vigorous, climbing growth.

Indy 500 Gr, *or*, 1976, *(Aztec × Queen Elizabeth seedling) × (Independence × Scarlet Knight seedling)*; Williams, J.B.; Krider Nursery. Bud tapered; flowers brilliant orange-red, dbl. (32 petals), medium-high to flat, large (4½-5 in.); very fragrant; foliage large, glossy, dark, reddish; vigorous, upright growth.

Infantania F, *w*, 1953, *Baby Alberic × Seedling*; Heers; Langbecker. Flowers snow-white, sometimes tinged green, dbl., small, borne in large clusters; very fragrant.

Infante Beatrice HT, *ob*, 1930, *Marie Adélaide × Seedling*; Guillot, M. Flowers orange-yellow, tinted reddish gold, base golden, dbl.; very fragrant; vigorous growth.

Infante Maria Cristina HT, *ob*, 1930, Gaujard. Bud pointed; flowers coppery, tinged carmine; fragrant; foliage reddish bronze; vigorous growth.

Inferno HT, *ob*, 1982, (AROkunce); *Zorina × Yankee Doodle*; Christensen, J.E.; Armstrong Nursery. Flowers orange blend, well-formed, large; slight fragrance; foliage medium, dark, semi-glossy; upright, bushy growth.

Ingar Olsson F, *mr*, 1931, *Else Poulsen × Ophelia*; Poulsen, S. Flowers brilliant cerise-red, semi-dbl., cupped blooms in clusters; slightly fragrant; foliage leathery; vigorous, rather compact growth.

Inge Horstmann HT, *rb*, 1964, Tantau, Math. Bud long, red, reverse white tinged pink; flowers cherry-red, high-centered; long stems; very fragrant; vigorous, bushy growth.

Ingrid Bergman® HT, *dr*, 1984, (POUlman); *Seedling × Seedling*; Poulsen, D.T.; John Mattock, Ltd., 1985. Flowers dark red, dbl. (35 petals), medium; slight fragrance; foliage medium, dark, semi-glossy; upright growth. GM, Belfast, 1985, Madrid, 1986; Golden Rose of The Hague, 1987.

Ingrid Stenzig Pol, *dp*, 1951, (Pink Triumph); *Orange Triumph sport*; Hassefras Bros.; B&A. Flowers rose-pink, buttercup form, small, borne in large clusters.

Ink Spots HT, *dr*, 1985, *Seedling × Seedling*; Weeks, O.L. Flowers dark red, dbl. (35 petals), medium; slight fragrance; foliage large, dark, semi-glossy; upright, bushy, spreading growth.

Inka® HT, *op*, 1978, (TANtreika); Tantau, 1981. Bud pointed; flowers salmon, dbl., large; slightly fragrant; foliage large, glossy; upright, bushy growth.

Inner Glow Min, *rb*, 1990, (PIXinner); *Ann Moore × Rainbow's End*; Chaffin, Lauren M.; Pixie Treasures Miniature Roses, 1991. Bud ovoid; flowers red with golden yellow base, yellow reverse, red veining towards outer edges, holds color as it ages, dbl. (40 petals), high-centered, exhibition, medium blooms borne singly; slight fragrance; foliage medium, medium green, semi-glossy; prickles hooked, tan; fruit round, medium green; bushy, medium growth.

Inner Wheel F, *pb*, 1984, (FRYjasso); *Pink Parfait × Picasso*; Fryer's Nursery. Flowers carmine edged rose pink, dbl. (22 petals), large; slight fragrance; foliage medium, dark red, matt; bushy growth.

Innisfree F, *yb*, 1964, *(Karl Herbst × Masquerade) × Circus*; Dickson, P.; A. Dickson. Flowers yellow, orange and pink, dbl. (22 petals), medium blooms in clusters; vigorous, tall growth.

Innocence HT, *w*, 1921, Chaplin Bros. Flowers white, stamens reddish, semi-dbl. (12 petals), slightly waved, large (5 in.), borne in clusters; fragrant; foliage dark; vigorous growth.

Innocence, Climbing Cl HT, *w*, 1938, Armstrong, J.A.; Armstrong Nursery.

Innocencia® F, *w*, 1987, (KORenbon); *Lorena sport*; Kordes, W., 1986. Flowers white, dbl. (26-40 petals), medium; no fragrance; foliage medium, medium green, matt; bushy growth.

Innocent Blush Min, *lp*, 1989, (RENblush); *Paul Shirville × Party Girl*; Rennie, Bruce F.;

Rennie Roses, 1990. Bud ovoid; flowers pale blush pink, reverse white, aging white, dbl. (40 petals), high-centered, exhibition, medium, borne usually singly and in sprays of 5-7; no fragrance; foliage medium, medium green, matt; prickles straight, medium, yellow; fruit none observed; upright, medium growth.

Innovation Minijet Min, *my*, 1986, (MEIjette; French Liberty); *(Rumba × Carol Jean) × (Zambra × Darling Flame)*; Meilland, M.L.; SNC Meilland & Cie, 1987. Flowers medium yellow, dbl. (over 40 petals), medium; slight fragrance; foliage small, light green, glossy; bushy growth.

Innoxa Femille HT, *dr*, 1983, (HARprincely); *Red Planet × Eroica*; Harkness, R. Flowers dark red, dbl. (50 petals), borne singly, sometimes 3 per cluster; slightly fragrant; foliage large, semi-glossy; dark prickles; medium, bushy growth.

Inoa F, *mr*, 1958, *Gruss an Teplitz × Pioupiou*; Arles; Roses-France. Flowers bright velvety red; vigorous growth.

Insel Mainau® F, *dr*, 1959, Kordes, R. Bud ovoid; flowers deep crimson, dbl., large blooms in clusters (up to 5); slightly fragrant; foliage leathery, dark; low, compact growth. ADR, 1960.

Inspecteur Jagourt F, *m*, 1932, *Mrs. Henry Winnett × Eblouissant*; Soupert & Notting. Bud glowing red; flowers purplish pink to china-rose, large white stamens, full (25-30 petals), large; large panicle; foliage glossy; vigorous growth.

Inspector Rose HT, *rb*, 1969, *Piccadilly sport*; Fryer's Nursery. Flowers maroon-red, reverse yellow, dbl. (35 petals), long, pointed; foliage coppery bronze-red; very free growth.

Inspektor Blohm HMsk (S), *w*, 1942, *Joanna Hill × Eva*; Kordes. Flowers white, very dbl., large corymb; very fragrant; foliage abundant, gray-green, vigorous, well branched growth; recurrent bloom.

Inspiration LCl, *mp*, 1946, *New Dawn × Crimson Glory*; Jacobus; B&A. Flowers pink, semidbl., large; fragrant; foliage large, glossy; moderate growth.

Instituteur Sirdey HT, *dy*, 1905, PernetDucher. Flowers deep yellow.

Insulinde HT, *yb*, 1923, *Mr. Joh. M. Jolles × Melody*; Van Rossem. Flowers clear yellow shaded golden yellow, dbl.; slightly fragrant.

Insulinde HT, *op*, 1923, *Ophelia × Jonkheer J.L. Mock*; Leenders, M. Flowers pink and salmon, dbl.; fragrant.

Interama F, *dr*, 1976, (IntRUma); *Kohima × (Europeana × Kimona)*; deRuiter. Flowers dark red, semi-dbl. (18 petals), large (3 in.); foliage large, glossy, dark; bushy growth.

INTerfire F, *ob*, 1992, (Orange Fire®; Darthuizer Orange Fire); *Orange Wave × Seedling*; Ilsink, Peter; Pekmez, 1987; Interplant B.V.; Kordes, 1988. Flowers very bright orange, dbl. (15-20 petals), urn-shaped, large (8 cms) blooms borne in sprays of 7-12; slight fragrance; foliage large, medium green, matt; upright growth.

INTergeorge Min, *mp*, 1992, (Carmela; Georgeous); *Candy Rose × Eyeopener*; Ilsink, Peter; Interplant B.V., 1990. Flowers pink, semidbl. (6-8 petals), cupped, small (3 cms) blooms borne in sprays of 3-8; slight fragrance; foliage small, dark green, glossy; bushy, low (30-40 cms) growth.

INTerjada F, *dp*, 1986, *Seedling × Seedling*; Interplant. Flowers deep pink, dbl. (35 petals), medium blooms in sprays; slightly fragrant; foliage medium, dark, semi-glossy; upright growth; greenhouse variety.

INTerleer F, *ob*, 1982, (Leersum 700); *Lichtkönigin Lucia × Marlena*; Interplant, 1979. Flowers light orange-yellow, semi-dbl., medium blooms in clusters; slight fragrance; foliage medium, light green, matt; many, small prickles; upright growth.

Intermezzo HT, *m*, 1963, *Grey Pearl × Lila Vidri*; Dot, S.; Minier & McGredy. Bud ovoid; flowers deep lavender, dbl. (25 petals), medium (3½ in); fragrant; foliage dark, glossy; moderately tall, compact growth.

INTermoto F, *dp*, 1985, (Joy); *Amruda × Seedling*; Interplant. Flowers deep pink, dbl. (35 petals), small blooms in clusters; no fragrance; foliage medium, medium green, semi-glossy; upright growth; greenhouse variety.

International Herald Tribune® F, *m*, 1984, (HARquantum; Viorita®; Violetta); *Seedling × ((Orange Sensation × Allgold) × R. californica)*; Harkness, R., 1985. Flowers violet-purple, dbl. (20 petals), cupped, flat, mini-flora, medium blooms in trusses; fragrant; foliage medium, medium green, semi-glossy; low, bushy growth. Geneva Rose D'Or; GM, Geneva, 1983, Monza, 1984 & Tokyo.

INTerorge F, *w*, 1983, (Georgette); *Seedling × Bordure Rose*; Interplant. Flowers white, dbl. (35 petals), large; slight fragrance; foliage large, medium green, semi-glossy; upright.

Interpool HT, *rb*, 1960, (Verdi); *Cafougnette × Independence*; Dorieux; Pin. Bud ovoid; flowers brick-red, reverse veined darker, dbl., medium; fragrant; foliage dark, glossy; very vigorous, bushy growth.

INTersina HT, *lp*, 1984, *Seedling × Red Success*; Interplant. Flowers light pink, dbl. (35 petals), large; no fragrance; foliage large, medium green, semi-glossy; upright growth; greenhouse variety.

INTertwik Min, *ly*, 1992, (Twinkle); *McShane × Seedling*; Ilsink, Peter; Interplant B.V., 1989. Flowers light yellow, does not fade, dbl. (10 petals), urn-shaped, small (5 cms) blooms borne singly; slight fragrance; foliage medium, medium green, matt; upright, low (40 cms) growth.

Interview HT, *dp*, 1968, (Interflora); *((Baccará × White Knight) × (Baccará × Jolie Madame)) × (Baccará × Paris-Match)*; Meilland. Flowers deep pink, dbl. (40 petals), high-centered, large; slightly fragrant; foliage leathery; vigorous, upright growth; greenhouse variety.

Intervilles® LCl, *mr*, 1968, *Étendard × Seedling*; Robichon; Ilgenfritz Nursery. Bud ovoid; flowers red, semi-dbl., cupped, large; fragrant; foliage dark, glossy; vigorous, climbing growth.

INTerway HT, *w*, 1992, (Milky Way); *Esmeralda × True Love*; Ilsink, Peter; Interplant B.V., 1991. Flowers white with hint of pink on reverse/edge, dbl. (20 petals), urn-shaped, large (10 cms) blooms borne in sprays of 1-10; slight fragrance; foliage large, dark green, glossy; upright, medium (100-120 cms) growth.

Intimité HT, *ob*, 1956, *Beauté × Seedling*; Delforge. Bud long; flowers golden orange shaded yellow and chamois, dbl., open, large; slightly fragrant; foliage glossy, dark; vigorous, bushy growth.

Intrigue F, *m*, 1982, (JACum); *White Masterpiece × Heirloom*; Warriner; J&P, 1984. Flowers reddish purple, dbl. (20 petals), large; very fragrant; foliage medium, dark, semi-glossy. AARS, 1984.

Invincible F, *dr*, 1983, (RUntru; Fennica); *Rubella × National Trust*; deRuiter; Fryer's Nursery, 1982. Bud large; flowers dark red, dbl. (20 petals), large; slight fragrance; foliage large, medium green, glossy; upright growth.

Invitation HT, *ab*, 1961, *Charlotte Armstrong × Signora*; Swim & Weeks; C-P. Bud long, pointed; flowers rich salmon-pink, base yellow, dbl. (30 petals), high-centered, large (4¹/₂ in.); very fragrant (spicy); foliage leathery, glossy; vigorous, compact, bushy growth.

Iobelle HT, *pb*, 1962, *Dean Collins × Peace*; Buck; Iowa State University. Bud ovoid; flowers ivory-white edged and overspread deep pink, high-centered, cupped, large; fragrant (fruity); foliage dark, glossy; vigorous, upright, compact growth.

Iode F, *dr*, 1974, *Lichterloh × Red Pinocchio*; Schloen, J. Bud ovoid; flowers dark red, semi-dbl., cupped, large; slightly fragrant; foliage glossy; vigorous, upright growth.

Iolanthe HT, *rb*, 1940, Gaujard. Flowers bright red, reverse yellow, semi-dbl., large; vigorous growth.

Ion Phillips HT, *dy*, 1934, Dickson, A. Flowers rich yellow, large, full; vigorous growth.

Iona Herdman HT, *dy*, 1914, McGredy; Flowers brilliant yellow, dbl.; slightly fragrant. GM, NRS, 1913.

Ione Min, *ly*, 1989, *Seedling × Seedling*; Jerabek, Paul E., 1990; Bud ovoid; flowers white with pale yellow center, very dbl. (50 petals), exhibition, medium, borne singly and in sprays of 2-5; slight fragrance; foliage medium, medium green, semi-glossy; prickles very few, very small, light green; fruit none observed; bushy, medium growth.

I Promise Min, *pb*, 1986, (LYOpri); *Seedling × Seedling*; Lyon; M.B. Farm Mini Roses. Flowers pink, reverse pale yellow, dbl. (28 petals), high-centered, exhibition, medium, borne usually singly; spicy fragrance; foliage medium, medium green, semi-glossy; few, small prickles; fruit globular, very small, red-gold; low, bushy.

Ipsilanté G (OGR), *m*, 1821, Flowers light lilac pink, full, flat, quartered, very large; vigorous.

Iranja® F, *or*, 1984, (LENira); *Little Angel × (Floradora × Angelina Louro)*; Lens, Louis. Flowers orange-red, dbl. (35 petals), 2 in. blooms in clusters of 3-24; no fragrance; foliage small, brilliant green; hooked, red-green prickles; low, bushy growth.

Ireland Hampton HT, *pb*, 1934, *Étoile de Feu × Seedling*; Hillock. Flowers flame-pink suffused gold, base gold, dbl., cupped, large; fragrant (spicy); foliage glossy; vigorous, compact growth.

Ireland Hampton, Climbing Cl HT, *pb*, 1936, Hillock.

Irene F, *pb*, 1941, *Seedling × Permanent Wave*; Leenders, M. Flowers rose-white, reverse pure white, semi-dbl.; fragrant.

Irène Bonnet Cl HT, *mp*, 1920, Nabonnand, C. Flowers hermosa pink, full; fragrant.

Irene Churruca HT, *ly*, 1934, (Golden Melody); *Mme. Butterfly × (Lady Hillingdon × Souv. de Claudius Pernet)*; La Florida. Bud pointed, yellow; flowers light buff, fading cream, well-formed, large; very fragrant.

Irene Curie HT, *mr*, 1952, *Seedling × Lawrence Johnston*; San Remo Exp. Sta. Bud very long, pointed; flowers scarlet, dbl. (20 petals), large; foliage glossy; very vigorous, bushy growth.

Irene of Denmark F, *w*, 1948, (Irene von Danemark; Irene au Danmark); *Orléans Rose × (Mme. Plantier × Edina)*; Poulsen, S.; C-P, 1950. Bud pointed; flowers white, dbl. (40 petals), cupped, large (3 in.); fragrant; foliage dark; vigorous, upright, bushy growth; (21).

Irene Thompson HT, *yb*, 1921, McGredy. Flowers deep ruddy gold shaded bronze or coppery, dbl.; very fragrant. GM, NRS, 1919.

Irene Watts Ch (OGR), *w*, 1896, Guillot, P. Bud soft apricot-orange; flowers white, dbl., with a button eye.

Irene's Choice HT, *mp*, 1978, *Karl Herbst × Blue Moon*; Ellick; Excelsior Roses. Flowers azalea-pink, dbl. (35-40 petals), full, large (4-5 in.); slightly fragrant; very free growth.

Irene's Delight HT, *lp*, 1982, *Admiral Rodney × Red Lion*; Varney, E. Flowers light pink, dbl., high-centered, large; very fragrant; foliage medium, dark, semi-glossy; upright.

Irina F, *dr*, 1969, *Tropicana × Europeana*; Grabezewski; Flowers dark crimson-red, semi-dbl., large; foliage soft, glossy; moderate, bushy growth.

Iris HSpn (OGR), *w*, *R. spinosissima variety (or hybrid)*. Flowers white, dbl.; fruit black, shining; foliage finely divided; dense, shrubby (3-4 ft.) growth.

Iris Patricia Green HT, *mr*, 1928, Pemberton. Bud pointed; flowers cherry-red; fragrant; foliage dark.

Iris Squire F, *mp*, 1966, *Seedling × Queen Elizabeth*; Bees. Flowers soft rose, large (4-5 in.); foliage dull; tall, vigorous growth.

Iris Webb F, *r*, 1988, (CHEWell); *Southampton × (Belinda × (Elizabeth of Glamis × (Galway Bay × Sutters Gold)))*; Warner, C.H.; LeGrice Roses, 1990. Flowers tan, fading to slate gray, dbl. (15-25 petals), medium, fragrant; foliage medium, dark green, semi-glossy; bushy growth.

Irish Afterglow HT, *ob*, 1918, *Irish Fireflame* sport; Dickson, A. Flowers very deep tangerine, passing to crushed strawberry.

Irish Charity HT, *rb*, 1927, McGredy; H&S; Dreer. Bud intense fiery scarlet with golden sheen; flowers rosy scarlet, dbl.

Irish Charm HT, *ab*, 1927, McGredy; H&S; Dreer. Bud pointed; flowers base golden apricot passing to blush-pink, dbl., high-centered; fragrant; foliage dark, leathery; vigorous growth.

Irish Courage HT, *op*, 1927, McGredy; Bud pointed; flowers soft shrimp-pink to salmon, dbl., high-centered; fragrant; foliage rich green, leathery, glossy; vigorous growth.

Irish Elegance HT, *ob*, 1905, Dickson, A.; Flowers bronze orange-scarlet, single (5 petals), large; vigorous growth; (21).

Irish Engineer HT, *mr*, 1904, Dickson, A. Flowers dazzling scarlet, single, large.

Irish Eyes F, *yb*, 1974, *Seedling × Gemini*; Byrum; J.H. Hill Co. Bud ovoid; flowers

yellow edged red, dbl. (45 petals), high-centered, large (2½-3 in.); slightly fragrant; vigorous.

Irish Fireflame HT, *ob*, 1914, Dickson, A. Flowers orange to old-gold, veined crimson, anthers light fawn, single (5 petals), large (5 in.); very fragrant; foliage dark, glossy; compact, bushy growth. GM, NRS, 1912.

Irish Fireflame, Climbing Cl HT, *ob*, 1916, Dickson, A.

Irish Glory HT, *pb*, 1900, Dickson, A.; Flowers silvery pink, reverse crimson, semi-dbl. (10 petals), large; fragrant; very vigorous growth.

Irish Gold HT, *my*, 1966, (Grandpa Dickson); *(Kordes' Perfecta × Governador Braga da Cruz) × Piccadilly*; Dickson, A.; J&P. Bud ovoid; flowers yellow, dbl. (33 petals), high-centered, very large (7 in.); fragrant; foliage dark, glossy, leathery; vigorous, upright, bushy growth. GM, RNRS PIT, 1965; GM, RNRS, 1965, The Hague, 1966, Belfast, 1968 & Portland, 1970.

Irish Heartbreaker Cl Min, *rb*, 1990, (SEAheart); *Rise 'n' Shine × (Oonagh × Siobhan)*; McCann, Sean, 1991. Flowers red blend, full (26-40 petals), small blooms; slight fragrance; foliage medium, medium green, semi-glossy; upright growth.

Irish Hope HT, *dr*, 1927, McGredy; H&S; Dreer. Bud pointed; flowers rosy crimson shaded maroon, dbl., high-centered, large; very fragrant; foliage dark, leathery; vigorous growth.

Irish Lady Min, *pb*, 1991, *Kathy Robinson sport*; Schmidt, Richard; Michigan Mini Roses, 1991. Flowers pink blend, full (26-40 petals), small; slight fragrance; foliage small, dark green, glossy; bushy growth.

Irish Mist F, *op*, 1966, (Irischer Regen; Irish Summer); *Orangeade × Mischief*; McGredy, S., IV; McGredy. Flowers orange-salmon, well-formed, large (4½ in.) blooms in clusters; slightly fragrant; foliage dark; dense growth.

Irish Morn HT, *pb*, 1927, McGredy; H&S; Dreer. Flowers pink, center coral, dbl.; fragrant.

Irish Rover HT, *op*, 1970, *Violet Carson × Tropicana*; McGredy. Flowers salmon-pink, dbl. (36 petals), large (4 in.); slightly fragrant; foliage coppery, dark; vigorous.

Irish Sweetness HT, *rb*, 1927, McGredy; H&S; Dreer. Bud pointed; flowers crimson suffused scarlet, dbl., high-centered, large; very fragrant; foliage dark, leathery; vigorous growth.

Iroquois S, *dp*, 1932, *Pythagoras × R. cinnamomea*; Central Exp. Farm. Flowers deep mauve-pink, semi-dbl.; fragrant; foliage leathery; vigorous, bushy, compact; non-recurrent.

Irresistible Min, *w*, 1989, (TINresist); *Tiki × Brian Lee*; Bennett, Dee; Tiny Petals Nursery, 1990. Bud ovoid; flowers near white with pale pink center, dbl. (43 petals), high-centered, exhibition, medium, borne singly and in sprays of 3-5; moderate, spicy fragrance; foliage medium, medium green, semi-glossy; prickles straight, yellow with red; fruit globular, green to yellow-brown; upright, tall growth.

Isa HT, *lp*, 1931, *Abol seedling*; Evans, F.&L. Flowers light pinkish cream, full, well shaped; fragrant; vigorous growth.

Isa Murdock HSpn (OGR), *w*, 1953, *R. spinosissima altaica × Dbl. white spinosissima*; Skinner. Flowers white, sometimes tinged with pink, dbl.; foliage spinosissima type; many prickles; height 3ft.; non-recurrent bloom.

Isabel de Ortiz HT, *pb*, 1962, (Isabel Ortiz); *Peace × Kordes' Perfecta*; Kordes, R.; J&P, 1965. Flowers deep pink, reverse silvery, dbl. (38 petals), well-formed, large (5 in.); fragrant; foliage dark, glossy; upright growth. GM, Madrid, 1961 & NRS, 1962.

Isabel Llorach HP (OGR), *yb*, 1929, *Frau Karl Druschki × Benedicte Seguin*; Dot, P. Flowers nankeen yellow, tinted red, semi-dbl.; fragrant.

Isabella HT, *ob*, 1964, *Queen Elizabeth × Pink Lustre*; Leenders, J. Flowers orange, star shaped.

Isabella Gray N (OGR), *dy*, 1854, *Chromatella seedling*; Gray, Andrew. Flowers golden yellow, more fragrant, but otherwise similar to parent.

Isabella Skinner S, *mp*, (*R. laxa × Tea*) × *Floribunda Seedling*; Prior to 1965. Flowers pink, dbl., well-formed; bushy growth; blooms on new wood all summer.

Isabella Sprunt T (OGR), *my*, 1855, *Safrano sport*; Sprunt; Buchanan, 1865. Flowers sulphur-yellow.

Isabelle de France HT, *or*, 1956, *Peace × (Mme. Joseph Perraud × Opera)*; Mallerin; Hémeray-Aubert. Bud pointed; flowers vermilion, dbl., high-centered, large; slightly fragrant; vigorous, upright growth.

Isella Min, *lp*, 1973, (*Baccará × Generosa*) × *Miss Italia*; Bartolomeo, Embriaco. Flowers light pink, dbl. (22 petals), cupped, small, borne singly and several together; no fragrance; foliage small, green; pale pink prickles; vigorous, compact, upright growth.

Isis F, *w*, 1973, *Vera Dalton × Shepherdess*; Mattock. Flowers ivory-white, dbl. (40-45 petals), large (4-5 in.); fragrant; compact growth.

Isobel HT, *pb*, 1916, McGredy. Bud pointed; flowers light rose-pink, shaded apricot, single (5 petals), cupped, large; slightly fragrant; foliage rich green, soft. GM, NRS, 1915.

Isobel Derby HT, *pb*, 1992, (HORethel); *Champagne Cocktail × ((Honey Favorite × Dr. A.J. Verhage) × Pot of Gold)*; Horner, Colin P.; Golden Fields Nursery, 1992. Flowers peach pink, reverse lighter pink, aging deeper pink, dbl., urn-shaped, large (120 cms) blooms borne singly or in sprays of 5-7; moderate, fruity fragrance; foliage medium, medium green, glossy; bushy, medium growth.

Isobel Harkness HT, *dy*, 1957, *McGredy's Yellow × Phyllis Gold*; Norman; Harkness & Armstrong Nursery. Flowers bright yellow, dbl. (32 petals), large (6in.); fragrant; foliage dark, leathery, semi-glossy; vigorous, upright, bushy growth.

Ispahan D (OGR), *mp*, (Isfahan; Pompon des Princes); Cult. before 1832. Flowers bright pink, loosely dbl.; very fragrant; foliage small; blooms over long season.

Italia HT, *dr*, 1959, *Baccará × Poinsettia*; Valentino. Bud ovoid; flowers cardinal-red and cherry-red, dbl., cupped to open, large; long, strong stems; fragrant; foliage leathery, dark; bushy, upright growth.

Italian Pink S, *mp*, 1959, *Cocorico × Yellow Holstein*; Leenders, J. Bud short, pointed; flowers begonia-pink, dbl., open, large, borne in clusters; fragrant; foliage dark; vigorous, upright, well branched growth.

Italie Impériale HT, *m*, 1936, Capiago. Flower purplish garnet-red, large; vigorous growth.

Italienisches Doerfchen F, *or*, 1967, *Highlight × Seedling*; Haenchen; Teschendorff. Bud ovoid; flowers orange-red, single, open, small, borne in clusters; slightly fragrant; foliage small, leathery; vigorous, bushy, low growth.

Ivanhoe HT, *rb*, 1928, Easlea. Bud pointed; flowers brilliant scarlet to rich crimson, dbl., high-centered, large; very fragrant; foliage glossy; vigorous growth.

Ivany F, *rb*, 1975, *Masquerade × Rumba*; Staikov, Prof. Dr. V.; Kalaydjiev and Chorbadjiiski. Flowers orange-yellow, shaded pink on petal edges, aging red, dbl. (50 petals), cupped, medium blooms in clusters of 5-30; foliage dark, glossy; vigorous.

Ivora F, *w*, 1986, (INTercream); *Amruda × Seedling*; Interplant. Flowers near white, dbl. (35 petals), medium blooms in clusters; slight fragrance; foliage medium, light green, matt; upright growth; greenhouse variety.

Ivory T (OGR), *w*, 1901, *Golden Gate sport*; Dingee & Conard. Flowers ivory-white, dbl., large; fragrant; vigorous growth.

Ivory Charm Cl F, *w*, 1968, *Ivory Fashion sport*; Earing. Bud ovoid; flowers white, semi-dbl., open, large; very fragrant; foliage glossy, leathery; vigorous, climbing growth.

Ivory Fashion F, *w*, 1958, *Sonata × Fashion*; Boerner; J&P. Bud ovoid; flowers ivory-white, semi-dbl. (17 petals), well-formed, large (4-4½ in.) blooms in clusters; fragrant; foliage leathery; vigorous, upright growth. AARS, 1959.

Ivory Fashion, Climbing Cl F, *w*, 1964, Williams, J.B.

Ivory Palace Min, *w*, 1990, (MORivory); *Sheri Anne × Pinocchio*; Moore, Ralph S., 1982; Sequoia Nursery, 1991. Bud ovoid; flowers ivory white, white reverse, aging similar color, very dbl. (60+ petals), high-centered, medium, borne in sprays of 3-8; slight fragrance; foliage medium, medium green, semi-glossy; bushy, medium growth.

Ivory Queen HT, *w*, 1954, *Edina × McGredy's Ivory*; Fletcher; Tucker. Bud ovoid; flowers ivory-cream, large (5-6 in.); fragrant; foliage dark, glossy; vigorous, bushy growth.

Ivory Queen Gr, *w*, 1965, *Queen Elizabeth sport*; Delforge. Flowers ivory.

Ivory Splendor Min, *w*, 1991, *Rise 'n' Shine × Seedling*; Gruenbauer, Richard, 1984; Flowers 'n' Friends Miniature Roses, 1993. Bud rounded; flowers white, pale yellow center, white reverse, aging white, dbl. (35 petals), high-centered, large; slight, fruity fragrance; foliage medium, medium green, matt; upright, tall growth.

Ivory Tip Top F, *lp*, 1976, *Tip Top sport*; Fryer's Nursery. Flowers ivory-pink, semi-dbl. (12-16 petals), full, medium (2-2½ in.); slightly fragrant; low, compact, bushy growth.

Ivory Tower HT, *w*, 1979, *Colour Wonder × King's Ransom*; Kordes, R.; Armstrong Nursery. Bud very long, pointed; flowers ivory-white, shaded light pink and light yellow, dbl. (35 petals), high-centered, large (5½ in.); fragrant; upright, bushy growth.

Ivory Triumph F, *w*, 1961, *Goldilocks × Seedling*; Abrams, Von; Peterson & Dering. Bud pointed; flowers ivory, semi-dbl. (12 petals), open, large (3-4 in.), borne in clusters; slightly fragrant; foliage leathery, light green; upright, compact growth.

Ivresse HT, *rb*, 1958, *Peace × Spectacular*; Combe; Japan Rose Society. Flowers clear red, reverse silvery, large; vigorous growth.

Ivy Alice R, *op*, 1927, *Excelsa sport*; Letts. Flowers soft pink to blush-salmon, splashed car-mine when fading, dbl., cupped, borne in very large clusters; slightly fragrant; foliage glossy, light; very vigorous, climbing (6 ft.) growth.

Ivy Evans HT, *mr*, 1926, *George C. Waud seedling × Gen. MacArthur*; Evans. Flowers light cerise; fragrant.

Ivy May HT, *pb*, 1925, *Mme. Butterfly sport*; Beckwith. Bud pointed; flowers rose-pink, base and edges amber, dbl.; fragrant; foliage dark; vigorous growth.

I. X. L. R. R, *dp*, 1925, *Tausendschön × Veilchenblau*; Coolidge. Flowers magenta; straight, thornless canes (1 in.diam.); very vigorous growth; chiefly valuable as an understock.

Iwara Misc OGR (OGR), *w*, (R. × *iwara* Siebold ex Regel; *R. yesoensis* Makino); *R. multiflora × R. rugosa*; Cult. prior to 1830. Flowers white, single, small.

I Zingari HT, *ob*, 1925, Pemberton. Flowers orange-scarlet, semi-dbl., corymb, stems claret; foliage dark.

JACaby HT, *or*, 1979, *South Seas × Tonight*; Warriner, W.A.; J&P. Flowers orange-red, large; slight fragrance; foliage large, medium green; upright, bushy growth.

JACage HT, *yb*, 1981, *Seedling × Spellbinder*; Warriner, W.A.; J&P. Flowers yellow blend, dbl. (35 petals), medium; slight fragrance; foliage medium, dark, leathery; upright, bushy growth.

JacaKOR® HT, *mp*, 1985, (Jacaranda; Jackaranda); *(Mercedes × Emily Post) × Seedling*; Kordes, W. Flowers mauve-pink, dbl. (35 petals), large; very fragrant; foliage large, medium green; upright growth.

JACal HT, *or*, 1984, *Spellbinder × Futura*; Warriner, W.A.; J&P. Flowers orange-red, dbl. (35 petals), large; no fragrance; foliage medium, dark, semi-glossy; upright growth.

JACalp HT, *or*, 1980, *Seedling × Medallion*; Warriner, W.A.; J&P. Flowers brick red, dbl. (50 petals), large; slight fragrance; foliage large, dark, leathery; upright.

JACant F, *r*, 1985, (Topaz); *Seedling × Intrigue*; Warriner; J&P. Flowers tan, dbl. (35 petals), medium; slight fragrance; foliage medium, medium green, semi-glossy; upright growth.

JACice HT, *w*, 1984, (Moonlight); *Coquette × Seedling*; Warriner, W. A.; J&P. Flowers white, dbl. (35 petals), medium; no fragrance; foliage large, medium green, matt; upright growth; greenhouse variety.

JACinal F, *mp*, 1985, (Debutante); *Bridal Pink × Zorina*; Warriner, W.A.; J&P. Flowers medium pink, dbl. (20 petals), small; slight fragrance; foliage medium, medium green, matt; bushy growth; greenhouse variety.

Jack Folly HT, *w*, 1976, Buss, H., Nursery. Bud ovoid; flowers cream color, dbl. (40 petals), opening cupped, very large (5½ in.); foliage dull, leathery; spreading growth.

Jack Frost F, *w*, 1962, *Garnette* × *Seedling*; Jelly; E.G. Hill Co. Bud pointed; flowers white to creamy, dbl. (42 petals), high-centered, sweetheart, medium; fragrant; foliage dark; vigorous, upright growth; greenhouse variety.

Jack Horner Min, *mp*, 1955, *Margo Koster* × *Tom Thumb*; Robinson, T. Flowers bright pink, dbl. (50 petals); slightly fragrant; no prickles; height 4-8 in.

Jack McCandless HT, *rb*, 1935, McGredy. Bud long, pointed, carmine and yellow; flowers amber-yellow, veined red, dbl., high-centered; slightly fragrant; foliage small, glossy, dark.

Jack of Hearts F, 1968, Waterhouse Nurs. Flowers cardinal red, semi-dbl., cupped, trusses; foliage dark, glossy; low, bushy; free bloom.

Jack O'Lantern Gr, *yb*, 1960, *Circus* × *Golden Scepter*; Swim & Weeks. Bud ovoid; flowers gold and yellow blend, dbl. (25 petals), high-centered, large (4½ in.); slightly fragrant; foliage leathery; vigorous, tall, bushy.

Jackie™ Min, *ly*, 1955, *Golden Glow* × *Zee*; Moore, R.S.; Sequoia Nursery. Flowers straw-yellow changing to white, dbl. (60 petals), high-centered, small (1½ in.); fragrant; foliage glossy; vigorous, dwarf (12 in.), bushy, spreading growth.

Jackie Clark HT, *dr*, 1990, *White Masterpiece* × *Red Planet*; Wambach, Alex, 1985; Alex Wambach, 1989. Bud pointed; flowers dark red, very dbl. (35 petals), high-centered, exhibition, large (3½ in.) blooms borne singly; heavy fragrance; foliage medium, dark green, matt, disease resistant; prickles curved down, pink; vigorous, upright growth.

Jackie, Climbing Cl Min, *ly*, 1957, *Golden Glow* × *Zee*; Moore, R.S.; Sequoia Nursery. Not a sport of Jackie. Flowers soft yellow to creamy white, dbl. (60 petals), small (1-1½ in.); fragrant; foliage semi-glossy, leathery; height to 10 ft.

Jackman's White HT, *w*, (Brookdale Giant White); Brookdale-Kingsway; Bosley Nursery, about 1940. Flowers creamy white, high-centered, very large; vigorous growth; very hardy for this type; thought to be an old variety, possibly Ethel Malcolm.

Jackpot Min, *dy*, 1984, (MORjack); *Little Darling* × *Sunspray*; Moore, R.S.; Moore Min. Roses, 1985. Flowers deep yellow, dbl. (40+ petals), small; fragrant; foliage small, medium green, matt; vigorous, bushy, spreading growth.

Jack's Fantasy Min, *yb*, 1986, (BILfan); *Little Darling* × *Over the Rainbow*; Bilson, Jack M., Jr. & Bilson, Jack M., III. Flowers yellow blushed with orange-red from edge, reverse medium yellow, aging bright, colors soften then fade, dbl. (21 petals), exhibition, medium, borne usually singly and in sprays of 3-4; slight fragrance; foliage medium, medium green, semi-glossy; few, beige prickles slightly sloped downward; no fruit; upright, bushy, medium growth.

JAClam F, *dr*, 1986, (Carmen); *Seedling* × *Samantha*; Warriner, W.A.; J&P. Flowers deep red, very little fading, dbl. (30 petals), high-centered, small, borne usually singly; no fragrance; foliage medium, dark green, semi-glossy; upright, bushy growth.

JACnel HT, *dy*, 1992, (Sundance); *Seedling* × *Emblem*; Warriner, William; Bear Creek Gardens (J&P), 1991. Flowers deep yellow, very full (41+ petals), large (7+ cms) blooms borne mostly singly; fragrant; foliage large, dark green, semi-glossy; some prickles; tall (180-120 cms), upright growth.

JACnon HT, *ob*, 1985, *Baccará* × *Seedling*; Warriner, W.A.; J&P. Flowers orange blend, dbl. (40+ petals), medium; slight fragrance; foliage large, medium green, matt; upright, bushy growth.

Jacotte LCl, *ab*, 1920, *R. wichuraiana* × *Arthur R. Goodwin*; Barbier. Bud ovoid, orange and yellow; flowers deep coppery yellow, tinted coppery red, semi-dbl., open, cupped, large (3 in.); long, strong stems; fragrant; foliage leathery, glossy, dark; very vigorous, climbing growth.

Jacqueline HT, *mr*, 1961, *Topper* × *Seedling*; J.H. Hill Co. Bud short, pointed; flowers turkey-red, dbl. (30 petals), high-centered, large (4-4½ in.); fragrant; foliage glossy; vigorous, well-branched growth.

Jacqueline du Pré® S, *w*, 1988, (HARwanna); *Radox Bouquet* × *Maigold*; Harkness, R.; R. Harkness & Co., Ltd., 1989. Flowers creamy blush to white, semi-dbl. (15 petals), cupped, loose, large, borne singly or in sprays of 3-5; moderate, musk fragrance; foliage medium, dark green, glossy; prickles small, dark; fruit oval, medium, green to orange; tall, spreading growth; repeats.   GM, LeRoeulx, 1988.

Jacqueline Dufier HT, *dr*, 1957, *Dicksons Red* × *Ena Harkness*; Kemp, M.L. Flowers crimson shaded black, dbl. (25 petals), high pointed, large (4 in.); slightly fragrant; foliage bronze; vigorous growth.

Jacqueline Sternotte HT, *rb*, 1974, Delforge, S. Bud ovoid; flowers red and white, very dbl. (51 petals), full, large (4½ in.); fragrant.

Jacques Carroy Pol, *m*, 1929, Turbat. Flowers carmine, slightly tinted purple, center velvety, borne in clusters of 15-20.

Jacques Carteau HT, *ly*, 1957, Privat. Bud long; flowers creamy yellow, medium; foliage glossy; moderate growth.

Jacques Cartier P (OGR), *lp*, 1868, Moreau-Robert. Flowers clear rose, center darker. Due to confused labeling, the rose now grown as Jacques Cartier must be exhibited as Marchesa Boccella in ARS rose shows.

Jacques Hackenburg HT, *pb*, 1919, *Jonkheer J.L. Mock × Marquise de Sinéty*; Leenders, M. Flowers deep rose-pink and carmine, opening flesh-white, dbl.; very fragrant.

Jacques Latouche HT, *pb*, 1935, *Souv. de Claudius Pernet × Director Rubió*; Mallerin; H. Guillot. Flowers orange-pink in spring, red in summer, reverse yellow, dbl., cupped, very large; slightly fragrant; foliage glossy; vigorous growth.

Jacques Porcher HT, *rb*, 1914, Guillot, P. Flowers blended tints of carmine, saffron and deep yellow, dbl.; fragrant.

Jacques Vincent HT, *rb*, 1908, *Mme. J.W. Budde × Souv. de Catherine Guillot*; Soupert & Notting. Flowers coral-red, center golden; vigorous growth.

JACtan LCl, *r*, 1986, (Butterscotch); *(Buccaneer × Zorina) × Royal Sunset*; Warriner; J&P. Flowers tannish-orange, dbl. (25 petals), cupped to loose, medium blooms in clusters of 3-5; slightly fragrant; foliage medium, medium green, semi-glossy; fruit none.

Jadis HT, *mp*, 1974, (JACdis; Fragrant Memory); *Chrysler Imperial × Virgo*; Warriner; J&P. Flowers medium pink, dbl., high-centered, large; very fragrant; foliage large, light, leathery; vigorous, upright, bushy.

Jägerbataillon Sp (OGR), *lp*, *R. canina strain*; Klinken. Almost thornless; once popular as an understock.

J. A. Gomis HT, *rb*, 1933, *Sensation × Souv. de Claudius Pernet*; Camprubi. Flowers crimson-red and yellow, dbl., cupped, medium; slightly fragrant; foliage dark, glossy; upright growth.

Jam Session Min, *op*, 1986, (ZIPjam); *Poker Chip × Anytime*; Zipper, H.; Magic Moment Min. Roses. Flowers coral pink, yellow reverse, dbl. (20 petals), small blooms borne singly or in small sprays; no fragrance; foliage small, medium green, matt; upright growth.

Jamaica HT, *mr*, 1965, *(Charlotte Armstrong × Floradora) × Nocturne*; Lindquist; Howard Rose Co. Bud ovoid; flowers cherry-red, semi-dbl., cupped, large; fragrant; foliage dark, glossy, leathery; vigorous, upright growth.

Jamboree F, *rb*, 1964, *Masquerade × Seedling*; Gregory. Flowers cherry-red, reverse lighter, dbl. (26 petals), flat, medium (1½-2 in.), borne in clusters; foliage glossy, light green; free growth.

James Appleby F, *ob*, 1963, *Orangeade sport*; Wood. Flowers orange-scarlet flecked deep crimson, semi-dbl., medium, borne in clusters; vigorous growth.

James Bond 007 HT, *op*, 1966, *Seedling × Fragrant Cloud*; Tantau, Math. Flowers coral-pink, pointed; foliage glossy; bushy growth.

James Bougault HP (OGR), *w*, 1887, (James Bourgault); Renault. Flowers rosy white.

James Ferris HT, *w*, 1927, Hall. Flowers creamy white; vigorous growth.

James Gibson HT, *mr*, 1928, McGredy. Bud pointed; flowers crimson-scarlet, dbl., high-centered, large; slightly fragrant; foliage dark, leathery; vigorous, bushy growth. GM, NRS, 1929.

James Mitchell M (OGR), *dp*, 1861, E. Verdier. Flowers pink, fully dbl., small; very heavily mossed; early bloom.

James Rea HT, *dp*, 1930, McGredy. Bud pointed; flowers rich carmine or rose-pink, dbl., high-centered, very large; very fragrant; foliage light, leathery; vigorous, bushy growth. GM, NRS, 1929.

James Smile® HT, *pb*, 1987, *Sea Pearl sport*; Rogin, Josip. Flowers china-pink, reverse pink-yellow blend, semi-dbl. (40 petals), cupped, loose, medium, borne i sprays of 3; moderate, spicy fragrance; foliage medium, medium green, semi-glossy; rare, small, brown prickles; fruit rounded, medium, pink-red; upright, medium growth.

James Veitch M (OGR), *m*, 1865, Verdier, E. Flowers violet-slate shaded fiery red, full, medium blooms in corymbs; moderately vigorous growth.

James Walley HT, *ab*, 1923, *Ophelia × Seedling*; Easlea. Flowers apricot and fiery salmon, dbl., large; fragrant; foliage olive-green, leathery; vigorous growth.

Jamie™ Min, *lp*, 1992, (MOGajam); *Party Girl × Fairlane*; Moglia, Thomas; Gloria Dei Nursery, 1993. Flowers light pink, full (26-40 petals), HT type, outer petals horizontal at exhibition stage, medium (4-7 cms.) blooms borne in small clusters; slight fragrance; foliage medium, medium green, semi-glossy; some prickles; medium (45-50 cms.), spreading growth.

Jan Abbing HT, *rb*, 1933, *Columbia × Étoile de Hollande*; Tantau. Bud pointed; flowers salmon-red shaded yellow, cupped, large; slightly fragrant; foliage leathery, dark; vigorous growth.

Jan Böhm HP (OGR), *mr*, 1928, *Hugh Dickson × King George V*; Böhm. Flowers velvety fiery red, dbl. (40 petals); fragrant; vigorous growth; recurrent bloom.

Jan Guest HT, *pb*, 1975, *Fragrant Cloud × Irish Gold*; Guest. Flowers carmine-pink with yellow reverse, dbl. (43 petals), large (4 in.); foliage glossy; vigorous, upright growth.

Jan H. Meyer HT, *mr*, 1954, *Tawny Gold × Gaudia*; Leenders, M. Flowers cinnabar-red, well formed, large; vigorous growth.

Jan Spek® F, *dy*, 1966, *Cläre Grammerstorf × Faust*; McGredy, S., IV; McGredy. Flowers deep yellow, dbl. (44 petals), flat, large (3 in.) blooms in clusters; slightly fragrant; foliage dark, glossy.   GM, Belfast, 1968 & The Hague, 1970.

Jan Steen HT, *mr*, 1923, *Mev. Dora van Tets × Gruss an Dresden*; Spek. Flowers brilliant scarlet-red, semi-dbl.; slightly fragrant.

Jan van Riebeeck HT, *m*, 1952, Leenders, M. Flowers carmine, dbl., large; fragrant; vigorous growth.

Jan Wellum Min, *dr*, 1986, (Vancouver Centennial); *Shrub Seedling × Dwarfking '78*; Fischer, C.&H.; Alpenflora Gardens. Flowers dark red, dbl. (20 petals), large blooms borne singly and in sprays of 3-5; slight, fruity fragrance; foliage medium, medium green, matt; small, straight, near-white prickles; fruit small, globular; spreading growth.

Janal HT, *dp*, 1978, *Charles Mallerin × (Duet × Kordes' Perfecta)*; Dawson, G.; Rainbow Roses. Bud pointed; flowers deep pink, dbl. (55 petals), exhibition blooms borne usually singly; strong fragrance; foliage bronze-red to dark green; hooked red prickles; vigorous.

Jane HT, *ob*, 1956, *Signora × Mrs. Edward Laxton*; Mee; Sanday. Flowers coppery orange suffused pink, dbl. (24 petals), well formed, medium (3½ in.); fragrant; foliage dark; vigorous, upright growth.

Jane Asher Min, *mr*, 1988, (PEApet); *Seedling × Seedling*; Pearce, C.A.; The Limes New Roses, 1987. Flowers scarlet, aging slightly paler, very dbl., rounded, small, borne in sprays of 4-40; patio; no fragrance; foliage small, medium green, semi-glossy; prickles straight, average, red; bushy, low growth.

Jane Carrel HT, *yb*, 1940, Gaujard. Bud pointed; flowers yellow shaded orange, dbl., medium; fragrant; very vigorous, bushy growth.

Jane Jackson F, *ob*, 1976, *Tip Top sport*; Jackson, J.R. Flowers strawberry-orange, dbl.; low, vigorous, bushy growth.

Jane Lazenby F, *mp*, 1959, *Alain × Mme. Henri Guillot*; McGredy, S., IV; McGredy. Flowers rose-pink, dbl. (25 petals), flat, large (3½ in.); fragrant; foliage dark; very vigorous, bushy growth.

Jane Pauley HT, *ob*, 1992, *Elizabeth Taylor × Fortuna*; Weddle, Von C.; Hortico, Inc., 1993. Flowers orange, reverse orange, aging orange pink, dbl. (35 petals), exhibition, high-centered, very large (6½") blooms borne singly; moderate fragrance; foliage large, medium green, semi-glossy; upright, medium growth.

Jane Probyn HT, *dp*, 1978, *Red Devil sport*; Anderson, K. Flowers deep pink.

Jane Rogers HT, *ab*, 1991, *Fragrant Cloud × Diamond Jubilee*; Mander, George. Flowers apricot blend, full (26-40 petals), large blooms borne singly, sometimes in small clusters; slight fragrance; foliage medium, medium green, semi-glossy; medium, spreading growth.

Jane Thornton HT, *rb*, Bees, about 1940. Flowers velvety crimson shaded maroon; very fragrant.

Janet HT, *ab*, 1915, Dickson, A. Flowers golden fawn, shaded copper and rose, fading, dbl.; fragrant. GM, NRS, 1916.

Janet Frazer F, *op*, 1937, *Mme. Léon Cuny × (Orange Sweetheart × Cinnabar)*; McGredy. Flowers shrimp-pink and yellow, semi-dbl., large (3½ in.) blooms in clusters; slightly fragrant; foliage light green.

Janet Morrison Cl HT, *dp*, 1936, *Black Boy × Seedling*; Clark, A.; NRS Victoria. Flowers deep pink, semi-dbl., large blooms with long stems; fragrant; vigorous.

Janet's Pride E (OGR), *pb*, 1892, *Probably a natural hybrid of R. eglanteria and R. damascena*; Found in a hedge row in Cheshire, England; Paul. Flowers white, edged carmine-rose, semi-dbl.; vigorous; non-recurrent bloom. Erroneously identified Clementine.

Janette Murray HT, *op*, 1985, *Daily Sketch seedling × Montezuma*; Bell, R.J.; Brundrett & Sons. Flowers orange pink, dbl. (35 petals), large blooms borne singly; slight fragrance; foliage large, medium green, semi-glossy; vigorous growth.

Janice Min, *mp*, 1971, *(R. wichuraiana × Floradora) × Eleanor*; Moore, R.S.; Sequoia Nursery. Bud ovoid; flowers medium pink, dbl., small; foliage small, glossy, leathery; vigorous, dwarf, upright, bushy growth.

Janice Tellian Min, *op*, 1979, *Fairy Moss × Fire Princess*; Moore, R.S.; Sequoia Nursery. Bud pointed; flowers light coral-pink, dbl. (40 petals), globular, high-centered, small (1 in.); slightly fragrant; foliage small; dwarf, bushy, compact growth.

Janida HT, *rb*, 1955, *Crimson Glory* × *Baby Château*; Robichon. Bud long, pointed, blood-red veined maroon; flowers orange, dbl.

Janine Astle F, *mp*, 1971, *Charlotte Elizabeth* × *Grand Slam*; Hunt. Flowers clear pink, dbl. (22 petals), high-centered, large (3 in.); slightly fragrant; foliage bluish green; vigorous, upright growth.

Janna Min, *pb*, 1970, *Little Darling* × *(Little Darling* × *(R. wichuraiana* × *Miniature seedling))*; Moore, R.S.; Sequoia Nursery. Bud pointed; flowers pink, reverse white, dbl., small; foliage leathery; dwarf, bushy growth.

Jantar HT, *dr*, 1966, Grabezewski. Bud elongated; flowers dark crimson, shaded darker, large; vigorous, upright growth.

Jantzen Girl Gr, *mr*, 1961, *Carrousel* × *(Chrysler Imperial* × *Seedling)*; Abrams, Von; Peterson & Dering. Bud ovoid; flowers red, dbl. (38 wavy petals), high-centered, large (4-5 in.) blooms in clusters; slightly fragrant; foliage glossy; upright growth.

Japonica A strain of *R. multiflora*, probably indistinguishable from it; popular as an understock.

Japonica Thornless A prickle-free strain of *R. multiflora* selected as an understock.

Jardins de Bagatelle® HT, *w*, 1986, (MEImafris; Sarah); *(Queen Elizabeth* × *Eleg)* × *MEIdragelac*; Meilland, M.L.; SNC Meilland & Cie, 1987. Flowers white, very dbl. (over 40 petals), large; very fragrant; foliage large, medium green, semi-glossy; upright growth. GM, Genoa, 1987.

Jarvis Brook HT, *rb*, 1928, Low. Flowers carmine, reverse orange, dbl.; fragrant.

Jaunâtre HSem (OGR), *ly*, *R. sempervirens hybrid*. Flowers yellowish white; fragrant.

Jaune Bicolor Sp (OGR), *yb*, 1633, *R. foetida bicolor* sport. Flowers yellow streaked red.

Jaune Desprez N (OGR), *yb*, 1830, (Desprez à Fleur Jaunes; Noisette Desprez); *Blush Noisette* × *Parks' Yellow Tea-scented China*; Desprez. Flowers warm yellow shaded peach and apricot, dbl., flat; fragrant; vigorous (to 20 ft.) growth.

Jaune d'Or T (OGR), *ob*, 1864, Oger. Flowers coppery yellow, full, globular, large.

Java F, *ob*, 1955, *Francais* × *Seedling*; Mallerin; EFR. Bud ovoid; flowers orange-red, dbl. (40-45 petals), medium, borne in clusters of 4-5; slightly fragrant; foliage bronze; vigorous, upright, bushy growth. GM, Geneva, 1954.

Jawahar HT, *w*, 1980, *Sweet Afton* × *Delhi Princess*; Div. of Veg. Crops & Floriculture. Flowers creamy white, dbl. (47 petals), high-centered blooms borne 2-6 per cluster; very fragrant; foliage light green, glossy; straight, brown prickles; vigorous, bushy growth.

Jay Jay HT, *w*, 1971, *Peace* sport; Kern Rose Nursery. Flowers white, edged pink, dbl., high-centered, very large; slightly fragrant; foliage large, dark, leathery; very vigorous, bushy growth.

Jaybo Min, *rb*, 1988, *Rise 'n' Shine* × *Seedling*; Bridges, Dennis; Bridges Roses. Flowers very bright red, yellow at base, fading to pink, semi-dbl. (22 petals), urn-shaped, medium, borne in sprays of 4-6; slight, fruity fragrance; foliage medium, dark green, glossy; prickles long, pointed, pink; bushy, medium growth.

Jazz F, *ob*, 1960, *Masquerade* × *Seedling*; deRuiter; Gregory. Flowers orange-yellow flushed crimson, dbl. (26 petals), medium (2 in.), borne in clusters; slightly fragrant; foliage dark, glossy; vigorous growth.

Jazz Fest F, *mr*, 1971, *Pink Parfait* × *Garnette*; Armstrong, D.L.; Armstrong Nursery. Bud long, pointed; flowers medium red, semi-dbl., medium; slightly fragrant; foliage large, leathery; vigorous, upright, bushy growth.

Jazz Time™ Cl Min, *dp*, 1985, (MINacco); *Little Darling* × *Little Chief*; Williams, E.D.; Mini-Roses, 1986. Flowers deep pink, dbl. (35 petals), small blossom clusters; slight fragrance; foliage small, dark, semi-glossy; upright, bushy (4-5 ft.) growth.

J. B. Clark HP (OGR), *dr*, 1905, *Lord Bacon* × *Gruss an Teplitz*; Dickson, H. Flowers deep scarlet, shaded blackish crimson, dbl. (25 petals), high-centered, large; fragrant; very prickly; vigorous (8-10 ft.), bushy, almost climbing growth.

J. B. Meilland HT, *ob*, 1941, *Mme. Joseph Perraud* × *(Charles P. Kilham* × *Margaret McGredy)*; Meilland, F. Flowers orange, reverse golden yellow, very full, large; fragrant; very vigorous growth.

J. C. Thornton HT, *mr*, 1926, *K. of K.* × *Red-Letter Day*; Bees. Bud pointed; flowers glowing crimson-scarlet, dbl.; slightly fragrant; foliage light olive-green, glossy, leathery; vigorous, branching growth. GM, NRS, 1928.

Jean Bach Sisley Ch (OGR), *pb*, 1889, Dubreuil. Flowers silvery rose, outer petals salmon-rose veined carmine; fragrant; growth moderate.

Jean Bodin M (OGR), *lp*, 1847, Vibert. Flowers light rose-pink, center quartered; not very mossy; vigorous growth.

Jean Bostick HT, *my*, 1936, (Yellow Condesa de Sastago); *Condesa de Sástago sport*; Bostick. Flowers deep yellow, sometimes splotched red, dbl. (50 petals), globular, large; very fragrant; foliage leathery, glossy; very vigorous growth.

Jean Campbell HT, *pb*, 1964, *Ethel Sanday seedling × Lady Sylvia*; Sanday. Flowers blush-pink suffused apricot, dbl. (28 petals), well formed, large (4½ in.); fragrant; foliage dark; upright growth.

Jean C. N. Forestier HT, *rb*, 1919, *Seedling × Mme. Edouard Herriot*; Pernet-Ducher. Flowers carmine, slightly tinted orange and yellow, dbl., very large; foliage glossy, bronze; very vigorous growth. GM, Bagatelle, 1919.

Jean Cote HT, *yb*, 1936, Gaujard; J&P. Flowers old-gold, center deeper, full, very large; foliage brilliant green; vigorous growth.

Jean de la Lune F, *dy*, 1965, (DELbut; DELcro; YelloGlo; Moon Magic); *(Orléans Rose × Goldilocks) × (Fashion × Henri Mallerin seedling)*; Delbard-Chabert; Cuthbert. Flowers deep yellow, dbl., cupped blooms in clusters; slightly fragrant; foliage matt; low growth.

Jean du Tilleux HT, *mp*, 1980, *King of Hearts × Golden Masterpiece*; Winchel, Joseph; Kimbrew-Walter Roses. Bud long; flowers medium lavender pink, dbl. (30 petals), exhibition blooms borne singly; slight fragrance; foliage deep green, waxy; slightly hooked prickles; medium, vigorous growth.

Jean Ducher T (OGR), *op*, Prior to 1889. Flowers salmon to peachy pink, globular; fragrant. Among the hardiest of the Teas.

Jean Gaujard® HT, *mr*, 1977, (GAUvitor); *Canasta × Rose Gaujard*; Gaujard. Flowers brilliant red, dbl. (40 petals); vigorous growth.

Jean Girin R, *pb*, 1910, Girin. Flowers bright rose-pink, base rosy white, stamens forming a yellow eye, dbl., small; vigorous, climbing growth; profuse bloom, sometimes repeated.

Jean Guichard R, *pb*, 1905, *R. wichuraiana × Souv. de Catherine Guillot*; Barbier. Bud bronzy crimson; flowers copper-pink; vigorous, climbing growth.

Jean Kathryn F, *pb*, 1973, *Memoriam × Gavotte*; Ellick. Flowers neyron rose, reverse white, dbl. (45 petals), very full, large (4 in.); very fragrant; foliage light; very vigorous growth.

Jean Kenneally™ Min, *ab*, 1984, (TINeally); *Futura × Party Girl*; Bennett, Dee; Tiny Petals Nursery. Flowers pale to medium apricot, dbl. (22 petals), HT form, small; slight fragrance; foliage medium, medium green, semi-glossy; upright, bushy. AOE, 1986.

Jean Lafitte LCl, *mp*, 1934, *R. setigera seedling × Willowmere*; Horvath; J&P. Bud pointed; flowers Willowmere pink, dbl., cupped, large; fragrant; foliage leathery; very vigorous, climbing (8-10 ft.) growth; very hardy.

Jean Lapeyre S, *my*, 1960, Gaujard. Flowers yellow, well formed; foliage bronze; vigorous, bushy growth; recurrent bloom

Jean Lhoste R, *rb*, 1926, *Alexandre Girault × Gerbe Rose*; Congy; Cochet-Cochet. Flowers rosy carmine, base flesh-white, dbl., large, borne in clusters of 50-100.

Jean Liabaud HP (OGR), *dr*, 1875, *Baron de Bonstetten × Seedling*; Liabaud. Flowers crimson-maroon, shaded scarlet, dbl. (60 petals), large; fragrant; vigorous; some recurrent bloom.

Jean Lorthois HT, *pb*, 1879, Ducher, Vve. Flowers rose-pink, center darker, reverse silvery, well formed, large.

Jean MacArthur HT, *mr*, 1942, *Joanna Hill × California*; Hill, J.H., Co. Bud long, pointed, begonia-red; flowers pink, dbl. (30-40 petals), high-centered, large (3½-4 in.); slightly fragrant; foliage leathery, wrinkled, dark; vigorous, upright growth; a florists' variety, not distributed for outdoor use.

Jean McGregor Reid HT, *w*, 1962, *Peace sport*; Sunter; Ross & Son. Flowers cream, large; fragrant; foliage dark, glossy; vigorous growth.

Jean Mermoz Pol, *mp*, 1937, (Jean Marmoz); *R. wichuraiana × Seedling*; Chenault; Hémeray-Aubert. Flowers ruddy pink, very full, imbricated, small blooms in long clusters; slightly fragrant; foliage glossy, dark; vigorous.

Jean Muraour F, *w*, 1935, *Gruss an Aachen sport*; Vogel, M. Flowers pure white, center light yellow.

Jean Rameau B (OGR), *dp*, 1918, *Mme. Isaac Pereire sport*; Darclanne; Turbat. Flowers iridescent rose.

Jean Renton HT, *my*, 1940, Clark, A. Flowers yellow; vigorous growth.

Jean Rose Min, *pb*, 1987, (TINjean); *Electron × Fairest of Fair*; Bennett, Dee; Tiny Petals Nursery. Flowers peach-pink with yellow base, reverse soft yellow, fading light pink, dbl. (20-25 petals), urn-shaped, medium, borne usually singly; slight fragrance; foliage medium, medium green, semi-glossy; few, slender, small, reddish prickles; fruit globular, medium, brown; upright, medium growth.

Jean Rosenkrantz HP (OGR), *or*, 1864, Portemer Fils. Flowers very bright coral red, full, large; very fragrant.

Jean Sisley HT, *m*, 1879, *Adam × Emilie Hausburg*; Bennett. Flowers lilac-rose, large; moderate growth.

Jean Soupert HP (OGR), *dr*, 1875, *Charles Lefèvre × Souv. du Baron de Sémur*; Lacharme. Flowers crimson-maroon, full, large; fragrant.

Jean Thomson Harris F, *op*, 1976, *(Fragrant Cloud × Heidelberg) × (Heidelberg × Kingcup)*; Cocker. Flowers salmon, shaded orange, dbl. (30 petals), large (4 in.).

Jean Webb HT, *rb*, 1966, *Bettina sport*; Marks. Flowers cochineal, reverse light bronze, large (4 in.); fragrant; foliage dark; vigorous growth.

Jeanie HT, *w*, 1959, *Condesa de Sástago × Mme. Edmond Labbé*; Eddie; Wyant. Flowers cream to pink, dbl. (66 petals), high-centered, large (4-4½ in.); fragrant; foliage dark; vigorous, spreading growth.

Jeanie Williams Min, *rb*, 1965, *Little Darling × Magic Wand*; Moore, R.S.; Sequoia Nursery. Flowers orange-red, reverse yellow, dbl., small; slightly fragrant; foliage leathery; vigorous, bushy.

Jeanine Defaucamberge Pol, *pb*, 1931, *Merveille sport*; Turbat. Flowers bright salmon-pink, passing to light pink, very dbl., peony form, large; foliage slender.

Jeanine Weber HT, *ob*, 1954, *Soestdijk × Mary Hart*; Leenders, M. Flowers orange, large; fragrant; vigorous growth.

Jeanne Cabanis HT, *rb*, 1922, Guillot, P. Bud coral-red; flowers bright rose-carmine, reverse silvery, center coppery rose, dbl.

Jeanne d'Arc A (OGR), *w*, 1818, Vibert. Flowers creamy flesh fading to ivory-white, dbl., large; dense bush (to 5 ft.).

Jeanne d'Arc N (OGR), *w*, 1848, Verdier, V. Flowers creamy white, dbl.; vigorous.

Jeanne d'Arc Pol, *w*, 1909, *Mme. Norbert Levavasseur sport*; Levavasseur. Flowers pure milky white; fragrant.

Jeanne de Montfort M (OGR), *mp*, 1851, Robert. Bud heavily mossed, dark carmine; flowers clear pink, edged silver, semi-dbl., flat blooms in large clusters; fragrant; foliage emerald-green; tall, vigorous growth.

Jeanne Drivon P (OGR), *w*, 1883, Schwartz, J. Flowers white, faintly shaded pink, very dbl.; fragrant.

Jeanne Excoffier HT, *pb*, 1921, *Mme. Philippe Rivoire × Mme. Edouard Herriot*; Buatois. Flowers daybreak-pink, inside buff, dbl.

Jeanne Hachette M (OGR), *m*, 1851, Robert. Flowers slaty violet.

Jeanne Lajoie Cl Min, *mp*, 1975, *(Casa Blanca × Independence) × Midget*; Sima; Mini-Roses. Bud long, pointed; flowers medium pink, dbl. (40 petals), high-centered, small (1 in.); slightly fragrant; foliage small, glossy, dark, embossed; upright, bushy growth. AOE, 1977.

Jeanne Lallemand LCl, *pb*, 1954, *Mrs. Pierre S. duPont × George Dickson*; Buatois. Flowers pink, reverse salmon-pink, dbl. (40-50 petals), large; very vigorous growth; very free, recurrent bloom.

Jeanne Lassalle LCl, *mp*, 1936, Lassalle; Vially. Flowers pink, borne in clusters of 50-60 on long, stiff stems; foliage broad, light; vigorous (5 ft.) growth; free, recurrent bloom.

Jeanne Mermet Pol, *w*, 1909, Mermet. Flowers white; vigorous growth.

Jeanne Nicod HT, *w*, 1929, Schwartz, A. Flowers white, center tinted cream, dbl.

Jeanne Richert R, *w*, 1929, *Léontine Gervais × Seedling*; Walter, L. Flowers cream, center red-brown, borne in large clusters; foliage glossy; very vigorous, climbing growth.

Jeanne Saultier HT, *pb*, 1927, *Louise Catherine Breslau × Mme. Edouard Herriot*; Laperrière. Flowers salmon-rose, reverse reddish pink, base yellow, dbl.; fragrant.

Jeannette G (OGR), *dp*, Descemet. Flowers bright light red, fading light rose-pink, dbl.

Jeannie Deans E (OGR), *dr*, 1895, Penzance. Flowers scarlet-crimson, semi-dbl.; foliage fragrant; vigorous growth; very free seasonal bloom.

Jeannie Dickson HP (OGR), *pb*, 1890, Dickson, A. Flowers rose-pink, edged silvery pink, full (45 petals), high-centered, large; vigorous growth; moderate bloom.

Jeannine Min, *lp*, 1992, (FROneen); *Baby Katie × Seedling*; Frock, Marshall J. Flowers light pink aging to white with a few red spots, similar to Royal Highness, dbl. (30 petals), high-centered, exhibition, slow to open, holds well, medium (4+ cms) blooms borne usually singly; heavy fragrance; foliage medium, medium green, semi-glossy; medium (40-50 cms), upright growth.

Jeannine Michelle Min, *dy*, 1989, (FROjean); *Rise 'n' Shine × Seedling*; Frock, Marshall J. Bud pointed; flowers deep gold-yellow, aging to pale yellow, dbl. (30 petals), high-centered, exhibition, medium, borne usually singly and in sprays of 2-5; moderate, fruity fragrance; foliage medium, medium green, semi-glossy; prickles straight, tan; fruit none observed; upright, bushy, medium, hardy growth.

Jeanny Soupert Pol, *w*, 1913, *Mme. Norbert Levavasseur × Petite Léonie*; Soupert & Notting. Flowers soft flesh-white, borne in large clusters; moderately vigorous growth.

Jean's Dream HT, *pb*, 1971, *My Choice × (Seedling × Memoriam)*; Ellick. Flowers orient pink to azalea-pink, dbl. (30 petals), exhibition form, very large (6 in.); foliage large; vigorous, upright, bushy growth.

JELcanodir F, *dy*, 1976, *Seedling 1-61-ys × Golden Garnette*; Jelly; Universal Plants. Flowers aureolin-yellow, dbl. (30 petals), full, large (2½-3 in.); slightly fragrant; vigorous, upright growth; almost continuous bloom in glasshouse.

JELeit F, *w*, 1971, *Seventeen × Jack Frost*; Hill, E.G., Co.; Meilland. Flowers white, dbl. (30-35 petals), globular, large (3 in.); slightly fragrant; foliage large, dull, leathery; vigorous, upright growth.

Jelico HT, *or*, 1973, *Baccará × (Forever Yours × Seedling)*; Jelly; Universal Plants. Flowers vermilion, reverse crimson, dbl. (35 petals), cupped, large (5 in.); slightly fragrant; foliage large, dark.

Jelly Bean™ Min, *rb*, 1981, (SAVabean); *Seedling × Poker Chip*; Saville, F. Harmon; Nor'East Min. Roses, 1982. Bud ovoid, pointed; flowers red-yellow blend, dbl. (20 petals), high-centered, micro-mini blooms borne 1-6 per cluster; moderate, spicy fragrance; foliage small; no prickles; very compact, tiny growth.

JELrandoli F, *rb*, 1976, *San Francisco × Little Leaguer*; Jelly; Universal Plants. Flowers vermilion-red, base cardinal-red, dbl. (35 petals), full, large (3-3½ in.); slightly fragrant; foliage large; vigorous, upright growth.

Jema HT, *ab*, 1981, *Helen Traubel × Lolita*; Perry, Astor; Perry Roses, 1982. Bud ovoid; flowers apricot, dbl. (45 petals), large blooms borne singly; fragrant; foliage medium, light green; small, triangular, straw prickles; tall, vigorous growth.

Jennie Anne™ Min, *rb*, 1986, (KINjen); *Gingersnap × Charmglo*; King, Gene; AGM Miniature Roses, 1987. Flowers red, reverse yellow, fading light yellow with red edge, dbl. (16 petals), high centered, exhibition, medium, borne usually singly or in sprays of 3-5; no fragrance; foliage medium, medium green, matt; straight, small, white prickles; fruit oval; bushy, medium growth.

Jennie June™ HT, *mr*, 1989, (TANjenju); *Seedling × Seedling*; Rosen Tantau; Bear Creek Gardens, 1990. Bud ovoid; flowers medium

red, reverse lighter with some bluing, dbl. (50 petals), high-centered, large, borne usually singly; slight fragrance; foliage large, medium green, semi-glossy; prickles short, narrow, hooked down, red-green; upright, spreading, medium growth.

Jennie Robinson Min, *op*, 1983, (TRObette); *Rumba × Darling Flame*; Robinson, Thomas; Thomas Robinson Ltd. Flowers orange flushed pink, dbl. (35 petals), patio, small; fragrant; foliage small, dark, glossy; bushy growth.

Jennifer HT, 1954, *(Mrs. Henry Bowles × Phyllis Gold) × Edina.*; Fletcher; Tucker. Flowers pale flesh pink, large (4-5 in.); very fragrant; foliage dull green; vigorous growth. RULED EXTINCT 1/85 ARM.

Jennifer F, 1959, *Independence × Fashion*; Fryer's Nursery; An improved Fashion, but darker. RULED EXTINCT 1/85 ARM.

Jennifer™ Min, *pb*, 1985, (BENjen); *Party Girl × Laguna*; Benardella, Frank; Nor'East Min. Roses. Flowers light pink, white reverse, dbl. (35 petals), HT form, small; very fragrant; foliage medium, dark, semi-glossy; bushy, spreading growth. AOE, 1985.

Jennifer Hart HT, *dr*, 1981, (AROart); *Pink Parfait × Yuletide*; Swim, H.C. & Christensen, J.E.; Armstrong Nursery, 1982. Bud ovoid, pointed; flowers dark red, dbl. (45 petals), high-centered, medium blooms borne singly; mild tea fragrance; foliage medium, medium green, semi-glossy; medium, upright, bushy growth.

Jennifer Jay HT, *pb*, 1977, *Christian Dior sport*; Thomas, A.S. Flowers light to medium pink.

Jennifer Joy Min, *lp*, 1985, (POULjenjoy); *Mini-Poul × Seedling*; Oleson, M.&P.; Ludwigs Roses, 1983. Flowers light pink, dbl. (75 petals), mini-flora, medium blooms in clusters; no fragrance; foliage light green; compact, low, bushy growth.

Jennifer-Betty Kenward HT, *or*, 1985, (LANbet); *Mildred Reynolds × Whisky Mac*; Sealand Nursery. Flowers orange-red, dbl. (35 petals), medium; slight fragrance; foliage medium, medium green, glossy; spreading growth.

Jenny Brown HT, *or*, 1974, *(Pink Favorite × Dorothy Peach) × Dainty Bess*; Parkes; Rumsey. Bud long, pointed; flowers salmon-pink, center paler, single (5 petals), open, large (4 in.), very fragrant; foliage glossy; very vigorous growth.

Jenny Duval HCh (OGR), Flowers rosy blush. This rose is apparently no longer in cultivation. G.S. Thomas reports that the rose which he imported from Bobbink & Atkins and described under this name in The

Old Shrub Roses is actually Président de Seze.

Jenny Fair HT, *mp*, 1967, *Tropicana × Seedling*; Gregory. Flowers pink, globular; fragrant; foliage dark; slender, upright growth.

Jenny Wren F, *ab*, 1957, *Cécile Brunner × Fashion*; Ratcliffe. Bud salmon-red; flowers creamy apricot, reverse pale salmon, dbl., small blooms in large, loose sprays; very fragrant; foliage dark.

Jenny's Dream HT, *dp*, 1980, *Red Devil sport*; Beckett, Ian. Flowers deep pink.

Jens Munk HRg (S), *mp*, 1974, *Schneezwerg × Frau Dagmar Hartopp*; Svejda; Canada Dept. of Agric. Bud ovoid; flowers medium pink, yellow stamens, dbl. (25 petals), large (3 in.); very fragrant; upright, bushy growth.

Jerry Gr, *pb*, 1987, *Seedling × Seedling*; Jerabek, Paul. Flowers white, flushing carmine red, reverse carmine, grading to white, fading deeper, dbl. (25+ petals), cupped, medium, borne in sprays of 3-5; heavy, sweet fragrance; foliage medium, medium green, semi-glossy; medium, red-brown prickles, hooked downward; fruit small, rarely sets; bushy, tall growth. ARC TG (S), 1986.

Jerry Desmonde HT, *mp*, 1959, *Lord Rossmore × Karl Herbst*; Norman; Harkness. Flowers rose-pink, reverse silvery, dbl. (50 petals), well formed, large (5 in.); foliage dark, glossy; vigorous, upright growth.

Jersey Beauty R, *ly*, 1899, *R. wichuraiana × Perle des Jardins*; Manda, W.A. Flowers pale yellow, fading white, single, large blooms in clusters; very fragrant; foliage very glossy; vigorous, climbing; non-recurrent.

Jersey Queen HT, *ob*, 1920, *Mme. Mélanie Soupert × Queen Mary*; Le Cornu; Jersey Nursery. Flowers flame-orange, edged rose, reverse lemon, dbl.

Jerusalem F, *w*, 1983, (HOLje); *(Queen Elizabeth × Seedling) × Moriah*; Holtzman, Arnold; Gandys Roses. Flowers cream, dbl. (40 petals), exhibition, large blooms in sprays of 5-8; fragrant; foliage medium, light green, matt; fruit ovoid, small, green; upright, bushy growth.

Jesmond Dene F, *op*, 1975, *Arthur Bell × Betty May Wood*; Wood. Flowers pastel salmon-pink, full, large (3½ in.); very fragrant; vigorous, upright growth.

Jessica R, *pb*, 1910, Walsh. Flowers cream-white, center light rose, large.

Jessie Pol, *rb*, 1909, *Phyllis sport*; Merryweather. Flowers bright crimson, fading rose-pink, center white, semi-dbl., small (1½ in.), borne in ¬lusters; slightly fragrant; foliage small, soft, glossy; bushy growth.

Jessie Anderson S, *dp*, *(Old Crimson China × R. canina) × Souv. d'Alphonse Lavallée*. Flowers deep rose, dbl., well formed, large; blooms continuously on new wood.

Jessie Brown Min, *mp*, 1978, *Fairy Moss × Fairy Moss*; Dobbs; Small World Min. Roses. Bud mossy; flowers medium pink, semi-dbl. (15 petals), loosely formed, small (½ in.); foliage small; bushy growth.

Jessie Clark LCl, *mp*, 1915, *R. gigantea × Mme. Martignier*; Clark, A.; NRS Victoria. Flowers rosy pink, becoming lighter, single, very large; foliage dark, leathery; very vigorous growth; early spring bloom.

Jessie Mathews HT, *yb*, 1982, (BEEjes); *Ernest H. Morse × Rosenella*; Bees, Ltd. Flowers light yellow, petals edged pink, dbl. (35 petals), medium; slight fragrance; foliage medium, light green, semi-glossy; bushy growth.

Jessie Segrave HT, *rb*, 1937, Mee; Beckwith. Flowers scarlet on deep chrome base, with pencil markings on inside, dbl. well formed; vigorous growth.

Jessika® HT, *op*, 1971, (TANjeka; Jehoca; Jehoka; Jessica); *Colour Wonder × Piccadilly*; Tantau. Bud long, pointed; flowers peach-salmon, medium; fragrant; vigorous, upright growth.

Jet HT, *dr*, 1948, *Pink Princess × Crimson Glory*; Brownell. Bud long, pointed; flowers red to very dark red, dbl., large; fragrant; foliage glossy, dark; vigorous, bushy, compact growth.

Jet Fire F, *or*, 1964, *Sumatra × Fashion*; Schloen, J.; Ellesmere Nursery. Bud ovoid; flowers orange-red, dbl., cupped, large; fragrant (spicy); foliage dark, glossy, vigorous, upright, bushy growth.

Jet Flame® Min, *m*, 1984, (LENpen; Jet Flame Nirpaysage); *New Penny × Violet Hood*; Lens, Louis. Flowers lavender-purple, dbl. (30 petals), rosette, micro-mini, small blooms in clusters of 3-100; no fragrance; foliage very small, brilliant dark green; no prickles; bushy, spreading growth. GM, Paris, 1984.

Jet Spray® Min, *m*, 1984, (LENcara; LEN 4); *New Penny × Seedling*; Lens, Louis. Flowers purple-pink, dbl. (21 petals), rosette, small; slight fragrance; foliage very small, dark; no prickles; bushy, spreading growth.

Jet Trail Min, *w*, 1964, *Little Darling × Magic Wand*; Moore, R.S.; Sequoia Nursery. Bud pointed; flowers white, sometimes tinted pale green, dbl. (40 petals), small; bushy (12-14 in.)growth.

Jet Trail Min, *w*, 1964, *Little Darling × Magic Wand*; Moore, R.S.; Sequoia Nursery. Bud pointed; flowers white, sometimes tinted pale green, dbl. (35-45 petals), small; bushy (12-14 in.).

Jeune Fille F, *op*, 1964, *Rose Gaujard seedling* × *Vendome*; Gaujard. Flowers bright salmon-pink, dbl., medium, borne in clusters; fragrant; foliage leathery; very vigorous, bushy growth.

Jeune Henry C (OGR), *mp*, Vibert, prior to 1815. Flowers vivid rose.

Jeunesse HT, *mp*, 1959, *(Independence* × *Tonnerre)* × *Michèle Meilland*; Laperrière; EFR. Flowers bright pink, dbl.; moderately bushy growth.

Jewel HT, *dr*, 1938, *Better Times sport*; Grillo. Flowers velvety red, dbl. (50 petals), large (5 in.); fragrant.

Jewel Box Min, *pb*, 1984, (MORbox); *Avandel* × *Old Master*; Moore, R.S.; Moore Min. Roses. 1983. Flowers light to deep pink blend, reverse lighter, dbl. (20 petals), small; slight fragrance; foliage small, medium green, semi-glossy; bushy growth.

Jewel's Delight™ Min, *mp*, 1989, (MINbaco); *Tom Brown* × *Twilight Trail*; Williams, Ernest D. Flowers medium pink, dbl. (33 petals), small; fragrant; foliage small, medium green, glossy; bushy growth.

Jezebel HT, *mp*, 1964, *Queen Elizabeth* × *Pink Lustre*; Leenders, J. Flowers pink, dbl., strong stems.

J. F. Barry HT, *my*, 1912, *Arthur R. Goodwin sport*; Piper. Flowers light daffodil-yellow.

J. F. Müller F, *dr*, 1929, *Rodhatte sport*; Müller, J.F. Flowers dark red, large; foliage dark; bushy, dwarf growth.

J. G. Glassford HT, *dr*, 1921, Dickson, H. Bud pointed; flowers deep crimson, high-centered, very large; fragrant; very vigorous, branching growth.

J. H. Bruce HT, *mr*, 1937, *H.V. Machin* × *Marion Horton*; Bees. Flowers crimson-scarlet, dbl., high-centered, very large; foliage glossy; vigorous, bushy growth. GM, NRS, 1936.

J. H. Pemberton HT, *mr*, 1931, Bentall. Flowers scarlet; fragrant (damask); vigorous growth.

J. H. Van Heyst HT, *yb*, 1936, *Comtesse Vandal* × *Edith Nellie Perkins*; Leenders, M. Bud pointed; flowers yellowish flesh, reverse pink; vigorous growth.

Jian Min, *mr*, 1965, *Juliette* × *Oakington Ruby*; Williams, E.D.; Mini-Roses. Bud ovoid; flowers medium red, reverse lighter, dbl., very small; foliage narrow, leathery; very vigorous, bushy, dwarf growth.

Jill F, *mr*, 1939, *(Else Poulsen* × *Seedling)* × *((Seedling (single red)* × *Étoile de Hollande)* × *Daily*

Mail Scented Rose); LeGrice. Flowers cerise-scarlet, semi-dbl., open, borne in clusters on long stems; slightly fragrant; vigorous, bushy growth.

Jill Darling HT, *rb*, 1937, Austin & McAslan. Flowers rich cerise, reverse cinnamon-yellow; fragrant; foliage glossy; vigorous growth.

Jim Dandy™ Min, *rb*, 1988, (BENjim); *Rise 'n' Shine* × *Marina*; Benardella, Frank; Nor' East Miniature Roses, 1989. Bud pointed; flowers medium red, reverse yellow flushed red, aging lighter, high-centered, exhibition, medium, borne usually singly and in sprays of 3-5; slight, spicy fragrance; foliage medium, medium green, semi-glossy; prickles none: fruit none; upright, bushy, medium growth. AOE, 1989.

Jim Todd HT, *rb*, 1940, Mallerin; A. Meilland. Flowers nasturtium-red, reverse touched yellow, semi-dbl., cupped, large; very vigorous, bushy growth.

Jiminy Cricket F, *op*, 1954, *Goldilocks* × *Geranium Red*; Boerner; J&P. Bud ovoid; flowers coral-orange to pink-coral, dbl. (28 petals), cupped, large (3-4 in.) blooms in clusters; fragrant (rose geranium); foliage glossy; vigorous, upright, bushy. AARS, 1955.

Jimmy Greaves HT, *m*, 1971, *Dorothy Peach* × *Prima Ballerina*; Gandy. Flowers red-purple, reverse silver, dbl. (55 petals), exhibition, large (5 in.); slightly fragrant; foliage large; erect, bushy growth.

Jimmy Savile F, *ob*, 1988, (PEApolly; Jimmy Saville); *Seedling* × *Seedling*; Pearce, C.A.; Rearsby Roses, 1988. Flowers coppery-orange, aging lighter, dbl. (25-30 petals), cupped, loose, medium, borne usually singly; moderate, fruity fragrance; foliage medium, medium green, matt; bushy, low growth.

Jingles F, *mp*, 1956, *Goldilocks* × *Garnette*; Boerner; J&P. Bud ovoid; flowers pink overcast deep rose-pink, dbl. (35-40 petals), cupped to open, large (2½-3 in.); fragrant; foliage leathery, dark green; vigorous, upright, bushy growth; a forcing variety for greenhouse use.

Jitterbug Min, *ob*, 1992, (JACminno); *Caribe* × *Impatient*; Warriner, William A.; Bear Creek Gardens, Inc., 1993. Flowers orange, slightly lighter on reverse, nicely formed, open, moderately full (15-25 petals), very heavy petal substance, very slight quelling, medium (4-7 cms) blooms borne in small clusters; slight fragrance; foliage medium, dark green, glossy; some prickles; tall (60-75 cms), upright, bushy growth.

J. K. Tyl LCl, *mp*, 1936, Brada; Böhm. Flowers bright pink, cactus form; vigorous growth; very free bloom.

J. K. B. Roos HT, *m*, 1933, Leenders, M. Bud pointed; flowers pale reddish lilac, shaded salmon-flesh, dbl., large; very fragrant; very vigorous growth.

J. Michel HT, *dy*, 1930, *Seedling* × *The Queen Alexandra Rose*; Felberg-Leclerc. Flowers dark golden yellow, full, large; foliage leathery; vigorous growth. RULED EXTINCT 1/87.

J. Michael™ Min, *or*, 1987, (KINmike); *Poker Chip* × *Watercolor*; King, Gene; AGM Miniature Roses. Flowers orange-red, aging lighter, dbl. (18 petals), high-centered, exhibition, large, borne usually singly; mini-flora; moderate, fruity fragrance; foliage large, light green, matt; straight, medium, white-green prickles; upright, tall growth.

J. M. López Picó HT, *dr*, 1947, *Editor McFarland* × *Comtesse Vandal*; Camprubi. Bud long, pointed; flowers crimson, dbl., high-centered, large; slightly fragrant; upright growth.

J. M. López Picó, Climbing Cl HT, *dr*, 1954, Camprubi.

J. N. Hart HT, *dp*, 1924, *George Dickson* × *Edith Cavell*; Chaplin Bros. Flowers rose-pink, dbl.; fragrant.

Joan HMsk (S), *ob*, 1919, *Trier* × *Perle des Jeannes*; Pemberton. Bud peach; flowers copper, semi-dbl., borne in clusters.

Joan Alder HT, *pb*, 1950, Moss. Bud long; flowers salmon-pink tinted mauve; foliage dark; very vigorous growth.

Joan Austin Min, *pb*, 1981, (MORdeb); *Avandel* × *Seedling*; Moore, R.S.; Moore Min. Roses. Bud pointed; flowers light to medium pink, white stripes, dbl. (38 petals), high-centered blooms borne singly, sometimes 3 or more per cluster; very fragrant; foliage small, medium green, semi-glossy to matt; very bushy, compact growth.

Joan Ball Min, *mp*, 1987, (TROball); *Orange Sensation* × *Seedling*; Robinson, Thomas, 1989. Flowers medium pink, dbl. (30 petals), high-centered, small blooms in sprays of 3-6; fruity fragrance; foliage small, dark, glossy; short, thin, red-brown prickles; upright, bushy growth.

Joan Bell HT, *dp*, 1985, *Portland Trailblazer sport*; Bell, John C. Flowers deep pink.

Joan Cant HT, *pb*, 1929, Cant, B.R. Bud pointed; flowers salmon-pink, reverse brighter, dbl., very large; very fragrant; foliage light, leathery; vigorous, bushy growth.

Joan Davis HT, *ab*, 1927, *Ophelia seedling*; Allen. Flowers salmon-apricot shaded cerise-pink, base yellow, dbl.; very fragrant.

Joan Elizabeth HT, *yb*, 1949, Fletcher; Tucker. Bud long, pointed; flowers golden yellow, reverse flushed pink, dbl. (30 petals), well formed, large (5 in.); fragrant; foliage dark, glossy; vigorous growth.

Joan Fittall HT, *yb*, 1946, *Luis Brinas* × *Seedling*; Moss; F. Mason. Bud long, pointed; flowers bronze and gold fading to pink, semi-dbl., open, medium; slightly fragrant; foliage leathery; vigorous, bushy growth.

Joan Frueh HT, *lp*, 1924, *Ophelia* × *General-Superior Arnold Janssen*; Frueh. Flowers shell-pink, dbl.; fragrant.

Joan Howarth HT, *pb*, 1924, *Lyon Rose* × *Mme. Abel Chatenay*; Bees. Flowers shell-pink shaded carmine, dbl., very large; fragrant.

Joan Knight Cl HT, *dr*, 1928, Knight, J. Flowers dark red; vigorous growth.

Joan Longer™ S, *w*, 1991, (WILktwo); *Queen Elizabeth* × *Ivory Fashion, Climbing*; Williams, J. Benjamin, 1971; The Scott Arboretum of Swarthmore College, 1991. Bud pointed; flowers blush pink opening to ivory with a hint of coral pink in center, semi-dbl., cupped, medium blooms borne in sprays of 5-9; moderate, damask fragrance; foliage large, dark green, semi-glossy; upright, bushy, tall growth.

Joan Margaret Derrick Pol, *dr*, 1953, *Golden Salmon sport*; Derrick. Flowers carmine-red, semi-dbl. (15 petals), small; vigorous growth.

Joan Ross HP (OGR), *pb*, 1933, *Frau Karl Druschki* × *Paul Neyron*; Nicolas. Bud pointed; flowers blush, reverse light pink, dbl., very large; slightly fragrant; vigorous growth; profuse, non-recurrent bloom.

Joanna Bridge HT, *yb*, 1916, Hicks. Flowers canary-yellow shaded strawberry, semi-dbl., borne on large trusses; vigorous growth.

Joanna Hill HT, *ly*, 1928, *Mme. Butterfly* × *Miss Amelia Gude*; J.H. Hill Co. Bud long, pointed; flowers creamy yellow, base flushed orange, dbl. (48 petals), large; fragrant; foliage leathery; vigorous growth.

Joanna Hill, Climbing Cl HT, *yb*, 1935, Howard Rose Co.

Joanna Troutman HT, *ob*, 1929, *Mme. Alexandre Dreux seedling*; Vestal. Bud pointed; flowers orange-yellow, semi-dbl., open; fragrant; foliage bronze, glossy.

Joanne HT, *op*, 1985, *Courvoisier* × *Princesse*; Poole, Lionel. Flowers medium shrimp pink, dbl. (43 petals), high-centered, exhibition, large blooms borne singly; slight fragrance; foliage large, dark, semi-glossy; large, dark brown prickles; fruit large, globular, orange; medium, upright growth.

Joannes Ginet HT, *pb*, 1929, *The Queen Alexandra Rose sport*; Gaujard. Flowers white, tinted cream, edged oriental red.

João Moreira da Silva HT, *my*, 1959, *Mme. Marie Curie* × *Dr. Manuel Alves de Castro*; Moreira; da Silva. Flowers yellow; fragrant (damask).

João Pereira da Rosa HT, *rb*, 1936, *Angèle Pernet* × *Mme. Méha Sabatier*; Moreira; da Silva. Flowers brilliant red shading orange and yellow, dbl., cupped, large; foliage light, soft; vigorous growth.

Joaquin Aldrufeu HT, *m*, 1897, Aldrufeu. Flowers garnet-purple, reverse violet to magenta, dbl.; slightly fragrant; foliage light green; moderate growth.

Joaquin Mir HT, *dy*, 1940, *Mrs. Pierre S. duPont* × *Senora Gari*; Dot, P. Flowers golden yellow, dbl., cupped, large; foliage glossy, dark; upright growth.

Joasine Hanet P (OGR), *m*, Vibert, prior to 1882. Flowers deep rose tinged with violet, full, quartered, medium; fragrant; heavy bloomer; very hardy.

Jocelyn F, *r*, 1970, LeGrice. Flowers mahogany aging purplish-brown, full, large (3 in.).

Jodrell Bank HT, *pb*, 1967, *Charles F. Warren sport*; Dale, F. Flowers light pink, reverse rose-pink.

Joe Roscoe HT, *mp*, 1971, *Karl Herbst* × *Tzigane*; Wright & Son. Flowers rose-red, dbl. (62 petals), large (6 in.); fragrant.

Joe-Joe™ Min, *ob*, 1985, (KINjoe); *Seedling* × *Rise 'n' Shine*; King, Gene; AGM Min. Roses. Flowers orange-yellow, reverse yellow, dbl. (25 petals), cupped, medium blooms borne singly; slight fragrance; foliage medium, dark, matt; straight, light yellow to brown prickles; bushy, spreading growth.

Joëlle® HT, *w*, 1986, (KRItiban; Joella); *Seedling* × *Seedling*; Kriloff, M. Flowers white, aging light pink, dbl., well-formed; foliage glossy.

Jofitali F, *rb*, 1976, *Sonia sport*; DeWitte; Meilland. Flowers rose-bengal, center cardinal-red.

Johanna Ofman HT, *dp*, 1962, *Pink Sensation sport*; Ofman. Flowers carmine-pink, dbl., large; very fragrant.

Johanna Röpcke R, *op*, 1931, (Johanna Ropke); *Dorothy Perkins* × *Ophelia*; Tantau. Bud pointed; flowers salmon-pink, resembling Ophelia but smaller, dbl., cupped, small, borne in clusters; foliage dark, bronze; very vigorous, climbing growth.

Johanna Tantau Pol, *w*, 1928, *Dorothy Perkins* × *Ophelia*; Tantau. Flowers white, center pinkish yellow, dbl., large, borne in clusters; foliage dark, leathery; bushy, dwarf growth.

Johannes Boettner F, *mr*, 1943, *Baby Château seedling* × *Else Poulsen*; Kordes. Flowers light crimson, dbl., high-centered, very large, borne in clusters; slightly fragrant; vigorous, bushy, compact growth.

Johannesburg Sun HT, *dy*, 1987, (KORdoubt); *Seedling* × *Seedling*; Kordes, W., Sohne; Ludwigs Roses, 1988. Flowers deep golden yellow, dbl. (22 petals), large, borne singly; moderate fragrance; foliage glossy, deep green; prickles concave, brown; tall, upright growth.

Johanniszauber HT, *dr*, 1926, *Château de Clos Vougeot* × *Seedling*; Tantau. Bud pointed; flowers dark velvety blood-red, very dbl.; vigorous growth.

John Abrams F, *op*, 1976, *Vera Dalton* × *Sarabande*; Sanday. Flowers vermilion and salmon, semi-dbl. (15 petals), large (3 in.).

John Allen Sp (OGR), *lp*, 1944, Wright, P.H. (Collected from a wild stand of *R. suffulta* in southern Saskatchewan near the ND border, by John Allen, Battleford, Sask, Canada.) Similar to Woodrow but with more pollen; height 18 in.; recurrent bloom.

John A. Allison Gr, *lp*, 1973, *Queen Elizabeth* × *Montezuma*; Golik; J. Schloen. Bud ovoid; flowers light pink, very dbl., large; slightly fragrant; very vigorous, upright growth.

John Bradshaw Min, *dp*, 1985, (HARquisp); *Seedling* × *Esther's Baby*; Harkness; White Rose. Flowers light rose red, dbl. (24 petals), flat, rosette (starry-shaped) blooms in clusters; slight fragrance; foliage small, semi-glossy; low, bushy growth.

John Bright HP (OGR), *mr*, 1878, Paul, G. Flowers bright crimson, medium.

John Cabot K (S), *mr*, 1978, *R. kordesii* × *Seedling*; Svejda; Canada Dept. of Agric. Bud ovoid; flowers medium red, dbl. (40 petals), medium (2½ in.) blooms in clusters; fragrant; foliage yellow-green; vigorous, upright, medium growth.

John Church F, *or*, 1964, *Ma Perkins* × *Red Favorite*; McGredy, S., IV; McGredy. Flowers orange-scarlet, dbl. (30 petals), well-formed, large (3½ in.) blooms in clusters; fragrant; vigorous growth.

John Cook HT, *pb*, 1917, *La France* × *Seedling*; Krüger; Ketten Bros. Bud dark pink; flowers La France pink, reverse very dark, dbl.; fragrant.

John Cranston M (OGR), *m*, 1861, Verdier, E. Flowers crimson, shaded purple, full, expanded, medium; vigorous growth.

John Cronin HT, *dp*, 1935, Clark, A.; NRS Victoria. Flowers deep pink, dbl., globular, large; fragrant; vigorous growth.

John C. M. Mensing HT, *mp*, 1924, (Pink Ophelia); *Ophelia sport*; Eveleens. Flowers deep bright rose-pink, dbl., open, large; very fragrant; vigorous growth.

John Davis K (S), *mp*, 1986, *(R. kordesii × Seedling) × Seedling*; Svejda, F.; Agric. Canada. Flowers medium pink, yellow at base, dbl. (40 petals), 3½ in. blooms in clusters of up to 17; strong, spicy fragrance; foliage glossy, leathery; straight prickles; trailing growth; recurrent bloom.

John Davison HT, *dr*, 1919, McGredy. Flowers rich velvety crimson, dbl.; fragrant.

John Dijkstra F, *dr*, 1965, (Letkis); *Olala × Paprika*; Buisman. Bud ovoid; flowers dark red, semi-dbl., medium, borne in clusters; foliage dark.

John Downie HT, *ob*, 1921, *Lyon Rose sport*; Dobbie. Flowers salmon.

John Edward Reed HT, *dy*, 1950, *Talisman sport*; Reed. Bud long, pointed; flowers buttercup-yellow, dbl. (32 petals), large (5½-6 in.); fragrant; vigorous, upright growth.

John E. Sleath HT, *rb*, 1937, Mee; Beckwith. Flowers carmine-red, suffused vermilion-orange; vigorous growth.

John Franklin S, *mr*, 1980, *Lilli Marleen × Seedling*; Svejda, F.; Agriculture Canada. Bud ovoid; flowers medium red, dbl. (25 petals), borne several together; fragrant; foliage round; yellow-green prickles with purple hues; upright, bushy growth.

John Fraser M (OGR), *rb*, 1861, Granger. Flowers bright red, shaded crimson and purple, full, large; shy growth.

John F. Kennedy HT, *w*, 1965, (JFK; President John F. Kennedy); *Seedling × White Queen*; Boerner; J&P. Bud ovoid, tinted greenish; flowers white, dbl. (48 petals), high-centered, large (5-5½ in.); fragrant; foliage leathery; vigorous.

John Greenwood F, *mr*, 1976, *Marlena × Fragrant Cloud*; Lea. Flowers bright red, dbl. (25 petals), full, large (2½ in.); slightly fragrant; foliage large, dark; vigorous, free growth.

John Grow M (OGR), *mp*, 1859, Laffay. Flowers clear pink.

John Hart HT, *mp*, 1922, Hicks. Flowers cherry-pink, dbl.; slightly fragrant.

John Henry HT, *mr*, 1925, Beckwith. Bud rosy scarlet; flowers rich pink; slightly fragrant.

John Hopper HP (OGR), *pb*, 1862, *Jules Margottin × Mme. Vidot*; Ward. Flowers bright rose edged lilac, center carmine, dbl. (70 petals), semi-globular, large; very fragrant; vigorous, upright, bushy growth; occasional recurrent bloom.

John Hughes F, *ab*, 1986, (SANphyllis); *City of Gloucester × Bristol Post*; Sanday, John. Flow-

ers soft apricot, semi-dbl. (6-14 petals), medium; slight fragrance; foliage medium, dark green, glossy; bushy growth.

John H. Ellis HT, *dp*, 1948, McGredy. Flowers deep rose-pink, dbl. (48 petals), well formed, large; free, bushy growth.

John Keynes HP (OGR), *dr*, 1865, Verdier, E. Flowers red shaded maroon, dbl. (48 petals); very fragrant; vigorous growth.

John Kidman HT, *my*, 1969, *Radar × Allgold*; Fankhauser. Bud ovoid; flowers lemon-yellow, dbl., camellia form, very large; very fragrant; foliage leathery; vigorous, tall, compact growth.

John Lawrence F, *my*, 1990, *Seedling × Sunsprite*; Bracegirdle, D.T., 1984. Bud pointed; flowers canary yellow, fading as it ages, dbl. (18 petals), flat shaped, medium, borne in sprays of 5-7; moderate, spicy fragrance; foliage medium, glossy; medium, upright growth.

John McNabb HRg (S), *mp*, 1932, *R. rugosa kamtchatica × R. beggeriana*; Skinner. Flowers pink, dbl.; profuse mid season bloom, sometimes continuing later.

John Moore HT, *yb*, 1939, Gaujard. Flowers buff shaded gold, dbl. (47 petals), well shaped, high-centered, very large; fragrant; foliage dark.

John Morley HT, *dp*, 1945, *Joanna Hill × J.C. Thornton*; Duehrsen; California Roses. Bud long, pointed; flowers glowing pink, dbl., high-centered, very large; fragrant; foliage dark, leathery; vigorous, bushy growth.

John Russell HT, *dr*, 1924, Dobbie. Flowers glowing crimson flushed deeper, very dbl., well-shaped, large; vigorous. GM, Bagatelle, 1924.

John Russell, Climbing Cl HT, *dr*, 1930, Ketten Bros.

John Square Cl HT, *dy*, 1937, *Souv. de Claudius Pernet sport*; Square. Flowers sunflower-yellow, center deeper, dbl., cupped, very large; foliage glossy, dark; vigorous, climbing (6-8 ft. in season) growth.

John S. Armstrong Gr, *dr*, 1961, *Charlotte Armstrong × Seedling*; Swim; Armstrong Nursery. Bud ovoid to urn-shaped; flowers dark red, dbl. (40 petals), high-centered to cupped, large (3½-4 in.); slightly fragrant; foliage leathery, semi-glossy, dark; tall, bushy growth. AARS, 1962.

John S. Bloomfield HT, *ab*, 1964, *Ma Perkins × Burnaby*; Fankhauser. Bud ovoid; flowers deep apricot flushed pink, dbl., open, large; slightly fragrant; compact growth.

John Wallace Pol, *dr*, 1941, *Marianne Kluis Superior sport*; Kluis; Klyn. Flowers deep red, dbl., open, large; foliage large, leathery, glossy; bushy growth.

John Waterer® HT, *dr*, 1970, *King of Hearts* × *Hanne*; McGredy, S., IV; McGredy. Flowers dark red, dbl. (44 petals), classic form, large (4 in.); fragrant.

Johnnie Walker HT, *ab*, 1983, (FRYgran); *Sunblest* × *(Arthur Bell* × *Belle Blonde)*; Fryer's Nursery, Ltd., 1982. Flowers buff apricot, dbl. (20 petals), well-formed, large; very fragrant; foliage medium, medium green, matt; vigorous, bushy growth.

John-Paul II HT, *ob*, 1984, (JACange); *Apricot Parfait* × *Futura*; J&P; McConnell Nursery. Flowers orange blend, dbl. (40+ petals), very large; no fragrance; foliage medium, dark, semi-glossy; upright growth.

Joia F, *yb*, 1962, *Seedling* × *Virgo*; Moreira; da Silva. Flowers yellow shaded carmine.

Joie de Vivre HT, *pb*, 1949, Gaujard; Wheatcroft Bros. Flowers pink, base gold, dbl., well shaped, very large; fragrant; foliage bronze green; moderately vigorous growth.

Joker HT, *ob*, 1958, *Peace* × *Karl Herbst*; Lens. Flowers orange-red, reverse lighter; slightly fragrant; foliage glossy.

Jolanda HT, *dp*, 1959, Malandrone. Bud long, pointed; flowers rose, cupped; vigorous, upright, bushy growth.

Joli Coeur F, *dr*, 1963, *Rose Gaujard* × *(Seedling* × *Josephine Bruce)*; Gaujard. Bud globular; flowers dark crimson, dbl., medium; fragrant; foliage dark; symmetrical growth.

Jolie Madame HT, *or*, 1958, *(Independence* × *Happiness)* × *Better Times*; Meilland, F.; URS, 1958; C-P, 1960. Bud ovoid; flowers vermilion-red, dbl. (65 petals), cupped, large (4-4½ in.); slightly fragrant; foliage leathery, glossy; vigorous, upright, bushy growth.

Jolie Princesse F, *pb*, 1955, *Peace* × *Independence*; Gaujard. Flowers pink, shaded ocher, dbl., borne on large trusses; fragrant; foliage leathery, bronze; very vigorous, bushy.

Jolly Pol, *m*, 1934, *Miss Edith Cavell* × *Tip-Top*; Leenders, M. Flowers carmine-purple, center white, single, borne in clusters; slightly fragrant; foliage sparse, dark; dwarf growth.

Jolly Good F, *pb*, 1973, *Cupid's Charm* × *Lucky Piece*; Fuller; Wyant. Bud ovoid; flowers salmon-pink, dbl. (55 petals), large (3½ in.); fragrant; foliage glossy, dark leathery; bushy, compact growth.

Jolly Roger F, *or*, 1973, *Spartan* × *Angelique*; Armstrong, D.L.; Armstrong Nursery. Bud ovoid, pointed; flowers bright reddish orange, semi-dbl., cupped, medium; slightly

fragrant; foliage wrinkled; growth moderate, bushy.

Jonetsu HT, *mr*, 1978, *(Kagayaki* × *Prima Ballerina)* × *Kagayaki*; Suzuki; Keisei Rose Nursery. Bud pointed; flowers dark scarlet, dbl. (30-35 petals), high-centered, very large (4½ -6 in.); fragrant; foliage dark, leathery; vigorous growth.

Jonkheer G. Sandberg HT, *my*, 1936, (J.G. Sandberg); *Christine* × *Mrs. Wemyss Quin*; Buisman; Armstrong Nursery, 1941. Flowers clear yellow, dbl.; foliage dark, leathery; vigorous growth.

Jonkheer J. L. Mock HT, *pb*, 1910, *(Mme. Caroline Testout* × *Mme. Abel Chatenay)* × *Farbenkönigin*; Leenders, M. Bud pointed; flowers silvery rose-white, reverse carmine-pink, bluing slightly, sometimes muddy, dbl., high-centered, large; fragrant; foliage dark, leathery; vigorous growth. GM, Bagatelle, 1911.

Jonkheer J.L. Mock, Climbing Cl HT, *pb*, 1923, Timmermans.

Jonkheer Mr. G. Ruys de Beerenbrouck HT, *ob*, 1919, *Mme. Mélanie Soupert* × *Joseph Hill*; Timmermans. Flowers pure orange-yellow fading clear yellow, dbl.; vigorous growth.

Jonquille F, *dy*, 1982, (DELjonq); *(Peace* × *Marcelle Gret)* × *(Velizy* × *Jean de la Lune)*; Delbard, G. Flowers deep yellow, dbl. (35 petals), large; no fragrance; foliage medium, medium green, matt; bushy growth.

Josef Angendohr F, *dp*, 1982, *Dame de Coeur* sport; Angendohr, Hans-Werner; Baumschulen Angendohr. Flowers deep pink.

Josef Peter HT, *m*, 1929, *Ruth* × *Frank W. Dunlop*; Ketten Bros. Flowers pale blush, reverse mauve-rose, dbl.; fragrant.

Josef Rothmund E (OGR), *ob*, 1940, (Joseph Rothmund); *Joanna Hill* × *Magnifica*; Kordes. Bud small, ovoid, orange-red; flowers light red with pinkish yellow, very dbl., borne in clusters; very fragrant; foliage bronze, leathery; very vigorous growth; profuse, non-recurrent bloom.

Josef Strnad HT, *rb*, 1932, *Aspirant Marcel Rouyer* × *Toison d'Or*; Böhm; J&P, 1934. Flowers dark red, with traces of yellow, orange and rose, dbl., cupped, very large; fragrant; foliage leathery, glossy, dark, bronze; very vigorous, bushy, branching growth.

Josefina de Salgado HT, *dp*, 1963, (Joséphine de Salgado); *Queen Elizabeth* × *Peace*; Dot, S. Flowers bright pink, dbl. (30 petals), large, somewhat weak stems; fragrant; very vigorous growth.

Joseph Arles Cl HT, *rb*, 1964, *Aloha* × *Gaby-chette*; Arles; Roses-France. Flowers vermilion-red, reverse silvery white; fragrant; foliage leathery; vigorous, climbing growth.

Joseph Baud HT, *yb*, 1919, *Rayon d'Or* × *Seedling*; Gillot, F. Flowers golden yellow and orange-yellow, dbl.; very fragrant.

Joseph Courbis HT, *pb*, 1958, *Margaret McGredy* × *Emma Wright*; Arles; Roses-France. Flowers carthamus-pink to orange-red, dbl. (48 petals); foliage dark, glossy; vigorous, upright growth.

Joseph F. Lamb S, *dr*, 1988, *Prairie Star* × *(Dornroschen* × *Peace)* × *Music Maker* × *(Music Maker* × *Topsi)*; Buck, Dr. Griffith J., 1989. Bud ovoid, pointed; flowers dark red, reverse lighter, aging darker, dbl. (23 petals), cupped, loose, medium, borne singly and in sprays of 5-15; moderate, fruity fragrance; foliage medium, medium green, semi-glossy; prickles awl-like, small, tan to reddish brown; fruit yellow-orange; upright, bushy, low, winter hardy growth.

Joseph Hill HT, *pb*, 1903, Pernet-Ducher. Bud pointed; flowers pink shaded salmon, reverse coppery pink, dbl.; slightly fragrant.

Joseph Liger R, *yb*, 1909, *R. wichuraiana* × *Irene Watts*; Barbier. Flowers canary-yellow, edged and washed light pink, reverse cream-white, borne in clusters of 20-30; vigorous, climbing growth.

Joseph Lowe HT, *op*, *Mrs. W.J. Grant sport*. Flowers salmon-pink; often regarded as synonymous with Lady Faire.

Joseph Pernet d'Annemasse HT, *op*, 1934, Pernet-Ducher; Gaujard. Bud pointed; flowers salmon, dbl.; foliage glossy, dark, bronze; very vigorous growth.

Josephine Min, *w*, 1969, *(R. wichuraiana* × *Carolyn Dean)* × *Jet Trail*; Moore, R.S.; Sequoia Nursery. Flowers white or soft pink, dbl., micro-mini, small; foliage small, glossy; dwarf, bushy.

Josephine Bruce HT, *dr*, 1949, *Crimson Glory* × *Madge Whipp*; Bees, 1949; Totty, 1953. Flowers crimson, dbl. (24 petals), large (5-6 in.); slightly fragrant; foliage dark; vigorous, branching growth.

Joséphine Guyet B (OGR), *dr*, 1873, (Mme. Joséphine Guyet); Touvais. Flowers deep red; recurrent.

Joséphine Marot HT, *lp*, 1894, Bonnaire. Flowers white washed pink.

Josephine Spiecker HT, *ob*, 1939, Verschuren-Pechtold; Harkness; Bentley. Flowers deep orange to yellow, very dbl., globular; foliage glossy, dark bronze; vigorous, bushy growth.

Josephine Thomas HT, *ob*, 1924, H&S; Dreer. Flowers orange-salmon to cream-flesh, very dbl., high-centered; slightly fragrant; foliage leathery; vigorous, bushy growth.

Josephine Vestal HT, *lp*, 1923, *Ophelia* × *Seedling*; Hill, E.G., Co.; Vestal. Flowers soft pink, dbl., high-centered; fragrant; very vigorous, bushy growth.

Joseph's Coat® LCl, *rb*, 1969, *Buccaneer* × *Circus*; Armstrong, D.L. & Swim; Armstrong Nursery, 1964. Flowers yellow and red, dbl., large (3 in.) blooms in clusters; slightly fragrant; foliage dark, glossy; vigorous, pillar growth; recurrent bloom. GM, Bagatelle, 1964.

Joshua™ Min, *pb*, 1989, (MOGajosh); *Loving Touch* × *Rainbow's End*; Moglia, Tom; Gloria Dei Nursery. Bud pointed; flowers clear, deep pink with yellow at base, reverse lighter to white, dbl. (20 petals), exhibition, medium, borne usually singly and in sprays of 3-4 on long stems; slight fragrance; foliage medium, medium green, semi-glossy; prickles hooked, small, red; fruit none observed; upright, medium growth.

Josysigal HT, *mr*, 1975, Delforge, S. Flowers medium red, dbl. (60 petals), cupped, large; very fragrant.

J. Otto Thilow HT, *mp*, 1927, *Hadley* × *Souv. de H.A. Verschuren*; Verschuren; H&S; Dreer. Bud pointed, well shaped; flowers rich glowing rose-pink, dbl., high-centered, large; very vigorous growth.

J. Otto Thilow, Climbing Cl HT, *mp*, 1933, Howard Rose Co.

Jour d'Été HT, *mr*, 1964, *Coup de Foudre* × *Berthe Mallerin*; Combe; Vilmorin-Andrieux. Bud very long; flowers bright red, open; vigorous growth.

Journey's End HT, *ob*, 1978, *Doreen* × *Vienna Charm*; Gandy. Flowers Indian orange, dbl. (37 petals), pointed, large (6 in.); slightly fragrant; foliage large, glossy; vigorous, upright.

Jouvencelle HT, *pb*, 1969, *Prima Ballerina* × *Helen Traubel*; Gaujard. Flowers salmon-pink suffused red, dbl. (50 petals); foliage reddish.

Jove F, *or*, 1968, *Vera Dalton* × *Paprika*; Harkness. Flowers scarlet, semi-dbl. blooms in clusters; slightly fragrant; foliage glossy; low growth.

Jovita® F, *or*, 1975, *Jove* × *Tip Top*; Harkness; Hauser. Flowers orange-red, medium blooms in large clusters; slightly fragrant; foliage bright green; medium, bushy growth.

Jovita Pérez HT, *ob*, 1929, *Mme. Butterfly* × *Souv. de Claudius Pernet*; Munné, B. Flowers coppery salmon, shaded coral, dbl., cupped; long, strong stems; fragrant; foliage soft, dark; vigorous, compact growth.

Joy HT, *pb*, 1929, Beckwith. Bud tangerine-red; flowers rose-pink suffused tangerine, base yellow, dbl., high-centered; fragrant; foliage leathery; vigorous, branching growth.

Joy O'Brien Gr, *op*, 1969, *Queen Elizabeth × Seedling*; Verschuren; Stassen. Flowers pink shaded orange-salmon, dbl., large; fragrant; foliage dark; vigorous growth.

Joy Owens HT, *mr*, 1977, (MACred); *Electron × Pharaoh*; McGredy, S., IV; McGredy Roses International. Bud ovoid; flowers medium red, classic HT form, large (4 in.); foliage very dark; moderate, bushy growth.

Joy Parfait F, *lp*, 1965, *Pink Parfait sport*; McIlroy. Flowers light pink.

Joyance HT, *mr*, 1939, *Regina Elena sport*; Grillo. Flowers velvety red, dbl. (50 petals), camellia shape, large (4 in.); fragrant; foliage leathery, dark; very vigorous, upright growth.

Joybells F, *mp*, 1961, (Joy Bells); *Seedling × Fashion*; Robinson, H. Flowers rich pink, dbl. (30 petals), camellia-shaped, large (3½ in.) blooms in clusters; fragrant.

Joyce HT, *dr*, 1953, *George Dickson × Étoile de Hollande*; Cant, F. Flowers dark velvety crimson, dbl. (24 petals), pointed, medium; fragrant; foliage leathery; vigorous growth.

Joyce Claire F, *dp*, 1965, *Queen Elizabeth × Seedling*; Tonkin. Bud globular; flowers deep pink, dbl., open, small; slightly fragrant; foliage glossy; very vigorous, upright growth.

Joyce Fairey Cl HT, *dp*, 1929, Clark, A.; NRS Victoria. Flowers soft red; pillar growth.

Joyce Longley HT, *ob*, 1958, *Opera sport*; Court. Flowers in sunset shades.

Joyce Northfield HT, *ob*, 1977, *Fred Gibson × Vienna Charm*; Northfield. Flowers deep orange, dbl., high-pointed, large (3-4 in.); slightly fragrant; foliage dark; vigorous, upright.

Joyce Riley F, *ob*, 1978, *Paddy McGredy × Arthur Bell*; Wood. Bud well formed; flowers vermilion, yellow-salmon, dbl. (25 petals), full, medium (2½ in.); slightly fragrant; foliage dark, leathery; vigorous, upright growth.

Joyce Robinson HT, *op*, 1945, *Rose Berkley sport*; Selwood; Rosecraft Nursery. Flowers peach-pink, high-centered; fragrant; foliage dark, leathery; vigorous, bushy growth.

Joycie™ Min, *ob*, 1988, (MORjoyc); *(Little Darling × Yellow Magic) × Gold Badge*; Moore, Ralph S.; Sequoia Nursery. Flowers orange-apricot, reverse lighter, dbl., high-centered, exhibition, small, borne singly or in sprays of 3-5; moderate, fruity fragrance; foliage

small, medium green, semi-glossy; prickles slender, small, brown; fruit globular, orange; bushy, medium growth.

Joyena LCl, *m*, 1964, *Blossomtime × Seedling*; Mason, P.G. Flowers spirea-red, reverse tyrian purple, high-centered, borne in small clusters; fragrant; foliage dark, bronze, leathery; vigorous growth.

Joyeux Noël HT, *or*, 1960, *(Floradora × Independence) × (La Vaudoise × Léonce Colombier)*; Delbard-Chabert. Bud long, pointed; flowers orange-red, dbl. (30-35 petals), well formed, medium; fragrant; foliage bronze, leathery; vigorous, bushy growth.

Joyful HT, *pb*, 1931, Vestal. Bud pointed; flowers pink, reverse streaked red, base red and orange; vigorous growth.

Joyous F, *pb*, 1939, *Else Poulsen sport*; deRuiter; J&P. Flowers rose-pink, reverse slightly darker; vigorous, bushy growth.

Joyous Cavalier HT, *mr*, 1926, *Red-Letter Day × Clarice Goodacre*; Archer. Bud pointed; flowers brilliant red, dbl. (25-30 petals), open, large; slightly fragrant; foliage dark, glossy; very vigorous growth.

J. P. Connell S, *my*, 1987, *Arthur Bell × Von Scharnhorst*; Svejda, Felicitas; Agriculture Canada, 1986. Flowers pale, medium yellow at inner petals, yellow-white on upper petals, dbl. (30-70 petals), high-centered, large, borne 1-8 per cluster; very fragrant, tea scent; foliage abundant, dark yellow-green, wide ovate, double serrate; no prickles; bushy, winter hardy growth; repeat bloom.

J. S. Baar HT, *dr*, 1934, Mikes; Böhm. Flowers pure dark carmine-red, dbl.; long, strong stems; very fragrant; foliage leathery; vigorous, bushy growth.

J. S. Fay HP (OGR), *rb*, 1905, *Prince Camille de Rohan × Souv. de Pierre Notting*; Walsh. Flowers dark crimson tipped scarlet, dbl.; vigorous growth.

Juan Maragall HT, *mr*, 1960, *Chrysler Imperial × Buccaneer*; Dot, S. Flowers bright strawberry-red, dbl. (35 petals), large; long, strong stems; very fragrant; vigorous, compact growth.

Juan Pich HT, *m*, 1921, Leenders, M. Flowers purplish wine-red, dbl.; fragrant.

Juan Quevedo HT, *ly*, 1921, *Entente Cordiale × My Maryland*; Leenders, M. Flowers cream-yellow, dbl.; fragrant.

Juana de Darder HT, *yb*, 1947, *Souv. de Claudius Pernet × (Sensation × Souv. de Claudius Pernet)*; Munné, M. Flowers deep yellow shaded salmon, cupped, strong stems; slightly fragrant; foliage bright green; vigorous growth.

Juanita G (OGR), *pb*, Flowers pink edged paler, full, medium.

Juanita Ch (OGR), *pb*, 1885, Robert. Flowers pink spotted white.

Jubilant F, *lp*, 1967, *Dearest* × *Circus*; Dickson, A. Flowers flesh pink, medium (2½ in.) blooms in clusters; fragrant; foliage glossy.

Jubilee HP (OGR), *m*, 1897, *Victor Hugo* × *Prince Camille de Rohan*; Walsh. Flowers purple, shaded maroon, dbl., large; fragrant; moderate growth; some recurrent bloom.

Jubilee HT, *w*, 1930, (Allen's Jubilee); *Paul's Lemon Pillar* × *Aspirant Marcel Rouyer*; Allen. Bud pointed; flowers cream, tinged salmon-pink and indian yellow, center coral-pink, dbl., high-centered, large; very fragrant; vigorous growth.

Jubilee Celebration F, *pb*, 1977, *Elizabeth of Glamis* × *Prima Ballerina*; Smith, E.; Wheatcroft, 1976. Flowers pink shaded salmon, dbl. (20 petals), large (4 in.); very fragrant; foliage matt, green; growth moderate.

Jubilee Sunset Min, *ob*, 1991, (TALjub); *Baby Katie* × *Poker Chip*; Taylor, Pete & Kay; Taylor's Roses, 1992. Flowers bright vivid orange, yellow eye, reverse creamy yellow, bright yellow stamens, moderately full (15-25 petals), medium (4-7 cms) blooms borne mostly singly; slight fragrance; foliage medium, medium green, semi-glossy; some prickles; low (40 cms), upright, bushy growth.

Judie Darling Cl Min, *pb*, 1979, Sudol. Flowers marbled pink, dbl. (45-50 petals), reflexed, small (1-1½ in.); fragrant; vigorous, climbing growth.

Judith HT, *rb*, 1938, LeGrice. Flowers glowing cerise, reverse golden yellow, dbl., globular; very fragrant (fruity); foliage glossy, bronze; vigorous, bushy growth.

Judith Black HT, *dr*, 1930, Clark, A.; Hazlewood Bros. Bud pointed; flowers rich dark red flushed fiery red, dbl., globular; fragrant; foliage soft; dwarf growth.

Judith I. B. Hall HT, *pb*, 1953, *Crimson Glory* × *Sterling*; Balcombe Nursery. Flowers pink, base orange, dbl. (32 petals), large (5 in.); very fragrant; very vigorous growth.

Judy HT, *mr*, 1940, *Jewel sport*; Grillo. Flowers cerise-red, dbl. (55 petals), large (4 in.); fragrant.

Judy Fischer Min, *mp*, 1968, *Little Darling* × *Magic Wand*; Moore, R.S.; Sequoia Nursery. Bud pointed; flowers rose-pink, dbl., small; foliage dark, bronze, leathery; vigorous, bushy, low growth. AOE, 1975.

Judy Garland F, *yb*, 1977, (HARking); ((*Tropicana* × *Circus*) × (*Sabine* × *Circus*)) × *Pineapple Poll*; Harkness, 1978. Flowers yellow, petals edged orange-red, dbl. (35 petals), medium-large, borne singly or several together; slight fragrance; foliage semi-glossy; medium, bushy.

Judy Hart HT, *mp*, 1958, *Pink Delight (HT) sport* × (*Senator* × *Florex*); Motose; G.B. Hart. Bud ovoid; flowers medium pink, dbl. (30-40 petals), large (4-5 in.); very fragrant; foliage leathery; vigorous, bushy growth; a greenhouse variety.

Jujnoberejnaia F, *dr*, 1955, (River's South Bank); *Independence* × *Vaterland*; Klimenko. Flowers velvety red, well shaped, medium.

Jules Closen R, *dr*, 1935, *Excelsa sport*; Opdebeeck. Flowers darker and more dbl.

Jules Finger T (OGR), *rb*, 1879, *Catherine Mermet* × *Mme. de Tartas*; Ducher, Vve. Flowers vivid red fading light red, shaded silvery, full, very large; vigorous growth.

Jules Gaujard HT, *ob*, 1928, *Jean C. N. Forestier* × *Seedling*; Pernet-Ducher; Gaujard. Flowers bright orange-red flushed carmine, cupped, very large; very fragrant; foliage bright green; very vigorous growth.

Jules Margottin HP (OGR), *mp*, 1853, *Probably La Reine seedling*; Margottin. Flowers carmine-rose, dbl. (90 petals), rather flat, large; slightly fragrant; vigorous; recurrent.

Jules Tabart HT, *pb*, 1920, *Seedling* × *Mme. Edouard Herriot*; Barbier. Flowers silvery salmon-pink, center coppery coral-pink, dbl.; fragrant.

Julia Ann Bostick Pol, *pb*, 1935, *Ideal sport*; Bostick. Flowers apple-blossom-pink, base white, single, cupped, small; fragrant; dwarf growth.

Julia Bartet HT, *yb*, 1920, *Lyon Rose* × *Georges Schwartz*; Schwartz, A. Flowers dark canary-yellow, fading pale straw-yellow, dbl.; slightly fragrant.

Julia Clements F, *mr*, 1957, Wheatcroft Bros. Flowers bright red, single, large (3 in.), borne in clusters; foliage dark, glossy; very vigorous growth.

Julia, Countess of Dartrey HT, *rb*, 1927, Hall; McGredy. Bud pointed; flowers tyrian rose, base yellow, dbl., high-centered, very large; very fragrant; foliage dark, leathery, glossy; very vigorous growth. GM, NRS, 1925.

Julia Mannering E (OGR), *lp*, 1895, Penzance. Flowers pearly pink, yellow stamens, single to semi-dbl. blooms borne along the cane; fragrant; vigorous; summer bloom.

Juliana Rose Pol, *op*, 1920, *Orléans Rose sport*; Den Ouden. Flowers pale salmon.

Julia's Rose® HT, r, 1976, *Blue Moon* × *Dr. A.J. Verhage*; Wisbech Plant Co. Bud long, pointed; flowers parchment and copper shades, dbl. (22 petals), pointed, small (2½ in.); slightly fragrant; foliage reddish; upright. GM, Baden-Baden, 1983.

Julie HT, dr, 1970, *Seedling* × *Red American Beauty*; Kordes, R.; Kordes. Bud ovoid; flowers dark red, dbl., cupped, large; very fragrant; foliage dark, soft; upright.

Julie Ann™ Min, or, 1984, (SAVaweek); *Zorina* × *Poker Chip*; Saville, F. Harmon; Nor'East Min. Roses. Flowers orange-red, dbl. (20 petals), high-centered, HT-form, small; fragrant; foliage small, medium green, semiglossy; upright, bushy growth. AOE, 1984.

Julie Anne Ashmore HT, yb, 1985, *Peace sport*; Owen, F. Flowers deep yellow, suffused with pink throughout.

Julie de Mersan M (OGR), mp, 1854, (Julie de Mersent); Thomas. Flowers rose shaded blush.

Julie Delbard® F, ab, 1986, (DELjuli); *(Zambra* × *(Orange Triumph* × *Floradora)) × ((Orléans Rose* × *Goldilocks) × (Bettina* × *Henri Mallerin))*; Delbard, 1976. Flowers apricot with yellow and orange hues, dbl. (28 petals), HT-form, large; no fragrance; vigorous, bushy growth. GM, Madrid, 1976.

Julie d'Étanges G (OGR), m, Flowers rosy lilac, edged blush, full, cupped, large; erect, vigorous.

Julie Sharp F, w, 1976, *Evelyn Fison sport*; Sharp. Flowers white, pink edge maturing to scarlet, dbl. (25-30 petals), full, cupped, large (3½ in.); slightly fragrant; foliage matt green; vigorous, upright growth.

Julie Strahl HT, rb, 1928, *Lady Greenall* × *Gorgeous*; Leenders Bros. Flowers nasturtium-red, passing to golden yellow, dbl.; very fragrant.

Julien Potin HT, ly, 1927, (Golden Pernet); *Souv. de Claudius Pernet* × *Seedling*; Pernet-Ducher; Dreer. Bud golden, pointed; flowers primrose-yellow, dbl., high-centered to cupped, large; fragrant; foliage bright green; vigorous. GM, Portland, 1929.

Julien Potin, Climbing Cl HT, dy, 1935, Bostick.

Julienne HT, mp, 1940, *Jewel sport*; Grillo. Flowers silvery pink.

Julie's Choice Min, pb, 1990, (RENjulie); *Seedling* × *Seedling*; Rennie, Bruce; Rennie Roses, International, 1991. Flowers pink blend, full (26-40 petals), small, borne in small clusters; slight fragrance; foliage small, medium green, glossy; bushy growth.

Juliet HP (OGR), pb, 1910, *Capt. Hayward* × *Soleil d'Or*; Paul, W. Bud globular, golden yellow; flowers rich rosy red to deep rose, reverse old-gold, dbl., large; fragrant; foliage curiously curled; vigorous growth; occasionally recurrent bloom.

Juliet Staunton Clark HT, w, 1933, *Juliet sport*; Robichon. Flowers white, center blush-white, turning white, very dbl., large; fragrant.

Juliette Min, mr, Lamb Nursery. A miniature Gruss an Teplitz; Flowers brilliant crimson-scarlet, dbl. (30 petals); foliage bright red in fall; vigorous (10-12 in.) growth.

Juliette E. van Beuningen HT, dp, 1937, (Mme. Juliette); *Dame Edith Helen* × *Mrs. Sam McGredy*; Buisman. Bud pointed; flowers bright pink, semi-dbl., open, very large; foliage leathery, dark.

Julischka® F, mr, 1974, (TANjuka); Tantau; Horstmann. Bud long, pointed; flowers bright red, semi-dbl., medium; slightly fragrant; foliage glossy, bronze. GM, NZ, 1976.

Julius Fabianics de Misefa T (OGR), mr, 1902, Geschwind. Flowers crimson.

Julius Gofferje HT, pb, 1930, Schmidt, J.C. Flowers peach-pink on yellow ground, dbl.; foliage bright green; vigorous growth.

July Glory R, dp, 1932, Chaplin Bros. Flowers rich rose-pink, dbl., small, borne in large clusters; foliage glossy; vigorous growth.

Jumping Jack Flash Min, yb, 1992, (TALjum); *Party Girl* × *Poker Chip*; Taylor, Pete & Kay; Taylor's Roses, 1993. Flowers yellow edged with deep pink to red, creamreverse, tipped with deep pink to red on edges, moderately full (15-25 petals), HT form, medium (4-7 cms) blooms borne mostly singly; slight fragrance; foliage medium, medium green, semi-glossy; few prickles; medium (42 cms), upright, bushy growth.

June HT, pb, 1937, Archer. Bud pointed; flowers shell-pink, center darker, well shaped; fragrant; vigorous growth.

June Aberdeen F, ob, 1977, *Anne Cocker* × *(Sabine* × *Circus)*; Cocker. Flowers salmon, dbl. (20 petals), medium (2½ in.); slightly fragrant; foliage dark.

June Boyd HT, rb, 1924, McGredy. Flowers salmon-carmine, base yellow, opening to bright peach-blossom-pink, dbl.; fragrant.

June Bride Gr, w, 1957, *(Mme. Butterfly* × *New Dawn)* × *Crimson Glory*; Shepherd; Bosley Nursery. Bud pointed, greenish white tipped pink; flowers creamy white, dbl. (30 petals), high-centered to cupped, large (4 in.) blooms in clusters of 3-7; fragrant; foliage leathery, crinkled; vigorous, upright growth.

June Bride Gr, *w*, 1957, *(Mme. Butterfly × New Dawn) × Crimson Glory*; Shepherd; Bosley Nursery. Bud pointed, greenish white tipped pink; flowers creamy white, dbl. (30 petals), high-centered to cupped, large (4 in.), borne in clusters of 3-7; fragrant; foliage leathery, crinkled; very vigorous. upright growth; profuse, recurrent bloom.

June Flame HT, *ob*, 1949, Fletcher; Tucker. Bud small, tight; flowers bright orange-flame shaded copper; very early bloom.

June Laver™ Min, *dy*, 1987, (LAVjune); *Helmut Schmidt × Gold Mine*; Laver, Keith, 1985; Springwood Roses, 1988. Flowers dark yellow, aging cream, dbl. (20-25 petals), high-centered, exhibition, large, borne usually singly or in sprays of 3-4; no fragrance; foliage large, dark green, matt; prickles small, short, green; fruit rounded, light orange-red; bushy, medium, compact growth.

June Morn LCl, *rb*, 1939, *Mme. Gregoire Staechelin × Souv. de Claudius Pernet, Climbing*; Nicolas; J&P. Bud ovoid; flowers carmine-red, reverse touched gold, dbl., high-centered, large (5 in.); vigorous, climbing (8 ft.) growth; some recurrent bloom.

June Opie F, *ab*, 1958, *Masquerade × Seedling*; Kordes; Morse. Flowers apricot shaded salmon-pink, semi-dbl., large (3 in.), borne on trusses; slightly fragrant; foliage leathery; very free, upright growth.

June Park HT, *dp*, 1958, *Peace × Crimson Glory*; Park; Sanday; Nonin. Flowers rose-pink, dbl. (40 petals), large (4½-5 in.); very fragrant; foliage dark; vigorous, spreading growth. GM, NRS, 1959.

June Patricia HT, *lp*, 1966, *Peace × Ena Harkness*; Lens. Flowers silvery pink, full, medium (3 in.); fragrant; foliage dark, glossy; moderate growth.

June Time Min, *lp*, 1963, *(R. wichuraiana × Floradora) × ((Étoile Luisante seedling × Red Ripples) × Zee)*; Moore, R. S.; Sequoia Nursery. Flowers light pink, reverse darker, dbl. (75 petals), small, in clusters; foliage glossy; bushy, compact (10-12 in.).

June Way HT, *mp*, 1977, *Pink Favorite × Chrysler Imperial*; Atkiss; Wyant. Flowers medium pink, dbl. (33 petals), cupped, large (4-5 in.); slightly fragrant; foliage glossy; spreading growth.

June Wedding HT, *w*, 1977, *Bewitched sport*; Graham; South Forrest Rose Nursery. Bud pointed; flowers white, tinted yellow, dbl. (27 petals), high-centered, large (4 in.); slightly fragrant; foliage glossy, dark; upright growth.

Juneen HT, *my*, 1967, *Burnaby × Burnaby seedling*; Mason, P.G. Flowers yellow, high-centered; slightly fragrant; compact growth.

Junior Bridesmaid F, *mp*, 1962, *Stoplite × Lovelight*; Jelly; E.G. Hill Co. Bud short, pointed; flowers medium pink, dbl. (35petals), sweetheart, medium (2 in.); slightly fragrant; foliage leathery; vigorous, upright growth; greenhouse variety.

Junior Gilbert HT, *or*, 1954, Mallerin; EFR. Flowers orange-red, cupped; vigorous growth.

Junior Miss F, *pb*, 1943, *Joanna Hill × Heidekind*; Duehrsen; California Roses. Bud well formed; flowers pink and yellow, semi-dbl., high-centered, medium, borne in clusters; slightly fragrant; foliage glossy; vigorous, bushy growth.

Junior Prom F, *dr*, 1962, *Orange Sweetheart × Lovelight*; Jelly; E.G. Hill Co. Bud ovoid; flowers crimson, dbl. (30-45 petals), open, medium (1½-2 in.); fragrant; vigorous, upright growth; for greenhouse use.

Junior Van Fleet S, *lp*, 1923, *Dr. W. Van Fleet × Frau Karl Druschki*; Kemp, J.A. Flowers flesh-pink, dbl.; fragrant; non-recurrent bloom.

Juno HCh (OGR), *lp*, 1847, Laffay. Flowers pale rose, full, globular, very large. This rose has also been classed as a Hybrid Bourbon; probably identical to the Juno recently distributed as a Centifolia.

Juno HT, *mp*, 1950, *Duquesa de Peñaranda × Charlotte Armstrong*; Swim; Armstrong Nursery. Bud ovoid; flowers soft medium pink, dbl. (30 petals), high-centered, large; slightly fragrant; foliage bright, leathery, wrinkled, glossy; moderate upright, bushy growth.

Juno C (OGR), *lp*, Prior to 1832. Flowers blush pink, very dbl., globular; arching shrub.

Junon® HT, *or*, 1978, (GAUcova); *Tanagra × Dora*; Gaujard. Bud full; flowers orange-red, dbl. (45 petals), medium (3 in.); foliage large, brownish; bushy growth.

Jupiter *R. spinosissima* hybrid. Flowers bright pink, dbl.; foliage finely divided; fruit black, shining; dense, shrubby (3-4 ft.) growth.

Jupon Rose® F, *op*, 1982, (LENniro); *Little Angel × Pernille Poulsen*; Lens, Louis. Flowers light salmon pink, dbl. (28 petals), cupped, medium blooms in clusters of 3-24; slight fragrance; foliage dark; hooked, reddish-green prickles; upright, bushy growth.

Just Buddy™ Min, *ly*, 1985, (KINbud); *New Day × Rise 'n' Shine*; King, Gene; AGM Min. Roses, 1986. Flowers light yellow, dbl. (45 petals), exhibition, mini-flora, large blooms borne singly; slight fragrance; foliage medium, light green, matt; straight, light brown prickles; no hips; medium upright, bushy growth.

Just For You Min, *dp*, 1990, (MORyou); *Orangeade × Rainbow's End*; Moore, Ralph S., 1986; Sequoia Nursery, 1991. Bud pointed; flowers dark pink to light red, lighter reverse, aging lighter, dbl. (35 petals), high-centered, exhibition, medium, borne singly or in sprays of 3-5; slight fragrance; foliage medium, medium green, semi-glossy; bushy, medium growth. AOE, 1991.

Just Joey HT, *ob*, 1972, *Fragrant Cloud × Dr. A.J. Verhage*; Cants of Colchester. Flowers buff-orange, dbl. (30 petals), classic form, large (5 in.); very fragrant; foliage glossy, leathery; growth moderate. GM, James Mason, 1986.

Just Judy HT, *lp*, 1992, *Mischief × Simba*; Poole, Lionel, 1994. Flowers light pink, full (26-40 petals), medium to large (4-7+ cms) blooms borne mostly singly; slight fragrance; foliage medium, dark green, semi-glossy; some prickles; upright (0-8 m) growth.

Just Lucky HT, *w*, 1984, *Typhoo Tea × Pascali*; Bridges, Dennis A.; Bridges Roses, 1985. Flowers white, dbl. (35 petals), well-formed, large; very fragrant; foliage medium, dark, glossy; bushy growth.

Just Magic Min, *pb*, 1989, (TRObic); *(Parkdirector Riggers × New Penny) × (Parkdirector Riggers × New Penny) × Seedling*; Robinson, Thomas, Ltd., 1992. Bud rounded; flowers cream to deep pink, reverse cream tinged pink, aging often strongly, dbl. (21 petals), cupped, loose, small, borne in sprays of 3-7; moderate, damask fragrance; foliage small, dark green, glossy; prickles very thin, pointed, reading brown; fruit spheroid, orange; upright, bushy, medium growth.

Justa Little Goofy F, *or*, 1992, (RENgoofy); *Seedling × Seedling*; Rennie, Bruce; Rennie Roses. Flowers orange-red, full (26-40 petals), medium (4-7 cms) blooms borne mostly singly; fragrant; foliage medium, medium green, semi-glossy; some prickles; medium, bushy growth.

Justina HT, *mp*, Similar to Mme. Butterfly but more highly colored; salmon-pink, tinted apricot and gold; fragrant.

Justine C (OGR), *m*, 1822, Vibert. Flowers pale lilac-pink, very dbl., medium.

Justine HT, *ly*, 1935, *Joanna Hill × Sweet Adeline*; Hill, J.H., Co. Bud orange; flowers creamy yellow, base dark orange, reverse almost white, dbl. (30-35 petals), large; foliage dark, leathery; vigorous growth; a florists' variety, not distributed for outdoor use.

Justine Ramet C (OGR), *m*, 1845, Vibert. Flowers purplish-rose, full, medium.

Justino Henriques HT, *yb*, 1926, *Louise Catherine Breslau sport*; deFreitas; P. Guillot. Flowers yellow tinted orange, stamens carmine, dbl.; fragrant.

Justizrat Dr. Hessert HT, *pb*, 1919, *Gen. MacArthur × Tip-Top*; Lambert, P. Bud carmine-red; flowers salmon-pink shaded red and yellow, dbl.; fragrant.

Jutlandia R, *mp*, 1913, *Mme. Norbert Levavasseur × Dorothy Perkins*; Poulsen, D. Flowers pink, full; vigorous growth.

Jutul F, *dp*, 1982, *New Dawn × Moulin Rouge*; Lundstad, A.; Agricultural Univ. of Norway. Flowers deep pink, semi-dbl. (14 petals), cupped, small blooms in clusters of 7-9; slightly fragrant; foliage dark, glossy; curved, red-brown prickles; vigorous growth.

J. W. Fargo Sp (OGR), *mp*, *R. arkansana variety*. Flowers wild-rose-pink, borne in clusters; well branched (20 in.) growth; non-recurrent bloom.

Kabuki® HT, *dy*, 1968, (MEIgold; Golden Prince); *(Monte Carlo × Bettina) × (Peace × Soraya)*; Meilland, M.L.; URS; C-P. Flowers deep yellow, dbl. (45 petals), high-centered, medium; fragrant; foliage bronze, glossy, leathery; vigorous, upright growth.

Kagayaki F, *rb*, 1970, (Brilliant Light); *(Aztec seedling × (Spectacular × Aztec)) × Cover Girl seedling*; Suzuki; Keisei Rose Nursery. Flowers brilliant scarlet and yellow, dbl., high-centered, large; slightly fragrant; foliage glossy, dark; vigorous, upright growth.

Kaikoura® Min, *ob*, 1978, (MACwalla); *Anytime × Matangi*; McGredy, S., IV. Flowers orange, dbl. (27 petals), patio, medium; slightly fragrant; foliage glossy, dark; vigorous, bushy.

Kaileen F, *ob*, 1991, (JACmar); *Marina sport*; Nakashima, Tosh; Bear Creek Gardens, 1992. Flowers bright orange, yellow reverse, full (26-40 petals), medium (4-7 cms) blooms borne in small clusters; slight fragrance; foliage medium, dark green, glossy; some prickles, light green to yellow; upright (180 cms) growth.

Kaiserin Auguste Viktoria HT, *w*, 1891, (K.A. Viktoria); *Coquette de Lyon × Lady Mary Fitzwilliam*; Lambert, P. Bud long, pointed; flowers snowy white, center tinted lemon, very dbl. (100 petals), well-formed; very fragrant; foliage rich green, soft.

Kaiserin Auguste Viktoria, Climbing Cl HT, *w*, 1897, Dickson, A.

Kalahari HT, *op*, 1971, *Uncle Walter × (Hamburger Phoenix × Danse de Feu)*; McGredy, S., IV. Flowers salmon-pink, dbl. (25 petals), high-pointed, large (4 in.); slightly fragrant; foliage glossy, dark.

Kalavalla F, *mp*, 1935, *Else Poulsen × Seedling*; Poulsen, S. Flowers pink, dbl., borne in large clusters; vigorous growth.

Kaleidoscope F, *ob*, 1972, *Circus × Redgold*; Fryer, G.; Fryer's Nursery. Flowers orange and yellow, dbl. (28 petals), large (3 in.); slightly fragrant; foliage glossy.

Kalmia R, *w*, 1911, Walsh. Flowers white, upper half of petals tinged pink, single, borne in clusters; foliage dark, glossy; vigorous, climbing growth; resembles the mountain laurel in foliage and profusion of bloom, hence its name.

Kamchin HT, *mp*, 1972, *Carina sport*; Kammeraad; Meilland. Flowers neyron rose, outside rose, dbl. (45 petals), cupped, large (4-5 in.), cupped; slightly fragrant; foliage dull, dark; vigorous growth.

Kamion Min, *or*, 1988, *Starina × Seedling*; Schoen-Jones, Helen; Justice Miniature Roses, 1988. Flowers bright orange-red, reverse matt finish, clear, golden stamens, semi-dbl. (12 petals), high-centered, loose, large, borne in sprays of 8-15; no fragrance; foliage large, dark green, glossy; prickles curved, small, reddish; fruit oval, large, light orange; upright, tall, sturdy growth.

Kammersanger Terkal F, *ob*, 1971, (Hartina); *Tropicana × Zorina*; Tantau; Ahrens & Sieberz. Bud small, globular; flowers pure orange, dbl., medium; slightly fragrant; foliage glossy; dwarf, bushy growth.

Kana HT, *dr*, 1982, *Ginger Rogers × Chiyo*; Ota, Kaichiro. Flowers dark red, dbl. (38 petals), high-centered, large blooms borne 1-3 per stem; no fragrance; foliage medium green; small prickles, slanted downward; tall, bushy growth.

Kanakangi HT, *ab*, 1968, *Mme. Charles Sauvage × Seedling*; Pal; Indian Agric. Research Inst. Bud globular; flowers gold and apricot, semi-dbl., open, medium; very fragrant; foliage leathery; moderate, bushy, open growth.

Kanarie HT, *dy*, 1919, *Golden Star × Melody*; Verschuren. Flowers clear dark yellow, dbl.

Kanegem F, *or*, 1985, *Ludwigshafen am Rhein × Satchmo*; Rijksstation Voor Sierplantenteelt, 1982. Flowers orange-red, dbl. (42 petals), high-centered to cupped, large blooms borne 1-7 per cluster; no fragrance; foliage dark, glossy; upright growth.

Kan-pai HT, *dr*, 1983, (Kampai); *(Yu-ai × (Happiness × American Beauty)) × Pharoah*; Suzuki, S.; Keisei Rose Nursery, 1980. Flowers deep red, dbl. (48 petals), high-centered blooms borne 1-3 per cluster; fragrant; foliage me-

dium, dark; upright growth. GM, Rome, 1983.

Kapai® F, *or*, 1977, (MACgam); *Madame Bollinger × Tombola*; McGredy, S., IV. Flowers orange-red, dbl. (30 petals), medium (3½ in.); very fragrant; foliage small; low, bushy.

Kapiti F, *mp*, 1991, (MACglemil); *Sexy Rexy × Eyeopener*; McGredy, Sam; Sam McGredy Roses International, 1992. Flowers medium pink, semi-dbl. (6-14 petals), medium (4-7 cms) blooms; slight fragrance; foliage medium, medium green, semi-glossy; spreading growth to 60 cms.

Kara Min, *mp*, 1972, (Dear One); *Fairy Moss × Fairy Moss*; Moore, R.S.; Sequoia Nursery. Bud long, mossy; flowers light to medium pink, single, micro-mini, mini-moss, small; foliage small, soft; vigorous, dwarf, bushy growth.

Kardinal® HT, *dr*, 1934, *Château de Clos Vougeot seedling × Seedling*; Krause. Flowers scarlet-red, sometimes tipped blackish, cupped, large; vigorous, compact, bushy.

Kardinal Piffl HT, *ob*, 1925, *(Mme. Edouard Herriot × Rayon d'Or) × Mme. Charles Lutaud*; Leenders Bros. Flowers red-orange, reverse golden yellow, dbl., very large; fragrant; good foliage. GM, Bagatelle, 1926.

Kardinal Schulte HT, *mr*, 1926, *(Jonkheer J.L. Mock × Radiance) × Commandeur Jules Gravereaux*; Leenders Bros. Flowers brilliant scarlet-red, dbl.; fragrant.

Karel Hynek Mácha HT, *dr*, 1936, Brada; Böhm. Flowers velvety red, well shaped.

Karen S, *w*, *R. primula × R. spinosissima cultivar*. Flowers creamy white flecked red, very dbl., well shaped; fragrant; bushy, erect (5 ft.) growth; non-recurrent bloom.

Karen F, *my*, 1961, *Goldilocks × Fashion*; Borgatti; Sgaravatti. Flowers straw-yellow shaded ocher-yellow, dbl. (30-35 petals), large (3 in.); bushy growth.

Karen Marie HT, *yb*, 1973, *Kordes' Perfecta sport*; Gates. Flowers cream and yellow, flushed pink, dbl. (40 petals), full, large (4 in.); very fragrant; foliage glossy, dark; free growth.

Karen Poulsen F, *mr*, 1932, *Kirsten Poulsen × Vesuvius*; Poulsen, S., 1932; J&P, 1933. Flowers scarlet, single blooms in huge trusses; vigorous; (28). GM, NRS, 1933 & Portland, 1935.

Karen Poulsen, Climbing Cl F, *mr*, Roger.

Karl Förster HSpn (OGR), *w*, 1931, *Frau Karl Druschki × R. spinosissima altaica*; Kordes. Bud pointed; flowers snow-white, dbl., high-centered, large; slightly fragrant; foliage wrinkled, light; vigorous (7 ft.) growth; repeat bloom.

Karl Herbst HT, *mr*, 1950, (Red Peace); *Independence × Peace*; Kordes. Flowers dull dark scarlet, dbl. (60 petals), well-shaped, large; very fragrant; vigorous growth. GM, NRS, 1950.

Karl Weinhausen F, *dr*, 1942, *Baby Château × (Heidekind × Ingar Olsson)*; Tantau. Flowers dark red tinted salmon, semi-dbl. (20 petals), rosette form, large, borne in clusters of 12-15; slightly fragrant; vigorous, upright growth.

Karlea HT, *pb*, 1965, O'Brien. Flowers pink and salmon, base yellow, dbl., full; slightly fragrant; foliage glossy; vigorous, upright growth.

Karlian HT, *mr*, 1991, *Pristine × Loving Memory*; Alde, Robert O. Flowers medium red, full, medium blooms borne mostly singly; very fragrant; foliage medium, medium green, semi-glossy; medium, upright, compact growth.

Karlsruhe K (S), *dp*, 1957, Kordes. Bud ovoid; flowers deep rose-pink, very dbl., cupped, large blooms in large clusters; slightly fragrant; foliage glossy; vigorous, climbing growth; repeat bloom.

Karoo HT, *lp*, Elton Farm Nursery. Flowers bright pink, high-centered, large; vigorous growth. RULED EXTINCT 2/88.

Karoo F, *or*, 1988, (POUlkaro; Karoo Rose); *Seedling × Seedling*; Poulsen Roser ApS; Ludwig's Roses, 1988. Flowers orange-red, aging watermelon-pink, dbl. (32 petals), medium, borne in sprays of 1-15; no fragrance; foliage medium, medium green, very hardy; prickles concave, yellow-brown; neat, medium, densely branched growth.

Kasbah HT, *dp*, 1977, *Seedling × Tropicana*; Takatori; Japan Rose Nursery. Bud pointed; flowers dark pink, reverse lighter, very dbl. (80-110 petals), cupped, medium (3½ in.); fragrant; foliage leathery; upright growth.

Kashmir Cl F, *m*, 1973, *Magenta × Royal Tan*; Thomson. Bud ovoid; flowers clear mauve, dbl., full, medium; slightly fragrant; foliage glossy, leathery; vigorous, climbing growth.

Kassel LCl, *or*, 1957, *Hamburg × Scarlet Else*; Kordes, R.; Morse. Bud ovoid; flowers orange-scarlet, semi-dbl., large blooms in clusters to 10; fragrant; foliage dark, glossy; vigorous growth; recurrent bloom; not dependably hardy.

Kätchen von Heilbronn Pol, *dr*, 1922, *Freudenfeuer × Seedling*; Kiese. Flowers very dark red, dbl., small.

Kate Edwards HT, *m*, 1963, *Condessa de Mayalde* sport; Edwards. Flowers magenta.

Käte Felberg HT, *pb*, 1930, *Seedling × Mrs. Wemyss Quin*; Felberg-Leclerc. Bud pointed; flowers creamy white, reverse violet-rose, full, large; fragrant; vigorous growth.

Kate Moulton, Climbing Cl HT, *pb*, 1928, *Miss Kate Moulton* sport; Opdebeeck.

Kate Mull HT, *op*, 1934, Easlea. Flowers crushed strawberry and coppery rose, fairly full.

Kate Rainbow HT, *pb*, 1935, Beckwith. Flowers blend of glowing pinks and gold, full, well formed, very large; very fragrant; foliage glossy, leathery; very vigorous growth.

Käte Schmid R, *dp*, 1931, *Fragezeichen × Tausendschön*; Vogel, R., Jr.; Kordes. Flowers deep rose-pink, dbl., very large, borne in clusters on long stems; slightly fragrant; foliage light; very vigorous, climbing growth.

Kate Smith HT, *pb*, 1954, (*Break o' Day × Golden Rapture) × Ballet*; Boerner; J&P. Bud ovoid; flowers apricot overcast grenadine-pink, dbl. (35-40 petals), high-centered, large (4½-5 in.); very fragrant; foliage glossy; vigorous growth.

Katelyn Ann F, *mp*, 1992, *Seedling × Seedling*; Williams, Michael C., 1987; Roses Unlimited, 1992. Flowers deep pink, reverse pale pink with hint of yellow, aging pale pink, cupped with button eye, very dbl. (60 petals), medium (6 cms) blooms borne in sprays of 3-5; old garden look; heavy fragrance; foliage medium, dark green, glossy; medium, upright growth.

Katharina Zeimet Pol, *w*, 1901, (White Baby Rambler); *Étoile de Mai × Marie Pavie*; Lambert, P. Flowers pure white, dbl., small blooms in clusters of 25-50 on short stems; fragrant; foliage small, rich green; dwarf, bushy growth.

Katharine Pechtold HT, *ob*, 1934, *Roselandia × Charles P. Kilham*; Verschuren-Pechtold; Dreer; H&S. Bud old-gold and bronzy orange; flowers coppery orange, flushed rose and gold, semi-dbl.; fragrant (clove pink); foliage leathery; vigorous, bushy growth.

Katharine Worsley F, *mr*, 1962, Waterhouse Nursery. Flowers bright oriental red, dbl. (28 petals), large (3½ in.), borne in large, well-spaced clusters; moderate, bushy growth.

Käthe Duvigneau S, *mr*, 1942, *Baby Château × R. roxburghii*; Tantau. Flowers glistening red tinted salmon, semi-dbl. (15 petals), large blooms in clusters of 12-15; slightly fragrant; foliage leathery, glossy, bright green; vigorous, upright growth.

Kathe von Saalfeld T (OGR), 1914, Eibel.

Katherine Cook HT, *mr*, 1927, *Crusader* × *Seedling*; Cook, J. Flowers cherry-red, dbl.; fragrant.

Katherine Harbour HT, *mp*, 1973, *Queen Elizabeth* × *Comtesse Vandal*; Aloe Vera Nursery. Bud ovoid; flowers pink, tinted apricot, dbl., open, large; fragrant; foliage glossy; vigorous, upright growth.

Katherine Loker F, *my*, 1978, (AROkr); *Zorina* × *Dr. A.J. Verhage*; Swim & Christensen; Armstrong Nursery, 1979. Bud pointed; flowers medium golden yellow, dbl. (28 petals), classic form, imbricated, large (3½ in.); slightly fragrant; upright, spreading growth.

Katherine McCarty Min, *yb*, 1991, *Poker Chip* × *Rise 'n' Shine*; Gruenbauer, Richard, 1984; Flowers 'n' Friends Miniatures Roses, 1993. Bud ovoid; flowers yellow center, then white, with coral edges, reverse same, coral color spreads more prevalent with age, very dbl. (60 petals), exhibition, medium; moderate, damask fragrance; foliage medium, dark green, matt; bushy, medium growth.

Katherine Mock HT, *my*, 1943, *Pres. Herbert Hoover sport*; Mock. Flowers yellow.

Katherine T. Marshall HT, *mp*, 1943, (K.T. Marshall); *Seedling* × *Chieftain*; Boerner; J&P. Flowers deep rose-pink, flushed yellow, dbl. (22 petals), cupped, large (5 in.); slightly fragrant (spicy); foliage leathery; vigorous, upright growth. AARS, 1944.

Kathleen HMsk (S), *lp*, 1922, *Daphne* × *Perle des Jeannes*; Pemberton. Flowers blush-pink, single, small blooms in large clusters; slightly fragrant; vigorous (6 ft.) growth; recurrent bloom.

Kathleen HMult (OGR), *pb*, 1907, Paul, W. Flowers soft rose with white eye, single.

Kathleen HT, *lp*, 1934, Dickson, A. Bud very long; flowers light yellowish salmon, large; slightly fragrant; vigorous, free branching growth.

Kathleen Ferrier F, *op*, 1952, *Gartenstolz* × *Shot Silk*; Buisman. Flowers deep salmon-pink, semi-dbl. (18 petals), medium (2½ in.) blooms in small clusters; fragrant; foliage dark, glossy; vigorous, upright growth.

Kathleen Harrop B (OGR), *lp*, 1919, *Zephirine Drouhin sport*; Dickson, A. Flowers soft shell-pink; (21).

Kathleen Jermyn HT, *or*, 1988, (LEGneed); *Royal Dane* × *Alexander*; LeGrice, E.B.; E.B. LeGrice Roses, Ltd. Flowers orange-red, dbl., urn-shaped, loose, medium, borne usually singly; slight fragrance; foliage large, dark green, semi-glossy; bushy, medium growth.

Kathleen Joyce F, *lp*, 1970, *Paddy McGredy* × *Ice White*; McGredy, S., IV. Flowers soft pink, dbl. (30 petals), large (4 in.); very fragrant.

Kathleen Kaye HT, *mp*, 1959, *Directeur Guérin* × *Mirandy*; Kemp, M.L. Flowers rich rose-pink, dbl. (60 petals), large (5 in.); very fragrant; foliage dark; vigorous growth.

Kathleen Kennedy HT, *op*, 1939, Dickson, A. Flowers light salmon-carmine, shaded orange, well formed, large; strong stems; fragrant; vigorous growth.

Kathleen King HT, *dp*, 1930, Marriott. Flowers carmine-pink, well formed, high-centered, large; very fragrant; vigorous growth.

Kathleen Kirkham F, *pb*, 1985, (KIRkit); *Manx Queen* × *Seedling*; Kirkham, Gordon W. Flowers pink blend, semi-dbl., medium; fragrant; foliage medium, medium green, semiglossy; upright growth.

Kathleen Mills HT, *pb*, 1934, LeGrice. Bud long, pointed; flowers pale pink tinted silvery, reverse deep pink, semi-dbl., large; very fragrant; foliage leathery; vigorous.

Kathleen Nash HT, *mr*, 1944, *Pink Delight sport*; Spera; Rose Farms Corp. Bud urn shaped; flowers bright cerise, dbl. (28 petals), globular, large (4 in.); very fragrant; foliage leathery, dark; vigorous growth.

Kathleen O'Rourke HT, *op*, 1976, *Fragrant Cloud* × *Red Planet*; Dickson, P.; A. Dickson. Flowers soft orange-pink, dbl. (38 petals), exhibition, large (4 in.); fragrant; foliage large, matt.

Kathleen Peden HT, *dr*, 1959, *Crimson Glory* × *Charles Mallerin*; Peden. Bud long pointed; flowers crimson, dbl., high-centered, large; very fragrant; foliage leathery, dark; very vigorous, upright growth.

Kathleen Wiggin Cl HP (OGR), *w*, 1932, *Frau Karl Druschki seedling*; Wiggin. Bud long pointed, opening one at a time on each cluster; flowers white, sometimes tinged pink, very dbl., large, borne in clusters on long stems; slightly fragrant; foliage glossy, heavy; vigorous, climbing (12-15 ft.) growth.

Kathryn S, *ab*, 1986, *Wind Chimes* × *Yellow HT*; Eggeman, H.W. Bud copper; flowers apricot, aging to buff, copper stamens, dbl. (25 petals), open form, large (4-5 in.); fruity fragrance; foliage semi-glossy; vigorous growth.

Kathryn Bailey F, *w*, 1992, *Gene Boerner sport*; Bailey, Dr. Edwin; Bailey's Plant Farm, 1993. Flowers white, full (26-40 petals), medium (4-7 cms) blooms; slight fragrance; foliage light green, glossy; some prickles; medium tall, upright growth.

Kathryn Gram F, *ab*, 1945, *Talisman* × *Seedling*; Moore, R.S.; Sequoia Nursery. Bud urn shaped; flowers apricot, large; fragrant; bushy, low growth.

Kathy Min, *mr*, 1970, *Little Darling* × *Magic Wand*; Moore, R.S.; Sequoia Nursery. Bud pointed; flowers medium red, dbl., small; fragrant; foliage small, leathery; moderate, dwarf, bushy growth.

Kathy Fiscus F, *mp*, 1950, *Seedling* × *Baby Château*; Duehrsen; Elmer Roses Co. Bud ovoid; flowers deep flesh-pink, dbl. (45 petals), open, medium, borne in clusters; fragrant; foliage leathery; very vigorous, upright, bushy growth.

Kathy Robinson Min, *pb*, 1968, *Little Darling* × *Over the Rainbow*; Williams, E.D.; Mini-Roses. Flowers pink, creamy reverse, dbl. (26 petals), high-centered, small (1 in.); slightly fragrant; foliage small, glossy, dark, embossed; upright, bushy growth.

Katie LCl, *mp*, 1959, *New Dawn* × *Crimson Glory*; O'Neal; Wyant. Bud long, pointed; flowers medium pink, reverse darker, semi-dbl. (17 petals), cupped, large; very fragrant; foliage glossy; vigorous growth; recurrent bloom.

Katrina HT, *op*, 1964, *Baccará sport*; Samtmann; C-P. Bud pointed; flowers orange-scarlet, dbl., cupped, medium; slightly fragrant; foliage glossy, leathery; bushy, vigorous growth; a greenhouse variety.

Kauth Sp (OGR), *lp*, (Kauff); *R. canina strain*; Used as an understock.

Kay F, *or*, 1971, *Queen Elizabeth* × *Numéro Un*; Delforge. Bud ovoid; flowers vermilion, dbl., cupped, large; slightly fragrant; foliage large, bronze; vigorous, upright growth.

Kay Barnard HT, *lp*, 1974, *South Seas* × *Queen Elizabeth*; Dingle. Bud long, pointed; flowers pale pink, high-centered; fragrant; upright growth.

Kazanlik D (OGR), *dp*, (*R. damascena trigintipetala*) (Dieck) R. Keller; Trigintipetala). Cult. prior to 1850. Flowers deep pink, dbl. (30 petals); grown chiefly in S.E. Europe for making attar; (28).

Keely Min, *or*, 1988, *Party Girl* × *Seedling*; Bridges, Dennis; Bridges Roses, 1989. Bud pointed; flowers bright, orange-red, reverse slightly darker, aging color fades slightly, dbl. (20 petals), high-centered, exhibition, medium, borne usually singly; foliage medium, medium green, semi-glossy; prickles straight, pointed, medium, red; bushy, medium growth.

Keepsake HT, *dr*, 1941, *Anne Leygues seedling*; Clark, A. Flowers deep red; fragrant. RULED EXTINCT 7/81.

Keepsake HT, *pb*, 1981, (KORmalda; Esmeralda, Kordes' Rose Esmeralda); Kordes Sohne; John Mattock, Ltd. Bud ovoid; flowers deep pink blended with lighter pink shades, dbl. (40 petals), reflexed, large blooms borne 1-3 per cluster; moderate fragrance; foliage dark; large, stout prickles; vigorous, bushy growth. GM, Portland, 1987.

Kees Knoppers Pol, *w*, 1930, *Mev. Nathalie Nypels sport*; Leenders, M. Flowers flesh-white, semi-dbl., open, large, borne in clusters; foliage rich green; vigorous, bushy growth.

Kegon HT, *mr*, 1976, *Gruss an Berlin* × *Christian Dior*; Onodera, T.; S. Onodera. Bud pointed; flowers deep red, dbl. (30 petals), high-centered, very large (5 in.); foliage leathery; tall growth.

Kei Min, *lp*, 1980, *Seedling* × *Seedling*; Lyon, Lyndon. Bud ovoid, pointed; flowers light pink, dbl. (33 petals), blooms borne 1-3 per cluster; slight fragrance; foliage tiny, dark; straight prickles; very compact, bushy growth.

Kelli Ann Min, *w*, 1981, *Patricia Scranton* × *(Patricia Scranton* × *Fairy Moss)*; Dobbs, Annette. Flowers white, dbl. (35 petals), small; slight fragrance; foliage small, medium green, matt; bushy growth.

Kelly-Leigh Min, *yb*, 1981, (STEkelly-Leigh); *Ko's Yellow* × *Seedling*; Stephens, Paddy. Flowers white and gold, semi-dbl., medium; no fragrance; foliage medium, medium green, glossy; bushy growth.

Kenmore HT, *dy*, 1971, *Jane Lazenby* × *Golden Delight*; Macara; Sanday. Flowers deep yellow, dbl. (36 petals), large (4½ in.); slightly fragrant; foliage glossy.

Kenora Duet F, *ab*, 1976, *Duet sport*; Tresise. Bud long, pointed; flowers salmon-pink, semi-dbl., open, medium; slightly fragrant; foliage glossy; vigorous, bushy growth.

Kentfield Pol, *mp*, 1922, *Cécile Brunner* × *Seedling*; Diener. Flowers soft cameo-pink to deeper pink, dbl., small; slightly fragrant.

Kentucky Derby HT, *dr*, 1972, (AROder); *John S. Armstrong* × *Grand Slam*; Armstrong, D.L.; Armstrong Nursery. Flowers dark red, dbl., high-centered, large; slightly fragrant; foliage large, glossy, leathery; vigorous, upright, bushy growth.

Kerry Gold F, *yb*, 1967, *Circus* × *Allgold*; Dickson, A. Flowers canary-yellow, outer petals veined red, globular, large (3 in.) blooms in clusters; foliage dark.

Kerry MacNeil F, *mr*, 1967, *Orangeade* × *Anna Wheatcroft*; Vincent. Flowers bright vermilion; free growth.

Kerryman® F, *pb*, 1971, *Paddy McGredy × (Mme. Léon Cuny × Columbine)*; McGredy, S., IV; McGredy. Flowers salmon and pink, dbl. (24 petals), large (4½ in.); slightly fragrant.

Kersbergen Pol, *mr*, 1927, *Miss Edith Cavell sport*; Kersbergen. Flowers bright currant-red.

Kesri F, *or*, 1969, *Orangeade, Climbing × Open pollination*; Singh; Gopalsinamiengar. Bud ovoid; flowers orient orange, dbl., open, small; slightly fragrant; foliage leathery; vigorous growth.

Ketje HT, *mr*, 1938, *Mrs. Sam McGredy × E.G. Hill*; Lens. Bud pointed; flowers brilliant red mixed dark pink, very full, well formed; foliage bronze; very vigorous growth.

Kev Min, *dy*, 1991, (TALkev; K.T.); *Azure Sea × Party Girl*; Taylor, Pete & Kay; Taylor's Roses. Flowers deep yellow, full, medium blooms borne mostly singly; no fragrance; foliage medium, medium green, semi-glossy; medium, upright growth.

Kew Beauty HT, *dr*, 1918, Therkildsen. Flowers crimson, dbl.; fragrant.

Kew Rambler R, *mp*, 1913, *R. soulieana × Hiawatha*. Flowers pink, center paler, single, borne in clusters; foliage gray-green; height to 15 ft.

Keystone LCl, *dy*, 1904, Dingee & Conard. Flowers deep lemon-yellow.

Ki Ki Paquel F, *or*, 1960, *Super-Congo × Independence*; Moreira; da Silva. Flowers bright brick color.

Kia Ora F, *or*, 1962, *Independence × Independence*; Mason, P.G. Flowers orange-scarlet, dbl. (35 petals), large; foliage glossy, dark; vigorous, bushy, compact growth.

Kiboh F, *rb*, 1986, (Lovita; Gypsy Carnival; Gypsy; Kibo); *Liberty Bell × Kagayaki*; Suzuki, S.; Keisei Rose Nursery. Flowers orange-red, reverse yellowish, dbl. (50 petals), cupped, large blooms in clusters of 3-5; slight fragrance; foliage dark, semi-glossy; prickles slanted downward; vigorous, upright growth. GM, The Hague, 1985.

Kickapoo HT, *rb*, 1990, (Daisy Mae × First Prize) × Seedling; Stoddard, Louis, 1991. Bud ovoid; flowers yellow, outer petals red, white reverse aging to light red blend, dbl. (20 petals), urn-shaped, large (5 in.) blooms borne singly; slight fragrance; foliage medium, medium green, dull; prickles straight, green aging to tan; fruit round, green to light yellow; bushy, medium, slightly spreading growth.

Kiddy Pol, *mr*, 1967, *Mme. Dieudonne × Seedling*; Delforge. Bud pointed; flowers dark red, becoming brighter, single, cupped, medium; foliage glossy; vigorous, upright growth; abundant, recurrent bloom.

Kidwai HT, *mp*, 1933, (Kidway); Pernet-Ducher; Gaujard; Dreer; H&S. Bud long, pointed; flowers salmon-rose, lower half of petals golden yellow, semi-dbl., large; slightly fragrant; foliage leathery, dark, bronze, glossy; very vigorous, bushy growth.

Kiese HCan (OGR), *mr*, 1910, *Général Jacqueminot × R. canina*; Kiese. Flowers bright red, semi-dbl.

Kiftsgate Sp (OGR), *w*, 1954, (Filipes Kiftsgate); *A form of R. filipes*; E. Murrell. Flowers creamy white, single (5 petals), borne in large clusters; fragrant; very vigorous, sprawling growth.

Kilimanjaro HT, *w*, 1977, (HERaro); *Seedling × Pascali*; Herholdt, J.A. Bud pointed; flowers pure white, dbl. (35-38 petals), large (4½-5 in.); fragrant; foliage rich green; vigorous growth.

Killarney HT, *mp*, 1898, *Mrs. W.J. Grant × Charles J. Grahame*; Dickson, A. Bud long, pointed; flowers bright medium pink, dbl., loose, large; very fragrant; foliage bronze.

Killarney Brilliant HT, *dp*, 1914, *Killarney sport*; Dickson, A. Bud long, pointed; flowers brilliant pink to rosy carmine, dbl., open; fragrant; foliage rich green, soft.

Killarney, Climbing Cl HT, *mp*, 1908, Reinberg.

Killarney Double Pink HT, *mp*, 1935, *Killarney Double White sport*; Vestal. Flowers sparkling shell-pink.

Killarney Double White HT, *w*, 1912, *Killarney sport*; Budlong; A.N. Pierson. Flowers snowy white; long a standard white rose for indoor growing.

Killarney Double White, Climbing Cl HT, *w*, 1935, Howard Rose Co.

Killarney Queen HT, *dp*, 1912, *Killarney sport*; Budlong. Flowers tyrian rose, brighter than Killarney.

Kilworth Gold HT, *dy*, 1977, *Whisky Mac sport*; Gandy. Flowers golden yellow.

Kilworth Pride F, *dr*, 1955, *Better Times × Floribunda seedling*; deRuiter; Gandy. Flowers dark red, semi-dbl., medium blooms in clusters; foliage bronze; dwarf, bushy.

Kim F, *my*, 1971, (Orange Sensation × Allgold) × Elizabeth of Glamis; Harkness, 1973. Flowers yellow, dbl. (28 petals), large (3 in.); slightly fragrant; foliage small, light green, matt; dwarf growth.

Kim Pol, *mp*, 1956, *Independence × Salmon Perfection*; Buyl Frères. Flowers geranium-rose, small, borne in clusters; vigorous growth.

Kimberley Anne HT, *w*, 1983, *Virgo* × *Secret Love*; Evans, F. David. Flowers white, dbl. (35 petals), large; very fragrant; foliage medium, medium green, matt; upright growth. ARC TG (B), 1985.

Kimberly Min, *ab*, 1986, (MICkim); *Party Girl* × *Sheri Anne*; Williams, Michael C.; The Rose Garden. Flowers apricot, dbl. (24 petals), urn-shaped, exhibition, medium blooms borne usually singly; fruity fragrance; foliage medium, medium green, semi-glossy; no prickles; fruit globular, small, orange; upright, medium growth.

Kimono® F, *pb*, 1961, *Cocorico* × *Frau Anny Beaufays*; deRuiter; Horstmann. Flowers salmon-pink, dbl. (30 petals), large (3 in.) blooms in broad clusters; fragrant; vigorous, bushy growth.

Kim's Cream™ F, *w*, 1991, (RUPkimcrm); *Lavender Pinocchio* × *Lavender Pinocchio*; Rupert, Kim L., 1992. Bud ovoid, pointed; flowers cream with coffee and gold tints, opening cream, tint remains in cool weather, red stamen, full (26-40 petals), large (7+cms), flat blooms borne in small clusters; very fragrant (spicy); foliage leathery, medium, medium green, semi-glossy; some prickles; low (45-50 cms), bushy, compact, vigorous growth.

KINbelle Min, *dp*, 1988, (Rosa Belle); *Vera Dalton* × *Party Girl*; King, Gene; AGM Miniature Roses. Flowers deep pink to yellow-cream at base, dbl. (21 petals), high-centered, exhibition, medium, borne usually singly or in sprays of 3-5; foliage medium, medium green, matt; prickles straight with hook, few, dark brown; no fruit; bushy, medium growth.

Kind Regards F, *mr*, 1956, Kordes. Flowers crimson-red, dbl., very large, borne in clusters; vigorous, bushy growth.

King Arthur F, *op*, 1967, *Pink Parfait* × *Highlight*; Harkness. Flowers salmon-pink, dbl., large (3½ in.) blooms in clusters; slightly fragrant; foliage glossy.

King Boreas F, *my*, 1941, *Golden Glow* × *Seedling*; Brownell. Flowers pure yellow shading to nearly white, very dbl. (100 petals), recurved, medium; fragrant; vigorous.

King Crimson S, *dr*, 1991, (JACshur); *Razzle Dazzle* × *Seedling*; Warriner, William A.; Bear Creek Gardens, Inc. Flowers dark red, semi-dbl. (6-14 petals), large; no fragrance; foliage large, dark green, semi-glossy; tall, upright, bushy growth.

King George V HP (OGR), *dr*, 1912, Dickson, H. Flowers crimson, dbl. (40 petals), high-centered, large, borne on strong stems;

fragrant; very vigorous, open growth; sparse, intermittent bloom.

King Midas LCl, *my*, 1942, Nicolas; J&P. Bud long, pointed; flowers clear yellow, dbl. (20 petals), cupped, large (4-5 in.) blooms in clusters of 4-6; slightly fragrant; foliage large, leathery, dark; vigorous, climbing or pillar (8-10 ft.) growth; repeat bloom.

King o' Kings HT, *mr*, 1973, *My Love* × *Duftwolke*; Anderson's Rose Nursery. Flowers red, dbl. (35-40 petals), high-centered, large (6 in.); very fragrant; foliage dark.

King of Hearts HT, *mr*, 1968, *Karl Herbst* × *Ethel Sanday*; McGredy, S., IV; Edmunds. Bud long, pointed; flowers red, dbl., high-centered, medium; foliage dark, leathery; vigorous, bushy growth.

King of Scots HSpn (OGR), *dp*, *R. spinosissima hybrid*; Lee, prior to 1848. Flowers deep pink, dbl.; fruit black, glossy; foliage finely divided; dense, shrubby (3-4 ft.) growth; profuse, early bloom.

King of the Prairies HSet (OGR), *mr*, 1843, *R. setigera hybrid*; Feast. Flowers bright red.

Kingaroy HT, *dr*, 1979, *Seedling* × *Red Lion*; Perry, Astor, 1981. Bud long, pointed; flowers dark red, dbl. (30 petals), urn-shaped blooms borne singly; slight fruity fragrance; foliage medium, matt; small prickles; medium growth.

Kingcup HT, *my*, 1953, *Mrs. Sam McGredy* × *Ellinor LeGrice*; LeGrice. Flowers buttercup-yellow, dbl. (40 petals), well formed, large (4 in.); very fragrant (fruity); foliage dark, glossy; very free growth.

Kingi F, *pb*, 1983, (MURki); *Liverpool Echo* × *Una Hawken*; Murray, Nola. Flowers yellow flushed rose pink, dbl. (35 petals), large; slight fragrance; foliage dense, dark; large, red prickles; bushy growth.

KINgig Min, *mp*, 1987, (Giggles); *Vera Dalton* × *Rose Window*; King, Gene; AGM Miniature Roses. Flowers light pink, reverse light to dark pink, fading to creamy pink, dbl. (18 petals), high-centered, exhibition, medium, borne singly or in sprays of 3-5; slight fragrance; foliage medium, medium green, matt; slightly crooked, white prickles; fruit oval, green; upright, tall growth.

King's Ransom® HT, *dy*, 1961, *Golden Masterpiece* × *Lydia*; Morey; J&P. Bud ovoid; flowers clear golden yellow, dbl. (38 petals), high-centered, large (5-6 in.); fragrant; foliage leathery, glossy; vigorous, upright growth. AARS, 1962.

King's Row S, *yb*, 1965, *Easter Parade* × *Herrenhausen*; Whisler; Germain's. Flowers yellow becoming rose-red, dbl., medium, borne in clusters; fragrant; foliage bronze, leathery; vigorous (4 ft.), compact growth.

Kinkaku HT, *dy*, 1975, *Seedling × Peace*; Okamoto, K.; K. Hirakata Nursery. Flowers golden yellow, dbl. (38 petals), high-centered, large blooms borne usually singly; slight fragrance; foliage medium, light green; brown prickles; medium, bushy growth.

Kinugasa HT, *lp*, 1984, *Michèlle Meilland × (Michelle Meilland × Anne Letts)*; Shibata, T.; K. Hirakata Nursery. Flowers light pink, dbl. (45 petals), high-centered, large blooms borne usually singly; fruity fragrance; foliage medium, light green; brown, hooked prickles; medium, bushy growth.

Kiora F, *mr*, 1989, *Liverpool Echo × John Church*; Cattermole, R.F.; South Pacific Rose Nursery. Bud pointed; flowers light vermillion shading to darker petal edges, dbl. (26 wide petals), flat, small, borne in sprays of 3-5; no fragrance; foliage dark green, shiny, veined; upright, bushy growth.

Kirsi HT, *rb*, 1967, *Rose Gaujard sport*; Palmer, H.E.; Edmunds. Flowers cream-white edged pink, becoming red over white, dbl., large; very vigorous growth.

Kirsten Poulsen F, *mr*, 1924, *Orléans Rose × Red Star*; Poulsen, S. Flowers bright scarlet, single, borne in clusters; slightly fragrant; foliage leathery; vigorous.

Kirsten Poulsen Improved F, *mr*, 1938, Radmore. Flowers scarlet, single, borne on trusses; foliage dark; free growth; free bloom.

Kirsty Jane F, *or*, 1979, (SIMkayjay); *Orangeade seedling × Megiddo*; Simpson, J.W. Bud ovoid; flowers orange-red, dbl. (28 petals), fluted blooms borne 3-10 per cluster; no fragrance; foliage medium, glossy; straight brown prickles; bushy, vigorous growth.

Kiskadee F, *my*, 1973, *Arthur Bell × Cynthia Brooke*; McGredy. Flowers bright yellow, dbl. (25 petals), HT form, large (3½ in.); slightly fragrant; foliage dark.

Kismet HT, *my*, 1930, *Talisman sport*; Nicolas; J&P. Flowers clear yellow, center deeper, dbl., cupped, large; very fragrant; foliage light, glossy.

Kiss Min, *ob*, 1980, *Seedling × Seedling*; Lyon, Lyndon. Bud ovoid, pointed; flowers Indian orange, reverse lighter, dbl. (28 petals), HT-form, blooms borne 1-3 per cluster; fruity fragrance; foliage small, medium green; straight prickles; strong, upright growth.

Kiss 'n' Tell Min, *ab*, 1985, (SEAkis); *Rise 'n' Shine × (Sally Mac × New Penny)*; McCann, S., 1989. Flowers apricot, dbl. (35 petals), flat, small; slight fragrance; foliage small, medium green, semi-glossy; bushy growth.

Kiss the Bride Min, *w*, 1987, (SEAwhi); *Rise 'n' Shine × White Bouquet*; McCann, S., 1990. Flowers white, dbl. (20 petals), small blooms borne singly and in clusters of 4-6; spicy fragrance; foliage medium, medium green, semi-glossy; bushy growth.

Kissin' Cousin S, *op*, 1978, *((Ophelia × Prairie Princess) × Tiki) × ((Corbeille Royale × American Heritage) × Hawkeye Belle)*; Buck; Iowa State University. Bud ovoid, pointed; flowers pink to coral-pink, dbl. (28 petals), high-centered, large (4-5 in.); slightly fragrant; foliage large, dark, leathery; vigorous, upright, spreading growth.

Kitana HRg (S), *m*, 1927, *Tetonkaha × Rose Apples*; Hansen, N.E. Flowers deep lavender-pink, semi-dbl.; very fragrant; fruit red, profuse; non-recurrent bloom.

Kitchener of Khartoum HT, *mr*, 1917, (K. of K.); Dickson, A. Flowers dazzling velvety scarlet, 10 petals, medium (3 in.); very fragrant; vigorous, branching growth. GM, NRS, 1916.

Kitty Hawk Min, *pb*, 1986, *Watercolor × Seedling*; Bridges, Dennis A. Flowers deep pink, reverse lighter pink, dbl. (29 petals), high-centered, exhibition, medium blooms borne singly; slight fragrance; foliage large, medium green, semi-glossy; medium, long, red prickles; medium, upright growth.

Kitty Kingsbury HT, *mp*, 1930, *Abol seedling*; Evans. Flowers shell-pink; fragrant; vigorous growth.

Kitty Kininmonth LCl, *dp*, 1922, *Seedling × R. gigantea*; Clark, A.; Hackett. Flowers deep pink, golden stamens, semi-dbl., cupped, very large; slightly fragrant; foliage dark, wrinkled; few prickles; vigorous, climbing growth; some recurrent bloom.

Kiwi HT, *w*, 1989, *Judith Morton × (Pascali × Blue Moon)*; Cattermole, R.F.; South Pacific Rose Nursery. Bud pointed; flowers creamy pink opening to creamy white, dbl. (32 wide petals), reflexed, pointed, medium, borne usually singly; slight fragrance; foliage dark green, shiny; prickles needle-like, red to light brown; tall, upright growth.

Kiwi Belle F, *pb*, 1983, *Silent Night × Irish Mist*; Cattermole, R.F. Flowers tan apricot to pink, dbl. (40 petals), globular, large blooms in clusters of 3-5; strong fragrance; foliage bronze green when young, turning light green; brown prickles; upright, spreading.

Kiwi Charm HT, *pb*, 1971, *Kordes' Perfecta × Champagne*; Lindquist; Bell Roses. Bud ovoid; flowers creamy yellow, edged pink, semi-dbl., high-centered, large; fragrant; foliage glossy, leathery; vigorous, bushy growth.

Kiwi Delight HT, *yb*, 1983, *Peace* × *(Peer Gynt* × *Irish Mist)*; Cattermole, R.F. Flowers golden yellow, petals edged deep pink, aging pink overall, dbl. (40 petals), globular, large blooms borne singly; strong fragrance; foliage bronze green turning dark green, glossy; gray-brown, very small and large prickles; upright, bushy growth.

Kiwi Gold HT, *yb*, 1984, *(Pink Parfait* × *Pink Parfait)* × *Waipounamu*; Cattermole, R.F. Bud pointed; flowers light yellow, reverse edges of petals flushed pink, dbl. (22 petals), exhibition blooms borne singly and up to 5 per cluster; very fragrant; foliage light green, glossy; very few, light brown prickles; upright growth.

Kiwi Queen HT, *yb*, 1983, *Peer Gynt* × *Command Performance*; Cattermole, R.F. Flowers yellow, shaded orange and pink, dbl. (44 petals), exhibition, large; slight fragrance; foliage medium green; light brown prickles; upright, spreading growth.

Kiyosumi HT, *m*, 1979, *Seedling* × *Sterling Silver*; Onodera, T.; S. Onodera. Bud slender; flowers clear light purplish blue, dbl. (25 petals), high-centered, medium (3 in.); slightly fragrant; foliage light green, leathery; upright growth.

Klaus Störtebeker HT, *mr*, 1962, Kordes, R. Flowers medium red, dbl. (40 petals), well-formed, large (5 in.); foliage dark; low, bushy growth.

Kleine Leo HT, *mr*, 1921, *Farbenkönigin* × *Gen. MacArthur*; Timmermans. Flowers brilliant red shaded dark red, full.

Kleiner Alfred Pol, *or*, 1904, *Anna-Maria de Montravel* × *Shirley Hibberd*; Lambert, P. Bud garnet-red; flowers orange-red, well formed, medium; foliage glossy; dwarf growth.

Klerksdorp Horizon HT, *rb*, 1987, (KORmowe); *Seedling* × *Seedling*; Kordes, W., Sohne; Ludwigs Roses, 1988. Flowers tomato-red, reverse golden yellow, dbl. (32 petals), large, borne 1-3 per cluster; no fragrance; foliage medium green, large; prickles concave, reddish-brown; upright, medium, free-flowering growth.

Kletternde Ruby R, *mr*, 1946, *Ruby sport*; Kordes. Bud globular; flowers scarlet, dbl., small, borne in clusters; slightly fragrant; foliage dark, wrinkled; very vigorous, trailing growth.

Klondyke R, *my*, 1911, Paul. Flowers soft yellow, center deeper, passing to ivory-white, dbl., large, borne in clusters; very vigorous, climbing growth.

Klondyke HT, *my*, 1934, *Lady Forteviot sport*; LeGrice. Flowers clear golden yellow.

Kluis Scarlet F, *mr*, 1931, *Lafayette sport*; Kluis, R. Flowers brilliant red; very free growth.

Klyn's Orange Pol, *or*, (Kluis Orange); Kluis. Flowers orange-scarlet, dbl., small, borne in dense clusters; foliage light green; dwarf growth.

Klyn's Yellow HT, *my*, 1948, *McGredy's Yellow* × *Seedling*; Klyn. Bud pointed; flowers clear yellow, dbl., open, large; fragrant; foliage glossy; very vigorous, compact growth.

Koa Min, *op*, 1978, *Persian Princess* × *Gene Boerner*; Rovinsky & Meredith; Kingsdown Nursery; Miniature Plant Kingdom. Bud ovoid; flowers coral-pink, dbl. (44 petals), high-centered, small (1 in.); slightly fragrant; tall, open, leggy growth.

Koba HT, *or*, 1979, (MEIroverna); *((Seedling* × *Rouge Meilland)* × *Independence)* × *Queen Elizabeth*; Meilland, M.L.; Meilland. Flowers scarlet, dbl. (40 petals), fully cupped, medium; foliage dark; very vigorous, upright growth.

Ko-Choh F, *ob*, 1983, *(Rumba* × *Olympic Torch)* × *Allgold*; Suzuki, S.; Keisei Rose Nursery. Flowers orange, reverse yellow shaded orange, dbl. (45 petals), high-centered, small, borne 3-5 per cluster; fragrant; foliage dark, semi-glossy; small prickles; low, compact.

Koha HT, *rb*, 1983, *Silent Night* × *(Josephine Bruce* × *Irish Mist)*; Cattermole, R.F. Flowers medium red, reverse lighter, dbl. (32 petals), exhibition, large; faint fragrance; foliage light, glossy, veined; brown prickles; upright, branching growth.

Kohima F, *rb*, 1972, *Orange Sensation* × *Mischief*; Ellick; Excelsior Roses. Flowers fire-red to orange, reverse cream, dbl. (45-50 petals), very full, large (4 in.); very fragrant; vigorous growth.

Koh-I-Noor HT, *pb*, 1973, (Memoriam × Peace) × My Choice; Ellick. Flowers white, center deep pink, dbl. (60 petals), very full, large (5 in.); very fragrant; foliage glossy, dark; vigorous growth.

Kojo no Tsuki LCl, *dy*, 1975, *(Souv. de Jacques Verschuren* × *Thais)* × *Amarillo*; Teranishi; Itami Bara-en. Bud circular; flowers deep yellow, dbl. (35 petals), high-centered, large (4½-5 in.); slightly fragrant; foliage light; vigorous, climbing growth.

KoKo Min, *yb*, 1982, Meredith, E.A. & Rovinski, M.E.; Casa de Rosa Domingo. Bud globular; flowers pale yellow, aging orange-red on petal edges, dbl. (55 petals), medium blooms borne singly; fragrant; foliage medium, medium green, matt; thin, triangular, light brown prickles; low, bushy growth.

Kokulensky Sp (OGR), *lp*, *R. canina selected strain*; Kokulensky. Used as an understock but declining in popularity on account of rust susceptibility.

Koldinghus F, *dp*, 1968, *Pernille Poulsen × Seedling*; Poulsen, N.D.; Poulsen. Flowers deep rose, dbl. (23 petals), open, medium (2-2½ in.); slightly fragrant; foliage dark, glossy; upright growth.

Kolibre F, *mr*, 1946, *Mev. Nathalie Nypels × Seedling*; Leenders, M.; Longley. Bud long, pointed; flowers red, semi-dbl. (20 petals), large (3 in.), small trusses; very fragrant; foliage bronze; moderately vigorous growth.

Kolkhoznitsa HT, *m*, 1957, *Peace × Mirandy*; Sushkov & Besschetnova. Flowers lilac-pink, dbl. (45 petals), large; fragrant; foliage dark; very vigorous, compact growth.

Köln am Rhein K (S), *op*, 1956, (Cologne); Kordes. Flowers deep salmon-pink, dbl., large blooms in clusters; fragrant; foliage dark, glossy; vigorous, climbing growth; recurrent bloom.

Kölner Karneval HT, *m*, 1964, (KORgi; Blue Girl, Cologne Carnival); Kordes, R. Flowers silvery lilac-blue, dbl. (40 petals), well-formed, large (5½ in.); foliage dark; vigorous, bushy. GM, Rome, 1964.

Komfort F, *mp*, 1967, Tantau, Math. Flowers salmon-pink, semi-dbl., large, borne in clusters (to 20); foliage glossy; very vigorous, bushy growth.

Kommerzienrat W. Rautenstrauch HFt (OGR), *mp*, 1909, *Léonie Lamesch × R. foetida bicolor*; Lambert, P. Flowers pure salmon-pink, center yellow, reverse lighter, semi-dbl., borne in clusters; slightly fragrant.

Kommodore F, *mr*, 1959, (The Commodore); Tantau, Math. Flowers blood-red, dbl., well-formed, large blooms in clusters; vigorous, low growth.

Konfetti HT, *pb*, 1965, Tantau, Math. Bud globular; flowers claret-rose, reverse light cream, dbl. (40-45 petals), well formed, large (5 in.); strong stems; foliage dark, leathery; bushy, upright growth.

Königin Beatrix® HT, *ob*, 1983, (HetKORa; Queen Beatrix); *Seedling × Patricia*; Kordes, W. Flowers orange, dbl. (35 petals), exhibition, large; very fragrant; foliage medium, medium green, semi-glossy; upright, bushy growth.

Königin Carola HT, *pb*, 1904, *Mme. Caroline Testout × Viscountess Folkestone*; Türke. Bud pointed; flowers satiny rose-pink, reverse silvery white, dbl., very large; slightly fragrant; foliage dark, leathery; vigorous growth.

Königin Luise HT, *w*, 1927, *Frau Karl Druschki × Sunburst*; Weigand, C. Flowers white, dbl., high-centered, very large; slightly

fragrant; foliage dark, leathery, glossy; vigorous, bushy growth.

Königin Viktoria von Schweden HT, *yb*, 1919, *Mme. Segond Weber × Mrs. Joseph Hill*; Ries; Teschendorff. Flowers light saffron-yellow, aging to pale salmon-pink, dbl.

Königin von Dänemark A (OGR), *mp*, 1826, (Belle Courtisanne; Queen of Denmark); *Probably R. alba × Damask hybrid*. Flowers flesh-pink, center darker, very full, medium; fragrant; vigorous growth; non-recurrent bloom.

Königsberg HT, *mr*, 1940, *Mrs. Henry Winnett × Marechal Petain*; Weigand, L.; Teschendorff. Flowers scarlet-red.

Koningin Astrid HT, *mr*, 1935, (Queen Astrid); Leenders, M. Bud long, pointed, nasturtium-red; flowers reddish apricot and bronze, dbl., very large; foliage dark, bronze; vigorous growth.

Koningin Juliana F, *mp*, 1948, *Poulsen's Pink × Mrs. Pierre S. duPont*; Buisman. Flowers salmon-pink becoming light yellow with salmon, dbl., large, borne in clusters; fragrant; foliage glossy; blooms late.

Konrad Adenauer® HT, *dr*, 1955, (Konrad Adenauer Rose); *Crimson Glory × Hens Verschuren*; Tantau, Math.; J&P, 1954. Bud globular; flowers blood-red, dbl. (35 petals), cupped, large (4 in.); very fragrant; foliage light green, glossy; vigorous, upright growth.

Konrad Glocker HT, *dr*, 1962, Kordes, R. Flowers dark red, dbl., large (3 in.); foliage dark; vigorous, bushy, low growth.

Konrad Henkel® HT, *mr*, 1983, (KORjet; Avenue's Red); *Seedling × Red Planet*; Kordes, W. Flowers medium red, dbl. (35 petals), exhibition, large; fragrant; foliage large, medium green, semi-glossy; upright, bushy growth.

Kon-Tiki F, *mr*, 1971, *Aztec × Paprika*; Inst. of Orn. Plant Growing. Bud ovoid; flowers bright red, semi-dbl., cupped, large; foliage glossy, dark; vigorous, upright growth.

Kootenay HT, *lp*, 1917, Dickson, A. Flowers primrose-color; a larger Kaiserin Auguste Viktoria.

Koppies HT, *lp*, 1979, *Tropicana × Wendy Cussons*; Perry, Astor. Bud ovoid; flowers light pink, dbl. (35 petals), classic HT-form, blooms borne usually singly; fruity fragrance; foliage medium, matt; short, recurved prickles; vigorous, tall growth.

Koralle F, *mr*, 1942, *Else Poulsen sport*; Koopman; Krause; Tantau & C-P. Flowers light red; slightly fragrant.

KORantel HT, *yb*, 1985, (Tarantella); *Colour Wonder × Wiener Charme*; Kordes, W.;

Horstmann, 1979. Flowers creamy yellow, petals edged and marked with pink, dbl. (54 petals), high-centered, large blooms borne singly; foliage medium, medium green, glossy; light brown prickles; upright growth.

Kordes' Brillant® S, *ob*, 1983, (KORbisch; Kordes' Brilliant); *Sympathie seedling × Seedling*; Kordes, W., 1982. Flowers orange, dbl. (35 petals), large; slight fragrance; foliage medium, medium green, glossy; upright, bushy growth.

Kordes' Perfecta HT, *pb*, 1957, (KORalu; Perfecta); *Golden Scepter × Karl Herbst*; Kordes; A. Dickson; McGredy, 1957; J&P, 1958. Bud urn-shaped; flowers cream tipped and then flushed crimson, suffused yellow, dbl. (68 petals), high-centered, large (4½-5 in.); very fragrant; foliage dark, leathery, glossy; vigorous, upright growth. GM, NRS, 1957 & Portland, 1958; PIT, 1957.

Kordes' Perfecta, Climbing Cl HT, *pb*, 1962, Japan Rose Soc.

Kordes' Perfecta Superior HT, *mp*, 1963, (Perfecta Superior); *Kordes' Perfecta sport*; Kordes, 1963; Wyant, 1966. Flowers bright pink.

KORhanbu HT, *op*, 1985, (KORprill; Belami); *(Prominent × Carina) × Emily Post*; Kordes, W. Flowers orange pink, dbl. (35 petals), large; fragrant; foliage medium, dark, glossy; upright, bushy growth.

KORicole F, *w*, 1985, (Nicole); *Seedling × Bordure Rose*; Kordes, W., 1984. Flowers white with pink petal edges, dbl. (35 petals), large; slight fragrance; foliage large, dark, semi-glossy; upright growth.

KORinter LCl, *op*, 1982, (Rosanna); *Coral Dawn × Seedling*; Kordes, W. Flowers orange pink, dbl. (35 petals), large; fragrant; foliage medium, medium green, glossy; upright growth.

KORiver S, *dr*, 1985, (Heidikind; Esterel); *The Fairy × Seedling*; Kordes, W. Flowers dark red, dbl. (20 petals), medium; slight fragrance; foliage small, medium green, glossy; upright, bushy growth.

KORizont LCl, *dp*, 1985, (Summer Wine); Kordes, W.; John Mattock. Flowers deep pink, red stamens, single (5 petals), large; fragrant; foliage large, medium green, semi-glossy; upright growth.

KORlingo HT, *mr*, 1986, (Kardinal; Kordes' Rose Kardinal); *Seedling × Flamingo*; Kordes, W., 1985. Flowers medium red, dbl. (35 petals), large; slight fragrance; foliage medium, dark, semi-glossy; upright growth.

KORmetter F, *op*, 1985, (Trier 2000; Anna Livia; Sandton Smile); *(Seedling × Tornado) × Seedling*; Kordes, W. Flowers orange pink, dbl. (20 petals), large; slight fragrance; foliage medium, medium green, semi-glossy; bushy growth. GM, Orleans, 1987.

Körner HMsk (S), *yb*, 1914, *Trier × Eugénie Lamesch*; Lambert, P. Bud reddish; flowers orange-yellow tinted salmon, dbl., borne in clusters.

Koro HT, *mr*, 1983, *Pink Parfait seedling × Red Planet*; Cattermole, R.F. Flowers scarlet, dbl. (32 petals), exhibition, large; strong fruity fragrance; foliage medium green; reddish prickles; upright growth.

Korona® F, *or*, 1955, (KORnita); Kordes; Morse. Flowers orange-scarlet, dbl. (20 petals), medium (2½ in.) blooms in large trusses; slightly fragrant; vigorous, upright growth. GM, NRS, 1954.

Korona, Climbing Cl F, *or*, 1957, Kordes.

Koronet HT, *ob*, 1941, *Julien Potin × Bright Wings*; Mallerin; A. Meilland & C-P. Bud globular, lemon shaded orange; flowers orange, reverse deep primrose, dbl. (40-50 petals), high-centered, becoming cupped, large (4½ in.); foliage dark, glossy, leathery; vigorous, upright, bushy, open growth.

Korovo HT, *mp*, 1931, *Mrs. T. Hillas × Étoile de Hollande*; Leenders, M. Bud pointed; flowers peach-blossom-pink and coppery old-rose, dbl. (30 petals), large; fragrant; foliage thick; vigorous growth.

KORpek HT, *mr*, 1985, *Seedling × Seedling*; Kordes, W.; Paul Pekmez. Flowers medium red, dbl. (20 petals); no fragrance; foliage dark, glossy; upright growth; greenhouse variety.

Korrigan F, *lp*, 1972, *Seedling × (Orléans Rose × Eden Rose)*; Poulsen, N.D.; Poulsen. Bud globular; flowers light pink, dbl. (25 petals), medium (2-2½ in.); slightly fragrant; foliage glossy, dark, leathery; vigorous, bushy growth.

KORtexung® F, *mp*, 1987, (Fleurop; Europa) *(Seedling × Banzai) × (Mercedes × Carol)*; Kordes, W., 1985. Flowers medium pink, dbl. (40+ petals), medium; slight fragrance; foliage medium, medium green, matt; bushy growth.

KORtime F, *my*, 1985, (Golden Times); *New Day × Minigold*; Kordes, W., 1976. Flowers medium yellow, dbl. (40+ petals), medium; very fragrant; foliage medium, dark, semi-glossy; bushy growth; greenhouse variety.

KORwerk Min, *mp*, 1982, (Zwergkönigin '82; Dwarf Queen '82); *KORkonig × Sunday Times*; Kordes, W. Flowers medium pink, dbl. (35 petals), medium; slight fragrance; foliage small, medium green, glossy; bushy.

Ko's Yellow Min, *yb*, 1978, (MACkosyel); *(New Penny × Banbridge) × (Border Flame ×*

Manx Queen); McGredy, S., IV; McGredy Roses International. Flowers yellow, edges marked red, fading to cream, dbl. (39 petals), classic form, medium; foliage dark, glossy; bushy growth.

Koster's Orléans Pol, *mr*, 1920, *Orléans Rose sport*; Koster, M. Flowers brilliant scarlet-red.

Kostior Arteka F, *or*, 1955, (Campfire Arteka); *Independence × Seedling*; Klimenko. Flowers coral-red tinted orange, large; slightly fragrant.

Koto HT, *dy*, 1972, *Lydia seedling × Peace seedling*; Suzuki; Keisei Rose Nursery. Bud ovoid; flowers pure deep yellow, dbl., high-centered, large; fragrant; foliage glossy, dark, leathery; vigorous, upright growth.

Kotobuki HT, *yb*, 1990, *Souma sport*; Ogura Rose Nurseries, 1985. Bud pointed; flowers creamy to creamy yellow, creamy yellow reverse with light pink at fringe, moderately full (30-35 petals), high-centered, large, borne usually singly; slight to moderate fragrance; foliage dark green, glossy; medium growth.

Kovalam HT, *w*, 1976, *(Amberlight × Traumland) × Western Sun*; Viraraghaven; Gopalsinamiengar. Bud globular; flowers cream-white, dbl. (20-25 petals), cupped, large (4 in.); very fragrant; foliage wrinkled; moderate, bushy growth.

Koyo F, *rb*, 1989, *Masquerade × Matador*; Kikuchi, Rikichi, 1990. Bud ovoid; flowers vermillion, reverse orange-yellow, dbl. (17-20 petals), cupped, small, borne in sprays of many blooms; slight fragrance; foliage dark green, glossy; prickles ordinary; spreading growth.

Koza HRg (S), *dp*, 1927, *(R. rugosa × La France) seedling × La Mélusine*; Hansen, N.E. Flowers deep pink, semi-dbl.; vigorous (over 7 ft.); extremely hardy.

Krakow HT, *dr*, Grabezewski. Bud ovate; flowers dark red, very dbl.

Kralj Alexander I HT, *dr*, 1935, *Capt. Kilbee Stuart × Jan Böhm*; Böhm. Flowers velvety blood-red, reflexes fiery red, full, very large; very fragrant; vigorous growth.

Kralj Petar II HT, *pb*, 1936, Brada. Flowers salmon-pink, reverse carmine, with coppery sheen; fragrant.

Kralj Tomislav HT, *mr*, 1931, *Dora Stober × Étoile de Hollande*; Leenders, M. Bud long, pointed; flowers solferino red, dbl., open, high-centered, very large; vigorous growth.

Kraljica Marija HT, *ly*, 1935, *Frau Karl Druschki × Golden Ophelia*; Brada; Böhm. Flowers creamy yellow to creamy white, full, large; very fragrant.

Kranenburg F, *dp*, 1963, *Pinocchio × Ma Perkins*; Verschuren, A.; van Engelen. Flowers very dark pink, dbl. (32 petals), borne in clusters; foliage glossy, dark; bushy growth.

Krasavitza Festivalia HT, *yb*, 1955, (Festival Beauty); *(Peace × Crimson Glory) × Poinsettia*; Klimenko. Flowers yellow edged raspberry-red, dbl. (28 petals), medium; foliage glossy, light green; spreading growth.

Krásná Uslavanka HT, *ob*, 1930, *Mrs. Beckwith × Arthur Cook*; Böhm. Flowers orange-rose, reverse dark orange-yellow; fragrant; very vigorous, bushy growth.

Krasnaia Moskva HT, *dr*, 1955, (Red Moscow); *Peace × Crimson Glory*; Klimenko. Flowers dark velvety red, medium; slightly fragrant.

Krasnokamenka F, *mr*, 1955, (Red Stone); *Independence × Kirsten Poulsen*; Klimenko. Flowers crimson-red, semi-dbl. (12 petals), medium; foliage dark, glossy; upright growth.

Krasnyi Mak F, *mr*, 1955, (Red Poppy); *Independence × Kirsten Poulsen*; Klimenko. Flowers scarlet, dbl. (26 petals), medium, on short stems; slightly fragrant; foliage glossy, light green; upright growth.

Krioga F, *lp*, 1986, *Seedling × Orange Garnet*; Kriloff, M. Flowers light pink, dbl. (35 petals), medium blooms in clusters; foliage dense; bushy growth.

Kristi HT, *mp*, 1976, *White Satin × Bewitched*; Swim & Ellis; Armstrong Nursery. Bud ovoid, pointed; flowers clear medium pink, dbl. (45 petals), large (5 in.); fragrant (spicy); foliage large; vigorous, upright growth; greenhouse variety.

Kristin™ Min, *rb*, 1992, (BENmagic); *DICmickey × Tinseltown*; Benardella, Frank; Nor'East Miniature Roses, 1993. Flowers white/red bicolor, dbl. (27-30 petals), high-centered, exhibition, does not open beyond ½ open stage, medium (4 cms.) blooms borne usually singly and in clusters of 3-5; no fragrance; foliage large, dark green, semi-glossy; upright, bushy, medium growth. AOE, 1993.

Kristina av Tunsberg F, *or*, 1972, *Charleston × Toni Lander*; Lundstad; Norges Landbrukshogskole. Bud long, pointed; flowers orange-red, very dbl., high-centered, large; slightly fragrant; foliage glossy, dark; vigorous, bushy growth.

Kronprincessin Viktoria B (OGR), *w*, 1887, *Souv. de la Malmaison sport*; Vollert. Flowers milk-white, center tinted yellow.

Kronprinsesse Ingrid F, *mp*, 1936, *Else Poulsen × Dainty Bess*; Poulsen, S.; Poulsen; C-P,

1942. Bud long, pointed; flowers deep rose-pink, semi-dbl, open; slightly fragrant; foliage dark; vigorous growth.

Kumbaya F, *my*, 1981, *Chatterbox × Allgold*; Sanday, John; Sanday Roses, Ltd. Bud pointed; flowers bright medium yellow, dbl. (22 petals), borne up to 15 per cluster; slight fragrance; foliage deep green; slightly hooked, red prickles; low, bushy growth.

Kunigunde F, 1960, Horstmann. Flowers pink, dbl. (35 petals), high-centered, large; fragrant; vigorous growth.

Kurt Scholz HT, *mr*, 1934, *Cathrine Kordes × W.E. Chaplin*; Kordes. Bud pointed; flowers blood-red with some crimson, dbl., high-centered, very large; slightly fragrant; foliage leathery; vigorous, bushy growth.

Kutno Pol, *m*, 1965, *Margo Koster seedling*; Wituszynski. Flowers lavender-pink, full; growth low; best in autumn.

Kwinana F, *rb*, 1962, *Orange Triumph × Seedling*; Riethmuller; Hazlewood Bros. Bud ovoid; flowers crimson overlaid carmine, single, open, borne in clusters on strong stems; fragrant; foliage leathery; vigorous, tall growth.

Kynast HT, *mr*, 1917, Krüger. Flowers amaranth-red.

Kyo-Maiko F, *op*, 1974, *Sarabande seedling × Ruby Lips seedling*; Suzuki; Keisei Rose Nursery. Bud ovoid; flowers deep bright salmon-orange, dbl., cupped, small; slightly fragrant; foliage small, glossy, light; moderate, dwarf, bushy growth.

Kyria F, *lp*, 1976, (Pitica); *Sonia sport*; Royon. Flowers light pink.

Kyson Cl HT, *mr*, 1940, *New Dawn × Allen Chandler*; Eacott; R. Murrell. Flowers bright red, single, open, very large, borne in clusters on short, strong stems; slightly fragrant; foliage leathery, glossy, dark; very vigorous, climbing (7 ft. or more) growth; recurrent bloom.

La Bella HT, *dr*, 1976, *Liebeszauber × Herz As*; Kordes; Horstmann. Bud large, ovoid; flowers dark red, dbl., globular; slightly fragrant; foliage glossy, dark; very vigorous, upright growth.

La Belle Distinguée E (OGR), *mr*, (La Petite Duchesse; Lee's Duchess; Scarlet Sweet Brier); Prior to 1837. Flowers bright crimson, fully dbl., small; foliage dainty, fragrant; compact growth; non-recurrent bloom.

La Belle Irisée HT, *ob*, 1943, *Mme. Joseph Perraud × Seedling*; Gaujard. Bud ovoid, coppery; flowers clear orange-yellow, dbl., globular, medium; slightly fragrant; foliage leathery; dwarf growth.

La Belle Marie T (OGR), *dp*, *Old Blush × Mme. Laurette Messimy*; Tillotson. Flowers pink, veined darker, reverse deep rose, center incurved, medium; fragrant (fruity); foliage smooth, pointed; vigorous, tall growth.

La Belle Sultane G (OGR), *dr*, (Gallica Maheca; Violacea); ca. 1795. Flowers deep crimson, becoming violet, base white, almost single.

La Belle Suzanne T (OGR), *lp*, *Old Blush × Mme. Laurette Messimy*; Tillotson. Flowers light pink suffused white; fragrant; foliage smooth, pointed; vigorous, tall growth.

La Biche N (OGR), *w*, 1832, Trouillet. Flowers white, center flesh, very dbl., cupped, large.

La Brillante HP (OGR), *mr*, 1862, Verdier, V. Flowers bright crimson, well formed, large.

La Caille M (OGR), *mp*, 1857, Robert et Moreau. Flowers bright rose-pink.

La Canadienne HT, *ob*, 1967, *Royal Sunset × Sierra Sunset*; Morey; Country Garden Nursery. Bud long, pointed; flowers orange to shrimp and cream, semi-dbl., large; very fragrant; foliage dark, bronze, glossy; vigorous, bushy growth.

La Champagne HT, *ob*, 1919, Barbier. Bud long, pointed; flowers light coppery red, base yellow, edged light pink, dbl. (25 petals), globular, large; fragrant; foliage rich green, leathery; vigorous growth.

La Couronne Tendre G (OGR), *lp*, Flowers flesh-pink, dbl., small.

La Fiamma R, *ob*, 1909, Walsh. Flowers flame, single, borne in very large clusters; vigorous, climbing (15 ft.) growth.

La Florida HT, *mp*, 1932, La Florida. Flowers salmon, well formed; strong stems; foliage glossy; very vigorous growth.

La Follette S, *mp*, *R. gigantea × Seedling*; Busby, prior to 1867. Flowers pink and carmine; fragrant; vigorous (to 20 ft.) growth; half-hardy; (14).

La Fontaine F, *my*, 1961, *Mme. Charles Sauvage × Fashion*; Meilland, M.L.; C-P. Bud pointed, ovoid; flowers barium yellow, dbl. (20-25 petals), high-centered to cupped, large (3½-4 in.), borne in clusters; slightly fragrant; foliage leathery, dark; vigorous, bushy growth.

La France HT, *lp*, 1867, *The parentage quoted, Mme. Victor Verdier × Mme. Bravy, has never been substantiated by records*; Guillot Fils; Guillot was of the opinion that it was a Mme. Falcot seedling. Bud long, pointed; flowers silvery pink, reverse bright pink, dbl. (60 petals), large; very fragrant; vigorous growth. Considered to be one of the first Hybrid Teas introduced, and the prototype of the class.

La France, Climbing Cl HT, *lp*, 1893, Henderson, P.

La France de '89 HT, *rb*, 1889, *Reine Marie Henriette* × *La France*; Moreau-Robert. Bud long, pointed; flowers bright red, sometimes striped white, full, very large; very vigorous growth.

La France Striped HT, *pb*, 1956, *La France sport*; Hennessey. Flowers deep pink to red, and white to blush; fragrant.

La France Victorieuse HT, *dp*, 1919, Gravereaux; M. Guillot. Flowers silvery carmine-pink, inside tinted yellow, dbl.; fragrant.

La Giralda HT, *mp*, 1926, *Frau Karl Druschki* × *Mme. Edouard Herriot*; Dot, P. Flowers pink.

La Joconde HT, *my*, 1920, *Arthur R. Goodwin sport*; Croibier. Flowers pure golden yellow. RULED EXTINCT 2/88.

La Joconde HT, *or*, 1988, (DELjacq; Joconde); *(Tropicana* × *(Rome Glory* × *Impeccable))* × *(Spartan* × *MEIger)*; Delbard & Chabert, 1989. Flowers orange-red, dbl. (40 petals), well-shaped, large; no fragrance; upright, vigorous growth.

La Jolie HT, *mr*, 1956, *Independence* × *Hens Verschuren*; Buyl Frères. Bud long, pointed; flowers geranium-red, dbl. (30-35 petals), dbl.; very vigorous growth.

La Jolla HT, *pb*, 1954, *Charlotte Armstrong* × *Contrast*; Swim; Armstrong Nursery. Bud long, pointed; flowers soft pink veined deeper, center cream and gold, dbl. (65 petals), high-centered, large (5 in.); fragrant; foliage dark, glossy; upright growth.

La Madelon de Paris F, *lp*, 1962, *Cécile Brunner* × *Seedling*; Robichon. Flowers bright pink, dbl., well formed, medium, borne in clusters of 6-8; vigorous growth.

La Maréchale Pétain HT, *mr*, 1927, *Col. Leclerc* × *Château de Clos Vougeot*; Sauvageot; F. Gillot. Flowers carmine, dbl.; fragrant.

La Marne Pol, *pb*, 1915, *Mme. Norbert Levavasseur* × *Comtesse du Cayla*; Barbier. Flowers blush white, edged vivid pink, single blooms in large, loose clusters; vigorous.

La Marseillaise® HT, *dr*, 1986, (DELgeot; Isobel Champion); *((Gloire de Rome* × *Impeccable)* × *(Rouge Meilland* × *Soraya))* × *(MEIsar* × *Walko)*; Delbard, 1976. Bud large, ovoid; flowers dark red, dbl. (40 petals), well-formed, large; fragrant; vigorous, bushy growth.

La Mascotte Cl HT, *dy*, 1933, *Reine Marie Henriette* × *Laurent Carle*; Schwartz, A. Flowers deep saffron-yellow, passing to straw-yellow, slightly tinted salmon, full, large; foliage dark, glossy.

La Mélusine HRg (S), *dp*, 1906, Späth. Flowers pinkish red, dbl., large, borne in large clusters; very fragrant; very vigorous growth.

La Mie au Roy HT, *yb*, 1927, *Duchess of Wellington* × *Pax Labor*; Bernaix, P. Flowers yellow, salmon and copper, dbl.

La Mortola Sp (OGR), *w*, 1954, *Form of R. moschata nepalensis*; Hanbury; Sunningdale Nursery. Flowers white, single (5 petals), large (3 in.) blooms in trusses; very fragrant; foliage downy gray-green; very vigorous, climbing growth.

La Neige M (OGR), *w*, 1905, *Blanche Moreau sport*; Moranville. Flowers pure white, dbl., medium; foliage turns purple; vigorous.

La Noblesse C (OGR), *lp*, 1856, Flowers soft pink, full; very fragrant; bushy growth; later bloom than most Centifolias.

La Paloma® F, *w*, 1959, *Yellow Rambler* × *Goldene Johanna Tantau*; Tantau, Math. Flowers creamy white, dbl., well-formed blooms in clusters (to 30); foliage dark, glossy.

La Parfaite HT, *op*, 1956, *R.M.S. Queen Mary* × *Lady Sylvia*; Buyl Frères. Bud pointed; flowers bright salmon-pink, dbl. (40-50 petals), large; vigorous, bushy growth.

La Parisienne HT, *or*, 1937, *Lucy Nicolas* × *Charles P. Kilham*; Mallerin; A. Meilland; C-P. Bud long, pointed, deep coral-red; flowers orange-coral, semi-dbl., open, very large; slightly fragrant; foliage glossy, dark; very vigorous growth.

La Perle R, *ly*, 1905, Fauque. Flowers pale yellow to white.

La Plus Belle des Ponctuées G (OGR), *pb*, Flowers deep rose, spotted pale rose, flat.

La Pologne HT, *or*, 1938, Chambard, C. Flowers orange-carmine, cupped, very large; foliage bronze; vigorous growth.

La Promise HT, *mr*, 1956, *Seedling* × *Betty Uprichard*; Buyl Frères. Bud long, pointed; flowers brick-red, semi-dbl.; tall growth.

La Ramée F, *dr*, 1949, *Holstein* × *Alain*; Meilland, F. Flowers crimson, semi-dbl. (13 petals), borne in clusters; foliage dark, bronze; vigorous growth.

La Reine HP (OGR), *mp*, 1842, (Reine des Francais; Rose de la Reine); Laffay. Flowers glossy rose-pink, dbl. (78 petals), cupped, large; fragrant; vigorous growth.

La Reine Victoria B (OGR), *mp*, 1872, (Reine Victoria); Schwartz, J. Flowers rich pink, dbl., well-formed, cupped; foliage soft green; slender, upright (to 6 ft) growth; repeat bloom.

La Rose Tatouée HT, *m*, 1956, (The Rose Tattoo); *Opera seedling* × *(Opera* × *Seedling)*; Gaujard. Flowers salmon-pink tipped and spotted lavender, semi-dbl., large; slightly fragrant; foliage leathery; very vigorous, upright growth.

La Rosée Pol, *w*, 1920, Turbat. Flowers sulphur-white, passing to pure white, then to soft pink, borne in clusters of 25-30.

La Scala HT, *rb*, 1964, *(Mme. Henri Guillot × Mirandy)× Peace*; Lindquist. Flowers reddish orange, dbl., cupped, large; very fragrant; foliage leathery; upright, open growth. GM, Rome, 1961.

La Sevillana® F, *or*, 1978, (MEIgekanu); *((MEIbrim × Jolie Madame) × (Zambra × Zambra)) × ((Tropicana × Tropicana) × (Poppy Flash × Rusticana))*; Meilland, M.L.; Meilland, 1982. Bud conical; flowers vermilion, semi-dbl. (13 petals), medium; foliage bronze; vigorous, bushy growth. ADR, 1979.

La Sirène HP (OGR), *m*, 1867, (La Syrène); Soupert & Notting. Flowers dark reddish-purple.

La Somme HT, *or*, 1919, *Mme. Caroline Testout × Rayon d'Or*; Barbier. Flowers deep coral-red tinted copper, turning salmon, semi-dbl.; fragrant.

La Stupenda HT, *pb*, 1966, *Aztec × First Love*; Taylor, L.R. Bud long, pointed; flowers pink, reverse darker, very dbl., large; slightly fragrant; foliage glossy; upright, bushy growth.

La Sylphide T (OGR), *m*, Prior to 1848. Flowers pink tinted lavender, deeper in fall, semi-dbl.; tall.

La Tosca HT, *pb*, 1901, *Josephine Marot × Luciole*; Vve. Schwartz Flowers shell-pink, center and reverse darker, dbl., large (4 in.); fragrant; foliage rich green, leathery; vigorous, bushy growth.

La Tour d'Auvergne G (OGR), *or*, 1842, Vibert. Flowers deep rosy crimson, flecked carmine, dbl., incurved, large.

La Vaudoise HT, *mr*, 1946, Heizmann, E.; A. Meilland. Bud oval; flowers blood-red touched brilliant scarlet, dbl., medium; fragrant; foliage leathery; vigorous, bushy growth.

La Vie HT, *dr*, 1931, *Talisman sport*; Groshens. Flowers crimson to scarlet, base orange to carmine, fading to red.

La Ville de Bruxelles D (OGR), *dp*, 1849, (Ville de Bruxelles); Vibert. Flowers pink, full, flat, quartered, center incurved, large; foliage glossy, light green; height 5 ft.

La Virginale HP (OGR), *w*, 1858, (Mme. Liabaud); Lacharme. Flowers white with flesh center, dbl., medium; delicate habit.

La Voulzie F, *dr*, 1953, *Brise Parfumée × Alain*; Robichon. Flowers garnet-red, semi-dbl.,

very large, borne in clusters of 8-15; very vigorous growth.

Labareda F, *mr*, Moreira; da Silva. Flowers bright red.

L'Abondance N (OGR), *w*, 1877, Moreau & Robert. Flowers pure white.

Lac La Nonne HRg (S), *dp*, 1950, *R. rugosa plena × R. acicularis*; Bugnet; P.H. Wright. Bud pointed, deep red; flowers very deep pink, semi-dbl., medium (2-3 in.); fragrant; foliage light; vigorous (7-8 ft.) growth; hardy.

Lace Cascade LCl, *w*, 1992, (JACarch); *Iceberg × Prairie Fire*; Warriner, William; Bear Creek Gardens. Flowers white, full (26-40 petals), large (7.5-8.0 cms) blooms borne in small and large clusters; fragrant; foliage large, medium green to dark green, semi-glossy, mildew tolerant; some prickles; tall (150-160 cms), upright, spreading growth; basal shoots.

Lachs Pol, *or*, 1943, *Dick Koster sport*; Kordes. Flowers glowing orange-red, dbl., medium; slightly fragrant; foliage glossy; upright, bushy growth.

Lacre F, *mr*, 1963, *Concerto × Seedling*; Moreira; da Silva. Flowers bright red, semi-dbl., loose.

Laddie HT, *or*, 1926, McGredy; Beckwith. Flowers deep carmine, flushed orange and scarlet, base orange; bushy growth.

Ladies Choice HT, *pb*, 1969, *Liberty Bell × Prima Ballerina*; Anderson's Rose Nursery. Flowers cerise, reverse silvery, dbl., high pointed, large; very fragrant; foliage light green; free growth.

Ladies' Choice, Climbing Cl HT, *pb*, 1975, *Ladies' Choice sport*; Anderson's Rose Nursery. Flowers cerise, reverse silvery, dbl., high-pointed, large; very fragrant; foliage light green.

Ladies' View Min, *yb*, 1990, (SEAview); *You 'n' Me × Amber Queen*; McCann, Sean. Flowers yellow blend, moderately full (15-25 petals), small; slight fragrance; foliage small, medium green, semi-glossy; bushy growth.

Lady HT, *mp*, 1983, *Song of Paris × Royal Highness*; Weeks, O.L., 1984. Flowers medium pink, dbl. (35 petals), medium; foliage large, medium green, matt to semi-glossy; upright, compact growth.

Lady Alice Stanley HT, *pb*, 1909, McGredy. Bud pointed; flowers pale flesh-pink, reverse coral-rose, dbl. (75 petals), large; fragrant; foliage rich green, leathery; branching growth.

Lady Anderson HT, *pb*, 1920, Hall. Flowers coral pink to flesh pink and yellow, dbl.

Lady Ann Min, *mp*, 1961, *(R. wichuraiana × Floradora) × Little Buckaroo*; Moore, R.S.; Sequoia Nursery. Bud pointed; flowers rose-pink, dbl. (42 petals), cupped, medium (1¼ in.); fragrant; foliage leathery, glossy, dark; vigorous, bushy, low growth.

Lady Ann Kidwell Pol, *dp*, 1948, *Cécile Brunner × Seedling*; Krebs; Marsh's Nursery. Bud pointed; flowers deep pink, dbl., star-shaped, medium; slightly fragrant; foliage glossy; vigorous, upright growth.

Lady Ashtown HT, *pb*, 1904, *Mrs. W.J. Grant seedling*; Dickson, A. Bud pointed; flowers carmine-pink, base yellow, dbl. (43 petals), high-centered, large; slightly fragrant; foliage rich green, soft; vigorous, bushy growth.

Lady Ashtown, Climbing Cl HT, *pb*, 1909, Bradley.

Lady Baillie HSpn (OGR), *ly*, *R. spinosissima hybrid*; Lee, prior to 1848. Flowers pale sulphur, semi-dbl.; fruit black, glossy; foliage finely divided; dense, shrubby (3-4 ft.) growth; profuse, early bloom; possibly one parent of Harison's Yellow.

Lady Barbara LCl, *ob*, 1987, *Red Planet × (Elizabeth of Glamis × (Galway Bay × Sutter's Gold))*; Warner, C.H. Flowers tangerine, dbl. (20 petals), medium; fragrant; foliage medium, medium green, semi-glossy; upright growth.

Lady Barnby HT, *pb*, 1930, Dickson, A. Bud pointed; flowers glowing pink, shaded red, dbl., high-centered, large; fragrant; foliage rich green, leathery; bushy, low growth.

Lady Barnett HT, *dr*, 1957, Verschuren; Blaby Rose Gardens. Flowers crimson, reverse darker, high-centered; fragrant; vigorous, upright growth.

Lady Battersea HT, *pb*, 1901, (Red Niphetos); *Mme. Abel Chatenay × Liberty*; Paul. Flowers cherry-blossom, base orange, dbl.

Lady Be Good Min, *mp*, 1990, (SEAgood); *Kiss 'n' Tell × (Irish Mist × Matangi)*; McCann, Sean, 1991. Flowers medium pink, moderately full (15-25 petals); slight fragrance; foliage small, medium green, semi-glossy; bushy growth.

Lady Beatty HT, *lp*, 1918, Chaplin Bros. Flowers blush-pink, well formed; fragrant; vigorous growth.

Lady Beauty HT, *pb*, 1984, *Lady × Princess Takamatsu*; Kono, Yoshito, 1986. Bud ovoid; flowers light pink flushed yellow, reverse deeper, dbl. (33 petals), high-centered, large; slight fragrance; foliage medium, medium green, glossy; few sickle-shaped prickles; vigorous, upright growth.

Lady Belper HT, *ob*, 1948, *Mev. G.A. van Rossem × Seedling*; Verschuren; Gregory. Flowers bronze-orange shaded light orange, dbl. (38 petals), semi-globular, high-centered,

large (4 in.); fragrant; foliage glossy, dark; vigorous growth.

Lady Betty HT, *ab*, 1930, *Sunburst × Mrs. Aaron Ward*; Bees. Bud pointed; flowers apricot-pink, veined red, semi-dbl., high-centered; slightly fragrant.

Lady Beverley F, *lp*, *Independence sport*; Owens. Flowers clear pink.

Lady Bird F, *yb*, 1966, *Seedling × Rumba*; Hill, J.H., Co. Flowers yellow shaded red at edge, dbl., small, borne in clusters; slightly fragrant; foliage leathery; vigorous, bushy growth; for greenhouse use.

Lady Bird Johnson HT, *or*, 1971, *Montezuma × Hawaii*; Curtis, E.C.; Texas Rose Research Foundation. Bud long, pointed; flowers orange-red, dbl., medium; fragrant; vigorous, upright growth.

Lady Bissett HT, *ob*, 1928, Lilley. Flowers bright orange, reverse apricot.

Lady Blanche R., *w*, 1913, Walsh. Flowers snow-white, dbl., borne in large clusters; very fragrant; very vigorous, climbing growth; free bloom, sometimes repeated in fall.

Lady Bountiful LCl, *mr*, 1938, *American Pillar seedling*; Tait; B&A. Flowers scarlet-rose, center white, single, open, large, borne in clusters; foliage leathery, dark; very vigorous, climbing or trailing growth.

Lady Braye HT, *dp*, 1960, Verschuren; Gandy. Flowers deep rose-pink, long, pointed; foliage dark.

Lady Cahn HT, *ab*, 1937, Gaujard. Bud long, pointed; flowers rich apricot-yellow, veined darker, dbl. (40-50 petals), large; long, strong stems; vigorous growth.

Lady Canada HT, *mp*, 1927, *Mme. Butterfly × Premier*; Dale. Flowers bright rose, dbl.; fragrant.

Lady Carolina S, *lp*, 1990, *Lady Gay sport*; Jeremias, Lephon L. Bud ovoid; flowers blush pink, same reverse, aging to white, 35-40 petals, decorative, small blooms borne in sprays of 15-70; slight fragrance; foliage average, dark, glossy; prickles small, hooked, reddish-brown; fruit sound, very small, red; bushy, spreading, hedge-type, medium growth; repeats.

Lady Castlereagh T (OGR), *yb*, Flowers rosy yellow, well formed; vigorous growth.

Lady Catherine HT, *or*, 1973, *Montezuma × Rubaiyat*; Von Koss; Kern Rose Nursery. Bud urn shaped; flowers orange-red, dbl. (32-45 petals), high-centered, large (3½-4 in.); slightly fragrant; foliage leathery; vigorous, upright, compact growth.

Lady Charles Townshend HT, *ob*, 1931, *The Queen Alexandra Rose × Shot Silk*; Daniels

Bros. Flowers orange, overlaid salmon, dbl., globular, large; vigorous, bushy growth.

Lady Charmion HT, *mr*, 1923, *Lyon Rose × Gen. MacArthur*; Bees. Flowers bright cherry-carmine, dbl.; fragrant.

Lady Craig HT, *ly*, 1922, Dickson, H. Flowers cream-yellow, center apricot-yellow, full, well formed, large; fragrant; vigorous, free branching growth.

Lady Cromwell HT, *dr*, 1956, Verschuren; Gandy. Flowers crimson, base gold, dbl., large; foliage bronze; vigorous growth.

Lady Cunliffe Owen HT, *pb*, 1932, *Mrs. A.R. Barraclough sport*; Ley. Flowers salmon and cream, base yellow, flushed carmine-rose, dbl., high-centered, outer petals reflexed, large; fragrant; foliage leathery; vigorous growth.

Lady Curzon HRg (S), *mp*, 1901, *R. macrantha × R. rugosa rubra*; Turner. Flowers pink, single, large; fragrant; arching, prickly canes; vigorous growth; (21).

Lady Dallas Brooks HT, *mp*, 1955, *Peace sport*; Downes. Flowers pink.

Lady Dawson Bates HT, *yb*, 1939, McGredy. Flowers golden yellow, flushed pink, high-centered, opening cupped; fragrant; vigorous growth.

Lady Diana HT, *lp*, 1986, *Sonia × Caress*; Hoy, Lowell L.; Joseph H. Hill Co., 1983. Flowers light pink, dbl. (37 petals), high-centered, medium blooms in sprays of 3-4; slight fragrance; foliage medium, medium green, matt; short, hooked prickles; fruit ovoid, orange; tall, upright growth; greenhouse variety.

Lady Dixon HT, *ab*, 1919, Dickson, A. Flowers rich apricot, flushed salmon-pink, dbl.; fragrant.

Lady Dixon-Hartland HT, *pb*, 1923, Cant, B.R. Flower centers deep salmon, outer petals pale pink, high-centered; vigorous growth.

Lady Duncan HRg (S), *pb*, 1900, *R. wichuraiana × R. rugosa*; Dawson; Eastern Nursery. Flowers rich glowing pink, center and stamens yellow, single, medium (3 in.); foliage glossy; trailing (6 ft.) growth; non-recurrent bloom.

Lady Dunleath HT, *w*, 1913, Dickson, A. Flowers ivory-white edged yellow, dbl., small; fragrant.

Lady Edgeworth David HT, *mp*, 1939, *Seedling × Betty Uprichard*; Fitzhardinge; Hazlewood Bros. Bud long, pointed; flowers malmaison rose shaded soft pink, dbl., open, large; fragrant; foliage glossy; vigorous growth.

Lady Eleanore Cl HT, *yb*, 1923, *Gruss an Teplitz × Barbara*; Dreer. Flowers light yellow-cream splashed rose, center golden to copper.

Lady Elgin HT, *yb*, 1954, (MEmaj; Thaïs); *Mme. Kriloff × (Peace × Geneve)*; Meilland, F.; URS, 1954; C-P, 1957. Bud ovoid; flowers buff-yellow washed pink, dbl. (40 petals), cupped, large; fragrant; foliage dark, leathery; vigorous, upright, bushy growth.

Lady Elphinstone HT, *yb*, 1921, *Mme. Edouard Herriot sport*; Dobbie. Flowers indian yellow to clear rose, semi-dbl.

Lady Emily Peel N (OGR), *w*, 1862, *Blanche Lafitte × Sappho*; Lacharme. Flowers white, tinged with blush.

Lady English HT, *or*, 1934, Cant, B.R. Flowers bright cerise, center orange, dbl., open, very large; long stems; slightly fragrant; foliage glossy, bronze; vigorous growth.

Lady Eve Min, *op*, 1978, *Neue Revue × Sheri Anne*; Rovinski & Meredith; Casa de Rosa Domingo. Bud globular; flowers creamy white, edged coral-pink, dbl. (40 petals), high-centered, 1½-2 in.; slightly fragrant; vigorous, upright, tall, spreading growth.

Lady Evelyn Guinness HT, *mp*, 1932, *Ophelia sport*; Evans. Flowers pink.

Lady Fairbairn HT, *mp*, 1929, *Mme. Abel Chatenay × Seedling*; Clark, A.; NRS New South Wales. Flowers bright pink, dbl. (40 petals); vigorous, upright growth.

Lady Faire HT, *mp*, 1907, *Mrs. W.J. Grant sport*; Bentley. Flowers salmon-pink.

Lady Fairfax HT, *ob*, 1930, Cant, F. Flowers rose and orange-cerise, flushed orange to yellow, well formed; long stems; fragrant; foliage light green; vigorous growth.

Lady Florence Stronge HT, *lp*, 1925, McGredy. Bud pointed; flowers pale flesh, base pink and gold, dbl., high-centered, very large; slightly fragrant; foliage leathery, glossy; vigorous, bushy growth.

Lady Forteviot HT, *yb*, 1926, Cant, B. R., 1928. Flowers golden yellow to deep apricot, dbl., high-centered, large; very fragrant; foliage bronze, glossy; vigorous, bushy growth; (28). GM, NRS, 1927.

Lady Forteviot, Climbing Cl HT, *yb*, 1935, Howard Rose Co.

Lady Fraser HT, *mr*, 1941, *War Paint seedling*; Clark, A. Flowers rich red.

Lady Frost HT, *dp*, 1935, *Lady Alice Stanley × Dr. Herbert Hawkesworth*; Bees. Flowers deep rose, dbl., very large; very fragrant; foliage leathery; vigorous, bushy.

Lady Gay R, *op*, 1905, *R. wichuraiana × Bardou Job*; Walsh. Flowers orange-pink, dbl., medium blooms in clusters; foliage small, dark, glossy; vigorous climbing (12-20 ft.); very similar to Dorothy Perkins, but blooms later and is more resistant to mildew.

Lady Georgia HT, *pb*, 1973, *Miss Hillcrest × Peace*; Curtis, E.C.; Kimbrew. Flowers pink, base blending to ivory, dbl., full, medium; fragrant; foliage dark, leathery; very vigorous, bushy growth.

Lady Godiva R, *lp*, 1908, *Dorothy Perkins sport*; Paul. Flowers cameo-pink.

Lady Gowrie Cl HT, *my*, 1938, *Sunburst, Climbing × Rev. F. Page-Roberts*; Fitzhardinge; Hazlewood Bros. Bud long, pointed; flowers maize and champagne-yellow, very dbl., large; long stems; fragrant; foliage leathery, glossy, dark; very vigorous, climbing growth; intermittent bloom.

Lady Grade HT, *or*, 1982, (Lady Kathleen Grade); *Tropicana × Seedling*; Gregory, C. Flowers vermilion, dbl. (35 petals), large; fragrant; foliage large, medium green, semi-glossy; bushy growth.

Lady Greenall HT, *yb*, 1911, Dickson, A. Flowers saffron-yellow, edges tinted shell-pink, dbl.; fragrant.

Lady Greenall, Climbing Cl HT, *yb*, 1923, Lippiatt.

Lady Gwendoline Colvin Cl HT, *pb*, 1918, Chaplin Bros. Flowers apricot-salmon, shaded chrome-yellow, outer petals stained carmine, dbl.; fragrant; height 6-10 ft.

Lady Hailsham HT, *or*, 1951, *McGredy's Sunset sport*; Knight's Nursery. Bud pointed; flowers orange flushed red, dbl. (30 petals), medium (3 in.); very fragrant; foliage glossy; vigorous growth.

Lady Hamilton HSpn (OGR), *lp*, *R. spinosissima hybrid*. Flowers rosy blush, semi-dbl.; dwarf growth; profuse, non-recurrent bloom.

Lady Harriet HT, *op*, 1992, (WILherb); *Carla × Sonia*; Williams, J. Benjamin, 1993. Flowers coral and peach blend, deep orange washings on petals, full (26-40 petals), long cutting canes; large (7+ cms) blooms borne mostly singly; very fragrant; foliage large, dark green, semi-glossy; few prickles; tall (4-5 ft.), upright, bushy growth.

Lady Helen HT, *mp*, 1970, *Margaret × (McGredy's Ivory × Peace)*; McTeer, G.; Waterhouse Nursery. Flowers soft clear pink, dbl. (30 petals), pointed, large (5 in.); very fragrant; foliage glossy, dark; bushy growth.

Lady Helen Maglona HT, *dr*, 1926, Dickson, A. Bud pointed; flowers bright crimson-red to scarlet-red, center deeper, dbl., high-centered, very large; very fragrant; foliage leathery; vigorous, bushy growth. GM, NRS, 1926.

Lady Helen Stewart HP (OGR), *dr*, 1887, Dickson, A. Flowers bright crimson shaded scarlet, full; very fragrant; vigorous growth.

Lady Hillingdon T (OGR), *yb*, 1910, *Papa Gontier × Mme. Hoste*; Lowe & Shawyer. Bud long, pointed; flowers deep apricot-yellow, semi-dbl.; fragrant; foliage bronze; bushy growth; sometimes as hardy as a Hybrid Tea; (21).

Lady Hillingdon, Climbing Cl T, *yb*, 1917, Hicks.

Lady Hudson HT, *ab*, 1930, Chaplin Bros. Flowers deep apricot, dbl., large; vigorous growth.

Lady Huntingfield HT, *my*, 1937, *Busybody × Seedling*; Clark, A.; NRS Victoria. Flowers rich golden yellow, reverse lighter, dbl., globular, large; long stems; fragrant; vigorous, bushy growth.

Lady Iliffe HT, *mr*, 1976, *Saul × Wendy Cussons*; Gandy. Flowers tyrian rose, dbl. (38 petals), large (5 in.); very fragrant; foliage large.

Lady in Red Min, *rb*, 1988, (SEAlady); *Rise 'n' Shine × Siobhan*; McCann, Sean, 1990. Flowers red with touch of white at base of petals, dbl. (15-25 petals), small; slight fragrance; foliage small, medium green, semi-glossy; bushy growth.

Lady Inchiquin HT, *or*, 1922, Dickson, A. Flowers orange-vermilion, very dbl., high-centered, globular, large; slightly fragrant; foliage leathery, rich glossy green; very vigorous, bushy growth. GM, NRS, 1920.

Lady Jane HT, *dy*, 1992, *Dorothe × Helmut Schimdt*; Poole, Lionel, 1993. Flowers deep yellow, full (26-40 petals), large (7+ cms) blooms borne mostly single; slight fragrance; foliage medium, medium green, semi-glossy; some prickles; medium (75 cms), upright growth.

Lady Johnstone LCl, *dp*, 1922, *R. gigantea × Beauté Lyonnaise*; Nabonnand, P. Bud yellow; flowers reddish pink, turning lilac-rose, stamens yellow, single, large; fragrant; vigorous, climbing growth.

Lady Kathryn Min, *m*, 1989, *Lavender Jade × Angel Face*; Jolly, Marie; Rosehill Farm, 1991. Bud pointed; flowers lavender, aging brown, dbl. (22 petals), urn-shaped, exhibition, medium, borne usually singly and in sprays of 3-4; moderate, damask fragrance; foliage medium, medium green, semi-glossy, disease resistant; prickles none observed; fruit round, green-brown; upright, medium, vigorous growth.

Lady Lauder HT, *yb*, 1931, Morse. Flowers deep canary-yellow, reverse flushed crimson, dbl., cupped, long stems; foliage thick, light; very vigorous growth.

Lady Layton HT, *my*, 1932, *Joanna Hill sport*; Layton. Bud long, pointed; flowers light sunflower-yellow, deepening as it opens, large; fragrant; vigorous growth.

Lady Leconfield HT, *w*, 1939, Burbage Nursery; C-P. Bud long, pointed, cream, flushed pink; flowers cream-white, dbl. (25-30 petals), cupped; very fragrant; foliage leathery; vigorous, bushy growth.

Lady Le-Ru HRg (S), *dp*, 1963, *R. rugosa hybrid × Hybrid Tea Seedling*; Lothrop. Bud round; flowers deep pink, dbl. (50 petals), cupped, large (3½-4 in.), long stems; fragrant; thornless; moderate, open (2½ ft.) growth; free, non-recurrent bloom; hardy.

Lady Leslie HT, *rb*, 1929, McGredy. Flowers rosy scarlet to scarlet-carmine suffused saffron-yellow, dbl., high-centered, large; foliage dark, leathery, glossy; vigorous growth.

Lady Liberty HT, *w*, 1986, *Lady Diana sport*; DeVor, Tom, 1987. Flowers clear white, yellow at base, dbl. (35 petals), high-centered, large, borne usually singly or in sprays of 1-2, on extremely long stems; slight fragrance; foliage medium,, medium green, semi-glossy; straight, medium, light yellow prickles; fruit globular, medium green; upright, profuse growth.

Lady Like HT, *ob*, 1971, *Seedling × Tropicana*; Tantau; Ahrens & Sieberz. Bud globular; flowers dark orange, dbl., large; slightly fragrant; vigorous, upright.

Lady Lilford HT, *my*, 1930, *Independence Day sport*; Gregory. Flowers clear yellow, center deep golden yellow; slightly fragrant; foliage rich green, glossy; vigorous, bushy, branching, compact growth.

Lady Lou HT, *ob*, 1948, *Pink Princess × Shades of Autumn*; Brownell. Bud long, pointed; flowers coral-peach, dbl. (50 petals), high-centered, large to medium; fragrant; foliage glossy, light; vigorous, dwarf growth.

Lady Luck HT, *pb*, 1956, *Tom Breneman × Show Girl*; Miller, A.J.; Elmer Roses Co. Bud long, pointed; flowers blends of pale to rich pink, dbl. (38 petals), high-centered, large (4-4½ in.); very fragrant (damask); foliage dark, leathery; vigorous, upright, bushy.

Lady Mandeville HT, *my*, 1941, *Seedling × Mrs. Sam McGredy*; McGredy; J&P. Flowers yellow, flushed amber, dbl. (35 petals), well-formed, large (5 in.); slightly fragrant (fruity); foliage dark, bronze; branching, moderate growth.

Lady Mann HT, *pb*, 1940, *Lorraine Lee × Seedling*; Clark, A. Flowers rosy salmon.

Lady Margaret Stewart HT, *ob*, 1926, Dickson, A. Bud long, pointed; flowers golden yellow shaded and streaked orange and red, dbl., high-centered, very large; fragrant; foliage sage-green, leathery; vigorous, bushy growth. GM, NRS, 1926; Bagatelle, 1928.

Lady Marine HT, *or*, 1981, *Seedling × Tropicana*; DeLashmutt; Roseway Nursery. Flowers dark orange-red, dbl. (53 petals), urn-shaped to high-centered, borne 1-3 per cluster; fragrant; foliage dark, leathery; medium, reddish prickles; medium growth.

Lady Martha Bruce HT, *mp*, 1925, Ferguson, W. Flowers pink, outer petals tinged peach-blossom-pink.

Lady Mary Elizabeth HT, *dp*, 1927, Dickson, A. Bud pointed; flowers brilliant carmine-pink, dbl., high-centered, large; very fragrant; vigorous, bushy growth.

Lady Mary Fitzwilliam HT, *lp*, 1882, *Devoniensis × Victor Verdier*; Bennett. Flowers flesh-color, globular, large; very fragrant; vigorous growth; a famous parent rose.

Lady Mary Ward HT, *ob*, 1913, McGredy. Flowers orange, shaded deeper, dbl.; fragrant. GM, NRS, 1912.

Lady Maureen Stewart HT, *dr*, 1920, Dickson, A. Flowers velvety blackish scarlet-cerise, reflex orange-maroon, dbl.; fragrant.

Lady Maysie Robinson HT, *pb*, 1956, *Seedling × Peace*; Kordes. Flowers deep pink, center white, dbl. (22 petals), cupped, large; fragrant; foliage dark, glossy; vigorous, upright, bushy growth.

Lady Miller HT, *dr*, 1940, Clark, A. Flowers dark-red, well-formed; fragrant.

Lady Mitchell HT, *mr*, 1990, (HARyearn); *Dr. Darley × Silver Jubilee*; Harkness, R.; R. Harkness & Co., Ltd., 1991. Bud pointed; flowers deep rose-red, reverse to rose-red, paling with age, very dbl. (50 petals), cupped to reflexed, medium blooms borne usually singly or in sprays of 3; moderate fragrance; foliage medium, medium green, semi-glossy; prickles slightly declining, medium, green; bushy, low to medium growth.

Lady Mond HT, *w*, 1920, Paul, W. Flowers deep cream, outer petals shaded rose.

Lady Moyra Cavendish HT, *mr*, 1939, McGredy. Bud long, pointed; flowers bright strawberry-red, flushed crimson, dbl., high-centered; slightly fragrant; foliage glossy, dark; bushy growth.

Lady Nutting HT, *mp*, 1938, Wheatcroft Bros. Flowers soft salmon-pink, high-centered, large; foliage leathery, dark; vigorous growth.

Lady of Sky HT, *or*, 1974, *Queen Elizabeth × Seedling*; Gregory. Flowers orange-red, dbl.

(35 petals), high-centered; slightly fragrant; foliage dark; vigorous, upright growth.

Lady of Stifford F, *or*, 1982, *Matador sport*; Warley Rose Gdns., 1981. Flowers orange-red.

Lady of the Dawn® F, *lp*, 1984, (INTerlada); *INTerdress × Stadt den Helder*; Interplant. Flowers light pink, semi-dbl., large; slight fragrance; foliage large, medium green, matt; upright growth.

Lady Penzance E (OGR), *op*, 1894, (R. × *penzanceana* Rehder); *R. eglanteria × R. foetida bicolor*; Penzance. Flowers coppery salmon-pink with yellow stamens, single; foliage dark, fragrant (apple); very vigorous; summer bloom. The name *R. × penzanceana* is frequently but wrongly applied to all Penzance hybrids.

Lady Pirrie HT, *ab*, 1910, Dickson, H. Bud pointed; flowers apricot-yellow, reverse coppery, dbl., large; fragrant; vigorous, bushy growth. GM, NRS, 1909.

Lady Pirrie, Climbing Cl HT, *ab*, 1938, Seedling.

Lady Plymouth T (OGR), *w*, 1914, Dickson, A. Bud long, pointed; flowers deep ivory-cream, very faintly flushed, dbl., large; fragrant; foliage rich green, leathery; vigorous, bushy growth; many canes. GM, NRS, 1913.

Lady Rachel Verney HT, *mp*, 1935, *Annie Laurie × Lord Charlemont*; Bees. Flowers rose, base lemon, dbl., cupped, large; foliage glossy, bronze; vigorous, bushy growth.

Lady Reading Pol, *mr*, 1921, *Ellen Poulsen sport*; Van Kleef. Flowers clear red.

Lady Roberts T (OGR), *ab*, 1902, *Anna Olivier bud sport*; Cant, F. Flowers rich reddish apricot, base coppery red, edges shaded orange, dbl.; fragrant; vigorous growth.

Lady Rose® HT, *op*, 1979, (KORlady; *Seedling × Traumerei*; Kordes, W., Sons. Bud long, pointed; flowers orange-pink, dbl. (34 petals), high-centered, large (5 in.); fragrant; vigorous, upright, bushy growth. GM, Belfast, 1981.

Lady Roundway HT, *ab*, 1923, Cant, B.R. Flowers bright apricot-orange, fading to creamy buff, semi-dbl., open; slightly fragrant; vigorous, but stubby growth. GM, NRS, 1923.

Lady Sackville HT, *w*, 1933, Cant, B.R. Bud pointed; flowers pure white, dbl., high-centered, very large; fragrant; foliage leathery, bronze; very vigorous growth.

Lady Seton HT, *lp*, 1966, *Ma Perkins × Mischief*; McGredy, S., IV; McGredy. Flowers light pink, dbl. (35 petals), large (4½ in.); very fragrant; vigorous, tall growth.

Lady Somers HT, *lp*, 1930, *Comte G. de Rochemur × Scorcher*; Clark, A.; NRS Victoria. Flowers fresh pink, tinted flesh, full; slightly fragrant; foliage wrinkled, light; bushy growth.

Lady Sonia S, *my*, 1961, *Grandmaster × Doreen*; Mattock. Flowers golden yellow, dbl. (20 petals), large (4-4½ in.); foliage dark; vigorous, upright, branching growth.

Lady Stanley T (OGR), *dr*, Bud long; flowers crimson, full, very large; fragrant.

Lady Stuart HCh (OGR), *lp*, 1851, Portemer. Flowers flesh pink to blush; leaflets 5-7.

Lady Sunblaze™ Min, *lp*, 1986, (MEIlarco; Peace Meillandina; Lady Meillandina Peace Sunblaze); *(Fashion × Zambra) × Belle Meillandina*; Meilland, Mrs. M.L., 1987. Flowers pale orient pink to light coral pink, very full (over 40 petals), medium; no fragrance; foliage, small, dark green, glossy; bushy growth.

Lady Sunshine HT, *my*, 1965, *Belle Étoile × (Michèle Meilland × Tawny Gold)*; Lens; Spek. Bud ovoid; flowers yellow, very dbl., large; very fragrant; foliage dark.

Lady Susan Birch HT, *ab*, 1934, Cant, B.R. Bud pointed; flowers apricot, full, high-centered, large; fragrant; foliage glossy, dark; vigorous, bushy growth.

Lady Suzanne HT, *w*, 1985, *Lady × x Flaming Beauty*; Bridges, Dennis A.; Bridges Roses. Flowers creamy white, dbl. (32 petals), exhibition, large; slight fragrance; foliage large, dark, glossy; bushy growth.

Lady Sydney Eardley-Wilmot HT, *mp*, 1925, Chaplin Bros. Flowers coppery reddish salmon, tinted fawn and apricot, semi-dbl.; fragrant.

Lady Sylvia HT, *lp*, 1926, *Mme. Butterfly sport*; Stevens, W. Flowers light pink.

Lady Sylvia, Climbing Cl HT, *pb*, 1933, Stevens, W.; Low.

Lady Tervueren Pol, *mr*, 1969, *Allotria × Seedling*; Buisman. Flowers red, dbl., medium to small; foliage dark.

Lady Trent HT, *ob*, 1940, (Julia Ferran); *Rosieriste Gaston Lévêque × Federico Casas*; Dot, P.; Wheatcroft Bros. Flowers coppery orange, dbl. (46 petals), high-centered, large; fragrant; foliage dark, glossy; vigorous growth.

Lady Ursula HT, *pb*, 1908, Dickson, A.; Flowers pink fading lighter, reverse cameo-pink, base lemon, very dbl., high-centered, large; slightly fragrant; foliage dark, leathery, glossy; vigorous, bushy growth.

Lady Venables Vernon HT, *lp*, 1922, *Mrs. Amy Hammond × Sir Alexander N. Rochfort*; Jersey Nursery. Flowers soft flesh-color, overlaid blush; fragrant.

Lady Vera HT, *pb*, 1974, *Royal Highness* × *Christian Dior*; Smith, R.W.; Brundrett. Flowers silvery pink, reverse rose-pink, full; slightly fragrant; vigorous growth.

Lady Verey HT, *mp*, 1922, Hicks. Flowers rose-pink, dbl.; fragrant.

Lady Violet Astor HT, *dp*, 1933, Cant, B.R. Flowers deep rose-pink, full, high-centered, very large; slightly fragrant; foliage leathery; vigorous growth.

Lady Wakefield HT, *ab*, 1926, Cant, B.R. Flowers bright apricot; fragrant.

Lady Waterlow Cl HT, *pb*, 1903, *La France de '89* × *Mme. Marie Lavalley*; Nabonnand, G. Flowers salmon-pink edged carmine, full, large; vigorous (8-10 ft.) growth.

Lady Wenlock HT, *lp*, 1904, Bernaix, P. Flowers china-pink tinted apricot.

Lady Willingdon HT, *lp*, 1928, *Ophelia* × *Premier*; Dale. Flowers very light pink, dbl., large; fragrant; foliage rich green, glossy; vigorous growth.

Lady Woodward HT, *lp*, 1959, *Heinrich Wendland* × *Elli Knab*; Riethmuller. Bud long, pointed; flowers pink veined, dbl., high-centered, large; fragrant; foliage dark, glossy; vigorous, upright, bushy growth.

Lady Worthington Evans HT, *dr*, 1926, Dickson, A. Bud pointed; flowers deep crimson shaded blackish, semi-dbl., high-centered; fragrant; foliage bronze, leathery; vigorous, bushy growth. GM, NRS, 1926.

Lady X HT, *m*, 1965, (MEIfigu); *Seedling* × *Simone*; Meilland, M.L.; C-P, 1966. Bud long, pointed; flowers mauve, dbl., high-centered, large; slightly fragrant; foliage leathery; vigorous, upright. GM, Portland, 1968.

Lady X, Climbing Cl HT, *m*, 1976, Takatori; Japan Rose Nursery.

Lady Zia HT, *or*, 1959, *Peace* × *Independence*; Park; Harkness. Flowers light orange-scarlet, dbl. (50 petals), well-formed, large (5-6 in.); fragrant; foliage dark, glossy; vigorous. GM, NRS, 1959.

Ladybug Min, *mr*, 1992, (MORbug); *Sheri Anne* × *Cherry Magic*; Moore, Ralph S.; Sequoia Nursery, 1993. Flowers medium red, semi-dbl. (6-14 petals), small (0-4 cms) blooms borne in small clusters; slight fragrance; foliage small, medium green, semi-glossy; few prickles; low (30-40 cms), bushy, compact growth; fast repeat.

Ladylove HT, *mp*, 1926, *Ophelia* × *Seedling*; McGredy; Beckwith. Flowers light rose-pink fading hydrangea-pink, flushed apricot, full, well shaped; very fragrant; foliage dark; very vigorous growth.

Lafayette F, *dp*, 1924, (Joseph Guy; August Kordes); *Rodhatte* × *Richmond*; Nonin; H&S; Dreer. Flowers bright cherry-crimson, semi-dbl., cupped, large blooms in clusters (up to 40); slightly fragrant; foliage rich green, glossy; vigorous, bushy growth.

L'Africaine LCl, *dr*, 1953, *Guinée* × *Crimson Glory*; Mallerin; EFR. Flowers garnet shaded coppery, well formed, large, borne in clusters on strong stems; very vigorous growth; abundant early bloom, not recurrent.

Lafter HT, *yb*, 1948, (V for Victory × *(Général Jacqueminot* × *Dr. W. Van Fleet))* × *Pink Princess*; Brownell. Bud pointed; flowers salmon-yellow, dbl. (23 petals), large (4 in.); fragrant; vigorous, upright, branching growth.

Lagerfeld™ Gr, *m*, 1986, (AROlaqueli; Starlight); *Blue Nile* × *(Ivory Tower* × *Angel Face)*; Christensen; Armstrong Roses, 1985. Flowers silvery lavender, dbl. (30 petals), high-centered, exhibition, 4-5 in. blooms in sprays of 5-15; intense fragrance; foliage medium, medium green, matt; medium, light brown prickles, hooked downward; fruit large, orange, globular; tall, upright, bushy growth.

Lagerfeuer® F, *mr*, 1958, (Feu de Camp); *Red Favorite* × *Kathe Duvigneau*; Tantau, Math. Bud pointed; flowers velvety scarlet, dbl., large blooms in clusters; slightly fragrant; foliage leathery, dark; vigorous, upright growth.

Lagoon F, *m*, 1970, *Lilac Charm* × *Sterling Silver*; Harkness, 1973. Flowers lilac, reverse darker, gold stamens, single (7 petals), medium (2½ in.); fragrant; foliage glossy.

Laguna HT, *or*, 1974, *Hawaii* × *Orange Delbard*; Kordes; Horstmann. Bud large, long, pointed; flowers orange-red, dbl., cupped; fragrant; foliage glossy; vigorous, upright growth.

Laila F, *ob*, 1968, *Orangeade seedling*; Abdullah. Flowers bright orange, dbl., well formed, borne on trusses; slightly fragrant; foliage glossy; vigorous growth.

Lake Como F, *m*, 1968, *Lilac Charm* × *Sterling Silver*; Harkness. Flowers lilac, semi-dbl., blooms in trusses; very fragrant.

Lakeland HT, *lp*, 1976, *Fragrant Cloud* × *Queen Elizabeth*; Fryer, G.; Fryer's Nursery. Flowers soft shell-pink, dbl. (36 petals), large (5-6 in.); slightly fragrant.

Lal HT, *pb*, 1933, *Commonwealth* × *Florence L. Izzard*; Easlea. Bud long, pointed; flowers deep salmon pink, suffused yellow; very fragrant; foliage dark; vigorous growth.

Lalima HT, *mr*, 1978, *Picture* × *Jour d'Été*; Pal, Dr. B.P.; K.S.G. Sons. Flowers medium red, dbl. (50 petals), high-centered, large blooms borne singly; strong fragrance; foliage large; vigorous, upright growth.

Lallita HT, *mp*, 1929, *Prés. Briand* × *Seedling*; Mallerin. Flowers rose, dbl., very large; long, strong stems; slightly fragrant; foliage rich green, leathery.

Lamarque N (OGR), *w*, 1830, *Blush Noisette* × *Parks' Yellow Tea-scented China*; Marechal. Flowers pure white, center lemon-yellow, dbl., blooms in clusters; very fragrant; vigorous, climbing growth; long, trailing shoots.

Lamartine HT, *op*, 1943, Meilland, F. Flowers pearly pink shaded orange, dbl.

Lamia HT, *or*, 1918, Easlea. Bud rich apricot; flowers intense reddish orange, semi-dbl.; vigorous growth. GM, NRS, 1918.

Lampion F, *or*, 1957, *Fanal* × *Käthe Duvigneau*; Tantau, Math. Bud pointed; flowers blood-red shaded orange, single (5 petals), open, large, borne in large clusters; slightly fragrant; foliage dark, leathery, glossy; dwarf, bushy growth.

Lamplighter Cl HT, 1948, *Talisman* × *Gold Rush*; Duehrsen; California Roses. Flowers blend similar to Talisman and Autumn, dbl., globular, large; very fragrant; foliage leathery; very vigorous, climbing (10-15 ft.) growth.

Lamplighter HT, *pb*, 1950, *Sam McGredy* × *Seedling*; McGredy. Flowers salmon-rose, reverse gold, dbl. (37 petals), high-centered, very large; slightly fragrant; foliage bronze; vigorous growth.

Lamplighter HT, *yb*, 1959, *Peace* × *Yellow Perfection*; Hill, J.H., Co. Bud long, pointed; flowers mimosa-yellow, dbl. (55-60 petals), high-centered to open, large (4-4^1/$_2$ in.); strong stems; fragrant; foliage dark, semi-glossy, leathery; vigorous, upright growth; for greenhouse use.

Lancashire HT, *mr*, 1950, *Christopher Stone* × *Seedling*; Wright, R. Flowers fiery red; very fragrant.

Lancashire Lass HT, *mr*, 1939, Archer. Bud well shaped, crimson; flowers scarlet-cerise, semi-dbl.; fragrant; foliage glossy, dark; vigorous growth.

Lancashire Life F, *or*, 1984, (RUIlanca); *Robert Stolz* × *Diablotin*; DeRuiter, G.; Fryer's Nursery. Flower scarlet, semi-dbl., medium blooms in clusters; slight fragrance; foliage medium, medium green, semi-glossy; bushy growth.

Lancaster Cl HT, *mr*, 1962, *Pres. Eisenhower* sport; Hicks, S.J.; C-P. Bud ovoid; flowers medium rose-red, dbl. (35-40 petals), high-centered, large (5 in.); very fragrant; foliage leathery, dark; vigorous growth.

Lancastrian HT, *mr*, 1965, *Ena Harkness* × *Seedling*; Gregory. Flowers crimson-scarlet, dbl. (40 petals), large (3^1/$_2$-4 in.); very fragrant; foliage light green, glossy; vigorous, upright growth.

Lance Hird HT, *mp*, 1973, *Seedling* × *Greetings*; Wood; Wood Roses. Flowers deep pink, reverse lighter, dbl. (20-30 petals), full, large (4 in.); slightly fragrant; free growth.

Lancier HT, *dr*, 1959, *Karl Herbst* × *Seedling*; Mallerin; Vilmorin-Andrieux. Flowers crimson-red.

Lancôme® HT, *dp*, 1986, (DELboip); *(Dr. Albert Schweitzer* × *(Michèle Meilland* × *Bayadere))* × *(MEImet* × *Present Filial)*; Delbard, 1973. Flowers deep pink, dbl. (28 petals), high-centered, exhibition, large; no fragrance; vigorous, upright, bushy growth; greenhouse variety.

Lander Gold Min, *my*, 1986, (MICgold); *Rise 'n' Shine* × *Little Jackie*; Williams, Michael C.; The Rose Garden. Flowers medium yellow, dbl. (36 petals), high-centered, medium blooms borne usually singly; fruity fragrance; foliage medium, medium green, semi-glossy; very few, small, straight prickles; fruit none; medium, bushy growth.

LANdia HT, *ab*, 1988, (Anne Diamond); *Mildred Reynolds* × *Arthur Bell*; Sealand Nursery, Ltd. Bud pointed; flowers apricot, reverse pink, aging apricot, dbl. (38 petals), urn-shaped, medium, borne in sprays of 3-4; foliage medium, dark green, semi-glossy; prickles slightly hooked, brown; upright, bushy growth.

Landour Cl HT, *w*, 1978, *Self seedling of Peace*; Thakur; Doon Valley Roses. Bud oval; flowers white, dbl. (40 petals), high-centered, very large (6-6^1/$_2$ in.); fragrant (fruity); foliage large, glossy, dark, leathery; upright growth; intermittent bloom.

Laneii M (OGR), *mr*, 1845, (Lane; Lane's Moss); Laffay, 1845; Int. into England by Lane & Son, ca. 1846. Bud large, globular, well-mossed; flowers rosy crimson, occasionally tinted purple, full, globular, large; foliage large, bright green, 5 leaflets; free of mildew; difficult to propagate from cuttings; robust growth.

Langford LCl, *dp*, *R. setigera seedling*; Preston; Central Exp. Farm. Flowers nearly red, dbl.; free bloom; needs protection in cold areas.

Langford Light Min, *w*, 1985, (LANnie); *Ballerina* × *Little Flirt*; Sealand Nursery, 1984. Flowers white, bright yellow stamens, semi-dbl., small; fragrant; foliage medium, dark, matt; bushy growth.

Langley HT, *dy*, 1942, *Mrs. Sam McGredy* × *Phyllis Gold*; Eacott; Ley. Bud streaked red; flowers clear deep yellow, edges flushed old-gold, dbl. (50 petals), large (4-5 in.); fragrant; foliage bronze, dark; a greenhouse variety.

Langley Gem F, *dp*, 1939, *Karen Poulsen* × *R. moyesii*; Eacott; R. Murrell. Flowers scarlet-cerise, single, open, borne in clusters on strong stems; foliage leathery, bronze; various growth.

Lanvin™ HT, *ly*, 1986, (AROlemo); *Seedling* × *Katherine Loker*; Christensen; Armstrong Nursery, 1985. Flowers light yellow, dbl. (30 petals), high-centered, exhibition, medium blooms in sprays of 3-5; fragrant; foliage medium, dark green tinted red, semi-glossy; medium, straight, light brown to red prickles; fruit none; medium, upright; bushy.

Lapponia® F, *op*, 1978, (TANnipola); Tantau. Bud broadly ovoid; flowers medium salmon-pink, dbl. (25 petals); slightly fragrant; bushy, upright growth.

Lara HT, *op*, 1967, *Tropicana* × *Romantica*; Kriloff; Cramphorn's Nursery. Flowers salmon-carmine, dbl. (38 petals), well-formed, large; slightly fragrant; foliage dark, glossy; vigorous, tall growth.

Larado Min, *mr*, 1991, (SPOlar); *Tobo Yellow* × *Seedling*; Spooner, Ray; Oregon Miniature Roses, 1992. Flowers bright, clear red with small white eye in center, semi-dbl. (6-14 petals), compact, small (0-4 cms) blooms borne singly; micro-mini; no fragrance; foliage small, medium green, semi-glossy; low (15 cms), bushy growth.

Largo d'Haendel HT, *dp*, 1947, (Handel's Largo); Mallerin; URS. Flowers reddish apricot to salmon-carmine.

Larissa® F, *mr*, 1987, (KORdodo); *(Seedling* × *Marina)* × *Rumba*; Kordes, W., 1989. Flowers medium red, dbl. (26-40 petals), medium; no fragrance; foliage small, medium green, semi-glossy; spreading growth.

Larry Burnett HSpn (OGR), *w*, 1925, *R. acicularis* × *R. spinosissima*; Skinner. Flowers blush-white, center deeper, semi-dbl, cupped, large (3½ in.), short stems; very fragrant; foliage small, rich green, soft; vigorous, bushy, spreading growth; profuse bloom; very hardy.

Larry's Surprize Min, *dy*, 1990, (RENlarry); *Golden Rule* × *Rise 'n' Shine*; Rennie, Bruce; Rennie Roses International, 1991. Flowers deep yellow, semi-dbl. (6-14 petals), small, borne mostly singly; slight fragrance; foliage small, light green, matt; bushy (15 in.) growth.

Las Vegas HT, *pb*, 1957, *Charlotte Armstrong* × *Mission Bells*; Whisler; Germain's. Bud long, pointed; flowers salmon-pink, reverse darker, dbl. (25-30 petals), high-centered to open, large (5 in.); slightly fragrant; foliage leathery; vigorous, bushy growth. RULED EXTINCT 6/80.

Las Vegas® HT, *ob*, 1981, (KORgane); *Ludwigshafen am Rhein* × *Feuerzauber*; Kordes, W. Bud large, pointed; flowers deep orange, reverse lighter, dbl. (26 petals), blooms borne 1-3 per cluster; fragrant; foliage green, slightly glossy; brown prickles; vigorous, upright, bushy growth. GM, Genova, 1985 & Portland, 1988.

Lasker HT, *pb*, 1979, *South Seas* × *Oregold*; Perry, Astor. Bud very long; flowers pink blend, dbl. (40 petals), classic HT blooms borne singly; fragrant; foliage glossy; curved prickles; tall growth.

Lassie HT, *pb*, 1946, *Picture sport*; Tuttle Bros. Nursery. Bud long, pointed; flowers shell-pink, base canary-yellow, dbl., high-centered; fragrant; foliage leathery; vigorous, compact growth.

Latan HT, 1979, *Lady* × *x Bronze Masterpiece*; Williams, J.B.; J.B. Williams & Associates. Bud long; flowers light lavender-tan, dbl. (43 petals), high-centered, large (4½-5½ in.); very fragrant; foliage leathery; upright, bushy growth.

Lathom Chapel F, *w*, 1973, *Orange Sensation* × *Sutter's Gold*; Ellick. Flowers buff-cream, blended to white, dbl. (20-25 petals), full, large (4 in.); very fragrant; vigorous growth.

Lathom Park F, *dp*, 1972, *Orange Sensation* × *Ballet*; Ellick. Flowers carmine, dbl. (40 petals), full, large (4in.); slightly fragrant; foliage glossy, light; vigorous growth.

Lathom Sunrise F, *ob*, 1973, *(Orange Sensation* × *Ballet)* × *Sutter's Gold*; Ellick. Flowers orange-flame, dbl. (25-30 petals), full, large (4 in.); very fragrant; vigorous growth.

Lathom Sunset HT, *ob*, 1973, *Karl Herbst* × *Mischief*; Ellick. Flowers orange-yellow, pink and red, dbl. (20-25 petals), full, large (4½ in.); fragrant; vigorous growth.

Lathom Twilight HT, *m*, 1973, *Karl Herbst* × *Mischief*; Ellick. Flowers deep purple to indian lake, dbl. (28-30 petals), full, large (5 in.); very fragrant; foliage dark; vigorous growth.

Laughter Lines F, *pb*, 1986, (DICkerry); *(Pye colour* × *Sunday Times)* × *Eyepaint*; Dickson, Patrick. Flowers pink blend, semi-dbl. (6-14 petals), large; slight fragrance; foliage small, medium green, semi-glossy; bushy growth. GM, RNRS, 1984.

Laura HT, *op*, 1969, *((Happiness × Independence) × Better Times) × (Baccará × White Knight)*; Meilland, M.L.; C-P. Flowers coral-pink, dbl., high-centered, large; fragrant; foliage leathery; vigorous, upright, bushy growth.

Laura Anne HT, *op*, 1992, (COCclarion); *((Sabine × Circus) × Maxi) × Harriny*; Cocker, James; James Cocker & Sons, 1990. Flowers pink flushed orange, full (26-40 petals), large (7+ cms) blooms borne in large clusters; fragrant; foliage large, medium green, glossy; some prickles; bushy (76.20 cms) growth.

Laura Ashley Cl Min, *m*, 1989, (CHEWharla); *Marjorie Fair × Nozomi*; Warner, C.H.; R. Harkness & Co., Ltd., 1991. Bud pointed; flowers lilac-mauve pink, reverse pink, aging same, single, loose, small, borne in sprays of 10-30; moderate fruity fragrance; foliage small, medium green, semi-glossy; prickles hooked, small, brown; fruit oval, small, red; spreading, low growth.

Laura Ford® Cl Min, *my*, 1989, (CHEWarvel; Normandie); *Anna Ford × (Elizabeth of Glamis × (Galway Bay × Sutter's Gold))*; Warner, C.H., 1990. Bud pointed; flowers medium yellow, reverse lighter yellow, aging pink flushes, dbl. (22 petals), high-centered, small, borne in sprays of 5-10; slight, fruity fragrance; foliage small, light green, glossy; prickles straight, small, infrequent, light brown; fruit round, large, average; upright, bushy, tall growth.

Laura Towill HT, *yb*, 1929, *Phantom × Buttercup*; Towill. Flowers copper-yellow, becoming copper-pink, semi-dbl.; slightly fragrant.

Lauré Davoust HMult (OGR), *lp*, 1834, (Marjorie W. Lester); Laffay. Flowers clear pink, fading to flesh, then white, dbl., cupped, small blooms in clusters; non-recurrent.

Lauré Soupert R, *ly*, 1927, *Tausendschön × George Elger*; Soupert; Notting. Flowers yellowish white to pure white, dbl., small blooms in clusters of 80-100 on strong stems; very fragrant; foliage small, glossy; vigorous, climbing or trailing growth; recurrent bloom.

Laureate F, *m*, 1989, *Baby Talk × Angel Face*; Jobson, Daniel J. Bud pointed; flowers lavender with pink highlights, aging lighter, dbl. (33 moderately ruffled petals), urn-shaped, exhibition, medium, borne in sprays of 3-5; slight fruity fragrance; foliage medium, dark green, glossy, disease resistant; prickles straight, medium, red; fruit none observed; upright, bushy, medium, winter-hardy growth.

Laurelle F, *m*, 1966, *Rumba × Lavender Princess*; Harris, J.R.; Paulen Park Nursery. Flowers lavender-pink, base veined lemon, dbl.,

borne in clusters; fragrant; foliage glossy; vigorous, bushy growth.

Lauren Elizabeth HT, *m*, 1991, (ORTlae); *Moonlight × Seedling*; Ortega, Carlos, 1992. Flowers mauve blend, full, large blooms borne mostly singly; very fragrance; foliage large, dark green, matt; tall, upright growth.

Laurent Carle HT, *mr*, 1907, Pernet-Ducher. Flowers brilliant velvety carmine, dbl., open, large; very fragrant; foliage rich green, soft; bushy growth.

Laurent Carle, Climbing Cl HT, *mr*, 1923, Rosen, L.P.

Laurent Carle, Climbing Cl HT, *mr*, 1924, Mermet.

Laurie HT, *lp*, 1970, *Princesse sport*; Scott, D.H. Flowers creamy pale pink, tipped salmon, dbl. (28 petals), full, large (5 in.); fragrant; foliage matt green; vigorous growth.

Lavaglut® F, *dr*, 1978, (KORlech; Intrigue; Lavaglow); *Gruss an Bayern × Seedling*; Kordes, W., Sons, 1979. Flowers dark red, dbl. (24 petals), globular, medium (2½ in.) blooms in clusters; slightly fragrant; foliage glossy; vigorous, upright, bushy growth.

LAValier Min, *dp*, 1989, *Loving Touch × (Honest Abe × Seedling)*; Laver, Keith G.; Springwood Roses. Bud pointed; flowers deep mauve-pink, reverse medium pink, dbl. (50 petals), cupped, small, borne singly; no fragrance; foliage small, medium green, matt, disease resistant; prickles straight, small, light brown; fruit round, red; upright, bushy, low, prolific growth.

LAValuck Min, *dp*, 1989, *Blueblood × Julie Ann*; Laver, Keith G.; Springwood Roses. Bud pointed; flowers vivid, deep cherry pink, aging fuchsia, dbl. (28 petals), urn-shaped, small, borne singly; no fragrance; foliage small, medium green, matt, long sepals, disease resistant; prickles none; fruit ovoid, orange-red; bushy, low growth.

LAVamaze Min, *lp*, 1989, *Loving Touch × Potluck*; Laver, Keith; Springwood Roses. Bud ovoid; flowers light pink with deeper center, reverse light pink, very dbl. (80 petals), exhibition, full, small, borne singly; moderate fragrance; foliage small, medium green to red, disease resistant; prickles straight, narrow, red; fruit round, orange-red; bushy, low growth.

LAVbound Min, *op*, 1989, *June Laver × Black Jade*; Laver, Keith G.; Springwood Roses. Bud pointed; flowers coral to orange-pink, outer petals pink-apricot, reverse pink with yellow base, dbl. (53 petals), high-centered, exhibition, medium, borne singly; no fragrance; foliage medium, medium green, semi-glossy, disease resistant; upright, bushy, low, prolific growth.

Laveena HT, *yb*, 1969, *Kiss of Fire* × *Seedling*; Laveena Roses. Bud long, pointed; flowers yellow tinged pinkish, dbl., high-centered, large; foliage glossy; vigorous, upright, compact growth.

Lavendale Min, *m*, 1989, *Lavender Jade* × *Angel Face*; Jolly, Marie; Rosehill Farm, 1990. Bud pointed; flowers deep lavender, dbl. (40 petals), high-centered, exhibition, medium, borne singly; heavy fragrance; foliage medium, medium green, semi-glossy; prickles none; fruit round, greenish-brown; upright, bushy, medium, vigorous growth.

Lavender Bird HT, *m*, 1964, Herholdt, J.A.; Herholdt's Nursery. Bud long, spiral, pointed; flowers lavender-pink, dbl., well formed, large; fragrant (lavender); vigorous growth.

Lavender Blue HT, *m*, 1982, (LEOlavblu); *Silver Star* × *Kolner Karneval*; Leon, Charles F., Sr. Flowers lavender, darker edges, dbl. (40+ petals), high-centered, large; very fragrant; foliage medium, dark, semi-glossy; upright, bushy growth.

Lavender Charm HT, *m*, 1964, *Brownie* × *Sterling Silver*; Boerner; J&P. Flowers persian lilac, dbl. (45-50 petals), cupped, large (4½-5 in.); very fragrant; foliage dark, leathery; vigorous, bushy growth.

Lavender Dream® S, *m*, 1984, (INTerlav); *Yesterday* × *Nastarana*; Interplant, 1985. Flowers deep lilac pink, semi-dbl. (16 petals), medium blooms in clusters; no fragrance; foliage medium, light green, matt; few medium prickles; bushy growth; repeat bloom. ADR, 1987.

Lavender Garnette F, *m*, 1958, *Grey Pearl seedling* × *Garnette*; Boerner; J&P. Bud globular; flowers lavender, dbl. (35-45 petals), open, medium; fragrant; foliage leathery; vigorous, bushy growth; a greenhouse variety.

Lavender Girl F, *m*, 1958, *Fantastique* × *(Ampere* × *(Charles P. Kilham* × *Capucine Chambard))*; Meilland, F.; C-P. Flowers rosy purple, reverse magenta, changing to lavender, dbl. (35-42 petals), cupped, large (3½ in.), borne in clusters; fragrant (spicy); dwarf, bushy growth.

Lavender Jade™ Min, *m*, 1987, (BENalav); *Rise 'n' Shine* × *Laguna*; Benardella, Frank; Nor'East Miniature Roses, 1987. Flowers lavender-white bicolor-mauve blend, dbl. (32-35 petals), high-centered, exhibition, large, borne usually singly; heavy, damask fragrance; foliage medium, dark green, semiglossy; short, straight prickles; fruit none observed; upright, tall growth for a miniature.

Lavender Jewel Min, *m*, 1978, *Little Chief* × *Angel Face*; Moore, R.S.; Sequoia Nursery. Bud pointed; flowers clear lavender-mauve, dbl. (38 petals), high-centered, small (1 in.); slightly fragrant; foliage dark; compact, bushy growth.

Lavender Lace Min, *m*, 1968, *Ellen Poulsen* × *Debbie*; Moore, R.S.; Sequoia Nursery. Flowers lavender, dbl., high-centered, small; fragrant; foliage small, glossy; vigorous, bushy dwarf growth. AOE, 1975.

Lavender Lace, Climbing Cl Min, *m*, 1971, Rumsey.

Lavender Lady F, *m*, 1956, *Seedling* × *Lavender Pinocchio*; LeGrice. Flowers pastel mauve, semi-dbl., large, borne in clusters; fragrant; vigorous, upright growth.

Lavender Lassie HMsk (S), *m*, 1960, Kordes; Morse. Flowers lilac-pink, dbl., medium (3 in.) blooms in large clusters; very fragrant; very vigorous, tall growth.

Lavender Love F, *m*, 1964, *Fashion* × *Floradora*; Daugherty; Wyant. Flowers lavender, medium; low growth.

Lavender Mist LCl, *m*, 1981, (Mystic Mauve); *Angel Face* × *Allspice*; Christensen; Armstrong Nursery. Bud ovoid; flowers mauve, dbl. (35 petals), borne mostly 3 per cluster; slight tea fragrance; foliage large; medium prickles, hooked downward; vigorous, long arching canes.

Lavender Pearl HT, *m*, 1976, *Blue Moon* × *Grandpa Dickson*; Shaw. Flowers lavender center shading to pearl, dbl. (40 petals), full, medium (3½ in.); fragrant (lemon); foliage small; moderate, bushy growth.

Lavender Pinocchio F, *m*, 1948, *Pinocchio* × *Grey Pearl*; Boerner; J&P. Bud ovoid, light chocolate-olive-brown; flowers pink-lavender, dbl. (28 petals), large (3-3½ in.) blooms in clusters; fragrant; vigorous, bushy, compact growth.

Lavender Princess F, *m*, 1959, *World's Fair seedling* × *Lavender Pinocchio seedling*; Boerner; J&P. Bud ovoid; flowers lavender, lightly overcast purplish lilac, dbl. (25 petals), open, large (3½-4 in.), borne in large clusters; fragrant (fruity); foliage leathery; vigorous, upright growth.

Lavender Queen HT, *m*, 1951, Raffel; Port Stockton Nursery. Bud pointed, touched red; flowers pinkish, lavender, dbl. (20-35 petals), cupped, large (5-6 in.); fragrant; vigorous growth.

Lavender Simplex™ Min, *m*, 1984, (MINtco); *Angel Face* × *Yellow Jewel*; Williams, E.D.;

Mini-Roses. Flowers lavender, purple stamens, single (5 petals), small blooms borne singly; fragrant; foliage small, dark, semi-glossy; upright, bushy growth.

Lavender Star™ Min, *m*, 1988, (MINauco); *Seedling × Lavender Simplex*; Williams, Ernest, 1989. Flowers mauve blended lavender-tan, single (5 petals), small; very fragrant; foliage small, dark green, semi-glossy; upright, bushy, dense growth.

Lavender Sweetheart™ Min, *m*, 1984, (WILlash); *Double Feature × Miniature seedling*; Williams, J.B.; J.B. Williams & Assoc. Flowers deep blue lavender, dbl. (20 petals), HT form, small, borne singly; very fragrant; foliage small, dark, semi-glossy; bushy growth.

Lavendula F, *m*, 1965, *Magenta × Sterling Silver*; Kordes, R.; McGredy. Flowers lavender, large (4 in.) blooms in clusters; very fragrant; foliage dark.

Lavina HT, *mp*, 1962, *Queen Elizabeth × Anne Letts*; Reynolds, W.H. Flowers buff-pink, dbl. (60 petals), high-centered, large; fragrant; foliage dark, leathery; vigorous.

Lavinia Harrison HT, *mp*, 1988, *Duet × Seedling*; Harrison, G. Flowers medium, shell pink with light undertones, dbl. (30-35 petals), large, borne in sprays of 1-3; slight fragrance; foliage red to light green, aging dark green; prickles pyramid, red-brown; vigorous growth.

LAVjoy Min, *pb*, 1989, (Enjoy); *(Moulin Rouge × Seedling) × Party Girl*; Laver, Keith G.; Springwood Roses, 1990. Bud pointed; flowers blush pink edged deeper pink, reverse white, dbl. (22 petals), high-centered, small, borne singly; no fragrance; foliage small, medium green, disease resistant; prickles straight, very small, sparse, light brown; fruit ovoid, orange; upright, low growth.

LAVlemo Min, *my*, 1989, *Dorola × Genevieve*; Laver, Keith G. Bud ovoid; flowers lemon yellow, deeper in center, dbl. (28 petals), high-centered, medium, borne usually singly; foliage small, medium green, matt; prickles beige; fruit ovoid, green; upright, bushy, medium growth.

LAVlow Min, *ob*, 1991, *(Painted Doll × June Laver) × Potluck Yellow*; Laver, Keith G.; Springwood Roses. Flowers orange yellow, full, small blooms borne in small clusters; no fragrance; foliage small, medium green, semi-glossy; few prickles; low, compact growth.

LAVmoth Min, *pb*, 1988, (Fair Genie); *Breezy × June Laver*; Laver, Keith; Springwood Roses, 1990. Bud pointed; flowers light orange in center with pink outer petals, reverse pink with yellow base, golden anthers, dbl. (33 petals), high-centered, exhibition, small,

borne singly; moderate fragrance; foliage small, medium green, glossy; prickles slender, straight, almost white, translucent; fruit ovoid, orange; upright, bushy, low, strong growth.

LAVsans Min, *dp*, 1986, (Sans Souci); *Rise 'n' Shine × Ontario Celebration*; Laver, K.; Springwood Miniature Roses. Flowers deep fuchsia pink, fading slightly, dbl. (40 pointed, recurved petals), high-centered, exhibition, medium, borne usually singly; slight fragrance; foliage medium, light green, matt; many, very fine, light brown prickles; fruit oblong, narrow, red; bushy, medium growth.

LAVsho Min, *lp*, 1984, *Mighty Mouse × Fairy Rose*; Laver, Keith. Flowers light pink, dbl. (20 petals), small blooms in large clusters; slight fragrance; foliage small, light green, glossy; spreading growth.

LAVsno Min, *w*, 1984, *Ice Princess × Sue Lawley*; Laver, Keith. Flowers white, dbl. (40+ petals); no fragrance; foliage small, medium green, matt; upright, bushy growth.

LAVtrek Min, *dy*, 1989, (King Tut); *June Laver × Genevieve*; Laver, Keith G.; Springwood Roses. Bud pointed; flowers rich, deep yellow, reverse medium yellow, dbl. (45 petals), exhibition, small, borne singly; moderate fragrance; foliage small, dark green, disease resistant; prickles curved down, light brown; fruit ovoid, orange-red; upright, low, compact growth.

Lawinia® LCl, *mp*, 1982, (TANklewi; TANklevi; Lavinia); Tantau, M., 1980. Flowers medium pink, dbl. (20 petals), cupped, large; fragrant; foliage large, medium green, semi-glossy; spreading (to 8 ft.) growth.

Lawrence Johnston LCl, *my*, 1923, (Hidcote Yellow); *Mme. Eugène Verdier × R. foetida persiana*; Ducher. Flowers yellow, semi-dbl., large blooms in clusters; fragrant; very vigorous, climbing (to 30 ft.); repeat bloom.

Lawrence Johnston HT, *yb*, 1946, *Souv. de Denier van der Gon × Brazier*; San Remo Exp. Sta. Bud pointed; flowers yellow edged red and salmon, semi-dbl., large; fragrant; foliage light green; vigorous, upright, bushy growth. GM, Rome, 1954.

Lawrence of Arabia HT, *yb*, 1938, Dickson, A. Flowers indian yellow, flushed coppery rose, full, large; vigorous, bushy growth.

Laxton's Standard HT, *mp*, 1926, Laxton Bros. Flowers clear cerise-pink.

Lazy Daze Min, *m*, 1991, (TALdaz); *Azure Sea × Seedling*; Taylor, Pete & Kay; Taylor's Roses, 1992. Flowers light lavender, reverse slightly darker, white base, very full (41+ petals), medium (4-7 cms) blooms borne mostly singly; blooms sometimes quarters; slight fragrance; foliage small, medium green, semi-glossy; some prickles; low (30 cms), compact growth.

Le Cid HRg (OGR), *mr*, 1908. Flowers dazzling crimson, large; vigorous.

Le Havre HP (OGR), *mr*, 1870, Eudes. Flowers vermilion, imbricated, large; vigorous.

Le Loiret Pol, *mp*, 1920, Turbat. Flowers very brilliant pink to salmon-rose, borne in clusters of 10-15.

Le Mexique R, *lp*, 1912, *Dorothy Perkins × Marie Pavie*; Schwartz, A. Flowers pale silvery rose, semi-dbl., medium, borne in clusters; slightly fragrant; vigorous, climbing growth.

Le Nankin T (OGR), *yb*, 1871, Ducher. Flowers yellow shaded coppery, well formed; fragrant.

Le Pactole T (OGR), *ly*, 1845, *Lamarque × Yellow Tea*; Miellez. Flowers pale yellow, full, large.

Le Pink Min, *lp*, 1986, (JAClip); *Seedling × Watercolor*; Warriner; J&P. Flowers light pink, dbl. (40 petals), cupped, crowded, small blooms in sprays of 3-20; slight damask fragrance; foliage small, light green, matt; long, thin prickles; numerous on peduncle; very dense, bushy, upright, medium growth.

Le Ponceau Pol, *dr*, 1912, *Gruss an Teplitz × Mme. Norbert Levavasseur*; Hémeray-Aubert. Flowers deep garnet-red, semi-dbl., small.

Le Progrès HT, *my*, 1903, Pernet-Ducher. Flowers yellow; very vigorous growth.

Le Rêve LCl, *ly*, 1923, *Mme. Eugène Verdier × R. foetida persiana*; Pernet-Ducher. Bud pointed; flowers pale yellow, semi-dbl., large; fragrant; foliage rich green, glossy; vigorous, climbing growth.

Le Rigide R, *mp*, 1920, Turbat. Flowers neyron pink, semi-dbl., borne in clusters of 25-30; vigorous growth.

Le Vésuve Ch (OGR), *pb*, 1825, Laffay. Flowers carmine shading to pink, very full, large; vigorous growth; (14).

Lea Ann Gr, *w*, 1976, *Queen Elizabeth × Ivory Fashion*; Patterson; Patterson Roses. Bud long, pointed; flowers clear white, dbl. (25-30 petals), high-centered, large (4 in.); fragrant; foliage soft; vigorous growth.

Leader HT, *mr*, 1924, *Premier sport*; Hill, E.G., Co. Flowers red.

Leading Lady HT, *lp*, 1935, Dickson, A. Flowers flesh-pink, flushed peach-blossom, full, high-centered, large; very fragrant; foliage deep green, leathery; vigorous, bushy growth. GM, NRS. 1934. RULED EXTINCT 1/85.

Leading Lady HT, *mp*, 1985, (JAClopi); *Seedling × Seedling*; Warriner; J&P. Flowers me-

dium pink, dbl. (35 petals), large; slight fragrance; foliage large, light green, matt; upright growth; greenhouse variety.

League of Nations HT, *m*, 1929, *Frau Felix Tonnar × Solliden*; Leenders, M. Flowers reddish lilac, shaded salmon-pink, semi-dbl.; fragrant.

Lealand Jewel S, *dp*, 1963, *Athabasca seedling*; Erskine. Flowers deep pink, fading quickly, semi-dbl. (15 wide petals; 14).

Leander® S, *ab*, 1983, (AUSlea); *Charles Austin × Seedling*; Austin, David; David Austin Roses, 1982. Flowers apricot, very dbl. (closely packed petals), flat, small blooms in clusters; fragrant; foliage medium, medium green, semi-glossy; spreading growth.

Leaping Salmon LCl, *op*, 1983, (PEAmight); *((Vesper × Aloha) × (Paddy McGredy × Maigold)) × Prima Ballerina*; Pearce, C.A.; Limes Rose Nursery, 1986. Flowers salmon pink, dbl. (20 petals), large; fragrant; foliage large, medium green, semi-glossy; upright (to 8-10 ft.).

Léda D (OGR), *w*, (Painted Damask); Cult. before 1827. Flowers white to blush, edged crimson, dbl., medium; fragrant; foliage dark; compact (3 ft.) growth; sometimes recurrent bloom; hardy. See also Pink Leda.

Leda S, *lp*, 1960, *R. laxa hybrid*; Skinner. Flowers pale pink, shallow cupped, borne in clusters of 4-5; very fragrant; foliage dark; fruit large, red, apple-like; bushy (5 ft.) growth.

Lee G (OGR), *lp*, 1823, Vibert. Flowers blush, shaded flesh, very dbl., expanded, large; abundant early bloom.

Leenders' Bergfeuer F, *mr*, 1959, *Independence × Fashion*; Leenders, J. Bud long; flowers scarlet, semi-dbl., large; fragrant; foliage dark, glossy.

Leenders' Flamingo F, *ob*, 1960, *Cocorico × Ma Perkins*; Leenders, J. Bud ovoid; flowers bright coral-peach, semi-dbl., open, large, borne in clusters; fragrant; vigorous, bushy growth.

Leenders' Pink F, *mp*, 1959, *Goldilocks × Mrs. Inge Poulsen*; Leenders, J. Flowers bright pink, dbl., large, borne in heavy clusters; slightly fragrant; foliage dark, leathery, glossy.

Legacy HT, *pb*, 1963, *Mrs. Bryce Allan sport*; Hamilton; Junior Legacy Club. Flowers rose-pink streaked white, dbl., large; very fragrant; foliage leathery; moderate growth.

Legacy Jubilee HT, *yb*, 1974, *Great Venture × Fred Streeter*; Dawson, G.; Neil. Bud long, pointed; flowers yellow, edged red, dbl., large; very fragrant; foliage large, glossy; vigorous, upright growth.

Legend HT, *mr*, 1992, (JACtop); *Grand Masterpiece × Seedling*; Warriner, William; Bear

Creek Gardens. Flowers medium red, very full (41+ petals), high-centered, large (7+ cms) blooms borne mostly singly; very fragrant; foliage medium, dark green, semi-glossy; very small prickles on peduncle; tall (120-140 cms), upright, bushy growth.

Legendary HT, *lp*, 1962, Abrams, Von; Peterson & Dering. Bud long, pointed; flowers soft pink, dbl. (55 petals), high-centered, large (5½ in.); fragrant; foliage leathery; vigorous, upright growth.

LEGglow HT, *ob*, 1981, (Can Can, Can-Can); *Just Joey × (Superior × Mischief)*; LeGrice, E.B., 1982. Flowers orange, dbl. (24 petals), large; very fragrant; foliage large, dark, semi-glossy; bushy.

Legion HT, *dp*, 1920, (American Legion); *Milady seedling × Hadley*; Towill. Flowers deep cerise-red, dbl.; fragrant.

Légion d'Honneur® F, *mr*, 1974, (DELsamar); *(Souv. de J. Chabert × (Walko × Souv. de J. Chabert)) × ((Tamango × Gay Paris) × (Zambra × Jean de la Lune))*; Delbard. Flowers medium red, dbl. (55 petals), well-formed, cupped, medium; light fragrance; low, bushy growth. GM, Geneva, 1974.

Leicester Abbey HT, *mr*, 1986, (NOSab); *(Gavotte × E.H. Morse seedling) × Erotika*; Greensitt, J.; Nostell Priory Rose Gardens. Flowers medium red, very full (over 40 petals), large; fragrant; foliage large, dark green, glossy; bushy growth.

Leigh Ann™ Min, *pb*, 1986, *Poker Chip × Rise 'n' Shine*; Jolly, M.; Rosehill Farm, 1987. Flowers pink, reverse cream, yellow center, fading to light pink, dbl. (34 petals), cupped, high-centered, exhibition, medium, borne usually singly or in sprays of 3-6; slight fragrance; foliage medium, medium green, semi-glossy; bayonet-shaped, pinkish brown prickles; fruit round, red-orange; upright, medium, vigorous growth.

Leigh-Lo HT, *mp*, 1979, (HARpurl); *Elizabeth Harkness × Red Devil*; Harkness, 1981. Bud pointed; flowers rose-bengal, dbl. (42 petals), urn-shaped, large; slightly fragrant; foliage large; vigorous, upright growth.

Leila Francis HT, *pb*, 1948, *Earl Haig × Crimson Glory*; Francis; F. Mason. Bud ovoid; flowers two-toned pink, dbl., high-centered, large; very fragrant; foliage leathery; vigorous, bushy growth.

Leipzig HMsk (S), *or*, 1939, *Eva × Mermaid*; Kordes. Flowers orange-scarlet, semi-dbl., open, borne inclusters on long, strong stems; foliage leathery, glossy, wrinkled; vigorous, bushy growth; recurrent bloom.

Leitrim Glory HT, *dy*, 1976, *Whisky Mac sport*; Hughes. Flowers deep yellow, dbl. (28-30 petals), full, large (5 in.); fragrant; foliage bronze, matt green.

Lele HT, *dr*, 1939, *Marquise d'Andigne × Pres. Herbert Hoover*; San Remo Exp. Sta. Bud pointed; flowers dark red, veined, dbl. (30 petals), very large; strong stems; fragrant; foliage bright green; very vigorous growth.

Lelia Laird Min, *ob*, 1979, *Contempo × Sheri Anne*; Bennett, Dee; Tiny Petals Nursery, 1980. Bud long, pointed; flowers orange-red with yellow eye and reverse, dbl. (38 petals), high-centered blooms borne 1-4 per cluster; tea fragrance; foliage medium green with red edging; long, thin, red prickles; upright growth.

L. E. Longley HT, *mr*, 1949, *Pink Princess × Crimson Glory*; Longley, L.E.; Univ. of Minn. Flowers red, semi-dbl., open, large to medium; fragrant; foliage glossy, dark, bronze; very vigorous, bushy growth.

Lemania HT, *dr*, 1937, Heizmann, E.; Meilland, A. Bud almost black; flowers velvety blackish red, dbl., well formed, very large; very fragrant; vigorous growth.

Lemon Beauty HT, *w*, 1932, Cant, B.R. Flowers creamy white, quickly fading to paperwhite, base lemon-yellow, well formed, large; fragrant (fruity); foliage light.

Lemon Chiffon HT, *my*, 1954, *Soeur Thérèse × Golden Dawn*; Swim; Arp Nursery Co. Bud long, pointed; flowers lemon-yellow, dbl. (40 petals), high-centered to open, large (3-4 in.); very fragrant (spicy); compact, bushy growth. RULED EXTINCT 9/86.

Lemon Delight Min, *my*, 1978, *Fairy Moss × Goldmoss*; Moore, R.S.; Sequoia Nursery. Bud mossy, long, pointed; flowers medium yellow, semi-dbl. (10 petals), mini-moss, small (1½ in.); slightly fragrant; bushy, upright growth.

Lemon Drop Min, *ly*, 1954, *(R. wichuraiana × Floradora) × Zee*; Moore, R.S.; Sequoia Nursery. Flowers light yellow, dbl. (25 narrow petals), very small (¾ in.); foliage very small; very prickly; dwarf (6 in.) growth.

Lemon Elegance HT, *my*, 1960, Jones; Hennessey. Bud long, pointed; flowers lemon-yellow, dbl. (38 petals), well-shaped, large (4½-5 in.); fragrant; foliage leathery; vigorous, tall growth.

Lemon Fluff Min, *my*, 1985, (CURlem); *(Seedling × Rise 'n' Shine) × Summer Butter*; Curtis, Thad; Hortico, Inc. Flowers medium yellow, dbl. (20 petals), HT form, small blooms borne singly and in clusters; no fragrance; foliage small, medium green, matt; upright, bushy growth.

Lemon Glow HT, *my*, 1964, *Sunlight* × *Golden Masterpiece*; Schwartz, E.W.; Wyant. Bud long, pointed; flowers lemon-yellow, dbl. (55 petals), high-centered, large (6-7 in.); fragrant; foliage soft; vigorous, upright growth.

Lemon Ice HT, *my*, 1960, *Leonard Barron sport*; Kern Rose Nursery. Bud pointed; flowers lemon-yellow, dbl. (65 petals), large (4 in.); slightly fragrant; foliage leathery, dark; vigorous, bushy, compact growth.

Lemon Mist Min, *w*, 1991, *Rise 'n' Shine* × *Seedling*; Gruenbauer, Richard, 1984; Flowers 'n' Friends Miniature Roses, 1993. Bud ovoid; flowers white with yellow center, aging white, very dbl. (50 petals), high-centered, medium; slight, fruity fragrance; foliage medium, medium green, matt; upright growth.

Lemon Ophelia HT, *my*, 1922, *Ophelia sport*; Leenders, M. Flowers lemon-yellow, dbl.; fragrant.

Lemon Sherbet HT, *ly*, 1973, *Florence sport*; Kern Rose Nursery. Bud ovoid; flowers white, center light yellow, dbl. (35 petals), exhibition, large (4 in.); slightly fragrant; foliage large, leathery; upright growth.

Lemon Spice HT, *ly*, 1966, *Helen Traubel* × *Seedling*; Armstrong, D.L.; Armstrong Nursery. Bud long, pointed; flowers light yellow, dbl., high-centered, large; very fragrant; foliage dark, leathery; vigorous, spreading growth.

Lemon Surprise F, *my*, 1978, *Allgold* × *Elizabeth of Glamis*; Slack. Flowers lemon, semi-dbl. (12 petals); fragrant (spicy); foliage glossy; low, upright growth.

Lemon Swirl F, *ly*, 1992, (RENswirl); *Seedling* × *Sunsprite*; Rennie, Bruce; Rennie Roses. Flowers light yellow, moderately full (15-25 petals), medium (4-7 cms) blooms borne in small clusters; slight fragrance; foliage medium, light green, glossy; few prickles; tall, upright growth.

Lemon Twist Min, *dy*, 1988, (FOUtwist); *Gold Badge* × *Great Day*; Jacobs, Betty; Four Seasons Rose Nursery. Bud pointed; flowers deep yellow, dbl. (25 petals), high-centered, exhibition, medium, borne usually singly and in sprays of up to 3; slight, tea fragrance; foliage medium, medium green, glossy; prickles slightly declining, long, red to brown; bushy, medium growth.

Lemon Yellow F, *my*, 1977, *Orange Sensation* × *King's Ransom*; Gandy. Flowers lemon-yellow, dbl. (21 petals), 2 in. blooms; slightly fragrant; foliage dark; bushy growth.

Lemonade F, *w*, 1974, *Nancy West sport*; Haynes Roses. Flowers cream, dbl. (25 petals), large (4½ in.); slightly fragrant; foliage matt.

Len Turner F, *rb*, 1984, (DICjeep; Daydream); *Electron* × *Eyepaint*; Dickson, Patrick. Flowers ivory petals flushed and edged carmine, dbl. (35 petals), large; slight fragrance; foliage medium, medium green, glossy; bushy, very compact growth.

Lena T (OGR), *ab*, 1906, Dickson, A. Flowers apricot, edged yellow.

LENana S, *lp*, 1984, (Flash); *R. multiflora nana* × *Seedling*; Lens, Louis. Flowers light pink, dbl. (22 petals), 1½ in. blooms in clusters of 3-50; light fragrance; foliage small, dark; hooked, green prickles; bushy, spreading growth.

L'Enchantresse G (OGR), *mp*, 1829, (Grande Henriette). Flowers clear pink, full, large. Evidently a Belgian variety introduced into France from Brussels in 1829.

Leni Neuss HT, *pb*, 1933, *Lilly Jung* × *Baronesse M. van Tuyll van Serooskerken*; Leenders, M.; C-P. Bud pointed; flowers hydrangea-pink, reverse reddish old-rose, full, very large; fragrant; very vigorous, bushy growth.

LENobit HMsk (S), *pb*, 1982, (Poesie); *Ballerina* × *Moonlight*; Lens, Louis, 1985. Flowers white shaded pink, dbl. (20 petals), 2 in. blooms in clusters of 5-32; very fragrant; foliage large, leathery, dark; hooked, light brown prickles; bushy, spreading growth.

LENrag F, *r*, 1980, (Ragtime); *Little Angel* × *Goldtopas*; Lens, Louis. Flowers brownish red, dbl. (25 petals), HT form, medium blooms in clusters of 7-18; slightly fragrant; foliage brownish-green; low, bushy growth.

LENsun Min, *yb*, 1983, (Sunnyside '83); *Little Angel* × *(Rosina* × *Seedling)*; Lens, Louis. Flowers yellow, spotted red, dbl. (20 petals), small blooms in clusters of 3-22; fruity fragrance; foliage small; small, hooked, green prickles; bushy growth.

Léon Chenault HT, *pb*, 1931, Pernet-Ducher; Gaujard. Flowers carmine-rose shaded salmon, base deeper, dbl., very large; very fragrant; foliage dark; very vigorous growth.

Leonard Barron HT, *op*, 1931, *Schoener's Nutkana* × *Souv. de Mme. Boullet*; Nicolas; C-P. Bud pointed; flowers salmon-copper and shell-pink, dbl., very large; fragrant; foliage leathery; bushy growth. ARS David Fuerstenberg Prize, 1933.

Léonce Colombier HT, *mr*, 1943, *Charles P. Kilham* × *(Charles P. Kilham* × *Capucine Chambard)*; Meilland, F.; Meilland, A. Bud oval; flowers brilliant geranium-red, stamens yellow, dbl., cupped, medium; slightly fragrant; foliage leathery; very vigorous, bushy growth.

Leonie F, *mp*, 1964, (Dazzler); *Queen Elizabeth × Circus*; Leenders, J. Flowers pink, dbl.; vigorous growth.

Léonie Lambert HT, *lp*, 1913, *Frau Karl Druschki × Prince de Bulgarie*; Lambert, P. Flowers silver-pink, shaded yellow and flesh, well shaped, large; fragrant; very vigorous growth.

Léonie Lamesch Pol, *ob*, 1899, *Aglaia × Kleiner Alfred*; Lambert, P. Flowers light coppery red, center yellow, edges flecked darker, semi-dbl.; foliage rich green, soft; vigorous, bushy growth.

Léonor de March HT, *dr*, 1957, *J.M. Lopez Pico × Poinsettia*; Camprubi. Bud long, pointed; flowers deep blood-red, dbl., large; fragrant; foliage glossy; upright growth. GM, Rome, 1958.

Léonora HT, *mr*, 1921, Paul, W. Flowers brilliant velvety red, center brighter, dbl.

Léontine Contenot HT, *yb*, 1935, *Joanna Hill × Souv. de Claudius Pernet*; Ketten Bros. Bud pointed; flowers sunflower-yellow bordered pink and yellow, dbl. (45-50 petals), high-centered, large; foliage quaker green; vigorous growth.

Léontine Gervais LCl, *ab*, 1903, *R. wichuraiana × Souv. de Catherine Guillot*; Barbier. Bud coppery red; flowers salmon-orange and yellow, large blooms in clusters of 3-10; fragrant; foliage dark, glossy; very vigorous, climbing growth; non-recurrent bloom.

Léopold I HP (OGR), *dr*, 1863, *Général Jacqueminot seedling*; Van Assche. Flowers deep red, dbl., well formed, large.

Léopold Lambotte HT, *mr*, 1944, *Grenoble × National Flower Guild*; Meilland, F. Bud long, pointed; flowers scarlet-red; fragrant; very tall growth.

Léopoldine d'Orléans R, *w*, 1828, *R. sempervirens hybrid*; Jacques. Flowers white shaded rose, dbl., medium.

Leora Stewart HT, *op*, Wilber. Flowers orange-pink; very fragrant; long continued bloom; a greenhouse variety.

Leotilde Minguez HT, *rb*, 1961, *Pres. Herbert Hoover × Vicky Marfa*; Dot, P. Flowers carmine, shaded vermilion and yellow, dbl. (30 petals), large; upright growth.

Leprechaun F, *yb*, 1971, *(Easter Parade × Masquerade) × Little Darling*; Adams, M.R. Bud ovoid; flowers red, reverse yellow, dbl., globular, small; fragrant; foliage glossy; growth moderate, upright.

Les Amis de Lille HT, *pb*, 1928, *Golden Emblem × Prés. Bouché*; Ketten Bros. Bud lincoln red on pale buff ground; flowers palebuff, edges and reverse suffused salmon-pink.

Les Amis de Troyes HT, *mp*, 1935, *Feu Joseph Looymans × Seedling*; Vially. Flowers china-pink, passing to carmine-pink, baseochre-yellow, full, well formed, large; vigorous growth.

Les Rosati HFt (OGR), *mr*, 1906, *Reported to be R. foetida persiana × Seedling (HP × T); also reported as R. foetida persiana sport.*; Gravereaux. Flowers bright carmine.

Les Sjulin Gr, *pb*, 1981, *Country Dancer × ((Dornröschen × Peace) × Pink Peace)*; Buck; Iowa State University. Flowers coral pink, reverse light red, dbl. (28 petals), urn-shaped to imbricated blooms borne 1-8 per cluster; old rose fragrance; foliage medium, dark olive green, leathery; awl-like prickles; erect, bushy growth.

Les Sylphides HT, *op*, 1960, *Margaret sport*; Watkins Roses. Flowers pink shading to yellow and orange, well shaped; long stems; very fragrant; foliage reddish; very vigorous growth.

Lesja Jean HT, *lp*, 1990, *Seedling × Seedling*; Weddle, Von C., 1989. Bud pointed; flowers light pink, very dbl. (37 petals), high-centered, exhibition, large blooms borne usually singly; moderate fragrance; foliage medium, medium green, semi-glossy; prickles medium, light; upright, medium growth.

Lesley Anne Min, *op*, 1987, (FRYminiles); *Seedling × Seedling*; Fryers, Gareth. Flowers pale peach-pink, pale yellow base, fading slightly paler, dbl. (45 petals), cupped, large, borne usually singly or in sprays of 3-6; no fragrance; foliage medium, light green, matt; thin, small, pointed, light brown prickles; fruit oval, orange-red; upright growth.

Lesley Dudley HT, *op*, 1932, (Leslie Dudley); McGredy. Flowers warm carmine-pink shaded orange, full, well shaped, large; very fragrant; foliage dark; vigorous, bushy growth. GM, NRS, 1931.

Lesley Johns HT, *dp*, 1972, *Soraya × Seedling*; Gregory. Flowers deep pink, dbl. (32 petals), high-pointed, large (5-6 in.); fragrant; foliage dark, glossy.

Leslie Evans HT, *dr*, 1927, *J.B. Clark × Red-Letter Day*; Evans; Beckwith. Flowers rich dark velvety crimson, semi-dbl.; vigorous growth.

Leslie G. Harris HT, *mr*, 1970, *Tropicana Seedling*); Gregory. Flowers crimson-scarlet, dbl. (27 petals), pointed, large (4 in.); very fragrant; moderate growth.

Leslie Holland HT, *dr*, 1911, Dickson, H. Flowers deep velvety crimson, full, large; fragrant. GM, NRS, 1909.

Leslie Pidgeon HT, *ob*, 1922, Dickson, H. Flowers orange-buff, suffused terra-cotta, semi-dbl.; fragrant.

Leslie Wheal F, *yb*, 1977, *Zorina sport*; Buss; H. Buss Nursery. Bud ovoid; flowers cream-yellow, dbl. (25-35 petals), cupped, small (1½ in.); foliage light green; compact growth.

Lessing HMsk (S), *rb*, 1914, *Trier × Entente Cordiale*; Lambert, P. Flowers reddish rose streaked white, center citron-yellow, dbl., small, borne in large clusters; fragrant; foliage large, light.

Lestra Hibberd HT, *dy*, 1935, *Joanna Hill × Sweet Adeline*; Hill, J.H., Co. Bud dark yellow; flowers amber-yellow to orange-yellow, dbl., large; strong stems; fragrant; foliage leathery; vigorous, compact growth.

Letchworth Garden City® F, *op*, 1972, (HARkover; Garden City); *(Sabine × Pineapple Poll) × (Circus × Mischief)*; Harkness, 1979. Flowers medium salmon-pink, dbl. (20 petals), medium (2½ in.); fragrant (spicy); foliage medium green, semi-glossy; vigorous, bushy growth. GM, Monza, 1978.

Letitia HT, *dr*, 1949, *Crimson Glory × Southport*; Bees. Bud long, pointed; flowers crimson, dbl. (35 petals), large (5-6 in.); foliage dark; very vigorous growth.

L'Etna Ch (OGR), *mp*, 1825, Laffay. Flowers pink, becoming brighter, very full, medium.

Letty Coles T (OGR), *w*, 1876, *Mme. Mélanie Willermoz sport*; Keynes. Flowers white, center pink.

Leuchtfeuer HCh (OGR), *mr*, 1909, (President Taft); *Gruss an Teplitz × Cramoisi Superieur*; Türke. Flowers bright red; fragrant.

Leuchtstern R, *pb*, 1899, *Daniel Lacombe × Crimson Rambler*; Schmidt, J.C. Flowers deep rose pink, center white, single, medium blooms in clusters; slightly fragrant; height 8-10 ft.

Leverkusen K (S), *ly*, 1954, *R. kordesii × Golden Glow*; Kordes. Bud long, pointed; flowers light yellow, dbl., high-centered, large blooms on long sprays; slightly fragrant; foliage glossy, light green; vigorous, creeper or pillar (to 8 ft.); recurrent bloom.

Leveson Gower B (OGR), *op*, 1845, (Leweson Gower; Leverson Gower; Souv. de la Malmaison Rose); Béluze. Flowers rose shaded salmon, full, cupped, very large; robust; mildews; has some Tea rose characteristics; evidently confused with Souv. de la Malmaison Rouge (Gonod, 1880) and Souv. de Leveson Gower (Guillot, 1852), both dark red roses.

Lewiston HT, *my*, 1981, *Red Lion × King's Ransom*; Perry, Astor, 1982. Flowers medium yellow, dbl. (40 petals), high-centered, pointed, large blooms borne singly; heavy fruity fragrance; foliage large, glossy; vigorous, tall growth.

Ley's Perpetual Class unknown, Grown prior to 1938 by F. Ley, Windlesham, Surrey, and thought to be a rediscovered old rose; int. Graham Thomas, Sunnindale Nurseries, ca. 1958. Flowers pale yellow, fully dbl., cupped; fragrant; vigorous, climbing (to 15 ft.).

Li Burés HT, *rb*, 1929, *Château de Clos Vougeot × Souv. de Claudius Pernet*; Dot, P.; C-P. Flowers rose-red and yellow mixed (very variable), dbl., cupped; slightly fragrant; very vigorous, bushy growth.

Libby Min, *rb*, 1978, *Overture × Perla de Alcañada*; Rovinski; Casa de Rosa Domingo. Bud ovoid; flowers white, edged red, dbl. (20 petals), high-pointed to flat, small (1-1½ in.); foliage glossy; upright, compact growth.

Libby's Gold HT, *yb*, 1977, *Apollo sport*; Carpenter. Bud long, slender; flowers yellow blend, dbl. (40 petals), large (5 in.); slightly fragrant; foliage dark; upright, compact growth.

Liberté F, *dr*, 1946, (Crimson Masse); *Florentina × Seedling*; Leenders, M. Flowers brilliant crimson-red, dbl., large.

Liberty HT, *dr*, 1900, *Mrs. W.J. Grant × Charles J. Grahame*; Dickson, A. Flowers brilliant velvety crimson, full, large; very fragrant; foliage dark; vigorous growth.

Liberty, Climbing Cl HT, *dr*, 1908, May.

Liberty Bell HT, *pb*, 1963, (Freiheitsglocke); Kordes, R.; A. Dickson; McGredy. Flowers deep pink, silver reverse, dbl., large.

Libia HT, *w*, 1934, Borgatti. Flowers milkwhite, center creamy yellow, very dbl., large; vigorous growth.

Libretto HT, *dp*, 1966, *Elli Knab × Seedling*; Verschuren, A.; van Engelen. Bud ovoid; flowers pink-red, dbl., medium, borne in clusters; foliage dark.

Lichterloh® F, *mr*, 1955, *Red Favorite × New Dawn*; Tantau. Bud ovoid; flowers velvety blood-red, semi-dbl., medium blooms in clusters; slightly fragrant; foliage leathery, dark, glossy; vigorous, upright (3 ft.) growth.

Lichtkönigin Lucia® S, *my*, 1985, (KORlilub); *Zitronenfalter × Cläre Grammerstorf*; Kordes, W., 1966. Flowers medium yellow, semi-dbl. (18 petals), cupped, medium blooms borne 3-5 per cluster; moderate fragrance; foliage medium, dark, glossy; bushy, tall growth. ADR, 1968.

Lída Baarová HT, *mp*, 1934, (Lida Paar); *Ophelia seedling*; Böhm. Bud pointed; flowers rosy salmon, dbl., cupped, large; foliage glossy; vigorous, bushy growth.

L'Idéal N (OGR), *mr*, 1887, Nabonnand, G. Flowers geranium to turkey-red, base indian yellow, semi-dbl.; vigorous, climbing growth.

Lidka Böhmova HT, *mp*, 1929, (Lidka Böhm); *Una Wallace sport*; Böhm. Flowers salmon-pink, tips veined reddish, base golden yellow, dbl., large; very fragrant; foliage soft, bronze; very vigorous, bushy growth.

Lido di Roma HT, *yb*, 1968, (DELgap); *(Chic Parisien × Michèle Meilland) × (Sultane × Mme. Joseph Perraud)*; Delbard-Chabert. Bud long, pointed; flowers deep yellow, shaded red, dbl., high-centered, large; slightly fragrant; foliage glossy, leathery; vigorous, upright, bushy growth. GM, Japan, 1968.

Liebesbote HT, *dr*, 1935, *Hadley × Miss C.E. van Rossem*; Weigand, C.; Pfitzer. Bud pointed; flowers velvety dark red, dbl., high-centered, very large; very fragrant; foliage soft; very vigorous, bushy growth.

Liebeszauber HT, *mr*, 1959, (Charme d'Amour); *Detroiter × Crimson King*; Kordes. Flowers velvety red, cupped, large; very fragrant; foliage dark; vigorous, upright growth.

Liesbeth van Engelen HT, *w*, 1960, *Briarcliff × Seedling*; Verschuren, A.; van Engelen. Flowers creamy white edged lilac-pink, dbl.; fragrant; foliage dark, glossy; upright growth.

Lieutenant Chauré HT, *dr*, 1909, *Liberty × Étoile de France*; Pernet-Ducher. Flowers velvety crimson-red, shaded garnet, dbl., cupped, very large; fragrant; foliage rich green, leathery; vigorous, bushy growth.

Lieutenant Colonel A. Fairrie HT, *my*, 1930, *Rev. F. Page-Roberts × Mme. Ravary*; Bees. Bud pointed; flowers primrose, base deep yellow, dbl., high-centered; large; fragrant (apple).

Lieutenant Colonel Desmaires F, *ob*, 1967, *Rondo × Fashion seedling*; Boerner; J&P. Bud ovoid; flowers orange and yellow, dbl., borne in clusters; fragrant; foliage leathery; vigorous, low growth.

Lieven Gevaert HT, *mr*, 1974, Delforge, S. Bud ovoid; flowers medium red, dbl. (30 petals), large (4 in.); fragrant; foliage dark.

Lifeboat Jubilee HT, *mr*, 1974, *Karl Herbst × (Karl Herbst × Crimson Glory)*; Sanday. Flowers scarlet, shaded crimson, dbl. (20 petals), classic form, large (4 in.).

Lifestyle Min, *pb*, 1992, (MORdarain); *Little Darling × Rainbow's End*; Moore, Ralph S.; Sequoia Nursery, 1993. Flowers pink blend, color holds well, moderately full (15-25 petals), medium (4-7 cms) blooms mostly singly; slight fragrance; foliage medium, medium green, semi-glossy; few prickles; medium (35-45 cms), upright, bushy, rounded growth.

Lifirane HT, *mp*, 1976, *Sweet Promise sport*; Zwemstra; Meilland. Flowers neyron rose, dbl. (20-25 petals), full, high-centered, medium (3 in.); slightly fragrant; foliage dull; vigorous, upright growth.

Light Editor McFarland HT, *lp*, 1950, *Editor McFarland sport*; Thomasville Nursery. Flowers light pink.

Lijnbaanroos F, *ly*, 1961, *Schneewittchen × Koningin Juliana*; Buisman. Bud yellow; flowers creamy yellow, semi-dbl., borne in clusters; foliage dark; vigorous, upright growth.

Li'l Alleluia™ Min, *rb*, 1990, (KINlu); *((B.C. × Scamp) × Tamango) × Magic Carrousel*; King, Gene; AGM Miniature Roses. Flowers wine to silver with yellow base, moderately full (15-25 petals), small, borne mostly singly; fragrant; foliage medium, medium green, matt; upright, tall growth.

Li'l Rip™ Min, *w*, 1992, (MOGarip); *Loving Touch × Cupcake*; Moglia, Thomas; Gloria Dei Nursery, 1993. Flowers white with yellow center, full (26-40 petals), small (0-4 cms.) blooms borne in small clusters; slight fragrance; foliage small, medium green, matt; few prickles; medium (35-45 cms.), narrow, upright growth.

Li'l Touch™ Min, *ab*, 1992, (MOGatouch); *Loving Touch × Prima Donna*; Moglia, Thomas; Gloria Dei Nursery, 1993. Flowers apricot, yellow stamens showing, moderately full (15-25 petals), open, circular outline, small (0-4 cms.) blooms, somewhat similar to Loving Touch but smaller, borne mostly singly; slight fragrance; foliage medium, medium green, matt; some prickles; medium (40-50 cms.), upright growth.

Lila Tan HT, *m*, 1961, *Grey Pearl × Simone*; Dot, P. Flowers violet-cobalt, dbl. (30 petals), medium; vigorous, spreading growth.

Lila Vidri HT, *m*, 1958, *(Seedling × Prélude) × Rosa de Friera*; Dot, S. Bud pointed; flowers lilac, dbl. (30 petals), high-centered, strong stems; fragrant; upright, compact growth.

Lilac Airs HT, *lp*, 1988, (SANlilac); *Fred Gibson × Whisky Mac*; Sanday, John; John Sanday Roses, Ltd. Flowers soft, lilac pink, yellow at base, reverse silver at base, very dbl. (36 petals), exhibition, large, borne usually singly; heavy, damask fragrance; foliage large, medium green, semi-glossy; prickles long, fairly straight, medium brown, matt; bushy, tall, strong growth.

Lilac Charm F, *m*, 1962, LeGrice; Wayside Gardens Co., 1952. Bud pointed; flowers pastel mauve, anthers golden, filaments red, single (5-8 petals), flat, large (4 in.) blooms in clusters; fragrant; foliage dark; upright, compact growth. GM, NRS, 1961.

Lilac Dawn F, *m*, 1964, *Lavender Pinocchio × Frolic*; Swim & Weeks; Armstrong Nursery. Bud pointed; flowers lavender-pink to lilac, dbl. (43 petals), medium (2½ in.) blooms in clusters; fragrant (lilac); foliage leathery, light green; vigorous, bushy growth.

Lilac Rose HT, *lp*, 1962, *Karl Herbst × Chrysler Imperial*; Sanday. Flowers pink tinted lilac, dbl. (28 petals), large (5 in.); fragrant; foliage dark; vigorous, upright growth.

Lilac Snow HT, *w*, 1985, *Admiral Rodney sport*; Williams, H.; P. Loaney. Flowers white, strong lilac tinge to inside petals.

Lilac Time Min, *m*, 1955, *Violette × Zee*; Moore, R.S.; Sequoia Nursery. Flower lilac-pink to light red, becoming lilac tinted, dbl., small; dwarf (10 in.) growth.

Lilac Time HT, *m*, 1956, *Golden Dawn × Luis Brinas*; McGredy. Flowers lilac, dbl. (33 petals), high-centered, medium (3½ in.); fragrant; foliage light green; growth moderate.

Lilette Mallerin HT, *m*, 1937, *Charles P. Kilham × Unnamed R. foetida bicolor seedling*; Mallerin; A. Meilland. Bud pointed, yellow; flowers mauve-red to mauve pink, deepening in cooler weather, reverse yellow, dbl., cupped, large; slightly fragrant; foliage glossy; vigorous growth.

Lilette Mallerin Improved HT, *m*, 1942, *Lilette Mallerin sport*; J&P. Bud pointed; flowers mauve-red, reverse yellow, dbl. (25 petals), cupped to high-centered, large; foliage bronze, glossy; vigorous, upright, bushy growth.

Lilian HT, *dy*, 1931, Cant, B.R. Flowers golden yellow, dbl., cupped, very large; very fragrant; foliage bronze, glossy; vigorous, bushy growth. RULED EXTINCT 12/85.

Lilian Austin® S, *op*, 1981, *Aloha × The Yeoman*; Austin, David, 1973. Bud globular; flowers orange-pink, dbl. (33 petals), flat blooms borne 1-5 per cluster; fragrant; foliage glossy, dark; hooked, brown prickles; spreading growth.

Lilian Bootle HT, *dp*, 1973, *Margaret × Seedling (red)*; Bootle. Flowers cerise, dbl. (35 petals), high-centered, large (4½-5 in.); fragrant; foliage matt green; compact, bushy growth.

Lilian Nordica HT, *w*, 1898, *Margaret Dickson × Mme. Hoste*; Walsh. Flowers white, dbl., large; fragrant; vigorous growth.

Liliana HT, *pb*, 1956, *Edith Krause × Fashion*; Camprubi. Flowers soft pink, reverse carmine. GM, Geneva, 1956   RULED EXTINCT 12/85.

Liliana Gr, *w*, 1977, *Queen Elizabeth × Seedling*; Staikov, Prof. Dr. V.; Kalaydjiev and Chorbadjiiski. Flowers white, dbl. (50 petals), large; foliage light green, leathery; vigorous, tall, upright growth.

Lilibet F, *lp*, 1953, (Fairy Princess); *Floradora × Pinocchio*; Lindquist; Howard Rose Co. Bud ovoid; flowers light pink, dbl. (30 petals), large (2½-3½ in.) blooms in clusters; fragrant (spicy); foliage glossy; low, bushy. AARS, 1954.

Lillan Min, *pb*, 1958, *Ellen Poulsen × Tom Thumb*; deVink. Flowers rose pink, white center, semi-dbl., small; very dwarf growth.

Lillebror Min, *mr*, 1978, Hubner; O. Baum. Flowers red, dbl.; dwarf, bushy growth.

Lilli Marleen® F, *mr*, 1959, (KORlima; Lili Marlene; Lilli Marlene); *(Our Princess × Rudolph Timm) × Ama*; Kordes, R.; McGredy, 1959 & J&P, 1961. Bud ovoid; flowers medium red, dbl. (25 petals), cupped, large (3 in.); fragrant; foliage leathery; vigorous. ADR, 1960; Golden Rose of The Hague, 1966.

Lilli Marleen, Climbing® Cl F, *mr*, 1983, (PEKlimasar; Grimpamt Lilli Marleen; Lili Marlene, Climbing; Lilli Marlene, Climbing; Pekmez, Paul.

Lillian French HT, *pb*, 1985, *Miss Hillcrest × Bishop Darlington*; French, Richard. Flowers light to medium pink, reverse deep pink, very dbl. (50-120 petals), quartered form, large blooms borne 1-5 per cluster; moderate fragrance; foliage medium, medium green, semi-glossy; large prickles pointed downward; upright, bushy growth.

Lillian Gibson HBlanda (S), *mp*, 1938, *R. blanda × Red Star*; Hansen, N.E. Flowers rose-pink, dbl. (40 petals), large (3 in.); very fragrant; vigorous growth; non-recurrent bloom; very hardy.

Lillian Gish F, *ly*, 1985, *Queen Elizabeth × Allgold*; French, Richard. Flowers very pale yellow, dbl. (35 petals), large blooms borne singly and in small clusters; slight fragrance; foliage medium, medium green, semi-glossy; few, straight prickles; upright growth.

Lillian Gomez-Mena Cl HT, *pb*, 1927, Chambard, C. Flowers salmon-cream, reverse carmine, dbl.; very fragrant.

Lillian Moore HT, *dy*, 1917, Dickson, H. Flowers deep yellow; fragrant.

Lillie Bell HT, *dp*, 1979, *Pink Peace × Miss All-American Beauty*; Williams, J.B.; Central Mississippi Rose Soc. Bud ovoid to pointed; flowers deep pink to cerise-red, dbl. (34 petals), ruffled, large (4½-5 in.); fragrant; foliage large; upright growth.

Lillie Dawber HT, *dr*, 1952, Kordes. Flowers scarlet overlaid crimson, dbl. (25 petals), cupped, large (5 in.); fragrant; foliage dark; free growth.

Lilly Jung HT, *my*, 1925, Leenders, M. Flowers golden yellow, dbl.; fragrant.

Lily de Gerlache HT, *dp*, 1971, *Kordes' Perfecta* × *Prima Ballerina*; Inst. of Orn. Plant Growing. Bud long, pointed; flowers rose-red, dbl., cupped, large; very fragrant; foliage glossy, bronze, leathery; growth moderate, upright, bushy.

Lily Kemp HT, *dp*, 1928, *Mme. Butterfly* × *Capt. Ronald Clerk*; Morse. Flowers deep cherry-cerise, dbl.; fragrant.

Lily Mertscherscky N (OGR), *m*, 1878, Nabonnand. Flowers violet-red.

Lily Pons HT, *ly*, 1939, *Glenn Dale* × *Stargold*; Brownell. Flowers yellow center, shading to white outer petals, dbl. (50 petals), high-centered, large; fragrant; foliage glossy.

Lily the Pink HT, *lp*, 1992, *HT Seedling* × *HT Seedling*; Scrivens, L., 1991. Flowers light pink, very full (41+ petals), large (7+ cms) blooms borne mostly singly; slight fragrance; foliage medium, medium green, semi-glossy; some prickles; tall (800 cms), upright growth.

Lily White HT, *w*, 1950, (Starbright); *Starlite sport*; Hartgerink; J&P. Bud ovoid; flowers white, dbl. (40 petals), high-centered, large (4½ in.); slightly fragrant; foliage glossy; vigorous, upright growth; a greenhouse cut flower.

Limburgia HT, *rb*, 1921, Leenders, M. Flowers glowing deep carmine, reverse lilac-white, dbl.; fragrant.

Limelight F, *r*, 1959, *Enterprise sport*; Morse. Flowers vermilion splashed golden, semi-dbl., borne in clusters; slightly fragrant; vigorous growth. RULED EXTINCT 5/85.

Limelight HT, *ly*, 1984, (KORikon; Golden Medaillon); *Peach Melba* × *Seedling*; Kordes, W., 1984. Flowers light yellow, dbl. (35 petals), high-centered, large; very fragrant; foliage medium, dark, semi-glossy; upright, bushy, spreading growth.

Limerick Min, *rb*, 1991, (ZIPlime); *Tamango* × *Jennifer*; Zipper, Herbert; Magic Moment Miniatures. Flowers red with white reverse, moderately full (15-25 petals), exhibition form, medium (4-7 cms), blooms borne in small clusters; slight fragrance; foliage medium, dark green, glossy; few prickles; medium (40 cms), spreading growth.

Limited Edition HT, *mr*, 1984, (JACref); *Seedling* × *Seedling*; J&P; McConnell Nursery. Flowers medium red, dbl. (40+ petals), large; no fragrance; foliage medium, medium green, semi-glossy; upright growth.

Lincoln Cathedral HT, *ob*, 1985, (GLAnlin; Sarong); *Silver Jubilee* × *Royal Dane*; Langdale, G.W.T. Flowers outer petals pink, inner ones

orange, yellow reverse, dbl. (28 petals), large; slight fragrance; foliage medium, medium green; glossy; many, reddish prickles; bushy growth. GM, RNRS, 1985.

Lincolnshire Poacher HT, *yb*, 1992, (GLAreabit); *Silver Jubilee* × *Woman and Home*; Langdale, G.W.T., 1993. Flowers yellow flushed apricot and pink, full (26-40 petals), large (7+ cms) blooms borne mostly singly; slight fragrance; foliage medium, medium green, semi-glossy; some prickles; medium (80 cms-1 m), bushy growth.

Linda Campbell HRg (S), *mr*, 1990, (MORten); *Anytime* × *Rugosa Magnifica*; Moore, Ralph S., 1985; Wayside Gardens, 1991. Bud pointed; flowers medium red, blooms slightly lighter reverse, aging medium red, semi-dbl. (25 petals), cupped, medium, borne in sprays of 5-25; no fragrance; foliage large, dark green, semi-glossy; upright, bushy, medium growth; fast repeat.

Linda Christine F, *pb*, 1980, *Molly McGredy sport*; Taylor, W.J. Flowers cerise, silver reverse.

Linda Guest HT, *ab*, 1984, ((*Golden Jewel* × *Mischief*) × *Red Planet*) × *Valencia*; Guest, M.M. Flowers apricot, dbl. (20 petals), exhibition, large; slight fragrance; foliage medium, medium green, matt; bushy growth.

Linda Lou™ F, *ob*, 1987, *Golden Slippers* × *Roman Holiday*; Harvey, Bob; Kimbrew-Walter Roses, 1988. Flowers orange-yellow-red, dbl. (30 petals), high-centered, medium, borne in sprays of 1-8; moderate fragrance; foliage medium, dark green; medium growth. ARC TG (S), 1987.

Linda Porter HT, *op*, 1957, (Miguel Aldrufeu); *Senateur Potie* × *Poinsettia*; Dot, P.; B&A. Bud ovoid; flowers salmon-pink, dbl. (55 petals), globular, large (5-6 in.); very fragrant; foliage leathery; vigorous, upright growth.

Lindbergh Pol, *mr*, 1927, *Orléans Rose sport*; Croibier. Flowers bright geranium-red.

Lindsey HT, *op*, 1972, *Whisky Mac sport*; Watkins Roses. Flowers salmon-pink, shaded copper, pointed, medium (3-4 in.); fragrant; foliage large; free growth.

Linette Pol, *dp*, 1922, Turbat. Bud reddish apricot; flowers shrimp-carmine-pink, passing to soft rose-pink, large, borne in clusters of 6-10.

Linville Min, *w*, 1989, *Seedling* × *Seedling*; Bridges, Dennis A.; Bridges Roses, 1990. Bud pointed; flowers light pink, aging white, dbl. (28 petals), high-centered, exhibition, large, borne usually singly; slight, fruity fragrance; foliage medium, medium green, semi-glossy; prickles straight, medium, deep pink; upright, medium growth.

Liolà HT, *w*, 1960, *Peace × (Baiser × Marguerite Chambard)*; Giacomasso. Flowers ivory edged crimson, dbl.; very vigorous growth.

Lionel Barrymore F, *my*, 1956, *Duchess of Atholl × Orange Everglow*; Silva; Booy Rose Nursery. Bud urn shaped; flowers yellow, center deeper, very dbl., cupped, large (3-3½ in.); strong stems; very fragrant; foliage dark; bushy growth.

Lipstick F, *rb*, 1940, Verschuren; Dreer. Flowers deep cerise shaded salmon, semi-dbl., cupped, small (2 in.) blooms in clusters; slightly fragrant; foliage glossy, dark; vigorous (3 ft.), bushy growth.

Lipstick 'n' Lace Min, *rb*, 1991, (CLElips); *Seedling × Seedling*; Clements, John; Heirloom Old Garden Roses, 1992. Flowers cream, shaded lipstick red, full (26-40 petals), high-centered, exhibition, medium (4-7 cms) blooms borne in small clusters; fragrant; foliage medium, medium green, matt; no prickles; medium (30 cms), upright, compact growth.

Lisa Colfax F, *ob*, 1975, *Mignonne × Sherry*; Parkes; Rumsey. Bud ovoid; flowers vermilion, overlaid brown, dbl., high-centered, medium; very fragrant; foliage leathery; very vigorous growth.

Lisa Maree HT, *dp*, 1989, *Esther Geldenhuys sport*; Cowper, Mrs. Maree; Cherry Wood's Nursery, 1989. Flowers deep pink, reverse lighter.

Lisbeth Prim HT, *or*, 1934, *Hadley × Lady Inchiquin*; Felberg-Leclerc. Flowers coppery red, fading lighter, full, large; very fragrant; vigorous growth.

Lisbeth Stellmacher Pol, *or*, 1919, *Aglaia × Marie van Houtte*; Lambert, P. Bud coppery orange-red; flowers coppery red with golden yellow, striped pink, dbl., small; very fragrant.

Lisboa HT, *dr*, 1953, *Barcelona × Crimson Glory*; Moreira; da Silva. Flowers red shaded darker, large; very vigorous growth.

Lise Chiavassa HT, *mr*, 1931, *Mme. Philippe Rivoire × Yves Druhen*; Buatois. Flowers carmine, dbl., cupped, very large; very fragrant; foliage glossy; vigorous growth.

Liselle HT, *ob*, 1982, (RUlis; Royal Romance); *Whisky Mac × Matador*; DeRuiter, G., 1980; Fryer's Nursery, 1981. Flowers orange-peach, dbl. (35 petals), well-formed, large; fragrant; foliage large, dark, semi-glossy; bushy growth.

Lissy Horstmann HT, *mr*, 1943, *Hadley × Heros*; Tantau; C-P. Flowers brilliant scarlet-crimson, dbl. (28 petals), cupped, large; foliage leathery; vigorous.

Little Amigo Min, *mr*, 1983, (TINamigo); *Futura × Orange Honey*; Bennett, Dee; Tiny Petals Nursery. Flowers medium red, dbl. (35 petals), HT form, small; no fragrance; foliage small, medium green, semi-glossy; upright growth.

Little Angel F, *mr*, 1961, Verschuren; Blaby Rose Gardens. Flowers salmon becoming scarlet, dbl. (30 petals), borne in large clusters; foliage dark, glossy; moderate growth.

Little Artist® Min, *rb*, 1982, (MACmanly; MACmanley; Top Gear); *Eyepaint × Ko's Yellow*; McGredy, Sam. Flowers open with hand-painted marks becoming solid medium red, off-white in base half and reverse, semi-dbl., mini-flora, small; slight fragrance; foliage small, medium green, semi-glossy; upright growth.

Little Ballerina Min, *pb*, 1988, (CURbal); *Little Darling × Little Pioneer*; Curtis, Thad; Oregon Miniature Roses, 1988. Flowers white flushed pink, very dbl. (34-40 petals), urn-shaped, exhibition, medium, borne singly; slight fragrance; foliage medium, medium green, semi-glossy; prickles none; fruit none; bushy, medium growth.

Little Beauty F, *mp*, 1935, (Crown of Jewels); *E.G. Hill seedling × Polyantha*; Howard, F.H.; Dreer. Flowers bright cerise-pink, fading to pink, very dbl., small; slightly fragrant; foliage leathery; vigorous, bushy growth, blooming in wreath form when well grown.

Little Betty HBlanda (S), *lp*, 1940, *Betty Bland × R. nitida*; Wright, P.H. Flowers soft pink, small; height 3 ft.; non-recurrent bloom.

Little Breeze Min, *ob*, 1981, *Anytime × Elizabeth of Glamis*; McCann, Sean. Bud long, slender; flowers orange-red, fading to pink, semi-dbl. (17 petals), loose blooms borne singly; fragrant; foliage large, dark, glossy; straight, gray prickles; vigorous.

Little Bridesmaid HT, *lp*, Archer. Flowers shrimp-pink, well shaped.

Little Buckaroo Min, *mr*, 1956, (*R. wichuraiana × Floradora*) × (*Oakington Ruby × Floradora*); Moore, R.S.; Sequoia Nursery. Flowers bright red, dbl. (23 petals), small; fragrant (fresh apple); foliage bronze, glossy, leathery; height 14-16 in.

Little Cameo F, *pb*, 1981, *Lara × Seedling*; Strahle, Robert; Carlton Rose Nursery. Bud medium, pointed; flowers pink blend with cream outer petals, dbl. (26 petals), blooms borne mostly singly; slight fragrance; foliage medium green, leathery; straight, short, red prickles; vigorous, upright growth; greenhouse variety.

Little Carol Min, *dp*, 1989, (TINcarol); *Sonia × Jean Kenneally*; Bennett, Dee; Tiny Petals Nursery. Bud ovoid; flowers deep magenta-pink, reverse slightly lighter, dbl. (38 petals), high-centered, exhibition, medium, borne singly and in sprays of 3-5; slight, spicy fragrance; foliage medium, dark green, semi-glossy; disease resistant; prickles hooked slightly downward, red, few; fruit globular, green to brown; upright, tall growth.

Little Chameleon Min, *pb*, 1977, *Little Amy × Seedling*; Lyon. Bud pointed; flowers rose-pink to red, dbl. (30 petals), small (1½ in.); slightly fragrant; upright growth.

Little Charm Min, *mp*, 1984, (LYOlit); *Seedling × Seedling*; Lyon, Lyndon. Flowers medium pink, semi-dbl., small; no fragrance; foliage small, medium green, semi-glossy; upright, bushy growth.

Little Chief Min, *dp*, 1971, *Cotton Candy × Magic Wand*; Moore, R.S.; Sequoia Nursery. Bud long, pointed; flowers deep pink, semi-dbl., small; foliage small, glossy, leathery; growth moderate, dwarf, bushy.

Little Compton Creeper LCl, *dp*, 1938, Brownell. Flowers deep rose-pink, single, borne in open clusters; fruit yellow-orange to red; foliage glossy, dark.

Little Curt Min, *dr*, 1971, *Red Seedling × Westmont*; Moore, R.S.; Sequoia Nursery. Bud long, pointed; flowers deep velvety red, semi-dbl., medium; foliage dark, leathery; vigorous, upright, bushy growth.

Little Darling F, *yb*, 1956, *Capt. Thomas × (Baby Château × Fashion)*; Duehrsen; Elmer Rose Co. Bud ovoid; flowers blend of yellow and soft salmon-pink, dbl. (27 petals), well-formed, medium (2½ in.); fragrant (spicy); foliage dark, glossy, leathery; very vigorous, spreading growth. GM, Portland, 1958; ARS David Fuerstenberg Prize, 1964.

Little Dickens Min, *ob*, 1979, *(Ma Perkins × Sheri Anne) × Over the Rainbow*; Schwartz, E.W.; Nor'East Min. Roses. Bud ovoid; flowers orange-red and yellow, dbl. (25 petals), cupped, small; slightly fragrant; foliage small; compact growth.

Little Dorrit Pol, *mp*, 1930, *Coral Cluster sport*; Reeves. Flowers glowing pink.

Little Dorrit, Climbing Cl Pol, *mp*, 1935, Letts.

Little Dot Pol, *lp*, 1889, Bennett. Flowers soft pink, flaked deeper on the outer petals; clusters; very dwarf.

Little Embers F, *rb*, 1988, *Rise 'n' Shine × Prominent*; McFarland, John. Flowers cerise to yellow, reverse yellow with cerise on tips, aging red, dbl. (25 petals), high-centered, exhibition, small, borne usually singly; foliage medium, medium green, matt; prickles long, narrow, small, light green; fruit none; upright, low growth.

Little Eskimo Min, *w*, 1981, (MORwit; MORwhit); *(R. wichuraiana × Floradora) × Jet Trail*; Moore, R.S.; Moore Min. Roses. Bud long, pointed; flowers near white, dbl. (55 petals), blooms borne 3-7 per cluster, sometimes singly; little or no fragrance; foliage small, semi-glossy, leathery; long, slender prickles; vigorous, bushy, upright growth.

Little Fireball Min, *or*, 1968, *(R. wichuraiana × Floradora) × New Penny*; Moore, R.S.; Sequoia Nursery; Mini-Roses. Bud ovoid; flowers bright coral-red, dbl., small; fragrant; foliage small, glossy; bushy, compact, low growth.

Little Flirt Min, *rb*, 1961, *(R. wichuraiana × Floradora) × (Golden Glow × Zee)*; Moore, R.S.; Sequoia Nursery. Bud pointed; flowers orange-red, reverse yellow, dbl. (42 petals), small (1½ in.); fragrant; foliage light green; vigorous, bushy (12-14 in.).

Little Gem M (OGR), *dp*, 1880, Paul, W. Bud heavily mossed; flowers bright deep pink, dbl., small blooms in clusters; very fragrant; dwarf, compact growth.

Little Girl Cl Min, *op*, 1973, *Little Darling × Westmont*; Moore, R.S.; Sequoia Nursery. Bud long, pointed; flowers coral-salmon-pink, dbl., medium; foliage glossy; bushy, climbing growth.

Little Guy Min, *mr*, 1980, *Magic Wand × Violette*; Moore, Ralph; Moore Min. Roses. Flowers medium red, reverse lighter, semi-dbl., small blooms in clusters of 3-7; no fragrance; foliage small, medium green, semi-glossy; fruit none; low, bushy growth.

Little Huzzy Min, *rb*, 1991, (TINhuzzy); *Futura × Pucker Up*; Bennett, Dee; Tiny Petals Nursery, 1992. Flowers white with striping of pink to medium red over most upper surfaces of petals, full (26-40 petals), HT form, medium (4-7 cms) blooms borne mostly singly; long cutting stems; fragrant; foliage small, medium green, semi-glossy; disease resistant; some prickles; tall (60-80 cms), upright growth.

Little Jackie™ Min, *ob*, 1982, (SAVor); *(Prominent × Sheri Anne) × Glenfiddich*; Saville, F. Harmon; Nor'East Min. Roses. Flowers light orange-red, yellow reverse, dbl. (20 petals), small; very fragrant; foliage medium, medium green, semi-glossy; vigorous. AOE, 1984.

Little Jewel Min, *dp*, 1980, (COCabel); *Wee Man × Belinda*; Cocker, James. Flowers deep pink, dbl. (34 petals), patio, blooms borne

6-12 per cluster; slight fragrance; foliage small, glossy, dark; straight prickles; low, compact growth.

Little Joe HT, *dr*, 1921, *Red-Letter Day* × *H.V. Machin*; Looymans; Prior. Flowers crimson-red, single.

Little John Min, *rb*, 1959, *Baby Masquerade sport*; Mason, F. Bud pointed; flowers scarlet, center white, semi-dbl. to dbl., high-centered, medium, borne in clusters; slightly fragrant; foliage soft; vigorous, bushy (12-15 in.).

Little Joker Min, *pb*, 1958, Spek. Flowers rose-pink, center cream, well-shaped; bushy.

Little Juan Min, *mr*, 1966, *Juliette* × *Seedling*; Williams, E.D.; Mini-Roses. Flowers medium red, reverse lighter, dbl., small; slightly fragrant; foliage small, leathery; vigorous, dwarf.

Little Juliet HT, *yb*, 1924, *F.J. Looymans seedling* × *Seedling*; Looymans; Prior. Flowers apricot and peach on yellow ground, dbl.; slightly fragrant.

Little Lady Pol, *w*, 1967, *Schneewittchen* × *Baby Faurax*; Harkness. Flowers blush to ice-white, dbl. (70 petals), small; slightly fragrant; dwarf growth.

Little Leaguer F, *dr*, 1962, *Garnette seedling* × *Yuletide*; Jelly; E.G. Hill Co. Bud ovoid; flowers dark red, dbl. (28-40 petals), cupped, medium (2-2½ in.); slightly fragrant; vigorous, upright growth; for indoor forcing.

Little Lighthouse Min, *rb*, 1991, (CLElight); *Robin Red Breast* × *Little Artist*; Clements, John; Heirloom Old Garden Roses, 1992. Flowers bright red with yellow to white eye, single (5 petals), exhibition, small (0-4 cms) blooms borne in small clusters; no fragrance; foliage small, medium green, semi-glossy; some prickles; low (18 cms), bushy, spreading, compact, ground cover growth.

Little Linda Min, *ly*, 1976, *Gold Coin seedling* × *Seedling*; Schwartz, E.W.; Nor'East Min. Roses. Bud high-pointed; flowers yellow, semi-dbl. (17 petals), high-centered, micro-mini, small (1 in.); slightly fragrant; compact growth.

Little Liza Min, *mp*, 1975, *Fairy Moss* × *Fairy Moss*; Saville; Nor'East Min. Roses. Bud mossy; flowers rose-pink, semi-dbl. (15 petals), small (½-1 in.); low, very compact.

Little Love Min, *mp*, 1977, *Little Amy* × *Seedling*; Lyon; L. Lyon Greenhouses. Bud pointed; flowers rose-pink, dbl. (25-30 petals), open, small (1½ in.); slightly fragrant; foliage tiny; very low, compact growth.

Little Magician™ Min, *yb*, 1989, (WILmag); *Circus* × *Magic Carrousel*; Williams, J. Benjamin; White Rose Nursery, 1990. Bud

ovoid; flowers light yellow with orange-red blend, dbl. (32 petals), high-centered, loose, small, borne usually singly and in sprays of 1-3; slight, damask fragrance; foliage small, medium green, semi-glossy; prickles none; fruit none observed; low, winter-hardy growth.

Little Marvel Min, *or*, 1988, (RUIgerdan); *Seedling* × *Seedling*; DeRuiter, G.; Fryers Nursery, Ltd., 1987. Flowers bright orange-scarlet, semi-dbl. (6-14 petals), small; slight fragrance; foliage small, medium green, semi-glossy; bushy growth.

Little Melody Min, *pb*, 1979, *Neue Revue* × *Sheri Anne*; Strawn, Leslie; Tiny Petals Nursery. Bud globular; flowers soft peach-yellow blend, dbl. (38 petals), exhibition blooms borne singly; fragrant; foliage medium green; light brown prickles, curved downward; compact, bushy growth.

Little Mike Min, *dr*, 1967, ((*R. wichuraiana* × *Floradora*) × *Seedling*) × *Little Buckaroo*; Moore, R.S.; Sequoia Nursery. Bud ovoid; flowers deep red, dbl., high-centered, small; foliage dark, glossy, leathery; vigorous, dwarf growth.

Little Miss Muffett F, *pb*, 1940, *Else Poulsen* × *Étoile de Hollande*; LeGrice; C-P. Bud pointed, cerise; flowers bright rose-pink, reverse deeper, semi-dbl., open, large, borne in clusters on strong stems; slightly fragrant; vigorous, bushy growth.

Little Nell HT, *yb*, 1933, Archer. Flowers deep cream, center apricot, reverse primrose, well shaped; very fragrant; foliage glossy, dark; vigorous growth.

Little Nugget Min, *my*, 1992, (SUNgold); *Lorena* × *Firefly*; Schuurman, Frank B.; Riverland Nurseries, Ltd., 1991. Flowers golden yellow, moderately full (15-25 petals), patio, small (0-4 cms.); slight fragrance; foliage small, medium green, semi-glossy; bushy growth.

Little One S, *rb*, 1988, (SANone); *(Sarabande* × *Seedling)* × *Circus*; Sanday, John; John Sanday Roses. Flowers red with white eye, single (5 petals), borne in sprays of 12-20; no fragrance; foliage medium, medium green, glossy; prickles average, light brown; bushy, low growth; repeats.

Little Opal Min, *lp*, 1992, (SUNpat); *White Dream* × *Dicky Bird*; Schuurman, Frank B.; Riverland Nurseries, Ltd., 1991. Flowers light pink, moderately full (15-25 petals), patio, small (0-4 cms.) blooms; slight fragrance; foliage small, medium green, glossy; upright growth.

Little Paradise™ Min, *m*, 1988, (WEKlips); *Shocking Blue* × *Helen Boehm*; Carruth, Tom;

Weeks Roses, 1991. Flowers deep lavender, blushing purple, reverse deep lavender, aging lighter, dbl. (20 petals), high-centered, exhibition, medium, borne usually singly; slight fragrance; foliage small, dark green, semiglossy, disease resistant; prickles nearly straight, small, yellow-brown; fruit none; upright, medium, vigorous, abundant growth.

Little Peaces Min, *yb*, 1985, (TINpeaces); *Electron × Fairest of Fair*; Bennett, Dee; Tiny Petals Nursery. Flowers yellow, edged pink, dbl. (33 petals), HT form, medium; slight fragrance; foliage medium, medium green, semi-glossy; compact, bushy growth.

Little Pearl Min, *lp*, 1992, (SUNpearl); *Innocent × MACfrabro (Firefly)*; Schuurman, Frank B.; Riverland Nurseries Ltd. Flowers light pink, full (26-40 petals), small (0-4 cms.) blooms; slight fragrance; foliage small, medium green, glossy; few prickles; medium (50 cms.), upright growth.

Little Pim® Min, *mr*, 1984, (LENnop); *Miniature seedling × Ruth Leuwerick*; Lens, Louis. Flowers medium red, dbl. (24 petals), rosette, small blooms in clusters of 3-32; no fragrance; foliage dark; hooked, greenish-brown prickles; bushy growth.

Little Pink F, *pb*, 1965, *Little Darling × Seedling*; Castleberry. Flowers pink, center creamy pink, very dbl., high-centered, small; slightly fragrant; foliage glossy; vigorous, compact growth.

Little Pioneer Min, *mr*, 1986, (CURneer); *(Rise 'n' Shine × Summer Butter) × Sheri Anne*; Curtis, Thad; Hortco, Inc. Flowers medium red, gold stamens, dbl. (35 petals), HT form, small blooms borne singly and in clusters; fragrant; foliage small to medium, medium green, matt; upright, bushy growth.

Little Pooh Min, *or*, 1979, *Anytime × Seedling*; Fong, William P. Bud slim, pointed; flowers orange-red, single (5-6 petals), flat blooms borne 5-6 per cluster; fragrant; foliage heavy, thick; triangular prickles; upright growth.

Little Prince Min, *or*, 1982, (COCcord); *Darling Flame × (National Trust × Wee Man)*; Cocker, J.; Cocker & Sons, 1983. Flowers orange-red, yellow eye, semi-dbl., patio, small; slight fragrance; foliage medium, medium green, semi-glossy; upright, bushy growth.

Little Princess Pol, *ob*, 1937, Knight, G.; Beckwith. Flowers pale salmon-coral, dbl., well-formed; vigorous, bushy growth.

Little Princess F, *mp*, 1955, *Garnette sport*; Sodano, J. Flowers rose-pink, reverse lighter, dbl. (50-75 petals), cupped, medium (2 in.), borne on long stems; fragrant; vigorous growth.

Little Rascal Min, *mr*, 1981, *Sheri Anne × Rise 'n' Shine*; Jolly, Betty; Rosehill Farm. Flowers medium red, shading to yellow at base, reverse lighter, dbl. (34 petals), high-centered, exhibition blooms borne usually singly; slight fragrance; foliage tiny, light green; slightly hooked prickles; compact, bushy growth.

Little Red Min, *or*, 1975, *New Penny × Coloranja*; Lens; Spek. Bud ovoid; flowers red-orange, semi-dbl. (18-22 petals), pompon shape, small ('/₂ in.); slightly fragrant; foliage glossy; compact growth.

Little Red Devil Min, *mr*, 1980, (AROvidil); *Gingersnap × Magic Carrousel*; Christensen; Armstrong Nursery. Bud ovoid, pointed; flowers medium red, dbl. (44 petals), imbricated small ('/₂ in.) blooms borne 1-8 per cluster; slightly fragrant; foliage small, semiglossy, irregularly serrated; small, narrow prickles; vigorous, bushy, fairly tall growth.

Little Red Monkey F, *mr*, 1954, *Donald Prior × Seedling*; Ratcliffe. Flowers bright red, very dbl., short stiff petals, borne singly and in sprays; bushy growth.

Little Russel Min, *mr*, 1982, (TRObric; TRObic); *Marlena × New Penny*; Robinson, Thomas; T. Robinson, Ltd., 1983. Flowers medium red, dbl. (20 petals), small; no fragrance; foliage small, dark, glossy; bushy growth.

Little Scotch Min, *ly*, 1958, *Golden Glow (LCl) × Zee*; Moore, R.S.; Sequoia Nursery. Bud long; flowers straw-yellow to white, dbl. (55 petals), medium (1½ in.); fragrant; foliage leathery; vigorous, bushy (12 in.) growth.

Little Showoff Cl Min, *yb*, 1960, *Golden Glow × Zee*; Moore, R.S.; Sequoia Nursery. Bud pointed; flowers bright yellow, sometimes tinted red, dbl. (30 petals), high-centered, small (1½ in.); fragrant; upright (to 4 ft.).

Little Shrimp® F, *lp*, 1984, (LENlit); *Little Angel × (Little Angel × Spartan)*; Lens, Louis. Flowers light shrimp-pink, dbl. (40 petals), rosette, 2 in. blooms in clusters of 3-24; slight fragrance; foliage small; hooked, brownish-red prickles; bushy growth.

Little Sir Echo Min, *mp*, 1977, *Ma Perkins × Baby Betsy McCall*; Schwartz, E.W.; Nor'East Min. Roses. Bud long, pointed; flowers medium pink, dbl. (48 petals), high-centered, small (1-1½ in.); fragrant; foliage matt, green; compact, upright growth.

Little Sir Echo, Climbing Cl Min, *mp*, 1985, *Little Sir Echo sport*; Watterberg, Leah.

Little Sizzler™ Min, *mr*, 1988, (JACiat; Patio Jewel); *Seedling × Funny Girl*; Warriner, William; Bear Creek Gardens, 1989. Bud ovoid, pointed; flowers medium red, dbl. (38 petals), cupped, large, borne usually singly and in sprays of 16-20; foliage large, dark green, semi-glossy; prickles hooked downward, reddish-brown; bushy, medium growth.

Little Slam® Min, *dr*, 1990, (KINslam); *((B.C. × Scamp) × Red Ace) × Scamp*; King, Gene; AGM Miniature Roses, 1989. Flowers deep red, moderately full (15-25 petals), small, borne mostly singly; no fragrance; foliage small, medium green, semi-glossy; bushy, low growth.

Little Smiles Min, *yb*, 1978, *Q17a × Redgold*; Lyon. Bud ovoid; flowers chinese yellow vermilion, semi-dbl. (12 petals), small (1 in.); fragrant (spicy); compact growth.

Little Squirt Min, *dy*, 1984, (TINsquirt); Bennett, Dee; Tiny Petals Nursery, 1983. Flowers deep yellow, semi-dbl. (14 petals), HT form, micro-mini, very small; slight fragrance; foliage small, medium green, semi-glossy; upright, compact growth.

Little Starburst™ Min, *yb*, 1991, *Prominent × Rise 'n' Shine*; Williams, J. Benjamin, 1988. Flowers orange-red washing on golden yellow, very full, small blooms borne mostly singly and in small clusters; slight fragrance; foliage small, medium green, semi-glossy; low, bushy growth.

Little Stephen HT, *mp*, 1971, *Gavotte × Seedling*; Sanday. Flowers glowing pink, dbl. (40 petals), high-centered, medium (3 in.); fragrant; foliage matt; upright growth.

Little Sunset Min, *pb*, 1967, *Seedling × Tom Thumb*; Kordes. Flowers salmon-pink on yellow, star-shaped blooming clusters; foliage small, light green.

Little Sunshine Pol, *my*, 1915, *R. multiflora nana × Soleil d'Or*; Cumming; A.N. Pierson. Flowers creamy yellow, varying to deep golden yellow, occasionally flecked crimson, dbl., medium (1½-2 in.), panicle; dwarf growth.

Little 't' Min, *w*, 1988, (TRAt); *Cinderella × Seedling*; Travis, Louis, 1989. Bud pointed; flowers white tinged pale pink, reverse white, dbl. (50+ petals), cupped, small, borne in sprays of 4-6; no fragrance; foliage small, medium green, matt; prickles none: fruit none; bushy growth.

Little Tease Min, *pb*, 1988, (ZIPtease); *High Spirits × Charmglo*; Zipper, Herbert; Magic Moment Miniature Roses, 1989. Flowers yellow to cream at base, suffused with clear pink, darker at edges, exhibition, small, borne singly; no fragrance; foliage small, medium green, semi-glossy; bushy, compact growth.

Little Tiger Min, *rb*, 1989, (MORshaki); *Golden Angel × Pinstripe*; Moore, Ralph S.; Sequoia Nursery. Bud short, pointed; flowers red, yellow and white stripes of varying patterns, reverse with more yellow, aging to white and red-pink, very dbl. (90+ petals), high-centered, medium, borne usually singly and in sprays of 3-5; no fragrance; foliage small, medium green, matt; prickles average, slender, inclined downward, brown; bushy, low, rounded growth.

Little Tyke Min, *pb*, 1986, (RENyke); *Julie Ann × Red Love*; Rennie, Bruce; Rennie Roses. Flowers medium pink, white reverse, dbl. (25 petals), loose form; small blooms borne singly; no fragrance; foliage small, medium green, matt; small, reddish prickles; fruit small; small, bushy, very compact growth.

Little Vegas Min, *mr*, 1985, (SPOvegas); *(Rise 'n' Shine × Prominent) × Red seedling.*; Spooner, Raymond A.; Oregon Min. Roses, Inc., 1984. Flowers medium red, dbl. (20 petals), HT form, small; slight fragrance; foliage small, medium green, semi-glossy; bushy growth.

Little Wallace F, *pb*, 1952, *Elfe (F) sport*; Beall; Beall Greenhouse Co. Bud very long; flowers light pink, center yellow, dbl. (25 petals), high-centered, medium blooms inclusters; slightly fragrant; foliage leathery, dark; vigorous growth.

Little Woman Min, *pb*, 1986, (DIClittle); *Memento × (Liverpool Echo × Woman's Own)*; Dickson, P. Flowers pink blend, moderately full (15-25 petals); patio; fragrant; foliage, small, medium green, semi-glossy; bushy growth.

Little Wonder F, *or*, 1975, *Duftwolke × Ena Harkness*; Huber. Bud pointed; flowers orange-red, dbl. (22-28 petals), shallow, large (3½-4 in.); fragrant (spicy); foliage small; upright to spreading growth.

Littlest Angel Min, *my*, 1976, *Gold Coin seedling × Miniature seedling*; Schwartz, E.W.; Nor'East Min. Roses. Bud short, pointed; flowers medium to deep yellow, dbl. (28 petals), high-centered, micro-mini, small (½ in.); slightly fragrant; foliage small; low, compact, bushy growth.

Littlest Spartan Min, *rb*, 1992, (GRUlit); *Red Ace × Seedling*; Gruenbauer, Richard; Flowers 'n' Friends Miniature Roses. Flowers medium red and yellow, moderately full (22-30 petals), small (2½ cms.) blooms borne mostly singly; no fragrance; foliage medium, medium green, semi-glossy; some prickles; low (20-30 cms.), upright, bushy growth.

Live Wire™ Min, *dp*, 1988, (SAVawire); *(Rise 'n' Shine × Sheri Anne) × Rainbow's End*; Saville, F. Harmon; Nor'East Miniature

Roses. Flowers deep cardinal red-pink, reverse darker, aging lighter, semi-dbl. (27-30 petals), cupped, loose, small, profuse, borne usually singly; micro-mini; no fragrance; foliage small, medium green, semi-glossy; prickles thin, straight, dark gray-purple; fruit none; bushy, low, compact growth.

Lively HT, *dp*, 1959, *Wellworth × Ena Harkness*; LeGrice. Flowers rose pink, dbl. (32 petals), large (4-6 in.); very fragrant; foliage dark, glossy; vigorous, compact, low growth.

Lively Lady F, *or*, 1969, *Elizabeth of Glamis × Tropicana*; Cocker. Flowers vermilion, dbl., large; slightly fragrant; foliage dark, glossy.

Liverpool Echo F, *op*, 1971, (Liverpool); *(Little Darling × Goldilocks) × Munchen*; McGredy, S., IV; McGredy. Flowers salmon, dbl. (23 petals), HT form, large (4 in.); slightly fragrant; foliage light; tall growth. GM, Portland, 1979.

Liverpool Remembers HT, *or*, 1992, (FRYstar; Beauty Star); *Corso × Seedling*; Fryer, Gareth; Roses by Fred Edmunds, 1990. Flowers vermillion, full (26-40 petals), large (7+ cms) blooms borne mostly singly; foliage medium, medium green, glossy; many prickles; tall (240 cms), upright growth.

Liverton Lady Cl HT, *mp*, 1978, *Bantry Bay × Sympathie*; Warner; Bradley Nursery. Flowers pink, semi-dbl. (16-20 petals), large (3-4 in.); slightly fragrant; foliage small, glossy; tall, climbing growth.

Living HT, *rb*, 1957, *Charlotte Armstrong × Grande Duchesse Charlotte*; Lammerts; Consolidated Nursery. Flowers reddish orange, reverse copper streaked red, dbl. (24 petals), high-centered, large (5-6 in.); spicy fragrance; foliage leathery, semi-glossy; vigorous.

Living Bouquet Min, *ly*, 1991, (LAVlinger; Yellow Festival); *Loving Touch × (Dorola × Genevieve)*; Laver, Keith, 1986; Springwood Miniature Roses. Bud ovoid; flowers light yellow, very dbl. (40-50 petals), flat, full, medium blooms borne in sprays of 3-5; no fragrance; foliage medium, light green, semi-glossy; bushy, compact, semi-upright growth.

Living Coral HT, *op*, 1974, *Queen of Bermuda × Tropicana*; Golik; Dynarose. Bud ovoid; flowers soft coral-pink, dbl. (28 petals), high-centered, large (5 in.); fragrant (fruity); foliage glossy; moderate growth.

Living Fire F, *ob*, 1972, *Tropicana × Seedling*; Gregory, 1973. Flowers orange, suffused orange-red, dbl. (33 petals), rosette form, medium (2½ in.); fragrant; foliage dark.

Lizabeth's Lullabye HT, *yb*, 1991, (WIRcurob); *Queen Elizabeth × Song of Paris*; Robbins, William C., 1990. Flowers yellow with pink tips, moderately full (35-40 petals), large; fragrant; foliage large, dark green, glossy; upright, tall growth.

Lizzie Molk S, *pb*, 1983, Rusnock, Ann M. Flowers light pink, white center, dbl. (20 petals), medium blooms in clusters; very fragrant; foliage medium, blue-green, glossy; spreading growth; does not repeat.

L. J. de Hoog HT, *mr*, 1934, *Hadley × Hawlmark Scarlet*; Leenders Bros. Flowers scarlet-red, full, well formed, large; slightly fragrant; vigorous, bushy growth.

Ljuba Rizzoli® HT, *dr*, 1980, (Via Romana); Dot, Simon; Barni-Pistoia, Rose. Bud pointed; flowers dark red, dbl. (25 petals), cupped blooms borne singly; very fragrant; foliage large, dark, matt; purple-green prickles; upright, bushy growth.

Lleida HT, *rb*, 1936, *Edouard Renard × Condesa de Sástago*; Dot, P.; A. Meilland. Flowers bright red, reverse yellow; very fragrant; very vigorous growth.

Lloyd Center Supreme Gr, *pb*, 1990, (TWOloy); *Brion × Seedling*; Twomey, Jerry, 1988; DeVor Nursery, 1990. Bud pointed; flowers light pink with yellow base, dark pink blending to yellow reverse, aging very light pink, dbl. (25 petals), high-centered, large, borne in sprays of 4-7; fruity fragrance; foliage medium, dark green, glossy; upright, bushy, medium growth.

Loads of Pink F, *mp*, 1991, (FIAlopi); *Fred Loads sport*; Fiamingo, Joe, 1991. Flowers medium pink, semi-dbl. (6-14 petals), medium (4-7 cms) blooms borne in large clusters; fragrant; foliage medium green, semi-glossy, disease resistant; some prickles; tall, upright, very vigorous growth.

Lobo HT, *rb*, 1987, *Kordes' Perfecta × Gavotte*; Perry, Astor, 1989. Flowers red-purple, reverse white, dbl. (26-40 petals), exhibition, large; very fragrant; foliage large, dark green, matt; upright growth.

L'Obscurité M (OGR), *dr*, 1848, Lacharme. Flowers dark garnet-crimson, semi-dbl., large.

Locarno Pol, *or*, 1926, *Orléans Rose sport*; deRuiter. Flowers orange-red, large, borne in huge clusters; vigorous, bushy growth.

Locomotion HT, *yb*, 1965, *R.M.S. Queen Mary × Lady Sylvia*; Verschuren, H.A.M.; Ravensberg. Flowers salmon tinted peach, becoming citron-yellow; foliage dark, leathery; vigorous, bushy growth.

Lodestar HT, *pb*, 1953, *Diamond Jubilee seedling × Serenade*; Boerner; J&P. Bud ovoid to globular; flowers buff-pink, center peach, dbl. (35-40 petals), large (4½-5 in.); very fragrant (spicy); foliage leathery; bushy growth.

Lodewijk Opdebeek HT, *dr*, 1921, *Jonkheer J.L. Mock* × *Mev. Dora van Tets*; Leenders, M. Flowers oxblood-red, reverse rose, dbl.; fragrant.

Loeta Liggett HT, *pb*, 1984, *Duet sport*; Liggett, Myron T. Flowers light pink, darker pink reverse, often with salmon center.

Lois Min, *mp*, 1985, (TINlois); *Deep Purple* × *Plum Duffy*; Bennett, Dee; Tiny Petals Nursery. Flowers medium lilac pink, dbl. (40+ pointed petals), HT form, medium; fragrant; foliage medium, medium green, semi-glossy; upright, bushy growth.

Lois Crouse HT, *lp*, 1937, *Mme. Butterfly seedling*; Moore, R.S.; Brooks & Son. Bud pointed; flowers light pink, suffused salmon, dbl., peony form, large; foliage dark; vigorous, bushy growth.

Lois Maney LCl, *op*, 1953, *R. maximowicziana pilosa* × *Templar*; Maney; Iowa State College. Flowers salmon-pink, dbl., large (4-5 in.); slightly fragrant; foliage leathery; very vigorous (25 ft.) growth; abundant, non-recurrent bloom.

Lola Vendrell HT, *pb*, 1957, *Serafina Longa* × *Mme. Kriloff*; Bofill; Toree Blanca. Flowers soft pink streaked deeper, dbl. (40 petals), well formed, large; long stems; fragrant; foliage glossy; vigorous growth.

Lolette Dupain R, *pb*, 1918, *Casimir Moulle* × *Mme. Norbert Levavasseur*; Lottin. Flowers yellowish rose, reverse silvery rose, dbl., borne in clusters; vigorous growth; sometimes recurrent bloom.

Loli Creus HT, *dp*, 1953, *Cynthia* × *Manuelita*; Dot, P. Flowers carmine, well formed, large; strong stems; foliage glossy; very vigorous growth.

Lolita® HT, *ab*, 1973, (KORlita; LitaKOR); *Colour Wonder* × *Seedling*; Kordes, R.; Dicksons of Hawlmark, 1972. Flowers golden bronze, dbl. (28 petals), large (5 in.); fragrant. ADR, 1973.

Lolita HT, *w*, 1937, *Frau Karl Druschki* × *Hybrid Tea Seedling*; Croibier. Flowers white, center cream, dbl., globular, very large; foliage leathery; vigorous growth.

Lollipop Min, *mr*, 1959, *(R. wichuraiana* × *Floradora)* × *Little Buckaroo*; Moore, R.S.; Sequoia Nursery. Flowers bright red, dbl. (35 petals), small (1-1½ in.); slightly fragrant; foliage glossy; vigorous (14 in.), bushy growth.

Lollo HT, *rb*, 1949, *Lele* × *Crimson Glory*; San Remo Exp. Sta. Bud pointed; flowers purplish red, reverse crimson-carmine, dbl. (32-36 petals), well formed; strong stems; fragrant; foliage dark; vigorous, bushy growth.

London Pride HT, *op*, 1954, Ratcliffe. Flowers deep salmon-pink shaded coral, high-centered; fragrant; upright growth.

London Starlets HT, *ob*, 1959, *Mission Bells* × *Jiminy Cricket seedling*; Maarse, G. Flowers orange to orange-red, dbl. (50 petals), well shaped, large; long, strong stems; fragrant; vigorous growth.

London Town HT, *op*, 1955, *Peace* × *Charles Gregory*; Letts. Flowers salmon-pink, base buff, well formed, medium; fragrant (fruity); vigorous growth.

Lone Star HT, *mr*, 1925, *Étoile de France seedling*; Buller; Hillje. Flowers velvety cardinal-red, semi-dbl., large; fragrant; vigorous, upright growth.

Lone Star State HT, *pb*, 1943, *Texas Centennial sport*; Collins. Flowers darker than parent, irregularly striped white.

Long John Silver LCl, *w*, 1934, *R. setigera seedling* × *Sunburst*; Horvath; J&P. Bud pointed; flowers silvery white, dbl., cupped, very large blooms in clusters; fragrant; foliage large, leathery; vigorous, climbing growth.

Longchamp F, *mr*, 1960, Laperrière; EFR. Flowers bright red cerise, semi-dbl., medium, borne in clusters; foliage glossy; vigorous, symmetrical growth.

Longwood LCl, *mp*, 1914, *American Pillar* × *Seedling*; Wintzer. Flowers pink, semi-dbl.

Longworth Rambler LCl, *mr*, 1880, Liabaud. Flowers light crimson, semi-dbl.; vigorous growth.

Looping® LCl, *ob*, 1977, (MEIrovonex); *((Zambra* × *Zambra)* × *(Malcair* × *Danse des Sylphes)* × *(Cocktail* × *Cocktail))* × *Royal Gold*; Meilland, M.L.; Meilland. Bud conical; flowers orange-coral, dbl. (40 petals), flat-cupped, medium; slightly fragrant; foliage dark; vigorous, climbing growth; spring bloom.

Lord Allenby HT, *dr*, 1923, Dickson, A. Flowers bright crimson, dbl., high-centered, very large; slightly fragrant; foliage rich green, leathery; dwarf, sturdy growth.

Lord Bacon HP (OGR), *dr*, 1883, Paul, W. Flowers deep crimson shaded scarlet, full, globular, large; vigorous growth.

Lord Baden-Powell HT, *ob*, 1937, Leenders, M. Bud orange striped red; flowers saffron-yellow, very dbl., large; fragrant; vigorous, bushy, compact growth.

Lord Calvert HT, *dr*, 1919, *Radiance* × *Hoosier Beauty*; Cook, J. Flowers dark velvety red, dbl.; very fragrant.

Lord Castlereagh HT, *dr*, 1927, Dickson, A. Bud pointed; flowers dark blackish crimson, semi-dbl., open; very fragrant; foliage dark, leathery; vigorous, bushy growth.

Lord Charlemont HT, *dr*, 1922, McGredy. Bud long, pointed; flowers clear deep crimson, dbl., high-centered, well shaped, large; very fragrant; foliage dark, leathery; bushy growth.

Lord Charlemont, Climbing Cl HT, *dr*, 1932, Hurcombe.

Lord Clyde HP (OGR), *dr*, 1863, Paul. Flowers bright crimson, well formed, large.

Lord Fairfax HT, *dp*, 1925, Gray, W.R. Flowers cherry-rose-pink, long stems; fragrant; foliage leathery; good habit.

Lord Frederick Cavendish HP (OGR), *mr*, 1883, Frettingham. Flowers bright scarlet.

Lord Houghton of Sowerby HT, *op*, 1989, (HARtubond); *Silver Jubilee* × *Basildon Bond*; Harkness, R. & Co., Ltd., 1990. Bud pointed; flowers warm, reddish, salmon-pink, reverse deeper, high-centered, exhibition, large, borne singly; slight, spicy fragrance; foliage large, dark green, glossy; prickles broad based, large, reddish; fruit none observed; upright, medium growth.

Lord Kitchener HT, *dp*, 1918, Chaplin Bros. Flowers bright carmine-rose, dbl.; very fragrant.

Lord Lambourne HT, *yb*, 1925, McGredy. Bud pointed; flowers buttercup-yellow, edged carmine-scarlet, dbl., high-centered, very large; fragrant; foliage light, leathery, glossy; very vigorous, bushy growth.

Lord Lonsdale HT, *ab*, 1933, Dickson, A.; H&S; Dreer. Bud pointed; flowers deepest orange-yellow, dbl., high-centered, large; fragrant; foliage glossy, light; vigorous, bushy growth. GM, NRS, 1931.

Lord Louis HT, *dp*, 1981, *Pink Favorite* × *Seedling*; Gregory, C.; C. Gregory & Sons. Bud pointed; flowers light crimson, dbl. (30 petals), blooms borne several together; fragrant; foliage mid-green, glossy; vigorous growth.

Lord Macaulay HP (OGR), *dr*, 1874, Paul, W. Flowers crimson, globular.

Lord Penzance E (OGR), *yb*, 1894, *R. eglanteria* × *Harison's Yellow*; Penzance. Flowers soft rosy yellow, paler at base, yellow stamens, single, blooms in clusters; fragrant; foliage small, dark, fragrant; very vigorous growth; summer bloom.

Lord Raglan HP (OGR), *dr*, 1854, *Geant des Batailles seedling*; Guillot Père. Flowers bright velvety crimson, very full, very large.

Lord Rossmore HT, *w*, 1930, Hall; McGredy. Flowers creamy white shaded rose toward edge, dbl., high-centered, large; fragrant; foliage dark olive-green, leathery; vigorous growth. GM, NRS, 1928.

Lord Stair HT, *dr*, 1930, Smith, T. Bud pointed; flowers velvety crimson-scarlet, dbl., high-centered, large; fragrant; foliage dark, leathery; very vigorous, bushy growth.

Lordly Oberon S, *lp*, 1983, (AUSron); *Chaucer* × *Seedling*; Austin, David; David Austin Roses, 1982. Flowers light pink, very dbl., cupped, large; very fragrant; foliage large, medium green, matt; upright growth.

L'Oréal Trophy HT, *ob*, 1981, (HARlexis; Alexis); *Alexander sport*; Harkness, R., 1982. Flowers orange. GM, Bagatelle; Belfast, 1984; Golden Rose of Courtrai, 1986.

Loree F, *w*, 1969, *Frolic* × *Seedling*; Pal; Son. Bud long, pointed; flowers white tinted pink, dbl., cupped, small; slightly fragrant; foliage leathery; vigorous, bushy, compact growth.

Lorelei S, *ab*, 1947, *Joanna Hill* × *Harison's Yellow*; Fisher, R.C. Bud ovoid; flowers peach-pink, center yellow, semi-dbl., large (3-4 in.); very fragrant; foliage leathery, dark; vigorous, upright growth; non-recurrent bloom.

Lorena® F, *mp*, 1984, (KORenlo; Lorina); *Angelique* × *Seedling*; Kordes, W., 1983. Flowers medium salmon-pink, dbl. (35 petals), HT form, large; no fragrance; foliage medium, medium green, semi-glossy; upright growth.

Lorenzo Pahissa HT, *op*, 1941, *Seedling* × *Mari Dot*; Pahissa. Flowers coral, full, very large; fragrant; foliage abundant; very vigorous, upright growth. GM, Bagatelle, 1941.

Loretta® F, *mp*, 1987, (KORenpi); *Lorena sport*; Kordes, W., 1986. Flowers medium pink, dbl. (26-40 petals), medium; no fragrance; foliage medium, medium green, matt; bushy growth.

Loretto LCl, *pb*, 1922, *Jersey Beauty* × *Seedling*; Clark, A.; Brundrett. Flowers reddish, center white, semi-dbl., medium blooms in clusters; fragrant; few prickles; vigorous, climbing.

Lori Ann F, *yb*, 1990, *Judy Garland* × *Sutter's Gold*; Schneider, Peter, 1987. Flowers bright amber yellow, flushed orange and pink, reverse yellow, aging golden yellow with orange, dbl. (20 petals), loose, cupped, large, borne usually singly or in sprays of 3-5; moderate, fruity fragrance; foliage medium, medium green, semi-glossy, slightly elongated and narrow; slightly spreading, medium growth.

Lori Nan Min, *dp*, 1965, (*R. wichuraiana* × *Floradora*) × (*Seedling* × *Zee*); Moore, R.S.; Sequoia Nursery. Bud globular; flowers rose-red, dbl., small; foliage glossy, leathery; moderate growth.

Lorna HT, *op*, 1936, Cant, B.R. Bud pointed; flowers salmon, dbl., high-centered; foliage leathery, glossy, light; vigorous, bushy.

Lorna Anderson HT, *mr*, 1940, Clark, A. Flowers red, well-formed; fragrant.

Lorna Doone F, *mr*, 1972, *Red Dandy* × *Lilli Marleen*; Harkness. Flowers medium red, dbl. (24 petals), large (4 in.); slightly fragrant; foliage dark, glossy.

Lorna May F, *rb*, 1958, *Poulsen's Pink* × *Käthe Duvigneau*; deRuiter; Blaby Rose Gardens. Flowers crimson-red, center white, single, medium (2 in.), large trusses; foliage light green; vigorous growth.

Lorraine HT, *op*, 1945, *Peace* × *Mme. Mallerin*; Meilland, F. Flowers salmon-carmine touched red, full, large; vigorous growth.

Lorraine Lee T (OGR), *pb*, 1924, *Jessie Clark* × *Capitaine Millet*; Clark, A.; Hackett. Bud pointed; flowers rosy apricot-pink, dbl., cupped; fragrant; foliage rich green, leathery, glossy; vigorous growth; (14).

Lorraine Lee, Climbing Cl T (OGR), *pb*, 1932, McKay.

Lorraine Stebbings Min, *w*, 1985, *Cinderella* × *Popcorn*; Morey, Dr. Dennison. Flowers white, dbl. (23 petals), small blooms borne singly; slight honey fragrance; foliage small, glossy; upright, bushy growth.

Los Angeles HT, *op*, 1916, *Mme. Segond Weber* × *Lyon Rose*; Howard, F.H.; H&S. Bud pointed; flowers coral-pink, base gold, dbl., large; very fragrant; foliage leathery; vigorous, spreading growth. GM, Bagatelle, 1918.

Los Angeles Beautiful Gr, *yb*, 1967, *Queen Elizabeth* × *Rumba*; Lammerts; Germain's. Flowers yellow blended with coral and scarlet, dbl., high-centered, medium; slightly fragrant; foliage dark, leathery, vigorous, upright, compact growth.

Los Angeles, Climbing Cl HT, *pb*, 1925, H&S.

Los Tejas HT, *mr*, 1968, *Chrysler Imperial* × *Happiness*; Patterson; Patterson Roses. Bud globular; flowers red, dbl., high-centered, large; fragrant; foliage leathery; vigorous, upright.

Lotte Günthart HT, *mr*, 1964, *Queen Elizabeth* × *Bravo*; Armstrong, D.L.; Armstrong Nursery. Bud ovoid; flowers bright red, very dbl. (90 petals), peony form, large; foliage leathery; tall, upright, bushy growth.

Lou-Celina S, *dr*, 1979, *(Venture* × *((Cecilia* × *China Belle)* × *Suzanne))* × *(Paula* × *Soeur Kristin)*; James, John; Historical Roses, 1986. Flowers dark red, dbl. (50 petals), large; fra-

grant; foliage medium, dark red-green, semi-glossy; upright; repeats.

L'Ouche HCh (OGR), *pb*, 1901, Buatois, 1891. Flowers rose shaded yellow.

Louisa Jane HT, *m*, 1976, *Baronne Edmond de Rothschild sport*; Ross, A.; A. Ross & Son. Flowers center soft white, shading to mauve-pink.

Louisa Schultheis HT, *op*, 1925, *Golden Ophelia* × *Ruhm von Steinfurth*; Schultheis, A. Flowers pink and salmon, center darker, dbl. (32-36 petals); slightly fragrant.

Louis Bourgoin HT, *lp*, 1921, *Jonkheer J.L. Mock* × *Frau Karl Druschki*; Gillot, F. Flowers flesh-pink passing to silvery pink, dbl.; slightly fragrant.

Louis de Funès® HT, *ob*, 1987, (MEIrestif; Charleston 88); *(Ambassador* × *Whisky Mac)* × *(Arthur Bell* × *Kabuki)*; Meilland, Mrs. Marie-Louise, 1983. Flowers orange capucine reverse cadmium yellow, dbl. (15-25 petals), large; slight fragrance; foliage medium, dark green, glossy; upright, strong growth.

Louise HT, *mp*, 1924, *Isobel* × *Seedling*; Prince. Bud pointed; flowers rose-pink shaded cerise, dbl., large; very fragrant; foliage dark, leathery; vigorous growth.

Louise Abdy F, *mp*, 1964, *Donald Prior* × *McGredy's Yellow*; Abdy. Flowers pink, base yellow, single (6 petals), large (4 in.); fragrant; foliage dark; vigorous growth.

Louise Baldwin HT, *ob*, 1919, McGredy. Bud pointed; flowers rich orange, tinted soft apricot, dbl., high-centered; very fragrant; vigorous growth.

Louise Catherine Breslau HT, *op*, 1912, *Seedling* × *Soleil d'Or seedling*; Pernet-Ducher. Flowers shrimp-pink shaded reddish coppery orange, reverse chrome-yellow; dbl.; fragrant; foliage dark, bronze, leathery; bushy growth.

Louise Catherine Breslau, Climbing Cl HT, *op*, 1917, Kordes.

Louise Cretté HP (OGR), *w*, 1915, *Frau Karl Druschki* × *Kaiserin Auguste Viktoria, Climbing*; Chambard, C. Flowers snow-white, center creamy white, dbl. (55 petals), high-centered, well-formed, very large (6-7 in.); fragrant; foliage dark; vigorous, bushy growth.

Louise Criner HT, *w*, 1919, *Seedling* × *Louise Cretté*; Chambard, C. Flowers snow-white, center creamy, dbl.; few thorns.

Louise de Vilmorin HT, *ab*, 1944, Gaujard. Bud ovoid; flowers orange-yellow, very dbl., very large; slightly fragrant; foliage glossy, dark; dwarf.

Louise Estes HT, *pb*, 1991, *Seedling* × *Miss Canada*; Winchel, Joseph F.; Coiner Nursery, 1992. Bud pointed; flowers pink blend, reverse white, aging medium pink, dbl. (35 petals), medium (10 cms), high-centered, exhibition blooms borne usually singly; moderate, fruity fragrance; foliage medium, medium green, matt, disease resistant; upright, medium growth; quick repeat. ARC TG (S), 1991.

Louise Gardner HT, *yb*, 1987, (MACerupt); *Freude* × *Sunblest seedling*; McGredy, Sam; McGredy Roses International, 1988. Flowers yellow blend, dbl. (15-25 petals), large; slight fragrance; foliage medium, medium green, matt; upright, bushy growth.

Louise Gaujard HT, *op*, 1941, *Mme. Joseph Perraud* × *Seedling*; Gaujard. Flowers coppery pink shaded coral, very dbl., open, cupped, very large; fragrant; foliage light green; vigorous, upright growth.

Louise Hopkins R, *lp*, 1923, *Trier sport*; Hopkins. Flowers white, center shell-pink, very dbl.; vigorous, climbing (20 ft. or more); non-recurrent bloom.

Louise Joly HT, *or*, 1922, *Seedling* × *Mme. Edouard Herriot*; Buatois. Flowers coral-red, shaded shrimp-pink, dbl.; fragrant.

Louise Krause HT, *ob*, 1930, *Mrs. Beckwith* × *Souv. de H.A. Verschuren*; Krause. Flowers reddish orange, passing to golden yellow, dbl., large; slightly fragrant; foliage dark, glossy; vigorous, bushy growth.

Louise le Cardonnel HT, *yb*, 1939, *Seedling* × *Mev. G.A. van Rossem*; Mallerin; Meilland, A. Bud globular; flowers yellow tinted coral, full, very large, stiff stems; very vigorous growth.

Louise Mack Min, *dr*, 1992, *Seedling* × *Seedling*; Jerabek, Paul, 1984. Flowers dark red, dbl. (30 petals), high-centered, medium (3 cms) blooms borne usually singly; slight fragrance; foliage medium, dark green, semi-glossy; medium, spreading growth.

Louise Méhul G (OGR), *pb*, Parmentier. Flowers light red, spotted white, flat, large.

Louise Odier B (OGR), *dp*, 1851, (Mme. de Stella); Margottin. Flowers bright rose-pink, full, well-formed; (28).

Louise Peyrony HP (OGR), *dp*, 1844, *La Reine seedling*; Lacharme. Flowers deep pink shaded carmine, full, very large; fragrant; moderate growth.

Louise Pigné T (OGR), *mp*, 1905, *Mme. Eugène Résal* × *Mme. Lombard*; Pigné. Flowers china-pink, base buff-yellow, very full, petals crinkled, very large; fragrant; very vigorous growth.

Louise Verger M (OGR), *lp*, 1860, Robert et Moreau. Flowers bright pink, full, medium.

Louise Walter Pol, *pb*, 1909, *Tausendschön* × *Rosel Dach*; Walter, L.; P. Lambert. Flowers white and flesh-pink, dbl., open; foliage small, rich green; very dwarf growth. Sometimes wrongly called and quite distinct from Baby Tausendschön.

Louis Gimard M (OGR), *mp*, 1877, Pernet Père. Flowers bright pink, full, very large blooms on long stems; well-mossed; vigorous growth.

Louis Jolliet K (S), *mp*, 1991, (*R. kordesii* × *Open pollinated Max Graf*) × (*R. kordesii* × (*Red Dawn* × *Suzanne*) × *Champlain*)); Ogilvie, Ian S.; Agriculture Canada, 1992. Flowers medium pink, full (26-40 petals), medium; slight fragrance; foliage medium, medium green, semi-glossy; spreading, low growth.

Louis Kahle HT, *mr*, 1922, *Lieutenant Chaure* × *Étoile de France*; Kiese. Flowers bright cherry-red; very fragrant.

Louis Pajotin HT, *op*, 1940, *Souv. de Claudius Pernet* × *Margaret McGredy*; Mallerin; Meilland, A. Flowers coral, stamens yellow, very full, large; long, stiff stems; very vigorous growth.

Louis Pajotin, Climbing Cl HT, *op*, 1959, Pajotin-Chédane.

Louis Philippe Ch (OGR), *rb*, 1834, (Louis Philippe d'Angers); Guérin. Flowers dark crimson with edges of center petals blush, aging crimson, dbl., globular, medium; bushy.

Louis Philippe, Climbing Cl Ch, *rb*.

Louis Rödiger LCl, *ob*, 1935, *Daisy Hill* × (*Charles P. Kilham* × *Mev. G.A. van Rossem*); Kordes. Bud pointed; flowers orange shaded yellow and red, semi-dbl., open, very large; fragrant (fruity); foliage leathery, wrinkled, dark; very vigorous, climbing trailing growth.

Louis van Houtte HP (OGR), *dr*, *Général Jacqueminot* × *Seedling*; Lacharme, before 1866. Flowers crimson-maroon, dbl. (40 petals), well-formed, large; very fragrant; some recurrent bloom.

Louis van Tyle *m*, Class and originator unknown. Flowers light crimson, shaded black or purple, semi-dbl., small.

Louis Walter HT, *ab*, 1938, *Mrs. Pierre S. duPont seedling* × *Charles P. Kilham*; Mallerin. Flowers golden orange-yellow, full, large; foliage clear green, glossy; vigorous growth. Not to be confused with Louise Walter.

Louis XII T (OGR), *m*, Flowers violet, cupped.

Louis XIV Ch (OGR), *dr*, 1859, Guillot Fils. Flowers dark crimson, dbl. (25 petals), medium; very fragrant; foliage sparse; moderate growth.

Louisiana HT, *w*, 1969, *Seedling × Seedling*; Weeks. Flowers creamy white, dbl. (38 petals), high-centered, medium (3-4 in.); slightly fragrant; foliage dark, leathery; upright growth.

Louisiana Purchase HT, *dp*, 1954, *Charlotte Armstrong × Piccaninny*; Swim; Stark Bros. Bud long, pointed; Flowers rich cerise, dbl. (20-25 petals), cupped, large (4-5 in.); very fragrant(damask); foliage dark, leathery; very vigorous, upright growth.

Louisville Lady HT, *pb*, 1986, *Osiria × Seedling*; Weddle, Von C. Flowers bright pink, silver reverse, dbl. (35 petals), exhibition, medium; very fragrant; foliage medium, dark, semi-glossy; bushy growth.

Louqsor® HT, *ab*, 1967, (DELcraf; DELcraft; Louksor); *Dr. Albert Schweitzer × Provence*; Delbard-Chabert. Flowers apricot, dbl., globular, medium; slightly fragrant; foliage glossy; vigorous, bushy growth.

Lourdes HT, *dy*, 1959, *V for Victory × (New Dawn sport × Copper Glow sport)*; Brownell; Stern's Nursery. Bud ovoid; flowers golden yellow, dbl. (35-50 petals), large (4-5 in.); fragrant; foliage leathery, glossy, dark; vigorous growth; hardy for the class.

Louvre® HT, *ab*, 1967, (DELfat); *Souv. de J. Chabert × (Walko × Souv. de J. Chabert)*; Delbard-Chabert. Bud long, pointed; flowers rosy apricot, dbl., medium; slightly fragrant; foliage bronze, glossy; moderate, upright growth.

Lovable HT, *lp*, 1979, (*Helen Traubel × Michèle Meilland*) × ((*Blanche Mallerin × Peace × (Peace × Virgo)*)) Leon. Bud long, pointed; flowers light pink, dbl. (30 petals), high-centered, large (4½-6 in.); fragrant; vigorous, upright, bushy growth.

Lovania S, *or*, 1978, *Robin Hood × (New Penny × Coloranja)*; Lens, 1977. Bud ovoid; flowers bright red-orange, semi-dbl. (18-22 petals), pompon shape, small (1½ in.); fragrant (fruity); foliage dark; vigorous, upright, climbing growth; recurrent bloom.

Love Cl HT, *or*, 1935, *Hadley × Ami Quinard*; Caron, B.; H. Guillot. Flowers scarlet, semi-dbl., open, long stems; fragrant; foliage dark; vigorous, climbing (6½-10 ft), bushy growth. RULED EXTINCT 1/79.

Love Gr, *rb*, 1980, (JACtwin); *Seedling × Redgold*; Warriner; J&P. Bud short, pointed; flowers bright red, reverse silvery white, dbl. (35 petals), exhibition, medium (3½ in.); upright growth. AARS, 1980; GM, Portland, 1980.

Love Affair HT, *dr*, 1970, *Seedling × Forever Yours*; Jelly; E.G. Hill Co. Bud short pointed; flowers brilliant red, very dbl., high-centered,

large; fragrant; foliage large, dark, leathery; vigorous, upright growth.

Love Bug Min, *ob*, 1986, *Heartland × Seedling*; Bridges, Dennis, 1987. Flowers orange, white base, reverse orange veining to white base, fades slightly, semi-dbl. (14 petals), high-centered, exhibition, medium, borne usually singly; slight fragrance; foliage medium, medium green, semi-glossy; short, small, pink prickles, hooked slightly downward; bushy, medium growth.

Love Call HT, *pb*, 1989, *Lady × x Wini Edmunds*; Bridges, Dennis A.; Bridges Roses, 1990. Bud ovoid; flowers deep pink, lighter at base, reverse light pink, dbl. (50 petals), high-centered, exhibition, large, borne singly; moderate, damask fragrance; foliage medium, dark green, glossy; prickles pointed slightly downward, medium, light green; upright, tall growth.

Love Dove Min, *w*, 1982, (LYOve); *Seedling × Seedling*; Lyon, Lyndon. Flowers near white, dbl. (35 petals), high-centered, HT form, medium; very fragrant; foliage medium, medium green, semi-glossy; low growth.

Love Letter® F, *w*, 1977, *Pink Parfait × Rosenelfe*; Lens, 1980. Flowers creamy white, dbl. (30-35 petals), cupped, large (3-3½ in.), very fragrant; foliage glossy, dark; vigorous, bushy, upright growth.

Love Note Min, *pb*, 1990, (ZIPnote); *Tamango × Cupcake*; Zipper, Herbert, 1986; Magic Moment Miniatures, 1991. Flowers deep pink, light red going to cream at base, reverse deep pink, at tip mostly cream, aging same, dbl. (35 petals), urn-shaped, high-centered, exhibition, large blooms borne usually singly; slight fragrance; foliage large, medium green, semi-glossy; prickles straight, small, light brown; fruit round, medium, orange; bushy, tall growth.

Love Song HT, *pb*, 1955, (Liebeslied); *Peace × Orange Nassau*; Fisher, G.; C-P. Bud ovoid; flowers neyron rose, reverse yellow, dbl. (45 petals), cupped, large (4½-5 in.); very fragrant; foliage dark, glossy; vigorous, upright growth.

Love Story® HT, *ob*, 1974, (TANvery); Tantau; Horstmann, 1972. Bud ovoid; flowers orange, dbl., cupped, large; slightly fragrant.

Love Token F, *mp*, 1964, Gregory. Flowers peach-pink, dbl. (28 petals), well formed, medium (2 in.); foliage dark, glossy; vigorous growth.

Love Torch™ Min, *rb*, 1992, (MINabeco); *Starburst × Over the Rainbow*; Williams, Ernest. Bud long, pointed; flowers red, orange and yellow blend, holds color well, full (26-40 petals), heavy substance, small (0-4 cms) blooms borne singly; slight fragrance; foliage small, dark green, glossy; some prickles; low (30 cms), upright, bushy growth; hardy.

Loveglo™ Min, *op*, 1983, (MINjco); *Little Darling × Over the Rainbow*; Williams, E.D.; Mini-Roses. Flowers light coral pink and cream, dbl. (40+ petals), high-centered, small; fragrant; foliage small, dark, glossy; bushy growth.

Loveliest HT, *lp*, 1956, *Charlotte Armstrong × Juno*; Leon. Bud ovoid; flowers clear rose-pink, dbl., high-centered, large; very fragrant; foliage leathery, light green; vigorous, upright growth.

Lovelight F, *mp*, 1959, *Garnette × Seedling*; Jelly; E.G. Hill Co. Bud short, pointed; flowers medium pink, dbl. (33 petals), high-centered to flat, large; slightly fragrant; vigorous, upright growth; greenhouse variety.

Loveliness R, *lp*, 1935, Chaplin Bros. Flowers pale pink, white spot at base, dbl., round, large, borne in large trusses; foliage light; vigorous, climbing growth.

Lovely HT, *dp*, 1936, H&S; Dreer. Bud pointed; flowers carmine-pink, semi-dbl., high-centered, large; fragrant (violet); foliage soft; vigorous, compact growth.

Lovely Lady HT, *mr*, 1934, *Better Times sport*; Asmus. Bud long, pointed; flowers pure rose-red, very dbl., high-centered, large; long, strong stems; very fragrant; foliage leathery; very vigorous, open hart. RULED EXTINCT 10/86.

Lovely Lady HT, *mp*, 1986, (DICjubell; Dickson's Jubilee); *Silver Jubilee × (Eurorose × Anabell)*; Dickson, P. Flowers medium pink, dbl. (35 petals), large; fragrant; foliage medium, mid-green, glossy; bushy.

Loverly F, *ab*, 1986, *Restless Native × Apricot Nectar*; Stoddard, Louis. Flowers apricot, semi-dbl., medium; fragrant; foliage medium, medium green, semi-glossy; bushy growth. ARC TG (S), 1985.

Lovers' Meeting HT, *ob*, 1980, *Seedling × Egyptian Treasure*; Gandy, O.L. Bud pointed; flowers bright orange, dbl. (25 petals), high-centered blooms borne singly and in clusters; fragrant; foliage bronze; short prickles; strong, upright growth.

Lovers Only Min, *rb*, 1989, (SEAlove); *Rise 'n' Shine × Siobhan*; McCann, Sean. Flowers cherry red, with straw-yellow bicolor, reverse fades to creamy yellow, dbl. (15-25 petals), sepals are fancy, recurving only slightly, small; slight fragrance; foliage medium, medium green, glossy; prickles pubescent on peduncle; upright, compact growth.

Loving Memory HT, *mr*, 1983, (KORgund; KORgund '81; Burgund '81; Red Cedar); *Seedling × Red Planet seedling*; Kordes, W., 1981. Flowers medium red, dbl. (40+ petals), high-centered, exhibition, large; slight fragrance; foliage medium green, semi-glossy; upright, bushy.

Loving Touch™ Min, *ab*, 1983, *Rise 'n' Shine × First Prize*; Jolly, Nelson F.; Rosehill Farm, 1982. Flowers apricot, dbl. (25 petals), high-centered, mini-flora, medium blooms borne usually singly; slight fragrance; foliage medium, medium green, semi-glossy; fruit globular; bushy, spreading growth. AOE, 1985.

Lovita HT, *mr*, 1965, *Baccará × (Independence × Peace)*; Meilland; Moerheim, 1965 & C-P, 1967. Bud ovoid; flowers bright red, dbl., large; foliage dark; vigorous, upright growth; for greenhouse use.

Lowell Thomas HT, *dy*, 1943, (Botaniste Abrial); *Mme. Mélanie Soupert × Nonin*; Mallerin; A. Meilland & C-P, 1943. Bud long, pointed; flowers rich yellow, dbl. (38 petals), high-centered, large (4-4½ in.); foliage leathery; vigorous, upright, bushy, compact growth. GM, Portland, 1944; AARS, 1944.

Lowell Thomas, Climbing Cl HT, *dy*, 1954, Armstrong, J.A.; Armstrong Nursery.

Loyal Rosarian HT, *mr*, 1990, (LEOloyros); *Red Planet × Red Devil*; Leon, Charles F.; Oregon Grown Roses, 1990-91. Bud ovoid; flowers medium red becoming darker red as it ages, dbl. (36-42 petals), high-centered, exhibition, large blooms borne usually singly; heavy fragrance; foliage medium, leathery, green; fruit large, germinates rapidly; upright, bushy, tall growth.

Loyalist S, *lp*, 1773, *Possibly R. damascena × R. virginiana*; Originator unknown; Brought to America in 1773 by John Cameron of Scotland and to Canada in 1776. Flowers pale rose fading almost white, very dbl., cupped; fragrant; bushy, densely branched; blooms well in June; repeats little.

L.R. May HT, *dr*, 1935, Chaplin Bros. Flowers scarlet-crimson, paling to silvery pink, base orange, well formed, large; vigorous growth.

Lubov Chevtsova HT, *lp*, 1956, *Cathrine Kordes × Peace*; Sushkov. Flowers light pink, base tinted orange, large (5 in); strong stems; foliage glossy; upright growth.

Lubra HT, *dr*, 1938, *Ophelia, Climbing seedling × Black Boy*; Fitzhardinge; Hazlewood Bros. Bud long, pointed; flowers dark crimson, , dbl., high-centered; very fragrant; foliage leathery, dark; vigorous growth.

Luc Varenne F, *mr*, 1959, *Alain × Montrouge*; Delforge. Bud oval; flowers scarlet, semi-dbl., open, medium, borne in clusters; foliage dark, glossy; vigorous, bushy growth.

Lucetta® S, *ab*, 1992, (AUSemi); Austin, David; David Austin Roses, 1983. Flowers pale peach, semi-dbl. (6-14 petals), large (13 cms) blooms borne in small clusters; fragrant; foliage medium, medium green, semi-glossy; some prickles; medium (120 cms), spreading growth.

Lucia Zuloaga HT, *rb*, 1932, *Duquesa de Peñaranda × F. Cambo*; Dot, P.; C-P, 1934. Flowers velvety brownish scarlet with a golden undertone, semi-dbl., open, very large; fragrant (fruity); foliage glossy, dark.

Lucie Fernand-David HT, *w*, 1924, Chambard, C. Flowers white, center slightly tinted cream, dbl.; very fragrant.

Lucie Marie HT, *yb*, 1930, Dickson, A. Bud pointed; flowers buttercup-yellow veined apricot-orange and shaded salmon-cerise, dbl., high-centered, large; fragrant; foliage dark, leathery, glossy; vigorous, compact, bushy growth.

Lucie Nicolas Meyer HT, *dp*, 1922, *Jonkheer J.L. Mock × Seedling*; Gillot, F. Flowers dark pink, edged lighter, dbl.; fragrant.

Lucile R, *lp*, 1911, Walsh. Flowers flesh-pink, base tinged rosy salmon, dbl., borne in clusters; foliage large, rich green, glossy; vigorous, climbing growth.

Lucile Barker HT, *ab*, 1922, Hicks. Bud pointed; flowers apricot-yellow, semi-dbl., high-centered; fragrant; foliage bronze; vigorous growth.

Lucile Hill HT, *dp*, 1939, *(Senior × De Luxe) × Sweet Adeline*; Hill, J.H., Co. Bud long, pointed, rose-red; flowers spinal-pink, dbl., very large; long stems; slightly fragrant; foliage leathery; very vigorous, compact growth; abundant indoor bloom.

Lucile Rand HT, *pb*, 1930, Pernet-Ducher; Gaujard. Bud pointed; flowers brilliant carmine, shaded yellow and orange, dbl., very large; very fragrant; very vigorous, semi-climbing, bushy growth.

Lucile Supreme HT, *dp*, 1941, *Lucile Hill sport*; Hill, J.H., Co. Flowers rose-red, dbl. (25-35 petals), very large (6 in.); a florists' variety, not distributed for outdoor use.

Lucilla F, *ab*, 1992, *Conservation sport*; Stainthorpe, Eric; Battersby Roses, 1993. Flowers apricot blend, semi-dbl. (6-14 petals), small (0-4 cms.) blooms borne in small clusters; slight fragrance; foliage small, medium green, semi-glossy; some prickles; low (35 cms.), compact growth.

Lucille Ball HT, *ab*, 1991, (JACapri); *Hello Dolly × Seedling*; Christensen, Jack; Bear Creek Gardens, 1993. Flowers apricot, amber blend, full (26-40 petals), good petal substance, large (7 cms) blooms borne mostly singly; fragrant; foliage medium, medium green, semi-glossy; some prickles; tall (145-160 cms), upright, bushy growth.

Lucille Ross LCl, *w*, 1940, *Dr. W. Van Fleet sport*; Ross; Roselawn Gardens. Flowers white, center golden, semi-dbl., open; slightly fragrant; vigorous, climbing (20-40 ft.) growth.

Lucinda HT, *dp*, 1927, *Columbia sport*; Heacock. Flowers dark pink.

Luciole T (OGR), *dp*, 1886, Guillot Fils. Bud long; flowers carmine-rose, base coppery yellow, large; very fragrant.

Luciole R, *rb*, 1923, *Hiawatha × Seedling*; Nonin. Flowers bright scarlet, center white, single, small; slightly fragrant; vigorous, climbing growth.

Lucky F, *dr*, 1962, *Goldilocks × Independence*; Leenders, J. Flowers deep velvety red, semi-dbl. (13 petals), large (3 in.).

Lucky Beauty HT, *pb*, 1970, *Kordes' Perfecta × Lucky Piece*; Fuller; Wyant. Bud ovoid; flowers pink, yellow reverse, very dbl. (90 petals), high-centered, large; fragrant; vigorous, upright, bushy growth.

Lucky Charm F, *yb*, 1961, Robinson, H.; Lowe. Flowers bright yellow tipped red, semi-dbl. (18 petals), large (3½-4 in.), borne in clusters of 6-10; very fragrant; foliage glossy; vigorous growth.

Lucky Choice HT, *w*, 1985, *American Heritage × Sodōri-Himé*; Ota, Kaichiro. Flowers creamy white, flushed light pink in center, dbl. (35 petals), high-centered, large blooms borne 1-3 per stem; slight fragrance; foliage large, medium green, few, small, slender prickles; upright growth.

Lucky Lady Gr, *lp*, 1966, (ARMlu); *Charlotte Armstrong × Cherry Glow*; Armstrong, D.L. & Swim; Armstrong Nursery. Bud long, pointed; flowers light pink, reverse darker, dbl. (28 petals), high-centered, large; slightly fragrant; foliage dark, glossy; vigorous, upright growth. AARS, 1967.

Lucky Piece HT, *pb*, 1962, *Peace sport*; Gordon; Wyant. Flowers copper, pink and gold blend.

Lucky Star HT, *yb*, 1936, *Souvenir sport*; Armacost; Armacost & Royston. Flowers golden yellow, suffused flame-scarlet.

Lucy Cl HT, *dp*, 1936, Williams, A.H. Flowers brilliant carmine, well formed, large; foliage glossy; very vigorous, climbing growth.

Lucy Ashton E (OGR), *w*, 1894, Penzance. Flowers pure white, edged pink, single; foliage dark, fragrant; vigorous growth; seasonal bloom. (42).

Lucy Bertram E (OGR), *rb*, 1895, Penzance. Flowers dark shining crimson, center white, single; foliage dark, fragrant; very vigorous growth; seasonal bloom.

Lucy Constable HT, *pb*, 1924, Lilley. Flowers silver pink, reverse deep salmon pink; fragrant.

Lucy Cramphorn HT, *or*, 1960, (Maryse Kriloff); *Peace × Baccará*; Kriloff; Cramphorn's Nursery. Flowers signal-red, dbl. (40 petals), well-formed, large (5 in.); fragrant; foliage glossy; vigorous, upright growth.

Lucy Marguerite HT, *yb*, 1978, *Val De Mosa × Denise-Anne*; Ellick; Excelsior Roses. Flowers buttercup-yellow, diffused red, dbl. (35-40 petals), full, large (4 in.); fragrant; foliage small, glossy, dark.

Lucy Nicolas HT, *r*, 1935, *Odette Foussier × Cécile Walter*; Mallerin; H. Guillot & C-P. Bud pointed; flowers coppery salmon, dbl., high-centered, large; foliage glossy, bronze; very vigorous growth.

Lucy Thomas Cl HP (OGR), *mp*, 1924, *Ulrich Brunner Fils × Georg Arends*; Nabonnand, P. Flowers pink, center brighter, semi-dbl.; rarely recurrent bloom.

Lucyle HT, *mp*, 1933, Vestal. Flowers glowing pink, dbl., very large; very fragrant; foliage leathery, dark; vigorous, bushy growth.

Ludmilla® HT, *m*, 1968, (LAPmau); *(Peace × Independence) × Heure Mauve*; Laperrière; EFR. Bud ovoid; flowers mauve, semi-dbl., medium; slightly fragrant; foliage glossy; vigorous, upright growth.

Ludwig Möller HP (OGR), *ab*, 1914, *Frau Karl Druschki × Maréchal Niel seedling*; Kiese. Flowers bright amber-yellow, fading white.

Ludwig Oppenheimer HT, *dr*, 1932, *Villa Pia × Capitaine Georges Dessirier*; Leenders Bros. Bud pointed; flowers crimson-scarlet, full, large; fragrant; foliage dark; vigorous growth.

Ludwigshafen am Rhein® F, *dp*, 1975, (KORludwig; Ludwigshafen); *Seedling × Pink Puff*; Kordes. Bud ovoid; flowers deep pink, dbl. (45 petals), high-centered, large (4 in.); fragrant; foliage soft; vigorous, upright, bushy growth. ADR, 1973.

Luis Brinas HT, *ob*, 1934, *Mme. Butterfly × Federico Casas*; Dot, P.; C-P. Bud long, pointed; flowers rose-orange, dbl., cupped, large; fragrant; foliage soft; vigorous. GM, Bagatelle, 1932; Portland, 1934.

Luis Desamero Min, *ly*, 1989, (TINluis); *Tiki × Baby Katie*; Bennett, Dee; Tiny Petals Nursery, 1988. Bud ovoid; flowers pastel yellow, dbl. (28 petals), high-centered, exhibition, medium, borne usually singly and in sprays of 3-5; slight, fruity fragrance; foliage medium, medium green, semi-glossy; prickles straight & tapering, pale yellow, reddish base; fruit globular, green to yellow-orange; upright, bushy, tall growth.

Luisa Fernanda de Silva HT, *rb*, 1946, Dot, P. Flowers reddish passing to purplish and then yellowish red, base yellow; fragrant; foliage dark, glossy; vigorous growth.

Luise Lilia HT, *dr*, 1912, Lambert, P. Flowers dark red; very fragrant; moderate growth.

Lullaby Pol, *w*, 1953, *(R. soulieana × Mrs. Joseph Hiess) × Cécile Brunner*; Shepherd; Bosley Nursery. Bud ovoid; flowers white, center flushed pink, dbl. (75 petals), cupped, medium (1½-2 in.) blooms in loose clusters; slightly fragrant; foliage dark, leathery; vigorous, bushy, compact growth.

Lullaby F, *dp*, 1957, Bishop; Baker's Nursery. Flowers rich rose-pink, semi-dbl., camellia shape to almost flat, large (3 in.), borne in clusters (to 28); vigorous growth.

Lulu HT, *op*, 1919, Easlea. Bud very long, pointed, deep orange-red; flowers salmon-pink, single (8 petals), large; slightly fragrant; foliage glossy; bushy, compact growth.

Lulu F, *ob*, 1973, *Zorina × Seedling*; Kordes. Flowers orange-pink, dbl., high-centered, medium; slightly fragrant; foliage glossy, dark, bronze; vigorous, upright, bushy growth.

Luluette Min, *mp*, 1986, *Fairy Moss × Fairy Moss*; Fischer, C.&H.; Alpenflora Gardens. Flowers medium pink, single, small blooms borne singly and in small sprays; no fragrance; foliage small, medium green, semi-glossy; small, straight, red prickles; low, compact, tiny growth.

Lumière HT, *yb*, 1944, Mallerin; A. Meilland. Flowers golden yellow suffused capucine-red, large; foliage dark, leathery; vigorous growth.

Lumina F, *or*, 1955, *Fanal × Alpine Glow*; Tantau, Math. Flowers orange-scarlet, dbl. (25 petals), rosette shape, medium (2½ in.) blooms in large trusses; foliage dark; vigorous growth.

Luminator Pol, *dr*, 1938, *Lady Reading sport*; Smith, J.; Eddie. Flowers scarlet-crimson; vigorous growth.

Luminion® F, *or*, 1975, (KORmiora; Rosi Mittermeier); *Hurra × Peer Gynt*; Kordes; Vilmorin. Bud globular; flowers orange-red, dbl. (34 petals), cupped, large (3 in.); fragrant;

foliage glossy, dark; vigorous, upright, bushy growth.

Luminosa HT, *or*, 1964, Mondial Roses. Bud long, pointed; flowers vermilion, dbl. (52 petals), high-centered, large; strong stems; foliage dark, glossy; vigorous, upright, bushy growth.

Luminous Pol, *or*, 1932, *Gloria Mundi sport*; deRuiter; J&P. Flowers brilliant scarlet tinted orange, dbl., cupped, small; slightly fragrant; foliage small, light, wrinkled; dwarf growth.

Lum's Double White HT, *w*, 1930, *Killarney Double White sport*; Lum; Totty. Flowers pure white, semi-dbl., high-centered, very large; fragrant; foliage dark, leathery; vigorous growth.

Luna HT, *ly*, 1918, *Harry Kirk × Sunburst*; Poulsen, S. Bud pointed; flowers pale yellow, dbl., high-centered, large; strong stems; very fragrant; foliage dark; very vigorous, bushy growth.

Luna Park LCl, *or*, 1964, *Gladiator × Seedling*; Croix, P. Flowers red shaded orange, large; vigorous, climbing growth; recurrent bloom.

Lunelle HT, *lp*, 1955, (George Sand); *Young France × Signora*; Meilland, F. Flowers pale pink, dbl. (50 petals), high-centered, very large; very fragrant; vigorous growth.

Luray F, *mr*, 1958, *Patty's Pink sport*; Masek; Carlton Rose Nursery. Flowers rose-red, dbl. (40-45 petals), medium (2-3 in.); fragrant; foliage leathery, glossy; vigorous, bushy growth.

Lustige HT, *rb*, 1973, (LuKOR; Jolly); *Peace × Brandenburg*; Kordes. Bud ovoid; flowers copper-red, reverse yellow, dbl., cupped, large; fragrant; foliage large, glossy, leathery; vigorous, upright growth.

Lustre HT, *mp*, 1926, *Ophelia × Hoosier Beauty*; Hill, E.G., Co.; Amling Bros. Flowers rose-pink, semi-dbl., large; fragrant.

Lutetia HT, *yb*, 1961, *The Optimist × Tudor*; deRuiter. Flowers coppery yellow, dbl. (28 petals), medium; vigorous, upright growth.

Luther Russell F, *op*, 1956, *Korona sport*; Morse. Flowers salmon, semi-dbl, borne several together; foliage olive-green.

Luvvie Min, *pb*, 1979, *Little Darling × Over the Rainbow*; Bennett, Dee; Tiny Petals Nursery, 1980. Bud ovoid; flowers soft to deep coral pink, dbl. (38 petals), exhibition, micro-mini, very small blooms borne singly; slight fragrance; foliage small, deep green with red peduncle and petiole; straight, thin, red prickles; low, bushy growth.

Luxembourg M (OGR), *dr*, *Probably a hybrid with R. gallica variety*. Flowers crimson, not very mossy; vigorous growth.

Luxembourg, Climbing Cl HT, *op*, 1932, *Marie Adélaide sport*; Wight. Flowers pinkish orange, base deep yellow; very vigorous, climbing growth.

Luxury HT, *rb*, 1968, *Seedling × Suspense*; Patterson; Patterson Roses. Flowers light red, reverse white, dbl., high-centered, large; fragrant; foliage soft; moderate growth.

Lycoris M (OGR), *pb*, Flowers light rosy red spotted white, dbl., flat, large.

Lydia HT, *dy*, 1949, *Phyllis Gold × Seedling*; Robinson, H.; Baker's Nursery. Bud long, pointed; flowers intense saffron-yellow, very dbl., high-centered, medium; fragrant; foliage dark, leathery, glossy; vigorous, bushy growth.

Lydia® S, *ob*, 1973, (Clubrose Lydia); *Seedling × Circus*; Kordes. Bud ovoid; flowers deep orange, reverse yellow, semi-dbl., cupped, medium; fragrant; foliage glossy, dark, leathery; very vigorous, upright, climbing growth.

Lydia HT, *op*, 1933, *Briarcliff × Florex*; Verschuren; Dreer; H&S. Bud pointed; flowers bright orange-rose, very dbl., large; fragrant; foliage glossy; vigorous, bushy.

Lykkefund R, *w*, 1930, *Seedling from R. helenae, Barbier's form, possibly crossed with Zephirine Drouhin*; Olsen. Flowers cream color, semi-dbl., blooms in clusters; very fragrant; foliage dark, glossy; no prickles; vigorous growth.

Lynda Hurst HT, *mp*, 1938, *Mme. Abel Chatenay × Seedling*; Clark, A.; NRS Victoria. Flowers pink, dbl., large; vigorous growth.

Lynette HT, *w*, 1985, (KORlyn); *Clivia × MEItakilor*; Kordes, R.; Ludwigs Roses Pty., Ltd., 1983. Bud long, pointed; flowers cream blended with coral pink, dbl., well-formed, large blooms in clusters of 1-5; no fragrance; foliage dark; straight, brown prickles; tall, upright.

Lynn Anne Min, *ob*, 1981, *Rise 'n' Shine × Sheri Anne*; Saville, F. Harmon; Nor'East Min. Roses. Bud short, pointed; flowers orange-yellow blend, dbl. (38 petals), high-centered to flat blooms borne singly and in large sprays; fragrant; foliage medium; long, thin prickles; vigorous, upright, compact growth.

Lynne Gold™ Min, *my*, 1983, (MORlyn); *Ellen Poulsen × Yellow Jewel*; Moore, R.S.; Moore Min. Roses. Flowers medium yellow, dbl. (20 petals), micro-mini, small; slight fragrance; foliage small, medium green, semiglossy; bushy, spreading growth.

Lyon Rambler R, *dp*, 1909, *Crimson Rambler seedling*; Dubreuil. Flowers bright rose-pink, flushed carmine.

Lyon Rose HT, *op*, 1907, *Mme. Mélanie Soupert* × *Soleil d'Or seedling*; Pernet-Ducher. Flowers shrimp-pink, center coral-red shaded yellow, dbl. (44 petals), large; fragrant; (28). GM, Bagatelle, 1909.

Lyon Rose, Climbing Cl HT, *op*, 1924, Ketten Bros.

Lyric S, *mp*, 1951, *Sangerhausen* × *Seedling*; deRuiter; J&P. Bud ovoid; flowers rose-pink, dbl. (28 petals), cupped, medium blooms in large clusters; fragrant; foliage leathery; vigorous (4 ft.), upright growth; good for hedge and border.

Lyrical F, *pb*, 1989, *Snow White* × *Yesterday*; Jobson, Daniel J. Bud pointed; flowers salmon pink shading to cremate base, semi-dbl. (11 petals), flat, medium, borne in sprays of 5-7; moderate, spicy fragrance; foliage medium, dark green, glossy, disease resistant; prickles hooked downward, red; fruit none observed; upright, bushy, low, winter-hardy growth.

Lys Assia F, *mr*, 1958, *Spartan* × *Hens Verschuren*; Kordes, R. Flowers deep orange-scarlet, semi-dbl. (20 petals), high-centered, large (4 in.), borne in small clusters; slightly fragrant; foliage glossy; vigorous, upright, bushy growth.

Lysbeth-Victoria F, *lp*, 1978, *Pink Parfait* × *Nevada*; Harkness. Flowers light shell-pink, semi-dbl. (11 petals), large (4½ in.); slightly fragrant; foliage matt; growth moderate.

Mabel Dot Min, *or*, 1966, *Orient* × *Perla de Alcañada*; Dot; Minier. Flowers rose-coral, dbl., small blooms in clusters; foliage small, bronze.

Mabel Drew HT, *w*, 1911, Dickson, A. Flowers deep cream, center canary-yellow, dbl., borne in clusters; fragrant. GM, NRS, 1910; Bagatelle, 1913.

Mabel Francis HT, *my*, 1943, *Leading Lady* × *Southport*; Bees. Flowers rose-pink, dbl. (35-40 petals), large (5 in.); fragrant; foliage light green; free growth.

Mabel Jackson HT, *ab*, 1924, *Edith Part* × *Queen Mary*; Easlea. Flowers apricot and pink, dbl.; very fragrant.

Mabel Lynas HT, *dr*, 1926, McGredy. Bud pointed; flowers crimson-scarlet, base yellow, dbl., large; strong stems; fragrant; foliage glossy; very vigorous, bushy growth. GM, NRS, 1924.

Mabel Morrison HP (OGR), *w*, 1878, *Baroness Rothschild sport*; Broughton. Flowers flesh-white, becoming pure white, sometimes tinged pink in autumn, dbl. (30 petals), cupped, well-formed; stout, erect growth; seasonal bloom.

Mabel Morse HT, *my*, 1922, McGredy. Bud pointed; flowers bright golden yellow, full, well shaped, large; foliage dark, bronze; bushy growth. GM, NRS, 1921.

Mabel Morse, Climbing Cl HT, *my*, 1931, Moulden.

Mabel Morse, Climbing Cl HT, *my*, 1932, Ley.

Mabel Prentice HT, *mp*, 1923, Lippiatt. Flowers clear rose-pink.

Mabel Stewart LCl, *dr*, 1942, Clark. Bud almost black; flowers velvety crimson, semi-single.

Mabel Turner HT, *pb*, 1923, Dickson, H. Bud pointed; flowers blush, center and reverse rosy carmine, high-centered, very large; slightly fragrant; foliage olive-green; vigorous growth.

Mabelle Stearns S, *mp*, 1938, (Maybelle Stearns); *Mrs. F.F. Prentiss* × *Souv. de Georges Pernet*; Horvath; Wayside Gardens Co. Flowers peach-pink with silvery reflex, dbl. (55 petals), blooms in clusters; very fragrant; foliage small, glossy, dark; height 2 ft., spreading (6-8 ft.) growth; recurrent bloom; hardy.

Mab Grimwade HT, *yb*, 1937, *Souv. de Gustave Prat* × *Seedling*; Clark, A.; NRS Victoria. Flowers rich chrome, shaded yellow, center apricot, dbl.

MACarom HT, *ly*, 1988, (Goldie); *Seedling* × *Golden Gate*; McGredy, Sam. Flowers pale yellow, dbl. (26-40 petals), large; very fragrant; foliage large, medium green, glossy; upright growth.

Macbeth HT, *dr*, 1921, *Richmond* × *Admiral Ward*; Bees. Bud pointed; flowers deep crimson, shaded darker, dbl., high-centered, large; very fragrant; foliage dark, bronze; vigorous, bushy, compact growth.

MACbigma F, *pb*, 1988, (Redhot; Red Hot); *Eyepaint* × *Ko's Yellow*; McGredy, Sam. Flowers pink blend, hand painted, dbl. (15-25 petals), medium; slight fragrance; foliage small, medium green, semi-glossy; bushy growth.

MACcourlod Min, *pb*, 1984, (Ragtime); *Mary Sumner* × *Seedling*; McGredy, Sam; McGredy Roses Ltd., 1982. Flowers pink blend, dbl. (40+ petals), small; slight fragrance; foliage small, dark, matt; bushy growth.

MACfrabro Min, *ob*, 1985, (Firefly); *Mary Sumner* × *Ko's Yellow*; McGredy, S. Flowers orange blend, dbl. (20 petals), small; slight fragrance; foliage small, dark, glossy; bushy.

MACmelan Min, *op*, 1988, (Melanie); *Seaspray* × *Wanaka*; McGredy, Sam; Sealand Nursery, 1989. Bud ovoid; flowers light salmon-pink, reverse lighter, dbl. (23 petals), cupped, small, borne in sprays of 20-25; slight fragrance; foliage small, medium green, semi-glossy; prickles straight, red-brown; bushy, low growth.

MACponui HT, *pb*, 1988, (Pinky); *Freude* × *Typhoo Tea*; McGredy, Sam. Flowers pink blend, dbl. (26-40 petals), large; slight fragrance; foliage large, dark green, glossy; upright growth.

MACsatur HT, *mp*, 1988, (MACnaru; Penthouse); *Seedling* × *Ferry Porsche*; McGredy, Sam. Flowers medium pink, dbl. (15-25 petals), large; fragrant; foliage large, medium green, matt; bushy growth.

MACseatri HT, *pb*, 1987, (Happy Days); *(Poulsen seedling* × *Picasso)* × *Paradise*; McGredy, Sam; Sam McGredy Roses International, 1988. Flowers pink blend, dbl. (15-25 petals), medium; slight fragrance; foliage medium, medium green, matt; bushy growth.

MACspice Min, *m*, 1983, (MACspike); *Anytime* × *Gartendirektor Otto Linne*; McGredy, Sam. Flowers mauve, semi-dbl., small; slight fragrance; foliage small, medium green, semiglossy; spreading growth.

MACsupcat HT, *yb*, 1989, (Miriam); *Sexy Rexy* × *Yabadabadoo*; McGredy, Sam, 1990. Flowers yellow blend, dbl. (20 petals), medium; slight fragrance; foliage medium, dark green, semi-glossy; bushy growth.

MACvolar F, *or*, 1987, (Volare); *Julischka* × *Matangi*; McGredy, Sam; Sam McGredy Roses International, 1988. Flowers orange-red, dbl. (15-25 petals), medium; slight fragrance; foliage large, medium green, glossy; upright growth.

MACwhaka S, *mp*, 1987, (Gwen Swane); *MACbroey* × *Snow Carpet*; McGredy, Sam; Sam McGredy Roses International, 1988. Flowers medium pink, dbl. (26-40 petals), medium; slight fragrance; foliage small, medium green, matt; spreading growth.

MACyefre HT, *yb*, 1987, (Solitaire; Chartreuse); *Freude* × *Benson & Hedges Gold*; McGredy, Sam, 1978; Sealand Nursery, 1987. Flowers yellow tinted pink, reverse yellow, fading without blanching, dbl. (25 petals), cupped, large, borne in sprays of 2-3; slight fragrance; foliage medium, dark green, semiglossy; slightly hooked, large, reddish-brown prickles; no fruit; bushy, strong growth. RNRS PIT, 1985.

Madam President F, *pb*, 1975, (Madame President); *Seedling* × *Handel*; McGredy, S., IV; Avenue Nursery. Bud long, pointed; flowers blend of pink shades, dbl. (70 petals), HT-form, large (4 in.); slightly 2 fragrant; bushy.

Mme. Abel Chatenay HT, *pb*, 1895, *Dr. Grill* × *Victor Verdier*; Pernet-Ducher. Bud pointed; flowers pale pink, center deeper, reverse carmine-pink, dbl., medium (3 in.); fragrant; foliage bronze when young.

Mme. Abel Chatenay, Climbing Cl HT, *pb*, 1917, Page; Easlea.

Mme. A. Bouchayer HT, *op*, 1927, Siret-Pernet. Flowers shrimp-pink, base indian yellow.

Mme. Achille Fould T (OGR), *yb*, 1903, Lévêque. Flowers yellow, shaded carmine rose and salmon, full, globular, very large.

Mme. Achille Villey HT, *or*, 1939, *Charles P. Kilham* × *Mrs. Aaron Ward*; Colombier. Flowers coral-red, tinted yellow, dbl.; foliage dark; very vigorous growth.

Mme. Adolphe Lafont HT, *ab*, 1921, *Joseph Hill sport*; Croibier. Flowers deep apricot-red tinted buff, semi-dbl.; very fragrant.

Mme. A. Galland HT, *pb*, 1928, *Pharisäer* × *(Constance* × *Hybrid Tea Seedling)*; Mallerin; Laperrière. Flowers rose-pink, shaded shrimp-pink, dbl.; very fragrant.

Mme. Agathe Nabonnand T (OGR), *lp*, 1886, (Agathe Nabonnand); Nabonnand, G. Flowers rosy flesh tinted amber, petals shell-like, very large.

Mme. Albert Barbier HP (OGR), *ob*, 1925, *Frau Karl Druschki* × *Seedling*; Barbier; Dreer. Flowers salmon, tinted nankeen yellow, center darker, dbl. (50 petals), cupped, large; slightly fragrant; vigorous, bushy growth; recurrent bloom.

Mme. Albert Bernardin T (OGR), *w*, 1904, Mari. Flowers white, shaded with carmine, center yellow.

Mme. Albert Gilles HT, *op*, 1934, *Seedling* × *Jean C.N. Forestier*; Guillot, H.; Mallerin. Flowers light coral-pink, very dbl., very large.

Mme. A. Labbey HP (OGR), *pb*, 1843, Flowers pink and lilac, medium or small. A collector's item.

Mme. A. Lerche HT, *mp*, 1928, *Mme. L. Hot* × *Mrs. Henry Winnett*; Bernaix, P. Flowers china-rose shaded carmine, reverse silvery rose, dbl.

Mme. Alexandre HT, *rb*, 1926, Walter, L. Flowers crimson-vermilion-red, shaded velvety purple, dbl.

Mme. Alexandre Charvet HT, *or*, 1943, *Charles P. Kilham* × *(Charles P. Kilham* × *Mme. Joseph Perraud)*; Meilland, F.; A. Meilland. Bud long, pointed; flowers orange-red, edged lilac, dbl., cupped, medium; slightly fragrant; foliage leathery; moderate growth.

Mme. Alexandre Dreux HT, *my*, 1921, *Rayon d'Or* × *Primerose*; Soupert; Notting. Bud pointed; flowers golden yellow, full, large.

Mme. Alfred Carrière N (OGR), *w*, 1879, Schwartz, J. Flowers pale pinkish white, full, globular, large; very fragrant; vigorous, climbing growth; recurrent; (21).

Mme. Alfred de Rougemont HP (OGR), *lp*, 1862, *Blanche Lafitte* × *Sappho (Vibert's)*; Lacharme. Flowers white tinted pink, medium; vigorous growth.

Mme. Alfred Ponnier HT, *w*, 1920, Bernaix, P. Flowers white.

Mme. Alfred Schisselé HT, *m*, 1930, *Frau Felix Tonnar* × *Angèle Pernet*; Leenders, M. Flowers lilac-white, center coppery orange, dbl., large; fragrant; foliage bronze.

Mme. Alice Garnier R, *pb*, 1906, *R. wichuraiana* × *Mme. Charles*; Fauque. Flowers bright rose, center yellow to light pink, small; very fragrant (sweet); foliage dark, glossy.

Mme. André Charmet HT, *mp*, 1921, *Mme. Mélanie Soupert* × *Mme. Maurice de Luze*; Croibier. Flowers carnation-pink, dbl., fragrant.

Mme. André de Halloy HT, *ob*, 1929, *Gloire de Hollande* × *Benedicte Seguin*; Ketten Bros. Flowers orange, reverse salmon-pink, very dbl.; slightly fragrant.

Mme. André Dulin HT, *op*, 1959, *Opera* × *Ville de Gand*; Gaujard. Flowers bright coppery pink, dbl., large; fragrant; vigorous, bushy growth.

Mme. André Gillier HT, *rb*, 1934, *Padre* × *Seedling*; Reymond; Vially. Bud pointed; flowers coppery red, shaded yellow, semi-dbl., cupped; slightly fragrant.

Mme. André Leroy HP (OGR), *mp*, 1864, Trouillard. Flowers salmon-rose, dbl., large; vigorous.

Mme. André Saint HP (OGR), *w*, 1926, *Frau Karl Druschki* × *Benedicte Seguin*; Barbier. Flowers milk-white to pure white, center clear chamois, dbl.; fragrant; few thorns; stocky.

Mme. Angélique Veysset HT, *lp*, 1890, Veysset. Flowers pink tinted white, full, large.

Mme. Annette Aynard HT, *w*, 1919, *Mme. Caroline Testout* × *Prince de Bulgarie*; Leenders, M. Flowers milk-white edged pink, passing to amber-yellow, dbl.; fragrant.

Mme. Anth. Kluis Pol, *op*, 1924, Kluis; Kluis & Koning. Flowers salmon-pink tinted orange, semi-dbl., large, borne in clusters.

Mme. Antoine Mari T (OGR), *pb*, 1901, Mari, A. Flowers rosy flesh, shaded lilac and rose, full, large; fragrant; opens well; (14).

Mme. Antoine Montagne HT, *lp*, 1930, Richardier. Flowers flesh-pink, with reflexes of old ivory.

Mme. Armand Souzy HT, *rb*, 1945, *Charles P. Kilham* × *(Charles P. Kilham* × *Margaret McGredy)*; Meilland, F. Flowers geranium-red and saffron-yellow, very large.

Mme. A. Roure HT, *yb*, 1932, *Wilhelm Kordes* × *Mev. G.A. van Rossem*; Lens. Flowers brilliant chrome-yellow shaded salmon, to a maranth-red, dbl.; fragrant.

Mme. Arthaud HT, *ob*, 1938, *Charles P. Kilham* × *(K. of K.* × *Mari Dot)*; Mallerin. Flowers deep orange, very dbl., large; slightly fragrant; vigorous growth.

Mme. Arthur Oger Cl B (OGR), *mp*, 1899, Oger. Flowers brilliant pink, dbl., very large; very vigorous, climbing growth.

Mme. Auguste Chatain HT, *op*, 1940, Mallerin; A. Meilland. Bud very long; flowers coral-salmon, full, well formed, large; very vigorous growth. GM, Bagatelle, 1939.

Mme. Auguste Choutet LCl, *ob*, 1901, *William Allen Richardson* × *Kaiserin Auguste Viktoria*; Godard. Flowers orange-yellow.

Mme. Auguste Nonin R, *dp*, 1914, *Dorothy Perkins* × *Blush Rambler*; Nonin. Flowers deep shell-pink, center white, semi-dbl., cupped, small, borne in clusters; slightly fragrant; foliage large, glossy; very vigorous, climbing (15-20 ft.), open growth.

Mme. Autrand HT, *ob*, 1922, *Mme. Caroline Testout* × *Prince de Bulgarie*; Leenders, M. Flowers coppery orange, dbl.; very fragrant.

Mme. Bardou Job HT, *ly*, 1913, *Prince de Bulgarie sport*; Dubreuil. Flowers canary-yellow, center chrome-yellow, semi-dbl.; slightly fragrant.

Mme. Barthélemy Levet T (OGR), *ly*, 1979, Levet, A. Flowers canary-yellow.

Mme. Bérard Cl T (OGR), *ob*, 1872, *Mme. Falcot* × *Gloire de Dijon*; Levet, F. Flowers salmon-yellow shaded salmon-rose, dbl., cupped, large; fragrant.

Mme. Berthe de Forge HT, *op*, 1935, Chambard, C. Flowers orange-coral, tinted coppery salmon, cupped, very large; foliage bronze.

Mme. Blytha Pearkes HT, *ab*, 1968, *Karl Herbst* × *Lady Hillingdon*; Blakeney; Eddie. Flowers light apricot blushed yellow and pink, dbl., medium; bushy, compact growth.

Mme. Boll HP (OGR), *dp*, 1859, Boll, Daniel; Boyeau. Flowers carmine-rose, large; recurrent; 5 leaflets per leaf; vigorous.

Mme. Bollaert HT, *rb*, 1938, *Ami F. Mayery* × *Seedling*; Chambard, C. Bud long, coppery red; flowers carmine, shaded nasturtium-red, dbl., cupped, very large; strong stems; very fragrant; very vigorous, bushy growth.

Madame Bollinger F, *op*, 1972, *(Little Darling × Goldilocks) × Bobbie Lucas*; McGredy, S., IV; McGredy. Flowers deep orange-salmon, dbl. (25 petals), HT form, large (3 in.); slightly fragrant; free growth.

Mme. Bravy T (OGR), *w*, 1846, (Adèle Pradel; Alba Rosea; Danzille; Joséphine Maltot; Mme. Denis; Mme. de Sertot); Guillot Père. Flowers creamy white shaded blush, dbl.; fragrant.

Mme. Butterfly HT, *lp*, 1918, *Ophelia sport*; Hill, E.G., Co. Flowers light creamy pink.

Mme. Butterfly, Climbing Cl HT, *lp*, 1926, Smith, E.P..

Mme. Byrne N (OGR), *w*, 1840, *Lamarque Seedling*; Buist. Flowers cream color, center rose, dbl., large.

Mme. Camille T (OGR), *lp*, 1871, Guillot Fils. Flowers aurora-pink, veined, with white reflections, full, well formed, large; fragrant.

Mme. Camille Laurens HT, *or*, 1956, *Peace × Happiness*; Dorieux; Pin. Flowers crimson-red tinted orange, well formed; strong stems; fragrant; foliage bright green.

Mme. Caristie Martel HT, *ly*, 1916, Pernet-Ducher. Flowers pure sulphur-yellow, center deeper, large (5-6 in.). GM, Bagatelle, 1917.

Mme. Carnot N (OGR), *yb*, 1889, *William Allen Richardson Seedling*; Moreau-Robert. Flowers golden yellow tinged orange, center darker, very dbl., globular, large; fragrant; vigorous, climbing growth.

Mme. Caroline Schmitt N (OGR), *yb*, 1878, (Caroline Schmitt); *Solfaterre Seedling*; Schmitt. Flowers salmon-yellow, full; recurrent bloom.

Mme. Caroline Testout HT, *mp*, 1890, *Mme. de Tartas × Lady Mary Fitzwilliam*; Pernet-Ducher. Bud pointed; flowers bright satiny rose, center darker, edged soft carmine-pink, dbl., large; fragrant; foliage rich green, soft; vigorous, bushy growth. Once planted by the thousands along the streets of Portland, Oregon. (28).

Mme. Caroline Testout, Climbing Cl HT, *mp*, 1901, Chauvry.

Mme. Ceccaldi HT, *op*, 1938, *Soeur Thérèse Seedling*; Chambard, C. Bud long; flowers salmon-carmine-pink, shaded vermilion, dbl., very large, strong stems; very vigorous growth.

Mme. Célina Noirey T (OGR), *lp*, 1868, Guillot Fils. Flowers soft pink, reverse purple, very dbl., large; fragrant.

Mme. Chaban Delmas HT, *mr*, 1957, Privat. Flowers bright red, well formed, large; foliage bright green.

Mme. C. Chambard HT, *lp*, 1911, *Frau Karl Druschki × Prince de Bulgarie*; Chambard, C. Flowers rosy flesh-pink, shaded salmon, base yellow, dbl. (72 petals); fragrant.

Mme. Chamouton-Murgue HT, *op*, 1925, *Seedling × Mrs. Edward Powell*; Chambard, C. Flowers orange-carmine, shaded vermilion, dbl., cupped, very large; fragrant; foliage dark; vigorous, erect, branching growth.

Mme. Charles T (OGR), *yb*, 1864, *Mme. Damaizin × Seedling*; Damaizin. Flowers yellow, center salmon.

Mme. Charles Allizon HT, *w*, 1928, *Mme. Vittoria Gagnière × Lady Pirrie*; Schwartz, A. Flowers rosy white, edges tinted yellow, dbl.

Mme. Charles Détreaux B (OGR), *mr*, Flowers bright carmine-red, large.

Mme. Charles Dubreuil HT, *pb*, 1911, *Pharisäer sport*; Guillot, P. Flowers salmon-rose, reverse shaded carmine, dbl.

Mme. Charles Frederic Worth HRg (S), *dp*, 1889, (C.F. Worth); Vve. Schwartz Flowers rosy carmine, fading, semi-dbl., large, borne in large clusters; fragrant; vigorous growth; profuse early bloom, but sparse in summer and fall.

Mme. Charles Guillaud HT, *op*, 1943, Mallerin. Flowers orange-pink with fiery tints.

Mme. Charles Haas HT, *w*, 1930, *Mme. Abel Chatenay × Golden Emblem*; Ketten Bros. Flowers amber-white, tinted flesh-white, full (60-70 petals), high-centered, large; fragrant; foliage leathery; vigorous, free branching growth.

Mme. Charles Joly HT, *op*, 1942, Chambard, C. Flowers bright salmon shaded coppery yellow.

Mme. Charles Lejeune LCl, *lp*, 1924, *Mme. Caroline Testout × Lady Ashtown*; Vandevelde. Flowers soft pink.

Mme. Charles Lutaud HT, *yb*, 1912, *Seedling × Marquise de Sinéty*; Pernet-Ducher. Flowers chrome-yellow, blending to rosy scarlet at edge, dbl. GM, Bagatelle, 1913.

Mme. Charles Lutaud, Climbing Cl HT, *yb*, 1922, Guillot, P..

Mme. Charles Magny HT, *rb*, 1941, *Mme. Joseph Perraud × Seedling*; Gaujard. Flowers coppery red and golden yellow, very dbl., cupped, very large; fragrant; vigorous, bushy growth.

Mme. Charles Mallerin HT, *ob*, 1939, *Lucy Nicolas × Brazier*; Mallerin; A. Meilland; C-P. Flowers orange-salmon, dbl., cupped, large;

slightly fragrant; foliage leathery, dark; vigorous growth.

Mme. Charles Meurice HP (OGR), *dr*, 1878, Meurice. Flowers velvety dark red, dbl., well formed, large; bushy growth.

Mme. Charles Rouveure HT, *dy*, 1946, Mallerin; A. Meilland. Flowers deep yellow, dbl. (36 petals), large (4-5 in.); fragrant (fruity); foliage dark; free growth.

Mme. Charles Sauvage HT, *yb*, 1949, (Mississippi); *Julien Potin × Orange Nassau*; Mallerin; URS. Flowers yellow tinted saffron, center orange-yellow, dbl. (30 petals), well-shaped, large (5 in.); slightly fragrant; bushy growth.

Mme. Charles Singer T (OGR), *dp*, 1916, Nabonnand, C. Flowers garnet, becoming dark velvety purple-garnet, dbl.; vigorous growth.

Mme. Charles Truffant HP (OGR), *lp*, 1878, Verdier, E. Flowers satiny rose, large; vigorous.

Mme. Charles Wood HP (OGR), *mr*, 1861, (Dinsmore); Verdier, E. Flowers fiery scarlet, dbl. (45 petals), large; fragrant; moderate growth.

Mme. Chédane-Guinoiseau T (OGR), *ly*, 1880, *Safrano × Seedling*; Lévêque. Flowers canary-yellow.

Mme. Cheine Duguy HT, *pb*, 1929, Schwartz, A. Flowers cerise-red, shaded scarlet, dbl.

Mme. Chiang Kai-shek HT, *ly*, 1942, *Joanna Hill × Sir Henry Segrave*; Duehrsen; H&S. Bud long, pointed; flowers lemon yellow, turning lighter, dbl. (27 petals), high-centered, large (5-5½ in.); fragrant; foliage leathery, glossy, dark; vigorous, upright, compact growth. AARS, 1944.

Mme. Clara d'Arcis HT, *pb*, 1931, (Clara d'Arcis); *Julien Potin × Seedling*; Gaujard; C-P. Flowers brilliant rose-pink, base yellow, dbl., large; fragrant (spicy); foliage dark, leathery.

Mme. Claude Olivier HT, *op*, 1939, *Soeur Thérèse × R. foetida bicolor Seedling*; Mallerin; A. Meilland. Bud long, pointed; flowers coral, tinted nasturtium-yellow, dbl., high-centered, very large; strong stems; slightly fragrant; foliage leathery; very vigorous, bushy growth.

Mme. Cochet-Cochet HT, *op*, 1934, *Mrs. Pierre S. duPont × Cécile Walter*; Mallerin; C-P. Bud very long; flowers coppery rose-pink, tinted coral, dbl. (30 petals), cupped, large; fragrant; foliage glossy; vigorous growth. GM, Bagatelle, 1932.

Mme. Colette Martinet HT, *yb*, 1915, Pernet-Ducher. Flowers old-gold shaded orange-yellow, dbl.; fragrant.

Mme. Constant Soupert T (OGR), *yb*, 1905, *Souv. de Pierre Notting × Duchesse Marie Salviati*; Soupert & Notting. Flowers yellow shaded peach.

Mme. Cordier HP (OGR), *m*, 1903, Leroy. Flowers bright lilac-pink, full, large.

Mme. Couibes HT, *ab*, 1938, *Charles P. Kilham × Rochefort*; Meilland, F. Flowers salmon, center apricot, edged lighter, passing to golden coral-pink, full, well formed; long stems; fragrant; foliage fresh green; vigorous, bushy growth.

Mme. Crespin HP (OGR), *m*, 1862, Damaizin. Flowers rose shaded violet.

Mme. C. Richardier HT, *my*, 1924, Richardier. Flowers yellow, passing to clear yellow, dbl.

Mme. Croibier HT, *op*, 1935, (Mme. Jean Croibier); *Seedling × Mme. Nicolas Aussel*; Gaujard. Flowers bright salmon, dbl., open, very large; foliage leathery; very vigorous growth. GM, Rome, 1936.

Mme. Crombez T (OGR), *op*, 1888, Nabonnand, G. Flowers rosy buff tinted bronze, dbl., well formed; fragrant.

Mme. Cusin T (OGR), *rb*, 1881, Guillot Fils. Flowers crimson, center yellowish white, full, well formed.

Mme. Damaizin T (OGR), *w*, 1858, Damaizin. Flowers creamy white shaded salmon, dbl., poorly formed, very large.

Mme. d'Arblay HMsk (S), *w*, 1835, *R. multiflora × R. moschata*; Wells. Flowers soft flesh changing to white, semi-dbl., borne in large clusters; fragrant.

Mme. David T (OGR), *lp*, 1895, Pernet Père. Flowers pale flesh, center darker, very dbl., flat; fragrant.

Mme. de Bauvoire HT, *lp*, 1922, *Mme. Vittoria Gagniere × Lady Ashtown*; Schwartz, A. Flowers pinkish white, center pale pink, dbl.

Mme. de Carbuccia HT, *mr*, 1941, *Admiral Ward × Mme. Méha Sabatier*; Kriloff; A. Meilland. Bud long, pointed; flowers bright crimson-red, dbl., medium; very fragrant; foliage leathery; very vigorous, upright growth.

Mademoiselle de Dinant F, *w*, 1966, *Purpurine × Lavender Pinocchio*; Lens. Bud globular; flowers creamy white, dbl. (22 petals), open, large (3-3½ in.); very fragrant (fruity); foliage light green; vigorous, spreading growth.

Mme. de la Rôche-Lambert M (OGR), *m*, 1851, Robert. Flowers dark reddish purple, full, globular, large; moderate growth.

Mme. de Pompadour HT, *rb*, 1945, Gaujard. Flowers coppery red and bright yellow, dbl., globular, medium, borne on short stems; slightly fragrant; foliage dark, glossy; vigorous, bushy growth.

Mme. de Sancy de Parabère Bslt (OGR), *lp*, 1874, (Mme. Sancy de Parabère); Bonnet. Flowers clear soft pink, outer petals larger than inner ones, which tend to form a rosette, large (5 in.); little fragrance; no prickles; very early, non-recurrent bloom; very hardy. Said to have been introduced before 1845; possibly confused with an earlier Boursault.

Mme. de Sévigné B (OGR), *pb*, 1874, Moreau-Robert. Flowers bright rose in center, edges lighter, full, large blooms in clusters; vigorous.

Mme. de St. Joseph T (OGR), *lp*, Flowers fawn shaded salmon, full, large; very fragrant; moderate growth.

Mme. de Tartas T (OGR), *lp*, 1859, (Mme. de Thartas); Bernède. Flowers blush-pink, full, cupped, large; vigorous, sprawling growth. Important ancestor of many Hybrid Teas.

Mme. de Vatry T (OGR), *dp*, 1855, Guérin. Flowers deep pink, center lighter, full, large; fragrant; vigorous growth; recurrent bloom.

Mme. de Watteville T (OGR), *yb*, 1883, Guillot Fils. Flowers lemon edged pink, dbl., large.

Mme. Denise Gallois HT, *pb*, 1941, Sauvageot. Flowers salmon shaded yellow.

Mme. Désiré Giraud HP (OGR), *pb*, 1853, *Baronne Prévost sport*; Van Houtte. Flowers blush-white striped rose.

Mme. Desmars HT, *yb*, 1929, *Ophelia × Constance*; Mallerin; H. Guillot, 1932. Bud long; flowers golden yellow, tinted nasturtium-red, full, high-centered, very large; slightly fragrant; foliage glossy; vigorous, bushy growth.

Mme. Desmary HT, *yb*, 1950, *Aspirant Marcel Rouyer × Emma Wright*; Moulin-Epinay; Vilmorin-Andrieux. Flowers ocher-yellow tinted orange, dbl. (30-35 petals); foliage bright green; vigorous growth.

Mme. Desprez B (OGR), *mp*, 1831, Desprez. Flowers rosy lilac, full, cupped.

Mme. Desprez Ch (OGR), *w*, Flowers white.

Mme. Devoucoux T (OGR), *my*, 1874, Ducher, Vve. Flowers bright yellow, well formed, full.

Mme. Didkowsky HT, *rb*, 1943, Mallerin; A. Meilland. Flowers fiery red, reverse golden yellow.

Mme. Dieudonné HT, *rb*, 1949, (Mme. L. Dieudonné); *(Mme. Joseph Perraud × Brazier) × (Charles P. Kilham × Capucine Chambard)*; Meilland, F. Flowers rose-red, reverse gold, dbl. (30 petals), high-centered, large (4-5 in.); fragrant; foliage dark, glossy; vigorous growth.

Mme. Dieudonné, Climbing Cl HT, *rb*, 1959, Anderson.

Mme. Dimitriu® Pol, *mp*, 1967, (DELcrip); *Chic Parisien × Provence*; Delbard-Charbert. Bud globular; flowers pink tinted lighter, dbl., large, borne in clusters of 5-10; foliage bronze, glossy; vigorous, bushy growth. GM, Geneva & Rome, 1967.

Mme. Driout Cl T (OGR), *pb*, 1902, Thirat, J. Flowers bright rose, striped carmine, full, large; very vigorous, climbing growth.

Mme. Dubost B (OGR), *lp*, 1890, Pernet Père. Flowers flesh, center rose.

Mme. Dubroca T (OGR), *pb*, 1882, Nabonnand, G. Flowers salmon shaded carmine, full, large.

Mme. Edmée Metz HT, *pb*, 1901, *Mme. Caroline Testout × Ferdinand Jamin*; Soupert & Notting. Flowers rosy carmine shaded salmon, dbl.

Mme. Edmond Gillet HT, *yb*, 1921, *Mme. Edmond Rostand × Marquise de Sinéty*; Pernet-Ducher. Flowers reddish nankeen yellow, slightly shaded carmine at tips, dbl.

Mme. Edmond Labbé HT, *rb*, 1938, *Souv. de Claudius Pernet × Hybrid Tea Seedling*; Mallerin; A. Meilland. Bud pointed; flowers orange-red, reverse golden yellow, dbl., large; long stems; slightly fragrant; very vigorous growth. GM, Bagatelle, 1938.

Mme. Edmond Raynal HT, *ly*, 1927, Sauvageot; F. Guillot. Flowers yellowish cream, center salmon, dbl.; very fragrant.

Mme. Edmond Rostand HT, *pb*, 1912, *Seedling × Prince de Bulgarie*; Pernet-Ducher. Flowers pale flesh, center shaded salmon and reddish orange-yellow, dbl.; fragrant.

Mme. Edouard Estaunié HT, *yb*, 1936, *Seabird × Souv. de Claudius Pernet*; Buatois. Bud long; flowers nankeen yellow, center reddish, edges and reverse flesh-pink, dbl., well formed, very large; long stems; fragrant; very vigorous growth.

Mme. Edouard Herriot HT, *ob*, 1913, (Daily Mail Rose); *Mme. Caroline Testout × HT*; Pernet-Ducher. Bud pointed; flowers coral-red shaded yellow and bright rosy scarlet, passing to prawn-red, semi-dbl., large; fragrant; foliage bronze, glossy; vigorous, spreading, branching growth. GM, NRS, 1913.

Mme. Edouard Herriot, Climbing Cl HT, *ob*, 1921, (Daily Mail Rose, Climbing); Ketten Bros..

Mme. Edouard Ory M (OGR), *dp*, 1854, Robert. Flowers bright carmine-pink, full, globular.

Mme. Elie Dupraz HT, *mr*, 1948, Gaujard. Bud large; flowers brilliant red, dbl., high-centered, medium; fragrant; foliage dark, glossy; very vigorous, bushy growth.

Mme. Elisa de Vilmorin HP, *mr*, 1864, (Mme. Eliza de Vilmorin); Lévêque. Flowers dark carmine, dbl. (30 petals), large; upright, bushy growth; sparse bloom.

Mme. Emile Daloz HT, *pb*, 1934, *Frau Karl Druschki × Souv. de Georges Pernet*; Sauvageot, H.; Sauvageot; C-P. Flowers satiny purplish pink, reverse bright rose-pink, dbl., globular, very large; very fragrant; foliage leathery, glossy; very vigorous, bushy growth.

Mme. Emile Mayen HT, *ly*, 1924, Chambard, C. Flowers sulphur-yellow passing to cream, dbl.

Mme. Emile Thierrard HT, *yb*, 1919, *Mrs. Aaron Ward × Joseph Hill*; Turbat. Flowers chamois-yellow and pink, stamens pure yellow, dbl.; fragrant.

Mme. Emilie Charron T (OGR), *mp*, 1895, Perrier. Flowers china-pink, cupped, large; very vigorous growth.

Mme. Emilie van der Goes HT, *op*, 1925, *Columbia × Irish Fireflame*; Verschuren. Bud pointed, orange-yellow and rosy shadings; flowers more pink than bud, semi-dbl., large; fragrant; foliage bronze, leathery; bushy growth.

Mme. Ernest Calvat B (OGR), *mp*, 1888, (Mme. Ernst Calvat; Pink Bourbon); *Mme. Isaac Pereire sport*; Vve. Schwartz Flowers pink shaded darker.

Mme. Ernest Charles HT, *or*, 1933, *Mme. Edmond Rostand × Severine*; Buatois. Bud large, long; flowers coral-red, reverse shrimp-red, dbl., cupped; fragrant; foliage leathery, glossy, bronze; vigorous, bushy growth.

Mme. E. Rocque R, *m*, 1918, *Veilchenblau × Reine des Violettes*; Lottin. Flowers violet, sometimes striped white, passing to amethyst, dbl., borne in clusters.

Mme. E. Terracol HT, *yb*, 1940, *Julien Potin × Soeur Thérèse*; Meilland, F.; A. Meilland. Bud globular; flowers pure yellow, base orange, dbl., very large; slightly fragrant; foliage leathery; very vigorous, upright growth.

Mme. Etienne T (OGR), *mp*, 1887, Bernaix, A. Flowers rose, well formed; vigorous growth.

Mme. Eugène Mallet N (OGR), *yb*, 1875, Nabonnand, G. Flowers pink and yellow, dbl.; fragrant; moderate, climbing growth.

Mme. Eugène Moreau HT, *my*, 1925, Richardier. Flowers yellow, dbl.; vigorous growth.

Mme. Eugène Picard HT, *my*, 1932, *Ariel sport*; Gillot, F.; C-P. Flowers yellow.

Mme. Eugène Résal Ch (OGR), *pb*, 1894, *Mme. Laurette Messimy sport*; Guillot, P. Flowers bright pink shaded reddish orange, base yellow.

Mme. Eugène Verdier HP (OGR), *lp*, Verdier, E., before 1866. Flowers silvery pink, full, globular, large; fragrant; vigorous growth.

Mme. Eugénie Boullet HT, *pb*, 1897, Pernet-Ducher. Flowers pink tinted yellow; fragrant.

Mme. Falcot T (OGR), *my*, 1858, Guillot Fils. Flowers nankeen yellow passing to clear yellow, dbl., large; fragrant.

Mme. Faurax-Lille HT, *mr*, 1933, *Cuba × Sir David Davis*; Reymond; Vially. Bud pointed; flowers bright vermilion-red passing to geranium-red, dbl., large.

Mme. Fearnley Sander HT, *m*, 1921, *Gen. MacArthur × Rayon d'Or*; Ketten Bros. Flowers carmine, deepening to purple, base yellow, dbl.

Mme. Fernand Gentin HT, *op*, 1939, *Seedling × Brazier*; Mallerin; A. Meilland. Bud long, pointed; flowers copper shaded coral, semi-dbl., cupped, large; slightly fragrant; vigorous growth.

Mme. Fernand Gregh HT, *yb*, 1955, *Padre × Madeleine Pacaud*; Robichon. Flowers canary-yellow shaded coppery, large; slightly fragrant; foliage glossy; vigorous growth.

Mme. Fojo HT, *ob*, 1937, Dot, P.; H. Guillot. Flowers orange, well formed, large, strong stems; vigorous growth.

Mme. Forest HT, *mp*, 1928, *Lieutenant Chaure × Mrs. George Shawyer*; Walter, L. Flowers pink.

Mme. Fraculy HT, *dy*, 1929, *Ophelia × Constance*; Siret-Pernet. Flowers deep golden yellow, dbl.; long, strong stems; foliage dark, glossy; vigorous growth.

Mme. Franck Augis® HT, *ob*, 1969, (LAPlam); *Magicienne × Seedling*; Laperrière; EFR. Bud ovoid; flowers clear orange, dbl., high-centered, medium; slightly fragrant; foliage glossy; vigorous, bushy growth.

Mme. François Bollez HT, *op*, 1934, Gillot, F. Flowers coral-pink, center brighter, tinted orange, dbl., very large; fragrant; foliage dark, bronze; very vigorous growth.

Mme. François Graindorge Pol, *pb*, 1922, Grandes Roseraies. Flowers dark reddish pink shaded magenta, base tinged lilac, large, borne in clusters of 40-50; vigorous growth.

Mme. François Hot HT, *pb*, 1928, *Lady Pirrie × Mme. de Bauvoire*; Schwartz, A. Flowers salmon shaded coppery rose, edged lighter, base salmon-yellow.

Mme. François Royet R, *mr*, 1926, *Crimson Rambler* × *Général Jacqueminot*; Royet. Flowers bright red.

Mme. Gabriel Hanra HT, *rb*, 1929, *The Adjutant* × *K. of K.*; Ketten Bros. Flowers strawberry-red, shaded carmine-purple, dbl.; slightly fragrant.

Mme. Gabriel Luizet HP (OGR), *lp*, 1877, Liabaud. Flowers light silvery pink, edged lighter, dbl. (34 petals), cupped, large; fragrant; vigorous growth; non-recurrent bloom.

Mme. Gaston Doumergue Pol, *lp*, 1934, *Probably Gloria Mundi sport*; Levavasseur. Flowers soft salmon.

Mme. Gaston Mestreit Pol, *lp*, 1922, *Jeanny Soupert* × *Katharina Zeimet*; Soupert & Notting. Flowers very soft flesh-white, borne in clusters.

Mme. Gaston Nocton Pol, *w*, 1928, *Amaury Fonseca* × *Jeanny Soupert*; Soupert & Notting. Flowers white, center flesh-pink, opening pure white, borne in clusters; dwarf growth.

Mme. Georges Brédif HT, *rb*, 1955, Privat. Flowers red mottled garnet, well formed; strong stems; fragrant.

Mme. Georges Bruant HRg (S), *w*, 1887, *R. rugosa* × *Sombreuil*; Bruant. Bud pointed; flowers white, loose, large blooms in clusters; fragrant; recurrent bloom; (14).

Mme. Georges Cozon HT, *pb*, 1929, *Mme. Charles Lutaud* × *Hybrid Tea Seedling*; Laperrière. Flower shrimp-pink, reverse yellow.

Mme. Georges Delbard HT, *or*, 1959, *Impeccable* × *Mme. Robert Joffet*; Delbart-Chabert. Flowers bright red suffused orange, dbl. (35-45 petals), large (5 in.); long, strong stems; fragrant; foliage dull green; very vigorous growth. RULED EXTINCT 4/85.

Mme. Georges Delbard® HT, *dr*, 1982, (DELadel; Madame Delbard®); *(Tropicana* × *Samourai)* × *(Tropicana* × *(Rome Glory* × *Impeccable))*; Delbard, G.; Roseraies Delbard, 1980. Flowers dark red, dbl. (40 petals), high-centered, exhibition, large; no fragrance; foliage large, medium green, semiglossy; upright growth.

Mme. Georges Droin HT, *op*, 1930, Gaujard, Jules. Flowers orange-shrimp-pink; foliage bronze; very vigorous growth.

Mme. Georges Landard HT, *lp*, 1925, *Mme. Abel Chatenay* × *Lyon Rose*; Walter, L.; Lamesch. Color and form similar to Mme. Abel Chatenay; foliage glossy.

Mme. Georges Petit HT, *mr*, 1928, *Gen. MacArthur* × *Mme. Edouard Herriot*; Ketten Bros.

Bud pointed; flowers bright purple-red to velvety crimson-red, full, high-centered, large; very fragrant; very vigorous growth.

Mme. Georges Renoard HT, *dy*, 1987, (DELreno); *(Peace* × *Marcelle Gret)* × *Legion d'Honneur Seedling*; Delbard-Chabert, 1988. Flowers deep yellow, dbl. (35-40 petals), long, large; fragrant; foliage clear, matt; upright, half divergent, vigorous growth.

Mme. G. Forest-Colcombet HT, *dp*, 1928, *Hadley sport*; Mallerin; Grandes Roseraies. Flowers deep carmine, strongly tinted scarlet.

Mme. G. Hekkens HT, *dr*, 1929, *Gloire de Holland* × *Hawlmark Crimson*; Faassen-Hekkens. Flowers velvety dark red (nearly as dark as Château de Clos Vougeot), single, open; very fragrant; foliage glossy.

Mme. Ghys R, *m*, 1912, *Crimson Rambler* × *Seedling*; Ghys; Decault. Flowers lilac-rose, borne in clusters; height 6-10 ft.

Mme. Gilberte Janaud F, *mp*, 1957, Privat. Flowers bright pink tinted salmon, very dbl., well formed; dwarf growth.

Mme. Gillet Lafond HT, *pb*, 1930, *Frau Felix Tonnar* × *Angèle Pernet*; Leenders, M. Flowers salmon-white, center old-rose, semi-dbl., large; fragrant; foliage light, leathery; vigorous growth.

Mme. Gina Demoustier HT, *mr*, 1920, *Étoile de France* × *Seedling*; Laperrière. Flowers pure garnet-red, dbl.; very fragrant.

Mme. Grégoire Staechelin LCl, *pb*, 1927, (Spanish Beauty); *Frau Karl Druschki* × *Château de Clos Vougeot*; Dot, P.; C-P, 1929. Flowers delicate pink, reverse stained crimson, ruffled, very large; fragrant; foliage heavy, large, dark; fruit pear-shaped; vigorous (13-14 ft.) growth; non-recurrent bloom. GM, Bagatelle, 1927; ARS John Cook Medal, 1929.

Mme. Gustave Soupert HT, *pb*, 1928, *Augustus Hartmann* × *Souv. de Georges Pernet*; Soupert & Notting. Flowers purplish pink, center brighter, reverse silvery carmine, dbl.; fragrant.

Mme. Hardy D (OGR), *w*, 1832, Hardy. Flowers pure white, occasionally tinged fleshpink, green pip, full, cupped, large blooms in clusters; very fragrant; vigorous growth.

Mme. Hector Leuillot HT, *yb*, 1903, Pernet-Ducher. Bud pointed; flowers golden yellow on carmine ground, dbl.; fragrant.

Mme. Hélène Duché HT, *pb*, 1921, *Mme. Caroline Testout* × *Reine Emma des Pays-Bas*; Buatois. Flowers soft rose with silvery reflexes, edged carmine, dbl.

Mme. Hélène Parmentier HT, *or*, 1935, *Seedling* × *Angèle Pernet*; Sauvageot. Bud long;

flowers clear nasturtium-red, shaded orange, passing to pink, reverse yellow, semi-dbl., cupped, long stems; fragrant; foliage glossy, wrinkled, bronze; vigorous, bushy growth.

Mme. Henri Bonnet HT, *pb*, 1948, *Elite × Seedling*; Boerner; J&P. Bud ovoid; flowers deep salmon-pink suffused golden orange, dbl., high-centered, large; fragrant; foliage leathery; vigorous, upright, compact growth.

Mme. Henri Gravereaux HT, *yb*, 1926, *Mrs. Aaron Ward × Seedling*; Barbier. Flowers coppery yellow tinted bronze-yellow, veined orange, dbl.; fragrant.

Mme. Henri Grimm HT, *lp*, 1934, *Mme. Charles Detreaux × Mme. Edouard Herriot*; Buatois. Bud long; flowers pinkish white tinged carmine, edged crimson, base yellow, dbl., high-centered, very large; very fragrant; foliage leathery, dark; vigorous, bushy growth.

Mme. Henri Guillot HT, *rb*, 1938, *Rochefort × R. foetida bicolor Seedling*; Mallerin; A. Meilland; C-P. Flowers orange-coral-red, dbl. (25 petals), large; slightly fragrant; foliage glossy; vigorous, bushy growth.   GM, Bagatelle, 1936; Portland, 1939.

Mme. Henri Guillot, Climbing Cl HT, *rb*, 1942, Meilland, F..

Mme. Henri Guillot, Climbing Cl HT, *rb*, 1947, Van Barneveld; C-P.

Mme. Henri Laforest HT, *my*, 1942, Gaujard. Bud pointed; flowers golden yellow, semi-dbl., very large; fragrant; foliage glossy; very vigorous, upright growth.

Mme. Henri Lustre HT, *rb*, 1924, *Mme. Edouard Herriot × Yves Druhen*; Buatois. Flowers purplish garnet tinted currant-red, dbl., high-centered, very large; slightly fragrant; foliage leathery; very vigorous, bushy growth.

Mme. Henri Paté HT, *ly*, 1929, *Souv. de Claudius Pernet × Seedling*; Pernet-Ducher; Gaujard. Bud pointed; flowers sulphur-yellow, semi-dbl., very large; very fragrant; foliage bronze; very vigorous, bushy growth.

Mme. Henri Pelley HT, *ly*, 1928, Richardier. Flowers transparent cream-yellow.

Mme. Henri Perline HP (OGR), *mr*, 1887, Vilin. Flowers crimson-red; fragrant.

Mme. Henri Queuille HT, *op*, 1928, Pernet-Ducher; Gaujard. Bud long; flowers bright shrimp-pink, center deeper, reverse coppery gold, semi-dbl.; fragrant; foliage bronze; very vigorous growth.

Mme. Henri Thiebaut HT, *op*, 1931, Chambard, C. Bud pointed; flowers salmon-coral base coral-orange, dbl., very large; strong stems; very fragrant; foliage bright green; vigorous growth.

Mme. Hermann Haefliger S, *dr*, 1951, *R. foetida bicolor Seedling × Charles P. Kilham*; Hauser. Flowers dark red, large; foliage dark; vigorous growth.

Mme. Herriot Panachée HT, *yb*, 1921, *Mme. Edouard Herriot sport*; Cassegrain; Flowers coral and golden yellow.

Mme. Hippolyte Dumas HT, *pb*, 1924, Guillot, P. Flowers flesh tinted salmon-pink, base yellow, dbl.; slightly fragrant.

Mme. Honoré Defresne Cl T (OGR), *my*, 1886, *Mme. Falcot Seedling*; Levet, F.; Flowers golden yellow, full, large; very fragrant; vigorous growth.

Mme. Hoste T (OGR), *w*, 1887, Guillot Fils. Flowers yellowish-white, globular, imbricated, large; vigorous growth.

Mme. Isaac Pereire B (OGR), *dp*, 1881, Garçon. Flowers deep rose-pink shaded purple, full, large; fragrant; vigorous growth.

Mme. Jacques Privat HT, *mr*, 1959, Privat, J. Bud long; flowers red, slightly fragrant; foliage glossy; vigorous growth.

Mme. Jean Dupuy T (OGR), *yb*, 1902, Lambert, P. Bud long, pointed; flowers golden yellow washed pink, full, large; fragrant; vigorous growth.

Mme. Jean Gaujard HT, *yb*, 1938, *Julien Potin × Seedling*; Gaujard; J&P. Bud long, pointed; flowers creamy yellow, reverse shaded orange and carmine-pink, dbl., very large; foliage leathery, light; very vigorous, bushy growth.

Mme. Jean Paquel HT, *ly*, 1934, *Alice Stern × Lilly Jung*; Walter, L.; Amis des Roses. Bud long, pointed; flowers yellow, passing to cream; foliage glossy.

Mme. Jean Raty HT, *w*, 1932, *Mme. Abel Chatenay × Seedling*; Ketten Bros. Bud pointed; flowers amber-white, edges tinted peach-blossom, full, well formed, large; fragrant.

Mme. Jenny R, *mp*, 1926, Nonin. Flowers satiny rose, cupped, small, borne in clusters; fragrant; foliage dark; vigorous, climbing growth.

Mme. Jenny Gillemot HT, *ly*, 1905, Pernet-Ducher. Bud pointed; flowers light saffron-yellow, dbl., high-centered, large; fragrant.

Mme. J. M. Fructus HT, *pb*, 1935, Chambard, C. Flowers satiny carmine, shaded salmon, base yellow, dbl., cupped, well formed; foliage dark; very vigorous growth.

Mme. Joannes Beurrier HT, *op*, 1942, Gaujard. Bud pointed; flowers bright orange-pink, reddish reflections, very dbl., very large; fragrant; foliage glossy, bronze; very vigorous, bushy growth.

Mme. Joseph Jullien HT, *pb*, 1938, *Ami F. Mayery* × *Seedling*; Chambard, C. Flowers coppery carmine, dbl., cupped, very large; fragrant; foliage slightly bronze.

Mme. Joseph Perraud HT, *yb*, 1934, (Sunburst); *Julien Potin* × *Seedling*; Gaujard. Flowers yellow, center deeply tinted coppery, dbl. (33 petals), large; fragrant; foliage glossy. GM, Bagatelle, 1934.

Mme. Joseph Perraud, Climbing Cl HT, *yb*, 1945, Marsh's Nursery.

Mme. Joseph Schwartz T (OGR), *w*, 1880, (White Duchesse de Brabant); *Probably a Duchesse de Brabant sport*; Schwartz, J. Flowers white washed flesh-pink, full, medium; vigorous growth.

Mme. Jules Bouché HT, *w*, 1911, *Pharisäer* × *Seedling*; Croibier; Bud pointed; flowers white, center shaded primrose or pale blush, dbl. (34 petals), large; fragrant; tall.

Mme. Jules Bouché, Climbing Cl HT, *w*, 1938, California Roses.

Mme. Jules Fontaine-Lamarche HT, *mr*, 1936, *Sensation* × *E.G. Hill*; Soupert & Notting. Flowers velvety scarlet-red, dbl., large.

Mme. Jules Gouchault Pol, *op*, 1913, *Maman Turbat* × *George Elger*; Turbat; Teschendorff. Flowers bright pink, tinted coral and orange, dbl., cupped, borne in clusters; fragrant; bushy growth.

Mme. Jules Gravereaux Cl T (OGR), *ab*, 1901, *Rêve d'Or* × *Viscountess Folkestone*; Soupert & Notting. Flowers flesh, shaded peach or yellow, very dbl.; slightly fragrant; foliage large, dark, glossy; height 3-4 ft., bushy growth; recurrent bloom.

Mme. Jules Grolez HT, *mp*, 1896, *Triomphe de l'Exposition* × *Mme. Falcot*; Guillot, P. Bud long, pointed; flowers bright china-rose, dbl., high-centered; fragrant; bushy growth.

Mme. Jules Guérin HT, *ly*, 1931, Gaujard. Flowers deep cream, full, very large; very fragrant; foliage bronze.

Mme. Jules Thibaud Pol, *op*, *Cécile Brunner sport*. Flowers coral-pink.

Mme. Jules Walthery HT, *my*, 1924, Allen. Flowers yellow, outer petals becoming white.

Mme. Julia Daran HP (OGR), *mr*, 1861, Touvais. Flowers crimson.

Mme. Julien Potin HRg (S), *lp*, 1913, *R. rugosa* × *Gloire de Dijon*; Gravereaux; Cochet-Cochet. Flowers pure flesh-pink, dbl., flat, large; foliage very leathery; vigorous growth; recurrent bloom.

Mme. J.W. Büdde HT, *dp*, 1906, Soupert & Notting. Flowers bright carmine.

Mme. Kahn HT, *ly*, 1939, *Charles P. Kilham* × *Ville de Paris*; Colombier. Flowers canary-yellow, reverse slightly reddish; vigorous growth.

Mme. Kastlery HT, *mr*, 1934, *Mme. Adèle Gance* × *Mme. Caroline Testout*; Walter, L.; Amis des Roses. Bud long, pointed; flowers red, dbl., large; very vigorous growth.

Mme. Klatz M (OGR), *dp*, Flowers deep pink, quite large.

Mme. Knorr P (OGR), *mp*, 1855, Verdier, V. Flowers pink, full; fragrant.

Mme. Kriloff HT, *yb*, 1944, *Peace* × *Signora*; Meilland, F.; A. Meilland. Flowers clear saffron-yellow, veined reddish orange, dbl., globular, large; fragrant; foliage leathery; vigorous, bushy growth. GM, Bagatelle, 1944; NRS, 1948.

Mme. la Colonelle Desmaires F, *dr*, 1969, *Mercator* × *Alain*; Delforge; Flowers dark red, dbl., large; slightly fragrant; foliage soft, bronze; moderate growth.

Mme. la Générale Ardouin HT, *rb*, 1927, Chambard, C. Flowers coppery carmine shaded chrome-yellow, dbl., fragrant.

Mme. Laffay HP (OGR), *mr*, 1839, Laffay. Flowers bright crimson, full; very fragrant; very vigorous growth.

Mme. Lajotte HT, *pb*, *Rome Glory* × *Marie-Rose Toussaint*; Gaujard. Flowers bright salmon, reverse yellow, dbl., large; very vigorous, bushy growth.

Mme. Lanquetin HT, *ab*, Ofman; Pin. Flowers apricot.

Mme. Lauras HT, *mr*, 1954, *Rome Glory* × *Mme. Elie Dupraz Seedling*; Gaujard. Flowers bright red, dbl., medium; slightly fragrant; foliage leathery; very vigorous growth.

Mme. Laurette Messimy Ch (OGR), *dp*, 1887, *Rival de Paestum* × *Mme. Falcot*; Guillot Fils. Bud long; flowers rose-pink, base shaded yellow, dbl., large; vigorous growth.

Mme. Lauriol de Barny B (OGR), *lp*, 1868, Trouillard. Flowers silvery pink, full, quartered, large; fragrant (fruity); height 5-6 ft.; rarely repeats.

Mme. le Guelinel HT, *mr*, 1959, *Mme. Kriloff* × *Marrakech*; Gaujard, R.; G. Truffaut. Flowers red, large; very fragrant.

Mme. Legras de St. Germain A (OGR), *w*, 1846, Flowers white, center rich cream, fully dbl., large; foliage gray-green; few prickles; vigorous (6-7 ft.) growth.

Mme. Léon Cuny HT, *mr*, 1955, *Peace* × *Seedling*; Gaujard. Bud long, pointed; flowers bright red, veined purple, dbl., high-centered, very large; fragrant; foliage dark, bronze; upright growth.

Mme. Léon Février T (OGR), *pb*, 1884, Nabonnand, G. Flowers silvery rose shaded crimson, full, well formed; very fragrant.

Mme. Léon Guinotte HT, *pb*, 1924, *Mme. Edouard Herriot × Old Gold*; Verschuren. Flowers glistening pink shaded yellow.

Mme. Léon Pain HT, *pb*, 1904, *Mme. Caroline Testout × Souv. de Catherine Guillot*; Guillot, P. Bud pointed; flowers silvery flesh-pink, center orange-yellow, reverse salmon-pink, dbl. (45 petals); fragrant; vigorous, bushy growth.

Mme. Léon Pin HT, *ob*, 1954, *Louise de Vilmorin × Capucine Seedling*; Gaujard; Flowers soft orange, dbl., medium; slightly fragrant; foliage dark, leathery; upright growth.

Mme. Léon Troussier HT, *op*, 1941, Mallerin; A. Meilland. Flowers coral, base golden yellow.

Mme. Léon Volterra HT, *mp*, 1958, *Ambassadeur Nemry × Tawny Gold*; Leenders, M. Flowers salmon-pink, dbl., well shaped; very fragrant; vigorous growth. GM, Bagatelle, 1957.

Mme. Léonce Colombier HT, *ly*, 1926, Richardier. Flowers center straw-yellow passing to white, reverse light rose, dbl.

Mme. L. Hot HT, *pb*, 1926, *Gorgeous × Rosomane Narcisse Thomas*; Bernaix, P.; Flowers reddish salmon, shaded salmon-rose and chrome-yellow, dbl.

Mme. Line Renaud HT, *mr*, 1956, *Crimson Glory × Seedling*; Mondial Roses. Flowers velvety red; very fragrant; foliage bright green.

Mme. Loeben Sels HT, *w*, 1879, Soupert & Notting. Flowers silvery white shaded rose, full, flat, large; moderate growth.

Mme. Lombard T (OGR), *op*, 1878, (Mme. Lambard); *Mme. de Tartas Seedling*; Lacharme. Flowers rosy salmon, center darker, sometimes rosy flesh, very dbl., large; fragrant; vigorous growth.

Mme. Louis Laperrière HT, *mr*, 1951, *Crimson Glory × Seedling*; Laperrière; EFR. Flowers rich scarlet, dbl. (48 petals), well-formed, medium; very fragrant; foliage dark; upright, bushy growth. GM, Bagatelle, 1950.

Mme. Louis Lens, Climbing Cl HT, *w*, 1935, *White Briarcliff sport*; Lens.

Mme. Louis Lévêque HP (OGR), *dp*, 1864, Lévêque. Flowers carmine-rose, full, very large; moderate growth.

Mme. Louis Lévêque M (OGR), *mp*, 1898, Lévêque. Flowers brilliant salmon-pink, full, globular, large, stems well-mossed; fragrant. Sometimes blooms in fall. A pink form was introduced in 1903.

Mme. Louis Lévêque T (OGR), *yb*, 1892, Lévêque. Flowers yellow washed pink, full; moderate growth.

Mme. Louisa Cointreau HT, *mr*, 1957, *Crimson Glory × Symbole*; Robichon. Flowers garnet-red, dbl.; slightly fragrant; vigorous growth.

Mme. Louise Trémeau HT, *op*, 1931, *(Frau Karl Druschki × Mme. Edouard Herriot) × (Mrs. Edward Powell × R. foetida bicolor)*; Mallerin; C-P. Flowers pink, shaded nasturtium-red, center brighter, dbl., open, cupped, large; slightly fragrant; vigorous growth.

Mme. L. Pradel® HT, *ob*, 1967, (LAPav); *Magicienne × Seedling*; Laperrière; EFR. Flowers clear orange, dbl., high-centered, medium; slightly fragrant; foliage bronze, glossy, leathery; vigorous, upright growth.

Mme. Lucien Perrier HT, *rb*, 1938, Gaujard. Bud long; flowers coppery red, lighter on opening, dbl., open, very large; fragrant; foliage glossy, dark; vigorous growth.

Mme. Lucien Villeminot HRg (S), *lp*, 1901, *Conrad Ferdinand Meyer × Belle Poitevine*; L'Hay. Flowers pale pink, full, globular, large; fragrant; vigorous growth.

Mme. Mallerin HT, *rb*, 1924, *Mrs. Edward Powell × Seedling*; Chambard, C. Flowers crimson-scarlet shaded vermilion; very fragrant.

Mme. Marcel Delanney HT, *pb*, 1916, Leenders, M. Flowers pale pink or soft rose, shaded hydrangea-pink, dbl.; fragrant. GM, Bagatelle, 1915.

Mme. Margottin T (OGR), *my*, 1866, Guillot Fils. Flowers lemon-yellow, dbl., large.

Mme. Marguerite Lagières HT, *w*, 1955, Privat. Flowers cream, base golden yellow, dbl., very large; strong stems; foliage glossy; vigorous growth.

Mme. Marie Curie HT, *dy*, 1943, (Québec); Gaujard; J&P. Flowers clear yellow, dbl. (25 petals), high-centered, large (5 in.); slightly fragrant; foliage leathery, dark; vigorous, bushy, compact growth. AARS, 1944.

Mme. Marie Eberlin HT, *w*, 1923, *Comtesse Mélanie de Pourtales × Capt. Christy*; Walter, A.; Bacher. Flowers cream, passing to white, base light yellow, dbl.

Mme. Marie Lavalley HT, *pb*, 1881, Nabonnand, G. Flowers bright rose tinted white.

Mme. Marius Dévigne HT, *pb*, 1930, Reymond. Bud long; flowers salmon-pink, reverse vivid carmine, globular, large.

Mme. Martignier Cl T (OGR), *m*, 1904, Dubreuil. Flowers red tinted purplish, on yellow ground.

Mme. Masson HP (OGR), *dr*, 1856, Masson. Flowers pure crimson-rose; fragrant; vigorous, compact growth; free bloom during long season.

Mme. Maurice Baudot HT, *ob*, 1941, *Mme. Joseph Perraud × Seedling*; Gaujard. Flowers bright orange, semi-dbl., high-centered, medium; fragrant; foliage dark; very vigorous, bushy growth.

Mme. Maurice Capron HT, *ab*, 1914, Guillot, P. Flowers deep apricot-yellow tinted salmon.

Mme. Maurice Cazin HT, *rb*, 1931, *Gen. MacArthur × Hadley*; Schwartz, A.; Bud pointed; flowers dark scarlet, reverse clear reddish crimson, full, large.

Mme. Maurice de Luze HT, *pb*, 1907, *Mme. Abel Chatenay × Eugène Fürst*; Pernet-Ducher. Flowers rose-pink, center carmine.

Mme. Maurice Kuppenheim T (OGR), *ab*, 1877, Ducher, Vve. Flowers salmon-yellow, full, large.

Mme. Maurin T (OGR), *ob*, 1853, Guillot. Flowers creamy white, shaded with salmon, full, large.

Mme. Méha Sabatier HT, *rb*, 1916, *Seedling × Château de Clos Vougeot*; Pernet-Ducher. Flowers deep red, with white stripes in some petals, dbl.

Mme. Mélanie Soupert HT, *yb*, 1905, Pernet-Ducher. Bud pointed; flowers salmon yellow, suffused pink and carmine, semi-dbl., large; fragrant; vigorous growth.

Mme. Mélanie Willermoz T (OGR), *lp*, 1849, Lacharme. Flowers white tinted pink; fragrant.

Mme. Mercier de Molin HT, *rb*, 1921, *Comte G. de Rochemur × Liberty*; Schwartz, A. Flowers fiery red, tinted crimson, edges slightly tinged rose-pink, dbl.; fragrant.

Mme. Michel Dufay HMoy (S), *rb*, 1932, *George Dickson × R. moyesii*; Sauvageot. Flowers maroon, reverse purplish garnet, full, cupped, large; slightly fragrant; foliage dark; very vigorous, bushy; non-recurrent bloom.

Mme. Millerand HT, *w*, 1926, *Pharisäer × Mme. Henriette Schissele*; Walter, L. Flowers rosy white, shaded salmon, dbl.

Mme. Miniver HT, *ob*, 1947, *Joanna Hill × Charles P. Kilham*; Vilmorin-Andrieux. Bud pointed; flowers orange-red tinted apricot, base yellow, dbl., large; vigorous growth.

Mme. Moisans LCl, *mp*, 1955, *Lady Sylvia × Seedling*; Robichon; Pin. Flowers hortensia-pink, dbl.; fragrant; foliage glossy; recurrent bloom.

Mme. Morand Andrée HT, *dr*, 1957, Privat. Flowers blackish red, very large; foliage dark; vigorous growth.

Mme. Moreau M (OGR), *pb*, 1872, Moreau-Robert. Flowers rose, edged white, full, large.

Mme. Moser HT, *pb*, 1889, Vigneron; Flowers pink to rosy white, full, large; very fragrant.

Mme. Mouseur-Fontaine HT, *yb*, 1931, *Sunburst × Primerose*; Soupert & Notting. Bud pointed; flowers sulphur-yellow, center saffron-yellow, dbl., large; slightly fragrant.

Mme. Nicolas Aussel HT, *ob*, 1930, Pernet-Ducher; Gaujard. Bud pointed; flowers salmon shaded carmine and ocher, dbl., large; foliage dark; vigorous. GM, Portland.

Mme. Nicolas Boudler HT, *pb*, 1934, *Souv. de Georges Pernet × Gloire de Dijon*; Boudler. Bud round; flowers rose, reverse shaded yellow, dbl., large.

Mme. Noël HT, *rb*, 1939, Chambard, C. Flowers vermilion-red, reverse carmine-yellow, dbl., cupped, very large; foliage dark; vigorous growth.

Mme. Noël le Mire HT, *rb*, 1934, *George Dawson × Dance of Joy*; Sauvageot. Flowers brilliant crimson-red with yellow reflections, semi-dbl., cupped, globular, borne in clusters on strong stems; fragrant; dwarf growth.

Mme. Norbert Levavasseur Pol, *mr*, 1903, (Red Baby Rambler); *Crimson Rambler × Gloire des Polyantha*; Levavasseur; Flowers crimson-red, center lighter, bluing badly, semi-dbl., cupped, small blooms in large clusters; slightly fragrant; foliage glossy, dark; bushy, dwarf growth.

Mme. Ocker Ferencz T (OGR), *yb*, 1892, Bernaix, A. Flowers yellow washed pink.

Mme. Ofman HT, *or*, 1954, Ofman. Bud long, pointed; flowers orange-red, very dbl., high-centered, large; strong stems; fragrant; foliage dark, glossy; vigorous, upright, bushy growth; a forcing variety.

Mme. Orève HT, *ob*, 1926, Chambard, M.; Flowers rose-salmon, center coppery salmon; fragrant.

Mme. Paquel HT, *my*, 1945, Mallerin; A. Meilland. Flowers chrome-yellow, full, well formed; wood and foliage reddish.

Mme. Paul Bouju HT, *ob*, 1930, Chambard, C. Bud long, pointed; flowers carmine-orange, cupped, very large; foliage bronze.

Mme. Paul Duringe HT, *mp*, 1934, Chambard, C. Flowers deep coral, large; very vigorous growth.

Mme. Paul Marchandeau HT, *w*, 1928, Barbaras. Flowers white, base deep yellow, dbl.; fragrant.

Mme. Paul Ollivary HT, *dp*, 1924, *Mme. Mélanie Soupert × Emma Wright*; Schwartz, A. Bud pointed; flowers coppery salmon, reverse shaded yellow, nearly single, large.

Mme. Paul Parmentier HT, *ob*, 1919, *Le Progrès × Lyon Rose*; Gillot, F.; Flowers salmon-yellow shaded flesh, copper and daybreak-pink, dbl.

Mme. Paul Rottier F, *rb*, 1957, Buisman. Flowers red shaded orange, borne in large clusters; moderate growth.

Mme. Pauline Labonté T (OGR), *op*, 1852, Pradel. Flowers salmon-pink, full, large; fragrant; vigorous growth.

Mme. P. Doithier HT, *pb*, 1920, Chambard, M. Flowers glossy pink, shaded shrimp-pink.

Mme. Philippe Rivoire HT, *ab*, 1908, Pernet-Ducher. Flowers apricot-yellow, center nankeen yellow, reverse red, full, globular, large; vigorous growth.

Mme. Pierre Cochet N (OGR), *yb*, 1891, *Rêve d'Or Seedling*; Cochet, S.; Flowers saffron-yellow, shaded scarlet, center apricot, dbl.; very fragrant; vigorous, climbing growth.

Mme. Pierre Euler HT, *rb*, 1907, (Mme. P. Euler; Mme. Paul Euler); *Antoine Rivoire × Killarney*; Guillot, P. Flowers silvery vermilion-pink, dbl.; fragrant.

Mme. Pierre Forestier HT, *ob*, 1933, Chambard, C. Flowers orange, shaded shrimp-carmine to satiny china-pink, cupped, very large; fragrant.

Mme. Pierre Koechlin HT, *op*, 1936, *Seedling × The Queen Alexandra Rose*; Sauvageot; C-P. Flowers salmon-pink, dbl., high-centered, globular, very large; slightly fragrant.

Mme. Pierre Oger B (OGR), *pb*, 1878, *La Reine Victoria sport*; Oger; C. Verdier. Flowers blush, reverse tinged rosy lilac.

Mme. Pizay HT, *op*, 1920, *Seedling × Mme. Mélanie Soupert*; Chambard, C. Flowers light salmon.

Mme. Plantier HAlba (OGR), *w*, 1835, *Thought to be R. alba × R. moschata*; Plantier. Flowers creamy white changing to pure white, green pip, very dbl., flat blooms in clusters; fragrant; foliage small, 7 leaflets; vigorous, spreading, bushy (about 5 ft.) growth; non-recurrent bloom.

Mme. Plumecocq HT, *dy*, 1931, *Roselandia × Ville de Paris*; Lens. Flowers golden yellow, center brighter.

Mme. Plumecocq HT, *pb*, 1954, *Peace × Seedling*; Gaujard. Flowers bright pink, reverse silvery, dbl., high-centered, very large; foliage bronze; vigorous, upright growth.

Mme. Raoul Fauran HT, *m*, 1934, Sauvageot. Flowers carmine shaded velvety purple, reverse light purple, semi-dbl., cupped, very large; fragrant; foliage leathery, dark; vigorous, bushy growth.

Mme. Ravary HT, *ob*, 1899, Pernet-Ducher. Flowers orange-yellow, dbl.; fragrant; vigorous, bushy growth.

Mme. Raymond Chevalier-Appert HT, *rb*, 1917, *Gen. MacArthur × Richmond*; Guillot, P. Flowers cerise-red, edged lighter, dbl.; very fragrant.

Mme. Raymond Poincaré HT, *pb*, 1919, (La Rose de Mme. Raymond Poincaré; Mme. Poincaré;) Gravereaux; Kieffer & Sons. Flowers pale pink and salmon, center yellow, dbl.; slightly fragrant. GM, Bagatelle, 1915.

Mme. Rémond T (OGR), *yb*, 1882, Lambert, E. Flowers sulphur-yellow, edged red, very dbl.; fragrant.

Mme. Renahy HP (OGR), *dp*, 1889, Guillot et fils. Flowers carmine.

Mme. René Cassin HT, *pb*, 1962, (DELtaf); *Mme. Armand Souzy × Impeccable*; Delbard-Chabert. Flowers cyclamen-pink, reverse silvery, dbl. (24 petals), high-centered, large (5 in.); fragrant; foliage dark, glossy; vigorous, upright growth. GM, Lyon; Bagatelle, 1962.

Mme. René Coty HT, *rb*, 1955, *Peace × Brazil*; Meilland, F.; URS. Bud globular; flowers persian red, reverse yellow, dbl., very large; long, strong stems; fragrant; foliage glossy, leathery; vigorous, upright growth. GM, Bagatelle, 1954.

Mme. René Lefèvre HT, *yb*, 1938, *Elizabeth of York × Mme. Henri Paté*; Robichon. Bud long, pointed, sulphur-yellow, edged cerise; flowers golden yellow, flushed carmine, semi-dbl., open, large; foliage leathery, bronze.

Mme. Robert HT, *yb*, 1917, Chambard, C. Flowers nankeen yellow with chamois reflexes, dbl.

Mme. Robert Fortin HT, *m*, 1935, *Mme. Caroline Testout × Yves Druhen*; Buatois. Flowers carmine-purple, full, cupped, large; very fragrant; very vigorous growth.

Mme. Robert Joffet F, *rb*, 1956, Delbard-Chabert. Flowers salmon to geranium, reverse carmine-pink, semi-dbl., well formed, large.

Mme. Robert Martin HT, *pb*, 1943, *Charles P. Kilham × Mme. Joseph Perraud*; Meilland, F.; A. Meilland. Bud long, pointed; flowers pink, center coral, very dbl., very large; slightly fragrant; foliage leathery; vigorous, bushy growth.

Mme. Robert Perrier HT, *ob*, Orard; Flowers coppery, stamens saffron, semi-dbl., large.

Mme. Roberte Huet HT, *rb*, 1960, Hémeray-Aubert. Flowers velvety scarlet, reverse raspberry-red, base gold, dbl., regular form; strong stems; slightly fragrant; foliage glossy, slightly bronze; vigorous growth.

Mme. Rochefontaine HP (OGR), *pb*, Flowers rosy flesh to clear pink, full, large; fragrant.

Mme. Roger Douine HT, *rb*, 1926, *Souv. de Claudius Denoyel × Mme. Edouard Herriot*; Reymond. Flowers crimson, shaded scarlet, dbl.

Mme. Roger Verlomme HT, *pb*, 1951, Mallerin. Flowers ocher edged flesh-pink, very dbl., very large; very vigorous growth. GM, Geneva, 1951.

Mme. Saportas G (OGR), *dp*, Flowers bright rosy red, full, large; very fragrant.

Mme. Schmitt HT, *ab*, 1922, Schwartz, A. Flowers salmon-pink, shaded peach-blossom-pink, dbl.

Mme. Schultz N (OGR), *yb*, Flowers pale yellow, center darker, full, medium; very fragrant; vigorous growth.

Mme. Schwaller HT, *mp*, 1886, Bernaix. Flowers pink, large; vigorous growth.

Mme. Scipion Cochet T (OGR), *pb*, 1872, *Anna Olivier × Duchesse de Brabant*; Bernaix, A. Flowers pale pink to white, center yellow, full, cupped, large; fragrant; vigorous.

Mme. Scipion Cochet HP (OGR), *m*, 1873, Cochet, S. Flowers purplish pink edged soft pink, full, cupped, center petals wrinkled; vigorous growth.

Mme. S. Croza HT, *ab*, 1935, *Sunburst Seedling*; Laperrière. Bud long; flowers flesh-pink, dbl., high-centered, very large; long stems; foliage leathery; vigorous growth.

Mme. Segond Weber HT, *op*, 1907, *Antoine Rivoire × Souv. de Victor Hugo*; Soupert & Notting. Flowers clear salmon-pink, dbl., open; long, strong stems; fragrant; bushy growth. GM, Bagatelle, 1909.

Mme. Segond Weber, Climbing Cl HT, *op*, 1911, Ardagh.

Mme. Segond Weber, Climbing Cl HT, *op*, 1929, Reymond.

Mme. Soledad de Ampuera de Leguizamon HT, *pb*, 1928, *General-Superior Arnold Janssen × Mrs. E.G. Hill*; Soupert & Notting. Flowers hydrangea-pink, reverse carmine-rose, dbl.; very fragrant.

Mme. Soupert M (OGR), *mr*, 1851, Moreau-Robert. Flowers well mossed, red.

Mme. Spotti HT, *m*, 1955, Privat. Flowers pink striped mauve, very full; foliage glossy; very vigorous growth.

Mme. Steinbach HT, *pb*, 1934, *Mrs. Pierre S. duPont × Cécile Walter*; Caron, B.; Bud very long; flowers coppery pink tinted coral, full, very large.

Mme. Suzanne Hervé HP (OGR), *dr*, 1936, *Baron Girod de l'Ain Seedling*; Hervé; Vially. Bud very long, pointed; flowers velvety red, heavily streaked maroon; very fragrant; vigorous growth.

Mme. Taft Pol, *dp*, 1909, *Crimson Rambler × Mme. Norbert Levavasseur*; Levavasseur. Flowers ruby-pink full, medium; vigorous, bushy growth.

Mme. Taha Hussein HT, *rb*, 1939, *Charles P. Kilham × Betty Uprichard*; Colombier. Flowers indian red, reverse darker, semi-dbl.; vigorous growth.

Mme. Trottier HT, *yb*, 1937, Leenders, M. Flowers yellowish flesh, very dbl., large; vigorous, bushy growth.

Mme. Van de Voorde HT, *mr*, 1928, *Mme. Méha Sabatier × K. of K.*; Mallerin; C-P. Bud pointed; flowers brilliant scarlet, semi-dbl., cupped, large; very fragrant; very vigorous growth.

Mme. Vannier HT, *or*, Orard. Flowers coppery red, dbl., cupped, large.

Madame Verbelen HT, *dr*, 1973, Delforge, S. Flowers dark red, dbl. (65 petals), cupped, full, large (4½ in.); very fragrant.

Mme. Verdier HP (OGR), *ab*, 1840, Verdier, V. Flowers pale flesh; foliage gray-green.

Mme. Victor Bozzola HT, *mp*, 1935, *Kardinal Piffl × Mme. Edouard Herriot*; Soupert, C. Bud pointed; flowers bright coral-pink, well formed, large.

Mme. Victor Lottin R, *rb*, 1921, Lottin; Resembles Excelsia, but flowers darker and closer together; blooms much earlier. Flowers dark red, shaded crimson; vigorous, climbing growth.

Mme. Victor Rault HT, *w*, 1920, *Mme. Mélanie Soupert × Lyon Rose*; Croibier; Flowers white tinted salmon, center yellow, dbl.

Mme. Victor Verdier HP (OGR), *mr*, 1863, *Senateur Vaisse × Seedling*; Verdier, E.; Flowers clear light crimson, dbl. (75 petals), flat, large; very fragrant; vigorous; seasonal bloom.

Mme. Vidot HP (OGR), *ab*, 1854, Couturier; E. Verdier. Flowers flesh-white.

Mme. Villate HT, *ob*, 1936, *Korovo × Seedling*; Walter, L. Flowers orange with yellow, dbl.; foliage glossy.

Mme. Vincent Auriol HT, *yb*, 1951, *Trylon × Seedling*; Caron, B.; URS. Bud long; flowers golden coral, dbl., peony form, large; slightly fragrant; foliage glossy; vigorous growth. GM, Bagatelle, 1948.

Madame Violet HT, *m*, 1981, *((Lady × x Sterling SIlver) × (Lady × x Sterling Silver)) × Self*; Teranishi, K., 1985; Itama Rose Nursery. Flowers lavender, dbl. (45 petals), high-centered, exhibition, medium blooms borne singly; no fragrance; foliage medium, medium green, semi-glossy; medium; reddish light-green prickles; tall, upright growth.

Mme. Virgilio Pirola HT, *mr*, 1939, *Charles P. Kilham × Étoile de Hollande*; Lens. Bud long, pointed; flowers very bright red, full, fragrant; foliage dark; vigorous, bushy growth. GM, Bagatelle, 1939.

Mme. Visseaux HT, *op*, 1936, *Odette Foussier × Elvira Aramayo*; Mallerin; C-P. Bud long; flowers orange-pink, base yellow, dbl., open, large (4-5 in.); slightly fragrant.

Mme. Vittoria Gagnière HT, *w*, 1909, *Anna Chartron × Mrs. W.J. Grant*; Vve. Schwartz Flowers white tinted pink.

Mme. Wagram, Comtesse de Turenne T (OGR), *pb*, 1894, Flowers bright satiny rose suffused with darker rose, very large; fragrant; vigorous growth.

Mme. Walter Baumann HT, *rb*, 1934, *Mlle. Franziska Krüger × Gwynne Carr*; Reymond; Vially. Bud long; flowers carmine, base yellow, dbl., open.

Mme. W.C. Whitney HT, *lp*, 1894, Flowers flesh-pink, very fragrant.

Mme. Welch T (OGR), *ob*, 1878, *Devoniensis × Souv. d'un Ami*; Ducher, Vve.; Flowers coppery orange-yellow, reverse pale yellow, very dbl., well formed, large.

Mme. William Paul M (OGR), *dp*, 1869, Moreau-Robert. Flowers bright rose, full, cupped, large; recurrent.

Mme. Yves Latieule HT, *my*, 1949, (Nankin); *Mme. Joseph Perraud × Léonce Colombier*; Meilland, F. Flowers primrose-yellow, dbl. (70 petals), large (5 in.); slightly fragrant; foliage glossy, dark; vigorous growth. GM, NRS, 1950.

Mme. Zöetmans D (OGR), *w*, 1830, Marest. Flowers pale flesh, dbl.

Madcap F, *mr*, 1954, *Independence × Crimson King*; Kordes; Stark Bros. Bud urn-shaped; flowers scarlet-red, dbl. (20-25 petals), cupped, large (4½ in.); fragrant; foliage leathery; bushy growth.

Madcap HT, *rb*, 1955, *Grand Duchesse Charlotte sport*; Ratcliffe. Bud dark red; flowers flame-scarlet striped yellow, or orange without stripe.

Maddalena HT, *op*, 1934, *Julien Potin × J.C. Thornton*; San Remo Exp. Sta. Bud pointed to ovoid; flowers salmon-pink, reverse begonia-rose, dbl. (30-32 petals), cupped, very

large; long stems; fragrant; foliage light green, glossy, leathery; very vigorous, upright, bushy growth.

Madeleine Lemaire R, *op*, 1923, *Mrs. F.W. Flight × Seedling*; Nonin. Flowers bright salmon-pink, semi-dbl., medium.

Madeleine Monod HT, *op*, 1939, Chambard, C. Bud long; flowers salmon-carmine, dbl., very large; fragrant; foliage bronze; vigorous growth.

Madeleine Pacaud HT, *op*, 1922, Chambard, C. Flowers silvery rose, tinted salmon.

Madeleine Selzer R, *ly*, 1926, (Yellow Tausendschön); *Tausendschön × Mrs. Aaron Ward*; Walter, L. Flowers pale lemon, fading white; few prickles; vigorous growth.

Madeleine Weidert R, *mp*, 1928, *Tausendschön × Rosel Dach*; Walter, L. Flowers rose-pink.

Madeline E (OGR), *w*, (Emmeline). Flowers creamy white edged pink, semi-dbl.

Madeline Correy HT, *dp*, 1971, *Minnie Watson × Sterling Silver*; Watson. Bud globular; flowers cerise, dbl., full, medium; fragrant (lemon); foliage glossy, dark; moderate growth.

Madeline Spezzano Min, *mp*, 1985, (TINmad); *Sonia × Beauty Secret*; Bennett, Dee; Tiny Petals Nursery. Flowers medium pink, dbl. (45 petals), HT form, mini-flora, medium; slight fragrance; foliage large, medium green, semi-glossy; upright, bushy growth.

Madelon HT, *or*, 1983, (RUImeva); *Varlon × MEIgenon*; deRuiter, G.; Fryer's Nursery, Ltd. 1981. Flowers orange-red, dbl. (20 petals), medium, slight fragrance; foliage medium, medium green, semi-glossy; upright growth; greenhouse variety.

Madelyn Lang Cl Min, *dp*, 1970, *Little Darling × Little Chief*; Williams, E.D.; Mini-Roses. Bud slightly ovoid; flowers deep pink, dbl. (40 petals), small (1 in.); foliage small, glossy, dark, embossed; upright growth.

Mademoiselle F, *dp*, 1950, *Goldilocks × Marionette*; Boerner; J&P. Bud ovoid; flowers rose-red, dbl. (50-60 petals), large (3½ in.); very vigorous, branching growth; best adapted for forcing.

Mlle. Alice Furon HT, *ly*, 1896, *Lady Mary Fitzwilliam × Mme. Chedane-Guinoisseau*; Pernet-Ducher. Flowers yellowish white.

Mlle. Annie Wood HP (OGR), *mr*, 1866, (Annie Wood); Verdier, E. Flowers clear red, full, large; fragrant; recurrent bloom.

Mlle. Bep van Rossem HT, *my*, 1926, *Seedling × Souv. de Claudius Pernet*; Van Rossem. Flowers deep canary-yellow, dbl.

Mlle. Bonnaire N (OGR), *w*, 1859, Pernet Père. Flowers white, center sometimes pink, full; growth moderate.

Mlle. Claire Andruejol HT, *lp*, 1920, *Comte G. de Rochemur × Mme. Maurice de Luze*; Schwartz, A. Flowers pale pink tinted carmine, dbl.; slightly fragrant.

Mlle. Claudine Perreault T (OGR), *mp*, 1885, Lambert, E. Flowers rose flesh, center darker, full, very large; free bloom.

Mlle. de Morlaincourt HT, *pb*, 1934, *Cécile Walter × Korovo*; Walter, L.; Amis de Roses. Flowers pink and yellow.

Mlle. Eugénie Verdier HP (OGR), *mp*, 1869, Guillot Fils. Flowers clear silvery pink, reverse silvery white, dbl. (40 petals), large; fragrant; vigorous, upright growth.

Mlle. Franziska Krüger T (OGR), *op*, 1880, *Catherine Mermet × Gén. Schablikine*; Nabonnand, G. Flowers coppery yellow and pink, center often green, very dbl., large blooms on weak stems; fragrant; hardy for this class; (14).

Mlle. Hélène Gambier HT, *op*, 1895, (Helen Gambier); Pernet-Ducher. Flowers salmon-pink to coppery rose, dbl., large; very fragrant.

Mlle. Henriette Martin HT, *w*, 1936, Reymond; Vially. Flowers white, shaded ivory, edges lightly tinted pale pink; fragrant.

Mlle. Irene Hennessy HT, *or*, 1923, *George C. Waud × Seedling*; Guillot, P. Flowers bright vermilion-orange, dbl.; fragrant.

Mlle. Jeanne Lenail Pol, *mr*, 1924, *Mrs. W.H. Cutbush × Mme. Taft*; Schwartz, A. Flowers bright ruby-red shaded carmine, full, large.

Mlle. Marie Louise Bourgeois M (OGR), *lp*, 1891, Corboeuf. Flowers light pink, edged white; very similar to Blanche Moreau.

Mlle. Marie Mascuraud HT, *w*, 1909, Bernaix, P. Flowers white tinted flesh.

Mlle. Marie Moreau T (OGR), *w*, 1880, Nabonnand, G. Flowers silver-white flushed crimson, well formed.

Mlle. Marthe Carron R, *w*, 1931, *R. wichuraiana sport × R. wichuraiana*; Mermet. Flowers white, slightly tinted pink on opening, borne in clusters of 40-50; vigorous growth.

Mlle. Marthe Moisset HT, *my*, 1935, *Mme. Henri Queuille × Seedling*; Ducroz. Flowers chrome-yellow on ocher ground, cupped, very large; fragrant; foliage glossy, dark; vigorous, erect, bushy growth.

Mlle. Maurand HP (OGR), *lp*, Flowers pale flesh.

Mlle. Simone Beaumez HT, *w*, 1907, Pernet-Ducher. Flowers flesh-white, center sometimes tinted saffron-yellow, dbl.; fragrant.

Mlle. Sontag G (OGR), *dp*, Flowers deep pink, reverse pale blush.

Mlle. Stella Mallerin HT, *w*, 1926, Chambard, C. Bud pointed; flowers white, center slightly shaded cream, dbl., cupped, very large; fragrant.

Mlle. Yvette Bouquil F, *yb*, 1955, Privat. Flowers yellow edged orange; bushy growth.

Madette HT, *op*, 1922, Guillot, P. Flowers coppery orange-pink.

Madge Elliott HT, *lp*, 1964, *Queen Elizabeth × Seedling*; Darvall; G. Knight. Flowers light pink, center shaded apricot, full, medium; slightly fragrant; foliage dark, leathery; very vigorous, upright growth.

Madge Prior F, *pb*, 1934, Prior. Flowers brilliant claret, white eye, single, borne in large clusters; foliage dark; vigorous growth.

Madge Taylor HT, *dp*, 1930, *Rhea Reid Seedling × Seedling*; Clark, A.; Hazlewood Bros. Flowers deep pink, full, globular, large; slightly fragrant; foliage light; vigorous growth.

Madge Whipp HT, *or*, 1936, *Lady Charmion × J.C. Thornton*; Bees. Flowers bright scarlet, dbl.; fragrant; foliage leathery; vigorous, bushy growth.

Madge Wildfire HT, *or*, 1932, Dobbie. Bud pointed; flowers indian red, very dbl., high-centered, very large; fragrant; foliage leathery; vigorous growth. GM, NRS, 1933.

Madhatter Min, *my*, 1988, (TINhat; G'Day); Gidday *Autumn × Avandel*; Bennett, Dee; Tiny Petals Nursery. Flowers medium yellow, aging paler, dbl. (25-30 petals), cupped, exhibition, medium, borne usually singly or in sprays of 3-5; moderate, damask fragrance; foliage medium, medium green, semi-glossy; prickles hooked slightly downward, reddish; fruit globular, green to brown; bushy, medium growth.

Madhosh HT, *rb*, 1975, Indian Agric. Research Inst. Bud globular; flowers deep magenta-red, streaked mauve, dbl. (45 petals), large (4½ in.); slightly fragrant; foliage leathery; vigorous, bushy, compact growth.

Madhumati HT, *mp*, 1973, *General MacArthur × Seedling*; Pal, Dr. B.P.; IARI. Flowers medium pink, dbl. (55 petals), high-centered, large blooms borne singly; highly scented; foliage medium, medium green, smooth; brown prickles; vigorous, upright, bushy.

Madhura F, *yb*, 1979, *Kiss of Fire × Goudvlinder*; Pal, Dr. B.P.; K.S.G. Sons. Bud pointed; flowers yellow blend, dbl. (70 petals), high-centered blooms borne 3-6 per cluster; fragrant; foliage glossy; vigorous, upright, bushy growth.

Madison T (OGR), *w*, 1912, *(Perle × The Bride) × Meteor*; Brant-Hentz. Flowers pure white.

Madoka F, *rb*, 1977, *(Zambra × Peace) × Cherry Brandy*; Teranishi, K.; Itami Bara-en. Flowers red blend, dbl. (25 petals), high-centered, medium (2-2½ in.); slightly fragrant; foliage glossy, dark; upright growth.

Madonna HT, *w*, 1908, *Mlle. Alice Furon × Marie van Houtte*; Cook, J. Flowers white.

Madras HT, *pb*, 1981, *seedlng × Seedling*; Warriner; J&P. Bud ovoid; flowers rose with yellow and light pink reverse, dbl. (48 petals), borne singly; fragrant; foliage large, leathery; prickles hooked downward; medium, spreading growth.

Madrigal HT, *dp*, 1950, *(Mme. Joseph Perraud Seedling × Seedling) × (Mme. Joseph Perraud Seedling × R. foetida bicolor)*; Gaujard. Bud long, pointed; flowers brilliant salmon-pink flushed coppery, dbl., very large; fragrant (spicy); vigorous growth.

Maestro HT, *dr*, 1957, *Crimson Glory × Charles Mallerin*; Delforge. Bud oval; flowers deep velvety red, dbl., open, large; very fragrant; foliage dark, glossy; vigorous, bushy growth. RULED EXTINCT 2/81.

Maestro® HT, *rb*, 1981, (MACkinju; MACinju); *Picasso Seedling × Seedling*; McGredy, Sam, 1980. Bud ovoid; flowers medium red, painted white, reverse lighter red and white (cool temperatures needed to produce painting; painting and color combinations variable), dbl. (28 petals), blooms borne 4-6 per cluster; slight fragrance; foliage matt, olive green; narrow, red prickles; upright, bushy growth.

Ma Fiancée HT, *dr*, 1922, *Gen. MacArthur Seedling × Red-Letter Day*; Van Rossem. Flowers dark crimson, often nearly black, dbl.; very fragrant.

Ma Fille HT, *ob*, 1960, *Berthe Mallerin × Seedling*; Mallerin; EFR. Flowers orange, dbl. (45 petals), large; slightly fragrant; foliage glossy; vigorous, bushy, symmetrical growth.

Magali HT, *dp*, 1952, *Charles P. Kilham × Brazier*; Mallerin; Meilland-Richardier. Flowers carmine, dbl. (35-40 petals), open, medium; slightly fragrant; foliage abundant, leathery; very vigorous, upright, bushy growth.

Magali Bonnefon HT, *pb*, 1916, *Mme. Abel Chatenay sport*; Nabonnand. Flowers pink, reverse bright salmon-pink, semi-dbl.; fragrant.

Magdalena de Nubiola HT, *op*, 1932, *Li Bures × Mari Dot*; Dot, P.; C-P. Flowers salmon-rose, semi-dbl.; slightly fragrant.

Magenta Pol, *m*, 1916, Barbier. Flowers violet-red, semi-dbl.; dwarf.

Magenta HT, *m*, 1954, (Kordes' Magenta); *Yellow Floribunda × Lavender Pinocchio*; Kordes. Bud ovoid; flowers rosy magenta to soft deep mauve, full, large blooms in large clusters; very fragrant; foliage dark, leathery; vigorous, upright, bushy growth.

Magenta HT, *mr*, 1934, Leenders, M. Bud pointed; flowers crimson-carmine, dbl., large; very fragrant; foliage glossy, dark; vigorous, bushy.

Magic HT, *pb*, 1954, *Thornless Beauty sport*; Grillo. Bud globular; flowers silver-pink, full (75 petals), open, large (5½ in.); fragrant; foliage leathery; very vigorous, upright growth. RULED EXTINCT 11/88.

Magic HT, *mr*, 1988, *MACvolar × Tonight*; Strahle, Robert; Carlton Rose Nursery, 1987. Bud pointed; flowers medium red, dbl. (24 petals), high-centered, medium, borne usually singly; foliage medium, medium green, matt; prickles slender, straight, medium, light green; fruit pear shaped, medium, orange; upright, tall growth.

Magic Carpet LCl, *yb*, 1941, *Coral Creeper × Stargold*; Brownell. Flowers yellow, splashed orange, scarlet and rose, semi-dbl., high-centered, globular, large, borne in clusters on strong stems; foliage small, bronze, leathery, glossy; vigorous, climbing or trailing growth.

Magic Carrousel® Min, *rb*, 1972, (MORrousel; MOORcar); *Little Darling × Westmont*; Moore, R.S.; Sequoia Nursery. Flower petals white, edged red, dbl., high-centered, small; slightly fragrant; foliage small, glossy, leathery; vigorous, bushy growth. AOE, 1975.

Magic Charm HT, *mp*, 1966, *Mount Shasta × Granada*; Aufill. Flowers medium pink, dbl., high-centered, medium; vigorous growth.

Magic Dragon Cl Min, *dr*, 1969, *((R. wichuraiana × Floradora) × Seedling) × Little Buckaroo*; Moore, R.S.; Sequoia Nursery. Bud short, pointed; flowers dark red, dbl., small; foliage leathery; very vigorous, upright growth.

Magic Fire® F, *or*, 1967, (LAPneuf); Laperrière; EFR. Bud pointed; flowers bright orange-red, semi-dbl., high-centered, small; foliage glossy; vigorous, bushy growth.

Magic Mist Min, *mr*, 1980, *Tom Brown × Little Chief*; Williams, E.D.; Mini-Roses. Bud pointed; flowers medium red, veined darker, dbl. (47 petals), high-centered blooms borne usually singly; fragrant; foliage small, medium to dark green, glossy; thin, tan prickles; bushy, spreading growth.

Magic Moment HT, *mr*, 1964, Buyl Frères; Cuthbert. Bud pointed; flowers scarlet to geranium-red, dbl., high-centered, large; fragrant.

Magic Moon Gr, *ob*, 1970, *Little Darling × Golden Scepter*; Schwartz, E.W.; Wyant. Bud ovoid; flowers deep salmon, reverse silver, very dbl., medium; slightly fragrant; foliage large, leathery; vigorous, upright growth.

Magic Mountain F, *yb*, 1973, *Circus × Texan*; Armstrong, D.L.; Armstrong Nursery. Bud ovoid; flowers yellow blend, dbl., high-centered, large; slightly fragrant; foliage glossy, dark, leathery; vigorous, bushy growth.

Magic Red F, *mr*, 1942, *Henri Pauthier × Dance of Joy*; Kordes; J&P. Flowers medium red, dbl. (45 petals), globular, large blooms in clusters; slightly fragrant; foliage leathery, glossy; vigorous, bushy growth.

Magic Splendor Min, *dr*, 1983, (LYOma); *Baby Betsy McCall × Seedling*; Lyon, Lyndon. Flowers dark red, dbl. (35 petals), small blooms in clusters; no fragrance; foliage medium, medium green, semi-glossy; upright, bushy growth.

Magic Touch HT, *lp*, 1974, *Tropicana × Queen of Bermuda*; Golik; Dynarose. Bud ovoid; flowers soft pink, dbl. (32 petals), high-centered, large (5 in.); fragrant; foliage glossy; moderate growth.

Magic Wand Cl Min, *dp*, 1957, *Éblouissant × Zee*; Moore, R.S.; Sequoia Nursery. Flowers light red, semi-dbl. (20 petals), small (1 in.) blooms in clusters; foliage small, dark; fruit orange; arching (to 4 ft.) growth.

Magicienne HT, *or*, 1957, *Comtesse Vandal × (Peace × Independence)*; Laperrière; EFR. Flowers geranium-red, dbl. (30 petals), well formed; foliage bronze; dwarf, bushy growth.

Magitta® HT, *mr*, 1982, (TANattigam); Tantau, M., 1981. Flowers medium red, dbl. (20 petals), large; slight fragrance; foliage medium, medium green, semi-glossy; upright growth.

Magna Charta HP (OGR), *mp*, 1876, (Casper); Paul, W. Flowers bright pink, suffused carmine, dbl., globular, very large; fragrant; foliage thick, rich green; vigorous, compact growth; some recurrent bloom.

Magnafrano HT, *mr*, 1900, *Magna Charta × Safrano*; Van Fleet; Conard; Jones. Flowers rich crimson-rose, dbl., large; very fragrant.

Magnifica E (OGR), *m*, 1916, (*R. eglanteria duplex* Weston; *R. rubiginosa magnifica*); *Lucy Ashton self seedling*; Hesse. Flowers purplish red, semi-dbl. Extensively used by Kordes and others in hybridizing.

Magnificence HT, *op*, 1954, *Peace Seedling*; Gaujard; McGredy. Flowers salmon-pink tinted yellow, dbl., high-centered, large; fragrant; foliage dark; vigorous, bushy growth.

Magnifique Pol, *lp*, 1928, *Orléans Rose sport*; deRuiter; Sliedrecht & Co. Flowers clear pink, semi-dbl., open, cupped, large, borne in clusters; foliage rich green, glossy; vigorous growth.

Magrana F, *or*, 1954, *Méphisto × Alain*; Dot, P. Flowers orange-red, dbl., well formed; vigorous growth.

Mahadev F, *or*, 1975, *Seedling × (Seedling × Seedling)*; Viraraghaven. Bud long, pointed; flowers orange-red, dbl. (20 petals), full, open, small (1½ in.); slightly fragrant; foliage glossy; vigorous, tall, bushy growth.

Mahagona HT, *pb*, 1956, (Mahogany); *Golden Rapture × Hens Verschuren*; Kordes; McGredy. Bud pointed; flowers dull orange-scarlet, open, very large; fragrant; foliage leathery, wrinkled; very vigorous, upright, bushy growth.

Mahaja HT, *dp*, 1936, *Rose Hill sport*; Carbaugh; Johnstown Greenhouses. Bud long, pointed; flowers deep rose-pink, center rose-red, base yellow, dbl., high-centered, large (4 in.); long stems; fragrant; foliage glossy; vigorous growth.

Maharajah HP (OGR), *mr*, 1931, Cant, B.R. Flowers velvety crimson, golden anthers, single to semi-dbl., large blooms in clusters; fragrant; foliage dark, bronze, leathery.

Mahina HT, *ab*, 1952, *Peace × Fred Edmunds*; Meilland, F. Flowers reddish apricot, reverse golden yellow, dbl. (35 petals), large; fragrant; oliage leathery; very vigorous, bushy growth. GM, Bagatelle, 1952.

Maid Marian HT, *pb*, 1920, Therkildsen. Flowers carmine-rose, reverse silvery pink, dbl.

Maid Marion R, *w*, 1909, Walsh. Flowers white, tipped pink, center filled with yellow stamens, single, slightly incurved, very large, borne in large clusters; foliage large, glossy; vigorous growth.

Maid Marion HMsk (S), *w*, 1930, Pemberton; Bentall. Flowers white opening blush, semi-dbl., borne in very large clusters; vigorous (3-4 ft.) growth.

Maid of Gold Cl HT, *my*, 1936, *Golden Emblem, Climbing × Seedling*; Raffel; Port Stockton Nursery. Bud globular, reddish; flowers golden yellow, very dbl., large; foliage glossy; vigorous, climbing (12 ft.), compact growth; profuse, intermittent bloom.

Maid of Honour F, *op*, 1951, (Schleswig); *Crimson Glory × Holstein*; Kordes; Morse. Bud long, pointed; flowers salmon-pink, single, open, large, borne in trusses; fragrant; foliage leathery, glossy, light green; vigorous, upright growth. (28). RULED EXTINCT 1/86.

Maid of Honour HT, *yb*, 1986, (Maid of Honor); *Folklore × Seedling*; Weddle, Von C.; Hortico, 1984. Flowers yellow, light pink center, dbl. (40+ petals), large blooms borne singly and in clusters; fragrant; foliage large, dark, semi-glossy; tall, upright growth.

Maid of Kent HT, *op*, 1929, *Ophelia × Mrs. W.J. Grant*; Archer. Flowers soft salmon-pink; fragrant.

Maid of Orleans F, *ob*, 1977, *Val De Mosa × Tropicana*; Ellick. Flowers orange-flame blend, dbl. (40 petals), full, large (4 in.); slightly fragrant; foliage glossy, dark; very free growth.

Maiden Voyage F, *pb*, 1992, (MAClocker); *Sexy Rexy × New Year*; McGredy, Sam IV; Cooperative Rose Growers, 1992. Flowers pink blend, moderately full (15-25 petals), medium (4-7 cms) blooms borne in small clusters; slight fragrance; foliage medium, medium green, glossy; medium (3½'), bushy growth

Maiden's Blush HAlba (OGR), *w*, 1797, (Small Maiden's Blush); *Presumed to be a natural hybrid of R. alba × R. centifolia*; Kew. Flowers soft blush, dbl., globular, medium; fragrant; vigorous (to 8 ft.) growth; non-recurrent bloom. Often referred to as Small Maiden's Blush to distinguish it from Great Maiden's Blush, which see.

Maids of Jubilee Min, *pb*, 1989, (TALmaid); *Azure Sea × Miniature Seedling*; Taylor, Pete & Kay; Taylor's Roses. Bud pointed; flowers bright deep pink with cream base in center, reverse cream and pink blend, fading lighter, dbl. (25-30 petals), high-centered, exhibition, medium, borne singly, good substance; no fragrance; foliage medium, dark green, semi-glossy; prickles yellowish-green; upright, bushy, medium growth.

Maidy® Min, *rb*, 1984, (KORwalbe); *Regensberg × Seedling*; Kordes, W. Flowers red blend, dbl. (20 petals), medium; no fragrance; foliage small, medium green, semi-glossy; bushy growth.

Maigold S, *dy*, 1953, *Poulsen's Pink × Frühlingstag*; Kordes. Flower bronze-yellow, semi-dbl. (14 petals), cupped, large (4 in.); very fragrant; foliage glossy; bushy (5 ft.), pillar or shrub growth; non-recurrent bloom. (Also reported as McGredy's Wonder × *Frühlingsgold*.)

Mainauperle® HT, *dr*, 1969, (KORmai); *Seedling × Americana*; Kordes, R. Bud ovoid; flowers dark red, dbl., high-centered, large; very fragrant; foliage large, dark, leathery; vigorous, upright, bushy growth. ADR, 1966.

Mainz HT, *my*, 1930, *Kardinal Piffl sport*; Leenders Bros. Flowers citron-yellow, dbl., very large; fragrant.

Mainzer Wappen S, *or*, 1963, (Mainzer Rad); Kordes, R. Bud pointed; flowers red tinted orange, dbl. (25 petals), large (3½ in.) blooms in clusters (up to 20); fragrant; foliage dark; bushy, upright (5 ft.) growth.

Maisie Gowie HT, *?*, 1968, Gowie. Very fragrant; foliage dark, leathery; bushy growth.

Maison Pernet-Ducher HT, *my*, 1934, Pernet-Ducher; Gaujard. Bud pointed; flowers golden yellow, veined copper, dbl., large; foliage glossy, dark; very vigorous, bushy.

Maja F, *mr*, 1959, *Independence × Signal Red*; deRuiter; Horstmann. Flowers cinnabar-red, dbl. (30 petals), cupped, borne in broad clusters; vigorous, bushy growth.

Maja Mauser F, *or*, 1970, *Evelyn Fison × Seedling*; Poulsen, N.D.; Poulsen. Flowers dark orange-red, dbl. (20 petals), large (4 in.); slightly fragrant; foliage glossy, dark; bushy, upright growth.

Majestade HT, *w*, 1957, *Mme. Marie Curie × Peace*; Moreira da Silva. Flowers cream-white, base deep yellow, well formed; very vigorous growth.

Majesté® HT, *op*, 1966, (DORma); *Radar × Eclipse*; Dorieux; Vilmorin. Bud oval; flowers salmon, dbl., large; fragrant; foliage glossy, leathery; very vigorous, upright growth.

Majestic HT, *or*, 1955, *Peace × Seedling*; Gaujard. Bud long, purplish; flowers cinnabar-red, dbl., open, large; fragrant; vigorous growth.

Major Frank Hayes HT, *dr*, 1934, *Joan Howarth × J.C. Thornton*; Bees. Flowers crimson, center darker, dbl., high-centered, very large; very fragrant; foliage leathery, dark; vigorous growth.

Major Shelley HT, *mr*, 1939, *Mrs. J.D. Eisele × Crimson Glory*; Howard, F.H.; H&S. Bud pointed; flowers rich crimson-scarlet, dbl. (35 petals), high-centered, large (5-6 in.); foliage leathery, dark; very vigorous, bushy growth.

Majorca HT, *mr*, 1938, *Aribau × Angels Mateu*; Dot, P.; C-P, 1941. Flowers scarlet, dbl., cupped, large; foliage glossy, bronze; vigorous, bushy growth.

Majorca HT, *op*, 1958, Buyl Frères. Bud short, thick; flowers rose-salmon, dbl. (52 petals); moderate growth.

Majorette® HT, *op*, 1967, (MEIdad; Minna Lerche Lerchenborg); *Zambra × Fred Edmunds*; Meilland; URS. Bud pointed; flowers coppery salmon, dbl., high-centered, large; slightly fragrant; foliage dark, leathery; vigorous, upright growth. GM, Bagatelle, 1966.

Majorette® Min, *mr*, 1986, (MEIpiess; Majorette 86); *Magic Carrousel × (Grumpy × Scarletta)*; Meilland, M.L., 1985. Flowers medium cardinal-red, moderately full (15-25 petals), medium; mini-flora; no fragrance; foliage small, medium green, semi-glossy; fruit produced in autumn; bushy growth.

Make Believe™ Min, *m*, 1986, (MORmake); *Anytime × Angel Face*; Moore, R.S., 1980; Moore Min. Roses, 1985. Flowers mauve and white blend, reverse red-purple, 10 petals, medium blooms in sprays of 3-5; no fragrance; foliage medium, dark, semi-glossy; very few, hooked, dark brown prickles; fruit small, orange, globular; upright, bushy growth.

M. A. Keessen Pol, *dp*, 1923, *Ellen Poulsen sport*; Keessen. Flowers darker.

Mala Rubinstein HT, *mp*, 1971, *Sea Pearl × Colour Wonder*; Dickson, A. Flowers pink, dbl. (45 petals), high-pointed, large (5½ in.); fragrant; foliage large, matt. Edland Fragrance Medal, 1972; GM, Belfast, 1973.

Malaga Cl HT, *dp*, 1971, *(Hamburger Phoenix × Danse de Feu) × Copenhagen*; McGredy, S., IV. Flowers reddish pink, dbl. (36 petals), classic form, large (4½ in.); very fragrant; foliage glossy, dark.

Malaguena S, *mp*, 1976, *Tickled Pink × Country Music*; Buck; Iowa State University. Bud ovoid, long, pointed; flowers medium pink, dbl. (28 petals), shallowly-cupped, large (4½ in.); slightly fragrant; foliage large, dark, leathery; erect, bushy growth.

Malahat HT, *rb*, 1987, (BETahat); *Pristine × Shockling Blue*; Betts, J.; Wisbech Plant Co., 1988. Flowers scarlet, reverse white, fading slightly, dbl. (40 petals), exhibition, medium, borne usually singly; heavy fragrance; foliage medium, red-brown to dark green, glossy; fruit round, medium, brown; bushy, vigorous growth.

Mälar-Ros HT, *dr*, 1932, *Hadley × Fragrance*; Kordes. Bud pointed; flowers glowing ruby-red indoors, dark blood-red with crimson outdoors, dbl., high-centered, very large; fragrant; very vigorous, bushy growth.

Malcolm HT, *dp*, 1979, *Hector Deane × Chopin*; Ellick; Excelsior Roses. Flowers carmine, dbl. (35-40 petals), full, large (4-5 in.); slightly fragrant; foliage large, glossy, dark; vigorous, free growth.

Malcolm Sargent HT, *mr*, 1987, (HARwharry; Natascha); *Herbstfeuer × Trumpeter*; Harkness, R., 1988. Flowers shining, bright crimson, dbl. (25 petals), urn shaped, loose, medium, borne usually singly; slight, spicy fragrance; foliage medium, dark green, glossy, pointed, narrow, small, reddish-green

prickles; fruit rounded, medium, green; bushy, medium growth. GM, Belfast, 1990.

Malek-Adel G (OGR), *lp*, (Melik El Adel). Flowers soft pink, dotted white, large.

Malesherbes G (OGR), *m*, 1834, Vibert. Flowers purple, spotted.

Malia Min, *mp*, 1992, *Seedling (Pink 1172) × Rosa Maria*; Mansuino, Dr. Domenico, 1988. Flowers medium pink, very full (41+ petals), small 0-4 cms) blooms borne singly; no fragrance; foliage small, medium green, semi-glossy; some prickles; bushy (100-150 cms) growth; highly recurrent bloom.

Malibu F, *or*, 1959, *Charlotte Armstrong × Independence*; Morey; J&P. Bud pointed, ovoid; flowers coral-orange-red, becoming lighter, dbl. (35 petals), high-centered to flat, large (4-4½ in.); very fragrant; foliage leathery; vigorous, bushy, upright growth.

Malinovka F, *dp*, 1956, (Raspberry Wine); *Staatspräsident Päts × Independence*; Sushkov. Flowers raspberry-red, medium; slightly fragrant.

Malkarsiddha HT, *lp*, 1989, *Century Two sport*; Patil, B.K.; K.S.G. Sons, 1987. Flowers light pink.

Malmesbury HT, *my*, 1980, *Vera Dalton × Parasol*; Sanday. Bud pointed; flowers medium yellow, dbl. (23 petals), blooms borne singly and several together; slight fragrance; foliage medium green; slightly hooked prickles; compact, bushy growth.

Malton HCh (OGR), *mr*, 1830, (Fulgens); Guérin. Flowers bright crimson. A parent of some of the early Hybrid Perpetuals.

Malva F, *m*, 1935, Leenders, M. Flowers mauve, center white, semi-dbl., open, large; foliage large, glossy, light; very vigorous, bushy growth.

Malvina C (OGR), *lp*, 1841, Verdier, V. Flowers pale pink, edged lighter, very dbl., well-formed, large blooms in clusters.

Mama de Meyer HT, *w*, 1931, *Duchess of Wellington × Aspirant Marcel Rouyer*; Lens. Flowers cream, center salmon, dbl., well formed, large; vigorous growth.

Mama Lamesch HT, *op*, 1922, *Frau Oberprasident von Grothe × Mme. Edouard Herriot*; Lambert, P. Flowers orange-rose, center deeper, reverse reddish rose, dbl.; fragrant.

Mama Mia Min, *mp*, 1986, (ZIPmia); *Sheri Anne × Sparrieshoop*; Zipper, H.; Magic Moment Min. Flowers medium pink, dbl. (40+ petals), exhibition, blooms borne singly or in 3's; slightly fragrant; foliage medium, medium green, matt; upright, bushy.

Mama Pechtold HT, *op*, 1938, *Katherine Pechtold × Briarcliff*; Pechtold. Bud long, pointed; flowers rosy salmon, dbl.; long, strong stems; foliage bronze; vigorous growth.

Maman HT, *or*, 1963, *(Rome Glory × La Vaudoise) × Impeccable*; Delbard-Chabert. Flowers orange-vermilion, dbl. (30-40 petals), well formed, large (4-5 in.); slightly fragrant; foliage bright green; bushy growth. GM, Geneva, 1962.

Maman Chérie HT, *pb*, 1980, (DELmanche); *Gay Paris × (Baccará × Impeccable)*; Delbard, G. Flowers pink blend, dbl., blooms in clusters.

Maman Cochet T (OGR), *pb*, 1893, *Marie van Houtte × Mme. Lombard*; Cochet, S. Bud pointed; flowers pale pink, center deeper, base lemon-yellow, dbl., high-centered, large (to 4 in.); fragrant; foliage dark, leathery; vigorous, bushy growth.

Maman Cochet, Climbing Cl T (OGR), *pb*, 1909, Upton, 1909; H&S, 1915.

Maman Dental HT, *mp*, 1921, *Mme. Caroline Testout sport*; Dental. Flowers pure rose-pink.

Maman Geneviève F, *or*, 1960, Hémeray-Aubert. Flowers red tinted orange; bushy growth.

Maman Levavasseur Pol, *dp*, 1907, (Baby Dorothy); *Mme. Norbert Levavasseur sport*; Levavasseur. Flowers bright crimson-pink, dbl.

Maman Pineau HT, *dr*, 1976, (GODilofter); *Maryse Kriloff × Uncle Walter*; Godin. Bud pointed; flowers dark red-purple, dbl. (26-28 petals), deeply cupped, medium (3-3½ in.); slightly fragrant; foliage bronze; vigorous growth.

Maman Turbat Pol, *pb*, 1911, *Mme. Norbert Levavasseur × Katharina Zeimet*; Turbat. Flowers china-rose shaded lilac, reverse almost white, semi-dbl., large, borne in clusters of 30-50; foliage dark, soft; bushy growth.

Mambo F, *op*, 1971, *Tropicana × Zorina*; Tantau. Bud ovoid; flowers salmon-pink, dbl., medium; slightly fragrant; dwarf, bushy growth.

Mambo Gr, *mr*, 1960, *Charlotte Armstrong × Seedling*; Swim; Weeks. Bud ovoid; flowers currant-red to cardinal-red, dbl., high-centered, medium; slightly fragrant; foliage dark, leathery; vigorous, tall, bushy growth.

Ma Mie HT, *yb*, 1955, *Peace × Seedling*; Laperrière; EFR. Flowers yellow, edge tinted pink, dbl. (50 petals), well formed, very large; foliage bright green; very vigorous, upright growth.

Mamie Serpa F, *w*, 1955, *Goldilocks × Snowbird*; Serpa. Bud ovoid, creamy; flowers white, dbl. (50 petals), open, medium (2½ in.); slightly fragrant; foliage dark, soft; vigorous, bushy, compact growth; a greenhouse variety.

Mamille HT, *my*, 1976, *Peer Gynt × Valencia*; Kordes; Vilmorin. Bud long, pointed; flowers medium yellow, dbl. (35 petals), high-centered, large (4½ in.); fragrant; foliage soft; vigorous, upright growth.

Mamita HT, *mr*, 1958, *Dicksons Red × Unamed Seedling*; Robichon. Flowers garnet-red, large; very fragrant; vigorous growth.

Mamy Blue® HT, *m*, 1984, (DELblue); *((Holstein × Bayadère) × (Prélude × St. Exupery)) × Seedling*; Delbard, G., 1991. Flowers mauve, dbl. (35 petals), high-centered, large; foliage medium, dark; bushy growth; greenhouse variety.

Mana F, *yb*, 1989, *Liverpool Echo × Arthur Bell*; Cattermole, R.F.; South Pacific Rose Nursery. Flowers creamy yellow, edges flushed pink, dbl. (35 fimbriated petals), large, borne in sprays of 5-7 and up to 24; good fragrance; foliage medium green, glossy, veined; prickles light brown; upright growth.

Mána Böhmová R, *w*, 1925, (Manja Böhm); *Tausendschön sport*; Böhm. Flowers greenish white.

Mandalay HT, *my*, 1942, (Helvétia); *Soeur Thérèse × Feu Joseph Looymans*; Mallerin; A. Meilland; J&P. Flowers clear yellow, dbl. (40 petals), open, very large (6 in.); long stems; fragrant; foliage leathery; very vigorous, upright growth.

Mandarin F, *mr*, 1951, *Lilette Mallerin sport × Red F Seedling*; Boerner; J&P. Bud ovoid; flowers mandarin-red, semi-dbl. (18 petals), high-centered, medium (3-4 in.) blooms in large clusters; fragrant; foliage leathery, glossy; vigorous (3½-4 ft.), upright growth.

Mandarin HT, *my*, 1946, *Betty Uprichard × Ville de Paris*; Robichon. Flowers golden yellow; very fragrant; foliage glossy; vigorous growth.

Mandarin Delight Min, *ob*, 1989, (FOUmande); *Party Girl × Gingersnap*; Jacobs, Betty A.; Four Seasons Rose Nursery. Bud pointed; flowers soft, light mandarin orange, reverse lighter, aging peach in cooler weather, apricot in warm, dbl. (24 reflexing petals), urn-shaped, exhibition, medium, borne singly and in sprays of up to 10; slight fragrance; foliage medium, medium green, semi-glossy; prickles needle, medium, red to tan; no fruit; bushy, medium growth.

Manda's Triumph R, *w*, 1899, *R. wichuraiana × Pâquerette*; Horvath; W.A. Manda. Flowers pure white, very dbl., borne in clusters of 10-12; very vigorous growth.

Mandrina F, *or*, 1964, (Mandarine); *Moulin Rouge × Frau Anny Beaufays*; deRuiter;

Carlton Rose Nursery. Flowers orange-red, dbl. (30 petals), large (2½-3 in.) blooms in clusters; foliage dark; vigorous, bushy growth; greenhouse variety.

Mandy F, *ly*, 1963, *Pinocchio × Sweet Repose*; Robinson, H. Flowers creamy yellow to soft peach, dbl., large; foliage coppery; very free growth.

Mandy Jo HT, *pb*, 1970, *Pink Favorite sport*; Abrahams. Flowers pale biscuit, flushed light pink, dbl. (22 petals), full, large (4½ in.); slightly fragrant; foliage very glossy, bright green; vigorous growth.

Maneca HT, *lp*, 1929, Pernet-Ducher; Gaujard. Flowers light pink, dbl.; fragrant.

Manetti N (OGR), *lp*, 1835, (*R. × noisettiana manettii* (Crivelli ex Rivers) Rehder; *R. chinensis manettii* hort.; *R. manettii* Crivelli ex Rivers); Rivers, 1835, from S. Manetti, Monza Bot. Gdn., Italy. Flowers pink, 2 in. diam.; vigorous shrub growth with red shoots; widely grown understock.

Manhattan HT, *or*, 1936, (Passion Rose); *Souvenir sport*; Asmus. Bud urn shaped; flowers jasper-red to coral-red, base yellow, dbl., cupped, very large; very fragrant; very vigorous growth.

Manifesto HT, *op*, 1920, McGredy. Flowers flesh-pink, tinged salmon, dbl.; fragrant.

Manille HT, *yb*, 1951, *Pierre × Lumière*; Mallerin; Vilmorin-Andrieux. Flowers golden yellow edged red, dbl. (40-50 petals), globular, very large; very fragrant; foliage leathery, bronze; vigorous, upright growth.

Manit HT, *dr*, 1990, (UMSdad); *Seedling × Olympiad*; Umsawasdi, Dr. Theera, 1991. Flowers dark red, semi-dbl. (6-14 petals), medium, borne mostly singly; no fragrance; foliage medium, medium green, matt; upright, bushy, tall (150-180 cms) growth.

Manitou HT, *rb*, 1957, Swim; Kordes. Flowers coppery red, reverse golden yellow, dbl., well formed, very large; upright, bushy growth.

Manjana F, *op*, 1969, *Orange Sensation × (Pink Parfait × Lavender Pinocchio)*; deRuiter. Flowers salmon-pink-apricot, high-centered; free growth.

MANlissa LCl, *dp*, 1991, *Morgengruss × Whisky Mac*; Mander, George, 1992-93. Flowers deep pink, moderately full (15-25 petals), large blooms borne in small clusters; very fragrant; foliage medium, dark green, glossy; tall, upright, bushy growth.

Mannequin F, *mp*, 1961, (*Peace × Cinnabar*) × *Fashion*; Lens. Flowers pink; slightly fragrant; vigorous, upright growth; a greenhouse variety.

Mannheim® S, *dr*, 1959, *Rudolph Timm × Fanal*; Kordes, R., 1958. Flowers crimson, dbl., large blooms in clusters; upright (3 ft.), bushy growth; recurrent bloom.

Manning's Blush E (OGR), *w*, Cult. before 1799. Flowers white faintly flushed pink, fully dbl., very small; foliage fragrant (apple); height 4-5 ft.

Manon HT, *ab*, 1924, *Christine × Mrs. Farmer*; Bernaix, P. Flowers yellow mixed with apricot, semi-dbl.

Manosque HT, *mr*, 1958, Buyl Frères. Flowers red, well formed; very fragrant; moderately vigorous growth.

Manou Meilland® HT, *m*, 1979, (MEItulimon); *(Baronne Edmond de Rothschild × Baronne Edmond de Rothschild) × (Ma Fille × Love Song)*; Meilland, M.L., 1980. Bud conical; flowers mauve-pink, dbl. (50 petals), fully cupped, medium; slightly fragrant; foliage glossy, dark; vigorous, bushy growth. GM, New Zealand, 1980.

MANprincess HT, *lp*, 1991, (*Tiffany × Pascali*) × *Super Sun*; Mander, George. Flowers light pink, very full (41+ petals), large blooms borne mostly singly; slight fragrance; foliage medium, light green, semi-glossy; tall, upright growth.

MANpurpearl F, *m*, 1992, *Rise 'n' Shine × MANpurple*; Mander, George, 1992-93. Flowers purple/cream bicolor, mauve color intensifies with sun and aging, full (26-40 petals), large (7+ cms) blooms borne in small clusters; slight fragrance; foliage medium, dark green, semi-glossy; very few prickles; medium (80-100 cms), bushy growth.

MANpurple HT, *m*, 1991, *Mount Shasta × Super Sun*; Mander, George. Flowers purple/cream bicolor, full (15-25 petals), large blooms borne mostly singly; slight fragrance; foliage medium, dark green, glossy; medium, bushy growth.

MANsopas Cl F, *op*, 1991, *Shades of Pink × Pascali*; Mander, George. Flowers medium pink shaded coral and cream, full (26-40 petals), medium blooms borne in small clusters; slight fragrance; foliage medium, dark green, glossy; tall, upright, bushy growth.

Mansuino Rose HT, *mr*, 1964, (Generosa); Mansuino, Q.; Carlton Rose Nursery. Flowers crimson to spirea-red, dbl. (35 petals), flat-cupped, small to medium blooms on thin stems; slightly fragrant; foliage small, dark.

Manu Mukerji HT, *my*, 1972, *Fragrant Cloud sport*; Friends Rosery. Flowers medium yellow.

Manuel Pinto d'Azevedo HT, *pb*, 1954, *Seedling × Peace*; Moreira da Silva. Flowers deep rose-pink, reverse lighter, dbl. (48 petals), large (4 in.); fragrant; foliage dark, glossy, leathery; vigorous, upright growth.

Manuela® HT, *mp*, 1968, Tantau, Math. Flowers medium pink, dbl. (30 petals), high-centered, large; fragrant; foliage glossy; vigorous, upright, bushy growth.

Manuelita HT, *or*, 1947, *Cynthia × Vive la France*; Dot, P. Flowers orange-red, large; very vigorous growth.

Manx Queen F, *ob*, 1963, (Isle of Man); *Shepherd's Delight × Circus*; Dickson, P.; A. Dickson. Flowers rich gold flushed bronze red, semi-dbl. (18 petals), medium blooms in large clusters; fragrant; foliage dark; bushy, compact growth.

Many Moons F, *my*, 1985, *Chinatown × Maigold*; Stoddard, Louis. Flowers deep yellow to light yellow, dbl. (35 petals), large; fragrant; foliage medium, medium green, matt; upright, bushy, tall, arching growth.

Many Summers HT, *ob*, 1975, *Arthur Bell × Belle Blonde*; Fryer, G.; Fryer's Nursery. Flowers orange-copper, dbl. (30 petals), full, large (6 in.); very fragrant; vigorous.

Maori Doll Min, *yb*, 1977, *Yellow Doll sport*; Bell Roses; Sequoia Nursery. Flowers buff, yellow center.

Maori Lullaby F, *pb*, 1963, *Traumland × Seedling*; Mason, P.G. Flowers carmine-rose, base light yellow to white, semi-dbl. (10-12 petals), large (3-3½ in.), borne in clusters; foliage bronze, leathery; bushy, low, compact growth.

Maori Moon F, *pb*, 1974, *Bengali × (Pink Parfait × King Boreas)*; Clayworth. Bud pointed; flowers pink, center cream, semi-dbl. (10 petals), cupped to flat, large (3½ in.); slightly fragrant; foliage light, aging darker; upright, compact, bushy growth.

Maorilander HT, *mr*, 1956, *Crimson Glory × Peace*; Mason, P. Bud ovoid, pointed; flowers crimson, lighter reverse, dbl., high-centered, large; fragrant; foliage bronze, leathery; bushy growth.

Ma Perkins F, *pb*, 1952, *Red Radiance × Fashion*; Boerner; J&P. Bud ovoid; flowers sparkling salmon shell-pink, dbl. (25 petals), cupped, large (3½ in.); fragrant; foliage rich green, glossy; vigorous, bushy growth. AARS, 1953.

Marama HT, *w*, 1979, (SIMaramam); *Lady Helen × Seedling*; Simpson, J.W. Bud pointed; flowers white, dbl. (45 petals), exhibition blooms borne singly; very fragrant; foliage large, medium green, semi-glossy; dark brown prickles; bushy, medium growth.

Maranta F, *yb*, 1974, Tantau; Ahrens; Sieberz. Bud globular; flowers yellow, red, semi-dbl.; medium; slightly fragrant; foliage soft; upright, bushy growth.

Marathon F, *op*, 1956, *Fashion × Hybrid Tea Seedling*; Mondial Roses. Flowers salmon-rose, semi-dbl., large (4 in.), borne in clusters; moderate, compact growth.

Marbrée P (OGR), *rb*, 1858, Robert et Moreau. Flowers red marbled white, fully dbl., large.

Marc Guillot F, *dr*, 1955, *Happiness × Demain*; Mallerin; EFR. Bud ovoid; flowers dark scarlet-red, dbl. (25-35 petals), cupped, medium; slightly fragrant; foliage dull green, leathery; vigorous, upright growth.

Marcel Boivin HT, *op*, 1954, *Souv. de Claudius Pernet × Château de Clos Vougeot*; Buatois. Flowers coral-pink, base yellow, dbl. (50-60 petals), very large; fragrant; vigorous growth.

Marcel Bourgouin G (OGR), *m*, (Le Jacobin); Corboeuf, 1899. Flowers velvety rich scarlet-purple mottled violet. Needs rich soil and good cultivation.

Marceline HT, *rb*, 1928, *Frau Karl Druschki × Yves Druhen*; Buatois. Flowers crimson, edge and reverse violet-rose, dbl.

Marcelle Auclair F, *or*, 1964, *Soleil de Lyon × Seedling*; Robichon; Ilgenfritz Nursery. Flowers orange-red, semi-dbl., high-centered, medium, borne in clusters of 5-8; very fragrant; foliage glossy, leathery; vigorous, upright growth.

Marcelle Gret HT, *my*, 1947, *Peace × Prinses Beatrix*; Meilland, F. Bud long, pointed; flowers saffron-yellow, dbl. (28 petals), large (6 in.); fragrant; foliage dark; vigorous growth. GM, Geneva, 1948.

Marcelle Gret, Climbing Cl HT, *my*, 1957, Brenier Frères.

Marcelle Petit F, *op*, 1958, *Pinocchio × Independence*; Arles; Roses-France. Flowers glowing salmon-pink; foliage glossy; vigorous growth.

Märchenland F, *ob*, 1951, (Exception); *Swantje × Hamburg*; Tantau, 1946. Flowers bright rose tinted salmon, semi-dbl. (18 petals), large blooms in clusters of 40; fragrant; foliage dark; vigorous, upright growth.

Marchesa Boccella HP (OGR), *lp*, 1842, (Marquise Boccella; Marquise Boçella); Desprez. Flowers delicate pink, edges almost blush, full, compact, large; petals smaller but more numerous than other Hybrid Perpetuals; flower stems stiff, erect; dwarf, robust habit.

Marchioness of Linlithgow HT, *dr*, 1929, Dobbie. Flowers deep blackish crimson, dbl., open, large; foliage soft, bronze; vigorous growth. GM, NRS, 1930.

Marchioness of Londonderry HP (OGR), *lp*, 1893, Dickson, A. Flowers pale pink, full (50 petals), high-centered, very large; fragrant; very vigorous growth.

Marchioness of Lorne HP (OGR), *pb*, 1889, Paul, W. Flowers rich rosy pink shaded darker, full, cupped, large; very fragrant; vigorous growth.

Marchioness of Ormonde HT, *ly*, 1918, Dickson, H. Flowers clear wheat-straw color, center deep honey-yellow, dbl.

Marcia HT, *op*, 1952, *Étoile de Hollande × Raffel's Yellow*; Raffel; Port Stockton Nursery. Flowers pink to coral, base yellow, well shaped, large; foliage glossy; vigorous, upright growth.

Marcia Coolidge HT, *pb*, 1927, *Gen. MacArthur Seedling*; Coolidge. Flowers very light pink, reverse darker, stamens dark crimson, semi-dbl.; very fragrant.

Marcia Gandy HT, *rb*, 1957, Verschuren; Gandy. Flowers crimson to rose-red, reverse rose-opal; very fragrant; vigorous growth.

Marcia Stanhope HT, *w*, 1922, *Frau Karl Druschki Seedling*; Lilley. Flowers pure white, dbl. (25 petals), globular, large; very fragrant; foliage leathery. GM, NRS, 1924.

Marco R, *w*, 1905, *R. wichuraiana × Souv. de Catherine Guillot*; Guillot, P. Flowers white, center coppery.

Marco Polo HT, *lp*, 1971, *Memoriam × Elizabeth Fankhauser*; Fankhauser. Flowers soft dawn-pink, dbl., high-centered, large; fragrant; foliage glossy; vigorous, upright growth.

Mardi Gras HT, *dr*, 1953, *Crimson Glory × Poinsettia*; Jordan, G.L.; J&P. Bud ovoid; flowers deep velvety red, dbl. (33 petals), high-centered, large (5 in.); fragrant; foliage leathery; vigorous, upright, bushy growth. GM, Baden-Baden, 1953.

Mardi Gras, Climbing Cl HT, *dr*, 1956, Kordes.

Marechal Carmona HT, *op*, Moreira da Silva. Flowers salmon-pink with reddish tones.

Maréchal Davoust M (OGR), *mp*, 1853, Robert. Flowers bright rose, cupped, large.

Maréchal de Villars B (OGR), *dp*, Flowers deep rose shaded violet, cupped.

Maréchal Foch Pol, *dp*, 1918, (Red Orléans Rose); *Orléans Rose* sport; Levavasseur. Flowers cherry-red to pink, semi-dbl., open, borne in compact clusters; fragrant; vigorous, bushy growth.

Maréchal Lyautey HT, *dr*, 1931, *Hadley × Laurent Carle*; Croibier. Flowers deep red, very dbl., high-centered, large; very fragrant; foliage thick, dark, bronze; very vigorous, bushy growth.

Maréchal Niel N (OGR), *my*, 1864, *Said to be a Chromatella Seedling*; Pradel. Bud long, pointed; flowers golden yellow, dbl., large blooms on weak stems; very fragrant; foliage rich green; very vigorous, climbing growth; (14).

Maréchal Pétain HT, *yb*, 1926, Reymond. Flowers soft pink on yellow ground.

Marella HT, *pb*, 1961, (*Happiness × Independence*) × *Better Times*; Meilland, M.L.; URS. Bud globular; flowers pink-red, dbl. (35 petals), large; slightly fragrant; foliage glossy, leathery; vigorous growth.

Maren S, *mr*, 1988, (WILgmar); *Red Fountain × Red Fountain*; Gimpel, W.F., 1989; J. Benjamin Williams & Associates, 1989. Flowers deep scarlet red with velvet overtones, dbl. (26-40 petals), large; slight fragrance; foliage large, dark green, semi-glossy, leathery, disease resistant; upright, spreading, vigorous, free standing growth.

Marfil HT, *w*, 1962, *White Knight × Angelis*; Dot, P. Flowers ivory-white, large, strong stems; tall growth.

Margaret HT, *pb*, 1954, *May Wettern Seedling × Souv. de Denier van der Gon*; Dickson, A. Flowers bright pink, reverse silvery pink, dbl. (70 petals), well-shaped; fragrant; vigorous. GM, NRS, 1954.

Margaret Amos HT, *dp*, 1952, *McGredy's Scarlet Seedling*; McGredy. Flowers strawberry-red, dbl. (25 petals), high-centered, large; slightly fragrant; foliage dark reddish green; very free growth.

Margaret Anderson LCl, *w*, 1931, (Broomfield Novelty); Thomas; H&S. Flower centers deep cream, outer petals cream-flesh, dbl., very large; fragrant; foliage thick, leathery; very vigorous, climbing growth; recurrent bloom.

Margaret Anne Baxter HT, *w*, 1927, *Harry Kirk Seedling*; Smith, T. Bud pointed; flowers white, sometimes tinted flesh, very dbl. (88 petals), large; fragrant; foliage thick, leathery, glossy, bronze; vigorous, bushy growth. GM, NRS, 1927.

Margaret Belle Houston HT, *dr*, 1929, Vestal. Flowers velvety crimson, dbl., very large; fragrant; foliage light, leathery.

Margaret Chase Smith HT, *dr*, 1966, *Red Duchess × Queen Elizabeth*; Brownell, H.C.

Bud long, pointed; flowers dark red, dbl., large; fragrant; vigorous, upright growth.

Margaret Daintry F, *dr*, 1988, (HORmartim); *Red Planet × (Blessings × (Parkdirektor Riggers × Honey Favorite))*; Horner, Colin P.; Rosemary Roses, 1988. Flowers crimson-scarlet, dbl. (15-25 petals), large, borne singly and in clusters; very fragrant; foliage medium, dark green, glossy; bushy growth.

Margaret Dickson HP (OGR), *w*, 1891, *Lady Mary Fitzwilliam × Merveille de Lyon*; Dickson, A. Flowers white, center pale flesh, dbl. (65 petals), well-formed, cupped, large; slightly fragrant; foliage dark; vigorous growth; occasional recurrent bloom.

Margaret Dickson Hamill HT, *yb*, 1915, Dickson, A. Flowers straw-yellow, flushed salmon, dbl., petals shell-shaped, large; slightly fragrant; foliage dark, leathery; bushy growth. GM, NRS, 1914; Bagatelle, 1917.

Margaret Egerton HT, *dp*, 1931, Chaplin Bros. Flowers rosy cerise passing to carmine, base yellow, well formed; fragrant; vigorous growth.

Margaret Elbogen Pol, *w*, 1936, Brada; Böhm. Flowers pinkish white; very fragrant; very vigorous growth.

Margaret Herbert HT, *lp*, 1956, Harrison; Much like Michèle Meilland, but flower opens wide.

Margaret Horton HT, *ab*, 1921, Hicks. Bud pointed; flowers apricot-yellow, dbl., open, high-centered, large; foliage leathery, glossy, light; vigorous growth.

Margaret Isabel HT, *w*, 1983, *Strawberry Ice × Redgold*; Summerell, B.L. Flowers oyster white, cream center, delicately flushed pink petal edges, dbl. (45 petals), exhibition, large; strong fragrance; red-brown prickles; upright growth.

Margaret Jean Min, *dp*, 1978, *Fairy Moss × Fairy Moss*; Dobbs, Annette; Small World Min. Roses. Bud ovoid; flowers deep pink, dbl. (40 petals), blooms borne 4-8 per cluster; slight fragrance; foliage small, dark; very few prickles; bushy, vigorous growth.

Margaret Law F, *ob*, 1981, *Princess Michiko × Gold Gleam*; McTeer, Gilbert; Bridgemere Nursery. Flowers luminous orange, pink on outer petals, dbl. (25 petals), HT-form, borne 3-23 per cluster; very fragrant; foliage dark, glossy; hooked, red prickles; vigorous.

Margaret McDowell HT, *mr*, 1992, (SEAdow); *(Ruby Wedding × (Seedling × Oonagh)) × (Seedling × Oonagh)*; McCann, Sean, 1993. Flowers medium red, full (26-40 petals), medium (4-7 cms.) blooms; slight fragrance; foliage medium, medium green, semi-glossy;

some prickles; medium (36 in), upright growth.

Margaret McGredy HT, *or*, 1927, McGredy. Flowers orange-scarlet, dbl. (35 petals), high-centered, large; fragrant; foliage light, leathery, glossy; vigorous growth. GM, NRS, 1925.

Margaret McGredy, Climbing Cl HT, *or*, 1936, Dixie Rose Nursery.

Margaret Mercer HT, *yb*, 1977, *Pink Favorite × Peace*; Mercer. Flowers pale yellow, edged light pink, very dbl. (53-65 petals), full, large (4½ in.); fragrant; foliage glossy, dark; vigorous growth.

Margaret Merril® F, *w*, 1977, (HARkuly); *(Rudolph Timm × Dedication) × Pascali*; Harkness, 1978. Flowers blush white, dbl. (28 petals), high-centered, full, large (4 in.); very fragrant. GM, Geneva, Monza; Rome, 1978; Edland Fragrance Medal, 1978; RNRS James Mason Medal, 1990

Margaret Molyneux HT, *my*, 1909, Dickson, A. Flowers canary-yellow; fragrant.

Margaret Moore Jacobs HT, *mp*, 1968, *Tiffany × Pink Masterpiece*; Fuller; Wyant. Bud ovoid; flowers pink, dbl., cupped, large; very fragrant; foliage glossy; vigorous, bushy growth.

Margaret M. Wylie HT, *pb*, 1921, (Mrs. A.J. Wylie); Dickson, H. Flowers flesh, edges heavily flushed deep rosy pink, dbl.; very fragrant. GM, NRS, 1920.

Margaret Roberts F, *dp*, 1976, *Elizabeth of Glamis × Wendy Cussons*; Wood. Flowers cerise, dbl. (20-25 petals), full, large (3½ in.); very fragrant; foliage small, dark; moderate, free growth.

Margaret Ruth HT, *w*, 1969, *Anne Letts × Christian Dior*; Taylor, L.R. Flowers creamy white, center pale pink, dbl., high-centered, large; slightly fragrant; foliage glossy, leathery; vigorous, upright, bushy growth; intermittent bloom.

Margaret Spaull HT, *ob*, 1928, *Ophelia × Seedling*; Cant, B.R. Flowers variable orange and lilac, dbl.; fragrant.

Margaret Telfer Min, *w*, 1992, (SEAtel); *Kiss the Bride × Margaret Merril*; McCann, Sean. Flowers white, moderately full (15-25 petals), medium (4-7 cms) blooms borne in small clusters; slight fragrance; foliage small, medium green, semi-glossy; some prickles; low (14"), upright growth.

Margaret Thatcher F, *rb*, 1983, (TAKsun); *Bridal Pink sport*; Takatori, Yoshiho; Sunao; Japan Rose Nursery. Flowers striped red and white.

Margaret Turnbull Cl HT, *yb*, 1931, Clark, A.; NRS New South Wales. Flowers soft pink on amber ground, dbl., cupped, large; slightly fragrant; foliage wrinkled, light; vigorous, pillar growth.

Margaret van Rossem HT, *op*, 1946, Van Rossem. Flowers coppery salmon, center old-gold; moderate growth.

Margarete Gnau HT, *ob*, 1930, *Mrs. Charles Lamplough × Souv. de H.A. Verschuren*; Krause. Flowers creamy white on orange ground, dbl., high-centered, very large; slightly fragrant; foliage leathery; very vigorous growth.

Margarete Herbst Pol, *dr*, 1934, Herbst. Flowers dark blood-red, dbl.; foliage ruby-red when young; vigorous, bushy growth; late bloom; recurrent.

Margaretha Mühle HT, *pb*, 1925, *Mme. Caroline Testout × Mrs. W.J. Grant*; Mühle; F.J. Grootendorst. Flowers clear satiny pink with silvery reflex, dbl.; fragrant.

Margarethe van de Mandere F, *dp*, 1952, Leenders, M. Flowers raspberry-red, single, large; very vigorous growth.

Margarita Riera HT, *op*, 1924, *Mme. Ravary × Mme. Edouard Herriot*; Dot, P. Flowers brilliant rose-salmon, base yellow, dbl.; slightly fragrant.

Margherita Croze HT, *m*, 1914, *Étoile de France × Earl of Warwick*; Ketten Bros. Flowers carmine-purple changing to purple-rose, base shaded deep rose-pink, dbl.; fragrant.

Margie Burns HT, *mp*, 1968, Carrigg. Flowers rose-pink, reverse tyrian rose, dbl., high-centered, large; fragrant; foliage leathery; very vigorous, upright, bushy growth.

Margo Koster Pol, *ob*, 1931, (Sunbeam); *Dick Koster sport*; Koster, D.A. Flowers salmon.

Margo Koster, Climbing Cl Pol, *ob*, 1962, (Sunbeam, Climbing); Golie; Crombie Nursery.

Margo Koster Superior Pol, *ob*, 1956, *Dick Koster sport*; Koster, D.A. Flowers deep salmon-pink.

Margo's Baby Pol, *yb*, 1987, *Margo Koster sport*; Partain, Joe L., 1988. Flowers creamy ivory, salmon edges, aging dark edge, dbl. (30 petals), cupped, small, borne in sprays of 10-20; no fragrance; foliage small, medium green, glossy; prickles few, medium, light green; upright, bushy, low, vigorous growth; winter hardy.

Margo's Sister Pol, *lp*, 1954, *Margo Koster sport*; Ratcliffe. Flowers shell pink.

Margot Amos HT, *op*, Bud high, pointed; flowers coral-pink flushed strawberry, large; foliage glossy, bronze.

Margot Anstiss HT, *lp*, 1947, Norman; Harkness. Flowers glossy satin-pink, dbl. (40-45 petals), large (6 in.); fragrant; vigorous, branching growth.

Margot Asquith HT, *mr*, 1934, *Betty Uprichard × K. of K.*; Prince. Flowers shining cerise-red, well formed; fragrant; very vigorous growth.

Margot Fonteyn HT, *op*, 1964, *Independence × Ma Perkins*; McGredy, S., IV; Fisons Horticulture. Flowers salmon-orange, dbl. (40 petals), large (4 in.); very fragrant; very free growth.

Margraten F, *mr*, 1949, *Donald Prior × World's Fair*; Leenders, M. Flowers currant-red, semi-dbl. (16 petals), flat, large (3-4 in.), borne in trusses; slightly fragrant; foliage light green; vigorous, bushy growth.

Margrethe Möller HT, *dp*, 1914, *Lady Mary Fitzwilliam × Seedling*; Poulsen, D. Flowers deep cerise-rose, dbl., well formed; fragrant.

Marguerite Amidieu de Clos HT, *my*, 1926, *Souv. de Claudius Pernet × Golden Emblem*; Ketten Bros. Flowers buttercup-yellow, dbl.; fragrant.

Marguerite Carels Cl HP (OGR), *mp*, 1922, *Frau Karl Druschki × Gen. MacArthur*; Nabonnand, P. Flowers neyron pink, center darker, dbl., large; vigorous, climbing growth; recurrent bloom.

Marguerite Chambard HT, *or*, 1928, Chambard, C. Bud pointed; flowers geranium-red to vermilion, high-centered, very large; slightly fragrant; foliage dark; very vigorous, bushy growth.

Marguerite Guillard HP (OGR), *w*, 1915, *Frau Karl Druschki sport*; Chambard, C. Flowers white, stamens yellow, semi-dbl. (20 petals), flat.

Marguerite Heitzmann HT, *or*, 1930, *Frau Karl Druschki × Mme. Edouard Herriot*; Buatois. Flowers salmon-pink, stamens golden yellow, dbl., cupped, very large; fragrant; foliage leathery; very vigorous growth.

Marguerite Hilling HMoy (OGR), *mp*, 1959, (Pink Nevada); *Nevada sport*; Hilling. Flowers medium pink.

Marguerite Moulin HT, *pb*, 1938, (*Mme. Edouard Herriot × Mrs. Aaron Ward) × Mme. Caroline Testout*; Moulin; Hamonière. Flowers lilac-pink, center salmon, very dbl., cupped, large; fragrant; vigorous, bushy growth.

Margy Pol, *mr*, 1936, Sauvageot; C-P. Flowers brilliant red, semi-dbl., open; fragrant (spicy); foliage small, soft; bushy growth.

Mari Dot HT, *ab*, 1927, *O. Junyent × Jean C.N. Forestier*; Dot, P.; C-P. Flowers bright salmon to salmon-pink, base yellow, borne in clusters of 3-5 on long, strong stems; fragrant; foliage glossy; very vigorous growth.

Maria HT, *rb*, 1974, *Rina Herholdt × Seedling*; Staikov, Prof. Dr. V.; Kalaydjiev and Chorbadjiiski. Flowers red, yellow reverse, dbl. (60 petals), large blooms borne singly; tea fragrance; foliage dark, glossy; vigorous growth.

Maria F, *or*, 1965, *Seedling × Border Beauty*; Gregory. Flowers orange-scarlet, single (10 petals), large (3 in.), borne in large clusters; slightly fragrant; foliage very large, dark, leathery; vigorous, upright growth.

Maria Antonia Camprubi HT, *mp*, 1956, *Peace × Rosa Munné*; Munné, M. Flowers soft carmine, well formed, large; very fragrant; vigorous growth.

Maria Burnett Min, *yb*, 1980, *Little Darling × Patricia Scranton*; Miniature Plant Kingdom. Bud globular; flowers light yellow, edged pink, dbl. (70 petals), globular, small; slightly fragrant; foliage light green; low growth.

Maria Cinta HT, *op*, 1967, *Duet × (Soraya × Chrysler Imperial)*; Dot, S.; Minier. Bud long, pointed; flowers coral, dbl. (28 petals), large; fragrant; foliage glossy, bronze; low, compact growth.

Maria de Mello HT, *dr*, 1935, *Mme. Gabriel Hanra × Mrs. John Bell*; Ketten Bros. Bud pointed; flowers bright velvety carmine-purple, dbl. (40-45 petals), cupped, large; foliage bronze quaker green; vigorous, branching growth.

Maria Delforge Pol, *mp*, 1959, *Orange Triumph × Ma Perkins*; Delforge. Bud oval; flowers pink, dbl., rosette form, medium, borne in clusters; slightly fragrant; foliage glossy; vigorous, bushy, low growth.

Maria Graebner S, *mp*, (R. × *mariae-graebneriae* Ascherson & Graebner); *R. palustris × R. virginiana*; Orig. ca. 1880. Flowers pink, a few borne all summer; foliage orange and red in fall; fruit subglobose, red; 5 ft. growth.

Maria Guarro HT, *dp*, 1935, Château de Clos Vougeot × Li Bures; Dot, P. Bud pointed; flowers pink in spring, blood-red in summer, very dbl., high-centered, large; slightly fragrant; foliage glossy, dark; very vigorous growth.

Maria Isabel HT, mr, Camprubi. Flowers deep strawberry-red, base yellow, high-centered; foliage dark; vigorous growth.

Maria Leonida HBc (OGR), *w*, 1829, (R. × *leonida* Moldenke); *Hybrid of ordinary Tea and R. bracteata*; Lemoyne. Flowers flesh, anthers purplish, very dbl.; strong tea fragrance.

Maria Lisa R, *pb*, 1936, Liebau. Flowers clear rose, center white, stamens yellow, single,

open, small, borne in clusters; foliage dark, leathery; very vigorous, climbing or trailing growth; profuse, non-recurrent bloom.

Maria Mathilda® Min, w, 1980, (LENmar); Miniature Seedling × *(New Penny × Jour de Fete)*; Lens, Louis. Flowers white, shaded pink, dbl. (24 petals), small blooms in clusters of 3-24; very fragrant; foliage very dark, glossy; hooked, brownish-red prickles; upright, bushy growth. Rose d'or a La Haye, 1981; Golden Rose of The Hague, 1981.

Maria Peral HT, *yb*, 1941, Dot, P. Flowers yellow suffused red, dbl., large; very vigorous.

Maria Reid HT, *dp*, 1924, *Mme. Caroline Testout × George C. Waud*; Ferguson, W. Flowers dark rose-pink tinted peach, base yellow, dbl.

Maria Serrat HT, *op*, 1946, *Mrs. Pierre S. du-Pont × Baronesa de Ovilar*; Munné, M. Flowers salmon-pink, base yellow, reverse deep yellow.

Maria Stern HT, *ob*, 1969, *Tip Toes × Queen Elizabeth*; Brownell, H.C.; Stern's Nursery. Bud pointed; flowers orange, dbl. (43 petals), globular, large; fragrant; vigorous, upright.

Maria Teresa® S, *lp*, 1984, (LENmacra); *Seedling × R. macrantha*; Lens, Louis. Flowers light pink, dbl. (28 petals), cupped, medium blooms in clusters of 32; very fragrant; foliage light green; hooked, brownish-green prickles; bushy growth; recurrent.

Maria Teresa Bordas HT, *mp*, 1953, *Sensation × Peace*; Bordas. Bud ovoid; flowers rose-pink, very dbl., high-centered, very large; fragrant; foliage dark, glossy; very vigorous, upright, bushy growth.

Mariale HT, *ab*, 1956, *Souv. de Jacques Verschuren* sport; de Boer. Flowers orange-yellow, semi-dbl.; slightly fragrant; vigorous growth.

Marian Anderson HT, *dp*, 1964, *Queen Elizabeth × Merry Widow*; Lammerts; Germain's. Flowers deep pink, semi-dbl., high-centered, large; spicy fragrance; foliage glossy; vigorous, tall, compact.

Marian Colthorpe HT, *op*, 1946, Wheatcroft Bros. Flowers coral shaded lemon and pink.

Mariandel® F, *mr*, 1986, (KORpeahn; Carl Philip Kristian IV; The Times Rose); *Tornado × Redgold*; Kordes, W.; John Mattock Ltd., 1985. Flowers scarlet crimson-red, semi-dbl. (6-14 petals), medium; slight fragrance; foliage medium, dark green, semi-glossy, disease resistant; bushy growth. RNRS PIT, 1982; Golden Rose of the Hague, 1990

Marianna Rolfs Cl HT, *lp*, 1926, Walter, L. Flowers silvery pink, slightly full.

Marianne HT, *yb*, 1933, *Sybil × Sunstar*; Krause. Flowers mixture of copper-yellow, pink and red, high-centered, large; fragrant; vigorous, bushy growth.

Marianne Kluis Superior Pol, *mr*, 1930, *Greta Kluis Superior sport*; Kluis & Koning. Flowers deep violet-red.

Marianne Powell HT, *dr*, 1986, *Kerryman × Red Dandy*; Powell, G. Flowers dark red, very full (50 petals), large; fragrant; foliage large, dark green, glossy; upright growth.

Mariano Vergara T (OGR), *mr*, 1896, Aldrufeu. Flowers magenta-red with vermilion reflections, dbl., large; vigorous growth.

Maribell HT, *rb*, 1987, *(Sea Pearl × Zorina) × Lovita*; Gressard, J.; Delbard's Nursery, 1988. Flowers carmine red, reverse silver white, dbl. (40-45 petals), large; light fragrance; upright, vigorous growth.

Marica HT, *mp*, 1964, Mondial Roses. Flowers bright pink, dbl., large; strong stems; slightly fragrant; vigorous, symmetrical growth.

Marica Cl Min, *pb*, 1989, *Ginza Komachi sport*; Kono, Yoshito. Flowers pink, reverse white.

Marie Adélaïde HT, *yb*, 1912, (Grande Duchesse de Luxembourg; Luxembourg); *Mme. J.W. Budde × Lyon Rose*; Soupert & Notting. Bud pointed; flowers coppery yellow, center deeper, dbl., high-centered, large; slightly fragrant; foliage bronze, soft; vigorous, spreading growth.

Marie Antoinette G (OGR), *m*, Vibert, prior to 1848. Flowers lilac-rose, full, large.

Marie Antoinette HT, *mp*, 1968, *Queen Elizabeth × Chrysler Imperial*; Armstrong, D.L.; Armstrong Nursery. Bud long, pointed; flowers pink, reverse darker, dbl., cupped, large; slightly fragrant; foliage dark, glossy; very vigorous, upright growth.

Marie Baumann HP (OGR), *mr*, 1863, *Alfred Colomb Seedling*; Baumann. Flowers carmine-red, full (55 petals), globular, large; fragrant; foliage dark; vigorous growth.

Marie Brissonet Pol, *lp*, 1913, Turbat. Flowers flesh-rose borne in pyramidal clusters of 75-100.

Marie Bugnet S, *w*, 1963, *(Thérèse Bugnet × Seedling) × F.J. Grootendorst*; Bugnet; Skinner. Bud long, pointed; flowers snow white, dbl., large (3 in.); very fragrant; foliage light green, rugose; vigorous (3 ft.), bushy, compact growth; recurrent bloom.

Marie-Chantal F, *mp*, 1959, *Peace × Fernand Arles*; Gaujard. Flowers bright pink, semi-dbl., open, large; slightly fragrant; foliage glossy; vigorous, bushy growth.

Marie-Claire HT, *or*, 1938, *(Charles P. Kilham × Duquesa de Peñaranda) × (Charles P. Kilham × Margaret McGredy*; Meilland, F. Bud deep orange-red; flowers golden coral-red, passing

to orange-yellow, full, large, strong stems; fragrant; foliage bronze, glossy; very vigorous, compact growth.

Marie-Claire, Climbing Cl HT, *or*, 1944, (Grimpant Marie-Claire); Meilland, F..

Marie de Blois M (OGR), *mp*, 1852, Robert. Flowers pink tinted lighter, large.

Marie de Bourgogne M (OGR), *mp*, 1853, Robert. Flowers pink, dbl., large.

Marie de Saint Jean P (OGR), *w*, 1869, (Marie de St. Jean); Damaizin. Flowers white, full, large.

Marie Dietrich LCl, *yb*, 1928, *Léontine Gervais × Eugénie Lamesch*; Walter, L. Flowers yellowish red, passing to white.

Marie d'Orléans T (OGR), *mp*, 1883, Nabonnand, G. Flowers bright pink shaded darker, full, flat, large; vigorous growth.

Marie Dougherty F, *dr*, 1976, *Sarabande × Sarabande*; Linscott. Bud long, slender; flowers dark red, single (5 petals), large (3½ in.); slightly fragrant (tea); foliage glossy; moderate, bushy growth.

Marie Dutour F, *op*, 1962, *Aloha × (Gloire du Midi × Edith de Martinelli)*; Arles; Roses France. Flowers reddish salmon, well formed, large.

Marie Eads Pol, *mr*, 1991, *Baby Faurax × Verdun*; Eads, C.E. Bud rounded; flowers medium red with blue overtones, reverse light red, dbl. (25 petals), small blooms borne in sprays of 10-25; no fragrance; foliage medium, medium green, semi-glossy with fringed stipples; bushy, low growth; repeats.

Marie Elizabeth F, *yb*, 1965, *Cläre Grammerstorf × Cavalcade*; McGredy, S., IV; McGredy. Flowers yellow shaded rose-pink, dbl. (28 petals), flat, large (3 in.); very fragrant; foliage dark, heavily veined; vigorous growth.

Marie Faist HT, *op*, 1925, *Mme. Edmond Rostand × Mrs. T. Hillas*; Berger, V.; Faist. Flowers shell-pink tinted salmon, center darker, with orange, dbl.; very fragrant.

Marie-France HT, *my*, 1957, *Feu Pernet-Ducher × Léonce Colombier*; Dorieux; Pin. Bud apricot shaded orange; flowers pure yellow, semi-dbl., large; very vigorous growth.

Marie Gouchault R, *mr*, 1927, Turbat. Flowers clear red passing to brilliant salmon-rose, dbl., small, borne in large clusters of 30-40; very vigorous growth; blooms much earlier than Dorothy Perkins; sometimes recurrent.

Marie Greene HT, *mr*, 1941, Clark, A. Flowers rich red; fragrant.

Marie Guillot T (OGR), *w*, 1874, Guillot Fils. Flowers white, tinged yellow, dbl., large, strong stems; very fragrant; vigorous growth.

Marie Guillot, Climbing Cl T (OGR), *w*, 1898, Dingee; Conard.

Marie Henriette Gräfin Chotek R, *dr*, 1911, Lambert, P. Flowers dark crimson, full, large, borne in clusters; very vigorous, climbing growth.

Marie-Jeanne Pol, *w*, 1913, Turbat. Flowers pale blush-cream borne in clusters of 40-60; no prickles; height 2-3 ft.

Marie Lambert T (OGR), *w*, 1886, (Snowflake; White Hermosa); *Mme. Bravy* sport; Lambert, E. Flowers pure white.

Marie Lavier HT, *yb*, 1935, *Souv. de Claudius Pernet* × *Mme. Edouard Herriot*; Buatois. Bud brownish yellow; flowers reddish nankeen yellow to salmon-yellow, rather full, large; fragrant; vigorous, bushy growth.

Marielle F, *mp*, 1963, *Independence* × *Seedling*; deRuiter. Flowers deep rosy pink, dbl. (25 petals), large (4 in.) blooms in large clusters; fragrant; foliage dark; vigorous.

Marie Louise D (OGR), *mp*, Before 1813. Flowers mauve-pink, very dbl., large; very fragrant; bushy, shrubby (about 4 ft.) growth. Grown in the gardens of Malmaison in 1813.

Marie-Louise Poncet HT, *op*, 1929, Gaujard. Flowers coppery rose to pale coppery pink, reverse carmine-salmon.

Marie-Louise Sondaz HT, *w*, 1967, *Rose Gaujard* × *Peace*; Gaujard. Flowers cream shaded red, dbl., very large; fragrant; foliage dark; very vigorous, upright growth.

Marie Lünnemann HT, *my*, 1920, *Pharisäer* × *Laurent Carle*; Timmermans. Flowers clear pink, dbl.; fragrant.

Marie Maass HT, *w*, 1928, *Kaiserin Auguste Viktoria* × *Maréchal Niel*; Maass. Flowers pure white to ivory-white, dbl., very large; very fragrant; vigorous, bushy growth.

Marie Menudel HP (OGR), *op*, 1927, Barbier. Flowers rose-pink, tinted salmon, dbl., large; fragrant.

Marie Pavié Pol, *w*, 1888, Allégatière. Flowers white, center flesh, dbl., medium (2 in.) blooms in clusters; foliage large, rich green; no prickles; vigorous, bushy growth.

Marie-Rose Pol, *mp*, 1930, *Marie-Jeanne* sport; Truffaut, T.A.; Turbat. Flowers ruddy pink, dbl., carnation shaped, large, borne in clusters of 30-40; foliage glossy; very vigorous growth.

Marie-Rose Besson HT, *lp*, 1939, *Souv. de Claudius Pernet* × *Seedling*; Mallerin; A. Meilland. Bud long, pointed, yellow, tinted coral; flowers light pink, tinted coral-orange, dbl., large; long stems; slightly fragrant; foliage glossy; vigorous growth.

Marie-Rose Toussaint HT, *lp*, 1946, Gaujard. Flowers satiny pink, very large; strong stems; fragrant; foliage dark, leathery; vigorous, bushy growth.

Marie Shields™ Min, *mp*, 1988, (MORmari); *Avandel* × *(Rumba* × *Floribunda Seedling)*; Moore, Ralph S.; Sequoia Nursery. Flowers medium pink, reverse pink veined white, very dbl. (over 50 petals), high-centered, small, borne usually in sprays or clusters; slight fragrance; foliage small, medium green, semiglossy; prickles slightly hooked, small, brown; bushy, medium growth.

Marietta® F, *yb*, 1985, (TANatiram); Tantau, M. Flowers yellow blend, dbl. (20 petals), medium; no fragrance; foliage medium green, glossy; upright.

Marietta Silva Tarouca R, *mp*, 1925, *Colibri* × *Crimson Rambler*; Originated in the Dendrological Gardens of Graf Silva Tarouca at Pruhonice. Flowers bright rose, large, borne in clusters; foliage rich green; very vigorous, climbing growth.

Marie Tudor G (OGR), *dp*, Variously described as cherry-red, cerise, and salmon-pink blotched rose.

Marie van Houtte T (OGR), *pb*, 1871, (Mlle. Marie van Houtte); *Mme. de Tartas* × *Mme. Falcot*; Ducher. Flowers deep cream, tinged pink, base buff-yellow, very dbl., high-centered, large; fragrant; foliage rich green, leathery; vigorous, bushy, sprawling; (14).

Marie van Houtte, Climbing Cl T (OGR), *pb*, 1936, Thomasville Nursery.

Marie Verbrugh F, *op*, 1954, *Ambassadeur Nemry* × *Souv. de Claudius Pernet*; Leenders, M. Flowers yellow-salmon, reverse coral, dbl., well formed, large; very fragrant; bushy growth.

Marie Young HT, *or*, Flowers brilliant orange-red, well formed.

Marigold HT, *op*, 1955, *Peace* × *Mme. Joseph Perraud*; Lens. Bud long, pointed; flowers salmon-yellow lightly washed pink, dbl. (52 petals), high-centered, large (6 in.); very fragrant; foliage leathery, glossy, bright green; vigorous, upright growth.

Marijke Koopman HT, *mp*, 1979, Fryer, G.; Fryer's Nursery. Bud long, pointed; flowers medium pink, dbl. (25 petals), borne 3-5 per cluster; fragrant; foliage dark, leathery; red prickles; vigorous, medium-tall, upright growth. GM, The Hague, 1978.

Mariko HT, *ly*, 1992, (DEVdorado); *Seedling* × *Seedling*; Marciel, Stanley G.; Jeanne A.; DeVor Nurseries, Inc. Flowers light yellow, full (26-40 petals), large (7+ cms) blooms borne mostly single; fragrant; foliage large, dark green, semi-glossy; some prickles; tall (210 cms), upright growth.

Marilyn Min, *lp*, 1955, *Perla de Montserrat × Bambino*; Dot, M. Flowers light pink, base purplish, dbl. (60 petals), small blooms in clusters; very compact growth.

Marilyn HT, *ab*, 1954, *May Wettern × Phyllis Gold*; Fletcher; Tucker. Bud long, pointed; flowers apricot-pink veined red; very fragrant; foliage dull, green; vigorous growth.

Marilyn Gowie F, Color not reported, 1968, Gowie; Flowers borne in trusses; foliage bronze; bushy growth.

Marimba® F, *mp*, 1965, *Garnette sport*; Dekkers; Verbeek. Flowers medium pink.

Marime Min, *mr*, 1992, (MORmarme); *Anytime × Happy Hour*; Moore, Ralph S.; Sequoia Nursery. Flowers excellent medium red, semi-dbl. (6-14 petals), good form, medium (4-7 cms) blooms borne mostly singly; no fragrance; foliage medium, medium green, semi-glossy; few prickles; medium (35-45 cms), upright, bushy growth.

Marina® F, *ob*, 1974, (RinaKOR); *Colour Wonder × Seedling*; Kordes, 1975. Bud long, pointed; flowers orange, base yellow, dbl.; fragrant; foliage glossy, dark, leathery; vigorous, upright growth. AARS, 1981.

Marina Fontcuberta HT, *dp*, 1924, *Entente Cordiale × Laurent Carle*; Dot, P. Flowers brilliant carmine, center rose-carmine, dbl.; very fragrant.

Marion F, *op*, 1956, (Salmon Sensation); *Duchess of Rutland × Fashion*; deRuiter. Flowers pink tinted salmon, semi-dbl., medium; bushy growth.

Marion F, *pb*, 1956, (Salmon Sensation); *Duchess of Rutland × Fashion*; deRuiter. Flowers pink tinted salmon, semi-dbl., medium; bushy growth.

Marion Cran HT, *or*, 1927, McGredy. Bud buttercup-yellow, flushed cerise; flowers scarlet veined orange and yellow, dbl., high-centered; foliage bronze, leathery, glossy; very vigorous, bushy growth.

Marion Dingee HT, *dr*, 1889, *((Comtesse de Caserta × Général Jacqueminot) × Maréchal Niel) × (Pierre Notting × Safrano)*; Cook, J. Flowers crimson.

Marion Harkness® HT, *yb*, 1979, (HARkantabil); *((Manx Queen × Prima Ballerina) × (Chanelle × Piccadilly)) × Piccadilly*; Harkness. Flowers canary-yellow, flushed orange-red, dbl. (24 petals), large (3½ in.); slightly fragrant; bushy growth.

Marion Horton HT, *my*, 1929, *Gorgeous × Sunstar*; Bees. Flowers primrose-yellow.

Marion Lawrie HT, *mp*, 1976, *Kordes' Perfecta sport*; Lawrie. Flowers pink, base gold, very dbl. (75 petals), very full, large (4 in.); slightly fragrant; foliage dark, leathery.

Marion R. Hall HT, *dp*, *Crimson Glory × Sterling*; Balcombe Nursery. Flowers bright cerise-red, semi-dbl. (20 petals), well formed, large (5 in.); vigorous growth.

Marionette F, *w*, 1944, *Pinocchio sport*; DeVor, P.; J&P. Bud cream-yellow; flowers white, dbl. (25-30 petals), small (1½ in.), borne in clusters; fragrant; vigorous, bushy growth.

Mariposa Pol, *or*, 1927, *Orange King sport*; Allen. Flowers deeper orange-red.

Marista HT, *rb*, 1975, *Sarah Arnot × Rina Herboldt*; Staikov, Prof. Dr. V.; Kalaydjiev and Chorbadjiiski. Flowers medium red, whitish reverse, dbl. (75 petals), large blooms borne singly; tea fragrance; foliage dark, glossy; upright growth.

Marita F, *ob*, 1961, *Masquerade × Serenade*; Mattock. Flowers copper-orange, heavily veined yellow, dbl. (30-40 petals), medium, borne in trusses; foliage coppery; growth very free, straggly.

Maritime Bristol HT, *ob*, 1983, (SANtang); *City of Gloucester × Seedling*; Sanday, John; Sanday Roses Ltd. Flowers tangerine, dbl. (35 petals), large; fragrant; foliage medium, dark, semi-glossy; upright, bushy growth.

Maritime Heir S, *dp*, 1986, *Thérèse Bugnet × R. nitida*; James, John. Flowers lavender pink, dbl. (40 tight, frilled petals), carnation-like, large; heavy fragrance; foliage small, light green, disease resistant; fine prickles; upright, bushy, very hardy growth; occasional repeat.

Marjolin Ch (OGR), *dr*, Flowers deep crimson-purple, cupped.

Marjoline HT, *rb*, 1949, *Boudoir × Léonce Colombier*; Meilland, F. Flowers cardinal-red, reverse indian yellow, dbl. (40 petals), cupped, very large (6 in.); slightly fragrant; vigorous, upright growth.

Marjorie Anderson F, *mp*, 1973, *Fragrant Cloud × Sea Pearl*; Dickson, P.; Dicksons of Hawlmark. Flowers medium pink, dbl. (26 petals), large (5½ in.); fragrant; foliage very large, matt.

Marjorie Atherton HT, *my*, 1977, *Mt. Shasta × Peace*; Bell, R.J.; Brundrett. Bud ovoid; flowers medium yellow, dbl.; foliage light, leathery; vigorous, upright, bushy.

Marjorie Bulkeley HT, *yb*, 1921, Dickson, H. Flowers buff, flushed rose-pink, passing to silvery pink, dbl.; fragrant. GM, NRS, 1920.

Marjorie Conn F, *lp*, 1981, *Bon Bon × Seedling*; Berry, Howard. Bud ovoid; flowers light pink, semi-dbl. (14 petals), blooms in clusters of 5-7; slight fragrance; foliage dark; brown prickles, hooked down; bushy growth.

Marjorie Ellick F, *w*, 1978, *(Spion-Kop × Ena Harkness) × (Sam Ferris × Karl Herbst)*; Ellick; Excelsior Roses. Flowers rowanberry, very dbl. (95 petals), very full, large (4-6 in.); foliage glossy, light; very vigorous, free growth.

Marjorie Fair® S, *rb*, 1978, (HARhero; Red Ballerina; Red Yesterday); *Ballerina × Baby Faurax*; Harkness, 1977. Flowers medium red, white eye, single (5 petals), small (1 in.) blooms in very large clusters; slight fragrance; foliage small, light green, semi-glossy; dense, bushy growth. GM, Rome, 1977; Baden-Baden, 1979.

Marjorie Foster R, *dr*, 1934, Burbage Nursery. Flowers deep blood-red, dbl., small; vigorous growth.

Marjorie LeGrice HT, *ob*, 1949, *Mrs. Sam McGredy × Président Plumecocq*; LeGrice. Flowers orange and yellow, dbl. (30 petals), pointed, large (5 in.); fragrant; foliage glossy; vigorous growth.

Marjorie LeGrice, Climbing Cl HT, *ob*, 1956, Tantau.

Marjorie Proops HT, *dr*, 1969, *Red Dandy × Ena Harkness*; Harkness. Flowers crimson, dbl., high-centered; fragrant.

Marjory Palmer Pol, *mp*, 1936, *Jersey Beauty × Seedling*; Clark, A.; NRS Victoria. Flowers rich pink, dbl., blooms in clusters; very fragrant; bushy, compact growth.

Mark One™ Min, *or*, 1982, (SAVamark; Apricot Sunblaze; Mark 1); *Sheri Anne × Glenfiddich*; Saville, F. Harmon; Nor'East Min. Roses. Flowers brilliant orange-red, dbl. (43 petals), cupped blooms borne singly and up to 10 per cluster; spicy fragrance; foliage very glossy; long, thin prickles, soft on peduncles; compact, bushy growth.

Mark Sullivan HT, *op*, 1942, (Président Chaussé); *Luis Brinas × Brazier*; Mallerin; A. Meilland; C-P. Flowers gold flushed and veined rose, dbl. (33 petals), high-centered to cupped, large (4-4½ in.); fragrant; foliage dark, leathery; glossy; vigorous, upright.

Mark Sullivan, Climbing Cl HT, *ob*.

Marlena F, *mr*, 1964, *Gertrud Westphal × Lilli Marleen*; Kordes, R.; A. Dickson; McGredy, 1964; J&P, 1967. Flowers crimson scarlet, semi-dbl. (18 petals), flat, patio, medium blooms in clusters; low, compact bushy growth. GM, Baden-Baden, 1962; Belfast, 1966; ADR, 1964.

Marmalade HT, *ob*, 1977, *Arlene Francis × Bewitched*; Swim & Ellis; Armstrong Nursery. Bud long, pointed; flowers bright orange,

reverse deep yellow, dbl. (30 petals), large (5 in.); very fragrant (tea); foliage large, glossy, dark; upright growth.

Marmalade Mist™ HT, *op*, 1990, Lammerts, Dr. Walter, 1981; DeVor Nurseries, Inc., 1991. Bud pointed; flowers medium salmon pink, with lighter salmon pink reverse, aging to medium pink, dbl. (25 petals), cupped, large blooms borne singly; slight, fruity fragrance; foliage large, dark green, semi-glossy; prickles deep plum and brown; upright, medium growth.

Marmion HT, *pb*, 1934, Dobbie. Flowers pale rose flushed orange, reverse salmon-pink, dbl.; fragrant; vigorous, branching growth.

Marques de Narros HT, *ob*, 1951, La Florida. Flowers salmon-pink, pointed; thornless.

Marquesa de Aguilar HT, *mr*, 1955, *Comtesse Vandal × Caprice*; Bofill; Torre Blanca. Bud ovoid; flowers cardinal-red to begonia pink, dbl. (60 petals), high-centered, large; fragrant; foliage glossy; vigorous growth.

Marquesa de Bolarque HT, *my*, 1945, *Shot Silk × Julien Potin*; Camprubi. Bud long, pointed; flowers lemon-yellow, dbl., high-centered, large; slightly fragrant; foliage dark, glossy; vigorous growth.

Marquesa de Casa Valdés HT, *or*, 1955, *Peace × Poinsettia*; Dot, P. Bud pointed; flowers scarlet-red slightly shaded orange, dbl. (35-40 petals), high-centered, large; fragrant; foliage dark; very vigorous, compact growth.

Marquesa de Goicoerrotea HT, *ab*, 1947, *Eclipse × Joanna Hill*; Dot, P. Flowers amber-yellow, well formed; slightly fragrant; upright growth.

Marquesa del Vadillo HT, *pb*, 1945, (Spanish Main); *Girona × Condesa de Sástago*; Dot, P. Flowers neyron pink, reverse silvery pink, open, large (5 in.); fragrant; foliage glossy, dark; upright growth.

Marquise d'Andigné HT, *dr*, 1927, *(Lieutenant Chaure × George C. Waud) × Laurent Carle*; Leenders Bros. Flowers velvety scarlet-crimson, dbl.; very fragrant.

Marquise de Barbentane HT, *ab*, 1928, *Mrs. Farmer × Severine*; Fugier. Flowers apricot-yellow, shaded orange and sunflower-yellow, dbl.

Marquise de Castellane HP (OGR), *dp*, 1869, Pernet Pere. Flowers dark rose-pink, full, well formed, large; fragrant; moderate growth.

Marquise de Ganay HT, *mp*, 1910, *Liberty × La France*; Guillot, P. Flowers silvery rose, dbl.; fragrant.

Marquise de Sinéty HT, *yb*, 1906, Pernet-Ducher. Flowers golden yellow, shaded bronzy red, dbl.; fragrant. Winner of the first Bagatelle Gold Medal; GM, Bagatelle, 1907.

Marquise de Sinéty, Climbing Cl HT, *yb*, 1912, Griffon.

Marquise de Vivens T (OGR), *dp*, 1886, Dubreuil. Flowers carmine, base yellowish, full, large.

Marquise Litta de Bréteuil HT, *mr*, 1893, Pernet-Ducher. Flowers red.

Marr Pol, *op*, Origin unknown. Flowers coral overcast orange, cupped, small (1 in.), borne in clusters; thornless; rangy habit (10-12 in.); sometimes classed as Miniature.

Marrakech HT, *dr*, 1945, *Rome Glory × Tassin*; Meilland, F. Flowers oxblood-red shaded bright scarlet, dbl., well formed, very large; upright, vigorous growth.

Marriotta Min, *dp*, 1989, (MACcricke); *Seaspray × Little Artist*; McGredy, Sam; McGredy Roses International, 1989; Oregon Mini. Roses, 1990. Flowers deep pink, dbl. (20 petals), small blooms with side buds and sprays; slight fragrance; foliage small, medium green, semi-glossy, resistant toblackspot and mildew; bushy growth.

Mars HT, *op*, 1927, Chaplin Bros. Flowers deep coral; fragrant.

Marshall P. Wilder HP (OGR), *dr*, 1885, *Général Jacqueminot × Seedling*; Ellwanger; Barry. Flowers bright deep red, dbl., globular, large; very fragrant; vigorous, tall growth.

Marta Min, *or*, 1983, *Persian Princess × Anytime*; Dobbs; Small World Min. Roses. Flowers orange-red, dbl. (20 petals), small; slight fragrance; foliage small, light green, matt; upright growth.

Martha Pol, *pb*, 1906, *Thalia × Mme. Laurette Messimy*; Lambert, P. Flowers coppery rose, dbl., blooms in clusters of 7-20; dwarf growth.

Martha Bugnet HRg (S), *mr*, 1959, ((R. *rugosa kamtchatica × R. rugosa amblyotis × R. rugosa plena) × F.J. Grootendorst*. Bud long, pointed; flowers purplish red, semi-dbl., open, large; weak stems; very fragrant; foliage dark rugosa type; fruit very large; vigorous, bushy (5-6 ft. tall and broad) growth; abundant, recurrent bloom.

Martha Drew HT, *w*, 1919, McGredy. Flowers creamy white, center rose, dbl.; fragrant. GM, NRS, 1919.

Martha Kordes F, *dp*, 1941, *Hedwig Fulda × Holstein*; Kordes. Flowers light capucine-red, becoming pink, semi-dbl., open, medium, borne in clusters; slightly fragrant; vigorous, upright growth.

Martha Lambert Pol, *rb*, 1939, *Frans Leddy × Paul's Scarlet Climber*; Lambert, P.; C-P. Flow-

ers brilliant scarlet with small yellow eye, single, small, borne in clusters on strong stems; slightly fragrant; foliage glossy; vigorous, bushy growth; recurrent bloom.

Martha Washington A plant has been grown under this name for many years in the flower garden at Mount Vernon. It is first evidenced in documents dated 1889. This plant can be identified botanical with *Rosa roxburghii* Trattinnick. Propagations of this plant were sold as souvenirs at Mount Vernon between 1890 and 1900 and again from 1932 to 1935. Commercial nurseries offered plants of many varieties and types between 1890-1900. Among them were: a vigorous climber with flowers and foliage identical with Old Blush, a climber with very pale pink flowers of Noisette type and a trailer.

Martha's Choice HT, *dp*, 1977, *Gavotte × Prima Ballerina*; Bailey. Bud high-centered; flowers deep pink, dbl. (37 petals), full, large (5 in.); slightly fragrant.

Marthe Ancey HT, *w*, 1932, (Mme. Martha Ancey); *Souv. de Claudius Pernet × Mme. Mélanie Soupert*; Schwartz, A. Flowers cream, tinted salmon-pink, center with straw-yellow reflections, full, large; vigorous growth.

Martian Glow F, *mr*, 1972, *Joseph's Coat × Dorothy Wheatcroft*; Gandy. Flowers red, reverse lighter, semi-dbl. (10 petals), small (1½ in.) blooms in clusters; slightly fragrant; foliage semi-glossy, medium green; vigorous, spreading.

Martian Sunrise S, *or*, 1979, *Paddy McGredy × Heidelberg*; Taylor, Thomas E. Bud ovoid; flowers orange-red, dbl. (43 petals), urn-shaped, high-centered, cupped blooms borne singly or 3-5 per cluster; slight fragrance; foliage light to medium green, semi-glossy; semi-hooked prickles; upright, bushy growth; repeats well.

Martin Faassen HT, *dp*, 1965, *Baccará × Seedling*; Verbeek. Bud ovoid; flowers pink-red, dbl., medium, borne in clusters; foliage dark.

Martin Frobisher HRg (S), *lp*, 1968, *Schneezwerg × Seedling*; Svedja; Canada Dept. of Agric. Bud ovoid; flowers light pink, center darker, dbl., medium; very fragrant; foliage light green; vigorous, tall growth; (14).

Martin Martin HT, *w*, 1985, (SEAmar); *Jimmy Greaves × Irish Gold*; McCann, S. Flowers cream, petals tipped red, high-centered, large; foliage large, dark, semi-glossy; upright growth.

Martine Hémeray F, *or*, 1958, (Orange Triumph × Mme. Edouard Herriot) × Seedling; Gaujard, R.; Hémeray-Aubert. Flowers china-red, dbl., well formed; slightly fragrant; foliage leathery.

Martone Min, *pb*, 1989, *Queen City* × *Seedling*; Bridges, Dennis A.; Bridges Roses, 1990. Bud pointed; flowers medium pink, lighter at base, reverse light pink, dbl. (30 petals), high-centered, exhibition, medium, borne singly; slight, damask fragrance; foliage medium, medium green, semi-glossy; prickles straight, medium, deep pink; upright, medium growth.

Marty F, *mr*, 1991, (PEAsweet); *Seedling* × *Sweetheart*; Pearce, C.; Rearsby Roses, 1991. Flowers dusty red, very full (41+ petals), HT type, medium (4-7 cms) blooms borne in small clusters; slight fragrance; foliage small, medium green, semi-glossy; few prickles; low (40-60 cms), bushy growth.

Marty's Triumph™ Min, *op*, 1984, (BISmar); *Little Darling* × *Seedling*; Bischoff, Francis J., 1985. Flowers bright coral pink, white reverse, dbl. (28 petals), flat, small blooms borne singly or in clusters; slight fragrance; foliage medium, dark, semi-glossy; pale green, straight prickles; upright, bushy growth.

Marushka HT, *dy*, 1984, *Kabuki* × *Seedling*; Staikov, Prof. Dr. V.; Kalaydjiev and Chorbadjiiski. Flowers deep yellow, dbl. (35 petals), exhibition, medium blooms borne 1-3 per stem; foliage dark, leathery, glossy; vigorous, bushy growth.

Marvlous HT, *mr*, 1937, Cant, B.R. Flowers crimson, dbl., open, large; very fragrant; foliage leathery; very vigorous growth.

Mary HT, *ob*, 1931, Bentall. Flowers buff and orange; fragrant; vigorous growth.

Mary Pol, *op*, 1947, *Orange Triumph sport*; Qualm; Spek. Flowers orange-cerise, borne in small clusters; vigorous growth.

Mary Adair Min, *ab*, 1966, *Golden Glow* × *Zee*; Moore, R.S.; Sequoia Nursery. Flowers buffy apricot, dbl., small; fragrant; foliage light green, soft; vigorous, bushy, dwarf.

Mary Ann F, *dp*, 1959, *Garnette sport*; Restani. Bud ovoid; flowers rose-red, dbl. (60-78 petals), high-centered to flat, medium (2 in.); slightly fragrant; foliage dark; upright growth; for greenhouse use.

Mary Barnard F, *op*, 1978, *(Karl Herbst* × *Sarabande)* × *Ernest H. Morse*; Sanday. Bud ovoid; flowers deep salmon-pink, semi-dbl. (18 petals), large (3½ in.); very fragrant; foliage dark; low, vigorous growth.

Mary Beaufort HT, *lp*, 1969, *Gavotte* × *(Ethel Sanday* × *Crimson Glory)*; Sanday. Flowers light peach-pink, well shaped, small; very fragrant; compact, low growth.

Mary Bell Min, *w*, 1987, *Cherish* × *Rise 'n' Shine*; Bell, Charles E., Jr.; Kimbrew-Walter Roses,

1987. Flowers white, full (26-40 petals), small, moderate fragrance; foliage medium, medium green, semi-glossy, disease resistant; bushy, hardy growth.

Mary Bostock HT, *lp*, 1952, Clark, A. Flowers shell-pink tinted white, dbl. (60 petals), blooms on strong stems; vigorous growth.

Mary Campbell F, *ob*, 1992, (HORlovequeen); *Lovers Meeting* × *Amber Queen*; Horner, Heather, 1993. Flowers orange, semi-dbl. (6-14 petals), medium (4-7 cms) blooms borne in small clusters; slight fragrance; foliage medium, medium green, semi-glossy; some prickles; medium (80 cms), bushy growth.

Mary Carver HT, *lp*, 1950, *Red Radiance sport*; Chick. Bud globular; flowers shell-pink, dbl. (80 petals), cupped, large (5 in.); very fragrant; foliage leathery, light green; vigorous, upright growth; blooms all season in Australia.

Mary Clark Min, *lp*, 1981, *Janna* × *Gene Boerner*; Hooper, J.C. Flowers light pink, dbl. (55 petals), medium; faint fragrance; foliage mid-green; straight, light yellow prickles.

Mary Clay HT, *dr*, 1951, *Kardinal* × *Crimson Glory*; Kordes; Morse. Flowers blood-red, dbl. (40-45 petals), large (6 in.); very fragrant; foliage very heavy, dark; very free growth.

Mary, Countess of Ilchester HT, *mp*, 1909, (Countess of Ilchester); Dickson, A. Flowers deep rose-pink, dbl., open, large; fragrant; foliage rich green, leathery, glossy; very vigorous, bushy growth.

Mary Delahunty HT, *dr*, 1990, *(Daily Sketch* × *Impeccable)* × *Red Planet*; Bell, R.J., 1985; Treloars Roses Pty., Ltd., 1990. Bud pointed; flowers dark red, full (35-40 petals), large, borne usually singly; damask fragrance; foliage dark green, glossy; bushy, tall growth.

Mary DeVor F, *mr*, 1967, (Douchka); *Christian Dior* × *Rumba*; Lammerts; Amling-DeVor Nursery. Flowers cardinal-red, dbl. (35 petals), sweetheart, medium; fragrant; foliage leathery; vigorous, upright growth; greenhouse variety.

Mary Donaldson HT, *mp*, 1983, (CANana); *Kathleen O'Rourke* × *Seedling*; Cants of Colchester, 1984. Flowers medium salmon-pink, dbl. (40+ petals), exhibition form, medium; very fragrant; foliage large, dark, glossy; upright growth.

Mary Dutton HT, *op*, 1949, *Crimson Glory* × *Mrs. Sam McGredy*; Bees. Bud long, pointed; flowers salmon-pink, dbl. (40 petals), large (6 in.); slightly fragrant; foliage glossy; very vigorous growth.

Mary Edith Min, *w*, 1991, (TALmar); *Azure Sea* × *Seedling*; Taylor, Pete & Kay; Taylor's

Roses. Flowers white, tipped with pink edges, flower turns darker pink, tints with age, full, medium blooms borne mostly singly; fragrant; foliage medium, medium green, semi-glossy; low, upright, bushy growth.

Mary Egerton F, *rb*, 1982, *Fragrant Cloud × Prominent*; Lea, R.F.G. Flowers white, petals edged orange-red, spreading with age, reverse white, dbl. (35 petals), large; foliage large, dark, glossy; upright, bushy growth.

Mary Elizabeth Min, *lp*, 1982, *Fairy Moss × Fairy Moss*; Dobbs; Small World Min. Roses. Flowers light pink, dbl. (29 petals), small; slight fragrance; foliage small, light green, matt; bushy growth.

Mary Guthrie Pol, *mp*, 1929, *Jersey Beauty × Scorcher*; Clark, A.; NRS Victoria. Flowers rich pink, single, small blooms in large clusters; fragrant; foliage light; bushy (2½ ft.) growth.

Mary Hart HT, *mr*, 1931, *Talisman sport*; Hart, G.B. Flowers medium red.

Mary Hart, Climbing Cl HT, *mr*, 1937, Western Rose Co..

Mary Hart, Climbing Cl HT, *mr*, 1942, Meilland, F..

Mary Haywood Min, *mp*, 1957, *(R. wichuraiana × Floradora) × Oakington Ruby*; Moore, R.S.; Sequoia Nursery. Flowers bright pink, base white, dbl. (50 petals), small (1 in.); fragrant; foliage glossy; very compact (10 in.), bushy growth.

Mary Helen Tanner HT, *dp*, 1932, *Templar sport*; Tanner. Flowers carmine, stems white or pinkish.

Mary Hicks R, *dr*, 1927, Hicks. Flowers deep scarlet, semi-dbl., borne in clusters; fragrant; foliage light; vigorous, climbing growth.

Mary Hill HT, *w*, 1916, *Ophelia × Sunburst*; Hill, E.G., Co. Flowers cream, center deep orange, dbl.

Mary Hill Min, *pb*, 1990, (MORhill); *Little Darling × Golden Angel*; Moore, Ralph S.; Sequoia Nursery. Bud pointed; flowers medium pink, yellow reverse, aging lighter, dbl. (30-35 petals), high-centered, decorative, medium, borne singly or in sprays of 3-5; moderate, fruity fragrance; foliage medium, medium green, semi-glossy; prickles slender, straight, small, brownish; upright, bushy, medium growth.

Mary Jean HT, *ab*, 1990, (HARyen; Mary-Jean); *Dr. Darley × Amber Queen*; Harkness, R.; R. Harkness & Co., Ltd., 1991. Bud ovoid to pointed; flowers apricot blend, dbl. (37 petals), cupped, large blooms borne usually singly; sweet fragrance; foliage medium to large, oval, medium green, semi-glossy; prick-

les slightly decurved, medium, green; bushy, medium growth.

Mary Jo HT, *my*, 1958, *Seedling × Orange Delight*; Hill, J.H., Co. Bud short, pointed; flowers maize-yellow, dbl. (30-35 petals), high-centered to open, medium (3½ in.), borne on strong stems; slightly fragrant; foliage leathery; vigorous, upright, bushy growth; a florists' variety, not distributed for outdoor use.

Mary Kate Min, *dp*, 1977, *Fairy Moss × Fairy Moss*; Dobbs; Small World Min. Roses. Bud mossy; flowers light red, dbl. (29 petals), flat, small (1 in.); slightly fragrant; foliage dark, soft; vigorous, upright growth.

Mary Kay™ Min, *lp*, 1984, (MINoco); *Tom Brown × Over the Rainbow*; Williams, Ernest; Mini-Roses. Flowers light pink, dbl. (35 petals), small; slight fragrance; foliage small, dark, glossy; upright, bushy growth.

Mary Kittel HT, *dr*, 1975, *(Chrysler Imperial × Night 'n' Day) × Night 'n' Day*; Harvey, R.E.; Kimbrew-Walter Roses. Bud pointed; flowers dark red, dbl. (35 petals), high-centered, large (5 in.); very fragrant; foliage large, glossy; vigorous growth.

Mary Lovett LCl, *w*, 1915, *R. wichuraiana × Kaiserin Auguste Viktoria*; Van Fleet; J.T. Lovett. Flowers snow-white, dbl., large; fragrant; vigorous, climbing (to 10-12 ft.) growth; some repeat bloom.

Mary Lynn HT, *dr*, 1987, (RENlynn); *(Electron × Watercolor) × Lavonde*; Rennie, Bruce F.; Rennie Roses, 1988. Flowers maroon red, reverse lighter, aging darker, semi-dbl. (15 petals), high-centered, medium, borne usually singly or in sprays of 3-5; heavy, damask fragrance; foliage medium, medium green, semi-glossy; prickles hooked, medium, red-brown; fruit oblong, medium, yellow; upright, tall growth.

Mary Lyon™ Gr, *w*, 1988, (WILmtho); *(Mount Shasta × Sonia) × (White Masterpiece × Ivory Fashion)*; Williams, J. Benjamin. Flowers pure chalk white, dbl. (26-40 petals), medium; very fragrant; foliage large, dark green, semi-glossy, thick, disease resistant; upright, hardy growth.

Mary L. Evans HRg (S), *dp*, 1936, *Hansa × R. macounii*; Wright, P.H. Flowers deep wild-rose-pink; very similar to Tekonkaha but growth more spreading; non-recurrent bloom.

Mary Malva HT, *lp*, 1971, *(Pascali × Charlotte Armstrong) × Lilac Charm*; Lens, 1972. Bud long, pointed; flowers light pink, dbl. (18-24 petals), high-centered, large (3½-4½ in.); fragrant (spicy); foliage dark, leathery; upright growth.

Mary Mangano Min, *op*, 1989, *Petite Folie sport*; Papandrea, John T. Flowers deep coral pink.

Mary Margaret McBride HT, *mp*, 1942, *Sunkist × Olympiad*; Pernet-Ducher; Nicolas; J&P. Bud long, pointed; flowers salmon-pink, dbl. (42 petals), high-centered, large (4-5 in.); fragrant; foliage dark, leathery, glossy; vigorous, upright, bushy growth. AARS, 1943; ARS David Fuerstenberg Prize, 1945.

Mary Marques HT, *or*, 1955, *Mediterranea × Suzanne Balitrand*; Bofill; Torre Blanca. Bud long, pointed; flowers orange-red tinted yellow, dbl. (40 petals), high-centered, medium; slightly fragrant; upright growth.

Mary Marshall Min, *ob*, 1970, *Little Darling × Fairy Princess*; Moore, R.S.; Sequoia Nursery. Bud long, pointed; flowers orange, base yellow, dbl., cupped, small; fragrant; foliage small, leathery; vigorous, dwarf, bushy growth. AOE, 1975.

Mary Marshall, Climbing Cl Min, *ob*, 1983, (MINico); Williams, E.D.; Mini-Roses, 1982.

Mary McHutchin R, *mr*, 1935, Cant, B.R. Flowers crimson, semi-dbl., cupped, borne in clusters; slightly fragrant; foliage large, leathery; vigorous, climbing (6-8 ft.) growth.

Mary Merryweather HT, *dy*, 1925, *Marquise de Sinéty × Lady Hillingdon*; Merryweather. Bud pointed; flowers deep golden yellow, semi-dbl., cupped; fragrant; foliage glossy; vigorous, bushy growth.

Mary Mine Gr, *op*, 1973, *Queen Elizabeth × Buccaneer*; Harkness. Flowers salmon-pink to light rose, dbl. (27 petals), large; slightly fragrant.

Mary Monro HT, *pb*, 1921, Pemberton. Flowers carmine-pink, flushed saffron-yellow, dbl.; fragrant.

Mary Mulligan HT, *or*, 1944, Mallerin; A. Meilland. Bud long, pointed; flowers flame, full, cupped; fragrant; vigorous growth.

Mary Murray HT, *ab*, 1930, Prior. Flowers deep apricot-yellow becoming lighter, dbl. (30 petals); foliage glossy, bronze; vigorous growth.

Mary Nish HT, *w*, 1928, (White Radiance); *Red Radiance sport*; Pacific Rose Co. Flowers white, center tinted shell-pink, dbl., very large; fragrant; foliage rich green, soft, glossy; vigorous, bushy growth.

Mary Pickford HT, *ab*, 1923, *Grange Colombe Seedling × Souv. de Claudius Pernet*; H&S. Bud pointed, orange-yellow; flowers pale yellow, center deeper, dbl., large; very fragrant; foliage bronze; vigorous, bushy growth.

Mary Pope F, *yb*, 1965, *Seedling × Independence*; Sanday. Flowers golden yellow suffused

pink, edged darker, dbl. (25 petals), large (3 in.), borne in clusters; foliage glossy, dark; vigorous growth.

Mary Poppins HT, *mp*, 1967, *Hallmark sport*; Morey; Country Garden Nursery. Flowers medium pink.

Mary Rand HT, *w*, 1965, *Caprice × Scandale*; Latham. Flowers cream, edged rose-pink, well formed, large (3½ in.); foliage glossy, light green; vigorous growth.

Mary Ratcliffe HT, *pb*, 1958, Ratcliffe. Flowers soft pink, reverse darker; fragrant.

Mary Robertson Pol, *mr*, 1969, *Paprika × Seedling*; Buisman. Bud ovoid; flowers red, dbl., medium; foliage dark.

Mary Rose® S, *mp*, 1983, (AUSmary); *Seedling × The Friar*; Austin, David; David Austin Roses. Flowers medium pink, very dbl., cupped, large; very fragrant; foliage medium, medium-green, matt; upright, bushy growth; recurrent.

Mary Russell HT, *mr*, 1940, Clark, A. Flowers red, well formed, large.

Mary Sheffield F, *mr*, 1986, (DEBrah); *Doris Tysterman × Admiral Rodney*; Bracegirdle, D.T., 1987. Flowers medium red, moderately full (15-25 petals), medium; fragrant; foliage small, medium green, glossy; spreading growth.

Mary Sumner F, *or*, 1976, (MACstra); *Seedling × Seedling*; McGredy, S., IV; McGredy Roses. Flowers orange-red, semi-dbl. (15 petals), medium (3 in.); slightly fragrant; tall, upright growth.

Mary Wallace LCl, *mp*, 1924, *R. wichuraiana × Pink Hybrid Tea*; Van Fleet; ARS. Bud long, pointed; flowers warm rose pink, semi-dbl., cupped, very large; fragrant; foliage glossy, rich green; vigorous, climbing (8-12 ft.) growth; seasonal bloom. A famous dooryard rose.

Mary Warren Cl HT, *mp*, 1931, *Mrs. Frank Guthrie × Scorcher*; Clark, A.; NRS New South Wales. Flowers pink, semi-dbl., open, large; slightly fragrant; foliage soft, large, dark; vigorous, pillar growth; recurrent bloom.

Mary Washington N (OGR), *w*, Supposed to have been originated by George Washington; Registered by Frank L. Ross, Nashville, Tenn. A plant has been grown under this name in the flower garden at Mount Vernon for many years. It is first evidenced in documents dated in 1891. Flowers white tinted pink, fading to white, dbl., blooms in clusters of 7-9; fragrant; very vigorous growth.

Mary Webb® S, *ab*, 1985, (AUSwebb); *Seedling × Chinatown*; Austin, David, 1984. Flowers apricot, dbl. (40+ petals), cupped, very large;

very fragrant; foliage large, light green, matt; bushy growth.

Mary Wheatcroft HT, *ob*, 1945, *Mrs. Sam Mc-Gredy* × *Princess Marina*; Robinson, H.; Wheatcroft Bros. Bud high-pointed; flowers deep copper; foliage bronze.

Mary Wise HT, *rb*, 1982, (HERmawi); *Madelaine* × *(Seedling* × *Apogee)*; Herholdt, J.A. Flowers medium red and gold with red reverse, dbl. (40 petals), large; no fragrance; foliage medium green, semi-glossy; bushy growth.

Maryellen Min, *pb*, 1981, (LEMmar); *Darling Flame* × *Seedling*; Lemrow, Dr. Maynard. Flowers deep pink, yellow center, single (5 petals), blooms borne 3 or more per cluster; no fragrance; foliage small, deep green; triangle-shaped prickles; upright.

Maryke-Marika F, *ob*, 1973, *Colour Wonder* × *Zorina*; Kordes. Bud medium, ovoid; flowers orange, base yellow, dbl., globular; slightly fragrant; foliage glossy; vigorous, upright growth.

Marylea Johnson Richards HT, *ab*, 1992, (WILlea); *Royal Highness* × *Command Performance*; Williams, J. Benjamin. Flowers light pink with peach tones, full (26-40 petals), medium (4-7 cms) blooms borne mostly singly and in small clusters; very fragrant; foliage medium, dark green, semi-glossy; few prickles; medium (3-4 ft.), upright, bushy growth.

Marylène HT, *mp*, 1965, *Mignonne* × *Queen Elizabeth*; Gaujard. Bud long, pointed; flowers pearl-pink, dbl., medium; fragrant; foliage dark, glossy; upright growth.

Mary's Pink HT, *mp*, 1952, *Better Times sport*; Spanbauer. Bud long, pointed; flowers neyron rose, dbl. (32 petals), large (4-4½ in.); slightly fragrant; foliage leathery; vigorous, compact, bushy growth.

Marysa Pol, *w*, 1936, Brada; Böhm. Flowers pure white; fragrant (lily-of-the-valley); vigorous growth.

Marytje Cazant Pol, *ab*, 1927, (Marie Casant; Mary Casant); *Jessie sport*; Van Nes. Bud globular; flowers coral-pink, blooms in large clusters; dwarf growth.

Masarykova Jubilejni HT, *dr*, 1931, (Jubilaire de Masaryk; Jubilee; Masaryk's Jubilee; Masaryk's Jubileums-Rose); *Blanta sport*; Böhm. Flowers velvety red shaded black, single, very large; slightly fragrant; foliage dark, glossy; vigorous growth.

Mascotte HT, *mp*, 1951, *Michèle Meilland* × *Pres. Herbert Hoover*; Meilland, F. Bud pointed; flowers Hermosa pink, dbl. (35 firm petals), large (4 in.); fragrant; foliage dark; vigorous.

Masked Ball HT, *pb*, 1966, *Masquerade* × *Peace*; Schwartz, E.W.; Wyant. Bud globular; flowers scarlet and gold, dbl., large; fragrant; foliage dark, glossy; vigorous, bushy growth.

Masquerade F, *rb*, 1949, *Goldilocks* × *Holiday*; Boerner; J&P. Bud small, ovoid, yellow; flowers bright yellow turning salmon-pink and then dark red, semi-dbl. (17 petals), medium (2½ in.) blooms in clusters of 19-25; slightly fragrant; foliage leathery, dark; vigorous, bushy, compact growth; (28). GM, NRS, 1952.

Masquerade, Climbing Cl F, *rb*, 1958, Dillian; Gregory.

Massabielle HT, *w*, 1958, Guillot, M. Flowers white, well formed, large; upright growth.

Master David HT, *pb*, 1949, Cox. Flowers pink, reverse carmine, dbl. (25 petals), pointed, large (4 in.); fragrant; almost thornless; vigorous growth.

Master Hugh Sp (OGR), *dp*, 1970, *R. macrophylla Seedling*; Mason, L.M.; Sunningdale Nursery. Flowers rich rose-pink, single (5 petals), medium (2½-3 in.) blooms in clusters; slightly fragrant.

Master John Cl HT, *or*, 1944, *Ednah Thomas* × *Golden Rapture*; Duehrsen; California Roses. Flowers fiery orange-red, base gold, dbl., globular, large; very fragrant; foliage glossy, dark; very vigorous, climbing growth; profuse spring bloom, then scattered until fall.

Ma Surprise S, *w*, 1872, *Probably R. roxburghii* × *R. odorata*; Guillot Fils. Flowers white tinged salmon, full, large; fragrant.

Matador F, *ob*, 1972, (KORfarim; Esther O'Farim; Esther Ofarim); *Colour Wonder* × *Zorina*; Kordes, R.; J&P, 1970. Bud ovoid; flowers light scarlet and orange, reverse gold, dbl., high-centered, medium; slightly fragrant; foliage large, dark, leathery; vigorous growth.

Matador HT, *dr*, 1935, *Charles P. Kilham Seedling* × *Étoile de Hollande*; Van Rossem; J&P. Bud long, pointed; flowers scarlet-crimson, shaded darker, very dbl., cupped, large; fragrant; foliage leathery, dark; vigorous, bushy growth. GM, Portland, 1940.

Matador, Climbing Cl HT, *dr*, 1938, Western Rose Co..

Matangi® F, *rb*, 1974, (MACman); *Seedling* × *Picasso*; McGredy, S., IV. Bud ovoid; flowers orange-red, silver eye and reverse, dbl. (30 petals), large (3½ in.); slightly fragrant; foliage small; bushy growth. GM, Rome, 1974, Belfast, 1976; Portland, 1982; RNRS PIT, 1974.

Matchless HT, *dp*, 1926, *Premier sport*; Duckham-Pierson Co. Flowers cerise-pink, dbl.; upright, bushy growth.

Mateus Rose HT, *pb*, 1973, *Pink Parfait × Mme. Butterfly*; Winship. Flowers peach, reverse pale pink, dbl. (20 petals), large (4 in.); slightly fragrant.

Mati Bradová HT, *dp*, 1934, *Gorgeous × Gen. MacArthur*; Brada; Böhm. Flowers dark rose-pink, sometimes almost carmine, full, very large; fragrant; foliage glossy, dark; very vigorous, bushy growth.

Matilda® F, *w*, 1988, (MEIbeausai; Seduction; Charles Aznavour; Pearl of Bedfordview); *MEIgurami × Nirvana*; Meilland, A.; SNC Meilland; Cie. Flowers white edged pink, dbl. (15-20 petals), large; no fragrance; foliage medium, dark green, semi-glossy; upright, low, compact, proliferous growth. GM, Bagatelle; Courtrai, 1987.

Matilda Campbell HT, *dp*, 1952, Campbell. Bud ovoid; flowers bengal rose, very dbl., high-centered, large (5-6½ in.); very fragrant; foliage glossy; vigorous, bushy growth.

Matson Modesty HT, *lp*, 1946, *Mrs. Sam McGredy × Heinrich Wendland*; Prosser. Flowers pale pink, dbl. (60 petals), large (4 in.); fragrant; vigorous growth.

Matterhorn® HT, *w*, 1965, (ARMma); *Buccaneer × Cherry Glow*; Armstrong, D.L.; Swim; Armstrong Nursery. Flowers white, dbl., high-centered, medium to large; foliage leathery; very tall, upright growth. GM, Portland, 1964; AARS, 1966.

Matthias Meilland® F, *mr*, 1988, (MEIfolio); *(Mme. Charles Sauvage × Fashion) × (Poppy Flash × Parador)*; Meilland, M.L.; SNC Meilland; Cie, 1985. Flowers medium red, dbl. (15-25 petals), large; no fragrance; foliage medium, dark green, glossy, disease resistant; upright, floriferous growth.

MATtnot LCl, *lp*, 1987, (Elizabeth Heather Grierson); *Bonfire Night × Dreaming Spires*; Mattock, John; The Rose Nurseries, 1986. Flowers soft pink, dbl. (15-25 petals), medium; fragrant; foliage medium, dark green, semi-glossy; upright growth.

Maturity HT, *mp*, 1973, *Fragrant Cloud × Lively*; LeGrice. Flowers rose-pink, dbl. (50 petals), full, pointed, very large (7 in.); foliage large, dark; free growth.

Maud HT, *pb*, 1921, Paul, W. Flowers salmon-pink.

Maud Betterton HT, *mp*, 1960, Gregory. Flowers rose-pink, dbl., medium; vigorous growth.

Maud Cole F, *m*, 1968, *Lilac Charm × Africa Star*; Harkness. Flowers mauve-purple, dbl.; fragrant; foliage dark, glossy.

Maud Cuming HT, *op*, 1923, Dickson, A. Bud pointed; flowers coral-pink, shaded peach and orange, dbl., high-centered, very large; slightly fragrant; foliage dark, glossy; vigorous, bushy growth.

Maud E. Gladstone Pol, *pb*, 1926, *Orléans Rose × Edward VII*; Bees. Bud pointed; flowers malmaison pink, shaded coraland chrome-yellow, dbl., globular, small; fragrant; foliage rich green, leathery, glossy; vigorous, bushy growth.

Maud Nash HT, *mr*, 1942, Clark, A. Flowers rich red; upright growth.

Maud Nunn F, *ly*, 1988, (DRIsconun); *Rise 'n' Shine × Rise 'n' Shine*; Driscoll, W.E. Bud pointed; flowers creamy yellow, aging paler lemon yellow, semi-dbl. (16 petals), high-centered, loose, small, borne in sprays; slight fragrance; foliage medium green, semi-glossy; prickles green; bushy, medium growth.

Mauna Loa HT, *mr*, 1937, H&S. Flowers bright red, dbl., large; foliage heavy.

Maupertuis M (OGR), *mp*, 1868, Moreau-Robert. Flowers rosy-pink.

Maureen MacNeil F, *op*, 1967, *Anna Wheatcroft × Orangeade*; Vincent. Flowers salmon, borne in clusters; moderate growth.

Maureen Thompson HT, *dr*, 1949, Cant, B.R.; Bosley Nursery. Bud pointed; flowers dark red, dbl. (35 petals), medium (3 in.); fragrant; foliage leathery; very vigorous growth.

Maurice Bernardin HP (OGR), *mr*, 1861, (Ferdinand de Lessups; Exposition de Brie); *Général Jacqueminot × Seedling*; Granger. Flowers bright crimson, moderately full, large blooms in clusters; very fragrant; vigorous.

Maurice Chevalier® HT, *mr*, 1959, (DELtre); *Incendie × (Floradora Seedling × Independence)*; Delbard-Chabert. Bud long; flowers rich red shaded garnet, dbl. (25 petals), large; fragrant; foliage glossy; vigorous growth.

Maurice Vilmorin HP (OGR), *rb*, 1868, Lédéchaux. Flowers garnet-crimson to purple-maroon, dbl.; fragrant; profuse bloom, sometimes repeated.

Mauricette Sistau Pol, *w*, 1925, Turbat. Flowers pure white to rosy white, full, large, borne in clusters of 25-50; thornless.

Maurine Neuberger™ Min, *mr*, 1989, (SPOmaur); *(Prominent × Zinger) × Centerpiece*; Spooner, Ray; Oregon Miniature Roses. Bud pointed; flowers medium red, dbl. (30 petals), high-centered, exhibition, medium, borne singly; moderate fragrance; foliage medium, medium green, matt; prickles needlelike, light brown; fruit ovoid, light green; upright, medium growth.

Mauve Melodee® HT, *m*, 1962, *Sterling Silver × Seedling*; Raffell; Port Stockton Nursery. Bud long, pointed, purple; flowers rosemauve, semi-dbl. to dbl. (17-25 petals), large (4½-5 in.); fragrant; foliage dark, leathery; vigorous, upright growth.

Mavis Campbell HT, *dp*, 1942, Clark, A. Bud long, deep pink; vigorous, tall growth.

Mavourneen S, *rb*, 1984, *(Tickled Pink × Prairie Princess) × El Catalá*; Buck; Iowa State University. Bud medium-large, ovoid, pointed; flowers medium red, white reverse, dbl. (23 petals), large blooms borne 1-10 per cluster; light fragrance; foliage large, leathery, semiglossy, dark; awl-like, tan prickles; erect, bushy growth; repeat bloom.

M. A. Willett HT, *op*, 1959, *Picture × Tahiti*; Kernovske; Langbecker. Bud globular; flowers pink to salmon-pink, base coppery, dbl., large; fragrant; foliage leathery; moderate, upright growth.

Max Colwell Min, *or*, 1969, *Red Floribunda Seedling × (Little Darling × Miniature Seedling)*; Moore, R.S.; Sequoia Nursery. Bud long, pointed; flowers orange-red to red, dbl. (25 petals), small (1½ in.); slightly fragrant; foliage leathery; bushy, spreading.

Max Graf HRg (S), *pb*, 1919, *Probable hybrid of R. rugosa × R. wichuraiana*; Bowditch. Flowers bright pink, center golden, single, medium; foliage glossy, rugose; vigorous, bushy, trailing; non-recurrent bloom; rarely produces seed; valuable hardy groundcover; (14).

Max Haufe E (OGR), *lp*, 1939, *Joanna Hill × R. eglanteria hybrid*; Kordes. Bud long, pointed, dark pink; flowers light pink, semidbl., large; foliage large, leathery, light; very vigorous (5-7 ft.), trailing growth; seasonal bloom.

Max Krause HT, *yb*, 1930, *Mrs. Beckwith × Souv. de H.A. Verschuren*; Krause; J&P. Flowers reddish orange, opening golden yellow, dbl., very large; fragrant; foliage dark, glossy; vigorous growth.

Max Krause, Climbing Cl HT, *yb*, 1940, Moreira da Silva.

Max Schmeling F, *or*, 1973, *Seedling × Seedling*; Tantau; Ahrens; Sieberz. Bud ovoid; flowers orange-red, dbl., large; slightly fragrant; foliage large, glossy; upright, bushy growth.

Max Vogel HT, *op*, 1929, *Fritz Maydt × Lilly Jung*; Leenders, M. Flowers coppery orange, very dbl., large; very fragrant; foliage bronze.

Maxi F, *rb*, 1971, *(Evelyn Fison × (Tantau's Triumph × R. macrophylla coryana)) × (Hamburger Phoenix × Danse de Feu)*; McGredy, S., IV; McGredy. Flowers red, white eye, semi-dbl. (12 petals), large (3 in.); slightly fragrant; free growth.

Maxim F, *op*, 1961, Tantau, Math. Bud ovoid; flowers salmon-pink, dbl., large, borne in broad clusters; foliage leathery; vigorous, bushy growth.

Maxime Corbon R, *rb*, 1918, *R. wichuraiana × Léonie Lamesch*; Barbier. Flowers dark coppery red turning apricot-yellow, dbl., borne in clusters; fragrant; foliage rich green, glossy, leathery; vigorous, climbing and trailing growth (8-18 ft.); abundant seasonal bloom.

Maximin Chabuel HT, *op*, 1943, Mallerin; A. Meilland. Flowers orange-pink.

Maxine F, *rb*, 1958, *Pinocchio × Crimson Glory*; Silva; Booy Rose Nursery. Bud globular, creamy pink; flowers camellia-red becoming maroon flecked pink and white, dbl. (37-40 petals), flat rosette form, medium, borne in clusters; fragrant; foliage leathery, glossy; very vigorous, low, bushy growth.

Maxistar HT, *or*, 1975, *Fragrant Cloud × Pharaon*; Huber. Bud round; flowers orange-red, very dbl. (70-80 petals), shallow, very large (5½-6 in.); foliage dark, leathery; vigorous, upright growth.

May Banks T (OGR), *ly*, 1938, *Lady Hillingdon sport*; Banks. Flowers lemon-yellow.

May Lyon HT, *mp*, 1982, (COCbay); *((Anne Cocker × Arthur Bell) × National Trust) × Silver Jubilee*; Cocker, J.; Cocker; Sons, 1983. Flowers medium pink, dbl. (35 petals), large; slight fragrance; foliage large, medium green, glossy; bushy growth.

May Martin HT, *ly*, 1918, *Ophelia sport*; Martin; Forbes Co. Flowers pure canary-yellow, center darker, semi-dbl.

May Queen R, *mp*, 1898, *R. wichuraiana × Champion of the World*; W.A. Manda. Flowers pink, very dbl., quartered; fragrant (fruity); height to 25 ft.

May Queen R, *lp*, 1898, Flowers lilac-pink, semi-dbl., flat, large; very fragrant; foliage glossy; vigorous, climbing or groundcover; profuse bloom, occasionally repeated.

May Robinson F, *op*, Form of Else Poulsen. Flowers bright salmon-pink.

May Taylor HT, *dp*, 1966, *Tassin × Ballet*; Taylor, L.R. Flowers deep rose-pink, dbl., high-centered, large; slightly fragrant; foliage soft; vigorous, bushy growth.

May Wettern HT, *mp*, 1928, Dickson, A. Bud pointed; flowers rosy pink, dbl., high-centered, large; fragrant; foliage rich green, leathery; vigorous, bushy growth. GM, NRS, 1928.

May Woolley F, *ab*, 1976, *Fairlight* × *Arthur Bell*; Wood. Flowers bronze-apricot to peach, dbl. (25-25 petals), full, cupped, large (2½-3 in.); very fragrant; foliage small, glossy; moderate, free, growth.

Maya F, *or*, 1986, *Zorina* × *Lara*; Kriloff, M. Flowers orange-red, blooms in clusters; foliage dense, bright; low growth.

Maya Lee HT, *or*, 1992, *Seedling* × *Seedling*; Jerabek, Paul E. Flowers orange-red, very full (50 petals), long stems, large (7+ cms) blooms borne mostly singly; very fragrant; foliage medium, medium green, semi-glossy; many prickles; medium (100+ cms), upright growth.

Mayday F, *lp*, 1957, *(Pinocchio Seedling* × *Hybrid Tea Seedling)* × *Fashion*; Boerner; J&P. Bud ovoid; flowers white overcast pink, dbl. (25-30 petals), cupped, large (3 in.), borne in flat clusters; fragrant; foliage rich green, leathery; vigorous, bushy growth; for greenhouse use.

Mayet HT, *mr*, 1951, *Condesa de Sástago* × *Mme. Henri Guillot*; Dot, P. Flowers crimson-red passing to neyron pink, base yellow, dbl. (30 petals), well formed; very fragrant; foliage olive-green; vigorous growth.

Mayfair HT, *dp*, 1935, Bentall. Flowers deep pink, well formed, large; fragrant; foliage bronze; very vigorous growth.

Mayflower HT, *pb*, 1958, *Eden Rose* × *Seedling*; Gregory. Flowers light cerise, reverse silvery pink, dbl. (30 petals), large (4 in.); very fragrant; foliage glossy; vigorous growth.

Maylina Cl HT, *w*, 1916, (Mrs. Charles E.F. Gersdorff); *White climbing rose* × *Killarney*; Gersdorff. Flowers silvery white, reverse killarney pink to shell-pink, dbl., cupped, very large; fragrant (spicy); foliage large, soft; vigorous, climbing (15 ft.), fairly compact growth; abundant, intermittent bloom.

Mayor Baker HT, *or*, 1928, *Mons. Paul Lédé* × *Hadley*; Thomas. Flowers terra-cotta to scarlet, base light orange; semi-dbl.; fragrant; vigorous growth.

Mayor Cermák HT, *dr*, 1932, *Mrs. Henry Winnett* × *Vaterland*; Böhm; J&P. 1934. Flowers very dark red, shaded purple, large; vigorous, branching growth.

Maytime S, *pb*, 1975, *Elegance* × *Prairie Princess*; Buck; Iowa State University. Bud ovoid, pointed; flowers carmine-rose, base yellow, single (6-10 petals), shallowly-cupped, large (3½-4 in.); fragrant; foliage dark, leathery; upright, bushy; repeat bloom.

Maytime LCl, *lp*, 1953, *R. maximowicziana pilosa* × *Betty Uprichard*; Maney; Iowa State

College. Flowers flesh-pink, reverse rose-pink, single, large (5-6 in.), borne in clusters of 5; slightly fragrant; foliage leathery; vigorous growth; profuse, non-recurrent bloom; (21).

Maywood HT, *mr*, 1924, *Charles K. Douglas* × *(Killarney* × *Ophelia)*; Hill, J.H., Co.; Amling Co. Flowers bright red, dbl.; fragrant.

Maywood Red HT, *mr*, 1923, *Premier* × *Seedling*; Hill, E.G., Co.; J.H. Hill Co. Flower medium red; fragrant.

Mazeppa G (OGR), *rb*, Prior to 1848. Flowers red, edged and marbled with white.

Mazowsze HT, *dp*, 1966, *Marella Seedling*; Grabezewski. Bud oblong; flowers deep pink edged lighter, dbl.; foliage leathery; very vigorous growth.

Mazurka F, *mp*, 1965, Verbeek. Bud ovoid; flowers pink, dbl., medium, borne in clusters; slightly fragrant; foliage dark.

Mazzini HT, *w*, 1925, *Mme. Butterfly* × *Gladys Holland*; Easlea. Flowers blush-white suffused pink, dbl.; fragrant.

M.B. HT, *rb*, 1941, *Dr. W. Van Fleet hybrid* × *Frau Karl Druschki hybrid*; Brownell. Flowers red shading to pink, overlaid orange and yellow, semi-dbl. to dbl. (25 petals), open, large; long stems; vigorous, compact, upright growth.

McGredy's Coral HT, *op*, 1936, McGredy. Flowers coral-pink, overlaid salmon, shaded copper, high-centered, large; foliage dark cedar-green; very vigorous, branching growth.

McGredy's Gem HT, *lp*, 1933, McGredy. Bud pointed; flowers creamy pink, base yellow, deepening to rose-pink edges, dbl. (25-40 petals), cupped; slightly fragrant; very vigorous growth.

McGredy's Ivory HT, *w*, 1930, (Portadown Ivory); *Mrs. Charles Lamplough* × *Mabel Morse*; McGredy; Dreer. Bud long, pointed; flowers creamy white, base yellow, dbl. (28 petals), high-centered, large; fragrant (damask); foliage dark, leathery, glossy; vigorous growth. GM, NRS, 1928.

McGredy's Ivory, Climbing Cl HT, *w*, 1939, Raffel; Port Stockton Nursery.

McGredy's Orange HT, *ob*, 1936, (Golden Thoughts; Morning Glory; Sunglow); *Mrs. Sam McGredy sport*; McGredy. Flowers deep indian yellow, reverse orange, flushed salmon, dbl., high-centered; fragrant; foliage dark, bronze; vigorous growth.

McGredy's Peach HT, *op*, 1933, McGredy. Bud pointed; flowers creamy yellow, washed salmon, cupped, very large; slightly fragrant; foliage glossy, dark; vigorous growth. GM, NRS, 1932.

McGredy's Pillar HT, *or*, 1935, McGredy. Flowers terra-cotta; fragrant.

McGredy's Pink HT, *lp*, 1936, McGredy; J&P. Flowers bright rose, outer petals pearly cream and pink, base saffron-yellow, well shaped, large; very fragrant; foliage dark; vigorous, branching growth.

McGredy's Pride HT, *op*, 1936, *Angèle Pernet × Mrs. Charles Lamplough*; McGredy; J&P. Bud long, pointed; flowers orange and salmon-pink, flushed saffron-yellow, reverse yellow and pink, dbl., large; fragrant. GM, NRS, 1936.

McGredy's Salmon HT, *ab*, 1940, *Mrs. Henry Morse × Seedling*; McGredy; J&P. Bud pointed; flowers apricot-salmon, dbl., strong stems; slightly fragrant; foliage dark, wrinkled; vigorous, compact growth.

McGredy's Scarlet HT, *mr*, 1930, McGredy. Flowers medium red, dbl. (35 petals), high-centered, medium; slightly fragrant; foliage leathery, glossy; vigorous.

McGredy's Sunset HT, *ob*, 1936, *Margaret McGredy × Mabel Morse*; McGredy; J&P. Bud long, pointed; flowers chrome-yellow shading to scarlet, reverse clear buttercup-yellow, dbl. (40 petals), globular, flat; fragrant; foliage glossy, bronze; vigorous.

McGredy's Sunset, Climbing Cl HT, *ob*, 1957, Shamburger, P..

McGredy's Triumph HT, *dp*, 1934, (Maurice); *Admiration × Seedling*; McGredy; J&P. Flowers soft rose flushed orange, dbl., high centered, very large, strong stems; fragrant; foliage dark reddish bronze, glossy; vigorous, branching; (28). GM, NRS, 1932.

McGredy's Triumph, Climbing Cl HT, *dp*, 1948, Simmonds Nursery.

McGredy's Wonder HT, *ob*, 1934, McGredy. Flowers coppery orange, flushed orange-red, reverse orange-red, semi-dbl., cupped, large; fragrant (fruity); foliage glossy, olive-green; vigorous growth.

McGredy's Yellow HT, *my*, 1933, *Mrs. Charles Lamplough × (The Queen Alexandra Rose × J.B. Clark)*; McGredy, 1934. Bud long, pointed; flowers bright buttercup-yellow, dbl. (30 petals), cupped, large; slightly fragrant; foliage glossy, bronze; vigorous. GM, NRS, 1930; Portland, 1956.

McGredy's Yellow, Climbing Cl HT, *my*, 1937, Western Rose Co..

Me Darling F, *pb*, 1971, *Evelyn Fison × Dearest*; Anderson's Rose Nursery. Flowers cream suffused pink, dbl. (37 petals), HTform, large (3½-4 in.), slightly fragrant; foliage glossy, light.

Meadow Dancer Min, *lp*, 1991, *Judy Fischer sport*; Gruenbauer, Richard, 1984; Flowers 'n' Friends Miniature Roses, 1990. Bud ovoid; flowers light pink, dbl. (45 petals), cupped, medium; no fragrance; foliage medium, medium green, semi-glossy; spreading, tall growth.

Meadow Ruby S, *mr*, 1978, *Prairie Princess × (Queen Elizabeth × Borealis)*; James, John. Flowers medium red, dbl. (40 petals), HT form, large blooms borne singly; fragrant; foliage leathery; long, red prickles; vigorous, upright growth; repeats.

Mécène G (OGR), *pb*, 1845, Vibert. Flowers white, striped with rose, dbl., compact, medium; shoots very smooth; erect, moderate growth.

Mechak HT, *dr*, 1979, *Samourai × Seedling*; Pal, Dr. B.P.; Arand Roses. Flowers very dark red, dbl. (20 petals), high-centered; no fragrance; foliage medium, dark, smooth; brown prickles; upright growth.

Mechtilde von Neuerburg E (OGR), *mp*, 1920, Boden. Flowers pink, semi-dbl., small (1 in.) blooms in corymbs; foliage typical sweet briar; fruit large, crimson; vigorous growth; very hardy.

Meda LCl, *op*, 1942, *(R. setigera × Mme. Butterfly) × Golden Dawn*; Horvath; Wayside Gardens Co. Flowers shrimp-pink, dbl. (40-60 petals), open, imbricated, large (3½-4 in.), long stems; very fragrant; foliage large, leathery; very vigorous, climbing (10-12 ft.) growth.

Medallion® HT, *ab*, 1973, *South Seas × King's Ransom*; Warriner; J&P. Bud long, pointed; flowers light apricot, dbl., very large; fragrant; foliage large, leathery; vigorous, upright growth. GM, Portland, 1972; AARS, 1973.

Mediator HT, *op*, 1949, Totty. Flowers coral-pink shading to salmon base, dbl. (45 petals), high-centered, medium; foliage soft, dark green; vigorous, bushy growth.

Medina HT, *w*, 1918, *Sunburst sport*; White Bros.; American Bulb Co.; White Bros., 1923. Flowers white.

Mediterranea HT, *pb*, 1943, *Signora sport*; Dot, P. Flowers carmine with yellow, passing to pink with white markings, dbl. (40 petals), high-centered, large (5 in.); fragrant; upright growth.

Medley HT, *lp*, 1962, *Hybrid Tea Seedling × Pageant*; Boerner; J&P. Bud pointed; flowers bright salmon-pink, reverse flushed yellow, dbl. (35-40 petals), semi-cupped, large (5-5½ in.); fragrant; foliage leathery; vigorous, upright growth.

Méduse® HT, *m*, 1981, (GAUtara; GAUdengi); *Chenonceaux × Tropicana*; Gaujard, Jean; Roseraies Gaujard, 1980. Flowers lavender red, dbl. (35 petals); fragrant; foliage large, dark, semi-glossy; upright growth.

Meg Cl HT, *ab*, 1954, *Probably Paul's Lemon Pillar × Mme. Butterfly.*; Gosset; Harkness. Flowers salmon-apricot, stamens red, single (10 peals), large (to 5½ in.) blooms in large clusters; fragrant; foliage dark, glossy; vigorous growth; recurrent bloom. GM, NRS, 1954.

Meg Merrilies E (OGR), *dp*, 1894, *R. eglanteria × HP or B*; Penzance; Keynes, Williams & Co. Flowers rosy crimson, single; fragrant; foliage very fragrant; very vigorous (10 ft.) growth; summer bloom.

Me-Gami HT, *op*, 1980, *Seedling × Fragrant Cloud*; Suzuki, S.; Keisei Rose Nursery. Flowers medium salmon-pink, dbl. (33 petals), high-centered, large; medium fragrance; foliage dark, leathery; upright growth.

Megan HT, *pb*, 1981, *Daily Sketch × Seedling*; Adams, Dr. Neil D. Bud pointed; flowers white with pink petal edges, HT form, blooms borne 3-5 per cluster; fragrant; foliage medium green, glossy; broad, slightly hooked prickles; upright, strong growth. ARC TG (B), 1981.

Megan Dolan HT, *mp*, 1989, (DEVnovia; Megan); *Angel × Independence '76*; Marciel, Stanley G.; DeVor Nursery. Bud urn-shaped; flowers medium pink, 18 petals, cupped, small, borne singly; sweetheart; slight, spicy fragrance; foliage medium, dark green; prickles declining, copper brown with olive green tinges; upright, tall growth.

Megan Louise HT, *pb*, 1981, *Red Lion × Silver Lining*; Erich Welsh Roses; Australian Rose Society; Roy Rumsey Ltd. Bud ovoid; flowers silvery pink, deep pink petal edges, dbl. (48 petals), high-centered, large blooms borne 1-5 per cluster; strong fragrance; foliage matt, green, tough; red-brown prickles; short, bushy growth.

Megastar HT, *or*, 1980, Sohne, W. Kordes; Barni-Pistoia, Rose. Bud globular; flowers orange-red, dbl. (40 petals), cupped blooms borne singly; strong, fruity fragrance; foliage light green; curved yellow-brown prickles.

Megiddo F, *or*, 1970, *Coup de Foudre × S'Agaro*; Gandy. Flowers orange-red, dbl. (25 petals), large (4½ in.); slightly fragrant; foliage large, olive-green; upright.

MEIbalbika® F, *mr*, 1984, (Iga 83 Munchen; Meilland Rosiga '83; Munchen 83; Rose Iga; The Wyevale rose); *MEIgurami × (Cruosa × City of Leeds)*; Meilland, Mrs. Marie; Meilland & Son, 1981. Flowers medium red, dbl. (20 petals), large; foliage medium, dark, semi-glossy.

MEIbiranda HT, *rb*, 1978, (Candia); *Matador × (Tropicana × Flirt)*; Meilland, M.L.; Meilland Et Cie. Flowers red and yellow blend, dbl. (38 petals), high-centered, large; light fragrance; foliage large, light green; greenhouse variety.

MEIbleri HT, *w*, 1985, (Alliance); *Rustica × Youki San*; Meilland, M.L., 1981; Meilland Et Cie, 1984. Flowers white, semi-dbl., large; no fragrance; foliage medium, dark, matt; upright.

MEIbrico HT, *op*, 1986, (Bettina '78); *(Jolie Madame × Sunlight) × (Lady Elgin × Dr. A.J. Verhage)*; Paolino; URS, 1974. Flowers coral, dbl. (30 petals), large (4 in.); slightly fragrant; foliage dark, leathery; vigorous growth.

MEIcapula Gr, *mp*, 1981, (Fiorella; Fiorella '82; Marion Foster); *(Queen Elizabeth × Nirvana) × (Tropicana × MEInaregi)*; Meilland, Marie L.; Meilland Et Cie. Flowers medium pink, dbl. (35 petals), large; slight fragrance; foliage medium, dark, matt; upright growth.

MEIdirapo HT, *dr*, 1975, *(Queen Elizabeth × (Peace × Michèle Meilland)) × (Baccará × Seedling)*; Paolino; Meilland. Flowers red to purple, dbl. (25 petals), full, cupped, large (3½-4 in.); slightly fragrant; vigorous growth; free bloom in greenhouse.

MEIdomonac S, *mp*, 1985, (Bonica; Bonica '82; Demon); *(R. sempervirens × Mlle. Marthe Carron) × Picasso*; Meilland, M.L.; Meilland Et Cie, 1981; C-P, 1987. Flowers medium pink center, lighter at edges, dbl. (40+ petals), medium; no fragrance; foliage small, dark, semi-glossy; bushy growth. ADR, 1983; AARS, 1987.

MEIdragelac HT, *or*, 1985, (Laura '81; Natilda); *(Pharaoh × Colour Wonder) × ((Suspense × Suspense) × King's Ransom)*; Meilland, M.L., 1974; Meilland Et Cie, 1981. Flowers orange-red, lighter reverse, dbl. (30 petals), large; slight fragrance; foliage small, dark, semi-glossy; medium growth. GM, Japan, 1981.

MEIdujaran F, *mr*, 1980, (Pimlico; Pimlico '81); *(Tamango × Fidélio) × (Charleston × Lilli Marleen)*; Meilland, M.L.; Meilland Et Cie. Flowers medium red, dbl. (35 petals), large; no fragrance; foliage large, dark, glossy; bushy growth. GM, Belfast, 1983.

MEIfikalif HT, *or*, 1980, (Allegeo '80); *(Diorette × Tropicana) × (Seedling × (Diorette × Tropicana))*; Meilland, M.L.; Meilland Et Cie. Flowers orange-red, dbl. (35 petals), large; no fragrance; foliage medium, medium green, semi-glossy; greenhouse variety.

MEIfluney Min, *dp*, 1984, *(Alain × Fashion) × (Rumba × (Zambra × Cinderella))*; Meilland, M.L.; Meilland Et Cie. Flowers deep pink, dbl. (40+ petals), medium; no fragrance; foliage medium, medium green, matt; bushy growth.

MEIfota HT, *mp*, 1981, *Seedling × (((Zambra × (Baccará × White Knight)) × Golden Garnette) × Seedling)*; Meilland, M.L.; Meilland Et Cie. Flowers medium pink, dbl. (20 petals), large; slight fragrance; foliage medium, dark, semi-glossy; upright growth.

MEIgandor HT, *ab*, 1977, (Sabrina); *(Sweet Promise × Golden Garnette) × ((Zambra × Suspense) × (King's Ransom × Whisky Mac))*; Meilland, M.L.; Meilland Et Cie. Flowers apricot-orange, dbl. (35 petals), large; upright growth; greenhouse variety.

MEIgerium HT, *or*, 1975, *(Romantica × Tropicana) × ((Show Girl × Baccará) × Romantica)*; Paolino; URS. Flowers light vermilion-red, dbl. (35 petals), full, large (4-4½ in.); foliage glossy; very vigorous growth.

MEIglusor Min, *dp*, 1988, (Concertino); *(Anytime × Julita) × Lavender Jewel*; Meilland, A.; SNC Meilland; Cie. Flowers cardinal-pink, dbl. (26-40 petals), medium; no fragrance; foliage small, medium green, semi-glossy; bushy, compact growth.

Meilland Decor Arlequin® S, *rb*, 1986, (MEIzourayor; Decor Arlequin); *((Zambra × Zambra) × (Suspense × Suspense)) × Arthur Bell*; Meilland, M.L.; Meilland Et Cie, 1977. Flowers strawberry-red and yellow, semi-dbl. (18 petals), cupped, medium; foliage dark; very vigorous, upright growth. GM, Rome, 1975.

MEIlontig S, *w*, 1987, (Repens Meidiland); *Swany × New Dawn*; Meilland, Mrs. Marie-Louise, 1985. Flowers white, single (5 petals), medium; no fragrance; foliage medium, light green, glossy; spreading, strong growth; poor blooming; can be propagated on own roots.

MEImalyna HT, *mr*, 1984, (Rouge Meilland; New Rouge Meilland); *((Queen Elizabeth × Karl Herbst) × Pharoah) × Antonia Ridge*; Meilland, M.L.; Meilland Et Cie, 1982. Flowers medium red, dbl. (40+ petals), large; no fragrance; foliage large, dark, semi-glossy; upright growth.

Mein Rubin HT, *dr*, 1984, *(Helene Schoen × Charles Mallerin) × (Helene Schoen × Charles Mallerin)*; Teranishi, K.; Itami Rose Nursery. Flowers dark red, dbl. (35 petals), urn-shaped, well-formed, medium blooms borne usually singly; foliage medium, medium green, semi-glossy; medium, lavender prickles; medium, bushy growth.

MEInarval HT, *my*, 1974, (Sun King; Sun King '74); *(Soroya × Signora) × King's Ransom*; Paolino; URS, 1972. Flowers medium yellow, dbl. (30 petals), high-centered, large; foliage small; vigorous, upright growth.

MEIpinjid Min, *mp*, 1985, (Classic Sunblaze; Duc Meillandina; Duke Meillandina); *Pink Meillandina sport*; Meilland, M.L.; SNC Meilland; Cie. Flowers medium pink.

MEIrandival HT, *yb*, 1980, *Meibiranda sport*; Meilland, M.L.; Meilland Et Cie. Flowers yellow blend.

MEIranoga Min, *or*, 1975, (Brilliant Meillandina); *Parador × (Baby Bettina × Duchess of Windsor)*; Meilland, M.L.; Meilland Et Cie. Flowers orange-red, semi-dbl. (15 petals), cupped to flat, medium blooms in clusters of 3-20; no fragrance; foliage dark, semi-glossy.

MEIridorio HT, *yb*, 1984, (Gilbert Bécaud); *(Peace × Mrs. John Laing) × Bettina*; Meilland, M.L.; Meilland Et Cie, 1979. Flowers orange and yellow blend, dbl. (45 petals), large; slight fragrance; foliage bronze, matt; upright growth.

MEIrilocra HT, *ab*, 1984, (Capella; Zambra '80); *Seedling × Banzai*; Meilland, M.L.; Meilland Et Cie, 1979. Flowers apricot, dbl. (35 petals), large; slight fragrance; foliage medium, dark, matt; greenhouse variety.

MEIrinlor HT, *my*, 1975, *Golden Garnette × ((Golden Garnette × Bettina) × Dr. A.J. Verhage)*; Paolino; URS. Flowers medium yellow, semi-dbl. (15-18 petals), large (4 in.); foliage dark.

MEIrodium HT, *rb*, 1976, (Red Success); *(Tropicana × MEIalto) × ((MEIbrem × Zambra) × Tropicana)*; Paolino; URS. Flowers blood-red, base cardinal-red, dbl. (40-45 petals), very full, large (4-4½ in.); slightly fragrant; foliage large; vigorous, upright growth.

MEIrov Min, *mr*, 1975, (Meillandina); *Rumba × (Dany Robin × Fire King)*; Paolino; URS. Flowers currant-red, dbl. (20 petals), cupped, then imbricated, small (1½ in.); foliage matt; vigorous growth.

Meisterstuck F, *mr*, 1940, *Holstein × Kardinal*; Kordes. Bud ovoid; flowers velvety crimson, dbl., cupped, large, borne in clusters; fragrant; foliage dark, glossy; upright, bushy growth.

MEItabifob HT, *my*, 1977, (Cocktail '80); Meilland, M.L.; Meilland. Bud elongated; flowers yellow, dbl. (20 petals), high-centered, large (5 in.); slightly fragrant; foliage dark; very vigorous growth.

MEItiloly HT, *yb*, 1976, (Mascotte '77); *(MEIrendal × (Rim × Peace)) × Peace*; Paolino;

All That Jazz™

Shrub orange-pink 1991 (TWOadvance)
Gitte × *Seedling*
Hybridized by Jerry Twomey
Photograph courtesy of DeVor Nurseries, Inc.
AARS, 1992

Aunt Gerry

Hybrid Tea light yellow 1992
Lanvin Sport
Hybridized by John & Jennifer Sheldon
Photograph courtesy of Trophy Roses

Child's Play

Miniature white 1991 (SAVachild)
(Yellow Jewel × Tamango) × Party Girl
Hybridized by F. Harmon Saville
Photograph courtesy of Nor'East Miniature Roses
AOE, 1993; AARS, 1993

Editor Tommy Cairns

Hybrid Tea pink blend 1991
Seedling × *Seedling*
Hybridized by Joseph F. Winchel
Photograph courtesy of Coiner Nursery

Figurine™

Miniature white 1991 (BENfig)
Rise 'n' Shine × *Laguna*
Hybridized by Frank Benardella
Photograph courtesy of Weeks Roses
AOE, 1992

Fountain Square™

Hybrid Tea white 1984 (JACmur)
Pristine sport
Hybridized by Muriel E. Humenick
Photograph courtesy of Fountain Square

Legend

Hybrid Tea medium red 1992 (JACtop)
Grand Masterpiece × *Seedling*
Hybridized by William Warriner
Photograph courtesy of Jackson & Perkins

Living Bouquet

Miniature light yellow 1991 (LAVlinger; Yellow Festival)
Loving Touch × *(Dorola* × *Genevieve)*
Hybridized by Keith Laver
Photograph courtesy of Springwood Miniature Roses

Lucille Ball

Hybrid Tea apricot blend 1991 (JACapri)
Hello Dolly × *Seedling*
Hybridized by Jack Christensen
Photograph courtesy of Jackson & Perkins

Mary Lyon™

Grandiflora white 1988 (WILmtho)
(Mount Shasta × Sonia) × (White Masterpiece × Ivory Fashion)
Hybridized by J. Benjamin Williams
Photograph courtesy of J. B. Williams & Associates

MEIdomonac

Shrub medium pink 1985 (Bonica; Bonica '82; Demon)
(R. sempervirens × Mlle. Marthe Carron) × Picasso
Hybridized by Marie-Louise Meilland
Photograph courtesy of Conard-Pyle Co.
ADR, 1983; AARS, 1987

Midnight Magic™

Hybrid Tea dark red 1984 (WILmnmg)
(Chrysler Imperial × Mister Lincoln) ×
(Christian Dior × Josephine Bruce)
Hybridized by J. Benjamin Williams
Photograph courtesy of J. B. Williams & Associates

Mikado™

Hybrid Tea red blend 1987 (Koh-Sai; Kohsai)
Fragrant Cloud × *Kagayaki*
Hybridized by Seizo Suzuki
Photograph courtesy of Conard-Pyle Co.
AARS, 1988

Palmetto Sunrise

Miniature orange blend 1992 (MICpal)
Orange Honey × *Miniature Seedling*
Hybridized by Michael C. Williams
Photograph courtesy of The Mini Rose Garden
AOE, 1993

Peace

Hybrid Tea yellow blend 1945 (Gioia; Gloria Dei; Mme. A. Meilland)
((George Dickson × Souv. de Claudius Pernet) ×
(Joanna Hill × Charles P. Kilham)) × Margaret McGredy
Hybridized by Francis Meilland
Photograph courtesy of Conard-Pyle Co.
GM, Portland 1944; AARS, 1946; GM, NRS, 1947; ARS National GM
Cert., 1947; Golden Rose of The Hague, 1965

Princess Alice ®

Floribunda medium yellow 1985 (HARtanna; Brite Lites; Zonta Rose
Judy Garland ✕ *Anne Harkness*
Hybridized by R. Harkness
Photograph courtesy of Weeks Roses
GM, Dublin, 1984

Princesse de Monaco®

Hybrid Tea white 1982 (MEImagarmic; Grace Kelly; Preference;
Princess Grace; Princess of Monaco)
Ambassador × Peace
Hybridized by Marie-Louise Meilland
Photograph courtesy of Conard-Pyle Co.

Rush ®

Shrub pink blend 1983 (LENmobri)
(Ballerina × Britannia) × R. multiflora
Hybridized by Louis Lens
Photograph courtesy of R.O.S.E. Pekmez International
GM, Monza; GM, Rome, 1982, GM, Bagatelle 1986

Secret™

Hybrid Tea pink blend 1992 (HILaroma)
Pristine × Friendship
Hybridized by Daniel Tracy
Photograph courtesy of Conard-Pyle Co.

Sheer Elegance™

Hybrid Tea orange-pink 1989 (TWObe)
Pristine × Fortuna
Hybridized by Jerry Twomey
Photograph courtesy of DeVor Nurseries, Inc.
AARS, 1991

Spinning Wheel™

Shrub red blend 1991
Handel × *Love*
Hybridized by J. Benjamin Williams
Photograph courtesy of J. B. Williams & Associates

The Temptations™

Hybrid Tea pink blend 1990 (WEKaq)
Paradise × Admiral Rodney
Hybridized by Joseph Winchel
Photograph courtesy of Weeks Roses
American Rose Center Trial Grounds, Gold, 1989

Touch of Class™

Hybrid Tea orange-pink 1984 (KRIcarlo; Maréchal le Clerc;
Marachal Le Clerc)
Micäela ✕ (Queen Elizabeth ✕ Romantica)
Hybridized by Michel Kriloff
Photograph courtesy of the American Rose Society
AARS, 1986; GM, Portland, 1988

Windmill™

Shrub red blend 1992 (WILwind)
Handel × *(Love* × *Double Feature)*
Hybridized by J. Benjamin Williams
Photograph courtesy of J. B. Williams & Associates

URS. Flowers yellow, edged cardinal-red, dbl. (40 petals), large (4½ in.); slightly fragrant; foliage glossy; vigorous growth. GM, Belfast, 1979.

MEItoflapo F, mp, 1980, (((Jack Frost × (Zambra × (Baccará × White Knight))) × ((Zambra × (Baccará × White Knight)) × Seedling); Meilland, M.L.; Meilland Et Cie. Flowers medium pink, dbl. (29 petals), large; no fragrance; foliage small, dark, semi-glossy; greenhouse variety.

Meiwonder Pol, mr, 1965, Marianne Kluis Superior sport; Grootendorst, F.J. Bud globular; flowers red, dbl., small, borne in clusters.

Melanie S, dr, 1946, R. rubrifolia × Gruss an Teplitz; Wright, P.H. Flowers deep red, semi-dbl.; foliage reddish; non-recurrent bloom; hardy (to about -15).

Melanie HT, dp, 1958, Sterling × Mme. Auguste Chatain; Combe; Japan Rose Soc. Bud long; flowers carmine-pink, dbl.; vigorous growth.

Melanie de Montjoie HSem (OGR), w, R. sempervirens hybrid; Jacques. Flowered pure white, large; vigorous growth.

Mélanie Soupert T (OGR), w, 1881, Gloire de Dijon Seedling; Nabonnand, G. Flowers white.

Melba F, yb, 1963, Masquerade × Independence Seedling; Sanday. Flowers soft cream and peach, dbl., well formed, small, borne in clusters; foliage light green; spreading growth.

Melglory F, mr, 1982, Lilli Marleen × Patricia; Rijksstation Voor Sierplantenteelt. Flowers medium red, dbl. (23 petals), large blooms in clusters of 4-16; no fragrance; foliage dark, matt; upright growth.

Melgold HT, dy, 1980, Sunblest × Souv. de Jacques Verschuren; Rijksstation Voor Sierplantenteelt. Flowers deep yellow, dbl. (62 petals), cupped, large blooms in cluster of 1-6; no fragrance; foliage dark, matt; prickles reddish-green; upright growth.

Melinda HT, rb, 1980, (RUlimpa; Impala); Whisky Mac × Criterion; DeRuiter, G.; Fryer's Nursery. Flowers scarlet, gold reverse, dbl. (35 petals), large; fragrant; foliage medium, dark, glossy; upright growth.

Melinda Claire Min, m, 1990, (TAYmel); Charmglo × Charmglo; Taylor, Thomas E., 1988; Michigan Miniature Roses, 1990. Bud pointed; flowers reddish magenta, yellow stamens, semi-dbl. (15 petals), high-centered, exhibition, small to medium blooms borne usually singly or in sprays of 3-5; slight to moderate fragrance; foliage medium, medium green, semi-glossy; prickles curved

downward, small, widely spaced, brownish; fruit globular, medium, orange.

Melinda Marie F, lp, 1972, Sarabande × Sarabande; Linscott. Bud ovoid; flowers clear light pink, dbl. (20-25 petals), semi-flat, large (3 in.); slightly fragrant; foliage dark, leathery; bushy growth.

Mélisande HT, lp, 1964, Mondial Roses. Bud long; flowers soft pink, reverse darker, dbl., well formed, large; long, strong stems; fragrant; foliage dark; vigorous, symmetrical growth.

Melissa HT, mp, 1975, Seedling 1968-1 × Sedling 167-d; McDaniel; Carlton Rose Nursery. Flowers medium pink, dbl. (27-32 petals), globular, large (4 in.); slightly fragrant; foliage leathery; very vigorous, upright, bushy growth.

Melissa McCartney F, dp, 1991, Cherish sport; Troyer, Ray & Pat. Bud ovoid; flowers deep pink, holds color well, does not fade, very dbl. (36 petals), high-centered, medium (5") blooms borne usually singly; slight fragrance; foliage medium, dark green, glossy, slight red tinge to new growth; bushy, low (70 cms) growth.

Melita R, mp, 1934, Thelma sport; Easlea. Flowers carnation-pink, dbl., large; foliage glossy, light; vigorous, climbing growth. GM, NRS, 1933.

Mellow Glow HT, pb, 1989, Thriller × Wild Cherry; Bridges, Dennis A.; Bridges Roses, 1990. Bud ovoid; flowers medium pink, reverse creamy yellow, dbl. (52 petals), high-centered, medium, borne usually singly; heavy, damask fragrance; foliage medium, medium green, semi-glossy; prickles pointed slightly downward, large, yellow; bushy growth.

Mellow Yellow HT, my, 1968, Piccadilly sport; Waterhouse Nursery. Flowers sunflower-yellow, edged pink, urn shaped; free growth.

Melody HT, pb, 1946, Joanna Hill × Miss C.E. van Rossem; Lammerts; Armstrong Nursery. Bud urn-shaped; flowers deep pink, edged lighter, dbl. (35 petals), large; fragrant; low, bushy growth.

Melody Lane Min, m, 1991, (MIClane); Lavender Jewel × Party Girl; Williams, Michael C.; The Rose Garden; Mini Rose Nursery, 1992. Flowers mauve, full (26-40 petals), small (0-4 cms) blooms borne in small clusters; no fragrance; foliage small, medium green, semi-glossy; low (6 cms) growth.

Melody Maker F, or, 1990, (DICqueen); Anisley Dickson × Wishing; Dickson, Patrick; Dickson Nurseries, Ltd., 1991. Flowers orange-red, very full petals, large blooms;

slight fragrance; foliage medium, dark green, semi-glossy; bushy growth. ROTY, 1991.

Melo-melo-day Cl F, *mp*, 1955, *Demure sport*; Motose. Bud ovoid; flowers cameo-pink, dbl. (40 petals), cupped, medium (2-2½ in.); fragrant; climbing (10-15 ft.) growth.

Melrose HT, *rb*, 1963, *Silver Lining* × *E.G. Hill*; Dickson, A. Flowers creamy white flushed cherry-red, dbl. (35 petals), medium (3½ in.); fragrant; foliage dark, leathery; vigorous, bushy growth.

Melvena HT, *op*, 1971, *Daily Sketch* × *Impeccable*; Dawson, G. Bud ovoid; flowers salmon-pink, dbl., full, medium; fragrant; foliage leathery; vigorous, upright growth.

Melvin F, *rb*, 1980, *Seedling* × *Seedling*; Jerabek, Paul. Bud pointed; flowers ivory, flushed red, aging darker red, dbl. (30 petals), high-centered blooms borne 1-11 per cluster; little fragrance; foliage medium green; triangular, hooked prickles; medium, dense growth. ARC TG (B), 1980.

Mémé Buy HT, *or*, 1935, Chambard, C. Flowers coppery coral-red, lightly streaked golden yellow, very dbl., cupped, large; foliage bronze; very vigorous growth.

Mémée Arles HT, *dr*, 1955, *Peace* × *Emma Wright*; Arles; Roses-France. Flowers deep red tinted vermilion; foliage glaucous green.

Mémée Azy HT, *pb*, 1921, *Étoile de France* × *Le Progrès*; Gillot, F. Flowers pink shaded carmine, bordered whitish, stamens orange-yellow, dbl.; slightly fragrant.

Mémée Chanteur F, *dr*, 1959, *Karl Herbst* × *Pioupiou*; Arles; Roses-France. Bud ovoid; flowers deep crimson, dbl., cupped, large, borne in clusters; slightly fragrant; foliage dark, leathery; vigorous, upright growth.

Memento® F, *rb*, 1978, (DICbar); *Bangor* × *Anabell*; Dickson, P.; Dickson Nursery. Bud globular; flowers salmon-red, dbl. (22 petals), cupped, large (3 in.); foliage sage green; bushy growth. GM, Belfast, 1980.

Memoriam HT, *lp*, 1961, *(Blanche Mallerin* × *Peace)* × *(Peace* × *Frau Karl Druschki)*; Abrams, Von; Peterson; Dering. Bud long, pointed; flowers pastel pink to nearly white, dbl. (55 petals), high-centered, large (6 in.); fragrant; foliage dark, leathery; moderately tall growth. GM, Portland, 1960.

Memories HT, *dy*, 1977, *Spanish Sun* × *Hoosier Gold*; Byrum; J.H. Hill Co. Bud short, pointed, ovoid; flowers empire-yellow, dbl. (25-30 petals), full, high-centered, small (2½ -3 in.); very fragrant (tea); foliage large, glossy; vigorous, upright, bushy growth; continuous bloom in greenhouse.

Memory HT, *pb*, 1932, Cant, B.R.; J&P. Bud pointed; flowers light pink to deeper pink, base yellow, dbl., high-centered, very large; very fragrant; foliage rich green, leathery; vigorous, compact growth. GM, NRS, 1932.

Memory Lane Min, *lp*, 1973, *(Pinocchio* × *William Lobb)* × *Little Chief*; Moore, R.S.; Sequoia Nursery. Bud ovoid; flowers rose-pink, very dbl., small; slightly fragrant; foliage leathery; vigorous, dwarf, bushy growth.

Memphis Heritage Gr, *pb*, 1969, *Queen Elizabeth* × *Happiness*; Patterson; Patterson Roses. Bud long, pointed; flowers pink blended with gold, dbl., high-centered, large; fragrant; very vigorous, compact growth.

Ménage A (OGR), *w*, 1847, Vibert. Flowers flesh, full, cupped, medium. Raised at Angers.

Mendel F, *mr*, 1946, *Florentina* × *Seedling*; Leenders, M.; Longley. Bud pointed; flowers cherry-red, semi-dbl. (15 petals), large (4 in.), borne in trusses; fragrant; foliage reddish green; vigorous, bushy growth.

Mennie d'Agnin F, *mr*, 1962, *Independence* × *Fashion*; Orard. Flowers vermilion-red, large.

Mentor S, *mp*, 1959, *Tallyho* × *New Dawn*; Wyant. Bud globular; Flowers light pink, reverse darker, dbl., medium; very fragrant; foliage dark, glossy; very vigorous (6 ft.), bushy, upright growth; recurrent bloom.

Menut Min, *dp*, 1956, *Rouletii* × *Perla de Alcañada*; Dot, S. Flowers carmine, semi-dbl. (20 petals), small; dwarf, bushy, compact growth; abundant, inter mitten bloom.

Méphisto F, *or*, 1951, *Francais* × *Seedling*; Mallerin; EFR. Flowers geranium-red, semi-dbl., medium, borne in clusters; foliage leathery; vigorous, upright, bushy growth.

Mercator HT, *dr*, 1962, *Chrysler Imperial* × *Tango*; Delforge. Flowers deep red, dbl., large; very fragrant; foliage dark.

Mercedes® F, *or*, 1974, (MerKOR; Merko); *Anabell* × *Seedling*; Kordes, R.; J&P, 1975. Bud ovoid; flowers bright scarlet, dbl. (33 petals), very high-centered; slightly fragrant; foliage large, leathery; greenhouse variety.

Mercedes G (OGR), *lp*, 1847, Vibert. Flowers white and lilac, changing to pale pink, dbl., large.

Mercedes Gallart Cl HT, *dp*, 1932, *Souv. de Claudius Denoyel* × *Souv. de Claudius Pernet*; Munné, B.; J&P. Flowers deep pink, base yellow, dbl., very large; very fragrant; foliage glossy; very vigorous, climbing growth; recurrent bloom.

Mercedes Juncadella HT, *op*, 1933, *Frau Karl Druschki* × *Angèle Pernet*; Munné, B. Flowers salmon-orange.

Mercedes Mendoza HT, *or*, 1962, *Asturias* × *Grand'mère Jenny*; Dot, S. Flowers orange-red, dbl. (30 petals), large; foliage glossy; vigorous.

Merci F, *mr*, 1974, Warriner; J&P. Bud ovoid, long, pointed; flowers medium red, dbl., medium; slightly fragrant; foliage dark, leathery; vigorous growth.

Mercurius LCl, *op*, 1940, *(Doubloons* × *a Damask rose)* × *Clio*; Horvath; Wayside Gardens Co. Flowers light coral-pink, semi-dbl., cupped, large, borne in clusters; foliage glossy; vigorous, climbing growth; profuse seasonal bloom.

Mercury F, *or*, 1967, *Independence* × *Paprika*; Sanday. Flowers orange-scarlet edged mahogany, borne in clusters; foliage dark; low, bushy growth.

Meredith LCl, *lp*, 1984, *(Charlotte Armstrong* × *New Dawn)* × *Araby*; Thomson, Richard. Flowers light pink to almost white, dbl. (20 petals), HT form, large blooms on long stems; fragrant; foliage large, dark, semi-glossy; upright (to 12 ft.) growth; repeats.

Meredith Anne Min, *pb*, 1983, (TINmere); *Sonia* × *Tea Party*; Bennett, Dee; Tiny Petals Nursery. Flowers salmon-pink, soft pink reverse, dbl. (23 petals), HT form, small blooms in clusters of 3-5 or more; brown to pale yellow prickles; vigorous growth.

Meredith Hughes Min, *op*, 1984, *Anne Scranton* × *Patricia Scranton*; Dobbs, Annette. Flowers medium coral pink, dbl. (40+ petals), HT form, medium; slight fragrance; foliage medium, medium green, glossy; bushy growth.

Merit F, *mp*, 1952, *Garnette sport*; Domilla; Twin Nursery. Bud short, pointed; flowers brilliant rose, reverse lighter, base white, dbl. (50-90 petals), opening flat, medium (1½-2 in.), borne in clusters of 3-8; very fragrant; foliage leathery, dark; very vigorous, bushy growth.

Merit Min, *ob*, 1989, (SPOmerit); *(Prominent* × *Zinger)* × *Miniature Seedling*; Spooner, Ray; Oregon Miniature Roses. Bud pointed; flowers brilliant orange, yellow base, reverse yellow, dbl. (17 petals), high-centered, exhibition, small, borne singly; no fragrance; foliage small, dark green, semi-glossy; prickles needle-like, brown; no fruit; bushy, low growth.

Merle Blanc S, *lp*, 1985, (LENisur); *Ballerina* × *Surf Rider*; Lens. Flowers blush pink, dbl. (22 petals), 2 in. blooms in clusters of 3-22; very fragrant; foliage dark; hooked, brownish-green prickles; tall, spreading growth; recurrent bloom.

Merlin F, *pb*, 1967, *Pink Parfait* × *Circus*; Harkness. Flowers yellow, pink and red, dbl., medium (2½ in.) blooms in clusters; slightly fragrant; foliage glossy.

Mermaid HBc (OGR), *ly*, 1918, *R. bracteata* × *a Double yellow Tea rose*; Paul, W. Flowers creamy yellow, amber stamens, single (5 petals), large (5-6 in.); fragrant; foliage dark, glossy; vigorous, climbing, pillar or trailer (6-9 ft.) growth; dependably recurrent bloom; tender in cold regions. GM, NRS, 1917.

Merrie Miss HT, *mp*, 1966, *Pink Favorite* × *Margaret*; Fuller; Wyant. Bud long, ovoid; flowers soft rose-pink, dbl. (60 petals), high-centered, large (4 in.); very fragrant; foliage dark, matt; upright, bushy growth.

Merrimac™ Min, *dr*, 1989, (KINmac); *(Alain* × *Scamp)* × *Lilli Marleen*; King, Gene; AGM Miniature Roses. Bud pointed; flowers dark red, deeper at tips, 18 petals, high-centered, exhibition, medium, borne usually singly and in sprays of 2-3; slight, fruity fragrance; foliage medium, medium green, matt; prickles straight, small, red; fruit ovoid, orange; upright, medium growth.

Merriment Min, *yb*, 1986, *Rise 'n' Shine* × *Seedling*; Bridges, Dennis A. Flowers bright yellow tipped red, reverse yellow edged red, (8 petals), medium blooms borne usually singly; slight fragrance; foliage large, medium green, semi-glossy; medium, long, pink prickles; tall upright growth.

Merry Christmas Min, *mr*, 1977, *Red Can Can* × *Seedling*; Lyon; Lyon Greenhouses. Bud pointed; flowers currant-red, single (5 petals), open, medium (2 in.); slightly fragrant; foliage dark; upright, compact, branching growth.

Merry England HP (OGR), *mr*, 1897, Harkness. Flowers satiny light red, shaded carmine, dbl. (50 petals); very fragrant; vigorous growth.

Merry Heart Gr, *rb*, 1960, *El Capitan* × *Seedling*; Swim; C.R. Burr. Bud ovoid; flowers orient red, dbl. (30 petals), high-centered to cupped, large (3½-4 in.), borne in small clusters; slightly fragrant; foliage glossy, dark; vigorous, upright growth.

Merry Widow Gr, *dr*, 1958, *Mirandy* × *Grande Duchesse Charlotte*; Lammerts; Germain's. Bud long, pointed; flowers velvety crimson, dbl. (23 petals), cupped, large (6 in.); very fragrant (spicy); foliage dark, glossy; vigorous growth.

Merry-Go-Round HT, *op*, 1950, *Talisman* × *R.M.S. Queen Mary*; Fisher, G.; Arnold-Fisher Co. Bud pointed, becoming urn shaped, orange; flowers orange and pink blend, dbl.

(25 petals), large (5 in.); foliage dark, leathery; tall, compact growth.

Merryweather's Crimson HT, *mr*, 1958, Merryweather. Flowers bright crimson, well formed, strong stems; fragrant; vigorous, bushy growth.

Merveille de Lyon HP (OGR), *w*, 1882, *Baroness Rothschild sport*; Pernet Père. Flowers pure white, tinted satiny rose, dbl., cupped, large (4 in.); vigorous; some recurrent bloom.

Merveille des Jaunes Pol, *yb*, 1920, Turbat. Flowers bright coppery golden yellow, dbl., borne in clusters; dwarf growth.

Merveille des Rouges Pol, *rb*, 1911, Dubreuil. Flowers deep velvety crimson, center whitish, semi-dbl., cupped, borne in large clusters; dwarf growth.

Meryl Jane Gaskin HT, *pb*, 1948, *Rose Berkeley sport*; Mee; Fryer's Nursery. Flowers shell-pink edged deeper pink, dbl. (48 petals), well formed, large (5-6 in.); very fragrant; free, branching growth.

Messestadt Hannover F, *mr*, 1962, (Hannover); Kordes, R. Flowers medium red, dbl., large blooms in clusters; foliage light green, glossy; moderate growth.

Messire LCl, *mr*, 1963, *Seedling × Spectacular*; Laperrière; EFR. Flowers bright red, semi-dbl. (10-15 petals), medium (3 in.), borne in clusters of 6-7; foliage bronze; moderately vigorous growth; profuse, recurrent bloom.

Messire Delbard® Cl HT, *dr*, 1986, (DELsire; Grandessa); *(Spectacular × Guinée) × ((Tenor × Fugue) × (Delbard's Orange Climber × Gloire de Dijon))*; Delbard, 1976. Flowers deep crimson red, dbl. (38 petals), well-formed, large; slightly fragrant; foliage large; vigorous (to 9 ft.) growth.

Meteor® F, *or*, 1959, *Feurio × Gertrud Westphal*; Kordes, R.; A. Dickson; McGredy. Flowers orange-scarlet, dbl. (40 petals), cupped, patio, large (3 in.) blooms in clusters (up to 10); foliage light green; vigorous, bushy, low growth. ADR, 1960.

Meteor HT, *mr*, 1887, Bennett. Flowers crimson-carmine, dbl., open; slightly fragrant; foliage small, soft; few thorns; dwarf growth; recurrent bloom.

Meteor N (OGR), *dp*, 1887, Geschwind. Flowers deep rose tinted carmine-purple, full, large; fragrant; vigorous growth.

Meteor, Climbing Cl HT, *mr*, 1901, Dingee; Conard.

Metis HNit (S), *mp*, 1967, (Simonet); *R. nitida × Thérèse Bugnet*; Harp; Morden Exp. Farm. Bud ovoid; flowers soft rose, dbl. (35 petals), flat, medium (2½-3 in.); slightly fragrant; foliage small, glossy; spring bloom.

Metropole HT, *mp*, 1961, *Sidney Peabody × Peace*; deRuiter; Blaby Rose Gardens. Flowers pink, dbl. (45 petals), globular, large (4-6 in.); fragrant; foliage matt, green; vigorous.

Mevrouw Amélie Müller HT, *yb*, 1927, *Golden Ophelia × Golden Emblem*; Verschuren. Flowers old-gold, shaded orange, dbl.; fragrant.

Mevrouw A. del Court van Krimpen HT, *lp*, 1917, *Seedling × Prince de Bulgarie*; Leenders, M. Flowers flesh-white and pale pink, tinted copper, dbl.; fragrant.

Mevrouw A.H. de Beaufort HT, *pb*, 1934, *Morgenglans × Gooiland Beauty*; Van Rossem. Flowers clear salmon-pink, dbl., large; fragrant; foliage bronze, glossy; vigorous growth.

Mevrouw Boreel van Hogelanden HT, *w*, 1918, *Mme. Léon Pain × Mme. Antoine Mari*; Leenders, M. Flowers flesh-white shaded carmine and pink, dbl., very fragrant.

Mevrouw C. van Marwijk Kooy HT, *w*, 1921, *Mme. Caroline Testout × Mrs. Aaron Ward*; Leenders, M. Flowers white, center indian yellow, sometimes coppery orange, dbl.; fragrant.

Mevrouw Dora van Tets HT, *mr*, 1913, *Farbenkönigin × Gen. MacArthur*; Leenders, M. Flowers velvety deep crimson, dbl.; fragrant. GM, Bagatelle, 1914.

Mevrouw Dr. L. Crobach HT, *pb*, 1928, *Pink Pearl × Red Star*; Leenders, M. Flowers carmine, base salmon, dbl.; fragrant.

Mevrouw D. A. Koster Pol, *mr*, 1934, *Dick Koster sport*; Koster, D.A. Flowers bright red.

Mevrouw G. de Jonge van Zwynsbergen HT, *pb*, 1923, *Mme. Mélanie Soupert × George C. Waud*; Leenders, M. Flowers pale flesh, center flesh-pink and salmon, dbl.

Mevrouw G. A. van Rossem HT, *ob*, 1929, (Mrs. G.A. van Rossem); *Souv. de Claudius Pernet × Gorgeous*; Van Rossem; C-P. Flowers orange and apricot on golden yellow, veined red, reverse often dark bronze, dbl., large; very fragrant; foliage very large, dark, bronze, leathery; vigorous growth; (28).

Mevrouw G. A. van Rossem, Climbing Cl HT, *ob*, 1937, (Mrs. G.A. van Rossem, Climbing); Gaujard.

Mevrouw Lala Philips HT, *or*, 1931, *Elvira Aramayo sport*; Leenders Bros. Flowers brilliant orange-toned shrimp-red, full, well formed, large; foliage dark; vigorous growth.

Mevrouw L. C. van Gendt HT, *ab*, 1925, *Seedling × Golden Emblem*; Van Rossem. Flowers salmon-apricot on yellow ground, dbl.; fragrant.

Mevrouw Nathalie Nypels Pol, *mp*, 1919, (Nathalie Nypels); *Orléans Rose × (Comtesse du Cayla × R. foetida bicolor)*; Leenders, M. Flowers rose-pink, semi-dbl., medium; very fragrant; dwarf, spreading growth; (14).

Mevrouw Smits Gompertz HT, *op*, 1917, *Lady Wenlock × (Mme. J.W. Büdde × Souv. de Catherine Guillot)*; Leenders, M. Flowers yellowish salmon and coppery orange shaded lilac, dbl.; very fragrant.

Mevrouw Welmoet van Heek HT, *dp*, 1933, Buisman. Flowers carmine-red, well formed; foliage dark; vigorous, bushy growth.

Mexicali Rose F, *yb*, 1957, *(Herrenhausen Seedling × Golden Rapture) × Easter Parade*; Whisler; Germain's. Bud short, pointed, yellow suffused red; flowers deep yellow turning deep rose-pink, then cerise-red, dbl. (65-70 petals), open, large (3 in.), borne in clusters; slightly fragrant (spicy); foliage dark; vigorous, upright growth.

Mexicana HT, *rb*, 1966, *Kordes' Perfecta × Seedling*; Boerner; J&P. Bud ovoid; flowers red, reverse silvery, dbl. (33 petals), high-centered, large; fragrant; foliage dark, glossy, leathery; vigorous, upright growth.

Mexico F, *or*, 1944, *Baby Château × Helgoland*; Krause; J&P. Bud globular, deep carmine; flowers deep scarlet, suffused orange, semi-dbl. (18 petals), cupped, large (4 in.), borne in clusters on strong stems; fragrant; foliage leathery; vigorous, bushy growth.

M. Geier HT, *dp*, 1929, *Augustus Hartmann × Admiral Ward*; Felberg-Leclerc. Flowers fiery dark carmine, shaded darker, dbl.

Mhairi's Wedding HT, *w*, 1983, *Dalvey × Virgo*; MacLeod, Major C.A.; Christies Nursery. Flowers white, dbl. (35 petals), flat; fragrant; foliage large, dark, matt; upright.

Mia Maid HT, *mp*, 1953, *Charlotte Armstrong × Signora*; Swim; Mt. Arbor Nursery. Bud ovoid; flowers phlox-pink, dbl. (40-50 petals), open, large (3½-4 in.); fragrant; foliage leathery, glossy; upright, compact growth.

Mia Snock HT, *ly*, 1925, *Mrs. T. Hillas × Mrs. Wemyss Quin*; Leenders, M. Flowers lemon-yellow, dbl.

Miami HT, *yb*, 1953, *Mme. Joseph Perraud × Fred Edmunds*; Meilland, F.; C-P. Flowers orange, veined, reverse yellow, dbl. (25 petals), long, pointed, large (5 in.); slightly fragrant; foliage dark; very vigorous, branching growth.

Miami Holiday Min, *rb*, 1976, *Seedling × Over the Rainbow*; Williams, E.D.; Mini-Roses. Bud pointed; flowers red, reverse yellow, dbl. (60 petals), small (1-1½ in.); fragrant; foliage small, glossy; upright, bushy growth.

Micaëla HT, *or*, 1986, (Trudor); *Manola × Seedling*; Kriloff, M. Flowers orange-red, fading to dark carmine red, blooms in clusters; vigorous growth.

Micaela G (OGR), *lp*, 1864, Moreau-Robert. Flowers blush, very dbl., compact, medium; erect growth.

Michael Saunders HT, *pb*, 1879, *Adam × Mme. Victor Verdier*; Bennett. Flowers deep pink and coppery red, well formed, medium; fragrant; moderate growth.

Michèle F, *op*, 1970, *Seedling × Orange Sensation*; deRuiter. Flowers deep salmon-pink, dbl. (25 petals), large; fragrant; foliage light green; bushy growth.

Michèle Meilland HT, *lp*, 1945, *Joanna Hill × Peace*; Meilland, F. Flowers light pink shaded lilac, center salmon, dbl., large; vigorous growth.

Michèle Meilland, Climbing Cl HT, *lp*, 1951, (Grimpant Michèle Meilland); Meilland, F..

Micheline HT, *dp*, 1953, *Edouard Renard × Luis Brinas*; de Basso, Mata. Flowers deep salmon-pink, base darker, dbl. (30-35 petals); foliage dark.

Michigan HT, *pb*, 1948, *Mme. Joseph Perraud × Vive la France*; Mallerin; URS. Flowers salmon-carmine, reverse indian yellow, dbl., very large; bushy growth.

Micki HT, *or*, 1982, *Fragrant Cloud × Tropicana*; James, John. Flowers light tangerine, dbl. (36 petals) HT form; fragrant; foliage dark, glossy, leathery; small, brown prickles; vigorous, upright growth.

Micky HT, *op*, 1951, *Lulu × Vesuvius*; Houghton, D.; Elmer Roses Co. Bud long, pointed; flowers coral-pink, single (9 petals); slightly fragrant; foliage leathery; few thorns; very vigorous, upright, bushy growth.

Micmac S, *w*, *R. rubrifolia × R. rugosa*; Central Exp. Farm. Flowers white, borne in clusters; foliage deep purplish red; open habit (4 ft.); non-recurrent bloom; hardy.

Micrugosa S, *lp*, (*R. × micrugosa* Henkel; *R. vilmorinii* Bean; *R. wilsonii* A.T. Johnson); *R. roxburghii × R. rugosa*; Orig. prior to 1905. Flowers light pink, single 3-4 in. in diam.; fruit orange-red; depressed-globose prickles, about 1¾ in. diameter.

Micrugosa Alba S, *w*, *R. roxburghii × R. rugosa*; Raised by C.C. Hurst after 1900. Flowers white, single, otherwise similar to Micrugosa.

Micurin LCl, *mr*, 1936, Böhm. Flowers bright red, semi-dbl., globular, very large, borne in large clusters; foliage dark, soft; vigorous, climbing growth; abundant seasonal bloom.

Midas Touch HT, *dy*, 1992, (JACtou); *Brandy* × *Friesensohne*; Christensen, Jack E.; Bear Creek Gardens, 1994. Flowers deep yellow, moderately full (15-25 petals), large (7+ cms) blooms; fragrant; foliage large, medium green, matt; small prickles on peduncle; tall (150-160 cms), upright, bushy growth. AARS, 1994.

Middlesbrough Pride HT, *pb*, 1986, (NOSmid); *Prima Ballerina* × *E.H. Morse*; Greensitt, J.A.; Nostell Priory Rose Gardens, 1984. Flowers pink blend, full (26-40 petals), medium; fragrant; foliage medium, medium green, semi-glossy; bushy growth.

Middlesex County F, *op*, 1990, (BOSanne); *Anne Harkness* × *Greensleeves*; Bossom, W.E., 1985. Bud pointed; flowers golden peach, semi-dbl. (10 petals), flat, medium, borne in sprays of 20-36; slight fragrance; foliage medium, medium green, glossy; tall, upright, very vigorous growth.

Midget Min, *mr*, 1941, *Ellen Poulsen* × *Tom Thumb*; deVink; C-P. Bud pink; flowers carmine-red, dbl. (20 petals), micro-mini, small (¹/₂ in.); slightly fragrant; foliage fern-like; dwarf.

Midinette HT, *mp*, 1962, *Pink Spiral* × *Seedling*; Delforge. Flowers cyclamen-pink, dbl., well formed; fragrant; vigorous growth.

Midnight HT, *dr*, 1956, *Gay Lady* × *Texas Centennial*; Swim; Armstrong Nursery. Bud urn shaped; flowers currant-red to cardinal-red, dbl. (23-30 petals), high-centered to open, large (3¹/₂-4¹/₂ in.), borne on long, strong stems; very fragrant; foliage dark, glossy; vigorous, compact growth.

Midnight Magic™ HT, *dr*, 1984, (WILmnmg); *(Chrysler Imperial* × *Mister Lincoln)* × *(Christian Dior* × *Josephine Bruce)*; Williams, J.B., 1986. Flowers dark red, dbl. (35 petals), exhibition, large; slight fragrance; foliage large, dark, semi-glossy.

Midnight Rendezvous Min, *dr*, 1985, *Scarlet King* × *Big John*; Hardgrave, Donald L.; Rose World Originals. Flowers dark red, dbl. (27 petals), small; slight fragrance; foliage small, dark, semi-glossy; bushy growth.

Midnight Sun HT, *dr*, 1921, *Star of Queensland* × *Red-Letter Day*; Grant; Kershaw. Flowers deep crimson flushed velvety black, semi-dbl.

Midnite Sun HT, *yb*, 1955, *Sutter's Gold* × *R. wichuraiana Seedling*; Brownell. Flowers buttercup-yellow edged red, becoming lighter, dbl. (40 petals), large (5 in.); fragrant; bushy growth.

Midsummer HT, *mp*, 1947, *Heinrich Wendland* × *Lady Sylvia*; Prosser. Flowers pink, semi-

dbl. (20 petals), high-centered, large (4-5 in.); fragrant (fruity); foliage leathery, dark.

Midwest Living® Min, *ob*, 1991, (KINliv); *Evelyn Fison* × *Party Girl*; King, Gene; Michigan Miniature Roses, 1992. Bud globular; flowers orange, full (26-40 petals), slight ruffle to petal edges, good substance, holds well, medium (4-7 cms) blooms borne singly or in small clusters; slight fragrance; foliage medium, medium green, semi-glossy; few prickles; bushy, spreading, medium (46 cms), healthy, vigorous growth.

Mie Min, *mr*, 1980, *Red Can Can* × *Seedling*; Lyon. Bud long, pointed; flowers medium red, semi-dbl. (18 petals), cupped blooms borne several together; slight fragrance; foliage very tiny, medium green; tiny, curved prickles; very compact.

Mien de Jonge F, *mr*, 1969, *Sumatra* × *Seedling*; Verschuren, A.; Stassen. Bud ovoid; flowers scarlet, semi-dbl., cupped, large; fragrant; vigorous, bushy growth.

Mies Bouwman F, *op*, 1973, *Lijnbaanroos* × *Seedling*; Buisman. Bud round; flowers salmon-reverse yellow; slightly fragrant; foliage glossy, dark; vigorous, bushy growth.

Mieszko Pol, *lp*, 1966, Grabezewski. Flowers pale pink, small; foliage small, light green; low growth.

Mieze Pol, *ob*, 1909, *Petite Léonie* × *R. foetida bicolor*; Lambert, P. Flowers orange-yellow, borne in small clusters; vigorous growth; very hardy.

Mieze Schwalbe Pol, *mr*, 1927, *Frau Rudolf Schmidt sport*; Lohse & Schubert. Flowers rose-red.

Mighty Mouse F, *rb*, 1980, (MACmigmou; Painted Star); *Anytime* × *Eyepaint*; McGredy, Sam. Flowers scarlet, white eye, 7-12 petals, blooms borne 20 per cluster; slight fragrance; foliage dark, very long, pointed; slightly hooked, red prickles; sets orange-red hips; tall, spreading growth.

Mignardise Pol, *mr*, 1971, *Luc Varenne* × *Seedling*; Delforge. Bud ovoid; flowers red, single, open, large; slightly fragrant; foliage large, leathery; vigorous, upright growth.

Mignonette Pol, *lp*, 1880, *Dbl. Fld. Multiflora* × probably *China or Tea*; Guillot Fils. Flowers rose, sometimes blush white bordered with wine-red spots, dbl., small (1 in.) blooms in short, full panicles of 50, resembling the Chinas; foliage dark green above, reddish beneath, glossy, 5-7 leaflets; branches dark red; hooked, red prickles; very dwarf, bushy growth.

Mignonne HT, 1962, *Mme. Butterfly* × *Fernand Arles*; Gaujard; Ilgenfritz Nursery, 1966. Bud long, pointed; flowers bright salmon-pink, dbl. (80 petals), large; fragrant; foliage leathery; very vigorous growth.

Mikado Ch (OGR), *dy*, 1929, Dobbie. Flowers deep golden yellow; vigorous growth. RULED EXTINCT 2/87.

Mikado™ HT, *rb*, 1987, (Koh-Sai; Kohsai); *Fragrant Cloud × Kagayaki*; Suzuki, Seizo, 1976; Keisei Rose Nursery, 1987; C-P, 1987-88. Flowers brilliant luminous light scarlet, suffused with yellow at base, fading darker, dbl. (25 petals), high centered, exhibition, medium, borne usually singly; slight fragrance; foliage medium, medium green, glossy; slightly recurved, medium green prickles, tinged purple, aging straw; fruit rounded, dull, orange-red; upright, tall growth. AARS, 1988.

Mikulás Ales HT, *lp*, 1936, Bojan. Flowers rosy salmon-white; very fragrant; very vigorous growth.

Mil Lamp HT, *w*, 1991, *Admiral Rodney sport*; Colclasure, C.E., 1989. Flowers white with pink border, moderately full (15-25 petals), medium; very fragrant; foliage medium, medium green, semi-glossy; bushy growth.

Milady HT, *dp*, 1914, *Richmond × J.B. Clark*; Towill; A.N. Pierson. Flowers deep pink, dbl., high-centered; fragrant; foliage small, soft; dwarf, sparse bloom.

Milagros de Fontcuberta HT, *m*, 1968, *(Sterling Silver × Intermezzo) × (Sterling Silver × Simone)*; Dot, S.; Rosas Dot. Bud pointed; flowers violet-mauve, dbl. (50 petals), medium; fragrant; upright, compact growth.

Milan F, *rb*, 1986, *Seedling × Seedling*; Jerabek, Paul. Flowers red, silver or yellow reverse, dbl. (28 petals), medium; slightly fragrant; foliage medium, medium green, semi-glossy; upright, bushy growth.

Milano R, *op*, 1923, Ingegnoli. Bud very long, pointed; flowers nasturtium-pink on indian yellow ground, dbl., borne in large clusters; fragrant; foliage glossy; vigorous, climbing (10 ft.) growth.

Mildewfree Else Poulsen F, *pb*, 1937, *Else Poulsen × Dainty Bess*; Poulsen, S. Flowers pink slightly tinged yellow, single, medium.

Mildred Cant HT, *mr*, 1935, Cant, B.R. Bud pointed; flowers bright crimson, dbl., high-centered, very large; very fragrant; foliage leathery; vigorous, open growth.

Mildred Grant HT, *w*, 1901, *Niphetos × Mme. Mélanie Willermoz*; Dickson, A. Flowers silvery white, tinted pink at edge, dbl., high-centered; very large; vigorous growth. GM, NRS, 1898.

Mildred Reynolds F, *mr*, 1966, *Peace × Seedling*; Dorieux; Bees. Flowers cardinal-red, cupped, large (3 in.), borne in large, compact clusters; slightly fragrant; foliage glossy.

Milestone HT, *rb*, 1983, (JACles); *Sunfire × Spellbinder*; Warriner; J&P, 1985. Flowers medium red, silvery red reverse, opening to coral-pink, shading lighter toward center, aging darker, dbl. (40+ petals), cupped, large; slight fragrance; foliage large, medium green, semi-glossy; upright growth.

Milkana HT, *rb*, 1974, *Tallyho × Spartan*; Staikov, Prof. Dr. V.; Kalaydjiev and Chorbadjiiski. Flowers brick-red, outer petals shaded pink, dbl. (50 petals), large; foliage dark, glossy; vigorous, upright, tall growth.

Milkmaid N (OGR), *w*, 1925, *Crepuscule × Seedling*; Clark, A.; Brundrett. Flowers white tinted fawn, semi-dbl., small blooms in clusters; fragrant; foliage rich green; very vigorous, climbing growth.

Milky Way R, *w*, 1900, Walsh. Flowers pure white, tips lightly tinged pink, stamens yellow, single to semi-dbl., very large, borne in large clusters; fragrant; foliage glossy; vigorous, climbing growth; seasonal bloom. RULED EXTINCT 9/86.

Milkyway Gr, *w*, 1986, *Seedling × Seedling*; Ohlson, J. Flowers white with yellow stamens, semi-dbl. (21 petals), cupped, loose, medium, borne singly; slight fruity fragrance; foliage small, medium green, semi-glossy; straight, small, greenish-yellow prickles; spreading, medium growth.

Milledgeville Sp (OGR), *mp*, 1842, *R. setigera natural variation*; Found in Georgia. Flowers carmine, over 5 petals.

Millicent S, *mp*, 1928; *R. rubrifolia × R. × harisonii*; Central Exp. Farm. Flowers light coral-red fading to flesh-pink, reverse yellowish; foliage dark green veined red-brown; fruit flattened, globe shape, light red; medium tall growth; non-recurrent bloom; hardy.

Millie Pol, *rb*, 1937, Russ. Flowers light cherry-red, base yellow, borne in clusters on strong stems; foliage dark.

Millie Perkins HT, *mr*, 1960, *Ena Harkness × Chrysler Imperial*; Maarse, G. Flowers velvety red, dbl., well formed, large; long, strong stems; vigorous growth.

Millie Walters™ Min, *op*, 1983, (MORmilli); *Little Darling × Galaxy*; Moore, R.S.; Moore Min. Roses, 1984. Flowers deep coral pink, dbl. (45 petals), slight fragrance; foliage small, medium green, matt; upright, bushy growth.

Milord F, *dr*, 1961, *Opera* × *Ville de Gand*; Gaujard. Flowers dark red, dbl., large, borne in clusters; foliage dark; vigorous growth.

Milord HT, *mr*, 1962, *Rubaiyat* × *Karl Herbst*; McGredy, S., IV; McGredy. Flowers crimson-scarlet, dbl. (35 petals), well formed, large (5-6 in.); very fragrant; foliage dark; upright growth.

Milou F, *dr*, 1964, Mondial Roses. Flowers dark vermilion-red, semi-dbl., medium; vigorous, low growth.

Milrose® F, *mp*, 1965, (DELbir); *Orléans Rose* × *(Francais* × *Lafayette)*; Delbard-Chabert. Flowers rose pink, semi-dbl., cupped, medium blooms in clusters of 5-15; slightly fragrant; foliage light green, glossy; vigorous, bushy growth. GM, Baden-Baden, 1964.

Milva® F, *m*, 1983, (TANavlim); Tantau, M. Flowers mauve, dbl. (35 petals), medium; slight fragrance; foliage medium, medium green, semi-glossy; upright growth; greenhouse variety.

Mimi Min, *mp*, 1965, (MEIdesi); *Moulin Rouge* × *(Fashion* × *Perla de Montserrat)*; Meilland, M.L.; URS. Bud ovoid; flowers medium pink, dbl. (33 petals), shallow-cupped, small (1-1½ in.) blooms in clusters; slightly fragrant; foliage leathery; vigorous, bushy (14 in.).

Mimi Coertse Gr, *mp*, 1963, *Queen Elizabeth* × *Constantia*; Herholdt, J.A.; Herholdt's Nursery. Bud pointed; flowers bright rose-pink, dbl., high-centered, large (4 in.); foliage glossy; upright.

Mimi Pink™ F, *lp*, 1985, (JELdaniran; Mimi Rose); *Seedling* × *Misty Pink*; Jelly, Robert G.; Universal Plants, 1980; E.G. Hill Co., 1985. Flowers light pink, reverse darker, dbl. (35 petals), sweetheart, large; no fragrance; foliage medium, dark, semi-glossy; upright; cut flower.

Mimi Pinson Pol, *dp*, 1919, Barbier. Flowers clear crimson, passing to purplish rose and then to neyron pink.

Mimollet F, *lp*, 1975, *(Queen Elizabeth* × *Ethel Sanday)* × *Zambra*; Ota. Bud pointed; flowers bright light pink, dbl. (40 petals), high-centered, large (3-4 in.); foliage glossy; upright growth.

Min Jurgensen HT, *w*, 1973, *Pascali sport*; Bauer; Trewallyn Nursery. Flowers center buff, aging to pink edges, dbl., full, medium; slightly fragrant; foliage dark, soft; very vigorous, upright growth.

Mindor F, *yb*, 1976, *Faust* × *Mme. Lucky*; Station Exp. de Roses. Flowers deep yellow, slightly flushed orange, dbl. (30-60 petals), urn shaped, large (3 in.); foliage dark; vigorous, low growth.

Minerette Min, *lp*, 1982, (INTerminer); *Marlena Seedling* × *Seedling*; Interplant. Flowers light pink, semi-dbl., medium blooms in clusters; slight fragrance; foliage small, medium green, glossy; many small prickles; bushy. GM, Baden-Baden, 1984.

Minerve HT, *yb*, 1947, *Peace* × *Prinses Beatrix*; Meilland F. Flowers chrome-yellow shaded red, dbl. (36 petals), high pointed; fragrant; foliage thick, dark; vigorous, branching growth.

Ming Toy F, *dp*, 1947, Krebs; H&S. Bud globular; flowers deep rose-pink, dbl. (50 petals), medium (2 in.), large, loose trusses; fragrant; foliage leathery, dark; vigorous, upright, bushy growth.

Mini Magic Min, *rb*, 1988, (MICmag; MICmagic); *Baby Katie sport* × *Watercolor*.; Williams, Michael; The Rose Garden. Flowers white with red edges, reverse more red color, dbl. (35 petals), cupped, small, borne in sprays of 5-8; no fragrance; foliage small, medium green, semi-glossy; prickles straight, light green; slightly spreading, low growth.

Mini Pink Melodies Min, *mp*, 1991, *Seedling* × *Seedling*; Spooner, Ray. Flowers medium pink, moderately full (15-25 petals), small; slight fragrance; foliage small, medium green, semi-glossy; bushy growth.

Miniature Pol, *lp*, 1884, Alégatière. Flowers pink, becoming yellowish white, very full, very small; very fragrant; moderate growth.

Minigold F, *my*, 1970, *Whisky Mac* × *Zorina*; Tantau. Flowers yellow, dbl. (35 petals), pointed, medium (2½ in.); fragrant; foliage glossy, dark.

Minilights S, *my*, 1987, (DICmoppet; Goldfächer; Mini Lights); *White Spray* × *Bright Smile*; Dickson, Patrick, 1988. Flowers medium yellow, semi-dbl. (6-14 petals), small; slight fragrance; foliage small, dark green, glossy; spreading, compact growth.

Mini-Poul® Min, *pb*, 1978, *Darling Flame* × *Seedling*; Poulsen, N.D.; D.T. Poulsen. Flowers yellow and deep pink blend, dbl. (25 petals), small; no fragrance; foliage small, dark, glossy; compact growth.

Minisa HRg (S), *mr*, 1927, *R. rugosa* × *Prince Camille de Rohan*; Hansen, N.E. Flowers deep crimson, semi-dbl. (17 petals); very fragrant; bloom repeats; very hardy.

Minister Afritsch F, *or*, 1964, *Seedling* × *Signalfeuer*; Tantau; Starkl. Flowers orange-red, dbl., large; vigorous, bushy growth.

Minister Luns F, *dp*, 1968, *Märchenland* × *Florence Mary Morse*; Wijnhoven. Bud ovoid;

flowers pink-red, semi-dbl., medium; foliage dark.

Ministre des Finances Rasín HT, *dp*, 1930, (Minister Rasín); *Mme. Maurice de Luze* × *Hadley*; Böhm. Bud long; flowers carmine-rose, full, large; vigorous growth.

Minna E (OGR), *w*, 1895, Penzance. Flowers pure white, semi-dbl.; very vigorous growth.

Minna F, *mp*, 1930, *Gruss an Aachen sport*; Kordes. Flowers rosy pink, dbl., large, borne in clusters; slightly fragrant; foliage rich green, leathery; bushy, dwarf growth.

Minnehaha R, *lp*, 1905, *R. wichuraiana* × *Paul Neyron*; Walsh. Flowers pink fading white, dbl., small blooms in large clusters; slightly fragrant; foliage small, glossy, dark; climbing (15-20 ft.) growth; non-recurrent bloom.

Minnie Min, *rb*, *Starburst* × *Over the Rainbow*; Williams, E.D.; Mini-Roses, 1977. Bud long, pointed; flowers red and yellow blend, dbl. (40 petals), high-centered, small (1 in.); fragrant; foliage small, glossy; upright growth.

Minnie Dawson R, *w*, 1896, *Dawson* × *R. multiflora*; Dawson. Flowers pure white, borne in very large clusters.

Minnie Francis T (OGR), *dp*, 1905, Griffing Nursery. Flowers deep pink, open; vigorous growth.

Minnie Marcus HT, *pb*, 1984, *Queen Elizabeth* × *Windsounds*; Rodgers, Shafner R.; Neiman-Marcus. Flowers pink blend, dbl. (35 petals), large; slight fragrance; foliage large, dark, glossy; upright growth.

Minnie Pearl™ Min, *pb*, 1982, (SAVahowdy); *(Little Darling* × *Tiki)* × *Party Girl*; Saville, F. Harmon; Nor'East Min. Roses. Flowers light pink, reverse darker, high-centered, HT form, small; slight fragrance; foliage small, medium green, semi-glossy; upright growth.

Minnie Saunders HT, *mr*, 1921, Hicks. Flowers bright red, semi-single; vigorous growth.

Minnie Watson HT, *lp*, 1965, *Dickson's Flame* × *Dickson's Flame*; Watson. Bud globular; flowers light pink, semi-dbl.; slightly fragrant; foliage glossy; compact, bushy growth.

Minstrel F, *mr*, 1967, *Independence* × *Paprika*; Sanday. Flowers scarlet, near single; medium (2½ in.), borne in clusters; foliage dark, glossy; very free growth.

Mint Julep HT, *w*, 1983, (AROgresh); *White Masterpiece* × *Queen Elizabeth*; Christensen; Armstrong Nursery. Flowers pale green and pink blend, dbl. (35 petals), large; slight fragrance; foliage medium, medium green, semi-glossy; upright growth.

Minuet HT, *my*, 1930, *Joanna Hill sport*; Thompson's Sons, J.H. Flowers yellow, semi-

dbl., open, large; slightly fragrant; foliage leathery; vigorous growth.

Minuette F, *rb*, 1969, (LAMinuette; La Minuette); *Peace* × *Rumba*; Lammerts; DeVor Nursery. Bud ovoid; Flower petals ivory-white, tipped red, dbl., sweetheart, medium; slightly fragrant; foliage glossy, dark; vigorous growth.

Minx F, *ob*, 1955, *Pinocchio Seedling* × *Garnette*; Boerner; J&P. Bud globular; flowers orange-pink, dbl. (75-80 petals), flat, medium (2½ in.), borne in pyramidal clusters on strong stems; fragrant; vigorous, upright growth; for greenhouse use.

Mio Mac F, *dy*, 1973, Tantau; Horstmann. Bud ovoid; flowers coppery yellow, dbl., medium; slightly fragrant; foliage glossy; growth moderate, upright, bushy.

Miracle F, *op*, 1962, *Seedling* × *Fashion*; Verbeek; Ilgenfritz Nursery. Flowers soft coral, semi-dbl. to dbl. (16-35 petals), high-centered to flat, large (3 in.) blooms in large trusses; foliage glossy; vigorous growth. GM, Bagatelle, 1958.

Miragaia HT, *pb*, 1958, *Peace* × *Coimbra*; Moreira da Silva. Flowers lilac-pink.

Mirage Gr, *op*, 1966, *Peace* × *Circus*; Gaujard. Bud ovoid; flowers bright salmon shaded red, dbl., medium; very fragrant; foliage dark; very vigorous, bushy growth.

Miralba HCh (OGR), *m*, Prior to 1848. Flowers dark crimson-purple, nearly black, very dbl., small; vigorous, branching growth.

Miramar F, *or*, 1956, *Opera Seedling* × *Seedling*; Gaujard. Bud globular; flowers cinnabar shaded coppery, large; foliage dark; very vigorous growth.

Miranda P (OGR), *mp*, 1869, de Sansal. Flowers satiny pink, very dbl.

Miranda Jane F, *op*, 1972, *Orange Sensation* × *Red Dandy*; Cocker. Flowers salmon, dbl. (20 petals), HT-form, large (4 in.); fragrant.

Mirandy HT, *dr*, 1945, *Night* × *Charlotte Armstrong*; Lammerts; Armstrong Nursery. Flowers garnet-red, aging darker, dbl. (45 petals), globular, large (5-6 in.); very fragrant (damask); foliage leathery; vigorous, upright, bushy growth. AARS, 1945.

Mirandy, Climbing Cl HT, *dr*, 1961, Moore.

Mirato HT, *mp*, 1974, *Seedling* × *Seedling*; Tantau. Bud ovoid; flowers pink, dbl.; very fragrant; foliage large, glossy; upright, bushy growth.

Mireille HT, *mr*, 1952, *Opera* × *Seedling*; Gaujard. Flowers coppery crimson-red, dbl. (26 petals), large (4 in.); fragrant; foliage rich green; vigorous growth.

Mireille Mathieu F, *or*, 1973, (KORdehn); *Fragrant Cloud* × *Peer Gynt*; Kordes; Dehner & Co. Bud ovoid; flowers orange-red, dbl. (27 petals), high-centered, large (3½ in.); slightly fragrant; foliage soft; vigorous, upright, bushy growth.

Miriam HT, *my*, 1919, Pemberton. Flowers nasturtium-yellow, dbl.; slightly fragrant. GM, NRS, 1919.

Miriam's Climber LCl, *op*, 1950, *Seedling* × *Edith Nellie Perkins*; Rosen, H.R. Bud ovoid, apricot-pink; flowers peach-pink, lighter at tip, dbl. (30 or more petals), large, borne in clusters; very fragrant; foliage dark, soft; very vigorous, climbing (25 ft.) growth.

Miriana HT, *mr*, 1981, (MEIburgana); *((Seedling* × *Independence)* × *Suspense)* × *(((Alain* × *R. mutabilis)* × *Caprice)* × *Pharaoh)*; Meilland, M.L.; Meilland Et Cie, 1982. Flowers medium red, dbl. (40+ petals), large; no fragrance; foliage medium, dark, semi-glossy; upright growth.

Mirza F, *ob*, 1974, *Zorina* × *Samba*; Kordes; Willemse. Bud ovoid; flowers orange blend, dbl. (35 petals), cupped, large (4 in.); fragrant; foliage glossy; vigorous, upright, bushy.

Mischief HT, *op*, 1961, (MACmi); *Peace* × *Spartan*; McGredy, S., IV; McGredy. Flowers salmon-pink, dbl. (28 petals), large (4 in.); fragrant; foliage light green; vigorous, upright growth. GM, NRS, 1961; Portland, 1965; NRS PIT, 1961.

Miss Agnes C. Sherman T (OGR), *rb*, 1901, Nabonnand. Flowers rose, salmon and red.

Miss Alice de Rothschild T (OGR), *ly*, 1910, Dickson, A. Flowers light canary-yellow, center deeper, dbl.; fragrant.

Miss All Australian Beauty HT, *dp*, 1969, *Aztec* × *Impeccable*; Armbrust; Langbecker. Bud ovoid; flowers light red, reverse darker, dbl., medium; slightly fragrant; upright growth.

Miss All-American Beauty HT, *dp*, 1965, (MEIdaud; Maria Callas); *Chrysler Imperial* × *Karl Herbst*; Meilland, M.L; Wheatcroft Bros., 1965; C-P, 1967. Bud ovoid; flowers dark pink, dbl. (55 petals), cupped, large; very fragrant; foliage leathery; vigorous, bushy growth. GM, Portland, 1966; AARS, 1968.

Miss All-American Beauty, Climbing Cl HT, *dp*, 1969, (MEIdaudsar; Maria Callas, Climbing); Meilland; URS.

Miss Amelia Gude HT, *dy*, 1921, *Columbia* × *Sunburst*; Lemon. Flowers deep yellow center shading to cream, dbl. (35-40 petals); fragrant; foliage dark; vigorous growth.

Miss America HT, *pb*, 1938, *Joanna Hill* × *S.M. Gustave V*; Nicolas; J&P. Flowers light pink, flushed salmon and gold, dbl. (65 petals), large (6 in.); fragrant; foliage dark, leathery; vigorous.

Miss Annamarie Bally HT, *or*, 1926, *Aspirant Marcel Rouyer* × *Lamia*; Easlea. Flowers reddish copper, reverse suffused whitish fawn.

Miss Australia HT, *mp*, 1933, *Dame Edith Helen* × *Mme. Segond Weber*; Knight, G. Flowers pink, center salmon, dbl. (50 petals), globular, very large; very fragrant; foliage thick; very vigorous, bushy growth.

Miss Blanche HT, *w*, 1980, (Kojack); *Evening Star* × *Coquette*; Warriner; J&P. Bud long; flowers white, dbl. (38 petals), urn-shaped to high-centered blooms borne usually singly; very little fragrance; foliage large, dark, leathery; straight, reddish prickles; upright.

Miss Brisbane HT, *lp*, 1953, *Seedling* × *The Doctor*; Ulrick. Flowers shell-pink, dbl., cupped, medium; fragrant; foliage light green; vigorous growth.

Miss California HT, *dp*, 1933, *Dame Edith Helen sport*; Smith, J. Flowers deep glowing pink.

Miss Canada HT, *pb*, 1963, *Peace* × *Karl Herbst*; Blakeney; Eddie. Bud ovoid; flowers rose-madder, reverse silver, dbl., high-centered, large; slightly fragrant; foliage glossy, leathery; vigorous, upright, spreading growth.

Miss Clipper HT, *pb*, 1942, *Angèle Pernet* × *Pres. Herbert Hoover*; Lammerts; Armstrong Nursery. Bud long, pointed to ovoid; flowers pale salmon-pink shaded yellow, dbl. (25-30 petals), high-centered, large (3½-4 in.), strong stems; fragrant (spicy); foliage glossy, light; vigorous, upright, bushy growth.

Miss Conner HT, *ly*, 1920, Dickson, A. Flowers canary-yellow on lemon-yellow, dbl.; fragrant.

Miss Cynthia Forde HT, *dp*, 1909, Dickson, H. Flowers deep brilliant rose-pink, reverse lighter, dbl., large; long stems; fragrant; vigorous, bushy growth. GM, NRS, 1909.

Miss C. E. van Rossem HT, *mr*, 1919, *Leuchtfeuer (Türke)* × *Red-Letter Day*; Verschuren. Bud long, pointed; flowers crimson-scarlet shaded carmine and black, semi-dbl. to dbl., open, cupped, medium to small; slightly fragrant; foliage leathery, bronze, dark; vigorous, bushy growth.

Miss Daisy Min, *dy*, 1991, (JACflare); *Seedling* × *Sun Flare*; Warriner, William A.; Bear Creek Gardens, Inc. Flowers deep yellow, very full (41+ petals), small; slight fragrance; foliage small, dark green, glossy; low, bushy growth.

Miss Delightful F, *my*, 1966, (*Masquerade* × *Seedling*) × *Golden Scepter*; Sanday. Flowers bright yellow, dbl. (30 petals), rosette form, large (3 in.), borne in heavy clusters; fragrant; foliage glossy; vigorous, upright growth.

Miss Dovey™ Min, *ab*, 1985, (KINdov); *Anne Harkness × Rise 'n' Shine*; King, Gene; AGM Mini. Roses. Flowers deep apricot, dbl. (21 petals), high-centered, HT form, medium blooms borne usually singly; slight fragrance; foliage medium, medium green, semi-glossy; straight, reddish-brown prickles; set ships; upright, bushy growth.

Miss Edith Cavell Pol, *dr*, 1917, (Edith Cavell; Nurse Cavell); *Orléans Rose sport*; deRuiter; Spek. Flowers scarlet-crimson overlaid velvety crimson.

Miss England HT, *w*, 1936, Cant, B.R. Flowers creamy, dbl., very large; fragrant; foliage leathery, dark; vigorous, compact growth.

Miss Flora Mitten LCl, *lp*, 1913, *R. wichuraiana × R. canina*; Lawrenson. Flowers soft pink, stamens yellow, single, large (3 in.); vigorous growth.

Miss France Gr, *or*, 1955, (Pretty Girl); *Peace × Independence*; Gaujard. Flowers bright scarlet, dbl., globular, large; fragrant; foliage bronze; vigorous growth.

Miss Georgie HT, *ab*, 1980, *South Seas × Seedling*; Warriner; J&P. Flowers apricot, dbl. (35 petals), blooms borne usually singly; fragrant; foliage large, semi-glossy; long prickles; upright, compact growth.

Miss G. Mesman R, *mr*, (Baby Rambler, Climbing); *Mme. Norbert Levavasseur climbing sport*.

Miss Hawaii HT, *w*, 1976, *Hawaii sport*; Payne; Lone Star Nursery. Flowers creamy white, dbl. (30-35 petals), high-centered, large (5½-6 in.); very fragrant; foliage leathery; very vigorous growth.

Miss Helyett LCl, *pb*, 1909, (Miss Heylett); *R. wichuraiana × Ernest Metz*; Fauque. Flowers bright carmine-pink, center yellowish salmon-pink, dbl., open, large; slightly fragrant; vigorous, climbing (10-12 ft.) growth.

Miss Henriette Tersteeg HT, *pb*, 1922, *Mme. Abel Chatenay Seedling × Mrs. Joseph Hill*; Van Rossem. Flowers flesh and salmon-pink, dbl.; slightly fragrant.

Miss Hillcrest HT, *or*, 1969, *Peace × Hawaii*; Curtis, E.C.; Kimbrew. Flowers orange-red, dbl., high-centered, large; very fragrant (fruity); foliage glossy; vigorous, tall growth.

Miss House HP (OGR), *w*, 1838, House. Flowers satin white.

Miss Huntington HT, *ob*, 1971, *Ma Perkins × San Francisco*; Patterson; Patterson Roses. Bud ovoid; flowers bright orange, dbl., high-

centered, large; fragrant; foliage leathery; vigorous, upright growth.

Miss Ireland HT, *or*, 1961, (MACir); *Tzigane × Independence*; McGredy, S., IV; McGredy. Flowers orange-red, yellow reverse, dbl. (37 petals), large (5 in.); fragrant; foliage dark; vigorous, bushy growth.

Miss Jekyll R, *w*, Flowers white, dbl.; probably a descendent of the Ayrshire roses.

Miss Joan Cl HT, *op*, 1943, *Ednah Thomas × Golden Dawn*; Duehrsen; California Roses. Flowers copper-bronze and salmon-pink, dbl., globular, large; very fragrant; foliage dark, glossy; very vigorous, climbing growth.

Miss Kate Moulton HT, *pb*, 1906, *Mme. Caroline Testout × (La France × Mrs. W.J. Grant)*; Monson; Minneapolis Floral Co. Flowers rosy pink shaded rosy salmon, dbl.

Miss Kate Sessions LCl, *pb*, 1953, *Heart of Gold × Ednah Thomas*; Hieatt. Flowers deep rose-pink on white base, reverse shell-pink, dbl., open, large; fragrant; foliage light green, leathery; moderate, climbing growth; profuse, intermittent bloom.

Miss Koganei Cl Min, *rb*, 1985, *Nozomi × Seedling*; Asano, S. Flowers medium red, white eye, yellow stamens, single (7-10 petals), cupped; foliage small; few prickles; vigorous (to 3 ft.).

Miss Liberté HT, *ob*, 1984, (AROvulc; Harlequin; Miss Liberty); *(Camelot × First Prize) × Gingersnap*; Christensen; Armstrong Nursery. Flowers coral orange to dusty deep red, dbl. (35 petals), well-formed, large; slight fragrance; foliage large, dark, semi-glossy; upright, bushy growth.

Miss Liberty LCl, *mp*, 1956, *New Dawn × World's Fair, Climbing*; Boerner; Stuart. Bud ovoid; flowers tyrian rose, semi-dbl. (15-20 petals), cupped to flat, large (3½ in.), borne in large clusters on strong stems; fragrant; foliage dark, leathery; vigorous, climbing (10-12 ft.) growth; repeat bloom.

Miss Lolita Armour HT, *or*, 1919, Howard, F.H.; H&S. Flowers deep coral-red suffused coppery red, base yellow, dbl., cupped, very large; very fragrant. GM, Bagatelle, 1921.

Miss Lolita Armour, Climbing Cl HT, *or*, H&S, about 1925.

Miss Lowe Ch (OGR), *mr*, *Possibly Slater's Crimson China sport*. Flowers bright red, single; dwarf growth; recurrent bloom. Erroneously equated with 'Sanguinea,' which is double.

Miss Marion Manifold Cl HT, *mr*, 1913, (Marion Manifold); Adamson; Brundrett. Flowers velvety scarlet, shaded crimson, dbl., globular, large; fragrant; foliage large, leathery; vigorous, climbing (12 ft.) growth.

Miss May Marriott HT, *ab*, 1917, *Mme. Edouard Herriot sport*; Robinson, T. Flowers glowing apricot.

Miss Middleton F, *op*, 1963, *Independence × Masquerade*; Hill, A. Flowers coral-pink, dbl. (20 petals), cupped, large (2½-3 in.), borne in small clusters; foliage light green; low, bushy growth.

Miss M'liss F, *mp*, 1958, *Garnette × Garnette Seedling*; Jelly; E.G. Hill Co. Bud short pointed; flowers phlox-pink, dbl. (25-30 petals), high-centered to flat, large (2½-3 in.); slightly fragrant; very vigorous, upright growth; a greenhouse variety.

Miss Modesto HT, *my*, 1934, *Rev. F. Page-Roberts sport*; Brooks, L.L.; Brooks & Son. Flowers pure yellow, dbl., high-centered, very large; fragrant.

Miss Muffett Min, *mp*, 1955, *Baby Bunting × Tom Thumb*; Robinson, T. Bud rather mossy; flowers apple-blossom-pink, dbl. (80 petals), compact (4-6 in.) growth.

Miss Murine F, *dp*, 1937, *Seedling × Cécile Brunner*; Fitzgerald. Flowers deep pink, base yellow, dbl., small; upright, bushy growth.

Miss M. J. Spencer HT, *my*, 1920, Dickson, H. Flowers clear bright golden yellow, dbl.

Miss Pearl™ Min, *lp*, 1991, (HOOpearl); *Gene Boerner × Pacesetter*; Hooper, J.C.; AGM Miniature Roses. Flowers light pink, moderately full (15-25 petals), medium (4-7 cms) blooms borne mostly singly; extremely fragrant (spicy); foliage medium, medium green, matt; few prickles; tall (80 cms), upright growth.

Miss Perfect™ Min, *lp*, 1989, (JACmiss); *Over the Rainbow × Lavender Lace*; Warriner, William A.; Bear Creek Gardens. Bud ovoid, pointed; flowers light pink to near white at edge, reverse lighter, very dbl. (60+ petals), cupped, medium, borne in sprays of 25-35; slight fragrance; foliage medium, medium green, semi-glossy; prickles straight to slightly hooked downward, light yellow-green; spreading, low growth.

Miss Personality F, *pb*, 1972, *Pink Parfait × (Ophelia × Parkdirektor Riggers)*; Sherwood; F. Mason. Bud ovoid; flowers cerise-pink, white eye, semi-dbl., open, medium; slightly fragrant; foliage small, dark, leathery; vigorous, bushy growth.

Miss Rowena Thom HT, *pb*, 1927, *Radiance × Los Angeles*; H&S. Flowers fiery rose and rosy mauve, center washed gold, dbl. (50 petals), large (6 in.); very fragrant; vigorous.

Miss Rowena Thom, Climbing Cl HT, *pb*, 1937, Van Barneveld; California Roses.

Miss Talmadge HT, *dy*, 1927, *Constance sport*; Pacific Rose Co. Flowers deep yellow, dbl.; fragrant.

Miss Universe HT, *rb*, 1956, *(Peace × Seedling) × Seedling*; Gaujard. Bud long, pointed; flowers orange-red, reverse tinted copper, large; fragrant; foliage dark; vigorous.

Miss Willmott HT, *ly*, 1917, McGredy. Flowers soft sulphury cream, edges flushed pale pink, dbl., well formed; fragrant; vigorous growth. GM, NRS, 1916.

Miss Windsor HT, *mr*, 1967, *Tropicana sport*; Heron. Flowers medium red, dbl., high-centered, medium; very fragrant; foliage light green, leathery; very vigorous, upright growth.

Mission Bells HT, *pb*, 1949, *Mrs. Sam McGredy × Malar-Ros*; Morris; Germain's. Bud long, pointed; flowers vermilion-pink, dbl. (43 petals), high-centered, large (5 in.); fragrant; foliage dark, soft; vigorous, bushy growth. AARS, 1950.

Mission Supreme HT, *ab*, 1981, *City of Glouchester × Seedling*; Sanday, John. Bud pointed; flowers pale peach pink to apricot, dbl. (30 petals), blooms borne singly; fragrant; foliage deep green; straight, red-brown prickles; vigorous, bushy, medium growth.

Mississippi HT, *dr*, 1976, *Charlotte Armstrong × Mister Lincoln*; Williams, J.B. Bud pointed; flowers deep red, dbl. (38 petals), large (4½-5 in.); fragrant (damask); foliage dark; upright growth.

Mississippi Rainbow HT, *yb*, 1977, Graham; South Forrest Rose Nursery. Flowers yellow blend, dbl. (41 petals), full, large (4 in.); slightly fragrant; foliage thick, glossy; upright growth.

Missy Min, *mr*, 1978, *Seedling × Seedling*; Lyon. Bud pointed; flowers cardinal-red, dbl. (22 petals), small (1½ in.); slightly fragrant; foliage small; compact, bushy growth.

Mistee Min, *ly*, 1979, *Little Darling × Peachy White*; Moore, R.S.; Sequoia Nursery. Bud long, pointed; flowers white, tinted yellow, dbl. (28 petals), flat, small (1½ in.); fragrant; foliage small; bushy, upright growth.

Mister America LCl, *dr*, 1974, *(Paul's Scarlet Climber × Golden Climber) × Pinocchio*; Zombory; General Bionomics. Flowers blood-red, dbl., high centered, very large; fragrant; foliage leathery; very vigorous, climbing; abundant bloom.

Mr. Bluebird Min, *m*, 1960, *Old Blush × Old Blush*; Moore, R.S.; Sequoia Nursery. Bud ovoid; flowers lavender-blue, semi-dbl. (15 petals), small (1¼ in.); foliage dark; compact, bushy (10-14 in.) growth.

Mr. Chips HT, *yb*, 1970, *Grandma Dickson* × *Miss Ireland*; Dickson, A. Flowers yellow and orange, dbl., high-pointed, large; foliage glossy.

Mr. E. E. Greenwell F, *op*, 1978, (HARjoobily); *Jove* × *City of Leeds*; Harkness. Flowers rosy salmon, semi-dbl. (18 petals), flat, large (3 in.); vigorous, bushy, spreading growth.

Mr. Faithful F, *mp*, 1968, *Pink Parfait* × *Self*; Harkness. Flowers medium pink, dbl., blooms in trusses; fragrant.

Mr. Joh. M. Jolles HT, *ly*, 1920, *Frau Karl Druschki* × *Mrs. Joseph Hill*; Van Rossem. Flowers clear creamy yellow, shaded apricot and golden yellow, dbl.

Mr. J. Bienfait HT, *mr*, 1923, (J. Bienfait); *Mme. Léon Pain* × *Red-Letter Day*; Van Rossem. Flowers brick-red.

Mister Lincoln® HT, *dr*, 1964, *Chrysler Imperial* × *Charles Mallerin*; Swim & Weeks; C-P. Bud urn-shaped; flowers dark red, dbl. (35 petals), high-centered to cupped, large (4½-6 in.); very fragrant; foliage leathery, matt, dark; vigorous growth. AARS, 1965.

Mister Lincoln, Climbing Cl HT, *dr*, 1974, Ram.

Mr. McCawber F, *w*, 1988, (WHIcaw); *(French Lace* × *Simplex)* × *(Pristine* × *White Angel)*; White, James J. Bud pointed, white flushed pink; flowers white, semi-dbl. (15-17 petals), high-centered, exhibition, medium, borne in sprays of 8-10; slight fragrance; foliage medium, medium green, semi-glossy, disease resistant; prickles hooked, light brown; fruit globular, orange; upright, bushy, tall, prolific growth.

Mister Otis Min, *mr*, 1986, (CURmist); *Rise 'n' Shine* × *Fire Princess*; Curtis, Thad; Hortco, Inc. Flowers medium red, dbl. (35 petals), exhibition, small blooms borne singly; no fragrance; foliage small, medium green, matt; upright, bushy growth.

Mr. Pat HT, *dr*, 1966, *Red Jacket* × *Mirandy*; Patterson; Patterson Roses. Bud globular; flowers dark red, dbl., high-centered, large; very fragrant (spicy); foliage leathery; compact growth.

Mister Softee HT, *w*, 1964, Morton's Rose Nursery. Flowers creamy white edged pink, dbl. (40 petals), open, large (4½ in.); fragrant; foliage glossy, dark; very free growth.

Mr. Standfast HT, *w*, 1968, *Dr. A.J. Verhage* × *Kordes' Perfecta*; Harkness. Flowers cream, dbl., large; fragrant; foliage glossy.

Mr. Tall HT, *op*, 1958, *Vogue* × *Grande Duchesse Charlotte*; Wyant. Bud long, pointed; flowers

salmon-pink, single (7 petals), open, large (4 in.); very fragrant (cinnamon); foliage dark, leathery; vigorous, upright growth.

Mistica HT, *m*, 1966, *Sterling Silver* × *Intermezzo*; Dot; Minier. Bud ovoid; flowers lilac, dbl., cupped, very large; very fragrant; foliage dark; vigorous.

Mistress Pat Pol, *mp*, 1928, Lilley. Flowers chatenay pink; fragrant.

Misty HT, *w*, 1965, *Mount Shasta* × *Matterhorn*; Armstrong, D.L.; Armstrong Nursery. Bud ovoid, pointed; flowers creamy white, dbl. (35 petals), cupped to formal, large (4 in.); fragrant (tea); foliage large, leathery; vigorous, upright growth.

Misty Dawn Min, *w*, 1979, *Charlie McCarthy* × *Seedling*; Schwartz, E.W.; Nor'East Min. Roses. Bud ovoid, pointed; flowers pure white, dbl. (33 petals), cupped, small (1 in.); foliage small, dark; vigorous, compact, spreading growth.

Misty Delight HT, *mp*, 1990, *Blue Wonder* × *Seedling*; Christensen, Jack; Vaughan's Seed Co., 1991. Flowers medium pink, full (26-40 petals), borne mostly singly; foliage large, dark green, glossy; upright growth.

Misty Gold F, *my*, 1954, *Floribunda (Yellow, semi-dbl., self Seedling)*; Boerner; Stark Bros. Bud ovoid, pointed; flowers empire-yellow, dbl. (45-50 petals), cupped, large (3½-4 in.); fragrant; foliage glossy; vigorous growth.

Misty Morn HT, *ly*, 1949, *Seedling* × *Mrs. Charles Lamplough*; McGredy. Flowers pale lemon-yellow, dbl. (45 petals), pointed, large; slightly fragrant; foliage dark.

Mitcheltonii S, *mp*, 1966, *(R.* × *mitcheltonii)*; *R. multiflora* × *I.X.L.*; Armbrust. Flowers pink, single, small; foliage small, leathery; thornless; very vigorous, climbing growth; profuse spring bloom.

Mitsouko® HT, *yb*, 1970, (DELnat); *(Michèle Meilland* × *Chic Parisien)* × *Peace*; Delbard, G. Flowers yellow, petals edged red, dbl. (50 petals), large; fruity fragrance; foliage medium, clear green; bronze-red prickles; dense, bushy growth.

Mitzi HT, *yb*, 1956, *(Peace* × *Mme. Joseph Perraud)* × *(Mrs. Pierre S. duPont* × *Mrs. John Laing)*; Meilland, F.; URS. Flowers pearly tints flushed mauve-rose, dbl. (35 petals), well formed; strong stems; fragrant; foliage dark; upright, bushy growth. GM, Rome, 1956.

Miyabi HT, *w*, 1977, *(Amatsu-Otome* × *Samba)* × *(Kordes' Perfecta* × *American Heritage)*; Teranishi, K.; Itami Bara-en, 1976. Bud ovoid; flowers near white, dbl. (30 petals), high-centered, large (4-4½ in.); slightly fragrant; upright growth.

Miyagino Cl Min, *pb*, 1978, *Nozomi × Seedling*; Onodera, T.; S. Onodera. Bud rounded; flowers light pink, single (5 petals), flat, small; foliage tiny.

Moana® Min, *mp*, 1978, (MACbipi); *Seedling × New Penny*; McGredy, S., IV; Flowers rose-pink, dbl. (35 petals), small; slightly fragrant; foliage glossy, dark.

Model of Perfection F, *ob*, 1977, *Zorina × Arthur Bell*; Dickson, A. Bud globular; flowers yellow, pink and orange, dbl. (28 petals), large; slightly fragrant.

Modern Art® HT, *rb*, 1985, (POUlart; Prince de Monaco); *Seedling × Seedling*; Olesen, M. & P.; D.T. Poulsen, 1983. Flowers medium red, dark red petal edges, spreading with age, reverse lighter, dbl. (25 petals), well-formed, large blooms borne singly; slight fragrance; foliage medium, dark, matt; upright, bushy growth. GM, Rome, 1984.

Modern Times HT, *rb*, 1956, *Better Times sport*; Verbeek; Minier. Flowers red striped pink.

Modesty HT, *pb*, 1916, McGredy. Bud pointed; flowers white, center rose-pink, dbl., high-centered, large; very fragrant. GM, NRS, 1915.

Moeder des Vaderlands F, *mr*, 1956, (Mère de la Patrie; Mother's Country); *Ambassadeur Nemry × Cinnabar*; Leenders, M. Flowers bright vermilion-red; strong stems; vigorous growth.

Mogador D (OGR), *dr*, (Roides Pourpres); *Rose du Roi sport*. Flowers deeper in color; repeats sparingly. Sometimes wrongly called Crimson Superb.

Mohawk S, *m*, *R. rubrifolia × R. rugosa*; Central Exp. Farm. Flowers brighter than aster-purple, center white, single; foliage dull green; rounded, dwarf growth; profuse, non-recurrent bloom; hardy.

Mohican F, *mr*, 1961, *Garnette sport*; Thompson, J.H. Flowers dark rose-red.

Mohican HT, *mr*, 1937, *Seedling × Briarcliff*; J.H. Thompson's Sons. Bud long, pointed; flowers cherry-red, dbl., large; long stems; slightly fragrant; foliage leathery, glossy, dark; very vigorous growth.

Mohini F, *ob*, 1970, *Sea Pearl × Shola*; Div. of Vegetable Crops & Flori. Bud long, pointed; flowers chocolate-brown, base tinged yellow, dbl., full, medium; foliage glossy, dark; moderate, bushy growth.

Moïse G (OGR), *m*, 1828, Parmentier; Flowers rosy-carmine, shaded purplish slate, dbl., expanded, large; moderate upright growth.

Mojave HT, *ob*, 1954, *Charlotte Armstrong × Signora*; Swim; Armstrong Nursery. Bud long; flowers apricot-orange tinted red, prominently veined, dbl. (25 petals), high-centered, large (4-4½ in.); fragrant; foliage glossy; vigorous, upright growth. GM, Bagatelle; Geneva, 1953; AARS, 1954.

Mojave, Climbing Cl HT, *ob*, 1964, Trimper; Ruston.

Moje Hammarberg® HRg (S), *m*, 1931, Hammarberg; Stockholm Stads Gatukontor. Flowers reddish violet, dbl., large blooms on short, weak stems; very fragrant; fruit large, red; vigorous growth; recurrent bloom; hardy.

Molde® F, *or*, 1964, (TANnimoll; Mistigri); Tantau, Math. Flowers orange-red, dbl., medium blooms in clusters; foliage dark, glossy; bushy, low, compact. GM, Baden-Baden, 1964.

Molitor® HT, *or*, 1981, (GAUtira); *Junon × Tanagra*; Gaujard, J. Flowers deep orange-red, dbl. (35 petals), large; fragrant; foliage medium, dark, semi-glossy.

Mollie Claire™ Min, *w*, 1989, (KINclaire); *(Evelyn Fison × Magic Mist) × Baby Diana*; King, Gene; AGM Miniature Roses. Bud pointed; flowers white, pink edge blushing toward center, reverse white tipped pink, aging pinkblush to picotee, dbl. (28 petals), high-centered, exhibition, small, borne singly; no fragrance; foliage small, medium green, matt; prickles crooked, very few, white to brown; no fruit; bushy, low growth.

Molly Abdy HT, *rb*, 1957, *Southport × Seedling*; Abdy; Shepperson. Bud pointed; flowers deep scarlet to lighter red, dbl., medium; fragrant; vigorous growth.

Molly Bishop HT, *op*, 1951, Robinson, H. Bud long, pointed; flowers orange-pink, dbl., high-centered, large; very fragrant; foliage leathery, rich green; vigorous growth.

Molly Bligh HT, *pb*, 1917, Dickson, A.; Flowers deep pink, base deep orange; fragrant.

Molly Darragh HT, *pb*, 1930, McGredy. Bud pointed; flowers bright old-rose, base orange-yellow, dbl., high-centered, very large; fragrant.

Molly Doyle F, *pb*, 1963, *Étoile de Hollande × Queen Elizabeth*; Barter. Flowers old-rose-pink, base silvery white, single (6 petals), large (5 in.); very fragrant; foliage light green; low, bushy growth.

Molly Kirby F, *or*, 1980, *Matangi sport*; Wilson, George. Flowers vermilion.

Molly McGredy F, *rb*, 1969, (MACmo); *Paddy McGredy × (Mme. Léon Cuny × Columbine)*; McGredy, S., IV; McGredy. Flowers medium red, reverse silver, dbl. (35 petals), well-formed, large blooms in trusses; slightly fragrant; foliage dark, glossy. RNRS PIT,

1968; GM, RNRS, 1968, Belfast; Portland, 1971.

Molly Sharman-Crawford T (OGR), *w*, 1908, Dickson, A. Bud long, pointed; flowers greenish white, becoming whiter, very dbl., high-centered; fragrant; foliage sparse, rich green; bushy growth.

Molodost HT, *lp*, 1956, (Youth); *Staatspräsident Pats × Cathrine Kordes*; Sushkov. Flowers light pink, dbl. (37 petals), large (5 in.); strong stems; foliage dark; vigorous, upright growth.

Molodost Mira HT, *mr*, 1955, (Early Peace); *Peace × (Crimson Glory × Poinsettia)*; Klimenko. Flowers coral-red, dbl. (50 petals), well formed, large; fragrant; foliage dark; vigorous, well branched growth.

Momo HT, *dp*, 1987, *(Picnic × Kordes' Perfecta) × Christian Dior*; Ota, Kaichiro, 1988. Flowers deep pink, dbl. (35-40 petals), large, borne usually singly; slight fragrance; foliage medium, dark green; prickles pointed, straight; fruit medium, copper.

Mon Amour, Climbing Cl HT, *pb*, 1966, *Peace, Climbing × Caprice*; Coggiatti. Bud ovoid; flowers phlox-pink, reverse silver-rose, dbl., cupped, large; fragrant; foliage dark, leathery; very vigorous growth; profuse, intermittent bloom.

Mon Cheri™ HT, *rb*, 1981, (AROcher); *(White Satin × Bewitched) × Double Delight*; Christensen; Armstrong Nursery. Bud ovoid, pointed; flowers medium pink, suffusing to near yellow at base, aging to dark red, dbl. (38 petals), formal blooms borne singly, sometimes 3 per cluster; light, spicy fragrance; foliage semiglossy, medium green; short prickles; upright, medium growth. AARS, 1982.

Mon Pays Gr, *w*, 1983, (Rigobec); *Iceberg × Peace*; Gailloux, Gilles. Flowers white, dbl. (40+ petals), large; slight fragrance; foliage medium to large, medium green, glossy; upright.

Mon Petit Min, *dp*, 1947, *Merveille des Rouges × Pompon de Paris*; Dot, P.; URS. Flowers light red, dbl. (80 petals); foliage pointed; dwarf, compact growth.

Mona F, *mr*, 1957, *Rudolph Timm × Fanal*; Kordes, R.; Dehner & Co. Flowers light crimson, center lighter, dbl., high-centered, medium (2 in.), borne in large clusters; slightly fragrant; foliage light green; vigorous, upright, bushy growth.

Mona Lisa Cl HT, *pb*, 1956, *Mrs. Sam McGredy × ((Mrs. Sam McGredy × (Seedling × Capt. Thomas))*; Malandrone; Armstrong Nursery. Bud ovoid; flowers warm pink overcast cameo-pink, dbl. (35-40 petals), cupped to flat, large (4-4½ in.), borne singly and in

clusters; very fragrant; foliage dark, leathery; vigorous, bushy pillar or climbing (8-10 ft.) growth; free, recurrent bloom.

Mona Rosette F, *pb*, 1963, *Pink Rosette sport*; Manski; Paulen Park Nursery. Bud ovoid; flowers pink and white striped, dbl., cupped, medium, in clusters; foliage dark, leathery; bushy, low growth.

Mona Ruth Min, *mp*, 1959, *((Soeur Thérèse × Skyrocket) × (Seedling × Red Ripples)) × Zee*; Moore, R.S.; Sequoia Nursery. Flowers medium pink, dbl. (30 petals), small (1-1½ in.); slightly fragrant; foliage leathery; vigorous (12-14 in.), bushy growth.

Monarch HT, *mp*, 1926, Dobbie. Bud pointed; flowers silvery pink, dbl., high-centered, very large; fragrant.

Mönch F, *mp*, 1952, *Karl Weinhausen Seedling*; Tantau. Flowers pink, dbl., large; large corymbs; foliage dark, leathery; vigorous, upright growth.

Moncton HRg (S), *lp*, 1977, *Schneezwerg × R. chinensis*; Svedja; Canada Dept. of Agric. Bud ovoid; flowers light pink, dbl. (20 petals), medium (2 in.); very fragrant; foliage gray-green; upright, bushy growth.

Mondial Pink HT, *pb*, 1965, Mondial Roses. Flowers pink, base yellow, high-centered, medium; slightly fragrant; foliage glossy; a greenhouse variety.

Mondovision HT, *dp*, 1969, (DELbrat); *Dr. Albert Schweitzer × (Bayadère × Mme. Rene Cassin)*; Schweitzer; Trioreau. Flowers cyclamen-pink, dbl. (35-45 petals), large (4-5 in.); fragrant.

Moneta F, *pb*, 1969, *Garnette sport*; Freytag; Santhof. Bud ovoid; flowers pinkish red, very dbl., small; foliage dark.

Monette R, *w*, 1921, *R. wichuraiana × Yvonne Rabier*; Hémeray-Aubert. Flowers white, very dbl., small, borne in clusters; very fragrant; vigorous, climbing growth.

Monette Pol, *rb*, 1922, *Phyllis × Seedling*; Turbat. Flowers fiery red, passing to rose, with many white streaks, borne in clusters of 60-100.

Monika® HT, *pb*, 1985, (TANaknom; Monica); Tantau, M., 1986. Flowers pink blend, dbl. (35 petals), medium; slight fragrance; foliage medium, dark, glossy; upright growth.

Monique HT, *op*, 1949, *Lady Sylvia × Seedling*; Paolino; URS. Flowers medium salmon-pink, dbl. (25 petals), well-shaped, large; very fragrant; vigorous, upright growth. GM, NRS, 1950.

Mons. Boncenne HP (OGR), *dr*, 1864, (M Boncenne); Liabaud. Flowers deep crimson, dbl., medium; moderate growth.

Mons. Louis Ricard HP (OGR), *m*, 1894, *Simon de St. Jean × Abel Carrière*; Boutigny. Flowers blackish purple, shaded vermilion, full, cupped, large; fragrant; vigorous growth.

Mons. Paul Lédé HT, *pb*, 1902, Pernet-Ducher. Flowers carmine-pink, shaded yellow, full, cupped, large; fragrant.

Mons. Paul Lédé, Climbing Cl HT, *pb*, 1913, Low.

Mons. Rosier T (OGR), *pb*, 1887, Nabonnand. Flowers rose and yellow.

Mons. Tillier T (OGR), *op*, 1891, Bernaix, A. Flowers rosy flesh, shaded salmon-rose and purple-rose, fairly full, large, opening well, often imbricated; vigorous.

Mont Hamel LCl, *mp*, 1937, Constantin. Flowers pink, semi-dbl., globular, borne in clusters; foliage glossy; very vigorous, climbing growth.

Mont-à-camp HT, *yb*, 1928, Delobel; Flowers pure yellow, reverse shaded orange, full, very large; vigorous, upright growth.

Monte Carlo HT, *ob*, 1949, *Peace × Seedling*; Meilland, F.; URS. Flowers indian yellow suffused russet-orange, dbl. (45 petals), well shaped, large (5 in.); fragrant; foliage glossy; vigorous growth. GM, NRS, 1950.

Monte Cristo HP (OGR), *dr*, 1861, Fontaine. Flowers dark red, full (50 petals), globular, large; low growth.

Monte Igueldo HT, *dr*, 1944, *Étoile de Hollande × Majorca*; La Florida. Flowers velvety dark red, well formed, open; very fragrant; upright, open habit.

Monte Toro HT, *pb*, 1962, *Berthe Mallerin × Grand'mère Jenny*; Dot, S. Flowers strawberry-pink shaded red, dbl., large; fragrant.

Monterey HT, *rb*, 1933, *The Queen Alexandra Rose sport*; Lester Rose Gardens; Flowers light gold flushed rose, veined and edged crimson, reverse lemon-yellow, dbl., very large; fragrant (fruity).

Monterosa HT, *pb*, 1952, *Elettra × Superba Alcarda*; Giacomasso. Flowers deep rose, edged lighter, dbl. (40 petals), peony form; very vigorous growth. GM, Rome, 1952.

Montesquieu HT, *pb*, 1959, *Loli Creus × Tahiti*; Dot, S. Flowers deep rose shaded crimson, dbl. (45 petals), high-centered; strong stems; fragrant; very vigorous growth.

Montezuma Gr, *op*, 1955, *Fandango × Floradora*; Swim; Armstrong Nursery. Bud urn-shaped; flowers orange-pink, dbl. (36 petals), high-centered, large (3½-4 in.); slightlyfragrant; foliage leathery, semi-glossy; very vigorous, compact growth. GM, Geneva, 1955, NRS, 1956; Portland, 1957.

Monthly Rambler LCl, *dr*, 1926, *R. wichuraiana × Slater's Crimson China*; Laxton Bros. Flowers brilliant crimson-red, semi-dbl., large, borne in clusters; fragrant; blooms throughout summer and on young wood in autumn.

Monthyon G (OGR), *m*, (Montigny); Flowers slaty pink blotched purple, full, globular, large.

Montijo F, *dr*, 1954, *Méphisto × Magrana*; Dot, P. Bud ovoid; flowers crimson-red, dbl. (40 petals), medium; very vigorous growth.

Montmartre F, *m*, 1955, *Peace × Seedling*; Gaujard. Bud ovoid; flowers bright purplish red, full, large; fragrant; foliage dark, bronze; very vigorous growth.

Montparnasse, Climbing Cl HT, *ab*, 1980, *Montparnasse sport*; Kodoya, Y.; Ogura Rose Nursery. Flowers apricot, dbl. (34 petals), high-centered, large; slight fragrance; foliage coppery green, leathery, semi-glossy; bushy, vigorous growth.

Montreal® HT, *pb*, 1980, (GAUzeca); *Americana × Dora*; Gaujard, Jean. Bud long; flowers cream and pink blend, dbl. (45 petals), large; fragrant; foliage large, dark; green prickles.

Montrose HT, *dp*, 1916, *Red Seedling × Laurent Carle*; Cook, J. Flowers deep pink.

Montrouge F, *rb*, 1956, *Peace × Alain Seedling*; Gaujard. Flowers clear red, center tinted copper, semi-dbl., medium; slightly fragrant; foliage glossy; vigorous, bushy growth.

Montseny HT, *op*, 1944, *Mme. Butterfly × Jean C.N. Forestier*; Dot, P. Flowers salmon-pink, well formed, full (40 petals), high-centered; very fragrant; foliage glossy; upright growth.

Montserrat HT, *op*, 1954, *Comtesse Vandal × Angels Mateu*; Camprubi. Flowers orange-salmon-pink, dbl., cupped, large; fragrant; foliage dark, glossy; very vigorous, upright growth.

Monviso HT, *pb*, 1955, *Julien Potin × Monterosa*; Giacomasso. Bud pointed; flowers white streaked pink, dbl., large; strong stems; slightly fragrant.

Monymusk HMsk (S), *my*, 1954, *Pax × Phyllis Gold*; Ratcliffe. Flowers clear yellow, semi-dbl., large; fragrant; vigorous (3-4 ft.) growth; recurrent bloom.

Mood Music Min, *op*, 1977, *Fairy Moss × Goldmoss*; Moore, R.S.; Sequoia Nursery. Bud mossy; flowers orange to orange-pink, dbl. (45 petals), flat to rounded, mini-moss, small (1 in.); slightly fragrant; foliage small; upright, bushy growth.

Moon Glow LCl, *pb*, 1937, *Glenn Dale × Mrs. Arthur Curtis James*; Brownell; Flowers creamy primrose, center soft yellow, dbl. (60-75 petals), large (3 in.); strong stems; fragrant; vigorous growth.

Moon Maiden F, *ly*, 1970, *Fred Streeter × Allgold*; Mattock. Flowers creamy yellow, dbl. (55 petals), large (3¹/₂-4 in.); fragrant; foliage dark.

Moon Mist™ Min, *w*, 1985, (PIXimis); *The Optimist × Darling Flame*; Strawn, Leslie E.; Pixie Treasures Min. Roses. Flowers ivory tinged pale pink, dbl. (20 petals), well-formed, small; fragrant; foliage small, medium green, semiglossy; bushy growth.

Moonbeam HT, *dy*, 1950, *Seedling × McGredy's Yellow*; Robinson, H.; Baker's Nursery. Flowers deep golden yellow, high-centered, large; fragrant; foliage dark, glossy. RULED EXTINCT 4/92.

Moonbeam S, *ab*, 1992, (AUSbeam); Austin, David; David Austin Roses, 1983. Flowers apricot yellow, semi-dbl. (6-14 petals), medium (4-7 cms) blooms borne in small clusters; very fragrant; foliage medium, light green, semi-glossy; some prickles; medium (100 cms), bushy growth.

Moonbeam, Climbing Cl HT, *dy*, 1955, Kordes.

Moondrops HT, *op*, 1965, *Sunny Boy × Seedling*; Delforge. Bud ovoid; flowers rose-amaranth shaded salmon, single, open; very fragrant (spicy); vigorous growth.

Moonlight HMsk (S), *ly*, 1913, *Trier × Sulphurea*; Pemberton. Flowers lemon-white, prominent yellow stamens, single, blooms in small clusters; fragrant; foliage dark, glossy; vigorous (4-5 ft.), bushy growth; repeat bloom. GM, NRS, 1913.

Moonlight Lady Min, *w*, 1986, (SOCalp); *Pink Petticoat × Pink Petticoat*; Eagle, Barry & Dawn; Southern Cross Nursery, 1987. Flowers creamy white, center buff pink, dbl. (52 petals), HT form, small blooms borne 1-3 per cluster; slight fragrance; foliage medium, dark, semi-glossy; narrow, red prickles; upright growth.

Moonlight Magic HT, *m*, 1991, *Seedling × Seedling*; Burks, Larry; Co-Operative Rose Growers. Flowers lavender, moderately full, medium blooms borne mostly singly; slight fragrance; foliage medium, medium green, matt; medium, bushy growth.

Moonlight Mist HT, *w*, 1965, *Buccaneer × Golden Harvest*; Armbrust; Langbecker. Bud pointed; flowers ivory-white, dbl., very large; slightly fragrant; very vigorous growth.

Moonlight Niagara® HT, *or*, 1987, *Red Queen sport*; Rogin, Josip. Flowers orange, reverse pale orange, very dbl. (60 petals),

high-centered, loose, star-shaped, medium, borne singly; moderate, spicy fragrance; foliage large, dark green, matt; semi-thick, medium, brow-red prickles; fruit rounded, medium, orange-red; upright, tall growth.

Moonlight Sonata HT, *ab*, 1966, *Diamond Jubilee Seedling × (Goldilocks × Orange Nassau)*; Boerner; J&P. Bud ovoid; flowers apricot, dbl., cupped, large; fragrant; foliage dark, glossy; vigorous, upright, bushy growth.

Moonraker® F, *ly*, 1968, *Pink Parfait × Highlight*; Harkness. Flowers pale yellow to white, dbl., large blooms in clusters; slightly fragrant; foliage light green.

Moonsprite F, *ly*, 1956, *Sutter's Gold × Ondine*; Swim; Armstrong Nursery. Bud ovoid; flowers creamy white, center pale gold, dbl. (80 petals), cupped, medium (2-2¹/₂ in.) blooms in clusters; very fragrant; foliage leathery, semi-glossy; dwarf, bushy growth. GM, Baden-Baden, 1955; Rome, 1956.

Moose Range HRg (S), *mr*, 1944, *Hansa × Mary L. Evans*; Wright, P.H.; Nearly the same color as Hansa but less fall bloom.

MORain Min, *yb*, 1989, (Lucky Charm); *Rumba × Pinstripe*; Moore, Ralph S.; Sequoia Nursery. Bud ovoid; flowers yellow, reverse tinting red, aging to pink to red, lightly striped, dbl. (50-60 petals), high-centered, exhibition, small, borne in sprays of 3-5; no fragrance; foliage small, medium green, matt; prickles straight, small, brown; no fruit; bushy, spreading, low growth.

Morden Amorette S, *dp*, 1977, *(Independence × (Donald Prior × R. arkansana)) × (Fire King × (J.W. Fargo × Assiniboine))*; Marshall, H.H.; Agriculture Canada. Bud pointed; flowers deep pink, dbl. (28 petals), large (3 in.); foliage dark.

Morden Blush S, *lp*, 1988, *(Prairie Princess × Morden Amorette) × (Prairie Princess × (White Bouquet × (R. arkansana × Assiniboine)))*; Collicutt, L.M.; Marshall, H.H.; Agriculture Canada. Flowers light pink, fading to ivory, dbl. (51 petals), flat, small, borne in sprays of 1-5; foliage medium, medium green, matt; prickles straight; bushy, low, hardy growth; repeats.

Morden Cardinette S, *mr*, 1980, *(Prairie Princess × (White Bouquet × (J.W. Fargo × Assiniboine)) × (Adelaide Hoodless × (Independence × (Donald Prior × R. arkansana))*; Marshall, H.H.; Agriculture Canada. Bud ovoid; flowers cardinal red, dbl. (25 petals), blooms borne 1-5 per cluster, occasionally 15 per cluster; faint fragrance; foliage 7 leaflets, globuous, dark.

Morden Centennial S, *mp*, 1980, *Prairie Princess × (White Bouquet × (J.W. Fargo × Assiniboine))*; Marshall, H.H.; Agriculture Canada. Bud ovoid; flowers medium pink, dbl. (50 petals), blooms borne 1-15 per cluster; light fragrance; foliage 7 leaflets, dark, slightly glossy; slightly recurved prickles; typical shrub growth; flowers on new growth; repeat bloom.

Morden Fireglow S, *or*, 1989, *Seedling × Morden Cardinette*; Collicutt, L.M.; Marshall, H.H.; Agriculture Canada, 1991. Bud pointed; flowers red-orange, reverse red, dbl. (28 petals), cupped, loose, medium, borne in sprays of 1-5; slight fragrance; foliage medium, medium green, matt; prickles slight downward curve, tan; fruit globular, reflexed calyx; bushy, low, medium growth; repeats.

Morden Ruby S, *pb*, 1977, *Fire King × (J.W. Fargo × Assiniboine)*; Marshall, H.H.; Agriculture Canada. Bud ovoid; flowers pink blend, very dbl., large (2½-3½ in.); vigorous, irregular growth; heavy bloom.

More Vale Pride Gr, *mp*, 1957, *Ma Perkins × Overloon*; Ulrick. Flowers pink.

Morga HRg (S), *mp*, Flowers pink, dbl., blooms in clusters.

Morgenglans HT, *op*, 1916, Van Rossem. Flowers salmon-flesh, semi-dbl., slightly fragrant.

Morgengrüss K (S), *op*, 1962, (Morning Greeting); Kordes, R. Bud ovoid; flowers light pink tinted orange-yellow, dbl., large blooms in clusters; very fragrant; foliage glossy, light green; very vigorous (13-14 ft.), bushy growth.

Morgenluft F, *pb*, 1962, *La France × Seedling*; Verschuren, A.; van Engelen. Flowers dark pink, reverse lighter, dbl. (55-60 petals), borne in clusters; foliage dark buff-green; upright, bushy growth.

Morgenröte HT, *mp*, 1951, Burkhard. Flowers pink. RULED EXTINCT 12/85.

Morgenrot® S, *rb*, 1985, (KORheim); *(Marlena × Europeana) × ((Tropicana × Carina) × (Cläre Grammerstorf × Frühlingsmorgen))*; Kordes, W. Flowers red blend, single (5 petals), medium; slight fragrance; foliage small, dark, matt; bushy growth.

Morgensonne S, *my*, 1954, (Morgensen; Morning Sun); Kordes. Bud ovoid; flowers golden yellow, very large; fragrant; foliage glossy, light green; very vigorous, upright, bushy.

Moriah HT, *ob*, 1984, (GANhol); *Fragrant Cloud × Seedling*; Holtzman, Arnold; Gandy's Roses Ltd. Flowers creamy yellow, orange reverse, dbl. (35 petals), large; very fragrant; foliage large, dark, matt; bushy growth.

Morletii Bslt (OGR), *m*, 1883, (Inermis Morletii); Morlet. Flowers magenta, small to medium blooms in clusters; little fragrance; calyx glandular; receptacle smooth; branches plum-colored, without prickles; very hardy; 5 ft. Has been confused with Mme. de Sancy de Parabère and perhaps with an earlier Inermis (prior to 1844). (14).

MORmuri HBc (OGR), *lp*, 1989, (Muriel); *R. bracteata × Guinee*; Moore, Ralph S.; Sequoia Nursery. Bud ovoid; flowers light to medium pink, aging slightly lighter, semi-dbl. (15 petals), flat, large, borne singly and in sprays of 3-5; foliage large, medium green, semi-glossy; prickles sharp, pointed, average, brown; fruit short, oval, large, orange, prickly; spreading, tall growth.

Morning Dawn LCl, *lp*, 1955, *New Dawn Seedling × R.M.S. Queen Mary*; Boerner; J&P. Flowers silvery rose flushed salmon, dbl. (63 petals), high-centered, large (5 in.); fragrant (spicy); foliage dark, glossy, leathery; vigorous, pillar (6-8 ft.) growth.

Morning Glory Cl HT, *rb*, 1937, *Portadown Sally sport*; Beckwith. Flowers carmine, reverse sulphur-yellow stained carmine, dbl., well formed; fragrant; very vigorous, climbing growth.

Morning Jewel® LCl, *mp*, 1968, *New Dawn × Red Dandy*; Cocker. Flowers pink, semi-dbl., large; fragrant; foliage glossy; recurrent bloom. ADR, 1975.

Morning Joy HT, *ab*, 1968, *Mischief sport*; Williamson. Flowers creamy amber, reverse flushed coppery pink, well formed, full; slightly fragrant; foliage light green; vigorous, upright growth.

Morning Mist HT, *m*, 1950, Fisher, G.; Arnold-Fisher Co. Flowers lavender tinted gray, semi-dbl., (15-20 petals), high-centered, medium (3½ in.); fragrant; moderately vigorous, upright growth; primarily a greenhouse rose.

Morning Stars S, *w*, 1949, *(New Dawn × Autumn Bouquet) × (New Dawn × Inspiration)*; Jacobus; B&A. Bud ovoid; flowers white, dbl., cupped, medium (3 in.), clusters; fragrant; foliage glossy; upright, bushy, compact; free, recurrent bloom.

Morocco HT, *mr*, 1961, *Carrousel × Charles Mallerin*; Abrams, Von; Peterson & Dering. Bud pointed; flowers velvety red, dbl. (30 petals), high-centered, large (5 in.); fragrant; foliage glossy; vigorous, upright growth.

Mosaïque F, *yb*, 1960, *(Alain × Cinnabar) × Circus*; Lens. Flowers light yellowish pink, becoming red, semi-dbl., open; foliage light green; low, bushy growth.

Moschata Grandiflora HMsk (S), *w*, 1866, *R. moschata* × *R. multiflora*; Bernaix, A. Flowers white, prominent golden stamens, single, large; very fragrant; very vigorous growth.

Mosel R, *m*, 1920, *Mme. Norbert Levavasseur* × *Trier*; Lambert, P. Flowers bluish violet, center reddish violet, dbl.; slightly fragrant; sometimes recurrent bloom.

Mosellied HMsk (S), *m*, 1932, *(Geheimrat Dr. Mittweg* × *Tip-Top)* × *(Chamisso* × *Parkzierde)*; Lambert, P. Flowers purplish red, center white, stamens golden yellow, single, petals heart shaped; large, upright panicle; very fragrant; foliage dark; vigorous (about 6½ ft.), broad growth; non-recurrent bloom.

Moss Magic Min, *mp*, 1977, *Fairy Moss* × *Seedling*; Sudol. Bud cupped, mossy; flowers medium to dark pink, dbl. (48 petals), circular, flat, small (1 in.); foliage dark; spreading growth; profuse bloom, repeating well.

Mossman S, *mp*, 1954, *(R. acicularis* × *R. rugosa)* × *Moss rose*; Skinner. Flowers heavily mossed, pale dusty pink, very dbl., medium (2½ in.); vigorous (4 ft. through) growth.

Mossy Gem Min, *mp*, 1984, *Heidi* × *Violette*; Kelly, Martin. Bud small, mossy; flowers medium pink, outer petals fading, dbl. (40+ petals), small; slight fragrance; foliage medium, dark, semi-glossy; bushy growth.

Mossy Rose de Meaux M (OGR), *mp*, (Mossy de Meaux); *Rose de Meaux sport*; Reported in 1801; Same except mossy buds.

Mother HT, *pb*, 1939, *Memory sport*; Cant, B.R. Flowers white edged bright pink; very fragrant.

Mother and Baby® HT, *dr*, 1988, (SANbaby); *Bristol* × *(Lilac Rose* × *(Magenta* × *Crimson Glory))*; Sanday, John; John Sanday Roses, Ltd. Flowers dark red with a velvet sheen, some black marking, reverse deep red-matt, unfading, dbl. (48 petals), flat, quartered, medium, borne usually singly and sometimes in sprays; foliage medium, medium green, semi-glossy; prickles barbed, light brown; low growth.

Mother Marie Pol, *w*, 1954, *Garnette sport*; Podesta. Flowers white, center green, dbl. (40 petals), flat, small (1½-2 in.), borne in clusters; foliage light green.

Mothersday Pol, *dr*, 1949, (Fête des Mères; Morsdag; Muttertagers; Day); *Dick Koster sport*; Grootendorst, F.J. Flowers deep red, dbl., globular, medium blooms in clusters (up to 20); foliage glossy, small; dwarf growth. Good for forcing as pot plant.

Mother's Day HT, *w*, 1937, Knight, G. Flowers white, at times shaded pink, very large; very vigorous growth.

Mothersday, Climbing Cl Pol, *dr*, 1956, (Muttertag, Climbing); Kordes.

Mother's Day Orange Sport Pol, *ob*, 1958, *Mothersday sport*; Klyn. Flowers orange-yellow.

Mother's Love Min, *pb*, 1989, (TINlove); *Futura* × *Party Girl*; Bennett, Dee; Tiny Petals Nursery, 1988. Bud ovoid; flowers pastel pink, blending to soft yellow at base, dbl. (23 petals), high-centered, exhibition, medium, borne usually singly and in sprays of 3-5; slight, fruity fragrance; foliage medium, medium green, semi-glossy; prickles straight, tapering, reddish; fruit globular, green to yellow-brown; upright, bushy, medium growth.

Motrea F, *mr*, 1968, *Coronet sport*; Mosselman; Terreehorst. Bud ovoid; flowers light red, very dbl., small; foliage dark.

Motylek HT, *w*, 1954, (Butterfly Papilio); *Freiburg II* × *Golden Dawn*; Shtanko, I. Flowers cream, base yellow, dbl. (40-45 petals), high-centered, medium; fragrant; moderate growth with thin, strong shoots.

Moulin Rouge® F, *mr*, 1952, (Sans souci); *Alain* × *Orange Triumph*; Meilland, F.; URS. Flowers medium red, dbl. (20-25 petals), cupped, medium (2 in.) blooms in clusters; slightly fragrant; foliage glossy; upright, very bushy growth. GM, NRS; Geneva, 1952; NRS PIT, 1952.

Moulin Rouge, Climbing Cl F, *mr*, 1957, Mondial Roses; URS.

Mount Everest S, *mp*, *Hybrid of R. pendulina*. Flowers larger; fruit larger; greater vigor.

Mount Hobben HT, *mr*, 1981, *Duftzauber* × *Christian Dior*; Ota, Kaichiro. Flowers bright scarlet, dbl. (30 petals), high-centered, large blooms borne 1-3 per stem; no fragrance; foliage medium green; many, small prickles; tall, upright growth.

Mount Homan HT, *ab*, 1983, *Ginger Rogers* × *Sunblest*; Ota, Kaichiro. Bud ovoid; flowers apricot, dbl. (35 quilled petals), high-centered, large blooms borne 1-3 per stem; slight fragrance; foliage dark, semi-glossy; large prickles; tall, upright, bushy growth.

Mt. Rai HT, *w*, 1987, *(Golden Scepter* × *Narcissus)* × *Ginger Rogers*; Ota, Kaichiro, 1988. Flowers white, pale cream at center, aging pale pink at edges, dbl. (42 petals), urn-shaped, high-centered, large, borne usually singly; slight fragrance; foliage dark green, semi-glossy; prickles medium, downward-shaped, slightly dented, green; fruit medium, yellow-green; bushy, medium growth.

Mt. St. Helens Gr, *dp*, 1981, *Seedling* × *Queen Elizabeth*; Northwest Rose Growers. Bud long, pointed; flowers deep pink, dbl. (35 petals), urn-shaped blooms borne 1-3 per cluster; slight spicy fragrance; foliage dark, leathery; bronze prickles; growth 4-5 ft.

Mount Shasta Gr, *w*, 1963, *Queen Elizabeth × Blanche Mallerin*; Swim & Weeks; C-P. Bud long, pointed; flowers white, dbl., cupped, large (4½-5 in.); fragrant; foliage leathery, gray-green; vigorous, upright growth.

Mt. Tara HT, *or*, 1987, *Ginger Rogers × Duftzauber*; Ota, Kaichiro, 1988. Flowers orange-red, dbl. (35 petals), high-centered, large, borne usually singly; slight fragrance; foliage dark green, semi-glossy; prickles medium, downward-shaped, slightly dented, green; fruit medium, yellow-green; bushy, medium growth.

Mountain Haze F, *m*, 1967, *Amy Vanderbilt × Lilac Time*; Morey; Country Garden Nursery. Flowers lavender, reverse silver; dbl. (55-60 petals), high-centered, medium; fragrant; foliage dark, leathery; vigorous, low, spreading growth.

Mountain Mist S, *m*, 1989, *Yesterday × Yesterday*; Jobson, Daniel J. Bud pointed; flowers purple-lavender shading to white at base, single (5 petals), flat, small, borne in sprays of 10-35; heavy, vanilla fragrance; foliage small, light green, semi-glossy; prickles very few, red; fruit globular, red; spreading, medium (4x6'), prolific growth.

Mountain Music S, *pb*, 1984, *Sevilla × Tom Brown*; Buck; Iowa State University. Flowers pink and yellow blend, dbl. (23 petals), cupped, medium blooms borne 5-15 per cluster; fragrant; foliage leathery, semi-glossy; awl-like, tanprickles; vigorous, erect, bushy growth; repeat bloom; hardy.

Mountain Snow R, *w*, 1985, (AUSsnow); Austin, David. Flowers white, dbl. (20 petals), small blooms in large sprays; slight fragrance; foliage large, dark, semi-glossy; vigorous (to 20 ft.) growth.

Mountaineer HT, *op*, 1963, *Mrs. Sam McGredy × Crimson Glory*; Wyant. Bud long, pointed, orange-red; flowers orange-pink, reverse creamy yellow, dbl. (35 petals), high-centered, large (5 in.); fragrant; foliage glossy; vigorous growth.

Mountbatten® F, *my*, 1982, (HARmantelle); *Peer Gynt × ((Anne Cocker × Arthur Bell) × Southampton)*; Harkness, R. Flowers medium yellow, dbl. (45 petals), cupped, large blooms borne singly or several together; fragrant; foliage large, leathery, glossy; many, large prickles; upright, dense growth. GM, Orleans, Belfast, 1982; Courtrai, 1986; ROTY, 1982; Golden Rose of The Hague, 1986

Mountie™ Min, *mr*, 1984, (LAVcale; LAVacek; LAVcali); *Party Girl × Dwarfking '78*; Laver, Keith; Springwood Consultants Ltd., 1985. Flowers medium red, dbl. (35 petals), high-centered; no fragrance; foliage small, dark, semi-glossy; bushy growth.

Mountjoy Sp (OGR), *lp*, *R. setigera natural Variant*; Found in Ohio, about 1840. Flowers blush, center darker, over 5 petals.

Mourne Gold HT, *yb*, 1980, *Whisky Mac sport*; Kane Brothers. Flowers deep yellow, pink flush.

Mousha HT, *lp*, 1974, *Colour Wonder × King's Ransom*; Kordes; Willemse. Bud long, pointed; flowers light pink, dbl. (24 petals), high-centered, large (4 in.); foliage glossy, dark; vigorous, upright growth.

Mousseline M (OGR), *w*, 1881, Moreau-Robert. Flowers white, lightly marked with rose, to pure white, dbl., cupped; few prickles, not well mossed; repeat bloom. Name used erroneously as a synonym for Alfred de Dalmas.

Mousseux Ancien M (OGR), *pb*, Vibert. Flowers pink, center shaded darker, well mossed.

Mousseux du Japon M (OGR), *mb*, (Japonica; Moussu du Japon; Muscosa Japonica). Bud and stems heavily mossed; flowers purplish rose, quickly fading to lavender, many stamens, semi-dbl.; growth moderate.

Mozart HMsk (S), *pb*, 1937, *Robin Hood × Rote Pharisäer*; Lambert, P. Flowers deep pink with large white eye, single, small blooms in clusters; fragrant; vigorous, trailing or bushy growth; repeat bloom.

Mridula HT, *w*, 1975, *Queen Elizabeth × Sir Henry Segrave Seedling*; Indian Agric. Research Inst. Bud long, pointed; flowers white, center soft pink, dbl. (35 petals), high-centered, large (3½ in.); fragrant; foliage large, light, soft; very vigorous, upright, erect growth.

Mrinalini HT, *mp*, 1973, *Pink Parfait × Christian Dior*; IARI. Bud long, pointed; flowers medium pink, dbl., high-centered, very large blooms borne singly; fragrant; foliage medium, medium green, soft; vigorous, bushy growth.

Mrs. Aaron Ward HT, *yb*, 1907, Pernet-Ducher. Bud long, pointed; flowers yellow, occasionally washed salmon (quite variable), dbl., high-centered; fragrant; dwarf, compact.

Mrs. Aaron Ward, Climbing Cl HT, *yb*, 1922, Dickson, A..

Mrs. A. J. Allen HT, *pb*, 1930, *Richmond × Souv. de Mme. Boullet*; Allen. Flowers rich pink, base lemon-yellow, tipped almost white, dbl. large; slightly fragrant.

Mrs. Albert Nash HT, *dr*, 1929, Clark, A.; NRS Victoria. Flowers dark red; fragrant.

Mrs. Alfred Tate HT, *rb*, 1909, McGredy. Flowers coppery red shaded fawn, base shaded ochre; fragrant.

Mrs. Alfred West HT, *op*, 1922, Cant, F. Flowers salmon-pink, dbl.; very fragrant.

Mrs. Ambrose Ricardo HT, *yb*, 1914, McGredy. Flowers deep honey-yellow, overlaid brighter yellow, dbl.; fragrant.

Mrs. Amy Hammond HT, *pb*, 1911, *Mme. Abel Chatenay Seedling*; McGredy. Flowers cream and amber, sometimes flushed pink, base apricot, dbl.; fragrant. GM, NRS, 1910.

Mrs. Andrew Carnegie HT, *w*, 1913, *Niphetos × Frau Karl Druschki*; Cocker. Flowers white, center lightly tinted lemon-yellow, dbl.; slightly fragrant. GM, NRS, 1912.

Mrs. Anne Dakin LCl, *pb*, 1972, Holmes, R.; Albrighton Roses. Flowers salmon-pink, reverse cream, full, medium (3½ in.); slightly fragrant; foliage glossy; moderate, climbing growth.

Mrs. Anthony Spalding HT, *or*, 1934, McGredy. Flowers strawberry-red flushed orange, reverse shaded orange, full, well shaped, large; vigorous growth.

Mrs. Anthony Waterer HRg (S), *dr*, 1898, *R. rugosa × Général Jacqueminot*; Waterer. Flowers deep crimson, semi-dbl.; very fragrant; vigorous growth; hardy; (21).

Mrs. A. R. Barraclough HT, *mp*, 1926, McGredy. Bud long, pointed; flowers bright carmine pink, dbl., high-centered, large; slightly fragrant; vigorous.

Mrs. A. R. Barraclough, Climbing Cl HT, *mp*, 1935, Fryer's Nursery.

Mrs. Archie Gray HT, *ly*, 1914, Dickson, H. Flowers deep creamy yellow, opening light canary-yellow. GM, NRS, 1913.

Mrs. Arnold Burr HT, *w*, 1945, *Peace × Seedling*; Burr, A. Flowers pure white, very dbl., high-centered, large; fragrant; foliage glossy; vigorous, upright growth.

Mrs. Arthur Curtiss James LCl, *my*, 1933, (Golden Climber); *Mary Wallace × Seedling*; Brownell; J&P. Bud long, pointed; flowers medium yellow, semi-dbl. (18 petals), large; fragrant; foliage glossy; vigorous, climbing; non-recurrent.

Mrs. Arthur E. Coxhead HT, *dr*, 1911, McGredy. Flowers claret-red, shaded brighter red, dbl.; fragrant.

Mrs. Arthur Johnson HT, *yb*, 1920, McGredy. Flowers rich orange-yellow to chrome-yellow; slightly fragrant.

Mrs. Arthur Robert Waddell HT, *pb*, 1909, Pernet-Ducher. Bud long, pointed; flowers reddish salmon, reverse rosy scarlet, fading, semi-dbl., open, large; slightly fragrant (apricot); vigorous growth.

Mrs. Atlee HT, *op*, 1926, Chaplin Bros. Flowers silvery pink, shaded soft salmon; fragrant.

Mrs. A. W. Atkinson HT, *w*, 1918, Chaplin Bros. Flowers ivory-white, dbl.

Mrs. Bayard Thayer HT, *pb*, 1915, *Mrs. Charles E. Russell sport*; Waban Conservatories. Flowers clear silvery pink, reverse deep rose.

Mrs. Beatty HT, *my*, 1926, Cant, B.R. Flowers Maréchal Niel yellow, well formed; fragrant; foliage bronze; vigorous growth. GM, NRS, 1925.

Mrs. Beckwith HT, *my*, 1922, Pernet-Ducher. Bud long, pointed; flowers buttercup-yellow, edged lighter, semi-dbl., open; slightly fragrant; vigorous growth. GM, NRS, 1923.

Mrs. Belmont Tiffany HT, *yb*, 1918, *Sunburst sport*; Budlong; A.N. Pierson. Flowers golden yellow, base apricot-orange.

Mrs. Bertram J. Walker HT, *dp*, 1915, Dickson, H. Flowers bright cerise-pink, full. GM, NRS, 1914.

Mrs. Blamire Young HT, *op*, 1932, *Una Wallace sport*; Young. Flowers salmon pink, slightly more petals than parent.

Mrs. Bosanquet B (OGR), *lp*, 1832, (Mistress Bosanquet); Laffay. Flowers rosy flesh, very dbl.; vigorous growth.

Mrs. B. R. Cant T (OGR), *mp*, 1901, (Mrs. Benjamin R. Cant); Cant, B.R. Flowers silvery rose, base suffused buff, reverse deep rose, dbl., cupped; fragrant; vigorous growth.

Mrs. B. R. Cant, Climbing Cl T (OGR), *mp*, 1960, Hjort.

Mrs. Breedlove HT, *pb*, 1947, *Golden Dawn sport*; Breedlove; Breedlove Nursery. Bud ovoid; flowers pink, base yellow, very dbl., very large; fragrant; foliage leathery, dark; vigorous, bushy growth.

Mrs. Brownell HT, *rb*, 1942, Brownell. Flowers red to pink and coppery orange, semi-dbl., medium; fragrant (spicy).

Mrs. Bryce Allan HT, *dp*, 1916, Dickson, A. Flowers rose-pink, very dbl.; very fragrant. GM, NRS, 1916.

Mrs. Bullen HT, *rb*, 1917, Pernet-Ducher. Flowers crimson, shaded yellow, passing to carmine, full.

Mrs. Calvin Coolidge HT, *yb*, 1924, *Ophelia sport*; U.S. Cut Flower Co.; F.R. Pierson. Bud long, pointed; flowers golden yellow, deepening to rich orange, semi-dbl.; fragrant.

Mrs. Campbell Hall T (OGR), *ab*, 1914, Hall; A. Dickson. Flowers soft creamy buff, edged or suffused rose, center warm salmon, high-centered, large; very fragrant; foliage leathery, dark; vigorous growth.

Mrs. C. E. Prell HT, *rb*, 1938, *Gustav Gruner-wald* × *Betty Uprichard*; Fitzhardinge; Hazlewood Bros. Bud long, pointed; flowers dark cerise, reverse pink, stamens golden, dbl., very large; long stems; very vigorous growth.

Mrs. Chaplin HT, *pb*, 1918, Chaplin Bros. Flowers creamy pink, base shaded yellow.

Mrs. Charles Bell HT, *op*, 1917, (Mrs. C.J. Bell; Salmon Radiance; Shell-Pink Radiance); *Red Radiance sport*; Bell, Mrs. C.J.; A.N. Pierson. Flowers shell-pink, shaded soft salmon.

Mrs. Charles Bell, Climbing Cl HT, *op*, 1929, Thomasville Nursery.

Mrs. Charles E. Pearson HT, *ob*, 1913, McGredy. Flowers orange-apricot, flushed fawn and yellow, well formed; fragrant. GM, NRS, 1912.

Mrs. Charles E. Russell HT, *dp*, 1914, *Mme. Caroline Testout* × *(Mme. Abel Chatenay* × *Marquise Litta de Breteuil)*; Montgomery, A.; Waban Conservatories. Bud long, pointed; flowers rosy carmine, dbl., globular, large; long stems; fragrant; foliage leathery; vigorous growth.

Mrs. Charles H. Rigg HT, *my*, 1946, McGredy. Bud long, pointed; flowers lemon-yellow, full, large; fragrant; vigorous growth.

Mrs. Charles Lamplough HT, *ly*, 1920, *Frau Karl Druschki* × *Seedling*; McGredy. Flowers pale lemon-yellow, dbl., very large; fragrant; vigorous growth. GM, NRS, 1919.

Mrs. Charles Reed HT, *w*, 1914, Hicks. Flowers pale cream, tinted deep peach, base soft golden yellow, dbl.; very fragrant.

Mrs. Charles Steward HT, *mp*, 1959, Verschuren; Gandy. Flowers bright pink, dbl., large; very fragrant; foliage dark; vigorous growth.

Mrs. Charles Tennant HT, *yb*, 1936, Cant, F. Flowers clear primrose, shaded rich canary-yellow; fragrant; foliage bronze; vigorous growth.

Mrs. Claude Aveling HT, *rb*, 1929, *The Queen Alexandra Rose* × *Gorgeous*; Bees. Flowers scarlet-cerise, tinted orange, base buttercup-yellow, anthers very prominent, semi-dbl., large; fragrant (fruity).

Mrs. Clement Yatman HT, *dr*, 1927, Hicks. Flowers deep crimson, dbl.; very fragrant.

Mrs. C. L. Fitzgerald F, *pb*, 1937, *Seedling* × *Cécile Brunner*; Fitzgerald. Bud pointed; flowers deep pink, base apricot-yellow, dbl., small; slightly fragrant; foliage glossy; upright growth.

Mrs. Colville HSpn (OGR), *m*, *Probably R. spinosissima* × *R. pendulina*. Flowers bright crimson-purple, white eye, single; vigorous (4 ft.) growth.

Mrs. Cornwallis West HT, *w*, 1911, Dickson, A. Flowers white, center blush, very large, globular, imbricated; vigorous growth. GM, NRS, 1910.

Mrs. Courtney Page HT, *ob*, 1922, McGredy. Bud long, pointed; flowers orange-cerise, shaded carmine, dbl., high-centered, very large; strong stems; fragrant. GM, NRS, 1922.

Mrs. Curnock Sawday HT, *mp*, 1920, Hicks. Flowers satiny pink, dbl., slightly fragrant.

Mrs. C. V. Haworth HT, *ab*, 1919, *Mrs. Wemyss Quin* × *Hugh Dickson*; Dickson, A. Flowers cinnamon-apricot, passing to buff, semi-dbl.; very fragrant.

Mrs. C. W. Dunbar-Buller HT, *dp*, 1919, Dickson, A. Flowers deep rosy carmine, dbl., large; very fragrant.

Mrs. C. W. Edwards HT, *rb*, 1924, McGredy. Bud pointed; flowers crimson-carmine, base yellow, reverse veined yellow, dbl., high-centered, very large; long stems; fragrant; foliage dark, glossy; very vigorous growth.

Mrs. C. W. Thompson R, *dp*, 1920, U.S. Dept. of Agric.; Storrs & Harrison Co. Flowers deep pink, dbl., quilled, small, borne in clusters; vigorous, climbing growth; good seasonal bloom.

Mrs. Dan Prosser HT, *rb*, 1946, *Mrs. Sam McGredy* × *Heinrich Wendland*; Prosser. Flowers red shaded gold, dbl. (60 petals), globular, high-centered, large (5½ in.); foliage glossy, dark red when young.

Mrs. David Baillie HT, *dp*, 1912, Dickson, H. Flowers carmine, penciled deeper, dbl.; fragrant.

Mrs. David McKee HT, *ly*, 1904, *Frau Karl Druschki* × *Kaiserin Auguste Viktoria*; Dickson, A. Flowers creamy yellow, well formed, large; dwarf, compact growth.

Mrs. Douglas Copland HT, *mp*, 1945, Clark, A. Flowers pink, full; vigorous growth.

Mrs. Dudley Cross T (OGR), *yb*, 1907, (Dudley Cross); Paul, W. Flowers pale yellow, tinted in autumn with crimson, full; slightly fragrant; no prickles; vigorous growth.

Mrs. Dudley Fulton Pol, *w*, 1931, *Dorothy Howarth* × *Perle d'Or*; Thomas; Armstrong Nursery. Flowers silver-white, single, large, borne in large clusters; dwarf growth.

Mrs. Dunlop Best HT, *ab*, 1916, (Cleveland II); Hicks. Bud long, pointed; flowers reddish apricot, base coppery yellow, dbl. (28 petals), large; fragrant; foliage leathery, bronze, glossy; vigorous growth.

Mrs. Dunlop Best, Climbing Cl HT, *ab*, 1933, Rosen, L.P..

Mrs. E. Claxton HT, *pb*, 1928, Cant, F. Flowers light pink, shaded salmon and carmine.

Mrs. Edith Stanley HT, *w*, 1919, Easlea. Flowers creamy white, shaded indian yellow.

Mrs. Edward J. Holland HT, *op*, 1909, McGredy. Flowers salmon-rose, large; fragrant; moderately vigorous growth. GM, NRS, 1909.

Mrs. Edward Laxton HT, *ob*, 1935, *Mrs. Henry Bowles × Shot Silk*; Laxton Bros. Flowers flaming orange and old-rose, very dbl., high-centered, large; foliage leathery, dark; very vigorous growth.

Mrs. Edward Powell HT, *dr*, 1911, Bernaix, P. Flowers velvety crimson, dbl.; fragrant.

Mrs. E. Gallagher HT, *dr*, 1924, McGredy. Flowers dark crimson, fragrant.

Mrs. E. G. Hill HT, *w*, 1906, *Mme. Caroline Testout × Liberty*; Soupert & Notting. Flowers alabaster-white, reverse rose-coral, dbl., well shaped, large; fragrant; vigorous growth.

Mrs. E. J. Hudson HT, *mp*, 1923, *Mrs. W.J. Grant Seedling*; Lilley. Flowers bright pink, dbl.; slightly fragrant.

Mrs. E. J. Manners HT, *dr*, 1938, Burbage Nursery. Flowers deep velvety crimson, becoming darker, well shaped; long, strong stems; vigorous, branching growth.

Mrs. Elisha Hicks HT, *w*, 1919, *Frau Karl Druschki × Mme. Gabriel Luizet*; Hicks. Flowers flesh, nearly white, dbl.; very fragrant.

Mrs. E. M. Gibson HT, *dr*, 1940, *Countess of Stradbrooke × Seedling*; Clark, A. Flowers dark red.

Mrs. E. M. Gilmer HT, *mr*, 1927, (Dorothy Dix); *Seedling × Crusader*; Cook, J. Flowers red.

Mrs. Erskine Pembroke Thom HT, *my*, 1926, *Grange Colombe × Souv. de Claudius Pernet*; Howard, F.H.; H&S. Bud long, pointed; flowers clear yellow, dbl. (40 petals), well formed, large; fragrant; vigorous growth.

Mrs. Erskine Pembroke Thom, Climbing Cl HT, *my*, 1933, Dixie Rose Nursery.

Mrs. E. T. Stotesbury HT, *pb*, 1918, *(Joseph Hill × My Maryland) × Milady*; Towill. Flowers light cream-pink, reverse dark pink, very dbl.

Mrs. Eveline Gandy HT, *dr*, 1959, Verschuren; Gandy. Flowers dark velvety crimson-scarlet, dbl. (50 petals), well formed, large; very fragrant.

Mrs. E. Willis HT, *lp*, *Mme. Segond Weber Seedling*; Weightman. Flowers light pink, semi-dbl.; fragrant; growth moderate.

Mrs. E. Willis, Climbing Cl HT, *lp*, 1948, Wilson.

Mrs. E. Wood HT, *yb*, 1934, Dickson, A. Bud very long; flowers light buff-yellow, tinted yellowish salmon, becoming cream-yellow, well formed, large; very fragrant; vigorous growth.

Mrs. E. W. Sterling HT, *mp*, 1916, *Antoine Rivoire × Pink Seedling*; Cook, J. Flowers rose-pink.

Mrs. Farmer HT, *yb*, 1918, Pernet-Ducher. Bud pointed; flowers yellow, reverse reddish apricot, dbl.; fragrant.

Mrs. F. F. Prentiss LCl, *lp*, 1925, *(R. setigera × R. wichuraiana) × Lady Alice Stanley*; Horvath. Flowers pale pink, dbl., large; vigorous, climbing growth; extremely hardy. The ancestor of many of the Horvath Setigera hybrids.

Mrs. F. J. Jackson HT, *mr*, 1933, LeGrice. Bud pointed; flowers cerise, dbl.; slightly fragrant; foliage leathery, bronze; vigorous growth.

Mrs. F. J. Knight HT, *mr*, 1928, *Lord Charlemont sport*; Knight, J. Flowers velvety scarlet; fragrant.

Mrs. Foley Hobbs T (OGR), *pb*, 1910, Dickson, A. Flowers soft ivory-white, edges tinged clear pink, dbl.; fragrant; vigorous, upright growth.

Mrs. Forde HT, *pb*, 1913, Dickson, A. Flowers carmine-rose on soft rose-pink, base chrome-yellow, dbl.; fragrant. GM, NRS, 1913.

Mrs. Francis King HT, *ly*, 1934, *Lady Lilford × Leonard Barron*; Nicolas; J&P. Flowers cream-white shaded straw-yellow, dbl. (80 petals), high-centered, large; slightly fragrant; foliage leathery; vigorous, bushy growth.

Mrs. Frank Guthrie HT, *lp*, 1923, *R. gigantea Seedling × Seedling*; Clark, A.; Hazelwood Bros. Flowers deep flesh in autumn, pale in summer, semi-dbl.; fragrant; foliage dark, leathery.

Mrs. Frank J. Usher HT, *yb*, 1920, *Queen Mary × Seedling*; Dobbie. Flowers rich yellow, edged rosy carmine, very dbl.; weak stems.

Mrs. Frank Schramm HT, *pb*, 1934, *Briarcliff sport*; Schramm. Flowers bright glowing rose-pink, reverse slightly lighter; dbl., very large; long stems; fragrant; foliage leathery, dark; very vigorous growth.

Mrs. Frank Serpa Pol, *dp*, 1954, *Rouletii × China Doll*; Serpa; Port Stockton Nursery. Flowers deep pink, borne in clusters; dwarf (18 in.) growth.

Mrs. Frank Verdon HT, *my*, 1935, *Joan Horton × Marion Horton*; Bees. Flowers creamy yellow, dbl., very large; slightly fragrant; foliage leathery, dark; vigorous growth.

Mrs. Frank Workman HT, *dp*, 1911, Dickson, H. Flowers bright rose-pink.

Mrs. Franklin Dennison HT, *w*, 1915, McGredy. Bud long, pointed; flowers porcelain-white, veiled primrose-yellow, base ochre, dbl., high-centered, very large; fragrant.

Mrs. Franklin D. Roosevelt HT, *dy*, 1933, *Talisman sport*; Traendly; Schenck. Bud long, pointed; flowers golden yellow, dbl., globular, large; fragrant; foliage glossy; very vigorous growth.

Mrs. Fred Cook HT, *ob*, 1920, Easlea. Flowers light terra-cotta, edged silvery white, dbl.; not vigorous.

Mrs. Fred Danks HT, *m*, 1951, Clark, A.; NRS Victoria. Bud long, pointed; flowers pink tinted lilac, semi-dbl. (15 petals), large; fragrant; foliage leathery; very vigorous, upright, pillar growth.

Mrs. Fred H. Howard HT, *ob*, 1926, Dobbie. Flowers orange-apricot edged straw-yellow, dbl.; very fragrant.

Mrs. Fred L. Lainson HT, *pb*, 1934, *Talisman sport*; Scittine; Lainson. Bud long, pointed; flowers deep pink, almost red, base yellow and bronze, reverse orange, dbl., large; fragrant; foliage leathery, glossy, bronze; vigorous growth.

Mrs. Fred Poulsom HT, *mp*, 1920, *Edith Part × Seedling*; Therkildsen. Flowers vivid pink; thorny; vigorous growth.

Mrs. Frederick W. Vanderbilt HT, *or*, 1912, McGredy. Flowers deep orange-red, shaded apricot, dbl. GM, NRS, 1913.

Mrs. F. R. Pierson HT, *dr*, 1926, *Premier sport*; Pierson, F.R. Bud pointed; flowers crimson, shaded scarlet, dbl., very large; very fragrant.

Mrs. F. W. Flight LCl, *dp*, 1905, *Crimson Rambler × Seedling*; Cutbush. Flowers rose-pink, semi-dbl., borne in clusters; foliage large, rich green, soft; Pillar (6-8 ft.) growth; non-recurrent bloom.

Mrs. F.W. Sanford HP (OGR), *lp*, 1898, *Mrs. John Laing sport*; Curtis. Flowers pink tinged white.

Mrs. G. A. Wheatcroft HT, *pb*, 1926, *Lady Pirrie sport*; Wheatcroft Bros. Flowers coppery pink to silver-rose at tips, reverse soft salmon-pink to carmine, dbl.; very fragrant.

Mrs. George B. Easlea HT, *dp*, 1939, Easlea. Flowers sparkling carmine-pink, well formed, high-centered, very large; strong stems; very fragrant.

Mrs. George C. Thomas HMsk (S), *op*, 1925, *Mme. Caroline Testout, Climbing × Moon-light*; Thomas; B&A. Flowers salmon-pink, center orange, semi-dbl. medium (2-2½ in.); fragrant; climbing growth to 10 ft.; repeat bloom.

Mrs. George Geary HT, *ob*, 1929, *Red-Letter Day × Mrs. Wemyss Quin*; Burbage Nursery. Bud pointed; flowers orange-cerise, shaded cardinal, dbl. (35-40 petals), high-centered, very large; very fragrant; vigorous growth.

Mrs. George Marriott HT, *w*, 1918, McGredy. Bud long, pointed; flowers deep cream and pearl, suffused rose, full, high-centered, very large; fragrant. GM, NRS, 1917.

Mrs. George Shawyer HT, *pb*, 1911, *Mme. Hoste × Joseph Lowe*; Lowe; Shawyer. Flowers rosy pink, reverse pale pink, dbl., very large; slightly fragrant.

Mrs. George Shawyer, Climbing Cl HT, *pb*, 1918, Lindquist, E.J..

Mrs. Georgia Chobe HT, *lp*, 1937, *Miss Rowena Thom × Renault*; H&S. Bud long; flowers light pink, dbl., high-centered, large; foliage leathery, light; vigorous growth.

Mrs. G. M. Smith HT, *dr*, 1935, *Red-Letter Day × Mrs. J.J. Hedley-Willis*; Bees. Bud long, pointed; flowers deep crimson, dbl., cupped; slightly fragrant; vigorous growth.

Mrs. Harold Alston Cl HT, *mp*, 1940, Clark, A. Flowers pink.

Mrs. Harold Bibby HT, *pb*, 1936, Bees. Flowers soft pink veined red, outer petals silvery pink; fragrant; foliage dark.

Mrs. Harold Brocklebank HT, *w*, 1907, Dickson, A. Flowers creamy white, center buff, base soft yellow, dbl.; fragrant.

Mrs. Harold Brookes HT, *mr*, 1931, *Frau Oberhofgartner Singer × Firebrand*; Clark, A.; NRS Victoria. Flowers very bright red, dbl., cupped, large; fragrant; foliage light; vigorous, bushy growth.

Mrs. H. Cobden Turner HT, *rb*, 1948, *Ophelia × Seedling*; Mee; Fryer's Nursery. Flowers cherry-cerise flushed orange, base yellow, dbl. (26 petals), large (3-4 in.); very fragrant; foliage glossy; moderately vigorous growth.

Mrs. H. D. Greene HT, *rb*, 1918, *Joseph Hill sport*; Easlea. Flowers reddish bronze, becoming flame and coppery pink; fragrant.

Mrs. Henri Daendels HT, *ab*, 1931, (Merrouw Daendels); *Mrs. Henry Bowles × Rev. F. Page-Roberts*; Buisman. Flowers apricot shaded orange, reverse violet-pink, very dbl., large; strong stems; very fragrant; foliage bronze; very vigorous growth.

Mrs. Henri Daendels, Climbing Cl HT, *ab*, 1950, Buisman.

Mrs. Henry Balfour HT, *pb*, 1918, McGredy. Flowers ivory-white, base primrose, edge penciled rose, like a picotee; fragrant.

Mrs. Henry Bowles HT, *mp*, 1921, *Lady Pirrie* × *Gorgeous*; Chapin Bros. Flowers rosy-pink, flushed salmon, dbl. (50 petals), well formed, high-centered, large; foliage dark, glossy; vigorous.

Mrs. Henry Bowles, Climbing Cl HT, *mp*, 1929, Dobbie.

Mrs. Henry Morse HT, *pb*, 1919, McGredy. Bud long, pointed; flowers cream, tinted rose, marked and veined red, dbl., high-centered, large; fragrant; dwarf growth. GM, NRS, 1919.

Mrs. Henry Morse, Climbing Cl HT, *pb*, 1929, Chaplin Bros..

Mrs. Henry Winnett HT, *dr*, 1917, *Mrs. Charles E. Russell* × *Mrs. George Shawyer*; Dunlop. Bud long, pointed; flowers deep rich red, dbl., high-centered, large; fragrant; foliage leathery; vigorous growth.

Mrs. Henry Winnett, Climbing Cl HT, *dr*, 1930, Bernaix, P..

Mrs. Herbert Carter HT, *ab*, 1934, Cant, F. Flowers apricot-yellow, center deeper, veined bronze, full, well formed, large; fragrant; vigorous growth.

Mrs. Herbert Dowsett HT, *pb*, 1928, *Los Angeles* sport; Easlea. Flowers several shades deeper, otherwise similar to parent.

Mrs. Herbert Hawksworth T (OGR), *r*, 1912, Dickson, A. Flowers ecru on milk-white, dbl.; fragrant.

Mrs. Herbert Hoover HT, *mr*, 1928, *Ophelia* × *Hoosier Beauty*; Coddington. Bud long, pointed; flowers rich velvety red, dbl., very fragrant; foliage dark, leathery; vigorous growth.

Mrs. Herbert Nash HT, *dr*, 1925, Chaplin Bros. Flowers scarlet-crimson shaded deep crimson, very large; long, strong stems; fragrant; vigorous growth.

Mrs. Herbert Stevens HT, *w*, 1910, *Frau Karl Druschki* × *Niphetos*; McGredy. Bud long, pointed; flowers white, dbl., high-centered; fragrant; foliage light; vigorous, bushy growth.

Mrs. Herbert Stevens, Climbing Cl HT, *w*, 1922, (Grimpant Mrs. Herbert Stevens; Stevens); Pernet-Ducher.

Mrs. H. G. Johnstone HT, *pb*, 1930, *Mme. Caroline Testout* × *Mrs. George Shawyer*; Bees. Bud long; flowers rose-pink, base and edges rose, dbl., high-centered, very large; slightly fragrant; vigorous growth.

Mrs. Hilton Brooks HT, *yb*, 1929, Cant, F. Flowers saffron-yellow, base deeper, suffused pink and carmine, dbl.; fragrant.

Mrs. H. L. Wettern HT, *mp*, 1922, McGredy. Flowers vivid pink, dbl.; fragrant.

Mrs. H. M. Eddie HT, *w*, 1932, *Mrs. Charles Lamplough* × *Mev. G.A. van Rossem*; Eddie. Flowers creamy white, passing to purest white, dbl. (40-45 petals), high-centered, large (5-6 in.); slightly fragrant; foliage dark, leathery, glossy; vigorous, bushy growth.

Mrs. H. M. Eddie, Climbing Cl HT, *w*, 1944, Eddie.

Mrs. Hornby Lewis HT, *ob*, 1921, *Gorgeous* × *Mme. Mélanie Soupert*; Hicks. Flowers orange-yellow, very dbl.; fragrant.

Mrs. Hovey HSet (OGR), *w*, 1850, *R. setigera* × *Seedling*; Pierce. Flowers blush to almost white; hardier than Baltimore Belle, but otherwise similar.

Mrs. H. R. Darlington HT, *ly*, 1919, McGredy. Bud long, pointed; flowers clear creamy yellow, well formed, balling in wet weather, very large; long stems; fragrant; vigorous growth. GM, NRS, 1919.

Mrs. Hugh Dettmann Cl HT, *ab*, 1930, Clark, A.; NRS Victoria. Flowers bright apricot-yellow; good pillar growth.

Mrs. Hugh Dickson HT, *yb*, 1915, Dickson, H. Flowers deep cream, heavily suffused orange and apricot, dbl. (44 petals). GM, NRS, 1916.

Mrs. Inge Poulsen F, *pb*, 1949, (Fru Inge Poulsen); *Poulsen's Pink* × *Seedling*; Poulsen, S.; Poulsen, 1949, McGredy; C-P, 1952. Flowers pink with a yellow center, semi-dbl., open, medium; slightly fragrant; foliage light, matt; vigorous, compact (80 cms.) growth.

Mrs. James Garner HT, *ab*, 1931, Cant, F. Flowers buff, base orange; fragrant.

Mrs. James Lynas HT, *pb*, 1914, Dickson, H. Flowers pearly pink, reverse and edges flushed rosy peach, dbl.; fragrant. GM, NRS, 1913.

Mrs. James Shearer HT, *w*, 1923, *Seedling* × *Mme. Colette Martinet*; Ferguson, W. Flowers pure white, base yellow, full, high-centered, large; fragrant.

Mrs. James Williamson HT, *mp*, 1922, Dickson, H. Flowers clear pink, dbl.; fragrant.

Mrs. J. C. Ainsworth HT, *mp*, 1918, *Mrs. Charles E. Russell* sport; Clarke Bros. Flowers rose-pink, very dbl.; fragrant.

Mrs. J. D. Eisele HT, *pb*, 1933, *Premier Supreme* × *McGredy's Scarlet*; Howard, F.H.; H&S. Bud long, pointed; flowers brilliant cherry-pink, center shaded scarlet, dbl., very large; very fragrant; vigorous growth.

Mrs. J. D. Russell HT, *dr*, 1930, *Prince Camille de Rohan* × *Mrs. Aaron Ward*; Bees. Flowers deep crimson, center maroon, almost blackin certain lights, dbl., cupped; very fragrant.

Mrs. Jeannette G. Leeds HT, *rb*, 1942, *Joanna Hill* × *R.M.S. Queen Mary*; Hill, J.H., Co. Bud globular, jasper-red and apricot-buff; flowers venetian pink, dbl. (50-60 petals), large (5-6 in.); slightly fragrant; foliage dark, leathery; very vigorous, upright growth; a florists' variety.

Mrs. Jennie Deverman HT, *pb*, 1933, *Pres. Herbert Hoover sport*; Deverman. Flowers cerise edged silvery, base tinted gold.

Mrs. J. F. Redly HT, *lp*, Flowers pale flesh-pink, center tinted salmon, dbl. (40 petals), large; vigorous growth; lightly repeats in late summer.

Mrs. J. Heath HT, *yb*, 1924, McGredy. Flowers maize-yellow, tinted peach-red, center yellow, dbl.; fragrant.

Mrs. J. J. Hedley-Willis HT, *dr*, 1929, *Admiral Ward* × *Richmond*; Bees. Bud pointed; flowers dark crimson, center almost plum-black, dbl., high-centered; very fragrant.

Mrs. John Bell HT, *dr*, 1928, Bell, J.; Dobbie. Bud long; flowers carmine, dbl., cupped, large; fragrant.

Mrs. John Cook HT, *w*, 1920, *Ophelia* × *Seedling*; Cook, J.; A.N. Pierson. Bud long, pointed; flowers white, suffused soft pink, deepening in cool weather, dbl., cupped, large; fragrant.

Mrs. John Inglis HT, *dr*, 1920, McGredy. Flowers rich crimson, dbl.; very fragrant.

Mrs. John Laing HP (OGR), *mp*, 1887, *François Michelon* × *Seedling*; Bennett. Bud pointed; flowers soft pink, dbl. (45 petals), large; fragrant; foliage light; vigorous, rather dwarf growth; recurrent bloom; (28).

Mrs. John McNabb S, *w*, 1941, *R. beggeriana* × *R. rugosa*; Skinner. Bud with very long sepals; flowers white, very dbl.; fragrant; foliage large, dark, slightly rugose, prickly underneath, to 9 leaflets; few prickles; height 5 ft.; non-recurrent.

Mrs. John R. Allan HT, *lp*, 1920, Dickson, H. Flowers soft rosy pink, reverse darker, dbl. GM, NRS, 1920.

Mrs. Joseph Hiess Pol, *lp*, 1943, *Roserie* × *Seedling*; Shepherd; Klyn. Flowers Mary Wallace pink, base white, dbl. (40 petals), cupped, borne in clusters of 3-16 on strong stems; slightly fragrant; foliage leathery; vigorous, upright, bushy, compact growth.

Mrs. Joseph H. Welch HT, *mp*, 1911, McGredy. Flowers brilliant rose-pink, dbl., large; slightly fragrant; vigorous growth. GM, NRS, 1910.

Mrs. Joseph H. Welch, Climbing Cl HT, *mp*, 1922, Perkins, H.S..

Mrs. J. T. McIntosh HT, *ab*, 1935, McIntosh; Brundrett. Flowers creamy apricot, center deeper apricot, base golden yellow, full, well formed, large; vigorous growth.

Mrs. J. Wylie HT, *lp*, 1923, Dickson, H. Flowers silvery blush-pink.

Mrs. L. B. Coddington HT, *mp*, 1931, *Templar* × *Souv. de Claudius Pernet*; Coddington. Bud long, pointed; flowers pink, dbl., large; fragrant; foliage leathery; vigorous growth.

Mrs. L. B. Copeland F, *pb*, 1934, *Seedling* × *Cécile Brunner*; Fitzgerald. Flowers salmon-pink, veined, base yellow, dbl., globular, small; very fragrant; foliage dark, glossy; vigorous growth.

Mrs. Leslie Moss Cl HT, *dp*, 1944, Moss; Mason, F. Flowers carmine-pink, semi-dbl., medium; foliage leathery; vigorous, climbing growth.

Mrs. Lovell Swisher HT, *pb*, 1926, *Seedling* × *Souv. de Claudius Pernet*; Howard, F.H.; H&S. Bud pointed; flowers salmon-pink, edged flesh, dbl., well formed; fragrant; foliage bronze; very vigorous growth.

Mrs. Lovell Swisher, Climbing Cl HT, *pb*, 1930, H&S.

Mrs. Luther Burbank HT, *mp*, 1954, *Christopher Stone* × *Charlotte Armstrong*; Swim; Stark Bros. Bud long, pointed; flowers rose-pink, dbl. (34 petals), cupped, large (4-4½ in.); very fragrant (spicy); foliage leathery; vigorous growth.

Mrs. Mabel V. Socha HT, *my*, 1935, *Seedling* × *Souv. de Claudius Pernet*; H&S. Bud pointed; flowers pure lemon-yellow, dbl.; long, strong stems; very fragrant.

Mrs. MacDonald's Rose HRg (S), *dp*, *Apparently R. rugosa plena* × *R. acicularis*; Reid; P.H. Wright. Closely resembles Lac La Nonne; non-recurrent bloom.

Mrs. MacKellar HT, *my*, 1915, Dickson, A. Flowers deep citron or pure canary, passing to primrose, dbl.; fragrant.

Mrs. Mary D. Ward HT, *pb*, 1927, *Double Ophelia* × *Souv. de Claudius Pernet*; Ward, F.B. Flowers shell-pink and gold, reverse ivory-white; fragrant.

Mrs. Maynard Sinton HT, *pb*, 1909, McGredy. Flowers silvery white suffused pink, very large; fragrant; moderately vigorous growth. GM, NRS, 1909.

Mrs. M. H. Horvath HT, *ly*, 1940, *(Mme. Butterfly × Seedling) × Souv. de Claudius Pernet*; Horvath; Wayside Gardens Co. Bud long, pointed; flowers pale yellow, dbl. (40 petals), open, large; long stems; foliage glossy; very vigorous, upright growth.

Mrs. M. H. Walsh R, *w*, 1913, Walsh. Flowers pure snow-white, dbl, small, borne in clusters; foliage large, glossy; very vigorous, trailing growth.

Mrs. Mina Lindell Sp (OGR), *lp*, 1927, *A form of R. macounii*; Found by Mrs. Lindell, South Dakota; N.E. Hansen. Flowers light pink, semi-dbl. (10-12 petals); height to 4 ft.; non-recurrent; hardy.

Mrs. Miniver HT, *mr*, 1944, (Souv. de Louis Simon); Chambard, C.; J&P. Flowers scarlet-crimson, reverse slightly darker, dbl. (20 petals), cupped, large (5½-6 in.); fragrant; foliage soft; vigorous, upright, bushy, compact growth.

Mrs. M. J. Gillon HT, *dr*, 1974, *Tropicana × Prima Ballerina*; Rijksstation voor Sierplantenteelt. Bud ovoid; flowers red-purple, dbl. (37 petals), globular, large (4 in.); fragrant; foliage glossy, dark; upright growth.

Mrs. Mona Hunting HT, *yb*, 1916, Dickson, H. Flowers chamois-yellow, opening fawn, dbl.

Mrs. Moorfield Storey HT, *lp*, 1915, *Gen. MacArthur Seedling × Joseph Hill*; Waban Conservatories. Flowers shell-pink, center deeper, dbl.

Mrs. Muir MacKean HT, *dr*, 1912, McGredy. Flowers carmine-crimson, high-centered, large; very fragrant; vigorous growth.

Mrs. Murray Allison HT, *pb*, 1925, Prior. Flowers rose-pink, base carmine, dbl.; slightly fragrant.

Mrs. Myles Kennedy T (OGR), *pb*, 1906, Dickson, A. Flowers silvery white tinted buff, center and reverse pink, full, large; vigorous growth.

Mrs. Nieminen HT, *rb*, 1954, *Hens Verschuren × Poinsettia*; Buyl Frères. Flowers blood-red shaded scarlet, very dbl., well formed, large; slightly fragrant; bushy, compact growth.

Mrs. Norman Watson Cl HT, *dp*, 1930, *Radiance × Gwen Nash*; Clark, A.; Geelong Hort. Soc. Flowers deep cherry-pink, large; very vigorous, pillar growth.

Mrs. Norris M. Agnew HT, *ob*, 1934, *J.C. Thornton × Florence L. Izzard*; Bees. Bud pointed; flowers orange-cerise, dbl., large; slightly fragrant; foliage leathery, light; very vigorous growth.

Mrs. Oakley Fisher HT, *dy*, 1921, Cant, B.R. Flowers deep orange-yellow, single, blooms in clusters; fragrant; foliage dark, bronze, glossy; vigorous growth.

Mrs. Olive Sackett F, *mr*, 1931, *Else Poulsen sport*; Wirtz & Eicke; Spath. Flowers bright red, semi-dbl., well formed, medium (2-2½ in.); foliage bronze in autumn; vigorous growth.

Mrs. Oliver Ames HT, *my*, 1941, *Max Krause × Julien Potin*; Verschuren; Dreer. Bud long, pointed; flowers lemon-yellow, dbl. (63 petals), globular, large (3½-4 in.); long stems; very fragrant; foliage leathery; vigorous growth.

Mrs. Oliver Mee HT, *rb*, 1948, *Mrs. Charles Lamplough × Edith Mary Mee*; Mee; Fryer's Nursery. Flowers scarlet shaded gold, dbl. (35 petals), high-centered, large (5-6 in.); fragrant; foliage glossy, bronze; very vigorous growth.

Mrs. Oswald Lewis HT, *yb*, 1936, Cant, F. Flowers soft canary-yellow, outer petals edged flame, dbl., well formed; long stems; very fragrant; vigorous growth. GM, Bagatelle, 1935.

Mrs. Oswald Smeaton HT, *pb*, 1932, Easlea. Flowers ivory-cream, center and petal tips pink, full (50-60 petals), very large; long stems; fragrant; vigorous growth.

Mrs. Paul B (OGR), *lp*, 1891, Paul. Flowers blush-white shaded rosy peach, large.

Mrs. Paul Goudie HT, *yb*, 1932, (Shining Sun); McGredy. Flowers deep buttercup-yellow, edged carmine-scarlet, dbl., very large; fragrant (fruity).

Mrs. Paul J. Howard Cl HT, *rb*, 1938, *Miss Rowena Thom × Paul's Lemon Pillar*; Howard, F.H.; H&S. Bud long, pointed; flowers brilliant crimson, reverse flame-red, dbl. (30 petals), large (5 in.); long stems; fragrant (spicy); foliage large, bronze, leathery; very vigorous, climbing (12-15 ft.) growth.

Mrs. Paul M. Pierson HT, *pb*, 1930, *Premier sport*; Pierson, P.M. Bud long, pointed; flowers soft pink, reverse brighter, dbl., high-centered, very large; fragrant.

Mrs. Paul R. Bosley HT, *my*, 1941, *Mme. Joseph Perraud sport*; Bosley Nursery. Flowers apricot-yellow.

Mrs. Percy V. Pennybacker HT, *pb*, 1929, *Mme. Butterfly Seedling*; Vestal. Flowers peach-pink shaded silver, dbl., cupped; fragrant.

Mrs. Peter Blair HT, *yb*, 1906, Dickson, A. Flowers lemon-chrome, center golden yellow, well formed, large. GM, NRS, 1906.

Mrs. Philip Russell HT, *dr*, 1927, *Hadley × Red Letter Day*; Clark, A.; Hackett. Bud long, pointed; flowers dark red, shaded black, semi-dbl.; slightly fragrant; foliage glaucous green; vigorous, semi-climbing, pillar or large bush growth.

Mrs. Pierce HSet (OGR), *mp*, 1850, *R. setigera hybrid*; Pierce. Flowers pink, well formed.

Mrs. Pierre S. duPont HT, *my*, 1929, *(Ophelia × Rayon d'Or) × (Ophelia × (Constance × Souv. de Claudius Pernet))*; Mallerin; C-P. Bud long, pointed, reddish gold; flowers golden yellow, becoming lighter, dbl. (40 petals); fragrant (fruity); foliage rich green; moderate growth. GM, Bagatelle, 1929.

Mrs. Pierre S. duPont, Climbing Cl HT, *my*, 1933, Hillock.

Mrs. Prentiss Nichols HT, *dp*, 1923, *Ophelia × Seedling*; Scott, R. Flowers brilliant deep pink, dbl.; fragrant.

Mrs. Ramon de Escofet HT, *dr*, 1919, Easlea. Flowers flame-crimson, dbl., large.

Mrs. Redford HT, *ab*, 1919, McGredy. Flowers bright apricot-orange, semi-dbl.; very fragrant; foliage holly-like. GM, NRS, 1917.

Mrs. Reynolds Hole T (OGR), *pb*, 1900, Nabonnand, P.&C. Flowers carmine shaded purple rose, reverse carmine, full, large.

Mrs. Richard Turnbull LCl, *w*, 1945, Clark, A. Flowers white, handsome stamens, single, very large.

Mrs. Richards F, *pb*, 1968, *Ann Elizabeth × Circus*; Harkness. Flowers pink tinged apricot, single, blooms in trusses; fragrant; foliage dark, glossy.

Mrs. Robert Bacon HT, *ab*, 1934, *Talisman sport*; Bertanzel. Flowers golden apricot shading to coral, base yellow, very dbl., cupped, large; very fragrant.

Mrs. Robert Garrett HT, *mp*, 1900, *Comtesse de Caserta × Mme. Eugène Verdier*; Cook, J. Flowers pink.

Mrs. Robert Mitchell HT, *pb*, 1926, *St. Helena × Mrs. Redford*; Jersey Nursery. Flowers salmon-rose, overlaid coppery pink.

Mrs. Robert Peary Cl HT, *w*, 1898, *Kaiserin Auguste Viktoria sport*; De Voecht; De Wilde; Dingee & Conard. Flowers white.

Mrs. Rosalie Wrinch LCl, *lp*, 1915, *Frau Karl Druschki × Hugh Dickson*; Brown, W.&J. Flowers shell-pink, semi-dbl., large; vigorous, pillar (5-8 ft.) growth.

Mrs. Roy Green HT, *dr*, 1940, Clark, A. Flowers dark red, very large blooms on long stems.

Mrs. Russell Grimwade T (OGR), *mp*, 1938, *Lorraine Lee sport*; Grimwade. Flowers fuchsia-pink.

Mrs. R. B. McLennan HT, *pb*, 1924, *George C. Waud × Mme. Caristie Martel*; Easlea. Flow-

ers satiny rose suffused yellow, very dbl.; very fragrant.

Mrs. R. B. Moloney HT, *mr*, 1925, McGredy. Flowers brilliant carmine-red, dbl.; very fragrant.

Mrs. R. C. Bell HT, *mr*, 1920, *Gen. MacArthur × Château de Clos Vougeot*; Clark, A. Flowers bright red.

Mrs. R. G. Sharman-Crawford HP (OGR), *pb*, 1894, Dickson, A. Flowers rosy pink, outer petals tinted flesh, full (75 petals), cupped, large; fragrant; vigorous growth; recurrent bloom.

Mrs. R. M. Finch Pol, *mp*, 1923, *Orléans Rose × Seedling*; Finch. Flowers rosy pink, becoming lighter, dbl., medium blooms in large clusters; bushy growth.

Mrs. R. M. Finch, Climbing Cl Pol, *mp*.

Mrs. Sam McGredy HT, *op*, 1929, *(Donald Macdonald × Golden Emblem) × (Seedling × The Queen Alexandra Rose)*; McGredy. Bud pointed; flowers scarlet-copper-orange, reverse heavily flushed red, dbl. (40 petals), high-centered, large; fragrant; foliage glossy, reddish bronze; vigorous growth. GM, NRS, 1929; Portland, 1956.

Mrs. Sam McGredy, Climbing Cl HT, *op*, 1937, (Geneviève Genest); Buisman.

Mrs. Sam McGredy, Climbing Cl HT, *ob*, 1938, (Genevieve Genest); Guillaud.

Mrs. Sam McGredy, Climbing Cl HT, *ob*, 1940, Western Rose Co..

Mrs. S. Paton HT, *ob*, 1928, McGredy. Bud long, pointed; flowers orange-carmine, base orange, dbl., large; slightly fragrant.

Mrs. S. K. Rindge HT, *yb*, 1919, *Rayon d'Or × Frau Karl Druschki*; H&S. Bud long, pointed; flowers deep golden yellow, suffused soft pink with age, semi-dbl., cupped, very large; long stems; fragrant.

Mrs. S. T. Wright T (OGR), *ob*, 1914, *Harry Kirk sport*; Dickson, A. Flowers old gold, center suffused rose-pink on orange, dbl.; fragrant.

Mrs. S. W. Burgess HT, *ab*, 1925, *Mme. Mélanie Soupert × Joseph Hill*; Burgess, S.W. Flowers apricot-yellow, base deeper, dbl.; fragrant.

Mrs. Talbot O'Farrell HT, *rb*, 1926, McGredy. Flowers cerise flushed bronze, reverse old-gold, dbl.; fragrant.

Mrs. Theodore Roosevelt HT, *lp*, 1903, *La France Seedling*; Hill, E.G., Co. Flowers light pink, dbl., well shaped, very large; fragrant; vigorous, bushy growth.

Mrs. Theodore Salvesen HT, *op*, 1922, Dobbie. Flowers salmon-pink.

Mrs. Theonville van Berkel HT, *pb*, 1935, *Briarcliff × Mrs. Sam McGredy*; Buisman. Bud long, pointed; flowers pink, reverse flushed yellow, dbl., high-centered, large; very fragrant; foliage leathery, dark; vigorous growth.

Mrs. Tom Paul HT, *yb*, 1920, Dickson, H. Flowers saffron-yellow, suffused pink, dbl.

Mrs. Tom Smith HT, *mr*, 1924, Smith, T. Flowers glowing cerise, dbl., fragrant.

Mrs. Tom Whitehead HT, *ab*, 1938, *Mrs. Charles Lamplough × Seedling*; Whitehead; Beckwith. Flowers cream, center apricot-orange, outer petals veined, dbl., high-centered, very large; very vigorous growth.

Mrs. Tresham Gilbey HT, *op*, 1923, *Waltham Flame × Edith Cavell (HT)*; Chaplin Bros. Bud pointed; flowers coral-rose shaded salmon, dbl., very large; fragrant. GM, NRS, 1923.

Mrs. T. Hillas HT, *my*, 1913, Pernet-Ducher. Flowers pure chrome-yellow, dbl.

Mrs. T. B. Doxford HT, *rb*, 1932, Dickson, A. Bud pointed; flowers salmon-carmine to peach-blossom-pink, reverse old-rose, dbl., high-centered, large; slightly fragrant.

Mrs. T. J. English HT, *ab*, 1922, English. Flowers apricot and amber, tinted salmon-flesh, heavily veined; fragrant.

Mrs. U. M. Rose HT, *dp*, 1931, Vestal. Bud long, pointed; flowers cerise-pink, semi-dbl., cupped; very fragrant.

Mrs. van Beresteyn-Frowein HT, *op*, 1935, *Souv. de Claudius Pernet × Mrs. Henry Bowles*; Buisman. Flowers salmon, very dbl., large; fragrant; Foliage leathery, light; vigorous growth.

Mrs. Vandenbergh HT, *mr*, 1938, (Mevrouw S. van den Bergh, Jr.); *E.G. Hill × Étoile de Hollande*; Buisman. Flowers bright red, semi-dbl., high-centered; strong stems; foliage dark; vigorous growth.

Mrs. Wakefield Christie-Miller HT, *pb*, 1909, McGredy. Flowers blush, shaded salmon, reverse vermilion-rose, dbl.; foliage light, leathery; dwarf growth.

Mrs. W. A. Lindsay HT, *pb*, 1920, Dickson, H. Flowers peach-pink, center golden yellow, dbl.; fragrant.

Mrs. Wallace H. Rowe HT, *m*, 1912, McGredy. Flowers mauve, high-centered; vigorous growth.

Mrs. Walter Brace HT, *dp*, 1939, *Picture sport*; Beckwith. Flowers vivid cerise-rose-pink, slightly larger, obetter shape.

Mrs. Walter Burns F, *mp*, 1978, (((*Queen Elizabeth × Escapade*) × ((*Orangeade × Lilac Charm*) × (*Sterling Silver × Africa Star*))) ×

(*Cläre Grammerstorf × Frühlingsmorgen*); Harkness. Bud ovoid; flowers medium pink, very dbl. (100 small petals), flat, patio, medium (2½ in.); fragrant (musky), foliage medium, matt, dark; compact, bushy.

Mrs. Walter Easlea HT, *dr*, 1910, Dickson, A. Flowers crimson, dbl., large; fragrant.

Mrs. Walter Jones HT, *rb*, 1930, Cant, B.R. Flowers brilliant coral-red, shaded orange, dbl.

Mrs. Walter T. Sumner HT, *dp*, 1920, *Ophelia × Hadley*; Clarke Bros. Flowers carmine to deep rose-pink, semi-dbl. (12-18 petals), large; very fragrant.

Mrs. Walter T. Sumner, Climbing Cl HT, *dp*, 1932, Hazlewood Bros..

Mrs. Warren E. Lenon HT, *dr*, 1924, *Hoosier Beauty × Premier*; Hill, E.G., Co.; Vestal. Bud long, pointed; flowers crimson, dbl., globular, large; very fragrant; vigorous growth.

Mrs. Warren G. Harding HT, *dp*, 1923, *Columbia sport*; Pierson, A.N. Flowers dark pink.

Mrs. Wemyss Quin HT, *dy*, 1914, Dickson, A. Flowers deep yellow, dbl.; fragrant; bushy, branching growth. GM, Bagatelle, 1916.

Mrs. W. E. Nickerson HT, *pb*, 1927, McGredy; H&S; Dreer. Bud pointed; flowers silvery pink deeply shaded old-gold and salmon, dbl., large; fragrant.

Mrs. W. H. Cutbush Pol, *dp*, 1907, *Mme. Norbert Levavasseur sport*; Levavasseur. Flowers deep pink.

Mrs. Whitman Cross Cl HT, *ob*, 1943, *Nanjemoy × Marion Cran*; Cross, C.W.; B&A. Bud long, pointed; flowers orange-apricot, overlaid pinkish, reverse sometimes striped rose-pink, semi-dbl., open, large; fragrant; foliage glossy, soft; height 8-9 ft. as climbing or pillar, upright.

Mrs. William C. Egan HT, *lp*, 1922, H&S. Bud long, pointed; flowers soft pink, dbl. (35 petals); fragrant.

Mrs. William C. Egan, Climbing Cl HT, *lp*, 1933, Howard Rose Co..

Mrs. William Fife HT, *pb*, 1926, Dobbie. Flowers soft rose-pink, flushed blush-pink, dbl.; fragrant.

Mrs. Wm. G. Koning Pol, *w*, 1917, *Louise Walter sport*; Kluis & Koning. Flowers pure white, dbl., open, borne in clusters; slightly fragrant; vigorous, bushy growth.

Mrs. William R. Hearst HT, *dp*, 1915, *My Maryland sport*; Pierson, A.N. Flowers clear dark pink.

Mrs. William Sergent HT, *ab*, 1923, Dickson, H. Flowers apricot and peach, edges flushed rose-pink, dbl.

Mrs. William Sprott HT, *my*, 1938, *Portadown Glory × Mrs. Sam McGredy*; McGredy. Bud long, pointed; flowers yellow, dbl., large; slightly fragrant; foliage glossy, bronze; vigorous, compact growth.

Mrs. W. J. Grant HT, *lp*, 1895, (Belle Siebrecht); *La France × Lady Mary Fitzwilliam*; Dickson, A. Bud long, pointed; flowers light pink fading purplish, dbl.; fragrant.

Mrs. W. J. Grant, Climbing Cl HT, *lp*, 1899, (Belle Siebrecht, Climbing); Hill, E.G., Co..

Mrs. W. R. Groves HT, *dr*, 1941, Clark, A. Flowers deep red.

M. S. Hershey HT, *dr*, 1941, *Seedling × E.G. Hill*; Coddington; C-P. Bud long, pointed; flowers velvety crimson, dbl. (33 petals), cupped, large (4-4½ in.); slightly fragrant; bushy growth.

Mucaba HT, *pb*, 1962, *Marechal Carmona × Suzon Lotthe*; Moreira da Silva. Flowers pink stained carmine.

Muchacha® F, *or*, 1977, (MEIlutida); *(Frenzy × Frenzy) × (Sangria × Sangria)*; Meilland, M.L.; Meilland. Bud conical; flowers brilliant vermilion, semi-dbl. (12 petals), shallowly-cupped, medium; foliage dark; very vigorous, semi-shrub growth. GM, The Hague Gold Medal; Golden Rose of The Hague, 1976.

Mühle Hermsdorf R, *w*, 1928, *R. wichuraiana × Gruss an Zabern*; Dechant. Flowers pure white, dbl., all open at once.

Mulbarton LCl, *mr*, 1965, *Paul's Lemon Pillar × (Ena Harkness × Richmond)*; Hooney. Flowers red, full, large (4½ in.); fragrant; foliage coppery; vigorous growth.

Multnomah HT, *rb*, 1948, *Contrast × Charlotte Armstrong*; Swim; Peterson; Dering. Bud long, pointed; flowers carmine, base gold, semi-dbl. (18-22 petals), large (4-5 in.), slightly fragrant; foliage glossy, dark; vigorous, upright, compact growth; hardy in Pacific Northwest.

Mum Mum Min, *w*, 1986, *Seedling × Seedling*; McDaniel, Earl; McDaniel's Min. Roses. Flowers pure white, dbl. (55 petals), cupped, small blooms in clusters of 3-25; no fragrance; foliage light green, semi-glossy; short, curved, light green prickles; low, upright, bushy, spreading growth.

München HMsk (S), *dr*, 1940, *Eva × Reveil Dijonnais*; Kordes. Bud long, pointed; flowers scarlet-crimson, semi-dbl., large blooms in clusters; slightly fragrant; foliage dark, glossy; very vigorous, trailing growth; repeat bloom.

Münchener Fasching S, *mr*, 1963, Kordes, R. Bud ovoid; flowers bright red, dbl. (30 petals), blooms in large clusters (up to 40); foliage dark, glossy; vigorous, bushy (6-6½ ft.).

Munchkin Min, *pb*, 1986, *Watercolor × Seedling*; Bridges, Dennis, 1987. Flowers pink edging, white center, reverse slight pink edged on white, fades with age, dbl. (22 petals), high-centered, small, borne usually singly; slight fragrance; foliage medium, medium green, semi-glossy; short, pointed, small, tan prickles; bushy, low growth.

Munro's Improved Premier HT, *dp*, 1927, Munro; A strong-growing Premier Supreme.

Munster S, *pb*, 1958, Kordes; McGredy. Flowers soft pink shaded deeper, dbl. (28 petals), high-centered, large (3½ in.) blooms in trusses; slightly fragrant; foliage light green.

Murasaki no Sono F, *m*, 1984, *Tasogare × Seedling*; Kobayashi, Moriji. Flowers silver lilac, semi-dbl. (13 petals), flat, medium blooms borne 1-5 per cluster; slight fragrance; foliage light green; prickles slanted downward; vigorous, tall growth.

Muria HT, *op*, 1968, (MACmu); *Miss Ireland × Tropicana*; McGredy, S., IV; Spek. Bud long, pointed; flowers salmon-orange, dbl. (40 petals), classic form, large (4 in.); slightly fragrant; foliage light green; bushy growth; for forcing only.

Muriel HT, *dr*, 1929, Archer. Bud long, pointed; flowers brilliant velvety scarlet, semi-dbl.; strong stems.

Muriel Armitage HT, *dp*, 1972, *(Orange Sensation × Ballet) × Mischief*; Ellick; Excelsior Roses. Flowers deep rose-pink, very dbl. (60-70 petals), very full, large (5 in.); fragrant; foliage large, glossy, dark; vigorous, upright growth.

Muriel Dickson HT, *ob*, 1915, Dickson, H. Flowers reddish copper. GM, NRS, 1913.

Muriel Moore HT, *w*, 1916, *My Maryland* sport; Moore, F.M. Flowers white.

Muriel O'Leary HT, *pb*, 1979, *Honey Favorite × Rose Gaujard*; Murray, N. Bud long; flowers light and deep pink, dbl. (27 petals), well formed, 3 in.; slightly fragrant; foliage large, glossy; vigorous, upright growth.

Muriel Pasquill HT, *pb*, 1927, *Padre* sport; Pasquill. Flowers strawberry-pink, reverse golden yellow, semi-dbl.; very fragrant.

Muriel Wilson T (OGR), *ly*, 1923, Hall; Prince. Flowers rich lemon-cream, dbl.; slightly fragrant. GM, NRS, 1921.

Murphy's Law HT, *mp*, 1982, (SEAmurp); *Fragrant Cloud* × *(Prima Ballerina* × *Gavotte)*; McCann, Sean. Flowers medium pink, lighter reverse, dbl. (35 petals), large; slight fragrance; foliage medium, dark, matt; bushy growth.

Mur-Ray HT, *pb*, 1936, *Briarcliff sport*; Murray. Flowers darker pink, tinged salmon.

Murray Hill HT, *my*, 1939, *Joanna Hill sport*; Coddington. Flowers yellow.

Musashino HT, *op*, 1989, *Garden Party* × *Daimonji*; Takahashi, Takeshi. Bud ovoid; flowers orange-pink, changing to pink, dbl. (35 petals), urn-shaped, high-centered, large, borne usually singly; foliage medium green, oblong, semi-glossy; prickles few; upright, medium growth.

Muscosa Simplex M (OGR), *mp*, (*R. centifolia andrewsii* Rehder; *R. muscosa; simplex*); Cult. 1807; Similar to Centifolia Muscosa but flowers single; (28).

Musette F, *dr*, 1936, *Ingar Olsson* × *Johanniszauber*; Tantau. Flowers glowing light crimson, single, open, large, borne in clusters on strong stems; slightly fragrant; foliage leathery, wrinkled, dark; bushy growth.

Music Maker S, *lp*, 1973, Buck; Iowa State University. Flowers light pink, dbl., high-centered, medium; fragrant; foliage glossy, light, leathery; vigorous, dwarf, upright, bushy growth.

Musicale Gr, *rb*, 1964, *(Bravo* × *Nellie E. Hillock)* × *Iobelle*; Buck; Iowa State University. Bud long, pointed; flowers straw-yellow changing to cherry red, dbl., small; fragrant; foliage glossy, bronze; moderate, bushy growth.

Musician S, *rb*, 1953, *Hansa* × *Hazeldean*; Wright, P.H. Flowers bicolor, nearer red than yellow, with gray tones, semi-dbl. (20 petals), borne in small clusters; foliage modified rugose; non-recurrent bloom.

Musketeer HMsk (S), *w*, Lester Rose Gardens. Flowers white, stamens bright yellow, semi-dbl.; vigorous (20-25 ft.) growth; spring bloom.

Mutabilis Ch (OGR), *yb*, (*R. chinensis mutabilis* (Correvon) Rehder; *R. mutabilis* Correvon; Tipo Ideale); Prior to 1894. Flowers sulphur-yellow, changing to orange, red and finally crimson, about 2 in. diam; Erroneously identified with the Mutabilis (a Centifolia) painted by Redoute.

Mutter Brada HT, *ab*, 1934, *Lady Craig* × *Freifrau Ida von Schubert*; Brada. Flowers apricot-yellow and red, varying; very fragrant; vigorous growth.

My Angel F, *dp*, 1987, *Pink Parfait* × *Roman Holiday*; Pencil, Paul, 1988. Flowers deep pink, dbl. (15-25 petals), medium, borne singly or in sprays of 6-10; slight fragrance; foliage medium, medium green, matt; upright, hardy growth.

My Baby Min, *dp*, 1967, *Cinderella* × *R. rouletti*; Quackenbush. Bud ovoid; flowers deep pink, very dbl., cupped, small; slightly fragrant; foliage small, glossy, dark; moderate, dwarf growth.

My Choice HT, *pb*, 1958, *Wellworth* × *Ena Harkness*; LeGrice. Flowers pink, reverse pale yellow, dbl. (33 petals), large (4½-5 in.); very fragrant (damask); foliage leathery; vigorous, upright growth. GM, NRS, 1958; Portland, 1961.

My Delight Min, *lp*, 1983, (TINmyde); *Futura* × *Avandel*; Bennett, Dee; Tiny Petals Nursery, 1984. Flowers light pink, dbl. (30 petals), HT-form, small; slight fragrance; foliage medium, medium green, semi-glossy; upright, spreading growth.

My Dream HT, *dp*, 1970, *Pink Favorite* × *Karl Herbst*; Winchel; Country Garden Nursery. Bud long, pointed; flowers deep pink, dbl., high-centered, medium; slightly fragrant; foliage glossy; upright growth.

My Fair Lady F, *pb*, 1959, Wheatcroft Bros. Flowers rose-pink, reverse darker, semi-dbl., large, borne in large clusters; foliage glossy; tall growth.

My Fancy F, *or*, 1970, (MEIflorem); *(Dany Robin* × *Fire King)* × *Rumba*; Meilland; URS. Flowers dutch vermilion, dbl. (25-30 petals), imbricated, large (3 in.); slightly fragrant; foliage dull, dark; vigorous, upright, bushy growth.

My Friend F, *lp*, 1956, *Garnette Seedling* × *Summer Snow sport*; Motose. Bud ovoid; flowers apple-blossom-pink, dbl. (30 petals), flat, medium (2½ in.); slightly fragrant; dwarf, bushy growth.

My Gal Gale F, *lp*, 1958, *Pinocchio* × *Morning Star*; Marsh; Marsh's Nursery. Flowers soft pink, very dbl. borne in clusters; dwarf growth.

My Gina S, *mp*, 1973, *Dorothy Wheatcroft sport*; Shortland. Flowers medium pink.

My Girl F, *ob*, 1964, (Cunosa); *Dacapo* × *Floribunda Seedling*; deRuiter; Gregory. Flowers deep salmon, dbl. (30 petals), cupped to open, large, borne in clusters; foliage dark; vigorous growth. GM, The Hague, 1963.

My Guy F, *or*, 1986, *Rosalynn Carter* × *Dorothy Wheatcroft*; Milner, William, 1979. Flowers bright orange-red, fading darker, semi-dbl. (13 petals), cupped, medium, borne in sprays of 7-20; moderate fragrance; foliage medium, medium green, semi-glossy; medium, light brown, slightly hooked prickles; fruit round, medium, light green; bushy, medium growth.

My Honey Min, *ob*, 1991, (JUShoney); *Orange Honey sport*; Justice, Jerry, 1990; Justice Miniature Roses. Bud pointed; flowers orange with light yellow accent at base, acquires pinkish cast with age, dbl., urn-shaped, loose, medium blooms borne singly; no fragrance; foliage medium, dark green, semi-glossy; spreading, medium growth.

My Joy HT, *mp*, 1976, *Red Devil sport*; Wood. Flowers medium pink.

My Lady HT, *ab*, 1956, *Seedling* × *Peace*; Robinson, H. Bud pointed; flowers apricot flushed gold, dbl. (46 petals), high-centered, large (5 in.); fragrant; foliage dark, leathery; very vigorous, bushy growth.

My Love HT, *dr*, 1960, *Bayadere* × *Ena Harkness*; Anderson's Rose Nursery. Flowers deep red, dbl. (45 petals), high-centered, large; very fragrant; foliage dark; vigorous growth.

My Lucky Starr HT, *mr*, 1987, *Secret Love* × *Karl Herbst*; Evans, Dave. Flowers medium red, full (26-40 petals), large; no fragrance; foliage large, dark green, semi-glossy, leathery; spreading growth.

My Maryland HT, *pb*, 1908, *Madonna* × *Enchanter*; Cook, J. Flowers bright salmon-pink, edged paler, dbl., large; very fragrant; vigorous growth.

My Own Min, *rb*, 1977, (COOsyl); *(Scarlet Knight* × *Soeur Thérèse)* × *Willie Winkie*; Cook, Sylven S. Flowers red, yellow center, single (5 petals), small; fragrant; foliage medium, medium green, semi-glossy.

My Pleasure™ Min, *pb*, 1986, (KINpleas;); *Lavender Pinocchio* × *Seedling*; King, Gene, 1981; AGM Miniature Roses, 1987. Flowers lavender pink, reverse light pink, fading lighter pink, dbl. (45 petals), cupped, exhibition, medium, borne usually singly or in sprays of 5-7; moderate fruity fragrance; foliage medium, dark green, matt; straight, white prickles with brown tips; fruit oval, medium green; upright, medium growth.

My Prayer HT, *op*, 1953, *Seedling* × *The Doctor*; H&S. Bud long, pointed; flowers peach-pink, dbl. (25-30 petals), high-centered; large (5 in.); very fragrant; foliage leathery; vigorous, upright growth.

My Sunshine Min, *my*, 1986, (TINshine); *Sunsprite* × *Fool's Gold*; Bennett, Dee; Tiny Petals Nursery. Flowers medium yellow, aging soft orange, bright yellow stamens, single, tiny point on each petal, medium blooms borne usually singly and in sprays of 3-4; fragrant; foliage medium, medium green, semi-glossy;

small, reddish-brown prickles; fruit globular,½ in. diam., green; medium, upright, bushy growth.

My Valentine™ Min, *dr*, 1975, (MORmyval); *Little Chief* × *Little Curt*; Moore, R.S.; Sequoia Nursery. Flowers deep red, dbl. (65 petals), high-centered, small (1 in.); foliage small, glossy, tinted bronze; vigorous, bushy growth.

Myra LCl, *w*, 1926, *Dr. W. Van Fleet* × *Lady Roberts*; Wilber. Flowers creamy white, dbl., very large, borne in clusters of 2-3; slightly fragrant; foliage dark, bronze; vigorous, climbing growth. RULED EXTINCT 1/92.

Myra HT, *pb*, 1992, (BATtoo); *Matangi* × *Mood Music*; Stainthorpe, Avril E.; Battersby Roses, 1990. Flowers pink blend, moderately full (15-25 petals), medium (4-7 cms) blooms borne in small clusters; slight fragrance; foliage medium, dark green, glossy; many prickles; medium (75 cms), bushy growth.

Myriam® HT, *lp*, 1992, (COCgrand); *Typhoo Tea* × *Grandpa Dickson*; Cocker, James; James Cocker; Sons, 1991. Flowers light pink, very full (41+ petals), large (7+ cms) blooms borne mostly singly; very fragrant; foliage large, medium green, semi-glossy; some prickles; medium (76.20 cms), upright growth.

Myrianthes Renoncule HSem (OGR), *pb*, *R. sempervirens hybrid*. Flowers pale peach, dbl., large; free bloom; not dependably hardy.

Mystère HT, *dp*, 1969, *Première Ballerine* × *Femina Seedling*; Gaujard. Bud long; flowers scarlet pink, dbl. (45 petals). RULED EXTINCT 10/86.

Mysterium F, *yb*, 1963, *Masquerade* × *Kordes' Perfecta*; Kordes, R. Bud long, pointed; flowers golden yellow striped scarlet, dbl. (25 petals), large (3 in.), borne in clusters (up to 20); slightly fragrant; foliage glossy; bushy, spreading, low growth.

Mystery HT, *rb*, 1983, (HERmesy); *(Seedling* × *Southern Sun)* × *Southern Sun*; Herholdt, J.A. Flowers light orange-red, edged amber, golden reverse, dbl. (35 petals), large; slight fragrance; foliage large, medium green; semi-glossy; bushy growth.

Mystic Gem HT, *dp*, 1959, *Rod Stillman* × *Bravo*; Armbrust; Langbecker. Bud long, pointed; flowers reddish pink, dbl., high-centered, large to medium; slightly fragrant; foliage leathery; vigorous, upright growth.

Mystique™ HT, *mr*, 1989, (DEVstica); *Samantha* × *Royalty*; Marciel, Stanley G.; DeVor Nursery. Bud pointed, slender, tapering; flowers bright red, dbl. (28 petals), cupped, large, borne singly; sweetheart; heavy, musk fragrance; foliage large, medium green, semi-glossy; prickles declining, pale red with tinges of green; upright, tall growth.

Naarden Red HT, *rb*, 1932, *Étoile de Hollande × Charles P. Kilham*; Van Rossem. Bud pointed; flowers crimson-red shaded orange, dbl., high-centered, large; very fragrant.

Nacha Pobeda HT, *dr*, (Our Victory); Costetske. Flowers dark velvety red.

Nadia HT, *dr*, 1956, *Mme. G. Forest-Colcombet × Seedling*; Delforge. Flowers dark red; foliage light green.

Nadine F, *dr*, 1962, *Red Pinocchio × Seedling*; Schwartz, E.W.; Wyant. Bud long, pointed; flowers maroon-red, dbl. (38 petals), cupped, large (3 in.); very fragrant; foliage bronze, soft; vigorous, bushy growth.

Naïr HFt (OGR), *yb*, 1936, *R. foetida bicolor × R. wichuraiana Seedling*; Chambard, C. Bud long, yellow and carmine; flowers vermilion-red, reverse yellow, stamens yellow, semi-dbl., large; vigorous, bushy growth; recurrent bloom.

Nambour F, *w*, 1953, *Yvonne Rabier × Mrs. Tom Henderson*; Ulrick. Flowers white flushed pink, very dbl., medium, borne in clusters; foliage bronze; very vigorous growth.

Namenlose Schöne T (OGR), *w*, 1886, Deegen. Flowers white tinted blush, well formed, large; fragrant.

Namib Sunrise Min, *yb*, 1984, (MORlogen); *Rumba × Yellow Jewel*; Moore, R.S.; Ludwigs Roses Ltd. Flowers yellow blended with coral pink, dbl. (64 petals), medium blooms in clusters of 15; slight fragrance; foliage light; straight, light brown prickles; dense.

Nan Anderson F, *op*, 1970, Anderson's Rose Nursery. Flowers deep pink, coral sheen, dbl. (30 petals), large (2½-3 in.); slightly fragrant; foliage glossy, dark; low, bushy.

Nan Poole Min, *pb*, 1983, *Seedling × Libby*; Meredith, E.A.; Rovinski, M.E.; Casa de Rosa Domingo. Bud globular; flowers yellow and pink blend, giving an overall coral-pink effect, dbl. (25 petals), high-centered to flat, medium; fragrant; foliage small, dark, semi-glossy; thin prickles; low, spreading growth.

Nana Mouskouri F, *w*, 1975, *Redgold × Iced Ginger*; Dickson, A. Flowers white, dbl. (30 petals), well formed, large (2½ in.); fragrant.

Nancy F, *mr*, Flowers bright red, single, very small; foliage very glossy.

Nancy HT, *dr*, 1930, Ferguson, W. Flowers bright scarlet-crimson, semi-dbl.; slightly fragrant.

Nancy HT, *my*, 1934, *Mrs. T. Hillas × Souv. de Claudius Pernet*; Mallerin; H. Guillot. Flowers chamois-yellow, semi-dbl., cupped; slightly fragrant.

Nancy Bergh F, *pb*, 1968, *Independence × Impeccable*; Fankhauser; A. Ross & Son. Bud ovoid; flowers pink, reverse silver-pink, semi-dbl., open, large; very fragrant; foliage dark, glossy, leathery; vigorous, open growth.

Nancy Elizabeth HT, *w*, 1947, *Korovo × Florinda Norman Thompson*; Mason, F. Bud long, pointed; flowers cream, dbl., high-centered, large; fragrant; foliage glossy; vigorous, upright growth.

Nancy Hall Min, *pb*, 1972, *Mary Adair sport*; Moore, R.S.; Mini-Roses. Flowers peachy.

Nancy Hayward LCl, *mr*, 1937, *Jessie Clark × Seedling*; Clark, A.; NRS Victoria. Flowers rich bright cerise, single, large; very vigorous, climbing growth.

Nancy Lee HT, *mp*, 1879, *Alba Rosea × Edward Morren*; Bennett. Flowers satiny rose-pink, medium to small; highly fragrant; dwarf, slender growth; not vigorous ; mildews.

Nancy Lee HT, *pb*, 1879, *Mme. Bravy × Edward Morren*; Bennett. Flowers deep pink; very fragrant; weak growth.

Nancy Pretty R, *pb*, 1917, *Dorothy Perkins × Ellen Poulsen*; MacLellan. Flowers pink, reverse lighter, dbl., small, borne in clusters.

Nancy Reagan HT, *or*, 1967, *Orange Delight × Hawaii*; Morey; Country Garden Nursery. Flowers orange-scarlet, dbl. (28 petals), high-centered, large (5-5½ in.); very fragrant; foliage dark, bronze, glossy, leathery; vigorous, tall growth.

Nancy Shaw HT, *lp*, 1992, (WIWancy); *Peggy Lee × Seedling*; Wilke, William. Flowers pink, full (26-40 petals), medium (4-7 cms) blooms borne mostly singly; slight fragrance; foliage medium, medium green, semi-glossy; some prickles; upright, bushy, tall (4 ft.) growth.

Nancy Steen F, *pb*, 1976, *Pink Parfait × (Ophelia × Parkdirektor Riggers)*; Sherwood; F. Mason. Flowers blush pink, center pale cream, dbl. (30 petals), flat, large (3½ in.); fragrant; foliage glossy, dark, bronze, leathery.

Nancy West F, *yb*, 1970, *Elizabeth of Glamis sport*; Haynes. Flowers medium yellow, suffused peach.

Nancy West F, *yb*, 1970, *Elizabeth of Glamis sport*; Haynes. Flowers mid-yellow, suffused peach, dbl. (30 petals), HT form, large (4 in.); very fragrant; foliage light; vigorous growth.

Nancy Wilson HT, *mp*, 1940, Clark, A. Flowers pink.

Nancy Wilson, Climbing Cl HT, *mp*, 1959, Campton; Hazlewood Bros.

Nanda HT, *mp*, 1959, *Dame Edith Helen × Eternal Youth*; Sartore. Bud ovoid to urn shaped, claret-red; flowers light rose, large; vigorous growth.

Nandini HT, *pb*, 1983, *Kiss of Fire* × *Seedling*; Pal, Dr. B.P.; Laveena Roses. Bud long, pointed; flowers pink with creamy white reverse, dbl. (46 petals), high-centered, medium blooms borne singly; strong fragrance; foliage large, medium green, leathery; brown-gray, hooked prickles; compact growth.

Nanette G (OGR), *rb*, Prior to 1848. Flowers rosy crimson marbled with purple, green eye, very dbl., cupped, small, blooms later than other Gallicas; vigorous, upright growth.

Nanette LCl, *w*, 1926, Hicks. Flowers creamy white, dbl., large, borne in clusters.

Nanjemoy Cl HT, *mp*, 1937, *Mme. Gregoire Staechelin* × *Bloomfield Comet*; Cross, C.W. Bud long, pointed; flowers pink, semi-dbl., open, large; strong stems; foliage dark; vigorous, climbing growth; free, intermittent bloom.

Nantucket HT, *ab*, 1972, *Chantré sport*; Kern Rose Nursery. Flowers peach apricot, dbl., high-centered, large; slightly fragrant; foliage leathery; vigorous, upright growth.

Naomi HT, *ob*, 1926, Pemberton. Flowers coppery buff, dbl.; fragrant. RULED EXTINCT 1/88.

Naomi HT, *dr*, 1988, *Red Lion* × *Seedling*; Poole, Lionel, 1989. Flowers dark red, shaded very dark in center, fading to red-purple, dbl. (32 petals), high-centered, decorative, medium, borne usually singly; slight fragrance; foliage large, dark green, semi-glossy; prickles flat, medium, medium green; tall, spreading, upright growth.

Napoléon G (OGR), *m*, 1846, Hardy. Flowers bright rose, shaded purple, dbl., very large; erect, vigorous growth.

Narcisse T (OGR), *my*, 1859, (Enfant de Lyon); Avoux. Flowers yellow, full, large.

Narcisse de Salvandy G (OGR), *mp*, 1843, Van Houtte. Flowers deep rose-pink, prominent yellow stamens, flat, large blooms in clusters; large, spreading growth.

Narita Korinkaku HT, *dy*, 1978, *Burnaby* × *Montparnasse*; Kikuchi. Bud pointed; flowers light orange, dbl. (35-40 petals), high-centered, very large (5-6 in.); very fragrant; foliage glossy, dark; upright growth.

Narmada Lahari HT, *pb*, 1979, *Shree Dayananda sport*; Hardikar, Dr. M.N. Bud ovoid; flowers pink blend, very dbl. (90 petals), blooms borne singly; fragrant; foliage small, green; beak-shaped prickles; bushy, dwarf growth.

Narre Fragrance HT, *ob*, 1942, *Portadown Fragrance sport*; Brundrett. Flowers golden orange.

Narre Peace HT, *yb*, 1960, *Peace sport*; Brundrett; Identical with Dorothy Goodwin.

Narrow Water N (OGR), *lp*, Said to be a Nastarana sport; Daisy Hill Nursery, ca. 1883. Flowers darker pink.

Narvik HT, *op*, 1960, *Seedling* × *Praline*; Robichon. Bud long, pointed; flowers salmon-pink to coppery, dbl., large; long, strong stems; slightly fragrant; foliage leathery; vigorous growth.

Narzisse HT, *my*, 1942, *Golden Rapture* × *Golden Glory*; Krause; C-P. Bud long, pointed; flowers apricot to maize-yellow, dbl. (23 petals), high-centered, large; fragrant; foliage dark, leathery; vigorous, upright growth.

Nascapee S, *w*, 1946, (*Ross Rambler* × (*R. rugosa* × *R. eglanteria*)) × *Seedling*; Preston; Central Exp. Farm. Flowers white, single (5 petals), open; slightly fragrant; tall, vigorous growth; free, recurrent bloom; hardy.

Nastarana N (OGR), *w*, 1879, (*R. moschata nastarana* Christ; *R. pissartii* Persian Musk Rose); *Probably an early R. chinensis* × *R. moschata hybrid.* Flowers white tinged pink, semi-dbl., medium (2 in.) blooms in clusters on new wood; very vigorous growth; recurrent; (14).

Natali F, *dr*, 1973, (TANnali); *Seedling* × *Seedling*; Tantau; Horstmann. Bud ovoid; flowers dark red, semi-dbl., small; foliage glossy; dwarf, upright growth. RULED EXTINCT 4/85.

Natali® F, *mp*, 1981, (TANrotreili); Tantau, M. Flowers medium pink, dbl. (20 petals), large; slight fragrance; foliage medium, medium green, matt; greenhouse variety.

Natalie Boettner HT, *my*, 1909, *Frau Karl Druschki* × *Goldelse*; Boettner. Flowers sulphur-yellow, passing to cream-yellow, tinted flesh, dbl.

Natalie Ward F, *mp*, 1974, *Pink Parfait* × *Seedling*; Thomas, R.; Pattollo's Nursery. Bud HT type; flowers pink, base yellow, dbl. (20 petals), medium (2-2½ in.); slightly fragrant; foliage light; bushy growth; bloom repeats quickly; good florists' rose.

Natalka HT, *lp*, Costetske. Flowers light pink.

Natasha F, *my*, 1974, *Highlight* × *Masquerade*; Staikov, Prof. Dr. V.; Kalaydjiev and Chorbadjiiski. Flowers lemon yellow, fading white, very dbl. (135 petals), large blooms in clusters of 7-13; foliage dark, glossy; bushy growth.

National Beauty HT, *mr*, 1983, *The Alamo sport*; Burks, Joe J.; J.B. Roses, Inc. Same as parent except fewer petals (40), better form and deeper color.

National Emblem HT, *dr*, 1915, McGredy. Flowers velvety dark crimson, edged vermilion, dbl., high-centered; fragrant.

National Flower Guild HT, *mr*, 1927, *(Capt. F. Bald × K. of K.) × Mme. Van de Voorde*; Mallerin; C-P, 1930. Flowers pure scarlet-red, dbl., large; long stems; very vigorous.

National Trust HT, *dr*, 1970, (Bad Nauheim); *Evelyn Fison × King of Hearts*; McGredy, S., IV; McGredy. Flowers bright red, dbl. (53 petals), classic form, large (4 in.).

National Velvet™ HT, *dr*, 1988, (BURalp); *Poinsettia × National Beauty*; Burks, Larry; Co-Operative Rose Growers, 1990. Flowers dark, deep velvet red, semi-dbl. (35 petals), urn-shaped, high-centered, medium, borne usually singly or in sprays of 1-3; slight fragrance; foliage large, medium green, semi-glossy; prickles recurved, average, dark; fruit globular, average, orange; upright, tall growth.

Native Wedding HSuf (S), *lp*, 1979, *Restless Native × (Mount Shasta × R. suffulta)*; Stoddard, Louis. Bud short, pointed; flowers light pink, semi-dbl. (14 petals), cupped, blooms borne singly; slight fragrance; foliage broad, waved, medium green, semi-glossy, 5-7 leaflet; straight prickles; upright, medium growth; repeat bloom.

Naughty But Nice Min, *ab*, 1991, (TINnaughty); *Futura × Why Not*; Bennett, Dee, 1983; Tiny Petals Nursery, 1990. Bud ovoid; flowers soft apricot, dbl. (20-25 petals), high-centered, exhibition, medium; slight, damask fragrance; foliage medium, medium green, semi-glossy; bushy, tall growth.

Naughty Nancy F, *pb*, 1970, Cants of Colchester. Flowers cream to red, semi-dbl. (12 petals), medium (2 in.); slightly fragrant; foliage dull, matt green; moderate growth.

Naughty Patricia Min, *pb*, 1989, (BILpat); *Rise 'n' Shine × Redgold*; Bilson, Jack M., Jr.; Jack M. III. Flowers medium pink, edges blush, dbl. (29 petals), outer petals quill, exhibition, large, borne usually singly and in sprays of 3-5; slight, fruity fragrance; foliage large, medium green, matt; prickles slight downward slope, reddish-tan; fruit globular, medium, green with orange-red blotch; upright, tall growth.

Nautilus F, *op*, 1960, *Signal Red × Fashion*; deRuiter. Flowers coral-salmon, dbl. (30 petals), open, borne in clusters; slightly fragrant; vigorous growth.

Navajo HT, *dp*, 1958, *Hortulanus Büdde × E.G. Hill*; Malandrone; J&P. Bud long, pointed; flowers dark red to rose-red, dbl. (35-40 petals), high-centered, large (4½-5 in.); very fragrant; foliage leathery; vigorous, upright growth.

Navid F, *or*, 1985, *Roydon Hall × Trumpeter*; Payne, A.J. Flowers orange-red, semi-dbl., patio, medium; slight fragrance; foliage medium, medium green, semi-glossy; bushy.

Navigator LCl, *mp*, 1925, *R. soulieana × Radiance*; Verhalen; Verhalen Nursery Co., 1943. Bud globular; flowers radiance pink, dbl. (25 petals), cupped, large; long stems; foliage soft; very vigorous, climbing growth.

Nav-Sadabahar F, *pb*, 1980, *Sadabahar sport*; Division of Vegetable Crops & Floriculture. Bud pointed; flowers deep pink striped white, dbl. (20 petals), blooms borne 15 per cluster; no fragrance; foliage medium, green; straight, pink to brown prickles; medium, spreading, bushy growth.

Nayika HT, *pb*, 1975, Pal; Anand Roses. Bud pointed; flowers delft-rose, reverse and base darker, very dbl. (45 petals), high-centered, large (4 in.); slightly fragrant (tea); foliage leathery; moderate, upright, bushy growth.

Nazneen HT, *lp*, 1969, *Queen Elizabeth × Seedling*; Pal; Son. Bud ovoid; flowers very soft pink, very dbl., high-centered, large; fragrant; foliage light green, glossy; vigorous, upright growth.

Nazr-e-Nazar HT, *mp*, 1968, *Clovelly × Seedling*; Singh. Bud pointed; flowers light pink edges flushed darker, dbl., high-centered, large; slightly fragrant; foliage leathery; vigorous, upright, compact growth.

Ne Plus Ultra N (OGR), *w*, Flowers creamy white; fragrant.

Néala G (OGR), *dp*, 1822, Vibert. Flowers deep rose edged lighter, full, medium.

Near You Min, *w*, 1990, (SEAnear); *Rise 'n' Shine × (Elina × Royal Gold)*; McCann, Sean. Flowers white, moderately full (15-25 petals), medium blooms; slight fragrance; foliage small, medium green, semi-glossy; spreading growth.

Nearly Wild F, *mp*, 1941, *Dr. W. Van Fleet × Leuchtstern*; Brownell. Bud small, long, pointed; flowers rose-pink, single (5 petals); fragrant; bushy growth.

Nearly Wild, Climbing Cl F, *mp*, 1962, Burks; Co-Operative Rose Growers.

Nébuleuse® F, *dr*, 1971, *Ritz × Lilli Marleen*; Gaujard. Flowers deep crimson, full, medium; vigorous growth.

Nederland HT, *dr*, 1919, *General-Superior Arnold Janssen × George C. Waud*; Verschuren. Flowers deep glowing red, full (60 petals).

Neelamabari F, *dr*, 1975, *Blue Moon × Africa Star*; Indian Agric. Research Inst. Flowers deep red, dbl. (35 petals), large; foliage dark, glossy; vigorous, compact, bushy growth.

Nehru Centenary HT, *dr*, 1989, *Christian Dior × Avon*; Indian Agricultural Research Institute. Bud pointed; flowers dark red, reverse deeper, high-centered, 60 petals, large, borne singly; slight fragrance; foliage very large, dark green, dense; prickles hooked, brown; tall, upright growth.

Neige d'Avril R, *w*, 1908, Robichon. Flowers pure white, stamens yellow, nearly dbl., large, borne in pyramidal clusters; very vigorous, climbing (to 8 ft.) growth; early, seasonal bloom.

Neige Parfum HT, *w*, 1942, *Joanna Hill × (White Ophelia × Seedling)*; Mallerin; A. Meilland; J&P. Flowers white, sometimes tinted cream, dbl., large; very fragrant; foliage leathery; vigorous.

Neige Rose LCl, *pb*, 1955, Delbard-Chabert. Flowers center deep pink, becoming lighter at petal edges, large; slightly fragrant; very vigorous growth.

Neiges D'Été Min, *w*, 1984, (Rigobec 2; Summer's Snow); *Baby Masquerade sport × Baby Masquerade Seedling*; Gailloux, Gilles. Flowers white, dbl. (37 petals), small; no fragrance; foliage medium, medium green, glossy; upright growth.

Nejenka F, *m*, 1955, (Tender One); *Raised from Independence*; Klimenko. Flowers purplish pink, dbl. (57 petals), large; fragrant; foliage dark, glossy; upright growth.

Nell Gwyn HT, *or*, 1968, *Tzigane sport*; Cobley; Blaby Rose Gardens. Flowers orange-copper, globular; fragrant; upright growth.

Nellie Charlton HT, *mp*, 1923, *Mme. Abel Chatenay Seedling*; Lilley. Flowers silvery pink, reverse salmon-pink, dbl; very fragrant.

Nellie E. Hillock HT, *mp*, 1934, *Golden Dawn × Seedling*; Hillock. Flowers silvery pink, base deep gold, reverse old-rose, dbl. (60 petals), cupped, peony form; fragrant; foliage leathery, dark; low, spreading growth.

Nellie E. Hillock, Climbing Cl HT, *mp*, 1948, Buck; Lester Rose Gardens.

Nellie Maud Powell HT, *yb*, 1977, *Columbine sport × Kordes' Perfecta*; Powell. Flowers yellow edged red, very dbl. (75-80 petals), large (4-5 in.); very fragrant; foliage glossy; vigorous growth.

Nellie Parker HT, *w*, 1916, Dickson, H. Flowers creamy white, center darker, full, well shaped, large; vigorous, upright growth. GM, NRS, 1916.

Nelly Custis HMsk (S), *w*, A plant has been grown under this name in the flower garden at Mount Vernon for many years. By undocu-

mented tradition it is known as having been planted by General Washington and named for Mrs. Washington's granddaughter. Flowers white, dbl., borne in clusters of 7-9; fragrant; vigorous, upright growth.

Nelly Verschuren HT, *my*, 1918, *Seedling × Duchess of Wellington*; Verschuren. Flowers clear yellow; very fragrant.

Némésis Ch (OGR), *dr*, 1836, Bizard. Flowers purplish crimson, dbl., pompon form; dwarf growth; (14)

Nénette Leydier Pol, *mr*, 1924, Richardier. Flowers crimson-scarlet, base lighter.

Nenikujaku F, *pb*, 1984, *Masquerade × Matador*; Kikuchi, R. Flowers pink, blended with yellow and red, semi-dbl. (15 petals), cupped, medium blooms in clusters; fragrant; vigorous.

Nenita F, *w*, 1962, *Seedling × Virgo*; Moreira da Silva. Flowers white, dbl. (22 petals), large; fragrant; foliage light green; vigorous, low growth.

Neon F, *ob*, 1971, Waterhouse Nursery. Flowers intense orange, dbl. (26 petals), medium (2 in.); compact growth.

Neon HT, *mr*, 1936, Nicolas; Beckwith. Flowers crimson-scarlet, very dbl., large; fragrant; vigorous, branching growth.

Neon Lights F, *dp*, 1991, (JACout); *Intrigue × Impatient*; Warriner, William A.; Bear Creek Gardens, Inc., 1992. Flowers hot magenta pink, moderately full (15-25 petals), large blooms borne in small clusters; fragrant; foliage medium, medium green, semi-glossy; medium, bushy growth.

Nerissa HT, *ly*, 1912, Paul, W. Flowers cream-yellow, shaded white; dbl.; slightly fragrant.

Néron G (OGR), *rb*, 1841, Laffay. Flowers crimson, blotched and marbled violet.

Nestor G (OGR), *mr*, Prior to 1848. Flowers crimson, full, large; very vigorous growth.

Nestor Bolderdijk HT, *pb*, 1938, *Comtesse Vandal × Pres. Macia*; Leenders, M. Bud long, pointed; flowers pale ecru, reverse yellowish salmon, base golden, dbl., very large; foliage glossy; vigorous growth.

Neue Revue® HT, *rb*, 1962, (KORrev; News Review); *Colour Wonder × Seedling*; Kordes. Flowers yellow-white, touched dark red, dbl. (30 petals), well formed, large (4½ in.); very fragrant; foliage leathery; many large prickles; upright growth. ADR, 1969.

Neutron Sp (OGR), *m*, 1984, *Grown from neutron-irradiated seed of R. rugosa*; Lundstad, Arne; Agricultural University of Norway. Flowers purple, semi-dbl. (10 petals), shallow-cupped, 3 in. blooms borne singly or few per cluster; strong fragrance; foliage thick, rugose, shining, dark; straight, gray prickles; upright, dense growth; repeat bloom.

Nevada HMoy (S), *w*, 1927, *Reported to be La Giralda* × *R. moyesii hybrid*; Dot, P.; Perhaps *R. moyesii fargesii*, a tetraploid form, was used as the parent instead of *R. moyesii*. Bud ovoid, pink or apricot; flowers white, reverse sometimes splashed carmine, single, large blooms on short stem; vigorous (7 ft.), shrubby growth; heavy bloom usually repeated.

Neville Chamberlain HT, *ob*, 1940, *Charles P. Kilham* × *Mrs. Sam McGredy*; Lens; J&P. Bud ovoid; flowers salmon, center orange, dbl. (26 petals), high-centered, large (4 in.); foliage bronze; vigorous, tall growth. GM, Portland, 1941.

Neville Gibson HT, *mp*, 1982, (HARportly); *Red Planet* × *(Carina* × *Pascali)*; Harkness, R., 1983. Flowers medium pink, dbl. (40 petals), high-centered, exhibition, large; slight fragrance; foliage large, medium green, semiglossy; medium, upright. Geneva Rose d'Or; GM.

New Adventure Min, *w*, 1989, (MORshefran); *Sheri Anne* × *Safrano*; Moore, Ralph S.; Sequoia Nursery. Bud pointed; flowers creamy white, dbl. (25 petals), flat, medium, borne singly and in sprays of 3-5; no fragrance; foliage small, medium green, matt; frickles short, pointed, brownish-gray; fruit globular, orange; upright, bushy, medium growth.

New Beginning™ Min, *ob*, 1988, (SAVabeg); *Zorina* × *Seedling*; Saville, F. Harmon; Nor'East Miniature Roses, 1989. Flowers bright orange-yellow bicolor, very dbl. (40-50 petals), decorative, medium, borne usually singly or in sprays of 3-5; no fragrance; foliage medium, medium green, semi-glossy; no fruit; very few prickles; bushy, compact growth. 1989 AARS.

New Castle Min, *rb*, 1984, *Watercolor* × *Seedling*; Bridges, Dennis A. Flowers red, white reverse, dbl. (20 petals), small; no fragrance; foliage medium, dark, semi-glossy; upright growth.

New Century HRg (S), *pb*, 1900, *R. rugosa alba* × *Clotilde Soupert*; Van Fleet; Conard & Jones. Flowers flesh-pink, center light red, edges creamy, dbl.; fragrant; foliage wrinkled, light, tough; vigorous (4-5 ft.), bushy growth; intermittent blooom.

New Columbia HT, *mp*, 1924, *Columbia sport*; Hill, E.G., Co. Flowers true pink, deepening to glowing pink.

New Daily Mail F, *dr*, 1972, (Pussta); *Letkis* × *Walzertraum*; Tantau. Bud globular; flowers dark red, semi-dbl., large; vigorous, upright, bushy growth.

New Daily Mail, Climbing Cl F, *dr*, 1989, (Pussta, Climbing); *New Daily Mail sport*; Patil, B.K.; K.S.G. Son's Roses, 1987.

New Dawn LCl, *lp*, 1930, (Everblooming Dr. W. Van Fleet; The New Dawn); *Dr. W. Van Fleet sport*; Somerset Rose Nursery; Dreer. Flowers same as parent except repeat blooming.

New Day HT, *my*, 1977, (KORgold; Mabella); *Arlene Francis* × *Roselandia*; Kordes, R.; J&P. Bud ovoid, pointed; flowers mimosa-yellow, dbl. (30 petals), high-centered, large (4-5 in.); very fragrant; foliage large, light; upright growth.

New Face® S, *yb*, 1982, (INTerclem); Interplant, 1978. Flowers yellow edged pink, single (5 petals), small blooms in large clusters; slight fragrance; foliage medium, medium green, semi-glossy; many prickles; upright; repeat bloom.

New Gold Min, *dy*, 1977, *Yellow Jewel* × *Allgold*; Lyon; L. Lyon Greenhouses. Bud long, pointed; flowers buttercup-yellow, dbl. (20 petals), open, medium (2-2½ in.); very fragrant; foliage small, very dark; vigorous, upright growth.

New Haven Queen HT, *ob*, 1939, *Token sport*; Grillo. Bud pointed; flowers tangerine, dbl. (40 petals), medium (3½ in.); fragrant; foliage leathery; vigorous growth.

New Hope Min, *w*, 1988, *Party Girl* × *Seedling*; Bridges, Dennis; Bridges Roses, 1989. Bud pointed; flowers creamy white, slight pink edge, 19 petals, high-centered, exhibition, medium, borne usually singly; foliage medium, dark green, semi-glossy; prickles straight, pointed, medium, medium red; bushy, medium growth.

New Look F, *rb*, 1961, *Charles Gregory Seedling* × *Orange Triumph Seedling*; Gaujard; Gandy. Flowers maroon, reverse silver, dbl. (50 petals), large (3 in.) blooms in clusters; fragrant; foliage glossy, coppery; vigorous, bushy growth.

New Love HT, *rb*, 1968, *South Seas* × *Coronado*; Morey; Country Garden Nursery. Flowers cardinal-red, reverse golden yellow, dbl., high-centered, large; foliage glossy, bronze; vigorous, bushy growth.

New Mexico HT, *mr*, 1967, *Mount Shasta* × *Granada*; Aufill. Flowers red, dbl., high-centered, medium; fragrant; foliage bronze, leathery; very vigorous growth.

New Moonlight HT, *my*, 1935, *Sun Gold* × *Joseph Hill*; Elmer's Nursery. Flowers yellow, dbl., very large; long stems; foliage glossy; very vigorous growth.

New Orleans HT, *yb*, 1966, *Peace sport*; Tate. Bud ovoid; flowers yellow, veined light red, dbl., globular, large; fragrant; foliage glossy; vigorous, upright growth. RULED EXTINCT 2/87.

New Orleans™ Min, *mr*, 1987, (KINnor); *Evelyn Fison × Magic Mist*; King, Gene; AGM Miniature Roses. Flowers medium to dark red toward base, non-fading, reverse medium red, fading lighter red, dbl. (32 petals), cupped, exhibition, medium, borne usually singly or in sprays of 3-5; slight, spicy fragrance; foliage medium, medium green, matt; straight, small, red prickles; fruit oval, small, green; bushy, spreading, medium growth.

New Peace™ HT, *yb*, 1988, (AROnewp); *Gingersnap × Young Quinn*; Christensen, Jack; Michigan Bulb, 1988. Flowers yellow-cream with bright red margins aging larger red margin, dbl. (48-52 petals), urn-shaped, high-centered, loose, large, borne usually singly; slight fragrance; foliage medium, medium green, matt; prickles pointed, small, dark tan; upright, medium growth.

New Penny Min, *or*, 1962, *(R. wichuraiana × Floradora) × Seedling*; Moore, R.S.; Sequoia Nursery. Bud short, pointed; flowers orange-red to coral-pink, dbl. (20 petals), small (1½ in.); fragrant; foliage leathery, glossy; bushy, dwarf (10 in.) growth.

New Planet HT, *mp*, 1930, *Premier sport*; Cleveland Cut-Flower Co. Flowers bright rose-pink, center light pink, dbl.; very fragrant.

New Style HT, *mr*, 1962, *(Happiness × Independence) × Peace*; Meilland, Alain; URS. Bud oval; flowers crimson flushed brighter, dbl. (25 petals), large; long stems; slightly fragrant; foliage leathery, glossy; very vigorous, bushy growth.

New World F, *rb*, 1945, *Crimson Glory × Château de Clos Vougeot*; Jacobus; B&A. Flowers velvety red and crimson, reverse lighter, dbl.; very fragrant; foliage soft, glossy; bushy growth; (28).

New Year® Gr, *ob*, 1983, (MACnewye; Arcadian); *Mary Sumner × Seedling*; McGredy, S., 1982. Flowers orange and gold blend, dbl. (20 petals), medium; slight fragrance; foliage large, dark, glossy; upright growth. AARS, 1987.

New Yorker HT, *mr*, 1947, *Flambeau × Seedling*; Boerner; J&P. Flowers velvety bright scarlet, dbl. (35 petals), high-centered, large (4-4½ in.); fragrant (fruity); vigorous, bushy.

New Yorker, Climbing Cl HT, *mr*, 1951, Boerner.

Newport Fairy R, *pb*, 1908, (Newport Rambler); *R. wichuraiana × Crimson Rambler*; Gardner; Roehrs. Flowers very deep rosy pink, white eye, golden stamens, single, small blooms in clusters.

News® F, *m*, 1968, (LEGnews); *Lilac Charm × Superb Tuscany*; LeGrice. Flowers red-purple, semi-dbl., blooms in trusses; fragrant; foliage olive-green, glossy. GM, RNRS, 1970.

Newsace HT, *ab*, 1961, *Horace McFarland × Good News*; Wyant. Bud ovoid; Flowers light apricot, center darker, dbl. (70 petals), large (4 in.); strong stems; fragrant; foliage glossy; vigorous, upright growth.

Newsgate HT, *op*, 1964, *Paulien Verbeek × (Jolie Madame × Baccará)*; Verbeek. Flowers rose and persimmon-orange, base yellow, reverse darker, dbl. (50-58 petals), large (4 in.); foliage dark, glossy; vigorous growth.

Niagara HT, *mr*, 1952, *Crimson Glory × Seedling*; Davis; Garden Town Nursery. Bud long, pointed; flowers bright red, dbl., high-centered; very fragrant (fruity).

Niagara Mist HT, *pb*, 1968, *Tiffany × Mrs. A.R. Barraclough*; Davis; Wyant. Bud ovoid; flowers light pink, base yellow, dbl., high-centered, large; fragrant; foliage glossy, vigorous, upright growth.

Niagara Sunshine HT, *dy*, 1969, Davis; Wyant. Flowers chrome-yellow, dbl., globular, large; foliage glossy, light green; vigorous, upright growth.

Nice Day Cl Min, *op*, 1992, (CHEWsea; Patio Queen); *Seaspray × Warm Welcome*; Warner, C.H.; Warner, C.H., 1993. Flowers salmon pink, moderately full (15-25 petals), small (0-4 cms) blooms borne in large clusters; fragrant; foliage small, bronze turning medium green, glossy; few prickles; upright bushy, climbing growth.

Nicholas Sweetbriar Sp (OGR), *lp*, *R. eglanteria seed-grown strain*; Nicholas; Univ. of Neb., 1959. (Probably brought from Virginia to Kansas before 1875; seed brought to North Platte Exp. Sta. by Nicholas; introduced Univ. of Neb., 1959.) Flowers pink, small (1½ in.); foliage fragrant; fruit abundant, red; very thorny; height 6-8 ft. Appears to be adapted to conservation planting beyond the range of *R. multiflora*. Grows rapidly from seeds.

Nickelodeon Min, *rb*, 1989, (MACnickel); *Roller Coaster × (Freude × ((Anytime × Eyepaint) × Stars 'n' Stripes))*; McGredy, Sam, 1991. Flowers red blend, semi-dbl. (6-14 petals), small; patio; slight fragrance; foliage small, dark green, semi-glossy; bushy growth.

Nicky F, *or*, 1970, *Cyclamen × Fire King*; Institute of Ornamental Plant Growing. Bud medium, pointed; flowers orange-red, semi-dbl., cupped, large blooms in clusters; no fragrance; foliage medium, light green, sparse, leathery; vigorous, upright, bushy growth.

Nic-Noc Min, *mr*, 1978, *Anytime* × *Gruss an Bayern*; Poulsen, N.D.; D.T. Poulsen. Flowers medium red, lighter reverse, dbl. (20 petals), cupped blooms in clusters; slight fragrance; foliage small, dark, semi-glossy; sets seed; spreading growth.

Nicola F, *dp*, 1980, *Seedling* × *Seedling*; Gandy, Douglas L.; Gandy Roses Ltd. Flowers deep rose pink, single (8 petals), blooms borne 6-10 per cluster; slight fragrance; green prickles; bushy growth.

Nicole HT, *yb*, 1931, Gaujard; C-P. Bud long, pointed; flowers yellow, center coppery, shaded carmine; very fragrant; very vigorous growth. RULED EXTINCT 11/80.

Nicole, Climbing Cl HT, *yb*, 1933, Kordes.

Nicole Debrosse HT, *dr*, 1962, *Seedling* × *Baccará*; Croix, P.; Minier. Flowers dark red, shaded scarlet; vigorous growth.

Nicoletta HT, *mp*, 1969, *Carla sport*; deRuiter. Bud ovoid; flowers pink, dbl., medium; foliage dark.

Nicolina Min, *pb*, 1991, (ZIPnic); *(Dandy Lyon × Razzle Dazzle) × Pink Petticoat*; Zipper, Herbert; Magic Moment Miniatures, 1992. Bud ovoid; flowers coral pink shading to white, reverse pink edge, shading to creamy white with yellow undertones, edges age to deep coral pink shading to white, dbl. (25 petals), cupped, exhibition, small (3 cms), blooms borne usually singly; slight fragrance; foliage small, dark green, semi-glossy; upright, bushy, tall growth.

Nida Senff Pol, *mp*, 1946, Kersbergen. Flowers soft rosy pink, borne in large clusters.

Nigel Hawthorne S, *pb*, 1989, (HARquibbler); *H. persica × Harvest Home*; Harkness, R.; Co. Bud pointed; flowers pale salmon-rose, deep scarlet eye at base, reverse same, aging paling, single (5 petals), cupped, opening wide, medium, borne singly and in sprays; slight, spicy fragrance; foliage medium, medium green, semi-glossy; prickles thin, narrow, variable, dark to light; fruit plump, small, green, infrequent; spreading, low growth.

Nigger Boy HT, *dr*, 1933, *Hadley × Yves Druhen*; Knight, G. Bud long, pointed; flowers very dark velvety blackish maroon, dbl. (56 petals), high-centered, globular; very fragrant; foliage thick, glossy, bronze; low, compact growth. Named in Australia in honor of the Australian bushman; the name may be

unpleasing to Americans, but no offense is intended.

Night HT, *dr*, 1930, (Lady Sackville); McGredy. Bud long, pointed; flowers deepest blackish crimson, shaded maroon, dbl., high-centered; very fragrant; foliage dark, glossy; bushy growth.

Night, Climbing Cl HT, *dr*, 1936, Armstrong, J.A.; Armstrong Nursery.

Night Fire Min, *dr*, 1982, (LYOfi); *Seedling × Seedling*; Lyon, Lyndon. Flowers deep red, petals often edged black, dbl. (20 petals), small; fragrant; foliage medium, dark, semi-glossy; upright, bushy growth.

Night Lady Min, *rb*, 1983, *Seedling × Libby*; Meredith, E.A.; Rovinski, M.E.; Casa de Rosa Domingo. Flowers red, white reverse, dbl. (36 petals), high-centered, medium, borne singly; heavy fragrance; foliage medium, dark, semi-glossy; upright.

Night Light® LCl, *dy*, 1985, (POUllight); *Westerland × Pastorale*; Poulsen, N.D.; D.T. Poulsen, 1982. Flowers deep yellow, dbl. (27 petals), large blooms in sprays of 1-5; moderate fragrance; foliage large, dark, glossy; large, dark red prickles; bushy growth.

Night Music Min, *mp*, 1988, (ZIPmusic); *Tamango × Pink Petticoat*; Zipper, Herbert; Magic Moment Miniatures, 1989. Flowers deep pink, dbl. (over 40 petals), medium, borne singly and in sprays; very fragrant; mini-floral; foliage large, medium green, semi-glossy; upright growth.

Night 'n' Day HT, *dr*, 1968, *(World's Fair × Chrysler Imperial) × Happiness*; Swim & Weeks. Bud pointed; flowers dark red, dbl., large; fragrant; foliage dark, leathery; vigorous, tall, bushy growth.

Night Song S, *dr*, 1984, *(Rosali × Music Maker) × Meisterstuck*; Buck; Iowa State University. Flowers dark red, dbl. (33 petals), large blooms borne 1-10 per cluster; fragrant; foliage medium-large, dark bronze green, semi-glossy; awl-like, tan prickles; compact, erect, bushy growth; repeat bloom; hardy.

Night Time HT, *dr*, 1975, *Forty-niner × Oklahoma*; Weeks. Bud long, pointed; flowers dark black-red, dbl. (39 petals), high-centered; very fragrant; foliage dark, leathery; vigorous.

Nighthawk™ Min, *mr*, 1988, (DOHhawk; Night Hawk); *Quinella × Poker Chip*; Hardgrove, Donald L.; Nor'East Miniature Roses, 1989. Bud globular, pointed; flowers medium red, dbl. (22 petals), high-centered, medium, borne singly and in sprays of 3-5; heavy, damask fragrance; foliage medium, medium green; prickles straight, slanted down, medium, reddish-brown; upright, bushy, medium growth. AOE, 1989.

Nightingale HT, *pb*, 1970, (HERgale); *Rina Herholdt × Tiffany*; Herholdt, J.A.; Herholdt's Nursery. Flowers rich rose-red, blended lighter, dbl. (25 petals), high-centered, large; slightly fragrant; growth moderate.

Nigrette HT, *dr*, 1934, *Château de Clos Vougeot × Lord Castlereagh*; Krause; C-P. Flowers blackish maroon or plum color, varying with season and weather, dbl., medium; bushy growth.

Nigritella F, *dr*, 1953, Cazzaniga. Flowers red shaded darker, dbl.; dwarf, bushy growth.

Nikki F, *ob*, 1981, *Dusky Maiden × Eyepaint*; Bracegirdle, A.J. Flowers vermilion, white eye and reverse, semi-dbl., medium; no fragrance; foliage medium, medium green, semi-glossy; bushy growth.

Nil Desperandum HT, *ob*, 1979, *Gavotte × Montezuma*; Ellick; Excelsior Roses. Flowers indian orange, dbl. (25-30 petals), full, large (4 in.); foliage large, light matt green; very vigorous growth.

Niles Cochet T (OGR), *rb*, 1906, (Red Maman Cochet); *Maman Cochet sport*; California Nursery Co. Flowers cherry-red on outer petals, lighter within.

Nilsson Guy F, *dp*, 1930, *Lafayette sport*; Leenders, M. Flowers deep rose-pink, semi-dbl., open, large, borne in clusters.

Nimbus F, *m*, 1989, (LEGgrey); *Grey Dawn × Seedling*; LeGrice, E.B. Roses. Bud pointed; flowers lilac-gray, very dbl., cupped, medium, borne in sprays; slight fragrance; foliage medium, medium green, semi-glossy; bushy, medium growth.

Nimes F, *rb*, 1970, *Pampa × Piccadilly*; Gaujard. Flowers vermilion, reverse gold, dbl.

Nina Marshall HT, *dp*, 1966, *Serenade × Queen o' the Lakes*; Golik; Ellesmere Nursery. Flowers cerise, base gold, semi-dbl., cupped; slightly fragrant; foliage glossy; moderate growth.

Nina Poulsen F, *mr*, 1940, *Grethe Poulsen × Hybrid Tea red seedling*; Poulsen, S.; Poulsen. Flowers clear red, semi-dbl.; taller and more vigorous than Rodhatte.

Nina Rosa HT, *op*, 1946, *Frank Reader × Condesa de Sástago*; Robichon. Flowers coppery pink shaded yellow, dbl., very large; fragrant.

Nina Weibull® F, *dr*, 1962, *Fanal × Masquerade*; Poulsen, S. Flowers dark red, dbl., medium; foliage dark; compact, bushy growth.

Ninetta® F, *dp*, 1985, (TANattenin); Tantau, M. Flowers deep pink, dbl. (20 petals), medium; slight fragrance; foliage medium

green, semi-glossy; upright growth; greenhouse variety.

Ninie Vandevelde Pol, *mp*, 1924, Vandevelde. Flowers salmon.

Ninon Vallin HT, *ab*, 1936, Gaujard. Flowers apricot, reverse fresh yellow, dbl., large; foliage bright green; very vigorous growth.

Niobe F, *w*, 1942, *Rosenelfe sport*; J&P. Flowers white, center sometimes flushed light pink.

Niphetos T (OGR), *w*, 1843, Bougere. Bud pointed; flowers white, globular, large; very fragrant. Once a famous greenhouse rose.

Niphetos, Climbing Cl T (OGR), *w*, 1889, Keynes, Williams & Co..

Nippy HT, *yb*, 1932, Cant, B.R. Flowers canary-yellow, reverse splashed red; fragrant (fruity); foliage dark.

Niramol Min, *ab*, 1991, (UMSnira); *Loving Touch × Seedling*; Umsawasdi, Theera. Flowers apricot blend, moderately full, medium blooms borne mostly singly; no fragrance; foliage medium, medium green, semi-glossy; medium, bushy growth.

Nirvana® F, *lp*, 1977, (MEIrisouru); *(Pink Wonder × Kalinka) × Centenaire de Lourdes*; Meilland, M.L.; Meilland. Bud ovoid; flowers light pink, dbl. (20 petals), fully cupped, large; foliage glossy; bushy growth. GM, Geneva, 1975.

Nisette F, *dp*, 1967, *Garnette sport*; van't Kruis; deRuiter. Flowers pink-red, globular, borne in trusses; foliage small, dark; moderate growth.

Nishiki-E F, *ob*, 1981, (Nishikie); *(Sarabande × Amanogawa) × Kagayaki*; Suzuki, S.; Keisei Rose Nursery. Flowers orange-yellow, dbl. (38 petals), high-centered, medium blooms borne 2-5 per stem; foliage dark, semi-glossy; small prickles slanted downward; upright.

Nita Min, *ab*, 1987, *Seedling × Miniature*; McDaniel, Earl; McDaniel's Min. Roses. Flowers apricot, lighter apricot reverse, dbl. (55 petals), high-centered, exhibition, medium blooms borne singly; slight fragrance; foliage medium, dark, semi-glossy; few, light green prickles; medium, upright, bushy growth.

Nitouche® F, *pb*, 1974, *Seedling × Whisky Mac*; Poulsen, N.D.; Poulsen. Flowers silvery, deep salmon pink reverse, dbl. (25 petals), large (4 in.); slightly fragrant; foliage glossy, dark; bushy, upright growth.

Nivea HT, *w*, 1949, *Nuria de Recolons × Blanche Mallerin*; Dot, P. Bud long, pointed; flowers white, dbl., high-centered, medium; very fragrant; foliage sparse; dwarf growth.

Noah HT, *ob*, 1985, *Dr. A.J. Verhage sport*; Nevo, Motke; Maoz Haim Rose Nursery, 1976. Flowers orange.

Nobility HT, *lp*, 1961, (Elle); *Peace Seedling × Peace*; Boerner; J&P. Bud ovoid; flowers ivory lightly overcast pink, center deeper, dbl. (35-40 petals), high-centered; large (5-5½ in.); fragrant; foliage leathery; vigorous, upright growth.

Nobilo's Chardonnay® HT, *my*, 1984, (MACrelea; Chardonnay; Chardony); *Freude × (Wienerwald × Benson & Hedges Gold)*; McGredy, Sam. Flowers orange yellow, dbl. (35 petals), large; slight fragrance; foliage small, light green, glossy; bushy growth.

Noblesse HT, *or*, 1969, *Coloranja × Coloranja*; Spek; A. Dickson. Flowers orange-red, dbl. (28 petals), very large; slightly fragrant; foliage glossy; moderate growth.

Nocturne F, *dr*, Archer. Flowers dark red, dbl.; moderate growth.

Nocturne HT, *dr*, 1947, *Charlotte Armstrong × Night*; Swim; Armstrong Nursery. Bud long, pointed; flowers dark red, dbl. (24 petals), cupped, large (4½ in.); fragrant (spicy); foliage leathery, dark; vigorous, upright, bushy growth. AARS, 1948.

Nocturne, Climbing Cl HT, *dr*, 1955, Armstrong, J.A.; Armstrong Nursery.

Noëlla Nabonnand Cl T (OGR), *dr*, 1901, *Reine Marie Henriette × Bardou Job*; Nabonnand, G. Flowers velvety crimson-red, semi-dbl., large; fragrant; (21).

Noella Virebent Cl T, *lp*, 1922, *R. gigantea × Archiduc Joseph*; Nabonnand, P. Flowers flesh-pink, center brighter, semi-dbl.; fragrant; foliage dark, glossy; few thorns; very vigorous growth.

Nogawa HT, *w*, 1989, *Garden Party × Kordes' Perfecta*; Takahashi, Takeshi. Bud ovoid; flowers cream, fringed with pink, dbl. (30 petals), high-centered, large, borne usually singly; moderate fragrance; foliage medium, dark green, semi-glossy; prickles almost right-angled to stem; bushy, tall growth.

Noisette Rose (*R. × noisettiana* Thory; *R. indica noisettiana* Seringe; *R. moschata autumnalis* hort.); A group of hybrids between China Roses and Musk Roses and certain offspring of these hybrids.

Nokomis R, *dp*, 1918, *R. wichuraiana × Comte Raimbaud*; Walsh. Flowers dark rose-pink, dbl., larger than Lady Gay or Dorothy Perkins, borne in clusters of 5-30; very fragrant; foliage light, glossy; vigorous, climbing growth.

Non Plus Ultra R, *dr*, 1904, (Weigand's Crimson Rambler); *Crimson Rambler ×*

Blanche Rebatel; Weigand, C. Flowers dark red, dbl., small blooms in clusters; vigorous growth.

Nona HT, *op*, 1924, *Mme. Edouard Herriot × Constance*; Easlea. Bud long, pointed; flowers flame and pink (like Mme. Edouard Herriot, but deeper vermilion tint), semi-dbl., fragrant.

Nonin HT, *yb*, 1938, *Souv. de Claudius Pernet × Seedling*; Mallerin; A. Meilland. Flowers golden yellow, tinted coral-orange, dbl., very large; slightly fragrant; foliage glossy; vigorous growth.

Nora Cuningham Cl HT, *lp*, 1920, *Gustav Grunerwald Seedling*; Clark, A.; Hackett. Flowers flesh-pink, center paler, semi-dbl., cupped, large; long stems; fragrant; foliage wrinkled, light; vigorous. climbing growth; free bloom, sometimes recurrent.

Nora Henslow HT, *dp*, 1925, *Mme. Mélanie Soupert × Gen. MacArthur*; Evans; Beckwith. Flowers crimson-cerise, single; fragrant.

Nora Hooker F, *mr*, 1970, *Queen Elizabeth sport*; Hooker; Harkness. Flowers red, dbl. (22 petals), large (4 in.); slightly fragrant; free growth.

Nora Johnson HMoy (S), *dp*, 1957, *Believed to be R. willmottiae × R. moyesii*; Found in garden of A.T. Johnson in North Wales; Sunningdale Nursery. Flowers cerise, small; slightly fragrant; fruit small, bright; arching wands.

Norah Longley Pol, *ob*, 1948, *Cameo sport*; Longley. Flowers flame-orange, borne in trusses; foliage bright green; vigorous, branching growth.

Nordic Chant HT, *mp*, 1974, *Tropicana × Queen of Bermuda*; Golik; Dynarose. Bud long, pointed; flowers salmon-pink, dbl. (40 petals), high-centered, large (4½ in.); fragrant (spicy); foliage glossy, light; vigorous growth.

Nordlicht HT, *or*, 1910, *Mme. Caroline Testout × Luciole*; Kiese. Flowers coppery red.

Nordlicht F, *or*, 1957, (Northlight); *Bergfeuer × Gertrud Westphal*; Kordes, R.; R. Schmidt. Flowers deep cinnabar-red, dbl., high-centered, large, borne in small clusters; slightly fragrant; foliage leathery; very vigorous, low, bushy growth.

Norfolk Harmony HT, *dp*, 1940, *Comtesse Vandal × Mrs. Sam McGredy*; LeGrice. Bud long, pointed; flowers rosy cerise, dbl., high-centered, large; slightly fragrant; foliage glossy, dark; very vigorous, tall growth.

Norida F, *dp*, 1967, (*Pinocchio × Pinocchio*) × *Elsinore*; Poulsen; McGredy; DeVor Nursery. Flowers light crimson-scarlet, dbl., medium; greenhouse variety.

Norita® HT, *dr*, 1971, (COMsor; Norita-Schwarze Rose®); *Charles Mallerin × Seedling*; Combe; Kern Rose Nursery, 1966. Flowers very deep red, dbl., high-centered, large; fragrant; foliage dark, leathery; vigorous, bushy.

Norma HT, *mr*, 1976, *Clio × Credo*; Gaujard. Flowers brilliant red, dbl. (50 petals), large.

Norma Bennett F, *dr*, 1958, *Florence Mary Morse × Border Queen*; Bennett, H.; Waikato Rose Soc. Flowers crimson.

Norma Margaret Min, *pb*, 1989, (FROnorm); *Baby Katie × Seedling*; Frock, Marshall J., 1990. Bud pointed; flowers pink, blending with copper shading, reverse white with pink shading, aging deeper, dbl. (30 petals), high-centered, exhibition, large, borne usually singly and in sprays of 2-3; moderate fragrance; foliage medium, medium green, semi-glossy; prickles straight, medium, brown; no fruit; upright, medium growth.

Norman HT, *mr*, 1934, Dickson, A. Flowers, bright scarlet-red, well formed; fragrant; vigorous growth.

Norman Hartnell HT, *mr*, 1964, *Ballet × Detroiter*; Kordes, R.; Wheatcroft Bros. Flowers crimson-red, dbl. (21 petals), well formed, large; foliage dark; very vigorous growth.

Norman Lambert HT, *ob*, 1926, McGredy. Bud long, pointed; flowers deep salmon-orange, suffused bronze and yellow, base lighter, reverse buttercup-yellow, dbl., high-centered, large; slightly fragrant. GM, NRS, 1924.

Norman Rogers HT, *dp*, 1933, Chaplin Bros. Flowers deep rose-pink, base yellow, large.

Normandie R, *mp*, 1929, Nonin. Flowers salmon-pink; vigorous growth.

Norris Pratt® HT, *my*, 1964, *Mrs. Pierre S. duPont × Marcelle Gret*; Buisman. Flowers bright yellow, large; foliage leathery; growth moderate.

Norrköping HT, *mr*, 1961, *Karl Herbst × (Baccará × Golden Sun)*; Poulsen, S. Bud pointed; flowers scarlet, reverse darker; long stems; very vigorous growth.

Norseman F, *mp*, 1963, *seelding × Pinocchio*; Abrams, Von. Flowers pink, dbl., medium; very fragrant; foliage soft; vigorous, upright growth.

Northern Dancer HT, *ob*, 1965, *Tzigane sport*; Schloen; Ellesmere Nursery. Bud ovoid; flowers orange-yellow, edges flushed pink, dbl., large; slightly fragrant; foliage dark, glossy, leathery; vigorous, tall, compact growth.

Northern Lights® HT, *yb*, 1969, *Fragrant Cloud × Kingcup*; Cocker, 1971. Flowers lemon-cream, tinted pink, dbl. (50 petals), large (5 in.); very fragrant.

Northern States HSpn (OGR), *w*, 1952, *R. spinosissima × Irish Charm*; Shepherd; Kern Rose Nursery. Bud long, pointed; flowers white tinged pink and yellow, single (5 petals), open, large; fragrant; foliage leathery; bushy, compact (2½ ft.) growth; profuse, non-recurrent bloom; hardy; makes a good hedge.

Northland F, *mp*, 1991, (MACcarlto); *(Sexy Rexy × New Year) × West Coast*; McGredy, Sam; Sam McGredy Roses International, 1992. Flowers medium pink, full (26-40 petals), large (over 7 cms) blooms; slight fragrance; foliage large, medium green, semi-glossy; ultra healthy, bushy (100 cms) growth.

Northlander S, *mp*, 1985, *Baronne Prévost × ((Magnifica × Joanna Hill) × (Blanche Mallerin × R. laxa))*; James, John. Flowers medium pink, single (5 petals), medium (4 in.) blooms borne singly and in clusters of 3; fragrant; foliage medium, dark, matt; vigorous, upright (to 8 ft.) growth; repeat bloom.

North Star HT, *lp*, 1964, *Marcia Stanhope × Peace*; Golik; Ellesmere Nursery. Bud ovoid; flowers light silvery pink, dbl. (60 petals), very large (6 in.); very fragrant; foliage glossy; vigorous, medium growth.

Northumberland W.I. HT, *ab*, 1988, *Silver Jubilee × Doris Tysterman*; Thompson, R.; Battersby Roses, 1988. Flowers deep apricot, reverse lighter, dbl. (26-40 petals), medium; slight fragrance; foliage large, dark green, glossy; bushy growth.

Norwich Castle F, *ob*, 1980, *(Whisky Mac × Arthur Bell) × Seedling*; Beales, Peter, 1979. Flowers orange, dbl. (30 petals), borne 3-5 per cluster; faint fruity fragrance; foliage medium green, shiny, smooth; wedged prickles; vigorous, upright growth.

Norwich Cerise HT, *mr*, 1962, *Bettina sport*; Morse. Flowers cerise, dbl. (25-30 petals), large (4-5 in.); fragrant; vigorous growth.

Norwich Gold S, *ob*, 1962, Kordes; Morse. Bud well formed; flowers yellow shaded orange, dbl. (55 petals), large; fragrant; vigorous, upright growth.

Norwich Pink K (S), *dp*, 1962, Kordes; Morse. Flowers bright cerise, semi-dbl. (16 petals), large (4 in.); fragrant; vigorous, pillar, well branched growth.

Norwich Salmon K (S), *op*, 1962, Kordes; Morse. Flowers salmon-pink, dbl. (30 petals), medium blooms in clusters; fragrant; foliage glossy; vigorous, pillar, well branched growth.

Norwich Union F, *my*, 1975, *Arthur Bell × (Seedling × Allgold)*; Beales, 1976. Flowers yellow, cupped, large (3 in.); very fragrant; foliage glossy, leathery.

Nossa Senhora de Fátima HT, *rb*, Moreira da Silva. Flowers deep red, reverse golden yellow.

Nostalgia™ Min, *mp*, 1989, (SAVarita); *Rita × (Rise 'n' Shine × Sheri Anne)*; Saville, F. Harmon; Nor'East Miniature Roses, 1990. Bud ovoid; flowers medium pink, reverse lighter, aging lighter, dbl. (38 petals), cupped, centers quartered, medium, borne usually singly and in sprays of 3-5; no fragrance; foliage medium, medium green, semi-glossy; prickles thin, straight, medium, gray-purple to brown; no fruit; spreading, low growth.

Nottingham HT, *yb*, 1938, Robinson, H.; Wheatcroft Bros. Flowers clear yellow, center tinted orange; fragrant; vigorous growth.

Nottingham Forest F, *mr*, 1971, *Metropole × Diamant*; deRuiter; Geo. deRuiter. Flowers red, dbl. (28 petals), large (3½ in.); foliage dark; moderate, bushy growth.

Notturno® HT, *dr*, 1981, *Papa Meilland × Seedling*; Barni-Pistoia, Rose. Flowers dark purplish red, dbl. (35 petals); strong fragrance; foliage large, dark; reddish, hooked prickles; upright, bushy growth.

Nouveau Vulcain G (OGR), *m*, Flowers dark purple, very dbl., medium.

Nouvelle Étoile HT, *yb*, 1966, *Chic Parisien × Provence*; Delbard-Chabert; Cuthbert. Flowers creamy yellow, edged carmine-red, dbl. (40-48 petals), well shaped; free growth.

Nouvelle Europe F, *or*, 1964, (Neues Europa; New Europe); *Miss France × Vendome*; Gaujard. Flowers bright orange, dbl., medium; fragrant; foliage dark; vigorous, bushy growth. ADR, 1964.

Nouvelle Pivoine G (OGR), *m*, Flowers violet tinted, center vivid red, large.

Nouvelle Transparente G (OGR), *dp*, 1835, Miellez. Flowers rosy crimson, full, large; very fragrant.

Nova F, *or*, 1968, *Anne Elizabeth × Paprika*; Harkness. Flowers orange-red, semi-dbl., blooms in clusters; slightly fragrant; foliage dark, glossy.

Nova Lux HT, *yb*, 1955, *Julien Potin × Sensation*; Aicardi, D.; Giacomasso. Flowers chrome-yellow with red reflections; foliage glossy; very vigorous growth.

Nova Red Min, *mr*, 1964, *Seedling × Little Buckaroo*; Moore, R.S.; Sequoia Nursery. Bud pointed; flowers crimson, semi-dbl. (10 petals), small blooms in clusters; low (12 in.) growth.

Nova Zembla HRg (S), *w*, 1907, *Conrad Ferdinand Meyer sport*; Mees. Flowers light pink to white.

Novitchkova HT, *ob*, (Newcomer); Novitchkov. Flowers orange-yellow, medium; slightly fragrant; foliage dark, leathery; low growth.

Noweta F, *mr*, 1960, *Spice × Garnette Seedling*; Boerner; J&P. Bud ovoid; flowers rose-red, dbl., medium, borne in clusters; fragrant; foliage leathery; vigorous, upright, bushy growth; a greenhouse variety.

Nozomi Cl Min, *lp*, 1968, (Heideroslein Nozomi); *Fairy Princess × Sweet Fairy*; Onodera. Flowers pearl-pink, single, flat blooms in trusses; slightly fragrant; foliage small, glossy; trailing growth.

Nuance Min, *or*, 1992, *Pierrine sport*; White, Al; Giles Roses, 1991. Flowers orange-red, full (26-40 petals), small (0-4 cms) blooms borne mostly single; slight fragrance; foliage small, medium green, matt; few prickles; medium, upright growth.

Nubian LCl, *dr*, 1937, B&A. Flowers dark velvety red, dbl., high-centered, borne in huge clusters; slightly fragrant; foliage large, leathery; vigorous (6-8 ft.) growth; sometimes recurrent bloom.

Nugget F, *my*, 1973, *Yellow Pinocchio × Seedling*; Warriner; J&P. Bud ovoid; flowers yellow, very dbl., high-centered, small; slightly fragrant; foliage large, glossy, dark; vigorous growth.

Nuggets HT, *dy*, 1941, *Joanna Hill × Seedling*; Hill, J.H., Co. Bud short, pointed, buff-yellow; flowers pale orange-yellow, semi-dbl. (15-20 petals), open, small (2-3 in.); slightly fragrant; foliage small, dark, leathery; a florists' variety.

Nuits de Young M (OGR), *dr*, 1845, (Old Black); Laffay. Flowers reddish purple shading to dusky violet-maroon, well mossed, small.

Numa Fay HT, *pb*, 1938, Richard; A. Meilland. Flowers salmon-pink, edged pale pink, dbl., well formed, large; vigorous growth.

Numéro Un HT, *or*, 1961, Mallerin; EFR. Flowers scarlet-red passing to vermilion-red, dbl. (35-40 petals), globular, large (5 in.); foliage bronze, glossy; vigorous, bushy, symmetrical growth.

Nuntius Pacelli HT, *w*, 1929, *Mrs. David McKee × British Queen*; Leenders Bros.; C-P. Flowers white, center cream, full, large; very fragrant.

Nuntius Schioppa HT, *my*, 1931, *Los Angeles sport*; Leenders Bros. Flowers golden yellow, sometimes washed peach-blossom-pink.

Nur Mahal HMsk (S), *mr*, 1923, *Château de Clos Vougeot × Hybrid Musk Seedling*; Pemberton. Flowers bright crimson, semi-dbl., blooms in clusters on strong stems; fragrant (musk); foliage small; vigorous bush or pillar growth; recurrent bloom; (21).

Nuria de Recolons HP (OGR), *w*, 1933, *Canigo × Frau Karl Druschki*; Dot, P. Flowers white, very full, well formed; slightly fragrant; foliage dense; very short peduncle.

Nurjehan HT, *dp*, 1980, *Sweet Afton × Crimson Glory*; Division of Vegetable Crops & Floriculture. Bud long, pointed; flowers deep pink, dbl. (50 petals), high-centered blooms borne singly; very fragrant; foliage medium, dark green, coppery when young; straight prickles; medium, spreading growth.

Nutkhut F, *or*, 1969, *Rumba × Cocorico*; Pal; Son. Bud long, pointed; flowers coral-red, very dbl., globular, small; slightly fragrant; foliage leathery; very vigorous, bushy, open growth.

Nutneyron S, *mp*, *Paul Neyron × R. nutkana*; Schoener. Flowers pink, semi-dbl.; height 4 ft.; occasionally repeats sparingly. Used by Dr. J.H. Nicolas for breeding purposes.

Nutzwedel F, *mr*, 1937, *Else Poulsen sport*; Schmidt, K.; Kordes. Flowers light crimson.

Nymph F, *op*, 1953, *Fashion × Seedling*; Dickson, A. Flowers coral-salmon, dbl. (30 petals), large (3 in.), borne in trusses; fragrant; foliage dark, glossy; very free growth.

Nymphenburg HMsk (S), *op*, 1954, *Sangerhausen × Sunmist*; Kordes; Morse. Flowers salmon-pink shaded orange, semi-dbl., flat, very large blooms in clusters (up to 20); fragrant; foliage large, glossy; upright growth; recurrent bloom.

Nypels Perfection Pol, *pb*, 1930, Leenders, M. Flowers hydrangea-pink, shaded deep pink, semi-dbl., large blooms in clusters; vigorous, bushy growth.

Nyveldt's White HRg (S), *w*, 1955, *(R. rugosa rubra × R. cinnamomea) × R. nitida*; Nyveldt. Flowers snow-white, single, large; fruit orange-red.

O Sole Mio® HT, *my*, 1984, (DELosol); *(Peace × Marcelle Gret) × Velizy Seedling*; Delbard, G. Flowers medium yellow, dbl. (35 petals), well formed, large; no fragrance; foliage medium, medium green, glossy; greenhouse variety.

Oakington Ruby Min, *mr*, 1933, Bloom. Bud deep crimson; flowers ruby-crimson, white-eye, dbl., small (1-1/2 in.); dwarf (1 ft. or less) growth; (14).

Oakley HT, *pb*, 1937, Fairhead. Flowers bright rose, base deep red, tipped flesh-pink, large; very fragrant; vigorous growth.

Oakmont HP (OGR), *pb*, 1893, May. Flowers deep pink, reverse lighter, blooms in clusters; recurrent bloom.

Obélisque® LCl, *op*, 1967, (DELmot); *Spectacular × (Orange Triumph Seedling × Floradora)*; Delbard-Chabert. Flowers coppery orange-pink, semi-dbl., globular, medium; foliage bronze, glossy; vigorous, climbing growth; abundant, intermittent bloom. GM, Geneva, 1967.

Oberbürgermeister Dr. Külb HT, *op*, 1931, *Roselandia sport*; Nauheimer. Flowers flame-colored, passing to salmon.

Oberbürgermeister Heimerich HP (OGR), *mp*, 1929, *Frau Karl Druschki × Souv. de Claudius Pernet*; Weigand, C. Flowers fresh rose, some petals with reverse lighter, dbl.; slightly fragrant.

Obergärtner Wiebicke F, *mr*, 1950, *Johannes Boettner × Magnifica*; Kordes. Bud long, pointed; flowers light red, semi-dbl., open, very large, borne in clusters; fragrant; foliage glossy, light green; vigorous, bushy growth.

Oberhofgärtner A. Singer HP (OGR), *mr*, 1904, *Mme. Caroline Testout × Marie Baumann*; Lambert, H. Flowers carmine, center darker, full (40 petals); dwarf, compact growth.

Oberleutnant Immelmann HT, *lp*, 1936, Henniger. Flowers soft yellowish pink, center deeper, globular, petals incurved, somewhat frilled, large.

Oberon F, *ab*, 1955, *Nymph × Seedling*; Dickson, A. Flowers salmon-apricot, dbl. (38 petals), medium 2-2½ in.) blooms in trusses; slightly fragrant; bushy growth.

Obsession HT, *dr*, 1990, (DEVtinta); *Seedling × Seedling*; Marciel, Stanley G.; DeVor Nurseries, Inc. Bud high-centered; flowers dark red, dbl. (42 petals), cupped, imbricated, large blooms borne singly; very moderate fragrance; foliage medium, medium green, semi-glossy; prickles wing-shaped, reddish tinge; upright, tall growth.

Ocooch Mountain Rose S, *mp*, 1981, Hall, William W. Bud small, pointed; flowers medium pink, single (5 petals), blooms borne 3-4 per cluster; strong, spicy fragrance; foliage 9 leaflet, small, slightly rugose, medium green; straight, fine prickles; arching growth.

Octavie G (OGR), *lp*, Coquerel. Flowers light pink, edged blush, full, open, medium; vigorous, branching growth.

Octet S, *m*, 1977, *R. rudiuscula × R. subglauca*; Rowley; Royal National Rose Soc. Bud narrow, pointed; flowers pale purple, single (5 petals), medium (3 in.); slightly fragrant;

foliage gray-green; extremely vigorous growth; prolific bloom in summer only.

October HT, *ob*, 1980, *Seedling × Seedling*; Weeks, O.L. Bud long, pointed; flowers rich salmon orange, dbl. (30 petals), high-centered blooms borne singly and 2-3 per cluster; fragrant; foliage leathery, dark; long, hooked prickles; tall, upright.

Odeon HT, *op*, 1977, (GAUfrarner); *(Château de Chenonceaux × Mignonne) × Americana*; Gaujard. Bud globular; flowers coral-pink, dbl. (50 petals), globular, medium (3 in.); fragrant; foliage large, dark; vigorous growth.

Odéric Vital HP (OGR), *lp*, 1858, *Baronne Prévost sport*; Oger; Lighter colored than parent.

Odette Chène HT, *mp*, 1940, *Richmond, Climbing × Charles P. Kilham*; Colombier. Flowers pink, base coral; vigorous growth.

Odette Foussier HT, *mp*, 1924, Chambard, C. Flowers salmon-pink, inside chrome on yellow ground, dbl.; very fragrant.

Odette Foussier, Climbing Cl HT, *mp*, 1929, Chambard, C..

Odette Joyeux LCl, *op*, 1959, *Lady Sylvia × Seedling*; Robichon. Bud globular, coral-orange; flowers pink to lilac-pink, dbl., cupped, large; very fragrant; foliage leathery, glossy; very vigorous ; abundant, recurrent bloom.

Odorata HT, *pb*, 1928, *Sunburst × Ma Fiancee*; Van Rossem. Flowers carmine-pink, reverse white edged pink, base golden yellow, dbl.; very fragrant. Should not be confused with the species *R. × odorata*.

Odyssée F, *or*, 1979, (GAUzomi); *Pampa × Seedling*; Gaujard, Jean. Flowers orange-red, dbl. (25 petals), well formed blooms borne 3-5 per cluster; fragrant; foliage dark; small, brown prickles.

Œillet C (OGR), *lp*, 1800, DuPont. Flowers bright pink, dbl., medium; fragrant; vigorous growth.

Œillet Flamand G (OGR), *pb*, 1845, Vibert. Flowers pale pink striped white and brighter pink, very dbl., flat, medium; very fragrant; very vigorous growth.

Œillet Panachée M (OGR), *pb*, 1888, (Striped Moss); Verdier, C. Flowers pale pink striped deep pink, flat, petals quilled, small.

Œillet Parfait G (OGR), *pb*, 1841, Foulard. Flowers blush, striped light and dark red, dbl., flat, medium; dwarf growth.

Ogoniok F, *ob*, 1955, (Little Fire); *Raised from Independence*; Sushkov. Flowers fiery orange edged darker, medium; slightly fragrant.

Oh-Choh HT, *yb*, 1983, *(Rumba × Olympic Torch) × Wisbech Gold*; Suzuki, S.; Keisei Rose Nursery. Flowers yellow tinted rose, aging red, dbl. (38 petals), high-centered, large; fragrant; foliage dark, semi-glossy; small prickles, slanted downward; upright.

Ohio S, *mr*, 1949, *R. soulieana × Gruss an Teplitz Seedling*; Shepherd. Flowers bright red, semi-dbl.; height 4 ft; recurrent bloom; hardy.

Ohio Belle LCl, *lp*, 1974, *New Dawn × Seedling*; Jerabek; Wyant. Bud globular; flowers light pink, dbl. (53 petals), medium (3 in.); slightly fragrant; foliage glossy, dark; repeat bloom.

Ohl G (OGR), *m*, 1838, Flowers violet-purple, center bright red, dbl., large; vigorous growth.

Ohshima Rose HT, *or*, 1992, (COChuster); *(National Trust × Alexander) × Red Planet*; Cocker, James; James Cocker; Sons, 1991. Flowers orange-red, full (26-40 petals), medium (4-7 cms) blooms borne mostly singly; fragrant; foliage medium, medium green, matt; some prickles; tall (91.44 cms), upright growth.

Oirase HT, *mr*, 1973, *Red Lion × Christian Dior*; Ito. Bud ovoid; flowers medium red, dbl. (24 petals), high-centered, very large (5½ in.); fragrant; foliage glossy, dark; vigorous, upright growth; below-average bloom continuity.

Oiseau Bleu HT, *m*, 1970, Poulsen, N.D.; Vilmorin-Andrieux. Flowers mauve-rose, dbl. (30 petals), large (4-4½ in.); very fragrant; foliage large, glossy, dark; vigorous growth.

Oiseau de Feu F, *mr*, 1956, *Chant Indou × Peace*; Mallerin. Flowers scarlet-red, dbl. (35 petals), cupped to open, medium (2 in.) borne in clusters; slightly fragrant; bushy growth.

Ojibway LCl, *w*, 1946, *Ross Rambler × ((R. rugosa × R. eglanteria) × Seedling)*; Preston; Central Exp. Farm. Bud pointed; flowers white, semi-dbl. (12-15 petals), medium (3 in.), borne in clusters; slightly fragrant; foliage dark; vigorous, spreading growth; free, non-recurrent bloom; hardy.

O. Junyent HT, *mr*, 1924, (Olegario Junyent); *Frau Karl Druschki × Mme. Edouard Herriot*; Dot, P. Flowers coral-red, base yellow, semi-dbl.

Okaga HRg (S), *dp*, 1927, *Alika × Tetonkaha*; Hansen, N.E. Flowers deep pink, semi-dbl.; low, bushy growth; non-recurrent bloom; very hardy.

Oklahoma HT, *dr*, 1964, *Chrysler Imperial × Charles Mallerin*; Swim & Weeks; Weeks Wholesale Rose Grower. Bud ovoid, long, pointed; flowers very dark red, dbl. (48 petals), high-centered, large (4-5½ in.); very fragrant; foliage leathery, dark, matt; vigorous, bushy growth. GM, Japan, 1963.

Oklahoma, Climbing Cl HT, *dr*, 1968, Swim & Weeks; Weeks Wholesale Rose Grower.

Oklahoma, Climbing Cl HT, *dr*, 1972, Ross, A., & Son.

Olala® F, *mr*, 1956, (Oh La La; Ohlala); *Fanal × Crimson Glory*; Tantau, Math. Bud pointed; flowers blood-red, center lighter, semi-dbl., large blooms in clusters to 25; slightly fragrant; foliage leathery, dark, glossy; vigorous, bushy, upright. GM, Baden-Baden, 1955.

Olave Baden-Powell HT, *mr*, 1972, Tantau; Harry Wheatcroft Gardening. Flowers scarlet, large (5 in.); slightly fragrant; foliage dark, leathery.

Old Blush Ch (OGR), *mp*, (Common Monthly; Common Blush China; Old Pink Daily; Old Pink Monthly; Parsons' Pink China); Int. into Sweden in 1752 and into England before 1759. Flowers two-tone pink, semi-dbl., medium blooms in loose sprays; almost scentless; vigorous, upright growth; dependably recurrent.

Old Blush, Climbing Cl Ch (OGR), *mp*,

Old Faithful HT, *dy*, 1991, (JAChy); *Sunbright × Medallion*; Warriner, William A.; Bear Creek Gardens, Inc. Flowers deep yellow, full (26-40 petals), large; fragrant; foliage large, dark green, semi-glossy; upright, bushy growth.

Old Fashion Red HT, *mr*, 1947, *Pink Princess × Crimson Glory*; Brownell. Flowers spectrum-red fading blush, very dbl., high-centered, large; fragrant; foliage glossy; vigorous, bushy growth.

Old Fashioned Girl Min, *w*, 1992, (TINold); *Blue Ribbon × Miniature Seedling*; Bennett, Dee; Tiny Petals Nursery, 1993. Flowers soft lavender to white, full (26-40 petals), initially HT form, opening very full, cupped, similar to OGR's, medium (4-7 cms) blooms borne mostly single; very fragrant; foliage small, medium green, semi-glossy; some prickles; medium (60-80 cms), bushy growth.

Old Glory HT, *mp*, 1940, *Briardiff sport*; Hausermann. Flowers clear brilliant pink, dbl., large; fragrant. RULED EXTINCT 2/88.

Old Glory™ Min, *mr*, 1988, (BENday); *Rise 'n' Shine × Harmonie*; Benardella, Frank; Nor'East Miniature Roses, 1988. Flowers bright post office red, aging blood-red to crimson, dbl. (23-25 petals), exhibition, large, borne usually singly or in sprays of 3-5; mini-flora; no fragrance; foliage medium, medium green, semi-glossy; prickles long, thin, curved downward, gray-red; upright, tall, vigorous growth. AOE, 1988.

Old Gold HT, *or*, 1913, McGredy. Flowers vivid reddish orange, shaded coppery red and apricot, semi-dbl. (10 petals); short stems; fragrant; foliage dark. GM, NRS, 1912.

Old Master F, *rb*, 1974, (MACesp); *(Maxi × Evelyn Fison) × (Orange Sweetheart × Frühlingsmorgen)*; McGredy. Flowers carmine, white eye and reverse, semi-dbl. (15 petals), large (4½ in.); slightly fragrant; foliage semi-glossy, medium green; vigorous, bushy growth.

Old Port F, *m*, 1990, (MACkati); *((Anytime × Eyepaint) × Purple Splendour) × Big Purple*; McGredy, Sam; Sam McGredy Roses International, 1991. Flowers mauve, full (26-40 petals), medium blooms; fragrant; foliage medium, medium green, matt; bushy growth.

Old Red Boursault R, *mr*, Flowers pale red, semi-dbl., Boursault type, poorly formed, borne in large clusters; fruit nearly round; very vigorous growth.

Old Red Moss M (OGR), *mr*, Original name and date unknown. Flowers carmine-red; vigorous growth; heavy bloom; non-recurrent.

Old Smoothie HT, *mr*, 1970, *Night 'n' Day × (First Love Seedling × (Queen Elizabeth × Chrysler Imperial))*; Weeks. Flowers red, very dbl., high-centered, large; slightly fragrant; foliage large, glossy, leathery; vigorous, upright growth.

Oldcastle HT, *mp*, 1985, *Queen Elizabeth × Charlotte Armstrong*; LeMire, Walter; Roses by Walter LeMire. Flowers medium pink, dbl. (55 petals), high-centered, exhibition, large blooms borne singly; fragrant; foliage large, dark, glossy; medium, upright.

Olde English F, *dp*, 1974, *(Floradora × Independence) × Siren*; Orard; Harry Wheatcroft Gardening. Flowers light red, dbl. (30-35 petals), large (3-4 in.); slightly fragrant; foliage glossy, bronze; free growth.

Olden Days Pol, *mr*, 1989, (Olden Times); *Pink Polyantha Paul Crampel sport*; Vash, Ernest J.; Historical Roses, 1987. Flowers medium red, semi-dbl. (10 petals), small, borne in sprays of 36; slight fragrance; foliage small, light green, elliptical, slightly serrated, matt; disease resistant; prickles brown; bushy, compact growth.

Oldtimer HT, *ob*, 1969, (KORol; Coppertone; Old Time); Kordes, R.; McGredy. Flowers bronze, long, pointed; slightly fragrant.

Olé Gr, *or*, 1964, *Roundelay × El Capitan*; Armstrong, D.L.; Armstrong Nursery. Bud well shaped; flowers orange-red, dbl. (50 petals), high-centered to cupped, medium; fragrant; foliage glossy; vigorous growth.

Olé, Climbing™ Cl Gr, *or*, 1982, (AROhaiclo); Haight, George S.; Swim, H.C.; Armstrong Nursery.

Oleander Rose S, *op*, 1983, (INTerander); *Liverpool Echo × Seedling*; Interplant. Flowers salmon-pink, single (7 petals), small blooms in large clusters; slight fragrance; foliage medium, medium green, semi-glossy; very few, small prickles; upright growth; repeat bloom.

Olga Rippon F, *m*, 1992, (HORtyard); *Sexy Rexy × (Intermezzo × Baby Faurax) × (Tassin × Seedling)*; Horner, Colin P. Flowers purple/mauve, dbl., loose, medium (6 cms)blooms borne in sprays of 5-9; slight, spicy fragrance; foliage medium, medium green, semi-glossy; bushy, low growth.

Olive F, *mr*, 1982, (HARpillar); *((Vera Dalton × Highlight) × Seedling) × Dublin Bay*; Harkness, R. Flowers medium red, dbl. (36 petals), high-centered, large blooms in clusters; spicy fragrance; foliage large, dark, glossy; dark prickles; branching growth.

Olive Cook HT, *w*, 1934, Cant, F. Flowers white, base faintly tinged lemon-yellow, high-centered, large; fragrant; foliage glossy; vigorous growth.

Olive McKenzie HT, *yb*, 1970, *Daily Sketch × Manitou*; Dawson, G.; Brundrett. Bud long, pointed; flowers orange-yellow, marked red, dbl., large; fragrant; foliage large, dark; vigorous, upright, bushy growth.

Olive Moore HT, *lp*, 1927, Allen. Flowers pale rose-pink, reflexed silver-pink; very fragrant.

Olive Percival HT, *rb*, 1948, *California × Eternal Youth*; Howard, P.J. Bud long, pointed; flowers intense cherry-red, base gold, semi-dbl. (14-20 petals), cupped, large (3½-4 in.); very fragrant; foliage leathery, bronze; very vigorous, upright, free branching growth.

Olive Taylor Min, *rb*, 1988, (PEAp); *Seedling × Seedling*; Pearce, C.A.; The Limes New Roses. Flowers vermillion red with yellow eye, dbl. (20 petals), small; slight fragrance; foliage medium, dark green, glossy; bushy growth.

Olive Whittaker HT, *op*, 1920, Easlea. Flowers rich coppery rose to cerise and salmon.

Oliver Mee HT, *mp*, 1927, Dickson, S. Flowers deep salmon tinted fawn, becoming deep salmon-pink, full, high-centered, large; fragrant.

Olivers HT, *m*, 1963, *Pres. Herbert Hoover × Seedling*; Oliver, H. Flowers purple to pink, semi-dbl., medium; fragrant.

Ollie HT, *mr*, 1982, *(Pink Garnette × Pink Hat) × ((Frau Karl Druschki × McGredy's Yellow) × (Baronne Prévost × Gruss an Teplitz))*; James, John. Bud globular, pointed; flowers medium red, dbl. (45 petals), blooms borne singly; strong fragrance; foliage large, leathery, rounded; red brown prickles; vigorous, tall growth.

Olwyn HT, *mp*, 1946, Bird; F. Mason. Bud long, pointed; flowers pink, high-centered, medium; slightly fragrant; foliage leathery; vigorous, bushy growth.

Olympe Frescency T (OGR), *w*, Flowers white, becoming yellow.

Olympia HT, *mr*, 1935, *Johanniszauber × Hadley*; Tantau. Flowers bright red, dbl., large; long, strong stems; fragrant; vigorous growth.

Olympia HT, *my*, 1955, *Eclipse × Seedling*; Delforge. Bud bright yellow, well formed; bushy, semi-upright growth.

Olympiad HT, *rb*, 1931, (Mme. Raymond Gaujard); Pernet-Ducher; Gaujard; Dreer. Bud long, pointed; flowers blood-red, shaded copper and yellow, dbl., large; very fragrant. GM, Bagatelle, 1930 RULED EXTINCT 11/82.

Olympiad™ HT, *mr*, 1982, (MACauck; Olympiode); *Red Planet × Pharaoh*; McGredy, Sam, 1983; Armstrong Nursery, 1984. Flowers brilliant medium red, dbl. (35 petals), exhibition, large; slight fragrance; foliage large, medium green, matt; upright, bushy growth. AARS, 1984; GM, Portland, 1985.

Olympiad, Climbing Cl HT, *rb*, 1938, Raffel; Port Stockton Nursery.

Olympic Charm HT, *lp*, 1963, *Grand'mère Jenny × Claude*; Barter. Flowers silvery, reverse bright pink, dbl. (65 petals), well formed, large (3½ in.); very fragrant; foliage dark, glossy.

Olympic Dream HT, *pb*, 1984, (JACade; Home's Choice); *Seedling × Seedling*; J&P; McConnell Nursery. Flowers pink blend, dbl. (35 petals), large; slight fragrance; foliage large, dark, semi-glossy; upright growth.

Olympic Flame F, *or*, 1962, Brett. Bud pointed; flowers orange-vermilion, single (8 petals), large (3 in.) blooms in clusters; foliage glossy, bright green; vigorous, upright, bushy.

Olympic Glory HT, *dr*, 1984, (JACed; Home's Beauty); Seedling × Seedling; J&P; McConnell Nursery. Flowers dark red, dbl. (35 petals), medium; slight fragrance; foliage large, medium green, glossy; upright growth.

Olympic Gold Min, *ly*, 1983, *Rise 'n' Shine × Bonny*; Jolly, Nelson F.; Rosehill Farm. Flowers light yellow, dbl. (31 petals), exhibition, mini-flora, medium; slight fragrance; foliage medium, medium green, semi-glossy; upright, bushy growth.

Olympic Star HT, *mp*, 1959, *Picture sport*; Trebbin. Flowers cerise-pink; vigorous.

Olympic Torch HT, *rb*, 1966, (Sei-Ka; Seika); *Rose Gaujard* × *Crimson Glory*; Suzuki; Keisei Rose Nursery. Bud long, pointed; flowers white and red, becoming all red, dbl., high-centered, medium; foliage glossy, bronze, leathery; vigorous. GM, NZ, 1971.

Olympic Triumph F, *rb*, 1973, *Shiralee* × *Apricot Nectar*; Dickson, P.; Dicksons of Hawlmark. Flowers red and yellow, dbl., globular, large (4½ in.); foliage sage green; upright.

Olympisches Feuer® F, *ob*, 1971, (TANolfeu); *Ahoi* × *Signalfeuer*; Tantau; Dehener & Co. Bud ovoid; flowers orange, dbl., medium; slightly fragrant; upright growth.

Omar Khayyám D (OGR), *lp*, 1893, (Propagated from a rose growing on Edward FitzGerald's grave at Boulge, Suffolk, England, 1893, which was raised from seed of a rose growing on Omar Khayyam's grave in Nashipur.) Flowers light pink, very dbl., flat, curiously quartered, center incurved, small; fragrant; foliage small, downy; dense, prickly growth (to 3 ft.).

Omar Pacha B (OGR), *mr*, 1863, Pradel. Flowers bright cherry; vigorous ; recurrent bloom.

Ombrée Parfaite G (OGR), *m*, 1823, Vibert. Flowers variable, light pink to deep purple, often in the same flower, full, medium.

Ondella HT, *or*, 1979, (MEIvanama); *(Elegy* × *Arturo Toscanini)* × *(Peace* × *Demain)*; Meilland, M.L.; Meilland. Bud conical; flowers vermilion, dbl. (33 petals), large; foliage dark; vigorous, upright growth.

Ondine HT, *w*, 1936, (Odine); *Louise Criner* × *Souv. de Claudius Pernet*; Ketten Bros. Bud pointed; flowers creamy white, slightly tinted pink, dbl. (20-25 petals), high pointed, large; long, strong stems; foliage dark gray-green; very vigorous growth.

O'Neal's Bequest S, *yb*, 1986, O'Neal, Conrad; Paul Jerabek. Flowers yellow with pink petal edges, semi-dbl., medium; slight fragrance; foliage large, medium green, glossy; upright growth.

O'Neal's White LCl, *w*, 1961, *Blossomtime* × *New Dawn*; O'Neal; Wyant. Flowers white, large; vigorous growth.

Onkel Svend F, *rb*, 1978, *Sonia* × *Ernest H. Morse*; Poulsen, N.D.; D.T. Poulsen. Flowers medium red and silvery red blend, dbl. (23 petals), large blooms in sprays of 3-8; spicy fragrance; foliage medium, dark, matt; low, bushy, spreading growth.

Only Love HT, *dr*, 1986, (INTeronly); *Seedling* × *Caramba*; Interplant. Flowers dark red,

dbl. (35 petals), large; no fragrance; foliage medium, dark, semi-glossy; upright growth; greenhouse variety.

Only You HT, *mr*, 1970, *Carina sport*; Vahldiek-Bissingen; URS. Flowers rose-carmine.

Ontario Celebration Min, *or*, 1983, (LAVmount); *Nic-Noc* × *(Party Girl* × *Queen of the Dwarfs)*; Laver, Keith, 1984. Flowers orange-red, dbl. (35 petals), small; fragrant; foliage small, deep reddish green, semi-glossy; spreading, compact growth.

Onyx Flamboyant HT, *lp*, 1965, *Sultane* × *Queen Elizabeth*; Delbard-Chabert; Cuthbert. Flowers peach to shell-pink, high-centered, large (4 in.); slightly fragrant; foliage serrated; vigorous, bushy growth.

Oomaston Pride HT, *yb*, 1954, *Haisha sport*; C.W.S. Ltd. Hort. Dept.; Co-op. Wholesale Soc. Flowers buttercup-yellow suffused deep carnation-pink, full, large; foliage dark, glossy; very vigorous growth.

Oonagh HT, *mr*, 1990, (SEAoona); *Matangi* × *Gavotte*; McCann, Sean. Flowers medium red, full (26-40 petals), large blooms; slight fragrance; foliage medium, medium green, semi-glossy; very spreading growth.

Oor Wullie Min, *mp*, 1978, *New Penny sport*; Anderson's Rose Nursery. Flowers salmon-pink, dbl. (24 petals), full, medium; slightly fragrant; foliage glossy, leathery; free growth.

Opal HT, *mp*, 1934, (Lise Palais); *Julien Potin* × *R. foetida bicolor Seedling*; Gaujard; J&P, 1941. Flowers salmon to opal, dbl. (45 petals), high-centered, large (5½ in.); very fragrant; vigorous growth.

Opal Brunner Cl F, *lp*, Marshall, O.C., about 1948. Bud very small; flowers blush-pink to pale rose, dbl., borne in large clusters; slightly fragrant (musk); tall, pillar (10 ft.) growth.

Opal Gold HT, *ab*, 1936, *Joanna Hill sport*; Bate. Flowers apricot, changing to pink.

Opal Jewel Min, *mp*, 1962, *Mothersday* × *Rosy Jewel*; Morey; J&P. Bud ovoid; flowers pink, center darker, dbl. (45 petals), small (1 in.); slightly fragrant; foliage leathery; vigorous, compact (8-10 in.) growth.

Opal of Arz HT, *ob*, 1938, *Mary Wallace Seedling*; Brownell. Flowers variable orange shades, dbl.; fragrant.

Opaline HT, *pb*, 1922, *Louise Catherine Breslau* × *Frau Karl Druschki*; Lippiatt. Flowers pale pink, shaded carmine and old-gold.

Ophelia HT, *lp*, 1912, *Perhaps a chance Seedling of Antoine Rivoire.*; Paul, W. Bud long, pointed; flowers salmon-flesh, center tinted light yellow, dbl. (28 petals); fragrant; foliage leathery; vigorous growth. A famous parent rose.

Open Secret F, *ab*, 1987, (WEEpaint); *Eyepaint sport*; Weeks, Michael. Flowers peach to salmon-pink, sometimes flecked darker, shading to white base, single (5 petals), medium; fragrant; foliage medium, medium green, semi-glossy; bushy, tall growth.

Opera HT, *rb*, 1950, *La Belle Irisée* × *Seedling*; Gaujard; J&P. Bud long, pointed; flowers light scarlet-red, base yellow, dbl., large (6 in.); fragrant; foliage leathery, light green; vigorous, erect growth. GM, NRS, 1949.

Opera, Climbing Cl HT, *rb*, 1956, (Grimpant Opera); Armbrust.

Ophelia, Climbing Cl HT, *lp*, 1920, Dickson, A..

Ophelia Queen, Climbing Cl HT, *lp*, 1923, *Ophelia sport*; Westbury Rose Co..

Ophelia Supreme HT, *lp*, 1917, *Ophelia sport*; Dailledouze Bros. Flowers light rose-pink, center darker.

Ophirie N (OGR), *op*, 1841, Goubault. Flowers reddish copper, reverse rosy and fawn, very dbl., cupped; fragrant; vigorous growth

Oporto HT, *dr*, 1930, *Château de Clos Vougeot* × *Betty Uprichard*; Allen. Flowers port-wine-red, dbl., petals very leathery; slightly fragrant.

Oradour F, *dr*, 1955, *Happiness* × *Demain*; Mallerin; EFR. Flower dark red, full.

Orange Beauty Cl F, *op*, 1961, *Little Darling* × *Gertrude Raffel*; Raffel; Port Stockton Nursery. Flowers orange to salmon, dbl., high-centered, medium blooms in clusters; slightly fragrant; foliage glossy; vigorous (6-8 ft.) growth.

Orange Blossom Special™ Cl Min, *ob*, 1989, (JACmocl); *Zorina* × *Andrea*; Warriner, William A.; Bear Creek Gardens, 1990. Bud ovoid, sepals serrated; flowers coral orange, edges darker, reverse lighter coral pink, aging lighter pink, darker margin, very dbl. (55+ petals), high-centered, small, borne in sprays of 3-9; slight fragrance; foliage small, dark green, semi-glossy; prickles straight to hooked down, reddish-green; upright, bushy, tall growth.

Orange Bouquet F, *ob*, 1972, *Masquerade* × *Paris-Match*; Northfield. Flowers coppery orange, turning pink, dbl. (25 petals), rosette form, medium (2½ in.); fragrant; foliage dark; upright, free growth.

Orange Bunny® F, *or*, 1979, (MEIrianopur); *Scherzo* × *(Sarabande* × *Frenzy)*; Meilland, M.L.; Meilland Et Cie. Bud pointed; flowers orange-red, reverse darker, semi-dbl. (13 petals), cup-shaped, borne 1-25 per cluster; slight

fragrance; foliage bronze, matt, very dense; bushy growth.

Orange Cascade Cl Min, *ob*, 1979, *Yellow Seedling* × *Magic Wand*; Moore, R.S.; Sequoia Nursery. Bud pointed; flowers yellow-orange, dbl. (20 petals), small (1 in.); fragrant; foliage small, fern-like; slender, willowy growth.

Orange Charm Min, *or*, 1982, (MINdco); *Starburst* × *Over the Rainbow*; Williams, Ernest D.; Mini-Roses. Flowers orange-red, dbl. (40+ petals), well formed, small; slight fragrance; foliage small, medium green, glossy; bushy growth.

Orange Cheer Pol, *ob*, 1937, Letts. Flowers clear orange, almost dbl.; vigorous growth.

Orange Chiffon F, *ob*, 1966, *Little Darling* × *Goldmarie*; Mease; Wyant. Flowers orange-salmon, reverse silvery orange, dbl., cupped; medium; foliage dark, leathery; vigorous, bushy growth.

Orange Combe HT, *ob*, 1956, *Charlotte Armstrong* × *Seedling*; Combe; Delbard. Flowers orange, very full, globular; vigorous, upright growth.

Orange Cup F, *or*, 1965, *Cocorico* × *Seedling*; Pal; Indian Agric. Research Inst. Bud pointed; flowers orange-scarlet, single, open, medium, borne in clusters; very fragrant; foliage dark, glossy; vigorous, compact growth.

Orange Darling Cl Min, *ob*, 1979, Sudol. Flowers orange, dbl. (32 petals), small (1½ in.); slightly fragrant; foliage dark, leathery; climbing or pillar growth.

Orange Dawn F, *ob*, 1973, *Orange Sensation* × *Sutter's Gold*; Ellick. Flowers orange, tinted vermilion, dbl. (30-35 petals), full, large (4 in.); very fragrant; foliage glossy, dark; vigorous growth.

Orange Delbard HT, *or*, 1959, (Lady Russon); *Impeccable* × *Mme. Robert Joffet*; Delbard-Chabert. Flowers bright orange, dbl., well formed, large; strong stems; fragrant; vigorous growth.

Orange Delight HT, *ob*, 1950, (Meerzicht Glory; Queen Juliana); Verschuren-Pechtold; J&P. Bud urn shaped; flowers orange, reverse veined red, dbl. (30 petals), cupped, large (5½ -6 in.); very fragrant; foliage glossy, dark; vigorous, tall growth; a greenhouse cut flower.

Orange Delight, Climbing Cl HT, *ob*, 1957, Verschuren-Pechtold.

Orange Dot HT, *ob*, 1963, *Chrysler Imperial* × *Soraya*; Dot, P. Bud long; flowers carthamus-red, dbl. (50 petals), large; fragrant; bushy growth.

Orange Drop Min, *ob*, 1988, *Heartland × Seedling*; Bridges, Dennis; Bridges Roses. Flowers soft orange, white at base, reverse soft orange edging veined white to base, semi-dbl. (20 petals), high-centered, exhibition, medium, borne usually singly; foliage medium, medium green, semi-glossy; prickles long, very pointed, medium, light green; bushy, medium, vigorous growth.

Orange Elf Cl Min, *ob*, 1959, *Golden Glow (LCl) × Zee*; Moore, R.S.; Sequoia Nursery. Bud pointed; flowers orange, fading lighter, dbl. (25 petals), small; slightly fragrant; vigorous, climbing growth; trailer or ground cover.

Orange Elizabeth of Glamis F, *ob*, 1974, *Elizabeth of Glamis sport*; Thames Valley Rose Growers. Flowers orange-flame, dbl. (30 petals), large (3 in.); very fragrant; foliage glossy; compact, bushy growth.

Orange Everglow LCl, *ob*, 1942, *Copper Glow sport*; Brownell. Flowers orange slightly shaded red and yellow.

Orange Festival HT, *op*, 1961, *Souv. de Jacques Verschuren × Serenade*; Leenders, J. Flowers pink to coral-orange, small.

Orange Fire Min, *op*, 1974, *(R. wichuraiana × Floradora) × Fire Princess*; Moore, R.S.; Sequoia Nursery. Bud short, pointed; flowers orange, pink, carmine, rose, dbl. (40 petals), small (1 in.); foliage very glossy, leathery; upright growth.

Orange Flame HT, *or*, 1963, *Monte Carlo × Radar*; Meilland, M.L.; C-P. Bud ovoid, pointed; flowers orange-red, dbl. (33 petals), high-centered, large (4½-5 in.); fragrant; foliage leathery, glossy; vigorous.

Orange Garnet F, *or*, 1965, *(Garnette × Circus) × Spartan*; Swim & Weeks. Bud ovoid; flowers orange-red, dbl., small; foliage dark, leathery; vigorous, upright, bushy growth; greenhouse variety.

Orange Glory HT, *ob*, 1936, *Seedling × Charles P. Kilham*; Leenders, M. Flowers orange, semi-dbl., open, large; foliage leathery, light; vigorous growth.

Orange Glow Pol, *ob*, 1936, Verschuren; Dreer. Flowers bright golden orange, borne in large trusses.

Orange Goliath HT, *op*, 1975, *Beauté × Serenade*; Gandy. Bud long, pointed; flowers copper-orange, dbl. (26 petals), very large (8 in.); fragrant; foliage matt, green; vigorous.

Orange Honey Min, *ob*, 1979, *Rumba × Over the Rainbow*; Moore, R.S.; Sequoia Nursery. Bud pointed; flowers orange-yellow, dbl. (23 petals), high-centered to cupped, medium (1½ in.); fragrant (fruity); foliage matt, green; bushy, spreading growth.

Orange Ice F, *or*, 1963, *Fashion × Sumatra*; Thomson, R.; Tillotson. Bud ovoid; flowers light orange-red, dbl. (25 petals), cupped, large (3 in.) blooms in clusters; slightly fragrant; foliage leathery, dark; vigorous, upright, bushy growth.

Orange Ilseta® F, *ob*, 1985, (TANilvoba); *Ilseta sport*; Tantau, M. Flowers orange.

Orange Jade Min, *or*, 1991, *Black Jade sport*; Cole, Catherine W.; East Tennessee Miniature Roses, 1990. Flowers orange-red, full (26-40 petals), medium blooms borne mostly singly; slight fragrance; foliage medium, dark green, semi-glossy; upright, medium growth.

Orange Juice F, *ob*, 1986, (AROraju; Lady Glencora); *Katherine Loker × Gingersnap*; Christensen; Michigan Bulb. Flowers clear orange, dbl. (33 petals), high-centered, exhibition, medium blooms in sprays of 3-5; slight fragrance; long, red prickles; fruit ovoid, medium, orange-red; medium, upright, bushy growth.

Orange King Pol, *ob*, 1922, *Orléans Rose sport*; Cutbush. Flowers light coral-red, fading greenish, dbl., open, very small (¾ in.), borne in clusters; foliage glossy, dark; bushy, dwarf growth.

Orange Korona F, *or*, 1959, *Bergfeuer × Independence*; Morse. Flowers orange-scarlet, dbl. (20 petals), well formed, large (4 in.) blooms in clusters; slightly fragrant; foliage olive-green; vigorous, upright growth.

Orange Love™ Min, *pb*, 1986, (MINafco); *Tom Brown × Over the Rainbow*; Williams, Ernest; Mini-Roses. Flowers orange, reverse deeper orange to dark red, fading lighter, dbl. (45 petals), high-centered, exhibition, small, very heavy bloom, borne usually singly; slight fragrance; foliage small, dark green, semi-glossy; very few, short, light tan prickles; no fruit; upright, bushy, medium growth.

Orange Marmalade Min, *ob*, 1991, *Gingersnap × Orange Honey*; Williams, J. Benjamin, 1988. Flowers bronze with yellow blend, full, small blooms borne mostly singly and in small clusters; fragrant; foliage medium, light green, matt; low, upright, bushy growth.

Orange Marvel Pol, *op*, 1928, *Miss Edith Cavell sport*; Van der Vis. Flowers salmon-orange.

Orange Masterpiece F, *or*, 1970, *Seedling × Orange Sensation*; deRuiter. Flowers orange-red, dbl., small, borne in trusses; foliage dark; bushy growth.

Orange Meillandina, Climbing Cl Min, *or*, 1986, (MEIjikatarsar; Grimpant Orange Meillandina; Orange Sunblaze, Climbing);

Orange Meillandina sport; Meilland, M.L. Flowers orange-red, full (26-40 petals), medium; no fragrance; foliage small, medium green, matt; upright growth.

Orange Mist F, *ob*, 1957, *Ma Perkins × Seedling*; Boerner; J&P. Flowers orange-salmon to yellow-orange, dbl. (38 pointed petals), large (4 in.); fragrant; dwarf, bushy growth; greenhouse variety.

Orange Morsdag Pol, *ob*, 1956, (Orange Mothersday); *Mothersday sport*; Grootendorst, F.J. Flowers deep orange.

Orange Nassau HT, *ob*, 1941, *Mev. G.A. van Rossem × Seedling*; Verschuren; Dreer. Bud long, pointed; flowers two-toned coppery orange, reverse yellow, dbl., cupped; fragrant; foliage leathery.

Orange Nymph F, *or*, 1960, *Nymph sport*; Tulp; G. Maarse. Flowers orange-red, dbl., medium, borne in small clusters.

Orange Parfait HT, *ob*, 1982, Weeks, O.L.; Weeks Roses. Bud ovoid, pointed; flowers orange, yellow reverse, dbl. (45 petals), high-centered, large blooms borne singly; slight tea fragrance; foliage medium to large, bronze green, leathery; long, narrow prickles, hooked downward, reddish at base; vigorous.

Orange Perfection Pol, *or*, 1927, *Ideal sport*; Spek. Flowers orange-red.

Orange Pixie Min, *or*, 1978, *Little Chief × Fire Princess*; Moore, R.S.; Sequoia Nursery. Bud ovoid, pointed; flowers bright orange-red, dbl. (48 petals), high-centered, small (1 in.); foliage small, glossy, leathery; bushy, compact, upright growth.

Orange Queen Pol, *op*, 1923, *Orléans Rose sport*; Van Nes. Flowers salmon-orange.

Orange Rapture HT, *op*, 1935, *Rapture sport*; Schmidt, K.; Kordes. Bud long, pointed; flowers orange with pink, dbl., high-centered, large; fragrant.

Orange Rosamini® Min, *or*, 1988, (RUIseto); *Seedling × Red Rosamini*; DeRuiter, G.; DeRuiters Nieuwe Rozen B.V. Flowers orange-red, semi-dbl.; medium growth.

Orange Rosette Pol, *or*, 1941, *Gloire du Midi sport*; deRuiter; J&P. Flowers scarlet-orange, dbl. (30 petals), small (1¼ in.), borne in clusters; vigorous, compact growth; a florists' pot plant.

Orange Ruffels HT, *ob*, 1952, *(Dr. W. Van Fleet × Général Jacqueminot) × Lafter*; Brownell. Bud long, pointed; flowers orange to saffron-yellow, dbl. (40 frilled petals), high-centered, large (4-5 in.); fragrant; foliage dark, glossy; vigorous, compact growth.

Orange Rumba F, *ob*, 1962, *Rumba sport*; Zieger; C-P. Flowers orange; a greenhouse variety.

Orange Schoon HT, *ob*, 1938, *Katharine Pechtold sport*; Lens. Flowers pure orange.

Orange Sensation® F, *or*, 1961, deRuiter; Gregory. Flowers orange-red, dbl. (24 petals), large (3 in.) blooms in clusters; fragrant; foliage dark; vigorous, bushy growth. GM, NRS, 1961; Golden Rose of The Hague, 1968.

Orange Sherbert Min, *ob*, 1985, (LYOra); *Dandy Lyon × Seedling*; Lyon; MB Farms, Inc. Flowers orange, dbl. (35 petals), cupped, small blooms borne singly; fragrant; foliage medium, medium green, matt; upright growth.

Orange Silk F, *or*, 1968, *Orangeade × (Ma Perkins × Independence)*; McGredy, S., IV; Gregory. Flowers orange-vermilion, shallow-cupped, large blooms in large clusters; slightly fragrant; foliage dark, glossy.

Orange Smoke F, *ob*, 1964, *Orange Ruffels × (Eva × Guinée)*; Hennessey. Flowers orange, with blue haze in cool weather, large (3-4 in.); very vigorous growth.

Orange Sparkle F, *ob*, 1984, (KORsparko); *(Colour Wonder × Zorina) × Uwe Seeler*; Kordes, R.; Ludwigs Roses. Flowers bright orange, yellow stamens, semi-dbl., medium blooms in clusters of 1-5; fragrant; foliage very glossy; straight, brown prickles; tall, bushy.

Orange Sparks HT, *ob*, 1969, *Cherry Brandy sport*; Vasishth. Flowers orange-vermilion blend, striped gold, dbl., medium; foliage glossy, bronze; vigorous, bushy growth.

Orange Special F, *or*, 1957, *Salmon Perfection sport*; deRuiter; Blaby Rose Gardens. Flowers orange-scarlet, dbl. (30-35 petals), cupped, small (1½ in.), borne in large trusses; dwarf, bushy growth.

Orange Spice Min, *ob*, 1980, *Seedling × Seedling*; Lyon. Bud ovoid, pointed; flowers orange, deeper on petal edges, dbl. (23 petals), cupped blooms borne singly or several together; fragrant; foliage small, medium green; recurved prickles; bushy, upright growth.

Orange Splash F, *ob*, 1991, (JACseraw); *Seedling × Seedling*; Christensen, Jack; Bear Creek Gardens, 1992. Flowers bright orange to orange-red with white and lighter orange stripes and flecks, moderately full (15-25 petals), large (7+ cms) blooms borne in small clusters; fragrant; foliage large, dark green, glossy; some prickles; medium (75-90 cms), upright, bushy growth.

Orange Star™ Min, *ob*, 1987, (MINalco); *Miniature Seedling × Miniature Seedling*; Williams, Ernest; Mini-Roses. Flowers orange, reverse orange with yellow at base, non-fading, dbl. (35 petals), high-centered, outstanding exhibition, small, borne usually singly or in sprays of 3-5; heavy, damask fragrance; foliage small, medium green, semi-glossy; tan prickles, dilated at base; no fruit; bushy, spreading, medium growth.

Orange Starina Min, *ob*, 1981, *Starina sport*; Graff, Roy; Mini Roses. Flowers light orange.

Orange Sunblaze™ Min, *or*, 1982, (MEIjikatar; Orange Meillandina; Sunblaze); *Parador × (Baby Bettina × Duchess of Windsor)*; Meilland, M.L.; C-P, 1981. Flowers orangered, dbl. (35 petals), cupped, medium blooms borne 1-3 per cluster; slight fragrance; foliage small, light green, matt; straw-brown prickles; upright, bushy growth.

Orange Sunshine Min, *ob*, 1968, *Bit o' Sunshine sport*; Moore, R.S.; Sequoia Nursery. Flowers orange.

Orange Sweetheart F, *op*, 1952, *Pinocchio Seedling × Fashion*; Boerner; J&P. Bud ovoid; flowers orange-pink, dbl. (20-25 petals), cupped, large (3-3½ in.); slightly fragrant (fruity); foliage dark; upright, bushy growth.

Orange Tango HT, *or*, 1972, (DANorang); *Seedling × Seedling*; McDaniel; Carlton Rose Nursery. Flowers orange-red, very dbl., high-centered, large; slightly fragrant; foliage bronze; vigorous growth.

Orange Thérèse HT, *ob*, 1943, *Soeur Thérèse sport*; Howard Rose Co. Flowers orange-yellow.

Orange Triumph® Pol, *mr*, 1937, *Eva × Solarium*; Kordes; Dreer. Flowers medium red, semi-dbl., cupped, small blooms in clusters; slightly fragrant; foliage glossy; compact, bushy growth. GM, NRS, 1937.

Orange Triumph, Climbing Cl Pol, *mr*, 1945, Leenders, M., 1945; Koopmann, 1948.

Orange Triumph Improved Pol, *or*, 1960, *Orange Triumph sport*; Cant, F. Flowers orange, dbl., borne in large clusters.

Orange Triumph Superba Pol, *ob*, 1953, *Orange Triumph sport*; Maarse, J.D. Flowers clear orange.

Orange Twist Min, *ob*, 1986, (MORtwist); *Sungold sport*; Moore, R.S.; Moore Min. Roses, 1985. Flowers tannish-orange.

Orange Velvet LCl, *or*, 1986, *Tropicana, Climbing × Swarthmore*; Williams, J. Benjamin. Flowers bright orange-red, reverse orange-red to orange pink, fading to orange-pink, with dark velvet overlay on inside petals, dbl. (37 petals), high centered, exhibition, large, borne singly or in sprays of 3-5; moderate, damask fragrance; foliage large, dark green, glossy, dark waxed; fruit medium, rounded, medium bright orange; upright, tall, vigorous growth.

Orangeade® F, *or*, 1959, *Orange Sweetheart × Independence*; McGredy, S., IV; McGredy. Flowers bright orange-red, semi-dbl., blooms in clusters; slightly fragrant; foliage dark; very vigorous, bushy growth. GM, NRS, 1959; Portland, 1965.

Orangeade, Climbing Cl F, *or*, 1964, Waterhouse Nursery.

Orange-Red Supreme F, *or*, 1958, *Spice × Garnette Seedling*; Boerner; J&P. Bud ovoid; Flowers orange-red, dbl. (18-24 petals), open, large (2½-3 in.), borne in clusters; fragrant; foliage glossy, wrinkled; bushy growth; for pot forcing.

Orangina® F, *or*, 1983, (ORAmont); *Royal Occasion sport*; Orard, Joseph; Paul Pekmez. Distinction from parent not reported.

Oraniën F, *or*, 1962, *Highlight × Seedling*; Verschuren, A.; van Engelen. Flowers orangered, sometimes lined yellow, base light yellow, dbl. (42 petals), large; foliage dark; upright, compact, symmetrical growth.

Oratam S, *yb*, 1939, *Summer Damask × Souv. de Claudius Pernet*; Jacobus; B&A. Bud globular; flowers pink edged copper-pink, base and reverse yellow, dbl., large; very fragrant (damask); foliage leathery, dark, matt, yellow-green; vigorous (5-6 ft.), bushy growth; non-recurrent bloom.

Orchid Jubilee Cl Min, *m*, 1992, (MORclilav); *(Little Darling × Yellow Magic) × Make Believe*; Moore, Ralph S.; Sequoia Nursery, 1993. Flowers mauve blend, holds color well in heat, moderately full (15-25 petals), medium (4-7 cms) blooms borne in small clusters; no fragrance; foliage medium, medium green, matt; few prickles; tall (2meters), upright, climbing growth; profuse repeat bloom.

Orchid Masterpiece HT, *m*, 1960, *Golden Masterpiece × Grey Pearl Seedling*; Boerner; J&P. Bud ovoid, deep orchid; flowers lavender-orchid, dbl. (68 petals), large; fragrant (fruity); foliage leathery, dark; vigorous growth.

Oregold HT, *dy*, 1975, (TANolg; Miss Harp; Silhouette; Anneliesse Rothenberger); *Piccadilly × Colour Wonder*; Tantau; J&P, 1970. Flowers deep yellow, dbl., high-centered, large; slightly fragrant; foliage large, glossy, dark; vigorous, upright, bushy growth. AARS, 1975.

Oregon Centennial HT, *mr*, 1959, *Charles Mallerin × (Charles Mallerin × Chrysler Impe-*

rial); Abrams, Von; Peterson; Dering. Bud pointed; flowers rose-red, dbl. (30-35 petals), high-centered to cupped, large (4-5 in.); long, strong stems; fragrant (fruity); foliage dark; vigorous, upright, bushy growth.

Oregon Ophelia HT, *mp*, 1921, *Ophelia sport*; Clarke Bros. Flowers salmon, edged pink, base yellow, dbl.

Oregon Rainbow Min, *yb*, 1991, (CLErain); *Seedling × Seedling*; Clements, John; Heirloom Old Garden Roses. Bud high-pointed, exhibition; flowers golden yellow, shaded and edged red, full (26-40 petals), small (0-4 cms) blooms; no fragrance; foliage small, dark green, semi-glossy; medium (40 cms), bushy growth.

Orfeo, Climbing LCl, *dr*, 1963, *Curly Pink × Guinee*; Leenders, J. Flowers deep red, dbl., large; fragrant.

Orgueil de Lyon HP (OGR), *or*, 1886, Besson. Flowers vermilion.

Oriana HT, *rb*, 1970, Tantau; Wheatcroft & Sons. Flowers cherry-red, reverse white, dbl. (38 petals), large (5 in.); slightly fragrant; foliage glossy, dark.

Orient HT, *dr*, 1959, *Queen of Bermuda × Henri Mallerin*; Dot, S. Bud pointed; flowers crimson becoming vermilion, reverse vermilion with yellow base, dbl. (22 petals).

Orient Express HT, *or*, 1978, *Sunblest × Seedling*; Wheatcroft. Flowers deep orange-red, reverse lighter, dbl. (40 petals), large (4-5 in.); very fragrant; foliage bronze; vigorous growth.

Oriental Charm HT, *mr*, 1960, *(Charlotte Armstrong × Gruss an Teplitz) × (Mme. Butterfly × Floradora)*; Duehrsen; Elmer Roses Co. Bud globular; flowers medium red, semi-dbl. (11 petals), large (3-4 in.); slightly fragrant; foliage leathery, glossy, dark; vigorous, upright, bushy growth.

Oriental Glamour F, *mr*, 1972, *Coup de Foudre × Tropicana*; Gandy. Flowers orient red, semi-dbl. (15 petals), HT form, large (4-5 in.); slightly fragrant; foliage bronze; free growth.

Oriental Queen Ch (OGR), *or*, 1926, McGredy; Beckwith. Flowers brilliant orange-scarlet, base yellow, fading to vivid carmine, dbl. (26 petals); foliage dark; few thorns.

Oriental Simplex™ Min, *or*, 1987, (MINanco); *(Starburst × Over the Rainbow) × Little Chief*; Williams, Ernest; Mini-Roses. Flowers bright orange-red, reverse creamy yellow, aging deeper, non-fading, single (5 petals), flat, small, borne usually singly; no fragrance; foliage small, medium green, glossy; tan

prickles, declining, dilated at base; no fruit; upright, bushy, medium growth.

Orientale Cl HT, *ob*, 1946, *George Dickson × Mrs. Pierre S. duPont*; Robichon. Flowers coral, becoming old-rose; fragrant; foliage glossy; very vigorous growth; free, recurrent bloom; not dependably hardy.

Oriflamme R, *pb*, 1914, Paul. Flowers deep rose-pink, suffused coppery gold, dbl. (55 petals), medium (2½ in.); fragrant; vigorous, climbing growth.

Origami™ F, *pb*, 1987, (AROcharm); *Coquette × Zorina*; Christensen, Jack; Carruth, Tom; Armstrong Roses, 1991. Flowers clear, soft pink, dbl. (25 petals), high-centered, exhibition, outstanding form, medium, borne usually singly or in sprays of 2-4; moderate, spicy fragrance; foliage medium, medium green, semi-glossy; normal, light green-tan prickles; upright, bushy, medium growth.

Orihime HT, *pb*, 1983, *Confidence sport*; Itami Rose Nursery. Flowers light pink flushed rose pink, reverse pearly light pink.

Orimanda HT, *dr*, 1975, *Fragrant Cloud × Seedling*; Kordes; Willemse. Bud long, pointed; flowers dark red, dbl. (27 petals), high-centered to cupped, large (3½ in.); slightly fragrant; foliage glossy, dark; vigorous, upright, bushy growth.

Orinda S, *ly*, 1922, *Harison's Yellow × Seedling*; Central Exp. Farm. Flowers deep cream, dbl., medium; foliage soft, dark; vigorous (5 ft.), bushy growth; profuse, non-recurrent bloom.

Oriole R, *my*, 1912, *Aglaia Seedling*; Lambert, P. Flowers Maréchal Niel yellow, dbl.; vigorous, climbing growth.

Orion F, *mr*, 1968, *Pink Parfait × Red Dandy*; Harkness. Flowers scarlet, dbl., medium; slightly fragrant; foliage glossy.

Orlando Sunshine Min, *pb*, 1992, (MICada); *Miniature Seedling × Miniature Seedling*; Williams, Michael C.; The Mini Rose Garden. Flowers pink and yellow blend, moderately full (15-25 petals), medium (4-7 cms.) blooms borne mostly singly; slight fragrance; foliage large, medium green, semi-glossy; some prickles; medium (18-24"), bushy growth; bloom and foliage larger than average miniature, especially in spring and fall.

Orléans Improved Pol, *mp*, 1931, *Orléans Rose sport*; Norfolk Nursery. Flowers vivid rose-pink.

Orléans Rose Pol, *rb*, 1909, *Thought to be Mme. Norbert Levavasseur Seedling*; Levavasseur. Flowers vivid rosy crimson, center white, semi-dbl.; slightly fragrant; foliage glossy; vigorous, bushy growth; repeat bloom; (14).

Orléans Rose, Climbing Cl Pol, *rb*, 1913, Levavasseur.

Ormiston Roy S, *dy*, 1953, *R. spinosissima* × *R. xanthina*; Doorenbos. Flowers deep yellow, single, large; bushy (3 ft.) growth; non-recurrent bloom.

Orpheline de Juillet G (OGR), *m*, Prior to 1837. Flowers crimson-purple, base of petals fiery red with occasional streaks of this color in the petals, very dbl., expanded, large; erect, moderate growth.

Orpheus HT, *op*, 1963, *Montezuma* × *Seedling*; Verschuren, A.; Stassen. Flowers salmon-orange, dbl. (35-40 petals), medium; long stems; foliage glossy, dark; vigorous growth.

Orpington Gem HT, *or*, 1953, *Princess Marina* × *Alamein*; Buckwell. Bud long, pointed; flowers coppery orange shaded gold, dbl. (32 petals), medium (3 in.); very fragrant; foliage dark, leathery; vigorous growth.

Orpington Jewel HT, *op*, 1953, *Princess Marina* × *Picture*; Buckwell. Bud very long; flowers coral-pink shaded coppery, base orange, dbl. (30 petals), medium size (3 in.); very fragrant; foliage dark, leathery; vigorous growth.

Osiria HT, *rb*, 1978, *Snowfire* × *Seedling*; Kordes, W.; Willemse. Bud long, pointed; flowers dark red, white reverse, dbl. (50 petals), high-centered, large (4½ in.) blooms on short stems; very fragrant; vigorous, upright, bushy growth.

Oskar Cordel HP (OGR), *mp*, 1897, (Oscar Kordel); *Merveille de Lyon* × *Andre Schwartz*; Lambert, P. Flowers carmine, dbl. (40 petals), cupped, large; fragrant; vigorous, compact growth.

Oskar Scheerer S, *dr*, 1961, Kordes, R. Flowers velvety dark red, dbl., large blooms in large clusters; vigorous (6 ft.), well branched growth.

Osmunda Pol, *dr*, 1923, *Jessie sport*; Holland. Flowers dark carmine.

Ostara F, *mr*, 1964, *Highlight* × *Valeta*; deRuiter. Flowers bright red, dbl., medium, borne in clusters; foliage dark.

Oswald Sieper HT, *w*, 1933, *Mrs. Charles Lamplough* × *Ville de Paris*; Krause; C-P. Bud long, pointed; flowers creamy white, dbl., high-centered, very large; very fragrant; foliage glossy; vigorous growth.

Otago® Min, *or*, 1978, (MACnecta); *Anytime* × *Minuette*; McGredy, S., IV; McGredy Roses. Flowers orange-red, dbl. (35 petals), HT-form, medium; fragrant; bushy growth.

Othello F, *or*, 1961, *Ma Perkins* × *Cocorico*; Leenders, J. Flowers light orange-red, dbl. (22 petals), cupped, medium (2½ in.).

Othello HT, *mr*, 1963, *New Yorker* × *Seedling*; Verschuren, A.; Stassen. Flowers velvety bright red, dbl. (48-60 petals), large; fragrant; foliage dark; vigorous, upright, bushy growth.

Otohime HT, *or*, 1977, (Fancy Princess); *(Hawaii* × *Tropicana)* × *(Tropicana* × *Peace)*; Keisei Rose Nursery. Bud pointed; flowers orange-red, dbl. (58 petals), high-centered, very large (6-6½ in.); fragrant; foliage large, glossy, dark; vigorous.

Otome Pink HT, *pb*, 1967, *Amatsu-Otome sport*; Rumsey. Flowers salmon-pink, reverse buff-yellow.

Otto Krause HT, *dy*, 1931, *Mme. Caroline Testout* × *Souv. de Claudius Pernet*; Weigand, C. Flowers coppery yellow, dbl., high-centered, large; slightly fragrant; foliage soft, glossy, bronze, dark; vigorous growth.

Otto Miller HT, *mr*, 1968, (Chrysler Imperial × Independence) × (Mrs. Charles Russell × Happiness); Morey; Country Garden Nursery. Bud long, pointed; flowers deep red, dbl., high-centered, cupped, large (6 in.); slightly fragrant; foliage glossy, leathery; vigorous, upright growth.

Ouma Smuts F, *ly*, 1950, *Egalite* × *Vanessa*; Leenders, M. Flowers straw-yellow shaded rosy flesh; very fragrant.

Our Annie HT, *op*, 1937, Letts. Flowers vivid orange-cerise, dbl., globular, large; fragrant; foliage glossy; very vigorous growth.

Our Bob HT, *mr*, 1928, Dawes. Flowers velvety red, center golden; very fragrant.

Our Coral Pearl Min, *op*, 1991, (DOSpearl); *Minnie Pearl sport*; Osburn, Dr. William, 1992. Flowers coral-salmon-pink, full (26-40 quilling petals), medium (4-7 cms) blooms borne mostly singly; slight fragrance; foliage medium, medium green, semi-glossy; few prickles, tan, straight and sharp; medium growth.

Our Jubilee HT, *ob*, 1988, (COCcages; Country Heritage); *Yellow Pages* × *Silver Jubilee*; Cocker, James,; Sons, 1986. Flowers orange blend, dbl. (20 petals), medium; slight fragrance; foliage medium, medium green, semi-glossy; upright growth.

Our Lady F, *mr*, 1956, *Seedling* × *Soestdijk*; Leenders, M. Flowers carmine; fragrant; vigorous growth.

Our Love HT, *yb*, 1984, (ANDour); *Doris Tysterman sport*; Anderson Rose Nursery. Flowers yellow-orange.

Our Princess F, *dr*, 1949, (Crimson Glow); *Donald Prior × Orange Triumph*; Robinson, H.; Baker's Nursery. Flowers deep velvety crimson, semi-dbl., borne in large trusses; slightly fragrant; foliage glossy, dark; vigorous growth; (28).

Our Rosamond HT, *pb*, 1983, *Daily Sketch Seedling × Red Planet*; Bell, R.J.; Treloar Roses. Flowers silver and pink blend, dbl. (35 petals), exhibition, large blooms borne singly; slight fragrance; foliage medium, medium green, glossy; upright growth.

Our Shirley HT, *w*, 1989, *Judith Morton × Sylvia*; Wilson, George D. Bud pointed; flowers white, dbl. (28 petals), medium, borne singly; no fragrance; foliage small, medium, dark green; prickles long, slender, red; medium, upright growth.

Our Sweet Ann F, *op*, 1975, *Queen Elizabeth × Elizabeth of Glamis*; Horsfield. Flowers warm pink, with orange glow, dbl. (28 petals), full, large (3½-4 in.); very fragrant; foliage dark, leathery; vigorous, upright growth.

Our Town Min, *mp*, 1986, (ZIPtown); *Maytime × Sheri Anne*; Zipper, H.; Magic Moment Min. Flowers medium pink, semi-dbl., small blooms in small sprays; no fragrance; foliage small, medium green, semi-glossy; spreading growth.

Outsider F, *mr*, 1956, *Fanal × Red Favorite*; Tantau, Math. Bud ovoid; flowers bright blood-red, semi-dbl., open, medium, borne in clusters; slightly fragrant; foliage glossy; vigorous, upright growth.

Ovation HT, *or*, 1977, *First Prize × Seedling*; Weeks. Bud ovoid; flowers orange-red, dbl. (25 petals), high-centered, large (4-4½ in.); foliage dark, leathery; vigorous, upright.

Over the Rainbow Min, *rb*, 1972, *Little Darling × Westmont*; Moore, R.S.; Sequoia Nursery. Flowers red, yellow reverse, dbl., high-centered, small; slightly fragrant; foliage leathery; vigorous, bushy growth. AOE, 1975.

Over the Rainbow, Climbing Cl Min, *rb*, 1974, Rumsey.

Overloon F, *dp*, 1949, *Irene × Hebe*; Leenders, M. Flowers rosy pink, dbl., medium; vigorous growth.

Overton on Dee HT, *pb*, 1976, (*Ballet × Gavotte) × Orange Sensation*; Ellick. Flowers pink, reverse cream, dbl. (40 petals), very full, large (4½ in.); slightly fragrant.

Overture F, *m*, 1960, (*Seedling × Lavender Pinocchio) × Prélude*; LeGrice. Flowers lilac-lavender, semi-dbl. (18 petals), well formed, large (3-3½ in.), fragrant; foliage dark; vigorous, low growth.

Oxfam HT, *pb*, 1973, *Fragrant Cloud × Blue Moon*; Cobley; Harry Wheatcroft Gardening. Flowers deep pink, shaded lilac, dbl. (40 petals), large (5 in.); very fragrant; foliage dark; upright.

Oxford HT, *yb*, 1930, Prince. Flowers deep warm peach, tipped orange-gold, well shaped, large; fragrant.

Pacemaker HT, *dp*, 1981, (HARnoble); *Red Planet × Wendy Cussons*; Harkness. Bud pointed; flowers deep pink, dbl. (40 petals), large (4 in.) blooms borne singly, sometimes 3 per cluster; very fragrant; foliage large, semi-glossy; large, broad, dark prickles; vigorous, upright, bushy growth. GM, Belfast, 1983.

Pacesetter Min, *w*, 1979, (SAVapace); *Ma Perkins × Magic Carrousel*; Schwartz, E.W.; Nor'East Min. Roses. Bud long, pointed; flowers pure white, dbl. (46 petals), high-centered, medium (1½ in.); fragrant; foliage dark, matt; vigorous, compact growth. AOE, 1981.

Pacific HT, *lp*, 1927, *Los Angeles sport*; Pacific Rose Co. Flowers soft pink, semi-dbl.

Pacific F, *mr*, 1958, *Alain × Chanteclerc*; Gaujard. Flowers bright red, semi-dbl.; foliage bright green.

Pacific Belle HT, *mp*, 1989, (*Peer Gynt Seedling*) × *Josephine Bruce*; Cattermole, R.F. Bud pointed; flowers light pink, reverse deeper pink, dbl. (31 petals), reflexed, pointed, medium, borne usually singly; slight fragrance; foliage light green, veined, glossy; prickles pointed, light brown; bushy, branching, upright growth.

Pacific Darling Min, *pb*, 1991, *Winifred Coulter × Seedling*; Sudol, Julia. Flowers pink blend, semi-dbl. (6-14 petals), large blooms borne in large clusters; slight fragrance; foliage large, dark green, glossy; low, upright, bushy, compact growth.

Pacific Princess HT, *mp*, 1989, *Pink Parfait × Red Planet*; Cattermole, R.F.; South Pacific Rose Nursery, 1988. Bud tapering; flowers medium pink, very dbl. (56 petals), medium, globular, borne usually singly and in sprays of 3-4; strong fragrance; foliage dark green, semi-glossy, veined; upright, branching growth.

Pacific Sunset HT, *pb*, 1977, *Mme. Henri Guillot × California*; Fong; United Rose Growers. Bud deep pointed; flowers pink to orange-scarlet, semi-dbl. (12-16 petals), high-centered, large (5 in.); slightly fragrant; foliage dark; upright growth.

Pacific Triumph Pol, *mp*, 1949, *Orange Triumph sport*; Heers; Pacific Nursery. Flowers salmon-pink; very fragrant; growth like parent.

Pacifica® F, *ab*, 1983, (JACif); *Mercedes × Marina*; Warriner; J&P. Flowers apricot, dbl. (35 petals), medium; slight fragrance; foliage medium, light green, matt; upright, bushy growth; greenhouse variety.

Pacoima HT, *lp*, 1927, *William F. Dreer sport*; Pacific Rose Co. Flowers flesh tinted yellow, dbl.

Paddy McGredy F, *mp*, 1962, (MACpa); *Spartan × Tzigane*; McGredy, S., IV; J&P. Bud ovoid; flowers deep rose-pink, dbl. (33 petals), cupped, large (4 in.) blooms in clusters; fragrant; foliage leathery; vigorous, bushy growth. GM, NRS, 1961.

Paddy Stephens HT, *ob*, 1991, (MACclack); *Solitaire × (((Tombola × (Elizabeth of Glamis × (Circus × Golden Fleece))) × Mary Sumner) × Seedling)*; McGredy, Sam; Sam McGredy Roses International. Flowers orange blend, moderately full (15-25 petals), large blooms; slight fragrance; foliage large, dark green, red when young; bushy (100 cms) growth.

Padre HT, *rb*, 1921, Cant, B.R. Flowers bright coppery scarlet, flushed yellow, semi-dbl., well formed; fruity fragrance; vigorous growth.

Padre Américo HT, *mr*, 1956, *Crimson Glory × Peace*; Moreira da Silva. Flowers carmine-red; very fragrant.

Padre Cruz HT, *w*, 1956, *Branca × Peace*; Moreira da Silva. Flowers rosy white edged ruby.

Padre Mañanet HT, *dr*, 1957, *Charles Mallerin × (Satan × Mirandy)*; Dot, P. Flowers bright purple-garnet, reverse crimson-red, dbl. (30 petals), high-centered, large; strong stems; fragrant; upright growth.

Paeonia HP (OGR), *dr*, 1855, Lacharme. Flowers crimson, full, large; very fragrant.

Pagan Beauty F, *pb*, 1965, *Montezuma × Seedling*; Verschuren; Baby Rose Gardens. Flowers bright vermilion, reverse salmon-pink, dbl. (42 petals), globular, large (4-5 in.); foliage dark, leathery; vigorous growth.

Pageant HT, *rb*, 1953, *Hybrid Tea Seedling × Orange Nassau Seedling*; Boerner; J&P. Bud ovoid; flowers red, reverse yellow, dbl. (35-40 petals), high-centered, large (4½-5 in.); fragrant; foliage leathery; vigorous, upright growth.

Pagliacci Gr, *yb*, 1969, Abrams, Von; Edmunds. Bud pointed; flowers yellow, becoming cerise, semi-dbl., medium; fragrant; foliage glossy, bronze; vigorous, upright growth.

Paint Box F, *yb*, 1963, *Seedling × St. Pauli*; Dickson, P.; A. Dickson. Bud ovoid; flowers red and golden yellow, becoming deep red, single to semi-dbl., flat, large (3 in.) blooms in clusters; slightly fragrant; foliage dark; vigorous, upright growth.

Paintbrush Min, *ly*, 1975, *Fairy Moss × Goldmoss*; Moore, R.S.; Sequoia Nursery. Bud mossy; flowers soft yellow to white, 8-10 petals, mini-moss, small (1½ in.); foliage small, glossy, leathery; vigorous, upright, bushy growth.

Painted Desert HT, *op*, 1965, *Talisman sport*; Lone Star Rose Nursery. Bud long, pointed; flowers pink and copper, dbl., open; fragrant; foliage leathery; vigorous, upright growth.

Painted Doll™ Min, *ob*, 1985, (LAVpaint); *Party Girl × Dwarfking '78*; Laver, Keith. Flowers orange, reverse yellow, dbl. (35 petals), small; slight fragrance; foliage small, light green, matt; bushy growth.

Painted Lady HT, *mp*, 1931, (*Crusader × Premier*) × *Julien Potin*; Ward, F.B. Bud long, pointed; flowers bright cerise, base old-gold, dbl. (42 petals), large.

Painted Lady HT, *yb*, 1979, Herholdt, J.A. Bud pointed; flowers cream and gold, red tipped, dbl., large (4 in.); slightly fragrant; foliage glossy, bronze; bushy growth.

Painted Moon HT, *rb*, 1989, (DICpaint); *Bonfire × Silver Jubilee*; Dickson, Patrick; Dickson Nursery, 1990. Flowers red blend, dbl. (40 petals), cupped, large; slight fragrance; foliage medium, medium green, semi-glossy; upright, bushy, stocky growth.

Painter's Palette Min, *rb*, 1984, (MORpale); Moore, R.S.; Ludwigs Roses. Bud mossy; flowers creamy white, striped deep pink to deep red, dbl. (72 petals), medium blooms borne 3-12 per cluster; slight fragrance; foliage deep green, needle straight, brown prickles; shrubby growth.

Paint-Pot Min, *or*, 1984, (TRObglow); *Seedling × Darling Flame*; Robinson, Thomas; T. Robinson, Ltd. Flowers orange-red, dbl. (24 petals), medium; very fragrant; foliage small, medium green, semi-glossy; bushy growth.

Paisley Anniversary F, *dr*, 1987, (ANDpai); *Michèle × Smiling Through*; Anderson's Rose Nursery. Flowers dark red, dbl. (15-25 petals), medium; slight fragrance; foliage medium, dark green, glossy; upright growth.

Palacky HT, *ob*, 1936, *Mme. Mélanie Soupert × Sunburst*; Böhm. Flowers orange-yellow, single, open, large; very fragrant; foliage glossy; vigorous growth.

Paladin F, *or*, 1960, *Signal Red × Fashion*; deRuiter. Flowers orange-red, semi-dbl. to dbl., open, medium (2½ in.), borne in clusters; moderate growth.

Palatino F, *mr*, 1956, Buyl Frères. Flowers red, dbl.; very vigorous growth.

Pale Hands HT, *ab*, 1965, *McGredy's Ivory × Seedling*; Pal; Indian Agric. Research Inst. Bud pointed; flowers ivory-white to buff and peach, dbl., very large; fragrant; foliage leathery; vigorous, upright growth.

Pale Moon HT, *my*, 1967, *Ma Perkins × Peace*; Patterson; Patterson Roses. Flowers medium yellow, dbl., high-centered, large; fragrant; foliage glossy; vigorous, compact growth.

Paleface Gr, *w*, 1959, *Joanna Hill × Seedling*; Lindquist; Howard Rose Co. Bud ovoid; flowers nearly white, base naples yellow, semi-dbl. (15-25 petals), high-centered to cupped, large (3-5 in.); slightly fragrant; foliage leathery, semi-glossy; vigorous, upright growth.

Palette F, *yb*, 1960, *Masquerade × High Noon*; Leenders, J. Bud ovoid; flowers yellow to salmon-pink and then red, dbl., medium blooms in clusters; slightly fragrant; foliage glossy; compact growth.

Pallas HT, *dr*, 1975, *Chrysler Imperial × Shannon*; Murray; Hawken; Kennedy. Flowers garnet-red, reverse paler, dbl. (40 petals), high-centered; very fragrant (spicy); foliage large, dull, dark; tall growth.

Pallida Ch (OGR), *mp*, 1789, (Bengal Ordinaire); Kerr. Flowers clear rose.

Palm Springs F, *rb*, 1965, *Oriental Charm × Circus*; Duehrsen; Elmer Roses Co. Bud ovoid; flowers oriental red to light bronze, center yellowish pink, dbl. (50 petals); very fragrant; foliage bronze; vigorous, upright growth.

Palmetto Sunrise Min, *ob*, 1992, (MICpal); *Orange Honey × Miniature Seedling*; Williams, Michael C.; The Rose Garden & Mini Rose Nursery, 1993. Flowers orange with a yellow base, yellow reverse, opening orange, moderately full (15-25 petals), medium (4-7 cms) blooms borne mostly singly; foliage medium, medium green, semi-glossy; some prickles; upright (50 cms) growth.   1993 AOE.

Palmyre D (OGR), *lp*, 1844, Laffay. Flowers pale pink, Portland type; often repeats.

Paloma HT, *w*, 1968, *Mount Shasta × White Knight*; Swim & Weeks; Weeks Roses. Bud urn-shaped; flowers white, dbl., high-centered, large; foliage leathery, olive-green; vigorous, bushy growth. GM, Portland, 1971.

Paloma Blanca S, *w*, 1984, *Vera Dalton × ((Pink Princess × Lillian Gibson) × (Florence Mary Morse × (Josef Rothmund × R. laxa))*;

Buck; Iowa State University. Flowers ivory-white, dbl. (35 petals), cupped, medium blooms borne 3-10 per cluster; fragrant; foliage leathery, dark olive green; awl-like, tan prickles; erect, spreading, bushy, compact growth; repeat bloom; hardy.

Paloma Falcó HT, *op*, 1930, *Li Bures × Château de Clos Vougeot*; Dot, P.; C-P. Flowers coral-salmon, dbl.; fragrant.

Pam F, *yb*, 1962, *Masquerade × Seedling*; Annabel. Bud ovoid; flowers yellow edged red, becoming deep red, semi-dbl., cupped, small; slightly fragrant; moderate, bushy growth.

Památník Komenského LCl, *mp*, 1936, Bojan; Böhm. Flowers salmon-pink, large; fragrant; vigorous, climbing growth; free early bloom.

Památník Krále Jiřího HT, *dr*, 1936, (King George's Memorial); *Gorgeous × Gen. MacArthur*; Böhm. Bud pointed; flowers deep crimson, marked velvety purple, dbl., large; very fragrant; foliage glossy, dark; vigorous growth.

Pamela HT, *yb*, 1924, Therkildsen. Flowers canary-yellow and bright blush-pink shaded deep carmine; dbl.; fragrant.

Pamela Travers HT, *mp*, 1966, *Pink Favorite × Queen Elizabeth*; Morey; Country Garden Nursery. Flowers medium pink, full, large; very fragrant; foliage leathery; vigorous, upright.

Pamela's Choice HT, *my*, 1966, *Piccadilly sport*; Bardill Nursery. Flowers golden yellow, large (4½ in.); slightly fragrant; foliage bronze.

Pampa F, *mr*, 1971, *Colisee × Atlantic*; Gaujard. Bud pointed; flowers brilliant vermilion-red, full; foliage dark.

Pan America HT, *ob*, 1941, *Heinrich Wendland sport × Max Krause*; Boerner; J&P. Flowers deep orange suffused tawny yellow, becoming light gold, dbl. (30-40 petals), open, large (5½ in.); long stems; fragrant; foliage glossy, bronze; vigorous, upright, bushy, open growth.

Panaché Gr, *mp*, 1959, *Rubin (HT) × Cinnabar*; Lens. Flowers light salmon-pink, well formed, large; very fragrant; vigorous growth.

Panachée d'Angers D (OGR), *lp*, 1879, Moreau-Robert. Flowers light pink, anthers golden, semi-dbl.; spiny stems; vigorous growth.

Panachée de Lyon P (OGR), *pb*, 1895, *Rose du Roi sport*; Dubreuil. Flowers pink, variegated crimson.

Panachée d'Orléans HP (OGR), *pb*, 1854, *Baronne Prévost sport*; Dauvesse. Flowers blush-white striped deep rose.

Panama HT, *lp*, 1913, *Frau Karl Druschki* × *Seedling (pink)*; Cook, J. Flowers flesh edged lighter, dbl.; slightly fragrant.

Paname LCl, *mp*, 1959, *Spectacular* × *Seedling*; Delbard-Chabert. Flowers bright pink, reverse apricot tinted salmon, dbl., large; long, strong stems; slightly fragrant; well branched growth; free, recurrent bloom.

Panchu F, *mr*, 1966, Pal; Indian Agric. Research Inst. Bud globular; flowers ruby-red, semi-dbl., open, medium; foliage leathery; very vigorous, upright, compact growth.

Pandemonium F, *yb*, 1988, (MACpandem; Claire Rayner); *New Year* × *((Anytime* × *Eyepaint)* × *Stars 'n' Stripes)*; McGredy, Sam. Flowers yellow and red stripes, dbl. (26-40 petals); slight fragrance; foliage small, medium green, glossy; bushy growth.

Pandora HT, *my*, 1947, *Golden Rapture* × *R.M.S. Queen Mary*; Barké; Arnold-Fisher Co. Bud ovoid; flowers cream to deep yellow, dbl. (35-55 petals), high-centered, large (5 in.); fragrant; foliage dark, semi-glossy; very vigorous, tall growth; a greenhouse variety.

Paneera HT, *w*, 1983, *Seedling* × *Seedling*; Fumagalli, Niso. Flowers white, dbl. (35 petals), large; fragrant; foliage medium, dark, glossy; upright growth.

Pania HT, *lp*, 1968, *Paddy McGredy* × *(Kordes' Perfecta* × *Montezuma)*; McGredy. Flowers light pink, well-formed; slightly fragrant; foliage leathery. GM, NZ, 1970.

Panorama HT, *mp*, 1943, *Mrs. A.R. Barraclough* × *Seedling*; McGredy; J&P. Flowers rose-pink, reverse silvery pink, dbl. (30 petals), cupped, large (5 in.); fragrant; foliage glossy; vigorous, upright, compact growth.

Panorama Holiday F, *mp*, 1973, (Panorama); *Queen Elizabeth* × *Seedling*; Gregory. Flowers rose, dbl. (34 petals), pointed, large (3¹/₂ in.); fragrant; foliage glossy, dark.

Pantomime F, *dp*, 1965, *Ma Perkins* × *Karl Herbst*; McGredy, S., IV; McGredy. Flowers deep pink, dbl. (30 petals), high-centered, large (4 in.), in clusters; fragrant (fruity).

Papa Gontier T (OGR), *pb*, 1883, Nabonnand, G. Bud long, pointed; flowers bright pink, reverse carmine-red, semi-dbl., large; fragrant; foliage rich green; vigorous, bushy growth; intermittent bloom; long a standard forcing variety; (21).

Papa Gontier, Climbing Cl T (OGR), *pb*, 1904, Chevrier.

Papa Gouchault R, *dr*, 1922, *Rubin* × *Seedling*; Turbat. Bud long, pointed; flowers pure crimson-red, full, open, borne in clusters of 10-20 on long stems; slightly fragrant; foliage large, glossy; very vigorous, climbing growth.

Papa Hémeray Ch (OGR), *rb*, 1912, Hémeray-Aubert. Flowers red, center white, single, blooms in clusters; very vigorous growth.

Papa Hendrickx HT, *or*, 1964, *(Jolie Madame* × *R. rugosa rubra)* × *Seedling*; Mondial Roses. Bud long, pointed; flowers vermilion-orange, dbl. (45-50 petals), high-centered, large; foliage bronze; very vigorous, upright growth.

Papa Joao XXIII HT, *lp*, 1963, *Plaisir de France* × *La Jolla*; Moreira da Silva. Flowers pearl-pink.

Papa Klein HT, *or*, 1934, *Margaret Spaull* × *Norman Lambert*; Ketten Bros. Flowers reddish coppery orange, passing to salmon-pink, full, imbricated, large; fragrant; foliage cedar-green; very vigorous growth.

Papa Meilland® HT, *dr*, 1963, (MEIsar; MEIcesar); *Chrysler Imperial* × *Charles Mallerin*; Meilland, Alain; URS. Bud pointed; flowers dark velvety crimson, dbl. (35 petals), high-centered, large; very fragrant; foliage leathery, glossy, olive-green; vigorous, upright growth. GM, Baden-Baden, 1962; James Alexander Gamble Fragrance Medal, 1974.

Papa Meilland, Climbing® Cl HT, *dr*, 1970, (MEIsarsar; Grimpant Papa Meilland®); Stratford; Rumsey.

Papa Rouillard R, *mr*, 1923, *Léontine Grevais* × *Seedling*; Turbat. Flowers bright carmine, dbl., borne in long clusters of 15-25 on long stems; foliage rich green, glossy; thornless; very vigorous, climbing growth; abundant seasonal bloom.

Papa Schneider HT, *dr*, 1961, *Crimson Glory* × *Seedling*; Kriloff. Flowers dark red-purple, dbl. (25 broad petals), large; fragrant; foliage glossy; vigorous, upright growth.

Papageno® HT, *rb*, 1990, (MACgoofy); *Freude* × *((Anytime* × *Eyepaint)* × *Stars 'n' Stripes)*; McGredy, Sam; Sam McGredy Roses International, 1989. Flowers red blend (striped), moderately full (15-25 petals) large blooms; slight fragrance; foliage large, light green, matt; upright growth.

Paper Doll Min, *ab*, 1992, (JACfiseg; JACfiseq); *Fiddler's Gold* × *Sequoia Gold*; Zary, Keith; Bear Creek Gardens. Flowers light apricot with a hint of pale pink fading to light amber, then white, moderately full (15-25 petals), medium (4-7 cms) blooms borne in small clusters; no fragrance; foliage small, dark green, glossy; some prickles; low (45-60 cms), upright growth.

Papillon T (OGR), *pb*, 1881, Nabonnand. Flowers coppery salmon rose, semi-dbl., medium.

Papillon Rose F, *mp*, 1956, *White Briarcliff* × *(Lady Sylvia* × *Fashion)*; Lens. Flowers pink tinted salmon, dbl., high-centered, blooms in clusters; very fragrant; vigorous, bushy.

Papoose Cl Min, *w*, 1955, *R. wichuraiana* × *Zee*; Moore, R.S.; Sequoia Nursery. Bud pointed; flowers white, single, small (1 in.)blooms in clusters; foliage small, fern-like, semi-glossy; vigorous, spreading (to 3-4 ft.) growth; trailer or ground cover.

Paprika® F, *or*, 1958, (TANprik); *Märchenland* × *Red Favorite*; Tantau, Math. Bud long, pointed; flowers brick red, semi-dbl., large (3½ in.) blooms in large clusters; slightly fragrant; foliage leathery, glossy, olive-green; vigorous, upright growth. GM, NRS, 1959; Golden Rose of The Hague, 1961.

Pâquerette Pol, *w*, 1875, (La Pâquerette; Ma Pâqueretta); *Raised from open-pollinated seed of a dbl. fld. Multiflora. Considered to have a China or Tea rose in its background*; Guillot Fils. Flowers pure white, very dbl., cupped with imbricated petals, small (1 in.) blooms in broad clusters of up to 40, resembling a Noisette; slight fragrance; stems bright green; foliage glossy, 3-5 leaflets; very few prickles; very dwarf (12-15 in.), bushy growth. The first Polyantha.

Para Ti Min, *w*, 1949, (For You; Pour Toi; Wendy); *Eduardo Toda* × *Pompon de Paris*; Dot, P.; A. Meilland, 1946. Flowers white, base tinted yellow, semi-dbl. (about 15 petals); foliage glossy; very bushy (6-8 in.) growth.

Parade LCl, *dp*, 1953, *New Dawn seedlng* × *World's Fair, Climbing*; Boerner; J&P. Bud ovoid; flowers deep rose-pink, dbl. (33 petals), cupped, large (3½ in.); fragrant; foliage glossy; vigorous growth.

Parade Marshal F, *mr*, 1974, *Little Leaguer* × *Gemini*; Byrum; J.H. Hill Co. Flowers medium red, dbl. (25-30 petals), full, high-centered, medium (2-2½ in.); slightly fragrant; vigorous growth.

Paradis HT, *mr*, 1944, Gaujard. Bud pointed; flowers clear red, dbl., cupped, medium; slightly fragrant; foliage glossy; vigorous growth.

Paradise R, *pb*, 1907, Walsh. Flowers rose-pink, center white, tips of petals notched, single, large blooms in clusters; slightly fragrant; foliage glossy; vigorous, climbing (10-15 ft.) growth; non-recurrent bloom. RULED EXTINCT 1/79.

Paradise™ HT, *m*, 1978, (WEZeip; Burning Sky); *Swarthmore* × *Seedling*; Weeks; C-P. Bud long, pointed; flowers silvery lavender shading to ruby-red at edge, dbl. (28 petals), well-formed, large (3½-4½ in.); fragrant; foliage glossy, dark; upright growth. AARS, 1979; GM, Portland, 1979.

Parador® HT, *or*, 1978, (MEIchanso; Tchin-Tchin); *((Sarabande* × *Meikim)* × *(Alain* × *Orange Triumph))* × *Diablotin*; Paolino; URS. Flowers orange-red, dbl. (20 petals), flat, cupped, large (3½ in.); very vigorous growth. GM, Tokyo, 1978.

Paraglider S, *ob*, 1984, *(Country Dancer* × *Carefree Beauty)* × *Alexander*; Buck; Iowa State University. Bud ovoid, pointed; flowers light pink, reverse orange-red, dbl. (28 petals), cupped, medium-large blooms borne 1-10 per cluster; slightly fragrant; foliage medium, dark green tinted copper, leathery; awl-like, tan prickles; vigorous, bushy, spreading growth; repeat bloom; hardy.

Paragon Min, *mr*, 1982, (MACkosred); *Ko's Yellow* × *Little Artist*; McGredy, Sam. Flowers medium red, dbl. (35 petals); fragrant; foliage small, dark, glossy; bushy growth.

Paramount HT, *ab*, 1950, *Charlotte Armstrong* × *Glowing Sunset*; Swim; Paramount Nursery. Bud long, pointed; flowers orange-salmon-buff, dbl. (30 petals), high-centered, becoming flat, large (4-5 in.); slightly fragrant; foliage glossy; very vigorous, upright, bushy growth.

Parasol HT, *dy*, 1964, *Peace* × *Ethel Sanday Seedling*; Sanday. Flowers rich yellow, dbl. (28 petals), large (5 in.); fragrant; foliage dark; compact growth.

Pardinas Bonet HT, *yb*, 1931, *La Giralda* × *Souv. de Claudius Pernet*; Dot, P.; C-P. Flowers deep yellow, reverse red, dbl.; very fragrant.

Parel van Aalsmeer HT, *dr*, 1941, (Perle von Aalsmeer); *Better Times sport*; Verschuren. Flowers deep red.; a greenhouse variety.

Parfait F, *mr*, 1975, *Minuette sport*; Knight, C.; DeVor Nursery. Flowers red, sweetheart.

Paris Pol, *mr*, 1929, deRuiter. Flowers bright red; vigorous growth.

Paris Superior Pol, *mr*, *Paris sport*; deRuiter. Flowers have more lasting color than parent.

Pariser Charme® HT, *mp*, 1965, Tantau, Math. Bud ovoid; flowers pink, dbl. (28 petals), well-formed, large (5 in.) blooms in clusters (to 10); very fragrant; foliage dark, glossy; vigorous, upright growth. ADR, 1966.

Paris-Match HT, *dp*, 1957, *Independence* × *Grand'mère Jenny*; Meilland, F.; URS. Flowers carmine to rose, center darker, dbl.; foliage leathery; vigorous. GM, Bagatelle, 1956.

Park Avenue HT, *dr*, 1962, *Yuletide* × *San Fernando*; Jelly; E.G. Hill Co. Bud ovoid; flowers cardinal-red, dbl. (38-48 petals), open, large (3-4 in.); fragrant; foliage leathery, dark;

vigorous, upright growth; a greenhouse variety.

Park Royal F, *ob*, 1967, *Tropicana* × *Shepherd's Delight*; Eddie, J.H.; Sheridan Nursery. Bud ovoid; flowers coral-pink, center white, reverse silver, dbl., open, medium; slightly fragrant; foliage light green; vigorous, upright growth.

Parkdirektor Riggers® K (S), *dr*, 1957, *R. kordesii* × *Our Princess*; Kordes, R. Bud long, pointed; flowers velvety crimson, semi-dbl., medium blooms in clusters (up to 50); slightly fragrant; foliage dark, glossy, leathery; very vigorous, climbing growth; recurrent bloom. ADR, 1960.

Parkfeuer HFt (OGR), *or*, 1908, Lambert, P. Flowers bright scarlet, single; vigorous (6-8 ft.) growth; non-recurrent bloom.

Parkjuwel S, *lp*, 1956, (Park Jewell; Parkjewel); *Independence* × *Red Moss*; Kordes; Morse, 1950. Bud ovoid; flowers light pink, very dbl., cupped, very large; very fragrant; foliage leathery, wrinkled, light green; vigorous (4 ft.), bushy growth; non-recurrent bloom.

Parklane HT, *my*, 1961, *Peace* × *Dawn*; Jelly; E.G. Hill Co. Bud ovoid; flowers canary-yellow, dbl. (25-35 petals), high-centered, large (4½-5 in.); slightly fragrant; foliage glossy, vigorous, upright growth; a greenhouse variety.

Parks' Yellow Tea-scented China T (OGR), *my*, 1824, (*R.* × *odorata ochroleuca* (Lindley) Rehder; *R. indica ochroleuca* Lindley). Int. into England in 1824. Introduced as the original Tea rose. Flowers pale yellow, dbl.

Parkside Rose S, *dp*, Found near Parkside, Sask., Canada. Flowers deep pink, single; vigorous (6 ft.) growth.

Parkzauber C (OGR), *dr*, 1956, *Independence* × *Nuits de Young*; Kordes. Bud long, pointed; flowers dark crimson, dbl., large; fragrant; foliage dark, leathery; very vigorous (4 ft.), upright, bushy growth; non-recurrent bloom.

Parkzierde B (OGR), *dr*, 1909, Lambert, P. Flowers scarlet crimson, dbl., petals shell-shaped, blooms on long stems; fragrant; very vigorous growth; non-recurrent bloom.

Parmelia HT, *mr*, 1957, *Mme. Chiang Kai-shek* sport; Lennard. Bud long, pointed; flowers flamingo-red, dbl. (24-30 petals), high-centered, large (5-5½ in.); foliage dark, glossy, leathery; very vigorous, upright, compact growth.

Parsifal F, *op*, 1968, *Dacapo* × *Ballade*; deRuiter. Flowers coral-salmon, dbl. (34 petals), well shaped; vigorous, bushy growth.

Parthenon® HT, *pb*, 1967, (DELbro); *Chic Parisien* × *(Bayadère* × *Rome Glory)*; Delbard-Chabert. Flowers carmine-pink, reverse soft yellow, dbl., cupped, large; foliage bronze, glossy; vigorous, upright, bushy growth.

Party Doll F, *ab*, 1958, *Goldilocks Seedling* × *Fashion*; Boerner; J&P. Bud ovoid; flowers pink, dbl. (40 petals), cuppedto open, medium (2½ in.); fragrant; foliage leathery, glossy; vigorous, bushy growth; for pot forcing.

Party Dress HT, *ab*, 1961, *Gay Crusader* × *Seedling*; Robinson, H.; Lowe. Flowers deep apricot shaded buff-peach, dbl. (25 petals), high-centered, large (5 in.); fragrant; foliage glossy; vigorous, bushy, compact growth.

Party Girl Min, *yb*, 1979, *Rise 'n' Shine* × *Sheri Anne*; Saville. Bud long, pointed; flowers soft apricot-yellow, dbl. (23 petals), high-centered, small (1 in.); fragrant (spicy); compact, bushy growth. AOE, 1981.

Party Line™ Min, *op*, 1992, (MOGaline); *Party Girl* × *Fairlane*; Moglia, Thomas; Gloria Dei Nursery, 1993. Flowers coral, moderately full (15-25 petals), small (0-4 cms.) blooms borne in clusters of 6 or more on basal canes, higher up canes blooms singly or in small clusters; slight fragrance; foliage small, medium green, matt; few prickles; medium (45-50 cms.), compact growth.

Party Pink F, *mp*, 1956, *Seedling* × *Pinocchio Seedling*; Raffel; Port Stockton Nursery. Flowers bright pink, dbl. (30-50 petals), small (1½ in.), borne in clusters; fragrant; moderate growth.

Party Time HT, *yb*, 1986, *Perfume Delight* × *Half Time*; Weeks, O.L. Flowers lemon yellow with pink overlay, reverse lemon yellow, fading yellow with rose-red overlay, dbl. (45 petals), cupped, large, borne singly; moderate, fruity fragrance; foliage medium, medium green, semi-glossy; medium, reddish prickles, hooked downwards; upright, medium growth.

Partyglo™ Min, *yb*, 1984, (MINpco); *Little Darling* × *Over the Rainbow*; Williams, Ernest D.; Mini-Roses. Flowers yellow with pink petal edges, yellow reverse, dbl. (35 petals), high-centered, exhibition, small; slight fragrance; foliage small, dark, semi-glossy.

Parure HT, *dp*, 1965, *Michèle Meilland* × *Chic Parisien*; Delbard-Chabert; Cuthbert. Flowers carmine-rose, cupped, large (5 in.); slightly fragrant; foliage serrated; tall to moderate growth.

Parure d'Or® LCl, *yb*, 1968, (DELmir); *(Queen Elizabeth* × *Provence)* × *(Sultane Seedling* × *Mme. Joseph Perraud)*; Delbard-Chabert, 1970. Flowers golden yellow edged orange, single to semi-dbl., medium; foliage dark, glossy; vigorous, climbing growth; repeat bloom. GM, Bagatelle, 1968.

Parwana F, *yb*, 1974, *Seedling × Seedling*; Pal. Bud pointed; flowers golden yellow, edged plum-red, dbl. (37 petals), open, cupped, large (3 in.); slightly fragrant; foliage glossy, dark; vigorous growth.

Pasadena HT, *yb*, 1927, *The Queen Alexandra Rose sport*; Coolidge. Flowers golden yellow, edged flame, dbl.; fragrant. RULED EXTINCT 1/82.

Pasadena® HT, *or*, 1982, (KORland); *Mercedes × (Sweet Promise × (Miss Ireland × Zorina))*; Kordes, W., 1980. Flowers orange-red, dbl. (35 petals), high-centered, large; no fragrance; foliage large, medium green, matt; upright growth.

Pasadena Tournament F, *mr*, 1942, (Red Cécile Brunner); *Cécile Brunner × Seedling*; Krebs; Marsh's Nursery. Bud long, pointed; flowers velvety red, dbl. (36 petals), cupped, small; long stems; fragrant; foliage bronze; very vigorous, bushy growth.

Pasadena Tournament, Climbing Cl F, *mr*, 1945, (Red Cécile Brünner, Climbing); Marsh's Nursery.

Pascali® HT, *w*, 1963, (LENip; Blanche Pasca); *Queen Elizabeth × White Butterfly*; Lens; A. Dickson, 1963; Armstrong Nursery, 1968. Flowers creamy white, dbl. (30 petals), well-formed, medium; foliage dark; vigorous, bushy growth. GM, The Hague, 1963; Portland, 1967; AARS, 1969; World's Favorite Rose, 1991

Pascali, Climbing Cl HT, *w*, 1978, Anderson's Rose Nursery.

Pascaline® Min, *w*, 1984, (LENpas); *Miniature Seedling × (New Penny × Jour de Fête)*; Lens. Flowers white, dbl. (35 petals), urn-shaped to HT-form, medium blooms in clusters of 3-24; no fragrance; foliage dark gray-green; slightly hooked, brownish-red prickles; upright, bushy growth.

Pasita HT, *dr*, 1982, (KORsita); *Mercedes × Seedling*; Kordes, R.; Ludwigs Roses. Flowers bright dark red, dbl. (25 petals), flora-tea, medium blooms borne singly; slight fragrance; foliage glossy; straight, light brown prickles; medium-high, densely branched growth.

Paso Doble F, *or*, 1976, (MEIlanodin); Paolino; URS. Flowers geranium-red, 9 petals, large (3 in.); slightly fragrant; vigorous growth.

Passion Gr, *mr*, 1954, *Peace × Alain*; Gaujard. Bud long, pointed; flowers scarlet-cerise, dbl.

(36 petals), large (4 in.); fragrant; foliage dark; very vigorous, bushy growth.

Passport Cl HT, *dr*, 1940, Clark, A. Flowers dark red, well-formed; fragrant; vigorous growth.

Pastel HT, *ab*, 1961, *(Sutter's Gold × Seedling) × Fred Edmunds*; Abrams, Von; Peterson; Dering. Bud long, pointed; flowers creamy yellow and soft pink, dbl. (25 petals), high-centered, large (5 in.); strong stems; fragrant; foliage glossy, wrinkled; vigorous, upright growth.

Pastelina F, *w*, 1992, (SUNpaste); *White Dream × Freegold*; Schuurman, Frank B.; Riverland Nurseries, Ltd., 1991. Flowers near white, full (26-40 petals), medium (4-7 cms.) blooms; slight fragrance; foliage medium, medium green, glossy; upright growth; very suitable as spray rose for forcing.

Pasteur HT, *pb*, 1973, *Firmament × Femina*; Gaujard. Bud long; flowers brilliant pink, flushed red, dbl.; upright growth.

Pastorale® S, *pb*, 1970, (POUrale; Pastourelle); *Seedling × Royal Dane*; Poulsen, N.D. Flowers deep pink, yellow reverse, dbl. (25 petals), urn-shaped, large blooms in sprays of 1-10; slight fragrance; foliage large, leathery, dark, glossy; dark green prickles; very vigorous, upright, bushy growth.

Pastourelle HT, *op*, 1952, *Comtesse Vandal × Étoile d'Or*; Robichon. Flowers salmon-pink, very large; very free bloom.GM, Rome, 1953 RULED EXTINCT 12/85.

Pat Nixon F, *dr*, 1972, *Tamango × (Fire King × Banzai)*; Meilland; Stuart. Bud ovoid; flowers dark red, dbl., large; fragrant; foliage large, glossy, dark; vigorous, upright, bushy.

Pat Phoenix HT, *yb*, 1964, *(Wellworth × Clarice Goodacre) × Peace*; Latham. Flowers cream to yellow, flushed pink, base yellow, dbl. (40 petals), large (4½-5 in.); fragrant; foliage dark, leathery; very vigorous growth.

Pat Stewart HT, *dp*, 1976, *Red Devil × Honey Favorite*; Stewart, G. Flowers cerise to deep rose-pink, dbl. (26 petals), full, very large (5-5½ in.); slightly fragrant; foliage dark; vigorous, upright growth.

Patchwork Quilt Min, *ob*, 1990, *Rise 'n' Shine × Dandy Lyon*; Jolly, Marie, 1985; Rosehill Farm, 1991. Bud ovoid; flowers orange-yellow-pink blend, aging light orange, dbl. (60 petals), urn-shaped, medium, borne usually singly; slight fragrance; foliage small, medium green, matt; upright, bushy, medium growth.

Patience HT, *ob*, 1927, McGredy. Bud pointed; flowers scarlet-carmine shaded orange and orange-scarlet, dbl., high-centered, large; fragrant. GM, NRS, 1926.

Patience, Climbing Cl HT, *ob*, 1935, Shamburger, C.S..

Patience Strong HT, *mr*, 1969, *Basildon Belle × Red Dandy*; Trew; Basildon Rose Gardens. Flowers crimson-scarlet, dbl., pointed, large; foliage dull, gray-green; free growth.

Patio Dance™ Min, *rb*, 1984, (WILpada); *Winifred Coulter × White Gem*; Williams, J.B. Flowers medium red, white reverse, dbl. (20 petals), HT-form, small; slight fragrance; foliage medium, dark, glossy; strong, low, bushy growth.

Patio Gem Min, *op*, 1992, (SUNsalm); *Sexy Rexy × Firefly*; Schuurman, Frank B.; Riverland Nurseries, Ltd., 1991. Flowers orange blend, moderately full (15-25 petals), small (0-4 cms.); fragrant; foliage small, medium green, matt; spreading growth.

Patio Gold™ Min, *my*, 1984, (WILpago); *Patio Patty × Rise 'n' Shine*; Williams, J.B. Flowers medium yellow, dbl. (40+ petals), small; slight fragrance; foliage medium, dark, semi-glossy; low, compact, bushy growth.

Patio Jewel F, *m*, 1975, *Europeana × Angel Face*; Williams, J.B. Bud pointed; Flowers purple to clear amethyst, single (5-7 petals), open, medium (2½ in.); slightly fragrant; foliage leathery; very vigorous growth.

Patio Patty Min, *yb*, 1975, *(Circus × The Optimist) × (Little Darling × Starina)*; Williams, J.B. Bud pointed; flowers yellow, washed peach and orange, semi-dbl. (16 petals), globular, medium (2 in.); very fragrant; foliage small, reddish-green.

Patio Pearl F, *pb*, 1975, *Fairy Queen × The Optimist*; Williams, J.B. Flowers light pearl-pink, base deeper, semi-dbl. (18-20 petals), high-centered, small (1-1½ in.); slightly fragrant; foliage small, glossy, dark; vigorous growth.

Patio Ribbon F, *dr*, 1975, *Europeana × Red Favorite*; Williams, J.B. Bud ovoid; flowers velvety bright dark scarlet, semi-dbl. (16 petals), cupped, large (2½-3 in.); fragrant; foliage dark; strong growth.

Patio Snow™ S, *w*, 1984, (WILpasn); *Sea Foam × Charlie McCarthy*; Williams, J.B. Flowers white, dbl. (35 petals), small; fragrant; foliage small, medium green, semi-glossy; very compact, spreading growth; ground cover.

Patrice HT, *w*, 1985, *(Baccará × Generosa) × Zecchino d'Oro*; Bartolomeo, Embriaco. Flowers white, dbl. (25 petals), exhibition, large; slight fragrance; foliage medium, dark, semi-glossy; upright, bushy growth.

Patricia F, *ab*, 1972, (KORpatri; Kordes' Rose Patricia); *Elizabeth of Glamis sport*; Kordes;

Fermor. Flowers apricot, base shaded gold. GM, Orleans, 1979.

Patricia HT, *mr*, 1932, Chaplin Bros. Flowers carmine flecked pink, base orange-yellow; fragrant; foliage glossy, dark; vigorous growth.

Patricia Anne HT, *dp*, 1962, *Kordes' Perfecta sport*; Buzza. Flowers deep pink, reverse silvery pink, large (4-5 in.); fragrant; foliage dark, glossy; vigorous growth.

Patricia C. Oppmann F, *w*, 1981, *Seedling × Seedling*; Jerabek, Paul E. Bud pointed; flowers very light yellow, dbl. (43 petals), cupped blooms borne 1-7 per cluster; light fragrance; foliage glossy, medium green; slightly hooked prickles; vigorous, upright, dense growth. ARC TG (B), 1984.

Patricia Harknett HT, *dp*, 1961, *Lady Sylvia sport*; Harknett. Flowers deep pink, dbl. (23 petals), large (4 in.); fragrant; foliage bronze-red; vigorous growth.

Patricia Hyde F, *mp*, 1969, *Ann Elizabeth × Red Dandy*; Harkness. Flowers medium pink, semi-dbl., medium.

Patricia Macoun R, *w*, 1945, *R. helenae × Seedling*; Central Exp. Farm. Flowers white, dbl.; slightly fragrant; foliage dark, glossy; hardy.

Patricia Miller HT, *w*, 1978, *Queen Elizabeth sport × Queen Elizabeth sport*; Miller, J.; Treloar. Bud ovoid; flowers pure white, semi-dbl., open, large; slightly fragrant; foliage leathery; vigorous, bushy growth.

Patricia Neal HT, *mr*, 1963, *Better Times sport*; Macres; Paragon Greenhouses. Flowers bright cerise, dbl., high-centered, large; foliage dark, leathery; vigorous, tall growth; a greenhouse variety.

Patricia Piesse HT, *lp*, 1971, *Elizabeth Fankhauser × Memoriam*; Fankhauser. Flowers luminous light pink, dbl. (50-60 petals), high-centered, medium; fragrant; foliage glossy; vigorous, upright growth.

Patricia Scranton Cl Min, *yb*, 1977, *Fairy Moss × Fairy Moss*; Dobbs; Small World Min. Roses. Bud pointed; flowers light yellow, streaked red, semi-dbl. (17 petals), small (1½ in.); slightly fragrant; foliage glossy, dark, soft.

Patricia Watkins F, *lp*, 1947, *Karen Poulsen sport*; Watkins Roses. Flowers bright pink, single (5 petals), medium, borne in trusses; slightly fragrant; foliage dark; vigorous growth.

Patricia Weston LCl, *lp*, 1992, (REYpat); *Westerland × Perfume Delight*; Reynolds, Ted; Reynolds Roses. Flowers light pink, full (26-40 petals), large (7+ cms) blooms borne in small clusters; fragrant; foliage large, dark green, glossy; some prickles; medium (2 m.), upright growth.

Patrician HT, *mr*, 1977, *Fragrant Cloud × Proud Land*; Warriner; J&P. Bud ovoid, pointed; flowers cardinal red, dbl. (28 petals), high-centered, large (4-5 in.); very fragrant; foliage large, dark; very upright growth.

Patrick Anderson HT, *dp*, 1938, *John Henry × Portadown Fragrance*; McGredy; J&P. Bud long, pointed; flowers deep rose-pink, dbl., high-centered, large; very fragrant; foliage leathery; vigorous growth.

Patrick Vincent HT, *dr*, 1967, *Mirandy × F.W. Alesworth*; Vincent. Flowers crimson; very fragrant; foliage dark; free growth.

Patriot HT, *dr*, 1991, (JAClin); *Showstopper × Mister Lincoln*; Warriner, William A.; Bear Creek Gardens, Inc. Flowers dark red, full (26-40 petals), large (7+ cms) blooms borne mostly singly; slight fragrance; foliage large, dark green, semi-glossy to glossy; upright (150 cms), spreading growth.

Pat's Delight S, *mr*, 1987, (WILrss); *Queen Elizabeth × Chrysler Imperial*; Williams, J. Benjamin, 1987-88. Flowers crimson to light scarlet, semi-dbl. (16 petals), loosely cupped, opening flat, borne in sprays of 5-7; slight fragrance; foliage large, dark green, glossy; light green prickles, curving downwards; upright, strong, good branching growth.

Patsy HT, *w*, 1930, Dickson, H.; Morse. Bud pointed; flowers pure white, dbl., open, cupped, very large; slightly fragrant.

Patsy Cline™ HT, *m*, 1983, (AROcomu; AROcumu); *Angel Face × Double Delight*; Christensen; Armstrong Nursery. Flowers light lavender, petals edged ruby lavender, dbl. (35 petals), exhibition, large; very fragrant; foliage medium, dark, matt; upright, bushy growth.

Patty Lou Min, *pb*, 1953, (Petite); *Oakington Ruby × Oakington Ruby*; Moore, R.S.; Sequoia Nursery. Bud ovoid; flowers rose pink, reverse silvery pink, dbl. (55 petals), small (1 in.); fragrant; foliage small; dwarf (10-12 in.), bushy growth.

Patty Sue Min, *mp*, 1985, (TINpat); *Little Darling × Little Chief*; Bennett, Dee; Tiny Jewels Nursery. Flowers medium pink, dbl. (35 petals), HT form, medium; slight fragrance; foliage medium, medium green, matt; vigorous, upright growth.

Patty's Pink F, *lp*, 1960, (*Cécile Brunner × Mrs. R.M. Finch*) × *Self*; Spanbauer. Bud long, pointed; flowers rose-opal, reverse camellia-rose, dbl. (40-45 petals), high-centered to flat, medium (2½ in.); slightly fragrant; foliage

leathery, glossy; very vigorous, upright, compact growth.

Patty's Red F, *mr*, 1968, *Patty's Pink sport*; Paulen Park Nursery. Flowers cherry-red.

Paul Bigot R, *dp*, 1924, Turbat. Flowers bright rose, shaded vermilion, borne in clusters of 5-10; vigorous, climbing growth.

Paul Bouclainville HT, *yb*, 1930, *Mme. Charles Detreaux × Mme. Edouard Herriot*; Buatois. Flowers carmine on yellow ground, reverse pinkish white tinted yellow, semi-dbl., cupped; fragrant; very vigorous growth.

Paul Buatois Cl HT, *dr*, 1931, *Marie Baumann × Mme. Edouard Herriot*; Buatois. Flowers velvety red, base yellow passing to purplish carmine, dbl., cupped, very large; fragrant; foliage leathery; very vigorous, climbing growth.

Paul Bunyan Gr, *dr*, 1961, *Charles Mallerin × Carrousel*; Abrams, Von; Peterson; Dering. Bud long, pointed; flowers deep red, dbl. (55 petals), high-centered, large (5 in.); slightly fragrant; foliage leathery; very vigorous, upright growth.

Paul Crampel Pol, *or*, 1930, Kersbergen. Flowers deep orange-scarlet, brighter and larger than Gloria Mundi but not so dbl., blooms in large clusters; (14).

Paul Crampel, Climbing Cl Pol, *or*, 1934, Appleton.

Paul Crampel, Climbing Cl Pol, *or*, 1934, Vially.

Paul Crampel, Climbing Cl Pol, *or*, 1937, Tantau.

Paul Dauvesse R, *my*, 1933, Barbier. Bud long, golden yellow; flowers bright canary-yellow, dbl., large, borne in clusters of 4-8; vigorous, climbing growth.

Paul Délépine Pol, *mp*, 1933, *Yvonne Rabier × Dorothy Perkins*; Délépine; Pajotin-Chédane. Flowers brilliant rose-pink, dbl., globular, borne in clusters; foliage leathery, glossy; vigorous growth.

Paul Duvivier HT, *mr*, 1932, *Constance × Pax Labor*; Laperrière. Flowers carmine, base yellow, nearly full; very fragrant.

Paul Lafont HT, *ly*, 1920, *Mme. Maurice Capron × Seedling*; Guillot, P. Flowers golden yellow to white tinted yellow, dbl.; slightly fragrant.

Paul Lede Cl T, *ab*, 1913, Lowe. Flowers yellowish buff, center flushed carmine.

Paul Lucchini HT, *dr*, 1931, *Rhea Reid × Yves Druhen*; Buatois. Flowers purplish garnet, shaded velvety red, dbl., cupped; very fragrant; foliage bronze, leathery; vigorous growth.

Paul Monnier HT, *yb*, 1902, Buatois. Flowers light yellow shaded salmon.

Paul Nabonnand T (OGR), *mp*, 1878, Nabonnand, G. Flowers pink, dbl. cupped, large; vigorous growth.

Paul Neyron HP (OGR), *mp*, 1869, *Victor Verdier × Anna de Diesbach*; Levet, A. Flowers clear pink to rose-pink, full (50 petals), cupped, very large; fragrant; foliage large, rich green; vigorous growth; occasional recurrent bloom.

Paul Noël LCl, *pb*, 1913, *R. wichuraiana × Mons. Tillier*; Tanne. Flowers old rose and pale yellow, medium (2-3 in.) blooms in clusters of 4-6; vigorous, climbing.

Paul Perras HP (OGR), *lp*, 1870, (The Crepe Rose); Levet. Flowers pale rose, very dbl., compact, large; sets many hips; vigorous, pillar.

Paul Ploton R, *mr*, 1910, *R. wichuraiana × Mme. Norbert Levavasseur*; Barbier. Flowers bright red; blooms late.

Paul Revere HT, *mr*, 1940, *Talisman sport*; Roland. Flowers carmine, opening scarlet-crimson, dbl. (24-30 petals), cupped, large (4-5 in.); fragrant; vigorous, upright growth.

Paul Ricault C (OGR), *mp*, 1845, Portemer. Flowers rose-pink, fully dbl., flat, quartered; very fragrant; height to 5 ft.

Paul Shirville HT, *op*, 1981, (HARqueterwife; Heart Throb); *Compassion × Mischief*; Harkness, R., 1983. Flowers light salmon-pink, dbl. (30 petals), high-centered, medium-large blooms borne singly and in 3's; sweet fragrance; foliage large, dark, semi-glossy; large, reddish prickles; medium, bushy growth. Edland Fragrance Medal, 1982.

Paul Transon LCl, *op*, 1900, *R. wichuraiana × L'Idéal*; Barbier. Flowers bright pink, full, large blooms in clusters of 3-5 on short, strong stems; slightly fragrant; foliage glossy, dark; height 10 ft.

Paul Verdier HP (OGR), *dp*, 1866, Verdier, C. Flowers bright rose.

Paula Gr, *or*, 1980, *Radiation induced Queen Elizabeth sport*; James, John. Flowers dusty salmon.

Paula Clegg HT, *mr*, 1919, *Kaiserin Auguste Viktoria × Seedling*; Kiese. Flowers bright scarlet.

Paula Mayer HT, *pb*, 1929, *Mme. Edmée Metz × Betty Uprichard*; Leenders Bros. Flowers silvery carmine-pink, reverse yellowish pink, semi-dbl.; very fragrant.

Paule Delavey Pol, *ly*, 1957, Privat. Flowers creamy yellow; vigorous, bushy growth.

Paulette F, *ly*, 1934, *Léontine Gervais × Paul Monnier*; Buatois. Flowers saffron-yellow to yellowish white, very dbl., cupped, borne in clusters; very fragrant; foliage leathery, glossy; vigorous growth.

Paulette HT, *dp*, 1946, *Peace × Signora*; Meilland, F. Flowers bright rosy scarlet, center tinted salmon, very dbl., well formed, large; slightly fragrant; foliage rich green; tall growth.

Paulette Buffet HT, *lp*, 1921, *Jonkheer J.L. Mock × Seedling*; Gillot, F. Flowers pale flesh-pink, reverse silvery pink, dbl.; slightly fragrant.

Paulette Coquelet HT, *mr*, 1947, *Seedling × Daniel*; Mallerin; URS. Bud long; flowers salmon-red tinted bright coral, dbl., large; very vigorous growth.

Paulien Verbeek HT, *ob*, 1958, Verbeek. Flowers orange-yellow, dbl. (55 petals), large; very vigorous growth; a forcing variety.

Paulii S, *w*, (R. × *paulii* Rehder; R. *rugosa repens alba* Paul); R. *arvensis* × R. *rugosa*; Orig. shortly before 1903. Flowers white, yellow stamens, single, 2½ in. diameter, borne in corymbose; prostrate shrub growth.

Paulii Rosea S, *pb*, (R. × *paulii rosea* hort.; R. *rugosa repens rosea*); Possibly a Paulii sport; Orig. shortly before 1912. Flowers medium pink, white eye, yellow stamens, single.

Pauline Dawson R, *dp*, 1916, Dawson; Eastern Nursery. Flowers deep pink, single, large; vigorous, climbing growth.

Pauline Lancezeur HP (OGR), *dr*, 1854, Lancezeur. Flowers crimson shaded violet, full, large; recurrent bloom.

Paul's Carmine Pillar Cl HT, *mr*, 1895, (Carmine Pillar); Paul. Bud long, pointed; flowers carmine-red, single, open, large; slightly fragrant; foliage rich green; vigorous growth; very early bloom.

Paul's Early Blush HP (OGR), *lp*, 1893, (Mrs. Harkness); *Heinrich Schultheis sport*; Paul. Flowers blush.

Paul's Himalayan Musk Rambler R, *lp*, Flowers blush-lilac-pink, rosette form, blooms in clusters on thread-like stems; growth to 30 ft.

Paul's Lemon Pillar Cl HT, *ly*, 1915, *Frau Karl Druschki × Maréchal Niel*; Paul. Bud pale lemon-yellow; flowers pale sulphur-yellow to almost white, full, very large blooms on long, strong stems; very fragrant; vigorous growth; non-recurrent bloom; not dependably hardy. GM, NRS, 1915.

Paul's Pink HT, *lp*, 1978, *Snowsong Supreme × Pink Puff*; DeVor, P.; DeVor Nursery. Flowers soft pink, dbl. (28 petals), small; very fragrant; vigorous growth; greenhouse variety.

Paul's Scarlet Climber LCl, *mr*, 1916, *Paul's Carmine Pillar* × *Rêve d'Or*; Paul, W. Flowers vivid scarlet, shaded bright crimson, semi-dbl., medium blooms in large clusters; slightly fragrant; vigorous, climbing or pillar growth; sometimes slightly recurrent; very hardy; (21)   GM, NRS, 1915; Bagatelle, 1918.

Paul's Single White Perpetual HP (OGR), *w*, 1883, (Paul's Perpetual White); Paul. Flowers pure white, single, solitary or in small clusters; foliage light green; vigorous.

Pax HMsk (S), *w*, 1918, *Trier* × *Sunburst*; Pemberton. Flowers pure white, prominent golden anthers, semi-dbl., medium (3-4 in.) blooms in clusters of 25-50 on long, strong stems; very fragrant; foliage large, leathery; vigorous (4 ft.), bushy growth; recurrent bloom; (21)   GM, NRS, 1918.

Pax F, *w*, 1946, *Irene* × *Mme. Alexandre Dreux*; Leenders, M. Flowers white tinted greenish, semi-dbl., large; fragrant.

Pax Amanda HBlanda (S), *lp*, 1937, *Frau Georg von Simson* × *R. blanda*; Hansen, N.E. Flowers light pink, turning to white, semi-dbl. (17 petals), borne in clusters; vigorous (7 ft. stems), thornless; free, non-recurrent bloom; very hardy.

Pax Apollo HBlanda (S), *dp*, 1938, *R. sempervirens* × *R. blanda*; Hansen, N.E. Flowers deep pink, semi-dbl. (14 petals), borne in large clusters; vigorous (7 ft.), thornless growth; non-recurrent bloom; very hardy.

Pax Iola HBlanda (S), *lp*, 1938, *Anci Böhmova* × *R. blanda*; Hansen, N.E. Flowers clear shell-pink, passing to nearly white, semi-dbl. (25 petals), large, borne in large clusters; vigorous, pillar, thornless growth; non-recurrent bloom; very hardy.

Pax Labor HT, *yb*, 1918, *Beauté de Lyon* × *Seedling*; Chambard, C. Flowers pale golden yellow, slightly shaded coppery carmine, passing to sulphur-yellow, full, globular, large; vigorous growth.

Pax Labor, Climbing Cl HT, *yb*, 1929, Gaujard.

Paysagiste Faure-Laurent HT, *ob*, 1947, Gaujard. Flowers orange, reverse orange-yellow, dbl., large; slightly fragrant; foliage glossy, dark; vigorous growth.

Paz Vila HT, *mr*, 1931, *Jovita Perez* × *Jean C.N. Forestier*; Munné, B. Flowers red, dbl., large; fragrant; foliage glossy; vigorous growth.

Peace HT, *yb*, 1945, (Gioia; Gloria Dei; Mme. A. Meilland); *((George Dickson* × *Souv. de Claudius Pernet)* × *(Joanna Hill* × *Charles P. Kilham))* × *Margaret McGredy*; Meilland, F.; C-P. Flowers golden yellow edged rose-pink,

dbl. (43 petals), high-centered to cupped, large (6 in.); slightly fragrant; foliage large, very dark, leathery, glossy; very vigorous, tall, bushy growth.   GM, Portland, 1944; NRS, 1947; AARS, 1946; ARS National Gold Med.al Certificate, 1947; Golden Rose of The Hague, 1965

Peace, Climbing Cl HT, *yb*, 1950, (Mme. A. Meilland, Climbing; Gioia, Climbing; Gloria Dei, Climbing); Brandy; C-P.

Peace, Climbing Cl HT, *yb*, 1951, Kordes.

Peaceful HT, *pb*, 1956, *Seedling* × *Peace*; Boerner; J&P. Bud globular; flowers deep coral rose pink, reverse lighter, dbl. (50 petals), cupped, very large (5½-6 in.); fragrant; foliage leathery; vigorous, upright.

Peaceport HT, *op*, 1960, *Peace sport*; Rokos; Wyant. Flowers deep orange-pink.

Peach Beauty HT, *pb*, 1970, *Ma Perkins* × *Polynesian Sunset*; Boerner; Thomasville Nursery. Bud ovoid; flowers peach-pink, dbl., large; fragrant; foliage large, leathery; vigorous, bushy.

Peach Blossom F, *dp*, 1932, Chaplin Bros. Bud orange-red; flowers soft carmine-rose, semi-dbl., medium, borne in clusters of 6-12; vigorous growth.

Peach Brandy Min, *ab*, 1978, Schwartz, E.W.; Bountiful Ridge Nursery; Gulf Stream Nursery. Bud pointed; flowers apricot, dbl. (23 petals), high-centered, small; fragrant; compact, bushy growth.

Peach Elite Min, *ab*, 1986, (LYOlite); *Dandy Lyon* × *Seedling*; Lyon; MB Farm Min. Roses. Flowers peach, dbl. (26 petals), high-centered to loose form, large blooms borne singly; no fragrance; foliage large, medium green, matt; small prickles; fruit globular, medium, orange-red; upright growth.

Peach Fuzz™ Min, *ab*, 1990, (WEKhelen); *Fairy Moss* × *New Year*; Carruth, Tom; Weeks Roses, 1991. Bud pointed, moss; flowers apricot blend fading to pastel, dbl. (22 petals), high-centered, exhibition, medium, borne singly or in sprays of 3-7; mini-moss; heavy moss fragrance; foliage medium, dark green, glossy; prickles straight, yellow brown; bushy, rounded, full, medium growth.

Peach Glow F, *pb*, 1960, *Goldilocks* × *Fashion*; Boerner; J&P. Bud ovoid; flowers golden coral, base pink, dbl. (30 petals), cupped, large (3 in.); fragrant (spicy); foliage leathery; vigorous, upright, compact growth.

Peach Melba HT, *yb*, 1960, *Golden Scepter* × *Hazel Alexander*; Dicksons & Co. Flowers yellow marked flame and pink; fragrant; vigorous growth.

Peach Silks Min, *ab*, 1991, (CLEpeach); *Seedling* × *Seedling*; Clements, John; Heirloom Old Garden Roses. Flowers rich peach, moderately full (15-25 petals), small (0-4 cms) blooms borne in small clusters; no fragrance; foliage small, dark green, glossy; few prickles; tall (50 cms), upright growth.

Peach Treat HT, *pb*, 1968, *Beauté* × *Kordes' Perfecta*; Fuller; Wyant. Bud ovoid; flowers peach-pink, very dbl., large; very fragrant; foliage leathery; vigorous, bushy growth.

Peachblow HT, *lp*, 1942, *Mme. Butterfly* × *Yellow Seedling*; Coddington; C-P. Bud long, pointed; flowers light pink, dbl., large; fragrant; foliage glossy; vigorous.

Peaches and Cream HT, *ob*, 1936, *Seedling* × *Miss Rowena Thom*; H&S; Dreer. Flowers salmon shaded gold and rose-pink, very dbl., slightly fragrant; bushy. RULED EXTINCT 4/77.

Peaches 'n' Cream Min, *pb*, 1976, *Little Darling* × *Magic Wand*; Woolcock; Pixie Treasures. Bud tapering; flowers light peach-pink blend, dbl. (52 petals), high-centered, exhibition, small (1 in.); slightly fragrant; foliage dark; upright, spreading. AOE, 1977.

Peachy Min, *pb*, 1964, *Golden Glow* × *Zee*; Moore, R.S.; Sequoia Nursery. Flowers pink tinted yellow, dbl. (50 petals), small; fragrant; foliage light green, soft; vigorous, bushy (12 in.) growth.

Peachy Keen Min, *ab*, 1979, *Little Darling* × *Sheri Anne*; Bennett, Dee; Tiny Petals Nursery. Bud long, pointed; flowers soft apricot pink, 18-20 petals, small (1 in.); slightly fragrant; bushy, spreading growth.

Peachy White Min, *w*, 1976, *Little Darling* × *Red Germain*; Moore, R.S.; Nor'East Min. Roses. Bud long, pointed; flowers near white, often tinted pink, semi-dbl. (18 petals), small (1½ in.); fragrant; foliage leathery; upright, bushy growth. AOE, 1976.

Peacock HT, *op*, 1985, *Red Queen sport* × *Red Queen*; LeMire, Walter. Bud ovoid, pointed; flowers orange-coral, reverse cream, dbl. (50+ petals), high-centered, large (5½ in.) blooms borne usually singly; spicy fragrance; foliage large, dark, semi-glossy; fruit large, globular, orange-red; vigorous, upright, bushy growth.

Peak Performance HT, *dr*, 1991, *Seedling* × *Seedling*; Burks, Larry; Co-Operative Rose Growers. Flowers dark red, full, large blooms borne mostly singly; slight fragrance; foliage medium, dark green, matt; tall, bushy, spreading growth.

PEApost F, *mr*, 1989, (Carol Ann); *Geraldine* × *Seedling*; Pearce, C.A.; Rearsby Roses, 1990. Bud rounded; flowers scarlet, dbl. (42 petals), loose, medium, borne in sprays of 3-15; slight fragrance; foliage large, medium green, semi-glossy; prickles straight, large, red; spreading, medium growth.

PEAprince F, *ob*, 1988, (Olympic Spirit); *Seedling* × *Seedling*; Pearce, C.A.; Rearsby Roses, 1988. Flowers orange, reverse yellow, aging orange-brown, semi-dbl., cupped, medium, borne in sprays of 4-5; slight, fruity fragrance; foliage small, dark green, glossy; prickles pointed, medium, red; bushy, low growth.

Pearl HT, *lp*, 1879, *Adam* × *Comtesse de Serenye*; Bennett. Flowers light pink, very dbl., small; fragrant; weak growth.

Pearl HT, *w*, 1933, Bentall. Flowers white, shaded pink; fragrant.

Pearl Costin HT, *yb*, 1959, *Elli Knab* × *Amy Johnson*; Reithmuller. Bud long, pointed; flowers light yellow, center pink, semi-dbl. to dbl., cupped, large; slightly fragrant; foliage leathery, wrinkled; vigorous, upright, bushy growth.

Pearl Dawn Min, *mp*, 1975, *(Cécile Brunner* × *Perla de Montserrat)* × *Perla de Montserrat*; Saville; Nor'East Min. Roses. Bud short, pointed; flowers medium pink, dbl. (38 petals), micro-mini, small (1 in.); very compact, bushy growth.

Pearl Drift® S, *w*, 1981, (LEGgab); *Mermaid* × *New Dawn*; LeGrice, 1980. Flowers white flushed pink, semi-dbl. (18 petals), blooms borne several together; slight fragrance; foliage glossy, reddish to dark green; small, light brown prickles; vigorous, compact, spreading growth.

Pearl Harbor HT, *pb*, 1943, *Seedling* × *Miss Rowena Thom*; Howard, F.H.; H&S. Bud long, pointed; flowers light pink reverse china-rose, dbl. (45 petals), high-centered, medium (3-3½ in.); very fragrant; foliage leathery, dark; very vigorous, upright growth.

Pearl Meidiland™ S, *lp*, 1989, (MEIplatin; Perle Meillandécor); *(Sea Foam* × *MEIsecaso)* × *Sea Foam*; Meilland, Alain; C-P, 1989. Bud ovoid; flowers light pink, aging white, dbl. (30 petals), flat, medium, borne in sprays of 3-15; no fragrance; foliage medium, dark green, glossy; prickles small, reddish-brown; fruit globular, small, reddish; spreading, low growth; repeat bloom.

Pearl of Baltimore HT, *lp*, 1925, *Ophelia* × *Glorified La France*; Cook, J. Flowers shell-pink, center deeper, very dbl.; fragrant.

Pearl S. Buck HT, *yb*, 1940, *Joanna Hill* × *Étoile d'Or*; Kordes; J&P. Bud long, pointed, deep orange; flowers golden yellow suffused apricot, dbl. (45 petals), large (4½ in.); long stems; fragrant; foliage leathery, dark; vigorous, bushy growth.

Pearl Wilson Kissel HT, *dp*, 1954, *Red Columbia × Chrysler Imperial*; Kissel and Motose. Flowers bright red, dbl. (30-40 petals), large (4¹/₂ in.); fragrant; foliage leathery; vigorous, bushy growth.

Pearlie Mae Gr, *ab*, 1981, *Music Maker × (Queen Elizabeth × Country Music)*; Buck; Iowa State University. Bud ovoid, pointed; flowers yellow blended with pink, reverse pink, dbl. (35 petals), cupped blooms borne 1-8 per cluster; moderate fragrance; foliage leathery, semi-glossy, dark olive green, tinted copper; awl-shaped prickles; erect, bushy.

Pearly Peace HT, *lp*, 1959, *Peace sport*; Fryer's Nursery. Flowers soft pearl-pink.

Pearly Queen F, *lp*, 1963, *Queen Elizabeth sport*; North Hill Nursery. Flowers light pink, dbl. (22 petals), well formed, large (4 in.); fragrant; vigorous growth.

Pearly Shell HT, *pb*, 1972, *Pink Parfait × Michèle Meilland*; Sherwood. Flowers shell pink, center cream, dbl. (30 petals), high-centered, large; fragrant; foliage glossy; vigorous, upright growth.

Pearly White LCl, *w*, 1942, *Glenn Dale × Mrs. Arthur Curtiss James self Seedling*; Brownell. Bud long, pointed; flowers white tinted pearl, semi-dbl. (21 petals), open; long, strong stems; vigorous, climbing (to 20 ft.), upright growth.

PEAspecial Min, *lp*, 1989, (Audrey Gardner); *Seedling × Seedling*; Pearce, C.A.; Rearsby Roses, 1990. Bud rounded; flowers shell pink, reverse slightly darker, aging same, dbl. (45 petals), cupped, large, borne in sprays of 25-30; no fragrance; foliage small, medium green, semi-glossy; prickles pointed, red; no fruit; bushy, medium growth.

Peat Fire Flame HT, *op*, 1985, *Red Planet × Bonnie Anne*; MacLeod, Major C.A. Flowers pale orange, reverse salmon-pink, dbl (20 petals), medium; fragrant; Foliage medium, medium green, glossy; upright growth.

Pebble Mill F, *rb*, 1973, *Paddy McGredy × Seedling*; Gregory. Flowers magenta, reverse spirea-red, dbl. (28 petals), flat, large (3¹/₂ in.); fragrant; foliage dark.

Pechtold's Triumph F, *dr*, 1961, *Red Favorite × Frensham*; Verschuren-Pechtold. Flowers oxblood-red, semi-dbl, medium, borne in large clusters.

Pedrálbes HT, *w*, 1935, *Frau Karl Druschki × Souv. de Mme. Boullet*; Camprubi; J&P. Flowers cream to pure white, dbl. (30 petals), high-centered, large (5 in.); slightly fragrant; foliage dark, glossy; very vigorous growth.

Pedro Veyrat HT, *ab*, 1933, *Lí Burés × Bénédicte Seguin*; Dot, P.; C-P. Bud long, pointed; flowers apricot, dbl, cupped, large; fragrant.

Peep o' Day F, *op*, 1972, *(Pink Parfait × Highlight) × Orion*; Harkness; Mason, 1973. Flowers salmon, shaded orange, dbl. (28 petals), large; slightly fragrant; foliage dark.

Peep-Eye™ Cl Min, *mr*, 1992, (MINpeep); *Red Delight × Seedling*; Williams, Ernest. Flowers very distinct shade of medium red, with large clusters of golden yellow stamens, full (25 petals), small (0-4 cms) blooms borne in small clusters; slight fragrance; foliage small, dark green, glossy; some prickles; tall (4 ft.), upright, bushy growth.

Peeping Tom S, *dp*, 1968, *Kordes' Perfecta × Parade*; MacLeod. Flowers deep pink, dbl., pointed, large; slightly fragrant; foliage medium, medium green, matt; vigorous, tall; recurrent.

Peer Gynt® HT, *yb*, 1968, (KORol); *Colour Wonder × Golden Giant*; Kordes, R.; McGredy. Flowers yellow, outer petals edged red, dbl. (50 reflexing petals), large; slightly fragrant; vigorous, bushy growth. GM, Belfast, 1970.

Peerless HT, *mr*, 1935, *Better Times sport*; Hill, J.H., Co. Bud long, pointed; flowers bright velvety scarlet-carmine, dbl. (38-40 petals), large; a florists' variety.

Peggy HT, *dp*, 1934, *Ophelia × Red-Letter Day*; Bees. Bud long, pointed; flowers deep rose, dbl., high-centered; very fragrant; foliage glossy, light; vigorous growth.

Peggy Ann Landon LCl, *ob*, 1938, *Glenn Dale × ((Seedling × Seedling) × Mary Wallace)*; Brownell. Flowers yellow-orange, becoming lighter, dbl., high-centered, large (3¹/₂-5 in.); fragrant; long, strong stems; foliage large, leathery, glossy, dark; very vigorous, climbing (15-25 ft.) growth.

Peggy Astbury HT, *ab*, 1920, Easlea. Flowers soft amber to light yellow.

Peggy Bell HT, *ab*, 1929, Clark, A.; NRS New South Wales. Color like Betty Uprichard, but more free and vigorous.

Peggy England HT, *ab*, 1923, Lilley. Flowers cream-apricot, sometimes tinted carmine.

Peggy Grant Min, *lp*, 1954, *(Robinette × Mons. Tillier) × Zee*; Moore, R.S.; Sequoia Nursery. Flowers shell-pink, dbl. (25 petals), small; foliage light green; dwarf (5-6 in.), bushy growth.

Peggy Jane™ Min, *lp*, 1986, (SAVapeg); *Starina sport*; Utz, Peggy L.; Nor'East Min. Roses. Flowers light pink, with lighter petal edges and base.

Peggy Joan Reynolds S, *mp*, 1992, (REYpeg); *(Possibly HCh × R. gigantea)*; Reynolds, Ted,

1993. Flowers medium pink, single (5 petals), small (0-4 cms.) blooms borne in small clusters; slight fragrance; foliage medium, light green, semi-glossy, disease resistant; few prickles; upright (150 cms.) growth; very remontant, almost perpetual; (14) pliody; very hardy; Variety found growing wild in a small cemetery in New Zealand.

Peggy Lee HT, *lp*, 1982, (ARofeigel); *Century Two sport*; Feigel, John R.; Armstrong Nursery. Flowers pale pink.

Peggy Netherthorpe HT, *mp*, 1974, *(Voeux de Bonheur × Chic Parisien) × (Michèle Meilland × Mme. Joseph Perraud)*; Delbard; Harry Wheatcroft Gardening. Flowers pink, dbl. (35 petals), large (5 in.); slightly fragrant; foliage light.

Peggy Newton F, *my*, 1957, *Golden Glow × Goldilocks*; Boerner; Stuart. Flowers primrose-yellow, dbl. (40-50 petals), globular, large (2½-3 in.), borne in clusters; slightly fragrant; foliage small, leathery, glossy; dwarf, spreading growth.

Peggy Rockefeller™ HT, *dr*, 1992, (WILace); *Queen Elizabeth × Swarthmore*; Williams, J. Benjamin, 1991; New York Botanical Garden, 1991. Flowers bright crimson to cherry red with dark smokey red on edge of petals, dbl. (40 petals), large (4½-5 in.) blooms borne usually singly and in sprays of 3-5; moderate, spicy fragrance; foliage large, dark green, semi-glossy; few prickles; upright, bushy, medium growth.

Peggy T™ Min, *mr*, 1988, (KINtee); *Poker Chip × Rise 'n' Shine*; King, Gene; AGM Miniature Roses. Flowers medium red to white, circular base, reverse white, aging medium pinkish red, single (5 petals), medium, borne usually singly or in sprays of 5-10; foliage medium, medium green, matt; prickles straight with hook, white; no fruit; bushy, medium growth.

Peggy's Delight Min, *pb*, 1982, (MINcco); *Little Darling × Over the Rainbow*; Williams, Ernest D.; Mini-Roses. Flowers deep pink, white reverse, dbl. (40+ petals), small; slight fragrance; foliage small, dark, glossy; bushy growth.

PEKali HT, *ob*, *Seedling × Marina*; Pekmez, P. Flowers orange dbl. (35 petals), large; no fragrance; foliage large, glossy; upright growth.

PEKamecel F, *or*, 1984, *Seedling × Seedling*; Pekmez, Paul. Flowers orange-red, dbl. (20 petals); slight fragrance; foliage dark; upright growth.

PEKatan HT, *pb*, 1984, (Clo-Clo); *Emily Post × Bellona*; Pekmez, Paul. Flowers pink blend,

dbl. (20 petals); slight fragrance; foliage dark; upright growth; greenhouse variety.

PEKgold HT, *dy*, 1984, *Seedling × Seedling*; Pekmez, Paul. Flowers deep yellow, medium; fragrant; foliage dark, glossy; upright growth; greenhouse variety.

PEKinois Pol, *dr*, 1975, (Tapis Afghan); *Marlena × Lampion*; Pekmez. Bud round; flowers dark red, semi-dbl. (15 petals), cupped, small (1-2 in.); dwarf growth.

PEKlican HT, *dy*, 1984, *Seedling × Bellona*; Pekmez, Paul. Flowers deep yellow, dbl. (35 petals), large; fragrant; foliage medium, light green, matt; bushy growth.

PEKlipink F, *mp*, 1984, (Claridge®); *Seedling × Seedling*; Pekmez, Paul. Flowers medium pink, dbl. (35 petals), large; fragrant; foliage medium, light green, semi-glossy; upright growth.

PEKomegir F, *mp*, 1984, (Président Souzy); *Emily Post × Seedling*; Pekmez, Paul. Flowers medium pink, dbl. (20 petals); fragrant; upright growth; greenhouse variety.

Pelé Cl HT, *w*, 1979, *Seedling × Seedling*; Benardella, Frank. Bud ovoid; flowers white, dbl. (35 petals), large blooms borne 1-3 per cluster; soft, fruity fragrance; foliage medium green; triangular, hooked prickles; upright growth with long canes; repeat bloom. ARC TG (B), 1980.

Pélisson M (OGR), *dr*, 1848, (Mons. Pélisson); Vibert. Flowers velvety red, turning purple.

Pelton Lonnen HT, *my*, 1975, *Whisky Mac sport*; Wood. Flowers pure yellow, dbl. (28-30 petals), full, cupped; fragrant; foliage light; bushy, compact growth.

Pemberton's White Rambler R, *w*, 1914, Pemberton. Flowers white, dbl., rosette form, borne in clusters.

Pembridge HT, *ob*, 1934, *Roselandia sport*; Stevens, E. Flowers richer, deeper orange-yellow.

Penelope T (OGR), *rb*, 1906, Williams, J. Flowers dark red, center creamy white, full, high pointed.

Penelope HMsk (S), *lp*, 1924, *Ophelia × Seedling or possibly with William Allen Richardson or Trier*; Pemberton. Flowers shell-pink fading to white, center lemon, semi-dbl., medium blooms in clusters; fragrant; foliage dark; shrubby growth; recurrent bloom, good in autumn; (21). GM, NRS, 1925.

Penelope, Climbing Cl T (OGR), *rb*, 1932, Rosen, L.P.

Penelope Plummer F, *dp*, 1970, *Anna Wheatcroft × Dearest*; Beales; Intwood Lane Nursery, 1971. Bud orange; flowers vivid flamingo-pink, semi-dbl. (16 petals), semi-flat, large (4 in.); slightly fragrant; foliage dark; moderate growth.

Pennant LCl, *mp*, 1941, Clark, A. Flowers begonia-pink, dbl.; profuse, non-recurrent bloom.

Pennsylvania HT, *pb*, 1934, *Joanna Hill sport*; Neuner. Bud long, pointed; flowers salmon-pink, center apricot, outer petals striped dark pink, semi-dbl., high-centered, large; very fragrant.

Pennsylvanian HT, *ob*, 1953, *Luna* × *(Mrs. Pierre S. duPont* × *Mrs. Sam McGredy)*; Ohlhus; C-P. Bud pointed; flowers apricot-orange, dbl. (25-30 petals), large (4-5 in.); fragrant; upright, bushy growth.

Penny F, *rb*, 1973, *Sarabande* × *Circus*; Sanday. Flowers strawberry-red, base orange, semi-dbl. (17 petals), rosette form, medium (2 in.); fragrant; dwarf.

Penny Annie Min, *lp*, 1983, (BISfra); *Little Darling* × *Seedling*; Bischoff, Francis. Flowers light pink, dbl. (35 petals), HT form, small; no fragrance; foliage medium, medium green, matt; bushy growth.

Penny Candy™ Min, *ob*, 1981, (SAVplenti); *Rise 'n' Shine* × *Sheri Anne*; Saville, F. Harmon; Nor'East Min. Roses. Bud ovoid; flowers orange-yellow blend, dbl. (30 petals), cupped, micro-mini, blooms borne singly or several together; slight fragrance; foliage small; long, thin prickles; tiny, compact growth.

Penny Lane Min, *lp*, 1992, (TALpen); *Party Girl* × *Maids of Jubilee*; Taylor, Pete & Kay; Taylor's Roses, 1993. Flowers cream base blending to light pink, reverse same, full (26-40 petals), HT form, small (0-4 cms) blooms borne mostly singly; no fragrance; foliage small, medium green, semi-glossy; few prickles; medium (38 cms), upright, bushy growth.

Peony of Fragrance HP (OGR), *mp*, 1933, Pahissa. Flowers pink, peony-like, large; fragrant; recurrent bloom.

People F, *dr*, 1956, (The People); *Cinnabar* × *(Käthe Duvigneau* × *Cinnabar)*; Tantau. Flowers crimson shaded pink, dbl. (26 petals), flat, large, borne in large trusses; slightly fragrant; foliage light green; vigorous, bushy growth. GM, NRS, 1955.

Pepe HT, *rb*, 1961, *Amor* × *Sutter's Gold*; deRuiter; Blaby Rose Gardens. Flowers flame, base and reverse gold, dbl., large (4 in.); foliage dark, glossy; vigorous growth.

Pepita G (OGR), *pb*, Moreau. Flowers soft rosy pink striped white.

Pepita Min, *dp*, 1987, (KORkeilich); *LENpi* × *(Mercedes* × *Garnette)*; Kordes, W., 1985. Flowers deep pink, dbl. (26-40 petals), small; no

fragrance; foliage small, medium green, semi-glossy; spreading growth.

Pepper Pot F, *pb*, 1973, *Circus* × *Seedling*; Fryer's Nursery. Flowers rose-pink to red, splashed yellow, dbl. (24 petals), HT form, large (3 in.); slightly fragrant; foliage light.

Peppermint F, *rb*, 1964, *Jingles* × *Jingles*; Boerner; J&P. Bud ovoid; flowers red, reverse cream, dbl., cupped, medium; foliage leathery; vigorous, bushy; greenhouse variety.

Peppermint Candy Min, *w*, 1991, *Rose Parade* × *Easter Morning*; Williams, J. Benjamin, 1988. Flowers ivory with red blend, full (26-40 petals), small (0-4 cms) blooms borne mostly singly; very fragrant; foliage small, dark green, glossy; medium (12-28 inches), upright, bushy growth.

Peppermint Ice F, *w*, 1992, (BOSgreen); *Anne Harkness* × *Greensleeves*; Bossom, W.; E.B. LeGrice Ltd., 1991. Flowers creamy green, semi-dbl. (10 petals), cupped, medium (8 cms) blooms borne singly or in sprays of 3-5; slight fragrance; foliage medium, medium green, semi-glossy; upright, medium growth.

Peppermint Patty Min, *rb*, 1990, *Libby* × *Libby*; Gruenbauer, Richard, 1984; Richard Gruenbauer. Bud pointed; flowers white with red edging, same reverse, aging darker red, dbl. (33 petals), urn-shaped, medium, borne usually singly; slight, fruity fragrance; foliage medium, medium green, semi-glossy; prickles straight, very few, tan; fruit oblong, orange when ripe; very hardy, upright.

Peppermint Stripe Min, *rb*, 1991, *Roller Coaster* × *Seedling*; Spooner, Ray. Flowers red blend, moderately full (15-25 petals), small; very fragrant; foliage small, medium green, semi-glossy; bushy growth.

Peppermint Swirl™ HT, *rb*, 1989, (DEVmenta); *Seedling* × *Seedling*; Marciel, Stanley G.; DeVor Nursery. Bud slender, tapering; flowers currant red, reverse same, aging discolors slightly, dbl. (30 petals), cupped, large, borne singly; slight, spicy fragrance; foliage medium, dark green, semi-glossy; prickles declining, copper brown; upright, tall growth.

Peppermint Twist F, *rb*, 1992, (JACraw); *Pinstripe* × *Maestro*; Christensen, Jack; Bear Creek Gardens, 1992. Flowers red/white/ pink striped, very full (41+ petals), open flat to slightly cupped, large (7+ cms) blooms borne in small clusters; slight fragrance; foliage large, medium green, semi-glossy; some prickles on peduncle; sepals have glandular structures on back; medium (90-110 cms), upright, bushy growth.

Per Chance Min, *op*, 1985, (FLOper); *Red Can Can* × *Care Deeply*; Florac, Marilyn; MB Farm

Roses Inc. Flowers orange-red fading bright pink, single (5 petals), small blooms borne singly and in clusters; fragrant; foliage small, dark, matt; bushy growth.

Perchè Si? HT, *rb*, 1956, *Peace × Crimson Glory*; Giacomasso. Flowers carmine-red, reverse silvery white, well formed; foliage dark, glossy; very vigorous growth.

Percussion Min, *rb*, 1989, (ZIPcuss); *Sheri Anne × Deep Purple*; Zipper, Herbert; Magic Moment Miniatures, 1990. Bud ovoid; flowers dark red with touch of yellow at base, reverse white at base with red shadings, aging dark red, white reverse, dbl. (25 petals), high-centered, exhibition, large, borne usually singly and in sprays of 2-3; mini-flora; moderate, sweet fragrance; foliage medium, medium green, semi-glossy; prickles very small, tan; upright, tall growth.

Percy Izzard HT, *yb*, 1936, *May Wettern × Barbara Richards*; Robinson, H.; Wheatcroft Bros. Flowers maize-yellow, reverse buff flushed warm rose, dbl., high-centered, large; slightly fragrant; foliage leathery; vigorous growth.

Percy Pilcher F, *op*, 1961, Verschuren. Flowers salmon-orange, dbl., large, borne in large clusters.

Percy Thrower HT, *mp*, 1964, *La Jolla × Karl Herbst*; Lens; Gregory. Flowers rose-pink, dbl. (28 petals), well-formed, large (4-5 in.); fragrant; foliage glossy; vigorous, tall.

Perdita® S, *ab*, 1992, (AUSperd); *The Friar × (Seedling × Iceberg)*; Austin, David; David Austin Roses, 1983. Flowers blush apricot, very full (41+ petals), large (7+ cms) blooms borne in small clusters; very fragrant; foliage medium, medium green, semi-glossy; some prickles; medium (100 cms), bushy growth. Edland Fragrance Medal, 1984.

Perfect Moment™ HT, *rb*, 1989, (KORwilma; Jack Dayson); *New Day × Seedling*; W. Kordes Sohne; Bear Creek Gardens, 1991. Bud pointed; flowers red on outer half of petals, yellow on inner, reverse yellow with red blushing, dbl., cupped, exhibition, medium, borne usually singly; slight fragrance; foliage medium, medium green, semi-glossy; prickles broad at base, narrowing, hooked down, red to brown; upright, bushy, medium growth. AARS, 1991.

Perfect Potluck™ Min, *dy*, 1992, (LAVpet; LAVroy); *Showbound × (Party Girl × June Laver)*; Laver, Keith; Springwood Roses. Flowers golden yellow, moderately full (15-25 petals), small (0-4 cms) blooms borne in small clusters; slight fragrance; foliage medium, dark green, glossy; few prickles; low (30 cms), compact growth.

Perfecta Pol, *dr*, 1920, *Ellen Poulsen × Merveille des Rouges*; Spek. Flowers scarlet-crimson under glass, dark crimson in the open, dbl., large, borne in clusters; vigorous growth.

Perfection HT, *mp*, 1925, *Columbia sport*; Stielow Bros. Flowers pink.

Perfection Pol, *op*, 1932, *Marytje Cazant sport*; Prior. Flowers softer coral-pink.

Perfection F, *pb*, 1957, *Masquerade × Self*; Ulrick. Flowers pink turning red, reverse white.

Perfection des Blanches N (OGR), *w*, 1873, Schwartz, J. Flowers white, full, medium, borne in corymbs; vigorous growth.

Perfeita F, *or*, *Cocorico × Vogue*; Moreira da Silva. Flowers orange and carmine.

Perfume HT, *dr*, 1929, Marriott; Beckwith. Bud long, pointed; flowers velvety, fiery deep crimson, semi-dbl. (15 petals); very fragrant; vigorous growth.

Perfume Beauty™ HT, *mp*, 1991, (MEIniacin; Fragrant Lady); *MEllista × (Carina × Silvia)*; Meilland, Alain, 1990; C-P, 1990. Bud conical; flowers rose bengal, very dbl., cupped, medium blooms borne singly; moderate, heavy fragrance; foliage large, dark green; upright, tall growth.

Perfume Delight HT, *mp*, 1973, *Peace × ((Happiness × Chrysler Imperial) × El Capitan)*; Weeks; C-P. Bud long, pointed; flowers deep pink, dbl., cupped, large; very fragrant; foliage large, leathery; vigorous, upright, bushy growth. AARS, 1974.

Pergolèse P (OGR), *m*, 1860, Robert et Moreau. Flowers bright purplish crimson, shading to lilac, very full, medium; fragrant; occasionally recurrent bloom.

Perky Min, *dp*, 1958, *(R. wichuraiana × Floradora) × Oakington Ruby*; Moore, R.S.; Sequoia Nursery. Bud pointed; flowers pink, dbl., small (1 in.); very fragrant; foliage glossy; very bushy (12 in.), compact growth.

Perla de Alcañada Min, *dp*, 1944, (Baby Crimson; Pearl of Canada; Perle de Alcañada; Wheatcroft's Baby Crimson); *Perle des Rouges × Rouletti*; Dot, P.; A. Meilland. Bud small, ovoid; flowers carmine, semi-dbl. (18 petals); foliage dark, glossy; dwarf, very compact (6-10 in.) growth.

Perla de Alcañada, Climbing Cl Min, *dp*, Dot, P..

Perla de Montserrat Min, *pb*, 1945, *Cécile Brunner × Rouletti*; Dot, P.; A. Meilland. Bud small; flowers hermosa pink edged pearl, semi-dbl. (18 petals), blooms in clusters; dwarf, very compact growth.

Perla Rosa Min, *mp*, 1946, *Perle des Rouges × Rouletti*; Dot, P. Bud well-formed; flowers bright pink, very full; very compact (6-8 in.) growth.

Perla Rosa, Climbing Cl Min, *mp*, 1947, Dot, P.

Perle Pol, *w*, 1920, Easlea. Flowers white.

Perle Angevine Pol, *lp*, 1920, *Jeanne d'Arc × Mrs. W.H. Cutbush*; Délépine. Flowers pale rose, dbl., small, borne in clusters; few thorns.

Perle Blanche HT, *w*, 1981, (DELanche); *(Virgo × Peace) × (Goldilocks × Virgo)*; Delbard, G. Flowers white, dbl. (35 petals), large; no fragrance; foliage medium, medium green, semi-glossy; upright, bushy growth; greenhouse variety.

Perle de Lyon T (OGR), *dy*, 1872, Ducher. Flowers dark chrome-yellow, full, large.

Perle des Jardins T (OGR), *ly*, 1874, *Mme. Falcot Seedling*; Levet, F. Flowers straw-yellow, full, globular, large; very fragrant; foliage dark; slender growth. Once the most important yellow greenhouse rose.

Perle des Jardins, Climbing Cl T (OGR), *ly*, 1890, Henderson, J.

Perle des Panachées G (OGR), *m*, 1845, (Panachée Double); Vibert. Flowers white striped with lilac and violet or rose. This name has been used in recent times for other striped roses. See also *'Centifolia Variegata'*.

Perle des Rouges Pol, *dr*, 1896, Dubreuil. Flowers velvety crimson.

Perle d'Or Pol, *yb*, 1884, (Yellow Cécile Brunner); *Polyantha × Mme. Falcot*; Rambaux; Dubreuil. Flowers golden pink, very dbl., blooms in clusters; very fragrant; foliage rich green, soft; height 3 ft.; (14).

Perle d'Or, Climbing Cl Pol, *yb*, (Yellow Cécile Brünner, Climbing).

Perle Noire® HT, *dr*, 1986, (DELurt; Black Pearl); *((Impeccable × Papa Meilland) × (Gloire de Rome × Impeccable)) × ((Charles Mallerin × Gay Paris) × (Rouge Meilland × Soraya))*; Delbard, 1976. Flowers velvety dark red, dbl. (38 petals), well-formed, large; light fragrance; vigorous, bushy growth.

Perle vom Wienerwald R, *pb*, 1913, *Hélène × Crimson Rambler*; Praskac; Teschendorff. Flowers carmine-rose, reverse soft rose-pink, semi-dbl., medium (2 in.), borne in clusters of 50; vigorous. climbing growth.

Perle von Godesberg HT, *ly*, 1902, *Kaiserin Auguste Viktoria sport*; Schneider. Flowers cream, shaded lemon.

Perle von Heidelberg HT, *mr*, 1905, *La France sport*; Scheurer. Flowers silvery pink; very fragrant; vigorous growth.

Perle von Hohenstein Pol, *lp*, 1923, *Freudenfeuer × Seedling*; Kiese. Flowers carmine-red, semi-dbl., small, borne in clusters.

Perle von Remagen HT, *lp*, 1957, *R.M.S. Queen Mary × Peace*; Burkhard; Kordes; Tantau. Bud pointed; flowers soft pink, reverse tinted creamy white, full, high-centered, large; long stems; fragrant; foliage glossy, leathery; vigorous, upright growth.

Perle von Weissenstein G (OGR), *m*, (Perle de Veissenstein); Prior to 1846. Flowers brownish, center purple.

Perl-Ilseta® F, *w*, 1985, (TANilsepo); *Ilseta sport*; Tantau, M., 1984. Flowers pearly white.

Permanent Wave F, *mr*, 1932, (Duchess of Windsor; L'Indéfrisible; Mevrouw van Straaten van Nes; Mrs. Van Nes; Van Nes; *Else Poulsen sport*; Leenders, M.; J&P, 1935. Flowers bright carmine, semi-dbl., petals wavy, large blooms in clusters; slightly fragrant; foliage glossy, dark; vigorous, bushy growth. GM, Bagatelle, 1933; Rome, 1934.

Perneille Poulsen® F, *mp*, 1965, *Ma Perkins × Columbine*; Poulsen, N.D.; McGredy. Flowers light pink, semi-dbl. (18 petals), large (3½ in.) blooms in clusters; fragrant; foliage pointed, light green.

Pernetiana Pernet-Ducher. A name for a class of roses — originally Hybrid Perpetual × *R. foetida, but later crossed with Hybrid Teas; Soleil d'Or* (1900) was the first of these. Now completely merged with the Hybrid Teas, to which they have contributed a greatly widened color range.

Pernille Poulsen, Climbing Cl F, *mp*, 1980, Poulsen, N.D.; Vilmorin-Andrieux.

Pero d'Alenquer F, *dr*, *Seedling × Alain*; Moreira da Silva. Flowers dark velvety red, center lighter.

Perpetual Red S, *mr*, 1955, *Gruss an Teplitz × Seedling*; Gaujard. Flowers bright red, semi-dbl., open, medium; foliage abundant; very vigorous growth; recurrent bloom.

Perpetual White Moss M (OGR), *w*, (Quatre Saisons Blanc Mousseux; Rosier de Thionville); *Autumn Damask sport*; Laffay, prior to 1837. Buds very mossy; flowers white, dbl., medium blooms in large clusters; repeats sparingly in fall.

Perroquet LCl, *dy*, 1957, Robichon. Flowers deep yellow, large; slightly fragrant; foliage glossy; vigorous growth.

Perroquet F, *rb*, 1960, *Peace × (Cinnabar × Circus)*; Lens. Flowers red, reverse yellow, becoming dark red, well formed; foliage bronze; vigorous growth.

Persepolis HT, *dy*, 1986, (Truper); *Seedling × Seedling*; Kriloff, M. Flowers deep yellow, dbl. (25 petals); strong, tea fragrance; foliage clear green, glossy.

Persian Princess Min, *or*, 1970, *Baccará × Eleanor*; Moore, R.S.; Sequoia Nursery. Flowers coral-red, dbl., small; fragrant; foliage leathery, vigorous, bushy, dwarf (12-14 in.).

Personality HT, *yb*, 1960, *Peace × Sutter's Gold*; Morey; J&P. Bud ovoid; flowers golden yellow splashed red, dbl. (35-40 petals), large (4½ in.); very fragrant; foliage leathery, glossy; vigorous, upright growth.

Persuader HT, *mp*, 1960, *Golden Scepter × Southport*; Eacott. Flowers bright pink, dbl. (30 petals), high-centered, large; very fragrant; vigorous growth.

Persuasion F, *lp*, 1972, *Vera Dalton × Tropicana*; Sanday. Flowers pale blush-pink, base orange, dbl. (30 petals), HT form, large (3½ in.); fragrant; foliage glossy.

Persue de Gossart C (OGR), *dp*, Flowers velvety cerise, with garnet reflexes, dbl.

Peter Benjamin HT, *ab*, 1978, *Benjamin Franklin × Peter Frankenfeld*; Allender, Robert William. Flowers light apricot pink, dbl. (40 petals), exhibition, borne 2-3 per cluster; fragrant; foliage light; pear-shaped, red prickles; medium-tall growth.

Peter Frankenfeld® HT, *dp*, 1966, Kordes, R.; A. Dickson. Flowers rose-pink, well-shaped, large; slightly fragrant.

Peter Frankenfeld, Climbing Cl HT, *dp*, 1975, Allen, L.C.; Welsh.

Peter Goldman HT, *yb*, 1986, (DICname); *Silver Jubilee × Bright Smile*; Dickson, P. Flowers yellow blend, full (26-40 petals), medium; slight fragrance; foliage medium, medium green, glossy; bushy growth.

Peter Lawson HP (OGR), *dr*, 1862, Thomas. Flowers deep scarlet shaded purple.

Peter May HT, *mr*, 1958, *The Doctor × New Yorker*; Verschuren; Blaby Rose Gardens. Flowers scarlet, dbl., large; long stems; very fragrant; foliage leathery; very vigorous growth.

Peter Pan HT, *dr*, 1935, Knight, G. Flowers dark crimson, large; vigorous growth.

Peter Pan HT, *dr*, 1935, Knight, G. Bud long; flowers dark velvety crimson, large; vigorous growth.

Peter Piper HT, *or*, 1969, *Piccadilly sport*; Waterhouse Nursery. Flowers chinese orange, semi-dbl., urn shaped, large; bushy growth.

Peter Rosegger LCl, *op*, 1914, *Geheimrat Dr. Mittweg × Tip-Top*; Lambert, P. Flowers coral-pink, full, rosette form, borne in clusters of 5-15; foliage dark; vigorous, climbing growth; repeats.

Peter's Briarcliff HT, *mp*, 1940, *Sport of Briarcliff*; J&P. Flowers true unshaded rose-pink, long pointed, well formed; very fragrant; foliage dark; vigorous, free growth; a florists' variety.

Petit Canard® Min, *ly*, 1984, (LENcan); *Rosina × (Le Vesuve × Belle Étoile)*; Lens. Flowers light yellow, dbl. (20 petals), high-centered to cupped, small blooms in clusters of 12-22; light fragrance; foliage small; few, green prickles; bushy growth. GM, Paris, 1984.

Petit Constant Pol, *mr*, 1899, *Mignonette × Luciole*; Soupert & Notting. Flowers nasturtium-red, full, small; very fragrant; vigorous growth.

Petit Four® Min, *mp*, 1982, (INTerfour); *Marlena Seedling × Seedling*; Interplant. Flowers medium pink, semi-dbl., patio, medium blooms in clusters; fragrant; foliage small, medium green, glossy; many, small prickles; bushy growth.

Petit François F, *or*, 1957, *Alain × (Brazier × Léonce Colombier)*; Dorieux; Pin. Flowers orange-red, semi-dbl.; foliage glossy; very dwarf growth.

Petit Jean HT, *ob*, 1926, *White Killarney × Sunburst*; Vestal. Flowers deep orange-buff, shaded to yellow, edged peach-pink, full, well shaped, large; fragrant.

Petit Louis R, *op*, 1912, *Dorothy Perkins × Seedling*; Nonin. Flowers shrimp-pink, very dbl., small; slightly fragrant; vigorous, climbing growth.

Petit Poucet F, *mr*, 1955, *Cocorico × Seedling*; Combe. Flowers bright red, center tinted yellow, single, petals wavy; dwarf growth.

Petit Prince Pol, *mr*, 1956, Laperrière; EFR. Flowers geranium-red, borne in clusters of 8-10; very dwarf growth.

Petit René R, *mr*, 1925, Nonin. Flowers brilliant red, very dbl., small, borne inclusters; very fragrant; vigorous, climbing growth.

Petite Carrousel Min, *w*, 1985, *Thought to be Magic Carrousel × Seedling*; Michelis, Dorothy, 1991. Flowers ivory, coral pink petal edges, small blooms borne singly and in clusters; slight fragrance; foliage small, dark, semi-glossy; upright, tiny growth.

Petite de Hollande C (OGR), *mp*, (R. centifolia minor; Petite Junon de Holland); Prior to 1838. Flowers rose pink, dbl., small blooms in clusters; fragrant; moderate growth.

Petite Ecossaise HSpn (OGR), *lp*, R. spinosissima hybrid; Vibert. Flowers flesh, small; moderate growth; non-recurrent bloom.

Petite Folie® Min, *ob*, 1968, (MEIherode); *(Dany Robin × Fire King) × (Cricri × Perla de Montserrat)*; Meilland; URS. Flowers vermilion, reverse carmine, dbl., globular, small blooms in trusses; slightly fragrant (fruity); foliage leathery; vigorous growth. GM, Japan, 1969.

Petite Jeanne R, *mr*, 1912, *Dorothy Perkins Seedling*; Nonin. Flowers currant-red.

Petite Léonie Pol, *w*, 1893, *Mignonette × Duke of Connaught*; Soupert & Notting. Flowers pinkish white, small.

Petite Lisette C (OGR), *dp*, 1817, Vibert. Flowers rich rose, pompon-shaped, small (1 in.); foliage matt, green; height 3-4 ft.

Petite Louise R, *op*, Flowers salmon-pink.

Petite Odette R, *lp*, 1923, *Lady Godiva × Seedling*; Nonin. Flowers light pink, very dbl., borne in clusters; slightly fragrant; vigorous, climbing growth.

Petite Orléanaise C (OGR), *mp*, (Petite de Orléanaise). Flowers pink, full, pompon-shaped, small; vigorous, almost climbing.

Petite Penny F, *w*, 1987, (MACjocel; Dresselhuys); *(R. Crepuscule × Seedling) × Royal Occasion*; McGredy, Sam; Sam McGredy Roses International, 1988. Flowers white, semi-dbl. (6-14 petals), small; fragrant; foliage small, medium green, semi-glossy; bushy growth.

Petra F, *mr*, 1974, *Seedling × Taora*; Kordes; Dehner. Bud medium, globular; flowers blood-red, dbl.; slightly fragrant; foliage dark, leathery; moderate, bushy growth.

Petrine HT, *ob*, 1921, *Old Gold × Mme. Edouard Herriot*; Therkildsen. Flowers coral-red, shaded chrome-yellow, dbl.; slightly fragrant.

Petronella HT, *rb*, 1980, *Gail Borden × (Dalvey × Fragrant Cloud)*; MacLeod, Major C.A.; Christie's Nursery. Flowers red blend, dbl. (49 petals), pointed blooms borne singly; fragrant; foliage dark, glossy; straight, red prickles; compact growth.

Petticoat Min, *w*, 1981, (JACpet); *Bon Bon × Lemon Delight*; Warriner; J&P. Bud short; flowers white tinted pink, dbl. (55 petals); mild fragrance; foliage dark, small, pointed; very compact, spreading growth.

Petticoat Lane Min, *pb*, 1985, (SOCamp); *Pink Petticoat × Pink Petticoat*; Eagle, Barry; Dawn; Southern Cross Nursery. Flowers medium pink, deeper in center, light pink reverse, dbl. (28 petals), HT form, small blooms borne 1-3 per cluster; slight fragrance; foliage small, dark, semi-glossy; upright, very small growth.

Petula Clark HT, *mr*, 1963, *Purpurine × Lavender Pinocchio*; Lens. Flowers clear red, dbl., high-centered, well-formed; foliage bronze; vigorous, bushy growth.

Petula Clark, Climbing Cl HT, *mr*, 1967, Lens.

Pfälzer Gold® HT, *dy*, 1982, (TANälzergo); Tantau, M., 1981. Flowers deep yellow, dbl. (20 petals), large; no fragrance.

Pfander's Canina Sp (OGR), *lp*, *Selected strain of R. canina*; Pfander, prior to 1954. Used as an understock in Germany.

Pfuss Pfree F, *mp*, 1988, *Sea Foam × (Restless Native Seedling × Europeana)*; Stoddard, Louis, 1989. Bud ovoid, pointed; flowers light pink, reverse medium pink, dbl. (25 petals), cupped, full, small, borne in sprays of 4-6; slight fragrance; foliage medium, medium green, very glossy, black spot and mildew resistant; prickles straight, tan-brown; fruit round, deep orange; spreading growth.

Phaenomen HT, *op*, 1934, (Phenomenon); Chotkové Rosarium; Böhm. Flowers slightly rosy salmon, reverse light rosy red, dbl., very large; foliage dark; very vigorous growth.

Phantasy HT, *lp*, 1927, *Lady Alice Stanley × Royal (or Priscilla)*; Dunlop. Flowers medium light pink, base yellow, dbl.; fragrant.

Phantom HT, *ob*, 1920, *(Joseph Hill × My Maryland Seedling) × Lady Hillingdon*; Towill. Flowers coppery yellow, center lighter, semi-dbl.; fragrant. RULED EXTINCT 4/92.

Phantom S, *mr*, 1992, (MACcatsan); *Pandemonium × Eyeopener*; McGredy, Sam; Sam McGredy Roses International. Flowers scarlet red, semi-dbl. (6-14 petals), large (7+ cms) blooms; slight fragrance; foliage large, medium green, semi-glossy; spreading (80 cms) growth.

Pharaoh HT, *or*, 1967, (MEIfiga; Pharaon); *(Happiness × Independence) × Suspense*; Meilland, M.L.; URS, 1967; C-P, 1969. Bud ovoid; flowers bright orange-red, dbl., high-centered, large (5 in.); fragrant; foliage dark, glossy, leathery; vigorous, upright growth. GM, Geneva, Madrid; The Hague, 1967, Belfast, 1969.

Phare® LCl, *or*, 1961, (DELgo); *Spectacular × (Floradora × Seedling)*; Delbard-Chabert. Flowers bright orange-red, dbl. (33 petals), large (3 in.); foliage glossy, dark; vigorous (to 10 ft.) growth.

Pharisäer HT, *op*, 1903, *Mrs. W.J. Grant Seedling*; Hinner, W. Bud long, pointed; flowers rosy white, shaded salmon, dbl., high-centered blooms on long, weak stems; fragrant; foliage bronze; vigorous growth.

Pheidippides F, *mr*, 1979, *Sam Ferris × Chopin*; Ellick; Excelsior Roses. Flowers currant-red, dbl. (35 petals), full, large (4 in.); foliage light green; moderately vigorous, low growth.

Phelan's Flag HCh (OGR), *rb*, 1952, Phelan. Bud ovoid, greenish white flushed purplish red; Fl. unique virgin blooms (1) red, (2) pink, (3) white, (4) red edged light blue and quartered white mutate color to pink then lavender-blue, dbl. (75-100 petals), medium (2½-3 in.), clusters of 7; very fragrant; foliage dark; vigorous (6 ft. or more), with tendency to climb; semi-recurrent bloom.

Phénice G (OGR), *dp*, 1843, Robert. Flowers reddish rose, spotted, full, medium.

Philadelphia R, *dr*, 1904, *Crimson Rambler × Victor Hugo*; Van Fleet; Conard; Jones. Flowers scarlet-crimson, center lighter, dbl., borne in gigantic clusters; vigorous, climbing growth; mid-season bloom.

Philémon Cochet B (OGR), *mp*, 1895, Cochet, Sc. Flowers rose.

Philibert Boutigny HP (OGR), *mp*, Flowers silvery rose, very large; vigorous growth.

Philip Harvey F, *ob*, 1975, *Fragrant Cloud × Circus*; Harkness. Flowers salmon-red, shaded orange, dbl. (25 petals), very large (5 in.); fragrant; foliage glossy, dark.

Philippe F, *op*, 1959, (Bel Ami); *Cognac × Fashion*; Delforge. Bud oval; flowers peach-salmon, semi-dbl. (15 petals), medium, borne in clusters; foliage glossy; moderate growth.

Philippe Pétain HT, *dp*, 1940, Nabonnand, C. Flowers velvety carmine with coppery reflections, not turning blue, cupped, large; slightly fragrant; foliage bright chive-green.

Philomène Pollaert HT, *or*, 1925, *Gen. MacArthur Seedling × Old Gold*; Pollaert. Flowers crimson tinted orange, dbl.; very fragrant.

Phoebe HT, *w*, 1922, *Ophelia × Verna Mackay*; Cant, B.R. Flowers cream-white, sometime pure white, dbl.; slightly fragrant.   GM, NRS, 1921.

Phoebe's Choice™ Min, *pb*, 1987, (BILice); *Little Darling × Over the Rainbow*; Bilson, Jack M., Jr.; Bilson, Jack M. III. Flowers pink, edges yellow, reverse same, pink softens, white edges appear as it ages, dbl. (38 pointed petals), exhibition, medium, borne usually singly or in sprays of 3-4; no fragrance; foliage medium, medium green, glossy; reddish-green prickles, sloped downwards; fruit round, light orange & green; upright, bushy growth.

Phoebus HP (OGR), *mp*, 1837, Originator unknown. Flowers bright pink, shading lighter, full, large; fragrant; bushy growth.

Phoenix HT, *dp*, 1973, *Manitou × Grand Slam*; Armstrong, D.L.; Armstrong Nursery. Flowers light cerise, dbl., high-centered, large; fragrant; foliage large, glossy, leathery; vigorous, upright growth.

Phoenix First F, *dr*, 1959, *Our Princess × Pompon Beauty*; Kernovske; Langbecker. Bud

ovoid; flowers dark red shaded black, very dbl., small, borne in clusters; slightly fragrant; foliage leathery; bushy growth.

Phyllis Pol, *mr*, 1908, *Mme. Norbert Levavasseur × Seedling*; Merryweather. Flowers bright red, full, small, borne in large clusters; recurrent bloom.

Phyllis Bide Cl Pol, *yb*, 1923, *Perle d'Or × Gloire de Dijon*; Bide. Flowers pale gold, shaded pink, almost dbl., small blooms in long, loose clusters; height 6 ft.; dependably recurrent bloom; (14). GM, NRS, 1924.

Phyllis Burden HT, *op*, 1935, Cant, B.R. Bud long, pointed; flowers shrimp-pink and orange, dbl., large; foliage glossy, light; very vigorous growth.

Phyllis Gold HT, *my*, 1935, *Lady Florence Stronge × Julien Potin*; Robinson, H.; Wheatcroft Bros. Flowers butter-yellow, edged lighter, dbl., high-centered; slightly fragrant; foliage rich olive-green; very vigorous, branching growth. GM, NRS, 1933.

Phyllis Gold, Climbing Cl HT, *my*, 1949, Fryer's Nursery.

Phyllis Lucas HT, *ob*, 1961, *Bettina sport*; Wheatcroft Bros. Flowers orange shaded bronze, well shaped; fragrant.

Phyllis Poyser HT, *op*, 1962, *Golden Sun × Spartan*; Fankhauser. Bud long, pointed; flowers orange-pink, dbl. (50 petals), high-centered, large; very fragrant (spicy); foliage light green, soft, elongated; vigorous, compact, bushy growth.

Phyllis Shackelford™ Min, *ob*, 1987, (MORshack); *Anytime × Gold Badge*; Moore, Ralph S. Flowers orange, fading pink, dbl. (20 petals), cupped, exhibition, small borne usually singly; moderate, fruity fragrance; foliage small, medium green, semi-glossy; few, medium, brownish prickles, slightly hooked downwards; fruit rounded, medium, orange; upright, bushy, medium growth.

Phynelia HT, *mr*, 1928, Reeves. Flowers crimson-cerise, borne in clusters.

Pia Berghout Pol, *mp*, 1967, *Saskia × Seedling*; Buisman. Flowers pink, dbl., medium, borne in clusters; foliage dark.

Picador F, *mr*, 1964, *Oranien sport*; Verschuren, A.; van Engelen. Flowers cherry-red, dbl., borne in clusters; foliage glossy, dark; upright, compact growth.

Picardy HT, *dp*, 1967, *Rose Gaujard × Bayadère*; Trew; Willik Bros. Flowers rose-bengal, globular; fragrant; foliage dark, glossy; free growth.

Picasso F, *pb*, 1971, (MACpic); *Marlena × (Evelyn Fison × (Frühlingsmorgen × Orange Sweetheart))*; McGredy, S., IV; McGredy. Flowers deep pink, petal edges lighter, white eye and reverse, semi-dbl. (18 petals), large (3 in.); foliage small. GM, Belfast; NZ, 1973.

Picayune Ch (OGR), *lp*, Prior to 1859. Flowers light pink to white, dbl., small blooms in clusters. Possibly an old variety from France, still grown in the South.

Piccadilly® HT, *rb*, 1960, (MACar); *McGredy's Yellow × Karl Herbst*; McGredy, S., IV; McGredy. Flowers scarlet, base and reverse gold, dbl. (28 petals), high-pointed, large (4½ -5 in.); foliage dark, glossy; vigorous, upright, branching. GM, Madrid; Rome, 1960.

Piccadilly, Climbing Cl HT, *rb*, 1963, Mized, 1963; Sutton, 1972.

Piccadilly Sunset HT, *ob*, 1970, *Piccadilly sport*; Goodwin; The Valley Nursery. Flowers orange flushed apricot, reverse gold, dbl. (34 petals), high pointed, large (4-5 in.); slightly fragrant; foliage glossy, dark; moderate, upright growth.

Piccaninny HT, *dr*, 1941, *Night × Sanguinaire*; Lammerts; Armstrong Nursery. Bud long, pointed; flowers dark red, stamens yellow, single (5-6 petals), large; very fragrant; foliage dark, glossy; vigorous growth.

Picciola Ina Pol, *op*, 1937, Giacomasso. Flowers pure salmon, borne in clusters of 10-50; vigorous, bushy growth.

Piccola Es S, *lp*, 1983, *Seedling × Seedling*; Fumagalli, Niso. Flowers light pink, dbl. (20 petals), medium; slight fragrance; foliage medium, medium green, semi-glossy; bushy.

Piccolo F, *dr*, 1957, *Red Favorite × Käthe Duvigneau*; Tantau, Math. Bud ovoid; flowers velvety dark red, dbl., borne in clusters; slightly fragrant; foliage dark, leathery, glossy; moderate, bushy, growth. RULED EXTINCT 4/85.

Piccolo® F, *or*, 1985, (TANolokip; Piccola); Tantau, M., 1984. Flowers orange-red, dbl. (20 petals), patio, medium; no fragrance; foliage large, dark, glossy; upright growth.

Piccolo Pete S, *mr*, 1984, *Carefree Beauty × ((Peace × Dornröschen) × Country Music)*; Buck; Iowa State University. Flowers medium red, 7-10 petals, flat, 4 in. blooms borne 1-10 per cluster; fragrant; foliage large, leathery, dark olive green; slightly hooked, tan prickles; upright, bushy growth; repeat bloom; hardy.

Pick Me Up HT, *mr*, 1941, Clark, A. Flowers red, well-shaped.

Picnic F, *or*, 1966, (Pic-Nic); *South Seas × Seedling*; Warriner; J&P. Bud short, pointed; flowers orange-red, high-centered, large (3-3½ in.); slightly fragrant; foliage leathery; upright.

Pico HT, *rb*, 1962, Buyl Frères. Bud pointed; flowers salmon-red and canary-yellow, dbl.; foliage glossy; bushy growth.

Picotee F, *rb*, 1960, *Little Darling × Gertrude Raffel*; Raffel; Port Stockton Nursery. Flowers white, edged red, dbl. (24 petals), cupped to flat, large (2½-3½ in.) blooms in clusters; slightly fragrant; foliage dark, glossy; vigorous, upright, bushy growth.

Picture HT, *lp*, 1932, McGredy. Flowers light pink, dbl. (34 reflexed petals), high-centered; slightly fragrant; foliage glossy, dark; vigorous.

Picture, Climbing Cl HT, *lp*, 1942, Swim; Armstrong Nursery.

Picture Page HT, *lp*, 1953, *Picture × Mme. Butterfly*; Jordan, B.L. Flowers peach-pink shading to flesh-pink, base yellow, dbl. (23-25 reflexed petals), well formed, large (4 in.); slightly fragrant; foliage dark; very free growth.

Picturesque HT, *lp*, 1950, *Mrs. H.M. Eddie × Mrs. Sam McGredy*; Eddie. Bud long; flowers pale pink with pronounced red veining, dbl. (30-35 petals), high-centered, large; slightly fragrant; foliage leathery; vigorous, upright, bushy growth.

Pied Piper F, *mr*, 1969, *Garnette × Moulin Rouge*; Lindquist; Howard Rose Co. Flowers red, dbl., globular, small; foliage leathery; moderate, low growth.

Pierre HT, *yb*, 1945, *Soeur Thérèse × Lumière*; Mallerin; A. Meilland. Bud large, ovoid; flowers deep golden yellow edged red, very dbl.; foliage glossy; vigorous, upright, bushy growth.

Pierre Aguetant HT, *my*, 1938, Gaujard. Bud long, pointed; flowers chamois-yellow, dbl., open, very large; fragrant; foliage leathery; vigorous growth.

Pierre Bredy HT, *rb*, 1958, *Peace × Schéherazade*; Arles; Roses-France. Flowers currant-red, reverse silvery; foliage dark; low growth.

Pierre Cormier Pol, *or*, 1926, Turbat. Flowers brilliant scarlet-red, center lighter, borne in clusters of 10-20; dwarf growth.

Pierre de Ronsard® LCl, *pb*, 1987, (MEIviolin; Eden; Eden Rose 88; Grimpant Pierre de Ronsard; *(Danse des Sylphes × Haender) × Pink Wonder, Climbing*; Meilland, Mrs. Marie-Louise, 1985. Flowers cream white suffused with carmine pink, dbl. (40+ petals), old rose shape, large; slight fragrance; foliage medium, light green, semi-glossy; spreading growth; repeat bloom.

Pierre de St. Cyr B (OGR), *lp*, 1838, Plantier. Flowers glossy pale pink, very dbl., cupped, large; vigorous growth; a good weeping variety.

Pierre Gaujard HT, *rb*, 1944, Gaujard. Bud pointed; flowers fiery shades, dbl., very large; slightly fragrant; foliage glossy; vigorous growth.

Pierre Notting HP (OGR), *dr*, 1863, *Alfred Colomb Seedling*; Portemer. Flowers dark red, dbl. (42 petals), globular, large; fragrant; upright growth; not often recurrent.

Pierrette HT, *rb*, 1931, *Felix Laporte sport*; Tantau. Flowers blackish red streaked white, passing to steel-blue, very dbl., cupped, small; short stems; slightly fragrant; foliage small; dwarf growth.

Pierrette HT, *or*, 1945, *Texas Centennial sport*; Tantau. Flowers bright copper red, flecked brighter, dbl. (25 petals), large; very fragrant; upright, bushy growth.

Pierrine Min, *op*, 1988, (MICpie); *Tiki × Party Girl*; William, Michael; The Rose Garden. Flowers medium salmon pink, reverse slightly lighter, dbl. (40 petals), high-centered, exhibition, medium, borne singly; slight, damask fragrance; foliage medium, medium green, semi-glossy; serrated edges; prickles curved down slightly, light green; fruit round, green to orange-yellow; upright, medium growth.

Pierrot F, *rb*, 1971, *Poupee × Fillette*; Lens. Bud ovoid; flowers white marked red, becoming red, dbl. (30 petals), cupped, medium (2½ in.); fragrant (spicy); foliage leathery; vigorous, compact growth.

Pierson's Pink HT, *dp*, 1950, *Better Times sport*; Pierson, A.N. Bud long, pointed; flowers rose-pink, dbl. (32 petals), high-centered, large (5 in.); slightly fragrant; very vigorous, upright growth.

Piet Retief F, *dr*, 1950, *Irene × Donald Prior*; Leenders, M. Flowers dark morocco-red.

Piet Saverys F, *ob*, 1955, *Independence × Border King*; Buyl Frères. Flowers orange, semi-dbl.; bushy growth.

Pigalle HT, *m*, 1951, *Fantastique × Boudoir*; Meilland, F. Flowers reddish violet, dbl. (64 small petals), large (4 in.); slightly fragrant; foliage bronze; bushy growth.

Pigalle® F, *ob*, 1985, (MEIcloux; Chacok; Fakir; Jubilee 150; Pigalle 84); *Frenzy × ((Zambra × Suspense) × King's Ransom)*; Meilland, M.L.; Meilland Et Cie, 1984. Flowers yellow blended with orange and orange-red, dbl. (40 petals), large; no fragrance; foliage medium, medium green, semi-glossy; bushy growth.

Pigalle, Climbing Cl HT, *m*, Roses-France.

Pigmy Gold F, *dy*, 1953, Boerner; J&P. Bud ovoid; flowers golden yellow, dbl., small; fragrant; foliage dark, glossy; dwarf growth.

Pigmy Lavender F, *m*, 1961, *Lavender Pinocchio Seedling × Hybrid Tea Seedling*; Boerner; J&P. Bud ovoid; flowers lavender tinted pink, dbl. (30-35 petals), cupped, medium (2 in.); short, strong stems; fragrant; foliage leathery, dark; vigorous, dwarf growth.

Pigmy Red F, *dr*, 1953, *Chatter × Red Pinocchio*; Boerner; J&P. Bud ovoid; flowers deep red, white eye, dbl., small blooms in clusters; fragrant; foliage glossy; dwarf growth.

Pike's Peak S, *pb*, 1940, *R. acicularis × Hollywood*; Gunter; B&A. Bud long, pointed; flowers light bright red, center yellow, fading white, semi-dbl. (13 petals), large (3½ in.) blooms in clusters (to 17); foliage light wrinkled; very vigorous (6 ft.), bushy growth; non-recurrent bloom.

Pilar de Arburua HT, *op*, *Comtesse Vandal × Fashion*; Camprubi. Flowers salmon, dbl., high-centered, large; slightly fragrant; foliage dark reddish green; free growth.

Pilar Dot Min, *op*, 1964, *Orient × Perla de Alcañada*; Dot, P. Flowers coral, well-formed, small; vigorous, well-branched growth.

Pilar Landecho HT, *ob*, 1940, (Marquesa de Urquijo); *(Sensation × Julien Potin) × Feu Joseph Looymans*; Camprubi; A. Meilland. Bud long, pointed; flowers yellow, reverse dark coral-orange, dbl., high-centered, large; slightly fragrant; foliage dark, leathery; vigorous growth. GM, Bagatelle, 1938.

Pilar Landecho, Climbing Cl HT, *ob*, 1954, (Marquesa de Urquijo, Climbing); Folgado, Comes.

Pilarín Vilella HT, *or*, 1936, *Mrs. Pierre S. duPont × Lucia Zuloaga*; Dot, P. Flowers lacquer-red, dbl., cupped, large; very fragrant; foliage dark; vigorous growth.

Pilgrim HT, *dr*, 1970, *Seedling × Chrysler Imperial*; Armstrong, D.L.; Armstrong Nursery. Bud ovoid; flowers dark red, dbl., cupped, large; fragrant; foliage dark, leathery; vigorous, upright, bushy growth.

Pilgrim HT, *pb*, 1920, Montgomery Co.; A.N. Pierson. Bud long, pointed; flowers silvery pink reverse clear rose-pink, dbl., high-centered, large; fragrant; foliage leathery, rich green; vigorous, bushy growth.

Pilina Mata HT, *ob*, 1934, *Souv. de Claudius Pernet × Los Angeles*; Munné, B. Flowers orange-yellow.

Pillar of Fire Cl F, *or*, 1963, *Floradora, Climbing sport*; Shamburger, P.; C-P. Bud short, ovoid; flowers coral-red, dbl. (33 petals), cupped to flat, medium (2-2½ in.) blooms in cluster; slightly fragrant; foliage leathery, matt; vigorous.

Pillar Stratford Cl HT, *lp*, 1946, *Stratford sport*; Watkins, A.F.; Krider Nursery. Flowers silvery pink, base deeper, very dbl., large; very fragrant; vigorous, upright (8 ft.) growth.

Pillarbox F, *or*, 1986, (CHEWaze; Pillar Box Wardlip); *Alexander* × *(Galway Bay* × *Elizabeth of Glamis)*; Warner, C.H. Flowers vivid vermillion, moderately full (15-25 petals), medium; slight fragrance; foliage medium, medium green, semi-glossy; upright growth.

Pillow Talk F, *m*, 1980, *Plain Talk* × *Angel Face*; Weeks, O.L. Bud short, ovoid; flowers reddish lavender, dbl. (28 petals rolled outward), high-centered, cupped blooms borne singly or several together; moderate tea fragrance; foliage medium, thin, leathery, dark; long prickles, hooked downward; low to medium, rounded growth.

Pimpant F, *or*, 1963, *Seedling* × *Soleil*; Laperrière; EFR. Flowers bright orange-red, dbl. (25-30 petals), borne in clusters of 7-8; moderate, bushy growth.

Pimpernell F, *or*, 1954, *Seedling* × *(Poulsen's Pink* × *Golden Dawn)*; LeGrice. Flowers turkey-red, semi-dbl., borne in clusters; foliage dark.

Pinafore Pol, *ly*, 1959, *China Doll* × *Mrs. Dudley Fulton*; Swim; Roseway Nursery. Flowers pale yellow to white, tinged pink, single (5 ruffled petals), small (1½-2 in.), borne in large, rounded to flat clusters; foliage glossy; low, bushy, compact growth.

Piñata LCl, *yb*, 1978, Suzuki; J&P. Bud ovoid; flowers yellow overlaid vermilion, dbl. (28 petals), high-centered, medium (3 in.); slightly fragrant; semi-climbing growth.

Pineapple Poll F, *ob*, 1970, *Orange Sensation* × *Circus*; Cocker. Flowers orange-yellow, flushed red, dbl. (30 petals), medium (2½ in.); fragrant; foliage glossy.

Pinehurst Min, *pb*, 1988, *Rise 'n' Shine* × *Seedling*; Bridges, Dennis; Bridges Roses. Flowers light pink, fading lighter at base, reverse light pink to creamy white, fading to pink, very dbl. (60 petals), urn-shaped, medium, borne in sprays of 4-5; moderate, fruity fragrance; foliage medium, dark green, semi-glossy; prickles straight, medium, pink; bushy, medium, vigorous, neat growth.

Pingan F, *w*, 1980, *Seedling* × *(Ivory Fashion* × *Little Darling)*; Fong, William P.; Del Rose Nursery. Bud ovoid, pointed; flowers white with pink petal edges, semi-dbl. (13 petals), blooms borne 4-6 per cluster; fragrant; foliage large, leathery; long prickles; upright growth.

Pink Alicia HT, *mp*, 1968, *Fragrant Cloud* × *Gavotte*; Dale, F. Flowers pink, pointed; fragrant; spreading growth.

Pink Angel Min, *mp*, 1982, *Starina sport*; Hunton, Claude B. Flowers medium pink.

Pink Anne F, *mp*, 1951, *Anne Poulsen sport*; Cant, B.R. Flowers pink, borne in trusses; slightly fragrant; (28).

Pink Avalanche S, *mp*, 1988, (WILpavl); *Sea Foam* × *The Fairy*; Williams, J. Benjamin, 1989. Flowers coral pink to medium red, dbl. (15-25 petals), small, borne in sprays of 20-30; slight fragrance; foliage medium, medium green, glossy; spreading, compact growth.

Pink Beauty HT, *mp*, 1919, *Ophelia* × *My Maryland*; Cook, J. Flowers clear pink, semi-dbl., cupped, large; very fragrant.

Pink Bedder HT, *mp*, 1920, Paul, W. Flowers rose-pink, center yellow, borne in clusters.

Pink Belle HT, *dp*, 1974, *Fragrant Cloud* × *Elizabeth of Glamis*; Harkness; Morse Roses. Flowers deep rose pink, dbl. (28 petals), large; fragrant; foliage dark. RULED EXTINCT 11/83.

Pink Bells® Min, *dp*, 1983, (POUlbells); *Mini-Poul* × *Temple Bells*; Poulsen, D.T.; John Mattock Ltd. Flowers deep pink, dbl. (35 petals), small; slight fragrance; foliage small, medium green, semi-glossy; spreading growth; ground cover.

Pink Blush HT, *lp*, 1974, *Bridal Pink* × *Seedling*; Warriner; J&P. Bud long, pointed; flowers light pink, dbl. (30 petals), cupped, large (4-5 in.); slightly fragrant; foliage large, leathery; very free growth.

Pink Bountiful F, *mp*, 1945, *Juanita* × *Mrs. R.M. Finch*; Hill, J.H., Co.; J.H. Hill Co.; J&P. Bud short, pointed; flowers pink, dbl. (55 petals), large (3 in.) blooms in clusters; fragrant; foliage dark, leathery; vigorous, upright, much-branched growth.

Pink Bounty™ Min, *mp*, 1984, (MINsco); *Tom Brown* × *Over the Rainbow*; Williams, Ernest D.; Mini-Roses. Flowers medium pink, dbl. (35 petals), high-centered, small; slight fragrance; foliage small, medium green, semi-glossy; very dense, bushy growth.

Pink Bouquet F, *mp*, 1954, *Curly Pink* × *Free Gold*; Brownell. Flowers china-rose pink, slightly tinted yellow, dbl. (60-75 petals), high-centered to ovoid, large (3-4 in.); fragrant; foliage leathery; upright, open, compact growth. RULED EXTINCT 11/90.

Pink Bouquet Min, *lp*, 1990, (LAVquest; Pink Festival); *Loving Touch* × *Ontario Celebration*; Laver, Keith, 1987; Springwood Roses, 1991. Bud pointed; flowers white to luminous blush pink, white reverse, aging white, very dbl. (50-60 petals), flat, very full, medium, borne in sprays of 1-3; no fragrance; foliage small, dark green, matt; bushy, spreading, low growth.

Pink Brocade F, *lp*, 1977, *Spartan × Lilli Marlene*; Bees. Flowers light pink, very dbl. (70 petals), very full, large (3 in.); slightly fragrant; foliage glossy; small, compact growth.

Pink Butterfly HT, *dp*, 1926, *Mme. Butterfly sport*; Brown, A.C. Flowers bright cerise, base light buff.

Pink Cameo Cl Min, *mp*, 1954, (Cameo, Climbing); *(Soeur Thérèse × Skyrocket) × Zee*; Moore, R.S.; Sequoia Nursery. Flowers rose-pink, center darker, dbl. (23 petals), small (1¼ in.) blooms in clusters (to 20); slightly fragrant; foliage small, glossy, rich green; height 3-5 ft.

Pink Carpet™ Min, *mp*, 1983, (MINnco); *Red Cascade × Red Cascade*; Williams, Ernest D.; Mini-Roses. Flowers medium pink, dbl. (40+ petals), small blooms in large clusters; no fragrance; foliage small, light to medium green, glossy; low, spreading (to 6 ft.) growth; hanging basket.

Pink Cascade Pol, *lp*, 1945, *Mrs. Dudley Fulton × Tom Thumb*; Lammerts; Univ. of Calif. Flowers La France pink, very dbl., small, borne in clusters; slightly fragrant; foliage glossy; vigorous, bushy growth. RULED EXTINCT 12/81.

Pink Cascade Cl Min, *mp*, 1981, (MORcade); *(R. wichuraiana × Floradora) × Magic Dragon*; Moore, R.S.; Moore Min. Roses. Flowers medium pink, dbl. (35 petals), small; slight fragrance; foliage small, medium green, matt to semi-glossy; spreading (5-7 ft.) growth; similar to Red Cascade.

Pink Cavalcade F, *pb*, 1955, *Cavalcade sport*; Shamburger, C.S.; Stuart. Flowers deep pink, reverse light yellow to white, dbl. (28-32 petals), cupped, large (2½-3 in.), borne in pyramidal clusters; fragrant; foliage leathery, glossy, bronze; vigorous, bushy growth.

Pink Chameleon Pol, *pb*, 1945, *Mrs. Dudley Fulton × R. chinensis mutabilis*; Lammerts; Univ. of Calif. Bud rose-red; flowers venetian pink, darkening to purple, single, open, small, borne in clusters; slightly fragrant; foliage dark, glossy; very vigorous, bushy growth; abundant, recurrent bloom.

Pink Champagne HT, *mp*, 1956, *Seedling × Pink Bountiful*; Jelly; E.G. Hill Co. Bud long, pointed; flowers pink, dbl. (32-48 petals), high-centered, large (5-6 in.); fragrant; foliage leathery; vigorous, bushy growth.

Pink Charm F, *dp*, 1938, Kordes; Dreer. Flowers deep clear pink, very dbl.; short stems;

slightly fragrant; foliage leathery; bushy growth.

Pink Charmer Min, *mp*, 1984, (LYOpin); *Baby Betsy McCall × Seedling*; Lyon, Lyndon. Flowers medium pink, dbl. (20 petals), medium; fragrant; foliage small, medium green, semi-glossy; upright, bushy growth.

Pink Charming HT, *lp*, 1953, Leenders, M. Flowers pale pink, dbl. (36 petals), loosely formed, large (5½ in.); fragrant; vigorous growth.

Pink Cherub Min, *lp*, 1980, (MORfair); *Fairy Moss × Fairy Moss*; Moore, R.S.; Moore Min. Roses. Bud ovoid; flowers medium to light pink, often lighter at tips, dbl. (43 petals); little or no fragrance; foliage small, medium green, matt; straight, small prickles; compact, very bushy growth.

Pink Chiffon F, *lp*, 1956, *Fashion × Fantasia*; Boerner; J&P. Bud ovoid; flowers light pink, dbl. (53 petals), cupped to flat, large (3½-4 in.); very fragrant; foliage glossy; vigorous, bushy growth.

Pink Chimo® S, *mp*, 1992, (INTerchimp); *Seedling × Immensee*; Ilsink, Peter; Interplant B.V., 1990. Flowers medium pink, single (5 petals), cupped, small (2½-3 cms) blooms borne singly; no fragrance; foliage medium, medium green, semi-glossy; spreading, low (30 cms) growth; repeats.

Pink Christian Dior HT, *dp*, 1966, *Christian Dior sport*; Chang, Chi-Shiang. Bud ovoid; flowers light red and deep pink, dbl., high-centered, large; slightly fragrant; foliage glossy; very vigorous, upright growth.

Pink Cloud LCl, *mp*, 1952, *New Dawn × New Dawn Seedling*; Boerner; J&P. Bud ovoid; flowers rich pink, dbl. (28 petals), cupped, large blooms in clusters of 5-20; fragrant; foliage glossy; vigorous, climbing (6-8 ft.) growth; recurrent bloom.

Pink Clouds Cl Min, *dp*, 1956, *Oakington Ruby × R. multiflora*; Moore, R.S.; Sequoia Nursery. Flowers deep rose pink, single, small to medium blooms in clusters; very fragrant; foliage dark, glossy; vigorous (5-8 ft.) growth.

Pink Cluster F, *op*, 1938, Morse. Flowers salmon-pink, shaded gold, borne in clusters.

Pink Cocktail HT, *pb*, 1963, *Queen Elizabeth × Claude*; Barter. Flowers light pink, reverse darker, dbl. (38 petals), large (5 in.); slightly fragrant; foliage dark, glossy.

Pink Dawn HT, *mp*, 1935, *Joanna Hill × Seedling*; H&S; Dreer. Bud long, pointed; flowers medium pink, dbl. (60 petals), high-centered, large; very fragrant; foliage soft; vigorous.

Pink Dawn, Climbing Cl HT, *mp*, 1941, H&S.

Pink Delight Pol, *dp*, 1922, (Laxton's Pink Delight); Laxton Bros. Flowers rose-pink, single; fragrant.

Pink Delight HT, *op*, 1936, (Vierlanden); *Senator × Florex*; Kordes; J&P. Bud long, pointed; flowers deep salmon-pink, dbl., high-centered, large; very fragrant; foliage leathery, light green; vigorous growth.

Pink Diamond HT, *lp*, 1942, Howard, F.H.; Diamond State Nursery. Bud long pointed; flowers shell-pink, base yellow, dbl. (38 petals), cupped, large (3½-4 in.); foliage leathery; vigorous, upright growth.

Pink Diane F, *dp*, 1959, *Rosenelfe sport*; Sodano, A. Bud ovoid; flowers deep rose-pink, dbl. (50-55 petals), cupped, large (3½-4 in.); very fragrant (fruity); foliage leathery, glossy, dark; vigorous, upright growth.

Pink Diddy™ Min, *mp*, 1991, (KINdiddy); *((B.C. × Scamp) × Miss Dovey) × Tudelum*; King, Gene, 1986; AGM Miniature Roses, 1990. Bud pointed; flowers pink, dbl. (28 petals), cupped, medium; slight, fruity fragrance; foliage small, medium green, semi-glossy; bushy, spreading, low growth.

Pink Diëlma HT, *mp*, 1969, *Furore sport*; Tas. Bud ovoid; flowers pink, very dbl., medium; foliage dark.

Pink Dream HT, *pb*, 1951, *Mrs. Sam McGredy × R.M.S. Queen Mary*; McGredy. Flowers pink, inside rosy white, dbl. (45 petals), high-centered, very large (6-7 in.); slightly fragrant; foliage dark; vigorous growth.

Pink Druschki HT, *mp*, 1949, Longley. Flowers bright pink, dbl. (27 petals), well formed, large (5 in.); slightly fragrant; very vigorous growth.

Pink Duchess HT, *dp*, 1959, *Peace Seedling × Seedling*; Boerner; J&P. Bud ovoid; flowers rose-red, dbl. (38 petals), cupped, large (5-6 in.); fragrant; foliage glossy; vigorous, upright, bushy growth.

Pink Elegance HT, *lp*, 1960, *White Butterfly × Baccará*; Hoefer; Carlton Rose Nursery. Bud long, pointed; flowers bright pink, dbl., high-centered, medium; slightly fragrant; foliage glossy; very vigorous growth; a greenhouse variety.

Pink Elf Min, *pb*, 1982, (MORelfire); *Ellen Poulsen × Fire Princess*; Moore, R.S.; Moore Min. Roses. Flowers medium pink, blended with yellow, semi-dbl., small; no fragrance; foliage small, medium green, matt to semi-glossy; upright, bushy growth.

Pink Emperor HT, *mp*, 1958, *Peace × Crimson Glory*; Jones; Hennessey. Flowers clear pink,

dbl. (50-60 petals), large (4-5 in.); foliage glossy; vigorous, bushy growth.

Pink Empress HT, *mp*, 1991, (HADempress); *Smooth Sailing × Medallion*; Davidson, Harvey, 1984; Hortico, 1991. Flowers clean medium pink, dbl. (32-36 petals), urn-shaped, exhibition, large blooms borne usually singly or sprays of 1-3; moderate, fruity fragrance; foliage medium, medium green, glossy; bushy, medium growth.

Pink Eutin F, *mp*, 1962, *Eutin sport*; Lindquist; Howard Rose Co. Flowers medium pink.

Pink Favorite HT, *mp*, 1956, (Pink Favourite); *Juno × (Georg Arends × New Dawn)*; Abrams, Von; Peterson; Dering. Bud pointed; flowers neyron rose, dbl. (25 petals), loosely-cupped, large (3-4 in.); slightly fragrant; foliage very glossy, bright green; vigorous, upright, bushy growth. GM, Portland, 1957.

Pink Flair F, *mp*, 1966, *Verona × Escort*; Swim & Weeks; Carlton Rose Nursery. Bud urn shaped; flowers medium pink, dbl., small; foliage leathery; vigorous, bushy growth; for greenhouse use.

Pink Flamingo HT, *pb*, 1957, *Golden Dawn sport*; Kern Rose Nursery. Flowers rose-pink tinted lighter, dbl. (50 petals), medium (2½-3½ in.); very fragrant; foliage dark, leathery; dwarf, bushy growth.

Pink Floradora F, *op*, 1951, *Floradora sport*; Shamburger, P. Bud ovoid; flowers shrimp-pink, dbl. (35-40 petals), cupped, large (3 in.); slightly fragrant; foliage glossy, light green; bushy growth.

Pink Formal S, *pb*, 1978, (Queen Elizabeth × Gladiator) × (Aztec × Little Darling); Williams, J.B.; Krider Nursery. Bud pointed; flowers bright coral-pink, dbl. (23 petals), loosely-ruffled, large (3½-4 in.); fragrant; foliage leathery; vigorous, upright growth.

Pink Fragrance HT, *mp*, 1956, (Orange Triumph × Golden Rapture) × Peace; deRuiter; Ilgenfritz Nursery. Bud long, pointed; flowers rose-pink, dbl. (78-85 petals), open, large (4½-5 in.), borne in pyramidal clusters; fragrant (spicy); foliage glossy, leathery; very vigorous, bushy, upright growth.

Pink Frills F, *lp*, 1954, *Garnette sport*; Carlton Rose Nursery. Flowers light pink; a greenhouse variety.

Pink Frost HT, *mp*, 1954, *Charlotte Armstrong × Texas Centennial*; Swim; Arp Nursery Co. Bud ovoid; flowers rose, dbl. (38-45 petals), high-centered to cupped, large (4-5 in.); very fragrant; foliage glossy, leathery; vigorous, bushy growth.

Pink Frostfire Min, *lp*, 1968, *Frostfire sport*; Moore, R.S.; Sequoia Nursery. Flowers light pink.

Pink Frosting HT, *mp*, 1992, (RENfrost); *Seedling × Prima Ballerina*; Rennie, Bruce; Rennie Roses. Flowers medium pink, full (26-40 petals), large (7+ cms) blooms borne mostly singly; very fragrant; foliage large, medium green, matt; some prickles; tall, upright growth.

Pink Garland S, *mp*, 1935, *R. blanda × R. spinosissima cultivar*; Skinner. Flowers clear pink, semi-dbl., open, large (3-3½ in.); very fragrant; upright (3 ft.) growth; non-recurrent bloom.

Pink Garnette F, *dp*, 1950, *Garnette sport*; Schneeberg. Flowers tyrian rose.

Pink Garnette F, *dp*, 1951, *Garnette sport*; Boerner; J&P. Flowers deep pink.

Pink Garnette Supreme F, *mp*, 1946, *Garnette Supreme sport*; Perkins, C.H.; J&P. Flowers rose-pink, dbl. (35-40 petals), cupped, medium (2½ in.), borne in clusters; fragrant; foliage glossy, leathery; vigorous, upright growth; a greenhouse variety.

Pink Gem HT, *lp*, 1949, Fletcher; Tucker. Bud long, pointed; flowers pearl-pink, dbl. (30 petals), flat, large (4-5 in.); very fragrant; foliage bluish green; vigorous, tall growth.

Pink Gem Min, *lp*, 1974, *Scarlet Gem sport*; Meilland; C-P. Bud ovoid; flowers rose-pink, dbl., full, medium; slightly fragrant; foliage soft; moderate, upright, bushy growth.

Pink Glory HT, *mp*, 1960, *Ernie Pyle Seedling × Peace*; Boerner; J&P. Bud long, pointed; flowers clear pink, dbl. (25 petals), high-centered, large (5 in.); very fragrant; foliage leathery; vigorous, upright.

Pink Glow HT, *lp*, 1951, *((Schoener's Nutkana × Seedling) × Mrs. Pierre S. duPont × Home Sweet Home*,) Boerner; J&P. Bud globular; flowers rose-pink, dbl. (40 petals), cupped, becoming flat, large (5-5½ in.); fragrant; foliage leathery, glossy; vigorous, upright growth; a florists' variety.

Pink Golden Dawn HT, *mp*, 1938, *Golden Dawn sport*; Bostick. Flowers pink, dbl., large; fragrant.

Pink Gown HT, *lp*, 1971, *Vera Dalton × Tropicana*; Sanday. Flowers light clear pink, dbl. (20 petals), large (4 in.); foliage matt green; tall.

Pink Grootendorst HRg (S), *mp*, 1923, *F.J. Grootendorst sport*; Grootendorst, F.J. Flowers clear pink.

Pink Gruss an Aachen F, *op*, 1929, *Gruss an Aachen sport*; Kluis; Koning. Flowers light salmon-pink.

Pink Hadley HT, *mp*, 1928, *Hadley sport*; Knight, G. Flowers clear rose pink.

Pink Hat F, *pb*, 1980, *Radiation induced sport of Floribunda Seedling*; James, John. Bud pointed; flowers light pink, center deep pink, dbl. (24 petals), high-centered blooms borne singly or 3-7 per cluster; slight fragrance; foliage red turning dark green, glossy; red prickles; vigorous, upright, bushy growth.

Pink Heather Min, *lp*, 1959, *(R. wichuraiana × Floradora) × (Violette × Zee)*; Moore, R.S.; Sequoia Nursery. Flowers lavender-pink to white, dbl. (45 petals), very small blooms in clusters; foliage very small, glossy; vigorous (10-12 in.), bushy growth.

Pink Hedge HRg (S), *mp*, 1956, *(R. rugosa rubra × R. cinnamomea) × R. nitida*; Nyveldt. Flowers pink; foliage small, bronze; fruit red.

Pink Honey Min, *mp*, 1988, *Summer Spice × Seedling*; Bridges, Dennis; Bridges Roses. Flowers medium honey-pink, yellow at base, reverse light yellow at base, fading to light pink, semi-dbl. (20 petals), high-centered, exhibition, medium, borne usually singly; slight, fruity fragrance; foliage large, medium green, semi-glossy; prickles long, pointed, medium, pink; bushy, tall growth.

Pink Ice F, *w*, 1984, (ANDpin); *Seedling × Iceberg*; Anderson Rose Nursery. Flowers white with deep pink petal edges, dbl. (20 petals), medium; no fragrance; foliage medium, light green, semi-glossy; bushy growth.

Pink Jenny HT, *mp*, 1961, *Grand'mère Jenny sport*; Ruston. Flowers rose-pink.

Pink Jewel F, *mp*, 1940, *Crimson Glory × Holstein*; Kordes; Dreer. Flowers arbutus-pink, center camellia-pink, semi-dbl., cupped; slightly fragrant; foliage leathery; vigorous growth.

Pink Joy Min, *dp*, 1953, *Oakington Ruby × Oakington Ruby*; Moore, R.S.; Sequoia Nursery. Flowers deep pink, dbl. (30 petals), well-shaped, small (1 in.); fragrant (sweet violet); dwarf (12 in.), bushy growth.

Pink Karen Poulsen F, *mp*, 1936, *Karen Poulsen sport*; Poulsen, S. Flowers pink.

Pink Key HT, *mp*, 1920, *Francis Scott Key sport*; Pierson, F.R. Flowers pink.

Pink Kiss™ Min, *lp*, 1987, (MINakco); *Tom Brown × Anita Charles*; Williams, Ernest; Mini-Roses. Flowers light pink, non-fading, dbl. (40-45 petals), high-centered, exhibition, small, borne usually singly or in sprays of 3-5; no fragrance; foliage small, medium green, semi-glossy; tan-red prickles, dilated at base; no fruit; bushy, medium growth.

Pink Koster Pol, *mp*, *Margo Koster sport*; Koster, D.A. Flowers pink.

Pink La Sevillana® F, *mp*, 1984, (MEigeroka; Pink La Sevilliana; Pink Sevilliana; Rosy La Sevilliana); *La Sevillana sport*; Meilland, M.L.; Meilland Et Cie, 1985. Flowers medium pink. GM, Baden-Baden, 1985.

Pink Lace F, *pb*, 1961, *The Optimist × Korona*; Watkins Roses. Flowers light pink, becoming darker and then red; dbl. (20 petals), flat, medium (2-2½ in.); slightly fragrant; foliage dark; vigorous growth.

Pink Lady HT, *mp*, 1947, *Pink Delight sport*; Wiltgen; Premier Rose Gardens. Bud urn-shaped; flowers soft pink, reverse darker, semi-dbl. to dbl., medium (3½ in.); slightly fragrant; vigorous growth.

Pink Lafayette F, *mp*, 1925, *Lafayette sport*; Griffin. Flowers clear rose-pink.

Pink Léda D (OGR), *mp*, *Léda sport or vice-versa*; Prior to 1844. Flowers light to medium pink, crimson edging on petals.

Pink Lemonade HT, *yb*, 1986, (ARO-frichee); *Friendship × Rosy Cheeks*; Christensen; Armstrong Nursery. Flowers yellow turning bright pink, dbl. (35 petals), well-formed, large; fragrant; foliage large, medium green, semi-glossy; upright, bushy growth.

Pink Lorraine HT, *w*, 1972, *Milord × Farah*; Williams, J. Flowers pink, paling to white, base cream, dbl. (40 petals), very full, large (4½ in.); slightly fragrant; foliage matt green; vigorous, upright growth.

Pink Lustre HT, *lp*, 1957, *Peace × Dame Edith Helen*; Verschuren; J&P. Bud ovoid; flowers light pink, dbl. (48 petals), high-centered, large (5 in.); very fragrant; foliage dark, glossy, leathery; vigorous, upright growth.

Pink Magic HT, *dp*, 1952, *Better Times sport (white) × Snow White*; Hill, J.H., Co. Bud long, pointed, spinel-red; flowers phlox-pink, dbl. (40-45 petals), large (4 - 6 in.); very fragrant; foliage leathery; vigorous, upright growth.

Pink Maiden F, *mp*, 1965, *Spartan Seedling × Queen Elizabeth*; Boerner; Spek. Bud ovoid; flowers medium pink, dbl., large blooms in clusters; slightly fragrant; foliage dark.

Pink Mandy Min, *mp*, 1974, *Ellen Poulsen × Little Chief*; Moore, R.S.; Sequoia Nursery. Bud globular; flowers medium pink, dbl. (40 petals), small (1 in.); foliage very glossy, leathery; low, bushy, spreading growth.

Pink Marvel F, *dp*, 1958, *Rosemary Rose × (Cécile Brunner × Floribunda Seedling)*; deRuiter; C-P. Flowers spirea-red, dbl. (45-55 petals), flat, medium (2½ in.), borne in clusters; foliage leathery; bushy, compact growth; a forcing variety.

Pink Masterpiece HT, *pb*, 1962, *Serenade Seedling × Kate Smith*; Boerner; J&P. Bud ovoid, pointed; flowers La France pink, tinted shrimp-pink, dbl. (38 petals), high-centered, very large (6 in.); fragrant; foliage leathery; vigorous, upright growth.

Pink Meidiland® S, *pb*, 1984, (MEipoque; Schloss Heidegg); *Anne de Bretagne × Nirvana*; Meilland, M.L.; Meilland & Son, 1985. Flowers deep pink, white eye, single (5 petals), medium; no fragrance; foliage small, medium green, semi-glossy; bushy growth. ADR, 1987.

Pink Meillandina® Min, *mp*, 1982, (MEijidiro; Pink Sunblaze); *Orange Sunblaze sport*; Meilland, M.L.; Meilland Et Cie, 1980. Flowers medium pink.

Pink Meteor F, *mp*, 1964, *Meteor sport*; Timmermans Roses. Flowers medium pink.

Pink Mini-Wonder™ Min, *mp*, 1990, (MEiselgra); *(Anytime × Parador) × Mogral*; Selection Meilland, 1987; C-P, 1989. Bud rounded; flowers light rose bengal, reverse pale rose bengal, aging pale rose bengal, dbl. (39-42 petals), cupped, small, borne usually singly or in sprays of 1-2; no fragrance; foliage medium green, semi-glossy; prickles small, very few, green, aging tan; bushy, medium growth.

Pink Mist HT, *mp*, 1959, *Red Better Times sport*; Hill, J.H., Co. Bud pointed, ovoid; flowers phlox-pink, becoming darker, dbl. (25-35 petals), high-centered to open, large (4-5 in.); very fragrant; foliage dark, leathery; vigorous, bushy growth; a greenhouse variety.

Pink Montezuma Gr, *lp*, 1964, *Montezuma sport*; Williams, J.B. Flowers light pink, reverse blush-pink, dbl., high-centered, large; slightly fragrant; foliage dark, leathery; vigorous, bushy growth.

Pink Nymph F, *mp*, 1959, *Nymph sport*; Koster, D.A. Flowers clear pink.

Pink Nymph Min, *mp*, *R. chinensis minima sport*. Flowers pink, dbl.; (14).

Pink Ocean® Cl HT, *lp*, 1980, (HAVink); *Pink Showers × Alexander*; Verschuren; H.A. Verschuren. Flowers light pink, dbl. (20 petals), large; very fragrant; foliage medium, medium green; semi-glossy; upright (to 7 ft.).

Pink Ophelia HT, *mp*, 1916, *Ophelia sport*; Breitmeyer. Flowers rose-pink.

Pink Panther® HT, *pb*, 1982, (MEicapinal; Aachener Dom; Panthere Rose); *MEigurami × MEinaregi*; Meilland, M.L.; Meilland Et Cie, 1981. Flowers petals silvery pink, edged deep pink, dbl. (40+ petals), large; no fragrance; foliage medium, semi-glossy; upright growth.

Pink Parasol HT, *mp*, 1950, *Rapture* × *Rome Glory*; Fisher, G.; Arnold-Fisher Co. Bud long, pointed; flowers clear pink, dbl. (25-30 petals), very large (6 in.); slightly fragrant; foliage leathery, dark; very vigorous growth.

Pink Parfait Gr, *pb*, 1960, *First Love* × *Pinocchio*; Swim; Armstrong Nursery. Bud ovoid to urn-shaped; flowers outer petals medium pink, center blended pale orange, dbl. (23 petals), high-centered to cupped, large (3½-4 in.); slightly fragrant; foliage leathery, semi-glossy; vigorous, upright, bushy growth. GM, Baden-Baden; Portland, 1959; AARS, 1961; GM, NRS, 1962.

Pink Passion Min, *pb*, 1978, *Sweet and Low* × *Seedling*; Schwartz, E.W.; Bountiful Ridge Nursery. Bud pointed; flowers shell-pink and ivory, dbl. (26 petals), high-centered, small (1½ in.); fragrant; upright, bushy growth.

Pink Peace® HT, *mp*, 1959, (MEIbil); *(Peace × Monique)* × *(Peace × Mrs. John Laing)*; Meilland, F.; URS; C-P. Flowers dusty pink, dbl. (58 petals), large (4½-6 in.); very fragrant; foliage leathery; vigorous, tall, bushy growth. GM, Geneva; Rome, 1959.

Pink Peace, Climbing® Cl HT, *mp*, 1968, (MEIbilsar); Meilland; URS.

Pink Pearl Cl HT, *op*, 1913, *Irish Elegance* × *Una*; Hobbies. Flowers pink shaded salmon, single.

Pink Pearl HT, *mp*, 1924, *Ophelia* × *(Gen. MacArthur* × *Marie van Houtte)*; Leenders, M. Flowers neyron pink, base salmon, dbl.; long stems; very fragrant; vigorous growth.

Pink Pearl, Climbing Cl HT, *mp*, 1933, Dixie Rose Nursery.

Pink Perfection HT, *mp*, 1927, *Premier* × *Baroness Rothschild*; Ward, F.B. Flowers clear rose-pink, dbl. (45 petals); fragrant.

Pink Perfekta HT, *pb*, 1962, *Kordes' Perfecta* sport; Ross, A.; A. Ross & Son. Flowers deep pink, often edged red.

Pink Perpétué LCl, *mp*, 1965, *Spectacular* × *New Dawn*; Gregory. Flowers bright rose-pink, dbl. (32 petals), semi-globular, medium blooms in clusters; fragrant; foliage glossy, light green; vigorous growth; recurrent bloom.

Pink Pet Ch (OGR), *mp*, 1928, Lilley. Flowers bright pink, dbl.

Pink Petticoat Min, *pb*, 1979, *Neue Revue* × *Sheri Anne*; Strawn; Pixie Treasures. Bud pointed; flowers creamy white, edged coral-pink, dbl. (33 petals), exhibition, mini-flora, medium (1½-2 in.); slightly fragrant; foliage glossy, dark; tall, upright. AOE, 1980.

Pink Picotee® Min, *pb*, 1990, (KINpic); *(Vera Dalton* × *Fancy Pants)* × *Magic Carrousel*; King, Gene; AGM Miniature Roses. Flowers white to cream with dark pink picotee edge, full (26-40 petals), small, borne mostly singly; no fragrance; foliage medium, light green, matt; upright, spreading, medium growth.

Pink Polyanna™ S, *mp*, 1989, (JACship); *Zorina* × *Heidi*; Warriner, William A.; Bear Creek Gardens, 1990. Bud ovoid; flowers medium pink, reverse slightly darker, aging lighter, dbl. (45+ petals), high-centered, exhibition, small, borne in sprays of 9-13; moderate fruity fragrance; foliage small, medium green, glossy; prickles small, straight, red to brown; upright, bushy, medium growth; repeats.

Pink Poodle Min, *pb*, 1991, (MORpoodle); *(Little Darling* × *Yellow Magic)* × *Old Blush*; Moore, Ralph S.; Sequoia Nursery, 1992. Flowers pink changing to lighter pink to white, very full (41+ petals), typical china characteristics, medium (4-7 cms) blooms borne in small clusters; fragrant; foliage small, medium green, matt; few prickles; low (26-30 cms), upright growth.

Pink Popcorn™ S, *lp*, 1991, (WILpop); *R. chinensis minima* × *(Sea Foam* × *The Fairy) Seedling*; Williams, J. Benjamin, 1992. Flowers light pink to coral, semi-dbl. (6-14 petals), small (0-4 cms) blooms borne in large clusters in small grape like sprays; slight fragrance; foliage small, medium green, matt, disease resistant; few prickles; low (12-18 in.), compact, bushy growth.

Pink Porcelain Min, *lp*, 1983, (TINporce); *Futura* × *Avandel*; Bennett, Dee; Tiny Petals Nursery. Flowers light pink, dbl. (23 petals), HT form, small blooms borne singly and in clusters; slight fragrance; foliage small, medium green, semi-glossy; upright growth.

Pink Posy Min, *m*, 1982, (COCanelia); *Trier* × *New Penny*; Cocker, James; Cocker & Sons. Flowers lilac, dbl. (40+ petals), small; fragrant; foliage dark, matt; bushy growth.

Pink Powder Puff F, *mp*, 1965, Pal; Indian Agric. Research Inst. Bud ovoid; flowers soft pink, dbl., open, medium; foliage leathery; vigorous, upright, compact growth.

Pink Powderpuff Cl HBc (OGR), *lp*, 1990, (MORpuff); *Lulu* × *Muriel*; Moore, Ralph S., 1964. Bud pointed; flowers light pink, aging slightly lighter, very dbl. (100+ petals), high-centered, old garden rose type, large, borne heavy in spring; heavy, damask fragrance; foliage large, medium green, semi-glossy; tall, spreading, climbing growth; repeats.

Pink Pride HT, *lp*, 1959, *May Wettern* × *Peace*; Fletcher. Flowers silvery pink, dbl. (30-35 petals), high-centered, large (5-6 in.); very fragrant; foliage light green.

Pink Princess HT, *pb*, 1939, *(Dr. W. Van Fleet × Général Jacqueminot) × Break o' Day*; Brownell. Flowers deep rose pink to yellowish, dbl., high-centered, large; very fragrant; foliage dark, leathery, glossy; vigorous, bushy growth.

Pink Profusion HSet (OGR), *pb*, 1938, *Mrs. F.F. Prentiss × Lady Alice Stanley*; Horvath; Wayside Gardens Co. Flowers pale flesh-pink, reverse deep coral-rose, dbl. (80 petals), globular, small blooms in clusters on long, strong stems; slightly fragrant; foliage large, glossy; very vigorous growth; non-recurrent bloom.

Pink Prosperity HMsk (S), *lp*, 1931, Bentall. Flowers light pink, blooms in large trusses; fragrant (musk); very vigorous growth.

Pink Puff F, *lp*, 1965, *Pinocchio Seedling × (Red Pinocchio Seedling × Garnette)*; Boerner; J&P. Flowers soft pink, dbl.; fragrant; foliage leathery; vigorous, upright growth.

Pink Quill Min, *mp*, 1992, (WEEquill); *Mr. Bluebird × Seedling*; Weeks, Michael W.J. Flowers medium bright pink, semi-dbl. (6-14 petals), small (0-4 cms) blooms borne in large clusters; fragrant; foliage medium, dark green, bronze when young, semi-glossy; some prickles; tall (25 cms), spreading growth.

Pink Revelation F, *lp*, 1979, *Summer Snow sport*; Schramm, D. Flowers light pink.

Pink Rhapsody LCl, *op*, 1973, *(Heidelberg × Bonn) × Pink Parfait*; Ellick. Flowers deep vermilion-pink, dbl. (35-40 petals), full, large (4 in.); slightly fragrant; very vigorous growth.

Pink Rhythm Min, *op*, 1990, *Party Girl × Fashion Flame*; Jolly, Marie, 1984; Rosehill Farm, 1991. Bud pointed; flowers coral pink, white center, medium pink reverse, aging light pink, semi-dbl. (18 petals), high-centered, exhibition, loose, borne usually singly; fruity fragrance; foliage medium, medium green, matt; upright, spreading, medium growth.

Pink Ribbon Min, *lp*, 1966, *(R. wichuraiana × Floradora) × Magic Wand*; Moore, R.S.; Sequoia Nursery. Flowers soft pink, dbl., small; slightly fragrant; foliage glossy, light green; vigorous, bushy, dwarf growth.

Pink Ripples F, *lp*, 1956, *Red Ripples sport*; Sanders, H.T. Flowers pink, semi-dbl. (15-20 wavy petals), open, large (2½-3 in.), borne in clusters; slightly fragrant; very vigorous, upright, compact growth.

Pink Roamer R, *pb*, 1897, *R. wichuraiana × Cramoisi Superieur*; Horvath; W.A. Manda.

Flowers pink, center white, single; vigorous growth.

Pink Robusta® S, *mp*, 1987, (KORpinrob; The Seckford Rose); *(Zitronenfalter × Grammerstorf, Climbing) × Robusta*; Kordes, W., 1986. Flowers medium pink, semi-dbl. (16-14 petals), large; slight fragrance; foliage large, dark green, glossy; bushy, spreading growth.

Pink Rocket S, *pb*, 1949, *Skyrocket Seedling*; Longley, L.E.; Univ. of Minn. Bud ovoid; flowers deep pink suffused copper, single and semi-dbl., open, large; slightly fragrant; foliage glossy, bronze, dark; very vigorous, upright growth; profuse, non-recurrent bloom; hardy.

Pink Rosette F, *lp*, 1948, Krebs; H&S. Bud small, ovoid; flowers soft pink, dbl. (50 petals), cupped, rosette form, medium (2 in.) blooms in clusters; slightly fragrant; foliage leathery, dark; vigorous, dwarf, bushy growth.

Pink Royal HT, *mp*, 1928, *Columbia × Mme. Butterfly*; Vestal. Flowers glowing pink, dbl.; fragrant.

Pink Ruby HT, *mp*, 1966, *Rubaiyat sport*; Anstiss. Flowers pink, high pointed, large (4-4½ in.); fragrant; foliage light green; vigorous growth.

Pink Ruffles F, *mp*, 1977, *Frolic self Seedling × Pinafore*, Ellis; Mansion Nursery. Bud pointed; flowers rose-pink, single (5-7 petals), ruffled, large (3 in.); slightly fragrant (tea); foliage very glossy, dark; very bushy growth.

Pink Sandy™ Min, *pb*, 1990, (KINsandy); *(Vera Dalton × Rainbow's End) × Fancy Pants*; King, Gene; AGM Miniature Roses. Flowers light pink to light apricot center, aging deep pink edges, full (26-40 petals), small, borne mostly singly; slight fragrance; foliage small, medium green, matt; bushy, low growth.

Pink Satin F, *mp*, 1945, *Indiana × William F. Dreer*; Cross, Mrs. C.W.; B&A. Bud large; flowers clean rose-pink, showy stamens, semi-dbl., open, cupped; fragrant; foliage soft, light green; very vigorous, bushy, compact growth.

Pink Satin F, *lp*, 1974, *Seedling × Bridal Pink*; Warriner; J&P. Bud ovoid; flowers light pink, dbl. (30-35 petals), high-centered, large (4-5 in.); foliage large; vigorous.

Pink Secret Min, *mp*, 1982, (TRObina); *Beauty Secret sport*; Robinson, Thomas; T. Robinson Ltd. Flowers medium pink.

Pink Semi Sp (OGR), *lp*, *R. laxa form*. Flowers pink; resembles R. blanda in appearance.

Pink Shadow Min, *dp*, 1977, *Over the Rainbow × Over the Rainbow*; Williams, E.D.; Mini-

Roses. Bud plump, pointed; flowers dusty pink, reverse darker, dbl. (52 petals), small (1 in.); fragrant; foliage glossy; bushy, spreading growth.

Pink Sheri Min, *lp*, 1985, (RENeri); *Sheri Anne* sport; Rennie, Bruce F. Flowers light pink.

Pink Showers Cl HT, *lp*, 1974, *Carla × Golden Showers*; Verschuren, T.; Verschuren. Flowers light pink, dbl., large; vigorous, tall, climbing growth.

Pink Silk HT, *mp*, 1972, *Pink Parfait × Seedling*; Gregory. Flowers carmine-rose, dbl. (42 petals), high-centered, large (4 in.); fragrant. GM, NZ, 1974.

Pink Snow Cl F, *pb*, 1981, *Summer Snow, Climbing* sport; Reed, Harry, Jr. Flowers light pink shading to white in center, deeper on edges of petals.

Pink Soupert Pol, *mp*, 1896, *Clotilde Soupert Seedling*; Dingee; Conard. Flowers pink, in clusters; vigorous.

Pink Spice HT, *lp*, 1962, Abrams, Von; Peterson; Dering. Bud long, pointed; flowers light pink flushed yellow, dbl. (30 petals), high-centered to cupped, large (5 in.); very fragrant; foliage leathery, light green; vigorous, upright growth.

Pink Spiral HT, *dp*, 1953, McGredy. Flowers deep china-rose-pink, dbl., high pointed, large (4 in.); foliage cedar-green; very vigorous growth.

Pink Splendour HT, *mp*, 1951, *Sam McGredy × Crimson Glory*; McGredy. Flowers rose-pink, dbl. (48 petals), large (6-7 in.); very fragrant; foliage dark; very free growth.

Pink Star® S, *mp*, 1978, (INTerpink); *Yesterday × Seedling*; Interplant, 1977. Flowers medium pink, semi-dbl., medium; slight fragrance; foliage medium, light, semi-glossy; spreading.

Pink Supreme HT, *lp*, 1964, *Amor × Peace*; deRuiter. Flowers light pink, dbl. (23 petals), large (4-5 in.); very fragrant; foliage light green; vigorous, upright, well-branched growth. GM, Geneva, 1965; Belfast, 1967.

Pink Surprise Min, *mp*, 1980, *Seedling × Seedling*; Lyon. Bud ovoid, pointed; flowers medium pink, dbl. (48 petals), blooms borne singly or several together; fragrant; foliage tiny, medium green; curved prickles; compact, bushy growth.

Pink Sweetheart™ F, *mp*, 1986, (WILpksh); *(Carla × Sonia) × (Circus × Ma Perkins)*; Williams, J.B. Flowers medium coral pink, dbl. (35 petals), well-formed, small blooms borne singly; fragrant; foliage medium, medium green, semi-glossy; upright, dwarf.

Pink Symphony Min, *lp*, 1987, (MEItonje; Pink Symphonie; Pretty Polly; Sweet Sunblaze); *Darling Flame × Air France*; Meilland, Mrs. Marie-Louise. Flowers light cardinal pink, dbl. (26-40 petals), medium; slight fragrance; foliage medium, dark green, glossy, disease resistant; bushy growth.

Pink Talisman HT, 1943, *Talisman* sport; Howard Rose Co. Flowers orange to pink with pink predominating, large; upright growth.

Pink Tingle Min, *mp*, 1978, Lyon. Bud ovoid; flowers dawn-pink, dbl. (20 petals), cupped to recurved, small (1 in.); slightly fragrant; foliage tiny; compact growth.

Pink Torch® S, *mp*, 1987, (INTertor; Torche Rose); *(Mozart × Seedling) × (Seedling × Eyepaint)*; Interplant. Flowers medium pink, single, small blooms in large pyramidal sprays; slight fragrance; foliage medium, medium green, glossy; upright (to 4 ft.) growth.

Pink Triumph Min, *mp*, 1983, *Operetta × Bonny*; Jolly, Nelson F.; Rosehill Farm. Flowers medium pink, dbl. (48 petals), small blooms borne usually singly; fragrant; foliage small, medium green, semi-glossy; upright, bushy growth.

Pink Vogue F, *mp*, 1960, *Vogue* sport; Kelleher; Hazlewood Bros. Bud pointed; flowers pink, semi-dbl., medium, borne in clusters; fragrant; moderate, upright growth.

Pink Wave F, *mp*, 1983, (MATtgro); *Moon Maiden × Eyepaint*; Mattock, John, Ltd. Flowers soft medium pink, semi-dbl., medium; fragrant; foliage medium, medium green, semi-glossy; spreading growth; ground cover.

Pink Winks Min, *mp*, 1986, (FLOwin); *Baby Betsy McCall × Red Can Can*; Florac, Marilyn, 1987. Flowers medium pink, semi-dbl. (13 petals), urn-shaped, small, borne usually singly; no fragrance; foliage small, medium green, matt; bushy, low growth; (14).

Pink Wonder F, *lp*, 1970, (MEIhartfor; Kalinka); *Zambra × (Sarabande × (Goldilocks × Fashion))*; Meilland; URS. Flowers light pink, dbl. (28 petals), imbricated, large (3 in.); very fragrant; foliage large, glossy, leathery; vigorous, upright growth. GM, Madrid, 1969; Belfast, 1972.

Pink Wonder, Climbing Cl F, *lp*, 1976, (MEIhartforsar; Kalinka, Climbing); Meilland, M.L.; Meilland.

Pink-A-Boo F, *mp*, 1961, *Spartan × Pink Garnette*; Boerner; J&P. Bud ovoid; flowers medium pink, dbl. (33 petals), large (3-3½ in.) blooms in large clusters; fragrant; foliage leathery; vigorous, upright growth.

Pink-A-Ling Min, *w*, 1988, (ZIPpink); *Tamango* × *Avandel*; Zipper, Herbert; Magic Moment Miniatures, 1989. Flowers white edged deep pink, dbl. (over 40 petals), small, borne singly and in sprays; slight fragrance; foliage medium, dark green, glossy; upright growth.

Pinkces LCl, *yb*, 1962, *Doubloons sport*; Schmalz; Limpert. Bud pointed; flowers light yellow to pink, dbl. (30 petals), open, large (3½-4 in.); fragrant; foliage leathery; vigorous, tall, compact growth; abundant, non-recurrent bloom.

Pinkerton HT, *mp*, 1949, Eacott. Bud long, pointed; flowers pink shaded deeper, dbl. (30 petals), large (4 in.); fragrant; foliage light green; vigorous growth.

Pinkie Pol, *mp*, 1947, *China Doll* × *Seedling*; Swim; Armstrong Nursery. Flowers neyron rose, semi-dbl. (16 petals), cupped, medium (1¾-2½ in.) blooms in large trusses; very fragrant; foliage soft, glossy, mostly 7 leaflet leaves; similar to China Doll, which see; dwarf, bushy growth; (21). AARS, 1948.

Pinkie, Climbing Cl Pol, *mp*, 1952, Dering; Armstrong Nursery.

Pinocchio F, *op*, 1940, (Rosenmärchen); *Eva* × *Golden Rapture*, Kordes; J&P, 1942. Flowers pink suffused salmon, edged deeper, dbl. (30 petals), cupped, small (2 in.) blooms in long sprays; fragrant (fruity); foliage leathery; vigorous, bushy growth; (28). GM, Portland, 1942.

Pinocchio, Climbing Cl F, *pb*, 1951, Parmentier, J.; J&P.

Pinson LCl, *my*, 1909, *R. wichuraiana* × *Souv. de Catherine Guillot*; Barbier. Flowers chamois-yellow, tinted rosy white, semi-dbl., very large, borne in clusters of 7-10; vigorous, climbing growth; early bloom.

Pinstripe™ Min, *rb*, 1985, (MORpints); *Pinocchio* × *Seedling*; Moore, R.S.; Armstrong Roses, 1986. Flowers red with white stripes, dbl. (35 petals), well-formed, small; slight fragrance; foliage small, medium green, semi-glossy; low, mounded habit.

Pinta HT, *w*, 1973, *Ena Harkness* × *Pascali*; Beales. Flowers creamy white, dbl. (23 petals), large (3½ in.); fragrant (sweetbriar); foliage dark, matt.

Pin-up F, *dp*, 1959, *Else Poulsen* × *Seedling*; Fletcher. Flowers deep china-rose, semi-dbl. (16-18 wavy petals), medium, borne in clusters; foliage light green; low, bushy growth.

Pinwheel Min, *pb*, 1977, *Jeanie Williams sport*; Moore, R.S.; Sequoia Nursery. Flowers pink and yellow blend.

Pioneer HT, *mr*, 1970, LeGrice. Flowers red, dbl. (50 petals), very full, large (4 in.); very fragrant; foliage small, dark; very free growth.

Pionerka F, *ob*, 1955, (Woman Pioneer); Sushkov. Flowers reddish orange, medium; slightly fragrant; vigorous growth.

Pioupiou F, *mr*, 1958, *Alain* × (*Alain* × *Seedling*); Arles; Roses-France. Flowers cerise-red, large; very vigorous, bushy, low growth.

Pip Min, *mr*, 1977, *N74* × *Seedling*; Lyon. Bud pointed; flowers red, semi-dbl. (12-15 petals), cupped, small; slightly fragrant; foliage tiny; very compact, bushy growth. RULED EXTINCT 7/90.

Pip HT, *w*, 1990, (*Poker Chip* × *Helmut Schmidt*) × ((*Rise 'n' Shine* × *Granada*) × *Handel*)); Stoddard, Lou, 1991. Bud ovoid; flowers white rimmed pink, white reverse, aging same, dbl. (30 petals), high-centered, medium, borne singly; slight fragrance; foliage medium, light to medium green, matt; bushy, medium growth.

Pipe Dreams S, *mp*, 1984, *Countryman* × ((*Meisterstuck* × *Prairie Princess*) × (*Tickled Pink* × *Prairie Princess*)); Buck; Iowa State University. Flowers medium pink, reverse darker, dbl. (28 petals), cupped, large (5 in.) blooms borne 5-10 per cluster; intense clove fragrance; foliage leathery, medium olive green; awl-shaped, red-brown prickles; bushy, compact, upright growth; repeat bloom; hardy.

Pippa's Song S, *mp*, 1984, *Prairie Princess* × (*Queen Elizabeth* × (*Morning Stars* × *Suzanne*)); Buck; Iowa State University. Flowers medium pink, imbricated, medium (3 in.) blooms borne 3-10 per cluster; light fragrance; foliage medium, leathery, dark olive green; awl-shaped, tan prickles; shrubby, erect, bushy growth; repeat bloom; hardy.

Pipsqueak Min, *m*, 1986, *Blue Mist* × *Snow Magic*; Dobbs; Port Stockton Nursery. Flowers pinkish mauve, dbl. (40 petals), flat, quilled, small blooms in sprays of 5-20; no fragrance; foliage small, light green, matt; very small, brown prickles, hooked downward; no fruit; bushy, spreading growth.

Pirate Gold F, *dy*, 1972, *Dr. A.J. Verhage* × *Seedling*; deRuiter; Carlton Rose Nursery. Flowers deep yellow, dbl., globular, small; slightly fragrant; foliage glossy, leathery; vigorous, upright growth.

Pirbright F, *mp*, 1948, Norman. Flowers pink, semi-dbl., borne in trusses; slightly fragrant; foliage dark; vigorous growth.

Piroschka® HT, *mp*, 1972, (TANpika); *Fragrant Cloud* × *Dr. A.J. Verhage*; Tantau. Bud long, pointed; flowers pink, dbl., large; fragrant; moderate, upright growth.

Pirouette F, *pb*, 1968, *Ma Perkins* × *Radar*; Fankhauser; A. Ross & Son. Flowers pink tinged orange-red, dbl., open, medium; fragrant.

Pismi HT, *rb*, 1972, *Dame Edith Helen* × *Rote Rapture*; Pecollo. Bud ovoid; flowers solferino-purple to spirea-red, dbl., cupped, large; fragrant; foliage large, dark, leathery; vigorous, upright bushy growth.

Pitica F, *lp*, 1976, *Sonia sport*; Royon; Universal Plants. Flowers light pink, dbl. (25-30 petals), full, high-centered, large (4 in.); slightly fragrant.

Pittsburgh HP (OGR), *lp*, 1929, *(R. gigantea Seedling* × *Frau Karl Druschki)* × *Mrs. John Laing*; Schoener; B&A. Flowers flesh-pink, base yellow, dbl. (25 petals), globular, very large; long stems; slightly fragrant; foliage leathery; very vigorous growth.

Pius IX HP (OGR), *mp*, 1849, (Pie IX; Pius the Ninth; Pope Pius IX); Vibert. Flowers violet-rose, very full, flat; very fragrant; vigorous growth.

Pius XI HT, *w*, 1925, (Pope Pius XI); *Ophelia* × *Seedling*; Leenders, M. Bud long, pointed; flowers cream-white, center cream-yellow, dbl., very large; fragrant.

Pixie Min, *w*, 1940, (Little Princess; Princesita); *Ellen Poulsen* × *Tom Thumb*; deVink; C-P. Flowers white, center light pink, dbl. (55 petals), small blooms on short stems; slightly fragrant; foliage very small, soft; dwarf, compact growth.

Pixie, Climbing Cl Min, *w*, 1964, Ruston.

Pixie Delight™ Min, *w*, 1981, (WILbentur); *Ma Perkins* × *Easter Morning*; Williams, J.B.; C-P. Flowers white, dbl. (40+ petals); slight fragrance; foliage small, dark, semi-glossy; upright.

Pixie Gold Min, *my*, 1961, *Perla de Montserrat* × *(Rosina* × *Eduardo Toda)*; Dot, P.; C-P. Flowers mimosa-yellow, semi-dbl. (11 petals), small (1-1½ in.); foliage very small, thin, dark; bushy growth.

Pixie Pearl Min, *w*, Lamb Nursery. Flowers pearly white, very dbl., small, borne in clusters; vigorous, compact growth.

Pixie Rose Min, *dp*, 1961, (Pink Pixie); *Perla de Montserrat* × *Coralín*; Dot, P.; C-P. Flowers deep pink, dbl. (43 petals), high-centered to cupped, small (1 in.) blooms in irregular clusters; foliage very small, dark; dwarf, much-branched growth.

Pizzazz Min, *rb*, 1991, *Orange Honey* × *Loving Touch*; Jolly, Marie; Rosehill Farm, 1992. Bud ovoid; flowers various yellows, pink hues, aging to orange-red, dbl. (50 petals), medium (4 cms) blooms borne usually singly

or in sprays of 2-3; slight fragrance; foliage medium, medium green, semi-glossy; upright, spreading, medium growth.

Pizzicato S, *lp*, 1962, *Florence Mary Morse* × *(Josef Rothmund* × *R. laxa)*; Buck; Iowa State University. Bud ovoid, long, pointed; flowers light salmon-rose, dbl. (40 petals), cupped, medium (3-4 in.); fragrant; foliage leathery, bronze; vigorous, upright (3-4 ft.), bushy.

Placet S, *w*, 1981, *Probably R. multiflora hybrid*; Bevan, Mrs. Ruth M. Bud small, ovoid; flowers white, single (5 petals), blooms borne 40 or more per cluster; fragrant; foliage soft green, 7 leaflet; bushy growth; all summer bloom.

Placida HT, *mr*, 1959, *Crimson Glory* × *Una Wallace*; Cayzer. Bud ovoid; flowers crimson, dbl., large; slightly fragrant; foliage glossy, dark; vigorous, bushy, compact growth.

Plain Talk F, *mr*, 1964, *Spartan* × *Garnette*; Swim & Weeks; Weeks Wholesale Rose Grower. Flowers medium red, semi-dbl. to dbl., medium blooms in clusters; slightly fragrant; foliage dark, leathery; vigorous, bushy, low growth.

Plaisante F, *mp*, 1957, *Borderer* × *Seedling*; Riethmuller. Flowers bright pink, base and reverse lighter, semi-dbl.; fragrant; low growth.

Plaisir de France HT, *dp*, 1952, *Peace* × *Seedling*; Gaujard. Flowers bright deep coppery pink, dbl. (35 petals), very large (6 in.); fragrant; foliage glossy, dark; vigorous growth.

Plamya Vostoka F, *or*, 1955, (Flame of the East); *Independence* × *Kirsten Poulsen*; Klimenko. Flowers fiery red tinted darker, dbl. (30 petals), medium; fragrant; medium growth.

Platinum Lady Min, *m*, 1988, (LAVplat); *Seedling* × *Lavender Jade*; Laver, Keith; Springwood Miniature Roses, 1989. Bud pointed; flowers light lavender, reverse white, dbl. (21 petals), high-centered, exhibition, borne singly, very slow to open; no fragrance; foliage small, dark green, young foliage edged in red, semi-glossy; prickles slender "V" shape, red; fruit ovoid, orange; upright, bushy, medium growth.

Plato HSpn (OGR), *m*, *R. spinosissima hybrid*; Vibert. Flowers red-violet, dbl.; foliage finely divided; fruit black, glossy; dense, shrubby (3-4 ft.) growth; non-recurrent.

Playboy® F, *rb*, 1976, (Cheerio); *City of Leeds* × *(Chanelle* × *Piccadilly)*; Cocker. Flowers scarlet, gold eye, single, large (3½ in.); slightly fragrant; foliage glossy, dark. GM, Portland, 1989.

Playfair F, *w*, 1991, (WIWait); *Playgirl × Seedling*; Wilke, William. Flowers white, single, medium blooms borne in small clusters; slight fragrance; foliage medium, medium green, semi-glossy; medium growth.

Playful HT, *ab*, 1970, *Mischief sport*; Watson. Flowers light apricot, edged pink.

Playgirl™ F, *mp*, 1986, (MORplag); *Playboy × Angel Face*; Moore, R.S.; Moore Min. Roses. Flowers medium pink, yellow stamens, single, medium blooms borne usually singly and in sprays of 3-5; slight fragrance; foliage medium, medium green, semi-glossy; few, brown prickles; no fruit; upright, bushy growth.

Playgroup Rose® F, *yb*, 1986, (HORsun); *Prominent × Southampton*; Horner, Heather M. Flowers yellow, petals edged red, reverse pale yellow, dbl. (25 petals), cupped, medium blooms in sprays of 5-9; fragrant; foliage medium, light green, glossy; large, light brown prickles; fruit small, globular, orange; medium, bushy growth.

Playmate F, *rb*, 1986, (WEOkay); *Playboy × Seedling*; Fonda, Henry; Wee Ones Miniature Roses, 1986. Flowers vivid scarlet, yellow center, single (5 petals), large, borne usually singly; slight fragrance; foliage medium, dark green, glossy; upright, bushy growth.

Playtime™ F, *or*, 1989, (MORplati); *Playboy × Old Master*; Moore, Ralph S.; Sequoia Nursery, 1990. Bud pointed; flowers vibrant orange-red, aging slightly darker, single (5 petals), flat, medium, borne usually singly and in sprays of 3-5; slight fragrance; foliage medium, dark green, semi-glossy; prickles straight, slightly hooked, medium, light brown; fruit round, medium, orange-red; upright, bushy, medium growth.

Pleasantly Pink Min, *mp*, 1992, (LAVplease); *(June Laver × Rosamini Red) × (Dwarfking × Julie Ann)*; Laver, Keith G.; Springwood Roses. Flowers clear pink, very full (41+ petals), medium (4-7 cms) blooms borne in small clusters; fragrant; foliage medium, medium green, matt; some prickles; medium (30-35 cms), bushy growth.

Pleasure F, *mp*, 1988, (JACpif); *(Merci × Faberge) × Intrigue*; Warriner, William; Bear Creek Gardens, 1990. Bud ovoid, pointed; flowers coral pink, reverse lighter, dbl. (33 petals), cupped, large, borne in sprays of 3-7; slight fragrance; foliage medium, dark green, semi-glossy; prickles slightly hooked downward, reddish-brown; fruit globular; low, compact growth. 1990 AARS.

Plein Ciel HT, *mp*, 1964, *Seedling × Golden Rapture*; Mondial Roses. Bud pointed; flow-

ers pink, dbl., high-centered, large; fragrant; foliage dark, glossy; vigorous, well branched.

Pleine de Grâce S, *w*, 1985, (LENgra); *Ballerina × R. filipes*; Lens, 1983. Flowers creamy white, single (5 petals), small blooms in clusters of 12-24; very fragrant; foliage yellowish-green; bushy, spreading growth; non-recurrent bloom.

Plena HSem (OGR), *lp*, (Double White Noisette); *R. sempervirens hybrid*; Laffay. Flowers flesh, dbl.

Plentiful F, *dp*, 1961, LeGrice. Bud globular; flowers deep pink, dbl. (75 petals), flat, large (3-4 in.) blooms in large clusters; foliage light green; vigorous, bushy growth.

Plomin F, *dp*, 1951, *(Johanna Tantau × Karen Poulsen) × Stammler*; Tantau. Flowers dark rose, semi-dbl., well formed, large, borne in large clusters; very fragrant; foliage leathery; bushy, dwarf growth.

Pluie de Feu LCl, *or*, 1964, Mondial Roses. Flowers bright scarlet, semi-dbl., borne in clusters; vigorous growth.

Plukovnik Svec HT, *dr*, 1935, (Colonel Svec); *Pres. Jac. Smits × K. of K.*; Böhm. Bud long (over 3 in.), pointed; flowers blood-red, semi-dbl., large; fragrant; foliage small; vigorous, bushy growth.

Plum Cake HT, *dr*, 1986, (MURca); *(Chanelle × Sabine) × Pompadour*; Murray, N. Flowers deep plum red, dbl. (27 petals), pointed, borne in sprays of 3-7; slight fragrance; foliage medium, dark green, glossy; pointed, brown prickles; bushy, almost everblooming.

Plum Crazy HT, *m*, 1985, (AROgraju); *(Ivory Tower × Angel Face) × Blue Nile*; Christensen; Armstrong Nursery. Flowers deep lavender, dbl. (35 petals), well-formed, large; fragrant; foliage medium, dark, matt; bushy growth.

Plum Dandy™ Min, *m*, 1991, (JACliang); *Seedling × Angel Face*; Warriner, William A.; Bear Creek Gardens, Inc. (J&P). Bud ovoid, pointed; flowers medium lavender, lighter near petal base, same reverse, fades to light lavender with age, very dbl. (35 petals), cupped, large; moderate, fruity fragrance; foliage medium, medium green, semi-glossy; bushy, spreading, medium growth.

Plum Duffy Min, *m*, 1978, *Magic Carrousel × Magic Carrousel*; Bennett, Dee; Tiny Petals Nursery. Bud ovoid; flowers deep plum, dbl. (25 petals), exhibition, small (1½ in.); slightly fragrant; foliage dark; compact growth.

Plum Pudding™ Min, *m*, 1984, (WILplpd); *Angel Face × Seedling*; Williams, J.B. Flowers blue-lavender washed red and purple, dbl. (35 petals), small; fragrant; foliage small, dark, semi-glossy; upright, bushy growth.

Plzen HT, *dr*, 1930, (City of Pilsen; Stadt Pilsen); *Étoile de Hollande* × *Macbeth*; Böhm. Bud very long; flowers dark blood-red, semidbl., very large; very vigorous growth.

Poco Min, *pb*, 1986, *Heartland* × *Seedling*; Bridges, Dennis, 1987. Flowers pink, white center, fades slightly, dbl. (29 petals), urn-shaped, medium, borne usually singly; slight fragrance; foliage medium, medium green, semi-glossy; medium, light green prickles, pointed downwards; bushy, medium growth.

Podruga HT, *mp*, 1939, Girl Friend *Vaterland* × *Mme. Edouard Herriot*; Costetske. Flowers bright pink, base dark red, oval, irregular shape; low, rather weak growth.

Poëma R, *mp*, 1933, *Tausendschön* × *Farbenkönigin*; Brada; Böhm. Flowers bright pink, passing to La France pink, borne in clusters of 10-100; foliage bright, dark; vigorous (5-10 ft.) growth; recurrent bloom.

Poente F, *ob*, *Pinocchio* × *Goldilocks*; Moreira da Silva. Flowers orange and carmine.

Poète Jean du Clos HT, *op*, 1919, *Le Progres* × *Lyon Rose*; Gillot, F. Flowers pink, shaded salmon, dbl.; very fragrant.

Poetry Min, *rb*, 1990, (ZIPoet); *Libby* × *Deep Purple*; Zipper, Herbert, 1987; Magic Moment Miniatures, 1991. Bud pointed; flowers red with white at base, white reverse with some red at edges, aging red with white reverse and red at edges, dbl. (30 petals), urn-shaped, exhibition, medium, borne usually singly; slight fragrance; foliage small, medium green, semi-glossy; bushy, low growth.

Poinsettia HT, *mr*, 1938, *(Mrs. J.D. Eisele* × *Vaterland)* × *J.C. Thorton*; H&S; Dreer. Bud long, pointed; flowers bright scarlet, dbl. (28 petals), large; fragrant; foliage glossy; vigorous, compact growth. GM, Portland, 1940.

Poinsettia, Climbing Cl HT, *mr*, 1950, Thompson, D.L.; Rosemont Nursery Co.

Point Clear Min, *w*, 1991, (TALpoi); *Azure Sea* × *Party Girl*; Taylor, Pete & Kay; Taylor's Roses, 1992. Flowers white, reverse same, light yellow base, full (26-40 petals), small (0-4 cms) blooms borne mostly singly; slight fragrance; foliage small, medium green, semi-glossy; some prickles; low (40 cms), upright growth.

Poker® HT, *dp*, 1985, (HAVaps); *Red Planet* × *Sonia*; Verschuren, Ted; H.A. Verschuren. Flowers deep pink, semi-dbl. (11 petals), cupped, large blooms in sprays of 6-8; heavy fragrance; foliage medium, medium green, semi-glossy; fruit rounded; bushy, medium.

Poker Chip Min, *rb*, 1979, *Sheri Anne* × *(Yellow Jewel* × *Tamango Seedling)*; Saville. Bud

pointed; flowers red with yellow reverse, dbl. (28 petals), high-centered, medium; very fragrant; foliage glossy, dark; fruit large; vigorous, compact growth.

Pokornyana S, *lp*, (*R.* × *pokornyana* Kmet; *R. scopulosa* Briquet); *R. canina* × *R. glauca*; Cult. 1916. Flowers to 1³/₄ in. diameter; sepals appendage; leaflets doubly serrate. Hungary; (40).

Polar Bear HP (OGR), *w*, 1934, *Schoener's Nutkana* × *New Century*; Nicolas; J&P. Flowers white tinted blush, becoming pure white, very dbl., globular, large; very fragrant; foliage large, leathery, wrinkled; vigorous, bushy growth; recurrent bloom.

Polaris LCl, *w*, 1939, (*R. wichuraiana* × *R. setigera)* × *R. foetida bicolor*; Horvath; Wayside Gardens Co. Flowers pure snow-white, dbl., open, borne in clusters; very fragrant; foliage glossy, light; very vigorous, climbing (12-15 ft.) growth; profuse, non-recurrent bloom.

Polarstern® HT, *w*, 1982, (TANlarpost; Polar Star); Tantau, M. Flowers pale yellow to white, dbl. (35 petals), exhibition, medium; no fragrance; foliage medium, medium green, matt; bushy growth. ROTY, 1985.

Pôle Nord HT, *w*, 1944, Mallerin; A. Meilland. Bud long, pointed; flowers pure white, base tinted greenish; vigorous growth.

Poliarchus S, *w*, *Seedling* × *R.* × *Harisonii*; Central Exp. Farm. Flowers cream flushed salmon, fading rapidly; spreading shrub (4 ft.); non-recurrent bloom; hardy.

Polina HT, *dp*, 1984, *Mistica* × *Chenon*; Staikov, Prof. Dr. V.; Kalaydjiev and Chorbadjiiski. Flowers deep pink, dbl. (38 petals), large; foliage dark, leathery; bushy growth.

Polka F, *mp*, 1959, *Moulin Rouge* × *Fashion*; Meilland, M.L.; URS. Bud ovoid; flowers medium pink, dbl. (42 petals), high-centered to cupped, large (3-3¹/₂ in.) blooms in flat clusters; fragrant; foliage leathery; vigorous, bushy growth.

Polka Dot Min, *w*, 1956, *Golden Glow* × *Zee*; Moore, R.S.; Sequoia Nursery. Flowers ivory white, dbl., small; foliage dark, leathery; vigorous, dwarf (10 in.), bushy growth.

Polka Time S, *op*, 1984, *Bonfire Night* × *Countryman*; Buck; Iowa State University. Bud ovoid, pointed; flowers salmon tinted yellow, veined pink, dbl. (38 petals), imbricated, cupped, 5 in. blooms borne 1-10 per cluster; fragrant; foliage dark, leathery; awl-like, tan prickles; low, bushy, compact growth; repeat bloom; hardy.

Pollentia HT, *dp*, 1942, Dot, P. Bud large, long pointed; flowers satiny strawberry-red, dbl.

(40 petals), high-centered; very fragrant; foliage dark, glossy; upright, compact growth.

Pollmeriana Sp (OGR), *lp*, *R. canina selection*; Pollmer. Very vigorous, almost thornless; used as an under stock.

Polly HT, *w*, 1927, *Ophelia Seedling* × *Mme. Colette Martinet*; Beckwith. Bud long, pointed; flowers cream, center tinted pink or light orange, fading white, dbl. (38 petals), high-centered, large; very fragrant.

Polly Flinders Min, *w*, 1954, *Little Princess (Knight)* × *Fashion*; Robinson, T. Flowers cream tinted copper-orange, dbl. (30 petals), small (1 in.); foliage veined red.

Polly Perkins HT, *op*, 1967, Gregory. Flowers orange-cerise, pointed; fragrant; foliage dark; very free growth.

Polo Club™ HT, *yb*, 1986, (AROtigy); *Gingersnap* × *Young Quinn*; Christensen, Jack; Armstrong Roses, 1986. Flowers yellow bordered red, fading cream with pink edges, dbl. (36 reflexed petals), small to medium, borne usually singly or in sprays of 2-3; slight fragrance; foliage medium, dark green, semi-glossy; straight, small, few, greenish to light brown prickles; no fruit; upright, bushy, tall growth.

Polonaise HT, *mr*, 1961, *Carrousel* × *(Chrysler Imperial* × *Seedling)*; Abrams, Von; Peterson; Dering. Flowers bright red, dbl. (40-50 ruffled petals), high-centered, very large (6 in.); fragrant; foliage glossy; vigorous, upright, compact growth. RULED EXTINCT 1/85.

Polonaise S, *dp*, 1984, *San Francisco* × *Prairie Princess*; Buck; Iowa State University. Bud ovoid, pointed; flowers deep pink, dbl. (43 petals), imbricated, 3 in. blooms borne 5-10 per cluster; foliage leathery, dark green with reddish veination; awl-like, red-brown prickles; dwarf, upright, bushy growth; repeat bloom; hardy.

Polstjärnan R, *w*, 1937, (Polestar; The Polar Star; The Wasa Star; Wasastiernan; White Rose of Finland; White Star of Finland); *R. beggeriana hybrid*; Wasast-jarna. Flowers pure white, very small blooms in clusters; very vigorous (to 18 ft.) growth; non-recurrent bloom; very hardy.

Poly Peace F, *yb*, 1959, *Masquerade* × *Peace*; Leenders, J. Flowers golden yellow edged rose-pink, semi-dbl., high-centered to cupped, large; strong stems; slightly fragrant; foliage dark, glossy; very vigorous, tall, bushy growth.

Poly Prim F, *dy*, 1953, *Goldilocks* × *Golden Rapture*; Eddie. Flowers deep yellow, dbl. (70 petals), well shaped, large (3 in.) borne in clusters; fragrant; foliage dark, glossy; very vigorous, bushy growth. GM, NRS, 1954.

Polyana S, *dp*, 1925, *R. rugosa* × *Polyantha (Mme. Norbert Levavasseur)*; Skinner. Flowers pink; almost identical with F.J. Grootendorst.

Polyantha In the horticultural sense (as distinct from *R. polyantha* Siebold; Zuccarini), loosely applied to descendants of *R. multiflora* and cluster-flowered roses in general.

Polyantha Grandiflora HMult (OGR), *w*, (Gentiliana); 1888. Flowers white, single.

Polygold® F, *dy*, 1982, (TANlypolo); Tantau, M., 1978. Flowers deep yellow, semi-dbl., medium; no fragrance; foliage medium, light green, glossy; bushy growth.

Polynesian Pearl Gr, *lp*, 1977, *Seedling* × *Tropicana*; Takatori; Japan Rose Nursery. Bud ovoid; flowers shell-pink, dbl. (35-59 petals), high-centered, small (2 in.); fragrant (fruity); foliage leathery; upright growth.

Polynesian Sunset HT, *op*, 1965, *Diamond Jubilee Seedling* × *Hawaii*; Boerner; J&P. Bud long; flowers coral-orange, dbl., high-centered, large (6 in.); fragrant (fruity); foliage leathery; vigorous, bushy growth.

Pompadour HT, *dp*, 1979, *Molly McGredy* × *Prima Ballerina*; Murray, N.; Rasmussen's. Bud pointed; flowers deep pink, dbl. (43 petals), high-centered, large (5½ in.); very fragrant (fruity); foliage dark, glossy; bushy, compact growth.

Pompadour Red F, *dp*, 1951, *Orange Triumph* × *Anne Poulsen*; deRuiter; J&P. Bud globular; flowers rose-red, dbl. (30-35 petals), cupped, large (3½ in.); fragrant (fruity); vigorous growth; a florists' pot plant.

Pompon C (OGR), *w*, Flowers white, streaked lilac-pink, dbl., small.

Pompon G (OGR), *dr*, 1835, Joly. Flowers brilliant crimson.

Pompon G (OGR), *w*, 1858, (Pompon Panachée); Robert & Moreau. Flowers cream to white, striped dark pink, dbl., well-formed, flat; foliage very small; wiry, erect growth.

Pompon Beauty F, *or*, 1949, *Polyantha Seedling* × *Hybrid Tea Seedling*; deRuiter; Spek. Flowers scarlet, very dbl., borne in large trusses; vigorous growth; (28). GM, NRS, 1950.

Pompon Blanc Parfait A, *w*, 1876. Flowers blush-white, pompon form; almost without prickles; compact growth.

Pompon de Paris Ch (OGR), *mp*, 1839, *A variety of R. chinensis minima*; Originator unknown. Bud very pointed; flowers bright pink, dbl., very small. Said to be identical to 'Rouletii' except for differences due to culture.

Pompon de Paris, Climbing Cl Ch (OGR), *mp*.

Pompon de Saint-François C (OGR), *dp*, Flowers deep violet-pink, full, small; low, bushy growth. Considerable confusion exists with regard to this variety.

Pompon Rouge F, *mr*, 1971, *Reverence × Miracle*; Delforge. Bud ovoid; flowers brilliant red, very dbl., full, medium; foliage soft; dwarf, bushy growth.

Poncheau-Capiaumont HCh (OGR), *dr*, (Rose Ponceau; Rose Poncheaux; Rosa Poncheaux); Originator unknown. Prior to 1848. Flowers dark red, borne in clusters of 3; foliage curiously stiff, thick, deeply veined.

Ponctuée M (OGR), *pb*, 1847, (Ma Ponctuée); Moreau-Robert. Flowers rose, spotted white, semi-dbl., medium; moderate growth; recurrent; raised at Angers.

Ponderosa® F, *or*, 1970, (KORpon); *Seedling × Marlena*; Kordes, R.; Kordes. Bud globular; flowers red-orange, dbl., cupped, medium; slightly fragrant; foliage leathery; vigorous, dwarf, bushy growth. ADR, 1971.

Pontbriant HT, *mp*, 1948, *Mme. Joseph Perraud × Kidwai*; Gaujard. Flowers bright pink, dbl., very large; slightly fragrant; foliage leathery; vigorous growth.

Pontcarral HT, *dp*, 1943, *Charles P. Kilham × (Charles P. Kilham × Margaret McGredy)*; Meilland, F.; A. Meilland. Bud long, pointed; flowers strawberry-red, reverse dull yellow, semi-dbl. to dbl., cupped, medium; slightly fragrant; foliage leathery; moderate, bushy growth.

Ponte d'Arrabida HT, *op*, 1963, *Grand'mère Jenny × Seedling*; Moreira da Silva. Flowers salmon-pink veined deep pink.

Poornima HT, *ly*, 1971, *Fernand Arles × Seedling*; Pal, Dr. B.P.; K.S.G. Sons. Bud long, pointed; flowers light yellow, dbl. (46 petals), high-centered, large blooms borne singly; fragrant; foliage medium, medium green, smooth; bushy, tall growth.

Popcorn Min, *w*, 1973, *Katharina Zeimet × Diamond Jewel*; Morey; Pixie Treasures. Bud ovoid; flowers pure white, semi-dbl. (13 petals), small (1 in.); fragrant (honey); foliage glossy; upright growth.

Poppet F, *mp*, 1979, *Spartan × Arthur Bell*; Bees. Flowers medium pink, dbl. (60 petals), cupped, large (3½ in.); slightly fragrant; foliage light green, matt; upright growth.

Popping White Min, *w*, 1977, Lyon. Bud ovoid; flowers white, semi-dbl. (12 petals), small (1 in.); vigorous, compact growth.

Poppy HT, *op*, 1939, Archer. Flowers coral-pink, passing to shell-pink, dbl., petals serrated; fragrant; vigorous growth.

Poppy F, *or*, 1960, *Cocorico × Geranium Red*; Soenderhousen; Hoersholm Nursery. Flowers scarlet, semi-dbl., medium (2-2½ in.), borne in clusters; very vigorous growth.

Poppy Flash F, *or*, 1971, (MEIléna; Rusticana); *(Dany Robin × Fire King) × (Alain × Mutabilis)*; Meilland, 1972. Flowers vermilion, dbl. (20 petals), large (3 in.); slightly fragrant (fruity); vigorous, bushy growth. GM, Geneva, 1970; Rome, 1972.

Poppy Flash, Climbing Cl F, *or*, 1975, (MEIlénasar; Rusticana, Climbing); Paolino; URS.

Pops Min, *dp*, 1983, (TINpops); *Sheri Anne × Little Girl*; Bennett, Dee; Tiny Petals Nursery. Flowers deep pink, dbl. (20 petals), HT form, small; slight fragrance; foliage medium, medium green, semi-glossy; bushy growth.

Porcelain F, *lp*, 1985, *Dainty Maid × ((Tropicana × Anna Wheatcroft) × (Tropicana × Anna Wheatcroft))*; Gobbee, W.D. Flowers shell pink over cream, semi-dbl., medium; slight fragrance; foliage small, dark, semi-glossy; upright, bushy growth.

Porcelain Princess Min, *pb*, 1990, *Libby × Seedling*; Gruenbauer, Richard, 1984; Richard Gruenbauer. Bud rounded; flowers cream with pale pink edging, aging light pink, dbl. (35 petals), high-centered, exhibition, medium, borne in sprays of 2-3; no fragrance; foliage medium, dark green, semi-glossy; prickles straight, tan; fruit oblong, orange-red; bushy, medium growth.

Porcelina HT, *w*, 1983, (INTerval); *Seedling × Golden Times*; Interplant. Flowers cream with pink tint, dbl. (30 petals), medium blooms borne singly or in small clusters; fragrant; foliage large, dark, glossy; few prickles; upright growth; greenhouse variety.

Portadown HT, *dr*, 1928, McGredy. Bud long, pointed; flowers velvety deep crimson, dbl., high-centered, large; slightly fragrant; vigorous, bushy growth. GM, NRS, 1929.

Portadown Bedder HT, *op*, 1929, McGredy. Bud long, pointed; flowers scarlet-cerise on orange ground, reverse orange-yellow flushed cerise, dbl., high-centered; fragrant; foliage glossy, dark; vigorous, bushy growth.

Portadown Fragrance HT, *op*, 1931, McGredy. Bud long, pointed; flowers brilliant orange-salmon-pink, flushed orange-scarlet, dbl., high-centered; very fragrant; foliage thick, bronze; low, sprawling growth. GM, NRS, 1928.

Portadown Glory HT, *my*, 1932, McGredy. Flowers clear canary-yellow, dbl., well formed, large; fragrant; foliage glossy, bright; vigorous growth. GM, NRS, 1933.

Portadown Sally HT, *mr*, 1931, McGredy. Bud long, pointed; flowers crimson-carmine, base yellow, reverse sulphur-yellow, semi-dbl., high-centered; fragrant; foliage thick, glossy; vigorous growth.

Portchester Pink HT, *dp*, 1978, *Red Devil sport*; Poole. Flowers deep rose-pink; very fragrant.

Portia HT, *lp*, 1910, Paul, W. Flowers pale rose, center yellow.

Portia HT, *mr*, 1921, *Bridesmaid* × *Sunburst*; Bees. Flowers nasturtium-red, paling to pink, dbl.; fragrant.

Portland An old class of roses, taking its name from the first of the class, Duchess of Portland. Probably created by crosses between Autumn Damask and Slater's Crimson China. With the Hybrid Chinas and Boubons, they fathered the Hybrid Perpetuals.

Portland HT, *dp*, 1958, Lowe. Flowers rose-madder, dbl., large; fragrant; foliage dark, glossy; vigorous, symmetrical growth.

Portland Dawn Min, *pb*, 1988, (SEAtip); *Rise 'n' Shine* × *(Copper Pot* × *Maxi)*; McCann, Sean, 1989. Flowers veined pink and bronze, dbl. (20 petals), small; slight fragrance; foliage small, medium green, semi-glossy; bushy growth.

Portland Pink F, *dp*, 1957, *Pinocchio sport*; Murrel, E. Flowers glowing deep pink.

Portland Rose Festival HT, *rb*, 1992, (DORjure); *Osiria* × *Pharaon*; Dorieux, Francois; Roses by Edmunds, 1992. Flowers strawberry red, white reverse, exceptional form with clear sharply defined colors, full (26-40 petals), large (7+ cms) blooms borne mostly singly; fragrant; foliage large, dark green, glossy; some prickles; tall (150 cms), upright growth.

Portland Trailblazer HT, *dr*, 1975, (Big Chief); *Ernest H. Morse* × *Red Planet*; Dickson, A.; Edmunds, 1978. Flowers crimson, dbl. (28 petals), high-centered, large (5½ in.); fragrant; foliage large, matt, brittle.

Porto HT, *dr*, 1934, *Capt. F. Bald* × *Mrs. Edward Powell*; Mallerin. Flowers deep garnet tinted bright scarlet, dbl., large; slightly fragrant; foliage leathery; vigorous growth.

Portofino F, *rb*, 1964, *Miramar* × *Seedling*; Delforge. Flowers red, reverse deep yellow; low growth.

Portrait HT, *pb*, 1971, (MEYpink); Stéphanie de Monaco); *Pink Parfait* × *Pink Peace*; Meyer, C.; C-P. Bud ovoid; flowers medium pink and light pink blend, dbl., medium; fragrant; foliage glossy, dark; upright, bushy growth. AARS, 1972 (First amateur winner).

Portrait of Jenny F, *dr*, 1951, *Donald Prior Seedling*; Hope. Flowers crimson, dbl. (30 petals), medium (2 in.), borne in trusses; foliage dark; vigorous, bushy growth.

Portugal Pink HT, *dp*, 1959, *Independence* × *Seedling*; Mondial Roses. Bud globular; flowers deep pink, dbl., cupped, large; very fragrant; foliage leathery; vigorous, upright growth.

Postillon HT, *ab*, 1962, *Peace* × *Seedling*; Verbeek. Flowers coppery yellow, dbl., large; foliage glossy; moderate growth.

Posy F, *pb*, 1951, *Rosenelfe* × *Dusky Maiden*; LeGrice. Flowers clear pink, reverse deeper, dbl. (30 petals), large (3 in.) blooms in large clusters; slightly fragrant; foliage dark; dwarf growth.

Pot Black Min, *dr*, 1985, (PEAnut); *Seedling* × *Seedling*; Pearce, C.A.; Limes Rose Nursery. Flowers dark red, dbl. (40+ petals), small; no fragrance; foliage small, medium green, matt; bushy growth.

Pot o' Gold HT, *my*, 1980, (DICdivine); *Eurorose* × *Whisky Mac*; Dickson, P. Bud pointed; flowers medium yellow, dbl. (32 petals), flat blooms borne 7 per cluster; very fragrant; foliage mid-green with strong purple veins; brown prickles; bushy, medium growth.

Potifar HT, *ab*, 1979, (Wieteke van Dordt); *Royal Dane* × *Pjerrot*; Poulsen, N.D.; A. Grumet, 1979; Jan Spek, 1982. Flowers pale peachy orange, dbl. (25 petals), urn-shaped, large blooms borne usually singly; slight fragrance; foliage large, leathery, dark, matt; bushy.

Potluck™ Min, *dr*, 1984, (LAVpot); *Dwarfking '78* × *Little Liza*; Laver, Keith. Flowers dark red, dbl. (20 petals), small; no fragrance; foliage small, medium green, glossy; compact, bushy, tiny growth.

Potluck™ White Min, *w*, 1985, (LAVwyte); *Baby Katie* × *Mountie*; Laver, Keith, 1987. Flowers white, dbl. (35 petals); no fragrance; foliage small, light green, glossy; spreading growth.

Potluck™ Yellow Min, *my*, 1985, (LAVglo; Spicy Minijet; Yellow Mini-Wonder); *Rise 'n' Shine* × *Lemon Delight*; Laver, Keith, 1986. Flowers medium yellow, dbl. (20 petals); no fragrance; foliage small, medium green, semi-glossy; bushy growth.

Potluck™ Cream Min, *ly*, 1987, (LAVacre; LAVcream); *Cornsilk* × *Seedling*; Laver, Keith; Springwood Roses, 1988. Flowers light yellow center, cream edges, reverse cream with yellow base, dbl. (30 petals), high-centered, medium, borne usually singly and in sprays of 5-6; no fragrance; foliage medium, medium green, matt; prickles slender, brown; no fruit; bushy, low, very free flowering growth.

Potluck™ Gold Min, *my*, 1991, (LAVgold); *Dorola × Julie Ann*; Laver, Keith, 1987; Springwood Roses. Flowers yellow, dbl. (20 petals), opening flat, small, borne in sprays of 3-5; no fragrance; foliage small, medium green, semi-glossy; bushy, low, very dwarf growth.

Potluck™ Orange Min, *or*, 1989, (LAVjack; Orange Mini-Wonder); *Julie Ann × Potluck*; Laver, Keith, 1990. Bud ovoid; flowers intense, dark orange, dbl. (24 petals), compact, full, small, borne in sprays of 3-6; no fragrance; foliage small, medium green, matt; prickles straight, pointed, light brown; no fruit; bushy, low, symmetrical growth.

Potluck™ Pink Min, *mp*, 1992, (LAValot); *June Laver × Julie Ann*; Laver, Keith G.; Springwood Roses. Flowers rose pink, full (26-40 petals), small (0-4 cms) blooms borne mostly single; slight fragrance; foliage small, medium green, matt; few prickles; low (25-30 cms), compact growth.

Potluck™ Purple Min, *dr*, 1992, (LAVpup); *(June Laver × Painted Doll) × Springwood Purple*; Laver, Keith G.; Springwood Roses. Flowers fuchsia, moderately full (15-25 petals), small (0-4 cms) blooms borne in small clusters; micro-mini; no fragrance; foliage small, medium green, matt; few prickles; low (25-30 cms), compact growth.

Potluck™ Red Min, *dr*, 1988, (LAVmin); *Breezy × June Laver*; Laver, Keith; Springwood Roses, 1989. Bud pointed; flowers deep red, dbl. (35 petals), compact, full, small, borne singly; no fragrance; foliage small, dark green, young edged in red, matt; frickles none; fruit globular, orange-red; upright, low growth.

Potton Heritage HT, *rb*, 1986, (HARsprice); *Precious Platinum × Dr. A.J. Verhage*; Harkness, 1987. Flowers plum red, reverse straw-yellow, dbl. (32 petals), high-centered, large; fragrant; foliage large, dark, glossy; bushy, branching growth.

POUlaps S, *ly*, 1985, (Armorique Nirpaysage); *Seedling × Kalahari*; Olesen, M.&P.; Poulsen's Roses. Flowers creamy yellow, dbl. (20 petals), urn-shaped, large blooms in clusters of 1-5; fragrant; foliage large, leathery, dark, glossy; sets fruit; tall, upright, bushy growth.

POUlink Min, *mp*, 1988, (Pink Hit); *Seedling × Seedling*; Olesen, Mogens; Pernille; Poulsen Roser ApS, 1986. Flowers medium pink, semi-dbl. (6-14 petals), small; no fragrance; foliage small, medium green, semi-glossy; bushy, compact, even, abundant growth.

POUloni HT, *op*, 1977, (Benoni '75; Vision); Poulsen, N.D.; Poulsen's (Olesen); Weeks Roses, 1990. Flowers medium salmon red, dbl. (22 petals), well-formed, large blooms borne 1-3 per stem; slight fragrance; foliage dark, glossy; vigorous, spreading growth.

Poulsen's Bedder F, *lp*, 1948, (Poulsen's Grupperose); *Orléans Rose × Talisman*; Poulsen, S.; Poulsen; McGredy, 1948; C-P, 1952. Flowers clear pink, semi-dbl., large (3 in.) blooms in trusses; slightly fragrant; foliage bronze; vigorous, upright growth.   GM, Portland.

Poulsen's Copper F, *op*, 1940, *Grethe Poulsen × Souv. de Claudius Pernet*; Poulsen, S.; Poulsen; C-P, 1940; McGredy, 1946. Flowers rosepink to orange, base yellow, dbl. (25-35 petals), cupped, large (3-3½ in.), borne in clusters; slightly fragrant (spicy); foliage small, light green; vigorous growth.

Poulsen's Crimson F, *dr*, 1950, *Orange Triumph × (Betty Uprichard × Johanniszauber)*; Poulsen, S.; Poulsen; McGredy. Flowers dark red, single (6 petals), medium blooms in clusters; slight fragrance; foliage medium, dark, matt; vigorous, bushy growth.

Poulsen's Delight F, *lp*, 1948, (Fru Julie Poulsen); *Else Poulsen × Seedling*; Poulsen, S.; McGredy. Flowers apple-blossom-pink, single (5-7 petals), borne in trusses; foliage dark, glossy; vigorous, upright growth.

Poulsen's Fairy F, *my*, 1940, (Rodovrerosen); *Orléans Rose × Dainty Bess*; Poulsen, S.; Poulsen. Flowers pink, single, borne in large clusters; very vigorous, tall growth.

Poulsen's Jubilaeumsrose Min, *yb*, 1978, (POUljub); *Darling Flame × Seedling*; Poulsen, N.D. Flowers deep pink and yellow blend, dbl. (28 petals), medium blooms in clusters; slight fragrance; foliage dark, glossy; upright growth.

Poulsen's Park Rose S, *lp*, 1953, *Great Western × Karen Poulsen*; Poulsen. Flowers silvery pink, dbl., well-shaped, large (4-5 in.) blooms in trusses; vigorous (6 × 6 ft.) growth.

Poulsen's Peach F, *ab*, 1948, Poulsen, S. Flowers peach, semi-dbl., cupped, large blooms inclusters; slight fragrance; foliage medium, medium green, semi-glossy; medium, bushy growth.

Poulsen's Pearl F, *lp*, 1949, *Else Poulsen × Seedling*; Poulsen, S.; Poulsen, 1948. Flowers pearly pink, single (5 petals), blooms intrusses; foliage light; vigorous. RNRS, GM.

Poulsen's Pink F, *lp*, 1939, *Golden Salmon × Yellow HT*; Poulsen; Poulsen, 1939; C-P, 1942. Flowers soft pink with yellow base, semi-dbl., cupped blooms in clusters; slightly fragrant; foliage glossy, light green; vigorous.

Poulsen's Scarlet F, *dp*, 1941, *D.T. Poulsen* × *Red HT*; Poulsen, S. Flowers bright rose, dbl. (30 petals), medium (2½ in.) blooms in clusters; slightly fragrant; bushy.

Poulsen's Supreme F, *mp*, 1945, (Kelleriis-Rose); *Poulsen's Pink* × *Seedling*; Poulsen, S.; McGredy, 1953. Flowers pink, semi-dbl., large (3 in.), borne in trusses; foliage light green; very free growth.

Poulsen's Yellow F, *my*, 1938, *Mrs. W.H. Cutbush* × *Gottfried Keller*; Poulsen, S.; C-P, 1939. Bud ovoid; flowers medium yellow, semi-dbl., blooms in clusters; very fragrant; foliage glossy; (21). GM, NRS, 1937.

Pounder Star HT, *mr*, 1981, (MACnic; Karma); *John Waterer* × *Kalahari*; McGredy, Sam; Roses by Fred Edmunds, 1982. Bud long, pointed; flowers medium red, dbl. (20 petals), exhibition blooms borne singly; old rose to spicy fragrance; foliage dark, glossy; small, curved prickles; upright, medium growth.

Poupée F, *lp*, 1965, Lens. Flowers flesh-pink, dbl. (25-30 petals), cupped, large (3-3½ in.); slightly fragrant; foliage glossy; vigorous, upright growth.

Pour Vous Madame F, *dp*, 1961, Gaujard; Gandy. Flowers rose-red, reverse lighter, dbl. (25 petals), open, large (4 in.); slightly fragrant; foliage dark; vigorous growth.

Pourpre Ch (OGR), *m*, 1827, Vibert. Flowers deep purple.

Pourpre du Luxembourg M (OGR), *m*, 1848, Hardy. Flowers pink, opening to lilac-pink.

Powder Puff F, *lp*, 1959, *Masquerade* × *Masquerade Seedling*; Mason, A.L.; F. Mason. Flowers creamy light pink, becoming darker, dbl., open, medium; slightly fragrant; foliage glossy; bushy growth.

Poyntzfield HT, *ab*, 1977, *Bonsoir* × *Percy Thrower*; Simpson, J.W. Flowers apricot, dbl. (35 petals), large (5 in.); slightly fragrant; foliage glossy, reddish-green; vigorous growth.

Poznan HT, *dr*, 1966, Grabezewski. Bud ovoid; flowers vivid dark crimson, dbl., well formed, large; vigorous growth.

Praecox Sp (OGR), *w*, *R. sericea form*; Good garden form of *R. sericea*, which see.

Prairie Breeze S, *m*, 1978, *Dornröschen* × *(Josef Rothmund* × *R. laxa)*; Buck; Iowa State University. Bud ovoid, pointed; flowers tyrian purple, dbl. (25 petals), cupped, large (4½ in.); fragrant (spicy); foliage olive-green, leathery; upright, bushy, spreading; repeat.

Prairie Charm S, *op*, 1959, *Prairie Youth* × *Prairie Wren*; Morden Exp. Farm. Flowers bright salmon-coral, semi-dbl.; stems arching; foliage light green; height 4 ft.; free, non-urgent bloom; hardy on prairies.

Prairie Clogger S, *mr*, 1984, *Carefree Beauty* × *(Marlena* × *Pippa's Song)*; Buck; Iowa State University. Bud medium-small, ovoid, pointed; flowers medium red, 8-10 petals, shallow-cupped to flat, 2½ in. blooms borne 1-10 per cluster; fragrant; foliage leathery, dark olive green; awl-like, tan prickles; vigorous, erect, bushy growth; repeat bloom.

Prairie Dawn S, *mp*, 1959, *Prairie Youth* × *(Ross Rambler* × *(Dr. W. Van Fleet* × *R. spinosissima altaica))*; Modern Exp. Farm. Flowers glowing pink, dbl., medium (2-2½ in.); foliage dark, glossy; upright (5 ft.) growth; repeat bloom on current season's wood; hardy on prairies.

Prairie Fire S, *mr*, 1960, *Red Rocket* × *R. arkansana*; Phillips; Univ. of Minn. Bud pointed; flowers bright red, base white, semi-dbl. (9 petals), medium (2½-3 in.) blooms in clusters of 35-50 on long stems; fragrant; foliage glossy, dark; very vigorous, tall growth; recurrent.

Prairie Flower S, *rb*, 1975, *(Rose of Tralee* × *Queen Elizabeth)* × *(Morning Stars* × *Suzanne)*; Buck; Iowa State University. Bud ovoid, pointed; flowers cardinal-red, center white, single (7 petals), flat, medium (2-3 in.); slightly fragrant (old rose); foliage dark, leathery; erect, bushy growth; repeat bloom.

Prairie Harvest S, *ly*, 1985, *Carefree Beauty* × *Sunsprite*; Buck; Iowa State University, 1984. Flowers medium yellow, dbl. (43 petals), imbricated, large (4-5 in.) blooms borne 1-15 per cluster; fragrant; foliage leathery, glossy, medium, dark; tan prickles; upright, bushy growth; repeat bloom; hardy.

Prairie Heritage S, *op*, 1978, *(Vera Dalton* × *Prairie Princess)* × *(Apricot Nectar* × *Prairie Princess)*; Buck; Iowa State University. Bud ovoid, pointed; flowers peach to coral-pink, dbl. (50 petals), cupped, quartered, large (4-5 in.); fragrant; foliage dark, leathery; vigorous, upright, spreading, bushy growth; repeat bloom.

Prairie Joy S, *mp*, 1990, *Prairie Princess* × *Morden Cardinette*; Collicutt, L.M.; Agriculture Canada, 1990. Flowers medium pink, aging light to medium pink, dbl. (30-40 petals), borne singly or in sprays of 1-6; slight fragrance; foliage medium, medium green, matt, high resistance to powdery mildew and blackspot; tall, bushy growth; sparse, repeat bloom.

Prairie Lass S, *pb*, 1978, *(Hawkeye Belle* × *Vera Dalton)* × *(Dornröschen* × *(World's Fair* × *Applejack))*; Buck; Iowa State University. Bud ovoid, pointed; flowers claret-rose to rose-red, dbl. (28 petals), large (3½ in.); fragrant (spicy); foliage dark, leathery; vigorous, upright, spreading, bushy growth; repeat bloom.

Prairie Maid S, *w*, 1959, (*Ophelia* × *Turkes Rugosa Samling*) × *R. spinosissima altaica*; Morden Exp. Farm. Flowers cream, dbl. (25 petals); fragrant; compact (4 ft.) growth; intermittent bloom; hardy on prairies.

Prairie Moon LCl, *ly*, 1953, *R. maximowicziana pilosa* × *Autumn*; Maney; Iowa State College. Bud ovoid, deep yellow; flowers creamy yellow, dbl. (30-35 petals), large, borne in clusters of 4-5; fragrant; foliage glossy, dark, leathery; vigorous, climbing (15 ft.) growth; abundant, non-recurrent bloom.

Prairie Pinkie S, *op*, 1958, Skinner. Flowers deep coral-pink, loosely dbl.; very fragrant; foliage like *R. spinosissima*; upright (2½ ft.), bushy growth; midsummer bloom.

Prairie Princess S, *op*, 1972, *Carrousel* × (*Morning Stars* × *Suzanne*); Buck; Iowa State University. Bud ovoid, long, pointed; flowers light coral-pink, semi-dbl., large; slightly fragrant; foliage large, dark, leathery; vigorous, upright growth; repeat bloom.

Prairie Red Min, *rb*, 1980, *Seedling* × *Seedling*; Lyon. Flowers red-yellow blend, semi-dbl. (18 petals), blooms borne singly or several together; fragrant; foliage tiny, medium green; brownish prickles curved downward; bushy, upright growth.

Prairie Sailor HSpn (OGR), *yb*, 1946, Pedigree involved *Dr. W. Van Fleet, Turkes Rugosa Samling and R. spinosissima altaica*; Morden Exp. Farm. Flowers golden yellow deeply edged bright red, single; vigorous (6 ft.) growth; profuse, non-recurrent bloom; hardy on prairies.

Prairie Schooner™ Min, *rb*, 1986, (KINschoon); *Vera Dalton* × *Sheri Anne*; King, Gene; AGM Min. Roses. Flowers red, reverse yellow edged red, dbl. (22 petals), high-centered, exhibition, medium blooms borne singly and in sprays of 5-10; slightly fragrant; foliage small, dark, matt; straight, brown prickles; no fruit; upright growth.

Prairie Squire S, *mp*, 1984, *Countryman* × *Carefree Beauty*; Buck; Iowa State University. Flowers medium pink, dbl. (20 petals), cupped, large (4-5 in.) blooms borne 1-10 per cluster; light fragrance; foliage leathery, dark green, tinted copper; awl-like, tan prickles; vigorous, erect, bushy, spreading growth; repeat bloom; hardy.

Prairie Star S, *ly*, 1975, *Tickled Pink* × *Prairie Princess*; Buck; Iowa State University. Bud ovoid, pointed; flowers pale chrome-yellow,

tinted pink, dbl. (54 petals), cupped, large (3½-4 in.); fragrant (green apple); foliage dark, leathery; vigorous, erect, bushy growth; repeat bloom.

Prairie Sunset S, *yb*, 1984, *Bonfire Night* × (*Music Maker* × *Athlone*); Buck; Iowa State University. Flowers deep pink, reverse yellow, dbl. (38 petals), urn-shaped, large (4 in.) blooms borne 5-10 per cluster; fragrant; foliage moderately large, leathery, dark; tan prickles; erect, bushy, slightly spreading growth; repeat bloom; hardy.

Prairie Valor S, *mr*, 1984, ((*Dornröschen* × (*Josef Rothmund* × *R. laxa*)) × *Rose du Roi a Fleurs Pourpres*) × (*Music Maker* × *Topsi*); Buck; Iowa State University. Flowers medium red, dbl. (38 petals), cupped, large (4-5 in.) blooms borne 3-5 per cluster; damask fragrance; foliage leathery, dark; awl-like, brown prickles; upright, bushy growth; repeat bloom; hardy.

Prairie Wren S, *mp*, 1946, Pedigree involves *Ophelia, Turkes Rugosa Samling* & *R. spinosissima altaica*; Morden Exp. Farm. Flowers rich pink, semi-dbl., large; heavy, non-recurrent bloom; very hardy.

Prairie Youth S, *op*, 1948, ((*Ross Rambler* × *Dr. W. Van Fleet*) × *R. suffulta*) × ((*Dr. W. Van Fleet* × *Turkes Rugosa Samling*) × *R. spinosissima altaica*); Morden Exp. Farm. Flowers pure salmon-pink, semi-dbl., blooms in clusters; slightly fragrant; vigorous (6 ft.) growth; repeat bloom; completely hardy on prairies.

Praise of Jiro F, *or*, 1959, *Korona* × *Spartan*; Kordes, R. Bud ovoid; flowers orange-red, dbl. (30 petals), large, borne in clusters; slightly fragrant; foliage leathery; vigorous, upright, bushy growth.

Praline HT, *dr*, 1955, *Camelia* × *Seedling*; Robichon. Flowers carmine-purple to crimson; slightly fragrant; foliage glossy.

Präsent F, *ab*, 1969, (Present); *Highlight* × *Allgold*; Haenchen; Teschendorff. Flowers yellow-orange, reverse yellow, dbl. (27 petals), high-centered, large; fragrant; foliage dark, glossy, leathery; vigorous, upright, bushy growth.

Präsident Dr. H. C. Schröder HT, *mr*, 1959, *New Yorker* × *Seedling*; Kordes, R. Flowers velvety deep red, dbl., large; strong stems.

Präsident Hindenburg Pol, *mr*, 1927, *Greta Kluis* × *Seedling*; Bom; P. Lambert. Flowers carmine to deep red, base white, dbl.

Prattigosa HRg (S), *mp*, 1953, *R. prattii* × *R. rugosa alba*; Kordes. Bud long, pointed, red; flowers pink, single, very large; slightly fragrant; foliage leathery, light green; vigorous (3½ ft.), upright, bushy growth.

Precilla HT, *dy*, 1973, *Peer Gynt × Seedling*; Kordes. Bud ovoid; flowers deep golden yellow, dbl., cupped, medium; fragrant; foliage dark, leathery; vigorous, upright growth.

Precious HT, *pb*, 1985, *(Briarcliff × Carla Seedling) × Pink Parfait*; Dawson, Charles P. Flowers blend of light, medium and deep pink, reverse medium pink, dbl. (35 petals), exhibition, large; fragrant; foliage medium, medium green, semi-glossy; very few prickles; upright, bushy growth.

Precious Moments Min, *my*, 1982, (LYOpr); *Dandy Lyon × Seedling*; Lyon. Flowers medium yellow, dbl. (35 petals), medium; fragrant; foliage medium, medium green, semi-glossy; upright, bushy growth.

Precious Platinum HT, *mr*, 1974, (Opa Pötschke; Red Star); *Red Planet × Franklin Englemann*; Dicksons of Hawlmark. Flowers cardinal-red, full, high-centered, medium to large; slightly fragrant; foliage glossy, leathery.

Précoce M (OGR), *dp*, 1843, Vibert. Flowers rosy red, sometimes spotted, full, medium; very early bloom.

Prediction HT, *mp*, 1974, *Queen of Bermuda × Golden Giant*; Golik; Dynarose. Flowers luminous pink, dbl. (35 petals), high-centered, large (4 in.); slightly fragrant; foliage leathery; moderate growth.

Prélude HT, *m*, 1954, *Fantastique × (Ampere × (Charles P. Kilham × Capucine Chambard))*; Meilland, F.; URS. Flowers lilac-mauve, dbl. (25 petals), well formed, medium; strong stems; fragrant; foliage dense; vigorous, bushy growth.

Prema F, *pb*, 1970, *Sea Pearl × Shola*; Div. of Veg. Crops & Floriculture. Flowers soft pink, petals edged deep pink, dbl., high-centered, medium; foliage leathery; vigorous, upright.

Premier HT, *mr*, 1918, *Ophelia Seedling × Mrs. Charles E. Russell*; Hill, E.G., Co. Bud long, pointed; flowers dark velvety rose-red, veined darker, reverse lighter, dbl., open, large; very fragrant; foliage rich green, leathery; vigorous growth.

Premier, Climbing Cl HT, *mr*, 1927, Vestal.

Premier Bal HT, *w*, 1950, *Fantastique × Caprice*; Meilland, F. Flowers ivory edged carmine, dbl. (30-40 petals), cupped; very fragrant.

Premier Bal HT, *w*, 1955, *(Fantastique × Caprice) × Peace*; Meilland, F.; URS. Flowers ivory edged cyclamen-rose, picotee effect, dbl. (45 petals); very fragrant; vigorous, bushy growth. This variety replaces the one first distributed under this name.

Premier Supreme HT, *dp*, 1927, *Premier sport*; Zieger. Bud long, pointed; flowers deep rose-pink, almost scarlet, dbl., high-centered, very large; long stems; fragrant; foliage dark, leathery; very vigorous growth.

Présence HT, *lp*, 1970, (DELprat); *Dr. Albert Schweitzer × (Michèle Meilland × Bayadère)*; Delbard, G.; Society of Nurseries; G. Delbard. Flowers pink, lighter reverse, dbl. (38 petals), large; light, fruity fragrance; foliage medium, medium green, matt; upright, bushy growth.

Présent Filial HT, *pb*, 1956, *Verschuren's Pink × Seedling*; Delbard-Chabert. Bud long; flowers old rose tinted coppery yellow, center salmon-pink, reverse lighter, very dbl. (85 petals); foliage dense.

President Boone HT, *dr*, 1936, *Seedling × Miss Rowena Thom*; Howard, F.H.; H&S. Bud long, pointed; flowers scarlet-crimson, dbl., globular, large, stems sometimes weak; very fragrant; foliage leathery; vigorous growth.

Président Bouché HT, *or*, 1917, *Seedling × Lyon Rose*; Pernet-Ducher. Flowers coral-red, shaded carmine, large to medium; vigorous growth.

Président Bray HT, *op*, 1954, Privat. Flowers salmon-pink veined pink; strong stems; vigorous growth.

Président Briand HP (OGR), *op*, 1929, *(Frau Karl Druschki seedling × Lyon Rose) × (Frau Karl Druschki × Willowmere)*; Mallerin; C-P. Flowers pink suffused salmon, dbl., globular, very large; strong stems; fragrant; foliage wrinkled; vigorous, compact growth.

Président Chérioux HT, *rb*, 1923, Pernet-Ducher. Flowers red and salmon-pink, shaded yellow, dbl.; slightly fragrant. GM, Bagatelle, 1923.

Président Cochet-Cochet HT, *dr*, 1937, *Grenoble × Seedling*; Mallerin. Flowers deep garnet-red, tinted scarlet, dbl., very large; slightly fragrant; foliage leathery; very vigorous growth.

President Coolidge LCl, *dr*, 1925, *(R. setigera × R. wichuraiana) × Château de Clos Vougeot*; Horvath. Flowers glowing crimson, dbl.; very hardy.

Président de Sèze G (OGR), *m*, (Mme. Hébert); Prior to 1836. Flowers magenta center, paler at edges, very dbl., cup-shaped, becoming convex, blooms in clusters.

Président Deville HT, *mr*, 1929, *Fritz Maydt × Mme. J.W. Büdde*; Leenders, M. Flowers red, dbl.; fragrant. GM, Bagatelle, 1929.

Président Duhem Pol, *mr*, 1930, Reymond. Flowers bright red, dbl.; foliage dark; vigorous growth.

Président Dutailly G (OGR), *m*, 1888, Dubreuil. Flowers reddish purple, dbl.; very fragrant.

President Eisenhower HT, *mr*, 1953, *Seedling (Captivator × Red Delicious) sport*; Hill, J.H., Co.; C-P. Bud ovoid; flowers rose-red, dbl. (35-40 petals), high-centered to open, large (4-5 in.); very fragrant; foliage dark, leathery; vigorous, bushy growth.

Président Férier HT, *op*, 1938, Gaujard. Flowers reddish coppery pink, base tinted yellow, very full; very fragrant; foliage bright green; very vigorous growth.

President Franklin D. Roosevelt HT, *or*, 1933, *Templar sport*; Traendly; Schenck; S. Reynolds. Flowers velvety scarlet, full (35-40 petals), large; fragrant.

President F. A. des Tombe HT, *ab*, 1925, *Mr. Joh. M. Jolles × Golden Emblem*; Van Rossem. Flowers apricot on golden yellow ground, reverse peach, dbl.; fragrant.

Président Georges Feuillet LCl, *yb*, 1954, Vially. Flowers sulphur-yellow edged vermilion, reverse saffron, semi-dbl.

Président Henri Queuille HT, *mr*, 1952, *Rome Glory × Seedling*; Gaujard. Flowers carmine-red, dbl., very large; very fragrant; very vigorous, upright growth.

President Herbert Hoover HT, *pb*, 1930, *Sensation × Souv. de Claudius Pernet*; Coddington; Totty. Bud long, pointed; flowers orange, rose and gold, reverse lighter, dbl. (25 petals), large; fragrant (spicy); foliage leathery; vigorous, tall growth. GM, ARS Gertrude M. Hubbard, 1934; ARS John Cook Medal, 1935.

President Hoover, Climbing Cl HT, *pb*, 1931, Dixie Rose Nursery.

President Herbert Hoover, Climbing C l HT, *pb*, 1937, Cant, B.R..

President Jac. Smits HT, *dr*, 1928, *Étoile de Hollande × K. of K.*; Verschuren; Dreer. Bud long, pointed; flowers brilliant dark red, semi-dbl., large; fragrant; foliage bronze, leathery; very vigorous growth.

Président J. B. Croibier HT, *ob*, 1940, *Mrs. Pierre S. duPont × Talisman*; Colombier. Bud well shaped, pure orange; flowers dark orange, reverse yellow; foliage light green; very vigorous growth.

Président Leopold Senghor® HT, *dr*, 1979, (MEIluminac; President L. Senghor); *((Scarlet Knight × Samourai) × (Crimson Wave × Imperator) × (Pharaoh × Pharaoh)) × (Pharaoh × Pharaoh)*; Meilland, M.L.; Meilland. Bud conical; flowers dark red, dbl. (25 petals), fully cupped, large; foliage glossy, dark; vigorous, bushy growth.

President Lincoln HP (OGR), *dr*, 1863, Granger. Flowers dark red shaded crimson, full, large.

President Macia HT, *lp*, 1933, (P.M. Leenders); *(Ophelia × Gloire de Hollande) × (Ophelia × Sensation)*; Leenders, M. Flowers light pink, darker veining, dbl. (25 petals), large (6 in.); very fragrant; foliage dark; vigorous, bushy.

Président Magnaud Ch (OGR), *dr*, 1916, Nabonnand, C. Flowers dark red, semi-dbl, small.

Président Morel Journel HT, *rb*, 1934, *Mrs. Edward Powell × R. foetida bicolor hybrid*; Chambard, C. Flowers scarlet, reverse yellow, cupped, large; fragrant; foliage bronze; vigorous growth.

Président Pacaud HT, *yb*, 1946, *Mme. Joseph Perraud × Seedling*; Sauvageot, H.; Sauvageot. Flowers ochre-yellow shaded dark carmine-red and copper, dbl., well formed, large; foliage glossy.

Président Parmentier HT, *ab*, 1926, *Col. Leclerc × Le Progrès*; Sauvageot; Cochet-Cochet. Flowers apricot-pink, dbl., slightly fragrant.

Président Paul Martin HT, *my*, 1942, *Charles K. Douglas × Souv. de Georges Pernet*; Moulin-Epinay; Hamonière. Flowers purplish carmine-red, semi-dbl., large; vigorous growth.

Président Paulmier Pol, *dr*, 1932, Turbat. Flowers pure blood-red, passing to garnet, very full, well formed, borne in clusters of 20-25; dwarf growth.

Président Plumecocq HT, *yb*, 1931, (Director Plumecock); Gaujard; C-P. Flowers coppery buff and deep salmon, dbl. (34 petals), cupped, large; fragrant (fruity).

Président Poincaré HT, 1920, *(Beauté Inconstante × Mme. Caroline Testout × Mev. Dora van Tets)*; Grandes Roseraies. Flowers reddish magenta, center crimson, shaded yellow, reverse bright rose, dbl.; fragrant.

Président Seize F, *dp*, 1958, Delbard-Chabert. Bud long; flowers light red becoming darker, semi-dbl. (10-15 petals), large (4 in.); strong stems; foliage dark; upright growth.

President Sono HT, *ly*, 1972, *Burnaby × Montparnasse*; Kikuchi. Bud pointed; flowers cream-yellow, dbl. (45-50 petals), high-centered; very large (5-6 in.); very fragrant; foliage dark; upright growth.

Président Van Oost HT, *my*, 1934, *Souv. de Claudius Pernet × Ville de Paris*; Lens. Flowers golden yellow, edged deeper, dbl., large; long, strong stems; foliage glossy; vigorous growth.

Président Vignet HT, *dr*, 1911, Pernet-Ducher. Flowers deep carmine-red, full, large.

President Wilson HT, *op*, 1918, Easlea. Flowers shrimp-pink, dbl.

President W. H. Taft HT, *op*, 1908, McCullough. Bud long, pointed; flowers salmon-pink, dbl., high-centered, large; long, strong stems; fragrant; foliage glossy; vigorous growth.

Presidente Carmona HT, *dr*, 1937, *Hortulanus Büdde × Château de Clos Vougeot*; Moreira da Silva. Flowers blackish crimson, shaded salmon, dbl., cupped, large; very fragrant; foliage soft; vigorous, bushy growth.

Presidente Craveiro Lopes HT, *rb*, 1954, *Sirena × Peace*; Moreira da Silva. Flowers cherry, reverse yellow, dbl. (33 petals), medium; strong stems; fragrant; foliage dark; very vigorous, upright growth.

Presidential Gr, *lp*, 1960, *Charlotte Armstrong × (Charlotte Armstrong × Floradora)*; Lammerts; Germain's. Bud long, pointed; flowers light crimson, reverse china-rose, dbl., cupped, large (5½ in.); slightly fragrant; foliage leathery, glossy; vigorous, tall growth.

Presque Partout M (OGR), *dp*, Flowers rose, full, cupped, medium; vigorous growth.

Prestatyn Rover HT, *op*, 1929, *Alfred Colomb × Mrs. Wemyss Quin*; Lavender. Flowers salmon-pink, reverse darker, dbl.; slightly fragrant.

Prestige S, *mr*, 1957, *Rudolph Timm × Fanal*; Kordes, R.; Morse. Flowers light crimson, semi-dbl., large; foliage dense, dark; vigorous, bushy growth; recurrent bloom.

Presumida Min, *yb*, 1948, (Baby Talisman; La Presumida; Peter Pan); *Eduardo Toda × Pompon de Paris*; Dot, P. Flowers pumpkin-yellow to white, center yellowish, dbl., small; dwarf growth.

Pretoria HT, *or*, 1953, Moro. Bud long; flowers copper-red to orange, large; very vigorous growth. GM, Rome, 1953.

Pretty Baby Min, *pb*, 1982, *Baby Katie × Miniature Seedling*; Jolly, Betty; Rosehill Farm. Flowers light pink, reverse creamy pink, dbl. (35 petals), exhibition, medium; slight fragrance; foliage small, medium green, semiglossy; bushy, spreading growth.

Pretty Jessica S, *dp*, 1992, (AUSjess); *Wife of Bath × Seedling*; Austin, David; David Austin Roses, 1983. Flowers deep pink, very full (41+ petals), medium (4-7 cms) blooms borne in small clusters; very fragrant; foliage medium, dark green, semi-glossy; some prickles; low (65 cms), bushy growth.

Pretty 'n' Single Min, *dp*, 1990, (UMSpretty); *Nymphenburg × Libby*; Umsawasdi, Theera, 1986; Theera Umsawasdi. Flowers deep pink, single (5 petals), small blooms; very fragrant; foliage medium, dark green, semi-glossy; upright, bushy, tall growth.

Pretty Pink LCl, *dp*, 1968, *New Dawn × Spartan*; Patterson; Patterson Roses. Flowers deep pink, dbl., open, medium; very fragrant; foliage glossy; very vigorous, climbing growth; recurrent bloom.

Pretty Please Min, *lp*, 1985, *Bride's White × Miniature Seedling*; Epperson, Richard G. Flowers light pink, dbl. (25 petals), urn-shaped, small blooms borne usually singly; no fragrance; foliage medium, light green, semi-glossy; very thin, long, straight, light red prickles; medium, bushy growth.

Pretty Poly F, *mr*, 1954, *Mme. Butterfly × Our Princess*; Bishop; Baker's Nursery. Flowers cherry-red, flat, camellia shaped, borne in clusters; vigorous, upright growth.

Pretty Woman Min, *pb*, 1991, (MINabdco); *Tom Brown × Over the Rainbow*; Williams, Ernest D.; Mini-Roses, 1992. Flowers pink with yellow and orange, deeper at edges, aging darker, may be red in cool weather, color deepens with age, dbl. (26-40 petals), excellent substance, exhibition, small (4 cms) blooms borne mostly singly; fragrance; foliage small, medium green, glossy; few prickles; low (30 cms), bushy growth.

Preussen HT, *dr*, 1920, *Farbenkönigin × Richmond*; Löbner; Kordes. Flowers glowing dark blood-red, dbl.; very fragrant.

Prevue S, *w*, 1978, *(Tausendschön × (Perle d'Or × Old China)) × Safrano*; James, John. Flowers white, semi-dbl., medium; no fragrance; foliage medium, medium green, semi-glossy; bushy growth.

Pride 'n' Joy™ Min, *ob*, 1991, (JACmo); *Chattem Centennial × Prominent*; Warriner, William A., 1983; Bear Creek Gardens, Inc. (J&P), 1992. Bud ovoid; flowers bright, medium orange, reverse orange and cream, fades to salmon pink, dbl. (30-35 petals), urn-shaped, exhibition, medium; moderate, fruity fragrance; foliage medium, dark green, semi-glossy; bushy, spreading, medium growth. AARS, 1992.

Pride of Canada HT, *dp*, 1981, *Ena Harkness × Charlotte Armstrong*; Collins; Pan American Bulb Co. Bud long, ovoid; flowers deep pink, dbl. (34 petals), high-centered blooms borne in pairs; fragrant; foliage dark; small, brown prickles; tall growth.

Pride of Hurst Pol, *op*, 1926, *Coral Cluster* sport; Hicks. Flowers coral-pink, very dbl., small.

Pride of Leicester HT, *pb*, 1960, *R.M.S. Queen Mary × Seedling*; Verschuren; Blaby Rose Gardens. Flowers rose-pink, base yellow, dbl., high-centered, large; very fragrant; foliage light green; vigorous growth.

Pride of Maldon F, *ob*, 1990, (HARwonder); *Southampton* × *Wandering Minstrel*; Harkness, R.; R. Harkness & Co., Ltd., 1991. Bud pointed; flowers bright reddish-orange, light orange-yellow reverse, darkening of red tones with aging, single (10 petals), cupped to flat, medium, borne in sprays of 3-9; slight fragrance; foliage medium, dark green, glossy; prickles straight or slightly curved, medium to small, green; bushy, medium growth.

Pride of New Castle HT, *dr*, 1930, *Hoosier* × *Beauty Seedling*; Hill, E.G., Co.; Heller Bros. Flowers deep velvety crimson, dbl., large; very fragrant; vigorous, bushy growth.

Pride of Newark F, *lp*, 1966, *Joanna Hill* × *The Fairy*; Morey; Country Garden Nursery. Flowers shell-pink, dbl., cupped, large (4 in.); very fragrant; foliage glossy, bronze, leathery; very vigorous, upright, compact growth.

Pride of Oakland F, *mp*, 1977, *Pinocchio* × *China Doll*; Lindquist; Howard of Hemet. Bud pointed; flowers medium pink, dbl. (26 petals), rosette form, medium (2½ in.); fragrant (spicy); upright, spreading growth.

Pride of Pacific F, *op*, 1957, *Pinocchio* × *Maxine*; Silva. Flowers salmon-pink, dbl., borne in clusters of 4-7; symmetrical growth.

Pride of Reigate HP (OGR), *rb*, 1884, *Comtesse d'Oxford sport*; Brown, J. Flowers carmine, striped and mottled white; sparse bloom.

Pride of Sunnybank Gr, *mp*, 1957, *Ma Perkins* × *Charlotte Armstrong*; Ulrick. Flowers pink.

Pride of Waltham HP (OGR), *mp*, 1881, *Comtesse d'Oxford sport*; Paul, W. Flowers silvery rose, very dbl. (80 thick petals), large; fragrant; vigorous growth.

Pride of Wansbeck HT, *dp*, 1986, (NOSwan); *Christian Dior* × *Seedling*; Greensitt, J.A.; Nostell Priory Rose Gardens, 1979. Flowers light red, full (26-49 petals), medium; fragrant; foliage medium, medium green, semiglossy; bushy growth.

Pride of Washington HSet (OGR), *m*, 1849, *R. setigera hybrid*; Pierce. Flowers rosy violet, very dbl.

Prima S, *pb*, 1988, (HARwanted; Many Happy Returns); *Herbstfeuer* × *Pearl Drift*; Harkness, R.; R. Harkness & Co., 1990. Flowers blush white, reverse blush pink, aging blush to white, semi-dbl. (18 petals), cupped, large, borne in sprays of 3-11; moderate, fruity fragrance; foliage medium, medium green, semi-glossy; prickles straight, small, red; fruit

round, medium, red; spreading, medium growth; repeats. GM, Geneva, 1987.

Prima Ballerina® HT, *dp*, 1957, (Première Ballerine; Primaballerina; *Seedling* × *Peace*; Tantau, Math. Bud long, pointed; flowers cherry-pink, semi-dbl. (20 petals), medium to large; very fragrant; foliage leathery, light green.

Prima Donna HT, *mp*, 1944, *Heinrich Wendland* × *Seedling*; Dickson, A.; J&P. Bud pointed; flowers rich deep salmon-pink tinted buff, dbl. (45 petals), high-centered, large (5 in.); slightly fragrant; foliage glossy; vigorous, upright, open growth. RULED EXTINCT 1/85.

Prima Donna™ Gr, *dp*, 1984, (Toboné); *(Seedling* × *Happiness)* × *Prominent*; Shirakawa, Takeshi; Tosh Nakashima, 1983. Flowers deep fuchsia pink, dbl. (27 petals), exhibition, large; slight fragrance; foliage large, medium green, semi-glossy; bushy, spreading growth; greenhouse variety. AARS, 1988.

Primarosa HT, *dp*, 1950, Giacomasso. Bud long; flowers carmine, base yellow, streaked orange, very large; strong stems.

Primavera HT, *op*, 1936, *Julien Potin* × *Sensation*; Aicardi, D.; Robichon. Flowers salmon-pink, dbl., well formed; fragrant (musk); vigorous growth.

Prime Time Min, *my*, 1984, *Picnic* × *Rise 'n' Shine*; Hardgrove, Donald & Mary; Rose World Originals. Flowers medium yellow, dbl. (35 petals), high-centered, exhibition, medium; slight fragrance; foliage small, medium green, semi-glossy; upright, bushy.

Primerose HT, *my*, 1913, *Mme. Mélanie Soupert* × *Mrs. Peter Blair*; Soupert & Notting. Flowers melon-yellow, deeper in autumn, shaded apricot, dbl.; fragrant.

Primerose Sistau Pol, *pb*, 1925, Turbat. Flowers carmine, shaded yellow, cupped, medium, borne in clusters of 5-6; few thorns; half dwarf.

Primevère LCl, *yb*, 1929, (Primrose); *R. wichuraiana* × *Constance*; Barbier; Dreer, 1930. Flowers primrose-yellow to canary-yellow, dbl., large blooms in clusters of 4-5 on long stems; slightly fragrant; foliage rich green, glossy; very vigorous, climbing and trailer; non-recurrent bloom.

Primo Premio HT, *pb*, 1964, Giacomasso. Flowers rose suffused yellow, well formed, medium.

Primrose Bedder F, *my*, 1956, Kordes; Morse. Flowers primrose-yellow, dbl., borne in large trusses; slightly fragrant; foliage light green.

Prince Albert HP (OGR), *rb*, 1841, Laffay. Flowers carmine-rose changing to dark crimson, globular, large.

Prince Arthur HP (OGR), *mr*, 1875, (Triomphe de Caen); *Général Jacqueminot × Seedling*; Cant, B.R. Flowers deep crimson, dbl. (55 petals), medium; very fragrant; vigorous growth.

Prince Bernhard HT, *mr*, 1937, *Matador Seedling*; Van Rossem; J&P, 1941. Bud pointed; flowers shining red, shaded strawberry-red, full, well formed, large; very fragrant; foliage dark; vigorous growth. GM, Bagatelle, 1937.

Prince Camille de Rohan HP (OGR), *dr*, 1861, (La Rosière, Climbing); *Possibly Général Jacqueminot × Géant des Batailles hybrid*; Verdier, E. Flowers very deep velvety crimson-maroon, very dbl. (nearly 100 imbricated petals), cupped, well-formed, large blooms on rather weak stems; very fragrant; vigorous, upright growth; sometimes recurrent.

Prince Charles B (OGR), *m*, 1842, Flowers deep red-purple, fading to lavender, veined magenta, base of petals near white, semi-dbl., loose, crinkled; foliage large, dark; very few prickles; vigorous (to 5 ft.) growth; non-recurrent bloom.

Prince Charles du Luxembourg Ch (OGR), *dp*, Flowers bright carmine, cupped.

Prince Charlie HT, *op*, 1932, Dobbie. Bud long, pointed; flowers coral-pink, overlaid salmon, base orange, dbl., cupped, large; fragrant; foliage leathery, bronze tinted; vigorous, bushy growth.

Prince Charming Min, *mr*, 1953, *Ellen Poulsen × Tom Thumb*; deVink; T. Robinson. Flowers bright crimson, dbl., small (1 in.); foliage tinted red; dwarf (8-12 in.) growth.

Prince Charming S, *lp*, 1958, *Alika hybrid*; Skinner. Flowers pale blush-pink, dbl.; very fragrant; upright (2½ ft.), bushy growth; prolonged bloom

Prince Damask HT, *dr*, 1954, *Guinée × Seedling*; LeGrice. Flowers maroon, dbl. (30 petals), medium; very fragrant; foliage small, dark.

Prince de Bulgarie HT, *lp*, 1900, Pernet-Ducher. Bud long, pointed; flowers silvery flesh, center deeper, shaded salmon and saffron-yellow, dbl., cupped; fragrant; foliage bright green; vigorous growth.

Prince Engelbert Charles d'Arenberg HT, *or*, 1909, *Richmond × Étoile de France*; Soupert & Notting. Flowers scarlet, dbl.; fragrance.

Prince Félix de Luxembourg HT, *mr*, 1930, *Gen. MacArthur × George C. Waud*; Ketten Bros. Flowers carmine-red, shaded purplish, full (30-35 petals), large; fragrant; foliage dark; very vigorous, bushy growth.

Prince Henry F, *mp*, 1926, *St. Helena × Seedling*; Easlea. Bud long, pointed; flowers bright pink, passing to blush-pink, clusters of 18-20.

Prince Jean de Luxembourg Pol, *w*, 1926, *Jeanny Soupert × Miniature*; Soupert & Notting. Flowers pure white, dbl., very small, borne in immense clusters of 100-150; moderately dwarf.

Prince Meillandina® Min, *dr*, 1988, (MEIrutral; Prince Sunblaze;); Red Sunblaze *Parador × Mograb*; Meilland, A.; SNC Meilland; Cie. Flowers dark currant-red, dbl. (15-25 petals), medium; no fragrance; bushy growth.

Prince Noir HP (OGR), *m*, 1854, Boyau. Flowers dark velvety crimson-purple, not very dbl.; moderate growth.

Prince of Denmark HT, *mp*, 1964, *Queen Elizabeth × Independence*; McGredy, S., IV; Fisons Horticulture. Flowers rose-pink, dbl. (35 whorled petals), large (4 in.); free growth.

Prince of Peace HT, *yb*, 1985, (JACpop); *Bridal Pink × Seedling*; J&P; McConnell Nurs., Inc. Flowers yellow edged with pink, dbl. (35 petals), medium; slight fragrance; foliage medium, medium green, glossy; upright growth.

Prince of Wales HT, *mr*, 1921, Easlea. Bud long, pointed; flowers brilliant cherry-scarlet, semi-dbl; very fragrant.

Prince Tango® Pol, *or*, 1968, (DELgus); *(Orléans Rose × Goldilocks) × (Orange Triumph Seedling × Floradora*; Delbard-Chabert. Bud pointed; flowers mandarin color, semi-dbl., open, small; foliage bronze, glossy; moderate, bushy growth. GM, Madrid, 1968.

Prince Yugala HT, *dr*, 1923, Cant, F. Bud long, pointed; flowers deep velvety maroon, dbl.; slightly fragrant.

Princeps LCl, *mr*, 1942, Clark, A. Flowers red, very large; fragrant; pillar growth; non-recurrent bloom.

Princess Alexandra F, *yb*, 1962, *Masquerade × Seedling*; Cobley. Flowers creamy yellow suffused carmine-pink, dbl. (30-35 petals), medium, borne in trusses; fragrant; foliage dark, glossy; very vigorous growth.

Princess Alice® F, *my*, 1985, (HARtanna; Brite Lites; Zonta Rose); *Judy Garland × Anne Harkness*; Harkness, R; Weeks Roses, 1991. Flowers medium yellow, semi-dbl. (22-28 petals), medium blooms in large sprays; slight fragrance; foliage medium, medium green, semi-glossy; upright growth. GM, Dublin, 1984.

Princess Angela HT, *lp*, 1991, *Pristine × Granada*; Alde, Robert O. Flowers light pink, very full, large blooms borne mostly singly; slight fragrance; foliage medium, dark green, semi-glossy; tall, upright, bushy growth.

Princess Angeline HT, *mp*, 1945, *Charlotte Armstrong × Times Square*; Swim; Peterson; Dering. Flowers pink, dbl. (35-50 petals), cupped, becoming open, large (4½-5½ in.); very fragrant (damask); foliage leathery; vigorous, tall growth.

Princess Bonnie T (OGR), *dr*, 1897, *Bon Silène × William Francis Bennett*; Dingee; Conard. Flowers vivid crimson.

Princess Chichibu F, *pb*, 1971, *(Vera Dalton × Highlight) × Merlin*; Harkness. Flowers pink blend, dbl. (30 petals), large (2½-3 in.); slightly fragrant; foliage glossy, dark.

Princess Elizabeth of Greece HT, *my*, 1926, Chaplin Bros. Flowers golden yellow shaded terra-cotta, high-centered, well shaped; fragrant.

Princess Fair HT, *ab*, 1962, *Queen Elizabeth × (Crimson Glory, Climbing × Happiness)*; Moren; J&P. Flowers light apricot, dbl., cupped, large; fragrant; foliage glossy; vigorous, upright growth.

Princess Hohenzollern T (OGR), *rb*, Flowers peach-red to crimson, dbl., well formed, very large.

Princess Margaret of England HT, *mp*, 1968, (MEIlista; MEIlisia; Princesse Margaret d'Angleterre); *Queen Elizabeth × (Peace × Michèle Meilland)*; Meilland, M.L.; URS, 1969. Flowers phlox-pink, dbl., high-centered, large; slightly fragrant; foliage leathery; vigorous, upright. GM, Portland, 1977.

Princess Margaret of England, Climbing Cl HT, *mp*, 1969, Meilland; URS.

Princess Margaret Rose HT, *pb*, 1933, *Los Angeles Seedling × Seedling*; Cant, B.R. Bud long, pointed; flowers glowing pink suffused orange, dbl., cupped, large; fragrant; foliage leathery; vigorous growth.

Princess Marina HT, *ab*, 1938, Robinson, H.; Port Stockton Nursery. Flowers apricot, shaded salmon and copper, dbl., well shaped; stiff stems; slightly fragrant; vigorous growth.

Princess Michael of Kent® F, *my*, 1981, (HARlightly); *Manx Queen × Alexander*; Harkness, R. Flowers medium yellow, dbl. (38 petals), high-centered, large blooms borne 1-3 per cluster; fragrant; foliage medium large, mid-green, glossy; short, thick, red prickles; low, bushy growth.

Princess Michiko F, *ob*, 1966, *Circus × Spartan*; Dickson, A. Flowers coppery orange, yellow eye, semi-dbl. (15 petals), cupped, large (3 in.), in clusters; foliage glossy; bushy.

Princess Mikasa HT, *dp*, 1983, *(Red Lion × Samantha) × (Red Lion × Samantha)*; Teranishi, K.; Itami Rose Nursery. Flowers deep pink, dbl. (45 petals), urn-shaped, medium blooms borne singly; no fragrance; foliage large, medium green, semi-glossy; small, light green prickles; tall, bushy growth.

Princess Nagaka HT, *rb*, 1922, Pemberton. Flowers fiery red, shaded yellow, semi-dbl., small; slightly fragrant.

Princess of India HT, *rb*, 1980, (Indian Princess); *Tropicana × Granada*; Pal, Dr. B.P.; K.S.G. Sons. Flowers outer petals deep red, inner petals carmine, dbl. (35 petals), high-centered, large; highly fragrant; foliage medium to large, dark, smooth; brown to gray prickles; upright, bushy growth.

Princess Pearl F, *w*, 1960, *Carol Amling sport*; Beldam Bridge Nursery. Flowers white center blush, dbl. (40 petals), large (3 in.) borne in clusters; slightly fragrant; foliage leathery, dark; moderate growth.

Princess Royal HT, *mp*, 1935, Dickson, A. Flowers rose-pink to hydrangea-pink, petals shell shaped, very large; very fragrant; foliage dark, glossy; vigorous growth. RULED EXTINCT 4/92.

Princess Royal HT, *ab*, 1992, (DICroyal); *Tequila Sunrise × Seedling*; Dickson, Colin; Dickson Nurseries. Flowers apricot, full (26-40 petals), large (7+ cms) blooms borne mostly singly on very stiff, thorny stems; slight fragrance; foliage large, medium green, semi-glossy; many prickles; medium (88 cms), bushy growth.

Princess Takamatsu HT, *pb*, 1974, *Bonsoir × Christian Dior*; Kono. Bud globular; flowers pink blend, dbl. (50 petals), high-centered, very large (6 in.); slightly fragrant; vigorous, upright growth.

Princess van Orange Cl Pol, *or*, 1935, (Princesse d'Orange; Prinses van Orange); *Gloria Mundi, Climbing sport*; deRuiter; J&P.

Princess Victoria HT, *or*, 1920, McGredy. Flowers glowing scarlet-crimson shaded orange, passing to carmine, base orange, dbl.; very fragrant. GM, NRS, 1920.

Princess White F, *w*, 1956, *Orange seedling × Demure*; Boerner; J&P. Bud pointed; flowers white, dbl., flat, medium; strong stems; fragrant; foliage leathery; vigorous, upright, bushy growth; a florists' variety.

Princesse HT, *or*, 1964, *(Peace × Magicienne) × (Independence × Radar)*; Laperrière; EFR. Flowers geranium-red, dbl. (45 petals), globular, large (4-5 in.); vigorous, upright.

Princesse Adélaide M (OGR), *lp*, 1845, Laffay. Flowers pale pink, dbl.; fragrant; not very mossy; foliage dark, often variegated; vigorous growth.

Princesse Alice M (OGR), *m*, 1853, *Luxembourg Seedling*; Paul, W. Flowers violet-rose, not very mossy.

Princesse Alice de Monaco T (OGR), *yb*, 1893, Weber. Flowers cream-yellow edged pink.

Princesse Amédée de Broglie HT, *or*, 1936, *Charles P. Kilham Seedling × Colette Clément*; Mallerin; Meilland. Bud very long, fiery red; flowers nasturtium-red, deeper in autumn, well formed, large; foliage dark, glossy; vigorous growth. GM, Bagatelle, 1935.

Princesse de Bassaraba de Brancovan T (OGR), *pb*, 1900, Bernaix, A. Flowers flesh-pink, shaded copper.

Princesse de Béarn HP (OGR), *mr*, 1885, Lévêque. Flowers velvety poppy-red, full, globular, large; vigorous growth.

Princesse de Monaco® HT, *w*, 1982, (MEImagarmic; Grace Kelly; Preference; Princess Grace; Princess of Monaco); *Ambassador × Peace*; Meilland, M.L.; Meilland Et Cie, 1981. Flowers petals cream, edged pink, dbl. (35 petals), high-centered, exhibition, large; fragrant; foliage large, dark, glossy; upright, bushy growth.

Princesse de Nassau N (OGR), *ly*, 1835, (Princess of Nassau); Laffay. Bud yellowish, tinted pink; flowers creamy yellow, fading to cream, very dbl., cupped, medium blooms in large clusters; branches grow in zig-zag fashion. Probably identical with *R. moschata autumnalis* as described by G.S. Thomas in Climbing Roses Old and New.

Princesse de Sagan Ch (OGR), *dr*, 1887, Dubreuil. Flowers crimson shaded with purple, dbl., cupped, medium; vigorous growth.

Princesse Étienne de Croy T (OGR), *yb*, 1898, Ketten Bros. Flowers amber yellow, shaded deep rose pink and mauve rose to the edges, full, very large.

Princesse Ghika T (OGR), *mr*, 1922, *Gén. Schablikine × Papa Gontier*; Nabonnand, P. Flowers brilliant red with dark reflexes, full, large.

Princesse Ita HT, *yb*, 1943, *Julien Potin × Charles P. Kilham*; Meilland, F.; A. Meilland. Bud oval; flowers indian yellow edged red, semi-dbl. to dbl., open, medium; slightly fragrant; foliage leathery; vigorous, bushy growth.

Princesse Jaune HT, *my*, 1945, Fessel; A. Meilland. Flowers citron-yellow, full, large.

Princesse Joséphine-Charlotte Pol, *op*, 1945, *Orange Triumph sport*; Lens. Flowers bright pink suffused apricot-salmon, semi-dbl., cupped, small; slightly fragrant; very

vigorous, bushy growth; very good in semi-shade and under glass.

Princesse Lamballe A (OGR), *w*, Prior to 1848. Flowers white, sometimes tinted flesh, full, medium; vigorous, compact, branching growth.

Princesse Liliane HT, *mr*, 1954, *Happiness × Hens Verschuren*; Buyl Frères; Morse. Flowers blood-red, dbl. (25-30 petals), large (5 in.); foliage dark; vigorous, upright growth.

Princesse Louise HSem (OGR), *w*, 1829, Jacques. Flowers creamy white, back petals shaded with rose, dbl., cupped, large.

Princesse Louise HP (OGR), *w*, 1869, *Mme. Vidot × Virginal*; Laxton; G. Paul. Flowers blush, globular, medium; vigorous.

Princesse Louise Cl HT, *m*, 1924, *La France de '89 × Victor Hugo*; Nabonnand, P. Bud long, pointed; flowers rich purple, center tinted brilliant garnet, semi-dbl., large; fragrant; vigorous, climbing growth.

Princesse Margaretha Pol, *lp*, 1932, Poulsen, S. Flowers pale pink, dbl., medium blooms in clusters; no fragrance; foliage medium, medium green, semi-glossy; medium, bushy growth.

Princesse Marie HSem (OGR), *mp*, 1829, Jacques. Flowers bright pink, blooms in very large clusters.

Princesse Marie Clotilde Napoléon Pol, *w*, 1924, Opdebeeck. Flowers white shaded pink, base pale yellow, dbl., large; vigorous growth.

Princesse Marie José Pol, *w*, 1924, Opdebeeck. Flowers white shaded rose, base yellow, full, large; vigorous growth.

Princesse Marie José HT, *or*, 1925, Klettenberg-Londes; F.J. Grootendorst. Bud long, pointed; flowers orange-scarlet, dbl.; fragrant (fruity).

Princesse Marie-Astrid HT, *mp*, 1964, *(Mme. Edouard Herriot × R. rugosa rubra) × La Jolie*; Mondial Roses. Bud globular; flowers deep rose to camellia-pink, dbl., large; slightly fragrant; moderate, bushy growth.

Princesse Marie-Christine HT, *dr*, 1955, *Poinsettia × Ena Harkness*; Buyl Frères. Bud ovoid to long; flowers blood-red, dbl. (25-30 petals); vigorous, bushy growth.

Princesse Paoli HT, *mp*, 1966, Mondial Roses. Flowers bright pink, dbl., high-centered, large (5 in.); very fragrant; foliage glossy; vigorous growth.

Princesse Stéphanie T (OGR), *op*, 1880, *Gloire de Dijon Seedling*; Levet, A. Flowers salmon-yellow, full, large; fragrant; very vigorous growth.

Princesse Stéphanie de Belgique HT, *dp*, 1929, *Gen. MacArthur × Seedling*; Soupert & Notting; C. Soupert. Bud long, pointed; flowers carmine, center deeper, dbl.; very fragrant.

Princesse Verona S, *mp*, 1984, (Princess Verona); *Verona × Prairie Princess*; Buck; Iowa State University. Flowers medium pink, dbl. (30 petals), cupped, 4 in. blooms borne 1-15 per cluster; light fragrance; foliage leathery, dark olive green; awl-like, tan prickles; upright, bushy, compact growth; repeat bloom; hardy.

Princesse Yvonne Ghika HT, *w*, 1927, *Stadtrat Glaser Seedling*; Mühle. Flowers white, center salmon, dbl.; fragrant.

Principe di Napoli HT, *my*, 1937, Aicardi Bros. Bud long; flowers yellow, dbl., large; very fragrant; foliage clear green; vigorous growth.

Principe di Piemonte HT, *dr*, 1929, *Mrs. Edward Powell × Gen. MacArthur*; Giacomasso. Flowers crimson-red, large; very fragrant.

Principessa delle Rose HT, *mr*, 1953, (Principesse des Roses); *Julien Potin × Sensation*; Aicardi, D.; V. Asseretto. Bud long, pointed; flowers lilac-rose, dbl. (30-40 petals), cupped, large; fragrant; very vigorous, upright growth.

Prins Hamlet HT, *lp*, 1927, *Ophelia sport*; Mohr. Bud long, pointed; flowers light pink, base yellow, semi-dbl., open, high-centered, large; very fragrant; foliage light, leathery; vigorous, bushy growth.

Prins Willem-Alexander F, *ob*, 1970, *Tropicana × Europeana*; Verschuren. Flowers coral-vermilion, medium (2-3 in.); foliage dark, red when young; bushy growth.

Prinses Béatrix HT, *ob*, 1940, (Princesse Béatrice); *Heinrich Wendland × Max Krause*; Busiman; A. Meilland; Morse. Bud long, pointed; flowers terra-cotta, shaded light apricot, dbl., cupped, large; very fragrant (fruity); foliage leathery, bronze; vigorous, bushy growth.

Prinses Christina F, *mr*, 1945, *Lafayette × Donald Prior*; Buisman. Bud large; flowers clear carmine-red, dbl., borne in clusters; very vigorous growth.

Prinses Juliana HT, *dr*, 1918, *Gen. MacArthur × Marie van Houtte*; Leenders, M. Bud long, pointed; flowers deep crimson-red, shaded darker, dbl.; very fragrant; foliage dark; vigorous growth.

Prinsesse Astrid af Norge F, *ob*, 1958, *Pinocchio × Pinocchio*; Poulsen, S. Flowers bright orange, semi-dbl.; vigorous, upright growth.

Prinsesse Margrethe HT, *op*, 1963, *Queen Elizabeth × (Independence × Golden Scepter)*; Poulsen, S. Flowers dark salmon-orange; dbl.; strong stems; slightly fragrant; vigorous, upright growth.

Printemps HT, *pb*, 1948, *Trylon × Brazier*; Mallerin; URS. Bud long; flowers old-rose tinted light red, reverse yellow, dbl., large (4 in.); fragrant; foliage glossy, dark; very vigorous growth.

Printemps Fleuri R, *m*, 1922, *Étoile Luisante × Seedling*; Turbat. Flowers bright purple passing to carmine-pink, stamens yellow, semi-dbl., medium, borne in clusters of 10-15; slightly fragrant.

Prinz Max zu Schaumburg HT, *op*, 1934, *Frau Karl Druschki × Lyon Rose*; Schaumburg-Lippe. Flowers salmon-pink, dbl., large; very fragrant; vigorous growth.

Prinzessin Hildegard HT, *my*, 1917, *Frau Karl Druschki × Friedrich Harms*; Lambert, P. Flowers bright yellow, fading to cream-yellow, dbl.; fragrant.

Prinzessin Irrlieb F, *mr*, 1963, Kordes, R. Flowers velvety bright red, dbl., borne in large clusters; moderate, symmetrical growth.

Prinzessin M. von Arenberg HT, *w*, 1928, *Ophelia × Los Angeles*; Leenders, M. Flowers rosy white, shaded pale rose-pink, dbl.; very fragrant.

Prinzessin Tatiana Wasiltchikoff HT, *lp*, 1941, Späth. Flowers flesh-pink, dbl.; long stems; upright growth.

Priory Pride HT, *mp*, 1986, (NOStpri); *Pink Peace × Chicago Peace*; Greensitt, J.A.; Nostell Priory Rose Gardens, 1981. Flowers medium pink, dbl. (26-40 petals), medium; fragrant; foliage medium, medium green, semi-glossy; bushy growth.

Priory Rose HT, *mp*, 1986, (NOStros); *Seedling × Seedling*; Greensitt, J.A.; Nostell Priory Rose Gardens, 1976. Flowers medium pink, full (26-40 petals), medium; very fragrant; foliage medium, medium green, semi-glossy; upright growth.

Priscilla HT, *mp*, 1922, *Seedling × Ophelia*; Montgomery Co.; A.N. Pierson. Bud long, pointed; flowers pink, outer petals rose-pink, dbl., cupped, very large; fragrant; foliage leathery, glossy; vigorous growth.

Priscilla Burton® F, *rb*, 1978, (MACrat); *Old Master × Seedling*; McGredy; Mattock. Flowers deep carmine pink and white blend (with variable combinations), semi-dbl. (10 petals), medium (2½ in.); fragrant; foliage glossy, dark. RNRS PIT, 1976.

Prissy Missy Min, *mp*, 1965, *Spring Song × Seedling*; Williams, E.D.; Mini-Roses. Flowers medium pink, reverse lighter, very dbl., small; fragrant (spicy); vigorous, bushy, dwarf.

Pristine® HT, *w*, 1978, (JACpico); *White Masterpiece × First Prize*; Warriner; J&P. Bud long; flowers near white, shaded light pink, dbl. (28 petals), imbricated, large (5-6 in.); slightly fragrant; foliage very large, dark; upright growth. GM, Portland, 1979; Edland Fragrance Medal, 1979.

Priub HT, *ly*, 1990, (UMSpriub); *Seedling × Seedling*; Umsawasdi, Theera, 1986; Theera Umsawasdi. Flowers yellowish-cream turning to pure white, single (5 petals), large blooms; slight fragrance; foliage medium, medium green, semi-glossy; prickles many; vigorous, upright, tall growth.

Privet iz Alma-Aty HT, *op*, 1958, (Greetings from Alma-Aty); *Independence × Peace*; Sushkov; Besschetnova. Flowers pink tinted orange, dbl. (60 petals), large; fragrant; foliage dark, glossy; very vigorous growth.

Priyatama HT, *pb*, 1981, (The Beloved); *Inge Horstmann × Picasso*; Viraraghavan, M.S.; K.S.G. Sons. Bud ovoid; flowers pink, paler reverse, dbl. (35 petals), high-centered, medium blooms borne singly; foliage glossy, slightly wrinkled; red prickles; bushy growth.

Prodaná Nevesta S, *w*, 1934, Brada; Böhm. Flowers snow-white, center tinted yellow, borne in large clusters; very fragrant; foliage light, glossy; vigorous growth; non-recurrent bloom.

Professeur Bérard HT, *dp*, 1930, *Hadley × The Queen Alexandra Rose*; Laperrière. Flowers bright purple-carmine, base yellow, dbl., petals laciniated; very fragrant; foliage leathery, dark; very vigorous growth.

Professeur Déaux HT, *ly*, 1935, Pernet-Ducher; Gaujard. Flowers light yellow streaked chamois, dbl.; longstems; foliage glossy, dark, bronze; very vigorous growth.

Professeur Émile Perrot D (OGR), *mp*, 1931, Brought from Persia by Prof. Perrot; Turbat. Apparently identical with Kazanlik, which see.

Professeur Ganiviat T (OGR), *pb*, 1890, Perrier. Flowers salmon carmine, shaded carmine purple, very full, large.

Professeur Jean Bernard® HT, *dr*, 1990, (DELjaber); *(Charles Mallerin × Divine) × (Tropicana × (Rome Glory × Impeccable))*; Delbard & Chabert, 1989. Bud cupped; flowers dark red, 25-30 petals, very large bloom; light fragrance; foliage dark green, abundant; bushy growth.

Prof. Alfred Dufour F, *mr*, 1969, *Paprika × Coup de Foudre*; Cazzaniga. Flowers bright red, semi-dbl., medium; slightly fragrant; foliage light green; compact growth.

Prof. Bento Carqueja HT, *op*, 1936, *Ophelia × Mme. Edouard Herriot*; Moreira da Silva. Bud long, pointed; flowers pink and salmon, shaded coral-red, dbl., high-centered, large; foliage soft; vigorous growth.

Prof. Chris Barnard HT, *mr*, 1970, *Ena Harkness × Karl Herbst*; Fishner, P.; Eden Rose Nursery. Flowers blood-red, dbl. (40 petals), pointed, large (4 in.); slightly fragrant; foliage glossy; upright growth.

Prof. Costa Leite HT, *my*, 1955, *Peace × Julien Potin*; Moreira da Silva. Flowers yellow; very vigorous growth.

Prof. C. S. Sargent LCl, *my*, 1903, *R. wichuraiana × Souv. d'Auguste Metral*; Hoopes, Bro.; Thomas. Flowers yellow, center deeper, fading to cream, dbl.; foliage small, ornamental; vigorous growth; early bloom. Not the same as Sargent, originated by Jackson Dawson.

Prof. Dr. von Beck HT, *pb*, 1927, *Mme. Abel Chatenay × Farbenkönigin*; Ries. Flowers bright rose-pink, reverse carmine-red, dbl.; fragrant.

Professor Fred Ziady HT, *my*, 1986, (KORambo); *Lusambo × Deep Secret*; Kordes, R.; Ludwig Roses, 1985. Flowers clear medium yellow, very full (43 petals), star-shaped, borne singly; medium fragrance; foliage medium green; straight, dark brown prickles; medium, sturdy growth.

Professor Gnau HT, *w*, 1928, *Oskar Cordel × Seedling*; Tantau. Bud long, pointed; flowers creamy white; very fragrant.

Professor Ibrahim LCl, *mp*, 1937, *Daisy Hill × Talisman*; Krause. Flowers rose-pink, base yellow, large blooms in clusters of 4-5; very fragrant; very vigorous, climbing (over 13 ft.).

Prof. Leite Pinto HT, *mr*, 1960, *Buccaneer × La Jolla*; Moreira da Silva. Flowers cherry-red, center ochre.

Prof. N. E. Hansen HRg (S), *dr*, 1892, Budd. Flowers rich velvety red.

Profile Gr, *op*, 1987, (MACjilli); *Freude × (Arthur Bell Seedling × Sunsong)*; McGredy, Sam; Sam McGredy Roses International, 1988. Flowers orange blend, dbl. (26-40 petals), large; slight fragrance; foliage large, medium green, semi-glossy; upright growth.

Profusion HT, *dp*, 1939, Dickson, A. Bud long, pointed; flowers carmine, base orange-yellow, full; fragrant; vigorous growth.

Profusion HT, *op*, 1944, *Mme. Henri Guillot × Signora*; Meilland, F. Bud very long; flowers orange-salmon and carmine; foliage glossy.

Prolet S, *pb*, 1975, *Generál Stefánik × Bonn*; Staikov, Prof. Dr. V.; Kalaydjiev and Chorbadjiiski. Flowers brick, shaded deep pink, very dbl. (85 petals), medium; foliage light green; vigorous, upright, branching growth; non-recurrent.

Prolifera de Redouté C (OGR), *mp*, Prior to 1824; Resembles Cabbage Rose, except sepals are longer and more fringed; often bears another flower in center of blossom. See also Steeple Rose.

Prolifère M (OGR), *dp*, Prior to 1848. Flowers deep-rose, cupped, too full to open well at times, large; vigorous.

Prom Date Min, *dp*, 1989, (MORprom); *Sheri Anne × (Seedling × Fairy Moss)*; Moore, Ralph S.; Sequoia Nursery. Bud short, pointed; flowers deep pink, aging lighter, dbl. (38 petals), globular, medium, borne singly, profuse; no fragrance; foliage medium, medium green, matt; prickles straight, pointed, medium, gray to brown; fruit globular, orange; upright, bushy, medium growth.

Prom Night Min, *pb*, 1987, (ZIPpro); *Poker Chip × Libby*; Zipper, Herbert; Magic Moment Miniatures. Flowers creamy yellow, shading to pink with deep pink flushing the edges, very full (40+ petals), medium, sweetheart sized (mini-flora); slight fragrance; foliage large, medium green, matt; upright, bushy, candelabra-formed growth.

Promenade Min, *dr*, 1985, (LYOpro); *Red Can Can × Seedling*; Lyon; MB Farms, Inc. Flowers very dark red, dbl. (35 petals), informal, ruffled, small blooms borne singly and in clusters; no fragrance; foliage medium, dark, matt; bushy growth.

Promethean S, *rb*, 1985, *(Blanche Mallerin × Pink Hat) × R. multibracteata*; James, John. Flowers medium red, reverse darker, white eye, single (12 petals), medium; slight fragrance; foliage medium, light green, smooth, matt; bushy growth; repeats.

Prominent® Gr, *or*, 1971, (KORp); *Colour Wonder × Zorina*; Kordes, R.; Kordes. Bud long, pointed; flowers orange-red, dbl. (33 petals), cupped, large (3½ in.); slightly fragrant; foliage matt; upright growth. GM, Portland, 1975; AARS, 1977.

Promise Cl Ch (OGR), *op*, 1929, (Chin Chin); *Mme. Eugène Resal sport*; Cant, F. Flowers salmon-pink, stamens bright yellow, single, borne in large clusters; fragrant; foliage almost evergreen; vigorous, climbing growth; non-recurrent bloom.

Promise HT, *lp*, 1976, (JACis; Poesie); *South Seas × Peace*; Warriner; J&P. Bud ovoid; flowers light pink, dbl., high-centered, large; slightly fragrant; foliage large, glossy; vigorous. GM, Bagatelle, 1976.

Promise Me HT, *w*, 1969, (JELwhite); *Snowsong Supreme × Seedling*; Jelly; E.G. Hill Co. Flowers white, dbl. (45 petals), high-centered, large (4 in.); slightly fragrant (sweet briar); foliage matt, dark, leathery; vigorous, upright growth.

Promotion F, *mp*, 1966, *Seedling × Miracle*; Verbeek. Bud ovoid; flowers pink, dbl., medium, borne in clusters; fragrant; foliage dark.

Prosper Laugier HP (OGR), *mr*, 1883, Verdier, E. Flowers scarlet-red, dbl. (30 petals), cupped, large; tall growth; recurrent bloom.

Prosperity HMsk (S), *w*, 1919, *Marie-Jeanne × Perle des Jardins*; Pemberton. Bud creamy white flushed pale pink; flowers ivory white, semi-dbl., small to medium blooms in large clusters; fragrant; foliage glossy; vigorous, pillar (6-8 ft.); recurrent bloom; (21).

Prospero® S, *dr*, 1983, (AUSpero); *The Knight × Seedling*; Austin, David, 1982. Flowers dark red, dbl. (40+ petals), flat, large; very fragrant; foliage medium, dark, matt; weak, upright growth.

Proteiformis S, *w*, (R. × protieformis Rowley; R. × heterophylla Cochet, not Woods); *R. rugosa alba × Seedling*; 1894. A curiosity of great botanical interest, the foliage very diverse, becoming narrower and more fern-like toward the end of the season.

Proud Heritage Min, *dr*, 1986, *Red Beauty × Big John*; Jolly, Nelson; Rosehill Farm. Flowers dark red, dbl. (28 petals), exhibition, patio, large blooms in sprays of 2-3; slight fragrance; foliage medium, medium green, matt; light green to brown prickles, hooked downward; fruit globular, orange; upright, bushy growth.

Proud Land HT, *dr*, 1969, *Chrysler Imperial × Seedling*; Morey; J&P. Bud urn-shaped; flowers deep red, dbl. (60 petals), large; fragrant; foliage dark, leathery; vigorous, upright growth.

Proud Mary Gr, *or*, 1991, (TWOhave); *Seedling × Royalty*; Twomey, Jerry, 1983; DeVor Nursery, 1991. Bud pointed; flowers scarlet red, semi-dbl. (19-21 petals), medium; moderate, damask fragrance; foliage medium, dark green, semi-glossy; upright, bushy, medium growth.

Proud Titania S, *w*, 1983, (AUStania); *Seedling × Seedling*; Austin, David, 1982. Flowers white, dbl. (35 petals), flat; very fragrant; foliage small, medium green, semi-glossy; upright growth.

Provence HT, *ob*, 1945, Paolino; A. Meilland. Flowers orange, tinted copper and pink, well-formed; fragrant.

Prudence Cl HT, *op*, 1938, *Warrawee* × *Souv. de Claudius Pernet*; Fitzhardinge; Hazlewood Bros. Flowers salmon-pink, semi-dbl., cupped, large; very fragrant; very vigorous, climbing (10 ft.) growth; recurrent bloom.

Prudhoe Peach HT, *ab*, 1970, *Piccadilly sport*; Wood; Homedale Nursery. Flowers apricot-peach, dbl. (25 petals), full; foliage glossy, dark, leathery; free growth.

P'tit Pacha F, *rb*, 1965, *Seedling* × *Coup de Foudre*; Combe. Bud pointed; flowers geranium-red edged dark red, semi-dbl., large; moderate growth. GM, Madrid, 1963.

Puccini HT, *rb*, 1968, *Opera* × *Teenager*; Ellick. Flowers red, veined yellow, dbl. (26-33 petals), full, large (4-6 in.); very fragrant; foliage large, light; very vigorous growth.

Puccini's Daughter F, *ob*, 1972, *(Puccini* × *Peace)* × *Orange Sensation*; Ellick; Excelsior Roses. Flowers orange-flame, reverse streaked yellow, semi-dbl. (20-25 petals), full, large (4 in.); very fragrant; foliage glossy, dark; very vigorous, upright growth.

Puck HT, *mr*, 1921, *Lyon Rose* × *Gen. MacArthur*; Bees. Bud long, pointed; flowers cherry-crimson, dbl., fragrant.

Puck F, *or*, 1960, *Pour Toi* × *Margaret McGredy*; Leenders, J. Bud globular; flowers cinnabar-red, dbl., cupped, large; slightly fragrant; foliage leathery; moderate growth.

Pucker Up Min, *or*, 1984, (TINpuck); *Futura* × *Avandel*; Bennett, Dee; Tiny Petals Nursery, 1983. Bud small; flowers bright orange-red, semi-dbl. (23 petals), HT form, exhibition; slight fragrance; foliage medium, medium green, semi-glossy; upright, bushy growth.

Puerta del Sol® Cl HT, *my*, 1971, (DELglap); *(Queen Elizabeth* × *Provence)* × *(Michèle Meilland* × *Bayadere)*; Delbard. Flowers medium golden yellow, dbl. (28 petals), large; light fragrance; vigorous, climbing (to 9 ft.).

Puerto Rico F, *ob*, 1975, (DELsob; Sable Chaud; Sable Cloud); *Zambra* × *(Orange Triumph* × *Floradora)*; Delbard; Armstrong Nursery. Flowers orange, reverse blended with yellow, dbl., cupped, medium; slightly fragrant (spicy); foliage bronze, leathery; vigorous, bushy.

Pumila Min, *dp*, Origin unknown. Bud long, pointed; flowers bright pink to red, dbl.; almost thornless; dwarf (8-10 in.) growth.

Punch F, *dp*, 1960, *Luc Varenne* × *Lafayette*; Delforge. Flowers raspberry-red, semi-dbl., open, medium, borne in clusters; foliage glossy; moderate, bushy growth.

Punkin Min, *ob*, 1983, (TINkin); *Orange Honey* × *Orange Honey*; Bennett, Dee; Tiny Petals Nursery. Flowers orange with yellow eye, ages red, single (5 petals), blooms borne singly; no fragrance; foliage small, medium green, semi-glossy; upright growth.

Puppy Love Min, *ob*, 1978, (SAVapup); *Zorina* × *Seedling*; Schwartz, E.W.; Nor'East Min. Roses. Bud pointed; flowers pink, coral, orange blend, semi-dbl. (23 petals), high-centered, small (1½ in.); slightly fragrant; foliage matt; upright, compact growth. AOE, 1979.

Pure Love™ HT, *w*, 1988, (BURlov); *Queen Elizabeth* × *World Peace*; Perry, Anthony; Co-Operative Rose Growers, 1987. Flowers white, semi-dbl., urn-shaped, large, borne singly; slight fragrance; foliage medium, dark green, semi-glossy; prickles slight recurve, average, brown-green; fruit globular, average, gray-red; upright, medium growth.

Purezza R, *w*, 1961, (*R. banksiae* 'Purezza'); Tom Thumb × *R. banksiae lutescens*; Mansuino, Q. Flowers white, dbl., medium (1-2 in.) blooms in clusters of 39-50; fragrant; foliage leathery; very vigorous growth; recurrent bloom. GM, Rome, 1960.

Puritan HT, *w*, Flowers white, large; fragrant.

Purity LCl, *w*, 1917, *Seedling* × *Mme. Caroline Testout*; Hoopes, Bro.; Thomas. Flowers pure unshaded white, semi-dbl., well-formed, large; slightly fragrant; foliage light; heavy prickles; vigorous, climbing growth.

Purple Beauty HT, *m*, 1979, *Eminence* × *Tyrius*; Gandy. Flowers red-purple, dbl. (30 petals), exhibition, large (5 in.); fragrant; foliage leathery; vigorous, upright growth.

Purple Bengal Ch (OGR), *dr*, 1827, (Violet Bengal); Vibert. Flowers maroon shaded darker; (14).

Purple Dawn Min, *m*, 1991, (BRIdawn); *Party Girl* × *Seedling*; Bridges, Dennis; Bridges Roses. Flowers velvety mauve, long-lasting, urn-shaped, high-centered, exhibition with good substance, dbl. (25 petals), medium (4 cms) blooms borne usually singly or in sprays of 5-7; slight fragrance; foliage medium, dark green, semi-glossy; upright, tall growth.

Purple East HMult (OGR), *m*, 1900, *Crimson Rambler* × *Beauté Inconstante*; Paul. Flowers crimson-purple, semi-dbl., medium blooms in clusters; early bloom.

Purple Elf Min, *m*, 1967, *Violette* × *Zee*; Moore, R.S.; Sequoia Nursery. Flowers fuchsia-purple, dbl. (43 petals), small; foliage glossy; dwarf, bushy (10 in.) growth.

Purple Fantasy Min, *m*, 1982, *Blue Mist* × *Snow Magic*; Dobbs, Annette. Flowers deep purple, dbl. (40+ petals), small; no fragrance; foliage small, medium green, matt; bushy.

Purple Heart HT, *m*, 1946, *Crimson Queen × Self*; Moore, R.S.; Sequoia Nursery. Bud long, pointed; flowers dahlia-purple to blackish red-purple, semi-dbl., cupped, large; very fragrant; upright, bushy growth.

Purple Imp Min, *m*, 1967, *Baby Faurax × Red Imp*; Wiliams, E.D.; Mini-Roses. Bud ovoid; flowers magenta to purple, dbl., small; foliage small, narrow, glossy; vigorous, very compact growth.

Purple Majesty™ Min, *m*, 1987, (MINajco); *Tom Brown × Black Jack*; Williams, Ernest; Mini-Roses. Flowers mauve, edged red, reverse mauve, dbl. (40 petals), high-centered, exhibition, small, borne usually singly or in sprays of 3-5; foliage small, medium green, semi-glossy; tan, needle-like prickles, dilated at base; no fruit; bushy, medium growth.

Purple Popcorn™ S, *m*, 1991, (WILpurp); *R. chinensis minima × (Sea Foam × The Fairy) Seedling*; Williams, J. Benjamin, 1992. Flowers bluish purple, single (6-14 petals), small (0-4 cms) blooms borne in small, grape like clusters; slight fragrance; foliage small, medium green, matt, disease resistant; few prickles; low (12-18 in.), compact, bushy growth.

Purple Splendour F, *m*, 1976, *News × Overture*; LeGrice. Flowers glowing purple, dbl. (26 petals), large (4 in.); slightly fragrant; foliage dark; upright growth.

Purple Sunset Min, *m*, 1992, (MANpursun); *Rise 'n' Shine × MANpurple*; Mander, George, 1992-93. Flowers purple/cream bicolor, very attractive bicolor combination, semi-dbl. (15-25 petals), small (0-4 cms) blooms borne in small clusters; no fragrance; foliage small, dark green, glossy; few prickles; low (35-40 cms), upright growth.

Purple Tiger F, *m*, 1991, (JACpurr); *Intrigue × Pinstripe*; Christensen, Jack; Bear Creek Gardens, 1992. Flowers very deep purple with stripes and flecks of white and mauve-pink, dbl. (26-40 petals), large (7+ cms) blooms borne in small clusters; stems very glabrous (shiny); fragrant; foliage medium, medium green, glossy; nearly thornless; medium (70-90 cms), bushy growth.

Purpurea Sp (OGR), *m*, (Maheka; Purpuria); *R. roxburghii Seedling*; Buist, prior to 1844. Flowers purple-crimson or purplish-rose; no prickles on sepals or receptacle; foliage and growth habit typical of *R. roxburghii*.

Purpurea S, *dr*, 1822, (Purple Noisette); Laffay. Flowers purple-crimson, semi-dbl., poorly formed; Boursault type.

Purpurea Rubra M (OGR), *m*, Flowers violet-purple, full, well mossed, large; very fragrant.

Purpurine F, *m*, *(Peace × Seedling) × Fashion*; Lens; Galan. Bud long; flowers fuchsia-purple to rhodamine-purple, dbl.; slightly fragrant; foliage dark; vigorous, bushy growth.

Pusa Christina HT, *mp*, 1976, Indian Agric. Research Inst. Bud globular; flowers pink, very dbl. (50 petals), high-centered, medium (3 in.); slightly fragrant; foliage soft; vigorous, upright growth.

Pusa Sonia HT, *dy*, 1968, *McGredy's Yellow × Seedling*; Indian Agric. Research Inst. Bud long, pointed; flowers golden yellow, dbl. (24 petals), large; fragrant; foliage leathery; vigorous, upright growth.

Pusa Sonora HT, *pb*, 1984, *Queen Elizabeth × First Prize*; Division of Floriculture and Landscaping. Flowers rose pink, deeper reverse, single (5 petals), medium; no fragrance; foliage medium green; bushy, upright growth.

Pye Colour F, *mr*, 1972, *Marlena × Elizabeth of Glamis*; Dickson, A. Flowers turkey-red, dbl. (30 petals), ovate, medium (2 in.); slightly fragrant; foliage leathery; free growth.

Pygmae® Min, *or*, 1977, (Pygmy); *Anytime × Minuette*; Poulsen, N.D.; D.T. Poulsen. Bud globular; flowers bright orange-red, yellow center, semi-dbl. (13 petals), small (1 in.) blooms in clusters; foliage small, glossy, dark; low, compact, spreading, bushy.

Pythagoras HSpn (OGR), *pb*, *R. spinosissima hybrid*; Prior to 1848. Flowers light pink, flecked deep pink, semi-dbl.; foliage finely divided; fruit black, glossy; dense, shrubby (3-4 ft.) growth; early bloom.

Quadroon S, *dr*, Supposedly *Hansa × (Hansa × R. nitida)*; Wright, P.H. Flowers rich dark red, single, small; growth rather poor; nonrecurrent bloom.

Quaker Beauty HT, *ab*, 1936, *Joanna Hill sport*; Brookins. Bud long, pointed; flowers glowing apricot, high-centered, large; a forcing variety.

Quaker Maid F, *or*, 1959, *Orange Sweetheart × Pinocchio*; Hill, J.H., Co. Bud ovoid; flowers nasturtium-red, semi-dbl. (18-20 petals), flat, medium (1½-2 in.), borne in clusters; fragrant (spicy); foliage leathery; vigorous, upright, bushy growth; for greenhouse use.

Quaker Star Gr, *op*, 1991, (DICperhaps); *Ainsley Dickson × Seedling*; Dickson, Colin; Roses by Fred Edmunds, 1992. Flowers orange with silver reverse, aging to salmon with orange petal edges, very full (over 40 petals), large (over 7 cms) blooms borne mostly singly; no fragrance; foliage medium, dark green, glossy; few prickles, straight, small; upright, medium (120 cms) growth.

Quantock Star HT, *or*, 1968, *Tropicana sport*; Heard. Flowers vermilion shaded pink, dbl., small; fragrant; foliage variegated; free growth.

Quatre Saisons Blanche D (OGR), *w*, 1838, *Quatre Saisons sport*. Flowers white.

Queen Alexandra R, *mp*, 1901, Veitch. Flowers rosy pink, semi-dbl.; large corymbs.

Queen Ann HT, *dr*, 1949, *Better Times sport*; Spandikow. Bud long, pointed; flowers crimson, dbl., high-centered, medium; strong stems; vigorous growth.

Queen Beatrice HT, *lp*, 1909, *Mme. Abel Chatenay × Liberty*; Kramer. Flowers bright silvery pink, very dbl., large to medium; fragrant; vigorous growth.

Queen Bee S, *dr*, 1984, (*Rosali × Music Maker*) × (*Square Dancer × Tatjana*); Buck; Iowa State University. Flowers dark red, dbl. (35 petals), high-centered to cupped, 4-5 in. blooms borne 5-8 per cluster; old rose fragrance; foliage large, leathery, dark olive green; awl-like, brown prickles; erect, bushy, branching growth; repeat bloom; hardy.

Queen Charlotte HT, *op*, 1988, (HARubondee); *Basildon Bond × Silver Jubilee*; Harkness, R.; R. Harkness; Co., Ltd., 1989. Flowers deep salmon-red, yellow base, reverse pink-red, aging paler, semi-dbl. (23 broad petals), high-centered, exhibition, large, borne usually singly; slight fragrance; foliage large, dark green, semi-glossy; prickles recurved, medium, reddish-green; fruit ovoid, large, green; upright, tall growth.

Queen City Min, *ob*, 1986, *Rise 'n' Shine × Seedling*; Bridges, Dennis, 1987. Flowers orange, yellow base, fading lighter, semi-dbl. (20 petals), high-centered, exhibition, medium, borne usually singly; slight fragrance; foliage medium, medium green, semi-glossy; long, straight, medium, light colored prickles; bushy, medium growth.

Queen Dina Gr, *dr*, 1964, *Cocorico × Geranium Red*; Soenderhousen; Hoersholm Nursery. Flowers deep scarlet, dbl., large; foliage leathery; very vigorous, upright, bushy growth.

Queen Dorothy Bell HT, *dr*, 1940, *Oswald Sieper sport*; Stell; Stell Rose Nursery. Flowers velvety scarlet, very dbl., globular; very fragrant; foliage light, leathery; vigorous growth.

Queen Elizabeth® Gr, *mp*, 1954, (Queen of England; The Queen Elizabeth Rose); *Charlotte Armstrong × Floradora*; Lammerts; Germain's. Bud pointed; flowers medium pink, dbl. (38 petals), high-centered to cupped, large (3½-4 in.) blooms borne singly and in clusters; fragrant; foliage dark, glossy, leathery; very vigorous, upright, bushy growth. GM, Portland, 1954; NRS, 1955; AARS, 1955; NRS PIT, 1955; ARS (Gertrude M. Hubbard), 1957; ARS National Certificate, 1960.

Queen Elizabeth, Climbing Cl Gr, *mp*, 1957, (The Queen Elizabeth Rose, Climbing; Grimpant Queen Elizabeth); Whisler; Germain's, 1957; Wheatcroft Bros., 1960.

Queen Esther HT, *w*, 1984, *Golden Masterpiece × Peer Gynt*; Poole, Lionel. Flowers cream, pale pink petal edges, dbl. (35 petals), spiraled, large; slight fragrance; foliage medium, medium green, matt; many prickles.

Queen Fabiola Gr, *or*, 1961, (Fabiola); *Montezuma sport*; Hazenberg; Delbard.

Queen Frances Connally HT, *mr*, 1939, *Katharine Pechtold sport*; Stell; Stell Rose Nursery. Flowers spectrum-red, base lemon-chrome, reverse yellow edged red.

Queen Gertrude Anne Windsor HT, *dp*, 1936, *Francis Scott Key sport*; Dixie Rose Nursery. Flowers darker.

Queen Louise Boren HT, *op*, 1935, (*Emile Charles × La France*) × *Maréchal Niel*; Nicolas; Dixie Rose Nursery. Flowers pink suffused salmon, dbl., large; very fragrant; very vigorous growth.

Queen Lucia F, *op*, 1954, *Pinocchio × Tapis Rose*; Maarse, G. Flowers salmon-pink, dbl., pompon form, borne in large trusses; vigorous growth; a forcing variety.

Queen Mab Ch (OGR), *ab*, 1896, Paul, W. Flowers soft rosy apricot, center shaded orange, reverse tinted rose and violet, full, large.

Queen Margaret Hunt HT, *dr*, 1936, *Templar × Ami Quinard*; Nicolas; Dixie Rose Nursery. Bud long, pointed, spiral; flowers dark velvety crimson-maroon, stamens golden yellow, cupped, large; very fragrant; foliage leathery; very vigorous growth.

Queen Marie HT, *pb*, 1925, *Mme. Butterfly × Lamia*; Chervenka. Flowers rose-pink, reverse deeper pink, base bronze yellow, dbl.; fragrant.

Queen Marie of Jugoslavia HT, *my*, 1935, *Mme. Butterfly sport*; Hicks. Flowers bright yellow, slightly flushed pink.

Queen Mary HT, *yb*, 1913, Dickson, A. Flowers bright canary yellow, shaded red; fragrant. GM, NRS, 1913.

Queen o' the Lakes HT, *dr*, 1949, *Pink Princess × Crimson Glory*; Brownell. Bud ovoid, long, pointed; flowers dark red, dbl., high-centered, large; fragrant; foliage glossy; vigorous, bushy growth.

Queen o' the Lakes, Climbing Cl HT, *dr*, 1965, Brownell.

Queen of Bath HT, *dy*, 1931, *Souv. de Claudius Pernet* × *Cleveland*; Bees. Bud long, pointed; flowers deep buttercup-yellow, outer edged chrome-yellow, dbl., high-centered; very fragrant; foliage thick, glossy, bronze; vigorous growth.

Queen of Bedders B (OGR), *dp*, 1871, *Sir Joseph Paxton Seedling*; Noble. Flowers deep carmine, well-shaped; dwarf, compact growth.

Queen of Bermuda Gr, *or*, 1956, *(Independence* × *Orange Triumph)* × *Bettina*; Bowie; Bermuda Rose Nursery. Bud ovoid; flowers orange-vermilion, dbl. (35 petals), high-centered, large (4 in.) blooms in small clusters; fragrant (fruity); foliage glossy, bronze; vigorous, bushy growth.

Queen of Bourbons B (OGR), *pb*, 1834, (Bourbon Queen; Reine des Iles Bourbon; Souv. de la Princesse de Lamballe); Mauget. Flowers fawn and rose, cupped; very fragrant.

Queen of Fragrance HT, *lp*, 1915, Paul, W. Flowers shell-pink, tipped silver, dbl., well shaped, large; very fragrant; foliage soft; dwarf growth.

Queen of Hearts Cl HT, *mp*, 1920, *Gustave Grünerwald* × *Rosy Morn*; Clark, A.; NRS Victoria. Bud globular; flowers rich pink, dbl., cupped, large; fragrant; foliage dark; very vigorous, climbing growth.

Queen of the Belgians Ayr (OGR), *w*, *R. arvensis hybrid*; Prior to 1848. Flowers white, very dbl., small.

Queen of the Belgians HT, *op*, 1916, Hicks. Bud long, pointed; flowers salmon-pink, single to semi-dbl. GM, NRS, 1915.

Queen of the Dwarfs Min, *dp*, 1955, (Dwarf Queen; Zwergkönigin); Kordes. Flowers deep pink, dbl.; foliage rather coarse; height 10-12 in.

Queen of the Musks HMsk (S), *pb*, 1913, Paul. Bud coppery red; flowers deep blush and white, blooms in panicles; very fragrant; foliage dark ivy-green; recurrent bloom.

Queen of the Prairies HSet (OGR), *pb*, 1843, (Beauty of the Prairies; Prairie Belle); *Probably R. setigera* × *China*; Feast. Flowers bright pink, frequently striped white, dbl., globular, large blooms in clusters; fragrant; foliage large; vigorous, climbing growth; hardy.

Queen Thornless, Climbing Cl HT, *dp, Accidentally produced from budding of Étoile de Hollande to R. multiflora*; Kittle; Lincoln Nursery Co. Bud pointed; flowers deep pink, semi-dbl. (20-40 petals), high-centered,

large (3-4 in.); strong stems; fragrant; foliage leathery, dull green; thornless; vigorous, arching growth; intermittent bloom.

Queen Victoria HP (OGR), *lp*, 1850, *La Reine Seedling*; Fontaine; A. Paul. Flowers blush-pink, full, large.

Queen Wilhelmina HT, *ob*, 1942, *Hinrich Gaede sport*; Deverman. Flowers brilliant orange, base light orange-yellow.

Queenie F, *lp*, 1962, (Petite Reine); *Pinocchio Seedling* × *Spartan*; Boerner; J&P. Bud ovoid; flowers light pink, dbl. (33 petals), cupped, large (4 in.) blooms in clusters; fragrant; foliage leathery; vigorous, upright, bushy growth.

Queenie Robinson HT, *op*, 1924, Easlea. Bud long, pointed; flowers orange-cerise to flame-pink, semi-dbl.; fragrant.

Queenie's Love HT, *dp*, 1968, *Libretto* × *Mme. Butterfly*; Verschuren, A.; Stassen. Bud globular; flowers begonia-rose, dbl., medium; fragrant; foliage leathery; vigorous growth.

Queen's Knight S, *mp*, 1979, *Don Juan* × *R. laxa (Retzius)*; Stoddard, Louis. Bud short, conical; flowers medium pink, single (6-10 petals), shallow-cupped, blooms borne 3 per cluster; slight fragrance; foliage semi-glossy, deep green, 7 leaflet; hooked prickles; erect arches, self-supporting growth; profuse for 6 weeks; non-recurrent.

Queen's Scarlet Ch (OGR), *mr*, 1880, (Red Hermosa); Hallock; Thorpe. Flowers rich velvety scarlet, dbl., small; fragrant; foliage small; bushy, compact growth.

Queen's Visit HT, *dr*, 1955, *Crimson Glory sport* × *Crimson Glory*; Viney; Wynne. Bud long, pointed; flowers dark velvety red veined darker, dbl., high-centered, medium; fragrant; foliage leathery; vigorous growth.

Queensland Beauty HT, *pb*, 1934, *Golden Dawn sport*; Alderton; Williams. Flowers coppery pink.

Queenstown HT, *dr*, 1991, *Silent Night* × *Josephine Bruce*; Cattermole, R.F., 1975; South Pacific Roses, 1991. Bud pointed; flowers deep crimson to ruby red, cupped, dbl. (32 petals), large (12.5 cms) blooms borne up to 6 per cluster; some fragrance; foliage leather, mid-green, semi-glossy; upright, spreading growth.

Quicksilver HT, *m*, 1985, (AROstal); *Blue Nile* × *Brandy*; Christensen; Michigan Bulb. Flowers pale lavender gray, dbl. (25 petals), high-centered, exhibition, large blooms borne singly; fragrant; foliage large, dark, matt; medium; yellow-gray prickles; tall, upright, bushy growth.

Quo Vadis? HT, *pb*, 1961, *Peace × (Baiser × Seedling)*; Giacomasso. Bud oval; flowers silvery pink becoming red, dbl. (50-60 petals), large; slightly fragrant; very vigorous growth.

Raat-ki-Rani HT, *mr*, 1975, *Seedling × Samourai Seedling (open-pollinated)*; Indian Agric. Research Inst. Bud pointed; flowers velvety crimson-red, dbl. (30 petals), full, large (4½ in.); slightly fragrant; foliage glossy; vigorous, upright growth.

Rabbie Burns HT, *mr*, 1959, *Ena Harkness × Sutter's Gold*; Arnot; Croll. Bud long, pointed; flowers bright light red, semi-dbl.; very fragrant; foliage dark; vigorous, upright growth.

Rachel HT, *ob*, 1929, Pemberton. Flowers orange-buff, flushed carmine, full, high-centered, large; foliage dark; very vigorous growth. RULED EXTINCT 5/84.

Rachel S, *mp*, 1977, (BOOyol); Booth, Mrs. Rachel Y. Flowers medium pink, dbl. (35 petals), medium; delicate fragrance; foliage medium, medium green, matt; upright growth.

Rachel Bowes Lyon S, *yb*, 1981, (HARlacal); *Kim × ((Orange Sensation × Allgold) × R. californica)*; Harkness, R. Flowers peach pink, reverse yellow, semi-dbl. (14petals), flat, medium blooms in large clusters; fragrant; foliage small to medium, medium green; small prickles; low, bushy growth.

Rachel Crawshay HT, *op*, 1977, *Fragrant Cloud × Mary Mine*; Harkness. Flowers pink to orange-salmon, dbl. (30 petals), large (5 in.); slightly fragrant; foliage olive-green.

Rachel Townsend HT, *yb*, 1963, *Sultane sport*; Townsend; Townsend & Son. Flowers golden yellow tipped carmine, dbl. (30 petals), large (4-4½ in.); foliage dark, glossy; free growth.

Rachelle F, *mp*, 1976, *Antigua × Seedling*; Warriner; J&P. Bud long; flowers french rose, dbl. (30 petals), nearly flat, medium (2-3 in.); slightly fragrant; upright growth; abundant bloom in greenhouse.

Rada HT, *dr*, 1975, *Baccará × Seedling*; Staikov, Prof. Dr. V.; Kalaydjiev and Chorbadjiiski. Flowers dark red, dbl. (75 petals), large; foliage medium green, glossy.

Radames HT, *dr*, 1983, *Seedling × Seedling*; Fumagalli, Niso. Flowers dark red, dbl. (35 petals), large; very fragrant; foliage large, medium green, glossy; upright growth.

Radar HT, *or*, 1953, *Charles Mallerin × Independence*; Meilland, F.; URS. Bud long; flowers light geranium-red, dbl. (45 petals), well formed, large; fragrant; vigorous growth.

Radar, Climbing Cl HT, *or*, 1959, Meilland, M.L.; URS.

Radar Italiana HT, *or*, 1944, *Souv. de Denier van der Gon × Brazier*; San Remo Exp. Sta. Bud pointed; flowers nasturtium-red edged rose, dbl. (32-34 petals), large; fragrant; foliage bright green; vigorous, bushy growth.

Radcliffe Flame HT, *mr*, 1986, *Alec's Red × Grandpa Dickson*; Thomson, Colin, 1987. Flowers medium red, dbl. (26-40 petals), medium; no fragrance; foliage medium, dark green, matt; upright growth.

Radiance HT, *lp*, 1908, (Pink Radiance); *Enchanter × Cardinal*; Cook, J.; P. Henderson. Bud globular; flowers rose-pink, reverse lighter, semi-dbl. (23 petals), cupped, large; very fragrant (damask); foliage leathery; vigorous growth.

Radiance, Climbing Cl HT, *lp*, 1926, (Pink Radiance, Climbing); Griffing, W.D.

Radiance, Climbing Cl HT, *lp*, 1928, (Pink Radiance, Climbing); Catt.

Radiant HT, *or*, 1962, *Mrs. Sam McGredy × Fantasia*; Fletcher; Tucker. Bud spiral; flowers orange-flame, reverse shaded red, dbl. (30 petals), large (4-5 in.); slightly fragrant; foliage glossy; very free growth. RULED EXTINCT 9/87.

Radiant™ Min, *or*, 1987, (BENrad); *Sheri Anne × Sheri Anne*; Benardella, Frank; Nor'East Miniature Roses, 1988. Flowers brilliant orange-red, dbl. (23-27 petals), urn-shaped, exhibition, medium, borne singly; mini-flora; long, straight stems; moderate, spicy fragrance; foliage dark green, semi-glossy; prickles long, straight, pointed slightly downward, gray-red; fruit none; upright, tall growth.

Radiant Beauty HT, *mr*, 1934, *Francis Scott Key sport*; Cleveland Cut-Flower Co. Flowers deeper crimson than parent, not turning blue, dbl. (about 25 petals less than parent); fragrant.

Radiant Glow F, *or*, 1953, *Pinocchio × Seedling*; Quinn; Roseglen Nursery. Bud pointed; flowers bright orange-salmon tinted peach, dbl., cupped, medium, borne singly and in clusters; foliage leathery, light green; vigorous, upright growth.

Radiant Gold HT, *my*, 1985, (JACern); *Precilla × Sunshine*; J&P; McConnell Nursery. Flowers medium yellow, dbl. (35 petals), large; foliage large, dark, glossy; upright growth.

Radiant Superglaze HT, *w*, 1986, (NOStrad; Radiant Super Glaze); *Gavotte × Erotika*; Greensitt, J.A.; Nostell Priory Rose Gardens, 1982. Flowers near white, dbl. (40+ petals), large; fragrant; foliage large, dark green, glossy.

Radiation F, *mr*, 1960, *Poulsen's Pink* × *Pompadour Red*; deRuiter. Flowers red, semi-dbl., open, large (3-3½ in.), borne in clusters; foliage glossy; vigorous growth.

Radieuse HT, *mr*, 1955, Laperrière; EFR. Bud long; flowers clear red, dbl. (30-35 petals), well formed, large; vigorous, bushy growth.

Radiman F, *ly*, 1975, *Highlight* × *Masquerade*; Staikov, Prof. Dr. V.; Kalaydjiev and Chorbadjiiski. Flowers light yellow, dbl. (50 petals), cupped, medium blooms in clusters of 5-35; tea fragrance; foliage dark, glossy; vigorous growth.

Radio HT, *yb*, 1937, *Condesa de Sástago sport*; Dot, P.; C-P. Flowers yellow slightly tinted pink, striped and marked rose, dbl. (50 petals), cupped, large; fragrant (spicy); foliage wrinkled, light; vigorous growth.

Radio Lancashire F, *or*, 1987, *Dusky Maiden* × *Matangi*; Bracegirdle, A.J.; Rosemary Roses, 1987. Flowers orange-red, reverse slightly lighter, dbl. (38 petals), rosette, medium, borne in sprays of 12-15; slight, fruity fragrance; foliage medium, dark green, glossy; triangle-shaped, brown prickles; fruit round, orange; upright, medium growth.

Radium HT, *rb*, 1922, *Beauté Lyonnaise* × *Capt. Hayward*; Lippiatt. Flowers carmine, shaded coppery red.

Radome F, *lp*, 1966, *Queen Elizabeth sport*; Nicol; Minier. Flowers pale rose.

Radox Bouquet F, *mp*, 1980, (HARmusky; Rosika); *(Alec's Red* × *Piccadilly)* × *(Southampton* × *(Cläre Grammerstorf* × *Frühlingsmorgen))*; Harkness, R., 1981. Flowers soft medium pink, dbl. (30 petals), cupped blooms borne 1-3 per cluster; fragrant; foliage large, glossy, medium green; large, dark prickles; upright, rather open growth.

Radway Charm HT, *dp*, 1959, *Christopher Stone* × *McGredy's Wonder sport*; Waterhouse Nursery. Flowers deep pink, base deep yellow, semi-dbl. (20 petals); fragrant; vigorous growth

Radway Glow F, *op*, 1960, Waterhouse Nursery. Flowers coral-pink, semi-dbl. (14 petals), borne in large, open clusters; slightly fragrant; foliage dull green; vigorous growth.

Radway Jewel F, *dr*, 1960, Waterhouse Nursery. Flowers yellow, becoming orange and deep red, dbl. (40 petals), medium, borne in large clusters; foliage light green.

Radway Pink F, *mp*, 1965, *Margaret* × *Korona*; Waterhouse Nursery. Flowers rose-pink, dbl. (42 petals), large (3½ in.) borne in clusters; foliage dull green; very free growth.

Radway Scarlet F, *mr*, 1963, *Karl Weinhausen* × *Seedling*; Waterhouse Nursery. Flowers red; low growth.

Radway Sunrise S, *ob*, 1962, *Masquerade* × *Seedling*; Waterhouse Nursery. Flowers yellow, shading through orange to red, single (7 petals), large (3½-4 in.) blooms in clusters; slightly fragrant; foliage dark, glossy; very vigorous growth; recurrent bloom.

Rae Dungan HT, *yb*, 1971, *Daily Sketch* × *Fred Streeter*; Dawson, G. Bud long, pointed; flowers creamy yellow, edged deep pink, dbl., large; fragrant; foliage dark; vigorous.

Rafaela G. de Peña Pol, *ob*, 1938, Dot, P. Flowers pure orange, full; foliage bright green, leathery; vigorous, bushy growth.

Raffel's Pride HT, *mr*, 1937, *Talisman* × *Seedling*; Raffel; Port Stockton Nursery. Bud small; flowers oriental red, reverse gold-splashed, dbl., open; vigorous growth.

Raffel's Yellow HT, *my*, 1942, *Probably Mrs. Beatty* × *Maid of Gold*; Raffel; Port Stockton Nursery. Flowers pure yellow, dbl. (25-35 petals), well shaped, large; foliage bronze turning very dark; vigorous growth.

Raffles Bruce HT, *ab*, 1943, *Mrs. Sam McGredy* × *Aureate*; Bees. Flowers apricot and gold, medium (3-4 in.), well shaped; foliage dark; compact growth. GM, NRS, 1943.

Raggedy Ann F, *mr*, 1956, *Garnette* × *Sister Kenny*; Hill, J.H., Co. Bud short, pointed; flowers red, semi-dbl. (13 petals), medium blooms in clusters; slightly fragrant; foliage dark, leathery; vigorous, upright growth; greenhouse variety.

Ragtime F, *ab*, 1981, (PEAcap); *Vesper* × *Aloha*; Pearce, C.A.; Limes Rose Nursery. Flowers apricot pink, very dbl. (65 petals), blooms borne 10-15 per cluster; little fragrance; foliage small, mid-green, glossy; large, straight, red prickles; bushy growth.

Rainbow T (OGR), *pb*, 1889, *Papa Gontier sport*; Sievers. Flowers pink striped carmine.

Rainbow Bliss™ Min, *rb*, 1989, (DEVdicha); *Seedling* × *Scarlet Sunblaze*; Marciel, Stanley G.; DeVor Nursery. Bud slender, tapering; flowers white with cream inside with red edges, reverse same, aging discolors slightly, dbl. (45 imbricated petals), cupped, medium, borne singly; slight, damask fragrance; foliage small, dark green, glossy; prickles declining, brown-orange; upright, low growth.

Rainbow Cerise™ Min, *dp*, 1989, (DEVclavel); *Scarlet Sunblaze* × *Seedling*; Marciel, Stanley G.; DeVor Nursery. Bud tapering, slender; flowers deep pink, dbl. (45 petals), cupped, medium, borne singly; slight, fruity fragrance; foliage medium, dark green, glossy; bushy, medium growth.

Rainbow Crimson™ Min, *dr*, 1989, (DEVmesi); *Seedling × Seedling*; Marciel, Stanley G.; DeVor Nursery. Bud slender; flowers deep red, aging discolors slightly, dbl. (33 imbricated petals), cupped, small, borne singly; slight, damask fragrance; foliage medium, dark green, semi-glossy; prickles declining, slightly dark mauve; upright, low growth.

Rainbow Eclipse™ Min, *rb*, 1989, (DEVeclipsar); *Scarlet Sunblaze × Seedling*; Marciel, Stanley G.; DeVor Nursery. Bud pointed; flowers crimson-pink edges, center very light whitish-pink, fading to white, reverse same, dbl. (40 imbricated petals), medium, borne singly; slight fragrance; foliage small, dark green, glossy; prickles declining, rusty-brown; bushy, medium growth.

Rainbow Gold™ Min, *yb*, 1991, (DEVoro); *Amber Flash × Rhumba*; Marciel, Stanley C.; DeVor Nurseries. Flowers yellow-orange blend, full petals, medium blooms borne in small clusters; slight fragrance; foliage small, dark green, semi-glossy; upright, medium (53.5 cms) growth.

Rainbow Hot Pink™ Min, *dp*, 1989, (DEViente); *Orange Sunblaze × Seedling*; Marciel, Stanley G.; DeVor Nursery. Bud long, slightly urn-shaped; flowers deep pink, dbl. (35 imbricated petals), small, borne singly; foliage small, dark green, semi-glossy; prickles declining, mauve; bushy, medium growth.

Rainbow Pink™ Min, *dp*, 1989, (DEVrosado); *Seedling × Orange Sunblaze*; Marciel, Stanley G.; DeVor Nursery. Bud ovoid, pointed; flowers deep pink, dbl. (32 whole-imbricated petals), small, borne singly; slight, spicy fragrance; foliage medium, dark green, semi-glossy; frickles declining, purple; bushy, medium growth.

Rainbow Red™ Min, *mr*, 1989, (DEVrojo); *Scarlet Sunblaze × Rumba*; Marciel, Stanley G.; DeVor Nursery. Bud pointed; flowers medium red, dbl. (32 flat, imbricated petals), small, borne singly; slight, spicy fragrance; foliage small, dark green, glossy; prickles declining, brown with orange; bushy, medium growth.

Rainbow Shower LCl, *pb*, 1992, (LEEsho); *Altissimo × Playboy*; Little, Lee W.; Heirloom Old Garden Roses, 1992. Flowers shrimp pink suffused with yellow and darker pink edge, aging darker, single (5 petals), large (7+ cms) blooms borne in sprays of 5-7; slight fragrance; foliage medium, medium green, glossy, disease resistant; some prickles; tall (210 cms), upright, spreading growth.

Rainbow Stanford™ Min, *rb*, 1989, (DEVrico); *Candia × Seedling*; Marciel, Stanley G.; DeVor Nursery. Bud pointed, slender; flowers bright red, reverse same, aging discolors to a bright red-orange, semi-dbl. (15 imbricated, flattened petals), medium, borne singly; slight, fruity fragrance; foliage medium, dark green, glossy; prickles declining, reddish-brown; bushy, medium growth.

Rainbow Sunrise™ Min, *ob*, 1989, (DEVaurora); *Amber Flash × Rumba*; Marciel, Stanley G.; DeVor Nursery. Bud pointed; flowers orange with tinge of red, reverse same, aging turns to a pleasant pink tone, semi-dbl. (18 imbricated petals), small, borne singly; slight, spicy fragrance; foliage small, medium green, glossy; prickles sparse, declining, brown; bushy, medium growth.

Rainbow Surprise™ Min, *ab*, 1989, (DEVpresa); *Orange Sunblaze × Seedling*; Marciel, Stanley G.; DeVor Nursery. Bud slender, tapering; flowers medium coral, reverse light coral, aging pink, dbl. (30 imbricated petals), small, borne singly; slight, fruity fragrance; foliage small, dark green, glossy; prickles declining, mauve; bushy, medium growth.

Rainbow Yellow™ Min, *ob*, 1989, (DEVamarillo); *Seedling × Amber Flash*; Marciel, Stanley G.; DeVor Nursery. Bud pointed, urn-shaped; flowers tangerine orange, aging lighter, dbl. (55 imbricated petals), small, borne singly; heavy, fruity fragrance; foliage medium, medium green, matt; prickles declining, reddish-brown; bushy, medium growth.

Rainbow Yellow Parade™ Min, *dy*, 1990, (POUlwee; Yellow Parade (TM)); *Seedling × Texas*; Olesen, Pernille & Mogens N., 1985; DeVor Nurseries, Inc., 1990. Bud cupped, globular; flowers bright yellow, aging slightly, dbl. (28-30 petals), cupped, small, borne singly; slight, damask fragrance; foliage small, dark green, semi-glossy; no prickles; upright, low, compact growth. GM, The Hague, 1988.

Rainbow's End™ Min, *yb*, 1984, (SAValife); *Rise 'n' Shine × Watercolor*; Saville, F. Harmon; Nor'East Min. Roses. Bud small; flowers deep yellow, red petal edges, aging red all over, dbl. (35 petals), HT form; no fragrance; foliage small, dark, glossy; upright, bushy growth. AOE, 1986.

Raindrops™ Min, *m*, 1989, (SAVarain); *Sachet × Rainbow's End*; Saville, F. Harmon; Nor'East Miniature Roses, 1990. Bud ovoid; flowers light mauve-purple, light yellow at base, reverse lighter, semi-dbl. (24 petals), urn-shaped, small, borne in large sprays of 5-20; slight fragrance; foliage small, dark green, semi-glossy; prickles straight, slanted downward, small, gray-red; fruit none observed; upright, medium growth.

Rainy Day® HT, *mp*, 1982, (MACraida); *Trumpeter* × *Typhoon*; McGredy, Sam; McGredy International. Flowers medium pink, semi-dbl. (20 petals), large; slight fragrance; foliage large, dark, semi-glossy; bushy growth.

Raja of Nalagarh HT, *or*, 1977, *Samourai* × *Montezuma*; Pal; Gopalsinamiengar. Bud pointed; flowers red, dbl. (32 petals), high-centered, large (4 in.); slightly fragrant; foliage dark, leathery; vigorous, upright growth.

Rajbala F, *pb*, 1975, *Delhi Princess* × *Seedling*; Pal; Indian Agric. Research Inst. Bud pointed; flowers pink blend, single (10 petals), open, large (4 in.); foliage large, glossy, light; very vigorous, upright, compact growth.

Rajkumari HT, *dp*, 1975, *(Charles Mallerin* × *Delhi Princess)* × *Seedling*; Indian Agric. Research Inst. Bud pointed; flowers deep fuchsine-pink, very dbl. (70 petals), full, large (4 in.); foliage glossy, light; vigorous, compact growth.

Raketa HT, *op*, 1952, (Rocket); *Narzisse* × *Comtesse Vandal*; Shtanko, E.E. Flowers golden orange-pink, dbl. (50 petals), large (5 in.); foliage reddish bronze; vigorous, upright, compact growth.

Raktagandha HT, *or*, 1975, *Christian Dior* × *Carrousel seedling*; Indian Agric. Research Inst. Bud long, pointed; flowers vermilion, dbl. (35 petals), high-centered, medium (3 in.); slightly fragrant; foliage glossy; vigorous, upright growth.

Rallye Pol, *r*, 1966, *Cognac* × *Fashion*; Delforge. Bud ovoid; flowers cognac color with pink, dbl., large, borne in clusters; fragrant; foliage dark, glossy; vigorous, upright growth.

Ralph Leighty F, *w*, 1971, *Gene Boerner sport*; Leighty; McFadden. Bud ovoid; flowers near white, dbl., high-centered, medium; slightly fragrant; foliage light, soft; moderate, upright growth.

Ralph Tizard F, *ob*, 1979, (Ralph Tizzard); *Vera Dalton* × *Tropicana*; Sanday. Flowers pure salmon, dbl. (28 petals), pointed, large (4 in.); fragrant; foliage dark; vigorous growth.

Ralph's Creeper™ S, *rb*, 1988, (MORpapplay; Creepy; Highveld Sun); *Papoose* × *Playboy*; Moore, Ralph S.; Armstrong Roses, 1987. Flowers dark orange-red, bright yellow eye, reverse bright yellow to white, aging pinkish-red, semi-dbl. (15-18 petals), loose, medium, borne in sprays of 10-15; moderate apple blossom fragrance; foliage small, dark

green, matt; prickles normal, intermediate, tall; fruit round, orange-red; spreading, low growth; repeats.

Ramapo Min, *mp*, 1985, (ZIPram); *Maytime* × *Libby*; Zipper, Herbert; Magic Moment Min. Flowers medium pink, single (5 petals), small blooms borne singly; no fragrance; foliage small, medium green, matt; bushy growth.

Ramat-Gan F, *dy*, 1972, *Golden Masterpiece* × *Zorina*; Holtzman; Holtzman Rose Nursery. Bud urn-shaped; flowers deep lemon-yellow, dbl. (25 petals), cupped to urn-shaped, small (1 in.); fragrant; foliage light; moderate growth.

Rambling Rector R, *w*, Prior to 1912. Flowers white, semi-dbl., blooms in large clusters; fragrant; vigorous.

Ramón Bach HT, *ob*, 1938, *Luis Brinas* × *Condesa de Sástago*; Dot, P.; C-P. Flowers bright orange, edged lighter, reverse reddish gold, stamens bright yellow, very dbl. (80 petals), globular, large; very fragrant (fruity); foliage glossy, dark; vigorous growth.

Ramona HLaev (S), *mr*, 1913, (Red Cherokee); *Anemone sport*; Dietrich & Turner. Flowers carmine-crimson, single.

Rampa Pal HT, *pb*, 1975, *From mixed seeds*; Pal. Bud ovoid; flowers fuchsine-pink, reverse lighter, very dbl. (60 petals), high-centered, large (4½ in.); slightly fragrant; foliage glossy; moderate, upright, bushy growth.

Rampant HSem (OGR), *w*, 1830, Jacques. Flowers white; profuse bloom, sometimes in autumn.

Ran S, *mp*, 1972, *R. cinnamomea* × *R. helenae hybrida*; Lundstad; Norges Landbrukshogskole. Bud globular; flowers pink, semi-dbl., open, small; slightly fragrant; foliage small, light, soft; vigorous, upright growth.

Randall G (OGR), *mp*, (An old variety taken by early pioneers to western Canada.) Flowers pink, fading rapidly, more dbl.than Alika, well-shaped; not as hardy as Alika.

Rangitoto HT, *m*, 1992, (SUNtoto); *Champagne* × *Chantilly Lace*; Schuurman, Frank B.; Riverland Nurseries, Ltd., 1990. Flowers mauve, dbl. (over 40 petals), medium (4-7 cms.); slight fragrance; foliage medium, medium green, glossy; upright growth; cut flower.

Rangoli F, *op*, 1978, *Golden Slippers mutation*; Thakur; Doon Valley Roses. Bud tapered; flowers coral-pink, dbl. (25 petals), high-centered to cupped, large (3-3½ in.); slightly fragrant (fruity); foliage glossy; dwarf, bushy growth.

Rangshala HT, *ab*, 1969, *Margaret Spaull* × *Open pollination*; Indian Agric. Research Inst.

Bud pointed; flowers apricot, shaded peach and amber yellow, dbl., full, open, medium; foliage glossy; moderate growth.

Ranjana HT, *or*, 1975, *Samourai* × *Seedling*; Pal; Anand Roses. Bud pointed; flowers rose-opal, dbl. (38 petals), full; large (4½ in.); very fragrant; foliage dark, leathery; very vigorous, upright, bushy growth.

Ranunculus Musk Cluster HMsk (S), *w*, Flowers pure white, very dbl.; very vigorous growth.

Raphael M (OGR), *w*, 1856, Robert. Flowers well mossed, pinkish white; slightly recurrent bloom.

Rapperswil® HT, *or*, 1975, *Fragrant Cloud* × *Ena Harkness*; Huber. Bud globular; flowers orange-red, dbl. (30 petals), cupped, large (4 in.); very fragrant; foliage dark, leathery.

Rapture HT, *pb*, 1926, *Mme. Butterfly sport*; Traendly & Schenck. Flowers deeper pink, flushed gold at base; (28).

Rapture, Climbing Cl HT, *pb*, 1933, Dixie Rose Nursery.

Raquel Meller HT, *lp*, 1957, *Edith Krause* × *Fashion*; Camprubi. Flowers soft pink, dbl., cupped, large; very fragrant; foliage glossy. GM, Geneva, 1956.

Raspberry Delight HT, *rb*, 1979, *Carrousel* × *First Prize*; Taylor, Thomas E. Flowers medium red on outer petals shading to creamy coral on inner petals, dbl. (30 petals), urn-shaped, high-centered to cupped; raspberry fragrance; foliage medium green, semi-glossy; hooked prickles; upright, bushy growth.

Raspberry Ice Min, *rb*, 1988, (ZIPberry); *High Spirits* × *Charmglo*; Zipper, Herbert; Magic Moment Miniatures, 1989. Flowers white brushed with red, deeper red at petal edge, dbl. (40 petals), medium; mini-flora; no fragrance; foliage medium, dark green, semi-glossy; upright growth.

Raspberry Ruffles F, *dp*, 1991, (TALras); *Garnette* × *Seedling*; Taylor, Franklin "Pete" & Kay, 1987; Taylor's Roses, 1990. Bud pointed; flowers deep pink with white eye, deep pink reverse, aging lighter, semi-dbl. (18-20 petals), high-centered, exhibition, opens flat when fully open, medium, borne in sprays of 4-6; heavy fragrance; foliage medium, medium green, semi-glossy; upright, bushy, medium growth.

Rassvet HT, *pb*, 1955, (Daybreak); *Peace seedling*; Klimenko. Flowers soft pink, base creamy yellow, very dbl. (48 petals), medium; foliage dark; spreading growth.

Rathernice HT, *ob*, 1957, Bishop; Baker's Nursery. Flowers coppery orange; foliage coppery; moderate growth.

Raubritter HMacrantha (S), *lp*, 1936, *Daisy Hill* × *Solarium*; Kordes. Flowers light pink, dbl., globular, in clusters; fragrant; foliage leathery, wrinkled; vigorous, climbing.

Ravenswood Min, *yb*, 1992, *Rise 'n' Shine* × *Seedling*; Catt, Graeme Charles, 1989; F.D. Catt Wholesale Nursery. Flowers gold, outer petals flushed pink, semi-dbl. (18-20 petals), small (½ in.-12 mm) blooms borne 3-4 per cluster; light fragrance; foliage healthy; upright, bushy growth.

Raving Beauty HT, *mp*, 1948, Hill, J.H., Co. Bud ovoid, rose-red; flowers tyrian rose, dbl. (35-40 petals), globular, medium (3-4 in.); very fragrant; foliage leathery, dark; vigorous, upright growth.

Ray Adeline HT, *my*, 1989, *First Prize* × *King's Ransom*; Bevard, Harry D., 1990. Bud pointed; flowers medium yellow, dbl. (40 petals), high-centered, exhibition, medium, borne usually singly and in sprays of 2-4; moderate fragrance; foliage medium, dark green, semi-glossy; prickles straight, hooked down, light green; fruit small, light green; upright growth.

Ray Bunge Cl HP (OGR), *dp*, 1927, *Paul Neyron sport*; Bunge; Andrews Nursery Co., 1959. Flowers dark rose, reverse lighter, dbl. (30-40 petals), large (4-5 in.), borne singly or clusters of 7-8 on very long stems; slightly fragrant; foliage dark; very vigorous (15½ ft.); prolific early spring bloom, repeating later in season; quite hardy.

Ray of Sunshine S, *my*, 1989, (COCclare); *Sunsprite* × (*Clüre Grammerstorf* × *Frühlingsmorgen*); Cocker, James & Sons, 1988. Bud pointed; flowers medium yellow, semi-dbl. (15 petals), cupped, small, borne in sprays of 3-9; patio, slight, spicy fragrance; foliage small, dark green, glossy; prickles small, green; fruit round, small, green; bushy, low growth.

Raymond HT, *pb*, 1917, *Rayon d'Or seedling*; Pernet-Ducher. Bud long, pointed; flowers peach-blossom-pink, center salmon-carmine, dbl.

Raymond Chenault K (S), *mr*, 1960, *R. kordesii* × *Montezuma*; Kordes, R. Flowers bright red, semi-dbl. (16 petals), large (4 in.) blooms in clusters; fragrant; foliage dark, glossy; vigorous (9-12 ft.) growth.

Raymond Privat Pol, *m*, 1935, Privat. Flowers violet, dbl., borne in clusters; vigorous growth.

Rayon d'Or HT, *my*, 1910, *Mme. Mélanie Soupert* × *Soleil d'Or*; Pernet-Ducher. Flowers golden yellow, dbl.

Rayon d'Or HT, *my*, 1962, Combe. Flowers yellow, well formed.

Razzle Dazzle F, *rb*, 1977, (JACraz); Warriner; J&P. Flowers red, reverse white, dbl. (25 petals), medium (2½ in.); slightly fragrant; foliage dark, leathery; bushy growth. GM, Portland, 1978.

Razzmatazz Min, *or*, 1981, (JACmat); *Zorina × Fire Princess*; Warriner; J&P. Flowers orange-red, full, high-centered, in clusters; very little fragrance; foliage semi-glossy; upright.

Rea Silvia HT, *or*, 1958, *Baiser × (Peace × Seedling)*; Giacomasso. Flower fiery red.

Real Charmer Min, *lp*, 1992, (PIXichar); *Gene Boerner × Crissy*; Chaffin, Lauren; Pixie Treasures Miniature. Flowers light pink, full (26-40 petals), large (7+ cms) blooms borne in small clusters; fragrant; foliage large, medium green, semi-glossy; long season, heavy bloomer with excellent form, easy to propagate; tall (45 cms), upright growth.

Rebecca HT, *pb*, 1930, Pemberton; Bentall. Bud large, long, pointed; flowers silvery pink, reverse salmon-pink, dbl.; foliage dark, leathery; vigorous.

Rebecca® HT, *rb*, 1970, (TANrekta; Renica); *Konfetti × Piccadilly*; Tantau. Bud ovoid; flowers red, yellow reverse, dbl., well-formed, large; slightly fragrant; vigorous, upright.

Rebecca Claire HT, *op*, 1981, *Blessings × Redgold*; Law, Michael John, 1986. Flowers coppery orange edged light coral, dbl. (28 petals), blooms borne singly and in clusters of 3-7; very fragrant; foliage medium green, semi-glossy; medium brown prickles; vigorous, bushy growth. GM, RNRS, 1980; RNRS PIT, 1980; Edland Fragrance Medal, 1980.

Rebecca Gue B (OGR), *mp*, 1982, *Mme. Ernest Calvat sport*; Gue, Derek J. Flower distinction from parent not described.

Rebecca's Delight F, *mp*, 1974, *(Pink Parfait × Highlight) × Circus*; Harkness; Morse Roses. Flowers soft salmon pink, shaded darker, dbl. (24 petals), large; slightly fragrant; foliage light green; vigorous, upright growth.

Rebell HT, *ob*, 1974, (FAYbell); *Brandenburg × Seedling*; Kordes; Fey. Flowers dark orange, dbl., high-centered, large; very fragrant; foliage leathery; vigorous, upright.

Recompense HT, *dp*, 1957, *Charles P. Kilham × Polly*; Ratcliffe. Flowers deep pink, well shaped, medium; fragrant; moderate growth.

Recuerdo de Angel Peluffo HT, *rb*, 1928, *Mme. Edouard Herriot × Elvira Aramayo*; Soupert & Notting. Flowers cardinal-red, center garnet-red, dbl.; fragrant.

Recuerdo de Antonio Peluffo T (OGR), *yb*, 1910, *Mme. Mélanie Soupert × Mme. Constant Soupert*; Soupert & Notting. Flowers light yellow, edged pink, dbl.

Recuerdo de Blas Munné Cl HT, *rb*, 1948, *Maria Serrat × Recuerdo del Doctor Ferran*; Munné, M. Flowers carmine-red shaded cerise red; long, strong stems; slightly fragrant; foliage dark; very vigorous growth.

Recuerdo de Felio Camprubi HT, *rb*, 1931, *Hugh Dickson × Souv. de Claudius Pernet*; Camprubi. Flowers crimson suffused pink, reverse yellow suffused red, dbl., large; very fragrant; vigorous growth.

Recuerdo del Doctor Ferran HT, *rb*, 1935, *Sensation × K. of K.*; Munné, B. Bud long, pointed; flowers scarlet-crimson, shaded fiery red, very dbl., open, large; very fragrant; foliage dark; vigorous growth.

Red Ace Min, *mr*, 1980, *Rise 'n' Shine × Sheri Anne*; Saville, F. Harmon; Nor'East Min. Roses. Flowers medium red, semi-dbl. (23 petals), high-centered HT form, blooms borne usually singly; slight fragrance; long, thin, straight prickles; low, compact, bushy growth.

Red Admiral F, *mr*, 1940, Archer. Flowers scarlet, borne in clusters.

Red Alert Min, *mr*, 1990, (MORalert); *Orangeade × Rainbow's End*; Moore, Ralph S., 1986; Sequoia Nursery, 1991. Bud pointed; flowers medium red, slightly lighter reverse, aging similar, dbl. (35 petals), high-centered, exhibition, medium, borne usually singly or in sprays of 3-4; slight fragrance; foliage medium, medium green, semi-glossy; upright, bushy, medium growth.

Red American Beauty HT, *mr*, 1959, *Happiness × San Fernando*; Morey; J&P. Bud ovoid; flowers scarlet overcast rose-red, dbl. (30-35 petals), high-centered, large (4½-5 in.); long stems; very fragrant; foliage leathery, dark; vigorous, upright, bushy growth.

Red Arrow Min, *mr*, 1962, *(R. wichuraiana × Floradora) × Seedling*; Moore, R.S.; Sequoia Nursery. Flowers medium red, dbl. (40 petals), high-centered, small (1¼ in.) blooms in clusters; slightly fragrant; foliage leathery; vigorous, 12-18 in. growth.

Red Azteca HT, *mr*, 1990, (SELazteca); *Seedling × Seedling*; Select Roses, B.V.; DeVor Nurseries, Inc. Bud pointed, tapering, slender; flowers bright red, no fading, dbl. (30-35 petals), cupped, large, borne singly; foliage large, dark green, glossy; prickles reddish, with yellow tip; upright, tall growth.

Red Ballerina S, *mr*, 1976, *Ballerina × Evelyn Fison*; Fryer, G.; Fryer's Nursery. Flowers bright crimson, single (10 petals), full, small; slightly fragrant; foliage glossy.

Red Beauty Min, *dr*, 1981, *Starburst* × *Over the Rainbow*; Williams, Ernest D.; Mini-Roses. Flowers dark red, yellow hinge, dbl. (35 petals), exhibition, small to medium; slight fragrance; foliage small, dark, glossy; bushy growth.

Red Beauty HT, *mr*, 1929, *Matchless sport*; Dunlop; Liggit. Flowers red.

Red Bells® Min, *mr*, 1983, (POUlred); *Mini-Poul* × *Temple Bells*; Poulsen, D.T.; John Mattock, Ltd. Flowers medium red, dbl. (35 petals), small; slight fragrance; foliage small, medium green, semi-glossy; spreading growth; ground cover.

Red Better Times HT, *mr*, 1937, *Better Times sport*; Asmus. Flowers bright clear red.

Red Bird HT, *mr*, 1957, *Better Times sport*; Manda, Jr., E.A.; J&P. Flowers bright red; greenhouse variety.

Red Blanket® S, *dp*, 1979, (INTercel; INTercell); *Yesterday* × *Seedling*; Ilsink; Dickson Nursery. Flowers dull, deep pink, semi-dbl., small blooms in small clusters; slightly fragrant; foliage dark, glossy; many medium prickles; vigorous (to 3-4 ft.); ground cover; repeats.

Red Boy HT, *or*, 1939, *Charles K. Douglas* × *Pres. Herbert Hoover*; Hansen, N.J.; B&A. Bud long, pointed; flowers fiery orange-red, fading to dominant pink, single and semi-dbl., open; slightly fragrant; foliage dark, glossy; vigorous, bushy growth.

Red Brigand F, *or*, 1984, (SANtor); *Vera Dalton* × *Stephen Langdon*; Sanday, John; Sanday Roses Ltd. Flowers orange-red, semi-dbl. (20 petals), medium; slight fragrance; foliage large, dark, semi-glossy; short, slightly hooked prickles; bushy growth.

Red Button Min, *dr*, 1978, *(R. wichuraiana* × *Floradora)* × *Magic Dragon*; Moore, R.S.; Sequoia Nursery. Bud short, pointed; flowers deep red, full, small; foliage very small, glossy; bushy, compact, spreading growth.

Red Camellia F, *or*, 1943, *Baby Château* × *Folkestone*; Krause. Bud small; flowers orange-scarlet, dbl. (20-30 petals); slightly fragrant; foliage dark, leathery; vigorous, upright, bushy growth; a greenhouse variety.

Red Can Can Min, *mr*, 1977, *Seedling* × *Seedling*; Lyon. Bud pointed; flowers cardinal-red, dbl. (28 petals), medium (2 in.); fragrant (fruity); foliage dark; vigorous, upright.

Red Carpet Cl F, *dr*, 1971, *Don Juan* × *Red Favorite*; Williams, J.B. Bud ovoid; flowers dark scarlet, overlaid darker, dbl., globular, medium; foliage large, dark, leathery; very vigorous, climbing growth.

Red Carrousel Min, *dp*, 1984, *Magic Carrousel sport*; Rumsey, R.H.; Rumsey Ltd. Flowers deep pink.

Red Cascade Cl Min, *dr*, 1976, (MOORcap); *(R. wichuraiana* × *Floradora)* × *Magic Dragon*; Moore, R.S.; Sequoia Nursery. Bud pointed; flowers deep red, dbl. (40 petals), cupped, small (1 in.); slightly fragrant; foliage small, leathery; prostrate, bushy. AOE, 1976.

Red Cheer Min, *mr*, 1975, *Seedling* × *Seedling*; Lyon. Flowers cherry-red, dbl. (45 petals), full, small (1 in.); slightly fragrant; foliage very small, dark; compact, bushy growth.

Red Cheerful HT, *dr*, 1951, *Better Times sport*; Blixen; Woodlawn Gardens. Bud pointed; flowers deep red, dbl. (30-40 petals), high-centered, large (4½ in.); fragrant; foliage glossy, leathery, veined red; vigorous, upright growth.

Red Chief HT, *mr*, 1967, *Seedling* × *Chrysler Imperial*; Armstrong, D.L.; Armstrong Nursery. Flowers medium red, dbl. (35 petals), high-centered, large; very fragrant; foliage leathery; vigorous, upright, bushy growth.

Red Columbia HT, *mr*, 1920, *Columbia sport*; Hill, J.H., Co. Flowers rich velvety scarlet, dbl., large; very fragrant; foliage leathery; very vigorous growth.

Red Cross HT, *ob*, 1916, Dickson, A. Flowers orange-crimson-scarlet; fragrant.

Red Cushion F, *dr*, 1966, *Circus* × *Ruby Lips*; Armstrong, D.L.; Armstrong Nursery. Bud pointed; flowers dark red, semi-dbl., small blooms in clusters; slightly fragrant; foliage dark, glossy, leathery; vigorous, bushy growth.

Red Dandy F, *mr*, 1959, *Ena Harkness* × *Karl Herbst*; Norman; Harkness. Flowers cherry-red, dbl. (40 petals), large (3 in.); fragrant; vigorous, upright growth.

Red Dawn S, *mr*, 1957, *New Dawn* × *Seedling*; Simonet; Skinner. Flowers deep rose-red, well-formed; recurrent; hardy.

Red Delicious HT, *mr*, 1942, *Rome Glory* × *Chieftain*; Hill, J.H., Co. Bud carmine, shaded oxblood-red; flowers brilliant rose-red, dbl. (30-35 petals), large (4-6 in.); weak necks; very fragrant; foliage leathery, dark; vigorous, upright growth; a florists' variety, not distributed for outdoor use.

Red Delight HT, *mr*, *Pink Delight sport*; Avansino; Mortensen, about 1935. Flowers bright red; a greenhouse variety. RULED EXTINCT 11/86.

Red Delight™ Cl Min, *mr*, 1986, (MINaico); *Golden Song* × *Magic Mist*; Williams, Ernest; Mini-Roses, 1987. Flowers medium red, yellow at base, dbl. (33 petals), exhibition, small, borne singly and in sprays of 3-5; heavy, usually spicy fragrance; foliage small, dark green, semi-glossy; few, small, tan prickles, slanted downwards; fruit round, red; tall growth.

Red Det Min, *mr*, 1978, *(Marlena × Kim) × Little Buckaroo*; Harkness; Rosen-Union. Flowers medium red, dbl., flat, medium blooms in clusters; slightly fragrant; foliage small, deep green, glossy; vigorous, bushy growth.

Red Devil HT, *mr*, 1970, (DICam; Coeur d'Amour); *Silver Lining × Prima Ballerina*; Dickson, A.; J&P. Bud ovoid; flowers medium red, reverse lighter, dbl. (72 petals), high-centered, large; fragrant; foliage glossy; vigorous. GM, Japan, 1967, Belfast, 1969; Portland, 1970.

Red Dragon F, *mr*, 1970, *Anna Wheatcroft × Seedling*; Cants of Colchester. Flowers red, single (5 petals), large (3½-4 in.); slightly fragrant; vigorous growth.

Red Duchess HT, *mr*, 1942, *Pink Princess × Crimson Glory*; Brownell. Bud long, pointed; flowers red, dbl. (35-45 petal), high-centered, large (3½-5 in.); long, strong stems; fragrant; foliage glossy, bronze; vigorous, upright, bushy growth.

Red Duchess, Climbing Cl HT, *mr*, 1955, Brownell.

Red Echo Pol, *or*, 1932, *Echo × Hybrid Tea Seedling*; Kluis; Koning; J&P. Flowers vermilion tinted crimson, dbl., cupped; slightly fragrant; foliage dark, wrinkled; dwarf growth.

Red Elf Min, *dr*, 1949, *Eblouissant × Tom Thumb*; deVink; C-P. Bud ovoid; flowers dark crimson, dbl. (23 petals), small (¾-1 in.); slightly fragrant; foliage soft, tiny; vigorous, bushy, dwarf growth.

Red Ellen Poulsen Pol, *mr*, 1918, (Dunkelrote Ellen Poulsen); *Ellen Poulsen sport*; Poulsen, S. Flowers red.

Red Ember HT, *or*, 1953, Cant, F. Flowers flame, dbl. (30 petals), well formed, large (4-5 in.); fragrant; foliage glossy, dark; free growth.

Red Emblem F, *dr*, 1958, *Garnette seedling × Pageant*; Boerner; J&P. Bud ovoid; flowers deep red, dbl. (30-35 petals), open, medium (2½ in.); fragrant; foliage leathery; upright, bushy growth; a greenhouse variety.

Red Empress LCl, *mr*, 1956, (Impératrice Rouge; Robur); *(Holstein × Decor) × Self*; Mallerin; EFR; C-P. Bud ovoid; flowers cardinal-red, dbl. (33 petals), high-centered to loosely cupped, large (3½ in.) blooms borne singly

or 2 per stem; very fragrant; foliage leathery; vigorous, climbing growth; recurrent bloom.

Red Ensign HT, *mr*, 1947, *Crimson Glory × Southport*; Norman; Harkness. Flower crimson, dbl. (40-45 petals), high-centered, large (4-5 in.); very fragrant (damask); foliage dark; very vigorous growth. GM, NRS, 1943.

Red Explorer Cl Pol, *dr*, 1938, *Miss Edith Cavell sport*; Penny. Flowers deep brilliant crimson, borne in large clusters; vigorous, climbing growth; recurrent bloom.

Red Favorite F, *mr*, 1954, (TANschweigru; Holländerin; Red Favourite; Salut à la Suisse; Schweizer Grüss); *Karl Weinhausen × Cinnabar*; Tantau; C-P. Bud ovoid; flowers velvety oxblood-red, semi-dbl. (13 petals), medium (2½ in.) blooms in trusses; slightly fragrant; foliage dark, leathery, glossy; vigorous, bushy growth. ADR, 1950.

Red Favorite, Climbing Cl F, *mr*, Australia, 1958.

Red Favorite, Climbing Cl F, *mr*, 1964, Münster.

Red Finch Pol, *mp*, 1937, *Mrs. R.M. Finch sport*; Stielow, F.C. Flowers cerise, more cupped, more open, more dbl.than parent, borne in clusters.

Red Flare LCl, *dr*, 1954, *Reine Marie Henriette × Paul's Scarlet Climber seedling*; Mansuino, A.; J&P. Bud globular; flowers carmine overcast spectrum-red, dbl. (40 petals), cupped, large (4-4½ in.), borne singly and clusters; fragrant; foliage dark, glossy; height 7-8 ft.; profuse bloom repeated sparingly.

Red Flush Min, *mr*, 1978, Schwartz, E.W.; Nor'East Min. Roses. Bud ovoid; flowers medium red, dbl. (53 petals), cupped, small (1½ in.); foliage green, matt; very compact growth. AOE, 1979.

Red Fountain LCl, *dr*, 1975, *Don Juan × Blaze*; Williams, J.B.; C-P. Bud ovoid, pointed; flowers scarlet, dbl., cupped, medium; very fragrant; foliage large, dark, leathery; very vigorous, climbing growth.

Red Germain Min, *rb*, 1975, *(R. wichuraiana × Floradora) × (Oakington Ruby × Floradora)*; Moore, R.S.; Sequoia Nursery. Bud long, pointed; flowers red, reverse lighter, dbl. (25 petals), flat, small (1 in.); slightly fragrant; foliage small, leathery; vigorous, bushy.

Red Globe F, *mr*, 1971, Delforge. Bud ovoid; flowers red, dbl., full, large; foliage soft; moderate, bushy growth.

Red Glory F, *mr*, 1958, *Gay Lady × (Pinocchio × Floradora)*; Swim; Armstrong Nursery. Bud ovoid, pointed; flowers cherry to rose-red, single (11 petals), cupped to flat, large (2½-3½ in.) blooms in rounded clusters;

slightly fragrant; foliage leathery, semi-glossy; very vigorous, tall, bushy growth. Good as fence or hedge.

Red Guard HT, *rb*, 1935, Verschuren. Flowers dark blood-red, very full, well formed; very vigorous growth.

Red Halo F, *mr*, 1968, *Tabarin* × *Karl Herbst*; Oliver, W.G. Flowers crimson, flat, borne in trusses; slightly fragrant; foliage glossy; vigorous, bushy growth.

Red Hedge HRg (S), *mr*, 1958, *(R. rugosa rubra* × *R. cinnamomea)* × *R. nitida*; Nyveldt. Flowers red; fruit small, red; upright, compact growth.

Red Hill HT, *mr*, 1941, *E.G. Hill seedling*; Clark, A. Flowers red, well-formed, large.

Red Hit Min, *dr*, 1984, (POULhit); *Mini-Poul* × *Seedling*; Olesen, M.&P.; Poulsen's Roses. Flowers dark red, semi-dbl. (20 petals), small; no fragrance; foliage small, dark, matt; low, bushy, compact growth.

Red Hoover HT, *rb*, 1937, *President Herbert Hoover sport*; Lens. Flowers brilliant red, center salmon-red.

Red Imp Min, *dr*, 1951, (Maid Marion; Mon Tresor; Montresor); *Ellen Poulsen* × *Tom Thumb*; deVink; C-P. Bud ovoid; flowers deep crimson, dbl. (54 petals), very flat, micro-mini, small (³/₄-1 in.); slightly fragrant; upright, bushy, dwarf (9 in.) growth.

Red Jacket HT, *mr*, 1950, *World's Fair* × *Mirandy*; Swim; Stuart. Bud ovoid, pointed; flowers red, semi-dbl. (21 petals), urn-shaped, flat, large (3³/₄ in.); slightly fragrant; foliage leathery; upright, bushy growth.

Red Jewel Min, *or*, 1984, (INTerro); *Amanda* × *Seedling*; Interplant. Flowers orange-red, semi-dbl. (20 petals), small; no fragrance; foliage small, medium green, semi-glossy; bushy growth.

Red Knight LCl, *dr*, 1964, *Dr. Huey sport*; Booy, P.J.; Booy Rose Nursery. Flowers maroon, semi-dbl., globular, medium, very vigorous growth; recurrent bloom.

Red Lion HT, *mr*, 1964, *Kordes' Perfecta* × *Detroiter*; McGredy, S., IV; Spek. Flowers red becoming rose-red, dbl. (38 petals), high-centered, large (5 in.).

Red Love™ Min, *mr*, 1984, (MINqco); *Tom Brown* × *Over the Rainbow*; Williams, Ernest D.; Mini Roses. Flowers medium red, dbl. (35 petals), spiral form, small; slight fragrance; foliage small, dark, semi-glossy to glossy; upright, bushy growth.

Red Magic Min, *mr*, 1977, *Red Can Can* × *Seedling*; Lyon; L. Lyon Greenhouses. Bud pointed; flowers deep cherry-red, semi-dbl.

(10-15 petals), open, medium; slightly fragrant; vigorous, upright growth.

Red Maid F, *or*, 1975, *Vera Dalton* × *Stephen Langdon*; Sanday. Flowers coral-red, semi-dbl. (18 petals), large (3 in.).

Red Malmaison B (OGR), *mr*, Flowers bright velvety crimson, very full, large; very fragrant.

Red Margo Koster Pol, *mr*, Identical with Margo Koster but bright red.

Red Martini HT, *dr*, 1967, *Chrysler Imperial* × *Seedling*; Delforge. Bud ovoid; flowers dark red, dbl., large; slightly fragrant; foliage bronze; vigorous, bushy growth.

Red Masquerade F, *mr*, 1962, *Masquerade* × *Independence*; Hill, A. Bud pointed; flowers red becoming darker, single (10 petals), large (2¹/₂-3 in.) borne in clusters; vigorous growth.

Red Masterpiece HT, *dr*, 1974, (JACder); *(Siren* × *Chrysler Imperial)* × *(Carrousel* × *Chrysler Imperial)*; Warriner; J&P. Flowers deep red, dbl., high-centered, large; very fragrant; foliage large, dark, leathery; vigorous, upright growth.

Red Meidiland™ S, *rb*, 1989, (MEIneble; Rouge Meillandécor); *Sea Foam* × *(Picasso* × *Eyepaint)*; Meilland, Alain; C-P, 1989. Bud conical; flowers red with white eye, single (5 petals), cupped, medium, borne in sprays of 7-15; no fragrance; foliage medium, dark green, glossy, disease resistant; Prickles gray-brown; fruit globular, small, red; spreading, medium, very winter hardy growth; repeats.

Red Minimo™ Min, *dr*, 1991, (RUImired); *Seedling* × *Seedling*; DeRuiter, George; Bear Creek Gardens, 1987. Flowers red, semi-dbl. (15-25 petals), small blooms borne in small clusters; no fragrance; foliage small, dark green, semi-glossy; low, bushy growth.

Red Mini-Wonder™ Min, *dr*, 1990, (MEInofrai); *(Anytime* × *Parador)* × *Mogral*; Selection Meilland, 1987; C-P, 1989. Bud rounded; flowers currant red, cardinal red reverse, aging to dark red, very dbl. (40-43 petals), cupped, small, borne usually singly or in sprays of 1-3; foliage small, medium green, very dense, semi-glossy; prickles small, green to tan; bushy, low growth.

Red Moss M (OGR), *mr*, Flowers heavily mossed, reddish rose, large.

Red Moss, Climbing Cl M (OGR), *mr*, Foote; B&A.

Red Nearly Wild F, *mr*, 1960, *Nearly Wild* × *Seedling*; Brownell, H.C.; Brownell. Bud globular; flowers rose-red, single, cupped, small, borne in clusters; foliage soft; vigorous, bushy growth.

Red Opal F, *mr*, 1968, *Karl Herbst × Korona*; Northfield. Bud pointed; flowers red, reverse cerise, flat, borne in small clusters; foliage small, dark; free growth.

Red Parade F, *mr*, 1972, *(Frolic × Peace) × Texan*; Patterson; Patterson Roses. Bud ovoid; flowers carmine-red, dbl., cupped, high-centered, medium; fragrant; foliage glossy, bronze; vigorous, bushy growth.

Red Pearl HT, *mr*, 1970, *Josephine Bruce × Kordes' Perfecta*; Watkins Roses. Flowers bright red, dbl. (40 petals), pointed, large (5 in.); fragrant; foliage large, dark; very vigorous.

Red Pendant™ Min, *dr*, 1984, (MINvco); *Red Cascade × Red Cascade*; Williams, Ernest D.; Mini Roses. Flowers dark red, dbl. (35 petals), small; no fragrance; foliage small, medium green, very glossy; low, spreading growth.

Red Perfection™ HT, *dr*, 1986, (MAChaden); *Karma × Arturo Toscanini*; McGredy, Sam; Co-Operative Rose Growers, 1987. Flowers dark red, reverse slightly lighter, fading purple-red, semi-dbl. (50-60 petals), high-centered, exhibition, medium, borne singly; moderate, old rose fragrance; foliage large, dark green, semi-glossy; slightly recurved, average, green prickles; fruit globular, large, dark red; tall growth.

Red Petticoat F, *mr*, 1967, *Buisman's Triumph × Lilli Marlene*; Watkins Roses. Flowers blood-red, dbl., flat, short petaled, borne in trusses; foliage dark, glossy; very vigorous growth.

Red Pinocchio F, *dr*, 1947, *Yellow Pinocchio seedling × Donald Prior*; Boerner; J&P. Flowers velvety carmine-red, dbl. (28 petals), cupped, large (3 in.) blooms in clusters; fragrant; vigorous, bushy growth.

Red Pistols Min, *dy*, 1982, *Rise 'n' Shine × Seedling*; Ballmer, Gordon W.; Biotika International. Flowers deep golden yellow, semi-dbl. 15-20 petals, small; no fragrance; foliage medium green, matt; brown, needle-like prickles; upright, bushy growth.

Red Planet HT, *dr*, 1970, *Red Devil × Seedling*; Dickson, P.; A. Dickson. Flowers crimson, dbl. (30 petals), large (5½-6 in.); very fragrant; foliage glossy. GM, RNRS, 1969; RNRS PIT, 1969.

Red Plume F, *or*, 1966, *Masquerade × Independence seedling*; Sanday. Flowers bright scarlet, dbl. (35 petals), rosette form, large (3 in.), borne in clusters; foliage glossy; vigorous, bushy growth.

Red Premier HT, *dp*, 1924, *Premier sport*; Scott, R. Bud long, pointed; flowers bright car-

mine, dbl., large; very fragrant; foliage leathery; vigorous growth.

Red Pride F, *mr*, 1968, Verbeek. Bud ovoid; flowers red, dbl., small.

Red Provence C (OGR), *mr*, Original name, introducer and date unknown. Flowers clear crimson-red, cupped, large; very fragrant; low, spreading growth.

Red Queen HT, *mr*, 1968, (Liebestraum); *Colour Wonder × Liberty Bell*; Kordes; Buisman; McGredy. Bud ovoid; flowers red, dbl., large; foliage dark; vigorous, upright growth.

Red Radiance HT, *dp*, 1916, *Radiance sport*; Gude Bros. Flowers light crimson.

Red Radiance, Climbing Cl HT, *dp*, 1927, Pacific Rose Co.

Red Radiance, Climbing Cl HT, *dp*, 1929, Catt.

Red Rascal S, *mr*, 1986, (JACbed); *Seedling × Seedling*; Warriner; J&P. Flowers medium red, dbl. (35 petals), cupped, patio, small blooms in sprays of 2-5; slight fragrance; foliage small, medium green, semi-glossy; medium, red to brown prickles, hooked downward; medium, bushy growth; repeat bloom.

Red Reflection HT, *mr*, 1964, *Tropicana × Living*; Warriner; J&P. Bud ovoid, pointed; flowers red, high-centered, large (4-5 in.); slightly fragrant; foliage large, leathery; upright.

Red Rider Cl F, *rb*, 1970, *Circus × Danse de Feu*; Guest. Flowers red, base yellow, dbl. (50 petals), full, small (2-3 in.); foliage large, glossy; vigorous growth.

Red Riding Hood Min, *dr*, 1955, *Red Imp sport*; Robinson, T. Flowers brilliant dark red.

Red Ripples F, *dr*, 1942, (Willi Maass); *Hamburg × Anne Poulsen*; Krause; C-P. Bud globular; flowers deep red, semi-dbl., petals wavy, small blooms in large clusters; slightly fragrant; foliage leathery, glossy, wrinkled; upright, bushy.

Red Robin HT, *rb*, 1940, Brownell. Flowers red, tending toward scarlet; vigorous growth.

Red Rock HT, *mr*, 1973, (MEIlusam; Lusambo; Red Rocky); *(Royal Velvet × Chrysler Imperial) × Pharaoh*; Meilland; URS. Flowers cherry-red, dbl. (35 petals), open, imbricated, large (5 in.); slightly fragrant; very vigorous growth.

Red Rocket S, *mr*, 1949, *Skyrocket seedling*; Longley, L.E.; Univ. of Minn. Bud ovoid; flowers crimson, single to semi-dbl., large blooms in clusters; slightly fragrant; foliage large, dark, glossy, bronze; vigorous, upright growth; non-recurrent bloom.

Red Rosamini® Min, *dr*, 1988, (RUIredro); *Seedling × Seedling*; DeRuiter, G.; C-P, 1987. Flowers deep red, medium; medium growth.

Red Rose Marie HT, *rb*, 1938, *Rose Marie sport*; Mordigan Evergreen Nursery. Bud ovoid; flowers cerise-red, dbl., high-centered, large; slightly fragrant; foliage dark, leathery; vigorous, bushy growth.

Red Rover Min, *dr*, 1991, (LAVride; Red Rider); *Mountie sport*; Laver, Keith G., 1988; Springwood Miniature Roses, 1990. Bud pointed; flowers dark red, dbl., exhibition, loose blooms borne usually singly; no fragrance; foliage small to medium, dark green, semi-glossy to glossy; bushy, low growth.

Red Ruffles F, *dr*, 1960, *Improved Lafayette × Carrousel*; Abrams, Von; Peterson; Dering. Bud pointed; flowers dull dark red, dbl. (45 ruffled petals), cupped to flat, medium (2½ -3 in.), borne in large clusters; slightly fragrant; foliage dark, glossy; vigorous, bushy, compact growth.

Red Rum F, *mr*, 1976, *Handel × Arthur Bell*; Bees. Flowers red, shaded scarlet, semi-dbl. (24 petals), large (2½ in.); slightly fragrant; foliage dark; vigorous growth.

Red Sarong HT, *dr*, 1974, *Baccará × Golden Showers*; Golik; Dynarose. Bud ovoid; flowers deep red, dbl. (36 petals), high-centered, large (5 in.); fragrant; foliage dark, leathery; tall growth.

Red Shadows™ Min, *dr*, 1984, (SAVmore); *Tamango × Sheri Anne*; Saville, F. Harmon; Nor'East Min. Roses. Flowers dark red, dbl. (40+ petals), HT form, small; no fragrance; foliage small, medium green, semi-glossy; bushy, slightly spreading growth.

Red Simplicity S, *mr*, 1991, (JACsimpl); *Seedling × Sun Flare*; Warriner, William; Zary, Keith; Bear Creek Gardens, 1992. Flowers bright red, a bit of blackening near petal edges, semi-dbl. (15-25 petals), large blooms borne in small clusters; slight fragrance; foliage medium, medium green, semi-glossy; medium, upright, spreading growth.

Red Skelton HT, *or*, 1968, *Rose Queen × Charlotte Armstrong*; Whisler, D.; Germain's. Bud long, pointed; flowers vermilion, dbl., high-centered, large; fragrant; foliage bronze, leathery; vigorous, upright growth.

Red Sparkler HT, *rb*, 1967, *Scarlet Royal × Rouge Mallerin*; Buck; Iowa State University. Flowers red, striped pink and white, dbl. (55 petals), cupped, large (4-4½ in.); very fragrant (damask); foliage dark, leathery; upright growth.

Red Spice F, *dr*, 1958, *Spice × Garnette*; Boerner; J&P. Bud short, flat topped; flowers dark red, very dbl. (80-85 petals), cupped, medium (2-2½ in.); fragrant; foliage dark, leathery; vigorous, bushy growth; for pot forcing.

Red Splendor HT, *mr*, 1954, *Joyance sport*; Grillo. Flowers bright red, dbl. (55 petals), large (6 in.); fragrant; foliage leathery; vigorous, upright growth.

Red Splendour F, *dr*, 1982, (DAVona); *Europeana sport*; Davies, Gareth, 1979. Flowers deeper red.

Red Sprite F, *mr*, 1974, LeGrice. Flowers glowing red, dbl. (35 petals), medium (2-2½ in.); slightly fragrant; foliage small, glossy, dark; low growth.

Red Summit Min, *dr*, 1981, *Seedling × Seedling*; Lyon. Bud ovoid, pointed; flowers dark red, dbl. (33 petals), blooms borne usually singly; slight fragrance; long, thin, straight prickles; low, compact, bushy growth.

Red Sweetheart F, *rb*, 1944, *Intercrossing of Cécile Brunner seedlings*; Krebs; Marsh's Nursery. Bud pointed; flowers crimson-carmine, dbl. (25 petals), high-centered, small (1-1½ in.); strong stems; fragrant (spicy); foliage small, glossy; vigorous, bushy growth.

Red Tag Min, *rb*, 1978, *Seedling × Over the Rainbow*; Williams, E.D.; Mini-Roses. Bud ovoid, pointed; flowers medium red, white reverse, dbl. (48 petals), high-centered, small (1 in.); fragrant; foliage small, glossy, dark; upright, spreading growth.

Red Talisman HT, *rb*, 1931, *Talisman sport*; Amling Bros. Flowers deep cerise, base yellow.

Red Talisman, Climbing Cl HT, *rb*.

Red Tausendschön R, *rb*, 1931, Tausendschön sport; Walter, L. Flowers vivid red with white eye, but varies considerably.

Red Triumph Pol, *or*, 1956, *Orange Triumph sport*; Morse. Flowers orange-red.

Red Velvet F, *mr*, 1940, Kordes; Dreer. Bud ovoid; flowers vivid crimson, semi-dbl., cupped; slightly fragrant; vigorous, compact growth.

Red Wagon Min, *mr*, 1980, (MORdan); *Little Darling × Little Chief*; Moore, Ralph S.; Moore Min. Roses. Flowers medium red, semi-dbl. (23 petals), blooms borne 1-3 or more per cluster; little or no fragrance; foliage glossy; brown prickles; vigorous, bushy, rounded growth.

Red Wand Cl Min, *mr*, 1964, ((R. *wichuraiana × Floradora*) × *Orange Triumph*) × *Miniature Seedling*; Moore, R.S.; Sequoia Nursery. Flowers light crimson-red, dbl., small; vigorous, climbing (3½-4 ft.) growth.

Red Wave F, *mr*, 1964, *Carolyn Dean × Floribunda seedling*; Moore, R.S.; Sequoia

Nursery. Flowers red, tulip shaped, small; low growth; will bloom in pot.

Red Wine HT, *mr*, 1970, *Lilac Rose × Seedling*; Sanday, John. Flowers medium red, semi-dbl. (22 petals), high-centered, medium (3½ in.) blooms in clusters; slight fragrance; foliage medium green, matt; upright growth.

Red Wing HHug (S), *my*, *Probably R. sericea pteracantha × R. hugonis*. Flowers bright golden yellow; large, winged red prickles.

Red Wings F, *dr*, 1958, *(Improved Lafayette × Herrenhausen) × Lavender Pinocchio*; Boerner; J&P. Bud ovoid; flowers rich dark red, semi-dbl. (20 petals), cupped, large (3½ in.); fragrant; foliage dark, leathery; vigorous, upright, bushy growth.

Red Wonder F, *dr*, 1954, *Better Times × Floribunda seedling*; deRuiter; C-P. Bud globular; flowers dark red, dbl. (28 petals), cupped, large (3-3½ in.) blooms in large clusters; fragrant; foliage leathery, semiglossy; vigorous, bushy.

Redcap F, *mr*, 1954, *World's Fair × Pinocchio*; Swim; Armstrong Nursery. Bud ovoid; flowers medium red, semi-dbl. (18 petals), high-centered, medium (2½ in.) blooms in clusters; foliage leathery, semi-glossy; vigorous, upright, bushy growth.

Redcliffe F, *mr*, 1975, *Seedling × Sarabande*; Sanday. Flowers bright crimson, semi-dbl. (15 petals), large (3½ in.); slightly fragrant.

Redcoat F, *mr*, 1981, (Red Coat); *Seedling × Golden Showers*; Austin, David, 1973. Bud pointed; flowers medium red, single (10 petals), blooms borne 1-5 per cluster; slight fragrance; foliage dark; hooked, brown prickles; bushy growth.

Redcraze HT, *ob*, 1959, *Independence × Independence*; Doley. Bud long, pointed; flowers orange-scarlet, dbl., high-centered, medium; slightly fragrant; foliage glossy, dark; vigorous, bushy growth.

Redglo™ Min, *mr*, 1991, (MINabbco); *Starburst × Over the Rainbow*; Williams, Ernest D.; Mini-Roses, 1992. Flowers medium red, very color fast, velvety knapp, full (26-40 petals), exhibition, outstanding substance, small (0-4 cms) blooms borne mostly singly; slight fragrance; foliage small, dark green, semi-glossy; some prickles; low (36 cms), bushy growth.

Redgold F, *yb*, 1971, (DICor; Rouge et Or); *((Karl Herbst × Masquerade) × Faust) × Piccadilly*; Dickson, A.; J&P. Bud ovoid; flowers gold edged deep pink, dbl., medium blooms in large clusters; slightly fragrant; vigorous, upright growth.   GM, Portland, 1969; AARS, 1971.

Redgold, Climbing Cl F, *yb*, 1974, Lynch; J&P.

Redgold, Climbing Cl F, *yb*, 1984, (DICorsar; Rouge et Or, Climbing; Grimpant Rouge et Or); Pekmez, Paul.

Redhead Cl Min, *dr*, 1956, *((Soeur Thérèse × Skyrocket) × (Seedling × Red Ripples)) × Zee*; Moore, R.S.; Sequoia Nursery. Flowers blood-red; height 2½ ft.

Redhots Min, *dr*, 1982, *Seedling × Darling Flame*; Meredith, E.A.; Rovinski, M.E.; Rosa de Casa Domingo. Flowers dark red, semi-dbl. (22 petals), globular, high-centered to flat blooms borne singly; slight fragrance; foliage small, long, medium green, finely serrated; very small, tiny growth.

Rediffusion Gold F, *dy*, 1984, (HARquorgold); *(Orange Sensation × Allgold) × Sunsprite*; Harkness, R.; R. Harkness & Co. Flowers deep golden yellow, semi-dbl. (70 petals), medium blooms in clusters of 3-7; slight fragrance; foliage small, light green, matt; small prickles; medium, bushy growth.

Redipuglia HT, *w*, 1933, Ingegnoli. Bud long, pointed; flowers pinkish white, reverse golden rose, base chrome-yellow, full, large; vigorous growth.

Redland Court F, *ab*, 1982, *Red Maid × Sarabande*; Sanday, John; Sanday Roses, Ltd. Flowers soft apricot, semi-dbl. (20 petals), small; slight fragrance; foliage small, medium green, glossy; bushy growth.

Redlands Century™ HT, *or*, 1988, (BURcen); *World Peace × Command Performance*; Perry, Anthony; Co-Operative Rose Growers, 1988. Flowers medium orange-red, aging slightly lighter, semi-dbl., urn-shaped, medium, borne usually singly; slight fragrance; foliage medium, medium green, semi-glossy; prickles average, yellow-green; fruit globular, small, orange; upright, medium growth.

Red-Letter Day HT, *dp*, 1914, Dickson, A. Flowers velvety rose-red, white streak in center of inner petals, stamens cinnamon, semi-dbl., medium (3½ in.); short stems; foliage glaucous sage-green; vigorous growth. GM, NRS, 1913.

Redonda HT, *mr*, 1968, *Queen Elizabeth × Happiness*; Patterson; Patterson Roses. Bud globular; flowers red, dbl, large; fragrant; foliage leathery, wrinkled; vigorous, upright growth.

Redway HT, *mr*, 1951, *Ena Harkness × Seedling*; Waterhouse Nursery. Flowers crimson-carmine, high-centered; fragrant; foliage leathery; moderate, upright growth.

Redwood F, *rb*, 1988, (MACwoodma); *Old Master × Wienerwald*; McGredy, Sam. Flowers red blend, hand painted, semi-dbl. (14 petals), medium; slight fragrance; foliage large, dark green, glossy; bushy growth.

Redwood Empire Min, *or*, 1984, (MORwood); *Rumba × Sheri Anne*; Moore, R.S.; Moore Miniature Roses, 1983. Flowers orange-red, semi-dbl. (20 petals), small; slight fragrance; foliage small, medium green, semiglossy; upright, bushy growth.

Reflection HT, *yb*, 1952, *Mme. Henri Guillot sport*; Ratcliffe. Bud long, pointed; flowers amber, reverse streaked scarlet; fragrant; vigorous growth.

Reflets F, *or*, 1964, *Gertrud Westphal × Sarabande*; Croix, P. Flowers orange-red, single, large; upright growth.

Refresher LCl, *w*, 1929, Clark, A.; Hazlewood Bros. Flowers pure white, single, blooms in clusters; vigorous, climbing growth; early bloom.

Refulgence E (OGR), *mr*, 1909, Paul, W. Flowers scarlet, aging to crimson, semi-dbl., large; foliage very fragrant; vigorous growth.

Reg Willis HT, *dp*, 1966, *Golden Masterpiece × Karl Herbst*; McGredy, S., IV. Flowers deep rose-pink, base yellow, well-formed, large (4½ in.); slightly fragrant.

Regal Gold HT, *dy*, 1958, *Golden Rapture sport*; Dale; Amling-DeVor Nursery. Bud pointed; flowers clear golden yellow, dbl. (40-45 petals), open, large (5 in.); fragrant; foliage glossy, leathery; vigorous, upright, bushy growth; a greenhouse variety.

Regal Lady Min, *pb*, 1989, *Sassy Lassie × First Prize*; Jolly, Nelson; Rosehill Farm, 1991. Bud pointed; flowers white, edged pink, dbl. (27 petals), high-centered, exhibition, borne usually singly and in sprays of 3-5; slight fragrance; foliage medium, medium green, semi-glossy; prickles none observed; fruit round; upright, spreading, tall growth.

Regal Pink HT, *mp*, 1980, *Red Queen sport*; Thomas, Dr. A.S. Flowers medium pink.

Regalia HT, *rb*, 1964, *Rose Gaujard × Seedling*; Robinson, H. Flowers cherry-red, reverse silver, dbl. (60 petals), well-formed, large (5½ in.); foliage bronze.

Regatta HT, *w*, 1986, (JACette); *Bernadette × Coquette*; Warriner; J&P. Flowers white, dbl. (48 petals), high-centered, large blooms borne singly; very fragrant; foliage medium, medium green, matt; medium red to brown prickles, hooked downward; fruit none; medium, upright growth; greenhouse variety.

Régence® HT, *pb*, 1967, (LAPdul); Laperrière; EFR. Bud globular; flowers flesh color edged bright pink, dbl., open; foliage glossy; vigorous, bushy growth.

Regensberg® F, *pb*, 1979, (MACyoumis; MACyou; Buffalo Bill; Young Mistress); *Geoff Boycott × Old Master*; McGredy, S., IV; McGredy Roses International. Flower petals pink, edged white, white eye, yellow stamens, reverse whitish, semi-dbl. (21 petals), cupped to flat, patio, large (4½ in.); fragrant; low, bushy. GM, Baden-Baden, 1980.

Regina R, *w*, 1916, Walsh. Flowers creamy white tipped pink, single; large panicles; foliage large, glossy; vigorous, climbing growth.

Regina Badet HRg (S), *dp*, (*Général Jacqueminot × Empereur du Maroc) × R. rugosa*. Flowers deep pink, very dbl., large; very fragrant; foliage dark; bushy growth; repeated bloom.

Régina de Alvéar HT, *w*, 1922, *Mme. Mélanie Soupert × Mme. Segond Weber*; Sauvageot. Flowers white, center slightly shaded pink, dbl.; slightly fragrant.

Regina Elena HT, *mp*, 1938, *Briarcliff sport*; Grillo. Bud long, pointed; flowers darker rose-pink than Briarcliff, dbl. (50 petals), large (5 in.); fragrant; foliage dark.

Regina Pacis HT, *w*, 1945, *Nuria de Recolons × Ibiza*; Dot, P. Flowers white, high-centered, large (5 in.); very fragrant; foliage soft; branching growth.

Reginald Fernyhough HT, *op*, 1949, *Southport × Seedling*; Bees. Flowers pink lightly suffused orange, dbl. (35 petals), long, pointed, large (5 in.); very fragrant; foliage olive-green; very vigorous growth.

Regine™ Min, *pb*, 1989, (HEFqueen); *Little Darling × Party Girl*; Hefner, John; Kimbrew-Walter Roses, 1990. Flowers soft, light pink, silvery-pink reverse, dbl. (30 petals), small; slight fragrance; foliage medium, medium green, semi-glossy; bushy growth. AOE, 1990.

Regulus T (OGR), *pb*, 1860, Moreau-Robert. Flowers bright coppery pink, full, flat, medium; very fragrant.

Reichspräsident von Hindenberg HT, *pb*, 1933, *Frau Karl Druschki × Graf Silva Tarouca*; Lambert, P. Flowers dark pink to carmine, veined lighter, reverse darker, very dbl., large (to 6 in.); fragrant; foliage broad; very vigorous, bushy growth.

Reiko HT, *op*, 1963, *Spartan × Fred Streeter*; Teranishi; Itami Rose Nursery. Bud long, pointed; flowers bright coral-peach, dbl. (25 petals), high-centered to cupped, large (3½-4 in.); slightly fragrant; foliage dark, leathery; vigorous, upright growth.

Reims HT, *yb*, 1924, Barbier. Bud long, pointed; flowers bright nankeen yellow shaded fiery red, orange-apricot and copper.

Reina Maria Cristina T (OGR), *ob*, 1894, Aldrufeu. Flowers orange-yellow, very dbl., globular; foliage bronze; very vigorous, compact growth.

Reine Astrid HT, *rb*, 1937, Gaujard. Bud long, pointed; flowers bright deep coppery red, reverse golden yellow, dbl., cupped; fragrant; foliage glossy; vigorous growth.

Reine Blanche M (OGR), *w*, 1857, Robert. Flowers pure white, full, flat, large.

Reine Blanche M (OGR), *w*, 1858, Robert et Moreau. Flowers white, large, broad, flat; vigorous growth.

Reine de Castille B (OGR), *mp*, 1863, Pernet. Flowers bright rose, well-formed; vigorous.

Reine de Dänemark D (OGR), *lp*, (Queen of Denmark); *Possibly Damask × Centifolia hybrid*; Miellez, 1826. Flowers light pink, very dbl.

Reine de Portugal T (OGR), *yb*, 1869, Guillot Fils. Flowers coppery yellow shaded pink, very dbl., large.

Reine des Amateurs G (OGR), *m*, (Mme. Hébert); Hèbert, Mme. Flowers clear lilac, edged pale pink, well shaped, very large.

Reine des Belges HCh (OGR), *w*, 1867, *Globe Hip × R. chinensis*; Cochet. Flowers white; vigorous growth; sparse bloom.

Reine des Centfeuilles C (OGR), *mp*, 1824, From Belgium. Flowers clear pink, dbl., reflexed, very large; very vigorous growth.

Reine des Violettes HP (OGR), *m*, 1860, (Queen of the Violets); *Pius IX seedling*; Millet-Malet. Flowers violet-red, very dbl. (75 petals), large; very fragrant; foliage sparse; recurrent.

Reine d'Espagne HP (OGR), *mr*, 1861, Fontaine. Flowers brilliant red; foliage light; bushy.

Reine Elisabeth HT, *mr*, 1955, *Princesse Liliane × Ena Harkness*; Buyl Frères. Flowers velvety blood-red.

Reine Elizabeth Pol, *mr*, From Belgium. Flowers crimson, pompon shape, borne in clusters; compact, dwarf growth.

Reine Elizabeth HT, *rb*, 1925, Opdebeeck. Bud long, pointed; flowers coral-red, changing to prawn-red, tinted yellow, dbl., very fragrant.

Reine Emma des Pays-Bas T (OGR), *my*, 1879, Nabonnand, G. Flowers coppery yellow.

Reine Maria de Roumanie HT, *w*, 1927, *Stadtrat Glaser seedling*; Mühle. Bud long, pointed; flowers marble-white, center yellow, dbl.

Reine Maria Pia T (OGR), *dp*, 1880, *Gloire de Dijon seedling*; Schwartz, J. Flowers deep pink, center crimson, large; fragrant; very vigorous growth.

Reine Marie Henriette Cl HT, *mr*, 1878, *Mme. Bérard × Général Jacqueminot*; Levet, F. Flowers pure cherry-red, dbl., large; fragrant; vigorous, climbing growth.

Reine Olga de Wurtemberg N (OGR), *mr*, 1881, Nabonnand, G. Flowers bright red, full, large; fragrant; very vigorous, pillar growth.

Reinhard Bädecker HP (OGR), *my*, 1918, *Frau Karl Druschki × Rayon d'Or*; Kordes. Flowers clear golden yellow, dbl.; slightly fragrant.

Rejoice Gr, *pb*, 1985, *Little Darling × Color Magic*; McMillan, Thomas G. Flowers salmon-pink blended with yellow, dbl. (40 petals), HT form, large blooms in clusters of 1-6; fragrant; foliage large, medium green, glossy; tall, upright, bushy growth. ARC TG (G), 1985 (First Gold Winner).

Rekordblüher F, *mp*, 1965, Tantau, Math. Flowers rose-pink, semi-dbl., medium (2-3 in.), borne in large trusses; foliage dark, glossy; bushy growth.

Rektor Foerster HT, *pb*, 1936, *Golden Ophelia × Mme. Caroline Testout*; Weigand, C.; Pfitzer. Flowers solferino-pink, flushed yellow, dbl., high-centered, large; foliage leathery; vigorous growth.

Relief HT, *w*, 1919, *Kaiserin Auguste Viktoria × Sunburst*; Verschuren. Flowers ivory-white, center yellowish pink.

Rembrandt P (OGR), *or*, 1883, Moreau-Robert. Flowers vermilion.

Rembrandt HT, *ob*, 1914, *Frau Karl Druschki × Lyon Rose*; Van Rossem. Flowers salmon, tinted orange-red, dbl. (40 petals), well-formed, large; foliage leathery; vigorous.

Remember Me® HT, *ob*, 1984, (COCdestin); *Ann Letts × (Dainty Maid × Pink Favorite)*; Cocker. Flowers orange and yellow blend, semi-dbl. (20 petals), large; slight fragrance; foliage small, dark, glossy; bushy, spreading growth.

Remembrance HT, *yb*, 1953, *Fred Howard × Seedling*; Howard, A.P.; H&S. Bud ovoid; flowers soft yellow edged dawn-pink, dbl. (50 petals), high centered, large (4-5 in.); fragrant; foliage leathery, glossy, coppery green; vigorous, upright; profuse bloom. RULED EXTINCT 4/92.

Remembrance F, *mr*, 1992, (HARxampton); *Trumpeter × Southampton*; Harkness, R., 1983; R. Harkness & Co. Ltd. Flowers medium red, cupped, dbl. (32 petals), large (9 cms or less) blooms borne in sprays of 5-7; slight fragrance; foliage dark green, glossy; bushy growth.

Renae Cl F, *mp*, 1954, *Étoile Luisante × Sierra Snowstorm*; Moore, R.S.; Armstrong Nursery. Bud pointed; flowers pink, dbl. (43 petals), medium (2½ in.) blooms in clusters; very fragrant; foliage small, glossy; vigorous, climbing growth; recurrent bloom.

Renaissance® HT, *rb*, 1945, (GAUdino); Gaujard. Bud pointed; flowers red and gold, dbl., medium; slightly fragrant; foliage glossy; low growth. RULED EXTINCT 10/86.

Renaissance® HT, *ob*, 1986, *Seedling × Pampa*; Gaujard, Jean. Flowers brilliant orange, dbl., high-centered; moderate fragrance; foliage large; small prickles; fruit rounded.

Renate HT, *w*, 1925, *Kaiserin Auguste Viktoria seedling*; Berger, V. Flowers cream-white, dbl.; very fragrant.

Rendez-vous S, *mp*, 1981, (LUCdod); *R. wichuraiana × Alain Blanchard*; Lucas, C.C. Flowers medium pink, semi-dbl., medium; very fragrant; foliage medium, medium green, matt; bushy growth.

René André R, *ab*, 1901, *R. wichuraiana × L'Idéal*; Barbier. Bud coppery; flowers saffron-yellow, becoming pale pink and carmine, semi-dbl., medium (2-2½ in.) blooms in clusters; fragrant; very vigorous growth.

René Buatois LCl, *mp*, 1936, *Léontine Gervais sport*; Buatois. Flowers ruddy pink.

René d'Anjou M (OGR), *dp*, 1853, Robert. Flowers deep pink, veined, full, globular, small.

René Javey HT, *ab*, 1934, Gillot, F. Flowers clear apricot, reverse salmon-pink shaded yellow, passing to hermosa pink, dbl., very large; foliage clear bronze green.

Renée Brightman HT, *rb*, 1936, *Emma Wright seedling*; Hurran. Flowers brilliant scarlet, shaded orange, reverse striped yellow, dbl.; fragrant; vigorous growth.

Renée Danielle LCl, *my*, 1913, Guillot, P. Flowers jonquil-yellow to golden yellow, passing to white, medium, borne in clusters and singly; vigorous, climbing growth; sometimes blooms again in autumn.

Renée Wilmart-Urban HT, *pb*, 1908, Pernet-Ducher. Bud long, pointed; flowers salmon-flesh, edged carmine, dbl.; slightly fragrant.

Renegade Min, *mr*, 1986, (LYOren); *Seedling × Seedling*; Lyon; MB Farms Min. Roses. Flowers medium red, dbl. (52 petals), cupped, medium blooms borne usually singly; no fragrance; foliage medium, medium green, matt; small, green prickles; medium, upright growth.

Renny Min, *mp*, 1989, (MOReny); *Anytime × Renae*; Moore, Ralph S.; Sequoia Nursery. Bud pointed; flowers medium rose pink, reverse lighter, dbl. (25 petals), old fashioned, medium, borne in sprays of 3-7; moderate fragrance; foliage medium, medium green, matt; prickles none; fruit none; upright, bushy, low growth.

Reno Gr, *mp*, 1957, *Mrs. Sam McGredy × Mme. Henri Guillot*; Silva; Booy Rose Nursery. Bud urn-shaped; flowers coral-salmon, 16-20 wavy petals, globular, large (3-3½ in.) blooms in clusters; slightly fragrant; foliage bronze; vigorous growth.

Renoir Gr, *pb*, 1982, Hall, William W. Bud plump, pointed; flowers flesh pink with peachtones toward base, semi-dbl. (18 petals), borne 1-4 per cluster; tea fragrance; foliage 7-9 leaflet, dark, smooth; curved prickles; vigorous, upright to arching growth; repeat bloom.

Renoncule G (OGR), *mp*, Dupont, prior to 1867. Flowers rose.

Renoncule Pol, *dp*, 1913, Barbier. Flowers deep pink tinted lighter, buttercup form.

Renouveau de Provins® HT, *or*, 1966, (LAPdi); *Magicienne × Numero Un*; Laperrière; EFR. Bud ovoid; flowers geranium color, dbl. (36 petals), open, very large; foliage glossy; vigorous, bushy growth.

Renown HT, *or*, 1927, *Red-Letter Day × Mrs. Wemyss Quin*; Burbage Nursery. Flowers glowing orange-cerise, shaded cardinal, dbl.; very fragrant.

Repandia® S, *lp*, 1983, (KORsami; Kordes' Rose Repandia); *The Fairy × R. wichuraiana seedling*; Kordes, W.; Kordes Roses, 1982. Flowers light pink, semi-dbl., small; fragrant; foliage small, dark, glossy; low, spreading (to 5 ft.) growth; ground cover. ADR, 1986.

Resolut F, *or*, 1962, Tantau, Math. Bud oval; flowers orange-red, dbl. (30 petals), large (4-5 in.), borne in large sprays; slightly fragrant; foliage glossy; upright, bushy growth.

Resplenda HT, *w*, 1974, *Queen of Bermuda × Golden Giant*; Golik; Dynarose. Bud ovoid; flowers white, dbl. (30 petals), large (4 in.); fragrant (fruity); foliage glossy; moderate growth.

Restless Native S, *or*, 1973, *Orangeade × R. carolina*; Stoddard. Bud ovoid; flowers orange-scarlet, base white, single, 8-12 petals, cupped to flat, medium (2½ in.); foliage large, dark, leathery; vigorous, compact, bushy growth.

Resurrection® HT, *dp*, 1986, (KRIlexis); *Seedling × Seedling*; Kriloff, M. Bud red; flowers bright pink, large; sweet fragrance; foliage dark.

Retina Min, *mr*, 1980, *Seedling × Over the Rainbow*; Williams, Ernest D.; Kimbrew-Walter Roses. Flowers medium red, reverse lighter, base gold, dbl. (43 petals), blooms borne singly, sometimes 2-5 per cluster; very faint, fruity fragrance; foliage green, matt; straight, long, tan prickles; bushy, spreading growth.

Reus HT, *m*, 1949, *Cynthia × Manuelita*; Dot, P. Bud long, pointed; flowers magenta, dbl., high-centered, large; fragrant.

Rêve de Capri HT, *op*, 1953, *Pres. Herbert Hoover × Seedling*; Buyl Frères. Flowers salmon-orange and yellow; foliage bronze; compact, low.

Rêve d'Hélène HT, *mp*, 1959, *Michèle Meilland × Seedling*; Orard. Flowers bright pink edged silvery, large; foliage clear green; free growth.

Rêve d'Or N (OGR), *my*, 1869, *Mme. Schultz seedling*; Ducher, Vve. Flowers buff-yellow tinted lighter, dbl.; fragrant; foliage rich green; vigorous, climbing growth.

Rêve Rose F, *mp*, 1950, Mallerin; Vilmorin-Andrieux. Flowers pink, dbl. (60 petals), borne in large clusters.

Réveil HT, *yb*, 1924, *Mr. Joh. M. Jolles × Mrs. Wemyss Quinn*; Van Rossem. Flowers golden yellow, reverse striped red, dbl.; fragrant.

Réveil Dijonnais Cl HT, *rb*, 1931, *Eugène Fürst × Constance*; Buatois. Flowers cerise, large golden yellow center, reverse yellow streaked carmine, semi-dbl. (13 petals), cupped, large (to 5 in.) blooms in clusters on short stems; fragrant; foliage thick, glossy, bronze; vigorous, climbing growth. GM, Portland, 1929.

Reveille HT, *pb*, 1941, *Kidwai × Golden Main*; Nicolas; J&P. Flowers light salmon-buff-pink, center deeper pink, dbl. (40-50 petals), open, cupped, large; slightly fragrant; foliage dark, leathery; vigorous, upright, bushy, compact growth.

Revelation HT, *pb*, 1938, *Briarcliff sport*; Witter; Evans City Cut Flower Co. Bud long; flowers thulite-pink to rose-red, dbl. (35 petals), high-centered, large (4½-5 in.); fragrant; foliage dark; very vigorous growth.

Revenante G (OGR), *pb*, Miellez. Flowers light rose-pink, edged lilac.

Rev. David R. Williamson HT, *mr*, 1904, Dickson, A. Flowers dark crimson, globular; fragrant.

Rev. F. Page-Roberts HT, *yb*, 1921, *Queen Mary × Seedling*; Cant, B.R. Bud long, pointed; flowers yellow shaded red, dbl., large; very fragrant. GM, NRS, 1920.

Rev. F. Page-Roberts, Climbing Cl HT, *yb*, 1931, Beverley; W.B. Clarke.

Rev. H. d'Ombrain B (OGR), *mr*, 1863, Margottin. Flowers brilliant red; vigorous; recurrent.

Rev. James Sprunt Cl Ch (OGR), *mr*, 1856, *Cramoisi Superieur, Climbing sport*; Sprunt; P. Henderson, 1858. Flowers crimson-red, larger.

Rev. Williamson HT, *or*, 1921, Pernet-Ducher. Bud long, pointed; flowers coral-red, shaded carmine, dbl.

Révérence F, *mr*, 1962, *Orange Triumph × Seedling*; Delforge. Flowers geranium-red, dbl. (26 petals), carnation form, medium (2 in.), borne in large clusters; foliage dark, glossy; vigorous, upright growth.

Reverie HT, *ab*, 1925, *Mme. Mélanie Soupert × Jean C.N. Forestier*; Ketten Bros. Flowers apricot, reverse shrimp-pink veined rose, dbl.

Review HT, *mp*, 1951, *Mrs. Henry Bowles × Trigo*; Fletcher; Tucker. Flowers bright rose, reverse flesh, dbl. (50 petals), very large (6-7 in.); fragrant; foliage dull, green; medium, dwarf growth.

Revival HT, *ab*, 1980, *Folklore sport*; Barni-Pistoia, Rose, 1979. Flowers light apricot.

Reward HT, *yb*, 1934, Dickson, A. Bud long, pointed; flowers clear yellow shaded peach, medium; fragrant; foliage dark, glossy; vigorous, bushy growth.

Rex HT, *mr*, 1959, *Senior × Better Times*; Spanbauer. Bud long, pointed; flowers velvety cardinal-red, semi-dbl., cupped, large; slightly fragrant; foliage leathery, glossy; vigorous, upright growth; a greenhouse variety.

Rex Anderson HT, *w*, 1938, *Florence L. Izzard × Mrs. Charles Lamplough*; McGredy; J&P. Flowers ivory-white, dbl., very well-formed, large; fragrant (fruity); foliage gray-green; vigorous growth; shy bloom.

Rexy's Baby F, *lp*, 1992, (MACcarrib); *Sexy Rexy × (Freude × ((Anytime × Eyepaint) × Stars 'n' Stripes))*; McGredy, Sam; Sam McGredy Roses International. Flowers light pink, full (26-40 petals), medium (4-7 cms) blooms; slight fragrance; foliage small, medium green, glossy; bushy (90 cms) growth.

Reynolda House HT, *pb*, 1992, (WILangil); *Royal Highness × Command Performance*; Williams, J. Benjamin. Flowers light pink with ivory and coral blend, dbl. (26-40 petals), medium (4-7 cms) blooms borne mostly singly; very fragrant; foliage medium, dark green, semi-glossy, disease resistant; few prickles; medium (3-4 ft.), upright, bushy growth; winter hardy.

R. G. Casson HT, *pb*, 1923, Cant, B.R. Flowers rose and copper; fragrant.

Rhapsody HT, *ob*, 1951, *Lulu × Cecil*; Houghton, D.; Elmer Roses Co. Bud long, pointed; flowers orange, reverse terra-cotta, 20 petals, high-centered, medium; foliage leathery; vigorous, bushy. RULED EXTINCT 1/85.

Rhapsody HT, *mp*, 1985, (JACsod); *Seedling × Seedling*; Warriner; J&P. Flowers medium pink, semi-dbl. (20 petals), medium; slight fragrance; foliage medium, medium green, matt; greenhouse variety.

Rhea Reid HT, *mr*, 1908, *American Beauty seedling × Red seedling*; Hill, E.G., Co. Bud long, pointed; flowers crimson-red, dbl., high-centered; fragrant; foliage soft. GM, Bagatelle, 1908.

Rhea Reid, Climbing Cl HT, *mr*, 1914, California Nursery Co.

Rheinaupark® S, *mr*, 1983, (KOReipark); *(Gruss an Bayern × Seedling) × R. rugosa seedling*; Kordes; Kordes Roses. Flowers medium red, semi-dbl. (20 petals), large; slight fragrance; foliage large, dark, glossy; upright, bushy growth.

Rheingold HT, *my*, 1934, *Mrs. T. Hillas × Mabel Morse*; Leenders, M.; J&P. Flowers golden yellow, very dbl., large; very fragrant; foliage leathery, light; dwarf, bushy, compact growth.

Rhode Island Red LCl, *dr*, 1957, *Everblooming Pillar No. 73 × Seedling*; Brownell. Flowers dark red, dbl. (33 petals), cupped, large (4-5 in.); fragrant; foliage glossy.

Rhodoloque Jules Gravereaux T (OGR), 1908, Fontes.

Rhona HT, *mp*, 1984, *Anne Letts × (Dainty Maid × Pink Favorite)*; Gobbee, W.D. Flowers medium pink, semi-dbl. (20 petals), large; very fragrant; foliage medium, medium green, semi-glossy; bushy growth.

Rhonda LCl, *mp*, 1968, *New Dawn × Spartan*; Lissemore; C-P. Bud globular; flowers carmine-rose, dbl., large; slightly fragrant; foliage dark, glossy; vigorous, climbing growth.

Ria Wenning HT, *dp*, 1932, *Mme. Maurice de Luze × Red Star*; Leenders, M. Bud long, pointed; flowers carmine, semi-dbl.; fragrant; vigorous growth.

Ribatejo F, *w*, 1962, *Virgo × Seedling*; Moreira da Silva. Flowers white, center deep yellow.

Rich and Rare Min, *rb*, 1987, (SEArich); *(Rise 'n' Shine × Siobhan) × Beauty Secret*; McCann, S. Flowers scarlet, reverse white veined red, dbl. (35 petals), exhibition, small blooms borne singly; slight fragrance; foliage small, dark, semi-glossy; bushy growth.

Richard HT, *dr*, 1979, *Gavotte × Memoriam*; Ellick; Excelsior Roses. Bud long, pointed; flowers spinel-red, dbl. (25-30 petals), large (4-5 in.); very fragrant; foliage light green; bushy, upright growth.

Richard E. West HT, *my*, 1924, Dickson, A. Bud long, pointed; flowers yellow, dbl., large; very fragrant; foliage leathery; vigorous growth.

Richard Hayes S, *mp*, 1973, *Fred Loads sport*; Holmes, R.A.; Wonnacott. Flowers pink, large (4 in.); fragrant; foliage light; vigorous, tall, upright growth.

Richardson Wright HT, *pb*, 1931, *Radiance × Ville de Paris*; C-P. Flowers pearl with carmine dashes and lemon reflexes, large, globular; fragrant; foliage dark, leathery; vigorous growth.

Richmond HT, *mr*, 1905, (Everblooming Jack Rose); *Lady Battersea × Liberty*; Hill, E.G., Co. Bud long, pointed; flowers bright scarlet, varying greatly at times, dbl.; fragrant (damask); vigorous growth. A famous parent.

Richmond, Climbing Cl HT, *mr*, 1912, Dickson, A.

Ridgeway HT, *pb*, 1953, *Princess Marina × Vanessa*; Ratcliffe. Flowers salmon-pink shaded apricot, dbl., well shaped; strong stems; fragrant; foliage rather sparse; very vigorous growth.

Rifleman HT, *or*, 1979, *Tropicana × Orange Sensation*; Murray, N. Bud ovoid; flowers light vermilion, dbl. (35-43 petals), high-centered, large (3½ in.); slightly fragrant; tall, very vigorous, bushy growth.

Rigaudon F, *dr*, 1957, *(Independence × Seedling) × Seedling*; Combe; Japan Rose Society. Flowers dark red tinted geranium, dbl.; very dwarf, dense growth.

Right Royal HT, *mp*, 1979, *Scented Air × Anne Letts*; Hawken, U. Flowers silvery pink, dbl. (30 petals), large (4 in.); slightly fragrant; foliage dark; moderate growth.

Rigoletto F, *ab*, 1954, *Floribunda seedling × Souv. de Claudius Pernet*; Leenders, M. Flowers apricot-yellow tinted copper, semi-dbl., well formed, large; very fragrant; vigorous growth.

Rijswijk F, *ob*, 1964, *Goldmarie × Fata Morgana*; Buisman. Bud deep yellow; flowers orange-yellow, semi-dbl., borne in clusters; foliage dark, glossy; vigorous growth.

Riksbyggerosen F, *or*, 1969, *Irish Wonder × Seedling*; Poulsen, N.D.; Poulsen. Flowers orange-red, semi-dbl. (23 petals), open, large (3 in.); foliage glossy, light green; low, compact growth.

Rima HT, *lp*, 1964, *Prima Ballerina sport*; Samuels. Flowers light silvery pink.

Rimosa F, *my*, 1958, *Goldilocks × Perla de Montserrat*; Meilland, F.; URS. Flowers indian yellow to citron-yellow, semi-dbl.to dbl. (18-25 petals), well formed, medium, borne in clusters; fragrant; foliage leathery; upright, symmetrical, compact growth.

Rina Herholdt HT, *pb*, 1962, (HERani); *Peace × Seedling*; Herholdt, J.A.; Herholdt's Nursery. Bud long, pointed; flowers milky white, flushed deep pink at edges, darkening with age, dbl. (60 petals), semi-cupped, large (3½ -4 in.); fragrant; foliage leathery, glossy; vigorous, bushy growth.

Rina Herholdt, Climbing Cl HT, *pb*, 1973, Arora, Bal Raj; The Rosery.

Ring of Fire™ Min, *yb*, 1986, (MORfire); *Pink Petticoat × Gold Badge*; Moore, Ralph S. Flowers yellow blended orange, reverse yellow, fading lighter, very dbl. (60 petals), imbricated, medium, borne usually singly and in sprays; slight fragrance; foliage medium, medium green, semi-glossy; slender, sharp pointed, medium, green to brown prickles; fruit none; upright, bushy, vigorous growth. AOE, 1987.

Ringfield HT, *or*, 1977, *Ernest H. Morse × Fragrant Cloud*; Plumpton. Flowers deep vermilion, dbl. (30 petals), full, large (5 in.); slightly fragrant; vigorous growth.

Ringlet Cl HT, *pb*, 1922, *Ernest Morel × Betty Berkeley*; Clark, A.; Brundrett. Flowers white, tipped pink and lilac, single, small blooms in clusters; vigorous, climbing growth.

Rio Grande HT, *dr*, 1973, *Seedling × Seedling*; Tantau; Ahrens; Sieberz. Bud ovoid; flowers velvety dark red, dbl., medium; fragrant; foliage soft; moderate, upright, bushy growth.

Rio Rita HT, *w*, 1931, *Mme. Butterfly × Premier*; Hill, J.H., Co. Bud long, pointed; flowers white tinged pink, dbl., large; very fragrant; foliage glossy; vigorous growth.

Rio Rita Cl HT, *w*, 1935, *E.G. Hill sport*; Elmer's Nursery. Flowers velvety scarlet-crimson, dbl., cupped, very large; very fragrant; foliage glossy; very vigorous growth.

Rio Samba HT, *yb*, 1991, (JACrite); *Seedling × Sunbright*; Warriner, William; Bear Creek Gardens, 1993. Flowers medium yellow fading to peach-pink, moderately full (15-25 petals), large (7 cms) blooms borne mostly singly; slight fragrance; foliage medium, dark green, matt; some prickles; medium (110-120 cms), upright, bushy growth; AARS, 1993.

Ripples F, *m*, 1971, *(Tantau's Surprise × Marjorie LeGrice) × (Seedling × Africa Star)*; LeGrice. Flowers lilac-lavender, semi-dbl. (18 wavy petals), large (3½ in.); slightly fragrant; foliage small, green, matt.

Rise 'n' Shine Min, *my*, 1977, (Golden Meillandina; Golden Sunblaze); *Little Darling × Yellow Magic*; Moore, R.S.; Sequoia Nursery. Bud long, pointed; flowers rich medium yellow, dbl. (35 petals), high-centered, small (1½ in.); fragrant; bushy, upright growth. AOE, 1978.

Rise 'n' Shine, Climbing Cl Min, *my*, 1990, (MorKINshine); *Rise 'n' Shine sport*; King, Gene; Sequoia Nursery, 1990. Bud pointed; flowers medium yellow, aging lighter, dbl. (35 petals), high-centered, small, borne usually singly or in sprays of 3-5; slight fragrance; foliage medium, medium green, semi-glossy; prickles straight, inclined slightly downward, brown; fruit round, orange; upright, spreading, tall, climbing.

Rising Sun HT, *rb*, 1924, Hicks. Bud long, pointed; flowers rich copper, base old-gold, cactus dahlia form.

Risqué Gr, *rb*, 1985, *Bob Hope × Seedling*; Weeks, O.L.; Weeks Roses. Flowers medium red, light yellow reverse, semi-dbl. (20 petals), medium; no fragrance; foliage medium, dark, semi-glossy; upright, slightly spreading growth.

Rita F, *mp*, 1960, *Karl Herbst × Pinocchio*; Fryer's Nursery. Flowers rich pink, dbl., blooms in large clusters; fragrant; foliage glossy; vigorous growth.

Rita Jackson HT, *rb*, 1964, *Tzigane sport*; Jackson, F. Flowers red blend, dbl., high-centered, large; slightly fragrant; upright, bushy growth.

Rita Sammons Pol, *pb*, 1925, (Justine Silva); *Cécile Brunner sport*; Clarke, B.; Clarke Bros. Flowers deep rose-pink, opening pink, edged lighter.

Rittenhouse™ HT, *ob*, 1988, (WILhkpk); *Queen Elizabeth × Zorina*; Williams, J. Benjamin, 1989. Flowers fiery orange to copper blended, dbl. (26-40 petals), large; fragrant; foliage large, dark green, glossy, disease resistant; upright, vigorous, mass-blooming, winter hardy growth.

Ritter von Barmstede K (S), *mp*, 1959, Kordes. Flowers medium pink, 20 petals, medium (2 in.) blooms in clusters of 30-40; foliage glossy; vigorous (10-15 ft.) growth.

Ritz LCl, *mr*, 1955, *R. setigera × Seedling*; Horvath; Wyant. Flowers velvety red, single (11 petals), 3 in. blooms in clusters; vigorous (8-9 ft.); recurrent.

Ritz F, *mr*, 1961, Gaujard. Flowers bright scarlet, semi-dbl. (16 petals), large (3½ in.); slightly fragrant; foliage dark, glossy; vigorous, well branched growth.

Riva Ligure HT, *dp*, 1947, *Seedling × Crimson Glory*; San Remo Exp. sta. Bud pointed; flowers velvety carmine, dbl. (24-35 petals); very fragrant; foliage dark; vigorous, bushy growth.

Rival HT, *mr*, 1954, *Southport × The Rev. W.S. Crawford*; Fletcher; Tucker. Flowers cherry-scarlet, loosely formed, flat, large (4-5 in.); foliage bronze; free growth.

Rival de Paestum T (OGR), *w*, Prior to 1848. Bud tinged pink; flowers white, base blush and ivory, dbl.; foliage dark; moderate growth.

Rivers HP (OGR), *mr*, 1832, Laffay. Flowers bright crimson, full, large, borne in corymbs; vigorous growth; recurrent bloom.

Rivers' George IV HCh (OGR), *dr*, (George IV; King George IV); *Thought to be Damask × China*; Rivers, ca. 1817. Flowers vivid crimson, shaded with dark purple, loosely dbl., cupped; vigorous, branching; shoots tinged with purple; non-recurrent bloom.

Rivers' Musk HMsk (S), *mp*, Rivers, prior to 1925. Flowers rosy buff, small; very fragrant.

Riviera HT, *or*, 1939, *Luis Brinas × Catalonia*; Dot, P.; J&P, 1940. Bud globular, yellow; flowers orange-scarlet, reverse lighter, base yellow, dbl., open, cupped, large; foliage glossy, wrinkled, dark; very vigorous, bushy growth.

R. M. S. Queen Mary HT, *mp*, 1937, (Mrs. Verschuren); *Briarcliff × Mrs. Sam McGredy*; Verschuren; Dreer; J&P. Flowers salmon-pink suffused orange, dbl., cupped, very large; foliage leathery; vigorous growth.

Roadman HT, *w*, 1977, *Hawaii × Kordes' Perfecta*; Ota. Bud pointed; flowers near white, dbl. (40-50 petals), high-centered, very large (6 in.); foliage leathery; upright growth.

Roaming HT, *dp*, 1970, *Vera Dalton × Tropicana*; Sanday. Flowers reddish pink shades, dbl. (24 petals), pointed, large (3½ in.); foliage green, matt.

Rob Roy® F, *dr*, 1970, (COrob); *Evelyn Fison × Wendy Cussons*; Cocker, 1971. Flowers dark red, dbl. (30 petals), HT form, large (4½ in.); slightly fragrant; foliage glossy.

Robe d'Été F, *or*, 1966, (*Chatelaine × Mannequin*) × (*Montezuma × Floradora*); Lens. Flowers salmon-orange, semi-dbl. (22-24 petals), high-centered, large (3-3½ in.); slightly fragrant; foliage bronze; bushy, upright growth.

Robert P (OGR), *pb*, 1856, Robert. Flowers carmine, marbled white.

Robert Betten HT, *mr*, 1920, *Frau Karl Druschki × Corallina*; Schmidt, J.C. Flowers clear dark carmine-red, not turning blue, dbl.

Robert Bland S, *dp*, 1960, ((*Hansa × R. macounii*) × *Betty Bland*) × (*R. blanda × Betty Bland*); Wright, P.H. Flowers dark pink, dbl., open, small; foliage rich green; thornless; vigorous, bushy growth; non-recurrent bloom; quite hardy.

Robert Cotton HT, *w*, 1968, *Marcia Stanhope × Karl Herbst*; Golik; Ellesmere Nursery. Bud ovoid; flowers white, edges flushed pink, dbl., large; slightly fragrant; foliage glossy, serrated, leathery; moderate growth.

Robert Dubol HT, *mr*, 1946, Sauvageot, H.; Sauvageot. Flowers warm orient red, stamens golden, very dbl., high-centered.

Robert Duncan HP (OGR), *pb*, 1897, Dickson, A. Flowers purplish pink, sometimes flamed brilliant red, very dbl. (70 petals), well-formed, large blooms in clusters; fragrant; vigorous growth; repeat bloom.

Robert F. Kennedy HT, *mr*, 1968, *Chrysler Imperial × Ena Harkness*; Takatori; Parnass Rose Nursery. Flowers scarlet, high-centered; very fragrant; foliage dark; very vigorous, upright growth.

Robert Huey HT, *dp*, 1911, Dickson, A. Bud long, pointed; flowers carmine edged lighter, bluing slightly; dbl., fragrant; moderate growth.

Robert le Diable G (OGR), *m*, Prior to 1837. Flowers scarlet-pink aging to deep purple, center often green, fully dbl.; low, lax growth.

Robert Léopold M (OGR), *pb*, 1941, Buatois. Flowers salmon-flesh-pink edged light carmine, dbl., large.

Robespierre Pol, *pb*, 1975, Delforge, S. Bud full; flowers pink blend, very dbl. (88 petals), cupped, small (2½ in.); fragrant; foliage bronze.

Robin Min, *mr*, 1956, *Perla de Montserrat × Perla de Alcañada*; Dot, P.; C-P. Bud urn-shaped; flowers rich red, very dbl. (65 petals), flat, small (1¼ in.) blooms in clusters of 15; foliage leathery, green, matt; vigorous, dwarf (12 in.), bushy growth.

Robin Hood HMsk (S), *mr*, 1927, (Rob in des Bois); *Seedling × Miss Edith Cavell*; Pemberton. Flowers cherry-red, blooms in large clusters; vigorous (4-5 ft.), dense, compact; recurrent.

Robin Hood HT, *mr*, 1912, Hill, E.G., Co. Flowers soft bright rosy scarlet, changing to bright scarlet-crimson, dbl.; very fragrant.

Robin Red Breast Min, *rb*, 1983, (INTerrob; Robin Redbreast); *Seedling × Eyepaint*; Interplant, 1984. Flowers dark red, white eye, reverse silver, single, small blooms in clusters; no fragrance; foliage small, medium green, glossy; many, medium prickles; bushy growth.

Robinette R, *rb*, 1943, *Hiawatha* × *Hiawatha*; Moore, R.S.; Hennessey. Flowers amaranth-red, white eye, single, open, small, borne in clusters; very fragrant; foliage gloy; height 10-12 ft.

Robusta® S, *mr*, 1979, (KORgosa; Kordes' Rose Robusta); *Seedling* × *R. rugosa*; Kordes, W. Bud long, pointed; flowers medium red, single (5 petals), medium (2½ in.); fragrant; foliage dark, glossy, leathery; very vigorous, upright, bushy growth. ADR, 1980.

Roccana Diane F, *dp*, 1985, (KIRdex); *Pink Favorite* × *Attraction*; Kirkham, Gordon W. Flowers deep pink, semi-dbl. (20 petals), medium; slight fragrance; foliage large, dark, glossy; upright growth.

Rochefort HT, *ab*, 1936, *Mrs. Pierre S. duPont* × *Charles P. Kilham*; Mallerin; C-P. Flowers apricot, dbl., large; very fragrant (fruity); foliage leathery; vigorous. GM, Portland, 1935.

Rochelle Hudson HT, *rb*, 1937, *Isobel* × *Mme. Edouard Herriot*; Moore, R.S.; Brooks & Son. Bud long, pointed; flowers carmine, base yellow, orange undertone deepening with age, semi-dbl., open, large; slightly fragrant (fruity); foliage dark; vigorous growth.

Rochester F, *ab*, 1934, *Echo* × *Rev. F. Page-Roberts*; Nicolas; J&P. Flowers buff, reverse orange-carmine, dbl., medium; fragrant; foliage leathery; vigorous, bushy growth.

Rochester Cathedral S, *mp*, 1985, (HARroffen; HARoffen); *(Seedling* × *((Orange Sensation* × *Allgold)* × *R. californica))* × *Frank Naylor*; Harkness, R., 1987. Flowers medium pink, dbl. (58 petals), cupped, medium to large blooms in clusters; fragrant; foliage medium, dark, matt; medium, dense, spreading growth; repeat bloom.

Rocket HT, *mr*, 1935, *Dame Edith Helen* × *Scorcher*; Nicolas; J&P. Flowers brilliant scarlet, reverse crimson, dbl., high-centered, large; very fragrant; foliage leathery, dark, bronze; very vigorous growth.

Rocky™ S, *ob*, 1979, (MACkepa; Blushing Maid); *Liverpool Echo* × *(Evelyn Fison* × *(Orange Sweetheart* × *Frühlingsmorgen))*; McGredy, S., IV; McGredy Roses International. Bud ovoid; flowers coral orange, reverse whitish, dbl. (25 petals), medium; vigorous, tall, bushy growth.

Rococo F, *mr*, 1964, *Moulin Rouge* × *Fire Opal*; McGredy, S., IV; Spek. Flowers scarlet, semi-dbl. (15 petals), large (3 in.), borne in clusters; free growth; a greenhouse variety.

Rod Stillman HT, *lp*, 1948, *Ophelia* × *Editor McFarland*; Hamilton. Flowers light pink, base flushed orange, dbl. (35 petals), large; very fragrant; foliage dark; vigorous.

Roddy MacMillan HT, *ab*, 1982, (COCared); *(Fragrant Cloud* × *Postillion)* × *Wisbech Gold*; Cocker, James; Cocker & Sons. Flowers apricot, dbl. (35 petals), large; fragrant; foliage medium, medium green, semi-glossy; bushy growth.

Rodeo F, *or*, 1960, *Obergärtner Wiebicke* × *Spartan*; Kordes, R.; McGredy. Flowers bright scarlet, dbl., large (3 in.), borne in clusters (up to 10); slightly fragrant; foliage light green; bushy, low growth.

Rodeo Drive™ HT, *mr*, 1986, (AROcore; Sunset Strip); *Merci* × *Pharaoh*; Christensen, Jack; Armstrong Roses. Flowers bright deep red, dbl. (32 petals), high-centered, large, borne usually singly, slight fragrance; foliage medium to large, medium green, semi-glossy; many attenuated, medium, reddish prickles aging light brown; fruit none observed; bushy, medium growth.

Rödhätte F, *mr*, 1912, (Red Riding Hood); *Mme. Norbert Levavasseur* × *Richmond*; Poulsen, D.; Poulsen. Flowers clear cherry-red, semi-dbl., large blooms in large clusters; foliage rich green; bushy, compact growth.

Rödhätte, Climbing Cl F, *mr*, 1925, Grootendorst, F.J.

Roelof Buisman HT, *mr*, 1964, Kordes, R. Bud ovoid; flowers bright pure red, well-formed, large; vigorous, upright, bushy growth.

Roger Boudou Pol, *mr*, 1957, *Lafayette seedling*; Privat. Flowers very bright red.

Roger Lambelin HP (OGR), *rb*, 1890, *Fisher Holmes sport*; Vve. Schwartz Flowers bright crimson fading maroon, petals margined white, very distinct, dbl. (30 fringed petals), irregular; vigorous growth; recurrent bloom; (28).

Roger Lambelin Striped HP (OGR), *rb*, 1953, *Roger Lambelin sport*; Hennessey. Flowers deep maroon to pink stripes on white ground; recurrent bloom.

Roi Albert HT, *pb*, 1925, *Laurent Carle seedling* × *Mme. Abel Chatenay*; Klettenberg-Londes. Bud long, pointed; flowers bright carmine-rose, center tinted scarlet; very fragrant.

Roi Alexandre HT, *ob*, 1937, (King Alexander I; S.M. Alexander I); Gaujard. Flowers coppery orange, tinted salmon, dbl., very large; fragrant; foliage leathery, glossy, bronze; very vigorous growth.

Roi des Aunes S, *dp*, 1885, (Erlkönig); *Perhaps raised from De la Grifferaie*; Geschwind. Flowers carmine tinted red, full, globular, large; very vigorous; non-recurrent bloom.

Roi des Bengales F, *rb*, 1958, *(Hermosa × Gruss an Teplitz) × Independence*; Arles; Roses-France. Flowers grenadine-red; vigorous, low growth.

Roi des Cramoisis Ch (OGR), *mr*, Flowers bright red, cupped.

Roi des Pays-Bas C (OGR), *dp*, 1848, (Roi de Pays-Bas). Flowers deep pink, dbl., cupped, large.

Roi Soleil HT, *my*, 1962, *Peace × Independence seedling*; Dorieux; Le Blévenec. Bud long, pointed; flowers citron-yellow; very vigorous growth GM, Madrid, 1963.

Roklea® HT, *ob*, 1975, Tantau, M. Flowers bright orange, semi-dbl. (20 petals), high-centered, large; fragrant; foliage large, dark, semi-glossy; upright; greenhouse variety.

Roland F, *ob*, 1961, *Karl Weinhausen × Independence*; Leenders, J. Flowers salmon-orange-red; low growth.

Roller Coaster Min, *rb*, 1987, (MACminmo; Minnie Mouse); *(Anytime × Eyepaint) × Stars 'n' Stripes*; McGredy, Sam; Sam McGredy International, 1988. Flowers red blend (striped), semi-dbl. (6-14 petals); slight fragrance; foliage small, medium green, glossy; upright growth.

Román HT, *mp*, 1961, *Asturias × Rosa de Friera*; Dot, S. Flowers nilsson pink, becoming hermosa pink, dbl. (35 petals), large; very fragrant.

Roman Festival F, *pb*, 1968, *Queen Elizabeth × Sumatra*; Williams, J.B. Bud ovoid; flowers coral, base yellow, high-centered, medium, borne in clusters; slightly fragrant; foliage dark, glossy; vigorous, low, compact growth.

Roman Holiday F, *rb*, 1966, (LINro); *(Pinkie × Independence) × Circus*; Lindquist; Howard Rose Co. Bud ovoid; flowers orange turning blood-red, base yellow, dbl. (28 petals), high-centered, medium blooms in clusters; fragrant; foliage dark, leathery; vigorous, bushy, low. AARS, 1967.

Roman Triumph F, *mr*, 1977, *Jove × City of Leeds*; Harkness. Flowers medium red, semi-dbl. (13 petals), large; slightly fragrant; foliage glossy; upright, bushy growth.

Romana HT, *rb*, 1938, *Better Times sport*; Ringdahl. Bud long, pointed; flowers rose-red to light purple, dbl., open, large; foliage leathery, glossy, dark; very vigorous growth.

Romance HT, *my*, 1931, *Souv. de Claudius Pernet × Buttercup seedling*; Towill. Bud long, pointed; flowers golden yellow, shading toward lemon, dbl., open, large; fragrant; foliage thick; very vigorous growth. RULED EXTINCT 11/82.

Romance Cl HT, *lp*, 1933, *Isa sport*; Beckwith. Flowers shell-pink, fading to pale blush, large, not too full; very fragrant; vigorous, climbing growth. RULED EXTINCT 11/82.

Romance HT, *mp*, 1983, (JACrom); *Seedling × Prominent*; Warriner; J&P. Flowers medium salmon-pink, dbl. (35 petals), large; slight fragrance; foliage large, medium green, semi-glossy; upright growth; greenhouse variety.

Romantica HT, *mp*, 1962, *Baccará × White Knight*; Meilland, M.L.; URS. Bud oval; flowers phlox-pink, dbl. (40 petals), high-centered, large; slightly fragrant; foliage leathery, glossy; very vigorous, upright growth; a forcing variety.

Romany F, *op*, 1965, *Orangeade × Mischief*; McGredy, S., IV; Geest Industries. Flowers salmon, well formed, large (3½ in.), borne in clusters; slightly fragrant; free growth.

Rome Glory HT, *mr*, 1937, (Gloire de Rome; Gloria di Roma; Glory of Rome); *Dame Edith Helen × Sensation*; Aicardi, D.; J&P. Bud ovoid; flowers scarlet, reverse cerise, dbl. (55 petals), globular, large (4-5 in.); fragrant; vigorous, bushy growth.

Romeo HT, *yb*, 1918, *Edith Part seedling × Ophelia*; Therkildsen. Flowers indian yellow, suffused coppery pink; slightly fragrant.

Romeo LCl, *dr*, 1919, Easlea. Flowers deep red, dbl., well formed, borne in small clusters; vigorous, climbing growth.

Ron West HT, *pb*, 1985, *Admiral Rodney sport*; West, Ronald. Flowers white with deep pink petal edges.

Ronald George Kent F, *mp*, 1992, (BRandypink); *Pink Favorite × Piccasso*; Bracegirdle, A.J. Flowers medium pink, moderately full (15-25 petals), large (7+ cms) blooms borne in small clusters; slight fragrance; foliage large, dark green, semi-glossy; few prickles; medium (86 cms), bushy growth.

Ronald Healy HT, *pb*, 1932, Dobbie. Bud long, pointed; flowers old-rose, shaded salmon and yellow, dbl., high-centered; fragrant; foliage glossy; bushy growth.

Ronald Tooke HT, *dr*, 1927, *Col. Oswald Fitzgerald sport*; Morse. Flowers deep blackish crimson.

Ronde Endiablée F, *or*, 1963, Combe. Flowers geranium-red, edged darker, semi-dbl., large; foliage dark, glossy; moderate growth. GM, The Hague, 1964.

Rondo HT, *or*, 1955, *Danzig × (Crimson Glory × Floradora sister seedling)*; Tantau; J&P. Bud ovoid; flowers orange-red, semi-dbl. (15-20 petals), high-centered to flat, large (3½-4 in.);

fragrant (fruity); foliage dark, leathery; vigorous, upright, compact growth.

Ronny Temmer F, *mp*, 1974, Delforge, S. Bud ovoid; flowers pink, dbl. (44 petals), full, large (3½ in.); fragrant.

Ronsard HT, *rb*, 1937, *Conrad Ferdinand Meyer* × *R. foetida bicolor seedling*; Gaujard; J&P. Bud long, pointed, yellowish edged red; flowers brilliant red, reverse yellow and cream, semi-dbl., cupped; slightly fragrant; foliage leathery, dark; bushy growth.

Roosendaal F, *mr*, 1965, *Gartendirektor Glocker* × *Alpine Glow*; Buisman. Flowers red, dbl., medium; foliage dark.

Roquebrune HT, *ob*, 1959, Delforge. Bud oval; flowers ocher-yellow edged orange, dbl., medium; strong stems; slightly fragrant; foliage dark, glossy; moderate, bushy growth.

ROSA For several reasons it is not possible to give a standard, unambiguous list of rose species. There is a plethora of published names, many ill defined, which under the current International Code of Botanical Nomenclature (1961), with its insistence on priority of publication, defy analysis. Again, roses have been cultivated and hybridized for so long in gardens that the status and relationships of many garden favorites can only be conjectured. The limits of some "species" are imperfectly understood, and authorities differ widely in the interpretation given them. Linnaeus himself singled out the genus two centuries ago as a source of confusion, to which he added by giving latinized names to double-flowered garden hybrids like *Rosa centifolia* which do not — indeed, could not — exist independently in the wild.

The present list is at best a compromise, adapted from the most widely accepted existing sources (A. Rehder's "Manual of Cultivated Trees and Shrubs," Edn. 2, 1940, and "Bibliography of Cultivated Trees and Shrubs," 1949) with additions by G.H.M. Lawrence and G.D. Rowley. For fuller descriptions of the species and synonymy the reader is referred to these above-mentioned works and to the R.H.S. Dictionary of Gardening, Ed. F. J. Chittenden, IV, 1951 and Supplement, Ed. P. M. Synge, 1956. Also useful are the descriptions in W. J. Bean's "Trees and Shrubs Hardy in the British Isles," Edn. VII, III, 1951. Synonyms are indicated in italics and hybrids of recent origin (as distinct from hybrid species like the *Caninae*) are preceded by the sign ×. The present separation of "species" from the "garden roses" on the basis of latinized and non-latinized names respectively is a matter of convenience and leads to inconsistencies.

Thus, a rose found spontaneously growing in the wild may have only a cultivar name (e.g. Woodrow, a double sport of *R. suffulta* Greene), while many garden hybrids wrongly bear latinized names (e.g. *Rosa damascena* Miller). The worst offenders, such as Rehder's *R.* × *arnoldiana* and *R.* × *bruantii*, which do not even apply to single crosses but to families, are here treated as cultivar names and transferred to the general body of the book as synonyms.
— G. D. Rowley

(Additions and corrections by Peter S. Green of the Arnold Arboretum, Jamaica Plain, MA.)

R. acicularis Lindley Sp (OGR), *dp*, 1805, (Arctic Rose; *R. acicularis carelica* (Fries) Matsson; *R. acicularis taquetii* (Léveillé) Nakai; *R. carelica* Fries; *R. fauriei* Léveillé, partly; *R. korsakoviensis* Léveillé; *R. sayi* Schweinitz; *R. stricta* Macoun; Gibson). Flowers deep rose 1½-2 in. diam., solitary; fragrant; fruit usually pyriform,½-1 in. long; 3 ft. Spring. N. Am., NE Asia, N. Eu. *Cinnamomeae*; (28, 42, 56).

R. acicularis fennica Lallemant Sp (OGR), *dp*, (*R. acicularis gmelinii* Bunge; *R. gmelinii* Bunge); Tetraploid variant from Finland and Siberia; (28).

R. acicularis nipponensis (Crépin) Koehne Sp (OGR), *dp*, 1894, (*R. nipponensis* Crépin). Flowers 1½ in. diam.; petioles and pedicles bristly. Japan; (14, rarely 28).

R. acicularis sayi Rehder Sp (OGR), *dp*, (*R. acicularis bourgeauiana* Crépin; *R. bourgeauiana* Crépin; *R. sayi* Watson, not Schweinitz); Cult. prior to 1875. Flowers larger than *R. acicularis*, often 2½ in. diam.; fruit usually globular. Ont. to B.C. and CO; (42, 56).

R. acicularis sayi plena Lewis Sp (OGR), *dp*, Discovered in the wild by P.H. Wright in Saskatchewan, Canada. Usually 9 (sometimes 15) petals; (42).

R. agrestis Savi Sp (OGR), *lp*, (*R. sepium* Thuillier); *Allied to R. eglanteria*; Cult. 1878. Flowers pale pink or whitish, small. Eu., N. Afr. *Caninae*; (35, 42).

R. albertii Regel Sp (OGR), *w*, *Allied to R. willmottiae*; 1877. Flowers white, 1½ in. diam.; 3 ft. Songarica, Turkestan. *Cinnamomeae*.

R. amblyotis C.A. Meyer Sp (OGR), *mr*, Cult. 1917. Flowers red, 2 in. diam., solitary or few; fruit subglobose or pyriform, ½-1 in. diam., red. Kamchatka. *Cinnamomeae*; (14).

R. andreae Lange Sp (OGR), A little-known species from the Sachaline Islands; not. cult.; (14).

R. anemoneflora Fortune Sp (OGR), *w*, (*R. sempervirens anemoniflora* Regel; *R. triphylla* Roxburgh ex Hemsley); 1844. Flowers white, dbl., 1 in. diam., corymbose; leaflets 3, lanceolate; Climbing. E. China. *Synstylae*; (14).

R. arkansana Porter Sp (OGR), *mp*, (Arkansas Rose; *R. angustiarum* Cockerell; *R. arkansanoides* Schneider; *R. heliophila* Greene; *R. pratincola* Greene, not H. Braun; *R. rydbergii* Greene; *R. suffulta* Greene); Cult. 1880. Flowers medium pink, 1½ in. diam., in corymbs; 1½ ft. N. Am. *Cinnamomeae*; (28; rarely 14).

R. arkansana alba (Rehder) Lewis Sp (OGR), *w*, (*R. arkansanoides alba* (Rehder) Schneider; *R. heliophila alba* (Rehder) Rehder; *R. pratincola alba* Rehder; *R. suffulta alba* (Rehder) Rehder); 1901. Flowers white.

R. arkansana plena Lewis Sp (OGR), *lp*, Distributed by P.H. Wright, Woodrow, Saskatchewan, Canada, where the form is native. Up to 20 pink petals.

R. arvensis Hudson Sp (OGR), *w*, (Field Rose; *R. repens* Scopoli; *R. silvestris* Herrmann; *R. serpens* Wibel). Flowers white, 1½-2 in. diam., in few-flowered corymbs; scentless; fruit ovoid; deciduous; creeping. Summer. Eu. *Synstylae*; (14).

R. banksiae Aiton fil Sp (OGR), (Banks' Rose; Banksian Rose; Lady Banks' Rose; *R. banksiana* Abel); Cult. 1796. Flowers white or yellow, about 1 in. diam., on slender pedicels in many-flowered umbels; slightly fragrant; foliage evergreen; climbing (20 ft. or more) growth; early spring bloom. C. & W. China. *Banksianae*; (14). This entry refers to more than one clone.

R. banksiae banksiae Sp (OGR), *w*, (Banksiae Alba; *R. banksiae alba* hort.; *R. banksiae alba-plena* Rehder; White Banksia; White Lady Banks' Rose); William Kerr, 1807. Flowers white, dbl.; (14).

R. banksiae lutea Lindley Sp (OGR), *ly*, (*R. banksiae luteaplena* Rehder; Yellow Lady Banks' Rose); 1824. Flowers yellow, dbl.; (14).

R. banksiae lutescens Voss Sp (OGR), *my*, ca. 1870. Flowers yellow, single; (14).

R. banksiae normalis Regel Sp (OGR), *w*, 1796, but not distributed until 1877. Flowers white, single; wild form; (14).

R. banksiopsis Baker Sp (OGR), *mr*, 1907. Flowers red, 1 in. diam. borne in corymbs. W. China. *Cinnamomeae*; (14).

R. beggeriana Schrenk ex Fischer & Meyer Sp (OGR), *w*, (*R. cinnamomea sewerzowii* Regel; *R. lehmanniana* Bunge; *R. regelii* Reuter; *R. silverhjelmii* Schrenk); 1868. Flowers white, 1½ in. diam., borne in corymbs; fruit small,

globular, without sepals; dense (5 ft.) growth; late summer bloom. C. Asia. *Cinnamomeae*; (14).

R. bella Rehder & Wilson Sp (OGR), *mp*, *Allied to R. moyesii*; 1910. Flowers pink, solitary, 1¼-2 in. diam.; fruit ovoid, scarlet, ¾ in. long; 8 ft. N. China. *Cinnamomeae*; (28).

R. bella pallens Rehder & Wilson Sp (OGR), *lp*, 1910. Flowers pale pink.

R. billotiana Crépin Sp (OGR), Similar to *R. canina*, with fruit like *R. sherardii*. Eu. *Caninae*; rarely cult.; (28).

R. blanda Aiton Sp (OGR), *mp*, (Hudson's Bay Rose; Labrador Rose; *R. fraxinifolia* Lindley, not Borkhausen; *R. gratiosa* Lunell; *R. solandri* Trattinnick; *R. subblanda* Rydberg; *R. virginiana blanda* Koehne); 1773. Flowers pink, single, 2-2½ in. diam., borne usually several on smooth peduncles; fruit globular, sometimes elongated; 5 ft.; spring bloom; usually unarmed. N. N. Am. *Cinnamomeae*; (14, rarely 21, 28).

R. blanda carpohispida (Schuette) Lewis Sp (OGR), *mp*, (*R. blanda hispida* Farwell); Canes densely covered with fine bristles; (14); a giant triploid (21) form is Amurensis.

R. blanda willmottiana Baker Sp (OGR), *mp*, Cult. prior to 1910. Flowers bright coral-pink; stems red.

R. bracteata Wendland Sp (OGR), *w*, (Chickasaw Rose; Macartney Rose; *R. lucida* Lawrance, not Ehrhart; *R. macartnea* Dumont de Courset); 1793. Fl. white, 2-2¾ in. diam., borne 1 or few on short stalks; fol. half-evergreen, bright green, somewhat glossy above, almost glabrous beneath, resistant to blackspot, leaflets 5-9; fruit large, globular, orange-red, tomentose; Cl. growth. Spring-Fall bloom. China, naturalized in S.E. N. Am. Sometimes confused with *R. laevigata*. *Bracteatae*; (14).

R. britzensis Koehne Sp (OGR), *lp*, 1901. Flowers pale pink changing to white, 3-4 in. diam., borne 1-2 together; fruit brown, ovoid; 6 ft. Kurdistan. *Caninae*; (35).

R. californica Chamisso & Schlechtendahl Sp (OGR), *mp*, (California Wild Rose; *R. gratissima* Greene); Cult. 1878; Fl. pink, 1½ in. diam., borne few or several on slender pedicels in dense corymbs; usually has paired infrastipular prickles, which are often curved; fr. globose-ovoid, usually with a prominent neck; up to 8 ft. Summer bloom. A very variable species; may include *R. spithamea*, *R. spithamea sonomiensis*, *R. pinetorum*. W. N.Am. *Cinnamomeae*; (14, 28).

R. californica nana Bean Sp (OGR), *mp*, Habit very dwarf.

R. californica plena Rehder Sp (OGR), 1894, Geschwind. Flowers dbl. or partially so. Theano, (int. Geschwind, 1894) is said to be the same as this; (14).

R. canina Linnaeus Sp (OGR), *lp*, (Brier Bush; Dog Rose; *R. leucantha* Loiseleur; *R. pseudoscabrata* Blocki; *R. sphaerica* Grenier; *R. surculosa* Woods); Cult. prior to 1737. Flowers white or pinkish, 2 in. diam., blooms solitary or in few-flowered corymbs; fruit ovoid, orange-red or scarlet, glabrous; 10 ft. Summer bloom. Eu., occasionally naturalized in N. Am.; much used as understock. *Caninae*; (35, 42, 34).

R. canina andegavensis (Bastard) Desportes Sp (OGR), (*R. andegavensis* (Bastard)); Variation with glabrous, eglandular foliage, but glandular hispid peduncles; (35).

R. canina blondaeana (Ripart) Rouy Sp (OGR), (*R. blondaeana* Ripart); Leaflet teeth glandular-biserrate; sepals and pedicels glandular; (42).

R. canina exilis (Crépin) Keller Sp (OGR), *mp*, (*R. exilis* Crépin). Flowers pink, small, about 1 in. diam.; low growth.

R. canina inermis hort. Sp (OGR), Vigorous, almost unarmed Dog Rose popular as an understock under the names Clou, Croibier, Brög's Thornless and Gamon.

R. canina lutetiana (Léman) Baker Sp (OGR), (*R. lutetiana* Léman); Entire plant glabrous and eglandular; (35).

R. canina spuria (Puget) Wolley-Dod Sp (OGR), (*R. canina insignis* Wolley-Dod); Serrations almost entirely simple; petioles glandular; fruit large; (35).

R. carolina Linnaeus Sp (OGR), *mp*, (Carolina Rose; Pasture Rose; *R. humilis* Marshall; *R. parviflora* Ehrhart; *R. pensylvanica* Wangenheim; *R. pratensis* Rafinesque; *R. virginiana humilis* Schneider); Cult. 1826. Flowers bright pink, 2 in. diam., borne often solitary 3-6 ft. growth, spreading by means of suckers. Summer bloom. E. N. Am. *Carolinae*. Name erroneously given to *R. palustris nuttalliana*; (28; rarely 14).

R. carolina alba Rehder Sp (OGR), *w*, (*R. lyonii alba* Rehder; *R. virginiana alba* Willmott); Cult. 1880. Flowers white; (28).

R. carolina glandulosa (Crépin) Farwell Sp (OGR), *mp*, (*R. mexicana* Watson, not Willdenow; *R. parviflora glandulosa* Crépin; *R. sarrulata* Rafinesque); Cult. 1902; Leaflets glandular-serrate; leaf-stalk glandular; (28).

R. carolina grandiflora (Baker) Rehder Sp (OGR), *mp*, (*R. humilis grandiflora* Baker; *R. laxa* Lindley; *R. lindleyi* Sprengel; *R. obovata* Rafinesque); Cult. prior to 1870. Flowers

bright pink, 2 in. diam.; foliage larger than *R. carolina*; (28).

R. carolina plena (Marshall) Doris Lynes Sp (OGR), *mp*, (*R. pennsylvanica plena* Marshall); Similar to *R. carolina* Linnaeus but flowers dbl. and under favorable conditions the plant is recurrent.

R. carolina triloba (Watson) Rehder Sp (OGR), *mp*, (*R. humilis triloba* Watson). Flowers bright pink, petals 3-lobed.

R. carolina villosa (Best) Rehder Sp (OGR), *mp*, (*R. carolina lyonii* (Pursh) Palmer & Steyermark; *R. humilis villosa* Best; *R. lyonii* Pursh; *R. pusilla* Rafinesque); Cult. 1887; Foliage pubescent beneath; (28).

R. caudata Baker Sp (OGR), *mr*, *Allied to R. macrophylla*; ca. 1896. Flowers red, 2 in. diam., borne in few-flowered corymbs; fruit ovoid; 12 ft. China. *Cinnamomeae*; (14, 28).

R. cerasocarpa Rolfe Sp (OGR), *w*, Cult. 1914. Flowers white, 1-1¼ in. diam., borne in large corymbs; fruit globose, over⅓ in. diam., deep red. China. *Synstylae*; (14).

R. chavinii Rapin ex Reuter Sp (OGR), *mp*, (*R. montana chavinii* (Rapin ex Reuter) Christ); *Perhaps a derivative of R. canina × R. montana*; Cult. 1905. Flowers pink, 2 in. diam.; fruit ovoid, setose; 6-10 ft. Eu. Alps. *Caninae*; (42).

R. chinensis Jacquin Ch (OGR), (Bengal Rose; China Rose; *R. chinensis indica* Lindley) Koehne; *R. indica* Loureiro, not Linnaeus; *R. indica vulgaris* Lindley; *R. nankinensis* Loureiro; *R. sinica* Linnaeus); Cult. 1759. Flowers crimson or pink, rarely whitish, about 2 in. diam., borne usually several, less often solitary, on long stems, rarely short-stemmed; not or slightly fragrant; foliage evergreen or partially so; fruit obovoid or turbinate, about ¾ in. long; recurrent. China. *Indicae*; (14, 21, 28).

R. chinensis longifolia (Willdenow) Rehder Sp (OGR), (*R. indica longifolia* (Willdenow) Lindley; *R. longifolia* Willdenow); Int. 1820, but not now in cult. Leaflets very long and narrow, like a willow.

R. chinensis minima (Sims) Voss Ch (OGR), (*R. indica pumila* Thory; *R. laurentiae* Trattinnick; *R. lawranceana* Sweet; *R. semperflorens minima* Sims); Cult. 1815; A group of dwarf Chinas, sometimes called Fairy Roses (including "Angel Roses" (*R. × rehderiana*), grown from seed). Flowers white, pink or red, single and dbl., petals often pointed, up to 1½ in. diam.; height variable. See Rouletii and Pompon de Paris.

R. chinensis spontanea Rehder & Wilson Sp (OGR), *dr*, Not in cult. Flowers deep red or pink, single, borne usually solitary. C. China.

R. cinnamomea Linnaeus Sp (OGR), *m*, (Cinnamon Rose; *R. collincola* Ehrhart; *R. spinosissima* Rydberg, not Linnaeus); Cult. prior to 1600. Flowers purple, about 2 in. diam., borne solitary or few on short, naked pedicels; fragrant; fruit depressed-globular, scarlet; 6 ft. May-June. Eu., N.; W. Asia, sometimes escaped in N. Am. *Cinnamomeae*; (14, 28).

R. cinnamomea plena Weston Sp (OGR), *m*, (Double Cinnamon; *R. foecundissima* Muenchhausen; *R. majalis* Herrmann; Stevens Rose; Rose du Saint Sacrament; Whitsuntide Rose); *Double form of R. cinnamomea* Linnaeus; Cult. 1596. Flowers double.

R. clinophylla Thory Sp (OGR), *w*, (*R. involucrata* Roxburgh ex Lindley; *R. lindleyana* Trattinnick; *R. lyellii* Lindley); *Closely allied to R. bracteata*; Int. prior to 1817. Flowers white; tender. India. *Bracteatae*; (14).

R. collina Jacquin Misc. OGR (OGR), *mp*, probably *R. corymbifera* × *R. gallica*; Cult. 1788. *Allied to R. alba*; Flowers rose-colored, sepals shorter. Eu., W. Asia.

R. coriifolia Fries Sp (OGR), *lp*, (*R. canina coriifolia* (Fries) Dumortier; *R. frutetorum* Besser; *R. watsonii* Baker); Cult. 1878. *Allied to R. canina*; Flowers pink, short-pediceled, with large bracts; leaflets gray-green, downy; 5 ft. Eu., W. Asia. *Caninae*; (35).

R. coriifolia froebelii (P. Lambert) Rehder Sp (OGR), *w*, (*R. canina froebelii* Christ; *R. froebelii* Christ; *R. laxa* Froebel, not Retzius); Cult. 1890. Flowers white, small. The popular Laxa understock of uncertain derivation; (35).

R. corymbifera Borkhausen Sp (OGR), *w*, (*R. canina dumetorum* Desvaux; *R. collina* De Candolle, not Jacquin; *R. dumetorum* Thuillier; *R. saxatilis* Steven; *R. taurica* von Bieberstein); Cult. 1838. Flowers light pink to white, 1¼ -2 in. diam., borne 1-many; leaflets downy, otherwise like *R. canina*; fruit ovoid to subglobose, ³⁄₄ in. long. Eu., W. Asia, Afr. *Caninae*; (35, 42).

R. corymbulosa Rolfe Sp (OGR), *rb*, 1908. Flowers red with a white eye, ³⁄₄-1 in. diam., borne in dense, umbel-like corymbs; fruit globose; 6ft. W. China. *Cinnamomeae*; (14).

R. crocacantha Boulenger Sp (OGR), *w*, Int. 1917-19. Flowers white,¹⁄₂ in. diam., borne in many-fld. panicles; spines curved, yellow; fruit globose, ¹⁄₃ in. diam., red. W. China. *Synstylae*; (14).

R. cymosa Trattinnick Sp (OGR), *w*, (*R. amoyensis* Hance; *R. esquirolii* Léveillé & Vaniot; *R. fragariaeflora* Seringe; *R. indica* Linnaeus, partly; *R. microcarpa* Lindley, not

Besser nor Retzius; *R. sorbiflora* Focke); Int. 1904. Flowers white, small, borne in many-fld. corymbs; fruit red, small, globose. China. *Banksianae*; (14).

R. davidii Crépin Sp (OGR), *lp*, (Father David's Rose); 1908. *Allied to R. macrophylla*; Flowers pink, 1¹⁄₂-2 in. diam., borne in corymbs; fruit oblong-ovoid or ovoid, long-necked, ¹⁄₂-³⁄₄ in. long, scarlet; 10 ft. W. China. *Cinnamomeae*; (28).

R. davidii elongata Rehder & Wilson Sp (OGR), *lp*, (*R. parmentieri* Leveille); 1908. Flowers fewer; fruit large, to 1 in. long. China.

R. davurica Pallas Sp (OGR), *m*, (*R. willdenowii* Sprengel); 1910. *Allied to R. cinnamomea*; Straight instead of curved prickles and smaller leaflets; fruit ovate. N.E. Asia. *Cinnamomeae*; (14).

R. × dulcissima Lunell S, *R. blanda* × *R. woodsii*; Natural hybrid common in north-central N. Am.

R. dumalis Bechstein Sp (OGR), (*R. afzeliana* Fries; *R. glauca* Villars, not Pourret; *R. gypsicola* Blocki; *R. reuteri* (Godet) Reuter); Cult. 1872; *Close to R. canina*; Heavily armed, with bluish green glaucous leaflets; sepals long persistent. Eu., W. Asia. *Caninae*; (35).

R. ecae Aitchison Sp (OGR), *dy*, (*R. xanthina* Auth., not Lindley; *R. xanthina ecae* (Aitchison) Boulenger; 1880. Flowers deep yellow, 1-1¹⁄₄ in. diam., borne solitary, short-stalked; fruit obovoid, ¹⁄₃-¹⁄₂ in, long; upright, 4 ft. Afghanistan. *Pimpinellifoliae*; (14).

R. eglanteria Linnaeus Sp (OGR), *lp*, (Eglantine; *R. rubiginosa* Linnaeus; *R. suavifolia* Lightfoot; *R. walpoleana* Greene; Sweet Brier Rose; Sweetbriar); Possibly cult. prior to 1551. Flowers pink, single, 2 in. diam., borne solitary or in few-fld. corymbs; foliage glandular and fragrant (apple); many prickles; very vigorous to 8 ft. Eu., naturalized in N. Am., and common in pastures. *Caninae*; (35, 42).

R. elasmacantha Trautvetter Sp (OGR), *my*, (*R. pimpinellifolia elasmacantha* (Trautvetter) Crépin); Cult. 1868. Flowers light yellow, borne solitary; low glabrous shrub. Caucasus. *Pimpinellifoliae*; (28).

R. elegantula Rolfe Sp (OGR), *mp*, Cult. 1900. Flowers pink, with golden anthers, small; 5-10 ft. Summer; free bloomer. W. China. *Cinnamomeae*.

R. elymaitica Boissier & Haussknecht Sp (OGR), *mp*, (*R. albicans* Godet ex Boissier); 1900. Flowers pink, small, borne 1-3 together; fruit small, globular, dwarf, 3 ft. N. Persia. *Cinnamomeae*; (14, 28).

R. × engelmannii S. Watson S, *dp*, (*R. acicularis engelmannii* (S. Watson) Crépin; *R. bakerii* Rydberg, not Déséglise; *R. engelmannii* Crépin; *R. melina* Greene; *R. oreophila* Rydberg); Naturally occurring hybrid between *R. nutkana* and *R. acicularis*; 1891. CO to B.C.; (42).

R. fargesii Boulenger Sp (OGR), *w*, Cult. 1916. *Similar to R. moschata*; Flowers white, 1³/₄ in. diam., paniculate. W. China; *Synstylae*.

R. farreri Stapf Sp (OGR), *w*, Not in cult. Flowers pale pink to white, 1¹/₄-1¹/₂ in. diam.; fruit ovoid to ellipsoid, red. N.W. China. *Pimpinellifoliae*.

R. farreri persetosa Stapf Sp (OGR), *mp*, (Threepenny Bit Rose); 1914. Whole plant finely bristly; flowers pink, smaller; (14).

R. fedtschenkoana Regel Sp (OGR), *w*, Int. 1876. Flowers white, 1¹/₂-2 in. diam., borne 1-4 together. Turkestan. *Cinnamomeae*; (28).

R. filipes Rehder & Wilson Sp (OGR), *w*, 1908. *Allied to R. moschata*; Flowers white, about 1 in. diam., borne in large, loose corymbs; fragrant; fruit globose, ¹/₃-¹/₂ in. diam., scarlet; sarmentose; 15 ft. China. *Synstylae*; (14).

R. foetida Herrmann Sp (OGR), *my*, (Austrian Briar; Austrian Brier Rose; Austrian Yellow Rose; *R. chlorophylla* Ehrhart; *R. eglanteria* Miller, not Linnaeus; *R. lutea* Miller); Possibly int. prior to 1542. Flowers bright yellow, single, 2-2¹/₂ in. diam., borne sometimes several, but without bracts on the peduncle; sickly sweet odor; fruit globular, rarely set; 10 ft. Summer. Asia. *Pimpinellifoliae*, (28).

R. foetida bicolor (Jacquin) Willmott Sp (OGR), *rb*, (Austrian Copper Rose; *R. aurantiaca* Voss; *R. bicolor* Jacquin; *R. eglanteria punicea* Thory; *R. lutea bicolor* Sims; *R. lutea punicea* (Miller) R. Keller; *R. punicea* Miller); *R. foetida sport*; Int. prior to 1590. Flowers orange-scarlet within, yellow reverse; (28).

R. foetida persiana (Lemaire) Rehder Sp (OGR), *my*, (Persian Yellow Rose; *R. hemisphaerica plena*; Rehder; *R. lutea persiana* Lemaire; *R. lutea plena* hort. *R. foetida form*; 1837. Flowers double; (28).

R. foliolosa Nuttall ex Torrey & Gray Sp (OGR), *mp*, Cult. 1880. Flowers rose 1¹/₂ in. diam., borne solitary or in few-fld. clusters; fruit globose; 1¹/₂ ft. Spring. N. Am. *Carolinae*; (14).

R. foliolosa alba (Bridwell) Rehder Sp (OGR), *w*, Cult. 1919. Flowers white; (14).

R. forrestiana Boulenger Sp (OGR), *dp*, Cult. 1918. Flowers rose, 1 in. diam., borne solitary or few. W. China. *Cinnamomeae*.

R. × francofurtana Muenchhausen Misc. OGR (OGR), *m*, (*R. campanulata* Ehrhart; *R. francofurtensis* Roessig; *R. germanica* Gordon et al; *R. inermis* Thory; *R. turbinata* Aiton); Probably *R. cinnamomea* × *R. gallica*; Possibly int. prior to 1629. Flowers purple, single or dbl., 2-3 in. diam., borne 1-3 together; slightly fragrant; fruit turbinate; 6 ft. Summer; This entry refers to more than one clone; (21, 28).

R. gallica Linnaeus G (OGR), *dp*, (French Rose; Provins Rose; *R. austriaca* Crantz; *R. grandiflora* Salisbury; *R. olympica* Donn; *R. rubra* Lamarck; *R. sylvatica* Gaterau); Cult. prior to 1500. Flowers deep pink to crimson, 2-3 in. diam. on stout pedicels; fruit subglobose or turbinate, brick-red; 5 ft. Summer. C.; S. Eu., W. Asia, occasionally naturalized in N. Am. *Gallicanae*. The probable ancestor of garden roses in Eu.; (28).

R. gallica haplodonta (Borbas) Braun Sp (OGR), *dp*, Wild variety with simply serrate foliage and woolly styles.

R. gallica pumila (Jacquin) Seringe Sp (OGR), *dp*, (*R. austriaca pygmaea* Wallroth; *R. humilis* Tausch, not Marshall; *R. pumila* Jacquin); Cult. prior to 1824. Flowers red, single; dwarf; creeping rootstock; (28).

R. gallica velutinaeflora Sp (OGR), (*R. velutinaeflora* Déséglise); Cult. prior to 1872. Flowers described by Déséglise as deep velvety red; however, rose now in commerce is mauve-pink, large; fruit pyriform, reddish-orange; late Spring. France.

R. gentiliana Léveillé & Vaniot Sp (OGR), *w*, (*R. polyantha grandiflora* hort.; *R. wilsonii* hort., not Borrer); 1907. Flowers creamy white, semi-dbl., borne in dense clusters; fruit red; vagaries shrub with red glandular branches. China. *Synstylae*; (14).

R. gigantea Collett Sp (OGR), *w*, (*R. macrocarpa* Watt, not others; *R. × odorata gigantea* (Collett ex Crépin) Rehder & Wilson; *R. xanthocarpa* Watt ex Willmott); 1889. Flowers creamy white, large, 4-5 in. diam.; vigorous; climbing to 50 ft. S.W. China, Burma. *Indicae*, (14).

R. gigantea erubescens Focke Sp (OGR), *mp*, (*R. × odorata erubescens* (Focke) Robert; Wilson). Flowers pink. Perhaps the same as *R. chinensis grandiflora* Willmott. W. China.

R. giraldii Crépin Sp (OGR), *pb*, Cult. 1897. Flowers pink with white center, 1 in. diam., borne solitary or few; fruit ovoid, scarlet, ¹/₃-¹/₂ in. long; 6 ft. C. China. *Cinnamomeae*; (14).

R. giraldii venulosa Rehder & Wilson Sp (OGR), *pb*, 1907. Like *R. giraldii* Crépin, but leaflets firmer and nearly glabrous.

R. glauca Pourret Sp (OGR), *mp*, (*R. ferruginea* Déséglise, not Villars; *R. giraldii* Crépin; *R. ilseana* Crépin; *R. lurida* Andrews; *R. rubrifolia* Villars); Cult. prior to 1830. Flowers pink, 1½ in. diam., borne 1-3 together; foliage reddish; fruit subglobose, scarlet 6 ft.; Spring. Mts. of C.; S. Eu. *Caninae*; (28).

R. glomerata Rehder & Wilson Sp (OGR), *w*, 1908. Flowers white, 1 in. diam., borne in dense corymbs; fragrant; fruit subglobose, orange-red, about ⅓ in. diam.; sarmentose; 20 ft. W. China. *Synstylae*.

R. glutinosa Sibthorp & Smith Sp (OGR), *mp*, (Pine-Scented Rose; *R. calabrica* Burnat & Gremli; *R. ferox* Regel, not others; *R. libanotica* Boissier; *R. pulverulenta* von Bieberstein; *R. pustulosa* Bertolini); 1821. *Allied to R. eglanteria*; Flowers pink, small; pine-scented; fruit globose, small, dwarf, glandular. S.E. Eu., W. Asia. *Caninae*; (35, 42).

R. glutinosa dalmatica (Kerner) Borbas Sp (OGR), *mp*, (*R. dalmatica* Kerner); Cult. 1882; Fruit ellipsoid; (35, 42).

R. graciliflora Rehder & Wilson Sp (OGR), *mp*, 1908. Flowers pale rose, 1½ in. diam., borne solitary, but numerous along the stem. W. China. *Pimpinellifoliae*.

R. gymnocarpa Nuttall ex Torrey & Gray Sp (OGR), *lp*, (Little Woods Rose; *R. abietorum* Greene; *R. glaucodermis* Greene); 1893. Flowers pale pink, about 1 in. diam., borne solitary, on short lateral branchlets; fruit small, globose, orange-red; 10 ft.; early summer. After fertilization, the top of the hypanthium is shed, including sepals, petals, stamens and tops of pistils. W. N. Am. *Cinnamomeae*; (14).

R. hawrana Kmet Sp (OGR), *lp*, Cult. 1914. *Allied to R. pomifera*; Flowers pink, about 2 in. diam.; fruit globose, densely bristly. Hungary. *Caninae*; (28).

R. heckeliana Trattinnick Sp (OGR), *lp*, (*R. hackeliana* Nyman); *Allied to R. eglanteria.* Flowers pink, small, borne usually solitary; dwarf. S. Eu. *Caninae.*

R. helenae Rehder & Wilson Sp (OGR), *w*, (*R. floribunda* Baker, not Steven; *R. moschata helenae* (Rehder & Wilson) Cardot; *R. moschata micrantha* Crépin); 1907. Flowers white, 1½ in. diam., borne in many-fld. umbel-like corymbs 3-6 in. diam.; fragrant; fruit ovoid or oblong-obovoid, scarlet, about ½ in. long; 15 ft.; late spring. C. China. *Synstylae*; (14).

R. hemisphaerica Hermann Sp (OGR), *my*, (*R. glaucophylla* Ehrhart; *R. rapinii* Boissier & Balansa; *R. sulphurea* Aiton; Sulphur Rose); Int. before 1625. Flowers sulphur-yellow, nodding, fully dbl., cupped, borne usually solitary; foliage bluish-green; late spring. W. Asia. *Pimpinellifoliae*; (28).

R. hemisphaerica rapinii (Boissier) Rowley Sp (OGR), *my*, (*R. rapinii* Boissier); 1933. The wild single-fld. species; rare and difficult to cultivate. Turkey to Persia; (28).

R. hemsleyana Täckholm Sp (OGR), *lp*, (*R. macrophylla* Crépin, not Lindley; *R. setipoda* Rolfe, not Hemsley & Wilson); 1904. Flowers light pink, about 2 in. diam., corymbose; fruit ovoid, about 1 in. long, with a distinct neck; late spring. C. China. *Cinnamomeae*; (42).

R. henryi Boulenger Sp (OGR), *w*, (*R. gentiliana* Rehder & Wilson, not Léveillé & Vaniot); 1907. Flowers white, 1½ in. diam., corymbose; fragrant; fruit globose, about ⅓ in. diam., dark red. Summer. China. *Synstylae*; (14).

R. holodonta Stapf Sp (OGR), *lp*, (*R. moyesii rosea* Rehder & Wilson); 1908. *Allied to R. moyesii*; Tetraploid, with coarsely serrate leaves and light pink flowers. W. China. *Cinnamomeae*; (28).

R. horrida Fischer Sp (OGR), *w*, (*R. ferox* von Bieberstein, not others); 1796. Flowers white, 1½ in. diam., borne solitary or few; fruit subglobose, ⅓-½ in. across, dark red; low, prickly shrub with very small, roundish leaflets. S.E. Eu., W. Asia. *Caninae*; (35).

R. hugonis Hemsley Sp (OGR), *my*, (Father Hugo Rose; Father Hugo's Rose; Golden Rose of China; *R. xanthina* Crépin, not Lindley); 1899. Flowers yellow, single 2½ in. diam., borne solitary, on slender glabrous pedicels; fruit depressed-globose, deep scarlet; (see end papers); branches drooping; 6 ft.; early spring. C. China. *Pimpinellifoliae*; (14).

R. inodora Fries Sp (OGR), *w*, (*R. agrestis inodora* Keller; *R. caryophyllacea* Besser; *R. elliptica* Tausch; *R. graveolens* Grenier; *R. klukii* Besser); Cult. 1875. *Allied to R. eglanteria*; Flowers white or pink, 1-1½ in. diam.; fruit ovoid, bright red. Eu. *Caninae*; (35, 42).

R. × involuta Smith Misc. OGR (OGR), *w*, (*R. braunii* Keller; *R. coronata* Crépin; *R. doniana* Woods; *R. sabinii* Woods; *R. villosa* Smith, not Linnaeus); *R. spinosissima × R. tomentosa*; Orig. prior to 1800. Flowers whitish. Eu.; (42); This entry refers to more than one clone.

R. × involuta wilsonii (Borrer) Baker Misc. OGR (OGR), (*R. wilsonii* Borrer. not hort.); vigorous, shrubby hybrid from N. Wales, sometimes cult.; (42).

R. × jacksonii Willmott S, *mr*, *R. rugosa × R. wichuraiana*; Cult. prior to 1910. Flowers bright crimson; very free bloomer. The diploid hybrid of which *R. kordesii* is the tetraploid. This entry refers to more than one clone, including Lady Duncan; Max Graf; (14).

R. × **kochiana** Koehne S, *dp*, (*R. oxyacanthos* K. Koch, not von Bieberstein); *Possibly an F² from the cross R. palustris × R. spinosissima*; Orig. prior to 1869. Flowers deep rose, 1½ in. diam., borne solitary or 2-3; (14).

R. × **koehneana** S, *m*, *R. carolina* × *R. rugosa*; Orig. prior to 1893. Flowers purplish red, larger; similar to *R. carolina*; (21).

R. **kordesii** Wulff Sp (OGR), *dp*, 1952. A new species that arose in cult. as a result of spontaneous chromosome doubling in a *R. rugosa* × *R. wichuraiana* hybrid. (*R. × jacksonii* Max Graf); Flowers deep pink, semi-dbl., cup-shaped; foliage shining green; fruit elliptic-ovoid; (28).

R. **koreana** Komarov Sp (OGR), *lp*, 1917. Flowers white, flushed pink, 1 in. diam., borne solitary, but numerous along the stem; fruit ovoid, ½ in. long, orange-red. Korea. *Pimpinellifoliae*; (14).

R. **laevigata** Michaux Sp (OGR), *w*, (Cherokee Rose; *R. camellia* hort.; *R. cherokeensis* Donn; *R. hystrix* Lindley; *R. nivea* De Candolle; *R. sinica* Aiton, not Linnaeus; *R. ternata* Poiret; *R. triphylla* Roxburgh); 1759. Flowers white, rarely rose, 2½-3½ in. diam., borne solitary; fragrant; foliage glossy, leaflets 3; fruit large, obovoid, bristly, yellow, later turning brown; tall, climbing; early spring. China, naturalized in S.E. N. Am. Sometimes confused with *R. bracteata. Laevigatae*; (14).

R. **latibracteata** Boulenger Sp (OGR), *mp*, 1936. *Similar to R. webbiana*; Flowers in two's or corymbose; bracts broad; leaflets 7, up to 1 in. long. Yunnan.

R. **laxa** Retzius Sp (OGR), *w*, (*R. gebleriana* Schrenk; *R. soongarica* Bunge); Cult. ca. 1800. Flowers white, small; foliage small, light green; fruit oblong-ovoid, small. C. Asia. *Cinnamomeae*; (28).

R. **leschenaultii** Wight & Arnott Sp (OGR), *w*, (*R. moschata leschenaultii* (Wight & Arnott) Crépin); Cult. prior to 1829. *Similar to R. moschata*; Flowers larger, in few-fld. corymbs. India. *Synstylae*; (14).

R. **longicuspis** Bertoloni Sp (OGR), *w*, (*R. charbonneaui* Léveillé; *R. irridens* Focke; *R. lucens* Rolfe; *R. willmottiana* Léveillé); Cult. 1915. Flowers white, petals silky outside, 1½ in. diam., borne corymbose; foliage half-evergreen; fruit ovoid, scarlet, or orange-red; 20 ft.; tender. W. China. *Synstylae*; (14).

R. **luciae** Franchet & Rochebrune Sp (OGR), *w*, (*R. franchetii* (Koidzumi); *R. fujisanensis* (Makino) Makino; *R. hakonensis* Koidzumi; *R. jasminoides* Koidzumi; *R. luciae fujisanensis*

Makino); Int. 1880. *Allied to R. wichuraiana*; Somewhat less hardy; flowers smaller; habit more upright. E. Asia. *Synstylae*; (14).

R. **macounii** Greene Sp (OGR), *lp*, (*R. grosseserrata* E. Nelson; *R. naiadum* Lunell; *R. subnuda* Lunell; *R. woodsii* Lindley, 1826, not 1820); Int. prior to 1826. Flowers pale pink, small; fruit depressed-globose; low. N.W. Am. *Cinnamomeae*; (14, 21).

R. **macrantha** hort., not Desportes Sp (OGR), *lp*, Found near La Fleche, 1823. Flowers blush-pink, single, large; fruit ¾ in. diam., dull red, subglobose; lax, trailing shrub.

R. **macrophylla** Lindley Sp (OGR), *dp*, (*R. hoffmeisteri* Klotzsch; *R. hookeriana* Bertoloni); 1818. Flowers red, about 2 in. diam., borne 1-3 together; fruit oblong-ovoid, red, 1-1½ in. long. Himalayas. *Cinnamomeae*; (14, 28).

R. **macrophylla doncasterii** (Doncasterii) Sp (OGR), *dp*, 1930, Hurst, C.C.; Int. E. Doncaster of J. Burrell & Co., ca. 1930. *R. macrophylla form*; Probably raised by Dr. C.C. Hurst. Flowers deep pink; foliage purplish-green; stems plum colored; hips red, flagon-shaped, large; arching growth (6 ft.).

R. × **malyi** Kerner S, *mr*, *Possibly R. pendulina* × *R. spinosissima*; Orig. prior to 1869. Flowers bright red; foliage similar to *R. spinosissima*; (28).

R. × **marcyana** Bouller S, *m*, (*R. terebinthinacea* Besson); *R. gallica* × *R. tomentosa*. Flowers pink to light purple, 2½-3 in. diam., long-stalked; low, 2 ft., rarely 4 ft. Spontaneous in S. France; This entry refers to more than one clone; (21).

R. **marginata** Wallroth Sp (OGR), *lp*, (*R. humilis* Besser, not Marshall; *R. jundzillii* Besser; *R. trachyphylla* Rau; *R. zagrabiensis* Vukotinovics & Braun); Cult. 1870. Flowers pink, 2-2½ in. diam., borne solitary or few; fruit globose to ellipsoid, scarlet, sepalsdeciduous. Eu., W. Asia. *Caninae*; (42).

R. **marginata godetii** (Grenier) Rehder Sp (OGR), *lp*, (*R. godetii* Grenier; *R. jundzilli godetii* R. Keller). Flowers small; low shrub. E. France.

R. **marretii** Léveillé Sp (OGR), *mp*, (*R. rubrostipullata* Nakai); Cult. 1908. Flowers pink, 1½-2 in. diam., borne usually 3-6; stems dark purple; fruit subglobose, ⅓-½ in. diam. Saghalin. *Cinnamomeae*; (14).

R. **maximowicziana** Regel Sp (OGR), *w*, (*R. faureri* Leveille; *R. granulosa* Keller); Cult. prior to 1880. Flowers white, 1½ in. diam., borne in many-fld. corymbs; partially climbing. N.E. Asia. *Synstylae*; (14).

R. maximowicziana jackii (Rehder) Rehder Sp (OGR), *w*, (Jack Rose; *R. coreana* Keller, not *R. koreana* Komarov; *R. jackii* Rehder; *R., kelleri* Baker, not Dalla Torre & Sarntheim); 1905. Stems without bristles; (14).

R. maximowicziana pilosa (Nakai) Nakai Sp (OGR), *w*, (*R. jackii pilosa* Nakai); Cult. 1916; Leaf and flower stalks pubescent. Korea; (14).

R. micrantha Smith Sp (OGR), *lp*, (*R. floribunda* Steven, not Baker; *R. nemorosa* Libert ex Lejeune; *R. rubiginosa* Britton & Brown, not Linnaeus; *R. rubiginosa nemoralis* Thory); Cult. prior to 1800. *Allied to R. eglanteria*; Flowers pale pink, small; 6 ft. S. Eu., Medit. region, naturalized in N. Am. *Caninae*; (35, 42).

R. minutifolia Englemann Sp (OGR), Cult. 1910. Flowers pink or white, 1 in. diam., short-pediceled; fruit subglobose, hispid; 4 ft.; early spring. L. CA. *Minutifoliae (Hesperhodos)*; (14).

R. mollis Smith Sp (OGR), *dp*, (*R. heterophylla* Woods, not Cochet; *R. mollossima* Fries; *R. villosa* Linnaeus, in part; *R. villosa mollissima* Rau); 1818. Flowers deep pink, rarely white, 1½-2 in. diam., borne 1-3 together; fruit small; branchlets purple, more or less bloomy; 4 ft. Summer. Eu., W. Asia. *Caninae*; (28).

R. montana Chaix Sp (OGR), *lp*. Cult. 1872. *Allied to R. canina*; Flowers pink, 1½ in. diam., borne solitary or few; fruit oblong-ovoid, ¾ in.; vigorous. S. Eu., N. Afr. *Caninae*; (42?).

R. montezumae Humboldt & Bonpland ex Thory Sp (OGR), *dp*, Not known to be cult. Flowers pale red, 1½ in. diam.; 3 ft.; June. Mex., but probably not native. *Caninae*; (35).

R. moschata Herrmann Sp (OGR), *w*, (Musk Rose; *R. ruscinonensis* Grenier & Déséglise); 1540. Flowers white, 1½-2 in. diam., borne usually in 7 flowered corymbs; fragrant (musk); fruit ovoid, small. Summer-Fall. S. Eu., N. Afr. *Synstylae*; (14).

R. moschata abyssinica (Lindley) Rehder Sp (OGR), *w*, (*R. abyssinica* Lindley); *R. moschata form*; Not cult.; More prickly, tender. Abyssinia; (14).

R. moschata nepalensis Lindley Sp (OGR), *w*, (Himalayan Musk Rose; *R. brownii* Trattinnick; *R. brunonii* Lindley); 1822. Like *R. moschata* but foliage dull green, downy. Himalayas; (14).

R. moschata plena Weston Sp (OGR), *w*, (*R. moschata flore semipleno* Thory); Possibly cult. prior to 1596. Flowers dbl.; (14)

R. moyesii Hemsley & Wilson Sp (OGR), *mr*, (*R. fargesii* Osborn, not Boulenger; *R. macrophylla rubrostaminea* Vilmore); 1894, Re-int.

1903. Flowers deep blood-red through deep rose to light pink, 1¾-2½ in. diam., borne solitary or 2 together; fruit oblong-ovoid, narrowed into a neck, 2-2½ in. long, deep orange-red 10 ft. Summer. W. China. *Cinnamomeae*; (42).

R. moyesii fargesii Rolfe Sp (OGR), *mr*, (*R. fargesii* hort., not Boulenger); Cult. 1900?; Leaflets smaller, broad-oval to suborbicular; (28).

R. mulliganii Boulenger Sp (OGR), *w*, 1917-19. Flowers white, about 2 in. diam., corymbose; fruit ovoid, ½ in. long. W. China. *Synstylae*; (14).

R. multibracteata Hemsley & Wilson Sp (OGR), *lp*, (*R. reducta* Baker); 1910. Flowers pink, 1¼ in. diam., corymbose, with numerous crowded bracts, sometimes few or solitary; fruit ovoid, ⅓-½ in. long, orange-red; 6 ft. W. China. *Cinnamomeae*; (28).

R. multiflora Thunberg Sp (OGR), *w*, (Multiflora Japonica; *R. dawsoniana* Ellwanger; Barry ex Rehder; *R. franchetii paniculigera* (Makino) Koidzumi; *R. intermedia* Carrière; *R. linkii* Denhardt; *R. microcarpa* hort.; *R. multiflora thunbergiana* Thory; *R. polyantha* Siebold & Zuccarini; *R. thunbergii* Trattinnick; *R. thyrsiflora* Leroy ex Déséglise; *R. wichurae* K. Koch); ca. 1810. Flowers usually white, ¾ in. diam., or more, borne in many-fld. pyramidal corymbs; fruit small, globular; recurving or climbing branches. Summer. E. Asia, naturalized in N. Am. *Synstylae*; (14, 28).

R. multiflora calva Franchet & Savatier Sp (OGR), *w*, (*R. calva* (Franchet & Savatier) Boulenger); Pedicels glabrous.

R. multiflora carnea Thory Sp (OGR), *lp*, (*R. blinii* Léveillé; *R. florida* Poiret; *R. grevillii* Sweet; *R. lebrunei* Léveillé; *R. multiflora plena* Regel; *R. rubeoides* Andrews); 1804. Flowers light pink, dbl.; derived from *R. multiflora cathayensis*; (14).

R. multiflora cathayensis Rehder & Wilson Sp (OGR), *lp*, (*R. cathayensis* (Rehder & Wilson) Bailey; *R. uchiyamana* Makino); 1907. Flowers pink, about 1½ in. diam., borne in rather flat corymbs; wild single-fld. form. China; (14).

R. multiflora nana hort.; Pol, Cult. after 1875; Origin unrecorded but apparently descended from crosses between *R. multiflora* and China or Teas; A diverse group of hybrids (including Carteri), marketed as roses that bloom in 8-10 weeks from seed. Flowers white to pink, single to dbl., very small, in clusters; bushy, dwarf (1-2 ft.); recurrent.

R. multiflora roseiflora (Focke) Rehder Sp (OGR), *lp*, (*R. multiflora dawsoniana* hort.

Rochester, not *R. dawsoniana* Rehder). Flowers pink, semi-dbl., 1 in. diam.

R. multiflora watsoniana (Crépin) Matsumura Sp (OGR), *lp*, 1870, (Bamboo Rose; *R. watsoniana* Crépin); Int. from a Japanese garden in 1870. Curious variant with linear foliage like a Japanese maple and miniature flowers; probably a chimera. Seedlings reproduce normal *R. multiflora* only; (14).

R. murielae Rehder & Wilson Sp (OGR), *w*, 1904. Flowers white, about 1 in. diam., borne in 3-7 fld. corymbs; fruit ellipsoid, orange-red, ¹/₂ - ³/₄ in. long; 8 ft. W. China. *Cinnamomeae*; (28).

R. nanothamnus Boulenger Sp (OGR), *mp*, 1935. Ally of *R. webbiana* and perhaps only a variety. Flowers and foliage smaller. China, C. Asia. *Cinnamomeae*; (14).

R. nitida Willdenow Sp (OGR), *mp*, (*R. blanda* Pursh, not Aiton; *R. redutea rubescens* Thory; *R. rubrispina* Bosc ex Poiret; Shining Rose); Cult. 1807. Flowers bright pink, 1-2 in. diam., solitary, or in few-fld. corymbs on slender pedicels; 1¹/₂ ft. Summer. Newf. to MA. *Carolinae*; (14).

R. nitida spinosa Lewis Sp (OGR), *mp*, (*R. carolina setigera* Crépin); Stems with enlarged prickles. New England; E. Canada.

R. nutkana Presl Sp (OGR), *mp*, (Nutka Rose; *R. manca* Greene; *R. muriculata* Greene; *R. spaldingii* Crépin); ca. 1876. Flowers pink, 2-2¹/₂ in. diam., usually solitary; fruit globose, without a neck; 5 ft. Summer. AK to OR; UT. *Cinnamomeae*; (42).

R. nutkana hispida Fernald Sp (OGR), *mp*, (*R. macdougalii* Holzinger); Receptacle glandular-hispid.

R. obtusifolia Desvaux Sp (OGR), (*R. canina tomentella* (Léman) Baker; *R. inodora* Hooker, not Fries; *R. tomentella* Léman); Cult. 1905. Flowers white or rose, about 1¹/₄ in. diam., 1-few; leaflets 1¹/₂ in. long, tip rounded, 5-7; fruit ovoid, ¹/₂ - ³/₄ in. long; to 12 ft. Eu. *Caninae*; (35).

R. × odorata Sweet (*R. chinensis fragrans* (Thory) Rehder; *R. gechouitangensis* Léveillé; *R. indica fragrans* Thory; *R. indica odorata* Andrews; *R. indica odoratissima* Lindley; *R. oulengensis* Léveillé; *R. thea* Savi; *R. tongtchouanensis* Léveillé); *Derivatives of the cross R. chinensis × R. gigantea*; Cult. 1752 (Upsala), 1769 (Kew). Flowers white, light pink or salmon-pink or yellowish, dbl., (2-3¹/₂ in. diam., singly or 2-3 together on short stems. W. China. *Indicae*. This entry refers to several clones; (14, 21, 28). See also Fun Jwan Lo, Hume's Blush Tea-scented China and Tea Rose.

R. orientalis Dupont ex Seringe Sp (OGR), *lp*, (Cult. 1905). *Allied to R. eglanteria*; Flowers pink, solitary, short-pedicled; dwarf. S.E. Eu., W. Asia. *Caninae*; (35).

R. palustris Marshall Sp (OGR), *mp*, (*R. carolina* Auth., not Linnaeus; *R. caroliniana* Bigelow; *R. corymbosa* Ehrhart; *R. elongata* Roessig ex Stendel; *R. fragrans* Salisbury; *R. hudsoniana* Thory; *R. pensylvanica* Michaux; *R. salicifolia* Thory; *R. virginiana* Du Roi, not Miller; Swamp Rose); 1726. Flowers pink, about 2 in. diam., usually corymbose; 8 ft. Spring-Summer. Novia Scotia to MN, south to FL; MS, preferring swampy, moist ground. *Carolinae*; (14, rarely 28).

R. palustris inermis (Regel) Lewis Sp (OGR), *mp*, (*R. carolina inermis* Regel); Unarmed. Infrequent in E. N. Am.; (14)

R. palustris nuttalliana Rehder Sp (OGR), *mp*, (*R. carolina nuttalliana* Rehder; *R. nuttalliana* Paul ex Rehder). Flowers larger than *R. palustris*, appearing later and continuing until fall; (42?).

R. palustris scandens Sp (OGR), *mp*, (*R. hudsoniana scandens* Thory; Swamp Rose); Cult. prior to 1824. Flowers dbl. Spring.

R. pendulina Linnaeus Sp (OGR), *dp*, (Alpine Rose; *R. alpina* Linnaeus; *R. cinnamomea* Linnaeus, partly; *R. fraxinifolia* Borkhausen; *R. glandulosa* Bellardi); Cult. 1683. Flowers pink, single, to 2 in. diam., usually solitary or 2-5 together; fruit usually nodding, oblong or ovoid, with an elongated neck, scarlet; 3 ft. Spring. C.; S. Eu. *Cinnamomeae*; (28).

R. pendulina gentilis (Sternberg) R. Keller Sp (OGR), *dp*, (*R. gentilis* Sternberg). Flowers deep pink; low shrub with bristly branches.

R. pendulina oxyodon (Boissier) Rehder Sp (OGR), *mp*, (*R. oxyodon* Boissier); Cult. 1896. Flowers rose, solitary. *Caucasus*; (28).

R. pendulina pyrenaica (Gouan) R. Keller Sp (OGR), *mp*, (Pyrenees Rose; *R. pyrenaica* Gouan); Cult. 1815; Leaves glandular; dwarf; (28).

R. persetosa Rolfe Sp (OGR), *dp*, (*R. davidii persotosa* (Rolfe) Boulenger; *R. macrophylla acicularis* Vilmorin; *R. macrophylla gracilis* Vilmorin & Bois); 1895. Flowers deep pink, 1 in. diam., in large panicles. W. China. *Cinnamomeae*; (14).

R. phoenicia Boissier Sp (OGR), *w*, (*R. phoenica*); ca. 1885. *Allied to R. moschata*; Flowers in many-fld. pyramidal corymbs; not hardy. Asia Minor. *Synstylae*; (14).

R. pinetorum A. Heller Sp (OGR), *dp*, *Possibly part of the R. californica complex*; Not known to be cult. Flowers deep rose, 1¹/₂ in. diam., usually solitary; floral tube usually not glandular; leaflets doubly serrate, with gland-tipped teeth; may be taller than *R. spithamea*; 3 ft. CA. *Cinnamomeae.*

R. pisocarpa Gray Sp (OGR), *mp*, Int. ca. 1882. Flowers pink, about 1 in. diam., on short pedicels in several to many-fld. corymbs; fruit globose, with a very short neck. Summer. W.N. Am. *Cinnamomeae*; (14, 21).

R. × polliniana Sprengel Misc. OGR (OGR), w, 1820, (Polliniana); *R. arvensis × R. gallica*; Cult. 1820. Flowers white to pink, large, on long stems. This entry may refer to more than one clone; (21).

R. pomifera Herrmann Sp (OGR), *mp*, (Apple Rose; *R. hispida* Poiret; *R. villosa* Linnaeus, in part); 1771. Flowers pink, 1½-2 in. diam., 1-3 together; fruit ovoid or subglobose, to 1 in. diam., hispid; 6ft. Summer. Eu., W. Asia. *Caninae*; (28).

R. pouzinii Trattinnick Sp (OGR), *mp*, (*R. hispanica* Boissier & Reuter; *R. inconsiderata* Déséglise; *R. rubiginosa parvifolia* Willdenow); Cult. 1905. Flowers pink, small, 1-few; fruit ellipsoid, small; 3-6 ft. S. Eu., N. Afr. *Caninae*; (42).

R. praelucens Byhouwer Sp (OGR), *lp*, Not cult.; Near to *R. roxburghii*, but fruit less bristly, leaflets larger, fewer; velvety pubescent. China. Yunnan. *Microphyllae (Platyrhodon).*

R. prattii Hemsley Sp (OGR), *mp*, Cult. 1908. Flowers pink, ¾ in. diam., 1-3 together; fruit subglobose to ovoid, scarlet, ¼-⅓ in. long; 8 ft. W. China. *Cinnamomeae*; (14).

R. primula Boulenger Sp (OGR), *ly*, (Incense Rose; *R. ecae* Kanitz, not Aitchison *R. sweginzowii* Meyer, not Koehne; *R. xanthina* Auth., not Lindley; *R. xanthina normalis* Rehder & Wilson); 1910. Flowers yellowish white; foliage small, stiff, remarkably incense-scented; red prickles and thin, flexible stems; 2-4 ft.; very early Spring. Turkestan to N. China. *Pimpinellifoliae.* Cult. in America for a long time as *R. ecae* Aitchison—not the same; (14).

R. × pteragonis Krause S, *my*, *R. hugonis × R. sericea*; Cult. 1938; Habit of *R. sericea pteracantha*. Flowers rich yellow, 1½ in. diam., numerous. This entry refers to more than one clone; see also Red Wing; (14).

R. × rapa Bosc Misc OGR (OGR), *mp*, (*R. lucida plena* Rehder; *R. virginiana plena* Rehder); *R. virginiana × diploid*; Before 1820. Flowers bright pink, dbl.; (21). See also D'Orsay Rose; Rose d'Amour.

R. × reversa Waldstein & Kitaibel Misc OGR (OGR), *mr*, (*R. rubella* Smith); *R. pendulina × R. spinosissima*; Cult. 1820. Flowers red; foliage dark green; fruit obovoid, scarlet, pendulous. Eu.; (28)

R. roxburghii Trattinnick Sp (OGR), *mp*, (Burr Rose; Chestnut Rose; Chinquapin Rose *R. microphylla* Roxburgh ex Lindley, not Desfontaines; *R. roxburghii plena* Rehder); Cult. prior to 1814. Buds prickly, like a chestnut burr; flowers lilac pink, dbl., 2-2½ in. diam., borne often solitary, on short pedicels; fruit depressed-globose, 1-1½ in. diam. 6 ft. Spring-Summer. E. Asia. *Microphyllae (Platyrhodon)*; (14).

R. roxburghii hirtula (Regel) Rehder & Wilson Sp (OGR), *mp*, (*R. hirtula* (Regel) Nakai; *R. microphylla hirtula* Regel); Prior to 1880. Flowers lilac pink; foliage pubescent beneath. Japan; (14).

R. roxburghii normalis Rehder & Wilson Sp (OGR), *lp*, (Single Chestnut Rose); 1908. Flowers single; wild form; (14).

R. × rubrosa Preston S, *mp*, *R. glauca × R. rugosa*; Orig. prior to 1903. Flowers pink, large. Carmenetta, which see, is the favorite garden form. This entry refers to more than one clone; (28).

R. rubus Léveillé & Vaniot Sp (OGR), *w*, (Blackberry Rose; *R. ernestii* Stapf ex Bean); 1907. Flowers white, 1-1⅓ in. diam., borne in dense corymbs; fragrant; fruit subglobose, dark scarlet, about ⅓ in. diam.; climbing, 20 ft. C.; W. China. *Synstylae*; (14).

R. rubus nudescens (Stapf) Rowley Sp (OGR), *w*, (*R. ernestii nudescens* Stapf); Glabrous variety, the type being densely downy.

R. rudiuscula Greene Sp (OGR), *mp*, 1917. Flowers pink, about 2 in. diam., corymbose, few; stems very bristly; fruit globose,½ in. diam., red. N. Am. *Carolinae*; (28).

R. rugosa Thunberg Sp (OGR), *m*, (Hedgehog Rose; Japanese Rose; Kiska Rose; *R. ferox* Lawrance, not others; *R. regeliana* Linden & André; Ramanas Rose; Rugosa Rose; Tomato Rose); Cult. prior to 1799. Flowers purple or white, 2½-3½ in. diam., borne solitary or few; foliage rugose, shining, dark green; fruit depressed-globose, brick-red, to 1 in. diam.; 6 ft. Spring-Fall. N.E. Asia, sometimes escaped in N. US. *Cinnamomeae*; This entry refers to more than one clone; (14).

R. rugosa alba (Ware) Rehder Sp (OGR), *w*, (*R. rugosa albiflora* Koidzumi). Flowers white; (14).

R. rugosa albo-plena Rehder Sp (OGR), *w*, Flowers white, dbl.

R. rugosa chamissoniana C.A. Meyer Sp (OGR), (*R. coruscans* Wairz ex Link); Almost free of bristles; (14).

R. rugosa kamtchatica (Ventenat) Regel Sp (OGR), (*R. kamtchatica* Ventenat); ca. 1770. Smaller flowers and fruit than *R. rugosa*; (14).

R. rugosa plena Regel Sp (OGR), *m*, (*R. pubescens* Baker; *R. rugosa rebro-plena* Rehder). Flowers purple, dbl.; very hardy shrub on the prairies, where it is called Empress of the North; (14).

R. rugosa rosea Rehder Sp (OGR), *mp*, Flowers pink; (14).

R. rugosa rubra hort., not Rehder Sp (OGR), *m*, (*R. rugosa typica* hort.); The largest single-fld. form; flowers brilliant magenta-purple; very vigorous; (14).

R. rugosa rugosa Sp (OGR), *m*, (*R. rugosa thunbergiana* C.A. Meyer). Flowers purple; (14).

R. × salaevensis perrieri (Verlot) Christ S, *R. dumalis* × *R. pendulina*. Flowers rose-purple, borne 1-3 together. Switzerland.

R. salictorum Rydberg Sp (OGR), *mp*, Flower pink, 1½ in. diam., borne in corymbs; stems nearly spineless; leaflets ovate oblong, mostly 2 in. long, 5-7; fruit globose, about ½ in. diam.; about 12 ft. ID, NV. *Cinnamomeae*; (14).

R. saturata Baker Sp (OGR), *dr*, 1907. Flowers dark red, anthers purple, about 2 in. diam., borne solitary; fruit globose-ovoid, ¾ in. long, coral-red; 8 ft. C. China. *Cinnamomeae*; (28).

R. sempervirens Linnaeus Sp (OGR), *w*, (*R. alba* Allioni, not Linnaeus; *R. atrovirens* Viviani; *R. balearica* Persoon); Cult. 1629. Flowers white, 2 in. diam., borne in few-fld., rarely many-fld. corymbs; slightly fragrant; evergreen; fruit subglobose or ovoid, orange-red. Summer.S. Eu., N. Afr. *Synstylae*; (14, 21, 28).

R. sempervirens prostrata Desvaux Sp (OGR), *w*, (*R. prostrata* De Candolle); Fruit ovoid.

R. sempervirens scandens (Miller) De Candolle Sp (OGR), *w*, (*R. scandens* Miller); Cult. prior to 1750; Fruit subglobose.

R. serafinii Viviani Sp (OGR), *lp*, (*R. apennina* Woods; *R. seraphinii* Viviani); Cult. 1914. Flower pink, 1 in. diam., solitary, very short-stalked; fruit globose-ovoid; 1-3 ft. Medit. region. *Caninae*; (35).

R. sericea Lindley Sp (OGR), *w*, (*R. tetrapetala* Royle; *R. wallichii* Trattinnick); 1822. Flowers white with 4, or rarely 5 petals, 1½-2 in. diam.; fruit globose or turbinate; 12 ft. Early Spring. Himalayas, W. China. *Pimpenellifoliae*; (14).

R. sericea chrysocarpa (Rehder) Rowley Sp (OGR), *w*, (*R. omeiensis chrysocarpa* Rehder); Fruit bright yellow.

R. sericea denudata Franchet Sp (OGR), *w*, Branches unarmed.

R. sericea hookeri Regel Sp (OGR), *w*, Branches glandular. Kumaon.

R. sericea omeiensis (Rolfe) Rowley Sp (OGR), *w*, (*R. omeiensis* Rolfe); 1901. Flowers white, single (4 or 5 petals); leaflets more numerous; pedicel thickened, orange-yellow. W.China; (14).

R. sericea polyphylla Geier Sp (OGR), *w*, Leaflets numerous; pedicel thin; (14).

R. sericea pteracantha Franchet Sp (OGR), *w*, (*R. omeiensis pteracantha* (Franchet) Rehder & Wilson); 1890. Flowers white, single (4 or 5 petals); stems with large, wing-like prickles, deep red and semi-transparent when young; (14).

R. sertata Rolfe Sp (OGR), *mp*, (*R. orbicularis* Baker; *R. webbiana* Vilmorin; Bois, not Royle); 1904. Flowers rose or rose-purple, 2-2½ in. diam., solitary on short branchlets; 5 ft. C.; W. China. *Cinnamomeae*; (14).

R. setigera Michaux Sp (OGR), *dp*, (Prairie Rose; *R. fenestrata* Donn; *R. trifoliata* Rafinesque); 1810. Flowers deep rose, fading to whitish, about 2 in.diam., in few-fld. corymbs; almost scentless; fruit globular, ⅓ in. diam. branches recurving or climbing; 6 ft. Summer. N. Am. *Synstylae*; (14).

R. setigera inermis Palmer & Steyermark Sp (OGR), *dp*, 1923. Unarmed; leaves glabrous.

R. setigera serena Palmer & Steyermark Sp (OGR), *dp*, 1924. Unarmed; leaves pubescent; (14).

R. setigera tomentosa Torrey & Gray Sp (OGR), *dp*, (*R. cursor* Rafinesque; *R. kentuckensis* Rafinesque; *R. rubifolia* R. Brown ex Ait. fil.); 1800. Leaves tomentose beneath; (14).

R. setipoda Hemsley & Wilson Sp (OGR), *lp*, (*R. macrophylla crasseaculeata* Vilmorin); 1895. Flowers pale pink, about 2 in. diam., in loose corymbs; foliage sweetbrier-scented; fruit oblong-ovoid with a narrow neck, about 1 in. long, deep red; 10 ft. Summer. C. China. *Cinnamomeae*; (28, 42).

R. sherardii Davies Sp (OGR), *dp*, (*R. omissa* Déséglise; *R. subglobsa* Smith (1828)); Cult. 1933. Flowers deep pink, 1½-2 in. diam., several; fruit ovoid or pear-shaped, ½-¾ in. across. N.; C. Eu. *Caninae*; (28).

R. sherardii perthensis Harrison Sp (OGR), *dp*, Cult. 1900; Remarkable variety with densely glandular hispid fruit. Scotland; (35).

R. sicula Trattinnick Sp (OGR), (*R. seraphinii* Gussone, not Viviani); Cult. prior to 1894. Flowers deep red to whitish, 1-1¼ in. diam., solitary, rarely to 4, short-stalked; fruit small, globose; low, ½-2 ft. S. Eu., N. Afr. *Caninae*; (35).

R. sinowilsonii Hemsley Sp (OGR), *w*, 1904. Flowers white 1½ in. diam., in many-fld. corymbs; fruit subglobose, small, red; vigorous, climbing to 50 ft.; half hardy. China. *Synstylae*, (14).

R. sonomensis Greene Sp (OGR), *mp, Allied to R. californica;* Not known to be cult. Flowers bright pink, 1-1½ in. diam., in dense few-fld. corymbs; 1 ft. CA. *Cinnamomeae.*

R. soulieana Crépin Sp (OGR), *w,* 1896. Flowers white, 1½ in. diam., corymbose; fruit ovoid or subglobose, ⅓-½ in. long, orange-red; 12 ft. W. China. *Synstylae,* (14).

R. spinosissima Linnaeus Sp (OGR), *w,* (Altaica; Burnet Rose; *R. illinoensis* Baker; *R. pulchella* Salisbury; Scotch Rose); Cult. prior to 1600. Flowers cream, but white, yellow, pink or purple in garden forms, 11/4 -2 in. diam., solitary, but usually very numerous along the stems; fruit globular, black; 3-4 ft. Spring. Eu., W. Asia, occasionally naturalized in N. Am. *Pimpinellifoliae.* This entry refers to more than one clone; (28).

R. spinosissima altaica (Willdenow) Bean Sp (OGR), *w,* (Altaica; *R. altaica* Willdenow; *R. grandiflora* Lindley, not Salisbury; *R. sibirica* Trattinnick; *R. spinossissima baltica* hort.); ca. 1820. Flowers white, large; more vigorous than *R. spinosissima.* W. Asia; (28).

R. spinosissima andrewsii Willmott Sp (OGR), *mr,* Flowers red, dbl.; (28).

R. spinosissima bicolor Andrews Sp (OGR), *pb,* Cult. before 1832. Flowers pale pink becoming cream flushed with pink, semi-dbl., cupped, later rotate; (28).

R. spinosissima fulgens Bean Sp (OGR), *mp,* Flowers bright rose; (28).

R. spinosissima hispida (Sims) Koehne Sp (OGR), *my,* (*R. hispida* Sims, not others; *R. lutescens* Pursh); Prior to 1781. Flowers sulphur-yellow, rather large, 2½-3 in.diam.; (28, 29)

R. spinosissima inermis (De Candolle) Rehder Sp (OGR), *lp,* (*R. mitissima* Gmelin; *R. pimpinellifolia inermis* De Candolle; *R. spinosissima mitissima* (Gmelin) Koehne). Flowers pink; branches almost unarmed.

R. spinosissima lutea Bean Sp (OGR), *my,* Flowers bright yellow; (28).

R. spinosissima luteola Andrews Sp (OGR), *ly,* (*R. ochroleuca* Swartz); Similar to *R. spinosissima hispida.* Flowers pale yellow, 2 in. diam.; (28).

R. spinosissima myriacantha (De Candolle) Koehne Sp (OGR), *w,* (*R. myriacantha* De Candolle); Prior to 1820. Flowers white, blushed, small; (28).

R. spinosissima nana Andrews Sp (OGR), *w,* Flowers white, semi-dbl., 2 in. diam.; (28).

R. spinosissima pimpinellifolia (Linnaeus) Hooker Sp (OGR), *w,* (*R. pimpinellifolia* Linnaeus). Flowers white, with smooth pedicels; (28).

R. × spinulifolia Dematra S, *mp,* (*R. glabrata* Déséglise); *R. pendulina* × *R. tomentosa.* Flowers pink, 2-2½ in. diam., solitary or few. Summer. Switzerland; (28?).

R. spithamea S. Watson Sp (OGR), (California Ground Rose); *Possibly allied to R. californica;* Rarely cult. Flowers usually solitary; floral tube often covered with gland-tipped bristles; ⅓-1 ft. Found mostly in the Coast Range, CA. *Cinnamomeae,* (28?).

R. spithamea sonomiensis Sp (OGR), *Possibly not distinct from R. spithamea;* Leaflets often double serrate, with gland-tipped teeth.

R. stellata Wooten Sp (OGR), *m,* (*R. vernonii* Greene); 1902. Flowers deep rose-purple, 1¾ -2¼ in. diam., solitary; leaflets 3-5; fruit turbinate, galbrous or puberulent with scattered short bristles; plant covered in a fine felt of stellate hairs; young floral branches white to yellow, occasionally puberulent prickles; 2 ft. NM, Organ; San Andreas Mts. *Minutifoliae (Hesperhodos);* (14).

R. stellata erlansoniae Lewis Sp (OGR), *m,* Floral branches angled at nodes, with few or no internodal bristles.

R. stellata mirifica (Greene) Cockerell Sp (OGR), *m,* (*R. mirifica* Greene; The Gooseberry Rose); 1916. Floral branches gladrous with many internodal gland-tipped bristles and prickles and no murications; less commonly pubescent with basal hairs on internodal prickles; 4 ft. NM.; (14).

R. stellata mirifica mirifica Lewis Sp (OGR), *m,* Floral branches more or less straight; densely covered with internodal bristles.

R. stellata stellata Lewis Sp (OGR), *m,* Floral branches tomentose-woolly with long stellate hairs originating from many, short murications or obsolete gland-tipped bristles; internodal prickles few; infrequently branches pubescent with short hairs originating from internodal prickles and with fewer murications.

R. stylosa Desvaux Sp (OGR), *w,* (*R. systyla* Bastard); Cult. 1838. Flowers white or light pink, 1½-2 in. diam., few; styles exserted; intermediate between *R. canina* and *R. arvensis,* and perhaps a descendant of an ancient hybrid between them. Eu. *Caninae;* (35, 42, 28, 34).

R. subserrulata Rydberg Sp (OGR), *mp,* Cult. 1930. Flowers rose, about 2 in. diam., solitary; 2½ ft. MO to TX. *Carolinae;* (14, 28).

R. sweginzowii Koehne Sp (OGR), *mp*, 1909. Flowers pink, 1¾ in. diam., 1-3 together; fruit oblong, 1 in. long. N.W. China; *Cinnamomeae*; (42).

R. sweginzowii macrocarpa hort. Sp (OGR), *mp*, A superior garden form from Germany with showy flowers and fruit.

R. tomentosa Smith Sp (OGR), *lp*, (*R. cuspidata* von Bieberstein; *R. dimorpha* Besser); Cult. 1820. *Allied to R. pomifera*; Flowers pale pink, on longer pedicels; foliage grayish green, downy; fruit smaller. Eu. *Caninae*; (35).

R. tomentosa subglobosa (Smith) Carion Sp (OGR), *lp*, (*R. subglosa* Smith, 1824); Fruit subglobose; prickles hooked.

R. turkestanica Regel Sp (OGR), *my*, Cult. 1900. Flowers yellow, 1-3; fruit subglobose. Turkestan. *Pimpinellifoliae*.

R. tuschetica Boissier Sp (OGR), *mp*, (*R. pimpinellifolia tuschetica* Christ); ca. 1945. Differs from *R. glutinosa* in the leaflets ovate (not obovate nor elliptic) and the sepals long caudate and erect in fruit, not spreading. Mts. Daghestan, USSR. *Caninae*.

R. virginiana Miller Sp (OGR), *mp*, (*R. humilis lucida* (Ehrhart) Best; *R. lucida alba* hort.; *R. lucida* Ehrhart; *R. pennsylvanica* Andrews, not Wangenheim nor Michaux; Virginia Rose); Prior to 1807. Flowers bright pink, about 2 in. diam., usually few or solitary; fruit red, remaining plump until next spring 6 ft. Summer. Newfoundland to NY and PA. *Carolinae*; (28).

R. virginiana lamprophylla Rehder Sp (OGR), *mp*, 1881. Leaves lustrous.

R. wardii Mulligan Sp (OGR), *w*, (*R. sweginzowii inermis* Marquand & Shaw); *Related to R. sweginzowii*; Not cult.; Almost unarmed; flowers white, up to 3 together. S.E. Tibet.

R. wardii culta Mulligan Sp (OGR), *w*, Cult. 1924. Flowers smaller, 1¼ in. diam., pedicels often glandular. The garden form; (42).

R. webbiana Wallich ex Royle Sp (OGR), *mp*, (*R. unguicularis* Bertoloni); 1879. Flowers pink, large, mostly solitary; fruit ovoid. Himalayas to Afghanistan to Turkestan. *Cinnamomeae*; (14).

R. wichuraiana Crépin Sp (OGR), *w*, (Memorial Rose; *R. bracteata* hort., not Wendland; *R. luciae* Franchet & Rochebrune, in part; *R. luciae taquetiana* Boulenger; *R. luciae wichuraiana* (Crépin) Koidzumi; *R. mokanensis* Léveillé; *R. taquetii* Léveillé); 1891. Flowers white, 1½-2 in. diam., in few-fld. pyramidal corymbs; fragrant; fruit ovoid, to ½ in. diam.; half-evergreen; prostrate with creeping branches. Late Summer. E. Asia. *R. bracteata*

hort. is often misnamed — it is chiefly the above species. *Synstylae*; (14).

R. willmottiae Hemsley Sp (OGR), *m*, 1904. Flowers rose-purple, 1-1¼ in. diam., solitary, short-stalked, on short lateral branchlets; foliage fern-like; fruit subglobose, ⅓-½ in. long, bright orange-red; 5-10 ft. Spring. W. China. *Cinnamomeae*. Not to be confused with *R. willmottiana* Léveillé, which is *R. longicuspis*, nor with *R. blanda willmottiana* Baker; (14).

R. woodsii Lindley 1820 Sp (OGR), *mp*, (Mountain Rose; *R. deserta* Lunell; *R. fimbriatula* Greene; *R. macounii* Rydberg, not Greene; *R. maximilianii* Nees; *R. mohavensis* Parish; *R. pyrifera* Rydberg; *R. sandbergii* Greene; *R. woodsii mohavensis* (Parish) Jepson); Cult. 1880. Flowers pink, rarely white, 1½-2 in. diam., corymbose or solitary, on very short, smooth pedicels; fruit globose, with a short neck; 3 ft. Summer. Sask. to CO; MO. *Cinnamomeae*; (14).

R. woodsii fendleri (Crépin) Rehder Sp (OGR), *mp*, (*R. fendleri* Crépin; *R. poetica* Lunell); Cult. 1888. Flowers and fruit somewhat smaller than *R. woodsii*; slenderer and often taller. B.C. to W. TX; NM.; (14).

R. woodsii hispida Lewis Sp (OGR), *dp*, (*R. adenosepala* Wooten; Standley). Flowers deep pink; hips glandular. MT.; (14).

R. woodsii ultramontana Lindley (Watson) Taylor & MacBryde Sp (OGR), *mp*, (*R. californica ultramontana* S. Watson; *R. pisocarpa ultramontana* (S. Watson) Peck; *R. ultramontana* (S. Watson) Heller); Cult. 1888. Flowers medium pink, about 2 in. diam., clusters of 3-10; fruit subglobose, small; 5 ft. N. to W. N. Am. *Cinnamomeae*; (14).

R. xanthina Lindley Sp (OGR), *my*, (Manchu Rose; *R. xanthinoides* Nakai); 1906. Flowers yellow, dbl., 1¾ in. diam., solitary, short-stalked; 10 ft. N. China, Korea. *Pimpinellifoliae*; (14).

R. xanthina spontanea Rehder Sp (OGR), *my*, 1907. Flowers single; wild; (14).

R. yainacensis Greene Sp (OGR), (*R. myriadenia* Green; *R. yainacencis*); Cult. 1912; *Allied to R. nutkana*; Tetraploid; flowers more numerous; fruit smaller. OR.; (28).

Rosa Bonheur M (OGR), *mp*, 1852, (Mlle. Rosa Bonheur); Laffay. Flowers pink or bright rose, full, large; moderate growth.

Rosa d'Abril HT, *dp*, 1948, Dot, P. Flowers carmine, very dbl., globular, large; very vigorous growth.

Rosa de Friera HT, *pb*, 1956, *Rosa Gallart* × *Paulette*; Dot, P. Flowers violet-pink with carmine reflections, dbl. (35 petals), large; strong stems; very fragrant; vigorous growth.

Rosa Gallart HT, *mp*, 1935, *Seedling × (Li Bures × Rose Marie)*; Dot, P. Bud long, pointed; flowers rose-pink, dbl., cupped, large; fragrant; foliage glossy; vigorous growth.

Rosa Gruss an Aachen F, *yb*, 1930, *Gruss an Aachen sport*; Spek. Flowers satiny yellowish pink.

Rosa Mamie HT, *mr*, 1956, *Rome Glory sport*; Asseretto, V. Bud ovoid; flowers bright rose, dbl. (35 petals), large; long stems; fragrant; vigorous growth.

Rosa Mundi G (OGR), *pb*, (*R. gallica versicolor* Linnaeus; *R. gallica rosa mundi* Weston; *R. gallica variegata* Thory; *R. mundi*). *Sport of Apothecary's Rose.* Flowers striped white, pink, and red, semi-dbl., yellow stamens; Often confused in rose literature with 'York and Lancaster'; (28).

Rosa Munné HT, *rb*, 1952, *Maria Serrat × Paz Vila*; Munné, M. Flowers red to saffron-pink, dbl., large; very fragrant; foliage clear green; very vigorous growth.

Rosa Traum F, *mp*, 1974, *Fragrant Cloud × Seedling*; Kordes; Dehner & Co. Bud pointed; flowers pink, dbl. (32 petals), high-centered, medium (2½ in.); slightly fragrant; foliage glossy; vigorous, upright, bushy growth.

Rosa Vollendung F, *pb*, 1943, *Crimson Glory × Else Poulsen*; Kordes. Bud long, pointed; flowers salmon-pink, reverse capucine-red, dbl., large, borne in clusters; slightly fragrant; foliage leathery, wrinkled; vigorous, bushy growth.

Rosabel Walker HT, *mr*, 1922, Cant, F. Bud long, pointed; flowers brilliant velvety crimson, dbl., medium (3½ in.); fragrant; very vigorous, bushy, spreading growth.

Rosabella HT, *mr*, 1941, *Mrs. J.D. Russell × Julien Potin*; Giacomasso. Flowers red with cerise reflections, very large; long stems; foliage abundant.

Rosabella F, *op*, 1955, *Pinocchio seedling*; Maarse, G. Flowers salmon-pink shaded orange, very dbl., well shaped, borne in very large clusters; vigorous growth.

Rosabelle Barnett F, *op*, 1970, *Tropicana × Seedling*; Gregory. Flowers coral, dbl. (32 petals), globular, medium (2½ in.); slightly fragrant; foliage dark; very free growth.

Rosada Min, *op*, 1950, (Rosata); *Perla de Alcañada × Rouletii*; Dot, P.; URS. Flowers peach edged pink, dbl. (25 petals), cupped; foliage small, glossy; compact (7-8 in.) growth.

Rosalba HT, *pb*, 1934, *Souv. de Claudius Pernet × Willowmere*; Borgatti. Bud long, pointed, streaked carmine; flowers lilac-pink, center shaded salmon-pink, dbl., large; vigorous growth.

Rosaleda HT, *yb*, 1958, *Monte Carlo × Michèle Meilland*; Moreira da Silva. Flowers yellow and white, dbl., well formed, large; strong stems; fragrant; foliage dark; upright, bushy growth.

Rosaleen HMsk (S), *dr*, 1933, Bentall. Flowers dark red, dbl., large clusters; recurrent.

Rosaleen Dunn HT, *mr*, 1942, McGredy; J&P. Flowers crimson-red, semi-dbl. (22 petals), cupped, large (5½ in.); very fragrant; foliage dark; vigorous growth.

Rosali F, *mp*, 1971, (TANli); *Seedling × Junior Miss*; Tantau. Bud long, pointed; flowers pink, dbl., large; fragrant; vigorous, upright growth. RULED EXTINCT 4/85.

Rosali® F, *mp*, 1983, (TANilasor; Rosali '83); Tantau. Flowers medium pink, dbl. (20 petals); medium; no fragrance; foliage medium, medium green, glossy; bushy.

Rosalia HT, *dp*, 1954, Cant, F. Bud long, pointed, light cerise; long stems.

Rosalie Coral Cl Min, *ob*, 1992, (CHEWallop); *(Elizabeth of Glamis × (Galway Bay × Sutter's Gold)) × Anna Ford*; Warner, C.H., 1991. Flowers orange, moderately full (15-25 petals), small (0-4 cms) blooms borne in small clusters; slight fragrance; foliage small, medium green, glossy; few prickles; medium (175-190 cms), bushy growth.

Rosalie Richardson HT, *lp*, 1932, Evans. Flowers soft pink; very fragrant.

Rosalind HT, *op*, 1918, *Ophelia sport*; Pierson, F.R. Bud bright coral; flowers apricot-pink becoming shell-pink, dbl.; fragrant.

Rosalind Russell HT, *mp*, 1950, *Briarcliff × Regina Elena*; Grillo. Bud long, well formed; flowers bright pink, full (45-50 petals), high-centered, large (5 in.); fragrant; foliage dark, leathery; very vigorous, upright growth.

Rosalinda HT, *dp*, 1945, *Editor McFarland × Comtesse Vandal*; Camprubi. Flowers carmine, very dbl., well formed, large; fragrant; very vigorous growth.

Rosalinde F, *mp*, 1944, Krause. Flowers clear pink, dbl., blooms in large clusters.

Rosalpina HT, *pb*, 1953, *Signora × Seedling*; Giacomasso. Flowers coppery pink, dbl. (50 petals), very large; strong stems; foliage glossy; very vigorous growth.

Rosalynn Carter Gr, *or*, 1979, (RUprins; Prins Claus); *Seedling × Scania*; deRuiter; C-P, 1978. Flowers coral-red with orange tones, dbl. (30 petals), high-centered, large (3½-4 in.); fragrant(spicy); tall, vigorous, bushy, upright growth.

Rosamond HT, *op*, 1927, *Red-Letter Day* × *R. foetida bicolor*; Burbage Nursery. Flowers orange-salmon, stamens golden, single.

Rosamunde F, *pb*, 1941, *Seedling* × *Permanent Wave*; Leenders, M. Flowers salmon-carmine, reverse hydrangea-pink, dbl., large; fragrant.

Rosanna HT, *mp*, 1959, *Baccará* × *Gruss an Coburg*; Valentino. Bud urn shaped; flowers spinel-rose, open, medium to large; slightly fragrant; foliage leathery; vigorous, upright, compact growth. RULED EXTINCT 4/77.

Rosarium Ueteresen® LCl, *dp*, 1977, (KORtersen; Rosarium Uetersen; *Karlsruhe* × *Seedling*; Kordes, W. Bud ovoid; flowers deep pink, very dbl. (142 petals), medium (3 in.); fragrant; foliage large, glossy; vigorous, climbing growth.

Rose à Feuilles Luisantes M (OGR), *lp*, 1843, Vibert. Flowers soft pink edged blush, full, globular, medium, borne in clusters; fragrant; foliage glossy; branching growth.

Rose à Parfum de l'Hay HRg (S), *mr*, 1901, (Parfum de l'Hay); *(Summer Damask* × *Général Jacqueminot)* × *R. rugosa*; Gravereaux. Flowers cherry-carmine-red, turning blue in heat, full, globular, large; very fragrant; foliage not typically rugose; vigorous (5 ft.) growth; recurrent bloom.

Rose Aimée HT, *m*, 1955, *Peace* × *Seedling*; Gaujard. Flowers gold, flushed and splashed crimson, dbl., well formed; fragrant; very vigorous, bushy growth.

Rose Angle E (OGR), *mp*, (Rose Angle Blush); *R. arvensis hybrid*; Martin, prior to 1848. Flowers bright lilac rose, cupped; foliage very fragrant; very vigorous growth. Not to be confused with Angle (Ayr).

Rose Anne Cl HT, *ob*, 1938, *Francesca* × *Margaret McGredy*; Thomas; Armstrong Nurs. Flowers orange-apricot, base deeper yellow, semi-dbl., cupped; foliage large, glossy; very vigorous, climbing (15 ft.); recurrent bloom. RULED EXTINCT 4/77.

Rose Apples HRg (S), *dp*, 1906, Paul. Flowers carmine-rose, semi-dbl., large; fragrant; vigorous.

Rose Bampton HT, *dp*, 1940, *Charles P. Kilham* × *Margaret McGredy*; Van Rossem; J&P. Bud carmine; flowers bright china-red, dbl. (50 petals), camellia form, large (5½ in.); fragrant; foliage dark; vigorous growth.

Rose Bansal HT, *yb*, 1972, *Ambossfunken sport*; Friends Rosery. Flowers yellow, petal edges sometimes crimson.

Rose Berkley HT, *op*, 1928, (Souv. de Rose Berkley); McGredy. Bud long, pointed; flowers deep rosy salmon-pink suffused orange,

base orange, high-centered, large; slightly fragrant; foliage rich green, glossy; very vigorous growth.

Rose Bowl HT, *mr*, 1961, *Mardi Gras* × *Chrysler Imperial*; Morey; J&P. Bud urn shaped; flowers bright red, dbl. (35 petals), high-centered, large; long, strong stems; very fragrant; foliage leathery; vigorous, upright, bushy growth.

Rose Bradwardine E (OGR), *mp*, 1894, Penzance. Flowers clear rose-pink, single, blooms in graceful clusters; foliage very fragrant; vigorous growth; seasonal bloom.

Rose Bruford HT, *ab*, 1961, *Soraya sport*; Wheatcroft Bros. Flowers creamy peach, shaded rosy bronze.

Rose Céleste® Cl HT, *lp*, 1979, (DELroceles); *(Queen Elizabeth* × *Provence)* × *(Sultane* × *Mme. J. Perraud)*; Delbard. Flowers light pink, dbl. (33 petals), well-formed, cupped, large; fragrant; vigorous, climbing (to 9 ft.) growth.

Rose Charm HT, *mp*, 1934, *Talisman sport*; Scittine; Lainson. Flowers Sanguineous pink.

Rose Cheal HT, *mp*, 1970, *New Style* × *Scarlet Queen Elizabeth*; Herincx. Flowers rose-pink, dbl. (42 petals), spiral form, large (4-5 in.); fragrant; foliage glossy, dark; free growth.

Rose d'Amour Misc. OGR (OGR), *dp*, (St. Mark's Rose; *R. virginiana plena*; The St. Mark's Rose); *Thought to be R. virginiana hybrid*; Prior to 1759. Bud deep pink with long sepals; fls. deep pink, outer petals fading to pale pink, dbl.; flag.; receptacle wide, glandular; lfts. 5-7, rich green, marked with red on leafstalks and stipules; prickles of mixed sizes, scattered; stipules and lfts. wider than those of 'D'Orsay Rose,' with which this has been confused. Summer bloom; lax growth to 10 ft.

Rose d'Amour HT, *rb*, 1936, Gaujard. Flowers brown-red, reverse yellow, dbl., open, large; foliage glossy, dark; vigorous growth.

Rose Dawn HT, *pb*, 1924, *(Joseph Hill* × *Mrs. George Shawyer seedling)* × *Ophelia*; Towill. Bud long, pointed; flowers soft shell-pink, base yellow, dbl., high-centered, large; very fragrant; foliage light; vigorous growth.

Rose de France HT, *op*, 1942, Gaujard. Bud ovoid; flowers brilliant salmon tinted orange, dbl., very large; slightly fragrant; foliage glossy; dwarf growth.

Rose de los Andes Gr, *op*, 1974, *Duet sport*; Gutierrez. Bud ovoid; flowers pink-salmon-peach, dbl. (44-46 petals), large (4-4½ in.); vigorous growth.

Rose de Lyon HT, *ob*, 1945, Gaujard. Bud pointed; flowers orange-yellow, dbl., medium; fragrant; foliage glossy.

Rose de Meaux C (OGR), *mp*, (Pompon Rose; *R. centifolia pomponia* (Roessig) Lindley; *R. dijoniensis*; *R. pomponia* Roessig; *R. pulchella* Willdenow, not Salisbury); Cult. 1789. Flowers medium pink, dbl., 1½ in. diam., dwarf growth.

Rose de Meaux White C (OGR), *w*, (Le Rosier Pompon Blanc; White de Meaux); Before 1799. Flowers white with pink centers.

Rose de Rescht D (OGR), *dp*, (Brought to England by Miss Nancy Lindsay from Persia or France in the 1940's.) Flowers bright fuchsia-red, fading with lilac tints, very full, rosette form; very fragrant (damask); foliage dense; vigorous, compact; long-season bloom.

Rose des Maures G (OGR), *dr*, (Sissinghurst Castle); Re-int. 1947. Flowers deep plum-crimson, yellow stamens, semi-dbl. (17 petals), medium (2½ in.); fragrant; foliage thin; vigorous growth.

Rose des Peintres C (OGR), *mp*, Prior to 1838. Flowers bright pink, dbl.; fragrant; vigorous.

Rose d'Evian T (OGR), *pb*, 1895, Bernaix, A. Flowers pink, center carmine.

Rose d'Hivers D (OGR), *w*, Flowers whitish, center shell-pink, well-shaped.

Rose d'Or HT, *dy*, 1941, *Julien Potin × Seedling*; Gaujard; J&P. Bud pointed; flowers intense yellow, dbl. (35 petals), large (4½-5 in.); slightly fragrant; foliage dark, bronze, glossy; very vigorous growth.

Rose Dot HT, *rb*, 1962, *Baccará × Peace*; Dot, S. Flowers red, reverse white, dbl. (35 petals), large; very fragrant; foliage dark; vigorous, upright growth.

Rose du Barri HT, *pb*, 1940, Archer. Flowers salmon-pink, reverse carmine, single, large; fragrant; vigorous growth.

Rose du Ciel® HT, *pb*, 1966, (DELfror); *Chic Parisien × (Michèle Meilland × Bayadère)*; D-C. Flowers cream-white broadly edged carmine-pink, dbl., globular, large; foliage dark, glossy; vigorous, bushy growth.

Rose du Maître d'École G (OGR), *m*, Flowers soft pink to lilac, dbl., flat, very large.

Rose du Prince HT, *mr*, 1959, *Blanche Mallerin × Profusion*; Dorieux; Pin. Bud long, pointed; flowers strawberry-rose, dbl., large; slightly fragrant; foliage leathery, light green; vigorous, upright growth.

Rose du Roi P (OGR), *mr*, 1815, (Lee's Crimson Perpetual); Lelieur; Souchet. Flowers bright red shaded violet, semi-dbl., large; very fragrant; foliage clear green, slightly fluted; vigorous growth; remontant bloom. A parent of the first HP.

Rose du Roi à Fleurs Pourpres P (OGR), *m*, *Rose du Roi sport*; 1819. Flowers purplish; (28).

Rose du Roi Panaché P (OGR), *rb*, *Rose du Roi sport*; Prior to 1848. Flowers pale flesh striped crimson.

Rose Eutin F, *mp*, 1958, *Eutin sport*; Hennessey. Flowers rose-pink.

Rose Fukuoka HT, *pb*, 1983, *(Utage × Kordes' Perfecta) × Miss Ireland*; Ota, Kaichiro. Flowers blend of light, medium and deep pink, (deeper at petal edges), dbl. (27 petals), high-centered, large; slight fragrance; foliage small, dark, glossy; compact growth.

Rose Gaujard® HT, *rb*, 1957, (GAUmo); *Peace × Opera seedling*; Gaujard; Armstrong Nursery, 1964. Flowers cherry-red, reverse pale pink and silvery white, very dbl. (80 petals), high-centered to cupped, large (3-4 in.); slightly fragrant; foliage leathery, glossy; vigorous, bushy growth. GM, NRS, 1958.

Rose Gaujard, Climbing Cl HT, *rb*, 1964, (Grimpant Rose Gaujard); Nagashima.

Rose Gilardi™ Min, *rb*, 1987, (MORose); *Dortmund × ((Fairy Moss × (Little Darling × Ferdinand Pichard)) × Seedling)*; Moore, Ralph S., 1986. Flowers red and pink striped, reverse similar, aging well, semi-dbl. (12-15 petals), informal, small borne in sprays of 3-5; mini-moss; slight fragrance; foliage small, medium green, semi-glossy; slender, straight, small to medium, brownish prickles; bushy, spreading, medium growth.

Rose Hannes HT, *w*, 1982, (Hannes); *Pascali × Seedling*; Wheatcroft, Christopher; Timmerman's Roses. Flowers white, dbl. (40+ petals), large; fragrant; foliage medium, medium green; vigorous, upright growth.

Rose Hill HT, *dp*, 1928, *Columbia sport*; Hill, J.H., Co. Bud long, pointed; flowers darker than Briarcliff, dbl., high-centered, very large; fragrant.

Rose Hills Red Min, *dr*, 1978, *(R. wichuraiana × Floradora) × Westmont*; Moore, R.S.; Sequoia Nursery. Bud pointed; flowers deep red, dbl. (30 petals), small (1½ in.); foliage glossy, leathery; vigorous, upright growth.

Rose Impériale HT, *ob*, 1942, Gaujard. Flowers flame and gold, very dbl., globular, very large; fragrant; foliage dark, glossy; vigorous growth. GM, Bagatelle, 1941.

Rose Marie HT, *mp*, 1918, *Hoosier Beauty × Sunburst*; Dorner. Flowers clear rose-pink, dbl., cupped, very large; fragrant; foliage glossy, dark; vigorous growth.

Rose Marie, Climbing Cl HT, *mp*, 1927, Pacific Rose Co.

Rose Marie Reid HT, *mp*, 1956, *Charlotte Armstrong × Katherine T. Marshall*; Whisler; Germain's. Bud globular; flowers neyron rose, dbl. (48 petals), loosely cupped, large (5-6 in.); fragrant; foliage dark, leathery; vigorous.

Rose Merk HT, *or*, 1931, Cant, F. Flowers bright geranium-red; fragrant; vigorous growth.

Rose Moet HT, *my*, 1962, Dorieux; Pin. Flowers golden yellow, dbl., large; long, strong stems; foliage leathery.

Rose Nabonnand T (OGR), *pb*, 1883, Nabonnand, G. Flowers salmon-pink tinted yellow, large; very fragrant.

Rose Noble HT, *lp*, 1927, *Mme. Caroline Testout × Seedling*; Mühle. Bud long, pointed; flowers silvery pink, semi-dbl.; fragrant.

Rose Nuggets Min, *lp*, 1991, *Red Ace sport*; Michelis, Dorothy; Justice Miniature Roses, 1992. Bud pointed; flowers light pink, aging lighter, dbl. (30 petals), self-cleaning, many petaloids, high-centered, exhibition, small (4 cms) blooms borne singly; no fragrance; foliage small, dark green, glossy, frequently 7 leaflets; very full, bushy, low growth.

Rose of Clifton F, *yb*, 1978, *Vera Dalton × Parasol*; Sanday. Bud pointed; flowers gold edged peach-pink, dbl. (27 petals), large (3½ in.); slightly fragrant; foliage dark, matt; vigorous, upright growth.

Rose of Freedom HT, *mr*, 1948, *Charlotte Armstrong × Night*; Swim; Mt. Arbor Nursery. Bud ovoid; flowers medium red, dbl. (50 petals), large (3½-4½ in.); very fragrant; foliage leathery, dark; vigorous, upright, bushy growth.

Rose of Lidice HT, *yb*, 1961, *Tzigane sport*; Wheatcroft Bros. Flowers lemon-yellow shaded poppy red.

Rose of Torridge HT, *dp*, 1961, *Karl Herbst × Pink Charming*; Allen, E.M. Flowers deep pink, dbl. (36 petals), large (6 in.); fragrant; foliage glossy; vigorous growth.

Rose of Tralee S, *op*, 1964, *Leverkusen × Korona*; McGredy, S., IV. Flowers deep pink shaded salmon, dbl. (35 petals), large (4 in.) blooms in small clusters; slightly fragrant; foliage dark; very vigorous, bushy growth.

Rose Opal HT, *dp*, 1962, *Wellworth × Independence*; LeGrice; Wayside Gardens Co. Flowers pink-opal, dbl. (25-30 petals), well formed, large (4-5 in.); fragrant; foliage dark (reddish when young); vigorous, upright, bushy growth.

Rose Parade F, *pb*, 1974, *Sumatra × Queen Elizabeth*; Williams, J.B.; Howard Rose Co. Bud ovoid; flowers coral-peach to pink, dbl., cupped, large; fragrant; foliage large, glossy; vigorous, bushy, compact growth. AARS, 1975.

Rose Queen HT, *or*, 1962, *Chrysler Imperial × Seedling*; Whisler; Germain's. Bud globular; flowers orange-red, dbl. (38 petals), high-centered, large (4-5 in.); fragrant; foliage leathery, dark; vigorous, upright, bushy growth.

Rose Sherbet F, *dp*, 1962, *Gruss an Teplitz × Seedling*; Pal; Indian Agric. Research Inst. Bud globular; flowers deep rose-pink, dbl., medium; very fragrant; foliage glossy; vigorous, upright, open growth.

Rose Valmae S, *mr*, 1981, Watts, Mrs. M.A. Flowers medium red, dbl. (40 petals), decorative blooms borne 3 per cluster; faint fragrance; foliage light green, 7 leaflet; upright, medium growth.

Rose Window Min, *ob*, 1978, *Seedling × Over the Rainbow*; Williams, E.D.; Mini-Roses. Bud ovoid, pointed; flowers orange, yellow, & red blend, semi-dbl. 15-20 petals, small (1 in.); slightly fragrant; foliage small, dark; spreading, bushy growth.

Roseanna Cl Min, *dp*, 1976, *Little Darling × Seedling*; Williams, E.D.; Mini-Roses. Bud long, pointed; flowers deep pink, dbl. (50+ petals), high-centered, small (1-1½ in.); foliage glossy; tall, semi-climbing growth.

Roseate Cl HT, *mr*, 1931, Clark, A.; Ivanhoe Hort. Soc. Flowers red, semi-dbl., cupped, large; slightly fragrant; foliage wrinkled; vigorous, climbing growth; good as a pillar.

Roseford LCl, *lp*, 1981, *Seedling × Seedling*; Jerabek, Paul E. Bud ovoid; flowers light pink, slightly darker reverse, dbl. (28 petals), cupped blooms borne 6 per cluster; light fragrance; foliage dark, semi-glossy; straight, red prickles; bushy (can be grown as shrub); repeats well. ARC TG (B), 1986.

Roseglen Bouquet F, *pb*, 1953, *Pinocchio × Seedling*; Quinn; Roseglen Nursery. Flowers ivory-white edged deep pink, very dbl., high-centered, small; slightly fragrant; foliage dark, glossy, leathery; vigorous, upright growth.

Rösel Dach Pol, *mr*, 1907, Walter, L. Flowers cherry-rose, full, borne in upright clusters; dwarf, bushy growth.

Roseland Rosette F, *dp*, 1952, *Crimson Rosette sport*; Houghton, T.B. Bud globular; flowers deep rose-pink, dbl., small; vigorous, bushy growth.

Roselandia HT, *my*, 1924, *Golden Ophelia sport*; Stevens, W.; Low. Flowers darker and larger.

Roselandia, Climbing Cl HT, *my*, 1933, Lens.

Roselette F, *mp*, 1957, *Orange Triumph × Alain*; Lens. Flowers soft salmon-pink; foliage bright green; very vigorous growth.

Rosella F, *pb*, 1930, *Else Poulsen sport*; Prior. Flowers salmon-rose-pink, semi-dbl., ruffled, borne in large trusses; vigorous growth.

Rosella Cl HT, *pb*, 1931, *Mme. Edouard Herriot × Roger Lambelin*; Dot, P.; C-P. Bud long, pointed; flowers velvety carmine, base yellow, orange undertone, single, medium (2³/₄ in.), borne in clusters; slightly fragrant; foliage large, glossy; vigorous (8 ft. or more) growth.

Rosella Grace Cremer F, *dp*, 1957, *Garnette sport*; Cremer. Bud conical to ovoid; flowers dark tyrian rose, reverse lighter, dbl. (35-40 petals), rosette center, medium; fragrant; very vigorous, bushy growth.

Rosella Sweet HT, *op*, 1930, (Rosalie); Pernet-Ducher; Dreer. Flowers nasturtium-yellow suffused salmon-pink, large; very fragrant.

Rosemarie Hinner HT, *mp*, 1949, *Frau Karl Druschki × (Ellen × Una Wallace)*; Hinner, P.; Bauské Bros.; Hinner. Bud long, pointed; flowers pink, high-centered, large; fragrant; foliage leathery, light green; very vigorous, upright, bushy growth.

Rose-Marie Viaud HMult (OGR), *m*, 1924, *Veilchenblau seedling*; Igoult; Viaud-Bruant. Flowers same as parent except bluer and more dbl.

Rosemary Cl HT, *lp*, 1925, Cant, F. Bud long, pointed; flowers pink shaded old-gold, very dbl., high-centered; fragrant; foliage leathery; pillar growth; free, recurrent bloom.

Rosemary Min, *mp*, Flowers apple-blossom-pink.

Rosemary F, *dp*, 1955, *Garnette sport*; Schenkel; Amling-DeVor Nursery. Bud ovoid; flowers rose-pink, dbl. (55-60 petals), flat, medium (2¹/₂ in.), borne in clusters; fragrant; foliage leathery; vigorous, bushy growth.

Rosemary Clooney F, *ab*, 1985, *Vera Dalton × Elizabeth of Glamis*; French, Richard. Flowers creamy apricot, semi-dbl. (20 petals), medium blooms in clusters of 3-6; slight fragrance; foliage small, medium green, matt; small, red prickles; upright, bushy growth.

Rosemary Duncan F, *my*, 1964, *Pinocchio sport*; Duncan. Flowers yellow, edged lighter, dbl. (40 petals), medium; foliage glossy; vigorous, bushy growth.

Rosemary Eddie F, *mp*, 1956, *New Dawn × Fashion*; Eddie. Flowers bright pink, well formed.

Rosemary Gandy F, *yb*, 1957, (Flash); *Tabarin seedling × Jolie Princesse seedling*; Gaujard.

Flowers yellow and coppery, semi-dbl., cupped, medium; fragrant; foliage glossy, bronze; bushy growth.

Rosemary Harkness HT, *op*, 1985, (HARrowbond); *Compassion × (Basildon Bond × Grandpa Dickson)*; Harkness, R. Flowers orange-salmon, orange-yellow reverse, dbl. (35 petals), medium-large; very fragrant; foliage large, dark, semi-glossy; bushy growth. GM, Belfast, 1987; Belfast Fragrance Award, 1987.

Rosemary Rose F, *dp*, 1954, *Gruss an Teplitz × Floribunda seedling*; deRuiter; Gregory. Flowers deep pink, dbl., camellia-shaped, medium blooms in large trusses; fragrant; foliage coppery; vigorous, bushy growth. GM, NRS; Rome, 1954.

Rosemary Stone HT, *mp*, 1970, *Waltzing Matilda sport*; Stone. Flowers pink, very dbl., high-centered; slightly fragrant; foliage leathery; moderate, upright growth.

Rosendorf Ufhoven E (OGR), *dr*, 1949, *Gen. MacArthur × Magnifica*; Kordes. Flowers crimson, very dbl., globular, very large blooms on weak stems; slightly fragrant; foliage leathery, glossy, dark; vigorous, upright, bushy growth; non-recurrent.

Rosenelfe F, *mp*, 1939, (Rose Elf); *Else Poulsen × Sir Basil McFarland*; Kordes; Dreer. Bud long, pointed; flowers medium pink, dbl., high-centered, medium (2¹/₂ in.) blooms in clusters; fragrant; foliage leathery, glossy, light; vigorous, bushy growth.

Rosenella HT, *mp*, 1964, Mondial Roses. Flowers clear pink, reverse brighter; very fragrant.

Rosenkavalier F, *dp*, 1963, Verschuren, A.; Stassen. Flowers deep rose, dbl. (45 petals), borne in clusters; very fragrant; foliage dark; vigorous, upright, bushy growth.

Rosen-Lambert LCl, *dr*, 1937, *Fragezeichen × American Pillar*; Vogel, M.; P. Lambert. Flowers oxblood-red, dbl., very large; foliage large, bronze, leathery; vigorous, climbing (9 ft.) growth.

Rosenpfarrer Meyer HT, *or*, 1930, *Mme. Edouard Herriot × Louise Catherine Breslau*; Soupert; Notting. Flowers coral-red passing to prawn-red, semi-dbl.; slightly fragrant; very vigorous growth.

Rosenprinzessin HT, *mp*, 1975, *Nordia × Sans Souci*; Hetzel. Bud ovoid; flowers pink, dbl., large (3¹/₂-5 in.); fragrant; foliage glossy; upright growth.

Rosenresli® S, *dp*, 1987, (KORresli); *(New Dawn × Prima Ballerina) × Seedling*; Kordes, W., 1986. Flowers deep pink, dbl. (26-40 petals), large; very fragrant; foliage medium, dark green, glossy; upright, bushy, possibly climbing growth. ADR, 1984.

Rosenwunder E (OGR), *dp*, 1934, *W.E. Chaplin × Magnifica*; Kordes. Bud long, pointed; flowers rose-red, semi-dbl., cupped, very large; slightly fragrant; foliage large, leathery, glossy, wrinkled; very vigorous, bushy growth; non-recurrent bloom; (29).

Roseraie de l'Hay HRg (S), *dr*, 1901, *Said to be a sport or hybrid of R. rugosa rosea, but this is unlikely*; Cochet-Cochet. Flowers crimson-red changing to rosy magenta, full, large; very fragrant; foliage rugose; vigorous (4-5 ft.) growth; recurrent bloom.

Roserie R, *mp*, 1917, (Rosary); *Tausendschön sport*; Witterstaetter. Flowers tyrian pink, base white, darkening with age, semi-dbl., open, large (3³/₄ in.); slightly fragrant; foliage large, rich green, leathery, glossy; thornless; very vigorous, climbing growth.

Roseromantic® F, *w*, 1984, (KORsommer); *Seedling × Tornado*; Kordes, W. Flowers light pink to white, single (5 petals), large; slight fragrance; foliage small, dark, glossy; bushy, spreading growth. GM, Baden-Baden, 1982.

Rosetime Min, *dr*, 1989, (BENtem); *Rise 'n' Shine × Black Jade*; Benardella, Frank A.; Kimbrew-Walter Roses, 1989. Flowers medium red, brushed with dark red, dbl. (26-40 petals), upright, medium; slight fragrance; foliage medium, medium green, matt; upright growth.

Rosetone Min, *mp*, 1977, *Dream Dust × Little Chief*; Moore, R.S.; Sequoia Nursery. Bud ovoid, pointed; flowers pink, dbl. (60 petals), high-centered, small (1 in.); slightly fragrant; foliage small, dark, leathery; very bushy growth.

Rosetta Min, *rb*, 1991, (SPOrose); *Scamp × Seedling*; Spooner, Ray; Oregon Miniature Roses, 1992. Flowers white center, red on outer half of petals, dbl. (26-40 petals), small (0-4 cms) blooms borne singly and sprays; no fragrance; foliage small, medium green, semi-glossy, disease resistant; bushy (34 cms) growth.

Rosette Pol, *mr*, 1926, Grandes Roseraies. Flowers fuchsia-red, dbl., medium; semi-dwarf growth.

Rosette HT, *or*, 1934, Dickson, A. Flowers rose red, shaded orange, base yellow, full, well formed, large; fragrant; vigorous, bushy growth.

Rosette F, *op*, Archer. Flowers peach-pink, dbl., borne in clusters; vigorous growth.

Rosette Delizy T (OGR), *yb*, 1922, *Gen. Galliéni × Comtesse Bardi*; Nabonnand, P. Flow-

ers yellow, apricot reflexes, outer petals dark carmine, full, well-formed, large; vigorous.

Rosie™ Min, *pb*, 1987, (BENros); *Rise 'n' Shine × (Sheri Anne × Laguna)*; Benardella, Frank; Nor'East Miniature Roses, 1987. Flowers cream with pink edges, dbl. (30-33 petals), high centered, exhibition, excellent form, medium, borne in sprays of 3-8; slight fragrance; foliage medium, medium green, exceptional substance; long, thin, straight prickles; fruit none observed; upright, bushy, medium growth.

Rosier d'Or Pol, *ob*, 1969, (DELpli); *Zambra × (Orléans Rose × Goldilocks)*; Delbard; Trioreau. Flowers orange-yellow, shaded apricot-yellow, dbl. (20-28 petals), large (2¹/₂-3¹/₂ in.); slightly fragrant.

Rosier Gloriette Min, *op*, Flowers orange-salmon, rosette form.

Rosiériste Gaston Lévêque HT, *dp*, 1932, *Mme. Butterfly × Jean C.N. Forestier*; Dot, P. Bud long, pointed; flowers brilliant carmine, dbl., cupped, large; very fragrant; foliage dark; very vigorous growth.

Rosiériste Pajotin-Chédane Pol, *dr*, 1934, Délépine; Pajotin-Chédane. Flowers deep red, with white, thread-like markings, semi-dbl., cupped, borne in clusters on strong stems; slightly fragrant; foliage leathery; vigorous, bushy growth.

Rosina Min, *my*, 1951, (Josephine Wheatcroft; Yellow Sweetheart); *Eduardo Toda × Rouletii*; Dot, P.; URS, 1935. Flowers sunflower-yellow, semi-dbl. (16 petals), small blooms in clusters; slightly fragrant; foliage glossy, light; dwarf, compact growth.

Rosine HT, *pb*, 1935, Lens. Bud citron-yellow with red; flowers flesh-pink, base clear salmon, quite dbl.; foliage bronze.

Rosita HT, *lp*, 1956, *The Doctor × Seedling*; Delforge. Bud long; flowers soft pink, dbl., large; fragrant; foliage glossy; vigorous growth.

Roslyn HT, *dy*, 1929, *Souv. de Claudius Pernet × Buttercup*; Towill. Bud long, pointed, deep orange; flowers golden yellow, reverse darker orange, semi-dbl., large; slightly fragrant; vigorous, compact growth.

Roslyn, Climbing Cl HT, *dy*, 1937, Vestal.

Rosmari HT, *pb*, 1962, *Vigoro × First Love*; Dot, S. Bud pointed; flowers pink, reverse purplish, dbl. (30 petals); strong stems; vigorous, upright growth.

Rosmarin® Min, *pb*, 1965, *Tom Thumb × Dacapo*; Kordes, R. Flowers light pink, reverse light red, globular, small; slightly fragrant; foliage glossy, light green; dwarf, bushy.

Rosomane Narcisse Thomas T (OGR), *rb*, 1908, Bernaix, P. Flowers crimson suffused apricot-yellow.

Rosorum F, *or*, 1959, *Buisman's Triumph × Alpine Glow*; Buisman. Flowers orange-scarlet, semi-dbl., borne in large clusters; foliage dark, glossy; vigorous, upright growth.

Ross Gowie HT, *dr*, 1968, Gowie; Gandy. Flowers dark red, conical, large; slightly fragrant; vigorous, tall growth.

Ross Rambler R, *w*, 1938, P.H. Wright. Found by Norman Ross, Canada. Flowers similar to Semi. Height 9 ft; blooms all summer.

Rossana HT, *dr*, 1958, *Orange Delight × Tudor*; Buyl Frères. Flowers blood-red, dbl., well shaped, large; vigorous, spreading growth.

Rostock HMsk (S), *lp*, 1937, *Eva × Louise Catherine Breslau*; Kordes. Bud long, pointed; flowers light pink, dbl., high-centered, very large blooms in clusters; slightly fragrant; foliage leathery, glossy, dark; very vigorous, bushy growth; recurrent bloom.

Roswytha F, *mp*, 1968, *Carol sport*; van der Meyden. Bud ovoid; flowers pink, very dbl., small borne in clusters; foliage dark.

Rosy Carpet® S, *dp*, 1983, (INTercarp); *Yesterday × Seedling*; Interplant, 1984. Flowers deep pink, single (5 petals), medium blooms in clusters; fragrant; foliage medium, dark, glossy; many, medium prickles; spreading (to 4 ft.) growth; repeat blooming.

Rosy Cheeks HT, *rb*, 1975, *Seedling × Irish Gold*; Anderson's Rose Nursery, 1976. Flowers red, reverse yellow, dbl. (35 petals), very large (7 in.); very fragrant; foliage dark, glossy.

Rosy Cheeks, Climbing Cl HT, *rb*, 1985, (ANDros); Anderson's Rose Nursery.

Rosy Cushion® S, *lp*, 1979, (INTerall); *Yesterday × Seedling*; Ilsink. Flowers light pink, single (7-8 petals), small blooms in large clusters; slightly fragrant; foliage dark, glossy; many medium prickles; vigorous (3-4 ft.) growth; repeat bloom; ground cover.

Rosy Dawn Min, *yb*, 1982, *Magic Carrousel × Magic Carrousel*; Bennett, Dee; Tiny Petals Nursery. Bud ovoid; flowers yellow, petals edged deep pink, dbl. (28 petals), exhibition, medium; slight tea fragrance; foliage small, medium green, glossy.

Rosy Future F, *dp*, 1992, (HARwaderox); *Radox Bouquet × Anna Ford*; Harkness, R.; Harkness New Roses Ltd., 1991. Flowers carmine, moderately full (15-25 petals), small (0-4 cms) blooms borne in large clusters; patio; fragrant; foliage small, dark green, semi-glossy; few prickles; medium (60 cms), upright growth.

Rosy Gem Min, *mp*, 1971, (MEIradia; Lutin); *Scarlet Gem sport*; Meilland, 1973. Flowers pink.

Rosy Glow HT, *mp*, 1947, *Better Times sport*; Hill, J.H., Co. Bud long, pointed; flowers hermosa pink, dbl. (25-35 petals), high-centered, large (4-5 in.); very fragrant; foliage leathery; vigorous, bushy growth; a florists' variety, not distributed for outdoor use.

Rosy Jewel Min, *pb*, 1958, *Dick Koster sport × Tom Thumb*; Morey; J&P. Bud ovoid; flowers rose-red, reverse lighter, center white, dbl. (25 petals), small (1 in.); fragrant; low (6-8 in.), compact growth.

Rosy Life HT, *mp*, 1970, *Walko × Souv. de J. Chabert*; Delbard; Laxton; Bunyard Nursery. Flowers sparkling pink, dbl. (25 petals), full, medium (3-4 in.); slightly fragrant; foliage glossy; vigorous growth.

Rosy Mantle LCl, *mp*, 1968, *New Dawn × Prima Ballerina*; Cocker. Flowers pink, dbl., large; fragrant; foliage dark, glossy.

Rosy Morn LCl, *mp*, 1914, *Frau Karl Druschki seedling*; Clark, A. Flowers pink, large.

Rosy Morn HP (OGR), *op*, 1878, Paul, W. Flowers soft peach shaded salmon-pink, well formed, very large; slightly fragrant; very vigorous growth.

Rosy Morn Pol, *mp*, 1930, Burbage Nursery. Flowers rose-pink, large, borne in large clusters; fragrant; vigorous growth.

Rosy Wings HT, *dp*, 1962, *Pink Spiral × Seedling*; Delforge. Flowers pink shaded light red, dbl. (35 petals), globular, medium (2-2½ in.); fragrant; foliage dark, glossy; vigorous growth.

Rotarian HT, *mr*, 1921, *Ophelia × Seedling*; Lemon. Bud long, pointed; flowers bright cherry-crimson, full (35-40 petals); fragrant.

Rotary Jubilee HT, *yb*, 1971, *Queen Elizabeth × Peace*; Lindquist; Bell Roses. Bud ovoid; flowers yellow blend, creamy yellow, dbl., cupped, high-centered, large; fragrant; foliage large, glossy, dark, leathery; vigorous, bushy growth.

Rotary President F, *or*, 1975, *Fairlight × Summer Holiday*; Wood. Flowers deep vermilion, full, large (4 in.); very fragrant; foliage small, plum color, turning dark green; dwarf, bushy growth.

Rotary Rose HT, *dr*, 1990, (MEIrypoux); *(Mister Lincoln × Pres. Leopold Senghor) × Karl Herbst*; Meilland, Alain; Rotary Rose Co., 1989. Bud pointed; flowers dark red, dbl. (27 petals), cupped, high-centered, blooms borne usually singly; no fragrance; foliage medium green; prickles large, red; vigorous, upright growth.

Rotary-Lyon HT, *yb*, 1936, Chambard, C. Bud long, pointed, well formed, golden pink; flowers old-gold shaded carmine, reverse yellow, stamens deep yellow, dbl., cupped, very large; fragrant; foliage dark; very vigorous growth.

Rote Else Poulsen F, *dp*, 1934, *Else Poulsen sport*; Koopmann; Tantau. Flowers dark pink.

Rote Gabrielle Privat Pol, *mr*, 1940, *Gabrielle Privat sport*; Koopmann. Flowers red.

Rote Max Graf® K (S), *mr*, 1980, (KORmax; Red Max Graf); *R. kordesii × Seedling*; Kordes, W. Bud ovoid; flowers medium red, single (6 petals), blooms in clusters; fragrant; foliage small, leathery, matt; dark brown prickles; vigorous, trailing; ground cover.   GM, Baden-Baden, 1981.

Rote Mevrouw G.A. van Rossem HT, *or*, 1934, *Mev. G.A. van Rossem sport*; Kordes. Flowers nasturtium-red, reverse lightly tinted yellow, dbl., open, large; very fragrant; foliage glossy, dark; vigorous growth.

Rote Perle F, *dr*, 1962, Tantau, Math. Flowers deep red, dbl. (25 petals), medium (1½ in.); foliage dark; vigorous, bushy growth.

Rote Pharisäer HT, *mr*, 1927, *Pharisäer × George C. Waud*; Hinner, W. Bud very long, pointed; flowers red, full, well shaped, large; very fragrant; foliage reddish green, leathery; very vigorous growth.

Rote Rapture HT, *mr*, 1934, *Rapture sport*; Weber, J. Flowers bright cherry-red.

Rote Teschendorffs Jubiläumsrose Pol, *dp*, 1930, Grunewald; Teschendorff. Flowers dark crimson-pink to light red, dbl., large, borne in large clusters; vigorous growth.

Rotelfe HT, *dr*, 1922, *Château de Clos Vougeot × Ulrich Brunner Fils*; Tantau. Flowers very dark red. RULED EXTINCT 4/85.

Rotelfe® F, *mr*, 1985, (TANrecktor; TANreckertor); Tantau, M. Flowers medium red, semi-dbl., medium; no fragrance; foliage small, medium green, semi-glossy; spreading growth; ground cover.

Roter Champagner HT, *dp*, 1963, (Pétillante); Tantau, Math. Bud pointed; flowers red champagne color, dbl., large; long, strong stems; slightly fragrant; foliage bright green; vigorous, upright growth.

Rotes Meer Pol, *or*, 1960, *Orange Triumph × Seedling*; Verschuren, A.; van Engelen. Flowers orange-red, dbl., borne in large clusters; foliage glossy, dark; upright, bushy, symmetrical growth.

Rotorua F, *or*, 1963, *Independence × Spartan*; McGredy, S., IV; Avenue Nursery. Bud ovoid; flowers orange-scarlet, dbl. (27 petals), high-centered, large (3½ in.), borne in clusters on short, strong stems; slightly fragrant; foliage leathery, dark; very vigorous, bushy growth.

Rotraut Pol, *dr*, 1931, *Miss Edith Cavell sport*; Grunewald. Flowers dark red, full, borne in clusters; vigorous growth.

Rouge Pol, *mr*, 1934, Verschuren; J&P. Flowers brilliant scarlet-crimson, semi-dbl., open; strong stems; foliage leathery; dwarf growth.

Rouge Champion HT, *mr*, 1956, *Happiness × Princesse Liliane*; Buyl Frères. Flowers bright red, dbl. (40-50 petals); very vigorous growth.

Rouge de Paris F, *mr*, 1958, (Paris Red); *Floradora seedlings × Orange Triumph seedlings*; D-C; Stark Bros., 1964. Flowers light red, dbl. (35-45 petals), large (3 in.); foliage purplish; vigorous, bushy growth.

Rouge de Parme HT, *pb*, 1963, (*Peace × Fred Edmunds*) × *Buccaneer*; Dorieux; Le Blévenec. Flowers mauve-pink, dbl., high-centered, large; foliage dark, dull.

Rouge Dorieux® HT, *mr*, 1967, (DORmal); *Seedling × Ena Harkness*; Dorieux; Vilmorin. Bud pointed; flowers cherry-red, dbl., open, very large; slightly fragrant; foliage dark, glossy, leathery; vigorous, upright growth.

Rouge Dot HT, *mr*, 1962, *Baccará × Lydia*; Dot, S. Flowers currant-red, dbl. (40 petals); slightly fragrant; vigorous.

Rouge Mallerin HT, *mr*, 1934, (Henri Mallerin); *Mme. Van de Voorde × Lady Maureen Stewart*; Mallerin; C-P. Bud long, pointed; flowers brilliant red, dbl., high-centered, large; very fragrant (damask); compact growth.

Rougemoss F, *or*, 1972, *Rumba × Moss hybrid*; Moore, R.S.; Sequoia Nursery. Bud ovoid; flowers orange-red, dbl., medium; fragrant; foliage leathery; vigorous, dwarf growth.

Rouletii Ch (OGR), *mp*, 1922, (R. rouletii Correvon); *A variety of R. chinensis minima, said to have been in cultivation before 1818*; Correvon, 1922. Discovered growing in pots on window ledges of Swiss cottages by Major Roulet, 1918. Flowers rose-pink, dbl., less than ½ in. diam.; dwarf; recurrent; said to be identical to *Pompon de Paris* except for differences due to culture.

Roundabout Min, *mr*, 1985, (ZIPround); *Double Joy × Libby*; Zipper, Herbert; Magic Moment Min. Flowers medium red, dbl. (20 petals), small blooms borne usually singly; no fragrance; foliage medium, medium green, matt; bushy growth.

Roundelay Gr, *dr*, 1954, *Charlotte Armstrong* × *Floradora*; Swim; Armstrong Nursery. Bud ovoid; flowers dark red, dbl. (38 petals), high-centered to flat, medium-large; fragrant; foliage dark; very vigorous growth. GM, Geneva, 1954.

Rowena R, *dp*, 1912, Paul, W. Flowers carmine, changing to mauve-pink, dbl., small, borne in clusters; vigorous, climbing growth.

Roxana HT, *yb*, 1933, Dickson, A. Bud large, long, pointed; flowers orange-yellow and copper, semi-dbl., open; fragrant; foliage glossy, light; vigorous, bushy growth.

Royal Air Force HT, *m*, 1969, Laperrière. Flowers light lavender-blue, dbl. (35 petals), high-centered, large (6 in.); slightly fragrant; foliage dark, matt.

Royal Albert Hall HT, *rb*, 1972, *Fragrant Cloud* × *Postillon*; Cocker. Flowers wine-red, reverse gold, dbl. (32 petals), large (5 in.); very fragrant; foliage dark.

Royal Amethyst™ HT, *m*, 1989, (DEVmorada); *Angel Face* × *Blue Moon*; DeVor, Paul F.; DeVor Nursery. Bud pointed; flowers lavender, dbl. (32 petals), large, borne singly; heavy, fruity fragrance; foliage medium, medium green, glossy; prickles declining, henna; fruit globular, tangerine orange; upright, tall growth.

Royal Ascot® HT, *pb*, 1968, (DELsab); *Chic Parisien* × *(Grande Première* × *(Sultane* × *Mme. Joseph Perraud))*; D-C. Flowers pink, reverse shaded crimson, semi-dbl., high-centered to cupped, large; foliage glossy, leathery; vigorous, bushy growth.

Royal Baby F, *mr*, 1982, (DEBrad); *Generosa* × *Baby Darling*; Bracegirdle, Derek T.; Arthur Higgs Roses. Flowers medium red, semi-dbl. (20 petals), medium; slight fragrance; foliage small, medium green, semi-glossy; upright growth.

Royal Bath & West Gr, *lp*, 1977, *Seedling* × *Prima Ballerina*; Sanday. Flowers pastel pink, semi-dbl. (20 petals), large (4 in.); very fragrant; foliage green, matt.

Royal Beauty HT, *dr*, 1940, *Better Times sport*; Coddington. Flowers dark velvety red, dbl. (25 petals), high-centered, large (5 in.); fragrant (spicy); foliage bronze; a florists' variety.

Royal Bright HT, *my*, 1976, *Garden Party* × *(Bronze Masterpiece* × *Memoriam)*; Kono. Bud ovoid; flowers medium yellow, dbl. (40 petals), high-centered, very large (6 in.); slightly fragrant; vigorous, upright growth.

Royal Canadian HT, *mr*, 1968, *Seedling* × *Talisman*; Morey; J&P. Bud ovoid; flowers scarlet, dbl. (35 petals), cupped, large; fragrant; foliage glossy, leathery; vigorous, upright growth.

Royal Carpet™ Min, *mr*, 1984, (MINuco); *Red Cascade* × *Red Cascade*; Williams, E.D.; Mini-Roses. Flowers medium red, dbl. (40+ petals), small blooms in clusters; no fragrance; foliage small, dark, semi-glossy; spreading growth; ground cover.

Royal Chinook HT, *mr*, 1939, *Rapture sport*; Chase. Flowers brilliant rose-red.

Royal City Min, *dr*, 1989, (RENity); *Goldmarie* × *Pink Sheri*; Rennie, Bruce F.; Rennie Roses, 1990. Bud ovoid; flowers dark red, semi-dbl. (23 petals), urn-shaped, exhibition, medium, borne singly; no fragrance; foliage medium, medium green, semi-glossy; prickles hooked, medium, yellow; fruit globular, medium, orange-red; upright, tall growth.

Royal Dane® HT, *ob*, 1971, (POUmidor; Troika); *(Tropicana* × *(Baccará* × *Princesse Astrid))* × *Hanne*; Deutsche Rosen-registerstelle; N. Poulsen. Flowers orange, outer petals red, classic form, large (6 in.); very fragrant; foliage large, dark, glossy, leathery; vigorous, upright, bushy.

Royal Dawn LCl, *mp*, 1962, *Royal Sunset* × *Aloha*; Morey; J&P. Flowers coral-pink, dbl. (35 petals), large; fragrant; foliage dark, glossy; vigorous, climbing growth.

Royal Flare HT, *rb*, 1988, *Pristine* × *Standout*; Wambach, Alex. Flowers red and white blend, high-centered, large, borne singly; slight fragrance; foliage medium, dark green, disease resistant; prickles down-turned, dark green; upright, medium growth.

Royal Flush LCl, *pb*, 1970, *Little Darling* × *Suspense*; Fuller; Wyant. Bud ovoid; flowers cream, edges blending pink, semi-dbl., cupped, medium; fragrant; foliage dark, leathery; vigorous, upright, climbing growth; repeat bloom.

Royal Gold LCl, *my*, 1957, *Goldilocks, Climbing* × *Lydia*; Morey; J&P. Flowers golden yellow, dbl. (35 petals), cupped, large (4 in.) blooms borne singly and in clusters of 3-7; fragrant (fruity); foliage glossy; vigorous, pillar (5-7 ft.) growth.

Royal Highness HT, *lp*, 1962, (Königlicht Hoheit; Konigliche Hoheit); *Virgo* × *Peace*; Swim; Weeks; C-P. Bud long, pointed; flowers soft light pink, dbl. (43 petals), high-centered, large (5-5½ in.); very fragrant; foliage dark, glossy, leathery; tender, upright, bushy growth. GM, Portland, 1960; Madrid, 1962; AARS, 1963; AARS David Fuerstenberg Prize, 1964

Royal Lavender LCl, *m*, 1961, *Lavender Queen* × *Amy Vanderbilt*; Morey; J&P. Bud ovoid;

flowers lavender tinted gray and pink, dbl. (35 petals), cupped, large (3 in.) blooms in clusters; very fragrant; foliage leathery; vigorous (6-9 ft.) growth.

Royal Lustre HT, *op, Mrs. Sam McGredy ×* *Crimson Glory*; McGredy. Flowers orange-buff overlaid salmon, dbl. (45 petals), very large (6-7 in.); slightly fragrant; foliage coppery; very free growth.

Royal Mail F, *rb*, 1986, (ANDroi); *Seedling ×* *Manx Queen*; Anderson's Rose Nurseries. Flowers red with yellow petal edges, dbl. (20 petals), small; no fragrance; foliage small, medium green, glossy; upright, bushy growth.

Royal Marbrée G (OGR), *m*, Prior to 1846. Flowers lilac and purple, marbled (striped) pink, very dbl., medium.

Royal Occasion F, *or*, 1974, (Montana); *Walzertraum × Europeana*; Tantau. Bud long, pointed; flowers orange-scarlet, semi-dbl. (20 petals), large (3 in.); slightly fragrant; foliage glossy; upright growth. ADR, 1974.

Royal Perfection HT, *or*, 1964, *Rome Glory ×* *Bayadere*; Delbard; Laxton; Bunyard Nursery. Flowers orange-coral, semi-dbl. (20 petals), full, large (4½ in.); slightly fragrant; vigorous growth.

Royal Porcelain Cl HT, *mp*, 1992, (LEEpel); *Pele × Altissimo*; Little, Lee W.; Heirloom Old Garden Roses, 1992. Flowers medium pink, full (26-40 petals), high centered, exhibition, large (7+ cms) blooms borne in small clusters on strong upright laterals with 1-5 blooms; slight fragrance; foliage large, disease resistant; some prickles; tall (260 cms), upright, spreading.

Royal Princess Min, *pb*, 1981, *Seedling × Seedling*; Lyon. Bud ovoid; flowers pink and yellow blend, very dbl. (65 petals), blooms borne 1-3 per cluster; fruity fragrance; foliage dark, leathery; hooked, bronze prickles; upright, bushy growth.

Royal Queen Gr, *w*, 1965, *Queen Elizabeth sport*; Verschuren. Flowers greenish white.

Royal Red HT, *mr*, 1924, Hill, E.G., Co. Bud pointed; flowers intense crimson-scarlet, dbl., very large; fragrant; foliage leathery; vigorous growth.

Royal Red HT, *dr*, 1956, *Happiness sport*; Lowe. Flowers deep scarlet, well formed; moderate growth.

Royal Robe HBlanda (S), *mr*, 1946, *(R. rugosa × Hybrid Perpetual) × (R. multiflora × R. blanda)*; Wright, P.H. Flowers crimson, almost purple, semi-dbl., rather large; vigorous growth; non-recurrent bloom.

Royal Romance HT, *my*, 1974, *Pink Parfait ×* *seedling*; Fryer, G.; Fryer's Nursery. Flowers bright lemon-yellow, dbl. (30 petals), full, large (5 in.); fragrant; foliage leathery; very free growth.

Royal Ruby Min, *mr*, 1972, *Garnette × (Tom Thumb × Ruby Jewel)*; Morey; Pixie Treasures. Flowers red, base white, dbl., globular, small; slightly fragrant; foliage small, dark, leathery; vigorous, upright growth.

Royal Salute Min, *mr*, 1976, (MACros; Rose Baby); *New Penny × Marlena*; McGredy; Mattock. Flowers rose-red, dbl. (30 petals), small (1½ in.); foliage small, dark.

Royal Scarlet HT, *mr*, 1966, *McGredy's Scarlet × Christian Dior*; Kraus; Wyant. Bud ovoid; flowers scarlet-red, dbl., high-centered, large; fragrant; foliage glossy; vigorous, bushy.

Royal Scarlet Hybrid LCl, *mr*, 1926, Chaplin Bros.; No longer in cultivation. Name released for reuse.

Royal Scot HT, *yb*, 1928, Dobbie. Flowers golden yellow, edged crimson, semi-dbl., open; fragrant; foliage dark; vigorous growth.

Royal Show HT, *mr*, 1973, *Queen Elizabeth × Seedling*; Gregory. Flowers medium red, dbl. (27 petals), pointed, large (4 in.); slightly fragrant; foliage glossy; vigorous.

Royal Success™ HT, *mr*, 1987, (AROreroy; Royal Delight); *Red Success × Royalty*; Christensen, Jack; Carruth, Tom; Armstrong Roses, 1986. Flowers medium red, dbl. (30 petals), high-centered, exhibition, large, borne usually singly; foliage medium, medium green, semi-glossy; normal, light green to tan prickles; fruit none observed; upright, bushy, tall growth.

Royal Sunblaze™ Min, *my*, 1987, (SCHobitet; Royal Meillandina); *Seedling × Seedling*; Schwartz, Ernest; SNC Meilland; Cie, 1984. Flowers lemon yellow, dbl. (40+ petals), medium; mini-flora; no fragrance; foliage medium, medium green, semi-glossy; bushy growth.

Royal Sunset LCl, *ab*, 1960, *Sungold × Sutter's Gold*; Morey; J&P. Bud ovoid; flowers apricot, semi-dbl. (20 petals), cupped, large (4½-5 in.); fragrant (fruity); foliage leathery; vigorous (6 ft.) growth. GM, Portland, 1960.

Royal Tan HT, *m*, 1955, *Charles P. Kilham × Mrs. Sam McGredy*; McGredy. Flowers pale purple feathered violet and chocolate, high-pointed, large (5 in.); slightly fragrant; foliage dark; vigorous.

Royal Touch F, *rb*, 1983, (ANDroy); *Orange Sensation × Elizabeth of Glamis*; Anderson's Rose Nursery. Flowers red, reverse silver, semi-dbl. (20 petals), medium; slight fragrance; foliage medium, medium green, semi-glossy; upright growth.

Royal Velvet HT, *dr*, 1959,*(Happiness × Independence) × (Happiness × Floradora)*; Meilland, F.; C-P. Flowers rich, velvety cardinal-red, dbl. (55-65 petals), large (4-5 in.) blooms; vigorous, tall growth. RULED EXTINCT 3/86 ARM.

Royal Velvet™ HT, *dr*, 1986, (MEIlotup); *(Exciting × Suspense) × Duke of Windsor*; Meilland, M.L.; Wayside Gardens. Flowers dark red, dbl. (28 petals), high-centered, large blooms borne usually singly; slightly fragrant; large, straw-colored prickles; fruit globular, small, medium green; medium, bushy growth.

Royal Victoria Min, *op*, 1991, (LAVictor); *(Painted Doll × June Laver) × Mountie*; Laver, Keith G.; Springwood Roses. Flowers coral pink, white reverse, very full (41+ petals), small blooms borne mostly singly; fragrant; foliage small, medium green, semi-glossy; tall, upright, bushy growth.

Royal Visit HT, *op*, 1939, *Picture × Mrs. Pierre S. duPont*; Eddie. Flowers deep tangerine-orange, reverse coral passing to apricot, dbl.; slightly fragrant; oliage leathery, glossy, dark; bushy growth.

Royal Volunteer HT, *ob*, 1988, (COCdandy); *Yellow Pages × Alexander*; Cocker, James & Sons. Flowers orange-red and yellow blended, dbl. (26-40 petals), medium; slight fragrance; foliage medium, light green, semi-glossy; upright growth.

Royal Welcome HT, *rb*, 1955, *Crimson Glory × Peace*; Homan; G.A. Williams. Flowers velvety dark red, reverse deep rosy pink, well formed; very fragrant; foliage glossy; vigorous growth.

Royal William HT, *dr*, 1984, (KORzaun; Duftzauber '84); *Feuerzauber × Seedling*; Kordes, W. Flowers dark red, dbl. (35 petals), high-centered, large; fragrant; foliage large, dark, semi-glossy; upright, bushy growth.

Royal Worcester® S, *w*, 1992, (TRObroy); *Simon Robinson × Gina Louise*; Robinson, Thomas; Thomas Robinson Ltd., 1991. Flowers peachy cream, semi-dbl. (6-14 petals), large (7+ cms) blooms borne in large clusters of 5-69; fragrant; foliage medium, dark green, very glossy; some prickles; low to medium (60 cms), bushy, compact growth.

Royalet HT, *mr*, 1968, *Seedling × Chrysler Imperial*; Herholdt, J.A. Flowers crimson-red, dbl. (35-40 petals), large (4½-5½ in.); slightly fragrant; foliage dark; upright, bushy growth.

Royalglo™ Min, *m*, 1986, (MINadco); *Angel Face × Anita Charles*; Williams, Ernest; Mini-Roses. Flowers mauve, non-fading, dbl. (40 petals), high-centered, exhibition, small, borne usually singly; heavy, damask, sweet fragrance; foliage small, dark green, semi-glossy; few, long, light tan prickles; fruit none; bushy, medium growth.

Royalist HT, *mp*, 1954, *(Billy Boy × Blossom) × Mrs. Redford*; McGredy. Flowers deep rose-pink, dbl. (28 petals), high-centered, large; very fragrant; foliage dull green; very free growth.

Royalty HT, *dr*, 1976, *Forever Yours × Love Affair*; Jelly; E.G. Hill Co. Bud globular, pointed; flowers deep red, semi-dbl. (20 petals), large (4-4½ in.); slightly fragrant; foliage leathery; vigorous.

Royden F, *my*, 1989, *Liverpool Echo × Arthur Bell*; Cattermole, R.F.; South Pacific Rose Nursery. Flowers bright gold, fading quickly to white, dbl. (40 petals), cupped, large, borne in sprays of 3-4 and up to 20; strong fragrance; foliage light green, glossy; tall, upright growth.

Roydon Hall F, *mr*, 1983, *City of Leeds × (Paprika × Rose Gaujard)*; Scrivens, I. Flowers medium red, dbl. (35 petals); large; no fragrance; foliage medium, medium green, semi-glossy; bushy growth.

Roze Koningin HT, *mr*, 1938, *Lady Sylvia seedling × Étoile de Hollande*; Lens. Bud long, pointed; flowers medium red, passing to pink, dbl., well formed; large; fragrant; vigorous growth.

Rozenamateur A. Bok F, *mr*, 1961, *Prinses Christina × Käthe Duvigneau*; Buisman. Flowers bright red, single, borne in large clusters; foliage dark; vigorous, upright growth.

R. S. Hudson HT, *yb*, 1939, Wheatcroft Bros. Flowers yellow tinged red, large, well-formed; vigorous, upright growth.

Rubaiyat HT, *dp*, 1946, *(McGredy's Scarlet × Mrs. Sam McGredy) × (Seedling × Sir Basil*; McFarland) McGredy; J&P. Bud long, pointed; flowers rose-red, reverse lighter, dbl. (25 petals), high-centered, large (4½-5 in.); very fragrant; foliage dark, leathery; vigorous, upright growth.   GM, Portland, 1945; AARS, 1947.

Ruban Rouge F, *dr*, 1957, *Alain × Cinnabar*; Lens. Bud globular; flowers deep velvety red, borne in clusters; foliage dark, leathery; vigorous growth.

Rubella F, *dr*, 1972, *Kimono × Lilli Marleen*; deRuiter. Flowers deep red, dbl. (24 petals), large; bushy growth.

Rubens T (OGR), *w*, 1859, Robert; Moreau. Flowers white, shaded with rose, center bronzy yellow, full, cupped, large.

Rubens HT, *mr*, 1972, *Rose Gaujard* × *Miss France*; Gaujard. Bud pointed; flowers vermilion red, full, large; vigorous growth.

Rubies 'n' Pearl Min, *m*, 1992, (MANrupearl); *Rise 'n' Shine* × *MANpurple*; Mander, George, 1992-93. Flowers purple/cream bicolor, very attractive, very dark purple on inside of petals, full (15-25 petals), small (0-4 cms) blooms borne in small clusters; slight fragrance; foliage small, medium green, semiglossy; few prickles; low (40-50 cms), upright, bushy growth.

Rubin R, *mr*, 1899, *Daniel Lacombe* × *Fellemberg*; Schmidt, J.C. Flowers crimson to spinel-red, semi-dbl., medium, borne in clusters; fragrant; height 10-12 ft.

Rubin HT, *or*, 1956, *Mme. Henri Guillot* × *Grande Duchesse Charlotte*; Lens. Flowers orange-red, base yellow, semi-dbl., large; slightly fragrant; vigorous growth.

Rubin F, *dr*, 1962, Kordes; Dehner & Co. Bud long, pointed; flowers deep red, dbl., borne in broad clusters; foliage dark; bushy, compact, low growth.

Rubinette F, *dr*, 1971, *(Mandrina* × *Baccará)* × *(Mandrina* × *Baccara)*; deRuiter; Carlton Rose Nursery. Flowers deep red, dbl. (28 petals), large (3½ in.); slightly fragrant; foliage dark; vigorous, upright growth.

Rubis Pol, *rb*, 1926, *Merveille des Rouges* × *Jessie*; Nonin. Flowers bright ruby-red, center white, medium, borne in clusters; dwarf growth.

Rubis Cl HT, *mr*, 1948, *Seedling* × *Mme. G. Forest-Colcombet*; Mallerin; URS. Flowers blood-red, well formed, large; very fragrant; foliage bronze; vigorous growth.

Rubor HT, *mp*, 1947, *Cynthia* × *Director Rubió*; Dot, P. Flowers neyron pink, dbl.; fragrant; foliage dark; very vigorous growth.

Ruby Pol, *mr*, 1932, deRuiter; Sliedrecht & Co. Flowers glowing scarlet.

Ruby Dee Gr, *mr*, 1968, *Queen Elizabeth* × *Happiness*; Patterson; Patterson Roses. Bud ovoid; flowers medium red, dbl., high-centered, large blooms in clusters; fragrant; foliage dark, glossy; vigorous, upright.

Ruby Gem HT, *mr*, 1962, *Seedling* × *Red Favorite*; Leenders, J. Flowers bright red, dbl. (28 petals), large; slightly fragrant.

Ruby Glow LCl, *mr*, 1955, *Dream Girl* × *New World*; Jacobus; B&A. Bud short, oval; flowers spectrum-red, semi-dbl. (13-15 petals), open, medium (3 in.), borne in clusters; fragrant; foliage glossy; moderate pillar (7 ft.) growth.

Ruby Jewel Min, *mr*, 1958, *Dick Koster sport* × *Tom Thumb*; Morey; J&P. Bud ovoid; flowers

ruby-red, reverse lighter, dbl. (35-40 petals), open, small (½ in.); fragrant; foliage glossy; low (6-8 in.), compact growth.

Ruby Lips F, *mr*, 1958, *World's Fair* × *Pinocchio*; Swim; Armstrong Nursery. Bud ovoid, pointed; flowers bright cardinal-red, semi-dbl. (18 petals), loose form, large (3 in.) blooms in clusters; slightly fragrant; foliage semi-glossy; vigorous, semi-spreading, bushy.

Ruby Magic Min, *mr*, 1986, (MORrubi; MORuby); *Orangeade* × *Pinstripe*; Moore, R.S.; Moore Min. Roses. Flowers medium red, dbl. (20 petals), small to medium blooms borne usually singly and in sprays of 3-5; slight fragrance; foliage small to medium, medium green, semi-glossy; brown prickles; fruit usually none; medium, upright, bushy growth.

Ruby Manwaring HT, *dp*, 1932, *Betty Uprichard sport*; Longley. Flowers rich rosy cerise.

Ruby Pendant Min, *m*, 1979, *(Lotte Gunthart* × *Salvo)* × *Baby Betsy McCall*; Strawn, Leslie E.; Pixie Treasures Nursery. Bud pointed; flowers red-purple, dbl. (28 petals), exhibition, borne singly; slight fragrance; foliage reddish-green; needle-shaped prickles; vigorous.

Ruby Princess HT, *mr*, 1949, *Jewel sport*; Grillo. Flowers velvety red, dbl. (50 petals), large (5 in.); fragrant.

Ruby Queen R, *dp*, 1899, *R. wichuraiana* × *Queen's Scarlet*; Van Fleet; Conard; Jones. Flowers deep rose-pink, reverse lighter, dbl., small, borne in clusters of 3-6; slightly fragrant; height 10 ft.; non-recurrent bloom.

Ruby Star Min, *dr*, 1990, (UMStar); *High Spirits* × *seedling*; Umsawasdi, Dr. Theera, 1991. Flowers deep red, single (5 petals), small, borne mostly singly; no fragrance; foliage medium, dark green, semi-glossy; upright, bushy, tall (24 cms).growth.

Ruby Superior Pol, *mr*, *Ruby sport*; deRuiter. Flowers have more lasting color.

Ruby Talisman HT, *mr*, 1935, *Talisman sport*; Eddie. Flowers rich ruby-red, more shapely than parent, with reflexed petals.

Ruby Tuesday Min, *dr*, 1988, (RENruby); *Pink Sheri* × *Black Jack*; Rennie, Bruce F.; Rennie Roses, 1989. Flowers dark, velvety red, reverse lighter, aging darker, dbl. (25-30 petals), cupped, pom-pom, small, borne usually singly; no fragrance; foliage small, dark green, semi-glossy; prickles slightly hooked, small, brownish; fruit round, small, red-orange; bushy, low growth.

Ruby Ulrick F, *dp*, 1953, *Mrs. Tom Henderson* × *Gloria Mundi*; Ulrick. Flowers deep pink, base white, dbl., borne in clusters; foliage leathery; very vigorous growth.

Ruby Wedding HT, *dr*, 1979, *Mayflower × Seedling*; Gregory. Flowers deep red, dbl. (44 petals), medium (3-3½ in.); vigorous, spreading growth.

Rudelsburg R, *dp*, 1919, Kiese. Flowers shining carmine-rose, medium blooms in clusters; no prickles; vigorous, climbing growth.

Rudola F, *mr*, 1973, *Dacapo × Kimono*; deRuiter. Bud ovoid; flowers light geranium-red, semi-dbl., open, large; slightly fragrant; foliage leathery; very vigorous, bushy growth.

Rudolf Alexander Schröder HT, *w*, 1930, *Mrs. Herbert Stevens × Pius XI*; Kordes. Bud long, pointed; flowers white, center tinted lemon, dbl., high-centered, large; very fragrant; foliage leathery, light; vigorous growth.

Rudolf Schmidts Jubiläumsrose F, *my*, 1955, Kordes; R. Schmidt. Flowers golden yellow, semi-dbl, high-centered, large, borne in clusters; fragrant; foliage light green, glossy; very vigorous, upright, bushy growth.

Rudolf Schock HT, *mr*, 1968, *Josephine Bruce × Seedling*; Verschuren, A.; Stassen. Flowers bright currant-red, dbl., large; fragrant; foliage dark, leathery; vigorous growth.

Rudolf von Bennigsen LCl, *mp*, 1932, *(Geheimrat Dr. Mittweg × Souv. de Paul Neyron) × Mrs. Joseph Hill*; Lambert, P. Bud pointed; flowers rosy-pink, edges fading, large, borne in loose trusses of 5-20; foliage broad, dark, glossy; vigorous, bushy, semi-climbing growth; recurrent bloom.

Rudolph Kluis Pol, *mr*, 1922, *Ellen Poulsen sport*; Kluis; Koning. Bud globular; flowers pure vermilion-red, dbl.; fragrant; foliage rich green, glossy; bushy growth.

Rudolph Kluis Superior Pol, *mr*, 1928, *Ellen Poulsen sport*; Kluis. Flowers glowing scarlet; more compact growth than Rudolph Kluis.

Rudolph Timm F, *rb*, 1951, *(Johannes Boettner × Magnifica) × (Baby Château × Else Poulsen)*; Kordes; Wheatcroft Bros. Flowers white, reverse red, semi-dbl. (15-20 petals), open, small (2 in.), borne in trusses to 40; fragrant; foliage glossy, light green; very free growth; (28).

Rudolph Valentino HT, *op*, 1929, Pernet-Ducher; Dreer. Flowers lively shrimp-pink or coral-red, suffused golden coppery, dbl., very large; fragrant; vigorous growth.

Rufus Pol, *mr*, 1925, *Orléans Rose sport*; Allen. Flowers intense scarlet, dbl., borne in clusters; compact growth.

Ruga Ayr (OGR), *w*, (*R. × ruga* Lindley); *Thought to be R. arvensis × China or Tea*; Prior to 1830. Flowers flesh changing to creamy white, dbl., cupped, large blooms in several-fld. corymbs; a good seed bearer; trailing growth.

Rugosa Copper S, *ob*, 1955, *Conrad Ferdinand Meyer × Seedling*; Gaujard. Flowers coppery orange, large; vigorous growth; recurrent bloom.

Rugosa Magnifica HRg (S), *m*, 1905, Van Fleet. Flowers reddish lavender, gold stamens, dbl.; fragrant; hips orange-red; vigorous, spreading growth; very hardy.

RühKOR HT, *w*, 1984, (Athena); *Seedling × Helmut Schmidt*; Kordes, W., 1981. Flowers white, dbl. (35 petals), large; fragrant; foliage large, medium green, matt; upright, bushy growth; greenhouse variety.

Ruhm der Gartenwelt HP (OGR), *dr*, 1904, *American Beauty × Fracis Dubreuil*; Jacobs. Flowers dark red, full, large.

Ruhm von Steinfurth HP (OGR), *mr*, 1920, (Red Druschki); *Frau Karl Druschki × Ulrich Brunner Fils*; Weigand, C.; H. Schultheis. Bud long, pointed; flowers red, dbl. (34 petals), cupped, large; very fragrant; foliage dark, leathery; vigorous growth.

Rukhsaar HT, *w*, 1969, *Virgo × Open pollination*; Singh; Gopalsinamiengar. Flowers cream, center shell-pink, dbl., high-centered, medium; slightly fragrant; foliage glossy; moderate growth.

Rum Butter Min, *ab*, 1991, (TALrum); *Azure Sea × Seedling*; Taylor, Franklin Pete & Kay, 1987; Taylor's Roses, 1990. Bud pointed; flowers apricot with yellow base-bloom gives a lavender cast blended with apricot, darker reverse, aging lighter, semi-dbl. (12-16 petals), high-centered, exhibition, small, borne singly and in sprays of 4-5; no fragrance; foliage medium, medium green, semi-glossy; upright, bushy, medium growth.

Rum Candy Min, *r*, 1990, (UMSrum); *Twilight Trail × seedling*; Umsawasdi, Dr. Theera, 1991. Flowers brownish apricot, light apricot shaded light pink when fully open, semi-dbl. (6-14 petals), small, borne mostly singly; slight fragrance; foliage small, light green, matt; upright, bushy, low (18 cms) growth.

Rumba HT, *op*, 1956, *Talisman × Seedling*; Faassen-Houba. Bud long, pointed; flowers salmon-orange; long stems; very fragrant.

Rumba® F, *rb*, 1958, *Masquerade × (Poulsen's Bedder × Floradora)*; Poulsen, S.; McGredy, 1960; C-P, 1962. Bud ovoid; flowers poppy-red, center yellow, dbl. (35 petals), cupped, medium (2-2½ in.) blooms in clusters;

slightly fragrant (spicy); foliage dark, glossy, leathery; vigorous, bushy growth.

Rumba, Climbing Cl F, *rb*, 1972, Bansal; Bansal Roses.

Rumpelstilzchen S, *dr*, 1956, (Repelsteeltje); deRuiter; Willicher Baumschulen. Flowers deep red, single, small; dwarf growth.

Running Maid® S, *m*, 1985, (LENramp); *R. multiflora* × *(R. wichuraiana* × *Violet Hood)*; Lens, 1982. Flowers lilac-red, white eye, single (5 petals), 2 in. blooms in clusters of 3-32; very fragrant; foliage reddish-green; hooked, brown prickles; spreading growth; recurrent bloom; ground cover.

Rupert Brooke HT, *pb*, 1928, *Miss Cynthia Forde* × *Mrs. Wemyss Quin*; Easlea. Flowers fawn-pink to cream, dbl.; fragrant.

Rural Rhythm S, *lp*, 1984, *Carefree Beauty* × *The Yeoman*; Buck; Iowa State University. Flowers light pink, dbl. (30 petals), shallow-cupped, 4 in. blooms borne 1-5 per cluster; myrrh fragrance; foliage dark, leathery; awl-like, tan prickles; erect, bushy, spreading growth; repeat bloom; hardy.

Ruritania HT, *or*, 1972, *Miss Hillcrest* × *Hawaii*; Curtis, E.C.; Kimbrew. Bud ovoid; flowers orange-red, very dbl., full, medium; very fragrant; foliage dark, leathery; vigorous, upright growth.

Rusalka LCl, *dp*, 1934, *Tausendschön* × *Farbenkönigin*; Brada; Böhm. Flowers carmine to sunset-rose, base yellow, semi-dbl., high-centered, very large; foliage glossy, light; climbing growth; profuse, recurrent bloom.

Rush® S, *pb*, 1983, (LENmobri); *(Ballerina* × *Britannia)* × *R. multiflora*; Lens. Flowers pink, white eye, single (5 petals), 2 in. blooms in clusters of 3-32; fruity fragrance; foliage light green; hooked, brownish-green prickles; upright, bushy growth; recurrent. GM, Monza; Rome, 1982, Bagatelle, 1986.

Ruskin HRg (S), *dr*, 1928, (John Ruskin); *Souv. de Pierre Leperdrieux* × *Victor Hugo*; Van Fleet; ARS. Bud ovoid; flowers deep crimson, dbl. (50 petals), cupped, large; very fragrant; foliage large, rich green, leathery; vigorous, bushy (4-5 ft.); sparingly recurrent.

Russell Supreme HT, *lp*, 1927, *Mrs. Charles E. Russell* sport; Pacific Rose Co. Flowers light pink.

Russelliana HMult (OGR), *m*, (Old Spanish Rose; Russell's Cottage Rose Scarlet Grevillea; Souv. de la Bataille de Marengo); Prior to 1873. Flowers magenta-crimson fading to mauve, fully dbl., flat blooms in clusters; fragrant; foliage coarse; height to 20 ft.

Russet Beauty Min, *or*, 1983, (POUlrusset); *Mini-Poul* × *Seedling*; Olesen, M.&P.; Ludwigs

Roses. Flowers orange-red, dbl. (46 petals), small blooms in clusters of 3-15; foliage matt; straight, brown prickles; compact, bushy growth.

Rustica HFt (OGR), *yb*, 1929, *Mme. Edouard Herriot* × *Harison's Yellow*; Barbier. Flowers straw-yellow and gold, center apricot, reverse citron-yellow, semi-dbl., medium; fragrant; non-recurrent bloom. RULED EXTINCT 4/81.

Rustica® F, *yb*, 1981, (MEIvilanic; Stadt Basel; Ville de Bâle); *(Queen Elizabeth* × *Seedling)* × *Sweet Promise*; Meilland, M.L.; Meilland Et Cie. Bud very long; flowers yellow-peach blend, reverse buff yellow-orange, dbl. (35 petals), cupped blooms borne 1-14 per cluster; slight fragrance; foliage dark, semi-matt; half upright growth.

Ruth HT, *ob*, 1921, Pemberton. Flowers orange flushed carmine, full, cupped, high-centered, large; fragrant; vigorous, bushy growth.

Ruth G (OGR), *mr*, 1947, *Mary L. Evans* × *Alika*; Wright, P.H. Flowers medium red (less bright than Alika), more dbl. (than Alika); upright growth (to 7 ft.); non-recurrent; sterile.

Ruth, Climbing Cl HT, *ob*, Flowers light orange shaded to red at edges, very dbl., very large; very fragrant; foliage very large, glossy, olive-green; vigorous, climbing growth; recurrent bloom in cool, shady location; not hardy.

Ruth Alexander LCl, *ob*, 1937, *Myra* × *Constance Casson*; Wilber; Bertsch. Bud long, pointed; flowers orange, base yellow, semi-dbl., high-centered, large; fragrant; foliage leathery, glossy, bronze; vigorous, climbing growth.

Ruth Harker HT, *mp*, 1983, (HARpooh); *Fragrant Cloud* × *Compassion*; Harkness, R. Flowers medium pink, dbl. (46 petals), large blooms borne 1-4 per cluster; very fragrant; foliage large, medium green, matt to semi-glossy; slightly curved, reddish prickles; upright, bushy growth.

Ruth Hewitt F, *w*, 1963, *Seedling* × *Queen Elizabeth*; Norman; Harkness. Flowers white, dbl. (36 petals), cupped, large (4 in.), borne in open clusters; slightly fragrant; foliage dark; vigorous, compact growth.

Ruth Leuwerik F, *mr*, 1961, *Käthe Duvigneau* × *Rosemary Rose*; deRuiter; Gandy. Flowers bright red, dbl. (30 petals), large (3 in.) blooms in clusters; fragrant; foliage bronze; vigorous, bushy growth.

Ruth Shamburger F, *lp*, 1934, *Kirsten Poulsen* sport; Shamburger, C.S. Flowers light pink.

Ruth Staley Min, *mp*, 1989, (TINstaley); *Electron × Peachy Keen*; Bennett, Dee; Tiny Petals Nursery, 1991. Bud ovoid; flowers medium shell pink, reverse lighter, dbl. (25 petals), high-centered, exhibition, medium, borne singly and occasionally in sprays of 3-5; moderate, fruity fragrance; foliage medium, dark green, semi-glossy, disease resistant; prickles slender, straight, red; fruit globular, green to brown; upright, tall growth.

Ruth Turner Pol, *dp*, 1941, *Étoile Luisante × Sierra Snowstorm*; Moore, R.S.; California Roses. Flowers rose-pink, dbl., high-centered, small, borne in clusters of 5-10; fragrant; foliage glossy, pointed; vigorous, bushy growth.

Ruth Vestal Cl T (OGR), *w*, 1908, (Climbing Bride); *The Bride climbing sport*; Vestal. Flowers snow-white, well formed, very large; fragrant; vigorous growth; recurrent bloom.

Ruth Warner F, *m*, 1978, *Little Darling × Angel Face*; Warner, A.J. Flowers deep lavender, dbl. (48 petals), high-centered, medium, borne singly and in clusters up to 5; extremely fragrant; foliage dark, smooth; very few prickles; upright. ARC TG (B), 1983.

Ruth Woodward F, *or*, 1992, (DICpleasant); *Wishing × seedling*; Dickson Nurseries. Flowers orange-red, full (26-40 petals), large (7+ cms) blooms borne in small clusters; some prickles; foliage medium, medium green, semi-glossy; medium, bushy growth.

Ruthie Min, *w*, 1988, (TINruth); *Sonia × Little Melody*; Bennett, Dee; Tiny Petals Nursery. Flowers cream-white with pink blush on outer petals, aging paler blush, dbl. (25-30 petals), cupped, exhibition, medium, borne usually singly or in sprays 3-5; moderate, damask fragrance; foliage medium, medium green, semi-glossy, aging darker; prickles hooked slightly downward, yellow to reddish; fruit globular, green to brown; upright, tall growth.

Rutilant HT, *mr*, 1960, *Gloire de Cibeins × Independence*; Arles; Roses-France. Bud ovoid; flowers carthamus-red, semi-dbl., open, medium; slightly fragrant; foliage glossy; vigorous, bushy growth.

Ruzyne HT, *rb*, 1936, Mikes. Flowers carmine-red marked rose, large; fragrant.

R. W. Proctor F, *dp*, 1947, *Anne Poulsen sport*; Proctor. Flowers deep rose-pink, single (10-12 petals), large (4 in.), borne in trusses; slightly fragrant; foliage glossy; vigorous growth.

S'Aagaró HT, *mr*, 1959, *Angels Mateu × (Radar × Grand'mère Jenny)*; Dot, S. Bud long, pointed; flowers geranium-red, dbl. (30 pet-

als), high-centered, large; slightly fragrant; foliage dark, glossy; compact growth.

Saarbrücken S, *mr*, 1959, Kordes. Flowers scarlet-red, semi-dbl., large (3 in.) blooms in clusters (up to 20); foliage dark; vigorous, bushy (5 ft.) growth.

Sabaudia HT, *pb*, 1934, *R. foetida hybrid × Harison's Yellow*; Cazzaniga. Flowers pink with gold reflections, base light chrome-yellow, dbl., cupped, large; fragrant; foliage leathery, glossy, dark; vigorous, bushy growth.

Sabine HT, *ob*, 1958, *Dame Edith Helen × Seedling*; Buyl Frères. Flowers salmon, dbl. (40 petals), well formed; vigorous growth.

Sabine HT, *dp*, 1962, (Sabine Sinjen); Tantau, Math. Bud pointed; flowers cherry-red, dbl. (30 petals), high-centered, medium; very fragrant; foliage dark, glossy; upright, bushy growth.

Sabinia HT, *pb*, 1940, *Julien Potin × Sensation*; Aicardi, D.; Giacomasso. Bud ovoid; flowers dark eglantine-pink passing to reddish yellow, dbl., high-centered, large; fragrant; foliage dark, leathery; very vigorous, upright growth. GM, Rome, 1939.

Sabre Dance F, *rb*, 1975, *Mildred Reynolds × Arthur Bell*; Bees. Flowers scarlet, reverse gold, dbl. (40 petals), high-centered, large (4 in.); slightly fragrant; foliage dark; vigorous.

Sabrina HT, *rb*, 1960, *Grand Gala × Premier Bal*; Meilland, M.L.; URS. Flowers crimson, reverse amber-yellow marked crimson, dbl. (35 petals), high-centered, large (5 in.); very fragrant; foliage dark, leathery; vigorous, bushy growth.

Sacajawea F, *mr*, 1982, *(Baccará × Garnet) × Seedling*; Elliott, Charles P. Flowers medium red, semi-dbl. (20 ruffled petals), small blooms borne singly; slight fragrance; foliage medium, medium green, smooth; upright growth.

Sachet™ Min, *m*, 1986, (SAVasach); *Yellow Miniature Seedling × Shocking Blue*; Saville, F. Harmon; Nor'East Min. Roses. Flowers lavender, yellow stamens, dbl. (30 petals), urn-shaped to loose, mini-flora, large blooms borne usually singly; heavy damask fragrance; foliage small, dark, semi-glossy; medium, thin prickles; medium upright, bushy growth.

Sachsengruss HP (OGR), *lp*, 1912, (Tendresse); *Frau Karl Druschki × Mme. Jules Gravereaux*; Neubert; Hoyer; Klemm. Flowers soft flesh, well-formed, very large; vigorous.

Saclay F, *pb*, 1970, *Miss France sport*; Inst. National Agronomique; Commissariat a l'Energie Atomique. Flowers opal, dbl. (20-22 petals), full, cupped, medium (2-3 in.); slightly fragrant; foliage dull, sage-green; bushy growth.

Sadabahar F, *mp*, 1970, *Frolic × Open pollination*; Indian Agric. Research Inst. Bud pointed; flowers pink, semi-dbl., open, medium; foliage glossy, dark; very vigorous, bushy growth.

Sadaranga HT, *mp*, 1977, *Kronenbourg × Peace*; Hardikar. Bud ovoid; flowers medium pink, very dbl. (60 petals), globular, large (4½ in.); slightly fragrant; foliage glossy; vigorous, upright, compact growth.

Sadie Hawkins Min, *pb*, 1989, (SPOhawk); *Roller Coaster × Seedling*; Spooner, Ray; Oregon Miniature Roses, 1990. Bud globular; flowers medium pink with white stripes, reverse white, aging lighter, semi-dbl. (16 petals), urn-shaped, medium, borne usually singly and in sprays of 3-4; moderate, fruity fragrance; foliage medium, medium green, matt; prickles none; fruit globular, medium green; bushy, medium growth.

Sadler Min, *op*, 1983, (BIScof); *Fabergé × Darling Flame*; Bischoff, Francis; Kimbrew-Walter Roses. Flowers orange pink, dbl. (43 petals), HT form, exhibition, small; no fragrance; foliage medium green, matt; upright growth.

Safari F, *my*, 1966, Tantau, Math. Flowers yellow, semi-dbl. (22 petals), cupped, large, borne in trusses; vigorous, compact growth.

Safrano T (OGR), *ab*, 1839, Beauregard. Bud pointed; flowers saffron and apricot-yellow, semi-dbl., large; fragrant; vigorous growth.

Saga F, *w*, 1973, *Rudolph Timm × (Chanelle × Piccadilly)*; Harkness, 1974. Flowers creamwhite, single (12 petals), small (2½ in.) blooms in clusters; slightly fragrant.

Sahara HT, *w*, 1956, *Mrs. Wemyss Quinn × Mev. G.A. van Rossem*; Stevenson; Waterer. Bud golden yellow; flowers creamy buff, well shaped; very vigorous, upright growth; rather late bloom.

Saïd F, *rb*, 1964, *Aloha × Pioupiou*; Arles; Roses-France. Bud ovoid; flowers cinnabar-red, reverse dark red, dbl. (28 petals), cupped, medium, borne in clusters on short stems.

Sailoz Mookherjea F, *or*, 1974, *Seedling × Seedling*; Pal. Flowers cadmium-orange to orange-vermilion, dbl. (20 petals), high-centered, large (3 in.); slightly fragrant; very vigorous growth.

Saint Alban F, *mr*, 1977, *Marlena × Seedling*; Harkness. Flowers red, semi-dbl. (15 petals), large (3 in.); slightly fragrant; foliage glossy; dwarf.

St. Boniface F, *or*, 1982, (KORmatt); *Diablotin × Traumerei*; Kordes, W., 1980. Flowers or-

ange-red, dbl. (35 petals), patio, medium; slight fragrance; foliage medium, dark, semiglossy.

St. Bruno F, *dy*, 1985, (LANpipe); *Arthur Bell × Zambra*; Sealand Nursery. Flowers deep yellow, dbl. (35 petals), large; very fragrant; foliage medium, medium green, semi-glossy; bushy growth. Edland Fragrance Medal, 1986.

St. Cecelia S, *my*, 1987, (AUSmit; St. Cecilia); *Seedling × Seedling*; Austin, David. Flowers pale buff yellow, fading cream, dbl. (40 petals), cupped, medium, borne usually singly and in sprays of 3-12; moderate, myrrh fragrance; foliage small, medium green, matt; small, brown prickles; no fruit; bushy, low, medium growth; repeat bloom.

Saint-Exupéry® HT, *m*, 1961, (DELtos; DELvor; Waltz Time); *(Christopher Stone × Marcelle Gret) × (Holstein × Bayadère)*; D-C. Flowers mauve tinted silvery, dbl., high-centered, large (5 in.); slightly fragrant; vigorous, bushy growth.

Saint Fiacre Pol, *or*, 1965, *Reverence × Sumatra*; Delforge. Bud ovoid; flowers geranium-red, single, cupped, borne in clusters; vigorous, upright growth.

St. Helena HT, *ly*, 1912, Cant, B.R. Flowers creamy yellow, center pinkish. GM. NRS. 1912 RULED EXTINCT 6/83.

St. Helena F, *mp*, 1983, (CANlish; Union-Rose St. Helena); *Jubilant × Prima Ballerina*; Cants of Colchester. Flowers medium lilac pink, semi-dbl. (20 petals), medium; slight fragrance; foliage medium, medium green, semi-glossy; upright growth.

St. Hilaire Sp (OGR), *mp*, *R. blanda form*; No prickles.

St. Hughs HT, *my*, 1987, (KORhug); *Seedling × Seedling*; Kordes, W.; The Rose Nursery, 1986. Flowers creamy yellow, full (26-40 petals), large; fragrant; foliage medium, medium green, semi-glossy; upright, bushy growth.

St. Ingebert HP (OGR), *w*, 1926, *Frau Karl Druschki × Mme. Mélanie Soupert*; Lambert, P. Bud long, pointed; flowers white, center yellowish and reddish, dbl. (62 petals), large; slightly fragrant; vigorous.

St. John's Rose S, *lp*, (*R. centifolia sancta* Zabel; *R. sancta* Richard, not Andrews; *R. × richardii* Rehder); *R. gallica × R. phoenicia*; Cult. 1902. Flowers rose, 2-2½ in. diam. Abyssinia.

Saint Louis Gr, *w*, 1989, (MALnino); *Lifirane sport*; Maltagliati, Mark G.; C-P, 1989. Flowers white to ivory.

St. Lucia HT, *mp*, 1973, *Seedling × Seedling*; Tantau; Ahrens; Sieberz. Bud ovoid; flowers pink, dbl., medium; fragrant; foliage glossy; moderate, upright, bushy growth.

Saint Mary™ Min, *m*, 1986, (MORyettem); *Little Chief × Angel Face*; Moore, R, S.; Moore Min. Roses. Flowers deep red purple, dbl., cupped, small; slightly fragrant; foliage small, medium green, semi-glossy; small, brown prickles; fruit none; medium, upright, bushy growth.

St. Nicholas D (OGR), *dp*, 1950, *Spontaneous seedling (Possibly Damask × Gallica)*; Found in garden of R. James; Hilling, 1950. Flowers rich pink, semi-dbl.; vigorous, erect growth.

St. Pauli F, *yb*, 1958, *Masquerade × Karl Herbst*; Kordes, R. Flowers golden yellow edged red to pink, becoming fused, semi-dbl. (15 petals), open, large (3 in.) borne in large clusters; slightly fragrant; foliage dark, glossy; very vigorous, upright, bushy growth.

St. Prist de Breuze Ch (OGR), *rb*, 1838, Desprez. Flowers rich deep crimson with rose center, full, globular, medium.

St. Quentin HT, *rb*, 1986, (KRIleville); *Seedling × Tropicana*; Kriloff, M. Flowers red, silver petal edges; foliage dark, glossy.

Sai-Un HT, *ob*, 1980, *(Miss All-American Beauty × Kagayaki) × Seedling*; Suzuki, S.; Keisei Rose Nursery. Flowers yellow-orange shaded deep orange-red, dbl. (50 petals), large; fragrant; foliage dark, glossy; prickles slanted downward; upright growth.

Salam Aleik HT, *mr*, Origin and name uncertain. Flowers pure red, dbl., very large.

Salamander HP (OGR), *mr*, 1891, Paul, W. Flowers bright scarlet-crimson, dbl., cupped, large; upright growth; non-recurrent bloom.

Salambo HT, *mr*, 1959, Kordes, R.; Vilmorin-Andrieux. Flowers carthamus-red.

Salazar HT, *rb*, Moreira da Silva. Flowers bright velvety red with salmon reflections, petals waved.

Salden Monarch HT, *mp*, 1968, *Ballet × Seedling*; Carrigg. Flowers medium pink, dbl., large; foliage glossy; vigorous growth.

Salet M (OGR), *mp*, 1854, Lacharme. Bud well mossed; flowers rosy pink, full, flat, very large; vigorous growth; some recurrence.

Sallie Lewis HT, *ab*, 1924, *Mme. Charles Lutaud × Gladys Holland*; Morse. Bud long, pointed; flowers creamy apricot, center deeper, dbl.; very fragrant; similar to Souv. de Mme. Boullet.

Sally HT, *mp*, 1938, *Mrs. Charles Russell × Mme. Butterfly*; Spandikow; Eddie. Bud long, pointed; flowers pink, dbl., high-centered; long stems; foliage leathery; vigorous growth. RULED EXTINCT 3/81.

Sally F, *ab*, 1981, *Elizabeth of Glamis sport*; Walker, B.; Homeric Rose Nurseries. Flowers pale apricot, fading to ivory, with pink veins.

Sally Alder HT, *mp*, 1944, *Portadown × Seedling*; Moss; F. Mason. Bud long, pointed; flowers pink, semi-dbl., high-centered, medium; foliage dark; moderate, bushy growth.

Sally Holmes® S, *w*, 1976, *Ivory Fashion × Ballerina*; Holmes, R.; Fryer's Nursery. Flowers creamy white, single (5 petals), large (3¹/₂ in.) blooms in large clusters; slightly fragrant; foliage dark, glossy; vigorous, bushy growth. GM, Baden-Baden, 1980.

Sally Mac F, *ab*, 1981, *(Joyfulness × Paddy McGredy) × (Circus × Joyfulness)*; McCann, Sean; Hughes Roses. Flowers apricot pink blend, yellow at base, dbl. (40 petals), blooms borne 4 per cluster; fragrant; foliage medium, dark, glossy; hooked, red-brown prickles; vigorous, upright growth.

Sally Pigtail HT, *pb*, 1959, *Wilfred Pickles × Karl Herbst*; Mee. Flowers cream flushed rose-pink, dbl. (32 petals), high pointed, large; fragrant; free growth.

Sally Tite HT, *dr*, 1930, Dickson, S.; B&A; Armstrong Nursery. Flowers glowing crimson, dbl., high-centered, very large.

Salmon Arctic LCl, *lp*, 1954, (Everblooming Pillar No. 83); *Seedling × Break o' Day*, *Climbing*; Brownell. Flowers dawn-pink, very dbl. (90-100 petals), large (3¹/₂-4¹/₂ in.); growth like a Hybrid Tea, followed by 4-5 ft. canes that bloom the first season.

Salmon Beauty Pol, *op*, 1929, *Orange King sport*; Wezelenburg. Flowers peach-pink, passing to soft salmon, very dbl., medium, borne in clusters; slightly fragrant; dwarf growth.

Salmon Glory Pol, *op*, 1937, *Gloria Mundi sport*; deRuiter. Flowers pinkish salmon.

Salmon Glow F, *op*, 1970, *Vera Dalton × Seedling*; Sanday. Flowers salmon, dbl. (25 petals), full, large (3 in.); slightly fragrant; foliage matt green; compact, bushy growth.

Salmon Marvel F, *op*, 1958, *Red Pinocchio × Signal Red*; deRuiter; Blaby Rose Gardens. Flowers orange-salmon, dbl. (44 petals), rosette shape, large (2¹/₂-3 in.), borne in trusses; foliage dark, glossy, crinkled; bushy, upright growth.

Salmon Perfection F, *rb*, 1952, deRuiter; A. Dickson; McGredy. Flowers scarlet-red shaded orange, dbl. (25 petals), cupped, medium, borne in trusses; foliage dark, leathery; vigorous growth.

Salmon Queen Pol, *op*, 1923, *Juliana Rose sport*; Den Ouden. Flowers deep salmon.

Salmon Spray F, *pb*, 1923, *Orléans Rose, Climbing × Midnight Sun*; Grant; Kershaw. Flowers light salmon-pink, reverse carmine, semi-dbl., cupped, borne in clusters; fragrant; foliage rich green, leathery; very vigorous, bushy growth.

Salmon Sprite F, *op*, 1964, *Seedling × Jiminy Cricket*; LeGrice. Flowers salmon suffused strawberry, dbl. (40 petals), large (3 in.) blooms in cluster to 15; very fragrant; upright growth.

Salmone Gr, *lp*, 1968, *Queen Elizabeth sport*; Faassen-Houba. Bud ovoid; flowers light pink, medium., borne in clusters; foliage dark.

Salmonea Pol, *op*, 1927, Cutbush. Flowers salmon-pink.

Salmon-King F, *rb*, 1972, *Show Girl × Orange Sensation*; Ellick; Excelsior Roses. Flowers red, inside orange-red, dbl. (28-30 petals), full, high pointed, large (5 in.); very fragrant; foliage glossy; vigorous, bushy growth.

Salomé HT, *op*, 1945, Gaujard. Bud ovoid; flowers salmon-flesh-pink, dbl., medium; fragrant; foliage glossy; very vigorous, upright growth.

Salomé F, *pb*, 1958, Buyl Frères. Flowers rose-orange, dbl.; vigorous growth.

Salou F, *pb*, 1971, *Astoria × Tiffany*; Delforge. Bud long, pointed; flowers deep pink to flesh-pink, dbl., open, large; fragrant; foliage dark, leathery; very vigorous, upright growth.

Salsa HT, *dr*, 1990, (JACstop); *Showstopper × Seedling*; Warriner, William A.; Bear Creek Gardens. Bud ovoid, pointed; flowers dark red, very dbl. (30-35 petals), urn-shaped, high-centered, exhibition, large, borne singly; moderate damask fragrance; foliage medium, dark green, semi-glossy; few prickles; upright, tall growth.

Saltaire HT, *dr*, 1925, Dickson, A. Bud long, pointed; flowers deep velvety crimson, dbl.; very fragrant.

Saltatina F, *or*, 1974, *Zorina × Fillette*; Lens. Bud ovoid; flowers orange-copper to red, dbl. (18-22 petals), open, large (2½-3 in.); fragrant (spicy); foliage dark; bushy, spreading growth.

Saltwell Park F, *mr*, 1976, *Paddy McGredy × Arabian Nights*; Wood. Flowers very deep scarlet, semi-dbl. (20 petals), full, large (3 in.); slightly fragrant; foliage dark; moderate, upright growth.

Salutation LCl, *op*, 1972, *Salute × Mme. Isaac Pereire*; Oliver, W.G. Flowers salmon, dbl. (38 petals), full, small (2½ in.); very fragrant; foliage glossy, dark; very vigorous growth.

Salute F, *rb*, 1958, *Masquerade × Lady Sylvia*; McGredy, S., IV; McGredy. Flowers cherry and ocher bicolor, semi-dbl. (20 petals), small (1½ in.) borne in trusses; foliage dark, leathery; free growth.

Salvo HT, *mr*, 1959, *Happiness × Grand Gala*; Herholdt, J.A.; Herholdt's Nursery. Flowers velvety crimson, dbl. (45 petals), large (5 in.); fragrant; vigorous, bushy growth.

Sam F, *r*, 1981, (STEsam); *Brown Eye × Seedling*; Stephens, Paddy. Flowers russet, reverse cream, dbl. (20 petals); slight fragrance; foliage medium, dark, glossy; bushy.

Sam Ferris F, *ob*, 1967, *Heidleberg sport*; Ellick. Flowers orange-scarlet, full, borne in trusses; slightly fragrant; vigorous growth.

Sam McGredy HT, *yb*, 1937, *Delightful × Mrs. Charles Lamplough*; McGredy. Flowers dark cream, base sunflower-yellow, high-centered, large; slightly fragrant; foliage dark, leathery; vigorous. Not to be confused with Mrs. Sam McGredy. GN, NRS, 1935.

Samantha® HT, *mr*, 1974, (JACmantha; JACanth); *Bridal Pink × Seedling*; Warriner; J&P. Bud ovoid; flowers medium red, dbl., high-centered, flora-tea, medium; slightly fragrant; foliage leathery; vigorous, upright growth.

Samba® F, *yb*, 1964, (KORcapas); Kordes, R. Bud globular; flowers golden yellow touched red, becoming fiery red, medium blooms in clusters; foliage glossy; low, bushy growth.

Sammetglut F, *dr*, 1943, *Holstein × Kardinal*; Kordes. Bud long, pointed; flowers crimson, semi-dbl., open, very large, borne in clusters; slightly fragrant; foliage dark, leathery; very vigorous, upright, bushy growth.

Sammy HMsk (S), *dr*, 1921, *(Trier × Watta) × Gruss an Teplitz*; Pemberton. Bud small; flowers carmine, semi-single, borne in erect clusters; slightly fragrant; foliage glossy, bronze; very vigorous, bushy growth; recurrent bloom.

Samoa Sunset HT, *ob*, 1965, *McGredy's Sunset sport*; Lone Star Rose Nursery. Flowers chrome-yellow and copper-orange, dbl., open, large; fragrant; foliage glossy, bronze; vigorous, bushy, compact growth.

Samson™ Min, *mr*, 1986, (SAVasam; Sampson); *Sheri Anne × (Yellow Jewel × Tamango)*; Saville, F. Harmon; Nor'East Min. Roses. Flowers brilliant scarlet red, dbl. (28 petals), urn-shaped, medium blooms in sprays of 20-60; slight fragrance; foliage large, dark, semi-glossy; long, thin, prickles; tall, upright growth.

Samuel Marsden Ch (OGR), *mp*, 1989, *Slater's Crimson China sport*; Nobbs, Kenneth J., 1987. Flowers medium pink.

Samuel Pepys HT, *w*, 1934, Cant, B.R. Flowers white, center slightly shaded cream, dbl., globular, very large; fragrant; foliage leathery; bushy growth.

San Antonio Gr, *or*, 1967, *Roundelay × El Capitan*; Armstrong, D.L.; Armstrong Nursery. Bud ovoid; flowers orange-red, dbl., large; foliage dark, glossy, leathery; very vigorous, upright, bushy growth.

San Diego HT, *my*, 1968, *Helen Traubel × Tiffany*; Armstrong, D.L.; Armstrong Nursery. Bud ovoid; flowers light yellow, dbl. (50 petals), high-centered, large; fragrant; foliage leathery; vigorous, upright, bushy, compact growth.

San Fernando HT, *mr*, 1948, *Heart's Desire × (Crimson Glory × Poinsettia)*; Morris; Western Rose Co. Flowers scarlet, dbl. (30 petals), high-centered, large; very fragrant; vigorous, upright growth. AARS, 1948.

San Fernando, Climbing Cl HT, *mr*, 1951, Whisler; Germain's.

San Francisco HT, *mr*, 1962, *Dean Collins × Independence*; Lammerts; Germain's; Amling-DeVor Nursery. Bud ovoid; flowers signal-red, dbl. (40 petals), high-centered to cupped, large (4-5 in.); fragrant; foliage dark, glossy, leathery; vigorous, compact, branching.

San Gabriel HT, *op*, 1947, *Poinsettia × Seedling*; Morris; Germain's. Bud long, pointed; flowers deep salmon-pink, dbl. (45 petals), high-centered, large (5½ in.); fragrant; foliage dark, leathery; vigorous, bushy growth.

San Joaquin HT, *ob*, 1939, *Talisman sport*; Moore, R.S. Flowers glowing orange.

San José HT, *ob*, 1933, Vve. Denoyel; J&P. Bud ovoid; flowers orange-salmon suffused gold, dbl., very large; fragrant; foliage glossy; very vigorous growth.

San Jose Sunshine Min, *dy*, 1991, (FOUsun); *(Rise 'n' Shine × Redgold) × Summer Madness*; Jacobs, Betty A., 1987; Sequoia Nursery, 1991. Bud pointed; flowers deep golden yellow, aging light yellow with orange highlights, dbl. (25-30 petals), high-centered, exhibition, medium blooms borne usually singly or in sprays of up to 10; slight, fruity to tea fragrance; foliage medium, medium green, matt; bushy, spreading, medium to tall growth.

San Luis Rey HT, *dy*, 1947, *Lady Forteviot × Pedralbes*; Morris; Germain's. Bud ovoid; flowers deep saffron-yellow, dbl. (40 petals), cupped, large (4½ in.); very fragrant; foliage dark, glossy; bushy growth.

SANcharm HMoy (S), *lp*, 1985, (Pink Nevada); *Nevada sport*; Sanday, John, 1970. Flowers pale lilac pink.

Sanctus K (S), *w*, 1978, *Borealis × Borealis*; James, John. Flowers pure white, dbl. (36 petals), HT-form, large blooms borne singly; moderate fragrance; foliage large, dark, leathery; large, straight, rust-brown prickles; vigorous, upright, tall growth; repeat bloom.

Sandar HT, *rb*, 1946, *Charles P. Kilham × Lleida*; Laperrière. Flowers carmine, center yellow, dbl. (25 petals), large; foliage dark; very vigorous growth.

Sander's White Rambler R, *w*, 1912, Sander & Sons. Flowers white, rosette form, small blooms in large clusters; fragrant; foliage bright green, glossy; vigorous growth.

S. & M. Perrier HT, *pb*, 1936, *Magdalena de Nubiola × Pres. Cherioux*; Mallerin; C-P. Flowers very pale rose-pink, with orange glow, dbl. (60 petals), high-centered, large; slightly fragrant; foliage glossy; vigorous growth.

Sandolina de Major HT, *dp*, 1977, *Dr. A.J. Verhage × Königin der Rosen*; Kordes, W., Sons; Willemse. Bud ovoid; flowers deep pink, very dbl. (57 petals), cupped, large (4 in.); fragrant; vigorous, upright growth.

SandraRs HT, *op*, 1981, (SandKOR); *Mercedes × Seedling*; Kordes, W. Flowers salmon, dbl. (35 petals), high-centered, large; slight fragrance; foliage medium, medium green, matt; upright growth.

Sandringham F, *my*, 1955, Kordes; Morse. Flowers yellow, dbl. (30 petals), medium (2½ in.) blooms in large clusters; fragrant; foliage light green, glossy; vigorous, tall.

Sandringham Centenary HT, *op*, 1980, (Sandringham Century); *Queen Elizabeth × Baccará*; Wisbech Plant Co., 1981. Bud pointed; flowers deep salmon-pink, semi-dbl. (22 petals), blooms borne singly; fragrant; foliage dark, glossy; vigorous, upright growth.

Sands of Time™ Min, *r*, 1989, (MINazco); *Tom Brown × Twilight Trail*; Williams, Ernest D.; Mini-Roses. Flowers russet, dbl. (32 petals), exhibition, small; very fragrant; foliage small, medium green, glossy; upright, bushy growth.

Sangerhausen HMsk (S), *dp*, 1938, *Ingar Olsson × Eva*; Kordes. Bud long, pointed; flowers deep pink, semi-dbl., cupped, large blooms in large clusters; slightly fragrant; foliage large, leathery, wrinkled; vigorous (4-5 ft.), bushy growth; repeat bloom.

Sangria® F, *or*, 1966, (MEIestho); *Fire King × (Happiness × Independence)*; Meilland, M.L.; URS. Flowers orange-red, semi-dbl. (15 wavy petals), in large trusses; vigorous. GM, Geneva; The Hague, 1966.

Sanguinaire HRg (S), *pb*, 1933, *Bergers Erfolg* × *Capt. Ronald Clerk*; Gillot, F. Bud long, pointed; flowers brilliant oxblood-red with orange, stamens yellow, semi-dbl. (18 petals), open, large (4 in.); short stems; slightly fragrant; foliage glossy; shrub or pillar (6½ ft.) grwth; recurrent bloom.

Sanguinea Ch (OGR), *dr*, (Bengal Cramoisi Double; Blood-red China); Rose; La Sanguine; R. indica cruenta Prior to 1824. Flowers velvety, vivid purple crimson, very dbl., petals concave with white bases, globular, medium; branches, leaves, and flowered stalks very purple; weak, spreading growth. Erroneously equated with *Miss Lowe*, which is single.

Sankt Anton Pol, *mr*, 1971, *Alain* × *Seedling*; Delforge. Bud long, pointed; flowers brilliant red, single, open, small; slightly fragrant; foliage leathery; vigorous, upright growth; profuse, continuous bloom.

Sanmez F, *rb*, 1977, (SANdokan); Sande; Pekmez. Flowers red blend, dbl. (27-32 petals).

Sanremo HT, *mr*, 1962, *(Pink Delight* × *Rome Glory)* × *Baccará*; Mansuino, Q.; Carlton Rose Nursery. Bud ovoid, pointed; flowers cardinal-red, dbl. (20-30 petals), high-centered to cupped, large (5½-6 in.); strong stems; fragrant; foliage glossy; vigorous, upright, bushy growth.

Santa Anita HT, *mp*, 1932, *(Mrs. J.D. Eisele* × *Seedling)* × *E.G. Hill*; Howard, F.H.; H&S. Bud long, pointed; flowers medium pink, dbl. (22 petals), high-centered, large (3½-4 in.); fragrant; foliage light; vigorous, bushy growth.

Santa Anita, Climbing Cl HT, *mp*, 1946, Howard, F.H.; H&S.

Santa Catalina Cl F, *lp*, 1970, *Paddy McGredy* × *Heidelberg*; McGredy, S., IV; McGredy. Flowers light pink, semi-dbl. (18 petals), medium (3½ in.); slightly fragrant.

Santa Claus Min, *dr*, 1991, (POUlclaus); *Floribunda seedling* × *Miniature seedling*; Olesen, M.&P.; Weeks Roses, 1995. Bud long, well-formed; flowers even, clean dark red, moderately full (15-25 petals), medium (4-7 cms) blooms borne mostly singly; slight fragrance; foliage medium, dark green, glossy, sepal inside tinted red; few prickles; medium (50-60 cms), upright, bushy growth.

Santa Fé HT, *op*, 1967, *Mischief* × *Tropicana*; McGredy, S., IV; McGredy. Flowers deep salmon-pink, reverse lighter, dbl., large.

Santa Maria F, *mr*, 1969, *Evelyn Fison* × *(Ma Perkins* × *Moulin Rouge)*; McGredy, S., IV; McGredy. Flowers scarlet, blooms in trusses; slightly fragrant; foliage small.

Santa Rita HT, *op*, 1961, *Independence* × *Papillon Rose*; Lens. Flowers salmon-pink, well formed, large; vigorous growth.

Santa Rosa F, *op*, 1954, *Golden Salmon* × *Pinocchio*; Silva. Bud ovoid; flowers salmon-pink tipped brick, dbl., globular, small; very fragrant; foliage glossy, soft, bronze; vigorous, bushy growth.

Santa Tereza d'Avila HT, *op*, 1959, *Monte Carlo* × *Michèle Meilland*; Moreira da Silva. Flowers salmon-pink and orange, reverse gold, well-formed; fragrant; foliage glossy; vigorous growth. GM, Madrid, 1959.

Santana® LCl, *mr*, 1985, (TANklesant); Tantau, M., 1984. Flowers medium red, semi-dbl. (20 petals), medium; no fragrance; foliage large, medium green, glossy; upright.

Saonara HT, *mr*, 1962, *Baccará* × *Peace*; Borgatti; Sgaravatti. Flowers geranium-red, dbl.; strong stems; foliage dark; vigorous growth.

Sapho HT, *ob*, 1933, Gaujard. Flowers salmon, tinted coppery, dbl., very large; slightly fragrant; foliage leathery, glossy, dark; very vigorous growth.

Sappho T (OGR), *pb*, 1889, Paul, W. Flowers fawn shaded pink, center yellow; vigorous growth.

S. A. Prince Youssof Kamal HP (OGR), *rb*, 1922, *Souv. de Mme. Chédane-Guinoisseau* × *Ulrich Brunner Fils*; Nabonnand, P. Bud long, pointed; flowers crimson, streaked brilliant scarlet, semi-dbl., large; fragrant.

Sarabande® F, *or*, 1957, (MEIhand; MEIrabande); *Cocorico* × *Moulin Rouge*; Meilland, F.; URS, 1957; C-P, 1959. Flowers light orange-red, stamens yellow, semi-dbl. (13 petals), cupped to flat, medium (2½ in.)blooms in large trusses; slightly fragrant; foliage semi-glossy; low, bushy growth. GM, Bagatelle, Geneva; Rome, 1957; Portland, 1958; AARS, 1960.

Sarabande, Climbing® Cl F, *or*, 1968, (MEIhandsar); Meilland; URS. GM, Japan, 1968.

Saragat HT, *rb*, 1968, *Seedling* × *Seedling*; Malandrone. Flowers deep strawberry to cream, dbl., globular, large; very fragrant; foliage leathery; very vigorous growth.

Sarah Arnot HT, *mp*, 1957, *Ena Harkness* × *Peace*; Croll. Flowers warm rose-pink, dbl. (25 petals), large (4½ in.); fragrant; foliage leathery; vigorous, upright growth. GM, NRS, 1958.

Sarah Bacherach F, *mp*, 1965, *Harmonie* × *Buisman's Triumph*; Buisman. Flowers pink, dbl., medium; very fragrant; foliage dark.

Sarah Bernhardt Cl HT, *dr*, 1906, Dubreuil. Flowers scarlet-crimson, semi-dbl., very large.

Sarah Coventry F, *dr*, 1956, *Red Pinocchio* × *Garnette*; Boerner; Stuart. Bud ovoid; flowers cardinal-red, dbl. (40-45 petals), open, cupped, medium, borne in irregular clusters; fragrant; foliage bright green; vigorous, compact, bushy growth.

Sarah Darley HT, *dy*, 1938, Wheatcroft Bros. Flowers clear deep golden yellow, well shaped; foliage dark; vigorous growth.

Sarah Hill F, *mp*, 1956, *Garnette* × *Pink Bountiful*; Hill, J.H., Co. Bud short, pointed; flowers phlox-pink, dbl. (25-30 petals), open, large (2½-3 in.); slightly fragrant (spicy); foliage dark, leathery; vigorous, upright, bushy growth; a forcing variety for greenhouse use.

Sarah Jane HT, *pb*, 1971, *Rose Gaujard* sport; Heath, W.L. Flowers rose-pink, edged deeper, reverse white, dbl. (35 petals), full, large (4½-5 in.); slightly fragrant; foliage glossy; very vigorous, tall growth.

Sarah Lynn HT, *mp*, 1991, *Seedling* × *Prima Ballerina*; Ohlson, John. Flowers medium pink, full, medium blooms borne mostly singly; vigorous, strong stems; slight fragrance; foliage large, dark green, semi-glossy; medium, compact growth. ARC TG (B), 1991.

Sarah Maud HT, *dy*, 1934, Mallerin. Bud long; flowers golden yellow, large; foliage bright, dark; very vigorous growth.

Sarah Robinson Min, *ab*, 1982, (TRObinette); *Rumba* × *Darling Flame*; Robinson, Thomas. Flowers soft apricot, semi-dbl. (20 petals), small; very fragrant; foliage small, dark, glossy; compact, bushy growth.

Sarah Van Fleet HRg (S), *mp*, 1926, *Reported as R. rugosa × My Maryland, but chromosome number makes this improbable*; Van Fleet; ARS. Flowers wild-rose-pink, semi-dbl., cupped, large; very fragrant; foliage leathery, rugose; compact (6-8 ft.) growth; recurrent bloom.

Sarah Wright HT, *dp*, 1927, *Ophelia* × *Emma Wright*; Morse. Bud long, pointed; flowers rose-pink, dbl.; slightly fragrant.

Sarajean Min, *pb*, 1979, *Seedling* × *Over the Rainbow*; Williams, E.D.; Mini-Roses. Bud pointed; flowers peach-pink, dbl. (50 petals), globular, small (1 in.); fragrant; foliage small, bronze-green, glossy; upright, bushy growth.

Saratoga F, *w*, 1963, *White Bouquet* × *Princess White*; Boerner; J&P. Bud ovoid; flowers white, dbl. (33 petals), gardenia-shaped, large (4 in.) blooms in irregular clusters; very fragrant; foliage glossy, leathery; vigorous, upright, bushy growth. AARS, 1964.

Sardane F, *rb*, 1962, Laperrière; EFR. Bud long; flowers coral-red tinted silvery, dbl.

(35-40 petals), large (3 in.); foliage bright green; very bushy, compact growth.

Sargent LCl, *pb*, 1912, *(R. wichuraiana × Crimson Rambler)* × *Baroness Rothschild*; Dawson; Eastern Nursery. Flowers apple-blossomrose to pale pink, base amber-yellow, semidbl., large (3 in.), borne in clusters of 50-60; height 10-12 ft.

Sarie HT, *mp*, 1977, *Pink Favorite* × *Nightingale*; Herholdt, J.A. Flowers medium pink, dbl. (35 petals), large (4½-5 in.); slightly fragrant; foliage glossy, bright green; vigorous.

Sarie Mareis F, *mr*, 1950, *Irene* × *Donald Prior*; Leenders, M. Flowers glowing scarlet.

Saroor F, *or*, 1969, *Gertrud Westphal* × *Open pollination*; Singh; Gopalsinamiengar. Bud ovoid; flowers orange-scarlet, dbl., open, large; slightly fragrant; foliage large, leathery; upright growth.

Saskia F, *mp*, 1961, *Pinocchio* × *Gartenstolz*; Buisman. Flowers pink, single, borne in large clusters; foliage dark; bushy growth.

Sassy™ F, *dr*, 1985, (HILtaco); *Little Leaguer* × *Mary DeVor*; Jelly, Robert; E.G. Hill Co. Flowers dark red, semi-dbl. (20 petals), highcentered, sweetheart, small blooms borne usually singly; slightly fragrant; foliage small, medium green, matt; prickles only on peduncle; fruit small, globular, grayed red; upright growth; greenhouse variety.

Sassy Lassy Min, *yb*, 1975, *Seedling* × *Over the Rainbow*; Williams, E.D.; Mini-Roses. Bud pointed; flowers yellow and pink blend, dbl. (28 petals), small (1 in.); slightly fragrant; foliage small, bronze, glossy, leathery; upright, spreading.

Satan HT, *dr*, 1939, (Joyce Lomax; Satanas); *(Mme. Edouard Herriot × Angèle Pernet)* × *Mari Dot*; Pahissa; J&P. Flowers very dark red, reverse lighter, nearly dbl., high-centered, large; fragrant; foliage leathery; bushy growth.

Satchmo® F, *or*, 1970, *Evelyn Fison* × *Diamant*; McGredy, S., IV; McGredy. Flowers bright scarlet, dbl. (25 petals), HT form, large (3 in.); slightly fragrant. GM, The Hague, 1970.

Satellite® HT, *dr*, 1958, *Editor McFarland* × *William Harvey*; Priestly. Bud pointed; flowers deep crimson, dbl. (30 petals), high-centered, large (4½ in.); very fragrant; foliage dark, glossy; vigorous, upright, compact growth.

Satin Doll F, *ly*, 1986, (JACspif); *Pacifica* sport; Warriner; J&P. Flowers cream to pale apricot.

Satinette Pol, *w*, 1971, *Maria Delforge* × *Irene of Denmark*; Delforge. Bud ovoid; flowers white, dbl., cupped, large; slightly fragrant;

foliage large, light, leathery; vigorous, upright growth.

Satinglo F, *mp*, 1954, *Pinocchio seedling* × *Vogue*; Boerner. Bud globular; flowers glowing coral, dbl. (45-50 petals), cupped, medium, (2½ in.), borne in clusters; fragrant; foliage leathery, glossy; vigorous growth.

Satisfaction HT, *dp*, 1956, *Parfum* × *Seedling*; Verbeek. Flowers carmine-pink, dbl., large; very fragrant.

Satmir HT, *dr*, 1956, *Satan* × *Mirandy*; Dot, P. Flowers carmine-red, dbl.; long, strong stems; very vigorous growth.

Saturnia HT, *rb*, 1936, *Julien Potin* × *Sensation*; Aicardi, D.; Robichon; J&P. Bud long, pointed; flowers bright scarlet with gold, dbl. (20 petals), cupped, large; fragrant (fruity); foliage dark, glossy; vigorous growth. GM, Rome, 1933; Portland, 1938.

Saucy Sue F, *mp*, 1974, *Pink Parfait* × *Europeana*; Lowe. Flowers pink, dbl. (20-25 petals), full, large (3½ in.); fragrant; free growth.

Saudade d'Anibal de Morais HT, *dr*, 1935, *Sir David Davis* × *Pres. Jac. Smits*; Moreira da Silva. Bud velvety crimson; flowers salmony crimson-red, full; vigorous growth.

Saul HT, *dp*, 1970, *Tropicana* × *Sterling Silver*; Gandy. Flowers light rose-madder, dbl. (28 petals), large (4 in.); fragrant; foliage large, dark; upright growth.

SAVanin Min, *rb*, 1986, *Rise 'n' Shine* × *Zinger*; Saville, F. Harmon; SNC Meilland; Cie, 1986. Flowers medium red with yellow center, semi-dbl. (15-25 petals), small; slight fragrance; foliage small, medium green, semi-glossy; bushy growth.

Savannah HT, *ab*, 1980, *Seedling* × *Arizona*; Weeks, O.L. Bud ovoid, pointed; flowers soft apricot, dbl. (32 petals), cupped, borne singly or 2-3 per cluster; slight, spicy fragrance; foliage moderately leathery; long prickles, hooked down; vigorous, upright.

Savannah Miss Min, *ab*, 1990, (PIXanah); *Pounder Star* × *Ann Moore*; Chaffin, Lauren M.; Pixie Treasures Miniature Roses. Bud pointed; flowers dark apricot, edges lighter, medium apricot reverse, fading to soft pink, dbl. (40-50 petals), high-centered, medium, borne singly; moderate fragrance; foliage medium, medium green, semi-glossy; prickles needle-shaped, light tan; fruit globular, medium green; bushy, tall growth.

Save the Children F, *mr*, 1986, (HARtred); *Amy Brown* × *Red Sprite*; Harkness. Flowers bright red, semi-dbl. (20 wavy petals), cupped, patio, medium blooms in clusters; slightly fragrant; foliage dark, semi-glossy;

narrow, straight prickles; low, bushy, compact growth.

Saverne HT, *rb*, 1937, Heizmann, E; A. Meilland. Flowers nasturtium tinted brownish red, reverse tinted yellow, full, large; foliage bright, bronze.

Savoia HT, *m*, 1937, *Julien Potin* × *Sensation*; Aicardi, D.; Giacomasso. Bud pointed, rosy lilac; foliage glossy; vigorous growth.

Savoy Hotel HT, *lp*, 1987, (HARvintage; Integrity;); Vercors; Violette Niestlé *Silver Jubilee* × *Amber Queen*; Harkness, R., 1989. Flowers light phlox pink, reverse shaded deeper, dbl. (40 petals), high-centered, well-formed, exhibition, large, borne usually singly; slight fragrance; foliage medium, dark green, semi-glossy; small, reddish-green, fairly straight, narrow prickles; fruit rounded, average, green; bushy, medium growth. GM, Dublin, 1988.

SAVrojet Min, *dp*, 1986, (*Tamango* × *Yellow Jewel*) × *Watercolor*; Saville, F. Harmon; SNC Meilland; Cie, 1985. Flowers deep pink, semi-dbl. (15-25 petals), small; no fragrance; foliage small, medium green, semi-glossy; bushy growth.

Sayonara HT, *yb*, 1959, *Sunnymount sport*; Grillo. Bud long, pointed; flowers yellow blend tinted pink, dbl. (50 petals), large (5 in.); fragrant; foliage leathery; vigorous, upright growth.

Sazanami Min, *lp*, 1984, *Yorokobi seedling* × *Yellow Doll*; Suzuki, S.; Keisei Rose Nursery, 1982. Flowers soft pink, dbl. (60 petals), flat, small blooms borne 2-5 per cluster; fragrant; foliage dark, semi-glossy; prickles slanted downward; bushy growth. GM, Japan, 1980.

Scabrata S, *m*, *R. corymbifera* × *R. gallica*. Flowers rich pinkish purple, single, large; foliage downy.

Scabrosa HRg (S), *m*, 1950, (*R. rugosa scabrosa* hort.); Origin unknown; Harkness. Flowers mauve-pink, stamens light sulphur, single (5 petals), large (5 in.) blooms in clusters of 5 or more; fragrant (carnation); foliage light, glossy, soft; fruit large, bright red; very bushy (5 ft.) growth; recurrent bloom.

Scamp™ Min, *mr*, 1984, (SAVacamp); *Baby Katie* × (*Yellow Jewel* × *Tamango*); Saville, F. Harmon; Nor'East Min. Roses. Flowers medium red, dbl. (35 petals), HT-form, micromini, small; slight fragrance; foliage small, medium green, semi-glossy; compact, bushy growth.

Scandale HT, *pb*, 1958, *Peace* × *Opera*; Gaujard. Bud pink; flowers crimson shaded coppery, dbl. (25 petals), large (4 in.); long stems; fragrant; foliage glossy, dark; vigorous, upright growth.

Scandia Pol, *op*, 1951, *Margo Koster sport*; van de Water; van Nes. Flowers salmon-orange.

Scania F, *dr*, 1965, *Cocorico × Seedling*; deRuiter. Flowers deep red, well-formed, large (3½ in.); foliage matt.

Scaramouche F, *mr*, 1968, *Ma Perkins × Duet*; Fankhauser. Bud long, pointed; flowers coral-red, dbl. (30-35 petals), high-centered, large; slightly fragrant; foliage leathery; vigorous, compact, tall growth.

Scarlano HSet (OGR), *mr*, 1938, (Faust); *(R. setigera × Papoose) × Paul's Scarlet Climber*; Horvath; Wayside Gardens Co. Flowers cerise-red, semi-dbl., open, borne in clusters on short, strong stems; slightly fragrant; foliage leathery, dark; bushy (2½ ft.) growth; sometimes recurrent bloom.

Scarlet Adventurer HT, *dr*, 1957, Lowe. Flowers scarlet, dbl., medium; foliage dark.

Scarlet Beauty HT, *dr*, 1934, *Mme. Butterfly × Premier Supreme*; Vestal. Flowers crimson-scarlet, dbl., very large; slightly fragrant; vigorous growth.

Scarlet Bedder HT, *ob*, 1927, *Mme. Edouard Herriot × Gen. MacArthur*; Henderson, W.H. Flowers rich orange-scarlet; dwarf growth.

Scarlet Betty Uprichard HT, *dr*, 1930, *Betty Uprichard seedling*; Allen. Bud long, pointed, shaded black; flowers intense scarlet, semi-dbl., cupped; very fragrant; foliage thick, light; vigorous growth.

Scarlet Button Pol, *dr*, 1932, *Locarno sport*; Dreer. Flowers brilliant scarlet.

Scarlet Crampel Pol, *dr*, *Paul Crampel sport*. Flowers scarlet.

Scarlet Else F, *dr*, *Else Poulsen × Hybrid Tea seedling (red)*; Kordes, about 1925. Flowers scarlet, single (10-12 petals), large (3-4 in.), borne in trusses; slightly fragrant; foliage leathery; very free growth.

Scarlet Emperor HT, *mr*, 1961, *Karl Herbst × Fandango*; LeGrice; Wayside Gardens Co. Flowers scarlet-red, dbl., high-centered, large; vigorous, upright growth.

Scarlet Flame HT, *mr*, 1934, Burbank; Stark Bros. Flowers brilliant red, dbl., petals recurved and fringed, large; fragrant; very vigorous growth.

Scarlet Garnette F, *mr*, 1971, *Garnette sport*; Newberry. Flowers scarlet, dbl. (45 petals), globular, small; slightly fragrant; foliage dark; vigorous growth.

Scarlet Gem® Min, *or*, 1961, (MEIdo; Scarlet Pimpernel); *(Moulin Rouge × Fashion) × (Perla de Montserrat × Perla de Alcañada)*; Meilland, A.; C-P. Bud ovoid; flowers orange-scarlet, dbl. (58 petals), cupped, small (1 in.); slightly fragrant; foliage dark, glossy, leathery; bushy, dwarf (12-15 in.) growth.

Scarlet Glory HT, *ob*, 1925, Dickson, A. Bud long, pointed; flowers orange-scarlet, dbl., high-centered; slightly fragrant; foliage leathery, rich green.

Scarlet Glow HT, *dr*, 1945, *Briarcliff sport*; Sodano, A.; St. Leonards Farms. Flowers brilliant velvety scarlet.

Scarlet Knight Gr, *mr*, 1966, (MEIelec; Samourai); *(Happiness × Independence) × Sutter's Gold*; Meilland, M.L.; URS, 1966; C-P, 1967. Bud ovoid; flowers crimson-scarlet, dbl., cupped, large (4-5 in.); slightly fragrant; foliage leathery; vigorous, upright, bushy growth. GM, Madrid, 1966; AARS, 1968.

Scarlet Knight, Climbing Cl Gr, *mr*, 1972, (Samourai, Climbing); *Scarlet Knight sport*; Jack; A. Ross & Son.

Scarlet Lady Min, *mr*, 1990, *Anita Charles × Chris Jolly*; Jolly, Nelson F., 1983; Rosehill Farm, 1991. Bud ovoid; flowers medium red, aging light pink, dbl. (30 petals), cupped, exhibition, large, borne singly; no fragrance; foliage medium, dark green, semi-glossy; upright, medium growth.

Scarlet Leader Pol, *ob*, 1927, Wezelenburg. Flowers brilliant orange-scarlet, dbl., large, borne in clusters.

Scarlet Mariner F, *mr*, 1972, *Seedling × Showboat*; Patterson; Patterson Roses. Flowers bright scarlet-red, dbl., high-centered, medium; fragrant; foliage leathery; vigorous, bushy growth.

Scarlet Marvel F, *mr*, 1958, *Alain × Floribunda seedling*; deRuiter; C-P. Flowers orange-scarlet, dbl. (45-50 petals), medium (2½ in.), borne in flat clusters; foliage leathery; vigorous, compact growth; a forcing variety.

Scarlet Meidiland™ S, *mr*, 1987, (MEIkrotal; Scarlet Meillandécor); *MEItiraca × Clair Matin*; Meilland, Mrs. Marie-Louise; SNC Meilland; Cie, 1985. Flowers light cherry red, reverse dark carmine pink, semi-dbl. (15-25 petals), small; no fragrance; foliage medium, dark green, glossy; spreading growth.

Scarlet Moss™ Min, *mr*, 1988, (MORcarlet); *(Dortmund × Moss Miniature seedling) × (Dortmund × Moss Miniature striped seedling)*; Moore, Ralph S.; Sequoia Nursery. Flowers intense, scarlet-red, semi-dbl., open, small, borne in sprays of 3-10; mini-moss; no fragrance; foliage medium, medium green, glossy, leathery; prickles slender, various, green to brown; fruit round elongated, orange; very mossy sepals; attractive yellow stamens; upright, bushy, tall growth.

Scarlet Queen F, *dr*, 1939, *Dance of Joy × Crimson Glory*; Kordes; Morse. Bud long, pointed; flowers pure scarlet, dbl., open, large, borne in clusters on long stems; slightly fragrant; foliage glossy, leathery, bronze; vigorous, bushy growth.

Scarlet Queen Elizabeth® F, *or*, 1963, (DICel); *(Korona × Seedling) × Queen Elizabeth*; Dickson, P.; A. Dickson. Flowers flame-scarlet, dbl., globular, medium; slightly fragrant; foliage dark; vigorous, tall growth. GM, The Hague, 1973; Golden Rose of The Hague, 1973.

Scarlet Ribbon Cl Min, *dr*, 1961, *((Soeur Thérèse × Wilhelm) × (Seedling × Red Ripples)) × Zee*; Moore, R.S.; Sequoia Nursery. Bud ovoid; flowers red, sometimes almost maroon, dbl. (50 petals), high-centered, small (1¼ in.); slightly fragrant; vigorous (3 ft.) growth.

Scarlet Royal HT, *mr*, 1963, *Karl Herbst × Independence*; Park; Tantau. Flowers scarlet, base yellow, well formed; vigorous growth.

Scarlet Ruffles Min, *or*, 1990, *Poker Chip × Zinger*; Gruenbauer, Richard, 1984; Richard Gruenbauer. Bud pointed; flowers orange-red with yellow eye, aging to light red, single (8 petals), loose, large, borne in sprays of 2-5; heavy, spicy fragrance; foliage medium, dark green, glossy; prickles straight, slightly hooked downwards, tan; fruit oblong, gold and orange; spreading, medium growth.

Scarlet Sensation LCl, *dr*, 1954, (Everblooming Pillar No.73); *Seedling × Queen o' the Lakes*; Brownell. Bud high pointed, crimson; flowers rose-madder, dbl. (35 petals), large (3½-4½ in.) borne in clusters; fragrant; growth like a Hybrid Tea, followed by 4-5 foot canes that bloom the first season; free bloom.

Scarlet Sunblaze™ Min, *dr*, 1982, (MEIcubasi; Scarlet Meillandina); *Tamango × (Baby Bettina × Duchess of Windsor)*; Meilland, M.L.; C-P, 1980. Flowers dark red, semi-dbl., (20 petals), medium; no fragrance; foliage medium, dark, matt; bushy growth.

Scarlet Sunset F, *or*, 1970, *Orange Sensation × Seedling*; deRuiter; Geo. deRuiter. Flowers orange-red, semi-dbl. (12 petals), small, borne on trusses; foliage dark, leathery; moderate bushy growth.

Scarlet Triumph F, *rb*, 1951, *Orange Triumph sport*; Poulter. Bud ovoid; flowers deep scarlet, base yellow, semi-dbl., cupped, small, borne in clusters; slightly fragrant; foliage glossy, light green; vigorous, bushy growth.

Scarlet Waves F, *mr*, 1961, *(Florence Mary Morse × Border Queen) × Mrs. Inge Poulsen*; Bennett, H.; Pedigree Nursery. Flowers bright scarlet, ruffled petals; tall growth.

Scarlet Wonder F, *or*, 1958, *Signal Red × Fashion*; deRuiter; Blaby Rose Gardens. Flowers bright orange-scarlet, semi-dbl., flat, large (3 in.), borne in clusters; slightly fragrant; foliage dark, glossy; vigorous growth.

Scarletina Min, *or*, 1985, *Futura × Poker Chip*; Hardgrove, Donald L.; Rose World Originals. Flowers orange-red, dbl. (40+ petals), spiraled, medium blooms borne usually singly; fragrant; foliage small, medium green, semi-glossy; upright, bushy growth.

Scarlett O'Hara Pol, *rb*, 1947, *Gloria Mundi sport*; Klyn. Bud ovoid; flowers brilliant red, overcast orange, dbl., open, large, borne in clusters; slightly fragrant; foliage leathery; vigorous, bushy growth.   RULED EXTINCT 2/88.

Scarlett O'Hara™ Gr, *mr*, 1987, (AROresas); *Red Success × Mary DeVor*; Christensen, Jack; Carruth, Tom; Armstrong Roses, 1986. Flowers medium red, dbl. (35 petals), high-centered, exhibition, medium, borne usually singly; slight fragrance; foliage medium, medium green, semi-glossy; nearly thornless; upright, tall growth.

Scented Air F, *op*, 1965, *Spartan seedling × Queen Elizabeth*; Dickson, P.; A. Dickson. Flowers salmon-pink, dbl., well-formed, large (5 in.) blooms in clusters; very fragrant; foliage very large; vigorous growth. GM, The Hague, 1965; Belfast, 1967.

Scented Bowl HT, *dr*, 1965, *Gen. MacArthur × Seedling*; Pal; Indian Agric. Research Inst. Bud ovoid; flowers bright red, dbl., medium; very fragrant; foliage glossy; open, upright growth.

Scented Star HT, *lp*, 1973, *Fragrant Cloud × Spek's Yellow*; Lowe. Flowers coral-pink, dbl. (30-35 petals), classic form, large (5-5½ in.); very fragrant; foliage dark; moderate growth.

Sceptre HT, *ob*, 1923, McGredy. Flowers bright flame, base shaded orange, reverse dull yellow; low growth.

Schaffners Erfolg F, *mr*, *Red Favorite × Fanal*; Tantau. Flowers red, dbl. (30 petals), medium (2 in.), borne in trusses; vigorous, bushy growth.

Scharlachglut S, *dr*, 1952, (Scarlet Fire; Scarlet Glow); *Poinsettia × Alika*; Kordes. Flowers scarlet-crimson, single, large (5 in.); foliage dull green; vigorous (4-5 ft.), dense, spreading growth.

Scharnkeana S, *m*, (R. × scharnkeana Graebner); *R. californica × R. nitida*; Orig. prior to 1900. Flowers rose-purple, 1-5 together; 3 ft.

Schéhérazade HT, *mr*, 1942, Mallerin; A. Meilland. Bud large, oval; flowers fiery red, dbl., cupped; slightly fragrant; foliage dark, glossy; vigorous, bushy growth. GM, Rome, 1940.

Scherzo® F, *rb*, 1975, (MEIpuma); *Tamango × Frenzy*; Paolino; URS. Flowers bright scarlet, reverse white and crimson, dbl. (40 petals), high-centered, spiraled, large (3¹/₂ in.); foliage dark; vigorous, bushy growth. GM, Belfast, 1975.

Schiehallion HT, *mr*, 1982, *Red Planet × Bonnie Anne*; MacLeod, Major C.A. Flowers medium red, dbl. (50 petals), large (4¹/₂ in.); very fragrant; foliage medium, medium green, glossy; upright growth.

Schiller R, *mp*, 1913, *Trier × Lady Mary Fitzwilliam*; Lambert, P. Flowers clear pink, medium, borne in clusters.

Schleswig-Holstein HT, *rb*, 1921, *Mme. Edouard Herriot sport*; Engelbrecht. Flowers reddish yellow.

Schloss Mannheim® F, *or*, 1975, (KORschloss); *Marlena × Europeana*; Kordes. Flowers red-orange, dbl., globular; slightly fragrant; foliage dark, leathery; vigorous, upright, bushy. ADR, 1972.

Schloss Moritzburg F, *dr*, 1967, *Donald Prior × Seedling*; Haenchen; Teschendorff. Flowers dark red, semi-dbl., cupped, medium; slightly fragrant; foliage dark, leathery; vigorous growth.

Schloss Seutlitz HSpn (OGR), *ly*, 1936, *R. spinosissima hybrid*; Dechan. Flowers light yellow, semi-dbl., very large; moderate growth; very early bloom.

Schmid's Ideal Sp (OGR), *lp*, *R. canina strain*; R. Schmid. Selected thorny strain of *R. canina*, used as an understock.

Schneekopf HP (OGR), *w*, 1903, *Mignonette × Souv. de Mme. Sablayrolles*; Lambert, P. Flowers snow-white, regular form; vigorous growth; recurrent bloom.

Schneelicht HRg (S), *w*, 1894, Geschwind. Flowers pure white, single, large blooms in clusters; very vigorous, climbing growth; makes an impenetrable, prickly hedge; very hardy.

Schneeprinzessin HT, *w*, 1946, Meilland, F.; Pfitzer. Bud long; flowers white, large; very fragrant; vigorous growth.

Schneeschirm F, *w*, 1946, *Johanna Tantau × (Karen Poulsen × Stammler)*; Tantau, 1956. Flowers white, center tinted rose-yellow, single, large blooms in clusters of 8-40; slightly fragrant; foliage dark.

Schneewalzer F, *w*, 1972, (TANschneewa); Tantau. Bud ovoid; flowers white, dbl., large; moderate, upright growth.

Schneewittchen Pol, *ly*, 1901, *Aglaia × (Pâquerette × Souv. de Mme. Levet)*; Lambert, P. Flowers yellow fading to white.

Schneezwerg HRg (S), *w*, 1912, (Snow Dwarf; Snowdwarf); *Possibly R. rugosa × Polyantha hybrid*; Lambert, P. Flowers snow-white, stamens golden yellow, semi-dbl., flat blooms in clusters of 3-10; foliage glossy, rugose; fruit abundant, small, red; vigorous (3-4 ft.), spiny growth; recurrent bloom; (14).

Schoener's Musk HMsk (S), *w*, Schoener. Flowers milk-white, medium; enormous trusses; vigorous, pillar growth.

Schoener's Nutkana HNut (S), *mp*, 1930, *R. nutkana × Paul Neyron*; Schoener; C-P. Flowers clear rose-pink, single, large (4 in.) blooms in arching canes; fragrant; few prickles; vigorous, shrub (4-6 ft.) growth; non-recurrent bloom.

Schöne Münchnerin® F, *mr*, 1984, (KORleen; Bavarian Girl); *Sympathie × Tornado*; Kordes, W.; Kordes; Ludwig Roses. Flowers medium red, dbl. (22 petals), cupped, medium blooms borne 2-3 per cluster; slight fragrance; foliage medium, medium green, semi-glossy; medium, green prickles; bushy growth.

Schöne von Holstein Pol, *mp*, 1919, *Orléans Rose × Seedling*; Tantau. Flowers pure hermosa pink, dbl.

Schöne von Kaiserslautern F, *op*, 1957, *R.M.S. Queen Mary × Obergärtner Wiebicke*; Kordes. Bud long, pointed; flowers orange tinted salmon-red, dbl. (30 petals), high-centered, large (4 in.); strong stems; very fragrant; foliage dark, leathery; very vigorous, upright, bushy growth; free, intermittent bloom.

Schöne von Marquardt R, *rb*, 1928, *Sodenia sport*; Clauberg. Flowers bright dark red, variegated with white; vigorous, climbing growth.

Schonerts Meisterklasse HT, *or*, 1952, Leenders, M. Flowers salmon and coral-red, full, well formed, very large; fragrant; vigorous growth.

Schoolgirl LCl, *ab*, 1964, *Coral Dawn × Belle Blonde*; McGredy, S., IV; McGredy. Flowers orange-apricot, well-formed, large (4 in.); recurrent bloom.

Schubert® S, *pb*, 1984, (LENmor); *Ballerina × R. multiflora*; Lens. Flowers pink, white-eye, single (5 petals), 1 in. blooms in clusters of 7-60; slight fragrance; foliage small; very hooked, greenish-brown prickles; bushy, spreading growth; recurrent bloom.

Schwabenland HRg (S), *mp*, 1928, *R. rugosa seedling × Elizabeth Cullen*; Berger, V.; Pfitzer. Flowers amaranth-pink, dbl., open, large; fragrant; foliage large, rich green, leathery; vigorous (3 ft.) growth; profuse, recurrent bloom.

Schwäbische Heimat HT, *dr*, 1934, *Jonkheer J.L. Mock sport*; Pfitzer. Flowers deep amaranth-red, dbl.

Schweizer Gold HT, *ly*, 1975, (Swiss Gold); *Peer Gynt × King's Ransom*; Kordes; Horstmann. Bud ovoid; flowers light yellow, dbl., high-centered; fragrant; foliage large, light; vigorous growth. GM, Baden-Baden, 1972.

Schwerin HMsk (S), *dp*, 1937, *Eva × D.T. Poulsen*; Kordes. Bud long, pointed; flowers light crimson, open, cupped, large; clusters on long, strong stems; fragrant (musk); foliage large, leathery, glossy, bronze; very vigorous, bushy; profuse, intermittent bloom.

Scintillation S, *lp*, 1967, *R. macrantha × Vanity*; Austin, D.; Sunningdale Nursery. Flowers pink, semi-dbl., blooms in large clusters; very fragrant; foliage dark, matt; vigorous.

Scoop Jackson Gr, *dr*, 1983, (Canterbury; Fidelity); *Kalahari × John Waterer*; McGredy, Sam; Roses by Fred Edmunds. Flowers dark red, semi-dbl. (20 petals), large; light fragrance; foliage glossy; upright growth.

Scorcher Cl HT, *dr*, 1922, *Mme. Abel Chatenay × Seedling*; Clark, A.; Hackett. Flowers brilliant scarlet-crimson, semi-dbl., large (4 in.); slightly fragrant; foliage large, wrinkled; vigorous, climbing or pillar (to 10 ft.) growth; non-recurrent bloom.

Scotch Blend HT, *pb*, 1975, *Queen Elizabeth × Peace*; J&B Roses; Eastern Roses. Bud long, pointed; flowers pink blend, dbl. (35 petals), high-centered, large (5-6 in.); slightly fragrant; foliage dark, leathery; upright growth.

Scotland's Trust HT, *lp*, 1992, (COClands); *Sunblest × Prima Ballerina*; Cocker, James & Sons. Flowers light pink, silver reverse, semi-dbl. (15-25 petals), well shaped, medium (4-7 cms) blooms borne mostly singly; very fragrant; foliage medium, medium green, matt; some prickles; medium (16-20 cms), upright growth.

Scottish Special Min, *lp*, 1985, (COCdapple); *Wee Man × Darling Flame*; Cocker, Ann G., 1987. Flowers light pink, semi-dbl., patio, large; slight fragrance; foliage small, medium green, semi-glossy; bushy growth.

Scott's Columbia HT, *dp*, 1928, *Columbia sport*; Scott, R. Flowers clear bright pink.

Scrabo F, *op*, 1968, *Celebration × Elizabeth of Glamis*; Dickson, A. Flowers light salmon-pink, dbl., high-centered, large; fragrant; free growth.

Scudbuster Min, *or*, 1991, (CLEscrub; Patriot Flame); *Seedling × Seedling*; Clements, John; Heirloom Old Garden Roses, 1992. Flowers intense rocket flame orange, very full (41+ petals), high-centered, exhibition, small (0-4 cms) blooms borne mostly singly; slight fragrance; foliage small, dark green, semi-glossy; some prickles; medium (35 cms), upright growth.

Sea Foam® S, *w*, 1964, ((White Dawn × Pinocchio) × (White Dawn × Pinocchio)) × (White Dawn × Pinocchio); Schwartz, E.W.; C-P. Flowers white to cream, dbl., medium blooms in clusters; slightly fragrant; foliage small, glossy, leathery; vigorous, climbing trailer, semi-prostrate; recurrent. GM, Rome, 1963; ARS David Fuerstenberg Prize, 1968.

Sea Mist HT, *w*, 1960, *Helen Traubel × Golden Harvest*; Armbrust; Langbecker. Bud long, pointed; flowers cream, center golden, semi-dbl., high-centered, large; slightly fragrant; foliage leathery; vigorous growth.

Sea Nymph Min, *pb*, 1986, *Seedling × Seedling*; McDaniel, Earl; McDaniel's Min. Roses. Flower petals blush pink, edged coral, dbl. (48 petals), high-centered, exhibition, large blooms borne singly; no fragrance; foliage medium, medium green, semi-glossy; medium, curved prickles; upright, bushy growth.

Sea of Fire F, *or*, 1954, (Feuermeer); (Baby Château × Else Poulsen) × Independence; Kordes. Flowers orange-scarlet, semi-dbl., large (3 in.) blooms in small clusters; slightly fragrant; foliage dark, leathery; vigorous, upright, bushy growth.

Sea of Tranquility HT, *ab*, 1991, *Sylvia sport*; Keene's Rose Nursery. Bud classical; flowers delicate light pink in bud, opening to apricot pink blush, lighter reverse, holds color, dbl. (40-45 petals), high-centered, large (12 cms) blooms borne mostly singly; lightly perfumed, sweet fragrance; foliage light green, small, disease resistant; upright (up to 5'), non-spreading growth.

Sea Pearl F, *pb*, 1964, (Flower Girl); *Kordes' Perfecta × Montezuma*; Dickson, P.; A. Dickson. Bud long, pointed; flowers soft pink, reverse flushed peach and yellow, semi-dbl. (24 petals), well-formed, large (4½ in.) blooms in clusters; foliage dark; upright, bushy growth.

Sea Spray HMsk (S), *w*, 1923, Pemberton. Flowers stone-white, flushed pink, borne in clusters; height 3-5 ft.; non-recurrent bloom. RULED EXTINCT 12/82.

Seabird HT, *my*, 1913, Dickson, H. Flowers primrose-yellow; vigorous growth.

Seabreeze Min, *mp*, 1976, (LEMsea); *White Fairy* × *Seedling*; Lemrow; Nor'East Min. Roses. Bud short, pointed; flowers pink, dbl. (35 petals), small (1 in.); slightly fragrant; foliage light to medium green; very vigorous, bushy growth.

Seafair HT, *ab*, 1959, *Charlotte Armstrong* × *Signora*; Abrams, Von; Peterson; Dering. Bud long, pointed; flowers deep apricot, dbl. (45 petals), high-centered to cupped, large; slightly fragrant; foliage glossy; vigorous, upright, symmetrical growth.   RULED EXTINCT 4/86.

Seafarer F, *or*, 1986, (HARtilion); *Amy Brown* × *Judy Garland*; Harkness. Flowers orange-red, dbl. (30 petals), cupped, large blooms in clusters of 3-5; slightly fragrant; foliage medium, dark, glossy; medium, red prickles; fruit medium, green; medium, bushy growth.

Seager Wheeler HSpn (OGR), *lp*, 1947, *R. spinosissima altaica* × *Seedling*; Wheeler; P.H. Wright. Flowers light pink, dbl.; sets seed; height 6 ft.; non-recurrent; hardy.

Seagull R, *w*, 1907, Pritchard. Flowers pure white, stamens golden, single, blooms in large clusters; very vigorous growth.

Sealily Min, *pb*, 1984, (LEMlil); *Max Colwell* × *Seedling*; Lemrow, Dr. Maynard. Flowers white, petals edged pink, dbl. (35 petals), small; no fragrance; foliage medium, dark, semi-glossy.

Sealing Wax HMoy (S), *mp*, *R. moyesii hybrid*; Royal Hort. Soc. Flowers pink, large; fruit abundant, bright red; height 8 ft.

Search for Life™ HT, *mr*, 1988, (WILsfol); *Miss All-American Beauty* × *Mister Lincoln*; Williams, J. Benjamin. Flowers medium red, dbl. (26-40 petals), exhibition, large; slight fragrance; foliage large, dark green, semi-glossy; vigorous, hardy, abundant growth.

Seashell HT, *op*, 1976, (KORshel); *Seedling* × *Colour Wonder*; Kordes, R.; J&P. Bud short, pointed; flowers burnt-orange, dbl. (48 petals), imbricated, medium (3-4 in.); slightly fragrant; upright growth. AARS, 1976.

Seashell R, *mp*, 1916, Dawson. Flowers pink, semi-dbl., large, borne in large clusters; foliage glossy.

Seaspray Min, *pb*, 1982, (MACnew); *Anytime* × *Moana*; McGredy, Sam; John Mattock, Ltd. Flowers pale pink flushed red, semi-dbl., medium; fragrant; foliage medium, medium green, matt; bushy growth.

Second Chance HT, *pb*, 1988, *Carefree Beauty* × *Sonia*; Stoddard, Louis, 1991. Bud ovoid; flowers coral orange, tips orange-red, reverse deep pink, aging medium pink with red edges, dbl. (35 petals), urn-shaped, high-cen-

tered, large, borne usually singly and in sprays of up to 3; moderate, damask fragrance; foliage medium, medium green to maroon, semi-glossy, a bit rugose; bushy, slightly spreading growth.

Secret™ HT, *pb*, 1992, (HILaroma); *Pristine* × *Friendship*; Tracy, Daniel; C-P, 1994. Flowers light pink edged with deep pink, full (26-40 petals), large (7+ cms) blooms borne mostly single with strong stems for cutting; very fragrant; foliage large, medium green, semi-glossy; some prickles; tall (120-130 cms), bushy growth.

Secret Love HT, *dr*, 1973, *Seedling* × *Seedling*; Armstrong, D.L.; Armstrong Nursery. Bud ovoid; flowers deep red, dbl., high-centered, large; fragrant; foliage leathery; moderate, upright, bushy growth. AARS, 1994.

Secrétaire Belpaire HT, *op*, 1934, *Angèle Pernet* × *Mme. Edouard Herriot*; Lens. Flowers brilliant salmon-pink, dbl., large; foliage bright bronze; vigorous growth.

Secretaire J. Nicolas HP (OGR), *m*, 1883, Schwartz. Flowers purple.

Secretaris Zwart HT, *dp*, 1918, *Gen. MacArthur* × *Lyon Rose*; Van Rossem. Flowers bright rose, reverse silvery rose.

Sedgebrook HT, *lp*, 1986, (MURse); *(Chanelle* × *Prima Ballerina)* × *Deep Secret*; Murray, Nola. Flowers very pale pink, almost white, dbl. (47 petals), classic form; very strong fragrance; foliage large, medium green, flat; pointed, brown prickles; low growth.

Seduction Pol, *mp*, 1927, Turbat. Flowers peach-blossom-pink, dbl., large, borne in clusters of 50-60; few thorns; dwarf growth.

Seefeld F, *rb*, 1958, *Fashion* × *Orange Triumph*; Delforge. Bud oval; flowers red tinted lighter, dbl., open, medium, borne in large clusters; foliage glossy; very vigorous, bushy growth.

Seftopolis Gr, *dp*, 1977, *Queen Elizabeth* × *Seedling*; Staikov, Prof. Dr. V.; Kalaydjiev and Chorbadjiiski. Flowers deep pink, dbl. (36 petals), large; Foliage glossy, leathery; vigorous growth.

Seion HT, *my*, 1987, *Grandpa Dickson* × *Sunblest*; Yokota, Kiyoshi, 1988. Flowers medium yellow, dbl. (35-40 petals), high-centered, large; moderate fragrance; foliage light green; prickles few; fruit medium, pale orange; upright, medium growth.

Sekel S, *yb*, 1984, *Lichterloh* × *Zitronenfalter*; Lundstad, Arne; Agricultural Univ. of Norway. Flowers light yellow, bright red blend, single (11 petals), 3½ in. blooms in clusters of 21; slight fragrance; foliage dark, leathery; vigorous, upright growth.

Seki-Yoh HT, *or*, 1975, *Miss France × Christian Dior*; Suzuki, S.; Keisei Rose Nursery. Flowers orange-red, dbl. (52 petals), high-centered, large; slightly fragrant; foliage dark, leathery; semi-glossy; upright, compact growth.

Selandia R, *mp*, 1913, *Mme. Norbert Levavasseur × Dorothy Perkins*; Poulsen, D. Flowers pink, full; vigorous growth.

Selfridges HT, *dy*, 1984, (KORpriwa; Berolina); Kordes, W.; John Mattock. Flowers amber yellow, dbl. (35 petals), large; fragrant; foliage medium, medium green, semi-glossy. ADR, 1986.

Selina HMsk (S), *dp*, 1992, (REYsel); *Cornelia × Trier*; Reynolds, Ted; Reynolds Roses, 1992-1993. Flowers deep pink, single (5 petals), small (0-4 cms) blooms borne in small clusters; slight fragrance; foliage small, medium green, semi-glossy; few prickles; medium, spreading growth.

SELstar HT, *my*, 1989, (Christina); *Eliora × Seedling*; Select Roses B.V.; DeVor Nursery, 1991. Bud pointed; flowers bright lemon-yellow, does not fade, dbl. (43 petals), cupped to globular, large, borne singly; no fragrance; foliage large, dark green, glossy; prickles declining, light red; upright, tall growth.

Selvetta® HT, *pb*, 1982, Cazzaniga-Como; Barni-Pistoia, Rose. Flowers light pink, petals edged salmon, dbl. (40 petals), large; no fragrance; foliage medium, dark, matt; upright growth.

Selwyn Bird HT, *or*, 1969, *Fragrant Cloud × Stella*; Cocker. Flowers salmon-cerise, dbl. (35 petals), high-centered; fragrant; foliage dark, glossy; vigorous growth.

Selwyn Toogood Min, *mp*, 1983, *Heidi × Seedling*; Eagle, P.B. & D.; Southern Cross Nursery. Flowers medium pink, dbl. (33 petals), high-centered, small; light moss on stems; slight fragrance; foliage small, light green; bushy, upright growth.

Semi Sp (OGR), *w*, 1913, (Grown from seed collected from *R. laxa* Retzius, by N.E. Hansen on the dry steppes of Semipalatinsk, Siberia, 1913.) Flowers white, small; fruit bright red; tall (8 ft.); blooms all summer. Altai Mtns., central Siberia, & extending westward to the Semipalatinsk region. The name, Semi is an abbreviation of Semipalatinsk; very hardy.

Semiramis HT, *yb*, 1957, *Capistrano × (Peace × Crimson Glory)*; Motose. Bud pointed; flowers rose, center buff or amber, dbl. (35-45 petals), high-centered, large (5 in.); very fragrant (raspberry); foliage dark, glossy; vigorous growth.

Sénateur Amic LCl, *mr*, 1924, *R. gigantea × Gen. MacArthur*; Nabonnand, P. Bud long, pointed; flowers brilliant carmine, nearly single; very vigorous growth.

Sénateur Mascuraud HT, *ly*, 1909, Pernet-Ducher. Flowers light yellow, center darker, dbl.; fragrant.

Sénateur Potié HT, *ob*, 1937, *Mme. Butterfly × Carito MacMahon*; Dot, P. Flowers orange-yellow, semi-dbl., cupped, large; foliage glossy, bronze; vigorous growth.

Sénateur Vaisse HP (OGR), *rb*, 1859, *Seedling × Général Jacqueminot*; Guillot Père. Flowers red, shaded darker, dbl. (32 petals), large; very fragrant; upright growth; occasionally recurrent bloom.

Senator HT, *mr*, 1926, *Red Columbia × Premier*; Florex Gardens. Bud long, pointed; flowers brilliant scarlet, dbl.; very fragrant.

Senator Burda® HT, *dr*, 1988, (MEIvestal; Victor Hugo; Dreams Come True; Spirit of Youth); *(Karl Herbst × (Royal Velvet × Suspense)) × Erotika*; Meilland, M.L.; SNC Meilland; Cie. Flowers brilliant currant-red, dbl. (26-40 petals), large; very fragrant; foliage large, medium green, semi-glossy; upright, strong, floriferous growth.

Senator Joe T. Robinson HT, *dr*, 1938, *Harvard × David O. Dodd*; Vestal. Bud long, pointed; flowers dark crimson, semi-dbl. and dbl., cupped; very fragrant; foliage leathery; vigorous growth.

Seneca Queen HT, *pb*, 1965, *(Serenade seedling × Fashion) × Golden Masterpiece*; Boerner; J&P. Flowers apricot-pink, reverse darker, dbl. (50 petals), high-centered, large (6 in.); fragrant; foliage leathery; vigorous growth.

Sénégal Cl HT, *dr*, 1944, Mallerin; A. Meilland. Flowers very dark red; very vigorous growth.

Senff Sp (OGR), *lp*, *R. canina* strain; Senff. Selected, almost thornless strain of *R. canina*, used as an understock; propagation by seed.

Senhora da Graça HT, *rb*, Moreira da Silva. Flowers red with carmine reflections.

Senior HT, *rb*, 1932, *Richmond × Général Jacqueminot*; Spanbauer; Hill Floral Products Co. Bud pointed; flowers scarlet-crimson, dbl., open; long stems; fragrant; foliage thick; very vigorous growth.

Senior Prom HT, *dp*, 1964, *Pink Princess × Queen Elizabeth*; Brownell, H.C.; Brownell. Bud long, pointed; flowers deep pink, dbl. (38 petals), high-centered, large (4½ in.); foliage dark, glossy; vigorous, upright growth.

Señor Philippe LCl, *m*, Flowers lilac-pink, center paler, dbl.; vigorous growth.

Señora de Bornas HT, *mr*, 1955, *J.M. Lopez Pico × Concerto*; Camprubi. Flowers vermilion-red, very dbl., cupped, medium; very fragrant; foliage glossy; vigorous, upright growth.

Señora de Carulla F, *mr*, 1961, Torre Blanca. Flowers cerise-red. GM, Madrid, 1961.

Señora Gari HT, *yb*, 1935, *Mari Dot × Constance*; Dot, P.; C-P. Bud long, pointed; flowers deep orange-yellow, dbl., high-centered, very large; fragrant; sprawling growth.

Señora Leon de Aujuria HT, *ob*, 1935, La Florida. Flowers orange; foliage glossy; vigorous growth.

Señorita F, *rb*, 1991, (JACdor); *Seedling × Matador*; Warriner, William; Bear Creek Gardens, 1992. Flowers orange-red to red on top of petal with a yellow petal base and a yellow tan reverse, semi-dbl. (26-40 petals), medium (4-7 cms) blooms borne in large clusters; slight fragrance; foliage medium, dark green, semi-glossy; many prickles; upright (75 cms), bushy growth.

Señorita Carmen Sert HT, *yb*, 1917, *Marquise de Sinéty seedling*; Pernet-Ducher. Flowers indian yellow, shaded pale pink, edged bright carmine, dbl.

Señorita de Alvarez HT, *mp*, 1931, Cant, B.R. Bud long, pointed; flowers glowing salmon, single, cupped, very large; very fragrant; foliage leathery, dark; vigorous growth. GM, NRS, 1930.

Sensass Delbard® Cl HT, *mr*, 1986, (DELmoun; Sensass); *(Danse du Feu × (Orange Triumph × Floradora)) × Tenor seedling*; , unnamed Delbard, 1973. Flowers bright velvety red, dbl. (28 petals), cupped, large; no fragrance; vigorous, climbing (to 10 ft.) growth.

Sensation HT, *mr*, 1922, *Hoosier Beauty × Premier*; Hill, J.H., Co. Bud long, pointed; flowers scarlet-crimson, dbl. (36 petals), open, large (5 in.); fragrant; foliage dark; free, branching growth.

Senta Schmidt Pol, *ob*, 1930, *Suzanne Turbat sport*; Schmidt, R. Flowers coppery orange, semi-dbl.; foliage small, soft, light; dwarf growth.

Sentinel HT, *pb*, 1934, Clark, A.; Wyant. Flowers velvety cerise, reverse silvery cerise, dbl., cupped, large; very fragrant; foliage glossy; vigorous growth.

Sentry HT, *dr*, 1948, Fletcher; Tucker. Bud long, pointed; flowers clear crimson, dbl. (25 petals), large (4-5 in.); very fragrant; dwarf, compact growth.

September Days Min, *dy*, 1976, *Rise 'n' Shine × Yellow Jewel*; Saville; Days Inn. Bud pointed; flowers deep yellow, dbl. (40 petals), high-centered, reflexed, micro-mini, small (1½ in.); fragrant; foliage glossy; upright, compact growth.

September Eighteenth HT, *pb*, 1991, (WILsept); *Carla × Queen Elizabeth*; Williams, J. Benjamin, 1992. Bud ovoid; flowers shell pink, reverse deep coral pink, aging light pink, dbl., high-centered, exhibition, medium blooms borne usually singly or in sprays of 3-4; heavy, damask fragrance; foliage large, light green, semi-glossy; medium, bushy growth.

September Morn HT, *pb*, 1913, *Mme. Pierre Euler sport*; Dietrich; Turner. Flowers flesh-pink, center deeper, large; fragrant; vigorous growth.

September Song Gr, *ab*, 1981, *(Vera Dalton × Prairie Princess) × (Apricot Nectar × Prairie Princess)*; Buck; Iowa State University. Bud ovoid; flowers apricot, dbl. (28 petals), cupped blooms borne singly and in clusters of 5-8; fruity fragrance; foliage dark, tinted with copper, semi-glossy, leathery; thin, awl-like prickles; erect, bushy growth.

September Wedding HT, *mp*, 1964, *Montezuma sport (through radiation)*; Schloen, J.; Ellesmere Nursery. Bud ovoid; flowers deep pink, reverse darker, dbl., high-centered, large; fragrant; foliage dark, glossy; vigorous, tall, compact growth.

Sequoia HT, *ob*, 1939, Verschuren-Pechtold; Dreer. Flowers ripe pumpkin-flesh shaded apricot, dbl., globular; slightly fragrant; foliage leathery, bronze; vigorous growth.

Sequoia, Climbing Cl HT, *ob*, 1940, Swim; Armstrong Nursery.

Sequoia Gold™ Min, *my*, 1986, (MORsegold); *(Little Darling × Lemon Delight) × Gold Badge*; Moore, Ralph S. Flowers medium yellow, fading lighter, dbl. (30 petals), high-centered, exhibition, medium, borne usually singly and in clusters of 3-7; moderate, fruity fragrance; foliage medium, medium green, glossy; slender, medium, pale green-brown prickles; fruit round, orange; bushy, spreading growth. AOE, 1987.

Sequoia Jewel Min, *mr*, 1989, (MORsewel); *Sheri Anne × Paul Neyron*; Moore, Ralph S.; Sequoia Nursery, 1990. Bud rounded; flowers medium red, dbl. (33 petals), cupped, medium, borne in sprays of 3-7; slight fragrance; foliage medium, medium green, matt; prickles straight, short, brown; fruit round, medium, orange-red; upright, bushy, medium growth.

Serafina Longa HT, *dp*, 1933, *Mme. Butterfly × Mme. Abel Chatenay*; La Florida. Flowers old-rose, heavily veined, well formed, large; fragrant; vigorous growth.

Seraphine HSet (OGR), *pb*, 1840, (Seraphim); *R. setigera hybrid*; Prince Nursery. Flowers soft pink, center darker, very dbl.

Serenade HT, *ob*, 1949, *Sonata* × *R.M.S. Queen Mary*; Boerner; J&P. Bud ovoid; flowers coral-orange, dbl. (28 petals), cupped, large (4-4½ in.); slightly fragrant; foliage glossy, leathery; vigorous, upright growth.

Serendipity S, *ob*, 1978, *(Western Sun* × *Carefree Beauty)* × *(Apricot Nectar* × *Prairie Princess)*; Buck; Iowa State University. Bud ovoid, pointed; flowers orange to buttercup-yellow, semi-dbl. (23 petals), shallowly-cupped, large (4-5 in.); fragrant; foliage dark, glossy, leathery; vigorous, upright, spreading, bushy growth.

Serene HT, *w*, 1940, Mallerin; C-P. Bud long, pointed, light buff; flowers shining silvery white, dbl. (30-40 petals), open, very large; foliage sparse, soft; vigorous, upright growth.

Serenissima LCl, *m*, 1980, Takatori, Y.; Barni-Pistoia, Rose. Bud pointed; flowers light lilac, dbl. (38 petals); strong fragrance; foliage large, light green, matt; straight, reddish-green prickles; upright growth; recurrent.

Sérénité HT, *my*, 1946, Gaujard. Bud pointed; flowers chrome-yellow, large; stiff stems; foliage reddish; very vigorous growth. RULED EXTINCT 7/86.

Sérénité® HT, *my*, 1986, *John Armstrong* × *Tanagra*; Gaujard, Jean. Flowers coppery-yellow, dbl., high-centered, borne singly; heavy fragrance; foliage large, medium green; large prickles; fruit rounded; tall growth.

Serge Basset HT, *dr*, 1918, Pernet-Ducher. Flowers brilliant garnet-red, dbl.

Sergeant Pepper Min, *or*, 1992, (KORtenses); *Seedling* × *Lavaglut*; W. Kordes Sohne; Bear Creek Gardens, Inc., 1992. Flowers orange-red, semi-dbl. (6-14 petals), medium (4-7 cms) blooms borne in small clusters; no fragrance; foliage small, dark green, glossy; some prickles; low (45-60 cms), upright, bushy, spreading growth.

Sergent Ulmann HT, *dr*, 1930, *Grenoble* × *Mme. Van de Voorde*; Mallerin. Bud long, pointed; flowers deep garnet, lightened with scarlet, semi-dbl., open, very large; slightly fragrant; foliage leathery, bronze; vigorous growth.

Serratipetala Ch (OGR), *pb*, 1912, (*R. chinensis serratipetala*; Rose Oeillet de Saint Arquey Vilfray); Similar to Slater's Crimson China, but petals fringed; outer petals crimson, inner ones light pink; stamens long, curled, carmine, not numerous.

Setina Cl Ch (OGR), *lp*, 1879, *Hermosa, Climbing sport*; P. Henderson.

Seven Seas F, *m*, 1973, *Lilac Charm* × *Sterling Silver*; Harkness. Flowers lilac, dbl. (26 pet-als), large (4 in.); fragrant; foliage large, glossy.

Seven Sisters HMult (OGR), *pb*, 1817, (*R. cathayensis platyphylla* (Thory) Bailey; *R. multiflora platyphylla* (Thory) Rehder & Wilson; *R. platyphylla* (Thory) Takasima, not Rau; *R. thoryi* Trattinnick; Seven Sisters Rose); 1817. Flowers pale rose to crimson, much larger than *R. multiflora*.

Seventeen F, *pb*, 1959, *Pinocchio seedling* × *Fashion seedling*; Boerner; J&P. Bud ovoid; flowers pink-coral, semi-dbl. (20-25 petals), cupped, large (3½ in.), borne in pyramidal clusters; very fragrant; foliage dark, leathery; vigorous, upright growth.

Seventh Heaven HT, *dr*, 1966, *Seedling* × *Chrysler Imperial*; Armstrong, D.L.; Swim; Armstrong Nursery. Flowers dark red, dbl., high-centered, large; foliage glossy; upright, bushy.

Séverine HT, *rb*, 1918, Pernet-Ducher. Flowers coral-red, passing to shrimp-red, semi-dbl.; foliage bronze; vigorous growth.

Severn Vale HT, *ob*, 1967, *Beauté sport*; Sanday. Flowers salmon, high-centered, large (4½ in.); free growth.

Sevilliana S, *pb*, 1976, *(Vera Dalton* × *Dornröschen)* × *((World's Fair* × *Floradora)* × *Applejack)*; Buck; Iowa State University. Bud ovoid, pointed; flowers light claret-rose, yellow from base, semi-dbl. (15 petals), slightly cupped, large (3½-4 in.); fragrant (spicy); foliage tinted copper, leathery; upright, bushy growth.

Sexy Rexy® F, *mp*, 1984, (MACrexy; Heckenzauber); *Seaspray* × *Dreaming*; McGredy, Sam. Flowers medium pink to light pink, dbl. (40+ petals), medium blooms in large clusters; slight fragrance; foliage small, light green, glossy; bushy growth. GM, New Zealand, 1984; Auckland, 1990.

Sfinge HT, *rb*, 1954, *Julien Potin* × *Sensation*; Aicardi, D.; Giacomasso. Flowers deep red edged rose; long stems; vigorous, upright growth.

Shabnam F, *w*, 1976, *Baby Sylvia* × *Seedling*; Indian Agric. Research Inst. Bud ovoid; flowers white, center pinkish, very dbl. (85 petals), open, small (2 in.); foliage soft; upright, open growth.

Shades of Autumn HT, *rb*, 1943, *Golden Glow* × *Condesa de Sástago*; Brownell. Flowers red to pink with some yellow, center yellow, dbl., large; very fragrant; foliage glossy, leathery; vigorous, compact, upright, bushy growth.

Shades of Pink™ F, *pb*, 1985, *Robin Hood* × *Pascali*; Mander, George. Flowers pink with white eye, dbl. (33 petals), imbricated, large (3½ in.), in clusters of 10-50; no fragrance; foliage medium green, glossy; curved, hooked prickles; bushy, upright growth.

Shadow Dance F, *rb*, 1969, *Pink Parfait × Crimson Glory*; Fankhauser. Bud ovoid; flowers silver-pink edged red, dbl. (30-35 petals), small; very fragrant; foliage glossy, leathery; vigorous, low, compact growth.

Shady Charmer Min, *yb*, 1989, (MICshade; MICshady); *Party Girl × Anita Charles*; Williams, Michael C.; The Rose Garden, 1990. Bud ovoid; flowers light yellow base with light pink edges, aging cream, dbl. (43 petals), high-centered, exhibition, medium, borne usually singly; slight, spicy fragrance; foliage medium, dark green, semi-glossy; prickles straight, very few, small, light green; fruit none; bushy, medium growth.

Shady Flame Min, *or*, 1981, *Prominent × Zinger*; Jolly, Betty; Rosehill Farm. Flowers orange-red, dbl. (35 petals), high-centered blooms borne usually singly; slight fragrance; foliage small, light green; straight prickles; compact, bushy growth.

Shady Lady Min, *dy*, 1981, *(Prominent × Zinger) × Puppy Love*; Jolly, Betty; Rosehill Farm. Flowers yellow-orange, dbl. (35 petals), high-centered blooms borne mostly singly; fragrant; foliage tiny, green; no prickles; upright, bushy growth.

Shady Lane HT, *pb*, 1990, *Thriller × Just Lucky*; Bridges, Dennis A.; Bridges Roses. Bud ovoid; flowers deep pink to white base, aging deeper pink, dbl. (35 petals), high-centered, exhibition, large, borne usually singly; heavy, damask fragrance; foliage medium, dark green, semi-glossy; prickles medium, pointed downwards, light green; upright, medium growth.

Shaida HT, *or*, 1976, *(Fandango × Fillette) × Coloranja*; Lens. Bud long, pointed; flowers red-orange-salmon, dbl. (28-32 petals), high-centered, large (3½-4½ in.); slightly fragrant; foliage dark, leathery; vigorous, upright growth.

Shailer's Provence C (OGR), *lp*, (Gracilis); *An atypical Centifolia hybrid*; Shailer; Prior to 1799. Flowers lilac-pink, base white, inner petals rolled and wrinkled, full, cupped blooms often borne in 3's; fragrant; foliage small; vigorous (4-5 ft.)growth.

Shakespeare Festival Min, *my*, 1979, *Golden Angel × Golden Angel*; Moore, R.S.; Sequoia Nursery. Bud pointed; flowers clear yellow, dbl. (45 petals), high-centered, medium (1½ in.); fragrant (tea); foliage green, matt; bushy, compact growth.

Shalimar R, *yb*, 1914, *Minnehaha sport*; Burrell. Flowers creamy blush, picotee edge of bright rose-pink, borne in immense, pyramidal clusters; vigorous, climbing growth.

Shalom® F, *or*, 1973, (Flammenmeer); *Korona seedling × Korona seedling*; Poulsen, N.D.; Poulsen. Bud globular; flowers orange-red, semi-dbl. (23 petals), large (3½-4 in.); foliage dark; vigorous, upright growth.

Shangri-La HT, *mp*, 1945, *Mrs. J.D. Eisele × Pres. Herbert Hoover*; Howard, F.H.; H&S. Bud long, pointed; flowers silvery pink, dbl. (35 petals), open, large (3½-4½ in.); long stems; very fragrant; foliage leathery; very vigorous, upright, bushy growth.

Shannon® HT, *mp*, 1965, (MACnon); *Queen Elizabeth × McGredy's Yellow*; McGredy, S., IV; McGredy. Bud ovoid; flowers medium pink, dbl. (58 petals), large (5 in.); foliage dark, rounded; vigorous growth.

Shantung® F, *pb*, 1988, (DELchine); *(Orléans Rose × Goldilocks) × Bordure Rose seedling*; D-C. Flowers mottled pink, cream and red, semi-dbl. (22 petals), flat, large; slight fragrance; foliage matt; vigorous growth.

Sharada Gr, *lp*, 1983, (Saroda); *Gamma ray induced somatic sport of Queen Elizabeth*; Gupta, Dr. M.N., Datta, Dr. S.K.; Nath, P.; National Botanical Research Institute. Flowers light pink.

Shari HT, *pb*, 1992, *Sweetie Pie sport*; Perry, Astor; Hortico Inc., 1993. Flowers, growth, and foliage same as Swarthmore; color is lighter, petals do not burn, dbl. (26-40 petals), large blooms; slight fragrance; foliage medium, medium green, matt; upright (185 cms) growth.

Sharon HT, *lp*, 1962, *Golden Rapture × Happiness*; Spandikow. Bud long, pointed; flowers soft pink edged lighter, base light yellow, reverse darker pink, dbl. (35-40 petals), high-centered, large (5½ in.); foliage leathery, dull; vigorous, upright growth.

Sharon Lorraine F, *rb*, 1978, *Seedling × Seedling*; Bossom, W.E. Bud pointed; flowers ivory yellow, aging red, reverse red, dbl. (40 petals), blooms borne 30-36 per cluster; foliage dark, semi-glossy; long, red prickles; medium, upright (2-2½ ft.) growth.

Sharon Louise HT, *w*, 1968, *Queen Elizabeth × Virgo*; Parkes. Bud ovoid; flowers near white, center pale pink, dbl., medium; slightly fragrant; foliage dark, leathery; vigorous, tall, bushy growth.

Sharon Muxlow Min, *op*, 1980, *Anytime × Persian Princess*; Dobbs; Min. Plant Kingdom. Bud globular; flowers bright coppery orange, dbl. (25 petals), flat, small (1 in.); foliage leathery; upright growth.

Shasta F, *w*, 1962, *Paul's Lemon Pillar* × *Fashion*; Schwartz, E.W.; Wyant. Bud pointed; flowers white, semi-dbl. (23 petals), large (4 in.) blooms in clusters; fragrant; foliage leathery; vigorous, bushy growth.

She F, *or*, 1962, *(Independence* × *Fashion)* × *Brownie*; Dickson, P.; A. Dickson. Flowers salmon-opal, base lemon, semi-dbl. (19 petals), medium (2½ in.), borne in clusters; slightly fragrant; moderate, bushy growth.

Sheelagh Baird Pol, *pb*, 1934, Cant, F. Flowers shell-pink, overlaid rich rose pink, base yellow, full, large blooms in large trusses; vigorous growth.

Sheer Bliss HT, *w*, 1985, (JACtro); *White Masterpiece* × *Grand Masterpiece*; Warriner; J&P, 1987. Flowers white with pink center, dbl. (35 petals), exhibition, large blooms borne singly; moderate, spicy fragrance; foliage medium, medium green, matt; medium brown prickles; medium, upright, bushy growth. GM, Japan, 1984; AARS, 1987.

Sheer Delight F, *or*, 1992, (HARwazzle); *Bobby Dazzler* × *Little Prince*; Harkness, R.; Harkness New Roses, Ltd., 1991. Flowers orange-red, semi-dbl. (15-25 petals), small (0-4 cms) blooms borne in large clusters; patio; no fragrance; foliage small, light green, semi-glossy; few prickles; low (40 cms), bushy growth.

Sheer Elegance™ HT, *op*, 1989, (TWObe); *Pristine* × *Fortuna*; Twomey, Jerry; DeVor Nursery, 1990. Bud pointed; flowers soft pink with dark pink edges, dbl. (43 petals), cupped, large, borne singly; moderate, musk fragrance; foliage large, dark green, glossy; prickles slightly curved, red with green; upright, tall growth. AARS, 1991.

Sheerwater HT, *ly*, 1977, *My Choice* × *Premier Bal*; Plumpton. Flowers beige to cream, veined carmine, dbl. (35 petals), full, large (5 in.); fragrant; foliage dark, matt green; free growth.

Sheila Pol, *op*, 1930, *An improved Golden Salmon with orange-salmon flowers.*; Walsh, J.; Beckwith. An improved Golden Salmon with orange-salmon flowers; particularly useful as a pot plant for forcing.

Sheila Bellair HT, *op*, 1937, *Miss Mocatta* × *Seedling*; Clark, A.; NRS Victoria. Flowers salmon-pink, semi-dbl., large; bushy growth.

Sheila MacQueen F, *w*, 1988, (HARwotnext); *Greensleeves* × *Letchworth Garden City*; Harkness, R., & Co., Ltd. Flowers chartreuse green with apricot tint at certain seasons, dbl. (24 petals), cupped, medium, borne in sprays of 3-9; slight, peppery fragrance; foliage medium, medium green, semi-glossy; prickles broad, straight, green; fruit rounded, medium, green; upright, medium growth.

Sheila Wilson HT, *mr*, 1910, Hall; A. Dickson. Flowers light scarlet; vigorous growth.

Sheila's Perfume F, *yb*, 1982, (HARsherry); *Peer Gynt* × *(Daily Sketch* × *(Paddy McGredy* × *Prima Ballerina))*; Sheridan, John; Harkness, 1985. Flowers yellow, petals edged red, semi-dbl. (20 petals), large blooms borne singly; very fragrant; foliage medium, dark, semi-glossy; medium, bushy growth. Edland Fragrance Medal, 1981.

Shelby Wallace R, *op*, 1929, *Cécile Brunner, Climbing seedling*; Moore, R.S. Flowers light salmon-pink, semi-dbl., small; slightly fragrant.

Shell Beach Min, *w*, 1983, (TRObeach); *Simon Robinson* × *Simon Robinson*; Robinson, Thomas. Bud soft pink; flowers creamy white, dbl. (28 petals), medium blooms in clusters; slight fragrance; foliage small, medium green, semi-glossy; bushy growth.

Shell Queen Gr, *lp*, 1961, *Queen Elizabeth sport*; Allen, L.C. Flowers shell pink, fading white.

Shellbrook Rose Sp (OGR), *dr*, *R. acicularis form*; Found near Shellbrook, Sask., Canada. Flowers deep red; fruit long, bottle-shaped.

Shelly HT, *pb*, 1987, *Francine sport*; Melville Nurseries Pty., Ltd., 1988. Flowers pale pink with cyclamen-pink shading, reverse fleck & stripe with pale pink-silver, semi-dbl. (20-25 petals), decorative, large, borne in sprays of 5-6; light, sweet fragrance; foliage dark green, glossy, disease resistant; prickles slightly hooked, beige-cream; medium growth.

Shelly Renee™ Min, *pb*, 1988, (SAVashel); *Spice Drop sport*; Saville, F. Harmon; Nor'East Miniature Roses, 1989. Flowers salmon pink, reverse peach, aging light pink to white.

Shenandoah LCl, *dr*, 1935, *Étoile de Hollande* × *Schoener's Nutkana*; Nicolas; C-P. Bud long, pointed; flowers crimson, semi-dbl., high-centered, large; very fragrant; foliage large, glossy; vigorous, climbing (10 ft.) growth.

Shepherdess F, *yb*, 1967, *Allgold* × *Peace*; Mattock. Flowers yellow flushed salmon, dbl., large (3½-4 in.) blooms in clusters; slightly fragrant; foliage dark, glossy, leathery; vigorous.

Shepherd's Delight F, *rb*, 1956, *Masquerade seedling* × *Joanna Hill*; Dickson, A. Flowers flame and yellow, semi-dbl. (15 petals), large (3 in.) blooms in trusses; slightly fragrant; foliage dark; vigorous growth. GM, NRS, 1958.

Sheri Anne Min, *or*, 1973, (MORsheri); *Little Darling* × *New Penny*; Moore, R.S.; Sequoia Nursery. Bud long, pointed; flowers orange-red, base yellow, semi-dbl. (17 petals), small (1-1½ in.); fragrant; foliage glossy, leathery; upright, bushy growth. AOE, 1975.

Sherry F, *r*, 1960, *Independence × Orange Sweetheart*; McGredy, S., IV; McGredy. Flowers dark sherry color, semi-dbl. (14 petals), medium (2½ in.) blooms in clusters; slightly fragrant; foliage dark; vigorous growth.

Shimmering Dawn F, *mp*, 1965, Verschuren. Bud rose-pink; flowers blush-pink, large (3 in.), borne in clusters; fragrant; foliage dark, glossy; very vigorous growth.

Shimmering Silk HT, *rb*, 1968, *Ena Harkness × Molly Doyle*; Barter. Flowers cerise tinted silvery pink, dbl., large; foliage dark; vigorous, upright growth.

Shining Coral HT, *pb*, 1992, (HADcoral); *Shining Ruby × (Honey Favorite × (Little Darling × Traviata))*; Davidson, Harvey; C & L Valley Rose Co., 1992-93. Flowers coral pink, semi-dbl. (22-24 petals), cupped, medium (10 cms) blooms borne in sprays of 1-3; moderate, fruity fragrance; foliage large, dark green, very glossy; medium, bushy growth.

Shining Flare HT, *or*, 1992, (HADflare); *Shining Ruby × (Smooth Sailing × Futura)*; Davidson, Harvey; C & L Valley Rose Co., 1992-93. Flowers orange-red, dbl. (24-26 petals), cupped, medium (11 cms) blooms borne in sprays; slight, fruity fragrance; foliage medium, dark green, very glossy; bushy, medium growth.

Shining Hour™ Gr, *dy*, 1989, (JACyef); *Sunbright × Sun Flare*; Warriner, William A.; Bear Creek Gardens, 1991. Bud ovoid; flowers deep, bright yellow, dbl. (33 petals), cupped, high-centered, medium, borne usually singly and in sprays of 3-5; moderate, fruity fragrance; foliage large, dark green, semi-glossy; prickles fairly long, hooked downward, red to yellow; upright, bushy, medium growth. AARS, 1991.

Shining Ruby HT, *mr*, 1992, (HADruby); *Pink Favorite × Simon Bolivar*; Davidson, Harvey; C & L Valley Rose Co., 1992-93. Flowers medium red, fading to blue, dbl. (24-26 petals), cupped, large (14 cms) blooms borne in sprays; moderate, spicy fragrance; foliage large, dark green, very glossy; bushy, medium growth.

Shining Star HT, *my*, 1945, (Mme. P. Olivier; Trylon); *Soeur Thérèse × Feu Pernet-Ducher*; Mallerin; C-P. Bud long, pointed; flowers vivid chrome-yellow, dbl., large; fragrant (fruity); foliage dark, leathery.

Shining Sun HT, *yb*, 1932, *Charles P. Kilham × Julien Potin*; Van Rossem. Bud long, pointed, golden yellow splashed scarlet; flowers yellow deepening to reddish center, dbl.; very fragrant; foliage thick, bronze; vigorous growth.

Shinju HT, *lp*, 1976, *Royal Highness × Garden Party*; Harada, Toshiyuki. Bud large, ovoid; flowers light pink, paler at petal edges, dbl. (28 petals), high-centered, large blooms borne 1-3 per stem; fragrant; foliage medium green, leathery; many, medium prickles, slanted downward; vigorous, upright growth.

Shin-sei HT, *dy*, 1979, (Shinsei); *(Ethel Sanday × Lydia) × Koto*; Suzuki; Keisei Rose Nursery, 1978. Bud pointed; flowers deep yellow, dbl. (38 petals), high-centered, well-formed, large blooms borne singly; fragrant; foliage medium large, medium green, glossy; prickles slanted downward; upright, bushy growth.

Shin-Setsu LCl, *w*, 1972, *(Blanche Mallerin × Neige Parfum) × New Dawn seedling*; Suzuki; Keisei Rose Nursery. Bud ovoid; flowers white, center soft cream, very dbl., high-centered, large; fragrant; foliage glossy, dark; very vigorous, climbing growth.

Shiralee HT, *yb*, 1965, *Seedling × Kordes' Perfecta*; Dickson, P.; A. Dickson. Flowers yellow flushed orange, dbl. (36 petals), high-centered, large (5½ in.); fragrant; vigorous, tall growth. GM, Japan, 1964.

Shire County HT, *op*, 1989, (HARsamy); *Amy Brown × Bonfire Night*; Harkness, R. & Co., Ltd., 1990. Bud ovoid; flowers peach on primrose yellow base, reverse salmon rose on primrose yellow base, aging deeper, dbl. (33 petals), cupped, medium, borne usually singly; moderate fragrance; foliage medium, medium green, semi-glossy; prickles decurved, medium, reddish; bushy, medium growth.

Shirley HT, *rb*, 1933, Dickson, A. Bud shaded russet; flowers light prawn-red, base yellow; very fragrant; vigorous growth.

Shirley Hibberd T (OGR), *my*, 1874, Levet, F. Flowers yellow, small.

Shirley Holmes HT, *ob*, 1958, *McGredy's Yellow × Ethel Sanday*; Mee; Edenvale Nursery. Bud long, pointed; flowers golden orange, dbl. (30 petals), large (4 in.); very fragrant; vigorous, bushy growth.

Shirley Laugharn HT, *yb*, 1974, *Granada × Garden Party*; Swim; Laugharn. Bud ovoid; flowers creamy yellow, edged pink, dbl. (35 petals), large (5 in.); fragrant (fruity); foliage dark; very vigorous, upright, slightly spreading growth.

Shirley Rose HT, *pb*, 1966, *Eden Rose sport*; Lawrence. Flowers cream and carmine, loose, large (5 in.); slightly fragrant; foliage dark; upright growth.

Shirley Temple HT, *ly*, 1936, *Joanna Hill* sport; Engle; Wyant. Flowers light yellow, edged lemon-yellow.

Shi-un HT, *m*, 1984, (Shiun); *(Blue Moon × Twilight) × (Red American Beauty × Happiness)*; Suzuki, S.; Keisei Rose Nursery. Flowers deep lilac purple, reverse deeper, dbl. (33 petals), high-centered, medium blooms borne singly; fragrant; foliage dark, leathery, semi-glossy; prickles slanted downward; vigorous, upright, bushy growth.

Shizu no Mai HT, *lp*, 1990, *Jana × Madame Violet*; Ohtsuki, Hironaka, 1986. Flowers light pastel pink, full (32-35 petals), high-centered, large, borne usually singly; slight fragrance; foliage medium, dark green, semi-glossy; sturdy, upright growth.

Shocking Pol, *rb*, 1967, *Red Favorite × Alain*; Hémeray-Aubert; McGredy. Flowers dark red, reverse lighter, high-centered, large (3 in.), borne in clusters; slightly fragrant; foliage dark, glossy; very low, erect growth.

Shocking Blue® F, *m*, 1974, (KORblue); *Seedling × Silver Star*, Kordes, 1985. Bud very large; flowers lilac-mauve, dbl., high-centered; very fragrant; foliage dark, glossy, leathery; vigorous.

Shocking Pink HT, *mp*, 1968, *Pink Sensation* sport; McCannon; DeVor Nursery. Flowers medium pink, dbl., cupped, large; very fragrant; foliage leathery; vigorous, upright growth; a greenhouse variety.

Shola F, *or*, 1969, *Anna Wheatcroft × Open pollination*; Indian Agric. Research Inst. Bud pointed; flowers sparkling orient red, dbl., full, medium; foliage leathery; vigorous, dwarf growth.

Shona F, *op*, 1982, (DICdrum); *Bangor × Anabell*; Dickson, Patrick. Flowers medium coral pink, semi-dbl. (23 petals), medium blooms in clusters; slight fragrance; foliage medium, medium green, semi-glossy; bushy growth.

Shooting Star Min, *yb*, 1972, *Rumba × (Dany Robin × Perla de Montserrat)*; Meilland; C-P. Bud ovoid; flowers yellow, tipped red, dbl., cupped, small; slightly fragrant; foliage small, light, soft; vigorous, dwarf growth.

Shootout Min, *ab*, 1981, *Tiki × Darling Flame*; Borst, Jim; Kimbrew-Walter Roses. Bud ovoid; flowers apricot-orange, dbl. (28 petals), blooms borne singly; very slight fragrance; foliage medium green; long, triangular, light green prickles; vigorous, bushy growth.

Short 'n' Sweet Min, *dp*, 1984, (TINshort); *Sheri Anne × Seedling*; Bennett, Dee; Tiny Petals Nursery. Flowers deep pink, dbl. (35 petals), very small; no fragrance; foliage medium, medium green, semi-glossy; bushy, spreading growth.

Shortcake™ Min, *rb*, 1991, (KEIbelmi); *Seedling × Seedling*; Keisei Rose Nurseries, Inc., 1981; Bear Creek Gardens (J&P), 1991. Bud ovoid, pointed; flowers red, white reverse, red color pales with age, blues slightly, dbl. (30-35 petals), cupped, large; no fragrance; foliage large, dark green, glossy; upright, bushy, tall growth.

Shot Silk HT, *pb*, 1924, *Hugh Dickson seedling × Sunstar*; Dickson, A. Flowers cherry-cerise, shading to golden yellow at base, dbl. (27 petals), high-centered; very fragrant; foliage glossy, slightly curled; vigorous. GM, NRS, 1923.

Shot Silk, Climbing Cl HT, *pb*, 1931, Knight, C.

Show Garden LCl, *mp*, 1954, (Pink Arctic); *Seedling × Queen o' the Lakes*; Brownell. Flowers crimson to rose-bengal, then magenta, dbl. (43 petals), large (4-5 in.); growth like a HT, followed by 4-5 ft. canes that bloom the first season.

Show Girl HT, *mp*, 1946, *Joanna Hill × Crimson Glory*; Lammerts; Armstrong Nursery. Bud long, pointed; flowers rose-pink, 15-20 petals, high-centered, large (3½-4½ in.); fragrant; foliage leathery; vigorous, upright, bushy growth. GM, NRS, 1950.

Show Girl, Climbing Cl HT, *mp*, 1949, Chaffin; Armstrong Nursery.

Show 'n' Tell Min, *ob*, 1988, (FOUtell); *Rocky × (Matangi × Honey Hill)*; Jacobs, Betty; Four Seasons Rose Nursery. Fl. bright, velvety orange-red, white border, reverse white, aging deeper, showing hand painting in cool weather, dbl. (30 petals) high centered, exhibition, large, borne usually singly or in sprays of up to 4; slight, spicy fragrance; foliage medium, medium green, semi-glossy, disease resistant; spreading, tall growth.

Showbiz F, *mr*, 1983, (TANweieke; Bernhard Daneke Rose; Ingrid Weibull); Tantau, M., 1981. Flowers bright medium red, semi-dbl. (20 petals), medium; no fragrance; foliage medium, dark, semi-glossy; bushy growth. AARS, 1985.

Showboat F, *yb*, 1965, *Carrousel × Seedling*; Patterson; Patterson Roses. Bud ovoid; flowers deep yellow on pink to cream ground, dbl. (30 petals), medium (2½ in.); fragrant; foliage leathery; moderate, bushy growth.

Showcase Min, *ab*, 1986, *Rise 'n' Shine × Over the Rainbow*; Stoddard, Louis. Flowers apricot, dbl. (35 petals), small; slight fragrance; foliage small, light green, semi-glossy; bushy.

Shower of Gold R, *my*, 1910, *Jersey Beauty* × *Instituteur Sirdey*; Paul. Flowers golden yellow, rapidly fading to pale yellow, dbl., rosette-shaped; foliage glossy, fern-like; very vigorous, climbing growth.

Showoff LCl, *mr*, 1952, *Blaze sport*; Moffet; Earl May Seed Co. Flowers scarlet, very dbl., cupped, medium to large, borne in large clusters; vigorous growth; profuse, recurrent bloom.

Showpiece HT, *mr*, 1958, Ratcliffe. Flowers bright scarlet; fragrant.

Showstopper HT, *dr*, 1981, (JACsho); *Seedling* × *Samantha*; Warriner; J&P. Bud pointed; flowers deep red, dbl. (33 petals), spiral blooms borne singly or 3-4 per cluster; very little fragrance; foliage large; long prickles; strong, upright, bushy growth.

Showtime HT, *mp*, 1969, *Kordes' Perfecta* × *Granada*; Lindquist; Howard Rose Co. Flowers pink, dbl., high-centered, large; fragrant (fruity); foliage glossy, leathery; vigorous, bushy.

Shree Dayananda HT, *dp*, 1979, *Scarlet Knight* × *Festival Beauty*; Hardikar, Dr. M.N. Bud ovoid; flowers deep pink, very dbl. (90 petals); fragrant; foliage small, green; beak-shaped prickles; bushy, dwarf growth.

Shreveport™ Gr, *ob*, 1981, (KORpesh); *Zorina* × *Uwe Seeler*; Kordes, R.; Armstrong Nursery. Bud ovoid, pointed; flowers orange, dbl. (50 petals), high-centered blooms borne 1-3 per cluster; slight tea fragrance; foliage large; small prickles, hooked downward; tall, upright, vigorous growth. Named in honor of the home city of ARS. AARS, 1982.

Shropshire Lass S, *lp*, 1968, *Mme. Butterfly* × *Mme. Legras de St. Germain*; Austin, D. Flowers blush-pink, single (5 petals), large (5 in.); fragrant; summer bloom.

Shu-getsu HT, *dy*, 1982, (Shugetsu); *Seiko* × *King's Ransom*; Suzuki, S.; Keisei Rose Nursery. Flowers deep yellow, dbl. (38 petals), high-centered, large; fragrant; foliage large, dark, glossy; large, straight prickles; upright, bushy growth.

Shun'yo HT, *ob*, 1982, *(Golden Sun* × *Summer Holiday)* × *(Garden Party* × *Narzisse)*; Kono, Yoshito. Flowers light yellow orange, dbl. (33 petals), high-centered, large; slight fragrance; foliage glossy, sickle-shaped prickles; vigorous, upright growth.

Shu-oh HT, *or*, 1982, (Shuo); *San Francisco* × *Pharaoh*; Suzuki, S.; Keisei Rose Nursery. Flowers orange-red, cupped, medium; fragrant; foliage dark, semi-glossy; prickles slanted downward; upright growth.

Shy Beauty Min, *mp*, 1985, (LYOshy); *Seedling* × *Seedling*; Lyon; MB Farms, Inc. Flowers medium pink, dbl. (55 petals), small blooms borne singly; slight fragrance; foliage medium, medium green, semi-glossy; bushy growth.

Shy Girl Min, *w*, 1988, (JACwhim); *Petticoat* × *Red Minimo*; Warriner, William; Bear Creek Gardens. Bud ovoid, pointed; flowers white, very dbl. (80 petals), high-centered, medium, borne usually singly and in sprays of 2-4; slight fragrance; foliage medium, dark green, semi-glossy; prickles straight, short; fruit none; upright, spreading, low growth.

Shy Maiden F, *rb*, 1984, (ANDshy); *Iceberg seedling* × *Iceberg*; Anderson Rose Nursery. Flowers white with red petal edges, dbl. (35 petals), large; slight fragrance; foliage medium, light green, glossy; bushy growth.

Si Min, *w*, *Perla de Montserrat* × *(Anny* × *Tom Thumb)*; Dot, P. Flowers rosy white, micromini, small; dwarf growth.

Si Bemol® Min, *m*, 1980, (LENmol); *(Little Angel* × *Le Vesuve)* × *Mr. Bluebird*; Lens, 1983. Flowers lilac blue and white, dbl. (30 petals), small blooms in clusters of 3-24; light fragrance; foliage dark; few, green prickles; bushy growth.

Sibelius HT, *mr*, 1958, *New Yorker* × *Étoile de Hollande*; Verschuren; Blaby Rose Gardens. Flowers velvety crimson, dbl., high-centered; vigorous growth.

Sidi-Brahim HT, *dy*, 1953, *Feu Pernet-Ducher* × *Mme. René Lefebvre*; Robichon. Flowers jonquil-yellow, dbl.; strong stems; slightly fragrant.

Sidney Peabody Gr, *dp*, 1955, *Rome Glory* × *Floribunda seedling*; deRuiter; Gandy. Flowers reddish pink, dbl. (36 petals), well formed, large (3½ in.), borne in clusters; slightly fragrant; foliage dark, leathery; very vigorous growth.

Sierra Dawn HT, *pb*, 1967, *Helen Traubel* × *Manitou*; Armstrong, D.L.; Armstrong Nursery. Bud long, pointed; flowers bright pink blend, dbl., high-centered, large; fragrant; foliage dark, bronze, leathery; vigorous, upright, bushy growth.

Sierra Glow HT, *pb*, 1942, *Crimson Glory* × *Soeur Thérèse*; Lammerts; Armstrong Nursery. Bud ovoid; flowers shrimp-pink, reverse strawberry-pink, dbl. (33 petals), high-centered, large (3½-4½ in.); fragrant; foliage leathery; vigorous, bushy, spreading growth.

Sierra Gold HT, *my*, 1960, *Queen Elizabeth* × *Tawny Gold*; Lammerts; Amling-DeVor Nursery. Bud urn shaped; flowers indian yellow, dbl (45-55 petals), high-centered, large (4-4½ in.); slightly fragrant; foliage leathery, semi-glossy; upright, compact growth; a greenhouse variety.

Sierra Snowstorm S, *ly*, 1936, *Gloire des Rosomanes* × *Dorothy Perkins*; Moore, R.S.; Henderson's Exp. Gardens and Brooks & Son. Bud long, pointed, cream and yellow; flowers white, single, open, small (2 in.) borne in clusters; very fragrant; foliage large, leathery, glossy, light; vigorous (5-6 ft.), bushy, arching growth; abundant, recurrent bloom.

Sierra Sunrise Min, *yb*, 1980, (MORliyel); *Little Darling* × *Yellow Magic*; Moore, R.S.; Sequoia Nursery. Bud medium, pointed; flowers soft yellow, petals tipped pink, dbl. (43 petals), cupped to high-centered, borne singly or 3-5 per cluster; slight fragrance; foliage medium, medium green; long, straight prickles; vigorous, bushy, upright growth. GM, NZ, 1984.

Sierra Sunset LCl, *yb*, 1961, *(Capt. Thomas* × *Joanna Hill)* × *Mme. Kriloff*; Morey; J&P. Bud pointed; flowers blend of yellow, peach, orange and red, dbl. (40 petals), high-centered, large (6 in.), in clusters; very fragrant (fruity); foliage glossy; vigorous (6-8 ft.) growth.

Siesta F, *or*, 1966, *Sarabande* × *Dany Robin*; Meilland; URS. Flowers light vermilion on cream base, dbl., large; foliage glossy, leathery; very free growth.

Sif LCl, *ob*, 1969, *Traumland* × *Royal Gold*; Lundstad. Flowers tangerine-orange, dbl. (25 petals), cupped, large; foliage dark, glossy; vigorous, climbing growth.

Signal Red Pol, *mr*, 1949, *DeRuiter's Herald* × *Polyantha seedling*; deRuiter; Gandy. Flowers scarlet, rosette-shaped, medium (2 in.) blooms in large trusses; foliage glossy, bronze; vigorous, bushy growth; (28).

Signalfeuer® F, *or*, 1959, (Fire Signal); *Lumina* × *Cinnabar seedling*; Tantau, Math. Flowers cinnabar to orange, dbl., blooms in clusters; bushy growth.

Signe Relander HRg (S), *dr*, 1928, *R. rugosa hybrid* × *Orléans Rose*; Poulsen, S.; Poulsen. Flowers bright dark red, dbl., small blooms in clusters; vigorous (6½ ft.) growth; recurrent bloom. Similar to Grootendorst Supreme.

Signet HT, *dp*, 1938, *Premier* × *Talisman*; Montgomery Co. Bud long, pointed; flowers deep pure pink, dbl., high-centered, large; very fragrant; foliage leathery; very vigorous growth.

Signora HT, *ob*, 1936, (Signora Piero Puricelli); *Julien Potin* × *Sensation*; Aicardi, D.; J&P. Bud long, pointed; flowers orange-apricot, suffused gold, outer petals magenta-pink, dbl.

(27 petals), cupped, large; fragrant; foliage glossy; vigorous. GM, Portland, 1937.

Silberlachs F, *op*, 1944, (Silver Salmon); *Rosenelfe* × *Hamburg*; Tantau. Flowers pale salmon, single (6-8 petals), shell shaped, borne in clusters of 3-10; slightly fragrant; foliage light green; upright, bushy growth.

Silent Night HT, *yb*, 1969, *Daily Sketch* × *Hassan*; McGredy. Flowers creamy yellow suffused pink, well-formed; slightly fragrant. GM, Geneva, 1969.

Silhouette® HT, *pb*, 1984, (Silver Medal); Warriner; J&P, 1980. Bud long, pointed; flowers white, petals edged pink, dbl. (25 petals), large (4-5 in.); foliage light green; upright growth.

Silk Hat™ HT, *m*, 1986, (AROsilha; AROsilma); *Ivory Tower* × *(Night 'n' Day* × *Plain Talk)*; Christensen; Armstrong Nursery, 1985. Flowers red purple, cream reverse, dbl. (45 petals), high-centered, exhibition, large blooms borne usually singly; fragrant; foliage large, medium green, matt; fruit none; medium, upright, bushy growth.

Silk Sash HT, *pb*, 1971, *Memoriam* × *Elizabeth Fankhauser*; Fankhauser. Flowers pastel pink, reverse silvery pink, very dbl. (85 petals), high-centered, very large; slightly fragrant; foliage dark, leathery; vigorous, upright growth.

Silva® HT, *pb*, 1964, (MEIcham); *Peace* × *Confidence*; Meilland, A.; URS. Bud long, pointed; flowers yellowish salmon shaded bright rose, dbl. (38 petals), high-centered, large (5½ in.); slightly fragrant; foliage dark, glossy, leathery; vigorous, upright growth. GM, The Hague, 1964.

Silva Graça HT, *ob*, 1956, *Michèle Meilland* × *Comtesse Vandal*; Moreira da Silva. Flowers salmon and yellow shaded pink, well shaped.

Silvabella HT, *pb*, 1967, *Dr. Debat* × *Eden Rose*; Guiseppe, M. Flower deep pink, reverse carmine-pink, dbl., cupped, large; slightly fragrant; foliage leathery; upright, bushy growth.

Silver Anniversary™ HT, *m*, 1990, (JAClav; Heather); *Crystalline* × *Shocking Blue*; Christensen, J.E., 1985; Bear Creek Gardens, 1990. Flowers medium lavender, reverse medium lavender, spot of yellow at base, aging paler, but still good lavender color to petal drop, dbl. (25-30 petals), urn-shaped, exhibition, large, borne singly; long, straight, sturdy stems average 24-32 in. long; heavy, damask fragrance; foliage large, very dk. green, semi-glossy-glossy; tall, upright, bushy growth.

Silver Beauty F, *m*, 1956, *La France seedling*; Verschuren; Gandy. Flowers silvery rose-madder; vigorous, bushy growth.

Silver Bell F, *lp*, 1976, (Gin no suzu); *Gene Boerner* × *Seedling*; Takatori; Japan Rose Nursery. Bud ovoid; flowers soft light pink, dbl. (35 petals), high-centered, small (2 in.); foliage glossy; vigorous, upright growth.

Silver Charm F, *m*, 1968, *Lilac Charm* × *Sterling Silver*; LeGrice. Flowers lavender-blue, semi-dbl., large blooms in large trusses; fragrant; foliage dark; vigorous, low growth.

Silver Columbia HT, *pb*, 1924, *Columbia sport*; Leonard. Flowers clear silver-pink.

Silver Dawn LCl, *w*, 1942, *Silver Moon* × *Silver Moon*; Zombory. Flowers creamy white, center deeper, stamens golden yellow, very dbl. (90-100 petals), open, large; foliage large, leathery, glossy, dark; vigorous (10-12 ft.), compact, climbing growth.

Silver Enchantment HT, *rb*, 1971, *Tropicana* × *Seedling*; Gregory. Flowers rich red, reverse silver, dbl. (36 petals), conical, large; fragrant; foliage dark; very free growth.

Silver Fox HT, *w*, 1992, (DEVspilio); *Seedling* × *Seedling*; Marciel, Stanley G. & Jeanne A.; DeVor Nurseries, Inc. Flowers white, dbl. (26-40 petals), large (7+ cms) blooms borne mostly single; slight fragrance; foliage large, dark green, semi-glossy; some prickles; tall (210 cms), upright growth.

Silver Gem F, *m*, 1969, deRuiter. Flowers silver-mauve, semi-dbl., large, borne in trusses; foliage dark, leathery; bushy growth.

Silver Jubilee HT, *yb*, 1937, Dickson, A. Flowers light golden yellow, base chrome, edged canary, dbl., very large; fragrant; foliage very large, glossy; vigorous growth. RULED EXTINCT 4/77.

Silver Jubilee® HT, *pb*, 1978, ((*Highlight* × *Colour Wonder*) × (*Parkdirektor Riggers* × *Piccadilly*)) × *Mischief*; Cocker. Flowers silvery pink, reverse darker, dbl. (33 petals), high-centered, large (5 in.); slightly fragrant; foliage glossy; vigorous. RNRS PIT, 1977; GM, RNRS, 1977; Belfast, 1980.

Silver Jubilee, Climbing Cl HT, *pb*, 1983, Cocker.

Silver Lady F, *m*, 1991, *Azure Sea* × *Seedling*; Taylor, Pete & Kay; Taylor's Roses, 1993. Flowers pale lavender, with a hint of darker lavender on edges of petals, reverse same, semi-dbl. (15-25 petals), large (7+ cms) blooms borne singly and in small clusters; no fragrance; foliage medium, medium green, semi-glossy; some prickles; medium (90 cms), upright, bushy growth.

Silver Lining HT, *pb*, 1958, *Karl Herbst* × *Eden Rose seedling*; Dickson, A. Flowers silvery rose, dbl. (30 petals), large (5 in.); very fra-

grant; vigorous. GM, NRS, 1958; Portland, 1964.

Silver Moon LCl, *w*, 1910, *Reputedly (R. wichuraiana* × *Devoniensis)* × *R. laevigata*; Van Fleet; P. Henderson. Bud long, pointed; flowers creamy white, base amber, stamens darker, semi-dbl. (20 petals), large (4½ in.) blooms in clusters; slightly fragrant; foliage large, dark, leathery, glossy; very vigorous (to 20 ft. or more); non-recurrent bloom.

Silver Phantom Min, *m*, 1988, (RENhom; Melissa Joyce); *Shocking Blue* × *Angelglo*; Rennie, Bruce F.; Rennie Roses, 1989. Bud pointed; flowers silver-lavender, dbl. (33 petals), high-centered, exhibition, large, borne usually singly; slight, licorice fragrance; foliage medium, dark green, semi-glossy; prickles hooked, medium, light tan-red to dark; fruit globular, medium, yellow-orange; upright, bushy, tall growth.

Silver Princess HT, *ob*, 1934, Burbank; Stark Bros. Bud salmon-yellow to delicate pink; flowers almost ivory-white, tinged pink, semi-dbl., very large; vigorous growth.

Silver Shadows HT, *m*, 1984, ((*Soir d'Automne* × *Music Maker*) × *Solitude*) × ((*Blue Moon* × *Tom Brown*) × *Autumn Dusk*); Buck; Iowa State University. Flowers light blue-lavender, dbl. (33 petals), cupped, large blooms borne 3-5 per cluster; very fragrant; foliage large, dark, leathery; awl-like, tan prickles; upright, bushy growth; repeat bloom; hardy.

Silver Slippers Min, *m*, 1991, (PIXislip); *Deep Purple* × *Jennifer*; Chaffin, Lauren M.; Pixie Treasures Miniature Roses, 1992. Bud slender; flowers unique silvery lavender, dbl. (26-40 petals), medium (4-7 cms) blooms borne mostly singly; fragrant; foliage medium, medium green, semi-glossy; medium (30 cms), bushy growth.

Silver Spoon HT, *m*, 1985, *Louisiana* × *Seedling*; Weeks, O.L.; Weeks Roses, Inc. Flowers mauve, dbl. (35 petals), large; no fragrance; foliage large, medium green, semi-glossy; upright, bushy, spreading growth.

Silver Star® HT, *m*, 1966, (KORbido); *Sterling Silver* × *Magenta seedling*; Kordes, R.; McGredy. Flowers lavender, dbl., well-formed, large (5 in.); very fragrant; foliage dark.

Silver Tips Min, *pb*, 1961, (*R. wichuraiana* × *Floradora*) × *Lilac Time*; Moore, R.S.; Sequoia Nursery. Bud pointed; flowers pink, reverse and tips silvery, becoming soft lavender, dbl. (50 petals), small (1 in.); slightly fragrant; foliage leathery; vigorous, bushy (10-12 in.) growth.

Silver Wedding HT, *w*, 1921, *Ophelia sport*; Amling Co. Flowers almost identical to parent.

Silver Wings HT, *w*, 1943, McGredy. Bud long, pointed; flowers ivory-white, dbl., high-centered, large; slightly fragrant; foliage glossy; vigorous, upright, bushy growth.

Silverado HT, *m*, 1987, (AROgrewod); *(Ivory Tower × Angel Face) × Paradise*; Christensen; Armstrong Nursery. Flowers soft silver blushed ruby, reverse white, dbl. (28 petals), high-centered, exhibition, large blooms borne usually singly; slightly fragrant; foliage medium, dark, matt; large prickles, hooked slightly downward; medium, bushy growth.

Silverelda HT, *pb*, *Heinrich Wendland × Nancy Wilson*; Riethmuller. Flowers veined silvery buff-pink, edged lighter, base yellow, dbl. (35 petals); slightly fragrant; foliage glossy; vigorous, compact growth.

Silvery Moon HT, *m*, 1982, (LEOsilmu); *Silver Star × Blue Moon*; Leon, Charles F., Sr. Flowers lilac, dbl. (35 petals), large; very fragrant; foliage medium, medium green, leathery, matt; sets seed; upright growth.

Silvia HT, *yb*, 1920, (Yellow Ophelia); *Ophelia sport*; Pierson, F.R. Flowers sulphur-yellow shading to white.

Silvia Leyva HT, *mr*, 1933, *Mrs. C.W. Edwards × Mari Dot*; Dot, P.; C-P. Flowers cardinal-red, dbl., cupped, large; fragrant; foliage glossy; vigorous growth.

Simerose HT, *rb*, 1939, *Charles P. Kilham × (Charles P. Kilham × Margaret McGredy)*; Meilland, F. Bud long; flowers nasturtium-red, reverse golden yellow; vigorous growth.

Simon Bolivar HT, *or*, 1966, *Roundelay × El Capitan*; Armstrong, D.L.; Armstrong Nursery. Bud ovoid; flowers bright orange-red, dbl. (40 petals), high-centered, large; slightly fragrant; foliage dark, glossy, leathery; vigorous, upright, bushy growth.

Simon de St. Jean HP (OGR), *m*, 1861, Liabaud. Flowers velvety purple.

Simon Dot HT, *or*, 1978, (DOTsurodo); *Pharaoh × Rose Dot*; Dot, S. Flowers orange-red, dbl. (35 petals), deeply cupped, large (5 in.); very fragrant; foliage dark, upright growth.

Simon Fraser S, *mp*, 1992, (*Bonanza × (Arthur Bell × (Red Dawn × Suzanne))) × (Single Kordesii × (Red Dawn × Suzanne) × Champlain)))*; Ogilvie, Ian; Agriculture Canada, 1992. Flowers medium pink, single to semi-dbl. (6-14 petals), medium (4-7 cms) blooms borne in small clusters; slight fragrance; foliage dark green, semi-glossy; some prickles; low (60 cms), upright growth; extremely winter hardy.

Simon Robinson Min, *mp*, 1982, (TRObwich); *R. wichuraiana × New Penny*; Robinson, Thomas. Flowers medium pink, single (5 petals), small blooms in clusters of 10-60; fragrant; foliage small, dark, glossy; compact, low, bushy growth.

Simona HT, *ab*, 1979, (TANmosina); Tantau, M. Flowers apricot, semi-dbl. (20 petals), large; fragrant; foliage large, medium green, matt; upright; greenhouse variety.

Simone HT, *w*, 1924, *Mme. Caroline Testout × Paul Monnier*; Buatois. Flowers flesh-white, center deeper pink, passing to creamy white, dbl.; fragrant.

Simone HT, *m*, 1957, (Mauve Mallerin; Parme); *(Peace × Independence) × Grey Pearl*; Mallerin; Hémeray-Aubert. Bud ovoid; flowers pastel lilac, dbl. (50 petals), high-centered to cupped, large (6 in.); fragrant; foliage leathery, dark, glossy; vigorous growth.

Simone Damaury HT, *dr*, 1925, *Liberty × Gen. MacArthur*; Soupert; Notting. Bud long, pointed; flowers brilliant crimson, semi-dbl.; very fragrant.

Simone de Chevigné HT, *pb*, 1924, Pernet-Ducher. Flowers flesh-pink, shaded yellow, dbl.

Simone de Nanteuil HT, *pb*, 1925, *Ophelia × Mme. Vittoria Gagnière*; Schwartz, A. Bud long, pointed; flowers rosy white, tinted carmine-pink, reverse flesh, dbl.; fragrant.

Simone Guérin HT, *my*, 1929, *Constance × Hybrid Tea seedling*; Mallerin. Flowers coral-yellow, semi-dbl., high-centered, large; slightly fragrant; foliage glossy, dark; vigorous growth.

Simone Labbé HT, *ab*, 1922, *Le Progrès × Lady Greenall*; Ketten Bros. Bud long, pointed; flowers apricot-yellow, passing to clear saffron-yellow, dbl.; very fragrant.

Simone Mayery HT, *yb*, 1937, Chambard, C. Bud long, pointed, cream-yellow, shaded carmine-pink; flowers cream, center dark yellow, cupped, very large; foliage bronze; vigorous growth.

Simonet's Double Pink Rugosa HRg (S), *mp*, *R. macounii × Mme. Georges Bruant*; Simonet; P.H. Wright. Flowers pink, very dbl., smaller than Hansa; non-recurrent bloom; hardy.

Simple Simon Min, *mp*, 1955, (*R. multiflora nana × Mrs. Pierre S. duPont) F² × Tom Thumb*; de Vink; T. Robinson. Flowers carmine-rose, base yellow, dbl.

Simplex Min, *w*, 1961, (*R. wichuraiana × Floradora) × Seedling*; Moore, R.S.; Sequoia Nursery. Bud long, pointed, apricot; flowers white, single (5 petals), small (1½ in.) blooms in small clusters; slightly fragrant; foliage leathery; vigorous, bushy (12-14 in.).

Simplicity F, *mp*, 1978, (JACink); *Iceberg* × *Seedling*; Warriner; J&P, 1979. Bud long, pointed; flowers medium pink, semi-dbl. (18 petals), flat, large (3-4 in.); slightly fragrant; bushy, upright growth. GM, NZ, 1976.

Simplicity HT, *w*, 1909, Dickson, H. Flowers pure white, single, open; slightly fragrant; foliage glossy, rich green.

Simply Divine F, *rb*, 1978, *Elizabeth of Glamis* × *Evelyn Fison*; Anderson's Rose Nursery. Flowers red blend, semi-dbl. (18 petals), large (3½ in.); slightly fragrant; foliage dark.

Simpson's Red HT, *dr*, 1977, *Red Lion* × *Grande Amore*; Simpson, J.W.; Lower Rangitikei Rose Soc. Flowers dark red, dbl. (40 petals), medium (3½in.); slightly fragrant.

Sinbad HT, *op*, 1964, *Pink Lustre* × *Circus*; Leenders, J. Flowers salmon-pink.

Sincerely Yours Min, *mr*, 1991, (MORdort); *Sheri Anne* × *Dortmund*; Moore, Ralph S.; Sequoia Nursery, 1992. Flowers medium red, single to semi-dbl. (6-14 petals), medium (4-7 cms) blooms borne in small clusters; no fragrance; foliage medium, medium green, semi-glossy; some prickles; medium (20-24 cms), bushy growth. AOE, 1992.

Sincerity HT, *ob*, 1940, *Comtesse Vandal seedling* × *Mrs. Sam McGredy*; LeGrice. Bud long, pointed; flowers flesh, shaded amber and orange, dbl., large; slightly fragrant; foliage dark, leathery; vigorous, compact growth.

Sindoor F, *or*, 1980, *Sea Pearl* × *Suryodaya*; Division of Vegetable Crops and Floriculture. Bud long, pointed; flowers orange-red, semi-dbl. (23 petals), blooms borne singly or 15 per cluster; no fragrance; foliage large, glossy, coppery when young; straight prickles, bending downward; upright, tall growth.

Singalong Min, *op*, 1988, (MACsingal); *(Anytime* × *Eyepaint)* × *New Year*; McGredy, Sam. Flowers salmon-orange and yellow, dbl. (26-40 petals), medium; patio; slight fragrance; foliage small, medium green, glossy; bushy growth.

Single Bliss Min, *pb*, 1980, *Seabreeze* × *Baby Betsy McCall*; Saville, F. Harmon; Nor'East Min. Roses. Bud short, pointed; flowers deep pink and white, single (5 petals), flat blooms borne 5-30 per cluster; little fragrance; foliage very small, very glossy; straight prickles; very compact, bushy growth.

Single Charm Min, *pb*, 1990, (UMScharm); *Jennifer* × *Seedling*; Umsawasdi, Dr. Theera. Flowers hand-painted white with pink edge, single (5 petals), small, borne mostly singly;

no fragrance; foliage small, medium green, matt; tall, upright, bushy growth.

Single's Better™ Min, *mr*, 1985, (SAVabet); *(Yellow Jewel* × *Tamango)* × *((Little Chief* × *Sarabande)* × *Lemon Delight)*; Saville, F. Harmon; Nor'East Min. Roses. Bud mossy; flowers medium red, yellow tinge, single (5 petals), mini-moss, small; slight fragrance; foliage medium, medium green, semi-glossy; bushy growth.

Siobhan F, *rb*, 1984, (SEAsio); *Maxi* × *Copper Pot*; McCann, Sean. Flowers red, reverse yellow, semi-dbl. (20 petals), HT form, medium; slight fragrance; foliage medium, dark bronze, semi-glossy; upright growth.

Sioux Beauty S, *rb*, 1927, *Tetonkaha* × *American Beauty*; Hansen, N.E. Flowers bright rose, center dark crimson, very dbl. (100 petals); fragrant; non-recurrent bloom; hardy;

Sir Min, *ab*, 1992, (JOLsir); *Olympic Gold* × *Rise 'n' Shine*; Jolly, Marie; Rosehill Farm, 1993. Flowers apricot, single to semi-dbl. (6-14 petals), small (0-4 cms) blooms; fragrant; foliage medium, dark green, semi-glossy; few prickles; medium growth.

Sir Alexander N. Rochfort HT, *ob*, 1917, *Lady Alice Stanley* × *Marquise de Sinéty*; Le Cornu. Flowers flesh, center darker.

Sir Arthur Streeton HT, *mp*, 1940, Clark, A. Flowers pink, well formed.

Sir Basil McFarland HT, *ob*, 1931, McGredy. Bud long, pointed; flowers orange-salmon-pink, flushed yellow, dbl., high-centered; fragrant; foliage thick; vigorous growth.

Sir Billy Butlin HT, *or*, 1969, (Sir William Butlin); *Bettina* × *Majorca*; Gandy. Flowers red-orange, dbl. (30 petals), cupped, large; slightly fragrant; foliage bronze; vigorous, upright growth.

Sir Cedric Morris LCl, *w*, 1980, *R. glauca* × *Seedling*; Morris, Sir Cedric; Peter Beales, 1979. Bud small, globular; flowers white, single (5 petals), blooms borne 20-40 per cluster; slight fragrance; foliage elongated, large; large prickles; very vigorous growth; summer bloom only in large quantity.

Sir Dallas Brooks HT, *mr*, 1962, *Ena Harkness* × *Charles Mallerin*; Smith, R.W.; T.G. Stewart. Bud long, pointed; flowers medium red, dbl., high-centered, large; fragrant; foliage leathery; vigorous, upright, open growth.

Sir David Davis HT, *rb*, 1926, McGredy. Bud long, pointed; flowers deep glowing crimson, base light yellow, dbl., high-centered; very fragrant; foliage dark, leathery; vigorous growth.

Sir David Reid HT, *mr*, 1941, Dickson, A. Flowers crimson-red, dbl. (25 petals), flat, large; fragrant.

Sir Galahad F, *dp*, 1967, *Pink Parfait × Highlight*; Harkness. Flowers deep pink, dbl., medium; slightly fragrant; foliage glossy.

Sir Harry HT, *my*, 1989, *Irish Gold × (Pink Favorite × Golden Autumn)*; Bracegirdle, A.J.; Gregory's Roses, 1989. Bud ovoid; flowers medium yellow, dbl. (30 petals), high-centered, medium, borne usually singly; slight fruity fragrance; foliage medium, dark green, glossy; prickles triangular, brown; fruit round, orange; bushy, medium growth.

Sir Harry Pilkington HT, *mr*, 1974, (TANema; Melina); *Inge Horstmann × Sophia Loren*; Harry Wheatcroft Gardening. Flowers red, dbl. (30 petals), well-formed, large (4-5 in.); slightly fragrant; foliage dark.

Sir Henry Segrave HT, *ly*, 1932, Dickson, A. Bud long, pointed; flowers light primrose-yellow, dbl., high-centered, large; very fragrant; foliage leathery. GM, NRS, 1932.

Sir Joseph Paxton B (OGR), *dr*, 1852, Laffay. Flowers deep red tinted violet, well-formed, medium.

Sir Lancelot F, *ab*, 1967, *Vera Dalton × Woburn Abbey*; Harkness. Flowers apricot-yellow, semi-dbl., large (3-4 in.); slightly fragrant; foliage light green, glossy.

Sir Thomas Lipton HRg (S), *w*, 1900, *R. rugosa alba × Clotilde Soupert*; Van Fleet; Conard; Jones. Flowers white, dbl., cupped; fragrant; foliage dark, leathery; vigorous (6-8 ft.), bushy growth; recurrent bloom.

Sir Walter Raleigh HT, *ob*, 1919, *Lady Pirrie × Seedling*; Le Cornu. Bud long, pointed; flowers coppery reddish salmon, reverse deep crimson, dbl.; fragrant.

Sir Winston Churchill HT, *op*, 1955, *Seedling × Souv. de Denier van der Gon*; Dickson, A. Flowers salmon-pink shaded orange, dbl. (48 petals), high-centered, large (5 in.); fragrant; foliage dark, glossy; very vigorous growth. GM, NRS, 1955.

Siren F, *or*, 1953, *(Baby Château × Else Poulsen) × Independence*; Kordes; J&P. Bud ovoid; flowers bright scarlet-red, semi-dbl. (18 petals), cupped, large (3-3½ in.) blooms in clusters; fragrant; foliage leathery; vigorous, compact growth. GM, NRS.

Sirena HT, *rb*, 1941, *Saturnia × Anemone*; Aicardi, D.; Giacomasso. Bud ovoid; flowers cardinal-red, center shaded yellow, dbl., cupped, very large; very fragrant; foliage leathery; very vigorous growth.

Sirius Cl HT, *mr*, 1939, *Seedling × Lubra*; Fitzhardinge; Hazlewood Bros. Bud long,

pointed; flowers cherry-red, center lighter, dbl., large; very fragrant; vigorous, climbing (15 ft.), open habit; intermittent bloom.

Sirocco F, *or*, 1971, *Independence × Orangeade*; Delforge. Bud globular; flowers vermilion-red, very dbl., cupped, large; slightly fragrant; foliage dark, leathery; vigorous, bushy growth.

Sister Kenny F, *mr*, 1954, *Baby Château × Red Delicious*; Hill, J.H., Co.; H&S. Bud ovoid; flowers scarlet, single (10-12 petals), flat, medium, borne in clusters; slightly fragrant; foliage leathery; very vigorous, upright growth.

Sister Susan HT, *r*, *Mrs. Sam McGredy × Soeur Thérèse*; Oliver, F. Bud ovoid, yellow stained crimson; flowers cream tinted flesh, center copper-orange, base yellow, dbl. (48 petals), high-centered, medium; slightly fragrant; foliage leathery, glossy, dark; vigorous, spreading growth.

Sitting Bull HSet (OGR), *dp*, Horvath. Flowers deep pink, semi-dbl.; height 6-8 ft.; nonrecurrent bloom; not hardy.

Sitting Pretty Min, *pb*, 1986, (TINsit); *Sonoma × Mabel Dot*; Bennett, Dee; Tiny Petals Nursery. Bud ovoid, lacy sepals; flowers apricot pink, yellow base, dbl. (38 petals), high-centered, exhibition, medium blooms borne usually singly and in sprays of 3-4; heavy damask fragrance; foliage medium, medium green, semi-glossy; small, red prickles; fruit globular, ½ in. diam., yellowish-green; medium, upright, bushy growth.

Six Flags Gr., *mr*, 1962, (Manja; Manja Mourier); *First Love × Roundelay*; Swim; Five M Nursery; Poulsen. Flowers cherry-red, dbl. (25-30 petals), high-centered to cupped, large (3½-4 in.); foliage slender, leathery, semi-glossy; vigorous, upright, spreading growth.

Sizzle Pink™ HT, *dp*, 1989, (DEVcali); *Seedling × Seedling*; Marciel, Stanley G.; DeVor Nursery. Bud slender, tapering; flowers deep pink, dbl. (25 petals), cupped, large, borne singly; sweetheart; slight fragrance; foliage large, dark green, matt; prickles declining, olive green; upright, tall growth.

Sizzler Min, *or*, 1975, *Sheri Anne × Prominent*; Saville; Nor'East Min. Roses. Flowers orange-red, dbl. (28 petals), high-centered, small (1-1½ in.); fragrant (spicy); vigorous, upright, spreading growth.

Sjoukji Dijkstra Pol, *mr*, 1966, *Chatter × Paprika*; Buisman. Bud ovoid; flowers scarlet, semi-dbl., medium, borne in large clusters; compact growth.

Skaggarak F, *mr*, 1970, *Irish Wonder × Seedling*; Poulsen. Flowers medium red, semi-dbl. 18-20 petals, large (3½-6 in.); slightly fragrant.

Skarlagen General MacArthur HT, *dr*, 1930, *General MacArthur × Seedling*; Poulsen, S.; Poulsen's Roses. Flowers scarlet, dbl., large; slight fragrance; foliage medium, dark, semi-glossy; upright growth.

Skinner's Rambler R, *lp*, 1955, *R. maximowicziana × Seedling*; Skinner; Univ. of NH. Bud long, pointed; flowers pale pink, single (5 petals), open, small, borne in clusters of 10-40; slightly fragrant; foliage soft green; very vigorous, climbing (20 ft. annually).

Skogul F, *dp*, 1969, *Lichterloh × Lumina*; Lundstad. Flowers rose-madder, semi-dbl. (18 petals), open, borne in clusters; foliage dark, glossy; vigorous growth.

Skylark F, *mp*, 1958, *Carol Amling sport*; DeVor, P.; Amling Roses. Bud urn shaped; flowers pink, reverse darker, dbl. (55-65 petals), high-centered to flat, medium (2½ in.), borne in clusters of 3-15; foliage glossy; very vigorous, upright growth.

Skylon HT, *rb*, 1952, *Mme. Henri Guillot sport*; Lowe. Bud very long, pointed; flowers orange shaded peach, veined red, dbl. (26 petals), large (5½-6 in.); foliage glossy; very free growth.

Skyrocket HMsk (S), *dr*, 1934, (Wilhelm); *Robin Hood (HMsk) × J.C. Thornton*; Kordes. Bud long, pointed; flowers dark red, semi-dbl., medium blooms in clusters of 50; fragrant; foliage large, glossy, leathery; vigorous, bushy (6-8 ft.) growth; recurrent bloom.

Slater's Crimson China Ch (OGR), *mr*, (Chinese Monthly Rose; Crimson China Rose; Old Crimson China; *R. bengalensis* Persoon; *R. chinensis semperflorens* (Curtis) Koehne; *R. diversifolia* Ventenat; *R. indica semperflorens* (Curtis) Seringe; *R. semperflorens* Curtis); A specimen dated 1733 is in the British Museum; ca. 1790. Flowers cherry red, usually solitary, on slender stems.

Slava™ HT, *rb*, 1987, (WILslav); *Garden Party × Love*; Williams, J. Benjamin, 1988-89. Flowers scarlet red, reverse ivory white, dbl. (34 petals), high-centered, exhibition, large, borne singly or in sprays of 1-3; damask fragrance; foliage large, dark green, glossy, disease resistant; medium, few, yellow-green prickles, hooked downwards; fruit rounded, medium, pumpkin-orange; upright, bushy, tall growth.

Sláva Böhmova HT, *rb*, 1930, *Covent Garden × Golden Emblem*; Böhm. Bud long; flowers salmon-red, base golden yellow, full, large; foliage blood-red, mahonia-like.

Slavia R, *w*, 1934, *Tausendschön × Seedling*; Brada; Böhm. Flowers rosy white, borne in large clusters; very fragrant; vigorous growth; recurrent bloom.

Slávuse HT, *w*, 1936, Brada. Flowers white, cactus dahlia form.

Sleeping Beauty HT, *w*, 1966, *(Frau Karl Druschki × Rex Anderson) × Virgo*; Morey; Country Garden Nursery. Bud long, pointed; flowers white, dbl., high-centered, large; fragrant; foliage leathery; vigorous, upright growth.

Sleepy Pol, *mp*, 1955, (Baldwin); *(Orange Triumph × Golden Rapture) × Polyantha seedling*; deRuiter; Gregory; Willicher Baumschulen. Flowers medium pink, dbl., very small blooms in trusses.

Sleepy Time Min, *op*, 1973, *Ellen Poulsen × Fairy Princess*; Moore, R.S.; Sequoia Nursery. Bud long, pointed; flowers soft peach to soft salmon-pink, dbl., small; slightly fragrant; foliage small, light, leathery; vigorous, dwarf, upright, bushy growth.

Sleigh Bells HT, *w*, 1950, *Capt. Thomas × Eternal Youth*; Howard, P.J.; H&S. Bud ovoid, cream; flowers white, center creamy, dbl. (40 petals), open, large; very fragrant; foliage leathery, glossy; very vigorous, upright growth.

Small Fantasy Min, *lp*, 1982, *Snow Magic × Blue Mist*; Dobbs, Annette. Flowers light pink, dbl. (40+ petals), small; slight fragrance; foliage small, light green, semi-glossy; bushy growth.

Small Slam Min, *dr*, 1984, (LAVlinc); *Nic Noc × Party Girl*; Laver, Keith. Flowers dark red, dbl. (40+ petals), small; slight fragrance; foliage small, dark, semi-glossy; bushy growth.

Small Talk F, *my*, 1963, *Yellow Pinocchio × Circus*; Swim; Weeks; Weeks. Flowers medium yellow, dbl. (33 petals), high-centered to flat, medium (2½ in.) blooms in large clusters; slightly fragrant; foliage leathery, glossy, dark; compact, low growth.

Small Virtue Min, *w*, 1986, *Party Girl × Snow Bride*; Jolly, Marie; Rosehill Farm, 1983. Flowers white, dbl. (48 petals), high-centered, exhibition, small blooms borne singly and in sprays of 2-7; slight fragrance; foliage small, medium green, semi-glossy; medium pink prickles; fruit not observed; low, bushy growth.

Small Wonder Min, *pb*, 1983, *Futura × Orange Honey*; Hardgrove, Donald L.; Rose World Originals. Flowers light pink, darker reverse, dbl. (40+ petals), high-centered, exhibition, small blooms borne singly; no fragrance;

foliage small, medium green, semi-glossy; upright, bushy growth.

Small World Min, *or*, 1975, *Little Chief* × *Fire Princess*; Moore, R.S.; Sequoia Nursery. Bud pointed; flowers rich orange-red, semi-dbl. (21 petals), flat, medium (2½ in.); foliage small, glossy, leathery; dwarf, compact growth.

Smarty® S, *lp*, 1979, (INTersmart); *Yesterday* × *Seedling*; Ilsink; Dickson Nursery. Flowers light pink, single (7 petals), small (2 in.) blooms in clusters; foliage bright green, matt; many, small prickles; vigorous growth; repeat bloom; ground cover.

S. M. Gustave V HP (OGR), *dr*, 1922, *Frau Karl Druschki* × *Avoca*; Nabonnand, P. Bud long, pointed, brilliant crimson; flowers carmine, reflexes crimson, dbl. (30 petals), well formed, cupped, very large; fragrant; vigorous growth.

Smiles F, *lp*, 1937, *Echo* × *Rev. F. Page-Roberts*; Nicolas; J&P. Flowers light salmon-pink, semi-dbl., medium blooms in clusters; slightly fragrant; foliage leathery; bushy.

Smiles Min, *my*, 1984, (JACsmi); *Spanish Sun* × *Calgold*; Warriner; J&P. Flowers medium yellow, dbl. (35 petals), medium; slight fragrance; foliage small, light green, semi-glossy; upright, bushy growth.

Smiley F, *ob*, 1979, *Arthur Bell* × *Little Darling*; Murray, N. Bud pointed; flowers orange, apricot, yellow, semi-dbl. (21 petals), shapely, medium (2½ in.); foliage matt green; tall, vigorous, upright growth.

Smiling Through F, *or*, 1976, *Orange Sensation* × *Mme. Louis Laperrière*; Anderson's Rose Nursery. Flowers orange to red, dbl. (27 petals), large (3 in.); slightly fragrant; foliage glossy, light.

Smiling Through F, *or*, 1976, *Orange Sensation* × *Mme. Louis Laperriere*; Anderson's Rose Nursery. Flowers orange to red, dbl. (27 petals), full, large (3 in.); slightly fragrant; foliage glossy, light; very free bloom; repeating well.

Smith's Parish T (OGR), *rb*, Well established in Bermuda. Flowers creamy white, occasionally with a red stripe on a few petals, with rare occurrences of all red blooms, dbl., medium; foliage light green. Possibly identical to or descended from Five-Colored Rose.

SMItling F, *or*, 1983, (Lady Taylor); *Elizabeth of Glamis* × *Topsi*; Smith, Edward; C. Gregory & Son, 1984. Flowers vermilion, dbl. (35 petals), patio, medium; slight fragrance; foliage medium, medium green, matt; bushy growth.

Smits' Briar HRg (S), no color reported, *R. rugosa* × *R. canina*; Smits. Vigorous understock, little used now.

Smoke Signals™ Min, *m*, 1989, (MINaxco); *(Tom Brown* × *(Rise 'n' Shine* × *Watercolor))* × *Twilight Trail*; Williams, Ernest D.; Mini-Roses. Flowers smoky, lavender-gray, dbl. (33 petals), exhibition, small; very fragrant; foliage small, medium green, glossy; upright, bushy growth.

Smoky HT, *rb*, 1968, Combe; J&P. Flowers smoky oxblood-red shaded burgundy, dbl., medium; vigorous, upright growth.

Smoky Mountain Min, *m*, 1988, *Black Jade* × *Seedling*; Bridges, Dennis; Bridges Roses, 1989. Bud pointed; flower deep mauve, semi-dbl. (24 petals), high-centered, exhibition, medium, borne usually singly; slight fragrance; foliage medium, dark green, semi-glossy; prickles straight, pointed, small, tan; upright, medium growth.

Smooth Angel HT, *ab*, 1986, (HADangel); *Smooth Sailing* × *Royal Flush*; Davidson, Harvey; Gurney Seed. Flower petals apricot blending to cream at edges, dbl. (36 petals), cupped, large blooms borne usually singly; foliage medium, medium green, matt; no prickles; fruit none; medium, bushy, spreading growth.

Smooth Lady HT, *mp*, 1986, (HADlady); *Smooth Sailing* × *((Polly* × *Peace)* × *Circus)*; Davidson, Harvey; Gurney Seed. Flowers medium pink, semi-dbl. (21 petals), urn-shaped to loose, medium blooms in clusters of 1-3; spicy fragrance; foliage large, medium green, very glossy; no prickles; fruit medium, orange, globular; tall, upright, bushy growth.

Smooth Melody F, *rb*, 1990, (HADmelody); *Royal Flush* × *Smooth Lady*; Davidson, Harvey, 1979; Hortico; C&L Valley Rose Co., 1990-91. Bud ovoid; flowers red to white center, white reverse with red on outer edge, aging darker, dbl. (26 petals), urn-shaped, loose, medium, borne in sprays of 3-4; heavy, fruity fragrance; foliage medium, dark green, semi-glossy; thornless; fruit round, rarely sets seed.

Smooth Perfume HT, *lp*, 1990, (HADperfume); *(Smooth Sailing* × *Medallion)* × *Blue Moon*; Davidson, Harvey, 1979; Hortico; C&L Valley Rose Co., 1990-91. Bud pointed; flowers light pink to very light mauve on edge, dbl. (28-30 petals), urn-shaped, exhibition, large, borne usually singly; heavy fragrance; foliage medium, medium green, semi-glossy; thornless; bushy, medium growth.

Smooth Prince HT, *mr*, 1990, (HADprince); *Smooth Sailing* × *Old Smoothie*; Davidson, Harvey, 1979; Hortico; C&L Valley Rose Co.,

1990-91. Bud ovoid; flowers medium red, dbl. (26-28 petals), urn-shaped, exhibition, large, borne usually singly; slight, fruity fragrance; foliage medium, medium green, semi-glossy; thornless; fruit oblong, rarely sets seed.

Smooth Romance HT, *w*, 1992, (HADromance); *Smooth Sailing × Portrait*; Davidson, Harvey, 1984; Hortico Inc., 1991. Flowers cream with tinge of pink in center, urn shaped, exhibition, dbl. (42-45 petals), large (12 cms) blooms borne usually singly on straight, upright stems; good cut; moderate fragrance; foliage medium, medium green, glossy; thornless; fruit willnot set seed; upright, bushy, tall growth; fast repeat.

Smooth Sailing Gr, *w*, 1977, *Little Darling × Pink Favorite*; Davidson; Burgess Seed & Plant Co. Flowers cream color, dbl. (30 petals), large (4 in.); slightly fragrant; foliage dark, glossy; tall growth.

Smooth Talk F, *w*, 1987, *Seedling × Seedling*; Weeks, O.L.; Weeks Roses, 1988. Flowers ivory-white, aging bright white, dbl. (25 petals), high-centered, exhibition, medium, abundant, borne in sprays of 3-7; slight fragrance; foliage medium, medium green, semi-glossy; prickles pointed, small, yellow-brown; upright, bushy, low, compact growth.

Smooth Velvet HT, *dr*, 1986, (HADvelvet); *(Smooth Sailing × ((Polly × Peace) × Circus)) × Red Devil*; Davidson, Harvey; Gurney Seed. Flowers dark red, dbl. (42 petals), cupped, large blooms borne usually singly; slight damask fragrance; foliage light green, matt; no prickles; fruit medium, orange, globular; tall, upright growth.

Smuts Memory HT, *dr*, 1950, *Sensation × World's Fair*; Leenders, M. Flowers brilliant deep crimson-red.

Snappie HT, *rb*, 1989, *Lady × x Wini Edmunds*; Bridges, Dennis A.; Bridges Roses, 1990. Bud pointed; flowers medium red with yellow at base, reverse creamy-yellow, aging to deep pink, dbl. (52 petals), high-centered, medium, borne usually singly; foliage medium, dark green, semi-glossy; prickles curved slightly downward, medium, deep pink; upright, medium growth.

Sneezy Pol, *dp*, 1955, (Bertram); deRuiter; Gregory; Willicher Baumschulen. Flowers neyron rose, single, small.

Sneprincesse Pol, *w*, 1953, *Mothersday sport*; Bang. Bud ovoid; flowers pure white, dbl., cupped, small, borne in clusters; slightly fragrant; foliage light green, glossy; moderate, upright, bushy growth.

Sneprinsesse® Pol, *w*, 1946, *Dick Koster sport*; Grootendorst, F.J. Flowers white.

Sno Min, *w*, 1982, *Seedling × Gold Pin*; Meredith, E.A.; Rovinski, M.E.; Casa de Rosa Domingo. Flowers white, dbl. (48 petals), high-centered, medium blooms in clusters of 1-3; very fragrant; foliage narrow, light green, matt; sprawling growth.

Snodoll Min, *w*, 1986, (TRAsno); *Yellow Doll × Yellow Doll*; Travis, Louis. Flowers white, dbl. (30-40 crinkled, translucent petals), borne singly; slight, fruity fragrance; foliage small, medium green, semi-glossy; bowed, white prickles; fruit none; upright growth.

Snookie Min, *ob*, 1984, (TINsnook); *Torchy × Orange Honey*; Bennett, Dee; Tiny Petals Nursery. Flowers deep orange, blushing red with age, dbl. (33 petals), very small; slight fragrance; foliage medium green, semi-glossy; bushy, tiny growth.

Snoopy HT, *rb*, 1973, *Paddy McGredy × Rose Gaujard*; Cadle's Roses. Flowers carmine, reverse silver, dbl. (28 petals), urn shaped, very large; fragrant (spicy); foliage large, glossy.

Snövit Pol, *w*, 1946, *Dick Koster sport*; Grootendorst, F.J. Flowers pure white.

Snow Ballet® S, *w*, 1977, (Claysnow; Snowballet); *Sea Foam × Iceberg*; Clayworth; Harkness, 1978. Flowers pure white, dbl. (45 petals), cupped, large (4 in.); slightly fragrant; foliage small, dark, glossy.   GM, Baden-Baden, 1980.

Snow Bride Min, *w*, 1982, (Snowbride); *Avandel × Zinger*; Jolly, Betty; Rosehill Farm. Flowers white, semi-dbl. (20 petals), high-centered, exhibition; slight fragrance; foliage medium, medium green, semi-glossy; bushy growth. AOE, 1983.

Snow Carpet® Min, *w*, 1980, (MACcarpe; Blanche Neige); *New Penny × Temple Bells*; McGredy, S., IV. Flowers white, dbl. (55 petals), small; slightly fragrant; spreading. GM, Baden-Baden, 1982.

Snow Cream HT, *w*, 1986, *Garden Party × Portrait*; Bridges, Dennis A.; Bridges Roses. Flowers cream, yellow stamens, single (11 petals), medium blooms in clusters of 4-6; slight fragrance; foliage medium, dark, glossy; medium, red, hooked prickles; medium, upright growth.

Snow Crystal HT, *w*, 1978, *Sonia × Pascali*; Verschuren, Ted; H.A. Verschuren. Flowers white, semi-dbl. (20 petals), large; slight fragrance; foliage large, light green, semi-glossy; cut flower.

Snow Fairy F, *w*, 1963, *Virgo × Katharina Zeimet*; Camprubi; C-P. Bud pointed; flowers white, semi-dbl. (18 petals), cupped, medium blooms in clusters; fragrant; foliage dark, glossy, leathery; vigorous, bushy growth.

Snow Flurry F, *w*, 1952, *Seedling × Red Ripples*; Moore, R.S.; Marsh's Nursery. Bud small, long, pointed, tinted pink in cool weather; flowers white, semi-dbl., open, borne in clusters; fragrant; foliage leathery, glossy, dark; vigorous, bushy growth.

Snow Hedge HRg (S), *w*, 1963, *(R. rugosa rubra × R. cinnamomea) × R. nitida*; Nyveldt. Flowers pure white, single, medium; fruit red; upright, compact growth.

Snow Infant Min, *w*, 1989, (Koyuki); *Katharina Zeimet × Seedling*; Yamasaki, Kazuko. Bud ovoid; flowers light green, reverse white, aging white, dbl. (40 petals), small, borne in sprays of 10-20; no fragrance; foliage small, light green, semi-glossy; prickles small, light green; fruit ovoid, small, red; upright, medium growth.

Snow Magic Min, *w*, 1976, *From unnamed seedling*; Moore, R.S.; Sequoia Nursery. Bud short pointed, light pink; flowers white, dbl. (40 petals), medium; slightly fragrant; foliage small, soft; bushy growth.

Snow Princess F, *w*, 1991, (LAVpert); *Regensberg × June Laver*; Laver, Keith G.; Springwood Roses, 1992. Flowers white, full (26-40 petals), medium (4-7 cms) blooms borne in large clusters; no fragrance; foliage large, dark green, glossy; some prickles; bushy, low (45 cms), compact growth.

Snow Shower Min, *w*, 1992, (JACwade); *Immensee × Roller Coaster*; Warriner, William & Zary, Keith; Bear Creek Gardens, 1993. Flowers white, dbl. (41+ petals), small (0-4 cms) blooms borne in small clusters; no fragrance; foliage small, medium to dark green, glossy; some prickles; low (15-20 cms), ground cover, spreading 60-75 cms across.

Snow Spray F, *w*, 1957, *Gartendirektor Otto Linne × Gartendirektor Otto Linne*; Riethmuller. Flowers pure white, stamens yellow, dbl.; fragrant; dwarf growth.

Snow Twinkle™ Min, *w*, 1987, (MORsno); *(Little Darling × Yellow Magic) × Magic Carrousel*; Moore, Ralph S. Flowers white, dbl., high-centered, small, borne usually singly; slight fragrance; foliage small, medium green, matt; small, brown prickles; fruit round, orange; bushy, medium growth.

Snow White HT, *w*, 1941, *Joanna Hill × White Briarcliff*; Hill, J.H., Co. Bud long, pointed; flowers white, dbl., high-centered, large; fragrant; foliage leathery, dark; vigorous, bushy, compact growth.

Snow White Min, *w*, 1955, *Little Princess × Baby Bunting*; Robinson, T. Flowers white tinted blush, dbl., micro-mini, small (1 in.) blooms in clusters; low (3-6 in.), spreading growth.

Snow White Pol, *w*, *Dick Koster sport*. Flowers white.

Snow White HT, *w*, 1938, *White Ophelia × Nuria de Recolons*; Dot, P. Flowers white, well formed, large; very fragrant.

Snow White, Climbing Cl HT, *w*, Cant, F.

Snow Wonder Min, *w*, 1980, *Red Can Can × Baby Betsy McCall*; Lyon. Bud ovoid, pointed; flowers white, dbl. (48 petals), blooms borne 3-5 per cluster; light fragrance; foliage tiny, medium green; tiny, curved prickles; vigorous, bushy growth.

Snowball R, *w*, 1901, Walsh. Flowers white, dbl.

Snowbank F, *w*, 1937, *Mrs. E.P. Thom × Gloria Mundi*; Nicolas; J&P. Flowers white tinted blush, changing to white, dbl. (30 petals), cupped, large (3½ in.); slightly fragrant; foliage leathery, dark; dwarf growth.

Snowbird HT, *w*, 1936, *Chastity × Louise Crette*; Hatton; C-P. Bud long, pointed; flowers white, center creamy, dbl., high-centered; very fragrant; foliage leathery; vigorous, compact, bushy growth.

Snowbird, Climbing Cl HT, *w*, 1949, Weeks.

Snowblush Min, *rb*, 1991, (CLEsnob; CLEsnow); *Minuette × Seedling*; Clements, John; Heirloom Old Garden Roses, 1990. Flowers purest white, edges red, very full (41+ petals), exhibition, high-centered, medium (4-7 cms) blooms borne mostly singly; no fragrance; foliage medium green, matt; some prickles; tall (50 cms), upright growth.

Snowbound Min, *w*, 1989, (LAVaway); *Tabris × June Laver*; Laver, Keith G.; Springwood Roses, 1990. Bud ovoid; flowers ivory, reverse white, aging white, dbl. (55 petals), urn-shaped, small, borne usually singly; slight fragrance; foliage small, dark green, matt, disease resistant; prickles straight, narrow, greenish-brown; fruit round, yellow-orange; bushy, low, compact growth.

Snowdance F, *w*, 1971, *Orange Sensation × Iceberg*; deRuiter. Flowers white, dbl. (36 petals), large (3 in.); slightly fragrant; moderate, bushy growth.

Snowdrift R, *w*, 1913, Walsh. Flowers pure white, dbl., small blooms in clusters of 20-30; foliage very large, light; vigorous (8-12 ft.) growth. RULED EXTINCT 1/85.

Snowdrift™ S, *w*, 1986, (WILsnod); *Sea Foam × The Fairy*; Williams, J.B. Flowers white, dbl. (35 petals), small blooms in large sprays;

slight fragrance; foliage medium, dark, semi-glossy; low, spreading growth; repeat bloom.

Snowfall™ Cl Min, *w*, 1988, (LEMfall); *Jeanne Lajoie × Seedling*; Lemrow, Dr. Maynard; Nor'East Miniature Roses, 1988. Flowers white, dbl., cupped, decorative, medium, borne usually singly or in sprays of 2-5; no fragrance; foliage medium, medium green, semi-glossy; prickles short, pointed, small; fruit none; spreading, tall, profuse, hardy growth.

Snowfire HT, *rb*, 1970, *Detroiter × Liberty Bell*; Kordes, R.; J&P. Bud ovoid; flowers bright red, reverse white, dbl., large; slightly fragrant; foliage large, dark, leathery; vigorous.

Snowflake T (OGR), *w*, 1890, Strauss & Co. Flowers white.

Snowflake R, *w*, 1922, Cant, F. Flowers pure white, dbl., blooms in clusters; very fragrant; foliage dark, glossy; vigorous, climbing growth. GM, NRS, 1921.

Snowflake Min, *w*, 1977, *Chipper sport*; Ludwig Roses.

Snowflakes Min, *w*, 1954, *(R. wichuraiana × Floradora) × Zee*; Moore, R.S.; Sequoia Nursery. Flowers white, dbl., small; dwarf (6 in.) growth.

Snowgoose F, *w*, 1986, (BARshiflo); *Seaspray × Iceberg*; Barrett, F.H. Flowers white, semi-dbl. (20 petals), small blooms in clusters; no fragrance; foliage medium, medium green, semi-glossy; upright growth.

Snowhite Climber LCl, *w*, 1938, Burbank; Stark Bros. Flowers white, dbl., large; long, strong stems; vigorous. climbing growth.

Snowline® F, *w*, 1970, (Edelweiss); Poulsen, N.; McGredy. Flowers white, dbl. (31 petals), large (3 in.); slightly fragrant. ADR, 1970.

Snowman HT, *w*, 1983, (MATjo); *(Peer Gynt × Isis) × Lady Seton*; Mattock, John. Flowers white, dbl. (40+ petals), large; fragrant; foliage large, dark, semi-glossy; upright, bushy.

Snowsong HT, *w*, 1961, *Snow White (Hill) × Snow White seedling*; Jelly; E.G. Hill Co. Bud long, pointed; flowers white, base yellow, semi-dbl. (20 petals), large (4½ in.); slightly fragrant (sweetbrier); foliage dark, glossy; moderately vigorous, upright growth.

Snowsong Supreme HT, *w*, 1965, *Snowsong × White Butterfly*; Jelly; E.G. Hill Co. Bud long, pointed; flowers white, base greenish, high-centered, medium; fragrant; moderate growth; greenhouse variety.

Snowstorm HMsk (S), *w*, 1907, *R. moschata × Climber*; Paul. Flowers pure white, semi-dbl., small blooms in clusters of 6-20; vigorous; recurrent.

Soaring Wings HT, *ob*, 1978, (KORwings); *Colour Wonder × Seedling*; Kordes, W., Sons; Ludwig Roses. Bud ovoid; flowers deep dusky orange, dbl. (64 petals), high-centered, exhibition, large; fragrant; foliage medium green, matt; vigorous, upright, bushy growth.

Sobhag F, *ob*, 1972, *Orangeade × Seedling*; Bansal, O.P.; Bansal Roses. Bud urn shaped; flowers orange, semi-dbl., open, medium; fragrant; foliage glossy, dark, leathery; vigorous, bushy growth.

SOCotra Min, *ob*, 1985, (Orange Spice); *Over the Rainbow × Over the Rainbow*; Eagle, Barry & Dawn; Southern Cross Nursery. Flowers orange, yellow reverse, dbl. (25 petals), small blooms in clusters of 1-3; slight fragrance; foliage small, medium green; very few prickles; short, compact, very bushy growth.

Socrates T (OGR), *pb*, 1858, Robert et Moreau. Flowers deep rose tinged fawn, dbl., large.

Sodenia R, *rb*, 1911, Weigand, C. Flowers bright carmine changing to deep pink, dbl., small, borne in large clusters; vigorous, climbing growth.

Sodōri-Himé HT, *w*, 1975, (La Blancheur); *White Knight × White Prince*; Onodera, T.; S. Onodera. Flowers white, dbl. (30 petals), high-centered, large (4½ in.); slightly fragrant; foliage dark; bushy.

Soestdijk F, *ob*, 1949, *Vanessa × Seedling*; Leenders, M. Flowers deep orange, base buttercup-yellow, semi-dbl., medium; fragrant; vigorous, compact growth.

Soeur Kristin K (S), *my*, 1978, *Blanche Mallerin × (R. kordesii × (Van Bergen × Soeur Thérèse))*; James, John. Flowers medium yellow, semi-dbl. (20 petals), large blooms borne singly; slight fragrance; foliage medium, medium green, glossy; semi-spreading; repeats.

Soeur Marie-Ange F, *w*, 1957, Privat. Flowers snow-white, very dbl.; bushy, dwarf growth.

Soeur Thérèse HT, *yb*, 1931, (Sister Thérèse); *(Général Jacqueminot × Juliet) × Souv. de Claudius Pernet*; Gillot, F.; C-P. Bud long, pointed; flowers golden yellow flushed and edged carmine, dbl. (25 petals), cupped, large; slightly fragrant; foliage leathery, bronze; vigorous, bushy growth.

Soeur Thérèse, Climbing Cl HT, *yb*, 1953, Shira.

Soft Scent F, *pb*, 1988, (RENscent); *Paul Shirville × California Girl*; Rennie, Bruce; Rennie Roses, 1990. Bud ovoid; flowers pink blend, reverse light pink, dbl. (48 petals), urn-shaped, high-centered, medium, borne usually singly and in sprays of 3-5; sweetheart; heavy, spicy fragrance; foliage medium, dark green, semi-glossy; prickles straight, medium, red; fruit elongated, medium, orange; bushy, medium growth.

Soft Steps Min, *pb*, 1986, (FLOsof); *Avandel* × *Seedling*; Florac, M.; MB Farms Min. Roses. Flowers creamy, petal edges pink, dbl. (33 petals), cupped, medium, borne singly; no fragrance; foliage medium, medium green, semi-glossy; small, reddish prickles; tall, upright.

Soft Touch Min, *ab*, 1984, (JACouch); *Bridal Pink* × *Fire Princess*; Warriner; J&P. Flowers apricot blend, semi-dbl., medium; slight fragrance; foliage medium, medium green, semi-glossy; cut flower.

Softee Min, *w*, 1983, (MORfree); *Seedling* × *Seedling*; Moore, R.S.; Moore Min. Roses, 1982. Flowers creamy white, dbl. (35 petals), small; slight fragrance; foliage small to medium, medium green, matt; no prickles; bushy, spreading growth.

Softly Softly F, *pb*, 1977, (HARkotur); *White Cockade* × *((Highlight* × *Colour Wonder)* × *(Parkdirektor Riggers* × *Piccadilly))*; Harkness, 1980. Flowers pink and creamy pink, dbl. (35 petals), large (5 in.); slightly fragrant; foliage leathery.

Sogno HT, *mr*, 1973, Calvino. Bud ovoid, globular; flowers orient red to geranium-lake, dbl., open, cupped, medium; slightly fragrant; foliage large, dark, leathery; vigorous, upright, bushy growth.

Soir d'Automne HT, *m*, 1966, *(Sterling Silver* × *Intermezzo)* × *(Sterling Silver* × *Simone)*; Dot; Minier. Bud long, pointed; flowers violet, dbl., cupped, medium; fragrant; foliage light green, leathery; vigorous growth.

Solaria HT, *or*, 1976, *(Anabell* × *Zorina)* × *Seedling*; Kordes, W., Sons; Barni. Bud long, pointed; flowers orange-red, dbl., deeplycupped; foliage dark; upright growth.

Solarium R, *w*, 1925, Turbat. Flowers velvety vermilion-red, stamens yellow, single, very large, borne in clusters of 30; foliage rich glossy green; very vigorous, climbing growth.

Soldier Boy LCl, *mr*, 1953, *Seedling* × *Guinée*; LeGrice. Flowers scarlet, single, large; vigorous, pillar growth; repeat bloom.

Soldier's Pride HT, *dr*, 1987, *Red Planet* × *Cläre*; MacLeod, C.A. Flowers dark red, full (26-40 petals), medium; slight fragrance; foliage medium, dark green, semi-glossy; upright growth.

Soleil® F, *or*, 1958, (MALso); Mallerin; EFR. Flowers bright vermilion, dbl. (29 petals), large (3 in.) blooms in clusters; foliage clear green; dwarf, bushy growth.

Soleil de France HT, *yb*, 1931, *Souv. de Claudius Pernet* × *Seedling*; Mermet; J&P. Flowers sun-yellow, center reddish, dbl., large; fragrant; foliage thick; vigorous growth.

Soleil de Lyon F, *op*, 1955, Robichon; Pin. Flowers salmon-pink; vigorous growth.

Soleil de Rustica LCl, *dy*, Cognet. Flowers golden yellow, large.

Soleil d'Or HFt (OGR), *yb*, 1900, *Said to be F² seedling of Antoine Ducher* × *R. foetida persiana*;. Pernet-Ducher. Bud long, pointed; flowers orange-yellow to ruddy gold, shaded nasturtium-red, dbl., large; fragrant; foliage rich green; vigorous, Noted for being the foundation of the Pernetiana class, which is now included in the HT class. See Pernetiana.

Soleil d'Orient Cl HT, *rb*, 1935, *Frau Karl Druschki* × *Mme. Edouard Herriot*; Croibier. Bud long, pointed; flowers indian red, shaded yellow, dbl., very large; long stems; foliage glossy; vigorous, climbing (6 ft.) growth; abundant, non-recurrent bloom.

Soleil Levant LCl, *ob*, 1956, *Spectacular* × *Seedling*; Mondial Roses. Flowers orange, single, borne in clusters.

Solfaterre N (OGR), *my*, 1843, *Lamarque seedling*; Boyau. Flowers medium yellow, dbl., large; slightly fragrant; vigorous.

Solid Gold HT, *my*, 1982, (LEOnoro); *(Royal Gold seedling* × *Golden Giant)* × *(Bright Gold* × *Phyllis Gold seedling)*; Leon, Charles F. Flowers golden yellow, dbl. (36 petals), large, borne 3-6 per cluster; very fragrant; foliage dark, glossy; vigorous.

Solistka Baleta HT, *yb*, 1955, (Prima Ballerina); *(Peace* × *Crimson Glory)* × *Poinsettia*; Klimenko. Flowers soft lemon-yellow edged pink, large; fragrant.

Solitaire F, *mp*, 1970, *Queen Elizabeth* × *Elysium*; Cants of Colchester. Flowers coral-pink, reverse silvery, dbl. (25 petals), large (3 in.); fragrant; foliage glossy, dark; vigorous growth.

Solitude™ Gr, *ob*, 1991, (POUlbero); *Selfridges* × *Seedling*; Olesen, M.&P.; C-P, 1992. Flowers orange-yellow bicolor, dbl. (26-40 petals), medium (4-7 cms) blooms borne in large clusters; slight fragrance; foliage medium, medium green, semi-glossy; medium (110 cms), bushy growth; AARS, 1993.

Soller HT, *my*, 1949, *Eduardo Toda* × *Senateur Potie*; Dot, P. Bud long, pointed; flowers yellow, very dbl., very large; foliage glossy, bronze; bushy growth.

Solliden HT, *rb*, 1924, *(Mme. Mélanie Soupert* × *George C. Waud)* × *Mme. Edouard Herriot*; Leenders, M. Bud long, pointed; flowers carmine, reverse shaded ocher, semi-dbl., open, large; slightly fragrant; foliage dark; vigorous growth.

Solo® Cl HT, *mr*, 1956, *Crimson Glory* × *Seedling*; Tantau, Math. Flowers dark red, full, well-formed, large blooms in large clusters; slightly fragrant; foliage dark, leathery; vigorous.

Solus S, *or*, 1967, *Kathleen Ferrier* × *Dickson's Flame*; Watkins Roses. Flowers bright orange-scarlet, semi-dbl. (19 petals), medium (2¹/₂ in.) blooms in clusters; slightly fragrant; foliage dark, glossy, leathery; very vigorous growth.

Solvang HT, *dr*, 1988, (POUlvang); *Vision* × *Seedling*; Olesen, Mogens; Pernille; Poulsen Roser ApS, 1987. Flowers dark red, single to semi-dbl. (6-14 petals), large; slight fragrance; foliage large, dark green, glossy; prickles average; bushy, vigorous growth.

Soma HT, *m*, 1980, *Chandrama* × *Surekha*; Division of Vegetable Crops & Floriculture. Bud long, pointed; flowers mauve blend, dbl. (40 petals), blooms borne 8 per cluster; no fragrance; foliage dark, leathery; straight prickles; bushy growth.

Sombrero F, *pb*, 1962, *Masquerade* × *Rubaiyat*; McGredy, S., IV; McGredy. Flowers cream flushed pink, dbl. (25 petals), well-formed, large (4 in.); slightly fragrant; foliage light green; vigorous.

Sombreuil Cl T (OGR), *w*, 1850, (Colonial White); *Gigantesque seedling*; Robert. Flowers creamy white, often tinted pink, dbl., flat, well-formed, large; vigorous growth.

Someday Soon Min, *ly*, 1992, (SEAsoon); *Miniature seedling* × *Antique Silk*; McCann, Sean; Justice Miniature Roses, 1993. Flowers light yellow framed in creamy white outer petals, reverse creamy white with yellow base, aging to nearly white, dbl. (52 petals), high-centered, exhibition, medium (3.5 cms) blooms borne singly; slight spicy fragrance; foliage medium, light green, matt, highly serrated; upright, medium growth.

Something Else™ Min, *rb*, 1991, (SAVapie); *(Yellow Jewel* × *Tamango)* × *Party Girl*; Saville, F. Harmon; Nor'East Miniature Roses, 1985. Flowers white with very contrasting red edge, dbl., cupped, medium blooms borne usually singly; slight fragrance; foliage small, medium green, semi-glossy; upright, bushy, medium growth.

Sommerduft® HT, *dr*, 1985, (TANfudermos; Summer Fragrance); Tantau, M., 1986. Flowers dark red, semi-dbl. (20 petals), medium-large; fragrant; foliage medium, dark, semi-glossy; upright.

Sommermärchen F, *dp*, 1945, *Prof. Gnau* × *Baby Château*; Tantau. Flowers dark rose, single, shell shaped, large, borne in clusters of 12-18; slightly fragrant; foliage light green, leathery; upright, vigorous, bushy growth.

Sommertraum F, *pb*, 1960, *Masquerade* × *Seedling*; Verschuren, A.; van Engelen. Flowers pink, red and yellow, semi-dbl., borne in clusters; foliage dark.

Sommet LCl, *or*, 1960, Mallerin; Hémeray-Aubert. Flowers orange-red, dbl., well formed; foliage bright green; vigorous growth.

Sonata HT, *pb*, 1942, Van Rossem; J&P. Bud long, pointed; flowers red becoming lively pink, reverse darker, dbl. (30 petals), high-centered, large (4 in.); fragrant (fruity); foliage glossy; vigorous, bushy growth.

Sonata in Pink Min, *pb*, 1991, (JOLson); *Chris Jolly* × *Chattem Centennial*; Jolly, Marie; Rosehill Farm, 1992. Flowers medium pink fading to light pink, semi-dbl. (24 petals), small (3 cms) blooms borne mostly singly; slight fragrance; foliage medium, medium green, semi-glossy; few prickles; medium (44 cms), upright growth.

Sonatina F, *lp*, 1982, *Red Maid* × *Sarabande*; Sanday, John; Sanday Roses. Flowers light pink, dbl. (35 petals), small; slight fragrance; foliage medium, dark, semi-glossy.

Song Bird Gr, *w*, 1978, *Tammy sport*; Ryan; J. Hill Co. Flowers white.

Song of Paris HT, *m*, 1964, (Saphir); *(Holstein* × *Bayadère)* × *Prelude*; D-C; Armstrong Nursery. Flowers silvery lavender, dbl., high-centered, large (4 in.); fragrant; foliage leathery; upright.

Songfest Min, *mp*, 1987, (ZIPson; Sonata); *Queen Elizabeth* × *Baby Katie*; Zipper, Herbert; Magic Moment Miniatures. Flowers medium pink, dbl. (40+ petals), exhibition, small, borne singly; no fragrance; foliage small, medium green, matt; bushy, compact growth.

Sonia Gr, *pb*, 1974, (MEIhelvet; Sonia Meilland; Sweet Promise); *Zambra* × *(Baccará* × *White Knight)*; Meilland; C-P. Bud long; flowers pink suffused coral to yellow, dbl. (30 petals), high-centered, large (4-4¹/₂ in.); very fragrant (fruity); foliage glossy, dark, leathery.

Sonia HT, *rb*, 1938, *(R. multiflora* × *R. canina)* × *Hortulanis Budde*; Horvath; Wayside Gardens Co. Flowers cherry-red, center orange, semi-dbl., camillia form; short stems; slightly fragrant; foliage glossy, dark; vigorous, bushy growth; hardy.

Sonia, Climbing Cl Gr, *pb*, 1976, (MEIhelvetsar; Grimpant Sonia Meilland; Sonia Meilland); Climbing; Sweet Promise, Climbing Meilland, M.L.; Meilland.

Sonja Henie HT, *pb*, 1949, *Briarcliff Supreme* × *Rosemarie Hinner*; Hinner, P.; Bauské Bros.; Hinner. Bud long, pointed to ovoid; flowers pink, reverse darker, very dbl., high-centered, very large; foliage leathery, dark; vigorous, upright growth.

Sonnengold HT, *dy*, 1936, *Lilian* × *Sir Basil McFarland*; Kordes. Bud long, pointed; flowers golden yellow, dbl., high-centered, large; slightly fragrant; foliage leathery, glossy, light; bushy growth.

Sonnenkind® Min, *dy*, 1987, (KORhitom; Perestroika); *Seedling* × *Goldmarie*; Kordes, W., 1986. Flowers deep yellow, dbl. (40+ petals), medium; slight fragrance; foliage small, medium green, semi-glossy; bushy growth.

Sonnenlicht HFt (OGR), *my*, 1913, *Lady Mary Fitzwilliam* × *Harison's Yellow*; Krüger; Kriese. Flowers canary-yellow, semi-dbl.; fragrant; vigorous growth; non-recurrent bloom.

Sonnenröschen® F, *dy*, 1977, (KORsonn); *Arthur Bell* × *Yellow seedling*; Kordes, W., Sons, 1978. Bud ovoid; flowers deep yellow, dbl. (40 petals), cupped, large (4 in.); slightly fragrant; foliage glossy; vigorous, bushy growth.

Sonnet HT, *lp*, 1961, *Golden Masterpiece* × *Spartan*; Boerner; J&P. Bud ovoid; flowers light salmon-pink, dbl. (58 petals), cupped, large (5 in.); fragrant; foliage leathery; vigorous, upright growth; greenhouse variety.

Sonnychild HT, *yb*, 1949, (Zonnekeild); Lowe. Flowers yellow, reverse edged scarlet, semi-dbl. (20 petals), large (6 in.); fragrant; foliage glossy; vigorous growth.

Sonoma F, *mp*, 1973, *Sumatra* × *Circus*; Armstrong, D.L.; Armstrong Nursery. Flowers medium salmon-pink, dbl., high-centered, medium; fragrant; foliage leathery; vigorous, upright, bushy growth.

Sonora F, *yb*, 1962, *Orange Mist* × *Mayday*; Boerner; J&P. Bud ovoid; flowers buff-yellow flushed to pink, dbl. (30 petals), cupped, large (3½-4 in.); fragrant; foliage leathery; vigorous, upright growth; greenhouse variety.

Sonrisa HT, *dr*, 1969, *Mister Lincoln* × *Night 'n' Day*; Swim & Weeks; Weeks Wholesale Rose Grower. Flowers deep crimson-red, dbl. (48 petals), high-centered, medium-large; very fragrant (damask); foliage dark, leathery; vigorous, upright growth.

Sophia HT, *pb*, 1988, *First Prize* × *Dolce Vita*; Weddle, Von C.; Hortico, 1987. Flowers medium pink with persimmon-orange, dbl. (27 petals), high-centered, exhibition, large, borne usually singly; moderate, fruity fragrance; foliage large, dark green, glossy; prickles none; fruit: none; upright, tall growth.

Sophia Fleur F, *ly*, 1978, *Elizabeth of Glamis sport*; Timmermans Roses. Flowers creamy yellow.

Sophia Loren® HT, *mr*, 1967, Tantau, Math. Flowers medium red, dbl. (33 petals), well-formed, large; foliage glossy; vigorous, upright.

Sophia's Song™ HT, *op*, 1989, (DEVloren); *Emily Post* × *Prominent*; Marciel, Stanley G.; DeVor Nursery. Bud slender, tapering; flowers coral, dbl. (32 petals), high-centered, large, borne singly; slight, fruity fragrance; foliage medium, dark green, semi-glossy; prickles declining, copper brown with pea green tinges; upright, tall growth.

Sophie de Bavière A (OGR), *mp*, Vibert. Flowers clear pink, full, very regular, medium.

Sophie de Marsilly A (OGR), *pb*, Prior to 1848. Flowers blush with rose center, full, globular, large blooms which need clear, dry weather to open well; more prickly than most Albas; vigorous, upright.

Sophie MacKinnon HT, *dr*, 1937, *John Cromin* × *Seedling*; Clark, A.; NRS Victoria. Flowers deep red, dbl., large; vigorous growth.

Sophie Ortlieb HP (OGR), *mp*, 1933, *Georg Arends* × *Seedling*; Walter, L. Bud long, pointed; flowers silvery pink, dbl., very large; foliage wrinkled; very vigorous, open habit.

Sophie Thomas Cl HT, *my*, 1931, (Bloomfield Loveliness); *Seedling climbing* × *Los Angeles*; Thomas; H&S. Flowers deep yellow, passing to lighter yellow but not cream, dbl., large; long, strong stems; fragrant; foliage good; vigorous growth.

Sophie's Perpetual Ch (OGR), *pb*, Classification and origin uncertain, prior to 1928; Re-int. Humphrey Brooke, 1960. Flowers pale pink, overlaid with deep pink and cerise red, globular; foliage dark green; few prickles; 8 ft.

Sophisticated Lady Gr, *lp*, 1985, *Queen Elizabeth* × *Arlene Francis*; Epperson, Richard G. Flowers light pink, dbl. (25 petals), high-centered, exhibition, medium blooms borne usually singly; slight, fruity fragrance; foliage medium, medium green, semi-glossy; medium, hooked, dull red prickles; upright, tall growth.

Sophocle HT, *m*, 1974, *Rose Gaujard* × *Credo*; Gaujard. Flowers purple-red, large.

Soprano F, *or*, 1961, *Mannequin × Aztec*; Lens. Flowers orange-red, dbl., large; fragrant; vigorous growth.

Soraya® HT, *or*, 1955, (MEIjenor; MEjenor); *(Peace × Floradora) × Grand'mère Jenny*; Meilland, F.; URS. Bud pointed; flowers orange-red reverse crimson-red, dbl. (30 petals), cupped, large; slightly fragrant; foliage glossy; vigorous, bushy growth.

Soraya, Climbing® Cl HT, *or*, 1960, (MEIjenorsar; MEjenorsar; Grimpant Soraya); Barni; URS.

Sorcier LCl, *ob*, 1958, *Seedling × Spectacular*; Hémeray-Aubert. Flowers bright orange; foliage bronze; vigorous growth; recurrent bloom.

Soroptimist HT, *dy*, 1958, *Golden Scepter × Seedling*; Verbeek. Flowers orange-yellow, dbl. (40 petals), well formed, large (4 in.); foliage glossy; vigorous growth; a forcing variety.

Souma HT, *mp*, 1977, Souma Rose Soc. Flowers medium pink, dbl. (45 petals), high-centered, large (6 in.); slightly fragrant; foliage glossy, dark; vigorous, upright.

Soupert et Notting M (OGR), *dp*, 1874, Pernet Père. Flowers deep pink, globular, very large; not very mossy; very fragrant; 5 leaflets per leaf; dwarf; recurrent.

Source d'Or LCl, *yb*, 1913, Turbat. Flowers amber-yellow, edged creamy yellow, very dbl., large, borne in clusters on short stems; very fragrant; foliage glossy, dark; height 6-8 ft.; abundant, non-recurrent bloom.

Sourire de France HT, *ob*, 1940, *Ampère × (Charles P. Kilham × Capucine Chambard)*; Meilland, F.; A. Meilland. Bud oval; flowers orange, base ocher-yellow, dbl., open, medium; slightly fragrant; foliage leathery, glossy; vigorous, bushy growth.

South Orange Perfection R, *pb*, 1899, *R. wichuraiana × Cramoisi Superieur*; Horvath; W.A. Manda. Flowers blush-pink, turning white, rosette form borne in clusters; fragrant; very hardy. One of the first *R. wichuraiana* hybrids.

South Pacific™ F, *dy*, 1988, (AROnesuf); *Sunsprite × Seedling*; Christensen, Jack; Bear Creek Gardens, 1988. Flowers deep yellow, color holds well, dbl. (26 petals), cupped, medium, borne in sprays of 4-6; slight fragrance; foliage medium, medium green, glossy; prickles hooked slightly downward, medium, few, green to tan; fruit none; bushy, medium growth.

South Seas HT, *op*, 1962, (Mers du Sud); *Rapture × Hybrid Tea Climbing seedling*; Morey; J&P. Bud ovoid; flowers coral-pink, dbl. (48 petals), cupped to flat, very large (6-7 in.); fragrant; foliage leathery; vigorous, upright growth.

Southampton F, *ab*, 1971, (Susan Ann); *(Ann Elizabeth × Allgold) × Yellow Cushion*; Harkness, 1972. Flowers apricot, dbl. (28 petals), large (3 in.); fragrant; foliage glossy. GM, Belfast, 1974.

Southend Jubilee F, *dp*, 1965, McCreadie. Flowers deep pink, semi-dbl., flat, medium (2½ in.), borne in clusters; very vigorous, bushy growth.

Southern Beauty HT, *pb*, 1926, *Columbia sport*; Rowe. Flowers deep rose-pink, edged light pink.

Southern Belle HT, *pb*, 1981, *Pink Parfait × Phoenix*; Swim; Ellis; Armstrong Nursery. Bud ovoid, long, pointed; flowers deep pink, white reverse, dbl. (28 petals), spiraled blooms borne singly or up to 3 per cluster; light fragrance; foliage large, semi-glossy; long, narrow prickles; medium, upright, spreading growth.

Southern Charm Min, *yb*, 1992, (BRIcharm); *Baby Katie × Seedling*; Bridges, Dennis A.; Bridges Roses. Flowers shades of light yellow and pink, pink intensifying with sun, full (25-40 petals), medium (4-7 cms) blooms borne in small clusters of 3-5; slight fragrance; foliage large, medium green, semi-glossy; no prickles; medium (40-45 cms), upright, bushy, slightly spreading growth.

Southern Cross HT, *mp*, 1931, *Joseph Hill × Gen. MacArthur*; Clark, A.; Ballarat Hort. Soc. Flowers pink, dbl., globular; fragrant; bushy growth.

Southern Delight Min, *yb*, 1991, (MORdashin); *Little Darling × Rise 'n' Shine*; Moore, Ralph S.; Sequoia Nursery, 1992. Flowers yellow edged with red, aging to pink and yellow, moderately full (15-25 petals), medium (4-7 cms) blooms borne in small clusters; slight fragrance; foliage medium, medium green, semi-glossy; few prickles; medium to tall (22-24 cms), upright, bushy growth.

Southern Lady HT, *pb*, 1988, *Lady × x Flaming Beauty*; Bridges, Dennis; Bridges Roses, 1989. Bud pointed; flowers light pink, center flesh tones, reverse slightly darker pink, dbl. (40 petals), high-centered, exhibition, borne usually singly; moderate fragrance; foliage medium, dark green, semi-glossy; prickles downward pointed, medium, tan; upright, medium growth.

Southern Spring Min, *m*, 1988, *Twilight Trail × Seedling*; Bridges, Dennis; Bridges Roses, 1989. Bud ovoid; flowers light mauve shaded pink, reverse lighter mauve edges, darker base, aging mauve to pink edges, dbl. (65 petals), urn-shaped, medium, borne usually singly; moderate fragrance; foliage medium, dark green, matt; prickles slightly downward pointed, medium, tan; bushy, low growth.

Southport HT, *mr*, 1933, *(George Dickson × Crimson Queen) × Souv. de George Beckwith*; McGredy. Bud long, pointed; flowers bright scarlet, semi-dbl. (18 petals), cupped; fragrant; vigorous growth. GM, NRS, 1931.

Southport, Climbing Cl HT, *mr*, 1946, Howard Rose Co.

Souvenance HT, *m*, 1965, *Seedling × Sterling Silver*; Lens. Bud very long, pointed; flowers deep lavender-lilac, dbl. (25-30 petals), high-centered, large (3½-4½ in.); very fragrant; foliage dark; moderately vigorous growth.

Souvenir HT, *dy*, 1930, *Talisman sport*; Pierson, A.N. Bud pointed; flowers golden yellow, dbl. (36-42 petals); fragrant; foliage glossy; vigorous growth.

Souv. d'Adolphe Turc Pol, *op*, 1924, Turc, 1926. Flowers clear salmon-pink.

Souv. d'Alexandre Bacot HT, *mr*, 1958, *Crimson Glory × Independence*; Arles; Roses-France. Flowers geranium-red, dbl. (50 petals), large; slightly fragrant; very vigorous growth.

Souv. d'Alexandre Bernaix HT, *dr*, 1926, *Étoile de Hollande × Gen. MacArthur*; Bernaix, P. Flowers crimson-scarlet, shaded darker, dbl., cupped, globular, very large; foliage purplish green; vigorous growth.

Souv. d'Alphonse Lavallée HP (OGR), *dr*, 1884, C. Verdier. Flowers dark velvety crimson to maroon; fragrant; height to 6 ft.

Souv. d'Angèle Opdebeeck HT, *my*, 1926, *Golden Ophelia × Golden Emblem*; Verschuren. Bud long, pointed; flowers canary-yellow, dbl.; fragrant.

Souv. d'Anne Frank F, *ob*, 1960, *Rêve de Capri × Chanteclerc*; Delforge. Flowers orange tinted yellow and salmon, semi-dbl. (17 petals), open, medium, abundant bloom, borne in clusters; foliage glossy, dark; moderate, bushy growth.

Souv. d'Antonin Poncet HT, *dr*, 1921, *Mme. Maurice de Luze × Lady Ashtown*; Schwartz, A. Bud long, pointed; flowers carmine, flecked paler, dbl.

Souv. d'Auguste Legros T (OGR), *mr*, 1890, Bonnaire. Flowers red-crimson, large.

Souv. d'Auguste Métral HT, *dr*, 1895, Guillot, P. Flowers crimson.

Souv. de Amand Opdebeeck HT, *yb*, 1936, Belge; Opdebeeck. Bud long, pointed; flowers yellowish apricot-pink, edged pink, dbl.,

high-centered, very large; fragrant; foliage leathery, bronze; very vigorous growth.

Souv. de Ben-Hur HT, *mr*, 1960, *Ena Harkness × Charles Mallerin*; Verschuren; Blaby Rose Gardens. Bud pointed; flowers crimson-scarlet, dbl., large (5 in.); very fragrant; very vigorous growth.

Souv. de Béranger HP (OGR), *mp*, 1857, Bruant. Flowers rose, full, large; moderate growth.

Souv. de Brod HSet (OGR), *rb*, 1886, (Erinnerung an Brod); Geschwind. Flowers cerise through crimson to purple, dbl., quartered, large; fragrant.

Souv. de Catherine Fontaine HT, *yb*, 1934, *Souv. de Jean Soupert × Mme. Edouard Herriot*; Soupert, C. Bud long, pointed; flowers brownish yellow, center brick-red, reverse coral-red, very large; fragrant.

Souv. de Catherine Guillot T (OGR), *rb*, 1895, Guillot, R. Flowers coppery carmine, center shaded orange, full, large; very fragrant; weak growth.

Souv. de Charles Gouverneur HT, *pb*, 1927, Chambard, C. Bud long, pointed; flowers flesh-pink, center salmon-orange, very large; fragrant.

Souv. de Charles Laemmel HT, *yb*, 1919, *Frau Karl Druschki × Soleil d'Or*; Gillot, F. Flowers golden yellow, streaked orange and shaded pink; very fragrant.

Souv. de Christophe Cochet HRg (S), *mp*, 1894, Cochet-Cochet. Flowers pink, semi-dbl., large; fragrant.

Souv. de Claude Vially HT, *rb*, 1931, Reymond. Bud long, pointed; flowers light red, tinted pink and aurora.

Souv. de Claudius Denoyel Cl HT, *dr*, 1920, (Denoyel); *Château de Clos Vougeot × Commandeur Jules Gravereaux*; Chambard, C. Bud long, pointed; flowers rich crimson-red, tinted scarlet, dbl., cupped, very large; fragrant; vigorous, climbing; sparse, recurrent bloom.

Souv. de Claudius Pernet HT, *my*, 1920, *Constance × Seedling*; Pernet-Ducher. Bud long, pointed; flowers pure sunflower-yellow, center deeper, dbl. (28 petals), large; long, strong stems; fragrant; foliage glossy, rich green; vigorous growth. GM, Bagatelle, 1920.

Souv. de Claudius Pernet, Climbing Cl HT, *my*, 1925, Western Rose Co.

Souv. de Claudius Pernet, Climbing Cl HT, *my*, 1932, Schmidt, J.C.

Souv. de Claudius Pernet, Climbing Cl HT, *my*, 1933, Gaujard.

Souv. de Clermonde HT, *pb*, 1925, Pernet-Ducher. Flowers salmon-rose, center darker, shaded yellow, semi-dbl.; fragrant.

Souv. de Denier van der Gon HT, *rb*, 1935, *Roselandia* × *Souv. de Claudius Pernet*; Verschuren-Pechtold. Bud long, pointed; flowers reddish yellow to golden yellow, full, large; fragrant; very vigorous growth.

Souv. de E. Guillard HT, *rb*, 1912, *Beauté Inconstante* × *Le Progrès*; Chambard, C. Flowers reddish yellow shaded coppery carmine, dbl., large; fragrant; very vigorous, branching growth. GM, Bagatelle, 1914.

Souv. de Francis Borges HT, *ob*, 1932, *Mme. Léon Pain* × *Seedling*; Chambard, C. Flowers flesh, center orange, very large; fragrant; vigorous growth.

Souv. de François Gaulain T (OGR), *rb*, 1889, Guillot. Flowers crimson and violet.

Souv. de François Graindorge HT, *yb*, 1928, *Bénédicte Seguin* × *Lady Hillingdon*; Grandes Roseraies. Bud long, pointed; flowers ocher-yellow, base indian yellow, dbl.; fragrant.

Souv. de François Mercier HT, *ob*, 1923, *Antoine Rivoire sport*; Laperrière. Bud long, pointed; flowers light coppery rose, edged deeper, dbl.; fragrant.

Souv. de François Richardier HT, *rb*, 1923, Richardier. Flowers bright carmine-pink, tinted cherry.

Souv. de F. Bohé HT, *op*, 1922, *Willowmere* × *Seedling*; Chambard, C. Bud long, pointed; flowers orange-salmon, dbl. (35 petals).

Souv. de Gabriel Luizet HT, *yb*, 1922, *Mme. Mélanie Soupert seedling* × *Lyon Rose*; Croibier. Flowers sulphur-yellow tinted salmon, passing to deep rich yellow and later straw-yellow, dbl. Not to be confused with Mme. Gabriel Luizet (HP).

Souv. de Gabrielle Drevet T (OGR), *op*, 1884, Guillot Fils. Flowers salmon-pink, base coppery, large, well formed; very fragrant.

Souv. de Gaston Commagères HT, *ob*, 1954, Privat. Flowers orange-ivory veined yellow, edge veined pink, very full; vigorous, bushy growth.

Souv. de George Beckwith HT, *pb*, 1919, *Seedling* × *Lyon Rose*; Pernet-Ducher. Bud long, pointed; flowers shrimp-pink, tinted chrome-yellow, base deeper, dbl. (55 petals), globular, very large; fragrant; foliage glossy; very vigorous growth.

Souv. de George Knight HT, *my*, 1926, *Rayon d'Or sport*; Knight, J. Flowers nanking yellow.

Souv. de Georges Pernet HT, *op*, 1921, *Seedling* × *Mme. Edouard Herriot*; Pernet-Ducher. Flowers medium salmon-pink, dbl. (31 petals), large; very fragrant; foliage dark, bronze; vigorous. GM, Bagatelle, 1921.

Souv. de Georges Pernet, Climbing Cl HT, *op*, 1927, Pernet-Ducher.

Souv. de Gilbert Nabonnand T (OGR), *pb*, 1920, Nabonnand, C. Flowers in summer: yellow base edged carmine-pink; in autumn: very deep begonia pink and yellow base, edged apricot, dbl.; very fragrant; vigorous growth; (28).

Souv. de Gustave Prat HT, *ly*, 1909, Pernet-Ducher. Flowers pure light sulphur-yellow, dbl.

Souv. de Gustave Schickelé HT, *yb*, 1927, *Mme. Edouard Herriot* × *Duchess of Wellington*; Ketten Bros. Bud long, pointed; flowers chrome-yellow, reverse bright rosy scarlet, shaded apricot, dbl.

Souv. de Henri Faassen HT, *pb*, 1929, *Betty Uprichard* × *(Mrs. George Shawyer* × *Los Angeles)*; Faassen-Hekkens. Bud long, pointed; flowers deep pink, base orange-yellow, semi-dbl., open, large; very fragrant; foliage bronze; very vigorous growth.

Souv. de Henri Venot HT, *mr*, 1931, *Lord Charlemont* × *Red Star*; Lens. Flowers brilliant red, very dbl.; very fragrant; foliage dark; vigorous growth.

Souv. de H.A. Verschuren HT, *yb*, 1922, *Seedling* × *Golden Ophelia*; Verschuren. Bud long, pointed; flowers yellow to orange-yellow, dbl. (38 petals), well-formed, large; fragrant; vigorous.

Souv. de Jacques Verschuren HT, *op*, 1950, *Katharine Pechtold* × *Orange Delight*; Verschuren-Pechtold. Bud long, pointed; flowers apricot-salmon, dbl., large; fragrant; foliage leathery, dark; vigorous, bushy growth.

Souv. de Jean Croibier HT, *pb*, 1921, *Mme. Mélanie Soupert* × *Lyon Rose*; Croibier. Flowers bright salmon-pink shaded chamois, center coral-red shaded yellow, dbl.; slightly fragrant.

Souv. de Jean Ginet HT, *mr*, 1935, Brenier, E.C.; Buatois. Flowers scarlet-red, base coppery, reverse golden yellow.

Souv. de Jean Soupert HT, *my*, 1929, *Ophelia* × *Feu Joseph Looymans*; Soupert & Notting. Bud long, pointed; flowers golden yellow, semi-dbl, cupped, very large; very fragrant; foliage bronze; vigorous growth.

Souv. de Jeanne Balandreau HP (OGR), *mr*, 1899, Vilin. Flowers medium red.

Souv. de John E. Knight HT, *ob*, 1928, Knight, J. Flowers terra-cotta, salmon-pink and flesh streaked yellow; fragrant; foliage dark; vigorous growth.

Souv. de Josefina Plà HT, *mr*, 1929, *Étoile de Hollande* × *Mme. Butterfly*; Munné, B. Flowers bright red, semi-dbl., large; fragrant; vigorous growth.

Souv. de Joseph Besson HT, *rb*, 1931, Brenier, E.C. Flowers reddish orange, base yellow.

Souv. de Jules Nicolas Mathieu Lamarche Pol, *rb*, 1934, *Éblouissant* × *Petit Constant*; Soupert, C. Flowers cardinal-red, base yellow, single, very small; large panicles.

Souv. de J. Chabert F, *mr*, 1956, (Bobbie Robbie; Pépite); *Français* × *Seedling*; D-C. Flowers medium red, dbl., well-formed, large blooms in clusters of 3-6; foliage dark, bronze; vigorous, low growth.

Souv. de J. Mermet R, *dr*, 1934, Mermet. Flowers silvery carmine, large, borne in clusters; foliage bright, bronze; very vigorous growth; recurrent bloom.

Souv. de J.B. Weibel HT, *dr*, 1930, *Seedling of Mrs. Bullen* × *Edouard Mignot*; Sauvageot; F. Gillot, 1930; C-P, 1933. Flowers carmine, dbl., cupped, very large; slightly fragrant; foliage dark; very vigorous, bushy growth.

Souv. de la Malmaison B (OGR), *lp*, 1843, (Queen of Beauty and Fragrance); *Mme. Desprez* × *Tea*; Béluze. Flowers creamy flesh, center rosy shaded, dbl., often quartered, very large; very fragrant (spicy); dwarf, bushy (2 ft.) growth; repeat bloom. A famous and influential rose.

Souv. de la Malmaison, Climbing Cl B (OGR), *lp*, 1893, Bennett.

Souv. de la Reine d'Angleterre HP (OGR), *mp*, 1855, *La Reine* × *Seedling*; Cochet Frères. Flowers bright pink, full, large; very vigorous growth; recurrent bloom.

Souv. de Laffay HP (OGR), *mr*, 1878, Verdier, E. Flowers crimson-red.

Souv. de l'Aviateur Métivier R, *ly*, 1913, *R. wichuraiana* × *Mme. Ravary*; Tanne. Flowers clear yellow, passing to white, dbl.; vigorous, climbing growth.

Souv. de l'Aviateur Olivier de Montalent R, *rb*, 1913, *R. wichuraiana* × *Anna Olivier*; Tanne. Flowers dull rose, base salmon, dbl., borne in clusters; foliage very glossy, dark; vigorous, climbing growth; profuse bloom, rarely recurrent.

Souv. de Lilette HT, *w*, 1937, Chambard, C. Bud very long; flowers snow-white, large; very fragrant; foliage slightly bronze; compact, bushy growth.

Souv. de Lucienne Valayer HT, *pb*, 1938, Chambard, C. Bud long; flowers soft pink, shaded light salmon, cupped, very large; fragrant; vigorous, bushy growth.

Souv. de Madeleine Rouillon HT, *ob*, 1929, *Manon* × *Elvira Aramayo*; Bernaix, P. Bud long, pointed; flowers orange, base yellow, dbl.; fragrant.

Souv. de Marcelle Balage HT, *pb*, 1930, (Marcella Baldge); *Willowmere* × *Mme. Pizay*; Bernaix, P. Bud long, pointed; flowers satiny flesh-pink, center slightly tinted salmon, dbl., cupped, very large; very fragrant; foliage dark.

Souv. de Maria Clotilde HT, *ly*, 1934, *Mme. Abel Chatenay* sport; Carneiro; Ketten Bros. Bud long; flowers amber-white, often passing to light yellow, center sometimes flesh-pink, full, large; fragrant; vigorous growth.

Souv. de Marie Finon HT, *ab*, 1924, Croibier. Flowers apricot-yellow passing to clear yellow shaded salmon. dbl.; very fragrant.

Souv. de Marie Thérèse Privat Pol, *mr*, 1935, Privat. Flowers bright vermilion, very full, well formed, borne in clusters of 40-50; foliage bright green; dwarf, good habit.

Souv. de Marie-Thérèse HT, *w*, Chabanat; Roses-France. Flowers ivory-white; slightly fragrant; low growth.

Souv. de Marques Loureiro HT, *rb*, 1912, *Mons. Paul Lédé* × *Mme. Hoste*; Ketten Bros. Flowers light red shading to rose, tinted yellow and purple, dbl.

Souv. de Maurice Chevalier Gr, *dr*, 1980, (DELsouche); *(Walko* × *Impeccable)* × *(Papa Meilland* × *(Baccará* × *Michèle Meilland))*; Delbard, G. Flowers dark red, semi-dbl., blooms in clusters.

Souv. de Mlle. Juliet de Bricard Pol, *dp*, 1934, *Cécile Brunner* × *Yvonne Rabier*; Délépine; Pajotin-Chédane. Flowers pale rosy pink, very dbl., globular; slightly fragrant; foliage glossy, dark; vigorous, bushy growth.

Souv. de Mme. Achille van Herreweghe HT, *dr*, 1936, Van Herreweghe-Coppitters. Flowers carmine-red; vigorous growth.

Souv. de Mme. Augustine Gillot HT, *op*, 1920, *Frau Karl Druschki* × *Lyon Rose*; Gillot, F. Bud long, pointed; flowers salmony flesh-pink, base salmon-yellow, reverse silvery flesh-pink; slightly fragrant.

Souv. de Mme. A. Hess HT, *pb*, 1936, *Seedling* × *Ami F. Mayery*; Chambard, C. Bud long, pointed; flowers shrimp-pink, center deep coral, cupped, very large; fragrant; foliage bronze; very vigorous, bushy growth.

Souv. de Mme. Boullet HT, *dy*, 1921, *Sunburst* × *Seedling*; Pernet-Ducher. Bud long, pointed; flowers deep yellow, full, well-formed, large; vigorous, spreading growth.

Souv. de Mme. Boullet, Climbing Cl HT, *dy*, 1930, H&S.

Souv. de Mme. Canel HT, *rb*, 1932, Gillot, F. Flowers carmine-orange, very full, large; foliage pointed, bronze; robust, bushy growth.

Souv. de Mme. Chédanne-Guinoiseau HP (OGR), *mr*, 1900, Chédanne-Guinoiseau. Flowers bright geranium red, full, very large.

Souv. de Mme. C. Chambard HT, *op*, 1931, Chambard, C.; C-P. Flowers coral-rose-pink, center flushed gold, semi-dbl., cupped, large; fragrant; vigorous growth.

Souv. de Mme. C. Chambard, Climbing Cl HT, *op*, 1935, Armstrong, J.A.

Souv. de Mme. Durand HT, *yb*, 1954, Privat. Flowers naples yellow, base bright yellow, edges veined pink, full, globular; strong stems; foliage glossy.

Souv. de Mme. Eugène Verdier HT, *w*, 1894, *Lady Mary Fitzwilliam × Mme. Chédanne-Guinoiseau*; Pernet-Ducher. Flowers white, base saffron-yellow.

Souv. de Mme. Gauthier-Dumont HT, *mr*, 1921, Guillot, P. Bud long, pointed; flowers scarlet.

Souv. de Mme. H. Thuret HP (OGR), *pb*, 1922, *Frau Karl Druschki × Lyon Rose*; Texier; P. Nabonnand. Flowers salmon-pink, center shrimp-red, edged chrome, cupped, well-formed, petals recurved, very large; foliage rich green; very vigorous growth.

Souv. de Mme. Jules Pages R, *pb*, 1937, *Phyllis Bide × Éblouissant*; Reiter; Stocking. Flowers deep pink shaded orange and red, dbl., open, small; slightly fragrant; vigorous, climbing or pillar growth; free, intermittent bloom.

Souv. de Mme. Kreuger HT, *op*, 1919, *Mme. Mélanie Soupert × Willowmere*; Chambard, C. Flowers pure salmon-orange, passing to coppery pink, dbl.

Souv. de Mme. Lefèbvre HT, *rb*, 1929, Richardier. Flowers oriental red, passing to pink, golden yellow and red; vigorous growth.

Souv. de Mme. Léonie Viennot Cl T (OGR), *yb*, 1898, Bernaix, A. Flowers yellow shaded pink, very full; vigorous growth.

Souv. de Mme. Levet T (OGR), *ob*, 1891, Levet, F. Flowers orange-yellow.

Souv. de Mme. Louise Cretté HT, *yb*, 1924, *Mme. Edouard Herriot seedling*; Cretté; C. Chambard. Flowers golden yellow, shaded coral and red, dbl.

Souv. de Mme. Morin-Latune HT, *dp*, 1920, Bernaix, P. Bud long, pointed; flowers cream-rose, dbl.

Souv. de Mme. Pidoux HT, *yb*, 1926, *Seedling × Mrs. Aaron Ward*; Chambard, C. Bud long, pointed; flowers chrome-yellow, reverse pink, cupped.

Souv. de Mme. Sablayrolles T (OGR), *ab*, 1891, Bonnaire. Flowers apricot-pink.

Souv. de Mme. Salati-Mongellaz HP (OGR), *dp*, 1937, *Frau Karl Druschki × Seedling*; Croibier. Bud long, pointed; flowers satiny rose-pink, dbl., very large; foliage dark; very vigorous growth.

Souv. de Norah Lindsay LCl, *mp*, Flowers bright pink, stamens golden, single, very large; vigorous, pillar growth.

Souv. de Nungesser HT, *dr*, 1927, *Mme. Maurice de Luze × Laurent Carle*; Croibier. Flowers brilliant deep carmine-red, dbl.; fragrant.

Souv. de Paul Grandclaude HT, *yb*, 1923, *Mme. Mélanie Soupert × Beauté de Lyon*; Sauvageot. Bud large, long, pointed; flowers yellow, shaded pink and in autumn light brown, semi-dbl.

Souv. de Paul Neyron T (OGR), *yb*, 1871, *Ophirie seedling*; Levet, A. Flowers salmon-yellow edged pink, semi-globular, large; very fragrant; very vigorous growth.

Souv. de Philémon Cochet HRg (S), *w*, 1899, *Blanc Double de Coubert sport*; Cochet-Cochet. Flowers white, center rose.

Souv. de Pierre Guillot HT, *ob*, 1928, *Marie Adélaide × Seedling*; Guillot, M. Bud long, pointed; flowers coral-orange blend, dbl.

Souv. de Pierre Ketten HT, *rb*, 1928, *Mme. Mélanie Soupert × Pilgrim*; Ketten Bros. Bud long, pointed; flowers bright rose, inside pink, base chrome-yellow, dbl. (30-35 petals); very fragrant.

Souv. de Pierre Leperdrieux HRg (S), *mr*, 1895, Cochet-Cochet. Flowers bright red; fruit large; very vigorous growth.

Souv. de Pierre Notting T (OGR), *yb*, 1902, *Maréchal Niel × Maman Cochet*; Soupert & Notting. Bud long, pointed; flowers sunflower-yellow tinted apricot and coppery yellow, edged rose, very dbl.; slightly fragrant; foliage rich green, soft.

Souv. de Pierre Vibert M (OGR), *rb*, 1867, Moreau-Robert. Flowers dark red, shaded carmine and violet, full, large; moderate growth; sometimes recurrent.

Souv. de Prosper Fraissenon HT, *m*, 1927, Richardier. Bud long, pointed; flowers geranium-red tinted violet

Souv. de Raymond Gaujard HT, *yb*, 1943, Gaujard. Bud ovoid; flowers golden yellow, reverse often veined red, dbl., open, medium; fragrant; foliage dark, glossy; vigorous, upright growth.

Souv. de René Grognet HT, *ob*, 1921, Chambard, C. Bud long, pointed; glowers coppery orange-yellow, shaded carmine.

Souv. de R. B. Ferguson HT, *pb*, 1922, *Seedling* × *Constance*; Ferguson, W. Flowers shell-pink and apricot, sometimes shaded rose-pink and cerise; slightly fragrant.

Souv. de St. Anne's B (OGR), *lp*, *Souv. de la Malmaison sport*; Hilling, 1950. Discovered in garden of Lady Ardilaun, near Dublin, Ireland, prior to 1916. Flowers blush-pink, nearly single; recurrent.

Souv. de S. A. Prince T (OGR), *w*, 1889, (The Queen); *Souv. d'un Ami sport*; Prince. Flowers white.

Souv. de Thérèse Lovet T (OGR), *dr*, 1886, *Adam* × *Seedling*; Lovet, A.

Souv. de Victoire Landeau HP (OGR), *pb*, 1884, Moreau-Robert. Flowers pale pink to mauve rose, full, globular, large.

Souv. de Victor Hugo T (OGR), *pb*, 1886, *Duchesse de Brabant* × *Regulus*; Bonnaire. Flowers china-pink, center salmon-pink, dbl., large; very fragrant.

Souv. de Victor Landeau B (OGR), *mr*, 1890, Moreau-Robert. Flowers vivid red.

Souv. de William Wood HP (OGR), *dr*, 1864, Verdier, E. Flowers dark velvety red, full (37 petals), cupped, large; fragrant; vigorous growth; sometimes recurrent.

Souv. d'Elise Vardon T (OGR), *w*, 1855, Marest. Flowers creamy white, center yellowish, full, globular, very large.

Souv. d'Emile Mayrisch HT, *dr*, 1932, Ketten Bros. Flowers dark crimson-garnet, dbl. (35-40 petals), well formed, large; stiff stems; vigorous growth.

Souv. d'Emmanuel Buatois HT, *rb*, 1932, *Mme. Edouard Herriot* × *Souv. de Claudius Pernet*; Buatois. Bud long, pointed; flowers coral-red shaded shrimp-red, reverse clear rose, base golden yellow, dbl., very large; fragrant; foliage leathery, bronze; vigorous growth.

Souv. d'Ernest Thébault R, *dr*, 1921, Thebault. Flowers dark red, dbl., borne in clusters of 10-20; vigorous, climbing growth.

Souv. de. H. A. Verschuren, Climbing Cl HT, *yb*, 1927, H&S.

Souv. du Baron de Sémur HP (OGR), *m*, 1874, *Charles Lefèvre* × *Seedling*; Lacharme. Flowers deep purple-red shaded fiery red and black, full, large; vigorous growth.

Souv. du Capitaine Crémona HT, *rb*, 1928, *Admiration* × *Gorgeous*; Bernaix, P. Flowers salmon-carmine over yellow ground, dbl.; fragrant.

Souv. du Capitaine Fernand Japy HT, *mr*, 1922, *Le Progrès* × *Les Rosati*; Sauvageot. Flowers red, dbl.; slightly fragrant.

Souv. du Capitaine Ferrand HT, *rb*, 1939, Gaujard. Bud long, well formed; flowers nasturtium-red, reverse golden yellow; erect, vigorous growth.

Souv. du Docteur Albert Reverdin HT, *rb*, 1930, *George C. Waud* × *Mrs. Edward Powell*; Bernaix, P. Bud long, pointed; flowers brilliant carmine, shaded vermilion, very dbl., large; strong stems; fragrant; foliage dark; vigorous growth.

Souv. du Docteur Jamain HP (OGR), *dr*, 1865, *Charles Lefèvre* × *Seedling*; Lacharme. Flowers plum shaded deep crimson, dbl.; fragrant; moderate growth.

Souv. du Papa Calame HT, *pb*, 1921, *Jonkheer J.L. Mock sport*; Gillot, F. Bud long, pointed; flowers carmine-pink, reverse silvery pink, stamens salmon, dbl.

Souv. du Président Carnot HT, *lp*, 1894, *Seedling* × *Lady Mary Fitzwilliam*; Pernet-Ducher. Bud long, pointed; flowers flesh-pink, center shell-pink; fragrant. Notable as one of the parents of Dr. W. Van Fleet.

Souv. du Président Carnot, Climbing Cl HT, *lp*, 1926, Grandes Roseraies.

Souv. du Président Plumecocq HT, *rb*, 1958, *Seedling* × *Peace*; Laperrière; EFR. Flowers bright red, reverse marked silvery, dbl., large; fragrant; foliage bronze; very vigorous, well branched growth.

Souv. du Reverend Pére Planque HT, *ob*, 1932, *Seedling* × *Souv. de Georges Pernet*; Bel. Flowers orange-chrome-yellow, fading lighter; foliage very glossy; very vigorous growth.

Souv. du Sénateur Bazire R, *m*, 1918, *Veilchenblau* × *Bordeaux*; Lottin. Flowers violet, center violet-rose, semi-dbl., borne in clusters of 25-50.

Souv. du Sergent Cretté HT, *yb*, 1921, *Mme. Mélanie Soupert* × *Seedling*; Chambard, C. Bud long, pointed; flowers coppery golden yellow, shaded carmine, cupped, very large; foliage bronze; very vigorous growth.

Souv. d'un Ami T (OGR), *lp*, 1846, Belot-Defougère. Flowers pale rose tinged salmon, dbl., cupped, very large; very fragrant; vigorous growth.

Souv. of Miami HT, *dr*, 1925, Cook, J. Flowers red.

Souv. of Stella Gray T (OGR), *ob*, 1907, Dickson, A. Flowers deep orange splashed apricot, salmon and crimson, semi-dbl., small to medium; fragrant.

Souv. of the Old Rose Garden HT, *pb*, 1929, Cant, B.R. Flowers silvery pink, brighter inside, dbl., globular, very large; strong stems; very fragrant; foliage glossy, light; vigorous growth. GM, NRS, 1928.

Souv. of Wootton HT, *mr*, 1888, *Bon Silène × Louis van Houtte*; Cook, J. Flowers rich velvety red, dbl., very large; very fragrant; foliage dark, leathery; vigorous growth.

Souv. of Wootton, Climbing Cl HT, *mr*, 1899, Butle.

Souviens-Toi F, *yb*, 1986, (KRIprile); Kriloff, M. Flowers medium yellow, petals edged and washed carmine, dbl. (38 petals), large; fragrant; foliage matt.

Sovereign HT, *dy*, 1922, *Queen Mary × Seedling*; Cant, B.R. Flowers deep yellow and old-gold, open, cupped; very fragrant (fruity); foliage glossy, dark, bronze; vigorous growth.

Sovrana HT, *ob*, 1930, *Julien Potin × Signora seedling (yellow)*; Aicardi, D.; Giacomasso. Flowers orange streaked yellow, well formed, large; very vigorous, upright growth.

Sox Min, *rb*, 1986, (MICsox); *Baby Katie × Angel Darling*; Williams, Michael C.; The Rose Garden. Flowers medium red, small white eye, single (7 petals), 1 in. blooms borne usually singly; no fragrance; foliage medium, dark; small, straight prickles; fruit small, globular, orange; medium, upright growth.

Soyécourt HT, *rb*, 1921, *Gen. MacArthur × George C. Waud*; Jersey Nursery. Flowers blood-red, overlaid orange.

Space Girl LCl, *dr*, 1966, *Queen Elizabeth × Étoile de Hollande*; Barter. Flowers dark crimson, dbl., very large; fragrant; foliage dark; vigorous, climbing growth.

Space Invader S, *lp*, 1990, (DICrocky); *Seedling × Temple Bells*; Dickson, Patrick; Dickson Nurseries, Ltd. Flowers light pink, full (26-40 petals), large blooms; fragrant; foliage medium, medium green, semi-glossy; spreading growth.

Space Walk™ Min, *m*, 1991, (MINabcco); *Seedling × Twilight Trail*; Williams, Ernest D.; Mini-Roses, 1992. Flowers mauve-tan/yellow, russet reverse, full (26-40 petals), small (4 cms) blooms borne mostly singly; very fragrant; foliage small, dark green, semi-glossy; few prickles; low (30 cms), bushy growth.

Spaethiana S, *m*, (*R. × spaethiana* Graebner); R. palustris × R. rugosa; Cult. 1902. Flowers purple, large, corymbose; (21).

Spanish Dancer Min, *or*, 1986, (MORliz); *Sarabande × Little Chief*; Moore, R.S.; Moore Min. Roses, 1980. Flowers orange-red, semi-dbl. (18 petals), small blooms in sprays of 5-7; slight fragrance; foliage medium, medium green, semi-glossy; small, brown prickles; fruit none; medium, bushy, spreading growth.

Spanish Eyes F, *op*, 1981, *Prominent sport*; Takatori; Japan Rose Nursery. Flowers orange-salmon, reverse yellow.

Spanish Gold HT, *dy*, 1960, Fletcher; Tucker. Flowers straw-yellow; tall, bushy growth.

Spanish Orange F, *ob*, 1966, deRuiter; Gregory. Flowers orange, very dbl., small (1½ in.) borne in clusters; fragrant; foliage dark, glossy; very free growth.

Spanish Rhapsody S, *pb*, 1984, *Gingersnap × Sevilliana*; Buck; Iowa State University. Flowers deep pink, tinted orange and freckled red, dbl. (30 petals), shallow-cupped, large blooms borne 1-8 per cluster; raspberry fragrance; foliage medium-large, leathery, dark olive green; awl-like prickles; upright, bushy, branching growth; repeat bloom; hardy.

Spanish Sun F, *dy*, 1966, *Yellow Pinocchio × Golden Garnette climbing seedling*; Boerner; J&P. Flowers deep yellow, dbl., large; very fragrant; foliage glossy, leathery; vigorous, bushy growth.

Spanky Min, *yb*, 1986, *Rise 'n' Shine × Seedling*; Bridges, Dennis A.; Bridges Roses. Flowers bright yellow, shaded pink to red, reverse yellow, aging pink, dbl., high-centered, miniflora, medium blooms borne usually singly; slight fragrance; foliage large, medium green, semi-glossy; few, pink, small prickles; medium, upright growth.

Sparkels HT, *rb*, 1956, *Briardiff sport*; Webber. Bud urn shaped; flowers red striped white, dbl. (35-50 petals), high-centered, medium; very fragrant; foliage leathery.

Sparkie Min, *mr*, 1957, (*R. wichuraiana × Floradora*) × *Little Buckaroo*; Moore, R.S.; Sequoia Nursery. Flowers bright red, becoming darker, single (6 petals), blooms in clusters; foliage glossy; vigorous (12-16 in.) growth.

Sparkle HT, *pb*, 1949, *Pink Princess × Shades of Autumn*; Brownell. Bud pointed, ovoid; flowers white turning cream, rose-pink and yellow toward center, dbl., high-centered, large; fragrant; foliage glossy, light green; vigorous, upright, bushy growth.

Sparkle Plenty F, *ob*, 1976, *Ma Perkins × Engagement*; Patterson; Patterson Roses. Bud ovoid; flowers bright orange, dbl. (25 petals), high-centered to open, large (3 in.); fragrant; foliage dark, leathery, wrinkled; vigorous growth.

Sparkler Pol, *mr*, 1929, *Golden Salmon sport*; deRuiter; Sliedrecht & Co. Flowers red.

Sparkling Burgundy F, *dr*, 1965, *Queen Elizabeth* × *Carrousel*; Williams, J.B. Flowers burgundy-red, dbl., open, medium, borne in clusters; fragrant; foliage dark, leathery, glossy; vigorous, upright growth.

Sparkling Orange™ HT, *ob*, 1989, (DEVilk); *Sonia* × *Prominent*; Marciel, Stanley G.; DeVor Nursery. Bud tapering; flowers vermillion, reverse scarlet, aging to rose, dbl. (23 imbricated petals), large, borne singly; sweetheart; heavy, musk fragrance; foliage large, dark green, glossy; prickles variation, reddish-brown; upright, tall growth.

Sparkling Scarlet Cl F, *mr*, 1970, (MEIhaiti; MEIhati; Iskra); *Danse des Sylphes* × *Zambra*; Meilland; URS. Flowers scarlet-red, semidbl. (13 petals), small (2½ in.); fragrant (fruity); foliage large. GM, Paris, 1969.

Sparrieshoop S, *lp*, 1953, *(Baby Château* × *Else Poulsen)* × *Magnifica*; Kordes. Bud long, pointed; flowers light pink, gold stamens, single (5 broad, wavy petals), large (4 in.); very fragrant; foliage leathery; very vigorous (5 ft.), upright, bushy; repeat bloom. GM, Portland, 1971.

Spartan F, *or*, 1955, (Aparte); *Geranium Red* × *Fashion*; Boerner; J&P. Bud pointed; flowers orange-red to reddish coral, dbl. (30 petals), high-centered, large (3-3½ in.) blooms borne singly and in clusters; very fragrant; foliage dark, leathery, glossy; vigorous, bushy growth. NRS PIT, 1954; GM, NRS, 1954; Portland, 1955; AARS David Fuerstenberg Prize, 1957; ARS National Gold Certificate, 1961

Spartan Blaze Min, *rb*, 1991, *Poker Chip* × *Rise 'n' Shine*; Gruenbauer, Richard, 1984; Flowers 'n' Friends Miniature Roses, 1991. Bud ovoid; flowers red with yellow reverse, dbl., high-centered, medium blooms borne usually singly; slight fragrance; foliage medium, medium green, semi-glossy; upright growth.

Spartan, Climbing Cl F, *or*, 1960, (Grimpant Spartan); Kordes.

Spartan, Climbing Cl F, *or*, 1964, Martinez; J & P.

Spartan Dawn Min, *yb*, 1990, *Rise 'n' Shine* × *Hokey Pokey*; Gruenbauer, Richard, 1984; Richard Gruenbauer. Bud rounded; flowers yellow with orange edges, reverse yellow to cream to orange, aging apricot, dbl. (30 petals), loose, medium, borne singly; no fragrance; foliage medium, medium green, matt; few or no prickles; fruit round, flat on top, orange-red; bushy, medium growth.

Späth's Jubiläum F, *or*, 1970, (Späth 250); *Castanet* × *Seedling*; Kordes. Bud ovoid; flowers orange-red, dbl. (22 petals), high-centered,

large (2½ in.); slightly fragrant; foliage dark, soft; vigorous, upright, bushy growth.

Speaker Sam HT, *yb*, 1962, *Peace sport*; Dean; Arp Nurs. Co. Flowers light yellow edged red.

Special Angel Min, *m*, 1992, *Jean Kenneally* × *(Rise 'n' Shine* × *Acey Deucy)*; Stoddard, Lou; Bridges Roses, 1992. Flowers mauve, tipped in pink, moderately full (15-25 petals), high-centered, small (0-4 cms) blooms borne mostly single; slight fragrance; foliage medium, dark green, semi-glossy; few prickles; tall (60-70 cms), upright, bushy growth.

Special Guest HT, *mr*, 1992, *Jan Guest sport*; Guest, M., 1990. Flowers crimson, very full (41+ petals), large (7+ cms) blooms borne mostly singly; slight fragrance; foliage medium, medium green, semi-glossy; many prickles; medium (70 cms), bushy growth.

Special Merit HT, *mr*, 1990, *Seedling* × *First Prize*; Wambach, Alex A. Bud pointed; flowers medium red, very dbl. (30 petals), high-centered, large, borne singly; foliage medium, dark green, semi-glossy; medium, upright, bushy growth.

Spectabile HSem (OGR), *m*, (Spectabilis); *Possibly R. sempervirens* × *Noisette hybrid*; Prior to 1846. Flowers bright rosy lilac, cupped petals "curiously incised" (notched); vigorous, climbing; occasionally repeats in autumn.

Spectacular LCl, *or*, 1953, (Danse du Feu; Mada); *Paul's Scarlet Climber* × *R. multiflora seedling*; Mallerin; EFR, 1953; J&P, 1956. Bud ovoid; flowers scarlet-red, dbl. (33 petals), cupped to flat, medium blooms in clusters; fragrant; foliage glossy, bronze; vigorous, climbing (8-10 ft.) growth; recurrent bloom.

Speechless™ Min, *ob*, 1986, (KINspeech); *Seedling* × *Watercolor*; King, Gene; AGM Miniature Roses, 1987. Flowers dark to light orange, fading darker, dbl. (30 petals), high-centered, exhibition, medium, borne usually singly; no fragrance; foliage dark green, semi-glossy; medium, hooked, red prickles, with brown tips; fruit oval, medium, green; upright, bushy growth.

Spellbinder HT, *pb*, 1975, (WARdido; Oratorio); *South Seas* × *Seedling*; Warriner; J&P. Bud ovoid; flowers ivory to crimson, dbl., high-centered, large; slightly fragrant; foliage large, dark, leathery; vigorous.

Spellbound HT, *dr*, 1949, *Better Times sport*; Sodano, J.; Amling-DeVor Nursery. Flowers deep velvety red, becoming darker, dbl. (25-30 petals), very large (5½-6 in.); fragrant; foliage dark; thorn less; very vigorous, upright growth; a greenhouse variety.

Spellcaster Gr, *m*, 1991, (JACangel); *Seedling* × *Angel Face*; Warriner, William; Bear Creek

Gardens, 1992. Flowers lavender and deep mauve, full (26-40 petals) with heavy substance, large (7+ cms) blooms borne mostly singly or in small clusters; fragrant; foliage large, dark green, glossy; some prickles; tall (145-160 cms), upright, spreading, very full, uniform growth.

Spencer HP (OGR), *lp*, 1892, *Merveille de Lyon sport*; Paul, W. Flowers soft pink.

Sphinx HT, *lp*, 1967, *Rose Gaujard × Gail Borden*; Gaujard. Flowers bright pink tinted lighter, dbl., very large; fragrant; foliage leathery; vigorous, bushy growth.

Spice F, *or*, 1954, *(Goldilocks × Floradora) × Floribunda seedling*; Boerner; J&P. Bud globular; flowers scarlet-red, dbl. (53 petals), cupped, large (3 in.) blooms in clusters; fragrant; foliage glossy; vigorous, compact, upright growth; greenhouse variety.

Spice Drop™ Min, *op*, 1982, (SAVswet; SAVasweet); *(Sheri Anne × Glenfiddich) × (Moss seedling × (Sarabande × Little Chief))*; Saville, F. Harmon; Nor'East Min. Roses. Flowers light salmon-pink, dbl. (35 petals), HT form, micro-mini, small; slight fragrance; foliage small, medium green, glossy; tiny growth.

Spiced Coffee HT, *r*, 1990, (MACjuliat; Old Spice); *Harmonie × Big Purple*; McGredy, Sam; McGredy Roses International, 1991. Flowers pale lavender with brown overtones, full (15-25 petals), large blooms; very fragrant; foliage medium, medium green, matt; upright growth.

Spinning Wheel™ S, *rb*, 1991, *Handel × Love*; Williams, J. Benjamin, 1992. Flowers cherry red with ivory striping, full, large blooms borne in large clusters; slight fragrance; foliage large, dark green, semi-glossy; tall, upright, spreading growth.

Spion-Kop F, *mr*, 1968, *Evelyn Fison × Orange Sensation*; Ellick. Flowers signal-red, dbl. (30-35 petals), full, large (3-5 in.); slightly fragrant; foliage light, bronze, matt green; vigorous growth.

Spirit of Glasnost HT, *pb*, 1991, (JACara); *Seedling × Seedling*; Warriner, William A.; Bear Creek Gardens. Flowers coral pink and ivory blend, full (26-40 petals), large blooms borne mostly singly; fragrant; foliage medium, dark green, semi-glossy; upright, spreading growth.

Spirit of Peace HT, *yb*, 1992, (JACstine); *Pristine × Seedling*; Warriner, William A.; Bear Creek Gardens, Inc. Flowers apricot yellow opening with pink tinge where sun strikes the opening petal, full (26-40 petals), large (7+ cms) blooms borne mostly singly; slight fragrance; foliage medium, dark green, semi-

glossy; some prickles; tall (170-180 cms), upright, spreading growth.

Spirit of Pentax F, *or*, 1990, (HARwex); *Alexander × Remember Me*; Harkness, R.; R. Harkness & Co., Ltd. Bud pointed; flowers bright red, bright orange-red reverse, aging deeper, dbl. (21 petals), high-centered to rounded, medium, borne in sprays of 3-7; slight fragrance; foliage small to medium, dark green, glossy; prickles straight, narrow, small to medium, medium green; upright, medium growth.

Spirit of '76 Gr, *or*, 1971, *Queen Elizabeth × San Francisco*; Whisler, D.; Gro-Plant Industries. Bud ovoid; flowers orange-red, dbl., medium; fragrant; foliage large, glossy, dark; vigorous, upright growth.

Spitfire HT, *mr*, 1943, *Better Times × Colleen Moore*; Hill, J.H., Co. Bud oxblood-red; flowers carmine, dbl. (25-30 petals), open, small (2-3 in.); short stems; fragrant; foliage dark, leathery; vigorous, upright, much branched growth; a florists' variety, not distributed for outdoor use. RULED EXTINCT 6/86.

Spitfire Improved HT, *dr*, 1949, *Spitfire sport*; Hill, J.H., Co. Bud medium, short-pointed, ovoid; flowers velvety dark carmine, semi-dbl., globular, large (4-5 in.); very fragrant; foliage leathery, dark; vigorous, upright, bushy growth; a florists' variety, not distributed for outdoor use. RULED EXTINCT 6/86.

Spitfire Min, *mr*, 1986, *Seedling × Seedling*; McDaniel, Earl; McDaniel's Min. Roses. Flowers medium red, dbl. (38 petals), high-centered, large blooms borne singly; no fragrance; foliage, medium, medium green, matt; thin, light green prickles; upright, bushy growth.

Splendens G (OGR), *mr*, Flowers glistening crimson, semi-dbl.

Splendens Ayr (OGR), *w*, (Ayrshire Splendens; Myrrh-scented Rose); *R. arvensis hybrid*; Prior to 1837. Bud crimson; flowers pale flesh to creamy blush, dbl., globular, large; fragrant (myrrh); good seed bearer; pendulous habit.

Splendor HT, *OR*, 1933, *La Maréchale Pétain × Souv. de Claudius Pernet*; Sauvageot; C-P. Bud long, pointed; flowers orange-carmine, dbl., cupped; fragrant; foliage leathery, glossy; vigorous growth.

Splendor HT, *mr*, 1940, *Better Times sport*; Abrams. Bud long; flowers rose-red, reverse slightly lighter, full, pointed, large (4-5 in.); very fragrant; foliage dark.

Spode HT, *ob*, 1972, *Diorama × Fragrant Cloud*; Fryer's Nursery. Flowers orange-scarlet, flushed cream, dbl. (35 petals), long, pointed, large (6 in.); very fragrant; foliage glossy, dark.

Spong C (OGR), *mp*, 1805. Flowers rose-pink, richer in center, rosette form, larger than Rose de Meaux; dwarf, compact (to 4 ft.) growth; early bloom.

Spot 'o Gold Min, *my*, 1992, (WEE Spot; WEEspot); *Rise 'n' Shine × Seedling*; Weeks, Michael W.J. Flowers medium yellow, yellow stamens, single (5 petals), small (0-4 cms) blooms borne in small clusters; slight fragrance; foliage medium, medium green, semi-glossy; some prickles; bushy (15 cms) growth.

Spotlight HT, *my*, 1969, *Seedling × Piccadilly*; Dickson, A. Flowers peach and gold, globular; fragrant; foliage dark; free growth.

Spray Cécile Brunner Pol, *pb*, 1941, *Cécile Brunner sport*; Howard Rose Co. Bud long, pointed; flowers bright pink on yellow, edged clear pink, center yellowish, dbl.; fragrant; foliage sparse, soft, dark; bushy growth. The rose sold as Bloomfield Abundance appears to be this.

Spring Beauty Min, *pb*, 1982, (MINeco); *Little Darling × Over the Rainbow*; Williams, E.D.; Mini-Roses. Flowers pastel pink and yellow blend, dbl. (35 petals), small; slight fragrance; foliage small, medium green, glossy; upright growth.

Spring Bouquet Min, *pb*, 1985, (TINspring); *Portrait × Party Girl*; Bennett, Dee; Tiny Petals Nurery. Flowers crimson pink, blended with yellow, HT form, medium; fragrant; foliage medium, medium green, semi-glossy; upright, bushy growth.

Spring Fever HT, *ob*, 1985, (AROcant); *Gingersnap × Brandy*; Christensen; Armstrong Roses. Flowers apricot, pink and orange blend, dbl. (35 petals), large; slight fragrance; foliage large, dark, semi-glossy.

Spring Frolic Min, *my*, 1978, *(Little Darling × Gold Coin) × Golden Angel*; Williams, E.D.; Mini-Roses. Bud ovoid; flowers medium yellow, dbl. (70 petals), pompon-shaped, small (1 in.); very fragrant; low, compact, spreading growth.

Spring Frost Min, *w*, 1978, Schwartz, E.W.; Bountiful Ridge Nursery. Flowers pure white, semi-dbl. (17 petals), ruffled, small (1 in.); slightly fragrant; foliage small; low, very compact.

Spring Hill's Freedom S, *mr*, 1989, (TWOfree; S.H. Freedom); *Samantha × Seedling*; Twomey, Jerry; DeVor Nursery, 1990. Bud ovoid; flowers medium, scarlet red, dbl. (35 petals), cupped, medium, borne singly; slight, musk fragrance; foliage medium, medium green, semi-glossy; prickles slightly curved, red-purple; upright, medium growth.

Spring Melody™ Min, *ob*, 1983, (MINmco); *Little Darling × Over the Rainbow*; Williams, E.D.; Mini-Roses. Flowers orange, dbl. (35 petals), small; slight fragrance; foliage small, bronze green, semi-glossy; bushy growth.

Spring Song Min, *pb*, 1957, *(R. wichuraiana × Floradora) × Thumbelina*; Moore, R.S.; Sequoia Nursery. Flowers pink tinted salmon, dbl., small blooms in clusters; foliage glossy; bushy growth.

Spring Song S, *dp*, 1954, *Gartendirektor Otto Linne seedling*; Riethmuller. Flowers rich carmine-pink, semi-dbl.; fragrant; vigorous, tall growth.

Spring Time™ Min, *w*, 1990, (WILspring); *Easter Morning (F²) × Toy Clown*; Williams, J. Benjamin; White Rose Nurseries, Ltd., 1990. Bud pointed; flowers ivory with light red edge, dbl. (26 petals), high-centered, exhibition, small, borne usually singly; heavy damask fragrance; foliage small, dark green, semi-glossy; bushy, low growth.

Springfields F, *ob*, 1978, (DICband); *Eurorose × Anabell*; Dickson, A. Flowers orange, red, gold, dbl. (48 petals), cupped, large (3 in.); slightly fragrant.

Springtime F, *lp*, 1935, *Miss Rowena Thom × Seedling*; Howard, F.H.; Dreer. Flowers wild-rose-pink, center white, semi-dbl., cupped, borne in clusters; slightly fragrant; foliage leathery; bushy growth. RULED EXTINCT 7/90.

Springvale HT, *w*, 1975, *Mme. A. Meilland sport*; Miller, J. Flowers white to pink, very dbl. (50 petals), high-centered, large (4 in.); slightly fragrant; foliage dark.

Springwood™ Coral Min, *or*, 1987, (LAVscent); *Helmut Schimdt × Potluck*; Laver, Keith, 1986; Springwood Roses, 1990. Flowers coral-pink, turning slightly white at stem, dbl. (23 petals), loose, large, borne in sprays of 3-4; heavy fragrance; foliage large, light green, matt; prickles curved, red; fruit round, light orange; bushy, medium growth.

Springwood™ Gold Min, *my*, 1989, (LAVtynine); *Rise 'n' Shine × June Laver*; Laver, Keith; Springwood Roses. Bud pointed; flowers deep, buttery yellow, reverse lighter, dbl. (20 petals), high-centered, exhibition, medium, borne usually singly; slight fragrance; foliage small, medium green, semi-glossy; prickles very narrow, straight, green; fruit globular, light orange; upright, bushy, medium growth.

Springwood™ Pink Min, *dp*, 1992, (LAVdusk); *Maurine Neuberger × (June Laver × Ontario Celebration)*; Laver, Keith G.; Springwood Roses. Flowers deep pink, moderately full (15-25 petals), small (0-4 cms) blooms borne in small clusters; slight fragrance; foliage medium, medium green, matt; some prickles; low (30-40 cms), spreading growth; suitable for pots.

Springwood™ Purple Min, *dp*, 1990, (LAVpurr); *June Laver × (Small Slam × Mountie)*; Laver, Keith, 1988; Springwood Roses, 1991. Flowers fuchsia, dbl. (25-30 petals), loose, medium to large, borne in sprays of 3; no fragrance; foliage large, medium green, semiglossy; bushy, spreading, medium, very compact growth.

Springwood™ Red Min, *dr*, 1988, (LAVred); *Small Slam × Mountie*; Laver, Keith G.; Springwood Roses, 1990. Flowers deep red, aging slightly lighter, dbl. (40 petals), urn-shaped, small, borne usually singly; no fragrance; foliage small, medium green, matt; prickles slightly recurved, light yellow-green; fruit ovoid, orange; bushy, low growth.

Springwood White™ Min, *w*, 1991, (LAVsnow; White Festival); *Loving Touch × June Laver*; Laver, Keith; Springwood Roses. Flowers white, very full (41+ petals), medium (4-7 cms) blooms borne mostly singly; no fragrance; foliage small, medium green, matt; few prickles; low (22 cms), bushy growth.

Sprint F, *mr*, 1961, *Jolie Princesse × Chanteclerc*; Gaujard. Bud oval; flowers bright red, semi-dbl. (12 petals), open, medium (2½ in.), borne in clusters; slightly fragrant; foliage glossy, dark; vigorous growth.

Spun Gold HT, *my*, 1941, *Seedling × Portadown Glory*; McGredy; J&P. Flowers gold, dbl. (27 petals), high-centered, large (4½ in.); foliage glossy, leathery; vigorous, bushy, fairly compact growth.

Spunglass HT, *w*, 1989, (DEVlass; Spun GlassTM); *Seedling × Angel*; Marciel, Stanley G.; DeVor Nursery. Bud pointed; flowers white, dbl. (50 petals), cupped, very large, borne singly; slight, spicy fragrance; foliage large, dark green, glossy; prickles declining, pea green; upright, tall growth.

Sputnik F, *or*, 1958, *Jiminy Cricket × Gloria Mundi*; Maarse, G. Flowers orange-red, semi-dbl., large trusses of 25-30; low, bushy growth.

Square Dancer S, *dp*, 1973, *Meisterstuck × ((World's Fair × Floradora) × Applejack)*; Buck; Iowa State University. Bud ovoid; flowers deep pink, dbl., cupped, large; fragrant; foliage large, dark, leathery; vigorous, upright, bushy growth; repeat bloom.

Squatter's Dream S, *my*, 1923, *Seedling from R. gigantea seedling*; Clark, A.; Hackett. Flowers medium yellow, becoming lighter, semi-dbl.,

cupped; fragrant; foliage dark bronze-green; no prickles; dwarf, bushy growth; recurrent bloom.

Srebra F, *pb*, 1975, *Highlight × Masquerade*; Staikov, Prof. Dr. V.; Kalaydjiev and Chorbadjiiski. Flowers pink, shaded mauve, dbl., medium blooms in clusters of 5-20; tea fragrance; foliage dark, glossy; bushy growth.

S. S. Pennock HT, *pb*, 1922, *Lieutenant Chaure × Mrs. George Shawyer*; Kordes. Flowers light rose-pink, with sulphur-yellow sheen (under glass, clear rose-pink), dbl; fragrant.

S. S. Pennock, Climbing Cl HT, *pb*, 1932, Lens; J&P.

Staatspräsident Päts HT, *my*, 1937, (President Pats); *Ophelia × Souv. de Claudius Pernet*; Weigand, C.; Späth. Bud long, pointed; flowers amber-yellow, very varying, dbl., very large; very fragrant; foliage leathery, dark; vigorous growth.

Staccato F, *mr*, 1959, *Cantate sport*; van de Water; Klyn. Bud ovoid; flowers vermilion-red, semi-dbl. (14-20 petals), open, medium; moderately vigorous, bushy growth.

Stacey F, *yb*, 1965, Verschuren, A.; Blaby Rose Gardens. Flowers maize-yellow tinted blush, dbl. (25-30 petals), large (4-5 in.), borne in clusters; fragrant; foliage dark, glossy, leathery; vigorous growth.

Stacey Sue Min, *lp*, 1976, *Ellen Poulsen × Fairy Princess*; Moore, R.S.; Sequoia Nursery. Bud short, pointed; flowers soft pink, dbl. (60 petals), small (1 in.); slightly fragrant; foliage small, glossy; bushy growth.

Stad Darmstadt Pol, *mr*, 1966, *Red Favorite × The Doctor*; deRuiter. Bud ovoid; flowers bright red, semi-dbl., small, borne in clusters; foliage dark.

Stad den Haag F, *mr*, 1969, *Evelyn Fison × (Spartan × Red Favorite)*; McGredy. Flowers scarlet, semi-dbl. (20 petals), open, large; slightly fragrant; foliage glossy; free growth.

Stadt den Helder F, *mr*, 1979, (INTerhel); *Amsterdam × (Olala × Diablotin)*; Interplant. Flowers medium red, dbl. (20 petals), medium; slight fragrance; foliage large, dark, matt; upright growth.

Stadt Kiel® S, *mr*, 1962, Kordes, R. Flowers cinnabar-red, dbl. (30 petals), medium blooms in large clusters; slightly fragrant; foliage dark; very vigorous, bushy growth.

Stadt Rosenheim® S, *or*, 1961, Kordes, R. Flowers orange-red, dbl., medium blooms in clusters (up to 10); fragrant; foliage glossy, light green; vigorous, upright growth. ADR, 1960.

Stadtrat Glaser HT, *yb*, 1910, Kiese. Flowers sulphur-yellow edged soft red.

Stadtrat Meyn Pol, *mr*, 1919, *Orléans Rose* × *Seedling*; Tantau. Flowers luminous brick-red, full, large.

Stagecoach™ Min, *op*, 1986, (KINcoach); *Vera Dalton* × *Orange Honey*; King, Gene; AGM Miniature Roses, 1987. Flowers medium salmon pink, dbl. (18 petals), high-centered, exhibition, medium, borne usually singly or in sprays of 3-5; slight fragrance; foliage medium, light green, matt; straight, white prickles; fruit oval, green; upright, spreading growth.

Stainless Steel HT, *m*, 1991, (WEKblusi); *Blue Nile* × *Silverado*; Carruth, Tom; Weeks Roses, 1995. Flowers clean, silvery grey lavender, full (26-40 petals), well-formed, large blooms borne mostly singly and some clusters; very fragrant (sweet); foliage large, medium green, semi-glossy; some prickles; tall to medium (130-150 cms), vigorous growth.

Stämmler HP (OGR), *mp*, 1933, *Victor Verdier* × *Arabella*; Tantau; C-P. Flowers rose-pink, very dbl., high-centered, large; very fragrant; foliage glossy; vigorous.

Stämmler HP (OGR), *mp*, 1933, *Victor Verdier* × *Arabella*; Tantau; C-P. Flowers rose-pink, very dbl., high-centered, large; very fragrant; foliage glossy; vigorous growth.

Standing Pol, *dr*, 1969, *Atlantic* × *Seedling*; Delforge. Flowers dark red, dbl., open, medium; slightly fragrant; foliage dark, glossy; vigorous growth.

Standout HT, *rb*, 1977, *Tiffany* × *Suspense*; Weeks; Weeks Wholesale Rose Grower. Bud ovoid, pointed; flowers red, white reverse, dbl. (40 petals), high-centered, medium (3-4 in.); slightly fragrant (tea); vigorous, upright growth.

Stanley Gibbons HT, *op*, 1976, *Fragrant Cloud* × *Papa Meilland*; Gregory. Flowers salmon-orange, dbl. (28 petals), pointed, large (4 in.); fragrant; foliage glossy, dark.

Stanley Matthews HT, *dr*, 1964, *(Independence* × *Crimson Glory)* × *Happiness*; Latham. Flowers crimson-scarlet, dbl. (26 petals), large (4½-5 in.); fragrant; foliage glossy, light green; vigorous growth.

Stanwell Perpetual HSpn (OGR), *w*, 1838, *Thought to be a repeat-blooming Damask* × *Spinosissima*; Lee. Flowers blush, dbl., medium; slightly fragrant; foliage very small; many prickles; moderate, spreading growth; recurrent bloom; (28).

Stanza F, *lp*, 1969, Pal; Gopalsinamiengar. Bud ovoid; flowers light pink, center darker, semi-dbl., open, medium; slightly fragrant; foliage glossy, dark; very vigorous, bushy growth.

Star Child® F, *rb*, 1987, (DICmadder; Tangeglow); *Eyepaint* × *(Liverpool Echo* × *Woman's Own)*; Dickson, Patrick, 1988. Flowers red blend, semi-dbl. (6-14 petals), small, borne on strong straight stems; slight fragrance; foliage small, medium green, glossy; bushy, prolific growth.

Star Delight HRg (S), *mp*, 1990, (MORstar); *Yellow Jewel* × *Rugosa Magnifica*; Moore, Ralph S., 1989; Sequoia Nursery. Bud pointed; flowers rose pink, white base, silvery pink reverse, single (5 petals), flat, medium, borne usually singly and in sprays of 3-5; slight fragrance; foliage medium, olive to bluish-green, semi-glossy; upright, bushy, tall growth; repeats.

Star of Bethlehem R, *w*, 1947, *Innocence* × *Silver Moon*; Fisher, R.C. Flowers white, stamens red, single (5 petals), medium (3-3½ in.); foliage glossy; less rampant than Silver Moon; moderate bloom.

Star of Persia HFt (OGR), *my*, 1919, *R. foetida* × *Trier*; Pemberton. Flowers bright yellow, stamens golden, semi-dbl., medium; vigorous (8-10 ft.) growth.

Star of Queensland HT, *w*, 1909, *Étoile de France* × *Earl of Dufferin*; Williams, J. Flowers creamy white, dbl. (40 petals), high-centered, medium; foliage grayish green; vigorous, bushy growth.

Star of Thailand HT, *w*, 1977, *Mount Shasta* × *Pascali*; Chinprayoon; Chavalit Nursery. Flowers creamy white, dbl. (40 petals), high-centered, medium; foliage grayish green; vigorous, bushy growth.

Star of Waltham HP (OGR), *mr*, 1875, Paul, W. Flowers carmine-crimson, full, semi-globular, medium; fragrant; foliage very large; smooth green wood with occasional red prickles; dwarf to medium growth.

Star Twinkle Min, *pb*, 1978, *Fairy Moss* × *Fire Princess*; Moore, R.S.; Sequoia Nursery. Bud pointed; flowers pink, coral and orange, single (5 petals), small (1 in.); foliage glossy; bushy, compact growth.

Starbright HT, *w*, 1962, *Princess White* × *Hybrid Tea seedling*; Boerner; J&P. Bud ovoid; flowers white, dbl. (43 petals), high-centered, large (4 in.); fragrant; foliage glossy, dark; vigorous, upright growth; greenhouse variety.

Starburst Gr, *rb*, 1969, *Zambra* × *Suspense*; Meilland, M.L.; C-P. Bud ovoid; flowers red and yellow, dbl., high-centered, medium; slightly fragrant; foliage glossy; vigorous, bushy.

Stardance™ Min, *w*, 1982, (WILblank); *Ma Perkins* × *(Charlie McCarthy* × *Easter Morning)*; Williams, J. Benjamin; C-P. Flowers white, deep yellow stamens, dbl. (35 petals), mini-flora; slight fragrance; foliage small, medium green, semi-glossy; compact growth.

Stardust HT, *w*, 1939, *Better Times sport*; Florex Gardens. Flowers rose-red. RULED EXTINCT 5/92.

Stardust HT, *w*, 1992, (DEVstar); *Coquette × Seedling 64022-39*; Marciel, Stanley & Jeanne; DeVor Nursery. Flowers full (26-40 petals), large (7+ cms) blooms borne mostly singly; no fragrance; foliage large, medium green, semi-glossy; some prickles; tall (230 cms), upright growth.

Starfire Gr, *mr*, 1958, *Charlotte Armstrong × (Charlotte Armstrong × Floradora)*; Lammerts; Germain's. Bud urn-shaped; flowers medium red, dbl. (28 petals), high-centered to cupped, large (to 5 in.) blooms in clusters; fragrant; foliage glossy; vigorous, tall, bushy growth. AARS, 1959.

Stargazer F, *ob*, 1977, *Marlena × Kim*; Harkness. Flowers orange-red, yellow eye, single (9 petals), patio, small to medium blooms in large clusters; slight fragrance; foliage medium, medium green, matt; medium, bushy growth.

Starglo Min, *w*, 1973, *Little Darling × Jet Trail*; Williams, E.D.; Mini-Roses. Bud long, pointed; flowers white, dbl., high-centered, small; slightly fragrant; foliage small, leathery; vigorous, bushy growth. AOE, 1975.

Stargold HT, *my*, 1936, *Mary Wallace self × (Seedling × Seedling)*; Brownell; Inter-State Nursery. Bud long, pointed; flowers yellow, often splashed red, dbl. (32 petals), high-centered; long, strong stems; very fragrant; foliage dark, glossy; branching, upright growth.

Starina® Min, *or*, 1965, (MEIgabi; MEIgali); *(Dany Robin × Fire King) × Perla de Montserrat*; Meilland, M.L.; C-P. Flowers orange-scarlet, dbl., small; foliage glossy; vigorous, dwarf growth. GM, Japan, 1968; ADR, 1971.

Starina, Climbing Cl Min, *or*, 1981, *Starina sport*; Asami, Hitoshi.

Stark Whitecap F, *w*, 1959, *Glacier × Garnette*; Boerner; Stark Bros. Flowers pure white, dbl. (30-35 petals), cupped, large (3 in.), borne in large clusters; fragrant; foliage glossy; vigorous, upright growth.

Starkrimson HT, *dr*, 1961, *Happiness × San Fernando*; Morey; Stark Bros. Flowers scarlet-red, dbl. (48 petals), cupped to flat, large (4½ in.); very fragrant; foliage leathery; vigorous, upright growth.

Starla Min, *w*, 1990, (PIXarla); *Honor × Rainbow's End*; Chaffin, Lauren M.; Pixie Treasures Miniature Roses, 1991. Bud pointed; flowers white, semi-dbl. (20-25 petals), high-centered, medium, borne singly; slight, fruity

fragrance; foliage medium, medium green, semi-glossy; prickles needle-shaped, tan; bushy, medium growth.

Starlet F, *my*, 1957, *Goldilocks × Seedling*; Swim; Armstrong Nursery. Bud pointed; flowers medium yellow, dbl. (60 petals), high-centered, medium (2½ in.) blooms in clusters; slightly fragrant; foliage dark, leathery, glossy; vigorous, compact, upright.

Starlight HT, *my*, 1934, Wood & Ingram. Flowers orange and buff; fragrant; vigorous growth. RULED EXTINCT 3/87.

Starlite HT, *w*, 1942, *Seedling × White Briarcliff*; Nicolas; J&P. Bud long, pointed; flowers clear white, center tinted cream, dbl. (40 petals), high-centered, large; foliage dark, soft; vigorous, upright, bushy growth. RULED EXTINCT 3/87.

Starlight HT, *my*, 1987, *Devotion × Benson & Hedges Gold*; Guest, M. Flowers medium yellow, full (26-40 petals), medium; slight fragrance; foliage large, light green, matt; bushy growth.

Stars 'n' Stripes Min, *rb*, 1975, *Little Chief × (Little Darling × Ferdinand Pichard)*; Moore, R.S.; Sequoia Nursery, 1976. Bud long, pointed; flowers evenly striped red and white, dbl. (21 petals), high-centered blooms in clusters; sweet fragrance; foliage light to medium green; bushy, upright growth.

Starscent HT, *pb*, 1976, *Silver Star × Peter Frankenfeld*; Parkes; Rumsey. Flowers rich pink, base yellow, dbl. (20 petals), large (4½ in.); very fragrant; foliage dull, blue-green; upright growth.

Starshine HT, *yb*, 1971, *Peace × Condesa de Sástago*; Hamm; Five M Nursery. Flowers pink and yellow blend, dbl., globular, very large; slightly fragrant; foliage glossy; vigorous, bushy growth.

Starstruck Min, *ob*, 1986, (TINstar); *October × Orange Honey*; Bennett, Dee; Tiny Petals Nursery. Flowers deep golden orange with petals edged red, reverse medium red, aging deep orange red, dbl. (32 petals), star-shaped, medium blooms borne singly; slight fragrance; foliage medium, medium green, semi-glossy; small, thin, reddish prickles; fruit globular, 3/8 in. diam., brownish; low, spreading growth.

Startler HT, *or*, 1955, *Hector Deane × Mary Wheatcroft*; Robinson, H. Flowers orange-scarlet, base rich yellow, well formed; vigorous growth.

State of Maine HT, *w*, 1930, *Lady Ursula sport*; de Bree. Flowers white, center slightly tinged greenish, very dbl., high-centered, large; slightly fragrant.

Stately HT, *lp*, 1930, *Souv. de Gustave Prat* × *Seedling*; Clark, A.; Hackett. Bud long, pointed; flowers pale flesh, center deeper, dbl., high-centered, well-shaped, large; slightly fragrant; vigorous growth.

Statesman HT, *dr*, 1991, *seedling* × *seedling*; Burks, Larry; Co-Operative Rose Growers. Flowers dark red, full, large blooms borne mostly singly; slight fragrance; foliage medium, medium green, matt; medium, bushy growth.

Steadfast HT, *ob*, 1939, *Mme. Auguste Choutet* × *Seedling*; Clark, A.; T.G. Stewart. Flowers amber, flushed yellow and pink, semi-dbl.; vigorous growth.

Steeple Rose C (OGR), *dp*, *Perhaps Prolifera de Redouté sport.* Flowers rich rosy crimson with large green bud in center, full, globular, large.

Stefanovitch Cl HT, *dr*, 1943, *Lemania sport*; Meilland, F. Flowers dark red, dbl., large; very fragrant; vigorous growth; recurrent bloom.

Steino HT, *my*, 1965, *Golden Rapture sport*; Stein. Bud ovoid; flowers yellow, dbl.; slightly fragrant; foliage dark.

Stella® Gr, *w*, 1958, *Horstmann's Jubilaümsrose* × *Peace*; Tantau, Math. Bud ovoid; flowers blush, edged deep pink on outer petals, dbl. (36 petals), high-centered, large 4-5 in.), in clusters; slightly fragrant; foliage dark, leathery; vigorous, upright. GM, NRS, 1960.

Stella Duce F, *dr*, 1956, Leenders, M. Flowers dark crimson-red, stamens deep gold; fragrant; vigorous growth.

Stella Elizabeth Min, *w*, 1983, *Seedling* × *Seedling*; Moore, R.S.; Roy H. Rumsey. Flowers creamy white, petals edged light pink, dbl. (35 petals), small; slight fragrance; foliage small, medium green, semi-glossy; bushy growth.

Stella Mattutina HT, *lp*, 1951, *Numa Fay* × *Asso Francesco Baracca*; Giacomasso. Flowers flesh-pink, dbl. (35 petals), well formed, large; foliage glossy; vigorous growth.

Stella Pacis HT, *ob*, 1946, *Julien Potin* × *Mme. G. Forest-Colcombet*; Giacomasso. Flowers combination of orange, salmon, red and yellow, large; vigorous growth.

Stella Polaris HRg (S), *w*, 1890, Jensen. Flowers silvery white, single, large; foliage dark; vigorous (4 ft.) growth; recurrent bloom.

Stellmacher S, *mr*, 1937, *D.T. Poulsen* × *Stämmler*; Tantau. Flowers bright red, dbl. well formed; umbels; fragrant; abundant, recurrent bloom; hardy.

Stephan Pol, *mp*, 1967, *Maria Delforge* × *Arc-en-Ciel*; Delforge. Bud ovoid; flowers cyclamen-pink, full, large, borne in clusters; slightly fragrant; foliage glossy; vigorous, upright growth.

Stephanie Cl HT, *lp*, 1973, *Coral Dawn* × *Titian*; Gatty. Flowers light pink, semi-dbl., open, large; slightly fragrant; foliage glossy; vigorous, climbing growth; profuse, repeated bloom.

Stephanie Ann Min, *mp*, 1978, Lyon. Bud long, pointed; flowers neyron rose, semi-dbl. (16 petals), small (1 in.); slightly fragrant; foliage tiny; upright, bushy growth.

Stephanie Diane HT, *mr*, 1971, *Fragrant Cloud* × *Cassandra*; Bees. Flowers scarlet-red, dbl. (50 petals), exhibition, large (5 in.); moderately vigorous, upright growth.

Stephen Foster LCl, *mp*, 1950, *Seedling* × *Black Knight*; Rosen, H.R. Bud ovoid; flowers pink, semi-dbl. (20 petals), recurved, large (3½-4 in.); vigorous, upright growth, spreading to 15 ft. or more.

Stephen Langdon F, *dr*, 1969, *Karl Herbst* × *Sarabande*; Sanday. Flowers deep scarlet, semi-dbl., large; slightly fragrant; foliage dark; vigorous, compact growth.

Stephens' Big Purple HT, *m*, 1985, (STEbigpu; Big Purple; Nuit d'Orient; Stephens' Rose Big Purple); *Seedling* × *Purple Splendour*; Stephens, Pat; Sam McGredy, 1986. Flowers purple, dbl. (35 petals), large; very fragrant; foliage large, medium green, matt; upright growth.

Stereo F, *or*, 1972, *Baccará* × *(Olé* × *Independence)*; Lens; Spek. Bud long, pointed; flowers pure orange, dbl. (18-24 petals), open, large (3-3½ in.); slightly fragrant; foliage brownish, leathery; bushy growth.

Sterling HT, *mp*, 1933, *Mme. Butterfly* × *Seedling*; Hill, E.G., Co. Bud long, pointed; flowers brilliant pink, base yellow, dbl. (35 petals), large; fragrant; foliage glossy; vigorous. GM, Portland, 1938; ARS Gertrude M. Hubbard, 1939.

Sterling Silver HT, *m*, 1957, *Seedling* × *Peace*; Fisher, G.; J&P. Bud long, pointed; flowers lilac, becoming lighter, dbl. (30 petals), high-centered to cupped, medium (3½ in.); very fragrant; foliage dark, glossy; vigorous, upright growth.

Sterling Silver, Climbing Cl HT, *m*, 1963, Miyawaki.

Stern von Prag HRg (S), *dr*, 1924, *R. rugosa seedling* × *Edward Mawley*; Berger, V.; Faist. Flowers dark blood-red, dbl., large; fragrant; foliage large, dark; very vigorous, bushy growth.

Steve Silverthorne HT, *pb*, 1991, (FULsteve); *Dorothy Anne* × *Headliner*; Fulgham, Mary, 1992. Flowers white with pink blushing, full, large blooms borne mostly singly; slight fragrance; foliage large, medium green, semi-glossy; medium, upright growth.

Stevie Min, *w*, 1992, (BUStev); *Frau Karl Druschki × Miniature seedling*; Buster, Larry S. Bud 6/10 cms. opening to 3+ cms; flowers white, very full (53 petals), well formed, small (0-4 cms) blooms borne mostly singly; slight fragrance; foliage small, medium green, matt; some prickles; low(42 cms.), upright, compact growth.

Stirling Castle F, *mr*, 1978, *(Anne Cocker × Elizabeth of Glamis) × (Orange Sensation × The Optimist)*; Cocker. Flowers bright scarlet, 18-20 petals, large (3 in.); slightly fragrant; foliage matt; low, compact.

Stockton Beauty HT, *pb*, 1948, *Banner sport*; Raffel; Port Stockton Nursery. Bud long, pointed; flowers deep salmon-pink, base yellow, dbl., open, large; fragrant; foliage soft; very vigorous, bushy growth.

Stockton Red Cl HT, *mr*, 1962, Raffel; Port Stockton Nursery. Flowers clear red, well formed; very long stems; vigorous growth.

Stokes HT, *op*, 1982, *Susan Massu × Yellow seedling*; Perry, Astor; Perry Roses. Flowers peach, reverse salmon, dbl. (35 petals), exhibition, large; slight, fruity fragrance; foliage medium green, matt; medium-tall growth.

Stolen Moment Min, *m*, 1990, (SEAmom); *Kiss 'n' Tell × (Aunty Dora × Charles de Gaulle)*; McCann, Sean. Flowers mauve blend, semi-dbl. (6-14 petals), small; slight fragrance; foliage small, medium green, semi-glossy; bushy growth.

Stoplite F, *mr*, 1955, *Garnette × Seedling*; Jelly; E.G. Hill Co. Flowers rose-red, dbl. (45-55 petals), medium; fragrant; vigorous, upright growth; for greenhouse use.

Stormly HT, *op*, 1966, *(Eclipse × Michèle Meilland) × Baccará*; Caranta, M.&H. Flowers coral, reverse red-pink, oval, cupped; foliage dull; tall growth.

Strange Music Min, *rb*, 1986, (MORmum; Striped Meillandina); *Little Darling × (Fairy Moss × (Little Darling × Ferdinand Pichard))*; Moore, R.S.; Moore Min. Roses, 1982. Bud mossy; flowers red, striped white, reverse near white, dbl. (50 petals), high-centered, mini-moss, medium blooms in clusters of 5-7; no fragrance; foliage medium, medium green, matt; small to medium, straight, brown prickles; bushy, spreading growth.

Stratford HT, *op*, 1936, *(Emile Charles × La France) × Maréchal Niel*; Nicolas; Dixie Rose Nursery. Bud long-pointed, ovoid; flowers luminous pink tinted salmon, very dbl.; long

stems; very fragrant; foliage leathery; very vigorous, bushy growth.

Strawberry HT, *mr*, 1950, *McGredy's Pink × Phyllis Gold*; Fletcher; Tucker. Flowers strawberry, reverse deep flesh, dbl. (35-40 petals), large (5½-6 in.); foliage light green; vigorous, compact growth.

Strawberry Blonde Gr, *or*, 1966, *Ma Perkins × Spartan*; Armstrong, D.L.; Armstrong Nursery. Bud urn-shaped; flowers light orange-red, dbl. (25 petals), high-centered, medium; fragrant (spicy); foliage dark, leathery; very vigorous, upright, bushy growth.

Strawberry Cream F, *pb*, 1972, Ellick; Excelsior Roses. Flowers strawberry-pink, streaked cream, dbl. (45 petals), very full, medium (3 in.); very fragrant; foliage light; vigorous, low growth.

Strawberry Crush F, *mr*, 1974, *Bridal Pink × Franklin Engelmann*; Dickson, A. Flowers medium red, full, large (3 in.); slightly fragrant; foliage red when young.

Strawberry Delight Min, *pb*, 1989, (RENerry); *Little Darling × California Dreaming*; Rennie, Bruce F.; Rennie Roses, 1990. Bud pointed; flowers white with medium pink freckles, reverse white with pink edges, dbl. (28 petals), high-centered, exhibition, medium, borne singly; no fragrance; foliage medium, dark green, semi-glossy; prickles straight, medium, brown; fruit none observed; spreading, medium growth.

Strawberry Fair F, *mr*, 1966, *Orangeade × Seedling*; Gregory. Flowers scarlet, dbl., medium (2 in.) blooms in clusters; slightly fragrant; foliage dark; vigorous, bushy.

Strawberry Ice F, *w*, 1975, *((Goldilocks × Virgo) × (Orange Triumph × Yvonne Rabier)) × Fashion*; Bees; Flower petals cream-white, edged pink, dbl. (22 petals), large (3-3½ in.); foliage dark; compact, bushy growth. GM, Madrid, 1974.

Strawberry Kiss Min, *rb*, 1991, (CLEkiss); *Seedling × Seedling*; Clements, John; Heirloom Old Garden Roses, 1990. Flowers white edged red, moderately full (15-25 petals), exhibition, small (0-4 cms) blooms borne mostly singly; no fragrance; foliage small, light green, semi-glossy; some prickles; medium (35 cms), upright, bushy growth.

Strawberry Social F, *mr*, 1979, *Pink Parfait × Chrysler Imperial*; Taylor, Thomas E. Bud ovoid; flowers medium red, dbl. (23 petals), high-centered blooms borne 3-7 per cluster; slight fragrance; foliage medium green, semi-glossy; hooked prickles; upright to spreading, bushy growth.

Strawberry Sundae Min, *w*, 1985, (LEOstra); *(Kathy Robinson × Seedling) × (Kathy Robinson × Seedling)*; Léon, Charles F., Sr. Flowers ivory flushed pink, dbl. (35 petals), medium; slight fragrance; foliage medium, light to medium green, semi-glossy; bushy, spreading growth.

Strawberry Swirl Min, *rb*, 1978, *Little Darling × Miniature seedling*; Moore, R.S.; Sequoia Nursery. Bud ovoid, pointed; flowers red mixed with white, dbl. (48 petals), high-centered, mini-moss, small (1 in.); bushy growth.

Stretch Johnson S, *rb*, 1988, (MACfirwal; Rock 'n' Roll); Tango *Sexy Rexy × Maestro*; McGredy, Sam; McGredy Roses International. Flowers orange blend, semi-dbl. (6-14 petals), medium; slight fragrance; foliage large, medium green, semi-glossy; bushy growth. GM, RNRS, 1988.

String of Pearls F, *w*, 1985, (Meg '81); *Meg, Climbing × Sunsprite*; Gandy's Roses, Ltd.; Rearsby Roses, Ltd. Flowers near white, semi-dbl., medium; slight fragrance; foliage medium, dark, semi-glossy; dwarf, bushy growth.

Striped Radiance HT, *pb*, 1919, *Radiance sport*; Vestal. Flowers distinctly striped white.

Stripez HT, *pb*, 1942, *Better Times sport*; Janssen; Premier Rose Gardens. Flowers striped and variegated.

Stroller F, *rb*, 1968, *Manx Queen × Happy Event*; Dickson, A. Bud loose; flowers cerise, reverse gold, dbl., large blooms in trusses; foliage matt.

Stuart's Quarry HT, *pb*, 1977, *Silver Lining × Anne Letts*; Bailey. Bud high centered; flowers pale bluish pink, reverse silver, dbl. (30 petals), full, large (4 in.); fragrant; foliage small, glossy, dark; bloom repeats quickly.

Studienrat Schlenz Cl HT, *mp*, 1926, *Mrs. Aaron Ward × Frau Karl Druschki*; Lambert, P. Flowers rose-pink, reverse pink, dbl., large; fragrant; height 6½-8 ft.; non-recurrent bloom.

Sturdy Gertie HT, *op*, 1949, *Pink Princess × Peace*; Taylor, C.A. Flowers coral-pink, dbl. (30 petals), medium; fragrant (raspberry); foliage small, dark, glossy, somewhat ribbed.

Stuttgart HT, *my*, 1928, *Edith Cavell × Mrs. Franklin Dennison*; Berger, V.; Pfitzer. Bud long, pointed; flowers pure yellow, medium, fragrant.

Stylish HT, *pb*, 1953, Robinson, H. Flowers rose-pink, base yellow, high-centered, large (5-6 in.); fragrant; foliage dark, glossy, vigorous growth.

Su Excelencia Señora de Franco F, *mr*, 1956, *Cocorico × Independence*; Camprubi.

Bud long, pointed; flowers red, dbl., cupped, medium; slightly fragrant; foliage dark, glossy; vigorous, upright growth.

Subaru F, *mr*, 1977, *Masquerade × Permanent Wave*; Kikuchi. Bud pointed; flowers red, single (5 petals), small (1½ in.); slightly fragrant; foliage dark; low growth.

Sublime HT, *op*, 1931, *Talisman sport*; Amling Co. Bud long, pointed; flowers orange-salmon, suffused scarlet, semi-dbl.; long stems; fragrant; very vigorous growth.

Substitut Jacques Chapel HT, *pb*, 1922, *Mme. Mélanie Soupert × Lyon Rose*; Bernaix, P. Flowers peach-blossom-pink, edged rose-pink, bases haded citron-yellow; very fragrant.

Succes HCan (OGR), *lp*, 1954, *R. canina seedling*; deRuiter. Flowers pinkish white, single, blooms in trusses; foliage dark, glossy; used for understock.

Succès Fou HT, *mr*, 1963, *Walko × Souv. de J. Chabert*; D-C. Bud long; flowers deep cherry-red, well formed; vigorous growth.

Sue Belle Min, *ob*, 1992, (TALsue); *Party Girl × Poker Chip*; Taylor, Pete; Kay; Taylor's Roses, 1993. Flowers orange with yellow eye, yellow stamens, aging to pink, semi-dbl. (6-14 petals), mostly has 5, medium (4-7 cms) blooms borne mostly singly; slight fragrance; foliage small, medium green, semi-glossy; some prickles; medium (40 cms), upright, bushy growth.

Sue Jo™ Min, *r*, 1989, (MINavco); *Tom Brown × Twilight Trail*; Williams, Ernest D.; Mini-Roses. Flowers russet, outside petals tan-lavender, inside petals golden-amber, dbl. (33 petals), small; very fragrant; foliage small, medium green, glossy; upright, bushy growth.

Sue Lawley F, *rb*, 1980, (MACspash; MAC-splash; Spanish Shawl); *((Little Darling × Goldilocks) × ((Evelyn Fison × (Coryana × Tantau's Triumph)) × (John Church × Elizabeth of Glamis))) × (Evelyn Fison × (Orange Sweetheart × Frühlingsmorgen)*; McGredy, Sam. Flowers medium red, petals edged light pink all around, 19 petals, blooms borne 7 per cluster; slight fragrance; foliage matt, red when young; small, straight prickles; bushy growth. GM, NZ, 1981.

Sue Leat HT, *pb*, 1983, *Golden Slippers × Anne Letts*; Summerell, B.L. Flowers medium pink on outer half of petals, golden yellow on lower half, dbl. (20 petals), medium; medium fragrance; brown prickles; upright growth.

Sue Ryder® F, *op*, 1980, (HARlino); *Southampton × ((Highlight × Colour Wonder) × (Parkdirektor Riggers × Piccadilly)*; Harkness, 1983.

Flowers salmon orange, reverse shaded yellow, dbl. (20 petals), cupped, medium blooms in large clusters; little fragrance; foliage medium, mid-green, semi-glossy; small prickles; vigorous, medium, bushy growth.

Suffolk HT, *w*, 1983, *Garden Party* × *Yellow seedling*; Perry, Astor; Perry Roses, 1984. Flowers white with pink petal tips, dbl. (40+ petals), high-centered, urn-shaped, large; slight fragrance; foliage large, medium green, matt; upright growth.

Sugandhini HT, *lp*, 1969, *Margaret Spaull* × *Seedling*; Indian Agric. Research Inst. Bud pointed; flowers light pink, dbl., full, medium; very fragrant; foliage glossy, light; bushy growth.

Sugar Babe Min, *lp*, 1978, Lyon. Bud long, pointed; flowers light pink, semi-dbl. (16 petals), small (1 in.); slightly fragrant; foliage bronze; compact growth.

Sugar Bear Min, *w*, 1986, *Heartland* × *Seedling*; Bridges, Dennis, 1987. Flowers white, dbl. (18 petals), high-centered, medium, borne singly; slight fragrance; foliage medium, medium green, semi-glossy; straight, pointed, medium, light green prickles; upright, medium growth.

Sugar Candy Pol, *mp*, 1951, Proctor. Flowers pink, dbl., very small; compact growth; profuse, recurrent bloom.

Sugar Elf Cl Min, *pb*, 1974, Moore, R.S.; Sequoia Nursery. Bud long, pointed; flowers pink and gold blend, semi-dbl. (15 petals), small (1 in.); slightly fragrant; foliage glossy, leathery; bushy, spreading growth.

Sugar 'n' Spice Min, *lp*, 1985, (TINspice); *Futura* × *Avandel*; Bennett, Dee; Tiny Petals Nursery. Flowers light peach-pink, dbl. (28 petals), HT form, medium; slight fragrance; foliage medium, medium green, semi-glossy; upright, bushy growth.

Sugar Plum HT, *mp*, 1954, (Prelude); *Crimson Glory* × *Girona*; Swim; Breedlove Nursery. Bud ovoid; flowers tyrian rose, dbl. (55 petals), high-centered to flat, large (4-5 in.); fragrant (spicy); foliage dark, glossy, leathery; vigorous, upright, bushy growth.

Sugar Sweet F, *pb*, 1973, *Wendy Cussons* × *Prima Ballerina*; Sanday. Flowers soft pink, reverse yellow and pink, semi-dbl. (13 petals), HT form, large (3-4 in.); fragrant; foliage green, matt. Edland Fragrance Medal, 1974.

Sukumari F, *w*, 1983, *Gamma ray induced somatic mutation of America's Junior Miss*; Gupta, Dr. M.N. & Datta, Dr. S.K.; National Botanical Research Institute. Flowers rosy white.

Sulcova Kladenska Pol, *lp*, 1936, Sulc. Flowers bright pink; vigorous growth.

Sulphurea T (OGR), *ly*, 1900, Paul, W. Flowers sulphur-yellow.

Sultan of Zanzibar HP (OGR), *m*, 1875, Paul. Flowers purplish maroon, globular, medium.

Sultane HT, *rb*, 1946, *J.B. Meilland* × *Orange Nassau*; Meilland, F. Bud long, pointed; flowers vermilion, reverse gold, dbl. (40 quilled petals), large (5 in.); slightly fragrant; foliage leathery, bronze.

Suma no Ura HT, *mr*, 1980, *(Rob Roy* × *Himatsuri)* × *Seedling*.; Teranishi, K.; Itami Rose Nursery. Flowers crimson, dbl. (40 petals), high-centered, exhibition, medium blooms borne usually singly; no fragrance; foliage small, medium green, semi-glossy; large, reddish-brown prickles; medium, bushy growth.

Sumatra F, *or*, 1956, *Olga* × *Fashion*; Mallerin; C-P. Bud ovoid; flowers signal-red, dbl. (26 petals), globular, large (3 in.) blooms in pyramidal clusters; fragrant; foliage leathery; moderate, upright growth.

Summer Beauty™ Min, *dy*, 1986, (MINahco); *Seedling* × *Seedling*; Williams, Ernest; MiniRoses. Flowers deep yellow, dbl. (35 reflexed petals, some quilling), high-centered, exhibition, small, borne usually singly or in sprays of 3-5; moderate fragrance; foliage small, dark green, semi-glossy; very few, thin, short, light prickles; fruit none; upright, bushy, medium growth.

Summer Blossom F, *mp*, 1971, *Orange Sensation* × *Kimono*; deRuiter. Flowers soft geranium-pink, open, medium (2-3 in.); upright, bushy growth.

Summer Breeze Min, *op*, 1991, (TALsum); *Baby Katie* × *Poker Chip*; Taylor, Pete & Kay; Taylor's Roses, 1992. Flowers light orange-pink, ages lighter, yellow base, reverse slightly darker, full (26-40 petals), small (0-4 cms) blooms borne mostly singly or in small clusters; slight fragrance; foliage medium, medium green, semi-glossy; some prickles; low (40 cms), spreading growth.

Summer Butter Min, *dy*, 1979, *Arthur Bell* × *Yellow Jewel*; Saville; Nor'East Min. Roses. Bud ovoid, pointed; flowers deep yellow, dbl. (22 petals), cupped, small (1-1½ in.); very fragrant (spicy); foliage glossy; vigorous, compact growth.

Summer Cloud Min, *w*, 1989, (ZIPcloud); *Roundabout* × *Erfurt*; Zipper, Herbert; Magic Moment Miniatures, 1990. Bud ovoid; flowers white with hint of pink, dbl. (65 petals), urn-shaped, exhibition, large, borne singly and in sprays of 3-4; slight fragrance; foliage medium, medium green, semi-glossy; prickles straight, small, few, light brown; fruit globular, medium, brown-orange; bushy, medium growth.

Summer Crest HT, *dp*, 1982, (HERcres); *Miss All-American Beauty* × *Seedling*; Herholdt, J.A. Flowers deep pink, dbl. (40+ petals), large; slight fragrance; foliage medium, medium green, semi-glossy.

Summer Damask D (OGR), (Damask Rose; *R. belgica* Miller; *R. calendarum* Borkhausen; *R. damascena* Miller; *R. gallica damascena* Voss; *R. polyanthos* Roessig; Int. to Eu. from Asia Minor in 16th Century. Flowers red, pink or white, sometimes striped, dbl., borne usually in corymbs; very fragrant; fruit ovoid; 5 ft. Summer bloom; garden origin. *Gallicanae*.

Summer Dawn Pol, *mp*, 1950, *Margo Koster* sport; Proctor. Flowers soft rose-pink; foliage small, dainty.

Summer Days HT, *ly*, 1976, *Fragrant Cloud* × *Dr. A.J. Verhage*; Bees. Flowers pale yellow, dbl. (36 petals), high-centered, full, large (3½ in.); fragrant; vigorous.

Summer Dream HT, *ab*, 1986, (JACshe); *Sunshine* × *Seedling*; Warriner; J&P, 1987. Flowers apricot pink, dbl. (30 petals), high-centered, exhibition, medium blooms borne singly; slight, fruity fragrance; foliage medium, medium green, matt; upright, tall.

Summer Fashion F, *yb*, 1986, (JACale; Arc de Triomphe); *Precilla* × *Bridal Pink*; Warriner; J&P, 1985. Flower petals light yellow edged pink, pink spreading with age, dbl. (20 petals), large blooms borne singly or in small clusters; fragrant; foliage large, medium green, semi-glossy.

Summer Fields F, *dp*, 1971, *Tropicana* × *Goldmarie*; Mattock. Flowers light scarlet, semidbl. (17 petals), large (5 in.); fragrant; foliage red when young, then green, matt.

Summer Frost F, *w*, 1962, *Princess White* × *Golden Masterpiece*; Boerner; Home Nursery Products Corp. Bud ovoid; flowers white, dbl. (30-35 petals), cupped, large (4½ in.); fragrant; foliage leathery, dark; vigorous, bushy, compact growth.

Summer Glory HT, *my*, 1961, *Dr. van Rijn* × *Seedling*; Leenders, J. Flowers lemon, well formed, large; upright growth.

Summer Holiday® HT, *or*, 1967, *Tropicana* × *Seedling*; Gregory. Flowers vermilion, dbl. (48 petals), high-centered; fragrant; foliage semi-glossy; very vigorous growth.

Summer Joy R, *dp*, 1911, Walsh. Bud pure white; flowers dark rose-pink, dbl., borne in clusters; foliage large, glossy; vigorous, climbing (18-20 ft.) growth.

Summer Love F, *ab*, 1986, (FRAnluv); *Pink Parfait* × *Cynthia Brooke*; Cowlishaw, Frank. Flowers light apricot, dbl. (27 petals), high-centered to flat, large blooms in clusters of 5-10; spicy fragrance; foliage large, dark, semi-glossy; upright growth.

Summer Madness™ Min, *my*, 1987, (FOUmad); *Party Girl* × *Sun Flare*; Jacobs, Betty; Four Seasons Rose Nursery. Flowers medium golden yellow, gold stamens, fading white, deeper in cool weather, dbl. (20-25 reflexed petals), long sepals, high-centered, exhibition, medium, borne usually singly or in sprays of up to 7; slight, fruity tea fragrance; foliage medium. medium green, matt; long, red to light brown prickles; fruit round, small, orange-red; bushy, medium growth.

Summer Magic Min, *op*, 1989, *Fashion Flame* × *Anita Charles*; Jolly, Marie; Rosehill Farm, 1991. Bud ovoid; flowers light pink blended apricot, reverse cream center, pink edging, very dbl. (150 petals), high-centered, medium, borne usually singly and in sprays of 2-4; slight, fruity fragrance; foliage small, medium green, matt; prickles none observed; bushy, spreading, medium growth.

Summer Meeting F, *my*, 1968, *Selgold* × *Circus*; Harkness. Flowers yellow, dbl. (45 petals), large blooms in trusses; slightly fragrant; foliage glossy; compact, bushy growth.

Summer Perfume LCl, *mr*, 1962, *Coral Dawn* × *Cocorico*; Leenders, J. Flowers vermilion-red, semi-dbl. (19 petals); very fragrant.

Summer Promise HT, *ly*, 1969, Abrams, Von; United Rose Growers. Flowers light yellow, dbl., high-centered, very large; slightly fragrant; foliage glossy; vigorous growth.

Summer Queen HT, *w*, 1964, *Queen Elizabeth* sport; Delforge. Flowers ivory-white, center tinted pink.

Summer Rainbow HT, *pb*, 1966, *Peace* × *Dawn*; Jelly; C-P. Bud ovoid; flowers pink, reverse yellow, dbl., high-centered, large; slightly fragrant; foliage glossy, leathery; vigorous, bushy growth.

Summer Scent Min, *mp*, 1989, (RENsum); *Paul Shirville* × *Seedling*; Rennie, Bruce F.; Rennie Roses, 1990. Bud ovoid; flowers medium pink with white center, reverse lighter, dbl. (30 petals), high-centered, medium, borne singly; moderate, spicy fragrance; foliage medium, dark green, glossy; prickles straight, small, few, brown; fruit none observed; bushy, low growth.

Summer Sérénade® F, *ab*, 1986, (SMItfirst); *(Seedling* × *Zambra)* × *Baby Bio*; Smith, Edward; Wheatcroft Roses, 1987. Flowers apricot to gold, fading to cream, semi-dbl. (25 petals), urn-shaped, medium, borne in sprays of 5-25; slight fragrance; foliage medium, dark green, glossy; medium, pointed, brown prickles; fruit round, small, orange, upright, medium growth. GM, Bagatelle; Geneva, 1986.

Summer Snow F, *w*, 1938, *Summer Snow, Climbing sport*; Perkins, C.H.; J&P. Flowers white, large (3½ in.) blooms in large clusters; slightly fragrant; foliage light green; bushy growth; heavy, recurrent bloom.

Summer Snow, Climbing Cl F, *w*, 1936, *Tausendschön seedling*; Couteau; J&P. Flowers white, semi-dbl., cupped, medium (2 in.) blooms in large clusters; slightly fragrant; foliage leathery; vigorous, pillar (8-10 ft.); sparse recurrent bloom.

Summer Song F, *ob*, 1962, (Chanson d'Été); *Seedling × Masquerade*; Dickson, P.; A. Dickson. Flowers orange and yellow, semi-dbl. (12 petals), large blooms in clusters; slightly fragrant; foliage glossy; low, bushy growth.

Summer Spice Min, *ab*, 1983, *Sheri Anne × Seedling*; Bridges, Dennis, 1984. Flowers light apricot, dbl. (35 petals), medium; fragrant; foliage medium, medium green, semi-glossy; spreading growth.

Summer Sunshine HT, *dy*, 1962, (Soleil d'Été); *Buccaneer × Lemon Chiffon*; Swim; Armstrong Nursery. Bud ovoid; flowers deep yellow, dbl. (25 petals), high-centered to cupped, large (3½-5 in.); slightly fragrant; foliage leathery, dark, semi-glossy; vigorous, upright, well-branched growth.

Summer Surprise Min, *mp*, 1991, *Libby × Seedling*; Gruenbauer, Richard, 1984; Flowers 'n' Friends, 1990. Bud rounded; flowers pink with yellow stamens, slightly darker reverse, aging light pink, very dbl. (60 petals), mum shaped, medium; no fragrance; foliage small, medium green, matt; bushy, low growth.

Summer Symphony Min, *yb*, 1984, *Lady Eve × Little Darling*; Hardgrove, Donald & Mary; Rose World Originals. Flowers yellow blend, dbl. (40+ petals), high-centered, large; very fragrant; foliage medium, medium green, semi-glossy; bushy, spreading.

Summer Tan F, *lp*, 1979, *Golden Slippers × Picasso*; Sheridan, J. Flowers flesh-pink; vigorous, compact growth.

Summer Wind S, *op*, 1975, *(Fandango × Florence Mary Morse) × Applejack*; Buck; Iowa State University. Bud ovoid, pointed; flowers orange-pink, single to semi-dbl., flat, large (3½-4 in.); fragrant (spicy clove); foliage dark, leathery; moderately vigorous, erect, bushy.

Summerdale Min, *dy*, 1991, (TALdal); *Rise 'n' Shine × Seedling*; Taylor, Pete & Kay, 1986; Taylor's Roses, 1990. Bud pointed; flowers deep yellow, aging lighter, very dbl. (30-35 petals), cupped, loose, medium, borne usually singly and in sprays of 3-4; no fragrance; foliage small, medium green, matt; bushy, low growth.

Summerrose S, *lp*, 1981, (INTersum); *Yesterday × Seedling*; Interplant. Flowers light pink, single (6-8 petals), 2 in. blooms in large clusters; fragrant; foliage medium, medium green, matt; many, long prickles; spreading growth; ground cover.

Summertime HT, *mp*, 1957, *Diamond Jubilee × Fashion*; Boerner; J&P. Bud ovoid; flowers cameo-pink overcast rose-pink, dbl. (65-70 petals), high-centered, large (4-4½ in.), borne in irregular clusters; very fragrant; foliage glossy, olive-green; bushy growth.

Summerwine HT, *mp*, 1974, *Tiffany × South Seas*; Warriner; J&P. Bud ovoid, pointed; flowers medium pink, dbl. (45 petals), large (4-6 in.); slightly fragrant; foliage leathery.

Sun Blush HT, *yb*, 1981, *Circus × Summer Sunshine*; Anderson Rose Nursery. Flowers yellow blend, dbl. (37 petals), high-centered blooms borne singly or 4 per cluster; slight fragrance; foliage mid-green; broad based, dark red prickles; upright growth.

Sun City HT, *yb*, 1985, (KORsun; KORgater); *((New Day × Minigold) × Seedling) × MEItakilor*; Kordes, R.; Ludwig's Roses. Flowers deep yellow with red petal edges, red spreading, dbl. (32 petals), star-shaped, large blooms in clusters of 1-3; slight fragrance; foliage deep green, red when young, leathery; dark brown prickles; upright, tall growth.

Sun Drops Min, *my*, 1986, (LYOdro); *Seedling × Redgold*; Lyon; MB Farms Min. Roses. Flowers medium yellow, dbl. (35 petals), cupped, medium blooms borne usually singly; slight fragrance; foliage medium, medium green, matt; very small, reddish prickles; low, bushy growth.

Sun Flare F, *my*, 1981, (JACjem; Sunflare); *Sunsprite × Seedling*; Warriner; J&P, 1983. Bud pointed; flowers medium yellow, dbl. (30 petals), flat, borne 3-12 per cluster; very light fragrance; foliage small, glossy; reddish prickles; low, compact. GM, Japan, 1981; Portland, 1985; AARS, 1983.

Sun Flare, Climbing Cl F, *my*, 1987, (JAClem); *Sun Flare sport*; Warriner; J&P.

Sun Flare, Climbing™ Cl F, *my*, 1987, (BURyellow; Yellow Blaze); *Sun Flare sport*; Burks, Joe; Co-Operative Rose Growers, 1987-88. Flowers medium yellow, fading lighter, semi-dbl., cupped, medium, borne in sprays of 3-7;

slight fragrance; foliage medium, medium green, semi-glossy; short, yellow-green prickles, slightly curved; fruit globular, medium, orange-red; spreading, tall growth.

Sun Glory HT, *dy*, 1987, (JACmey); *Golden Emblem* × *Seedling*; Warriner, William; J&P. Flowers deep yellow, dbl. (30 petals), high-centered, medium, borne singly; slight, fruity fragrance; foliage medium, medium green, matt; long, red prickles, pointed slightly downwards; fruit none; upright growth.

Sun Glow HT, *op*, 1934, *Talisman sport*; Florex Gardens. Bud long, pointed; flowers dark coral-pink, dbl., high-centered, large; long, strong stems; fragrant; foliage glossy; very vigorous growth.

Sun God HT, *pb*, 1930, *Seedling* × *Mme. Edouard Herriot*; Klyn; Wayside Gardens Co. Flowers shrimp-pink, yellow, and orange-copper, very dbl.; short stems; fragrant; foliage leathery, bronze; dwarf growth.

Sun Gold HT, *my*, 1935, Elmer's Nursery. Flowers pure yellow, dbl., large; slightly fragrant; foliage glossy, dark; very vigorous growth. RULED EXTINCT 3/83.

Sun Honey Min, *my*, 1983, (MORhoney); *Orange Honey sport*; Moore, R.S.; Moore Min. Roses. Flowers medium yellow.

Sun King® HT, *my*, 1954, *Peace* × *Duchesse de Talleyrand*; Meilland, F.; C-P. Bud long, pointed; flowers bright lemon-yellow, dbl. (45 petals), high-centered, large (3½ in.); fragrant; foliage dark, glossy, leathery; vigorous, upright growth.

Sun Princess Min, *lp*, 1984, (LAVsun); *(Dwarfking '78* × *Starina)* × *Lemon Delight*; Laver, Keith. Flowers light salmon-pink, dbl. (35 petals), small; slight fragrance; foliage small, medium green, semi-glossy; bushy, spreading growth.

Sun Sparkle Min, *yb*, 1984, (LYOsun); *Dandy Lyon* × *Seedling*; Lyon. Flowers yellow blended red, dbl. (20 petals), small; fragrant; foliage small, medium green, semi-glossy; upright, bushy growth.

Sun Up HT, *lp*, 1951, *Break o' Day (HT) sport*; Brownell. Flowers china-pink, dbl., large; fragrant; vigorous growth.

Sun Valley HT, *dy*, 1952, (Yukon); *Soeur Thérèse* × *Mark Sullivan*; Whisler; Germain's. Bud ovoid; flowers golden yellow, dbl. (30-35 petals), open, large (4-5 in.); very fragrant (spicy); foliage dark, leathery; vigorous, upright growth.

Sunbeam Min, *my*, 1957, *(Tom Thumb* × *Polly Flinders)* × *Golden Scepter*; Robinson, T. Flowers yellow; very fragrant; dwarf (14-18 in.) growth.

Sunbeam® HT, *ab*, 1987, (KORdoselbla); Kordes, W. Flowers apricot, dbl. (26-40 petals), large; slight fragrance; foliage large, dark green, semi-glossy; bushy growth.

Sunbird™ Min, *my*, 1988, (POULnish); *MiniPoul* × *Seedling*; Poulsen Roser ApS; C-P, 1987. Flowers medium yellow opening to light yellow, fading to light pastel yellow, dbl. (25-30 petals), exhibition, medium, borne usually singly; no fragrance; foliage medium, dark green, matt, convex, straw to light maroon; fruit ovoid, few, pale orange-red; bushy, medium growth.

Sunblest HT, *dy*, 1970, (Landora); *Seedling* × *King's Ransom*; Tantau. Flowers yellow, dbl. (38 petals), large (5 in.); slightly fragrant; foliage glossy. GM, Japan, 1971; NZ, 1973.

Sunbonnet F, *dy*, 1967, *Arlene Francis* × *(Circus* × *Sweet Talk)*; Swim & Weeks; Weeks Wholesale Rose Grower. Bud pointed; flowers bright greenish yellow, dbl., high-centered, medium; fragrant; foliage dark, leathery; vigorous, low, bushy growth.

Sunbonnet Sue S, *yb*, 1984, *Gold Dot* × *Malaguena*; Buck; Iowa State University. Flowers yellow stippled with scarlet, dbl. (25 petals), large blooms borne 1-10 per cluster; fragrant; foliage large, leathery, semi-glossy, medium green; small, awl-like, brown prickles; upright, bushy growth; repeat bloom; hardy.

Sunbright® HT, *my*, 1984, (JACjel); *Seedling* × *New Day*; Warriner, William A; J&P. Bud long, pointed; flowers medium yellow, dbl. (28 petals), flat, large (4 in.); slightly fragrant; upright.

Sunburst HT, *dy*, 1912, Pernet-Ducher. Bud long, pointed; flowers variable yellow, toward orange, dbl., cupped. GM, NRS, 1912.

Sunburst, Climbing Cl HT, *dy*, 1914, Howard Rose Co.

Sunburst, Climbing Cl HT, *dy*, 1915, Low.

Sunburst Jewel HT, *rb*, 1979, *Muchacha* × *Seedling*; Herholdt, J.A. Bud pointed; flowers red, reverse pale gold, dbl. (35 petals); bushy growth.

Sundance F, *yb*, 1954, *Poulsen's Supreme* × *Eugène Fürst*; Poulsen, S.; Poulsen; McGredy. Flowers orange-yellow changing to bright rose-pink, dbl. (22 petals), medium (2½ in.) blooms in trusses; slightly fragrant; foliage light green, matt, thin; vigorous, tall (4 ft.), upright, uneven growth. GM, NRS, 1954.

Sunday Best LCl, *rb*, 1924, *Frau Karl Druschki* × *Seedling*; Clark, A.; NRS Victoria. Bud long, pointed; flowers brilliant red, center white, single blooms in clusters; slightly fragrant; foliage wrinkled; vigorous, climbing growth; long seasonal bloom.

Sunday Brunch Min, *yb*, 1984, (MORday); *Rumba* × *Peachy White*; Moore, R.S.; Moore Min. Roses, 1983. Flowers soft creamy yellow, petal tips becoming pink, which spreads with age, dbl. (20 petals), small; fragrant; foliage small to medium, medium green, semi-glossy; vigorous, upright, bushy growth.

Sunday Lemonade HT, *lp*, 1986, (MOLsunlem); *Lemon Spice sport*; Molder, W.A.; Rose Acres. Flowers light pink, dbl. (30 petals), high-centered, exhibition, medium blooms borne usually singly; heavy, fruity fragrance; foliage medium, dark, matt; medium, amber prickles, hooked downward; upright, medium-tall growth.

Sunday Press HT, *mr*, 1970, Kordes; McGredy. Flowers medium red, dbl. (53 petals), classic form, large (4¹/₂ in.).

Sunday Times F, *dp*, 1972, (Shrubby Pink); McGredy; Kordes. Flowers deep rosy pink, dbl., globular, medium; slightly fragrant; foliage light; moderate, dwarf growth.

Sunderland Supreme HT, *lp*, 1986, (NOSsun); *Paul Neyron* × *Royal Highness*; Greensitt, J.A.; Nostell Priory Rose Gardens, 1980. Flowers light pink, full (26-40 petals), medium; slight fragrance; foliage medium, medium green, semi-glossy; upright growth.

Sundial™ HT, *my*, 1987, (AROlyme); *(Golden Wave* × *(American Heritage* × *First Prize))* × *((Camelot* × *First Prize)* × *Yankee Doodle)*; Christensen, Jack; Armstrong Roses, 1986. Flowers medium, bright yellow, dbl. (30 petals), high-centered, exhibition, medium, borne usually singly; slight, spicy fragrance; foliage medium, medium green, glossy; many, normal, small and large, light green-tan prickles; fruit none; upright, bushy, medium growth.

Sundown HT, *mp*, 1934, *Talisman sport*; Scittine; Lainson. Bud globular; flowers pink, dbl. (35-40 petals), medium (3¹/₂ in.); very fragrant; foliage glossy; very vigorous growth.

Sundowner Gr, *ab*, 1978, (MACcheup; MACche); *Bond Street* × *Peer Gynt*; McGredy, S., IV; Edmunds. Flowers golden orange, dbl. (35 petals), classic form, large (4 in.); very fragrant; foliage leathery; tall, upright growth. AARS, 1979.

Sundra® F, *dr*, 1968, (GAisu); *Club* × *Lilli Marlene*; Gaujard. Bud pointed; flowers dark red, semi-dbl., cupped, large; very fragrant; foliage glossy; vigorous, bushy growth.

Sundust Min, *yb*, 1977, *Golden Glow* × *Magic Wand*; Moore, R.S.; Sequoia Nursery. Bud pointed; flowers light apricot, dbl. (23 pet-

als), small (1¹/₂ in.); fragrant (fruity); foliage small, light; low, bushy, compact growth.

Sunfire F, *or*, 1974, (JACko); *Tropicana* × *Zorina*; Warriner; J&P. Bud ovoid; flowers mandarin-red, dbl., high-centered, medium; slightly fragrant; foliage large, leathery; vigorous, upright, bushy growth.

Sungirl F, *yb*, 1981, *Charleston* × *Seedling*; Barni-Pistoia, Rose. Flowers deep yellow, light red on petal tips, dbl. (25 petals); no fragrance; foliage medium, deep green, glossy; reddish-green prickles; upright growth.

Sunglo F, *or*, 1976, *Woburn Abbey sport*; Kuramoto, H.; J&P. Bud ovoid; flowers orange-red, dbl. (25 petals), open to flat, large (3 in.); slightly fragrant (fruity).

Sungold Cl HT, *my*, 1939, *Margaret Anderson* × *Souv. de Claudius Pernet, Climbing*; Thomas; Armstrong Nursery. Bud long, pointed; flowers bright golden yellow, dbl., large; foliage glossy, dark; vigorous (15-18 ft.) growth. RULED EXTINCT 3/83.

Sungold Min, *ob*, 1983, (MORlem; Sun Gold); *Rumba* × *Lemon Delight*; Moore, R.S.; Moore Min. Roses, 1982. Flowers yellow overlaid with orange on outer half of petals, reverse light yellow, dbl. (20 petals), small blooms in clusters; no fragrance; foliage small, medium green, matt to semi-glossy; upright, bushy growth.

Sunil Gavaskar F, *m*, 1985, *(First Rose Convention* × *Scarlet Knight)* × *Ena Harkness*; Hardikar, Dr. M.N. Flowers mauve, dbl. (60 petals), cupped, 3 in. blooms in clusters of 7 or more; no fragrance; foliage large, dark, leathery; light green, needle-like prickles; dwarf, bushy growth.

Sunkissed HT, *my*, 1980, *Minigold* × *Precilla*; Tantau, M.; J&P. Bud ovoid, pointed; flowers yellow-orange, blooms borne singly; very little fragrance; foliage leathery; long, light green prickles, hooked down; upright growth.

Sunkist™ HT, *yb*, 1932, *Joanna Hill sport*; Hill, E.G., Co. Flowers orange-copper; slightly longer bud and more petals than parent.

Sunlight HT, *my*, 1956, (Grisbi); *(Eclipse* × *Ophelia)* × *Monte Carlo*; Meilland, F.; URS, 1956; C-P, 1958. Bud ovoid; flowers yellow, dbl. (45 petals), high-centered to cupped, large (4 in.); fragrant; foliage leathery; vigorous, upright, bushy growth.

Sunlight, Climbing Cl HT, *my*, 1963, (Grisbi, Climbing); Meilland, M.L.; URS.

Sunlit HT, *ab*, 1937, Clark, A.; NRS Victoria. Flowers rich apricot, dbl., globular; compact growth.

Sunmist F, *ly*, 1940, *(Eva × Golden Rapture) × Hede*; Kordes; Dreer. Bud pointed; flowers clear light sulphur-yellow, semi-dbl., open; slightly fragrant; foliage leathery; vigorous growth.

Sunningdale HT, *mp*, 1929, Hicks. Bud long, pointed; flowers reddish carmine passing to cherry-pink, dbl., high-centered; fragrant.

Sunny F, *my*, 1952, *Seedling × Goldilocks*; Moore, R.S.; Marsh's Nursery. Bud pointed, yellow overlaid red; flowers lighter yellow, semi-dbl., open, small; fragrant; foliage leathery, glossy; vigorous, upright, bushy growth.

Sunny Boy HT, *pb*, 1961, *Mme. Butterfly × The Queen*; Delforge. Flowers buff-pink, tinted gold and lilac, center darker, well formed; fragrant; foliage bronze.

Sunny California HT, *my*, 1936, *Feu Joseph Looymans sport*; Hanshaw, E. Bud long, pointed; flowers yellow like Ville de Paris, dbl., cupped, very large.

Sunny Child® Min, *dy*, 1984, (HAVychi); *Gold Bunny × Seedling*; Verschuren, Ted; H.A. Verschuren. Flowers deep yellow, single (8 petals), small; slight fragrance; foliage medium, light green; no prickles; spreading, low growth.

Sunny Days HT, *my*, 1939, Verschuren; Dreer. Bud long, pointed; flowers chrome-yellow at edges; dbl., high-centered, large; slightly fragrant; foliage leathery, dark; vigorous growth. RULED EXTINCT 11/86.

Sunny Day™ Min, *dy*, 1986, (SAVasun); *Golden Slippers × Rise 'n' Shine*; Saville, F. Harmon; Nor'East Miniature Roses, 1987. Flowers bright yellow, fading lighter, slight red blush on outer petals in full sun, dbl. (30 petals), high-centered, exhibition, small, borne usually singly or in sprays of 3-12; slight, spicy fragrance; foliage small, dark green, semiglossy; long, thin prickles, angled slightly downwards; fruit none; upright, bushy, low growth.

Sunny Honey F, *yb*, 1972, *Happy Event × Elizabeth of Glamis*; Dickson, P. Flowers yellow-pink blend, reverse red, dbl. (22 petals), large (4 in.); fragrant; foliage large, dark.

Sunny Jersey HT, *ab*, 1928, *Mme. Edouard Herriot sport*; Le Cornu. Flowers bronze, apricot, salmon and orange.

Sunny June S, *dy*, 1952, *Crimson Glory × Capt. Thomas*; Lammerts; Descanso Distributors. Bud pointed; flowers deep canary-yellow, single (5 petals), slightly cupped to flat, medium 3-3½ in.) blooms in large clusters; slightly fragrant (spicy); foliage dark, glossy; upright, compact, pillar or shrub (8 ft.) growth.

Sunny Maid F, *my*, 1949, *(Golden Rapture × Fred Walker) × Seedling*; Fletcher; Tucker. Flowers bright yellow, single (6-8 petals), large (4 in.), borne in large clusters; foliage glossy, light green; very vigorous, upright growth.

Sunny Meillandina® Min, *ob*, 1986, (MEIponal; Sunblaze; Sunny Sunblaze); *(Sarabande × Moulin Rouge) × (Zambra × Meikim)*; Meilland, M.L.; Meilland, 1985. Flowers yellow-orange, dbl. (35 petals), medium; no fragrance; foliage small, dark, matt; bushy growth.

Sunny Morning Min, *my*, 1974, *Golden Glow × Peachy White*; Moore, R.S.; Sequoia Nursery. Bud long, pointed; flowers medium to creamy yellow, dbl. (35 petals), flat, small (1-1½ in.); fragrant; bushy, upright growth.

Sunny San Joaquin F, *rb*, 1962, *Little Darling × Gertrude Raffel*; Raffel; Port Stockton Nursery. Flowers cerise-red, reverse tinted ivory; well shaped, borne in large clusters; slightly fragrant; tall growth.

Sunny South HT, *pb*, 1918, *Gustav Grünerwald × Betty Berkeley*; Clark, A.; NRS Victoria. Flowers pink flushed carmine, base yellow, semi-dbl., cupped, large; fragrant; foliage rich green; very vigorous growth.

Sunny Today F, *dy*, 1970, *(Summer Sunshine × Gold Cup) × Isobel Harkness*; Whisler, D.; Gro-Plant Industries. Flowers clear deep yellow, dbl., high-centered, medium; fragrant; foliage glossy, dark; moderate, bushy growth.

Sunnydew Min, *dy*, 1978, *Yellow Doll × Seedling*; Schwartz, E.W.; Bountiful Ridge Nursery. Bud ovoid; flowers yellow, semi-dbl. (18 petals), high-centered, small (1 in.); slightly fragrant; well-branched, spreading growth.

Sunnymount HT, *my*, 1936, *Joanna Hill sport*; Grillo. Bud sharp pointed but short; flowers buttercup-yellow, dbl. (50 petals), large; very fragrant; foliage leathery; vigorous growth.

Sunnyside HT, *op*, 1949, *Yellow Gloria sport*; Andre; Andre Greenhouses. Bud pointed, orange; flowers pink shaded orange, dbl. (24-30 petals), high-centered, large (4½-5 in.); slightly fragrant; very vigorous growth.

Sunnyside® Min, *yb*, 1963, *(Purpurine × Miniature seedling) × Rosina*; Lens. Flowers yellow, becoming pink and then red; vigorous growth.

Sun-Ray HT, *my*, 1932, Bentall. Flowers golden yellow, semi-dbl.; fragrant; vigorous growth.

Sunrise HT, *mp*, 1939, *Pilarín Vilella × Rosa Gallart*; Dot, P. Bud long, pointed; flowers salmon, dbl., open, large; foliage glossy, bronze; vigorous, bushy growth.

Sunrise-Sunset HT, *pb*, 1971, *Tiffany* × *(Seed-ling* × *Happiness)*; Swim & Weeks; Weeks Roses. Flowers blended pink, cream and lavender, dbl., high-centered, large; slightly fragrant; foliage glossy, light to dark, leathery; vigorous.

Sunset T (OGR), *dy*, 1883, *Perle des Jardins sport*; Henderson, P. Flowers orange-yellow.

Sunset Cl HT, *yb*, 1947, *Faience sport*; Marsh; Marsh's Nursery. Flowers peach and apricot, reverse yellow, dbl. (45-60 petals), cupped, large (5 in.); slightly fragrant; vigorous growth.

Sunset Glory HT, *ab*, 1947, *McGredy's Sunset sport*; Boerner; J&P. Bud ovoid; flowers golden yellow overlaid dusty rose-pink, dbl. (35-40 petals), cupped, large (4-4½ in.); fragrant (fruity); vigorous, upright, compact growth.

Sunset Jubilee HT, *pb*, 1973, *Kordes' Perfecta* × *Pink Duchess seedling*; Boerner; J&P. Bud ovoid; flowers medium pink, tinted lighter, dbl., high-centered, large; slightly fragrant; foliage large, light, leathery; vigorous, upright, bushy growth.

Sunset Song HT, *ab*, 1981, (COCasun); *(Sabine* × *Circus)* × *Sunblest*; Cocker, J. Bud pointed; flowers golden amber, dbl. (46 petals), HT-form, borne 1-5 per cluster; slight fragrance; foliage large, glossy, light olive green; beak-shaped, red-brown prickles; upright.

Sunshine HT, *yb*, 1918, Chaplin Bros. Bud long, pointed; flowers golden yellow, shaded apricot, dbl.; fragrant.

Sunshine Pol, *ob*, 1927, *George Elger* × *William Allen Richardson*; Robichon; Cutbush. Bud ovoid; flowers golden orange, dbl., small blooms in clusters; fragrant; foliage glossy; dwarf growth; (14).

Sunshine Girl Min, *my*, 1985, (PIXisun); *Sunsilk* × *Rise 'n' Shine*; Woolcock, Edward P.; Pixie Treasures Min. Roses. Flowers medium yellow, dbl. (35 petals), HT-form to multi-star shaped, small; slight fragrance; foliage small, medium green, semi-glossy; upright.

Sunshine Princess F, *yb*, 1983, (ANDsun); Andersons Rose Nursery. Flowers yellow blend, dbl. (20 petals), medium; slight fragrance; foliage medium, medium green, semi-glossy; bushy growth.

Sunshower F, *my*, 1974, *Golden Showers* × *Prairie Fire*; Golik; Dynarose. Bud ovoid; flowers bright yellow, semi-dbl. (16 petals), ruffled, medium (2½ in.); foliage glossy, light; moderate growth.

Sunsilk F, *my*, 1974, *Pink Parfait* × *Redgold seedling*; Fryer, G.; Fryer's Nursery. Flowers lemon-yellow, dbl. (30 petals), large (5 in.);

slightly fragrant; foliage dark. GM, Belfast, 1976.

Sunsmile™ Min, *my*, 1988, (JACmiy); *Spanish Sun* × *Calgold*; Warriner, William; Bear Creek Gardens, 1989. Bud ovoid; flowers medium yellow, dbl. (48 petals), high-centered, medium, borne singly and in sprays of 2-3; slight fragrance; foliage medium, medium green, semi-glossy; prickles straight to slightly hooked downward, brown; bushy, spreading, compact, vigorous growth.

Sunsong Gr, *ob*, 1966, (Dorrit); *Folie d'Espagne* × *(Zambra* × *Danish Pink)*; Soenderhousen; Armstrong Nursery. Bud globular; flowers orange to coral blend, dbl. (63 petals), informal, large (3 in.); slightly fragrant (tea); foliage glossy, leathery; upright, bushy growth.

Sunsplash™ Min, *dy*, 1989, (JACyim); *Rise 'n' Shine* × *Sun Flare*; Warriner, William A.; Bear Creek Gardens. Bud ovoid, pointed; flowers deep yellow, aging pale yellow, dbl. (43 petals), cupped, high-centered, exhibition, borne in sprays of 18-21; slight fragrance; foliage medium, medium green, very glossy, attractive; prickles long, slightly hooked downward, red to green-tan; tall, upright, spreading growth.

Sunspot F, *my*, 1965, *Golden Anniversary* × *Masquerade*; Fisher, G.; C-P. Flowers mimosa-yellow, dbl., cupped, large, borne in clusters; foliage leathery; vigorous, bushy growth.

Sunspray™ Min, *dy*, 1981, (AROrasp); *Gingersnap* × *Magic Carrousel*; Christensen; Armstrong Nursery. Bud ovoid, long, pointed; flowers bright deep yellow, semi-dbl. (16 petals), borne singly or several per cluster; slight tea fragrance; foliage semi-glossy, dark; straight prickles; vigorous, upright growth.

Sunsprite F, *dy*, 1977, (KORresia; Friesia); *Seedling* × *Spanish Sun*; Kordes, R.; J&P. Bud ovoid; flowers deep yellow, dbl. (28 petals), flat, large (3 in.); very fragrant; foliage light; upright growth. GM, Baden-Baden, 1972.

Sunsprite, Climbing Cl F, *dy*, 1989, *Sunsprite sport*; Kroeger, Henry, 1990.

Sunstar HT, *or*, 1921, *Mrs. C.V. Haworth* × *Hugh Dickson*; Dickson, A. Bud long, pointed; flowers orange and red, semi-dbl.; very fragrant; foliage light green; vigorous, bushy growth. GM, NRS, 1917; Bagatelle, 1923.

Sunstar, Climbing Cl HT, *or*, 1925, Dickson, A.

Sunstone HT, *yb*, 1957, *Bridget* × *Marcelle Gret*; Fletcher; Tucker. Bud long; flowers bright yellow splashed red, large (6 in.); strong stems; slightly fragrant; foliage glossy, bronze; vigorous, tall growth.

Sunstrike F, dy, 1974, *Spanish Sun* × *(Buccaneer* × *Zorina)*; Warriner; J&P. Bud small, pointed, ovoid; flowers deep yellow, dbl., high-centered, medium; slightly fragrant; foliage large, light, leathery; very vigorous, bushy growth.

Sunstruck Min, yb, 1978, *Redgold* × *Seedling*; Lyon. Bud long, pointed; flowers aureolinyellow and signal-red, dbl. (20 petals), medium (2 in.); very fragrant; foliage dark; upright growth.

Suntan HT, dy, 1939, *Nanjemoy* × *Mrs. Pierre S. duPont*; Hansen, N.J.; B&A. Flowers deep orange-yellow, fading slowly, dbl. (35 petals), large; strong stems; foliage leathery, dark, bronze. RULED EXTINCT 4/92.

Suntan HT, lp, 1940, *Mrs. Franklin D. Roosevelt sport*; Yoder. Bud long, pointed; flowers buff-salmon, base yellow, reverse light coral-red, dbl. (25 petals), cupped, medium (3½ in.); fragrant; vigorous, upright growth. Was not int. RULED EXTINCT 4/92.

Suntan™ Min, r, 1992, (INTerbronzi); *Seedling* × *The Fairy*; Ilsink, G. P., 1983; Interplant B.V., 1989. Flowers bronze, little fading, urn-shaped, dbl. (30 petals), small (4 cms) blooms borne in sprays of 5-8; slight fragrance; foliage small, dark green, glossy; upright, bushy, low (30 cms) growth.

Suntan Beauty™ Min, r, 1989, (MINawco); *(Angel Face* × *Golden Angel)* × *Yellow Jewel*; Williams, Ernest D.; Mini-Roses. Flowers tan with rosy highlights, dbl. (33-45 reflexed petals), exhibition, small; very fragrant; foliage small, dark green, glossy, disease resistant; bushy growth.

Super Aribau HT, dr, 1960, *Aribau* × *Director Rubió*; Dot, P. Flowers crimson-carmine, reverse silvery crimson, dbl. (24 petals), large; strong stems; very fragrant; upright, vigorous growth.

Super Chief HT, mr, 1976, *Queen Elizabeth* × *Happiness*; Patterson; Patterson Roses. Bud globular; flowers bright red, aging darker, very dbl. (60-65 petals), high-centered, large (5 in.); slightly fragrant; foliage dark; vigorous growth.

Super Congo HT, dr, 1950, *Congo* × *Léonce Colomber*; Meilland, F. Bud ovoid; flowers velvety dark blood-red, dbl. (30 petals), medium; slightly fragrant; foliage dull green; upright growth.

Super Gamusin HT, m, 1962, *Grey Pearl* × *Tristesse*; Dot, P. Flowers chamois to mauve.

Super Star Supreme HT, or, 1982, *Tropicana sport*; U.S. Patent Sales, Inc. Flowers deeper color.

Super Sun HT, my, 1967, *Piccadilly sport*; Bentley. Flowers maize-yellow.

Super Tabarin F, ob, 1963, *Faust* × *Tabarin*; Gaujard. Flowers coppery, reverse orange, semi-dbl.; vigorous growth.

Superb HT, lp, 1924, *Mme. Caroline Testout* × *Willowmere*; Evans. Flowers pale pink, tinted blush.

Superb Pol, dr, 1927, deRuiter. Flowers crimson, dbl.

Superb, Climbing Cl Pol, dr, 1933, Guillot, P.

Superb Tuscan G (OGR), m, (Superb Tuscany; Tuscany Superb); *Tuscany seedling*; Rivers, prior to 1837; Similar to Tuscany but flowers fuller and plant larger; good seedbearer.

Superba HSet (OGR), lp, 1843, *R. setigera seedling*; Feast. Flowers blush, borne in large clusters.

Superba HMoy (S), dr, *Charles P. Kilham* × *R. moyesii*; Van Rossem. Flowers dark crimson, dbl., large; no fruit; vigorous habit of *R. moyesii*.

Superba Sp (OGR), w, *R. multiflora strain*; Selected Dutch strain of *R. multiflora* used as an understock.

Superba HT, dp, 1940, *Julien Potin* × *Seedling*; Aicardi, L.; Giacomasso. Flowers intense rose with yellow reflections, very large; long stems; very fragrant.

Superga HT, lp, 1956, *Savoia sport*; Giacomasso. Flowers rose-pearl, high pointed; long stems; slightly fragrant; foliage dark, glossy; very vigorous growth.

Superglo Min, or, 1985, (SPOglo); *((Prominent* × *Rise 'n' Shine)* × *Trumpeter)* × *Chattem Centennial*; Spooner, Ray. Flowers orange-red, semi-dbl., small; slight fragrance; foliage small, medium green, semi-glossy; bushy growth.

Super-Harrington HT, dr, 1938, *Tassin* × *Victoria Harrington*; Brown, John; A. Meilland. Bud oval; flowers dark crimson, mottled scarlet, dbl., medium; fragrant; foliage leathery; vigorous, upright growth.

Superior F, ab, 1968, *Masquerade* × *Amberlight*; LeGrice. Flowers apricot-yellow, semi-dbl., blooms in trusses; slightly fragrant; foliage dark, glossy; vigorous, low growth.

Supra™ HT, dy, 1980, (MEIrobidor; Carte d'Or); *((Zambra* × *(Baccará* × *White Knight)* × *Golden Garnette))* × *Seedling*; seedling Meilland, M.L.; Meilland Et Cie. Flowers deep yellow, dbl. (20 petals), flora-tea, large; no fragrance; foliage medium, dark, semi-glossy; upright growth; cut flower.

Supreme HT, *my*, 1963, *Golden Masterpiece ×* *Ethel Sanday*; LeGrice. Flowers lemon-yellow, dbl. (40-45 petals), well formed, large (4½-5 in.); fragrant; foliage dark, leathery, glossy; vigorous, tall growth.

Supreme Rendezvous HT, *pb*, 1961, *Day of Triumph sport*; Langbecker. Flowers cream to pale pink, edged carmine.

Supreme's Sister F, *mp*, 1960, Jones; Hennessey. Bud red; flowers coppery salmon to salmon-pink, dbl. (42 petals), medium; foliage leathery, bronze; low, bushy growth.

Surabhi HT, *mp*, 1975, *Oklahoma × Delhi Princess*; Indian Agric. Research Inst. Bud long, pointed; flowers phlox-pink, very dbl. (80 petals), high-centered; very fragrant; foliage glossy, dark; upright, compact growth.

Surain HT, *mp*, 1985, *Seedling × Forever Yours*; Elliott, Charles P. Flowers medium pink, dbl. (35 petals), exhibition, large; slight fragrance; upright growth.

Surekha HT, *or*, 1969, *Queen Elizabeth × Open pollination*; Indian Agric. Research Inst. Bud pointed; flowers coral-red, dbl., full, large; foliage dark, leathery; very vigorous, upright growth.

Surf Rider S, *w*, 1968, *Ivory Fashion × Ballerina*; Holmes, R.A.; Fryers Nursery. Flowers creamy white, dbl. (25 petals), medium blooms in large trusses; fragrant (musk); foliage bright, glossy; very vigorous, erect growth.

Surfer Girl Min, *or*, 1988, (RENfer); *Pink Sheri × Paul Shirville*; Rennie, Bruce; Rennie Roses. Flowers light orange-red, salmon, reverse lighter, dbl. (25-30 petals), high-centered, medium, borne usually singly; moderate, spicy fragrance; foliage medium, medium green, matt; prickles hooked, medium, transparent yellow-brown; fruit round, small, yellow-orange; bushy, medium growth.

Surf's Up Min, *ob*, 1984, (LEMsur); *Avandel × Seedling*; Lemrow, Dr. Maynard W. Flowers orange, yellow reverse, dbl. (35 petals), HT-form, small blooms borne singly; no fragrance; foliage small, medium green, semi-glossy; upright growth.

Surfside Min, *pb*, 1988, (MICsurf); *Tiki × Party Girl*; Williams, Michael; The Rose Garden. Flowers medium pink to creamy yellow to creamy white, dbl. (24 petals), high-centered, medium, borne usually singly; no fragrance; foliage large, light green, semi-glossy; prickles curved down, very few, red-green; fruit round, medium, green to orange-yellow; upright, medium growth.

Surkhab HT, *m*, 1976, Pal; Anand Roses. Bud globular; flowers tyrian purple, reverse silvery amaranth, very dbl. (76 petals), cupped,

large (4 in.); very fragrant; foliage leathery; very vigorous, upright, compact growth.

Surpasse Tout G (OGR), *mr*, (Cérisette la Jolie); Cult. before 1832. Flowers rosy crimson, fading cerise-pink, dbl.; height 3-4 ft.

Surprise HT, *mp*, 1925, *Frau Karl Druschki × Mme. Edouard Herriot*; Van Rossem. Flowers salmon-pink, dbl., cupped; slightly fragrant.

Surrey S, *lp*, 1985, (KORlanum; Sommerwind); *The Fairy × Seedling*; Kordes, W. Flowers light pink, semi-dbl., medium; slight fragrance; foliage small, medium green, semi-glossy; bushy growth.

Surville HT, *mr*, 1924, *Mme. Edouard Herriot seedling*; Croibier. Flowers indian red, shaded cerise, dbl.

Surya Kiran F, *or*, 1979, *Flamenco × Orangeade*; Pal, Dr. B.P.; Friends Rosery. Bud pointed; flowers orange-red, 19 petals, blooms borne 2-14 per cluster; slight fragrance; foliage large, glossy; hooked prickles; tall, upright, vigorous, open growth.

Suryodaya F, *ob*, 1968, *Orangeade × Seedling*; Indian Agric. Research Inst. Bud ovoid; flowers bright orange, semi-dbl., medium; foliage dark, leathery; very vigorous, upright growth.

Susan F, *mr*, 1955, *Donald Prior × Our Princess*; Robinson, H. Flowers crimson, semi-dbl., well-formed blooms in large clusters; foliage dark; bushy, compact growth.

Susan Elizabeth HT, *pb*, 1989, (SCHuprak); *Pristine × Akebono*; Schlueter, Barry; Schlueter Rose Culture. Bud ovoid; flowers cream tipped with very deep purple-pink, reverse cream to pale yellow at base, aging broadening of picotee, dbl. (40 petals), high-centered, exhibition, medium, borne singly; slight, fruity fragrance; foliage medium, medium green, semi-glossy; prickles slightly recurved, sparse, red; fruit none observed; upright, medium growth.

Susan Hampshire HT, *lp*, 1972, (MEInatac); *(Monique × Symphonie) × Miss All-American Beauty*; Paolino; URS. Flowers light fuchsia-pink, dbl. (40 petals), globular, large (5½ in.); very fragrant; foliage matt; vigorous, upright growth.

Susan Hayward Cl HT, *lp*, 1967, *Fontanelle × Gen. MacArthur*; Hayward. Flowers light pink, center and reverse darker, dbl., high-centered, large; foliage dark, glossy; vigorous, climbing, open habit.

Susan Louise S, *lp*, 1929, *Belle Portugaise seedling*; Adams; Stocking. Bud very long, pointed, deep pink; flowers flesh-pink, semi-dbl.; slightly fragrant; vigorous (4-5 ft.), bushy growth; recurrent bloom.

Susan Massu HT, *yb*, 1970, (KORad; Susan); *Colour Wonder* × *Liberty Bell*; Kordes, R.; Kordes. Bud ovoid; flowers light yellow and salmon blend, dbl., cupped, large; fragrant; foliage glossy, dark, leathery; vigorous, upright. GM, Baden-Baden, 1968.

Susan Noel Min, *ab*, 1986, *Rise 'n' Shine* × *Orange Honey*; Jolly, Nelson; Rosehill Farm. Flowers light apricot, very dbl. (80 petals), urn-shaped, small blooms borne usually singly; slight fragrance; foliage small, medium green, semi-glossy; small, slightly hooked, gray-orange prickles; fruit small, globular; medium, upright growth.

Susana Marchal HT, *or*, 1953, *Cynthia* × *Vive la France*; Dot, P. Bud pointed; flowers coral-red, semi-dbl. (18 petals), high-centered, large; strong stems; foliage clear green; upright growth.

Susane Dot Cl HT, *dr*, 1963, *Queen Elizabeth* × *Peace, Climbing*; Dot, S. Flowers crimson, dbl. (32 petals), large; fragrant; vigorous.

Susie HT, *mp*, 1955, *Mme. Butterfly* × *Sally*; Spandikow. Flowers pink, base yellow, dbl. (45-50 petals), high-centered, large (4-6 in.); slightly fragrant; foliage leathery; vigorous, bushy growth. RULED EXTINCT 11/90.

Su-Spantu F, *m*, 1962, *Alain* × *Independence*; Borgatti; Sgaravatti. Flowers purplish pink, dbl. (25 petals), borne in clusters of 7-8; upright growth.

Suspense HT, *rb*, 1960, (MEIfan); *Henri Mallerin* × *(Happiness* × *Floradora)*; Meilland, F.; URS, 1960; C-P, 1961. Bud ovoid; flowers turkey-red, reverse yellow-ocher, dbl. (58 petals), high-centered, large (4½-5 in.); slightly fragrant; foliage leathery, dark, glossy; vigorous, upright, bushy growth.

Sutter's Gold HT, *ob*, 1950, *Charlotte Armstrong* × *Signora*; Swim; Armstrong Nursery. Bud orange overlaid indian red; flowers golden orange, often with red on outer petals, dbl. (33 petals), high-centered, large (4-5 in.); very fragrant; foliage dark, leathery; very vigorous, upright growth. GM, Portland, 1946; Bagatelle, 1948; Geneva, 1949; AARS, 1950; James Alexander Gamble Rose Fragrance Medal, 1966

Sutter's Gold, Climbing Cl HT, *ob*, 1950, Weeks; Armstrong Nursery.

Sutton Place™ Gr, *op*, 1991, *Queen Elizabeth* × *(Carla* × *Command Performance)*; Williams, J. Benjamin, 1992. Flowers light pink with salmon pink edge, single, large blooms borne mostly singly and in small clusters; very fragrant; foliage large, dark green, semiglossy; tall, upright, bushy growth.

Suzan Ball F, *ab*, 1957, *Tom Breneman* × *Fashion*; Warriner; H&S. Bud conical; flowers salmon-coral, dbl. (25 petals), high-centered to loosely open, large (2½-3½ in.), borne in clusters; fragrant (spicy); foliage dark; vigorous, upright growth.

Suzanne HSpn (OGR), *op*, 1950, *Second generation R. laxa* × *R. spinosissima*; Skinner. Flowers pale coral-pink, very dbl.; foliage small, dark; height 4 ft.; recurrent bloom.

Suzanne Albrand Pol, *mr*, 1930, Turbat. Flowers bright red, large, borne in large clusters; foliage glossy; vigorous growth.

Suzanne Balitrand HT, *or*, 1942, Mallerin; A. Meilland. Flowers coral edged fiery red, stamens yellow.

Suzanne Blanchet T (OGR), *lp*, 1885, Nabonnand, G. Flowers flesh-pink, large; very fragrant.

Suzanne Carrol of Carrolton HP (OGR), *mp*, 1924, *Frau Karl Druschki* × *Mme. Gabriel Luizet*; Nabonnand, P. Flowers light satiny rose and salmon, semi-dbl., large; vigorous growth.

Suzanne Hester Cl HT, *w*, 1950, *Marie Maass* sport; Hester. Bud ovoid; flowers white, base tinted yellow, dbl. (30 petals), high-centered, very fragrant; foliage glossy; vigorous growth.

Suzanne Meyer Pol, *w*, 1926, *Tausendschön* × *Rosel Dach*; Walter, L. Flowers white shaded soft pink, center bright rose-pink, medium; medium growth.

Suzanne Michela HT, *my*, 1932, *Mme. la Générale Ardouin* × *Seedling*; Chambard, C. Bud long, pointed; flowers pure chrome-yellow, dbl., cupped, very large; fragrant; very vigorous.

Suzanne Miller Pol, *mr*, 1927, Wezelenburg. Flowers clear bright cherry-red, dbl., medium, borne in clusters; low, bushy growth.

Suzanne Turbat Pol, *ob*, 1919, *Petit Constant seedling* × *Seedling*; Turbat. Flowers coral-red, shaded shrimp-pink, dbl., cupped, medium, borne in clusters of 10-20; slightly fragrant; dwarf growth.

Suzanne Villain HT, *pb*, 1935, *(Rev. Williamson* × *Gorgeous)* × *Mrs. John Bell*; Ketten Bros. Flowers peach-blossom-pink suffused cherry-red, reverse salmon-pink, dbl. (60-65 petals), large; foliage rich green; vigorous, bushy growth.

Suzanne-Marie Rodocanachi HP (OGR), *mp*, 1883, *Victor Verdier seedling*; Lévêque. Flowers dark rosy cerise, shaded and bordered lighter, full (45 petals), well formed, globular, very large; profuse bloom, somewhat recurrent.

Suzon Lotthé HT, *pb*, 1951, *Peace* × *(Signora* × *Mrs. John Laing)*; Meilland, F.; C-P. Bud peach; flowers pearl-pink, flushed deeper toward edge, dbl. (60 petals), high-centered, large (4 in.); very fragrant (damask); foliage dark; very vigorous growth.

Suzon Lotthé, Climbing Cl HT, *pb*, 1964, Trimper; Ruston.

Suzy Min, *mp*, 1990, (BRIsuzy); *Party Girl* × *seedling*; Bridges, Dennis, 1986; Bridges Roses, 1991. Bud pointed; flowers medium pink, near white at base blending to light pink, lightens slightly with age, dbl. (38-40 petals), high-centered, exhibition, medium, borne usually singly or in sprays of 3-5; slight fragrance; foliage medium, dark green, semi-glossy; bushy, medium growth. AOE, 1991.

Suzy Q™ Min, *mp*, 1991, (JAChill); *Rose Hills Red* × *Baby Ophelia*; Warriner, William A.; Zary, Keith, 1985; Bear Creek Gardens (J&P), 1992. Bud ovoid; flowers medium shell pink, deeper color at petal margins, very dbl. (40-45 petals), cupped, medium; no fragrance; foliage medium, dark green, glossy; upright, bushy, medium growth.

Svatopluk Cech LCl, *dy*, 1936, Brada; Böhm. Flowers orange-yellow; very fragrant; vigorous growth; recurrent bloom.

Svaty Václav HT, *w*, 1936, Berger, A. Flowers white, center yellowish, large; very fragrant.

Svetla Albena F, *yb*, 1974, *Highlight* × *Masquerade*; Staikov, Prof. Dr. V.; Kalaydjiev and Chorbadjiiski. Flowers opening yellow orange, aging red, very dbl. (85 petals), medium blooms in large clusters of 10-30; foliage dark; vigorous, upright growth.

Svornost Pol, *dr*, 1935, *Orléans Rose sport*; Böhm. Flowers pure dark red, with fiery streaks, borne in large clusters.

Swagatam HT, *ab*, 1989, *Surkhab sport*; Patil, B.K.; K.S.G. Son's Roses, 1987. Flowers light pink, reverse apricot.

Swami HT, *lp*, 1973, *Scarlet Knight* × *Festival Beauty*; Hardikar. Bud long, pointed; flowers light pink, very dbl. (100 petals), high-centered, very large (5 in.); fragrant; very vigorous, upright growth.

Swan Lake LCl, *w*, 1968, (Schwanensee); *Memoriam* × *Heidelberg*; McGredy. Flowers white, center tinged pinkish, dbl. (50 petals), well-formed, large; slightly fragrant.

Swansdown HT, *w*, 1928, Dickson, A. Bud large, long, pointed; flowers creamy white, center deeper cream, spiral form, full; slightly fragrant; foliage olive-green; fairly vigorous growth.

Swansong Min, *w*, 1988, (SEAswan; Swan Song); *(Rise 'n' Shine* × *Party Girl)* × *Margaret*

Merril; McCann, Sean. Flowers white, dbl. (15-25 petals), small; very fragrant; foliage small, medium green, semi-glossy; bushy growth.

Swantje F, *w*, 1936, *Johanna Tantau* × *(Prof. Gnau* × *Joanna Hill)*; Tantau. Flowers snow-white, dbl., very large, borne in clusters; foliage glossy, light; very vigorous, bushy growth.

Swany® Min, *w*, 1978, (MEIburenac); *R. sempervirens* × *Mlle. Marthe Carron*; Meilland, M.L.; Meilland, 1977. Bud ovoid; flowers pure white, very dbl. (95 petals), flat, cupped, large; foliage glossy, bronze; very vigorous, spreading growth.

Swany River HT, *w*, 1981, (Fredagh of Bellinchamp); *Pascali* × *Seedling*; Herholdt, J.A. Flowers white, dbl. (40+ petals), large; fragrant; foliage medium, dark, semi-glossy; upright growth.

Swarthmore HT, *pb*, 1963, (MEItaras); *(Independence* × *Happiness)* × *Peace*; Meilland, A.; C-P. Flowers shades of pink blended, dbl. (50 petals), high-centered, large (4 in.); slightly fragrant; foliage dark, leathery; vigorous, tall, bushy growth.

Swarthmore, Climbing Cl HT, *pb*, 1973, Thomas, A.S.; A. Ross & Son.

Swati Pol, *w*, 1968, *Winifred Coulter* × *Seedling*; Indian Agric. Research Inst. Bud pointed; flowers white, edged deep pink, semi-dbl., open, small; foliage dark, leathery; moderate, bushy growth.

Swedish Doll Min, *op*, 1976, *Fire King* × *Little Buckaroo*; Moore, R.S.; Sequoia Nursery. Bud long, pointed; flowers orange-pink, dbl. (28 petals), small (1½ in.); slightly fragrant; foliage glossy, leathery; vigorous, upright, branched growth.

Sweepstakes HT, *op*, 1979, (MACaft; Margaret Trudeau); *Prima Ballerina* × *Ginger Rogers*; McGredy, S., IV; Armstrong Nursery. Bud long, pointed; flowers coral-orange to salmon-pink, dbl. (35 petals), imbricated, high-centered, large (3½-5 in.); fragrant; upright, spreading, bushy growth.

Sweet Min, *my*, 1980, *Seedling* × *Seedling*; Lyon. Bud long, pointed; flowers medium yellow, dbl. (50 petals), blooms borne 1-3 per cluster; fragrant; foliage tiny, glossy, deep green; tiny, curved prickles; compact, bushy growth.

Sweet Adeline HT, *mp*, 1929, *Rapture* × *Souv. de Claudius Pernet*; Hill, J.H., Co. Bud long, pointed; flowers rose-pink, semi-dbl., large; fragrant; a florists' variety, not distributed for outdoor use.

Sweet Afton HT, *w*, 1964, *(Charlotte Armstrong* × *Signora)* × *(Alice Stern* × *Ondine)*; Armstrong,

D.L.; Swim; Armstrong Nursery. Flowers near white, reverse pale pink, dbl., high-centered, large (4½-5 in.); very fragrant; foliage leathery; tall, spreading, bushy growth.

Sweet Allison Min, rb, 1985, *Bonny × (Tiki × Seedling)*; Jolly, Nelson F.; Rosehill Farm. Flowers orange-red shading to yellow or white, reverse cream, deeper orange-red on petal edges, dbl. (35 petals), mini-flora, large blooms borne singly or in clusters of 4-5; slight fragrance; foliage medium, medium green, semi-glossy; upright, bushy growth.

Sweet and Low F, pb, 1962, *Pinocchio × Sweet Fairy*; Schwartz, E.W.; Wyant. Bud globular; flowers salmon-pink, center lighter, dbl. (36 petals), small, borne in large clusters; slightly fragrant; foliage glossy, bronze; compact, low growth.

Sweet Briar Queen F, mp, 1960, *Rosemary sport*; Schenkel; H.R. Schenkel, Inc. Flowers rose-pink, dbl. (45-50 petals), flat, medium (2 in.), borne in flat clusters; fragrant; foliage maroon when young, leathery; vigorous, branching growth.

Sweet Butterfly Min, m, 1989, (LAVstar); *(Dwarfking × Baby Katie) × (Small Slam × Mountie)*; Laver, Keith G.; Springwood Roses. Bud rounded; flowers mauve pink, semi-dbl. (12-15 petals), flat, pointed, open, loose, medium, star-like form, borne singly; heavy fragrance; foliage medium, medium green, matt; prickles short, pointed, beige; fruit globular, yellow; bushy, low growth.

Sweet Caress F, mp, 1958, *Pigmy Red × Demure*; Boerner; J&P. Bud ovoid; flowers rose-pink, dbl. (55-60 petals), large; fragrant; foliage leathery, glossy; vigorous, upright growth; for pot forcing.

Sweet Chariot™ Min, m, 1984, (MORchari; Insolite); *Little Chief × Violette*; Moore, R.S.; Moore Min. Roses. Flowers lavender to purple blend, dbl. (40+ petals), small blooms in clusters of 5-20; very fragrant; foliage small, medium green, matt; upright growth.

Sweet Charity HT, w, 1967, Park, F.; Moulton-Jones. Flowers waxy white, sometimes marked pink, semi-dbl., medium; fragrant; foliage dark, glossy; vigorous, upright growth.

Sweet Cherry HT, mr, 1960, (Cherry Glow); *Margaret × Karl Herbst*; Dickson, A. Flowers cherry-red and yellow, high-centered, large.

Sweet Dreams HT, pb, 1977, (Kojo); *Jrn. No. 8 seedling × Royal Highness*; Takatori; Japan Rose Nursery. Bud long, pointed; flowers light pink, reverse deep pink, dbl. (45-50 petals), high-centered, very large (6 in.); slightly fragrant (tea); foliage dark; vigorous, very upright growth.

Sweet Fairy Min, lp, 1946, *Tom Thumb × Seedling*; de Vink; C-P. Flowers light pink, dbl. (57 petals), cupped, micro-mini, very small (1 in.); fragrant; foliage small, dark; vigorous, dwarf (6-8 in.) growth.

Sweet Harmony F, pb, 1962, *Peace × Masquerade*; Gaujard; Gandy. Flowers canary-yellow edged crimson-pink, dbl. (36 petals), large (3½ in.), borne in clusters; fragrant; foliage glossy, light green; vigorous growth.

Sweet Home HT, dp, 1969, *(Jolie Madame × Baccará) × (Baccará × Jolie Madame)*; Meilland, M.L.; URS. Flowers deep pink, dbl. (35 petals), high-centered to cupped, large; slightly fragrant; foliage leathery; vigorous.

Sweet Inspiration F, mp, 1991, (JACsim); *Sun Flare × Simplicity*; Warriner, William; Bear Creek Gardens, 1993. Flowers medium pink with some cream coloration at petal base on both sides of petals, full (26-40 petals), large (7+ cms) blooms borne in large clusters; foliage medium, medium green, matt; few prickles; upright (85-100 cms), bushy growth; AARS, 1993.

Sweet Interlude HT, pb, 1989, *Pristine × Olympiad*; Wambach, Alex A. Bud pointed; flowers white center with pink edging, dbl. (32 petals), high-centered, exhibition, large, borne singly, slow opening; heavy fragrance; foliage medium green, disease resistant; prickles moderate, brown; upright, bushy, medium growth.

Sweet Keri HT, lp, 1988, *Judith Marten × Folklore*; Wilson, G.D. Flowers light pale pink, dbl. (44 petals), high-centered, large, borne singly; no fragrance; foliage medium green, large; prickles triangular, red; medium, upright growth.

Sweet Lavender R, pb, 1912, Paul. Flowers blush, edged mauve, single, borne in large clusters.

Sweet Lavinia HT, my, 1967, *Golden Scepter × Peace*; McTeer, F. Flowers medium yellow, high-centered; very fragrant; foliage glossy.

Sweet Lelanie HT, lp, 1967, *Charlotte Armstrong × Seedling*.; Duehrsen; Elmer Roses Co. Flowers light pink, base yellow, dbl., globular, large; fragrant; foliage wrinkled, bronze; vigorous, upright.

Sweet Love HT, mp, 1980, *Queen Elizabeth × Duke of Windsor*; Rijksstation Voor Sierplantenteelt. Flowers medium pink, very dbl. (90 petals), flat, medium-large blooms borne 1-7 per cluster; no fragrance; foliage matt, dark; red prickles; upright growth.

Sweet Magic Min, ob, 1986, (DICmagic); *Peek A Boo × Bright Smile*; Dickson, P. Flowers orange blend, moderately full (15-25 petals), small; patio; no fragrance; foliage small, medium green, glossy; bushy growth. ROTY, 1987.

Sweet Maid HT, *lp*, 1950, Moss. Bud pointed; flowers porcelain-pink, semi-dbl.; very fragrant.

Sweet Mandarin Min, *ob*, 1978, *Sweet and Low × Gypsy Moth seedling*; Schwartz, E.W.; Bountiful Ridge Nursery. Bud pointed; flowers light orange, semi-dbl. (16 petals), flat, small; fragrant; foliage small, soft; compact growth.

Sweet Memorie HT, *mp*, 1937, *Mrs. C.W. Edwards × Rose Marie*; Hieatt. Flowers pink, base yellow, reverse purplish, semi-dbl., cupped, large; very fragrant; foliage leathery; vigorous growth.

Sweet Memory F, *lp*, 1991, *Hana-Gasumi × (Lady × x Paradise)*; Yasuda, Yuji, 1992. Bud pointed; flowers light pink, dbl. (30 petals), urn-shaped, high-centered, 10 cms blooms; moderate fragrance; foliage medium, medium green, matt; bushy, medium growth.

Sweet Mimi® HT, *mp*, 1981, (HAUmi); *Tropicana × Elizabeth Harkness*; Hauser, Victor; Roseraies Hauser. Flowers medium pink, dbl. (20 petals), large; fragrant; foliage medium, reddish green, semi-glossy; bushy growth.

Sweet Mystery Min, *ob*, 1986, (FLOmyst); *Care Deeply × Red Can Can*; Florac, Marilyn, 1987. Flowers deep orange fading to pink, dbl. (90 petals), cupped, medium, borne usually singly; moderate, damask fragrance; foliage medium, dark green, semi-glossy; few, green prickles; bushy, medium growth; (21).

Sweet 'n' Pink HT, *dp*, 1976, *(Prima Ballerina × Seedling) × Seedling*; Weeks; Weeks Roses. Bud ovoid, pointed; flowers deep pink, dbl. (48 petals), high-centered, large (4-4½ in.); very fragrant; foliage dark; upright, branching.

Sweet Nell F, *ob*, 1983, (COCavoter); *Anne Cocker × (Mischief × ((Sabine × Circus) × (Tropicana × Circus)))*; Cocker, Alexander M.; Cocker & Sons, 1984. Flowers orange, dbl. (35 petals), large; slight fragrance; foliage medium, medium green, semi-glossy; upright.

Sweet Pickins Min, *lp*, 1987, (TINsweet); *Futura × Party Girl*; Bennett, Dee; Tiny Petals Nursery. Flowers pale pink, dbl. (35-40 petals), urn-shaped, medium, borne usually singly; micro-mini; moderate fruity fragrance; foliage medium, medium green, semi-glossy; slender, straight, small, reddish prickles; fruit globular, medium, brown; upright, bushy, medium growth.

Sweet Prince HT, *pb*, 1988, *Honey Favorite × Granada*; Stoddard, Louis. Flowers deep pink, petals edged medium red, dbl. (20 petals), 3½ in. blooms borne singly; very fragrant; foliage large, dark, matt; heavily prickled; bushy growth.

Sweet Raspberry Min, *dp*, 1984, *Little Rascal × Cinderella*; Jolly, Nelson F.; Rosehill Farm. Flowers deep purplish pink, dbl. (28 pointed petals), urn-shaped to flat, small; slight fragrance; foliage small, medium green, matt; bushy growth.

Sweet Seventeen HT, *lp*, 1923, *Frau Karl Druschki × Bardou Job*; Clark, A.; NRS Victoria. Flowers light pink, semi-dbl.; fragrant; foliage light, wrinkled; bushy, dwarf growth.

Sweet Seventeen Gr, *mp*, 1960, *Fred Howard × Cocorico*; Leenders, J. Flowers pink, small; vigorous growth.

Sweet Shaddow HT, *mr*, 1963, *Queen Elizabeth × Étoile de Hollande*; Barter. Flowers scarlet, edged darker, dbl. (22 petals), large (4½ in.); fragrant; foliage dark; vigorous growth.

Sweet Shirley Min, *mp*, 1991, (CLEshir); *Tweedle Dee × Seedling*; Clements, John; Heirloom Old Garden Roses. Flowers medium pink, lighter reverse, moderately full (15-25 petals), exhibition, small (0-4 cms) blooms borne mostly singly; slight fragrance; foliage small, medium green, semi-glossy; some prickles; bushy (40 cms), spreading growth.

Sweet Sixteen HT, *pb*, 1943, *Mrs. Sam McGredy × Pres. Herbert Hoover*; Lammerts; Armstrong Nursery. Bud long, pointed; flowers salmon-pink, base yellow, 16-20 petals, large (4-5 in.); very fragrant; vigorous, upright, bushy growth.

Sweet Song F, *mp*, 1971, (MEIhivano); *Fidélio × Bettina*; Meilland. Flowers medium pink, dbl. (35 petals), large (4½ in.); fruity fragrance; bushy.

Sweet Sue HT, *op*, 1940, *Joanna Hill × Night*; Lammerts; Armstrong Nursery. Bud long, pointed, flame to blood-red; flowers coral-pink, stamens maroon, single, open to cupped; fragrant (spicy); vigorous growth.

Sweet Sue Min, *lp*, 1979, *Pink Ribbon × Pink Ribbon*; Bennett, Dee; Tiny Petals Nursery. Bud ovoid; flowers light pink, semi-dbl. (13 petals), exhibition, very small blooms in clusters of 10-25; foliage small, dark; bushy growth.

Sweet Sultan Cl HT, *dr*, 1958, (Swet Sultain); *Independence × Honour Bright*; Eacott; LeGrice. Flowers crimson shaded maroon, single (5 petals), large (4 in.) blooms in trusses; very fragrant; vigorous, pillar growth.

Sweet Sunshine Min, *my*, 1981, (MORsun); *Rumba* × *Yellow Jewel*; Moore, R.S.; Moore Min. Roses. Flowers medium yellow, dbl. (20 petals), small; very fragrant; foliage small, medium green, semi-glossy; upright, bushy growth.

Sweet Surrender HT, *mp*, 1983, *Seedling* × *Tiffany*; Weeks, O.L.; Weeks Roses. Flowers medium silvery pink, dbl. (40 petals), cupped, large; very strong tea fragrance; foliage dark, leathery. AARS, 1983.

Sweet Talk F, *ly*, 1964, *Frolic* × *Lavender Pinocchio*; Swim & Weeks; Weeks Roses. Flowers lemon to white, dbl., medium blooms in clusters; fragrant; foliage light green, leathery; low, uniform, bushy growth.

Sweet Thoughts HT, *lp*, 1965, *Kordes' Perfecta* × *Show Girl*; Cant, F. Flowers light pink, large (5 in.); slightly fragrant; vigorous growth.

Sweet Twilight Cl HT, *ly*, 1954, *Tawny Gold* sport; Motose. Flowers buff-yellow, center darker, dbl. (25 petals), high-centered, large (4-5½ in.); fragrant (fruity); vigorous (15-30 ft.) growth; abundant, recurrent bloom.

Sweet Velvet F, *mr*, 1969, *Leverkusen* × *S'Agaro*; Martin, J.; Gandy. Flowers red, dbl., large; fragrant; foliage small, leathery, glossy; moderate growth.

Sweet Vivid Min, *pb*, Flowers pink, yellow center, dbl., well-formed; fragrant; vigorous.

Sweet Vivien F, *pb*, 1961, *Little Darling* × *Odorata (HT)*; Raffel; Port Stockton Nursery. Bud ovoid; flowers pink, center light yellow, semi-dbl. (17 petals), large (3 in.) blooms in clusters on short stems; slightly fragrant; foliage small, dark, glossy; fruit large, pear-shaped; very compact, bushy growth.

Sweetheart R, *w*, 1901, *R. wichuraiana* × *Bridesmaid*; Walsh. Bud rose-pink; flowers white, very dbl., medium (2½ in.); fragrant; foliage glossy, dark; vigorous, climbing growth. RULED EXTINCT 4/80.

Sweetheart HT, *mp*, 1980, (COCapeer); *Peer Gynt* × *(Fragrant Cloud* × *Gay Gordons)*; Cocker, J. Bud ovoid; flowers medium pink, yellow base, dbl. (52 petals), high-centered blooms borne singly; fragrant; foliage large, medium green; vigorous, upright growth. Belfast Fragrance Award, 1982.

Sweetie Pie HT, *lp*, 1971, *Swarthmore sport*; Hyde. Flowers light pink, outer edges darker.

Sweetness HT, *mp*, 1919, McGredy. Flowers intense rose-pink, shaded scarlet, well formed; fragrant.

Sweetness HT, *ab*, 1937, Dickson, A. Bud long, pointed; flowers apricot-yellow shaded pink, dbl., spiral, reflexed petals, large; fra-

grant; foliage glossy; very vigorous growth. GM, NRS, 1935.

Sweetwaters HT, *op*, 1987, (MACsweetwa; Freshie); *((Sympathie* × *Red Lion)* × *Pharaoh)* × *(Tombola* × *(Elizabeth of Glamis* × *(Circus* × *Golden Fleece)))* × *Ferry Porsche*; McGredy, Sam; Sam McGredy Roses International, 1986. Flowers medium salmon-pink, dbl. (26-40 petals), large; slight fragrance; foliage large, dark green, glossy; upright, tall, very big growth.

Swinger Min, *my*, 1984, *Anita Charles* × *Orange Honey*; Jolly, Nelson F.; Rosehill Farm. Flowers medium yellow, dbl. (35 petals), high-centered, medium blooms borne usually singly; slight fragrance; foliage medium, medium green, semi-glossy; spreading growth.

Swingtime F, *rb*, 1961, *Little Darling* × *(Red Pinocchio* × *Masquerade)*; Morgan; Carlton Rose Nursery. Bud pointed; flowers crimson, reverse buff-white, dbl. (40 petals), globular, cupped, medium; fragrant (sweetbrier); vigorous, upright growth.

Swiss Bliss Min, *my*, 1988, *Anytime* × *Seedling*; Lemrow, Dr. Maynard W. Flowers yellow, aging lighter, dbl. (45-50 petals), decorative, small, borne singly or in sprays of 3-5, prolific; slight fragrance; foliage small, medium green, matt, serrated; prickles reddish-brown; upright, bushy, medium growth.

Swiss Fire® HT, *or*, 1975, (HUBar); *Fragrant Cloud* × *Ena Harkness*; Huber. Bud globular, flowers orange-red, dbl. (50 petals), large (4-4½ in.); slightly fragrant; foliage dark; upright.

Swiss Lass Min, *rb*, 1987, (LEMswi); *Seedling* × *Seedling*; Lemrow, Dr. Maynard. Flowers red, reverse almost all white, very full (40+ petals), medium; slight fragrance; foliage small, medium green, semi-glossy; upright growth.

Sword of Hope HT, *mr*, 1964, Abrams, Von; Peterson; Dering. Bud long, pointed; flowers medium red, dbl. (45 petals), high-centered, large (5-6 in.); fragrant; foliage glossy; vigorous, upright growth.

Sybil HT, *mp*, 1921, *Sunburst* × *Mary, Countess of Ilchester*; Bees. Bud long, pointed; flowers silvery salmon-rose, center orange-salmon, very dbl.; fragrant.

Sybil Thorndike HT, *mr*, 1975, *Liebeszauber* × *Seedling*; Kordes; Harry Wheatcroft Gardening. Flowers red, dbl. (25 petals), full, large (5 in.); slightly fragrant; foliage dark.

Sydney HCh (OGR), *mp*, 1977, *Old Blush* × *Frau Dagmar Hartopp*; Svejda; Canada Dept. of Agric. Bud ovoid; flowers phlox-pink, dbl. (20 petals), cupped, large (3-3½ in.); very fragrant; foliage rugose, yellow-green; bushy, spreading growth; abundant bloom in protected location.

Sydonie HP (OGR), *mp*, 1846, (Sidonie); Dorisy. Flowers rose, very full, quartered, medium; red prickles; vigorous.

Sylt K (S), *dr*, 1981, (KORylt; Kordes' Rose Sylt); *R. kordesii* × *Seedling*; Kordes, W. Flowers dark red, semi-dbl., medium; slight fragrance; foliage medium, dark, glossy; spreading growth.

Sylvan Sunset HT, *pb*, 1979, *Swarthmore* × *First Prize*; Taylor, Thomas E. Bud pointed; flowers pink blend, dbl. (28 petals), high-centered; slight fragrance; foliage medium green, semi-glossy; hooked prickles; vigorous, upright, tall, bushy growth.

Sylvander S, *my*, *R. Xharisonii open-pollinated seedling*; Central Exp. Farm. Flowers clear yellow, single, large; dwarf (2-3 ft.) growth.

Sylvia HT, *my*, 1949, *Golden Gleam sport*; Foster. Flowers buttercup-yellow, dbl. (25 petals); fragrant (fruity). RULED EXTINCT 1/79.

Sylvia R, *ly*, 1911, Paul, W. Flowers pale lemon-yellow, passing to white, dbl.; fragrant; moderate growth.

Sylvia Dot F, *lp*, 1965, *Queen Elizabeth* × *Orient*; Dot, S.; Minier. Bud pointed; flowers salmon, dbl. (30 petals), high-centered, medium; slightly fragrant; foliage glossy, bronze; upright, dense growth.

Sylvia Groen HT, *pb*, 1935, *Pres. Herbert Hoover sport*; Groen. Flowers coral-rose, shaded crimson; vigorous, upright growth.

Sylvia Louise HT, *op*, 1973, *Ena Harkness, Climbing seedling*; Shaw, H.C.W. Flowers pink and orange blend; foliage glossy.

Symbole S, *mr*, 1945, *Mev. G.A. van Rossem* × *Roseraie de l'Hay*; Robichon; Vilmorin-Andrieux. Bud thick, pointed; flowers carmine, well shaped, very large; long, strong stems; slightly fragrant; vigorous growth.

Sympathie® K (S), *mr*, 1964, Kordes, R. Flowers velvety dark red, well-formed; very fragrant; foliage glossy, dark; very vigorous (9-12 ft.) growth. ADR, 1966.

Symphonette Min, *pb*, 1973, *Cécile Brunner* × *Cinderella*; Morey; Pixie Treasures. Bud ovoid; flowers light pink, reverse deep pink, dbl., small; fragrant; foliage small, glossy, leathery; vigorous, dwarf, bushy growth.

Symphonie HT, *pb*, 1951, *Peace* × *(Signora* × *Mrs. John Laing)*; Meilland, F.; C-P. Bud pointed, ovoid to globular; flowers shades of pink, veined carmine-pink, dbl. (25 broad petals), high-centered, large (4½-5 in.); foliage glossy, leathery; vigorous, upright, bushy growth. GM, NRS, 1949.

Symphonie, Climbing Cl HT, *pb*, Elmer Roses Co., about 1952.

Symphony HP (OGR), *lp*, 1935, *Frau Karl Druschki* × *Souv. de Claudius Pernet*; Weigand, C.; P.J. Howard. Bud long, pointed; flowers light pink, dbl., high-centered, large; foliage leathery, dark.

Syr S, *dr*, 1977, *Stadt Rosenheim* × *Sangerhausen*; Lundstad; Agricultural Univ. of Norway. Bud pointed, ovoid; flowers dark red, dbl. (23 petals), high-centered, large (4 in.); slightly fragrant; foliage glossy, dark; very vigorous, upright growth.

Syracuse HT, *mr*, 1930, *Mme. G. Forest-Colcombet* × *Aspirant Maumejean*; Mallerin; C-P. Bud crimson; flowers scarlet-crimson, dbl., large; slightly fragrant; foliage dark, leathery; vigorous growth.

Ta Ta Min, *mp*, 1988, (MINatco); *Tom Brown* × *Over the Rainbow*; Williams, Ernest. Flowers medium pink, dbl. (33 petals), small; no fragrance; foliage small, medium green, semi-glossy, dense; bushy growth.

Tabarin F, *mp*, 1956, *Opera* × *Masquerade*; Gaujard. Bud oval; flowers salmon-pink flushed yellow and copper-orange to red, semi-dbl., large (3-4 in.), borne in large clusters; slightly fragrant; foliage light green; vigorous, bushy growth.

Tablers' Choice F, *rb*, 1974, *(Ann Elizabeth* × *Allgold)* × *(Tropicana* × *Piccadilly)*; Harkness. Flowers deep red, yellow reverse, dbl. (38 petals), large (4 in.); slightly fragrant; foliage glossy.

Tabriz HT, *lp*, 1986, *Belle Epoque* × *Seedling*; Kriloff, M. Flowers soft pink, large; slight fragrance; few prickles.

Tache de Beauté® F, *op*, 1982, (LENpic); *Little Angel* × *Picasso*; Lens. Flowers orange-pink, dbl. (22 petals), high-centered, 2 in. blooms in clusters of 3-24; light fragrance; foliage dark; hooked, brown prickles; upright, bushy growth.

Tackholmii S, *mp*, (*R. balsamea* hort., not Keller; *R. hibernica* Hooker, not Templeton nor Smith; *R.* × *tackholmii* Hurst); Garden hybrid; Cult. before 1922. Flowers pink, solitary or few; vigorous, erect, shrub growth; early flowering.

Tacoma HT, *ab*, 1921, *Mme. Butterfly* × *Honeymoon*; Chervenka. Bud long, pointed; flowers flaming apricot, dbl.; fragrant.

Taconis® F, *or*, 1968, *Ruth Leuwerik* × *City of Nottingham*; deRuiter. Flowers orange-scarlet, in trusses; slightly fragrant; foliage glossy; vigorous. GM, Baden-Baden, 1968.

Taffeta HT, *pb*, 1947, *Mrs. Sam McGredy* × *Pres. Herbert Hoover*; Lammerts; Armstrong Nursery. Bud urn-shaped; flowers pink-yellow blend, dbl. (20 petals), medium (3-3½ in.); fragrant; foliage leathery, glossy, bronze-green; vigorous, upright. AARS, 1948.

Taffeta, Climbing Cl HT, *pb*, 1954, Armstrong, J.A.; Weeks.

Taffy Min, *yb*, 1988, (BAKtaf); *Seedling × Seedling*; Baker, Larry. Flowers soft, pastel butter yellow, tipped light pink, reverse pure butter yellow, dbl. (33 petals), high-centered, exhibition, small, borne usually singly or in sprays of 3-5; slight fragrance; foliage small, medium green, matt; prickles nearly straight, small, light brown; bushy, low, compact, full growth.

Tag-a-long Min, *rb*, 1992, (MORcoat); *Seedling (Little Darling × Yellow Magic) × Make Believe*; Moore, Ralph S.; Sequoia Nursery, 1993. Flowers contrast of reddish lavender against white, semi-dbl. (6-14 petals), medium (4-7 cms) blooms, somewhat on the larger side, best when fully open, borne in small clusters; no fragrance; foliage medium, medium green, new foliage bronze, matt; few prickles; medium (30-40 cms), upright, bushy growth.

Tagore F, *my*, 1955, *Pinocchio seedling*; Maarse, G. Flowers yellow-ocher, reverse shaded orange, borne in clusters; compact growth.

Tahiti HT, *yb*, 1947, *Peace × Signora*; Meilland, F. Flowers amber-yellow suffused carmine, large (6 in.); very fragrant; foliage glossy, dark.

Tahore HT, *mp*, 1958, *Peace × Seedling*; Buyl Frères. Flowers rose, dbl. (45-50 petals), high-centered, large; strong stems; fragrant; foliage glossy; vigorous, upright growth.

Taiga® F, *mp*, 1972, (TANtiga); *Geisha × Junior Miss*; Tantau. Bud globular; flowers pink, dbl., medium; vigorous, upright growth.

Tai-Gong F, *or*, 1974, (Apachi); *Klaus Storte-beker × Seedling*; Kordes. Bud long, pointed; flowers orange to red, dbl. (28 petals), high-centered, large (3½ in.); slightly fragrant; foliage glossy, dark; vigorous, upright growth.

Taj Mahal HT, *dp*, 1972, *Manitou × Grand Slam*; Armstrong, D.L.; Armstrong Nursery. Flowers deep pink, dbl., high-centered, large; fragrant; foliage large, leathery; vigorous, upright, bushy growth.

Takao HT, *yb*, 1975, (*Masquerade × Lydia*) × (*Montezuma × Miss Ireland*); Okamoto, K.; K. Hirakata Nursery. Flowers deep yellow, aging scarlet, dbl. (33 petals), high-centered, medium blooms borne usually singly; damask fragrance; foliage medium, medium green; deep brown prickles; medium, bushy growth.

Takapuna® Min, *op*, 1978, (MACtenni); *New Penny × ((Cläre Grammerstorf × Cavalcade) × Elizabeth of Glamis)*; McGredy, S., IV; McGredy Roses International. Flowers light peach-pink, dbl. (37 petals), medium; very fragrant; tall, spreading growth.

Takatori Prominent F, *op*, 1981, *Prominent sport*; Takatori; Japan Rose Nursery. Flowers orange-salmon.

Talisman HT, *yb*, 1929, *Ophelia × Souv. de Claudius Pernet*; Montgomery Co. Bud pointed; flowers golden yellow and copper, dbl. (25 petals), flat, medium; fragrant; foliage light green, leathery, glossy; vigorous growth. GM, ARS (Gertrude M. Hubbard) 1929; ARS John Cook Medal, 1932.

Talisman, Climbing Cl HT, *yb*, 1930, Western Rose Co.

Talisman, Climbing Cl HT, *yb*, 1932, Dixie Rose Nursery.

Talisman No. 5 HT, *yb*, *Talisman form*. Flowers deeper color; good growth; free bloom; a florists' variety.

Tall Story® F, *my*, 1984, (DICkooky); *Sunsprite × Yesterday*; Dickson, P.; Dickson Nursery. Flowers medium yellow, semi-dbl., medium; slight fragrance; foliage medium, light green, glossy; spreading growth.

Tallulah HT, *yb*, 1983, (BEElah); *Astral × Piccadilly*; Bees. Flowers gold with deep pink petal edges, dbl. (20 petals), large; slight fragrance; foliage medium, dark, semi-glossy; bushy.

Tallyho HT, *dp*, 1948, *Charlotte Armstrong × Seedling*; Swim; Armstrong Nursery. Bud urn-shaped; flowers deep pink, dbl. (35 petals), high-centered, large (3½-4 in.); very fragrant (spicy); foliage leathery; vigorous, upright, bushy growth. AARS, 1949; ARS David Fuerstenberg Prize, 1951.

Tallyho, Climbing Cl HT, *dp*, 1952, Armstrong, J.A.; Armstrong Nursery.

Tam o'Shanter F, *yb*, 1969, *Orange Sensation × Circus*; Cocker. Flowers yellow and red, dbl., borne in clusters; slightly fragrant; low, compact growth.

Tama HT, *op*, 1989, *Red Lion × Garden Party*; Sato, Kohi. Bud pointed; flowers salmon-pink, fringed with pink, reverse creamy yellow, dbl. (35 petals), urn-shaped, high-centered, large, borne in sprays of 2-3; slight fragrance; foliage dark green; prickles small, lower part hollow; upright, tall growth.

Tamango® F, *dr*, 1967, (MEIdanu); (*Alain × Mutabilis*) × (*Radar × Caprice*); Meilland, M.L.; Wheatcroft Bros. Flowers dark red, dbl. (35 petals), large blooms in large clusters; slightly fragrant.

Tamara HT, *mr*, 1966, *Parel van Aalsmeer × Independence*; Mondial Roses. Flowers geranium-red, dbl., high-centered; foliage dark; very vigorous growth.

Tamarisk HT, *mp*, 1954, *Mme. Butterfly × Signora*; Ratcliffe. Flowers clear rose-pink, camellia shaped; very fragrant; foliage leathery, dull green; very vigorous growth.

Tambourine F, *rb*, 1958, *Independence seedling × Karl Herbst*; Dickson, A. Flowers cherry-red, base yellow, reverse light burnt-orange, dbl. (25 petals), large (3½ in.), borne in clusters; slightly fragrant; foliage dark, veined; vigorous, tall, bushy growth.

Tammy Pol, *lp*, 1972, *Seventeen × Jack Frost*; Byrum. Flowers light pink, dbl., high-centered, medium; fragrant; foliage large, leathery; vigorous, upright, bushy growth.

Tamora S, *ab*, 1992, (AUStamora); *Chaucer × Conrad Ferdinand Meyer*; Austin, David; David Austin Roses, 1983. Flowers apricot yellow, very full (41+ petals), deeply cupped, old rose form, medium (4-7 cms) blooms borne in small clusters; very fragrant (unusual myrrh); foliage small, dark green, semiglossy; some prickles; medium (90 cms), bushy growth.

Tampa Bay™ Min, *ob*, 1989, (KINbay); *(Arthur Bell × Orange Honey) × Baby Diana*; King, Gene; BDK Nursery, 1988. Bud pointed; flowers orange, edges aging darker, dbl. (18 petals), high-centered, exhibition, medium, borne singly; slight, fruity fragrance; foliage medium, medium green, matt; prickles straight, red; fruit ovoid, orange; upright, medium growth.

Tampico HT, *or*, 1976, *South Seas × Hawaii*; Warriner; J&P. Bud ovoid, long, pointed; flowers coral-pink, dbl., large; slightly fragrant; foliage large, leathery; vigorous, upright.

Tam-Tam F, *my*, 1961, *Goldilocks seedling × Demure seedling*; Boerner; J&P. Bud ovoid; flowers yellow flushed pink, dbl. (35-40 petals), cupped, large (3 in.); fragrant; foliage glossy; vigorous, upright growth; a greenhouse variety for cut-flower purposes. RULED EXTINCT 1/88.

Tam-Tam Min, *lp*, 1988, *(Nozomi × Nozomi) × Bo-Peep*; Onodera, Toru F. Flowers light pink, dbl. (18-20 petals), flat with inner petals upright, borne in large clusters; slight fragrance; foliage small, light green; fruit longated, orange.

Tanagra® HT, *or*, 1969, (GActa); *Queen Elizabeth × Tropicana*; Gaujard. Bud long,

pointed; flowers orange-red, dbl., large; fragrant; foliage soft; vigorous, upright growth.

TANaloap HT, *mr*, 1982, (Paola); Tantau, M., 1981. Flowers medium red, dbl. (20 petals), large; slight fragrance; foliage large, dark, matt.

TANamola F, *w*, 1985, (La Paloma '85; The Dove); Tantau, M. Flowers white, dbl. (20 petals), medium; no fragrance; foliage medium, light green, glossy; upright.

TANbeedee F, *ob*, 1971, (Belinda); *Seedling × Zorina*; Tantau. Bud ovoid; flowers copper to orange, dbl., medium; fragrant; vigorous, upright, bushy growth.

TANcary HT, *yb*, 1976, (Canary); Tantau; Krussmann, 1972. Flowers yellow, petals marked orange, dbl., well-formed, medium; fragrant.

Tane F, *r*, 1979, (SIMetna); *(Orangeade × Megiddo) × (Seedling × Jocelyn)*; Simpson, J.W. Bud pointed; flowers russet, dbl. (38 petals), HT-form, blooms borne 4-10 per cluster; no fragrance; foliage small, dark, very glossy; short, straight, dark brown prickles; vigorous, upright growth.

TANezamor S, *mp*, 1985, (Romance; Romanze); Tantau, M.; Tantau Roses, 1984. Flowers medium pink, dbl. (20 petals), medium; slight fragrance; foliage medium, dark, semi-glossy; bushy growth. GM, Baden-Baden, 1985; ADR, 1986.

Tanger HT, *rb*, 1949, *Condesa de Sástago × Peace*; Dot, P. Bud ovoid; flowers crimson, reverse yellow, dbl. (60 petals), large; fragrant; moderate, compact growth.

Tangerine HT, *op*, 1942, *Capt. Glisson × R.M.S. Queen Mary*; Hill, J.H., Co. Bud globular, coral-red; flowers light salmon-orange, dbl. (30-35 petals), large (3½-4 in.); strong stems; slightly fragrant; foliage dark, leathery; vigorous, very upright, well branched growth; a florists' variety, not distributed for outdoor use.

Tangerine Contempo F, *ob*, 1983, *Gamma ray induced somatic Contempo sport*; Gupta, Dr. M.N.; Datta, Dr. S.K.; National Botanical Research Institute. Flowers tangerine orange.

Tangerine Mist F, *ob*, 1987, (RENist); *(Avandel × Seedling) × Gold Mine*; Rennie, Bruce F.; Rennie Roses, 1988. Flowers orange, semi-dbl. (15 petals), high-centered, medium, borne singly; moderate, fruity fragrance; foliage medium, light green, glossy; prickles straight, medium, red-brown; fruit round, small, orange; upright growth.

Tangier HT, *rb*, 1955, *Katharine Pechtold × R.M.S. Queen Mary*; Parmentier, J. Bud long, pointed; flowers peach-red to scarlet-copper, dbl. (60 petals), high-centered, medium; slightly fragrant; vigorous, bushy growth.

Tango HT, *mr*, 1937, *Seedling × Talisman*; H&S. Flowers scarlet, reverse bronze, base shaded old-gold; vigorous growth.

Tango HT, *mr*, 1955, *The Doctor × Karl Herbst*; Delforge. Bud long; flowers tango-red, dbl., open, large; fragrant; foliage dark, glossy; vigorous, bushy growth.

Tango Rose HT, *ob*, 1978, (DELtanga); *(Belle Rouge × (Gloire de Rome × Gratitude)) × ((Dr. Schweitzer × Tropicana) × (Ena Harkness × Quebec))*; Delbard. Bud pointed; flowers salmon-orange, dbl. (35-40 petals), large; foliage matt green; bushy growth.

Tania Verstak HT, *mr*, 1962, *Charlotte Armstrong × Happiness*; Armbrust; Langbecker. Flowers rich red, dbl., large; slightly fragrant; foliage light green, soft; vigorous, upright growth.

TANnireb HT, *mp*, 1985, Tantau, M. Flowers medium pink, dbl. (20 petals), large; slight fragrance; foliage medium, dark, semi-glossy; upright.

TANryrandy HT, *ob*, 1985, (Cherry Brandy '85); Tantau, M. Flowers orange, dbl. (35 petals), large; no fragrance; foliage large, medium green, glossy; upright.

TANsinnroh HT, *ab*, 1984, (Frohsinn '82; Joyfulness); Tantau, M., 1982. Flowers apricot and orange blend, dbl. (35 petals), large; slight fragrance; foliage large, dark, glossy.

Tant Mieux S, *ob*, 1984, (Saskabec); *R. gallica × Maria Stern*; Wright, Percy; Gilles Gailloux. Flowers tangerine, yellow center, single (5 petals), medium blooms in clusters; no fragrance; foliage medium, medium green, glossy; bushy growth.

Tantallon HT, *mp*, 1934, Dobbie. Flowers salmon-pink, base yellow, reverse cerise-red touched orange, dbl.; foliage glossy, dark; dwarf, stocky growth.

Tantau's Delight F, *or*, 1951, *Cinnabar × Käthe Duvigneau*; Tantau. Bud long, pointed; flowers orange-red, semi-dbl., open, large, borne in clusters; slightly fragrant; foliage dark, glossy; vigorous, bushy growth.

Tantau's Surprise F, *mr*, 1951, (Tantau's Ueberraschung); *Bouquet × Hamburg*; Tantau. Flowers blood-red, dbl. (40 petals), large, borne in clusters of 5-8; slightly fragrant; foliage dark, glossy; upright growth.

Tantivvy Pol, *mr*, 1954, *Gloire du Midi sport*; Ratcliffe. Flowers crimson-scarlet, semi-dbl., rosette form; compact, bushy growth.

Tanya HT, *ob*, 1959, (Majeure); *Peace × (Peace × Orange Nassau)*; Combe; Vilmorin-Andrieux;

J&P. Bud pointed; flowers deep orange to apricot-orange, dbl. (48 petals), high-centered, large (5 in.); fragrant; foliage leathery, glossy; vigorous, upright growth.

Tanya Kim HT, *my*, 1975, *Whisky Mac sport*; Marks. Flowers clear yellow, dbl. (24 petals), full, large (4½ in.); very fragrant; foliage glossy.

Taora® F, *or*, 1968, (TANta); *Fragrant Cloud × Schweizer Grüss*; Tantau. Bud long, pointed; flowers orange-red, dbl., large; foliage glossy; very vigorous, bushy growth. ADR, 1969.

Tapestry HT, *rb*, 1958, *Peace × Mission Bells*; Fisher, G.; C-P. Bud pointed; flowers red, yellow and pink, dbl. (38 petals), high-centered to cupped, large (4½-6 in.); spicy fragrance; foliage glossy; upright, bushy.

Tapis Blanc Pol, *w*, 1927, Turbat. Flowers pure white, center tinted cream, dbl., large, borne in clusters of 12-15; bushy, dwarf.

Tapis Jaune® Min, *my*, 1973, (RUgul; Gulletta); *Rosy Jewel × Allgold*; deRuiter. Flowers yellow, dbl. (20 petals), small (1½ in.); foliage small, glossy, dark; low, compact growth.

Tapis Rose F, *mp*, 1950, *Pinocchio × Mme. Jules Gouchault*; Meilland, F.; C-P. Bud ovoid; flowers rose-pink, dbl. (40 petals), high-centered, becoming cupped, medium (2-2½ in.), borne in clusters; fragrant; foliage leathery, dark; vigorous, upright, bushy growth; (27).

Tapis Rouge F, *mr*, Improvement on Lafayette, with more lasting, bright red color; more compact and dwarf.

Tapis Volant® S, *pb*, 1982, (LENplat); *(R. luciae × Seedling) × (R. multiflora × Ballerina)*; Lens. Flowers white-pink blend, semi-dbl., 2 in. blooms in clusters of 7-35; fruity fragrance; foliage reddish green; hooked, reddish-brown prickles; spreading; recurrent; ground cover. GM, Kortrijk, 1987.

Tara Allison Min, *or*, 1987, (MACwaiwer; Tara); *Wanaka × Eyepaint*; McGredy, Sam; Justice Miniature Roses, 1986. Flowers orange-red, semi-dbl. (6-14 petals), small; slight fragrance; foliage small, medium green, semi-glossy; bushy growth.

Tara Red HT, *dr*, 1974, *Peace × Charles Mallerin*; Golik; Dynarose. Bud ovoid; flowers carmine-red, becoming very dark, dbl. (38 petals), high-centered, very large (6 in.); fragrant; foliage leathery; tall growth.

Taranga® F, *mr*, 1982, (TANagnarat); Tantau, M., 1981. Flowers medium red, semi-dbl., medium; no fragrance; foliage medium, medium green, semi-glossy; bushy.

Tarantella® HT, *dy*, 1936, *Charles P. Kilham × Pres. Herbert Hoover*; Tantau. Flowers deep golden yellow, dbl., cupped, large; slightly fragrant; foliage light, wrinkled; vigorous, bushy growth.

Tarantelle HT, *or*, 1965, *(Beauté × Ma Fille) × Magicienne*; Laperrière; EFR. Flowers orange-red, dbl. (40 petals), well-formed; foliage bronze; vigorous, bushy growth.

Tarde Gris HT, *m*, 1966, (Evening Light); *(Sterling Silver × Intermezzo) × (Sterling Silver × Simone)*; Dot, S.; Roses Dot. Flowers soft lilac, dbl. (25 petals), large; fragrant; foliage dark; upright.

Target F, *rb*, 1986, (JACrim); *Prominent × Seedling*; Warriner; J&P. Flowers white with red petal edges, dbl. (25 petals), high-centered, medium blooms borne usually singly; no fragrance; foliage medium, medium green, semi-glossy; straight, large and small prickles; upright, bushy, medium growth; greenhouse variety.

Taro HT, *my*, 1977, *Edith Krause × Narzisse*; Ota. Bud oval; flowers medium yellow, dbl. (35 petals), high pointed, very large (5½ in.); foliage dark, leathery; vigorous, upright growth.

Tarragona HT, *ab*, 1945, *Duquesa de Peñaranda × Federico Casas*; Dot, P. Flowers apricot-yellow, dbl. (25-35 petals), high-centered, open; slightly fragrant; foliage glossy; upright growth.

Tartufe F, *mr*, 1956, *Pompadour Red × Independence*; Buyl Frères. Flowers dark geranium-red, dbl. (28 petals); moderate growth.

Tarzan LCl, *mr*, 1955, D-C. Flowers coppery carmine, dbl.; fragrant; foliage bronze; very vigorous growth; free, recurrent bloom.

Tasman Min, *dp*, 1983, (MURta); *Smiley × ((Pink Parfait × Una Hawken) × Anytime)*; Murray, Nola. Flowers deep pink, dbl. (17 petals), flat, small; no fragrance; foliage medium, dark, leathery; compact growth.

Tasogare F, *m*, 1977, *Gletscher × (Sterling Silver × Gletscher)*; Kobayashi. Bud cupped; flowers mauve, semi-dbl. (18 petals), flat, large (2½-4 in.); fragrant; foliage glossy; vigorous, spreading.

Tassin HT, *mr*, 1942, *National Flower Guild × Lemania*; Meilland, F.; A. Meilland. Bud ovoid; flowers medium red, dbl., large; very fragrant; foliage leathery; vigorous, upright.

Tassin, Climbing Cl HT, *mr*, Moreira da Silva.

Taste of Honey F, *ob*, 1977, *Elizabeth of Glamis* sport; Young, S.A. Bud ovoid; flowers honey color, aging pink, dbl., open, large; very fragrant; foliage leathery; vigorous, upright growth.

Tata Centenary HT, *rb*, 1974, *Pigalle* sport; Pradhan, Rauf, Murmu, Ghosh. Flowers

deep carmine, striped pale yellow, reverse buff.

Tatjana® HT, *dr*, 1970, (KORtat; Rosenthal); *Liebeszauber × Präsident Dr. H.C. Schroder*; Kordes, R.; Kordes. Bud long, pointed; flowers dark red, dbl., cupped, large; very fragrant; foliage leathery, soft; vigorous, upright growth.

Tattletale Min, *mp*, 1988, (ZIPtale); *High Spirits × Charmglo*; Zipper, Herbert; Magic Moment Miniatures, 1989. Flowers deep pink, dbl. (33 petals), small, borne singly and in sprays; no fragrance; foliage small, dark green, semi-glossy; bushy, compact growth.

Taupo® F, *op*, 1978, (MACmisech); *Liverpool Echo × Irish Mist*; McGredy, S., IV; McGredy. Flowers light rose-salmon, dbl. (40 petals), flora-tea, large (5 in.); tall.

Tauranga Centennial F, *or*, 1982, *Arthur Bell × (Alexander × Sympathy)*; Wareham, Phyllis E. Flowers orange-red, center yellow, dbl. (22 petals), large blooms in cluster of 3, sometimes 4-5; slight fragrance; light brown prickles; upright growth.

Taurinia HT, *mp*, 1942, *Julien Potin × Sensation*; Aicardi; Giacomasso. Bud ovoid; flowers bright salmon-pink, very dbl., cupped, large; fragrant; foliage leathery; very vigorous growth.

Tauro F, *dr*, 1958, *Poinsettia × Alain*; Bofill; Torre Blanca. Bud globular; flowers ox-blood-red, dbl., large, borne in clusters; foliage glossy; upright growth.

Taurus Min, *or*, 1978, *Baby Masquerade × (Spion-Kop × Evelyn Fison)*; Ellick; Excelsior Roses. Bud pointed, ovoid; flowers vermilion, dbl. (35-40 petals), full, large (2-3 in.); foliage dark; compact, upright growth.

Tausendschön HMult (OGR), *pb*, 1906, (Thousand Beauties); *Daniel Lacombe × Weisser Herumstreicher*; Schmidt, J.C. Flowers deep rose-pink, center white (a third of petals white), dbl., cupped, large blooms in large clusters; slightly fragrant; foliage soft; no prickles; climbing (8-10 ft.) growth.

Tawny Gold HT, *dy*, 1951, *Vanessa × Burgemeester van Oppen*; Leenders, M.; J&P. Bud pointed; flowers tawny gold, dbl. (25 petals), well-shaped, high-centered, large (5 in.); very fragrant; foliage leathery; bushy, compact growth.

Tawny Superior HT, *my*, 1958, Leenders, M. Flowers golden yellow.

Taxi F, *rb*, 1969, *Isabelle de France × Basildon Belle*; Trew; Basildon Rose Gardens. Flowers mandarin red, reverse soft rose, dbl., pointed, large; foliage dark, matt.   RULED EXTINCT 12/85.

Tennessee™ Min, *op*, 1988, (KINtenn); *Kiskadee* × *Orange Honey*, King, Gene; AGM Miniature Roses. Flowers coral to white, reverse light coral to white, aging darker coral, dbl. (18 petals), high-centered, exhibition, medium, borne usually singly or in sprays of 3-5; foliage medium, light green, matt; prickles straight, light green; fruit oval, large, orange; upright, tall growth.

Tennessee Belle LCl, *mp*, Flowers bright rosy blush, dbl., large, borne in clusters; fragrant; vigorous, climbing growth.

Ténor LCl, *mr*, 1963, (DELcap); D-C. Flowers velvety red, semi-dbl., blooms in clusters of 6-20; very vigorous growth; early bloom.

Tentation® HT, *op*, 1968, (DORteam); *Touggout* × *Flaminaire*, Dorieux; Vilmorin. Bud pointed; flowers carmine-pink to orange, dbl., large; slightly fragrant; foliage glossy; vigorous, upright.

Teodora HT, *mr*, 1983, *Honey Favorite* × *Command Performance*, Stoddard, Louis; Barni-Pistoia, Rose. Flowers medium red, dbl. (30 petals), cupped, large; light fragrance; foliage large, brownish-green, matt; reddish-green prickles; upright growth.

Tequila® F, *ob*, 1982, (MEIgavesol); *Poppy Flash* × *(Rumba* × *(Meikim* × *Fire King))*, Meilland, M.L.; Meilland Et Cie. Flowers light yellow, overlaid with orange, stained carmine on outer petals, dbl. (20 petals), large; slight fragrance; foliage medium, dark, matt; bushy.

Tequila Sunrise HT, *rb*, 1988, (DICobey; Beaulieu); *Bonfire Night* × *Freedom*; Dickson, P.; Dickson Nursery, 1989. Flowers red blend, dbl. (40 petals); slight fragrance; foliage medium, medium green, glossy; bushy growth. GM, RNRS, 1988.

Tequilla Sunset™ F, *ob*, 1991, (WILsun); *Redgold* × *Tropicana*; Williams, J. Benjamin, 1976; Paramount Nursery Packaging Co., 1992. Bud ovoid; flowers brilliant orange and yellow blend, dbl. (32 quilled petals), urn-shaped, medium blooms borne in sprays of 3-7; moderate, fruity fragrance; foliage medium, medium green, semi-glossy; upright, bushy, medium growth.

Teresa Finotti-Masieri HT, *m*, 1929, *George C. Waud* × *Souv. de Gabriel Luizet*, Ketten Bros. Bud long, pointed; flowers brilliant purple-rose, rosy scarlet reflexes, bordered yellow.

Teresa Ozores Cl HT, *lp*, 1957, *Frau Karl Druschki* × *Lady Sylvia*; Camprubi. Bud ovoid; flowers soft pearly pink, dbl., cupped, large; very fragrant; vigorous growth.

Terrell Anne F, *lp*, 1991, (GREtag); *Gene Boerner sport*; Greenwood, Chris. Bud ovoid; flowers light pink, full (26-40 petals), high-centered, medium (4-7 cms) blooms borne in small clusters; slight fragrance; foliage medium, medium green, glossy; some prickles; medium (90 cms), upright growth.

Terry O' F, *rb*, 1976, *Redgold sport*; Hughes; Hughes Roses. Flowers dark red, reverse copper yellow.

Teschendorffs Jubiläumsrose Pol, *dr*, 1928, *Orléans Rose sport*; Teschendorff. Flowers vivid rosy crimson, darker than Orléans Rose and more brilliant.

Tesco Bernstein F, *dy*, 1972, *Cognac* × *Allgold*; Haenchen; Teschendorff. Bud ovoid; flowers brownish yellow, semi-dbl., open, globular, medium; slightly fragrant; foliage glossy, dark, leathery; vigorous, bushy growth.

Tesco Blickfang F, *or*, 1972, *Dicksons Flame* × *Circus*; Haenchen. Bud ovoid; flowers dark vermilion-red, dbl., large; slightly fragrant; foliage dark, soft; vigorous, upright, bushy growth.

Tesco Brennpunkt F, *or*, 1972, *Highlight* × *Dicksons Flame*; Haenchen; Teschendorff. Bud ovoid; flowers bright vermilion-red, semi-dbl., open, medium; slightly fragrant; foliage dark, soft; vigorous, upright growth.

Tesco Goldteppich F, *my*, 1972, *Cognac* × *Allgold*; Haenchen; Teschendorff. Bud ovoid; flowers yellow, semi-dbl., cupped, medium; slightly fragrant; foliage glossy, dark, leathery; vigorous, bushy growth.

Tesco Lichtblick S, *ob*, 1972, *Yellow Holstein* × *Heidelberg*; Haenchen; Teschendorff. Flowers pink and orange-pink on yellow ground, dbl., high-centered, large; slightly fragrant; foliage glossy, leathery; vigorous, upright growth; abundant, continuous bloom.

Tesco Romanze F, *pb*, 1972, *Märchenland* × *Seedling*; Haenchen; Teschendorff. Bud globular; flowers pink, center white, semi-dbl., open, small; slightly fragrant; foliage small, glossy, dark, leathery; vigorous, dwarf, bushy growth.

Tesorino® Min, *lp*, 1982, *Seedling* × *Seedling*; Barni-Pistoia, Rose. Flowers light pink, dbl. (20 petals), small; no fragrance; foliage small, light green, matt; light green prickles; spreading growth; ground cover.

Tess R, *mp*, 1939, Beckwith. Flowers neyron pink, passing to deeper pink, center brighter, dbl., large, borne in large clusters on strong stems; slightly fragrant; foliage large, rich green; very vigorous growth. RULED EXTINCT 11/91.

Tess Min, *lp*, 1991, (CLEtest; CLEtess); *Cupcake* × *Seedling*; Clements, John; Heirloom Old Garden Roses, 1992. Flowers flesh pink, semi-dbl. (6-14 petals), exhibition, small (0-4 cms) blooms borne mostly singly; no fragrance; foliage small, medium green, semi-glossy; few prickles; medium (30 cms), bushy growth.

Teton Beauty HRg (S), *dp*, 1927, *Tetonkaha × American Beauty*; Hansen, N.E. Flowers rich pink to crimson, dbl. (65 or more petals), cupped; fragrant; foliage rugosa-like; recurrent bloom; very hardy.

Tetonkaha HRg (S), *dp*, 1912, *R. macounii × Rugosa hybrid*; Hansen, N.E. Flowers deep rich pink, semi-dbl., medium; very fragrant; vigorous (6 ft. tall and wide); profuse, non-recurrent bloom; hardy.

Tewantin Cl HT, *dp*, 1953, *Editor McFarland × Self*; Ulrick. Bud globular; flowers deep pink, dbl., large; long stems; fragrant; vigorous (12 ft.) growth.

Texan F, *mr*, 1956, (The Texan); *Improved Lafayette × Peace*; Lindquist; Howard Rose Co. Bud ovoid; flowers rose-red, dbl. (23 petals), high-centered to flat, large (3½-4 in.), borne singly and in clusters; fragrant; foliage dark, leathery; vigorous, upright.

Texas Min, *my*, 1984, (POUltex; Golden Piccolo); *Seedling × Seedling*; Poulsen, D.T.; Weeks Roses, 1990; John Mattock Ltd. Flowers medium yellow, semi-dbl., mini-flora, small; slight fragrance; foliage small, medium green, matt.

Texas Centennial HT, *rb*, 1935, *Pres. Herbert Hoover sport*; Watkins, A.F.; Dixie Rose Nursery. Flowers vermilion-red with some gold, center lighter. GM, Portland, 1935.

Texas Centennial, Climbing Cl HT, *rb*, 1936, Dixie Rose Nursery, 1936; Armstrong Nursery, 1942.

Texas Girl™ HT, *yb*, 1991, (MEIcijas); *Lovely Girl sport*; Meilland, Alain; C-P, 1991. Flowers creamy yellow, full (26-40 petals), large; slight fragrance; foliage large, medium green; tall, upright growth.

Texas Gold HT, *my*, 1935, *Pres. Herbert Hoover sport*; Wolfe. Flowers golden yellow occasionally tinged pink, dbl., large; very fragrant.

Texas Queen HT, *mp*, 1965, *Tip Toes sport*; Leidy; Wilson Nursery. Flower base cream, shading to light and darker pink, very dbl. (100 petals), large; very fragrant; foliage light green, soft; vigorous, almost thornless growth.

Texas Sunrise Min, *yb*, 1990, (UMStex); *Arizona Sunset sport*; Umsawasdi, Dr. Theera, 1991. Flowers yellow at times with pinkish edge, moderately full (15-25 petals), small, borne mostly singly; no fragrance; foliage medium, medium green, semi-glossy; upright, bushy growth.

Texas Wax S, *lp*, *Appears to be a hybrid of R. chinensis × R. multiflora*; Introduced from Texas as an understock.

T. F. Crozier HT, *dy*, 1918, Dickson, H. Flowers deep canary-yellow, fading, dbl.

Thalia HMult (OGR), *w*, 1895, (White Rambler); *R. multiflora × Pâquerette*; Schmitt; P. Lambert. Flowers white, dbl., small blooms in clusters; early bloom.

Thanet Ballerina HT, *w*, 1973, *Prima Ballerina sport*; Court. Flowers pearl-white, blushed pink; fragrant; foliage rich green; vigorous growth.

Thanksgiving HT, *ob*, 1965, *Fred Howard × Seedling*; Warriner; Great Western Rose Co. Bud ovoid; flowers bronze shades, reverse orange-red, dbl. (38 petals), high-centered, medium (3½ in.); foliage dark, leathery; vigorous growth.

The Adjutant HT, *mr*, 1922, Pemberton. Bud long, pointed; flowers bright red, dbl.; very fragrant.

The Alamo HT, *mr*, 1959, *Happiness × Independence*; Meilland, F.; Co-Operative Rose Growers. Bud ovoid; flowers cardinal red, very dbl. (110 petals), large (3½-4½ in.); slightly fragrant; foliage leathery; vigorous, upright, bushy growth.

The Allies Pol, *w*, 1930, Heers. Flowers white suffused pale pink, dbl., open, small, borne in clusters; slightly fragrant; foliage small, glossy; dwarf, bushy growth.

The Australian Bicentennial HT, *mr*, 1987, *Daily Sketch seedling × Red Planet*; Bell, R.J.; Roy H. Rumsey, Pty. Ltd., 1988. Flowers medium to deep red, full (30 petals), well-formed, borne usually singly; very fragrant; foliage medium, medium green, glossy, disease resistant; curved, green prickles; tall, branching, average growth; Named in commemoration of the Australian Bicentennial and the World Federation Rose Convention, 1988.

The Bairn HT, *dy*, 1976, *Arthur Bell × Seedling*; Wood. Flowers golden yellow, dbl. (40-50 petals), very full, medium (3½ in.), foliage dark, leathery; dwarf growth.

The Beacon R, *rb*, 1922, Paul, W. Flowers bright fiery-red with white-eye, as in American Pillar, single, sometimes semi-dbl., borne in large clusters; vigorous, climbing (to 8 ft.) growth.

The Bishop C (OGR), *m*, Name, classification and origin uncertain. Flowers unusual shade of cerise-magenta, fading bluish purple, flat, rosette form; slender, upright (4-5 ft.) growth; early bloom.

The Bishop HT, *dr*, 1937, Dickson, A. Flowers bright crimson, full, large; very fragrant; foliage dark; vigorous growth. GM, NRS, 1937.

The Bride T (OGR), *w*, 1885, *Catherine Mermet sport*; May. Flowers white tinged pink.

The Bride HT, *w*, 1963, *White Swan* × *Seedling*; Herholdt, J.A.; Herholdt's Nursery. Bud pointed, ivory-white; flowers white, dbl. (30 petals), well formed; foliage glossy.

The Chief HT, *ob*, 1940, (Chief); *Charles P. Kilham* × *Pres. Herbert Hoover*; Lammerts; Armstrong Nursery. Bud long, pointed; flowers flame, coral and copper, dbl. (35 petals), large (4-6 in.); very fragrant; vigorous, bushy, spreading growth. AARS, 1940.

The Countryman® S, *mp*, 1987, (AUSman); *Seedling* × *Comte de Chambord*; Austin, David. Flowers medium pink, dbl. (40 petals), rosette, medium, borne usually singly and in sprays of 3-5; heavy, damask fragrance; foliage medium, medium green, matt; hooked, small, pale prickles; fruit ovoid, medium, red; spreading, medium growth; repeat bloom.

The Coxswain HT, *pb*, 1985, (COCadilly); *(Tropicana* × *Ballet)* × *Silver Jubilee*; Cocker, Alexander; Cocker & Sons. Flowers cream and pink blend, dbl. (35 petals), large; very fragrant; foliage medium, medium green, semi-glossy; bushy growth.

The Daniel™ HT, *dr*, 1989, (WILdan); *Chrysler Imperial* × *Queen Elizabeth*; Williams, J. Benjamin; The Peninsula Nursery, 1990. Bud ovoid; flowers dark velvety red, reverse burgandy, dbl. (36 petals), high-centered, medium, borne usually singly; no fragrance; foliage large, dark green, semi-glossy; prickles few; fruit none observed; upright, medium growth.

The Dazzler Cl HT, *mr*, 1955, *Dainty Bess, Climbing seedling*; Marsh's Nursery. Flowers bright red, single, petals ruffled; profuse, recurrent bloom.

The Doctor HT, *mp*, 1936, *Mrs. J.D. Eisele* × *Los Angeles*; Howard, F.H.; Dreer. Flowers satiny pink, dbl. (25 petals), well-formed, large (to 6 in.); very fragrant; foliage soft, light; dwarf, bushy growth. GM, NRS, 1938.

The Doctor, Climbing Cl HT, *mp*, 1950, Dyess; Reliance Rose Nursery.

The Dowager Countess of Roden HT, *lp*, 1919, *Viscountess Enfield* × *George C. Waud*; Paul, W. Flowers bright silvery pink, dbl.

The Duke HT, *rb*, 1956, *Applause* × *Peace*; Abrams, Von; Peterson; Dering. Bud globu-

lar; flowers carmine-red, reverse gold, dbl. (55 petals), high-centered, large (5-6 in.) blooms in clusters of 3-15; slightly fragrant; foliage semi-glossy; vigorous, open growth.

The Fairy Pol, *lp*, 1932, (Fairy; Feerie); *Paul Crampel* × *Lady Gay*; Bentall, Ann; J.A. Bentall. Flowers pink, dbl., small blooms in clusters; foliage glossy, small; compact, spreading; recurrent; hardy.

The Farmers Wife F, *lp*, 1962, *Queen Elizabeth* × *Spartan*; Boerner; J&P. Bud ovoid; flowers light pink, dbl. (38 petals), cupped, large (4½ in.) blooms in clusters; very fragrant; foliage leathery, glossy; upright, moderate growth.

The Fisherman's Cot F, *op*, 1990, (HARwicklow); *Radox Bouquet* × *Anna Ford*; Harkness, R.; R. Harkness & Co., Ltd., 1991. Bud pointed; flowers light salmon pink, aging to deeper pink, dbl. (28 petals), cupped, medium, borne in sprays of 3-9; moderate, sweet, slightly pungent fragrance; foliage small to medium, dark green, semi-glossy.

The Flower Arranger F, *ab*, 1984, (FRYjam); *Seedling* × *Seedling*; Fryer's Nursery. Bud large; flowers peach, semi-dbl., well-formed; slight fragrance; foliage large, dark, glossy; upright growth.

The Friar S, *lp*, 1969, *Ivory Fashion* × *Seedling*; Austin, D. Flowers blush, edged white, 10 petals, medium; very fragrant; foliage dark; repeat bloom.

The Garden Editor® Min, *dy*, 1988, (MINasco); *Gold Badge* × *Yellow Jewel*; Williams, Ernest. Flowers deep yellow, dbl. (33 petals), small; fragrant; foliage small, medium green, glossy; upright, bushy growth.

The Garland Misc. OGR (OGR), *w*, 1835, (Wood's Garland); *R. moschata* × *R. multiflora*; Wells. Flowers faint yellow, pink, and white, semi-dbl., medium blooms in large, long clusters; fragrant (musk); moderate climbing (8 ft.) growth; mid-season bloom.

The General HT, *mr*, 1920, Pemberton. Flowers blood-red, flushed lighter, dbl., globular, large; fragrant (damask); foliage dark, bronze, leathery; vigorous, low growth.

The Gentleman HT, *yb*, 1958, *Seedling* × *Irish Fireflame*; Hay; Marsh's Nursery. Bud long; flowers creamy yellow flushed pink, semi-dbl.; very fragrant.

The Indian HT, *dr*, 1939, *Sensation* × *Seedling*; Clark, A.; Brundrett. Flowers very dark red, semi-dbl., large; vigorous growth.

The Jester Gr, *yb*, 1960, (Leerder's Harlequin); *Masquerade* × *High Noon*; Leenders, J.; British Hort. Co. Flowers yellow changing to red, dbl., compact, borne in clusters; slightly fragrant; foliage dark.

The Knight S, *dr*, 1969, *Chianti* × *Seedling*; Austin, D. Flowers crimson turning purple and mauve, dbl. (80 petals), flat, medium; fragrant; foliage dark; repeat bloom.

The Master Cutler HT, *mr*, 1954, *The Doctor* sport; Liberty Hill Nurs. Flowers cherry-red shaded rose, dbl., well formed, very large; very fragrant; vigorous growth.

The Miller S, *mp*, 1981, *Baroness Rothschild* × *Chaucer*; Austin, David, 1970. Bud globular; flowers medium pink, dbl. (40 petals), rosette-shaped blooms borne 1-4 per cluster; fragrant; foliage medium green; hooked, red prickles; upright, bushy growth; repeats.

The Mountie F, *mr*, 1949, *Springtime* × *World's Fair*; Eddie. Flowers cherry-red, semi-dbl. (12-15 petals), medium, borne in huge trusses; fragrant; foliage leathery, glossy, light green; bushy growth.

The Old Fashioned Rose HT, 1930, Archer. Flowers deep crimson, dbl., fragrant; very vigorous.

The Optimist F, *yb*, 1955, (Sweet Repose); *Golden Rapture* × *Floribunda seedling*; deRuiter; Gandy, 1955; C-P, 1956. Bud ovoid; flowers maize-yellow tinged carmine, becoming carmine, dbl. (27 petals), high-centered to cupped, large (3 in.) blooms in large clusters; fragrant; foliage dense, leathery, parsley-green; vigorous, upright, bushy. GM, NRS, 1955.

The Princess Elizabeth HT, *ob*, 1927, *The Queen Alexandra Rose* sport; Wheatcroft Bros. Flowers orange-yellow, edged deep cerise, dbl., large; fragrant.

The Prioress S, *lp*, 1969, *La Reine Victoria* × *Seedling*; Austin, D. Flowers blush to white, yellow stamens, dbl. (24 petals), cupped, medium; fragrant; repeat bloom.

The Queen HT, *ob*, 1954, Lowe. Bud pointed; flowers orange suffused salmon, dbl. (26-30 petals), medium; fragrant; very free growth.

The Queen Alexandra Rose HT, *rb*, 1918, (Queen Alexandra); McGredy. Flowers bright red, reverse shaded old-gold, base orange, dbl., large (5 in.); fragrant; foliage glossy, dark; bushy growth. GM, NRS, 1917.

The Queen Alexandra Rose, Climbing Cl HT, *rb*, 1929, Lindecke; Kordes.

The Queen Alexandra Rose, Climbing Cl HT, *rb*, 1931, Harkness.

The Queen Mother F, *mp*, 1959, *Nymph* sport; Stedman. Flowers soft rosy pink, dbl. (45-50 petals), large (3½ in.), borne on large trusses; fragrant; foliage glossy, light green; vigorous growth.

The Rajah HT, *dr*, 1937, *Red-Letter Day* × *Seedling*; Clark, A.; NRS Victoria. Flowers deep red, full; bushy growth.

The Reeve® S, *dp*, 1981, *Lilian Austin* × *Chaucer*; Austin, David, 1979. Bud globular; flowers deep pink, dbl. (58 petals), cupped blooms borne 1-5 per cluster; very fragrant; foliage red, turning to green; hooked, red prickles; spreading, shrubby growth; repeats.

The Senator HT, *mr*, 1980, *Seedling* × *Suspense*; Weeks, O.L. Bud ovoid, long; flowers bright medium red, dbl. (46 petals), petals loosely rolled outward, blooms borne usually singly; slight, musk fragrance; foliage large, leathery, wrinkled, dark; long, narrow-based, brown prickles, curved down; tall, upright growth.

The Squire® S, *dr*, 1976, *The Knight* × *Château de Clos Vougeot*; Austin, David, 1977. Bud globular; flowers very dark red, very dbl. (120 petals), rosette-shaped blooms borne 1-3 per cluster; strong fragrance; foliage dark; straight prickles; open, bushy growth.

The Stork HT, *mp*, 1952, *Seedling* × *The Doctor*; Whisler; Germain's. Bud long, pointed; flowers carmine-rose, dbl. (28 petals), high-centered, large (5-5½ in.); slightly fragrant; foliage leathery; bushy growth.

The Sun F, *op*, 1972, (*Little Darling* × *Goldilocks*) × *Irish Mist*; McGredy, S., IV; McGredy. Flowers salmon-orange, semi-dbl. (15 petals), large (3½ in.); slightly fragrant. GM, Madrid, 1973.

The Surgeon HT, *mp*, 1956, *The Doctor* seedling; Verschuren; Blaby Rose Gardens. Flowers darker rose-pink, more dbl., more vigorous than The Doctor.

The Temptations™ HT, *pb*, 1990, (WEKaq); *Paradise* × *Admiral Rodney*; Winchel, Joseph; Weeks Roses, 1993. Bud pointed; flowers pink blend, medium pink reverse, aging slightly lighter, dbl. (35 petals), high-centered, exhibition, medium, borne usually singly; moderate, fruity fragrance; foliage medium, dark green, semi-glossy, disease resistant; prickless lightly hooked, medium, green; fruit oval, medium, orange; upright, tall growth. ARC TG (G), 1989.

The Venerable Bede F, *yb*, 1973, *John Church* × *Bobby Shafto*; Wood; Homedale Nursery. Flowers yellow to cherry, dbl. (20-30 petals), full; large (3-3½ in.); slightly fragrant; foliage small, glossy; moderate, free growth.

The Wallflower LCl, *mr*, 1901, (Wallflower); *Crimson Rambler* × *Beauté Inconstante*; Paul. Flowers bright red, semi-dbl., large, borne in large clusters; vigorous growth; late bloom.

The Wife of Bath S, *pb*, 1969, (Wife of Bath); *Mme. Caroline Testout* × (*Ma Perkins* × *Con-*

stance Spry); Austin, D. Flowers deep rose-pink, reverse blush, semi-dbl., cupped, medium; very fragrant; foliage small; repeat bloom.

The Yank HT, *mr*, 1942, *Chieftain × Lucile Hill*; Hill, J.H., Co. Flowers rose-red, dbl. (55-60 petals), very large; long, strong stems; very fragrant; foliage leathery, dark; very vigorous, upright, much branched growth; a florists' variety, not distributed for outdoor use.

The Yeoman S, *op*, 1969, *Ivory Fashion × (Constance Spry × Monique)*; Austin, D. Flowers salmon-pink, dbl. (50 petals), flat, medium; very fragrant; recurrent.

Thea Russel F, *mr*, 1954, *Ambassadeur Nemry × Cinnabar*; Leenders, M. Flowers bright red; fragrant; vigorous growth.

Theda Mansholt Gr, *my*, 1966, *Peace × Garden Party*; Buisman. Bud ovoid; flowers yellow, dbl., medium; slightly fragrant; foliage dark; upright growth.

Thelma R, *op*, 1927, *R. wichuraiana × Paul's Scarlet Climber*; Easlea. Flowers coral-pink, suffused carmine-red, semi-dbl. large (3 in.) blooms in clusters of 3-10; slightly fragrant; few prickles; vigorous, climbing growth.

Thelma Amling Pol, *w*, 1942, *Mrs. R.M. Finch sport*; Amling Bros.; J.H. Hill Co. Bud globular; flowers white, semi-dbl., small; short stems; slightly fragrant; foliage small, leathery; vigorous, bushy growth.

Thelma Bader HT, *ob*, 1956, *seedling × (Independence × Fashion)*; Latham. Flowers orange-scarlet to salmon-pink, semi-dbl. (20 petals), medium (3 in.); slightly fragrant; foliage dark, glossy; moderately vigorous growth.

Thelma Walton HT, *pb*, 1970, *Red Devil sport*; Walton; Cooke. Flowers deep pink, lightly edged silver, very dbl., high-centered, very large; slightly fragrant; foliage glossy, dark; vigorous, upright growth.

Theodora HT, *dr*, 1984, *Apricot Nectar × Dame de Coeur*; Staikov, Prof. Dr. V.; Kalaydjiev and Chorbadjiiski. Flowers dark red, semi-dbl. (16 petals), large.

Theodore Roosevelt HT, *dr*, 1987, (BURred); *Alamo sport*; Burks, Larry; Co-Operative Rose Growers, 1986-87. Flowers deep red, fading slightly lighter, semi-dbl. (6-14 petals), high-centered, exhibition, medium, borne singly; slight fragrance; foliage large, medium green, semi-glossy; average, light yellow-green prickles; fruit globular, large, dark red; upright, tall growth.

Theresa Morley HT, *dp*, 1928, *Mme. Segond Weber × Lady Battersea*; H&S. Flowers brilliant carmine-cerise, dbl., fragrant

Thérèse Bauer HSet (OGR), *mp*, 1963, *(Hansa × R. setigera) × R. setigera*; Ludwig; Kern Rose Nursery. Flowers medium pink, semi-dbl., open, large, borne in clusters; slightly fragrant; very vigorous, upright growth; profuse.

Thérèse Bonnaviat HT, *lp*, 1934, *Mrs. Arthur Robert Waddell × Seedling*; Chambard, C. Bud long, pointed; flowers clear pink, center coppery pink, very large; fragrant; foliage purplish green; very vigorous growth.

Thérèse Bugnet HRg (S), *mp*, 1950, *((R. acicularis × R. rugosa kamtchatica) × (R. amblyotis × R. rugosa plena)) × Betty Bland*; Bugnet; P.H. Wright. Bud conical but square-tipped; flowers red aging pale pink, dbl. (35 petals), large (4 in.); fragrant; vigorous; repeat bloom.

Thérèse Schopper HT, *mr*, 1933, *(Charles P. Kilham × Mev. G.A. van Rossem) × Lady Forteviot*; Kordes. Bud long, pointed, blood-red; flowers nasturtium-red, reverse yellow, semi-dbl., high-centered, open, large; fragrant; foliage leathery, dark; vigorous growth.

Thérèse Zeimet-Lambert HT, *dp*, 1922, *Richmond × Mrs. Aaron Ward*; Lambert, P. Bud long, pointed; flowers deep rose, yellow ground, base orange, dbl., high-centered, large; very fragrant; foliage glossy, bronze; vigorous growth.

Theresette S, *mp*, 1986, *Arctic Glow × Thérèse Bugnet*; James, John. Flowers deep soft pink edged white, full (26-40 frilly petals), carnation-like, medium, borne in clusters; fragrant; foliage small, medium green, semi-glossy, disease resistant; bushy, hardy, compact, dwarf growth.

Think Pink Min, *mp*, 1983, (TINthink); *Electron × Little Chief*; Bennett, Dee. Flowers medium pink, golden stamens, dbl. (28 petals), small; strong apple fragrance; foliage small, medium green, semi-glossy; bushy growth.

Thirza HT, *or*, 1932, Bentall. Flowers orange-scarlet; fragrant.

Thisbe HMsk (S), *ly*, 1918, *Daphne sport*; Pemberton. Flowers chamois-yellow, full, rosette-shaped blooms in large clusters; very fragrant; vigorous, bushy; recurrent.

Thomas A. Edison HT, *pb*, 1931, Bernaix, P.; C-P. Bud long, pointed; flowers two-toned pink, dbl., cupped, very large; fragrant; very vigorous growth.

Thomas Mills HP (OGR), *dp*, 1873, Verdier, E. Flowers rosy crimson, full, cupped, large; fragrant; vigorous; non-recurrent bloom.

Thor LCl, *dr*, 1940, *(Alpha × R. xanthina) × Pres. Coolidge*; Horvath; Wayside Gardens Co.

Bud ovoid; flowers crimson, dbl. (58 petals), large (4-5 in.); slightly fragrant (damask); foliage large, leathery, dark; vigorous, climbing (8-10 ft.) growth.

Thor Supreme LCl, *dr*, 1951, Horvath; Wyant. Flowers dark crimson edged deeper, large (4 in.); very fragrant (damask); foliage large, leathery, dark; vigorous, climbing growth; fairly abundant

Thora Hird F, *w*, 1988, (TonyBRAc); *Chinatown × Picasso*; Bracegirdle, A.J.; Rosemary Roses, 1987. Flowers white deepen to cream in center with pink veins, very dbl. (40 petals), loose, medium, borne in sprays of 5-6; moderate, sweet fragrance; foliage medium, dark green, semi-glossy; prickles straight, brown; fruit round, amber; bushy, medium growth.

Thora McCrea HT, *mr*, 1986, *Pink Parfait × Crimson Glory*; Summerell, B.L. Flowers medium red, dbl. (20-25 petals), exhibition; mild fragrance; foliage dark green; red-brown prickles; well-shaped, upright, medium growth.

Thornfree Wonder HMult (OGR), *w*, 1985, (NOBal); *Tausendschön × Seedling*; Nobbs, K.J. Flowers peach pink, fading to white, semi-dbl. (14 petals), cupped to flat blooms in clusters (up to 14); slight fragrance; no prickles; spreading; long canes; summer bloom.

Thornless Beauty HT, *dr*, 1938, *Better Times sport*; Grillo. Bud long, pointed, dark crimson-red; flowers light crimson-red, dbl. (50 petals), large (4 in.); long, strong, thornless stems; fragrant; foliage leathery; vigorous growth.

Thornless Blush HT, *lp*, 1954, *Rosalind Russell sport*; Grillo. Bud globular; flowers blush-pink, dbl. (70 petals), high-centered, large (4½ in.); thornless stems; fragrant; foliage leathery; very vigorous, upright growth.

Thornless Fringedale HT, *lp*, 1955, *Thornless Beauty sport*; Grillo. Flowers light pink, dbl. (25 petals), large (4 in.); thornless stems; fragrant.

Thornless Glory LCl, *lp*, 1935, Izzo. Flowers clear pink, semi-dbl. (20 petals), large (3 in.); long, thornless stems; slightly fragrant; vigorous, climbing growth; early summer bloom.

Thornless Mirage HT, *mr*, 1955, *Jewel sport*; Grillo. Flowers red suffused blush-pink, dbl. (25 petals), large (5 in.); thornless stems; fragrant.

Thornless Premier HT, *mp*, 1955, *Victory Stripe sport × Jewel*; Grillo. Bud globular, pointed; flowers rich pink, dbl. (75 petals), large (4½ in.); thornless stems; fragrant.

Thornless Victory Stripe HT, *rb*, 1955, *Victory Stripe sport × Jewel*; Grillo. Bud long, pointed; flowers dark red and blush-pink, striped, dbl. (50 petals), large (5 in.); thornless stems.

Thriller HT, *pb*, 1986, *Lady × x Flaming Beauty*; Bridges, Dennis, 1987. Flowers white center, pink edges, reverse slight pink edging, pink highlights with sun, dbl. (28-30 petals), high-centered, exhibition, large, borne singly; heavy, fruity fragrance; foliage medium, dark green, glossy; medium, long, light green prickles, pointed downwards; upright, medium, strong growth.

Thumbelina Min, *rb*, 1954, *Éblouissant × Zee*; Moore, R.S.; Sequoia Nursery. Flowers cherry-red, white eye, semi-dbl., small; foliage dark, glossy; dwarf (6-8 in.), bushy.

Thunder Cloud Min, *or*, 1979, *Little Chief × Fire Princess*; Moore, R.S.; Sequoia Nursery. Bud ovoid; flowers orange-red, dbl. (70 petals), small (1-1½ in.); foliage glossy, leathery; dwarf, bushy, upright growth.

Thunderbird F, *mr*, 1958, *Skylark sport*; DeVor, P.; Amling Roses. Bud urn-shaped; flowers rose-red, dbl. (48 petals), high-centered, medium (2½ in.) blooms in clusters of 3-8; vigorous, spreading growth.

Thunderbolt HT, *pb*, 1990, (BRIbolt); *Lady × Flaming Beauty*; Bridges, Dennis, 1980; Bridges Roses, 1991. Bud ovoid; flowers pink blend, white reverse, color intensifies with age, turning almost red in some cases, dbl. (45 petals), urn-shaped, medium, borne singly; slight fragrance; foliage medium, dark green, matt; bushy, medium growth.

Thusnelda HRg (S), *mp*, 1886, *R. rugosa alba × Gloire de Dijon*; Müller, F. Flowers rose, semi-dbl.; vigorous growth; non-recurrent bloom.

Tiara F, *w*, 1960, *Chic × Demure seedling*; Boerner; J&P. Bud ovoid; flowers white, dbl. (48 petals), cupped, large (3 in.) blooms in clusters; fragrant; foliage leathery; vigorous, bushy growth; greenhouse variety.

Tickle Me Pink Min, *mp*, 1989, (PIXink); *Osiria × Magic Carrousel*; Chaffin, Lauren M.; Pixie Treasures. Bud pointed; flowers medium pink to soft cream at base, reverse cream blush, aging darker, dbl. (33 mottled petals), urn-shaped, medium, borne singly; moderate, spicy fragrance; foliage small, medium green, semi-glossy; prickles needle-like, light tan; fruit globular, medium green, rare; bushy, low growth.

Tickled Pink HT, *mp*, 1963, *Queen Elizabeth × Fashion*; Lammerts; Germain's; Amling-DeVor Nursery. Bud long, pointed; flowers medium pink, dbl. (38 imbricated petals), high-centered, medium; fragrant (spicy); upright, bushy growth.

Tick-Tock Min, *ob*, 1973, *New Penny × Elizabeth of Glamis*; McGredy, S., IV; McGredy. Flowers salmon-pink, shaded orange, semidbl. (10 petals), open, medium (2 in.); slightly fragrant; free growth.

Tidewater Min, *w*, 1991, (BRItide); *Jennifer × Seedling*; Bridges, Dennis, 1988; Bridges Roses. Bud pointed; flowers white with slight pink tints, dbl. (30-32 petals), high-centered, exhibition, medium (6 cms) blooms borne usually singly; long stems for cutting; moderate fragrance; foliage medium, medium green, matt; bushy, spreading, medium growth.

Tiergartendirektor Timm F, *dp*, 1944, *Sweetness × Hamburg*; Kordes. Bud long, pointed; flowers carmine-pink, semi-dbl., open, very large, borne in clusters; slightly fragrant; foliage dark, glossy; very vigorous, upright growth.

Tiffany HT, *pb*, 1954, *Charlotte Armstrong × Girona*; Lindquist; Howard Rose Co. Bud long, pointed; flowers pink-yellow blend, dbl. (28 petals), high-centered, large (4-5 in.); very fragrant; foliage dark; vigorous, upright growth. GM, Portland, 1954; AARS, 1955; ARS David Fuerstenberg Prize, 1957; James Alexander Gamble Rose Fragrance Medal, 1962

Tiffany, Climbing Cl HT, *pb*, 1958, (Grimpant Tiffany); Lindquist; Howard Rose Co.

Tiffany Lynn Min, *pb*, 1985, *(Tiki × Seedling) × Party Girl*; Jolly, Nelson F.; Rosehill Farm. Flowers light to medium pink at edges, blending to white in center, dbl. (21 petals), high-centered, mini-flora, large; slight fragrance; foliage medium, medium green with red edges, semi-glossy; prickles slanted downward; upright, bushy growth.

Tiffie Min, *lp*, 1979, *Little Darling × Over the Rainbow*; Bennett, Dee; Tiny Petals Nursery. Bud long, pointed; flowers soft pink, sometimes apricot, 15-20 petals, high-centered blooms borne singly; lilac fragrance; foliage medium green; large, red prickles; upright.

Tifton HT, *yb*, 1983, *Fire Magic × Oregold*; Perry, Astor; Perry Roses. Flowers brilliant yellow, petal tips red, red spreading with age, dbl. (40+ petals), high-centered, large; fragrant; foliage large, medium, semi-glossy; bushy growth.

Tiger Belle F, *ob*, 1962, *Orange Sweetheart × Lovelight*; Jelly; E.G. Hill Co. Bud ovoid; flowers light signal-red, dbl. (25-35 petals), cupped, medium (2-2½ in.); moderate growth; a greenhouse variety.

Tiger Butter Min, *dy*, 1982, (PIXiter); *Sunblest × Over the Rainbow*; Strawn, Leslie E.; Pixie Treasures. Flowers deep yellow, dbl. (20 petals), small; slight fragrance; foliage small, dark, semi-glossy; upright, bushy growth.

Tiger Stripes Min, *yb*, 1992, (CLEtig); *Seedling × Seedling*; Clements, John K.; Heirloom Old Garden Roses, 1991. Flowers unusual striped color combination, yellow, striped orange, full (26-40 petals), small (0-4 cms.) blooms borne in small clusters; no fragrance; foliage small, medium green, semi-glossy; few prickles; low (25 cms.), bushy, compact growth.

Tiger Tail F, *ob*, 1991, (JACtiger; JACtang); *Matangi × Pinstripe*; Christensen, Jack E.; Bear Creek Gardens, 1992. Flowers deep orange, white or cream colored stripes, cream colored reverse, and a small eye at the center, full (26-40 petals), medium blooms borne in small clusters; no fragrance; foliage medium, medium green, glossy; medium, bushy growth.

Tiglia S, *yb*, 1962, *Ma Perkins × High Noon*; Leenders, J. Flowers creamy yellow tinged pink, dbl.; fragrant; recurrent bloom.

Tigris S, *yb*, 1986, (HARprier); *Hulthemia persica × Trier*; Harkness, 1985. Flowers yellow, dark red eye, dbl., small (1 in.); little fragrance; foliage small, light green, variable in shape; gooseberry-like prickles; compact, rounded growth. See Hulthemia.

Tiki F, *pb*, 1964, *Mme. Léon Cuny × Spartan*; McGredy, S., IV; McGredy. Flowers light pink and white blend, dbl. (30 petals), well-formed, flora-tea, large (3½ in.); foliage dark; vigorous.

Till Uhlenspiegel E (OGR), *rb*, 1950, *Holstein × Magnifica*; Kordes. Bud pointed; flowers bright red, white eye, single (5 petals), medium blooms in clusters; foliage large, glossy, dark reddish-green; tall (to 10 ft.), arching; non-recurrent.

Tillicum HT, 1924, *Général Jacqueminot × Old Gold*; Wilber. Flowers deep rose-pink shaded orange, dbl.; slightly fragrant.

Tim Page HT, 1920, Page; Easlea. Flowers rich daffodil yellow; fragrant.

Times Square HT, *ob*, 1943, *Mrs. Sam McGredy × Pres. Herbert Hoover*; Lammerts; Armstrong Nursery. Bud peach; flowers orange, center golden yellow, large; very fragrant; foliage leathery, glossy; vigorous growth.

Timmie Arkles F, *lp*, 1954, *Mrs. R.M. Finch × (Improved Lafayette seedling × Rochester seedling)*; Boerner; J&P. Flowers light pink, dbl., large (3 in.) blooms in flat clusters of 30-40; fragrant (fruity); vigorous growth.

Timm's Jubilaümsrose F, *or*, 1975, *Marlena × Europeana*; Kordes; Timm. Bud globular; flowers orange-red, dbl. (27 petals), globular, medium (2 in.); slightly fragrant; foliage soft; vigorous, upright, bushy growth.

Timothy Berlen Min, *ob*, 1986, *Anita Charles × Poker Chip*; Jolly, M.; Rosehill Farm, 1988. Flowers orange, yellow center, reverse yellow fading dark pink, semi-dbl. (20 petals), high-centered, exhibition, medium, borne usually singly or sprays of 2-3; slight fragrance; foliage small, medium green, semi-glossy; bayonet-shaped, light pink prickles; fruit round, green to yellow-orange; upright, spreading, low growth.

Timothy Eaton HT, *op*, 1968, *Radar × Mischief*; McGredy. Flowers salmon-pink, well-formed; slightly fragrant.

Tina Turner HT, *ob*, 1992, *Silver Jubilee × Doris Tysterman*; Thompson, R.; Battersby Roses, 1990. Flowers orange blend, full (26-40 petals), medium (4-7 cms) blooms borne mostly singly; fragrant; foliage large, dark green, glossy; some prickles; bushy (60 cms) growth.

Tineke HT, *w*, 1989, *Seedling × Seedling*; Select Roses B.V.; DeVor Nursery, 1990. Bud pointed; flowers creamy white, dbl. (53 petals), cupped, large, borne singly; no fragrance; foliage large, dark green, semi-glossy; prickles yellow-green with reddish tip; upright, tall growth.

Tineke van Heule® F, *lp*, 1985, (LENtini); *Seedling × City of Belfast*; Lens. Flowers light pink, 7-12 petals, medium blooms in clusters of 3-12; slightly fragrant; foliage large, leathery, greenish-brown; few, reddish-brown prickles; upright, bushy.

Tinker Bell Min, *mp*, 1954, *Ellen Poulsen × Tom Thumb*; deVink; C-P. Bud ovoid; flowers bright rose-pink, dbl. (60 petals), cupped, small (1½ in.); foliage small, leathery; dwarf (8 in.), bushy growth.

Tintin F, *or*, 1964, Mondial Roses. Flowers cinnabar-red, semi-dbl., cupped, large, borne in large clusters; moderate growth.

Tiny Bubbles™ Min, *w*, 1989, (JACbub); *Zorina × Funny Girl*; Warriner, William A.; Bear Creek Gardens, 1990. Bud ovoid; flowers ivory, near white, fading to white, dbl., cupped, medium, borne usually singly and in sprays of 3; no fragrance; foliage medium, medium green, semi-glossy; prickles straight, slightly angled downward, green-yellow; upright, spreading, medium growth.

Tiny Flame Min, *or*, 1969, *(R. wichuraiana × Floradora) × New Penny*; Moore, R.S.; Sequoia Nursery. Flowers coral-orange-red, dbl., micro-mini, very small; foliage very small; dwarf (6 in.), bushy growth.

Tiny Jack Min, *mr*, 1962, *(R. wichuraiana × Floradora) × (Oakington Ruby × Floradora)*; Moore, R.S.; Blue Ribbon Plant Co. Bud pointed; flowers medium red, dbl. (28 petals), cupped, small (1-1½ in.); slightly fragrant; foliage leathery, dark; vigorous, bushy (12-14 in.) growth.

Tiny Jill Min, *mp*, 1962, *(R. wichuraiana × Floradora) × Little Buckaroo*; Moore, R.S.; Blue Ribbon Plant Co. Bud pointed; flowers medium pink, dbl. (45 petals), high-centered, small (1½ in.); fragrant; foliage glossy; vigorous, bushy (12-14 in.) growth.

Tiny Love Min, *dr*, 1980, *Seedling × Seedling*; Lyon. Bud ovoid; flowers dark red, semi-dbl. (11 petals), cupped blooms borne 1-3 per cluster; strong fragrance; foliage dark; straight prickles; open, bushy growth.

Tiny Petals Min, *rb*, 1992, (TINypetals); *San Antonio × Jean Kenneally*; Bennett, Dee; Tiny Petals Nursery, 1993. Flowers orange-red with cream reverse, full (15-25 petals), HT form, small (0-4 cms) blooms borne mostly singly; long stems; foliage small, dark green, semi-glossy, disease resistant; some prickles; medium (60-80 cms), bushy growth.

Tiny Stars Min, *rb*, 1986, (TRAstar); *Magic Carrousel × Magic Carrousel*; Travis, L.R. Flowers white with red narrow edges, semi-dbl. (12 petals), cupped, small, borne usually singly and in sprays of 3-4; micro-mini; no fragrance; foliage small, medium green, matt; almost thornless; fruit none; bushy, low growth.

Tiny Tears Min, *mp*, 1979, *Pink Ribbon × Pink Ribbon*; Bennett, Dee; Tiny Petals Nursery. Bud ovoid; flowers pink, single (5 petals), micro-mini, very small blooms in clusters of 10-25; foliage glossy, dark; trailing growth.

Tiny Tim F, *my*, 1943, *Golden Glow × Shades of Autumn*; Brownell. Bud long, pointed; flowers clear yellow, dbl. (23 petals), open, high-centered, small; foliage glossy; moderately vigorous, compact to open growth.

Tiny Tot Min, *mp*, 1955, Robinson, T. Flowers deep cerise-pink; very dwarf growth.

Tiny Visions Min, *rb*, 1981, *Seedling × Seedling*; Lyon. Bud long; flowers crimson with white center, single (5 petals), slightly cupped blooms borne singular several together; fragrant; foliage dark, apple-scented; very tiny, hooked, brown prickles; very tiny, bushy growth.

Tiny Warrior Min, *rb*, 1975, *Starburst × Little Chief*; Williams, E.D.; Min-Roses. Bud ovoid; flowers red blend, dbl. (34 petals), flat, small (1 in.); slightly fragrant; foliage small, glossy, very dark, embossed; upright, bushy growth.

Tip Toes HT, *op*, 1948, *(Général Jacqueminot × Dr. W. Van Fleet) × Anne Vanderbilt*; Brownell. Bud pointed; flowers salmon-pink, shading to yellow at base, semi-dbl., high-centered, large; fragrant; foliage glossy; vigorous, upright growth.

Tipper™ Min, *mp*, 1987, (JOLtip); *Chris Jolly × Chattem Centennial*; Jolly, Marie; Rosehill Farm, 1988. Flowers medium pink, aging lighter, dbl. (32 petals), exhibition, medium, long lasting, borne singly; slight fragrance; foliage medium, medium green, semi-glossy; prickles bayonet, light brown; fruit round, orange; upright, medium growth. AOE, 1989.

Tipperary HT, *my*, 1917, *Mrs. Aaron Ward seedling*; McGredy. Bud long, pointed; flowers golden yellow, semi-dbl.; fragrant.

Tipsy HT, *dp*, 1969, *Basildon Belle × Seedling*; Trew; Basildon Rose Gardens. Flowers soft rose, reverse geranium-red, dbl., pointed, large; foliage dark, dull; free growth.

Tip-Top® Pol, *w*, 1909, (Baby Doll); *Trier × R. foetida bicolor seedling*; Lambert, P. Flowers white, tipped tyrian rose, aging white and pale yellow, reverse white, dbl., medium; bushy, dwarf growth.

Titania Ch (OGR), *rb*, 1915, Paul, W. Flowers deep salmon-red, shaded clear yellow, dbl., small; dwarf, bushy growth.

Titania Pol, *lp*, 1938, *Mev. Nathalie Nypels × Seedling*; Leenders, M. Flowers salmon-flesh to rosy white, very dbl., large; very fragrant; foliage leathery, dark; vigorous, bushy growth.

Titi Parisien F, *dr*, 1959, *Français seedlings × (Orange Triumph seedlings × Floradora)*; Delbard-Chabert. Flowers crimson, center lighter, stamens ivory, single (5 petals), large (3 in.); bushy, low growth.

Titian F, *dp*, 1950, Riethmuller. Flowers deep pink, dbl., large blooms in clusters; vigorous, tall.

Titian, Climbing Cl F, *dp*, 1964, Kordes.

Tivoli F, *mp*, 1955, *Poulsen's Supreme × (Souv. de Claudius Denoyel × Hvissinge-Rose)*; Poulsen, S.; McGredy. Flowers warm rose-pink, center yellow, dbl. (24 petals), well formed, large (3 in.), borne in clusters; fragrant; foliage dark, glossy; very vigorous growth.

Tiziana F, *op*, 1969, *Papillon Rose × Gay Paris*; Cazzaniga. Bud pointed; flowers copper-pink, semi-dbl., large; slightly fragrant; foliage light green; vigorous, compact growth.

Tobago® F, *ab*, 1961, (DELtogo); *Avalanche × (Zambra × Orange Sensation)*; Delbard, G. Flowers yellow apricot, outer petals aging pink, dbl. (35 petals), large; fragrant; foliage medium, dark, semi-glossy; upright. Geneva Rose d'Or.

Tobo™ Min, *dy*, 1989, (KINbo); *Arthur Bell × Rise 'n' Shine*; King, Gene; AGM Miniature Roses. Bud pointed; flowers deep yellow, dbl. (32 petals), high-centered, exhibition, medium, borne usually singly and in sprays of 2-3; slight, fruity fragrance; foliage medium, light green, matt; prickles straight, slight crook, red to brown; fruit ovoid, green; upright, bushy, medium growth.

Toccata F, *or*, 1959, *Independence × Cinnabar*; Lens. Flowers orange-red, well-formed blooms in large clusters; low growth.

Toccata HT, *mp*, 1963, *Karl Herbst × Seedling*; Sanday. Flowers light rose edged darker, reverse silvery, becoming redder, dbl. (27 petals), large (5 in.); fragrant; vigorous growth.

Today™ Gr, *ob*, 1989, (MACcompu); *(Typhoo Tea × (Yellow Pages × Kabuki)) × ((Yellow Pages × Kabuki) × (MACjose × Typhoon))*; McGredy, Sam; Co-Operative Rose Growers, 1990. Bud ovoid; flowers light orange blending to yellow, dbl. (33 petals), cupped, urn-shaped, medium, borne usually singly and in sprays of up to 3; slight fragrance; foliage medium, dark green, glossy; prickles recurved, medium, brown; fruit globular, medium, orange-red; bushy, medium growth.

Toddler F, *pb*, 1977, *Seedling × Seedling*; LeGrice. Flowers pink, reverse deeper, semi-dbl. (19 petals), medium (2 in.); foliage small, dark; very low, bushy growth.

Todoroki HT, *dr*, 1977, *(Pharaon × Kagayaki) × Yu-Ai*; Keisei Rose Nursery. Bud pointed; flowers dark red, dbl. (33 petals), high-centered, large (6½ in.); slightly fragrant; foliage dark; vigorous growth.

Toffee Min, *ob*, 1992, (SEAtoff); *Bloomsday × Miniature seedling*; McCann, Sean; Justice Miniature Roses, 1993. Flowers bright orange, medium yellow eye, dark orange stamens, reverse orange with slight yellow at base, aging with slight pink cast, semi-dbl. (18 petals), self-cleaning, urn-shaped, loose, medium (2.75 cms) blooms borne singly; slight fruity fragrance; foliage medium, medium green, semi-glossy, disease resistant; bushy, medium growth.

Toison d'Or HT, *ab*, 1921, Pernet-Ducher. Flowers apricot-yellow, shaded orange-red, dbl. GM, Bagatelle, 1922.

Token HT, *yb*, 1933, *Mme. Butterfly × Premier Supreme*; Montgomery Co. Bud ovoid; flowers glowing orange, dbl., open, large; strong stems; fragrant; foliage glossy; vigorous growth.

Token Glory HT, *or*, 1957, *Token Supreme sport*; Grillo. Bud pointed; flowers orange, dbl. (40 petals), large (4 in.); long stems; fragrant; foliage dark, leathery; very vigorous, upright, bushy growth.

Token Supreme HT, *ob*, 1940, *Token sport*; Grillo. Flowers deep orange, dbl. (35 petals), large (5 in.); fragrant.

Tokyo Cl F, *my*, 1972, *Salute × Canary Bird*; Oliver, W.G. Flowers yellow, single (5 petals), medium (3 in.); foliage light; vigorous growth; profuse May-June bloom.

Tom Barr HT, *op*, 1932, McGredy. Bud long, pointed; flowers salmon and scarlet, suffused yellow and orange, dbl., high-centered, large; fragrant; vigorous growth.

Tom Breneman HT, *dp*, 1950, *Mauna Loa × R.M.S. Queen Mary*; Howard, F.H.; H&S. Bud ovoid; flowers rose-pink, dbl. (30-40 petals), globular, large (4-4½ in.); very fragrant; foliage leathery, dark; very vigorous, upright growth.

Tom Breneman, Climbing Cl HT, *dp*, 1954, H&S.

Tom Brown F, *r*, 1964, *Seedling × Amberlight*; LeGrice. Flowers orangy-brown, reverse brownish-red, dbl. (32 petals), well-shaped, large (3 in.); very fragrant; foliage leathery, dark; vigorous, bushy growth.

Tom Maney LCl, *mp*, 1953, *R. maximowicziana pilosa × K. of K.*; Maney; Iowa State College. Bud ovoid; flowers rose-pink, dbl. (35-40 petals), cupped, large (4-5 in.), borne in clusters of 3-4; fragrant; foliage leathery, dark; vigorous, climbing (15-20 ft.) growth; non-recurrent bloom; quite hardy.

Tom Pilliby F, *or*, 1963, Combe. Flowers orange-red, semi-dbl., in large clusters; slightly fragrant; vigorous.

Tom Thumb Min, *rb*, 1936, (Peon); *Rouletii × Gloria Mundi*; de Vink; C-P. Flowers deep crimson, center white, semi-dbl., small (1 in.); foliage leathery, light green; very dwarf growth.

Tom Tom F, *dp*, 1957, *Improved Lafayette × Floradora*; Lindquist; Howard Rose Co. Bud ovoid; flowers deep pink, dbl. (25 petals), high-centered to flat, large (3-3½ in.) blooms in clusters; slightly fragrant (spicy); foliage dark; vigorous, upright, bushy.

Tom Tom, Climbing Cl F, *dp*, 1962, Lindquist; Howard Rose Co.

Tom Wood HP (OGR), *mr*, 1896, Dickson, A. Flowers cherry-red, full, cupped, large; fragrant.

Tomás Batâ HP (OGR), *dr*, 1932, *Fisher Holmes × Prince Camille de Rohan*; Böhm. Flowers dark red shaded crimson, passing to maroon, full, large; fragrant; foliage leathery, glossy, dark; very vigorous growth.

Tombola F, *dp*, 1967, *Amor × (Ena Harkness × Peace)*; deRuiter. Flowers deep pink, large (4 in.); very fragrant; foliage dark, glossy; vigorous, upright, bushy growth.

Tomboy Min, *mp*, 1988, (ZIPboy); *Maytime × Poker Chip*; Zipper, Herbert; Magic Moment Miniatures, 1989. Flowers medium pink, single (5 petals), small; no fragrance; foliage small, dark green, semi-glossy; upright, spreading growth.

Tomkins Red F, *dr*, 1943, *(Dr. W. Van Fleet × Général Jacqueminot) × Nigrette*; Brownell. Bud long, pointed; flowers deep velvety crimson turning maroon, semi-dbl. (18 petals), open, borne in clusters on long stems; fragrant; foliage dark, glossy; vigorous, compact, upright growth.

Tommy Bright F, *mr*, 1961, *Chatter seedling × Garnette Supreme*; Boerner; J&P. Bud ovoid; flowers scarlet-red, dbl. (35-40 petals), cupped, large (3½ in.); strong stems; fragrant; foliage leathery; very vigorous, upright growth; a greenhouse variety for cut-flower purposes.

Tommy Thompson HT, *or*, 1974, *Queen o' the Lakes × Tropicana*; Golik; Dynarose. Bud ovoid; flowers orange-red, dbl. (50 petals), high-centered, large (5 in.); fragrant (spicy); foliage glossy, very dark; moderate growth.

Tommy Tucker Min, *lp*, 1955, *Rouletii × Tom Thumb*; Robinson, T. Flowers silvery pink, dbl., small (1 in.), borne in clusters.

Tonehime HT, *w*, 1983, *Mizuho × Sodōri-Himé*; Kikuchi, Rikichi. Flowers white, creamy center, dbl. (30 petals), high-centered, large blooms borne usually singly; slight fragrance; foliage small, dark, glossy; few prickles; vigorous, slender, tall growth.

Tonga HT, *ob*, 1955, Lowe. Flowers deep golden orange, outer petals veined bronze and scarlet, dbl., well formed, medium; very fragrant; foliage dark, leathery; vigorous, upright growth.

Toni Corsari F, *dr*, 1961, *Red Favorite × Seedling*; Delforge. Flowers velvety deep red, semi-dbl., medium, borne in large clusters; fragrant; bushy, low growth.

Toni Lander F, *ob*, 1958, *Independence × Circus*; Poulsen, S. Flowers salmon-orange, dbl. (22 petals), large (3 in.), borne in large clusters; slightly fragrant; foliage dark; bushy growth. GM, Madrid, 1960.

Tonia HT, *m*, 1992, (FRANcibel); *Lagerfeld × Remember Me*; Franklin-Smith, Roger, 1995. Flowers light lavender/mauve with deeper tones (silvery lavender) at edges, full (26-40 petals), large (7+ cms.) blooms borne in small clusters; very fragrant; foliage medium, medium green, matt; some prickles; upright (175-180 cms.), vigorous growth.

Tonight HT, *mr*, 1972, *Seedling × Forever Yours*; Warriner. Bud ovoid; flowers bright red, dbl., high-centered, large; slightly fragrant; foliage leathery; vigorous.

Tonnerre® F, *dr*, 1953, (Not); *Holstein × Français*; Mallerin; EFR, 1952. Flowers deep velvety red, dbl. (24 petals), large (3 in.) blooms in large clusters; foliage dark; vigorous, bushy growth.

Tonner's Fancy LCl, *w*, 1928, *R. gigantea seedling × Seedling*; Clark, A.; Gill; Searle. Flowers white, tinted pink in bud, dbl., globular, large; fragrant; vigorous, climbing growth.

Tony Jacklin F, *op*, 1972, McGredy, S., IV; McGredy. Flowers orange-salmon, dbl. (30 petals), HT-form, flora-tea, large (4 in.); slightly fragrant. GM, Madrid, 1972; Portland, 1986.

Tony Peace HT, *ab*, 1964, *Peace sport*; Brundrett. Flowers buff-yellow to apricot.

Tony Spalding HT, *dr*, 1933, McGredy. Flowers brilliant crimson, semi-dbl., high-centered; very fragrant; foliage glossy; very vigorous growth.

Tooth of Time Min, *w*, 1989, (RENtime); *Party Girl × Paul Shirville*; Rennie, Bruce F.; Rennie Roses, 1990. Bud pointed; flowers white with cream, dbl. (25 petals), urnshaped, small, borne usually singly and in sprays of 3-5; slight, spicy fragrance; foliage small, dark green, semi-glossy; prickles hooked downward, medium, light yellow; fruit none observed; bushy, medium growth.

Tootsie F, *pb*, 1990, (GREtoots); *Angel Face × Old Master*; Greenwood, Chris, 1985; Armstrong Garden Centers, 1991. Flowers deep pink painted white, reverse mostly white, aging with a slight fading of pink, semi-dbl. (20 petals), loose, medium, borne in sprays of 5-7; slight fragrance; foliage medium, dark green, glossy, disease resistant; upright, bushy, rounded, medium growth.

Top Choice Min, *op*, 1985, *Gingersnap × Baby Katie*; Hardgrove, Donald L.; Rose World Originals. Flowers medium salmon-pink, dbl. (36 petals), medium; slight fragrance; foliage small, medium green, semi-glossy; dense, spreading, bushy growth.

Top Gun™ Min, *pb*, 1990, (KINgun); *(Rainbow's End × Vera Dalton) × Vera Dalton*; King, Gene, 1985; AGM Miniature Roses, 1991. Bud ovoid; flowers peony pink, yellow base, apricot yellow reverse, dbl. (28 petals), high-centered, exhibition, medium, borne usually

singly; no fragrance; foliage medium, medium green, semi-glossy; tall, upright growth.

Top Hat F, *ab*, 1968, *Ma Perkins × Garden Party*; Fankhauser; A. Ross & Son. Bud ovoid; flowers apricot-blush, dbl., high-centered, medium; fragrant; foliage small, dark, glossy; compact, low growth.

Top Secret Min, *mr*, 1971, *Beauty Secret sport*; Moore, R.S.; Sequoia Nursery. Flowers medium red.

Topaz Pol, *yb*, 1937, *Joanna Tantau × (Prof. Gnau × Julien Potin)*; Tantau; C-P. Flowers lemon-yellow, petals edged cream, reverse lemon and cream, very dbl., high-centered, small; slightly fragrant; foliage small, leathery; dwarf, spreading growth.

Topaz Jewel™ HRg (S), *my*, 1987, (MORyelrug; Gelbe Dagmar Hastrup; Rustica 91; Yellow Fru Dagmar Hartopp); *Golden Angel × Belle Poitevine*; Moore, Ralph S.; Moore Miniature Roses; Wayside Gardens, 1987. Flowers medium yellow fading to cream, dbl. (25+ petals), cupped, large, borne in sprays of 5-8 or more; moderate, fruity fragrance; foliage large, medium green, rugose, matt; slender, fairly long, brown prickles in variable sizes; fruit none; upright, bushy, spreading, vigorous growth; repeats.

Topaze Orientale HT, *yb*, 1965, *Sultane × Queen Elizabeth*; D-C; Cuthbert. Flowers maize-yellow to light pink, dbl., high-centered, large (5-6 in.); fragrant; tall.

Topeka F, *mr*, 1978, *Vera Dalton × Seedling*; Wisbech Plant Co. Bud long, pointed; flowers medium red, dbl. (21 petals), flat, large (3 in.); foliage glossy; vigorous, upright growth.

Topper HT, *mr*, 1959, *Pink Bountiful × Sister Kenny*; Hill, J.H., Co. Bud short, pointed; flowers signal-red to crimson, dbl. (25-30 petals), high-centered to open, medium (3-3½ in.); long, strong stems; slightly fragrant; foliage dark, leathery; vigorous, upright growth; for greenhouse use.

Toprose F, *dy*, 1992, (COCgold; Dania); *((Chinatown × Golden Masterpiece) × Adolph Horstmann) × Yellow Pages*; Cocker, James; James Cocker & Sons, 1988. Flowers bright yellow, full (26-40 petals), large (7+ cms) blooms borne in large clusters; slight fragrance; foliage large, medium green, glossy; some prickles; medium (76.20 cms), upright growth. GM, Baden-Baden, 1987.

Topsi® F, *or*, 1971, *Fragrant Cloud × Signalfeuer*; Tantau. Bud ovoid; flowers orange-scarlet, semi-dbl., patio, medium; slightly fragrant; moderate, dwarf. GM, RNRS, 1972; RNRS PIT, 1972.

Topsi's Friend F, *lp*, 1981, *Dreamland × Topsi*; Anderson's Rose Nursery. Flowers light pink, semi-dbl. (15 petals), rosette blooms borne 5 per cluster; no fragrance; foliage light green, glossy; green prickles; upright growth.

Torch R, *or*, 1942, *Climbing sport of orange Polyantha seedling*; deRuiter. Flowers scarlet-orange, white eye, semi-dbl. (15 petals), small (1½ in.) blooms in clusters; slightly fragrant; foliage glossy, dark; vigorous, climbing (6-8 ft.) growth.

Torch of Liberty™ Min, *or*, 1986, (MORtorch); *Orangeade × Golden Angel*; Moore, R.S.; Moore Min. Roses, 1985. Flowers orange-red, silver reverse, dbl. (20 petals), small; slight fragrance; foliage small, medium green, semi-glossy; upright, bushy growth.

Torch Song HT, *or*, 1959, *(Peace × Floradora) × Grand'mère Jenny*; Meilland, F.; C-P. Bud ovoid; flowers vermilion, dbl. (30-35 petals), high-centered, large (5 in.); slightly fragrant; foliage dark, leathery; vigorous, upright, bushy growth.

Torchlight F, *or*, 1951, *Dusky Maiden × Holstein*; LeGrice. Flowers brilliant orange-scarlet shaded deeper, single (5-8 petals), large (3½ in.), borne in clusters to 30; fragrant; foliage dark; vigorous growth.

Torchy F, *or*, 1969, *Heat Wave × Spartan*; Armstrong, D.L.; Armstrong Nursery. Bud pointed to urn-shaped; flowers brick-orange, dbl., high-centered, medium; fragrant; foliage leathery; moderate, bushy growth.

Toreador HT, *pb*, 1919, Paul, W. Flowers rosy red, reverse golden yellow, semi-dbl.

Toresky F, *lp*, 1931, *Perle d'Or × Antoine Rivoire*; Padrosa. Flowers light pink with white eye, dbl., cupped, borne in large clusters; slightly fragrant; foliage wrinkled, light; dwarf growth.

Toresky, Climbing Cl F, *lp*, 1956, Torre Blanca.

Torino F, *mp*, 1960, *Seedling × Cocorico*; Mansuino, Q. Flowers spinel-rose, small to medium; vigorous growth.

Tornado® F, *or*, 1973, (KORtor); *Europeana × Marlena*; Kordes, R.; Kordes. Flowers orange-red, semi-dbl., globular, medium; slightly fragrant; foliage leathery; vigorous, bushy. ADR, 1972.

Torrero F, *ob*, 1961, *Ma Perkins × Cocorico*; Leenders, J. Flowers pink-orange-red, semi-dbl. (18 petals), flat, large (3 in.).

Torvill & Dean HT, *pb*, 1985, (LANtor); *Grandpa Dickson × Alexander*; Sealand Nurseries, Ltd., 1984. Flowers pink, yellow reverse, dbl. (35 petals), medium; slight fragrance; foliage medium, dark, semi-glossy; upright growth.

Tosca F, *or*, 1972, *Seedling × Ginger*; Warriner; J&P. Bud long, pointed; flowers orange-red, dbl., open, medium; slightly fragrant; foliage large, leathery; very vigorous, upright growth.

Toscana HT, *dp*, 1954, Cazzaniga; Fedi. Flowers deep pink, dbl.; fragrant; vigorous growth.

Total Recall™ Min, *or*, 1984, (SAVacall); *Zorina × Baby Katie*; Saville, F. Harmon; Nor'East Min. Roses. Flowers orange-red, dbl. (40+ petals), medium; no fragrance; foliage small, medium green, semi-glossy; bushy growth.

Totote Gelos HT, *w*, 1915, Pernet-Ducher. Bud long, pointed; flowers flesh-white, center shaded chrome-yellow, dbl.

Tottie F, *mr*, 1961, *Alain × Fashion*; Borgatti; Sgaravatti. Flowers purplish red, dbl. (35-40 petals), large (3 in.), borne in clusters of 6; vigorous, bushy growth.

Totty's Red HT, *dr*, 1926, *Premier sport*; Totty. Flowers crimson-scarlet.

Touch o' Midas™ Cl Min, *yb*, 1985, (MINabco); *Little Darling × Over the Rainbow*; Williams, E.D.; Mini-Roses. Flowers deep yellow, petals edged deep pink, dbl. (35 petals), small blooms borne singly or in small clusters; slight fragrance; foliage small, dark, semi-glossy; upright (to 5 ft.) growth.

Touch of Class™ HT, *op*, 1984, (KRIcarlo; Maréchal le Clerc; Marachal Le Clerc); *Micaela × (Queen Elizabeth × Romantica)*; Kriloff, M.; Armstrong Nursery. Flowers medium pink, shaded coral and cream, dbl. (33 petals), exhibition, large; slight fragrance; foliage large, dark, semi-glossy; upright, bushy growth. AARS, 1986; GM, Portland, 1988.

Touch of Elegance HT, *w*, 1988, (LEOtoelg); *(Gavotte × Buccaneer) × Miniature seedling*; Léon, Charles; John Carrigg, 1987. Bud pointed; flowers white with creamy yellow center, dbl., high-centered, exhibition, large, borne in sprays of 1-3; slight fragrance; foliage medium, medium green, semi-glossy; upright, tall growth.

Touch of Fire Min, *ob*, 1988, (RENfire); *Tangerine Mist × California Girl*; Rennie, Bruce F.; Rennie Roses, 1989. Bud ovoid; flowers orange-yellow, reverse light orange, aging apricot-orange, dbl. (25 petals), urn-shaped, small, borne singly; moderate, spicy fragrance; foliage small, medium green, semi-glossy; prickles straight, small, orange-red; fruit none; bushy growth.

Touch of Kiwi HT, *yb*, 1989, *Kiwi Queen* × *Command Performance*; Cattermole, R.F.; South Pacific Rose Nursery. Bud tapering; flowers creamy yellow, 1/4 in. wide orange margin on petals, widening as flower ages, creamy reverse aging red, dbl. (up to 60 imbricated petals), medium, borne usually singly and in sprays of 2-3; very slight fragrance; foliage medium green; prickles pointed, light brown, varying size; upright growth.

Touch of Magic HT, *or*, 1977, *San Francisco* × *Peace*; Patterson; Patterson Roses. Bud globular; flowers orange-red, dbl. (40-45 petals), high-centered, large (5 in.); very fragrant; very vigorous growth.

Touch of Raspberry™ HT, *dp*, 1989, (DEVicio); *Love Affair* × *Paul's Pink*; Marciel, Stanley G.; DeVor Nursery. Bud slender, tapering; flowers deep pink, dbl. (30 petals), cupped, large, borne singly; slight, fruity fragrance; foliage large, dark green, semiglossy; prickles declining, light lime green with mauve tinges; upright, tall growth.

Touch of Velvet HT, *rb*, 1988, (LEOvelv); *(First Prize* × *Gypsy)* × *Seedling*; Léon, Charles; John Carrigg, 1987. Bud pointed, long; flowers magenta red with lighter tones, dbl. (31 petals), high-centered, exhibition, borne usually singly and in sprays of 1-3; moderate fragrance; foliage medium, dark green, semiglossy; upright, tall growth.

Touch of Venus HT, *w*, 1971, *Garden Party* × *Sweet Afton*; Armstrong, D.L.; Armstrong Nursery. Flowers near white, center shaded pink, dbl., high-centered, large; very fragrant; foliage large, leathery; vigorous, upright growth.

Touchdown Min, *mr*, 1988, *Sheri Anne* × *Anita Charles*; Jolly, Nelson; Rosehill Farm, 1989. Bud ovoid; flowers medium red, reverse red with white center, aging bluish, dbl. (40 petals), urn-shaped, small, borne singly; no fragrance; foliage small, medium green, matt; prickles none; fruit none; low, upright growth.

Touch-Up Min, *pb*, 1989, (FOUtouch); *Scarlet Knight* × *(Matangi* × *Honey Hill)*; Jacobs, Betty A.; Four Seasons Nursery. Bud pointed; flowers medium pink with cream border, reverse cream, hand-painted, dbl. (30 petals), cupped, exhibition, medium, borne usually singly and in sprays of up to 3; moderate, tea fragrance; foliage medium, medium green, matt; prickles straight, large, red to tan; fruit round, medium, russet-orange; upright, bushy, tall growth.

Touggourt F, *or*, 1959, *(Gruss an Teplitz* × *Independence)* × *(Floradora* × *Independence)*; Arles; Roses-France. Bud globular; flowers orange-shrimp-pink, dbl., open, large; foliage dark, leathery; vigorous, bushy growth.

Tour de France F, *OR*, 1963, *(Alain* × *Orange Triumph)* × *Seedling*; Mondial Roses. Flowers deep orange-scarlet shaded blood-red, semidbl., large to medium; vigorous, bushy growth.

Tour de Malakoff C (OGR), *m*, 1856, Soupert & Notting. Flowers mauve-pink shaded purple, heavily veined, center green, loose papery petals, large; fragrant; sprawling (7 ft.).

Tourbillon F, *rb*, 1959, (French Cancan); *Michèle Meilland* × *(Incendie* × *(Floradora* × *Orange Triumph))*; Delbard-Chabert. Flowers red, reverse silvery pink, dbl. (30-35 petals), well formed, large (3-4 in.), borne in clusters of 6-8; very vigorous, bushy growth. RULED EXTINCT 4/85.

Tourbillon F, *pb*, 1981, (DELnolli); *Zambra* × *((Orléans Rose* × *Goldilocks)* × *(Spartan* × *Fashion))*; Delbard, G. Flowers deep pink, yellow reverse, dbl. (20 petals), large; fragrant; foliage small, medium green, semi-glossy; upright growth.

Tourmaline® HT, *pb*, 1965, (DELfri); *Michèle Meilland* × *Chic Parisien*; D-C; Cuthbert. Flowers creamy white, widely edged carmine, dbl. (28 petals), high-centered, large; foliage light green; moderate growth. GM, Madrid, 1965.

Tournament of Roses Gr, *mp*, 1988, (JACient; Berkeley;); Poesie *Impatient* × *Seedling*; Warriner, William A.; J&P Co., 1989. Flowers light coral pink, reverse deep pink, aging coral pink, dbl., high-centered, large, borne usually singly or in sprays of 3-6; no fragrance; foliage large, dark green, semi-glossy, disease resistant; prickles large; upright, bushy, medium growth. AARS, 1989.

Town Crier HT, *ly*, 1961, *Peace* × *Yellow Perfection*; Hill, J.H., Co. Bud ovoid; flowers straw-yellow, dbl. (33 petals), high-centered, large (5-6 in.); fragrant; foliage dark, glossy; vigorous, upright, well-branched growth.

Town Talk F, *or*, 1966, *(Circus* × *Garnette)* × *Spartan*; Swim; Weeks; Weeks Roses. Bud ovoid; flowers orange-red, dbl., cupped, small; foliage dark, leathery; moderate growth.

Town Talk, Climbing Cl F, *or*, 1975, Weeks, V.E.; Weeks Roses.

Townsend HSpn (OGR), *mp*, *R. spinosissima hybrid*. Flowers pink, dbl.; non-recurrent bloom.

Townswoman HT, *rb*, 1973, *Seedling* × *Piccadilly*; Anderson's Rose Nursery. Flowers red-purple, reverse silver, dbl. (35 petals), globular, large (5 in.); very fragrant; foliage light; free growth.

Toy Balloon Min, *dr*, 1979, *Fairy Moss × Fire Princess*; Moore, R.S.; Sequoia Nursery. Bud ovoid, pointed; flowers dark red, dbl. (48 petals), high-centered, medium (1½ in.); slightly fragrant; foliage dark; bushy, spreading growth.

Toy Clown Min, *rb*, 1966, *Little Darling × Magic Wand*; Moore, R.S.; Sequoia Nursery. Flowers white edged red, semi-dbl., small; foliage small, leathery; bushy, dwarf growth. AOE, 1975.

Toy Soldier Min, *rb*, 1985, (CURtoy); *Pink Parfait × Over the Rainbow*; Curtis, Thad; Hortco, Inc. Flowers red-white blend, dbl. (20 petals), medium; no fragrance; foliage medium, medium green, semi-glossy; bushy growth.

Toyland Min, *mr*, 1977, Lyon. Bud ovoid; flowers indian red, semi-dbl. (10 petals), small (1 in.); slightly fragrant; foliage tiny; compact, bushy growth.

Tracey Wickham Min, *yb*, 1984, *Avandel × Redgold*; Welsh, Eric; Rose Hill Roses. Flowers bright yellow, petals edged bright red, dbl. (30 petals), HT-form, patio, small, in clusters of 3- 5; very strong fragrance; foliage medium, medium green, semi-glossy; upright.

Trade Winds HT, *rb*, 1964, *(Multnomah × Seedling) × (Carrousel × Seedling)*; Abrams, Von; Edmunds. Bud long, pointed; flowers dark red, reverse silver, dbl. (55 petals), high-centered, large (5 in.); very fragrant; foliage glossy; vigorous, tall growth.

Tradition HT, *mr*, 1965, *Detroiter × Don Juan*; Kordes, R.; McGredy. Flowers scarlet-crimson, dbl. (35 petals), large (4½ in.); a greenhouse variety.

Trafalgar Square F, *mp*, 1965, Van den Akker Bros. Flowers pink, dbl., large; vigorous growth.

Trailblazer F, *or*, 1975, *Albert × Orange Sensation*; Harvey, R.E.; Kimbrew-Walter Roses. Bud long, pointed; flowers orange-red, dbl. (22 petals), high-centered, medium (2½ in.); slightly fragrant; foliage glossy.

Trakiika HT, *dr*, 1974, *Tallyho × Spartan*; Staikov, Prof. Dr. V.; Kalaydjiev and Chorbadjiiski. Flowers dark red, dbl. (25 petals), cupped, large; fragrant; foliage dark; vigorous, upright, bushy growth.

Tranquility Cl Pol, *op*, *Princess van Orange sport*; Radmore. Flowers coral-salmon, rosette form, small, borne in trusses; foliage light green; vigorous growth. RULED EXTINCT 11/82.

Tranquillity HT, *ab*, 1982, (BARout; Handout; Tranquility); *Whisky Mac × Pink Favorite*; Barrett, F.; John Mattock, Ltd. Flowers pale apricot, peach and yellow blend, dbl. (35 petals), medium blooms borne singly; slight fragrance; foliage medium, dark, glossy; upright growth.

Träumerei® F, *ob*, 1974, (KORrei; ReiKOR; Dreaming; Reverie); *Colour Wonder × Seedling*; Kordes. Bud long, pointed; flowers orange, dbl., cupped, medium; very fragrant; foliage leathery; vigorous, upright, bushy growth.

Traumland F, *lp*, 1958, (Dreamland); *Cinnabar Improved × Fashion*; Tantau, M. Flowers light peach-pink, dbl. (20 petals), well-formed blooms in clusters; slightly fragrant; foliage dark, leathery; upright, bushy growth.

Travemünde® F, *mr*, 1968, (KORrantu); *Lilli Marleen × Ama*; Kordes; Buisman. Bud ovoid; flowers red, dbl., medium; foliage dark. ADR, 1966.

Traverser LCl, *yb*, 1928, Clark, A. Flowers yellow and cream, well-shaped blooms in clusters; vigorous, climbing growth.

Traverser LCl, 1928, Clark, A. Flowers yellow and cream, well shaped, clusters; vigorous, climbing.

Travesti F, *yb*, 1965, *Orange Sensation × Circus*; deRuiter. Flowers yellow to carmine-red, dbl. (38 petals), cupped, medium, in clusters; fragrant; foliage dark; vigorous, bushy.

Traveston Cl HT, *dr*, 1953, *Black Boy × Editor McFarland*; Ulrick. Bud long, pointed; flowers crimson, semi-dbl., medium; vigorous growth.

Traviata HT, *rb*, 1962, *Baccará × (Independence × Grand'mère Jenny)*; Meilland, Alain; URS, 1962; C-P, 1963. Bud ovoid, pointed; flowers bright red blending to white base, dbl. (30 petals), high-centered, large (4½ in.); fragrant; foliage leathery; vigorous, bushy.

Treasure HT, *ab*, 1929, *Golden Rapture × Fred Walker*; Fletcher; Tucker. Bud pointed; flowers apricot-pink, dbl., large (6 in.); foliage glossy, dark; very vigorous growth.

Treasure Chest HT, *my*, 1968, *Charlotte Armstrong × Fred Howard*; Whisler, D.; Germain's. Bud ovoid; flowers yellow, dbl., high-centered, large; slightly fragrant; foliage glossy; vigorous, upright growth.

Treasure Gold HT, *my*, 1950, *Pink Princess × Free Gold (HT)*; Brownell. Bud ovoid, pointed; flowers yellow, some petals splashed red, dbl. (38 petals), large (4 in.); fragrant; upright, branching growth.

Treasure Island HT, *op*, 1938, *Comtesse Vandal × Mme. Nicolas Aussel*; Raffel; Port Stockton Nursery. Bud long, pointed; flowers light salmon, reverse flaming coppery pink, base orange, dbl., high-centered, large; fragrant; foliage leathery, bronze; vigorous growth.

Treasure Island, Climbing Cl HT, *op*, 1941, Hennessey.

Treasure Isle F, *op*, 1967, *Seedling × Treasure Island*; Raffel; Port Stockton Nursery. Flowers salmon-pink, reverse coppery, dbl., small; fragrant; foliage glossy; vigorous, bushy.

Treasure Trove R, *ab*, 1977, *Kiftsgate × China (possibly Old Blush)*; Treasure. Flowers apricot, mauve-pink and cream, dbl. (23 petals), cupped, medium (1½-2 in.); very fragrant; vigorous.

Tribute HT, *dp*, 1983, (JACrose); *Seedling × Seedling*; Warriner; J&P. Bud long, pointed; flowers deep pink, dbl. (30 petals), loose form, large blooms borne singly; light fragrance; foliage large; reddish prickles, hooked down; upright growth.

Tricentenaire HT, *mp*, 1949, *Charles P. Kilham × Neville Chamberlain*; Lens. Bud long, pointed; flowers pink, center deeper, dbl. (25 petals), high-centered, medium; fragrant; foliage leathery, small; vigorous growth.

Tricia LCl, *lp*, 1942, *New Dawn seedling*; O'Neal. Bud long, pointed; flowers flesh-pink to ivory-pink, dbl., high-centered; very fragrant; foliage dark, glossy; vigorous (about 8 ft. in season) growth; hardy.

Tricia's Joy LCl, *op*, 1973, *Mme. Caroline Testout, Climbing × Blessings*; McKirdy, J.M.; John Sanday Roses. Flowers deep coral pink, dbl. (35 petals), large; fragrant; foliage medium, dark, semi-glossy; vigorous growth (to 18 ft.).

Tricolore G (OGR), *pb*, 1827, (Reine Marguerite); Lahaye Père. Flowers lilac-pink, fringed at edges, dotted and mottled white.

Tricolore HMult (OGR), *pb*, 1863, *R. multiflora × Seedling*; Robert et Moreau. Flowers lilac-pink, similar to Tricolore (G), blooms in small clusters; more vigorous than the preceding.

Tricolore de Flandre G (OGR), *pb*, 1846, Van Houtte. Flowers pale blush, striped bright pink, fading to mauve, dbl., small; fragrant.

Trier® HMult (OGR), *w*, 1904, *Probably Aglaia self seedling*; Lambert, P. Flowers rosy white, base straw-yellow, semi-dbl.; fragrant; height 6-8 ft.; (14).

Trigo HT, *ab*, 1931, Dickson, A. Bud long, pointed; flowers indian yellow, reverse apricot, tinted cerise, dbl., high-centered, large; very fragrant; foliage thick, bronze, glossy; vigorous growth. GM, NRS, 1931.

Trilby HT, *op*, 1927, Dobbie. Flowers rich salmon, dbl.

Trinity T (OGR), *w*, Well established in Bermuda. Flowers pale pink to white, gold stamens, semi-dbl., large (4 in.) nodding blooms borne usually singly; foliage dark; vigorous, spreading growth.

Trinity HT, *pb*, 1976, *Korovo × Seedling*; de Freitas. Flowers variegated pink and yellow, dbl., globular, medium; very fragrant; vigorous, upright, compact growth.

Trinket Min, *mp*, 1965, *(R. wichuraiana × Floradora) × Magic Wand*; Moore, R.S.; Sequoia Nursery. Flowers phlox-pink, dbl., micromini, small; foliage glossy; vigorous, bushy, dwarf.

Trintago HT, *mr*, 1962, *Souv. de Jacques Verschuren × Charles Mallerin*; Leenders, J. Flowers cardinal-red, dbl., well formed.

Trio F, *pb*, 1966, *Kordes' Perfecta × Shot Silk*; Dickson, A. Flowers gold and pink, well-formed, large; slightly fragrant.

Triomphe Angevin Pol, *mr*, 1934, Délépine; Pajotin-Chédane. Flowers cerise-red, semi-dbl., cupped, borne in clusters; slightly fragrant; foliage glossy; very vigorous growth.

Triomphe Briard F, *op*, 1958, *Seedling × Fashion*; Robichon. Flowers coral, dbl., borne in clusters; fragrant; foliage glossy; moderate growth.

Triomphe de Bolwyller HSem (OGR), *w*, *R. sempervirens hybrid*; Baumann, prior to 1837. Flowers white, center tinted yellow, globular, large; fragrant.

Triomphe de la Guillotière S, *w*, 1872, *Probably R. roxburghii × R. odorata*; Guillot Fils. Flowers white tinged pink.

Triomphe de la Malmaison HT, *dp*, 1946, Gaujard. Flowers dark satiny pink, very large, petals reflexed; very fragrant; foliage dark; vigorous growth.

Triomphe de la Terre des Roses HP (OGR), *mp*, 1864, Guillot Père. Flowers violaceous pink, full, large; moderately vigorous growth.

Triomphe de Laffay HCh (OGR), *w*, Prior to 1837. Flowers delicate flesh, changing to white, very dbl., expanded, large; pendulous habit.

Triomphe de l'Exposition HP (OGR), *mr*, 1855, Margottin. Flowers cherry-red, full (55 petals), large; vigorous, bushy growth; recurrent.

Triomphe du Luxembourg T (OGR), *pb*, Hardy; Prior to 1848. Flowers salmon-buff shaded rose.

Triomphe Orléanais Pol, *mr*, 1912, Peauger. Flowers cherry-red, semi-dbl., small (1½-2 in.) blooms in large clusters; slightly fragrant; foliage leathery, glossy, bright; vigorous growth.

Triomphe Orléanais, Climbing Cl Pol, *mr*, 1922, Turbat.

Tristesse HT, *m*, 1953, (Tristeza); *Charles P. Kilham × Betty Uprichard*; Camprubi. Flowers gray-mauve, dbl. (30-40 petals), flat, medium; slightly fragrant; foliage glossy; vigorous growth.

Triton HT, *yb*, 1978, *Colour Wonder × Tzigane*; Dickson, P. Flowers white to light yellow, petals edged pink, dbl. (47 petals), large; upright growth.

Triumphant HSet (OGR), *w*, 1850, *R. setigera × Seedling*; Pierce. Flowers white tinted flesh, dbl.

TRObspread S, *yb*, 1992, (Unforgettable); *Snow Carpet × Woodland Sunbeam*; Robinson, Thomas; Thomas Robinson Ltd., 1994. Flowers amber, moderately full (15-25 petals), large (7+ cms) blooms borne in large clusters; fragrant; foliage small to medium, dark green, glossy; some prickles; medium (90 cms), bushy, spreading (hemisphere shape) growth; repeats.

Trocadero HT, *mr*, 1964, *Karl Herbst × Seedling*; Delforge. Bud pointed, bright red; foliage bronze; vigorous growth.

Troika, Climbing Cl HT, 1964, Thomas, A.S.; Rumsey.

Troilus S, *ab*, 1992, (AUSoil); *(Duchesse de Montebello × Chaucer) × Charles Austin*; Austin, David; David Austin Roses, 1983. Flowers creamy apricot, very full (41+ petals), large (7+ cms) blooms borne in large clusters; very fragrant; foliage large, dark green, semi-glossy; some prickles; medium (110 cms), upright growth.

Troja HT, *w*, 1927, *Mrs. Herbert Stevens sport*; Mikes; Böhm. Bud long, pointed, cream-yellow; flowers creamy white, full; fragrant; vigorous, bushy growth.

Trojan Gr, *yb*, 1961, *Sutter's Gold × (Mme. Henri Guillot × Seedling)*; Abrams, Von; Peterson & Dering. Bud long, pointed; flowers pastel pink, reverse yellow, dbl. (40 petals), high-centered, large (5 in.); fragrant; foliage leathery; upright growth.

Trojan Victory HT, *dr*, 1986, (KORperki); *Seedling × Uwe Seeler*; Kordes, R.; J&P. Bud ovoid; flowers deep red, dbl. (50 petals), high-centered, exhibition, medium blooms borne singly; damask fragrance; foliage medium, medium green, semi-glossy; medium prickles, hooked downward; medium, spreading growth.

TROpat F, *or*, 1992, (Temptation); *Orange Sensation × Seedling*; Robinson, Thomas; Thomas Robinson Ltd. Flowers orange red, single (5 petals), large (7+ cms) blooms borne in small clusters; fragrant; foliage medium, medium green, semi-glossy; some prickles; low (70 cms), dense, bushy, compact growth.

Trophée LCl, *mr*, 1968, *Valenciennes × Étendard*; Robichon; Ilgenfritz Nursery. Flowers medium red; foliage glossy; vigorous, climbing growth.

Tropical Sunrise Gr, *dy*, 1992, (JOHillgold); *Golden Fantasie × Seedling*; Hoy, Lowell (Joseph H. Hill Co.); DeVor Nurseries. Flowers deep yellow aging to medium yellow, semi-dbl. (21 petals), high centered, medium (10 cms) blooms borne singly and in sprays of 1-3; slight fragrance; foliage medium, medium green, semi-glossy; upright, medium growth.

Tropicana HT, *or*, 1960, (TANorstar; Super Star); *(Seedling × Peace) × (Seedling × Alpine Glow*; Tantau, Math.; J&P, 1962. Bud pointed; flowers coral-orange, dbl. (33 petals), well-formed, large (5 in.); very fragrant (fruity); foliage dark, glossy, leathery; vigorous, upright growth. NRS PIT, 1960; GM, NRS, 1960, Portland, 1961; ARS (National Certificate), 1967; AARS, 1963

Tropicana, Climbing Cl HT, *or*, 1971, (TANgostar; TANgosar; Super Star, Climbing); Boerner; J&P.

Tropique LCl, *or*, 1956, (DELjis); D-C. Flowers orange-red, dbl.; foliage dark.

Troubadour R, 1911, Walsh. Flowers bright red, shaded maroon, dbl., large clusters; foliage large, glossy, dark; vigorous, climbing; free seasonal bloom. RULED EXTINCT.

Troubadour HT, 1956, Buyl Frères. Flowers rose-copper, dbl., large; strong stems; fragrant; moderate growth; free bloom. RULED EXTINCT.

Truby King F, *dp*, 1965, *Border Queen × Helen Traubel*; Harris, L.M.; Cutler. Flowers carmine, semi-dbl., open, large, borne in large clusters; very fragrant; foliage leathery, glossy, bronze; vigorous, tall growth.

True Love HT, *dr*, 1970, Delbard; Laxton; Bunyard Nursery. Flowers deep red, dbl. (30 petals), large (3½-4 in.); slightly fragrant; foliage glossy; moderately vigorous growth.

Truly Fair F, *w*, 1953, Ratcliffe. Flowers cream, center apricot, semi-dbl., small, borne in sprays of 4-5; fragrant; bushy growth.

Truly Yours HT, *ob*, 1972, *Miss Ireland × Stella*; Robinson, H. Flowers coral-salmon to orange, dbl. (44 petals), globular, large (5 in.);

very fragrant; foliage large; vigorous, upright. Edland Fragrance Medal, 1971.

Trumpet F, *my*, 1962, *Goldilocks × Capt. Thomas*; Abrams, Von; Peterson; Dering. Bud pointed; flowers yellow, semi-dbl. (15-22 petals), large (4 in.), borne in clusters; fragrant; foliage glossy; vigorous, upright growth.

Trumpeter® F, *or*, 1977, (MACtrum); *Satchmo × Seedling*; McGredy, S., IV; McGredy Roses International. Bud ovoid; flowers orange-red, dbl. (39 petals), cupped, large (3½ in.); slightly fragrant; foliage medium green, glossy; bushy, compact. GM, NZ, 1977, Portland, 1981; James Mason RNRS Medal, 1991.

Tsukiakari HT, *w*, 1984, *Utage × Anne Letts*; Ota, Kaichiro. Flowers creamy white, dbl. (35 petals), high-centered, globular, large blooms borne 1-3 per stem; no fragrance; foliage medium green, semi-glossy; medium prickles; bushy growth.

Tucker's Folly HT, *pb*, 1951, Fletcher; Tucker. Flowers glowing cerise overlaid orange, dbl. (35-40 petals), very large (6-7 in.); foliage bronze; very vigorous growth.

Tucker's Yellow HT, *dy*, *Max Krause sport*; Tucker. Flowers deep golden yellow.

Tudelum™ Min, *dp*, 1986, (KINlum); *Baby Katie × Watercolor*; King, Gene; AGM Miniature Roses, 1987. Flowers deep pink to lighter shades, petal edges darken on opening, fading deeper pink on edges, dbl. (30 petals), high-centered, exhibition, medium, borne usually singly or in sprays of 3-5; no fragrance; foliage medium, medium green, matt; straight, medium, light pink prickles; fruit none; upright, bushy, medium, vigorous growth.

Tudor HT, *mr*, 1953, (Pechtold's Flame); *Katharine Pechtold × Crimson Glory*; Verschuren-Pechtold; J&P. Flowers spectrum-red overcast scarlet-red, dbl. (20-25 petals), high-centered to flat, large (5 in.); long stems; fragrant; vigorous growth.

Tudor Prince Gr, *mr*, 1959, (Prince Philip); *Independence × Buccaneer*; Leenders, J. Bud long, pointed, chestnut; flowers bright red shaded geranium-red, dbl. (30-40 petals), large; foliage glossy, dark; vigorous, upright growth.

Tudor Victory HT, *dr*, 1987, *Queen Elizabeth × John Waterer*; Bracegirdle, D.T., 1988. Flowers dusky, dark red, reverse medium red, aging purple, dbl. (27 petals), high-centered, medium, borne in sprays of 2-3; slight, damask fragrance; foliage large, medium green, semi-glossy; prickles straight, large, red; upright, tall growth.

Tuhua R, *ab*, 1979, *Iceberg × Tausendschön*; Murray, N. Bud small, pointed; flowers apricot, 11 petals, blooms borne 3-5 per cluster; no fragrance; foliage small, glossy; small, red-brown prickles; vigorous, lax, tall growth; early bloomer with some repeat.

Tupperware HT, *pb*, 1981, *(Pink Peace × Queen Elizabeth) × (Kordes' Perfecta × Peace)*; Williams, J. Benjamin; Tupperware Home Parties. Bud ovoid, pointed; flowers carmine pink, reverse silver, dbl. (65 petals), high-centered to flat, borne 1-5 per cluster; fragrant; foliage large, dark, glossy; medium prickles; vigorous, upright growth.

Turenne HP (OGR), *dr*, 1861, *Général Jacqueminot sport*; Verdier, V. Flowers maroon; vigorous growth. This name has been applied to at least four varieties of doubtful class and questionable characteristics.

Türkes Rugosa Sämling HRg (S), *pb*, 1923, *Conrad Ferdinand Meyer × Mrs. Aaron Ward*; Türke; Teschendorff. Bud long, pointed; flowers peach-pink on yellow ground, semi-dbl., large; strong stems; very fragrant; foliage dark, leathery; vigorous (2½-3 ft.)growth.

Turlock High Min, *my*, 1991, (CLElock); *Rise 'n' Shine × Seedling*; Clements, John; Heirloom Old Garden Roses, 1992. Flowers bright yellow, full (26-40 petals), small (0-4 cms) blooms borne mostly singly; wonderfully fragrant; foliage small, dark green, semi-glossy; some prickles; medium (40 cms), upright, bushy growth.

Tuscany G (OGR), *m*, (The Old Velvet Rose); Prior to 1820. Flowers velvety blackish-crimson to deep purple, semi-dbl., large blooms with conspicuous yellow stamens; vigorous, upright growth. Perhaps identical to Gerard's *Velvet Rose* (1596).

Tutti-Frutti Min, *yb*, 1991, (JACtutti); *Fool's Gold × Pinstripe*; Christensen, Jack E., 1984; Bear Creek Gardens (J&P), 1991. Bud ovoid, pointed; flowers yellow with red-orange stripes, dbl. (25-30 petals), cupped, medium; slight fragrance; foliage medium, dark green, semi-glossy; bushy, spreading, medium growth.

Tutu Min, *pb*, 1978, *Over the Rainbow × Seedling*; Rovinsky; Meredith; Kingsdown Nursery. Bud ovoid; flowers pink and rose, dbl. (40 petals), high-centered, small (1 in.); slightly fragrant; upright, bushy growth.

Tutu Mauve F, *m*, 1963, D-C. Flowers magenta shaded mauve and rose, dbl. (30 petals), well-formed, large (4 in.); bushy, low. GM, Madrid, 1962.

Tutu Petite F, *pb*, 1967, *Rudolph Timm × Seedling*; Samuels. Flowers pink, reverse darker, semi-dbl., blooms in clusters; slightly fragrant; foliage glossy, light; compact, bushy.

Tuxedo HT, *dr*, 1988, (ARObrisp); *Portland Trailblazer* × *Olympiad*; Christensen, Jack; Bear Creek Gardens, 1988. Bud ovoid; flowers dark red, dbl. (45 petals), urn-shaped, large, borne singly; foliage medium, medium green, semi-glossy; prickles broad, hooked downward, red-brown; upright growth.

TV Times HT, *dr*, 1970, *Gallant* × *(Brilliant* × *Seedling)*; Dickson, A. Flowers crimson, dbl. (35 petals), ovate, very large (5½ in.); fragrant; foliage very large, dull; very free growth.

Tweedle Dee Min, *op*, 1987, (TINtwee); *Deep Purple* × *Cupcake*; Bennett, Dee; Tiny Petals Nursery, 1986. Flowers coral pink, reverse lighter, dbl. (35-40 petals), urn-shaped, small, borne usually singly; micro-mini; slight fragrance; foliage small, medium, semi-glossy; no prickles; Fruit globular, small, brown; upright, bushy, low growth.

Tweetie Min, *lp*, 1973, *Perle d'Or* × *Fairy Princess*; Moore, R.S.; Sequoia Nursery. Bud ovoid, long, pointed; flowers soft pink, dbl., small; slightly fragrant; foliage small, light, leathery; moderate, dwarf, bushy growth.

Twice as Nice HT, *rb*, 1984, *Peace* × *Mirandy*; Patterson, Randell E. Flowers white blending to red at edges, dbl. (40 petals), large; very fragrant; foliage large, dark, semi-glossy.

Twilight HT, *m*, 1955, *Grey Pearl* × *Lavender Pinocchio*; Boerner; J&P. Bud pointed; flowers lavender-lilac, reverse silvery, dbl. (30-35 petals), high-centered, large (4½ in.); fragrant; foliage dull green; bushy, upright growth.

Twilight Beauty Min, *m*, 1977, *Angel Face* × *Over the Rainbow*; Williams, E.D.; Mini-Roses. Bud long, pointed; flowers red-purple, dbl. (40 petals), high-centered, small (1-1½ in.); fragrant; bushy, spreading growth.

Twilight Dream Min, *m*, 1992, (MINdream); *Tom Brown* × *Twilight Beauty*; Williams, Ernest. Flowers mauve, good color stability, very full (41+ petals), high-centered, heavy substance, small (0-4 cms) blooms borne mostly singly; very fragrant; foliage small, dark green, glossy; few prickles; low (30 cms), bushy growth; hardy; good repeat.

Twilight Trail™ Min, *m*, 1985, (MINxco; MINsco); *Angel Face* × *Anita Charles*; Williams, E.D.; Mini-Roses. Flowers lavender-tan, dbl. (35 petals), small; very fragrant; foliage small, dark, semi-glossy; upright, bushy growth.

Twilight Zone Min, *mr*, 1985, *Scarlet Knight* × *Big John*; Hardgrove, Donald L.; Rose World Originals. Flowers medium red, dbl. (60 petals), well-formed, medium; no fragrance;

foliage small, dark, semi-glossy; bushy, dense growth.

Twin Pinks Min, *pb*, 1991, (CLEtwin); *Seedling* × *Seedling*; Clements, John; Heirloom Old Garden Roses. Flowers two-tone pink, moderately full (15-25 petals), exhibition, small (0-4 cms) blooms borne in small clusters; slight fragrance; foliage small, medium green, semi-glossy; some prickles; low (30 cms), bushy, compact growth.

Twinkie Min, *lp*, 1974, *(R. wichuraiana* × *Floradora)* × *Eleanor*; Moore, R.S.; Sequoia Nursery. Bud pointed; flowers light clear pink, dbl. (40 petals), small (1 in.); foliage small, glossy; upright, very bushy growth.

Twinkle Toes Min, *mr*, 1982, (LYOto); *Merry Christmas* × *Seedling*; Lyon. Flowers medium red, semi-dbl., small; no fragrance; foliage small, medium green, semi-glossy; very compact growth.

Twinkle Twinkle Min, *ab*, 1981, *Contempo* × *Sheri Anne*; Bennett, Dee; Tiny Petals Nursery. Bud pointed; flowers white with apricot petal edges, aging dark pink, dbl. (23 petals), blooms borne singly; very faint tea fragrance; foliage medium green, semi-glossy; very fine, curved prickles; slender, straight, upright growth.

Twinkles Min, *w*, 1954, *Perla de Montserrat* × *Polyantha seedling*; Spek; J&P. Bud flesh; flowers white, dbl. (43 petals), small; fragrant; dwarf (8 in.), compact.

Two-Timer Min, *ob*, 1990, (MORswiss); *Orangeade* × *Pinstripe*; Moore, Ralph S., 1982; Sequoia Nursery, 1991. Bud ovoid; flowers orange-red with lighter shades of orange and white striped, similar to slightly lighter reverse, aging similar but less intense, dbl. to very dbl. (up to 70 petals), high-centered, medium, borne usually singly or in sprays of 3-5; no fragrance; foliage medium, medium green, semi-glossy; bushy, spreading, low growth.

Twyford HT, *op*, 1939, Waterer. Bud long; flowers bright salmon-pink, base gold, reverse deep salmon flushed orange; fragrant; foliage dark, reddish; vigorous growth.

Tyler™ HT, *rb*, 1988, (Sebago); *(Tamango* × *Red Planet)* × *First Prize*; Poor, Cuyler. Flowers red blend, dbl. (15-25 petals), large; slight fragrance; foliage medium, dark green, matt; upright growth.

Tynwald HT, *ly*, 1979, (MATTwyt); *Peer Gynt* × *Isis*; Mattock. Bud ovoid; flowers cream, center yellow, dbl. (60 petals), large (5 in.); fragrant; bushy, upright growth.

Typhoo Tea HT, *rb*, 1974, (Doux Parfum; Été Parfumé); *Fragrant Cloud* × *Arthur Bell*;

McGredy, S. Flowers medium red, silver reverse, dbl. (50 petals), classic form, large (5 in.); fragrant; foliage small, glossy.

Typhoon HT, *ob*, 1972, (Taifun); *Dr. A.J. Verhage × Colour Wonder*; Kordes, R.; McGredy. Flowers salmon, shaded yellow, dbl. (35 petals), large (4 in.); very fragrant.

Tyriana HT, *dp*, 1963, *(Happiness × Independence) × Paris-Match*; Meilland, Alain; URS; Wheatcroft Bros. Bud pointed, ovoid; flowers rose-pink, dbl. (40 petals), well formed, large (4½-5 in.); fragrant; foliage leathery, dark; vigorous, upright growth.

Tyrius HT, *m*, 1972, *Bettina × Prima Ballerina*; Gandy. Flowers tyrian purple, dbl. (20 petals), large (5 in.); slightly fragrant; foliage glossy, bronze.

Tzigane HT, *rb*, 1951, (Tiz); *Peace × J.B. Meilland*; Meilland, F.; URS, 1951; Hennessey, 1956. Bud ovoid; flowers rose-red, reverse yellow, dbl., cupped to cactus-formed, large; fragrant; foliage dark, glossy, leathery; upright, bushy growth.

Tzigane, Climbing Cl HT, *rb*, 1958, Lagoona Nursery; Roseglen Nursery; Wheatcroft Bros., 1958; URS, 1960.

Uetersen® S, *mr*, 1939, (Zenith); *K. of K. × Stämmler*; Tantau. Flowers glowing red, semi-dbl.; upright, bushy growth; recurrent bloom.

Uhland HMsk (S), *yb*, 1916, *Geheimrat Dr. Mittweg × Tip-Top*; Lambert, P. Flowers reddish yellow, petals fringed, borne in clusters of 3-15; foliage pointed, like Tip-Top.

Ukrainskaia Zorka F, *mr*, 1955, (Ukrainian Dawn); *Independence × Seedling*; Klimenko. Flowers bright cinnamon-red, medium; slightly fragrant.

Ulmer Münster® S, *dr*, 1981, (KORtello); *Sympathie × Seedling*; Kordes, W., 1982. Flowers dark red, dbl. (35 petals), large; slight fragrance; foliage large, dark, glossy.

Ulrich Brunner Fils HP (OGR), *dp*, 1881, (Ulrich Brunner); *Variously reported as Anna de Diesbach sport or seedling and/or Paul Neyron sport*; Levet, A. Flowers geranium-red to carmine, full (30 petals), cupped, large; very fragrant; vigorous.

Ulrick's Buttercup F, *ly*, 1953, *Yvonne Rabier × Baby Alberic*; Ulrick. Bud ovoid; flowers light yellow, dbl., cupped, medium, borne in clusters; very fragrant; foliage bronze; very vigorous, bushy growth.

Ulrick's Gem F, *pb*, *Mrs. Tom Henderson × Self*; Ulrick. Flowers deep pink and white, very dbl., borne in clusters; foliage glossy; very vigorous, bushy growth.

Ulrick's Smokie F, *m*, 1953, *Mrs. Tom Henderson × Tip-Top*; Ulrick. Bud long, pointed; flowers smoky mauve, background white, very dbl., large, borne in clusters; very fragrant; foliage light green; bushy growth.

Ulrick's Yellow HT, *my*, 1953, *Mrs. Pierre S. duPont × Lady Hillingdon*; Ulrick. Bud globular; flowers yellow, center darker, dbl., cupped, medium; very fragrant; foliage light green; bushy growth.

Ulster Gem HT, *my*, 1917, Dickson, H. Bud long, pointed; flowers canary-yellow, single, large; slightly fragrant. GM, NRS, 1916.

Ulster Monarch HT, *r*, 1951, *Sam McGredy × Mrs. Sam McGredy seedling*; McGredy. Flowers apricot shaded buff, dbl. (50 petals), high-pointed, medium; slightly fragrant; foliage glossy, bright green; upright growth.

Ulster Queen F, *ob*, 1960, *Cinnabar × Independence*; McGredy, S., IV; McGredy. Flowers salmon-orange, dbl. (25 petals), well formed, large (3 in.), borne in clusters; slightly fragrant; vigorous growth.

Ulster Volunteer HT, *mr*, 1918, Dickson, H. Flowers brilliant cherry-red, base clear white, single, large (5-6 in.).

Una HCan (OGR), *ly*, 1900, *Tea × R. canina*; Paul. Flowers buff-yellow becoming creamy white, single and semi-dbl.; vigorous growth; non-recurrent bloom.

Una Hawken F, *ly*, 1972, *Arthur Bell × Arthur Bell*; Murray, N.; Rasmussen's. Bud ovoid; flowers butter-yellow to cream, dbl., cupped, medium; fragrant; foliage glossy, leathery; vigorous, upright, bushy growth.

Una Wallace HT, *dp*, 1921, McGredy. Flowers soft, even-toned cherry-rose, dbl., well formed; long, strong stems; fragrant; vigorous growth. GM, NRS, 1920.

Uncle Joe HT, *dr*, 1972, (El Toro; Toro); *(Mirandy × Charles Mallerin) × Seedling*; Kern Rose Nursery, 1971. Flowers dark red, very dbl., high-centered, very large; foliage large, dark, leathery; very vigorous, upright, tall growth.

Uncle Sam HT, *dp*, 1965, *Charlotte Armstrong × Heart's Desire*; Warriner; J&P. Flowers deep rose-pink, high-centered, large; fragrant; foliage dark, leathery, glossy; vigorous, tall growth.

Uncle Walter HT, *mr*, 1963, (MACon); *Detroiter × Heidelberg*; McGredy, S., IV; McGredy. Flowers crimson-scarlet, dbl. (30 petals), high-centered, large (5 in.); foliage leathery, coppery; vigorous, tall growth.

Undine HT, *ob*, 1901, *L'Ideal × Sunset*; Jacobs. Flowers dark orange, medium; fragrant; upright, bushy growth.

Unforgettable HT, *mp*, 1991, (JAChyp); *Honor × American Dawn*; Warriner, William; Bear Creek Gardens, Inc., 1992. Flowers medium pink, full (26-40 petals), large (7+ cms) blooms borne mostly singly; very fragrant; foliage large, dark green, semi-glossy; tall (140 cms), upright, spreading growth.

Unique Ch (OGR), *w*, Laffay. Flowers white edged pink, compact.

Unique LCl, *op*, 1928, *Tip-Top × Hybrid Perpetual*; Evans. Flowers bright fawn-orange-salmon; vigorous growth; recurrent bloom.

Unique Blanche C (OGR), *w*, 1775, (Blanche Unique; Vièrge de Clery; White Provence); *Resembles Cabbage Rose, of which it is presumed to be a sport.* Flowers white, sometimes tinged pink, dbl., large; fragrant.

Unique Moss M (OGR), *w*, 1844, *Unique Blanche sport*; Robert. Flowers pure white, occasionally tinted pink, full, well-mossed, large; shoots very spiny.

Unique Panachée C (OGR), *w*, 1821, *Unique Rouge sport*; Caron. Flowers white, faintly striped rose and lilac, dbl., globular, large; vigorous growth.

Unique Rouge C (OGR), *mp*, Prior to 1821. Flowers bright pink, medium.

United Nations F, *op*, 1949, *Mev. Nathalie Nypels × Rosamunde*; Leenders, M. Flowers salmon-pink, dbl. (26 petals), open, medium, borne in clusters; fragrant; foliage glossy; very vigorous, bushy growth.

Unity HT, *dp*, 1956, *Red Ensign sport*; Sansum. Flowers deep pink, reverse slightly darker, dbl. (45 petals), well shaped, large (5½ in.); very fragrant; foliage dark; vigorous, upright growth.

Universal Favorite R, *mp*, 1898, *R. wichuraiana × Pâquerette*; Horvath; W.A. Manda. Flowers soft rose, dbl., borne in large clusters; fragrant; vigorous, climbing growth.

Université d'Orléans Pol, *mr*, 1966, *Seedling × Ronde Endiablee*; Hémeray-Aubert. Bud globular; flowers red, semi-dbl., cupped, borne in large clusters; vigorous growth.

Unn F, *dp*, 1972, *Rimosa × Fidélio*; Lundstad. Bud ovoid; flowers deep pink, semi-dbl., open, medium; slightly fragrant; foliage glossy; dwarf, moderate growth.

Unser Stolz HT, *dr*, 1960, *Ena Harkness × Seedling*; Verschuren, A.; van Engelen. Flowers bright crimson-scarlet, dbl., large; foliage leathery, dark, glossy; upright growth.

U. P. Hedrick HSpn (OGR), *mp*, 1932, *R. spinosissima altaica × Betty Bland (probably)*; Central Exp. Farm. Flowers pink, single, open, large; fragrant; foliage soft, dark; vigorous (6

ft.), bushy, compact growth; profuse, non-recurrent bloom.

Upstart Min, *mr*, 1984, (JACup); *Merci × Fire Princess*; Warriner; J&P. Flowers medium red, semi-dbl., small; slight fragrance; foliage small, medium green, semi-glossy; upright.

Uptown Min, *m*, 1991, (TALuptown); *Azure Sea × Party Girl*; Taylor, Pete & Kay; Taylor's Roses, 1992. Flowers lavender, edges darker violet, reverse lighter, yellow base, full (26-40 petals), exhibition, medium (4-7 cms) blooms borne mostly singly; no fragrance; foliage medium, medium green, semi-glossy; some prickles; medium (46 cms), upright, bushy growth.

Urania HP (OGR), *dr*, 1906, *American Beauty × Suzanne-Marie Rodocanachi*; Walsh. Flowers bright crimson, dbl.; recurrent bloom.

Urdh HP (OGR), *mp*, 1933, *Victor Verdier × Papa Lambert*; Tantau; C-P, 1930. Bud long, pointed; flowers medium pink, dbl. (45 petals), high-centered, large; very fragrant; vigorous.

Ursula® HT, *mr*, 1968, (LAPon); *Jeunesse × (Peace × Independence)*; Laperrière; EFR. Bud ovoid; flowers clear red, dbl., open, medium; slightly fragrant; foliage glossy; vigorous, upright growth.

Uschi F, *dp*, 1972, *Marimba sport*; Tantau. Flowers dark pink, dbl., full, medium; slightly fragrant; foliage glossy, dark; vigorous, bushy growth.

Usha F, *dr*, 1975, *Orangeade × Seedling*; Indian Agric. Research Inst. Bud ovoid; flowers deep red, dbl. (35-40 petals), open, small (1½ in.); foliage soft; compact, bushy growth.

UT Tyler Rose Gr, *ob*, 1984, *Seedling × Seedling*; Weeks, O.L.; University of Texas at Tyler. Flowers orange, dbl. (35 petals), medium; slight fragrance; foliage large, medium green, matt; upright growth. Grown for campus beautification only.

Utage HT, *w*, 1977, *Edith Krause × Bridal Robe*; Ota. Bud pointed; flowers white, dbl. (30-35 petals), high centered, very large; foliage leathery; vigorous, upright.

Utro Moskvy HT, *mp*, 1952, (Morning in Moscow; Moscow Morn); *Frau Karl Druschki × Independence*; Shtanko, E.E. Flowers soft rose tinted carmine, dbl. (60 petals), large; slightly fragrant; foliage leathery, grayish; spreading growth. GM, International Exhibition, 1961.

Uttam HT, *lp*, 1969, *Elite × Open pollination*; Indian Agric. Research Inst. Bud pointed; flowers pastel pink, dbl., full, large; foliage glossy; vigorous, upright growth.

Uwe Seeler® F, *ob*, 1970, (KORsee; Gitta Grummer; Orange Vilmoria; Orange Vilmorin Rainer Maria Rilke; Reiner Maria Rilke); *Queen Elizabeth × Colour Wonder*; Kordes, R.; Kordes. Bud ovoid; flowers salmon-orange, semi-dbl., high-centered, large; fragrant; foliage large, glossy, bronze, leathery; vigorous, upright, bushy growth.

V for Victory HT, *ly*, 1941, *Golden Glow × Condesa de Sástago*; Brownell. Bud ovoid, long, pointed; flowers yellow faintly tinted orange, dbl. (45 petals), high-centered; very fragrant; foliage glossy; vigorous, bushy, compact to open growth.

Vabene HT, *my*, 1977, (MEItrogana); *Arthur Bell × (MEIgold × Kabuki)*; Meilland, M.L.; Meilland. Bud conical; flowers yellow, dbl. (30 petals), high-centered, medium; slightly fragrant; very vigorous, upright growth.

Vagabonde F, *ob*, 1962, *Mannequin × Fashion*; Lens. Bud long, pointed; flowers salmon-orange, dbl. (25 petals), high-centered, medium blooms in clusters of 3 or more; foliage dark, glossy; vigorous, bushy growth.

Vahine HT, *or*, 1964, Combe; Vilmorin-Andrieux. Flowers dark cardinal-red tinted orange; strong stems; vigorous, upright growth.

Vainqueur HT, *m*, 1937, *Sensation seedling*; Heizmann, E.; A. Meilland. Bud ovoid, dark red; flowers velvety purple, reverse dark red, very dbl., very large; long, strong stems; fragrant; foliage bright green; very vigorous growth.

Val De Mosa HT, *my*, 1968, *La Jolla × Cynthia Brooke*; Ellick. Flowers yellow, very dbl., (70 petals); fragrant; foliage dark, glossy; vigorous growth.

Vale of Clwyd F, *pb*, 1983, (BEEval); *Handel × Arthur Bell*; Bees Ltd. Flowers yellow, pink petal edges, dbl. (35 wavy petals), medium; no fragrance; foliage large, medium green, glossy; upright growth.

Valencia HT, *ab*, 1967, *Golden Sun × Chantré*, Kordes, R.; J&P. Flowers apricot-orange, dbl., high-centered, large; fragrant; foliage glossy, leathery; vigorous, upright growth.

Valenciennes LCl, *dr*, 1960, *Paul's Scarlet Climber × Seedling*; Robichon. Bud long, pointed; flowers dark red, semi-dbl., medium, borne in clusters; slightly fragrant; foliage dark, glossy; very vigorous growth.

Valentine F, *mr*, 1951, *China Doll × World's Fair*; Swim; Armstrong Nursery. Flowers bright red, semi-dbl. (18 petals), medium (2½ -3 in.) blooms in large clusters; slightly fragrant; foliage dark olive-green; spreading, bushy, compact growth.

Valentine Heart F, *mp*, 1989, (DICogle); *Shona × Pot o' Gold*; Dickson, Patrick; Dickson Nursery, 1990. Flowers medium pink, dbl. (15-25 petals), large; very fragrant; foliage large, medium green, glossy, purple when young; bushy growth.

Valerie F, *w*, 1932, Chaplin Bros. Bud pointed, yellow; flowers cream, large, borne in large clusters; foliage glossy, dark; bushy growth. GM, NRS, 1931.

Valerie Boughey HT, *op*, 1960, (Val Boughey); *Tzigane sport*; Fryer's Nursery. Flowers coppery salmon-pink, dbl. (36 petals), high pointed, very large (6 in.); fragrant; foliage leathery, glossy; vigorous, upright growth.

Valerie Jeanne Min, *dp*, 1980, (SAVaval); *Sheri Anne × Tamango*; Saville, F. Harmon; Nor'East Min. Roses. Bud globular; flowers deep magenta pink, dbl. (58 petals), high-centered, flat blooms borne 1-20 per cluster; slight fragrance; foliage very glossy; long, straight, thin prickles; vigorous, upright growth. AOE, 1983.

Valerie Purves HT, *mp*, 1940, Clark, A. Flowers pink, well formed; fragrant; vigorous growth.

Valeta F, *or*, 1960, *Signal Red × Fashion*; deRuiter. Flowers red shaded vermilion, dbl., open, borne in clusters (up to 20); foliage dark; vigorous growth.

Valiant HT, *mr*, 1948, *Poinsettia × Satan*; Boerner; J&P. Bud long, pointed; flowers bright red, dbl. (30 petals), high-centered, large; fragrant; foliage dark, leathery; vigorous, upright, branching growth.

Valldemosa F, *mr*, 1956, *Magrana × Radar*; Dot, M. Flowers fiery red, dbl. (20 petals), globular, large; foliage glossy; vigorous, open growth.

Valrose LCl, *w*, 1964, Mondial Roses. Flowers white suffused pink at edges, semi-dbl., medium, borne in clusters of 3-5; recurrent bloom.

Valstar HT, *dp*, 1962, Mondial Roses. Flowers deep pink, dbl., well formed, large; strong stems; very fragrant; foliage leathery.

Vamp Min, *dr*, 1981, *Fairy Moss × Fairy Moss*; Gatty, Joseph. Flowers dark red, single (5 petals), cupped blooms borne 3 per cluster; no fragrance; foliage dark; pointed prickles; angular habit.

Van Artevelde G (OGR), *dp*, Flowers deep pink, very dbl., petals imbricated in whorls, large.

Van Bergen S, *ly*, 1980, *(R. wichuraiana × Baronne Prévost) × Fun Jwan Lo*; James, John. Bud pointed; flowers light yellow fading to white, dbl. (48 petals), blooms borne 3, 5, 7 per cluster; mild, fruity fragrance; foliage small, glossy, dark; hooked, red prickles; vigorous, compact, bushy growth; repeat bloom.

Van Rossem's Jubilee HT, *op*, 1937, Van Rossem. Flowers bright carmine or coral; foliage glossy, bronze; vigorous growth.

Vanamali HT, *m*, 1978, *Lady* × *x ((Gruss an Teplitz* × *Seedling)* × *(Lake Como* × *Angel Face));* Viraraghaven. Bud long, pointed; flowers orchid-mauve, dbl. (35-40 petals), full, high-centered, very large (6 in.); fragrant; foliage dark, leathery; tall, vigorous, bushy growth.

Vanda Beauty HT, *dy*, 1971, *Gertrude Gregory* × *Seedling*; Gregory. Flowers deep yellow, dbl. (28 petals), pointed, large (3½ in.); fragrant; foliage glossy, dark; very free growth.

Vandael M (OGR), *m*, 1850, Laffay. Bud well mossed; flowers rich purple, edged lilac, full, large; vigorous growth.

Vanessa HT, *pb*, 1946, *Arch. Reventós* × *Lord Baden-Powell*; Leenders, M.; Longley. Bud ovoid; flowers coral, reverse yellow, dbl. (25 petals), large (4½ in.); very fragrant; foliage bright green; vigorous growth.

Vanguard HRg (S), *op*, 1932, *(R. wichuraiana* × *R. rugosa alba)* × *Eldorado*; Stevens, G.A.; J&P. Flowers orange-salmon, dbl., large; fragrant; foliage light, very glossy; vigorous (to 10 ft.) growth. ARS Dr. W. Van Fleet Medal, 1933; ARS David Fürstenberg Prize, 1934

Vanity HMsk (S), *dp*, 1920, *Château de Clos Vougeot* × *Seedling*; Pemberton. Flowers rose-pink, near single, blooms in very large sprays; very fragrant; foliage rich green, leathery; very vigorous (to 8 ft.), bushy growth; recurrent bloom; (21).

Vanity Fair HT, *lp*, 1942, *Better Times* × *Golden Rapture*; Roberts; Totty, 1944. Bud long, pointed; flowers cameo-pink, semi-dbl. (19 petals), high-centered, large; long stems; slightly fragrant; foliage soft; very vigorous, upright growth.

Vanto Pol, *dr*, *Dick Koster sport*; Vanto. Flowers dark red.

Variegata di Bologna B (OGR), *rb*, 1909, Bonfiglioli. Flowers white, striped purplish red, dbl., globular, large blooms in clusters of 3-5; fragrant; vigorous (6-8 ft.) growth.

Variety Club F, *yb*, 1965, *Columbine* × *Circus*; McGredy, S., IV; McGredy. Flowers yellow marked rose-red, dbl. (48 petals), well-formed blooms in clusters; slightly fragrant; foliage dark.

Varlon HT, *mr*, 1973, (Ilona); *Miracle* × *(Romantica* × *Edith Piaf)*; Verbeek. Flowers medium red, dbl. (40 petals), large (4-4½ in.); slightly

fragrant; foliage glossy, leathery, bushy growth.

Vasant HT, *yb*, 1980, *Sweet Afton* × *Delhi Princess*; Division of Vegetable Crops & Floriculture. Bud pointed; flowers yellow edged pink, high-centered blooms borne 10 per cluster; slight, spicy fragrance; foliage dark; straight, brown prickles; upright, bushy growth.

Vasco da Gama F, *mr*, *Pinocchio* × *Alain*; Moreira da Silva. Flowers velvety red.

Vassar Centennial HT, *pb*, 1961, *Helene de Roumanie* × *Confidence*; Meilland, M.L.; C-P. Flowers peach to shell-pink, dbl. (30 petals), high-centered to cupped, large (4½-5 in.); fragrant; foliage dark, leathery; upright, branching growth.

Vater Rhein HT, *dr*, 1922, *Kynast* × *Seedling*; Kiese. Flowers very dark red, dbl.; very fragrant.

Vaterland HT, *dr*, 1928, *National Emblem* × *Earl Haig*; Berger, V.; Pfitzer. Flowers dark red with coppery reflexes, dbl., large; fragrant; foliage bronze, leathery; vigorous growth.

Vatertag® Pol, *ob*, 1959, (Father's Day; Fête des Pères; Jour des Pères; Orange Muttertag); *Mothersday sport*; Tantau, Math. Flowers salmon-orange.

Vatican® HT, *ab*, 1967, (DELop); *Grande Première* × *(Sultane* × *Mme. Joseph Perraud)*; D-C. Bud ovoid; flowers apricot-yellow shaded carmine, dbl., high-centered, medium; slightly fragrant; foliage glossy; moderate, bushy growth.

Vedette HT, *mr*, 1951, *(Frau Karl Druschki* × *George Dickson)* × *Seedling*; Gaujard. Flowers brilliant red, dbl. (28 petals), large; fragrant; foliage leathery.

Veilchenblau HMult (OGR), *m*, 1909, (Blue Rambler; Blue Rosalie; Violet Blue); *Crimson Rambler* × *Erinnerung an Brod*; Schmidt, J.C. Flowers violet, petals streaked with white, center white, yellow stamens, semi-dbl., cupped, small (1¼ in.) blooms in large clusters on short stems; fragrant; foliage large, pointed, glossy, light; very few prickles; vigorous, climbing (10-15 ft.) growth; has been used as an understock.

Veldfire HT, *ab*, 1987, (KORgust; Wurzburg; Sunsation); *Seedling* × *Seedling*; Kordes, W., Sohne; Ludwigs Roses, 1988. Flowers orange, reverse chrome-yellow, dbl. (38 petals), large, borne singly; moderate fragrance; foliage glossy, medium green; prickles concave, yellow-brown; upright, well-branched, free-flowering growth.

Velizy® HT, *ab*, 1973, (DELsamour); *((Peace × Marcelle Gret) × (Michèle Meilland × Tahiti)) × (Peace × Grand Première)*; Delbard. Flowers apricot, dbl. (30 petals), well-formed, large; light fragrance; bushy, branching growth.

Velluto HMoy (S), *dr*, 1934, *R. moyesii × J.C. Thornton*; San Remo Exp. Sta. Bud long, pointed; flowers velvety dark crimson, stamens red, semi-dbl., medium; foliage dark; intermittent bloom.

Velour F, *mr*, 1967, *Garnette seedling × Hawaii seedling*; Boerner; J&P. Bud ovoid; flowers medium red, dbl., flat; fragrant; foliage glossy; vigorous, upright, bushy growth.

Velsheda HT, *lp*, 1936, Cant, F. Flowers softest rose-pink, dbl., well formed, large; strong, erect stems; fragrant; foliage dark; vigorous growth.

Velutina G (OGR), *m*, 1810, Van Eeden. Flowers velvety purple shaded violet, golden stamens, three rows of petals.

Velvet Beauty HT, *mr*, *Happiness × New Yorker*; Fisher, G.; Arnold-Fisher Co. Bud high pointed; flowers currant-red, dbl. (40-55 petals), high-centered to cupped, large (5-5½ in.); fragrant (clove); vigorous, upright growth; a greenhouse variety for florists' use.

Velvet Dreams Min, *dr*, 1982, (LYOet); *Seedling × Seedling*; Lyon. Flowers dark red, semidbl., small; slight fragrance; foliage small, medium green, semi-glossy; very miniature, upright, bushy growth.

Velvet Flame HT, *dr*, 1973, (MEImaur; Joséphine Baker); *Tropicana × Papa Meilland*; Meilland; URS. Flowers dark red, dbl. (30 petals), large (5-5½ in.); slightly fragrant; foliage dark; vigorous growth.

Velvet Fragrance HT, *dr*, 1988, (FRYperdee); *Seedling × Seedling*; Fryers Nursery, Ltd. Flowers deep crimson, dbl. (over 40 petals), large; very fragrant; foliage large, dark green, semiglossy; upright growth. Edland Fragrance Medal, 1987; Baden-Baden Fragrance Prize, 1990.

Velvet Hour HT, *dr*, 1978, LeGrice. Flowers oxblood-red, dbl. (44 petals), full, medium (3 in.); fragrant; foliage dark; vigorous, upright growth.

Velvet Mist™ HT, *m*, 1990, (Fragrant Lavendar); *Blue Ribbon × Shocking Blue*; Christensen, Jack, 1984; Flowers of the Month, 1990. Flowers deep lavender, borne usually singly, dbl. (25-35 petals), high-centered, medium, moderate to heavy, fruity fragrance; foliage large, medium green, matt, disease resistant; upright, bushy, medium to tall growth.

Velvet Queen HT, *dr*, 1965, *Fandango × Seedling*; Herholdt, J.A. Flowers blood-red,

pointed, large (4 in.); fragrant; moderate growth.

Velvet Times HT, *dr*, 1960, *Better Times sport*; Peters; J&P. Bud pointed; flowers rose-red, dbl. (40-50 petals), high-centered, large (4½-5 in.); very fragrant; foliage leathery; vigorous, upright growth; a greenhouse variety.

Velvetier HT, *dr*, 1946, *Pink Princess × Crimson Glory*; Brownell. Bud long, pointed; flowers deep velvety red, dbl. (28-35 petals), high-centered, large (4-5 in.); fragrant; foliage glossy; vigorous, upright growth; hardy for the class.

Velvia F, *mr*, 1992, (HARxample); *Dr. Darley × Trumpeter*; Harkness, R.; Harkness New Roses Ltd., 1991. Flowers medium red, full (26-40 petals), large (7+ cms) blooms borne in small clusters; slight fragrance; foliage medium, dark green, semi-glossy; some prickles; medium, bushy growth.

Vendôme F, *ob*, 1957, (GAUra); *Comtesse Vandal × (Fashion × Vogue)*; Gaujard. Bud long; flowers bright salmon, dbl., medium; fragrant; foliage dark, glossy; bushy growth.

Venezuela F, *op*, 1957, *Joanna Hill × Pinocchio*; Silva. Flowers salmon, edged dull red; very vigorous growth.

Venise HT, *rb*, 1946, *Joanna Hill × Margaret McGredy*; Meilland, F. Flowers red with silvery white reverse flushed salmon-carmine, dbl., large; spreading growth.

Venlo F, *or*, 1960, *Cinnabar × Fashion*; Leenders, G. Bud pointed; flowers orange-red, semidbl, flat, medium, borne in compact clusters; slightly fragrant; foliage dark; moderate, compact growth.

Venture S, *mp*, 1984, *(Charlotte Armstrong × (Cecilia × China Belle)) × Prevue*; James, John. Flowers medium pink, semi-dbl., medium blooms in clusters; fragrant; foliage medium, light green, glossy; upright, slender growth.

Venus HP (OGR), *m*, 1895, Schmidt, J.C. Flowers carmine purple.

Venus HT, *dp*, 1921, *J. Barriot × Sunburst*; Bees. Bud long, pointed; flowers carmine, edge flushed cream, very dbl.; fragrant. GM, NRS, 1922.

Venus F, *w*, 1955, *Pinocchio seedling*; Maarse, G. Flowers pure white, well shaped, borne in large trusses on long stems; vigorous, bushy growth.

Venusic® HT, *my*, 1966, (DELdra); *(Queen Elizabeth × Provence) × (Mme. Joseph Perraud × Bayadère;)* D-C. Flowers saffron-yellow, dbl., globular to cupped, medium; fragrant; foliage dark, glossy; vigorous, upright, bushy growth.

Venusta Pendula Ayr (OGR), *w*, 1928, *R. arvensis hybrid*; Origin unknown; Re-int. Kordes, 1928. Bud pink; flowers blush white, fading to creamy white, semi-dbl., small blooms in clusters (up to 20); nearly scentless; vigorous (to 15 ft.) growth; early flowering.

Venu-Vaishali HT, *pb*, 1970, *Astrée sport*; Deshpande. Bud ovoid; flowers light pink, striped white, base yellow, dbl., full, large; foliage large, soft; very vigorous, upright growth.

Vera HT, *op*, 1922, Paul, W. Flowers deep salmon, shaded coral-red, dbl.

Vera Allen HT, *op*, 1939, Dickson, A. Flowers salmon-pink, full, well formed, large; very fragrant; compact growth.

Vera Cruz HT, *pb*, 1938, *Frank Reader × Johanniszauber*; Moreira da Silva. Bud long, pointed; flowers pink shaded mauve, flushed red and yellow, dbl., high-centered, large; slightly fragrant; foliage soft; vigorous growth.

Vera Dalton F, *mp*, 1961, *(Paul's Scarlet Climber × Paul's Scarlet Climber) × (Mary × Queen Elizabeth)*; Norman; Harkness. Bud pointed; flowers soft pink, dbl. (24 petals), cupped, large (4 in.) blooms in clusters; fragrant; foliage glossy, dark; vigorous, bushy.

Vera Johns® Gr, *or*, 1977, (KORvera); *Seedling × Prominent*; Kordes, R.; Ludwig Roses. Bud ovoid, pointed; flowers orange-red, dbl. (40 petals), high-centered, large; slightly fragrant; foliage glossy, dark, leathery; vigorous, upright growth.

Verastella HT, *mp*, 1954, Giacomasso. Flowers rose, center deeper; strong stems; vigorous growth.

Vercors HT, *or*, 1946, *(Mme. Arthaud × Mme. Henri Guillot) × (Comtesse Vandal × Brazier)*; Mallerin; A. Meilland. Flowers brilliant orient red, dbl., globular, large; fragrant; vigorous growth.

Verdun Pol, *mr*, 1918, Barbier. Flowers vivid carmine-red, dbl., large blooms in clusters of 25-50; vigorous, dwarf growth.

Verena F, *dr*, 1973, *Lucy Cramphorn × Inge Horstmann*; Hetzel; GAWA. Bud ovoid; flowers dark velvety red, center lighter, dbl., medium; very fragrant; foliage glossy, bluish green; upright, bushy growth.

Vermillon HT, *or*, 1929, *Constance × Paul's Scarlet Climber*; Barbier; Dreer. Flowers scarlet tinged orange, base yellow, semi-dbl.; slightly fragrant.

Verna Mackay HT, *ly*, 1912, Dickson, A. Flowers buff to bright lemon-yellow.

Verona F, *lp*, 1963, *Spartan × Garnette*; Swim; Weeks. Bud long, pointed to urn-shaped; flowers light pink, dbl. (42 petals), high-centered, large (2½-3 in.); foliage leathery, dark;

vigorous, bushy growth; abundant bloom; greenhouse variety.

Veronica HT, *w*, 1950, Prosser. Bud pale yellow; flowers snow-white, dbl. (32 petals), imbricated, large (4½ in.); very fragrant; vigorous growth.

Veronique F, *mr*, 1961, *Sumatra × Philippe*; Delforge. Flowers bright raspberry-red, single (9 petals), large (4 in.), borne in clusters; foliage dark, glossy; vigorous, bushy growth.

Versailles® HT, *lp*, 1967, (DELset; Castel); *(Queen Elizabeth × Provence) × (Michèle Meilland × Bayadère)*; D-C. Bud ovoid; flowers soft pink, dbl., cupped, medium; slightly fragrant; foliage dark, glossy, leathery; vigorous, upright, bushy growth. GM, Baden-Baden, 1965, Bagatelle; Geneva, 1966.

Verschuren's Pink HT, *op*, 1950, *Mme. Butterfly × Pink Pearl*; Verschuren; Gregory. Flowers salmon-pink with darker reflections, dbl. (42 petals), high-centered, reflexed, large (3-4 in.); fragrant; foliage glossy, dark; very vigorous growth. GM, NRS, 1949.

Very Busy Min, *pb*, 1973, *Perle d'Or × Fairy Princess*; Moore, R.S.; Sequoia Nursery. Bud long, pointed; flowers pink and yellow, dbl., small; slightly fragrant; foliage small, leathery; dwarf, bushy growth.

Vesenii Aromat HT, *or*, 1955, (Spring Fragrance); *Crimson Glory × Peace*; Klimenko. Flowers red tinted orange, base lighter, dbl. (73 petals), medium; slightly fragrant; foliage dark, glossy; very vigorous, spreading growth.

Vesper F, *ob*, 1966, LeGrice. Flowers orange, reverse burnt orange, dbl., medium blooms in clusters; slightly fragrant; foliage small, blue-gray; moderate growth.

Vesta F, *mr*, 1946, *Irene × Donald Prior*; Leenders, M. Flowers currant-red, semi-dbl.; fragrant.

Vestal's Coral Gem HT, *op*, 1939, *Betty Uprichard seedling*; Vestal. Flowers soft salmon-pink, reverse glowing carmine with coppery sheen, dbl., large; foliage leathery, light; vigorous growth.

Vestal's Red HT, *mr*, 1937, Vestal. Flowers clear red, dbl., cupped, large; slightly fragrant; foliage leathery, light; vigorous growth.

Vestal's Torchlight HT, *rb*, 1939, *Pres. Herbert Hoover × Seedling*; Vestal. Bud long, pointed; flowers red and gold, dbl., open, large; slightly fragrant; foliage leathery, bronze; vigorous growth.

Vesuvius HT, *dr*, 1923, McGredy. Bud long, pointed; flowers dark velvety crimson, single (6 petals), large; fragrant; foliage light, leathery; vigorous growth.

Vesuvius F, or, 1963, Vilmorin-Andrieux. Flowers geranium-red, large; very vigorous growth. GM, Bagatelle, 1963.

Vevey HT, my, 1953, Heizmann & Co. Flowers sun-yellow, dbl., large.

Via Mala® HT, w, 1977, (ViaKOR); Silver Star × Peer Gynt; Kordes, W., Sons. Bud long, pointed; flowers white, dbl. (33 petals), high-centered, large (4 in.); slightly fragrant; foliage glossy, dark, leathery; vigorous, upright, bushy growth.

Vianden HT, pb, 1932, George C. Waud × Ruth; Ketten Bros. Flowers reddish old-rose and pink, reverse ocher-yellow and raw sienna, very dbl. (90-100 petals), large; very fragrant; vigorous, bushy growth.

Vicki Kennedy HT, pb, 1976, Queen Elizabeth × Red Lion; Murray; Hawken; Rasmussen's. Bud globular; flowers deep rose-pink, center yellow, dbl. (53 petals), large (4 in.); slightly fragrant; foliage large, bronze, upright, bushy growth.

Vickie Thorne HT, lp, 1972, Prima Ballerina sport; Thorne. Flowers light pink, dbl. (25 petals), large (4-4½ in.); very fragrant; foliage dark; vigorous growth.

Vick's Caprice HP (OGR), pb, 1891, Archiduchesse Elisabeth d'Autriche sport; Vick. Flowers lilac-rose, striped white and carmine, dbl., cupped, large; fragrant; medium growth; repeat bloom. A once-famous oddity.

Vicky HT, or, 1972, Canasta × Peace; Gaujard. Bud long, pointed; flowers orange-vermilion; fragrant.

Vicky Marfá HT, mp, 1958, (Soraya × Ellinor LeGrice) × Henri Mallerin; Dot, S. Bud ovoid; flowers begonia-pink, center yellow, dbl. (32 petals), high-centered, large; strong stems; fragrant; upright, compact growth.

Vicomte Maurice de Mellon HT, ab, 1921, Earl of Warwick × Sunburst; Ketten Bros. Flowers apricot and yellowish salmon with coppery reflexes, washed pink, dbl.; fragrant.

Vicomtesse de Bernis T (OGR), op, 1884, Nabonnand, G. Flowers coppery rose to fawn and deep salmon, full, large; very fragrant.

Vicomtesse de Chabannes LCl, rb, 1921, Buatois. Flowers purplish crimson, center white, forming a distinct eye, semi-dbl., large; vigorous, climbing growth.

Vicomtesse Pierre du Fou Cl HT, op, 1923, L'Ideal × Joseph Hill; Sauvageot. Flowers red aging to deep coral pink, dbl., large; very fragrant; foliage large, glossy, bronze; vigorous, climbing growth; recurrent bloom.

Victor HT, dp, 1918, Ophelia seedling × Killarney Brilliant; Hill, E.G., Co. Bud long, pointed; flowers deep rose, often red, semi-dbl.; very fragrant.

Victor Ferrant HT, dp, 1933, C.W. Cowan × Pres. Cherioux; Ketten Bros. Flowers carmine changing to purplish pink, base indian yellow, dbl. (60-70 petals), very large; slightly fragrant; vigorous growth.

Victor Hugo HP (OGR), dr, 1884, Charles Lefèbvre × Seedling; Schwartz, J. Flowers carmine-red shaded purple, dbl. (30 petals), globular, medium; fragrant; vigorous.

Victor Magnin Pol, mr, 1930, Van Gelderen. Flowers bright red, dbl., borne in large clusters; vigorous growth.

Victor Mayer HT, dr, 1921, Buatois. Bud long, pointed; flowers blood-red, reflexes deeper.

Victor Teschendorff HT, w, 1920, Frau Karl Druschki × Mrs. Aaron Ward; Ebeling; Teschendorff. Flowers almost pure white on pale greenish yellow ground, dbl., high-centered, very large; long stems; fragrant; foliage glossy, dark; vigorous growth.

Victor Verdier HP (OGR), dp, 1859, Jules Margottin × Safrano; Lacharme. Flowers bright rose, center carmine, dbl. (50 petals), globular, large; fragrant; vigorous growth.

Victor Waddilove HT, dp, 1923, McGredy. Bud long, pointed; flowers bright carmine-pink, base yellow, very dbl., large.

Victoria HT, dp, 1924, Isobel × Seedling; Prince. Bud long, pointed; flowers deep rose-pink, center darker, dbl.; very fragrant.

Victoria F, pb, 1946, Irene × Donald Prior; Leenders, M. Flowers carmine, center white, semi-dbl., large; fragrant.

Victoria HT, ly, 1947, Golden Dawn × Phyllis Gold; Robinson, H.; Baker's Nursery. Flowers pale lemon-yellow, large; fragrant; foliage dark; vigorous growth.

Victoria Cl F, or, Seedling × Alain; Moreira da Silva. Flowers clear geranium-red.

Victoria de los Angeles HT, or, 1952, (Victoria); Cynthia × Manuelita; Dot, P. Bud ovoid; flowers velvety geranium-red, dbl. (35 petals), medium; fragrant; vigorous, compact growth.

Victoria Harrington HT, rb, 1931, Diadem × Hadley; Thomas; H&S. Flowers very dark red shaded orange-brown, center lighter, dbl. (38 reflexed petals), large; very fragrant (spicy); foliage leathery, dark; vigorous growth.

Victoria Harrington, Climbing Cl HT, rb, 1938, Mordigan Evergreen Nursery.

Victoria Hyland HT, op, 1973, Seedling × Colour Wonder; Golik; Dynarose. Bud ovoid;

flowers red-pink to coral, dbl. (34 petals), large (4 in.); fragrant (fruity); foliage glossy; moderate, compact growth.

Victoria Regina HT, *yb*, 1938, *Nellie E. Hillock* × *Golden Dawn*; Hillock. Flowers golden yellow, reverse brownish yellow, sometimes blushed peach, dbl. (40 petals), very large; vigorous, compact growth.

Victoriana F, *ob*, 1977, LeGrice. Flowers orange, reverse silver, dbl. (28 petals), large (5 in.); slightly fragrant; foliage dark.

Victory LCl, *dp*, 1918, *Dr. W. Van Fleet* × *Mme. Jules Grolez*; Undritz. Flowers deep pink, center darker, dbl., large; fragrant; vigorous, climbing growth.

Victory HT, *dr*, 1920, McGredy. Flowers scarlet-crimson, dbl.; fragrant. GM, NRS, 1919.

Victory Red HT, *dp*, 1939, *Pink Delight sport*; Elliott. Flowers rose-red.

Victory Stripe HT, *rb*, 1942, *Jewel sport*; Grillo. Flowers cerise-red variegated white and light pink, dbl. (50 petals), large (5 in.); fragrant.

Victory Year HBlanda (S), *mp*, 1951, *Betty Bland* × *Seedling*; Wright, P.H. Bud ovoid; flowers clear pink, semi-dbl., open, medium; slightly fragrant; foliage leathery; very vigorous, upright growth; profuse, non-recurrent bloom.

Vidiago HT, *mr*, 1962, *Baccará* × *(S'Agaró* × *Peace)*; Dot, S. Flowers currant-red, reverse geranium-red, dbl. (26 petals), large; very vigorous growth.

Vidyut F, *dp*, 1983, *Europeana sport*; Yadava, U.N.; Tata Electric Co. Flowers deep pink.

Vienna Charm, Climbing Cl HT, *ob*, 1972, Gandy, D.L.; Gandy.

Vienna Maid F, *my*, 1957, deRuiter; Blaby Rose Gardens. Flowers empire-yellow, dbl. (30 petals), medium (2½ in.), borne in large clusters; foliage dark, glossy; moderately bushy growth.

Vierländerin F, *mp*, 1983, (KORvila); *(Zorina* × *Zorina)* × *Rosenelfe*; Kordes, W.; Kordes Roses, 1982. Flowers medium salmon-pink, dbl. (35 petals), large; fragrant; foliage medium, medium green, matt; upright growth; cut flower.

View® Pol, *dp*, 1980, (LENvie); *Britannia* × *R. multiflora*; Lens. Flowers deep pink, (7-15 petals), (2 in.) blooms in clusters of 3-32; no fragrance; foliage greenish-brown; hooked, brown prickles; low, bushy growth. GM, The Hague, 1978.

Vigane HT, *rb*, 1962, Buyl Frères. Flowers red and light yellow bi-color, dbl.

Vigilant HT, *dr*, 1941, *Night seedling*; Clark, A. Flowers very dark red.

Vigoro HT, *op*, 1953, *Ophelia* × *Federico Casas*; Dot, P. Flowers salmon-pink, dbl. (30 petals), high-centered, large; fragrant; foliage clear green; very vigorous, upright, compact growth.

Viking HT, *dr*, 1968, *Volcano* × *Happiness*; Moro; Ball. Bud ovoid; flowers crimson, dbl. (45-50 petals), large (4½-5½ in.); fragrant; foliage leathery, dark; vigorous, upright growth.

Viking Queen LCl, *mp*, 1963, *White Dawn* × *L.E. Longley*; Phillips; Univ. of Minn. Flowers medium to deep pink, dbl. (60 petals), globular, large (3-4 in.) blooms in large clusters; very fragrant; foliage dark, glossy, leathery; vigorous growth; recurrent bloom.

Viktoria Adelheid HT, *yb*, 1932, *Charles P. Kilham* × *Mev. G.A. van Rossem*; Kordes. Flowers golden yellow edged and shaded nasturtium-red, dbl., large; fragrant; foliage leathery, glossy; dwarf growth.

Vilia F, *op*, 1960, Robinson, H.; Gregory. Flowers bright coral-pink, single, medium (2½ in.), borne in large clusters; fragrant; foliage dark, glossy; moderate growth. GM, NRS, 1958.

Villa de Bilbao HT, *mr*, 1933, *O. Junyent* × *Margaret McGredy*; La Florida. Flowers cardinal-red, dbl., cupped, large; vigorous growth.

Villa de Madrid HT, *or*, 1965, *Baccará* × *Peace*; Dot, S.; C-P. Flowers vermilion-red to poppy-red, dbl. (60 petals), large; strong stems; fragrant (musk); upright growth. GM, Madrid, 1961.

Villa de Sitges HT, *op*, 1930, *Frau Karl Druschki* × *Mme. Edouard Herriot*; Munné, B. Flowers pink shaded salmon; very vigorous, spreading growth.

Villa Pia HT, *dr*, 1926, *Prés. Vignet* × *Château de Clos Vougeot*; Leenders Bros. Bud long, pointed; flowers velvety deep red, almost black, dbl.; fragrant.

Village Maid G (OGR), *pb*, (Belle Rubine; La Belle Villageoise; La Rubanée; La Villigeoise; Panachée Double); Prior to 1829. Flowers white, striped pink and purple (stripes varying in width, sometimes only one of the darker colors predominating), full, cupped, large.

Villandessa HT, *ob*, 1977, *Peer Gynt* × *Seedling*; Kordes, W., Sons; Willemse. Bud long, pointed; flowers orange-blend, dbl. (33 petals), high-centered, large (4½ in.); slightly fragrant; vigorous, upright, bushy growth.

Ville d'Angers HT, *mr*, 1934, *Souv. de Georges Pernet* × *Souv. de Claudius Denoyel*; Delaunay. Bud long, pointed; flowers pure currant-red, semi-dbl., cupped, large; foliage leathery, dark; vigorous, bushy growth.

Ville de Bordeaux HT, *dr*, 1955, Privat. Bud long; flowers dark scarlet-red, dbl.; fragrant; very vigorous growth.

Ville de Brest HT, *or*, 1942, Gaujard. Flowers fiery orange veined reddish copper, semi-dbl., globular, medium; slightly fragrant; foliage bronze, glossy; vigorous growth.

Ville de Chalons HT, *or*, 1938, Champion. Flowers reddish orange shaded darker, dbl.

Ville de Gand HT, *op*, 1951, *Georges Chesnel seedling × (Mme. Joseph Perraud seedling × R. foetida bicolor)*; Gaujard. Flowers deep salmon, dbl. (25 petals), well formed, large (3½ in.); fragrant; foliage bronze; very vigorous, upright growth. GM, Geneva, 1950.

Ville de Malines HT, *yb*, 1929, Lens. Bud long, pointed, yellow shaded cherry-red; flowers orange to pink shaded yellow; vigorous growth.

Ville de Nancy HT, *pb*, 1940, *Souv. de Claudius Pernet × Federico Casas*; Gillot, F.; C-P. Bud long, pointed, old-rose shaded gold; flowers buff-pink, edges penciled white, reverse light pink, base yellow, dbl. (50-55 petals), cupped, large; slightly fragrant; foliage leathery, dark; vigorous, upright growth.

Ville de Paris HT, *my*, 1925, *Souv. de Claudius Pernet × Seedling*; Pernet-Ducher. Flowers clear bright yellow, dbl., globular, large; slightly fragrant; foliage reddish green, glossy; vigorous, growth. GM, Bagatelle, 1925.

Ville de Paris, Climbing Cl HT, *my*, 1935, Armstrong, J.A.

Ville de Paris, Climbing Cl HT, *my*, Cognet.

Ville de Prague HT, *or*, 1940, Chambard, C.; Orard. Bud long, bright coral-red; flowers scarlet and copper, very large; foliage bright green; bushy growth.

Ville de Saverne HT, *or*, 1937, Heizmann, E. Flowers orange-scarlet, tinted brownish red, reverse tinted yellow, quite full, well formed, very large.

Ville de Valenciennes HT, *or*, 1954, *Peace × Seedling*; Gaujard. Flowers orange-copper, dbl., well formed, very large; fragrant; vigorous growth.

Ville de Zurich® F, *or*, 1967, *Miss France × Nouvelle Europe*; Gaujard. Flowers orange-red, dbl. (25 petals), well-formed; fragrant; foliage bright green; vigorous, bushy growth.

Ville d'Ettelbruck S, *dr*, 1983, (LENivill); *Satchmo × Skyrocket*; Lens. Flowers deep red, dbl. (20 petals), 2 in. blooms in clusters of 5-18; fruity fragrance; foliage dark, leathery;

hooked, green prickles; upright, bushy growth.

Ville du Havre HT, *w*, 1931, *K. of K. × Souv. de Claudius Pernet*; Cayeux, H.; Turbat. Flowers cream-white, washed rose-pink, base yellow, very dbl.; foliage dark; very vigorous growth.

Ville du Perreux F, *pb*, 1988, (DELrula); *Seedling × (Milrose × Legion d'Honneur)*; D-C. Flowers pink with white and cream, dbl. (28 petals), long, large; slight fragrance; foliage bright; bushy, vigorous growth.

Vim HT, *mp*, 1963, *Charlotte Armstrong × Applause*; Wyant. Bud pointed; flowers pink, single (5 large petals), medium; foliage soft; moderate, bushy growth; moderate bloom.

Vin Rosé HT, *mp*, 1969, *Revelry × Hawaii*; Boerner; J&P. Bud long, pointed; flowers light coral-pink, dbl. (30-35 petals), high-centered, large; slightly fragrant; foliage glossy; vigorous, upright growth.

Vincent Godsiff Ch (OGR), *mr*, Well established in Bermuda. Flowers deep luminous rosy-red, yellow stamens, semi-dbl. (10 petals), cupped, 2 in.; foliage dark; compact, upright (to 3 ft.) growth.

Vincent van Gogh Pol, *or*, 1969, *Allotria × Hobby*; Buisman. Bud ovoid; flowers orange-red, dbl., medium; foliage dark.

Vincenz Bergers Weisse HT, *w*, 1943, (Vinzens Berger's Weisse); *Mrs. Sam McGredy × Seedling*; Berger, V.; Kordes. Bud long, pointed, sulphur; flowers white, dbl., open, high-centered, very large; fragrant; foliage glossy, bronze; very vigorous, upright growth.

Vino Delicado HT, *m*, 1972, *Seedling × Mauve Melodee*; Raffel; Port Stockton Nursery. Bud long, pointed; flowers mauve, edged purple-red, dbl., well-formed, large; slightly fragrant; foliage large, leathery; upright growth.

Vintage Visalia F, *mp*, 1992, (MORlu); *Pink Petticoat × Lulu*; Moore, Ralph S.; Sequoia Nursery, 1993. Flowers medium pink, reverse of outer petals deeper pink than inside surface, excellent bud and open flower, very full (41+ petals), beautiful old garden rose form, large (7+ cms) blooms borne mostly single; slight fragrance; foliage large, medium green, semi-glossy; few prickles; medium (50-60 cms), upright, bushy growth.

Vintage Wine Cl HT, *rb*, 1982, (POUllack; Kirsch, Climbing; Lakeland Princess); *Royal Dane × Arthur Bell*; Poulsen, Niels; Roses by Fred Edmunds, 1983. Flowers burgundy red, straw-yellow reverse, dbl. (40 petals), exhibition, large; light old rose fragrance; foliage large, moss green; prickles red when new, then tan; pillar (8-10 ft.) growth.

Viola HT, *m*, 1955, *Orange Triumph × Peace* seedling; Gaujard. Flowers lilac-pink, dbl., very large; very fragrant; foliage leathery; vigorous, upright growth.

Violacée M (OGR), *m*, 1876, Soupert; Notting. Flowers purple, shaded violet to grayish pink, full, large.

Violaine HT, *m*, 1968, *Eminence × Simone*; Gaujard; Ilgenfritz Nursery. Bud long, pointed; flowers mauve, dbl., high-centered, large; very fragrant; foliage leathery; tall, vigorous.

Violet Carson F, *op*, 1964, (MACio); *Mme. Léon Cuny × Spartan*; McGredy, S., IV; McGredy. Flowers peach-pink, reverse silvery, dbl. (35 petals), well-formed, medium blooms in large clusters; fragrant; foliage dark, glossy; compact, bushy growth.

Violet Dawson HT, *m*, 1991, (RESone); *Paradise × Seedling*; Sheldon, John & Jennifer. Flowers mauve blend, full, medium blooms borne in small clusters; fragrant; foliage medium, dark green, disease resistant; medium, bushy growth; winter hardy.

Violet Fontaine S, *m*, 1972, *Seedling × Seedling*; Tantau; Ahrens; Sieberz. Bud ovoid; flowers violet-purple, dbl., large; slightly fragrant; foliage large, soft; vigorous, upright, bushy growth; abundant, continuous bloom.

Violet Hood S, *m*, 1976, *Robin Hood × Baby Faurax*; Lens, 1975. Bud ovoid; flowers dark violet, semi-dbl. (18 petals), pompon shape, small (1 in.); very fragrant; foliage ribbed, brownish; very vigorous, overhanging growth; recurrent bloom.

Violet Liddell HT, *pb*, 1904, Schwartz, A. Flowers light pink to white, center and reverse coppery salmon.

Violet Messenger LCl, *lp*, 1974, *Spek's Yellow, Climbing × Masquerade*; Cadle's Roses. Flowers shell-pink, base yellow, dbl. (30 petals), reflexed, large (6 in.); very fragrant; foliage large, matt green.

Violet Parncutt HT, *yb*, 1923, Easlea. Bud small, pointed; flowers brownish gold, semi-dbl.

Violet Queen HP (OGR), *m*, 1892, Paul, G. Flowers marbled crimson and violet.

Violet Queen HT, *m*, 1970, *Seedling × Violette Dot*; Northfield. Flowers deep violet-pink, dbl. (35-40 petals), pointed, large (4 in.); very fragrant; foliage dark; upright, free growth.

Violet Simpson HT, *op*, 1930, Simpson; Laxton Bros.; H&S. Flowers vivid prawn-pink, base yellow, dbl.; fragrant; foliage purple.

Violet Wilton HT, *mp*, 1930, *Gen. MacArthur × Mme. Charles Lutaud*; Ketten Bros. Bud

very long, pointed; flowers bright rose-pink on flesh-white ground, tinted yellow, full (35-40 petals), large; fragrant; vigorous growth.

Violetera HT, *m*, 1980, (Embruixada); Dot, Simon; Barni-Pistoia, Rose. Bud ovoid; flowers reddish-mauve, dbl. (30 petals), shallow-cupped blooms borne singly to 3 per cluster; strong fragrance; foliage medium, light green, matt; curved, reddish-green prickles; bushy growth.

Violetta HT, *m*, 1957, *Peace × Guinée*; Croix, A. Flowers mauve; very fragrant; foliage glossy; vigorous growth.

Violette HMult (OGR), *m*, 1921, Turbat. Flowers pure deep violet, very dbl., blooms in large clusters; vigorous growth.

Violette Bouyer HP (OGR), *w*, 1881, *Jules Margottin × Sombreuil*; Lacharme. Flowers pinkish white, cupped, large; fragrant.

Violette Dot HT, *m*, 1960, *Rosa de Friera × Prélude*; Dot, S. Flowers ageratum-blue, semi-dbl. (20 petals), medium; strong stems; fragrant; spreading growth.

Violine S, *m*, 1985, (LENdadi); *(Little Angel × Picasso) × Skyrocket*; Lens. Flowers lilac, pink, white blend, dbl. (20 petals), 2 in. blooms in clusters of 5-28; fruity fragrance; foliage light green; few, small, brown prickles; upright, bushy growth.

Violinista Costa HT, *rb*, 1936, *Sensation × Shot Silk*; Camprubi. Flowers red to deep purplish red, well-formed, large; fragrant; vigorous growth; (28).

Violoncelliste Albert Fourès HT, *ab*, 1920, *Joseph Hill × Seedling*; Croibier. Flowers orange-yellow, shaded buff-yellow, dbl.

Víra HRg (S), *mr*, 1936, Böhm. Flowers bright red; very fragrant; very vigorous growth.

Virgen de Farnés HT, *mp*, 1960, *Queen Elizabeth × Virgo*; Dot, M. Flowers bright rose, reverse lighter, dbl. (26 petals), well formed; strong stems; very fragrant; vigorous growth.

Virginia LCl, *ob*, 1934, *Magnafrano × Eldorado*; Nicolas; C-P. Flowers brilliant flame, suffused gold, dbl., open, large; fragrant; foliage large, dark; vigorous, climbing (9 ft.) growth; non-recurrent bloom.

Virginia Dare HT, *dp*, 1934, *Joanna Hill × Seedling (dark red)*; Thompson's, J.H., Sons. Bud long, pointed; flowers deep cerise-pink, dbl., large; long stems; fragrant; foliage leathery, dark; very vigorous growth.

Virginia Lee Min, *yb*, 1989, (MIClee); *Rise 'n' Shine × Baby Katie*; Williams, Michael C.; The Rose Garden. Bud ovoid; flowers creamy yellow with pink border, reverse creamy yellow, aging pink, dbl. (30 petals), cupped, medium, borne usually singly; no fragrance; foliage medium, dark green, glossy; prickles straight, green; fruit globular, green to orange-yellow; slightly spreading, medium growth.

Virginia Reel S, *dp*, 1975, *Tickled Pink* × *Prairie Princess*; Buck; Iowa State Univ. Bud ovoid, pointed; flowers light red, dbl. (40 petals), cupped, large (4-4½ in.); fragrant; foliage large, dark, leathery; erect, bushy growth.

Virgo HT, *w*, 1947, (Virgo Liberationem); *Blanche Mallerin* × *Neige Parfum*; Mallerin; Meilland-Richardier. Flowers white, sometimes blush-pink, dbl. (30 petals), high-centered, large (5 in.); slightly fragrant; foliage dark, leathery; vigorous growth. GM, NRS, 1949.

Virgo, Climbing Cl HT, *w*, 1957, Mondial Roses.

Virolay HT, *ob*, Camprubi. Flower edges orange-red, base deep yellow, high-centered, large; very fragrant; vigorous growth.

Vi's Violet Min, *m*, 1991, (MORvi); *Seedling* × *Angel Face*; Moore, Ralph S. Flowers soft lavender, full, small, slight fragrance; foliage small, medium green, matt; upright, bushy, compact growth.

Visa HT, *mr*, 1972, (MEIred); *(Baccará* × *Queen Elizabeth)* × *Lovita*; Meilland. Flowers turkey-red, dbl. (38 petals), high-centered, large (5 in.); slightly fragrant; foliage large, leathery; vigorous, upright growth.

Viscount Southwood HT, *pb*, 1949, *Walter Bentley* × *Aribau*; Cobley; Harkness. Flowers china-pink shaded creamy peach to copper, dbl. (35-40 petals), high-centered, large (4-5 in.); vigorous growth.

Viscountess Charlemont HT, *mp*, 1937, McGredy. Bud salmon-rose; flowers satiny rose-pink, base deep buttercup-yellow, dbl., large; very fragrant; foliage dark cedar green; branching growth. GM, NRS, 1936.

Viscountess Devonport HT, *dy*, 1923, Hicks. Flowers rich indian yellow, dbl.

Viscountess Enfield HT, *pb*, 1910, *Seedling* × *Soleil d'Or seedling*; Pernet-Ducher. Flowers coppery old-rose, shaded yellow.

Viscountess Falmouth HT, *pb*, 1879, *Adam* × *Soupert et Notting*; Bennett. Flowers mottled pink, dbl., globular, very large; fragrant; dwarf, thorny growth.

Viscountess Folkestone HT, *pb*, 1886, Bennett. Flowers creamy silver-pink, center deep salmon-pink, dbl.; fragrant.

Vision® HT, *pb*, 1967, *Kordes' Perfecta* × *Peace*; Dickson, A. Flowers gold and pink, dbl., large (5½ in.); slightly fragrant; foliage glossy

Vital Spark F, *ab*, 1982, (COCacert); *(Anne Cocker* × *(Sabine* × *Circus))* × *Yellow Pages*; Cocker, James; Cocker & Sons. Flowers gold, flushed coral, dbl. (35 petals), medium; slight fragrance; foliage medium, medium green, semi-glossy; bushy growth.

Vittonville-Rose HT, *ob*, 1945, Mallerin; A. Meilland. Flowers orange, base yellow, reverse lighter; vigorous growth.

Viuda Verdaguer HT, *ob*, 1934, *Shot Silk* × *Mari Dot*; Dot, P. Flowers orange, dbl., open, very large; foliage glossy, dark; very vigorous growth.

Viva F, *dr*, 1974, (JACiv); *Seedling* × *Seedling*; Warriner; J&P. Bud ovoid; flowers dark red, dbl., high-centered, medium; slightly fragrant; foliage glossy, dark; vigorous, upright growth. GM, Portland, 1984.

Vivacé F, *or*, 1974, *Klaus Störtebeker* × *Seedling*; Kordes. Flowers orange-red, dbl., high-centered, large; slightly fragrant; foliage large, leathery; very vigorous, upright growth.

Vivacious F, *mp*, 1971, *Tropicana* × *Seedling*; Gregory. Flowers phlox-pink, dbl. (35 petals), large (4 in.); fragrant; very free growth.

Vivacious Dianne HT, *or*, 1989, (CHRisjevans); *Voodoo* × *Hello Dolly*; Christensen, Jack E. Flowers orange-red, dbl. (33 petals), medium; slight fragrance; foliage medium, medium green, semi-glossy; upright, bushy growth.

Vivaldi S, *mr*, 1984, (LENmobar); *R. multiflora seedling* × *(Seedling* × *Robin Hood)*; Lens. Flowers medium red, single (5 petals), 1 in. blooms in clusters of 7-50; foliage small; very hooked, greenish-brown prickles; bushy, spreading growth.

Vivastella HT, *dp*, *Julien Potin* × *Sensation*; Aicardi, D.; Giacomasso. Flowers laque de Robbie color (possibly carmine), well shaped.

Vive la France HT, *rb*, 1944, *Shining Star* × *Mme. Arthaud*; Mallerin; A. Meilland. Bud pointed, well formed; flowers purplish red, reverse yellow, dbl., large; slightly fragrant; foliage glossy; vigorous growth. GM, Bagatelle, 1943.

Vivian Morelle T (OGR), *w*, Bud cream; flowers snow-white; profuse bloom.

Vivid B (OGR), *m*, 1853, Paul, A. Flowers brilliant magenta to magenta-pink, fully dbl.; fragrant; foliage glossy; robust, prickly growth; height to 6 ft.

Vivid F, *or*, 1951, LeGrice. Flowers brilliant orange-scarlet, single (5-7 petals), large (3½ in.), borne in huge clusters; compact growth.

Vivid Mason HT, *dp*, 1934, *Premier* × *Mme. Alexandre Dreux*; Mason, J.A.; McLellan Co.

Flowers vivid dark pink, base yellow, dbl., large; foliage leathery, glossy; very vigorous growth.

Vivien HT, *dp*, 1922, Paul, W. Flowers deep rose-pink, dbl.; very fragrant.

Vivien Leigh HT, *mr*, 1963, *Queen Elizabeth × Detroiter*; McGredy, S., IV; Fisons Horticulture. Flowers crimson, dbl. (35 petals), high-centered, large (5 in.); fragrant; foliage dark; very free growth.

Vixen Min, *or*, 1988, (JACormin); *Petticoat × Red Minimo*; Warriner, William; Bear Creek Gardens, 1990. Bud ovoid, pointed, green with reddish-brown; flowers red-orange with yellow base, aging red-orange to pink orange, dbl. (28 petals), cupped, medium, borne in sprays of 5-35; no fragrance; foliage medium, medium green, semi-glossy, small; prickles small, straight, reddish-brown; bushy, spreading, low growth.

Vlam HT, *or*, 1956, *Tawny Gold × Sarie Mareis*; Leenders, M. Flowers fiery red, dbl.; fragrant; vigorous growth.

Vltava LCl, *m*, 1936, *Veilchenblau × Seedling*; Böhm. Flowers violet, passing to purplish red, dbl., globular, large, borne in clusters; foliage glossy; very vigorous, climbing growth.

Voeux de Bonheur HT, *pb*, 1960, (Bon Voyage); *Michèle Meilland × Chic Parisien*; D-C. Flowers creamy white, petals edged cerise-pink, reverse white, dbl., high-centered, large; very fragrant; foliage dark, glossy; vigorous growth.

Vogue F, *pb*, 1951, *Pinocchio × Crimson Glory*; Boerner; J&P. Bud ovoid; flowers cherry-coral, dbl. (25 petals), high-centered, large (3½-4½ in.) blooms in clusters; fragrant; foliage glossy; vigorous, upright, bushy, compact growth; (28). GM, Portland; Geneva, 1950; AARS, 1952.

Voie Lactée Cl HT, *w*, 1949, *Frau Karl Druschki × Julien Potin*; Robichon. Bud globular, creamy white; flowers white, dbl., large; very fragrant; foliage glossy; very vigorous, climbing growth.

Vol de Nuit HT, *m*, 1983, (DELrio; Night Flight); *(Holstein × (Bayadère × Prélude)) × Saint-Exupery*; Delbard, G., 1970. Flowers deep lilac, dbl. (33 petals), large; very fragrant; foliage medium, light green, matt; bronze-red prickles; bushy growth. GM, Rome, 1970.

Volare HT, *dr*, 1976, McDaniel; Carlton Rose Nursery. Bud ovoid; flowers bright red, dbl. (38-44 petals), high-centered, large (3½ in.); flora-tea; slightly fragrant; foliage leathery; bushy, upright growth.

Volcano HT, *dp*, 1950, *Charles P. Kilham × Rome Glory*; Moro; J&P. Bud long, pointed; flowers cherry-red, dbl. (25 petals), cupped, very large (6½ in.); fragrant (fruity); foliage dark; vigorous, upright growth.

Volunteer F, *yb*, 1985, (HARquaker); *Dame of Sark × Silver Jubilee*; Harkness, R., 1986. Flowers yellow blend, dbl. (35 petals), large; slight fragrance; foliage medium, light, glossy; bushy.

Von Hötzendorf HP (OGR), *pb*, 1916, *Frau Karl Druschki × Beauté de Lyon*; Schmidt, J.C. Flowers golden rose-pink, richly tinted coppery red, dbl.; fragrant; vigorous growth.

Von Liliencron HFt (OGR), *pb*, 1916, *Geheimrat Dr. Mittweg × Mrs. Aaron Ward*; Lambert, P. Flowers yellowish light pink with white, reverse salmon-pink, stamens yellow, dbl., high-centered, small, borne in clusters; fragrant; foliage glossy, dark, bronze; vigorous (6 ft.) growth; profuse bloom, sometimes recurrent.

Von Scharnhorst S, *ly*, 1921, *Frau Karl Druschki × Gottfried Keller*; Lambert, P. Flowers yellow to yellowish-white, semi-dbl.; slightly fragrant; vigorous (6-8 ft.); recurrent.

Voodoo™ HT, *ob*, 1984, (AROmiclea); *((Camelot × First Prize) × Typhoo Tea) × Lolita*; Christensen; Armstrong Nursery, 1986. Flowers salmon, yellow, orange and red blend, dbl. (35 petals), exhibition, large; rich fragrance; foliage medium, dark, very glossy; upright, bushy, tall growth. AARS, 1986.

Voorburg F, *op*, 1959, *Sangerhausen × Vogue*; Buisman. Flowers salmon-pink, semi-dbl., borne in large clusters; foliage bronze to dark; vigorous growth.

Vorbergii HFt (OGR), *ly*, (R. × *harisonii vorbergii* Rehder; *R. vorbergli* Graebner ex Spaeth); *R. foetida × R. spinosissima*. Flowers pale yellow, single.

Vox Populi HT, *dr*, 1945, Mallerin. Flowers velvety dark red, semi-dbl.

Vulcain HP (OGR), *dr*, 1861, Verdier, V. Flowers rich dark crimson, well formed.

Vulcain Pol, *mr*, 1921, Turbat. Flowers deep cherry-red, dbl.; vigorous growth.

Vulcana LCl, *dr*, 1964, Mondial Roses. Flowers blood-red, semi-dbl., borne in clusters; vigorous growth.

Vulcania HT, *mr*, 1948, *Matador × Principe di Piemonte*; Giacomasso. Bud long; flowers purplish red, well formed, very large; foliage dark.

Vuurbaak F, *or*, 1946, *Florentina × World's Fair*; Leenders, M.; Longley. Flowers scarlet, semi-dbl. (15 petals), open, large (4 in.), borne in clusters; foliage reddish green; vigorous, upright growth.

V. Viviand Morel T (OGR), *dr,* Flowers rich crimson shaded dark red and carmine, full, large.

Wabash Dawn S, *op,* 1978, *(Queen Elizabeth × Gladiator)* × *(Aztec × Little Darling)*; Williams, J.B.; Krider Nursery. Bud tapered; flowers bright orange-pink, dbl. (34 petals), high-centered, large (4-4½ in.); very fragrant; foliage large, glossy; vigorous, upright growth; repeat bloom.

W. A. Bilney HT, *ab,* 1927, Easlea. Flowers pale apricot suffused cerise, reverse yellow tinted pink, large, not very full; slightly fragrant; foliage dark, leathery; vigorous growth.

Wadei HRg (S), *mp, R. rugosa × Seedling.* Flowers pink, single; foliage rich green; weak, prostrate growth; of curiosity value only.

Wagbi F, *ob,* 1981, (BleBAR); Barrett, F.H.; John Mattock, Ltd. Bud pointed; flowers orange-pink, dbl. (20 petals), flat blooms borne 3-5 per cluster; fragrant; foliage large, dark; large, red prickles; vigorous, upright growth.

Wageningen Pol, *my,* 1968, *Golden Giant × Peace*; Buisman. Bud ovoid; flowers yellow, dbl., medium; foliage dark.

Waiheke™ Gr, *op,* 1986, (MACwaihe; Waikiki); *Tony Jacklin × Young Quinn*; McGredy, Sam, 1985; Co-Operative Rose Growers, 1987. Flowers coral-pink fading lighter, semi-dbl. (30 petals), high-centered, exhibition, medium, borne in sprays of 5-9; slight, spicy fragrance; foliage medium, dark green, glossy; small, green prickles; fruit ovoid, small, tan-orange; upright, bushy growth.

Waikato HT, *mr,* 1990, (MAChoro); *Candella × Auckland Metro*; McGredy, Sam; Sam McGredy Roses International. Flowers medium red, moderate (15-25 petals), large blooms; fragrant; foliage large, medium green, matt; bushy growth.

Waipounamu HT, *yb,* 1982, *Peace × Blue Moon*; Cattermole, R.F. Flowers creamy yellow, shaded mauve-pink on outer petals, dbl. (50 petals), exhibition blooms in clusters of 3; very fragrant; foliage bronze green, glossy; upright growth.

Waitmata® Min, *rb,* 1978, (MACweemat; Wąitemata; Wee Matt); *Wee Man × Matangi*; McGredy, S., IV; McGredy Roses Int., 1980. Flowers red blend, dbl. (42 petals), medium; slightly fragrant; foliage light green, glossy; bushy growth.

Waitziana S, *dp,* (*R. × waitziana* Trattinnick); *R. canina × R. gallica*; Cult. 1874. Flowers deep rose, about 2½ in. diam., often solitary.

Waldfee HP (OGR), *mr,* 1960, Kordes, R. Flowers blood-red, dbl., camellia-shaped, large (4 in.) blooms in small clusters; fragrant; foliage glossy; vigorous, tall (10 ft.), dense growth; recurrent bloom.

Waldtraut Nielsen M (OGR), *dp,* Flowers clear deep pink, large.

Walko F, *dr,* 1957, (DELde); *(Incendie × Holstein) × Rouge Chabert*; D-C. Flowers dark crimson, dbl. (23 petals), blooms in clusters of 6-8; fragrant.

Walküre HT, *w,* 1919, *Frau Karl Druschki × Mme. Jenny Gillemot*; Ebeling. Bud long, pointed; flowers cream-white, center ocheryellow, dbl.

Walkyrie HT, *dr,* 1959, *Happiness × Volcano*; Moro. Bud urn shaped or ovoid; flowers dark red, low-centered, large; bushy growth.

Walsham Gold HT, *my,* 1965, LeGrice; Wayside Gardens Co. Flowers yellow with burnished gold and copper overtones in cool weather.

Walter HT, *dp,* 1949, *Charles P. Kilham × Comtesse Vandal*; Lens. Bud long, pointed; flowers pink, reverse vivid rosy red, semi-dbl. (20 petals), open, very large; very fragrant; foliage bronze, leathery; very vigorous, bushy growth.

Walter Bentley HT, *op,* 1938, *Mrs. Sam McGredy × Dame Edith Helen*; Robinson, H.; Wheatcroft Bros. Bud long, pointed; flowers coppery orange shaded pink, dbl., high-centered, very large; slightly fragrant; foliage leathery, glossy, dark, bronze; vigorous growth. GM, NRS, 1937.

Walter C. Clark HT, *dr,* 1917, Paul, W. Bud long, pointed; flowers deep maroon-crimson, shaded black, dbl., high-centered, large; very fragrant; foliage dark, leathery; vigorous growth.

Walter Rieger S, *dp,* 1977, *Carina × Molde*; Hetzel. Bud pointed; flowers pink to reddish, dbl., medium; slightly fragrant; foliage glossy; vigorous growth; continuous bloom.

Walter Ross HT, *my,* 1970, *Mme. Marie Curie × King's Ransom*; Morey; General Bionomics. Bud ovoid; flowers yellow, dbl., high-centered, large; fragrant; foliage large, glossy, dark, bronze, leathery; vigorous, upright, bushy growth.

Walter Speed HT, *dy,* 1909, Dickson, A. Flowers deep lemon-yellow, passing to milk-white, dbl.

Waltham Bride LCl, *w,* 1905, Paul, W. Flowers snow-white, dbl., medium; fragrant.

Waltham Climber No. 1 Cl HT, *mr*, 1885, *Gloire de Dijon seedling*; Paul, W. Flowers rosy crimson, dbl., imbricated, large; very fragrant; vigorous, climbing growth; recurrent bloom.

Waltham Climber No. 2 Cl HT, *or*, 1885, Paul, W. Flowers flame-red, tinted crimson, dbl., large; recurrent bloom.

Waltham Climber No. 3 Cl HT, *mr*, 1885, Paul, W. Flowers deep rosy crimson, dbl., imbricated, large; very fragrant; vigorous, climbing growth; recurrent bloom.

Waltham Crimson HT, *dr*, 1922, Chaplin Bros. Flowers deep crimson.

Waltham Cross HT, *dr*, 1927, Chaplin Bros. Flowers glowing crimson-scarlet, semi-dbl.

Waltham Flame HT, 1921, Chaplin Bros. Flowers deep terra-cotta, shaded bronzy orange.

Waltham Rambler R, *dp*, 1903, Paul, W. Flowers deep rosy pink, center paler, stamens bright yellow, single, borne in clusters; vigorous, climbing growth; early bloom.

Waltham Scarlet HT, *dr*, 1914, Paul, W. Flowers crimson-scarlet, single.

Waltzing Matilda HT, *rb*, 1965, *Christian Dior sport*; Jack; Girraween Nursery. Flowers red splashed light to dark pink, dbl., well shaped, large; vigorous growth.

Walzertraum HT, *mr*, 1968, Tantau, M. Flowers red, dbl.; foliage dark.

Wanaka® Min, *or*, 1978, (MACinca; Longleat; Young Cale); *Anytime* × *Trumpeter*; McGredy, S., IV; McGredy Roses International. Flowers orange-red, dbl. (40 petals), small; slightly fragrant; foliage light green; low, bushy growth.

Wanda HT, *mp*, 1953, *Pink Bountiful* × *Celebrity*; Hill, J.H., Co. Bud short, pointed; flowers rose, dbl. (28-30 petals), high-centered to flat, large (3½-4½ in.); very fragrant; foliage leathery; vigorous, upright growth; a forcing variety.

Wanderin' Wind S, *lp*, 1973, *Dornröschen* × *Andante*; Buck; Iowa State University. Flowers two-toned light pink, dbl., high-centered, medium; very fragrant; foliage large, glossy, dark, leathery; very vigorous, upright, bushy growth.

Wandering Minstrel F, *op*, 1986, (HARquince; Daniel Gelin); *Dame of Sark* × *Silver Jubilee*; Harkness. Flowers pink shaded orange, dbl. (28 petals), large blooms in clusters; slightly fragrant; foliage dark green, glossy; medium, bushy growth.

Wapex Pol, *my*, 1968, *Golden Showers* × *Fata Morgana*; Buisman. Bud pointed; flowers yellow, semi-dbl., medium, borne in clusters; foliage dark.

War Dance Gr, *or*, 1962, *Roundelay* × *Crimson Glory*; Swim; Weeks; C-P. Bud ovoid; flowers dark orange-red, dbl. (34 petals), high-centered to cupped, large (4-4½ in.); foliage leathery; vigorous, bushy growth.

War Paint LCl, *mr*, 1930, *Rhea Reid seedling* × *Seedling*; Clark, A.; Hackett. Flowers medium red, dbl., globular, large; slightly fragrant; vigorous, pillar or climbing (8 ft.) growth.

Warana Festival HT, *mp*, 1962, *Christian Dior sport*; Jack; Langbecker. Flowers rich pink, base rich apricot, dbl., well formed; vigorous growth.

Warleyensis S, *mp*, (*R.* × *warleyensis* Willmott); *R. blanda* × *R. rugosa*; Orig. prior to 1910. Flowers pink; (14).

Warm Rain Min, *mr*, 1985, *Fragrant Cloud* × *Orange Honey*; Hardgrove, Donald; Rose World Originals. Flowers medium coral red, dbl. (70 petals), high-centered, medium; slight fragrance; foliage small, medium green, semi-glossy; vigorous, upright, bushy.

Warm Welcome Cl Min, *or*, 1992, (CHEWizz); *Elizabeth of Glamis* × *(Galway Bay* × *Sutter's Gold)* × *Anna Ford*; Warner, C.H., 1991. Flowers orange vermilion, semi-dbl. (6-14 petals), small (0-4 cms) blooms borne in small clusters; fragrant; foliage small, dark green, semi-glossy; few prickles; tall (200+ cms), upright growth.

Warrawee HT, *mp*, 1935, *Padre* × *Rev. F. Page-Roberts*; Fitzhardinge; C-P. Bud long, pointed; flowers flesh-pink shaded rose-pink, dbl. (30 petals), high-centered, large; fragrant; foliage glossy; vigorous growth.

Warrior F, *or*, 1977, *City of Belfast* × *Ronde Endiablee*; LeGrice. Flowers scarlet-red, dbl. (32 petals), large (3-4 in.) blooms in trusses; slightly fragrant; foliage light green, semi-glossy.

Warszawa HT, *ob*, 1957, *Carioca sport*; Grabczewski. Flowers bright orange, reverse golden yellow; foliage dark, glossy.

Wartburg R, *mp*, 1910, *Tausendschön*; Kiese. Flowers pink to magenta, dbl., cupped, twisted and reflexed petals, borne on strong stems; fragrant; foliage large, light, soft; very vigorous, climbing (15-20 ft.) growth.

Warwhoop Min, *or*, 1973, *Baccará* × *Little Chief*; Williams, E.D.; Mini-Roses. Bud ovoid; flowers brilliant orange-red, very dbl., small; slightly fragrant; foliage small, glossy, dark; vigorous, bushy growth.

Warwick Castle® S, *dp*, 1992, (AUSlian); *The Reeve* × *Lilian Austin*; Austin, David; David Austin Roses, 1986. Flowers pink, very full

(41+ petals), large (7+ cms) blooms borne in small clusters; fragrant; foliage small, medium green, matt; some prickles; low (75 cms), spreading growth.

Wasagaming HRg (S), *mp*, 1939, *(R. rugosa × R. acicularis) × Gruss an Teplitz*; Skinner. Flowers clear rose, dbl.; fragrant; vigorous (3 ft.) growth; recurrent bloom.

Waskasoo HRg (S), *dr*, 1963, *Little Betty × Hansa*; Erskine. Flowers dark red, dbl. (50 long petals), not clustered; growth typical rugosa; (14).

Watchung HT, *yb*, 1932, *Pres. Herbert Hoover sport*; Didato. Flowers yellow tipped pink, dbl. (24-26 petals), medium (3½ in.).

Water Music LCl, *dp*, 1982, *Handel × Seedling*; Bell, Ronald J. Flowers deep pink, darker on petal edges, dbl. (20 petals), medium; slight fragrance; foliage dark, medium, glossy; spreading, climbing growth.

Watercolor Min, *mp*, 1975, (Watercolour); *Rumba × (Little Darling × Red Germain)*; Moore, R.S.; Sequoia Nursery. Bud long, pointed; flowers bright pink, dbl. (26 petals), high-centered, small (1½ in.); slightly fragrant; foliage small, glossy, leathery; vigorous, upright, bushy.

Waverland® HT, *yb*, 1982, (LENway); *Peer Gynt × Peace*; Lens. Flower petals deep yellow, edged orange-red, dbl. (30 petals), exhibition, large, borne singly and in clusters of 3-7; very fragrant; foliage dark, leathery; large; brown prickles; upright, bushy. GM, Monza, 1980.

Waverley F, *dr*, Norman. Flowers crimson-scarlet, dbl. (22 petals), large (3½ in.), borne in trusses; slightly fragrant; foliage glossy, dark; vigorous, bushy, compact growth.

Waverley Triumph Pol, *mp*, 1951, *Orange Triumph sport*; Poulter. Flowers bright pink, base yellow, semi-dbl., cupped, small, borne in clusters; slightly fragrant; foliage glossy, light green; vigorous, bushy growth.

Waves HT, *mp*, 1944, (Admiral); *Seedling (deep salmon) × Lucie Marie*; Dickson, A.; J&P. Bud ovoid; flowers rose-pink, dbl. (35 petals), open, cupped, large (4½ in.); very fragrant; foliage dark, leathery, wrinkled; vigorous growth.

Wavria F, *or*, 1973, *Europeana sport*; Lens. Flowers orange-crimson.

Wayside Garnet Min, *dr*, 1956, *Oakington Ruby sport*; Wayside Gardens Co. Flowers garnet-red, dbl., small; dwarf, compact growth.

W. C. Gaunt HT, *dr*, 1916, Dickson, A. Bud long, pointed; flowers velvety crimson-scarlet, reflexed petals tipped scarlet, reverse crimson-maroon, full; fragrant.

W. E. Chaplin HT, *dr*, 1929, Chaplin Bros. Flowers crimson, deepening to maroon, dbl., high-centered, large; vigorous growth. GM, NRS, 1930.

W. E. Chaplin, Climbing Cl HT, *dr*, 1936, Heizmann, E.

Wedded Bliss™ Min, *mp*, 1985, (SAVawed); *(Yellow Jewel × Tamango) × Nozomi*; Saville, F. Harmon; Nor'East Min. Roses. Flowers medium pink, semi-dbl., medium blooms in clusters; slight fragrance; foliage small, medium green, glossy; very spreading; ground cover.

Weddigen HT, *lp*, 1916, Lambert, P. Flowers silver-pink; fragrant.

Wedding Bells R, *w*, 1906, *Crimson Rambler × Seedling*; Walsh. Flowers white, outer half of petals soft pink, semi-dbl., cupped, borne in clusters on short stems; foliage light; very vigorous, climbing (12-15 ft.) growth.

Wedding Day R, *w*, 1950, *R. sinowilsonii × Seedling*; Stern, F.C. Flowers yellow to white flushed pink, single, blooms in huge clusters; very fragrant; height to 20 ft.; (14).

Wedding Pink HT, *lp*, 1990, (JACbip); *Bridal White sport*; Nakashima, Tosh; Bear Creek Gardens, Inc., 1990. Bud ovoid; flowers light pink, reverse slightly paler pink, very dbl, urn-shaped, exhibition, large, borne singly; slight fragrance; foliage medium, dark green, matt; prickles long, very narrow, reddish-brown; upright, tall growth.

Wedding Ring HT, *my*, 1956, *Ville de Paris × Mrs. Sam McGredy*; Shepherd; Bosley Nursery. Bud long, pointed; flowers golden yellow, dbl. (25-35 petals), large (4-4½ in.); slightly fragrant; foliage dark, glossy, leathery; vigorous, upright, compact growth.

Wedding Song HT, *w*, 1971, *Virgo × Ivory Fashion*; Whisler, D.; Gro-Plant Industries. Flowers white; slightly fragrant; upright growth.

Wee Barbie Min, *w*, 1980, (JELbar); *Seedling × Seedling*; Jellyman, J. Bud globular; flowers cream-white, dbl. (43 petals), blooms borne 10-20 per cluster; fragrant; foliage dark; bushy growth.

Wee Beth Min, *ob*, 1981, *Orange Silk × Fairy Moss*; Cherry, R.; Welsh; Roy Rumsey Pty., Ltd. Bud pointed, mossy; flowers salmon-pink, semi-dbl. (11 petals), blooms borne 3-20 per cluster; sweetbrier fragrance; foliage small, dark, bristles on reverse; red prickles; bushy growth.

Wee Butterflies Pol, *pb*, 1989, *The Fairy × Seedling*; Jerabek, Paul E., 1990. Bud pointed; flowers medium pink with white eye, single (5 petals), small, borne in sprays of 3-35;

slight fragrance; foliage medium, light green, glossy; prickles straight, pink; fruit round, small, red; bushy, low growth.

Wee Jock® Min, *mr*, 1980, (COCabest); *National Trust* × *Wee Man*; Cocker, J. Bud pointed; flowers medium red, dbl. (50 petals), patio, blooms borne 9-15 per cluster; slight fragrance; foliage small, fairly glossy, medium green; red prickles; low, compact growth.

Wee Lass Min, *mr*, 1974, *Persian Princess* × *Persian Princess*; Moore, R.S.; Sequoia Nursery. Bud pointed; flowers blood-red, semi-dbl. (18 petals), small ('/₂-1 in.); foliage small, dark; upright, bushy growth.

Wee Man Min, *mr*, 1974, (Tapis de Soie); *Little Flirt* × *Marlena*; McGredy. Flowers scarlet, semi-dbl. (14 petals), medium (2 in.); slightly fragrant; foliage glossy, dark.

Wee Topper Min, *mr*, 1988, (ANDwee); *Starina sport*; Anderson's Rose Nursery. Flowers medium red, dbl. (15-25 petals), small; slight fragrance; foliage small, light green, semi-glossy; bushy growth.

Weihenstephan S, *dp*, 1964, Kordes. Flowers rich pink, semi-dbl., blooms in large clusters; vigorous (4½ ft.) growth.

Weisse aus Sparrieshoop S, *w*, 1962, Kordes. Flowers white, medium; fragrant.

Weisse Gruss an Aachen F, *w*, 1944, *Gruss an Aachen sport*; Vogel. Bud ovoid; flowers snow-white, very dbl., large, borne in clusters; fragrant; upright, bushy growth.

Weisse Immensee® S, *w*, 1983, (KORweirim; Kordes' Rose Weiss Immensee; Lac Blanc; Partridge); *The Fairy* × *R. wichuraiana seedling*; Kordes, W.; Kordes Roses, 1982. Bud light pink; flowers white, single (5 petals), small; very fragrant; foliage small, dark, glossy; spreading (10 ft.) growth; ground cover.

Weisse Max Graf® S, *w*, 1983, (KORgram); *Seedling* × *R. wichuraiana seedling*; Kordes, W.; Kordes Roses. Flowers white, semi-dbl., medium; very fragrant; foliage small, dark, glossy; spreading (10 ft.) growth; ground cover.

Weisse Repandia® S, *w*, 1982, (KORiant); *The Fairy* × *R. wichuraiana seedling*; Kordes, W.; Kordes Roses. Flowers white, semi-dbl., small; slight fragrance; foliage small, dark, glossy; spreading (7 ft.) growth; ground cover.

Weisser Herumstreicher R, *w*, 1895, *Daniel Lacombe* × *Pâquerette*; Schmidt, J.C. Flowers pure white, full, large, borne in clusters; vigorous, climbing growth.

Welch Sp (OGR), *w*, *R. multiflora strain*; Mt. Arbor Nursery. Selected thornless strain of *R. multiflora* used as an understock.

Welcome HT, *mp*, 1948, Dickson, A. Bud ovoid; flowers glistening rose-pink, dbl. (35 petals), high-centered, very large; slightly fragrant; foliage leathery; vigorous, upright, bushy growth.

Welcome Guest HT, *ab*, 1984, *Jan Guest sport*; Cox, Arthur George. Flowers apricot with a tinge of pink around edges of petals.

Welcome Home F, *mr*, 1984, (ANDwel); *Orange Sensation* × *Michelle*; Anderson Rose Nursery. Flowers medium red, dbl. (20 petals); foliage medium, light green, semi-glossy; upright growth.

Welcome Stranger F, *my*, 1968, *Ophelia, Climbing* × *Allgold*; Fankhauser; A. Ross & Son. Flowers yellow, single, large; very fragrant; foliage extra large, glossy, leathery; very vigorous, compact growth.

Wellesley HT, *dp*, 1905, *Bridesmaid* × *Liberty*; Montgomery, A. Flowers dark rosy pink, dbl., large; fragrant.

Wellington G (OGR), *m*, Int. prior to 1848. Flowers crimson-purple, cupped.

Wellworth HT, *pb*, 1949, *Léontine Contenot* × *Golden Dawn*; LeGrice. Flowers peach shaded gold, dbl. (40 petals), pointed, large (5 in.); very fragrant; foliage grayish green; vigorous growth.

Wendelien F, *mr*, 1946, *Donald Prior* × *Seedling*; Leenders, M.; Longley. Flowers cardinal-red, dbl. (22 petals), globular, large (4 in.), borne in clusters; slightly fragrant; foliage bright green; vigorous, branching growth.

Wendy Pol, *mp*, 1949, *Tip-Top* × *Dorothy Perkins*; Heers; Pacific Nursery. Flowers pink, dbl., open, medium, borne in clusters; fragrant; foliage soft, light green; moderately vigorous, upright growth. RULED EXTINCT 11/91.

Wendy F, *mp*, 1991, (ZIPwen); *Wendy Cussons* × *High Spirits*; Zipper, Herbert; Magic Moment Miniatures, 1992. Flowers medium pink, moderately full (15-25 petals), exhibition, medium (4-7 cms) blooms borne in small clusters; very fragrant; foliage medium, dark green, semi-glossy; few prickles; medium (75 cms), upright growth.

Wendy Barrie Pol, *op*, 1936, Beckwith. Flowers orange-salmon, dbl., well formed; vigorous, dwarf growth.

Wendy Cussons HT, *mr*, 1963, *Believed to be Independence* × *Eden Rose*; Gregory; Ilgenfritz Nursery. Bud long, pointed; flowers rose-red, dbl. (30 petals), high-centered, large (5-6 in.); very fragrant; foliage leathery, glossy, dark; vigorous, well-branched growth. NRS

PIT, 1959; GM, NRS, 1959; Portland, 1964; Golden Rose of The Hague, 1964

Wendy Cussons, Climbing Cl HT, *mr*, 1967, Follen; Gregory.

Wendy Pease HT, *yb*, 1986, (DEBraf); *John Waterer × Tenerife*; Bracegirdle, D.T. Flowers yellow blend, dbl. (35 petals), medium; slight fragrance; foliage medium, medium green, semi-glossy; upright growth.

Wenlock® S, *mr*, 1985, (AUSwen); *The Knight × Glastonbury*; Austin, David, 1984. Flowers medium red, dbl. (40+ petals), large; very fragrant; foliage large, dark, semi-glossy; vigorous.

Werner Dirks LCl, *w*, 1937, *Mrs. Pierre S. duPont × Daisy Hill*; Kordes. Bud long, pointed; flowers ivory-white, dbl., high-centered, very large, borne in clusters on long, strong stems; fragrant; foliage large, leathery, wrinkled; very vigorous, climbing growth.

Werner Teschendorff F, *op*, 1949, *Swantje × Hamburg*; Tantau; Teschendorff. Bud ovoid; flowers orange-pink, dbl., cupped, medium, borne in clusters; slightly fragrant; foliage glossy; vigorous, upright, bushy growth.

Wesnianka HT, *w*, 1941, (Spring); *Mme. Butterfly × Mrs. T. Hillas*; Costetske. Flowers white, base carmine-yellow.

West Coast® HT, *mp*, 1987, (MACnauru; Penthouse; Metropolitain); *((Yellow Pages × Kabuki) × Golden Gate) × (Poulsen seedling × Picasso)*; McGredy, Sam; Sam McGredy Roses International, 1986. Flowers medium pink, dbl. (15-25 petals), large; slight fragrance; foliage large, light green, matt; bushy growth.

Westbroekpark F, *or*, 1968, *Orange Sensation × Kimono*; deRuiter. Flowers orange-red, dbl., medium, borne in clusters; foliage dark.

Westerland® F, *ab*, 1969, (KORwest; KORlawe); *Friedrich Worlein × Circus*; Kordes. Bud ovoid; flowers apricot-orange, dbl. (20 petals), cupped, large (3 in.); very fragrant; foliage large, dark, soft; vigorous, upright, bushy growth; repeat bloom. ADR, 1974.

Western Gold HT, *my*, 1932, *Talisman sport*; Western Rose Co. Flowers clear yellow.

Western Sun® HT, *dy*, 1965, *Golden Scepter seedling × Golden Sun*; Poulsen, N.D. Flowers deep yellow, dbl. (40 petals), large (5 in.); foliage dark.

Western Sunlight HT, *ab*, 1989, (HADsun); *((Honey Favorite × Irish Mist) × (San Francisco × Prima Ballerina)) × Just Joey*; Davidson, Harvey; Hortico, Inc., 1990. Bud pointed; flowers apricot-orange, aging to yellow, dbl. (31 petals), high-centered, exhibition, large, borne usually singly and in sprays of 2-3; slight, fruity fragrance; foliage medium, dark

green, glossy, serrated; prickles hooked downward, light brown; fruit inverted, orange, does not set seed readily; upright, medium growth.

Western Sunset F, *yb*, 1958, *Maxine × Masaquerade*; Silva. Bud pointed; flowers yellow tipped pink, becoming pink and then mahogany-red, dbl. (35 petals), cupped, medium (1½-2 in.), borne in clusters; foliage leathery; vigorous, upright growth.

Westfalengruss F, *mr*, 1978, Hubner; O. Baum. Bud ovoid; flowers fire-red, dbl., medium; foliage glossy; low, bushy growth.

Westfalenpark® S, *ab*, 1987, (KORplavi; Chevreuse; Kordes' Rose Westfalenpark; *Seedling × Las Vegas*; Kordes, W., 1986. Flowers apricot, dbl. (26-40 petals), large; fragrant; foliage large, dark green, glossy; bushy, spreading growth.

Westfield Beauty HT, *ab*, 1923, *Lady Pirrie × Mme. Edouard Herriot*; Morse. Bud long, pointed; flowers deep coppery apricot, tinted golden and salmon-pink, dbl.; fragrant.

Westfield Flame HT, *or*, 1925, *Mme. Edouard Herriot × Diadem*; Morse. Bud long, pointed; flowers very deep flame, dbl.; slightly fragrant.

Westfield Gem HT, *dr*, 1925, *Col. Oswald Fitzgerald sport*; Morse. Flowers dark maroon-crimson, dbl.; slightly fragrant.

Westfield Scarlet HT, *mr*, 1931, *Lady Inchiquin sport*; Morse. Flowers clear scarlet, dbl., open, very large; slightly fragrant; foliage leathery, dark; bushy growth. GM, NRS, 1932.

Westfield Star HT, *w*, 1922, *Ophelia sport*; Morse. Flowers cream, fading white.

Westminster HT, *rb*, 1960, *Gay Crusader × Peace*; Robinson, H. Flowers red, gold reverse, dbl. (35 petals), loosely-formed, large; very fragrant; foliage dark; vigorous, tall. GM, NRS, 1961.

Westmont Min, *mr*, 1958, *(R. wichuraiana × Floradora) × (Oakington Ruby × Floradora)*; Moore, R.S.; Sequoia Nursery. Bud pointed; flowers bright red, semi-dbl. to dbl., small (1½ in.); foliage leathery, semi-glossy; vigorous (12-18 in.), bushy.

Westward Ho! HT, *rb*, 1964, *Karl Herbst × Pink Charming*; Allen, E.M.; Sanday. Flowers mahogany-red, reverse silver, dbl. (42 petals), large (4½ in.); fragrant; foliage very dark; vigorous, upright, compact growth.

Wettra F, *mr*, 1976, *Pink Puff × Barcarolle*; Rijksstation Voor Sierplantenteelt. Flowers medium red, dbl. (20 petals), cupped, large blooms borne 4-15 per cluster; no fragrance;

foliage dark, matt; red prickles; upright growth.

W. E. Wallace HT, *dy*, 1922, *Gorgeous sport*; Dickson, H. Flowers deep golden yellow, dbl., well formed, large; fragrant. GM, NRS, 1922.

We Zair C (OGR), *pb*, Flowers two-tone pink.

W. Freeland Kendrick LCl, *lp*, 1920, (Bloomfield Endurance); *Aviateur Bleriot* × *Mme. Caroline Testout*; Thomas; B&A. Flowers flesh, center peach, very dbl., large; fragrant; foliage dark, bronze, leathery, glossy; vigorous, semi-climbing growth; non-recurrent bloom.

W. G. Pountney F, *or*, 1964, *Moulin Rouge* × *Mrs. Inge Poulsen*; Bennett, H.; Pedigree Nursery. Flowers scarlet; tall growth.

W. H. Cotton HT, *ab*, 1946, *Mrs. Beatty* × *Mrs. Sam McGredy*; Cobley; Leicester Roses. Flowers orange shaded gold, large; foliage dark; vigorous, upright growth.

W. H. Dunallan HT, *mr*, 1939, *Edith Clark* × *Seedling*; Clark, A.; NRS Victoria. Flowers very rich bright red, flushed darker, semi-dbl.; vigorous growth.

Wheatcroft Giant HT, *lp*, 1962, Wheatcroft Bros. Flowers pearly pink, well-formed, large; vigorous growth.

Whickham Highway F, *r*, 1992, (HORmasbrick); *Mary Sumner* × *(Prominent* × *Southampton)*; Horner, Heather, 1993. Flowers brick red, semi-dbl. (6-14 petals), medium (4-7 cms) blooms borne in large clusters; slight fragrance; foliage medium, medium green, glossy; some prickles; tall (120 cms), upright growth.

Whimsical Min, *pb*, 1980, *Tiki* × *Baby Betsy McCall*; Strawn, Leslie E.; Pixie Treasures Nursery. Bud pointed; flowers either light pink or deeper peach-pink on same plant at same time, dbl. (48 petals), exhibition blooms borne singly; no fragrance; foliage medium green; no prickles; upright, bushy growth.

Whipped Cream Min, *w*, 1968, *(R. wichuraiana* × *Carolyn Dean)* × *White King*; Moore, R.S.; Sequoia Nursery. Bud pointed, ivory; flowers white, dbl., small; foliage light green, leathery; vigorous, bushy, dwarf growth.

Whippet HT, *pb*, 1973, Scott, D.H. Flowers salmon-pink, reverse lighter, dbl. (35 petals), high-centered, large (5 in.); slightly fragrant; moderate growth.

Whisky F, *yb*, 1964, *Cognac* × *Arc-en-Ciel*; Delforge. Flowers yellow shaded orange-bronze, dbl., open, large, borne in clusters; slightly fragrant; foliage glossy, light green; very vigorous, upright growth.

Whisky Gill HT, *ob*, 1972, *Whisky Mac sport*; Cobley. Flowers burnt-orange to bright orange.

Whisky Mac HT, *yb*, 1967, (TANky; Whisky); Tantau, Math. Bud ovoid; flowers bronze-yellow, dbl. (30 petals), well-formed, large; very fragrant; foliage glossy; vigorous, upright, bushy.

Whisky Mac, Climbing Cl HT, *yb*, 1985, (ANDmac; Whisky, Climbing); Anderson Rose Nursery.

Whisper F, *lp*, 1971, *Queen Elizabeth* × *Monique*; Cants of Colchester. Flowers pale pink, semi-dbl. (10 petals), large (3-3½ in.); slightly fragrant; foliage light; vigorous.

Whistle Stop Min, *rb*, 1988, (MACmosco); *Mighty Mouse* × *Hurdy Gurdy*; McGredy, Sam, 1989. Flowers red blend (striped), semi-dbl. (6-14 petals), small; slight fragrance; foliage small, medium green, semi-glossy; bushy growth.

White Aachen F, *ly*, 1937, *Grüss an Aachen sport*; Western Rose Co. Flowers buff-yellow to pure white.

White Alaska HT, *w*, 1960, *White Ophelia* × *Seedling*; Hartgerink; Armacost; Royston. Bud long, pointed; flowers pure white, dbl. (20 petals), high-centered to cupped, large (4½-5 in.); slightly fragrant; foliage leathery, dark; vigorous, upright.

White Angel Min, *w*, 1971, *(R. wichuraiana* × *Floradora)* × *(Little Darling* × *Red Miniature seedling)*; Moore, R.S.; Sequoia Nursery. Flowers white, dbl., high-centered, small; slightly fragrant; foliage small, light; vigorous, dwarf, bushy growth. AOE, 1975.

White Avalanche S, *w*, 1988, (WILwavl); *Sea Foam* × *The Fairy*; Williams, J. Benjamin, 1989. Flowers cream, opening to pure white, dbl. (15-25 petals), small, borne in clusters; slight fragrance; foliage medium, medium green, glossy, disease resistant; spreading, compact, uniform, winter hardy growth.

White Baby Star Min, *w*, 1965, *Baby Gold Star sport*; Spring Hill Nursery; Wyant.

White Baroness HP (OGR), *w*, 1888, *Baroness Rothschild sport*; Paul. Flowers white.

White Bath M (OGR), *w*, (Clifton Moss; R. centifolia albo-muscosa; R. muscosa alba; Shailer's White Moss); Cult. 1810; Like Centifolia Muscosa but flowers white; (28).

White Beauty HT, *w*, 1965, *The Doctor sport*; Brooks, M.L.; Texas Rose Research Found. Flowers pure white.

White Bells® Min, *w*, 1983, (POULwhite); *Mini-Poul* × *Temple Bells*; Poulsen, D.T.; John Mattock, Ltd., 1980. Flowers white, dbl. (35 petals); slight fragrance; foliage small, medium green, semi-glossy; spreading growth; ground cover.

White Bougère T (OGR), *w*, 1898, Dunlop. Flowers pure white.

White Bouquet F, *w*, 1956, *Glacier × Pinocchio seedling*; Boerner; J&P. Bud ovoid; flowers white, dbl. (45 petals), gardenia-shaped, large (4¹/₂ in.) blooms in irregular clusters; fragrant (spicy); foliage dark, glossy; bushy growth. AARS, 1957.

White Briarcliff HT, *w*, 1932, (Mme. Louis Lens); *(Briarcliff × Kaiserin Auguste Viktoria) × (Briarcliff × Mrs. Herbert Stevens)*; Lens; J&P. Bud long, pointed; flowers pure white, dbl., high-centered, large; fragrant; foliage leathery; vigorous growth.

White Butterfly HT, *w*, 1954, *Ophelia × Curly White*; Spanbauer. Bud long, pointed; flowers white, inner petals pale chartreuse, dbl. (24 petals), center cupped, large (3¹/₂-4¹/₂ in.); fragrant; foliage leathery; vigorous, compact growth; greenhouse variety. ARS John Cook Medal, 1957.

White Cap F, *w*, 1954, *Seedling × Break o' Day, Climbing*; Brownell. Flowers white, dbl. (60 petals), large (3¹/₂-4 in.); fragrant.

White Cécile Brunner Pol, *w*, 1909, *Cécile Brunner sport*; Fraque. Flowers white, sulphur yellow and buff.

White Charm F, *w*, 1958, *Pinocchio × Virgo*; Swim & Weeks. Bud long, pointed; flowers white, base yellow-green, semi-dbl. (17-22 petals), high-centered to cupped, large (2¹/₂-3 in.); fragrant; foliage leathery; bushy, upright growth; a greenhouse variety. RULED EXTINCT 10/88.

White Charm™ Min, *w*, 1988, (MINaqco); *Tom Brown × Over the Rainbow*; Williams, Ernest. Bud long; flowers white, dbl. (33 petals), high-centered, small; very fragrant; foliage small, medium green, glossy; bushy growth.

White Chatillon Pol, *w*, (Chatillon White); *Probably a Chatillon Rose sport*. Bud pale pink, fading to white.

White Christmas HT, *w*, 1953, *Sleigh Bells × Seedling*; H&S. Bud long, pointed; flowers pure white, dbl., high-centered, medium; fragrant; foliage leathery, light green; moderate, upright growth.

White Cloud™ Min, *w*, 1988, (SAVacloud); *Buttons 'n' Bows sport*; Saville, F. Harmon; Nor'East Miniature Roses. Flowers white with pale pink.

White Clouds Cl HT, *w*, 1953, *Frau Karl Druschki × Kaiserin Auguste Viktoria*; Silva. Bud long, pointed; flowers white, dbl. (50 petals), large (4¹/₂ in.); very fragrant; foliage

leathery, dark; vigorous growth. RULED EXTINCT 8/88.

White Cockade LCl, *w*, 1969, *New Dawn × Circus*; Cocker. Flowers white, dbl., large; fragrant; foliage glossy; vigorous, low, climbing growth.

White Columbia, Climbing Cl HT, *w*, 1934, Clark's Rose Nursery.

White Cross LCl, *w*, 1950, *Mrs. Arthur Curtis James sport*; Hester. Bud ovoid; flowers white, center tinted lemon, very dbl., large; fragrant; foliage leathery, glossy; very vigorous growth.

White Dawn® LCl, *w*, 1949, *New Dawn × Lily Pons*; Longley, L.E.; Univ. of Minn. Flowers white, dbl. (35 petals), gardenia-shaped, medium blooms in clusters; fragrant; foliage glossy; very vigorous, climbing growth; recurrent bloom.

White Delight HT, *w*, 1989, (JACglow); *White Masterpiece × Futura*; Warriner, William A.; Jackson; Perkins, 1990. Bud ovoid, pointed; flowers white with pink blush, dbl. (38 petals), high-centered, large, borne usually singly; slight fragrance; foliage medium, dark green, matt; prickles hooked, medium, brown; upright, medium growth.

White Demure F, *w*, 1952, *Demure sport*; Boerner. Bud ovoid; flowers white, dbl. (30-35 petals), flat, medium (2-2¹/₂ in.); slightly fragrant; foliage leathery; vigorous, compact, bushy growth; a greenhouse variety.

White Dian Min, *w*, 1965, *Dian sport*; Moore, R.S.; Sequoia Nursery. Flowers white, sometimes light pink.

White Dorothy R, *w*, 1908, (White Dorothy Perkins); *Dorothy Perkins sport*; Cant, B.R. Flowers creamy white.

White Dream® Min, *w*, 1985, (LENblank; LENvir); *Seedling × Seedling*; Lens, 1982. Flowers white, dbl. (36 petals), exhibition, small blooms in clusters of 3-28; light fragrance; hooked, greenish-brown prickles; low, bushy growth.

White Duchess HT, *w*, 1964, Herholdt, J.A.; Herholdt's Nursery. Bud spiral, pointed; flowers snow-white, medium; strong stems; foliage glossy; vigorous growth.

White Elfe F, *w*, 1954, *Rosenelfe sport*; Holmes, V.E.; Mortensen, Avansino. Bud pointed; flowers white faintly tinted pink, dbl. (40-45 petals), high-centered to cupped, medium (2-2¹/₂ in.), borne in clusters of 3-7; slightly fragrant; foliage dark, leathery; vigorous growth.

White Ensign HT, *w*, 1925, McGredy. Flowers white, very dbl., large; slightly fragrant;

foliage leathery, dark, glossy; vigorous growth.

White Fairy Min, *w*, 1952, Sequoia Nursery. Flowers white, very dbl., small blooms in clusters.

White Feather Min, *w*, 1980, (MORfeat); *(R. wichuraiana × Floradora) × Peachy White*; Moore, R.S.; Moore Min. Roses. Flowers white, semi-dbl. (15 petals), loose form, small blooms in clusters of 3-5; slight fragrance; foliage small, light green, semi-glossy; very few prickles; fruit none; medium, bushy growth.

White Finch Pol, *w*, 1937, *Mrs. R.M. Finch sport*; Stielow, F.C. Flowers white, tinted pink.

White Forcer Pol, *w*, 1926, *Jesse sport*; Spek. Flowers white; larger flowers and trusses than parent.

White Garnette F, *w*, 1952, *Pinocchio seedling × Garnette*; Boerner; J&P. Flowers white tinged cream, dbl. (30-35 petals), medium (2 in.), borne in clusters; slightly fragrant; foliage rich green; bushy growth; a florists' variety.

White Gem® Min, *w*, 1976, (MEIturusa); *Darling Flame × Jack Frost*; Meilland; C-P. Bud long; flowers soft ivory, shaded pale tan, very dbl. (90 petals), medium (1½ in.); slightly fragrant; foliage large, glossy, dark; upright, bushy growth.

White Gene Boerner F, *w*, 1978, *Gene Boerner sport*; Takatori; Japan Rose Nursery. Flowers white.

White Gold LCl, *w*, 1943, *Glenn Dale × Mrs. Arthur Curtiss James*; Brownell. Bud long, pointed; flowers white, center yellow, dbl., high-centered, petals reflexed; foliage dark, glossy; vigorous, climbing (20 ft.) growth.

White Grootendorst HRg (S), *w*, 1962, *Pink Grootendorst sport*; Eddy. Flowers white.

White House HT, *w*, 1951, *McGredy's Yellow × Frau Karl Druschki*; Silva. Bud high-centered to ovoid; flowers satiny white; foliage thick, light green.

White Jewel F, *w*, 1957, *Starlite seedling × Glacier seedling*; Boerner; J&P. Flowers white, dbl. (33 petals), cupped, large (4 in.) blooms in clusters; fragrant; vigorous, bushy growth; greenhouse variety.

White Joy HT, *w*, 1952, Spanbauer. Bud pointed; flowers pure white, dbl. (55-65 petals), flat, large (4-5 in.); fragrant; foliage leathery; bushy, upright growth.

White Killarney HT, *w*, 1909, *Killarney sport*; Waban Conservatories. Flowers white; fragrant.

White King Min, *w*, 1961, *Golden Glow × Zee*; Moore, R.S.; Sequoia Nursery. Bud pointed, ovoid; flowers cream-white, dbl. (45 petals), small (1½ in.); fragrant; foliage leathery; bushy (12 in.) growth.

White Knight HT, *w*, 1955, (MEban; Message); *(Virgo × Peace) × Virgo*; Meilland, F.; URS, 1955; C-P, 1957. Bud long, pointed; flowers clear white, dbl. (33 petals), high-centered, large (4 in.); foliage leathery, light green; vigorous, upright growth. AARS, 1958.

White Knight, Climbing Cl HT, *w*, 1959, Komatsu; Kakujitsuen.

White Knight, Climbing Cl HT, *w*, (Message, Climbing), 1965, Meilland; URS.

White Lightnin'™ Gr, *w*, 1980, (AROwhif); *Angel Face × Misty*; Swim; Christensen; Armstrong Nursery. Bud ovoid, pointed; flowers clear white, dbl. (30 petals), large (3½-4 in.); very fragrant; foliage glossy; upright, bushy growth. AARS, 1981.

White Love HT, *w*, 1973, *Frau Karl Druschki × (Peace × seedling)*; Buisman. Bud long; flowers ivory-white, large; very fragrant; foliage dark; bushy growth.

White Ma Perkins F, *w*, 1962, *Ma Perkins sport*; McDonald; Hennessey. Bud long, pointed; flowers white, dbl. (20-40 petals), large (3½ in.), borne in clusters; very fragrant; foliage light green; very vigorous, upright growth.

White Madonna Min, *w*, 1973, *(R. wichuraiana × Floradora) × (Little Darling × red Miniature)*; Moore, R.S.; Sequoia Nursery. Bud long, pointed; flowers white to pale pink, dbl. (33 petals), small (1 in.); slightly fragrant; foliage glossy, leathery; upright, bushy.

White Maman Cochet T (OGR), *w*, 1896, (White Cochet); *Maman Cochet sport*; Cook, J. Flowers white, often flushed pink.

White Maman Cochet, Climbing Cl T (OGR), *w*, 1907, Knight, G.; Leedle & Co., 1911.

White Masterpiece HT, *w*, 1969, (JACmas); Boerner; J&P. Bud long, pointed; flowers white, dbl., high-centered, very large; large peduncle; slightly fragrant; upright.

White Meidiland™ S, *w*, 1986, (MEIcoublan; Alba Meidiland; Blanc Meillandécor); *Temple Bells × MEIgurami*; Meilland, Mrs. M.L., 1987. Flowers white, very full (over 40 petals), large; no fragrance; foliage medium, dark green, glossy; spreading growth.

White Meillandina Min, *w*, 1984, (MEIblam; Yorkshire Sunblaze); *Katharina Zeimet × White Gem*; Meilland, M.L.; Meilland Et Cie, 1083. Flowers white, semi-dbl., medium; no fragrance; foliage small, light green, semi-glossy; bushy growth.

White Mimollet F, *w*, 1984, *Mimollet sport*; Ota, Kaichiro. Flowers white.

White Mini-Wonder™ Min, *w*, 1988, (MEIzogrel; MEIsogel; Spot Minijet); *White Gem × Cinderella*; Meilland, A.; SNC Meilland; Cie. Flowers white, very dbl. (over 40 petals), small; no fragrance; foliage small, medium green, matt; bushy growth.

White Mite Min, *w*, 1991, (FROmite); *Baby Katie × Seedling*; Frock, Marshall J. Flowers white, full (26-40 petals), small, micro-mini blooms; slight fragrance; foliage small, medium green, semi-glossy; upright growth.

White Mountains R, *w*, 1958, *Skinner's Rambler × Skinner's Rambler*; Risley. Bud globular; flowers white, becoming greenish, dbl., small, borne in clusters; foliage glossy; vigorous growth; profuse, intermittent bloom; quite hardy.

White Mrs. Flight HMult (OGR), *w*, 1916, *(White Flight) Mrs. F.W. Flight sport*; T. Rockford. Flowers pure white.

White Mystery HT, *w*, 1982, (DEVabe); *Paul's Pink sport*; DeVor, Paul F.; DeVor Nursery. Flowers white.

White Nun HT, *w*, 1968, *Virgo × Seedling*; Pal; Indian Agric. Research Inst. Flowers white, dbl., open, medium; foliage glossy; vigorous, upright growth.

White Ophelia HT, *w*, 1920, *Ophelia sport*; Cleveland Cut-Flower Co.; E.G. Hill Co.; Cleveland Cut-Flower Co. Flowers white, center faintly tinted pink, becoming white, semi-dbl., well formed; fragrant.

White Orléans Pol, *w*, 1920, *Orléans Rose sport*; Van Eyk. Flowers white.

White Pearl HT, *w*, 1948, Totty. Bud long, pointed; flowers glistening white, dbl. (45-50 petals), open, well formed, large; slightly fragrant; foliage large, soft; very vigorous, upright growth. RULED EXTINCT 4/85.

White Pet Pol, *w*, 1879, (Little White Pet); Henderson, P. Flowers white, dbl., small blooms in large clusters; very dwarf growth.

White Pet, Climbing Cl Pol, *w*, 1894, Corboeuf.

White Pillar LCl, *w*, 1958, *William F. Dreer × Seedling*; Hay; Marsh's Nursery. Flowers white, very dbl.; pillar (8 ft.) growth.

White Pinocchio F, *w*, 1950, *Mrs. R.M. Finch × Pinocchio*; Boerner; J&P. Bud ovoid; flowers white, dbl. (50 petals), globular, medium (2½ in.); fragrant; vigorous growth.

White Prince HT, *w*, 1961, *(Blanche Mallerin × Peace) × (Peace × Frau Karl Druschki)*; Abrams, Von; Peterson; Dering. Bud

pointed; flowers creamy white, dbl. (50-80 petals), nearly globular, large (5-6 in.); slightly fragrant; foliage leathery, glossy; vigorous, upright growth.

White Queen HT, *w*, 1958, *Starlite seedling × Glacier seedling*; Boerner; J&P. Flowers white, center creamy, dbl. (30 petals), cupped to flat, large (5 in.); fragrant; foliage leathery; vigorous, upright growth.

White Queen Elizabeth F, *w*, 1965, (Blanc Queen Elizabeth); *Queen Elizabeth sport*; Banner; North Hill Nursery. Flowers pure white, large (4 in.), borne in clusters; fragrant; foliage light green, leathery; vigorous growth.

White Radox Bouquet S, *w*, 1988, *Radox Bouquet sport*; Melville Nurseries, 1989. Bud small, rounded; flowers white with pink tinge in center, very dbl. (50 petals), large, borne in sprays of 5 or more; fragrant; foliage dark green, leathery; prickles hooked, small, beige; tall, shrub to semi-climber growth.

White Rain Min, *w*, 1991, (MORcas); *Papoose × Renae*; Moore, Ralph S.; Sequoia Nursery, 1992. Flowers white, moderately full (15-25 petals), small (0-4 cms) blooms borne in large clusters; fragrant; foliage small, light green, semi-glossy; some prickles; low (22 cms), spreading, ground cover growth.

White Rose of York A (OGR), *w*, (Bonnie Prince Charlie's Rose; Jacobite Rose; La Rose de York; *R. alba* Linnaeus; *R. procera* Salisbury; *R. usitatissima* Gateau); *Probably R. corymbifera × R. gallica*; Cult. before 1597. Flowers white, more or less dbl., borne usually several together; fragrant; fruit ovoid, scarlet; 6 ft. Summer bloom.

White Satin HT, *w*, 1965, *Mount Shasta × White Butterfly*; Swim; Weeks; Carlton Rose Nursery. Bud urn-shaped; flowers white, center greenish yellow, dbl., large; fragrant; foliage light gray-green, leathery; vigorous, tall growth; greenhouse variety.

White Seduction Pol, *w*, *Seduction sport*. Flowers white.

White Sheen F, *w*, 1959, *Ma Perkins seedling × Demure seedling*; Boerner; J&P. Bud ovoid; flowers white, dbl. (25-30 petals), medium (2 in.), borne in clusters; very fragrant; foliage dark, glossy; upright growth; for pot forcing; no longer being sold.

White Spray F, *w*, 1968, *Seedling × Iceberg*; LeGrice. Flowers pure white, well-formed, small blooms in clusters; fragrant.

White Star HT, *w*, 1920, *Ophelia sport*; Morse. Flowers ivory-white, base shaded lemon-yellow; very fragrant.

White Success HT, *w*, 1985, (JELpirofor); *Bridal Pink × Seedling*; Jelly; E.G. Hill Co. Flowers white, dbl. (55 petals), high-centered, large blooms borne singly; no fragrance; foliage large, dark, semi-glossy; medium, straight prickles; upright growth; greenhouse variety.

White Swan HT, *w*, 1951, *Kaiserin Auguste Viktoria seedling* × *White seedling*; Verschuren-Pechtold; J&P. Bud ovoid; flowers pure white, dbl. (30 petals), high-centered, large (4½-5 in.); fragrant; foliage glossy, dark; vigorous, upright growth.

White Sweetheart F, *w*, 1941, *Rosenelfe sport*; J&P. Flowers white flushed blush-pink when half open, dbl., high-centered, small; short, strong stems; slightly fragrant; foliage leathery; vigorous, upright, bushy growth; a greenhouse cut flower.

White Tausendschön R, *w*, 1913, *Tausendschön sport*; Paul, W. Flowers white, sometimes flaked pink.

White Wings HT, *w*, 1947, *Dainty Bess* × *Seedling*; Krebs; H&S. Bud long, pointed; flowers white, anthers chocolate-colored, single (5 petals), medium (3½ in.) blooms in large clusters; fragrant; foliage leathery, dark; vigorous, upright, bushy growth.

Whiteout Min, *w*, 1988, (MACwhitout); *Sexy Rexy* × *Popcorn*; McGredy, Sam; Justice Miniature Roses, 1990. Flowers white, dbl. (20 petals), small; slight fragrance; foliage small, medium green, semi-glossy; bushy growth.

Whitley Bay F, *w*, 1988, (HORharryplus); *Champagne Cocktail* × *(Colour Wonder* × *(Vera Dalton* × *Piccadilly))*; Horner, Colin P.; Battersby Roses, 1990. Bud ovoid; flowers cream with pink splashes, reverse cream, cupped, loose, medium, borne in sprays of 6-8; slight fragrance; foliage medium, medium green, semi-glossy; prickles medium, brown; fruit ovoid, medium, yellow; spreading, medium growth.

Whoopi™ Min, *rb*, 1991, (SAVawhoop); *(Yellow Jewel* × *Tamango)* × *Party Girl*; Saville, F. Harmon; Nor'East Miniature Roses, 1992. Flowers red and white blend, red edges suffuse more of each petal as bloom ages, dbl. (28-32 petals), high-centered, exhibition, medium (4 cms) blooms borne usually singly or in sprays of 3-10; slight, spicy fragrance; foliage medium, dark green, semi-glossy; bushy, medium growth.

Why Not Min, *rb*, 1983, (MORwhy); *Golden Angel* × *Seedling*; Moore, R.S.; Moore Min. Roses. Flowers medium red, yellow eye, single (7 petals), small; slight fragrance; foliage small, medium green, matt to semi-glossy; upright, bushy growth.

Whytewold S, *w*, 1961, *R. laxa hybrid*; Skinner. Flowers white, dbl., cupped; height 3 ft.; non-recurrent bloom.

Wichmoss R, *lp*, 1911, *R. wichuraiana* × *Salet*; Barbier. Bud long, pointed, mossed; flowers pale blush-pink fading to white, semi-dbl., small (2 in.) blooms in clusters of 6-15; slightly fragrant; foliage dark, leathery; vigorous, climbing growth.

Wiener Blut F, *or*, 1961, Horstmann. Bud globular; flowers salmon-red, dbl. (30 petals), borne in clusters; very fragrant; vigorous, upright growth.

Wiener Charme® HT, *ob*, 1963, (KORschaprat; Charme de Vienne; Charming Vienne; Vienna Charm); *Chantré* × *Golden Sun*; Kordes, R.; McGredy, 1963; J&P, 1965. Bud pointed; flowers coppery, orange, dbl. (27 petals), high-centered, large (6 in.); fragrant; foliage dark; vigorous, tall.

Wiener Walzer F, *mr*, 1965, (Pur Sang); Tantau, Math. Bud pointed; flowers velvety bright red, dbl. (25-30 petals), large; foliage glossy; very vigorous, upright growth.

Wienerwald HT, *op*, 1974, (Vienna Woods); *Colour Wonder* × *Seedling*; Kordes. Bud long, pointed; flowers pink to light orange, dbl., large; fragrant; foliage large, dark, leathery; vigorous, upright, bushy growth.

Wijhe F, *or*, 1961, *Seedling* × *Alpine Glow*; Buisman. Flowers orange-red, dbl., borne in clusters; foliage dark; moderate growth.

Wilberforce C (OGR), *dr*, *Probably R. centifolia* × *R. gallica*; About 1840. Flowers dark crimson, full, large.

Wild Cherry HT, *mr*, 1984, *King of Hearts* × *Granada*; Bridges, Dennis A.; Bridges Roses, 1985. Flowers medium red, dbl. (38 large petals), large; fragrant; foliage large, dark, glossy; bushy growth.

Wild Child S, *lp*, 1982, *R. rugosa rubra* × *Dortmund seedling*; Hall, William W. Bud small, pointed; flowers light pink, single (5 petals), blooms borne 3-15 per cluster; tea fragrance; foliage small, light green, 9 leaflet, slightly rugose; curved, thin prickles; vigorous, erect, some arching growth; repeat bloom.

Wild Flame HT, *or*, 1973, *Granada* × *South Seas*; Meyer, C.; Ball. Bud ovoid; flowers orange-red, dbl., medium; fragrant; foliage leathery; vigorous, upright growth.

Wild Ginger Gr, *ob*, 1976, *(Queen Elizabeth* × *Ruth Hewitt)* × *Lady Elgin*; Buck; Iowa State University. Bud ovoid, pointed; flowers orange blend, dbl. (33 petals), large (4-4½ in.); fragrant (fruity); foliage dark, leathery; upright, bushy growth.

Wild Honey HT, *ab*, 1977, Weeks. Bud long, pointed; flowers coral and peach, dbl. (45 petals), large (3-5 in.); very fragrant (spicy); foliage leathery; tall, vigorous growth.

Wild One Min, *mr*, 1982, (LYOwe); *Merry Christmas* × *Seedling*; Lyon. Flowers medium red, lighter center, semi-dbl., medium; no fragrance; foliage medium, dark, semi-glossy; bushy, upright growth.

Wild Spirit S, *mr*, 1985, *Alika* × *R. moyesii*; James, John. Flowers bright medium red, single (5 petals), small; fragrant; foliage small, dark, matt; vigorous, upright, branched growth; non-recurrent bloom; fertile.

Wild Thing Min, *ob*, 1992, (TINwild); *Gingersnap* × *Baby Katie*; Bennett, Dee; Tiny Petals Nursery, 1993. Flowers bright orange-yellow, moderately full (15-25 petals), medium (4-7 cms) blooms borne mostly single; fruity fragrance; foliage small, medium green, semi-glossy, disease resistant; some prickles; medium (60-80 cms), bushy growth.

Wildest Dreams Min, *yb*, 1992, (TALwil); *Poker Chip* × *Seedling*; Taylor, Pete & Kay; Taylor's Roses, 1993. Flowers yellow blending to deep pink edges, aging lighter, reverse yellow base spreading to cream and deep pink blend, moderately full (15-25 petals), medium (4-7 cms) blooms borne mostly singly and in small clusters; no fragrance; foliage small, medium green, semi-glossy; few prickles; medium (40 cms), upright, bushy growth.

Wildfeuer S, *mr*, 1953, Kordes. Flowers fiery red, semi-dbl., large (4½ in.); bushy.

Wildfire F, *mr*, 1955, *World's Fair* × *Pinocchio*; Swim; Armstrong Nursery. Bud ovoid; flowers bright red, 8-10 petals, large (3 in.) blooms in clusters; slightly fragrant; foliage leathery; vigorous, bushy, compact growth.

Wildwood HT, *op*, 1937, H&S. Bud long, pointed; flowers gold, salmon and bronze, semi-dbl.; very fragrant; foliage glossy, wrinkled; vigorous growth.

Wilf Taylor HT, *ab*, 1981, *Gavotte* × *Red Lion*; Bracegirdle, A.J. Flowers apricot, dbl. (35 petals), exhibition, large; slight fragrance; foliage large, dark, matt; upright growth.

Wilfred Norris HT, *mp*, 1972, *Tropicana* × *Elizabeth of Glamis*; Harkness. Flowers medium salmon-pink, dbl. (23 petals), large; foliage matt.

Wilfred Pickles HT, *op*, 1939, *Mrs. Charles Lamplough* × *Edith Mary Mee*; Mee; Fryer's Nursery. Flowers peach shaded gold, dbl. (26 petals), well formed, large (6 in.); stems red; fragrant; foliage glossy, dark; very vigorous growth.

Wilfrid H. Perron Min, *mp*, 1987, (LAVshrimp); *(Dwarfking '78* × *Baby Katie)* × *Painted Doll*; Laver, Keith, 1988. Flowers clear shrimp-pink, aging paler, very dbl. (70-80 petals), large, borne singly; no fragrance; foliage very small, medium green, matt; prickles straight out, very slender, greenish-red; fruit round, green-red, very rare set; bushy, low growth.

Wilhelm Hansmann K (S), *dr*, 1955, (William Hansmann); Kordes. Bud ovoid; flowers deep crimson, dbl., high-centered, large blooms in clusters; slightly fragrant; foliage dark, leathery; very vigorous growth; recurrent bloom.

Wilhelm Kordes HT, *op*, 1922, *Gorgeous* × *Adolf Koschel*; Kordes, H. Bud long, pointed; flowers salmon, copper and golden blend, dbl., high-centered, large; fragrant; foliage bronze, leathery, glossy; bushy growth.

Wilhelm Kordes, Climbing Cl HT, *op*, 1927, Wood; Ingram.

Wilhelm Teetzmann F, *mr*, 1943, (Advance Guard); *Holstein* × *Crimson Glory*; Kordes. Flowers intense crimson, semi-dbl., open, large (3½ in.), borne in clusters; very vigorous, upright, bushy growth; (28).

Wilhire Country F, *ob*, 1981, (Willhire Country); *Elizabeth of Glamis* × *Arthur Bell*; Beales, Peter; Beales Roses, 1979. Flowers orange blend, 25 petals, flat-topped blooms borne 6-8 per cluster; strong fragrance; foliage glossy, round, dark; broad, hooked, brown prickles; tall, upright.

Will Alderman HRg (S), *mp*, 1954, *(R. rugosa* × *R. acicularis)* ×*Seedling*; Skinner. Flowers clear rose-pink, dbl., well-shaped, large; very fragrant; erect (4 ft.), bushy growth; repeat bloom.

Will Rogers HT, *dr*, 1936, *Seedling* × *(Hadley* × *Crimson Glory)*; Howard, F.H.; H&S. Flowers velvety maroon-crimson, base almost black, burning in sun, dbl. (65 petals), medium (3 in.); very fragrant (damask); foliage leathery, light; vigorous growth.

Will Rogers, Climbing Cl HT, *dr*, 1940, H&S.

Will Scarlet HMsk (S), *mr*, 1948, *Skyrocket* sport; Hilling; Wayside Gardens Co., 1956. Flowers scarlet.

William Allen Richardson N (OGR), *yb*, 1878, *Rêve d'Or seedling*; Ducher, Vve. Bud pointed; flowers orange-yellow, usually white at petal edges, dbl., medium to large; very vigorous, climbing (12 ft.) growth; early bloom, repeating; (14).

William Baffin K (S), *dp*, 1983, *R. kordesii seedling*; Svedja, Felicitas; Agriculture Canada. Bud ovoid; flowers deep pink, dbl. (20 petals), blooms in clusters of 30; no fragrance; foliage glossy; vigorous, climbing growth.

William Bowyer HT, *mr*, 1924, *Hadley* × *Hoosier Beauty*; Chaplin Bros. Bud long, pointed; flower velvety red; very fragrant.

William Carter HT, *dp*, 1957, *Red Ensign sport*; Carter. Flowers deep pink; fragrant; very vigorous growth.

William Cobbett F, *dp*, 1968, *Dorothy Wheatcroft sport*; Seale Rose Gardens. Flowers claret-rose, semi-dbl., borne in trusses; slightly fragrant; vigorous growth.

William C. Egan LCl, *lp*, 1900, *R. wichuraiana* × *Général Jacqueminot*; Dawson; Hoopes, Bro.; Thomas. Flowers flesh-pink, very dbl., large, borne in large clusters on long stems; fragrant; foliage bright, glossy; vigorous, semi-climbing growth; non-recurrent bloom.

William E. Nickerson HT, *or*, 1928, *Priscilla* × *William F. Dreer*; Easlea. Flowers glowing orange-cerise, dbl., large; fragrant; foliage light; vigorous growth.

William Francis Bennett HT, *mr*, 1880, Bennett. Bud long; flowers crimson, full, large; fragrant.

William F. Dreer HT, *lp*, 1920, *Mme. Segond Weber* × *Lyon Rose*; H&S. Flowers shell-pink, base yellow, sometimes suffusing the entire flower, dbl., high-centered, large; fragrant.

William F. Ekas HT, *op*, 1935, *Souvenir sport*; Cremer. Bud cupped; flowers salmon-orange, suffused pink, full (45-50 petals), large (4 in.); fragrant.

William Godfrey S, *lp*, 1954, *Altalaris* × *Hybrid Perpetual*; Skinner. Bud white; flowers pale pink, very dbl., well shaped, large; moderately vigorous, erect growth; intermittent bloom all season.

William Harvey HT, *mr*, 1948, *Crimson Glory* × *Southport*; Norman; Harkness. Flowers scarlet, dbl., high-centered, large (4-6 in.); very fragrant; vigorous, bushy growth.

William III HSpn (OGR), *m*, *R. spinosissima hybrid*. Flowers magenta-crimson, changing to rich plum, fading to dark lilac-pink, semi-dbl., small; fragrant (spicy); foliage tiny, dark.

William Jesse HP (OGR), *mr*, 1840, Laffay. Flowers red suffused violet, full, large.

William Leech HT, *yb*, 1988, (HORtropic; Sir William Leech); *Royal Dane* × *Piccadilly*; Horner, Calvin L.; Battersby Roses, 1989. Bud ovoid; flowers yellow edged red, reverse light yellow, dbl., high-centered, exhibition, large, borne usually singly; slight fragrance; foliage medium, medium green, glossy; prickles medium, red; fruit ovoid, large, orange; bushy, medium growth.

William Lobb M (OGR), *m*, 1855, (Duchesse d'Istrie; Old Velvet Moss); Laffay. Flowers dark crimson-purple, reverse lilac-pink, fading to grayish-lavender, semi-dbl., large; very mossy; extremely prickly; vigorous growth.

William Moore HT, *mp*, 1935, McGredy. Bud long, pointed; flowers soft, even-toned pink, becoming deeper, dbl., cupped, large; very fragrant; foliage soft, light; bushy growth.

William Notting HT, *rb*, 1904, *Mme. Abel Chatenay* × *Antoine Rivoire*; Soupert; Notting. Flowers salmon-red, center brighter, dbl.; fragrant.

William Orr HT, *mr*, 1930, McGredy. Bud long, pointed; flowers crimson-scarlet, dbl. (45 reflexed petals), high-centered, large; very fragrant; foliage light, glossy, leathery; vigorous growth.

William R. Smith T (OGR), *pb*, 1908, (Blush Maman Cochet; Charles Dingee; Jeannette Heller; Maiden's Blush; President Smith; President Wm. R. Smith); *Maman Cochet* × *Mme. Hoste*; Bagg; E.G. Hill Co.; P. Henderson. Bud pointed; flowers center pale pink, outer petals creamy flesh, base citron-yellow, dbl.; foliage rich green, leathery; vigorous growth.

William Shakespeare® S, *dr*, 1987, (AUSroyal); *The Squire* × *Mary Rose*; Austin, David. Flowers deep crimson-purple, fading rich purple, dbl., rosette, small, borne in sprays of 3-7; heavy, damask fragrance; foliage large, dark green, semi-glossy; broad based, straight, medium, red prickles; no fruit; upright, tall growth; repeat bloom.

William Shean HT, *mp*, 1906, Dickson, A. Bud long, tapering; flowers clear rose-pink, veined darker, dbl. (45 shell-shaped petals), very large. GM, NRS, 1906.

William Silva HT, 1951, *Étoile de Hollande* × *Radiance*; Silva; vigorous growth; heavy roots; few prickles at base; fast growing; sometimes used as understock.

William the Fourth HSpn (OGR), *lp*, *R. spinosissima hybrid*. Flowers light pink, very dbl.; very dwarf growth; non-recurrent bloom.

William Thomson Pol, *pb*, 1921, *Maman Turbat* × *Ellen Poulsen*; Leenders, M. Flowers salmon-carmine and bright rose, small, borne in clusters; compact, bushy growth.

William Walker HT, *dy*, 1984, (DEBraro); *Western Sun* × *Circus*; Bracegirdle, D.T. Flowers deep yellow, dbl. (20 petals), medium; no fragrance; foliage medium, medium green, semi-glossy; upright growth.

William Wright Walcott HT, *lp*, 1921, *Richmond sport* × *Ophelia*; McGorum. Flowers light pink, outer petals darker, dbl.

William's Double Yellow HSpn   (OGR), *my*, 1828, (Double Yellow Scots Rose); *R. foetida is considered to be one of the parents*; Williams, John. Flowers pine-yellow with green carpels, semi-dbl., small (2 in.); very fragrant (sweet); foliage tiny, dark; growth free but spindly; very free bloom in spring.

Williamsburg HT, *lp*, 1965, *Contrast × Queen Elizabeth*; Howard, A.P.; Great Western Rose Co. Bud long, pointed; flowers rose-pink, dbl., cupped, medium; fragrant; foliage dark, glossy; vigorous, upright growth.

Willie Mae Min, *mr*, 1966, *(R. wichuraiana × Carolyn Dean) × Little Buckaroo*; Moore, R.S.; Mini-Roses. Flowers red, dbl., small; slightly fragrant; foliage dark, glossy, leathery; vigorous, bushy, dwarf growth.

Willie Winkie Min, *lp*, 1955, *Katharina Zeimet × Tom Thumb*; de Vink; T. Robinson. Flowers light rose-pink, dbl., globular, micromini, small.

Williwaw HT, *m*, 1978, *Silver Lining × Duke of Windsor*; Melle. Bud pointed; flowers red-purple, yellow at base, dbl. (60 petals), cupped; fragrant; foliage glossy, dark; hooked prickles; upright growth.

Willowmere HT, *op*, 1913, *Seedling × Lyon Rose*; Pernet-Ducher. Bud long, pointed; coral-red; flowers rich shrimp-pink, center yellow, dbl., cupped; foliage light; spreading growth.

Willowmere, Climbing   Cl HT, *op*, 1924, Mermet.

Willy Chapel HT, *yb*, 1930, Delhaye. Flowers coppery yellow, shaded salmon and shrimp-pink; vigorous growth.

Willy Den Ouden Pol, *or*, 1938, Den Ouden. Flowers intense orange, rosette form, small, borne on trusses; dwarf, compact growth.

Wilshire HT, *mp*, 1991, *Don Juan sport*; Woodard, Joe, 1983; Kimbrew-Walter Rose Growers, 1991. Bud pointed; flowers medium pink, dbl. (25 petals), high-centered, exhibition, medium; moderate fragrance; foliage medium, medium green, glossy; upright, tall growth. ARC TG (B), 1985.

Wiltshire Pride HT, *rb*, 1988, (SANwife); *Bristol × Piccadilly*; Sanday, John; John Sanday Roses, Ltd., 1989. Flowers scarlet with yellow at base, reverse yellow with red edging, aging redder, dbl. (28 petals), exhibition, medium, borne usually singly; slight fragrance; foliage large, dark green, semi-glossy; prickles slightly hooked, dark brown; upright, tall growth.

Wimi® HT, *pb*, 1982, (TANrowisa); Tantau, Math., 1983. Flowers shiny pink, silver reverse, dbl. (20 petals), well-formed, large; very fragrant; foliage large, dark, semi-glossy; bushy growth.

Wind Chimes HMsk (S), *mp*, Lester, prior to 1946; Lester Rose Gardens, ca. 1949. Flowers rosy pink, small (1 in.) blooms in clusters; very fragrant; vigorous (15-20 ft.) growth; recurrent bloom.

Wind Song HT, *ab*, 1968, *Royal Sunset × Sierra Sunset*; Morey; Country Garden Nursery. Flowers orange, dbl., large; fragrant; foliage leathery; bushy growth.

Windekind F, *mr*, 1974, *Colour Wonder × Geisha*; Inst. of Orn. Plant Growing. Bud pointed; flowers red, dbl. (34 petals), cupped, large (3 in.); foliage matt, dark; upright.

Windermere LCl, *dp*, 1932, Chaplin Bros. Flowers carmine-rose, semi-dbl., blooms in large clusters; vigorous growth.

Windjammer Min, *dp*, 1982, (SAVswat); *Sheri Anne × Watercolor*; Saville, F. Harmon; Nor'East Min. Roses. Flowers deep pink, reddened by sun, dbl. (35 petals), small; slight fragrance; foliage medium, medium green, semi-glossy.

Windmill S, *rb*, 1992, (WILwind); *Handel × (Love × Double Feature)*; Williams, J. Benjamin, 1994. Flowers burgundy with ivory white on reverse bi-color, single (5 recurling petals), large (7+ cms) blooms borne singly and in small clusters; slight fragrance; foliage medium, medium green, semi-glossy; few prickles; medium (3-5'), bushy, spreading growth.

Windrush® S, *ly*, 1985, (AUSrush); *Seedling × (Canterbury × Golden Wings)*; Austin, David, 1984. Flowers light yellow, semi-dbl., large; very fragrant; foliage medium, light green, matt; vigorous, branching growth.

Windsor HT, *mr*, 1929, Chaplin Bros. Flowers rich crimson-scarlet; fragrant; vigorous growth.

Windsor Charm HT, *lp*, 1978, *First Prize sport*; Lemire. Bud long, tulip shaped; flowers light pink to ivory, dbl. (27-30 petals), very large (5-5½ in.); slightly fragrant; foliage leathery; vigorous, bushy growth.

Windsounds HT, *lp*, 1976, *First Prize sport*; Scoggins; American Rose Foundation. Flowers light pink. Named for the Windsounds at the American Rose Center.

Windy City Min, *dp*, 1974, *Little Darling × (Little Darling × (R. wichuraiana × Seedling;)* Moore, R.S.; Mini-Roses. Flowers deep pink, reverse lighter, dbl., high-centered, small; slightly fragrant; foliage small, bronze; upright, bushy growth.

Winefred Clarke HT, *my*, 1964, *Peace × Lydia*; Robinson, H. Flowers yellow, dbl. (34 petals), high-centered, large (5½ in.); foliage dark, glossy.

Winged Fellowship F, *or*, 1988, (HORwingfel); *Guitare* × *Prominent*; Horner, Heather M.; Rosemary Roses, 1989. Bud ovoid; flowers vermillion orange, reverse lighter, dbl. (28 petals), urn-shaped, medium, borne in sprays of 5-7; slight fragrance; foliage medium, medium green, matt; prickles small, brown; fruit globular, medium, red-orange; bushy, medium growth.

Wini Edmunds HT, *rb*, 1973, *Red Lion* × *Hanne*; McGredy, S., IV; Edmunds. Flowers red, reverse white, dbl., high-centered, large; fragrant; foliage dark, leathery; vigorous, upright.

Winifred HT, *yb*, 1930, Chaplin Bros. Flowers deep yellow, shaded peach to old-gold, full, large; vigorous growth. RULED EXTINCT 4/81.

Winifred Gr, *mp*, 1981, *Queen Elizabeth* × *Seedling*; Jerabek, Paul E. Bud pointed; flowers bright medium pink, dbl. (23 petals); light fragrance; foliage reddish when young; slightly hooked, red prickles; vigorous, tall growth.

Winifred Coulter F, *rb*, 1962, *Baby Château* × *Contrast*; Kemple; Van Barneveld. Bud pointed; flowers vermilion-scarlet, reverse silvery, dbl. (23 petals), flat, large (2½-3 in,) blooms in clusters; very fragrant; foliage leathery, glossy, dark; vigorous, bushy growth. ARS David Fuerstenberg Prize, 1968.

Winkfield Crimson Emperor LCl, *dr*, 1958, *Red Empress* × *Surprise*; Combe; Winkfield Manor Nursery. Flowers dark crimson, dbl. (27 petals), large (3½ in.), borne in clusters; slightly fragrant; foliage leathery; vigorous, pillar growth; recurrent bloom.

Winners All HT, *dp*, 1990, *Cherry Brandy sport*; Rearsby Roses, Ltd., 1986; Rearsby Roses, Ltd. Bud ovoid; flowers carmine pink with a touch of orange in center, dbl., cupped, loose, large, borne usually singly; slight, fruity fragrance; foliage medium, medium green, semi-glossy; bushy, medium growth.

Winnie Davis HT, *mp*, 1902, *Kaiserin Auguste Viktoria* × *Mrs. W.J. Grant*; Nanz; Neuner. Bud long, pointed; flowers pink with lighter reflexes, semi-dbl.; fragrant.

Winnie Renshaw Min, *lp*, 1991, (RENwinnie); *Lavonde* × *Party Girl*; Rennie, Bruce; Rennie Roses International. Flowers light pink, moderately full, small blooms borne in small clusters; fragrant; foliage small, medium green, semi-glossy; medium growth.

Winning Colors™ Gr, *ob*, 1989, (TWOwin); *Gingersnap* × *Marina*; Twomey, Jerry; DeVor

Nursery, 1990. Bud ovoid; flowers orange-yellow blend, very dbl. (60 petals), cupped, medium, borne singly; moderate, musk fragrance; foliage medium, dark green, glossy; prickles declining, yellow-green; upright, medium growth.

Winnipeg Parks S, *dp*, 1990, *(Prairie Princess* × *Cuthbert Grant)* × *(Seedling* × *Morden Cardinette)*; Collicutt, Lynn M., 1981; Agriculture Canada, 1991. Bud pointed; flowers dark pink-red, dark pink reverse, aging dark pink, semi-dbl. (22 petals), cupped, medium, borne singly or in sprays of 1-4; slight fragrance; foliage medium, medium green, matt; medium, bushy growth; repeats.

Winsome HT, *dp*, 1924, *Premier* × *Hoosier Beauty*; Hill, E.G., Co.; Vestal. Flowers cherry-rose, dbl.; slightly fragrant. RULED EXTINCT 1/85.

Winsome Cl HT, *mr*, 1931, Dobbie. Bud long, pointed; flowers cherry-red, dbl., large; very fragrant; foliage leathery; very vigorous growth. RULED EXTINCT 1/85.

Winsome™ Min, *m*, 1984, (SAVawin); *Party Girl* × *Shocking Blue*; Saville, F. Harmon; Nor'East Min. Roses, 1985. Flowers red-purple, dbl. (40+ petals), high-centered, HT form, mini-flora, medium blooms borne singly and in sprays; no fragrance; foliage medium, dark, semi-glossy; upright, bushy growth. AOE, 1985.

Winsome Native HSuf (S), *w*, 1979, *Gene Boerner* × *R. suffulta*; Stoddard, Louis. Bud ovoid, pointed; flowers white, dbl. (20 petals), cupped, borne singly; no fragrance; foliage finely serrated, 5 leaflet; no prickles; rounded, medium growth; sparse, repeat bloom.

Winter King S, *dp*, 1985, *((McGredy's Scarlet* × *Polly)* × *Frau Karl Druschki)* × *Northlander*; James, John. Flowers bright deep pink, semi-dbl. (11 petals), medium blooms borne singly; very fragrant; foliage medium, dark, leathery, matt; compact, branching growth; repeat bloom; hardy.

Winter Magic™ Min, *m*, 1986, (FOUmagic); *Rise 'n' Shine* × *Blue Nile*; Jacobs, Betty A.; Four Seasons Rose Nursery. Flowers light lavender-gray, golden stamens, dbl. (30 petals), cupped, large blooms borne usually singly and in small sprays; citrus tea fragrance; foliage medium, medium green, semi-glossy; red, slender, straight, medium prickles; fruit medium, orange-red, globular; medium, upright, bushy growth.

Wintonbury Parish Min, *w*, 1988, (BERpar); *Poker Chip* × *Lady X*; Berg, David. Flowers white with top third of petal light red, semi-dbl. (14 petals), high-centered, medium, borne usually singly; slight fragrance; foliage medium, medium green, semi-glossy; prickles curved, large, light greenish-white; upright, medium growth.

Wintoniensis HMoy (S), *mp*, (*R.* × *wintoniensis* Hillier); *R. moyesii* × *R. setipoda*; 1935. Flowers rosy pink, blooms in clusters; foliage with sweetbrier (apple) fragrance; general appearance like *R. moyesii.*

Wisbech Gold HT, *yb*, 1964, *Piccadilly* × *Golden Star*; McGredy, S., IV; McGredy. Flowers golden yellow edged pinkish, dbl. (35 petals), cupped, well-formed, large (4 in.); fragrant; vigorous, compact growth.

Wise Portia S, *m*, 1983, (AUSport); *The Knight* × *Seedling*; Austin, David, 1982. Flowers mauve, dbl. (40+ petals), large; very fragrant; foliage medium, dark, semi-glossy; bushy growth.

Wishing F, *mp*, 1985, (DICkerfuffle; Georgie Girl); *Silver Jubilee* × *Bright Smile*; Dickson, P.; Dickson Nursery Ltd., 1984. Flowers medium peachy pink, dbl. (35 petals), large; slight fragrance; foliage medium, medium green, semi-glossy; bushy growth.

Witchcraft F, *yb*, 1961, *Masquerade* × *Seedling*; Verschuren; Blaby Rose Gardens. Bud ovoid; flowers yellow, reverse scarlet, dbl. (45-50 petals), medium (2-2½ in.), borne in large clusters; fragrant; foliage dark, glossy; vigorous growth.

Witching Hour F, *dr*, 1967, *Rapture* × (*F.W. Alesworth* × *Charles Mallerin*); Morey; Country Garden Nursery. Bud ovoid; flowers dark red, almost black, dbl., medium; vigorous, bushy, compact growth.

With Love HT, *yb*, 1983, (ANDwit); *Grandpa Dickson* × *Daily Sketch*; Andersons Rose Nursery. Flowers yellow, petal edges pink; fragrant; foliage medium, medium green, semi-glossy; upright growth.

Wit's End Min, *rb*, 1988, (SEAwit); *Rise 'n' Shine* × *Siobhan*; McCann, Sean, 1989. Flowers red with yellow reverse, dbl. (20 petals), small, borne in sprays of 3-5; slight fragrance; foliage small, medium green, semi-glossy; bushy growth.

Wizo® HT, *ob*, 1968, (KRIwi); *Tropicana* × (*Gamine* × *Romantica*); Kriloff; Domaine Agricole de Cronenbourg. Flowers salmon-red, reverse darker, dbl. (40 petals), high-centered; foliage reddish-green, matt.

Woburn Abbey F, *ob*, 1962, *Masquerade* × *Fashion*; Sidey; Cobley; Harkness, 1962; J&P, 1964. Bud ovoid; flowers orange, dbl. (25 petals), cupped, large (3½ in.) blooms in clusters; fragrant; foliage dark, leathery; moderate growth.

Woburn Gold F, *dy*, 1970, *Woburn Abbey sport*; Robinson, H. Flowers gold.

Wolfe's Glorie Pol, *op*, 1943, *Orléans Rose sport*; Wolf, Van der; Hage. Flowers salmon-pink to deep orange; vigorous growth; a greenhouse variety.

Wolfgang von Goethe HP (OGR), *pb*, 1933, *Frau Karl Druschki* × *Souv. de Claudius Pernet*; Weigand, L. Bud very long; flowers delicate bright yellowish pink, full, high-centered, very large; vigorous growth.

Woman and Home HT, *ob*, 1976, *Apricot Silk* × *Piccadilly seedling*; Gregory. Flowers orange, dbl. (33 petals), pointed, large (5 in.); slightly fragrant; foliage glossy, dark.

Woman's Day HT, *or*, 1966, *Queen Elizabeth* × *Karl Herbst*; Armbrust; Langbecker. Bud ovoid; flowers scarlet-orange, semi-dbl., high-centered, medium; foliage leathery; vigorous, upright growth.

Woman's Own® Min, *mp*, 1973, *New Penny* × *Tip-Top*; McGredy, S., IV; McGredy. Flowers pink, dbl. (45 petals), small (1½ in.); slightly fragrant; foliage dark.

Woman's Realm HT, *mr*, 1966, *Chrysler Imperial seedling*; Gregory. Flowers scarlet, large (3½-4 in.); slightly fragrant; foliage glossy; upright growth.

Woman's Value HT, *pb*, 1984, (KORvalue); (*Sonia* × ((*Dr. A.J. Verhage* × *Colour Wonder*) × *Zorina*)) × *Asso di Cuori*; Kordes, R.; Ludwigs Roses Ltd. Flowers cream with shades of rose and coral, dbl. (42 petals), star-shaped blooms borne singly or 7-15 per cluster; slight fragrance; foliage glossy, deep green; straight, brown prickles; medium, bushy, well-branched growth.

Wonder of Woolies F, *ab*, 1978, *Arthur Bell* × *Elizabeth of Glamis*; Bees. Flowers deep apricot, dbl. (30 petals), large (4½ in.); very fragrant; vigorous growth.

Wonderstar F, *my*, 1960, *Goldilocks* × *Seedling*; Mondial Roses. Flowers bright yellow, semi-dbl., large; low, bushy growth.

Wood Lawn HT, *mp*, 1985, (FIAlawn); *Fontainebleau sport*; Fiamingo, J. Flowers clear medium pink.

Woodland Sunbeam Min, *my*, 1984, (TRObgold); *Orange Sensation* × *Calay*; Robinson, Thomas. Flowers medium yellow, dbl. (23 petals), patio, medium; very fragrant; foliage small, dark, glossy; few prickles; vigorous, bushy growth.

Woodlands Lady Min, *mp*, 1984, (TRObsa); *Seedling* × *New Penny*; Robinson, Thomas. Flowers medium salmon-pink, semi-dbl. (15 petals), small blooms in large clusters; slight fragrance; foliage small, dark, glossy; compact, bushy growth.

Woodlands Sunrise Min, *yb*, 1982, (TRObsun); *Rumba × Darling Flame*; Robinson, Thomas. Flowers yellow blend, dbl. (35 petals), small; slight fragrance; foliage small, dark, glossy; upright, bushy growth.

Woodrow Sp (OGR), *mp*, *R. suffulta natural variant*; Hunt, Miss Alice; P.H. Wright, 1936. Collected in the wild near Woodrow, Sask., Canada by Miss Alice Hunt, about 1925. Flowers pink, dbl. (60 petals); low growth; fall bloom.

Work of Art Cl Min, *ob*, 1989, (MORart); *Yellow Climbing Miniature seedling × Gold Badge*; Moore, Ralph S.; Sequoia Nursery. Bud short; flowers orange blend, reverse slightly more yellow, dbl. (35 petals), urn-shaped, high-centered, exhibition, medium, borne in sprays of 3-5; slight fragrance; foliage medium, bronze aging to medium green, semiglossy; prickles slender, nearly straight, average, brown, few; fruit globular, medium, orange; upright, spreading, tall growth.

World Peace™ HT, *pb*, 1987, (BURworpe); *First Prize × Gold Glow*; Perry, Anthony, 1972; Co-Operative Rose Growers, 1989. Flowers pink blend suffused with cream, tips of petals tinged dark pink, dbl. (30-35 petals), high-centered, exhibition, large; moderate, fruity fragrance; foliage large, medium green, semiglossy, disease resistant; average prickles; fruit globular, orange; upright, tall growth.

World's Fair F, *dr*, 1939, (Minna Kordes); *Dance of Joy × Crimson Glory*; Kordes; J&P. Flowers deep crimson fading to scarlet, semidbl. (19 petals), large (4 in.) blooms in clusters; fragrant (spicy); foliage leathery; vigorous, bushy growth. AARS, 1940.

World's Fair, Climbing Cl F, *dr*, 1941, J&P.

World's Fair Salute HT, *mr*, 1964, *Mardi Gras × New Yorker*; Morey; J&P. Bud ovoid; flowers crimson-red, dbl. (33 petals), high-centered, large (5½ in.); fragrant; foliage leathery; vigorous, upright growth.

Worthington Sp (OGR), *lp*, *R. setigera natural variation*; Found in Ohio, about 1840. Flowers clear pink, over 5 petals.

Worthwhile HT, *ob*, 1973, *Gavotte × Vienna Charm*; LeGrice. Flowers orange, reverse lighter, dbl. (33 petals), pointed, large (5-6 in.); slightly fragrant; foliage matt, olive-green.

Wow! Min, *ob*, 1985, (PIXiwow); *Ann Cocker × Seedling*; Strawn, Leslie E.; Pixie Treasures Min. Roses. Flowers bright orange, dbl. (35 petals), small; slight fragrance; foliage small, dark, glossy; bushy growth.

W. R. Hawkins HT, *op*, 1948, *Crimson Glory seedling × Silver Jubilee*; Toogood. Bud ovoid; flowers tango-pink, very dbl., high-centered, large; very fragrant; foliage glossy; vigorous, upright growth.

Wright's Salmon HT, *op*, 1960, *Opera sport*; Wright & Son. Flowers salmon, dbl. (32 petals), high-centered, large (5 in.).

Wynanda F, *mp*, 1968, *United Nations × Seedling*; Heidemij. Bud ovoid; flowers pink, dbl., medium; slightly fragrant; foliage dark.

Wyralla HT, *dr*, 1949, *Lemania × Ami Quinard*; Heers; Pacific Nursery. Bud ovoid; flowers dark red, semi-dbl., high-centered, large; vigorous, bushy growth.

Xavier Olibo HP (OGR), *dr*, 1865, *Général Jacqueminot sport*; Lacharme. Flowers velvety crimson shaded purplish.

Xerxes S, *yb*, 1989, (HARjames); *H. persica × Canary Bird*; Harkness, R. & Co., Ltd. Bud pointed; flowers rich yellow with scarlet red eye at base, reverse yellow, aging tones muted, single (5 petals), cupped to flat, medium, borne usually singly; slight fragrance; foliage small, grayish-green, matt; prickles narrow, small, reddish; fruit none observed; upright, medium to tall growth.

Yabadabadoo® HT, *dy*, 1981, (MACyaba); *Yellow Pages × Bonfire Night*; McGredy, Sam. Flowers deep yellow, dbl. (20 petals), large; slight fragrance; foliage medium, medium green, semi-glossy; bushy growth.

Yachiyo-Nishiki F, *ob*, 1986, (*Maxim × MyoJoh*) *× Fragrant Cloud*; Suzuki, S.; Keisei Rose Nursery, 1984. Flowers orange, reverse yellow, dbl. (28 petals), medium, borne 2-5 pet stem; medium fragrance; foliage dark green, semi-glossy; prickles curved downwards; upright, compact growth.

Yametsu-Hime Min, *pb*, 1961, *Tom Thumb × Seedling*; Hebaru; Itami Rose Nursery. Flowers white edged pink, semi-dbl., small; foliage glossy, light; dwarf growth.

Yamini Krishnamurti HT, *m*, 1969, *Sterling Silver, Climbing × Open pollination*; Singh; Gopalsinamiengar. Flowers lilac, dbl., high-centered, medium; slightly fragrant; foliage glossy; moderate growth.

Yanina F, *op*, 1964, *Fashion × Queen Elizabeth*; Yeoman & Sons. Flowers salmon-pink, semi-dbl. (16 petals), large; fragrant; foliage glossy; vigorous growth.

Yanka S, *mp*, 1927, (*Tetonkaha × Gruss an Teplitz*) *× La Mélusine*; Hansen, N.E. Flowers pink, semi-dbl., borne in clusters; height 3-4 ft.; non-recurrent bloom; very hardy.

Yankee Doodle® HT, *yb*, 1965, (YanKOR); *Colour Wonder × King's Ransom*; Kordes, R.;

Armstrong Nursery. Bud urn-shaped; flowers apricot to peachy pink and butter-yellow, dbl. (75 petals), imbricated, large (4 in.); slightly fragrant (tea); foliage glossy, dark; upright, bushy growth. AARS, 1976.

Yantai Min, *yb*, 1989, (TINtai); *Portrait × Party Girl*; Bennett, Dee; Tiny Petals Nursery, 1988. Bud ovoid; flowers pastel yellow, deeper yellow in center and highlights of pastel pink, dbl. (28 petals), high-centered, exhibition, borne usually singly and in sprays of 3-5; moderate, fruity fragrance; foliage medium, medium green, semi-glossy; prickles hooked downward, yellow to red; bushy, spreading, tall, vigorous growth.

Yaroslavna HT, *mp*, 1958, (Famous Cliff); *La Parisienne × Peace*; Sushkov; Besschetnova. Flowers pink, dbl. (60 petals), large; fragrant; foliage dark; vigorous growth.

Yashwant HT, *rb*, 1986, *Suspense sport*; Patil, B.K.; KSG Sons, 1985. Flowers red, striped white and yellow, reverse yellow, striped red, dbl. (55-60 petals), high-centered, large; slight fragrance; foliage glossy; pale, green prickles, curving downwards; vigorous, upright, bushy growth.

Yasnaya Poliana HT, *op*, 1958, (Bright Meadow); *Independence × Luna*; Shtanko, I. Flowers salmon-pink, dbl. (45-50 petals), well formed, large; fragrant; foliage dark; vigorous, compact growth.

Yatkan S, *mp*, 1927, *Probably Gruss an Teplitz × La Mélusine*; Hansen, N.E. Flowers pure, dbl., medium (2½ in.); non-recurrent bloom; very hardy.

Yawa HBlanda (S), *op*, 1940, *Anci Bohmova × R. blanda*; Hansen, N.E. Flowers light coral-pink, dbl. (58 petals), medium (2 in.), borne in clusters of 4-12 on 8-12 in. stems; fragrant; tall, wide spreading (pillar to 9 ft.) growth; free, non-recurrent bloom; very hardy.

Yeller Rose O'Texas HT, *dy*, 1986, *Arizona sport*; Wambach, A.A. Flowers deep yellow, full (26-40 petals), medium, very fragrant; foliage medium, medium green, semi-glossy; upright growth.

Yello Yo Yo F, *dy*, 1980, *Arlene Francis × Seedling*; Weeks. Bud slender, long; flowers deep yellow, dbl. (20 petals), high-centered blooms borne singly and in clusters; slight tea fragrance; foliage medium green; upright growth.

Yellow Altai HSpn (OGR), *my*, 1950, *R. spinosissima altaica × Persian Yellow*; Wright, P.H. Flowers bright yellow, becoming lighter, small, borne in clusters; foliage light green, soft; stems reddish brown; vigorous (7 ft.), upright growth; profuse, non-recurrent bloom; hardy (to -60).

Yellow Bantam Min, *ly*, 1960, *(R. wichuraiana × Floradora) × Fairy Princess*; Moore, R.S.; Sequoia Nursery. Bud pointed, yellow; flowers yellow to white, dbl. (25 petals), micromini, very small (½ in.); slightly fragrant; foliage glossy; bushy (10 in.) growth.

Yellow Bantam, Climbing Cl Min, *ly*, 1964, Rumsey.

Yellow Beauty HT, *my*, 1945, *Golden Rapture sport*; Ruzicka's. Bud longer, more pointed, clear golden yellow; more uniform growth; a florists' variety, not distributed for outdoor use.

Yellow Bedder HT, *ly*, 1923, *Mr. Joh. M. Jolles × Mme. Edouard Herriot*; Van Rossem. Flowers clear yellow to cream, dbl.; slightly fragrant.

Yellow Belinda F, *dy*, 1972, (TANyellda); *Tanbeedee sport*; Tantau. Bud long, pointed; flowers orange-yellow, dbl., medium.

Yellow Bird HT, *dy*, 1974, *Sunlight × Arthur Bell*; McGredy. Bud ovoid; flowers deep yellow, dbl. (42 petals), large (3½ in.); slightly fragrant; upright growth.

Yellow Butterfly HT, *ob*, 1927, *Mme. Butterfly sport*; Scott, R. Flowers orange-yellow. RULED EXTINCT 1/89.

Yellow Butterfly S, *ly*, 1989, (MORwings); *Ellen Poulsen × Yellow Jewel*; Moore, Ralph S.; Sequoia Nursery. Bud pointed; flowers light yellow, aging to near white, single (5 petals), informal, medium, borne in sprays of 3-7; no fragrance; foliage medium, light green, semi-glossy; prickles slender, inclined downward, small, brownish; fruit ovoid, small, yellowish-orange; bushy, spreading, medium, clean growth.

Yellow Button® S, *yb*, 1975, *Wife of Bath × Chinatown*; Austin, David. Bud globular; flowers medium yellow, deeper in center, very dbl. (90 petals), flat, rosette blooms borne 1-15 per cluster; slight fragrance; foliage dark; straight, red prickles; bushy; repeats.

Yellow Charles Austin® S, *ly*, 1981, *Charles Austin sport*; Austin, David, 1979. Flowers light yellow.

Yellow Cluster F, *my*, 1949, *Golden Rapture × Polyantha seedling*; deRuiter; Spek. Flowers mimosa-yellow; spreading growth.

Yellow Contempo F, *dy*, 1983, *Contempo somatic sport, gamma ray induced*; Gupta, Dr. M.N., Datta, Dr. S.K.; Banerji, Shri B.K.; National Botanical Research Institute. Flowers deep yellow.

Yellow Creeping Everbloom LCl, *my*, 1953, *((Orange Everglow × New Dawn) × Seedling) × Free Gold*; Brownell. Flowers yellow; very vigorous, pillar or ground cover; recurrent bloom.

Yellow Curls HT, *my*, 1947, *Golden Glow* × *Self*; Brownell. Flowers yellow, dbl., open; fragrant; foliage glossy; vigorous growth.

Yellow Cushion F, *my*, 1966, *Fandango* × *Pinocchio*; Armstrong, D.L.; Armstrong Nursery, 1962. Bud pointed; flowers yellow, dbl., large blooms in small clusters; fragrant; foliage glossy, leathery; vigorous, bushy growth.

Yellow Doll Min, *ly*, 1962, *Golden Glow* × *Zee*; Moore, R.S.; Sequoia Nursery. Bud pointed; flowers yellow to cream, dbl. (55 narrow petals), high-centered, small (1½ in.); fragrant; foliage leathery, glossy; vigorous, bushy (12 in.) growth.

Yellow Doll, Climbing Cl Min, *ly*, 1976, Kirk; Sequoia Nursery.

Yellow Dot HT, *ob*, 1938, *Rapture* × *Betsy Ross*; Hill, J.H., Co. Bud short, pointed; flowers light orange-yellow, reverse coral-red, dbl., small; short stems; foliage soft, dark; vigorous growth; a florists' variety, not distributed for outdoor use.

Yellow Faïence HT, *my*, 1942, *Faïence sport*; C-P. Flowers lemon-yellow.

Yellow Fairy® S, *my*, 1988, (POUlfair); *Texas* × *The Fairy*; Olesen, Mogens; Pernille; Poulsen Roser ApS. Flowers medium yellow, semi-dbl. (6-14 petals), small, slight fragrance; foliage small, light green, semi-glossy; spreading, compact, hardy, abundant growth. GM, Madrid, 1988.

Yellow Fontaine S, *my*, 1972, *Seedling* × *Seedling*; Tantau; Ahrens; Sieberz. Bud ovoid; flowers yellow, dbl., large; slightly fragrant; foliage large, glossy; vigorous, upright growth; free, continuous bloom.

Yellow Gloria HT, *my*, 1936, *Talisman sport*; Bertanzel. Bud long, pointed; flowers golden yellow, base saffron, dbl., high-centered, large; fragrant; long, strong stems; foliage leathery; vigorous growth.

Yellow Gold HT, *dy*, 1957, Boerner; J&P. Bud ovoid; flowers deep golden yellow, dbl. (30-35 petals), cupped, large (5 in.); strong stems; very fragrant; foliage leathery, glossy; vigorous growth; a forcing variety for greenhouse use.

Yellow Hit Min, *dy*, 1988, (POUllow); *Seedling* × *Seedling*; Olesen, Mogens; Pernille; Poulsen Roser ApS. Flowers deep yellow, dbl. (15-25 petals), small; slight fragrance; foliage small, dark green, semi-glossy; bushy, compact, even growth. GM, International, 1986.

Yellow Hoover HT, *my*, 1933, *Pres. Herbert Hoover sport*; Western Rose Co. Flowers pure yellow.

Yellow Jacket S, *dy*, 1992, (JACyepat); *Seedling* × *Seedling*; Christensen, Jack; Bear Creek Gardens, 1992. Flowers deep yellow, full (26-40 petals), medium (4-7 cms) blooms borne mostly singly or small clusters; patio; slight fragrance; foliage medium, dark green, glossy, very disease resistant; some prickles; very vigorous, medium (75-90 cms), upright, bushy growth.

Yellow Jewel Min, *my*, 1973, *Golden Glow* × *(Little Darling* × *Seedling)*; Moore, R.S.; Sequoia Nursery. Bud long, pointed; flowers clear yellow, red eye, semi-dbl., medium; fragrant; foliage small, glossy, leathery; dwarf, bushy growth.

Yellow Joanna Hill HT, *my*, 1932, *Joanna Hill sport*; White, C.N.; White Bros. Bud long, pointed; flowers yellow, dbl. (28 petals), well formed; long stems; slightly fragrant; foliage light; vigorous growth.

Yellow Magic Min, *my*, 1970, *Golden Glow* × *(Little Darling* × *Seedling)*; Moore, R.S.; Sequoia Nursery. Bud long, pointed; flowers yellow, semi-dbl., small; fragrant; foliage small, glossy, dark, leathery; vigorous, dwarf, upright, bushy growth.

Yellow Meillandina Min, *yb*, 1982, (MEItrisical; Yellow Sunblaze); *(Poppy Flash* × *(Charleston* × *Allgold))* × *Gold Coin*; Meilland, M.L.; Meilland Et Cie, 1980. Flowers yellow, petals edged pink, dbl. (20 petals); fragrant; foliage medium, dark, semi-glossy; bushy growth.

Yellow Mellow Min, *my*, 1984, *Rise 'n' Shine* × *Seedling*; Bridges, Dennis A.; Bridges Roses, 1985. Flowers medium yellow, dbl. (35 petals), small; slight fragrance; foliage large, dark, glossy; bushy growth.

Yellow Miniature Min, *my*, 1961, *Rosina seedling*; Wayside Gardens Co. Flowers bright yellow, small.

Yellow Mme. Albert Barbier HP (OGR), *my*, 1937, *Mme. Albert Barbier sport*; Lens. Flowers sunflower-yellow.

Yellow Moss M (OGR), *dy*, 1932, *Old Moss* × *Hybrid Tea*; Walter, L.; J&P. Bud ovoid, slightly mossed, deep yellow; flowers yellow, edges tinted pink, semi-dbl., cupped; fragrant; foliage thick; vigorous growth; free, intermittent bloom.

Yellow Necklace Min, *ly*, 1965, *Golden Glow* × *Magic Wand*; Moore, R.S.; Sequoia Nursery. Bud pointed; flowers straw-yellow, dbl., small; fragrant; foliage leathery; vigorous, dwarf growth.

Yellow Pages HT, *yb*, 1971, *Arthur Bell* × *Peer Gynt*; McGredy, S., IV; McGredy, 1972.

Flowers yellow, dbl. (50 petals), classic form, large (4 in.); fragrant; foliage small, glossy.

Yellow Perfection HT, *ly*, 1952, *Pearl Harbor × Golden Rapture*; Hill, J.H., Co. Bud long, pointed, lemon-yellow; flowers canary-yellow, dbl. (25-30 petals), high-centered, medium; slightly fragrant; foliage leathery, dark; vigorous, upright growth; a greenhouse variety.

Yellow Petals HT, *my*, 1971, *King's Ransom × Dorothy Peach*; Robinson, H. Flowers yellow, dbl. (30 petals), high-centered, large (5½ in.); fragrant; foliage large, light.

Yellow Pigmy F, *my*, 1964, *Seedling × (Éblouissant × Goldilocks)*; Moore, R.S.; Sequoia Nursery. Flowers yellow, dbl., small; fragrant; foliage small, glossy; dwarf, spreading growth; will bloom in pots.

Yellow Pinocchio F, *my*, 1949, *Goldilocks × Marionette*; Boerner; J&P. Bud ovoid; flowers apricot-yellow, fading to cream, dbl. (45 petals), cupped, large (3 in.) blooms in clusters; fragrant; foliage dark; vigorous, bushy growth; (28).

Yellow Pinocchio, Climbing Cl F, *my*, 1959, Palmer.

Yellow Queen Elizabeth Gr, *my*, 1964, *Queen Elizabeth sport*; Vlaeminck; Fryer's Nursery. Flowers orange-yellow.

Yellow Ribbon F, *dy*, 1977, (DICalow); *Illumination × Stroller*; Dickson, P.; A. Dickson. Flowers deep golden yellow, dbl. (23 petals), cupped, medium; slightly fragrant; foliage medium green, semi-glossy; vigorous, compact, bushy growth.

Yellow River HT, *my*, 1972, *Bettina sport*; Timmermans Roses. Flowers yellow, dbl. (30 petals), pointed, large (3½ in.); slightly fragrant; foliage glossy; vigorous growth.

Yellow Ruffels HT, *my*, 1953, *Orange Ruffels sport*; Brownell. Flowers yellow, dbl. (35-50 wavy petals), large (4-5 in.); fragrant; foliage dark, glossy; compact growth.

Yellow Sástago HT, *my*, 1939, (Yellow Condesa de Sástago); *Condesa de Sástago sport*; Howard Rose Co. Flowers yellow.

Yellow Sea LCl, *my*, 1977, *Seedling × Ivory Fashion*; Fong; United Rose Growers. Bud long, pointed; flowers lemon-yellow, semi-dbl. (18-20 petals), high-centered, very large (6 in.); very fragrant (honey spice).

Yellow Shot Silk HT, *my*, 1944, *Shot Silk sport*; Beckwith. Flowers yellow.

Yellow Star F, *my*, 1965, deRuiter. Flowers yellow, well shaped, medium; foliage glossy; moderate growth; for greenhouse use.

Yellow Sweetheart F, *my*, 1952, *Pinocchio × Seedling*; Boerner; J&P. Bud pointed; flowers

lemon-yellow, reverse sulphur-yellow, dbl. (35 petals), globular, becoming flat, large (3½-4 in.); foliage leathery; vigorous, branching growth; a greenhouse cut flower.

Yellow Sweetheart, Climbing Cl F, *ly*, 1952, *Étoile Luisante seedling × Goldilocks*; Moore, R.S.; Marsh's Nursery. Flowers apricot-yellow to creamy -yellow, dbl. (26 petals), high-centered, small; fragrant; foliage leathery, glossy; vigorous, climbing (12 ft.) growth.

Yellow Talisman HT, *ly*, 1929, *Talisman sport*; Amling Co. Flowers yellow.

Yellow Talisman HT, *ly*, 1935, *Talisman sport*; Eddie. Flowers pale sulphur-yellow.

Yellow Talisman, Climbing Cl HT, *ly*, Stocking.

Yellow Tiffany HT, *yb*, 1976, *Tiffany sport*; Floradale Nurs. Flowers yellow tinted pink.

Yellow Wings S, *my*, 1986, ((Will Scarlet × Sutter's Gold) × Paula) × Golden Wings; James, John. Flowers light-medium yellow, fading to cream, moderately full (16 petals), large, borne in clusters; fragrant; foliage medium, light green, glossy, disease resistant; straight, brown prickles; bushy growth.

Yellowcrest HT, *ly*, 1935, LeGrice. Bud small, pointed; flowers clear canary-yellow, dbl.; foliage light, glossy, small; vigorous growth.

Yellowhammer F, *my*, 1956, (Yellow Dazzler; Yellow Hammer); *Poulsen's Yellow × Seedling*; McGredy. Flowers golden yellow to light yellow, dbl. (48 petals), large (3 in.) blooms in clusters; fragrant; foliage dark, glossy; vigorous, bushy growth; greenhouse variety. GM, NRS, 1954.

Yellowstone HT, *my*, 1969, *Seedling × Seedling*; Weeks. Bud pointed; flowers soft tawny yellow to lighter yellow, dbl. (38-44 petals), full, large (3½-4 in.); fragrant (tea); foliage glossy, dark, leathery; tall, upright growth.

Yesterday® Pol, *mp*, 1974, (Tapis d' Orient); *(Phyllis Bide × Shepherd's Delight) × Ballerina*; Harkness. Flowers lilac pink, golden stamens, semi-dbl. (13 petals), small (1½ in.) blooms in trusses; slightly fragrant; foliage small, glossy; bushy growth with polyantha characteristics. GM, Monza, 1974; Baden-Baden, 1975; ADR, 1978.

Yesterday Reef HT, *w*, 1984, *(Tiffany × Sunblest) × Irish Gold*; Stoddard, Louis. Flowers white, faintly tinted pink and yellow, dbl. (35 petals), exhibition, large; slight fragrance; foliage large, medium green, matt; narrowly upright growth.

Yesterday's Garden S, *pb*, 1992, (MORshakrug); *Shakespeare Festival × Belle Poitevine*; Moore, Ralph S.; Sequoia Nursery, 1993. Flowers pink blend, very full (41+ petals), medium (4-7 cms) blooms borne in small clusters; no fragrance; foliage medium, medium green, semi-glossy; tall to medium (over 50 cms), upright, bushy, spreading growth; good garden shrub for screening/mass planting/barriers.

Yoimatsuri F, *ob*, 1989, *Masquerade* × *Subaru*; Kikuchi, Rikichi, 1990. Bud ovoid; flowers orange and yellow tinged, single (5 petals), cupped, medium, borne in sprays of many; moderate fragrance; foliage small, light green, glossy; prickles ordinary; spreading, medium growth.

Yolande d'Aragon HP (OGR), *m*, 1843, Vibert. Flowers bright purple-pink, very full, large

York and Lancaster D (OGR), *pb*, (*R. damascena variegata* Thory; *R. damascena versicolor* Weston; York et Lancastre); Cult. prior to 1629. Flower petals blush white and light pink, sometimes all one color or the other, or mixed (but not striped), loosely dbl.; foliage downy light gray-green; mixed prickles; tall growth. Often confused in rose literature with *Rosa Mundi*.

Yorkshire Bank HT, *w*, 1979, (RUTrulo; True Love); *Pascali* × *Peer Gynt*; DeRuiter, G.; Fryer's Nursery. Flowers white, dbl. (36 petals), blooms borne 3-5 per cluster; fragrant; foliage bright green; pointed, brown prickles; vigorous, medium, bushy growth. GM, NZ; Geneva, 1979.

Yorkshire Lady HT, *ly*, 1992, ((*Red Lion* × *Royal Highness*) × *Yellow Petals*) × *Piccadilly*; Thompson, Robert; Battersby Roses, 1992. Flowers light yellow, full (26-40 petals), classical high-pointed, medium (4-7 cms) blooms borne mostly single; fragrant; foliage medium, medium green, glossy; few prickles; upright (95-100 cms) growth.

Yosemite HT, *ob*, 1934, *Charles P. Kilham* × *Mrs. Pierre S. duPont*; Nicolas; J&P. Bud long, pointed; flowers scarlet-orange, reverse suffused carmine, dbl., cupped; fragrant; foliage leathery; vigorous growth.

You 'n' Me Min, *w*, 1985, (SEAyou); *Avandel* × *Party Girl*; McCann, Sean, 1987. Flowers white, light apricot center, dbl. (40+ petals), high-centered, small; slight fragrance; foliage small, medium green, semi-glossy; bushy growth.

Youki San® HT, *w*, 1965, (MEIdona; Mme. Neige); *Lady Sylvia* × *White Knight*; Meilland; URS; Wheatcroft Bros. Flowers white, dbl. (40 petals), large; very fragrant; foliage light green; tall growth. GM, Baden-Baden, 1964.

Young France HT, *lp*, 1945, (Jeune France); *Joanna Hill* × *Mme. Joseph Perraud*; Meilland, F.; C-P. Bud long, pointed; flowers apple-

blossom-pink, base flushed orange, tipped silvery pink, high-centered, large; fragrant; foliage soft, dark; vigorous, upright growth.

Young Love Min, *ob*, 1980, *Seedling* × *Seedling*; Lyon. Bud medium-long, pointed; flowers orange, yellow-center, semi-dbl. (18 petals), borne 1-3 per cluster; very fragrant; foliage tiny, dark; tiny, curved prickles; compact, bushy growth.

Young Quinn® HT, *my*, 1975, (MACbern; Yellow Wonder); *Peer Gynt* × *Kiskadee*; McGredy, Sam. Bud small, short; flowers medium yellow, dbl. (28 petals), borne singly; slight fragrance; foliage heavily veined, dark; upright, tall growth. GM, Belfast, 1978.

Young Venturer F, *ab*, 1979, (MATsun); *Arthur Bell* × *Cynthia Brooke*; Mattock. Bud ovoid; flowers rich apricot, dbl. (30 petals), large (4½ in.); very fragrant; foliage dark, glossy, leathery; vigorous, upright growth.

Youpi Min, *my*, 1966, *R. wichuraiana* × *Pour Toi*; Lens. Bud ovoid; flowers lemon-chrome, semi-dbl. (12-19 petals), cupped, small (1 in.); fragrant (fruity); foliage light green; vigorous, compact growth.

Yours Truly HT, *mp*, 1945, *Seedling* × *Texas Centennial*; Morris; Germain's. Bud long, pointed; flowers rose-pink, base golden yellow, dbl. (48 petals), open, large (4½ in.); very fragrant (spicy); foliage leathery; very vigorous, upright growth.

Youth HT, *w*, 1935, *Souv. de Claudius Pernet* × *My Maryland*; Cook, J.W. Bud ovoid; flowers creamy, suffused pink, dbl. (60 petals), high-centered, very large; long stems; fragrant; foliage dark.

Yu-Ai HT, *rb*, 1970, *Sarabande seedling* × *Peace seedling*; Suzuki; Keisei Rose Nursery. Bud ovoid; flowers bright red, base yellow, dbl., cupped, large; slightly fragrant; foliage dark, leathery; very vigorous, bushy growth.

Yuhla S, *mr*, 1927, *Wild rose from Lake Oakwood* × *Général Jacqueminot*; Hansen, N.E. Flowers crimson, semi-dbl. (20 petals, 26 petaloids); non-recurrent bloom; very hardy.

Yuki-Matsuri HT, *w*, 1989, (*Dolce Vita* × *Royal Highness*) × *Nobility*; Yokota, Kiyoshi. Bud ovoid; flowers white, dbl. (42 petals), urn-shaped, high-centered, large, borne usually singly; moderate fragrance; foliage medium, dark green, glossy; prickles sparse; fruit large, light orange; medium growth.

Yuletide HT, *mr*, 1956, *Hill Crest* × *Silver Kenny*; Hill, J.H., Co. Bud ovoid; flowers currant-red, dbl. (43 petals), high-centered, large (3½ -4½ in.) blooms; slightly fragrant; foliage leathery, semi-glossy; vigorous, upright, bushy growth; greenhouse variety.

Yumeotome Min, *lp*, 1989, *Miyagino sport*; Tokumatsu, Kazuhisa. Bud ovoid; flowers pink changing to white, dbl. (38 petals), slight fragrance; foliage small, dark green; prickles lower part hollow, about 15 on a stem; bushy growth.

Yusai HT, *yb*, 1989, *(American Heritage seedling × Christian Dior) × Miss Ireland*; Ota, Kaichiro. Bud ovoid; flowers bright yellow with reddish fringe, reverse changing to red with sunshine, dbl. (30 petals), urn-shaped, high-centered, large, borne in sprays of 2-3; foliage medium, dark green with bronze tinge, slightly denticulated, glossy; bushy, spreading growth.

Yuzen Gr, *pb*, 1982, (Yuzen); *Seedling × Confidence*; Suzuki, S.; Keisei Rose Nursery. Flowers pink, blending deeper at petal edges, dbl. (50 petals), urn-shaped to high-centered, large, borne 2-5 per stem; fragrant; foliage dark, glossy; prickles slanted downward; upright.

Yvan Mission Pol, *mp*, 1922, *Jeanny Soupert × Katharina Zeimet*; Soupert & Notting. Flowers peach-blossom-pink, borne in large clusters.

Yves Druhen HT, *dr*, 1920, *Gen. MacArthur × Château de Clos Vougeot*; Buatois. Flowers dark velvety red, dbl.; very fragrant.

Yves Piaget® HT, *dp*, 1985, (MEIvildo; Queen Adelaide; The Royal Brompton Rose); *((Pharaoh × Peace) × (Chrysler Imperial × Charles Mallerin)) × Tamango*; Meilland, M.L.; Meilland Et Cie, 1983. Flowers deep pink, dbl. (40+ petals), large; very fragrant; foliage medium, dark, semi-glossy; upright growth.

Yvette HT, *op*, 1921, *Mrs. T. Hillas × Mme. Edouard Herriot*; Buatois. Flowers salmon-yellow.

Yvonne R, *pb*, 1921, Cant, F. Flowers blush-pink, base deep pink shaded yellow, dbl., cupped, high-centered; fragrant; foliage dark, glossy; very vigorous growth. GM, NRS, 1920.

Yvonne Carret HT, *ob*, 1961, Gaujard. Flowers orange-red, reverse golden yellow, dbl. (25 petals), large (4½ in.); foliage bright green.

Yvonne d'Huart HT, *rb*, 1932, *Mme. Mélanie Soupert*; Ketten Bros. Bud long, pointed; flowers coral-red to lincoln red, base chrome yellow, full, large; slightly fragrant; very vigorous growth.

Yvonne Millot HT, *ab*, 1936, *(Pharisäer × Constance) × Feu Joseph Looymans*; Mallerin; C-P. Bud pointed; flowers apricot-yellow, dbl., high-centered, large; slightly fragrant; foliage glossy; vigorous growth.

Yvonne Plassat HT, *or*, 1941, *Mme. Edouard Herriot × Mrs. Aaron Ward × Emma Wright*; Moulin-Epinay; Nonin. Flowers coppery orange to glowing red, dbl.

Yvonne Printemps HT, *or*, 1939, Gaujard. Bud long, almost red; flowers orange, veined copper, reverse bright yellow.

Yvonne Rabier Pol, *w*, 1910, *R. wichuraiana × a Polyantha*; Turbat. Flowers pure white, center slightly tinted sulphur, dbl., blooms in clusters; foliage rich green, glossy; vigorous growth; recurrent bloom; (14).

Yvonne Vacherot HT, *w*, 1905, *Antoine Rivoire × Souv. d'un Ami*; Soupert & Notting. Bud long, pointed; flowers porcelain-white, strongly flushed rose-pink, dbl., imbricated, high-centered, large; vigorous growth.

Yvonne Virlet HT, *my*, 1936, Walter, L. Flowers golden yellow, full, large.

Zaïd S, *rb*, 1937, *R. foetida bicolor × R. wichuraiana seedling*; Chambard, C. Bud bright yellow and copper-red; flowers coppery flame-red, semi-dbl.; foliage glossy, bright green; vigorous growth; non-recurrent bloom.

Zaida HT, *op*, 1922, Lippiatt. Flowers pale coral-pink, dbl., large.

Zambra® F, *ob*, 1961, (MEIalfi); *(Goldilocks × Fashion) × (Goldilocks × Fashion)*; Meilland, M.L.; URS, 1961; C-P, 1964. Bud ovoid; flowers orange, reverse yellow, semi-dbl. (13 petals), flat, large (2½-3 in.) blooms in clusters; slightly fragrant (sweetbrier); foliage leathery, glossy, light green; vigorous, well-branched growth. GM, Bagatelle; Rome, 1961.

Zambra, Climbing® Cl F, *ob*, 1969, (MEIalfisar); Meilland; URS.

Zani S, *mr*, 1927, *(R. rugosa × Anna de Diesbach) × Tetonkaha*; Hansen, N.E. Flowers dark crimson, with a white streak through center petals, semi-dbl.; height 6-8 ft.; non-recurrent bloom; very hardy.

Zansho HT, *rb*, 1975, *Garden Party × Christian Dior*; Takahashi. Bud ovoid; flowers scarlet and yellow, dbl. (45 petals), high-centered, very large (6 in.); slightly fragrant; foliage dark, leathery; upright, bushy growth.

Zanzibar F, *mr*, 1964, *Paradis × Circus*; Leenders, J. Flowers bright red.

Zara Hore-Ruthven HT, *mp*, 1932, *Mme. Abel Chatenay × Scorcher*; Clark, A.; NRS South Australia. Flowers rich pink, dbl., cupped, large; slightly fragrant.

Zauberlehrling F, *op*, 1963, Kordes, R. Flowers light salmon, dbl., well formed, large; strong stems; bushy, low growth.

Zborov Pol, *dr*, 1935, *Corrie Koster sport*; Böhm. Flowers blood-red, very dbl., borne in large clusters; foliage glossy, dark; vigorous growth.

Zee Cl Min, *mp*, 1940, *Carolyn Dean × Tom Thumb*; Moore, R.S. Flowers pink, very small; foliage very small; nearly thorn less; height 30 in; recurrent bloom. The parent or grandparent of all Climbing Minuature varieties originated by R.S. Moore. Not in commerce.

Zelda Lloyd Min, *mp*, 1988, (TINzel); *Deep Purple × Blue Mist*; Bennett, Dee; Tiny Petals Nursery. Flowers medium pink, reverse deep pink, single (5 petals), cupped, medium, borne usually singly or in sprays of 3-5; slight, fruity fragrance; foliage medium, medium green, semi-glossy; prickles hooked slightly downward, reddish; fruit globular, green to yellow-brown; filaments pink with golden yellow anthers; bushy, medium growth.

Zélia Pradel N (OGR), *w*, 1860, (Estelle Pradel); Pradel. Flowers pure white, full, large.

Zena HT, *dr*, 1986, *Seedling × New Style*; Plumpton, E. Flowers dark crimson, dbl. (25 petals), large blooms borne singly or several together; slight fragrance; foliage medium, medium green, semi-glossy; upright growth.

Zenaitta Pol, *rb*, 1991, *Seedling × Seedling*; Jerabek, Paul E., 1985. Bud ovoid; flowers bright medium red with small white area at petal base, dbl., cupped, small blooms borne in sprays of 3-65; no fragrance; foliage small, medium green, glossy; bushy, medium growth.

Zenobia M (OGR), *mp*, 1892, Paul, W. Bud well mossed; flowers satiny pink, full, large; fragrant; vigorous.

Zéphirine Drouhin B (OGR), *mp*, 1868, Bizot. Bud long, pointed; flowers rose, base white, semi-dbl., large; fragrant; foliage soft, light; no prickles; vigorous, semi-climbing; recurrent.

Zephyr F, *yb*, 1961, *Goldilocks × Seedling*; Verschuren; Blaby Rose Gardens. Flowers yellow tipped pink, dbl. (64 petals), large (2½-3 in.), borne in clusters; foliage glossy, light; very vigorous growth.

Zeus LCl, *my*, 1959, *Doubloons × Seedling*; Kern Rose Nursery. Bud long, pointed; flowers yellow, dbl. (25 petals), high-centered, medium; slightly fragrant; foliage leathery, dark; vigorous (15-20 ft.) growth.

Zika S, *lp*, 1927, *(R. rugosa × Anna de Diesbach) × Tetonkaha*; Hansen, N.E. Flowers shell-pink, semi-dbl.; fragrant; non-recurrent bloom; very hardy.

Zingaro F, *mr*, 1964, *Masquerade × Independence seedling*; Sanday. Flowers bright crimson, semi-dbl. (12 petals), medium (2 in.), borne in clusters; foliage dark; compact, low growth.

Zinger Min, *mr*, 1978, *Zorina × Magic Carrousel*; Schwartz, E.W.; Nor'East Min. Roses. Bud long, pointed; flowers medium red, semi-dbl. (11 petals), flat, small (1½ in.); fragrant; very vigorous, spreading growth. AOE, 1979.

Zita Pol, *mr*, 1965, *Amoureuse × Seedling*; Delforge. Bud ovoid; flowers red shaded dark geranium, single, open; foliage dark, leathery.

Zitkala HBlanda (S), *mr*, 1942, *R. blanda × Amadis*; Hansen, N.E. Flowers brilliant velvety red, dbl. (25 petals), large (3 in.); very fragrant; red wood, almost thornless; non-recurrent bloom; very hardy.

Zitronenfalter® S, *my*, 1956, *Märchenland × Peace*; Tantau, Math. Bud ovoid; flowers golden yellow, dbl. (20 petals), large blooms in clusters; fruity fragrance; foliage dark, leathery; few, curved prickles; fruit globular, slightly flattened top; upright, bushy; repeats.

Zitronenfalter HSpn (OGR), *ly*, 1940, *(R. spinosissima altaica × Star of Persia) × Golden Ophelia*; Berger, V.; Teschendorff. Flowers brimstone color.

Zitronenjette® HT, *my*, 1987, (KORjoni); *Sutter's Gold × Sunblest*; Kordes, W., 1986. Flowers medium yellow, dbl. (15-25 petals), large; very fragrant; foliage large, medium green, glossy; spreading growth.

Zizi F, *dr*, 1963, *Walko × Souv. de J. Chabert*; D-C. Flowers garnet-red, semi-dbl. (15 petals), medium, borne in clusters of 3-10; fragrant; vigorous, bushy growth.

Zlatá Praha HT, *my*, 1931, (Das Goldene Prag); *Kardinal Piffl sport*; Böhm. Flowers golden yellow.

Zlaty Dech HT, *ob*, 1936, *Admiration × Talisman*; Böhm. Bud long, pointed; flowers orange-yellow, brown, red and gold shadings, semi-dbl., cupped, large; fairly fragrant; foliage glossy, light; vigorous growth.

Zodiac F, *mr*, 1961, *Red Favorite × Seedling*; Verschuren; Blaby Rose Gardens. Flowers red, dbl. (74 petals), camellia-shape, large (2⅓-3 in.), borne in large clusters; foliage leathery, light green; very vigorous growth.

Zodiac F, *pb*, 1963, *Masquerade × Karl Herbst*; Kordes, R. Flowers begonia-pink, base yellow, dbl., borne in clusters of 25-30; low, bushy growth.

Zoé M (OGR), *mp*, 1861, (Moussue Partout); Pradel. Flowers rose-pink, globular; well-mossed.

Zola S, *dy*, 1979, *Spek's Yellow × Magenta*; Sanday. Bud pointed; flowers golden yellow, semi-dbl. (18 petals), medium (2½ in.); very fragrant; foliage dark; vigorous, upright.

Zola Budd F, *rb*, 1986, (KORzola); *New Day × ((Dr. A.J. Verhage × Colour Wonder) × Zorina)*; Kordes, R.; Ludwig Roses, 1985. Flowers white with ruby red, single (5-7 petals), borne 1-3 per cluster; slight fragrance; foliage deep green, leathery; straight, light brown prickles; vigorous, bushy, densely-branched growth.

Zonnekind HT, *my*, 1941, *Arch. Reventos × Amalia Jung*; Leenders, M. Flowers buttercup-yellow, dbl., large; fragrant.

Zora F, *yb*, 1974, *Masquerade × Rumba*; Staikov, Prof. Dr. V.; Kalaydjiev and Chorbadjiiski. Flowers yellow, deep pink petal edges, aging deep pink, semi-dbl. (18 petals), medium blooms in clusters of 5-30; foliage dark; vigorous growth.

Zorina F, *or*, 1963, (Rozorina); *Pinocchio seedling × Spartan*; Boerner; J&P. Bud ovoid; flowers orange-red, dbl. (25 petals), cupped, large (3 in.); fragrant; foliage glossy; vigorous, upright growth; greenhouse variety. GM, Rome 1964.

Zukunft F, *or*, 1951, *Lafayette sport*; Verschuren. Flowers scarlet-red.

Zulu Queen HT, *dr*, 1939, *(Cathrine Kordes × E.G. Hill) × Fritz Hoger*; Kordes; J&P. Bud long, pointed; flowers dark maroon, dbl., high-centered, large; fragrant; foliage leathery; vigorous, bushy growth.

Zulu Queen, Climbing Cl HT, *dr*, 1961, Moore.

Zulu Warrior F, *rb*, 1980, *Arthur Bell × Flaming Peace*; Hawken, Una. Flowers burgundy red, silver reverse, semi-dbl. (9 petals), blooms borne 3-20 per cluster; slight fragrance; foliage dark, tough; large, reddish prickles; medium growth.

Zweibrücken K (S), *dr*, 1955, *R. kordesii × Independence*; Kordes. Bud ovoid; flowers deep crimson, dbl., large blooms in large clusters; slightly fragrant; foliage dark, leathery; very vigorous, climbing growth; recurrent bloom.

Zwemania Gr, *or*, 1974, *Sweet Promise sport*; Zwemstra; Meilland. Flowers light vermilion, dbl. (25-30 petals), full, high-centered; fragrant (fruity); foliage dark; very vigorous growth.

Zwergenfee® Min, *or*, 1979, (KORfee; Dwarf Fairy); *Miniature seedling × Träumerei*; Kordes, W. Bud globular; flowers orange-red, dbl. (29 petals), cupped, medium (2 in.); fragrant; foliage small, glossy; dwarf, vigorous, upright growth.

Zwerg-Rubin Pol, *mr*, 1924, *Rubin seedling × Erna Teschendorff*; Schmidt, J.C. Flowers bright ruby-red, cupped, small, borne in clusters; dwarf growth.

Appendix I
Cross Reference of Synonyms to Official Entries

This listing provides a valuable key to locate the main descriptive record in the body of the main text for those cultivars where only an alternate name or synonym is known. The reference to the official registered name appears in bold face.

-A-

A.G.A. Ridder van Rappard see **A.G.A. Rappard**
A.R.S. Centennial see **American Rose Centennial**
Aachener Dom see **Pink Panther®**
Abalard see **Abaillard**
Abraham Darby see **AUScot**
Ace of Hearts see **Asso di Cuori®**
Adéle Pradel see **Mme. Bravy**
Admiral see **Waves**
Adolph Horstmann see **Adolf Horstmann®**
Advance Guard see **Wilhelm Teetzmann**
Adventure see **Aventure**
Ænnchen Müller see **Annchen Müller**
Agathe Nabonnand see **Mme. Agathe Nabonnand**
Agrippina see **Cramoisi Supérieur**
Agrippina, Climbing see **Cramoisi Supérieur, Climbing**
Air France Meillandina® see **Air France**
Airain see **Châtelet**
Alba Meidiland™ see **White Meidiland**
Alba Meillandécor see **Alba Meidiland**
Alba Rosea see **Mme. Bravy**
Alberich® see **Happy**
Alchemist see **Alchymist**
Alchymiste see **Alchymist**
Alexander Laquemont see **Alexandre Laquement**
Alexander MacKenzie see **A. MacKenzie**
Alexandra see **Alexander**
Alexis see **L'Oréal Trophy**

Alfie™ see **Alfi**
All Gold® see **Allgold**
All In One see **Exploit**
Allegro '80 see **MEIfikalif**
Allen's Jubilee see **Jubilee**
Alliance see **MEIbleri**
Alpenglühen see **Alpine Glow**
Alpine Rose see **R. pendulina** Linnaeus
Altaica see **R. spinosissima** Linnaeus
Altaica see **R. spinosissima altaica** (Willdenow) Bean
Altesse see **Anticipation**
Altus see **Altissimo**
Amanda™ see **Amanda Marciel**
Amanda see **Amruda**
Amber Light see **Amberlight**
Amberlight see **Fyvie Castle**
America's Choice see **H.C. Andersen**
American Independence™ see **Air France**
American Legion see **Legion**
Ames Climber see **Ames 5**
Ami des Jardins see **Finale**
Amoretta® see **Amorette**
Amour Ardent see **Burning Love**
Anci Böhm see **Anci Böhmova**
Anemone Rose see **Anemone**
Angela® see **Angelica**
Angelina Lauro see **Angeline Lauro**
Angelique® see **AnKORi**
Anisley Dickson see **Dicky**
Anna Livia see **KORmetter**
Anna-Maria de Montravel see **Anne-Marie de Montravel**
Anna Von Diesbach see **Anna de Diesbach**
Annabelle see **Anabell**
Anne Diamond see **LANdia**
Anne Marie see **Anne Marie Trechslin**

Anne-Mette Poulsen see **Anne Poulsen**
Anneliesse Rothenberger see **Oregold**
Annie Mueller see **Annchen Müller**
Annie Wood see **Mlle. Annie Wood**
Anvil Sparks see **Ambossfunken**
Apachi see **Tai-Gong**
Aparte see **Spartan**
Apothecary's Rose of Provins see **Apothecary's Rose**
Apple Rose see **R. pomifera** Herrmann
Apricot Prince see **Gingersnap**
Apricot Midinette see **Apricot Medinette**
Apricot Sunblaze see **Mark One**
Arc de Triomphe see **Summer Fashion**
Arcadian see **New Year**
Arctic Rose see **R. acicularis** Lindley
Ardennes see **Eye Appeal**
Arkansas Rose see **R. arkansana** Porter
Arles see **Fernand Arles**
Armorique Nirpaysage see **POUlaps**
Armosa see **Hermosa**
Arnaud Delbard® see **First Edition**
Arnoldiana see **Arnold**
Arturo Toscanini see **Elegy**
As de Coeur see **Herz As**
Ash Wednesday see **Aschermittwoch**
Astrid Späth see **Frau Astrid Späth**
Athena see **RühKOR**
Atkins Beauty see **Center Gold**
Atoll see **Clarita**

Atom Bomb see
  Atombombe
Atomflash see Atombombe
Audace® see Carefree Beauty
Audrey Gardner see
  PEAspecial
August Kordes see Lafayette
Austrian Briar see R. foetida
  Herrmann
Austrian Brier Rose see R.
  foetida Herrmann
Austrian Copper Rose see R.
  foetida bicolor (Jacquin)
  Willmott
Austrian Yellow Rose see R.
  foetida Herrmann
Autumn Fire see Herbstfeuer
Avenue's Red see Konrad
  Henkel
Ayrshire Splendens see
  Splendens
Azulabria see Blue Peter

-B-

Baby Carnaval see Baby
  Masquerade
Baby Carnival see Baby
  Masquerade
Baby Crimson see Perla de
  Alcañada
Baby Doll see Tip-Top
Baby Dorothy see Maman
  Levavasseur
Baby Herriot see Étoile
  Luisante
Baby Mascarade® see Baby
  Masquerade
Baby Maskarade see Baby
  Masquerade
Baby Maskerade® see Baby
  Masquerade
Baby Rambler, Climbing see
  Miss G. Mesman
Baby Talisman see Presumida
Baby Tausendschön see Echo
Baby Vougeot see Baby
  Château
Bad Nauheim see National
  Trust
Bad Naukeim see National
  Trust
Baldwin see Sleepy
Bamboo Rose see R.
  multiflora watsoniana
  (Crépin) Matsumura
Banks' Rose see R. banksiae
  Aiton fil

Banksiae Alba see R.
  banksiae banksiae
Banksian Rose see R.
  banksiae Aiton fil
Banzai '76 see Banzai
Baron Sunblaze see Baron
  Meillandina
Baroness Henrietta Snoy see
  Baronne Henriette de
  Snoy
Baroness Henriette Snoy see
  Baronne Henriette de
  Snoy
Baronne Adolphe de
  Rothschild see Baroness
  Rothschild
Baronne de Rothschild® see
  Baronne Edmond de
  Rothschild
Baronne de Rothschild,
  Climbing® see Baronne
  Edmond de Rothschild,
  Climbing
Bavarian Girl see Schöne
  Münchnerin
Baveria see Gruss an
  Bayern
Beaulieu see Tequila Sunrise
Beauty of Glazenwood see
  Fortune's Double Yellow
Beauty of the Prairies see
  Queen of the Prairies
Beauty Star see Liverpool
  Remembers
Bekola see Aalsmeer Gold
Bel Ami see Philippe
Belami see KORhanbu
Belinda see TANbeedee
Belinda's Rose see Belinda's
  Dream
Bella Epoca see Bel Ange
Belle Ange see Bel Ange
Belle Courtisanne see
  Königin von Dänemark
Belle de Baltimore see
  Baltimore Belle
Belle de Londres® see
  Compassion
Belle Epoque see Bel Ange
Belle of Portugal see Belle
  Portugaise
Belle Rubine see Village
  Maid
Belle Siebrecht see Mrs. W.J.
  Grant
Belle Siebrecht, Climbing see
  Mrs. W.J. Grant,
  Climbing

Belle Sunblaze see Belle
  Meillandina
Belle Villageois see
  Centifolia Variegata
Bellringer see Bell Ringer
Bengal Cramoisi Double see
  Sanguinea
Bengal Ordinaire see
  Pallida
Bengal Rose see R. chinensis
  Jacquin
Benoni '75 see POUIoni
Benson & Hedges Special see
  Dorola
Berkeley see Tournament of
  Roses
Bernhard Daneke Rose see
  Showbiz
Berolina see Selfridges
Bertram see Sneezy
Bettina '78 see MEIbrico
Betty Herholdt see Bettie
  Herholdt
Bharami see Bharani
Big Cabbage of Holland see
  Gros Choux d'Hollande
Big Chief see Portland
  Trailblazer
Big Purple see Stephen's Big
  Purple
Bijou des Prairies see Gem of
  the Prairies
Bijou d'Or see Golden
  Jewel
Bizarre Triomphante see
  Charles de Mills
Blaby Jubilee see Dries
  Verschuren
Black Pearl see Perle Noire
Blackberry Rose see R. rubus
  Léveillé & Vaniot
Blackboy see Black Boy
Blanc Dot see Blanche Dot
Blanc Lafayette see Dagmar
  Späth
Blanc Meillandécor see
  White Meidiland
Blanc Queen Elizabeth see
  White Queen Elizabeth
Blanche Neige see Snow
  Carpet
Blanche Pasca® see Pascali
Blanche Superbe see Blanche
  de Belgique
Blanche Unique see Unique
  Blanche
Blaze Superier see
  Demokracie

Blood-red China Rose see **Sanguinea**

Bloomfield Endurance see **W. Freeland Kendrick**

Bloomfield Improvement see **Ednah Thomas**

Bloomfield Loveliness see **Sophie Thomas**

Blooming Easy see **Bloomin' Easy**

Blue Carpet see **Cosette**

Blue Danube see **Blauwe Donau**

Blue Girl see **Kölner Karneval**

Blue Monday see **Blue Moon**

Blue Monday, Climbing see **Blue Moon, Climbing**

Blue Perfume see **Blue Parfum**

Blue Rambler see **Veilchenblau**

Blue Rosalie see **Veilchenblau**

Blue Sky see **Aozora**

Bluenette® see **Blue Peter**

Blush Maman Cochet see **William R. Smith**

Blush Musk see **Fraser's Pink Musk**

Blushing Maid see **Rocky**

Blushing Rose see **Coy Colleen**

Bobbie Robbie see **Souv. de J. Chabert**

Bon Voyage see **Voeux de Bonheur**

Bonica see **MEIdomonac**

Bonica '82 see **MEIdomonac**

Bonne Nouvelle see **Good News**

Bonnie Prince Charlie's Rose see **White Rose of York**

Bordure de Nacre see **Bordure Nacre**

Botaniste Abrial see **Lowell Thomas**

Boule de Nanteuil see **Comte Boula de Nanteuil**

Bouquet de la Marie see **Aimeé Vibert**

Bourbon Queen see **Queen of Bourbons**

Bradley Graig see **Bradley Craig**

Brasier see **Brazier**

Brennende Liebe see **Burning Love**

Brier Bush see **R. canina** Linnaeus

Bright Meadow see **Yasnaya Poliana**

Brilliant see **Detroiter**

Brilliant Light see **Kagayaki**

Brilliant Meillandina see **MEIranoga**

Brite Lites® see **Princess Alice**

Britestripes see **Britestripe**

Bronce Masterpiece see **Bronze Masterpiece**

Brookdale Giant White see **Jackman's White**

Broomfield Novelty see **Margaret Anderson**

Bucks Fizz see **Gavno**

Buffalo Bill see **Regensberg**

Burgund '81 see **Loving Memory**

Burgundy Rose see **Burgundian Rose**

Burkhard see **Grumpy**

Burkhardt see **Grumpy**

Burnet Rose see **R. spinosissima** Linnaeus

Burning Sky see **Paradise**

Burr Rose see **R. roxburghii** Trattinnick

Bushveld Dawn see **Cary Grant**

Butterfly Papilio see **Motylek**

Butterscotch see **JACtan**

Buttons see **DICmickey**

-C-

C.F. Worth see **Mme. Charles Frederic Worth**

C.W.S.® see **Canadian White Star**

California Ground Rose see **R. spithamea** S. Watson

California Wild Rose see **R. californica** Chamisso & Schlechtendahl

Calypso see **Blush Boursault**

Cameo, Climbing see **Pink Cameo**

Campanela® see **Campanile**

Campfire Arteka see **Kostior Arteka**

Can Can see **LEGglow**

Can-Can see **LEGglow**

Canadiana see **Imperial Gold**

Canary see **TANcary**

Candia see **MEIbiranda**

Candy Stick see **Candystick**

Canterbury see **Scoop Jackson**

Capella see **MEIrilocra**

Cardinal Richelieu see **Cardinal de Richelieu**

Caribia see **Harry Wheatcroft**

Caribia, Climbing see **Harry Wheatcroft, Climbing**

Carl Philip see **Mariandel**

Carmargue see **Telford's Promise**

Carmela® see **INTergeorge**

Carmen see **JAClam**

Carmine Pillar see **Paul's Carmine Pillar**

Carnival see **Carnaval**

Carol see **Carol Amling**

Carol Ann see **PEApost**

Carolin see **Coralin**

Carolina Rose see **R. carolina** Linnaeus

Caroline de Berry see **Foliaceé**

Caroline Schmitt see **Mme. Caroline Schmitt**

Carolyn see **Coralin**

Carte d'Or see **Supra**

Casper see **Magna Charta**

Castel see **Versailles**

Castilian see **Autumn Damask**

Céleste see **Celestial**

Centennaire de Lourdes see **Centenaire de Lourdes**

Centifolia Muscosa see **Communis**

Centre Piece see **Centerpiece**

Cevennes see **Heidesommer**

Chacok see **Pigalle**

Champagner® see **Antique Silk**

Champneys' Rose see **Champneys' Pink Cluster**

Chanson d'Été see **Summer Song**

Chanterelle see **Cynthia**

Chapeau de Napoléon see **Crested Moss**

Chardonnay see **Nobilo's Chardonnay**

Chardony see **Nobilo's Chardonnay**

Charles Aznavour see **Matilda**

Charles Dingee see **William R. Smith**

Charleston 88 see Louis de
  Funs
Charm see Charme
Charme d'Amour see
  Liebeszauber
Charme de Vienne see
  Wiener Charme
Charming Vienne see Wiener
  Charme
Chartreuse see MACyefre
Chasing Rainbows see
  Chasin' Rainbows
Château see Baby Château
Chateau de Versailles® see
  Guy Laroche
Chatillon White see White
  Chatillon
Cheerie see Chérie
Cheerio see Chérie
Cheerio see Playboy
Cherie Michelle see Cheré
  Michelle
Cherokee Rose see R.
  laevigata Michaux
Cherry Brandy '85 see
  TANryrandy
Cherry Glow see Sweet
  Cherry
Chestnut Rose see R.
  roxburghii Trattinnick
Chevreuse see Westfalenpark
Chickasaw Rose see R.
  bracteata Wendland
Chief see The Chief
Chin Chin see Promise
China Rose see R. chinensis
  Jacquin
Chinese Monthly Rose see
  Slater's Crimson China
Chinquapin Rose see R.
  roxburghii Trattinnick
Chipmonk see Chipmunk
Christina see SELstar
Christoph Colombus see
  Christopher Columbus
Christophe Colomb® see
  Christopher Columbus
Christophe Colomb see
  Cristoforo Colombo
Cinnamon Rose see R.
  cinnamomea Linnaeus
City of Alexandria see
  Alexandria Rose
City of Birmingham see
  Esprit
City of Pilsen see Plzen
City of Warwick see Grand
  Marshall

Claire Rayner see
  Pandemonium
Claire Rose® see AUSlight
Clara Bow, Climbing see
  Clara Bow
Clara d'Arcis see Mme. Clara
  d'Arcis
Claridge® see PEKlipink
Classic Sunblaze see
  MEIpinjid
Claysnow see Snow Ballet
Cleveland II see Mrs.
  Dunlop Best
Clifton Moss see White Bath
Climbing Geheimrat
  Duisberg see Golden
  Rapture, Climbing
Climbing Spek's Yellow see
  Golden Scepter,
  Climbing
Climbing Bride see Ruth
  Vestal
Clo-Clo see PEKatan
Cloth of Gold see
  Chromatella
Clubrose Lydia see Lydia
Cocktail '80 see MEItabifob
Coeur d'Amour see Red
  Devil
Colibre see Colibri
Cologne see Köln am Rhein
Cologne Carnival see Kölner
  Karneval
Colonel Svec see Plukovník
  Svec
Colonial White see
  Sombreuil
Colorbreak see Brown
  Velvet
Colourama see Colorama
Colysée see Colisée
Common Blush China see
  Old Blush
Common Monthly see Old
  Blush
Common Moss see
  Communis
Comte de Nanteuil see
  Comte Boula de
  Nanteuil
Comtesse d'Alcantara see
  Home & Country
Comtesse de Labarathe see
  Duchesse de Brabant
Comtesse de Mortemart see
  Comte de Mortemart
Comtesse Ouwaroff see
  Duchesse de Brabant

Comtesse Risa du Parc see
  Comtesse Riza du Parc
Comtesse Vandale see
  Comtesse Vandal
Comtesse Vandale, Climbing
  see Comtesse Vandal,
  Climbing
Concertino see MEIglusor
Concorde see Forever
  Yours
Constanze Spry see
  Constance Spry
Coppertone see Oldtimer
Coquette see Bertram Park
Cornelia Cook see Cornélie
  Koch
Corona de Oro see Gold
  Crown
Cosmopoliet see
  Cosmopolitan
Cosmopolit see
  Cosmopolitan
Côte Rôtie see Grand Amour
Cottage Maid see Centifolia
  Variegata
Coucher de Soleil see Coral
  Sunset
Countess Vandal see
  Comtesse Vandal
Countess Vandal, Climbing
  see Comtesse Vandal,
  Climbing
Countess of Ilchester see
  Mary, Countess of
  Ilchester
Countess of Oxford see
  Comtesse d'Oxford
Country Heritage see Our
  Jubilee
Coupe d'Or see Gold Cup
Couronne d'Or see Gold
  Crown
Coventry Cathedral see
  Cathedral
Creepy see Ralph's Creeper
Crested Provence Rose see
  Crested Moss
Cri-Cri® see Cricri
Crimson Boursault see
  Amadis
Crimson China Rose see
  Slater's Crimson
  China
Crimson Glow see Our
  Princess
Crimson Maman Cochet see
  Balduin
Crimson Masse see Liberté

Crimson Midinette see
Crimson Medinette
Crisette la Jolie see Surpasse
Tout
Cristata see Crested Moss
Cristobal Colon see
Christopher Columbus
Cristoforo Colombo see
Christopher Columbus
Crown of Jewels see Little
Beauty
Crucencia see Hot Pewter
Crucenia see Hot Pewter
Cuisse de Nymphe see Great
Maiden's Blush
Cuisse de Nymphe Emue see
Great Maiden's Blush
Cunosa see My Girl
Cygne Blanc see White Swan
Cymbelene see Cymbaline
Cymbeline see Cymbaline

-D-

Daily Mail Rose see Mme.
Edouard Herriot
Daily Mail Rose, Climbing
see Mme. Edouard
Herriot, Climbing
Dallas see Cora Marie
Dama di Cuori see Dame de
Coeur
Damas de Yuste see
Freiheitsglocke
Damask Rose see Summer
Damask
Dame Vera see Dame Vera
Lynn
Dania see Toprose
Daniel Gelin see Wandering
Minstrel
Danina see Cara Mia
Danse du Feu see Spectacular
Danzille see Mme. Bravy
Darling see Cream Delight
Darthuizer Orange Fire see
INTerfire
Das Goldene Prag see
Zlatá Praha
Day Break see Daybreak
Daybreak see Rassvet
Daydream see Len Turner
Daylight see Day Light
Dazzler see Leonie
Dear One see Kara
Dearest One see Cara Mia
Debutante see JACinal

Decor Arlequin see Meilland
Decor Arlequin
Decor Rose see Anne de
Bretagne
Decorat see Freude
Degenhard see Doc
Delicia® see Elegant Beauty
Delta see Break o' Day
Dembrowski see Dembrosky
Demon see MEIdomonac
Denoyel see Souv. de
Claudius Denoyel
Desprez Fleur Jaunes see
Jaune Desprez
Diantheflora see Fimbriata
Dianthiflora see Fimbriata
Dickson's Jubilee see Lovely
Lady
Dinsmore see Mme. Charles
Wood
Director Plumecock see
Président Plumecocq
Direktör Benschop see City
of York
Direktör Rikala see Frau
Astrid Späth
Dixie Dream see Festival
Docteur F. Debat see Dr.
Debat
Dr. Dick see Doctor Dick
Dr. F. Debat see Dr. Debat
Dr. F.G. Chandler see
Dickson's Red
Dr. Faust see Faust
Dr. R. Maag® see
Colorama
Dr. Wolfgang Pöschl see
Canadian White Star
Dog Rose see R. canina
Linnaeus
Donatella see Granada
Doncasterii see R.
macrophylla doncasterii
Dorothy Dix see Mrs. E.M.
Gilmer
Dorrit see Sunsong
Dorus Rijkers see Doris
Ryker
Double Cherokee see
Fortuniana
Double Cinnamon see R.
cinnamomea plena
Weston
Double Else Poulsen see
Else's Rival
Double French Rose see
Apothecary's Rose

Double Mme. Butterfly see
Annie Laurie
Double White see Elegans
Double White Noisette see
Plena
Double Yellow Scots Rose see
William's Double Yellow
Douce Symphonie see
Debut
Douchka see Mary DeVor
Doux Parfum see Typhoo
Tea
Dovedale see Dove
Dream Boat see Dreamboat
Dreamgirl see Dream Girl
Dreaming see Träumerei
Dreamland see Traumland
Dreams Come True see
Senator Burda
Dreamtime see Dream
Time
Dresselhuys see Petite Penny
Duc de Angoulême see
Duchesse d'Angoulême
Duc de Rohan see Duchesse
de Rohan
Duc de Wellington see Duke
of Wellington
Duc Meillandina see
MEIpinjid
Duchess of Windsor see
Permanent Wave
Duchesse de Portland see
Duchess of Portland
Duchesse d'Istrie see William
Lobb
Dudley Cross see Mrs.
Dudley Cross
Duftgold see Fragrant
Gold
Duftwolke see Fragrant
Cloud
Duftzauber '84 see Royal
William
Duke Meillandina see
MEIpinjid
Duke Wayne see Big Duke
Dunkelrote Ellen Poulsen see
Red Ellen Poulsen
Dwarf Fairy see
Zwergenfee
Dwarf King see Dwarfking
Dwarf Queen see Queen of
the Dwarfs
Dwarf Queen '82 see
KORwerk
Dyna see Bingo

-E-

E. Veyrath Hermanos see E.
Veyrat Hermanos
Early Peace see Molodost
Mira
Easter Morn see Easter
Morning
Eberwein see Dopey
Edelweiss see Snowline
Eden see Pierre de Ronsard
Eden Rose 88 see Pierre de
Ronsard
Edith Cavell see Miss Edith
Cavell
Edwardian Lady see Edith
Holden
Eglantine see R. eglanteria
Linnaeus
Eiffelturm see Eiffel Tower
El Toro see Uncle Joe
Elfin® see Alfi
Elise Boëlle see Elisa Boëlle
Elizabeth Heather Grierson
see MATtnot
Elle see Nobility
Embruixada see Violetera
Emmanuelle see Emanuel
Emmeline see Madeline
Ena Baxter see COCbonne
Enfant de Lyon see Narcisse
English Garden® see AUSbuff
Enjoy see LAVjoy
Erica see Eyeopener
Erinnerung an Brod see
Souv. de Brod
Erlkönig see Roi des Aunes
Eroica see Erotika
Eroika see Erotika
Erotica see Erotika
Esmeralda see Keepsake
Estelle Pradel see Zélia
Pradel
Esterel see KORiver
Esther O'Farim see Matador
Esther Ofarim see Matador
Estralia see Estrellita
Estrellita de Oro see Baby
Gold Star
Été Parfum see Typhoo Tea
Eterna Giovanezza see
Eternal Youth
Eugénie de Guinoiseau see
Eugénie Guinoiseau
Europa see KORtexung
Europe 92® see DELsulan
Evening Light see Tarde
Gris

Everblooming Dr. W. Van
Fleet see New Dawn
Everblooming Jack Rose see
Richmond
Everblooming Pillar No. 12
see Eternal Flame
Everblooming Pillar No. 73
see Scarlet Sensation
Everblooming Pillar No. 83
see Salmon Arctic
Exception see Märchenland
Exposition de Brie see
Maurice Bernardin
Eye of the Dragon see
Dragon's Eye
Eye Opener® see Eyeopener
Eye Paint see Eyepaint

-F-

F. Cuixart see Francesca de
Cuixart
F.K. Druschkii see Frau Karl
Druschki
F.R.M. Undritz see Gen.
John Pershing
F.W. Mee see Fred W. Mee
Fabiola see Queen Fabiola
Fair Opal see Fire Opal
Fairy see The Fairy
Fairy Hedge see Baby Jayne
Fairy Princess see Lilibet
Fairy Red see Fairy Damsel
Fairy Tale Queen see Bride's
Dream
Fakir see Pigalle
Famous Cliff see
Yaroslavna
Fancy Princess see Otohime
Fanny Bias see Gloire de
France
Fantasque see Fantastique
Father David's Rose see R.
davidii Crépin
Father Hugo Rose see R.
hugonis Hemsley
Father Hugo's Rose see R.
hugonis Hemsley
Father's Day see Vatertag
Faust see Scarlano
Favorite see Favori
Fée des Neiges see Iceberg
Feerie see The Fairy
Félicité Bohan see Félicité
Bohain
Felicity II see Buttons 'n'
Bows
Fellemberg see Fellenberg

Fellowship see De Greeff's
Jubilee
Fellowship see HARwelcome
Fennica see Invincible
Ferdi see Ferdy
Ferdinand de Lessups see
Maurice Bernardin
Festival Beauty see
Krasavitza Festivalia
Fête des Mères see
Mothersday
Fête des Pères see Vatertag
Feu d'Artifice see Feuerwerk
Feu de Buck see Ferdinand
de Buck
Feu de Camp see Lagerfeuer
Feuermeer see Sea of Fire
Feuerwerk® see Firework
Fidelity see Scoop Jackson
Field Rose see R. arvensis
Hudson
Filipes Kiftsgate see Kiftsgate
Finnstar® see Finstar
Fiorella see MEIcapula
Fiorella '82 see MEIcapula
Fire Magic see Feuerzauber
Fire Pillar see Bischofsstadt
Paderborn
Fire-Rider see Feuerreiter
Fire Signal see Signalfeuer
Firefly see Holstein
Firefly see MACfrabro
Fireworks, Climbing see Feu
d'Artifice
First Class see Class Act
Fisher & Holmes see Fisher
Holmes
Fivre d'Or see Golden Giant
Flame Dance see
Flammentanz
Flame Dancer see
HARdancer
Flame of the East see Plamya
Vostoka
Flamingo see HERfla
Flammenmeer see Shalom
Flammette see Crimson
Gem
Flash see LENana
Flash see Rosemary Gandy
Flavia see Fleurette
Fleurop® see KORtexung
Flore see Flora
Florian see Tender Night
Florian, Climbing see
Tender Night, Climbing
Flower Girl see Sea Pearl
Fontaine see Fountain

Fontaine Blue see Fontainebleau
For You see Para Ti
Fortuné Besson see Georg Arends
Fortune's Five-colored Rose see Five-Colored Rose
Fortuneana see Fortuniana
Foster's Melbourne Cup see Foster's Wellington Cup
Four Seasons see Autumn Damask
Fragrant Charm see Duftzauber
Fragrant Lady see Perfume Beauty
Fragrant Lavendar see Velvet Mist
Fragrant Memory see Jadis
Francofurtana see Empress Josephine
Frank Leddy see Frans Leddy
Frau Dagmar Hastrup see Frau Dagmar Hartopp
Fred W. Alesworth see F.W. Alesworth
Fredagh of Bellinchamp see Swany River
Free Gold® see Freegold
Freiheitsglocke see Liberty Bell
French Cancan see Tourbillon
French Liberty see Innovation Minijet
French Rose see R. gallica Linnaeus
Freshie see Sweetwaters
Friendship see HAVipip
Friesia see Sunsprite
Frohsinn '82 see TANsinnroh
Fru Dagmar Hastrup see Frau Dagmar Hartopp
Fru Inge Poulsen see Mrs. Inge Poulsen
Fru Julie Poulsen see Poulsen's Delight
Fulgens see Malton
Fulton MacKay see COCdana
Furedaiko see Fure-Daiko

-G-

G'Day see Madhatter
Gabrielle see Gabi
Gabrielle see Gabriella

Gabrielle Noyelle see Gabriel Noyelle
Gallica Grandiflora see Alika
Gallica Maheca see La Belle Sultane
Galsar see Gallivarda
Garden City see Letchworth Garden City
Garden Magic see Gartenzauber
Garnette Carol see Carol Amling
Garnette Pink see Carol Amling
Garnette Red see Garnette
Gartenzauber '84 see Gartenzauber
Gavolda see Cricri
GAxence see Éminence
Gelbe Dagmar Hastrup see Topaz Jewel
Gén. Jacqueminot see Général Jacqueminot
General Jack see Général Jacqueminot
Generosa see Mansuino Rose
Geneviève Genest see Mrs. Sam McGredy, Climbing
Gentiliana see Polyantha Grandiflora
George IV see Rivers' George IV
George Sand see Lunelle
Georgeous® see INTergeorge
Georgette see INTerorge
Georgie Girl see Wishing
Geranium see Independence
Gerbe d'Or see Casino
Germania see Charme
Giant of Battles see Géant des Batailles
Gidday see Madhatter
Giesebrecht see Bashful
Gigantea Cooperi see Cooper's Burmese
Gilbert Bécaud see MEIridorio
Gin no suzu see Silver Bell
Gioia see Peace
Gioia, Climbing see Peace, Climbing
Gitane see Bright Wings
Gitta Grummer see Uwe Seeler
Gloire de Bordeau see Belle de Bordeaux
Gloire de Bordeaux see Belle de Bordeaux

Gloire de l'Exposition de Bruxelles see Gloire de Bruxelles
Gloire de Paris see Anna de Diesbach
Gloire de Rome see Rome Glory
Gloire des Mousseux see Gloire des Mousseuses
Gloire des Perpetuelles see Flon
Gloria Dei see Peace
Gloria Dei, Climbing see Peace, Climbing
Gloria di Roma see Rome Glory
Glory of Paris see Anna de Diesbach
Glory of Rome see Rome Glory
Goddess see Desse
Gold Bunny® see Gold Badge
Gold Crest see Golden Crest
Gold Fever see Baby Sunrise
Gold Heart see Burnaby
Gold Krone see Gold Crown
Gold of Ophir see Fortune's Double Yellow
Gold Star see Goldstar
Gold Star see Goldstern
Gold Topaz see Goldtopas
Golden Anniversary see Firstar
Golden Butterfly see Goudvlinder
Golden Climber see Mrs. Arthur Curtiss James
Golden Girls see Golden Beauty
Golden Heart see Burnaby
Golden Medaillon see Limelight
Golden Meillandina see Rise 'n' Shine
Golden Melody see Irene Churruca
Golden Pernet see Julien Potin
Golden Piccolo see Texas
Golden Pride see Gold Coast
Golden Prince see Kabuki
Golden Rambler see Alister Stella Gray
Golden Rambler see Easlea's Golden Rambler
Golden Rider see Goldener Reiter

Gruss an Worishofen see Bad
Wörishofen
Gulletta see Tapis Jaune
Gwen Swane see MACwhaka
Gypsy see Kiboh
Gypsy Carnival see Kiboh
Gypsy Lass see Gipsy Lass

-H-

H.G. Hastings see Harry G.
Hastings
H.P. Pinkerton see
Cleveland
Haendel® see Handel
Hallelujah see Allelulia
Hamburger Phonix® see
Hamburger Phoenix
Hanabusa see Hana-Busa
Hanagasumi see
Hana-Gasumi
Hanamigawa see
Hanami-Gawa
Handel® see Handel
Handel's Largo see Largo
d'Haendel
Handout see Tranquillity
Hannes see Rose Hannes
Hannover see Messestadt
Hannover
Hans Christian Andersen see
H.C. Andersen
Happy Anniversary see
Heureux Anniversaire
Happy Days see MACseatri
× ardii see × H. hardii (Cels)
Rowley
Harisonii see Harison's
Yellow
Harison's Salmon see
Harison Salmon
Harkness Marigold see
HARtoflax
Harlequin see Miss Liberté
Harold Ickes see Crepe
Myrtle
Harry® see Harry
· Wheatcroft
Hartina see Kammersanger
Terkal
Harukaze see Haru-Kaze
Harvest Home see Harvest
Home
Heart Throb see Paul
Shirville
Heather see Silver
Anniversary
Heckenzauber see Sexy Rexy

Hedgehog Rose see R. rugosa
Thunberg
Heideroslein Nozomi see
Nozomi
Heidetraum™ see Flower
Carpet
Heidi Kabel see
Holsteinperle
Heidikind see KORiver
Helen Gambier see Mlle.
Hélène Gambier
Helen Gould see Balduin
Helsingör see Elsinore
Helvétia see Mandalay
Henri Foucquier see Henri
Fouquier
Henri Mallerin see Rouge
Mallerin
Herald see DeRuiter's Herald
Herz-Dame see Dame de
Coeur
Herzblut see
yCommonwealth
Herzog von Windsor® see
Duke of Windsor
Hi Teen see Designer's
Choice
Hidcote Yellow see Lawrence
Johnston
Highveld Sun see Ralph's
Creeper
Himalayan Musk Rose see R.
moschata nepalensis
Lindley
Holländerin see Red Favorite
Holstein 87 see Esprit
Home's Beauty see Olympic
Glory
Home's Choice see Olympic
Dream
Home's Pride see Firstar
Homecoming see
Home-Coming
Honey Favourite see Honey
Favorite
Honey Sweet see
Honeysweet
Honeybunch see Honey
Bunch
Honeymoon see Honigmond
Honorine Lady Lindsay see
Hon. Lady Lindsay
Honour see Honor
Hoosier Glory see Eutin
Hotshot see Hot Shot
Houston see Cathedral
Hudson's Bay Rose see R.
blanda Aiton

Hulthemia berberifolia
(Pallas) Dumortier see H.
persica (Michaux)
Bornmueller
× Hulthemia persica see H.
persica (Michaux)
Bornmueller
Hungarian Rose see
Conditorum
Hypathia see Hypacia

-I-

Ideal Home see Idylle
Iga 83 Munchen see
MEIbalbika
Ile de France see Adoration
Ilona see VARlon
Ilsetta see Ilseta
Impala see Melinda
Imperator® see Crimson
Wave
Impératrice Josephine see
Empress Josephine
Impératrice Rouge see Red
Empress
Incense Rose see R. primula
Boulenger
Indian Meillandina see
Carol-Jean
Indian Princess see Princess
of India
Indian Sunblaze see
Carol-Jean
Indica Major see Fun Jwan
Lo
Inermis Morletii see Morletii
Ingrid Weibull see Showbiz
Insolite see Sweet Chariot
Integrity see Savoy Hotel
Interbec see Espoir
Interflora see Interview
Intrigue see Lavaglut
Intruma see Interama
Irene au Danmark see Irene
of Denmark
Irene von Danemark see
Irene of Denmark
Irischer Regen see Irish Mist
Irish Beauty see Elizabeth of
Glamis
Irish Summer® see Irish Mist
Irish Wonder see Evelyn
Fison
Isabel Ortiz see Isabel de
Ortiz
Isfahan see Ispahan
Iskra see Sparkling Scarlet

Isle of Man see Manx Queen
Isobel Champion see La
  Marseillaise

-J-

J. Bienfait see Mr. J.
  Bienfait
J.G. Sandberg see Jonkheer
  G. Sandberg
Jacaranda® see JacaKOR
Jack Dayson see Perfect
  Moment
Jack Rose see Général
  Jacqueminot
Jack Rose see R.
  maximowicziana jackii
  (Rehder) Rehder
Jackaranda see JacaKOR
Jacobite Rose see White Rose
  of York
James Bourgault see James
  Bougault
Japanese Rose see R. rugosa
  Thunberg
Japonica see Mousseux du
  Japon
Jaqueline see Baccará
Jarlina see Bellevue
Jean Marmoz see Jean
  Mermoz
Jeannette Heller see William
  R. Smith
Jehoca see Jessika
Jehoka see Jessika
Jessica see Angle
Jessica see Jessika
Jet Flame Nirpaysage® see Jet
  Flame
Jeune Fille see Brocade
Jeune France see Young
  France
Jeunesse Éternelle see Eternal
  Youth
JFK see John F. Kennedy
Jimmy Saville see Jimmy
  Savile
Joan Anderson see Else
  Poulsen
Joan Brickhill® see Golden
  Fantasie
Jockey see Horrido
Joconde see La Joconde
Joella® see Jolle
Johanna Ropke see Johanna
  Röpcke
John Ruskin see Ruskin
Jolly see Lustige

Joseph Guy see Lafayette
Joseph Rothmund see Josef
  Rothmund
Joséphine Baker see Velvet
  Flame
Joséphine Beauharnais see
  Belle de Ségur
Josephine Maltot see Mme.
  Bravy
Josephine Wheatcroft see
  Rosina
Jour des Pères see Vatertag
Joy Bells see Joybells
Joyce Lomax see Satan
Joy® see INTermoto
Joyfulness see Frohsinn
Joyfulness see TANsinnroh
Jubilaire de Masaryk see
  Masarykova Jubilejni
Jubilee see Masarykova
  Jubilejni
Jubilee 150 see Pigalle
Julia Ferran see Lady Trent
Julie de Mersent see Julie de
  Mersan
Junior Miss see America's
  Junior Miss
Justine Silva see Rita
  Sammons

-K-

K.A. Viktoria see Kaiserin
  Auguste Viktoria
K. of K. see Kitchener of
  Khartoum
K.T. see Kev
K.T. Marshall see Katherine
  T. Marshall
Kalinka see Pink Wonder
Kalinka, Climbing see Pink
  Wonder, Climbing
Kampai see Kan-pai
Kardinal see KORlingo
Karma see Pounder Star
Karolyn see Coralin
Karoo Rose see Karoo
Katherine Mansfield see
  Charles de Gaulle
Kauff see Kauth
Kelleriis-Rose see Poulsen's
  Supreme
Kibo see Kiboh
Kidway see Kidwai
Kiki Rose® see
  Caterpillar
King Alexander I see Roi
  Alexandre

King George IV see Rivers'
  George IV
King George's Memorial see
  Památnik Krále Jiriho
King Tut see LAVtrek
Kirsch, Climbing see Vintage
  Wine
Kiska Rose see R. rugosa
  Thunberg
Klaus Groth see Claus
  Groth
Kleopatra see Cleopatra
Kluis Orange see Klyn's
  Orange
Koh-Sai see Mikado
Kohsai see Mikado
Kojack see Miss Blanche
Kojo see Sweet Dreams
Königin der Rosen® see
  Colour Wonder
Konigliche Hoheit see Royal
  Highness
Königlicht Hoheit see Royal
  Highness
Konrad Adenauer Rose® see
  Konrad Adenauer
Kordes' Brilliant see Kordes'
  Brillant
Kordes' Harmonie see
  Harmonie
Kordes' Magenta see
  Magenta
Kordes' Rose Anabel see
  Anabell
Kordes' Rose Angelique see
  AnKORi
Kordes' Rose Bella Rosa see
  Bella Rosa
Kordes' Rose Champagner
  see Antique Silk
Kordes' Rose Delicia see
  Elegant Beauty
Kordes' Rose Esmeralda® see
  Keepsake
Kordes' Rose Florentine® see
  Florentina
Kordes' Rose Holstein see
  Esprit
Kordes' Rose Immensee® see
  Immensee
Kordes' Rose Kardinal see
  KORlingo
Kordes' Rose Lady Rose see
  Lady Rose
Kordes' Rose Pasadena see
  Pasadena
Kordes' Rose Patricia see
  Patricia

Kordes' Rose Repandia® see
Repandia
Kordes' Rose Robusta® see
Robusta
Kordes' Rose Sylt® see
Sylt
Kordes' Rose Sylvia see
Congratulations
Kordes' Rose Weiss
Immensee see Weisse
Immensee
Kordes' Rose Westfalenpark®
see Westfalenpark
Kordes' Sondermeldung see
Independence
Koyuki see Snow Infant
Krause's Rote Joseph Guy see
Feuerschein
Kristian IV see Mariandel
Kronenbourg see Flaming
Peace
Krásná Azurea see Generál
Stefánik

-L-

L'Arlésienne see Fred
Edmunds
L'Indéfrisible see Permanent
Wave
La Belle Villageoise see
Village Maid
La Blancheur see
Sodōri-Himé
La Coquette de Lyon see
Coquette de Lyon
La Mienne see Flon
La Minuette see Minuette
La Paloma '85 see TANamola
La Pâquerette see Pâquerette
La Passionata see Betsy Ross
La Petite Duchesse see La
Belle Distinguée
La Presumida see Presumida
La Rose see Dr. Debat
La Rose de Mme. Raymond
Poincaré see Mme.
Raymond Poincaré
La Rose de York see White
Rose of York
La Rosire, Climbing see
Prince Camille de
Rohan
La Royale see Great
Maiden's Blush
La Rubane see Village Maid
La Sanguine see
Sanguinea

La Seduisante see Great
Maiden's Blush
La Syrne see La Sirne
La Tour d'Argent™ see Guy
Laroche
La Villiageoise see Village
Maid
La Virginale see Great
Maiden's Blush
Labrador Rose see R. blanda
Aiton
Lac Blanc see Weisse
Immensee
Lac Rose® see Immensee
Lady Banks' Rose see R.
banksiae Aiton fil
Lady Brisbane see Cramoisi
Supérieur
Lady Brisbane, Climbing see
Cramoisi Supérieur,
Climbing
Lady Eve Price see Caprice
Lady Glencora see Orange
Juice
Lady Kathleen Grade see
Lady Grade
Lady Meillandina see Lady
Sunblaze
Lady Russon see Orange
Delbard
Lady Sackville see Night
Lady Taylor see SMItling
Lafayette, Climbing see
Auguste Kordes
Lakeland Princess see
Vintage Wine
Lakeland's Pride see Double
Feature
Landora see Sunblest
Lane see Laneii
Lane's Moss see Laneii
Laser Beam see Funkuhr
Laura '81 see MEIdragelac
Lavaglow see Lavaglut
Lavinia see Lawinia
Laxton's Pink Delight see
Pink Delight
Le Jacobin see Marcel
Bourgouin
Le Rosier Pompon Blanc see
Rose de Meaux White
Lee's Crimson Perpetual see
Rose du Roi
Lee's Duchess see La Belle
Distinguée
Leerder's Harlequin see The
Jester
Leersum 700 see INTerleer

Len 1 see Bouquet Fait
Leslie Dudley see Lesley
Dudley
Letkis see John Dijkstra
Leverson Gower see Leveson
Gower
Leweson Gower see Leveson
Gower
Liberty Bell see
Freiheitsglocke
Lida Paar see Lída Baarová
Lidka Böhm see Lidka
Böhmová
Liebesglut see Crimson King
Liebeslied see Love Song
Liebestraum see Red Queen
Lied see Bouquet
Lien Budde see Caroline
Budde
Lili Marlene see Lilli
Marleen
Lili Marlene, Climbing see
Lilli Marleen, Climbing®
Lilli Marlene see Lilli
Marleen
Lilli Marlene, Climbing see
Lilli Marleen, Climbing®
Lise Palais see Opal
Little Bit o' Sunshine see Bit
o' Sunshine
Little Devil see Diablotin
Little Devil, Climbing see
Diablotin, Climbing
Little Fire see Ogoniok
Little Princess see Pixie
Little Silver see Eloquence
Little White Pet see White
Pet
Little Woods Rose see R.
gymnocarpa Nuttall ex
Torrey & Gray
Liverpool® see Liverpool
Echo
Longleat see Wanaka
Lorina see Lorena
Louis Philippe see
Grandissima
Louis Philippe d'Angers see
Louis Philippe
Louksor see Louqsor
Lovita see Kiboh
Lowea berberifolia (Pallas)
Lindley see H. persica
(Michaux) Bornmueller
Lübeck see Hansestadt
Lübeck
Lübecker Rotspon see Glad
Tidings

Lucky Charm see MORain
Ludwigshafen see
  Ludwigshafen am Rhein
Luise Kiese see Frau Luise
  Kiese
Lund's Jubilum see Baby
  Blaze
Lusambo see Red Rock
Lustrous see Celebrity
Lutin see Rosy Gem
Luxembourg see Fanny
  Blankers-Koen
Luxembourg see Marie
  Adélaïde

-M-

M Boncenne see Mons.
  Boncenne
Ma Pâqueretta see Pâquerette
Ma Ponctuée see Ponctuée
Mabella see New Day
Macartney Rose see R.
  bracteata Wendland
Mada see Spectacular
Mme. A. Meilland see Peace
Mme. A. Meilland, Climbing
  see Peace, Climbing
Mme. Cécile Brunner see
  Cécile Brunner
Mme. Cécile Brunner,
  Climbing see Cécile
  Brunner, Climbing
Mme. de Sertot see Mme.
  Bravy
Mme. de Stella see Louise
  Odier
Mme. de Thartas see Mme.
  de Tartas
Madame Delbard® see Mme.
  Georges Delbard
Mme. Denis see Mme. Bravy
Mme. Eliza de Vilmorin see
  Mme. Elisa de Vilmorin
Mme. Ernst Calvat see Mme.
  Ernest Calvat
Mme. Eugène Marlitt see
  Eugène E. Marlitt
Mme. Eugène Marlitt see
  Eugène E. Marlitt
Mme. Ferdinand Jamin see
  American Beauty
Mme. Hébert see Président
  de Séze
Mme. Hébert see Reine des
  Amateurs
Mme. Jean Croibier see
  Mme. Croibier

Mme. Joséphine Guyet see
  Joséphine Guyet
Mme. Juliette see Juliette E.
  van Beuningen
Mme. L. Dieudonn see Mme.
  Dieudonn
Mme. Lambard see Mme.
  Lombard
Mme. Liabaud see La
  Virginale
Mme. Louis Lens see White
  Briarcliff
Mme. Martha Ancey see
  Marthe Ancey
Mme. Neige see Youki San
Mme. Neumann see Hermosa
Mme. P. Euler see Mme.
  Pierre Euler
Mme. P. Olivier see Shining
  Star
Mme. Paul Euler see Mme.
  Pierre Euler
Mme. Paula Guisez see Heat
  Wave
Mme. Poincaré see Mme.
  Raymond Poincaré
Madame President see
  Madam President
Mme. Raymond Gaujard see
  Olympiad
Mme. Sancy de Parabére see
  Mme. de Sancy de
  Parabére
Mme. Teresa Estaban see
  Coral Fiesta
Mlle. Cécile Bunner see
  Cécile Brunner
Mlle. Cécile Brunner,
  Climbing see Cécile
  Brunner, Climbing
Mlle. Marie van Houtte see
  Marie van Houtte
Mlle. Rosa Bonheur see Rosa
  Bonheur
Magic de Feu see
  Feuerzauber
Magie des Jardins see
  Gartenzauber
Magneet see Feuerwerk®
Magnolia Rose see
  Devoniensis
Magnolia Rose see
  Devoniensis
Maheka see Purpurea
Mahogany see Mahagona
Maid of Honor see Maid of
  Honour
Maid Marion see Red Imp

Maiden's Blush see Great
  Maiden's Blush
Maiden's Blush see William
  R. Smith
Mainzer Rad see Mainzer
  Wappen
Mainzer Fastnacht see Blue
  Moon
Mainzer Fastnacht, Climbing
  see Blue Moon, Climbing
Maja Mauser see Cara Mia
Maja Oetker see Coronation
  Gold
Majeure see Tanya
Majorette 86 see Majorette
Malicorne® see Beverly Hills
Manchu Rose see R.
  xanthina Lindley
Mandarine see Mandrina
Manja see Six Flags
Manja Böhm see Mána
  Böhmová
Manja Mourier see Six Flags
Manola see Fred Cramphorn
Many Happy Returns see
  Prima
Marachal Le Clerc see Touch
  of Class
Marcella Baldge see Souv. de
  Marcelle Balage
Marchal le Clerc see Touch
  of Class
Marchenkonigin® see Bride's
  Dream
Margaret Thatcher see
  Flamingo
Margaret Trudeau see
  Sweepstakes
Maria Callas see Miss
  All-American Beauty
Maria Callas, Climbing see
  Miss All-American
  Beauty, Climbing
Maria Teresa de Esteban see
  Coral Fiesta
Maribel see COCdana
Marie Casant see Marytje
  Cazant
Marie de St. Jean see Marie
  de Saint Jean
Marion Foster see MEIcapula
Marion Manifold see Miss
  Marion Manifold
Marjorie W. Lester see Lauré
  Davoust
Mark 1 see Mark One
Marquesa de Urquijo see
  Pilar Landecho

Marquesa de Urquijo, Climbing see **Pilar Landecho, Climbing**

Marquise Boccella see **Marchesa Boccella**

Marquise Boçella see **Marchesa Boccella**

Mary Casant see **Marytje Cazant**

Mary-Jean see **Mary Jean**

Maryse Kriloff see **Lucy Cramphorn**

Masaryk's Jubilee see **Masarykova Jubilejni**

Masaryk's Jubileums-Rose see **Masarykova Jubilejni**

Mascotte '77® see **MEItiloly**

Math Altry see **Dresden**

Maurice see **McGredy's Triumph**

Mauve Mallerin see **Simone**

Maxima see **Alba Maxima**

Maybelle Stearns see **Mabelle Stearns**

Medal of Honor see **American Spirit**

Meerzicht Glory see **Orange Delight**

Meg '81 see **String of Pearls**

Megan see **Megan Dolan**

Meidiland Alba see **Alba Meidiland**

Meilland Decor Rose see **Anne de Bretagne**

Meilland Rosiga '83 see **MEIbalbika**

Meillandina see **MEIrov**

Melanie see **MACmelan**

Melanie Lemaire see **Hermosa**

Melik El Adel see **Malek-Adel**

Melina see **Sir Harry Pilkington**

Melissa Joyce see **Silver Phantom**

Memorial Rose see **R. wichuraiana Crépin**

Merko see **Mercedes**

Merrouw Daendels see **Mrs. Henri Daendels**

Mers du Sud see **South Seas**

Message see **White Knight**

Messagere see **Bettie Herholdt**

Métro see **Auckland Metro**

Metropolitain see **West Coast**

Mevrouw S. van den Bergh, Jr. see **Mrs. Vandenbergh**

Mevrouw van Straaten van Nes see **Permanent Wave**

Michel Hidalgo see **Hidalgo**

Michéle Torr® see **Honor**

Midas see **Dorothe**

Mignon see **Cécile Brunner**

Mignon, Climbing see **Cécile Brunner, Climbing**

Miguel Aldrufeu see **Linda Porter**

Mildred Scheel see **Deep Secret**

Milky Way see **INTerway**

Mimi Rose see **Mimi Pink**

Mini Lights see **Minilights**

Mini Metro see **Finstar**

Minister Rasín see **Ministre des Finances Rasín**

Minna Kordes see **World's Fair**

Minna Lerche Lerchenborg® see **Majorette**

Minnie Mouse see **Roller Coaster**

Minuette see **Darling Flame**

Minuetto see **Darling Flame**

Miramar see **Almirante Américo Tomás**

Miriam see **MACsupcat**

Miss Annie Crawford see **Annie Crawford**

Miss Dovie see **Miss Dovey**

Miss Harp see **Oregold**

Miss Heylett see **Miss Helyett**

Miss Liberty see **Miss Liberté**

Miss Pam Ayres see **Bonanza**

Mississippi see **Mme. Charles Sauvage**

Mistigri see **Molde**

Mistress Bosanquet see **Mrs. Bosanquet**

Mon Tresor see **Red Imp**

Mona Lisa see **Australian Gold**

Monica® see **Monika**

Mons. E.Y. Teas see **E.Y. Teas**

Mons. Pélisson see **Pélisson**

Montagny see **Flaminaire**

Montana see **Royal Occasion**

Montigny see **Monthyon**

Montresor see **Red Imp**

Moon Magic see **Jean de la Lune**

Moonlight see **JACice**

Moorcap see **Red Cascade**

Morgensen see **Morgensonne**

Morning Blush see **Duquesa de Peñaranda**

Morning Glory see **McGredy's Orange**

Morning Greeting see **Morgengrüss**

Morning in Moscow see **Utro Moskvy**

Morning Sun see **Morgensonne**

Morsdag see **Mothersday**

Moscow Morn see **Utro Moskvy**

Moss Rose see **Centifolia Muscosa**

Mossy de Meaux see **Mossy Rose de Meaux**

Mother's Country see **Moeder des Vaderlands**

Mountain Rose see **R. woodsii Lindley 1820**

Mousseau Ancien see **Communis**

Mousseline see **Alfred de Dalmas**

Moussu du Japon see **Mousseux du Japon**

Moussue Partout see **Zo**

Mère de la Patrie see **Moeder des Vaderlands**

Mrs. A. Hudig see **Flaming June**

Mrs. A.J. Wylie see **Margaret M. Wylie**

Mrs. Annie Beaufays see **Frau Anny Beaufays**

Mrs. Benjamin R. Cant see **Mrs. B.R. Cant**

Mrs. C.J. Bell see **Mrs. Charles Bell**

Mrs. Charles E.F. Gersdorff see **Maylina**

Mrs. de Graw see **Champion of the World**

Mrs. DeGraw see **Champion of the World**

Mrs. G.A. van Rossem see **Mevrouw G.A. van Rossem**

Mrs. G.A. van Rossem, Climbing see **Mevrouw G.A. van Rossem, Climbing**

Mrs. Harkness see **Paul's Early Blush**

Mrs. Jones see **Centenaire de Lourdes**

Parkay see Dorola
Parkjewel see Parkjuwel
Parme see Simone
Parsons' Pink China see Old
   Blush
Partridge see Weisse
   Immensee
Parvifolia see Burgundian
   Rose
Passion Rose see Manhattan
Pastourelle see Pastorale
Pasture Rose see R. carolina
   Linnaeus
Patio Cloud see Fluffy
Patio Flame see Apricot
   Medinette
Patio Jewel see Little Sizzler
Patio Prince see Crimson
   Medinette
Patio Queen see Nice Day
Patriot Flame see Scudbuster
Paul de Fontainne see Deuil
   de Paul Fontaine
Paul Fromont see Boudoir
Paul Holtge see Grace Moore
Paul's Perpetual White see
   Paul's Single White
   Perpetual
Peace Meillandina® see Lady
   Sunblaze
Peace Sunblaze see Lady
   Sunblaze
Peach Melba see Gitte
Peanut Butter & Jelly see
   Chipmunk
Pearl of Bedfordview see
   Matilda
Pearl of Canada see Perla de
   Alcañada
Peaudouce see Elina
Pechtold's Flame see Tudor
Peek a Boo see Brass Ring
Pénélope® see GAUbiroc
Penelope Keith see Freegold
Penthouse see MACsatur
Penthouse see West Coast
Peon see Tom Thumb
Pépite see Souv. de J.
   Chabert
Perestroika see Sonnenkind
Perfect Peace see Dorothy
   Goodwin
Perfecta see Kordes'
   Perfecta
Perfecta Superior see Kordes'
   Perfecta Superior
Perle de Alcañada see Perla
   de Alcañada

Perle de Veissenstein see
   Perle von Weissenstein
Perle Meillandécor® see Pearl
   Meidiland
Perle von Aalsmeer see Parel
   van Aalsmeer
Persian Musk Rose see
   Nastarana
Persian Yellow Rose see R.
   foetida persiana
   (Lemaire) Rehder
Peter Pan see Presumida
Peter Wessel see Glad Tidings
Petit Marquis see Esprit
Petite see Patty Lou
Petite de Orléanaise see
   Petite Orléanaise
Petite Junon de Holland see
   Petite de Hollande
Petite Red Scotch see Double
   Dark Marbled
Petite Reine see Queenie
Pharaon® see Pharaoh
Pheasant see Heidekönigin
Phenomenon see Phaenomen
Phoebe see HARvander
Phoebe's Frilled Pink see
   Fimbriata
Phoenix see HARvee
Pic-Nic see Picnic
Piccola see Piccolo
Pie IX see Pius IX
Pigalle 84 see Pigalle
Pillar Box Wardlip see
   Pillarbox
Pillar of Gold see E. Veyrat
   Hermanos
Pimlico see MEIdujaran
Pimlico '81 see MEIdujaran
Pine-Scented Rose see R.
   glutinosa Sibthorp &
   Smith
Pink Angel see Angel Pink
Pink Arctic see Show
   Garden
Pink Bourbon see Mme.
   Ernest Calvat
Pink Cherokee see Anemone
Pink Drift see Caterpillar
Pink Elizabeth Arden see
   Geisha
Pink Favourite see Pink
   Favorite
Pink Festival see Pink
   Bouquet
Pink Hit see POUlink
Pink La Sevilliana see Pink
   La Sevillana

Pink Moss see Communis
Pink Nevada see Marguerite
   Hilling
Pink Nevada see SANcharm
Pink Ophelia see John C.M.
   Mensing
Pink Pixie see Pixie Rose
Pink Radiance see Radiance
Pink Radiance, Climbing see
   Radiance, Climbing
Pink Sevilliana see Pink La
   Sevillana
Pink Sunblaze™ see Pink
   Meillandina
Pink Symphonie® see Pink
   Symphony
Pink Triumph see Ingrid
   Stenzig
Pinky see MACponui
Pitica see Kyria
Pius the Ninth see Pius IX
Pixie Hedge see Baby Jayne
Pixie Pearl see Estrellita
Planten un Blomen see
   Cherrio
Poesie see LENobit
Poesie see Promise
Poesie see Tournament of
   Roses
Point du Jour® see Goldstar
Polar Star see Polarstern
Polestar see Polstjärnan
Polliniana see R. ×
   polliniana Sprengel
Pompon de Bourgogne see
   Burgundian Rose
Pompon de Burgogne see
   Burgundian Rose
Pompon de Panachée see
   Pompon
Pompon des Princes see
   Ispahan
Pompon Panachée see
   Pompon
Pompon Perpetual see
   Bernard
Pompon Rose see Rose de
   Meaux
Pope Pius IX see Pius IX
Pope Pius XI see Pius XI
Porcelain see Flamingo
Portadown Ivory see
   McGredy's Ivory
Portland Rose see Duchess
   of Portland
Poulsen's Grupperose see
   Poulsen's Bedder
Pour Toi see Para Ti

Prairie Belle see Queen of the Prairies

Prairie Rose see R. setigera Michaux

Preference see Princesse de Monaco

Prelude see Sugar Plum

Premier Amour see First Love

Premiére Ballerine see Prima Ballerina

Present see Présent

President see Adam

Président Charles Hain see Amelia Earhart

Président Chauss see Mark Sullivan

President John F. Kennedy see John F. Kennedy

President L. Senghor® see Président Leopold Senghor

Président Nomblot see Horace McFarland

President Pats see Staatspräsident Päts

President Smith see William R. Smith

President Souzy see PEKomegir

President Taft see Leuchtfeuer

President Wm. R. Smith see William R. Smith

Pretty Girl see Miss France

Pretty Polly see Pink Symphony

Preziosa see Indian Song

Prima Ballerina see Solistka Baleta

Primaballerina® see Prima Ballerina

Primrose see Primevre

Prince Abricot see Gingersnap

Prince de Monaco see Modern Art

Prince Eugène see Eugène de Beauharnais

Prince Igor® see Frenzy

Prince Philip see Tudor Prince

Prince Sunblaze see Prince Meillandina

Prince Wasiltchikoff see Duchess of Edinburgh

Princesita see Pixie

Princess Grace see Princesse de Monaco

Princess of Monaco see Princesse de Monaco

Princess of Nassau see Princesse de Nassau

Princess Verona see Princesse Verona

Princesse Batrice see Prinses Beatrix

Princesse Batrice see Prinses Batrix

Princesse des Roses see Principessa delle Rose

Princesse d'Orange see Princess van Orange

Princesse Margaret d'Angleterre® see Princess Margaret of England

Prins Claus see Rosalynn Carter

Prinses van Orange see Princess van Orange

Progress see Fortschritt

Provence Rose see Cabbage Rose

Provins Rose see R. gallica Linnaeus

Pétillante see Roter Champagner

Pur Sang see Wiener Walzer

Puregold see Fanion

Purple Noisette see Purpurea

Purpuria see Purpurea

Pussta see New Daily Mail

Pussta, Climbing see New Daily Mail, Climbing

Pygmy see Pygmae

Pyrenees Rose see R. pendulina pyrenaica (Gouan) R. Keller

-Q-

Quatre Saisons see Autumn Damask

Quatre Saisons Blanc Mousseux see Perpetual White Moss

Québec see Mme. Marie Curie

Queen Adelaide see Yves Piaget

Queen Alexandra see The Queen Alexandra Rose

Queen Astrid see Koningin Astrid

Queen Beatrix see Königin Beatrix

Queen Juliana see Orange Delight

Queen of Beauty and Fragrance see Souv. de la Malmaison

Queen of Colors see Farbenkönigen

Queen of Denmark see Königin von Dänemark

Queen of Denmark see Reine de Dänemark

Queen of England see Queen Elizabeth

Queen of Hearts see Dame de Coeur

Queen of Roses see Colour Wonder

Queen of the Violets see Reine des Violettes

-R-

Radiant Super Glaze see Radiant Superglaze

Ragged Robin see Gloire des Rosomanes

Ragtime see LENrag

Ragtime see MACcourlod

Rainer Maria Rilke see Uwe Seeler

Ralph Tizzard see Ralph Tizard

Ramanas Rose see R. rugosa Thunberg

Raspberry Ice see Hannah Gordon

Raspberry Wine see Malinovka

Record see Décor

Red Ace see Amruda

Red Baby Rambler see Mme. Norbert Levavasseur

Red Ballerina see Marjorie Fair

Red Cécile Brunner see Pasadena Tournament

Red Cécile Brunner, Climbing see Pasadena Tournament, Climbing

Red Cedar see Loving Memory

Red Cherokee see Ramona

Red Coat see Redcoat

Red Dorothy Perkins see Excelsa

Red Druschki see Ruhm von Steinfurth

Red Favourite see Red Favorite

Red Festival see Festival Rouge

Red Garnette see Garnette

Red Gruss an Coburg see Clotaria

Red Hermosa see Queen's Scarlet

Red Hot see MACbigma

Red La France see Duchess of Albany

Red Maman Cochet see Balduin

Red Maman Cochet see Niles Cochet

Red Marechal Niel see Grossherzog Ernst Ludwig

Red Max Graf see Rote Max Graf

Red Moscow see Krasnaia Moskva

Red Moss see Henri Martin

Red 'n' White Glory see Candystick

Red New Dawn see Étendard

Red Niphetos see Lady Battersea

Red Orléans Rose see Maréchal Foch

Red Peace see Karl Herbst

Red Pixie see Heinzelmännchen

Red Poppy see Krasnyi Mak

Red Prince® see Fountain

Red Prolific see Clos Vougeot

Red Rider see Red Rover

Red Riding Hood see Rödhätte

Red Robin see Gloire des Rosomanes

Red Rocky see Red Rock

Red Rose of Lancaster see Apothecary's Rose

Red Soldier see Fusilier

Red Star see Precious Platinum

Red Stone see Krasnokamenka

Red Success see MEIrodium

Red Sunblaze see Prince Meillandina

Red Yesterday see Marjorie Fair

Redhot see MACbigma

Reina Elisenda see Independence

Reine Blanche see Hebe's Lip

Reine des Bordures see Border Queen

Reine des Couleurs see Farbenkönigen

Reine des Francais see La Reine

Reine des Iles Bourbon see Queen of Bourbons

Reine des Neiges see Frau Karl Druschki

Reine des Roses see Colour Wonder

Reine Marguerite see Tricolore

Reine Victoria see La Reine Victoria

Reiner Maria Rilke see Uwe Seeler

Rendez-vous see Day of Triumph

Renica see Rebecca

Repelsteeltje see Rumpelstilzchen

Repens Meidiland see MEIlontig

Rev. Floris Ferwerda see Ben Stad

Reverie see Trumerei

Rigobec see Mon Pays

Rigobec 2 see Neiges D'Été

Rigobec 3 see Danse Azteque

Rim see Happiness

Rimosa 79 see Gold Badge

River's South Bank see Jujnoberejnaia

Rob in des Bois see Robin Hood

Robbie Burns see AUSburn

Robin Redbreast see Robin Red Breast

Robur see Red Empress

Rock 'n' Roll see Stretch Johnson

Rocket see Raketa

Rodin see Anticipation

Rodovrerosen see Poulsen's Fairy

Roi de Pays-Bas see Roi des Pays-Bas

Roi des Bordures see Border King

Roi des Pourpres see Mogador

Romance see TANezamor

Romantique Meillandina see Candy Sunblaze

Romanze see TANezamor

R. abietorum Greene see R. gymnocarpa Nuttall ex Torrey & Gray

R. abyssinica Lindley see R. moschata abyssinica (Lindley) Rehder

R. acicularis bourgeauiana Crépin see R. acicularis sayi Rehder

R. acicularis carelica (Fries) Matsson see R. acicularis Lindley

R. acicularis engelmannii (S. Watson) Crépin see R. × engelmannii S. Watson

R. acicularis gmelinii Bunge see R. acicularis fennica Lallemant

R. acicularis taquetii (Léveillé) Nakai see R. acicularis Lindley

R. adenosepala Wooten & Standley see R. woodsii hispida Lewis

R. afzeliana Fries see R. dumalis Bechstein

R. agrestis inodora Keller see R. inodora Fries

R. alba Allioni, not Linnaeus see R. sempervirens Linnaeus

R. alba Linnaeus see White Rose of York

R. alba incarnata (Miller) Weston see Great Maiden's Blush

R. alba maxima see Alba Maxima

R. alba rubicunda Willmott see Great Maiden's Blush

R. alba rubicunda plena Roessig see Great Maiden's Blush

R. alba semi-plena see Alba Semi-plena

R. alba suaveolens Dieck see Alba Suaveolens

R. albicans Godet ex Boissier see R. elymaitica Boissier & Haussknecht

R. alpina Linnaeus see R. pendulina Linnaeus

R. altaica Willdenow see R.
spinosissima altaica
(Willdenow) Bean
R. amoyensis Hance see R.
cymosa Trattinnick
R. andegavensis (Bastard) see
R. canina andegavensis
(Bastard) Desportes
R. × anemonoides Rehder see
Anemone
R. angustiarum Cockerell see
R. arkansana Porter
R. apennina Woods see R.
serafinii Viviani
R. arkansanoides Schneider see
R. arkansana Porter
R. arkansanoides alba (Rehder)
Schneider see R.
arkansana alba (Rehder)
Lewis
R. arvensis ayreshirea Seringe
see Ayrshire Rose
R. arvensis capreolata (Neill)
Bean see Ayrshire Rose
R. × aschersoniana Graebner
see Aschersoniana
R. atrovirens Viviani see R.
sempervirens Linnaeus
R. aurantiaca Voss see R.
foetida bicolor (Jacquin)
Willmott
R. austriaca Crantz see R.
gallica Linnaeus
R. austriaca pygmaea Wallroth
see R. gallica pumila
(Jacquin) Seringe
R. bakerii Rydberg, not
Déséglise see R. ×
engelmannii S. Watson
R. balearica Persoon see R.
sempervirens Linnaeus
R. balsamea hort., not Keller
see Tackholmii
R. banksiae alba hort. see R.
banksiae banksiae
R. banksiae alba-plena Rehder
see R. banksiae banksiae
R. banksiae lutea plena Rehder
see R. banksiae lutea
Lindley
R. banksiae 'Purezza' see
Purezza
R. banksiana Abel see R.
banksiae Aiton fil
R. belgica Miller see Summer
Damask
R. bengalensis Persoon see
Slater's Crimson China

R. bicolor Jacquin see R.
foetida bicolor (Jacquin)
Willmott
R. bifera Persoon see Autumn
Damask
R. bifera semperflorens
Duhamel de Courset see
Autumn Damask
R. blanda Pursh, not Aiton
see R. nitida Willdenow
R. blanda hispida Farwell see
R. blanda carpohispida
(Schuette) Lewis
R. blinii Léveillé see R.
multiflora carnea
Thory
R. blondaeana Ripart see R.
canina blondaeana
(Ripart) Rouy
R. borboniana Chaix see
Bourbon Rose
R. × borboniana Desportes see
Bourbon Rose
R. bourgeauiana Crépin see R.
acicularis sayi Rehder
R. boursaultii hort. see
Boursault Rose
R. bracteata hort., not
Wendland see R.
wichuraiana Crépin
R. bracteata alba odorata see
Alba Odorata
R. braunii Keller see R. ×
involuta Smith
R. brownii Trattinnick see R.
moschata nepalensis
Lindley
R. brunonii Lindley see R.
moschata nepalensis
Lindley
R. burgundensis Weston see
Burgundian Rose
R. burgundica Ehrhart see
Burgundian Rose
R. calabrica Burnat & Gremli
see R. glutinosa Sibthorp
& Smith
R. calendarum Borkhausen see
Summer Damask
R. californica ultramontana S.
Watson see R. woodsii
ultramontana Lindley
(Watson) Taylor &
MacBryde
R. × calocarpa (André)
Willmott see Calocarpa
R. calva (Franchet & Savatier)
Boulenger see R.

multiflora calva
Franchet & Savatier
R. camellia hort. see R.
laevigata Michaux
R. campanulata Ehrhart see R.
× francofurtana
Muenchhausen
R. canina borboniana Thory
see Bourbon Rose
R. canina coriifolia (Fries)
Dumortier see R.
coriifolia Fries
R. canina dumetorum Desvaux
see R. corymbifera
Borkhausen
R. canina froebelii Christ see
R. coriifolia froebelii (P.
Lambert) Rehder
R. canina insignis Wolley-Dod
see R. canina spuria
(Puget) Wolley-Dod
R. canina tomentella (Léman)
Baker see R. obtusifolia
Desvaux
R. × cantabrigiensis Weaver see
Cantabrigiensis
R. capreolata Neill see
Ayrshire Rose
R. carelica Fries see R.
acicularis Lindley
R. carnea Dumont de Courset
see Great Maiden's Blush
R. carolina Auth., not
Linnaeus see R. palustris
Marshall
R. carolina inermis Regel see
R. palustris inermis
(Regel) Lewis
R. carolina lyonii (Pursh)
Palmer & Steyermark see
R. carolina villosa (Best)
Rehder
R. carolina nuttalliana Rehder
see R. palustris
nuttalliana Rehder
R. carolina setigera Crépin see
R. nitida spinosa Lewis
R. caroliniana Bigelow see R.
palustris Marshall
R. caryophyllacea Besser see R.
inodora Fries
R. cathayensis (Rehder &
Wilson) Bailey see R.
multiflora cathayensis
Rehder & Wilson
R. cathayensis platyphylla
(Thory) Bailey see Seven
Sisters

R. centifolia Linnaeus see
Cabbage Rose
R. centifolia albo-muscosa see
White Bath
R. centifolia andrewsii Rehder
see Muscosa Simplex
R. centifolia bullata hort. see
Bullata
R. centifolia cristata Prevost see
Crested Moss
R. centifolia minima hort. see
Centifolia Minima
R. centifolia minor see Petite
de Hollande
R. centifolia muscosa see
Communis
R. centifolia muscosa (Aiton)
Seringe see Centifolia
Muscosa
R. centifolia muscosa cristata
(Prevost) Hooker see
Crested Moss
R. centifolia parvifolia
(Ehrhart) Rehder see
Burgundian Rose
R. centifolia pomponia
(Roessig) Lindley see
Rose de Meaux
R. centifolia provincialis see
Apothecary's Rose
R. centifolia sancta Zabel see
St. John's Rose
R. centifolia simplex Thory see
Ciudad de Oviedo
R. centifolia variegata see
Centifolia Variegata
R. charbonneaui Léveillé see R.
longicuspis Bertoloni
R. cherokeensis Donn see R.
laevigata Michaux
R. chinensis fragrans (Thory)
Rehder see R. × odorata
Sweet
R. chinensis indica (Lindley)
Koehne see R. chinensis
Jacquin
R. chinensis manettii hort. see
Manetti
R. chinensis mutabilis
(Correvon) Rehder see
Mutabilis
R. chinensis pseudindica
(Lindley) Willmott see
Fortune's Double Yellow
R. chinensis semperflorens
(Curtis) Koehne see
Slater's Crimson
China

R. chinensis serratipetala see
Serratipetala
R. chinensis viridiflora
(Lavallée) Schneider see
Green Rose
R. chlorophylla Ehrhart see R.
foetida Herrmann
R. cinnamomea Linnaeus,
partly see R. pendulina
Linnaeus
R. cinnamomea sewerzowii
Regel see R. beggeriana
Schrenk ex Fischer &
Meyer
R. collina De Candolle, not
Jacquin see R.
corymbifera Borkhausen
R. collincola Ehrhart see R.
cinnamomea Linnaeus
R. × cooperi see Cooper's
Burmese
R. coreana Keller, not R.
Koreana Komarov see R.
maximowicziana jackii
(Rehder) Rehder
R. coronata Crépin see R. ×
involuta Smith
R. coruscans Wairz ex Link see
R. rugosa
chamissoniana C.A.
Meyer
R. × coryana Hurst see
Coryana
R. corymbosa Ehrhart see R.
palustris Marshall
R. cursor Rafinesque see R.
setigera tomentosa
Torrey & Gray
R. cuspidata von Bieberstein
see R. tomentosa
Smith
R. dalmatica Kerner see R.
glutinosa dalmatica
(Kerner) Borbas
R. damascena Miller see
Summer Damask
R. damascena bifera hort., not
Regel see Autumn
Damask
R. damascena rubrotincta see
Hebe's Lip
R. damascena semperflorens
(Duhamel de Courset)
Rowley see Autumn
Damask
R. damascena trigintipetala
(Dieck) R. Keller see
Kazanlik

R. damascena variegata Thory
see York and Lancaster
R. damascena versicolor
Weston see York and
Lancaster
R. davidii persetosa (Rolfe)
Boulenger see R.
persetosa Rolfe
R. dawsoniana Ellwanger &
Barry ex Rehder see R.
multiflora Thunberg
R. deserta Lunell see R.
woodsii Lindley 1820
R. dijoniensis Roessig see Rose
de Meaux
R. dimorpha Besser see R.
tomentosa Smith
R. diversifolia Ventenat see
Slater's Crimson
China
R. doniana Woods see R. ×
involuta Smith
R. dumetorum Thuillier see R.
corymbifera Borkhausen
R. × dupontii Déséglise see
Dupontii
R. ecae Kanitz, not Aitchison
see R. primula Boulenger
R. eglanteria Miller, not
Linnaeus see R. foetida
Herrmann
R. eglanteria duplex Weston
see Magnifica
R. eglanteria punicea Thory see
R. foetida bicolor
(Jacquin) Willmott
R. ehrhartiana Trattinick see
Burgundian Rose
R. elliptica Tausch see R.
inodora Fries
R. elongata Roessig ex Stendel
see R. palustris
Marshall
R. engelmannii Crépin see R.
× engelmannii S. Watson
R. ernestii Stapf ex Bean see
R. rubus Léveillé &
Vaniot
R. ernestii nudescens Stapf see
R. rubus nudescens
(Stapf) Rowley
R. esquirolii Léveillé & Vaniot
see R. cymosa Trattinnick
R. exilis Crépin see R. canina
exilis (Crépin) Keller
R. fargesii hort., not
Boulenger see R. moyesii
fargesii Rolfe

R. fargesii Osborn, not
Boulenger see **R. moyesii**
Hemsley & Wilson

R. fauriei Léveillé, partly see
R. acicularis Lindley

R. fauriei Léveillé see **R.
maximowicziana** Regel

R. fendleri Crépin see **R.
woodsii fendleri**
(Crépin) Rehder

R. fenestrata Donn see **R.
setigera** Michaux

R. ferax Lawrance, not others
see **R. rugosa** Thunberg

R. ferax Regel, not others see
R. glutinosa Sibthorp &
Smith

R. ferax von Bieberstein, not
others see **R. horrida**
Fischer

R. ferruginea Déséglise, not
Villars see **R. glauca**
Pourret

R. filipes 'Brenda Colvin' see
Brenda Colvin

R. fimbriatula Greene see **R.
woodsii** Lindley 1820

R. floribunda Baker, not
Steven see **R. helenae**
Rehder & Wilson

R. floribunda Steven, not
Baker see **R. micrantha**
Smith

R. florida Poiret see **R.
multiflora carnea** Thory

R. foecundissima
Muenchhausen see **R.
cinnamomea plena**
Weston

R. foetida harisonii Rehder see
Harison's Yellow

R. fortuneana Lemaire see
Fortuniana

R. fortuniana hort. see
Fortune's Double Yellow

R. × fortuniana Lindley see
Fortuniana

R. fragariaeflora Seringe see **R.
cymosa** Trattinnick

R. fragrans Salisbury see **R.
palustris** Marshall

R. franchetii (Koidzumi) see
R. luciae Franchet &
Rochebrune

R. franchetii paniculigera
(Makino) Koidzumi see
R. multiflora Thunberg

R. francofurtana Thory (not
Muenchhausen) see
Empress Josephine

R. francofurtensis Roessig see
R. × francofurtana
Muenchhausen

R. fraxinifolia Borkhausen see
R. pendulina Linnaeus

R. fraxinifolia Lindley, not
Borkhausen see **R.
blanda** Aiton

R. freudiana (Graebner) see
Dupontii

R. froebelii Christ see **R.
coriifolia froebelii** (P.
Lambert) Rehder

R. frutetorum Besser see **R.
coriifolia** Fries

R. fujisanensis (Makino)
Makino see **R. luciae**
Franchet & Rochebrune

R. gallica agatha see **Agathe
Roses**

R. gallica agatha (Thory)
Loiseleur see **Agatha**

R. gallica centifolia Regel see
Cabbage Rose

R. gallica conditorum Dieck see
Conditorum

R. gallica damascena Voss see
Summer Damask

R. gallica grandiflora see
Alika

R. gallica macrantha hort. ex
Rehder see **Gallica
Macrantha**

R. gallica maxima hort. see
Apothecary's Rose

R. gallica officinalis Thory see
Apothecary's Rose

R. gallica plena Regel see
Apothecary's Rose

R. gallica remensis Wallroth
see **Burgundian Rose**

R. gallica rosa mundi Weston
see **Rosa Mundi**

R. gallica variegata Thory see
Rosa Mundi

R. gallica versicolor Linnaeus
see **Rosa Mundi**

R. gebleriana Schrenk see **R.
laxa** Retzius

R. gechouitangensis Léveillé see
R. × odorata Sweet

R. gentiliana Rehder &
Wilson, not Léveillé &
Vaniot see **R. henryi**

R. gentilis Sternberg see **R.
pendulina gentilis**
(Sternberg) R. Keller

R. germanica Gordon et al see
R. × francofurtana
Muenchhausen

R. giraldii Crépin see **R.
glauca** Pourret

R. glabrata Déséglise see **R. ×
spinulifolia** Dematra

R. glandulosa Bellardi see **R.
pendulina** Linnaeus

R. glauca Villars, not Pourret
see **R. dumalis** Bechstein

R. glaucodermis Greene see **R.
gymnocarpa** Nuttall ex
Torrey & Gray

R. glaucophylla Ehrhart see **R.
hemisphaerica** Hermann

R. gmelinii Bunge see **R.
acicularis fennica**
Lallemant

R. godetii Grenier see **R.
marginata godetii**
(Grenier) Rehder

R. grandiflora Lindley, not
Salisbury see **R.
spinosissima altaica**
(Willdenow) Bean

R. grandiflorai Salisbury see
R. gallica Linnaeus

R. granulosa Keller see **R.
maximowicziana** Regel

R. gratiosa Lunell see **R.
blanda** Aiton

R. gratissima Greene see **R.
californica** Chamisso &
Schlechtendahl

R. graveolens Grenier see **R.
inodora** Fries

R. grevillii Sweet see **R.
multiflora carnea** Thory

R. grosseserrata E. Nelson see
R. macounii Greene

R. gypsicola Blocki see **R.
dumalis** Bechstein

R. hackeliana Nyman see **R.
heckeliana** Trattinnick

R. hakonensis Koidzumi see **R.
luciae** Franchet &
Rochebrune

R. × harisonii Rivers see
Harison's Yellow

R. × harisonii vorbergii Rehder
see **Vorbergii**

R. headleyensis see
Headleyensis

R. heliophila Greene see R. arkansana Porter

R. heliophila alba (Rehder) Rehder see R. arkansana alba (Rehder) Lewis

R. hemisphaerica plena Rehder see R. foetida persiana (Lemaire) Rehder

R. × heterophylla Cochet, not Woods see Proteiformis

R. heterophylla Woods, not Cochet see R. mollis Smith

R. hibernica Hooker, not Templeton nor Smith see Tackholmii

R. × hibernica Templeton see Hibernica

R. × highdownensis Hillier see Highdownensis

R. hillieri (Hillier) see Hillier Rose

R. hirtula (Regel) Nakai see R. roxburghii hirtula (Regel) Rehder &Wilson

R. hispanica Boissier & Reuter see R. pouzinii Trattinnick

R. hispida Poiret see R. pomifera Herrmann

R. hispida Sims, not others see R. spinosissima hispida (Sims) Koehne

R. hoffmeisteri Klotzsch see R. macrophylla Lindley

R. hookeriana Bertoloni see R. macrophylla Lindley

R. hudsoniana Thory see R. palustris Marshall

R. hudsoniana scandens Thory see R. palustris scandens

R. humilis Besser, not Marshall see R. marginata Wallroth

R. humilis Marshall see R. carolina Linnaeus

R. humilis Tausch, not Marshall see R. gallica pumila (Jacquin) Seringe

R. humilis grandiflora Baker see R. carolina grandiflora (Baker) Rehder

R. humilis lucida (Ehrhart) Best see R. virginiana Miller

R. humilis triloba Watson see R. carolina triloba (Watson) Rehder

R. humilis villosa Best see R. carolina villosa (Best) Rehder

R. hystrix Lindley see R. laevigata Michaux

R. illinonensis Baker see R. spinosissima Linnaeus

R. ilseana Crépin see R. glauca Pourret

R. incarnata Miller see Great Maiden's Blush

R. inconsiderata Déséglise see R. pouzinii Trattinnick

R. indica Linnaeus, partly see R. cymosa Trattinnick

R. indica Loureiro, not Linnaeus see R. chinensis Jacquin

R. indica cruenta see Sanguinea

R. indica fragrans Thory see R. × odorata Sweet

R. indica longifolia (Willdenow) Lindley see R. chinensis longifolia (Willdenow) Rehder

R. indica noisettiana Seringe see Noisette Rose

R. indica ochroleuca Lindley see Parks' Yellow Tea-scented China

R. indica odorata Andrews see R. × odorata Sweet

R. indica odoratissima Lindley see R. × odorata Sweet

R. indica pumila Thory see R. chinensis minima (Sims) Voss

R. indica semperflorens (Curtis) Seringe see Slater's Crimson China

R. indica vulgaris Lindley see R. chinensis Jacquin

R. inermis Thory see R. × francofurtana Muenchhausen

R. inodora Hooker, not Fries see R. obtusifolia Desvaux

R. intermedia Carrire see R. multiflora Thunberg

R. involucrata Roxburgh ex Lindley see R. clinophylla Thory

R. irridens Focke see R. longicuspis Bertoloni

R. × iwara Siebold ex Regel see Iwara

R. jackii Rehder see R. maximowicziana jackii (Rehder) Rehder

R. jackii pilosa Nakai see R. maximowicziana pilosa (Nakai) Nakai

R. jasminoides Koidzumi see R. luciae Franchet & Rochebrune

R. jundzillii Besser see R. marginata Wallroth

R. jundzilli godetii R. Keller see R. marginata godetii (Grenier) Rehder

R. kamtchatica Ventenat see R. rugosa kamtchatica (Ventenat) Regel

R. kelleri Baker, not Dalla Torre & Sarntheim see R. maximowicziana jackii (Rehder) Rehder

R. kentuckensis Rafinesque see R. setigera tomentosa Torrey & Gray

R. klukii Besser see R. inodora Fries

R. korsakoviensis Léveillé see R. acicularis Lindley

R. l'heritierana Thory see Boursault Rose

R. laurentiae Trattinnick see R. chinensis minima (Sims) Voss

R. lawranceana Sweet see R. chinensis minima (Sims) Voss

R. laxa Froebel, not Retzius see R. coriifolia froebelii (P. Lambert) Rehder

R. laxa Lindley see R. carolina grandiflora (Baker) Rehder

R. lebrunei Léveillé see R. multiflora carnea Thory

R. lehmanniana Bunge see R. beggeriana Schrenk ex Fischer & Meyer

R. × leonida Moldenke see Maria Leonida

R. leucanthai Loiseleur see R. canina Linnaeus

R. × l'heritierana Thory see Boursault Rose

R. libanotica Boissier see **R. glutinosa** Sibthorp & Smith

R. lindleyana Trattinnick see **R. clinophylla** Thory

R. lindleyi Sprengel see **R. carolina grandiflora** (Baker) Rehder

R. linkii Denhardt see **R. multiflora** Thunberg

R. longifolia Willdenow see **R. chinensis longifolia** (Willdenow) Rehder

R. lucens Rolfe see **R. longicuspis** Bertoloni

R. luciae Franchet & Rochebrune, in part see **R. wichuraiana** Crépin

R. luciae fujisanensis Makino see **R. luciae** Franchet & Rochebrune

R. luciae taquetiana Boulenger see **R. wichuraiana** Crépin

R. luciae wichuraiana (Crépin) Koidzumi see **R. wichuraiana** Crépin

R. lucida alba hort. see **R. virginiana** Miller

R. lucida Ehrhart see **R. virginiana** Miller

R. lucida Lawrance, not Ehrhart see **R. bracteata** Wendland

R. lucida plena Rehder see **R. × rapa** Bosc

R. lurida Andrews see **R. glauca** Pourret

R. lutea Miller see **R. foetida** Herrmann

R. lutea bicolor Sims see **R. foetida bicolor** (Jacquin) Willmott

R. lutea hoggii Don see **Harison's Yellow**

R. lutea persiana Lemaire see **R. foetida persiana** (Lemaire) Rehder

R. lutea plena hort. see **R. foetida persiana** (Lemaire) Rehder

R. lutea punicea (Miller) R. Keller see **R. foetida bicolor** (Jacquin) Willmott

R. lutescens Pursh see **R. spinosissima hispida** (Sims) Koehne

R. lutetiana Léman see **R. canina lutetiana** (Léman) Baker

R. lyellii Lindley see **R. clinophylla** Thory

R. lyonii Pursh see **R. carolina villosa** (Best) Rehder

R. lyonii alba Rehder see **R. carolina alba** Rehder

R. macartnea Dumont de Courset see **R. bracteata** Wendland

R. macdougalii Holzinger see **R. nutkana hispida** Fernald

R. macounii Rydberg, not Greene see **R. woodsii** Lindley 1820

R. macrantha Desportes see **Gallica Macrantha**

R. macrocarpa Watt, not others see **R. gigantea** Collett

R. macrophylla Crépin, not Lindley see **R. hemsleyana** Täckholm

R. macrophylla acicularis Vilmorin see **R. persetosa** Rolfe

R. macrophylla crasseaculeata Vilmorin see **R. setipoda** Hemsley & Wilson

R. macrophylla rubrostaminea Vilmore see **R. moyesii** Hemsley & Wilson

R. majalis Herrmann see **R. cinnamomea plena** Weston

R. manca Greene see **R. nutkana** Presl

R. manettii Crivelli ex Rivers see **Manetti**

R. × mariae-graebneriae Ascherson & Graebner see **Maria Graebner**

R. maximilianii Nees see **R. woodsii** Lindley 1820

R. melina Greene see **R. × engelmannii** S. Watson

R. mexicana Watson, not Willdenow see **R. carolina glandulosa** (Crépin) Farwell

R. microcarpa hort. see **R. multiflora** Thunberg

R. microcarpa Lindley, not Besser nor Retzius see **R. cymosa** Trattinnick

R. microphylla Roxburgh ex Lindley, not Desfontaines see **R. roxburghii** Trattinnick

R. microphylla alba odorata see **Alba Odorata**

R. microphylla hirtula Regel see **R. roxburghii hirtula** (Regel) Rehder & Wilson

R. × micrugosa Henkel see **Micrugosa**

R. mirifica Greene see **R. stellata mirifica** (Greene) Cockerell

R. mitissima Gmelin see **R. spinosissima inermis** (De Candolle) Rehder

R. mohavensis Parish see **R. woodsii** Lindley 1820

R. mokanensis Léveillé see **R. wichuraiana** Crépin

R. montana chavinii (Rapin ex Reuter) Christ see **R. chavinii** Rapin ex Reuter

R. moschata autumnalis hort. see **Noisette Rose**

R. moschata flore semipleno Thory see **R. moschata plena** Weston

R. moschata helenae (Rehder & Wilson) Cardot see **R. helenae** Rehder & Wilson

R. moschata leschenaultii (Wight & Arnott) Crépin see **R. leschenaultii** Wight & Arnott

R. moschata micrantha Crépin see **R. helenae** Rehder & Wilson

R. moschata nastarana Christ see **Nastarana**

R. moschata nivea Lindley see **Dupontii**

R. moyesii rosea Rehder & Wilson see **R. holodonta** Stapf

R. multiflora dawsoniana hort. Rochester, not R. dawsoniana Rehder see **R. multiflora roseiflora** (Focke) Rehder

R. multiflora platyphylla (Thory) Rehder & Wilson see **Seven Sisters**

R. multiflora plena Regel see
R. multiflora carnea
Thory
R. multiflora thunbergiana
Thory see **R. multiflora**
Thunberg
R. mundi see **Rosa Mundi**
R. muriculata Greene see **R.**
nutkana Presl
R. muscosa Aiton see
Centifolia Muscosa
R. muscosa alba Thory see
White Bath
R. muscosa simplex Andrews
see **Muscosa Simplex**
R. mutabilis Correvon see
Mutabilis
R. myriacantha De Candolle
see **R. spinosissima**
myriacantha (De
Candolle) Koehne
R. myriadenia Green see **R.**
yainacensis Greene
R. naiadum Lunell see **R.**
macounii Greene
R. nankinensis Loureiro see **R.**
chinensis Jacquin
R. nemorosa Libert ex Lejeune
see **R. micrantha**
Smith
R. nipponensis Crépin see **R.**
acicularis nipponensis
(Crépin) Koehne
R. nivea De Candolle see **R.**
laevigata Michaux
R. × noisettiana Thory see
Noisette Rose
R. × noisettiana manettii
(Crivelli ex Rivers)
Rehder see **Manetti**
R. nuttalliana Paul ex Rehder
see **R. palustris**
nuttalliana Rehder
R. obovata Rafinesque see **R.**
carolina grandiflora
(Baker) Rehder
R. ochroleuca Swartz see **R.**
spinosissima luteola
Andrews
R. × odorata erubescens (Focke)
Robert & Wilson see **R.**
gigantea erubescens
Focke
R. × odorata gigantea (Collett
ex Crépin) Rehder &
Wilson see **R. gigantea**
Collett

R. × odorata ochroleuca
(Lindley) Rehder see
Parks' Yellow
Tea-scented China
R. × odorata pseudindica
(Lindley) Rehder see
Fortune's Double
Yellow
R. officinalis (Thory)
Kirschleger see
Apothecary's
Rose
R. olympica Donn see **R.**
gallica Linnaeus
R. omeiensis Rolfe see **R.**
sericea omeiensis (Rolfe)
Rowley
R. omeiensis chrysocarpa
Rehder see **R. sericea**
chrysocarpa (Rehder)
Rowley
R. omeiensis pteracantha
(Franchet) Rehder &
Wilson see **R. sericea**
pteracantha Franchet
R. omissa Déséglise see **R.**
sherardii Davies
R. orbicularis Baker see **R.**
sertata Rolfe
R. oreophila Rydberg see **R. ×**
engelmannii S.
Watson
R. oulengensis Léveillé see **R. ×**
odorata Sweet
R. oxyacanthos K. Koch, not
von Bieberstein see **R. ×**
kochiana Koehne
R. oxyodon Boissier see **R.**
pendulina oxyodon
(Boissier) Rehder
R. parmentieri Leveille see **R.**
davidii elongata Rehder
& Wilson
R. parviflora Ehrhart see **R.**
carolina Linnaeus
R. parvifolia Ehrhart, not
Pallas see **Burgundian**
Rose
R. parviflora glandulosa
Crépin see **R. carolina**
glandulosa (Crépin)
Farwell
R. × paulii Rehder see **Paulii**
R. × paulii rosea hort. see
Paulii Rosea
R. pennsylvanica Andrews, not
Wangenheim nor

Michaux see **R.**
virginiana Miller
R. pennsylvanica plena
Marshall see **R. carolina**
plena (Marshall) Doris
Lynes
R. pensylvanica Michaux see
R. palustris Marshall
R. pensylvanica Wangenheim
see **R. carolina Linnaeus**
R. × penzanceana Rehder see
Lady Penzance
R. phoenica see **R. phoenicia**
Boissier
R. pimpinellifolia see **R.**
spinosissima Linnaeus
R. pimpinellifolia Linnaeus see
R. spinosissima
pimpinellifolia
(Linnaeus) Hooker
R. pimpinellifolia elasmacantha
(Trautvetter) Crépin see
R. elasmacantha
Trautvetter
R. pimpinellifolia inermis De
Candolle see **R.**
spinosissima inermis
(De Candolle) Rehder
R. pimpinellifolia tuschetica
Christ see **R. tuschetica**
Boissier
R. pisocarpa ultramontana (S.
Watson) Peck see **R.**
woodsii ultramontana
Lindley (Watson) Taylor
& MacBryde
R. pissartii see **Nastarana**
R. platyphylla (Thory)
Takasima, not Rau see
Seven Sisters
R. poetica Lunel see **R.**
woodsii fendleri
(Crépin) Rehder
R. × pokornyana Kmet see
Pokornyana
R. polyantha Siebold &
Zuccarini see **R.**
multiflora Thunberg
R. polyantha grandiflora hort.
see **R. gentiliana** Léveillé
& Vaniot
R. polyanthos Roessig see
Summer Damask
R. pomifera duplex see
Duplex
R. pomponia Roessig see **Rose**
de Meaux

R. pomponia Thory ex Redouté, not Roessig see **Burgundian Rose**

R. pratensis Rafinesque see **R. carolina Linnaeus**

R. pratincola Greene, not H. Braun see **R. arkansana Porter**

R. pratincola alba Rehder see **R. arkansana alba (Rehder) Lewis**

R. procera Salisbury see **White Rose of York**

R. prostrata De Candolle see **R. sempervirens prostrata Desvaux**

R. × protieformis Rowley see **Proteiformis**

R. provincialis Miller see **Apothecary's Rose**

R. × pruhoniciana Schneider see **Hillier Rose**

R. pseudindica Lindley see **Fortune's Double Yellow**

R. pseudoscabrata Blocki see **R. canina Linnaeus**

R. × pteragonis cantabrigiensis (Weaver) Rowley see **Cantabrigiensis**

R. pubescens Baker see **R. rugosa plena Regel**

R. pulchella Salisbury see **R. spinosissima Linnaeus**

R. pulchella Willdenow, not Salisbury see **Rose de Meaux**

R. pulverulenta von Bieberstein see **R. glutinosa Sibthorp & Smith**

R. pumila Jacquin see **R. gallica pumila (Jacquin) Seringe**

R. punicea Miller see **R. foetida bicolor (Jacquin) Willmott**

R. pusilla Rafinesque see **R. carolina villosa (Best) Rehder**

R. pustulosa Bertolini see **R. glutinosa Sibthorp & Smith**

R. pyrenaica Gouan see **R. pendulina pyrenaica (Gouan) R. Keller**

R. pyrifera Rydberg see **R. woodsii Lindley 1820**

R. rapinii Boissier see **R. hemisphaerica rapinii (Boissier) Rowley**

R. rapinii Boissier & Balansa see **R. hemisphaerica Hermann**

R. reclinata Thory see **Boursault Rose**

R. reducta Baker see **R. multibracteata Hemsley & Wilson**

R. redutea rubescens Thory see **R. nitida Willdenow**

R. regeliana Linden & André see **R. rugosa Thunberg**

R. regelii Reuter see **R. beggeriana Schrenk ex Fischer & Meyer**

R. remensis De Candolle see **Burgundian Rose**

R. repens Scopoli see **R. arvensis Hudson**

R. × richardii Rehder see **St. John's Rose**

R. rouletii Correvon see **Rouletii**

R. roxburghii plena Rehder see **R. roxburghii Trattinnick**

R. rubella Smith see **R. × reversa Waldstein & Kitaibel**

R. rubeoides Andrews see **R. multiflora carnea Thory**

R. rubicans Roessig see **Great Maiden's Blush**

R. rubifolia R. Brown ex Ait. fil. see **R. setigera tomentosa Torrey & Gray**

R. rubiginosa Britton & Brown, not Linnaeus see **R. micrantha Smith**

R. rubiginosa Linnaeus see **R. eglanteria Linnaeus**

R. rubiginosa magnifica see **Magnifica**

R. rubiginosa nemoralis Thory see **R. micrantha Smith**

R. rubiginosa parvifolia Willdenow see **R. pouzinii Trattinnick**

R. rubra Lamarck see **R. gallica Linnaeus**

R. rubrifolia Villars see **R. glauca Pourret**

R. rubrispina Bosc ex Poiret see **R. nitida Willdenow**

R. rubrostipullata Nakai see **R. marretii Léveillé**

R. × ruga Lindley see **Ruga**

R. rugosa albiflora Koidzumi see **R. rugosa alba (Ware) Rehder**

R. rugosa calocarpa André see **Calocarpa**

R. rugosa rebro-plena Rehder see **R. rugosa plena Regel**

R. rugosa repens alba Paul see **Paulii**

R. rugosa repens rosea see **Paulii Rosea**

R. rugosa scabrosa hort. see **Scabrosa**

R. rugosa thunbergiana C.A. Meyer see **R. rugosa rugosa**

R. rugosa typica hort. see **R. rugosa rubra** hort., not Rehder

R. ruscinonensis Grenier & Déséglise see **R. moschata Herrmann**

R. rydbergii Greene see **R. arkansana Porter**

R. sabinii Woods see **R. × involuta Smith**

R. salicifolia Thory see **R. palustris Marshall**

R. sancta Richard, not Andrews see **St. John's Rose**

R. sandbergii Greene see **R. woodsii Lindley 1820**

R. sarrulata Rafinesque see **R. carolina glandulosa (Crépin) Farwell**

R. saxatilis Steven see **R. corymbifera Borkhausen**

R. sayi Schweinitz see **R. acicularis Lindley**

R. sayi Watson, not Schweinitz see **R. acicularis sayi Rehder**

R. scandens Miller see **R. sempervirens scandens (Miller) De Candolle**

R. × scharnkeana Graebner see **Scharnkeana**

R. scopulosa Briquet see **Pokornyana**

R. semperflorens Curtis see **Slater's Crimson China**

R. semperflorens Duhamel de Courset in part see **Autumn Damask**

R. semperflorens minima Sims
see R. chinensis minima
(Sims) Voss

R. sempervirens anemoniflora
Regel see R.
anemoneflora Fortune

R. sepium Thuillier see R.
agrestis Savi

R. seraphinii Gussone, not
Viviani see R. sicula
Trattinnick

R. seraphinii Viviani see R.
serafinii Viviani

R. serpens Wibel see R.
arvensis Hudson

R. setipoda Rolfe, not
Hemsley & Wilsonsee R.
hemsleyana Täckholm

R. sibirica Trattinnick see R.
spinosissima altaica
(Willdenow) Bean

R. silverhjelmii Schrenk see R.
beggeriana Schrenk ex
Fischer & Meyer

R. silvestris Herrmann see R.
arvensis Hudson

R. sinica Aiton, not Linnaeus
see R. laevigata Michaux

R. sinica Linnaeus see R.
chinensis Jacquin

R. solandri Trattinnick see R.
blanda Aiton

R. soongarica Bunge see R.
laxa Retzius

R. sorbiflora Focke see R.
cymosa Trattinnick

R. × spaethiana Graebner see
Spaethiana

R. spaldingii Crépin see R.
nutkana Presl

R. sphaerica Grenier see R.
canina Linnaeus

R. spinosissima Rydberg, not
Linnaeus see R.
cinnamomea Linnaeus

R. spinosissima baltica hort. see
R. spinosissima altaica
(Willdenow) Bean

R. spinosissima mitissima
(Gmelin) Koehne see R.
spinosissima inermis
(De Candolle) Rehder

R. stricta Macoun & Gibson
see R. acicularis Lindley

R. suavifolia Lightfoot see R.
eglanteria Linnaeus

R. subblanda Rydberg see R.
blanda Aiton

R. subglobsa Smith, 1824 see
R. tomentosa
subglobosa (Smith)
Carion

R. subglobsa Smith, 1828 see
R. sherardii Davies

R. subnuda Lunell see R.
macounii Greene

R. suffulta Greene see R.
arkansana Porter

R. suffulta alba (Rehder)
Rehder see R. arkansana
alba (Rehder) Lewis

R. sulphurea Aiton see R.
hemisphaerica Hermann

R. surculosa Woods see R.
canina Linnaeus

R. sweginzowii Meyer, not
Koehne see R. primula
Boulenger

R. sweginzowii inermis
Marquand & Shaw see R.
wardii Mulligan

R. sylvatica Gaterau see R.
gallica Linnaeus

R. systyla Bastard see R.
stylosa Desvaux

R. × tackholmii Hurst see
Tackholmii

R. taquetii Léveillé see R.
wichuraiana Crépin

R. taurica von Bieberstein see
R. corymbifera
Borkhausen

R. terebinthinacea Besson see
R. × marcyana
Bouller

R. ternata Poiret see R.
laevigata Michaux

R. tetrapetala Royle see R.
sericea Lindley

R. thea Savi see R. × odorata
Sweet

R. thoryi Trattinnick see
Seven Sisters

R. thunbergii Trattinnick see
R. multiflora Thunberg

R. thyrsiflora Leroy ex
Déséglise see R.
multiflora Thunberg

R. tomentella Léman see R.
obtusifolia Desvaux

R. tongtchouanensis Léveillé see
R. × odorata Sweet

R. trachyphylla Rau see R.
marginata Wallroth

R. trifoliata Rafinesque see R.
setigera Michaux

R. triphylla Roxburgh see R.
laevigata Michaux

R. triphylla Roxburgh ex
Hemsley see R.
anemoneflora Fortune

R. turbinata Aiton see R. ×
francofurtana
Muenchhausen

R. uchiyamana Makino see R.
multiflora cathayensis
Rehder & Wilson

R. ultramontana (S. Watson)
Heller see R. woodsii
ultramontana Lindley
(Watson) Taylor &
MacBryde

R. unguicularis Bertoloni see
R. webbiana Wallich ex
Royle

R. usitatissima Gaterau see
White Rose of York

R. velutinaeflora Déséglise see
R. gallica velutinaeflora

R. vernonii Greene see R.
stellata Wooten

R. villosa Linnaeus, in part
see R. mollis Smith

R. villosa Linnaeus, in part
see R. pomifera
Herrmann

R. villosa Smith, not
Linnaeus see R. ×
involuta Smith

R. villosa mollissima Rau see
R. mollis Smith

R. vilmorinii Bean see
Micrugosa

R. virginiana Du Roi, not
Miller see R. palustris
Marshall

R. virginiana alba Willmott
see R. carolina alba
Rehder

R. virginiana blanda Koehne
see R. blanda Aiton

R. virginiana humilis
Schneider see R. carolina
Linnaeus

R. virginiana plena see Rose
d'Amour

R. virginiana plena Rehder see
R. × rapa Bosc

R. viridiflora Lavalée see
Green Rose
R. vorbergii Graebner ex
Spaeth see Vorbergii
R. × *waitziana* Trattinnick see
Waitziana
R. × *waitziana macrantha*
(Desportes) Rehder see
Gallica Macrantha
R. wallichii Trattinnick see R.
sericea Lindley
R. walpoleana Greene see R.
eglanteria Linnaeus
R. × *warleyensis* Willmott see
Warleyensis
R. watsoniana Crépin see R.
multiflora watsoniana
(Crépin) Matsumura
R. watsonii Baker see R.
coriifolia Fries
R. webbiana Vilmorin & Bois,
not Royle see R. sertata
Rolfe
R. wichurae K. Koch see R.
multiflora Thunberg
R. willdenowii Sprengel see R.
davurica Pallas
R. willmottiana Léveillé see R.
longicuspis Bertoloni
R. wilsonii A.T. Johnson see
Micrugosa
R. wilsonii Borrer. not hort.
see R. × involuta
wilsonii (Borrer) Baker
R. wilsonii hort., not Borrer
see R. gentiliana Léveillé
& Vaniot
R. × *wintoniensis* Hillier see
Wintoniensis
R. woodsii Lindley, 1826, not
1820 see R. macounii
Greene
R. woodsii mohavensis (Parish)
Jepson see R. woodsii
Lindley 1820
R. xanthina Allard see Allard
R. xanthina Auth., not
Lindley see R. primula
Boulenger
R. xanthina Auth., not
Lindley see R. ecae
Aitchison
R. xanthina 'Canary Bird' see
Canary Bird
R. xanthina Crépin, not
Lindley see R. hugonis
Hemsley

R. xanthina ecae (Aitchinson)
Boulenger see R. ecae
Aitchison
R. xanthina normalis
Rehder & Wilson see R.
primula Boulenger
R. xanthinoides Nakai see R.
xanthina Lindley
R. xanthocarpai Watt ex
Willmott see R. gigantea
Collett
R. yainacencis see R.
yainacensis Greene
R. yesoensis (Franchet &
Savatier) Makino see
Iwara
R. zagrabiensis Vukotinovics &
Braun see R. marginata
Wallroth
Rosa Belle™ see KINbelle
Rosa berberifolia Pallas see H.
persica (Michaux)
Bornmueller
Rosa × *hardii* Cels see × H.
hardii (Cels) Rowley
Rosa × *mitcheltonii* see
Mitcheltonii
Rosa persica Michaux see H.
persica (Michaux)
Bornmueller
Rosa Poncheaux see
Poncheau-Capiaumont
Rosa simplicifolia Salisbury see
H. persica (Michaux)
Bornmueller
Rosabell see COCceleste
Rosali '83® see Rosali
Rosalie see Rosella Sweet
Rosanna see KORinter
Rosarium Netersen® see
Rosarium Ueteresen
Rosary see Roserie
Rosata see Rosada
Rose Angle see Angle
Rose Angle Blush see Rose
Angle
Rose Baby see Royal Salute
Rose de la Reine see La Reine
Rose des Quatre Saisons see
Autumn Damask
Rose du Matin see Chloris
Rose du Saint Sacrament see
R. cinnamomea plena
Weston
Rose Elf see Rosenelfe
Rose Feuilles de Laitue see
Bullata

Rose Iga see MEIbalbika
Rose Oeillet de Saint Arquey
see Serratipetala
Rose of Castille see Autumn
Damask
Rose Ponceau see
Poncheau-Capiaumont
Rose Poncheaux see
Poncheau-Capiaumont
Rosenmrchen see Pinocchio
Rosenthal see Tatjana
Rosi Mittermeier see
Luminion
Rosier de Thionville see
Perpetual White Moss
Rosika see Radox Bouquet
Roslyne® see Bordure Rose
Rosy La Sevilliana see Pink
La Sevillana
Rosy Meillandina see Air
France
Rosy Morn see Improved
Cécile Brunner
Rouge et Or see Redgold
Rouge et Or, Climbing see
Redgold, Climbing
Rouge Meilland see
Happiness
Rouge Meilland see
MEImalyna
Rouge Meilland, Climbing
see Happiness, Climbing
Rouge Meillandécor® see
Red Meidiland
Rouge Prolific see Clos
Vougeot
Roy Rumsey see Firefall
Royal Delight see Royal
Success
Royal Meillandina see Royal
Sunblaze
Royal Romance see Liselle
Royale see Belle Époque
Rozorina see Zorina
Rubrotincta see Hebe's Lip
Rubus coronarius see Easter
Rose
Rubus rosaefolius coronarius
see Easter Rose
Rugosa Rose see R. rugosa
Thunberg
Russell's Cottage Rose see
Russelliana
Rustica 91 see Topaz Jewel
Rusticana see Poppy Flash
Rusticana, Climbing see
Poppy Flash, Climbing

-S-

Schlosser's Brilliant see Detroiter

S.H. Freedom see Spring Hill's Freedom

S.M. Alexander I see Roi Alexandre

Sabine Sinjen see Sabine

Sable Chaud see Puerto Rico

Sable Cloud see Puerto Rico

Sabrina see MEIgandor

Salmon Sensation see Marion

Salmon Charm see Ginger Rogers

Salmon Sensation see Marion

Salmon Radiance see Mrs. Charles Bell

Saluté la Suisse see Red Favorite

Sam Buff see Afterglow

Samaritan see Fragrant Surprise

Samoa see Fred Cramphorn

Samourai, Climbing see Scarlet Knight, Climbing

Samourai see Scarlet Knight

Sampson see Samson

San Rafael Rose see Fortune's Double Yellow

Sandringham Century see Sandringham Centenary

Sandton Smile see KORmetter

Sans Souci see Moulin Rouge

Sans Souci see LAVsans

Saphir see Song of Paris

Sarah see Jardins de Bagatelle

Saroda see Sharada

Sarong see Lincoln Cathedral

Saskabec see Tant Mieux

Satanas see Satan

Satellite® see DELsatel

Scala see Clubrose Scala

Scarlet Glow see Scharlachglut

Scarlet Meillandécor see Scarlet Meidiland

Scarlet Fire see Scharlachglut

Scarlet Meillandina see Scarlet Sunblaze

Scarlet Pimpernel see Scarlet Gem

Scarlet Sweet Brier see La Belle Distinguée

Scarlet Grevillea see Russelliana

Schleswig see Maid of Honour

Schloss Heidegg see Pink Meidiland

Schneewittchen see Iceberg

Schwanensee see Swan Lake

Schweizer Gruss see Red Favorite

Scotch Rose see R. spinosissima Linnaeus

Scout see Boy Scout

Seafirst see Dr. McAlpine

Sebago see Tyler

Seduction see Matilda

Sei-Ka see Olympic Torch

Seika see Olympic Torch

Sensass see Sensass Delbard

Senteur Royale® see Duftrausch

Sentimental see Eva Gabor

Seraphim see Seraphine

Serpent Vert® see Green Snake

Seven Sisters Rose see Seven Sisters

Shafter see Dr. Huey

Shailer's White Moss see White Bath

Shell-Pink Radiance see Mrs. Charles Bell

Shi Tz-mei see Crimson Rambler

Shining Sun see Mrs. Paul Goudie

Shining Rose see R. nitida Willdenow

Shinsei see Shin-sei

Shiun see Shi-un

Show Off see AROwago

Showoff see AROwago

Shrubby Pink see Sunday Times

Shugetsu see Shu-getsu

Shuo see Shu-oh

Sidonie see Sydonie

Siegeslied see Bouquet

Signora Piero Puricelli see Signora

Silhouette see Oregold

Silver Medal see Silhouette

Silver Salmon see Silberlachs

Simba see Helmut Schmidt

Simonet see Metis

Sincera see Amistad Sincera

Single Chestnut Rose see R. roxburghii normalis Rehder & Wilson

Sir William Butlin see Sir Billy Butlin

Sir William Leech see William Leech

Sissi see Blue Moon

Sissi, Climbing see Blue Moon, Climbing

Sissinghurst Castle see Rose des Maures

Sister Thérèse see Soeur Thérèse

Small Maiden's Blush see Maiden's Blush

Smith's Parish see Five-Colored Rose

Snow Dwarf see Schneezwerg

Snow Queen see Frau Karl Druschki

Snowball see Angelita

Snowballet® see Snow Ballet

Snowbride see Snow Bride

Snowdrop see Amorette

Snowdwarf see Schneezwerg

Snowflake see Marie Lambert

Soleil d'Été see Summer Sunshine

Solitaire see MACyefre

Sommerwind see Surrey

Sonata see Songfest

Sondermeldung see Independence

Sonia Meilland see Sonia

Sonia Meilland, Climbing see Sonia, Climbing

Soukara-Ibara see Crimson Rambler

Souv. de Louis Simon see Mrs. Miniver

Souv. de Rose Berkley see Rose Berkley

Souv. de la Bataille de Marengo see Russelliana

Souv. de la Princesse de Lamballe see Queen of Bourbons

Souv. de l'Imperatrice Josephine see Empress Josephine

Souvenir de Adolphe Turc see Souv. d'Adolphe Turc

Souvenir de la Malmaison Rose see Leveson Gower

Spanish Shawl see Sue Lawley

Spanish Beauty see Mme. Grégoire Staechelin

Spanish Main see Marquesa del Vadillo

Spectabilis see Spectabile
Spek's Yellow see Golden
  Scepter
Spicy Minijet see Potluck
  Yellow
Spirit of Youth see Senator
  Burda
Spot Minijet see White
  Mini-Wonder
Spring Gold see
  Frühlingsgold
Spring Fragrance see Vesenii
  Aromat
Spring Morning see
  Frühlingsmorgen
Spring see Wesnianka
Springs 75 see Dolly
Späth 250® see Späth's
  Jubiléum
Spun Glass™ see Spunglass
St. Cecilia see St. Cecelia
St. Mark's Rose see Rose
  d'Amour
Stadt Basel see Rustica
Stadt Pilsen see Plzen
Starbright see Lily White
Starlight see Lagerfeld
Stephens' Rose Big Purple see
  Stephen's Big Purple
Stevens, Climbing see Mrs.
  Herbert Stevens,
  Climbing
Stevens Rose see R.
  cinnamomea plena
  Weston
Stéphanie de Monaco see
  Portrait
Strawberry Ice see Bordure
  Rose
Striped Meillandina see
  Strange Music
Striped Moss see OEillet
  Panachée
Sulphur Rose see R.
  hemisphaerica Hermann
Summer Fragrance see
  Sommerduft
Summer Wine see KORizont
Summer's Snow see Neiges
  D'Été
Sun Gold see Sungold
Sun King see MEInarval
Sun King '74 see MEInarval
Sunbeam see Margo Koster
Sunbeam, Climbing see
  Margo Koster, Climbing
Sunblaze see Sunny
  Meillandina

Sunblaze see Orange
  Sunblaze
Sunburnt Country see Ave
  Maria
Sunburst see Mme. Joseph
  Perraud
Sundance see JACnel
Sunflare see Sun Flare
Sunglow see McGredy's
  Orange
Sunny Sunblaze see Sunny
  Meillandina
Sunnyside '83 see LENsun
Sunsation see Veldfire
Sunset Glow see
  Canarienvogel
Sunset Strip see Rodeo Drive
Super Derby see Easter
  Bonnet
Super Star see Tropicana
Super Star, Climbing see
  Tropicana, Climbing
Super-Dupont see Dolly
  Madison
Superb Tuscany see Superb
  Tuscan
Surprise Party see Charisma
Susan see Susan Massu
Susan Ann see Southampton
Swamp Rose see R. palustris
  scandens
Swamp Rose see R. palustris
  Marshall
Swan Song see Swansong
Swan see AUSwhite
Sweet Promise see Sonia
Sweet Dream see FRYminicot
Sweet Repose see The
  Optimist
Sweet Promise, Climbing see
  Sonia, Climbing
Sweet Sunblaze see Pink
  Symphony
Sweet Brier Rose see R.
  eglanteria Linnaeus
Sweet Symphony see Debut
Sweetbriar see R. eglanteria
  Linnaeus
Sweetheart Rose, Climbing
  see Cécile Brunner,
  Climbing
Sweetheart Rose see Cécile
  Brunner
Swet Sultain see Sweet
  Sultan
Swiss Gold see Schweizer
  Gold
Sylvia see Congratulations

-T-

Taifun see Typhoon
Tangeglow see Star Child
Tango see Stretch Johnson
Tantau's Ueberraschung see
  Tantau's Surprise
Tantau's Triumph see
  Cinnabar
Tapis Afghan see Pekinois
Tapis de Soie see Wee Man
Tapis d'Orient see Yesterday
Tapis Rouge see Eyeopener
Tapis Persan see Eyepaint
Tara see Tara Allison
Tarantella see KORantel
Tarragona see Diputacion de
  Tarragona
Tchin-Tchin® see Parador
Teardrop see Tear Drop
Teeny-Weeny see Buttons 'n'
  Bows
Temptation see TROpat
Ten Sisters see Crimson
  Rambler
Tender One see Nejenka
Tendresse see Sachsengruss
Tendresse® see DELjofem
Testa Rossa see
  Holsteinperle
Thaïs see Lady Elgin
The Apothecary's Rose of
  Provins see Apothecary's
  Rose
The Conductor see Dirigent
The Jacobite Rose see Alba
  Maxima
The Cambridge Rose see
  Cantabrigiensis
The Crepe Rose see Paul
  Perras
The Gooseberry Rose see R.
  stellata mirifica (Greene)
  Cockerell
The St. Mark's Rose see Rose
  d'Amour
The Commodore see
  Kommodore
The Beloved see Priyatama
The Old Velvet Rose see
  Tuscany
The Engineers Rose see
  Crimson Rambler
The Lady see FRYjingo
The Seckford Rose see Pink
  Robusta
The Rose Tattoo see La Rose
  Tatoue

The World see Die Welt
The Hunter see Hunter
The Texan see Texan
The Farquhar Rose see
  Farquhar
The Queen Elizabeth Rose,
  Climbing see Queen
  Elizabeth, Climbing
The Mouse see Grey Pearl
The Queen see Souv. de S.A.
  Prince
The Queen Mother see
  August Seebauer
The People see People
The Queen Elizabeth Rose
  see Queen Elizabeth
The Dove see TANamola
The Royal Brompton Rose
  see Yves Piaget
The Wasa Star see Polstjärnan
The Polar Star see
  Polstjärnan
The Wyevale Rose see
  MEIbalbika
The New Dawn see New
  Dawn
The Alexandria Rose see
  Alexandria Rose
The Dragon's Eye see
  Dragon's Eye
The Times Rose see
  Mariandel
The Edwardian Lady see
  Edith Holden
Thoresbyana see Bennett's
  Seedling
Thousand Beauties see
  Tausendschön
Threepenny Bit Rose see R.
  farreri persetosa Stapf
Tidbit Rose see Conditorum
Tipo Ideale see Mutabilis
Tiz see Tzigane
Toboné see Prima Donna
Tocade see Arizona
Toison d'Or see Golden
  Fleece
Tomato Rose see R. rugosa
  Thunberg
Top Gear see Little Artist
Topaz see JACant
Toque Rouge® see Asso di
  Cuori®
Torche Rose® see Pink Torch
Toro see Uncle Joe
Tour Eiffel see Eiffel Tower
Touraine see H.C. Andersen
Toynbee Hall see Bella Rosa

Tranquility see Tranquillity
Trier 2000 see KORmetter
Trigintipetala see
  Kazanlik
Triomphe de Caen see
  Prince Arthur
Tristeza see Tristesse
Troika see Royal Dane
Trudor see Micaëla
True Love see Yorkshire
  Bank
Truper see Persepolis
Trylon see Shining Star
Turner's Crimson Rambler
  see Crimson Rambler
Tuscany Superb see Superb
  Tuscan
Twinkle® see INTertwik

-U-

Ukrainian Dawn see
  Ukrainskaia Zorka
Ulrich Brunner see Ulrich
  Brunner Fils
Unforgettable see
  TRObspread
Union-Rose St. Helena® see
  St. Helena

-V-

Vaire see Château de Vaire
Val Boughey see Valerie
  Boughey
Valerie Swane see Crystalline
Van Nes see Permanent
  Wave
Vancouver Centennial see
  Jan Wellum
Velvet Lustre see Happy Day
Velvet Beauty see
  Barkhatnaia Krasavitsa
Velvet Robe see Atombombe
Verbesserte Tantau's Triumph
  see Cinnabar Improved
Vercors see Savoy Hotel
Verdi see Interpool
Veronica see Flamingo
Veronika see Flamingo
Via Romana see Ljuba
  Rizzoli
Vice-President Curtis see
  Autumn Queen
Victor Hugo® see Senator
  Burda
Victoria see Victoria de los
  Angeles

Vienna Charm see Wiener
  Charme
Vienna Woods see
  Wienerwald
Vierlanden see Pink Delight
Ville de Ble see Rustica
Ville de Chine see Chinatown
Ville de Grenoble see
  Grenoble
Ville de Bruxelles see La Ville
  de Bruxelles
Vinzens Berger's Weisse see
  Vincenz Bergers Weisse
Violacea see La Belle Sultane
Violet Bengal see Purple
  Bengal
Violet Blue see Veilchenblau
Violetta see International
  Herald Tribune
Violette Niestl see Savoy
  Hotel
Viorita® see International
  Herald Tribune
Virge de Clery see Unique
  Blanche
Virginia R. Coxe see Gruss
  an Teplitz
Virginia Rose see R.
  virginiana Miller
Virginia R. Coxe, Climbing
  see Gruss an Teplitz,
  Climbing
Virgo Liberationem see Virgo
Vision Blanc® see Ice White
Vision see POUloni
Vivacity see Temperament
Voeux de Bonheur see Bon
  Voyage
Volare see MACvolar

-W-

Waikiki see Waiheke
Waitemata see Waitmata
Wallflower see The
  Wallflower
Walsh's Rambler see America
Waltz Time see
  Saint-Exupéry
Wasastiernan see Polstjärnan
Watercolour see Watercolor
Wave of Flame see Ho
  No-o-no-nami
Waves of Flame see Ho
  No-o-no-nami
Wax Rose see Duchesse
  d'Angoulême
Wee Matt see Waitmata

Appendix II
List of Non-Registered Roses

Many cultivars of importance in the world remain, as yet, unregistered. This listing provides confirmation of their status. In some cases, there is a cross reference to a second alternate name and/or more popular names.

-A-

Abbe Berleze
Abigaile®
Achantha
Addo Heritage
Adele Hue
Adelfi
Adiantifolia
Aditya
Adora
Adrien Mercer®
Adrienne de Cardoville
Aebleblomst
AEnnchen von Tharau
After Glow
Afterglow
Agatha Christie or Ramira
Agathe Fatima
Agnes Bernauer®
Agni
Agnihotri
Ahalya
Aimable Rouge
Akashi
Akashsundari
Akers Spring Noisette
Aladin®
Albert-Georg Pluta Rose®
Albert la Blotais
Albert Poyet
Albino®
Alessa
Alexandra®
Alexandre Pelletier
Alezane®
Alfons Lavalle
Alina®
Alinka (HT or)
Alinka (HT rb)
All in One
Alliance, Climbing
Al Moise Bourbon/Noisette
Alpina Maheca or Belle
    Sultane
Amadeus®
Amalia®

Amara
Amaroela
Amazon
Ambridge Rose
Ambroise Pare
Amerlock®
Ametista®
Ami Clement®
Ami des Jardins®
Amourette®
Amulett®
Andenken an Alma de l 'Aigle
Andenken an Gustav Frahm
Andrea
Andromeda®
Anemone Ancienne or
    Ornement de la Nature
Anena
Angel Face, Climbing
Angela
Angela Merici
Angelus
Anika®
Anima Renata®
Anita
Anjani
Anjou Nirpaysage®
Anna®
Anna Angelera
Anna Pavlova
Annie Vibert
Annie Girardot®
Annie's Red
Annie's Song
Ans
Anthony Meilland®
Antico Amore®
Antike 89®
Antonia
Anvil Sparks, Climbing
Apart
Appassionata®
Apple Blossom Koster
Apricot
Apricot Gem
Apricot Hit®
Aquitaine Nirp®

Arabia®
Arakvathi
Arbelle®
Ardiente
Arianna™
Arielle®
Arielle Dombasie, Grimpant®
Arlessiene
Armida
Armida (A)
AROcruby or Park Place
AROkish or Bel Air
AROkonic or Velvet Arrow
AROkris or Golden Wedding
AROplumi or Fragrant Plum
AROsumo or Morning Sun
AROtigny or Cherry Gold
AROwillip or Strawberry
    Fayre
Arromanches
Arrowtown
Artiste®
ASAblue or Blue Magic
Asha
Ashirwad
Ashwini 189
Asso di Cuori, Climbing®
Astra (BENstar)
Astra (F)
Astra Desmond
Astrea®
Astree, Climbing
Astrid Spath Striped
Astrid Lindgren®
Atago
Atena®
Atida
Augustine Halem
Aunt Belle's Tea
Aurelia™
AUSap or Queen Nefertiti
AUSbells or Bow Bells
AUSbloom or The Dark Lady
AUSblossom or Peach
    Blossom
AUSbord or Gertrude Jekyll
AUSbreak or Jayne Austin

AUScat or Winchester
    Cathedral
AUScountry or Country
    Living
AUScrim or L.D. Braithwaite
AUSdimindo or Bibi
    Maizoon
AUSfin or Financial Times
    Centenary
AUSglisten or Cottage Rose
AUSglobe or Brother Cadfael
AUSleap or Sweet Juliet
AUSlilac or Lilac Rose
AUSnun or The Nun
AUSpot or Potter & Moore
AUSram or Francine Austin
AUSreef or Sharifa Asma
AUSren or Charles Rennie
    MacKintosh
AUSsemi or The Herbalist
AUSspry or Sir Walter
    Raleigh
AUStin or Financial Times
    Centenary
Austragold®
Australian Centre Gold
AUSvariety or Kathryn
    Morley
AUSvelvet or The Prince
AUSwalker or The Pilgrim
Autumn Leaves
Avalanche
Aveu
Awayuki
Ayaori
Azteka

-B-

Baby Sun
Baby Shower
Badener Gold®
Bakewell Scots Briar
Baldock Festival
Ballade®
Balwant
Banco 86®
Banksiae de Costello
Banquise®
Banzai 83®
BARamad or Amadeus
BARanam or Antico Amore
BARapp or Appassionata
BARasd or Rapsodia
Barbara®
Barbara Worl
Barbara's Rose
BARbrio or Briosa

BARcam or Campanela
BARcast or Castore
BARdim or Midi
BARdon or Donna Marella
    Agnelli
BARemp or Maia
BARfiob or Fiocco Bianco
BARfra or Frasquita
BARgold or Golden Dance
BARimp or Impulse
BARinas or Rinascimento
Barkarole®
BARkel or Helen Keller
BARleo or Eleonora
BARlev or Rita Levi
    Montalcini
BARlioc or Clio
BARlit or Elite
BARmand or Mandarina
BARmast or Dorabella
BARmezz or Brunella
BARmont or Moment
BARmut or Ornella Muti
BARnec or Mirella
BARnerio or Orione
Barock®
Baron J.B. Gonella
Baronesse®
Baronne Surcouf®
BARorp or Astrea
BARpess or La Favorita
BARpoll or Polluce
BARpris or Primo Sole
BARred or Red Sea
Barricade®
BARros or Rosellana
BARsib or Sibilla
BARsilv or Silver Queen
BARsin or Talia
BARsor or Eros
BARten or Atena
BARvir or Andromeda
BARwast or Wall Street
BARzos or Tersicore
Bassino®
Basye's Purple Rose
Basye's Myrrh Scented Rose
Batavia Rose or Rose Chou
Bayerngold®
Bayreuth
Bayreuth or Bayreuth
Beauce Nirpaysage® or
    Palmengarten Frankfurt
Beauty Show or Shoba
Bebe Lune
Becketts Single
Bel Air (AROkish) HT
Bel Air (HT)

Bella Weiß®
Belle au Bois Dormant
Belle Helene
Belle Herminie
Belle Nanon
Belle sans Flatterie
Belle Sultane
Bellissima®
Bellona
Belmont
Belvedere
BENburgun or Ans
Bengale Rouge
BENimbro or Imbroglio
BENstar or Astra
BENtintot or Tiny Tot
Berenice®
Berliner Luft®
Bernadette
Bernina®
Bernstein-Rose®
Besancon®
Beth
Betty Sheriff
Bewitched, Climbing
Beyut
Bhanu
Bharati
Bhavani
Bhivaji Patil
Bianca®
Bibi Maizoon
Bibiche®
Bicolette
Bicolore Incomparable
Biddulph Grange
Big Dream
Bio-Kor
Bipontina
Black Delight
Blanc Pur
Blaue Adria
Blaze Improved
Blaze Superior
Blessings, Climbing®
Bloemfontein
Blondie®
Blue Crystal
Blue Delight
Blue Girl, Climbing
Blue Magic
Blue Ocean
Blue Parade®
Blue Sky®
Blue Sky (Cel Blau)
Bobikopf
Bobino
Bonbon Hit®

Bordure d 'Or®
Bordure Vermillon®
Bordure Vive®
Bordurella®
Borsalino®
Bouquet Parfait®
Bouquet Tout Fait
Bouquetterie
Bow Bells
Braserade, Grimpant®
Braunwald®
BRIarcouf or Baronne
  Surcouf
Bridal Sonia™
Bright Beauty
Bright Imp
Bright Pink Garnette
Bright Sky
Bright Spark
BRIletjui or Juillet
Brilliant Hit®
Brinessa®
Briosa®
BRIsines or Riviere de
  Diamant
Brother Cadfael
Browsholme Rose
Brunella®
Bubble Bath
Bubikopf®
Buoy
Burg Baden
Burghausen®
Burning Glow
Bushfire
Buttercup
Butterfly

-C-

Cadillac
Caldwell Pink
Calliope®
Calypso®
Camaieux, Solid Reversion
Camellia Rose
Cameo Cream or Caroline
  de Monaco
Camp David
Canary Island
Candelabra
Candida or The Nun
CANdoodle or Lady Rachel
Candy Flo
Canina Bitetiana
CANlloyd or Lloyds of
  London
Cannes Festival®

CANplant or Prunella
CANson or Dame Wendy
CantaPEK or Miss Paris
Cantilena Moravica
Capitaine Dyel de Graville
Capitaine Sisolet
Capitole®
Caporosso
Cappanella®
Capreolata Ruga
Capri Sun®
Caprice de Meilland
Caramella®
Carat®
Carinella
Carlita®
Carmen®
Carmosine
Carol-Joy
Carol Minimo
Carole Anne
Caroline de Monaco®
Cascade
Cassandre, Grimpant®
Castore®
Catherine Deneuve®
Cathie Irwin
Cauvery
Cecile Lens®
Cel Blau or Blue Sky
Celebration Days
Celica™
Cels Multiflora
Centifolia Foliacea
Centifolia Major
Centifolia Muscosa Rubra
Cesonie
Chaitra
Chamois Dore®
Chandralekha
Chandrika
Chantefleur®
Charlemagne
Charles Monselet®
Charles Rennie MacKintosh®
Charlie Chaplin®
Charlotte Brownell
Charlotte Rampling®
Charlotte Searle
Charm of Paris
Charmi or Charmy
Charming Mix
Charming Rosamini
Charmy
Chateau de la Juvenie
Chateau de Namur
Cheerio®
Chenonceaux®

Cherie Noire®
Cherry Gold
Cherryade
CHEWba or Lady Barbara
CHEWsea or Patio Queen
Chicago Peace, Climbing
Chidori
Chitrarajini
Chorus, Climbing
Christel von der Post®
Christin™
Christine Lanson
Christophe Colomb®
Ciel Bleu®
Cilla
Cimarosa®
Cindy
Circus Clown
Cisco
City of Christchurch
City of Hope
City of Ichalkaranji
City of Lucknow
City of Panjim
City of Pretoria
Claire Jolly
Claire Truffant
Clara
Claudia Augusta
CLEamour or Glamour Girl
CLEclown or Circus Clown
CLEcurio or Royal Harlequin
CLEgold or Golden Intensity
CLEhob or Frodo
Clemence Raoux
Clementina Carbonieri
Clio (HT)
Clio® (BARlioc)
Clive Lloyd
Cloverdene
COCaquil or Cockadoo
COCcopna or Coppa Nob
COCember or Roxburghe
  Rose
COCfoster or Regal Red
Cockadoo
Cocktail 80
Coco®
Cocorico® (MEllano)
Cocorico® (MEllasso)
Colibre 79
Collegiate
Columbian Climber
Colombina®
Colvilei
COMbar or Barricade
Comic de Tarn-et-Garonne
Comte Boel

Comte de Falloux
Comtesse®
Comtesse de Barbantane
Comtesse de Galard Bearn
Comtesse de Gaylord Bearn
   or Comtesse de Galard B
Comtesse de Leusse
Concerto™
Copelia® or Copelia 76®
Coppa Nob
Copper Arch
Copper Gem
Cora®
Coral Fiesta, Climbing
Coral Floc
Coral Island
Coral Midinette
Coral Rosamini
Coralie
Corne Herholdt
Cottage Rose
Cotton Candy
Coucou®
Countess of Home
Country Living
Crackerjack
Cricket, Climbing
Crimean Night
Crimson Blush
Crimson Cascade
Crimson Gallica
Crimson Queen
Crimson Rosamini
Criterion, Climbing
Crumble Bar
Cuisse de Nymphe Emue

-D-

Daily Express
Dainty Minimo
Dame Bridget
Dame Wendy
Dandenong
Daniel Boone
Daniela®
Dapple Dawn
Darlow's Enigma
D-Artagnan®
Dart's Dash
Dart's Red Dot®
David Whitfield
Davidoff
Dearest, Climbing
Debbie Thomas
Deborah®
Deccan Delight
Deccan Deluxe

Decora
DELblue or Mamy Blue
DELbojaune or Bordure d'Or
DELbover or Bordure
   Vermillon
DELboviv or Bordure Vive
DELcart or Le Roouge et Le
   Noir
DELcreme or Regine Crespin
DELfib or Bebe Lune
DELgold or Lord Gold
Delicate Beauty
Delicious
Delight
Delore
DELredi or Renata Tebaldi
Delta queen
DELteb or Huguenot 300
Deneb
Denise Grey®
Denise Hilling
Dentella
Dentelle de Bruxelles®
Dentelle De Malines®
Descemet
Desgaches
Destin
Destin, Climbing
Destiny®
Deutsche Welle®
DEVale or Bridal Sonia
De Valis Paul
Devil's Dance
DEVine or Dolores
DEVoran or Karen
Diadem®
Diane de Poitiers
DICkindle or Lemon Honey
DICknowall or Collegiate
Dickson's Wonder
DICnifty
DICplay or New Horizon
DICquasar
DICqueue
DICracer or Duchess of York
Diletta®
Dil-Ki-Rani
Dilruba
Disco
Djamilla
Doctor Abrahams
Dr. Briere
Dr. Mors
Dr. M.S. Randhawa
Dr. R. R. Pal
Dolcezza®
Dolores™
Domila®

Don Bosco®
Don's Blue
Donau
Donna Marella Agnelli®
Doorenbos Selection
DORache or Adrien Mercer
Dorandi
DORapri or Mango
Dorbella®
DORbin or Jericho
DORdeli or Starion
DORflo or Bibiche
DORgold or Coucou
DORiste or Artiste
DORjure or Julien Renoard
DORnapa or Flushing
   Meadow
Dorothea Furrer®
DORpobi or Alezane
DORpurp or Parc des Princes
DORsafr or Open d'Australie
DORtive or Pierre Troisgros
DORto or Sika
DOTcris or San Valentino
DOTebro or Spanish Breeze
DOTflo or Patio Delight
DOTraner or Jardinero Ortiz
DOTrenodi or Jardinero
   Ortiz
Double Plum Hybrid China
Double Time
Dream
Druschky Rubra
Duc de Crillon
Duchess of York
Duchesse de Berry
Duchesse de Cambridge
Duchesse de Savoie®
DUCmar or Marquisette
Duftes Berlin®
Duftparadies
Dukat®
Dunwich Rose
Durgapur Delight
Dutch Beauty
Dwarf
Dwarf Pavement

-E-

Echo
Ecole d 'Ecully®
Edith de Murat
Edna Walling
Eldorado
El Dorado Tea
Elegance
Elegans

Eleganta
Elegante Gallica
Eleonor
Eleonora®
Eleusine
Eliana®
Elida
Elite®
Elwina®
Emily Louise
Eminence, Climbing
Emotion (B)
Emotion® (President
   Kekkonen)
Emotion (Souvenir d 'Aline
   Fontaine)
Empress Michiko
Enghien
English Elegance®
English Violet
English Wedding Day
Enric Palau
Ernest H Morse, Climbing
Eros®
Eskimo®
Essex
Estima
Etoile Rouge®
Eugene E. Marlitt or Maggie
Eugenie Verdier
Euro 92
Europe Sensation
Eva de Grossouvre
Evelyn®
Evening Sentinel
Everglow
Evergold
Ever Gold
Exciting
Exciting or Roter Stern

-F-

Fabulous
Fairfield Blaze
Fairy Dance®
Fairysnow
Fama®
Fandango, Grimpant®
Fanny Essler
Fanny's La France
Fanton
Favorite
Favourite Rosamini
Fedtschenkoana Flore Pleno
Fee®
Felicia Teichmann
Fenja

Fennet
Ferline®
Fernant Point
Fiery Hedge
Fiery Sunsation or
   Mainaufeuer
Fil d 'Ariadne®
Financial Times Centenary
Fiocco Bianco®
Fiord
Firebrite
Firelight
Fire Robe
Firestar(F)
First Lady®
First Red®
Fishel Zahof
Flacon de Neige
Flametta
Flaminaire
Flaming Rosamini
Flaming Torch
Flamingo Meidiland
Fleur d 'Orchidee
Flirt®
Floral Choice
Florange
Florence®
Florizel
Fluorescence
Flushing Meadow®
Forever
Foxi®
Fragrant Charm
Fragrant Garden
Fragrant Magenta
Fragrant Plum
Frances Phoebe
Francine Austin®
Francis Moreau
Francis Phoebe or Frances
   Phoebe
Frankfurt
Frasquita®
Frederik Mey
Freisinger Morgenrote
Fresh Cream
Fresh Hit®
Fresh Pink (MACpinderal)
Fridolin
Frilly Dilly (Min)
Frisson Frais®
Frodo
Fruhlingstunde
Fruite®
FRYchambi or Daily Express
FRYclimbdown or Crimson
   Cascade

FRYdarkey or Biddulph
   Grange
FRYevenest or Evening
   Sentinel
FRYholiday or Tonight
FRYmartor or Marianne
   Tudor
FRYmaxicot or Summer
   Dream
FRYministar or Top Marks
FRYprincess or Julie Cussons
FRYrelax or Pensioners Voice
FRYrhapsody or Langdale
   Chase
FRYshrewby or Shrewsbury
   Show
FRYstassi or Rosaletta
FRYsweetie or Mary Gamon
FRYtango or The Observer
FRYtranquil or Golden
   Moments
FRYtrooper or Liverpool
   Daily Post
FRYvivacious or Julie
   Andrews
Fuchsia Meillandecor®
Fulgurante®

-G-

GAesca or Scala
Gala™
GAlioca or Chenonceaux
Galopi
GANa or David Whitfield
Garden Perfume
Gardens of the World
Garibaldi
Garnette Apricot
Garnette Rose
Garnette White
Garnette Yellow
Gartenarchitekt Gunther
   Schulze®
GAUhari or Amara
Gaujard 985
GAUrama or Arbelle
GAUtara or Simone Merieux
GAUvara or Serenite
GAUvila or Renee Collomb
GAUzimar or Berenice
GAUzimi or Lisima
Gavina
GAybar or Barbara
Geisha
Ge Korsten
Gemma
General Allard

Gentle Kiss
Gentle Maid
George Cuvier
George Sand
Georges de Cadonel
Georgetown Tea
Gerdo
Gerry Hughes
Gertrude Jekyll®
Geschwind Orden
Geschwind's Nordlandrose
Geschwind's Schonste
Giant Pink
Gil Blas
Gina
Gina Lollobrigida®
Ginevra
Ginger Meggs
Ginrei
Giriji
G.K. Rose
Glad Rags
Glamour Girl
Gletscherfee®
Gloire d 'Olivet
Gloriette (Min)
Gloriette® (S)
Glory of Edsell
Glowry™
G. Nabonnand
Godavari
GODin or Aladin
GODocally or Savane
GODomeve or Perle d'Anjou
GODotreve or Cherie Noire
GODpico or Aladin
Goldbeet®
Gold Bunny, Climbing
Gold Rush (JACrus)
Gold Rush (Min)
Golden Afternoon
Golden Blush
Golden Cascade
Golden Colonel
Golden Dance®
Golden Elf
Golden Flame®
Golden Gloves
Golden Heart®
Golden Hit®
Golden Holstein®
Golden Intensity
Golden Medaillon
Golden Mist
Golden Moments
Golden Monica®

Golden Mozart
Golden Penny
Golden Queen
Golden Quill
Golden Rosamini
Golden Scepter, Climbing
Golden Wedding
Goldfassade
Goldika®
Goldquelle®
Goldstein®
Goliath (HT ob Wheatcroft)
Goliath (HT dr)
Gomathi
Gourdault
Graceland
Grafin Marie-Henriette
   Chotek
Graf Lennart®
Grand Chateau® or Barkarole
Grand Trianon®
Grande Amore
Granny®
Granny Grimmetts
Great Ormond Street
Greenalls Glory
Grisbi™
Gruss an Maiengrun
Guernsey Love
Guitare, Climbing
Gulab Nagree Nashik or
   Rose city of Nashik
Gulgong Gold
Gulzar
Gypsy®

-H-

H 275
Hafiz®
Hagoromo
HakuCho
Hampshire
Happensdans
Happenstance
Harlekijn
Harlekin®
Harley Nirpaysage®
Harmonie
HARsuma or Suma
Har Tabor
HARtbrad or Gentle Kiss
HARtellody or Baldock
   Festival
Haruyo
Harvest Song

HARvilac or Gentle Maid
HARvissa or Juliet Ann
HARward or Fairy Dance
HARwigwam or Indian
   Summer
HARwilla or Emily Louise
HARyoricks or Pat James
HARyup
Haynesville Pink Cluster
Hedgefire
Heidelinde®
Heideschnee®
Heidi®
Helen Ann
Helen Keller®
Helen Knight
Helen Traubel, Climbing
Helene de Gerlache®
Helga®
Hello Dolly
Hemavathy
HERbeau or Southern Sun
Herbiz
HERclov or Cloverdene
HERdame or Corne Herholdt
HERdominec or
   Johannesburg Centennial
Heriflor
HERlav or Fragrant Charm
Hermosa, Climbing
Heroine de Vaucluse
HERpot or Kristo Pienaar
Hertfordshire
HERtroci or Potch Pearl
HERves or Springtime
Hidden Depths
Higoromo
HILpet or Christin
HILtag or Gala
Himmelsauge
Hiogi
Hojun
Hokkaido
HOLfairy or Fairy Snow
Holterman's Gold
Homage
Homestead Hybrid China
Home Sweet Home, Climbing
Hondo
Honeycup®
Honeysweet
Horticolor®
Hot Chocolate
Hot Spot
Hotel Royal®
Huguenot 300

Huilito
Hunslet

-I-

Ico Ambassador
Ico Delight
Ico Deluxe
Ico Pearl
Ico Trimurthi
Idole
Ilios
Illisca®
Illumination
Imbroglio
Imp
Improved Haute Pink
Impulse® (BARimp)
Independance du
   Luxembourg
Indian Pearl
Indian Summer
   (HARwigwam)
Indian Summer
   (PEAperfume)
Indigoletta
Indraman
Inspiration
INTERdort or Peeping Tom
INTERgol or Golden
   Rosamini
INTERhenk or White
   Minimo
INTERhyro or Borsalino
INTERim or Red Trail
INTERmunder or Dart's Red
   Dot
INTERniki or Nikita
INTERonly or Only Love
INTERpin or Pink Fire
INTERprince or Princess
INTERval or Porcelina
Intrepide
Invention
Irene®
Irish Brightness
Iskra 82®
Ispahan
Ita Buttrose
Ivory Beauty

-J-

JACaebi or Rendez-Vous
JACanne or Roxanne
JACap or Amazon
JACcoeur or Gardens of the
   World

JACdash
JACfed
JACgolf or Sun Up
JAClay or Treasure Trove
JACoh
JACprov or Improved Haute
   Pink
Jacqueline Nebout®
Jacquenetta or Jaquenetta
Jacques Esterel
Jacquot
JACspri or Eldorado
JACster or North Star
JACter
JACwhif or Pearlita
James Mason
Janet B. Wood
Janina®
Janine Herholdt
Jaquenetta
Jardinero Ortiz®
Jawani
Jayne Austin
Jay's Hudson Hybrid
   Perpetual
Jean
Jean Adrien Mercer® or
   Adrien Mercer
Jean Bach Sisley
Jean Monnet®
Jean Rosenkrantz
JELdaniran or Mimi Pink
Jellona
Jenny Charlton
Jericho®
Jezza Belle
Jhb Garden Club
Jisraela Amira
Joan Ball
Joaquina Munoz
Jody
Jogan
Johannes XXIII
Johannesburg Centennial
Johannisfeuer®
John Wright
Jolanda d 'Aragon
Jolie Comtoise®
Jolly Dance
Jorianda
Joro
Joseph Goudreau
Joseph Sauvageot®
Josephine Bruce, Climbing
Josephine de Beauharnais
Jour de Fete
Joybells
Juillet®

Jules Jorgensen
Julette
Julia®
Julie Andrews
Julie Cussons
Julien Renoard®
Juliet Ann
Juliette
Juwena®

-K-

Kaina
Kakwa
Kaladi
Kalinka™ (MElfrony)
Kamaladevi Chattopadhayay
Kambala
KAMchim or Carlita
Kanak
Kanchi
Kanva
Kanyakumari
Karen™
Karine Sauvageot®
Karl Herbst, Climbing
Karl Hochst®
Kasturirangan
Katharina Sophia®
Kathleen
Kathleen's Rose
Kathryn Morley
Kathy Reid
Katy Road Pink
Kean
KEIjourna or Aurelia
Keith Kirsten
KEIzoubo or Pareo
Kent®
Kessy®
Kingswood College
KIRkitt or Kathleen's Rose
KIRmac or Greenalls Glory
KIRpink or Owens Pride
KIRscot or Graceland
KIRshow or Clive Lloyd
Kirsten
Kiss
Kiss of Fire
Kocho
Koliam
Komala
Kookaburra
Koralle®
KORam or Ami des Jardins
KORbalem or Little Lemmy
KORbaxand or Alexandra
KORbolak or Melody

LAPran or Longchamp 80
LAPruni or Banquise
La Quatre Saisons Continue
Laque de Chine
Las Casas
Laser™
Laura (HBour)
Laura™ (MElvouplix)
Laura Jane
Laure Charton
Laurence Olivier or Wapiti
Lavande
Lavender
Lavender Blue
Lavender Crystal™
Lavender Friendship
Lavender Meillandina
Lavender Midinette
Lavender Pink Pam
Lavender Pink Parfait
Lavender Pixie
La Virginale
L.D. Braithwaite®
Leah
LEBbet or Favorite
LEGram or Pink Fountain
Lemon Blush
Lemon Honey
Lemon Light
Lemon Rosamini
Lemon Time
Lena®
LENbrac or Pink Surprise
LENcil or Cecile Lens
LENfil or Fil d'Ariane
LENpaga or Harley
LENpaya or White Spray
LENpi or Pink Delight
LENrav or Ravel
LENray or Pink Spray
Lenzburger Duft
Leon Lecomte
Leopold Ritter
Lerna
Le Rosier Eveque
Le Rouge et Le Noir®
Lesdain
Leventina®
L'Eveque or Le Rosier Eveque
Ley's Perpetual Yellow
Liane®
Libretto
Liebeszauber®
Lilac Minimo
Lilac Pink Moss
Lilac Rose
Linburn Light
Linda

Lindaraja®
Lindee
Lisa
Lisburn Light
Lisette de Beranger
Lisima®
Literary Giant
Little Angel®
Little Bo-Peep
Little Lemmy®
Little Lemon Spice
Little Len
Little Mabel
Little Purple
Little Red Hedge
Little White Pet, Climbing
Liverpool Daily Post
Livia™
Lloyds of London
Lola Montes
Longchamp® or Longchamp
    80®
Longwind
Lord Gold®
Lord Ian
Lorenzo Pahissa, Climbing
Louise d'Arzens
Louisiana, Climbing
Lovely Girl™
Lovely Louise
Lovely Red Polyantha
Love's Spring or Spek's
    Centennial
Lovita
Luarca
Luberon®
Lucens Erecta
Lucia®
Lucinde®
Lucretia
Ludmila Lopato®
Lumen®
Luminesse
Lutin®
Lysa

-M-

Maaike
MacGregor
MACgremly or Tiger
MAChana
MACivy or Spek's Centennial
MACkankaf or Raspberry
    Red
MACkung or Austragold
MAClutker or Oriola
MACmatan or Ten Ten

MACmooblu or Moody Blues
MACosred or Parabon
MACpinderal or Fresh Pink
MACtrampol or Remuera
Mme. Adelaide Ristori
Mme. Antoine Rebe
Mme. Auguste Rodrigues
Mme. Berkeley
Mme. Bruno Coquatrix®
Mme. Chevalier
Mme. Cornelissen
Mme. Denise Gallois
Mme. de Soubeyran
Mme. de Villars
Mme. Dore
Mme. Edmund Laport
Mme. Fernandel®
Mme. Francois Pittet
Mme. Gilbert Dubois
Mme. Jules Finger
Mme. Juliette Guillot
Mme. Letuve de Colnet
Mme. L. Ladoire
Mme. Nerard
Mme. Olymphe Teretschenko
Mme. R. Gravereaux
Mme. Sachi
Mme. Segond Weber Cerise
Mme. Souveton
Mme. Yvette Gayraud
Mme. Yvonne Chaverot
Madeleine Rivoire®
Mademoiselle™
Mlle. Augustine Guinoisseau
Mlle. Blanche Lafitte
Mademoiselle de Dinant
Mlle. Marie Dirvon
Madness at Corsica or
    Napoleon
Magali®
Maggie
Magia Nera®
Magic
Magic Carpet
Magic Fire 83®
Magic Moments
Magic Sunblaza™
Magicienne 78®
Magie d 'Orient
Mahadani
Mahalaxmi
Maharani
Mahina
Maia®
Mainaufeuer®
Maiwunder
Maiwunder® or Maywonder
Majolika®

Make-up®
Malak
Malakarsiddha
Maleica®
Malibu
Mamy Blue®
Mamy Laperriere®
Mandarin®
Mandarina®
Mandelon
Mandy®
Maneca
Mango®
Manhattan Blue®
Manmatha
Manyo
Maos 2
Marcella (HT dp RVS)
Marcella (HT yb LeGrice)
Marchioness of Salisbury
Marechal du Palais
Margaret's Pink Rambler
Margaret Watson
Marguerite D'Anjou
Marguerite Defforey®
Marianne Tudor
Marie Accarie
Marie-Antoinette Rety®
Marie-Cecile
Marie Christina
Marie Dermar
Marie-Francoise Saignes
Marieken
Marie Palit
Marie Robert
Marietta Silva Tarouca
Marita
Marlyse®
Marondo
Marquise de Balbiano
Marquisette®
Martha
Martha Gonzales
Mary Dresselhuys®
Mary Gammon
Mary Hailsham
Mary Hayley Bell
Mary MacKillop
Mary Manners
Mary Queen of Scots
Mary Woolley
Matangi, Climbing
Matchball®
MATTdor or
    Northamptonshire
MAUkeole or Vent des Indes
Maurice Lepelletier
Maywonder

McCartney Rose or The
    McCartney Rose
McClinton Tea
Megami
MEIalzonite or Lady Meilland
MEIbalani or Retro
MEIbaltaz or Anthony
    Meilland
MEIblonver or White Majesty
MEIcairma or Niccolo
    Paganini
MEIcauf or Amalie
MEIcelna or Tino Rossi
MEIchevil or Mimi Pink
MEIchoiju or Jacqueline
    Nebout
MEIcorval or Mimi Red
MEIcubal
MEIdanover or Colibre 79
MEIdenji or Cassandre,
    Grimpant
MEIfarent or Solidor
MEIfersi or Michel Lis Le
    Jardinier
MEIflarol or Pareo
MEIfota or Celica
MEIfrony or Kalinka
MEIfructoz or Fruite
MEIgidak or Petite Pink
MEIgosar or Prince Igor,
    Grimpant
MEIgoufin or Magali
MEIgovin or Snow
    Meillandina
MEIgrelou or Grisbi
MEIgro-Nurisar or Rimosa,
    Climbing
MEIgrouge or Preference
MEIgurami or Coppelia 76
MEIhirvin or Charlotte
    Rampling
MEIhourag or Arielle
    Dombasie, Grimpant
MEIjade or Fandango,
    Grimpant
MEIjason or Lovely Girl
MEIjulitasar or Chorus,
    Climbing
MEIkola or Livia
MEIkruza or Arianna
MEIlano or Cocorico
MEIlasso or Cocorico
MEIlauf or Amalia
MEIlenangal or Mitzi 81
MEIliaxi or Schuss
MEIlicafal or Cannes Festival
MEIlivar or Gina Lollobrigida
MEIloise or Reve de Paris

MEIluminacsar or President
    Leopold Senghor, Climb
MEImandinan or Mahina
MEInagre or Wapiti
MEInaregi or Romantica 76
Meine Oma or Granny®
MEInitpar or Caramella
MEInivoz or Paul Ricard
Mein Munchen
MEInoiral or Deborah
MEIpal-JELpin or Mimi Pearl
MEIpelta or Fuchsia
    Meillandecor
MEIpierar or Caroline de
    Monaco
MEIplovon or Mademoiselle
MEIpobil or Rendez-Vous
MEIpraserpi or Catherine
    Denueve
MEIpsilon or Yakimour
MEIridol or Irene
MEIrolour or Concerto
MEIrotego or Minijet
MEIsecaso or Lutin
MEIsevari or Coral Island
MEIsolroz or Flamingo
    Meidiland
MEIsourayor or Decor
    Arlequin
MEIspola or Preview
Meissa
MEIsunaj or Mme. Fernandel
MEItiraca or Bordurella
MEItixia or Revolution
    Francaise
MEItosier
MEItrosra or Iskra 82
MEIvouplix or Laura
MEIwiran or Mimi White
MEIxapic or Pink Arianna
MEIxerul or Peche
    Meillandina
MEIxetal or Denise Grey
MEIzalitaf or Spectra
MEIzeli or The McCartney
    Rose
Melanie
Melanie Waldor
Melflor
Melgold
Melodee
Melodie Lane
Melody
Melrose
Menja
Merry Go Round
Merveille de la Brie
Metanoia®

Mexico
Michel Bonnet
Micheline
Michelle Joy
Michel Lis Le Jardinier
Mickey Mouse
Mic Mac
Micrantha Sepium or R.
  micranthosepium
Midi®
Mikado
Mimi Pearl
Mimi Pink™ (MEIchevil)
Mimi Red™
Mimi White™
Minerette®
Minette
Minijet®
Mini Nicole
Minuette, Climbing
Mirage
Mirandolina®
Mirato®
Mireille Mathieu®
Mirella®
Miss Aalsmeer
Miss Paris®
Miss Reus
Miss Universe, Climbing
Mr. C.A. Thompson
Mr. G.M. Cope
Mistraline®
Misty (if not Misty Dawn)
Misty Pink
Mitzi® or Mitzi 81®
Miwaku
Modesty
Moment®
Monarch
Monna Lisa®
Monna Lisa, Climbing®
Monsieur A. Maille
Montblanc
Monte Cassino
Monte Rosa
Monty's White Tea
Moody Blues
Moondrops®
Morena®
Morgensonne 88®
Morgenstern®
Morinaye
Morning Blush
Morning Sun
Morton Goree
Moth
Mother's Value
Mouna®

Mount Shasta, Climbing
Mt. Vernon Purple Noisette
Mrinalini
Mrs. F. Hope Thompson
Mrs. K.B. Sharma
Mrs. Maxine E. Frack
Mrs. O.G. Orpen
Mrs. Wood's Lavender-Pink
  Noisette
Munchner Herz®
Munot®
Musimara®
Musk-a-Plenty
My Granny or Granny
My Little Boy
My Love, Climbing
My Ouma or Granny®
My Way
Myra Stegmann
Mystic

-N-

Naas Botha
Napoleon
Narmada
Nartaki
Natacha®
Natchitoches Noisette
Nathalie
Neela
Neena
Nefertiti
Neige d'Ete
Neon
Netravathy
New Ave Maria
New Blaze
Newcomer®
New Horizon
New Pink Favourite
New Rosmarin 90
New Star
Niagara White Star
Niccolo Paganini®
Nicolas Briant
Night Life
Night's Musk
Nikita
Nipponensis × Rugosa
Noack's Uberraschung®
Noblesse
Nona (HT)
Nona® (F)
Norah Cruickshank
Norfolk
Northamptonshire
Northern Yellow

North Star
Nozomi Pearl
Nu Gold
Nuit d 'Ete® or Marianne
  Tudor
Nursing Centenary

-O-

Ocho
Octavius Weld
Odee Pink
Old Black
Old Gay Hill
Old Lilac or Lilac Rose
Old Yellow Scotch
Olga®
Olga Nys
Olga Tschechowa®
Olivet
Omi Oswald®
Onda Rose®
Onex
Only Love
Opaline, Grimpant®
Open d'Australie®
Orana Gold
Orange Flame
Orange Flare
Orange Floribunda
Orange Juwel®
Orange Koster
Orange Queen
Orange Sauvageot
Orange Sensation, Grimpant
Orange Supreme
Orange Wave®
ORApal®
ORAred or Romy Schneider
ORAroro or Sourire d
  'Enfant
Orchid Masterpiece,
  Climbing
Orement de la Nature or
  Ornament de la Nature
Oriola
Orion
Orione®
Ornament de la Nature
Ornella Muti®
Ornement des Bosquets
Osiana
Oudtshoorn Joy
Our Sweet Ann
Out of Africa
Owens Pride
Oyster Pearl
Oz Gold

-P-

Pablito
Paganini (S)
Paganini® F or Niccolo
 Paginini
Pahadi Dhun
Pakeka
Paljas®
Palmengarten Frankfurt®
Pamela® (TANlepam)
Pamina®
Pampa
Pam's Pink
Papa Pirosha
Papillon (G)
Papillon (Ch)
Papst Johannes or Johannes
 XXIII
Parabon
Paradise, Climbing
Paradisea®
Paray
Parc des Princes®
Paree Red
Paree Salmon
Paree White
Pareo® (MEIflarol)
Pareo™ (KEIzoubo)
Parfum de Franche-Comte®
Parfy F
Park Place
Parktown's Pride
Park Wilhelmshohe
Parly II®
Passaya
Pastel Delight
Patchwork
Patchwork, Climbing
Patio Delight
Patio Pearl
Patio Queen
Pat James
Paul McCartney or The
 McCartney Rose
Paul Ricard®
Pavillon de Pregny
Peach Blossom
Peach Meillandina
Peach Sunblaze or Peach
 Meillandina
Peach Surprise
Peachy
PEApatio or Royal Flush
PEAperfume or Indian
 Summer
Pearl
Pearlita

Peche Meillandina®
Peeping Tom®
PEKblout or Roussillon
 Nirpaysage
PEKbord or Lorraine
 Rosapaysage
PEKcoubeach
PEKcoubo or Bo
PEKcoucan or Star 2000
PEKcoucinq
PEKcouet or Ludmila Lopato
PEKcouetam
PEKcouflash or Mouna
PEKcougel or Anna
PEKcougelosia or Olga
PEKcougraine or Natacha
PEKcouguver or Modesty
PEKcoujaca or Lady
 Casablanca
PEKcoujenny or First Red
PEKcoujoux
PEKcouketch
PEKcouliane or Julia
PEKcoulune
PEKcoumage
PEKcoupample
PEKcoupassy
PEKcoural or Tikana
PEKcousilia
PEKcouvarpo
PEKcouvite
PEKcram or Jean Monnet
PEKerose
PEKminou or Etoile Rouge
PEKmiwhite or Perce Neige
PEKomecli or Marlyse
PEKpus or Sophia
PEKsolred or Ile de France
 Rosapaysage
PEKspocre or Sari
PEKtarampe or Alsace
 Rosapaysage
Penelope
Pensioners Voice
Penthouse
Peonia
Pepino®
Pepite d 'Or
Perce Neige®
Percy Thrower, Climbing
Perfumer
Perle d'Anjou®
Perle des Blanches
Perle von Heidelberg,
 Climbing
Petite Pink™
Petite Pink Scotch
Petit Rat de l'Opera®

Petro
Philip Robinson
Phil's Hot Pink Perpetual
 Damask
Phloxy®
Picaninni
Pierette®
Pierre Troisgros®
Pinata
Pinctata Aurea
Pincushion
Pink Arianna™
Pink Bouquet
Pink Charm or Penthouse
Pink Cover®
Pink Cup Hybrid Perpetual
Pink Cushion (if not The
 Fairy)
Pink Delight®
Pink Fire®
Pink Fountain
Pink Fringe®
Pink Hit®
Pink Ilseta®
Pink Love
Pink Magic®
Pink Mermaid
Pink Minimo
Pink Mothers' Day
Pink Parade®
Pink Pearl or Fee
Pink Perfecture (if not Pink
 Perpetue)
Pink Pet, Climbing
Pink Pillar
Pink Princess
Pink Reflection®
Pink Showers
Pink Spray® (LENray)
Pink Spray (Pol)
Pink Sunsation
Pink Surprise (S)
Pink Surprise (LENbrac)
 (HRg)
Pink Surprise Nirpaysage® or
 Pink Surprise
Pink Wave
Pink & White®
Pirandello®
Pirette Pavement
Pirouette
Plein Soleil®
Poblet
Point de Avignon
Polisiedame
Pol Kor
Polluce®
Pol Yellow

Pompeii
Poppius
Porcelina
Porthos®
Porthos, Climbing
Portland from Glendora or
 Glendora Portland
Potch Pearl
Potluck White 192
Potter & Moore
POULage or Mirage
POULamb or Apricot Hit
POULave or Sussex
POULbol or Blue Parade
POULbon or Bonbon Hit
POULbright
POULbril or Brilliant Hit
POULbufi or Bushfire
POULcar or Pink Parade
POULcov or Kent
POULcover or Pink Cover
POULcrack or Crackerjack
POULdotage or Addo
 Heritage
POULfan or Jhb Garden
 Club
POULfolk or Norfolk
POULfre or Fresh Hit
POULglow or Everglow
POULgold or Golden Hit
POULkir or Kirsten
POULlen or Little Bo-Peep
POULnoz or Essex
POULpearl or Patio Pearl
POULrise or Peach Surprise
POULrohill or Rose Hill
POULshine or Rutland
POULstar or Starlight Parade
POULvic or Victory Parade
POULvue or Victor Borge
POUvision or Springs 75
Precious Michelle
Preference™
Prelude™
President Gaupin
President Leopold Senghor,
 Climbing®
President Viard
President Willermoz
Prestige de Bellegarde
Preview™
Pride of Ichalkaranji
Pride of Nagpur
Pride of Park
Primo Sole®
Prince Albert
Prince Igor, Grimpant®
Prince Napoleon

Princess
Princess Margaret
Princess Marie or Belvedere
Princess Michiko, Climbing
Princess of Wales
Princesse de Lamballe
Princesse de Monaco,
 Climbing
Priti
Prive™
Priyadarshini
Prof. Kurt Lotz-Rose Wildlife
 or Wildlife
Professor le Crenier
Profondo Rosso®
Prophyta
Proserpine
Protima
Provence®
Provence Pink
Prunella
Puccini®
Pucelle de Lille
Puerto Rico
Pulsar®
Purple China
Purple Climber
Purple Leaf Rose
Purple Minimo
Purple Pavement
Pushkala
Pushkarani
Pyrenees Nirpaysage®

-Q-

Quatre Saisons d'Italie
Quatre Saisons Rose
Queen Elizabeth Abricot
Queen Elizabeth Blush
Queen Elizabeth Lilas
Queen Elizabeth Rouge
Queen Margarethe
Queen Mother
Queen Nefertiti®
Queen of Bermuda or Roter
 Stern
Queenie
Quinella
Quintet

-R-

Raf Braeckman
Rainbow (S)
Rainbow Pot of Gold
Rainbow Robe
Raissa®

Raja Surendra Singh of
 Nalagarh
Rajhans
Rajni
Ramira®
Randfontein Gold
Randilla® Juane
Randilla® Rose
Randilla® Rouge
Rapsodia®
Rare Edition
Rashmi
Raspberry Ice
Raspberry Parfait
Raspberry Red
Raspberry Ripple
Ratan
Ratnaar
Ravel®
Rebekah
Red And White Delight
Red Blush
Red Det 80®
Red Diadem®
Red Dot® or Dart's Red Dot
Red Fan
Red Lady®
Red Meillandina®
Red Mercedes
Red Moss Rambler
Red Mozart or Rote Mozart
Red Nella
Red Nelly
Red Parfum, Grimpant®
Red Recker
Red Ribbon®
Red Roulette
Red Sea®
Red Trail
Regal Red
Regatta®
Regina
Regine Crespin®
Regula
Reine de Saxe
Reine des Belges
Reine des Mousseuses
Reine des Vierges
Reine du Danemark
Reine Lucia
Release®
Remuera
Remy Martin®
Renata Tebaldi®
Rendan
Rendez-vous
Rendez-Vous®
Rene Marie

Renee Collomb®
Retro®
Reve de Paris®
Reve de Valse®
Reveil
Revolution Francaise®
Rhodes Rose
Richard Buckley
Richard Tauber®
Rimosa, Climbing®
Rinascimento®
Rita Levi Montalcini®
Riverside Red
Riverview Centennial
Riviere de Diamant®
Robert Perpetual
Robert Pineau
Robina
Robinetta
Robusta
Roby
Rodina
Roi de Nains
Roi de Siam CIT
Rojale
Rokoko®
Roland Garros®
Romain
Romantica® or Romantica 76®
Romy Schneider®
R. arvensis plena discovered 1982
R. canina alba
R. canina 'Brags'
R. canina "deep pink selection"
R. × cannabifolia
R. carolina humilis grandiflora plena
R. corymbifera laxa
R. ecae 'Helen Knight' or Helen Knight
R. haematodes
R. hemisphaerica 'Flore Pleno'
R. hypoleuca
R. iliensis (may be R. illinoensis)
R. longicuspis erecta
R. luciae onoei
R. lutea bicolor atropurpurea
R. macrophylla rubricaulis
R. micranthosepium
R. moschata nana
R. multiflora adenochaeta
R. multiflora 'Double White'
R. multiflora grandiflora
R. multiflora 'Great White'
R. multiflora 'Pastel Pink'

R. multiflora 'Spring Shower'
R. multiflora thornless
R. nitida 'Defender'
R. omeiensis atrosanguinea
R. palustris plena
R. pendulina 'Bourgogne'
R. pimpinellifolia rubra
R. × prattigosa
R. rouletti, Climbing
R. rugosa augustrioribus
R. rugosa germanica
R. rugosa regeliana
R. rugosa regeliana rubra
R. × rugotida
R. sericea pteracantha atrosanguinea
R. setigera 'Female-hips'
R. setigera variegata
R. spinosissima 'Cherry Red'
R. spinosissima 'Crimson Purple'
R. spinosissima 'Double Blush'
R. spinosissima 'Double Pink'
R. spinosissima 'Double White'
R. spinosissima 'Irish Rich Marbled'
R. spinosissima lutea maxima
R. spinosissima 'Marbled Pink'
R. spinosissima 'Marbled White'
R. spinosissima maxima lutea
R. spinosissima repens
R. spinosissima 'Scotch Pink'
R. spinosissima 'Scotch White'
R. spinosissima 'Scotch Yellow'
R. spinosissima 'Single Cherry'
R. spinosissima 'Single Lilac'
R. spinosissima 'Single Sherry'
R. spinosissima 'Single White'
R. tomentosa cinerascens
R. villosa recondita
R. wichuraiana 'Double White'
R. wichuraiana grandiflora
R. wichuraiana poteriifolia
R. wichuraiana thornless
R. wichuraiana variegata
R. xanthina 'Karl Jones'
Rosaletta
Rosamunde®
Rosarama
Rosazwerg or Dwarf Pavement
Rosa Zwerg
Roschen Albrecht®
Rose a Parfum de Grasse
Rose Bleue
Rose Chou (Rose Chou de Hollande)

Rose Chou de Hollande or Rose Chou
Rose City of Nashik
Rose de Puteaux
Rose de Schelfhout
Rose Edouard
Rosegarden
Rose Hill
Rosellana®
Rose Memorial Noisette
Rosenau
Rosendorf Schmitshausen
Rosendort Sparrieshoop®
Rosenfee®
Rosenfest
Rosenreigen®
Rosenrot®
Rosenstadt Zweibrucken®
Rosentanz® or Biddulph Grange
Roseraie de Blois®
Rose Royale
Rose Wettriana
Rosier de Damas
Rosmarin 89®
Rosy Cheeks
Rote Flame®
Rote Krimrose
Rote Mozart®
Roter Stern
Rotes Meer
Roulette®
Roussillon Nirpaysage®
Roxane®
Roxanne
Roxburghe Rose
Royal Bassino
Royal Blush
Royal Dot
Royal Flush
Royal Harlequin
Royal Smile
Royal Swan or Rajhans
Roypinpro or Sweet Sonia
Rubezahl
Rubina®
RUbrispa or Bright Spark
Ruby
Rugelda®
Rugspin
RUIcarmi or Carol Minimo
RUIcharo or Charming Rosamini
RUIdriko or Vivaldi
RUIfaro or Favourite Rosamini
RUIfifty or Dainty Minimo
RUIforto or Coral Minimo

RUIklena or Purple Minimo
RUImarso or Sweet Rosamini
RUImeys or Idole
RUInanny or Rosy Minimo
RUIpiko or Pink Minimo
RUIpova or Splendid
    Rosamini
RUIrupo or Scarlet Rosamini
RUIsalro or Salmon
    Rosamini
RUIseto or Orange Rosamini
RUIsta or Estima
RUItapaf or Crimson
    Rosamini
RUIwita or White Rosamini
Rustlers' Skyrocket
Ruth Leuwerik, Climbing
Ruth's Pink Musk Cluster
Rutland
Rythmic®

-S-

Sachalin
Sadlers Wells
Sahasradhara
St. Albans Gem
St. Dunstan's Rose
St. Thomas China
Sainte-Genevieve
Saiun
Sakura Gasumi
Salita®
Salmon
Salmon Polyantha
Salmon Rosamini
Salmon Sorbet
Salmon Sunsation
Sandeepini
Sandra Kim®
Sandrine
Sanka
Santa Rosa
San Valentino®
Saphir®
Sappho
Sarah, Duchess of York or
    Duchess of York
Sari®
Sarie Marais
Saroja
Saturday®
SAUblim or Atida
SAUkar or Karine Sauvageot
Savane®
Savine
Savkar
Sayonara®

Scabrosa Alba
Scala®
Scandinavian
Scarlet Rosamini
Scarlet Showers
Scarletta®
Scented Cloud (if not
    Fragrant Cloud)
Schleswig 87®
Schnee-Eule®
Schneekoppe
Schneesturm®
Schneewalzer®
Schone Berlinerin®
Schuss®
Schwarzwaldmadel®
Schweizer Woche®
Scipion Cochet
Scotch Yellow
Secret Garden Musk Climber
Secret Garden Noisette
Seika, Climbing
Seiko
Selene
Senateur Lafollette
Sentinel
Serape, Climbing
Serenite®
Shady Lady
Shanti Pal
Sharifa Asma®
Shimsha
Shirpa
Shoba
Show Yellow
Showy Gold
Shrewsbury Show
Shunpo
Shuzao Red
Sibelius®
Sibilla®
Sibylle
Sica or Sika
Siddartha
Sika®
Sila®
Silk Button
Silky Mist
Silva™ (KEIromo)
Silver Cloud
Silver Pink®
Silver Queen (HP)
Silver Queen® (BARsilv)
Silver River®
Silver Wedding
SIMcho or Hot Chocolate
Simone Merieux®
Simplex Rambler, Climbing

Simplicity
Simply Delightful
SIMsilko or Silky Mist
SIMway or Jenny Chariton
SIMzu or Zuma
Single Pink
Sinjun
Sinoia®
Sinsetu
Sir Clough
Sir C. V. Raman
Sirenetta®
Sir Frederick Ashton
Sir Glaugh or Sir Glough
Sir Henry®
Sir Walter Raleigh®
Sisi Ketten
Skyline®
Snowdon
Snowflakes
Snow Meillandina
Snow Pavement
Snow Sunblaze or Snow
    Meillandina Snow White
SOCalp or Moonlight Lady
Sococ
Softie, Climbing
Solidor®
So Lovely
Somasila
Sommermond®
Sommermorgen®
Sophia®
Sophie
Sourire d'Antan®
Sourire d'Enfant®
Sourire d'Orchidee
Sousyun
Southern Sun
Souvenir®
Souv. d'Alma de l 'Aigle or
    Andenken an Alma de l'
Souv. de J.B. Guillot
Souv. de la Malmaison Rouge
Souv. de MacKinley
Souv. de Mme. Auguste
    Charles
Souv. de Mme. Breuil
Souv. de Mme. Breuill or
    Souv. de Mme. Breuil
Souv. de Mme. Bruel or
    Souv. de Mme. Breuil
Spanish Breeze
Spectra™
Spek's Centennial
Spicy Minijet
Spielplatz DRS®
Spinnaker

Splendid Rosamini
Sprayer
Springs 75
Springtime (HHug)
Springtime (HERves) HT
Sprinter®
Srinivasa
Stadt Eltville®
Stadt Luzern
Star 2000®
Starion®
Starlight
Starlight Parade®
Starlina
STARqueli or Remy Martin
Star Trail or Colibre 79
Stefanie
Stephanie de Monaco,
    Climbing
Sternenflor®
Strauchmaskerade
Strawberry Fayre
Strawberry Ice, Climbing
Striking
String of Pearls (Min)
Striped Mary Rose
Stromboli
Suffolk
Sugandha
Sukanya
Sultan Qaboos
Sultane, Climbing
Suma
Summer Blush
Summer Breeze (S)
Summer Breeze (F)
Summer Dream
Summer Lady®
Summer Sunshine, Climbing
Summer Time
Sun Baby
Suncluster
Sunmaid®
Sunrose
Sunset
Sun Up
Super Excelsa®
Supriya
Surkhab
Surpassing Beauty of
    Woolverstone
Survivor
Sushma
Sussex
Suvarnrekha
Sweet Honesty
Sweet Juliet®
Sweet Minimo

Sweet Rosamini
Sweet Sonia™
Sweet Sensation
Sweet Sunsation
Sybil Hipkin
Sylvaine
Sylvie Vartan®
Symphony (AUSlett)

-T-

1320
33682-A
Table Mountain
Tabris
Taihape Sunset
Talia®
Tamara®
Tambrabarani
TANaluma or Amulett
TANarocus or Cora
TANatulp or Albert-Georg
    Pluta Rose
TANavit or Tina
TANcandy or Cotton Candy
TANceila or Maleica
TANchyo
TANdalaum or Traumland
TANdirpkrap or Parktown's
    Pride
TANedallab or Ballade
TANeitber or Bernstein-Rose
TANekily or Lady Like
TANelaigib or Abigaile
TANellelog or Goldquelle
TANelliv or Stadt Eltville
TANelorak or Barkarole
TANemita or Tea Time
TANemrac or Carmen
TANerou or Juwena
TANeselbon or Noblesse
TANessemoc or Comtesse
TANessenor or Baronesse
TANetorde or Red Diadem
TANettahn or Manhattan
    Blue
TANettelur or Roulette
Tangerine
Tangerine Tango
TANibara or Arabia
TANija or Janina
TANilknip or Pink Ilseta
TANipep or Pepino
TANkeijoli or Majolika
TANkobi or Bubikopf
TANkorab or Barock
TANlepam or Pamela
TANmeda or Diadem

TANmurse or Schneesturm
TANnus or Capri Sun
TANokor or Rokoko
TANonibla or Albino
TANope or Tip Top
TANosyl or Calypso
TANracta or Carat
TANre or Reve de Valse
TANrezlaw or Schneewalzer
TANrikas or Saphir
TANrised or Schone
    Berlinerin
TANrosilb or Naas Botha
TANsirk or Keith Kirsten
Tantaliser
TANtatuk or Dukat
TANtocirpa or Apricot
TANtrossali or Alina
TANyab or Bayerngold
TANydal or Summer Lady
TANyssek or Kessy
Tapti
Tarang
Taubie Kushlik
Tea Time®
Tender Blush
Tennesor
Tennyo
Tenshi
Ten Ten
Tenth Rose Convention
Teresina
Tersicore®
Texas (if not Texas
    Centennial)
Thalassa
Thalia (KORtape) F
Thalia (HT)
Thalia Remontant
Thalie La Gentillle
Thari®
The Dark Lady
The Fairy, Climbing
The Faun®
The Gift
The Herbalist
The McCartney Rose®
The Moth or Moth
The Nun
The Observer
The Pilgrim
The Prince
The Valois Rose
Thiona
Thornhem
Thornless Beauty
Thugabhadra
Ticino®

Tickled Pink
Tiger®
Times Square
Tina®
Tino Rossi®
Tiny Tot
Tipsy Imperial Concubine
Tip Top®
Tip Top, Climbing
Tipu's Flame
Toby Tristam
Tojo®
Tommy's Orange
Tonight
Tonsina
Top Marks
Tosca
Toscana
Traumland®
Travera
Treasure Trove
Trianon
Triomphe de la Ducher
Triomphe des Noisettes
Trulyr or Parly II
TSCHaka or Charlie Chaplin
Tullamore
Twinkler

-U-

UHLater or Pierette
Uncle Bill
Uncle Buck
Unermudliche
Unica Alba
Unknown Anna's Image

-V-

Valencia®
Vamshadhara
Vanamali
Variegata di Bologna
    Reversion or Victor
    Emmanuel
Variegata di Bologna Rouge
Variegata di Bologna
    Spontaneous Reversion
Vasavi
Vascade
Velvet Arrow
Velvet Rosamini

Venere®
Vent des Indes®
Venus
Vera Johns
Verdi
Verschuren
Vicomte Fritz de Cussy
Vicomtesse du Fou (if not
    Vicomtesse Pierre du Fou)
Vicomtesse d 'Avesnes
Victor Borge
Victor Emmanuel
Victory Parade®
Ville d'Arcis
Ville de Londres
Ville de Troyes®
Ville de Villeurbanne
Ville du Roeulx
Vindonissa®
Visveswaraya
Vivaldi
Viva Romana
Vlammenspel
Vogelpark Walsrode
Vydehi

-W-

Waanrode
Wall Street®
Walter Butt
Wapiti®
Warley Jubilee
Warwickshire
Weetwood
Weisse Ilseta
Weisse Nelkenrose
Weisse New Dawn
Weisser Engel
W.E. Lippiat
Wembley Stadium
Wetteriana
Wheato
White Bella Rosa or Bella
    Weisse
White Blush
White Chipper
White Christmas, Climbing
White Cloud
White Cover or Kent
White Dick Koster or
    Blanche Neige
White Dog

White Fleurette®
White Gold
White Hedge
White Junior Miss
White Koster or Blanche
    Neige
White Magic®
White Majesty™
White Mary Rose
White Masterpiece, Climbing
White New Dawn
White Nights
White Simplicity®
White Spray®
White Surprise Nirpaysage®
    or White Surprise
Wickwar
Wildenfelsgelb
Wildflower or Wild Flower
Wildlife
Wilfred Laurier
William And Mary
Winchester Cathedral®
Woody
Woolverstone Church Rose
    or Surpassing Beauty
WRIpic or Picaninni

-Y-

Yakimour®
Yardley English Rose
Yellow Blush
Yellow Hammer, Grimpant
Yellow Koster
Yellow Mothers' day
Yellow Mozart
Yellow Patio
Yellow Pixie
Yellow Sunbeam
Yeshwant
Young At Heart
Young Mistress
Yugiri

-Z-

Zaire
Zigeunerblut
Zola Budd
Zorina, Climbing
Zuma
Zwergkonig 78®

Appendix III
Hybridizers, Introducers, Nurseries and Others

This historical listing of hybridizers, introducers, nurseries and others involved in the rose registration process and/or publication has been assembled for the first time to provide the reader and rose scholars with a master reference list. In some cases, the individuals have passed on or the companies are no longer in existence. However, this list captures the rich tapestry of tradition these individuals have woven on an international level over the past 50 years.

-A-

A World of Roses
P O Box 90332
Gainesville FL 32607

Abbey Rose Gardens
Burnham
Bucks England SL1 8NJ

Abbotsford Nursery, Inc.
605 rue Principale
St. Paul d'Abbotsford
Quèbec Canada JOE 1AO

Abdullah, Mrs. Aslam
Rawalpindi West Pakistan

Abdy, Sidney
Sherwood
Nottingham England

Abrahams, C.J.
Alwoodley
Leeds England

Abrams, F.B.
Ossing NY

Acton Beauchamp Roses
Worcester England WR6 5AE

Adam & Craigmile
Aberdeen Scotland

Adams, Charles E.
San Jose CA

Adams, Dr. Neil D.
1028 Shorey Road
Chehalis WA 98532

Adamson
Gardener to J.C. Manifold
Victoria Australia

AGM Miniature Roses, Inc.
P.O. Box 6065 McDonald Ln.
Highway 165 South
Monroe LA 71211

Agriculture Canada
Research Branch
Ottawa Research Station
Ottawa Ont. Can. KIA OC6

Agriculture Canada
Research Station
P.O. Box 3001
Morden Manitoba Canada
ROG 1JO

Agricultural University of Norway
Department of Dendiology
& Nursery
P.O. Box 16
N-1432 AAS-NLH Norway

Ahrens & Sieberz
Holstein Germany

Aicardi Bros.
San Remo Italy

Aicardi, Dominico
Villa Minerva
San Remo Italy

Aicardi, Luigi
San Remo Italy

Albrighton Roses
Albrighton Wolverhampton
Staffs. England

Alde, R. O.
5215 Drake Terrace
Rockville MD 20853

Alderton & Williams
Brisbane Queenlands
Australia

Aldous, J.
Iowa City IA

Aldrufus, Joaquin
Barcelona Spain

Alégatière
Lyon France

Allen, A.J. & C.
Norwich England

Allen, E.F.
Copdock Suffolk
England

Allen, E.M.
Bideford North Devon
England

Allen, J.
Battleford Sask. Canada

Allen, L.C.
Eastwood NSW
Australia

Allender, R.W.
1-A Hawker Avenue
Preston 3072
Melbourne Victoria Australia
00016

Aloe Vera Nurseries
Harlingen TX

Alpenflora Gardens
17985-40th Avenue
Surrey BC Canada V3S 4N8

Amand Roses
Gandhinage Tonk Road
Janipur 302015 India

American Association of Nurserymen, Inc.
1250 Eye Street N.W.
Suite 500
Washington DC 20005

American Beauty Roses
110 West Elm Street
Tipp City OH 45371

American Beauty Roses
6523 North Galena Rd.
Peoria IL 61656

American Bulb Co.
New York NY

American Horticultural
 Society
7931 East Boulevard Drive
Alexandria VA 22308

American Rose Foundation
P O Box 30,000
Shreveport LA 71130-0030

American Rose Society
P O Box 30,000
Shreveport LA 71130-003

Amling, Albert F. Co.
Maywood IL

Amling Bros.
Santa Ana CA

Amling, Clarence M.
Santa Ana CA

Amling, Clarence Roses, Inc.
Santa Ana CA

Amling-Devor Nursery
California

Amling, Martin C.
Pana IL

Anderson, E.S.
206 Harding Ave.
Princeton IN 47670

Anderson Garden Center
5700 Monroe Street
Sylvania OH 43560

Anderson, K.
35 Mendip Grove
Gunthorpe Peterborough
England PE4 6TX

Anderson, P. & J Ltd.
Grandhome Aberdeen
Scotland

Anderson's Nursery
3630 Highway 60 East
Bartow FL 33830

Anderson's Rose Nurseries
Friarsfield Road
Cults. Aberdeen Scotland
AB1 9QT

Andre Greenhouses, Inc.
Doylestown PA

Andre, Thomas J.
Doylestown PA

Andres Floral Co.
New Philadelphia OH

Andrews Nursery Co.
Fairbault MN

Angendohr, Hans Werner
Happelter 4054 Nettletal
Germany

Annabel, E.E.
129 Dennis Street
Lakemba Australia

Anstiss, L.A.
West Willow Hants.
England

Antique Rose Emporium
Route 5, Box 143
Brenham TX 77833

Appleton, W.R.
Belgrade Leicester England

Appleyard, R.
Gisborne New Zealand

Apuldram Roses
Apuldram Lane
Dell Quay
Chichester West Sussex
England PO20 7EF

Arbor Nursery
3885 Napa Vallejo High
Vallejo CA 94590

Archer, W.E.B. & Daughter
Sellindge Ashford Kent
England

ARF
P.O. Box 30,000
Shreveport LA 71130-0030

Argentina Rose Society
Buenos Aires, Argentina

Arles, Fernand
Feyzin Isère France

Armacost & Royston, Inc.
West Los Angeles CA

Armacost, Walter
West Los Angeles CA

Armbrust, F.J.
15 Pascoe St.
Mitchelton Queensland
Australia

Armstrong, D.L.
California

Armstrong J.A.
California

Armstrong Nursery
Ontario CA

Armstrong, Philip M.
Dalton PA

Armstrong's Roses
West-Winds
15 Knockboy Road
Broughshane Co. Antrim
Northern Ireland

Arnold-Fisher Co.
Woburn MA

Arnot, David M.
Broughty Ferry Dundee
Scotland

ARP Nursery Co.
Tyler TX

ARS
P.O. Box 30,000
Shreveport LA 71130-0030

Artistic Landscape Designs
2079 Bank Street
Ottawa Ont. Canada 8A8 KIV

Asami, Hitoshi
558 Hashikadani Tojo-Cho
Kado-Gun
Hyogo-Ken 673-13 Japan

Asmus, E.R. Sr.
Closter NJ

Asociaciòn Argentina de
 Rosicultura
Peru 630
5° piso Dep. 20
1068 Buenos Aires Argentina

Asociaciòn Uruguaya de la
 Rosa
L. Cavia 3099 Apt. 11
Montevideo Uruguay

Associazione Italiana della
 Rosa
Villa Reale
20052 Monza Italy

Asseretto, Angelo
San Remo Italy

Asseretto, Vincenzo Cav.
San Remo Italy

Astolat Nursery Ltd.
Guildford Surrey England

Atkiss, Lincoln
Newtown Square PA

Attfield, Brian Barratt
106 Shakespeare Street
Cambridge Hamilton New
Zealand

Aubin Nurseries, Ltd.
P.O. Box 1089
Carman Manitoba Canada
ROG OJO

Aufill, L.
Albuquerque NM

Australia Rose Society
Australia

Austin, David Roses, Ltd.
Bowling Green Lane
Albrighton Nr. Wolverhampton
England WV7 3HB

Austin, Robert
Glasgow Scotland

Avansino, Mortenson
San Francisco CA

Avenue Nursery
Avenue North
Levin New Zealand

-B-

B&A
East Rutherford NJ

Babb, J.T.
The Croft, Coton Hill
Milwich Stafford England
ST18 OEH

Bagg, Richard
Bridgeton NJ

Bailey, John
Tupsley Herts. England .

Bailey Nurseries Ltd.
1325 Bailey Road
St. Paul MN 55119

Baines, E.
London England

Baker, Larry
11715 Rio Hondo Pkwy.
El Monte CA 91732

Baker's Nursery, Ltd.
Codsall Wolverhampton
England

Bakker, John & Son
R.R. 3, St. Catharines
Ont. Canada L2R 7P9

Balcombe Nursery
Swallowfield Berkshire
England

Ball Seed Co.
250 Town Road
West Chicago IL 60185

Ballarat Horticultural
Society
Ballarat Victoria Australia

Ballin, Donald & Paula
249 Barberry Road
Highland Park IL 60035

Ballmer, Gordon W.
4391 Elmwood Court
Riverside CA 92506

Balzer, J.W.
Steinfurth Germany

Bancroft, Hon. George
Historian
Washington DC

Banerji, Shri B.K.
Rana Pratap Marg.
Lucknow 226001 UP India

Banks, Mrs.
Australia

Banner, Charlford
Bromsgrove Worsc. England

Bansal, O.P.
New Delhi India

Bansal Roses
New Delhi India

Barbaras, E.
Reims Marne France

Barbier & Co.
Orléans France

Barclay, Hilary M.
7 Lassock Avenue
Findor 5023 South Australia

Bardhill Nurseries
Stapleford Notts. England

Barké, Harvey E.
Amherst MA

Barker, E. A.
56 Grafton Road
Ruphden Northants England

Barni Nursery
Italy

Barni-Pistoia
Italy

Barni, Vittoria
P.O. Box 105
51100 Pistoia
Pistoia 4 Italy

Barrett, F.F.
47 Malford Road
Headington Oxford England

Barter, William
Corringham Essex England

Basildon Gardens
Basildon Essex England

Bass, Henry
Livermore CA

Bate, W.G.
Newton Falls OH

Battersby Roses
Pear Tree Cottage
Old Battersby, Great Ayton
Cleveland England TS9 6LU

Bauer, K.A.
Bundaberg Queensland
Australia

Baum, Floyd F.
Knoxville TN

Baum, Oswald
2200 Elmshorn West
Germany

Baumann, A.N.
Bolwyller France

Baumschuler Angendohr,
Happelter
4054 Nettetal
Germany

Bauské Bros. & Hinner
Woodstock IL

Bay of Plenty Rose Society,
Inc.
R.D. 2
Te Puke New Zealand

Bazeley, B.L.
England

BDK Nursery
P.O. Box 628
Apopka FL 32704-0628

Beales, P.
Interwood Lane Nurseries
Norwich England

Beales, Peter
Peter Beales Roses
London Road
Attleborough Norfolk
England NR17 1AY

Beall Greenhouse Co.
Vashon WA

Beall, Wallace M.
Vashon WA

Bear Creek Gardens
P.O. Box 1020
Somis CA 93066-1020

Beaverlodge Nursery Ltd.
Box 127
Beaverlodge Alberta Canada
TOH OCO

Beck, Leon, S.A.
Rosieriste en Alsace
2 bis route d'Oberhausbergen
B.P. 2
67037 Strasbourg Cedex
France

Beckett, Ian C.
Gorran Chackmore
Buckingham England MK18 5JE

Beckwith, G. & Sons
Haddesdon Herts England

Bees of Chester
England

Bees, Teemana Ltd.
England

Begault, A.-Pigné
Maine-et-Loire France

Begonia, F.B.
Livermore CA

Begonia, Paul B.
San Jose CA

Beggren, Carl
Vallingby Sweden

Beijing Rose Society China
A2 Wanshousi Haidian
Beijing China

Beldam Bridge Nurseries
Chobham Woking Surrey
England

Belden, Wade
Leroy OH

Belgium Rose Society
Belgium

Bell, John
Bearsden Dumbartonshire
Scotland

Bell, John C.
33 Elmhurst Avenue
Melton Mowbray
Leicestershire England

Bell, Mrs. C.J.
Washington DC

Bell, Ronald J.
King Road
Harkaway Victoria 3808
Australia

Bell Roses Ltd.
P.O. Box 21144
Auckland 8 New Zealand

Beltran, Gabriel
Santa Ana CA

Béluze, Jean
Lyon Rhône France

Benardella, Frank
266 Orangeburgh Road
Old Tappan NJ 07675

Benary, Ernst
Erfurt Germany

Bennett, Dee
489 Minot Avenue
Chula Vista CA 92010

Bennett, H.
Point Wells Matakana
Northland New Zealand

Bennett, Henry
Schepperton England

Bennett, J.A.
Hamilton New Zealand

Bennett, V.G.T.
Wellsprings Gloucester
England

Bennetts Nursery
1028 Madison
Daytona Beach FL 32014

Bentall, J.A.
Havering Romford Essex
England

Bentley, Walter
Bentley & Sons Ltd.
The Nurseries
Loughborough Road
Wanlip Leicester England
LE7 8PN

Bents Nurseries & Garden
  Centre
Warrington Road
Glazebury Nr. Leigh
Lancs England WA3 5AT

Berckmans, J.P. Co.
Atlanta GA

Berg, David
11 Oxbow Lane
Bloomfield CT 06002

Berger, Adolf
Pockau bei Aussig
Czechoslovakia

Berger, Vincinz
Bad-Harzburg Germany

Bermuda Rose Society
P.O. Box PG 162
Paget 6 Bermuda

Bernaix, P.
Villeurbanne-Lyon
Rhône France

Bernal, Joseph
Bogota Columbia

Bernard, C.
Edwalton Nottingham
England

Bernède, H.B.
Bordeaux France

Berry, Howard
5217 Washington Avenue
Gulfport MS 39501

Bertanzel, C.F.
Roslyn NY

Bertsch, R.C. Co.
Auburn WA

Beschnidt, William
Zwenkau-Leipzig Germany

Besschetnova, Mrs. M.V.
USSR

Betzel, Irwin L.
Eugene OR

Bevan, Mrs. Ruth M.
Laver Mead Stour Row
Shaftesbury Dorset England
SP7 0QH

Bide, S. & Sons Ltd.
Alma Nurseries
Farnham Surrey England

Bilson, Jack M. Jr.
127 Gable Road
Paoli PA 19301

Bilson, Jack M. III
127 Gable Road
Paoli PA 19301

Bingley Lane Nurseries
Stannington Sheffield Yorks.
England

Binny, D.H.
Campden Glos. England

Biotika International
4391 Elmwood Court
Riverside CA 92506

Bird, S.R.
Australia

Biron, E.
Mont-Saint-Aignan
Seine-Inf France

Bischoff, Francis
1726 N. Bosart Avenue
Indianapolis IN 46218

Bishop, Ernest
Codsall Wolverhampton
England

Bizard, Angerrs
Maine-et-Loire France

Blaby Rose Gardens, Ltd.
Blaby Leicester England

Blakemore, R.
Coseley West Midlands
England

Blakeney, Frederick
Burnaby BC Canada

Blazey, Daniel J.
5232 Pawnee Road
Toledo OH 43613

Blixen, Harris H.
Edwardsville IL

Bloom, C.R.
Oakington Cambridge
England

Blue Ribbon Plant Co.
Hollywood CA

Bobbink & Atkins
East Rutherford, N.J.

Bodley, R.M.
Sandy OR

Boema, M.
Groningen Holland

Boer Bros.
Biezen Boskoop Holland

Boerner, E.S.
New York

Boettner, Johannes
Frankfort Germany

Bofill, F.
San Feliu de Llobregat
Barcelona Spain

Böhm, Jan
Blatna-Cechy Czechoslovakia

Bombay Rose Society
Bombay India

Bone, John & Son
New Zealand

Bonfiglioli, A.
Garisenda Italy

Bonnaire
Lyon Rhône France

Bonnet, A. & Fils
Nantes France

Booth, Rachel
Ivy Cottage
Collycroft Clifton
Ashbourne Derby
England DE6 2GN

Bootle, A.W.
Selsey Sussex
England

Booy, Herman
San Jacinto CA

Booy, Peter
J. Rose Nursery
San Jacinto CA

Bordas, Juan
Barcelona Spain

Borgatti, Giovanni
Bologna Spain

Borst, James
Louisiana

Bos, Henry
Melrose Park IL

Bosley Nursery
Mentor OH

Bostick, J.A.
Rose Hill Farm
Tyler TX

Bossom, William Edward
27 Brodie Road
Enfield Middlesex England

Boudler, Joseph
Mamer Luxembourg

Boughen Nurseries
Valley River
Manitoba Canada ROL 2BO

Bountiful Ridge Nursery
Maryland

Boutigny
Rouen France

Bowditch, James H.
Pomfret Center CT

Bowie, Cdr. E.D.
Burmuda Rose Nurseries
Paget East Bermuda

Boxall, W.A.
Winchmore Hill England

Boyau
Angers Maine-et-Loire France

Boytard, Camille
Orléans France

Brada, Dr. Gustav
Czechoslovakia

Brady, Lee A.
Tyler TX

Bracegirdle, A.J.
109 Peel Brow
Ramsborrom
Gr. Manchester England

Bracegirdle, Derek T.
Wyndham 9 Baulk Lane
Kneesail Newark
Notts England NG22 OAA

Bradley Nursery
Great Barley Arrish
Liverton Newton Abbott
Devon England

Bradshaw, J. & Son
Herne Herne Bay
Kent England CT6 7LJ

Breedlove, Jesse
Tyler TX

Breedlove Nursery
Tyler TX

Breitmeyer, J. Sons
Detroit MI

Brenier Freres
Auberives-sur-Vareze
Isere France

Brett, Canberra
Australia

Brewer, Mrs. Doris
Balwyn Victoria Australia

Bridgemere Nurseries
England

Bridges, Dennis
Bridges Roses
Rt. 2 Box 348 A-1
Lawndale NC 28090

British Horticultural Co.
Ltd.
Walton Peterborough
England

Brix, Felix
Kotxschenbroda-Dresden
Germany

Broadley, C.
Darra Queensland Australia

Brög, R.
Reichenbach Germany

Brook, Kate Nursery
R.R. 1
Hardwick VT 05843

Brookdale-Kingsway Ltd.
150 Duke Street
Bowmanville Ont. Canada
L1C 2W3

Brookins, H.B.
Orchard Park NY

Brooks, L.L.
Modesto CA

Brooks, M.L.
Winona TX

Brooks & Son
Modesto CA

Brookville Nursery
5300 Northern Boulevard
Glen Head NY 11545

Brown, A.C.
Springfield IL

Brown, Edythe M.
P.O. Box 28411
Menphis TN 38128

Brown, Harry G.L.S.
52 Couchmore Avenue
Esher Surrey England
KT10 9AU

Brown, W. & K
Eastfield Peterborough
England

Brown, William
35 Simonside Avenue
Stakeford Choppington
Northland England

Brownell, Mr. & Mrs.
Walter D.
Little Compton RI

Brownell, H.C.
Little Compton RI

Bruant, G.
Portiers France

Brundrett, Allen
Brundrett Road
Narre Warren North
P.O. Box 1
Victoria 3804 Australia

Brundrett, S. & Sons (Roses)
Pty. Ltd.
Brundrett Road
Narre Warren North
P.O. Box 1
Victoria 3804 Australia

Buatois
Dijon Côte d'Or France

Buchanan's Nursery
5108 Western Boulevard
Raleigh NC 27606

Buck, Dr. Griffith J.
1108 Scott Street
Ames IA 50010

Buckingham, S.
P.O. Box 127
Kumeu New Zealand

Buckley Nursery & Garden
Center
Rt. 2 Box 199
646 North River Road
Buckley WA 98321

Buckwell, A.A. & Sons
St. Mary Cray
Kent England

Budd, Prof. J.L.
Iowa

Budlong & Sons Co.
Auburn RI

Bugnet, George
Legal Alberta Canada

Buisman, G.A.H. & Son,
Ltd.
Postbus 43
8180 AA Heerde
Holland

Buist, Robert
Philadelphia PA

Buller, Miss H.
Alvin TX

Bunge, Rev. W.W.
Rochester NM

Burage Nursery
Leicestershire England

Burbank, Luther
California

Burdett, H.J.
5100 4th Street
Port Arthur TX 77643

Burgess, S.W.
Tunbridge Kent England

Burgess Seed & Plant
Company
905 Four Seasons Road
Bloomington IL 61701

Burks, Joe
P.O. Box 4400
Tyler TX 75712

Burks, Larry
P.O. Box 4400
Tyler TX 75712

Burnett, E.M.
Wanganui New Zealand

Burpee, W. Atlee Company
300 Park Avenue
Warminster PA 18974

Burr, Arnold
Rockville MD

Burr, C.R. Co.
Manchester CT

Burrell, J.& Co.
Cambridge England

Burrows, Rose
Meadowcroft Dale
Abbey
Derby England
DE7 4PQ

Burston Nursery
c/o RNRS
St. Albans England

Burwell Nurseries
4050 East Main Street
Columbus OH 43213

Bushby
Gardener to Lord Brougham
Cannes France

Busheyfields Nursery
Herne Herne Bay
Kent England

Buss, H.E. Nursery
5 Allen Street, Florida Park
1710 Transvaal
South Africa

Butner's Old Mill Nursery
806 South Belt Highway
St. Joseph MO 64507

Butter, M.E.
Battle Sussex England

Buyl, Frères
Cherscamp Schellebelle
Belgium

Buzza, A.E.
Bowdon Cheshire England

Byland's Nurseries, Ltd.
1600 Byland Road
Kelowna BC Canada VIZ 1H6

Byrum, Roy L.
Indiana

-C-

Cadey, Charles
Tyler TX

Cadle's Roses
Thames Oxon England

Cairns, Thomas
3053 Laurel Canyon Blvd.
Studio City CA 91604

Caldwell & Sons, Ltd.
The Nurseries
Chelford Road
Knutsford, Cheshire,
England WA16 8LX

California Nursery Co.
Niles CA

California Roses Inc.
Puente CA

Caluya, Frederick L.
Newman CA

Calvino, S.
San Remo Italy

Campbell, H.R.
El Segundo CA

Camprubi, Nadal Cipriano
Barcelona Spain

Camprubi, Rosas
Domingo Carlos
Barcelona Spain

Campton, D.
Carlingford NSW Australia

Canadian Department of
Agriculture
Ottawa Ont. Canada

Canadian Ornamental
Plant Foundation
Carlisle Ont. Canada

Canadian Rose Society
20 Portico Drive
Scarborough Ont. Canada
M1G 3R3

Cannor Nurseries, Ltd.
48291 Chilliwack Central Rd.
R.R. 1
Chilliwack BC Canada
V2P 2H3

Cant, B.R.
England

Cant, Frank
England

Cants of Colchester, Ltd.
305 Mile End Road
Colchester Essex England
C04 5EB

Capiago
Como Italy

Caranta, M.& H.
Antibes France

Carbaugh, Keller
Lower Yoder Township PA

Carlton Rose Nursery
Carlton OR 97111

Carman, Elbert S.
River Ridge NJ

Caron
Gardener at Rouen France

Caron, Bertha
Mme. Charles Mallerin
Isère France

Carpenter, O.B.
Orient OH

Carrette, Dr. Ch.
Ronchin-les-Lille France

Carrigg, John & Sons
Canby OR

Carroll Gardens, Inc.
P.O. Box 310
444 East Main Street
Westminster MD 21157

Carter, F. & Sons
Wokingham Berkshire
England

Cartier, M.
France

Cartwright, Jimmy D.
6373 Duchess Drive
Rubidoux CA 92509

Casa de Rosa Domingo
12757 Barrett Lane
Santa Ana CA 92705

Cassegrain, René
Orléans France

Castleberry, W.P.
Auburndale FL

Catt, H.J.
NSW Australia

Cattermole, R.F.
11 Howe Street
New Brighton Christchurch
New Zealand

Cayeux, H.
Le Havre France

Cayeux, Henri
Lisbon Botanical Garden
Lisbon Portugal

Cayzer, C.E.
Leongatha Victoria Australia

Cazzaniga-Como
Italy

Cazzaniga, F.G.
Vimodrone Milan Italy

Central Experimental Farm
Horticultural Section
Ottawa Canada

Central Mississippi Rose
  Society
Mississippi

Chabert, Andre
France

Chaffin, C.W.
California

Chaffin, Laurie
California

Chambard, C.
Parilly-Vnissieux-les-Lyon
Rhône France

Chambard, M.
Lyon-Monplaisir France

Champney, John
Charleston SC

Chan, Dr. A.
Ottawa Canada

Chaplin Bros. Ltd.
Waltham Cross England

Chaplin, H.J.
Cheshunt Herts England

Chaplin & Sons
Bedford England

Charles, John Nurseries Ltd.
64 Derby Road Risley
Derby England DE7 3SU

Chase, Clarence A.
Eugene OR

Chase Gardens
Eugene OR

Chauvry
Bordeaux France

Chavalit Nursery
187 Nakornsawan Street
Bangkok Thailand

Chenault, R.
Orléans France

Chenoweth, E.B.
Mt. Vernon WA

Cherry, R.
Australia

Chervenka, F.A.
Sumner WA

Chessum, Paul
21 High Street Gt. Barford
Bedford England MK44 3JH

Chichester Roses Ltd.
Chalder Farm
Sidlesham Chichester
West Sussex England P020
7RN

Chick, W.
Queensland Australia

China Rose Society
Beijing, China

Chinprayoon, Chavalit
187 Nakornsawan Street
Bangkok Thailand

Chi-Siang, Chang
Taiwan Rose Center
Yuan-Lin Chang-hua Taiwan

Chorbadjiiski
Bulgaria

Chotkove Rosanium
Czechoslovakia

Christensen, Jack E.
1285 N. San Antonio Avenue
Ontario, CA 91762

Christie, T. & W. (Forres)
  Ltd.
The Nurseries
Forres Moray Scotland
IV36 OEA

CIOPORA
B.P. 2
67037 Strasbourg France

Circle S. Nursery
Rt. 1 Box 155
Lindale TX 75771

Claire's Garden Center
Haviland Hollow Road
Patterson NY 12563

Clark, Alister
Australia

Clarke Bros.
Portland OR

Clarke Bros. Nursery
Jacksonville TX

Clarke, W.B. & Co.
San Jose CA

Clarks' Rose Nursery
Jacksonville TX

Classic Nursery
Rt. 3
Belmont Road
Athens GA 30605

Clayworth, W.
New Zealand

Clements, J.
Heirloom OGRs
24062 Riverside Drive NE
St. Paul OR 97137

Cleveland Cutflower Co.
Newton Falls OH

Cley Nurseries Ltd.
64 Derby Road Risley
Derby England DE7 3SU

Cobley, Alfred
Earl Shilton
Leicester England

Cochet-Cochet
Coubert Seine-et-Marne
France

Cochet, Frères
Grisy-Suisnes Seine-et-Marne
France

Cochet, P.
Grisy-Suisnes Seine-et-Marne
France

Cochet, Scipion
Soubert Seine-et-Marne France

Cocker, Alexander M.
Scotland

Cocker, Ann G.
Scotland

Cocker, James
James Cocker & Sons
Whitemyres Lang Stracht
Aberdeen Scotland AB9 2XH

Coddington, L.B.
Murray Hill NJ

Coggiatti, Stelvo
Rome Italy

Cognet, Mme. Olivet
Loire France

Coiner Nursery
John Mellon
3000 B Street
P O Box 7217
LaVerne CA 91750

Cole Nursery Co.
Painesville OH

Collier, H.L.
Seattle WA

Collin, W.C.
Scraptoft Leicester England

Collin, W.H., & Sons
(Roses) Ltd.
Manor House Knossington
Oakham Leics England
LE15 8LX

Collins, Canada

Collins, Margaret
Portland OR

Colombier, L.
Macon Saone-et-Loire France

Combe, Maurice
Grenoble France

Comes, Folgado
Aldaya Valencia Spain

Comley, Ivan F.
Salisbury South Australia

Commissariat a l'Energie
Atomique
Paris France

Conard-Pyle Co.
West Grove, PA

Concord Floral Co.
Concord Ont.
Canada

Cone, Dr.
Whitby Yorkshire England

Congy, M.
Trilport Seine-et-Marne
France

Conklin, H.A.
West Corvina CA

Conrad & Jones
West Grove, PA

Consolidated Nursery Inc.
Tyler TX

Conyers, H.B.
Urbana OH

Cook, John
Baltimore MD

Cook, Joseph William
John Cook, Inc.
Baltimore MD

Cook, Sylven S.
420 E. Bowser Avenue
Chesterton IN 46304

Cook, Thomas N.
Watertown MA

Cooke, K.R.
Holder Hill South Australia

Coolidge, D.W.
East Pasadena CA

Cooling, G. & Sons
Bath England

Cooper, F.
Cerincester Glos England

Co-Operative Rose Growers
P.O. Box 4400
Tyler TX 75712

Corboeuf
Orléans France

Corn Hill Nursery Ltd.
Rte. 890 (Corn Hill) R.R. 2
Anagance
New Brunswick Canada
EOE 1AO

Correvon, Henri
Geneva Switzerland

Costetske, N.D.
USSR

Cottage Garden
Queens L.I. NY

Country Bloomers Nursery
RR 2 Box 33-B
Udall KS 67146

Country Garden Nursery
555 Irwin Lane
Santa Rosa CA 95401

Court, Mark
Pyson's Road Broadstairs
Kent England CT10 2LA

Cowlishaw, Frank
7 Ashley Road
Breedon on the Hill
Derby England DE7 1AZ

Cox, Arthur George
P.O. Box Oakridge
Stroud Glos. England

Cox, G.
Slough Bucks England

C-P
Star Roses
Rosehill Road
West Grove PA 19390

Cralle, Dorothy L.
4121 Prospect Avenue
Yorba Linda CA 92686

Cramphorn's Nursery
Sudbury Suffolk England

Crane, Jasper E.
Wilmington DE

Cremer, F.E.
Hanover PA

Croibier, J. & Fils
Saint-Tous Rhône
France

Croix, A.
Montbrison Loire France

Croix, Paul
Bourg-Argental Loire
France

Croll, D. & W., Ltd.
Broughty Ferry
Dundee Scotland DD5 2PP

Cross, Dr. C. Whitman
Chevy Chase MD

Cross, Mrs. C. Whitman
Washington DC

Crouch, J.
Brisbane Queensland
Australia

Cummings, Alex
Bristol Nurseries
Briston CT

Cummings, Peter
14267 Whickey Hill Road
Hubbard OR 97032

Curtis, F.C.
Dallas TX

Curtis, R.F.
Torrance CA

Curtis, Thad
3400 Bella Vista
Midwest City OH 73110

Cutbush, W.H. & Son, Ltd.
Barnet Herts England

Cuthbert, R.& G.
Waltham Cross Herts
England

Cutler, H.G. & Sons
New Lynn Auckland
New Zealand

-D-

Dahlgren, Edward
Boone IA

Dahlledouze Bros.
Brooklyn NY

Dale Estates Ltd.
Toronto Canada

Dale, F.
Coongleton Cheshire
England

Dalhousie Nurderies
Broughty Ferry
Dundee Scotland DD5 2PP

Damaizin
Lyon Rhône France

Dannegger, Emil R.
Milford DE

Daniels Bros. Ltd.
Norwich England

Darvall, Dr. Roger
Carlingford NSW Australia

Datta, Dr. D.S.
Rana Pratap Marg
Lucknow 226001 UP India

Daugherty, William
Cleveland OH

Davidson, Harvey
#3 El Verano Road
Orinda CA 94563

Davies, Gareth
Lonicera Station Road
Talybont-on-Usk Brecon
Powys England

Davis, C.A.
Grand Isle NY

Davison, G.H.
25 Welbeck Road Sheepwash
Choppington
Northumberland England

Dawnay, Mrs. Evelyn
Rose Cottage Canwick Road
Washingborough
Lincoln England LNU 1H5

Dawson, George
Harkaway Victoria Australia

Dawson, Jackson
Arnold Arboretum
Jamaica Plain MA

Deamer, F
Great Warley
Brentwood Essex England

Dean, L.A.
Tyler TX

de Boer, A.S.
Aalsmeer Holland

de Bree, Victor
Richmond ME

Dechant, Ernst
Hohenstein-Ernstthal
Germany

de Coninck-Dervaes &
Pomona
Maldegem Belgium

Deering, E.P.
Scappoose OR

de Freitas, J.F.
Auburn Australia

Dehner & Co.
Rain, Germany

Dekkers, W. & Son
Aalsmmer Holland

DeLashmutt
Oregon

Delaunay, F.
Angers France

Delbard-Chabert
Georges Delbard &
Andre Chabert
France

Delbard, Georges S.A.
16 Quai de la Megisserie
75038 Paris Cedex 01 France

Délépine, Paul
Carrères Angers France

Delforge, Hipp & Fils
Belsele (Waas) Belgium

Delforge, S.
Belsele (Waas) Belgium

Delobel, Marcel
Somme-les-Lille
France

Del Rose Nursery
Nuestro Road
Yuba City CA 95991

Delves, Peter
Woolhouse Nursery
Redford Midhurst
Sussex England GU29 0QH

De Marco Green Tree
Nursery
East Branch NY 13756

De Mott, Monroe F.
Clinton NJ

Dene, Jesmond Nursery and
Garden Centre
P.O. Box 511
Pietermaritzburg 3200
Republic of South Africa

Dennison, Franklin
Cranford Leamington
England

Den Ouden, H. & Son
Old Farm Nurseries
Boskoop Holland

Denoyel, Mme. or Vve.
Venissieux France

Dental, J.B.
Alpes Maritimes France

De Puy, Dr. Herman
Tacoma WA

de Ruiter, George
Hazerswoude Holland

de Ruiter, George
Widmerpool Nottingham
England

Desamero, Luis
3053 Laurel Canyon Blvd.
Studio City CA 91606

Descanso Distributors
Livermore CA

Descemet, M.
St. Denis France

Deshpande, R.K.
Parrati Poona India

Desprez
Yèbels France

Deutsche Rosen-Registerelle
Dortmund West Germany

Deverman, Harry
Clifton NJ

de Vink, J.W. & Sons
Boskoop Holland

DeVor Nursery
P.O. Box 1269
Freedom CA 95019

DeVor, Paul F.
California

DeVor, Thomas R.
California

DeVor, William L.
California

De Witte, W.
Rijsenhout Holland

Diamond State Nursery
Little Silver NJ

Dickson, Alex
Northern Ireland

Dickson, A.P.C.
Northern Ireland

Dickson, Hugh Ltd.
Belfast Ireland

Dickson Nursery Ltd.
Milecross Road Newtownards
County Down Northern
Ireland BT23 4SS

Dicksons of Hawlmark
Northern Ireland

Dickson, Patrick
Northern Ireland

Dickson, Sandy
Belfast Ireland

Dickson & Sons, Ltd.
Northern Ireland

Dicksons & Co.
Edinburgh Scotland

Didato, James
Middlesex NJ

Diener, Richard Nursery
Oxnard CA

Dietrich & Turner
Montebello CA

Dillan, C.J.
Kenton
Newcastle on Tyne
England

Dingee & Conrad
West Grove PA

Dingle, J.M.
Victoria Australia

Division of Floriculture &
Landscape
India

Division of Vegetable Crops
& Floriculture
India

Dixie Rose Nursery
Tyler TX

Dobbie & Co. Ltd.
Edinburgh Scotland

Dobbs, Annette
2817 Sheridan Way
Stockton CA 95207

Dobson, Beverly R.
215 Harriman Road
Irvington NY 10533

Doley, N.
Bexley North
Sidney Australia

Domaine Agricole de
Cronenbourg
Strasbourg France

Domilla, Silvo
San Lorenzo CA

Donner, F. & Sons Co.
Lafayette IN

Donovan's Roses
P.O. Box 37,800
Shreveport LA 71133-7800

Doon Valley Roses
1-A Lakshmi Road
Dehran Dun
India

Doorenbos, S.A.G.
The Hague Holland

Dorieux, F., Roseraies
GAEC
42840 Montagny (Loire)
France

Dot, G.F.
Spain

Dot, Marino M.
Spain

Dot, Pedro
Spain

Dot, Simon S.
Spain

Dot, Vivers
Doctor Fleming 21
Apartado 273
Vilafranca del Penedes
Barcelona Spain

Downham, H.C. Nursery
Co., Ltd.
626 Victoria Street
Strathroy Ont. Canada
N7G 3C1

Downes, Mrs. Rupert
Malvern Australia

Doyle, John
Springfield OH

Dramm, E.R.
Elmhurst IL

Dreer, Henry A. Inc.
Philadelphia PA

Driscoll, W.E.
72 Kelvin Road
Beechdale Estate
Walsall England WS2 7DR

Dubreuil
Lyon Rhône France

Ducher & Vve.
Lyon Rhône France

Duckham-Pierson Co.
Madison NJ

Ducroz, J.
Villeurbanne-Lyon Rhône
France

Duehrsen, Carl G.
Montebello CA

Duffey, L.B.
Logan OH

Duncan & Davies
P.O. Box 340
New Plymouth
New Zealand

Duncan, Walter
Eastwood
South Africa

Dundee Nursery
16800 Highway 55
Plymouth NY 55446

Dunlop, John H. & Son Ltd.
Toronto Ont. Canada

Dunstan
Bundaberg Queensland
Australia

Dunstrathraven Roses Ltd.
14706 Old Henry Road
Anchorage KY 40223

Dunton Nursery
Biggleswade Beds England

Dupont, Andre
Founder of Rose Collection
at Luxembourg Palace
Paris France

Dwight, Robert & Son, Rose
    Nurseries
Altear Road Gt. Altear
Formby Moerseyside England

Dyess, J.L.
Tyler TX

Dynarose, Ltd.
Brooklin Ont. Canada

-E-

Eacott, S.
Langley Bucks England

Eads, C.E.
2623 State St.
Granite City IL 62040

Eagle, Barry & Dawn
P.O. Box 12009
Christchurch New Zealand

Earing, Elsie A.
Schenectady NY

Earing, F.A.
Schenectady NY

Easlea, Walter & Sons Ltd.
Eastwood Leigh-on-Sea Essex
England

Eastern Nurseries Inc.
Holliston WA

Eastern Roses
New Jersey

Ebben, Roeland N.V.
Cuyk Holland

Ebeling, F.
Bernburg Germany

Eddie, H.M. & Sons
Vancouver BC Canada

Eddie, J.H.
Vancouver BC Canada

Eddy, Paul
Howard Lake MN

Eden Rose Nursery
Noor der Paarl Cape
South Africa

Edenvale Nursery
Tarlton Transvaal
South Africa

Edmunds Roses
Philip & Kathy Edmunds
Roses by Fred Edmunds
6235 SW Kahle Rd.
Wilsonville OR 97070

Edwards, P.B.
Upper Burnie Tasmania
Australia

EFR
Edition Française de Roses
Champagne-au-Mont-d'Or
Rhône France

Egmont Roses
P.O. Box 3162
New Plymouth New Zealand

Eichholz, Henry
Waynesboro PA

Ellesmere Nursery
Brooklin Ont. Canada

Ellice, R.G.
Harlow Essex England

Ellick, Charles W.
2 Mere-Close Skelmersdale
Lancashire England WN8RN

Elliott, Charles P.
2208 Monterey Avenue
Santa Clara CA 95051

Elliott, John S.
Dover NH

Ellis, A.E.
Wasco CA

Ellis, A.W.
Wasco CA

Ellis, T.L.
Great Barley Arrish
Liverton Newton Abbott
Devon England

Ellwanger & Barry
Rochester NY

Elm Park Garden Centre
Aldermaston Rd. Pamber End
Busingstoke Hants England

Elmer, Constance A.
Elmer Roses
San Gabriel CA

Elmer Roses
San Gabriel CA

Elmer's Nursery
San Jose CA

Elton Farm Nursery
Johannesburg South Africa

Embriaco, Bartolomeo
via Grossi Bianchi 303
18030 Poggio di Sanremo IM
Italy

Emlong Nurseries, Inc.
Stevensville MI 49127

Engall, R.
Epping NSW Australia

Engelbrech, H.
Elmshorn Germany

England, Bernard
c/o RNRS
St. Albans Herts. England

England Rose Society
Hertfordshire England

English, T.J. & Son
Barnwood Gloucester
England

Epperson, Richard G.
4590 Del Mar Avenue
San Diego CA 92107

Erskine, Robert
Carlos Alberta Canada

Esser, L., & Son
Grange Farm Nursery
Barton Road (B1441) Wisbech
Cambs England PE13 4TH

Evans City Cut Flower Co.
Evans City PA

Evans, F. David
482 Winston Place
Springfield OR 97477

Evans, Frederick
Brighton England

Everitt, D.
England

Excelsior Rose Hybridizers
2 Mere-Close Skelmersdale
Lancashire England
WN8RN

-F-

Faassen-Herkens, J.H.
Tegelen Holland

Faassen-Houba, M.J.
Tegelen Holland

Fairhead, W.H.
Loughton England

Fankhauser, D.A.
Jetty & Eastbourne Rds.
Rosebud
Victoria Australia

Farmer Seed & Nursery Co.
P.O. Box 129
Fairbault MN 55012

Farquar, R.& J.
Boston MA

Farr, C.
West End Woking England

Fauque & Fils
Orléans France

Feast, Samuel & John
Baltiimore MD

Federation of Rose Societies
of South Africa
5 Douglas Street Waverley
Johannesburg 2090
South Africa

Fedi, Shi Raffaello
Pistoria Italy

Feigel, John R.
823 Lombard Avenue
Evansville IN 47715

Felbergs-Leclerc, J.
Trier Germany

Ferguson, R.C.
Dunfermline Scotland

Ferguson, William
Dunfermline Scotland

Fermor, E.R.
Maidstone Kent
England

Fernbank Science Center
156 Heaton Park Drive N.E.
Atlanta GA 30307

Ferndale Ridge Nursery
South Africa

Ferris, Earl Nursery &
Garden Center
811 Fourth Street N.E.
Hampton IA 50441

Fey, Chr.
West Germany

Fiamingo, J.
Weatlawn 178 Ember Lane
East Molesey
Surrey England KT8 OB5

Field Bros.
Washington DC

Field, Henry Seed &
Nursery Co.
Shenandoah IA 51602

Finch, R.M.
Concord NSW
Australia

Fischel, Reuben Roses
Nursery
Schadmont Dvora 15240
Lower Galilee Israel

Fischer, C. & H.
17985-40th Avenue Surrey
BC Canada V3S 4N8

Fisher, Gladys (Mrs. Gordon)
Woburn MA

Fisher, P.
Constantia Cape South Africa

Fisher, R.C.
Rochester NY

Fisons Horticulture, Ltd.
Felixstowe Suffolk England

Fitzgerald, Charles L.
Hawthorne CA

Fitzhardinge, Mrs. H.C.
Warrawee NSW Australia

Five M Nursery
Tyler TX

Fletcher, Norman H.
Farmingdon Berkshire
England

Flora World
Highland Park IL

Florac, Marilyn
Jamison Hill Road
Clinton Corners NY 12514

Floradale Nurs. Ltd.
P.O. Box 2073 Beacon Bay
East London England

Florex Gardens
North Wales PA

Flower of the Month Inc.
Grand Rapids MI

Flower World of America,
Inc.
1655 Imperial Way
Mid-Atlantic Park
West Deptford NJ 08086

Flowers 'n' Friends
Greenhouse
Miniature Roses
9590 100th Street S.E.
Alto MI 49302

Follen, Hugh
Wiebach England

Fonda, Henry
3662 Moore Street
Los Angeles CA 90066

Fong, William P.
Nuestro Road
Yuba City CA 95991

Fontane
Clamart France

Foot, Mrs. Harriet
Marblehead MA

Fortune, Robert
English Botanist
London England

Foster
Devenport England

Foulard
Le Mans France

Fountain Square Nursery,
Inc.
Diamond Springs, CA

Four Season's Nursery &
Landscaping
P.O. Box 776
Chesteron IN 46304

Franc, Godfrey C.
Englewood CO

France Rose Society
Lyon Cedex 3, France

Frances' Old Fashioned
Roses
Frances Grate
472 Gibson Ave.
Pacific Grove CA 93950

Francis, Dr. R.S.R.
Hastings New Zealand

Franklin Park Garden
Center
1777 E. Broad St.
Columbus OH 43203

French, Richard
238 W. Daniels Road
Palatine IL 60067

Freud
Berlin-Kopenich Germany

Freuh, Charles & Sons
Saginaw MI

Freytag, Bernard
Handorf bei Münster West
Germany

Friends Rosery
B-110 Mahamagar
Lucknow 226 006 India

Frock, Marshall J.
4325 Phoenix Drive
Springfield OH 45503

Fryer, Gareth R.
Manchester Road
Knutsford Cheshire England
WA16 0SX

Fryer's Nursery Ltd.
Manchester Road
Knutsford Cheshire England
WA16 0SX

Fugier, Henri
Saone-et-Loire
France

Fulgham, Mary
5335 Braeburn
Bellaire TX 77401

Fuller, Mrs. Clayton W.
1201-28th St. N.
St. Petersburg FL 33713

Fumagalli, Niso
Via Missouri 8
20052 Monza Milano Italy

-G-

Gailloux, Gilles
1030 St. Alexandre
Longuevil Quèbec Canda
J4H 3H1

Galan, Ets. Jose
Valencia Spain

Gamon
Lyon Rhône France

Gandy, F. Douglas
England

Gandy, O.L.
Gandy, England

Gandy's Roses Ltd.
North Kilworth Nr.
Lutterwoth
Leics. England LE17 6HZ

Garçon
Rouen Seine-Inf France

Garden Town Nursery
Eggertsville NY

Gardner
Newport Nurseries
Newport RI

Gardner, B.C.
Los Banos CA

Garelta, Mrs. J.
c/co NRS New Zealand
Wellington New Zealand

Garrison, C.G.
Shreveport LA

Garwood, St. Clair
Xenia OH

Gates, H.
Putnoe Bedford England

Gateshead Metropolitan
   Borough Council
Department of Parks Services
Saltwell Park Office
Saltwell Road South
Gateshead England NE9 6DU

Gatty, Joseph
451 North Lillian Street
Stockton CA 95205

Gatty, M.B.
Howrah Tas Australia

Gatwared, E.E.
Cambridge
England

Gaujard, Jean
38 route de Lyon 69320
Feyzin Isère France

Gaujard, Raymond
Orléans Loiret France

G.A.W.A.
Bad Godesberg West Germany

Geary, G.
Burbage Nurseries
Leicestershire England

Geduldig, Philipp
Kohlscheid bei Aachen
Germany

Geelong Horticultural
   Society
Australia

Geest Industries Inc.
Spaulding Lincolnshire
England

Geiger, William A.
North Wales PA

Geltsendeger, P.P.
USSR

General Bionomics
Santa Rosa CA

Germain Seed & Plant Co.
Los Angeles CA

Germany Rose Society
Baden Baden, Germany

Gersdorff, Charles E.F.
Washington DC

Geschwind, G.
Karpona Hungary

Gesellschaft Schweizeriacher
   Rosenfreunde
c/o Ingenieurachule ISW
Gruntal CH-8820 Wadenswil
Switzerland

Getz Edgemore Nursery
R.R. 2
Morton IL 61550

Geytenbeeks Nursery
Cudlee Creek
South Australia

Ghosh, P.
New Delhi India

Giacomasso, Fratelli
Turin Italy

Gillot, Francis
Trepillot-Besançon Doubs
France

Girin, G.
Saint-Romain-de-Popey
Rhône France

Girraween Nursery
69 Kavanagh Street
Upper Mt. Gravatt Brisbane
Queensland 4122 Australia

Giuseppe, M.
Mortara Pavia Italy

Gloria Dei Nursery
36 East Road
High Falls Park
High Falls NY 12440

Gobbee, W.D.
92 Culverden Road
Balham London England
SW12

Godard
Thoissey France

Godfrey, S.S.
Sydenham England

Godin, Maurice
France

Godly's Roses
Dunstable Road
Redbourn St. Albans
Herts England AL3 7PS

Golden State Nursery
Atlanta GA

Golie, Lu Verne P.
Union City PA

Golik, A.
Ellesmere Nurseries Ltd.
Brookin Ont Canada

Good & Reese
Springfield OH

Goodinsons Rose Ltd.
Bingley Lane Nursery
Stannington Sheffield Yorks
England

Goodwin, C.H.
Kimberley Notts England

Gopalaswamiengar, K.S.
177 V Main Road
Charmarajpet Bangalore
560 018 India

Gordon, Winifred L.
East Springfield PA

Gosset, Dr. A.C.V.
Cornborough Liphook Hants
England

Gould, L.C.
Chicago IL

Gowie, W.L.
Grahamstown
South Africa

Grabczewski, J.L.
Warsaw Poland

Graf, A.B.
Rutherford NJ

Graff, Roy
Cottage 115 2422 Camillia Dr.
Hopkinsville KY 42240

Graham, R. Merrell
Hattiesburg MS

Grandes Roseraies du Val
de la Loire
Orléans France

Granger
Grisy-Suisnes Seine-et-Marne
France

Grant, Patrick
Macksville N.S.W.
Australia

Gravereaux, Jules
Roserie de l'Haÿ
Paris France

Gray, Alexander Hill
Bath England

Gray, Andrew
Charleston SC

Gray, W.R.
Oakton VA

Great Britain Rose Society
Hertfordshire
England

Great Western Rose Co.
Pomona CA

Green Acres Landscape
Growers
P.O. Box 3278
1616 East Francis Suite B
Ontario CA 91761

Green Acres Rose Nursery
Stapleford Abbotts England

Greenbauer Nursery
9590-100th Street S.E.
Alto MI 49302

Greene, H.L.
Portland OR

Greenfield, P.L.
Hightae Plant Nursery
16 Coronation Street
Takapuna Auckland 9
New Zealand

Greenhead Roses
Greenhead Nursery
Old Greenock Road
Inchinnan Renfrew Scotland

Greenmantle Nurs.
3010 Ettersburg Road
Garberville CA 95440

Greensitt, I.
Nostell Wakefield England
WF4 IQE

Greensitt, J.A.
Nostell Wakefield England
WF4 IQE

Greenway, C.D.
Letton Hereford
England

Greenwood, Chris
4222 N. Harlan
Baldwin Park CA 91706

Greff, Nikolai P.
225 26th Avenue
San Mateo CA 94403

Gregory, C. & Son, Ltd.
The Rose Gardens
Stapleford Nottingham
England NG9 7JA

Griffin, J. Bruce
Philadelphia PA

Griffing Nurseries
Beaumont TX

Griffing, W.D.
MacClenny FL

Griffiths, Trevor Ltd.
No. 3 R.D.
Timaru New Zealand

Grillo, Nicolas
Milldale CT

Groen, C.J.
Montebello CA

Grootendorst, F.J. & Sons
Boskoop Holland

Grootendorst, Rien
Boskoop Holland

Gro-Plant Industries
Shafter CA

Groshens & Morrison
Roslyn PA

Groshens, Victor
Roslyn PA

Gruenbauer, Richard
Flowers 'N Friends
Miniature Roses
9590 100th Street SE
Alto MI 49302

Grumer, A.
2285 Leopoldsdorff am
Marchfeld Austria

Gubonenk, F.R.
USSR

Gude, A.E.
Rockville MD

Gude Bros.
Washington DC

Gue, Derek John
The Folly Oakridge
Stroud Glos. England

Guérin, Modeste
Paris France

Guerteen & Ritson, Ltd.
Horley Surrey
England

Guest, M.M.
28 Longmyrd Way
Dunley Park
Stourport-on-Severn Worcs.
England

Guillaud, Vve. A. & Fil
Grand Lemps Isère France

Guillot Fils
J.-B. Guillot
Lyon-Monplaisir
France

Guillot, Henri
Saint-Marcellin Isère France

Guillot, Marc
Sain-Priest Isère France

Guillot, Pere
Lyon France

Guillot, Pierre
Lyon-Monplaisir France

Guinoiseau B
Angers France

Guinoiseau Fils
Angers France

Gulf Stream Nursery, Inc.
Wachapreague VA 23480

Gunn & Sons, Ltd.
Olton Warwickshire England

Gunter, Dr. N.C.
Pueblo CO

Gupta, Dr. M.N.
Rana Pratap Marg
Lucknow 226001 UP India

Gupta, S.C.
6/25 S.P. Mukherjee Rd. A Zone
Durgapur 4 (LB) India

Gurney Seed & Nursery Co.
Yankton SD 57079

Gürtler, A
Miskolc Hungary

Gutierrez, Dr. B.
Bogota Columbia

-H-

Hackett & Co.
Adelaide Australia

Haenchen, Dr. Eckart
Cossebaude bei Dresden
Germany

Hage, W.C. & Co.
Boskoop Holland

Hahn, John L.
San Jose CA

Haight, George S.
California

Hall, Dr. J. Campbell
Monaghan Ireland

Hall, William W.
417 East 2nd Street
Richland Center WI 53581

Hallman Orchards and
    Nursery
Box 1218
Ganges BC Canada VOS 1RO

Hamblin, Stephen F.
Lexington MA

Hamilton, R.T.
399 Lower Heidelberg Road
Heidelberg Victoria Australia

Hamlin Nursery
Rt. 1 Box 91700
Beaumont TX 77706

Hamm, J.
Lindale TX

Hammann, Ferd.
Kassel Germany

Hamoniere, Marc
Ivry Seine France

Hanbury, Cecil
La Mortola Italy

Handley Rose Nurseries
Lightwood Road Marsh Lane
Sheffield, England S31 9RG

Handover, P.
Hemel Hempstead
Herts England

Hansen, C.B.
California

Hansen, Dr. N.E.
State College Brookings ND

Hansen, Neils J.
Washington DC

Harada, Dr. Tomin
2-5-1 Funairi-Minami
Hiroshima Japan

Harada, Dr. Toshiyuki
Japan

Harbour, Eric Roland
19 Teesdale Avenue
Isleworth Middlesex England
TW7 6AP

Hardgrove, Donald & Mary
1656 N. Second Street
El Cajon CA 92021

Hardikar, Dr. M.N.
41/14 Erandawane Karve
Road
Pune 411-004 India

Hardy, M.
Luxembourg Gardens
Paris France

Harison, George Folliott
New York NY

Harkness, R. & Co.
The Rose Gardens
Hitchin Hertfordshire
England SG4 0JT

Harp, H.F.
Morden Manitoba Canada

Harris, J.R.
Toogoolawah Queensland
Australia

Harris, L.M.
Kerikeri North Auckland
New Zealand

Harrison, George
14 Chifley CRS
Dandenong Victoria Australia

Harrison, L.R.
Cambridge England

Harrison's Antique &
    Modern Roses
P.O. Box 527
Canton MS 39046

Hart, G.B. Inc.
Rochester NY

Hart, George B.
Rochester NY

Hart, L.P.
Everson WA

Hartgerink, Conrad
West Los Angeles CA

Harvey, Ida D.
Schoolfield VA

Harvey, R.E.
Irving TX

Haselmos, Bob, Roses
535 Tomarack Circle
Lompoc CA 93436

Hassefras Bros.
Hazerwoude Holland

Hastie, W.G.
Glen Waverley Victoria
Australia

Hasting's
434 Marietta Street N.W.
P.O. Box 4274
Atlanta GA 30302-4274

Hatton, R. Marion
Harrisburg PA

Hauenstein AG
Baumschulen Rosenkulturen
8197 Rafz Switzerland

Hauser, Susan
Switzerland

Hauser, Victor
Switzerland

Hausermann, C. Co.
Melrose Park IL

Halevi, Anya Malka
1338 Jessie
San Francisco CA 94103

Hawker, N.
Erdington Birmingham
England

Hawker, Una
Palmerston North
New Zealand

Hay, Oscar F.
Marsh's Nursery
Pasadena CA

Haynes, F. & Partners
(Roses)
10 Heather Road
Kettering Northamptonshire
England NN16 9TR

Hayward, Alfred E.
Wonthaggi North Victoria
Australia

Hazenberg, G.
Lille Belgium

Hazlewood Bros.
Epping NSW Australia

Heacock, Joseph Co.
Wyncote PA

Heard, A.E.
Wachet West Somerset
England

Heath, H.
Swallowfield Berkshire
England

Heath, W.L.
Newbury Berks England

Hebaru
Japan

Heers, C.W.
Manley Queensland Australia

Hefner, John
145 Crosby Drive
Indianapolis IN 46227

Heidemij, Kon. Ned.
Arnhem Holland

Heirloom Old Garden Roses
24062 Northeast Riverside Dr.
St. Paul OR 97137

Heinsohn, Franz
Germany

Heizmann & Co.
Vevey Switzerland

Heizmann, E.
Vevey
Switzerland

Heller Bros.
New Castle IN

Hemeray-Aubert
Orléans Loiret France

Henderson, Peter & Co.
New York NY

Henderson, William H.
Fresno CA

Henderson's Experimental
Gardens
Fresno CA

Hendrickx, Ignace
Maldegem Belgium

Hennessey, Roy
Scappoose OR

Henson, H.
England

Henson, T.H.
England

Herholdt, J.A.
Herholdt's Nursery
P.O. Box 17
Eikenhof 1872 South Africa

Herinex, D.J.R.
Teddington Middlesex
England

Heritage Rose Foundation
1512 Gorman St.
Raleigh NC 27606

Heritage Rose Gardens
16831 Mitchell Creek Road
Fort Bragg CA 95437

Heron, Alex
Windsor Ont. Canada

Hershey Nursery
Pennsylvania

Hesse, H.A.
Baumschulen Weener Ems
Germany

Hester, Addison R.
Washington DC

Hetzel, Elisha J.
Hurst Berkshire England

Hetzel, Karl
7519 Oberderdingen
West Germany

Heyes, Alex & Janice
433 Scoresby Road
Ferntree Gully
Victoria 3156 Australia

Hicks, J.S.
Tyler TX

Hieatt, Forrest L.
San Diego CA

Higgs, Arthur (Roses)
Water Lane Farm, North
Hykeham Lincoln England

Higgs, R.H. & Sons Ltd.
Castle Grove Nursery
Scotts Grove Road
Chobham Woking Surrey
England GU24 8DY

High Country Rosarium
1717 Downing Street
Denver CO 80218

Highfield Nurseries
Whitminster Gloucester
England GL2 7PL

Highlands Hardware &
Nursery
684 Dearborn Street
Aurora CO 80011

Hildebrandt, John T.
Melrose Park IL

Hill, A.
Rhodes Middleton
Manchester England

Hill Crest Greenhouses
Newtown PA

Hill, E.G. Co., Inc.
446 N.W. 18th Street
Richmond IN 47374

Hill, E.H.
c/o RNRS
St. Albans
England

Hill, Ernest
England

Hill Floral Products Co.
Richmond IN

Hill, Joseph H. Co.
2700 Peacock Road
Richmond IN 43734

Hill Park Nurseries
Kingston By Pass (A309)
Surbiton Surrey
England KT6 5HN

Hillcrest Gardens
Weston MA

Hillier Nurs.
Winchester, Ltd.
Ampfield House
Ampfield Romsey Hants.
England S05 9PA

Hilling, T. & Co., Ltd.
Chobham Working
Surrey England

Hillje, Miss Meta
Alvin TX

Hillock, V.S.
Arlington TX

Hills Nurseries
Netherton Road
Appleton NR
Abingdon Oxon England
OX13 5QN

Hilltop Nursery
Box 975 Nichols Lane
Gallatin TN 37066

Hinner, Peter
Woodstock Il

Hinner, W. Wilhelm
Trier Germany

Hirakata, Keihan Nurs.
1-5 Ikagakotobuki-Cho
Hirakata-Shi Osaka 573 Japan

Hiroshima Rose Nurseries
K Tagashira 2-2
Kami-tenmacho
Nishi-ku Hiroshima City
Japan

Hiscox, Jesse F.
East Patchogue NY

Historical Roses, Inc.
1657 West Jackson Street
Painesville OH 44077

Hjort, A.P.
Georgia

Hjort, S.C.
Georgia

Hobbies, Ltd.
Dereham England

Hofmann, Harry
Jacksonville IL

Holland Rose Society
Deurne, Holland

Hollinger, Franc
8695 Harvie Road
R.R. 10
Surrey BC Canada V3S 5X7

Holmes, Mazwell A.
San Leandro CA

Holmes, R.A.
Stockport Cheshire England

Holmes, Victor E.
San Bruno CA

Holtzman, Arnold
37 Givat Avia
Yehud Israel

Homan, C.A.
Roseneath Runcorn Australia

Homan, H.J.
Kingsville MD

Home Nursery Products
    Corp.
Newark NY

Homedale Nursery
Prudhoe on Tyne
Northamberland England

Homeric Rose Nurseries
Algar Kirk
Boston Lincolnshire England
PE20 2BE

Homestead Nurseries
Wright Road
Clayburn BC Canada VOX
1E0

Hooker, W.J.
Winchester Hants England

Hooney, C.H.
Portersw Bar Hers England

Hooper, John Clint
3151 Douglass
Memphis TN 38111

Hoopes Bros. & Thomas Co.
West Chester PA

Hope, William
Shaw Heath
Knutsford
Cheshire England

Hopkins, A.D.
Mineral Wells WV

Horner, A.D.
Dunmow Essex England

Horner, Colin P.
21 Rainsford Road
Stansted Essex England
CM24 8DU

Horner, Heather M.
21 Rainsford Road
Stansted Essex England
CM24 8DU

Horsfield, T.
North Barnsley Yorks
England

Horstmann & Co.
Elmshorn Holstein Germany

Hortco, Inc.
10901 N.E. 23rd Street
Oklahoma City OK 73141

Hortico
Spalding Lincs England

Hortico, Inc.
723 Robson Road R.R. 1
Waterdown
Ont. Canada L04 2H0

Horvath, M.H.
Mentor OH

Hosp, F.P.
Riverside CA

Hough, Robin
915 Oak Vista Court
Friendswood TX 77546

Houghton, Douglas
Arcadia CA

Houghton, T.B.
Roseneath
Runcorn
Queensland Australia

Houle, Raymond
R.R. 1 St. Albert Compte
Athabaska
Quèbec Canada J0A 1E0

House, Bernice L.
Texas

House of Meilland
Antibes, France

House of Wesley
2200 E. Oakland Dept. 41
Bloomington IL 61701

Hoverman John & Sons, Inc.
Route 17
Rochelle Park NJ 07662

Howard, A.P.
Sierra Madre CA

Howard, Fred H.
see H&S

Howard, Paul J.
Los Angeles CA

Howard Rose Co.
Paul W. Howard
Hemet CA

Howard & Smith
see H&S

Hoy, Lowell L.
1311 North C Street
Richmond IN 47374

H&S
Howard & Smith
Montebello CA

Huber, Richard AG
5605 Dottikon AG
Switzerland

Hubner, Siegfied
4972 Lohne
West Germany

Huck, Arnold
Dresden-Gostritz Germany

Hudson's Landscape
    Nursery
3609 Walton Way Ext.
Augusta GA 30909

Hughes, G.T. Roses
Ireland

Humenick, Muriel E.
6641 Crystal Boulevard
Diamond Springs CA 95619

Hunt, E.
Heage Derbys. England

Hunt, W. Henry
441 Somerset Drive
Birmingham AL 35206

Hunter, John
Thornton Fife England

Hunton, Claude B.
Rt. 7 Box 164
Claremore OK 74017

Hurst, Dr. C.C.
Botanic Garden
Cambridge England

Hyde, R.W.
Crystal River FL

-I-

IARI
Indian Agricultural Research
Institute
Division of Vegetable Crops
& Floriculture
New Delhi 110-012 India

Ilgenfritz Nursery Inc.
Monroe MI

Ilsink, Peter
Broekweg 3 P.O. Box 2
3956 ZR (N.E.) Leersum
Holland

Indian Agricultural
Research Institute
India

Indian Rose Federation
438 Pushpam-106th Road
Chembur Bombay 400-071
India

Ingegnoli, Fratelli
Milano Italy

Institute National
Agronomique
Paris France

Institute of Ornamental
Plant Growing
Melle Belgium

Interplant B.V.
Broekweg 3 P.O. Box 2
3956 ZR (N.E.) Leersum
Holland

Inter-State Nurseries, Inc.
Hamburg, IA 51640

Intwood Nurseries
Swardeston Norwich England
NR14 8EA

Iowa State College
Ames, IA

Iowa State University
Dept. of Horticulture
Ames IA 50011

IRAR
International Registration
Authority for Roses
P.O. Box 30,000
Shreveport LA 71130-0030

Isso, Patsy A.
Glen Head NY

Israel Rose Society
The Wohl Rose Park of
Jerusalem
Kiryat Ben-Gurion
P.O.B. 1312
Jerusalem 91012 Israel

Italy Rose Society
Monza, Italy

Itami Bara-en
Japan

Itami Rose Nursery Ltd.
161 Ikenoue
Gogazuka Itami-Shi
Hyogo-Ken 664 Japan

Ito, R.
Tokyo Japan

Iufer, Mrs. Ernest
Iufer Nursery Co.
P.O. Box 3241
Salem OR 97302

Ivanhoe Horticultural
Society
Victoria Australia

-J-

Jack, John
69 Kavanagh Street
Upper Mt. Gravatt Brisbane
Queensland 4122 Australia

Jackman, George & Son Ltd.
Woking Surrey England

Jack's Mini Roses
1530 Lillie Drive
Bosque Farms NM 87068

Jackson, F.
Bassendean Australia

Jackson, J.R.
Wink Hill Staffordshire
England

Jackson & Perkins Company
Medford, OR

Jacobs, Betty A.
525 Butler Road
Bakersfield CA 93304

Jacobs, O.
Weitendorf Mecklenburg
Germany

Jacobus, Martin R.
Ridgefield NJ

Jacotot
Dijon France

Jamain, Hippolyte
Paris France

James, John
2601 Joseph Street
Avon OH 44011

James, R.
Richmond Yorkshire
England

Janssen, George
Chicago IL

Japan Rose Nursery
1078 Kataoka Nadasaki-Cho
Kojima-Gun Okayama Pref.
709-12 Japan

Japan Rose Society
4-12-6 Todoroki Setagaya-Ku
Tokyo 158 Japan

Jaques, A.A.
Gardener at Château de
Neuilly France

J&B Roses
Jolly & Borst
West Long Branch NJ

J.B. Roses, Inc.
960 G Street
P.O. Box X
Wasco CA 93280

Jelly, Robert G.
446 N.W. 18th Street
Richmond IN 47374

Jellyman, J.S.
129 Summer Street
Stroud Glos. England
GL5 1PQ

Jerabek, Paul E.
10763 Beechwood Drive
Kirtland OH 44026

Jeremias, Dr. Charles &
Lephon L.
Bynum Manor Roses
2103 Johnstone St.
Newberry SC 29108

Jersey Nurseries Ltd.
Jersey Channel Island

Jobson, Daniel J.
42 Elm Ave.
Newport News VA 23601

Johns, A. & Sons
Houghton NSW
Australia

Johnson, G.E.
Clinton NJ

Johnson, Walter E.
Reading MA

Johnstown Greenhouses
Johnstown PA

Joliffe, Hazel R.
423 Sunnyside Avenue
Ottawa IL 61350

Jolly, Betty
Maryland

Jolly, Marie
Maryland

Jolly, Nelson F.
Maryland

Joly
Pont-Carré France

Jones, C. & K.
Barrow Lane
Tarvin Chester England
CH3 8EN

Jones, J.A.
Little Rock AR

Jordan, B.L.
Crowborough Sussex England

Jordan, G.L.
Urbana IL

J&P
Jackson & Perkins Company
P.O. Box 1028 1 Rose Lane
Medford OR 97501

Jung, J.W. Seed & Nursery
Co.
335 S. High Street
Randolph WI 53957-0001

Junior Legacy Club
Melbourne Australia

Justice, J.
Justice Miniature Roses
5947 SW Kahle Rd.
Wilsonville OR 97070

-K-

Kakujitsuen
Japan

Kalaydjiev
Bulgaria

Kallay, Joseph W.
Painesville OH

Kammeraad, H.
Aalsmeer Holland

Kane Brothers
92 Dundrinner
Castlewellan England

Kashimoto
Japan

Kaucher, Ruth
Newtown PA

Kawai, Siniti
Tokyo Japan

Keene's Rose Nursery
11 Hezlett Road
Kellyville NSW Australia 2153

Keener Classics
205 East Edgewood
Friendswood TX 77546

Keessen, J.
Aalsmeer Holland

Keisei Rose Nurseries, Inc.
1-12-1 Oshiage
Sumida-Ka Tokyo 131 Japan

Keisei Rose Research
Institute
755 Owadashinden
Yachiyo-Shi (City)
Chiba-Ken (Pref.) 276 Japan

Kelleher, Mrs. J.
North Ryde Australia

Kelly Brothers Nurseries,
Inc.
650 Maple Street
Dansville NY 14437

Kelly, J.A.W.
Burwood Victoria Australia

Kelly, Martin & Norma
36 East Road High Falls Park
High Falls NY 12440

Kemble-Smith Co.
Boone IA

Kemp, J.A.
Little Silver NJ

Kemp, M.L.
Halstead Essex England

Kemper Nursery
Rt. 1 Box 9
Farnham VA 22460

Kemple, William H.
San Diego CA

Kennedy, T.
Wangagui New Zealand

Keren-Zur
Baruch
Keren-Zur Nursery
Beit Lehem
Haglilit Israel 36G15

Kern, Joseph J. Rose Nursery
Box 33
Mentor OH 44060

Kersbergen
Boskoop Holland

Kershaw, G.W.
Wahroonga NSW Australia

Kessler, Henry
Red Bank NJ

Ketten Bros.
Luxembourg

Kew Gardens
London England

Keynes, John
Salisbury England

Keynes, William & Co.
Salisbury England

Kiese, Herm. & Co.
Vieselbach-Erfurt Germany

Kikuchi, Rikichi
Japan

Kimbrew-Walter Rose
Growers
Rt. 2 Box 172
Grand Saline TX 75140

King, Benson E. (Gene)
3711 Caddo
Monroe LA 71203

Kingsdown Nursery
Santa Rosa CA

Kinsman, A.N. Inc.
Austin MN

Kirk, J.
Whittier CA

Kirkham, Gordon W.
Rose Cottage
Heaton Park Prestwich
Manchester England
M25 5SW

Kissel, Brim
Fairport NY

Kistler, Robert H.
Houston TX

Kittle, Wilfred
Pittsburgh PA

Klimenko, Mrs. V.N.
Nikita Botanical Garden
Yalta USSR

Klinken, J.
Silesia

Kluis, Anthony
Boskoop Holland

Kluis & Koning
Boskoop Holland

Klyn, Gerad K. Inc.
Mentor OH

Knight, A.T.
West Clandon
Surrey England

Knight, C.
Livermore CA

Knight, C.R.
Parklea NSW Australia

Knight, George & Sons
Homebush NSW Australia

Knight, John E. & Son
Wolverhampton England

Knights Nurseries
Hailsham Sussex England

Knupper Nursery
1801 North Rand Road
Palatine IL 60067

Kobayashi, Moriji
1056 Takanagi-Cho
Sano-Tochigi Japan

Koch, Anthony
Baltimore MD

Kokulensky
Berlin Germany

Komaba, R.N. Rose Nursery
1-2-2 Komaba
Meguroku Tokyo 153 Japan

Komatsu
Japan

Kono, Yoshito
Japan

Kordes, Hermann
West Germany

Kordes, Peter
West Germany

Kordes, Reimer
West Germany

Kordes, Wilhelm Sohne
Rosenstrasse 54
D 2206 Klein
Offenseth-Sparrieshoop
West Germany

Koster, D.A.
Boskoop Holland

Koster, M.M. & Sons
Boskoop Holland

Kraats, Jan
Boskoop Holland

Kramer, E.F.
Washington DC

Kraus, Max
Haslohe Holstein Germany

Kraus, V. Nurseries, Ltd.
Carlisle Ont. Canada
L0R 1H0

Krebs, Alfred
Montebello CA

Kreis, Franz A. Wwe.
Niederwalluf am Rhein
Germany

Kress, Edward
Baltimore MD

Krider Nursery, Inc.
P.O. Box 29
Middlebury IN 46540

Krieter, Otto
Chicago IL

Kriloff, Michel
Chemin des Brusquets
Quartier Saint-Maymes
06600 Antibes France

Kroeger, Henry
Fountain Square
7115 Greenback Lane
Citrus Heights CA 95621

Krowka, M.
Des Plaines IL

Krüger, Dr. D.
Freiburg Baden Germany

Krussmann, Dr. G.
West Germany

Kumar, S.
Trivandrum Kerala India

Kuramoto, H.
Salinas CA

Kuramoto, S.
San Lorenzo CA

KSG's Roses
177 V Main Road
Charmarajpet
Bangalore 560 018 India

-L-

Lacharme, Francois
Lyon Rhône France

La Florida
Eugenio Fojo
Bertendona Bilbao
Spain

Laffay, M.
Bellevue France

Lagoona Nursery
Brisbane Queensland
Australia

Laison, Fred L.
Council Bluffs IA

Lakeland Nurseries Sales
Unique Merchandise Mart
Bldg. 4
Hanover PA 17333

Lamb Nurseries
E. 101 Sharp Avenue
Spokane WA 99202

Lambert, Elie
Lyon Rhône France

Lambert, Peter
Trier Germany

Lamesch, J.B.
Doimmeldange Luxembourg

Lammerts, Dr. W.E.
Livermore CA

Lane
Berkhamsted England

Langbecker, C. & Sons
Bundaberg Queensland
Australia

Langdale, G.W.T.
18 Broadway
Copperfield Lincoln England
LN2 1SH

Laporte, J.A. Flowers
R.R. 1
Cumberland Ont. Canada
K0A 1S0

Laperriere, J.
Route Nationale 6 Chesnes
38 Saint-Quentin-Fallavier
France

Lartay
Bordeaux Gironde France

Latham, W.H.
Weston nr. Crewe Shewshire
England

Laugharn, H.F. Jr.
Los Angeles CA

Laveena Roses
Meerut India

Lavender, Joseph
Prestatyn Flintshire Wales

Laver, Keith G. & June
R.R. No. 3
Caledon East
Ont. Canada L0N 1E0

Law, Michael J.
15 Mallard Hill
Brickhill Bedford England
MK41 7QR

Lawrence, W.J.
Knaphill Woking
England

Lawrenson, T.A.
Newcastle-on-Tyne England

Lawrie, J.M.
Haqddington East Lothian
Scotland

Lawyer Nursery Inc.
950 Highway 200
West Plains MT 59859

Laxton Bros. Ltd.
Bedford England

Laxton & Bunyard Nursery
Brampton Huntingdon
England

Layham Nurseries &
    Garden Centre
Summerfield Straple
Canterbury Kent England
CT3 1LD

Layton, J.G.
Olean NY

Lea, R.F.G.
Duxford Mill
Nr. Cambridge England
OB2 4PT

Leal, N.A.
Turramurra NSW Australia

Le Blévenec, Ets. H.
Bois-Colombes Seine France

Le Cornu, Philip
High View
Jersey
Channel Islands

Lédéchaux
Villecresne France

Le Duc, Emil J.
Danville PA

Lee, J.
Hammersmith England

Leenders Bros.
Steyl-Tegelen Holland

Leenders, Gebr.
Steyl Holland

Leenders, Jan Export
    Nurseries
Tegelen Holland

Leenders, M. & Co.
Tegelen Holland

Lees, H.
Kewsbury Yorks England

LeGrice, E.B. Roses
Norwich Road North
Walsham
Norfolk England NR28 0DR

Leidy, Charles
Austin TX

Leighty, R.S.
Gainesville OH

Lemire, Leo
343 Watkins
Windsor Ont. Canada
N9C 2X9

Lemire, Walter
Roses by Walter Lemire
R.R. 1
Oldcastle Ont. Canada
N0R 1L0

Lemon, Fred H. & Co.
Richmond IN

Lemrow, Dr. Maynard W.
10135 Tres Lagos Court
Spring Valley CA 95078

Lennard, T. Barrett
Australia

Lens, Louis
Mechelbaan 147
B-2860 O.L.V. Waver Belgium

Leon, Charles F., Sr.
14134 NE Siskiyou Ct.
Portland OR 97230

Leonard, A.M., Inc.
6665 Spiker Road
Piqua OH 45356

Lester Rose Gardens
Watsonville CA

Letts, G.F. & Sons
Semer Suffolk England

Letzeburger Rosenferenn
51 Ave. du 10
Septembre Luxembourg

Levavasseur & Sons
Orléans Loiret France

Lévêque, P.
Ivry France

Levet, Antoine
Lyon Rhône France

Levet, Francois
Lyon Rhône France

Ley, F.
Windlesham Surrey
England

L'Haÿ
Roseraie de l'Haÿ
Bourg-la-Reine France

Liabaud, Jean
Lyon Rhône France

Liberty Hill Nurseries
Stannington Sheffield
England

Liggett, Myron T.
Liggett's Rose Nursery
1206 Curtiss Avenue
San Jose CA 95125

Liggit, C. U. Co.
Philadelphia PA

Lille, Leonard
Lyon-Villeurbanne
France

Lilley, George
Cippenham Slough Bucks
England

Limberlost Roses
7304 Forbes Avenue
Van Nuys CA 91406

Limes Rose Nursery
Kelly Lifton
Devon England PL16 0HQ

Limpert, Anthony S.
Rochester NY

Lincoln Nursery Co.
Pittsburgh PA

Lindecke, Herm
Remagen Germany

Lindner, Richard
South Africa

Lindquist, Robert V., Jr.
P.O. Box 413
43135 Acacia
Hemet CA 92343

Lindquist, Robert V., Sr.
26119 Dumont Road
Hemet CA 92343

Linscott, T.D.
Loomis CA

Lippiatt, W.E.
Otahuhu Auckland
New Zealand

Lissemore, J.D.
Tenafly NJ

Little Gems Nursery
2972 Unberland Drive
Dovaville GA 30340

Loaney, P.
Australia

Lobner, Max
Bonn Germany

Lociteim Roses
P.O. Box 25
Arcturus Zimbabwi
South Africa

Logee's Greenhouses
55 North Street
Danielson CT 06239

Lohberg, Henry
Lomira WI

Lohse & Schubert
Augermund
Germany

Lone Star Nursery
Tyler TX

Longley, George & Sons
Rainham Kent England

Longley, Dr. L.E.
University of Minnesota
St. Paul MN

Looymans, P.J. & Co.
Oudenbosch Holland

Lorenzen, Frederick C.
2080 Maple Street
Wantagh NY 11793

Lothop, Grover C.
Mobridge SD

Lottin, Victor
Avranches Manche
France

Lovett, J.T. Nursery
Little Silver NJ

Lovett, L.C.
Diamond State Nurseries
Little Silver NJ

Low, Stuart & Co.
Enfield Middlesex England

Lowe, Malcolm M.
Lowe's Own Root Rose Nursery
6 Sheffield Road
Nashua NH 03062

Lowe & Shawyer
Uxbridge
England

Lowe, William & Son, Ltd.
Beeston
Nottington England

Lower Rangitikei Rose
Society
New Zealand

Lowman, Abner
Elmira NY

Lucas, C. C.
Dodpits House
Nr. Yarmouth Isle of Wight
England

Lucknow, H.A.L.
India

Ludwig, C.F.
Beloit WI

Ludwig's Roses Ltd.
P.O. Box 28165 Sunnyside
0132 Pretoria Republic of
South Africa

Luigi, Lorenzi
Ventimiglia Italy

Lum, Carleton
Chastham NJ

Lundstad, Arne
Agricultural
Universitry of Norway
Dept. of Dendiology & Nursery
P.O. Box 16
N-1432 AAS-NLH
Norway

Luxembourg Rose
Society
Luxembourg

Lykke, Ellen & Hugo
Honebjergvej 31 Soby
8543 Horslet Denmark

Lynch, T.
Wasco CA

Lyon, Lyndon Greenhouse
14 Mutchler Street
Dolgeville NY 13329-0249

-M-

Maarse, G.
Aalsmeer Holland

Maarse, J.D. & Zonen B.V.
Handels Kwekerijen
Oosteinderweg 489
1432 B.J. Aalsmeer Holland

Maass, Conrad
Rellingen Germany

Macara, Rev. A.
Ervine Ayrshire
England

MacHugh Nusery
Eltopia WA 99330

Mackay, Ian F.
West Chicago IL

MacLellan, Alexander
Newport RI

Macleod, Major C.A.
Elm Cottage Dalvey
Forres England IV36 OSP

Macres, Thomas
Patchogue NY

Magic Moment Minatures
P.O. Box 499
Rockville Center NY 11571

Maitland Nursery
R.R. 1
Brockville Ont. Canada

Malandrone Michele
Italy

Mallerin, Charles
Varces Allieres-et-Risset Isère
France

Maltagliati, Mark
Ninomiya Nursery Co.
506 Brookside Drive
Richmond CA 94801

Manawatu Rose Society
New Zealand

Manda, E.A. Jr.
Pleasant Hill MO

Manda, W.A.
South Orange NJ

Mander, George
2232 Gale Avenue
Coquitlam
BC Canada V3K 2Y8

Maney, Prof. T.J.
Ames IA

Manisuno, Ada
Poggio, San Reno Italy

Manisuno, Quinto
Poggio, San Reno
Italy

Mansion Nursery
Wasco CA

Maoz Haim Rose Nursery
10845 Maoz
Haim Israel

Marciel Stanley C.
607 St. Andrews Drive
Aptos CA 95003

Maréchal
Angers France

Marest
Paris France

Margottin, M.
Bourg-la-Reine France

Mari, Antoine
Nice Alpes-Maritimes France

Marks, H. Esq.
Waterend Hemel Hemstead
Herts England

Marlin, G.
Pennant Hills NSW Australia

Marriott, George
Carlton
Nottingham England

Marsh, Edward E.
Pasadena CA

Marshall, H.H.
Resarch Station
P.O. Box 3001 Morden
Manitoba Canada ROG 1JO

Marshall, James
Scarlsbrick Ormaskirk
England

Marshall, Dr. O.C.
Watsonville CA

Marsh's Nursery
Pasadena CA

Martin
Dundee Scotland

Martin & Forbes
Portland OR

Martin, J.
Rugby
Warwickshire England

Martin, W.A.
Ashburton Victoria Australia

Martinez, John
Glendale AZ

Masek, Raymond
Kirkwood MO

Mason, A.L.
Fielding
New Zealand

Mason, Frank & Sons Ltd.
P.O. Box 155
Feilding New Zealand

Mason, J.A.
Burlingame CA

Mason, L.M.
Fincham Kings Lynn
Norfolk England

Mason, P.
Auckland New Zealand

Mata de Basso
Gavá Barcelona Spain

Maton, Paul
Pana IL

Matthews, T.J.
Wanganui New Zealand

Mattock, John Ltd.
The Rose Nurseries
Nuneham Courtenay
Oxford England OX9 9PY

Mattock, R.H.
England

Mauget
Orléans Loiret France

May, Earl Seed & Nursery
Co.
Shenandoah IA 51603

May, H.B.
Summit NJ

Mayhew, I.T.
Newton Abbot Devon
England

Mayle, William John
504 Falmer Road
Woodingden Brighton Sussex
England

MB Farm Miniature Roses,
Inc.
Jamison Hill Road
Clinton Corners NY 12514

McCann, Sean
173 Clonkeen Road
Blackrock Co. Dublin Ireland

McCannon, Charles A.
Mount Clemens MI

McCarthy, Rosemary
Stapleford Lane
Toton Beeston
Nottingham England

McClung, H.L. Nursery
Tyler TX

McConnell Nurseries, Inc.
Port Burwell
Ont. Canada N0J 1TO

McCorkle Nurseries
1757 Gordon Highway
Augusta GA 30904

McCreadie, K.
Southend-on-Sea England

McCullough, J. Charles
Seed Co.
Cincinnati OH

McCummings, Edward
West Grove PA

McDaniel, Earl E.
McDaniel's Miniature Roses
7523 Zemco Street
Lemon Grove CA 92045

McDaniel, G.K.
California

McDonald, William C.
San Angelo TX

McFadden, S.E. Jr.
Somerville TN

McGorum, Robert T.
Natick MA

McGredy, P.
New Zealand

McGredy, Samuel IV
New Zealand

McGredy, Samuel
New Zealand

McGredy, Samuel & Son,
Ltd.
Royal Nurseries
Portadown Ireland

McGredy Roses
International
130-B Beach Road
Castor Bay Auckland 9 New
Zealand

McGuire, Lou Patio &
Garden Shop, Inc.
1200 State Line Road
West Southaven MS 38671

McIntosh, J.T.
Prahran Australia

McIntyre, James
James McIntyre Roses
Rose Cottage
Main Street
North Leverton
Retford Notts. England
DN22 0AN

McKenzie, T.U.
Clan New Zealand

McKirdy, J.M.
Cambooya Furnace
Argyll Scotland

McLellan, E.W. Co.
Colma CA

McMillan, Thomas G.
3962 Longmeadow Drive
Trenton MI 48183

McTeer, F.
Madeley Crew
Cheshire England

McTeer, Gilbert
10 John Offley Road
Madeley Crew
Cheshire England

McTureous Rose Nursery
Rt. 1 Box 14
Umatilla FL 32784

Mea Nursery
P.O. Box 668
Lindale TX 75771

Meadowlands Nursery Ltd.
7370 Mississauga Road
R.R. 3 Mississauga
Ont. Canada L5M 2B3

Mease, Frank
Maugansville MD

Meilland, Alain
France

Meilland & Co., SNC
France

Meilland, Francis, France

Meilland Et Cie
134 BD. Francis Meilland
06601 Antibes France

Meilland, Mrs. Marie-Louise
France

Meilland-Richardier
50 rue Depèret
69160 Tassin-la-Demi-Lune
France

Meilland Roses
France

Mell, A.J. & Son
Forrestville Western Australia

Mellinger's Inc.
2310 West South Range Road
North Lima OH 44452-9731

Melville Bros.
Purley Reading England

Melville Nurseries Pty, Inc.
Melville Nurseries
40 Mason Mill Road
Carmel 6076
Western Australia

Meneve, Ivan
Ministerie Van Landbouw
Caritasstraat
9230 Melle Belgium

Mercer, A.
Markinch Fife England

Meredith, Earnest A.
12757 Barrett Lane
Santa Ana CA 92705

Mee, Oliver
Wilmslow Cheshire England

Mermet, Louis
Lyon-Montplaisir Rhône
France

Merritt Frank
Hamilton MT

Merryweather, H. & Sons Ltd.
Southwell Notts England

Mesman, Nicholas
Madison OH

Meyer, C.
Cleves OH

Meyer, E.F.H.
Nahoon Valley East London
England

Meyer, H.M.
Harlingen TX

Michelis, Dorothy
P.O. Box 369
Auburn CA 95603

Michell, Henry F. Co.
Philadelphia PA

Michigan Bulb Company
1950 Waldorf N.W.
Grand Rapids MI 49550

Michigan Miniature Roses
45951 Hull Rd.
Belleville MI 48111

Middlebrooks, F.L.
Forest Park GA

Miellez
Esquermess France

Mike's Roses
6807 Smithway Drive
Alexandria VA 22307

Miles Gardener
Pomological Institute
Troja Czechoslovakia

Miller, A.I.
St. John's Hill, Seven Oaks
Kent England

Miller, Andrew J.
Montebello CA

Miller, Dr. Frederick
46 Manchester Lane
Stony Brook NY 11790

Miller, J.
Victoria Australia

Milner, William
58 Broadway
West Dormanstown
Redcar Cleveland England

Miniature Plant Kingdom
4125 Harrison Grade Road
Seabastopol CA 95472

Miniature Plant World
45638 Elder Avenue
Box 7 Sardis
British Columbi Canada
V2R 1A5

Miniature Rose Company,
200 Rose Ridge
Greenwood SC 29647

Minier, Ets.
Angers Maine-et-Loire France

Mini Farm
Rt. 1, Box 501
Bon Aqua TN 37025

Mini Rose Nursery
P.O. Box 873
Guelph Ont. Canada
N1H 6M6

Mini-Roses
P.O. Box 4255 Station A
Dallas TX 75208

Mini Roses of Texas
P O Box 267
Denton TX 76202

Minneapolis Floral Co.
Minneapolis MN

Miyawaki, H.
Hiroshima Japan

Mizen, F. & G. Ltd.
Effingham Surrey England

Moffet, William B.
Gustine CA

Moglia. Tom
34 Donna Lane West
Wallkill NY 12589

Mohr
Copenhagen Denmark

Molder, Wiley A.
5506 San Juan Avenue
Citrus Heights CA 95610

Molina, M.
Santa Ana CA

Moller, V.A.
Queensland Australia

Mondial Roses
Malegem Belgium

Mondial Roses
Orléans France

Mon Reve Nursery
Magaliesburg Transvaal
South Africa

Montebello Rose Co., Inc.
California

Montgomery, Alex
Hadley MA

Montgomery Co.
Hadley MA

Moore, Frank
Chatham NJ

Moore Nursery & Floral Co.
Tyler TX

Moore, Ralph S.
Moore Miniature Roses
2519 E. Noble Avenue
Visalia CA 93277

Moorhouse, L.
Skelmanthorne Yorks.
England

Morden Experimental Farm
Morden Manitoba Canada

Morden Nurseries, Ltd.
P.O. Box 1270 Morden
Manitoba Canada ROG 1JO

Mordigan Evergreen
    Nursery
San Fernando CA

Moreau, F.
Lyon Rhône France

Moreau-Robert
Angers France

Moreira da Silva, Alfredo &
    Fos. Lda.
Rua de D. Manuel 11
55-4000 Porto Portugal

Morey, Dr. Dennison
555 Irwin Lane
Santa Rosa CA 95401

Morgan, William P.
Indianapolis IN

Morlet
Avon France

Moro, Luciano
San Remo Italy

Morris, Sir Cedric
England

Morris, Theodore
Van Nuys CA

Morse, Henry & Sons
Brundall Norwich England

Morse Roses
Herdfordshire
England

Morton's Rose Nursery
Wilmslow Cheshire England

Moss, Leslie
New Zealand

Mosselman & Terreehorst
Aalsmeer Holland

Motose, Dr. Thomas E.
Fairport NY

Moulden, Dr. A.
Unley South Africa

Moulin, H.
Epinay-sur-Orge Seine-et-Oise
France

Moulin-Epinay
Seine-et-Oise France

Moulton-Jones, Mrs. A.E.
Wambeeral NSW Australia

Mt. Arbor Nursery
Shenandoah IA

Mount, George & Sons
Canterbury England

Muellers Nursery
Rt. 4 Box 121, South Avenue
Chippewa Falls WI 54729

Mungia, F.A., Sr.
P.O. Box 338
McFarland CA 93250

Mühle, Arpad
Temesvar Roumania

Müller, Dr. F.
Weingarten Germany

Müller, J.F.
Rellingen Germany

Münch & Haufe
Dresden-Leuben Germany

Munger, Mrs. Clark
Zeneth WA

Munné, Blas
Gavá Barcelona Spain

Munné, Manuel y Joaquin
Gavá Barcelona Spain

Münster, J.
Ellerhoop Germany

Murley, John J.
37 Anderson Street, Bendigo
Victoria 3550 Australia

Murmu, L.C.
New Delhi India

Murray & Hawken
Auckland New Zealand

Murray, Nola
73 Anzac Parade
Wanganui New Zealand

Murray, William B.
Atco NJ

Murrell, Edwin Ltd.
Shrewbury England

Murrell, R.
Hemel Hempstead
Herts England

Myer & Samtmann
Chestnut Hill
Philadelphia PA

-N-

Nabonnand, Clement
Alpes-Maritimes
France

Nabonnand, Gilbert
Golfe Juan
Alpes-Maritimes
France

Nabonnand, Paul
Golfe Juan
Alpes-Maritimes
France

Nagashima
Japan

Nakashima, K. Nursery
1548 Daily Court
San Leandro CA 94577

Nakashima, Toshio
1548 Daily Court
San Leandro CA 94577

Nanz & Neuner
Louisville KY

Nath, P.
Rana Pratap Marg
Lucknow 226001 UP India

National Botancial
    Research Institute
Rana Pratap Marg
Licknow 226001 UP India

National Rose Society of
    Australia
271-B Belmore Road
North Balwyn
Victoria 3104 Australia

National Rose Society of
    New Zealand
P.O. Box 66
17 Erin Street
Bunnythorpe
Palmerston North
New Zealand

Nauman Nursery
4101 Pennsylvania Avenue
Dubuque IA 52001

Nederlandse
    Rozenvereniging
Kievitweg 5 5752 PT Deurne
Holland

Neil, J.
Victoria Australia

Neiman-Marcus
Maine & Ervay
Dallas TX 75201

Neosho Nurseries
P.O. Box 550
Neosho MO 64850

Neuhoff, H.
Elmshorn Germany

Neuner, Harry A.
Erie PA

Nevo, Motke
10845 Maoz
Haim Israel

Newberry, C. & Son
Knebworth
Herts England

New Zealand Nurserymen's
Association
Box 31-045
Lower Hutt New Zealand

New Zealand Plant
Varieties Journal
Lincoln, New Zealand

New Zealand Rose Society
New Zealand

Nicol
Lannion
Cote du Nord France

Nicolas, J.H.
New York

Ninomiya Nursery Co.
506 Brookside Drive
Richmond CA 94801

Nipoti, Poggio
San Reno Italy

Noack, A.
Berlin Germany

Nobbs, Kenneth J.
R.D. 2 Tekauwhata Road
00226 New Zealand

Noisette, Philip
Charleston SC

Nonin, Auguste & Fils
Chatillon
Seine France

Nor'East Miniature Roses
58 Hammond Street
Rowley MA 01969

Norfolk Nursery
Dereham England

Norges Landbruks-hogskole
Vollebekk Norway

Norman, A.
Wisteria Mormandy
Surrey England

Northern Ireland Rose
Society
Belfast, Northern Ireland

Northfield, G.
5 Manor Park Histon
Cambridge England CB4 4JT

North Hill Nursery
Chilham
Surrey England

Northwest Rose Growers
1567 Guild Road
Woodland WA 98674

Norweigian Rose Society
Postboks 9008
Vaterland 0134
Oslo 1 Norway

Nostell Priory Rose Gardens
Nostell Nr. Wakefield
West Yorkshire England
WF4 1QE

Notcutts, Nurseries, Ltd.
Woodbridge
Suffolk England IP12 4AF

Novitchkov
USSR

NRS
National Rose Society
NSW Australia

NRS
National Rose Society
of South Australia

NRS
National Rose Society
Victoria Australia

Nyveldt, A.A.
Boskoop Holland

-O-

Obertello, Orlando
Oakland CA

O'Brian, J.E.
Rockhamton
Queensland Australia

O'Briens Nursery
1111 Memorial Blvd.
Murfreesboro TN 37130

O'Connell, Mrs. N.
Penshurst
NSW Australia

Ofman, A.
Aalsmeer Holland

Ogawa, Isamu
Japan

Ogden, Edna C.
30 Rosemont Drive
Little Rock AR 72204

Oger, A.
Caen France

Ogilvie, William Donald
Belmont
104 High Street
West Matling Maid Store
Kent England ME19 6NE

Ohata, Hatsuo
Japan

Ohlhus, George
West Grove PA

Ohlson, John
1695 Matheson Road
Concord CA 94521

O.K. Roses
Ferriby High Road
North Ferriby
North Humberside England
HU14 3LA

Olds, L.L. Seed Company
Madison WI 53707

Olesen, Mogens & Pernille
Olesen
Postbox 44 Kellerisvej 64
3490 Kvistgaard
Denmark

Oliver, F.
Buffalo NY

Oliver, H.
Bramshott
Liphook
Hants England

Oliver, W.G.
Slough
Bucks England

O'Neal, Conrad
Encinitas CA

Onodera, F.T.
Motobuto
Urawa Japan

Onodera, Susumu S.
48 Kami-Okubo
Urawa 338 Japan

Onodera, Dr. Toru F.
48 Kami-Okubo
Urawa 338 Japan

Opdebeeck, A. Sons
Putte-lez-Malines
Belgium

Orard, J.,
Feyzin Isere France

Oregon Miniature Roses Inc.
8285 S.W. 185th Avenue
Beaverton OR 97007

Ormerod, M.
Blackburn
Lancs. England

Orr, Rudolph F.
Rt. 1 Box 21 A
Edgemoor SC 29712

Ortega, Carlos
537 Brookside Drive
Richmond CA 94801

Osburn, Dr. William
4831 Broad Brook Drive
Bethesda MD 20814

Ota, Kaichiro,
Japan

Ottawa Research Station,
    Research Branch
Ottawa Ont. Canada
K1A 0C6

Owen, Fred
4 Whitewalls
Hewelsfield St. Brinuels
Glos. England GL15 6UN

Owen, Richard Nursery
2300 E. Lincoln Street
Bloomington IL 61701

Owens, H.B.
Tathra NSW Australia

-P-

Pacific Nursery
Manly Queensland Australia

Pacific Rose Co.
Los Angeles CA

Padella Rose Co.
Los Angeles CA

Padilla, John Robert
San Francisco CA

Padrosa, José
San Justo Desvern
Barcelona Spain

Page, Courtney
Hayward's Heath
Sussex England

Pajotin-Chedane
Maitre-Ecole
Angers France

Pal, Dr. B. P.
P-11
Hauzkhas Enclave New
Delhi 16 India

Pallek, Carl & Son Nurseries
Box 137
Virgil Ont. Canada LOS 1TO

Palmer, A. W. & Sons
    Garden Centers, Ltd.
P. O. Box 1 Glen Eden
Auckland New Zealand

Palmer, Harry E.
Portland OR

Palmer, R. & Co.
West Pennant Hills
NSW Australia

Pan American Bulb Co.
13700 100th Avenue
Surry BC Canada

Paolino, Marie-Louise,
    France

Papandrea, John
995 Old Northern Road
Dural 2158 Australia

Paramount Nursery
West Grove PA

Parhissa, Lorenzo
San Feliu de Llobregat
Barcelona Spain

Park, Bertram
Pinner
Middlesex England

Park, Mrs. Frances
Wamberal
NSW Australia

Park, George W. Seed Co.
254 Cokebury Road
Greenwood SC 29647

Parkes, M.H.
Dural
NSW Australia

Parmentier
Enghien Belgium

Parmentier, J. Roses
Bayport L.I. NY

Parnass Rose Nursery
Kataoka
Nadasaki-cho
Kojima-gun
Okayama-ken
Japan

Partain, Joe
58 Ward Circle
Aiken SC 29801

Pasley, M.J.H.
Karori
Wellington
New Zealand

Pasquil, Thomas
North Vancouver BC
Canada

Patil, B.K., Bangalore,
India

Patterson, J.W.
Patterson Roses
6518 Kernel Street
Houston TX 77087

Patterson, Randell E.
4905 Glenlea Drive
Texarkana AR 75502

Pattoloo's Nursery
Hastings New Zealand

Paul, George & Son
Cheshunt Herts England

Paul, William & Son Ltd.
Waltham Cross
Herts England

Paulen Park Nursery
Lindah Road
Tinana Maryborouth
Queensland Australia

Pavlick, Mike
1820 Washington Street
Allentown PA 18104

Pawsey, Roger
305 Mile End Road
Colchester Essex England
CO4 5EB

Payless Nursery
400 Hamilton Street
Carlsbad NM 88220

Payne, A. J.
42 Linden Avenue
Kidderminster England
DY10 3AA

Payne, R.
Tyler TX

Pearce, C.A.
Kelly Lifton Devon England
PL16 OHQ

Pearson, R.T.
c/o RNRS
St. Albans England

Pecollo, I.
San Remo Italy

Peden, G.H.
Epping N.A.
West Australia

Pedigree Nursery
New Zealand

Peirce, E.A.
Wathan MA

Pekmez, Paul
La Petite Pierre
67290 Loingen seer Moder
France

Pemberton, Rev. J.H.
Havering atte-Bower
Essex England

Pencil, Paul S.
5665 Dietrick Jordan Pike
Springfield OH 45502

Pennine Nurseries
J. & W. Blackburn, Ltd.
Pennine Nurseries
Shelley Huddersfield England
HD8 8LG

Penny, Antoine
Clermont-Ferrand
Puy-de-Dome France

Penzance, Lord
Eashing Park England

Pepinieres Charevoix, Inc.
C.P. 818 La Malbaie Cte.
Charlevoix
Quèbec Canada GOJ 1JO

Pepinieres Et Roseraies G.
Delbard
Cedex France

Pepinieres Et Roseraies
Gaujard
Isère France

Pepinieres Louis Lens
Mechelbaan 147
B-2860 O.L.V. Waver Belgium

Pepinieres Raymond Houle
R.R. 1 St. Albert
Compte Atabaska Quèbec
Canada JOA 1EO

Perennial Garden
128 108th Street
Saskatoon Sask. Canada S7N 1P4

Perkins, C.H.
Newark NY

Perkins, H.S.
Portland OR

Permenter, Mrs. P.S.
Los Alamitos CA

Pernet-Ducher, Joseph
Venissieux-les-Lyon
Rhône France

Pernet, Père
Lyon Rhône France

Perron, W. H. & Co., Ltd.
515 Boulv. Labelle Laval
Quèbec Canada H7V 2T3

Perry, Anthony, 40734
Mayberry Avenue
Hemet CA 92344

Perry, Astor
Perry Roses
1201 Pineview Drive
Raleigh NC 27606

Peters, Lincoln & Norman
Hempstead NY

Peterson & Deering
Scappoose OR

Peterson, V.
Peterson's Planteskole
Love Denmark

Pfander, J.
Wurtemburg Germany

Pfitzer, Wilhelm
Stuttgart
Wurtemburg Germany

Phelan, Stephen Rice
Memphis TN

Phillip, B.
Aldermaston Road Pamber
End
Busingstoke Hants. England

Phillip, J. & Son, Ltd.
Aldermaston Road Pamber
End
Busingstoke Hants. England

Phillips, R.A.
Minneapolis MN

Philp, J.B. & Son Ltd.
Elm Park Garden Centre
Pamber End
Basingstoke Hants England
RG26 5QW

Pickering Nurseries, Inc.
670 Kingston Road (Highway
2)
Pickering Ont. Canada L1V
1A6

Pierce, Joshua
Washington DC

Pierson, A.N. Inc.
Cromwell CT

Pierson, F.R.
Tarrytown NY

Pierson, P.R.
Ossing NY

Pikiewicz, J.
Erie PA

Pin-Blanchon
Léon Pin-Michel
St.-Genis-Laval France

Pinchbeck, William E.
Guilford CT

Pineau, Jean Marc
Antibes France

Pixie Treasures Miniature
Roses
4121 Prospect Avenue
Yorba Linda CA 92686

Plant Adoption Center
12702 N. 56th Street
Temple Terrace FL 33617

Plant Hybridizers of
California
Sebastopol CA

Plant Varieties Office
P.O. Box 24
Lincoln New Zealand

Plantier
Lyon Rhône France

Plumpton, E.
9 Quatermaine House
Whitefield Woking England

Podesta, John A.
San Leandro CA

Polish Society of Rose
Fanciers
Warazawa B 6
Browiewakigo 19 Mt Poland

Poole, K.E.
c/o RNRS
St. Albans England

Poole, Lionel
13 Turnham Green
Penylan Cardiff Wales
England CF3 7DL

Poor, Cuyler
913 Lake Boone Trail
Raleigh NC 27607

Port Stockton Nursery
2910 East Main Street
Stockton CA 95205

Portchester Nurseries
Calais House St. Martins
Guerney CI England

Portemer
Gentilly France

Porter, J.M.
Houston TX

Portland Nursery
Shrewbury England

Portland Rose Society
Portland OR

Poulsen, Dines T.
Denmark

Poulsen, Niels Dines
Denmark

Poulsen Roser APS
Hillerodvej 49
DK-3480 Fredensborg
Denmark

Poulsen, Svend
Denmark

Poulsen's Planteskole APS
Denmark

Poulsen's Roses
Denmark

Powell, George
29 Front Street
Acomb York. England
402 3BW

Pradel, Henry
Lyon Rhône France

Pradhan, S.K.
India

Prairie Garden Center
Highway 1 North
Mt. Vernon VA 52314

Praskac, F.
Freundorf Czechoslovakia

Premier Rose Gardens
Des Plaines IL

Preston, Miss Isabella
Central Exp. Farm
Ottawa Canada

Priestley, J.L.
271-B Belmore Road
North Balwyn
3104 Victoria Australia

Primavera
Chemin de la Banne
83600 Frejus France

Prince, George
Longworth Berks England

Prince Nursery
Flushing NY

Prinz, Josef
Wolfsberg Austria

Prior, D. & Son
Colchester Essex England

Privat, B. & Fils
Ste.-Germaine-Bruges
France

Privat, J.
Ste.-Germaine-Bruges
France

Proctor, R.W. & Sons Ltd.
Chesterfield England

Prof. F. Roses
Benmore, Transvaal
South Africa

Proietti, Joseph
San Leandro CA

Prosser, D. & Son
Gloucester England

-Q-

Quackenbush, V.L.
Medford OR

Quaim, D.
Hazerswoude Holland

Quintin, G. H.
La Fontaine
St. Saviours Guernsey

Quétier
Meaux France

Quinn, L.
Rochdale Brisbane
Queensland Australia

-R-

Radmore, A.
Castle Lane
Bournemouth
England

Radway Roses, Ltd.
Skelmersdale
Lancs England

Raffel, Frank C.
Port Stockton Nursery
Stockton CA

Rainbow Roses
433 Scoresby Road
Ferntree Gully
Victoria 3156 Australia

Ram, Dr. B.
New Delhi India

Rambaud
Lyon Rhône France

Rasmussen's Ltd.
Wanganui New Zealand

Ratcliffe, R. & E.
Chilton Didcot
Berkshire England

Rauf, A.
India

Ravensberg, Maurice
Boskoop Holland

Ravine, M.D.
New Philadelphia OH

Rearsby Roses Ltd.
Melton Road
Rearsby Leicester England
LE7 8YP

Reasoner, E.
Wasco CA

Reed, Harry R. Jr.
2302 Northview Dr. S.W.
Roanoke VA 24015

Reed & Son
High Beach Loughton
Essex England

Reeces, A. & Co.
Old Catton
Norwich England

Reid, Dr.
Siilver Park
Sask. Canada

Reinberg, Peter
Chicago IL

Reinold, H.
Dortmund Germany

Reiter, V.
San Francisco CA

Reliance Nursery
Tyler TX

Remarks Orchard & Nursery
Box 129
Kingsville Ont. Canada
N94 2E8

Rennie, Burce F.
R.R. 2
Elora Ont. Canada
NOB 1SO

Restani, Albert J.
San Francisco CA

Reymond, L.
Lyon-Villeurbanne
Rhône France

Reynolds Rosery
New Zealand

Reynolds, Ted
C/O P.O. Waihola
South Otago
New Zealand

Reynolds', S. Farm
Norwalk CT

Reynolds, W.H.
Levin New Zealand

Rhodesia Rose Society
Rhodesia

Rice Bros.
Geneva NY

Richardier, C.
50 rue Depèret
69160 Tassin-la-Demi-Lune
France

Richmond Nursery
Richmond Ont. Canada
KOA 2ZO

Ries, Fr.
Durlach Germany

Riethmuller, F.L.
Turramurra
Sydney NSW Australia

Rijksstation voor
  Sierplantenteelt
Ministerie van Landvouw
Caritasstraat 17
9230 Melle Belgium

Ringdahl, Iva
Rome NY

Risley, E.B.
University of New Hampshire
Durham NH

Rivers, Thomas & Son Ltd.
Sawbridgeworth
Herts England

RNRS
Royal National Rose Society
Chiswell Green Lane
St. Albans
Hertfordshire England

Robert, M.
Biarritz
Basses-Pyrénées
France

Robert et Moreau
Angers France

Roberts, G.
c/o RNRS
St. Albans England

Roberts, P.D.
Long Eaton Notts
England

Roberts, Stanley B.
Madison NJ

Robichon, Marcel
Pithiviers Loiret France

Robins, W.
Shepparton Victoria
Australia

Robinson, H.
Australia

Robinson, Herbert
Burbage
Hinckley Tews England

Robinson, Thomas Ltd.
Calais House
St. Martins Guerney CI
England

Rock, Mrs. W. E.
Hitchin, Herts., England

Roddy's Miniature Roses,
  Inc.
407 Morris Avenue
Monroe, LA 71202

Rodgers, Shafner R.
1519 North St.
Augustine Callas TX 75217

Roehrs, Julius Co.
Rutherford NJ

Roeser
Crecy-en-Brie France

Roger, R.V., Ltd.
The Nurseries
Pickering North Yorkshire
England

Rokos, B.J.
Detroit MI

Roland, Phillip H.
Nahant MA

Rosas Dot
San Feliu de Llobregat
Barcelona Spain

Rose Acres
6641 Crystal Boulevard
Diamond Springs CA 95619

Rose Barni-Pistoia

Rosecroft Nursery
Langley Prairie BC Canada

Rose, Evelyn M.
15633 Horace Street
Granada Hills CA 91344

Rose Farm Corp
Madison NJ

Rose-France
Feyzin Isère France

Rose Garden & Mini Rose
  Nursery
P.O. Box 203
Cross Hill SC 29332

Roseglen Nursery
Rochdale Brisbane
Queensland Australia

Rosehill Farm
Gregg Neck Road, P.O. Box 406
Galena MD 21635

Rosehill Gardens, Inc.
9300 Holmes Street
Kansas City MO 64131

Rose Hill Roses
5 Kirra Street Erina
NSW 2250 Australia

Rose Hybridizers Association
3245 Wheaton Road
Horseheads NY 14845

Roseland Nursery
Norwich Road
North Walsham Norfolk
England NR28 0DR

Roselawn Gardens
Nashville TN

Rosemary Roses
The Nurseries
P.O. Box No. 15 Stapleford
Lane Toton
Beeston Nottingham
England NG9 5FD

Rosemont Nurseries
124 Stanton Road
Sandiacre Notts. England

Rosemont Nursery
Tyler TX

Rosemount Nursery
Hull England

Rosenbluth, E.M.
Wallingford PA

Rosen, H.R.
University Arkansas
Fayetteville AR

Rosenkultren
5605 Dottikon AG
Switzerland

Rosen, L.P. & Son
Carlingford NSW Australia

Rosenplanteskole
Honebjergvej 31 Soby
8543 Horslet Denmark

Rosen Tantau
Tornescher Weg 13
Postfach 1344
2082 Uetersen West Germany

Roseraies E. Tschanz
Route de Chavannes 61
1007 Lausanne Switzerland

Roseraies Gaujard, S.A.
38 Route de Lyon
69320 Feyzin Isere France

Roseraies Hauser
2028 Vaumarcus
Neuchatel-Suisse Switzerland

Roses of Yesterday & Today
802 Brown's Valley Road
Watsonville CA 95076-0398

Rose Society of Northern
Ireland
13 Glen Eber Park
Belfast Northern Ireland
BT4 2JJ

Rose Society of Zimbabwe
P.O. Box HG 366
Highlands Harare Zimbabwe
Rhodesia

Roseway Nursery
P.O. Box 269
1567 Guild Road
Woodland WA 98674

Rose World Originals
1656 N. Second Street
El Cajon CA 92021

Ross, A. & Son
St. Andrews Tce.
P.O. Box 23
Willunga 5th S.A. 5172
Australia

Ross, Mrs. Frank L.
Nashville TN

Ross Roses
St. Andrews Tce.
P.O. Box 23
Willunga 5th S.A. 5172
Australia

Roussel
Montpelier France

Rovinski, Margaret E.
12757 Barrett Lane
Santa Ana CA 92705

Rowe, Harry L.
Richmond VA

Rowley, A.D.
c/o RNRS
St. Albans England

Royal Horticultural Society
Wisley Surrey England

Royal National Rose Society
Chiswell Green Lane
St. Albans
Hertfordshire England
AL2 3NR

Royer, George
Versailles Seine-et-Oise France

Royon, R.
Mougins France

Ruehl-Wheeler Nursery Co.
San Jose CA

Rumwood Nurseries
Langley Maidstone
Kent England ME17 3ND

Rumsey, Roy H.
P.O. Box 1 Dural
NSW 2158 Australia

Rupert, Kim
16945 Blackhawk #4
Granada Hills CA 91344

Rusnock, Ann M.
6982 Hunter Place
Boulder CO 80301

Russ, George
Victoria Australia

Ruston, D.W.
Renmark
South Australia

Rusicka's Inc.
Chatham NJ

Ryan, Glen H.
Richmond IN

-S-

St. Bridget Nurseries, Ltd.
Old Rydon Lane
Exeter Devon England EX2
7JY

St. Leonards Farm
Newtown PA

Samtmann Bros.
Chestnut Hill
Philadelphia PA

Samtmann, Charles
Chestnut Hill
Philadelphia PA

Samuels, S.J.
New Zealand

Sanday, John (Roses) Ltd.
Over Lane
Almondsbury Bristol
England BS12 4DA

Sande, J.V.D.
England

Sanders, Harold T.
Tyler TX

Sanders & Sons
St. Albans England

Sandy, D.L. Roses Ltd.
North Kilworth
Rugby England

San Remo Stazione
Sperimentale di Floricoltura
San Remo Italy

Sansum, W.H.J.
Shirehampton Bristol
England

Saunders, Dr. W.
Central Experimental Farm
Ottawa Ont. Canada

Sauvageot, J. Roseraies
Doubs France

Sauvageot, H.
Doubs France

Savage Farms Nursery
P.O. Box 125 PL
McMinnville TN 37110

Savage Nursery Ltd.
Barkingside Essex England

Saville, F. Harmon
58 Hammond Street
Rowley MA 01969

Savoureux
Rouen France

Saxena, Major Prem
Dehra Dun India

Scenic Nursery
1313 Scenic Drive
Modesto CA 93555

Schaum & Van Tol
Hansa Nursery
Boskoop Holland

Schenkel, Herman R.
Lynchburg VA

Schenkel, H.R. Inc.
Lynchburg VA

Schloen, J.
Brooklin Ont.
Canada

Schloen, P.
Brooklin Ont. Canada

Schlueter Rose Culture
Barry Schlueter
18300 Anne Drive
Houston TX 77058

Schluter, O.L.
Baltimore MD

Schmalz, Charles E.
Rochester NY

Schmid, R.
Bad Kostritz
Fernruf Germany

Schmidt, J.C.
Erfurt Germany

Schmidt, Rudolf
Rellingen Holstein Germany

Schmitt
Lyono Rhône France

Schneeberg, Paul
Sayville NY

Schneider
Godesberg Germany

Schneider, Peter
P.O. Box 16035
Rocky River OH 44116

Schoener, Rev. George M.A.
University of Santa Clara
Santa Clara CA

Schoepfle, O.B.
Birmingham OH

Schramm, Dwayne
6035 North 8th Street
Fresno CA 93710

Schramm, Frank
Crystal Lake IL

Schraven, F.
Lottum Holland

Schulteis, Anton
College Point NY

Schulteis, H.
Steinfurth Germany

Schurr, E.
Edmonds WA

Schuurman, Frank Bart
231 Lincoln Road
Henderson New Zealand

Schwartz, Andre
Venissieux Rhône France

Schwartz, E.W.
Kingsville MD

Schwartz, J. & Vve.
Lyon France

Scittine, Peter
Council Bluffs IA

Scoggins, C.
Shreveport LA

Scott, D.H.
Beaconfield Bucks England

Scott, George John
Coburg Victoria Australia

Scott, Robert & Son Inc.
Sharon Hill PA

Scotts Nurseries (Merriott)
Ltd.
Merriott Somerset England
TA16 5PL

Scrivens, L.
67 James Road
Kidderminster Worcs.
England DY10 2TR

Sealand Nurseries, Ltd.
Sealand
Chester England CHI 6BA

Seale Rose Gardens
Farnham Surrey England

Searn
Antibes France

Sears-McConnell Nursery
Ontario, Canada

Selection Meilland
France

Selwood, Archie
Vancouver BC Canada

Senff
Zerbst Germany

Sequoia Nursery
California

Serpa, Frank
Rio Vista CA

Sgaravatti, B.
Saonara Padua Italy

Shailer, Henry
Little Chelsea England

Shamberger, C.S.
Tyler TX

Shamberger, P.
Tyler TX

Shamberger Rose Nursery
Tyler TX

Sharman, A.B.
Wisbech Camb. England

Sharp, W.T.
Kimberley Notts. England

Shaw, F.
Chapeltown Sheffield
England

Shaw, H.C.W.
21 Oakleigh Road
Uxbridge Middlesex England
UB10 9EL

Shaw, Dr. J.A.
4003 N. Pacific Avenue
Fresno CA 93705

Shaw Rose Trees
29 Vicarage Road
Willoughton Gainsborough
Lincs. England DN21 5SA

Sheldon, John and Jennifer
127 N. Evanston
Arlington Hts IL 60004

Shenandoah Nursery
Shenandoah IA

Shephard, David Alfred
Victor
1 Wolsey Road
Enfield Middlesex England

Shepherd, Roy & Ann
Medina OH

Shepperson, Sam
Bingham Nottinghamshire
England

Sheridan, John
28 Downhill Road
Catford London England SE6

Sheridan Nurseries, Ltd.
1116 Winston Churchill Blvd.
Oakville Ont. Canada
L6J 4Z2

Sheridan Road Nursery
3823 N. Sheridan Road
Peoria IL 61614

Sheridan, V.
Coral Gables FL

Sherwood Forest Nursery
2623 Harris Street
Eureka CA 95501

Sherwood, G.C.
20 Gordon Place
Levin New Zealand

Shibata, Tadashi
1-5 Ikagakotobuki-Cho
Hirakata-Shi Osaka 573
Japan

Shira, J.
Tyler TX

Shirakawa, Takeshi
20 Koyama Takenoya
Gamagorishi Aichi Japan

Shortland, J.C.
Pool-in-Wharfedale
Yorks England

Shropshire Roses Ltd.
Bridgnorth Road Shipley
Pattingham
Wolverhampton England

Shtanko, E.
USSR

Shtanko, Ivan
Central Botanical Garden
Moscow USSR

Shukla, R.
India

Sidey, George
Earl Shilton
Leicestershire England

Silva, William E.
Sebastopol CA

Silver Leaf Nursery
7655 San Gabriel Street
Atascadero CA 93422

Sima, E.P.
Seattle WA

Simmonds Nursery, Ltd.
Chipperfield
Herts England

Simonet, R.
Edmonton Alberta Canada

Simpson, J.
South Queensferry
NB Canada

Simpson, J.W.
New Zealand

Simpson, Nola M.
17 Montgomery Terrace
Palmerston North
New Zealand

Singh, Raja Surendra
New Delhi India

Singleton, C.H.
62 Te Rahu Road
Te Awamutu New Zealand

Siret-Pernet, Ch.
Lyon-Monplaisir France

Sitton, George D. Sr.
Lindale TX

Skinner, Dr. F.L.
Skinner's Nursery Ltd.
Dropmore
Manitoba Canada

Slack, G.
c/o RNRS
St. Albans England

Slacks Roses
White Post
Farnsfield Nottingham
England NG22 8HX

Slattery, P. Esq.
Clonmel County
Tipperary Ireland

Slidrecht & Co.
Boskoop Holland

Small, P.E. & Sons
West End Woking England

Smith, Edward
124 Stanton Road
Sandiacre Notts. England

Smith, John
Haywood CA

Smith, Percy E.
Boston
Lincolnshire England

Smith, R.W.
Australia

Smith, Robert L.
Smith's Greenhouse & Nursery
RFD 1 Box 145
Mitchell SD 57301

Smith, Thomas & Sons
Stranraer Scotland

Smith, W.H.
Orpington Kent England

Smith's Greenhouse &
Nursery
Mitchell SD

Smits, J.
Naarden Holland

S.N.C. Meilland & Cie
France

Société Delbard
16 Quai de la Mègisserie
75038 Paris Cedex 01 France

Sociète Francaise des Roses
Parc de la Tete d'Or
69459 Lyon
Cedex 3 France

Sociète Royale Nationale
"Les Amis de la Rose"
Mullenstraat 14
B 9762 Mullem
(Oudernaarde) Belgium

Sodono, Alphonso
Newtown PA

Sodono, Jimmy
Madison NJ

Soenderhousen, O.
Denmark

Somerset Rose Nursery
New Brunswick NJ

Son, K.S.G.
Bangalore India

Soria, C.
Livermore CA

Souma Rose Society
Tokyo Japan

Soupert, Constant
Luxembourg

Soupert & Notting
Luxembourg

South Africa Rose Society
Johannesburg, South Africa

Southern Cross Nurseries
Barry & Dawn Eagle
P.O. Box 12009
Chirstchurch
New Zealand

Southern Plant-It Garden
Center
3550 Concord
Beaumont TX 77703

South Forest Rose Nursery
Hattiesburg MS

Sovereign Nursery Stock
48 Springfield Road
Repton Derby England
DE6 6GP

Spanbauer, Frank
Spanbauer Greenhouses
Decatur IL

Spandikow, William
Spandikow Greenhouses
Hot Springs AR

Späth, L.
Berlin Germany

Spek, Jan Nurseries
21 JDE
155 Boskoop
The Netherlands

Spera, Louis
Madison NJ

Spicer, Mrs. W.E.
England

Spies, Mark C.
1059 North Montana Street
Arlington VA 22205

Spooner, Raymond A.
8285 S.W. 185th Avenue
Beaverton OR 97007

Spring Hill Nursery
110 West Elm Street
Tipp City OH 45371

Spring Hill Nursery
6523 North Galena Road
Peoria IL 61656

Springwood Miniature Roses
Box 255, Port Credit P.O.
Missassauga Ont. Canada
L5G 4L8

Spruce Arbor Ltd.
Box 1621
Sussex New Brunswick
Canada E0E 1P0

Sprunt, Rev. James M.
Kenansville NC

Square, John & Son
Painesville OH

Staikov, Prof.
Dr. V. Staikov
"Benkovski" str. 4
6100 Kazanlak Bulgaria

Stalder-Welte, E.R.
6045 Meggen Switzerland

Stanard, J.L.
Seattle WA

Stanek's Nursery & Garden Center
East 2929 27th Avenue
Spokane WA 99203

Staples, Murray Garden Center
Ace 1676-A
P.O. Box 1881
703 Knight Avenue
Waycross GA 31501

Star Roses
West Grove PA

Stark Bros. Nurseries & Orchards Co.
Louisiana MO 63353-0010

Starkl, J.
West Germany

Stassen, L. Jr. Ltd.
Hillegom Holland

Station Experimentale de Roses
De Coninck-Devaes
Asse-ter-Heide Belgium

Stebbings, H.E.
1116 Hyland Drive
Santa Rosa CA 95404

Stedman, E.W. Ltd.
Longthorp Peterborough
Northants England

Stein, K.C.
Poelkijk Holland

Stell, L.H.
Tyler TX

Stell Rose Nursery
Tyler TX

Stephens, Paddy
New Zealand

Stern, F.C.
Highdown Goring-by-Sea
Sussex England

Stern's Nursery
Geneva NY

Stevens, G.A.
Harrisburg PA

Stevens, Walter Ltd.
Hoddesdon
Hertfordshire England

Stevenson, Walter
Twyford
Berkshire England

Stewart, G.
Stanway Colchester
Essex England

Stewart, T.G.
Victoria Australia

Stielow Bros.
Niles Center IL

Stielow, F.C.
Niles Center IL

Stocking, C.H. Rose Nursery
785 N. Capitol Avenue
San Jose CA 95131

Stoddard, Louis A.
P.O. Box 1133
Edgewood MD 21040

Stokman, Messrs.
Aalsmeer Holland

Stone, B.J.T.
Balwyn Victoria Australia

Storrs & Harrison Co.
Painesville OH

Strahle, Glen
Carlton, OR 97111

Strange, J.F.
Gislingham Road
Finningham Stowmarket
Suffolk England LP14 4HY

Stratford, L.
Parramatta NSW Australia

Strawn, Leslie E.
10422 Morningside Drive
Garden Grove CA 92643

Stuart, C.W. & Co. Inc.
Newark NY

Stuppy Floral Co.
St. Joseph MO

Stytdd Nursery
Stonygate Lane Ribchester
Nr. Preston
Lancashire
England PR3 3YN

Sudol, J.
Alhambra CA

Summerell, B.L.
76 Canada Street
Morrinsville New Zealand

Sunbeam Nurseries, Ltd.
231 Lincoln Road
Henderson New Zealand

Sunningdale Nursery, Ltd.
Windlesham Surrey England

Sunter, Miss Helen
College Park South Australia

Sushkov, L.K.
USSR

Sutton, G.T.
Wisbech Cambs England

Suzuki, Seizo
755 Owadashinden
Yachiyo-Shi (City) Chiba-Ken
(Pref.) 276 Japan

Svejda, Dr. Felicitas J.
1356 Meadowlands Dr. E.
Nepean Ont. Canada K2E6K6

Swane's Nursery
Swane Bros. Pty. Ltd. Inc.
Galston Road (off Old Northern Road)
Dural 2158 NSW Australia

Sweet
Bristol England

Sweetbriar Nursery
2002 Sweetbriar Lane
Morganton NC 28655

Sweetbriar Roses
Sweetbriar Marks Hall Lane
Margaret Rodding
Dunmow Essex MG 1QT

Swim, Herbert
1329 College Way
Ont. CA 91762

Swim & Weeks
Chino CA

Switzerland Rose Society
Wädenswil Switzerland

Sykes, R.O.
Winston-Salem NC

-T-

Taiwan Rose Center
2 Alley 1 Lane 104 Chung
Cheng Shih Lin Taipei
Taiwan Republic of China

Takahashi, Kiyooki
2-15-24 Hondo
Musashino-Shi Tokyo 180
Japan

Takahashi, Takeshi
1-799 Owada-Cho
Omiya-Shi 330 Japan

Takatori, Sunao
1078 Kataska Hazakawa P.O.
Okayama-Ker 709-12 Japan

Takatori, Yoshiho
1078 Kataska Hazakawa P.O.
Okayama-Ker 709-12 Japan

Tamarack Roses
Vancouver BC Canada

Tanne, R.
France

Tanner, C.D.
Holland NY

Tantau, Math
Tornescher Weg 13
Postfach 1344
2082 Uetersen
West Germany

Tas, J.
Aalsmeer Holland

Tata Electric Cos.
Tata Vidyut Karyalaya
Murzban Road
Bombay 400-001 India

Tate, P.O. Nursery
Rt. 20 Box 436
Tyler TX 75708

Tavistock Nursery
R.R. 1
Tavistock Ont. Canada
N0B 2R0

Taylor, C.A.
Long Beach CA

Taylor, L.R.
Watsonia Victoria Australia

Taylor, Pete & Kay
24 Ridgeview Drive
P O Box 11272
Chickasaw AL 36671-0272

Taylor, Thomas E.
10353 Judd Road
Willis MI 48191

Taylor, W.J.
675 Third Avenue
Enfield Middlesex England

Taylor's Roses
Stockwell Gate Holbeach NR
Spalding Lincs England PE12
8AX

Taylor's Roses
Pete & Kay Taylor
24 Ridgeview Drive
P.O. Box 11272
Chickasaw AL 36671-0272

Teas Nurseries
Bellaire Spring
Houston TX

Ted Castle, Mr. & Mrs. A.W.
Milton MA

Temmerman, P.C.
Serskamp Belgium

Teranishi, Kikuo
168 Ikenoue
Gogazuka Itami-shi
Hyogo-ken 664
Japan

Teranishi, Tito
168 Ikenoue
Gogazuka Itami-shi
Hyogo-ken 664
Japan

Teschendorff, V.
Cossebaude Dresden
Germany

Texas Rose Research
    Foundation Inc.
Tyler TX

Thakur, Arpi
Dehra Dun India

Thames Valley Rose
    Growers
Laleham Staines
Middx England

Thanet Roses
Pyson's Road
Broadstairs Kent
England CT10 2LA

Therkildsen, K.
Kew Gardens
Southport
Lancashire England

Thomas, Dr. Alfred S.
340 Unikon Road
Balwyn Victoria 3103
Australia

Thomas, Capt. George C., Jr.
Beverly Hills CA

Thomas, R.
Hastings
New Zealand

Thomasville Nurseries, Inc.
P.O. Box 7
Thomasville GA 31799

Thompson, D.L.
Tyler TX

Thompson, J.H. Jr.
Kennett Square PA

Thompson, M.
178 Tyntyla Road Llwyny P.A.
Rhondda Mid Glamorgan
England

Thompson, Mrs. Mary L.
Van TX

Thompson's, J.K. Sons
Kennett Square PA

Thomson, Colvin
47 Upper Gynor Place
Ynyshir
Rhondda Mid Glamorgan
France

Thomson, Richard
415 Wister Road
Wynnewood PA 19096

Thorne, D.R.
Orpington Kent England

Thornley, T.
Skelmanthorpe Yorks
England

Tillotson's
California

Timm, J. & Co.
Elmshorn Holstein Germany

Timmermans, J.H.
Timmerman's Roses
Lawdham Lane
Woodborough
Nottingham England
NG14 6DN

Timmermans, Jos.
Herten Roermond Holland

Tiny Jewels Nursery
9509 N. Bartlett Road
Oklahoma City OK 73131

Tiny Petals Nursery
Pat & Sue O'Brien
489 Minot Avenue
Chula Vista CA 92010

Tokumatsu, K.
    (Yumeotome)
2-8-10 Hagiyamachio Higashi
Murayama City 189 Japan

Tonk, Karl H.M.
Tonk Nurseries
25 Hill Street
Richmond Nelson
New Zealand

Tonkin, R.R.
Box Hill North
Victoria Australia

Toogood, Douglas
Australia

Torre Blanca
San Feliu de Llobregat
Barcelona
Spain

Totty, Charles H. Co. Inc.
Madison NJ

Toussaint, Mille Fils
Lyon Rhône France

Touvais
Petit-Montrouge France

Towill, Edward
Roslyn PA

Townsend, Charles L.
Chilwell
Nottingham England

Townsend, James & Son
Lower Broadheath England

Traendly & Schenck
New York NY

Train, John & Sons
Benston Tarbolton
Ayrshire Scotland

Trauger, Fred
Albuquerque NM

Travis, Louis R.
Rt. 3 Box 3490-E Heck Road
Prosser WA 99350

Treloar Roses Pty. Ltd.
Keillers Road
Portland Victoria 3305
Australia

Tresise, A.C.
Rhodesia

Trew, C.A.
Basildon Essex England

Trewallyn Nursery
Australia

Trimper, E.L.
Renmark
South Australia

Trioreau, P.P.
Paris France

Trophy Roses
1308 N. Kennicott
Arlington Heights IL 60004

Trouillard
Angers France

Troyer, Ray/Pat
10762 NE Hoyt St.
Portland OR 99220

Truffaut, Georges
Versailles France

Tschanz, E.
Route de Chavannes 61
1007 Lausanne Switzerland

Tucker, R. & Sons Ltd.
Faringdon Berkshire England

Tulp, J.
Aalsmeer Holland

Turbat, E. & Co.
Orléans France

Turke, Robert
Meissen III
Saxony
Germany

Turley, Vivian G.
75 Ashen Drive
Dantford Kent England
DA1 3LZ

Turner, Charles
Slough England

Tuttle Bros. Nursery
Pasadena CA

Twin Nursery
San Lorenzo CA

Twomey, Jerry
194 Avocado St.
Leucadia CA 92024

Tysterman, W.E.
Lynn Road
Wisbech Cambs. England

Ty-Tex Rose Nursery
Tyler TX

-U-

Ulrick, L.W.
Sunnybank Brisbane
Queensland Australia

Umsawasdi, Theera
5531 Jason
Houston TX 77096

Undritz, F.R.M.
West New Brighton L.I. NY

United Kingdom Rose
Society
Hertfordshire England

United Rose Growers
P.O. Box E
Woodland WA 98674

United States Department
of Agriculture
(USDA) Permit Unit
PPQ Federal Bldg. Rm. 638
Hayattsville MD 20782.
(For importing roses from
foreign countries)

Universal Plants
France

Universal Rose Selections
France

University of California
Los Angeles CA

University of Minnesota
St. Paul MN

University of Nebraska
Lincoln NE

University of New
Hampshire
Durham NH

University of Saskatchewan
Saskatoon Canada

University of Texas at Tyler
3900 University Boulevard
Tyler TX 75701

URS
France

Uruguay Rose Society
Montevideo Uruguay

U.S. Cut Flower Co.
Elmira NY

U.S. Patent Sales, Inc.
960 G. Street
Wasco CA 93280

Utz, Peggy L.
1328 Mill Lane
New Albany IN 47150

-V-

Vahldiek-Bessingen
Bundesrepublick Germany

Valdezm, J.D.
Brentwood CA

Valentino, B.
Camporosso Italy

Valley Nursery
Kimberley Notts England

Van Barneveld, John H.
La Habra CA

Van Bourgondien Bros.
P.O. Box A
245 Farmingdale Road
Rt. 109
Babylon NY 11702

Van den Akker Bros.
Boskoop Holland

van der Meyden, W.J.L. &
Son
Tijsenhout Holland

van der Schilden, Teunis
Aalsmeer Holland

Van der Vis & Co.
Boskoop Holland

Van der Wolf, Nic
Boskoop Holland

van de Water, J.H.
Boskoop Holland

Van de Yssel, A.
Alpen ad Ryn Holland

van Englen, A.J.N.V.
Hillegom Holland

Van Fleet, Dr. Walter
Glenn Dale MD

Van Heerreweghe-
Coppitters, Ach.
Cherscamp Belgium

Van Houtte, Louis
Gand Holland

Van Nes
Boskoop Holland

Van Rossem, G.A.
Naarden Holland

Van Sante, W. & T.
Smetledestraat 52-B-9200
Wetteren Belgium

van't Kruis, N.
Aalsmeer Holland

Vanto, Mikko
Kaanaa Raisioas Finland

Van Veen, J.
Carlton OR

Van Veen, Jan
Hornweg 92 1432 GE
Aalsmeer Holland

Varney, E.
142 Workshop Road
Swallownest
Sheffield England S31 OWE

Vasishth, Maj. L.M.
Lucknow India

Veitch, J. & Sons
Kings Road
Chelsea England

Verbeek, G.
Hornweg 92 1432 GE
Aalsmeer Holland

Verbeek, G. & Zn.
Aalsmeer Holland

Verdier, Eugène
Paris France

Verdier, Victor
Paris France

Verein Deutscher
Rosenfreunde E.V.
Waldseetrasse 14
7570 Baden Baden Germany

Verhalen, Geo. F.
Scottsville TX

Verhalen Nursery Co.
Scottsville TX

Verschuren, Andries
Holland

Verschuren, H.A.M.
Holland

Verschuren, H.A. & Sons
St. Hubertsweg 7A Postbus 2
Haps Holland

Verschuren-Pechtold, Jac.
Verschuren-Pechtold
Holland

Verschuren, Ted
Holland

Vestal, Jos. W. & Son
Little Rock AR

Vétillard
Le Mans France

Via cava, Luigi
via. E. Baroni
2-17-16129 Genova Italy

Vially, P.
Villeurbanne Rhône France

Vibert, J.P.
Angers France

Vick, James
Rochester NY

Victoria Nurseries
Burbage Hinckley
Tews England

Vilmorin
Frankreich West Germany

Vilmorin-Andrieux
4 Quai de la Megisserie
Paris France

Vincent, G.C.
Hemingford Grey
Huntingdonshire England

Viney, E.A.
Surrey Road
Queensland Australia

Viraraghavan, M.S.
Hill View Fern Hill Road
Kodaikani
624 101 Tamil Nadu India

Vlaeminck
Schellebelle Belgium

Vogel, Max
Sangerhausen Germany

Vogel, R. Jr.
Sangerhausen Germany

Von Abrams, Gordon J.
Davis CA

Von Koss, F.
Mentor OH

-W-

Waban Conservatories
Natick MA

Walden, John K.
Bear Creek Gardens
P.O. Box 2000
Somis CA 93066

Walker, B.
Algar Kirk Boston
Lincolnshire England
PE20 2BE

Walker, D.R.
Huonville
Tasmania 7109 Australia

Walker, Miss Marjorie
Kernhill NSW Australia

Wallace, E.
Comrie Perthshire England

Walsh, M.H.
Woods Hole MA

Walsh, James & Sons Ltd.
Portadown England

Walter, A.
Saverne France

Walter, John C.
Rt. 2 Box 172
Grand Saline TX 75140

Walter, Louis
Saverne Bas-Rhin France

Wambach, Alex A.
111 Ridgewood Drive
Fredericksburg TX 78624

Ward
Ipswich England

Ward, F.B.
Bay City MI

Wareham, Phyllis Eveline
15 Ririnui Place Maungatapu
Tauranga New Zealand

Warley Rose Gardens, Ltd.
Warley Street Great Warley
Brentwood
Essex England CM13 3JH

Warmerdam & Co. Ltd.
Endfield Middlx
England

Warner, A.J.
3802 South Highlander
Orange TX 77630

Warner, C.H.
Great Barley Arrish Liverton
Newton Abbott
Devon England TQ12 6HN

Warren, Donald Roy
Burwood E. 13
Victoria Australia

Warriner, William A.
P.O. Box 808
Tustin CA 92680

Waterer, John Sons & Crisp
Ltd.
Twyford Berkshire England

Waterhouse Nursery Ltd.
Radway Green Cheshire
England

Waterhouse, W.P.
Radway Green Cheshire
England

Watkins, A.F.
Dixie Rose Nursery
Tyler TX

Watkins Roses Ltd.
Hampton-in-Arden
Solihull
Warwickshire England

Watson, R.
Australia

Watts, M.L.
Parklands
Northampton
England

Watts, Mrs. Mary A.
RD 1
Kaitaia New Zealand

Watterberg, Leah
1615 Adelita Dr. NE
Albuquerque NM 87111

Wayman, Robert
Bayside L.I. NY

Wayside Gardens
Hodges SC 29695-0001

Webber, Edward J.
Missoula MT

Weddle, Von C.
2801 Charlestown Road
New Albany IN 47150

Wedwick, C.D.
Nanticoke Ont. Canada

Wee Ones Miniature Roses
3662 Moore Street
Los Angeles CA 90061

Weeks, Michael W.J.
1 Hope Road South Benfleet
Essex England SS7 5JJ

Weeks, O.L.
11530 Vernon Ave.
Chino CA 91710

Weeks Roses
Tom Carruth
430 E. 19th Street
Upland CA 91786

Weigand, Christoph
Bad Soden a Taunus
Germany

Weigand, L.
Bad Soden a Taunus
Germany

Weiland & Risch
Chicago IL

Wells, Tunbridge
Kent England

Wells, Verlie W., Jr.
P.O. Box 157
Brighton TN 38011

Welsh, Eric T.
5 Kirra Street Erina
NSW 2250 Australia

Welter, Nicola
Trier Germany

West, Mrs. Olga
Leopard Mines
Que Que South Rhodesia

West, Ronald
29 Maddoxford Lane
Boorley Green Botley
Southampton England
S03 2DG

Westbury Rose Co.
Westbury L.I. NY

Western Rose Co.
Van Nuys CA

Westwood Garden Center &
Nursery
Mineral Springs Road
Dalton GA 30720

Wezelenburg, K. & Son
Hazerwoude Holland

Whartons Roses Ltd.
Harleston Norfolk
England

Wheatcroft Bros. Ltd.
England

Wheatcroft, Christopher A.
England

Wheatcroft Gardening
England

Wheatcroft, Harry
England

Wheatcroft & Sons, Ltd.
England

Wheatcroft Roses Ltd.
Edwalton
Nottingham England
NG12 4DE

Wheatley, R.G.
Upper Mt. Gravatt Australia

Wheeler, Dr. Seager
Rosthern Sask. Canada

Wheelers Nursery
Rt. 20 Box 399 Gray Highway
Macon GA 31211

Whisler, Milton L.
Shafter CA

Whistler, Dorothy
Shafter CA

White, Al
12609 Clock Tower Pkwy.
Bayonet Point FL 34667

White, James J.
1065 Lomita Boulevard, #216
Harbor City CA 90710

White, T. H.
Adelaide South Australia

White Bros. Roses Corp.
Medina NY

White, Charles N.
Medina NY

Whitehead, T.M.
Selkirk Scotland

Whittington, J.O. Sr.
15723 Parete Road
Jacksonville FL 32218

Wiggins, John H.
Attleboro MA

Wijnhoven, G. & Son
Wanssum Holland

Wilbur, Miss Rena E.
Seattle WA

Wilke, William
6443 Bayard St.
Long Beach CA 90815

Willemse
Holland

Williams, Dr. A.H.
Horsham Sussex
England

Williams, Ernest D.
1510 Lebanon Avenue
Dallas TX 75208

Williams, G. A.
Roseneath Nursery
Runcorn Brisbane
Australia